The Motion Picture Guide

★ ★ ★ ★ ★ ★ ★ ★ ★ ★ ★ ★ ★ ★ ★ ★ ★ ★ ★

1997 Annual

THE MOTION PICTURE GUIDE

★ ★ ★ ★ ★ ★ ★ ★ ★ ★ ★ ★ ★ ★ ★ ★ ★ ★ ★

1997 ANNUAL (THE FILMS OF 1996)

Editor : Edmond Grant
Associate Editor : Ken Fox
Editorial Assistant : Andrew Joseph

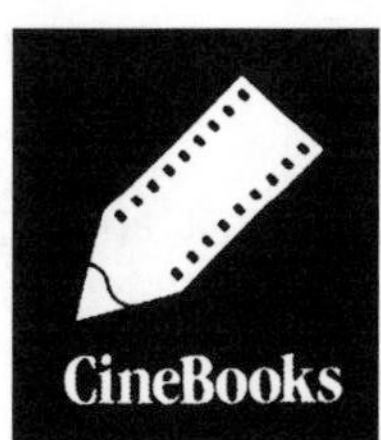

Published by CineBooks, a division of News America Publishing Incorporated,
620 Avenue of the Americas, 6th Floor, New York, NY 10011

First Edition
Printed in the United States
1 2 3 4 5 6 7 8 9 10

Library of Congress Catalog Number 8571145

ISBN: 0-933997-00-0 THE MOTION PICTURE GUIDE (10 Vols.)
ISBN: 0-933997-11-6 THE MOTION PICTURE GUIDE INDEX (2 Vols.)
ISBN: 0-933997-39-6 THE MOTION PICTURE GUIDE 1997 ANNUAL
(THE FILMS OF 1996)

TABLE OF CONTENTS

FOREWORD v

INFORMATION KEY ix

FILM REVIEWS. 3

ACADEMY AWARDS 429

OBITUARIES 433

INDICES

MASTER INDEX 477
FILMS BY COUNTRY 511
FILMS BY DISTRIBUTOR 517
FILMS BY STAR RATING 523
FILMS BY GENRE 527
FILMS BY MPAA RATING 535
FILMS BY PARENTAL RECOMMENDATION 539
NAMES INDEX. 543
REVIEW ATTRIBUTION 787
OUR CONTRIBUTORS 791

FOREWORD

The 1997 *Motion Picture Guide Annual*, covering films released during 1996, is the twelfth supplement to the original, twelve-volume *Motion Picture Guide*. It is also the most ambitious *Annual* to date, breaking all our previous records by reviewing no less than 669 films. Not only have we broadened our scope to include many more of the scores of straight-to-video productions that were released last year, but we have, we believe, set new standards in the quality and accuracy of our coverage.

Several people were integral to the production of this book. First and foremost is our tireless and dedicated Associate Editor, Ken Fox. We'd also like to single out Andrew Joseph who, as Editorial Assistant, did an exemplary job of dealing with the nuts-and-bolts work that is so necessary in the production of a book of this scope. Strengthening our team is a fine staff of contributing editors, including Joe Diliberto, Mary Jayne McKay, Derek A. Baker, Andrea Waitt, Meredith Mundy Wasinger, Suzanne Lander, Susan Pottinger, Penny Perkins, and Charles Cassady Jr. Ellen Crean, Angelo Virgona, M. Faust, and Kim Stitzel deserve special thanks for their excellent work in helping us maintain a consistent tone and format throughout the book. Frank Lovece and Joe Frazzetta produced an obituary section loaded with fascinating details about the year's departed and, as always, we salute Noel Harrington for his patience and expertise in turning our data into a book. We hope you enjoy the fruits of their labors and welcome your comments, which should be sent to us at the address on the copyright page.

Edmond Grant	Jo Imeson	Michelle Diliberto
Editor	Director	Business Manager

The Year in Review

On the whole, moviegoers encountered few surprises in 1996. A handful of brilliant and visionary works were released during the year, but the so-called "indie sweep" of the Oscars merely confirmed what had already been suspected by cinephiles around the world: These days, there's very little difference between high-gloss Hollywood product and the latest "hot" independent production.

The pendulum has indeed swung back—to 1969, when EASY RIDER's incredible box-office success convinced studio heads it could be highly profitable (and critically advantageous) to take a chance on modest, character-based films. A number of remarkable films emerged from this period of corporate largesse, but the even richer rewards reaped by the films of Steven Spielberg and George Lucas quickly had the moguls focusing on producing big-budget genre pictures.

In 1996, these dual legacies of the '70s found complete and utter compatability as INDEPENDENCE DAY and TWISTER swept the multiplexes, while at least one screen was usually set aside for a prestige independent title like THE ENGLISH PATIENT or FARGO. In fact, the term "independent" has become so distorted in the past few years that the current high-profile films bearing that label have little if nothing to do with the no-budget 8- and 16-millimeter efforts still being cranked out by truly independent souls around the world, not to mention the trailblazing dramas made outside conventional channels by the likes of John Cassavetes and Shirley Clarke.

Now that maverick distributors Miramax and Fine Line are owned by The Walt Disney Company and The Turner Corporation respectively, the entire complexion of the "indie" film world has changed; now low-budget, character-driven dramas and comedies have the feel of audition pieces. If a filmmaker can't dig up funding from a "mini-major" for his or her next feature, the solution appears to be attracting a "name"—Eric Stoltz, Parker Posey, Drew Barrymore, et al—to take a walk-on role. The most interesting manifestation of this phenomenon by far is an event called the Independent Spirit Awards. It was originally set up as an alternative to the Academy Awards with an eye towards honoring those working outside of Hollywood; this year, however, the nominations for the ISAs uncannily mirrored those of the Oscars, further blurring the lines between corporate moviemaking and the so-called "fringe".

But despite the co-opting of the independent film community by shrewd, *Last Tycoon*-like movie producers (whose reputations aren't diminished when they lose money on a critically-lauded film), not all mini-major releases were Gen-X relationship drama-dies (the unwatchable THE POMPATUS OF LOVE) or tepid character studies (the disappointing GIRLS TOWN). Several interesting and original works emerged from the broad spectrum of items branded "independent." The Coen brothers shook off the charming-but-squeaky-clean tone that pervaded THE HUDSUCKER PROXY (1994) and concocted FARGO, one of their finest blends of dippy farce and dark humor. Actor Billy Bob Thornton received much critical acclaim, and an Academy Award for Best Adapted Screenplay, for his SLING BLADE. Another performer-turned-director, Steve Buscemi, familiar from character turns in a number of recent independent landmarks, made his directing debut with TREES LOUNGE, a winning slice-of-life concerning the dead-end pursuits of a Long Island barfly.

And while Hollywood continues to hold to the notion, spawned in the '80s, that the only foreign films worthy of US release are prestige period pieces based on noted novels (like the picturesque but hollow THE HORSEMAN ON THE ROOF), some vital and innovative works from overseas did receive widespread distribution on these shores. The most notorious was TRAINSPOTTING, a grim but kinetic portrayal of a drug addict's attempts to kick his habit; unlike his American counterparts, Danny Boyle capably backed up his flashy direction with an involving story. Veteran filmmaker Mike Leigh's trademark naturalism was used at the service of a touching narrative in SECRETS AND LIES. Lars Von Trier turned to spiritual matters with his troubling chronicle of a religious believer's downward spiral in his superb BREAKING THE WAVES. The year's most impressive foreign release was the small-in-scope yet masterfully stylized CHUNGKING EXPRESS, which brought wider recognition to the immensely talented Wong Kar-Wai. Wong's work exudes an enthusiasm for cinema, but he is not following the same path as the genre-movie-addicted Quentin Tarantino (who made no film during 1996, but did start up Rolling Thunder, a cult-movie-oriented arm of Miramax promising an eccentric selection of "high" and "low" releases, starting off with CHUNGKING). Instead, Wong's films hearken back to the modest means and fresh ideas of the French New Wave and the passion for visual experimentation found in the early works of Martin Scorsese.

Scorsese detailed that very passion in his wonderful documentary A PERSONAL JOURNEY WITH MARTIN SCORSESE THROUGH AMERICAN MOVIES, which registered as a far more heartfelt project than his grandiose CASINO (1995). Other 1996 films from older "masters" included Nicolas Roeg's return to form with the aggressively obsessive

TWO DEATHS; Robert Altman's seemingly slight but resonant KANSAS CITY; Milos Forman's myth-making THE PEOPLE VS. LARRY FLYNT; and Pedro Almodovar's grandly entertaining melodramatic farce, THE FLOWER OF MY SECRET. Neil Jordan turned to historic spectacle with MICHAEL COLLINS, while Terence Davies delivered a well-cast but unfortunately thin adaptation of THE NEON BIBLE. Three '70s wunderkinds turned to Hollywood pap pure and simple, as Francis Ford Coppola directed the bittersweet JACK, Michael Cimino supplied the impenetrable SUNCHASER, and Brian De Palma crafted the big-budget blockbuster MISSION: IMPOSSIBLE.

A more recent crop of purebred independents turned out some of the year's most entertaining and thought-provoking features. John Sayles mixed social problems, western conventions, and the structure of a mystery in LONE STAR. Spike Lee made two very disparate movies: the playful GIRL 6 and the hard-hitting but awkwardly didactic GET ON THE BUS. Hal Hartley tried but failed at a peculiar experiment to remake the same love story three different ways in FLIRT. Abel Ferrara retreated further into a tough-guy existential haze in THE FUNERAL. Allison Anders went retro with her '60s rock tale GRACE OF MY HEART, while Woody Allen revisited '30s musical cliches in his uneven EVERYONE SAYS I LOVE YOU. Jane Campion tackled a literary classic with THE PORTRAIT OF A LADY, but her first feature, TWO FRIENDS (which received its first US release in 1996), better displayed her cinematic strong points. In the realm of the art-house circuit, the Brothers Quay impressed with their first live-action feature INSTITUTE BENJAMENTA; Rosa Von Praunheim humorously spoofed his own bad-boy reputation in NEUROSIA: 50 YEARS OF PERVERSITY; and Mark Rappaport once again examined the private life of a film star in FROM THE JOURNALS OF JEAN SEBERG. However, the best film made by a "veteran" indie director in 1996 was arguably Jim Jarmusch's DEAD MAN. An engrossing and intelligent evocation of the dark horse operas of the '40s and '50s—as well as the revisionist westerns made by Monte Hellman, Arthur Penn, and Altman—DEAD MAN proved that Kevin Costner's tediously "correct" westerns haven't killed off the genre entirely.

On the subject of fading genres, the films of 1996 did little to reverse the headlong slide of American comedies into oblivion. Ben Stiller's darkly humored THE CABLE GUY was the first Jim Carrey star vehicle to miss the $100-million mark domestically. (It did take in more than that amount worldwide, however.) Other non-events in the stagnant world of film comedy included the resounding failures of "Friends" star David Schwimmer's THE PALLBEARER and Demi Moore's satirically unsound STRIPTEASE (for which she was paid $12.5 million, reportedly the highest salary ever received by an actress); the dubious comic teaming of Whoopi Goldberg and Gerard Depardieu in BOGUS; the pleasant but disappointing reunion of a brilliant comedy team in KIDS IN THE HALL: BRAIN CANDY; the clumsy transfer of a successful TV series to the big screen in MYSTERY SCIENCE THEATER 3000: THE MOVIE; and the nightmare that is Tom Arnold (THE STUPIDS, BIG BULLY, CARPOOL). To add insult to injury, the ubiquitous Dan Aykroyd appeared in no less than *five* releases in 1996.

Still, a few comedies *did* manage to attract moviegoers. Among the surprise successes were the incredibly weak THE TRUTH ABOUT CATS AND DOGS and Eddie Murphy's fx-laden remake of THE NUTTY PROFESSOR. Not-so-surprisingly successful was THE BIRDCAGE, again a remake, but calculatingly borrowed from the French. And while some facile comedies like THE FIRST WIVES' CLUB, HAPPY GILMORE, and, strangely enough, MTV's BEAVIS AND BUTT-HEAD DO AMERICA may have done respectable business at the box office, one of the year's funniest films will probably only receive its just due in future years at camp afficionados' video parties. THE ISLAND OF DR. MOREAU had all the hallmarks of a cult movie: behind-the-scenes temper tantrums, overwrought performances, dialogue to howl over, and a narrative that appeared to disassemble itself as the film continued along.

On the action front, numerous films mimicked Tarantino's style (2 DAYS IN THE VALLEY, AMERICAN STRAYS), but the most significant developments both related to Hong Kong's influential action cinema. First, the success of John Woo's BROKEN ARROW, and second, the American-market breakthrough of international star Jackie Chan with the lively but routine RUMBLE IN THE BRONX. Chan's next 1996 vehicle, the 1992 film SUPERCOP (reviewed in the 1993 *Motion Picture Guide Annual*), was a far better example of Chan's physical and comedic talents, but it failed to duplicate RUMBLE's runaway success.

Formulaic action vehicles (that don't come within leagues of even Chan's meagerest efforts) make up a large chunk of the straight-to-video market, the other central phenomenon being incredibly dull "erotic thrillers." The movie fan who still firmly believes in the sanctity of a darkened auditorium wouldn't recognize their names, but the faces (and forms) of such straight-to-video staples as Don "The Dragon" Wilson, Frank Zagarino, David Bradley, Maria Ford, Julie Strain, and Shannons Tweed and Whirry are burned into the brains of late-night cable viewers. 1996 saw the release of no breakout straight-to-video hit like RED ROCK WEST (1994)—not surprising, considering the unbelievably low standards by which straight-to-video directors crank out their hackwork.

The central cinematic happening of the year, however, was a movie that was strictly manufactured to hit all the right buttons and, in the process, become a box-office blockbuster. INDEPENDENCE DAY (cloyingly dubbed "ID4" by its publicists) was little more than a war movie with a sci-fi overlay. Moviegoers voted their approval for the movie and made it the most successful film of the year (it later claimed the title of the second most popular film worldwide, right behind JURASSIC PARK). In its wake, Tim Burton's bright absurdist comedy with a similar alien-invasion theme, MARS ATTACKS!, was released to extremely disappointing returns, yet it supplied a welcome antidote to the pieties and overblown spectacle contaminating ID4. Whereas ID4 director Roland Emmerich and screenwriter Dean Devlin shamelessly played on the audience's heartstrings and patriotism, Burton and screenwriter Jonathan Gems took a patently humorous approach. And while some of ID4's defenders view the film as a genre spoof, a quick glance at any sequence in MARS ATTACKS!—including the lightweight, throwaway conclusion—supplies ample evidence of how a sci-fi parody *should* be handled. In fact, Burton and Gems delightfully deflate the notion of patriotism entirely when one character runs to surrender while holding aloft an American flag; a magazine is later shown to have proclaimed the fleeing coward as a hero on its cover.

By the spring of 1997, another blockbuster had come along to erase the inroads made by ID4—a little number called STAR WARS. Which, come to think of it, brings us right back to our discussion of how '90s Hollywood has been duplicating the patterns of the '70s. Perhaps another "Independence Day" has already come and gone for American low-budget filmmakers.

Edmond Grant
New York City
April 1997

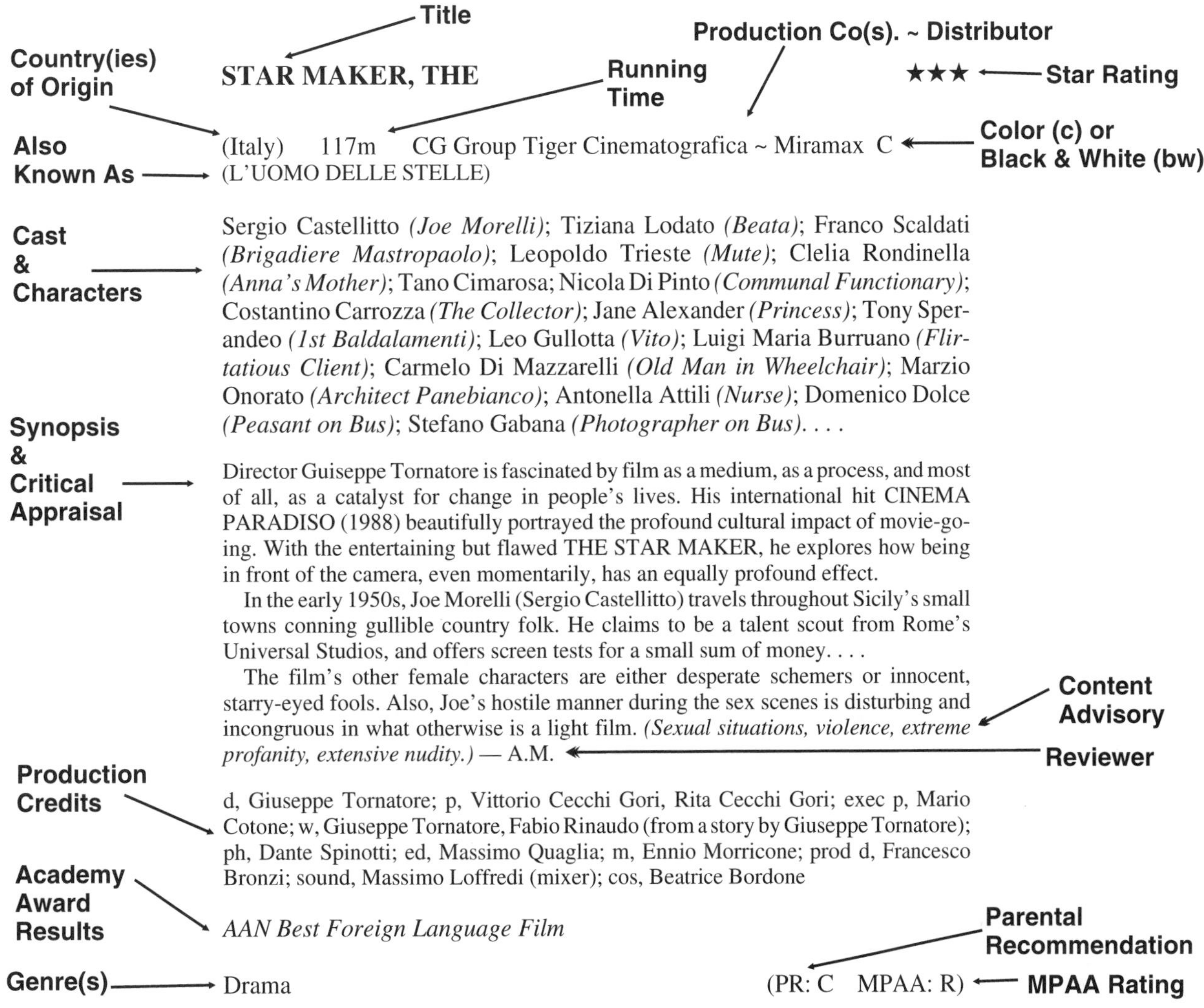

Title
Production Co(s). ~ Distributor
Country(ies) of Origin
STAR MAKER, THE
Running Time
★★★
Star Rating
Also Known As
(Italy) 117m CG Group Tiger Cinematografica ~ Miramax C
Color (c) or Black & White (bw)
(L'UOMO DELLE STELLE)
Cast & Characters
Sergio Castellitto (Joe Morelli); Tiziana Lodato (Beata); Franco Scaldati (Brigadiere Mastropaolo); Leopoldo Trieste (Mute); Clelia Rondinella (Anna's Mother); Tano Cimarosa; Nicola Di Pinto (Communal Functionary); Costantino Carrozza (The Collector); Jane Alexander (Princess); Tony Sperandeo (1st Baldalamenti); Leo Gullotta (Vito); Luigi Maria Burruano (Flirtatious Client); Carmelo Di Mazzarelli (Old Man in Wheelchair); Marzio Onorato (Architect Panebianco); Antonella Attili (Nurse); Domenico Dolce (Peasant on Bus); Stefano Gabana (Photographer on Bus). . . .
Synopsis & Critical Appraisal
Director Guiseppe Tornatore is fascinated by film as a medium, as a process, and most of all, as a catalyst for change in people's lives. His international hit CINEMA PARADISO (1988) beautifully portrayed the profound cultural impact of movie-going. With the entertaining but flawed THE STAR MAKER, he explores how being in front of the camera, even momentarily, has an equally profound effect.
In the early 1950s, Joe Morelli (Sergio Castellitto) travels throughout Sicily's small towns conning gullible country folk. He claims to be a talent scout from Rome's Universal Studios, and offers screen tests for a small sum of money. . . .
The film's other female characters are either desperate schemers or innocent, starry-eyed fools. Also, Joe's hostile manner during the sex scenes is disturbing and incongruous in what otherwise is a light film. (Sexual situations, violence, extreme profanity, extensive nudity.) — A.M.
Content Advisory
Reviewer
Production Credits
d, Giuseppe Tornatore; p, Vittorio Cecchi Gori, Rita Cecchi Gori; exec p, Mario Cotone; w, Giuseppe Tornatore, Fabio Rinaudo (from a story by Giuseppe Tornatore); ph, Dante Spinotti; ed, Massimo Quaglia; m, Ennio Morricone; prod d, Francesco Bronzi; sound, Massimo Loffredi (mixer); cos, Beatrice Bordone
Academy Award Results
AAN Best Foreign Language Film
Parental Recommendation
Genre(s)
Drama
(PR: C MPAA: R)
MPAA Rating

INFORMATION KEY

Titles
All entries are arranged alphabetically by title, with articles (A, AN, THE) appearing after the main title.

International Productions
When a film has been produced by a country or countries other than the US, these are noted in parentheses on the first line following the title.

Production Companies/Distributor
The film's production company or companies are listed first, with a tilde (~) separating them from the distributor.

Production Credits
The credits for the creative and technical personnel of a film include: d (director); p (producer); exp (exec. producer); asp (assoc. producer); cop (co-producer); w (writer); ph (cinematographer); ed (editor); m (music composer); md (music director); prod d (production designer); art d (art director); set d (set decorator); anim (animation); chor (choreography); sound; fx (special effects); casting; cos (costumes); makeup; stunts; tech (technical adviser).

Academy Award Results
Academy Award information is preceded by *AA,* for a winner, or *AAN,* for a nominee, followed by the category and the name of the recipient, where appropriate.

Genres
Each film is classified by up to three genres drawn from the following list: Action, Adventure, Animated, Biography, Children's, Comedy, Crime, Dance, Disaster, Docudrama, Documentary, Drama, Erotic, Fantasy, Historical, Horror, Martial Arts, Musical, Mystery, Opera, Political, Prison, Religious, Romance, Science Fiction, Sports, Spy, Thriller, War, Western.

Parental Recommendations
The parental recommendation (PR) provides parents with an indication of the film's suitability for children. The recommendations are as follows: AA – good for children; A – acceptable for children; C – cautionary, some scenes my be objectionable for children; O – objectionable for children.

A RESZLEG
(SEE: OUTPOST, THE)

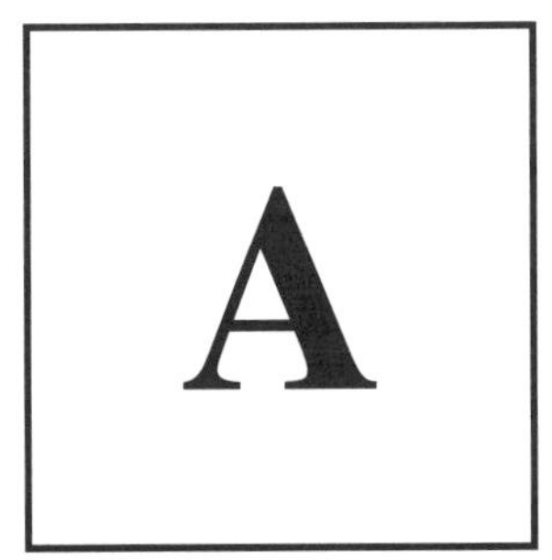

ABUSE ★★½
(U.S.) 93m Cinevista ~ Cinevista Home Video bw

Richard Ryder *(Larry Porter)*; Raphael Sbarge *(Thomas Carroll)*; Steve James *(Dr. Bennett)*; Kathy Gerber *(Kathy Logan)*; Jack Halton *(Professor Rappaport)*; Mickey Clark *(Laura)*; Maurice Massaro *(Mr. Carroll)*; Susan Schneider *(Mrs. Carroll)*; Luba Gregus *(Sara)*; Kathy Giotta *(Elaine)*; Tracy Vivat *(Amy)*; Billy Lux *(Aaron)*; Paul Peterson *(David)*; David Schacter *(Mark)*; Jean Garrett *(Dean Kincaid)*; Pam Poitier *(Samantha)*; Jeff Olmsted *(Richard)*; Jim O'Connor *(Frankie)*; Carol Siskind *(Telephone Operator)*; Ralph Penner *(Gym Teacher)*; Max Schmid *(Engineer)*; Keith Michl *(Detective)*; Dennis Baines *(Waiter)*; J. J. Davis *(Woman in Restaurant)*; John Kartovsky *(Man in Restaurant)*; Murray Rosenthal *(Man in Restroom)*; Jennifer Begansky *(Shelter Switchboard Operator)*

One long caterwaul for mercy, ABUSE is a raw indictment of child abuse. Thanks to its sporadic awkwardness, the viewer is offered the respite of a certain aesthetic distance from its often stomach-churning themes and situations.

At St. Matthew's Hospital, an intern notifies Larry Porter (Richard Ryder), a thesis candidate in film, about a teenager who has been rushed to the emergency room with evidence of parental beating. Larry senses that this battered 14 year old, Thomas Carroll (Raphael Sbarge), could be the centerpiece of his film about society's neglect of battered children.

Tentatively agreeing to meet Larry on Sundays, Thomas opens up to the older gay documentarian, not only revealing war stories about his punishing home life, but admitting that he, too, is gay. Thomas bonds with Larry, who still views the adolescent solely as a hot property for his project.

Ignoring his college's directive to edit Thomas out of the film for legal reasons, Larry begins a sexual affair with the vulnerable lad. But he doesn't know how to remove Thomas from an escalation of physical injuries, including cigarette burns.

After viewing a rough cut of Larry's film, Thomas finds the courage to strike his father. But his defiance only pushes his parents to worse abuses with a cigarette lighter. On the day of his movie's school showcase, Larry runs away with Thomas and abandons his promising career.

In a complex manner, ABUSE indicts domestic violence while questioning the sexual exploitation of the teenager by the older homosexual. To many viewers, the film presents a scenario in which Thomas is doomed either way.

Problematically, ABUSE is so prejudiced in favor of its own solution that it never sets up alternatives, such as Thomas running away alone or entering foster care. While outing the home-front abuse syndrome, the film enters a gray area in which adult Larry behaves irresponsibly toward an impressionable adolescent. Ultimately, the movie is a love story about two damaged souls, with the adult taking parental responsibility for the child.

The film suffers from a clumsy stab at documentary realism, with talking heads spouting psychobabble in Larry's film-within-a-film. Also, the script treats the parents as faceless monsters rather that giving them human dimensions. The whole project is further damaged by the rampant inferiority of performances.

Nevertheless, ABUSE is an important film because of its indictment of child victimization. It is a risk-taking love story that pierces societal norms and attitudes. *(Graphic violence, adult situations, sexual situations.)* — R.P.

d, Arthur J. Bressan Jr.; p, Steve McMillin, Arthur J. Bressan Jr.; exec p, Frederick Schminke; w, Arthur J. Bressan Jr.; ph, Douglas Dickinson; ed, Arthur J. Bressan Jr.; m, Shawn Phillips; art d, Robert Lisiecki; sound, Bruce Tovsky; makeup, Gigi Williams

Drama (PR: O MPAA: NR)

ADRENALIN: FEAR THE RUSH ★
(U.S.) 77m Largo Entertainment; Filmwerks ~ Legacy Releasing c

Christopher Lambert *(Lemieux)*; Natasha Henstridge *(Delon)*; Norbert Weisser *(Cuzo)*; Elizabeth Barondes *(Wocek)*; Xavier DeClie *(Volker)*; Craig Davis *(Suspect)*; Nicholas Guest *(Rennard)*; Andrew Divoff *(Sterns)*; Jon Epstein *(Waxman)*

Cops are on the trail of a mutant killer in a plague-ravaged society in this bottom-of-the-barrel futuristic horror thriller from schlockmeister Albert Pyun (CYBORG, NEMESIS).

America, 2007 A.D.—A deadly virus has wiped out Europe, and all recent immigrants to the US have been quarantined in a ghetto-like prison camp near Boston. Police officer Delon (Natasha Henstridge), has been imprisoned with her husband and child. After her husband is killed, she needs to obtain a special passport to leave the camp with her sick son. She buys one on the black market, but discovers that before she can leave she has to catch a crazed, cannibalistic killer who's stalking the camp and is carrying the virus.

Delon discovers a pile of hacked-up corpses in the bowels of an abandoned prison and calls for backup. Officer Lemieux (Christopher Lambert) arrives with two other cops. They continue their search and think they've trapped the maniac in an old jail cell. When Lemieux goes in to make sure, the killer shoots him, locks him up, and escapes. The killer ties Delon up and hangs her and Lemieux from the ceiling. He starts to torture Lemieux, but Delon kicks him in the head and manages to wriggle out of the ropes, grab a gun, and shoot the killer. Back outside, a government agent sees Delon's black-market passport. But instead of arresting her, he orders one of his men to escort Delon and her son across the border to safety.

Unlike most of Albert Pyun's direct-to-video productions, ADRENALIN: FEAR THE RUSH amazingly managed to scrape up a limited theatrical release, although distributor Dimension Films was obviously so ashamed of the movie that print ads carried the phony company name of "Legacy Releasing" (onscreen, Dimension is credited). One can hardly blame them for disowning the film, since it makes no sense at all and offers no entertainment value whatsoever.

For starters, the Boston-set film was shot in Slovakia, so almost everyone speaks with thick European accents and all the police cars blatantly read "Policia." For most of its brief (albeit not brief enough) running time, the movie follows its lead characters through dark, dank corridors, with the only illumination coming from flashlights that keep breaking. Glimpses of the killer consist of quick cuts to bloodshot eyes and rotting teeth. The dialogue (mainly profanity-laced screaming) is unintelligible due to the hyped-up sound mix which emphasises heavy breathing, ominous music, and the sounds of dripping water. The relentlessly prowling Steadicam and the grimy, grungy widescreen visuals only serve to emphasize that nothing is really going on, and the big showdown at the end is so poorly staged and underlit that it's impossible to tell what's happening.

As for the cast, Lambert looks like he's recovering from a bad hangover and seems so embarrassed to be in the movie at all that he mumbles his lines and is constantly swathed in darkness. Henstridge just sweats and grunts a lot and hides the natural charms she displayed in SPECIES by stubbornly remaining in uniform at all times. *(Graphic violence, extreme profanity.)* — M.S.

d, Albert Pyun; p, Tom Karnowski, Gary Schmoeller; exec p, Barr B. Potter, Paul Rosenblum; co-p, Mark Scoon; w, Albert Pyun; ph, George Mooradian; ed, Ken Morrisey; m, Tony Riparetti; art d, Nenad Pecur; set d, Laci Markic; sound, Lee Howell; fx, John McLeod, Marijan Karogian; cos, Shelly Boies; makeup, Maureen Wirgler; stunts, Kenny Bates

Horror/Thriller/Fantasy **(PR: O MPAA: R)**

ADVENTURES OF PINOCCHIO, THE ★★★

(U.K./Germany/France) 96m Savoy Pictures; Kushner-Locke Productions; Pangaea Holdings; Twin Continental Films; Allied Pinocchio Productions; Davis Films; Deiter Geissler Filmproduktion GmbH; Alta Vista Film GmbH; bibo film productions GmbH; Etamp Film Praha A.S.; A.B. Barandov A.S. ~ New Line c

Martin Landau *(Geppetto)*; Jonathan Taylor Thomas *(Pinocchio)*; Genevieve Bujold *(Leona)*; Udo Kier *(Lorenzini)*; Bebe Neuwirth *(Felinet)*; Rob Schneider *(Volpe)*; Corey Carrier *(Lampwick)*; Marcello Magni *(Baker)*; Dawn French *(Baker's Wife)*; Richard Claxton *(Saleo)*; Griff Rhys Jones *(Tino)*; John Sessions *(Schoolmaster)*; Jean-Claude Drouot *(Magistrate)*; Jean-Claude Dreyfus *(Foreman)*; Teco Celio *(Henchman)*; Wilfred Benaiche *(Henchman)*; Erik Averlont *(Zito)*; David Doyle *(Pepe the Cricket)*; Vladimir Koval *(Luigi)*; Daniela Tolkein *(Lampwick's Mother)*; Anita Zagaria *(Luigi's Wife)*; Lilian Malkina *(Woman in Laundry)*; Vaclav Vydra *(Infantino's Mother)*; Petr Bednar *(Growling Father)*; Stefan Weclawek *(Infantino)*; Zdenek Podhursky *(Cabineer)*; Jiri Kvasnicka *(Cabineer)*; Gorden Lovitt *(Big One Attendant)*; Jan Slovak *(Butler)*; Dean Cook *(Boy With Red Ball)*; Joe Swash *(Fighting Boy)*; Oliver Barron; Jake Court; Luke DeLeon; Kevin Dorsey; Thomas Orange; Sean Woodward *(Boys)*; Jiri Patocka *(Man With Donkey)*; Lida Vlaskova *(Woman In Bakery)*; Paavel Koci *(Puppeteer)*

Remaking Disney's 1940 animated classic PINOCCHIO was a formidable task, and this update, a combination of live action and animation, suffers in comparison to the original. THE ADVENTURES OF PINOCCHIO is an entertaining family film, bolstered by a wonderful performance by Martin Landau and incredible animatronic effects by Jim Henson's Creature Shop. But it just doesn't possess the magic or charm of the original.

Geppetto (Landau), a lonely old puppet maker, carves a little wooden boy out of an enchanted log he finds in the forest. The puppet, named Pinocchio for his source wood (pine) and his eyes (*occhio* is Italian for eye), is extraordinarily lifelike. He can walk without strings, talk, and has a talent for mimicry. But he isn't a real boy, which is what he wants more than anything in the world.

His curious nature soon gets Pinocchio into trouble. He demolishes a pastry shop, and Geppetto cannot afford to pay for the damages. Evil showman Lorenzini pays the fine and claims Pinocchio in exchange.

Pinocchio escapes from Lorenzini's puppet show and runs off with some schoolboys. The runaway boys are bound for Terra Magica, an amusement park where magical waters turn naughty boys into donkeys, to be sold at a premium by Lorenzini, the mastermind behind Terra Magica. Pinocchio manages to save himself and his friends, while Lorenzini is transformed into a sea monster by the same waters that turned the boys into donkeys.

Pinocchio returns home to learn that Geppetto has set out to sea to find him. Pinocchio follows and is swallowed by the sea monster, who has already gulped down Geppetto. Father and puppet are reunited in the monster's belly, and Pinocchio uses his wiles and his nose to get them out of trouble. Once back on land, Pinocchio gets his wish and turns into a real boy.

THE ADVENTURES OF PINOCCHIO, like the Disney cartoon, is based on the 1883 novel by Italian novelist Carlo Collodi. Collodi, a political journalist who began writing for children when he was past 50, created Pinocchio in the mold of Punchinello (better known as "Punch" of Punch and Judy), the Commedia del Arte's resident anarchist. The beloved children's tale which has enchanted generations of American children is a diluted version which lacks the social and political commentary of Collodi's novel.

Though the makers of THE ADVENTURES OF PINOCCHIO strove for a more honest adaptation of Collodi's work, the differences between Pinocchio's new adventures and the Disney classic aren't that glaring. Pinocchio is still an innocent at heart, and the moral of the story is the same: respect your elders and always tell the truth. The most notable difference, other than the live action format, is the name of Pinocchio's wisecracking companion, the cricket Pepe. Jiminy Cricket, something is amiss!

One of the film's biggest draws commercially was its young star, teen heartthrob Jonathan Taylor Thomas (of TV's "Home Improvement"), who provides Pinocchio's voice, and briefly appears in the flesh as Pinocchio turns into a real boy. Thomas's voice-over work rates high marks; he endows Pinocchio with the right mix of wonder and mischief. But he bears little physical resemblance to his wooden alter ego, making Pinocchio's transformation from puppet to real boy at the film's end almost a disappointment. Landau is perfectly cast as Geppetto. Genevieve Bujold is sublime as his love interest. Udo Kier and Bebe Neuwirth are choice villains, while Rob Schneider's buffoonery is neither funny nor frightening.

The film's real star is the animatronic Pinocchio created by Jim Henson's Creature Shop. Capable of a wide range of lifelike facial expressions (not to mention the nose which grows and grows), the puppet is an amazing achievement which on its own makes this film worth watching.— B.R.

d, Steve Barron; p, Raju Patel, Jeffrey Sneller; exec p, Sharad Patel, Peter Locke, Donald Kushner; assoc p, Jan Bilek; co-p, Michael MacDonald, Tim Hampton, Edward Simons, Samuel Hadida, Deiter Geissler; w, Sherry Mills, Steve Barron, Tom Benedek, Barry Berman (based on the novel by Carlo Collodi); ph, Juan Ruiz Anchia; ed, Sean Barton; m, Rachel Portman; prod d, Allan Cameron; art d, Ian Reade-Hill, Anthony Reading, Jiri Matolin; sound, Jean-Philippe Le Roux (recordist); fx, Angus Bickerton, Garth Inns, Jim Henson's Creature Shop; casting, Annette Benson, Irene Lamb; cos, Maurizio Millenotti; makeup, Walter Cossu; stunts, George Branche, Ladislav Lahoda

Children's/Fantasy **(PR: A MPAA: G)**

AFFAIR, THE ★★½

(U.K./U.S.) 105m BBC; HBO Showcase ~ Orion Home Video/HBO Home Video c

Courtney B. Vance *(Travis Holloway)*; Kerry Fox *(Maggie)*; Leland Gantt *(Barrett Owens)*; Beatie Edney *(Esther)*; Ciaran Hinds *(Edward Leyland)*; Rory Jennings *(David Leyland)*; Ned Beatty *(Col. Banning)*; Bill Nunn *(Sgt. Rivers)*; Fraser James *(Sonny)*; Adrian Lester *(Ray)*; Nicholas Selby *(Mr. Leyland)*;

Anna Cropper *(Mrs. Leyland)*; Rolf Saxon *(Capt. Marks)*; Todd Boyce *(Capt. Carlton)*; Michael J. Shannon *(Capt. Ford)*; Martin McDougall *(Dr. Hastings)*; Manning Redwood *(Military Judge)*

A wartime affair between an African-American soldier and a married Englishwoman has dire consequences in this drama inspired by true events. THE AFFAIR was originally broadcast on HBO, and later released to home video.

In 1944, the US military was still racially segregated. PFC Travis Holloway (Courtney B. Vance) is a soldier in an all-black unit that has been shipped to England to train in preparation for the invasion of Normandy. He befriends and then becomes romantically involved with Maggie Leyland (Kerry Fox). She's married; her husband, Edward (Ciaran Hinds), is an officer in the British Navy, but the union has been troubled since he had an affair. Travis and Maggie are careful to be very discreet, but his best friend Barrett (Leland Gantt) is discovered when he has a sexual fling with Esther (Beatie Edney), Maggie's friend and the town trollop, and Barrett is brutally beaten by white soldiers for it.

Edward comes home on leave and catches his wife with Travis, who is arrested and charged with rape. Under duress, Maggie testifies against her lover, believing he will only receive light punishment. The sentence is death by hanging, and when she learns of this, Maggie recants to Travis' commanding officer, Colonel Banning (Ned Beatty). D-Day will be soon, and Banning doesn't like Negroes anyway—especially not those with the temerity to sully white women—so he does nothing. Maggie is later informed by post of "her attacker's" execution.

In an epilogue scene set 50 years hence, Maggie meets with Barrett and professes that her love for Travis never died or diminished, just as he declared his devotion to her at the gallows. This is a testament to the depth of their romance, but the passion they felt is never effectively conveyed. Vance and Fox play the lovers as noble works of marble, never as lustful beings of flesh. Perhaps a burnished example of British restraint, or American trepidation at depicting inter-racial sexual relations, the affair is nonetheless a very tepid one and comes off as mostly a distraction from the movie's greater themes.

What's most interesting about THE AFFAIR is its frank portrayal of the racist abuse suffered by the black troops, and the irony of their going to Europe to fight for democracy when they are denied liberty in the United States. (This issue was also handled in another 1996 made-for-HBO feature, THE TUSKEGEE AIRMEN.) Holloway says he's willing and eager to fight because he optimistically believes once blacks prove themselves in battle, they will have to be accepted as "real" Americans. He, of course, underestimated the depth of white hatred and hypocrisy (and paid the price for it), as African-Americans would have to fight dearly at home for their rights. Race continues to be the most divisive issue facing American society, and a movie like THE AFFAIR is a document both of how far we've come and how much further we have to go. *(Profanity, violence, sexual situations.)* — P.R.

d, Paul Seed; p, David M. Thompson, John Smithson; exec p, Harry Belafonte; w, Pablo Fenjves, Bryan Goluboff; ph, Ivan Strasburg; ed, John Stothart; m, Christopher Gunning; prod d, Hugo Luczyc-Wyhowski; casting, Mary Colquhoun, Gail Stevens; cos, Frances Tempest; makeup, Jan Sewell

War/Romance/Drama **(PR: C MPAA: R)**

ALASKA ★★½

(U.S.) 104m Agamemnon Films; Castle Rock Entertainment ~ Columbia c

Thora Birch *(Jessie Barnes)*; Vincent Kartheiser *(Sean Barnes)*; Dirk Benedict *(Jake Barnes)*; Charlton Heston *(Perry)*; Duncan Fraser *(Koontz)*; Gordon Tootoosis *(Ben)*; Ben Cardinal *(Charlie)*; Ryan Kent *(Chip)*; Don S. Davis *(Sergeant Grazer)*; Dolly Madsen *(Mrs. Ben)*; Stephen E. Miller *(Trooper Harvey)*; Byron Chief Moon *(Chip's Father)*; Kristin Lehman *(Florence)*; Adrien Dorval *(Burly Fisherman)*

Though spectacularly photographed, ALASKA is a trite and formulaic children's adventure about two kids who search for their father, and battle poachers in the process, when his plane crashes in the Alaskan wilderness.

Following the death of his wife, Chicago airplane pilot Jake Barnes (Dirk Benedict) moves to Alaska with his 13-year-old daughter Jessie (Thora Birch), and his 15-year-old son Sean (Vincent Kartheiser). The family settles in the remote seaside village of Quincy, where Jake gets a job as a pilot for an air delivery service.

On a flight carrying emergency medical supplies into the mountains, Jake's plane crashes, and he's badly injured. The police search for him but can't find him, so Sean and Jessie set out to rescue him themselves, climbing mountains and glaciers, running rapids, and trekking across miles of uncharted land.

Meanwhile, a ruthless poacher named Perry (Charlton Heston), and his assistant Koontz (Duncan Fraser), have killed a mother polar bear and captured its cub, intending to sell the baby animal on the black market. During their trip, Sean and Jessie discover the poachers' camp and set the cub free. They christen the little bear "Cubby," and it joins them on their journey.

A friend of Jake's named Charlie (Ben Cardinal) sets off in a helicopter to look for the children and encounters the poachers, who intentionally point him in the wrong direction. Sean and Jessie fall out of their kayak and into a waterfall, and are rescued by a Native American, Ben (Gordon Tootoosis) and his son Chip (Ryan Kent).

Catching up to the children, the poachers shoot Cubby with a tranquilizer dart and take it on their helicopter. But the animal unexpectedly fights back, causing Perry to hit Koontz with a dart inadvertently. Koontz's rifle goes off and destroys their helicopter, allowing Cubby to escape.

Jessie and Sean finally find their father's plane, dangling on the edge of a mountain. As Sean tries to pull Jake out of the wreckage, his rope begins to slip, but Cubby arrives and pulls the rope up the mountain with his teeth. Charlie flies over the mountain in his helicopter and picks them all up, and they set Cubby free to live among the other polar bears.

ALASKA is an unsurprising, old-fashioned family film notable only for the natural beauty of its locations, and its outstanding cinematography of the majestic wilderness. Shot on location in Alaska and British Columbia, the film offers breathtaking panoramic views of the picturesque landscape as Sean and Jessie climb snowy mountains and kayak through raging rivers, with the camera often circling over them in dazzling, dizzying aerial shots.

The story contains all the expected elements of the children's adventure genre: cute and cuddly animals, caricatured villains, noble Native Americans who possess mystical wisdom and offer spiritual guidance, city kids who learn to appreciate nature and develop maturity through adversity, and a banal moral about "never quitting." Heston turns in an amusingly tongue-in-cheek performance as the rifle-toting poacher. He parodies his NRA-poster boy image by playing the character as a cold-blooded, vicious slaughterer of endangered animals (although he does make a subtle distinction by pointing out to his cohort that what they're doing "isn't hunting; it's business"). In another in-joke, the poachers deceive Charlie by telling him they're taking pictures for the Sierra Club's new calendar.

Fraser C. Heston (Charlton's son) directs the action competently, but the film would have benefited greatly if it had been cut by at least 20 minutes. All in all, ALASKA is not the worst of its genre, but it's far from the best, although the photography alone makes it worth seeing. *(Violence.)* — M.S.

d, Fraser C. Heston; p, Carol Fuchs, Andy Burg; assoc p, John Stronach; co-p, Gordon Mark; w, Andy Burg, Scott Myers; ph, Tony Westman; ed, Rob Kobrin; m, Reg Powell; prod d, Douglas Higgins; art d, Rex Raglan; set d, Tedd Kuchera; sound, Eric J. Batut (mixer); fx, Dean Lockwood; casting, Mary Gail Artz, Barbara Cohen; cos, Monique Prudhomme; makeup, Stan Edmonds; stunts, Betty Thomas

Adventure/Children's (PR: A MPAA: PG)

ALEX ★★½

(New Zealand/Australia) 92m Australian Film Finance Corp.; New Zealand Film Commision; New Zealand On Air; Isambard Productions Ltd. ~ Orion Home Video c

Lauren Jackson *(Alex Archer)*; Chris Haywood *(Mr. Jack)*; Josh Picker *(Andy Richmond)*; Catherine Godbold *(Maggie Benton)*; Elizabeth Hawthorne *(Mrs. Benton)*; Bruce Phillips *(Mr. Archer)*; May Lloyd *(Mrs. Archer)*; Patrick Smith *(Mr. Benton)*; Grant Tilly *(Cyril Upjohn)*; Greg Johnson *(Enderby)*; Alison Bruce *(Female Journalist)*

ALEX is an old-fashioned family film about a teenage girl who overcomes fierce competition and personal tragedy while struggling to make the 1960 New Zealand Olympic swimming team.

Expert swimmer Alex Archer (Lauren Jackson) is a six-foot-tall 15-year-old girl from Auckland who is training for the 1960 Olympics. After being beaten in a race by newcomer Maggie Benton (Catherine Godbold), Alex realizes that she'll have to work even harder to make the team. This may be harder than Alex knows, since Maggie's scheming mother is busy currying favor with the head of the swimming federation. In the meantime, Alex breaks her leg while playing hockey and must sit out for two painful months recovering, while Maggie quickly become the new contender. Alex continues to train after recovering, but loses to Maggie again in her first race. Soon afterward, Alex is shattered upon learning that her boyfriend Andy (Josh Picker) has been killed in a car accident. She responds by increasing her determination and rededicates herself to making the team for Andy.

Maggie and Alex go to the National Swimming Championships, which will determine which of the two is chosen for the Olympics. The night before the big race, Alex is so nervous she goes for a swim to relax. The next day, she's told by the judges that she's disqualified after someone reported that she had a late-night tryst with the pool manager. Alex denies the allegation and accuses Maggie's mother of spreading malicious lies. The qualifying committee votes to allow Alex to participate, but she has already run away in shame. Just as the race is about to begin without her, Alex shows up. After two false starts by Alex, Maggie jumps out to an early lead, but Alex makes up ground at the first turn and eventually wins the race.

ALEX is the kind of clean-cut, innocuous, "uplifting" tale of triumphing over adversity that usually shows up stateside as a TV-movie or "Afterschool Special." However, this 1993 production (released to US video in 1996) comes from a joint New Zealand-Australian venture and makes for adequate diversion for its intended audience of prepubescent girls. Overall, ALEX has a sincere, unpretentious quality, and Lauren Jackson gives an appealing performance as the athletic lead, convincingly portraying Alex's struggles as a gawky, overgrown girl grappling with her emerging femininity. Visually, the late '50s small-town atmosphere is nicely captured as are some of New Zealand's lovely beaches. — M.S.

d, Megan Simpson; p, Tom Parkinson, Phil Gerlach; assoc p, Alan Withrington; w, Ken Catran (based on the novel by Tessa Duder); ph, Donald Duncan; ed, Tony Kavanagh; m, Todd Hunter; prod d, Kim Sinclair; art d, Jill Cormack; sound, David Madigan; casting, Liz Mullane, Sheridan Jobbins, Heather Ogilvie; cos, Sara Beale; makeup, Jane Petersen, Fran Holley

Sports/Drama (PR: AA MPAA: NR)

ALL DOGS GO TO HEAVEN 2 ★★

(U.S./U.K.) 84m Metro-Goldwyn-Mayer Animation ~ MGM/UA c

VOICES OF: Charlie Sheen *(Charlie Barkin)*; Sheena Easton *(Sasha La Fleur)*; Ernest Borgnine *(Carface)*; Dom Deluise *(Itchy Itchiford)*; George Hearn *(Red)*; Bebe Neuwirth *(Anabelle)*; Adam Wylie *(David)*; Wallace Shawn *(Labradour MC)*; Hamilton Camp *(Chihuahua)*; Pat Corley *(Officer McDowell)*; Marabina Jaimes *(Officer Reyes)*; Tony Jay *(Reginald)*; Jim Cummings *(Jingles)*; Bobby DiCicco *(Thom)*; Annette Helde *(Claire)*; Kevin Michael Richardson *(St. Bernard/Officer Andrews)*; Steve Mackall *(Short Customs Dog)*; Dan Castellaneta *(Tall Customs Dog/Angel Dog #1)*; Maurice La Marche *(Lost and Found Officer)*

ALL DOGS GO TO HEAVEN 2 continues the adventures of Charlie Barkin, Itchy Itchiford, and the other canine characters from Don Bluth's popular 1989 animated feature, ALL DOGS GO TO HEAVEN. But even with lots of cinematic bells and whistles (i.e., music, comedy, drama, and action-adventure animation) this heavenly sequel unfortunately stays far too "down to Earth."

In the first HEAVEN, Charlie, a mischievous mongrel, earned his wings as a dog-angel by helping an orphan girl. In the sequel, Charlie (spoken by Charlie Sheen and sung by Jesse Corti) grows restless in Dog Heaven and seeks to return to Earth with his best friend, the recently deceased Itchy (the voice of Dom DeLuise). As luck would have it, Charlie and Itchy receive an assignment to retrieve Gabriel's Trumpet, which has fallen out of Heaven and landed in San Francisco. However, also on the trail of the precious instrument is Carface (the voice of Ernest Borgnine), a dog thief and Charlie's old nemesis.

Once Charlie and Itchy arrive in the City by the Bay, they are joined in their quest by a beautiful Irish setter named Sasha (the voice of Sheena Easton) and a young runaway boy, David (the voice of Adam Wylie). The group encounters many problems while tracking down the trumpet, most notably a run-in with a vicious cat named Red (the voice of George Hearn), who is plotting to steal the trumpet (with Carface's assistance) and trap all the Bay City dogs on Alcatraz. In the end, Charlie foils Red's scheme, convinces runaway David to return home, and leaves Earth—and Sasha—for good, restoring the trumpet to its rightful owner in Heaven.

Taking their cues from the first HEAVEN, co-directors Paul Sabella and Larry Leker make only slight alterations to the basic story structure—a storyline which, coincidentally, resembles the sequel to HOMEWARD BOUND, a live-action dog movie also set in San Francisco. Perhaps the biggest change between HEAVEN 1 and HEAVEN 2 are the voices of the cartoon canines; instead of Burt Reynolds, Loni Anderson, and Melba Moore, we hear Sheen, Easton, and Borgnine. (Only DeLuise returns as Itchy.) But it hardly matters, given that the big Broadway-style songs are totally forgettable, even when belted out by

Easton, Hearn, and Bebe Neuwirth (as a dog-vamp). Equally disappointing is the lack of imagination in the drawings. Moreover, the one bright spot in the animation, the transformation of the soothsayer into the devilish Red, will probably only serve to frighten children.

In a preemptive marketing strike, Disney re-released its 1988 animated dog musical, OLIVER AND COMPANY, at the same time MGM/UA launched ALL DOGS GO TO HEAVEN 2. However, Disney really had nothing to worry about—especially since neither dog movie comes close to being anything like a LION KING or a LITTLE MERMAID. — E.M.

d, Paul Sabella, Larry Leker; p, Paul Sabella, Jonathan Dern, Kelly Ward, Mark Young; w, Arne Olsen, Kelly Ward, Mark Young (from a story by Kelly Ward and Mark Young); ed, Michael Bradley, Thomas V. Moss, Tony Garber; m, Mark Watters; art d, Deane Taylor; anim, Todd Waterman, David Feiss; sound, Robert Deschaine (mixer), Dana Johnson-Porter (recordist); casting, Maria Estrada

Animated/Children's/Musical/Comedy (PR: A MPAA: G)

AMANDA AND THE ALIEN ★

(U.S.) 94m Retrofit Productions ~ Republic Pictures Home Entertainment c

Nicole Eggert *(Amanda)*; John Diehl *(Colonel Rosencrans)*; Michael Dorn *(Vint)*; Stacy Keach *(Emmitt Mallory)*; David Millbern *(LeBeau)*; Dan O'Connor *(Nick)*; Raymond Turner *(Mac)*; Alex Meneses *(Connie)*; J. Marvin Campbell *(Guard)*; Marcia Shapiro *(Shopper)*; Carol Ann Plante *(Jessica)*; Rene Weisser *(Shanda)*; Jessica Hahn *(TV Host)*; Michael Bendetti *(Charlie Nobles)*; Edwina Moore *(News Anchor)*; Brett Golov *(Slacker)*; Richard Speight Jr. *(Jo Jo)*; Johnny Caruso *(Beatnik Bob)*; Chadd Nyerges *(Dave)*; Allen Cutler *(Beret)*; Ryan Holihan *(Bellman)*; Ritch Brinkley *(Bubba)*; Cindy Morgan *(Holly)*; Liz Johnson *(Thelma)*

This exceedingly lightweight farcical romance is lit like an army training film and acted as if Shannen Doherty were the movie's dialogue coach. Pushing for laughs with a script that doesn't provide any, the flailing actors mug their way from here to eternity.

Unlike her tredy contemporaries, non-conformist Amanda (Nichole Eggert) prefers hanging out in her favorite coffee house to shopping mall spending sprees or rave parties. She feels she's as much of a misfit as an extraterrestrial visiting Earth. Meanwhile, FBI hotshot Emmitt Mallory (Stacy Keach) and junior officers Vint (Michael Dorn) and LeBeau (David Millbern) are trying to keep a pair of actual space aliens under wraps. After assuming the shape of government employee Connie (Alex Meneses), one alien escapes Mallory's custody and tries to pass as human at the coffee house Amanda frequents. Due to Connie's unusual behavior, Amanda realizes that she is actually an alien invader. Unafraid, Amanda encourages the clueless outer space creature to inhabit the body of her philandering boyfriend Charlie (Michael Bendetti). (Unfortunately, the space-creature's human hosts get obliterated each time the restless alien invades another earthling's body). Once the alien inhabits Charlie, Amanda falls passionately in love with this newly sensitized version of her boyfriend, and vows to drive the alien-Charlie to his contact point at the Hollywood sign in LA.

Tracked to a Bakersfield motel by Mallory's indomitable agents, Amanda dupes the Feds into believing she's the latest alien-inhabited earthling, thus enabling the alien to leave Charlie and take over agent Vint. A lift from a sympathetic trucker named Bubba (Ritch Brinkley) puts Amanda and Alien-Vint nearer his rendezvous point, but dogged FBI pursuit forces the alien to take control of Mallory's body. Aided once more by Bubba, Amanda must bid farewell to her alien amour who's beamed aboard a spaceship. Made confident by her close encounter, Amanda remains on Earth with a renewed interest in life and in her art career.

Taking those tabloid "I Slept With a Spaceman" stories to a level of comical incongruity, AMANDA AND THE ALIEN tries hard to lampoon the extra-terrestrial sighting craze. Apparently absent when God was passing out filmmaking finesse, this movie's perpetrators know little about manufacturing gossamer romance and absolutely nothing about building comedy sequences. A lampoonish souffle can't rise to the occasion when its ingredients include harsh lighting, grating soft-rock music, and bungled slapstick. Although principals Eggert and Bendetti exhibit some chemistry, the other thespians overdo their awareness of what's supposed to be amusing. Viewing this film is like watching Red Skelton or Benny Hill laughing at their own jokes—when they're not funny. Replete with masturbation gags, lunkhead FBI stereotypes, and cheesy creature special effects, AMANDA AND THE ALIEN offers viewers little solace, but does provide reformed PTL sinner Jessica Hahn with a cameo as a TV talk show hostess. *(Extreme profanity, extensive nudity, violence, sexual situations.)* — R.P.

d, Jon Kroll; p, Larry Estes; exec p, Miles Copeland III, Paul Colichman; assoc p, Cindy Morgan; co-p, Jonas Thaler; w, Jon Kroll; ph, Gary Tieche; ed, Brian Berdan; m, Jane Wiedlin, Michael Cozzi; prod d, M. Nord Haggerty; art d, Charley Cabrera; set d, Dawn Ferry; sound, D. J. Ritchie (mixer); fx, Gary Tunnicliffe; casting, Donald Paul Pemrick; cos, Wendy Range; makeup, Bernadette Harper; stunts, Jon Epstein

Science Fiction/Romance/Comedy (PR: C MPAA: R)

AMERICAN BUFFALO ★★★

(U.S.) 88m Capitol Films; Punch Productions; Prairie Oyster Productions; Samuel Goldwyn Company ~ Samuel Goldwyn Company c

Dustin Hoffman *(Teach)*; Dennis Franz *(Don)*; Sean Nelson *(Bobby)*

More than two decades after this three-character drama first hit the stage, AMERICAN BUFFALO comes to the screen, proving writer David Mamet a master at capturing the lowlife criminal mind at its seediest.

Junk shop owner Donny (Dennis Franz) has taken the teenaged Bobby (Sean Nelson) under his wing. When the always-scheming Teach (Dustin Hoffman) overhears the two discussing a heist, he wants in. Feeling ripped off by a customer who recently bought a buffalo-head nickel from him for $90, Donny now wants to break into the man's home and steal his entire coin collection. Teach convinces Donny that he'd be a better man to assist in the heist, since Bobby is too young to help. Long into the evening, the two discuss the particulars of the burglary—but they hit a road block when Donny wants another thief, Fletch, to come along. Meanwhile, the ousted Bobby continues to hit up Donny for cash, at one point even bringing in his own buffalo nickel to try to sell.

The next day, Bobby tells Donny and Teach that Fletch is in the hospital with a broken jaw. Suspicion rises and tempers flare among the conspirators, and Teach hits Bobby in the head with a telephone, thinking Bobby is covering something up. Bleeding from the ear, Bobby admits that he lied about knowing the coin collector's whereabouts; a phone call proves that Fletch is indeed in the hospital, exactly as Bobby explained. Their plans ruined, Teach throws a tantrum in the shop, overturning shelves. Finally, with their high hopes behind them, they prepare to take Bobby to the hospital.

Though its once-shocking barrage of expletives now seems tame and Michael Corrente's choppy direction often undercuts the verbal choreography, Mamet's portrait of two-bit thieves retains its potency. Tackling the role of Teach, first played by Robert Duvall in the 1970s Broadway production and later by Al Pacino in the 1980s off-Broadway revival, Hoffman proves to be a decidedly less charismatic hustler. Age plays a big part in this: both Pacino and Duvall took the role when they were in their 40s. At nearly 60, Hoffman seems more over-the-hill and desperate than the earlier, dangerously explosive incarnations. In fact, with his long greasy hair and weaselly demeanor, Hoffman's Teach seems like Ratso Rizzo's healthier older brother, especially when running off at the mouth with Mamet's jackhammer dialogue. Franz underplays his role effectively, while Sean Nelson (in his follow-up to FRESH) holds his own against Hoffman's splashier lead. The nicely-dressed, claustrophobic set provides plenty of props to heave about when the moment arises, and Pawtucket, Rhode Island lends the film a suitably depressed urban exterior. Though far from a definitive adaptation, this still gives us Mamet at his grittiest. Little is actually accomplished by these dead end characters, and that's the point of the drama—this is a world where talking in circles only hides the fact that life has already spiraled out of control. *(Extreme profanity, violence.)* — S.P.

d, Michael Corrente; p, Gregory Mosher; exec p, John Sloss; co-p, Sarah Green; w, David Mamet (based on his play); ph, Richard Crudo; ed, Kate Sanford; m, Thomas Newman; prod d, Daniel Talpers; set d, Jessica Lanier; sound, Ronald Judkins, Robert Jackson; casting, Billy Hopkins, Suzanne Smith, Kerry Barden; cos, Deborah Newhall; makeup, Brenda McNally

Drama/Crime **(PR: C MPAA: R)**

AMERICAN STRAYS ★★½

(U.S.) 93m Canned Pictures ~ Unapix Films c

Jennifer Tilly *(Patty Mae)*; Eric Roberts *(Martin)*; John Savage *(Dwayne)*; Luke Perry *(Johnny)*; Carol Kane *(Helen)*; Joe Viterelli *(Gene)*; James Russo *(Harv)*; Vonte Sweet *(Mondo)*; Sam Jones *(Exterminator)*; Brion James *(Otis)*; Toni Kalem *(Alice)*; Melora Walters *(Cindy)*; Scott Plank *(Sonny)*; Anthony Lee *(Omar)*; Stephanie Cushna *(Johnny's Girlfriend)*; Stace Williamson *(Johnny's Brother)*; Luana Anders *(Martha)*; Robert Fields *(Harry)*; Jack Kehler *(Walker)*; Charles Bailey-Gates *(Bob)*; Tom Eliot *(Timmy)*; Will Rothhaar *(Jordan)*; Jessica Perelman *(Daphne)*; Mike Horse *(Lead Cop)*; Patrick Warburton *(Cop #1)*; Mike Kaliski *(Cop #2)*; Leland Crooke *(Cop #3)*

AMERICAN STRAYS might have been considered a masterpiece had it preceded Quentin Tarantino's tales of bleak Americana. Unfortunately, the more it tries to be off-beat and original, the more it seems strained and imitative.

AMERICAN STRAYS looks at a number of twisted characters in the Southwest; most of them are on the road, and from frequent road signs we can see that they are in the vicinity of Red's Desert Oasis, a diner run by chipper Helen (Carol Kane). Dwayne (John Savage) is a vacuum cleaner salesman who murders anyone who will listen to his pitch. Martin (Eric Roberts), stressed out from having lost his job, is nearing a nervous breakdown as he drives his wife and two young children on a family vacation. A pair of Mafiosi (Joe Viterelli, James Russo) are on their way out of Las Vegas with a hostage in their trunk. A pair of younger gangsters, the drug-dealing kind (Vonte Sweet, Anthony Lee), decry the sad state of America as they drive through the desert. Sonny (Scott Plank) and Cindy (Melora Walters) are passionate young lovers with nowhere in particular to go. And Johnny (Luke Perry) has been abused by life so thoroughly and for so long that he decides to put an end to his life—but the sadistic hit man he hires (Sam Jones) enjoys his job so much he figures he'll make it last.

Dwayne nearly gives up his calling when he falls for Patty Mae (Jennifer Tilly). When he tells her that he was fired by the vacuum cleaner company years ago and that he is a serial killer, she reveals that she is also a killer, who specializes in salesmen; instead of killing each other, they join forces. Johnny is beaten and tortured by the hit man and his own brother (Stace Williamson), but when they decide to rape a girl they've picked up, Johnny finds a reason to live: he kills them and makes the girl his own. All of the other characters intersect at the diner, including Martin, who, with no money, is trying to shoplift food for his family. When police officers enter the diner, tensions explode into a gunfight and everyone is killed—except Martin and his family, who drive off uneasily.

Like PULP FICTION (1994) and RESERVOIR DOGS (1992), AMERICAN STRAYS features quirky characters in a harsh, hostile universe. Writer-director Michael Covert's story of how these unhappy oddballs meet at a southwestern diner is less intricately plotted than Tarantino's temporally-altered narratives, but delivers the same sort of violence-as-catharsis climax. When not lifting from Tarantino, Covert copies from David Lynch (the lovers on the run are right out of WILD AT HEART).

The best parts of AMERICAN STRAYS, then, come from the little touches by the all-star cast. Roberts shows off a comic side as the harried patriarch of a "typical" nuclear family on vacation. Savage and Tilly perform a tension-filled tango as the two sociopaths who have met each other's match; Viterelli and Russo bicker amusingly as gangster buddies; and Perry as a suicidal masochist effectively breaks out of his "Beverly Hills 90210" mold. Unfortunately, the scenes with Sweet and Lee as the edgy drug-dealers are ruined by the presence of a microphone that slips into frame.

AMERICAN STRAYS offers nothing new as dark satires of the American Dream go, but the efforts of the ensemble provide bits and pieces worth savoring. *(Graphic violence, nudity, sexual situations, adult situations, substance abuse, extreme profanity.)* — E.M.

d, Michael Covert; p, Rod Dean, Kirk Hassig, Douglas Textor; exec p, Frank Agrama; assoc p, Trudi Callon; w, Michael Covert; ph, Sean Mutarevic; ed, Rod Dean; m, John Graham; prod d, Paul Holt; art d, Denise Hudson; set d, Mary Gullickson; sound, Ben Patrick (mixer), Ron Long (mixer), Daryl Linkow (mixer); casting, Sheila Jaffe, Georgianne Walken; cos, Tanya Gill, Agda Lavadenz; makeup, Lydia Milars, Marina Tarpin, Linda Samodral

Crime/Thriller **(PR: C MPAA: R)**

AMERICA'S DREAM ★★★½

(U.S.) 86m Carrie Productions; HBO ~ FoxVideo c

Danny Glover *(Silas)*; Tate Donovan *(David)*; Tina Lifford *(Sarah)*; Daniel Tucker Kamin *(Mr. Harper)*; Wesley Snipes *(George Du Vaul)*; Norman D. Golden II *(Aaron)*; Jasmine Guy *(Elna Du Vaul)*; Rae'ven A'lyia Kelly *(Lara)*; Timothy Carhart *(Professor Daniels)*; Vaness Bell Calloway *(Miss Williams)*; Kevin Jamal Woods *(Clyde)*; Ruth Beckford *(Mrs. McClaren)*; Yolanda King *(Mrs. Crawford)*; Lorraine Toussaint *(Philomena)*; Susanna Thompson *(Beth Ann)*; Carl Lumbley *(Cal)*; Bennet Guillory *(Willie)*; Summer Ross Jefferson *(Young Philomena #1)*; Winter Elaine Jefferson *(Young Philomena #2)*; Amanda Addison *(Young Beth Ann)*

Three African-American directors adapt short stories by prominent African-American writers (Richard Wright, John Henrik Clarke, Maya Angelou) in this trilogy made for HBO.

"Long Black Song": Alabama, 1938. Farmer Silas (Danny Glover) leaves his wife Sarah (Tina Lifford) and infant daughter alone while he takes his crops to town. Lonely and bored, Sarah entertains the sales pitches of a young white peddler, David (Tate Donovan), and makes love to him. When he learns what has happened, the outraged Silas wants to take out all of his frustrations at the world on David, but Sarah convinces him not to let his anger get the better of him.

"The Boy Who Painted Christ Black": Georgia, 1948. A talented young student at a "colored" school submits a painting of Christ as a black man for a state-wide contest on the theme of ethnic pride. This creates a conflict for his school's principal, George Du Vaul (Wesley Snipes). After much soul-searching, Du Vaul agrees to enter the painting in the contest, even though it will cost him a promotion by offending his superiors.

"The Reunion": Chicago, 1958. When jazz musician Philomena (Lorraine Toussaint) spots a familiar face in the audience of the club where she is playing, it brings back memories of her unhappy childhood as the daughter of a domestic servant in a white household.

Aside from being strong works of fiction in their own rights, the short stories that comprise AMERICA'S DREAM combine into a satisfying whole, providing a portrait of African-American life in flux as the country moves from a rural to a city-based economy. Unusual for this kind of omnibus film, the segments are presented in reverse order of quality, with the best one opening the program. Of the three, "Long Black Song" is the one segment that could stand on its own. "The Boy Who Painted Christ Black" makes a strong point but has rather a didactic conclusion. "The Reunion," despite an excellent performance by Toussaint, is repetitious and goes on too long. As the conclusion of this trilogy, however, it has far more effect than it would on its own.

Handsomely produced and well-acted by a first-rate cast, AMERICA'S DREAM is a sterling example of the kind of niche filmmaking that cable television is able to provide. *(Violence, nudity, sexual situations, profanity.)* — M.F.

d, Kevin Rodney Sullivan, Bill Duke, Paris Barclay; p, David Knoller; exec p, Danny Glover, Carolyn McDonald; assoc p, C. Cory M. McCrum-Abdo; co-p, Ron Stacker Thompson, Ashley Tyler; w, Ron Stacker Thompson, Ashley Tyler (based on Richard Wright's story "Long Black Song," John Henrik Clarke's story "The Boy Who Painted Christ Black," and Maya Angelou's story "The Reunion"); ph, Karl Hermann; ed, Angelo Corrao, Monty DeGraff, Michael Schultz; m, Patrice Rushen; prod d, Anthony Cowley; casting, Janet Hirshenson, Jane Jenkins; cos, Winnie D. Brown; makeup, Abiiba S. Howell

Drama **(PR: C MPAA: NR)**

ANGELA ★★★½

(U.S.) 103m Tree Farm Pictures; RJK Productions ~ Tree Farm Pictures c

Miranda Stuart Rhyne *(Angela)*; Charlotte Blythe *(Ellie)*; Anna Thomson *(Mae)*; John Ventimiglia *(Andrew)*; Ruth Maleczech *(Sleepwalker)*; Vincent Gallo *(Preacher)*; Garrett Bemer *(Tom)*; Sara Caitlin Hall *(Anne)*; Hynden Walch *(Darlene)*; Henry Stram *(Man at Fair)*; Rodger L. Phillips *(Frank)*; Io Tillet Wright *(Sam)*; Wil McKnight *(Greg)*; Carl Nick Reighn *(Fair Attendant)*; Peter Facinelli *(Devil)*; Jack O'Connell *(Man at Bar)*; Nurith Cohn *(Makeover Woman)*; Constance McCord *(The Virgin Mary)*; Roxana Stuart *(Saleslady)*

In ANGELA, the directorial debut of Rebecca Miller, a young girl resorts to mystical, religious behavior in a sad attempt to protect herself and her sister from their mother's mental illness. Miller, who both wrote and directed ANGELA, was awarded the best new filmmaker prize at the 1996 Sundance festival for this wonderful portrayal of the confusion and fears of childhood.

Angela (Miranda Stuart Rhyne) and her younger sister Ellie (Charlotte Blythe) are the daughters of aging ex-musicians. Living under the heavy shadow of the fading beauty and manic-depression of their mother Mae (played by Anna Thomson), the girls are left to their own devices, despite the efforts of their caring and beleaguered father, Andrew (John Ventimiglia). After a token visit to church with her family, Angela decides that the path to redemption lies in ritual. She fills her younger sister's head with tales of a fallen angel who lives in their basement and waits to claim one of them. In order to resist him, they surround themselves with dolls and stuffed animals and await "the good angel," being careful not to step outside their protective teddy-bear circle. Angela warns Ellie of being absorbed into "the big nothing," a place that holds both fear and fascination for Angela. Ellie is dragged along on a series of strange ritualistic adventures into the night, but—while heavily influenced by her older sister's imagination—she remains somewhat reluctant and always less devoted.

The young girls spend most of their time alone in their room, indulging their fantasy of the fallen angel or eavesdropping on their parents through a floor vent. Through this vent, they witness many things, including their mother grieving to their father that she no longer feels anything for her daughters. Too young to understand their mother's illness, the girls are terrified and hurt.

After Mae is taken to a mental institution, the film truly begins to follow the surrealistic logic of childhood imagination. The girls are left with a pregnant babysitter who gives birth while they are in her care. They escape and wander about, being led aimlessly by a white horse. They meet a boy who belongs to a fundamentalist religious group and will be baptized that weekend. Nightfall finds them at a terrifying carnival, where Angela is nearly molested by a man she believes to be "the good angel." That weekend, Angela insists upon being baptized in the river with the young boy, and her father reluctantly indulges her desire. Later, Angela awakens her sister Ellie in the middle of the night, insisting that she finally has the solution to their fractured familial existence. She drags Ellie through the darkness back to the river and insists that they dunk themselves until they are purified. Angela is overzealous in her efforts and is dragged away by the river. When she drowns, Ellie magically rises up into the air, exhibiting Angela's conviction that the sacrifice of one will liberate the others.

Anna Thomson gives an excellent performance as the vulnerable and weary mother, Mae, at one moment nearly catatonic with depression, the next exhilarated and overly hopeful, insisting on restarting her singing career, or moving again, or painting the children's room. Miranda Stuart Rhyne is wonderful as Angela, the disoriented child, holding herself and supernatural forces responsible for the outcome of the family. Though the film often indulges in a romantic, adolescent fascination with madness, it ambitiously presents the consciousness and point of view of childhood, linking it with such sad films as THE SPIRIT OF THE BEEHIVE (1973) and CRIA (1976). Visually, ANGELA is interesting and provocative, recreating the gothic atmosphere of childhood—complete with gnarled trees, moonlit nights, cobwebbed basements, and beckoning symbols. *(Nudity, adult situations.)* — R.C.

d, Rebecca Miller; p, Ron Kastner; w, Rebecca Miller; ph, Ellen Kuras; ed, Melody London; m, Michael Rohatyn; prod d, Daniel

Talpers; set d, Caroline Seckinger; sound, Stefan Springman (mixer); fx, Drew Jiritano; casting, Pam Reece, Cindy Tolan; cos, Todd Thomas; makeup, Valerie Gatchell, Kelly Gleason; stunts, Roy Farfel

Drama **(PR: C MPAA: NR)**

ANGELS AND INSECTS ★★★

(U.K./U.S.) 116m Playhouse International Pictures ~ Samuel Goldwyn Company c

Mark Rylance *(William Adamson)*; Patsy Kensit *(Eugenia Alabaster)*; Kristin Scott Thomas *(Matty Crompton)*; Jeremy Kemp *(Sir Harald Alabaster)*; Douglas Henshall *(Edgar Alabaster)*; Saskia Wickham *(Rowena Alabaster)*; Chris Larkin *(Robin Swinnerton)*; Annette Badland *(Lady Alabaster)*; Lindsay Thomas *(Lady Alabaster's Maid)*; Michelle Sylvester *(Margaret Alabaster)*; Clare Lovell *(Elaine Alabaster)*; Jenny Lovell *(Edith Alabaster)*; Anna Massey *(Miss Mead)*; Oona Haas *(Alice Alabaster)*; Angus Hodder *(Guy Alabaster)*; Margery Golder *(Nurse)*; Paul Ready *(Tom)*; Naomi Gudge *(Martha)*; John Jenkins *(Ralph Blackwood)*; John Veasey *(Arthur)*; Clare Redman *(Amy)*; Jack Turney *(Newborn Twin)*; Elizabeth Turney *(Newborn Twin)*; Nicky Turney *(Wet Nurse)*; Alice Maitland *(Six-month-old Twin)*; Hannah Maitland *(Six-month-old Twin)*; Vita Haas *(Robert Edgar (One Year Old))*; Pam Smitham *(Midwife)*; Brett Harris *(Stable Lad)*

Philip Haas has taken a novella by the distinguished A. S. Byatt and turned it into one of the most intelligent costume films ever made. Actress Kristen Scott Thomas provides the passionate heart and soul of the piece.

Naturalist Will Adamson (Mark Rylance), survivor of a shipwreck off the coast of South America, comes to stay at the country estate of the Alabaster family in England. He is to help Lord Alabaster catalogue his vast collection of scientific specimens, as well as tutor his three youngest daughters. There are two older daughters, as well: Rowena (Saskia Wickham), and the eldest, the beautiful Eugenia (Patsy Kensit), with whom Will falls in love. Eugenia is depressed over the recent death of her fiance, and her parents privately despair that Rowena will most likely marry before her. Will woos Eugenia, at one point unleashing a gorgeous swarm of butterflies for her delight. She accepts his marriage proposal and he joins the family, over the objections of her snobby brother Edgar (Douglas Henshall), who considers Adamson an unworthy outsider. The couple soon have children.

Will busies himself on the estate, observing the progress of various armies of ants. He is accompanied by Matty Crompton (Kristen Scott Thomas), a poor relation of the Alabasters with a scientific bent of her own, who encourages Will to write a popular study of ants. Will and Eugenia's marriage begins to sour as she sequesters herself behind a locked bedroom door and he, indeed, begins to feel like an outsider. One evening while playing anagrams, Matty tries to tip him off to what's going on when she switches the letters of the word "insect" to read "incest," but Will fails to grasp her meaning. He is suddenly and mysteriously instructed to go to Eugenia's room one afternoon and surprises his wife in bed with her brother Edgar. Horrified, he realizes that this has been going on for years, and was the cause of Eugenia's fiance's suicide; the children he thought his were probably fathered by Edgar. Will and Matty confront one another with the desires they've suppressed, and with the royalties from their ant book, they decide to go to the Amazon together to continue their work.

Byatt's novella *Morpho Eugenia* is the basis for this intriguing film, a period piece filled with fascinating twists and turns. Byatt's trademark obsession with research provides much of the interest: Adamson and Matty mercifully have something to *do* besides sip tea and pose in Victorian costumes. Their field work involving the ants is every bit as compelling as what goes on in the marbled halls and, indeed, is something of a commentary on the human activity. The busy worker ants are like the regiment of anonymous, colorless, and silent servants who are always underfoot yet remain an unseen presence, turning their faces to the wall whenever their masters pass. And the fat, lazy queen ant finds her anthropomorphic equivalent in both Lady Alabaster (Annette Badland), a living mountain of beruffled, corpulent flesh, and her daughter Eugenia, who eventually metamorphoses into a replica of her mum. As adapted by Philip and Belinda Haas, the story unfolds at an absorbingly contemplative pace; you get to know each character intimately and feel what it's like to live on a vast estate that's like a private empire unto itself. It's anything but a dull costumer: there are heaving passions and febrile minds under those crinolines and waistcoats. The discovery of incest is a shocker, and staged as such. Bernard Zitzerman's adroit photography and Alexander Balanescu's potent music are additional boons.

It takes a while to warm to Rylance's Scottish accent and missionary demeanor, but he makes Adamson an appealing sobersides—you believe in the man's natural, simple goodness. Kensit is rather out of her depth as Eugenia. Tentative and mousy, she plays the role on one monotonously childish note. Henshall is appropriately caddish as Edgar; Badland is a memorably gross visual cartoon as Lady Alabaster, like an obscenely overgrown baby; and the wonderful Anna Massey plays the children's civic-minded governess. But it's Thomas who really makes the film worth seeing. Perfectly in period, she resembles an Ingres painting come to life and invests her role with a fierce, clear-eyed intelligence. *(Nudity, sexual situations, adult situations.)* — D.N.

d, Philip Haas; p, Joyce Herlihy, Belinda Haas; exec p, Lindsay Law; w, Belinda Haas, Philip Haas (based on the novella *Morpho Eugenia* by A.S. Byatt); ph, Bernard Zitzermann; ed, Belinda Haas; m, Alexander Balanescu; prod d, Jennifer Kernke; art d, Alison Riva; ch, Kim Brandstrup; sound, Colin Nicolson (recordist); casting, Celestia Fox; cos, Paul Brown; makeup, Sarah Monzani

AAN Best Costume Design: Paul Brown

Drama/Romance/Historical **(PR: C MPAA: R)**

ANIMAL INSTINCTS III: THE SEDUCTRESS ★

(U.S.) 90m Axis-Davis Joint Venture ~ A-Pix Entertainment c

Wendy Schumacher *(Joanna Coles)*; James Matthew *(Alex Sage)*; Marcus Grahm *(Stone Chill)*; John Bates *(Trick Willy)*; Anthony Lesa *(Shane Hooligan)*; Reanna Lynn Rossi *(Lolly Pop)*; Larry Butler *(Clay Majors)*; Sam Cupae *(Stone's Bodyguard)*; Brian Salatino *(Orlando)*; Tara Hayes *(Cleaning Woman)*; Jacqueline Lovell *(Cleaning Woman)*; Karen Chavis *(Party Waitress)*; Cher Willis *(Party Waitress)*; Michael Gradilone *(Party Waiter)*

To truly appreciate the flavor of tasty deep-dish eroticism like that of TWO MOON JUNCTION (1988), sex-vid connoisseurs should be forced to nibble at a soft core-manque like ANIMAL INSTINCTS III.

Not only is Joanna Coles (Wendy Schumacher) the talk show hosts' delight and a best-selling author, but she's also a libertine fond of having public sex at pool halls. Enjoying the roar of the crowd, this exhibitionist meets her match in record producer/artistic guru, Alex Savage (James Matthew), whose credentials include world-class voyeurism. Deceiving the world at large and new playmate, Joanna, into believing that he's gone blind, Alex coaxes uninhibited Joanna into becoming his mansion roomie. There he gets his kicks watching his duped, cheating girlfriend have sex with music clients whom he has hand-picked. As Alex salivates, horny Joanna does it with acid rocker Trick Willy (John Bates) and ghetto performer Shane Hooligan (Anthony Lesa). However, Alex goes too far when he career manages gangsta rapper Stone Chill (Marcus Grahm). Pretending he's left Alex's palatial digs, Stone Chill sexually debases Joanna, forces her to have sex with his bodyguard, then murders his lily-livered agent (Larry Butler) in full view of faux-blind Alex. Before Stone Chill can direct his homicidal impulses at Joanna, Alex throws a knife at the crazed rapper with deadly accuracy. Furious at Alex's fakery, Joanna takes a powder; with the sex games gone sour, the relationship was doomed anyway.

Sporting two unsympathetic, soul-dead characters played by a facetiously smirking James Matthew and a frozen-pouted Wendy Schumacher, ANIMAL INSTINCTS III is unlikely to stimulate any viewer's nether regions. The film quickly passes the point where perversion just seems silly. Not having the courage of its S&M convictions, this sexcapade camps it up with double-entendre character names such as "Trick Willy" and his groupie, "Lolly Pop," and with an over-indulgent series of interior monologues. ANIMAL INSTINCTS III also doesn't fly as provocative libido-enhancement because its steamy interludes are preposterously conceived and sexlessly acted; Matthew seems to be engaged in a Guinness record-book competition for non-stop preening, and Schumacher simulates sex like a life-sized rubber doll strapped to changing partners. Failing to address the immorality of Alex's antics, this sexist rubbish is so laughably bad that it's futile to condemn its sins against liberated women. *(Graphic violence, extreme profanity, extensive nudity, substance abuse, sexual situations.)* — R.P.

d, Gregory Hippolyte; p, Andrew Garroni; exec p, Walter Gernert; w, Selwin Harris; ph, Ernest Paul Roebuck; ed, Jody Fedele; m, Erik Lundmak, Daniel Walker; prod d, Le'Ce Edwards; set d, Lily Zuleta; sound, Bill Reinhardt (mixer); casting, Lori Cobe; cos, Julie Clark, Tim Jesneck; makeup, Inger Ostrom

Erotic **(PR: O MPAA: R)**

ANNA ★★★

(Russia/France) 100m Studio Three T; Camera One ~ New Yorker Films c

Anna Mikhalkov; Nikita Mikhalkov

Part poetic home movie, part Soviet history lesson, and part intellectual diatribe against the evil empire of godless Communism, ANNA is a moving and fascinating collage by director Nikita Mikhalkov in which he juxtaposes the growth of his daughter with the tumultuous changes of the USSR from 1980-91.

Beginning in 1980, Mikhalkov starts filming his six-year-old daughter, Anna, and asks her five questions: What scares you the most? What do you love the most? What do you hate the most? What do you want the most? What do you expect from life?

At first, Anna's responses are what one would expect from a child: she's scared of a witch, she hates borscht, and she wants a crocodile.

Mikhalkov explains that since home movies were illegal in the Soviet Union, he had to film clandestinely and had great difficulty obtaining film stock and other equipment. Mikhalkov then inserts scenes from his 1980 film OBLOMOV, about a little boy growing up in the Czarist empire, and news footage of Leonid Brezhnev and other Soviet leaders.

A year later, we see the Mikhalkovs watching Brezhnev's funeral on television, and Anna says she loves nature, hates evil people, wants to be intelligent, and is scared of fights. In 1982, the next Soviet leader, Yuri Andropov, dies, and there is another funeral. Mikhalkov is horrified to discover that Anna's answers are beginning to mimic the party line. Thirteen months later, Mikhail Gorbachev takes over and footage of the war in Afghanistan is shown, along with interviews of some dissident soldiers, and censored scenes from Mikhalkov's film, KINSHIP (1982).

Mikhalkov takes a break from filming for a couple years while he's working in Italy, and in 1987, he is on the set of DARK EYES in Rome, where he celebrates the birth of his new daughter, Nadia. Under Gorbachev, "perestroika" is the new buzzword, and Mikhalkov says that what it really means to the Russian people is that they now can do openly what they used to do in secret. He also laments the new influx of Western culture and the corrupt values of foreign videos, which Russians are now emulating, such as a nationally televised birthday party for a transvestite nightclub singer. A series of disasters are shown, which Mikhalkov claims is God's way of striking back at an amoral world: the Challenger explosion, Iranian fundamentalism, Chernobyl, the Armenian earthquake, and even the decadent fashion designs of Jean-Paul Gauthier.

In 1988, Mikhalkov's beloved mother dies, and the whole family gathers to mourn. Fourteen-year-old Anna is now afraid of war and the death of her relatives, and Mikhalkov reminisces about the New Year's Eve celebrations of his childhood. News footage shows the fall of the Berlin Wall, and the democratization of the newly capitalist Russia.

Boris Yeltsin comes to power when Anna is 16, and Mikhalkov observes that her answers now show a great distance between them. When she turns 17, Anna prepares to leave home to go to Switzerland and cries when her father asks her if she'll return. He says that he'd like to make a sequel to this film in 13 years, and he starts to ask the same five questions of his four-year-old daughter Nadia. As Anna walks down a hill, Mikhalkov bemoans the loss of her childhood and asks God to watch over her in her travels.

Mikhalkov (BURNT BY THE SUN), is the scion of a renowned and respected Russian family of artists, which includes his half-brother, director Andrei Konchalovsky. As such, his view of the USSR may be from the perspective of a privileged intellectual who has never really had to deal with the harsh realities of oppression and totalitarianism, but this doesn't detract from the validity of his argument, since the film is ultimately more interested in notions of personal integrity, belief in God, and the importance of family, than in being an educational documentary. It may be a highly subjective and idiosyncratic view of political history, yet that is precisely what makes it effective. Mikhalkov's philosophical commentary and the scenes of his family life are filled with an overwhelming sense of melancholy and nostalgia, which turn the film into a poignant family album with universal themes of memory and the loss of innocence.

Considering the onerous conditions under which it was filmed, ANNA is superb on a technical level, with masterly editing in the best tradition of Soviet montage, and a lyrical music score that adds a level of mysticism. *(Nudity, adult situations.)* — M.S.

d, Nikita Mikhalkov; p, Nikita Mikhalkov; co-p, Michel Seydoux; w, Nikita Mikhalkov, Serguei Mirochnitchenko (from an original idea by Nikita Mikhalkov); ph, Pavel Lebechev, Elisbar Karavaev, Vadim Ioussov, Vadim Alissov; ed, Eleonora Praskina; m, Eduard Artemyev

Documentary/Political **(PR: C MPAA: NR)**

ANNE FRANK REMEMBERED ★★★½

(U.K./U.S.) 122m Jon Blair Film Company; BBC; Disney Channel ~ Sony Pictures Classics c/bw

Kenneth Branagh *(Narrator)*; Glenn Close

Remarkably enough, ANNE FRANK REMEMBERED is the first eyewitness account of the life and enduring legacy of the brave teenage girl who kept the 20th Century's most poignant diary and died in a German concentration camp toward the end of WWII. Made with the cooperation of the Anne Frank House in Amsterdam, Jon Blair's Academy Award-winning documentary interlaces fragments of personal testimony, previously undisclosed letters, family photos, and brief (but haunting) home-movie footage of a carefree Anne Frank watching a wedding couple from the window of her Amsterdam home into a mosaic that is both informative and emotionally wrenching.

Blair—who received a British Academy Award for his 1983 documentary, SCHINDLER—begins the story in 1925 when Anne's parents, Otto and Edith Frank, were married in Germany, and traces the family history up to Otto's death in Switzerland in 1980. Anne, the younger of the couple's two daughters, received a diary on her 13th birthday, in 1942, nearly a decade after the Franks relocated to Holland in hopes of escaping Hitler's persecution of the Jews. Less than a month after Anne began keeping her journal, the Franks went into hiding in the cramped attic of an Amsterdam building. Filmmaker Blair was given unprecedented access to the hiding place and was allowed to re-create this "secret annex" nearly a half century after it sheltered the Franks and another Jewish family from the Nazis.

ANNE FRANK REMEMBERED uses Anne's journal as an essential source-text, but positions it relative to the larger landscape of the world outside. The film also shows that Anne—who had long addressed the journal as a secret, comforting friend—had already begun revising it, with an eye toward submitting it for publication. Learning of D-Day, she speculates in its pages that the family may be liberated soon and she can return to school for the next term. Instead, the residents of the secret annex were betrayed, taken prisoner, and sent to Auschwitz.

The witnesses who provide the film's oral history offer some of its most memorable moments. Death camp survivor Hanneli Goslar, Anne's friend from early childhood, attests to her "spicy" personality and enthusiasm for life. Otto Frank, filmed shortly before he died in 1980, speaks movingly about his family loss and Anne's legacy. Miep Gies, who was one of Otto's employees and brought food to the hiding place daily, recalls how she presented Otto with his daughter's writings upon news of her death. Bloeme Evers-Emden, a former classmate of Anne's sister Margot, remembers Mrs. Frank and the children at Auschwitz, before the girls were dispatched to the Bergen-Belsen concentration camp, where Anne and Margot, already weak and sick, died of typhus, days apart, only a month before the camp was liberated.

"In spite of everything," Anne wrote in her journal, "I still believe that people are really good at heart." ANNE FRANK REMEMBERED celebrates this extraordinary young girl whose hope and humanity put much of the world to shame. *(Adult situations.)* — E.K.

d, Jon Blair; p, Jon Blair; assoc p, Wouter Van Der Sluis; w, Jon Blair; ph, Barry Ackroyd; ed, Karen Steininger; m, Carl Davis; art d, Rein Van Der Pol; sound, Robert Edwards

AA Best Documentary Feature: Jon Blair

Documentary/Biography/Historical (PR: A MPAA: PG)

ANNIE O ★★½

(U.S./Canada) 93m Sugartime Entertainment ~ Hallmark Home Entertainment c

Coco Yares *(Annie Rojas)*; Robert Stewart *(Coach Will Cody)*; Chad Willett *("Wild" Bill Porter)*; Robert Luft *(Freddie Rojas)*; Suzanne Ristic *(Mama Rojas)*; Lenno Britos *(Papa Rojas)*; Nuno Antunes *(Mike Rojas)*; Will Sengotta *(Doug Frazier)*; Russell B. Porter *(Barry)*; Joely Collins *(Robin)*; Trevor Roberts *(Skylar Marston)*; Chris Wilding *(Buddy)*; Jorge Vargas *(Jose)*; Winston Brown *(Winston)*; Biski Gugushe *(Big Jim Brady)*; Russell B. Porter *(Barry)*; Lalaina Lindbjerg *(Brooke)*; Peter Flemming *(College Guy No. 1)*; J.B. Sugar *(College Guy No. 2)*; Richard Leacock *(College Guy No. 3)*; Aaron Pearl *(Chuck)*; Chris Bradford *(Bob)*; Erick Kennylside *(Craig Frazier)*; Alf Humphreys *(Parent No. 2)*; Bobby Stewart *(Parent No. 4)*; Rebecca Toolan *(Principal Aragon)*; Tony Sampson *(Heckler No. 1)*; William Sasso *(Heckler No. 2)*; Silvio Pollio *(D'Angelo)*; Peter Hanlon *(Burt Cameron)*; Sean Milliken *(Reporter No. 2)*; Jessica Pedlow *(Young Girl)*; Paul Norman *(Scorekeeper)*; Christopher Anthony Bickford *(Bruins Student)*; Curtis Bechdholt *(Fall Valley Player)*; Paul Stafford *(Fall Valley Coach)*; Sabrina Byrne *(Young Fan No. 1)*; Vinessa Antoine *(Young Fan No. 2)*

ANNIE O is a morale-building, made-for-TV drama that serves up a roster of fresh faces in this story of a teen athlete and her struggle to "make the team."

Years of practice have left Annie Rojas (Coco Yares) a basketball whiz equal to her hotshot brother Freddie (Robert Luft). But their Tacoma high school lacks a team for girls, so Annie's only chance to shine is to join the institution's all-male hoop team, the Greyhounds. Coach Cody (Robert Stewart) enthusiastically favors adding Annie to the lineup, as does team captain Bill Porter (Chad Willett). However, other uptight players, parents, and peers—including her own brother Freddie—grumble their displeasure, and Annie becomes a local *cause celebre*. The pressure hurts her performance in the season opener, but gradually Annie gets her nerve (and her shot) back. In the "Big Game" she makes an assist to Freddie, and the brother-sister act clinches the state championship for the Greyhounds.

Meanwhile, back in the town's political arena, supporters make the case that Annie, and not team captain Porter, deserves the title All-American. Solomon-like, Coach Cody uses a basket-shooting contest between Annie and Bill to decide the matter, with ticket sales going to establish a girls' varsity team.

There isn't much novelty in ANNIE O apart from an inversion of gender stereotypes in attitudes about Annie's desire to play basketball on the boy's team. Interestingly enough, patriarchal authorities like Coach Cody and Annie's own father have no objection to her athletic endeavors, while tradition-bound Mama Rojas (Suzanne Ristic) scolds, "You're a girl—you should be proud of it!" But by the end of the fourth quarter, even mother comes around. Yares is an appealing performer on and off the court, and the whole story passes the time pleasantly enough, especially if you're a young female athlete looking for fictional role models.— C.C.

d, J. Michael McClary; p, Larry Sugar; w, Jefferson Berlin, Mark Bryan; ph, Dick Quinlan; ed, Judy Andreson; m, John Bryant, Frank Hames; prod d, M. Kevin Ryan; art d, Lana Kozak

Children's/Sports (PR: AA MPAA: PG)

ANTONIA

(SEE: ANTONIA'S LINE)

ANTONIA'S LINE ★★

(Netherlands/Belgium/U.K.) 104m Antonia's Line International; Bergen Film; Prime Time; Bard Entertainment; NPS Televisie ~ First Look Pictures c (ANTONIA)

Willeke van Ammelrooy *(Antonia)*; Els Dottermans *(Danielle)*; Dora van der Groen *(Allegonde)*; Veerle van Overloop *(Therese)*; Jan Decleir *(Bas)*; Mil Seghers *(Crooked Finger)*; Marina de Graaf *(DeeDee)*; Jan Steen *(Loony Lips)*; Elsie de Brauw *(Lara)*; Thyrza Ravesteijn *(Sarah)*; Wimie Wilhelm *(Letta)*; Flip Filz *(The Curate)*; Fran Waller Zeper *(Olga)*; Reinout Bussemaker *(Simon)*; Jakob Beks *(Farmer Daan)*; Filip Peeters *(Pitte)*; Michael Pas *(Janne)*; Catherine ten Bruggencate *(Mad Madonna)*; Paul Kooij *(The Protestant)*; Leo Hogenboom *(The Village Priest)*; Esther Vriesendorp *(Therese, Age 13)*; Carolien Spoor *(Therese, Age 6)*; Dirk Zeelenberg *(Pier)*; Ellen Dikker *(Muisje)*; Truus te Selle *(Ma Ge)*; Erik de Bruyn *(Arend)*; Petra Laseur *(Mother Theodora)*; Michel van Dousselaere *(Blacksmith)*; Hans Man in't Veld *(The Professor)*; Johan Heldenbergh *(Tom)*; Victor Low *(Harry)*; Igor Corbeau *(Simon, Age 13)*; Carlo Van Dam *(Simon, Age 6)*; Lineke Rijxman *(Narrator)*

Winner of the 1996 Academy Award for Best Foreign Language Film, ANTONIA'S LINE is an overplotted multigenerational chronicle that makes one wonder just what the Academy members are thinking when they cast their votes.

Elderly Antonia (Willeke van Ammelrooy) wakes up one morning and decides that she has lived long enough and this will be the day of her death. She surveys her life, beginning at the end of WW II, when she returns to her rural hometown after an absence of 20 years. With her young daughter, Danielle (Els Dottermans), she has come to bury her mother and claim the family farm.

Antonia has decided to build a life on her own terms with no men. While her decision may seem odd to the town residents, it's an area not lacking in unusual characters. Danielle, though still young, has her own idiosyncrasies, including whimsical visions of the dead and inanimate cavorting with the living.

As the years go by, Antonia's farm becomes home to an assortment of misfits and outcasts. These include two refugees from a neighboring farm run by the ignorant bully, Daan (Jakob Beks), and his sons. Antonia has a better relationship with another neighbor, Farmer Bas (Jan Decleir), though she scorns his proposal of marriage.

Danielle goes to art school, then returns to her mother's farm to paint. She decides that she wants a child, though not a husband. At a home for unwed mothers, she and Antonia meet Letta (Wimie Wilhelm), a woman who openly enjoys her frequent pregnancies. She arranges a tryst between Danielle and her brother, leading to the birth of a daughter, Therese (Veerle van Overloop).

A prodigy with a talent for mathematics, Therese is educated on the farm by one of its residents, the misanthropic genius Crooked Finger (Mil Seghers). Antonia, who has come to enjoy a sexual relationship with Farmer Bas, continues to collect lost souls, and they and their children make the farm a community unto itself.

When she is old enough, Therese goes to college and has some unrewarding relationships. She returns to the farm, where some of the older residents have died, and has a child with one of Letta's sons. On the day of Antonia's death, Therese's daughter, Sarah (Thyrza Ravesteijn), has a vision of a banquet shared by all the past and present residents of the farm.

A succession of events does not a plot make, as ANTONIA'S LINE proves. At 105 minutes, the film plays like the severely edited highlights of an eight-hour miniseries. Gaps are filled in by a narrator who regularly announces "Time moved on like. . . " followed by some precious simile. Like the longest-ever Bob Dylan song, the film is filled with characters who consist of nothing but a funny name and a peculiar personality trait. None of them occupies enough screen time for the audience to take much interest in them.

At least it can be said that writer-director Marlene Gorris's film is less strident than her controversial A QUESTION OF SILENCE (1982). Gorris's conception of feminism is on the level of 8-year-old schoolchildren arguing that girls are better than boys. She clearly has axes to grind, particularly against organized religion, but lacks anything intelligent to say on the subject. *(Violence, extensive nudity, sexual situations.)* — M.F.

d, Marleen Gorris; p, Hans de Weers; co-p, Antonino Lombardo, Judy Counihan; w, Marleen Gorris; ph, Willy Stassen; ed, Michiel Reichwein, Wim Louwrier; m, Ilona Sekacz; art d, Harry Ammerlaan; sound, Dirk Bombey, Wim Post (mixer); fx, Steven van Couwelaar, Olivier de Laveleye; casting, Hans Kemna, Job Gosschalk; cos, Jany Temime; makeup, Jan Sewell

AA Best Foreign Language Film

Drama/Fantasy **(PR: C MPAA: NR)**

APART FROM HUGH ★★

(U.S.) 87m ~ Water Bearer Films bw

David Merwin *(Collin)*; Jennifer A. Reed *(Frieda)*; Steve Arnold *(Hugh)*; Harris M. Lynam *(David)*; J. P. McCollum *(Bus Driver)*; Doreen H. Lewis *(Coffee House Patron)*; M. Caroline Eddy *(Coffee House Patron)*; Crispyn Duplisia Suij *(Nancy)*; John Cajun Bryan *(Oliver Twist)*; Shorty Johnson *(Bartender)*; Russ Thorson *(Man at Table)*; Eric Heimbigue *(Bearded Pool Player)*; Kathy Milholland *(Patron)*; Shirley Murra *(Speaking Saleslady)*; Christine Reinhardt *(Saleslady)*; Annette Renee Le Roux *(Fran)*; Joe Diamond *(Charades Player)*; Kevan Daniel *(Grant)*; Graig Wunder *(William)*; Stephen M. Rondel *(Dolly)*; Tina Rorker *(Tina Rorker)*; Roy Mapes *(Poet)*; Deanna Elliot *(Deanna)*; Brian Sperber *(Husband)*; Kimberly Ann Johnson *(Lodi)*

Throughout film history, homosexuals have been tarred and feathered as predators (CRUISING), mascaraed and exploited as court jesters in the Kingdom of Straights (THE BIRDCAGE), or even Eve Ardened into the leading lady's neutered confidante (Roddy McDowall in FUNNY LADY). But whether victimized for cheap laughs or shock value, gays have never been portrayed as boring human beings. Not, that is, until APART FROM HUGH.

A young man, Collin (David Merwin), ponders the depth of his commitment to live-in lover Hugh (Steve Arnold). Oblivious to Collin's soul-searching and unaware of the shakiness of his relationship, lovestruck Hugh plans a first-year anniversary party. He graciously invites Collin's former roommate Frieda (Jennifer A. Reed), a free spirit currently involved in a *menage a trois* with a bisexual couple.

Upon arrival in town, flamboyant Frieda steadies her nerves at a local pub, shoplifts a pair of Goodwill pumps to complete her party ensemble, and greets the happy couple. Collin confesses to Frieda that he feels his own limited life experience makes him a poor match for well-rounded Hugh. Frieda downplays his misgivings and expresses her reluctance to become involved in Collin's departure plans. Although he temporarily leaves with Frieda, Collin sees the light and returns to Hugh. Hugh is none the wiser.

Exclaiming their flowery lines like high school debaters at a gay forensics tournament, Merwin and Arnold earnestly mouth the writer-director's distasteful pieties. APART FROM HUGH depicts Collin and Hugh like any highfalutin heterosexual couple who choose to express themselves in the manner of greeting-card verse. While this psycho-babbly drama deserves commendation for avoiding stereotypes, it replaces the customary energized negatives with puling positives. The gay couple's sensitivity is supposed to make the audience feel good, but the film makes you feel as if you've been forced into group therapy with inveterate party bores. What gives this touchy-feely guff the lie is quirky actress Reed. Her lively performance embodies the cheekiness and devil-may-care attitude that gays have had to develop in order to survive, relieving the audience from Collin's over-analyzed romantic vacillations. *(Extreme profanity, adult situations.)* — R.P.

d, Jon Fitzgerald; p, Jon Fitzgerald; co-p, Randall Allred; ph, Randall Allred; ed, Jon Fitzgerald, Randall Allred; m, James Clarke; prod d, Gerald Scott; makeup, Erin Wright, Ricoh Vigen

Drama **(PR: C MPAA: NR)**

ARRIVAL, THE ★★½

(U.S.) 109m LIVE Entertainment ~ Orion c

Charlie Sheen *(Zane Ziminski)*; Ron Silver *(Gordian)*; Lindsay Crouse *(Ilana Green)*; Teri Polo *(Char)*; Richard Schiff *(Calvin)*; Tony T. Johnson *(Kiki)*; Leon Rippy *(DOD #1)*; Buddy Joe Hooker *(DOD #2)*; Geoff Hanson *(Clark)*; Danna Garen *(Susan)*; Ami Rothschild *(Sunny)*; Kim Dawson *(Leslie)*; Amy Lemmon *(Tina)*; Danny Fendley *(Jeff)*; Stuart Gordon *(Biker)*; Carolyn Purdy-Green *(Liquor Store Woman)*; Jason Bach *(Dr. Johnson)*; Brad Mills *(Michael)*; Dean Minerd *(Hank)*; Bill Brochtrup *(Ace)*; Mark Kemble *(Detective Quig)*; Linda Ljoka *(Laura)*; David Schmoeller *(Dr. Carlyle)*; Steve Tietsort *(Cashier)*; Todd Jeffries *(Officer Barnes)*; Tom Crowl *(Government Official)*; Zatella Beatty *(Prostitute)*; Gregg Ostrin *(Pimp)*; Dick Bocelli *(Blood Doctor)*; Daniel J. Ljoka *(Prints Detective)*; Julie Reed *(Nurse)*; Patricia Rive *(Parking Lot Woman)*; Peter Manoogian *(Binocular Agent)*; Theadora Tolkin *(Mary)*; Adam Foster *(Nicky)*; Piyo *(Agent Williams)*; Flavio Fabrini *(Dr. Torres)*; Mark Rakenzes *(Lance)*; Rosemary Moritz *(Mary Ann Reynolds)*; Richard Pattee *(Waiter)*; Ruthann Mason *(Blood Nurse)*; Loni White *(Liz)*; Michele Bravo *(Murder Victim)*; Belinda Jensen *(Hooker)*; Anita Korf *(Street Walker)*; Nancy Howard *(Party Guest)*; Lauren Martin *(Young Mrs. Page)*; Monty Jordan *(SWAT Leader)*; Jarel McCaul; Bob Petracci; Marty Walsh; Mike Alessi; Dennis Murphy; Zimbo; Dana Bedard; Glenn Sharp *(Library Patrons)*

Overshadowed at the summer 1996 box-office by INDEPENDENCE DAY, THE ARRIVAL is a smaller-scale alien-invasion thriller that succeeds on its own modest terms.

Radio astronomer Zane Ziminski (Charlie Sheen) has been searching for signs of intelligent extraterrestrial life for years, and his obsession has caused friction between him and his girlfriend, Char (Teri Polo). Late one night, Zane picks up a brief but powerful signal and reports it to his NASA boss, Gordian (Ron Silver). To Zane's shock, Gordian is not only unimpressed by his claims, but fires him. Zane's suspicions are further inflamed when his partner, Calvin (Richard Schiff), informs him that government operatives are cleaning out their lab. Continuing to work on his own, with help from young neighbor Kiki (Tony T. Johnson), Zane traces the signals to Mexico. There he encounters scientist Ilana Green (Lindsay Crouse), who has been investigating strange pockets of global warming.

Ultimately, Zane discovers that aliens have arrived on Earth, and are using a Mexican power plant as a base to implement worldwide warming that will make the planet more hospitable for them. When Ilana is killed by scorpions placed in her room, Zane escapes back to the US, hoping to broadcast evidence of the alien conspiracy (in which Gordian is involved) from a giant satellite dish. He brings along neighbor Kiki and girlfriend Char, despite his suspicions that she, too, is part of the plot. However, Kiki proves to be the alien agent, and Gordian and his thugs soon arrive. Their "imploder" device destroys both the satellite dish and themselves; Kiki escapes and reverts to his alien form, and Zane and Char also get away, broadcasting the evidence of "the arrival" to the world.

Though it suffers from some occasional indulgences, THE ARRIVAL is generally a tense and involving paranoia story about "invasion." Writer-director David Twohy co-wrote THE FUGITIVE (1993), among other screenplays, so it's not surprising to find him tackling another man-on-the-run story. Although Sheen is no Harrison Ford (and tends to bug his eyes too much while making a point), he does emerge as a convincing Everyman hero to guide the audience through this tale of extraterrestrial takeover.

Eschewing the special effects spectacle of INDEPENDENCE DAY and its ilk, Twohy instead concentrates on small-scale effects and gritty suspense—for example, in the unexpectedly intense scene involving Crouse and the room full of scorpions. However, the best of these scenes involve the "imploder," sort of a Tornado-in-a-Ball that wipes whole rooms and buildings clean. Although derided by some critics as stop-motion throwbacks, the extraterrestrials themselves are quite convincing computer-generated beings, their alien appearance effectively revealed in gradual glimpses.

The supporting roles are unsurprising (and the character of Kiki seems gratuitous, his presence not making sense until the final revelation that she is an alien), but the actors acquit themselves well. Polo convincingly suggests her alienation from Zane and the possibility that she is an alien herself, while Silver, doing his best Christopher Walken, is appropriately smarmy as the key human villain. Though not as lavish as its big-studio brethren, THE ARRIVAL certainly has more on its mind than many of them. *(Violence, profanity.)* — M.G.

d, David Twohy; p, Thomas G. Smith, Jim Steele; exec p, Ted Field, Robert W. Cort; assoc p, Lorenzo O'Brien, David Tripet; co-p, Cyrus Yavner; w, David Twohy; ph, Hiro Narita; ed, Martin Hunter; m, Arthur Kempel; prod d, Michael Novotny; art d, Anthony Stabley; set d, Jaime Rivas; fx, Robin D'Arcy, Charles L. Finance; casting, Mary Jo Slater, Steven Brooksbank; cos, Mayes C. Rubeo; makeup, Todd Masters; stunts, Buddy Joe Hooker, Eddie Braun

Science Fiction/Thriller **(PR: C MPAA: PG-13)**

ASSAULT AT WEST POINT ★★

(U.S.) 94m Ultra Entertainment ~ Republic Pictures Home Video c

Samuel L. Jackson *(Richard Greener)*; Sam Waterston *(Daniel Chamberlain)*; Seth Gilliam *(Cadet Johnson Whittaker)*; John Glover *(Major Asa Bird Gardiner)*; Mason Adams *(Hyde)*; Eddie Bracken *(Dr. Charles Alexander)*; Brad Greenquist *(Dr. Beard)*; Peter Maloney *(William Michie)*; Scott Paetty *(Cadet George Burnett)*; Ken Garito *(Cadet Lewis Ostheim)*; Anthony Rapp *(Cadet Frederick Hodgson)*; John Wehr *(Cadet Blake)*; Al Freeman Jr. *(Old Whittaker)*

This courtroom drama, about one of the first black cadets at West Point, was produced for the Showtime cable network in 1994, and released on video in 1996. Despite strong source material and a quality cast, the film falls flat, as the performances and script seem perfunctory and rushed.

In 1880, Johnson Whittaker (Seth Gilliam) is found in his West Point room, tied up and covered in blood. Though it's obvious that he was attacked, the school's administration claims that he staged his own assault to avoid an upcoming exam. A trial is set; if Whittaker is found guilty of staging the assault, he will be expelled from West Point and jailed.

Daniel Chamberlain (Sam Waterston) is Whittaker's lawyer, and he is assisted by Richard Greener (Samuel L. Jackson), one of the first black graduates of Harvard Law School. From the beginning, Greener states that the trial "isn't about justice, but manipulation." Prosecuting attorney Major Asa Bird Gardiner (John Glover) is notorious for representing murderers and crooks, and in this case, his witnesses tell lie after lie on the stand.

Chamberlain's defense is careful and polite, but Greener argues that the defense must be bold, that they can't win unless the obvious racism in the case is clearly brought before the court. Not trusting Chamberlain to press the issue, Greener takes it into his own hands to collect evidence. When witnesses claim that Whittaker's injury caused little blood, Greener visits Whittaker's West Point room and finds a large bloodstain hidden under a rug. When a so-called handwriting expert testifies that Whittaker wrote an incriminating note, Greener travels to Virgina to find Hyde (Mason Adams), a lawyer who testifies that the expert is unqualified and dishonest.

Despite Greener's extra work and Whittaker's poise as a witness, the outlook is grim. The jury is composed of five men: if two find Whittaker not guilty, he will be freed. When the verdict is due, the only jury member known to be sympathetic to Whittaker is absent. Greener implores Chamberlain to object, but Chamberlain refuses. Whittaker is found guilty.

Many years later, Whittaker tells the tale. He appealed the trial, and though he was expelled, he did not have to go to jail. Despite the injustice of this incident, he lives a long, productive life.

ASSAULT AT WEST POINT is a true story, and some of the dialogue comes directly from court records. Unfortunately, the presentation of the story doesn't achieve much of a life of its own. Despite the presence of such talents as Jackson and Waterston, the acting is consistently bland; the characters speak their lines clearly, quickly, and without emotion. Their stilted speech style may be an attempt to mimic the tone of the 1880s, but modern language is included as well, implying that the filmmakers could not decide whether they wanted to make a pure period piece or a modernization. Only Adams appears to be having any fun with his role.

While the racism of the time is presented in a believable way, it's a shame that the exploration of that racism's many effects isn't taken further. ASSAULT AT WEST POINT may be historically accurate, but it would have been better if it had dug more deeply rather than simply presenting the case. *(Profanity, violence)* — A.M.

d, Harry Moses; p, Harry Moses; exec p, Bob Rubin, Bill Siegler; w, Harry Moses (based on the book *The Court-Martial of Johnson Whittaker* by John F. Marszalek); ph, Ken Kelsch; ed, Jay Freund; m, Terence Blanchard; prod d, Howard Cummings; art d, Jea Devoe; fx, Bob Shelley; casting, Leonard Finger, Stephanie Klapper; cos, Paul Simmons; makeup, Joseph P. Hurt

Drama/Historical **(PR: C MPAA: PG-13)**

ASSOCIATE, THE ★★½

(U.S.) 114m ATL Productions; Frederic Golchan Productions; Interscope Communications; Hollywood Pictures ~ Buena Vista c

Whoopi Goldberg *(Laurel Ayres)*; Dianne Wiest *(Sally)*; Eli Wallach *(Fallon)*; Tim Daly *(Frank)*; Bebe Neuwirth *(Camille)*; Austin Pendleton *(Aesop Franklin)*; Laine Kazan *(Cindy Mason)*; George Martin *(Walter Manchester)*; Kenny Kerr *(Charlie)*; Lee Wilkof *(Bissel)*; Helen Hanft *(Mrs. Cupchick)*; George Morfogen *(Plaza Manager)*; Zeljko Ivanek *(SEC Agent Thompkins)*; Miles Chapin *(Harry)*; Jean De Baer *(Loan Officer)*; Louis Turenne; William Hill *(Detective Templeton)*; Colleen Camp *(Detective Jones)*; Brian Tarantina *(Eddie)*; Jerry Hardin *(Harley Mason)*; John Short *(Harley's Associate)*; Thomas Wagner *(Harley's Associate)*; Johnny Miller *(Himself)*; Nicholas Kepros *(Dalton)*; Donald J. Trump *(Himself)*; Peter McRobbie *(Executive at Strip Club)*; Daryl Edwards *(Executive at Strip Club)*; Allison Janney *(Sandy)*; Frederick Rolf *(Carl Bode)*; Larry Gilliard Jr. *(Plaza Bellhop Thomas)*; Liana Pai *(Plaza Concierge Charlotte)*; Vincent Laresca *(Plaza Waiter Jose)*; Arthur French *(Plaza Men's Room Attendant)*; Kathleen McClellan *(Frank's Girlfriend)*; Robert Levine *(Door Slam Executive)*; John Rothman *(Jogging Track Executive)*; Jonathan Freeman *(Hockey Game Executive)*; Socorro Santiago *(Syntonex Worker)*; Bernie McInerney *(Client at Cutty/Ayres)*; Katherine Wallach *(Reporter)*; Leon Addison Brown *(Reporter)*; Sally Jessy Raphael *(Herself)*; Judith Calder *(Audience Member)*; Ted Brunetti *(Fallon's Messenger)*; Baxter Harris *(Disgruntled Investor)*; Craig Braun *(Disgruntled Investor)*; Rex Robbins *(Investor at 21 Club)*; Ira Wheeler *(Investor at 21 Club)*; Boris McGiver *(Plaza Reporter)*; Billy Jaye *(Plaza Reporter)*; Ginny Yang *(Funeral Reporter)*; Joel Blake *(Poker Player)*; Alberto Alejandrino *(Maitre d' at Peabody Club)*; The Roy Gerson Orchestra *(Fallon Ball Band)*

Another contender in the apparently endless stream of Disney remakes of French comedies, THE ASSOCIATE is a pleasant farce that eschews any big moments in favor of coasting comfortably on the charms of its star, Whoopi Goldberg.

Diligent Wall Street financial analyst Laurel Ayres (Whoopi Goldberg) is consistently overshadowed by her less able partner Frank (Tim Daly), who gets clients to sign deals she has prepared by showing them a good time. When he gets promoted over her, she quits and opens her own consulting business. Despite her contacts and abilities, Laurel is unable to get any decision-makers to meet with her. Frank's secretary Sally (Dianne Wiest) pulls a favor to get Laurel into a meeting with business tycoon Fallon (Eli Wallach) but when Laurel shows up, he won't take her seriously because she's a woman. Out of frustration, she invents on the spur of the moment an imaginary male partner named Robert Cutty. Fallon agrees to read "their" proposal, loves it, and pays a large commission.

Laurel rents and furnishes a large, masculine-looking office. She also hires Sally when Frank fires her. With recommendations from Fallon and the cachet of the mysterious genius Mr. Cutty, Laurel's agency is soon the toast of Wall Street. Trouble starts when the Securities and Exchange Commission demands to meet with Cutty, and Laurel responds by disguising herself as a middle-aged white man. She arranges a quiet meeting with the SEC, but tabloid reporters spot "Cutty" and chase her all over Manhattan before she can escape to her apartment. Soon after, Laurel and Sally stage Cutty's accidental "death," only to be arrested and charged with his murder. They are released when Frank, who has figured out the ruse, resurrects Cutty as a way of boosting his own reputation. When Cutty is named Man of the Year by a prestigious all-male club, Laurel frustrates Frank's plans by showing up in her disguise to accept the award. From the podium, she reveals her true identity and chastises the club for its sexism. Frank is fired, and ends up looking for a job at a new company run by Sally, who turns him down.

Adapted from a French film of the same title (which was barely released in the US), THE ASSOCIATE differs from its predecessor by making its leading character a woman who invents a male partner in order to deal with Wall Street sexism. (In the original, Michel Serrault created a charismatic partner to compensate for his own bland personality.) But compared to something like THE FIRST WIVES' CLUB, the male-female power clash central to the script's premise is so cartoonish that it's largely unmoving.

Surprisingly, given that Goldberg first came to fame by portraying diverse characters in her stage shows, the low point of the film comes when she appears as "Robert Cutty" in male drag. Resembling a wax statue of George Washington, the disguise is so stiff and lifeless that it seriously undermines the film's believability. Fortunately, the film spends little time with him and more with the cast of first-rate supporting actors. Sitcom star Tim Daly makes a wonderfully oily villain. Equally charming are Wallach as the tycoon Fallon, Austin Pendleton as a computer genius, Lainie Kazan as a gossip columnist, and Bebe Neuwrith as a Wall Street woman who plays the game the old-fashioned way. Donald Petrie's direction is typically bland, although the film gains much atmosphere from use of actual Manhattan locations (dressed up in their snowy, wintry finest).*(Nudity, adult situations, profanity.)* — M.F.

d, Donald Petrie; p, Frederic Golchan, Patrick Markey, Adam Leipzig; exec p, Ted Field, Scott Kroopf, Robert W. Cort, David Madden; co-p, Rene Gainville, Michael A. Helfant; w, Nick Thiel; ph, Alex Nepomniaschy; ed, Bonnie Koehler; m, Christopher Tyng; prod d, Andrew Jackness; art d, Phil Messina; set d, Jessica Lanier; sound, Rosa Howell-Thornhill (mixer); fx, Albert Griswold; casting, Mary Colquhoun; cos, April Ferry; makeup, Michael Germain; stunts, Jery Hewitt

Comedy **(PR: A MPAA: PG-13)**

... AT FIRST SIGHT ★★

(U.S.) 90m PRO FilmWorks; Trimark Pictures ~ Vidmark Entertainment c
(AKA: TWO GUYS TALKIN' ABOUT GIRLS)

Dan Cortese *(Joey Fortone)*; Jonathan Silverman *(Lenny Kaminsky)*; Allison Smith *(Rhonda Glick)*; Monte Markham *(Lester Glick)*; Kathleen Freeman *(Grandma)*; Pamela Segall *(Tracey)*; Susan Walters *(Cindy One)*; Shannon Sturges *(Cindy Four)*; Lisa Gorlitsky *(Cindy Five)*; Kristin Datillo-Hayward *(Angel)*; Mariangelo Pino *(Edith)*; Antoinette Peragine; Dee Dee Hemby; Jake Marley; Jay Lacopo

A meandering, thoughtless movie about empty-headed guys that masquerades as a hip, trendy film about cool guys, . . .AT FIRST SIGHT is perhaps the ultimate generic "guy-talk" feature.

Lenny Kaminsky (Jonathan Silverman), a young Long Island professional, encounters gamine Rhonda Glick (Allison Smith) at a planetarium and is smitten. "I think this girl is it," he confides to best pal Joey Fortone (Dan Cortese), a cocky East Coast Casanova who advises Lenny how to proceed. Throughout Rhonda-oriented escapades, Lenny senses that Joey's womanizing—with a succession of beauties all named Cindy —hides a secret heartache, but Lenny's attempt to match Joey with the Cindy of his dreams ends in disaster. Meanwhile, Rhonda proves to be neither as perceptive nor as deep as Lenny first fancied. That she doesn't dig Paul Simon concerts clinches the matter, and Lenny lets her drift away. Sadder and wiser, though not by much, Lenny and Joey start over with another pair of pretty girls.

Without much happening, the vacant plot desperately complicates itself with trivia like Lenny faking illness to avoid work, or Rhonda murmuring a stranger's name in her sleep—which turns out to be her dog.

Silverman and Cortese put a bit of life into their byplay, and the gag-filled closing credits suggest a good time was had by all behind the scenes. If only that same easy *bonhomie* trickled down to the viewer. The classic "guy-talk" picture is Barry Levinson's DINER, and the idea found broadcast success in the TV sitcom "Seinfeld"—which was copied by Silverman's own prime-time vehicle, "The Single Guy."

Given the temptation for tyro filmmakers to launch their careers in formulaic exploitation cheapies, it seems ungenerous to slam young auteurs like Steven Pearl who bravely venture into freeform. But really, there just isn't much going on here. *(Adult situations, sexual situations, profanity)* — C.C.

d, Steven Pearl; p, Craig Saavedra, Jonathan Baruch, Jonathan Komack Martin; exec p, Mark Amin, Richard Becker; assoc p, Steven Pearl; w, Ken Copel; ph, Glenn Kershaw; ed, Mary Jo Markey; m, Richard Gibbs; set d, Melanie Paizis; sound, Marshall Wiemer; casting, Russel Gray, Mark Tillman; cos, Susan Susan Kaufman

Comedy/Romance **(PR: C MPAA: R)**

AUF DER SONNENSEITE DES LEBENS

(SEE: MISSING PIECES)

AUGUST ★★

(U.K.) 93m Granada Film; Majestic Films; Newcomm ~ Samuel Goldwyn Company c

Anthony Hopkins *(Ieuan Davies)*; Kate Burton *(Helen Blathwaite)*; Leslie Phillips *(Professor Alexander Blathwaite)*; Gawn Grainger *(Dr. Michael Lloyd)*; Rhian Morgan *(Sian Blathwaite)*; Hugh Lloyd *(Thomas "Pocky" Prosser)*; Rhoda Lewis *(Mair Davies)*; Menna Trussler *(Gwen)*

Anthony Hopkins tosses his hat into the over-populated ring of actors-turned-directors with a botched adaptation of Anton Chekhov's *Uncle Vanya.* Changing the setting to Wales adds an attractive backdrop, but nothing more.

At the end of the 19th century, Professor Alexander Blathwaite (Leslie Phillips), a querulous old tyrant, and his young, American second wife, Helen (Kate Burton), come up from London to visit Alexander's estate in the north of Wales. The place is currently inhabited by Ieuan Davies (Anthony Hopkins), the manager of the estate and the brother of Alexander's first wife; his mother, Mair (Rhoda Lewis); Alexander's plain, lonely daughter, Sian (Rhian Morgan); and Gwen, the family housekeeper (Menna Trussler). Also in attendance is the local physician, Dr. Michael Lloyd (Gawn Grainger), an idealistic conservationist repelled by the industrial progress sweeping the countryside.

Alexander and his wife intend to impose their cosmopolitan ways on the slower country folk, but their visit elicits something far more damaging. Over the course of one pivotal August weekend, under the combined influences of heat, drink, indolence, and intimacy, secret loves are revealed. Ieuan drowns himself in liquor over his unrequited love for Helen while he rants about his meaningless existence. Sian silently longs for Dr. Lloyd. Lloyd harbors a hidden, drunken desire for Helen as well. Helen mourns the course her life has taken. Sian confesses her feelings for Lloyd to Helen. Lloyd himself begins to confess his love to Helen; Ieuan walks in on them and quickly departs. After Alexander announces that he is selling the estate, Ieuan lashes out at him. Alexander and Helen leave, as does Lloyd, who informs Sian that he will not be returning anytime soon. With all the visitors gone, Ieuan and Sian simply return to business as usual and work on the estate's books together.

In its attempt to translate the mercurial emotionalism of Chekhov's *Uncle Vanya* to the screen, AUGUST fails miserably, especially when compared to Louis Malle's magical cinematic take on the same play, VANYA ON 42ND STREET (1994). Hopkins's first-time direction is stagey and marred by visual cliches. For example, a mine explosion seen early in the film is both a contrived metaphor for "opening things out" and a needless attempt to provide socio-economic context.

Julian Mitchell's screenplay reads like a bad Freudian soap opera; his dialogue flattens every possible nuance, leaving no depths to be plumbed. Deep-seated melancholy is replaced with pinched repression (a fault aggravated by the Welsh setting) and plainly-stated confessions. Before long, one wishes everyone would just shut up and enjoy the gorgeous view.

As this displaced Vanya, Hopkins is in full prosciutto mode. Bleary-eyed, drunken closeups of the actor-director dominate the film, along with fits of animal explosiveness which come off as embarrassing and juvenile. For all his revelatory commotion, there's simply no reason to care about him. The same, unfortunately, holds true for the other characters. In her role as an American, Burton must regrettably stifle her own unimpeachable Welsh heritage; she reads her lines in flat Midwestern tones, presenting a woman completely drained of life and interest. She's a drab far cry from Julianne Moore, who was luminous in the parallel role of Yelena in VANYA ON 42ND STREET. In subsidiary parts, Lewis and Hugh Lloyd (as a garrulous neighbor) are more lively and compelling than anyone else.*(Sexual situations, adult situations, substance abuse, profanity.)* — D.N.

d, Anthony Hopkins; p, June Wyndham-Davies, Pippa Cross; exec p, Steve Morrison, Guy East; co-p, Janet Day; w, Julian Mitchell (adapted from his play, based on *Uncle Vanya* by Anton Chekhov); ph, Robin Vidgeon; ed, Edward Mansell; m, Anthony Hopkins; prod d, Eileen Diss; art d, Humphrey Bangham; sound, Rudi Buckle (recordist); casting, Carolyn Bartlett, Cheryl Nance, Wally Byatt; cos, Dany Everett

Drama **(PR: C MPAA: PG)**

AVENTURERA ★★★½

(Mexico) 101m Producciones Calderon ~ Shadowfax Film bw

Ninon Sevilla *(Elena Tejero)*; Tito Junco *(Lucio "Pretty Boy" Saenz)*; Andrea Palma *(Rosaura)*; Ruben Rojo *(Mario)*; Miguel Inclan *("El Rengo")*; Jorge Mondragon *(Facundo "Pacomio" Rodriguez)*; Maruja Grifell *(Cousuelo, Elena's Mother)*; Luis Lopez Somoza *(Ricardo)*; Maria Gentil Arcos *(Petra)*; Miguel Manzano; Armando Osorlo; Arturo Soto Urena; Jose Ruiz Velez

Originally released in 1950, this Mexican melodrama recounts the story of a woman's slide from bourgeois respectability to depravity and back again. No punches are pulled in the telling.

On the cusp of womanhood, pampered Elena (Ninon Sevilla) lives with her parents in Chihuahua. Her world is unhinged when she returns home early from dance class and finds her usually dour mother (Maruja Grifell) in the arms of a family friend. When her mother runs off with the man, her indulgent and sensitive father commits suicide, leaving Elena defenseless and penniless.

Elena moves to Ciudad Juarez and takes job after job, only to be subjected to constant harassment from lecherous bosses. Desperate and destitute, Elena runs into an old acquaintance, Lucio (Tito Junco), who offers to take her out for a night on the town. He takes her to a swinging cabaret, plies her with drug-laced champagne and sells her to the local madam, Rosaura (Andrea Palma).

Elena initially puts up a fight, but before too long, she is the star of the floor show. Her performance in a lavish harem musical number signals her acceptance of her straits and determination to thrive in the mercenary environment of the brothel. Elena quickly hardens into a salacious cabaret professional.

One night, she spots her mother's lover and breaks a bottle over his head, sparking a brawl that causes Rosaura to discipline her severely. Lucio strong-arms Rosaura into giving him Elena, then enlists her as a getaway car driver in a robbery. Rosaura finds out about the planned robbery and reports it to the police. Lucio is sentenced to serve 20 years, while Elena escapes to Mexico City, where she gets a job as a cabaret dancer.

Mario (Ruben Rojo), a rich, handsome, naive patsy, asks Elena to marry him. Just as she is about to dismiss him, she is faced with a blackmailer who knows about her involvement in the failed robbery. She marries Mario and accompanies him to Guadalajara to meet his wealthy family, She is shocked to discover that his mother is Rosaura, the Ciudad Juarez madam, leading a double life. The two women practically hiss when they are in the same room, and Elena sinks into a pattern of destructive behavior that jeopardizes the family's social status.

At her wit's end, Rosaura goes back to Ciudad Juarez and orders her henchman, "El Rengo" (Miguel Inclan), to kill Elena. At the same time, Lucio escapes from prison and attempts to kidnap Elena. But El Rengo, deeply in love with Elena, defies Rosaura and kills Lucio instead. Elena realizes how decent Mario is after all and goes back to him.

Many consider this previously "lost" film to be the finest example of the *cabaretera*, a Mexican sub-genre of the melodrama set in cabarets. Sevilla, a Cuban-born rhumba dancer, went on to star in three other films, also under Alberto Gout's direction.

The plot's pace is dizzying and presents a grim view of human nature. Its style is excessive and overwrought, running the gamut from the comical to the cruel. Yet the frantic action is riveting, combining elements of film noir, musicals, and women's pictures. The emotionally resonant, Greek chorus-like musical numbers complement the extravagant and campy dance performances, and adventurous moviegoers will be thankful that this film was rescued from the bin of oblivion. *(Adult situations.)* — S.C.

d, Alberto Gout; p, Pedro A. Calderon, Guillermo Calderon; w, Alvaro Custodio, Carlos Sampelayo (from a story by Alvaro Custodio); ph, Alex Phillips; ed, Alfredo Rosas Priego; m, Antonio Diaz Conde, Damaso Perez Prado; ch, Ninon Sevilla, Julien de Meriche; sound, Javier Mateos

Musical/Drama **(PR: C MPAA: NR)**

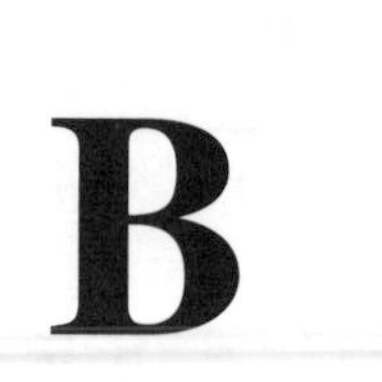

BACKLASH: OBLIVION 2 ★★
(U.S.) 83m Full Moon Entertainment ~ Full Moon Home Video c
(AKA: OBLIVION 2)

George Takei *(Doc Valentine)*; Julie Newmar *(Miss Kitty)*; Isaac Hayes *(Buster)*; Richard Joseph Paul *(Zack Stone)*; Jackie Swanson *(Mattie Chase)*; Andrew Divoff *(Jaggar)*; Meg Foster *(Stell Barr)*; Irwin Keyes *(Bork)*; Jimmie F. Skaggs *(Buteo)*; Carel Struycken *(Gaunt)*; Musetta Vander *(Lash)*; Maxwell Caulfield *(Sweeney)*; Jeff Weston *(Crowley)*; Brent Huff *(Long John)*; Michael C. Mahon *(Sidekick)*; Sam Irvin *(Stogie Joe)*

The sequel to 1994's OBLIVION picks up immediately where the first ended. Like its predecessor, it's an uneasy mix of STAR WARS (1977) and HIGH NOON (1952). It approaches western stereotypes with a sci-fi spin, and features a supporting cast of recognizable faces.

The planet Oblivion awaits the arrival of Sweeney (Maxwell Caulfield), who, despite his foppish English attire, is the deadliest bounty hunter in the sector. On this occasion, he's tracking down a corporate saboteur, but has no description to go on, except that she's female. Assuming that the beautiful but evil Lash (Musetta Vander) must be the culprit, he temporarily locks her up in the local hoosegow. In the meantime, Sweeney romances the town widow, Mattie Chase (Jackie Swanson), much to Marshall Zack Stone's (Richard Joseph Paul) displeasure, and the town's cyborg deputy, Stell Barr (Meg Foster), has her bionic arm upgraded by the drunken local doctor (George Takei).

When Miss Kitty (Julie Newmar), who runs the town's "cathouse," confesses to the Marshall that she is actually the wanted woman, Zack refuses to hand over Lash to Sweeney. Angered, the bounty hunter transforms into a hideous beast, just as a small army run by reptilian villain Jaggar (Andrew Divoff) invades the town. A final showdown is averted when Kitty announces her guilt, only to be apparently killed while saving the lives of Sweeney and Zack. After Sweeney departs, Miss Kitty makes a surprise appearance in the middle of her own funeral.

This OBLIVION adventure deposits its viewers into the world with little explanation, and it's no surprise, since both the first feature and its sequel were filmed in Romania at the same time. Unfortunately, instead of combining the western and sci-fi genres for fresh inspiration, the merging only gives the filmmakers twice as many cliches with which to work. Still, there is an appeal thanks to its odd cast, even if they are given little to do. The only actor to get any genuine laughs is the towering Carel Struycken (Lurch in THE ADDAMS FAMILY movies) as Gaunt, the town's mortician, who awaits every demise with a blissful smile. Vander lends the film some sex appeal as Lash, looking like a villainous Bettie Page in her dominatrix-style, black-vinyl attire.

The special effects are minimal, and even with its slight running time (and extensive flashback footage), the story feels padded. Likable yet lame-brained, this material seems better-suited to a Saturday-morning children's TV show. *(Violence.)* — S.P.

d, Sam Irvin; p, Vlad Paunescu, Oana Paunescu; exec p, Charles Band; co-p, Albert Band, Debra Dion, Peter David; w, Peter David (based on an original story idea by Charles Band; story by John Rheaume, Hreg Suddeth, Mark Goldstein); ph, Adolfo Bartoli; ed, Andy Horvitch; m, Pino Donaggio; prod d, Milo; fx, David Allen Productions; makeup, Michael S. Deak, Alchemyfx

Science Fiction/ Western/Comedy **(PR: A MPAA: PG-13)**

BAD LOVE ★
(U.S.) 93m Boomerang Productions ~ Benla Inc. c

Pamela Gidley *(Eloise)*; Tom Sizemore *(Lenny)*; Richard Edson *(Bubba)*; Joe Dallesandro *(Boss)*; Vyto Ruginis *(Evan)*; Seymour Cassel *(Uncle Bud)*; Jonathan David *(Man at Gas Station)*; Jordan Lund *(Mr. Cook)*; Jill Goldman *(Secretary)*; Barbara Pilavin *(Waitress)*; Margaux Hemingway *(Jackie)*; Jennifer O'Neill*(Ms. Alman)*; Pat Crawford Brown *(Woman in Pink)*; Debi Mazar *(Delores)*; Don Bajema *(Bartender)*; Julie Strain *(Amber)*; David Pesko *(Duane)*; Joe E. Tata *(Norm)*; Richard Ardi *(Jack)*; Kimberly Bolin *(Porn Actress 1)*; Rhonda G. Miller *(Porn Actress 2)*; Peter Spellos *(Mover)*; Paul Bollen *(Paul)*; Alisa Christensen *(Felicia)*; Kari French *(Jane)*; Blaire Tefkin *(Saleswoman)*; Reed Hollister *(Salesman)*

Tom Sizemore's abrasively edgy lead performance sets the tone for this meandering, low-key character study. Sizemore's character is such a loser-with-a-capital-L that this lower-depths drama quickly turns into an exploitation flick about the dangers of live-in relationships.

Unable to hold down a job, perpetual dreamer Lenny (Tom Sizemore) crashes at the apartment of his brother, Evan (Vyto Ruginis). Meanwhile, across town, hemmed in by office duties that include bedding her married boss (Joe Dallesandro), Eloise (Pamela Gidley) quits her dead-end position with few prospects lined up. Later, when Lenny screws up a gas-pumping job to drive Eloise (who is a total stranger to him) to an interview, all Eloise sees is Sir Galahad, not an impractical hustler. While Eloise lands a promising assignment as personal secretary to an actress, Ms. Alman (Jennifer O'Neill), drifter Lenny gets bounced from his new arcade-machine repair job. Things move quickly for these unhealthy star-crossed lovers: Eloise allows Lenny to move in with her, and immediately Lenny badgers Eloise about her past promiscuity. Hypocritically, he then takes temp work as a sound technician on a porno film. Arrested in a vice raid, Lenny prevails upon Eloise, now thoroughly disillusioned and destitute, for bail. With their resources strapped enough to make eviction a reality, Lenny persuades Eloise to participate in a staged burglary at Ms. Alman's. Unfortunately, the gag Lenny uses on robbery victim Alman chokes her to death. When Eloise phones 911, Lenny refuses to flee without her. Flashing a pistol at arriving policemen, Lenny is instantly executed, and Eloise is arrested.

An erotic drama without any sensual heat must be considered a failure. For a film like this to connect with the audience, it has to be foremost a sizzling love story. Here the principals seem more likely to get on each other's nerves than under each other's clothes. Unable to create a convincing portrait of sex as a form of insanity, the film leaves the viewer wondering why Eloise doesn't throw the schlub out and get on with her life. As for Sizemore, usually a brilliant actor (particularly in WHERE SLEEPING DOGS LIE), here he is so intent on perfecting his small-time character's tics that he loses sight of the bigger picture.

Mired in slice-of-life realism and the kind of semi-improvised acting that rings false, BAD LOVE ultimately leaves you with the feeling that you've just watched a dysfunctional relationship dissected on a talk show. This tale of a woebegone blunderer and the well-meaning masochist who takes him in (she just can't help herself when bad boy kisses her) has the impersonality of a radio shrink pigeonholing the emotional hang-ups of a lifetime in two-minute sound bytes. What THE BOOST (1988) was to cocaine, this cautionary fable is to addictive love. *(Graphic violence, extensive nudity, extreme profanity, sexual situations, substance abuse.)* — R.P.

d, Jill Goldman; p, Matt Devien, Jonathan Reiss; exec p, Cassian Elwes; assoc p, Andrei Schuth, Chris Beckman, David Andriole; co-p, Janet Levine; ph, Gary Tieche; ed, Esther Russell; m, Rick Cox; prod d, John Di Minico; art d, John Guedon; set d, Gina Goldman; sound, Craig Felburg; casting, Fern Cassel; cos, Marisa Aboitiz; makeup, Jill Fink; stunts, Ed Anders

Drama/Crime/Erotic **(PR: C MPAA: R)**

BAD MOON ★★

(U.S.) 82m Bad Wolf Productions; Morgan Creek Productions ~ Warner Bros. c

Michael Pare *(Ted Harrison)*; Mariel Hemingway *(Janet)*; Mason Gamble *(Brett)*

Surprisingly unsurprising, BAD MOON revisits but fails to revitalize that classic horror creature, the werewolf.

While on assignment in the jungles of Nepal, photojournalist Ted (Michael Pare) and his girlfriend are attacked by a ferocious man-beast. Only Ted survives the attack.

In the Pacific northwest, Ted's sister Janet (Mariel Hemingway) lives with her son Brett (Mason Gamble) and German shepherd Thor in a secluded house on the edge of a forest where a series of grisly murders have been committed. Janet receives a phone call from Ted, who since his return from Nepal has been living in his trailer at the other end of the forest. Not realizing that he is a werewolf who is responsible for the murders, she visits Ted and persuades him to come and stay at her house. Ted agrees, hoping his family's love (and the practice of tying himself to a tree before the moon rises) will cure him.

Everyone, especially Thor, notices that Ted seems different. Following Ted on one of his prowls in the forest, the dog discovers his secret. But when another murder is committed, the local police, having seen the dog's aggressive behavior toward Ted, blame Thor. Despite his efforts to restrain himself, Ted is finally overcome and attacks his sister's house. Thor fights back, tracks the werewolf into the woods, and, finding him reverted back to an injured but still living Ted, kills him.

Less than 80 minutes long, BAD MOON may have been trimmed prior to release, though it's hard to imagine what might be missing in a film whose sole virtue is its brevity. Aside from a few minor and arbitrary adjustments to standard cinema werewolf lore (i.e., Ted is affected by any moon, not merely a full one), BAD MOON is so perfunctory as to make you wonder why a major studio and name-value cast considered it worth their time.

Like all the best werewolves from Lawrence Talbot to AN AMERICAN WEREWOLF IN LONDON's David Kessler, Ted is a figure of some pity, a decent man who becomes a murderous beast against his will. But neither the script nor Pare's gloomy performance make much of this. As the tale wears on, sympathy falls to the dog Thor, who is almost made to pay the ultimate price for Ted's crimes. (Presumably this comes from the script's source, a novel entitled *Thor*.) Director-screenwriter Eric Red has some strong features to his credit, including COHEN AND TATE (1989) and the script for THE HITCHER (1986), but BAD MOON isn't one of them. *(Graphic violence, nudity, sexual situations.)* — M.F.

d, Eric Red; p, James G. Robinson; exec p, Gary Barber, Bill Todman Jr.; co-p, Jacobus Rose; w, Eric Red (based on the novel *Thor* by Wayne Smith); ph, Jan Kiesser; ed, Timothy O'Meara; m, Loek Dikker; prod d, Linda Del Rosario; set d, David Chiasson; sound, David Husby; casting, Michelle Allen; cos, Rita Riggs

Horror **(PR: C MPAA: R)**

BADKONAK-E SEFID

(SEE: WHITE BALLOON, THE)

BAJA ★

(U.S.) 92m Baja Brothers; Dream Entertainment ~ Republic Pictures Home Video c

Molly Ringwald *(Bebe)*; Donal Logue *(Axel)*; Chris Shearer *(Chris)*; Nelson Lyon *(Nelson)*; Michael A. Nickles *(Michael)*; Corbin Bernsen *(Stone)*; Rique Renaldo *(Hotel Manager)*; Wayne Duvall *(Husband)*; Karen S. Gregan *(Wife)*; Lance Henriksen *(Burns)*; Thomas G. Romero *(Barkeep)*; Julian Reyes *(Shorty)*; Roxanna Michaels *(Prostitute)*

Itching to be an existential thriller, BAJA sports a screenplay so self-important and characters so wafer-thin that it might better be described as "Sartre a la screen." Directed with irksome film school bravado, BAJA is covered with cinematic flashiness to distract attention from the fact that its slavishly-delivered ironies have been explored with greater depth in other, better movies.

On a downward spiral since her mother's death under questionable circumstances, heiress Bebe Stone (Molly Ringwald) takes up with a small-time drug courier, Axel (Donal Logue). When Nelson (Nelson Lyon), another drug dealer, rips them off, Axel shoots Nelson's representative, and the scared couple flees south of the border. Concurrently, Bebe's father Stone (Corbin Bernsen) (whom Bebe believes responsible for her mother's death) coaxes Bebe's ex-husband Michael (Michael A. Nickles) into trekking to Baja to help retrieve his hellion daughter. Meanwhile, a touchy hit man named Burns (Lance Henriksen) is hot on Axel and Bebe's trail, too. Cultivating Michael's friendship in Mexico, crafty Burns closes in on Axel whom he locates by terrorizing (then killing) Axel's Baja connection. What Bebe doesn't realize is that disgruntled Nelson isn't Burns' employer; her father is. So anxious is Burns to complete his assignment, he causes a church shoot-out that leaves innocent bystanders and the *policia* dead. While Bebe continues to turn a deaf ear to Michael's prudent counsel, resentful Axel turns on Michael. Courtesy of Burns, Axel is killed for blackmailing Stone with evidence of guilt in his wife's murder. With his job finally done, Burns leaves Bebe and Michael unharmed and flees homeward.

Unresolved plot issues surround this movie like buzzards circling a dead screenwriter in the Baja desert. (For instance, wouldn't Stone also want his daughter silenced? Why is Burns such a sloppy assassin? Wouldn't someone so nonchalant about human life wipe out Bebe and Michael as a matter of course?) A generous interpretation suggests BAJA's writer-director is after bigger game than simply updating a 40s film noir to the 90s drug culture; perhaps BAJA is intended as a philosophical statement about degrees of criminal culpability and the value judgments of the amoral. Even so, the film is padded with so many tourist shots you'd think BAJA had been commissioned by the Baja Chamber of Commerce. And for the final nail in the coffin, this sun-drenched bore can't even manage a car chase with any pep—something less pretentious action dramas can handle in their sleep.

Playing yet another quirky character who marches to a different drummer, Henriksen single-handedly keeps the plot mechanics whirring and the lofty soul-searching in its place. However, one does wonder how Henriksen's hit man character, Burns, stays in business given his propensity for shooting everyone in sight. Did the director consciously intend that the only fully dimensional, sympathetic character in his film be a sloppy assassin? *(Graphic violence, extreme profanity, extensive nudity, adult situations, substance abuse.)* — R.P.

d, Kurt Voss; p, Larry J. Rattner; exec p, Ehud Bleiberg, Yitzhak Ginzberg; assoc p, Lee Ann Groff; co-p, Russell Gray; w, Kurt Voss; ph, Denis Maloney; ed, Gail Yasunaga; m, Reg Powell; prod d, Elisabeth Scott; set d, Jodi Muller; sound, Jon Ailetcher; fx, Ron Trost, Rodney Nixon, Claire van der Poel, Gabriel Vasquez; casting, Russell Gray; cos, Kristen Anacker; makeup, Elizabeth Dahl; stunts, Kay Kimler

Crime/Thriller **(PR: O MPAA: R)**

BARB WIRE ★½
(U.S.) 90m Propaganda Films; Dark Horse Entertainment; Polygram ~ Gramercy Pictures c

Pamela Anderson *(Barb Wire)*; Temuera Morrison *(Axel Hood)*; Victoria Rowell *(Cora D)*; Jack Noseworthy *(Charlie Kopetski)*; Xander Berkeley *(Alexander Willis)*; Steve Railsback *(Colonel Pryzer)*; Udo Kier *(Curly)*; Andre Rosey Brown *(Big Fatso)*; Tony Bill *(Foster)*; Marc Collver *(Manny)*; Vanessa Lee Asher *(Emily)*; Jennifer Banko *(Spike)*; Shelly Desai *(Sharif)*; Clint Howard *(Schmitz)*; Ken Forsgren *(Greaseball)*; Neil Hunt *(Weasel)*; Henry Kingi *(Moe)*; Tiny "Zeus" Lister *(Bouncer)*; Marshall Manesh *(Sheik)*; John Paxton *(Smooth)*; Pee Wee Piemonte *(Frick)*; Loren Rubin *(Krebs)*; Michael Russo *(Santo)*; Harvey Shield *(Dad)*; Patti Tippo *(Mom)*; Dominique Vandenberg *(Frack)*; Al Wan *(China)*; Diane Warshay *(Maria)*; Nicholas Worth *(Reuben)*; Nils Allen Stewart *(Jack)*; Amir Aboulela *(Patron)*; Adriana Alexander *(Redhead)*; Ron Balicki *(Customs Agent No. 1)*; Candace Camille Bender *(Dancer)*; Alex Bookston *(Man in White Suit)*; Gil Borgos *(Old Man)*; Tina Cote *(Woman in Bar No. 1)*; Vinnie Curto *(Aide to Pryzer)*; Miles Dougal *(Goon No. 1)*; David Andriole *(Goon No. 2)*; Darrell Heath *(Soldier in Flashback)*; Diana Lee Insanto *(Customs Agent No. 2)*; Tiffany Lawrence *(Security Guard)*; Mary Anna Reyes *(Woman in Torture Room)*; Jeffrey Dean Rosenthal *(Bald Man)*; Joe Sagal *(Fred the Bartender)*; Diane Shay *(Stripper in Dressing Room)*; Lou Simon *(Passenger)*; Rene Stahl *(Woman in Bar No. 2)*; Teo *(Disc Jockey)*; Jack Wright *(Package Check Guy)*; Salvator Xuereb *(Young Soldier)*

Yet another comic book (er, "graphic novel") adapted for the big screen, BARB WIRE is sexier than TANK GIRL (1995) but dumber than any BATMAN sequel so far.

The artificially endowed Pamela Anderson Lee portrays the titular anti-heroine—a stripper who owns her own disco and just happens to be a part-time mercenary-bounty hunter. She has the ferocity of a cornered kitten, as she kicks, pouts, and shoots her way into and out of trouble.

She establishes her tough-as-Lee-Press-On-Nails attitude in the opening sequence by killing a drunken goon who calls her "Babe." The backstory involves a future wherein the US government has been perverted into a Nazi-like dictatorship of SS-uniformed rednecks at war with rebellious surfer dudes.

Barb is drafted against her will by a former lover (Temuera Morrison) to help him escape with his research scientist spouse (Victoria Rowell), who carries a secret genetic macguffin in her contact lenses. Barb must match wits with the evil Col. Pryzer (Steve Railsback) while the local law officer (Jack Noseworthy) with whom Barb has an uneasy alliance can only stand around making sarcastic comments.

Barb declares herself neutral and resists every effort by either side to get her involved. Her brave, bitter brother (Xander Berkeley), who was blinded in the Battle of Seattle, seeks the assistance of the local Rebel forces, only to find them slaughtered in a bloody massacre by jack-booted government storm troopers. Tortured, he does not crack and dies without telling them what they want to know.

Enraged over her brother's cruel death, Barb uses a combination of brute force and underworld connections to secure passage for two on the last plane to Switzerland. Double-crossed at the last minute, she's forced to flee a small army of motorcycle-riding pseudo-Nazis by driving a Winnebago outfitted with flame-throwers and machine guns.

All this leads to the final, drawn-out battle between Barb and Pryzer, in which he seals his fate by taunting her with the unforgivable four-letter word—babe.

The CASABLANCA-like plot line is not really a homage, as nothing inventive or clever is done with it. But it is a convenient, familiar hook on which to hang the flimsy characters and unspectacular stuntwork. The cast seems almost as bored as the writers clearly were, and even the usually surefire crowd-pleasing explosions and kung-fu kickfests are lifeless and uninspired. And yet somehow BARB WIRE manages to get just enough campy appeal out of Lee to keep the film rolling along, almost in spite of itself.

Donning or doffing some new variation on black leather and stiletto heels every five minutes, Lee fills the screen admirably, even if her acting is less colorful than her wardrobe. Pouty and sullen, she struts through the role so oblivious to the silliness of it all that she inadvertently wins the viewer over. A Barbie doll forced to play amongst the GI Joes, Lee puffs her expensively teased hair out of her face and sways her hips to whatever drumbeat the thudding story throws at her next. As a translation of the darkly nihilist comics on which it is based, BARB WIRE is an unmitigated failure, but as a showcase for Lee's unique talents, it's kind of adorable. *(Nudity, profanity, violence.)* — R.S.

d, David Hogan; p, Brad Wyman, Mike Richardson, Todd Moyer; exec p, Peter Heller; assoc p, Ray Manzella, Dennis Brody; w, Chuck Pfarrer, Ilene Chaiken (from a story by Ilene Chaiken); ph, Rick Bota; ed, Peter Schink; m, Michel Colombier; prod d, Jean-Philippe Carp; art d, Dins Danielsen; set d, Lisa Robyn Deutsch; sound, Vince Garcia (mixer); fx, John E. Gray, CB; casting, Rick Montgomery, Dan Parada; cos, Rosanna Norton; makeup, Donna L. Henderson; stunts, M. James Arnett

Action/Thriller/Science Fiction **(PR: A MPAA: R)**

BASQUIAT ★★½
(U.S.) 108m Build a Fort, Inc. ~ Miramax c

Jeffrey Wright *(Jean Michel Basquiat)*; Michael Wincott *(Rene Ricard)*; Benicio Del Toro *(Benny Dalmau)*; Claire Forlani *(Gina Cardinale)*; David Bowie *(Andy Warhol)*; Dennis Hopper *(Bruno Bischofberger)*; Gary Oldman *(Albert Milo)*; Christopher Walken *(The Interviewer)*; Willem Dafoe *(The Electrician)*; Jean Claude Le Marre *(Shenge)*; Parker Posey *(Mary Boone)*; Elina Lowensohn *(Annina Nosei)*; Paul Bartel *(Henry Geldzahler)*; Courtney Love *(Big Pink)*; Tatum O'Neal *(Cynthia Kruger)*; Chuck Pfeifer *(Tom Kruger)*; Rockets Redglare *(Rockets)*; Esther G. Schnabel *(Esther Milo)*; Jack Schnabel *(Jack Milo)*; Lola Schnabel *(Jacqueline Milo)*; Peter McGough *(Himself)*; David McDermott *(Himself)*; Michael Chow *(Himself — Mr. Chow)*; Olatz Maria Schnabel *(Christine)*; Stella Schnabel *(Stella)*; Steven Randazzo *(Maitre d' at Ballato's)*; Michael Badalucco *(Counterman at Deli)*; Francis Dumaurier *(Giorgio)*; Joseph R.

Gannascoli *(Guard at Hospital)*; Hope Clarke *(Matilde)*; Brian Wright *(Young Jean Michel)*; Tarmo Urb *(Lech)*; Denise Burse *(Mary on TV)*; Robert Alexander *(Band Guy)*; Vincent Laresca *(Vincent)*; Nemo *(Nemo)*; Paul Outlaw *(Paul)*; Leonard Jackson *(Jean Michel's Father)*; Dave Shelley *(Photographer)*; Fredrick Weller *(Frank)*; Rene Rivera *(Juan)*; Sam Rockwell *(Thug)*; Ron Brice; William Seymour *(Mr. Chow's Maitre d')*; Linda Larkin *(Fan)*; Julie Araskog *(Julie)*; Richard Butler; Joe Glasco; Steven Parenago; Jose Luis Ferrer; Irene Kiss; Richard the Ox *(Medieval Villagers)*

The New York art scene of the 1980s, with its huge bankrolls, instant celebrities and hungry collectors, has been a story just waiting to be told. But insider Julian Schnabel, who wrote, directed and partially financed BASQUIAT, may be too close to the action to tell the story well.

Tormented artist Jean-Michel Basquiat (Jeffrey Wright) begins his career as a graffiti artist whose work litters the streets of lower Manhattan under the pseudonym Samo. He lives in a cardboard box, plays in a rock band, hangs out with dubious friends, visits his mother in an insane asylum, and scribbles his images on every urban surface that crosses his path.

When critic Rene Ricard (Michael Wincott) encounters his work at a Lower East Side party, life takes a radical turn. The first dealer to court him, Annina Nosei (Elina Lowensohn), sets him up with a one-man show and a studio. When his work meets with critical success, every other dealer in town tries to steal him. For a time, he leads a charmed life, selling his work for staggering sums and hob-nobbing with the art world's elite, including Andy Warhol (David Bowie). After he has had his 15 minutes of fame, the media ignores him and the art world turns a cold shoulder. Shortly after Warhol's death, Basquiat begins to degenerate and is reduced to walking the streets of SoHo in a drug haze. He dies in 1988 of a heroin overdose at age 27.

Part of BASQUIAT's strange story includes its telling. In this case, Julian Schnabel, one of the sought-after painters of that decade, is able to partially finance this film and compete with Hollywood.

This illustrates the most striking aspect of that moment in art history. The avant garde, a word nearly synonymous with poverty and marginality, emerged from the shadows and got rich. Painters who only weeks before had searched the streets for materials and food were suddenly being interviewed by *Time* magazine and *Vanity Fair.* With this film, Schnabel tries to create the myth of an artist beaten down, not by art and failure, but by the art world and success.

Though it seems that Schnabel would have preferred to make himself the subject of this film, he fictionalizes himself in the character of Albert Milo (Gary Oldman), as a beacon of wisdom, tolerance, perseverance, and good advice.

It is easy to tell just whom Schnabel likes and dislikes. He delivers a particularly harsh treatment of mega-dealer Mary Boone (Parker Posey) as an aloof and dismissive dilettante. He seems to prefer his colleagues who already have been buried, giving perhaps the first fair rendition of Warhol and being downright sentimental in his treatment of Basquiat.

Schnabel focuses on the difficulties that Basquiat had in coping with his sudden change in fortune. He is depicted as arrogant, insecure and defensive about and uncomfortable with his position as the first black man to enter what until then had been a white history. Schnabel also focuses on the uneasiness and unhappiness of the art community, where egos clash and abuses of hierarchy play themselves out. Basquiat's friendship with Warhol is scrutinized, contrasting how the media played it, how the community interpreted it, and how these factors corrupted the authentic connection they had established.

Schnabel claims he took responsibility for this film because he didn't want a tourist to tell the tale later. Unfortunately Schnabel's insider view only harms the story. Not even his cast of famous friends, including cameos by Dennis Hopper, Courtney Love, Christopher Walken, Tatum O'Neal and William Dafoe, can revive this pedestrian film. Though Schnabel uses the techniques of independent film making, they are meaningless in the context of a traditional and sentimental narrative.

And that is the biggest disappointment of BASQUIAT: Schnabel's talents as a painter do not translate into film. *(Adult situations.)* — R.C.

d, Julian Schnabel; p, Jon Klik, Randy Ostrow, Joni Sighvatsson; exec p, Peter Brant, Joseph Allen, Michiyo Yoshizaki; co-p, Lech Majewski; w, Julian Schnabel (from a story written by Lech Majewski and developed by Michael Thomas Holman); ph, Ron Fortunato; ed, Michael Berenbaum; m, John Cale, Julian Schnabel; prod d, Dan Leigh; art d, C.J. Simpson; set d, Susan Bode; sound, Allan Byer (mixer); cos, John Dunn; makeup, Jennifer Aspinall; stunts, Jeff Ward

Biography/Drama **(PR: C MPAA: R)**

BATON ROUGE ★★★½

(Spain) 94m Modigil ~ Arenas Group/Meridian c

Carmen Maura *(Isabel Harris)*; Victoria Abril *(Dr. Ana Alonso)*; Antonio Banderas *(Antonio)*; Rafael Diaz *(Ramon Ramos)*; Francisco Guijar *(Leon Harris)*; Aldo Grillo *(False Leon Harris)*; Yayo Calvo *(Antonio's Dad)*; Pedro Diaz Del Corral *(Forensics Worker)*; Gracia Lleo *(Forensics Assistant)*; Fernando Melgosa *(Policia)*; Lupe Barrado *(Maribel)*; Jose Luis Baringo *(Hospital Director)*; Alberto Fernandez; Luis San Narciso; Ignacio Duran *(Card Players)*; Pilar Barrera *(Celandora)*; Paco Guijar; Laura Cepeda; Noel Molina; Angel de Andres Lopez

Hitchcock's influence lives on in this sometimes-mystifying, always-provocative thriller which eschews black comedy and edge-of-the-seat suspense for a slow, but steady, infusion of frissons.

Socialite Mrs. Isabel Harris (Carmen Maura) promotes her one-night stand Antonio (Antonio Banderas) to the status of live-in gigolo, despite her professed inability to tolerate intercourse. Allegedly suffering from a recurring rape nightmare, Mrs. Harris attempts to gain maximum value from Antonio's presence in her domain by undergoing treatment with a sex therapist, Dr. Ana Alonso (Victoria Abril). Rather than cure her client's neurosis, though, Alonso becomes involved with Antonio and entices him to frame Mrs. Harris for the murder of her wealthy ex-husband, Leon Harris (Francisco Guijar). Alonso assures gullible Antonio that they can extort more dough from the Harris family after they drive trusting Mrs. Harris around the bend. But with whom is ersatz love doctor Alonso really plotting?

Antonio keeps his end of the bargain by slipping out of a card game he's using as an alibi to meet Alonso right after she fatally stabs Mr. Harris in the boudoir. Unfortunately, Alonso always intended Antonio to be her patsy. Lying to every man she meets, Alonso also pretends to be a co-conspirator of Mrs. Harris's lawyer, who becomes Alonso's next casualty. With a legal agreement signed by Mrs. Harris and Antonio, Alonso implicates Antonio in Mr. Harris's slaying; she then plants the tire jack she used to kill the attorney inside Antonio's car. Alerted by the perfect symmetry of the frame-up, police question Alonso and suspect her of scheming with the Mrs. Harris (who claims she's innocent) to acquire free access to the late Mr. Harris's fortune.

When captured fall-guy Antonio escapes, the police shoot him but don't rush to apprehend him. After drowning treacherous

Mrs. Harris in her pool, Antonio denounces her lesbian lover, Alonso; he's buoyed by the realization that she can't touch Mrs. Harris's blood money. The criminals have done themselves in: Mrs. Harris is dead; Antonio is mortally wounded; and Alonso will face double-homicide charges.

Crime-film buffs will be held rapt by this intricately-maneuvered shell game involving a fertility clinic, multiple copies of a financial agreement, two unscrupulous sapphics, and a self-infatuated hustler who becomes a prize chump. Although there are occasions when the screenplay doesn't play fair in its attempts to blindfold and blindside the viewer, most of its calculated payoffs are sweet, such as the tricky doctor planting a second copy of a document in Antonio's car after the audience witnesses him tearing up what he believes is his only link to the crime.

Even if the elegantly directed BATON ROUGE (so named because of Antonio's dearest travel goal) weren't so icily entertaining, it would be indispensable because it provides a rare opportunity to see all three of director Pedro Almodovar's favorite stars in the same film. The bewitching Maura and lusty Abril are perfect foils for matinee-idol Banderas, whose sex appeal registers so much more forcefully in his native language. An adroitly handled movie about a nearly-perfect crime, BATON ROUGE doesn't care to create suspense with speculation about the female characters' chances of getting away with murder. Instead, the thrills emerge from discovering how they've perfected the art of deceiving men. Aside from the police chief, every male falls under their spell.

Any man tempted by the notion of killing for money is advised to take a gander at BATON ROUGE, which neatly epitomizes the rule that not only is the female deadlier than the male, she's smarter, too. *(Graphic violence, nudity, profanity, sexual situations, adult situations.)* — R.P.

d, Rafael Moleon; exec p, Eduardo Campoy, Edmundo Gil; assoc p, Antonio Llorens; w, Rafael Moleon, Agustin Diaz Yanes; ph, Angel Luis Fernandez; ed, Jose Salcedo; m, Bernardo Bonezzi; art d, Javier Fernandez; sound, Ricardo Steinberg, Daniel Goldstein; makeup, Gregorio Martinez

Thriller/Erotic/Crime (PR: C MPAA: NR)

BEASTMASTER 3: THE EYE OF BRAXUS ★

(U.S.) 92m Stu Segall Productions ~ MCA Universal Home Video c

Marc Singer *(Dar)*; Tony Todd *(Seth)*; Keith Coulouris *(Bey)*; Sandra Hess *(Shada)*; Casper Van Dien *(Tal)*; Patrick Kilpatrick *(Jaggard)*; Lesley-Anne Down *(Morgana)*; David Warner *(Lord Agon)*; Olaf Pooley *(Maldor)*; David Grant Wright *(Korum)*; Kimberly Stanphill *(Kala)*; Joey Zimmerman *(Pir)*; Gary Simpson *(Crimson Captain)*; Lance Rushing *(Crimson Warrior)*; Dar Thompson *(Guard)*; Michael S. Deak *(Braxus)*

This unaccountably popular series continues to waste the talent of star Marc Singer, who is required to do little more than thrust, parry, and flex his pecs. As usual, Singer's ancient-world Doctor Dolittle struts his legendary stuff in a juvenile adventure that could be categorized as a Steve Reeves movie without the guts.

Hoping to regain his waning powers, wizened Lord Agon (David Warner) saps the strength out of young, virile sacrificial victims and plots to lay his sorcerer's mitts on the magical gem, the Eye of Braxus. King Tal (Casper Van Dien) shares the Braxus-jewel artifact with his sibling Dar, the Beastmaster (Marc Singer). King Tal, captured by Agon, refuses to divulge Dar's whereabouts, despite torture inside the Shroud of Agony.

Meanwhile, King Tal's trusted bodyguard, Seth (Tony Todd), and Dar are betrayed by the Amazon Shada (Sandra Hess), who delivers them to a savage tribe but fails to steal Dar's Braxus gem-half.

Freed thanks to the combine cunning of Dar's trained lion, hawk and ferrets, Dar befriends Bey (Keith Coulouris), a callow acrobat in a traveling carnival. Seth reluctantly renews his acquaintance with Bey's boss, Morgana the Witch (Lesley-Anne Down). Morgana hatches a plot by which Dar might rescue King Tal. The plan includes Dar being delivered to Agon's crimson guard, on the theory that Dar will be able to rescue King Tal once he's inside the palace. Inside Agon's castle, adventuress Shada redeems herself by saving Dar from a pit of unfriendly animals.

Stymied before he can complete a rejuvenation treatment courtesy of a captured Bey, Agon does manage to acquire both pieces of the Eye of Braxus, which he fits into the forehead of a satanic idol. Although Agon transforms himself into a hellish creature with unlimited powers, Dar snatches the Braxus-gem from the statue and runs a sword through Agon's demonic manifestation, which Dar sends back to the pit of Hades. After Dar destroys the Eye of Braxus once and for all, peace is restored to the kingdom.

The thoroughly routine loin-cloth shenanigans of BEASTMASTER 3 will probably best be enjoyed by aggressive kids and young adults who thought YOR: THE HUNTER FROM THE FUTURE (1983) was a terrific movie. Despite some jollity here and there, BEASTMASTER 3 takes its legend-making seriously and doesn't resort to a tongue-in-cheek attitude. That's just as well, since the assembled cast wouldn't have had the flair to put it across anyway.

Whenever the script doesn't defeat the efforts of the athletic cast, the pinch-penny budget does. Unable to build a crescendo of suspense or to manufacture any dramatic conflict, BEASTMASTER 3 dishes out loud, sword-clanking action like mashed potatoes lumped onto a plastic cafeteria plate. *(Violence.)* — R.P.

d, Gabrielle Beaumont; p, David Wise, Lisa M. Cochran; exec p, Stu Segall, Sylvio Tabet; assoc p, Geraint Bell; w, David Wise (based on characters created by Dan Coscarelli and Paul Pepperman); ph, Michael Davis; ed, Ken Bornstein; m, Jan Hammer; prod d, Nigel Clinker; art d, Stephen Runningen; set d, Cecelia Rodarte; sound, Lee Archer (mixer); casting, Barbara Claman, Kerry Karsian; makeup, Keith Hall; stunts, Fernando Celis

Adventure/Children's/Action (PR: A MPAA: PG)

BEAUTE VOLEE

(SEE: STEALING BEAUTY)

BEAUTIFUL GIRLS ★★★

(U.S.) 112m Woods Entertainment; Miramax ~ Miramax c

Matt Dillon *(Tommy "Birdman" Rowland)*; Noah Emmerich *(Michael "Mo" Morris)*; Annabeth Gish *(Tracy Stover)*; Lauren Holly *(Darian Smalls)*; Timothy Hutton *(Willie Conway)*; Rosie O'Donnell *(Gina Barrisano)*; Max Perlich *(Kev)*; Martha Plimpton *(Jan)*; Natalie Portman *(Marty)*; Michael Rapaport *(Paul Kirkwood)*; Mira Sorvino *(Sharon Cassidy)*; Uma Thurman *(Andera)*; Pruitt Taylor Vince *(Stanley "Stinky" Womack)*; Anne Bobby *(Sarah Morris)*; Richard Bright *(Dick Conway)*; Sam Robards *(Steve Rossmore)*; David Arquette *(Bobby Conway)*; Adam LeFevre *(Victor)*; John Carroll Lynch *(Frank Womack)*; Sarah Katz *(Kristen Rossmore)*; Camille D'Ambrose *(Sharon's Mother)*; Martin Rubin *(Chip)*; Tom Gibis *(Peter the Eater)*; Allison Levine *(Waitress at Moonlight Mile)*; Earl R. Burt *(Bartender)*; Gregory Dulli *(Lead Singer, Afghan Wigs)*; Trent Nicholas Thompson *(Michael Morris, Jr.)*; Nicole Ranallo *(Cheryl Morris)*; Joyce Lacey *(Reunion Classmate #1)*; Matthew Nathan

Castens *(Reunion Classmate #2)*; Anne W. Erickson *(Coffee Shop Waitress)*; Ollie Osterberg *(Drinker #1)*; Sterling Robson *(Drinker #2)*; Edward Kaspszak *(Drinker #3)*; John Scurti *(Ticket Agent)*; Herbie Ade *(Bar Owner)*; Ben Gooding *(Customer)*; Frank Anello *(Irv)*

Ted Demme's Capra-esque direction and a fine ensemble cast distinguish this ebullient romantic comedy.

Lounge pianist Willie (Timothy Hutton) begs leave from his job to attend his high-school reunion in a small town in Minnesota. He joyously hooks up with old buddies Tommy (Matt Dillon), Paul (Michael Rapaport), and Kev (Max Perlich), but finds himself alienated from his woebegone widowed father and emotionally damaged brother. Their house remains sadly unchanged, a depressing repository of memories, but Willie's interest is at least piqued by a new next-door neighbor. Marty (Natalie Portman) is an angelic 13-year-old, half goofy adolescent, half intriguing Lolita, with a non-stop line of precocious chatter. Willie reluctantly tears himself away from their daily chats to deal with his pals, who are mired in troubled relationships.

Tommy's affair with bitchy, married Darian (Lauren Holly) is almost as bewildering to the guys as it is to his heartbroken girlfriend, Sharon (Mira Sorvino). Jan (Martha Plimpton) wants nothing more than to be rid of the misogynistic Paul, a difficult prospect who has a habit of using his snow plow to dump mountains of white stuff in front of her garage door. While the boys are hanging out in the neighborhood bar one day, in walks the dazzling Andrea (Uma Thurman), the visiting cousin of the barkeep (Pruitt Taylor Vince). The guys each try to make a play for her. All of them strike out, because she's already attached. Willie becomes momentarily torn between her and Marty, a situation made more urgent by the imminent arrival of his fiancee, Tracy (Annabeth Gish).

Tommy tries to break off with Darian, who refuses to go quietly. She crashes the surprise birthday party Sharon has thrown for Tommy and creates utter havoc. On the night of the reunion, Tommy is accosted by Darian's husband and his friends, and beaten to a pulp. Tommy's friends swear revenge, but are stopped in their tracks when they realize Tommy's affair threatens to break up Darian's family. Tommy and Sharon are happily reunited in the hospital, while Paul and Jan go their separate ways. Tracy arrives, and Willie bids a regretful farewell to the tearful Marty.

Director Demme, who previously demonstrated his skill with actors in THE REF (1994), shows here that he has a true gift for registering the warmth and intimacy that can spring up between "average" souls. He is ably assisted by scripter Scott Rosenberg, who has crafted a hybrid of hilariously nasty comedy, romantic idealism, and self-conscious mush.

The film provides a showcase for its stars, and while some of them shine, others can't quite meet the challenge. The very whitebread Hutton seems ill at ease with his blue-collar character. Dillon, in a surprisingly touching performance, is far more at home with Tommy's relaxed-yet-macho posture, and overpowers Hutton in every scene they share. Rapaport gives a knockout portrayal of the crew's unregenerate buffoon, getting the lion's share of the script's most trenchant lines.

Though Rosenberg's script places its focus on the male characters, some exceptional work is done by the distaff stars. With her knock-out performance as Gina, the group's self-named authority on the heinousness of men, it becomes clear that Rosie O'Donnell has honed her comic skill well enough to be considered a latter-day Joan Blondell. O'Donnell has a one-take tour-de-force shopping scene, during which she delivers a breathtaking rant against MTV, Madison Avenue, and the debilitating effects centerfold models have on American men. Thurman gives a lustrous performance as everybody's congenial dream girl. If O'Donnell's monologue is the comic high point of the movie, the two-character scenes that Thurman shares with Hutton and Dillon provide its emotional peaks. The latter ends on a lovely, rueful note, with Thurman spurning Dillon's come-ons to walk home alone in the snow.

As for the younger cast members, Portman takes center stage with a peformance that's riddled with keenly observed pubescent mannerisms that eventually coalesce into a deeply effective portrayal of a lovesick teenager. In her few scenes, Annabeth Gish makes such a deep impression that you readily believe how Willie's too-cliched Dad and goofball brother could instantly fall in love with her. *(Adult situations, sexual situations, substance abuse, profanity.)* — D.N.

d, Ted Demme; p, Cary Woods; exec p, Bob Weinstein, Harvey Weinstein, Cathy Konrad; assoc p, Scott Rosenberg, Joel Stillerman; co-p, Alan C. Blomquist; w, Scott Rosenberg; ph, Adam Kimmel; ed, Jeffrey Wolf; m, David A. Stewart; prod d, Dan Davis; art d, Peter Rogness; set d, Tracey A. Doyle; sound, James Thornton (mixer); fx, Dieter Sturm; casting, Margery Simkin; cos, Lucy W. Corrigan; makeup, Cindy J. Williams; stunts, Peter Bucossi

Drama/Comedy/Romance **(PR: C MPAA: R)**

BEAUTIFUL THING ★★★

(U.K.) 90m Channel Four; World Productions ~ Sony Pictures Classics c

Glen Berry *(Jamie Gangel)*; Linda Henry *(Sandra Gangel)*; Scott Neal *(Ste Pearce)*; Tameka Empson *(Leah)*; Ben Daniels *(Tony)*; Jeillo Edwards *(Rose)*; Anna Karen *(Marlene)*; Daniel Bowers *(Trevor Pearce)*; Garry Cooper *(Ronnie Pearce)*; Sophie Stanton *(Louise)*; Julie Smith *(Gina)*; Steven Martin *(Ryan McBride)*; Catherine Sanderson *(Kelly)*; Liane Ware *(Claire)*; John Benfield *(Rodney Barr)*; Marlene Sidaway *(Betty)*; Andrew Fraser *(Jayson)*; John Savage *(Lenny)*; Davyd Harries *(Brewery Official)*; Beth Goddard *(Brewery Official)*; Martin Walsh *(Bennett)*; Dave Lynn *(Drag Performer)*; Meera Syal *(Miss Chauan)*; Ozdemir Mamodeally *(Slasher)*

Slight yet sweet, this adaptation by Britain's Channel Four of a 1994 stage play is a paean to the hurt and the joyful flush of first love. That it involves two gay teens is almost beside the point.

Teenager Jamie Gangel (Glen Berry) lives in a crowded London housing estate with his unmarried mother, Sandra (Linda Henry). Sensitive yet smart-mouthed, he shares a contentious relationship with his careworn and equally tart-tongued mother, disapproving of her flirtations with much younger neo-hippie Tony (Ben Daniels). Their next-door neighbors are sassy Leah (Tameka Empson), who deals with life by getting stoned and channeling 1960s singer Mama Cass, and Ste Pearce (Scott Neal), Jamie's schoolmate. Ste suffers beatings from his brutal older brother, Trevor (Daniel Bowers) and their boozing, unmarried father Ronnie (Garry Cooper). Sandra often takes him in, and the boys bunk together. One night Jamie, who has accepted his homosexuality, rubs lotion onto the bruised Ste, who only ambivalently acknowledges his orientation, and, well, you know. Ste—confused and as scared by first love as he is of being gay—tries to avoid Jamie, but the other youth persists, and the two seem fine again, until Leah reveals that Trevor suspects. Sandra herself learns about the relationship from a school headmistress. She tails Jamie and Ste to a gay club, and later that night confronts her son. Despite her bewilderment, she nonetheless chooses to be supportive and tolerant. Sandra breaks up with Tony, and the boys come out by dancing cheek to cheek in the housing project plaza.

Playwright Jonathan Harvey adapted his own work, with Hettie Macdonald, who directed *Beautiful Thing* for the West End equivalent of off-Broadway, at the cinematic helm. Despite the specific environment (shot on location in London's Thamesmead area), one senses this story could well take place in Trailer Park, USA. Harvey's characters aren't noble archetypes but believable, complicated people (excepting Leah, whose purpose seems to be to provide saucy wisecracks). Macdonald's direction leans perilously toward the heavy-handed when songs comment on the action—such as "Make Your Own Kind of Music" laid atop a prototypic young-lovers romp with swirling, circular camerawork—yet her efforts have genuine feeling. Ben Daniels creates a highly likable Tony, smart yet a bit loopy in a determinedly fresh way.

BEAUTIFUL THING played the American art-theater circuit, its appeal to Yank audiences limited by the marble-mouthed, working-class accents of the characters, who use slang like "sort me out" and "a slapper never changes her knickers." Assuming you're not too "knackered" you should be able to follow the story just fine. *(Violence, nudity, profanity, substance abuse, adult situations.)* — F.L.

d, Hettie Macdonald; p, Tony Garnett, Bill Shapter; w, Jonathan Harvey; ph, Chris Seager; ed, Don Fairservice; prod d, Mark Stevenson; art d, Alison Wratten, Chrysoula Sofitsi; sound, John Midgley (mixer); casting, Gail Stevens, Andy Pryor; cos, Pam Tait; makeup, Elisa Johnson

Romance/Comedy/Drama **(PR: C MPAA: R)**

BEAVIS AND BUTT-HEAD DO AMERICA ★★

(U.S.) 80m MTV; Geffen Pictures ~ Paramount c

VOICES OF: Mike Judge *(Beavis/Butt-head/Tom Anderson/Van Driessen/Principal McVicker)*; Cloris Leachman *(Old Woman on Plane and Bus)*; Robert Stack *(Agent Flemming)*; Eric Bogosian *(Ranger at Old Faithful/Press Secretary/Lieutenant at Strategic Air Command)*; Richard Linklater *(Tour Bus Driver)*; Jacqueline Barba *(Agent Hurly)*; Pamela Blair *(Flight Attendant/White House Tour Guide)*; Kristofor Brown *(Man on Plane/Man in Confession Booth #2/Old Guy/Jim)*; Tony Darling *(Motley Crue Roadie #2/Tourist Man)*; John Doman *(Airplane Captain/White House Representative)*; Francis Dumaurier *(French Dignitary)*; Jim Flaherty *(Petrified Forest Recording)*; Tim Guinee *(Hoover Guide/ATF Agent)*; Earl Hofert *(Motley Crue Roadie #1)*; Toby Huss *(TV Thief #2/Concierge/Bellboy/Male TV Reporter)*; Sam Johnson *(Limo Driver/TV Thief #1/Man in Confession Booth #1/Petrified Forest Ranger)*; Rosemary McNamara *(Flight Attendant #2)*; Harsh Nayyar *(Indian Dignitary)*; Karen Phillips *(Announcer in Capitol)*; Dale Reeves *(President Clinton)*; Mike Ruschak *(Hoover Technician/General at Strategic Air Command)*; Gail Thomas *(Flight Attendant #3/Female TV Reporter)*

Those who are offended by the antics of MTV's moronic cartoon duo will find nothing in this feature film to change their minds. Unfortunately, fans won't find anything here that couldn't have been done as well or better on television.

Life loses all meaning for suburban teenagers Beavis and Butt-head after their television is stolen. The search for a replacement brings them to a local motel, where Muddy, a shady miscreant, mistakes them for the hit men he has hired to kill his wife, Dallas. This misunderstanding hinges on different interpretations of the phrase "do my wife." What Muddy doesn't tell them is that he and Dallas have been running a "Mom and Pop arms-smuggling operation," and that she has double-crossed him and taken off with a powerful but unstable miniature biological-warfare device. Muddy puts Beavis and Butt-head on a plane to Las Vegas, where Dallas is hiding.

After the plane almost crashes because of a disruption caused by Beavis's caffeine- and sugar-induced alter ego "Cornholio," the two arrive in Las Vegas. They find their way to Dallas's hotel room, expecting to have sex with her. She figures out what the situation is, and turns it to her own advantage. She secretly sews the weapon into Beavis's shorts, then puts the two on a bus to Washington DC, where she plans to meet them after she shakes the FBI agents on her trail.

After various distractions brought on by automatic urinals, a display of petrified wood, defecating donkeys, and a psychedelic near-death experience in the desert, Beavis and Butt-head arrive in Washington. They become separated at the White House. While FBI agents apprehend Butt-head, Beavis—who has again reverted to Cornholio—spots the trailer belonging to his vacationing neighbors, the Andersons. Overcome by the urge to masturbate, Beavis enters the trailer, which is soon surrounded by the FBI. But the feds mistakenly arrest Mr. Anderson, and Beavis and Butt-head are proclaimed heroes by President Bill Clinton. Returning home, they are reunited with their beloved television.

Every recent generation has had a pair of comic idiots to reflect the times, and Beavis and Butt-head probably will go down in history as emblematic of the 1990s. But the decision to expand them to the big screen seems to have been made solely from a financial point of view. All that distinguishes BEAVIS AND BUTT-HEAD DO AMERICA from an episode of the TV series are: better animation—a dubious improvement to a show whose very crudity is part of its appeal; and a long-form plot—also of questionable benefit for a show that parodies short attention spans. For better or worse, depending on your point of view, the levels of profanity and vulgarity are the same as on television: crude and sophomoric, but never explicit. And while gaining nothing, the film loses a major—if not the only—element of the show's appeal: the scenes of Beavis and Butt-head making fun of music videos. Those bits, perhaps because they are brief, have always been much funnier than the canned Catskills-humor of "Mystery Science Theater 3000," another TV show that foundered in an ill-advised attempt to move from television to movie houses.

There are still funny moments here, though most have little to do with the story line, including: the credit sequence, featuring Beavis and Butt-head as "Starsky and Hutch" wannabes; an outrageous visit to a church—those offended by the duo's mistaking confessional booths for Porta-Potties may be relieved to know that God gets the last word—and the guaranteed non-hit single "Lesbian Seagull," reprised under the end credits by Engelbert Humperdinck. Animation fans will want to see Beavis's hallucination, designed by Rob Zombie of the band White Zombie, in a style harkening back to warped 1960s illustrators like Ed "Big Daddy" Roth and Basil Wolverton. *(Adult situations, sexual situations, profanity.)* — M.F.

d, Mike Judge; p, Abby Terkuhle; exec p, David Gale, Van Toffler; co-p, John Andrews; w, Mike Judge, Joe Stillman (based on "MTV's Beavis and Butt-head" created by Mike Judge); ed, Terry Kelley, Gunter Glinka, Neil Lawrence; m, John Frizzell; art d, Jeff Buckland; anim, Yvette Kaplan, Choon Man Lee, Jae Joong Kim, Jun Nam Park, Jong Ho Kim, Rob Zombie, Chris Prynoski; sound, John Benson (design), John Lynn (design); fx, Normand Rompre, Dave Hughes; casting, Hughes Moss Casting

Animated **(PR: C MPAA: PG-13)**

BED OF ROSES ★★½

(U.S.) 87m Juno Pix, Inc.; New Line ~ New Line c

Christian Slater *(Lewis)*; Mary Stuart Masterson *(Lisa)*; Pamela Segall *(Kim)*; Josh Brolin *(Danny)*; Brian Tarantina *(Randy)*; Debra Monk *(Mom)*; Mary Alice *(Alice)*; Kenneth Cranham *(Simon)*; Ally Walker *(Wendy)*; Anne Pitoniak *(Grandma Jean)*; R.M. Haley *(Dad)*; Cass Morgan *(Aunt Meg)*; Gina Torres *(Francine)*; Nick Tate *(Fayard)*; Victor Sierra *(Jimmy)*; Michael Mantell *(Sam)*; Zachary Chaltiel *(Jason)*; Claire Mari Jacobs *(Lisa's Secretary)*; Paul Cassell *(1st Executive)*; Yvonne Zima *(Young Lisa)*; Desire Casado *(Amelia)*; Aldis Hodge *(Prince)*; Jessica Brooks Grant *(Queen)*; Jonathan Nocera *(King)*; Leah Pepper *(Sara)*; Donna Jean Fogel *(Student Teacher)*; S.A. Griffin *(Stanley)*; Edith Blume *(Mumuu Woman)*; Liz Sinclair *(Sad Woman)*; Al Cerullo *(Helicopter Pilot)*

Another first-rate performance by Mary Stuart Masterson highlights BED OF ROSES, a bittersweet but conventional romantic drama. Christian Slater is also appealing, but both stars have to work hard to keep viewers' interest from flagging in the second half of the story.

Lisa (Mary Stuart Masterson) is a young, hard-working Manhattan investment banker. The day after hearing that her father has died, Lisa receives a beautiful floral arrangement from a secret admirer. When her boss (Kenneth Cranham) gives Lisa a few days of vacation, Lisa uses her time to find out who sent the flowers. Her detective work pays off when Lewis Farrell (Christian Slater), a young Greenwich Village flower shop owner, admits to her that he sent the bouquet after seeing her crying in her window.

Lisa is charmed by Lewis and spends an entire day with him delivering flowers, but she runs away when they become more intimate. The next day, Lewis sends Lisa an endless series of rose bouquets to win her over. Lisa visits the flower shop to put a stop to the courtship, but she ends up falling in love instead. She is especially moved by Lewis's story about the death of his wife many years earlier. Lisa drops her sometime-boyfriend, Danny (Josh Brolin), and begins an affair with Lewis.

As Christmas approaches, Lewis invites Lisa to stay with his family over the holidays. Lisa's hesitation leads to a confession. Lisa explains that she does not know who her parents are and that her recently deceased father was actually a foster father who had molested her as a little girl. Lisa finally joins Lewis and his family for the holidays, but leaves abruptly when Lewis proposes marriage to her in front of his folks. Months pass before Lisa learns the value of what she has passed up. One day she appears suddenly on Lewis's doorstep, ready to start over again.

Masterson has proven that she is a talented and versatile actress in such films as BENNY AND JOON (1993) and IMMEDIATE FAMILY (1989). BED OF ROSES provides a decent showcase, giving her the focal role. She remains convincing in both the light comic scenes with Pamela Segall (who memorably plays her protective best friend), and in the high-powered dramatic moments toward the end. Slater, who meshes well with his co-star, maintains a steady, low-key approach (a la his underrated work in UNTAMED HEART [1993]) that is far more effective than the cocky persona he has displayed in some other films.

BED OF ROSES contains interesting performances, but its story line has few places to go after the romance gets fully under way—the Christmas episode in the second half seems like a toned-down rehash of HOME FOR THE HOLIDAYS. For a first directorial effort from writer Michael Goldenberg, however, at least BED OF ROSES commits no egregious errors; it plays it safe, but is also pleasant and proficiently made. *(Adult situations.)* — E.M.

d, Michael Goldenberg; p, Allan Mindel, Denise Shaw; exec p, Joseph Hartwick, Lynn Harris; assoc p, Kim Moarefi; co-p, Michael Haley; w, Michael Goldenberg; ph, Adam Kimmel; ed, Jane Kurson; m, Michael Convertino; prod d, Stephen McCabe; art d, Jefferson Sage; set d, Debra Schutt, Carolyn Cartwright; sound, Danny Michael (mixer); casting, Meg Simon; cos, Cynthia Flynt; makeup, Sharon Ilson

Romance/Drama/Comedy (PR: A MPAA: PG)

BEFORE AND AFTER ★★½

(U.S.) 108m Before & After Productions; Caravan Pictures; Hollywood Pictures ~ Buena Vista c

Meryl Streep *(Carolyn Ryan)*; Liam Neeson *(Ben Ryan)*; Edward Furlong *(Jacob Ryan)*; Julia Weldon *(Judith Ryan)*; Alfred Molina *(Panos Demeris)*; Daniel Von Bargen *(Fran Conklin)*; John Heard *(Wendell Bye)*; Ann Magnuson *(Terry Taverner)*; Alison Folland *(Martha Taverner)*; Kaiulani Lee *(Marian Raynor, Prosecutor)*; Larry Pine *(Dr. Tom McAnally)*; Ellen Lancaster *(Panos' Assistant)*; Wesley Addy *(Judge Grady)*; Oliver Graney *(T.J.)*; Bernadette Quigley *(T.J.'s Mom)*; Pamela Blair *(Dr. Ryan's Assistant)*; John Wylie *(Dr. Trygve Hanson)*; John Deyle *(Doctor #1)*; Tim Cavanaugh *(Young Policeman)*; John Webber *(Hardware Clerk)*; Jay Potter *(TV Reporter)*; Sharon Ullrick *(Female Bailiff)*; Robert Westenberg *(Journalist #1)*; Susan Pratt *(Journalist #2)*

Searching for meaning in a post-O.J. trial world, BEFORE AND AFTER tries to make points about the American justice system, but spoils a good mystery movie in the process.

The peaceful lives of the upper-middle-class Ryan family, Carolyn (Meryl Streep), Ben (Liam Neeson), and daughter Judith (Julia Weldon), are shattered when the police inform them that their teenaged son, Jacob (Edward Furlong), is being accused of the murder of his girlfriend, Martha Taverner (Alison Folland). After getting over the shock of the accusation and Jacob's disappearance, Carolyn and Ben argue over how to handle the situation: Carolyn disapproves of Ben destroying evidence from Jacob's car, while Ben wants to protect his son at all costs.

His parents are relieved when Jacob is tracked down and brought to a local youth detention center. The court allows Jacob to return home with his family, but he remains silent throughout the first few days of his awkward homecoming. Finally, Jacob tells his family the truth about what happened. He explains that he did kill Martha, but that it was an accident that arose out of a fight. With the help of their family lawyer (John Heard), the Ryans hire Panos Demeris (Alfred Molina), a crafty defense attorney who, with Ben, fabricates a story that absolves Jacob of all guilt.

But Jacob, Carolyn and Judith are uncomfortable with the lie and, each in their own way, fight to have the truth told—despite the potential consequences of imprisonment. Anxious to keep Jacob out of prison, Ben and Panos continue pressing their false version of events. Ultimately, Jacob insists on telling the truth in court and pleads with his father to support his decision. Jacob is declared not guilty, but gets a five-year sentence for his flight from the authorities. Ben gets a one-year sentence for destroying evidence.

Two years later, Jacob leaves jail on probation and is reunited with his parents.

The first half of BEFORE AND AFTER builds an intriguing case study of how a sudden calamity can expose the poorly-sealed divisions in a fragile nuclear family structure. Once the truth is revealed midway through, the film becomes a more traditional family melodrama with overstated allusions to the Old Testament. Ted Tally's screenplay also gets preachy about truth-telling and ends with the sappiest possible image of a reconstituted family unit.

Director Barbet Schroeder (BARFLY, REVERSAL OF FORTUNE) carefully creates atmosphere and suspense in the first half, but gets careless with the high-pitched theatrics of the second half. Even the uniformly solid cast seems to be straining for effect well before the conclusion. Streep and Neeson have one good scene, as they confront their son for the first time in the detention center. But most of their time together—especially in their brief sex scene—merely illustrates how poorly matched they are here. *(Violence, sexual situations, adult situations, profanity.)* — E.M.

d, Barbet Schroeder; p, Barbet Schroeder, Susan Hoffman; exec p, Roger Birnbaum, Joe Roth; assoc p, Jonathan Glickman; co-p, Chris Brigham; w, Ted Tally (based on the book by Rosellen Brown); ph, Luciano Tovoli; ed, Lee Percy; m, Howard Shore; prod d, Stuart Wurtzel; art d, Steve Saklad; set d, Gretchen Rau; sound, Tom Nelson (mixer); fx, John Milinac, Steve Kirshoff, Stuart Robertson; casting, Howard Feuer; cos, Ann Roth; makeup, Jean A. Black; stunts, Doug Coleman, Richard Blackwell

Drama **(PR: C MPAA: PG-13)**

BERKELEY IN THE 60S ★★★

(U.S.) 117m Kitchell Films ~ Pacific Arts/First Run Features c/bw

Susan Griffin *(Narrator)*; Jentri Anders; Frank Bardacke; Hardy Frye; John Gage; Jackie Goldberg; David Hilliard; Barry Melton; Mike Miller; Suzy Nelson; Ruth Rosen; Michael Rossman; Bobby Seale; John Searle; Jack Weinberg; Mario Savio; Todd Gitlin; Eldridge Cleaver; Joan Baez; Martin Luther King Jr.; Huey Newton; Allen Ginsberg; Ronald Reagan; The Grateful Dead

BERKELEY IN THE 60S provides an informative history of the rise of political activism on the University of California Berkeley campus, encompassing the movement from the student protest against the House on Un-American Activities Committee to the Memorial Day march on People's Park. Including recent interviews with key players, news footage, and a great music score, this historical study brings the decade and its significance to life without the nostalgia and romanticism that usually plague such pieces.

The first sparks of political activism appear on campus as early as May 1960 when students protest the paranoia and dubious nationalism of the House on Un-American Activities Committee. These protesting students were hosed down the stairs outside San Francisco City Hall by nervous powers-that-be. Filmed by the media, such televised images only served to drive like-minded and restless youth to the Berkeley campus.

This idealistic, young group finds its next battle in the civil rights movement. After a victory at the Sheraton Palace Hotel, in which the entire hotel industry is forced to curb discriminatory hiring practices, the student movement becomes unstoppable. The local community urges the university to crack down, but disciplinary actions only fan the flames of dissent and reinforce a centralized student base of power, unified on issues of free speech and democratic ideals. This new liberalism forms a serious critique of the reactionary nationalism and growing consumerism of 1950s America. Gradually, a population of privileged, middle-class youth comes to identify itself as a marginalized, oppressed population, and the spirit of revolution is born.

With confidence gained from civil rights victories, student activists turn their attention to the Vietnam War. Simultaneously, the San Francisco hippies emerge, asserting that the solution to the corruption of society lies not in political action, but in dropping out and adopting an anti-materialistic, communal, spiritual lifestyle based on freedom and experience. At first these two groups stand in opposition, but they both gradually adopt the characteristics of the other and cohere as a radical youth movement whose values and styles transverse the nation. The documentary covers the charismatic rise of the Black Panthers and the brutality of the Chicago Democratic convention, and ends with the Memorial Day March. In that action, 35,000 protesters marched to the site of the destruction of People's Park. In do doing, they saluted the broken symbol of building a utopian society where products are not artifacts of corporate profit, but rather useful tools in a decentralized, communal effort of cooperation and love.

This informative documentary addresses the finer details of a familiar movement, serving best to elucidate the lesser known trajectory of its history. BERKELEY IN THE 60S primarily succeeds thanks to the memories and insights of the leaders of the student movement, who prove to be better spokespersons than the rock stars and the typical "I was there" commentators from whom we usually hear. — R.C.

d, Mark Kitchell; p, Mark Kitchell; assoc p, Kevin Pina; ph, Stephen Lighthill; ed, Veronica Selver; m, Country Joe and the Fish

Documentary **(PR: A MPAA: NR)**

BEST OF THE BEST 3: NO TURNING BACK ★★

(U.S.) 102m Movie Group; Picture Securities LTD. ~ Buena Vista c

Phillip Rhee *(Tommy Lee)*; Gina Gershon *(Margo Preston)*; Christopher McDonald *(Jack Banning)*; Mark Rolston *(Donnie Hanson)*; Peter Simmons *(Owen Tucker)*; Dee Wallace Stone *(Georgia Tucker)*; Cristina Anzu Lawson *(Karen Banning)*; Michael Bailey Smith *(Tiny)*; Justin Brentley *(Luther Phelps)*; Andra Ward *(Reverend Phelps)*; Barbara Boyd *(Isabel)*; Kitao Sakurai *(Justin Banning)*; Cole McKay *(Bo)*; Steve Hulin *(Tre)*; Jack C. Thomas *(Mr. Morgan)*; John Robert Thompson *(Mayor)*; Howard Young *(Davey)*; George Wilson *(Shopkeeper)*; David Rody *(Arms Dealer)*; Jonathan McCurdy *(Owen's Brother)*

Surprisingly, given its genre origins, BEST OF THE BEST 3: NO TURNING BACK takes on the serious subject matter of hate groups co-opting government-weary small-town America. Not surprisingly, this also proves to be its greatest weakness. Although it earnestly targets the seduction of impressionable folks by White Supremacists, this action picture fumbles by portraying the encroaching Aryans as right-wing cartoons.

When Asian American Tommy Lee (Phillip Rhee) returns to his hometown to visit his sister Karen Banning (Cristina Anzu Lawson) and brother-in-law Sheriff Jack Banning (Christopher McDonald), he's disgusted that Liberty, USA has become a breeding ground for intolerance. The militia, headed by Donnie Hanson (Mark Rolston), has beaten to death an Afro-American, Reverand Phelps (Andra Ward), and later kills a bible-thumping White minister, who fronts for their organization, for espousing a segregationist view that the militia deems "too mild." Bonding with his nephew Justin (Kitao Sakurai) and Luther (the son of the late Reverend Phelps), pacifist Tommy Lee punches back when Hanson's goons threaten his family. While finding time to woo the town schoolmarm Margo Preston (Gina Gershon), who obstructs the militia's land expansion at a town-hall meeting, Tommy spearheads the campaign to douse the rising fires of the burning-cross mentality.

Pursued by motorcycling rednecks, Tommy Lee rescues Margo from gang rape but can't prevent the kidnapping of Justin and Luther. Inside the neo-KKK camp where Hanson is training an army with illegal weapons, Sheriff Banning and Tommy Lee create chaos with demolitions, free the children, and attempt a getaway in a school bus driven by Margo after the Sheriff is wounded. After sparing the life of a new racist recruit, Owen Tucker (Peter Simmons), Tommy Lee knocks the daylights out of, but no sense into, Donnie Hanson. When Hanson cowardly attempts to assassinate Tommy Lee, Owen shoots down his former wizard like a dog. With the power of the supremacist cabal defused, the townspeople soon restore order.

Those action buffs in the mood for mindless body-bashing should steer clear of this martial arts anomaly, which sorely tries to temper its violence with a contemplation of the side effects of misguided testosterone, hate, and racism. For all its admirable social concern, BEST OF THE BEST 3 can't overcome the hazards of speechifying, stereotyping, and amorphous direction. The cast, awkwardly headed by leading leg-man Rhee (who also directed), lends the ideal of tolerance a vital dimension, but can't help but emerge as paper-doll figures.

Although specific martial arts sequences (e.g., Rhee's solo salvation of his relatives outside the mini-mart) rate high on the adrenaline chart, the film lacks the skill to link its sundry climaxes in the kind of Hong Kong cinema trajectory that leaves an audience gasping for air. Reminiscent of classic Westerns like SHANE (1953) and neo-Westerns like WALKING TALL (1973), BEST OF THE BEST 3 delivers ample high-kicking but winds up a bloodier, Big Screen version of an episode of "Walker, Texas Ranger." *(Graphic violence, extreme profanity, sexual situations.)* — R.P.

d, Phillip Rhee; p, Peter E. Strauss, Phillip Rhee; exec p, Frank Giustra, Marlon Staggs; assoc p, Stacy Cohen; co-p, Deborah Scott; w, Deborah Scott, Barry Gray; ph, Jerry Watson; ed, Bert Lovitt; m, Barry Goldberg; prod d, William J. Perretti; art d, Virgil Sanchez; set d, Natali Pope; sound, Chat Gunter (mixer); fx, Larry Fioritto; casting, James Tarzia; cos, Renee Alaina Sacks; makeup, Wade Daily; stunts, Simon Rhee

Martial Arts/Action **(PR: O MPAA: R)**

BEWARE: CHILDREN AT PLAY ★★

(U.S.) 94m Troma Films ~ Troma, Inc. c

Michael Robinson *(John DeWolfe)*; Rich Hamilton *(Ross Carr)*; Robin Lilly *(Cleo Carr)*; Lori Tirgrath *(Julia DeWolfe)*; Jamie Krause *(Kara DeWolfe)*; Sunshine Barrett *(Mary Rose Carr)*; Mark Diekman *(Luke Domain)*; Mik Cribben *(Farmer Braun)*; Susan Chandler *(Mrs. Braun)*; Herb Klinger *(Franklin Ludwig)*; Lauren Cloud *(Dale Hawthorn)*; Lorna Courtney *(Amy Carr)*; Danny McClaughlin *(Grendel)*; Stephanie Jaworski *(Alice Allegari)*; Lee Kayman *(Josiah Modicah)*; Bernard Hocke *(Professor Randall)*; Eric Tonken *(Glenn Randall)*; Rick Bitzelberger *(Dr. Fish)*; Anne Grindley *(Witness)*; John Reischel *(Witness)*

This excursion into poverty-row horror is a combination of LORD OF THE FLIES (1990) and THE TEXAS CHAINSAW MASSACRE (1974), with ordinary children giving way to their most primitive urges and turning into feral, half-pint cannibals—as the special effects crew ladles on the gore. Made in 1989, this film sat on a shelf until 1996, when it finally received a straight-to-video release courtesy of Troma Team.

A father-son camping trip in the wilds of New Jersey goes awry when Professor Randall (Bernard Hocke) steps into a bear trap. His passing leaves eight-year-old Glenn (Eric Tonken) so traumatized that he disembowels the corpse, while repeating his father's last, feverish words, taken from *Beowulf:* "Gulp the blood, gobble the flesh." Ten years later, a tabloid-style novelist named John DeWolfe (Michael Robinson), his wife, Julia (Lori Tirgrath), and daughter, Kara (Jamie Krause), visit a sheriff friend, whose daughter is only one of a dozen recent disappearances of area youth. Unbeknownst to the adults, the children have all been recruited into the Woodies, a pack of forest-dwelling kids led by the teenaged Glenn, who believes himself to be the cannibalistic Grendel from *Beowulf.* Together, they lure several adults into the woods, slice them up and dig in. With most of the cast either killed or abducted, DeWolfe captures one of the Woodies and is taken to their campsite, which is decorated with human remains. Meanwhile, the rural townsfolk are convinced by religious fanatic Braun (Mik Cribben) that the youngsters are actually demons. They converge on the camp and slaughter everyone, including DeWolfe. The only survivor is Kara, who roams back into the woods in search of fresh blood.

Although rife with weaknesses that would sink any ordinary movie, this cruel, often tasteless item has everything a crude exploitation movie could ask for. There's an unconventional storyline, loads of shocking violence, community theater-level acting, and plenty of gaffes, such as the film's inability to get its star's name right (the opening credits list him as Michael Robinson, the end credits as Robertson). Though the idea of cannibal kiddies sounds like the makings of a sick comedy, it's all played with a straight face, and scriptwriter Fred Sharkey sneaks in some unexpected jabs at religious zealots when the vigilante townsfolk become more monstrous than any of the deluded children. When the ideas run dry, Cribben relies on a torrent of gruesome (albeit economical) special effects. Few horror movies have the audacity to shove a gun into a child's mouth and blow his brains out, on-screen, and since Troma had to substantially trim the picture in order to secure an R-rating, one can only imagine what it was like in its original form. *(Graphic violence, nudity, sexual situations.)* — S.P.

d, Mik Cribben; p, Ellen Wedner, Michael Koslow; exec p, Linda Sanford, Lawrence Littler; w, Fred Sharkey; ph, Mik Cribben; ed, Michael Cribben; prod d, Ellen Wedner; art d, Steven Mann; fx, Mark Dolson, Mark Kwiatek; makeup, Gregory Mosel

Horror **(PR: O MPAA: R)**

BEYOND DESIRE ★★

(U.S.) 87m Beyond Pictures; Atlantic ~ LIVE Entertainment c

William Forsythe *(Elvis Ray Patterson)*; Kari Wuhrer *(Rita)*; Leo Rossi *(Frank Zulla)*; Sharon Farrell *(Shirley)*; Frederick Malick Doumani Jr. *(Rocco)*; Billy Bastiani *(Leo)*; Dennis Hayden *(Lt. Davis)*; Natalia Lapina *(Jody)*; Russell Gannon *(Chauffeur)*; Tina Catharina Antman *(Dead Body)*; Gina Lapinto *(Undercover Cop)*; James Carrera *(Desert Joy Rider)*; Michael Carr *(Prison Guard)*

Only the easily-pleased will enjoy this silly saga about a prisoner of love who rights a wrong and salvages a call girl's bed-hopping existence. Professionally scripted with some neat betrayals, BEYOND DESIRE suffers from a regrettable tendency to milk its story line for laughs.

Released from prison after being framed for his girlfriend's murder, ex-con and ex-Marine Elvis Ray (William Forsythe) wonders why prison groupie Rita (Kari Wuhrer) offers him a lift in her flashy car. Willing to bed Rita but not trust her, Elvis is plunged back into a Las Vegas homicide whirlpool after Rita shoots two thugs sent by her boss—and Elvis's old nemesis—Frank Zulla (Leo Rossi). Elvis later learns that the two "hits" were faked to ensure his fearful silence. At an area whorehouse, inquisitive Elvis informs Madame Shirley (Sharon Farrell), the sister of his late girlfriend, Linda, that he did not bayonet Linda 26 times or run off with the skimmed profits Linda stole from Zulla.

Elvis is sex-starved enough to fall for Rita. He also aggravates Lt. Davis (Dennis Hayden), whom Elvis suspects of pocketing Zulla's missing fortune, so Elvis reopens the murder investigation single-handedly. Although Rita tries to wheedle information about the cash out of Elvis, he doesn't dig up buried treasure in the desert, but rather Marine artillery for his payback plan.

Setting his trap for Zulla, Elvis realizes that Rita truly loves him only after Zulla threatens to kill her for double-crossing him. With Shirley and his goons in tow, Zulla agrees to exchange Rita for money at Hoover Dam.

Incapacitating Zulla's gunsels and duping him into confessing to Linda's murder, Elvis waits for the police. Although Lt. Davis doesn't fork over his ill-gotten gain, he arrests Zulla for Linda's slaying and enables Elvis and Rita to start a new life.

Chugging along familiar Vegas back roads, this Forsythe vehicle represents a good case against the promotion of second bananas to starring roles. Aside from Forsythe's desire to showcase himself as a sexier Gary Busey, this flick is barely beyond mediocrity. Its prehistoric revenge motifs, crooked copper cliches, and heart-of-gold hooker stereotypes torment the audience, which overdoses on formula.

It's a toss-up as to whether there are more bullets flying or more bedroom innuendoes sailing past viewers' ears in BEYOND DESIRE.

Rossi has worked hard to establish himself as a lead in the RELENTLESS movies, and this movie forces him to parody his former low-life specialty.

The film goes far afield with its insistence on Forsythe's hunky hero status. Like a bizarre vanity production, BEYOND DESIRE allows its star to sing, make love often and boisterously, and hog the proceedings so robustly that the viewer wants to run for cover. *(Graphic violence, extreme profanity, extensive nudity, sexual situations, substance abuse.)* — R.P.

d, Dominique E. Othenin-Girard; p, Frank Cinelli; exec p, William Forsythe; assoc p, Juana Meyer; co-p, Ed Cathell III, Kristian Forland; w, Dale Trevillion; ph, Sven Kirsten; ed, Dan Duncan; m, Mark Holden; art d, Don McAllister; sound, Patrick Mitchell; fx, David J. Barker; casting, Bob Morones; cos, Jillian Ann Kreiner; makeup, Jim Sacca Jr.; stunts, Greg Anderson

Crime/Erotic/Action **(PR: C MPAA: R)**

BEYOND THE CALL ★★★½

(U.S.) 100m Showtime; Barnstorm ~ Hallmark Entertainment c

Sissy Spacek *(Pam O'Brien)*; David Strathairn *(Russell Cates)*; Arliss Howard *(Keith O'Brien)*; Janet Wright *(Fran)*; Lindsay Murrell *(Rebecca)*; Les Carlson *(Dan)*; Ken James *(Mel)*; Christina Collins *(Ruth)*; Andrew Sardella *(Mark)*; Wayne Downer *(Policeman No. 2)*; Diane D'Aquila *(Angela)*; Christine Reeves *(Policeman's Wife)*; Rufus Crawford *(Thibodeaux)*; Desmond Campbell; John Pearson; Jefferson Mappin; Kevin Rushton *(Guards)*; Dov Tiefenbach *(Mark's Friend)*; Craig Eldridge *(Policeman No. 1)*; Emily Andrews *(Teen Pam)*; Ross Ifull *(Teen Russell)*; Allan Chow; Steve Michalchuk *(Inmates)*; Shawn Lawrence *(Bartender)*; John Blackwood *(Regular)*; Caleb Marshall; D. Garnet Harding *(Soldiers)*

This made-for-cable film is an excellent example of the kind of issue-oriented script that deserves to be made even if it isn't the kind of thing on which the Hollywood studios could make any money.

In 1989, Connecticut housewife Pam O'Brien (Sissy Spacek) learns that her high school sweetheart Russell (David Strathairn) is on death row in a South Carolina prison. Despite the disapproval of her husband, Keith (Arliss Howard), Pam agrees to the request of Russell's sister that she go to South Carolina and attempt to persuade Russell to speak in his own defense at his clemency hearing.

Pam finds Russell quite different from the gentle boy she once knew. Although resigned to his fate, he agrees to appear at his clemency hearing if she will come back to lend her support. From a friend of Russell's, Pam learns that he has suffered from post-traumatic shock syndrome after serving in combat in Vietnam. Russell confirms this by telling her a few of the horrifying things he saw as a soldier, things he was afraid to talk about when he returned home.

Russell's appeal is turned down, despite mitigating circumstances surrounding his killing of a South Carolina policeman. Pam's visits to Russell upset Keith, who also served in Vietnam but feels he has been able to put it behind him. Pam persuades Keith to come to South Carolina with her, where Russell asks to talk to him. He discovers that Keith also has a guilty memory of the war that troubles him, and Russell advises him to tell Pam about it and let it go. Keith and Pam return home, and Russell dies in the electric chair.

One of four films released in the same year dealing with a condemned prisoner waiting to be executed (along with DEAD MAN WALKING, LAST DANCE, and THE CHAMBER), BEYOND THE CALL differs from the others. It is less a story of personal salvation than an exploration of a larger societal issue. And while none of these films overtly questions the justice of the death penalty, BEYOND THE CALL makes the best unspoken argument against it by showing how easily it can be misused by local courts and politicians too enamored of public opinion.

Even though the central issue here is the lingering effects of Vietnam on the people who went there, BEYOND THE CALL is still a death row story and as such offers a terrific part for Strathairn. Nearly as good is Howard, although his big breakdown scene where he reveals his own war trauma is damaged because it is pulled from his character too quickly. Spacek's role, is mostly reactive, calling for her to do little except look lovingly at whomever she's speaking to. *(Violence, profanity.)* — M.F.

d, Tony Bill; p, Helen Bartlett, Tony Bill, Doug Magee; exec p, Bob Christiansen, Rick Rosenberg; w, Doug Magee; ph, Jean Lapine; ed, Axel Hubert; m, George S. Clinton; prod d, Jeff Ginn; art d, Karen M. Clark; fx, Michael Kavanagh; casting, Beth Klein, Jon Comerford; cos, Lynne MacKay; makeup, Katherine Southern

Prison/Drama **(PR: A MPAA: R)**

BIG BULLY ★½

(U.S.) 90m Lee Rich Productions; Morgan Creek ~ Warner Bros. c

Rick Moranis *(David Leary)*; Tom Arnold *(Rosco "Fang" Bigger)*; Julianne Phillips *(Victoria)*; Carol Kane *(Faith)*; Jeffrey Tambor *(Art)*; Curtis Armstrong *(Clark)*; Faith Prince *(Betty)*; Tony Pierce *(Ulf)*; Don Knotts *(Principal Kokelar)*; Blake Bashoff *(Ben)*; Cody McMains *(Kirby)*; Harry Waters Jr. *(Alan)*; Stuart Pankin *(Gerry)*; Justin Jon Ross *(Young David)*; Michael Zwiener *(Young Fang)*; Tiffany Foster *(Young Victoria)*; Matthew Slowik *(Young Ulf)*; C.J. Grayson *(Young Alan)*; Grant Hoover *(Young Gerry)*; Bill Dow *(David's Father)*; Susan Bain *(David's Mother)*; Christine Willes *(Teacher—1970)*; Ingrid Torrance *(Fourth Grade Teacher)*; Tyler Van Blankenstein *(Freckle-Faced Kid)*; Doug Abrahams *(Guard)*; Lillian Carlson *(Old Woman)*; Matt Hill *(Teenager)*; Kate Twa *(Shop Clerk)*; Norma McMillan *(Mrs. Rumpert)*; Eryn Collins *(Kid No. 1)*; Tegan Moss *(Girl in Class)*; Gregory Smith *(Kid No. 2)*; Lois Dellar *(Teacher No. 1)*; Claire Riley *(Sympathetic Teacher)*; Alf Humphreys *(Teacher No. 1)*; Brent Morrison *(Stookie)*; Alexander Pollock *(Corky)*; Kyle Labine *(Stevie)*; Zachary Webb *(Kyle)*; Eric Pospisil *(Bobby)*; Miriam Smith *(Crying Teacher)*; Colum Cantillon *(Paul)*; Dawn Stofer *(Secretary)*; Steven Taylor *(Hallway Kid No. 1)*; Justin Goodrich *(Hallway Kid No. 2)*; Anthony Pavlokovic *(Hallway Kid No. 3)*; Andrew Wheeler *(Soldier)*; James Sherry *(Delinquent No. 1)*; Tommy Anderson *(Delinquent No. 2)*; Jacob Rupp *(Stunt Police No. 1)*; David Jacox Jr. *(Stunt Police No. 2)*; Tina Klassen *(Korean Lady in Bookstore)*; Tamara Stanners *(Connie)*; Helena Yea *(Connie TV Guest)*; Ray Fairchild *(Connie TV Guest)*

Promoted as a comedy, BIG BULLY is a peculiarly dark and depressing tale of a writer who returns to his hometown to confront a childhood bully.

In a prologue set in Hastings, Minnesota, circa 1970, Roscoe a.k.a. "Fang" (Michael Zwiener) constantly bullies Davey (Justin Jon Ross), his bookish 10-year-old classmate. On the day Davey and his family move out of the city, Davey takes revenge by telling school authorities that Fang stole a priceless moon rock from a school display.

Twenty-five years later, after hawking a novel on an unsuccessful book tour, David (Rick Moranis) accepts a teaching assignment from his former elementary school. Now 35 and divorced, David moves back to Hastings, where his own teenage son, Ben (Blake Bashoff) quickly starts picking on Kirby (Cody McMains), the son of the ineffectual shop teacher. David soon discovers that Kirby's father is none other than Roscoe, now called Ross (Tom Arnold).

David is surprised to find that Ross has become a meek character, but once Ross recognizes David as Davey and remembers the moon rock incident, he immediately transforms back into a "big bully." At home, Ross also changes from a henpecked, trailer-park husband into a dictatorial patriarch. As Ross begins pulling dangerous pranks on David, David tries to convince the school principal, Mr. Kokelar (Don Knotts) of his problem. David, meanwhile, also falls for the sex education instructor, Victoria (Julianne Phillips).

One night, Ross terrorizes David by chasing him through the town with a chainsaw. David runs from Ross until he reaches a bridge over a waterfall, on which he stops and finally confronts his nemesis. While struggling to stay balanced on the bridge, Ross admits that he always had wanted to be friends with David. Thanks to the help of their sons, who have already started to make friends with each other, David and Ross likewise pledge to start anew.

In a part that seems tailor-made for the late John Candy, Tom Arnold plays the title role in BIG BULLY opposite Rick Moranis's nerd-hero. Both portrayals totter between realism and cartoonism. Arnold's "Fang," for example, is a pathetic clown in one scene and a menacing monster in the next. Likewise, the direction by Steve Miner (FOREVER YOUNG; MY FATHER, THE HERO) alternates between loud farce and melodramatic thriller (particularly in the climatic footbridge confrontation). All of these genre devices are unnecessary, however, because the idea behind Mark Steven Johnson's screenplay is a good one. The film itself might have also been good had it developed its characters more intelligently and handled its subject matter more subtlely. But BIG BULLY compromises its theme about standing up against oppression by turning its characters into caricatures. Adults, let alone kids, will be more confused than amused.

In the cast, only Julianne Phillips escapes the foolishness in her small part, while the film's comic highlight—a mildly funny spoof of daytime TV talk shows—is totally unrelated to the main story. Technically, BIG BULLY seems patched together at times, but awkward editing is the least of this comedy-noir's problems. *(Violence, profanity.)* — E.M.

d, Steve Miner; p, Lee Rich, Gary Foster; exec p, Gary Barber, Dylan Sellers; w, Mark Steven Johnson; ph, Daryn Okada; ed, Marshall Harvey; m, David Newman; prod d, Ian Thomas; art d, Douglasann Menchions; set d, Lesley Beale; sound, Larry Sutton (mixer); fx, Dean Lockwood, Buena Vista Special Effects; cos, Monique Prudhomme; makeup, Victoria Down; stunts, J.J. Makaro

Comedy/Drama **(PR: A MPAA: PG)**

BIG NIGHT ★★★★

(U.S.) 107m Timpano Productions ~ Samuel Goldwyn Company c

Stanley Tucci *(Secondo)*; Tony Shalhoub *(Primo)*; Isabella Rossellini *(Gabriella)*; Ian Holm *(Pascal)*; Minnie Driver *(Phyllis)*; Marc Anthony *(Cristiano)*; Campbell Scott *(Bob)*; Allison Janney *(Ann)*; Liev Schreiber *(Leo)*; Pasquale Cajano *(Alberto)*; Gene Canfield *(Charlie)*; Tina Bruno *(Ida)*; Peter Appel *(Chubby)*; Karen Shallo *(Chubby's Wife)*; Alvaleta Guess *(Lenore)*; Tamar Kotoske *(Dean)*; Andre Belgrader *(Stash)*; Robert W. Castle *(Father O'Brien)*; Susan Floyd *(Joan)*; Dina Spybey *(Natalie)*; Seth Jones *(Jameson)*; Larry Block *(Man in Restaurant)*; Caroline Aaron *(Woman in Restaurant)*; Christine Tucci *(Woman Singer)*; Peter McRobbie *(Loan Officer)*; Jack O'Connell *(Man on Truck)*

Perhaps the most surprising delight of the year, this treatise on food and family warms the soul. Skillfully filmed, often eschewing dialogue altogether, it's a small classic.

Two brothers, Primo (Tony Shalhoub) and Secondo (Stanley Tucci), own the Paradise, an Italian restaurant that is dying on the vine due to lack of business. It's not the fault of the food—Primo is a super chef. Unfortunately, he's also an intractable purist when it comes to the preparation and presentation of his culinary masterpieces. Set in '50s New Jersey, the clientele is basically made up of the type of people who think "steak" when it comes to fine dining. This leads to endless disputes between Primo and Secondo, who desperately wants to succeed in his adopted country. Faced with foreclosure, Secondo turns in desperation to Pascal (Ian Holm), the rival owner of a wildly popular restaurant just across the street. Pascal is unable to lend him any money but has the bright idea of inviting his "good friend," recording star Louis Prima, to have dinner at the Paradise. The attendant positive publicity and word of mouth should undoubtedly make their fortune. Secondo excitedly withdraws every cent from his bank account and sets about preparing the feast of feasts. The real motivation behind this must, of course, be kept from Primo, who loathes brash Pascal's assimilist ways and everything he stands for. Also in on the scheme are Secondo's long-suffering, almost-fiancee (Minnie Driver) and Pascal's mistress (Isabella Rossellini), with whom Secondo is also spending time. The big night finally arrives. Primo inevitably discovers the ruse, throws a tantrum, but eventually acquiesces enough to serve up a legendary repast. One problem: Louis Prima never shows up. It seems that, in an effort to ruin the brothers so they'll be forced to come work for him, Pascal never called the star. The brothers have a violent confrontation, with Primo announcing his intention to return to Rome to work for their family. Secondo refuses to give up on America. However much he may disagree with his brother, his ultimate respect and love shine through when he tells off Pascal, saying that he will never be Primo's equal.

The brothers reunite over a shared, very simple, but lovingly prepared breakfast.

Co-directors Tucci and Campbell Scott have made a marvelously character-driven film every bit as elegant and nurturing as the cuisine it features so proudly. Their unstressed, laconic mastery at telling this modest story evinces itself in long, one-take sequences, devoid of dialogue, which recall the best achievements of silent movies. The script abounds with sharply specific observation and, always, a laugh or brusque moment of affection to ride over the rough spots. Ken Kelsch's camerawork has an inquisitive, gliding elan, laced with quirky moments of humor, like the desk lamp that annoyingly covers Pascal's face during a diatribe until he impatiently knocks it aside. Cooking comprises much of the salient action and proves to be compellingly photogenic. Nowhere is this more apparent than in the sublime final scene, which is as humanly touching as any ever rendered on screen. Primo's capable deliberation as he heats up the oil and cracks eggs for an omelette, while simultaneously going over the events of that hectic big night, have an uncanny suspense, shot as it is in real time without a single cut. One aches to hear what he's thinking, even as one wonders, "will the oil burn, the eggs singe?" Needless to say, all is carried off with exquisite timing and, by the time Primo sits down to eat and Secondo silently puts a conciliatory arm around him, the emotional impact is overwhelming.

The film contains a fully stocked gallery of wonderful performances. Tucci is edgy and intense as Secondo, a whiz at the comedy of frustration and the slow burn. The fact that BIG NIGHT is also one of the best film treatments of fraternal love is largely due to his suave, spiffily controlled acting. Shalhoub is a fitting contrast to him, alternately a Mussolini in the kitchen and painfully shy when it comes to talking to a woman he admires. Ian Holm revels in the vulgarity of Pascal, an ethnic caricature redeemed by its rambunctious high spirits and triumphant profanity. Isabella Rossellini delivers her strongest performance since BLUE VELVET, as his casually amoral mistress. Minnie Driver is completely convincing as an uncomplicated neighborhood gal who just wants to get hitched. *(Sexual situations, profanity, adult situations.)* — D.N.

d, Stanley Tucci, Campbell Scott; p, Jonathan Filley; exec p, Keith Samples, David Kirkpatrick; co-p, Elizabeth W. Alexander, Peter Liguori, Oliver Platt; w, Joseph Tropiano, Stanley Tucci; ph, Ken Kelsch; ed, Suzy Elmiger; m, Gary DiMichele; prod d, Andrew Jackness; art d, Jeffrey D. McDonald, David Stein; set d, Susan Raney; sound, William Sarokin (mixer); fx, Connie Brink; cos, Juliet Polcsa; makeup, Neal Martz; stunts, George Aguilar

Drama/Comedy **(PR: C MPAA: R)**

BIG SQUEEZE, THE ★★½

(U.S.) 82m Zeta Entertainment; Overseas Filmgroup ~ First Look Pictures c
(AKA: THREE IFS AND A MAYBE)

Peter Dobson *(Benny)*; Lara Flynn Boyle *(Tanya Mulhill)*; Danny Nucci *(Jesse)*; Luca Bercovici *(Henry Mulhill)*; Michael Chieffo *(Inspector)*; Sam Vlahos *(Father Sanchez)*; Valente Rodriguez *(Father Arias)*; Bert Santos *(Manny)*; Teresa Dispina *(Cece)*; Raye Birk *(Contractor)*; Angelina *(Estrada)*; Janet MacLachlan *(Bank Manager)*; Demetrius Navarro *(Young Man)*; Marita De Leon *(Young Woman)*; Tony Genaro *(Older Man)*; Gary Paul *(Mechanic)*; Laura Ceron *(Letter Carrier)*

Blandly titled, THE BIG SQUEEZE has its good points but is generally an odd, lukewarm stew of caper comedy and inspirational whimsy.

LA barmaid Tanya Mulhill (Lara Flynn Boyle) works hard to support herself and spouse Henry (Luca Bercovici), a minor-league ballplayer who damaged his knee and mostly mopes around or prays. Tanya accidentally learns that Henry received an insurance settlement in excess of $130,000 but hoards it in secret. When she demands half, Henry strikes her, and Tanya splits, moving in with Jesse (Daniel Nucci), a soulful groundskeeper who has long adored her from afar. Tanya asks Benny (Peter Dobson), a somewhat ineffectual con-man who frequents the bar, to help her bilk Henry out of the money she feels she deserves.

The barrio church Henry frequents needs $136,000 for earthquake repairs, so Benny, posing as the parish contractor, preys on Henry's conscience with a few stage-managed miracles, like Tanya returning without explanation to her husband's bed. Benny also plants a magnolia seed near the church, and replaces it by night with a succession of larger plants. News of the wonder draws pilgrims to the site (Jesse tells the priests the truth—but they keep quiet about it), and Henry finally withdraws all his savings from the bank. But when he gives the envelope to Benny the next day, they find only scrap paper inside; Tanya found the cache that morning, and, knowing Benny was going to rip her off anyway, took the cash for herself. She drives away with Jesse. A furious Henry chases Benny, and thus realizes that his leg is no longer crippled. Benny discovers the magnolia has grown several more yards without his intervention and is hailed as a miracle.

Writer/director Marcus DeLeon previously made the Latino-flavored suspense drama KISS ME A KILLER for Roger Corman. THE BIG SQUEEZE possesses a similar film noir dynamic of ruthless people deceiving each other for lust and money, but climaxes with divine intervention instead of murder. Actually, the viewer needs the patience of a saint to endure the slowly-paced narrative long enough for these greedy schemers and their relationships to get interesting (which, fortunately, they do). DeLeon rashly assumes the characters are instantly adorable but only Nucci, in a badly underwritten role, somehow manages to command sympathy from the outset. The film's studio-backlot theology is dubious, but its soundtrack boasts some catchy mariachi covers of old favorites like "Crimson and Clover," "Can't Take My Eyes Off of You," and "Come a Little Bit Closer." *(Violence, sexual situations, adult situations, substance abuse, profanity.)* — C.C.

d, Marcus De Leon; p, Zane W. Levitt, Mark Yellen, Liz McDermott; w, Marcus De Leon; ph, Jacques Haitkin; ed, Sonny Baskin; m, Mark Mothersbaugh; prod d, J. Rae Fox; art d, William Paine; set d, Traci Kirshbaum; sound, Don Gooch (mixer), Paul Ratajczak (mixer); casting, Laura Schiff; cos, Charmian Schreiner; stunts, Gary Paul

Crime/Comedy/Romance **(PR: C MPAA: R)**

BIG WARS ★★★

(Japan) 70m ~ Central Park Media/US Manga Corps c

VOICES OF: Hideyuki Tanaka *(Captain Akuh)*; Hiroko Emori *(Dasa)*; Yumi Touma *(Dr. Ree)*; Yuzuru Fujimoto *(Mikawa)*; Shinya Ohtaki *(Yutaka)*; Ikuya Sawaki; Toshiyuki Morikawa; Kouji Tsujitani; Masaharu Sato

On a "terraformed" Mars, Earth colonists battle a powerful alien race in this short but spectacular Japanese animated tale.

In the 24th century, armed forces defending Earth colonies on Mars confront an invasion by the superior forces of the Gods, an alien humanoid race of uncertain origin. The job is made harder by the Gods' "infection" of Earth colonists, a process in which the infected slowly turn against the Earth forces, committing acts of terrorism and sabotage before finally going mad.

Ground Force Captain Kanki Akuh is assigned a new ship named the Aoba. He encounters an old flame, intelligence officer Lt. Dasa Keligan, and resumes a torrid affair with her. When she scratches him during lovemaking, she repairs the wound with artificial skin. She turns out to be infected by the Gods and warns Akuh of their impending invasion. On the morning of the invasion, she holds him at gunpoint to prevent him from reporting to his ship. Akuh is forced to kill her. He later finds a taped message from her acknowledging her infection and revealing that she'd passed on crucial information to him.

On board the Aoba, the ship's doctor, Dr. Ree, inspects Akuh's wound and discovers a tiny computer chip planted under the artificial skin. The chip contains detailed information about the Gods' supership, the massive carrier Jigoku, which has so far laid waste to the Mars Defense Forces. With this information, the Earthlings are able to devise a plan to attack the carrier.

In stealth mode, the Aoba moves under the Jigoku. Akuh leads a force which drills into the enemy ship and engages the Gods in battle. Akuh and his surviving team members plant a nuclear device and set it off, miraculously escaping just in time in a captured enemy fighter craft.

BIG WARS is enhanced by its subplot of a romance between a military hero and a female colleague subverted by the enemy, and the situation's subsequent psychological effects. Throughout the action, Captain Akuh is haunted by Dasa, who appears to him at crucial points long after her violent death. However, the film suffers from its curious avoidance of any detail regarding the nature of the Gods, so we never learn exactly who the enemy is.

Based on a manga (comic book) by Yoshio Aramaki, BIG WARS offers spectacular scenes of interplanetary warfare, rivaled only by the same year's big live-action hit INDEPENDENCE DAY, scenes of which recall the earlier BIG WARS. The similarities are enough to provoke a slight suspicion that perhaps the INDEPENDENCE DAY effects designers managed to see BIG WARS first. *(Sexual situations, nudity, violence)* — B.C.

d, Toshifumi Takizawa; p, Tatsumi Yamashita, Yukio Kikukawa, Satoshi Dezaki; w, Kazumi Koide (based on the comic book by Yoshio Aramaki from a concept by Hideo Ogata); m, Michiaki Katoh; anim, Keizou Shimizu

Animated/Science Fiction (PR: C MPAA: NR)

BIO-DOME ★

(U.S.) 95m 3 Arts Entertainment; Weasel Productions; Motion Picture Corporation of America ~ MGM/UA c

Pauly Shore *(Bud Macintosh)*; Stephen Baldwin *(Doyle Johnson)*; William Atherton *(Dr. Noah Faulkner)*; Kylie Minogue *(Petra von Kant)*; Joey Adams *(Monique)*; Teresa Hill *(Jen)*; Dara Tomanovich *(Mimi Simkins)*; Patricia Hearst *(Doyle's Mother)*; Jeremy Jordan *(Trent)*; Kevin West *(T.C. Romulus)*; Denise Dowse *(Olivia Biggs)*; Henry Gibson *(William Leaky)*; Roger Clinton *(Professor Bloom)*; Taylor Negron *(Russell)*; Rose McGowan *(Denise)*; Channon Roe *(Roach)*; Trevor St. John *(Parker)*; Robbie Thibaut Jr. *(Young Doyle)*; Adam Weisman *(Young Bud)*; Brian Hayes Currie *(Guard)*; Butch McCain *(Reporter Joachim West)*; Courtney Mizel *(Screamer)*; Jack Black *(Tenacious D)*; Kyle Gass *(Tenacious D)*; Loomis *(Drummer)*; Joe Sib *(Singer)*; Soda Pop *(Guitarist)*; Burdie Cutlas *(Bassist)*; Rene Moreno *(Partier)*; Molly Bryant *(Bio-Dome Technician)*; Mark Burton *(Guy)*; Ben McCain *(Anchor Aries West)*; Katherine Kousi *(Vigilante)*; Elizabeth Guber *(Vigilante)*; Chloe Hult *(Vigilante)*; Tucker Smallwood *(Gates)*; Phil Lamarr *(Assistant)*; Paul Eiding *(Assistant)*; Andy Lucchesi *(SWAT Guy)*; Rodger Bumpass *(Narrator)*; Phil Proctor *(AXL)*; Cecile Krevoy *(Woman in Bandstand)*; Jordan Mayerson *(Kid Tourist)*; Jason Davis *(Kid Tourist)*

The indefatigable, unfunny Pauly Shore headlines BIO-DOME, a very unfunny comedy which costars the most abrasive of the Baldwin brothers, Stephen. While MGM surely meant to tap into the lucrative DUMB AND DUMBER market, the resulting film is another low point in the Shore canon (JURY DUTY, et al.).

Shore and Baldwin respectively play Bud and Doyle—best friends, college roommates, and slackers who will seize any excuse not to help clean waste on Earth Day. When their ecologically-conscious girlfriends, Monique (Joey Adams) and Jen (Teresa Hill), trick them into driving into the Arizona desert, they happen upon what appears to be the opening of an enormous, modern shopping mall.

Once inside, Bud and Doyle discover that they've entered—and compromised the integrity of—an experimental, environmentally-controlled scientific community called "Bio-Dome." What's more, they are sealed in for a year. The head of the project, Dr. Noah Faulkner (William Atherton), and his five assistant scientists are alarmed by the intrusion, but they try to make the best of it. Bud and Doyle, meanwhile, find themselves attracted to two of the women scientists (Dara Tomanovich, Kylie Minogue).

In the beginning, Bud and Doyle merely wreak havoc in the Dome. Then, they nearly destroy the project entirely by inviting their fellow college chums to a wild party in the Dome's ecologically-balanced desert. Just when it seems that their outrageous behavior has doomed the experiment to failure, Bud and Doyle—in an attempt to impress their girlfriends—save the day by performing a massive clean-up job.

With its 70's icons (Henry Gibson of LAUGH-IN and Patty Hearst in small parts), 80's music (Bow Wow Wow's "I Want Candy") and 90's slacker attitude ("Yo, dude, forget Earth Day, let's dance!"), BIO-DOME promises to be a light, enjoyable satire on clashing cultures and the trendier aspects of the contemporary environmental movement. Unfortunately, that promise goes wholly unfulfilled as BIO-DOME lacks the slightest cleverness. It is a sign of the film's quality that the unannounced cameo by Bill Clinton's younger brother Roger constitutes a highlight.

The main problem with "BIO-DUMB" is that it has been so specifically built around the dubious talents of Shore and Baldwin that it misfires before it even gets started. No other cast member (not even William Atherton as the lightweight nemesis) gets a chance to be funny, while the two stars make unfunny fools of themselves via unintelligible, homoerotic bathroom/sex jokes with food in their open mouths. When not engaged in such offputting behavior, our anti-hero duo is gleefully destroying the Bio-Dome environment in an anarchic style that is more unnerving than humorous to watch. Several scenes even appear to be deliberately cruel to animals. Such truly offensive political incorrectness must stop—as must the creation and exhibition of future Pauly Shore comedies. *(Violence, profanity, sexual situations, nudity.)* — E.M.

d, Jason Bloom; p, Brad Krevoy, Steve Stabler, Brad Jenkel; exec p, Michael Rotenberg, Jason Blumenthal, Adam Leff, Mitchell Peck; assoc p, Kip Koenig, Scott Marcano, Wayne Nelson Page, Jeff McCarthy, Jon Katzman; co-p, Dan Etheridge, Elaine Dysinger; w, Kip Koenig, Scott Marcano (from a story by Adam Leff, Mitchell Peck, and Jason Blumenthal); ph, Phedon Papamichael; ed, Christopher Greenbury; m, Andrew Gross; prod d, Michael Johnston; art d, Don Diers, Carl Stensel; set d, Amy B. Ancona; sound, William M. Fiege (mixer); fx, Lou Carlucci, FTS EFX,

Inc.; casting, Rick Montgomery, Dan Parada; cos, Mary Claire Hannan; stunts, Kurt Bryant

Comedy **(PR: C MPAA: PG-13)**

BIRDCAGE, THE ★★

(U.S.) 118m Icarus Productions; United Artists ~ MGM/UA c

Robin Williams *(Armand Goldman)*; Gene Hackman *(Senator Keeley)*; Nathan Lane *(Albert)*; Dianne Wiest *(Louise Keeley)*; Dan Futterman *(Val Goldman)*; Calista Flockhart *(Barbara Keeley)*; Hank Azaria *(Agador)*; Christine Baranski *(Katharine)*; Tom McGowan *(Harry Radman)*; Grant Heslov *(Photographer)*; Kirby Mitchell *(Chauffeur)*; James Lally *(Cyril)*; Luca Tommassini *(Celsius)*; Luis Camacho; Andre Fuentes; Anthony Richard Gonzalez; Dante Lamar Henderson; Scott Kaske; Kevin Alexander Stea *(The Goldman Girls)*; Tim Kelleher *(Waiter in Club)*; Ann Cusack *(TV Woman in Van)*; Stanley DeSantis *(TV Man in Van)*; J. Roy Helland *(Club Hostess)*; Anthony Giaimo *(Fishmonger)*; Lee Delano *(Bakery Man)*; David Sage *(Senator Eli Jackson)*; Mike Kinsley *(TV Host)*; Tony Snow *(TV Host)*; Dorothy Constantine *(Keeley's Maid)*; Trina McGee-Davis *(Black Girl on TV)*; Barry Nolan; Amy Powell; Ron Pitts; James Hill; Mary Major *(TV Reporters)*; Steven Porfido *(State Trooper)*; John D. Pontrelli *(Waiter in Cafe)*; Herschel Sparber *(Big Guy in Park)*; Francesca Cruz *(Katharine's Secretary)*; Brian Reddy *(TV Editor)*; Jim Jansen *(TV Editor)*; Al Rodrigo *(Latino Man in Club)*; Marjorie Lovett *(Matron)*; Sylvia Short *(Matron)*; James H. Morrison *(Pastor)*; Rabbi Robert K. Baruch *(Rabbi)*

Mike Nichols' THE BIRDCAGE is a slick, Americanized remake of the classic French stage and screen farce, LA CAGE AUX FOLLES, that is generally enjoyable, but instantly forgettable.

Armand Goldman (Robin Williams) and his "wife," Albert (Nathan Lane), live together in Miami's South Beach area, where Armand manages a gay nightclub called "The Birdcage," and Albert performs as a drag queen. Armand's son, Val (Dan Futterman), who was the result of one heterosexual experience 20 years earlier, shows up and announces he's engaged to Barbara Keeley (Calista Flockhart), the daughter of ultra right-wing US Sen. Kevin Keeley (Gene Hackman), who is the co-founder of the Coalition for Moral Order.

Barbara tells her parents that Val's mother is a housewife, and his father is a diplomat whose name is Coleman, so her parents won't know he's Jewish. When the other co-founder of the Coalition for Moral Order dies while in bed with an underage, black prostitute, Senator Keeley and his family decide to escape the scandal by driving down to Miami to meet Val's parents. But a reporter from a sleazy tabloid follows them.

Val pleads with his father to redecorate the house, send Albert away, and invite his birth mother, Katharine (Christine Baranski), over for their dinner with the Keeleys, and Armand reluctantly agrees. But Albert insists on staying and takes lessons on how to act "straight" from Armand. Realizing he will never pull it off, Albert gives in and agrees to leave. However, when the Keeleys arrive and Katharine is stuck in traffic, Albert suddenly appears in a wig and a dress and introduces himself as Val's mother. Albert immediately charms Senator Keeley with his conservative conversation.

Armand leaves a note on the door informing Katharine not to come upstairs, but the reporter takes it off, and Katharine shows up at the dinner, also introducing herself as Val's mother. Val decides to end the charade, and, taking off Albert's wig, he confesses the whole truth to Barbara's shocked and confused parents. When they try to leave, the Keeleys encounter an army of reporters waiting outside, and the only way they can elude them is for the senator to get into full drag regalia and sneak out by mingling with the nightclub's stage show. They successfully escape, and the wedding goes off without a hitch.

Making homosexuality safe for the malls of America, THE BIRDCAGE is another in a long line of Hollywood films that present a stereotyped and sanitized sitcom image of gays as being just a bunch of wacky, flamboyant characters who dance and sing all day. Although Williams' Armand is relatively restrained, Lane has a campy field day as the prissy Albert, who goes into hysterics at the drop of a hat. Hank Azaria's Guatemalan houseboy, Agador, is quite possibly the most outrageously cliched throwback since Ray Hedge's pansy character in the 1934 Three Stooges movie "Myrt and Marge." These characters are caught in a 1970s time warp where disco rules, everybody's happy, and there's no such thing as AIDS. This kind of thing was easier to take in 1978 when the original LA CAGE AUX FOLLES was released, but in 1996, it's a little hard to accept, even in a pure comedy. Undeniably, there are some real belly laughs, such as the scene in which Armand tries to teach Albert to act like a "macho" man, including a riotous imitation of John Wayne's walk. And the dinner-party sequence is a foolproof comic set piece. But there's something vaguely offensive about the whole movie, even as it goes out of its way to be tolerant and politically correct.

True farce, being an inherently theatrical convention, is an extremely difficult thing to do successfully on the screen, with most cinematic attempts coming off as forced, frenetic and stage-bound. In THE BIRDCAGE, Nichols' direction seems lethargic and disinterested, while he and writer Elaine May appear to have intentionally slowed down the pace and concentrated on Albert and Armand's relationship. But this only results in a protracted buildup to the inevitable dinner scene, which doesn't even occur until 75 minutes in. And this is a shame, since Hackman and Dianne Wiest, as his priggish wife, are clearly the best things in the movie, giving real performances as opposed to the vaudevillian caricatures on display elsewhere. Hackman is impeccable in his expressions of moral outrage and buffoonish bewilderment, and he is a sight to behold in a white wig and a sequined dress, boogying to "We Are Family." *(Profanity, adult situations.)* — M.S.

d, Mike Nichols; p, Mike Nichols; exec p, Neil Machlis, Marcello Danon; assoc p, Michele Imperato; w, Elaine May (based on the screenplay *La Cage Aux Folles* by Jean Poiret, Francis Veber, Edouard Molinaro, and Marcello Danon, adapted from the stage play by Jean Poiret); ph, Emmanuel Lubezki; ed, Arthur Schmidt; prod d, Bo Welch; art d, Tom Duffield; set d, Cheryl Carasik; ch, Vincent Paterson; sound, Gene Cantamessa (mixer); fx, Stan Parks, Syd Dutton, Bill Taylor, Illusion Arts, Inc.; casting, Juliet Taylor, Ellen Lewis; cos, Ann Roth; makeup, J. Roy Helland, Peter Owen, Cheri Minns; stunts, Jery Hewitt

AAN Best Art Direction: Bo Welch, Cheryl Carasik

Comedy **(PR: C MPAA: R)**

BITTER SUGAR ★★½

(Cuba) 102m Azucar Films S.A. ~ First Look Pictures/Susan Senk bw

Rene Lavan *(Gustavo)*; Mayte Vilan *(Yolanda)*; Miguel Gutierrez *(Dr. Tomas Valdez)*; Larry Villanueva *(Bobby)*; Luis Celeiro *(Mr. Garcia)*; Teresa Maria Rojas *(Belkis)*; Orestes Matacena *(Claudio)*; Caridad Ravelo *(Soraya)*; Jorge Pupo *(Yiyo)*; Augusto Feria *(Security Guard (Hotel))*; Felix German *(Security Guard (Beach))*

BITTER SUGAR details the growing political disillusionment of a young "New Cuban" living in contemporary Havana. This handsome-looking film tries hard to be realistic, but the main story is far too simplistic and reactionary to make an impact.

BITTER SUGAR tells the story of Gustavo (Rene Lavan), a graduate of the Lenin School in Havana. Gustavo lives at home with his father, Tomas (Miguel Gutierrez), a widowed psychiatrist, and his brother, Bobby (Larry Villanueva), a heavy-metal "Rockero." At one of Bobby's underground concerts, Gustavo meets Yolanda (Mayte Vilan), a beautiful dancer. Soon, Gustavo asks Yolanda out, but, on their first date, they realize they have opposite political views: Gustavo believes in Castro's regime while Yolanda dislikes what the government has done to her people. Despite their differences, however, Gustavo and Yolanda fall in love.

Over time, outside events begin to effect Gustavo's life profoundly. Just as Gustavo receives a scholarship to study aeronautical engineering in Prague, Bobby is arrested and beaten after a public demonstration against the government's confiscation of their equipment. Next, Gustavo and Yolanda are kicked out of a "tourist-only" hotel where only American dollars are accepted. Then Tomas quits his hospital job so that he can make more money as a piano player in the same hotel. Finally, Gustavo learns that Bobby has chosen a tragic form of protest against his oppressors—he has injected himself with AIDS-tainted blood.

Despite the difficulties facing his family, Gustavo still argues with Yolanda about the merits of the Castro government. Eventually, their political views drive them apart. Yet, life becomes even more challenging as Gustavo is forced to take a menial job at the Havana airport when he learns that his scholarship will be delayed. It is while performing his new job that Gustavo sees Yolanda with a wealthy foreigner, Claudio (Orestes Matacena), gets jealous and confronts the interloper.

Later, Yolanda and Gustavo reconcile when she tells him that Claudio means nothing to her. Gustavo proposes marriage and plans to join her in Miami, where she is sailing the next day. But after seeing Yolanda sail away, Gustavo decides to punish the government that has broken his spirit by assasinating the country's leader, Fidel Castro, during a rally. Tragically, however, Gustavo is killed by one of Castro's guards during the act of vengeance.

Aided by Claudio Chea's sleek, though never slick, black-and-white cinematography, Cuban-born director Leon Ichaso (CROSSOVER DREAMS, SUGAR HILL) shows a flair for composing images. Regrettably, however, the anti-Socialist, anti-Castro message of his story, co-written with Pelayo Garcia, and screenplay, co-written with Matacena, is telegraphed too early and too often.

The doomed romance between Gustavo and Yolanda—played by a miscast Vilan—becomes a vehicle for opposing political views and garners less interest than the dramatic subplot about Gustavo's brother. Even the film's sole humorous character, Gustavo's father—charmingly played by Gutierrez—turns into another ideological mouthpiece by his final scene, telling Gustavo, "The revolution is for sale, son."

BITTER SUGAR nicely captures a sense of uneasy squalor through its heartfelt visuals, but fans of the films of Tomas Gutierez Alea (MEMORIES OF UNDERDEVELOPMENT, STRAWBERRY AND CHOCOLATE) and the fiction of Oscar Hijuelos (*The Mambo Kings Play Songs of Love*) will find this a rudimentary socio-political critique. *(Violence, adult situations, profanity.)* — E.M.

d, Leon Ichaso; p, Leon Ichaso, Jaime Pina; exec p, Pelayo Garcia; assoc p, Claudio Chea, Mari Ichaso, Purita Carrillo, Julio Carillo; co-p, Lisa Rhoden; w, Leon Ichaso, Orestes Matacena (from a story by Leon Ichaso and Pelayo Garcia); ph, Claudio Chea; ed, Yvette Pineyro; m, Manuel Tejada; prod d, Liliana Soto

Drama **(PR: C MPAA: NR)**

BLACK DAY BLUE NIGHT ★★½

(U.S.) 97m Sandstorm Films; Capella Films ~ Republic Pictures Home Video c

Mia Sara *(Hallie Schrag)*; Gil Bellows *(Dodge)*; Michelle Forbes *(Rinda Wooley)*; J. T. Walsh *(Lt. John Quinn)*; Tim Guinee *(Bo Schrag)*; John Beck *(Chief Reed)*; F. J. Flynn *(Odell)*; Norman Patrick Brown *(Begay)*; Benjamin Lum *(Hop Chung)*; Kellye Nakahara-Wallett *(Fat Mama)*; Michael Holmes *(Bus Clerk)*; Thomas Redhouse *(Navajo Man)*; Caroline Barclay *(Dutton)*; Kirk Bailey *(Mayor's Assistant)*; Jack Leal *(Trooper #1)*

BLACK DAY BLUE NIGHT is a well-acted, modestly effective direct- to-video film noir about two women driving from Utah to Phoenix who pick up a mysterious hitchhiker who may or may not be on the lam from a robbery-murder rap.

Utah State police lieutenant John Quinn (J. T. Walsh) is investigating an armored car robbery in which a guard who was his best friend was killed. Two of the three robbers were also killed, but a third got away with a suitcase filled with over $1 million.

Meanwhile, a foul-mouthed, hard-boiled waitress named Rinda (Michelle Forbes) befriends a mousy woman named Hallie (Mia Sara), after Hallie catches her abusive husband Bo in a hotel room with Rinda.

Hallie and Rinda decide to drive to Phoenix. Along the way, they pick up a hitchhiker named Dodge (Gil Bellows) who's carrying a suitcase. At a gas station, Dodge tells an inquisitive cop that he's married to Rinda, who plays along with him. Dodge tells Rinda that there's nothing but old records in the suitcase, and that he wasn't involved in any crime. Quinn shows up at the gas station and finds a marked $20 bill from the robbery, and the owner tells him he got it from a woman driving an old red Cadillac.

Rinda, Dodge and Hallie drive to a remote canyon, and that night, Hallie and Dodge go skinny-dipping in the hot springs and make love while Rinda watches. The next day, Rinda decides to leave, and Hallie stays with Dodge.

Quinn finds Rinda after spotting her Cadillac at a diner, and he tells her about the marked $20 and that there's a $10,000 reward for capturing the robber. Angry that Dodge lied to her, Rinda agrees to show Quinn where Dodge is, and they're joined by a cop from the Navajo nation.

At the canyon, Quinn ambushes Dodge, handcuffs him, and holds his head under water to get him to tell where the money is. Dodge denies having any money and when the Navajo cop tries to get Quinn to let Dodge go, Quinn shoots the cop, then Rinda, killing them both. A flashback reveals that Quinn was a participant in the robbery and that he was the one who killed his ex-partner. Hallie tells Quinn that she has the money, then pulls out a gun and kills him.

Dodge and Hallie get the money from a bus station locker, then get a hotel room, but her husband Bo shows up while Dodge is out buying a new car, and he forces Hallie to drive away with him. Dodge sees them driving away and chases them to a railroad crossing, and Bo starts shooting at Dodge. As a speeding train approaches, Hallie intentionally drives the car onto the tracks so that Bo can't hurt Dodge, and the car is demolished by the train. Dodge gets out of his car and sees that Hallie is dead. He runs away screaming as a crop-dusting plane flies over him.

BLACK DAY BLUE NIGHT is a dark and moody little Southwestern noir in the RED ROCK WEST (1993) vein that's not half-bad, thanks to good performances and a thoughtful script that plays it straight with the rules of the genre. At the very least, it's a refreshing change from the scores of postmodern, ironic Tarantino wannabes, where quirky characters with cute names spout hipster dialogue as they blow people away, and the brutal violence is meant to be funny and cartoonish. Writer-director J. S. Cardone's solidly constructed script offers a number of twists and turns, and though most of them are fairly predictable, such as Quinn's true motive, they're still effective since the tongue-in-cheek attitude is kept to a minimum.

The crosses and double-crosses sometimes become confusing, and it's never really clearly explained how Hallie ended up with the money (Bo may have been involved in the robbery), but an honest attempt is made to give the characters some depth and background history, even if this results in some long, monotonous dialogue scenes. The parched and spooky desert milieu is nicely observed and the acting is superior for this kind of low-budget production, with Forbes, Sara, Bellows, and Walsh creating believable, substantial characters. Unfortunately, the ending is not really emotionally satisfying and seems arbitrary, despite remaining admirably true to the genre by not copping out with a clever, audience-pleasing twist which would allow Dodge and Hallie to drive into the sunset together with their suitcase full of cash. *(Violence, extreme profanity, nudity, sexual situations.)* — M.S.

d, J. S. Cardone; p, Carol Kottenbrook, Scott Einbinder; exec p, David Korda, Willi Baer; w, J. S. Cardone; ph, Michael Cardone; ed, Thomas Meshelski, Claudia Hoover; m, Johnny Lee Schell, Joe Sublett; prod d, Jerry Fleming; sound, Yehuda Maayan; fx, Richard Malzahn; casting, Elisa Goodman, Abra Edelman; cos, Bonnie Stauch; makeup, Carlann Matz

Mystery/Thriller **(PR: O MPAA: R)**

BLACK MOUNTAIN ★★★★

(China) 97m Xi'an Film Studio c
(AKA: BLACK MOUNTAIN ROAD, THE; HEI SHAN LU)

Ailiya *(The Woman)*; Xie Yuan *(Sixth Brother)*; Zhao Xiaorui *(Elder Brother)*; Han Guichen; Wang Anqing; Jin Lianhua; Zhao Gang; Wang Dawei; Guo Zhiqiang

A decrepit temple on a wild mountainside sets the stage for elemental power plays between a lone woman and six aggressive brothers in a tale illuminating the struggles between mankind and nature in wartime China.

Set around the Sino-Japanese War of 1894, the tale opens with a twilight shot of the haggard temple. Built by a foreign monk—who was ultimately burned alive inside by the villagers for having brought bad luck—it now serves as an inn for travelers. It is run by a young woman (Ailiya) who has only her vicious dog Luo to protect her. When six hungry peasant porters, all brothers, arrive, the woman feeds them and carves the black calluses off their feet with a knife as they gnaw their meat. When the brothers try to rape her, she calls to Luo.

There are bandits in the hills, and, when the men wage a victorious assault the following day, they return to the inn claiming ownership of the entire mountain. Elder Brother (Zhao Xiaorui) is wounded and remains behind as the rest set off to work in the morning. Once alone, he ties up the dog and rapes the woman. After the rape, the woman cleans clothes against a stone, repeatedly, pounding her wood stick against the rock. When Elder Brother throws off his own rags and orders her to wash them, Luo attacks. Without looking up at their desperate battle in the water, she continues to pound away rhythmically. He gradually dominates her by force, keeps the others away, and earns Luo's obedience. The woman responds by seducing Sixth Brother (Xie Yuan), the youngest and weakest, who has charmed her with the gift of a mirror.

One day, Sixth Brother returns from work alone and tells how he escaped abduction by the Japanese, who are building a road through the mountains. This adds both a military and economic dimension, because a road would ruin the men's livelihood.

When Elder Brother returns from gathering food, he finds Sixth Brother and the woman entangled, beats them mercilessly, and turns the place into a prison for Sixth Brother. The woman tries to stab Elder Brother but hesitates. As she is beaten, Sixth Brother angrily breaks his way out with an ax.

Their fight is interrupted by the return of the four other brothers, bearing news that their village has been sacked, their wives and children slain, and the Japanese are on the way to the temple. The defenders are no match for the enemy guns, and four brothers and the woman die in the shooting. When Sixth Brother tells Elder Brother of the woman's fate, they run to their deaths in the now-flaming temple. The film ends with the burning edifice at night on the mountainside.

Though there are no explicit shots of nudity, 1990's BLACK MOUNTAIN was banned by Chinese censors, allegedly for sexual content, and kept from release for three years.

Director Zhou Xiaomen, one of the younger of the so-called "Fifth Generation" of talented Chinese filmmakers who flourished in the late 1980s, repeatedly expresses a correlation between the natural and human orders with stunning visual juxtapositions. Images of fire dominate during moments of danger, and strong winds sweep the mountain during sexual encounters. Ambient sounds fill the audio track—fires crackling, tools pounding, winds blowing, people singing, water flowing, all reinforced intermittently by drums and simple instruments.

The archetypal characters are never even granted names—the woman is unknown and the brothers go only by order of hierarchy. There is simplicity and dramatic perfection to the relationships among the characters.

The fierce eroticism and brutishness captured in BLACK MOUNTAIN reveal the base-level complexities of power which traverse the realms of individual, gender, race, and nation. The Other, be it Woman, Japanese, or Brother, represents a challenge to be resolved, ultimately by conquest, fire, and even death.

Zhou's later ERMO (1994) also depicts an independent peasant woman in a changing China, and was less-vexing to Beijing bureaucrats. Portraying universal constants of human experience with a visceral, cinematic purity, BLACK MOUNTAIN is his harsh masterwork. *(Violence, adult situations, sexual situations.)* — R.C.

d, Zhou Xiaowen; w, Zhu Jianxin, Zhou Xiaowen; ph, Zhou Xiaowen; ed, Zhong Furong; m, Zhao Jiping; art d, Dou Guoxiang; sound, Hu Dongzhi; cos, Ren Zhiwen

Drama **(PR: C MPAA: NR)**

BLACK MOUNTAIN ROAD, THE

(SEE: BLACK MOUNTAIN)

BLACK OUT ★★

(U.S.) 98m Moonstone Entertainment; Midnight Heat Productions ~ Vidmark c

Brian Bosworth *(John Grey/Wayne Garret)*; Brad Dourif *(Thomas Payne)*; Claire Yarlett *(Jenny)*; Marta DuBois *(Sharon Grey)*; Jeremy Roberts *(Scar)*; Maria Barrientos *(Cindy)*; Lance LeGault; Sheila Wills; Thomas W. Poster; Roy Conrad; Brad Greenquist; David Gene Gibbs

Following his flashy stint on the football field (and the failure of his big-screen vehicle STONE COLD), athlete Brian Bosworth appeared as an action hero in weak, straight-to-video items like BLACK OUT.

An amnesiac after a car mishap, businessman John Grey (Brian Bosworth) must relearn everything about his life. But his nightmarish flashbacks to cellblock scenes and robberies don't square with the public John Grey, an Arizona bank executive.

He discovers he was once Wayne Garret, member of a fearsome criminal gang (who have, coincidentally, just burst out of prison). Grey's/Garret's incautious inquiries draw the attention of his former outlaw boss, Thomas Payne (Brad Dourif), who orders Garret killed for having been the state's witness at the trial. Hit men rub out the present Mrs. Grey (Marta DuBois), but Garret escapes.

Suspected of murdering his wife and with his memory still largely blank, fugitive Garret goes to California after Payne and finds refuge with waitress Jenny (Claire Yarlett). Garret locates a handy arms cache from his past, and he and Jenny invade the villain's lair. With the firefight finished and Payne slain, a federal agent brings the *deus ex machina* revelation that Garret was never a crook in the first place, but an undercover supercop who once infiltrated Payne's mob.

The premise of the amnesiac who knew too much gets a mild uplift from Allan Goldstein's direction and a soundtrack that is reminiscent of B-movie potboilers of yesteryear.

But when the gunfire starts, the filmmakers opt for action scenes in a lightweight, almost camp vein. Bosworth is really the main drag on the tale's overextended credibility, far more convincing as a beefy thug yelling "You want a piece of me?!" than a confused yuppie whining "What am I *doing*?" an instant later. One-time Oscar nominee (ONE FLEW OVER THE CUCKOO'S NEST) Dourif does a Christopher Walken bit as the dapper bad guy.

Despite the ingrained marketing bias toward huge guys with huge guns, it would have been more interesting to see all-pro thespian Dourif handle the duality of the disoriented hero and leave The Boz with the larger-than-life antagonist position he once practiced on the football field. *(Violence, substance abuse, profanity, sexual situations, nudity)* — C.C.

d, Allen A. Goldstein; p, Yakov Bentsvi, Ashok Amritraj, Steven Schoenberg; exec p, Gary Wichard, Ernst Stroh; assoc p, James Holt; w, Steven Schoenberg, Reuben Gordon; ph, Geoff Schaaf; ed, Kert Vander Meulen; m, Terry Plumeri; prod d, Arlan Jay Vetter; art d, James R. Zachary; casting, Kathy A. Smith; cos, Ron Talsky; stunts, Cole S. McKay

Thriller/Crime **(PR: C MPAA: R)**

BLACK ROSE OF HARLEM ★

(U.S.) 81m Concorde-New Horizons Corp. ~ New Horizons Home Video c
(AKA: MACHINE GUN BLUES)

Cynda Williams *(Georgia Freeman)*; Nick Cassavetes *(Johnny Verona)*; Joe Viterelli *(Costanza)*; Lawrence Monoson *(Joey)*; Richard Brooks *(Yancey)*; Richard T. Jones *(Cateye)*; Garrett Morris *(Fry Wisdom)*; Tony Burton *(Turner)*; Maria Ford *(Alba)*; Marcus Aurelius *(Newby)*; Eb Lottimer *(Lou)*

BLACK ROSE OF HARLEM (aka: MACHINE GUN BLUES) is a tedious low- budget gangster drama, with Cynda Williams as a black nightclub singer who falls for Italian mob enforcer Nick Cassavetes in 1931 Harlem.

Georgia Freeman (Williams) is a singer in a Harlem nightclub that Italian mob boss Costanza (Joe Viterelli) wants to take over. Costanza visits the club with his henchmen, Johnny (Nick Cassavetes) and Joey (Lawrence Monoson). Georgia and Johnny make eyes at each other.

Club co-owner Fry Wisdom (Garrett Morris) refuses to pay protection money to Costanza, and Joey shoots him dead. In the ensuing gunfight, Johnny saves Costanza's life. In gratitude, Costanza makes Johnny his #2 man and introduces him to his precocious daughter, Alba (Maria Ford). That night, Alba sneaks into Johnny's room and tries to make love to him, but he fantasizes about Georgia.

The nightclub is reopened with the help of new co-owner Yancey (Richard Brooks), and Georgia is a hit with her nightly performances. Soon, she and Johnny are having a torrid affair. Cateye (Richard T. Jones), a musician who's in love with Georgia, warns her to stay away from Johnny, but she doesn't listen.

Johnny suggests to Costanza that they take over the club, but the club's co-owner, Turner (Tony Burton), turns down Johnny's offer. Costanza sends Joey and his goons to take the place by force. Johnny warns Yancey and Turner that Joey's coming, and they ambush him, making him strip and humiliating him. Joey, convinced that Johnny tipped them off, tells Costanza that he saw Johnny in Alba's room. Johnny admits it, and Costanza makes him propose to her.

Joey kills Yancey and Turner, and Costanza takes over the club. After Johnny leaves Alba at the altar, Joey tells Costanza about his secret secret affair with Georgia. They catch Johnny and Georgia together at the club. A gunfight breaks out, and Costanza and Johnny are shot. Before Johnny dies, Georgia tells him she's pregnant. Joey's about to shoot Georgia when Cateye comes up behind him and shoots him. The movie ends with Georgia boarding a bus alone.

BLACK ROSE OF HARLEM is Roger Corman's attempt to meld aspects of THE COTTON CLUB, THE GODFATHER trilogy, THE UNTOUCHABLES, and countless other gangster classics. Unfortunately, the film violates Corman's First Commandment: Thou Shalt Not Bore. Consisting mostly of long conversations in the darkened nightclub, it lacks excitement and atmosphere.

Always eager to recycle excerpts from his old productions, Corman reuses stock footage from 1979's THE LADY IN RED for virtually all of the exterior shots and action montages.

Williams gives a decent, low-key performance, and she has a nice singing voice. But the movie is padded with her many musical numbers, which are shot in a flat, static style. Viterelli is an old hand at playing grotesque Mafiosi, and he's perfectly cast as Costanza, but Monoson shamelessly hams it up as the hotheaded Joey.

As for Cassavetes, he's smarmy and totally unconvincing as a 1930s tough guy. In a string of bad, direct-to-video productions, he has consistently demonstrated that, despite wonderful genes (from father John and mother Gena Rowlands), he's simply not a good actor. *(Nudity, sexual situations, graphic violence, extreme profanity.)* — M.S.

d, Fred Gallo; p, Mike Elliott; exec p, Roger Corman; assoc p, Michael Amato; co-p, Bill Bromiley Jr.; w, Charles Philip Moore (based on a story by Frances Doel); ph, John Aronson; ed, Brian Katkin; m, David Wurst, Eric Wurst; prod d, Nava; art d, Danielle Berman; sound, Christopher M. Taylor; fx, Greg Landerer; casting, Jan Glaser; cos, Tami Mor; makeup, Diana Ragland

Crime **(PR: O MPAA: R)**

BLACK SCORPION ★★

(U.S.) 90m Pacific Trust ~ New Horizons Home Video c
(AKA: OF UNKNOWN ORIGINS)

Joan Severance *(Darcy Walker/Black Scorpion)*; Rick Rossovich *(Lt. Stan Walker)*; Garrett Morris *(Argyle)*; Bruce Abbott *(Michael Russo)*; Stephen Lee *(Captain Strickland)*; Terri J. Vaughn *(Tender Lovin)*; Michael Wiseman *(Hacksaw)*; Brad Tatum *(Razor)*; Steven Kravitz *(Rookie No. 1)*; Darryl M. Bell *(E-Z Street)*; Casey Siemaszko *(Dr. Noah Goddard/Breathtaker)*; John Sanderford *(DA Thomas Aldridge)*; Shane Powers *(Cop No. 2)*; Ashley Peldon *(Little Darcy)*; Kimberly Roberts *(Nurse)*; Kyle Fredericks *(Orderly)*; Randy Ideishi *(Tong Leader)*; Paula Tricky *(Newscaster Leslie Vance)*; Heather O'Ryan *(Teenage Runaway)*; Rick Tyler Barnes *(Mugger)*; Vincent Chase *(Accountant)*; Anita Hart *(Scary Mary)*; Rosine "Ace" Hatem *(Connie the Crusher)*; Kurt Lott *(Security Guard No. 1)*; Anthony Kramme *(Security Guard No. 2)*; Rodman Flender *(Hank)*; Matt Roe *(Mayor)*; Janelle Hensley Paradee *(Babette)*; Rick Dean *(Wino)*; Mike Elliott *(Cop No. 1)*; Jonathan Winfrey *(Bar Patron)*; Greg Brazzel *(Guard in Store)*

The heroine of this 1995 "Roger Corman Presents" Showtime movie—the direct-to-video goddess Joan Severance—wears a black bustier, spike-heel thigh-high boots, a mask, and practically nothing else. This could very well have been the entire pitch that got this movie made. If that is all you're looking for, then BLACK SCORPION more than delivers.

Eighteen years after her police lieutenant father, Stan Walker (Rick Rossovich), accidentally kills a doctor, Darcy (Severance) has become a police detective. With her partner, Michael Russo (Bruce Abbott), they bust a killer pimp, E-Z Street, whom DA Thomas Aldridge (John Sanderford) lets off on a technicality. Later, Aldridge kills ex-Lt. Walker while he and Darcy commiserate in a bar. At the headquarters of BREATH (Bureau of Research and Engineering in Atmospheric Technologies for Health), an unnamed villain seems pleased by the TV news report. When Darcy subsequently threatens the "temporarily insane" Aldridge in his cell, she's suspended from the force.

Meanwhile, Tender Lovin, one of E-Z Street's prostitutes whom Darcy promised to help, gets cut up by the angry pimp. After Tender Lovin shows up at Darcy's apartment to blame her, Darcy straps on her sexy superhero outfit and goes off to met out justice. She confronts Easy Street, and kicks him out a window to his death. Later, she saves Tender Lovin from a mugger, and the hooker describes the vigilante as looking like a black scorpion.

The Black Scorpion fights crime, but the police want to stop her vigilantism—especially Russo, who wrestles with her one night in a clinch that ends with a kiss before she escapes. This causes complications when Darcy (as herself) wants to get romantic with Russo, because he now has a thing for the Black Scorpion. Later, after the two separately fight the villain, dubbed Breathtaker, the Black Scorpion arrives to throw Russo on his bed and have her way with him.

The Black Scorpion eventually defeats Breathtaker—discovering he's the doctor whom her father had apparently killed 18 years ago—and Russo discovers her real identity. But he soon forgets (thanks to a complicated sub-plot), and Darcy is reinstated into the force.

The "mood" of the film swerves from straight-forward police noir themes to cartoony superhero action. Given the hackneyed dialogue, and Severance's wooden delivery of it, the best thing about this film just might be its beautifully haunting theme music. However, the film does have one brilliant touch: that comic-book-fanboy dream of seeing Supergirl strip off her top and mount her man. Otherwise, the only breathtaking thing about BLACK SCORPION is the physique of its super-hero lead. *(Nudity, graphic violence, sexual situations.)* — F.L.

d, Jonathan Winfrey; p, Mike Elliott; exec p, Roger Corman, Lance H. Robbins; w, Craig J. Nevius; ph, Geoff George; ed, Tom Petersen, Gwyneth Gibby; m, Kevin Kiner; prod d, Nava, Eric Kahn; art d, Aaron Mays; set d, Cynthia Anne Slagter; sound, Bill Robbins (mixer), Thomas P. Boyle (mixer); fx, Perry Harovas, Bob Farnham; casting, Jan Glaser; makeup, Stephanie Massie; stunts, Patrick Statham, Cole McCay

Crime/Fantasy/Adventure (PR: O MPAA: R)

BLACK SHEEP ★

(U.S.) 91m Broadway Video; Paramount ~ Paramount c

Chris Farley *(Mike Donnelly)*; David Spade *(Steve Dodds)*; Tim Matheson *(Al Donnelly)*; Christine Ebersole *(Governor Tracy)*; Gary Busey *(Drake Sabitch)*; Grant Heslov *(Robbie Mieghem)*; Timothy Carhart *(Roger Kovary)*; Bruce McGill *(Neuschwender)*; Michael Patrick Carter *(Scott Colleary)*; Boyd Banks *(Clyde Spinoza)*; David St. James *(Motorcycle Cop)*; Skip O'Brien *(State Trooper)*; Branden R. Morgan *(Fan)*; "Gypsy" Spheeris *(Pocket Pool Lady)*; John Ashker *(Jim Blaine)*; William Howell *(Rastafarian)*; Austin Kottke *(Tough Kid)*; Toby Scott Ganger *(Tough Kid)*; Dylan Lucas *(Ricky)*; James Noah *(Mayor)*; Chris Owen *(Hal)*; Jonathan Everett Lewis *(Carl)*; Larita Shelby *(Reporter)*; Karen Kahn *(Anchor Woman)*; Laura Weekes *(TV Reporter)*; Tucker Smallwood *(Election Analyst)*; Mark Thomas McLaughlin; Steven Neil Turner; Matt David Lukin; Daniel Joe Peters *(Mudhoney)*; Kevin P. Farley *(Bouncer)*; John Farley *(Bouncer)*; Patrick Pankhurst *(Donald Tracy)*; Luke Dickinson *(Andrew Tracy)*; Fred Wolf *(Ronald Forte)*; Patricia Place *(Woman at Party)*; Annie O'Donnell *(Election Worker)*; Kathleen O'Malley *(Mrs. Oneacre)*; Jean Speegle Howard *(Elderly Woman)*; Drew Wilson *(Elderly Man)*; Michele Burkette *(Police Woman)*; Andrew Breymann *(Hillbilly Kid)*

BLACK SHEEP is baa-ad. "Saturday Night Live" stars Chris Farley and David Spade reprise their odd couple, slapstick shtick from TOMMY BOY (1995) with abysmal results.

Al Donnelly (Tim Matheson) is a gubernatorial candidate with good prospects for election. But the antics of his big-hearted, bigger-stomached brother, Mike (Chris Farley), are generating a lot of bad press. Political aide Steve Dodds (David Spade) is charged with keeping Mike out of trouble. This proves to be a more difficult task than anyone imagines, and the two don't get along at all.

When the corrupt incumbent, Governor Tracy (Christine Ebersole), frames Mike for arson, the oil-and-water duo escape to a remote cabin in the woods. Mike won't be kept down, though. On election eve, he shows up at a Rock The Vote concert, gets stoned, gets on stage, and delivers an incoherent spiel that ends with the rallying cry, "Kill Whitey!"

Al loses the election, but Mike uncovers proof of ballot fraud on Tracy's part. With Steve's help, Mike confronts Tracy and offers the evidence to the media. In the end, thanks to Mike, Al becomes Governor.

BLACK SHEEP follows the same formula as TOMMY BOY: put a fat slob and a sarcastic wiseguy together, send them on a road trip, hope for laughs. And its repetition only proves that sometimes once *is* enough. BLACK SHEEP's comic highlight has Spade and Farley arriving at the cabin, finding a bat inside, and struggling to get rid of it. The climax occurs when Spade covers Farley with a blanket and beats him mercilessly with a broom handle. Sadistic torture is funny when The Three Stooges do it (perhaps it's all that percussion). But Farley merely flails about wildly and screams like a maniac, whether he staples his hand or gets dragged behind a car. It is just painful to watch.

Speaking of scenes that are painful to watch, BLACK SHEEP also includes would-be poignant moments that show how much Mike, who's really just a little boy at heart, loves kids, and a forceful "Voting kicks ass!" message.

How this pro-vote admonition will go over with the movie's target audience of third and fourth graders is uncertain. *(Violence, substance abuse.)* — P.R.

d, Penelope Spheeris; p, Lorne Michaels; exec p, C.O. Erickson, Robert K. Weiss; assoc p, Eric Newman; co-p, Dinah Minot; w, Fred Wolf; ph, Daryn Okada; ed, Ross Albert; m, William Ross; prod d, Peter Jamison; art d, Chris Cornwell; set d, Linda Spheeris; sound, Willie Burton (mixer); fx, Richard M. Zarro; casting, Debora Aquila, Jane Shannon; cos, Jill Ohanneson; makeup, James L. McCoy; stunts, Shane Dixon

Comedy **(PR: C MPAA: PG-13)**

BLONDES HAVE MORE GUNS ★

(U.S.) 85m Troma Films ~ Troma, Inc. c

Michael McGaharn *(Harry Bates)*; Elizabeth Key *(Montana Beaver-Shotz)*; Richard Neil *(Dick Smoker)*; Gloria Lusiak *(Dakota Beaver)*; Andre Brazeau *(Captain Hook)*; David Myers *(Lyle Shotz)*; Brian York *(The Doctor)*; Bennie Buttner *(Dr. Hasselblad/Henry)*; Romana Lisa *(Patricia Martin)*; Derek Yee *(Tom Woo)*; Ron Meier *(Detective)*; Richard Myers *(Dahmer)*; Anderson Lim *(Short Cop)*; Elizabeth Conrad *(Athletic Cop)*; Paul Ferrari *(Security Guard)*; Carol Daly *(Lorena)*; Dianne Lanning *(Harry's Mother)*; Megan Bajon *(Harry's Sister)*; Antoinette Sandmann *(Mrs. Landers)*; Cathy Pizza *(Screaming Woman)*; Karl-Heinz Teuber *(Montana's Father)*; John Faris *(Telemarketer)*; Regis Demidio *(Television Producer)*

Troma Films strikes again with this low-budget spoof of cop thrillers, which parodies such big-budget hits as BASIC INSTINCT and INDECENT PROPOSAL. The story features a dim-witted cop on the trail of a deadly femme fatale. But the real star of this film is its scattershot barrage of sight gags and verbal puns, which aspire to a NAKED GUN-style wackiness.

A mysterious blonde has been tying her lovers to the bed and killing them with a chainsaw. When the fourth body is discovered, police detective Harry Bates (Michael McGaharn) is put on the case. Finding a wedding invitation on the latest victim, Harry and his partner, Dick Smoker (Richard Neil), go to the ceremony and take in the lovely bride, Montana Beaver-Shotz (Elizabeth Key), for questioning. Montana's twin half-stepsister (once removed), Dakota (Gloria Lusiak), comes to town and unsuccessfully tries to seduce Harry, who instead falls for the promiscuous Montana, even though her husband's fresh corpse is further proof of her guilt.

Afraid that Montana is the killer, the lovesick Harry transfers his affections to Dakota. But when a fresh body turns up at Dakota's home, she's taken in for questioning. She persuades her questioners of her innocence by uncrossing her legs and revealing that she is really a man—Montana's brother. Harry and Montana have sex, after which both Montana and Dakota are shot by Harry's ex-partner (who thinks he's a dog). Montana and Dakota both survive, while Harry discovers that the crazed, love-obsessed transvestite murderess is really his superior, Captain Hook. Appearing in drag, Hook ties Harry to the bed and pulls out his chainsaw, only to be shot by Smoker, who walks in on the bizarre scene.

If the preceding synopsis doesn't make much sense, there's a good reason. The filmmakers were more concerned with ladling on jokes than writing a coherent script. Even worse, most of the humor lays there like roadkill, and despite the movie's R-rated story line, its sense of humor is firmly entrenched in the fourth grade.

The wafer-thin narrative is padded with a few spicy sex scenes, but mostly, it's a rapid-fire array of laughless gags that range from the crude to the offensive to the merely asinine. There are gay jokes, infomercial take-offs, tired drug schtick, self-reflexive comments, and even if a joke falls flat the first time around, it's repeatedly beaten into the ground.

This is an amateurish comedy that dredges the bottom of the barrel, even by Troma's standards. *(Violence, nudity, sexual situations, substance abuse, profanity.) — S.P.*

d, George Merriweather; p, George Merriweather; exec p, Dennis Valovich, Ferris Suer; co-p, Lloyd Kaufman, Michael Herz; w, George Merriweather, Dan Goodman, Mary Guthrie; ph, Maximo Munzi; ed, Rick LeCompte; m, Joe Renzetti; sound, Bryan Matheson

Comedy **(PR: C MPAA: R)**

BLOOD & DONUTS ★

(Canada) 89m Feature Film Project; Daban Films ~ Malofilm c

Gordon Currie *(Boya)*; Justin Louis *(Earl)*; Helene Clarkson *(Molly)*; Fiona Reid *(Rita)*; Frank Moore *(Pierce)*; Hadley Kay *(Axel)*; David Cronenberg *(Stephen)*; J. Winston Carroll *(Bernie)*; Earl Pastko *(Junkie)*; Susan Koffman *(Old Lady)*; Charles Hayter *(Old Wino)*; Sam Malkin *(Hotel Clerk)*

This insipid horror spoof could be described as a vampire without dentures—it tries to sink its fangs into a farcical send-up of bloodsucker lore, but only succeeds in gumming up the works. Clumsily stalking the loopy spirit of AN AMERICAN WEREWOLF IN LONDON (1981), this chill-less, laugh-less creature feature lacks the Hollywood budget, the deft writing, and the spruced-up performers needed to create a bitingly witty parody.

Having rested in peace since the 1969 Moonwalk, genially philosophical vampire Boya (Gordon Currie) reawakens in the nerve-wracking 90s. Because a cabby, Earl (Justin Louis), shows friendly concern during a jaunt to the cemetery, late-night fare Boya returns the favor when Earl is roughed up by two mob leg-men, Pierce (Frank Moore) and Axel (Hadley Kay). Protective Boya's period of adjustment is complicated when he falls for Molly (Helene Clarkson), an acerbic donut shop waitress; this relationship is jeopardized by the appearance of Boya's former necking partner Rita (Fiona Reid), who demands Boya turn her into a full-fledged vampire. Although Boya saves Earl from another bruising lesson in late payments from Pierce and Axel, Earl freaks out at buddy Boya's otherworldly transformation and falls out of his window. With Boya's aid, Molly revives a dying Earl at the cemetery with the juice from jumper cables. Tired of mortal strife and hesitant about vampirizing Molly, Boya submits to daylight exposure while traveling in a car trunk and perishes from the sun's rays.

Pointless and daft, BLOOD & DONUTS exhibits such a slippery grasp of tone, it's difficult to fathom its creators' intentions; dull stretches of the movie resemble a tame historical romance with a bit of blood spattered on the bodices. Mired in too many love scenes devoid of co-star chemistry, this film also shifts gears and becomes, alternately, a loan shark flick take-off, a dumb-ass buddy-buddy comedy, and a riff on INTERVIEW WITH THE VAMPIRE (1994). Through it all, pop tunes pound at the audience like a stake driven into your MTV heart. (Anyone who doubts that music videos have had a deleterious effect on filmmaking should take a gander at this tune-filled turkey; like DANGEROUS MINDS (1995), this isn't a movie, it's an excuse to release a soundtrack album.) As acted by many Not-ready-for-Prime-time players and directed by Holly Dale as if it were a grade school Halloween pageant, BLOOD & DONUTS can only be recommended to children of the night who want to catch a glimpse of frightmeister David Cronenberg; the cult director is quite effective in a blackly comic cameo as a nasty Mafia nabob. *(Graphic violence, extreme profanity, adult situations, substance abuse.)* — R.P.

d, Holly Dale; p, Steven Hoban; exec p, Colin Brunton; assoc p, Stephen Fanfarra, Justine Whyte; w, Andrew Rai Berzins; ph, Paul Sarossey; ed, Stephen Fanfarra, Brett Sullivan; m, Nash the Slash; prod d, David Moe; art d, Ingrid Jurek; set d, Mava Ravins; sound, John Woolfson; fx, Michael Lennick, Sean Sampson; casting, Deirdre Bowen; cos, Emma England; makeup, Cathie Davies-Irvine; stunts, Dwayne McLean

Horror/Comedy/Romance (PR: O MPAA: R)

BLOODKNOT ★★½

(U.S.) 98m Chesler Productions; Perlmutter Productions ~ Showtime/Paramount Home Video c

Kate Vernon *(Kay Everett "Connie")*; Craig Sheffer *(Mike)*; Patrick Dempsey *(Tom)*; Margot Kidder *(Evelyn)*; Allan Royal *(Arthur)*; Ashley Ann Wood *(Gail)*; Krista Bridges *(Julie)*; Nancy Cser *(Connie)*; Dean McDermott *(Local Boy)*; Heidi Atherton *(Fran)*; Kate Trotter *(Phyllis)*; Penelope Gioris *(Check-out Girl)*; Victor Ertmanis *(Boater)*; Judah Katz *(Corporal)*; Kevin Hicks *(Paramedic)*

Engrossing trash, BLOODKNOT never underestimates the depths to which human nature can descend and never makes the miscalculation of peppering its escapism with either too much lovemaking or too much homicide.

Picking up lesbian soldier Connie (Nancy Cser) and murdering her is the first step in the payback plan of Kay Everett (Kate Vernon). Posing as the dead Connie, Kay next ingratiates herself into the Reeves family, which is mourning the loss in the Gulf War of Corporal Martin Reeves. Palming herself off as Martin's secret fiancee, Kay easily hoodwinks Martin's dad, Arthur (Allan Royal); his Mom, Evelyn (Margot Kidder); his jealous younger brother, Tom (Patrick Dempsey); and precocious younger sister, Gail (Ashley Ann Wood). However, she gains the enmity of family friend, Julie (Krista Bridges), whose estrangement from Tom is exacerbated by the flirtatious Kay. Bonding with Evelyn after rescuing Gail from a swimming mishap, Kay restores the family's will to thrive, them closes in for the kill.

She beds the gullible Tom and tries to eliminate Gail after a fire on a boat sends the child into a coma. Having been abandoned by Evelyn, daughter Kay has spent her formative years planning how to systematically destroy Evelyn's perfect new family. Wounding Tom with a knife, Kay fights off a vigilant Julie; yet, Evelyn can't deny a mother's feelings. The emotionally crippled Kay is carted off to a hospital for the criminally insane, so that her absentee mother, Evelyn, can save her from Julie's vengeance.

Usually, these psycho-slasher films don't offer much excuse for their loonies to run amok. Not only does BLOODKNOT provide its raving murderess with a believable motive, but it reinforces its standard revenge plot by concentrating on the killer's methodical ways. Polishing its bloodlust for viewers, BLOODKNOT shows how insanity can be corralled into a purpose; one marvels at Kay Everett's bottomless bag of dirty tricks. Parodying all those "Unsolved Mystery" segments in which adopted children are blissfully reunited with their birth mothers, BLOODKNOT builds up its arsenal of goosebumps by springing its "I'm home, Mommy" motive just before the climax. Fueled by a cast not content to walk through these variations on a homicidal theme, BLOODKNOT simmers with psychological embellishments without denying the audience its clamor for carve-ups.

Perhaps, the film inevitably disintegrates because the Reeves are easy pickings for Kay. Skewering smug platitudes about the indomitabile family unit, BLOODKNOT covers no new ground but manages to spook its audience. *(Graphic violence, extreme profanity, extensive nudity, sexual situations, substance abuse.)* — R.P.

d, Jorge Montesi; p, T. A. Baird; exec p, Lewis B. Chesler, David M. Perlmutter; assoc p, David Baird, John Morgan; co-p, Hank McCann, Kevin Kelly Brown; w, Randy Kornfield; ph, Philip Linsey; ed, George Roulston; m, Michel Rubini; prod d, Ed Hanna; sound, Bill McMillan; cos, Noreen Landry; makeup, Maribeth Knezev

Crime/Thriller (PR: C MPAA: R)

BLOODSPORT II: THE NEXT KUMITE ★

(U.S.) 86m FM Entertainment; Heidi Eckes Chantre ~ FM Entertainment c

Daniel Bernhardt *(Alex)*; Pat Morita *(David Leung)*; Donald Gibb *(Tiny)*; James Hong *(Sun)*; Lori Lynn Dickerson *(Janine)*; Philip Tan *(John)*; Ong Soo Han *(Demon)*; Nick Hill *(Sergio)*; Ron Hall *(Cliff)*; Master Lee Il Cho *(Head Judge)*; Lisa McCullough *(Kim)*; Chuay *(Chien)*; Steve Martinez *(Referee)*; Jeff Wolfe *(Flash/Fighter)*; Cliff Bernhardt *(Len)*; Nils Stewart *(Gorilla)*; Eric Lee *(Seng)*; Chad Stahelski; Earl White; Jerry Piddington; Richard Kee Smith; Eddie Eaton; Ken Harte; Pouono M. Poloa; Gokor Chivichyan; Dirk Bernhardt *(Fighters)*

Bearing only a token connection to its nominal predecessor, the 1988 Jean-Claude van Damme vehicle BLOODSPORT, BLOODSPORT II shows only the slightest interest in plot anyway.

In Bangkok, small-time crook Alex Cordo (Daniel Bernhardt) steals a priceless ceremonial sword from the home of David Leung (Pat Morita). Doublecrossed by his partner John (Philip Tan), he is captured by the police.

In a Thai prison, Alex is tutored by martial arts master Sun (James Hong). After a few years, his freedom is arranged by Leung, who wants him to help retrieve the sword by entering the Kumite, a secret martial arts competition held every five years in Hong Kong. No longer the dishonorable thief he once was, Alex agrees to do so.

With the help of trainer Tiny (Donald Gibb), Alex rises through the preliminary rounds of the Kumite. He is reunited with Janine (Lori Lynn Dickerson), who he met at Leung's house and who is now working for John. She arranges a meeting between the two ex-partners. Knowing that Alex is dangerous, John plans to doublecross him again, but instead is captured by the police when Alex turns the tables on him. After returning the sword to Leung (who arranges to have Sun freed), Alex bests the bestial Demon (Ong Soo Han) and wins the Kumite.

After the first half-hour, BLOODSPORT II more closely resembles a different Jean-Claude van Damme film, THE QUEST, since it consists almost entirely of brief fight sequences as Kumite contestants duke it out. Plot is sandwiched between these like the dialogue scenes in a porn movie, with little care or expectation that the audience will be much interested in them. Also like a porn film, the fighters are mostly anonymous bodies flailing away at each other. The only elements that break things up are the comically oversized Donald Gibb, the one link to the previous BLOODSPORT, and female fighter Lisa McCullough, whose opponents are so clumsy that you get little sense of what she might really be able to do. As for star Daniel Bernhardt, he has a better English accent than van Damme but little screen presence. *(Violence, profanity.)* — M.F.

d, Alan Mehrez; p, Alan Mehrez; exec p, Diane Mehrez, Jeffrey Konvitz; assoc p, Michael Criscione; co-p, Alexander Tabrizi; w, Jeff Schechter; ph, Jacques Haitkin; ed, Douglas Seelig; m, Steve Edwards; cos, Rattana Fungfuang; makeup, Amanda Llewellyn, Shecheep Nonjui

Martial Arts/Action **(PR: C MPAA: R)**

BLOODY WEEKEND
(SEE: LOADED)

BLUSH ★★
(China/Hong Kong) 119m Ocean Film Company; Beijing Film Studio ~ First Run Features c
(HONG FEN)

Wang Ji *(Qiuyi)*; Wang Zhiwen *(Lao Pu)*; He Saifei *(Xiao'e)*; Zhang Liwei *(Liu Qing)*; Wang Rouli *(Mrs. Pu)*; Song Xiuling *(Ruifeng)*; Xing Yangchun *(Mr. Zhang)*; Zhou Jianying *(Mrs. Zhang)*; Yin Jimei *(Wu Ma)*; Gu Zhifen *(Aunt)*; Zhu Jiyong *(Feng Lao Wu)*; Cao Lei *(Narrator)*

A melodramatic weeper and a guilty near-pleasure, the China-Hong Kong co-production BLUSH is a relatively frank adaptation of the novel *Hong Fen* by Su Tong (who wrote the novel that was the basis for 1991's RAISE THE RED LANTERN). Draped in the cloak of a Serious Political Statement about life after the 1949 Communist takeover, this is actually trashy, titillating soap opera running true to genre form: marriages of convenience, miscarried pregnancies, illegitimate children, attempted suicide, and enough tears to fill the Yangtze River.

"Liberated" by the Communists, tough yet regal prostitute Zhou Qiuyi (Wang Ji) and her best friend, Wang Xiao'e (He Saifei), are among those ejected from the Red Happiness Inn, where Xiao'e was born and raised. The two women are separated when they try to escape their rehabilitation center, and Xiao'e is caught.

Over the next several months or few years (the jumps in time being impossible to ascertain), Qiuyi takes up with a rich young john, Lao Pu (Wang Zhiwen), for whom she has fallen. After leaving him because of his caddishness, and under pressure from his domineering mother (Wang Rouli), she joins a Buddhist temple, ultimately thrown out for being pregnant with Lao's child. The stress makes her miscarry—or so the viewer is told by a narrator who gamely attempts throughout the film to describe scenes one never sees.

Meanwhile, Xiao'e half-heartedly attempts suicide, graduates from the center, and gets pregnant with the baby of Qiuyi's beloved Lao—a poorly paid accountant now that Communists have seized the family land.

Xiao'e marries Lao, bickers venomously, and continually threatens suicide. Lao, still carrying a torch for Qiuyi, embezzles money for her once he learns about his child. He's caught and executed. By this time, Qiuyi—according to the narrator—has married a teahouse owner. She helps the widowed Xiao'e raise her baby, and adopts the child after Xiao'e runs off with a man—again, according to the narrator.

Well-acted and handsomely shot, despite clearly not having the world's best film stock available, the oddly titled BLUSH showcases some attractive, eye-catching shot transitions. In particular, the emotional strain of working-class poverty comes through with unromanticized, uncompromising candor.

Yet director Li Shaohong relies overwhelmingly on stagey, static long or medium shots, displaying little camera movement; she reserves most close-ups for the one or two mildly sexual scenes. There's predictably no flesh seen other than a leg glimpsed through a slit skirt or a flash of hand or face on a dress-covered breast—remarkably daring by Beijing standards.

Much less remarkably, BLUSH ultimately comes down to Qiuyi's "Well, *duhh*" conclusion of, "How strange life is." *(Cantonese with English subtitles)* — F.L.

d, Li Shaohong; p, Chen Kunming, Jimmy Tan; exec p, Cheng Zhigu; w, Ni Zhen, Li Shaohong (based on the novel by Su Tong); ph, Zeng Nianping; ed, Zhou Xinxia; m, Guo Wenjing; art d, Chen Yiyun, Lin Chaoxing; set d, Wang Zesheng, Xie Xinsheng; sound, Wu Ling (recordist); cos, Liu Jianhua; makeup, Sun Hongkui, Sun Bin

Romance/Historical/Drama **(PR: C MPAA: NR)**

BOCA A BOCA
(SEE: MOUTH TO MOUTH)

BODY COUNT ★★
(U.S.) 93m West Side Studios Inc.; Toei Video ~ A-Pix Entertainment c

Brigitte Nielsen *(Sybil)*; Robert Davi *(Eddie Cook)*; Steven Bauer *(Vinnie Rizzo)*; Sonny Chiba *(Makato)*; Jan-Michael Vincent *(Detective Reinhardt)*; Cindy Ambuehl *(Janet Hood)*; Eliott Keener *(Capt. Hendricks)*; Lawrence Le John *(T. C.)*; Eric Codora *(Jake)*; Mario Opinato *(Joey Gianelli)*; Jim Chimento *(Bruce Gianelli)*; Anne McAuley *(Dani)*; Eric Weston *(Jensen)*; Celeste Mellerine *(Young Girl)*; Angela Johnson *(Katherine)*; Daniel Savitt; Talun Hsu *(Interpreters)*; Graham Timbes *(Buck)*; Benford Davis; Douglas Griffin *(Prison Guards)*; John McConnell *(Truck Driver)*; Lynn Gansar *(Reporter)*; Brent Pfaff; B. J. Greene; Barry Fletcher *(Cops)*; Eric Lutes *(Detective)*; Tonia Henderson *(Bartender)*

Astute use of New Orleans locales is about the only asset of BODY COUNT, a stereotypical film about slaying cops and vengeful felons.

When two goodfellas, the Gianelli brothers, are rubbed out, their murderer, Makato (Sonny Chiba), has trouble collecting his paycheck and maintaining his freedom. Not only was Makato hired for the hit by a member of the New Orleans police force, but that same vigilante cop set up Makato to get caught. Suffering the ignominy of incarceration, Makato vows to target the entire force until he punishes his betrayer. Sprung from jail by an escape expert, Sybil (Brigitte Nielsen), Makato flees after helping Sybil slaughter the guards at his outdoor work detail. Meanwhile, veteran cops Detective Cook (Robert Davi) and partner Detective Rizzo (Steven Bauer) resent the diligence of new superior officer, Janet Hood (Cindy Ambuehl), as she scratches for clues to uncover the cop linked to Makato's paid hit.

After initiating his vendetta by offing a stoolie, Makato slashes, torches, tortures, and pushes off of high places several members of the force, leaving Rizzo for dead. Eventually Hood and Cook deduce that Rizzo hired Makato to ice the Gianelli boys, because they kidnapped Rizzo's young daughter for a kiddie-porn sideline. At the hospital, Rizzo, in disgrace, pulls out his own life support. While Hood tangles with Sybil, who is eventually crushed to death under a compressor at a trolley barn, Cook grapples with Makato aboard a runaway trolley. At the last second, Cook hops off and Makato meets a fiery end as the trolley crashes into a fuel tanker.

Dependable action star Robert Davi brings his reserved masculinity to BODY COUNT, lending this clunky crimestopper some much needed class. Clever incorporation of photogenic

New Orleans locales cannot disguise the mechanics of a stereotypical revenge scenario. Instead of revving up the thrills with a police force counteroffensive, the film passively portrays the cops as sitting ducks, priming the audience for each of Makato's gruesome assaults as if this were a slasher flick instead of a cop drama. The aggressive violence depicted is often startling, but not satisfying. *(Graphic violence, extreme profanity, extensive nudity, adult situations, sexual situations, substance abuse.)* — R.P.

d, Talun Hsu; p, David Winters, Tony Vincent, Simon Tse; exec p, Diane Daou, Yoshinori Watanabe, Mitsuru Kurosawa; w, Henry Madden; ph, Blake Evans; ed, Tony Lanza, Steve Nielson; m, Don Peake; prod d, Quenby Tilley; art d, Joan Long; sound, Brian Tracy (mixer), Peter Bentley (mixer); casting, Patricia Rose; makeup, Amanda Poulsen-Wells; stunts, B. J. Davis, Ed Anders

Martial Arts/Action/Crime **(PR: C MPAA: R)**

BODY OF INFLUENCE 2 ★½

(U.S.) 87m Axis Films International; Black Rose Productions; Gernert/Garroni Productions ~ A-Pix Entertainment c

Jodie Fisher *(Leza Watkins)*; Daniel Anderson *(Dr. Thomas Benson)*; Jonathan Goldstein *(Rick Benson)*; Pat Brennan *(Walter Watkins)*; Stephen Poletti *(Lt. Murphy)*; Cheryl Lawyer *(Carrie)*; Clive Rees *(Nicky Diamond)*; Kim Gruenenfelder *(Jerry's Bartender)*; Landon Hall *(Girl at Club)*; Kelly Howard *(Flashback Woman)*; John LaForme *(Flashback Husband)*; Bart Baker *(Prescription Guy)*; Joyce Westergaard *(Tooth Woman)*; Shannon Randall *(Dream Stranger)*; Frank J. Coady *(Dream Stranger)*

Propelled initially by the lurid story of a shrink sexually obsessed by a patient, BODY OF INFLUENCE 2 goes on a twisted psycho-sexual journey that suffers from an incomprehensible plot thanks to shoddy direction and editing.

Dr. Thomas Benson's (Daniel Anderson) mysterious blonde patient Leza (Jodie Fisher) tells him about her dreams, involving leather-masked sex and her own death. Disturbed by his interest and his own sordid sexual visions, he recommends Leza see another shrink, but she plays a sympathy card with a tale of her vicious older husband Walter. The doctor and Leza become intimate, but the smitten Benson can't locate Leza outside the office because all her records have been faked. He eventually finds her at a kinky sex club. Leza warns that Walter must never find out about their liaison. Almost immediately, Walter (Pat Brennan) the husband—contrary to Leza's description, a young man—turns up and tells Benson he knows about the affair.

Benson's brother Rick (Jonathan Goldstein), a private detective, suspects that Leza wants Benson to kill her husband, and he investigates. He discovers that Leza has a master's degree in psychology and her husband has a $10 million life insurance policy. Leza begins to play Benson against his brother by claiming Rick raped her years ago, but Rick shows him photographs of Leza and her young, virile husband having sex. Rick goes snooping around Leza's estate and is beaten. Benson gets a call from Leza that is interrupted by a scream. He calls the police and rushes over to find a bloodied Leza, apparently dead. He grabs a bloody knife and is holding it when the cops rush in and arrest him for murder. Leza is alive and claims Benson killed both her husband and Rick in a jealous rage. She even has photographs of her sleeping with Rick.

Filled with sex scenes that are either sordid or intensely boring, BODY OF EVIDENCE 2 is long and confusing. The editing, which director Brian J. Smith may have intended as enhancement to the "mystery" here, blurs points of view, so it's hard to tell whether we are watching Benson's sexual fantasies, or Leza's, or Benson's interpretation of Leza's fantasies. There are unexplained story lines—including one involving Benson's rough sex past—but the greatest enigma is why Leza has chosen to victimize Benson with this clever frame-up finale. It's just one of many unanswered questions in a movie filled with holes. *(Nudity, sexual situations, adult situations.)* — S.K.

d, Brian J. Smith; p, Andrew W. Garroni, Brian J. Smith; exec p, Walter Gernert; w, Brian J. Smith; ph, Azusa Ohno; ed, Jody Fedele; m, Ron Sures; prod d, Michael Pearce; set d, Beth Ann Lundin; sound, Bill Reinhardt (mixer); casting, Lori Cobe; cos, Bonnie Stauch; makeup, Nacoma Whobrey

Mystery/Thriller **(PR: O MPAA: R)**

BOGUS ★½

(U.S.) 110m Beaux Gus Productions; New Regency Productions; Yorktown Productions ~ Warner Bros. c

Whoopi Goldberg *(Harriet)*; Gerard Depardieu *(Bogus)*; Haley Joel Osment *(Albert)*; Andrea Martin *(Penny)*; Nancy Travis *(Lorraine)*; Denis Mercier *(Antoine)*; Ute Lemper *(Babette)*; Sheryl Lee Ralph *(Ruth Clark)*; Barbara Hamilton *(Mrs. Partridge)*; Al Waxman *(School Principal)*; Elizabeth Harpur *(Ellen)*; Fiona Reid *(School Teacher)*; Kevin Jackson *(Bob Morrison)*; Richard Portnow *(M. Clay Thrasher)*; Mo Gaffney *(Travelers Aide—New Jersey)*; Sara Peery *(Travelers Aide—Las Vegas)*; Cynthia Mace *(Flight Attendant)*; Don Francks *(Dr. Surprise)*; Justine Johnston *(Woman in Plane)*; Frank Medrano *(Man in Plane)*; Philip Williams *(Airport Cop)*; Jackie Richardson *(Babysitter)*; Quancetia Hamilton *(Meter Maid)*; Jared Durand; Michael Vollans *(Boys in Playground)*; D. Ruby Son; Michael Ho; Fielding Horan *(Kids in Classroom)*; Dina Morrone *(Mom at Party)*; Stuart Hughes *(Airline Agent)*; Stan Coles *(Mr. Franklin)*; Yetunde Alabi *(Harriet Age 7)*; Jennifer Pisana *(Lorraine Age 7)*; Michael R. Sousa *(Strongman)*; Yvan Labelle *(Little Person)*; Damon D'Oliveira *(Office Worker)*; Csaba McZala *(Traffic Officer)*; Muguette Moreau *(Assistant to Dr. Surprise)*; Tabitha Lupien *(Girl at Party)*; Nicolette Hazenwinkel *(Wirewalker)*; Doug Gilmore *(Surprise Guest)*; Rebekah Abou-Keer; Kenner Ames; Shelley Bianchi; Heather Braaten; Roger Clown; David Dunlop; Alexei Fateyev; Vince Fera; Joe Gladman; Theresa Fung; Orville Heyn; Peter Jarvis; Lisa Renee Knight; Gigi De Leon; Kelly McIntosh; Jennifer Podemski; Simmi Raymond; Sonny Tran; Jason Twardowski *(Circus Characters)*

Gerard Depardieu and Whoopi Goldberg may be an odd pair to cast as co-stars, but interesting things could be done with such a combination. BOGUS, however, fails to take much advantage of that pairing.

The happy world of seven-year-old Albert (Haley Joel Osment) is destroyed when his mother, Lorraine (Nancy Travis), a performer in a Las Vegas circus, is killed in an automobile accident. With no living relatives, Lorraine's will names her childhood friend, Harriet (Whoopi Goldberg), as the boy's guardian. Feeling abandoned by his circus friends, Albert is sent off to live with Harriet in New Jersey.

Albert makes a new friend on the airplane, a large invisible Frenchman named Bogus (Gerard Depardieu). Bogus tries to coach Albert along in his new relationship, explaining that Harriet is nervous and will need time to adjust. However, a small child is the very last thing that Harriet needs or wants in her life. A woman who, by her own description, doesn't have a motherly bone in her body, Harriet devotes all of her time to the small restaurant-supply business she owns.

Harriet tries to take care of Albert, but she has unresolved problems from her own difficult childhood and has shut herself off emotionally from the world. After a particularly frustrating night in which she has had to retrieve Albert after he runs away to Atlantic City, Harriet voices her frustrations aloud, berating Bogus for not taking proper care of Albert—or of her when she needed help as a child. To her surprise, Bogus appears and reminds her of the magical elements of childhood, leading her in a ballroom dance.

With an opened heart, Harriet goes to Albert's bedroom, only to find that he has walked in his sleep out onto the fire escape. In his dream, his mother tells him to go to Harriet, who catches him on the roof. They agree to become a family, and Bogus leaves in search of someone else who needs his help.

There isn't anything terribly wrong with BOGUS; there just isn't much that's particularly memorable about it. It really isn't a children's movie, although it could have been, had it spent more time with the relationship between Albert and Bogus. In his best scenes, Gerard Depardieu demonstrates exactly the playful-but-protective, larger-than-life quality the role requires—if it wasn't written for him it could have been. It's certainly not a juvenile version of HARVEY (1950), although a clip from the James Stewart classic inevitably shows up.

The film succeeds best with Whoopi Goldberg's emotionally blocked businesswoman, although even that character is a bit underdrawn and suffers by competing for time with so much else in the film. BOGUS would have benefited from some judicious trimming—it's far too long, and director Norman Jewison's pacing is terrible. Apparently trying to evoke childish whimsy (as in Albert's dream of returning to the circus after he runs away), Jewison instead creates languor that brings the story grinding to a halt. The exception is the scene in which Bogus appears to Harriet and the two dance, a wonderful moment that makes one wish Depardieu and Goldberg had more chances to interact on-screen. . . in a better movie. *(Violence.)* — M.F.

d, Norman Jewison; p, Norman Jewison, Arnon Milchan, Jeff Rothberg; exec p, Michael Nathanson, Patrick Markey, Gayle Fraser-Baigelman; assoc p, Michael Jewison; w, Alvin Sargent (from a story by Jeff Rothberg and Francis X. McCarthy); ph, David Watkin; ed, Stephen Rivkin; m, Marc Shaiman; prod d, Ken Adam; art d, Alicia Keywan; set d, Hilton Rosemarin; sound, Bruce Cawardine (mixer); fx, Neil Trifunovich, Alan Munro, Richard Berman, VCE, Inc., Illusion Arts, Inc.; casting, Howard Feuer; cos, Ruth Myers; makeup, Michael Germain; stunts, Ted Hanlan

Comedy **(PR: A MPAA: PG)**

BOTTLE ROCKET ★★★

(U.S.) 93m Gracie Films; Boyle-Taylor Productions ~ Columbia c

Owen C. Wilson *(Didgnan)*; Luke Wilson *(Anthony Adams)*; Robert Musgrave *(Bob Mapplethorpe)*; Andrew Wilson *(Future Man)*; Lumi Cavazos *(Inez)*; James Caan *(Mr. Henry)*; Ned Dowd *(Dr. Nichols)*; Shea Fowler *(Grace)*; Haley Miller *(Bernice)*; Brian Tenenbaum *(H. Clay Murchison)*; Jenni Tooley *(Stacy Sinclair)*; Temple Nash *(Temple)*; Dipak Pallana *(Bookstore Employee)*; Darryl Cox *(Bookstore Manager)*; Stephen Dignan *(Rob)*; Julie Mayfield *(Wife in Motelroom)*; Don Phillips Jr. *(Husband in Motelroom)*; Anna Cifuentes *(Carmen)*; Donny Caicedo *(Rocky)*; Melinda Renna *(Anita)*; Richard Reyes *(Man in Bar)*; Julio Cedillo *(Man Outside Bar)*; Teddy Wilson *(Hector Mapplethorpe)*; Jim Ponds *(Applejack)*; Takayuki Kubota *(Rowboat)*; Kumar Pallana *(Kumar)*; Haskel Craver *(Jackson)*; Jill Parker-Jones *(Motel Manager)*; Nena Smarz *(Maid)*; Hector Garcia *(Freezer Guy)*; Daniel R. Padgett *(Freezer Guy)*; Russell Towery *(Cop)*; Ben Loggins *(Cop)*; Linn Mullin *(Detective)*

BOTTLE ROCKET marks the auspicious feature debut of director Wes Anderson. This lightweight road picture about a group of inept thieves has an uneven beginning but ends up charming and satisfying.

In Austin, Texas, Dignan (Owen Wilson) and Anthony (Luke Wilson) help each other escape from the mental institution in which they have been convalescing for some time. Back in their hometown, the duo enlist their friend Bob (Robert Musgrave) in a scheme to hold up a neighborhood bookstore.

After some group in-fighting, Dignan, Anthony and Bob carry out their crime and run away with the money. Later, on the road, they stop off at a motel to rest. During their stay, Anthony falls in love with Inez (Lumi Cavazos), a motel maid, and Bob abandons everyone one night. Dignan and Anthony finally leave the motel and hit the road again, but Dignan becomes furious when he learns that Anthony has given Inez most of their loot as a tip.

Dignan and Anthony split up over the "tip," but eventually they reunite with Bob in their hometown when Dignan introduces them to Mr. Henry (James Caan), a big-time thief posing as the head of a landscaping company. The three young men join Henry and his associates in the heist of a factory. The robbery goes awry, however, after one of Henry's men is accidentally shot and the police capture Dignan. Meanwhile, Henry double-crosses his team and robs from Bob's posh home during the factory heist.

Dignan goes to the state penitentiary without turning in his friends. After visiting Dignan in prison, Bob pursues a more peaceful existence, while Anthony joins Inez for less-tumultuous adventures.

Filmed mainly in Dallas, BOTTLE ROCKET captures the energy of Jean-Luc Godard's BREATHLESS by appropriating some of its stylistic strategies, including a clever use of jump cuts. Of course, BOTTLE ROCKET lacks the more bravura aspects—aesthetic and thematic—that made BREATHLESS a groundbreaker in 1959, but this new film is nearly on par with some of the other self-reflexive crime capers that have also been influenced by the French New Wave classic (including 1990's MIAMI BLUES). The focus on the troubled two-bit gangsters in all these films occasionally side-steps some larger moral questions, but the characters are, at least, refreshingly real.

After an awkward beginning, BOTTLE ROCKET picks up as a quirky, tense character study. Dignan and Anthony's overlapping-dialogue shtick in the first reel is off-putting, but, eventually, Owen and Luke Wilson (brothers playing best friends here) settle down to give strong, convincing performances. Cavazos (LIKE WATER FOR CHOCOLATE) brings a charming presence to her scenes as the unexpected love interest, and Caan, the one star in the cast, has a few welcome moments as the head gangster (playing off his role in THIEF).

At times the low-budget film slips technically (not all of the abrupt cutting seems deliberate), but some of Robert Yeoman's photography is sharp (especially in the edgy heist scenes) and Mark Mothersbaugh's score is highly pleasing.

BOTTLE ROCKET may not be profound work, but it shows off some genuine talent both behind and in front of the camera. *(Violence, sexual situations, adult situations, profanity.)* — E.M.

d, Wes Anderson; p, Polly Platt, Cynthia Hargrave; exec p, James L. Brooks, Richard Sakai, Barbara Boyle, Michael Taylor; assoc p, Michael Lang, Andrew Wilson; co-p, Ray Zimmerman, L.M. Kit Carson; w, Owen C. Wilson, Wes Anderson; ph, Robert Yeoman; ed, David Moritz; m, Mark Mothersbaugh; prod d, David Wasco; art d, Jerry N. Fleming; set d, Sandy Reynolds-

Wasco; sound, Stacy Brownrigg (mixer); fx, Randy E. Moore; casting, Liz Keigley; cos, Karen Patch; makeup, Manny Sarris Jr., Nena Smarz; stunts, Russell Towery

Comedy/Crime/Drama (PR: C MPAA: R)

BOUND ★★★½

(U.S.) 107m Dino De Laurentiis Communications; Spelling Films ~ Gramercy Pictures c

Jennifer Tilly *(Violet)*; Gina Gershon *(Corky)*; Joe Pantoliano *(Caesar)*; John P. Ryan *(Mickey Malnato)*; Christopher Meloni *(Johnnie Marconi)*; Richard Sarafian *(Gino Marzzone)*; Barry Kivel *(Shelly)*; Mary Mara *(Bartender)*; Peter Spellos *(Lou)*; Susie Bright *(Jesse)*; Margaret Smith *(Woman Cop)*; Ivan Kane *(Cop #1)*; Kevin M. Richardson *(Cop #2)*; Gene Borkan *(Roy)*

BOUND is a clever, exceptionally stylish twist on the edge-of-the-seat thriller. The story has its share of suspense and surprises, and the dual femmes fatales take THE LAST SEDUCTION (1994) one step further. Yet what makes BOUND stand out from the pack is the fast-paced and offbeat dialogue, slick characterizations and brash cinematography.

Corky (Gina Gershon), fresh from prison, is gritty and down-to-earth, and bursting with sly sexuality. Soon after she starts renovating a Chicago high-rise apartment, she meets neighbor Violet (Jennifer Tilly), who lives with mobster Caesar (Joe Pantoliano). Caesar has provided Violet with money and luxury, but she still can't resist turning a few tricks here and there. Her mind really isn't on men anyway, and she immediately falls for Corky.

Energized by the relationship and sick of the violence that Caesar has brought into her life, Violet decides to leave. That evening, $2 million dollars are supposed to be delivered to Caesar, and Violet and Corky scheme to steal the money and pin its theft on Caesar's rival, Johnnie Marconi (Christopher Meloni). Caesar is supposed to present the money to Mafia boss Gino Marzzone (Richard Sarafian), who happens to be Johnnie's father, so the women expect that Caesar will skip town to save his skin. Caesar may be a dim bulb, but the women underestimate him, and their carefully thought-out plan goes awry when he decides not to run for his life but to stay and prove Johnnie guilty of stealing the cash.

Caesar ends up killing Gino and searching for the money. Though at first he doesn't suspect Violet, her eagerness to keep in touch with Corky by phone gives her away. Caesar captures the two women and tortures them into giving him the money. They outsmart him and escape. Believing that Violet doesn't have it in her to kill him, Caesar tries to leave with the money. He's wrong, and she shoots him.

The story has twists and turns galore, and it is to the credit of first-time writers-directors Andy and Larry Wachowski that the suspense remains constant without stretching the plot's plausibility beyond the breaking point. The lesbian twist on the "young lovers dupe the rich boyfriend-husband" plot heightens suspense. It's not a gimmick though; the relationship is sexy, tender and believable. The Wachowski brothers obviously care about these characters. Even so, the audience knows that this is an American film, so sooner or later the women will be brought into crisis situations due to lack of physical strength (Caesar knocks out Corky and ties up both women) and due to emotional frailty (Violet can't stop herself from phoning Corky while Caesar is just a room away). Is using traditional "feminine" traits as a plot device sexist? Probably, but the dynamics between the women are genuine and exciting, and the audience is set up to root for them.

Bill Pope's cinematography is outstanding. In terms of plot and characterizations, it is a film noir, but it's the brightest one the audience will ever see. His decision to use black, white, flesh, red and gray almost exclusively gives the film a distinctive stark look, so splashes of blood and white paint take on tremendous significance. The majority of the film takes place in two adjoining apartments, where the walls, floors and furniture seem to take on lives of their own.

Gershon is a wonder as Corky. While publicity was given to the fact that a "lesbian expert" was consulted for the script, Gershon's method of preparing for her role by studying how classic male actors played their love scenes is what makes her performance unique and powerful. Pantoliano's Caesar is also a terrific creation. He's smarter than he looks, tougher than people expect, and likable enough to keep the conflict honest.

The sly and snappy dialogue in the first few scenes set the pace for the breathtaking action that will follow, but also immediately set BOUND apart from other thrillers with its intelligence and clever humor. The Wachowskis show remarkable depth for first-time directors. *(Graphic violence, adult situations, nudity, sexual situations, extreme profanity.)* — A.M.

d, Larry Wachowski, Andy Wachowski; p, Andrew Lazar, Stuart Boros; exec p, Larry Wachowski, Andy Wachowski; co-p, Jeffrey Sudzin; w, Larry Wachowski, Andy Wachowski; ph, Bill Pope; ed, Zach Staenberg; m, Don Davis; prod d, Eve Cauley; art d, Robert Goldstein, Andrea Dopaso; set d, Kristen Toscano Messina; sound, Felipe Borrero (mixer), Dane Davis (design); fx, Lou Carlucci; casting, Nancy Foy; cos, Lizzy Gardiner; makeup, Suzanne Rodier; stunts, Cliff Cudney

Crime/Thriller (PR: C MPAA: R)

BOY CALLED HATE, A ★★½

(U.S.) 96m Nickel Productions; Pacific Motion Pictures Association ~ Dove International c

Scott Caan *(Steve "Hate" Bason)*; Missy Crider *(Cindy)*; Elliott Gould *(Richard Wells)*; Adam Beach *(Billy Little Plume)*; James Caan *(Jim)*; Bryon Lee Nishold *(Cop)*; Kevin Richardson *(Staff Member)*; Duane Davis *(Ed Jenkins)*; Wade Allain-Marcus *(Cool Kid)*; Seth Isler *(Bartender)*; Stephanie Allain *(Waitress)*; Scott Patterson *(CHIPS Officer)*; Bradley Jay Lesley *(Moving Truck Driver)*; Buffalo Child *(Billy's Friend)*; Jon Proudstar *(War Bonnet Bartender)*; Brian Frejo *(Edwin)*; Frank Stonoma Salsedo *(Ted)*; Eric Siegel *(Golfer)*; Robert Harvey *(Male Golfer)*; Sheila Caan *(Female Golfer)*; Martin Marini *(Pro Shop Golfer)*; Ted Nye *(Hostage)*

It's a cliched equation: an aimless teenage car thief with a gun and a grudge; an abused, underage sexpot with an attitude; and a chance encounter on an empty road, followed inevitably by violence and a hopeless flight from the law. But A BOY CALLED HATE is handsomely mounted by writer-director Mitch Marcus, and newcomers Scott Caan (son of James) and Missy Crider turn in surprisingly nuanced performances as the bad teenagers in love.

Released into the custody of his alcoholic dad, Jim (James Caan), troubled teen Hate (Scott Caan) ankles his reformatory only to step into the arena of felonious assault. After rescuing a foul-mouthed damsel, Cindy (Missy Crider), outside a bar where she's being fondled by her guardian and uncle, Richard Wills (Elliott Gould), Hate hightails it with Cindy in the belief that he has murdered the pawing Mr. Wills.

Paranoid about capture, Hate guns down a highway patrolman who only wanted to return a purse Cindy had left in a diner. While the squabbling adolescents drive with no destination, a recovered Wills, who is an attorney, uses the media to blackball Hate and Cindy while camouflaging his own sexual guilt.

After they bond with kindred rebel Billy Little Plume (Adam Beach), the Native American troublemaker creates a diversion for authorities so Cindy and Hate can make a dash for the hills. Later, Billy drops the fugitives off at a golf course where a hostage situation develops after Hate is caught stealing a car by a member of the posh country club, Camelot. Pressuring Hate to turn himself in, Cindy then prepares to wait for her great love, a circumstance somewhat mitigated by the fact that Wills has been discredited publicly.

Writer-director Mitch Marcus's world view seems to be defined by film school on one side and Francis Ford Coppola's RUMBLE FISH (1983) on the other. Adults are ogres of varying degrees of evil, always ready to crucify the young on the cross of their bitterness and selfish rage.

But Marcus has a good eye and gets surprisingly good performances from his young leads—including Adam Beach, who makes Little Plume a genuinely sympathetic character—supported by some great turns from the middle-aged set. James Caan's appearance is brief, but he is memorable as Hate's bad dad, and Elliott Gould is stupendously sleazy as the abusive uncle who sets off the lethal chain reaction. *(Graphic violence, sexual situations, extreme profanity, substance abuse.)* — R.P.

d, Mitch Marcus; p, Steve Nicolaides; exec p, Tom Rowe, Tony Allard, Marjorie Skouras; assoc p, Sami Kassim; co-p, Bobby Duchowny; w, Mitch Marcus; ph, Paul Holahan; ed, Michael Ruscio; m, Pray For Rain; prod d, Caryn Marcus; art d, Mark Billerman; sound, Donny Blank, Roger Stevenson (mixer); fx, Danny Gill; casting, Susan Wieder, Kim Orchen; cos, Vanessa Vogel; makeup, Kathy Doss; stunts, Michael Papajohn

Crime/Drama (PR: O MPAA: R)

BOYS ★★

(U.S.) 88m Interscope Communications; Polygram; Touchstone ~ Buena Vista c

Winona Ryder *(Patty Vare)*; Lukas Haas *(John Baker, Jr.)*; Skeet Ulrich *(Bud Valentine)*; John C. Reilly *(Officer Kellogg Curry)*; Bill Sage *(Officer Bill Martone)*; Matt Malloy *(Bartender)*; Wiley Wiggins *(John Phillips)*; Russell Young *(John Van Slieder)*; Marty McDonough *(Teacher)*; Vivienne Shub *(Frances)*; Charlie Hofheimer *(John Cooke)*; Spencer Vrooman *(John Murphy)*; Christopher Pettiet *(Jon Heinz)*; Andy Davis *(Jonathan Marco)*; David Newsom *(Curt)*; James LeGros *(Fenton Ray)*; Catherine Keener *(Jilly)*; Maddie Corman *(Liz Curry)*; James Gardiner *(Kellogg Curry, Jr.)*; Cheryl Goode *(Beer Girl)*; Chris Cooper *(Mr. John Baker)*; Jessica Harper *(Mrs. John Baker)*; John J. Fitzpatrick *(Steve Hunt)*; Gregorio Rosenblum *(Dr. Paz)*; Miranda Syp *(Ellen Vare)*; Robert Carlton *(Tom Vare)*; John Reeves *(Phil Rains, Esq.)*; Carter McNeese *(Floor Waxer)*; Angela Hall *(Officer Julie Leroux)*; Bob Moore *(Officer Darryl Cane)*; David Paulson *(Lieutenant Love)*

After making a strong impression in a series of period films, Winona Ryder returned to the present in this muddled and ultimately laughable attempt at a coming-of-age drama.

After being questioned at her home by police regarding events at a party the night before, a young woman named Patty Vare (Ryder) goes riding on her horse, only to be thrown and knocked unconscious. She is discovered by a couple of students from a nearby boys' school; they tell a friend, senior John Baker Jr. (Lukas Haas), who smuggles Patty into his room. Chafing at his tedious classes and the corporate future his overbearing father has planned for him, John finds the idea of harboring Patty exciting, especially when she refuses to see a doctor or police. While attempting to keep her presence a secret, he finds himself falling in love with her.

The pair sneak out for a nighttime visit to a local carnival and wind up sleeping together in the nearby woods, but when John awakens, Patty is gone. Subsequently, he too is questioned by the police, and Patty again turns up at his dorm. It transpires that Patty had been driven away from the party by baseball player Bud Valentine (Skeet Ulrich), who drunkenly drove his car into a nearby pond; Patty escaped, but Bud drowned. John and Patty are brought to the local police station, and John's parents arrive to collect him. The pair manage to slip away from the adults who would restrain them, however, and drive off together.

BOYS went through an endless progression of title changes (including "The Secret Life of Boys," "The Girl in His Room," and "She's Not There") on the way to its delayed release, and that's not the only way in which confusion informs this movie. Despite the title, writer-director Stacy Cochran seems to have little idea how boys talk or behave, and the dorm situations play like material straight out of an '80s teen sex comedy, only pitched with deadly seriousness and sanitized language (in a few cases, the dialogue clearly has been overdubbed to eliminate the more severe profanities). As the film goes on, it slides from ineffectively earnest to downright laughable, with a ludicrous language-class scene played entirely in French and a climax dependent on the premise that a small rural police station requires an elevator.

Though she does her best, Ryder can't transcend her material, or the fact that she's simply miscast as the story's "older woman." In her scenes with Haas, she looks barely older than he is, and indeed looks so much like him that one half-expects a revelation that the two are actually brother and sister. Such a plot twist would certainly be no less convincing than anything else in BOYS. *(Adult situations, sexual situations, substance abuse, profanity.)* — M.G.

d, Stacy Cochran; p, Peter Frankfurt, Paul Feldsher, Erica Huggins; exec p, Ted Field, Robert W. Cort, Scott Kroopf; co-p, Rudd Simmons; w, Stacy Cochran (based on the short story "Twenty Minutes" by James Salter); ph, Robert Elswit; ed, Camilla Toniolo; m, Stewart Copeland; prod d, Dan Bishop; art d, Gary Kosko; set d, Dianna Freas; sound, David Kelson (mixer); fx, Matthew Vogel; casting, Todd Thaler; cos, Lucy W. Corrigan; makeup, Naomi Donne; stunts, Phil Neilson

Drama/Romance (PR: C MPAA: PG-13)

BOYS NEXT DOOR, THE ★★½

(U.S.) 100m Hallmark Hall of Fame ~ Hallmark Home Entertainment c

Nathan Lane *(Norman)*; Robert Sean Leonard *(Barry)*; Tony Goldwyn *(Jack)*; Michael Jeter *(Arnold)*; Courtney B. Vance *(Lucian)*; Mare Winningham *(Sheila)*; Elizabeth Wilson; Richard Jenkins; Lynne Thigpen; Caroline Aaron; Michael Hogan; Laura Bertram; Martha Burns; George R. Robertson; Jenny Robertson

A typically sentimental Hallmark made-for-TV movie about the mentally challenged, THE BOYS NEXT DOOR, though occasionally inspiring, suffers from an advanced case of theatricalism.

Jack (Tony Goldwyn), a devoted Chicago social worker, has neglected his spouse, trying to care for his four wacky charges. He makes sure that the sweetly simple Norman (Nathan Lane) controls his bottomless appetite for donuts; that the even simpler Lucian (Courtney B. Vance) is ready to appear in front of the state Senate to insure continued support for their group home; that the grade A schizophrenic Barry (Robert Sean Leonard) deals with the upcoming visit of his father; and that the flighty manic depressive Arnold (Michael Jeter) takes his medication and learns to stand up for himself at the supermarket.

With plenty of love and patience, Jack manages, more or less, to keep his "boys" under control. While Norman finds love with the developmentally disabled Sheila (Mare Winningham), Jack is summoned by his wife to appear at a marriage counselor's office. Soon after, to salvage his home life, Jack decides to take a new job leasing cars. How is he going to break this news to the boys?

The timing isn't great as Barry is re-institutionalized after his heartless father berates him. Jack comforts Barry, then informs the others about his new job. Crushed, the remaining threesome, at Arnold's prompting, go to the train station to catch the next train to Russia. Jack buys the three men, and his supervisor, round-trip tickets to nearby Milwaukee and tells them they're off to Russia. He does this to coax a more positive farewell out of them. The ploy works. The boys wave a tearful goodbye from the departing train as Jack embraces his wife.

Perhaps too aware of the awards lavished upon the RAIN-MANs and GUMPs of the world, Nathan Lane and Michael Jeter attempt to ham their way into our hearts. Though their broad performances are at times endearing, they sometimes turn annoying. Director John Erman should have explained that there's no need to play to the back row; it's television, not off-Broadway, where this piece got its start. The histrionics peak when the boys kill a rat, and then learn that the flushed rodent was their neighbor's pet hamster. The resulting chorus of bawls should never have made it out of the editing room.

On the flip side, Mare Winningham, in a supporting role, offers a classier, more realistic performance, and Courtney B. Vance's Lucian supplies the best reason to rent this video. When Jack takes Lucian, whose brain hasn't progressed past that of a 5-year-old's, to testify before the state Senate, the poor soul can barely string together a coherent sentence. Through a clever device, Jack fantasizes what an intelligent Lucian might say in the situation. Suddenly Lucian leaps to his feet and delivers an eloquent, riveting speech describing what it's like to go through life "mystified by faucets and radios, elevators and newspapers." He proclaims society's responsibility to care for his kind because "damaged though I may be, I shall not wither, because I am unique and irreplaceable and part of you all."

It's nothing short of remarkable to witness Vance's transformation from a simpleton to a brilliant spokesman for a people who can barely express themselves. — T.Y.

d, John Erman; p, John Erman; exec p, Richard Welsh, Brent Shields; co-p, Christopher Cook; w, William Blinn (based on a play by Tom Griffin); ph, Frank Tidy; ed, John W. Wheeler; m, John Kander; prod d, Karen Bromley; casting, Phyllis Huffman, Olivia Harris; cos, Arthur Roswell; makeup, Patricia Green

Comedy/Drama **(PR: A MPAA: PG)**

BREACH OF TRUST ★★

(U.S.) 96m Keystone Pictures ~ Republic Pictures Home Video c

Michael Biehn *(Casey)*; Matt Craven *(Rodney Powell)*; Leilani Sarelle Ferrer *(Madeline)*; Miguel Sandoval *(Carlos Sanchez)*; Kim Coates *(Palmer Davis)*; Ed Lauter *(Krueger)*; Ben Ratner *(Ellis)*; James Kidnie *(Goodwin)*; Vladimir Kulich *(Bracco)*; Jude Zachary *(Moser)*; Topaz Hasfal-Schou *(Lisa)*; C. Ernst Harth *(Doorman)*; Zdenek Juricek *(Zeke)*; Lizi Gal *(Jackie)*; Mitchell Davies *(Driver)*; Kyle Riefsnyder *(Valet)*; David Fredericks *(Phil)*; Melvin Cragg *(Hal)*

This occasionally incoherent crime thriller is distinguished mainly by the romantic chemistry of leads Michael Biehn and Leilani Sarelle Ferrer. Aside from this welcome star-power and a hard-bitten cynicism that informs the actions of both heroes and villains alike, BREACH OF TRUST is routine crook-chasing. It seems to improvise its wayward scenario as it goes along, and to escalate its violence whenever the plot gets too unwieldy.

Money-launderer Carlos Sanchez (Miguel Sandoval) could pay with his life if he botches a $40,000,000 transfer for his uptight client, Krueger (Ed Lauter). When disgruntled employee Palmer Davis (Kim Coates) tries to extort $2,000,000 from this deal, Carlos scurries to retrieve the account codes stolen by Davis. Carlos doesn't realize that his own accountant, Rodney Powell (Matt Craven), is Davis's silent partner.

At Davis's pad, Casey (Biehn), an ex-buddy whom Davis cheated out of money, and Madeline (Ferrer), an undercover cop posing as a hooker to investigate Davis, get caught in the crossfire when Davis is killed on Carlos's orders. Intercepting the code disk for Carlos's accounts, mercenary Casey and straight-laced Madeline narrowly escape Carlos's desperate pursuit. Learning of Davis's untimely death, Rodney sets up Madeline's crooked superior officer, Ellis (Ben Ratner), to throw suspicion off himself.

After Ellis is killed by a car bomb and Madeline herself is nearly killed in a parking garage, she decides to pool resources with Casey even though he operates outside the law. Figuring out Rodney's scam, Madeline decides to locate Carlos's mainframe (hidden in a sewer) and transfer his millions into an FBI account. When Carlos's men ice Rodney after he reveals Madeline's location, Casey sets up a Madeline-for-disk exchange at a cannery. However, once Madeline deliberately knocks over Carlos's personal computer, Krueger's last chance at laundering is doomed. Enraged, Carlos shoots Rodney's assistant, Hal (Melvin Cragg). Then, before Krueger pops Carlos, he informs him that he's just wiped out Carlos's entire family. Defeating Carlos's thugs, including main enforcer, Bracco (Vladimir Kulich), Madeline and Casey flee the crime-world rat race. But will they keep the millions for themselves?

Given its surging level of dishonor among thieves, BREACH OF TRUST should be a lot more potent. Without a scorecard, viewers may feel lost as the principals play hot potato with $40,000,000 worth of computer codes. Grounding all this not-so-grand larceny is the hate-you-love-you rapport between roguish soldier-of-fortune Casey and no-nonsense peacekeeper Madeline. Although the white-collar crooks, Davis and Powell, are a formidable pair of scoundrels, as embodied by Coates and Craven, it's Biehn and Ferrer who prevent BREACH OF TRUST from imploding from its own plot-devices.

Aside from the sparks struck by Biehn and Ferrer, this crime opus is best enjoyed as a non-stop series of narrow squeaks; each set-piece delivers excitement, but the mini-climaxes don't build to an explosive conclusion. *(Graphic violence, extreme profanity, extensive nudity, substance abuse, adult situations.)* — R.P.

d, Charles Wilkinson; p, Robert Vince, William Vince; exec p, Michael Strange; assoc p, Kelsey Howard; w, Gordon Basichis, Raul Inglis; ph, Michael Slovis; ed, Richard Martin; m, Graeme Coleman; prod d, Lynn Stopkewich; art d, Karen Brooks; set d, Darryl Deegan; sound, Jochen Schliessler (mixer); casting, Abra Edelman, Elisa Goodman; cos, Druh Ireland; makeup, Nicole Demers; stunts, Scott Ateah, Bill Ferguson

Crime/Thriller/Action **(PR: C MPAA: R)**

BREAKAWAY ★★

(U.S.) 95m Dash/Gardner Films ~ Century Film Partners Inc. c

Tonya Harding *(Gina)*; Teri Thompson *(Myra)*; Joe Estevez *(Grey)*; Tony Noakes *(Dan)*; Chris DeRose *(Carter)*; Michael Garganese *(Nicky)*; Ray Dash *(Anton)*; Rick Beatty *(Rick)*; Joe Hanlin *(Vince)*; Bela Lehoczki *(Drake)*; Pasquale Scuderi *(Bobby)*; Rhodes Short *(Al)*; Jimmy Paola *(Larry)*; William Lebanz *(Billy)*; Brian Carlton *(Toby)*; Dave Graubard *(Lou)*; David Tetreau *(Davey)*; Dominic Gironda *(Frank)*; Dyanne Stempel *(Gallery Owner)*; Sharon Young *(Myra's Sister)*; Joe Morrissey *(Jimmy)*; Jeff Keiser *(Beach Waiter)*; Merrill Eichenberger *(Big Ike)*

Not many action movies feature a hero named Myra in a frilly blouse. BREAKAWAY does, but don't expect it to become a trend, because there's nothing here you're likely to remember half an hour after the end credits have rolled.

Tired of doing deliveries for Los Angeles mobster Anton (Ray Dash), Myra (Teri Thompson) steals $300,000 of his money. Before she and her boyfriend, Carter (Chris DeRose), can leave town, Anton gets wise and sends his nephew, Nicky (Michael Garganese), to kill her. On the run, Myra ducks into the art gallery where mild-mannered anthropology professor Dan (Tony Noakes) is waiting to meet a blind date. Myra decides to use Dan as a cover and pretends to be his date. They lose Nicky and end up at a local motel.

Anton calls in a professional hitman, Grey (Joe Estevez), to help the incompetent Nicky. But when Grey kills Nicky for getting in his way once too often, Anton orders his men to kill Grey as well as Myra. Myra and Dan meet up with Carter at a secluded cabin in the woods, where Myra eventually tells Dan the truth. What she doesn't know is that Carter is two-timing her with Gina (Tonya Harding), the manager of the restaurant where he has hidden the money. Dan comes to Myra's aid when Carter reveals his true colors and helps her fight off Anton's forces. They are the only survivors of a climactic battle in which the money is presumed destroyed, although it actually has been found by Gina, who uses it to move to Fiji.

BREAKAWAY's trump card, aside from the inevitable exposure of its heroine's cosmetically-amplified bosom, is the casting of scandal-ridden professional skater Tonya Harding. (Had Andy Warhol been a little more prescient, he would have predicted a future in which everyone was famous for 90 minutes, the standard length of a made-for-video film.) Harding isn't on screen long enough to have much impact, though in a fight scene she handles herself well enough to suggest that she may have potential as an action heroine. (It's not like the job description generally calls for any thespian abilities.)

There's nothing in particular to recommend BREAKAWAY to potential viewers: the performers are bland, the sex perfunctory and the action scenes wholly without panache. (Joe Estevez' portrayal of a superhuman killing machine is strictly an exercise in wishful thinking.) Still, the script doles out its abundance of plot elements so regularly that it at least holds one's attention: one doesn't realize precisely how dull it is until it's over. *(Violence, nudity, sexual situations, profanity.)* — M.F.

d, Sean Dash; p, Eric Gardner, Sean Dash; exec p, Aron Schifman, Richard W. Munchkin; assoc p, Michael Muller; co-p, Jud Cremata; w, Eric Gardner, Sean Dash; ph, Carlos Montaner; ed, Eric Gardner; m, Robert Wait; prod d, John Tollotson; art d, Antonia Carew-Watts; fx, Larry Fioritto, Don Powers; cos, Michelle Michel; makeup, Margie Latinopolous

Action **(PR: O MPAA: R)**

BREAKING THE WAVES ★★★

(Denmark/Sweden/Norway/Netherlands/Finland/France/U.S./Iceland) 156m Zentrop a Entertainment; Trust Films; Liberator Productions; Argus; Northern Lights; La Sept; Swedish Television Drama; Media Investment Club; Nordic Film & Television Fund; VPRO Television ~ October Films c

Emily Watson *(Bess)*; Stellan Skarsgard *(Jan)*; Katrin Cartlidge *(Dodo)*; Jean-Marc Barr *(Terry)*; Udo Kier *(Man on the Trawler)*; Adrian Rawlins *(Doctor Richardson)*; Jonathan Hackett *(The Minister)*; Sandra Voe *(Bess' Mother)*; Mikkel Gaup *(Pits)*; Roef Ragas *(Pim)*; Phil McCall *(Grandfather)*; Robert Robertson *(Chairman)*; Desmond Reilly *(An Elder)*; Sarah Grudgeon *(Sybilla)*; Finlay Welsh *(Coroner)*; David Gallacher *(Glasgow Doctor)*; Ray Jeffries *(Man on Bus)*; Owen Kavanagh *(Man at Lighthouse)*; Bob Dogherty *(Man on Boat)*; David Bateson *(Young Sailor)*; Callum Cuthbertson *(Radio Operator)*; Gavin Mitchell *(Police Officer 1)*; Brian Smith *(Police Officer 2)*; Iain Agnew *(Praying Man 1)*; Charles Kearney *(Praying Man 2)*; Steven Leach *(Praying Man 3)*; Dorte Romer *(Nurse)*; Anthony O'Donnell *(Boy 1)*; John Wark *(Boy 2)*; Ronnie McKellaig *(Precentor)*

Lars Von Trier's BREAKING THE WAVES is a twisted fable about the miraculous powers of faith, sacrifice and unconditional love. Despite moments of undeniable brilliance, the film is almost sabotaged by a unsettling cinematic technique which is disconcerting at best and disastrous at worst.

A naive, young woman named Bess (Emily Watson) lives in a puritanical Presbyterian community in Scotland in the 1970s, where the women aren't allowed to speak in church and the pastor refuses to install church bells. Bess gets married to an earthy oil-rigger named Jan (Stellan Skarsgard), despite the objections of her family. At her wedding party, the two of them sneak into the bathroom and make love together for the first time. Bess goes to church and thanks God for sending her Jan. She constantly talks to God and He answers back through her own mouth. Jan and Bess have a blissful life together, but she cries whenever he tells her he'll be leaving soon to return to the oil rigs at sea. Bess's sister-in-law Dodo (Katrin Cartlidge) tells Jan that Bess is not right in the head and when Jan leaves for work, Bess gets hysterical and has to be medicated.

Bess goes home to live with her mother and begins to talk to God more frequently. She prays that Jan will come home soon. On the oil-rig, there is an accident and Jan is flown to a hospital. The doctors tell Bess that he'll probably be completely paralysed. Bess begins to have therapy sessions with a Dr. Richardson and tells him that the accident was her fault because she prayed for Jan to come home. Jan tells Bess that he wants to die unless she agrees to take lovers and tells him about them. She initially refuses, but finally gives in and goes to see Dr. Richardson to seduce him; he rejects her, so she gets on a bus and masturbates a man sitting in the back. Bess begins to dress like a hooker and picks up men around town, but when she goes out to a ship to service the sailors, she is attacked. Her mother kicks her out of the house, she's barred from the church, and the doctors try to have her committed.

Jan's condition worsens, and in a desperate act to save him, Bess goes back to the ship, where she is savagely beaten. She's taken to a hospital and dies, but Jan miraculously recovers and starts to walk on crutches. He steals her corpse and gives her a burial at sea. The next day, Jan and the other riggers are awakened by the deafening sound of church bells ringing. Above the oil rig two huge church bells are clanging above the clouds.

Von Trier has admitted that in the past he "had an almost fetishistic attraction to film technology." From the golden-sepia tone of THE ELEMENT OF CRIME (1984), to the hyper-stylization of ZENTROPA (1992), to the cinema verite surrealism of THE KINGDOM (1995), the form of his films have always been inextricably bound with their content. This was never more true than in BREAKING THE WAVES, where the chosen technique has been employed so relentlessly that the film is often literally hard to watch. The movie was intentionally filmed with a shaky hand-held camera, then transferred to video, and then transferred back to film, creating an unattractive and grainy electronic-looking image which is virtually drained of color. On top of that, the use of the Super 35 widescreen format involves optically extracting a widescreen image from the negative in the lab, which adds a further layer of graininess. Also, the editing constantly utilizes abrupt jump-cuts and other jarring effects. The result is an ordeal to sit through, akin to watching a three-hour CinemaScope home-video.

Von Trier has said that he didn't think audiences could tolerate the romantic and fantastical aspects of the film if it had been rendered with a conventional technique, so he chose a style that purposely worked against the story. He also admits the technique is just a theory on his part. Unfortunately, in practice, the result is extremely off-putting and distancing. That said, there is much to admire in BREAKING THE WAVES, particularly Emily Watson's fearless and star-making performance. The film is divided into seven chapters and an epilogue, and each chapter is introduced by beautifully designed, digitally-generated panoramic images, accompanied by ironic use of classic '70s rock songs by David Bowie, Jethro Tull, Elton John, et al. The ending is impressive and memorable, although it's a bit surprising to see the *enfant terrible* Von Trier aspiring to achieve a Carl Dreyer-like spiritual epiphany. *(Extensive nudity, sexual situations, extreme profanity, violence.)* — M.S.

d, Lars Von Trier; p, Vibeke Windelov, Peter Aalbaek Jensen; exec p, Lars Jonsson; co-p, Axel Helgeland, Peter Van Vogelpoel, Rob Langestraat, Marianne Slot; w, Lars Von Trier, Peter Asmussen; ph, Robby Mueller; ed, Anders Refn; m, Joachim Holbek; art d, Karl Juliusson; sound, Per Streit; fx, Morten Jacobsen, Lars Andersen; casting, Joyce Nettles; cos, Manon Rasmussen; makeup, Jennifer Jorfald, Sanne Gravfort; stunts, Terry Forrestal

AAN Best Actress: Emily Watson

Drama **(PR: O MPAA: R)**

BRITT ALLCROFT'S MAGIC ADVENTURES OF MUMFIE—THE MOVIE ★½

(U.K.) 110m Britt Allcroft (Mumfie) Ltd. ~ BMG Video c

Patrick Breen *(Storyteller)*

British producer Britt Allcroft gained international success with her children's TV show "Shining Time Station" (alias "Thomas the Tank Engine and Friends"). "Mumfie" was a friendly elephant brought to TV by Allcroft in 1995 and given overlong feature treatment here.

Kindly but restless, Mumfie searches for adventure, persuading a melancholy, unemployed scarecrow to come along. They meet a flying pig named Pinky, homesick for an island he can barely recall. RMS Whales, a whale who furnished himself as a luxury liner, is happy to take the trio to Pinky's island. There the benevolent Queen of Night has been usurped by her evil secretary, who locked away all flying pigs, along with laughter, dancing, singing, and similar fun. Foiling the Secretary of Night requires a complicated quest to the bottom of the sea, where a pirate gang have gotten its hands on a crucial enchanted diamond. But it's the Queen's long-lost Cloak of Dreams, which Scarecrow finds hidden in a thimble, that turns the Secretary of Night into an inert inkwell and restores the Queen of Night to her throne. Mumfie and Scarecrow perform a closing musical number that sums up the moral of it all: There's no place like home.

Most animated features, even those intended for grownups, like BEAVIS AND BUTT-HEAD DO AMERICA, seldom exceed 80 minutes. What justifies the (figuratively) colorless Mumfie getting nearly two hours? Not very much at all, as the plot wanders all over ocean, land, and sky, introducing numerous odd characters and time-killing songs (music by Larry Grossman, lyrics by John Kane). Furthermore, at least in the US-release version, narrator Patrick Breen provides nearly every voice, reinforcing the tedium. The animation is slightly interesting, with the Secretary of Night never clearly shown, and the hospitable RMS Whales is a whimsy on par with the "cat-bus" from MY NEIGHBOR TOTORO. His touristy sloganeering—"You'll find a welcome in Whales," punning Wales—hints at the British origin of the material. Perhaps something got lost in translation. End credits acknowledge an Oxford zoologist and a Harvard child psychologist for their input. However, consider the zoological viability of a small, bipedal, singing elephant who breathes underwater because he's "special," not to mention a flying pig and a talking, plush-interiored passenger whale; then ask yourself if the shrink was equally astute. — C.C.

d, John Laurence Collins; p, Britt Allcroft; w, Britt Allcroft, John Kane (based on works by Katherine Tozer); m, Larry Grossman; prod d, Bob Gould-Galliers; art d, Peter Moerhle

Children's/Animated/Fantasy **(PR: A MPAA: NR)**

BROKEN ARROW ★★★

(U.S.) 108m 20th Century Fox; Mark Gordon Company; Metropolis Entertainment ~ 20th Century Fox c

John Travolta *(Vic Deakins)*; Christian Slater *(Riley Hale)*; Samantha Mathis *(Terry Carmichael)*; Delroy Lindo *(Colonel Max Wilkins)*; Bob Gunton *(Pritchett)*; Frank Whaley *(Giles Prentice)*; Howie Long *(Kelly)*; Vondie Curtis-Hall *(Lt. Colonel Sam Rhodes)*; Jack Thompson *(Chairman, Joint Chief of Staff)*; Vyto Ruginis *(Johnson)*; Ousaun Elam *(Lt. Thomas)*; Shaun Toub *(Max)*; Casey Biggs *(Novacek)*; Jeffrey J. Stephen *(Shepherd)*; Joey Box *(Frakes)*; Jon W. Kishi *(Daly)*; Myke Schwartz *(Brandt)*; Jim Palmer *(Lt. Reed)*; Vince Deadrick Sr. *(Jim)*; Charlie Brewer *(McKeller)*; Gary Epper *(Miller)*; Mario Roberts *(Carl)*; J.N. Roberts *(Moss)*; Kurtwood Smith *(Secretary of Defense Baird)*; Daniel von Bargen *(Air Force General Creely)*; Bruce E. Holman *(Chairman Aid)*; Carmen Argenziano *(General Boone)*; James G. MacDonald *(Park Ranger Baker)*; French Stewart *(I.R. Crewman)*; Jim Moyle *(Pentagon Assistant)*; Chris Mulkey *(Major Hunt)*; Henry Murph *(Captain Johnson)*; Tom Waddell *(Captain Wright)*; Rosemary Schoppman *(Wanda)*

John Woo does it again: He turns an ordinary action-adventure picture into something special. BROKEN ARROW lacks the formal beauty of some earlier Woo epics, and barely suppresses its troubling subtext, but it more than delivers its share of adrenaline-pumping set pieces.

A "broken arrow" is the government term for a stolen nuclear device. Veteran US Air Force pilot Vic Deakins (John Travolta) plots to steal two nuclear bombs and sell them back to the government because he was passed over for a promotion. Deakins carries out his mission by ejecting his co-pilot, Riley Hale (Christian Slater), from a B-3 Stealth bomber during their routine night-flight maneuvers. Miraculously, Hale survives the low-level ejection, and joins forces with a park ranger, Terry Carmichael (Samantha Mathis).

Through cleverness and luck, Hale and Carmichael get one of the bombs back from Deakins and hide it in a copper mine. By accidentally detonating it underground, Hale and Carmichael partially derail Deakins's plan. Jumping aboard a freight train to stop Deakins from getting away with the second bomb, Hale discovers Deakins has gone crazy and killed his associates. Hale gets into a fistfight with Deakins, who plans to detonate the second device on the train. Hale stops Deakins just in time to prevent a deadly nuclear explosion above ground. He then reunites with Carmichael.

Despite a drastic studio re-cut, John Woo's previous Hollywood film, HARD TARGET (1993), revealed new stylistic possibilities for the moribund action-adventure genre. BROKEN ARROW's dusty-brown desert setting prevents the new film from looking as visually bold as HARD TARGET, or his earlier THE KILLER (1989) and BULLET IN THE HEAD (1990), but Woo's action sequences are as lively as ever. From the boxing-match opener to the train-fight climax—an homage, no doubt, to Robert Aldrich's EMPEROR OF THE NORTH (1973)—BROKEN ARROW remains eye-catching and pleasurably startling. Hans Zimmer's score is also better than usual for this sort of film, blending the motifs of Ennio Morricone and Angelo Badalamenti.

In the cast, Travolta seems to relish playing his first thoroughly bad bad-guy role in his first action picture. He tosses off lines like, "Would you mind not shooting at the thermonuclear weapons?" with glib ease. As the story's hero, Slater keeps pace with the fast-moving pyrotechnics. Most of the others in the cast fade into the background, although Mathis's Carmichael develops a pleasantly tough Howard Hawks-style romance with Slater's Hale.

This BROKEN ARROW bears no relation to the 1950 Jimmy Stewart western with the same title. The more intellectually minded may protest that BROKEN ARROW resembles either a techno-fascist version of Antonioni's ZABRISKIE POINT (1970)—right down to the apocalyptic explosions—or, worse, a remake of Clint Eastwood's FIREFOX (1982). Indeed, Hale dismisses the dangers of the nuclear explosion in the copper mine so lightly, one wonders if the effect here was supposed to be satirical. Fortunately, Woo's visual sense of humor elsewhere indicates a lighthearted sensibility at work. It's hard to be too offended by such a stylish comic strip. *(Violence, adult situations, profanity.)* — E.M.

d, John Woo; p, Mark Gordon, Bill Badalato, Terence Chang; exec p, Christopher Godsick, Dwight H. Little; co-p, Allison Lyon Segan; w, Graham Yost; ph, Peter Levy; ed, John Wright, Steve Mirkovich, Joe Hutshing; m, Hans Zimmer; prod d, Holger Gross; art d, William O'Brien; set d, Richard Goddard; sound, David Ronne (mixer); fx, Richard Thompson, Peter Crosman, Don Baker, Jacques Stroweis, Elliot Markman; casting, Donna Isaacson; cos, Mary Malin; makeup, Sharon Ilson; stunts, Alan Graf

Action/Adventure **(PR: C MPAA: R)**

BROTHER OF SLEEP ★★½

(Germany/Austria) 127m Perathon Film; B.A. Film; Kuchenreuther Filmprodukution; Iduna Filmprodution; DOR-Film ~ Sony Pictures Classics c
(SCHLAFES BRUDER)

Andre Eisermann *(Elias)*; Dana Vavrova *(Elsbeth)*; Ben Becker *(Peter)*; Angelika Bartsch *(Bruga)*; Michael Mendl *(Nulf)*; Eva Mattes *(Nulf's Wife)*; Peter Franke *(Seff)*; Michaela Rosen *(Seff's Wife)*; Detlef Bothe *(Lukas)*; Jochen Nickel *(Michael the Charcoal Burner)*; Jurgen Schornagel *(Curate Benzer)*; Paulus Manker *(Oskar)*; Lena Stolze *(Oskar's Wife)*; Heinz Emingholz *(Haintz)*; Martin Heesch *(Paul)*; Gilbert von Sohlern *(Albert)*; Birge Schade *(Franziska)*; Nadine Neumann *(Magdelena)*; Regina Fritsch *(Midwife)*; Ingo Naujoks *(Sergeant Hirsch)*; Herbert Knaup *(Choirmaster Goller)*; Conradin Blum *(Elias as a Child)*; Daniel Lins *(Peter as a Child)*; Michaela Pfeiffer *(Philipp as a Child)*; Robert Studer *(Fritz as a Child)*; Florian Wostry *(Lukas as a Child)*; Peter Fuchsl *(Paul as a Child)*; Ralph Sauerwein *(Albert as a Child)*; Natalie Winkel *(Franziska as a Child)*; Theresa Longoni *(Girl)*; Janina; Josefina *(Anna—2 Years Old)*; Robert Schneider *(Coachman)*

A 19th-century romantic triangle sets the stage for tragedy in BROTHER OF SLEEP, an ornate but conventional period drama.

In Eschberg, a remote Alpine village at the turn of the nineteenth century, a little boy named Elias Alder sets himself apart from the other children and angers the adults through his frequent daydreaming and precocious musical ability. Throughout his childhood, Elias has only one friend, Peter, another odd and lonely boy.

As an adult, Elias (Andre Eisermann) wins over the other villagers with his perfect pitch, beautiful singing voice, and magnificent organ-playing. But Peter (Ben Becker), who loves his strange and mysterious friend more than ever, grows jealous when his sister, Elsbeth (Dana Vavrova), also forms an attraction to Elias. Elias, meanwhile, does not notice any of the passions directed at him, for his only love is his music: when not sleeping on his magic rock, he plays the church organ, and eventually becomes the town organist.

Despite his rebuffs to Elsbeth, Elias shows remorse when he finds her making love to Lukas (Detlef Bothe), her fiance. Peter notices Elias's newfound feelings for his sister and, in a fit of jealousy, decides to kill Elsbeth. One night, he sets fire to her cottage, but Elsbeth escapes the flames that ultimately consume the entire village. Peter then allows the villagers to blame Michel (Jochen Nickel), a mystical charcoal-burner, for the holocaust. After the citizens kill Michel, they leave Eschberg en masse. Only Elias and Peter stay behind.

One day, Goller (Herbert Knaup), the choirmaster of nearby Feldberg, arrives in the village. Although his mission is to register the town organ, Goller is so impressed by Elias's playing that Goller invites him to take part in the organist competition at the Feldberg cathedral several miles away. Elias accepts the offer and his playing in Feldberg has a miraculous effect on the churchgoers, including Elsbeth and her baby. But, despite his success in the competition, Elias returns to Eschberg, where he expires on his magic rock—the one that had once opened his heart and soul to the sounds of the world.

BROTHER OF SLEEP most resembles the films of the high-pitched musician-composer-biography genre—it is even shot in 1950s-style CinemaScope. Like A SONG TO REMEMBER (1945), THE MUSIC LOVERS (1971) and the recent IMMORTAL BELOVED (1994), BROTHER OF SLEEP tells the story of a tragic hero and his tortured attempts to live for his music. Also, like these films, BROTHER OF SLEEP is lengthy (127 minutes), elaborately produced and filled with dramatic incident. Director Joseph Vilsmaier (LENINGRAD) and screenwriter Robert Schneider, who wrote the original novel, further draw upon the work of Ingmar Bergman, Peter Weir, Volker Schlondorff and especially Werner Herzog's HEART OF GLASS (1976) for artistic inspiration during the more mystical passages. Best of all, Rolf Zehetbauer (CABARET, LILI MARLEEN) contributes his characteristically stunning production design.

What goes wrong with BROTHER OF SLEEP is that it remains a pastiche of the aforementioned films without taking off in its own right. It's hard to care about stock characters caught up in a romantic melodrama when there is so little reflexivity about the traditions into which it is tapping. Also, the performances are only fair, but at least Eisermann, star of KASPAR HAUSER (1996), has the right haunted look for Elias. Ironically, some of the English subtitles seem jarringly anachronistic—"That woman is hot," one man says of Elsbeth—threatening to throw the film off-balance at times. These moments of perhaps unintended humor are rare in a film that is florid and dramatically overwrought, but oddly uncompelling. *(Violence, sexual situations, adult situations, profanity.)* — E.M.

d, Joseph Vilsmaier; p, Joseph Vilsmaier; w, Robert Schneider (based on his novel); ph, Joseph Vilsmaier; ed, Alexander Berner; m, Norbert J. Schneider, Hubert von Goisern; prod d, Rolf Zehetbauer; art d, Anja Muller, Walter Richarz; sound, Reinhold Kaiser (recordist); casting, Bernhard Kock, Barbara Vogel; cos, Ute Hofinger; makeup, Heiner Niehuse, Rith Philipp, Karin Schon

Drama **(PR: C MPAA: R)**

BUGGED ★★½

(U.S.) 82m RKA Cinema Creations, Inc. ~ Troma, Inc. c

Priscilla K. Basque *(Divine Hill)*; Ronald K. Armstrong *(Dave)*; Jeff Lee *(Steve)*; Derek C. Johnson *(Sam)*; Billy Graham *(Gunther)*; David McKay *(Lance)*; John Kilgore *(Dr. Craig)*; Jacqui Everett *(Dr. Young)*; Malachi B. Weir *(Bill)*; Harold W. Smith *(J&B Van Driver #1)*; Richard Horton *(J&B Van Driver #2)*; Casim Gomez *(Mutated Van Driver)*; Victor Villegas *(Mutated Van Driver)*; Karina Felix *(Tina)*; Virgil Wade *(Brian)*; Randy Miller; Al Woodley; Lauren R. Sack *(FDA Board Members)*; Mitzi Gary *(Divine's Mother)*

An entertaining low-budgeter with an agreeably goofy sense of humor, BUGGED puts a comic spin on the insects-amok subgenre.

Thanks to a van accident, some canisters of a genetic mutating agent get mixed up with pesticide being delivered to Dead and Buried Exterminators. Two of the company's workers, Dave (Ronald K. Armstrong) and Steve (Jeff Lee), are called to the suburban mansion of wealthy poet Divine Hill (Priscilla K. Basque) to deal with her cricket problem. While accidentally spraying the bugs with the DNA chemical, Steve puts the moves on Divine, who is more attracted to the lower-key Dave. After the pair leave, Divine is confronted by the now two-foot insects, and frantically calls Dead and Buried for help.

Dave and Steve return, joined by coworkers Sam (Derek C. Johnson) and Lance (David McKay) and their boss, Gunther (Billy Graham). The group soon find themselves under siege by the bugs, and Sam, Lance, Gunther, and Steve are killed by either the crickets or their own backfired attempts to destroy them. Dave and Divine are able to escape and set off an explosion that incinerates the insects, but Dave himself has been infected and threatens to mutate into a bug-man.

The opening 10 minutes of BUGGED aren't promising, detailing the creation of the mutating agent in the overexaggerated, ham-handed manner of much of Troma's product. But after that, the movie (released but not directly produced by Troma) finds its own, more relaxed style and significantly improves. While the monsters themselves are generally played straight, their mayhem seems influenced by the sensibility of old Warner Bros. cartoons. When the heroes attempt to lure the bugs into a trap by tossing a decoy into the woods, for example, the insects respond by throwing back a lure of their own—a whole roasting chicken on a string. The ensemble cast of exterminators has an easygoing, likable camaraderie, and Basque is a lovely and hardly defenseless presence in the midst of the craziness.

Refreshingly, although writer-director-star Armstrong and almost all of his cast are black, the movie never wears race on its sleeve or makes it an issue at any point. It's concerned solely with giggly, unpretentious entertainment—with special effects that are no better than they should be nor worse than one might expect—and as such serves as a promising calling card for Armstrong. *(Violence, extreme profanity.)* — M.G.

d, Ronald K. Armstrong; p, Gay Abel-Bey; exec p, Lloyd Kaufman, Michael Herz; w, Ronald K. Armstrong; ph, S. Torriano Berry; ed, Ronald K. Armstrong; m, Boris Elkins; sound, Sound Dimensions; fx, Angel L. Acevedo, Louis Zakarian, Craig Linberg; casting, Lisa Brown; cos, O. K. Uniforms; makeup, Henry Brown, Lisa Arrindell, Sunshine Martinez

Horror/Comedy **(PR: O MPAA: R)**

BULLETPROOF ★★

(U.S.) 85m Gold/Miller Productions; Robert Simonds Company; Brillstein-Grey Entertainment; Universal ~ Universal c

Damon Wayans *(Keats)*; Adam Sandler *(Moses)*; James Caan *(Colton)*; Jeep Swenson *(Bledsoe)*; James Farentino *(Capt. Jensen)*; Kristen Wilson *(Traci)*; Larry McCoy *(Detective Sulliman)*; Allen Covert *(Detective Jones)*; Bill Nunn *(Finch)*; Mark Roberts *(Charles)*; Mark Cassella *(Disneyland Cop)*; Andrew Shaifer *(Cop at Airport)*; Monica Potter *(Biker's Woman)*; Jonathan Loughran *(Rookie Cop)*; Steve White *(Veteran Cop)*; Gwen McGee *(Surgeon)*; Bill Capizzi *(Tommy)*; Charmaine Craig *(Waitress)*; Jill Holden *(Gruesome Lady)*; Renee Paidle *(Porn Woman)*; Adam Voughn *(Porn Man)*; Xander Berkeley *(Gentry)*; Sal Landi *(Cole)*; David Labiosa *(Rigo)*; Conrad Goode *(Biker)*; Maury Sterling *(Skinny Guy)*; Scott Hoxby *(Lindsay)*; Victor Aaron *(Hispanic Man)*; Jacqueline Dickerson *(Bartender)*; Donna M. Duffy *(Anesthesiologist)*; Janice Rivera *(Senorita)*; Loetta Ernest *(Senorita)*; Cindy Barrera *(Senorita)*; Ford Scott *(Arizona Highway Patrol)*; William Proctor *(Bad Guy)*; Garret T. Sato *(Bad Guy)*; Paule Stewart *(Moses' Mom)*

Primarily a vehicle for the narcissistic, goofball antics of "Saturday Night Live" alum Adam Sandler (with sporadic gunplay thrown in), BULLETPROOF is merely a poor cousin to its buddy-cop action film ancestors such as 48 HOURS and LETHAL WEAPON.

Looking to bring down drug kingpin Frank Colton (James Caan), LAPD detective John Carter (Damon Wayans) has gone undercover as thief "Rock Keats." In this guise he has befriended one of Colton's minions, Archie Moses (Adam Sandler). Moses considers "Rock" the only person he can trust, and has even taken him home to meet his mother. But before the Big Bust goes down, Carter's true identity is revealed, and the betrayed Moses shoots him in the head while escaping. During his rehab, Carter falls in love with his physical therapist, Tracy Flynn (Kristen Wilson).

Moses is apprehended in Arizona, and when he agrees to turn state's evidence against Colton, Carter is sent to retrieve him. After an ambush by Colton's men, the two former buddies are stranded in the desert. Moses convinces Carter that Colton has so many people in his pocket that no one, not even Carter's gruff captain (James Farentino), can be trusted.

Back in LA, Carter is contacted by Colton, who has kidnapped physical therapist Flynn and is offering to trade her for Moses. Carter throws out the rules, and arms Moses so they can team up and get Colton. When the bullets start flying, it's revealed Flynn was in Colton's employ all along. After Colton is killed, Carter, who now knows how betrayal feels, decides to be a friend, not a cop, and lets Moses go free.

BULLETPROOF is lowest common denominator filmmaking. Ignoring the rules of the genre, it mixes wacky comedy with anarchic violence, and in so doing takes the genre to a new low. Aping the dynamic of the LETHAL WEAPON movies, Wayans is stuck in the role of a by-the-book black cop who needs to loosen up. Even worse, in place of Mel Gibson's on-the-edge recklessness, we're offered Sandler's over-the-top, gooney man-child routine—in other words, HAPPY GILMORE gets to do some killin'.

The most noteworthy aspect of BULLETPROOF, however, is how it derives comedy by laying bare the homoerotic subtext of "the buddies" relationship. (In other words, all that buddy bickering was really a "defense mechanism" against their repressed libidinal desires.) To wit, Carter repeatedly denies accusations that he's "sweet on" Moses, who in turn is not at all coy about his feelings. In the film's comedic highlight, Moses serenades Carter from the shower with a ear-aching rendition of "I Will Always Love You." In response, Carter pokes the barrel of his gun into Moses' sudsy posterior. Some might view the intermixture of gay sex jokes and violence as an expression of homophobia; however, in the end, romance wins out as Carter and Moses (and his mom) join up in Mexico, presumably to live happily ever after. *(Violence, profanity, sexual situations.)* — P.R.

d, Ernest Dickerson; p, Robert Simonds; exec p, Brad Grey, Bernie Brillstein, Sandy Wernick, Eric L. Gold; assoc p, Janine Sherman; co-p, Ira Shuman, Jack Giarraputo; w, Joe Gayton, Lewis Colick (based on a story by Joe Gayton); ph, Steven Bernstein; ed, George Folsey Jr.; m, Elmer Bernstein; art d, Perry Andelin Blake, William F. Matthews; set d, Lisa Robyn Deutsch; sound, Jim Stuebe (mixer); fx, T. Brooklyn Bellissimo; casting, Joanna Colbert; cos, Marie France; makeup, Ann Pala; stunts, Tim A. Davison

Comedy/Action (PR: O MPAA: R)

BURIAL OF THE RATS ★

(U.S.) 77m Mosfilm; New Horizons ~ New Horizons Home Video c

Adrienne Barbeau *(Queen)*; Maria Ford *(Madeleine)*; Kevin Alber *(Bram Stoker)*; Olga Kabo *(Anna)*; Eduard Plaxin *(Mr. Stoker)*; Vladimir Kuleshov *(Constable)*; Leonid Timtsunik *(Verlaine)*; Maya Menglets *(Mme. Renaud)*; Katiya Batanova *(Danielle)*; Alexander Pyatkiv *(Pedophile Gambler)*; Nikolai Penkov *(Gambler No. 2)*; Elena Puzova *(Sleazy Prostitute)*; Inna Khokhlushkina *(Naked Prostitute)*; Pavel Ostroukhov *(Priest)*; Yuri Kutsunku *(New Priest)*; Sergei Gatkin *(Torturer)*; Dan Golden *(Man with Knife in Back)*; Vladimir Badov *(Prisoner)*; Amy Segal; Linnea Quigley; Nikki Fritz; Jay Copeland; Nora Genelin; Marie Laurin; Melina Wesley *(Rat Women)*; Eugeni Degtyarenko *(Coach Driver)*; Brian Katkin; John Gilbert *(Soldiers)*

Had the Soviets known that the fall of Communism would lead to films like this coproduction between Roger Corman's New Horizons and the Russian studio Mosfilm, they would have fought harder to win the Cold War.

While traveling through Eastern Europe, young Bram Stoker (Kevin Alber) and his father (Eduard Plaxin) are attacked by hooded figures who rob them and kidnap Bram. They take him to their castle, the home of a group of women who, under the leadership of their Queen (Adrienne Barbeau), use rats to terrorize men.

The Queen sentences Bram to a ritual death, but his life is spared when his captor Madeleine (Maria Ford), moved by his devotion to his father, fails to strike the killing blow. In his cell he tells her of his desire to be a writer, and she smuggles a pen and paper in to him.

Reading his description of one of their raids, the Queen decides that Bram's stories are perfect weapons to help strike terror into the hearts of their enemies. Deciding to join their cause, Bram helps them rescue Madeleine from the local prison where she is being tortured.

At his initiation ceremony, Bram is told to execute a hooded man. He is stopped from killing the man—his captured father—by the arrival of armed forces, who battle the rat women. Realizing her cause is lost, the Queen commands her rats to devour her. Madeleine is killed helping Bram and his father escape, and the older man advises his son to write about her so that she will live forever.

Movies just don't come any more foolish than this effort, whose sole distinction is the ability of its director and cast to play such risible material with straight faces. (Special credit goes to Barbeau's character, whose dialogue consists in large part of stuff like "I am the queen of vermin, the pied piper's twisted sister!") BURIAL OF THE RATS is simply an excuse to fill the screen with a few dozen women in patent leather push-up bras, high heel boots, and G-strings (or, in the case of the numerous dance scenes sprinkled through the film, even less). A few scenes reach an almost Monty Python-ish level of absurdity, as when the rat women storm the torture dungeon and randomly slaughter everyone in their path, including the prisoners. But the viewer has to work hard to find even that much to enjoy. *(Graphic violence, extensive nudity, sexual situations, adult situations, substance abuse, extreme profanity.)* — M.F.

d, Dan Golden; p, Anatoly Fradis; exec p, Roger Corman; assoc p, Felix Kleiman, Alex Kostich, Amy Segal; w, S. P. Somtow, Tara McCann, Adrie Hein (based on the writing of Bram Stoker); ph, Vladimir Klimov; ed, John Gilbert, Lorne Morris; m, Eduard Artemyev; prod d, Ludmila Kusakova; fx, Boris Martynov, Rafik Shatkov, John Buechler; casting, Laura Schiff, Marina Zaitseva; cos, Nelly Fomina, Tatyana Ilyevtseva; makeup, Nina Kolodkina

Thriller (PR: O MPAA: R)

BUTTERFLY KISS ★★½

(U.K.) 88m British Screen; Merseyside Film Production Fund; Dan Films Ltd. ~ CFP Distribution c

Amanda Plummer *(Eunice)*; Saskia Reeves *(Miriam)*; Kathy Jamieson *(Wendy)*; Des McAleer *(Eric)*; Lisa Jane Riley *(Danielle)*; Freda Dowie *(Elsie)*; Paula Tilbrook *(Ella)*; Fine Time Fontayne *(Tony)*; Elizabeth McGrath *(Waitress)*; Joanne Cook *(Angela)*; Shirley Vaughn *(Waitress)*; Paul Brown *(Gary)*; Emily Aston *(Katie)*; Ricky Tomlinson *(Robert)*; Katy Murphy *(Judith)*; Adele Lawson *(Wife)*; Jeffrey Longmore *(Husband)*; Suzy Yannis *(Motel Receptionist)*; Julie Walker *(Shop Assistant)*; Kelly *(Kelly)*

In many respects, despite the gender twist, BUTTERFLY KISS is just another road film about serial killers in love.

Miriam (Saskia Reeves), a shy and unremarkable gas station attendant, is pulled into the vortex of the life of the crazy and raging Eunice (Amanda Plummer). Dressed in prison garb and facing the camera in a stark setting, Miriam recounts the story of her lesbian affair with Eunice and their deadly travels across Britain.

They meet as Eunice is wandering from one gas-station convenience store to the next, clutching a packet of love letters and searching for her lost love. Repeatedly, she asks the clerk if her name is Judith and if the store carries a particularly piece of music about love. The wrong answer means death.

Miriam, immediately infatuated with Eunice's freedom and transgression, invites her to the home she shares with her disabled mother. Eunice proceeds to offer some religious advice to the mother and daughter. Later, she takes over the mother's bed and makes love to Miriam. Though Eunice has vanished by morning and leaves only the message, "You are not Judith," scrawled across the bathroom mirror in shaving lotion, Miriam quickly decides to leave everything behind.

On the road with Eunice, she finds herself trying to dispose of the bodies that keep appearing in the trunks of the various cars they steal. Though horrified by Eunice's bad habit of killing people, Miriam eventually indulges in the intoxication of murder.

When Eunice trusts that Miriam will do whatever she asks, she reveals her true aspiration: death. After instructing Miriam to kill her, they frolic through a field of sheep and come to the sea. While they are playing in the water Eunice suddenly shouts, "Now", and Miriam obeys. After several gasps for air Eunice's body goes limp, and the film ends to the sounds of Miriam's sobs.

BUTTERFLY KISS details Miriam's journey from a simple and timid clerk, to a devoted lover and murderer. The two women are polar opposites. As Miriam explains, Eunice is a Pisces and she, an Aires, forcing them to strive for a perfect balance so that one would not extinguish the other. The final image, of Eunice's death, unites the themes of absolution, sacrifice, and the failure of opposing forces to sustain harmony.

The voyage can now be interpreted as a journey through godforsakeness, and the final act one of redemption through love. At one point in the film the women simply begin to refer to each other as "me" for Miriam and "you" for Eunice, and it beomes evident that the subject of the film is not murder or freedom, but love.

Though Plummer gives a fierce and charged performance as Eunice, the characters and their relationship remain one dimensional. The meditative and lyrical vocals of a soundtrack dominated by the Cranberries is oddly incongruent with the subject of the film, and turns the combative into the sentimental. Ultimately, the film has an unfinished and hasty quality and falls short of its rather ambitious thematic goals. *(Nudity, adult situations, violence).* — R.C.

d, Michael Winterbottom; p, Julie Baines; assoc p, Sarah Daniel; w, Frank Cottrell Boyce (from an idea by Frank Cottrell Boyce and Michael Winterbottom); ph, Seamus McGarvey; ed, Trevor Waite; m, John Harle; art d, Rupert Miles; sound, Ronald Bailey (recordist); cos, Rachael Fleming; makeup, Maureen McGill

Drama **(PR: O MPAA: NR)**

BUVOS VADASZ
(SEE: MAGIC HUNTER)

CABLE GUY, THE ★★½

(U.S.) 91m Bernie Brillstein/Brad Grey; Licht/Mueller Film Corp. ~ Columbia c

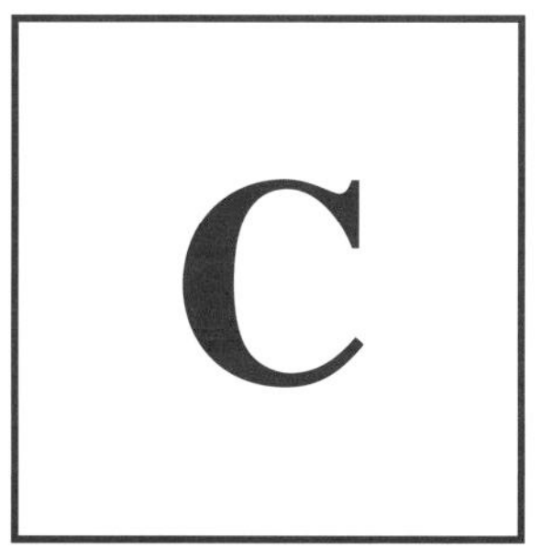

Jim Carrey *(Cable Guy)*; Matthew Broderick *(Steven)*; Leslie Mann *(Robin)*; Jack Black *(Rick)*; George Segal *(Steven's Father)*; Diane Baker *(Steven's Mother)*; Ben Stiller *(Sam Sweet)*; Eric Roberts *(Himself)*; Janeane Garofalo *(Medieval Waitress)*; Misa Koprova *(Heather)*; Andy Dick *(Medieval Host)*; Harry O'Reilly *(Steven's Boss)*; David Cross *(Sales Manager)*; Amy Stiller *(Steven's Secretary)*; Owen Wilson *(Robin's Date)*; Keith Gibbs; Tommy Hinkley; Shawn Michael Howard; Jeff Kahn; Suli McCullough; Jeff Michalski; Joel Murray; Andrew Shaifer *(Basketball Players)*; Cameron Starman *(Cable Boy)*; Kathy Griffin *(Cable Boy's Mother)*; Jeremy Applegate; Adam Consolo; Michael Fossat; Kennedy Kabasares; Robert L. Rasner *(Medieval Times Serfs)*; Paul Greco *(Raul)*; Aki Aleong; Dona Hardy; Lloyd Kino; Sara Lowell; Cynthia Mason; Michael Rivkin; Harper Roisman; Sandra Thigpen; Sean Whalen; Marty Zagon *(Karaoke Party Guests)*; Staci Flood; Mary Lee; Raydeen Revilla; Darlene Worley *(Karaoke Video Dancers)*; Cynthia Lamontagne *(Restaurant Hostess)*; James O'Connell *(Bathroom Attendant)*; Douglas Robert Jackson *(Bathroom Patron)*; Charles Napier *(Arresting Officer)*; Christopher Michael *(Arresting Officer)*; Charles Knox Robinson III *(Steven's Lawyer)*; John O'Donohue *(Prison Guard)*; Lydell M. Cheshier; Jason Larimore; Ahmad Reese; Emilio Rivera *(Jail Inmates)*; Bob Odenkirk *(Steven's Brother)*; Julie Hayden *(Steven's Sister)*; Annabelle Gurwitch *(Steven's Sister-in-Law)*; Blake Boyd *(Steven's Brother-in-Law)*; Lisa D'Agostino *(Newsroom Researcher)*; Tabitha Soren *(Herself)*; Rikki Klieman *(Herself)*; Robert Simels *(Himself)*; Leonard Turner *(Sam Sweet Judge)*; Carlo Allen *(Sam Sweet Court Judge)*; Conrad Janis *(Father "Double Trouble")*; Thomas Scott *(Sam at 8 years)*; Steven Scott *(Stan at 8 years)*; Christine Devine *(Anchor Woman)*; Mark Thompson *(Newsroom Reporter)*; Wendy Walsh *(Reporter Outside Courtroom)*; Marion Dugan *(Robin's Neighbor)*; Bill Beasley *(Nuclear Dad)*; Christine Beasley *(Nuclear Mom)*; Adam Beasley *(Nuclear Kid)*; Devon Beasley *(Nuclear Kid)*; Barbara Babbin *(Bar Patron)*; Frank Davis *(Bar Patron)*; Julian Reyes *(Bar Patron)*; Kyle Gass *(Couch Potato)*; David Bowe *(Helicopter Paramedic)*; Bobby Zajonc *(Pilot)*; Barbara Babbin *(Bar Patron)*

A dark and unsettling premise gets zany comedy treatment in THE CABLE GUY, a Jim Carrey vehicle, but the uneven quality of the film—and its disappointing performance at the box-office (given the overriding success of three preceding Carrey vehicles)—has less to do with mixed genres than it does with uncertain writing and direction.

Architect Steven Kovacs (Matthew Broderick) is dropped suddenly by his girlfriend, Robin (Leslie Mann), after proposing marriage. Steven moves into a new apartment in the city and waits a full day for the cable service technician to hook him up. Chip Douglas, "the cable guy" (Carrey), finally arrives, and before finishing his job, invites Steven to join him on a visit to the satellite dish where the electromagnetic signals converge. Steven's kind acceptance of Chip is reciprocated when Chip furnishes his new "preferred customer" with an array of free cable equipment. But Steven also acquires a friend he does not want: Chip is alternately goofy and menacing as he finagles his way into every area of Steven's life.

Chip initially helps Steven win back Robin, but he goes too far when he beats up one of Robin's dates in the men's room of a restaurant. Later, when one of Chip's schemes almost ruins Steven's own date with Robin, Steven breaks off his friendship with Chip. Feeling betrayed, Chip retaliates by inviting himself to Steven's parents' home, where he introduces the family to "Porno Password." Chip also sets up Steven on a charge of cable theft, which lands him in jail. Finally, Chip kidnaps Robin and takes her to the satellite dish, where he plans to kill her. But the police intervene in time and save Robin, while Chip falls into the satellite dish, but survives. As he's being taken aboard a rescue chopper, he finds a new friend in the attending paramedic.

Carrey has a field day playing a cable TV technician who obsessively tries to befriend one of his customers. Some may not think Carrey deserved the $20 million he was paid for the role, but Carrey's manic combination of pathos and misanthropy charge several scenes with more comic voltage than they otherwise would have contained. Unfortunately, even Carrey cannot re-route some unfunny detours into physical violence that pander to action-flick expectations. Director Ben Stiller shows more flair for setting up isolated jokes than shaping narrative.

Furthermore, Lou Holtz Jr.'s story and screenplay, a sort of homoerotic, noir reworking of MR. WRONG (1996) or PLAY MISTY FOR ME (1971), might have benefited from greater grounding in reality to offset the actions of Carrey's pitiful stalker. For example, Matthew Broderick and Leslie Mann are well cast as puppy-dog innocents in love, but their characters are just *too* naive and foolish (at least for Big City types) next to the Cable Guy's obvious machinations. Also, some critics disliked THE CABLE GUY for being too dark for a comedy, but in some ways, the film is not dark enough. Certainly, the tacked-on happy ending leaves much to be desired. But the film also carefully dances around the possible sexual motivations on the Cable Guy's part.

Despite these flaws, there are several things to like about THE CABLE GUY, including a load of lightweight TV and movie spoofs, amusing cameos by Janeane Garafolo, Eric Roberts, and director Stiller, and, most of all, Jim Carrey's unpredictable performance, which, in the tradition of the great stars, makes the most of even weak material. His best scene highlights his karaoke-singing "Somebody to Love," but his worst scene finds him pummeling his co-star while dressed in medieval garb. *(Violence, sexual situations, adult situations, profanity.)* — E.M.

d, Ben Stiller; p, Andrew Licht, Jeffrey A. Mueller, Judd Apatow; exec p, Brad Grey, Bernie Brillstein, Marc Gurvitz; co-p, William Beasley; w, Lou Holtz Jr.; ph, Robert Brinkmann; ed, Steven Weisberg; m, John Ottman; prod d, Sharon Seymour; art d, Jeff Knipp; set d, Maggie Martin; sound, Nelson Stoll (mixer); fx, Matt Sweeney, Sony Pictures Imageworks; casting, Juel Bestrop; cos, Erica Edell Phillips; makeup, Sheryl Leigh Ptak; stunts, Freddie Hice

Comedy/Thriller (PR: C MPAA: PG-13)

CALLING THE GHOSTS: A STORY ABOUT RAPE, WAR AND WOMEN ★★★½

(U.S.) 63m Bowery Productions; Indican Productons ~ Women Make Movies c

Jadranka Cigelj; Nusreta Sivac

In CALLING THE GHOSTS: A STORY ABOUT RAPE, WAR AND WOMEN, an almost flawless documentary, two women recall their experiences in a Serbian concentration camp.

Jadranka Cigelj, a Croatian divorcee living with her son, and her friend, Nusreta Sivac, a Muslim, reside in the Bosnian town of Prijedor. Both women are lawyers. In April 1992, anticipating a Serbian takeover of the town, Sivac's husband flees. Assuming that as a female she is immune to the atrocities of war, Sivac lingers behind, planning to join her husband in a few days. Soon both women are arrested and transported to a Serbian concentration camp in Omarska.

There they witness and endure unspeakable cruelties of every description administered in many cases by people who had been their neighbors. Murder, beatings, and rape are frequent occurrences. Malnutrition, disease, and the screaming of the tortured are everywhere. Cigelj recalls being raped over a 4-1/2-hour period by a group of men led by Zeljko Mejakic, the camp's commander of security. When horrifying rumors about the camps begin to circulate in the world press, most of Omarska's female inmates are released.

Cigelj and Sivac relocate to Zagreb, Croatia, where Sivac is reunited with her husband. After a period of psychological readjustment, both women devote themselves to aiding victims of the war and to the prosecution of Serbian war criminals. Through the efforts of Cigelj, Sivac, and others like them, a war crime trial is convened in The Hague, the Netherlands. One of the defendants is Zeljko Mejakic.

CALLING THE GHOSTS is as straightforward, lucid, and professional a documentary as one is likely to see. Wisely limiting its scope largely to the testimony of two brave women, among the many who might have been called on, the film avoids the pitfalls of intricate historical exposition in order to tell an important story in accessible terms. Totally free of poetic flourishes and hysterical rhetoric (for once, the word "genocide" is used with near accuracy), CALLING THE GHOSTS nonetheless pulls no punches in stating its case: that the Serb concentration camps not only existed, but they rivaled those of the Nazis in brutality; that they were part of a deliberate Serbian policy to conquer, humiliate, and rout—if not exterminate—the entire Muslim and Croatian populations; that rape is a war crime, not an unfortunate by-product of war; and that war and its criminals are victimizing women throughout the world as they have throughout history.

Discreet as its musical score is, CALLING THE GHOSTS probably should have done without it. Otherwise, this award-winning film (the first in a projected series of documentaries on violence toward women) is commendable in nearly every respect. It may sound insensitive to say so in this context, but the face and voice of Jadranka Cidelj, one of the movie's principal witnesses, have a dark resonance that many professional actresses would envy.

The film ends on a relatively light note of vindication, with its two heroines giggling as they mail a mischievous "wish-you-were-here" postcard from The Hague to their Serbian ex-colleagues in Prijedor. *(Adult situations.)* — D.T.

d, Mandy Jacobson, Karmen Jelincic; p, Mandy Jacobson; exec p, Anita Saewitz, Maury Soloman, Julia Ormond; assoc p, Thomas Halaczinsky; ph, Mario Delic; ed, Susanne Rostock; m, Tony Adzinikolov

Documentary **(PR: C MPAA: NR)**

CANNIBAL! THE MUSICAL ★★½

(U.S.) 97m ~ Troma Team Video c

Juan Schwartz *(Alferd Packer)*; Ian Hardin *(Shannon Bell)*; Matthew Stone *(James Humphrey)*; Jon Hegel *(Israel Swan)*; Jason McHugh *(Frank Miller)*; Dian Buchar *(George Noon)*; Toddy Walters *(Polly Pry)*; Robert Muratore *(Frenchy Cabazon)*; Andrew Kemler *(Preston Nutter)*; Edward Henwood *(The Cyclops)*

Filmed in 1993 as ALFERD PACKER: THE MUSICAL, this film was released to video three years later by Troma Team Video. Though its new title implies gory exploitation, the film is actually a satire of Hollywood musicals, telling the alleged true story of Alferd Packer, an 18th century pioneer accused of cannibalism.

The story begins in Lake City, Colorado, circa 1883, with Packer (Juan Schwartz) on trial, accused of murdering and eating the rest of his party. In a series of flashbacks, he gives reporter Polly Pry the real story, which began a decade earlier, when Packer was recruited to lead a quintet of miners from Utah to Colorado in the middle of the winter—where characters break into song at the most inopportune moments. Packer is heartbroken when his beloved horse, LeeAnn, runs off, and fearing that she was kidnapped by a trio of trappers, he foolheartedly takes his group in pursuit. Soon they're lost and hungry in the middle of the Rockies. When cohort Swan gets on the party's nerves, Bell kills him and divvies up his body for dinner. Soon Bell—a Mormon preacher—goes completely insane, slaughters the others, and is finally killed by Packer after several gruesome initial attempts go awry (these include a pick ax to the chest and a meat cleaver to the face). Since Packer is the only survivor, he's eventually jailed for the crimes. The story ends with a rousing musical number, as the entire town prepares for an all-singing, all-dancing hanging, only to have Polly save Packer at the last moment with a Governor's stay of execution.

Though it often resembles an overlong "Saturday Night Live" skit, a surprising amount of wit shines through this otherwise amateur endeavor. This is especially true when CANNIBAL! satirizes cheery Tinseltown musicals—from Packer's campfire love ballad to the missing LeeAnn ("There's nothing I couldn't do/When I was on top of you."), to a trio of trappers singing about the joy of skinning small defenseless animals. Unfortunately, things get rougher when the creators are obliged to create a coherent narrative. Lacking a real storyline, the laughs become scattered, going to supporting cast members such as Jon Hegel, who plays the eternal optimist in the group. For better or worse, director Trey Parker isn't afraid to scrape bottom for his humor, whether it's indulging in outlandish violence, or a touching love story of a man and his horse. It's this type of good-taste-be-damned charm that keeps CANNIBAL! afloat, despite its narrative gaps. *(Graphic violence.)* — S.P.

d, Trey Parker; p, Ian Hardin, Alexandra Kelly, Jason McHugh, Trey Parker, Matthew Stone; exec p, Alexandra Kelly, Andrew Kemler, Jason McHugh; assoc p, Edward Henwood; w, Trey Parker; ph, Robert Muratore, Chris Graves; ed, Ian Hardin ; m, Trey Parker, Rich Sanders; prod d, David Hedge; art d, Nathan Galie; ch, Diane Adamo, Philip S. Rosemund; fx, Tim Ornec

Musical/Comedy/Western **(PR: O MPAA: R)**

CANTERVILLE GHOST, THE ★★★

(U.S.) 91m Anasazi Productions ~ Hallmark Home Entertainment c

Patrick Stewart *(Sir Simon Canterville)*; Neve Campbell *(Ginny Otis)*; Joan Sims *(Mrs. Umney)*; Donald Sinden *(Mr. Umney)*; Cherie Lunghi *(Lucille Otis)*; Edward Wiley *(Hiram Otis)*; Daniel Betts *(Francis)*

Enjoyable if somewhat straightforward, THE CANTERVILLE GHOST updates Oscar Wilde's story and gives its star an opportunity to ham it up.

Teenaged Ginny (Neve Campbell) unhappily accompanies her family on an extended trip to England. Upon arriving, they settle in at Canterville Hall, a sprawling old manor. Over their first few nights, various eerie events occur. A ghost (Patrick Stewart) appears to Ginny and her brothers, though her parents cannot see him. Her father (Edward Wiley) blames Ginny for playing practical jokes and threatens to send her home. Ginny meanwhile meets Francis (Daniel Betts), a young duke, and begins to fall in love with him. Together they attempt to convince her father that the ghost exists.

Finding a hidden doorway, Ginny makes her way to the ghost's chamber. There she learns that he is the ghost of Sir Simon Canterville, who four centuries earlier was accused of murdering his wife. Sir Simon agrees to Ginny's plan of using a scene from Shakespeare's "Hamlet" to convince her father, as Simon claims to be the inspiration for the ghost of Hamlet's father. While doing the scene, however, Simon is overcome and disappears.

He later tells Ginny that he drove his wife to suicide while in a jealous rage. She can help his soul to rest by accompanying him to the realm of darkness and pleading for his freedom. After Ginny disappears with him, her family searches for her and her father becomes convinced that supernatural forces exist. They are able to pull Ginny back to the real world and together they find Simon's bones, which they inter next to his wife. Simon is thus able to rest happily and Ginny's family decides to remain in England.

The best reason for seeing THE CANTERVILLE GHOST is Stewart's performance. Clearly enjoying himself, he relishes the opportunity to frighten children, spout Shakespeare, and moon over his lost love. Among the other actors, Campbell and Betts convincingly portray teenage affection and Wiley is an obstinate but caring father.

Care was obviously taken in showing Canterville Hall and the surrounding countryside realistically. The script, while a bit cliched and predictable, successfully updates and expands Wilde's short story. The only other flaw is the film's low-rent special effects which clumsily show, for example, Stewart walking through a door. Otherwise, THE CANTERVILLE GHOST is enjoyable family fare. — K.Fr.

d, Syd Macartney; p, Robert Benedetti; exec p, Brent Shields, Richard Welsh; co-p, Patrick Stewart; w, Robert Benedetti (based on the story by Oscar Wilde); ph, Denis Lewiston; ed, Paul Martin Smith, Jim Oliver; m, Ernest Troost; prod d, Peter Mullins; art d, David Minty; sound, Brian Simmons; fx, Peter Hutchinson; casting, Lynn Kressel, Simone Reynolds; cos, Howard Burden; makeup, Steff Roeg

Children's/Fantasy **(PR: AA MPAA: NR)**

CAPTIVES ★★½

(U.K.) 100m BBC Films; Distant Horizons Productions ~ Miramax c

Julia Ormond *(Rachael Clifford)*; Tim Roth *(Philip Chaney)*; Richard Hawley *(Sexton)*; Jeff Nuttall *(Harold)*; Kenneth Cope *(Dr. Hockley)*; Keith Allen *(Lenny)*; Bill Moody *(Surgery Officer)*; Peter Capaldi *(Simon)*; Siobhan Redmond *(Sue)*; Christina Collingridge *(Katie)*; Victoria Scarborough *(Dental Nurse)*; Aedin Moloney *(Supermarket Checker)*; Tricia Thorns *(Prison Receptionist)*; Nathan Dambuza *(Moses)*; Colin Salmon *(Towler)*; Annette Badland *(Maggie)*; Cathy Murphy *(Companion)*; Mark Strong *(Kenny)*; Sandra James-Young *(Angie)*; Sharon Hines *(Melissa)*; Julian Maud *(Escort Officer/Newsreader)*; Anthony Kernan *(Blackie)*; Tony Curran *(Spider)*; Joe Tucker *(Con)*; James Hooton *(Trustee Prisoner)*; Steve Swinscoe *(Officer A)*; Catherine Sanderson *(Coffee-shop)*; David MacCreedy *(Officer B)*; Douglas McFerran *(Officer C)*; Shaheen Khan *(Estate Agent)*; Shend *(Gus)*; Gilbert Martin *(Bulldog Officer)*; Michael L. Blair *(Shaved Head/Hare Krishna)*; David Hounslow *(Detective)*

Filmed in 1994 for the BBC, this low-key British melodrama had a brief American release in 1996 to capitalize on the popularity of its two stars, Tim Roth and Julia Ormond. Stripping itself of the more melodramatic cliches associated with prison and romance tales, it emerges as a chilly character study of two desperate people involved in an increasingly dangerous relationship.

Rachel Clifford (Ormond) is a recently separated dentist who begins a part-time job conducting examinations at a London prison. One of her first patients is Philip Chaney (Roth), who is on his eighth year of a 10-year sentence. To Rachel's surprise, she later encounters Chaney at the supermarket, and he explains that he's let out one day a week to take college courses.

During his next prison dental appointment, Chaney slips her a note, asking if she could come to see him during visiting hours. Rachel changes her hairstyle so she won't be recognized by the guards, meets Chaney, and they become better friends—soon escalating to more overt sexual teasing while he's in her dentist's chair. Ignoring the no-fraternization rule, the two meet outside the prison walls, with Rachel risking her job, and Chaney risking his brief moments of freedom. Increasingly less discreet, the pair have sex in a ladies room stall. Rachel uncovers a newspaper article that describes Chaney's arrest for the murder of his wife. Distraught, she confronts him, and though he's at first furious that she went behind his back, he soon admits to his crime—hitting his wife and instantly killing her when he learned of her infidelity.

Towler (Colin Salmon), the cell block's drug dealer, gets wind of their relationship, and blackmails Chaney to get Rachel to sneak a parcel into the jail. Chaney's fear that Rachel's life will be in jeopardy if she refuses is confirmed when she's attacked in her home by an accomplice of Towler's. She reluctantly agrees, only to change her mind when she discovers the parcel contains a gun.

Chaney beats Towler, who again threatens Rachel's life. Panicked, Chaney admits everything to the prison authorities and asks them to protect Rachel. Rachel encounters Towler's brutal partner in a local cafe and shoots him with the gun. In the aftermath of the events, the two plan to continue their romance.

Mix a beautiful female dentist with a brooding but charismatic convict, and you've got all the makings of a generic made-for-TV movie. Luckily, director Angela Pope keeps her story steeped in realistic details and human complexities. For a while, she succeeds, especially when focusing on the budding romance between Chaney and Rachel. Though often bordering on the obsessive, they peel away the layers of their lives—just as they're soon peeling away each other's clothes. But once they consummate their relationship and the sexual tension is diffused, the film falters in plot twists that ring false.

The film's limited success is due to Roth and Ormond, who tackle their roles with an honesty that helps cover up the anemic script. Roth continues to excel as working class anti-heroes, having begun his career with similarly small but intense dramas, such as Mike Leigh's MEANTIME and Alan Clarke's MADE IN BRITAIN. But it's Ormond who truly shines, as a deeply hurt young woman who becomes more volatile when faced with her unraveling life. This film is intelligently handled and impeccably acted. It's a shame that the script isn't in the same league. *(Violence, sexual situations, profanity.)* — S.P.

d, Angela Pope; p, David M. Thompson; exec p, Anant Singh, Mark Shivas; assoc p, Ian Hopkins; w, Frank Deasy; ph, Remi Adefarasin; ed, Dave King; m, Colin Towns; prod d, Stuart Walker; art d, Diane Dancklefsen; sound, Stuart Moser (recordist), Richard Manton (recordist); fx, Stuart Brisdon; casting,

Gail Stevens; cos, Odile Dicks-Mireaux; makeup, Jan Sewell; stunts, Clive Curtis, Wayne Michaels

Drama/Romance/Prison (PR: C MPAA: R)

CARNOSAUR 3: PRIMAL SPECIES ★½

(U.S.) 81m New Horizons ~ New Horizons Home Video c

Scott Valentine *(Rance)*; Janet Gunn *(Dr. Hodges)*; Rick Dean *(Polchek)*; Rodger Halston *(Sanders)*; Anthony Peck *(Gen. Mercer)*; Terri J. Vaughn *(B. T. Coolidge)*; Billy Burnette *(Ferguson)*; Morgan Englund *(Rossi)*; Stephen Lee *(Sergeant)*; David Roberson *(Johnson)*; Justina Vail *(Proudfoot)*; Paul Darrigo *(Garcia)*; Robert Camilletti *(Nitz)*; Cyril O'Reilly *(Dolan)*; Jason Brawley *(Terrorist)*; Jonathan Winfrey *(Bob)*; Rodman Flender *(Nephew)*; Slade Barnett *(O'Donnell)*; Abraham Gordon *(Billings)*; Michael James McDonald *(Wilson)*; Bob McFarland *(Mulcowsky)*; Brian Currie *(Officer)*

While the first sequel to JURASSIC PARK (1993) was still in production, Roger Corman rushed this second sequel to his JURASSIC PARK knock-off CARNOSAUR (1993) to video stores—proving once again that quantity is no substitute for quality.

A group of terrorists hijacks an Army transport convoy and drives the vehicles to a Los Angeles dock. There, the trucks' contents—frozen flesh-eating dinosaurs—thaw out, come to life, and bloodily kill the terrorists, as well as some investigating cops. Rance (Scott Valentine) and his anti-terrorist squad are called in to take charge of the situation, but the monsters decimate his squad. Soon, he is told by General Mercer (Anthony Peck) and Dr. Hodges (Janet Gunn) that the dinosaurs are part of a genetic medical experiment and are to be taken alive, without being shot. Rance and his team (who have been joined by a detachment of marines) reluctantly comply and subdue one of the creatures, but it soon wakes up and escapes.

The dinosaurs take refuge in a docked, abandoned ship, and the soldiers board the vessel and head out to sea, hoping to freeze them in the ship's refrigeration compartment. Instead, the creatures pick the humans off one by one until only Rance and Dr. Hodges are left alive. They set off explosive charges and leap from the ship just before it blows up. Back on the dock, however, one dinosaur remains alive.

While director Jonathan Winfrey does demonstrate some aptitude for creative camerawork and editing transitions, CARNOSAUR 3 remains a slack, unscary exercise. One would think that more would be done with the monsters as the series went on, but this film may actually contain less dinosaur footage than either of its two predecessors. While this might be considered an advantage given the phoniness of John Carl Buechler's special effects, the one-dimensional characters and acting don't add much as compensation.

In addition to presenting one of the most incompetent anti-terrorist squads in film history (early on, they're stymied by having a stack of boxes knocked onto them), Scott Sandin's script boasts dialogue that's no more creative than "This guy's been carved up like a Thanksgiving turkey." It also actually manages to pillage the few key story points of ALIENS (the no-firing-weapons command, the discovery of an egg chamber) not already ripped off by CARNOSAUR 2. *(Graphic violence, profanity.)* — M.G.

d, Jonathan Winfrey; p, Roger Corman; w, Scott Sandin; ph, Andrea V. Rossotto; ed, Louis Cioffi; m, Kevin Kiner; prod d, Nava; art d, Mary Spain Winfrey; sound, Buck Robinson, William Smith, Joe Barnett, Jeffrey Whitcher; fx, John Carl Buechler, Magical Media Industries, Anthony Doublin; casting, Jan Glaser; cos, Maral Kalinian; makeup, Nicola Zvorsky

Horror/Action (PR: O MPAA: R)

CARPOOL ★

(U.S.) 90m Regency Enterprises; Arnon Milchan ~ Warner Bros. c

Tom Arnold *(Franklin Laszlo)*; David Paymer *(Daniel Miller)*; Rhea Perlman *(Martha)*; Rod Steiger *(Mr. Hammerman)*; Rachael Leigh Cook *(Kayla)*; Kim Coates *(Detective Erdman)*; Micah Gardener *(Bucky Miller)*; Mikey Kovar *(Andrew Miller)*; Colleen Rennison *(Chelsea)*; Jordan Warkov *(Travis)*

A comedy aimed at adolescents, CARPOOL stars David Paymer as an executive dad who gets stuck driving the kiddie carpool only to be car-jacked by a n'er-do-well carnival worker played by Tom Arnold. A multitude of car chases follow, but, on the whole, the laughs do not. The film's primary social value, it seems, is in conveying just how unpleasant an experience being trapped all day in a car with Arnold would be.

Disaster strikes on the day that ad exec Daniel Miller (Paymer) is set to make the most important pitch of his life, to prospective client Hammerman's Grocery: his wife gets sick, and he has to drive the carpool. Along with his young son Andrew (Mikey Kovar), and his teenage son Bucky (Micah Gardener), the passengers include precocious Chelsea (Colleen Rennison), pretty Kayla (Rachael Leigh Cook), and "that weird kid" Travis (Jordan Warkov), who pesters Miller to no end. Along the way, would-be bank robber Franklin Laszlo (Arnold), a down-on-his-luck carny, takes this gang hostage, and they lead the police on a chase through the streets of Seattle and a crowded shopping mall. Their principal pursuers are a detective (Kim Coates), and a determined meter-maid (Rhea Perlman). The kids don't like wet blanket Miller, who wouldn't let them listen to the Ramones, but they like Laszlo (who does). In fact, the youngsters like their kidnapper *so* much, that when he offers to let them go, they refuse.

Over the course of the day, Miller loosens up and realizes that he has devoted too much time to work and not enough time to his sons. Finally, the whole gang ends up helping Miller make a winning presentation for Mr. Hammerman (Rod Steiger), and when Miller is offered a big promotion, he quits. Instead, he and Hammerman, who has also been reminded of the importance of loving children, join Laszlo in the carnival business.

The situation in CARPOOL is not without comic potential. It's just that the script doesn't find much of it. Nor does the pedestrian direction enhance what little the script *does* offer (i.e., endless shots of people jumping out of an oncoming car's way do not a movie make). Even the two denouements—Miller quitting his job and he and Hammerman joining Laszlo's carnival—which are meant to be dramatic and heartwarming, are simply boring. As a children's movie, CARPOOL makes the deadly mistake of not providing personalities for the kids' characters. In fact, the kids barely register as more than faces in the seats behind Miller and Laszlo. In the end, adults accompanying children to CARPOOL will tire of this ride and be tempted to join in with the Ramones singing, "I Wanna Be Sedated!"*(Violence.)* — P.R.

d, Arthur Hiller; p, Arnon Milchan, Michael Nathanson; exec p, Fitch Cady; assoc p, Casey Grant; w, Don Rhymer; ph, David M. Walsh; ed, William Reynolds, L. James Langlois; m, John Debney; prod d, James D. Vance; art d, Sandy Cochrane; set d,

Dominique Fauquet-Lemaitre; sound, Larry Sutton; casting, Lynn Stalmaster; cos, Trish Keating; stunts, Conrad Palmisano

Comedy **(PR: A MPAA: PG)**

CARRIED AWAY ★★
(U.S.) 104m CineTel Films ~ Fine Line c

Dennis Hopper *(Joseph Svenden)*; Amy Irving *(Rosealee Henson)*; Amy Locane *(Catherine Wheeler)*; Julie Harris *(Joseph's Mother)*; Gary Busey *(Major Wheeler)*; Hal Holbrook *(Dr. Evans)*; Christopher Pettiet *(Robert Henson)*; Priscilla Pointer *(Lily Henson)*; Gail Cronauer *(Catherine Wheeler's Mother)*

In CARRIED AWAY, Dennis Hopper plays a school teacher who agonizes over leaving his straight-laced fiancee (Amy Irving) for a vampish student (Amy Locane), but even the full-frontal nudity of the three stars cannot enliven this hokey, hum-drum romantic triangle.

Set in the mid-1970s in an unidentified Midwestern state, CARRIED AWAY concerns the mid-life crisis of Joseph Svenden (Hopper), a middle-aged school teacher and farmer in the rural town of Howardsville. Joseph is a model citizen, the caretaker of his dying mother (Julie Harris), and, for six years, the fiance to Rosealee (Irving), a fellow teacher and widow of his best friend, who was killed in Vietnam. Rosealee is more than ready to marry, but Joseph delays his commitment when the state board threatens to shut down the two-room school house in which they teach.

During this same time, Joseph meets Catherine Wheeler (Locane), a new student in town, who makes immediate, obvious sexual advances. When Catherine and her father, Maj. Nathan Wheeler (Gary Busey), decide to rent a stable on Joseph's farm for Catherine's prize stallion, Joseph and Catherine use the space to initiate their passionate but secret love affair.

Joseph becomes increasingly frustrated by his dual existence, and, in a moment of drunken, emotional angst, insists that Rosealee engage in the same sort of lusty love-making that he has experienced with Catherine. Eventually, Rosealee and others in the town catch wind of the illicit romance, but most of the residents—even Catherine's father—are forgiving. Despite her pain, Rosealee remains Joseph's fiancee and stands by him during the school board tribunal. Catherine and her father, meanwhile, leave Howardsville.

Co-producer and star Amy Irving allowed her boyfriend, director Bruno Barreto (THE STORY OF FAUSTA, A SHOW OF FORCE), to photograph her in the buff in one of the many awkward and uncomfortable scenes in this film. Still, CARRIED AWAY is much more of a showcase for Locane, who plays a sort of disturbed Lolita. Locane's Catherine seduces Hopper's bespectacled schoolteacher by disrobing in most of her scenes, including a memorable interlude during which she masturbates on the roof of his car on a highway in broad daylight.

The sex scenes provide vivid distraction from the foolish dialogue of Ed Jones and Dale Herd (from a novel by Jim Harrison); most of CARRIED AWAY parrots old-fashioned melodrama doctrine. The film even sanctifies male philandering when Julie Harris, almost unrecognizable as Joseph's dying mother, says if cheating "made men bad, we'd all be lost." Even Gary Busey coming off drably; his showdown scene with Hopper is a big nothing.

CARRIED AWAY boasts a good cast, an interesting director and a potentially engrossing story, but there is nothing on screen that would make one believe it possesses any of these. *(Extensive nudity, sexual situations, adult situations, profanity.)* — E.M.

d, Bruno Barreto; p, Lisa M. Hansen, Paul Hertzberg; exec p, Bruno Barreto, Amy Irving, Robert Dattila; co-p, Catalaine Knell; w, Ed Jones, Dale Herd (based on the novel *Farmer* by Jim Harrison); ph, Declan Quinn; ed, Bruce Cannon; m, Bruce Broughton; prod d, Peter Paul Raubertas; art d, Jonathan Alexandre Raubertas; sound, David O. Daniel; casting, Wendy Kurtzman, Liz Keigley; cos, Grania Preston

Drama/Romance **(PR: O MPAA: R)**

CATWALK ★★
(U.S.) 95m Style TV Productions, Inc.
~ Arrow Releasing c

Christy Turlington; Kate Moss; Naomi Campbell; Jean-Paul Gaultier; Todd Oldham; Azzedine Alaia; John Galliano; Nino Cerruti; Karl Lagerfeld; Giorgio Armani; Isaac Mizrahi; Cindy Crawford; Helena Christiansen; Gianni Versace; Gianfranco Ferre; Valentino; Claudia Schiffer; Alberta Ferretti; Carla Bruni; Veronica Webb; Nadja Auerman; Francesco Clemente; Jaye Davidson; Arthur L Elgort; Yasmine LeBon; Oribe; Andre Leon Talley

Anyone expecting an in-depth dissection of *haute couture* will be disappointed by this vapid excuse to film of beautiful women in glamorous clothing. Only the most dedicated followers of fashion will be interested.

The experiences of model Christy Turlington are followed over the course of a spring season's worth of fashion shows in Milan, Paris, and New York. Various designers (and their divergent personalities) are introduced through on- and offstage footage, including speed-talker Karl Lagerfeld; offbeat Jean-Paul Gaultier; and icily serious Giorgio Armani. In one of the few scenes not relating to a fashion show, Turlington attends a party thrown by actor Jaye Davidson (THE CRYING GAME, STARGATE) on the arm of her beau, actor Christian Slater.

This cinematic puff piece (the title of which is model-slang for runway) is little more than a paean to Turlington's photogenic beauty and ability to wear anything from a towering Marie Antoinette wig (for Lagerfeld) to a draped sari and detachable nose rings (for Gaultier). Her face and figure recall the gamine delicacy of Audrey Hepburn, and she seems pleasant enough (though a few overheard cell-phone conversations with her agent reveal her iron-butterfly side when it comes to negotiations and scheduling).

If CATWALK reveals anything, it's that the fashion world is a cuckoo empire in which one model's adroit way with a crinoline earns her the sobriquet of "genius." However, like the world of high fashion itself, the film is not without a certain mindless appeal. Viewers in the market for behind-the-scenes, between-the-models bitchiness will be thrilled as model Helena Christiansen is nearly hooted out of the dressing room for defending actress Sharon Stone, who did little to impress Turlington and her compatriots with her guest walk-on at designer Valentino's show. And when British designer John Galliano instructs his models to pretend they're Anna Karenina escaping from Russia before sending these pale, distraught-looking women hurtling forth in his billowing hoopskirts (to a soundtrack of baying wolves, no less), some fashion victims may be compelled to grab their credit cards and go shopping immediately. *(Adult situations.)* — D.N.

d, Robert Leacock, Milton Moses Ginsberg; p, Sug Villa; exec p, Daniel Wolf, Donald Rosenfeld; assoc p, Helen Sayad; ph, Robert Leacock; ed, Milton Moses Ginsberg; m, Malcolm McLaren; sound, Michael Lonsdale

Documentary **(PR: A MPAA: NR)**

CAUGHT ★★★
(U.S.) 109m Sony Pictures Classics ~ Sony Pictures Classics c

Edward James Olmos *(Joe)*; Maria Conchita Alonso *(Betty)*; Arie Verveen *(Nick)*; Steven Schub *(Danny)*; Bitty Schram *(Amy)*; Shawn Elliot *(Santiago)*; Bernie Abbot; Tommy Abbot *(Peter)*; Sandra Kazan *(Bag Lady)*; Edward Pomerantz *(Man in Window)*; Joseph D'Onofrio *(Crack Dealing Kid)*; Angela Ali *(Cop)*; Gregory Lichtenson *(Cop)*; Dominick Oliveri *(Fish Dealer)*; Antonio Oliveri *(Big John)*; Dick Curry *(Yacht Salesman)*; Willo Varsi Hausman *(Yacht Sales Associate)*

CAUGHT is a steamy melodrama centered on the eternal romantic triangle and played out against the backdrop of a Jersey City fish market. Erotic, suspenseful, and, at times, darkly humorous, this well-acted drama plays like a contemporary version of a Greek tragedy, with flashes of film noir thrown in. It's a heady mix, even if the film's denouement disappoints.

One afternoon while running from the police, Nick (Arie Verveen), a handsome Irish drifter, literally stumbles into the modest fish shop owned by Joe (Edward James Olmos) and his restless wife Betty (Maria Conchita Alonso). Almost at once there's an attraction between Nick and the older Betty. When she offers him a job and a place to stay, the stage is set for trouble. Betty sets Nick up in the bedroom of her son Danny (Steven Schub), who is currently living in LA and pursuing a career as a stand-up comic. Joe is a trusting sort and, once Nick proves himself a good worker, he comes to think of him almost as the dutiful son that prodigal Danny never was. This suits Betty just fine, as she and Nick soon begin a torrid affair practically under the nose of an unsuspecting Joe. Once he's asleep, Betty and Nick meet up for clandestine sex in various rooms of the house—even in the bathroom shower. The fact that their affair is based on more than just cheap sex doesn't change the recklessness of what they are doing; in fact, they seem to be deliberately tempting fate. However, Joe carries on unaware and, happy with his new and improved family, seriously considers selling the storefront property to a real estate developer and retiring from the fish business.

Disaster strikes when Danny returns home unannounced with his wife Amy (Bitty Schram) and a serious cocaine habit. Danny, who's closer to his mother than any son really should be, is disturbed to find Nick ensconced in his bedroom and quickly suspects something's going on. His suspicions are confirmed one afternoon at a family picnic: Danny, seated at a table next to Nick and across from his mother, thrusts his foot between Betty's legs. Betty, of course, thinks it's Nick, and her obvious arousal is a dead giveaway. In Danny's cocaine-addled mind, Nick is also sleeping with Amy, and Danny can barely contain his jealousy. He hits upon a plan to remove Nick from the picture entirely. Having recently hit Betty up for a loan, Danny knows his mother occasionally "borrows" a little money from the stash Joe keeps hidden in the shop. Danny calls his father and hints that the beloved Nick has been stealing. Joe checks the freezer and discovers that there is fact money missing. He confronts Nick with the evidence in front of Betty, who not only admits that she took the money, but that she and Nick are lovers and plan to leave Jersey City together. The news causes Joe to go into cardiac arrest and, despite Nick and Betty's panicky efforts, he dies. Distraught and racked with guilt, Nick aimlessly wanders the Jersey City waterfront at night. Danny, insane with drugs and jealousy, steals up behind him and slits his throat, leaving him to bleed to death in the rain.

Veteran independent director Robert M. Young (SHORT EYES, EXTREMITIES) has long been acknowledged as a deft handler of actors and the performances in CAUGHT are uniformly strong. Irish newcomer Verveen has genuine charisma reminiscent of a young, brooding Marlon Brando. Olmos is characteristically sturdy and Alonso gets to play a full palette of sexual longing and deceit. But it's Schub who nearly steals the movie with his on-target take on a ruthlessly ambitious comic with a serious Oedipus complex. Once the stage is set for what should be a robust resolution, however, CAUGHT loses its nerve, and Young settles for a rather by-the-numbers action finale. *(Sexual situations, substance abuse, profanity.)* — E.K.

d, Robert M. Young; p, Richard Brick, Irwin Young; exec p, Jim Pedas, Ted Pedas, Bill Durkin, George P. Pelecanos; w, Edward Pomerantz; ph, Michael Barrow; ed, Norman Buckley; m, Chris Botti; prod d, Hilary Rosenfeld; casting, Kimberly Davis; cos, Hilary Rosenfeld; makeup, Nicki Lederman; stunts, Peter Bucossi

Romance/Drama/Erotic **(PR: C MPAA: R)**

CELESTIAL CLOCKWORK ★★★
(France/Venezuela/Belgium/Spain) 85m Miralta Films; Pandorados; International Network Group; Paradise Films; Mistral Films; Club D'Investissement Media; Bastille Films ~ October Films c

Ariadna Gil *(Ana)*; Arielle Dombasle *(Celeste)*; Evelyne Didi *(Alcanie)*; Frederic Longbois *(Armand)*; Lluis Homar *(Italo)*; Chantal Aimee *(Tina)*; Alma Rosa Castellanos *(Lucila)*; Dominique Abel *(Gaby)*; Hidegar Garcia Madriz *(Toutou)*; Oliver Granier *(Claude)*; Michel Debrane *(Grigorieff)*; Pedro Del Llano *(Mariano)*; Didier Azoulay *(Pierre-Jean)*; Philippe Beautier *(Herve)*

Filmmaker Fina Torres's wacky Cinderella fable is strictly for those who have a weakness for opera, astrology, magic realism, and sexual teasing.

Ana (Ariadna Gil) runs out on her wedding in Venezuela to seek her fortune as a singer in Paris. There, she falls in with a sorority of Latinas, who both help and harm her chances of stardom. To Ana's delight, her very first cab driver plays Rossini's high-soaring "La Cenerentola" on his radio, and they both happily sing along to it. A crusty old Russian vocal coach, Grigorieff (Michel Debrane), is enraptured by her voice and takes her on as a pupil for free.

Unknown to Ana, one of her roommates, Celeste (Arielle Dombasle), is her nemesis, bent on becoming a star through her dabblings in video, painting, and performance art. She even goes so far as to develop her voice so she can try out for Ana's dream role of Cenerentola, which is being cast by a famous director in town.

Ana moves in with a ditsy psychiatrist, Alcanie (Evelyne Didi), who offers her safe harbor when the immigration police come inquiring after her visa status. A gay clairvoyant, Armand (Frederic Longbois), even agrees to marry her so she can stay in the country. With the intervention of Toutou (Hidegar Garcia Madriz), a Puerto Rican shaman, Ana defeats the odds and ends up warbling Rossini to her heart's content.

Director Torres keeps the tone bubbly and light. It's a dream of Paris, as seen through a gamine's eyes. In its blithe insouciance and sudden outbreaks of music, it recalls the early work of Rene Clair and Jacques Demy.

A young girl's fantasy of romance and success in Paris is one of cinema's most venerable themes, and that tradition is divertingly upheld here. A huge poster of Maria Callas dominates Ana's bedroom. The highly eclectic music score percolates with Latin, classical and syntho-pop. Somewhat less successful are some video interpolations demonstrating Celeste's admittedly over-the-top work.

The movie is fleshed out with a raft of charming performances. Gil has a forlorn, waifish appeal, and she is pretty good at lip-synching the glorious sounds of Schubert lieder, which are sung by Elsa Maurus. The four-eyed Didi is amusingly frazzled, with her video-shrink techniques and wonder at her newfound sexuality. As a villainess, Arielle Dombasle is fiendishly pretty, like a malevolent Nina Hagen or a junior Cruella DeVil. Longbois is as lovable as a teddy bear in a role that just avoids veering into gay caricature. *(Sexual situations, adult situations, profanity.)* — D.N.

d, Fina Torres; p, Fina Torres; exec p, Gerard Costa; w, Fina Torres, Daniel Odier, Blanca Strepponi, Telsche Boorman, Yves Delaubre, Chantal Pelletier; ph, Ricardo Aronovich; ed, Christiane Lack, Catherine Trouillet; prod d, Claire Dague, Sandi Jelambi; sound, Claude Bertrand; fx, Eve Ramboz; cos, Ariadna Papio

Drama/Comedy/Fantasy **(PR: C MPAA: NR)**

CELLULOID CLOSET, THE ★★★

(U.S.) 102m Telling Pictures; HBO; Channel 4; ZDF/arte; Brillstein-Grey Entertainment ~ Sony Pictures Classics c/bw

Lily Tomlin *(Narrator)*; Tony Curtis; Armistead Maupin; Susie Bright; Whoopi Goldberg; Jan Oxenberg; Harvey Fierstein; Quentin Crisp; Richard Dyer; Jay Presson Allen; Arthur Laurents; Gore Vidal; Farley Granger; Stewart Stern; Paul Rudnick; Shirley MacLaine; Barry Sandler; Mart Crowley; Antonio Fargas; Tom Hanks; Ron Nyswaner; Daniel Melnick; Harry Hamlin; John Schlesinger; Susan Sarandon

THE CELLULOID CLOSET examines the ways in which homosexuality has been portrayed in Hollywood films. Based on a book by Vito Russo, the film is a kaleidoscopic, entertaining ride that covers a lot of territory.

Lily Tomlin handles the narration, which has been rather perfunctorily written by Armistead Maupin. Film clips beginning from the early silent days are interspersed with interviews with various interested figures. Some segments prove far more successful than others.

Clips from some films date from the pre-Hays Code era, when lax censorship enabled coverage of taboo subjects. Lesbian glamour reached a cinematic peak in the '30s with Marlene Dietrich, dressed in a tuxedo, exhibiting physical affection for women in MOROCCO and BLONDE VENUS. Her erotic rival, Greta Garbo, also weighed in by playing lesbian Swedish Queen Christina, announcing to her chancellor, "I shall die a bachelor!"

After the movie industry's adoption of the Hays Code and the creation of the Catholic Legion of Decency, such freedom came to a halt. Gays turned malevolent onscreen. A typical example is Judith Anderson's sublimely evil Mrs. Danvers in REBECCA. Of course, such figures of perversion always met with bad ends, often victims of murder or suicide. Hitchcock double-whammied the equation with ROPE, in which he had *two* gay murderers, based on Leopold and Loeb. When adapting a play or novel featuring an actual gay character, filmmakers were forced to change the defining orientation of that character, making him, say, a Jew (CROSSFIRE) or alcoholic (THE LOST WEEKEND) instead.

The 1950s continued this demonizing tradition with that prison crew of mean butch dykes in CAGED and Mercedes McCambridge, who played leathery mean mamas in both JOHNNY GUITAR and TOUCH OF EVIL. But, by the '60s, things were changing. TV and a slew of more sexually explicit foreign films had made serious inroads on Hollywood profits. To compete, American movies became more adult and the influence of the Hays Code began to wane. WALK ON THE WILD SIDE and ADVISE AND CONSENT contained serious gay subplots. Unfortunately, tragic fates still continued to dog homosexual characters: Shirley Maclaine hangs herself in THE CHILDREN'S HOUR; steely Barbara Stanwyck's paramour, Capucine, is shot in the finale on WALK ON THE WILD SIDE, and Don Murray's political career is ruined by sexual blackmail in ADVISE AND CONSENT.

Old habits die hard, for even in a supposedly more enlightened age, negative images still surface with disturbing regularity (the psychopathic murderers in CRUISING, THE FAN, BASIC INSTINCT).

By focusing primarily on Hollywood, producer-directors Rob Epstein and Jeffrey Friedman have managed to control their far-ranging, unwieldy topic. This focus, however, proves to be the film's major weakness as well. As incisive as they are about the old studio system's uneasy relationship with the subject, they're rather too complacent and tunnel-visioned in regard to present-day Hollywood. The final, "triumphant" montage has the queasy, self-congratulatory quality of one of those "Aren't we fabulous?" film sequences tailored for the Oscar ceremonies.

By skimming over the contributions of foreign films and, especially, independent films, the filmmakers have trivialized the subject. Films like PARTING GLANCES, THE WEDDING BANQUET, and R.W. Fassbinder's FOX AND HIS FRIENDS, reveal gay life with greater realism than such safe and sterile propositions as PHILADELPHIA, with its privileged, physically perfect role-model central couple who barely touch each other, yet cry and cry, and, of course, die.

The interviews are a decidedly mixed blessing. Gore Vidal inveighs with all his expatriate majesty, describing his subversive attempt to inject a homosexual relationship into BEN HUR, an in-joke that excluded star Charlton Heston. On a somewhat lower intellectual rung, Tony Curtis basks in his own vulgarity, describing donning drag in SOME LIKE IT HOT and "dropping the soap" in the notoriously censored bath scene with Olivier in SPARTACUS. Two feisty, veteran screenwriters, Arthur Laurents and Jay Presson Allen, are very enlightening as they reminisce about working in and around the system.

Shirley MacLaine and Susan Sarandon are both informative and funny, offering the actress's perspective. At the other end of the spectrum, there is the unspeakably annoying Susie Bright, billed in the press kit as "a noted commentator on human sexuality." Her observations are embarrassing in their inanity, whether she is commenting on Clifton Webb, deliciously acidulous in LAURA, or Dietrich at her most gloriously perverse. *(Adult situations, violence, sexual situations, profanity, nudity.)* — D.N.

d, Rob Epstein, Jeffrey Friedman; p, Rob Epstein, Jeffrey Friedman; exec p, Howard Rosenman, Bernie Brillstein, Brad Grey; assoc p, Michael Ehrenzweig, Wendy Braitman, Caryn Mendez; co-p, Michael Lumpkin; w, Armistead Maupin, Rob Epstein, Jeffrey Friedman, Sharon Wood (based on the book *The Celluloid Closet: Homosexuality in the Movies* by Vito Russo); ph, Nancy Shreiber; ed, Jeffrey Friedman, Arnold Glassman; m, Carter Burwell; art d, Scott Chambliss; sound, Pat Jackson

Documentary **(PR: C MPAA: R)**

CELTIC PRIDE ★½

(U.S.) 91m Hollywood Pictures; Caravan Pictures ~ Buena Vista c

Damon Wayans *(Lewis Scott)*; Daniel Stern *(Mike O'Hara)*; Dan Aykroyd *(Jimmy Flaherty)*; Gail O'Grady *(Carol)*; Adam Hendershott *(Tommy)*; Paul Guilfoyle *(Kevin O'Grady)*; Deion Sanders *(Himself)*; Bill Walton *(Himself)*; Christopher McDonald *(Coach Kimball)*; Gus Williams *(Derrick Lake)*; Ted Rooney *(Tony Sheppard)*; Vladimir Cuk *(Lurch)*; Keith Gibbs *(Terry Kirby)*; Joe Mingle *(Referee)*; Peter A. Hulne *(Pat Fitzsimmons)*; Patrick Hulne *(Tim Fitzsimmons)*; Will Lyman *(Rich Man)*; Darrell Hammond *(Chris McCarthy)*; Colton Russo *(Josh)*; Ed "The Machine" Regine *(Ralph)*; Bill McDonald *(Mr. Tanner)*; Belle McDonald *(Mrs. Tanner)*; Larry Bird *(Himself)*; Charles Broderick *(Drunken Fan)*; Jeffrey Ross *(Car Theft Victim)*; Scott Lawrence *(Ted Hennison)*; Steve Sweeney *(Nick)*; Tony V. *(Cabbie)*; Mary Klug *(Grandma)*; Marv Albert *(Himself)*; Charlie Haugk *(John 3:16 Guy)*; Bob Cousy *(Himself)*; Andy Jick *(Boston Garden Announcer)*; Connie Perry *(Suzy)*; Curt Frisk *(Big Jim Fulton)*; James Dickinson *(Basketball Player)*; George MacDonald *(Reporter)*; Charles Porter *(Bartender)*; Ed Logan *(Program Seller)*; Robert M. Curcuro *(Bobby)*; Nicole Brathwaite *(Kid in Gym)*; Michael Biase *(Bar Patron)*; Kevin Benton *(Security Guard)*; Maryanne Di Modica *(Waitress)*; Bob Haggerty *(Man in Bathroom)*

This comedy is notable only as a symptom of how far low Hollywood is prepared to go to cash in on the popularity of professional basketball. Absurd and uninvolving, CELTIC PRIDE is also severely short on laughs.

Mike O'Hara (Daniel Stern) and Jimmy Flaherty (Dan Aykroyd) are two rabid Boston Celtics fans with little interest in life's incidentals—such as family or work. With their team on the verge of another world championship, they find the Celtics' road to glory blocked by the superstar of the Utah Jazz, Lewis Scott (Damon Wayans). After witnessing Scott administer yet another drubbing in front of the home crowd at the Boston Garden, O'Hara and Flaherty are surprised to discover their nemesis partying at a local nightclub. Drunk, they hatch a scheme to assure the Celtics the championship by snatching Scott. They wake the next morning to the horrible realization that they've actually succeeded.

Though Scott is unapologetically self-centered and cocky, he's intelligent; after playing a number of psychological games on his inept kidnappers, he manages to escape. He opts not to press charges, as long as O'Hara and Flaherty very loudly and very publicly change their allegiance to the Utah Jazz. The superfans find themselves in the deathly position of have to preserve their freedom by rooting for the opposition. Ironically, they discover the grass is just as green (or in this case, purple and gold) on the other side of the fence.

The fundamental problem with the film is that its only sure audience is among basketball fans, but they are the most likely to sniff out its preposterousness. That a star of Jordanesque magnitude would be unlikely to go out on the town alone, or that Damon Wayans (who is not much taller than Aykroyd) is unconvincing as a physically dominant basketball player, or that a team saddled with a "ball-hog" star like Scott would be unlikely to make it all the way to finals, go unaddressed in Judd Apatow's screenplay. By comparison, a film like FORGET PARIS (1995), which is only incidentally about the sport but which cast real players, ends up as a more satisfying portrayal of the modern game.

More seriously, where Daniel Stern (DINER, HOME ALONE, CITY SLICKERS) is a credible supporting or ensemble player, he's got nothing to support in co-star Dan Aykroyd. Director Tom De Cerchio gets little more than hapless mugging out of Aykroyd, whose best work seems far behind him. CELTIC PRIDE's only interest may well be archaeological—it was shot in the old Boston Garden just before it was torn down. *(Violence, profanity.)* — N.N.

d, Tom De Cerchio; p, Roger Birnbaum; exec p, Judd Apatow, Charles J.D. Schlissel, Jonathan Glickman; assoc p, Michael Waxman, Katherine E. Beyda, Colin Quinn; w, Judd Apatow; ph, Oliver Wood; ed, Hubert De La Bouillerie; m, Basil Poledouris; prod d, Stephen Marsh; art d, Dina Lipton; set d, Jan K. Bergstrom; sound, Curt Frisk; fx, Guy Clayton, Erik Henry, VIFX; casting, Ferne Cassel; cos, Mary Claire Hannan; makeup, Carla Palmer, Whitney L. James; stunts, Rick Le Fevour

Comedy/Sports (PR: C MPAA: PG-13)

CEMETERY MAN ★★★★

(Italy/France) 100m Audifilm-Urania Film; K.G. Productions; Le Studio Canal Plus; Silvio Berlusconi Communications; Bibo TV and Film Productions
~ October Films c
(DELLAMORTE DELLAMORE)

Rupert Everett *(Francesco Dellamorte)*; Francois Hadji-Lazaro *(Ghaghi)*; Anna Falchi *(The Three "She")*; Mickey Knox *(Foreign Marshall)*; Clive Riche *(Doctor Verseci)*; Fabiana Formica *(Valentina)*; Katja Anton *(Thin Girl)*; Barbara Cupisti *(Magda)*; Pietro Genuardi *(New Mayor Civardi)*; Anton Alexander *(Franco)*; Stefano Masciarelli *(Mayor Scanarotti)*; Vito Passeri *(Ghigini)*; Alessandro Zamattio *(Claudio)*; Patrizia Punzo *(Claudio's Mother)*; Micha Kopman *(2nd Returner)*; Renato Donis *(Husband of "She")*; Claudia Lawrence *(Miss Chiaromondo)*; Francesca Gamba *(Hospital Nurse)*; Elio Cesari *(Nun)*; Maruizio Romoli *(Hospital Doctor)*; Maddalena Ischiale *(Stanza Franco Nurse)*; Maria Elena Fresu *(Hospital Sister)*; Stefano di Tomassi *(1st Boy Scout)*; Simone Ervini *(2nd Boy Scout)*; Flavio Marti *(3rd Boy Scout)*; Daniele Mezzoprete *(4th Boy Scout)*; Sandro Prati *(1st Boy on Square)*; Fabio Alberici *(2nd Boy on Square)*; Tiziano Nardoni *(3rd Boy on Square)*; Gianluca Gennaro *(4th Boy on Square)*; Marco Fiorentini *(Photographer)*; Fiorenzo Marsili *(Returning Priest)*; Rinaldo Zamperla *(Cyclist)*

Originally titled DELLAMORTE DELLAMORE (*Of Death and Love*), this darkly comic fantasy is equal parts morbid eroticism and gut-crunching violence, seasoned with fashionable Freudianism, fright-night archetypes, pulp nihilism and romantic iconography. In this film directed by Dario Argento protege Michele Soavi (THE CHURCH [1991], THE DEVIL'S DAUGHTER [1992]), style takes precedence over conventional storytelling, and the narrative is elegantly circular.

Brooding antihero Francesco Dellamorte (Rupert Everett) is the handsome caretaker of Buffalora cemetery and lives on the grounds with his assistant, the mute, grotesquely fat, bald and childlike Gnaghi (Francois Hadji-Lazaro). Dellamorte is on the phone with his friend, Franco (Anton Alexander), ignoring ominous scratching at the front door. The persistent visitor is a reanimated corpse, whom Dellamorte dispatches with a bullet to the brain. The dead are rising in Buffalora cemetery—Boy Scouts, bikers, businessmen, and babes—and sending the "returners" back to their graves is a nightly chore Dellamorte finds increasingly onerous.

At a funeral, Dellamorte glimpses the bewitching woman who will be known only as "She" (Anna Falchi). The young and succulent widow of an old man, she and Dellamorte fall in love amidst tombstones and sepulchers, and consummate their liaison atop her husband's grave by the icy light of the moon. Unfortunately, the husband chooses this moment to return and take a bite from his widow's flesh. She dies and returns, vines and dirt clinging to her hair. Dellamorte must kill her again. His heart is broken.

Dellamorte gets a second chance when "She" returns, this time in the guise of a local politician's starchy assistant. She adores him, she says, but she's pathologically afraid of sex. Dellamorte tries to persuade a local doctor to emasculate him, but the doctor only will go so far as providing a massive hypodermic needle filled with a castrating chemical. The concoction makes Dellamorte deathly ill, and when he eventually recovers, his beloved tells him that an amazing thing has happened. Her boss raped her, after which they "did it again, nicely." Her fear of sex cured, she's going to marry him, but wants to be friends. Once again, Dellamorte's heart is broken.

Gnaghi, meanwhile, has developed a crush on Valentina (Fabiana Formica), the mayor's spoiled daughter. She is killed in a motorcycle accident, and Gnaghi disinters her re-animated head: He dresses it in a wedding veil and installs it in his broken television. Their relationship is disrupted when her father comes to the cemetery and is attacked by his daughter's flying head.

In a vision, the figure of Death tells Dellamorte to stop killing the dead and start killing the living. Dellamorte complies, murdering people in the town square and at the local hospital. The crime spree baffles the local police.

Dellamorte meets the last incarnation of "She," who takes him home for a night of passionate sex. Later, while she's asleep, her roommate reveals that they are students, and they trade sex for money to pay their tuition. Dellamorte sets the house on fire, and he and Gnaghi get into their car and drive away from Buffalora. But the road ends abruptly, and as they stand at the edge, looking into the abyss below, Gnaghi becomes articulate, and Dellamorte is reduced to grunting. The camera pulls back to reveal that they're both figures in a snow globe.

Crammed with self-conscious allusions to everything from NIGHT OF THE LIVING DEAD (1968) to the pop surrealism of Rene Magritte and inspired by a hugely popular Italian comic-book series about an "investigator of nightmares" named *Dylan Dog,* this is the sort of richly textured genre movie Americans seem to have forgotten how to make. Soavi—who has also worked with Terry Gilliam (the influence of THE ADVENTURES OF BARON MUNCHAUSEN is especially clear in the visit from Death)—successfully balances his disparate influences, binding them together with unforgettable images of eerie, stylized beauty. British actor Everett was the model for the comic book Dylan Dog, so his casting could not be more appropriate. *(Nudity, violence.)* — M.M.

d, Michele Soavi; p, Tilde Corsi, Gianni Romoli, Michele Soavi; exec p, Conchita Airoldi, Dino Di Dionisio; assoc p, Michele Ray Gavras, Heinz Bibo; co-p, Conchita Airoldi, Dino Di Dionisio; w, Gianni Romoli (based on the *Dylan Dog* novel *Dellamorte Dellamore* by Tiziano Sclavi); ph, Mauro Marchetti; ed, Franco Fraticelli; m, Manuel De Sica; art d, Antonello Geleng; set d, Roberto Caruso; sound, Andrea Dallimonti (recordist), Angelo Raguseo (mixer); fx, Sergio Stivaletti; cos, Maurizio Millenotti, Alfonsina Lettieri; makeup, Gino Zamprioli, Enrico Iacaponi; stunts, Neno Zamperla

Horror/Fantasy **(PR: O MPAA: R)**

CHAIN REACTION ★★½

(U.S.) 106m Zanuck Company; Chicago Pacific Entertainment; 20th Century Fox ~ 20th Century Fox c

Keanu Reeves *(Eddie Kasalivich)*; Morgan Freeman *(Paul Shannon)*; Rachel Weisz *(Lily Sinclair)*; Fred Ward *(FBI Agent Ford)*; Kevin Dunn *(FBI Agent Doyle)*; Brain Cox *(Lyman Earl Collier)*; Joanna Cassidy *(Maggie McDermott)*; Chelcie Ross *(Ed Rafferty)*; Nicholas Rudall *(Dr. Alistair Barkley)*; Tzi Ma *(Lu Chen)*; Krzysztof Pieczynski *(Lucasz Screbneski)*; Julie R. Pearl *(Emily Pearl)*; Godfrey C. Danchimah Jr. *(Chidi Egbuna)*; Gene Barge *(James Washington)*; Nathan Davis *(Morris Grodsky)*; Aaron Williams *(Lab Techie #3)*; Daniel H. Friedman *(Video Dan)*; Johnny Lee Davenport *(Caleb Williams)*; James Sie *(Ken Lim)*; Joan Kohn *(Sarah Fine)*; Juan Ramirez *(Raymond Pena)*; Nydia Rodriguez Terracina *(Gabrielle Guerrera)*; Scott Benjaminson *(Stuart Showcroft)*; Ned Schmidtke *(Wisconsin Chief Schmidke)*; Randall Arney *(DC Technician)*; Noelle Bou-Sliman *(DC Technician)*; Joe Kosala *(Sergeant Joe Byczkowski)*; Ron Dean *(Sergeant Nick Zingaro)*; Miguel Nino *(Officer Miguel)*; Turk Muller *(Dane County Cop)*; Neil Flynn *(State Trooper Nemitz)*; Michael Skewes *(State Trooper Schwartz)*; Margaret Travolta *(Anita Fermi)*; Jacqueline Arthur *(Jackie Mann)*; Tom Mula *(Chicago Administrator)*; Denise Price *(Receptionist)*; Rick LeFevour *(Matthew Haig)*; Charley Sherman *(Justin Tidy)*; Gina Raffin *(Colleen Dryden)*; Pam Zekman *(Rita Bliss)*; Lisa Tejero *(Dolores Enrique)*; David Pasquesi *(Al Vanzetti)*; John Drummond *(Drummond)*; Catherine Lemkau *(TV Reporter)*; Tell Draper *(TV Reporter)*; Danny Goldring *(Clancy Butler)*; Eddie Bo Smith Jr. *(Yusef Reed)*; Michael Gaylord James *(Jim Gaylord)*; Ken Moreno *(Naldo Partida)*; Allen Hamilton *(Senator Phil Schmidt)*; Dick Cusack *(Senate Chairman)*; Nick Kusenko *(Staff Member Stennis)*; David Michael Gee *(Senate Guard)*; Stanley M. Span *(Firechief #1)*; Ann Whitney *(Barkley's Lawyer)*; Rich Komenich *(Bar Patron)*; Afram Bill Williams *(Bridge Controller)*; Will Zahrn *(Bridge Controller)*; John W. Hardy *(Train Porter)*; Mary Seibel *(Older Woman on Train)*; Nina Beesley *(Flower Shop Owner)*; Mike Shannon *(D.C. Flower Delivery Man)*; Billy Haynes *(Doorman)*; Walter Doggett *(Gate Guard)*; Jack Kandel *(Panhandler)*; Timothy Maxwell *(Homeless Husband)*; Leslie Mikol *(Homeless Wife)*; Rio Zavala *(Homeless Man)*; Mark Morettini *(Romano)*; Soseh Kevorkian *(Evelyn)*; Christopher Holloway *(Max Holloway)*; Jim Ortlieb *(Orbit)*; Cheryl Hamada *(Hamada)*; Mike Gray *(Swizlard)*; Joe Guastaferro *(Tunnel Foreman)*

Andrew Davis, who so ably directed THE FUGITIVE, here directs it again—and expands his boundaries, since CHAIN REACTION stars Keanu Reeves and Rachel Weisz as *two* framed people on the lam. Slick direction, a streamlined pace and razor-sharp editing add up to good, dumb fun, even though CHAIN REACTION lacks any kind of sensible or even comprehensible story.

Eddie Kasalivich (Reeves) works as a machinist on the University of Chicago's Hydrogen Energy Project. Led by idealistic Dr. Alistair Barkley (Nicholas Rudall) and funded mostly through a foundation headed by Paul Shannon (Morgan Freeman), the project is on the verge of perfecting a clean-burning hydrogen-energy machine fueled by water. Eddie serendipitously discovers a sound-wave frequency that stabilizes the energy reaction so that the hydrogen won't explode. America's freedom from the oil cartels seems imminent.

Later that night, after Barkley tries to share this earthshaking data with scientists on the Internet, evil men in black kill him and vandalize the lab. Eddie stumbles upon Barkley's corpse as the place is about to explode, and barely escapes the fiery mushroom cloud that levels eight city blocks.

During the ensuing investigation by FBI Agent Leon Ford (Fred Ward) and his assistant Agent Doyle (Kevin Dunn), a fax sent by an unknown party implicates two missing members of Barkley's team—Dr. Lu Chen (Tzi Ma) and young physicist Dr. Lily Sinclair (Weisz). Eddie has been framed as well—the police find $250,000 and a high-tech transmitter in his home. The platonic duo of Eddie and Lily turn to Shannon for help. He urges them to give themselves up, but agrees to have them speak with his lawyer first while they hide out in Wisconsin with Eddie's old friend, Maggie McDermott (Joanna Cassidy).

Unknown to Eddie and Lily (not to mention the FBI), Shannon is the one who had Barkley killed in order to prevent him from giving away the secret of his new technology. Shannon is the head of C-Systems, a secret research group controlled by multinational businesses, defense contractors, and the CIA. After getting the key sound-wave frequency that only Eddie knows, they plan to kill him and Lily and blame them for the destruction of Barkley's project.

Confused by the different forces pursuing them, Eddie and Lily narrowly escape from Wisconsin. Arranging a meeting with Shannon, they walk into a trap he has arranged for them. Lily is captured, but Eddie escapes.

Having taken an ID card from one of their pursuers, Eddie locates and infiltrates the C-Systems headquarters in Virginia, where Lily and Chen are being forced to continue Barkley's project.

Eddie eventually manages to sabotage C-Systems's computers and download their contents to the FBI; he also uploads the Hydrogen Project data, frequency and all, to scientists on the Internet. C-Systems explodes just as Barkley's lab did. Shannon kills his co-conspirators while escaping and later vanishes in a chauffeured limo with a secretary. Eddie and Lily are whisked away to spill all to the feds.

With the barest nod at plausibility, this film posits high-tech, high-security installations with computers that require no passwords. That's like a bank having vaults without locks. Furiously and determinedly simple-minded behind its high-science premise, CHAIN REACTION is overloaded with labels and signs for the slower members of the audience; at a critical point, Eddie finds a map that practically says "Villain's Secret Hideout Here!" And since the geniuses at C-Systems know the stabilizing factor is a sound frequency, why don't they just cycle through a range of them until they find the right one, rather than framing, kidnapping, and torturing people and getting the FBI on their backs?

Former second-unit director Davis continues to prove he's really good at filming people running, cars coming and going, and big metal things looking. . . really big and metallic. The film's screenplay, which was adapted by two writers from a story by three others, makes as much sense as such a melange suggests. The cast play along amiably: Reeves, who mercifully has little dialog, is an appealingly earnest presence here, though the biggest kudos go to Ward, the film's most casually charismatic presence (he's this film's answer to Tommy Lee Jones in THE FUGITIVE), and to a remarkably subtle and nuanced Freeman.

Though the film's story line is often impenetrable, CHAIN REACTION's slick visuals, non-graphic violence, and lack of sex scenes make it a enjoyable comic book-like tale of intrigue. *(Violence, adult situations)* — F.L.

d, Andrew Davis; p, Andrew Davis, Arne L. Schmidt; exec p, Erwin Stoff, Richard D. Zanuck; assoc p, Maher Ahmad, Carlos H. Sanchez, Teresa Tucker-Davies; w, Josh Friedman, J.F. Lawton, Michael Bortman (from a story by Arne L. Schmidt, Rick Seaman, and Josh Friedman); ph, Frank Tidy; ed, Donald Brochu, Dov Hoenig, Arthur Schmidt; m, Jerry Goldsmith; prod d, Maher Ahmad; art d, David J. Bomba; set d, Gene Serdena; sound, Robert R. Anderson Jr. (mixer), Randy Thom (design); fx, Roy Arbogast, James Reedy, Nick Davis; casting, Amanda Mackey, Kathy Sandrich; makeup, Hallie D'Amore; stunts, Walter Scott

Action/Adventure/Thriller **(PR: C MPAA: PG-13)**

CHAMBER, THE ★½

(U.S.) 110m Imagine Entertainment; Davis Entertainment ~ Universal c

Chris O'Donnell *(Adam Hall)*; Gene Hackman *(Sam Cayhall)*; Faye Dunaway *(Lee Bowen)*; Robert Prosky *(E. Garner Goodman)*; Raymond Barry *(Rollie Wedge)*; Bo Jackson *(Sgt. Packer)*; Lela Rochon *(Nora Stark)*; David Marshall Grant *(Governor McAllister)*; Nicholas Pryor *(Judge Slattery)*; Harve Presnell *(Attorney General Roxburgh)*; Richard Bradford *(Wyn Lettner)*; Greg Goossen *(J.B. Gullitt)*; Seth Isler *(Marvin Kramer)*; Millie Perkins *(Ruth Kramer)*; Sid Johnson *(Josh Kramer)*; Blake Johnson *(John Kramer)*; Josef Sommer *(Phelps Bowen)*; Leonard Vincent *(Lucas Mann)*; Bonita Allen *(Ms. Cooley)*; Dick Stilwell *(George Nugent)*; Gloria Jackson Winters *(Woman Guard)*; Greg Elam *(Joe Lincoln)*; Zaquarii Walters *(Quince Lincoln)*; Jane Kaczmarek *(Dr. Anne Biddows)*; Thom Gossom Jr. *(Bink)*; Jana Barraza *(Gate Attendant)*; Nick Brett *(Rally Skinhead)*; Curtis Epper *(Rally Skinhead)*; Craig Pinckes *(Rally Skinhead)*; Dan Beene *(Lead Sheriff)*; James Geralden *(Newscaster)*; Michelle Davison *(Professor Burns)*; Jack Conley *(White Guard)*; Stephanie Bell Flynt *(Newcaster on Air)*; Ruby Wilson *(Jessie)*; Joe Meek *(Senate Aide)*; Anthony Kopczynski *(Vistor's Room Guard)*; Ken Colquitt *(Vistor's Room Guard)*; Neil Barton *(Visitor's Room Guard)*; Gilbert Ivan Johnson *(Trustee)*; Jerry Gauny; Ed Siebert; Bob Rummler; Disraeli Ellison; Rod Phillips; Jeff Sanders; Richard T. Munoz; Clee Cottel *(Inmates)*; Ian Brady *(Deputy Executioner)*; Sam Bologna *(Deputy Executioner)*; Charles Swain *(Observation Cell Guard)*; Tony Scott Sherrom *(Governor's Aide)*

Lawyer-*cum*-best-selling author-*cum*-Hollywood brand name John Grisham was able to sell the movie rights to *The Chamber* when it was little more than an idea on paper. Apparently, he took this as license to concoct a very thriller-unfriendly tale about the defense of a murderous Klansman.

Jackson, Mississippi. Sam Cayhall (Gene Hackman) sits on death row for the 1967 bombing of a civil rights attorney's offices in which two children were killed. Adam Hall (Chris O'Donnell), a novice lawyer from up North, arrives to appeal the execution order. Although they have never met, Hall is Cayhall's grandson. Hall does not believe that the old man is innocent, nor is he sympathetic to racist beliefs. To him, the case is both an abstract, legal cause and a chance to get some answers about his family's tragic past—particularly his father's mysterious suicide. Hall doesn't even have the support of Cayhall, who considered his son a weakling and his grandson a traitor to "the cause."

Hall does have the secret support of Mississippi's governor McAllister (David Marshall Grant). Having gained office as the DA who successfully prosecuted Cayhall's case, McAllister now figures to make political hay out of staying Cayhall's execution—appeasing both anti-death penalty liberals and racist conservatives. He assigns his assistant, Nora Stark (Lela Rochon), to help Hall and to keep him informed of Hall's activities. An investigation reveals that the case has many secrets, and Hall starts thinking Cayhall may have confessed to protect others. Rattling bones in the family's dark closet upsets Hall's socialite aunt Lee (Faye Dunaway), who tells her nephew how Cayhall once shot a black neighbor in cold blood and got away with it. This murder was also witnessed by Lee's young brother—Hall's father—and guilt over it was the cause of his suicide. Stark gets Hall access to some secret government files identifying another man as the real bomber. These "Sovereignty Commission" files establish that these and other terrorist activities were ordered by state-sanctioned, anti-civil rights organizations.

Hall pleads Cayhall's case in court—arguing that Cayhall, a fourth generation Klansman, suffered from diminished capacity because he was raised in a racist culture—to no avail. The governor only thanks Hall for digging up the Sovereignty Commission files, which he will suppress and use as dirt on political opponents. Cayhall will die, but the truly guilty will go free. Though unrepentant for his crimes, Cayhall comes to recognize the pain he has caused his family. After grandson and grandfather share a reconciling hug, Cayhall is led to the gas chamber.

Earlier in 1996, another Grisham adaptation dealing with the defense of a racially motivated murder was a big hit with audiences. In A TIME TO KILL a black man who killed his daughter's white rapists is acquitted when his lawyer convinces a jury that the clear act of vigilante justice was justice, nonetheless. THE CHAMBER's cool and reasoned, liberal look at a racist criminal is like a photographic negative of A TIME TO KILL's emotional, hot-button pushing (with special emphasis on the word "negative").

Only in a high-minded, message drama such as DEAD MAN WALKING (1995) can the ethics of capital punishment be assessed with any dispassion. The "what if (pick a horrible crime) happened to your spouse or child?" identification from audiences that fuels its desire for final retribution is a thriller's bread and butter. Cayhall may have only been an accessory to the bombing, but he killed that one black man, probably did some other nasty stuff, and is an unrepentant racist. When Hall defends him by claiming that the state's sanction and encouragement of such actions mitigates them, it doesn't engender sympathy for poor ol' Sam; rather, it makes us want to see more "good ol' boys" rounded up and tossed in the gas chamber with him.

Presented with source material that didn't fit their pre-conception, Universal pressed the production to deliver a slick thriller like THE FIRM. Hired-on director James Foley's (FEAR) efforts to impose thriller mechanics on THE CHAMBER has resulted in a good-looking and stylish muddle. That also pretty well describes the predicaments of O'Donnell and Rochon, whose characters' developments were excised—he was supposed to step out of his family's shadow and find his own identity, she was supposed to be his love interest—and were left only to run through the plot's paces. *(Profanity, violence, adult situations.)* — P.R.

d, James Foley; p, John Davis, Brian Grazer, Ron Howard; exec p, David Friendly, Ric Kidney, Karen Kehela; assoc p, Karen Snow; w, Willaim Goldman, Chris Reese (based on the novel by John Grisham); ph, Ian Baker; ed, Mark Warner; m, Carter Burwell; prod d, David Brisbin; art d, Mark Worthington; set d, Lisa Fischer; sound, Jose Antonio Garcia (mixer); fx, Burt Dalton, Peter Montgomery; casting, Mali Finn; cos, Tracy Tynan; makeup, Leonard Engelman, Kevin Haney; stunts, Webster Whinery

Crime/Thriller/Drama **(PR: C MPAA: R)**

CHAMELEON ★★

(U.S.) 108m Rysher Entertainment ~ WarnerVision c

Anthony LaPaglia *(Willie Serling)*; Kevin Pollak *(Matt Gianni)*; Wayne Knight *(Stuart Langston)*; Melora Hardin *(Jill Hallman)*; Derek McGrath *(Morris Steinfeld)*; Andy Romano *(Giovanni Pazatto)*; Robin Thomas *(Jason Ainsley)*; Richard Brooks *(Tom Wilson)*; Tony Mandola *(Alberto Cortese)*; Marianne Muellerleile *(Betty Bowen)*

With Anthony LaPaglia starring as a master-of-disguise federal agent, CHAMELEON has commendable ambitions to rise above the usual straight-to-video level but is seriously undermined by sluggish pacing and gross overlength.

After DEA agents are ambushed during a raid, agent Matt Gianni (Kevin Pollak) suspects a leak in his office. He calls his boss Stuart Langston (Wayne Knight) and asks for a fresh agent to come in. Langston assigns Willie Serling (Anthony LaPaglia), a master-of-disguise expert who has gone over the edge since his wife and daughter were murdered by drug smuggler Alberto Cortese (Tony Mandola). Langston tells Serling to go undercover in prison to get the goods on a drug-smuggling, money-laundering operation possibly led by Cortese.

In jail, Willie poses as a computer expert to get a job which allows him to gather bank records on disk. Gianni pulls Willie out of jail and gets him a position at American Liberty Bank, where he poses as a British auditor to find out who is involved. His first suspect is Jill Hallman (Melora Hardin), whom he also dates, but he discovers that the real crook is another bank executive, Morris Steinfeld (Derek McGrath). Steinfeld realizes he's been found out and meets with bank president Jason Ainsley (Robin Thomas), who informs Cortese. Cortese knocks off Ainsley while a hit man rubs out Steinfeld and goes after Willie, but Willie shoots him first while disguised as a hobo.

Willie becomes haunted by nightmares about Cortese and his behavior gets more bizarre. Gianni tells Willie to quit, but Willie refuses. After Gianni orders busts at the prison and the bank, Willie goes back to the bank and transfers all of Cortese's money from an offshore account. Willie then confesses his real identity to Jill and leaves her. Cortese breaks into Jill's apartment and when he's about to kill her, Willie appears and shoots Cortese in the head repeatedly.

CHAMELEON is a surprisingly low-key, talky thriller that remains consistently watchable but doesn't really explore its intriguing premise involving disguise, identity, and personality transference. Every time it appears to be striving to transcend the genre by concentrating on Willie's psychology, it invariably falls back on its cliched revenge plot. Unfortunately, the plot lacks action or suspense, with a number of slow dialogue scenes lacking any apparent point.

Technically, the film is decently made, with special makeup effects that are quite effective and a cast that's generally above-average for a straight-to-video release. LaPaglia is an interesting actor, handling the various disguises and accents well, but just when it seems he's on the verge of giving a daring and original performance, he pulls back, just like the film. *(Violence, sexual situations, profanity.)* — M.S.

d, Michael Pavone; p, Michael Pavone, Dave Alan Johnson; exec p, Keith Samples; assoc p, Bernie Laramie, Gary Johnson; co-p, Tony Amatullo; w, Michael Pavone, Dave Alan Johnson; ph, Ross Berryman; ed, Joanne D'Antonio; m, John Debney; prod d, Dorian Vernacchio, Deborah Raymond; art d, Ken Lanson; sound, Mark Friedgen; fx, Kevin McCarthy; casting, Denise Chamian; cos, Sylvia Vega-Vasquez; makeup, Kevin Haney

Thriller **(PR: O MPAA: R)**

CHAMPAGNE SAFARI, THE ★★★½

(Canada) 94m Field Seven Films ~ Frist Run Features c/bw

Colm Feore *(Narrator)*; Jim Morris *(Narrator)*; David Hemblen *(Voice of Bedaux)*

Interesting but obscure individuals from the past make ideal documentary subjects. THE CHAMPAGNE SAFARI, a rich and refreshingly dispassionate portrait, does a first-rate job of resurrecting one of them: Charles E. Bedaux, the "Citizen Kane" of industrial management.

Born in a middle-class Paris suburb in 1886, Charles E. Bedaux emigrates to America at the age of 19 with one dollar to his name. After becoming a successful efficiency expert, he launches his own company in 1917 and becomes a multimillionaire within a decade. In the 1930s, he and his wife, Fern, embark on a series of far-flung expeditions, including an ambitious trek across Canada's uncharted Rocky Mountain region in 1934.

Throughout this period, Bedaux's European business interests entangle him deeper and deeper with Germany's Third Reich. In 1941, he convinces the German high command and France's Vichy government to sponsor the construction of a trans-Saharan railroad and fuel pipeline under his supervision. After the Allies invade North Africa, Bedaux is arrested and sent to Miami, where he is charged with treason. In February 1944, he commits suicide while awaiting trial.

Bedaux appeared to have the world by the tail. He made a fortune before he was 50. He was a pioneer in an exciting new field that he loved. He lived in a 114-room chateau in France's Loire Valley, where he hosted the wedding of the Duke of Windsor and Wallis Simpson. He adored his beautiful wife and she not only reciprocated, but got on well with his mistresses. He knew how to spend money and he knew how to have fun. Naturally, it all had to end badly. His fatal flaw was his egotistical refusal to recognize social iniquity, both in the brutality of Hitler and the inhumanity of super-efficient theories of industrial management.

A 1995 Canadian documentary released the following year in the US, THE CHAMPAGNE SAFARI was the result of 16 years of research, inspired in part by its director's discovery of 20 cans of nitrate film in a Paris basement. The film turned out to be a record of Bedaux's costly, bizarre, and rather foolhardy Canadian expedition of 1934. Shot by top Hollywood cinematographer Floyd Crosby on commission, this footage is used by THE CHAMPAGNE SAFARI's director, George Ungar, throughout his film. Unfortunately, its prominence is not justified by its value; Bedaux apparently staged a good deal of his "documentary" footage for possible use in a hypothetical Hollywood feature. It does, however, provide a thought-provoking microcosmic parallel to Bedaux's entire life: an exciting journey that doesn't end very well.

"I wish to go neither left nor right," Bedaux used to say. "I wish to go forward." In 1934, at least, he was smart enough to reverse his forward momentum before disaster struck—the "champagne safari" was aborted early.— D.T.

d, George Ungar; p, George Ungar; exec p, John Walker; assoc p, Gordon Martin, Harold Crooks; w, Steve Lucas, John Kramer, Harold Crooks; ph, Floyd Crosby, Kirk Tougas, Douglas Kiefer, Ray Dumas, Susan Gourley; ed, John Kramer; m, Normand Roger, Denis Chartrand; sound, Sylvia Poirier, Hank Bridgeman, Gary Marcuse, Peter Sawade, Art Lopez

Documentary **(PR: A MPAA: NR)**

CHASING BUTTERFLIES ★★½

(France/Germany/Italy) 115m France 3 Cinema; Sodaperaga ~ New Yorker Video c

Narda Blanchet *(Solange)*; Pierette Pompom Bailhache *(Valerie)*; Alexandre Tcherkassoff *(Henri de Lampadere)*; Thamar Tarassachvili *(Marie-Agnes de Bayonette)*; Alexandra Lieberman *(Helene von Zastro)*; Lilia Ollivier *(Olga)*; Emmanuel de Chauvigny *(Father Andre)*; Sacha Piatgorsky *(Maharajah)*; Anne-Marie Eisenschitz *(Marie)*; Francoise Tsouladze *(Yvonne)*; Maimouna N'Diaye *(Caprice)*; Yannick Carpentier *(Monsieur Carpentier)*; Otar Iosseliani *(The Ghost)*; Alexander Askoldov *(Drunk)*; Pascal Aubier *(Quarrelsome Man)*

Director Otar Iosseliani's leisurely style suits this movie's subject matter: the slow death of the French aristocracy in modern times. CHASING BUTTERFLIES grudgingly respects the plight of the outmoded upper class, but Iosseliani's gently satiric approach is so polite, the film soon becomes tiresome.

Far from big-city bustle, the inhabitants of a sleepy French town adhere to an outmoded, insular way of living. In her decaying yet still splendid chateau, Marie-Agnes (Thamar Tarassachvili) depends on the kindness of her bossy country cousin and allows the followers of Hare Krishna the run of her property because she enjoys their company. One antique at a time, Marie-Agnes sells furnishings to maintain the front of moneyed civility. Like Marie-Agnes, local landowners also must fend off a persistent magistrate who represents Japanese businessmen hankering to own mansions as impressive as that of Marie-Agnes. Despite this, the aging aristocrats still have time for preferred pastimes such as disputing property lines or entertaining a visiting maharaja, who counts his wealth in the company of blindfolded servants.

When Marie-Agnes dies, squabbling relatives descend for a reading of the will. Disinheriting most of them, Marie-Agnes bequeaths her estate to her sister, Helene Von Zastro (Alexandra Liebermann), whose daughter gives every indication of running through this inheritance quickly. After the Von Zastros unload the chateau on the Japanese, who modernize the surroundings, several townspeople accompany the maharaja on a train ride. These passengers are killed in a terrorist bombing, like one of the faraway events the townspeople used to hear reported on the radio.

That sudden climactic bomb-burst comes as quite a shock, given the director's penchant for quiet atmosphere; it provides heartbreaking closure to this exploration of lives devoted to the manners of generations past.

Dissecting the social pecking order of the village, Iosseliani expertly recreates a safety zone of politesse. The stumbling block in this measured approach is that the daily events of the dinosaur nobility are shaped almost in documentary form—a documentary that hasn't been sufficiently edited. Instead of focusing on a few characters, the director puts an entire class under a microscope. So it's difficult to tell who is who in the large cast. This is made even worse by the photography. The director shows a penchant for wide landscape shots and dawdling over vistas; even important character revelations are framed from a distance. When those greedy relatives come calling, however, viewers may face a crisis of differentiating the characters.

Since audiences may be conditioned for warm nostalgia, Iosseliani's clinical mindset and detachment could prove irritating. He doesn't give us a comfortable viewing experience about the ostrich-like attitudes of cute senior citizens as the film's conclusion shows so powerfully. When the golden-agers are ripped from life abruptly, the audience grieves for them and for the romanticized past they clung to. *(Violence.)* — R.P.

d, Otar Iosseliani; p, Martine Marignac; co-p, Guy Seligman, Maurice Tinchat, Luciano Gloor, Ettore Rosboch, Lilia Smecchia; w, Otar Iosseliani; ph, William Lubtchansky; ed, Otar Iosseliani; m, Nicolas Zourabichvili; art d, Emmanuel de Chauvigny; set d, Jean-Michel Simmonet; sound, Yekaterina Evans; cos, Charlotte David; makeup, Evelyne Byot

Drama **(PR: A MPAA: NR)**

CHEKIST, THE ★★★

(Russia) 90m Lenfilm Associates; Trinity Bridge Productions ~ Cinema Parallel c

Igor Sergheyev *(Srubov)*; Mikhail Wasserbaum *(Katz)*; Alexi Poluyan *(Pepel)*; Alexander Kharashkevich *(Boje)*; Igor Golovin *(Commandant)*

Decades before Germany's Gestapo became a synonym for terror and political murder, the first modern secret police was born on December 20, 1917, in Petrograd. In chilling detail, Alexander Rogozhkin's THE CHECKIST indicts Lenin's "Extraordinary Commission to Combat Counter-Revolution and Sabotage," which for 70 years provided the domestic force behind the Communist Party's words.

THE CHEKIST focuses on the early, heroic period of the Soviet secret police, abbreviated in Russian as "the Checka," and is thus an even stronger condemnation of the methods used to build what was once called the first socialist state.

In a richly furnished office, three men sit around reading off lists of names and crimes, quickly deciding on whether to execute the offenders. Two wear uniforms, while their nominal chief dresses like a bourgeois, in a suit and tie. Andrei Srubov (Igor Sergheyev) is a provincial Cheka chief somewhere in European Russia during the last year of the civil war.

While his uniformed colleagues, Katz and Pepel (Mikhail Wasserbaum and Alexi Poluyan), authorize executions and then spend the rest of their time with women or hobbies, Srubov dutifully watches the nightly executions, pacing back and forth as the executioners do their work. Some of the Chekists seem to enjoy their work, but one, Boje (Alexander Kharashkevich), tries to commit suicide. When a pretty young girl begs for her life, the Chekists waver until Srubov himself intervenes and shoots her down.

Srubov broods more and more deeply on the role of killing. At one execution, he doffs his clothes to join the next batch of victims. A quick gesture by an observant commandant (Igor Golovin) saves his life, but before long, he is reduced to a prospective victim in a mental hospital, where procedures are almost a facsimile of the Cheka's. The film ends with a fantasy image of Srubov and his comrades riding as if to a more open and honest battle, though they end up in a desolate field enclosed by mist.

The power of THE CHEKIST lies in the grisly details of the executioner's work, so fully captured by the camera: rats that scurry away when the killers test their guns, the wooden doors against which the victims must stand, the channels designed to drain away the blood, and the hoist for lifting the bodies into a waiting truck. Ironies abound in this script by Jacques Baynac. Srubov's father had been executed by Katz. Perhaps guilt-ridden, Katz indulges in gallows humor that is almost prophetic: "What is the fate of a Chekist who has killed 50 people? He is the 51st!"

Rogozhkin seems to revel in his new-found ability to criticize the Cheka's origins. He also uses his new freedom as a filmmaker to focus excessively on the nude bodies of the victims in a clear comparison to the agony of Christ. The script includes idiosyncrasies that make the Cheka look good, but only in comparison to Stalin's later enforcers. In one scene, a few suspects are released. In another, Srubov pardons an officer accused of mutiny to the cheers of his men. Still, the round of murders inures most of the characters to the petty crimes, mass suffering, and casual brutality around them. *(Violence, extensive nudity, sexual situations, adult situations.)* — L.R.

d, Alexander Rogozhkin; p, Oleg Konkov, Guy Seligmann; w, Jacques Baynac (based on *The Chip* by V. Zazubrin); ph, Valery Molgaut; ed, Tamara Denisova; m, Dimitry Pavlov; art d, Grigory Obratzov; sound, Nikolay Astakhov

Political/Historical/Drama **(PR: C MPAA: NR)**

CHILDREN OF FURY ★★½

(U.S.) 85m Concorde ~ New Horizons Home Video c
(AKA: IN THE LINE OF DUTY: SIEGE AT MARION)

Dennis Franz *(Bob Bryant)*; Kyle Secor *(Addam Swapp)*; Tess Harper *(Vickie Singer)*; Paul LeMat *(Doug Bodrero)*; Ed Begley Jr. *(Fred House)*; Norbert Weisser *(John Singer)*; Lindsay Ginter *(Woody Jackson)*; William H. Macy *(Ray Daniels)*; Rex Linn *(Sheriff Gray)*; Edward Wiley *(Donald Miller)*; Mike Westenskow *(Ronald Perkins)*; Mitch Carter *(Ian Walters)*; Oscar Rowland *(Otto Doeffer)*; Garwin Sanford *(Rossi)*; Jan Tanner *(Heidi Swapp)*; Monique Lanier *(Charlotte Swapp)*; Marcia Dangerfield *(Beth Bryant)*; Colette Kilroy *(Ann House)*; Michael Weatherred *(Timothy Singer)*; Timothy Shoemaker *(Jonathan Swapp)*; Richard Clark *(John Nielsen)*; Craig Clyde *(Nolan Douglas)*; Don Glover *(Josh Keller)*; Harry Murphy *(Gov. Bangerter)*

Despite some compelling performances and reasonable suspense, the fact-based TV drama CHILDREN OF FURY suffers from lapses in plot logic and an abundance of red herrings which undermine this story of an FBI standoff against a house of religious zealots in Marion, Utah.

When police kill religious polygamist John Singer at his ranch, his widow, Vickie (Tess Harper), and his children publicly vow revenge. After seeing the family on TV, avowed fundamentalist and polygamist Addam Swapp (Kyle Secor) insinuates himself into their circle. Soon he marries two of Singer's daughters and decides to carry on Singer's work. He arms the elder children and trains them to defy authority.

Swapp's intimidating tactics frighten the neighbors, but when police intercede, Swapp threatens them off his ranch at gunpoint. The cops arrest Swapp's brother while Swapp, in retaliation, bombs a town building. This act of aggression forces the local authorities to summon the FBI, led by chief agent Bob Bryant (Dennis Franz). He immediately orders a stakeout of Swapp's property and encourages Swapp to turn himself in. Swapp refuses, declaring that the family is waging war against the government and authorities in the name of God and their anointed prophet, John Singer.

Bryant then orders his men to employ tactics of psychological harassment by shutting off the family's electricity and water, shining floodlights into the house, and using a piercing siren. This only enrages Swapp, who steps up his violence against them. By the 12th day of the stakeout, Bryant gets permission to use aggressive force to end the siege. Using attack dogs as a diversion, the agents manage to shoot Swapp and swarm the house, where the others finally surrender.

First shown on TV as "In the Line of Duty: Siege at Marion," CHILDREN OF FURY's puzzling title change is just one of the many irritating loose ends plaguing the movie. Charles Haid's direction is so scattershot that it's difficult to keep track of which character is which and who's related to whom. Supporting players appear and disappear without explanation and dramatic moments fall flat with no resolution.

Fortunately, most of the performances are first-rate. Harper is scarily effective as the hellfire-and-brimstone Vickie. Though Secor doesn't seem capable of the kind of manic intensity that Powers Boothe displayed in the TV movie GUYANA TRAGEDY: THE STORY OF JIM JONES (1980), his hammy portrayal of the religious fanatic Swapp is diverting. But Franz's performance is unbearable. He walks through his role in a zombie-like trance, occasionally throwing in a mannerism left over from his "Andy Sipowicz" character on "NYPD Blue." *(Violence, adult situations.)* — D.O.

d, Charles Haid; p, Stephanie Hagen; exec p, Kenneth Kaufman, Tom Patchett; w, Rick Husky; ph, William Wages; ed, Andrew Doerfer; m, Gary Chang; prod d, Stephen Storer; art d, Nathan Haas; sound, Stephen Laneri (mixer); fx, Kevin McCarthy; casting, Beth Hymson; cos, Susie DeSanto; makeup, Kris Evans

Drama **(PR: C MPAA: PG-13)**

CHILDREN OF NOISY VILLAGE, THE ★★★
(Sweden) 88m ~ First Run Features c

Harald Lonnebro *(Olle)*; Linda Bergstrom *(Lisa)*; Anna Sahlin *(Anna)*; Ellen Demerus *(Britta)*; Henrik Larsson *(Bosse)*; Crispin Dickson Wendenius *(Lasse)*; Tove Edfeldt *(Kerstin)*; Elisabeth Nordkvist *(Mellengardes Maja)*; Ingwar Svensson *(Mellengardes Anders)*; Catti Edfeldt *(Soregardes Lisa)*; Bill Jonsson *(Soregardes Nisse)*; Anne Sophie Knape *(Norregardes Greta)*; Soren Petersson *(Norregardes Erik)*; Sigfrid Eriksson *(Farfar)*; Louise Raeder *(Pigan Agda)*; Peter Dywik *(Orangen Oskar)*; Olof Sjogren *(Skomakare Snall)*; Ewa Carlsson *(Froken)*; Lasse Stahl *(Handlare Emil)*; Willy Turesson *(Johani Kvarn)*

THE CHILDREN OF NOISY VILLAGE is a gentle Swedish film, for and about young kids. Set in rural 1930s Sweden, the screenplay by Astrid Lindgren (author of the popular *Pippi Longstocking* books), directed by Lasse Hallstrom (MY LIFE AS A DOG), is whimsical and innocent without being cloyingly sweet.

Olle (Harald Lonnebro), Lisa (Linda Bergstrom), Anna (Anna Sahlin), Britta (Ellen Demerus), Bosse (Henrik Larsson), Lasse (Crispin Dickson Wendenius) and Kerstin (Tove Edfelt), are children living in a small hamlet comprising North, South, and Middle farms. The school term has just ended, and summer fun beckons.

As Lisa narrates, the children help with chores on the farms, encounter local grownups, and indulge in good-natured mischief.

They are terrified by the drunk shoemaker, Mr. Kind, but befriend his dog, Svik. The miller, Oskar (Peter Dywik), tells them about a troll that haunts his mill, and they wait for him to appear. Lisa and Anna go to town to buy necessities, make up a song about sausage, and keep forgetting things and going back to the store, where they are plied with candy.

Bosse cares for Svik while Mr. Kind is laid up. The kids sleep in haylofts (boys and girls are separate) and scare each other. The boys "find" a treasure note and try to trick the girls into searching for the hoard, but the girls trick them instead. The boys find the treasure, a can of goat turds with an admonitory note from the girls; a reward for their dishonesty. The film ends with everyone returning to school.

NOISY VILLAGE is saved from becoming kitsch by the children, who are real and believable in their interactions. While weeding a field, the kids search for a game to pass the time. Bosse suggests a cussing contest: the girls veto him because the boys would win! NOISY VILLAGE is sunny and idyllic, but genuine. The beautiful cinematography, by Jens Fischer and Rolf Lindstrom, does ample justice to the Swedish countryside, and captures the nuances of the youngsters' mischievous moods. Adults are bit players in NOISY VILLAGE. The kids' ensemble acting is excellent: a large part of the film's small magic is their warmth and realism together.

Nothing much happens in NOISY VILLAGE. American kids, accustomed to hyperactive Saturday morning cartoons, may find it boring. Parents with young children, and those who limit their kids TV viewing, will find it relaxing family entertainment. Since it is dubbed, subtitles present no barrier to young viewers' enjoyment.— C.M.

d, Lasse Hallstrom; p, Waldemar Bergendahl; w, Astrid Lindgren; ph, Jens Fischer, Rolf Lindstrom; ed, Susanne Linnman; m, Georg Riedel; art d, Lasse Westfelt; casting, Catti Edfeldt; cos, Inger Pehrsson

Children's **(PR: AA MPAA: NR)**

CHILDREN OF THE CORN: THE GATHERING ★
(U.S.) 85m Dimension Pictures ~ Dimension Home Video c

Naomi Watts *(Grace Rhodes)*; Karen Black *(June Rhodes)*; Brent Jennings *(Donald Atkins)*; Samaria Graham *(Mary Anne)*; Jamie Renee Smith *(Margaret Rhodes)*; Brandon Kleyla *(Josiah)*; William Wingdom *(Dr. Rob Larson)*; Mark Salling *(James Rhodes)*; Toni Marsh *(Sandra Atkins)*; Lewis Flanagan III *(Marcus Atkins)*; Salle Ellis *(Jane Nock)*; Marietta Marich *(Rosa Nock)*; Jonathan Patterson *(Charlie McLellan)*; Joshua Patterson *(Scott McLellan)*; Kay Bower *(Janet McLellan)*; Evan Greenwalt *(Convulsive Boy)*; Adam Lidberg *(Michael)*; Libby Villari *(Michael's Mom)*; Bill Prael *(Concerned Father)*; Stephen Earnhart *(Willis)*; Jim Krieg *(Smits)*; Richard Gross *(Sheriff Biggs)*; Harrison Young *(Drifter)*

Having steadily improved through its first three installments, the Stephen King-inspired film series CHILDREN OF THE CORN takes a giant step back with this hackneyed entry, THE GATHERING.

College student Grace Rhodes (Naomi Watts) returns to her hometown of Grand Island, Nebraska to take care of her mother, June (Karen Black), who is raising Grace's younger sister and brother, Margaret (Jamie Renee Smith) and James (Mark Salling). June has been acting disturbed, as a result of being tormented by nightmares of a disfigured young boy named Josiah (Brandon Kleyla). As her visions foreshadowed, Josiah's spirit returns to life and kills a drifter. Meanwhile, at her job assisting Dr. Rob Larson (William Wingdom), Grace is unnerved by the severe, fever-like illness that seems to be sweeping the town's children. It's not long before the youngsters are behaving strangely and calling themselves by new, biblical names, while several local adults (including Dr. Larson) meet violent deaths.

Soon Grace—along with Donald Atkins (Brent Jennings), whose son is one of those afflicted—discovers that the "children of the corn" are under the sway of Josiah's spirit. It turns out that Josiah was a youthful traveling preacher with a demonic heart who was killed decades before by townspeople; he now seeks to be reborn in a ritual performed by the children, in which Margaret will be a sacrifice. With Donald's help, Grace rescues Margaret and destroys Josiah's ghost, restoring the youngsters to normal.

Eschewing any connection to the previous CHILDREN OF THE CORN films or King's original story, director and co-writer Greg Spence unfolds a tired tale of kiddy cultdom that just happens to be set among the cornfields of Nebraska (even though the story's Gothic religious underpinnings would seem more at home in the deep South). Overall, the film settles for genre cliches instead of any genuinely imaginative twists. A couple of gory jolts aside, the scares are predictable, as are the characters and plotting. Even the scenes of young children undergoing seizures and losing their teeth are more nauseating than frightening. Given such material, the performances can't rate high: Watts, so fetching as the sidekick in TANK GIRL (1994), is appealing but given little to do except go through the motions; Black gives her typical mannered, eccentric performance; and Kleyla brings no particular malice to the pint-sized villain. *(Graphic violence, adult situations, profanity.)* — M.G.

d, Greg Spence; p, Gary DePew; assoc p, Jake Eberle; w, Stephen Berger, Greg Spence (based on the short story "Children of the Corn" by Stephen King); ph, Richard Clabaugh; ed, Chris Cibelli; m, David Williams; art d, Carla Curry; sound, Mac Melson, Larry Scharf; fx, Wayne Beauchamp, Ken Wheatley;

casting, Donald Paul Pemrick; cos, Christine Radovanov; makeup, Gary Tunnicliffe, SOTA FX, Abiiba Howell

Horror **(PR: O MPAA: R)**

CHONGQING SENLIN
(SEE: CHUNGKING EXPRESS)

CHUNGKING EXPRESS ★★★★½
(Hong Kong) 100m Jet Tone ~ Rolling Thunder c
(CHONGQING SENLIN)

Brigitte Lin *(The Drug Dealer)*; Takeshi Kaneshiro *(Ho Chi-wu—Cop #223)*; Tony Leung Chiu-Wai *(Cop #663)*; Faye Wong *(Faye)*; Valerie Chow *(Air Hostess)*; "Piggy" Chan *(Manager of "Midnight Express")*; Guan Lina; Huang Zhiming; Liang Zhen; Zuo Songshen

Wong Kar-Wai's plaintively romantic chronicle of a few days in the lives of two heartbroken, Hong Kong policemen owes its mood and plot line to the anecdotal love stories recounted in the films of the French New Wave. The movie's impressive visual style blends the flashy cinematography of a music video with the playful experimentation found in the early works of Godard and Scorsese.

A mysterious woman (Brigitte Lin) wearing a blonde wig, sunglasses, and a raincoat, arranges a drug-smuggling deal which quickly goes awry when her couriers, a group of East Indian immigrants, suddenly disappear. She attempts to retrieve the packages of heroin with which she now believes the Indians have absconded—to the extent of briefly taking one of their children hostage—but she never recovers the goods.

Ho Chi-wu (Takeshi Kaneshiro), a policeman who frequents the Midnight Express fast-food counter, creatively obsesses on the recent loss of a relationship by purchasing cans of pineapple (his ex's favorite snack) dated with the month's end; he believes that his grief, and hope for reconciliation, should have "an expiration date."

He and the blonde eventually cross paths in a bar and spend an uneventful night together. With the dawn the two dispel their respective demons: He jogs in the rain to forget his lost love, and she kills her treacherous supplier, who's been stalking her since the smuggling job went sour.

Ho is seen at the Midnight Express, where Cop #633 (Tony Leung Chiu-wai), whose live-in stewardess girlfriend (Valerie Chow) has just left him, is picking up an envelope containing a farewell note and his apartment keys. When the heartbroken cop leaves the envelope behind, the eatery's waiflike counter-person, Faye (Faye Wong), takes advantage of the situation by visiting his apartment on a regular basis. Lovestruck, she cleans the place from top to bottom, plays with his possessions, and erases a phone message from his ex. After he begins to warm up to Faye—and after he discovers her leaving his apartment—he asks her out. He waits at the specified location, but she never shows up. A year later the two run into each other, and positions are reversed: he is now behind the Express counter, which he has purchased from the owner, and she is in uniform, having become a stewardess. They find there is hope for their future together.

Among the film's virtues is its small scope; the four leads are well delineated (with Lin's character remaining a fantasy figure of sorts) and each is allowed his or her own voice-over narration. The first narrative contrasts hard-boiled genre conventions against a more "realistic" tale of urban heartache; the second, lengthier, narrative maintains a whimsical (yet still incredibly poignant) approach, with Faye's look (ultra-short hairdo, slacks, striped shirt) qualifying her as a '90s variant on Jean Seberg's character in BREATHLESS (1960).

Lending an emotional resonance to the proceedings is Wong's use of a special technique, step-printing, to visually fragment certain actions. This process, which simulates slow motion, is complemented by a careful use of time-lapse photography to isolate the lovesick policemen in both space and time.

Wong also utilizes an evocative selection of popular hits, most of them Western in origin—including Dinah Washington's "What a Difference a Day Makes," a Cantonese rendition (by Wong, who is a Hong Kong pop star in real life) of the Cranberries' "Dreams," and Faye's anthem, the Mamas and the Papas "California Dreamin'"—to craft the film's reflective atmosphere. The four leads succeed in making their characters particularly endearing, with Kaneshiro and Leung effectively incarnating the film's themes of romantic fixation and eventual redemption.

The film garnered good notices at film festivals around the US, and then was chosen by Quentin Tarantino to be the first release for his Rolling Thunder arm of Miramax Films. *(Violence.)* — E.G.

d, Wong Kar-Wai; p, Chan Yi-Kan; exec p, Chan Pui-Wah; assoc p, Jacy Pang; w, Wong Kar-Wai; ph, Christopher Doyle, Lau Wai-Keung; ed, William Chang, Hai Kit-Wai, Kwong Chi-Leung; m, Frankie Chan, Roel A. Garcia, Michael Calasso; prod d, William Chang; art d, Qiu Weiming; sound, Liang Da (recordist), Liang Lizhi (recordist), Chen Weixiong (recordist); fx, Ding Yunda, Deng Weijue, Cheng Xiaolong; cos, Yao Huiming; makeup, Guan Lina

Drama/Romance/Comedy **(PR: C MPAA: R)**

CITIZEN RUTH ★★
(U.S.) 126m Lucky Guess; Independent Pictures; Miramax ~ Miramax c

Laura Dern *(Ruth Stoops)*; Swoosie Kurtz *(Diane Sieglar)*; Kurtwood Smith *(Norm Stoney)*; Mary Kay Place *(Gail Stoney)*; Kelly Preston *(Rachel)*; M. C. Gainey *(Harlan)*; Kenneth Mars *(Dr. Charlie Rollins)*; David Graf *(Judge Richter)*; Kathleen Noone *(Nurse Pat)*; Tippi Hedren *(Jessica Weiss)*; Burt Reynolds *(Blaine Gibbons)*; Lance Rome *(Ruth's Lover)*; Jim Kaal *(Tony Stoops)*; Shea Degan *(Arresting Officer)*; Vince Morelli *(ER Doctor)*; Marilyn Tipp *(Kathleen)*; Lois Nemec *(Sandy)*; Tim Vandeberghe *(Bail Clerk)*; Sebastian Anzaldo III *(Matthew Stoney)*; Alicia Witt *(Cheryl Stoney)*; Mick McDonald *(Party Dude)*; Okley Gibbs *(Norm's Manager)*; Roberta Larson *(Briana)*; Pam Carter *(Fran)*; Steven Wheeldon *(Kirk)*; Billie Barnhouse-Diekman; John Lapuzza *(Clinic Protesters)*; Susan Stern *(Cindy Lindstrom)*; Jeffrey L. Goos *(News Anchor)*; James Devney *(Officer Iverson)*; Tim Driscoll *(Officer Bundy)*; Caveh Zahedi *(Peter)*; David Hirsch *(Man in Motel Lobby)*; Gail Erwin *(Woman in Motel Lobby)*; Tony Wike *(Anecdote-telling Man)*; Sherry Josand Fletcher *(Helpful Registration Woman)*; Jim Delmont *(Press Conference Reporter)*; Dennis Grant *(Don Mattox)*; Will Jamieson *(Surveillance Guy)*; Jeremy Sczepaniak *(Eric)*; Delaney Driscoll *(Ruth's "Sister")*; R. D. "Cuz" O'Connell *(Biker)*; Judith Hart *(Sarah Schneider)*; Joan Pirkle *(Dr. Cary Milton)*; Lorie Obradovich *(Receptionist)*; Joan Hennecke *(Nurse)*; Mike Tourek *(Guy Hit by Toilet Lid)*; Katrina Christensen *(Ruth's Kid)*; John Bell *(Ruth's Kid)*; Jeff "J. J." Johnson; Fred Lovelace; Ed Morehouse; Jim Reinken; Wm. J. "Billy Bob" Muddle *(Harlan's Biker Friends)*

CITIZEN RUTH may be the first cinematic social satire on the subject of abortion. Such material is bound to offend, but what makes this "comedy" truly odious is the way it makes everyone look foolish for the sake of humor that just isn't funny.

Ruth Stoops (Laura Dern) is a homeless young midwestern woman who, during her umpteenth arrest for hazardous vapor inhalation, discovers she is pregnant for the fifth time. The judge in her case offers her a deal: if she has an abortion, he will reduce her charges. While considering the proposal in her jail cell, Ruth is joined by a group of "right-to-life" protesters, four housewives who take umbrage when they learn of the judge's offer.

Soon, Ruth is bailed out of jail and taken into the home of one of the wives, Gail (Mary Kay Place), whose husband, Norm (Kurtwood Smith), is a leader of a local right-to-life movement called the Baby Savers. While Gail and Norm shelter Ruth from the media and try to encourage her to have her baby, Ruth takes advantage of their hospitality. Unable to deal with Ruth's self-destructive ways, Norm Norm and Gail hand her over to their friend, Diane (Swoosie Kurtz). Diane gladly takes Ruth off their hands because she is actually a mole in the Baby Savers camp, a pro-choice veteran who wants Ruth to have her abortion and send a message to the conservative activists who block family planning clinics.

During her stay with Diane, Ruth becomes more confused than ever. The ever increasing media circus keeps her from stepping outside Diane's home, but she learns from television coverage that the country's right-to-life guru, Blaine Gibbons (Burt Reynolds), is offering a substantial financial reward if Ruth takes her pregnancy to term. Realizing that Ruth will be under the influence of the conservatives, Diane's war-veteran friend, Harlan (M.C. Gainey), ups the ante on Blaine's payment. Ruth secretly miscarries, but takes Harlan's money anyway, escaping from both groups of extremists to start a new life as a real estate investor.

CITIZEN RUTH begins somewhat promisingly with Frank Sinatra's rendition of "All the Way" accompanying Ruth's lousy sexual experience (the start of the trouble) in her boyfriend's grimy apartment. As Ruth, Dern appears to be parodying Jodie Foster's petulant "white trash" victim in THE ACCUSED, running up against a cruel society that turns a cold shoulder to her plight. But after a few minutes, the dark comedy becomes foolish, poorly timed and repetitious.

Clearly, first-time director and co-writer Alexander Payne is trying to satirize the fanaticism on both sides of the abortion debate, but he does so at the expense of developing the characters and story. The events that occur are more sad than funny, which leaves the cartoon-like depictions by the cast looking awkward at best. Payne's equitable misanthropy is also questionable, for it's easier to accept the anti-choice protesters as religious zealots than the pro-choice contingent as New Age lesbians (and no one with an opinion looks very good). CITIZEN RUTH aims to be THE MIRACLE OF MORGAN'S CREEK for the 1990s, but ends up no better than a sitcom episode. *(Violence, nudity, sexual situations, adult situations, substance abuse, extreme profanity.)* — E.M.

d, Alexander Payne; p, Cary Woods, Cathy Konrad; co-p, Andrew Stone; w, Alexander Payne, Jim Taylor; ph, James Glennon; ed, Kevin Trent; m, Rolfe Kent; prod d, Jane Ann Stewart; set d, Lisa Denker; sound, Jay Patterson; fx, Wes Clowers; casting, Lisa Beach; cos, Tom McKinley; makeup, Angela Margolis-Moos

Comedy/Drama **(PR: C MPAA: R)**

CITY HALL ★★★

(U.S.) 111m Ken Lipper Productions; Edward R. Pressman Corporation; Castle Rock ~ Columbia c

Al Pacino *(Mayor John Pappas)*; John Cusack *(Kevin Calhoun)*; Bridget Fonda *(Marybeth Cogan)*; Danny Aiello *(Frank Anselmo)*; Martin Landau *(Judge Walter Stern)*; David Paymer *(Abe Goodman)*; Tony Franciosa *(Paul Zapatti)*; Richard Schiff *(Larry Schwartz)*; Lindsay Duncan *(Sydney Pappas)*; Nestor Serrano *(Detective Eddie Santos)*; Mel Winkler *(Detective Holly)*; Lauren Velez *(Elaine Santos)*; Chloe Morris *(Maria Santos)*; Ian Quinlan *(Randy Santos)*; Roberta Peters *(Nettie Anselmo)*; Angel David *(Vinnie Zapatti)*; Larry Romano *(Tino Zapatti)*; Rob LaBelle *(Wakeley)*; Ray Aranha *(James Bone)*; Jaliyl Lynn *(James Bone, Jr.)*; John C. Vennema *(Peter Ragan)*; Steve Aronson *(Murray Safire)*; Jerome X. O'Donovan *(Seymour Harris)*; Mark Lonow *(Lenny Lasker)*; Murphy Guyer *(Captain Florian)*; John Finn *(Commissioner Coonan)*; Richard Gant *(Deputy Commissioner Samuels)*; Tamara Tunie *(Leslie Christos)*; Fran Brill *(Angie)*; Brian Murray *(Corporation Council)*; John Slattery *(Intel Detective—George)*; Benny Nieves *(Intel Detective—Jaime)*; Miguel Sierra *(Israel Torres)*; Sylvia Kauders *(Gussie)*; Brenda Thomas *(Clara)*; Gerry Vichi *(Milton)*; Ernest F. Hollings *(Senator Marquand)*; Jordan Baker *(Mrs. Marquand)*; Reverend Leonard Chapman *(Reverend Chapman)*; Tony Capone *(Billy—"Carousel")*; Jennifer Prescott *(Julie—"Carousel")*; Reverend Joseph Kelly S.J. *(Hospital Priest)*; Harry Bugin *(Morty the Waiter)*; Ron L. Cox *(Prosecutor)*; Kaity Tong; Amy Atkins; Brenda Pressley; Michael O'Looney; Carl White; Mary Murphy; Justin Ashforth; Charles Gemmill; Gina Rice *(Field Reporters)*; Roma Torre; Jack Cafferty; Lewis Dodley; Edward I. Koch *(Newscasters)*; Stanley Anderson *(Train Conductor)*; Sally Mayes *(Floyd Diner Waitress)*; Lucia Mendoza *(Elaine Santos' Sister)*; Geoffrey Wade *(Gracie Mansion Butler)*; Gloria K. Smith *(Female Vocalist—Soprano)*; James F. Gainer *(Male Vocalist—Bass)*

New York City's powerful political machinery is the star of CITY HALL, an involved and involving film in which some artistic gaffes, a lack of visual flair, and a limited sense of city life are compensated for by some good performances and admirable dramatic restraint.

On a Brooklyn street, a six-year-old African-American boy is killed in the crossfire between an off-duty cop and a drug dealer. Deputy Mayor Kevin Calhoun (John Cusack) soon becomes aware of the incident and informs his boss, the fiery, populist Mayor John Pappas (Al Pacino). Pappas assigns Calhoun to quell any suspicions about the episode, but in the process of the investigation, the idealistic Calhoun and an equally earnest attorney, Marybeth Cogan (Bridget Fonda), begin believing that a cover-up has taken place.

While Pappas reaches out to his African-American constituency during the church funeral for the boy, Calhoun and Cogan try to understand the unholy alliance between Pappas and Frank Anselmo (Danny Aiello), a Brooklyn political boss with Mafia ties who has been requesting pork barrel "goodies" in exchange for supporting BankExchange, a mayoral development project.

What Calhoun and Cogan finally realize is that Anselmo had put pressure on a well-regarded judge, Walter Stern (Martin Landau), to release the murderous drug dealer, a nephew of a Mafia don, on probation. Anselmo kills himself when the facts come to light, but Calhoun also learns—to his surprise—that his idol, Pappas, was aware of the crime all along. Sick of the corruption around him, Calhoun decides to run for office himself—as a reformer.

CITY HALL is reminiscent of John Sayles's CITY OF HOPE (1992), which also dealt with metropolitan politics and a variety of characters within a city hall setting. Together, the two films make a masterpiece, but individually, they suffer from opposite problems. Whereas CITY HALL features an interesting plot and generally realistic dialogue (courtesy of the all-star writing team of Ken Lipper, Paul Schrader, Nicolas Pileggi, and Bo Goldman), CITY OF HOPE has laughably bad dialogue. On the other hand, CITY OF HOPE's lively, even poetic camerawork far outclasses the stylistic choices of CITY HALL's director, Harold Becker. Had Sidney Lumet (on a good day) made CITY HALL, perhaps it would have been the masterpiece it should have been.

In any case, this dramatic re-working of several real New York City scandals from the last decade maintains interest without resorting to an overtly melodramatic style. The solid screenplay works similarly to Lumet's Q&A (1990), in that the plot twists and surprises come about naturally.

Best of all, four of the performers make their roles multi-dimensional: Pacino, Landau, Tony Franciosa (as a mafioso) and Aiello. Pacino and Aiello are particularly skillful at conveying the tragic dimensions of populist politicians who become corrupt (Anselmo's fondness for Rodgers and Hammerstein is a nice touch). Nominal leads Cusack (who played a similar part in TRUE COLORS, 1991) and Fonda give less-interesting performances in less-interesting roles, but they don't hurt the film.

The director's undistinguished visual style does, however. So do the various ethnic stereotype bits and nondescript, non-iconographic settings that make CITY HALL's New York seem like CITY OF HOPE's fictionalized city.

Only one scene, however, stands out as truly offensive and badly done—the mayor's rousing sermon (in front of a painting of Jesus!) during the church funeral for the young African-American victim. Given New York City's history of racial division and the fact that few recent New York mayors have been well-received in this setting, CITY HALL derails badly here. But it gets back on track in time to tell a most interesting tale in a mildly interesting way. *(Violence, profanity.)* — E.M.

d, Harold Becker; p, Edward R. Pressman, Ken Lipper, Charles Mulvehill, Harold Becker; assoc p, Thomas Mack; w, Ken Lipper, Paul Schrader, Nicholas Pileggi, Bo Goldman; ph, Michael Seresin; ed, Robert C. Jones, David Bretherton; m, Jerry Goldsmith; prod d, Jane Musky; art d, Robert Guerra; set d, Robert J. Franco; sound, Tod A. Maitland (mixer); fx, Steven Kirshoff; casting, John Lyons; cos, Richard Hornung; makeup, Bernadette Mazur; stunts, Mike Russo

Drama/Political/Crime (PR: C MPAA: R)

CLUBHOUSE DETECTIVES ★

(U.S.) 85m Silver State Productions ~ A-Pix c

Michael Ballam *(Michael)*; Michael Galeota *(Billy Rackman)*; Jimmy Galeota *(Kade Rackman)*; Suzanne Barnes *(Vicky Rackman)*; Christopher Ball *(Eddie)*; Thomas Hobson *(Jimmy)*; Alex Mirand *(J. J.)*; Lillian Cabal *(News Media)*; James Claffin *(Harvey)*; Thom Dillon *(Policeman)*; Alisa Harris *(Marcela)*; Carolyn Hurlburt *(Theater Woman)*

Once upon a time, there was an immaculately designed thriller entitled THE WINDOW (1949). Its boy-who-cried-wolf premise has been ripped off many times since, including this movie about a contingent of generic Little Rascals on the trail of a neighborhood murderer.

Overly curious Billy Rackman (Michael Galeota) spends his time dealing with his tagalong younger brother, Kade (Jimmy Galeota), running unsolicited interference between his mom (Suzanne Barnes) and her dates, and hanging out with his chums at their Blue Heaven Clubhouse. Billy witnesses next-door neighbor Michael (Michael Ballan), a well-known composer, strangling his lover Marcela (Alisa Harris) to death. Having plagiarized her musical composition, Michael eliminated Marcela to save his good name.

Billy's mom doesn't believe a word of her son's improbable tale. After snooping around the killer's house, Billy's suspicion that Marcela's corpse was stashed in a freezer proves unfounded. Michael stashes Marcela's body in a crawlspace and prepares to move out of town. But he has already slipped up, having given his piano student Kade some sheet music bearing Marcela's name. With the sporadic assistance of his buddies, Billy locates Marcela's body but gets cornered by a frantic Michael under the latter's porch. Fortunately, Kade saves the day by phoning 911 before turning up to protect older brother Billy from Michael, who's unable to escape.

Leaving to parents the question of whether digging up a corpse is really suitable comedic fodder for a children's video, other adult viewers are left with an inconsistent suspense comedy with kids who unmask a killer in their spare time rather than building a go-cart or winning the Little League game. Cast with a bevy of talentless players, CLUBHOUSE DETECTIVES washes over viewers of all ages in waves of undistinguished writing and direction, as unscary as it is unfunny. *(Violence, adult situations.)* — R.P.

d, Eric Hendershot; p, Eric Hendershot, Dicklyn Hendershot; exec p, Richard A. Malott; assoc p, Troy Rohovit; w, Eric Hendershot; ph, T.C. Christensen; ed, Michael Amundsen; m, Alan Williams; prod d, Steve Lee; set d, Rob Bennett; sound, Doug Cameron (mixer); casting, Shancy Pierce, Roz Soulam; cos, Camille Morris; makeup, Barbara Page; stunts, Fenton Quinn

Children's/Adventure/Thriller (PR: AA MPAA: PG)

COLD COMFORT FARM ★★★½

(U.K.) 95m BBC Films; Thames International ~ Gramercy Pictures c

Eileen Atkins *(Judith Starkadder)*; Kate Beckinsale *(Flora Poste)*; Sheila Burrell *(Ada Doom)*; Stephen Fry *(Mybug)*; Freddie Jones *(Adam Lambsbreath)*; Joanna Lumley *(Mrs. Smiling)*; Ian McKellen *(Amos Starkadder)*; Miriam Margolyes *(Mrs. Beetle)*; Rufus Sewell *(Seth)*; Ivan Kaye *(Reuben)*; Jeremy Peters *(Urk)*; Maria Miles *(Elfine)*; Christopher Bowen *(Charles Fairford)*; Louise Rea *(Meriam Beetle)*; Sophie Revell *(Rennet)*; Rupert Penry-Jones *(Dick Hawk-Monitor)*; Angela Thorne *(Mrs. Hawk-Monitor)*; Tim Myers *(Mr. Hawk-Monitor)*; Harry Ditson *(Earl P. Neck)*; Trevor Baxter *(Sneller)*; Frederick Jaeger *(Doctor Adolf Mudel)*; Pat Keen *(Aunt Gwen)*; Robert James *(Mr. McKnag)*; William Masson *(Bikki)*; Susannah Morley *(Mrs. Murther)*; Richard Bebb *(Hawk-Monitor Butler)*; William Osborne *(Coiffeur)*; Basil Hoskins *(Couturier)*; Allison Roberts *(Girl in Hayloft)*; Ninka Scott *(Tea Shop Waitress)*; Myfanwy Hill *(Young Ada Doom)*

COLD COMFORT FARM, directed by John Schlesinger, is a lively, satire set in rural 1930s England. Based on the 1932 novel by English author Stella Gibbons, it offers broad and familiar fare.

Suddenly orphaned at age 20, Flora Poste (Kate Beckinsale) finds herself with a mere 100 pounds a year income and few prospects. Pretty, clever, and determined to become a writer a la D.H. Lawrence, she refuses to go to work, preferring to find some distant relative who would be undoubtedly delighted to take her in. "I have such a lot in common with Jane Austen," Flora tells her best friend Mrs. Smiling (Joanna Lumley), "Neither of us could endure mess," and she's certain her organizational skills would be an asset to anyone. Unfortunately, aside from the amorous advances of amateur aviator Charles Fairford (Christopher Bowen), the only acceptable offer comes from the Starkadders, a grim clan living at Cold Comfort, a bleak Sussex farm. Upon her arrival, Flora is appalled by the disheveled homestead and its miserable inhabitants, all of whom appear quite mad. Flora's cousin Judith (Eileen Atkins) whiles away the hours dealing Tarot cards and bemoaning her fate; Judith's husband Amos (Ian McKellen) preaches terrifying fire-and-brimstone sermons at the Church of the Quivering Brethren; their two sons, Seth (Rufus Sewell), a handsome lothario with a yen for Hollywood glamour, and Reuben (Ivan Kaye), who fears Flora has come to steal the farm, spend most of their time seducing the local lasses; and young Elfine (Maria Miles), a Bloomsbury wanna-be, loves the son of the local gentry, Dick Hawk-Monitor (Rupert Penry-Jones), but is promised to her lecherous cousin Urk (Jeremy Peters). The whole lot are ruled by the tyrannical shut-in Ada Doom (Sheila Burrell), the ancient matriarch who, as a child, "saw something nasty in the woodshed," an incident she's never been quite able to forget, or explain. She convinces her wretched brood that they're living under some obscure Starkadder curse and are forbidden ever to leave Cold Comfort Farm. Flora has her work cut out for her.

Undaunted, Flora immediately sets about straightening up the Starkadders' doom-laden way of life and, with a little help from Mrs. Smiling, she's a smashing success. She hooks up depressed Judith with a world-famous psychoanalyst (Frederick Jaeger); convinces Amos to invest in a Ford van so he can travel around the country spreading the Gospel, thereby leaving the farm to Reuben; introduces Seth to a famous movie producer (Harry Ditson), who takes him to Hollywood; and finally works a bit of Henry Higgins-style magic on Elfina, transforming her into an acceptable addition to the gentile Hawk-Monitor family. Flora has even broken the crusty surface of Ada who, at Elfina and Dick's wedding at the refurbished Cold Comfort Farm, announces that she's leaving for a tour of France. With every loose end tied, Flora even manages to tidy up her own life when she agrees to leave Cold Comfort Farm in the cockpit of Charles Fairford's biplane.

This is your basic "fish out of water" tale, in the vein of city mouse in the country, though novelist Malcolm Bradbury's clever adaptation wisely avoids parable. While Gibbons' novel could be dry and earnest, its humor almost camouflaged, Schlesinger's film is outspoken and robust. Ironically, in light of the movie's emphasis on the rural, COLD COMFORT FARM's most memorable scenes are those that take place in London, where smart photography and witty production design dazzle the audience. Once back in the boondocks, the movie is lively enough, but its eager-to-please air steers clear of subtlety. Schlesinger has recruited a very talented cast, with Beckinsale charming as the dogged sophisticate on a mission; Atkins endowing Judith with formidable presence; McKellen amusingly homespun; Stephen Fry likeable as the eccentric writer Mybug, who becomes hopelessly smitten with Flora; and Lumley delightfully daft as Mrs. Smiling, a London socialite who happens to be a devoted collector of brassieres. *(Sexual situations, profanity.)* — E.K.

d, John Schlesinger; exec p, Richard Broke, Antony Root; assoc p, Joanna Gueritz; w, Malcolm Bradbury (based on the novel by Stella Gibbons); ph, Chris Seager; ed, Mark Day; m, Robert Lockhart; prod d, Malcolm Thornton; art d, Jim Holloway; sound, Jim Greenhorn (recordist); fx, Mike Kelt, Jeremy King; casting, Noel Davis; cos, Amy Roberts; makeup, Dorka Nieradzik

Drama/Romance/Comedy **(PR: C MPAA: PG)**

COLD FEVER ★★★★

(U.S./Iceland/Germany/Denmark) 85m
Icelandic Film Corp.; Pandora Film; Sunrise Inc.; Zentropa Entertainments; Icicle Films ~ Artistic License Films c

Masatoshi Nagase *(Atsushi Hirati)*; Lili Taylor *(Jill)*; Fisher Stevens *(Jack)*; Gisli Halldorsson *(Siggi)*; Laura Hughes *(Laura)*; Seijun Suzuki *(Grandfather)*

A young Japanese man's pilgrimage to honor his dead parents turns into a funny, odd, and even harrowing adventure in COLD FEVER, a little-seen independent release. Director Fridrik Thor Fridriksson introduces his native Iceland through this surprisingly engaging story.

In Tokyo, executive Atsushi Hirati (Masatoshi Nagase) looks forward to his annual Christmas vacation in sunny Hawaii. Atsushi's plans change, however, when his grandfather (Seijun Suzuki) requests that he perform a memorial ceremony for his parents at their death site in distant, cold Iceland. Atsushi wavers, but once he decides to go, he becomes determined, no matter what obstacles lie in his way.

Atsushi arrives in Iceland and rents a car to drive to the remote town. Along the route he meets an American psychic, Laura (Laura Hughes), who likes to photograph funerals, and he is helped by an elderly Icelandic couple when his car breaks down. Later on, he picks up a hitchhiking couple from the US, Jack (Fisher Stevens) and Jill (Lili Taylor). At first, Atsushi welcomes their company, but he quickly tires of their demanding, foul-mouthed manner. At a rest stop, Jack holds up a convenience store, makes a getaway, then throws Atsushi out of his car. Realizing too late that he had been transporting criminals, Atsushi has little choice but to walk the rest of the way through the empty, white wilderness.

After Atsushi finds a hotel for the night, he learns that he may not be able to get to his destination because of the ice cover in the mountains. But, in a nearby diner, he meets an elderly native, Siggi (Gisli Halldorsson), who promises to help him with the rest of his journey. Siggi's knowledge of the terrain enables Atsushi to arrive—finally—at his destination, where he performs the burial rites.

COLD FEVER's limited release in 1996 may have had something to do with its unusual setting and its mixing of cultures, yet these very elements make the film so winning. Like the work of Jim Jarmusch, with whom producer and co-writer Jim Stark often works, COLD FEVER benefits from delineating similarities and differences among people "thrown together" under strange (and strained) circumstances. The use of a young Japanese protagonist also may have put off some Western viewers, though, ironically, the character of Atsushi is more "Western" and accessible than many of the English-speaking oddballs he encounters. Masatoshi Nagase's performance is low-key and affecting, and director Fridriksson made an interesting choice in casting a noted filmmaker, Japanese maverick Seijun Suzuki, to play his grandfather.

The use of a Japanese protagonist also allows Fridriksson and Stark to indict the racist joking of "Jack and Jill" without overstating the point. Stevens and Taylor play this obnoxious couple with zest. Ultimately, Atsushi's journey merges with the viewer's because the beautiful but haunting tundra is just as new to him as it is to most viewers. Some of the other fellow travelers—Laura, a gravedigger, and, most of all, Siggi—offer philosophical musings that are alternately provocative and charming. Siggi's theory about ghosts and their predilection for islands is particularly interesting. COLD FEVER marks the end of Fridriksson's trilogy about mystical rites and spirits, which started with CHILDREN OF NATURE and MOVIE DAYS.

The flaws of COLD FEVER are minor and forgivable—a scene with a little girl apparition that owes too much to Jerzy Skolimowski's THE SHOUT (1978), and a overextended musical interlude in the diner. For most of the film, Hilmar Orn Hilmarsson's score sets the just the right, other-worldly mood.

This is one "road" picture that departs from the traditional route and finds its own, unique path. *(Substance abuse, mild profanity.)* — E.M.

d, Fridrik Thor Fridriksson; p, Jim Stark; exec p, Fridrik Thor Fridriksson, Christa Saredi, Reinhard Brundig, Peter Aalbaek Jensen; co-p, George Gund; w, Jim Stark, Fridrik Thor Fridriksson; ph, Fridrik Thor Fridriksson; ed, Steingrimur Karlsson; prod d, Arni Poll Johansson; sound, Kjartan Kjartansson

Comedy **(PR: A MPAA: NR)**

COLD LIGHT OF DAY ★★★

(Netherlands) 100m Meteor Film Productions; PolyGram; Capitol Films ~ PolyGram Video c

Richard E. Grant *(Victor Marek)*; Lynsey Baxter *(Milena Tatour)*; Perdita Weeks *(Anna Tatour)*; Simon Cadell *(Vladimir Kozant)*; James Laurenson *(Pavel Novak)*; Heathcote Williams *(Stephen Nuslauer)*; Thom Hoffman *(Alexi Berka)*; Gerard Thoolan *(Jan Pastorek)*; Roger Sloman *(Ludek Dittmayer)*; Elizabeth McKechnie *(Eva Pastorek)*; Joanna Dickens *(Old Lady at Gas Station)*; Jade Hope *(Jana Katsler)*; Vladimir Kulhavy *(Martin Wittman)*; Boudewijn de Groot *(Dog Owner)*; Robert Cavanagh *(Policeman at Caves)*; Natasa Hanusova *(Desk Policewoman)*; Marta Hrachovinova *(Schoolteacher)*; Nina Jirankova *(Headmaster)*; Nela Boudova *(Policewoman with Pictures)*; Amber Taylor *(Lady at Antiques Shop)*

Among the many serial killer movies crowding the video racks, THE COLD LIGHT OF DAY stands out as a creepy, disturbing piece of work.

In an Eastern European village, a young girl is found murdered and stripped naked in the woods. A vagrant is arrested for the crime, despite the protests of detective Victor Marek (Richard E. Grant) that they have the wrong man. When the suspect kills himself, the police close the case. Victor resigns from the force but continues to investigate on his own. Deducing that the killer traveled a certain roadway, Victor takes over operation of a gas station on the route and invites homeless mother and daughter Milena (Lynsey Baxter) and Anna (Perdita Weeks) to live with him in the adjoining house. Victor hopes young Anna's presence will attract the real killer, and sure enough, she catches the attention of the psycho, pediatrician Vladimir Kozant (Simon Cadell).

Victor gradually develops real feelings for Milena, who has become suspicious of his activities, and finds himself compelled to tell her the truth. Furious, Milena makes ready to leave with Anna, and Victor's former police colleagues arrive to take him away. At the same time, however, Kozant has lured Anna into the woods. Victor escapes from the cops and confronts him. Kozant takes Milena hostage, but Victor is able to outwit him and Milena shoots Kozant dead. Later, Victor and Milena are reconciled.

The character of a heroic cop protecting an innocent woman from a threatening psycho has become a cliche, but THE COLD LIGHT OF DAY adds a dark, compelling twist. Consumed by his pursuit of the madman, Victor initially thinks nothing of putting little Anna in danger and only confesses the truth to Milena when it is almost too late. Grant is perfect for the role, possessing both the necessary edge and also the innate humanity to keep Victor from becoming overly unsympathetic. Baxter holds her own as a strong-willed woman who is anything but a helpless heroine, and Cadell is genuinely frightening as the villain.

Dutch director Rudolf van den Berg, whose previous film THE JOHNSONS (1992) was more explicitly horrific, treads on some touchy ground in dealing with a child sex-killer. But his approach, while direct, remains unexploitative, and he creates several chillingly suggestive moments; the first we see of Kozant, for example, is his hands gently pressing on a little girl's bare stomach in his clinic. Van den Berg also brings a redeeming panache to such token scenes as the killer fetishistically fondling children's dolls and the climactic standoff between Victor and Kozant, who is given a depth of pathology not seen in most screen psychos.

The credits somewhat misstate the story's origins, citing the title of a German film also based on Friedrich Durrenmatt's book, which is actually titled *Das Versprechen* ("The Pledge").*(Violence, nudity, adult situations, profanity.)* — M.G.

d, Rudolf van den Berg; p, Chris Brouwer, Haig Balian; w, Doug Magee (based on the story "Es geschah am hellichten Tag" by Friedrich Durrenmatt); ph, Igor Luther; ed, Kant Pan; m, Stefan Truyman, Yves Elegeert; art d, Zdenek Fleming; sound, Roberto van Eijden, Jeremy Child; casting, Karen Lindsay Stewart; cos, Linda Bogers; makeup, Derrick Bosch, Dick Naostepad, Libuse Barlova

Thriller **(PR: O MPAA: R)**

COLONY, THE ★★½

(U.S.) 93m MCA Television ~ MCA/Universal Home Video c

John Ritter *(Rick Knowlton)*; Hal Linden *(Phillip Denning)*; Mary Page Keller *(Leslie Knowlton)*; Alexandra Picatto *(Dannielle Knowlton)*; Cody Dorkin *(Andy Knowlton)*; Marshall Teague *(Doug Corwin)*; Todd Jeffries *(Mike Knowlton)*; June Lockhart *(Mrs. Billingsley)*; John Wesley *(Jerry Franklin)*; Frank Bonner *(Frank Barnett)*; Michele Scarabelli *(Sandi Barnett)*; Shirley Spangler *(Mary)*; Don Gilvezan *(Steve)*; Douglas Rowe *(Forensics Officer)*; Cynthia Harrison *(Realtor)*; Steve Kronish *(Elisberg)*; Karen Kim *(Audrey Benson)*; Rance Howard *(Stan Benson)*; Vince Deadrick Jr. *(Bob Benson)*; Stacy Courtney *(Mrs. Benson)*; Lesley Woods *(Carol Knowlton)*; Edith Fields *(Peg Benson)*; Colby French *(Security Guard)*; Richie Fenner *(Bradley)*; Brandon Lawrence *(Matthew Barnett)*; James Castle Stevens *(Jogging Officer)*; Brett Harman *(Night Patrol Officer)*

Despite a smashing opening sequence (the faked accidental death of two defectors), THE COLONY is less a nail-biting thriller than a cogent Big-Brother-is-Watching melodrama. Pitched in a twilight world reminiscent of 1975's THE STEPFORD WIVES, this anti-corporate, rabble-rousing social critique makes a frightfully compelling case against suburban migration.

Rattled by the urban crime scene and mesmerized by visionary exec Phillip Denning (Hal Linden), for whom his company is developing a foolproof alarm system, Rick Knowlton (John Ritter) jumps at the chance to move his wife Leslie (Mary Page Keller), computer-wiz teenager Dannielle (Alexandra Picatto), and artistic young son Andy (Cody Dorkin) to the Denning's secure enclave known as the Colony. Embracing their posh community's environmental control at first, Rick and Leslie inevitably have misgivings about the rigid rules and biases. While Rick's brother Mike (Todd Jeffries), a police detective, investigates a car accident involving Bob Benson (Vince Deadrick Jr.) on the Colony's perimeters, Rick senses something more insidious than conformity at hand and discovers a buried wire in all the homes' electronics systems.

After a rebellious resident "commits suicide," and the family dog is surgically altered to prevent his barking, Rick is sufficiently spooked to leave the Colony even if it means Denning will keep the equity in his house. However, the Knowltons' speedy departure is delayed by the kidnapping of Andy. After

Knowlton's brother is nearly electrocuted on the Colony's security fence, Dannielle finds an incriminating disk, which the late-Benson had hid because it proved Denning was bugging every home in his model housing project. Imprisoning the Knowltons in their dream house, Denning is ironically executed by his private police force when they answer the Knowlton's break-in call and spot Denning holding a handgun.

By the time the plucky Knowltons survive their terrorism, the complacent audience will have retreated far from the edge of their seats. Telegraphing its shudders, THE COLONY is too stage-managed and sanitized to be scary; the thrills can't build if the audience is keyed into every twist ahead of time. Although short on jitters, this Chamber of Commerce horror tale does have its moments as the squabbling family falls back on its own splintering resources to defeat a well-organized messianic control freak. So, if one doesn't approach this film as a chiller-diller, but as a cautionary tale about the hazards of perfection, then the viewer can enjoy a contemporary soap opera about "being careful what you wish for."

If Ritter isn't up to the demands of his role, he at least makes an adequate Everyman. Likewise, the supporting cast adequately conveys the film's scariest notion: Creepy model citizens make excellent bogeymen. *(Violence, profanity.)* — R.P.

d, Rob Hedden; p, Fern Field; exec p, Kevin Kelly Brown; w, Rob Hedden; ph, David Geddes; ed, Barry B. Leirer; m, Dennis McCarthy; prod d, Vincent Jefferds; set d, Susan Cordova; sound, Garry Cunningham; casting, Mark Tillman; cos, Robert Moore; makeup, Phyllis Temple; stunts, Jeff Jensen

Thriller/Drama **(PR: C MPAA: PG-13)**

CONDITION RED ★★½

(U.S./Finland) 83m Beyond the Law Inc.; Oak Island Films; Marianna Films; Zweites Deutsches Fernsehen; Pyramide Productions; Finnish Film Foundation ~ Arrow Releasing c

James Russo *(Dan Cappelli)*; Cynda Williams *(Gidell)*; Paul Calderon *(Angel)*; Victor Argo; Dierdre Lewis; Monique Cintron; Andre Degass; Anna Minot

A flawed attempt at a prison noir, CONDITION RED promises something intriguing but fails to deliver on it. Based on a real-life story, it's just a simple tale of a driven woman, a bad guy, and a fall guy.

Volatile corrections officer Dan Capelli (James Russo) works in a Philadelphia prison. He lives, he claims, "between two worlds, one inside and one outside." Capelli feels just as much a prisoner as the inmates he is in charge of, as if here were in what correction officers call "Condition Red," a state of alarm. After one too many violent attacks upon the men he guards, Capelli is transferred to the women's section of the penitentiary. He develops an interest in beautiful and sensitive Gidell (Cynda Williams), a first-time offender. With few words exchanged, they begin a secret affair, full of broom-closet trysts. Gidell is offered parole in exchange for evidence against her cocaine-dealing boyfriend, Angel (Paul Calderon), but she refuses.

When Angel suspects Gidell of having a prison affair, he gets rough with her. In revenge, the hot-tempered Capelli beats Angel up. Capelli gets suspended, and the lovers dream of each other, but can't seem to communicate, even during their stolen phone calls. When Gidell tells Capelli she's pregnant by him, he impulsively busts her out. While holed up in a motel on their way to Mexico, Gidell betrays her captor-liberator by calling Angel. Angel orders Gidell to tie Capelli up and the three of them drive off.

Capelli breaks free and attacks Angel. Although he tries to leave Gidell, he is unable to. At the airport, the couple is once again found by Angel, who is being followed by some criminals who have a vested interest in his business. In a shoot-out, both Angel and Gidell are killed. Shocked but resigned, Capelli drives off to Mexico, a hunted but free man.

CONDITION RED has a haunting quality that brings to mind better prison pictures like ESCAPE FROM ALCATRAZ and MIDNIGHT EXPRESS. Despite the film's budgetary limitations, Ken Kelsch's bare-boned cinematography makes the film surprisingly memorable. Russo gives an impressively restrained performance, proving once again that he is a vastly under-appreciated actor.

Despite these positive aspects, however, the film falls apart by the end. Capelli and Gidell's relationship lacks any real dimension, and as a result the film never escapes its action-movie roots. *(Violence, sexual situations, substance abuse, profanity.)* — J.D.

d, Mika Kaurismaki; p, Kenneth Schwenker, Andre Degass; exec p, Michael Bambihill; assoc p, Klaus Heydemann; w, Andre Degass; ph, Ken Kelsch; ed, Mika Kaurismaki, Suzanne Pillsbury; m, Mauri Sumen; prod d, Jeff Cox; art d, Stacy Tanner; sound, Pekka Karjalainen, Kauko Lindfors; casting, Mike Lemon; cos, Fran Hurley, Karin Leonard

Prison/Crime/Romance **(PR: O MPAA: R)**

CONUNDRUM

(SEE: FRAME BY FRAME)

COURAGE UNDER FIRE ★★½

(U.S.) 120m Davis Entertainment Company; Fox 2000 Pictures ~ 20th Century Fox c

Denzel Washington *(Nat Serling)*; Meg Ryan *(Karen Walden)*; Lou Diamond Phillips *(Monfriez)*; Michael Moriarty *(General Hershberg)*; Matt Damon *(Ilario)*; Bronson Pinchot *(Bruno)*; Seth Gilliam *(Altameyer)*; Regina Taylor *(Meredith Sterling)*; Zeljko Ivanek *(Banacek)*; Scott Glenn *(Gartner)*; Tim Guinee *(Rady)*; Tim Ransom *(Boylar)*; Sean Astin *(Patella)*; Armand Darrius *(Robins)*; Mark Adair-Rios *(Bobcat 5)*; Ned Vaughn *(Chelli)*; Manny Perez *(Jenkins)*; David McSwain *(Egan)*; Sean Patrick Thomas *(Thompson)*; Ken Jenkins *(Joel Walden)*; Kathleen Widdoes *(Geraldine Walden)*; Christina Stojanovich *(Anne Marie Walden)*; Lucky Luciano *(Nathan Serling, Jr.)*; Erica C. Newman *(Joleen Serling)*; Jamal A. Mays *(Brian Serling)*; Ashlee Jordan Pryor *(Josie Serling)*; Michole White *(Maria)*; Jeffrey Waid *(Hillerman)*; Patrick Young *(Drill Team Commander)*; Jimmy Ray Pickens *(Soldier)*; Jack Watkins *(Coffee Sergeant)*; Matt Sigloch *(Cadre)*; James Paul *(Morse)*; Bruce McGill *(McQuillan)*; Rory J. Aylward *(Teegarden's Crew Chief)*; Kyle Mickaelian *(Refueler)*; Michael Dolan *(Orderly)*; John Roarke *(The President)*; Tom Schanley *(Questioner)*; Bob Apisa *(Iraqi Tank Commander)*; Daniel Gonzalez *(Laughing Gunner)*; Albert Hall *(Speaker)*; Richard Venture *(Don Boylar)*; Diane Baker *(Louise Boylar)*; Amy Hathaway *(Annie)*; Reed Frerichs *(Delinquent Soldier)*; Julius Carter *(Rowtero)*

Ethical decisions in war and peacetime get a real workout in COURAGE UNDER FIRE, but this film about the investigation into the death of a captain during the 1991 Persian Gulf conflict ends up romanticized and reactionary.

COURAGE UNDER FIRE tells two stories simultaneously: the events leading up to the death of Capt. Karen Walden (Meg Ryan) and the struggles of Lt. Col. Nathaniel Serling (Denzel Washington) to uncover the truth about her demise. Serling has never recovered from a "friendly fire" incident in which men under his command fired on and killed several of their own, mistaking them for Iraqis. The army hushed the incident up.

Back in Washington, Gen. Hershberg (Michael Moriarty) protects the guilt-plagued Serling by giving him a routine Pentagon job reviewing the Medal of Honor candidates of the year. There is pressure to speed through Walden's case because the White House is eager to name her the first female recipient of the Medal. But as he interviews the survivors of the Medevac chopper on which Walden was pilot, Serling discovers that the events surrounding the Captain's death are far from clear-cut.

The team's medic, Ilario (Matt Damon), tells Serling that Walden died heroically in combat. Gunner Monfriez (Lou Diamond Phillips) describes Walden as a scared, ineffectual leader who died in shame. A third survivor, Altameyer (Seth Gilliam), is so ill he is unable to contribute any information. Serling delays his report to Hershberg when he discovers that Ilario has gone AWOL and that Altameyer has tried to commit suicide. But Serling's tenacity takes its toll on him both professionally and personally: Hershberg threatens to expose his "friendly fire" incident if he doesn't submit his report immediately; and Serling's wife, Meredith (Regina Taylor), threatens to leave him if he doesn't stop his excessive drinking. Serling's investigation is further complicated by the presence of a nosy *Washington Post* reporter, Tony Gartner (Scott Glenn), who could expose the "friendly fire" episode.

Serling finally tracks down Ilario and gets the real story. Monfriez staged a mutiny which left Walden alone to die while the rest of the unit escaped onto a rescue chopper. The men agreed to keep the truth a secret to avoid a court martial, but all became wracked with guilt. After Serling confronts him with the real story, Monfriez kills himself, but Serling also sees a liberating side to telling the truth. He recommends Walden for the Medal, and new evidence acquits his judgment in the "friendly fire" incident. He returns to his family a renewed man.

COURAGE UNDER FIRE updates an old-fashioned war film for the 1990s. Director Edward Zwick (who did the 1989 Civil War film GLORY, also with Denzel Washington) and screenwriter Patrick Sheane Duncan would rather address lofty themes about the meaning of heroism and truth-telling than shed any light on the US-led massacre known as the Persian Gulf War (Brian De Palma's 1989 film CASUALTIES OF WAR had the same problem *vis a vis* Vietnam, but partly made up for it with directorial style).

Perhaps more disturbingly, Zwick and Duncan turn the "friendly fire" subplot into an occasion for bathos over a tragic loss, rather than an opportunity to question the entire notion of war.

Ideological problems aside, COURAGE UNDER FIRE tells its story fairly well, but lacks dramatic fire. The RASHOMON (1950) structure surrounding Walden's death lends mystery and suspense to the primary investigation, but only one of the stories holds any truth, so the effect of the subjective point-of-view experiment is negated. Washington strains to make Serling's inner turmoil convincing, but the scenes with his family (including a poorly used Taylor as his wife) are sketchy and his liberation from alcohol (thanks to Alka-Seltzer!) seems downright silly.

The other performers fare only slightly better: Ryan's part seems more a dramatist's tool than a flesh-and-blood character; Moriarty mumbles in an odd accent and Glenn is barely used. By default, then, the best work comes from the three young actors playing the soldiers—Damon, Gilliam, and Philips. COURAGE UNDER FIRE can't help but stimulate interest at times, but if Zwick and company wanted to show the moral complexities that occur at war, their film lacks the courage of its own convictions. *(Violence, profanity.)* — E.M.

d, Edward Zwick; p, John Davis, Joseph M. Singer, David T. Friendly; exec p, Joseph M. Caracciolo, Debra Martin Chase; w, Patrick Sheane Duncan; ph, Roger Deakins; ed, Steven Rosenblum; m, James Horner; prod d, John Graysmark; art d, Steve Cooper; set d, Rick Gentz; sound, Rudy Pi (recordist), Mark Harris (recordist), Lon E. Bender (design); fx, Peter Michael Sullivan; casting, Mary Colquhoun; cos, Francine Jamison-Tanchuck; makeup, Edna Sheen; stunts, Ron Stein

Drama/War **(PR: C MPAA: R)**

CRACKER: THE MADWOMAN IN THE ATTIC ★★★
(U.K.) 100m Granada Television; A&E ~ A&E Home Video c

Robbie Coltrane *(Fitz)*; Adrian Dunbar *(Kelly)*; Nicholas Woodeson *(Hennessy)*; Lorcan Cranitch *(DS Jimmy Beck)*; Christopher Eccleston *(DCI Bilborough)*; Geraldine Somerville *(DS Penhaligon)*; Jeffrey Robert *(Head of Psychiatry)*; Louise Downie *(Jacqui Appleby)*; Ian Mercer *(DC Giggs)*; Ron Meadows *(Roberts)*; Paul Copley *(Pathologist)*; Kerry Shale *(Crime Scene Expert)*; Vincent Paul Davies *(Taxi Driver)*; Barbara Flynn *(Judith Fitzgerald)*; Kieran O'Brien *(Mark Fitzgerald)*; Tess Thomson *(Kate Fitzgerald)*; Peter Faulkner *(Mike)*; Kathy Jamieson *(Jo)*; Paulette Constable *(Waitress)*; Kika Markham *(Ann Appleby)*; John Grillo *(Simon Appleby)*; Vanessa Kirkpatrick *(Newscaster)*; Julie Westwood *(PR Woman)*; Philippa Howell *(Dr. Turner)*; Alan David *(Hanrahan)*; Tony Xu *(Dr. Soroya)*

In the course of unraveling complex murder cases, the CRACKER mysteries allow viewers time to dissect the personal crises of their sleuths. Although THE MADWOMAN IN THE ATTIC isn't the most chilling of these imports (made for British TV), it's a confidently directed and sleekly scripted study of complicated crime-solvers.

Although Detective Chief Inspector Bilborough (Christopher Eccleston) can't quickly crack a series of railway attacks on young women, he resents the interference of police psychologist Fitz (Robbie Coltrane), a gambling addict who doesn't suffer fools gladly. Flanked by ambitious Detective Sergeant Penhaligon (Geraldine Somerville) and sexist Detective Sergeant Jimmy Beck (Lorcan Cranitch), Bilborough arrests an amnesiac, Kelly (Adrian Dunbar), who apparently jumped from the train on which the most recent victim, Jacqui Appleby (Louise Downie), was killed. While the cops mercilessly badger Kelly, Fitz uncovers Kelly's Catholic background. As Fitz's personal life deteriorates in debt and drinking, he takes custody of the accused, who turns out to have been a priest. Kelly wanders off at the racetrack when he spots a familiar face. That face belongs not to the murderer but to a petty thief who rolled Kelly after he'd been pushed from the speeding train by the real murderer.

Police get phone calls from the sex maniac who claims to be a priest to whom Kelly confessed his crimes. Although axed from the investigation, Fitz refuses to abandon Kelly's cause. Fitz narrows the possible murder candidates to those with Catholic backgrounds. After prodding Kelly's memory in his jail cell, Fitz scans the railway manifests for likely suspects. With sympathetic Penhaligon's unofficial cooperation, Fitz narrows the field to one suspect, a traveling health inspector, Hennessey (Nicholas Woodeson), whose schedule coincided with all of the killings. Backed up by Penhaligon, Fitz boards a train bound for Leeds and stops Hennessey from killing another woman. Cleared of charges and having recovered his memory, Kelly contentedly returns to his cloistered life in a monastery.

Despite their adherence to a formula (police psychologist messes up his private life while miscalculating crucial evidence, finally correcting his theory), the CRACKER mysteries are superior examples of their genre. Without stinting on the deductive aspects, these character studies also penetrate protagonist Fitz's Achilles' heel, highlight interdepartmental rivalries at the precinct, and examine social issues raised by the case. It's remarkable how much cogent psychological insight and astute sociological commentary can be squeezed into these crackerjack mysteries without sacrificing suspense or focus.

In addition to atmospheric direction and gutsy screenwriting, THE MADWOMAN IN THE ATTIC features superb acting. Coltrane is painfully good at conveying the ruins of his flawed character, and he is matched by a dazzling supporting cast. Prickly and paranoid, the British detectives here are scared professionals who mask uncertainty with arrogance. The stressed-out criminologists are as intensely motivated as the fastidious killer going about his bloody business. In THE MADWOMAN IN THE ATTIC, proving who-dun-it reveals as much about the psychologically battered crime-busters as it does about the psychotic killer. *(Graphic violence, profanity, adult situations, substance abuse.)* — R.P.

d, Michael Winterbottom; p, Gub Neal; exec p, Sally Head; w, Jimmy McGovern; ph, Ivan Strasburg; ed, Trevor Waite; m, Julian Wastall; prod d, Chris Wilkinson; art d, Deborah Morley; sound, Phil Smith (mixer); fx, Peter Brayham; casting, Gail Stevens; cos, Janty Yates; makeup, Helen King; stunts, Peter Brayham, Chris Webb

Mystery/Crime **(PR: C MPAA: NR)**

CRAFT, THE ★★★

(U.S.) 105m Red Wagon Productions; Columbia ~ Columbia c

Robin Tunney *(Sarah)*; Fairuza Balk *(Nancy)*; Neve Campbell *(Bonnie)*; Rachel True *(Rochelle)*; Skeet Ulrich *(Chris)*; Christine Taylor *(Laura Lizzie)*; Breckin Meyer *(Mitt)*; Nathaniel Marston *(Trey)*; Cliff De Young *(Mr. Bailey)*; Assumpta Serna *(Lirio)*; Helen Shaver *(Grace)*; Jeanine Jackson *(Jenny)*; Brenda Strong *(Doctor)*; Elizabeth Guber *(Laura's Friend)*; Jennifer Greenhut *(Laura's Friend)*; Arthur Senzy *(Vagrant)*; Endre Hules *(Monsieur Thepot)*; Mark Conlon *(Swimming Coach)*; Christine Louise Berry *(Stewardess)*; William Newman *(Street Preacher)*; Erin Tavin *(Homeless Mother)*; Rod Britt *(Priest)*; Brogan Roche *(Insurance Man)*; Rebecca McLaughlin *(Biology Teacher)*; Tony Genaro *(Bus Driver)*; Janet Rotblatt *(Homeroom Teacher)*; Jason Filardi *(Paramedic)*; Karyn J. Dean *(Whispering Girl)*; Danielle Koenig *(Whispering Girl)*; Janet Eilber *(Sarah's Mother)*; Esther Scott *(Nurse)*

A refreshingly intelligent teen horror film, THE CRAFT presents witchcraft as a source of youthful female empowerment.

Teenager Sarah Bailey (Robin Tunney), whose mother died in childbirth and who once attempted suicide, arrives at St. Benedict's Academy. Unable to fit in with her peers, she falls in with an outcast clique consisting of the white-trash Nancy (Fairuza Balk), withdrawn burn victim Bonnie (Neve Campbell), and Rochelle (Rachel True), the school's only black student. The three reveal that they have been experimenting with witchcraft, and that Sarah, who has demonstrated minor occult abilities, can serve as the fourth participant needed to invoke magic.

The quartet are successful, and begin using their newfound powers to take control of their lives. Sarah casts a hopeless love spell on insensitive jock Chris (Skeet Ulrich); Bonnie's burns magically heal; Rochelle causes the bitchy Laura (Christine Taylor), who has tormented her, to lose her hair. After Nancy gives her abusive stepfather a heart attack, she and her mother, Grace (Helen Shaver), find themselves the recipients of a sizable insurance windfall.

But while her three friends let their newfound power go to their heads, Sarah begins to have doubts, particularly after Nancy causes Chris's death. This leads the trio, under Nancy's direction, to turn on Sarah, tormenting her with frightening visions. But Sarah, whose mother also practiced "the craft," is able to withstand them, and has a violent, black-magic battle with Nancy. Nancy ends up raving in an asylum. When Bonnie and Rochelle arrive to apologize to Sarah, she gives them a supernatural reminder to watch their steps in future.

Proof that it can be more fun to have adolescent girls be the antagonists, instead of helpless victims, in a horror film, THE CRAFT benefits from a realistic approach to its subject. It marks a significant step up for director Andrew Fleming from his previous two features. He examines the emotional concerns of his youthful characters in a far less indulgent manner than in THREESOME, and his terror tactics largely avoid the gimmickry of his BAD DREAMS. While it's not as scary as one might hope, this film commendably has other things on its mind.

Like his script for FLATLINERS, co-writer Peter Filardi's story charts the progress of a group of young people who dabble in the unknown and get in over their heads. This time, however, the four girls revel in the power they've awakened within themselves, and the ways in which they exploit their abilities are both wickedly funny and calmly chilling. For the most part, the film is exaggerated neither in its presentation of occult practices (it employed the services of a witchcraft consultant) nor in its emotions. Not since CARRIE (or, venturing outside the genre, HEATHERS) has high school seemed so hellish, even before the supernatural shenanigans begin.

By the climax, the story ventures into more traditional horror-film territory, with Sarah and Nancy engaging in a special-effects fight to the death. The scene never goes too far over the top, though, and Balk is a sight to behold as Nancy becomes increasingly (and literally) wigged-out. The other three actresses hold their own with sympathetic, believable performances that help to securely anchor THE CRAFT, unlike so many other youth-appeal chillers, in the realm of the recognizable. *(Violence, substance abuse, adult situations, profanity.)* — M.G.

d, Andrew Fleming; p, Douglas Wick; exec p, Ginny Nugent; co-p, Lisa Tornell; w, Peter Filardi, Andrew Fleming (from a story by Peter Filardi); ph, Alexander Gruszynski; ed, Jeff Freeman; m, Graeme Revell; prod d, Marek Dobrowolski; art d, Gae S. Buckley; set d, Nancy Nye; sound, Jim Stuebe (mixer); fx, David Kelsey, Kelley R. Ray, Mageara Cameron, Robin Griffin, Sony Imageworks; casting, Pam Dixon; cos, Deborah Everton; makeup, Jeffrey Hamilton, Tony Gardner, Alterian Studios, Inc.; stunts, Glory Fioramonti

Drama/Horror/Fantasy **(PR: C MPAA: R)**

CRIMINAL HEARTS ★½

(U.S.) 88m ~ WarnerVision c

Kevin Dillon *(Rafe)*; Amy Locane *(Keli)*; Morgan Fairchild *(D.A.)*; M. Emmet Walsh *(Martin)*; Michael James McDonald *(Tierney)*; Don Stroud *(Thackler)*; Carlos Palomino *(Ramon)*; Chelsea Madison Ciu *(Letra)*; Michael Todd Curry *(Steve)*; Patricia Elliott *(Good Samaritan)*; Bob McFarland *(Officer Duane)*; Emile Levisetti *(Yuma Sheriff)*; Rodger Halston *(L.A. Police Detective)*; Kirk Fox *(AZ Highway Patrolman)*; Lisa Boyle *(Claire)*; Rodman Flender *(Delivery Boy)*

In the crime adventure CRIMINAL HEARTS, an innocent young woman is ripped from her staid lifestyle when she teams up with a wanted man. With the southwest desert as their backdrop, these "Bonnie and Clyde wannabes" take on corrupt lawmen in this frantic highway thriller.

Keli (Amy Locane) is driving to Phoenix to confront her cheating fiancee, when she picks up Rafe (Kevin Dillon), who, unbeknownst to her, has just robbed a gas station, getting a surprisingly large amount of cash. They soon end up sharing a bottle of wine, as well as a bed, and it's only when Amy discovers a pistol under his pillow, that she becomes suspicious. It turns out that Rafe is actually robbing these stores of illicit drug money, but since someone else is later on killing these store owners, their murders are also being blamed on him. Soon, two corrupt FBI agents, Martin (M. Emmet Walsh) and Tierney (Michael James McDonald), are on the trail, taking time out to eliminate everyone who knows about their secret drug operation. Along the way, Keli and Rafe infiltrate a US Border Patrol warehouse, become captured by Mexican drug runners and tied to a cactus in the middle of the desert. Keli eventually makes it home with the money, thinking Rafe is dead. The FBI men storm in, having found the still-alive Rafe, and Keli shoots both of the Feds. Luckily, she first captures their confession on her answering machine, thus proving the young lovers' innocence.

Though the story offers little new, writer/director David Payne tries to cover up that fact by keeping his characters running back and forth across the desert, or turning on each other at a moment's notice. Believability plays little part in the proceedings. Thankfully, as Rafe, Dillon's wise-ass demeanor helps make up for Locane's ludicrous role as Keli, which overnight transforms her from a gun-shy innocent to a crack-shot action heroine. Meanwhile, solid character actors M. Emmet Walsh and Don Stroud serve time in quirky, but painfully underwritten, roles. And Morgan Fairchild fans mustn't get their hopes up—-she receives less than one minute of screen time. Despite some effective seedy locales, this movie remains a convoluted crime hodgepodge that moves fast, leaves a trail of corpses, and doesn't have a fresh idea in its head. *(Violence, nudity, sexual situations.)* — S.P.

d, David Payne; p, Mike Elliott; exec p, Lance H. Robbins; w, David Payne; ph, Christopher Baffa; ed, Brian Katkin; m, Tyler Bates; prod d, Trae King; art d, Brian Massey

Action/Crime/Drama (PR: O MPAA: R)

CROCODILES IN AMSTERDAM ★★

(Netherlands) 88m Orthel Filmproductie ~ Water Bearer Home Video c

Joan Nederlof *(Gino)*; Yolanda Entius *(Nina)*; Hans Hoes *(Jacque)*; Moral Musters *(Jerry)*; Trudie Lute *(Charlotte)*; Jaap ten Holt *(Peter)*; Evert van der Meulen *(Adje)*; Truus te Selle *(Moeder)*; Olga Zuiderhoek *(Mevrouw Top)*; Gahit Olmez *(Alex)*; Khaldoun El Mecky *(Koos)*; Fried Mertens *(Mike)*; Carel Alphenaar *(Uncle Victor)*; Daria Mohr *(Theresa)*; Ed Pols *(Garageman)*; Nancy Gould *(Tourist)*; Lieneke Le Roux *(Inez)*

This contemporary screwball comedy quickly wears out its welcome as two lesbians assault Amsterdam with their fetching lack of logic. Imagine a film featuring two clones of the dippy heiress Katherine Hepburn played in BRINGING UP BABY (1938), and you'll have some idea of the nuclear-strength dithery charm aimed at the helpless audience.

By sweet-talking loans out of her Uncle Victor (Carel Alphenaar) and perpetually apartment-sitting, Gino (Joan Nederlof) ekes out a living through the generosity of friends and relatives. Committed to revolutionary acts of robbery with her amateur terrorist friends, fractious Nina (Yolanda Entius) finds difficulty in marshaling her gang that can't even *bomb* straight. Hoping to explore less explosive forms of thievery, Nina befriends Gino with a plan to burglarize Uncle Victor's fancy digs. But unfortunately for Nina, Gino doesn't quite get with the program. During the women's tempestuous courtship, flighty Gino agrees to participate in the robbery but gets sidetracked not only by a scheme to buy her own house but also the pursuit of her ex-lover Jacques (Hans Hoes). Gino does manage to furnish Nina with an alarm clock for one of Nina's dynamite bombs, but it turns out to be a dud; so does the break-in at Uncle Victor's when Gino defects at the last minute. Even after Nina's disappointed cohorts ostracize her, she forgives Gino. Without their old boyfriends and gang members in the way, the two women commit to a relationship with each other.

Thanks to the leading actresses' comic *esprit de corps* and a determinedly offbeat, consistently breezy tone, CROCODILES IN AMSTERDAM is a bearably nutty caper, but nothing more. Suffering from a cuteness overdose, the film gamely resurrects screwball comedy stereotypes but regretfully seals them in an oxygen-deprived atmosphere of repetitive escapades and flat dialogue. And while it's refreshing to see lesbians featured in the kind of formulaic romantic comedy reserved for straight characters, the screenplay offers little to support this role transference. Inevitably, the crackpot crook Nina and the spoiled-brat sponge Gino aren't lovable enough to allow the audience to indulge their nerve-grating antics. *(Violence, adult situations.)* — R.P.

d, Annette Apon; p, Rolf Orthel; exec p, Eric Hafkamp; assoc p, Jetse Sprey; w, Yolanda Entius, Annette Apon, Henriette Remmers; ph, Bernd Wouthuysen; ed, Danniel Daniel; m, Henk van der Meulen; prod d, Ruben Schwartz; set d, Marieken Verheyen; sound, Erik Lanhout (mixer); fx, Hary Wiessenhaan; casting, Jeanette Snik; makeup, Trudy Buren

Comedy (PR: C MPAA: NR)

CROSSCUT ★★

(U.S.) 90m Pavlic/Raimondi Pictures ~ A-Pix Entertainment c

Costas Mandylor *(Martin Niconi)*; Megan Gallagher *(Anna Hennessey)*; Casey Sander *(Max Dodger)*; Allen Cutler *(Jeff Hennessey)*; Jay Acovone *(Frank)*; Christopher Stanley *(Jerry)*; Zack Norman *(Sheriff Moreland)*; Greg Collins *(Victor)*; Jed Reghanti *(Joey)*; George Murdock *(Uncle Leo)*; Doug Spinuzza *(Conni Trentillo)*; Richard Manzullo *(Al)*; Richard Gross *(Wally)*; Paul Ennis *(Gordy)*; Walter Norman *(Ollie)*; Ed Smith *(Clyde)*; Elise Rothberg *(Angie)*; Chopper Bernet *(Johnny)*; Ed Vasgersian *(Mr. Trentillo)*; Chris Pavlic *(Logger)*; Chris Passaro *(Bartender)*

The derivative CROSSCUT substitutes cinematic bravado for imagination and can be filed under generic mob movie.

Lamenting the good old days when his Dad was a powerful Mafia don, mob loyalist Martin Niconi (Costas Mandylor) toes the mark for the Trentillo Family. When the Boss's psychotic son Conni (Doug Spinuzza) shoots thick-witted Victor (Greg Collins) in a fit of pique, Martin blows heir apparent Conni away. To escape mob vengeance, Martin hightails it to a family cabin in a Northern California hamlet, where his Uncle Leo (George Murdoch) agrees to wire funds. Posing as an itinerant logger, Martin befriends fatherless teen Jeff Hennessey (Allen Cutler), who has a plan to save his village from environmental restrictions. He also falls for Jeff's mom, Anna (Megan Gallagher). Martin's desire to remain inconspicuous piques the curiosity of Anna's brother-in-law, Max (Cassey Sander), who delves into Martin's mob past.

After brutalizing and slaying Uncle Leo, the Trentillo enforcers hunt Martin down. Rolling into town, the Mafiosi blast away the village bartender, thus riling Sheriff Moreland (Zack Norman), who dies trying to corner the gangsters at Martin's remote cabin. As Martin and Anna fend off the big city avengers, the townspeople rally to even the odds. Victorious, Martin and Anna survive and relocate, and Jeff saves the dying town with Martin's gift of Uncle Leo's cash transfer.

This Timberland GOODFELLAS (1990) is directed as if its excitement content had been strained through a sieve. Only the character of Uncle Max, with his paranoia about the Feds and his pseudo-incestuous interest is his sister-in-law, has any interesting creases in his personality. The other half-baked players, especially Gallagher's pristine widow, are fashioned with dull cookie cutters.

Stalled in the same violent low gear throughout, CROSSCUT never kicks into high, although the number of homicides make an undisturbed sleep unlikely for viewers. Contributing to the boredom is Mandylor, who seems more preoccupied with standing in a flattering key light than in hitting histrionic high notes. CROSSCUT possesses the thin flavor of Ragu poured over boxed pasta, a pale imitation of robust and unmistakably homemade Italian fare. *(Graphic violence, sexual situations, extreme profanity, extensive nudity, substance abuse.)* — R.P.

d, Paul Raimondi; p, Jane Raimondi; exec p, John Pavlic, Bobbie Pavlic; w, David Masiel, Paul Raimondi, Scott Phillips; ph, David Bridges; ed, Christopher Holmes; m, Christopher Tyng; art d, Kerry Longacre; sound, Marshall Wiemer; fx, Larry Fioritto; casting, Donald Paul Pemrick; cos, Cathryn Wagner; makeup, Ann Wiemer; stunts, Rawn Hutchinson, Winston Omega

Action/Crime (PR: C MPAA: R)

CROW: CITY OF ANGELS, THE ★

(U.S.) 85m Bad Bird Productions; Edward R. Pressman Film Corp. ~ Miramax c

Vincent Perez *(Ashe)*; Mia Kirshner *(Sarah)*; Richard Brooks *(Judah)*; Iggy Pop *(Curve)*; Thomas Jane *(Nemo)*; Vincent Castellanos *(Spider Monkey)*; Thuy Trang *(Kali)*; Eric Acosta *(Danny)*; Ian Dury *(Noah)*; Tracey Ellis *(Sybil)*; Beverley Mitchell *(Grace)*; Aaron Thell Smith *(Tattoo Customer)*; Alan Gelfant *(Bassett)*; Shelly Desai *(Hindu)*; Holley Chant *(Holly Daze)*; Kerry Rossall *(Zeke)*; Reynaldo Duran *(Priest)*; Danny Verduzco *(Boy in Church)*; Maria Julia Moran *(Old Lady in Church)*; Deftones *(Day of the Dead Band)*

A gratuitous sequel, this misbegotten revenge fantasy attempts to replicate the original CROW (1994) without its charismatic star or any of its emotional power.

In the desolate, crime-ridden Los Angeles of the future, young mechanic Ashe (Vincent Perez) and his little son, Danny (Eric Acosta), are gunned down by a gang of punks controlled by crime lord Judah Earl (Richard Brooks). Elsewhere in the city, tattoo artist Sarah (Mia Kirshner)—tormented by disturbing dreams she visualizes in paintings—is visited by a mysterious crow. Following it to the docks, she witnesses Ashe rising from the dead and takes him back to her loft. Realizing that he has been brought back to take care of unfinished business, she paints his face with garish makeup, and he sets out to avenge himself.

One by one, Ashe confronts, taunts, and kills Judah's henchmen. Curve (Iggy Pop), Judah's chief thug who has received a crow tattoo from Sarah, tries to warn his boss about the vengeful spirit that's come for them before he, too, is killed. Judah has Sarah kidnapped and brought to his tower hideaway; when the crow that guides Ashe arrives before him, Judah kills the bird and sets out to dispatch the now-weakened Ashe. In the midst of crowds celebrating the "Day of the Dead," Judah thrashes Ashe within an inch of his life before being interrupted by Sarah, whom he stabs to death. In a rage, Ashe calls down a flock of crows which tear Judah to pieces, then he returns to the netherworld.

One of the things that made the original CROW so memorable was a quality that does not lend itself to a sequel: it told a self-contained quest story that proceeded inexorably to a moving and cathartic ending. As if that wasn't enough, the death of star Brandon Lee during filming, which gave the movie an extra unintended resonance, should have precluded any attempts at a follow-up. But money—especially a $50 million box office gross—talks, and thus Miramax/Dimension served up this deadening, depressing, and wasteful rehash. David S. Goyer's script manages to shamelessly ape the original while missing its emotional impact, while director Tim Pope (like the first film's Alex Proyas, a music-video veteran) drenches the film in a yellowish visual scheme that's initially intriguing but becomes ugly to watch.

French actor Perez, chosen to take on the no-win assignment of following Lee, looks the part of the supernatural avenger but brings no particular panache to it. Kirshner, so memorable in EXOTICA (1995), is wasted in a role that gives her no depth or sizzle, and to which she responds with a markedly indifferent performance. (Originally, the script established her as the grown-up incarnation of the first film's young Sarah, but any such reference since has been jettisoned.) Brooks is among the least effective megalomaniacal villains in screen history, coming off more like a bored dilettante than an all-powerful crime lord. Only rocker Pop contributes any true sense of performing energy. The movie is full of gimmicky set pieces in place of real drama and, like all of Dimension's genre sequels, features an obviously altered ending that makes no sense. The one positive thing that can be said is that the film's rapid plunge at the box office would seem to indicate that a third CROW will not be inflicted upon audiences. *(Graphic violence, nudity, substance abuse, extreme profanity.)* — M.G.

d, Tim Pope; p, Edward R. Pressman, Jeff Most; exec p, Bob Weinstein, Harvey Weinstein, Alessandro Camon; assoc p, Gregory G. Woertz, Jeff Conner; co-p, Michael Flynn; w, David S. Goyer (based on the comic book series and comic strip by James O. Barr); ph, Jean-Yves Escoffier; ed, Michael Knue, Anthony Redman; m, Graeme Revell; prod d, Alex McDowell; art d, Gary Diamond, Charles Breen; set d, Anne Kuljian; sound, Joe Geisinger; fx, Roger Dorney, Bruno Van Zeebroeck; casting, Lora Kennedy; cos, Kirsten Everberg; stunts, Doug Coleman

Fantasy/Horror/Action (PR: C MPAA: R)

CRUCIBLE, THE ★★★½

(U.S.) 123m 20th Century Fox ~ 20th Century Fox c

Daniel Day-Lewis *(John Proctor)*; Winona Ryder *(Abigail Williams)*; Paul Scofield *(Judge Danforth)*; Joan Allen *(Elizabeth Proctor)*; Bruce Davison *(Reverend Parris)*; Rob Campbell *(Reverend Hale)*; Jeffrey Jones *(Thomas Putnam)*; Peter Vaughan *(Giles Corey)*; Karron Graves *(Mary Warren)*; Charlayne Woodard *(Tituba)*; Frances Conroy *(Ann Putnam)*; Elizabeth Lawrence *(Rebecca Nurse)*; George Gaynes *(Judge Sewall)*; Mary Pat Gleason *(Martha Corey)*; Robert Breuler *(Judge Hathorne)*; Rachael Bella *(Betty Parris)*; Ashley Peldon *(Ruth Putnam)*; Tom McDermott *(Francis Nurse)*; John Griesemer *(Ezekiel Cheever)*; Michael Gaston *(Marshal Herrick)*; William Preston *(George Jacobs)*; Ruth Maleczech *(Goody Osborne)*; Sheila Pinkham *(Goody Good)*; Peter Maloney *(Dr. Griggs)*; Kali Rocha *(Mercy Lewis)*; Taylor Stanley *(Joanna Preston)*; Lian-Marie Holmes *(Deliverance Fuller)*; Charlotte Melen *(Margaret Kenney)*; Carmella Mulvihill *(Hannah Brown)*; Jessie Kilguss *(Deborah Flint)*; Simone Marean *(Rachel Buxton)*; Amee Gray *(Lydia Sheldon)*; Anna V. Boksenbaum *(Sarah Pope)*; Mary Reardon *(Esther Wilkens)*; Alexander Streit *(Joseph*

Proctor); Michael McKinstry *(Daniel Proctor)*; Dorothy Brodesser *(Mrs. Griggs)*; Dossy Peabody *(Goody Sibber)*; Mara Clark *(Goody Barrow)*; Jane Pulkkinen *(Goody Bellows)*; Katrina Nevin *(Dorcas Bellows)*; Will Lyman *(Isaiah Goodkind)*; Karen MacDonald *(Townswoman)*; Sheila Ferrini *(Townswoman)*; June Lewin *(Townswoman)*; Ken Cheeseman *(Goat Owner)*; Steven Ochoa *(Putnam's Servant)*

One of the greatest works of the American stage comes, after more than 40 years, to the American screen with this adaptation penned by Arthur Miller himself. Bursting with powerful performances, THE CRUCIBLE is a brilliant and rich drama.

Salem, Massachusetts, 1692. Respected citizen John Proctor (Daniel Day-Lewis) has committed adultery with young Abigail Williams (Winona Ryder), his servant, and after this is discovered by his prim wife Elizabeth (Joan Allen), Abigail is discharged. The scorned maid enlists a dozen other girls in a voodoo ritual, during which Abigail calls for Elizabeth's demise. After Reverend Parris (Bruce Davison) spies "the coven" dancing in the woods, rumors begin to circulate about witchery. Reverend Hale (Rob Campbell), an expert in black matters, is summoned to investigate. Led by Abigail, the girls take the only avenue available: they confess to being influenced by Satan, and begin charging other townspeople with being in his league. Deputy Governor Danforth (Paul Scofield) arrives in Salem to adjudicate the witchcraft trials.

In Danforth's court, no claim of innocence or defense is accepted; once accused, one must confess, and thus be forgiven, or else face hanging. The charge of practicing witchcraft becomes an excellent means of exacting personal vengence. Prominent landowner Thomas Putnam (Jeffrey Jones) uses the charges to eliminate his neighbors and increase his holdings. Parris sees the independent-minded persons who have challenged his authority brought to trial. Proctor disdains the proceedings and stays away, until Abigail charges Elizabeth.

To save his wife and the other good people falsely accused, Proctor goes before Danforth, confesses his lechery with Abigail, and denounces the proceedings as hypocrisy. For standing against the court—its expressed purpose is doing God's will, so anyone against it is *ipso facto* against God—Proctor is sentenced to hang. The convictions of the Proctors and other well-regarded citizens turn public opinion against the trials, and against Abigail, who runs away. Even Hale quits the court in protest. Danforth and Parris implore Proctor to "confess" to witchery and close the episode, but he will not, and dies on the gallows.

When sex—America's favorite boogeyman—is unleashed in Puritan Salem, it's eros versus the ethos of repression. For John Proctor, the prototypical American, sex represents freedom and self-determination—for which he sees ample opportunity in the open vistas of the New World. Judge Danforth, the State, sees this also, but to him sex is a demon, and he seeks to nip desire in the bud. Proctor awakens Abigail's appetite for sex, but it's Danforth who perverts her lusty motivations into evil actions.

This depiction of mad authority cloaked in piety is famous as an allegory of McCarthyism in the 1950s. More importantly, THE CRUCIBLE is a great, timeless drama of the necessity for a man to take a principled stand against the ill wind of popular fascism.

Contemporary audiences weaned on happy endings may bemoan Miller's resolution of the battle between authority and autonomy. Proctor decides, somewhat ironically, that to affirm himself he must die a moral individual, rather than give sanction to an unjust State by living. The notion of someone choosing death over "life with a bad name" is a head-scratcher in our morally ambiguous culture. THE CRUCIBLE'spresentationof this unconventional, ethical heroism gives the story relevance far beyond the first blush of Red Scare allegory usually attributed to it.

Director Nicholas Hytner (THE MADNESS OF KING GEORGE) pulls Miller's spellbinding argument outside of the courtroom and infuses it with passionate kineticism. The film starts like a rifle-shot of erotic rage, and the intense pitch never lets up. Reunited from THE AGE OF INNOCENCE, Day-Lewis, the embodiment of rough-hewn nobility, and Ryder, a dervish of fierce emotionality, head a superb cast. All of the actors previously cited, as well as startling newcomer Karron Graves, who plays the wicked coward Mary Warren, give outstanding performances. *(Adult situations.)* — P.R.

d, Nicholas Hytner; p, Robert A. Miller, David V. Picker; assoc p, Mitchell Levin; co-p, Diana Pokorny; w, Arthur Miller (based on his play); ph, Andrew Dunn; ed, Tariq Anwar; m, George Funton; prod d, Lilly Kilvert; art d, John Warnke; set d, Gretchen Rau; sound, Michael Barosky (mixer); fx, Brian Ricci; casting, Donna Isaacson, Daniel Swee; cos, Bob Crowley; makeup, Naomi Donne; stunts, Walter Scott

AAN Best Supporting Actress: Joan Allen; *AAN Best Adapted Screenplay:* Arthur Miller

Drama **(PR: C MPAA: PG-13)**

CURDLED ★★★

(U.S.) 94m A Band Apart Productions; Tinderbox Films ~ Miramax c

Angela Jones *(Gabriela)*; William Baldwin *(Paul Guell)*; Bruce Ramsay *(Eduardo)*; Lois Chiles *(Katrina Brandt)*; Barry Corbin *(Lodger)*; Mel Gorham *(Elena)*; Daisy Fuentes *(Clara)*; Carmen Lopez *(Lourdes)*; Vivienne Sandaydiego *(Eva)*; Caridad Ravelo *(Joan)*; Sandra Thigpen *(Grace)*; Kelly Preston *(Kelly Hogue)*; Lupitz Ferrer *(Marie Clement)*; Sabrina Cowan *(Red Haired Waitress)*; Charles J. Tucker *(Sam the Barback)*; Alyssa Tacher *(Young Gabriela)*; Nattacha Amador *(Young Gabriela's Mother)*; Therese Marie Guitierez *(P.F.C.S. Spokesmaid)*; Jay Amor *(Falling Man)*

A wickedly morbid black comedy, CURDLED features one of the year's most memorably offbeat female leads.

Gabriela (Angela Jones) is a young Colombian woman living in Miami who has been obsessed with murder and death since childhood. Her particular interest is in the Blue Blood Killer—actually handsome bartender Paul Guell (William Baldwin)—who has been knocking off a series of rich women. His most recent victim, Katrina (Lois Chiles), has managed to scrawl his name on the floor, where it is covered up by her own blood. Gabriela takes a job with the Post Forensic Cleaning Service, which mops up after gruesome murders, and her enthusiasm for the work unnerves her partner, Elena (Mel Gorham). While cleaning up the site of Katrina's murder, Gabriela uncovers Paul's name, piquing her interest all the more.

During a subsequent date with Eduardo (Bruce Ramsay), Gabriela insists on bringing him to the crime scene—where Paul also has returned and is hiding in a closet. While Gabriela continues to examine the scene, Paul knocks Eduardo out and confronts her, leading her into a dance that is part seduction and part preparation for murder. She is able to fend him off, however, and it is Paul who ends up dying, and confirming Gabriela's suspicion that freshly severed heads are momentarily able to speak.

Sometimes a movie contains one scene that throws the entire film into focus, and crystallizes everything about it. Such is the case with CURDLED, once Gabriela has made her return trip to

Katrina's blood-spattered house. Left alone after Eduardo (unbeknownst to her) has been subdued by Paul, the murder-fixated Gabriela picks up a kitchen knife, turns on a tape player and dances her way through a reenactment of the victim's death throes, twisting and crawling from one patch of dried blood to another to the beat of her tango music. It's a breathtaking solo set piece, and when it occurs, one realizes that everything in the film, even the slow stuff that didn't seem important, has been building to this moment, and it's a stunner.

It's to Jones and director Reb Braddock's credit that here, as in the whole movie, they prevent Gabriela from becoming morbid, but turn her into one of the freshest, most original lead characters on the 1990s indie-thriller scene. Despite her preoccupation with blood and death, Gabriela remains charming and likable, with a devilish wit about herself. Braddock (who also scripted with John Maass) expanded this movie from a short film, and the pokey pacing makes this evident at times, but he and Jones keep one interested and intrigued throughout. Despite seeming somewhat miscast as a serial killer, Baldwin holds his own opposite Jones, and the final half hour showcasing their *tete-a-tete* is sharply played and leads to a perfect punch line.

CURDLED is one of the best of the black-comic thrillers to have sprung up in the wake of Quentin Tarantino's success, perhaps in part because it was executive-produced by Tarantino himself. Impressed by Braddock's short original, Tarantino cast Jones as a similar character (the cab driver Esmeralda) in PULP FICTION (1994) before supervising this movie. He also contributed a bit of his trademark self-referentialism to the feature: a TV true-crime show clip that contains an amusing FROM DUSK TILL DAWN (1996) in-joke. *(Graphic violence, adult situations, profanity.)* — M.G.

d, Reb Braddock; p, John Maass, Raul Puig; exec p, Quentin Tarantino; w, John Maass, Reb Braddock; ph, Steven Bernstein; ed, Mallory Gotlieb; m, Joseph Julian Gonzalez; prod d, Sherman Williams; set d, Karen Virgin; sound, Peter Devlin; casting, Yvonne Casas; cos, Beverly Nelson Safier; stunts, James Vickers

Comedy/Crime/Thriller (PR: C MPAA: R)

CURTIS'S CHARM ★★½

(Canada) 74m Curtis's Charm Productions; Rabid Dog Films ~ Strand Releasing c

Maurice Dean Wint *(Curtis)*; Callum Keith Rennie *(Jim)*; Rachel Crawford *(Cookie)*; Barbara Barnes-Hopkins *(Voodoo Ma)*; Aron Tager *(Park Worker)*; Hugh Dillon *(Spitting White Trash Thug)*; Trent Carr *(Thug)*; Dale Harrison *(Thug)*; Brian Clancy *(The Killer)*; John Dondertman *(Furry Pimp)*; Bruce McDonald *(Man in Restaurant)*; Bruno Bryniarski *(Dealer)*; Mary Sylwetser *(Hooker)*; Kei *(Junkie)*; Trevor Black *(Junkie)*; Mina Mushtaghi *(Teen)*; Guy Sanvido *(Patron)*; Conrod Ciandre *(Afro Junkie)*; Ross Redfern *(Exiting Man)*

Drug addiction gets a different sort of cinematic spin in CURTIS'S CHARM, a flaky, offbeat story about a recovering user helping his junkie friend. The lighter-than-usual approach is welcome and the cinematography is sublime, but CURTIS'S CHARM needs a bit more juice to sustain viewers.

The story begins when Jim (Callum Keith Rennie), a Caucasian and former heroin addict living in New York, hears from Cookie (Rachael Crawford), a waitress, that her husband, Curtis (Maurice Dean Wint), an African-American drug user, is missing. Jim thinks back over the previous day to figure out where Curtis might be. In a flashback, Curtis seems worried that his mother-in-law (Barbara Barnes-Hopkins) is using voodoo to seek vengeance upon his "wicked ways." When Jim first hears this, he dismisses Curtis's concerns as drug-related paranoia, but as the day wears on and he hears more odd stories about the peculiar events that are occurring in his friend's life, Jim is less sure.

As a favor to Curtis, Jim creates a "lucky charm" picture of a snake to ward off the evil forces of Curtis's mother. To his surprise, Jim notices that his placebo seems to contain magical properties that indeed protect Curtis. But, after parting at the end of the day, Curtis tries to use the charm toward continuing his habit. In doing so, he runs afoul of a white street gang, however, and is killed. In the end, Jim still does not realize what has happened to his Curtis, but he senses that a life force has been sucked out of the neighborhood.

CURTIS'S CHARM technically belongs to a genre of film that explores drug-addiction from the point of view of the addict. Like the Hollywood classics THE MAN WITH THE GOLDEN ARM (1955) and A HATFUL OF RAIN (1957), and the more recent independent efforts, JUMPIN' AT THE BONEYARD (1992) and SWEET NOTHING (1995), CURTIS'S CHARM looks at the world of the junkie with sympathy and compassion but without condoning the use of drugs. Yet, unlike these films, CURTIS'S CHARM eschews the melodramatic formulas that usually dominate the narrative structures. CURTIS'S CHARM is more interested in telling a story that happens to be about two drug users than trying to moralize one way or the other about drugs (the film could have influenced 1997's funny, hip-hop entry to the genre, GRIDLOCK'D).

Much of the cheeky amorality stems from the source material and Jim Carroll's real-life tales. In some ways, the film conveys Carroll's "street poetry" better than his official biopic, BASKETBALL DIARIES (1994). The mixture of gritty realism and hallucinogenic fantasy is brilliantly captured by Harald Bachmann's black-and-white photography. The final shots of the "missing" Curtis in all his favorite haunts leaves an indelible impression that supersedes anything in the dialogue.

It's a pity, then, that some of the script and most of the acting is not up to par. Rennie plays Jim as laid-back, to the point of somnambulism, while Wint plays Curtis on a manic one-note, which has the unfortunate effect of being forced and rarely funny; frankly, there hasn't been so much African-American eye-popping since the days of Mantan Moreland. And Crawford is so ineffectual as Cookie, one wishes her performance had been cut out altogether. The other parts are too minor to mention, including "Voodoo Ma" (Barnes-Hopkins), whose few images as a demonic witch plays into the hands of yet another African-American stereotype.

Writer-director John L'Ecuyer surely didn't mean to create a racist portrait, but it doesn't help that a story mostly about black people is told by a white person, no matter how "cool" Jim may be. Regrettably, too, Jim's remark that "all this dark synchronicity stuff was becoming tiresome" becomes—ultimately—an accurate critique of the film. *(Violence, adult situations, substance abuse, extreme profanity.)* — E.M.

d, John L'Ecuyer; p, Sandra Cunningham; exec p, Atom Egoyan, Patricia Rozema; assoc p, Carolynne Bell; w, John L'Ecuyer; ph, Harald Bachmann; ed, Craig Webster; m, Mark Korven; prod d, John Dondertman; sound, John Hazen; cos, Beth Pasternak

Drama/Comedy (PR: C MPAA: NR)

D3: THE MIGHTY DUCKS ★★½

(U.S.) 104m Gordon's Last Song Productions; Walt Disney ~ Buena Vista c

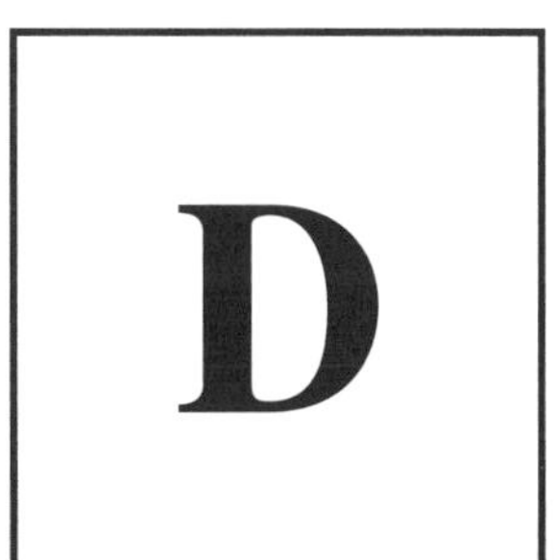

Emilio Estevez *(Gordon Bombay)*; Jeffrey Nordling *(Coach Orion)*; David Selby *(Dean Buckley)*; Heidi Kling *(Casey)*; Joshua Jackson *(Charlie)*; Joss Ackland *(Hans)*; Elden Ryan Ratliff *(Fulton)*; Shaun Weiss *(Goldberg)*; Vincent A. Larusso *(Banks)*; Matt Doherty *(Averman)*; Garette Ratliff Henson *(Guy)*; Marguerite Moreau *(Connie)*; Michael Cudlitz *(Cole)*; Christopher Orr *(Rick)*; Aaron Lohr *(Portman)*; Ty O'Neal *(Dwayne)*; Kenan Thompson *(Russ)*; Mike Vitar *(Luis)*; Colombe Jacobsen *(Julie)*; Justin Wong *(Ken)*; Scott Whyte *(Scott)*; Margot Finley *(Linda)*; Lynn Phillip Seibel *(Tom Riley)*; Benjamin Salisbury *(Josh)*; Eliza Coyle *(Angela Delaney)*; James Craven *(Mr. Barber)*; Claudia Wilkins *(Mrs. Madigan)*; Melissa Keller *(Mindy)*; Samantha Harris *(Cindy)*; Jack White *(Coach Wilson)*; Steven Brill *(Arcade Attendant)*; Mary Brill *(Jeannie)*; Jeannette Kerner *(Board Member)*; Herbert Brill *(Board Member)*; Mike Kelly *(Referee)*; Claire Bednarski *(Gabriella)*; Jerry Kerner *(Customer at Mickey's Diner)*; Bert Sandberg *(Customer at Mickey's Diner)*

The progressive aging of the young actors reprising their roles as members of the Mighty Ducks hockey team could ensure that this will stand as the final sequel to THE MIGHTY DUCKS (1992)—and not a moment too soon.

Having won the Junior Goodwill Games (as shown in the conclusion of D2: THE MIGHTY DUCKS (1994)), the team of young hockey players accept athletic scholarships to the prestigious Eden Hall Academy. Despite their scholarships, the teammates are welcomed with less-than-open arms. Snobbish elements in the school board and the student body feel these kids from "the wrong side of the tracks" have no place at Eden. But their biggest hurdle seems to be their new coach, Orion (Jeffrey Nordling). Determined to teach the team the long-term benefits of defensive play as opposed to their more flashy offensive style, Orion tries to break the team of its old habits by any means he can, beginning with stripping team captain Charlie (Joshua Jackson) of his title until he can prove he has earned it.

Gradually, the team comes to adopt Orion's teachings. The change in style affects their scoring, however, giving the school board a excuse to revoke their scholarships. Their place at Eden is secured thanks to the efforts of lawyer and former coach Gordon Bombay (Emilio Estevez). The team pulls together to regain its honor by beating the snooty Eden varsity team in a final, official showdown.

Strictly an exercise in squeezing the last drops out of a franchise while its young actors can still pass for children, D3 lacks most of the qualities that made its predecessors such hits. With Emilio Estevez on hand for no more than a glorified cameo (presumably his agent got a fat bonus for getting him sole above-the-title billing), what little plot there is involves team captain Charlie, who wants to be a hotshot scorer instead of a solid team player. D3's emphasis on the virtues of learning from one's mistakes is commendable, though less so than it might have been in a film that didn't make it look as though all these kids ever do is play hockey. Education receives such short shrift that the filmmakers would have been better off leaving it out entirely; when the topic is addressed, it's done so perfunctorily as to suggest that they were forced to shoehorn some schooling in amongst the body checks. The same is true of every other non-hockey-related element of the film, including the obligatory teen romances, family problems, and the personalities of most of the Ducks. This could almost be forgiven if the hockey scenes had any panache, which they sorely lack. These kids are supposed to be the Harlem Globetrotters of junior hockey, but that kind of fun and excitement can't be generated onscreen. *(Violence.)* — M.F.

d, Robert Lieberman; p, Jordan Kerner, Jon Avnet; exec p, Steven Brill, C. Tad Devlin; assoc p, Kathy L. Menzies; co-p, Elizabeth Guber Stephen; w, Steven Brill, Jim Burnstein (from a story by Kenneth Johnson and Jim Burnstein, based on characters created by Steven Brill); ph, David Hennings; ed, Patrick Lussier, Colleen Halsey; m, J.A.C. Redford; prod d, Stephen Storer; art d, Harry Darrow; set d, Robin Peyton; sound, Tim Cooney (mixer); fx, Paul Murphy; casting, Judy Taylor; cos, Kimberly A. Tillman; makeup, Cheryl Nick; tech, Jack White

Sports/Comedy/Children's (PR: A MPAA: PG)

DADETOWN ★★★½

(U.S.) 93m KHXT ~ Castle Hill c

Jim Pryor *(Tom Nickenback)*; Fred Worrell *(Ed Hubble)*; Edith Meeks *(Dorrie Daniel)*; Ford Slater *(Tom Dooley)*; Bill Garrison *(Bill Parsons)*; Carolynn Hannan *(Julie Parsons)*; Lucia Reed *(API Daughter)*; Norm Anderson *(Pete Nagler)*; Greg Rougeux *(Walter Smouth)*; David Phelps *(Tony Pitino)*; Loni Lodwig *(Judy Pitino)*; Sean Perry *(Steve Minning)*; Jonathan Shafer *(Bill Bowers)*; Kenneth Klumm *(Richard Arkin)*; Peter Kelly *(Martin Small)*; Pamela Storms *(Betty Small)*; Margie Geurin *(Woman on Bench)*; Marcia States *(Woman on Bench)*; Sharon Stevens *(Woman on Bench)*; Anessa Ansley *(Cheryl Broomfield)*; Michael Ansley-Purpura *(Broomfield Baby)*; Mary Matthewson *(Barlitz Child)*; Robert Matthewson *(Barlitz Child)*; Stephen Beals *(Dan Barlitz)*; Valerie Gilbert *(Joanna Barlitz)*; G. Gunny Gundrum *(Chief Andrew McNally)*; Bob Signoracci *(Mayor Ed Stalsolm)*; Frankie Earle *(Susan Chambers)*; Jim Burns *(Alan Chambers)*; Paul Drum *(Ethan Foley)*; Lydia Sobczyk *(Pitino's Daughter)*; Ed Cryer *(Angry Local in Park)*; John Webster *(API Man in Park)*; Sarah States *(API Daughter in Park)*; Mary Cushman *(Grieving Woman)*; Gerald Dolezar *(Stuart Newell)*; Dorothy Nixon *(May Newell)*; Jimi Celeste *(Dominic)*; Josephine Potenza *(Gorman Secretary)*; Melba LaRose *(Town Clerk)*; Jerry Lewkowitz *(Jerry—Arguing Employee)*; Terry Nardone *(David McRae)*; Judi Warden *(Bess Gluckman)*; Grant Gifford *(Teen at Playground)*; Christine Tipton *(Little Girl at Playgorund)*; Samantha Gifford *(Girl Lifting Beam)*; Mary Farmer *(Woman Driving Car)*; Jerry Jaffe *(Art Allen)*; Sal Cippola *(Hostile Man)*; Joseph Leone *(Louis—Man in Bar)*; Jonathan Douglas *(Officer Truman)*; Bill Gorman *(Man Arrested at Gas Station)*; Emery Cummings *(Man in Coffee Shop)*; Jeffrey White *(API Man in Parking Lot)*; Leonardo Doe *(Gorman Supervisor)*; Robert Wall *(Young Laid-Off Employee)*; Robert DelBono *(Depressed Employee)*; Jim Gifford *(Town Lawyer)*; Carl Cohen *(Richard Tyne)*; Brian Pienkoski *(Mark Simmons)*; Jack Creeden *(Glen Reading)*; Joe Iacona *(George)*; Don Macri *(Joseph Gorman)*; Edward Vigeant *(Gorman Bodyguard)*; Dan Blanchard *(Gorman Bodyguard)*; Scott Cramer *(Interviewer with Gorman)*; Diane Thomas *(Woman at Strike)*; Harrison Capiche *(Man at Strike)*; David Kinney *(Phil Stenerson)*; Gayle Stein *(Naomi Brabner)*; Don Ackley *(Tim—Worker at Strike's End)*; Gerald Baroody *(Ambulance Attendant)*; Beth King *(Ambulance Attendant)*; Jeff McNinch *(Doctor)*; Allison Karan *(TV Interviewer)*; Grant Monroy *(Phillip)*; Tyler LaCroix *(Tyler)*; Richard Stillman *(Luca—Dead Boy)*; Lisa Nicholas *(Luca's*

Mother); Gloria Gonyeo *(Rev. Gayle Kirkman)*; Tiffini Minatel *(Bea Wass)*; Chris Nardone *(McRae's Son)*

It is difficult to write about DADETOWN without revealing the startling secret that caps the film. Be that as it may, this documentary about the decay of smalltown America is worthwhile even with its ending known in advance.

DADETOWN introduces the viewer to a upper New York State community in 1994, economically dependent on the metal-bending facility that has been the town's backbone since its heyday in WWII. It is a major event when American Peripheral Imaging (API), a high-tech corporation, establishes its regional headquarters on the outskirts of the town. Beneath the forced smiles and words of inclusiveness, there exists a major rift between the blue-collar locals and the white-collar API families, who are slowly changing the face of Dadetown.

After lay-offs begin at the metal-bending factory, the threat of economic and social instability triggers an all-out war between the two communities. The mayor and town council become ineffectual in quelling the anger directed at API. Eventually, tensions climax in a strike at the metal plant, but while the protest rages on in the heart of the town, a small boy is fatally wounded in a shooting accident which is connected to the presence of guns at the strike. Finally, the factory closes, several former employees move out of Dadetown, and API effectively takes over the town. The surprise ending—the literal postscript—reveals that this "documentary" had been performed by a cast of actors.

Credit director Russ Hexter for creating this sharp-edged portrait of small-town America in the throws of modernization. In DADETOWN, Hexter draws upon the spirit of such documentaries as HARLAN COUNTY, USA (1976) and ROGER AND ME (1989) to expose the dark side of American capitalism and urbanization. But Hexter uses comparatively traditional documentary techniques to tell the sad tale of Dadetown, a New York State working-class community upset by the newly-arrived high-tech communications company that dramatically changes the town's economic and social life.

Only one significant aspect of Hexter's work is deliberately oblique—that it was a wholly created fiction—but it does not really mitigate the power of the film's statement. Suffice it to say that DADETOWN questions the very notion of the "documentary," in the tradition of Luis Bunuel's LAND WITHOUT BREAD (1932), Jim McBride's DAVID HOLTZMAN'S DIARY (1968) and Peter Greenaway's STAIRS ONE GENEVA (1994).

Sadly, after completing his debut feature, Russ Hexter died from an aortic aneurysm at the age of 27. DADETOWN, therefore, marks the end of a promising career, while also delivering a strong message about some of the harsh facts of modern Western life. *(Violence, profanity.)* — E.M.

d, Russ Hexter; p, Jim Carden; w, Russ Hexter, John Housley; ph, W.J. Gorman; ed, David Kirkman; prod d, J. Edward Vigeant

Drama **(PR: C MPAA: NR)**

DAENS ★★★½

(Belgium) 134m Favorite Films; Films Derives; Shooting Star Films; Titane ~ Orion c

Jan Decleir *(Adolf Daens)*; Gerard Desarthe *(Charles Woeste)*; Julia Ranaszkiewicz *(Nini)*; Antje DeBoeck *(Nette Scholliers)*; Michael Pas *(Jan De Meeter)*; Johan Leysen *(Schmitt)*; Idwig Stephane *(Eugene Borremans)*; Wim Meuwissen *(Pieter Daens)*; Jappe Claes *(Ponnet)*; Julien Schoenaerts *(Bishop Stillemans)*; Karel Baetens *(Jefke)*; Brit Alen *(Louise Daens)*; Brenda Bertin *(Marie)*; Alex Wilequet *(Monsignor Goossens)*; Rik Hancke *(Nuncio)*; Giovanni DiBenedetto *(Cardinal)*; Fred Van Kuijk *(Mayor Vanwambeke)*; Gerald Marti *(King Leopold II)*; Frank Vercruyssen; Koen Van Impe *(Baron De Bethune)*; Marilou Mermans *(Mother Scholliers)*; Mark Peeters *(Vandermmersch)*; Filip Van Luchene *(Lambrecht)*; Herbert Flack *(Vanlangenhove)*; Yves Degen *(Druwe)*; Marc Legein *(Cumont)*; Gaston Bertin *(Leirens)*; Max Schnur *(Old Man)*; Anna Grazyna Suchoka

Indignation about injustice is coupled with classic filmmaking in this handsomely mounted film about child labor exploitation in Aalst, Belgium in the late 19th century. Photographed as if Rembrandt himself were the cinematographer, DAENS deserved its 1992 Oscar nomination for Best Foreign Film. Painstakingly building a case for the liberation of the oppressed, this historical evocation is especially timely after 1996 news headlines revealed that child workers are still being victimized throughout the world.

Restless and prickly, Father Daens (Jan Decleir) exasperates Belgium Church officials with his secular meddling. Transferred to the impoverished region of Aalst, Daens shakes up the power structure by publishing an article in his brother's paper about pernicious working conditions at local mills. Their lives endangered by unhealthy work conditions, children like Nini (Julia Ranaszkiewicz) are also sexually abused by predators like shop foreman Schmitt (Johan Leysen). Nini's death ignites Daens's public advocacy of labor reform; however, the upper class, represented by Charles Woeste (Gerard Desarthe), retaliates by firing the men and hiring only lower-waged women and children. Fighting back, Daens discovers an immutable conspiracy between the Middle class, the governing royalty, and his own Catholic Church.

Thanks to Daens's advocacy, an investigative committee finally tours the factories, but the members don't speak the peasants' language. When another child dies in a textile machine accident, laborer and activist Nette (Antje DeBoeck) tries carrying the dead child to the visiting inspectors. Alerted by the gentry, government troops attack her and steal the proof of hazardous conditions: the corpse of the boy-worker. Further angering his Church, Daens then runs for office, an election he wins despite widespread corruption at the polls. Unfortunately, Daens's social strides are impeded by Woeste, who insists that religious leaders banish Daens to the Vatican. Abandoned by his Church for his progressive ideas, Daens eventually returns to Aalst with his support neutralized. Strikers have been starved into compliance, Nette has been raped by Schmitt, and Daens's brother's printing press has been vandalized. After a starving boy is killed while trying to steal meat from a circus animal, Daens finally removes his clerical collar and works alongside the poor, in the trenches of social disenfranchisement, until the time of his death.

Eschewing the typical Hollywood approach, DAENS follows the trajectory of history and views Daens's heroism matter-of-factly. Through this central figure's quiet dignity and stubbornness, we learn a history lesson about industrialized slavery made possible by the indifference of the monarchy, the greed of the middle class, and the power-lust of the Church. Although directed with restraint (i.e., the horror of squalor isn't dwelled upon), this disturbing film accrues power by piling up incremental details that make the tragedy of economic subjugation almost unbearable. DAENS also draws strength from a flawless period reconstruction.

If this film has a flaw, it lies in its scrupulous fidelity to so many incidents of Church-and-State miscreancy. Somehow the key figure of Daens gets lost, especially during the section about his exile in Rome. With narrative events repositioned, this banishment could have been realized by a brief montage. Dramatically, the film suffers by shifting its focus away from its zealous hero. After all, the movie is a cry of protest, but one that's uttered in the voice of a specific character. But when the elements of agitprop and biography are in synch, DAENS moves us as a soul-stirring indictment of social injustice, in a world where inhumane working conditions once thrived—and are still not extinct. *(Violence, profanity, sexual situations, adult situations.)* — R.P.

d, Stijn Coninx; p, Dirk Impens; exec p, Simon Zaleski; assoc p, Jean-Luc Ormiers, Hans Pos, Maria Peters, Dave Schram; w, Stijn Coninx, Francois Chevallier (based on the book *Pieter Daens* by Louis-Paul Boon); ph, Walther Vanden Ende; ed, Ludo Troch; m, Dirk Brosse; prod d, Allan Starski; art d, Hubert Pouille; set d, Frederick Huwaert; sound, Henri Morelle, Jean-Paul Loublier; casting, Continental Casting ; cos, Jan Tax; makeup, Winnie Gallis

Biography/Religious/Historical (PR: C MPAA: R)

DANGEROUS PASSION ★★½

(U.S.) 94m Davis Entertainment; Stormy Weathers Productions ~ LIVE Entertainment c

Billy Dee Williams *(Lou)*; Lonette McKee *(Meg)*; Carl Weathers *(Kyle Weston)*; Elpidia Carrillo *(Angela)*; Michael Beach *(Steve)*; L. Scott Caldwell *(Ruby)*; Charles Boswell *(Frank Carmen)*; Tony DiBenedetto *(Walt)*; Miguel Sandoval *(Sergeant Hidalgo)*; Daniel Ziskie *(Adelman)*; Nancy Fish *(Blake)*; Rudy Ramos *(Policeman)*; Shannon Wilcox *(Janet Gregton)*; Charles Stransky *(Senator Gregton)*; Bob Minor *(Security Guard No. 1)*; Nick Dimitri *(Security Guard No. 2)*; Michael Melon *(Ticket Buyer)*; Leon Delaney *(Rawlings)*; Brian Williams *(Intruder)*; Jason Keene *(Delivery Man)*; Peter Strong *(Officer No. 1)*; Charles Douglass *(Officer No. 2)*; Carl D. Parker *(Old Man)*

This is an expert retread of Hollywood crime formulas, infused with new life by a top-flight African-American cast. But the snugly constructed script stands on its own merits.

Millionaire Lou (Billy Dee Williams) values his antique cars more than his spirited wife, Meg (Lonette McKee). After he kills an intruder, Lou pressures his mechanic, Kyle (Carl Weathers), to take the fall for him. Kyle feels even more threatened after Lou forces him to witness the drowning of Lou's wheelchair-bound attorney, Mr. Adelman (Daniel Ziskie). Risking his well-being by dallying with Lou's mistreated spouse, Kyle clings to hopes that Lou will release a promised $30,000 payoff that would enable Kyle to buy Napa Valley land as an upright citizen.

Meanwhile, Lou hires a henchman, Frank Carmen (Charles Boswell), and Kyle finds out that Meg is pregnant and he s the father. Cashing in a luxury car given to him by the big boss, Kyle flees with Meg. After Frank fatally stabs Meg in a coffee shop, a frightened waitress-witness, Angela (Elpidia Carrillo), is sought by Lou's men and by Kyle, because only this illegal alien can clear him in Meg's slaughter. Although Kyle slays Frank, another henchman, Walt (Tony DiBenedetto), kidnaps Angela.

During a confrontation in Lou's warehouse, Kyle trades Lou a sports car (which has been rigged with explosives) for Angela. Kyle escapes with his life and his witness, but indications exist that auto-fancier Lou may yet buy his way out of the bloody mess.

DANGEROUS PASSION rings true even when its skirmishes seem improbable. The film doesn't merely pit its enamored fugitives against an implacable foe; it picks at their own insecurities as they turn on each other in waves of mistrust. Weathers more than fits the movie star bill as a handsome tuna swimming among barracudas like Lou. Matching McKee's enticing performance as the self-destructive Meg is Billy Dee Williams, whose Lou isn't just a grabby businessman but a collector of souls.

DANGEROUS PASSION is an invigorating peek into the dark recesses of the human spirit—until McKee is killed off. Afterward, this once-promising film moves into more conventional macho action territory. *(Graphic violence, extreme profanity, extensive nudity, sexual situations, substance abuse.)* — R.P.

d, Michael Miller; p, Paul Pompian; exec p, John Davis, Andrew Hill; co-p, Carl Weathers; w, Brian Taggert (based on an idea by Andrew Hill); ph, Steven Shaw; ed, Janet Bartels-Vandagriff; m, Rob Mounsey; art d, K. C. Fox; set d, Tori Nourafchan; sound, Edward Earl Rue (mixer); casting, Judith Weiner; makeup, Peggy Teague; stunts, Bob Minor

Crime/Action (PR: C MPAA: NR)

DARK SECRETS ★

(U.S.) 90m Midnight Productions ~ A-Pix Entertainment c

Julie Strain *(Mauri)*; Justin Carroll *(Justin Deville)*; Chanda *(Nancy Boyer)*; Tom Crowl *(Ben Burner)*; Joe Estevez *(Larry)*; William Knight *(Senator Kilburn)*; John Mappin *(Peter Day)*; Brenda Holiday *(Female Party Guest)*; Lori Wagner *(Woman With Senator)*; Kelly Nelson *(Greg)*; Monique Parent *(Claire Reynolds)*; Glitter *(Dominatrix)*; Cheryl Rixon *(Philipa)*; Clement von Franckenstein *(Clement)*; Doria Rone *(Leona)*; Ed Wasser *(Dennis Gary)*; Rico Buena *(Bum 1)*; Felix Castro *(Bum 2)*; Aldo Giraldi *(Bum 3)*

With its twisted sense of right and wrong, DARK SECRETS takes the position that any form of sexual perversion is morally superior to fatally stabbing a lover in the back.

Ambitious reporter Claire Reynolds (Monique Parent) goes undercover as a lingerie model to get an exclusive story on media mogul-sex club magnate Justin Deville (Justin Carroll). Of all the mannequins working for Justin's photographer-procurer, only Claire possesses a perfect blend of carnality and innocence—Justin regards her as marriage material.

After finding photos that could link Justin to a woman's murder, Claire slowly falls under the spell of Justin's erotic black magic. At his mansion, Justin blackmails a senator with an incriminating videotape. Meanwhile, at his pleasure palace, Justin introduces Claire to sensualists like Mauri (Julie Strain) who seduces her.

To test his potential wife's loyalty, Justin arranges for a TV producer to offer Claire a high-profile job in exchange for her feeding him juicy tidbits from Justin's shady empire. Conflicted, Claire takes the bait, not realizing that the murder photos were faked. So Claire gets her on-camera gig but not her man, and a saddened Justin continues searching for that perfect combination of schoolgirl and whore who is worthy of being his mate.

While this movie's anti-puritanical stand may be unassailable from one perspective, its artistic integrity, screenplay, and array of terrible acting are not. Never has sex been so explicitly reenacted in a non-X-rated excursion, yet seemed so unarousing and silly. Does anyone want to see a gruesomely overdeveloped naked woman being covered with Saran Wrap?

DARK SECRETS portrays Claire's exposure to back room dirty-doings in terms of Victorian melodrama, but instead of being harassed by a mustache-twirling villain, she's chased by horny hedonists. Of course, Claire's Big "O" is reserved for Justin, whom we're supposed to admire for his erotic openness, while we condemn Claire for selling him out. However, let's give this woman a break. After all, she suspected her fiance of murder; it's not her fault he only turned out to be guilty of hypocrisy, blackmail, and a God-complex. *(Violence, extreme profanity, extensive nudity, adult situations, sexual situations, substance abuse.)* — R.P.

d, John Bowen; p, William Witrock, Ron Lavery; exec p, Chuck Zane, Alejandra Mejia; w, Steve Tymon; ph, Keith Holland; ed, Baker Azul; m, Efrem Bergman; art d, John Acevedo; set d, Mary Hurte; sound, Al Samuels; casting, Sheila Thompson; cos, Gwen Lavery; makeup, Shirley Orme

Erotic/Drama (PR: O MPAA: NR)

DARKMAN III: DIE DARKMAN DIE ★★½

(U.S.) 87m Renaissance Pictures ~ MCA/Universal Home Video c

Jeff Fahey *(Rooker)*; Von Flores *(Johnny Lee)*; Arnold Vosloo *(Peyton Westlake/Darkman)*; Eric Hollo *(Paul Raney)*; Darlanne Fleugel *(Bridget Thorne)*; Gino Giacomini *(Beast)*; Roxann Biggs-Dawson *(Angela Rooker)*; Lance Paton *(Narrator)*; Nigel Bennett *(Nico)*; Suzanne Primeau *(Mother)*; Alicia Panetta *(Jenny Rooker)*; Bob Windsor *(Uncle Owen)*; Ronn Sarosiak *(Mack)*; Lorne Cossette *(Dr. Leonard)*; Peter Graham *(Joey)*; Diana Platts *(Reporter #1)*; Shawn Doyle *(Adam)*; Joanna Reece *(Reporter #2)*; Vieslav Krystyan *(Ivan)*; Walker Boone *(Sgt. Troy)*; Chris Adams *(Whit)*; Brian Paul *(Angry Guest)*; Rick Parker *(E. K.)*; Michelle Collins *(Nurse)*; Joel Bissonette *(Mayo)*; Denise Baillargeon *(Female Guest)*; John Novak *(Ryan Mitchell)*; Chris Bondy *(Gibson)*

Sam Raimi's unconventional superhero returns in DARKMAN III: DIE DARKMAN DIE. Like its predecessor, DARKMAN II: THE RETURN OF DURANT, this eager-to-please sequel manages to evoke some of the thrills that Raimi so deftly delivered with the original DARKMAN.

As in Raimi's EVIL DEAD films, DARKMAN III begins with a pre-credit sequence summarizing Dr. Peyton Westlake/Darkman's story thus far. Grotesquely burned and superhumanly strong, Westlake (Arnold Vosloos) works in his underground lab, trying to perfect the liquid skin that allows him to look normal. Frustratingly, the skin only lasts 99 minutes before dissolving.

Westlake thwarts a drug deal set up by the ruthless Peter Rooker (Jeff Fahey) and uses the money for his research. Still, his equipment is insufficient, and it seems fortuitous when Dr. Bridget Thorne (Darlanne Fleugel) tracks Westlake down and offers him the use of her well-equipped lab. Westlake breaks the 99 minute barrier, but before he can use his new skin, Thorne, who works for Rooker, renders him unconscious. Rooker and Thorne plan to build an army of supercrooks using steroids made from Westlake's adrenal glands. Darkman escapes, but not before Thorne synthesizes the steroid.

Attempting to recover his perfected skin formula, Westlake follows Rooker. He discovers that not only was the steroid experiment a success, but that the mobster plans to use his supercrooks to kill the crusading new district attorney. Using liquid skin to disguise himself as Rooker, Westlake enters the criminal's house to retrieve his formula. He is sidetracked by Rooker's neglected wife and daughter, however, who awaken in him feelings he had thought were long dead.

Westlake foils the assassination attempt and tracks Rooker to a warehouse, where he discovers that the crime boss is holding his own wife and daughter hostage. After doing away with the supercrooks, Darkman defeats Rooker, who has enhanced himself with the steroid. In the battle, the computer disk containing the liquid skin formula is destroyed, leaving only a small sample. Although there is just enough left to restore Westlake's face, he sacrifices his needs to help Rooker's daughter, whose face was badly burned during the fight. Although he has let Rooker's wife and daughter get close to him, Westlake realizes that he must return to his quest alone.

Returning for his second DARKMAN film, cinematographer-director Bradford May does an admirable job of sustaining Raimi's original vision. Although DARKMAN III lacks the quirky personality and whiz-bang pacing of the first film, May manages to slip in a few of Raimi's trademark hyper zooms and lightning edits to goose the action sequences.

Although original Darkman Liam Neeson's presence is missed, Vosloos does a nice job as the conflicted Westlake, and the film actually manages to develop the Darkman character. As the film begins, Westlake is a bitter loner, but his contact with Rooker's wife and daughter allow him to once again appreciate companionship. Fahey also deserves credit for creating a new nemesis for Darkman who is not simply a retread of the first two films' sinister Durant.

The production boasts impressive visuals in the form of blue screen pyrotechnics and various makeup effects.

It is clear that DARKMAN III is not a mere cash-in on the original's popularity, and that the intention is to continue Darkman's adventures in future films released directly to home video. Compared with the prospect of double digit installments of CRITTERS, PUPPETMASTER, or DOLLMAN, that doesn't seem like such a dark thing. *(Graphic violence, profanity).* — D.G.

d, Bradford May; p, David Roessell; exec p, Sam Raimi, Robert Tapert; assoc p, Bernadette Joyce; co-p, David Eick; w, Michael Colleary, Mike Werb (based on characters created by Sam Raimi); ph, Bradford May; ed, Daniel Cahn; m, Randy Miller, Danny Elfman; art d, Ian Brock; sound, Chaim Gilad; fx, John Gajdecki; cos, Noreen Landry

Action/Science Fiction (PR: C MPAA: R)

DAYLIGHT ★★½

(U.S.) 109m Daylight Productions; Joseph M. Singer Productions; Davis Entertainment ~ Universal c

Sylvester Stallone *(Kit Latura)*; Amy Brenneman *(Madelyne Thompson)*; Viggo Mortensen *(Roy Nord)*; Dan Hedaya *(Frank Kraft)*; Jay O. Sanders *(Steven Crighton)*; Karen Young *(Sarah Crighton)*; Claire Bloom *(Eleanor Trilling)*; Vanessa Bell Calloway *(Grace)*; Renoly Santiago *(Mikey)*; Colin Fox *(Roger Trilling)*; Danielle Harris *(Ashley Crighton)*; Trina McGee-Davis *(Latonya)*; Marcello Thedford *(Kadeem)*; Sage Stallone *(Vincent)*; Jo Anderson *(Boom)*; Mark Rolston *(Chief Dennis Wilson)*; Rosemary Forsyth *(Ms. London)*; Luoyong Wang *(Gem Dealer)*; Barry Newman *(Norman Bassett)*; Stan Shaw *(George Tyrell)*; Marc Chadwick; Candace Miller; Lee Oakes *(Grunges)*; Sakina Jaffrey *(Ms. Doctor)*; Albert Macklin *(Mr. Doctor)*; Tony Munafo *(Cannister Truck Driver)*; Joseph Ragno *(Dispatcher)*; Nestor Serrano *(Weller)*; Harold Bradley *(Police Chief)*; Stephen Nalewicki *(TB Marketing Executive)*; John Lees *(Jonno)*; Robert Sommer *(Father)*; Lenore Lohman *(Young Woman)*; Mark DeAlessandro; Lisa McCullough *(Cops)*; Penny Crone; Madison; Ed Wheeler; Dan Daily; Stephen James; Isis Mussenden *(Reporters)*

A throwback to the disaster movies of the mid-1970s, DAYLIGHT suffers from the same weaknesses as even the best of those films: empty spectacle, predictable scripts, and "all-star" ensembles of fine actors in dull roles. Aside from the improved special effects (by Industrial Light and Magic), DAYLIGHT could have been produced by Irwin (THE POSEIDON ADVENTURE, THE TOWERING INFERNO) Allen.

Trouble is brewing in the New York metro area when several truckloads of explosive toxic waste are unlawfully shipped through the Lincoln Tunnel (under the Hudson River between Manhattan and New Jersey). In mid-tunnel, a carful of thieves fleeing the city collides with the trucks, causing an explosion that seals the tunnel from both ends. Among those trapped are Madelyn (Amy Brenneman), a frustrated young playwright fed up with NY and on her way home; a macho sporting-goods magnate (Viggo Mortensen); an older couple grieving for their dead son (Claire Bloom, Colin Fox); a genial bridge and tunnel cop (Stan Shaw); and a busload of small-time felons on their way to prison. Fires and exhaust problems are rapidly depleting their oxygen supply, while the 80-year-old tunnel structure slowly disintegrates around them. Rescue squads are stymied, as punching into the wreckage will inevitably upset the air pressure inside, causing a fatal cave-in.

Just outside the tunnel at the time of the explosion is Kit Latura (Sylvester Stallone), former chief of New York's Emergency Rescue Service who was stripped of his position when a scapegoat was needed for an unavoidable but highly visible mishap. (Though blameless, he is still racked with guilt over the incident.) Having once run a study of what to do in case of a terrorist attack on the tunnel, Latura knows it intimately. After much arguing, city officials agree to let him try to make his way into the tunnel though the ventilation system.

Latura reaches the survivors and helps them stay alive, despite arguments over the best course of action. City bureaucrats, meanwhile, panicked at the prospect of snarled traffic the next morning and unable to make radio contact with Latura, abandon hope for any survivors and bring in demolition equipment to punch through the rubble. By following a pack of rats, Latura discovers a passage to the surface and leads the remaining survivors through it. But he and Madelyn are left behind when the passage collapses. After the others have escaped, they improvise a plan to blow a hole in the tunnel and let air pressure "blow" them to the surface of the river. A rescue boat picks them up in the river, and Latura is hailed as a hero.

Clearly, Leslie Bohem's script is not too troubled by issues of plausibility. Instead, it seems structured on the logic of a theme-park ride, with obstacles and last-minute rescues choreographed for the diversion of the glands of the viewer, not the mind or heart. Indeed, aside from the various survivors, Bohem makes little attempt to characterize anybody top-side—though the premise is ripe for tension both above and below, the film seems enamored of the artificial world it creates inside the Tunnel. It simply becomes man-against-worst-case-scenario, in the most obvious terms possible.

As is so often the case in the disaster genre, DAYLIGHT is a parable of very different kinds of Americans working together against a common threat. Perhaps it is a measure of how unlikely such collaboration seems that it takes a major disaster to make it believable. *(Violence, adult situations.)* — N.N.

d, Rob Cohen; p, John Davis, Joseph M. Singer, David T. Friendly; exec p, Raffaella De Laurentiis; assoc p, Tony Munafo; co-p, Hester Hargett, Herbert W. Gains; w, Leslie Bohem; ph, David Eggby; ed, Peter Amundson; m, Randy Edelman; prod d, Benjamin Fernandez; art d, Pier-Luigi Basile; set d, Giorgio Desideri; sound, Reinhard Stergar, Richard L. Anderson, David A. Whittaker; fx, Kit West, Industrial Light & Magic; casting, Margery Simkin; cos, Thomas Casterline, Isis Mussenden; makeup, Giannetto De Rossi; stunts, Paul Weston

AAN Best Sound Effects Editing:

Action/Adventure/Disaster (PR: C MPAA: PG-13)

DE AMOR Y DE SOMBRA

(SEE: OF LOVE AND SHADOWS)

DEAD COLD ★★½

(U.S.) 91m Image Organization; Ventana Productions ~ LIVE Entertainment c

Lysette Anthony *(Alicia)*; Chris Mulkey *(Eric Thornsen)*; Peter Dobson *(Kale)*; Michael Champion *(Bill Butler)*; Alina Thompson *(Sarah)*; Anneliza Scott *(Susan)*

Fooling the audience to good effect, DEAD COLD chills at just the right temperature; with its menage-a-trois twist, direct-to-vid viewers don't have to feel as if they're struggling to climb out of a snowdrift of obviousness.

After recuperating from a near-fatal car-jacking, screenwriter Eric Thornsen (Chris Mulkey) bundles up his supportive wife Alicia (Lysette Anthony) for a remote spot where he can forget urban anxiety and complete his novel. The rustic calm of this second honeymoon is marred by the appearance of a homicidal fugitive, Kale (Peter Dobson), also responsible for the car-jacking. Kale has warmed up for terrorizing the Thornsens by shooting Sarah (Alina Thompson), the daughter of local tourist cabin manager Bill Butler (Michael Champion). When Eric finds a frostbitten Kale on his doorstep, the good Samaritan takes in the viper despite Alicia's overstated wariness. Irredeemably vulgar, Kale proves to be a trying houseguest whose stay is prolonged by the inexplicable conk-out of Eric's auto. Failing to fully comprehend what he's up against, Eric is goaded into an evening of boozing which climaxes in Kale incapacitating him and dumping his body down a ravine. Returning to ravage the wife, Kale gets a warm reception from the spidery Alicia. . . for whom this is the second attempt on her unsuspecting hubby's life. While the lethal lovebirds count their insurance payments before they're hatched, hypothermic Eric trudges slowly cabin-ward. Putting two and two together while looking for his missing daughter, Bill Butler employs an accusatory tone that nets him a pitchforked response from Kale. When Eric stumbles back, after discovering Sarah's corpse, he's prepared to confront his wily mate, who improvises by fatally shooting Kale to cover her guilt. But wised up to his would-be widow, Eric defends himself from a vicious assault that builds up to Alicia's fatally falling onto an ax jutting from a tree stump below.

If only this sly escapade's middle section didn't sag like a mid-life gut, this otherwise trim film noir might have been a model tale of triangular betrayal. Despite the complacent cross-cutting between shivering Eric and the bickering spouse-exterminators before the climax, the movie must be saluted for its devious set-up and dazzling pay-off. By slyly beginning the film with Eric laying out a fictitious murder scenario for a script, DEAD COLD freezes the viewer into Eric's perspective and engages sympathy while establishing the gullibility that makes him a patsy for a doxy like Alicia. In the vein of KNIFE IN THE WATER (1962) and DEAD CALM (1989), the shifting loyalties inside that cramped cabin bristle with bottled-up erotic tension; this type of thriller suggests that only in close quarters are people unable to disguise their true colors. Perhaps the revelation about Kale and Alicia's teamwork should have been postponed; as it stands, DEAD COLD does drop the ball once we realize Alicia is a *belle dame sans merci.* But DEAD COLD is a reasonably gripping suspense package that often maxes thrills from its isolated setting. *(Extreme profanity, extensive nudity, graphic violence, adult situations, substance abuse, sexual situations.)* — R.P.

d, Kurt Anderson; p, Richard Brandes; exec p, Pierre David; assoc p, Lysette Anthony; co-p, Clark Peterson; w, Richard

Brandes (from a story by Kurt Anderson and Richard Brandes); ph, M. David Mullen; ed, Daniel Lowenthal; m, Richard Bowers; casting, Laura Schiff; prod d, Brian McCabe; sound, Adam Joseph; fx, Kevin McCarthy; cos, Nadine Haders; makeup, Roxy D'Alonzo

Thriller/Mystery **(PR: C MPAA: R)**

DEAD MAN ★★★★

(U.S./Germany/Japan) 121m 12-Gauge Productions; JVC; Newmarket Capital Group; Victor Company of Japan; Pandora Film ~ Miramax bw

Johnny Depp *(William Blake)*; Gary Farmer *(Nobody)*; Lance Henriksen *(Cole Wilson)*; Gabriel Byrne *(Charlie Dickinson)*; Robert Mitchum *(John Dickinson)*; John Hurt *(John Scholfield)*; Crispin Glover *(The Fireman)*; Michael Wincott *(Conway Twill)*; Eugene Byrd *(Johnny "The Kid" Pickett)*; Mili Avital *(Thel Russell)*; Billy Bob Thornton *(Big George Drakoulious)*; Iggy Pop *(Salvatore "Sally" Jenko)*; Jared Harris *(Benmont Tench)*; John North *(Mr. Olafsen)*; Alfred Molina *(Trading Post Missionary)*; Jimmie Ray Weeks *(Marvin, Older Marshall)*; Mark Bringelson *(Lee, Younger Marshall)*; Michelle Thrush *(Nobody's Girlfriend)*; Peter Schrum *(Drunk)*; Gibby Haines *(Man in the Alley)*; George Duckworth *(Man at End of Street)*; Richard Boes *(Man with Wrench)*; Mike Dowson *(Old Man with Wanted Posters)*; John Pattison *(Trading Post Man No. 1)*; Todd Pfeiffer *(Trading Post Man No. 2)*; Leonard Bowechop *(Mahah Villager)*; Cecil Cheeka *(Mahah Villager)*; Michael McCarty *(Mahah Villager)*; Thomas Bettles *(Young Nobody No. 1)*; Daniel Chas Stacy *(Young Nobody No. 2)*

In DEAD MAN, Jim Jarmusch contemplates "the western" and all that generic movie term implies. This sometimes daring, sometimes frustrating ode to cinematic and literary traditions develops an offbeat charm and lingers intensely in the memory.

In the 1800s, an accountant from Cleveland, William Blake (Johnny Depp), travels by train to the western town of Machine, where a job awaits him at the Dickinson Metalworks factory. When he arrives from his exhausting journey, William discovers that the job has been filled by someone else. He tries to complain, but John Dickinson (Robert Mitchum) sends him on his way. In despair, William spends his last coins at a local saloon, where he meets the beautiful Thel Russell (Mili Avital). William and Thel later make love but are interrupted by Dickinson's son, Charlie (Gabriel Byrne), Thel's former fiance. In a scuffle, Charlie kills Thel and shoots William, and William kills Charlie and flees to the wilderness.

The next day, William, now a wounded fugitive, is awakened by Nobody (Gary Farmer), a displaced Native American and avid reader of the English poet William Blake. Believing he has found the dead poet, Nobody feels he must return him to the world of the spirits where he belongs.

Meanwhile, Dickinson hires three famous killers to avenge the death of his son: Cole Wilson (Lance Henriksen), Conway Twill (Michael Wincott), and Johnny "The Kid" Pickett (Eugene Byrd). While Nobody tests William's courage along the dangerous western terrain, the three mercenaries hunt for William to claim their reward.

After painting William's face, Nobody leaves his partner, who effects his public myth as killer when he shoots two marshalls (Jimmie Ray Weeks, Mark Bringelson) who have heard about Dickinson's bounty. Nearby, Cole Wilson decides to kill his accomplices and search for William on his own. Eventually, William and Nobody are reunited on their journey to the coastal village of Makah. Along the way they are almost betrayed by a missionary (Alfred Molina), but the weary travelers finally arrive. The Makah elders present Nobody with a canoe to bury the dying William at sea. After sending William off in the canoe, Nobody has a shootout with Cole on shore. Both men fall, as William drifts away on the horizon.

Before its limited release, Miramax sat on DEAD MAN for a seeming eternity, despite the art-house cachet of director Jarmusch (STRANGER THAN PARADISE, MYSTERY TRAIN). Perhaps the distributors wanted to avoid a repeat of Gus Van Sant's EVEN COWGIRLS GET THE BLUES (1994) fiasco, but other than being another all-star revisionist western from a gifted but idiosyncratic art-film director, DEAD MAN has little in common with COWGIRLS. At least, DEAD MAN, whatever its flaws, claims a place as a "head" movie, a visual treat, and, ultimately, a haunting drama, too.

DEAD MAN gets away with its pretentious conceits by having self-reflexive fun with itself. The repeated references to the poetry and artwork of the real William Blake (1757-1827) are acknowledged by both Jarmusch and the story characters. The silly "all-star" allure is subverted by the relative brevity of the guest star appearances. (Indeed, some performers, including Crispin Glover playing a train fireman, are barely recognizable.) The digressions within the somber story are often odd or funny or both, including a camp fire scene with Billy Bob Thornton, Jared Harris and Iggy Pop (inexplicably in drag) as Bible-thumping animal skinners.

Finally, Jarmusch never forgets the pulp roots of the western genre, as evidenced in his casting of Robert Mitchum (icon of many a western) and visual quotations from Peckinpah, Lang, Leone and Fuller, among others.

DEAD MAN, however, contains some disappointing elements. The women characters fare no better here than in classic westerns. (Thel takes a bullet a la Frenchie in DESTRY RIDES AGAIN). By contrast, the depiction of racism towards the Native Americans and African Americans feels *too* modern. Some of the jokes fall flat, including the repeated Beckett-like play on Nobody's name and a gag involving a bear having sex with a man. On the technical side, Robby Mueller's black-and-white cinematography is beautiful, but the quick, frequent fades to black are annoying, and Neil Young's 70s-style score desperately needs some variations.

DEAD MAN will please Jarmusch followers as much as it will irritate old-fashioned western fans. Of course, that's part of the director's scheme—and he mostly succeeds with this allegorical, intellectual answer to DANCES WITH WOLVES (1990). *(Graphic violence, sexual situations, adult situations, substance abuse, extreme profanity).* — E.M.

d, Jim Jarmusch; p, Demetra J. MacBride; co-p, Karen Koch; w, Jim Jarmusch; ph, Robby Muller; ed, Jay Rabinowitz; m, Neil Young; prod d, Bob Ziembicki; art d, Ted Berner; set d, Dayna Lee; sound, Drew Kunin (mixer); fx, Lou Carlucci, FTS Effects, Jon Farhat, R/Greenberg Associates West, Inc.; casting, Ellen Lewis, Laura Rosenthal; cos, Marit Allen; makeup, Neal Martz, Steve Johnson's XFX

Western **(PR: C MPAA: R)**

DEAD TO RIGHTS ★★½

(U.S.) 93m Multimedia Motion Pictures ~ Vidmark c

Charles Donato *(Sgt. Mike Donato)*; Dana Delany *(Dina Donato)*; Xander Berkeley *(Russ Loring)*; Louis Giambalvo *(Hugh Halliday)*; Jenette Goldstein *(Judy McCartney)*; Marc Alaimo *(Detective Petsky)*; Tom Verica *(Bobby Keegan)*; Bonnie Bartlett *(Renata Donato)*; Richard Kuss *(Chief Stone)*; Patti Yasutake *(Dr. Stewart)*; Michael Cavanaugh *(Vinnie Stellino)*; Julianna McCarthy *(Adele Loring)*; Kim Weeks *(Andrea Loring)*; Charles

Hayward *(Detective Scott)*; Ian Patrick Williams *(Kim Lyle)*; Sam Vincent *(Towers)*; Sylvia Short *(Sister Margaret)*; Malechi Pearson *(Cal)*; Kathleen Coyne *(Sister Mary Ann)*; David Gautreaux *(Jake Bloomberg)*; Renee Golden *(Daily News Reporter)*; Gregory Itzin *(Cornell)*; Pirie Jones *(Times Reporter)*; David McClain *(Video Tech)*; Virginia Morris *(Jellinek)*; Tony Pandolfo *(Bert Harris)*; Robin Cahill *(USA Reporter)*; Ronald Pitts *(Reporter)*

Surprisingly brutal for a network TV presentation, this crime drama is saddled with a central domestic father-daughter dilemma that isn't nearly as engrossing as the ritual murder case that the father and daughter detectives must solve. Dampened by the overrated "sincerity" of star Dana Delany, DEAD TO RIGHTS occasionally transcends its serial killer subgenre.

At loggerheads with her father, Sgt. Donato (Charles Bronson), over the mystery-shrouded death of her brother, Tommy, superior officer Dina Donato (Dana Delany) doesn't leap at the chance to add her dad to her task force to solve a string of nun slayings. Unable to flush the smug killer out, the baffled detectives follow various leads, including an addict with a grudge against one of the victims. Dina is wracked with guilt when her pregnant sister-in-law, Judy (Jenette Goldstein), is fatally shot in the line of duty. Dina eventually narrows her focus to two likely suspects: Kim Lyle (Ian Patrick Williams), a cross-dressing photographer, and Russ Loring (Xander Berkeley), a yuppie broker.

While her associates concentrate on Lyle, Dina checks out Loring, and Sgt. Donato questions Loring's over-protective mother (Juliana McCarthy) about her son's broken engagement to a woman who intended to enter a convent. Rattling Loring's cage only emboldens this serial killer to taunt Dina and to stab his wife, Andrea (Kim Weeks), when she confronts him with damaging evidence. Cagily misleading Loring by claiming the police have arrested another man, Dina stalls for time at Loring's apartment until a search warrant is issued. When critically injured Andrea taps from the bedroom for help, Loring accosts Dina and drags her to the building's roof. There, Sgt. Donato fatally shoots nun-killer Loring. A grateful Dina can now forgive her father for his revelation about covering up the facts of her brother's drug-related death to spare the family.

DEAD TO RIGHTS captures the gritty details of a grinding police investigation. Its false starts and liberating breakthroughs make viewers feel as if they're really in the crimefighting trenches. Although the murderer's identity is revealed early, the suspense stems from witnessing the interlocking of such puzzle pieces as hidden motive, shifting modus operandi, and the hunt for a chink in the madman's psychological armor. Would that the trumped-up father-daughter conflict had the same dramatic force. Every time the screenplay cuts away to another bitter exchange between "Donato and Daughter" (the film's original title), the audience gets soggy from the soapsuds. Fortunately, the maniacal slayer is memorably limned by Xander Berkeley as a mega-arrogant sociopath who feels justified in symbolically murdering over and over again the woman who rejected him for God. In a brilliantly written and acted scene, we also meet the grotesquely indulgent mother who spawned this monster. Thanks to such grace notes, DEAD TO RIGHTS locks in viewer interest as it humanizes both cops and victims and makes the nun-terminator's motive both reprehensible and comprehensible. *(Graphic violence, profanity, adult situations.)* — R.P.

d, Rod Holcomb; p, Marian Brayton, Anne Carlucci; exec p, Neil Russell, Brenda Miao; w, Robert Roy Pool (based on the novel by Jack Early); ph, Thomas Del Ruth; ed, Christopher Nelson; m, Sylvester Levay; prod d, Richard Sherman; set d, Michael Wargo; sound, Kim Ornitz (mixer); casting, Karen Hendel; cos, Timothy D'Arcy; makeup, Marilyn Carbone

Crime/Drama **(PR: C MPAA: R)**

DEAD WEEKEND ★

(U.S.) 82m Retrofit Productions; IRS Media; Showtime Entertainment ~ Paramount Home Video c

Stephen Baldwin *(Weed)*; Alexis Arquette *(McHacker)*; David Rasche *(Payne)*; Tom Kenny *(Joe Blow)*; Bai Ling *(Amelia A)*; Affifi Alaouie *(Amelia B)*; Blair Valk *(Amelia C)*; Jennifer MacDonald *(Amelia D)*; Barbara Alyn Woods *(Amelia E)*; Sam Scarber *(General Mills)*; Marcos Antonio Ferraez *(Gonzolo)*; Clint Culp *(Overweight Soldier)*; Greg Wrangler *(TWF 1)*; Greg Collins *(TWF 2)*; David Millbern *(Medic 1)*; Joe Davis *(Trooper)*; Stacy Strauss *(Waitress)*; Jon Regnery *(TWF Soldier)*; Cindy Morgan *(Newscaster)*; Richard Speight Jr. *(Rebel 1)*; Craig Kvinsland *(TWF Soldier)*; Perry Lang *(Captain)*; Patrick Cupo *(Rebel 2)*; Nicholas Worth *(Hayden)*

A chameleon alien meets a sexually hyperactive human, who lubricates her every transformation. If they aren't making love, they're talking about it, but the only blip on the sexual radar screen comes from second unit shots of army combat.

In the future, True World Forces (TWF) has perfected martial law as a social panacea. When an extraterrestrial named Amelia threatens their grip on the populace, General Mills (Sam Scarber) fakes an earthquake in order to evacuate the city, orders his troops to gun down Amelia, and consolidate power by clearing the streets of radicals and criminals. His primary opponents are Joe Blow (Tom Kenny), a rebel DJ who transmits illegal broadcasts, and soldier boy Weed (Stephen Baldwin), who meets Amelia and can't put patriotism before lust.

Despite the disapproval of his friend Payne (David Rasche), Weed protects Amelia, who changes racial identities and shapes on contact. As the TWF scores a bullseye by poisoning Joe Blow and his resistance assistant, Amelia tells Weed that she suffers from a DNA-shifting disorder, aggravated by recreational sex. Desperate to return home for treatment, Amelia lectures the violent earthling soldiers before boarding her homebound spaceship with Weed.

The makers of DEAD WEEKEND were not bold enough to stretch the limits of sci-fi satire. Neither the plot nor the characters ever move from point A to point B. Bullets fly, gums flap, bodies writhe, and little happens. There is much talking to pad the film, and everyone winds up sounding like patients at an impotency clinic for Trekkies. One even tires of Baldwin bedding his one-woman UN.

With its anti-government patter and moronic debasement of sexual politics, DEAD WEEKEND is a comedy of Eros that may be fully appreciated only by immature young men who can't look at a woman without mentally unsnapping her brassiere. *(Violence, extreme profanity, extensive nudity, sexual situations.)* — R.P.

d, Amos Poe; p, Larry Estes; exec p, Paul Colichman, Miles Copeland III; assoc p, Cindy Morgan; co-p, Amos Poe, Damian Jones; w, Joel Rose (based on a story by Amos Poe); ph, Gary Tieche; ed, Fabienne Rawley; m, Steve Hunter; prod d, Wayne Beswick, Gustav Alsina; art d, Mark Cohen; set d, Dawn Ferry; sound, D. J. Ritchie; fx, Movie Arms Management; casting, Donald Paul Pemrick; cos, Wendy Range; makeup, Jennifer Montgomery; stunts, Tim Trella

Science Fiction **(PR: O MPAA: R)**

DEADLY OUTBREAK ★★

(U.S.) 94m Takeover; Goldbar Entertainment ~ LIVE Entertainment c

Ron Silver *(Colonel Baron)*; Jeff Speakman *(Dutton Hatfield)*; Rochelle Swanson *(Dr. Allie Levin)*; Jack Adelist *(Ramon)*; Jonathan Sagalle *(Gallo)*; Yehuda Elboim *(Lt. Epstein)*; Dan Turjeman *(Colonel Gideon)*; Yehuda Efroni *(Dr. Berg)*; Kevin Jones *(Hopper)*; Idan Alterman *(Ira)*; Bridget Marks *(Elaine)*; Yorman Yosephsberg *(Gunther)*; R. L. Noff *(Vartan)*; Larry Smith *(Dr. Stein)*; Michael Parlato *(Luther)*; Erin Rosenberg *(T. J.)*; Elan Frank *(Pilot)*; Eli Weizman *(Sergeant)*; Ron Shuki *(Arthunian)*; Jeri Hayman *(General Miller)*; Ami Dayan *(Dr. Abraham)*; Jack Widierker *(Dr. Dinkins)*; Yoram Gal *(Stanislav)*; Andray Kashkar *(Paklowsky)*; Harel Goldstein *(Air Controller)*; Olga Cohen *(Ms. Eli)*; Oded Greenstein *(Corporal Deon)*; Chaim Rinski *(Embassy Guard)*

This plague thriller threatens our immune system with little more than raging deja vu—with its resemblance to other merciless-microbes movies, including big-budget items like OUTBREAK and low-budget schlock like IRON EAGLE 4.

Headed for BBI, a top security lab in Israel, a plane load of scientists is intercepted and annihilated so that a group of anarchists can assume their identities. When UN peacekeeper Sgt. Dutton Hatfield (Jeff Speakman) greets the contingent led by wily Colonel Baron (Ron Silver), he doesn't realize Baron plans to extort a half-billion dollars under threat of unleashing BBI's deadly chemical warfare strain. After Baron and his troops wipe out BBI personnel, only three people can throw a monkey-wrench into Baron's plot to hold the world hostage: Hatfield; Ira (Idan Alterman), a lowly security guard; and Dr. Allie Levin (Rochelle Swanson), a research genius who whisks away an antidote to the bio-nightmare.

With the cooperation of inside man Dr. Berg (Yehudi Efroni), Baron kills more hostages and forces back Israeli commandos led by Colonel Gideon (Dan Turjeman). Rescuing Dr. Levin during the takeover of the facility and bedeviling Baron's assassin squad, Hatfield barely escapes incineration in a basement escape tunnel. Although Levin blocks surveillance transmissions, Baron kills Dr. Berg with nerve gas and tricks Hatfield out of the chemical warfare canister in exchange for a hostage. In a double cross, Baron orders the hostage slaughtered. Boarding an escape bus with Dr. Levin, three hostages, and his enforcer Ramon (Jack Adelist), Baron smugly drives toward freedom until Hatfield's helicopter intercepts the bus. Too late for the hostages who are killed in the melee, Hatfield saves Dr. Levin and the canister and slays Ramon. After Baron's bus plows into fuel canisters, Colonel Gideon shoots down Baron's just-arrived agent, enabling a wounded Hatfield to scotch Baron's pestilence plot.

Dedicated to mayhem in all its forms, DEADLY OUTBREAK is practically a filmic textbook on ways to destroy human life, but it lacks the escapist punch of some other direct-to-videos. Speakman's martial artistry is as flexible and crowd-pleasing as ever, but he's wasting his charm on a lackluster vehicle. Many action spectaculars demonstrate a similar disregard for humanity, but most of these direct-to-videos employ tongue-in-cheek undercurrents to float the rampant destruction to a cartoon level. DEADLY OUTBREAK is submerged in its own violence; because there's no compensatory directorial eclat or challenging screenplay, the nastiness quickly curdles. *(Graphic violence, extreme profanity, sexual situations, adult situations.)* — R.P.

d, Rick Avery; p, Harel Goldstein, Bill Barnett, David Goldstein; exec p, Avi Lerner, Danny Dimbort, Trevor Short; assoc p, Juanita Diana; co-p, Danny Lerner; w, Charles Morris, Harel Goldstein; ph, Avi Koren; ed, Alain Jakubowicz; m, Harvey Mason; prod d, Ariel Roshko; set d, Miguel Mirkin; sound, Eli Yarkoni; fx, Pini Klavir; cos, Laura Dinulesco; makeup, Mira Tal; stunts, Buck McDancer

Martial Arts/Action/Thriller (PR: C MPAA: R)

DEAR GOD ★★

(U.S.) 111m Steve Tisch Company; Rysher Entertainment; Paramount ~ Paramount c

Greg Kinnear *(Tom Turner)*; Laurie Metcalf *(Rebecca Frazen)*; Maria Pitillo *(Gloria McKinney)*; Tim Conway *(Herman Dooly)*; Hector Elizondo *(Vladek Vidov)*; Jon Seda *(Handsome)*; Roscoe Lee Browne *(Idris Abraham)*; Anna Maria Horsford *(Lucille)*; Kathleen Marshall *(Whispering Lady)*; Isadora O'Boto *(Hot Mary)*; Felix A. Pire *(Ramon)*; Donal Logue *(Webster)*; Sam McMurray *(Federal Prosecutor)*; Nancy Marchand *(Judge Kits Van Heynigan)*; Larry Miller *(State Judge)*; Rue McClanahan *(Mom Turner)*; Jack Sheldon *(Homeless Trumpeter)*; Coolio *(Gerard)*; Toby Huss *(Doubting Thomas Minister)*; Stephanie Niznik *(Emanda Maine)*; John Pinette *(Junior)*; Seth Mumy *(Joey McKinney)*; Greg Lewis *(Greek Bailiff)*; Sunny Hawks *(Greek Daughter)*; Timi Prulhiere *(Southern Tourist)*; Valerie Wildman *(Southern Tourist)*; Jennifer Perkins *(Information Booth Clerk)*; Rick Hill *(Parade Father)*; Barbara Marshall *(Sister Charlotte)*; Jane Morris *(Sarah Alcott)*; Tom Hines *(Theo)*; Jeff Michalski *(Otis)*; Shannon Wilcox *(Madame Zema)*; Joshua Iscovich *(Joey's Friend)*; Jill Lover *(Regular Customer)*; Seron Bellio *(Regular Customer)*; Leigh Molloy *(Regular Customer)*; Timothy Stack *(Cousin Guy The Postal Cop)*; William Wolff *(Doug Diamond)*; Sarina L. Ranftl *(Postal Window Clerk)*; Monica Campbell *(Postal Window Clerk)*; Sam Lima *(Postal Customer)*; Ellery King *(Postal Customer)*; Diane Frazen *(Postal Customer)*; Jennifer Peterson *(Postal Signer)*; Joy Rosenthal *(Rich Postal Customer)*; Adrienne Wilde *(Postal Cashier)*; Bud Markowitz *(Juggling Biker)*; Bonnie Aarons *(Prophet Woman)*; Steve Tisch *(Neighbor with Dog)*; Mariana Morgan *(Neighbor with Dog)*; Jack Klugman *(Jemi)*; Marvin Braverman *(Petting Zoo Man)*; Ellen Cleghorne *(Marguerite)*; Curtis Williams *(Marguerite's Son)*; Deborah Benson-Wald *(Juanita)*; Odette Yustman *(Angela)*; Marcus Toji *(Petting Zoo Kid)*; Yvonne Pollack *(Normandie Arms Tenant)*; Mona Lyden *(Crystal Fricker)*; Betty Carvalho *(Maid)*; Hope Alexander-Willis *(Female Minister)*; Mel Novak *(Sidewalk Minister)*; Dom Magwili *(Teacher)*; Don Feldstein *(Charlie at Bowl)*; Harvey Keenan *(Homeless Man)*; A. Kent Braverman *(Salvation Army Guy)*; Lori Sigrist *(Adult Twin Nurse)*; Terri Sigrist *(Adult Twin Nurse)*; Patrick Richwood *(Federal Clerk)*; Jim Meskimen *(State D.A.)*; Israel Juarbe *(Ernesto on Scaffold)*; Martin Garbus *(Assistant Prosecutor)*; Allan Kent *(Court Officer)*; Duane Matthews *(Court Officer)*; Carol Williard *(Court Photographer)*; Sean O'Bryan; Joanna Heimbold; Rebecca Holberg *(Undercover Cops)*; Renee Albert *(Camerawoman)*; Robert Malina *(News Video Cameraman)*; Jeris Lee Poindexter *(Local Newscaster)*; Dr. Joyce Brothers *(Herself)*; Erin Moran *(Celebrity in Parade)*; Elinor Donahue *(Celebrity in Parade)*

DEAR GOD aspires to keep company with MIRACLE ON 34TH STREET (1947) and IT'S A WONDERFUL LIFE (1946), but though it possesses a similar "feel good" sentimentality, it doesn't hold a candle to those Christmas classics.

Tom Turner (Greg Kinnear) is a charismatic LA con man who is arrested while trying to hustle money to pay off a gambling debt. To stay out of jail, Turner is forced to take a job in the dead letter department at the post office. At first, Turner dismisses as losers the authors of the volumes of undeliverable letters to Santa, Elvis, and God. Then he accidentally mails his pay to one of the writers, an indigent woman. He tries to retrieve the cash but cannot bring himself to take it back when he sees how much the woman and her family need it.

Tom's coworker, Rebecca (Laurie Metcalf), witnesses Tom's generosity and thinks Tom did the good deed on purpose. She and the other dead letter office employees want to help Tom on his "mission of mercy." They begin reading the Dear God mail and performing good deeds ranging from baby-sitting for over-burdened parents to rescuing a suicidal man (Jack Klugman).

The motley crew of miracle workers look to Tom as their leader, despite his protests that he is not the selfless man they think he is. Tom reluctantly takes charge of the group, which is tagged by the media as "the God Squad." They perform 12 acts of kindness before the postal authorities intervene, and Tom is arrested for tampering with the mail.

At Tom's trial, his coworkers and beneficiaries testify on his behalf, and the city's mail carriers rally outside the courthouse, chanting, "Tom in jail, no mail." Tom is found not guilty, and returns to his job at the post office a changed man.

Like a candied Christmas fruitcake, DEAR GOD has many fine ingredients, but combined they add up to a confection that no one really wants. In his first starring film role, Kinnear is more appealing than his material, displaying a natural charm and cocky verve. DEAR GOD is a dismal follow-up to his critically acclaimed debut in SABRINA (1995). The supporting cast all have their moments of inspired looniness, with Tim Conway doing what he does best, and Metcalf going way over the top, out-burlesquing even Conway. Director Garry Marshall appears to good advantage as the postmaster general, and Klugman is touching in a too-brief role.

Though DEAR GOD sprang from an amusing premise, the story by Warren Leight and Ed Kaplan is unimaginative and predictable. The script relies heavily on postal puns, few of which provide bona fide laughs. The drawn-out courtroom climax makes the film feel about 20 minutes too long, and Marshall's sitcom-style direction interjects sentimental moments into strings of pratfalls and one-liners. The final result is a treacly mess that neither tickles the funny bone nor lifts the spirit. *(Profanity.)* — B.R.

d, Garry Marshall; p, Steve Tisch; exec p, Mario Iscovich; assoc p, Angel Pine, Karen Stirgwolt; co-p, Ellen H. Schwartz, Kearie Peak; w, Warren Leight, Ed Kaplan; ph, Charles Minsky; ed, Debra Neil-Fisher; m, Jeremy Lubbock, James Patrick Dunne; prod d, Albert Brenner; art d, Gregory Bolton; set d, Garrett Lewis; sound, James E. Webb Jr. (mixer); fx, Tom Ward; casting, Carrie Frazier; cos, Deborah Hopper; makeup, Stephen Abrums; stunts, Gary Combs

Comedy **(PR: A MPAA: PG)**

DEATH ARTIST, THE ★

(U.S.) 79m New Horizons ~ New Horizons c

Anthony Michael Hall *(Walter Paisley)*; Justine Bateman *(Carla)*; Shadoe Stevens *(Maxwell)*; Sam Lloyd *(Leonard)*; Jesse D. Goines *(Art)*; Kin Shriner *(Lou)*; Sheila Traviss *(Mayolia)*; David Cross *(Charlie)*; Victor Wilson *(Cuff)*; Patrick Briston *(Link)*; Paul Bartel *(Older Man)*; Mink Stole *(Older Woman)*; Julianna McCarthy *(Mrs. Swicker)*; Will Ferrell *(Young Man)*; Alan Sues *(Art Buyer)*; Darcy DeMoss *(Alice)*; Jennifer Coolidge *(Stupid Girl)*; Stephen Burrows *(Carpenter)*; Jim Jackson *(Art Critic)*; Jennifer Judith Joyce *(Woman at Show)*; Michael James McDonald *(Dancer)*; Jim Wise; Scott Levy *(Sleazy Agent)*; Brendan Broderick *(Sleazy Agent)*; Deena Casiano *(Violinist)*; Markus Reinhardt *(Cellist)*

If nothing else, executive producer Roger Corman's dreary remake of his 1959 cult classic A BUCKET OF BLOOD proves that he has no particular reverence for his own work. Likewise, the audience should have no particular reverence for *this* film.

Dimwitted busboy Walter Paisley (Anthony Michael Hall) longs to be an artist like the poets and performers at the Jabberjaw, the coffeehouse where he works. Unable to create a sculpture, he covers a dead cat in clay and passes it off as an original work. The piece, "Dead Cat," is acclaimed by the hipsters who had once scorned him, as is "Murdered Man," the clay-covered body of a narcotics cop Walter accidentally kills.

Basking in his new fame and the attentions of cafe habitue Carla (Justine Bateman), Walter turns to murder for more raw material. When he discovers that Carla's attentions are merely platonic, he plans to make her his next model. But when the clay starts to flake off his sculptures, the bodies underneath are revealed to horrified viewers. One step ahead of his pursuers, Walter returns to his apartment, covers himself in plaster-of-Paris, and hangs himself, making of his own death his final (and best) work.

THE DEATH MASTER is so closely a word-for-word remake of A BUCKET OF BLOOD that original scriptwriter Charles B. Griffith probably has grounds to sue for full credit instead of the "based upon" credit he is given. On the other hand, it's unlikely that he'd actually *want* to. It's astonishing how the creators of THE DEATH MASTER could stick so slavishly to their source and still miss everything that made it a cult classic. With the exceptions of performances by Justine Bateman, hiding behind ugly glasses and a preposterous Italian accent, and Shadoe Stevens, as a pretentious poet, everything is played perfectly straight. The competent but uninspired production lacks any of the endearing and tacky ambiance that make the original such a period piece. *(Graphic violence, nudity, sexual situations, substance abuse, profanity.)* — M.F.

d, Michael James McDonald; p, Mike Elliott; exec p, Roger Corman, Lance H. Robbins; w, Brendan Broderick, Michael James McDonald (based on the screenplay by Charles B. Griffith); ph, Christopher Baffa; ed, Roderick Davis; m, David Wurst, Eric Wurst; prod d, Nava; art d, Danielle Berman; sound, Karla Hennessy (coordinator); casting, Jan Glaser; cos, Maral Kalinian; makeup, Stephanie Massie

Horror/Thriller/Comedy **(PR: O MPAA: R)**

DEATH BENEFIT ★★★

(U.S.) 89m MTE ~ MCA/Universal Home Video c

Peter Horton *(Steven Keeney)*; Carrie Snodgress *(Virginia McGinnis)*; Wendy Makkena *(Wynn Burkholder)*; Penny Johnson *(Sylvia Guzman)*; Elizabeth Ruscio *(LuAnn Wilkens)*; Belita Moreno *(Sarah West)*; Lee de Broux *(Mark Vandenburg)*; Nathan Lawrence *(Christian Keeney)*; James McAlpine *(B. J. McGinnis)*; Dean Norris *(Rod Montgomery)*; Jack Kehler *(Dick Coates)*; Glenn Morshower *(Tim O'Grady)*; Joan McMurtrey *(Dr. Susan Lindsay-Rhodes)*; Ben Slack *(Eddie)*; Rick Cicetti *(Parishioner)*; Dale Raoul *(Mrs. Greene)*; Brittany Ashton Holmes *(Cynthia Coates)*; Abraham Alvarez *(Judge)*

Rising head and shoulders above most made-for-cable offerings, this true-life crime story takes viewers step by step through the cracking of a bizarre murder case and demonstrates just how exciting the intricacies of brain power can be in the unraveling of a mystery.

High-powered corporate attorney Steven Keeney (Peter Horton) is blessed with a loving son, Christian (Nathan Lawrence), and a devoted lover, Wynn Burkholder (Wendy Makkena), but these relationships are jeopardized by a *pro bono* case that isn't even in his area of expertise. Approached by a grieving mom, LuAnn Wilkens (Elizabeth Ruscio), goodhearted Keeney checks out her routine insurance request, never realizing that he's opened up a Pandora's box that will consume his life. Many questions arise in Keeney's mind when he discovers that LuAnn's naive daughter had somehow fallen to her death during a suspiciously impromptu ocean-cliff expedition while staying with B. J. (James McAlpine) and Virginia McGinnis (Carrie Snodgress). Why was Melissa wearing high heels? Why was she slightly drugged? More importantly, why did the McGinnises take out a $30,000 life-insurance policy on Melissa, a virtual stranger?

Tenaciously, Keeney pieces together Virginia McGinnis's homicidal history that seems to have included killing her own daughter and other family members for profit. While his private and public lives disintegrate due to his absorption in the case, Keeney visits Virginia's ex-husband, Dick Coates (Jack Kehler), who supports Keeney's suspicions. But Coates kills himself before he can testify. The San Diego police agree to tackle the circumstantial case, but technical snafus severely limit the district attorney's evidence pool. Refusing to cave in, Keeney points out that a roll of film used by the McGinnises as an alibi also proves that wily Virginia snapped photos after B. J. pushed Melissa off the cliffs. Keeney's meticulously developed theory helps convict the heretofore unconvictable—and always unrepentant—Virginia and B. J.

What distinguishes this compact thriller is how it generates high-octane suspense not from the straightforward depiction of a scary crime but from the minutiae of detective work used to solve it. Breathtakingly, DEATH BENEFIT finds a visual equivalent to the thought processes of the dogged lawyer: the flashbacks to events surrounding Melissa's final moments bleed directly from quick shots of the crime-scene photos. The transitions between Keeney's insights into each photo and the reenactments of the corresponding moments are seamless.

If this reality-based terror tale has flaws, they are errors of omission. The viewer will want to know more about Melissa's personality and why it attracted the McGinnis duo. The film might also have benefited from devoting more screen time to Virginia, a character sketch brilliantly filled out by Snodgress in her few scenes. But essentially, DEATH BENEFIT *is* a Peter Horton vehicle, and Horton does it full-throttle justice. *(Violence, adult situations, profanity.)* — R.P.

d, Marc Piznarski; p, Tina Threadgil; exec p, Rick Rosenberg; co-p, Phillip Rosenberg, Derek Kavanaugh; w, Phillip Rosenberg (based on the novel by David Heilbroner); ph, Christopher Taylor; ed, Robert Frazen; m, Brian Adler; prod d, James Schoppe; set d, Kristin Peterson; sound, Walter Hoylman (mixer); fx, Russ Hesseyh; casting, Karen Hendel; cos, Jo Ynocencio; makeup, Cynthia Bachman; stunts, Joe Dunne

Drama/Thriller/Mystery (PR: C MPAA: PG-13)

DELLAMORTE DELLAMORE
(SEE: CEMETERY MAN)

DELTA OF VENUS ★★
(U.S.) 101m Venus Productions; Alliance Communications; Evzan Kolar Productions ~ Fine Line c

Costas Mandylor *(Lawrence)*; Audie England *(Elena)*; Eric Da Silva *(Marcel)*; Raven Snow *(Leila)*; Rory Campbell *(Miguel)*; Bernard Zette *(Donald)*; Emma Louise Moore *(Ariel)*; Daniel Leza *(Pierre)*; Stephen Halbert *(Harry)*; Dale Wyatt *(Millicent)*; Jiri Ded *(Priest)*; Valerie Zawadska *(Landlady)*; Marek Vasut *(Luc)*; Marketa Hrubesova *(Bijou)*; James Donahower *(Bandleader)*; Robert Davi *(The Collector)*; Wale *(Clairvoyant)*; Clive Revill *(Radio Announcer)*; Eva Duchkova *(Veiled Woman)*; Daniel Tichy *(Veiled Woman's Husband)*; Josef Nedorost *(Blindfolded Man)*; Roberta Hanley *(Opium Den Proprietor)*; Simon Nordfjord *(Young Man)*; Sona Navratilova *(Bound Woman)*; Marek Borinsky *(Bound Woman's Man)*; Milan Svanc *(Bound Woman's Man)*; Ladislav Polata *(Bound Woman's Man)*; Michaela Srbova *(Beautiful Woman)*; Andrea Nemcova *(Marcel's Secretary)*; Daniel Dvorak *(Middle-Aged Man)*; Oldrich Hruza *(Fisherman)*; Irena Hanova *(Society Woman)*; Edward Rychtarik *(Sailor)*; Zdenek Sedlacek *(Soldier)*; Petr Pechaty *(Shopkeeper)*; Pavel Chalupa *(Teenager)*; Petr Rocovsky *(Handsome Man)*; Radim Kalvoda *(Communist Member)*; Jan Laibl *(Father)*; Jana Stradalova *(Little Girl)*; Josef Kral *(Young Man)*; Rudolph Benes; Frantisek Svihlik; Karel Polisensky; Oldrich Stransky

In the tradition of his WILD ORCHID (1990) and RED SHOE DIARIES (1992), director Zalman King serves up DELTA OF VENUS, another mixture of light pornography and high-blown melodrama. The results this time are considerably more strained and tedious than before.

Paris, 1939. A naive young American writer, Elena (Audie England) seeks love, romance and adventure in the glamorous, seductive City of Lights. She meets Lawrence (Costas Mandylor), a more-established expatriate writer, who is about to return to the United States for a book tour. Before Lawrence leaves, Elena has a brief, passionate affair with him.

While Lawrence is gone, Elena receives a commission through her editor, Marcel (Eric Da Silva), to write erotic stories for an anonymous benefactor. Elena "researches" her stories by witnessing various Parisians act out their sexual fantasies, including a prostitute who gets hypnotized by a nude West African psychic, and a wealthy man who watches his wife have sex with another man. Elena participates in her own writing experiment by posing nude in an art class and by allowing herself to be raped by a Fascist brute.

The attack on Elena, however, symbolically sets the stage for the Nazi occupation of Paris in 1940. During the violent takeover of the city, Elena learns that Lawrence has been her anonymous benefactor all along, and he had never left Paris. Elena is furious at him for the deception, but later realizes that he has provided the strength for her to write. Elena forgives Lawrence as she sails back to America.

Inspired by the Anais Nin novel of the same name, King places his libidinous characters in the potentially tense, exciting setting of Paris before the occupation. Unfortunately, this backdrop is merely an excuse for showing off—and taking off—some stylish retro clothing. Meanwhile, the vapid writer-lover characters are unintentionally funny whenever they recite purple prose such as "she realized he had not only penetrated her body but also her very being." The leads are also incredibly dull whenever they engage in heated but artistically choreographed sex. Even the average made-for-TV adaptation of a Judith Krantz novel provides more zing than this phony, overlong romance.

At least King and cinematographer Eagle Egilsson create a seductive—if slightly anachronistic—atmosphere with stylish lighting. Yet, without the hung-over appeal of Mickey Rourke or the sexy innocence of Carre Otis (the WILD ORCHID pair), King can't sustain our interest in the glossy goings-on. Mandylor and England exhibit absolutely no chemistry, but at least England wears nice clothes.

Thus, despite the many quickly cut scenes of soft-porn lovemaking, this would-be camp piece of "erotica" remains about as sexy as a sewing machine. *(Violence, extensive nudity, sexual situations, adult situations, profanity.)* — E.M.

d, Zalman King; p, Evzen Kolar; exec p, Michael Nolin, Rolf Mittweg, Phillip L. Rosen; assoc p, Matthew Gayne, Janis Rothbard Chaskin; co-p, Tony Moskalyk; w, Elisa Rothstein, Patricia Louisianna Knop (based on the novel by Anais Nin); ph, Eagle Egilsson; ed, James Gavin Bedford, Marc Grossman; m, George S. Clinton; prod d, Zdenek Flemming; art d, Milan Stary, Daniel Dvorak; set d, Miloslav Dvorak; sound, Stephen Halbert (mixer); fx, Vaclav Krejcik, David Krejcik; casting, Sue Shawn; cos, Jolie Anna Jimenez; makeup, Lynn Rodgers

Erotic/Drama **(PR: O MPAA: NC-17)**

DEMOLITIONIST, THE ★½

(U.S.) 93m Planet Productions; Le Monde Entertainment; A-Pix ~ A-Pix Entertainment c

Nicole Eggert *(Alyssa Lloyd/The Demolitionist)*; Bruce Abbott *(Prof. Jack Crowley)*; Richard Grieco *(Mad Dog Burne)*; Susan Tyrrell *(Mayor Grimbaum)*; Peter Jason *(Higgins)*; Sarah Douglas *(Surgeon)*; Andras Jones *(Daniel Dupre)*; Heather Langenkamp *(Christy Carruthers)*; David Anthony Marshall *(One Eye)*; Jack Nance *(Father McKenzie)*; Josef Pilato *(Boxer)*; Tom Savini *(Roland)*; Nils Allen Stewart *(Hammerhead)*; Randy Vasquez *(Little Henry)*; Yvonne M. Cohrs *(First Mall Patron)*; Christopher Thunderwolf *(Second Mall Patron)*; James Mongold *(Arlis)*; Danny Hicks *(Krutchfield)*; Chris Cowell *(Executioner)*; Reggie Bannister *(Warden Timms)*; Jennifer Andersen; Tonya Hall; Naomi Jaramillo; Gina Lackey *(Dancers)*; Joelle Salers *(Biker Slut)*; Paul Muncz *(Skin)*; Shanah S. Elevins *(Makeup Artist)*; Gigi Moran *(Lab Assistant)*; Laser *(The Negotiator)*; Russ McGuire *(Ram)*; J. Wolf *(Wolf)*; Shay Burk *(Jermol)*; Michael Maranda *(Otto)*; Ryan Rowley *(Porkchop)*; Armand Medina *(Mortay)*; Richard French *(J. C.)*; Walter C. Hubbard *(The Hubb)*; Porter Jamison *(Swamp Rat)*; Derek Mears *(Chuck X)*; Larry Clark *(Second Reporter)*; Geoff Seaton *(Bank Guard)*; Randy Stofford *(Lipps)*; Greg Nicotero *(Elevator Punk)*; Gino Crognale *(Second Punk)*; Rosey Brown *(Big Frank)*; John G. Neuman *(Clean-Cut Biker)*; Bob Hurst *(Duffy)*; Bruce Campbell *(Gang Member)*

To the list of failed cinematic action heroines like TANK GIRL (1994) and BARB WIRE (1996), now add THE DEMOLITIONIST, an ambitious but fatally derivative and tepid sci-fi thriller.

In Metro City, where Mayor Grimbaum (Susan Tyrrell) has issued a no-guns edict, gang leader Mad Dog Burne (Richard Grieco) is rescued from his execution by his minions. He soon discovers that one of his followers, Alyssa Lloyd (Nicole Eggert), is an undercover cop and kills her.

She is brought back to life by Prof. Jack Crowley (Bruce Abbott) through the use of an experimental drug, as part of a program designed to turn her into an unstoppable warrior. Though she resists at first (the drugs give her horrific nightmares), she ultimately goes through with her training and emerges as a supercop dubbed the Demolitionist, who begins to wipe out Metro City's crime.

In the course of stopping a bank robbery, the Demolitionist's actions almost result in the death of an innocent young girl, and Mayor Grimbaum decides that she should be terminated—violently. But "Demo" is rescued by Crowley, who helps her recuperate and sends her back out on the street to destroy Mad Dog's gang. This she does, leading to a final confrontation with Mad Dog, whom she kills with an overdose of the drug that gives her life.

THE DEMOLITIONIST marks the directorial debut of Robert Kurtzman, who first conceived and was originally to helm 1996's FROM DUSK TILL DAWN. Unfortunately, the script by Brian DiMuccio and Dino Vindeni (from a story by Kurtzman and his wife Anne) amounts to a carbon copy of 1987's ROBOCOP, from its basic plot to individual scenes (Demo being blasted down by the cops she's supposedly in league with, a key villain's meltdown death, etc.). What DEMOLITIONIST lacks is its inspiration's satiric viewpoint, or enough of a budget to create any memorable action scenes.

Indeed, the film takes way too long to get to Demo's war on crime, frittering away nearly half its length on well-intentioned but ineffective character drama involving Alyssa's transformation and her relationship with Dr. Crowley. Genre fans will get a kick out of all the familiar faces in the supporting cast (Tyrrell, Tom Savini, Heather Langenkamp, Reggie Bannister, and an uncredited Bruce Campbell), but they're no substitute for the movie's lack of honest thrills or imagination. *(Graphic violence, nudity, sexual situations, extreme profanity.)* — M.G.

d, Robert Kurtzman; p, Donald P. Borchers; exec p, Robert Baruc, John Fremes; assoc p, John Esposito, Anne Kurtzman; w, Brian DiMuccio, Dino Vindeni (based on a story by Robert and Anne Kurtzman); ph, Marcus Hahn; ed, Paolo Mazzucato; m, Shawn Patterson; prod d, Charley Cabrera; art d, Leah Cabrera; sound, Patrick M. Griffith; fx, John Hartigan, KNB EFX Group, Flash Film Works; cos, Angela Dawn Alderson; makeup, Melanie Tooker

Science Fiction/Action/Thriller **(PR: O MPAA: R)**

DENISE CALLS UP ★★

(U.S.) 80m David Entertainment; Skyline Entertainment Partners; Dark Matter Productions ~ Sony Pictures Classics c

Alanna Ubach *(Denise)*; Tim Daly *(Frank)*; Caroleen Feeney *(Barbara)*; Dan Gunther *(Martin)*; Dana Wheeler-Nicholson *(Gale)*; Liev Schreiber *(Jerry)*; Aida Turturro *(Linda)*; Sylvia Miles *(Gale's Aunt Sharon)*; Jean Claude Lamarre *(The Cab Driver)*; Mark Blum *(Dr. Brennen)*; Hal Salwen *(Jerry as a Little Boy)*

DENISE CALLS UP represents what used to be dubbed a "Yuppie Comedy." This film about a handful of single white males and females looking for love in New York City tries to be witty and profound about modern relationships, but fails to live up to its hip, state-of-the-art premise.

In current-day Manhattan, several thirtysomething professionals are so busy, they only connect via telephone. The pregnant Denise (Alanna Ubach) calls up Jerry (Liev Schreiber) when she finds out that he donated the sperm she received from a sperm bank. Jerry feels great about the news, but never makes plans to see Denise. Jerry does find time, however, to tell his friend Martin (Dan Gunther) about the baby. Meanwhile, Martin awkwardly pursues Barbara (Caroleen Feeney) over the phone, and when Martin fails to keep his date with her, they have phone sex instead. Across town, Martin's friend, Frank (Tim Daly), tries to rekindle a romance with Gale (Dana Wheeler-Nicholson). Tragically, Gale dies in a car accident before they can meet. Soon after Gale's death, Denise gives birth. Frank calls all of Gale's friends to mourn her by coming to a New Year's Eve party. However, the friends (except for two) fail to show up at the party, proving how hard it is to establish true intimacy in the Big Apple today.

In the 1970s Woody Allen made modern romantic comedies like ANNIE HALL (1977). In the 1980s, Allen imitators made more modern romantic comedies. Now, in the 1990s, the imitators of the imitators are making modern romantic comedies like DENISE CALLS UP. To his credit, writer-director Hal Salwen, updates the genre with a clever gimmick: until the conclusion, the characters never meet in person, which gives the narrative a certain amount of tension. Also, Salwen plays off of John Guare's thesis about interpersonal relationships in SIX DEGREES OF SEPARATION (1993), as six initial strangers become united (through a death and a birth) over the course of the story.

Yet, what a shame it is that Salwen does so little with his high-tech alienation theme. Instead of the expected social satire, DENISE CALLS UP concentrates on dropping Woody Allen-type one-liners on a regular basis. And in another slavish nod to the Woodman, the Martin-Barbara romance in particular resembles the nervous and nebbishy Allen-Diane Keaton courtship boilerplate. The talented cast valiantly tries to make the material fresh, but Salwen encourages forced, theatrical performances from everyone. Of special note, though, is Sylvia Miles (as Gale's Aunt Sharon) who sticks out like a Fellini-esque gargoyle in the middle of this otherwise semi-realistic comedy-drama.

In the end, there is little to like about DENISE CALLS UP—but one day, no doubt, this film will be imitated, too. *(Nudity, sexual situations, adult situations, profanity.)* — E.M.

d, Hal Salwen; p, J. Todd Harris; exec p, John Davis, Stephen Nemeth; co-p, Michael Cozell; w, Hal Salwen; ph, Michael Mayers; ed, Gary Sharfin; prod d, Susan Bolles; set d, Catherine Pierson; sound, Matthew Sigal (mixer); casting, Sheila Jaffe, Georgianne Walken; cos, Edi Giguere; makeup, Marie Delprete

Comedy/Drama/Romance **(PR: C MPAA: PG-13)**

DENTIST, THE ★★½

(U.S.) 93m Novacaine Pictures ~ Vidmark c

Corbin Bernsen *(Dr. Feinstone)*; Linda Hoffman *(Brooke)*; Molly Hagen *(Jessica)*; Ken Foree *(Detective Gibbs)*; Virginia Keehen *(Sarah)*; Patty Toy *(Karen)*; Jan Hoag *(Candy)*; Christa Sauls *(April Reign)*; Tony Noakes *(Detective Sunshine)*; Earl Boen *(Marvin Goldblum)*; Lise Simms *(Paula Roberts)*; Michael Stadvec *(Matt)*; Christopher Kriesa *(Mr. Schaeffer)*; Joanne Baron *(Mrs. Saunders)*; Mark Ruffalo *(Steve Randers)*; Sal Viscuso *(Matthew Zeiger)*; Brian McLaughlin *(Jody)*; Aixa Maldonado *(Maria)*; Betsy Monroe *(Young Female)*; Brian Yuzna *(Attendant)*; Michael Guerin *(Student #1)*; Shanna Corinne *(Student #2)*; Michael Rodgers *(Nervous Patient)*; Diana Tash *(Opera Singer)*

A film that might have given the Marquis de Sade a few chuckles, THE DENTIST is a splatter film awash in outre violence. In addition to being visually repellent, however, this is a smartly conceived horror pic that shifts focus between reality and the protagonist's distorted perspective of reality.

Obsessed with cleanliness, upscale dentist Dr. Feinstone (Corbin Bernsen) embarks on a snowballing descent into madness. Pressure from the IRS widens the cracks in anal-retentive Feinstone's perception of normalcy; his discovery of an affair between his pristine wife, Brooke (Linda Hoffman), and his pool man drives him batty. Trailing the stud pool man to the home of his horny neighbor, Mrs. Roberts (Lise Simms), disturbed Feinstone shoots her watchdog. Losing his marbles at work, Feinstone injures a pediatric patient, overmedicates himself, sexually molests patient April Reign (Christa Sauls), and arouses the suspicions of dental hygienist Jessica (Molly Hagen).

Surprising his wife on their anniversary, Feinstone disfigures Brooke's face with the tools of his trade. The next time the pool man shows up, irate Feinstone slits his throat. At the office, Jessica's intervention prevents Mrs. Roberts from receiving unnecessary, damaging dental work. When meddling Jessica threatens to close down her boss's practice, Dr. Feinstone strangles her with April's discarded pantyhose. As cops investigate the dog-shooting at Mrs. Roberts, IRS official Marvin Goldblum (Earl Boen) forces delinquent taxpayer Feinstone into free dental work; Feinstone transforms Goldblum into a freak. When Feinstone's other assistant, Karen (Patty Toy), spots the mutilated tax collector, Feinstone also murders her. Meanwhile, the cops find the slain pool man and the deformed Brooke. After terrorizing a teenager set for braces-removal, Feinstone holds a college dental clinic at gunpoint. Finally, the police arrest Dr. Feinstone, the Sweeney Todd of dentists.

Without its far-out gross-outs, THE DENTIST might have been even more frightening, because the film constantly unbalances the audience by altering Dr. Feinstone's perceptions. We're inexorably drawn to the narrowing universe this madman inhabits, a world where the dentist feels honor-bound to purify the "unclean." Certainly, with its stomach-churning scenes of torture, THE DENTIST plays to wider thrill-seeking audiences; its grotesquerie is so outrageous, it becomes comical. And yet, THE DENTIST might have aspired to a subtler, less hokey domain, that of the psychological thriller, such as REPULSION (1965). In its state of Grand Guignol-overkill, this offbeat chiller is bound to offend those viewers who wish the offspring of Sam Raimi and Stuart Gordon would learn the use of filmmaking restraint. For more bloodthirsty fright fans, the biggest problem isn't the film's excessive violence, but its failure to call it quits when the film hits a horrifying peak. Prolonged by Dr. Feinstone's gun-toting visit to his teaching venue, the film should have ended at the dentist's clean-up campaign in his office. This creepy film causes one's goosebumps to break out because of one's latent paranoia about phobic professionals like Dr. Feinstone. *(Graphic violence, extreme profanity, adult situations, sexual situations, substance abuse.)* — R.P.

d, Brian Yuzna; p, Pierre David; exec p, Michael Stadvec, Mark Amin; assoc p, Sheri Bryant; co-p, Noel Zanitsch, Phillip Goldfine; w, Charles Finch, Stuart Gordon, Dennis Paoli; ph, Levie Isaacks; ed, Christopher Roth; m, Alan Howarth; prod d, William Ryder; art d, Robyn Buschmann; sound, Tony Smyles (mixer); casting, Carol Lefko; cos, Warden Neil; makeup, Patricia Gundlach, Anthony Ferrante; stunts, Kurt Bryant

Horror **(PR: O MPAA: R)**

DER BEWEGTE MANN

(SEE: MAYBE . . . MAYBE NOT)

DER FREISCHUTZ

(SEE: MAGIC HUNTER)

DERNIERE FRONTIERE

(SEE: OUTPOST, THE)

DESIRE ★★

(U.S.) 90m Westwind Productions ~ Monarch Home Video c

Martin Kemp *(Gordon Lewis)*; Kate Hodge *(Lauren Allen)*; Robert Miranda *(Nick Palermo)*; Deborah Shelton *(Grace Lantel)*; Mary Stavin *(Adrienne)*; Todd Joseph *(Kevin)*; Greg Daniel *(Police Captain)*; Carrie Hall *(Receptionist)*; Deborah Worthington *(Gordon's Assistant)*; Gere Baker *(Hostess)*; Rick Brian *(Photographer)*; Rodd Britt *(Cop Clerk)*; Jennifer Leigh Burton *(Cynthia)*; Carrie Chambers *(Nicole)*; O'Neal Compton *(Dockworker)*; Don Fischer *(Male Model)*; Joseph Ferreri *(Hot*

Dog Vendor); Evelyn Furtak *(Secretary)*; Melanie Good *(Kathleen)*; Mitchell Hankin *(Bartender)*; Carrie Janisse *(Female Model)*; Hugh Holub *(FBI Agent)*; Andrea Riave *(Nicole's Roommate)*; Thomas Schuler *(Lauren's Partner)*; Glen Naessens *(Flashback Killer)*; Marcia Shapiro *(Store Manager)*

Lurid rather than provocative, the erotic thriller DESIRE is one of those JAGGED EDGE-convolutions in which a heroine must weigh a man's bedroom virility vs. his homicidal potential. Is he a ladykiller or literally a lady killer? DESIRE can pat itself on its negligee-covered back for one reason: it juggles suspects skillfully enough to dupe viewers into guessing the killer's identity incorrectly.

LA is plagued by a series of brutal murders in which the female victims are doused with Desire perfume, the best-selling fragrance of Lantel Inc. As security chief for Lantel, ex-cop Lauren Allen (Kate Hodge) crosses paths with her former partner, Nick Palermo (Robert Miranda), while investigating these killings, which are a public relations nightmare for Lauren's boss, Grace Lantel (Deborah Shelton). Agreeing to go undercover as a moonlighter for the LAPD, Lauren pretends to order a personally designed scent from Grace's former associate, prime murder suspect Gordon Lewis (Martin Kemp), who's suing Grace over the ownership rights to Desire perfume.

Another possible perpetrator of the murders is delivery boy Kevin (Todd Joseph); his post as messenger for a posh Beverly Hills department store gave him access to the homes of all the victims. Although Palermo's gut instinct points to Gordon, Lauren falls for the debonair perfumer and can't accept his guilt wholeheartedly, despite damning evidence that leads to his arrest. Late one night, Lauren gets paged to Lantel headquarters, where she's shocked to find Grace murdered. Having meticulously framed Gordon, Grace's ex-lover, Adrienne (Mary Stavin), a saleswoman for the same store that employed Kevin, confesses to Lauren about her string of jealousy-motivated murders. Before Grace's dumped girlfriend can claim another victim, Lauren blasts her right out the window.

Although DESIRE neatly forestalls cluing us into the killer, the movie's actual barebones detective work is mundanely developed. Nor is the dangerous courtship of Gordon Lewis out of the ordinary. Too much time is wasted on the love-making flourishes of the smooth fragrance-meister, and not enough on shading this screenplay with psychological explanations for the behavior of the principal players. One gets the nagging feeling that this flick's producers approached their project by doling out portions of sex and violence without caring about how those two crowd-pleasing elements would intersect and support the storyline. It's hard to say which is less interesting: the standard, heavy-breathing mattress-wrestling; or the police search for fingerprints (which is duller crime-solving than the Barnaby Jones crew at their slowest).*(Graphic violence, extreme profanity, extensive nudity, sexual situations.)* — R.P.

d, Rodney McDonald; p, Rick Conrad; exec p, Thomas Schuler, Robert Mann; assoc p, Mitchell Hankin; co-p, Carol Schuler; w, Rodney McDonald; ph, John Huneck; ed, Michael Thibault; m, Richard Allen; prod d, Jane Cavedon; art d, Liz Cavedon; sound, Daniel Monahan (mixer); fx, Steve Petino; casting, Mary Margiotta, Margaret Margiotta; cos, Charmian Espinoza; makeup, Debra Wolski McNulty; stunts, Kurt Bryant

Erotic/Thriller **(PR: C MPAA: NR)**

DESOLATION ANGELS ★★★½

(U.S.) 94m McCann & Co. ~ Canosa Inc. c

Michael Rodrick *(Nick Adams)*; Jennifer Thomas *(Mary)*; Peter Bassett *(Sid)*; Shannon Gold *(Ralph)*; Mike Alpert *(Hank)*; Cheryl Clifford *(Donna)*; Linda Moran *(Sarah)*; Frank Olivier *(Otis)*; Quentin Crisp *(Beggar)*

A hard-hitting study of contemporary gender relations, DESOLATION ANGELS stands above other recent films on the topic. Though shaky at the start, this low-budget entry has a few surprises in store.

DESOLATION ANGELS is set in a lower middle-class section of Brooklyn, where the men maintain excessively macho fronts to mask their inner fears, doubts, and sensitivity. One such young man, Nick (Michael Rodrick), has graduated from college but works in a menial job for a local moving company. Nick's circle of friends includes his roommate, Ralph (Shannon Gold), his girlfriend, Mary (Jennifer Thomas), her roommate, Sarah (Linda Moran), his best friend from college, Sid (Peter Bassett), and Sid's girlfriend, Donna (Cheryl Clifford).

One night, Mary tells Nick that while he was away in Boston, Sid "came on" to her. Nick becomes furious at the news and immediately blames Mary for the incident. But when Nick learns from Sarah that Sid raped Mary, Nick explodes. Against Mary's wishes, Nick plots to get even with Sid by hiring a couple of professional thugs to beat him up. On the night of the intended beating, however, the gentle Ralph gets mistaken for Sid and is pummeled by the assailants. Nick feels sorry for his roommate, but cannot bring himself to admit his complicity. Later, Nick tries to retrieve the money he had paid to the thugs, but he is rebuffed and almost lands in his own fight with them.

Over the next few days, Nick obsesses about getting even with Sid. Disgusted with his brooding, Mary ends their relationship. Nick is hurt and surprised, but finally agrees to go on his way. When he sees Sid again, Nick confronts his former friend and they begin to fight. Thanks to their other friends, they stop in time to realize the futile nature of their aggressive behavior.

DESOLATION ANGELS looks at some of the same characters who populate THE POMPATUS OF LOVE, THE LOW LIFE, and BEAUTIFUL GIRLS, but in a grittier, more realistic milieu. Like these other films, DESOLATION follows a few confused and angry young men trying to cope with modern mores regarding love, sex, honor and, oh yes, how to make a living. Happily, DESOLATION ANGELS moves beyond the male point of view and tries to show the flaws in macho posturing and sexist assumptions. Nick's incremental realizations make his character far more interesting to watch than any of the pretentious "heroes" of those aforementioned men-in-bar films. In some ways, DESOLATION ANGELS charts the same territory as two classics, Ingmar Bergman's THE VIRGIN SPRING (1960) and Claude Chabrol's THIS MAN MUST DIE (1970); it's not as good, but it is sometimes just as gripping.

First-time helmer Tim McCann shows (for now) more strength as a writer than director. He also edited and co-produced this feature, which is "presented" by Jonathan Demme and Barbet Schroeder. While McCann's material is strong, his direction is amateurish. One might see Bazinian realism in the taxing long-takes of so many scenes, but they seem more the product of an inability to break down the shots properly (at least Matthew Howe's camera could have better framed the actors). Another sign of inexperience comes from the actors themselves, although the male leads, Michael Rodrick and Peter Bassett, are quite good. A foolish cameo from Quentin Crisp as a homeless beggar also throws the film off momentarily. Fortunately, most of DESOLATION ANGELS does not depend on careful aesthetic attributes to succeed. It's a good film in spite of itself. *(Violence, nudity, sexual situations, adult situations, substance abuse, extreme profanity).* — E.M.

d, Tim McCann; p, Tim McCann, Steve Olivieri; exec p, Jonathan Demme, Barbet Schroeder; assoc p, Sean McCann; w,

Tim McCann; ph, Matthew Howe; ed, Tim McCann; art d, Larry O'Neil; sound, Eric Susch; cos, Marianne Powell-Parker

Drama **(PR: O MPAA: NR)**

DEVOTION ★★★½

(U.S.) 123m Dancing Arrow Productions; Auntie Em Productions ~ Cinema Products Video c

Jan Derbyshire *(Sheila Caston)*; Kate Twa *(Julie Rosen)*; Cindy Girling *(Lynn Webster)*; Eileen Barrett *(Katie McRae)*; Steve Adams *(Bill Matthews)*; Sharon Heath; Michele Lonsdale Smith; Jane Sowerby

DEVOTION is an exceptionally honest love story. Although it is about love affairs between women, its universal themes and characterizations make it appealing to a wide audience. It is an intelligent, humorous and compassionate film.

Sheila (Jan Derbyshire) is a popular stand-up comic. She returns from a tour to her live-in lover, Julie (Kate Twa), an artist who owns and runs a gallery. On her first night back, Sheila gets her big break: she is asked to play an openly homosexual woman on a new television comedy. Her enthusiasm is crushed when she learns that the producer's wife is Lynn (Cindy Girling), the woman who broke Sheila's heart 15 years ago and hasn't been in contact with her since. When the two women were about 20 years old, they were best friends and roommates. Sheila fell in love with Lynn, kissed her, and got kicked out. After 14 years of marriage, Lynn is questioning her sexuality, and wonders if she made a mistake about Shiela.

Sheila, whose comedy routines about fear of intimacy mirror her own inability to communicate her feelings, had never let Julie know about Lynn, and still won't tell Julie what's going on. Julie, frustrated and hurt, moves out. Lynn leaves her husband, and she and Sheila attempt to start over again as lovers—but Sheila realizes that Lynn is her past, not her present. There will be no television show, but a warmer, more confident Sheila goes back to Julie, ready to move on with her life.

DEVOTION's story is not profound or unusual, but it is refreshingly open and genuine. Sheila and Julie's penultimate argument is as unflinchingly honest as you'll see in film, and the characters are brilliantly developed. Writer-director Mindy Kaplan's background as a therapist is evident, as she has keen insight into what drives people, and how certain life events can alter them permanently.

Sheila's stand-up routines are outstanding, and despite the often heavy emotions, DEVOTION has a joyous spirit. The performances are heartfelt and the casting is, for the most part, ideal. Derbyshire shows true star potential, and the bit roles are authentic and charming. Girling, unfortunately, overdoes the ice-queen image somewhat, but manages to show some passion when Lynn comes to terms with her own sexuality. The cinematic aspects of the film often take a back seat to the characterizations, but Kaplan's presentation of flashbacks, even the happy ones, in horror-movie fashion—slow motion, distorted voices, ominous music—is creative and effective.

The film's pace slows considerably as Shiela's life gets more complicated, and the maudlin aspects of the film detract from its appeal. While its happy ending is rewarding, the tearjerker elements that precede it aren't as well done as DEVOTION's humorous earlier scenes. *(Nudity, adult situations, sexual situations, profanity)* — A.M.

d, Mindy Kaplan; p, Arlene Battishill; exec p, Emily Decker; co-p, Pamela S. Curi, Lisa King; w, Arlene Battishill, Mindy Kaplan (based on the novel by Mindy Kaplan); ph, Mario Araya; ed, Mindy Kaplan; m, Arlene Battishill; prod d, Cathy Robertson; cos, Jenny Bernice

Drama/Romance **(PR: C MPAA: R)**

DIABOLIQUE ★★

(U.S.) 107m Marvin Worth Productions; Morgan Creek ~ Warner Bros. c

Sharon Stone *(Nicole Horner)*; Isabelle Adjani *(Mia Baran)*; Chazz Palminteri *(Guy Baran)*; Kathy Bates *(Shirley Vogel)*; Spalding Gray *(Simon Veatch)*; Shirley Knight *(Edie Danziger)*; Allen Garfield *(Leo Katzman)*; Adam Hann-Byrd *(Erik Pretzer)*; Donal Logue *(Video Photographer)*; Jeffrey Abrams *(Video Photographer)*; Diana Bellamy *(Ms. Vawze)*; Clea Lewis *(Lisa Campos)*; O'Neal Compton *(Irv Danziger)*; Bingo O'Malley *(Gannon)*; Stephen Liska *(PHP Officer)*; Jim Kisicki *(Rear-ender)*; Kevin Vinay *(Desantis)*; Cory Pattak *(Nunez)*; Kate Young *(Photo Shop Clerk)*; Sophia Salguero *(Maid)*; Hank Stohl *(Morgue Cop)*; Zachary Mott *(Howie)*; Jesse Sky Ross *(Hall Monitor)*

DIABOLIQUE gives Henri-Georges Clouzot's 1955 French classic a diabolically bad face-lift and makeover, completely losing all the positive elements of suspense and nearly all the mysticism of the original. Nonetheless, connoisseurs of camp will find lots to like here.

DIABOLIQUE updates the story to contemporary Pittsburgh, where two schoolteachers, the frail Mia (Isabelle Adjani) and the steely Nicole (Sharon Stone), plot to kill Mia's cruel, philandering husband, Guy (Chazz Palminteri), the headmaster of the boys's school at which they both work. Mia's motives for murder are obvious, but Nicole has had an open affair with Guy, and seems to participate out of loyalty to her friend. During a holiday weekend away from their remote academy, Mia finds the courage to poison Guy, but, in order to finish him off, the two women drown him in the bathtub. Later, Mia and Nicole hide the corpse in the school's murky swimming pool but are shocked when the pool is drained, and the body has disappeared.

Soon, other mysterious events occur, including the reappearance of Guy's suit, neatly hanging in Mia's room, attached to a roll of film that includes snapshots of Guy after the murder. Both women begin suspecting that someone might be trying to blackmail them, while Mia is convinced that Guy is still alive. When she checks out a body—that turns out to not be Guy's—in a faraway river, Mia attracts the interest of a nosy ex-detective, Shirley (Kathy Bates). Much to Nicole's annoyance, Shirley volunteers to find Guy by snooping around the school grounds.

Eventually, Nicole admits to Mia that her motive in helping kill Guy was financial—she knew where he kept his money. Mia orders Nicole to leave the school on the same night that Shirley gets closer to the truth. In order to scare Mia to death and wrest the school from her, Guy turns up very much alive. But his and Nicole's scheme to eliminate Mia unravels as Nicole gets second thoughts about following through with Mia's murder. Instead, Nicole saves Mia by tussling with Guy. Then, once again, both women kill him by drowning. Shirley sees the entire episode, but decides that Guy deserved to die and lets the women go free.

DIABOLIQUE is yet another lousy American remake of a 1950s French classic. Of course, Hollywood has been poorly remaking foreign films for decades, but it does seem as though a nadir has been reached. Two better American versions of the original LES DIABOLIQUES include GAMES (1967) and REFLECTIONS OF MURDER (1974). In fairness to DIABOLIQUE, perhaps it should be said that LES DIABOLIQUES isn't all that it's cracked up to be, at least compared to the film version of VERTIGO (1958)—by the same authors, Pierre Boileau and Thomas Narcejec. The combination of metaphysics and mysticism actually is stronger in Hitchcock, perhaps because Clouzot is too literal-minded for the subject matter. Even the famous bathtub climax was more imaginatively handled in William Castle's THE TINGLER (1959) a few years later.

Vera Clouzot, the director's wife and star of the original, threatened to sue Warner Bros. for remaking the film without securing the rights from her. But perhaps she also should have litigated against artistic ineptitude. This new DIABOLIQUE gets everything wrong when it comes to suspense and nearly abandons altogether the layer of mysticism of the original. Much of the unintended humor comes from the Don Roos screenplay, which more or less follows the original plot, but makes the women grotesque caricatures and rather foolish criminals who leave evidence everywhere. Director Jeremiah Chechik (BENNY AND JOON) handles practically every moment as indelicately as possible.

The waste of the usually lovely—but here, puffy and forlorn—Adjani in the Vera Clouzot role is only one of many sins. Casting Adjani was some agent's idea of adding a touch of French class, no doubt. Stone and Bates turn the occasion into a romp. Both toss off one-liners with gleeful tough-girl abandon. In Simone Signoret's role, Stone even gets to wear a batch of ludicrous leopard-skin outfits that suggest a spoof. Stone reportedly hated making the film and refused to promote it, but at least she *appears* to be having fun. At times, the viewer will, too, although not the kind of fun the filmmakers intended. *(Violence, nudity, sexual situations, adult situations, substance abuse, profanity.)* — E.M.

d, Jeremiah Chechik; p, Marvin Worth, James G. Robinson; exec p, Gary Barber, Bill Todman Jr., Chuck Binder, Jerry Offsay; co-p, Gary Daigler; w, Don Roos (based on the novel *Celle qui n'etait pas* by Pierre Bouileau and Thomas Narcejac); ph, Peter James; ed, Carol Littleton; m, Randy Edelman; prod d, Leslie Dilley; art d, Dennis Bradford; set d, Michael Seirton; sound, Dennis Maitland (mixer); casting, Jackie Burch; cos, Michael Kaplan; makeup, Joe Campayno

Thriller/Crime/Mystery **(PR: O MPAA: R)**

DIE EROTISCHE GESCHICHTEN
(SEE: TALES OF EROTICA)

DISPARA
(SEE: OUTRAGE)

DOGFIGHTERS, THE ★★
(U.S./Hungary) 96m Hess Kallberg Associates ~ Live Home Video c

Robert Davi *(Rowdy Welles)*; Alexander Godunov *(Lothar Krasna)*; Ben Gazzara *(Dick Althorp)*; Lara Harris *(Mike (Mikaela))*; Patricia Rive *(Louise)*; Geza Kaszas *(Dmitri)*; Kathleen Gati *(CIA Technician)*; Joszef Szekhelyi *(Nektar)*; Robin Dalglish *(Duncan)*; Karoly Korognai *(Customs Agent)*; Balazs Galko *(Stefan)*; Akos Istvan Sinko *(Rubelov)*; Tibor Felszeghy *(Elder)*; Marta Bako *(Old Woman)*; Rudolf Varszegi *(Alexei)*; Tamas Vavrik *(Merchant)*; Marta Kertesz *(Lothar's Lab Assistant)*; Andras Toth *(Cart Driver)*; Andras Fesos *(Henchman)*; David Gautreaux *(Rich)*; Istvan Kiraly *(Bus Driver)*; Barry Zetlin *(Lonnie)*

THE DOGFIGHTERS is as inconsequential a film as they come. However, this action work-out benefits from the presence of star Robert Davi. Cast against type as a high-flyin' secret agent man, Davi can't pull the film out of a quicksand of Russian Mafia stereotypes, but he does command the screen when he's on it, even during heady aerial sequences.

Having sufficiently annoyed the Pentagon Brass to drum him out of the military, iconoclastic legend Rowdy Welles (Davi) now wastes his talent on marijuana runs. By faking the death of one of Rowdy's one-night stands, CIA chief Dick Althorp (Ben Gazzara) blackmails the retired Welles into going undercover. His assignment: to capsize the black market empire of a Russian "Godfather," Lothar Krasna (Alexander Godunov).

As a reluctant soldier of fortune, Welles gets a cold reception from Krasna's Soviet enforcers who are scheming to manufacture plutonium bombs. Aided by a double agent named "Mike" (Lara Harris), who's bedding Krasna, Welles is finally outfitted by an unfortunate weapons monger, Nektar (Joszef Szekhelyi), who pays for his cooperation by being killed by Krasna's henchmen.

Fending off assorted assassination attempts, Welles infiltrates the nuclear facility and rescues hostage "Mike," vacating the premises just before they explode. However, the explosion doesn't prevent Krasna from completing his bomb. After shooting down Krasna and his home-made bomb in the air, Welles returns home. Realizing he was set up with a faked murder charge and that Althorp considered him a likely casualty of the operation, Welles finishes meting out international justice by punching out the wily CIA chief.

Despite the plethora of authentic Russkie accents, the "no-goodniks" in this assembly line film could just as easily be Mafia from Sicily, skinheads from Berlin, or ticket scalpers from Madison Square Garden. Like all interchangeable threats, the villains exist for the sole purpose of an Ugly American to polish off with xenophobic righteousness. Serving as propaganda for weekend warriors to watch at paramilitary getaways, films like THE DOGFIGHTERS never tire of exposing the dirty underwear of those indefatigable Commies. Going a step further, this particular celebration of All-American individuality (i.e., vigilantism) also satirizes the long arm of the CIA as a crypto-military dictatorship trying to run America—we all know that keeping America safe is the province of heroes like Welles with gripes against the government. If you don't have a high tolerance for this sort of qualified flag-waving then steer clear of THE DOGFIGHTERS. (And in doing so, you will also spare yourself the dismaying sight of a dissipated Godunov in one of his last roles.) *(Graphic violence, extreme profanity, substance abuse.)* — R.P.

d, Barry Zetlin; p, Kevin Kallberg, Oliver G. Hess; exec p, Kenneth J. Kallberg; assoc p, Richard Boehm; co-p, Paula Hammerel; w, Anthony Stark, Sean Smith (based on a story by Barry Zetlin and Richard Boehm); ph, Pierre Isaacks; ed, Dick Barry; m, Jimmie Haskell; prod d, Lorand Javor; set d, Agnes Menyhart; sound, Peter Meiselmann; casting, Dawn Steinberg; cos, Andrea Feschi; makeup, Katalin Jakots; stunts, Gyorgy Kives

Action/Spy/Martial Arts **(PR: O MPAA: R)**

DONOR UNKNOWN ★★
(U.S.) 93m Citadel Entertainment ~ MCA/Universal Home Video c

Peter Onorati *(Nick Stillman)*; Alice Krige *(Alice Stillman)*; Clancy Brown *(Nash Creed)*; Richard Portnow *(Hal Cooney)*; Sam Robards *(Dr. David Bausch)*; Leo Garcia *(Father Raul Arias)*; Christina Solis *(Gloria)*; Becky Herbst *(Danielle Stillman)*; John Dorman *(Dr. Bochman)*; Dan Martin *(Frank Donnelly)*; Irene Olga Lopez *(Carmen)*; Steven Culp *(Joel)*; Philip Lenkowsky *(Ray Haskell)*; Emilio Rivera *(Emilio)*; Denise Maria Toledo *(Marena)*; Robert Madrid *(Coyote)*; T. J. Castranovo *(Eddie)*; Laurie Ciarametaro *(Pretty Woman's Nurse)*; Lisa Lord *(Servant)*; Dian Kobayashi *(University President)*; Joe Marinelli *(Paolo)*; Mitchell Thomas Gibney *(Maitre D')*; Rene Carasco *(Bartender)*

DONOR UNKNOWN is yet another venture into Michael Crichton country. The film's preachy undercurrents about the sanctity of the American family and the rights of illegal aliens pull at a slender thread of suspense until this overburdened thriller snaps.

Workaholic Nick Stillman (Peter Onorati) busts fraudulent clients for his insurance investigation company but spends little time with his wife Alice (Alice Krige). Working at full throttle strains Nick's heart, and he nearly dies. Complying with the wishes of Nick's surgeon, Dr. Bausch (Sam Robards), Alice asks no questions when a healthy heart becomes available for transplant. Although the operation is a success, detail-oriented Nick frets that his donor Juan died in a police-pursuit car crash, whereas the late Juan's girlfriend Gloria (Christina Solis) insists illegal immigrant Juan never learned how to drive.

With the aid of a detective Ray Haskell (Philip Lenkowsky) and the background checking of barrio priest Father Arias (Leo Garcia), Nick learns that the couple posing as Juan's grieving parents are too young to have borne him. Doubts about Dr. Bausch's methods lead Nick to former cop Nash Creed (Clancy Brown), an organ harvester who collects coveted hearts, lungs, etc., by killing unwilling living donors. Slated to tout Bausch's proposed clinic at a fund-raiser, Nick refuses to quit digging for evidence even after Creed threatens Alice and their daughter, Danielle (Becky Herbst). Although weakened by organ-rejection drugs injected by a suspicious Dr. Bausch, Nick confronts an unrepentant Creed at his boat, shoots him, and drowns him in the bay. After publicly discrediting Dr. Bausch, Nick expires, knowing that his sacrifice will end the killing cycle where the disenfranchised are eliminated so the elite can have a second chance at life.

DONOR UNKNOWN assembles all the right ingredients for a chiller but leaves them unblended. Independent of each other, the medical chicanery, the illegal-alien exploitation, and the Stillmans' domestic dysfunction don't achieve any crescendo of suspense. The film implies that Nick's feverish search for justice connects with his bulldog nature, but the plucky claims investigator seems more at the mercy of grinding plot mechanics than inner demons. Instead of pushing Nick into a maelstrom of self-doubts, the film portrays his conspiracy-busting in the routine manner of a 1970s TV detective show. As a melodrama, DONOR UNKNOWN has its moments, but as a thriller, this movie could have used a transplant of healthy suspense. *(Graphic violence, profanity, adult situations.)* — R.P.

d, John Harrison; p, Leanne Moore, John Sutton III; exec p, David Ginsburg; w, John Harrison (based on the novel *Corazon* by William Mooney); ph, Zoltan David; ed, Harry B. Miller III; m, David Bergeaud; prod d, Sara Andrews; set d, Kurt Meisenbach; sound, Charles Kelly; fx, Kevin Pike; casting, Melissa Skoff; cos, Kathleen Detoro; makeup, Angela Nogaro; stunts, Tierre Turner

Thriller **(PR: C MPAA: R)**

DON'T BE A MENACE TO SOUTH CENTRAL WHILE DRINKING YOUR JUICE IN THE HOOD ★★★

(U.S.) 89m Island Pictures; Ivory Way ~ Miramax c

Shawn Wayans *(Ashtray)*; Marlon Wayans *(Loc Dog)*; Tracey Cherelle Jones *(Dashiki)*; Chris Spencer *(Preach)*; Suli McCullough *(Crazy Legs)*; Darrell Heath *(Toothpick)*; Helen Martin *(Loc Dog's Grandma)*; Isaiah Barnes *(Doo Rag)*; Lahmard Tate *(Ashtray's Father)*; Keenen Ivory Wayans *(Mailman)*; Keith Morris *(Dave the Crackhead)*; Craig Wayans *(Thug #1)*; Casey Lee *(Brithday Boy Thug)*; Joe "Nub" Scott *(Birthday Cake Boy)*; Kim Wayans *(Mrs. Johnson)*; Vivica Fox *(Ashtray's Mother)*; Lee Scott *(Flashback Girl)*; Marian Reynolds *(Flashback Mother)*; Tommy Morgan Jr. *(Car Jacker)*; Virginia Watson *(Loc Dog's Mom)*; Gabriel Alexander *(Jheri Curl Kid)*; Scott Randle *(Doughboy)*; Wesley Eugene *(Tre)*; Tedero Jones Jr. *(Ricky)*; Queline Young *(A.K.)*; Alex Thomas *(Al Dog)*; Reginald Green *(Gang Member)*; Samuel Monroe Jr. *(Sam)*; Kwame Ganon *(Driver with Curlers)*; Warren "Zubari" Washington *(Cellular Phone #1)*; Don "Mazi" Mitchell *(Cellular Phone #2)*; Benjamin Everitt *(The Man)*; Toshi Toda *(Korean Store Owner)*; Tamayo Otsuki *(Korean Woman)*; Ahmad Reese *(Low Rider Gangsta)*; Lester Barrie *(Preacher)*; Vivian "Rappin' Granny" Smallwood *(Sister Williams)*; Omar Epps *(Malik)*; Jeffery Anderson-Gunter *(Homeless Man)*; Cynthia Madvig *(Secretary)*; James Van Patten *(Harvard Man)*; Alan Abelew *(Recruiter)*; Michael Adler *(Man in White Coat)*; Don Reed *(Driving Instructor)*; Faizon Love *(Rufus)*; Bernie Mac *(Officer Self Hatred)*; Mik Scriba *(Officer with Bullhorn)*; Kirk Kinder *(Prison Guard)*; A.J. Jamal *(The Cellmate)*; Antonio Fargas *(Old School)*; La Wanda Page *(Old School's Mom)*; Yvette Wilson *(Nurse)*; Guy Torry *(Doo Rag's Father)*; Travon Jamar *(Drug Thug #1)*; Damien Wayans *(Cousin with Bag)*; Charles Edward Bennett *(Jiffy Pop)*; Paula Jai Parker *(Drunk Party Girl)*; Lisa Morgan *(Sabomboo)*; Tiara English *(La Quanda)*; Terri J. Vaughn *(Keisha)*; Xavier Cook *(Child Support Man)*; Mitchell Marchand *(Mitchell)*; J.W. Smith *(Detective Cliche)*; Kelly Vaughn *(Snowflake)*

Rude, crude, and often hilarious, DON'T BE A MENACE TO SOUTH CENTRAL WHILE DRINKING YOUR JUICE IN THE HOOD is a happy surprise from the Wayans ("In Living Color") family, and Miramax, which inexplicably failed to promote this raucous spoof of BOYZ N THE HOOD (1991), SOUTH CENTRAL (1992), MENACE II SOCIETY (1993), et al.

DON'T BE A MENACE. . . follows the generic plotline of all 'hood movies: a mother (Vivica Fox) returns her son, a young black man, Ashtray (Shawn Wayans), to the neighborhood where he grew up in South Central, Los Angeles, so that he will be reunited with his father (Lahmard Tate). Ashtray settles into the 'hood with the help of his old friends, Loc Dog (Marlon Wayans), Crazy Legs (Suli McCullough), and Preach (Chris Spencer).

At a party, Ashtray falls for Dashiki (Tracey Cherelle Jones), an unwed mother looking for a way out of South Central. Ashtray promises to join Dashiki in her journey and become a father to her many children, but he must first fight off a gang that is headed by a thug who had once been involved with Dashiki. With the help of Loc Dog's gun-toting Grandma (Helen Martin), Ashtray and his friends combat their enemies, leaving our hero free to leave the bleak urban landscape with Dashiki and her children.

Like Keenen Ivory Wayans' television series, "In Living Color," and his first feature, I'M GONNA GIT YOU SUCKA! (1988), DON'T BE A MENACE. . . parodies contemporary black culture with such gleeful abandon that it occasionally embodies the very racism it attempts to expose. On the other hand, most of the jokes are so broad and funny that almost anyone from any background will appreciate the irreverent sensibility, which has a sharper edge than Robert Townsend's similar HOLLYWOOD SHUFFLE (1987). Also, as with the AIRPLANE and the NAKED GUN films, the jokes are hit and miss, but the good ones make up for the bad. This is the sort of low-budget enterprise where technical glitches in dubbing and shadows from the camera don't hurt the fun.

Hot off their syndicated series, "The Wayans Brothers," co-writers and co-stars Shawn and Marlon Wayans take a minor swipe at Spike Lee's CLOCKERS (1995), but they save their best ammunition for the John Singleton canon, including Janet Jackson's pretentious poet-heroine in POETIC JUSTICE (1993), the campus fascists in HIGHER LEARNING (1995), and, of course, generous portions of the violent drug scene in BOYZ N THE HOOD. The sidebar shots at other genre films, including NINE 1/2 WEEKS (1986) and STAND BY ME (1986), seem oddly dated and out of step, but amusing, nonetheless. Still, some of the best jokes are less specific to a particular source, such as the pot-smoking Grandma's impromptu breakdance in church. DON'T BE A MENACE. . . is far from a total success, but, for better or worse, it sounds a riotous death knell for all "Hood" movies of the future. *(Violence, sexual situations, adult situations, substance abuse, extreme profanity.)* — E.M.

d, Paris Barclay; p, Keenen Ivory Wayans, Eric L. Gold; exec p, Mark Burg, Dan Genetti; assoc p, Cristal Rivera-Mitchell; co-p, Carrie Morrow; w, Shawn Wayans, Marlon Wayans, Phil Beauman; ph, Russ Brandt; ed, William Young, Marshall Harvey; m, John Barnes; prod d, Aaron Osborne; art d, Reiko Kobayashi; set d, Jeanne Lusignan; ch, Donovan; sound, Pat Toma (mixer); fx, Dean Miller; casting, Robi Reed-Humes, Tony Lee, Andrea Reed; cos, Valari Adams; makeup, Lyssa Wittun

Comedy **(PR: C MPAA: R)**

DON'T LET YOUR MEAT LOAF ★

(U.S.) 81m No Shuckin' No Jivin' Productions ~ Stardance c

Leander Sales *(Wei)*; Dana S. Hubbard *(Tony)*; Brad Albright *(Johnny)*; Khadijah Karriem *(Patryce)*; Freddy "Doc Ice" Reeves *(Chuck)*; Marilyn Sue Perry *(Paulette)*; Peter Cossack *(Frank)*; Andre Blake *(Cool Breeze)*; Tajamika Paxton *(Hollyweird)*; Michael Quarry *(Sweet Dreams)*; Damon Chandler *(Pops)*; Cecelia Antoinette *(Moms)*; Ronette von Briel *(Cutie Ann)*; Gwen Coleman *(Traffic Cop)*; Zae Smith *(Billy)*; Gerald Halfhide Jr. *(Jamal)*; Carlos Patterson *(Carlos)*; Glenn Reid *(Jesus)*; Stephanie Laughlin *(Bruce)*; Celvia Jones *(Jo)*; Frank Goode *(Mr. Shoeshine)*; Patrick Dean *(Sellout)*; Larry Johnson *(Muslim)*; Jake-Ann Jones *(Resa)*; Jalil Hutchins *(NY Driver)*; Tony W. Gentry *(Salesman EBI)*; Carmen Mathis *(Betty Boom)*; Mark Jones *(Car Theft Victim)*; Terez Mychelle *(Mishon)*; Sikay Tang *(Chinese Girl)*; Gloria Burroughs *(Elderly Woman)*; Salif Cisse *(Restaurant Owner)*; Mame Bougouma *(Wife of Restaurant Owner)*; Ali Abdul Watthaub *(Thug)*; Michael Jamison *(Thug)*; Steven Dye *(Roscoe)*; Chandra Pointer *(Sister)*; Rodney Green *(Derelict)*; Courtney *(Halliday)*; Martin Whitfield *(Mr. Washing Machine)*; Myla Whitfield; Freda Canty; Mookie Cannon *(Train Passengers)*

The kind of independent no-budget feature that deserves to be judged on its intentions rather than its technical shortcomings, DON'T LET YOUR MEAT LOAF still fails because it really doesn't seem to have any intentions other than to get a bunch of people into a movie.

Wei (Leander Sales), Tony (Dana S. Hubbard), and Johnny (Brad Albright) are Brooklyn homeys who perform at open mike night at the local comedy club. Their dream is to open a club of their own, to be owned and operated by comedians. But with no money or investors, their future looks dim. So does any future for Wei and his girlfriend Patryce (Khadijah Karriem), who has tried to put up with Wei's obsession about his club but breaks up with him when he forgets her birthday.

The three friends put on a street corner show that draws a crowd but no money. They fare a little better performing on subway trains, where the audiences can't walk away. They decide that the best way to raise money for their venture is to put on weekend shows for a few months in the backyard of the house owned by Wei's parents. Although no one shows up for opening night, Wei's father advises them not to abandon their dreams.

Producer-director-writer-editor-star Leander Sales may deserve credit for getting a movie together on what appears to have been a non-existent budget, but one has to wonder why he went to all the trouble. "Introducing great new talent," boasts the opening credits, and it wouldn't be a surprise to learn that everyone who invested in the film got to make an appearance: it is crammed with character bits that are as pointless as they are unamusing. Most of the film's dialogue consists of stale comic one-liners (typical sample: "Your mama's so old she was a waitress at the Last Supper"). So it's probably just as well that much of the dialogue is rendered inaudible by a combination of accents, poor voice projection, and intrusive street noises from the various on-location shots in Fort Greene and Crown Heights. *(Violence, nudity, sexual situations, substance abuse, profanity.)* — M.F.

d, Leander Sales; p, Leander Sales; co-p, Mark Kennerly; w, Leander Sales; ph, Floyd Rance III; ed, Leander Sales; m, Foster Bradley, Todd Cheek, Wendell Hanes; prod d, Anna Otis; art d, Anna Otis; sound, Leander Sales; casting, Tracey Moore; cos, Sheila Wade; makeup, Barry White, Joan Wilson

Comedy **(PR: O MPAA: NR)**

DOWN, OUT AND DANGEROUS ★★½

(U.S.) 90m USA Networks; Fast Track Films; Wilshire Court Productions ~ Paramount Home Video c

Richard Thomas *(Tim Willows)*; Bruce Davison *(Brad Harrington)*; Cynthia Ettinger *(Monica Harrington)*; Steve Hytner *(Grant Cromwell)*; Christine Cavanaugh *(Leslie McCoy)*; George DiCenzo *(Lance Fredericks)*; Jason Bernard *(Detective Danner)*; Melinda Culea *(CeCe Dryer)*; Stuart Pankin *(Calvin Burrows)*; Sarah MacDonnell *(Julie Harrington)*; Virginia Hawkins *(June)*; Lyla Graham *(Mrs. Lois Schmitz)*; Joe Nesnow *(Doc Spencer)*; Richard Narita *(Endo Tanaka)*; David J. Partington *(Old Mr. Walters)*; Michael Bayer *(Young Mr. Walters)*; Leonard Kelly-Young *(Businessman)*; Carole Wyand *(Judge)*; Rusty Schwimmer *(Bartender)*; David Jean-Thomas *(Man No. 1)*

Although DOWN, OUT AND DANGEROUS may be condemned as reactionary twaddle by advocates for the homeless, for mean-spirited thrill-seekers it's as much fun as stuffing oneself with a bag of cookies. Empty-calorie escapism, this tango between a decent suburbanite and a demented street person gets a lot of mileage out of the question: how much can that bum get away with?

White-collar worker Brad Harrington (Bruce Davison) toils at an office without getting the respect he deserves from a jittery boss, Lance Fredericks (George DiCenzo). At home, he deals with the needs of his wife Monica (Cynthia Ettinger) and with the pettiness of his neighbor Mr. Burrows (Stuart Pankin), who forces Brad to demolish backyard landscaping in a property-line dispute.

Seeking to help the less fortunate while clearing off branches, Brad employs Tim (Richard Thomas), a dispossessed sociopath with a low tolerance for the slurs of the gainfully employed. After a particularly nasty argument with Burrows turns violent, Brad knocks him unconscious. While Brad isn't looking, Tim kills Burrows with a blow to the head. Brad thinks himself responsible, and doesn't interfere when Tim helps him cover up the crime. Tim uses this leverage to wheedle his way into a job at Brad's firm.

Ingratiating himself with Fredericks and with a secretary, Leslie McCoy (Christine Cavanaugh), Tim horns in on one of Brad's key deals as Detective Danner (Jason Bernard) lays the groundwork for Brad's arrest for homicide. As Brad's lawyer pal, Grant Cromwell (Steve Hytner), checks out crazy Tim's past, Tim plants doubts in Monica's mind about Brad's fidelity and sabotages Brad's investment strategies so badly Brad ends up being fired. In addition to canceling Brad's credit cards, bloodthirsty Tim kills Mr. Fredericks and one of his employees, and implicates Brad in the crimes. While Grant tells police about Tim's homicidal past, Brad rids his life of this cancer by bashing Tim on the noggin with a wood shard after Tim has already stabbed himself during their struggle.

The unseemly incidents come fast and furious in this psychoflick. Tim's ingenious nibbling at the core of Brad's being is so incessant that viewers never have time to question the preposterousness of the plot's set-up. What is less persuasive is the cool maniac's campaign of total annihilation against Brad. Instead of showing how cagily Tim supplants Brad, the film opts for a slasherama approach with Tim self-destructing in his war against his benefactor.

Overlooking the overkill of Tim's hunger to squash unselfish Brad, horror fanciers will eat up the high body count. Reunited from LAST SUMMER (1969), Davison and Thomas make such formidable adversaries that audiences will never question the downward reversal of the two characters' fortunes. *(Graphic violence, adult situations.)* — R.P.

d, Noel Nosseck; p, Jack Roe; w, Carey Hayes, Chad Hayes; ph, Paul Maibaum; ed, Cari Coughlin; m, Mark Snow; prod d, Roy Alan Amaral; set d, Linda Lee Sutton; sound, Trevor Black (mixer); casting, Dan Shaner; cos, Sandi Culotta; makeup, Toby Lamm; stunts, Gary Davis

Thriller/Crime **(PR: C MPAA: R)**

DOWN PERISCOPE ★★

(U.S.) 90m Robert Lawrence Productions; 20th Century Fox ~ 20th Century Fox c

Kelsey Grammer *(Tom Dodge)*; Lauren Holly *(Emily)*; Rob Schneider *(Marty Pascal)*; Harry Dean Stanton *(Howard)*; Bruce Dern *(Admiral Graham)*; William H. Macy *(Captain Knox)*; Ken Hudson Campbell *(Buckman)*; Toby Huss *(Nitro)*; Duane Martin *(Jackson)*; Jonathan Penner *(Spots)*; Bradford Tatum *(Stepanak)*; Harland Williams *(Sonar)*; Rip Torn *(Admiral Winslow)*; James Martin Jr. *(Orlando Radioman)*; Jordan Marder *(Orlando Ensign)*; Matt Landers *(Orlando XO)*; Joseph Latimore *(Orlando Sonarman)*; Patton Oswalt *(Stingray Radioman)*; Joe Soto *(Helmsman)*; John Shepherd *(Young Sailor)*; Pierrino Mascarino *(Trawler Captain)*; Dennis Fimple *(Fisherman)*; Ancel Cook *(Fisherman)*; James Harper *(Supportive Admiral)*; Rudy Hornish *(Admiral #2)*; Tommy Terrell *(Admiral #3)*; Elliot Easton *(Secretary)*; Michael William Connors *(Orlando Young Sailor)*; Paul Tranghese *(Sailor #2)*; Mitch Danton *(Conn Tower Officer)*; Jackson Sleet *(Torpedo Man)*; Annie Talbot *(Singing Waitress)*; Eugene Daniel; Bob Dini; Andrew English; Steve Giralo; Robert Grochau; Jamie James; Joseph Keawkalaya; Todd Odom *(Singing Sailors)*

Comedy often provides the means by which artists deflate the pompous authority of institutions, such as the military in this case; sadly, DOWN PERISCOPE serves more as a Navy recruiting poster than a subversive submarine farce.

DOWN PERISCOPE opens with a heated discussion among the Navy's top brass concerning the impending promotion of Lt. Comdr. Thomas Dodge (Kelsey Grammer). While Admiral Winslow (Rip Torn) advocates for Dodge, Admiral Graham (Bruce Dern) warns of his reputedly eccentric behavior. They finally agree to test Dodge in a war game exercise to see if he deserves higher ranking.

Dismayed to discover that he has been assigned a submarine from the 1950s and a crew of oddballs and rejects, Dodge nevertheless proceeds, restoring the craft (called the Stingray) and quickly gaining the respect of his shipmates. Dodge's tasks also include integrating into the crew a female officer, Lt. Emily Lake (Lauren Holly), as part of an experiment to include women on submarines.

Against all odds, Dodge and his fellow officers succeed in the war games by escaping detection from Graham's nuclear-powered sub and reaching the contact points in the harbor. Much to Graham's chagrin, Admiral Winslow rewards Dodge with his promotion, including a new submarine and crew. But Dodge insists on carrying out his future missions with the wacky but talented Stingray crew, including his admiring new girlfriend, Emily.

Kelsey Grammer, of TV's "Cheers" and "Frasier" fame, makes his feature debut in this comedy about a motley crew of misfits subordinating their individuality for the sake of patriotism and patriarchy. Thus, the message of DOWN PERISCOPE is frightfully reactionary: honor thy country and thy father (and, while you're at it, don't question authority figures).

Of recent Hollywood B comedies, DOWN PERISCOPE mercifully tones down the level of excessive violence and bathroom humor (even though the biggest laugh here centers on passing gas), but the obligatory sexist smirking is alarmingly increased. What would be offensive by any contemporary standard is especially unnerving in the wake of recent real-life military sex scandals.

David S. Ward directs DOWN PERISCOPE proficiently, but is surprisingly better at handling the action-adventure portions than the comedy sequences. Usually reliable actors like Bruce Dern and Rip Torn merely shout their lines, while Grammer coasts through his role with minimal effort. DOWN PERISCOPE wants you to believe that Navy work is hip and fun. Hopefully, most viewers will not be fooled. *(Violence, profanity.)* — E.M.

d, David S. Ward; p, Robert Lawrence; exec p, Jack Cummins; co-p, Stanley Wilson; w, Hugh Wilson, Andrew Kurtzman, Eliot Wald (from a story by Hugh Wilson); ph, Victor Hammer; ed, William Anderson, Armen Minasian; m, Randy Edelman; prod d, Michael Corenblith; art d, Dan Webster; set d, Mickey S. Michaels; sound, William B. Kaplan (mixer), Paul Urmson (design); fx, Marty Bresin, Richard E. Hollander, VIFX, Jamie Price; casting, Ferne Cassel; cos, Luke Reichle; makeup, James R. Kail; stunts, Glenn Randall Randall

Comedy **(PR: C MPAA: PG-13)**

DRAGONHEART ★★½

(U.S.) 108m Universal ~ Universal c

Dennis Quaid *(Bowen)*; David Thewlis *(Einon)*; Sean Connery *(Voice of Draco)*; Pete Postlethwaite *(Gilbert)*; Julie Christie *(Aislinn)*; Dina Meyer *(Kara)*; Jason Isaacs *(Felton)*; Brian Thompson *(Brok)*; Lee Oakes *(Young Einon)*; Wolf Christian *(Hewe)*; Terry O'Neill *(Redbeard)*; Peter Hric *(King Freyne)*; Eva Vejmelkova *(Felton's Minx)*; Milan Bahul *(Swamp Village Chief)*; Sandra Kovacicova *(Young Kara)*; Kyle Cohen *(Boy in Field)*; Thom Baker *(Aislinn's Chess Partner)*; Ivo Kristof *(Horse Master)*

An engaging combination of light-hearted fantasy and magical drama, DRAGONHEART benefits from solid talent on both sides of the camera.

In the Dark Ages, seasoned knight Bowen (Dennis Quaid) trains the king's son, Einon (Lee Oakes), in the ways of the old code of King Arthur. During a peasant revolt, the king is killed and Einon gravely wounded, and the latter can only be saved with the help of a nearby dragon (voice of Sean Connery), who donates part of his heart to restore the young man.

Twelve years later, Einon (now played by David Thewlis) has become an arrogant, vicious ruler, and Bowen, believing the dragon's blood to be responsible for the boy's cruel demeanor, has devoted his life to slaying the magical beasts. He encounters the dragon who saved Einon—the last of his species—and they fight to a standoff. The two end up making a deal: Draco (as Bowen names him, after the constellation) terrorizes local villages, and Bowen pretends to slay him for a price.

Their scheme is soon revealed by Kara (Dina Meyer), the peasant girl who originally wounded Einon and who is now mounting another revolt against the king. She convinces Bowen to join the cause, although Draco reveals that the sharing of his heart with Einon links them; if Einon should die, so will Draco.

Kara is captured by Einon but freed by his mother, the queen Aislinn (Julie Christie), who in turn is murdered by Einon. The king then captures Draco and fights a lengthy duel with Bowen, who cannot bring himself to kill Einon and thus his friend. Ultimately, Draco convinces Bowen to sacrifice him. As Einon dies, Draco s spirit ascends to join his namesake constellation.

Breezier in tone than the gloomier and more visceral medieval adventures of the 1980s and 90s, DRAGONHEART is a film of many pleasures. Chief among them is Draco the dragon himself, who represents yet another striking advance in computer effects work. Not only is he completely convincing as a physical being, he has been given a completely convincing personality, too, as if someone taught one of the JURASSIC PARK dinosaurs how to act. It doesn't hurt that said personality is that of Connery, who does a wonderful job voicing the beast, and whose mannerisms have been skillfully transposed onto his fire-breathing on-screen alter ego.

Giving its monster such a distinct personality is one of the key differences between this film and dragon stories past—along with the fun subplot of having Draco and Bowen pulling their 10th-century scam and Draco's and Einon's link, which provides the film its pathos. The basic plot of the duo's battles against the ruthless king is more standard, though it helps that Thewlis's characterization is relatively fresh for this type of role: instead of an older, more tyrannical ruler, Einon is a spoiled, spiteful youth whose lack of maturity contributes to his villainy.

By making their dragon a figure of fun for a good portion of the running time, director Rob Cohen and writer Charles Edward Pogue let slip the opportunity to generate a true sense of awe and wonder until the final act. And while the leads are all fine, the supporting players are not as compelling; Meyer is better at action than emotion, while Christie and Pete Postlethwaite, as Bowen's monk sidekick, don't have enough to do. But overall, this is an entertaining and occasionally quite funny and dazzling fantasy. *(Violence, adult situations.)* — M.G.

d, Rob Cohen; p, Raffaella De Laurentiis; exec p, David Rotman, Patrick Read Johnson; assoc p, Herbert W. Gains, Kelly Breidenbach; co-p, Hester Hargett; w, Charles Edward Pogue (from a story by Charles Edward Pogue and Patrick Read Johnson); ph, David Eggby; ed, Peter Amundson; m, Randy Edelman; prod d, Benjamin Fernandez; art d, Maria Teresa Barbasso, Jano Svoboda; set d, Giorgio Desideri; sound, Reinhard Stergar (mixer), Geoff Rubay (designer); fx, Kit West, Phil Tippett, James Straus, John Baker, Scott Squires, Industrial Light & Magic; casting, Margery Simkin; cos, Thomas Casterline, Anna Sheppard; makeup, Giannetto De Rossi, Maurizio Silvi; stunts, Paul Weston

AAN Best Visual Effects: Scott Squires, Phil Tippett, James Straus, Kit West

Fantasy/Adventure **(PR: A MPAA: PG-13)**

DUNSTON CHECKS IN ★

(U.S.) 85m Freestyle Enterprises; Wizan/Black Films; The Movie Group; Fox Family Films ~ 20th Century Fox c

Jason Alexander *(Robert)*; Faye Dunaway *(Mrs. Dubrow)*; Eric Lloyd *(Kyle)*; Rupert Everett *(Rutledge)*; Graham Sack *(Brian)*; Paul Reubens *(La Farge)*; Glenn Shadix *(Lionel Spalding)*; Nathan Davis *(Victor)*; Jennifer Bassey *(Mrs. Dellacroce)*; Judith Scott *(Nancy)*; Bruce Beatty *(Murray)*; Danny Comden *(Norm)*; Steven Gilborn *(Artie)*; Lois de Banzie *(Mrs. Winthrop)*; Natalie Core *(Mrs. Feldman)*; Eugenia Hamilton *(Frau Biedermeyer)*; Michelle Bonilla *(Consuelo)*; Alexander Walters *(William)*; Toribio Prado *(Bernard)*; Bree Turner *(French Girl)*; Kevin Kraft *(Desk Clerk)*; Peter Siragusa *(Maintenance Man)*; Ernest Perry Jr. *(Doorman)*; Frank Kopyc *(Night Doorman)*; Lynne Marie Stewart *(Cucumber Woman)*; Marceline Hugot *(Mrs. Harrison)*; Cynthia Martells *(Ms. Pink)*; Michael McCarty *(Tex)*; Katherine Olsen *(Mrs. Tex)*; Cynthia Madvig *(Kimberly)*; Ken Patrick Martin *(Waiter)*; Karen Maruyama *(Telephone Operator)*; Ray K. Morris *(Maintenance Man #2)*; Rita Minor *(Maid #1)*; Victoria Kemsley *(Maid #2)*; Ray Chang *(Bellman #1)*; Nicholas Garr *(Bellman #2)*; Roderick Bascom *(Bellman #3)*; Paula Malcomson *(Bellman #4)*; Neriah Davis *(Ferrari Girl)*; Toni Perrotta *(Maid)*; Jim Ishida *(Bali Majestic Guest)*; Sunni *(Bali Majestic Clerk)*; Tracy Zahoryin *(Fashion Model)*

Given that it's a monkey movie, DUNSTON CHECKS IN is virtually assured of an audience, but its lack of spirited monkey-business will limit that audience to those with ages in the single digits.

Ten-year old Kyle (Eric Lloyd) and his teenage brother Brian (Graham Sack) live in the ritzy Majestic Hotel with their widower father, Robert Grant (Jason Alexander), the hotel's put-upon manager. While Kyle and Brian use the hotel as their personal playground (apparently they don't attend school), Grant tends to the demands of his snobby guests and answers to the hotel's heartless owner, Mrs. Dubrow (Faye Dunaway). Into the mix steps Lord Rutledge (Rupert Everett) with an orangutan named Dunston that he has trained as a jewel thief. Because Rutledge is mean to Dunston, the ape takes off and befriends Kyle. With Brian's help, Kyle struggles to conceal the mischievous Dunston, while Rutledge struggles to recapture him, and Grant struggles to keep a lid on all the strange goings-on. Meanwhile, Dubrow hires "animal control officer" Buck LaFarge (Paul Reubens) to shoot the orangutan, and Kyle implores his father to protect his hairy friend. It all comes to a head at the Crystal Ball, the social event of the season, where Dunston wreaks havoc, Rutledge is exposed as a criminal, Dubrow gets her comeuppance, Grant risks his job to side with his son, and Kyle saves Dunston from LaFarge.

Surprisingly (in the way getting clothes instead of toys for your birthday is surprising), DUNSTON CHECKS IN isn't just 90 minutes of an ape run amok in a fancy hotel—rather, the movie offers up bathos in place of monkeyshines. The story is a barebones version of a formula popularized in recent children's movies (such as FREE WILLY and MONKEY TROUBLE) where an animal helps mend a broken family. Sadly for DUNSTON, its narrative is so facile that it would be insulting if it weren't so pathetically ineffective. Positing a child's eye view of the world, the film is shot from low angles to exaggerate the perspective that the rare adult who isn't ignoring kids is instead leering menacingly at them. However, in the face of the success of Jim Carrey's films (which take gross-out humor to new lows), DUNSTON can claim to take the high road, since its star wears shorts so that no one will see his monkey butt.— P.R.

d, Ken Kwapis; p, Todd Black, Joe Wizan; exec p, Rodney Liber; assoc p, John T. Kretchmer; co-p, Jason Blumenthal; w, John Hopkins, Bruce Graham (from a story by John Hopkins); ph, Peter Collister; ed, Jon Poll; m, Miles Goodman; prod d, Rusty Smith; art d, Keith Neely; set d, Jim Samson; sound, Clark D. King (mixer); fx, John C. Hartigan, Craig Barron, Ultimate Effects; casting, Linda Lowy, John Brace; cos, Alina Panova; makeup, Patricia Messina; stunts, Walter Scott

Comedy/Children's (PR: A MPAA: PG)

ED ★½

(U.S.) 94m Longview Entertainment ~ Universal c

Matt LeBlanc *(Jack Cooper)*; Jayne Brook *(Lydia)*; Jack Warden *(Chubb)*; Bill Cobbs *(Tippet)*; Patrick Kerr *(Kirby Woods)*; Doren Fein *(Liz)*; Charlie Schlatter *(Buddy Halsten)*; Carl Anthony Payne II *(Stats Jefferson)*; James Caviezel *(Dizzy Anderson)*; Mike McGlone *(Oliver Barnett)*; Zacharias Ward *(Dusty Richards)*; Phillip Bruns *(Clarence)*; Curt Kaplan *(Randall "Zonk" Cszonka)*; Valente Rodriguez *(Jesus Rodriguez)*; Gene Ross *(Red)*; Paul Hewitt *(Bucky)*; Sage Allen *(Cooper's Mother)*; Stan Ivar *(Cooper's Father)*; Jim O'Heir *(Art)*; Rick Johnson *(Kurt "Crush" Bunyon)*; Leonard Kelly-Young *(Customer Joe)*; Troy Evans *(Bus Driver)*; Richard Gant *(Umpire—Sharks Game)*; Bill Capizzi *(Farley)*; Steve Eastin *(Shark's Manager)*; K.C. Corkery *(Little Boy—Banana Toss)*; Jaquita Green *(Little Girl)*; Ken Zavayna *(Peanut Man)*; Kevin Kraft *(Shortstop)*; Brad Hunt *(Carnie)*; Mark Cassella *(Security Guard)*; Joe Bucaro *(Goon #1)*; Noon Orsatti *(Goon #2)*; John-Clay Scott *(Banana Truck Driver)*; Jessica Pennington *(Nurse Rosa Cays)*; Tommy LaSorda *(LaSorda)*; Mitchell Ryan *(Abe Woods)*; Macka Foley *(Umpire—Championship Game)*; Michael Chieffo *(Dr. Joseph Middleton)*; Jay Caputo; Denise Cheshire *(Ed Sullivan)*; Gary Hecker *(Voice of Ed Sullivan)*

Likable sitcom star Matt LeBlanc strives for big-screen eminence in ED, but this sports comedy about a baseball rookie who befriends his team's mascot is stolen by LeBlanc's co-star. . . a monkey.

Farm boy Jack Cooper's (Matt LeBlanc) ability to pitch lightning-fast balls through tires lands him a place on the Santa Rosa Rockets baseball team. Unfortunately, Jack has never been able to bat successfully, and becomes incredibly nervous when playing baseball in public. The manager of the Rockets, Chubb (Jack Warden), hopes to help Cooper, so when the owners bring in a chimpanzee named Ed Sullivan to be a mascot, Chubb assigns him to live with Jack, who quickly discovers that Ed is a handful. Cooper begins to loosen up in public, however, inspired by the carefree example set by the chimp.

Between baseball practice and taking care of his new ward, Jack barely has time to field the romantic advances of his comely neighbor and single mom, Lydia (Jayne Brook). Back on the field, Jack and the team are astonished to find that Ed can play ball. At first, Chubb places Ed at third base, but later gives him a pitching spot, because, like Jack, he is a much better pitcher than hitter.

Ed becomes a celebrity, and the team makes their way into the championship game. The owner's son kidnaps Ed to sell him for a big profit. Jack looks for his abducted friend, finding him in time to play in the game. But Jack also discovers that he can play—and win—without his helpmate. Later, he celebrates his triumph with his new family, Lydia, her daughter. . . and Ed.

Only the fans of LeBlanc's saccharine smile on "Friends" will pay any attention to his lackluster performance here as a farm boy turned pro pitcher. Everyone else will have their eyes fixed on Ed, who is represented by an animatronic creature in certain scenes and played by two actors (Jay Caputo, Denise Cheshire) taking turns in a monkey suit in others. Unlike "Bonzo" or the monkey in Howard Hawks's 1952 classic, MONKEY BUSINESS, Ed is imbued with particularly human qualities, including the ability to play baseball, drive a van, and clean house in record time. Still, ED is peculiar as comedies go: sometimes, the monkey's mischief-laden devotion toward Jack recalls the creepy hero-monkey relationship in George Romero's MONKEY SHINES (1988), while the scene where Ed is tortured while wearing a clown suit resembles a Bruce Nauman installation.

Thanks to Ed, Jack learns to "stop and smell the roses" (harmless enough as morals go), but the film's subtext is disturbing: are the filmmakers and merchandisers of ED much different than the fictitious evil, greedy businessmen who buy the kidnapped Ed? Clearly, the advertisers plugging their wares in ED want the monkey to do for Reebok, Coke, and Budweiser what ET did for Reeses Pieces.

Another theme of the film is downright racist: by having Ed bond easily with the African-American characters, including an umpire who defends his presence on the field with anti-discriminatory discourse, ED reinforces the ancient association between simian creatures and dark-skinned humans. Given all this, ED can hardly be recommended; if you missed DUNSTON CHECKS IN in 1996 or have nostalgia for Clint Eastwood and the orangutan in EVERY WHICH WAY BUT LOOSE, ED will make a poor substitute indeed.— E.M.

d, Bill Couturie; p, Rosalie Swedlin; exec p, Bill Finnegan, Bill Couturie, Brad Epstein; assoc p, Kathryn Couturie, Ned Gusick; w, David Mickey Evans (from a story by Ken Richards and Janus Cercone); ph, Alan Caso; ed, Robert K. Lambert; m, Stephen D. Endelman; prod d, Curtis A. Schnell; art d, Michael L. Fox; set d, Crista Schneider; sound, Jacob Goldstein (mixer); fx, David Blitstein, Robert A. Grasmere Jr.; casting, Shari Rhodes, Joseph Middleton; cos, Robin Lewis; makeup, Dee Dee Altamura, Dave Nelson, Norman Tempia, Animated Engineering; stunts, Ernie Orsatti

Children's/Sports/Comedy (PR: AA MPAA: PG)

EDDIE ★★

(U.S.) 98m Eddieball, Inc.; Permut Presentations; Island Pictures; Hollywood Pictures ~ Buena Vista c

Whoopi Goldberg *(Edwina "Eddie" Franklin)*; Frank Langella *(Wild Bill Burgess)*; Dennis Farina *(Coach Bailey)*; Richard Jenkins *(Assistant Coach Zimmer)*; Lisa Ann Walter *(Claudine)*; John Benjamin Hickey *(Joe Nader)*; Troy Beyer *(Beth Hastings)*; John Salley *(Nate Wilson)*; Rick Fox *(Terry Hastings)*; Malik Sealy *(Stacy Patton)*; Mark Jackson *(Darren Taylor)*; Dwayne Schintzius *(Ivan Radovadovitch)*; Greg Ostertag *(Joe Sparks)*; Vernel Singleton *(Jamal Duncan)*; Marv Albert *(Himself)*; Chris Berman *(Himself)*; Aasif Mandvi *(Mohammmed)*; Johnny Williams *(Big Al)*; Albert Pisarenkov *(Mischa)*; Isiah Whitlock Jr. *(Rick)*; Walt Frazier *(Himself)*; Rudolph W. Giuliani *(Mayor of New York City)*; Edward Koch *(Former Mayor of New York City)*; Donald Trump *(Himself)*; Muijibur Rahman *(Himself)*; Sirajul Islam *(Himself)*; James K. Flynn *(MSG Announcer)*; Gary Payton *(Rumeal Smith)*; George O. Gore II *(Malik Jones)*; Zachary Simmons Glover *(Jerome)*; Jermaine Mauriece Butler *(Suli)*; Davenia McFadden *(Rae Jones)*; Lou Criscuolo *(Fred)*; Sylvia Harman *(Helen)*; Jonathan Marten *(Eric—Bag No.1)*; Ethan Edward Marten *(Keith—Bag No.2)*; Melrose Larry Green *(Colorful Fan)*; Norman "Max" Maxwell *(Fair Weather Fan)*; Moses Gibson *(Odell)*; Alexandra Adi *(ESPN Radio Announcer)*; Jim Gloster *(LA Bellhop)*; Kristian Damian *(Young Malik)*; Allan Lindo *(Young Jerome)*; Scott Owen Cumberbatch *(Young Suli)*; Ana Divac *(Party Girl)*; Julie Araskog *(Frazier Radio Announcer)*; Spud Webb *(Atlanta Hawks Player)*; Glenn "Doc" Rivers *(Atlanta Hawks Player)*; Jon Koncak *(Atlanta Hawks Player)*; Vlade Divac; Corie Blount; Cedric Ceballos; "Pig" Miller; Nick Van Exel *(Los Angeles Lakers)*; Kurt Rambis; John "Hot Rod"

Williams; Brad Daugherty; John S. Battle; Bobby Phills; Terrell Brandon *(Cleveland Cavaliers)*; Alex English *(Cleveland Cavaliers Head Coach)*; Rob Ryder *(Cleveland Cavaliers Assistant Coach)*; Dennis Rodman; Avery Johnson; Vinny Del Negro; J.R. Reid; Cory Alexander; Jack Haley *(San Antonio Spurs)*; Olden Polynice; Walt Williams; Randy Brown; Tyus Edney; Brian Grant; Mitch Richmond; Duane Causwell *(Sacramento Kings)*; Sam Mitchell *(Indiana Pacer)*; Dale Davis *(Indiana Pacer)*; Danny Manning; Joe Kleine; Danny Schayes; Elliot Perry; Wayman Tisdale *(Phoenix Suns)*; Larry Johnson; Muggsy Bogues; David Wingate; Scott Burrell; Joe Wolf *(Charlotte Hornets)*; Anthony Mason *(Pick-Up Player)*; Herb Williams *(Pick-Up Player)*; John Starks *(Pick-Up Player)*; David Dwyer; J. Don Ferguson; Mick McGovern; Jerry J. Heater; Zelton Steed *(Game Referees)*; Gary T. McTague; Patt Noday; Ron Clinton Smith; Steve Coulter; Dorothy Recasner Brown *(Locker Room Reporters)*; Al Trautwig *(NYC TV Reporter)*; John Di Maggio *(Construction Worker)*; Armand Dahan *(Street Vendor)*; Daniel D. Bannister; Tyrone Bell; Marcus P. Blucas; Demetrius Calip; Ray Lawson *(Bench Knicks)*; Gene Banks *(Knicks Assistant Coach)*; Bret Wood *(Knicks Trainer)*; Mitchell Gordon *(Dancing Knicks Fan)*; Alan Scott *(Rowdy Fan)*; Fabio *(Himself)*; Joseph Sinacori *(Joe the Cop)*; Rachel Pond *(Owner's Box Hostess)*; Beau Nix *(Game Scorer)*; Charles Martin *(St. Louis Businessman)*; George Halgas *(St. Louis Businessman)*; Anthony Lopez Sr. *(Youth Ref)*; Kim Delgado *(Businessman)*; Bernie Engel *(Elderly Fan)*; Joseph Anthony Battaglia *(Angry Fan)*; Thomas Nial *(Angry Fan)*; Jo-Ann Ebony *(Patton's Mama)*; Eartha D. Robinson *(Knicks Choreographer)*; Gene Anthony Ray; Ben Bagby; Michelle Bagby; Kimberly Marie Bailey; T'Fani Bose; Heather Atwood Brody; Debbie Caddell; Joy Davis; Michelle Fernandez; Felicia Fritz; Cezette Gregory; Sandy Heddings; Candy House; Arnella Jarrett; Heather Jones; Melissa Marlowe; Lia Panos; Nicole Price; Katrina Simmons; Shannon Spivey; Julie C. Wells; Tara Wood *(Dancers)*

When loud-mouthed New York Knicks fan Edwina "Eddie" Franklin (Whoopi Goldberg) is plucked from the cheap seats of Madison Square Garden and anointed head coach, she drags the apathetic players out of a slump, fires up the fans, and prevents the sale of the team, winning the love of New Yorkers from Joe Hardhat to Donald Trump. A thin story of an everywoman whose moxie helps virtuous New York win out over slickness and greed, EDDIE's few routine scenes of actual play do little to enliven this limp film.

The New York Knicks are in the midst of a serious losing streak, but limo driver Eddie Franklin hasn't given up on her beloved team. She is dispatched to the airport to pick up "Wild" Bill Burgess (Frank Langella), a Texas sports entrepreneur who has just bought the Knicks and believes that a little flashy marketing is all that is needed to turn them around. Eddie regales the new owner with her more substantive solutions to the team's problems.

Wild Bill's disconnection with the New York fans is clearly demonstrated at the game that night when his indoor fireworks display ignites Walt Frazier's jersey. There's also plenty of tension between the new owner and the nasty head coach, John Bailey (Dennis Farina). When Bailey quits, Wild Bill names Eddie head coach.

Eddie quickly notes that the players spend most of their energy seducing women and negotiating lucrative advertising deals. Veteran Nate Wilson (John Salley) advises her that she has the same problem as Bailey did: he doesn't care about the players as individuals. Eddie reaches out to some team members and benches the arrogant Stacy Patton (Malik Sealy). These moves launch the team on a winning streak.

Wild Bill makes Eddie an offer: if the Knicks go all the way, he will sell the team to St. Louis, where she will get a million dollar contract. At the deciding game, Eddie calls a time-out in the last ten seconds of play. She grabs a mike and announces that if the Knicks win, Wild Bill will sell the team. Fans and players stream onto the floor to join her, and Wild Bill faces the enraged crowd with his assurances that the Knicks will stay in New York. The team sweeps to victory and the players embrace their hero, Eddie.

EDDIE is a harmless fantasy, and a rare example of a sports film with a woman at the center. The character's intense love for her team is infectious. But ultimately it is hard to care about what happens in EDDIE because all of the characters are so thinly drawn. Goldberg plays her stock wisecracking tough gal with a warm heart. The team is made up of feeble stereotypes, from the huge dumb Russian who can't speak English ("Ivan make defense") to the slick former ghetto boy who has forgotten his humble roots. Langella's Texas tycoon is an odd cipher—at times, it seems he respects Eddie for her energy and genuine talent; at others, he seems to have utter contempt for her and anyone else who would stand in the way of his profit motive. The basketball scenes are a disappointment. Cameos by New York Mayor Rudy Guiliani, former mayor Ed Koch, and others are attempts to give EDDIE some genuine local texture, but the film remains bland to its core. *(Sexual situations, profanity.)* — N.Z.

d, Steve Rash; p, Mark Burg; exec p, Ron Bozman, Steven Zacharias, Jeff Buhai; co-p, Andrew Gunn; w, John Connolly, David Loucka, Eric Champnella, Keith Mitchell, Steve Zacharias, Jeff Buhai (from a story by John Connolly, David Loucka, Steve Zacharias, and Jeff Buhai); ph, Victor J. Kemper; ed, Richard Halsey; m, Stanley Clarke; prod d, Dan Davis; art d, Robert K. Shaw Jr.; set d, Roberta J. Holinko; ch, Eartha D. Robinson; sound, James E. Webb; casting, David Giella, Eddie Dunlop, Beth Chambers; cos, Molly Maginnis; makeup, Michael Germain; stunts, Gary Combs

Comedy/Sports **(PR: C MPAA: PG-13)**

EDIE & PEN ★★½

(U.S.) 98m Emby Eye ~ PolyGram Video c

Jennifer Tilly *(Edie)*; Stockard Channing *(Pen)*; Scott Glenn *(Harry)*; Stuart Wilson *(Victor)*; Chris Sarandon *(Max)*; Michael O'Keefe *(Ken)*; Michael McKean *(Rick)*; Randy Travis *(Pony Cobb)*; Joanna Gleason *(Maude)*; Beverly D'Angelo *(Barlady)*; Martin Mull *(Johnnie Sparkle)*; Louise Fletcher *(Judge)*; Wendy Mull *(Resident Witness)*; Carol Ann Susi *(Irma)*; Missy Hargreaves *(Rosalee)*; Jen Smart *(Wendy the Waitress)*; Kelly Wolf *(Leslie the Stewardess)*; Eric Swanson *(Hotel Clerk)*; Michael Landers *(Bellman)*; Charles "Chip" Lucia *(Barman)*; Dave Powledge *(Hefty Cowboy)*; Scott Burkholder *(Policeman)*; Philip Waller *(Teenager)*; Walter Bobbie *(Speeding Cabbie)*; Joe Nipote *(Socrates the Cabbie)*; Jack Conley *(Pianist)*; Lincoln Lageson *(Porter)*; Victoria Tennant *(Blonde with Dog)*

Bright performances elevate this inconsequential script about female bonding into diverting if unmemorable entertainment.

Reno Nevada, "Divorce capital of America," is the meeting place for two dissimilar women. Pen (Stockard Channing) is a middle-aged woman distraught by the end of her marriage to Victor (Stuart Wilson), who withheld emotional support and had an affair with a younger woman. Edie (Jennifer Tilly) is an outgoing younger woman divorcing the husband she hasn't seen in years in order to marry her new boyfriend.

Having completed their courtroom formalities, Edie and Pen strike up a conversation in a bar, mostly to evade the unwanted attentions of a trio of local cowboys. They also meet Harry (Scott

Glenn), a local pharmacist and philanderer whose wife has just left him.

After bonding with stories of their most embarrassing moments, Edie and Pen go out for a night on the town. But when Pen discovers that Edie's fiancee is her now ex-husband, she returns to her hotel room. Harry follows and tries to seduce her, but she falls asleep.

The next morning, everyone heads to the airport. Edie learns the truth about Pen and Victor, but decides to marry him anyway, even though he lied to her. Pen and Edie agree to remain friends, and Harry persuades Pen to stay with him in Reno.

"Why can't men love us the way we love them?" weeps one of the two title characters in a line of dialogue indicative of EDIE AND PEN's TV-movie feminism. The utter lack of irony, or even self-awareness, of giving this line to a woman who has just said that she wants nothing more from a man than a house and babies is typical of a genre that panders to its audience as relentlessly as Zalman King does to his.

That aside, EDIE AND PEN isn't nearly as strident as it might have been, which may mean it lacks the courage of its male-bashing convictions but at least makes it watchable. Jennifer Tilly plays pretty much the same role she always plays, and even if it's not much of a stretch, she continues to do it with buoyant charm. Better is Stockard Channing, an attractive actress too often made dowdy in movies that can't seem to believe that brains and beauty aren't mutually exclusive. If only this made-for-cable feature gave them something more substantive to do together, instead of wasting time with a gaggle of pointless celebrity cameos. *(Sexual situations, adult situations, profanity.)* — M.F.

d, Matthew Irmas; p, Matthew Irmas, Victoria Tennant; co-p, Susan Vanderbeek; w, Victoria Tennant; ph, Alicia Weber; ed, Michael Ruscio; m, Shawn Colvin; prod d, Jon Gary Steele; sound, L. Mo Weber; casting, Bruce H. Newberg; cos, Michelle Cole; makeup, Suzanne Rodier

Comedy/Drama **(PR: C MPAA: PG-13)**

ED'S NEXT MOVE ★★★

(U.S.) 88m Ed's Films ~ Orion Classics c

Matt Ross *(Eddie Brodsky)*; Callie Thorne *(Lee)*; Kevin Carroll *(Ray Obregon)*; Cathy Curtin *(Anne)*; Nina Sheveleva *(Elenka)*; Ramsey Faragallah *(Dr. Banarjee)*; Jimmy Cummings *(Lee's Boyfriend)*; Aunjanue Ellis *(Erica)*; R.E. Rodgers *(Officer Sanchez)*; Timothy Pilato *(Hospital Kid)*; Ramon Moses *(Greedy Roommate)*; Eric Weiner *(Sloppy Roommate)*; Joshua Astrachan *(Pot-Smoking Roommate)*; David Pittu *(Fiche Lock Roommate)*; Devin Eggleston *(Beach Blanket Roommate)*; Robert Margolis *(Hyper-Wary Tenant)*; Michael Huston *(Angry Actress)*; Voltaire *(Brush with Happiness Guy)*; Will Arnett *(Weather Video Guy)*; Joy Findlay *(Woman at Party)*; Veronika Korvin *(Performance Artist)*; Liz Tuccillo *(Numbers Woman)*; Rick Kaplan *(Bond Trader Jordan)*; Joseph Fuqua *(Bond Trader Bryce)*; Cynthia Kaplan *(Female Translator)*; Dale Carman *(Male Translator)*; Peter Jacobson *(Yalta Coffee Shop Owner)*; A.J. Brentano *("Nitty Gritty" Disputer)*; Reine Hewitt *(Girl #1 in Coffee Shop)*; Kelly Yusko *(Girl #2 in Coffee Shop)*; Ned Ringleh *(Nice Guy Salesman)*; Merrill Holtzman *(Nice Guy)*; Lisa Harris *(Woman Nice Guy Hits On)*; Helene Weintraub *(Cloisters Lady #1)*; Gloria Goldman *(Cloisters Lady #2)*; Steven Arvanites *(Bubble Wrap Sculptor)*; Haras Ginsberg *(Art Student)*; Conrad Wolfson *(Liquor Store Clerk)*; Roxanne Manzano *(Teacher)*; Andy Buelvas *(School Kid)*; Oliver Wadsworth *(Video Camera Guy)*

ED'S NEXT MOVE is a daffy, featherweight diversion about a Wisconsin romantic who moves to Manhattan. A surprise hit at the Sundance Film Festival, this genial relationship movie goes to the head of the Generation X comedy class and provides more amusement than similar 1996 films such as SHE'S THE ONE and THE TRUTH ABOUT CATS AND DOGS.

When his girlfriend, Anne (Cathy Curtin), breaks up with him because attentive Ed (Matt Ross) gives her claustrophobia, Ed boldly jump-starts his stalled life by heading for New York with nothing but a hopeful spirit, a job as a rice geneticist, and a list of his faults (a going-away present from Anne). After interviews with assorted kooks, Ed is relieved when Ray (Kevin Carroll) chooses him as his roommate. Ray is as worldly and cynical as Ed is lonely and determined to find Miss Right. At the Yalta Coffee Shop, Ed strikes up a conversation with Natalie (Callie Thorne), who calls herself "Lee," a hard-shelled Manhattan musician, who brushes him off. Tripping over his social graces at museums and galleries, Ed learns naivete isn't a commodity single women are lining up for.

When Ed and Lee both witness a hit-and-run accident, Ed uses the accidental meeting as an excuse to call Lee for a date. Although the tete-a-tete begins with promise, Lee's ardor is dampened by typical urban downers like finding mice caught in a glue trap. What Ed later discovers is that Lee's see-sawing affection stems from her long-standing, unhappy relationship with a neurotic musician (Jimmy Cummings).

When Casanova Ray gets unexpectedly dumped by his latest main squeeze, the appeal of bed-hopping suddenly sours. Ed and Ray attend a concert by Lee's alternative music band, and they both get decked by Lee's hot-headed lover. Finally wising up, Lee commits herself to goodhearted Ed.

ED'S NEXT MOVE has off-beat touches that only *seem* tangential to the story line; actually, they form the basis of its celebration of true love. Avoiding the facile mean-spiritedness that mars many contemporary comedies, this film's appeal arises not so much from how Ed wins over his Big Apple princess, but from how the setbacks he suffers en route cause him to mature.

In the capable hands of debuting writer-director John Walsh, the dating booby traps that ensnare Ed not only shore up his nerve, but also reveal to the audience how truly resilient Ed is. At first, he seems like the loser Anne rejected, but when he takes over Ray's apartment with Rube Goldberg devices or chases barefoot down the street after a ticketing sanitation worker, the viewer stops interpreting his persistence and enthusiasm negatively.

At times, one loses patience with the unoriginal plight of the "lonely guy," and some of its Manhattan vs. Midwest insights aren't fresh. But the movie improves as it becomes less a yarn about a small-town boy and more a tale of a stranger who refuses to adapt to his environment. Ed makes New York take him on his own terms. That's an act of heroism.

Due to the screenplay's loose construction, the writer-director is free to insert hilarious interludes that comment on Ed's courtship dilemmas. The drollest examples are a commercial for the "I'm a Nice Guy" ID, a plastic card that eases the reservations of potential pick-ups; and an inspired sequence in which two professional relationship translators clearly interpret what Anne and Ed are *not* telling each other in half-truths and cliches.

Cementing this comic odyssey is the low-key performance of Matt Ross, who makes Ed's obsessiveness seem attractive. Hired simply to read with auditioning actresses, Ross eventually was singled out for the lead role. It's an astute choice, because this talented actor effortlessly floats this charming bubble of a movie about the importance of being earnest.

In an era when comedies are vulgar and comic stars are over-hyped, the upbeat ED'S NEXT MOVE and the self-effacing Ross are throwbacks to a sweeter period when romantic comedies prided themselves on candle-lit mutual attraction and unforced peals of laughter. *(Extreme profanity, violence, sexual situations.)* — R.P.

d, John Walsh; p, Sally Roy; assoc p, Joshua Astrachan; w, John Walsh; ph, Peter Nelson; ed, Pamela Martin; m, Benny Golson; prod d, Kristin Vallow; art d, Jessica Kibel; set d, Michael Murphy; sound, William Tzouris (mixer); casting, Susan Shopmaker; cos, Maura Sircus; makeup, Jane Choi

Romance/Comedy **(PR: C MPAA: R)**

EL SILENCIO DE NETO
(SEE: SILENCE OF NETO, THE)

ELECTRA ★½
(U.S.) 87m Electra Film Productions ~ New Horizons Home Video c

Shannon Tweed *(Lorna Duncan/Electra)*; Joe Tab *(Billy Duncan)*; Sten Eirek *(Dr. Marcus Roach)*; Katie Griffin *(Mary Anne Parker)*; Lara Daans *(Karen)*; Dyanne Di Marco *(Gina)*; John Stoneham *(Howard Parker)*; Ed Sahely *(Dr. Bartholomew)*; Rod Wilson *(Roach Driver)*; Daniel Levinson *(Bug #1)*; Louise Martin *(Ellen Parker)*; Ron Sarosian *(Ron Thatcher)*; Todd Schroeder *(Wiley)*; Danny Lima *(Matt)*; Tig Fong *(Muscleman)*; Peter Schnidelhauer; Charles Seixas; John Stoneham Jr.; Robert Racki; Eric Bryson; Paul Rutledge; Anthony Tyukodi *(Thugs)*; Dirk K. Heinze *(Guard #3)*

How does one describe the perverse luster of this super-hero extravaganza that ends, rather optimistically, with an announcement for ELECTRA 2: THE SECOND COMING? One could remark that this comic-bookish adventure is a weird combination of SPANKING THE MONKEY (1995) and MODEL BY DAY (1994). Inspired by Greek mythology and Sigmund Freud, ELECTRA spotlights aberrant psychology the way the SUPERMAN series features the dreaded kryptonite.

Trapped in his wheelchair, diabolical entrepreneur Mr. Roach (Sten Eirik) pressures his toady, Dr. Bartholomew (Ed Sahely), to perfect a restorative remedy for his legs. When test subjects, captured by Roach's Amazon guards (Lara Daans and Dyanne Di Marco), expire, Bartholomew is forced to reveal the whereabouts of one human subject who has survived prolonged use of the mobility-restoring wonder drug. Suffering, as did his late father, from a rare, life-threatening anemia, Billy Duncan (Joe Tab) pops Daddy's top-secret, all-purpose pills, which endow him with super strength. Because teenage Billy can transmit both his blood malady and his mega-stamina sexually, he strives for self-denial. However, both his girlfriend, Mary Anne (Katie Griffin), and his provocative stepmother, Lorna (Shannon Tweed), are quite willing to risk sharing his predicament.

When Roach's predators attack the Duncan household, Herculean Billy defeats the thugs and learns about the plan to steal the Duncan family cure. Lorna flees to the ranch of Mary Anne's father, Parker (John Stoneham Jr.), who is murdered by Roach's female assassins. By the time that Billy and Mary Anne venture into Roach's domain, Roach has captured Lorna and siphoned off her forbidden desire for Billy into a device that transforms her into a wicked wonderwoman named Electra. Although Roach imprisons Billy and Mary Anne, Mary Anne bravely swallows one of Billy's miracle-capsules.

Consumed by lust, Electra straddles a manacled Billy, rapes him, and proceeds to pass on her sexually acquired powers to paraplegic Roach. Pharmaceutically strengthened to the max, Mary Anne dispatches her female guards, frees Billy, and vanquishes Electra. Outmaneuvering Roach, Billy crashes the cyber-nut's wheelchair into a computer console, thus causing Roach to explode from an overload of data. Electra flickers with signs of vengeful life after Billy and Mary Anne escape.

Hell hath no fury like a stepmother scorned! The problem with ELECTRA is that its writer and director exhibit more imagination than style. It's a fanciful but retrogressive action flick that diminishes its energy during every martial arts sequence; the brawlers seem to wait for each choreographed punch to land. However, as a libidinously incorrect fairy tale for adults, ELECTRA is quite juicy. This naughty fantasy successfully parodies mad scientist movies, revealing the drooling subtext driving all those hysteria-prone lab monsters butting into God's business. If Roach is a voyeur version of Dr. Frankenstein, then Lorna/Electra is the bride of Frankenstein born at a clinic for sex addicts. Deliberately crossing the bounds of propriety, ELECTRA toys with pseudo-incest as a catalyst. It doesn't matter that Lorna is Billy's *stepmother*; everyone behaves as if she has violated the handbook of motherhood. Thus, despite the seesawing predictability of the many villainous attack scenes, and despite some cosmically bad acting, ELECTRA tickles its audience by focusing on a trumped-up moral depravity. There are far less entertaining spectacles than a sci-fi fest in which everyone is motivated by and saturated with titillating sexuality. *(Graphic violence, extensive nudity, extreme profanity, adult situations, sexual situations.)* — R.P.

d, Julian Grant; p, Helder Goncalves, Julian Grant; exec p, Ashok Amritraj, Damian Lee; assoc p, Nadia Rajewski; co-p, John Gillespie; w, Lou Aguilar, Damian Lee; ph, Gerald R. Goozee; ed, Paul G. Day; m, Mitchell D. Krol; prod d, John Gillespie; art d, Janet Macleod; set d, Jim Lambie; sound, Henry Embry (mixer/recordist); fx, Brock Jolliffe; casting, Marjorie Lecker; cos, Judith England; makeup, Shannon Coplin, Traci Loader; stunts, John Stoneham Stoneham

Erotic/Crime/Fantasy **(PR: O MPAA: R)**

EMMA ★★★½
(U.K./U.S.) 120m Matchmaker Films; Haft Entertaiment; Miramax ~ Miramax c

Gwyneth Paltrow *(Emma Woodhouse)*; Toni Collette *(Harriet Smith)*; Alan Cumming *(Mr. Elton)*; Jeremy Northam *(Mr. Knightley)*; Ewan McGregor *(Frank Churchill)*; Greta Scacchi *(Mrs. Weston)*; Juliet Stevenson *(Mrs. Elton)*; Polly Walker *(Jane Fairfax)*; Sophie Thompson *(Miss Bates)*; Phyllida Law *(Mrs. Bates)*; James Cosmo *(Mr. Weston)*; Denys Hawthorne *(Mr. Woodhouse)*; Kathleen Byron *(Mrs. Goddard)*; Edward Woodall *(Robert Martin)*; Brett Miley *(Little Boy)*; Brian Capron *(John Knightley)*; Karen Westwood *(Isabella)*; Paul Williamson *(Footman)*; Rebecca Craig *(Miss Martin)*; Angela Down *(Mrs. Cole)*; John Franklyn Robbins *(Mr. Cole)*; Ruth Jones *(Bates Maid)*

This third adaptation of a Jane Austen novel to come to the big screen within a year's passage can rightly be considered "the Americanization of *Emma*." With a wonderfully comic cast, and featuring Gwyneth Paltrow's first star turn, EMMA has plenty of humor and charm, but will pique Austen's ardent fans.

England, 1816. In the village of Highbury, Emma Woodhouse (Paltrow) is the pretty and wealthy mistress of her domain, an insular world of strict social etiquette. Kind-hearted Emma bestows her charity on the town's poor, but in the opinion of Mr. Knightley (Jeremy Northam), her brother-in-law, who is as he is named, Emma is a meddling know-it-all because she fancies herself a matchmaker without peer. Ever-manipulative Emma convinces Harriet Smith (Toni Collette), her friend, a plainer girl of uncertain lineage, to refuse the proposal of one Robert Martin (Edward Woodall), a farmer whose social standing is neither high nor low enough to merit Emma's notice, and set her sights on the Reverend Elton (Alan Cumming). Unbeknownst to Emma, he has his sights set on her however, and when Mr. Elton reveals his true feelings, it's almost enough to shake Emma's confidence in the keenness of her insight. After Emma's rebuke, Mr. Elton retreats to Bath from whence he returns with an artfully immodest wife (Juliet Stevenson).

With the arrival in Highbury of Frank Churchill (Ewan McGregor), the dashing stepson of Emma's former governess (Greta Scacchi), Emma is presented for the first time with a man worthy of her own consideration. And with the arrival of Jane Fairfax (Polly Walker), the niece of the delightfully daffy Miss Bates (Sophie Thompson), Emma is presented with a rival for the adoration and attention she has always commanded. Emma thinks she might love Mr. Churchill because the thought of him fills her with boredom, but decides she doesn't, and promotes him for Harriet. But Harriet isn't interested—just as well since Mr. Churchill and Miss Fairfax were secretly engaged all along—because she's become infatuated with Knightley. This arouses such jealousy in Emma that she realizes her own love for the gentleman. Fortunately, he reciprocates her affections, and, in the end, Harriet becomes Mrs. Martin, and Emma weds Knightley.

A skillful storyteller, Jane Austen was also an incisive observer, reporter, and critic of her social milieu. To varying degrees, PERSUASION and SENSE AND SENSIBILITY (Austen adaptations from 1995) presented the folly *and* pain that were the result of class and gender oppression. EMMA shies away, downplaying these darker themes to the point where the elaborate dance of Austen's narrative becomes just fodder for a high-minded date movie. Writer and first-time director Douglas McGrath (who cowrote 1994's BULLETS OVER BROADWAY) plays up the jokes and heavily accentuates the punchlines, lest any go by his fellow, dullard Yanks.

Emma's naivete and self-delusion are displayed, but her character's politely destructive hubris and disconnectedness never emerge in the film. McGrath doesn't provide the audience any opportunity to feel ambivalently about Emma and, in turn, her world. What EMMA lacks that *Emma* has is an authorial voice that conveys critique or satire. Austen might cringe at the lack of irony in the trajectory of Emma and Knightley's romance in EMMA; by her telling, the couple's "certain happiness" was not so certain at all.

Paltrow has been a critic's darling ever since gaining notice in 1993's FLESH AND BONE. EMMA was her self-chosen vehicle to leading lady status, and was expected to be her star-making, breakthrough role; however, the film had too much of an art-house air about it to gain mass appeal. Nonetheless, Paltrow deserves praise for her excellent performance. Her Emma is at once girlish and poised, elegant and funny. Paltrow is the rare American actress that projects class—that she isn't overwhelmed by her British costars is an achievement itself. She, of course, looks gorgeous, and is positively luminous onscreen. Paltrow gets compared to Audrey Hepburn (it's something about the neck) by her admirers, but it appears her ROMAN HOLIDAY is at least another movie off.— P.R.

d, Douglas McGrath; p, Patrick Cassavetti, Steven Haft; exec p, Bob Weinstein, Harvey Weinstein, Donna Gigliotto; assoc p, Donna Grey; w, Douglas McGrath (based on the novel by Jane Austen); ph, Ian Wilson; ed, Lesley Walker; m, Rachel Portman; prod d, Michael Howells; art d, Sam Riley, Joshua Meath Baker; set d, Totty Whateley; ch, Sue Lefton; sound, Chris Munro (mixer); fx, Effects Associates; casting, Mary Selway, Sarah Trevis; cos, Ruth Myers; makeup, Tina Earnshaw, Susie Adams

AA Best Original Musical or Comedy Score: Rachel Portman; *AAN Best Costume Design:* Ruth Myers

Romance/Historical/Comedy **(PR: A MPAA: PG)**

ENGLISH PATIENT, THE ★★★

(U.K./U.S./Italy) 162m Saul Zaentz; Miramax ~ Miramax c

Ralph Fiennes *(Almasy)*; Juliette Binoche *(Hana)*; Willem Dafoe *(Caravaggio)*; Kristin Scott Thomas *(Katharine Clifton)*; Naveen Andrews *(Kip)*; Colin Firth *(Geoffrey Clifton)*; Julian Wadham *(Madox)*; Kevin Whately *(Hardy)*; Clive Merrison *(Fenelon-Barnes)*; Nino Castelnuovo *(D'Agostino)*; Hichem Rostom *(Fouad)*; Peter Ruhring *(Bermann)*; Geordie Johnson *(Oliver)*; Torri Higginson *(Mary)*; Lisa Repo-Martell *(Jan)*; Raymond Coulthard *(Rupert Douglas)*; Philip Whitchurch *(Corporal Dade)*; Lee Ross *(Spalding)*; Anthony Smee *(Beach Interrogation Officer)*; Matthew Ferguson *(Young Canadian Soldier)*; Jason Done *(Kiss Me Soldier)*; Roger Morlidge *(Sergeant, Desert Train)*; Simon Sherlock *(Private, Desert Train)*; Sebastian Schipper *(Interrogation Room Soldier)*; Fritz Eggert *(Interrogation Room Soldier)*; Sonia Mankai *(Arab Nurse)*; Rim Turki *(Aicha)*; Sebastian Rudolph *(Officer in Square)*; Thoraya Sehill *(Interpreter in Square)*; Sondess Belhassen *(Woman with Baby in Square)*; Dominic Mafham *(Officer, El Taj)*; Gregor Truter *(Corporal, El Taj)*; Salah Miled *(Bedouin Doctor)*; Abdellatif Hamrouni *(Ancient Arab)*; Samy Azaiez *(Kamal)*; Habib Chetoui *(Al Auf)*; Philipa Day *(Officer's Wife)*; Amanda Walker *(Lady Hampton)*; Paul Kant *(Sir Ronnie Hampton)*

Stuck between the blare of popular fiction and the quietude of internal drama, THE ENGLISH PATIENT is a sweeping story of love, war, and adultery set and shot in Italy and North Africa. The film swept the 1996 Oscars: out of its twelve nominations, it won nine, including Best Picture, Best Director (Anthony Minghella), Best Cinematography (John Seale), and Best Supporting Actress (Juliette Binoche).

In 1938, a cartographic expedition journeys into the Sahara Desert. Among its members are Hungarian Count Laszlo Almasy (Ralph Fiennes) and English newlyweds Katharine (Kristin Scott Thomas) and Geoffrey Clifton (Colin Firth). Almasy and Katharine begin a torrid affair. After war has erupted, Geoffrey learns of their liaison and tries to erase the entire triangle by crashing his plane in the desert. He dies in the attempt and his wife is badly injured, but Almasy survives unharmed. Almasy carries Katharine to a cave and promises to return for her, then walks to the nearest city, where he is mistaken for a German spy and taken prisoner. He escapes, purchases a plane, and flies back to the cave to find that Katharine has died. He loads her body into the plane and takes off, but is shot down by military fire.

Horribly burned and near death, Almasy is picked up by the Allies and placed in a ruined Italian monastery where he is cared for by Hana (Juliette Binoche), a Canadian nurse whose boyfriend has died in combat, and who believes herself to be a jinx to those she loves. Sharing the monastery are Kip (Naveen Andrews), a Sikh British army lieutenant with whom Hana begins an affair, and Caravaggio (Willem Dafoe), a former thief and Allied spy, who has lost his thumbs to a German interrogator. Caravaggio means to kill Almasy, whom he believes to be the informer responsible for the Axis takeover of Tobruk, but when Almasy tells him his true history, Caravaggio relents. After the surrender of Germany, Almasy dies and Hana returns to her Red Cross unit.

Rather than telling its story chronologically, THE ENGLISH PATIENT begins in the middle with the shooting down of Almasy's plane, and then proceeds to jump back and forth from the present (1945) to the past (1938 onward). By spotting the more energized and eye-catching material throughout, the filmmakers saved their movie from bogging down in its second half.

The story never bogs down, but it never really soars either, mainly because its principal characters don't precipitate much action. Instead, things happen to them. This may be true to life, but on this level of commercial cinema, at least, it's not good storytelling. Indeed the narrative vacuum created by Almasy, Katharine, and Hana forces viewers, particularly those who are not big fans of romance fiction, to pin all their hopes on the late-arriving Caravaggio, the morphine-addicted, thief-spy-avenging angel. But even he fails to deliver. His decision to abort his deadly mission after hearing Almasy's story, though not unwelcome, is handled in an extremely perfunctory and anticlimactic manner. Almost as disappointing is the romance of Hana and Kip, which neither develops nor concludes. It just peters out.

Ralph Fiennes appears to have had a lot less fun playing the dour early Almasy than the mortally burned and bedridden later Almasy—almost a separate role. Made up to look like one of the aged astronauts in 2001: A SPACE ODYSSEY (1968), Fiennes portrays the dying count with the breathiness and some of the sly wit of the late Olivier. The rest of the cast do the best they can with what they've been given.

To some extent, THE ENGLISH PATIENT is the victim of its own good taste. Apart from the crystalline photography of John Seale—which succeeds in being continuously involving without being inelegant—a modest and appealing turn by Naveen Andrews, and Juliette Binoche's exquisite complexion, the picture doesn't give its viewers much to remember.

There is one memorable moment, however. In an abandoned Italian church, Kip puts a flare in Hana's hands, ties her and himself to opposite ends of a giant pulley, climbs a mountain of sandbags, and throws himself off the top, hoisting a surprised and delighted Hana to the ceiling, where she finds herself face to face with a row of beautiful old paintings. Now *that's* what movies are all about. *(Violence, extensive nudity, sexual situations, profanity.)* — D.T.

d, Anthony Minghella; p, Saul Zaentz; exec p, Bob Weinstein, Harvey Weinstein, Scott Greenstein; assoc p, Paul Zaentz, Steve Andrews; w, Anthony Minghella (based on the novel by Michael Ondaatje); ph, John Seale; ed, Walter Murch; m, Gabriel Yared; prod d, Stuart Craig; art d, Aurelio Crugnola; set d, Aurelio Crugnola, Stephenie McMillan; sound, Walter Murch, Mark Berger, David Parker, Chris Newman (recordist), Ivan Sharrock (recordist); fx, Richard Conway, Dennis Lowe; casting, Michelle Guish, David Rubin; cos, Ann Roth; makeup, Fabrizio Sforza, Jim Henson's Creature Shop, Nigel Booth; stunts, Jim Dowdall

AA Best Picture; AA Best Director: Anthony Minghella; *AA Best Supporting Actress:* Juliette Binoche; *AA Best Art Direction:* Stuart Craig, Stephenie McMillan; *AA Best Cinematography:* John Seale; *AA Best Sound:* Walter Murch, Mark Berger, David Parker, Chris Newman; *AA Best Original Dramatic Score:* Gabriel Yared; *AA Best Costume Design:* Ann Roth; *AA Best Film Editing:* Walter Murch; *AAN Best Actor:* Ralph Fiennes; *AAN Best Actress:* Kristin Scott Thomas; *AAN Best Adapted Screenplay:* Anthony Minghella

Romance/Drama **(PR: C MPAA: R)**

ENTERTAINING ANGELS: THE DOROTHY DAY STORY ★★★

(U.S.) 110m Paulist Productions ~ Paulist Pictures c

Moira Kelly *(Dorothy Day)*; Martin Sheen *(Peter Maurin)*; Lenny Von Dohlen *(Forster)*; Heather Graham *(Maggie)*; Paul Lieber *(Mike Gold)*; Geoffrey Blake *(Floyd Dell)*; James Lancaster *(Eugene O'Neill)*; Boyd Kestner *(Lionel Moise)*; Tracy Walter *(Joe Bennett)*; Allyce Beasley *(Frankie)*; Melinda Dillon *(Sister Aloysius)*; Heather Smerling *(Tamara)*; Samantha MacLachlan *(Annie)*; Brian Keith *(Cardinal)*; Thom Adcox Hernandez *(Dan Irwin)*; Mary Greening *(Eleanor)*; Geoffrey Blake *(Floyd)*; Marianne Muellerleile *(German Landlady)*; Brian Libby *(Home)*; Kirsten Holmquist *(Irish Girl)*; Redmond Gleeson *(Irish Man)*; David Beron *(John)*; Renee Estevez *(Lilly)*; Paul Weaver *(Lou)*; John Michael Quinn *(Man)*; Larry Udy *(Man)*; Peggy Roeder *(Prison Matron)*; Val Bettin *(Mr. Breen)*; Gina Minervini *(Mrs. Matarazzo)*; Ana Mercedes *(Spanish Woman)*; Father Greg Apparrcel *(Priest—Baptism)*; Father Ellwood E. Kieser *(Priest—Confession)*; Pamela Shafer *(Tesse)*; Mary Ostrow *(Young Nurse)*; Jack Knight *(Eviction Landlord)*

Despite some surface clumsiness, this independently made biography of the woman who founded the Catholic Worker movement is a moving testament to the ability of one person to make a difference.

In 1917, Dorothy Day (Moira Kelly) is a journalist living a bohemian lifestyle while working for the New York socialist newspaper *The Call.* She becomes pregnant by her uncommitted lover. Fearful of losing him, she has an abortion, but he leaves to take a job in Chicago.

Distraught, Dorothy moves to then-rural Staten Island. She is brought out of her shell by Forster Batterham (Lenny Von Dohlen), a botanist with whom she falls in love and has a child. She also meets a nun (Melinda Dillon) whose work for the community sparks Dorothy's interest in Christianity. Dorothy and her daughter Tamara are baptized. Unwilling to be "caged up," Forster leaves.

In 1933, Dorothy and Tamara (Heather Smerling) return to Manhattan, moving into the lower East Side apartment of Dorothy's brother and sister-in-law. Dorothy is appalled at conditions in New York City. Public housing is scarce, and families are regularly evicted onto the streets; cholera and syphilis are at epidemic levels. Dorothy continues to write about urban conditions, but feels the need to do more.

One evening, she is visited by Peter Maurin (Martin Sheen), a Bible-quoting activist who teaches her about the relations of rich and poor. Peter becomes a regular guest in the Day apartment, bringing poor people in need of food and shelter. Unable to turn away anyone in need, Dorothy does what she can to take care of all of them.

Dorothy starts a newspaper, *The Catholic Worker,* to create a greater public awareness of social injustice. She also rents a storefront and opens a soup kitchen. Dorothy's efforts are received with mixed emotions by the local Catholic hierarchy, which dislikes the fact that she supports striking workers who are also supported by Communists. Dorothy comes close to giving up, but her fervor is renewed thanks to a chance encounter with an old friend who has fallen on hard times. An end title says that Dorothy continued working to amend unjust conditions until her death in 1980.

"Don't call me a saint," Dorothy Day was known to tell her admirers. "I don't want to be dismissed so easily." That advice should be heeded by viewers who might avoid this film for fear of being subject to religious proselytizing. Despite the fact that it was produced by a religious order (the Paulists, an order of Roman Catholic priests who specialize in serving those outside the Church and who also produced the excellent ROMERO), ENTERTAINING ANGELS is an inspirational film in the best sense of the word. Rather than regard religion as an end in itself, John Wells' script shows how religion and faith can serve as a guiding light for someone who wants to help those less fortunate neighbors who are beyond the purview of a mercantile society. At the very least, the film makes clear how disturbingly similar the America of the 1990s is to the US during the Great Depression.

ENTERTAINING ANGELS is not without its flaws. Some of the early scenes showing Day's life in bohemian Greenwich

Village border on the laughable (especially the forced profanities); Martin Sheen overacts, employing the most atrocious French accent this side of Monty Python; and the melodramatic handling of Day's abortion is rather preachy. But it would be a mistake to write this off as simply a "religious" film. ENTERTAINING ANGELS can be seen and enjoyed by people of all faiths, or of no faith at all. *(Adult situations, profanity.)* — M.F.

d, Michael Rhodes; co-p, Peter J. Burrell, Chris Donahue; w, John Wells; ph, Mike Fash; ed, George Folsey Jr., Geoffrey Rowland; prod d, Charles Rosen; art d, Mary Olivia McIntosh; sound, Edward Tise (mixer); casting, Cara Jones; cos, Gail Evan-Ivy

Biography/Drama **(PR: A MPAA: PG-13)**

ERASER ★★

(U.S.) 105m Arnold Kopelson Productions; Warner Bros. ~ Warner Bros. c

Arnold Schwarzenegger *(US Marshal John Kruger)*; James Caan *(Robert Deguerin)*; Vanessa Williams *(Lee Cullen)*; Robert Pastorelli *(Johnny C.)*; James Coburn *(Beller)*; Andy Romano *(Harper)*; James Cromwell *(Donahue)*; Danny Nucci *(Monroe)*; Nick Chinlund *(Calderon)*; Michael Papajohn *(Schiff)*; Joe Viterelli *(Tony)*; Mark Rolston *(J. Scar)*; John Slattery *(Corman)*; Robert Miranda *(Frediano)*; Roma Maffia *(Claire)*; Tony Longo *(Little Mike)*; Gerry Becker *(Morehart)*; John Snyder *(Sal)*; Melora Walters *(Darleen)*; Olek Krupa *(Sergei)*; Cylk Cozart *(Darryl)*; K. Todd Freeman *(Duton)*; Rocco Sisto *(Pauley)*; Gerald Berns *(Young Agent)*; Steve Ford *(Knoland)*; Ismael "East" Carlo *(Priest)*; Thomas J. Huff *(Somes)*; Rick Batalla *(Bartender)*; Michael Gregory *(Lieman)*; Patrick Kilpatrick *(Haggerty)*; James Short *(Crane Sniper)*; A.J. Nay *(Sniper 2)*; Camryn Manheim *(Nurse)*; Skipp Sudduth *(Watch Commander)*; Anthony Fusco *(Witsec Op)*; Gregory McKinney *(Witsec Op)*; Craig Barnett *(Clerk)*; Corey Joshua Taylor *(Officer)*; Rick Marzan *(Crawford)*; Brian Libby *(Perimeter Guy)*; Dan Wynands *(Perimeter Guy)*; David Wolos-Fonteno *(Security Official)*; Sonny H. King *(Security Guard)*; Edward Rote *(Security Guard)*; Michael Cameron *(Gate Guard)*; Tim Colceri *(Lobby Guard)*; Dieter R. Trippel *(Lobby Guard)*; Matthew Mahaney *(Vault Guard)*; Denis Forest *(Technician)*; Christopher Mankiewicz *(Zoo Guard)*; Michael Stone *(Zoo Killer 1)*; Kevin Fry *(Dock Guard)*; Sam Scarber *(Dock Guard)*; Richie Varga *(Secretary)*; Diana Morgan *(Female Reporter)*; Ben Shenkman *(Reporter)*; Dominic Marcus *(Reporter)*; Pat Collins *(Anchorman)*; Dorin Seymour *(Attorney)*; Clayton Landey *(Witsec Agent)*; Terry Beeman *(Dancer)*; Michael Gregory Gong *(Dancer)*; Sebastian LaCause *(Dancer)*; Frank Mintello *(Paramedic)*; Charles Chiquete *(Office Worker 1)*; Glenndon Chatman *(Glenndon)*; Camille Winbush *(Camille)*; Vic Polizos *(Hannon)*; James Clark *(Locomotive Engineer)*; David Bilson *(Pilot)*; Al Cerullo *(Pilot)*; Rick Shuster *(Pilot)*

Arnold Schwarzenegger tests his acting ability in ERASER and fails. He drags down the story of an agent protecting a woman in the Federal Witness Protection Program. Yet, the dark superproduction has its compensations.

John Kruger (Arnold Schwarzenegger) is an "eraser" for the U.S. government. In his specialized role, marshal Kruger uses elaborate, high-tech equipment (combined with good, old-fashioned combat ability) to make witnesses disappear and keep their pursuers at bay.

In his latest case, Kruger is assigned to Lee Cullen (Vanessa Williams), a government worker in Washington, D.C. who has uncovered a turncoat scheme within the defense industry. The traitors aim to deliver the ray gun, one of the most advanced weapons ever developed, into the hands of the Russian mafia.

Despite her initial reluctance to "disappear" from the world, Cullen goes along with Kruger's plan to hide her in New York City's Chinatown. But it becomes apparent that Cullen is not safe when her best friend, Claire (Roma Maffia), a reporter, is killed. Kruger suspects that a mole exists in the system and discovers that the traitor is his boss, Robert Deguerin (James Caan). With his identity uncovered, Deguerin and his thugs pursue Kruger and Cullen in New York.

In order to stop Deguerin's plans to sell the assault-style ray guns to government enemies, Kruger hires a former witness, Johnny C. (Robert Pastorelli), and several of his mafia friends to thwart the arms shipment at Baltimore harbor. By using the guns against Deguerin and his men, Kruger and his team succeed in obstructing the transfer.

Having grown closer to Cullen through the ordeal, Kruger plans to spend his future days close to the witness—after she testifies against her former employers.

If TRUE LIES restored Schwarzenegger's box-office luster (following the LAST ACTION HERO disaster), ERASER just barely sustains his rank. The chief problem is that ERASER demands a solid dramatic performance from the star, something he is apparently incapable of giving. TRUE LIES, as well as most of his other films, merely required a light comic portrayal within the context of the action-adventure parameters. Schwarzenegger's reading of his more "sensitive" lines in his love scenes with Vanessa Williams are laughably amateurish. He is obviously much more comfortable telling a crocodile "You're luggage!" before shooting it with a high-tech ray gun. Although the credits claim that no animals were harmed during the production, animal lovers probably will not fancy this Bronx Zoo set-piece.

Otherwise, ERASER's B-movie script (by Tony Puryear and Walon Green) keeps the action moving swiftly, if not always logically, over the course of 115 minutes. The highly generic material steals from both "lady-in-distress" thrillers and the "macho" adventures with which Schwarzenegger is more often associated. The special "X-ray" device of the ray gun is reminiscent of the monster's-eye view in the star's 1987 flick, PREDATOR. The cinematic cribbing even includes a high-security disk-theft sequence that looks amazingly similar to the one in MISSION IMPOSSIBLE (which was released just a few weeks before ERASER in 1996), and a zoo shoot-out sequence much like the finale of the Jackie Chan vehicle, FIRST STRIKE (which was released in Hong Kong six months earlier than this). Like other action pics of the time, ERASER continues the Cold War by making the bad guys "Commie bastards." Still, once one accepts the material's familiarity (and stupidity), the film becomes moderately enjoyable.

What really prevents ERASER from greater success—apart from the star's inept acting—is the patch-work quality of the production. Although it is clear that Warner Bros. spent a great deal of money on the film, ERASER contains some surprisingly cheap-looking special effects, which are displayed too long in the extended Panavision action sequences. Reportedly, ERASER had some post-production snafus, but much here could have been simply improved by the work of a talented editor. Ironically, a trouble-shooting "eraser" is just what this film needs. *(Violence, profanity.)* — E.M.

d, Chuck Russell; p, Arnold Kopelson, Anne Kopelson; exec p, Michael Tadross, Chuck Russell; assoc p, Frank Capra III; co-p, Caroline Pham, Stephen Brown; w, Tony Puryear, Walon Green (from a story by Tony Puryear, Walon Green, and Michael S. Cherunchin); ph, Adam Greenberg; ed, Michael Tronick; m, Alan Silvestri; prod d, Bill Kenney; art d, William Ladd Skinner;

set d, Garrett Lewis; sound, Robert Eber (mixer), Christopher Boyes (design), Alan Robert Murray, Bub Asman; fx, John Sullivan, Terry Frazee, Mass. Illusion, Warner Digital Effects, Industrial Light & Magic; casting, Bonnie Timmermann; cos, Richard Bruno; makeup, Jeff Dawn, Steve Johnson's XFXf; stunts, Joel Kramer

AAN Best Sound Effects Editing: Alan Robert Murray, Bub Asman

Action/Adventure/Thriller **(PR: C MPAA: R)**

ERNESTO CHE GUEVARA—THE BOLIVIAN DIARY ★★½

(France/Switzerland) 94m Cine-Manufacture; Les Films d'Ici bw

Robert Kramer *(Voice of Ernesto Che Guevara)*; Judith Burnett *(Narrator)*

A fascinating subject, Che Guevara's 11-month struggle in 1967 to incite revolution in Bolivia, gets thorough but plodding treatment in this French-Swiss documentary.

The film begins with information about Guevara's relationship to Fidel Castro within the Marxist Cuban government following their overthrow of dictator Fulgencio Batista in 1959. As the Cuban Minister of Industry, Guevara disagreed with the Soviets about the extent of their humanitarian commitments, and, in 1965, he split with Castro. He left Cuba for Africa, then returned to Bolivia incognito in 1966 to lead a guerrilla revolt on behalf of the poorest citizens in the jungle.

The rest of the film follows Guevara's daily journal entries during his difficult trek. Guevara and his men quickly discovered that Bolivian President Barrento had ordered their deaths, and, along the way, the guerrillas were ambushed by US soldiers. On October 9, 1967, Guevara was captured and executed by the Bolivian army, while the others in his command either retreated or were also killed.

Throughout ERNESTO CHE GUEVARA: THE BOLIVIAN DIARY, writer-director Richard Dindo admires the infamous Marxist rebel. Emphasizing Guevara's often-overlooked humanitarian concerns, Dindo addresses the circumstances that led up to Guevara's break with Fidel Castro in 1965. Then, Dindo retraces his journey through the Bolivian jungle by reading from diary entries, using a subjective camera from Guevara's point of view and interviewing some of the people who remember him.

Though nothing is inherently wrong with Dindo's straightforward (albeit politically slanted) concept, there are some problems with the results. He tells little about the man prior to the mid-1960s (for example, that Guevara was a medical doctor by training). Also, the monotonous voice-overs by the narrators (Robert Kramer "as Guevara" with Judith Burnett) drain the journey of drama. Dindo admirably avoids the melodramatic excesses that ruined CHE! (the infamous 1969 fiction film about Guevara), but perhaps some middle-ground could have been established between issuing dry facts and creating hysteria.

ERNESTO CHE GUEVARA serves its purpose as a sober, ultra-serious account of Guevara's last year and provides an antidote to 1996's overblown screen version of EVITA. But those looking for a more artistic, historical, or philosophical treatise may be disappointed. — E.M.

d, Richard Dindo; w, Richard Dindo; ph, Pio Corradi; ed, Richard Dindo, Georg Janett, Catherine Poitevin

Documentary **(PR: A MPAA: NR)**

ETZ HADOMIM TAFUS

(SEE: UNDER THE DOMIM TREE)

EVENING STAR, THE ★★

(U.S.) 129m Rysher Entertainment ~ Paramount c

Shirley MacLaine *(Aurora Greenway)*; Jack Nicholson *(Garrett Breedlove)*; Bill Paxton *(Jerry Bruckner)*; Juliette Lewis *(Melanie Horton)*; Miranda Richardson *(Patsy Carpenter)*; Ben Johnson *(Arthur Cotton)*; Scott Wolf *(Bruce)*; George Newbern *(Tommy Horton)*; Marion Ross *(Rosie Dunlop)*; Mackenzie Astin *(Teddy Horton)*; Donald Moffat *(Hector Scott)*; Jennifer Grant *(Ellen)*; China Kantner *(Jane)*; Shawn Taylor Thompson *(Bump)*; Jake Langerud *(Henry)*; Sharon Bunn *(Dolly)*; Clement Von Franckenstein *(Pascal Ferney)*; Antonia Bogdanovich *(Toni)*; Jimmie Lee Balthazar *(Jimmie Lee)*; Melinda Renna *(Nurse Susan)*; Mark Walters *(Dr. Faulkner)*; Ann Hardman-Broughton *(Lola Bruckner)*; Woody Watson *(James)*; Larry Elliott *(Billy)*; Donny Caicedo *(Joey)*; Connie Cooper *(Casting Assistant)*; Laura Cayouette *(Sitcom Actress Becky)*; John McCalmont *(Bernie Steinberg)*; John Bennett Perry *(Sitcom Dad)*; Mary Gross *(Sitcom Mom)*; Alex Morris *(Professor Warwick)*; Will Wallace *(Ticket Agent)*; Kim Terry *(Flight Attendant)*; Eileen Morris *(Nurse Margaret)*; Christopher Ballinger *(Bump—Age 9)*; Austin Samuel Hembd *(Bump—Age 7)*; Don Burgess *(Stage Manager)*; Steve Danton *(Minister B. Ramsey)*

This lugubrious sequel to 1983's TERMS OF ENDEARMENT tries to be the woman's film of all time but, judging from its overall lack of wit, vulgarity and brazen exploitation, it seems more geared toward morons of any stripe.

Fifteen years after the death of her daughter Emma, Aurora Greenway (Shirley MacLaine) is as stubborn as ever, driving her three grandchildren crazy with her meddling ways. Melanie (Juliette Lewis) has a slacker boyfriend Bruce (Scott Wolf), whom Aurora can't abide. Rebellious Tommy (George Newbern) is in jail on a possessions charge and could do without her regular visits and brownies. Teddy (Mackenzie Astin) is the easy-going sweetheart he was as a child; it's his girlfriend Jane (China Kantner) who bears Aurora's disapproval.

Aurora's faithful maid Rosie (Marion Ross), troubled by her boss's neuroticism, arranges for her to see a therapist, Jerry (Bill Paxton). At first resistant, Aurora soon finds herself falling for this younger man, to everyone's horror. Forever malingering on the sidelines is Patsy (Miranda Richardson), Emma's best friend, who interferes in the lives of Aurora's grandchildren, particularly Melanie. Patsy even takes up with Jerry herself when Aurora decides it's not working out. The women have an uneasy alliance, marked by frequent explosions.

Their problems are as nothing, however, compared to Rosie's sudden decision to marry next-door neighbor Arthur (Ben Johnson). Aurora is upset when Rosie refuses to stay in touch with her, but she eventually learns that Rosie is dying and doesn't want to be a burden. After Rosie's death, Aurora faces the problem of what to do with her ashes. Back into her life walks her great love, Garrett Breedlove (Jack Nicholson). They have a bittersweet reunion and he helps her scatter the ashes.

Meanwhile, the grandchildren's lives finally seem to be coming together. Melanie dumps Bruce and begins an acting career in television. Tommy gets out of jail, marries a girlfriend of Jane's, and gives Aurora a great-grandson. With everything falling so benignly into place, there seems to be nothing for Aurora to do but die, which she does, surrounded by her ever-loving and grateful family.

Many sequels are nothing more than efforts to capitalize on a previous success, but this one really takes the cake. TERMS OF

ENDEARMENT had some classic performances and James Brooks' savvy direction and writing. Adapted from Larry McMurtry's sequel to his original novel, EVENING STAR tries to milk a formula that by now is pretty much set in stone: win the audience's hearts for the characters by giving 'em chuckles galore and then, pow! Slam 'em with tragedy so they'll feel like they've gotten their money's worth.

Scripter-director Robert Harling's sole claim to fame is the play "Steel Magnolias." Such are the mysteries of Hollywood that the success of that one, admittedly effective but extremely manipulative work has made him a kingpin of the modern-day woman's film. He makes his directorial debut here and a heavier, more witless hand couldn't be imagined. The movie strains to be glossy entertainment like TERMS OF ENDEARMENT, yet is hideously photographed in the muddiest of tones. The music consists primarily of an ever-present wistful tinkle, augmented by the schmaltzy theme used back in 1984.

Without James Brooks' sure comic direction, MacLaine delivers a wayward, completely overwrought performance. We've seen it all before: the hysterical fits, oceanic sobbing, camp bitchery. Even appearing without makeup in the final scenes recalls the finale of POSTCARDS FROM THE EDGE (1990). Compounding the general air of movie star narcissism is Nicholson who, in a glorified cameo role (despite his co-star billing), gives one of his most mannered performances. With Harling's sycophantic help, Nicholson and MacLaine make complete caricatures of themselves.

The casting of perennially funky bad actress Lewis as Emma's daughter was a slovenly choice. Her screen persona has the wildness and certain nymphette qualities of sensuality Debra Winger (who played Emma) has evinced, but none of that fine actress's vivid empathy or intelligence. Richardson is an apt hammy match for MacLaine and more than holds her own in their endless scenes of competition. Her role is a one-note Texas rich bitch, but she at least is fitfully amusing and her performance seems more in control than anyone else's. *(Profanity, sexual situations, adult situations, brief nudity)* — D.N.

d, Robert Harling; p, David Kirkpatrick, Polly Platt, Keith Samples; co-p, Dennis Bishop; w, Robert Harling (based on the novel by Larry McMurtry); ph, Don Burgess; ed, Priscilla Nedd-Friendly, David Moritz; m, William Ross, Michael Gore; prod d, Bruno Rubeo; art d, Richard L. Johnson; set d, Rick Simpson; sound, Douglas Axtell; fx, Randy E. Moore; casting, Jennifer Shull; cos, Renee Ehrlich Kalfus; makeup, Mindy Hall; stunts, Russell Towery

Drama/Comedy (PR: C MPAA: PG-13)

EVERYONE SAYS I LOVE YOU ★★½

(U.S.) 97m Sweetland Films ~ Miramax c

Woody Allen *(Joe)*; Julia Roberts *(Von)*; Goldie Hawn *(Steffi)*; Tim Roth *(Charles Ferry)*; Alan Alda *(Bob)*; David Ogden Stiers *(Holden's Father)*; Drew Barrymore *(Skylar)*; Lukas Haas *(Scott)*; Natalie Portman *(Laura)*; Edward Norton *(Holden)*; Gaby Hoffmann *(Lane)*; Natasha Lyonne *(DJ)*; Vivian Cherry *(Nurse)*; Tommie Baxter *(Old Woman)*; Jeff Derocker *(Homeless Man)*; Kevin Hagan *(Doorman)*; Trude Klein *(Frieda)*; Itzhak Perlman *(Himself)*; Navah Perlman *(Pianist)*; Barbara Hollander *(Claire)*; John Griffin *(Jeffrey Vandermost)*; Waltrudis Buck *(Psychiatrist)*; Patrick Cranshaw *(Grandpa)*; Isiah Whitlock *(Cop)*; Edward Hibbert *(Harry Winston Salesman)*; Frederick Rolf *(Le Cirque Waiter)*; Timothy Jerome *(X-ray Room Doctor)*; Paolo Seganti *(DJ's Venice Date)*; Andrea Piedimonte *(Alberto)*; Robert Knepper *(Greg)*; Billy Crudup *(Ken)*; Robert Khakh *(Cab Driver)*; Scotty Bloch *(Holden's Mother)*; Ed Hodson *(Scott's Doctor)*; Michel Moinot *(Bob's Doctor)*; Diva Gray; Ami Almendral; Madeline Balmaceda *(Nannies)*; Cherylyn Jones; Tina Paul; Vikki Schnurr *(Mannequins)*; Kevin Bogue; Colleen Dunn; Pamela Everett; Susan Misner; Gregory Mitchell; Dana Moore; Troy Myers; Joe Orrach; Michael O'Steen; Tina Paul; Luis Martin Perez; Krissy Richmond *(Harry Winston Dancers)*; Daisy Prince; Linda Maurel-Sithole; Helen Miles; Arlene Martell *(Nurses)*; Rene Ceballos; Ruth Gottschall; Colton Green; Lisa Leguillou; Joe Locarro; Monica McSwain; Jill Nicklaus; Andrew Pacho; Luis Martin Perez; John Selya; Myra Lucretia Taylor; Jo Telford *(Hospital Dancers)*; Gerry Burkhardt; Eileen Casey; Shelley Frankel; Fred C. Mann III; Kathy Sanson; Valda Setterfield; Frank Pietri; Luis Martin Perez *(Ghost Dancers)*; Robert Walker; Devalle Hayes; Damon McCloud *(Rap Group)*; Tony Sirico; Ray Garvey *(Escaped Convicts)*; Tommy John; Lindsay Canuel; Richard Cummings; Kristen Pettet; Patrick Lavery; Christy Romano; Jonathan Giordano; Gabriel Millman *(Trick-or-Treat Children)*; Don Correia; Sean Grant; Roland Hayes; Darren Lee; Delphine T. Mantz; Joanne McHugh; John Mineo; Cynthia Onrubia; Luis Martin Perez; Willie Rosario; Nancy Ticotin; Jerome Vivona *(Groucho Party Dancers)*

Woody Allen pays tribute to 1930s Hollywood musicals in EVERYONE SAYS I LOVE YOU, a story of romance among New York City's upper crust. What should be a special treat, however, is just another Woody Allen movie with songs thrown in.

A wealthy, extended family headed by Bob (Alan Alda) and Steffi (Goldie Hawn) makes its home on the Upper East Side of New York City. DJ (Natasha Lyonne), Steffi's oldest daughter from a previous marriage, relates the family's various domestic dilemmas. Her half-sister Skylar (Drew Barrymore) gets engaged to mild-mannered Holden (Edward Norton) but finds more romantic interest in Charles (Tim Roth), a lascivious ex-con. Bob, a dyed-in-the-wool liberal, and DJ's half-brother Scott (Lukas Haas), a young conservative, clash over their differing political beliefs. DJ's youngest half-sisters Laura (Natalie Portman) and Lane (Gaby Hoffman) both fall in love with the same attractive teenage boy; Laura is crushed when the boy chooses Lane over her.

While on vacation in Venice, DJ escapes her family's travails and helps her biological father, Joe (Woody Allen), woo Von (Julia Roberts), an unhappily married woman. After much plotting to win her affections, Joe convinces Von to live with him in his garret in Paris, but Von eventually tires of her new lifestyle and goes back to her husband in New York. Similarly, Skylar tires of Charles the moment he returns to a life of crime and she renews her relationship with Holden. Laura and Lane resolve their sibling rivalry, and a blow to Scott's head turns him into a liberal. The entire clan meets Joe in Paris for a big New Year's Eve party; Steffi consoles her lonely ex-husband, but remains with her current husband.

Though warmly received by many upon its release, EVERYONE SAYS I LOVE YOU is a flawed, uneven attempt to reproduce Hollywood musical magic. Perhaps movie critics and Allen fans were relieved that New York's favorite son did not fall on his face a la Peter Bogdanovich-remember AT LONG LAST LOVE (1975)?—but here, Allen only *just* gets by with a circumspect approach. By filming in his safest visual style, Allen maintains his competency as a filmmaker, but the "tribute" regresses to some of the earliest, most conventional sound musicals rather than the more experimental Arthur Freed MGM pictures of the later "Golden Age." Ironically, Allen himself has been more innovative in his own work (notably THE PURPLE ROSE OF CAIRO); EVERYONE is more like the commercial HANNAH AND HER SISTERS set to music than a courageous new effort.

Indeed, the only creative energy comes from the *idea* of modern-day characters breaking into song-and-dance at the drop of a hat—a notion that was used to greater effect in Dennis Potter's dramatic British miniseries "Pennies from Heaven" (remade as a 1981 American feature). The final *pas de deux* between Allen and Hawn does contain some trick photography, but it's nothing compared to the Astaire-Kelly numbers it emulates.

Thus, the production never insults tradition, but neither does it soar as an original flight of fancy. Old musicals allowed viewers to imagine they could sing and dance like Astaire and Kelly, but no one in the cast—even the surprisingly effective Hawn—would inspire anyone with their tone-deaf renditions of the classic numbers (Roberts sang much better in the concurrent release, MICHAEL COLLINS, and Barrymore was reportedly so bad she had to be dubbed). Allen also overuses the leitmotif, "I'll Never Fall Again," and the bigger numbers look more like Mel Brooks's spoofs than classy homages—"Makin' Whoopee," for example, set in a hospital, uses sick and dying patients as performers (another echo of Potter's work, as a key musical number in THE SINGING DETECTIVE was set in a hospital ward).

As with SHADOWS AND FOG, Allen assembles a talented group of actors only to waste most of them. Allen himself really doesn't fit into this outing and his character seems almost grafted onto the proceedings. Occasionally, the director comes up with a well-timed gag but, for the most part, he passes up the chance to revise or tinker with old forms. *(Adult situations, profanity.)* — E.M.

d, Woody Allen; p, Robert Greenhut; exec p, Jean Doumanian, J.E. Beaucaire; co-p, Helen Roth; w, Woody Allen; ph, Carlo DiPalma; ed, Susan E. Morse; prod d, Santo Loquasto; art d, Tom Warren; set d, Elaine O'Donnell; ch, Graciela Daniele; sound, Gary Alper; fx, Connie Brink; casting, Juliet Taylor; cos, Jeffrey Kurland; makeup, Fern Buchner, Rosemarie Zurlo; stunts, Roy Farfel, Bill Anagnos

Musical/Comedy (PR: A MPAA: R)

EVERYTHING RELATIVE ★★★

(U.S.) 110m Big Sister Productions ~ Tara Releasing c

Ellen McLaughlin *(Josie)*; Olivia Negron *(Maria)*; Stacey Nelkin *(Katie)*; Monica Bell *(Victoria)*; Andrea Weber *(Luce)*; Gabriella Messina *(Gina)*; Carol Schneider *(Sarah)*; Malindi Fickle *(Candy)*; Mina Bern *(Grandma Kessler)*; Irma St. Paule *(Aunt Sadie)*; Lynn Cohen *(Mrs. Kessler)*; Harvey Fierstein *(The Moyle)*; Rabbi Sharon Kleinbaum *(The Rabbi)*; Andrew McCarthy *(Howard)*

In the tradition of THE BIG CHILL, EVERYTHING RELATIVE is a reunion movie with a 90s twist: the group that comes together after years apart are lesbians. Adventurous in its spirit and anti-chic in its style, EVERYTHING RELATIVE provides an excellent contemporary example of the growth and development of lesbian and gay cinema.

Long-time lovers Katie (Stacey Nelkin) and Victoria (Monica Bell) celebrate the birth of their baby (via insemination) by inviting friends and family to the bris. After the ceremony, the happy couple and five of their long-time college friends take off for a memory-lane weekend at Katie's family's lakeside cottage.

Luce (Andrea Weber) has never gotten over Sonia, the love of her life who died years ago in a car accident. Since then, she's drowned her sorrows in alcohol and quick affairs. On this occasion, she is joined by a much younger galpal, Candy (Malindi Fickle), a conservative investment banker who doesn't fit in with the group. After one too many awkward moments, Luce sends Candy back home, and focuses her antagonistic attention on Gina (Gabriella Messina). Gina has a sordid past as a hooker, but is now single, "respectable," and working as a singer in Hollywood. With Candy gone, sexual tension develops between Luce and Gina.

At the same time, Maria (Olivia Negron) is mourning the loss of her children in a custody battle with her ex-husband. Maria left her lover Josie (Ellen McLaughlin) eight years ago because she couldn't handle "the life" or Josie's drinking. While Maria rebounded into heterosexuality and reproduction (ending in divorce and custody battles), Josie got sober. Reunited for the first time since they broke up, Maria and Josie have a lot to get past, but clearly the time is right for a romantic reunion.

The final member of the group, Sarah (Carol Schneider), is the "token straight." Sarah works at Planned Parenthood but is depressed over the fact that she and her husband have been unable to have a baby.

EVERYTHING RELATIVE gives us a snapshot of the issues affecting these women—from Victoria, who is closeted at work and in much of her life, battling with her more "out" lover Katie, to Luce, facing drinking and intimacy issues in her own way. The outcomes of the film are predictable: Luce and Gina begin a romance, and Maria and Josie pick up where theirs left off. Katie and Victoria revel in their monogamy, and Sarah (apparently by osmosis and kismet) becomes pregnant.

Much like the word that has become synonymous with the real-life communication style of gay women, EVERYTHING RELATIVE is about *process*. First-time writer-director Sharon Pollack gives us a slice of life that is refreshingly sincere in response to the recent influx of "lesbian chic" material. The ensemble feel of the film rings true, but much of the dialogue is riddled with cliches. The characters are generally bland, especially when compared to their more politically-driven and passionate college-aged selves. However, a couple of the actresses—namely Nelkin as Mom Katie, and Bell as Katie's self-described "husband" Victoria—manage to give unexpected depth to their roles. Harvey Fierstein, the best-known performer in the cast, makes an early cameo as the wise-cracking moyle.

Like its characters, the film itself tries very hard and possesses its own unique charm. EVERYTHING RELATIVE is an "anti-slick" film for the 90s that revels in characters who are comfortable just being themselves—although it lacks the spontaneous "magic" of a less talky, more visual film. From a historical perspective, however, EVERYTHING RELATIVE will surely be remembered as a (closet) door-opening movie. *(Adult situations, sexual situations.)* — J.D.

d, Sharon Pollack; p, Sharon Pollack; exec p, Irene Sullivan; co-p, Patricia Larouziere; w, Sharon Pollack; ph, Zakaela Rachel Othmer; ed, Meredith Paige; m, Frank London; sound, Chen Harpaz (design); casting, Jack Bowdan

Romance/Comedy/Drama (PR: C MPAA: NR)

EVIL ED ★★

(Sweden) 88m ~ A-Pix Entertainment c

Johan Rudebeck *(Eddie)*; Per Lofberg *(Nick)*; Olof Rhodin *(Sam Campbell)*; Camela Leierth *(Mel)*; Cecilia Ljung *(Barbara)*; Nathalie Kankuja *(Emmy)*; Gert Fylking *(Nurse in Corridor)*; Mikael Kallaanvaara *(Tom McClane)*; Hans Wilhelmsson *(Welder/Patient in Waiting Room/Lunatic in Corridor)*; Anders Ek *(Janitor)*; Memory Garp *(Office Girl)*; Ulf Landergren *(Art Film Department Boss)*; Jenny Forslund *(Art Film Department Editor)*; Therese Malmer; Estelle Milburne; Sanna Hansson *(Splatter Department Bimbos)*; Niklas Hattstrom *(Splatter Department Hunk)*; Thomas Lewart *(Splatter Department Hunk)*; Vasa *(The John/Dr. Wrench)*; Monia Botngard *(Prostitute)*; Fredrik Johansson *(Dude in Theater)*; Gun Forss *(Senior Neighbor)*;

Fredrik Hauge *(Screamer/Medic)*; Johan Harnesk *(Screamer)*; Therese Malmer *(Sexy Patient)*; Goran Lundstrom *(Bandage Face/Medic)*; Estelle Milburne *(Secretary)*; Kelly Tainton *(White Demon)*; Danne Malmer *(Zip)*; Kim Sulocki *(Crackhead)*; Anders Jacobsson *(Car Driver)*; Jose Jimenez *(Police Officer/Paranoid Lunatic)*; Andreas Beskow *(Police Officer)*; Heming Kulo *(Medic)*; Lena Neogard *(Patient in Waiting Room)*; Pia Berg *(Patient in Waiting Room/Lunatic in Corridor)*; Magnus Wadling *(Patient in Waiting Room)*; Roger Olsson *(Dr. West)*; Carina Ristholm *(Nurse in Waiting Room/Lunatic)*; Asa Svegen *(Nurse in Waiting Room/Lunatic)*; Karin Hallheden *(Nurse in Waiting Room)*; Carina Sundgren *(Nurse in Waiting Room)*; Marie Bergenholtz *(Dr. Dinkenspiel/Demonic Doc)*; Hanna Elfvin *(Lunatic in Corridor)*; Sven-Erik Olsson *(Nurse)*; Robert Drose *(Psychiatric Ward Guard)*; Sten Grettve *(Lunatic)*; Jenny Wigge *(Lunatic)*; Joakim Lindman *(SWAT Team Lieutenant)*; Kurt Nilsson; Joel Rhodin; Hannes Rhodin *(SWAT Team)*; Kaj Steveman *(Mop Boy)*

Although occasionally inspired, this English-language horror-comedy from Sweden doesn't have the narrative facility to support its better moments.

Film editor Eddie (Johan Rudebeck) is transferred by his boss, Sam Campbell (Olof Rhodin), to their studio's Splatter and Gore Department. There, Eddie is to cut the more offensive scenes out of the company's "Loose Limbs" series of horror films so that they can be marketed to foreign countries.

At first, Eddie goes about his task as he would any other assignment. But, soon, viewing all the blood-spattered footage begins to take its toll. He hallucinates that food he's cutting up is dismembered body parts, and he starts seeing demons pursuing him and living in his refrigerator.

Eddie's pleas to be taken off the job fall on deaf ears, and ultimately he begins violently turning on others, from the studio's delivery boy to his wife Barbara (Cecilia Ljung) and daughter Emmy (Nathalie Kankuja). The insane Eddie ends up being taken to a nearby hospital for psychiatric treatment, but he escapes and begins a bloody rampage through the building. A SWAT team is called in, and the horror finally ends when one of them shoots Eddie's head off.

From its title and its anything-goes approach, this production was clearly influenced by the EVIL DEAD films that established director Sam Raimi and star Bruce Campbell as horror icons. But while those films were distinguished by their relentless momentum, EVIL ED has a poky pace that reduces it to a series of fun moments strung together by a story that would have been better served by the short-film format. There just aren't enough scares or laughs to support the slim plot, and though the movie rallies with the rousing hospital-set final act, it also serves to remind of what the preceding hour or so has lacked.

One can't fault the tyro filmmaking team behind EVIL ED on a technical level. Working on a very low budget in a country not known for its horror fare, they've put together an atmospheric movie with some excellent special effects. They also avoid making a gratuitous political statement out of their real-vs.-reel-violence theme, yet given the film's overall lack of content, its only real message seems to be that viewing too many horror flicks will turn one into a psychopath—which is, no doubt, hardly the statement the filmmakers intended. *(Graphic violence, nudity, profanity.)* — M.G.

d, Anders Jacobsson; p, Goran Lundstrom; w, Goran Lundstrom, Christer Ohlsson, Anders Jacobsson (based on a story by Bend Team); ph, Anders Jacobsson; ed, Anders Jacobsson; m, Henriksson & Lindh; sound, Deaf by Dawn, Anders Jacobsson, Doc, Kaj Steveman; fx, Goran Lundstrom; cos, Katharina Ljung; makeup, Goran Lundstrom, Fredrik Hauge, Sanna Hansson

Horror/Comedy **(PR: O MPAA: R)**

EVIL HAS A FACE ★★½

(U.S.) 92m Spinnaker Films ~ MCA/Universal c

Sean Young *(Gwen McGarrell)*; William R. Moses *(Tom Sawyer)*; Brighton Hertford *(Bria)*; Joe Guzaldo *(Radachek)*; Chelcie Ross *(Henry Willis McGarrell)*; Kate Buddeke *(Ellen)*; Suzanne Petri *(Phyliss)*; Dick Cusack *(Lester)*; Mary Seibel *(Degattis)*; Morgan McCabe *(Kohler)*; Jason Wells *(Skullington)*; Mike Houlihan *(Captain)*; Soseh Kevorkian *(Roommate)*; Richard Pickren *(Ted)*; Jason Zone Fisher *(Michael)*; Gary Mach *(Rescuer)*; James Eichling *(Bob)*; Sam Kitt *(Plainclothesman)*; James Chisem *(Lineup Cop)*; Everett Dean *(Hunter)*; Bridgett Baron *(Librarian)*; Stephen Cinabro *(Cop 1)*; Robert Mohler *(Cop 2)*; John Judd *(Cop 3)*

For much of its running time, EVIL HAS A FACE is a nifty suspense drama that doesn't leave the audience groaning at some crossroads of coincidence. Weaving the police sketch artist into its story line much more astutely than other crime-solving fare like THE SKETCH ARTIST (1992), this deft thriller features strong acting at its center with some keen psychological observations around its periphery.

Sketch artist Gwen McGarrell (Sean Young) doesn't relish her latest police assignment. The site of this missing-child case in Redmund, Minn., is too close to her hometown and the scene of her own childhood traumas. Although Gwen is treated respectfully by Redmund deputy sheriff Tom Sawyer (William R. Moses), her unconventional methods are disparaged by the FBI agents on the case.

Working from the memory of a girl Bria (Brighton Hertford) who has escaped from her abductor, Gwen produces a sketch that she releases to the media. Risking the scorn of the feds, Gwen then repudiates her drawing without revealing why: the face she sketched is that of her "late" stepfather, Henry Willis McGarrell (Chelcie Ross), who sexually abused Gwen thoughout her childhood.

Although circumstantial evidence pushes the FBI toward Skullington (Jason Wells), a recidivist molester, Tom agrees with Gwen's deduction that Bria's kidnapping is linked to a string of youngsters' murders. Gwen's investigation reveals that her stepfather did not die as she was told. After strangling her mother to death, McGarrell was imprisoned and released in 1993, when the child murders began.

The unbalanced Skullington turns up at Gwen's cabin with a grudge and is later killed while fleeing authorities. While the police are busy wrapping up the Skullington case, McGarrell menaces Gwen and Bria. Although he orders Bria into a closet, the resourceful child sneaks a gun into the taped hands of Gwen. Subsequently, Gwen wounds McGarrell. McGarrell closes in on Gwen and Bria, and Gwen manages to surprise McGarrell and stab him.

Among this thriller's plusses is its underlying insistence that victims can recover their self-respect. Gwen, not as helpless as she thought, saves Bria's life and her own before the cops storm her cabin. Enriched by the bond between Gwen and Bria, the film works as a catharsis in which Gwen empowers a child to fight back in a way she was never able to do in her own tainted childhood. In return, Bria enables the adult Gwen to exorcise her girlhood demons.

Despite the audience's interest in Gwen's psychological battle, the police work itself is rather routine, especially the old saw about the FBI looking down their noses at the small-town crime beat. More effective as a character-driven suspense drama than a standard nab-a-killer chiller, EVIL HAS A FACE is fine as melodrama and fair as criminology. *(Profanity, violence, sexual situations, adult situations)* — R.P.

d, Rob Fresco; p, John L. Roman; exec p, Sam Kitt; w, Rob Fresco; ph, Stephen Lighthill; ed, Andrew London; m, Joseph Vitarelli; prod d, Anthony Tremblay; set d, Michael Gianneschi; sound, David Obermeyer (mixer); fx, Sam Barkan; casting, Melissa Skoff; cos, Susan Kaufman; makeup, Anne Scheeley; stunts, Stacy Logan, James Fierro

Crime/Thriller **(PR: C MPAA: R)**

EVITA ★★★

(U.S.) 135m Cinergi Productions; Dirty Hands Productions; Hollywood Pictures ~ Buena Vista c

Madonna *(Eva "Evita" Peron)*; Antonio Banderas *(Che Guevara)*; Jonathan Pryce *(General Juan Domingo Peron)*; Jimmy Nail *(Agustin Magaldi)*; Victoria Sus *(Dona Juana)*; Julian Littman *(Brother Juan)*; Olga Merediz *(Blanca)*; Laura Pallas *(Elisa)*; Julia Worsley *(Erminda)*; Maria Lujan Hidalgo *(Young Eva)*; Servando Villamil *(Cipriano Reyes)*; Andrea Corr *(Peron's Mistress)*; Peter Polycarpou *(Domingo Mercante)*; Gary Brooker *(Juan Bramuglia)*; Mayte Yerro *(Julieta)*; Adrian Collado *(Carlos)*; Gabriel Kraisman *(Cinema Manager)*; Martin Drogo *(Young Juan)*; Venesa Weis *(Young Blanca)*; Veronica Ferrari Risler *(Young Elisa)*; Aldana Garcia Soler *(Young Erminda)*; Domingo Chiofalo *(Chivilcoy Priest)*; Ismael Osorio *(Juan Duarte Sr.)*; Lidia Leonor Catalano *(Estela Grisolia)*; John Coverdale; Roderick Hart; Ian Hill; Rob Levy; Teddy Peiro; Joe Townsend *(Junin Tango Band)*; Mark Ryan; Gordon Neville; Frederick Warder *(Waiters in Junin Bar)*; Albin Pahernik; Luca Tommassini; Denis Tremblay *(Eva's Dance Partners)*; Eva Vari *(Senora Magaldi)*; Zsanett Farkas *(Magaldi Child)*; Sergio Lerer *(Theatre Producer)*; Mara Bestelli; Monica Lairana; Bettina Menegazzo; Laura Miller *(Starlets at Audition)*; Marcelo Alejandro Auchelli *(Huevo)*; Luis Alday *(Emilio Kartulowicz)*; Luis Boccia *(Senor Jabon)*; Vera Fogwill *(Zaz Jingle Singer)*; Bettina Menegazzo *(Zaz Jingle Singer)*; Alfredo Martin *(Col. Anibal Imbert)*; Diego Leske; Francisco Napoli; Eduardo Ruderman; Fabian Stratas *(Eva's Admirers)*; David Henry *(President Rawson)*; Fernando Agustin Henin *(Eva's Co-star)*

Yes, Madonna *is* Eva Peron, in EVITA, Alan Parker's breathlessly paced film version of Andrew Lloyd Webber and Tim Rice's epically proportioned rock opera. More spectacle than movie, EVITA is all sound and fury, piecing together an impressionistic historical biography with a dazzling array of visual treats.

The illegitimate daughter of a married middle-class man, little Eva Duarte is banished from her father's funeral. Resolved to transcend the dull poverty of her youth, Eva, barely a young woman, uses a brief love affair with a loutish balladeer (Jimmy Nail) to transport her from the countryside to the big city, Buenos Aires. She forges an acting career from whatever connections her increasingly powerful parade of lovers can provide. Reaching the top of the ladder of available men, Eva meets politician Juan Peron (Jonathan Pryce) at a fundraiser. Their mutual attraction is based as much on a shared impulse toward empire-building as on erotic chemistry. The two are married.

Using her popular radio show to promote his political aspirations, Eva aids Peron's seduction of the working class, insuring his election as president. Unaccepted by the Argentinian elite due to her lower class background, Eva launches her own charitable organization, which is splashy enough to keep the poor hopeful, and Eva herself in designer gowns. But her efforts to improve living conditions for *los descamisados* are plagued by corruption, her penchant for self-aggrandizement, and indifference, even hostility, from her husband's cabinet regarding any progressive actions. Sent abroad to raise the Peron profile worldwide, Eva is greeted by adoring crowds in Franco's Spain, but is less welcome in Italy, where "They equate Peron with Mussolini, can't think why!" The trip tires her, and upon her return to Buenos Aires, she is diagnosed with the cancer that would soon cause her death at age 33. The film ends as it began—with a funeral; Eva's body lies in luxurious state for thousands of mourners to whom she is "Santa Evita."

Throughout the film, a narrator, apparently based on a mythologized version of revolutionary Che Guevara (Antonio Banderas), trails like a shadow behind Eva, explicating the political climate and events of the era that are the backdrop for Eva's every move, and which also provide fodder for his commentary and a bit of comic relief. Historical inaccuracy aside (Che and Eva never met in real life), his role is part court jester, part conscience of the nation. He witnesses her bedroom exploits, leads massive protest marches, and offers comfort to victims of earthquakes and Peron's brutal regime. Charming, cynical, and a one-man Greek chorus, he provides not only a great deal of EVITA's narrative cohesion by facilitating potentially disjointed transitions between scenes, but also its only clear political and moral point of view.

Plagued by two decades of fits and starts, once coveted by directors ranging from Oliver Stone to Ken Russell, and leading ladies from Bette Midler to Meryl Streep, EVITA finally landed in Parker's hands. One of the few contemporary directors with any musical experience (FAME), and possessing a slick touch with period detail, Parker is responsible for EVITA's stunning look and cunning casting, but his commitment to character development and to telling a coherent story is weak by comparison.

Nearly every word of dialogue in EVITA is performed as recitative singing typical of opera (a style rarely seen in filmed musicals, with the exception of THE UMBRELLAS OF CHERBOURG). Lacking the nerve to carry out this style fully, too many scenes melt into slick montages, resorting to the methods of music video and granting the film more repetition than rhythm. EVITA's soundtrack is enervatingly eclectic, even when Rice's lyrics slip from the awfully clever to the awfully cliched. Evoking their most original score (JESUS CHRIST SUPERSTAR), Webber slips in some rock-n-roll segues that Banderas tackles joyously, as in "And the Money Kept Rolling In (and Out)." Madonna handles vulnerable ballads like "Another Suitcase in Another Hall" delicately, and throws herself gamely into even the most ridiculously scored show tunes ("Rainbow High").

Despite the spectacular visual pleasures of EVITA, it cannot be forgotten that the story of Eva Duarte's marriage to Juan Peron and his tenure as the president of Argentina is based (however loosely) on fact. How many viewers (and soundtrack listeners) will pick up on the film's cursory—to put it mildly—history lessons? Does all the toe-tapping drown out references to government corruption and class struggle? Is the rise of Fascism obliterated, even glorified, by magnificent set design? It obviously makes little difference to Parker, Webber, and Rice. Still, as a portrait of how celebrity—specifically, political celebrity—is constructed, how public adoration can be manufactured, and the ambivalent adoration and loathing directed towards women in powerful positions, its lessons are unambiguous. At least on film, these lessons have rarely been made so glamorously. *(Violence, sexual situations, adult situations.)* — C.Ch.

d, Alan Parker; p, Robert Stigwood, Alan Parker, Andrew G. Vajna; assoc p, Lisa Moran; w, Alan Parker, Oliver Stone (based on the musical play *Evita*, lyrics by Tim Rice and music by Andrew Lloyd Webber); ph, Darius Khondji; ed, Gerry Hambling; m, Andrew Lloyd Webber; prod d, Brian Morris; art d, Jean-Michel Hugon, Richard Earl; set d, Philippe Turlure; ch, Vincent Paterson; sound, Ken Weston (recordist), Andy Nelson, Anna Behlmer; fx, Yves De Bono; casting, John Hubbard, Ros Hubbard; cos, Penny Rose; makeup, Sarah Monzani; stunts, Rocky Taylor

AA Best Original Song: Andrew Lloyd Webber (music), Tim Rice (lyrics); *AAN Best Art Direction:* Brian Morris, Philippe Turlure; *AAN Best Cinematography:* Darius Khondji; *AAN Best Film Editing:* Gerry Hambling; *AAN Best Sound:* Andy Nelson, Anna Behlmer, Ken Weston

Musical/Biography **(PR: C MPAA: PG)**

EXECUTIVE DECISION ★★½

(U.S.) 135m Warner Bros.; Silver Pictures ~ Warner Bros. c

Kurt Russell *(David Grant)*; Steven Seagal *(Lieutenant Colonel Austin Travis)*; Halle Berry *(Jean)*; John Leguizamo *(Rat)*; Oliver Platt *(Cahill)*; Joe Morton *(Cappy)*; David Suchet *(Nagi Hassan)*; B. D. Wong *(Louie)*; Len Cariou *(Secretary of Defense Charles White)*; Whip Hubley *(Baker)*; Andreas Katsulas *(Jaffa)*; Mary Ellen Trainor *(Allison)*; Marla Maples Trump *(Nancy)*; J. T. Walsh *(Senator Mavros)*; Ingo Neuhaus *(Doc)*; William James Jones *(Catman)*; Paul Collins *(Nelson)*; Nicholas Pryor *(Secretary of State Jack Douglas)*; Stanley Grover *(General Price)*; Eugene Roche *(Admiral Lewis)*; Ken Jenkins *(General Wood)*; Charles Hallahan *(General Sarlow)*; Dey Young *(Gail)*; Richard Riehle *(Air Marshal)*; Robert Apisa *(Demou)*; Granville Hatcher *(Ahmed)*; Chris Maher *(Kahlil)*; Jay Tavare; Ahmed Ahmed; Shaun Toub; Majed Ibrahim; Jon Huertas; Joey Naber *(Terrorists)*; Ray Baker *(747 Captain)*; Michael Milhoan *(747 First Officer)*; Julie Wright; Sunni Boswell *(Flight Attendants)*; Gregg Artz; Will Schaub *(Assistants to Senator Mavros)*; Yvonne Zima *(Little Girl)*; Marianne Muellerleile *(Diabetic Woman)*; Brad Blaisdell *(Beckings Institute Aide)*; Don Fischer *(Remora Pilot)*; John Rixey Moore *(Flight Instructor)*; Warren Munson *(American Ambassador)*; Lance August *(American Embassy Duty Officer)*; Maggie Egan *(CNN Reporter)*; James Victor *(Spider)*; Tim Kelleher *(Bulldog)*; David Birznieks *(Fire Fighter)*; Nick Jameson *(London Maitre D')*; Juan Fernandez *(London Bomber)*; Todd Jeffries *(Collins)*; Joe Cook; Ilia Volokh *(Chechens)*; Blair Valk *(Yugoslavian Girl)*; Joseph Makkar *(Arab Co-pilot)*; Damon Lee *(Translator)*; Jayne Walter *(London Hostess)*; Robert Londberg *(Diamond Smuggler)*; Edmond Brown *(FBI Agent)*; Michelle Boudreau *(Party Girl)*; Kurt Kohler *(MP)*; Jeffrey Senour; Dentis McDaniel; Bruce Ross; Leslie E. Smith; Kevin Eldridge; John Hardy *(Helicopter Pilots)*

An AIRPORT movie for the 1990s, EXECUTIVE DECISION energizes the macho action-picture genre with exciting set pieces, despite the fact there are more holes in the script than in the high-flying aircraft of the story.

Dr. David Grant (Kurt Russell), the head of a Washington, DC, anti-terrorist agency, becomes the point man of a dangerous mission to save the lives of innocent passengers when a group of Islamic militants hijack an Athens-to-DC flight and demands $50 million and the release of their apprehended superior. Grant also worries about a nerve gas the terrorists have on board, which could destroy the entire population of Washington. In an emergency meeting with the Secretary of Defense (Len Cariou), Grant tells the war council to keep the craft out of American air space at all costs. At the same meeting, Grant meets Lieutenant Colonel Austin Travis (Steven Seagal), an anti-terrorist operative who insists that Grant join his team of commandos on their planned midair raid of the airliner.

Grant and weapon designer Dennis Cahill (Oliver Platt) reluctantly join Travis and his men aboard an F-117 Stealth fighter plane. As the vehicle attaches to the bottom of the 747 undetected, Grant and the team crawl onto the plane, but Travis loses his life when the hatch closes too soon and the untested F-117 breaks away. Once inside—hiding in the cargo section—Rat (John Leguizamo) assumes the leadership role. He assigns Cappy (Joe Morton) and Louie (B.D. Wong) the role of finding and neutralizing the deadly chemicals, and Grant the role of spying on the terrorists in the main cabin by using small, high-tech cameras inserted in the ceiling and floor. Grant gets help from Jean (Halle Berry), a flight attendant who accidentally discovers the undercover agents during the hostage ordeal.

Finally, after many tense interludes, Grant and the others confront and kill the terrorists, who have not harmed the passengers but have killed the pilots. Grant then takes over at the cockpit and lands the plane to safety. Once back on terra firma, Jean thanks the heroic Dr. Grant for his bravery and suggests they get to know each other better.

In the midst of his anti-terrorist activities, John Leguizamo's "Rat" hopes that there's "a good movie on this flight," and, for much of its two-hour-plus length, EXECUTIVE DECISION delivers lively suspense. Former editor and first-time director Stuart Baird may lack the artistry of John Woo, but he knows how to put together a sequence of film. Notably, Baird brings visual clarity and coherence to the largely implausible premise and story development of Jim and John Thomas's screenplay.

Where Baird goes off course is in directing the actors, especially the passenger extras. Pros like Kurt Russell, Joe Morton, Halle Berry, and even Steven Seagal (in a virtual cameo) get by admirably, but David Suchet is permitted to overact as the chief villain, and there is even a hint of apparently unintended AIRPLANE-style parody in the casting of the hopelessly inept Marla Maples Trump as an airline attendant. Other flaws include an overly tricky globe-hopping opening sequence, an uneven use of special effects (including obvious miniatures and matte shots), and (like the DELTA FORCE films) the typical one-dimensional ethnic stereotyping of Arabs as terrorists. Action fans will probably be able to overlook these defects, but others may lament that, with more care, this elaborate PASSENGER 57-type thriller might have been much, much better. *(Violence, adult situations, profanity.)* — E.M.

d, Stuart Baird; p, Joel Silver, Jim Thomas, John Thomas; exec p, Steve Perry; assoc p, Spencer Martin; co-p, Karyn Fields; w, Jim Thomas, John Thomas; ph, Alex Thomson; ed, Dallas Puett, Frank J. Urioste, Stuart Baird; m, Jerry Goldsmith; prod d, Terence Marsh; art d, William M. Cruse; set d, Marvin March; sound, Clark David King (mixer); fx, Kenneth D. Pepiot, Peter Donen; casting, Amanda Mackey Johnson, Cathy Sandrich; cos, Louise Frogley; makeup, Dennis Liddiard; stunts, Dick Ziker

Action/Adventure **(PR: C MPAA: R)**

EXIT ★★

(U.S.) 81m IRS Media Inc.; Century Group Inc. ~ Republic Pictures Home Video c

Shannon Whirry *(Diane)*; David Bradley *(Charles)*; Joe Bucci *(Alex Becque)*; Fred Ottamano *(Sheriff Wilson)*; Scott Blake *(Eddie)*; Brad Long *(Kyle Wilson)*; Yeniffer Behrens *(Kindra)*; Glenn Scherer *(Anderson)*; Kevin Dean Hackett *(Nobby)*; Sheel *(Sheila)*; Nicole Hansen *(Nikki)*; Patrice DeGraff-Arenas *(Cherry)*; Perry Barnot *(Patrick)*; Gina La Marca *(Rita)*; Harold Bergman *(Mr. Versage)*; Peter Vallas *(Banks)*; J. Jason Winfield

(Deputy Jenkins); Robin Trapp *(News Reporter)*; Richard Theiss *(SWAT Guy)*; Scott Reinger *(Cab Driver)*; Joseph Marino *(Patron)*; Toni Lincoln; Angel Boris; Sabrina Sadoti; Shana Petrone *(Dancers)*

Straight-to-video sexpot Shannon Whirry tries to extend her market range in this suspense thriller, though not so far as to totally alienate her heavy-breathing fans.

When her boyfriend, the son of a local politician, proposes marriage, student Diane (Shannon Whirry) fears he will discover that she works part-time as a stripper. She resolves to make that night's performance her last. But while she's onstage, the club is robbed by armed bandits.

When the holdup goes awry and the building is surrounded by police, gang leader Charles (David Bradley) decides to hold the dancers and patrons hostage. Among the hostages is Alex (Joe Bucci), a former federal agent.

Working together, Diane and Alex are able to get most of the hostages into the club's freezer room (which locks from the inside). Enraged, Charles locks the outside as well and turns the room's thermostat to below freezing.

Diane is allowed to leave the club to accompany an injured hostage, as Charles tries to bargain with the police. She sneaks back into the club through an air vent in order to help the freezing hostages. When the club's power is cut off, she and Alex take advantage of the confusion to overcome Charles, setting him on fire with alcohol.

Diane's boyfriend and his father decide not to hold her former employment against her, while Alex declines a job offer from the sheriff, having decided from the evening's events that he prefers a quieter life.

A sort of overripe Jacqueline Bissett, Shannon Whirry has built a substantial following in a seemingly endless series of straight-to-video sexploitation features. If the title of this film doesn't seem to have much to do with the plot, maybe it can be understood as her attitude toward the nudie genre. So as a more "dramatic" actress, Whirry limits her fleshy exposure to a steamy love scene and one interrupted strip routine. The bare torso primarily displayed in EXIT belongs to male newcomer Joe Bucci, who spends a long stretch of the film tied like Samson to two dancers' poles. The symbolism is probably accidental, as the position seems to have been chosen because it provides maximum bicep distension.

EXIT is a serviceable thriller whose main problem, aside from the usual limits of a low-budget feature, is that it has too much plot and too little development: many things happen, but few are particularly interesting.*(Violence, nudity, sexual situations, profanity.)* — M.F.

d, Ric Roman Waugh; p, Michael Greenfield, Melanie Ray; exec p, Miles A. Copeland III; assoc p, Joel Wein; co-p, Jonathan Stathakis; w, Joe Augustyn, Brent V. Friedman, David Robinson; ph, David B. Nowell; ed, Dody Dorn; m, Kevin Kiner; prod d, Michael T. J. Fontana; art d, Greg Hamlin; fx, John Bosseau; casting, Donald Paul Pemrick; cos, Tami Richt, Elizabeth Jett; makeup, Juliet Loveland

Action/Erotic/Thriller **(PR: O MPAA: R)**

EXQUISITE TENDERNESS
(SEE: SURGEON, THE)

EXTREME MEASURES ★★
(U.S.) 118m Simian Films; Castle Rock ~ Columbia c

Hugh Grant *(Dr. Guy Luthan)*; Gene Hackman *(Dr. Lawrence Myrick)*; Sarah Jessica Parker *(Jodie Trammel)*; David Morse *(Frank Hare)*; Bill Nunn *(Burke)*; John Toles-Bey *(Bobby)*; Paul Guilfoyle *(Dr. Jeffrey Manko)*; Debra Monk *(Dr. Judith Gruszynski)*; Shaun Austin-Olsen *(Claude Minkins)*; Andre De Shields *(Teddy Dolson)*; J.K. Simmons *(Dr. Mingus)*; Peter Appel *(Detective Stone)*; Diana Zimmer *(Helen)*; Nancy Beatty *(Ruth Myrick)*; Gerry Becker *(Dr. Gene Spitelli)*; Gene Ruffini *(Izzy)*; Bill MacDonald *(Stone's Partner)*; D. Garnet Harding; Derwin Jordan; Simon Reynolds; Tara Rosling; Martin Roach; Bernard Browne; Sanjay Talwar *(ER Doctors)*; Christina Collins; Arlene Duncan; Cheryl Swarts *(ER Nurse)*; Peter Maloney *(Mr. Randall)*; Johnie Chase *(Cop)*; Noam Jenkins *(Criminal)*; Larissa Lapchinski *(Myrick's Daughter)*; Phallon Carpino *(Granddaughter)*; Ross Petty *(Dr. Garlock)*; Todd Stewart *(Shelter Supervisor)*; Lawrence Arancio *(Medical Examiner)*; Vincent Marino *(Janitor)*; Marcia De Bonis *(Pam)*; John Ventimiglia *(Detective Manning)*; John Heffernan *(Cartman)*; Raynor Scheine *(Half-Mole)*; John Trudell *(Tony)*; Nelson Vasquez *(Skicap)*; Vincent Laresca *(Patches)*; Denis Akiyama *(Professor Asakura)*; Kim Roberts *(Home Nurse)*; Gerry Quigley *(Party Guest)*; Teresa Yenque *(Neighbor)*; Chris Edwards *(Uniform Cop)*; David Eisner *(Guy's Lawyer)*; Dana Stevens *(Prosecutor)*; Michael J. Reynolds *(Judge)*; David Cronenberg *(Hospital Lawyer)*; Desi Moreno *(Toll Collector)*; Marc Gosselin *(Jodie's Brother)*; Jackie Richardson *(Triphase Nurse)*; Marium Carvell *(Triphase Nurse)*; Marilyn McDonald *(Mole Lady)*

Model Elizabeth Hurley produced this medical thriller starring her errant boyfriend, Hugh Grant, but it's too bad EXTREME MEASURES has a lot less zip than their 1995 tabloid exploits, involving Grant's tryst with a prostitute.

At the start of the picture, while Dr. Guy Luthan (Hugh Grant) busily saves lives in the emergency room of Gramercy Hospital, two nude men run from an unseen predator on the dark but busy streets of nighttime Manhattan. Eventually, one of the men, Claude Minkins (Shaun Austin-Olsen) stumbles into the medical facility, where Guy assumes the patient is suffering from exposure. But when Claude goes into mysterious convulsions and dies, Guy wishes to find out the cause.

Guy orders a battery of tests, but they produce unclear results. Then Claude's file and corpse disappear from the morgue. A senior staff member urges Guy to ignore the odd situation, but Guy becomes even more curious. Guy suspects that the renowned doctor, Lawrence Myrick (Gene Hackman), has some connection to the missing body, but before he can learn the truth, Guy gets suspended from his job for misusing drugs, a false charge.

Now on his own, but with the reluctant help of the senior nurse, Jodie Trammel (Sarah Jessica Parker), Guy tracks down Teddy Dolson (Andre De Shields), a former patient of Myrick's who explains that the famous doctor has been using invalids as guinea pigs for spinal nerve experiments. In a violent showdown with Myrick, Guy forces Myrick to admit to his unethical actions, then he kills him. Later, Guy discovers that Jodie was complicit in Myrick's activities, but the young doctor gets his job back and receives some solace from Myrick's widow, who relinquishes all her husband's files to him.

Grant continues patterning his career after his cinematic forebear, Cary Grant, an actor who also alternated comedies with dramas, including the 1950 medical thriller, CRISIS, after the 1948 medical comedy, EVERY GIRL SHOULD GET MARRIED. But, in fairness, the new Grant tones down his stammering gentleman bit and lends genuine humor and interest to the early ER-style scenes of EXTREME MEASURES, which is at least better than the medical comedy, NINE MONTHS (1995), Hugh Grant's first big Hollywood foray. Unfortunately, as the mystery unfolds, the generic qualities of EXTREME MEAS-

URES take hold, and the piece becomes a hodgepodge of COMA (1978), OUTBREAK (1995), and THE ISLAND OF DR. MOREAU (1996). Not even Hugh Grant can save a climax in which he must deliver a pious speech about medical ethics while performing action-hero tussling.

Still, the most cynical aspect of Tony Gilroy's screenplay is its implication that almost any person would morally sell out in order to cure themselves or their loved ones of a medical disability. In a way, the talented documentarian Michael Apted (7 UP) has himself sold out (to Hollywood, that is), but it's not the first time (witness CRITICAL CONDITION, another medical "comedy," and among other Apted stinkers). *(Violence, nudity, adult situations, profanity.)* — E.M.

d, Michael Apted; p, Elizabeth Hurley; exec p, Andrew Scheinman; co-p, Chris Brigham; w, Tony Gilroy (based on the book by Michael Palmer); ph, John Bailey; ed, Rick Shaine; m, Danny Elfman; prod d, Doug Kraner; art d, Tom Warren, Paul Denham Austerberry; set d, Alyssa Winter; sound, D. Bruce Carwardine (mixer), Tom Nelson (mixer); fx, Michael Kavanagh, Robert Hodgson, Chris Watts; casting, Linda Lowy, John Brace; cos, Susan Lyall; makeup, Donald J. Mowat, Gord Smith; stunts, Jery Hewitt

Thriller **(PR: C MPAA: R)**

EYE FOR AN EYE ★

(U.S.) 101m Paramount ~ Paramount c

Sally Field *(Karen McCann)*; Kiefer Sutherland *(Robert Doob)*; Ed Harris *(Mack McCann)*; Olivia Burnette *(Julie McCann)*; Alexandra Kyle *(Megan McCann)*; Joe Mantegna *(Detective Sergeant Denillo)*; Beverly D'Angelo *(Dolly Green)*; Darrell Larson *(Peter Green)*; Charlayne Woodard *(Angel Kosinsky)*; Philip Baker Hall *(Sidney Hughes)*; Keith David *(Martin)*; Wanda Acuna *(Hispanic Housewife)*; Geoffrey Rivas *(Hispanic Housewife's Husband)*; Armin Shimerman *(Judge Younger)*; Natalija Nogulich *(Susan Juke)*; Nicholas Cascone *(Howard Bolinger)*; Stella Garcia *(Maria)*; Justine Johnston *(Aunt McCann)*; Wayne Pere *(French Teacher)*; Joan Crowe *(Michelle)*; Ross Bagley *(Sean)*; Jane Morris *(County Clerk)*; Cynthia Rothrock *(Tina)*; Bobby J. Foxworth *(Man Following Karen)*; Manny Rodriguez *(Gun Instructor)*; Michael Podwal *(Pilates Instructor)*; Sierra Pecheur *(Teacher)*; Zack Eginton *(Obnoxious Boy)*; Kim Kim *(Shopkeeper)*; A.C. Weary *(Newscaster)*; Brenda Smith *(Waitress)*; Ron Dean *(Detective at McCann House)*; David Courier *(Crime Scene Policeman)*; Ellis E. Williams *(Crime Scene Policeman)*; David Barrera *(Precinct Officer)*; Scott Waara *(Detective)*; Tom Lillard *(Bailiff)*; Angela Paton *(Moderator)*; Donal Logue *(Tony)*; William Mesnick *(Albert Gratz)*; Rondi Reed *(Regina Gratz)*; Michael Buchman Silver *(Assistant)*; Eric Morris *(Columnist)*; Iris Field *(Office Staffer)*; Jeremy Eynon *(Office Staffer)*; Fort Atkinson *(Angry Man)*; Evelyn Parke *(911 Caller)*; Dolores Velazquez *(Hispanic Woman)*; Pablo Velazquez *(Hispanic Man)*; Patricia Belcher *(Quarreling Woman)*; Alesia Jones *(Quarreling Woman)*; Maurice Sherbanee *(TV Salesman)*; Bob Clendenin *(Hotel Clerk)*; Larry Polson *(Yelling Man)*; Sharon D. Chase; Janet Dey; Buzz Barbee; Nino Polito *(Mourners)*; Cherie Franklin; Francesca P. Roberts; Marie Chambers; Rolando Molina; Ernie Vincent; Teddy Vincent; Minnie Summers Lindsey

If you yearn to see two-time Academy Award-winner Sally Field at her most agonized in a plot older than Pearl White, laced with graphic scenes of women being raped an murdered, this is the film for you.

Karen McCann (Field) is a museum director who lives in a posh Los Angeles suburb. A stranger breaks into her home and rapes and murders her teenage daughter, Julie (Olivia Burnette). Detective Joe Denillo (Joe Mantegna) soon arrests the perpetrator, a lowlife delivery man named Robert Doob (Kiefer Sutherland). Despite an abundance of DNA evidence, Doob is acquitted on a technicality involving the mishandling of a sperm sample and immediately released. Karen tracks him down to his seedy flat and demands his arrest, but the police are powerless to help. After seeing Doob apparently stalking another victim, a young Hispanic woman, Karen is unable to get either the police or the potential victim to heed her warnings. She then decides to take matters into her own hands. She joins a victims' survivors' support group, learns how to use a gun during her lunch hour, and takes up martial arts. Doob becomes a ghastly obsession with her, despite the pleas of her husband Mack (Ed Harris), surviving daughter Megan (Alexandra Kyle), and her support group. The unrepentant Doob, meanwhile, smugly goes about his evil business: he rapes and kills the Hispanic woman and once again gets away with it, despite Karen's warnings. After sending her daughter and husband away, Karen lures Doob to her home. Knowing that she is entitled by law to shoot anyone who breaks into her house, she waits for him and shoots him dead. Although Denillo recognizes what Karen has done, he reports it as a simple case of self-defense.

EYE FOR AN EYE is a loaded potboiler of the crassest type. Given loftier material like FAR FROM THE MADDING CROWD (1967), SUNDAY, BLOODY SUNDAY (1971), or AN ENGLISHMAN ABROAD (1988), director John Schlesinger is capable of beautifully nuanced work. Throw him a script more pulpy and hysterical in tone, however, and tact flies out the window with all the subtlety of Doob's lifeless corpse falling on a quivering Karen moments after she's pumped him full of lead. The camera lingers over the brutalized and bloodied remains of the Hispanic victim, showing her none of the respectful restraint given Karen's privileged, white teen-aged daughter. Such offensive infelicities abound.

It's beyond the actors to save this film (those that aren't a factor in its demise, that is). Field runs the sorrowing, determined gamut, unable to overcome the unsuitability of her aging-Gidget face for the role of a tragic avenger. Harris plays her peripheral, supportive helpmate, a thankless assignment which might have been amusing for its role-reversal qualities in better circumstances. Mantegna in the "humane detective" role gives a performance that's pure pulp. Charlayne Woodard appears in a ridiculous subplot as a lesbian mother and gets to deliver the big line, "I was in those meetings investigating vigilante behavior. I'm with the FBI." Outfitted with every possible white-trash cliche—greasy pompadour, sleazy goatee, bicep tattoos and, in one of the film's most offensive touches, a garish crucifix—Sutherland barely even needs to give a performance: his wardrobe is as stacked against him as his character's name. *(Violence, substance abuse, adult situations, sexual situations, profanity.)* — D.N.

d, John Schlesinger; p, Michael I. Levy; assoc p, Kathryn Knowlton; co-p, Michael Polaire; w, Amanda Silver, Rick Jaffa (based on the novel by Erika Holzer); ph, Amir M. Mokri; ed, Peter Honess; m, James Newton Howard; prod d, Stephen Hendrickson; art d, David J. Bomba; set d, Jan K. Bergstrom; sound, Edward Tise (mixer); fx, Kevin Pike; casting, Mali Finn; cos, Bobbie Read; makeup, Robin L. Neal; stunts, Bobby J. Foxworth

Drama/Crime/Thriller **(PR: C MPAA: R)**

EYE OF VICHY, THE ★★★

(France) 110m FIT Production; Institut National de L'audiovisuel ~ First Run bw

(L'OEIL DE VICHY)

Robert Paxton *(Narrator)*

This documentary from director Claude Chabrol demonstrates how the old-fashioned compilation can still have a dramatic impact when skillfully edited with a carefully crafted narration. Using Vichy's own newsreels and songs, THE EYE OF VICHY shows the blend of opportunism and native fascism that made up the collaborationist government, undercut by brief references to the items not caught by offical cameramen at staged events.

Opening with a very quick montage of battle scenes, both real and fictional, the film gets to the establishment of a new authoritarian government headed by the revered WWI hero, Marshal Petain, whose emphasis on the sins that lead to the 1940 defeat often make him appear a not very forgiving Father Confessor. The Vichy newsreels stress German aid to France, although more cynical audiences might see the Nazi effort to save damaged oil refineries and railways as good military sense. More interesting is the emphasis on battles in North Africa between Vichy forces and the British, a sure winner for French emotions.

Most citizens in the first few years of German domination are not terribly bothered by the defeat. Only Jews and outright anti-fascists had anything to worry about, since the Vichy regime eagerly initiated anti-Semitic legislation and paramilitary organizations. The visit to Paris by the dreaded SS General Heydrich and the formation of the *Milice* are heralded in the newsreels. The Germans also cleverly use their French POWs as more than a million bargaining chips, releasing some here and there, but mostly exchanging them for laborers sent to Germany. That demand for labor eventually undermines Vichy's early popularity as Petain and Laval begin to conscript men to work in the Third Reich. The newsreels talk as much about bandits and criminals as about Allied bombing-raid victims.

Besides the outright racist slogans, there is even more talk about a common European link, uniting France with Germany against the foreign Anglo-Americans and Soviets. One very novel piece of propaganda is an animation that features a crassly bourgeois family talking of liberation in terms of food and delicacies, while an American bombing squadron piloted by the likes of Mickey Mouse, Donald Duck, and Popeye destroys their home. There are also rallies and meetings honoring the several thousand French volunteers in the German Army on the Russian front. As the war draws closer to French shores, the newsreels show the massive fortifications closest to the English coast and stress the letters written by children to their fathers still held in German POW camps.

Despite too much emphasis on Petain's official appearances before adoring crowds, THE EYE OF VICHY furthers the view of the collaborationist regime first pioneered by Marcel Ophuls in THE SORROW AND THE PITY (1970)—namely, that many Frenchmen cooperated wholeheartedly with the government—and uses some similar period footage. This Chabrol film, however, benefits from a narration co-scripted by the American expert on Vichy, Robert Paxton, and closes with the chilling statistic that at the war's close there were more Frenchmen in Germany than in 1940. From Goebbels' diaries, we know that the Nazi leaders seriously planned to annex Burgundy once their victory was certain, which weakens any revisionist arguments concerning the viability of a separate peace with Hitler. *(Adult situations, violence.)* — L.R.

d, Claude Chabrol; exec p, Jean-Pierre Ramsay Levi; w, Jean-Pierre Azema, Robert Paxton; ed, Frederic Lossignol; sound, Sophia Cerda

Documentary/Historical/War (PR: C MPAA: NR)

FAITHFUL ★½

(U.S.) 91m Tribeca Productions; Price Entertainment; Savoy Pictures ~ New Line c

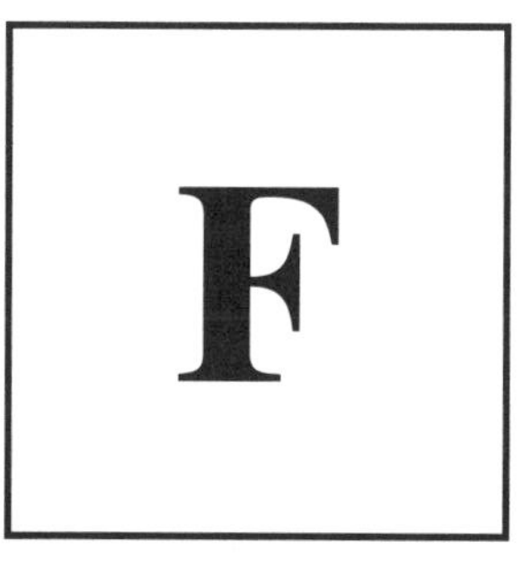

Cher *(Margaret)*; Chazz Palminteri *(Tony)*; Ryan O'Neal *(Jack)*; Paul Mazursky *(Dr. Susskind)*; Amber Smith *(Debbie)*; Elisa Leonetti *(Maria)*; Mark Nassar *(Maria's Boyfriend)*; Stephen Spinella *(Young Man at Rolls)*; Jeffrey Wright *(Young Man at Rolls)*; David Merino *(Little Tony)*; Steven Randazzo *(Tony's Father)*; Olinda Turturro *(Tony's Mother)*; Max Norat *(Jewelry Store Salesman)*; Allison Janney *(Saleslady)*; Chris O'Neill *(Priest)*; Michael Mulheren *(Foreman)*; Jerry Walsh *(Trucking Dispatcher)*; Gianna Ranaudo *(Teacher)*; Omar Sharif Scroggins *(Kid)*; Zakee Howze *(Kid)*; Paul Ronan *(Young Guy in Car)*; Steve Carreri *(Young Guy in Car)*

Noel Coward meets David Mamet in FAITHFUL, a high-pitched comedy of bad manners about a depressed wife, her philandering husband, and the hit man who comes between them.

Cher plays the rich, beautiful but lonely wife, Margaret O'Donnel, married to Jack O'Donnel (Ryan O'Neal), a New York trucking company owner. Suspecting her husband of having an affair with his secretary, Margaret becomes suicidal when Jack takes a business trip on the occasion of their 20th anniversary. Just as she is about to swallow a handful of pills, Margaret is interrupted by Tony (Chazz Palminteri), a thug who has broken into her posh estate.

Methodically, Tony ties Margaret to a chair in the living room and explains his presence: he is waiting for Jack to ring their number twice then hang up. The signal will permit Tony to murder Margaret, so that Jack can collect $5 million in insurance and establish an alibi. Margaret is incredulous. She cannot believe that Jack would want her dead, and, for the next hour, she argues with Tony about a variety of topics, including the sanctity of marriage and the joys of crunchy peanut butter. Margaret even confuses the mobster, making him think that perhaps she hired him to kill her and has now changed her mind.

Eventually, the discussion causes Tony to agonize over the death of his sister, a mob-hit casualty. Tony calls his psychiatrist, Dr. Susskind (Paul Mazursky), but gets greater comfort from Margaret instead. Finally, Tony and Margaret acknowledge their attraction to one another and make love in the upstairs bedroom.

Some time later that night, Jack returns home, surprised to find Margaret alive. While she avoids confronting Jack about the murder plot, Margaret seeks to measure her husband's love for her by engaging him in a verbal battle regarding their marriage. Suddenly, Tony reappears, still unsure of who planned the hit. After changing his mind a few times about who to kill, Tony finally murders Jack and leaves Margaret with the hope that they will someday meet again. Margaret, meanwhile, feels more contented from the experience.

Although based on star-screenwriter Palminteri's play of the same title, FAITHFUL also borrows the plot outline from 1993's THE REF (not to mention the even more interesting BULLETPROOF HEART). Yet, while THE REF dynamically combined comedy and suspense, FAITHFUL bogs down in its Anthony Shaffer-style plot twists, Neil Simon-esque dialogue, and static theatrical staging (camouflaged somewhat by Fred Murphy's elegant camera movements). Behind the scenes, the film's release was delayed several months while director Paul Mazursky feuded with his producers; he finally got his way, and the version released to the public was his original final cut.

FAITHFUL may not be as disastrous as other recent films by Mazursky (SCENES FROM A MALL, THE PICKLE), but matters are not helped by the distancing use of filters and shadows to disguise the advancing age of the stars, Cher (in a one-note "comeback" performance, her first since 1990's MERMAIDS) and O'Neal (heavy-set but lighter weight than ever). Mazursky himself even plays a psychoanalyst in a pointless and unfunny subplot that includes a typically racist cabdriver bit. Only Palminteri himself survives his own work and makes something amusing out of his character, but he's not very impressive either if one has seen him in any of his many similar film roles over just the last few years (A BRONX TALE, BULLETS OVER BROADWAY).

In fairness, FAITHFUL builds up to a conclusion that is not entirely predictable, but with the other triangle-romance duds released in 1996 (e.g. CARRIED AWAY, SHE'S THE ONE, FLIRT), infidelity is looking duller than ever on screen. *(Violence, sexual situations, adult situations, extreme profanity.)* — E.M.

d, Paul Mazursky; p, Jane Rosenthal, Robert De Niro; exec p, Peter Gatien, Dan Lauria; assoc p, Henry Bronchtein; co-p, Geoffrey Taylor; w, Chazz Palminteri (based on his play); ph, Fred Murphy; ed, Nicholas C. Smith; m, Phillip Johnston; prod d, Jeffrey Townsend; art d, Caty Maxey; set d, Justin Scoppa Jr.; sound, Bill Daly (mixer); fx, Steve Kirshoff, KFX; casting, Ellen Chenoweth; cos, Hope Hanafin; makeup, Michael Laudati; stunts, Peter Bucossi

Comedy/Drama **(PR: C MPAA: R)**

FAMILY THING, A ★★★

(U.S.) 109m Randa Haines/Todd Black Productions; Butchers Run Films; United Artists ~ MGM/UA c

Robert Duvall *(Earl)*; James Earl Jones *(Ray)*; Michael Beach *(Virgil)*; Irma P. Hall *(Aunt T.)*; Grace Zabriskie *(Ruby)*; Regina Taylor *(Ann)*; Mary Jackson *(Carrie)*; Paula Marshall *(Karen)*; James Harrell *(Earl, Sr.)*; Lauren Leigh Phillips *(Kindra)*; Ashleigh Jordan *(Danielle)*; David Keith *(Sonny)*; Saundra Quarterman *(Young Aunt T.)*; Patrice Pitman Quinn *(Willa Mae)*; Don James *(Junior Turner)*; Jim Sanderson *(Dr. Parks)*; Karla Harscheid *(Young Carrie Pilcher)*; Crystal Laws Green *(Maotis)*; Marquis Ramone Colquitt *(Little Raymond)*; Nathan Lee Lewis *(Brother Conners)*; Katherine Mitchell *(Woman in Apartment)*; Xander Berkeley *(Sunburned Man)*; Willo Hausman *(Waitress)*; Rufus Thomas *(Tommy)*; Richard Lexsee *(Truckjacker)*; Ramsey Harris *(Truckjacker)*; J. Antonio Moon *(Truckjacker)*; Meg Thalken *(Doctor)*; Jeri Boyle *(Old Lady)*; Tommy Bush *(Old Man)*; Jacqueline Williams *(Woman at Hospital)*; Wanda Christine *(Woman at City Hall)*; Roy Hytower *(Man at Gas Station)*; John Mikels *(Policemen)*; Asa Harris *(Woman Birthday Friend)*; Bernard Mixon *(Birthday Husband)*; Paulette McDaniels *(Birthday Girl)*; Phillip Edward Van Lear *(Club Manager)*; Antoine Roshell *(Young Man in Car)*; Greg Hollimon *(Man #2)*; Reginald C. Hayes *(Virgil's Friend)*; Andrew Love; Garry Goin; Paul D. Wilson; Ernie Adams; Tony Brown; Theotis Rogers; David Spencer *(Nightclub Band)*

A FAMILY THING proves that a Hollywood family melodrama with a racial theme need not be mawkish or overly manipulative.

Earl Pilcher Jr. (Robert Duvall), a middle-aged white Southerner, learns at his mother's deathbed that his real mother was a black maid, whom his father had impregnated and who died giving birth to him. Before she dies, Earl's mother urges him to seek out the half-brother he did not know he had. First Earl confronts his father, whose silence on the matter serves as confirmation of the truth. Then, to fulfill his mother's dying wish, Earl then sets out on a journey to find his brother.

Leaving his wife (Grace Zabriskie) and grown children behind, Earl travels from smalltown Arkansas to the busy, urban streets of Chicago, where (through some detective work) Earl finds his brother, a City Hall police officer named Ray Murdock (James Earl Jones). Ray, who blames Earl for their mother's death, surprises Earl by telling him that he wants nothing to do with him. But when Earl is beaten and robbed on his way out of town, Ray reluctantly helps him by putting him up in his modest home, where he lives with his grown son, Virgil (Michael Beach), and his blind but wily Aunt T. (Irma P. Hall).

For the next several days, as Earl recovers from his injuries, the brothers get to know each other, while keeping their secret from the other members of the household. Earl and Ray often argue over a variety of subjects, but they eventually grow closer thanks to Aunt T.'s guidance. Earl is able to help Virgil with his troubles involving his estranged wife, Ann (Regina Taylor), and their children. Virgil is angry when he learns Earl's true identity, but Aunt T. reveals she knew all along who he was. She helps supply closure to Earl's search by telling him the story of his birth, allowing him to return home with a new understanding about his family, his heritage, and himself.

What might have come off as a dramatic and sentimental version of THE JERK (1979), turns out to be a dignified—and often charming—account of a Caucasian man's discovery that his mother was African-American. Duvall (who also produced the film) and Jones are perfectly cast as half-brothers who only get to know each other in their late middle-age; they are well supported by Beach. Of the female cast members, Taylor and Zabriskie are wasted in small roles, but Hall steals the show as the irascible Aunt T.

Director Richard Pearce (A LONG WALK HOME) gives the actors plenty of space to do their thing, and the writing team of Tom Epperson and Billy Bob Thornton (SLING BLADE) provide dialogue that is generally on-target about racial issues.

Nonetheless, A FAMILY THING fumbles occasionally in its storytelling. The sepia-tone flashback climax about Ray's birth adds nothing to what has already been revealed. Aunt T.'s role as the blindness-as-insight metaphor has been done to death (from "Oedipus Rex" to *Native Son*). And Pearce is a better director of stirring monologues than action sequences. Fortunately, there are only a few action sequences in A FAMILY THING, a Hollywood film that is sufficiently compelling without such things. *(Violence, adult situations, nudity, profanity.)* — E.M.

d, Richard Pearce; p, Robert Duvall, Todd Black, Randa Haines; exec p, Michael Hausman; assoc p, Scott Ferguson; co-p, Brad Wilson; w, Billy Bob Thornton, Tom Epperson; ph, Fred Murphy; ed, Mark Warner; m, Charles Gross; prod d, Linda DeScenna; art d, Jim Nedza; set d, Ric McElvin; sound, Glenn Williams (mixer); fx, Rod Kiser; casting, Victoria Thomas; cos, Joe I. Tompkins; makeup, Linda Melazzo; stunts, Rick LeFevour

Drama/Comedy **(PR: C MPAA: PG-13)**

FAN, THE ★★

(U.S.) 120m Wendy Finerman Productions; Scott Free Productions; Mandalay Entertainment; TriStar ~ TriStar c

Robert De Niro *(Gil Renard)*; Wesley Snipes *(Bobby Rayburn)*; Ellen Barkin *(Jewel Stern)*; John Leguizamo *(Manny)*; Benicio Del Toro *(Juan Primo)*; Patti D'Arbanville *(Ellen Renard)*; Chris Mulkey *(Tim)*; Andrew J. Ferchland *(Richie Renard)*; Brandon Hammond *(Sean Rayburn)*; Charles Hallahan *(Coop)*; Dan Butler *(Garrity)*; Kurt Fuller *(Bernie)*; Michael Jace *(Scalper)*; Frank Medrano *(Leon the Bartender)*; Don S. Davis *(Stook)*; John Kruk *(Lanz)*; Stoney Jackson *(Zamora)*; Brad Henke *(Tjader)*; Drew Snyder *(Burrows)*; Edith Diaz *(Elvira)*; Walter Addison *(Detective Lewis)*; Wayne Duvall *(Detective Baker)*; Joe Pichler *(Sick Sean)*; James G. MacDonald *(Sick Sean's Dad)*; Tuesday Knight *(Nurse)*; Marla Sucharetza *(Angie)*; Nikki Lee *(Dawna)*; Marjorie Lovett *(Stanford Woman)*; Michael Andolini *(Man Behind Gil)*; M.C. Gainey *(Man Behind Man)*; Michael Bofshever *(Little League Coach)*; Kirk Ward *(The Giant Mascot)*; Eric Bruskotter *(Catcher)*; Kirk D. Terry *(Umpire)*; Abraham Flores *(Umpire)*; Dennis Neil Henderson *(Umpire)*; Aaron Neville *(Opening Game Singer)*; Jerry Saslow; Michael P. Byrne; Bret Lewis; Roger Lodge; Ron Pitts *(Reporters)*; Stanley DeSantis *(Stoney)*; Jack Black *(Broadcast Technician)*; Thomas Duffy *(Figgy)*; Don Fischer *(Cop)*; Vernon Guichard II *(Cop)*; Kim Robillard *(Jefferson Sporting Goods Clerk)*; Keith Leon Williams *(Stadium Offical)*; Chante Moore *(Primo Tribute Singer)*; Paul Herman *(Seedy Suit Guy)*; Robert Louis Kempf *(Baggage Attendant)*; Jesse Ibarra *(Padres Pitcher)*; Chris Fick *(Giants Left Fielder)*; Ben Hines *(Giants 1st Baseman)*; Rick Magnante *(Giants 3rd Base Coach)*; Carl Mergenthaler; Clayton Holt; Lennox Brown; Troy Cephers; Freeman White *(Bobby's Teammates)*; Bruce Hines *(Umpire—End Game)*; Adam Druxman *(Paparazzo)*; Kathy Stewart; Nikki Hart; Bo Daniels; Randal Salguero; Tracy Leanne Mandac *(Fans)*; Gregg Tome *(Detective Schmerg)*; Sonya Bertelson *(Waitress)*; Brian Freifield *(Art)*; Jennifer Stander *(Store Employee)*; Roy Conrad; Richard Riehle; Earl Billings; John Carroll Lynch; Tim Monsion; Ralph Bertelle; Norm Compton *(Shopkeepers)*

Slick, dark and stylish, THE FAN tells the not-uninteresting tale of a baseball fan's obsession with a star player. Unfortunately, what promises to be the film-noir thriller for the '90s strikes out with bases loaded.

Gil Renard (Robert De Niro), a sporting goods salesman, is "the fan." He has wildly supported Bobby Rayburn (Wesley Snipes), a celebrated centerfielder, since Rayburn's 1982 high-school championship game. At the beginning of the current season, Rayburn seems to have it all: he's a four-time League RBI player with a .310 lifetime batting average and a $40 million annual paycheck. As Rayburn returns to his home town to play for the San Francisco Giants, Renard excitedly greets his hero on a live radio call-in show, hosted by sports broadcaster Jewel Stern (Ellen Barkin).

Unfortunately, events take a downturn on opening day. Rayburn suffers an injury which handicaps him during subsequent games, and Renard, feeling obligated to attend the first match of the season, misses an appointment with an important client. Renard is soon fired from his job for his poor performance, while Rayburn's position as champ is routed by Juan Primo (Benicio Del Toro), a Giants rival.

Eventually, the unstable Renard becomes totally unhinged by his deteriorating relationship with his ex-wife and young son. As a way to "help" Rayburn during his career slump, Renard kills Juan Primo when Rayburn's cocky rival refuses his request to step aside as the new Giants star. Primo's death allows Rayburn to return to his old position, and he soon improves his game on the field. When Renard finally meets Rayburn, he is disappointed to find that his idol does not attribute his new success to Primo's death. As revenge for Rayburn's lack of gratitude, Renard kidnaps and threatens to kill Rayburn's son. Renard then gives Rayburn an ultimatum: he will return his child unharmed if he hits a home run during the next game. Rayburn fails to hit the homer, but, luckily, the police stop and kill the psychotic fan in time.

THE FAN should not be confused with the trashy but fun 1981 film of the same title, although the premise is similar. It's also like THE CABLE GUY (1996) without the jokes. The difference here is that director Tony Scott takes Phoef Sutton's screenplay (based on Peter Abraham's novel) all too seriously. The frequent use of slow motion, close-ups and somber music weighs down what could have been a tense, exciting movie. Scott's penchant for milking rain and smoke effects gives this thriller more atmosphere than thrills. A series of loud rock songs (mainly from the Rolling Stones), some not-so-subtle ad placements (like a Sony headphone in this Sony Pictures release), and several continuity errors also are distracting.

As usual, Robert De Niro makes his psychotic case study believable, but it's an act we're seen before—and better—in the unfairly neglected Scorsese film, THE KING OF COMEDY (1983). The best part of THE FAN comes late: when the doppelgangers, fan and star, finally meet. It's an edgy, humorous scene played out by two pros, but it stands alone. The other performers are well cast but not well used, including Ellen Barkin as the talk-radio host and John Leguizamo (Snipes's fellow transvestite traveler in TO WONG FOO, THANKS FOR EVERYTHING, JULIE NEWMAR) as Rayburn's fast-talking agent. (Interestingly, the film's "good-hearted" sexist rejoinders directed at Barkin's character contrast startlingly with the film's lack of mention of race as an issue.)

In an early scene in the film, Renard's boss tells his staff about the strategy of replacing cheap product with more of the same. Unintentionally, to be sure, this speech states the problem with Hollywood today and explains why this second-rate movie seems depressingly familiar. *(Violence, adult situations, extreme profanity.)* — E.M.

d, Tony Scott; p, Wendy Finerman; exec p, Bill Unger, James W. Skotchdopole, Barrie M. Osborne; assoc p, Greg Mooradian; co-p, Margaret French Isaac; w, Phoef Sutton (based on the novel by Peter Abrahams); ph, Dariusz Wolski; ed, Christian Wagner, Claire Simpson; m, Hans Zimmer; prod d, Ida Random; art d, Mayne Berke; set d, Claire Bowin; sound, Bill Kaplan (mixer); fx, Joe Ramsey; casting, Ellen Lewis; cos, Rita Ryack, Daniel Orlandi; makeup, Richard Snell, Kevin Yagher; stunts, Chuck Picerni Picerni, Steve Picerni

Thriller **(PR: C MPAA: R)**

FAR HARBOR ★½

(U.S.) 101m Castle Hill ~ Castle Hill c

Edward Atterton *(Frick)*; Jennifer Connelly *(Ellie)*; Dan Futterman *(Brad)*; Marcia Gay Harden *(Arabella)*; Andrew Lauren *(Trey)*; George Newbern *(Jordan)*; Tracee Ellis Ross *(Kiki)*; Jim True *(Ryland)*

FAR HARBOR is the story of a group of friends spending a weekend in the ritzy Long Island Hamptons coming to terms with their differences. Unfortunately, this pretentious romp focuses on characters who are more concerned with how things look and sound than how they feel. With no depth of character, this ensemble piece makes audiences feel nothing but bored—just like the people in FAR HARBOR.

Frick (Edward Atterton) is a pretentious London-born filmmaker who is attempting to get over his recent failures in Los Angeles. His ex-wife, Arabella (Marcia Gay Harden), is a high-powered Washington attorney. Her sister, Ellie (Jennifer Connelly), manages to cook four-star restaurant meals despite suffering from a mysterious ailment. Ellie's husband, Ry (Jim True), is the sensitive and well-to-do proprietor of a family business, who longs to live the life of a vineyard owner. Bradley (Dave Futterman), a yuppie doctor, brings his date, Kiki (Tracee Ellis Ross), a blunt hedonist, who feels perpetually left out of the loop. Jordan (George Newbern) is a quiet dairy farmer, while his boyfriend, Trey (Andrew Lauren), is a marriage-minded bisexual. In the middle of these folks's cozy cove is the one hundred and twenty foot yacht of David Spreckman, a powerful Hollywood filmmaker.

The boat assumes a great importance to all of the characters, especially Frick, who has given up all hope of commercial success as a filmmaker. Much to Frick's dismay, Ellie is writing a screenplay to take her mind off her mysterious problem, which we finally learn was brought on after her infant child fell out an open window and died. Although everyone offers Ellie sympathy, she believes that Frick is the only one who understands her. (It is possible that his marriage to Arabella failed, because Frick was in love with Ellie.) In a gesture of selflessness, Frick swims across the cove, with Ellie's script strapped to his body, to deliver her words to his nemesis, Spreckman. On the way, however, he injures himself and must be rushed to the hospital. Ellie responds by changing the title page of her screenplay, giving Frick authorship. The movie ends with her rowing to Mr. Spreckman's boat, presumably hand-delivering "Frick's" script to the movie mogul.

FAR HARBOR's indulgent metaphors and subject matter (a group of rich pals, one of them a Hollywood Player wannabe) would be enraging, if they weren't dully overshadowed by the bland glamour of Long Island's richest community. Nearly every shot mirrors a J. Crew catalogue or an Ikea commercial. About the only positive thing to say here is that first time writer-director John Huddles has snared some fine actors (Marcia Gay Harden is the best, with the least to do) as well as some controversial new faces: celebrity kids Tracee Ellis Ross (Diana's daughter) and Andrew Lauren (Ralph's heir) in their inauspicious big screen debuts. *(Adult situations.)* — J.D.

d, John Huddles; p, Gigi de Pourtales Davis; exec p, John Huddles, Gary Huddles, John Wolstenholme; assoc p, Colleen Hahn, Sarah Porter; co-p, Laura Barnett; w, John Huddles; ph, Tami Reiker; ed, Wilton Henderson, Margaret Guinee, Janice Keuhnelian; m, Christopher Tyng, Keola Beamer; prod d, Maggie Martin; art d, Don Marshall Maclean; set d, Susanna Bolton, Gail Bennett; sound, David Alverez (mixer); casting, Mikie Heilbrun, Lisa Essary; cos, Erin Folsey; makeup, Tracy Warbin

Drama **(PR: C MPAA: NR)**

FARGO ★★★½

(U.S.) 98m Working Title Films; PolyGram ~ Gramercy Pictures c

Frances McDormand *(Marge Gunderson)*; Steve Buscemi *(Carl Showalter)*; William H. Macy *(Jerry Lundegaard)*; Peter Stormare *(Gaear Grimsrud)*; Harve Presnell *(Wade Gustafson)*; John Carroll Lynch *(Norm Gunderson)*; Kristin Rudrud *(Jean Lundegaard)*; Tony Denman *(Scotty Lundegaard)*; Steve Park *(Mike Yanagita)*; Steven Reevis *(Shep Proudfoot)*; Warren Keith *(Reilly Diefenbach)*; Larry Brandenburg *(Stan Grossman)*; Bruce Bohne *(Lou)*; Cliff Rakerd *(Officer Olson)*; Jose Feliciano *(Himself)*; Bain Boehlke *(Mr. Mohra)*; Rose Stockton *(Valerie)*; Gary Houston *(Irate Customer)*; Sally Wingert *(Irate Customer's Wife)*; Kurt Schweickhardt *(Car Salesman)*; Larissa Kokernot *(Hooker #1)*; Melissa Peterman *(Hooker #2)*; Steve Edelman *(Morning Show Host)*; Sharon Anderson *(Morning Show Hostess)*; James Gaulke *(State Trooper)*; Michelle Suzanne Le Doux *(Victim in Car)*; Petra Boden *(Cashier)*; Wayne Evenson *(Customer)*; Jessica Shepherd *(Hotel Clerk)*; Peter Schmitz *(Airport Lot Attendant)*; Steve Shaefer *(Mechanic)*; Michelle Hutchinson *(Escort)*; David Lomax *(Man in Hallway)*; Don William Skahill *(Night Parking Attendant)*; Robert Ozasky *(Bismarck Cop #1)*; John Bandemer *(Bismarck Cop #2)*; Don Wescott *(Bark Beetle Narrator)*

Joel and Ethan Coen are born filmmakers, and FARGO, a well-made and involving character comedy, won them the Academy Award for Best Original Screenplay. Leading a fine cast, Frances McDormand won a Best Actress Oscar for her charming portrayal of a small-town sheriff.

Jerry Lundegaard (William H. Macy), the sales manager of a Minneapolis car dealership, hires two hoodlums, Carl Showalter (Steve Buscemi) and Gaear Grimsrud (Peter Stormare), to kidnap his wife, Jean (Kristin Rudrud). The deal: Jerry and the hoods are to split the $80,000 that his rich father-in-law, Wade Gustafson (Harve Presnell), will be required to pay in ransom. After snatching Jean, the kidnappers kill a suspicious state trooper (James Gaulke) and two unlucky witnesses. They proceed to a hideout in the woods as Marge Gunderson (Frances McDormand), the very pregnant sheriff of the town in which the triple murder took place, launches an investigation.

Jerry tells his father-in-law that the kidnappers have demanded $1 million. Gustafson insists on delivering it himself. When he and Carl meet at a parking lot to make the exchange, Carl is alone. Gustafson refuses to turn over the ransom money until his daughter is returned to him. Carl shoots Gustafson and as the latter lies dying, he shoots Carl in the face. Later, Carl pulls over to the side of the road, opens Gustafson's suitcase, and is surprised to find $920,000 more than he expected. He buries the bonus money and returns to the hideout, where he discovers that his partner has killed Jean. After Carl gives Gaear his $40,000 share, the two men squabble and Gaear kills Carl. Jerry ends up hiding Gustafson's body. Later, he panics after being questioned by Marge and goes on the run.

Ultimately, while driving through the woods, Marge spots a car that fits the description of the murderers' vehicle and she pulls into the driveway, where she surprises Gaear disposing of Carl and Jean Lundegaard's bodies. When he makes a break for it, she shoots him in the leg and brings him in. Shortly thereafter, Jerry is traced to a motel outside Bismarck, North Dakota, and then arrested.

Hardly a week passes without some hot new director being compared to Hitchcock, but the Coen brothers are the genuine article. The most precociously gifted filmmakers since Stanley Kubrick, they easily outweigh Kubrick and indeed Hitchcock, two first-rate minds, in the heart-and-soul department. The Coens are often accused of being cold-blooded. Perhaps it is their formal rigor and strong streak of sly, satirical wit that some viewers mistake for heartlessness, for their best work consistently resonates with feeling.

Ostensibly inspired by crimes committed in 1987, and offering the story of an unconventional sheriff in pursuit of a group of criminal foul-ups, FARGO would be a major accomplishment from virtually any other filmmaker. The Coens can and have done better, however. Yet, with style and humor to spare, the film remains an assured and amusing combination of crime caper and small-town slice-of-life.

The average filmmaker approaches regional material by instructing his players to drop their "g"s and leaving it at that. Native Minnesotans, the Coens are thoroughly familiar with the speech and behavior patterns of northern Midwesterners, and they have applied this know-how throughout FARGO—perhaps over-applied it: at moments, utterances of "yah" and "jeez" nearly swamp the performances. Nonetheless, this kind of regional sophistication, rare in the American cinema, is always very welcome.

Within a good cast are several standout players. Steve Buscemi is outstanding as a frustrated loser whom two independent witnesses, a prostitute and a bartender, are capable of recalling only as a "little guy. . . kind of funny-looking." William H. Macy, an actor who looks like he procured his face from a '50s family comic strip, is immediately sympathetic, almost too much so for the selfish weakling he plays here. Macy is a performer capable of effortlessly winning the kind of audience empathy and identification Jack Lemmon regularly sweats bullets to extract. In her early scenes, Kristin Rudrud's regionally dead-on portrayal of Jerry's nervous, well-meaning wife is so affecting that the compassion she elicits from the audience early on carries over into the post-kidnapping portion of the film, when her character is reduced to a whimpering, hooded figure. Oscar winner Frances McDormand strikes just the right note as Marge Gunderson. Though no Sherlock Holmes, Marge is a competent police officer as well as a thoroughly decent (if somewhat dull and naive) individual.

If FARGO leaves its viewers with anything conclusive, it's a suspicion that were all police chiefs women, the world might be a better place to live in. *(Graphic violence, nudity, sexual situations, extreme profanity.)* — D.T.

d, Joel Coen; p, Ethan Coen; exec p, Tim Bevan, Eric Fellner; w, Ethan Coen, Joel Coen; ph, Roger Deakins; ed, Roderick Jaynes; m, Carter Burwell; prod d, Rick Heinrichs; art d, Thomas P. Wilkins; set d, Lauri Gaffin; sound, Allan Byer (mixer); fx, Paul Murphy; casting, John Lyons; cos, Mary Zophres; makeup, John Blake; stunts, Jery Hewitt

AA Best Actress: Frances McDormand; *AA Best Original Screenplay:* Ethan Coen, Joel Coen; *AAN Best Picture; AAN Best Supporting Actor:* William H. Macy; *AAN Best Director:* Joel Coen; *AAN Best Cinematography:* Roger Deakins; *AAN Best Film Editing:* Roderick Jaynes

Crime/Drama/Comedy (PR: C MPAA: R)

FAST MONEY ★★★

(U.S.) 93m Stu Segall Productions ~ Orion c

Yancy Butler *(Francesca Marsh)*; Matt McCoy *(Jack Martin)*; Merritt Yohnka *(Brad)*; Clement Blake *(Joey)*; Andy Romano *(Bob)*; Buck Flower *(Window Washer)*; Naomi *(Gate Attendant)*; Roy Werner *(Supervisor)*; John Ashton *(Lt. Diego)*; Ron Johnson *(Agent Vargas)*; Trevor Goddard *(Regy)*; Jacob Witkin *(Sir Stewart)*; Al Lewis *(Poon)*; Lloyd Wessof *(Agent Johnson)*; Russell Solberg *(Agent Marsh)*; Ruta Aras *(Sheriff)*; Lisa Moore *(Isabel)*; Carole Cook *(Ester)*; Daniel Edward Mora *(Ernesto)*; Patrika Darbo *(Teebou)*

FAST MONEY, an unexpected diamond in the rough, occasionally floors its accelerator pedal to the max. At its best, it is a wind-in-your-hair highway ride, equal parts outlaw saga and white-collar liberation yarn; IT HAPPENED ONE NIGHT (1934) meets SOMETHING WILD (1986).

Having caused a major cop-car pileup, luxury-car-thief Francesca Marsh (Yancy Butler) latches onto journalist Jack (Matt McCoy), who is on his way to cover a karaoke convention.

Desiring a change of wheels, amoral Francesca "borrows" a flashy red sportscar—not realizing the stolen vehicle's trunk contains counterfeit plates and $2.7 million in cash. These ill-gotten gains belong to British crime king Sir Stewart (Jacob Witkin), and he orders his triggerman Regy (Trevor Goddard) to team up with bad cop Lt. Diego (John Ashton) to retrieve the goods and eliminate Francesca.

Adept at outsmarting the pitbullish Diego, Francesca wheedles Jack into further cooperation by pointing out the headline potential of their predicament. Entrapped by corrupt Feds on Stewart's payroll, Jack turns over the counterfeit plates, but streetwise Francesca rubs out the crooked officials before they can eliminate Jack.

Fleeing warrants for robbery and murder, the erstwhile Bonnie and Clyde flummox their trackers until Regy and Lt. Diego finally corner them at a roadside tavern. Increasingly rattled, Regy guns down a barmaid to show Jack and Francesca that he means business.

Francesca and Jack escape once more, lie low at the apartment of Jack's mom, and await passports arranged by Jack's newspaper editor. After these travel plans are cancelled by the murders of the editor and his companion, Regy and Diego chase the fugitives to the Mexican border.

Jack and Francesca stow away on an ice cream truck after Jack is wounded, hitch another ride, and attempt to cross the border on foot. Dropping the loot as Regy circles above in a copter, Jack uses Diego as a shield and shoots Regy right out of his whirlybird. Without money, Jack and Francesca cross the border.

Despite some misfires, FAST MONEY is fast-paced fun invigorated by the personality-plus Butler, who strikes sparks in the usually bland McCoy. Butler has enough cover-girl sensuality and sharp timing to rev up the engines of any direct-to-video movie. In FAST MONEY, a sort of thumbnail sketch for a slicker Hollywood blockbuster, Butler distracts viewers from massive doses of improbability.

The most serious hiccup in this madcap game of highway tag is that slaughter of the innocent barmaid. Although intended to underscore Regy's deadly volatility, the senseless act puts a heavy burden on a light entertainment. Overlooking that sharp swerve into Demme-land, action buffs and romantics can both enjoy this seduction of a contemporary Mr. Deeds by a service-road Lorelei. Car theft as an aphrodisiac is a new spin on the Hollywood dictum that crime can be rewarding but dangerous. *(Graphic violence, extreme profanity.)* — R.P.

d, Alexander Wright; p, Vince Ravine; exec p, Stu Segall, Martin W. Greenwald; co-p, Don Edmonds, Russell Solberg; w, Alexander Wright; ph, Thomas Jewett; ed, Ron Cabreros; m, Tony Riparetti; art d, Mark Zabonik; set d, Alison Howard; sound, Jon Ailetcher (mixer); fx, Kevin McCarthy; casting, Dorian Dunas; cos, Mari Helgenson; makeup, Joy Tilk; stunts, Russell Solberg

Action/Crime **(PR: C MPAA: R)**

FATALLY YOURS ★★

(U.S.) 90m Quantumquest Films ~ Monarch Home Video c

Rick Rossovich *(Danny/Jon)*; Sage Stallone *(Palermo's Son)*; Roddy McDowall *(Pauly)*; George Lazenby *(Grandinetti)*; Sarah MacDonnell *(Sara)*; Robert Gentili *(Sammy)*; Annie Fitzgerald *(Patricia)*; John Capodice *(Vince)*; Steven Langa *(Kip)*; Robbi Chong *(Bobbi)*; Ralph Monaco *(Mr. Palermo)*; Voyo Goric *(Leo)*; Joseph Pilato *(Francis)*; Al D'Andrea *(Peter)*; Chris Fiore *(Michael)*; James Walsh *(Auctioneer)*; John Hammill *(Chuck)*; Jack Jozefson *(Palermo Gangster)*; Judy Landon *(Chancy)*; Adam Dreschler *(Pizza Man)*; Lisa McCullough *(Roberta)*; Honey Lauren *(Flapper)*; Guerin Barry *(Louie)*; Patty Negri *(Party Girl)*; Mark Delassanoro *(Palermo Thug)*; Katherine Mariah *(Baby Sara)*

The fanciful FATALLY YOURS deserves credit for attempting something different: a gangland reincarnation thriller. But the writing isn't precise enough to balance the past and present, and the directing fails to stylize the time polarities—not to mention the multiple characters struggling within them.

In the the 1920s, Mafia princess Sara (Sarah MacDonnell) and her mob accountant hubby, Jon (Rick Rossovich), are attacked during a massacre aimed at her mobster father, Grandinetti (George Lazenby). Jon is mortally wounded, but, before he dies, an enemy gangster (Sage Stallone), son of rival gangleader Palermo (Ralph Monaco), threatens the accountant to get him to reveal the whereabouts of a cache of jewels. In turn, Palermo's son is killed by Sara's dying father.

In the 1990s, real estate agent Danny (Rick Rossovich) finds himself mysteriously drawn to a dilapidated property. Encouraged by his financial advisor, Kip (Steven Langa), Danny buys the property at a price so high that it jeopardizes the life of his father-in-law/business partner, Pauly (Roddy McDowall), whose gambling debts have depleted company resources. Ignoring Pauly's desperate insistence that he unload the white elephant quickly, Danny moves into the decaying property with his wife, Patricia (Annie Fitzgerald), and returns to working on a crime novel he hasn't touched in years. A principal figure in his novel, Sara Grandinetti, reaches out to Danny (who turns out to be the reincarnation of Jon); Sara the Ghost advises Danny on how to protect her granddaughter (Danny's wife) from Pauly's creditors who might harm Patricia to pay back her welshing father.

In the haunted house, Pauly's loanshark Sammy (Robert Gentili) finally intrudes to grab the long-buried gems, which he then refuses to relinquish to his boss, traitorous Kip (the reincarnation of Palermo's cutthroat son). The 1920s slaughter replays with new faces, as Sammy shoots Pauly and Kip, who manages to murder Sammy before expiring. Cleansed of the past, Danny publishes his book, and Sara's ghost rests in peace.

FATALLY YOURS, in attempting to dole out key clues during the unraveling of the present-day saga, makes two miscalculations: the 1920s flashbacks are too repetitive and foolishly linger on surface details, and the 1990s story line isn't invested with enough inherent thrills for a scenario dipping into real estate fraud and a string of thwarted, cover-up homicides. Also, the supernatural proceedings are both time-consuming and silly, as the much-too-sexy ghost of Grandma Sara invades Danny's sweaty dreams.

Even more devastating to plausibility is Danny's frozen attachment to his word processor. This would-be hero becomes a passive observer, who annoys his wife (and the audience) with his spooked stasis. Considerable reworking might have enabled this misfire to jazz up the neo-GODFATHER cycle, but it lacks the creative control to recycle decades-old terror as it reverberates with present-day paranoia. *(Graphic violence, extreme profanity, extensive nudity, adult situations.)* — R.P.

d, Tim Everitt; exec p, Jonathan Parker, Bruce Ditchfield; co-p, Darin McDaniel; w, Darin McDaniel; ph, Tim Everitt; ed, Tim Everitt; m, Scott Greer; art d, Jennifer McDaniel; set d, Melanie Sharp; sound, Robert Larrea (mixer); fx, Tassilo Baur; makeup, Valerie Joslin; stunts, Mark Werner

Mystery/Action/Crime **(PR: C MPAA: NR)**

FATE ★★★★

(Germany) 80m German Film and Television Academy; Deutsche Film und Fernsehnakademie Berlin ~ Goethe House New York/Anthology Film Archives c

Sanja Spengler *(Luba)*; Valerij Fedorenko *(Valera)*

In his feature film debut, FATE, director Fred Kelemen creates a challenging work that captures the despair of displaced immigrants in modern-day Germany. Kelemen's strong imagery and experimental style turn an elemental story into a provocative chronicle.

Valera (Valerij Fedorenko), a Russian musician, plays for his supper in a grimy subway station. A middle-class German man listens to the music for a while, then invites Valera back to his apartment to play for him.

During Valera's performance, the man grows increasingly hostile, insisting that Valera play only lighthearted polkas. Valera finally tries to leave, but the man refuses to pay him unless he drinks an entire bottle of vodka. Valera gulps down the liquor, takes the money, and then jumps into a nearby city fountain where he cries out in psychic pain.

Later, Valera walks into a bar, where he wins some money in a pool match. The other players get angry when Valera takes the money and leaves. Valera next visits his girlfriend, Luba (Sanja Spengler), a prostitute, but he is angered to discover her with a client. In a rage, Valera shoots the man dead. Valera flees, while Luba goes into shock.

Later, only half-dressed, Luba runs down her street, tripping in the rubble. When she gets up, she goes to a bar, where she is given drinks by the waitresses. After flirting and dancing with the men in the bar, Luba stumbles again, but, instead of helping her, the patrons of the bar rape her.

The next morning, Luba finds herself in a forest. She staggers through the woods until she reaches a landfill, where she hears Valera playing his accordion. The two are reunited, and are both nearly run over by a tractor. They emerge unscathed and go off together.

In the course of 80 very weighty minutes, FATE observes the lives of two Russian outcasts—a homeless street musician and his prostitute girlfriend—in searing, unblinking fashion. The other characters who appear are mostly native Germans who use and abuse the outsiders (as they also use and abuse themselves) in ways that symbolize a breakdown of all forms of social decency. (Thematically, FATE brings to mind 1995's similar LA RONDE-inspired films, KIDS and ECLIPSE, as well as the work of Jean Genet.)

What makes FATE more than a series of indulgently depressing vignettes is how the director depicts the existential angst. In 1994, Kelemen transferred his video production to grainy 16mm film stock, giving an already dark piece an appearance that recalls early German Expressionism. The crude look fittingly mirrors the souls of the characters.

One of many remarkable and haunting minute-long takes in the piece occurs as Valera—after being humiliated in the polka lover's apartment—cries out in the fountain, his black silhouette flanked by the water and lights. When the scene fades to black, his cry becomes muffled.

Elsewhere, Kelemen's use of hand-held cinema verite camerawork allays the stylization and creates many seemingly—and shockingly—authentic moments, including Luba's gang rape in the bar.

Some of FATE's images are difficult, even unpleasant, to watch, and the symbolism of the last shot is overemphatic, given what has come before. But all of FATE fits neatly into the canon of bitterly ironic work from Fassbinder, Herzog, and Wenders, the first masters of the New German Cinema. *(Graphic violence, nudity, sexual situations, adult situations, extreme profanity.)* — E.M.

d, Fred Kelemen; exec p, Christian Hohoff; co-p, Fred Kelemen; w, Fred Kelemen; ph, Fred Kelemen; ed, Fred Kelemen; prod d, Fred Kelemen; sound, Alejandra Carmona, Regina Krah; cos, Fred Kelemen

Drama **(PR: O MPAA: NR)**

FEAR ★★½

(U.S.) 95m Imagine Entertainment ~ Universal c

Mark Wahlberg *(David McCall)*; Reese Witherspoon *(Nicole Walker)*; William Petersen *(Steve Walker)*; Amy Brenneman *(Laura Walker)*; Alyssa Milano *(Margo Masse)*; Christopher Gray *(Toby)*; Tracy Fraim *(Logan)*; Gary John Riley *(Hacker)*; Jason Kristofer *(Terry)*; Jed Rees *(Knobby)*; Todd Caldecott *(Gary Rohmer)*; John Oliver *(Eddie Clark)*; David Fredericks *(Larry O'Brien)*; Ravinder Toor *(Counterman)*; Andrew Airlie *(Alex McDowell)*; Jo Bates *(Julie Masse)*; Will Sengotta *(Kid at Door)*; Harvey Gold *(Peterman)*

Despite a good cast and solid direction, FEAR won't raise a goosebump thanks to its "been there, done that" script which could be described in a Hollywood pitch as, "CAPE FEAR meets FATAL ATTRACTION for the CLUELESS set."

Bursting with teenage rebellion, 16-year-old Nicole Walker (Reese Witherspoon) goes to a "rave" with her wild friend Margo (Alyssa Milano). When violence erupts, Nicole is protected by David McCall (Mark Wahlberg), an older, hunky ne'er-do-well, with whom she quickly falls in love. Nicole brings David home to meet the family while he ingratiates himself, Eddie Haskell style, with her step-mother Laura (Amy Brenneman), he doesn't fool her father Steve (William Petersen). Daddy doesn't approve of David at all, which only makes Nicole want him more. Jealousy eventually drives David to reveal his true, crazy, violent nature, and Nicole decides to break it off; but when her father gives her an ultimatum to stop seeing David, it only serves to send her back into his muscular arms. Soon after, Nicole discovers David is having sex with Margo and finally tells him to get lost. But he won't be put off so easily. Psychopath David rounds up some of his murderous friends and they lay siege to the Walker home. Fortunately, architect Steve had designed the house with repelling an armed assault in mind, and after a protracted battle, David is killed.

FEAR starts out on fertile, interesting ground: a father and daughter, their relationship strained by divorce, her burgeoning sexuality making him nervous and possessive (and perhaps more); and a new boyfriend maliciously intent on displacing the father. Conflict, passion, threats—they are all there, but unfortunately FEAR doesn't do anything with them.

Witherspoon (THE MAN ON THE MOON) is perfectly cast with her innocent, blue eyes and baby doll face. As her father, Petersen (MANHUNTER) is talented enough to suggest complexities for his character that probably weren't on the page. Wahlberg (formerly known as rap artist Marky Mark) wears the combined image of lost puppy and fast-talking lothario like an old pair of the Calvin Klein briefs he once hawked. But just when Christopher Crowe's script should be adding plot complications and thematic layers, it takes a bad, sharp turn. (Watching the movie, you'll feel like a backup singer in a 1960s girl group—that is, the Leader of the Pack is skidding out of control, and all you can do is scream, "Look out! Look out! Look out!! Look out!!!") David suddenly turns into Travis Bickle, Nicole and Steve lose all credible dimension, and the overly violent third act fails to excite or thrill. Too bad—such a turn of events force us to file FEAR on the video shelf next to other teen-psycho misfires like POISON IVY and THE CRUSH. *(Violence, sexual situations, profanity.)* — P.R.

d, James Foley; p, Brian Grazer, Ric Kidney; exec p, Karen Kehela; assoc p, Karen Snow; w, Christopher Crowe; ph, Thomas Kloss; ed, David Brenner; m, Carter Burwell; prod d, Alex McDowell; art d, Richard Hudolin; set d, D. Fauquet-Lemaitre; sound, Eric J. Batut (mixer); fx, Tim Storvick, Peter Montgomery, Carolyn Soper, Buena Vista Visual Effects; casting, Debra Zane; cos, Kirsten Everberg; makeup, Victoria Down; stunts, Charles Andre

Thriller **(PR: O MPAA: R)**

FEELING MINNESOTA ★★

(U.S.) 95m Jersey Films ~ Fine Line c

Keanu Reeves *(Jjaks)*; Vincent D'Onofrio *(Sam)*; Cameron Diaz *(Freddie)*; Delroy Lindo *(Red)*; Courtney Love *(Waitress)*; Tuesday Weld *(Nora)*; Dan Aykroyd *(Ben)*; Levon Helm *(Bible Salesman)*

Highly unlikely to help the tourist industry of Minnesota, this grungy black comedy about hopeless losers trying to break out of their lifeless environment wastes an excellent cast in the service of a script that knows only what it doesn't want to do—not what it does.

At the urging of his mother (Tuesday Weld), petty thief Jjaks (Keanu Reeves) returns to his Minnesota home. The occasion is the wedding of his hated brother, Sam (Vincent D'Onofrio), to Freddie (Cameron Diaz), a B-girl at the sleazy club where Sam works as an accountant. Freddie has been forced into the marriage as punishment for embezzling from their boss, small-time mobster Red (Delroy Lindo).

At the backyard wedding reception, Freddie is instantly attracted to her new brother-in-law and lures him to an empty bathroom to consummate their flirtation. Jjaks and Sam fight, causing their mother to die of a heart attack.

Freddie persuades Jjaks to rob Sam and set off with her to Las Vegas. (Sam is the real embezzler; in love with Freddie, he reported her "crime" to Red in order to get her for his own.) They hit the road, but Sam tracks them down and shoots Freddie in a motel room while Jjaks is away. Jjaks returns to the room and passes out before noticing Freddie's body. When he comes to, he is convinced that he must have killed Freddie during a blackout, and disposes of her body in a field. Jjaks eventually discovers that Freddie is alive and in hiding, having faked her death in order to get away with the money. After settling the score with Sam, he hitchhikes to Las Vegas, where Freddie, now working as a dancer, welcomes him.

An end credit notes that FEELING MINNESOTA was "Developed at the Sundance Institute." If this is the developed version, we'd hate to see the rough draft. First-time writer-director Steven Baigelman obviously wanted to make a film free of Hollywood gloss, which explains the participation of producer Danny DeVito and his Jersey Films partners. Baigelman deserves credit for seeking and capturing the grimy ambiance of a small industrial city without giving the impression that he's holding his nose while doing so. The film never gets better than the wedding scene that opens it, where the band looks like slumming longshoremen and the groom can't stop adjusting his rented tux. Next to this, Las Vegas certainly looks like the land of milk and honey.

But having achieved a setting, Baigelman doesn't seem to know what to put in it. (Nor does he seem to know where to aim the camera most of the time, especially when he needs to punctuate a visual joke.) You can neither laugh at the characters nor feel anything for them. Jjaks (the odd name is the result of a misspelling on his birth certificate) is too passive to carry the film, yet Baigelman stops short of making him that standard noir victim, the man led to his destruction by a scheming woman. As far as the scheming woman part goes, Freddie seems to be improvising her actions; the plot element of having everyone think she's dead makes no sense whatsoever. And Sam is overplayed by the normally excellent Vincent D'Onofrio with a fatal lack of direction; is he supposed to be evil, stupid, mentally deficient, what? There are nice bits from the supporting cast, notably Delroy Lindo and Tuesday Weld; on the other hand, Courtney Love, Levon Helm, and Max Perlich are all wasted in cameo appearances. While FEELING MINNESOTA does have an excellent song score, it oddly omits the Soundgarden song "Outshine" that contributed the film's title. *(Violence, nudity, sexual situations, substance abuse, profanity.)* — M.F.

d, Steven Baigelman; p, Stacey Sher, Danny DeVito, Michael Shamberg; exec p, Erwin Stoff; co-p, Erin McLeod; w, Steven Baigelman; ph, Walt Lloyd; ed, Martin Walsh; prod d, Naomi Shohan; art d, Philip Messina; set d, Yvette Siegel; sound, Steve Nelson (mixer); casting, Francine Maisier; cos, Eugenie Bafaloukos

Crime/Comedy/Drama **(PR: O MPAA: R)**

FELONY ★

(U.S.) 93m Southern Star Studios ~ New Line Home Video c

Jeffrey Combs *(Bill Knight)*; Ashley Laurence *(Laura Bryant)*; Leo Rossi *(Kincade)*; Lance Henriksen *(Taft)*; Joe Don Baker *(Donovan)*; David Warner *(Cooper)*; Charles Napier *(Duke)*; Pat Gallagher *(Robby)*; Cory Everson *(Sondra)*; Red West *(Police Chief Edwards)*; John West *(Sgt. Monroe)*; Fred Lewis *(Lt. Hackett)*; Deke Anderson *(Dennis)*; Dave Scott *(The Transient)*

FELONY has gunplay and explosions, an obligatory strip club scene, and the mug of a you-know-his-face-but-not-his-name star (Lance Henriksen) on the box—all the markings of generic, direct-to-video, action fare.

After a dozen officers are gunned down in a drug raid that turned out to be an ambush, Bill Knight (Jeffrey Combs), the thrill-seeking cameraman of a "Cops"-style TV show, makes off with the videotape identifying the killers. A shoot-out, a chase, and a leap from a bridge later, Knight learns the killers are part of a renegade CIA unit selling drugs to fund covert operations. CIA villain Taft (Lance Henriksen) wants him dead and police detective Kincade (Leo Rossi) wants him in jail. There is also a mysterious Fed, Donovan (Joe Don Baker), with a secret agenda.

Not knowing what else to do, Knight heads for the soft arms of a beautiful nurse, Laura Bryant (Ashley Laurence). Unfortunately, it turns out she's working for Taft. More shooting, more chasing, and more leaping ensue. Knight arranges to sell the videotape to Taft, but it's really a trap to put the villain into the hands of the law. When it's all said and done, and Knight goes off with the forgiven Laura, Donovan learns that the resourceful lens-jockey is really a secret agent, too.

Writer-director David A. Prior's story of cops and double-crossing robbers exists in a world of plot implausibilities big enough to choke the average moviegoer. But that probably won't bother the juvenile mentality this escapist movie is intended to entertain. (Neither will the misogyny of the strip scene.) They might notice, however, that all the vehicles being crashed, shot, and blown up in this low-production-value effort are junkyard reclamations.

Prior keeps FELONY moving well for 90 minutes; it's just too bad he couldn't have slowed down to inject some atmosphere. The movie is set in New Orleans, but no one would ever guess it. Prior also should have elicited some acting from his cast, but perhaps it's just as well that he didn't bother. Very likely no effort would have overcome the handicap of lead Jeffrey Combs, a B-horror flick vet, who plays his scenes with all the dramatic urgency of a prop comic. *(Graphic violence, nudity, profanity.)* — P.R.

d, David A. Prior; p, Robert Willoughby, Ted Prior; exec p, Patrick F. Gallagher; w, David A. Prior; ph, Don E. Fauntleroy; ed, Tony Malanowski; m, Jan A. P. Kaczmarek; casting, Billy DaMota

Action/Thriller **(PR: C MPAA: R)**

FEMALIEN ★

(U.S.) 89m Surrender Cinema ~ Amazing Fantasy Entertainment c

Venesa Talor *(Kara)*; Jacqueline Lovell; Matt Shue; Kurt Schwoeble; Taylore St. Clair *(Gina/Meditation Woman)*; Michelle Barry *(Girl Cop/Theater Woman)*; Juan Carlos de Vasquez *(Frank)*; Kathleen Mozzatta *(Jean)*; Carlos San Miguel *(Harry)*; Holly Cat *(Celeste)*; Everett J. Rodd *(Paul)*; Leigh Matchett *(Debra)*; Bobbie Marie *(Girl Toy/Meditation Woman)*; Rob Lee *(Boy Cop)*; Summer Leigh *(Wheel Girl)*; Stu Gotz *(Dak)*; Stevi Conrad *(Angel)*; Roxanne Miller *(Rub Down Attendant)*; Stephanie Hudson *(Danielle)*; Skylar Nicholson *(Theater Woman/Meditation Woman)*; Bobby Young *(Theater Man/Meditation Man)*; Bobby Johnson *(Theater Man/Meditation Man)*; Adam Wilde *(Theater Man/Meditation Man)*

FEMALIEN dispenses with concern over plot, characters and dialogue to concentrate on function (bodily function, that is), offering more nudity and sex montages than two typical erotic videos combined.

Kara (Venesa Talor), a "collector" from another planet, has been sent to Earth to gather information about primitive sexual behavior. To aid her mission, Kara's been given a suitably gorgeous body and the power to arouse uncontrollable sexual desire in humans. First, she concentrates on observation. She watches a businessman have sex with his sunbathing wife, a male model and a female model "getting busy" at a shoot, two sexy saleswomen in a tryst at a lingerie shop, and a lesbian-themed performance art piece.

After meeting Sun, the hippie-chick owner of a diner, and Drew, a hunky cook, Kara decides to proceed with interaction. She and Drew make passionate love, and he reveals that Sun has lost the diner's deed to a lecherous massage parlor mogul. Kara uses her special powers to get the deed for Sun, but she doesn't want it; Sun's ready for some adventure in her life. Kara suggests sex with a femalien, and Sun eagerly agrees. In the end, Kara decides to continue her mission as part of a *menage a trois* with Sun and Drew.

If it had some fire and explosions (and better music), FEMALIEN would certainly be "the greatest movie ever made," according to Beavis and Butt-head, as it is wall-to-wall buxom babes, and sex montages. With its unusually high quotient of graphic, female nudity, shots of women fondling themselves, and scenes of lesbian sexual encounters, FEMALIEN makes no bones about being visual stimulation for autoerotic manipulation. And so, though it barely deserves description as narrative film, it does deserve some credit for being exactly what it needs to be, and nothing else. *(Extensive nudity, sexual situations.)* — P.R.

d, Sybil Richards; exec p, Pat Siciliano; w, Sybil Richards (based on a story by Randy Fontana); ph, Allen Smitty; ed, Barry Byrne; m, Ollie Wood; prod d, Karissa Chambers; sound, John Halaby, Douglas Salkin; cos, Roxanne Miller; makeup, Shutchai "Tym" Buacharern

Erotic/Science Fiction **(PR: O MPAA: R)**

FIDDLEFEST: ROBERTA GUASPARI-TZAVARAS AND HER EAST HARLEM VIOLIN PROGRAM

(SEE: SMALL WONDERS)

FINAL CUT, THE ★★½

(U.S.) 92m Keystone Entertainment ~ Republic Pictures Home Video c

Sam Elliott *(John Pierce)*; Amanda Plummer *(Rochstein)*; Charles Martin Smith *(Capt. Weldon Mamet)*; Matt Craven *(Lloyd)*; Anne Ramsay *(Sgt. Kathleen Hardy)*; George Touliatos *(Schulmann)*; Campbell Lane *(Kulkonne)*; Lisa Langlois *(Sara)*; Ray Baker *(Col. Forsythe)*; Lloyd Berry *(Loscalzo)*; Philip Granger *(Barron)*; Frank Cassini *(Bartender)*; Suki Kaiser *(Kate Amis)*; Akiko Morison *(Woman in Labor)*; Pamela Perry *(Nurse)*; Erich Anderson *(Talberg)*; John Hannah *(Gilmore)*; Mark High *(Anchorman)*; Mark Simms *(Franklin Dunn)*; Kelly Benson *(Dead Body)*; Rachel Hayward *(Barmaid)*; Brad Loree *(SWAT Cop)*; Jed Rees *(Morrisey)*; Greg Rogers *(Doctor)*; Jill Teed *(Daniels)*; Owen Walstrom *(Security Guard No. 2)*; Jude Zachary *(Jonathan Callowman)*; Mike Crestjo *(Driver)*; Weston MacMillian *(Police Officer)*; Tim O'Hallaran *(Security Guard No. 1)*; Patricia Schill *(Ticket Taker)*; Nelson K. Skalbania *(Mayo)*; Barbara Tyson *(Wailer)*

Can't get your hands on SPEED, BLOWN AWAY, DIE HARD 3, SUDDEN DEATH, and EXECUTIVE DECISION? Try THE FINAL CUT, an unimaginative amalgam from the director of 1994's NOSTRADAMUS.

The Seattle area is being peppered with expertly constructed bombs that continue to foil—and kill—the city's bomb squads. Desperate, police captain Mamet (Charles Martin Smith) calls in the FBI, led by one Colonel Forsythe (Ray Baker), while bomb squad sergeant Kathleen Hardy (Anne Ramsay) coaxes former bomb squad head John Pierce (Sam Elliott) out of retirement.

As the explosions keep coming, the FBI creates a profile of the people who possess the kind of expertise required to build such intricate bombs, as well as having access to materials. The name that keeps popping up is John Pierce. Smelling a frame-up, Pierce hides from the cops, while determining the real bomber is none other than Colonel Forsythe, a former Navy Seal instructor who has for years been left in the shadows while his students go on to get all the glory.

The inevitable confrontation comes in an office building's sub-basement, where the psychotic Forsythe has wired a living woman into a nefarious device called "the Human Bomb." With precious seconds slipping away, Pierce quickly kills Forsythe before helping Hardy disarm the Human Bomb.

Watching THE FINAL CUT is likely to prompt an overpowering sense of deja vu. Almost every element of the film has been borrowed from other movies. The notion of a bomb-crazy terrorist is to '90s movies as crashing airplanes and flaming buildings are to '70s movies. That's fine when it is done well, as in SPEED (1994) and EXECUTIVE DECISION (1996). But THE FINAL CUT steals the most trite elements from the most mediocre of the genre—from the sweaty, ticking-clock defusing scenes right down to the inevitable slow-motion explosion. Furthermore, THE FINAL CUT even steals from itself; the four scenes in which the police attempt to disarm bombs are nearly identical, including the bombs themselves.

Contributing to the film's wearying familiarity are Elliott and Smith, who each turn in the exact same performance we've seen them do a hundred times before. Ramsay is passable as the tough-but-vulnerable bomb squad computer guru, but is not good enough to make the audience forget her character in the TV sitcom "Mad about You." Viewers in need of a bomb fix would be better served by another viewing of SPEED. *(Violence, sexual situations, profanity.)* — B.T.

d, Roger Christian; p, Robert Vince, William Vince; exec p, Michael Strong III; assoc p, Kelsey T. Howard; w, Raul Inglis (based on a story by Crash Leyland); ph, Mike Southon; ed, Robin Russell; m, Ross Vanelli; prod d, John Dondertman; fx, Andrew Chamberlayne; casting, Leah Mallen, Audrey Skalbania; cos, Druh Ireland; makeup, Lisa Love; stunts, Scott J. Ateah

Action/Thriller **(PR: C MPAA: R)**

FINAL EQUINOX, THE ★
(U.S.) 93m Triad Studios ~ Monarch Home Video c

Joe Lara *(Lugar)*; Tina May Simpson *(Sandra)*; Gary Kasper *(Alon)*; Martin Kove *(Torman)*; Wolf Muser *(Commander Dreg)*; Ron Robbins *(Fremont)*; Rowdy Jackson *(Neil)*; Robin Joi Brown *(Piper)*; Vincent Klyn *(Lex)*; David Warner *(Shilow)*; Bruce Mercury *(Torman's Man No. 1)*

Combining crime drama with sci-fi, this direct-to-video pulls out all the stops for its fanciful climax, but prior to that bears the stamp of a filmmaker ordered to print only first takes.

In the near future, government agent Lugar (Joe Lara) tackles a perilous assignment. Someone has stolen a Peruvian artifact in great demand by the underworld, scientific circles, and worldwide military power structures. Of extra-terrestrial origin, the device, if opened, will turn all human life into vegetation. The thief is master criminal Torman (Martin Kove). Lugar breaks into Torman's operation via a brain-implanted tracking device that throws Torman's men off guard. Lugar is captured, manhandled, and dumped by the Torman gang and betrayed by his own employers. He gets a crash course in the outer space bomb's intricacies from quantum physicist Shilow (David Warner).

Caught in the middle of a free-for-all in which Shilow is shot and sent rolling down a hill with the alien contraption, Lugar finishes off Torman and his men and escapes by helicopter from the activated vegetator. Fortuitously, alien spaceships land on Earth in time to stop the greening effect.

Despite an outrageous climax that threatens to turn Earth into a literal garden party, this failed attempt at cross-pollination will satisfy neither crime nor sci-fi buffs. Actors sleepwalk or even crawl through their roles. Even when overlooking this thespian stupor, viewers are stuck with a taffy-pull of sticky plot resolutions, gummy dialogue, and rubbery direction. Slowly played scenes seem to be stretched beyond normal running times. Admittedly the slam-bang end-of-the-world conclusion with oceans and land masses overcome by plant life is nifty. With part of our planet saved, this "Miracle Grow" flick grinds to a halt on an upbeat image of a world with lots less people and lots more parks. *(Extreme profanity, extensive nudity, graphic violence, adult situations, substance abuse.)* — R.P.

d, Serge Rodnunsky; p, Dan Bates, Jimmy Lifton; exec p, Morton Salkind; assoc p, Rowdy Jackson; co-p, Serge Rodnunsky; w, Serge Rodnunsky; ph, Pierre Chemaly; ed, Miles Rodd; m, George Black; sound, Tom Weir (mixer), Art Wood (mixer), Jussi Tegelman (mixer); fx, Stargate Films Inc.; casting, Gerald Wolff; makeup, Joanne Fletcher; stunts, Gary Kasper

Science Fiction/Action **(PR: C MPAA: NR)**

FIRE ON THE MOUNTAIN ★★
(U.S.) 72m Gage & Gage Productions ~ First Run Features c

Fritz Benedict; Bill Bowerman; David Brower; Bill Hackett; Bob Lewis; John Hay; John Jay; Dev Jennings; Steve Knowlton; Morely Nelson; Robert Parker; Paul Petzoldt; Friedl Pfeifer; Peter Seibert

The US Army's 10th Mountain Division was the product and preserve of ski bums, refugee European sportsmen, wealthy amateurs, and mountaineers. Scripted and directed by Beth and George Gage, FIRE ON THE MOUNTAIN looks at the men who forged that new fighting unit, suffered high losses in WWII and went on to found the American ski industry. It has some intriguing wartime footage, yet fails to deliver a complete picture of the unit.

Charles Dole, creator of the National Ski Patrol, a volunteer rescue group, follows the success of Finnish ski troops against the Red Army and conveys his interest to high-up friends in Washington. A month before Pearl Harbor, America's first mountain regiment is activated. A number of famous European skiers, refugees from Austria and Norway, teach Americans the principles of modern skiing, but the US Army wants its troops trained in climbing and a host of other skills as well. The first snowmobiles, Vibram soles, mummy sleeping bags, and nylon climbing ropes are designed for, and tested by, the troops of the 10th Division.

As a result, they remain in training for a long time and do not see combat until the end of 1944, when shipped to Italy. The 10th Division, under General George Hays, is given the tough assignment of dislodging German alpine units entrenched in the Apennines. Their mountain-climbing skills are successfully stretched to the limit when they attack in mid-February 1945. Eventually, however, the division suffers high losses with a third of its number killed or wounded.

With war's end, many of the veterans return to the region around their old training base, Camp Hale, and help found such ski resorts as Aspen, Vail, and Snowmass. Another two veterans start the Nike shoe company, while a third pioneers the formation of the Sierra Club.

The film features some strikingly beautiful footage of snow-capped mountains and of troops in white camouflage suits skiing in formation. It also misuses some clips, suggesting that the Germans had to fight their way into Austria in 1938.

Filmmakers bring poignancy to the story with present-day interviews with veterans who remember the loss of comrades, especially since their long training and shared love of skiing had fostered deep friendships.

One curious gap is the total omission of the fact that the German armies in northern Italy, where the unit was fighting, capitulated a few days before the official end of the war. That was the achievement of Allen Dulles, who later served a decade as head of the Central Intelligence Agency. Dulles's superior officer in the Office of Strategic Services, Brigadier General Magruder, had a son in the 10th Mountain Division. *(Violence, adult situations.)* — L.R.

d, Beth Gage, George Gage; p, Beth Gage, George Gage; w, Beth Gage; ph, Kenneth Lehn; ed, Scott Conrad, Krysia Carter-Giez; m, Todd Barton

Documentary/War **(PR: A MPAA: NR)**

FIRST KID ★★
(U.S.) 101m Caravan Pictures; Walt Disney Pictures ~ Buena Vista c

Sinbad *(Sam Simms)*; Brock Pierce *(Luke Davenport)*; Blake Boyd *(Dash)*; Timothy Busfield *(Woods)*; Art La Fleur *(Morton)*; Robert Guillaume *(Wilkes)*; Lisa Eichhorn *(Linda Davenport)*; James Naughton *(President Davenport)*; Fawn Reed *(Susan Lawrence)*; Erin Williby *(Katie Warren)*; Zachery Ty Bryan *(Rob)*; Michael Krawic *(James)*; Bill Cobbs *(Speed)*; Jemar Jewann Jefferson *(Andre)*; Daniel Baron *(Yo-Yo)*; Joe Inscoe *(Peterson)*; J. Michael Hunter *(Clark)*; Tomas Arana *(Harold)*; Doug MacArthur Williams *(Eddie)*; Helen Hedman *(Teacher)*; Jonathan Cabot Wade *(Kid #1)*; Andrew T. Wood *(Kid #2)*; Lee Sparks *(Kid #3)*; Sonny Bono *(Congressman Sonny Bono)*; Henry Strozier *(General)*; Elisabeth Noone *(President's Secretary)*; Peyton Chesson-Fohl *(Roller Blade Kid)*; Heather Kirk *(Katie's Friend #1)*; Kristi Cobb *(Katie's Friend #2)*; Scott Evans *(Uniformed Agent)*; Bob Child *(Security Officer)*; Patsy Grady Abrams *(Cleaning Lady)*; Richard Trask *(Walter)*; Derek

Leonidoff *(Donut Kid)*; Sylvia "Small Frie" Cannon *(Coffee Kid)*; Melissa Johnston *(Reporter)*; Raynor Scheine *(Maintenance Worker)*; Melanie Hastings *(Local News Anchor)*; Steve Kmetko *(Famous News Anchor)*; Ricardo Miguel Young *("Inside Copy" Anchor)*; Mark Nassar *(Secret Service Agent #1)*; Robert Earl Stoudamire *(Little Boy)*; Stephanie Lloyd *(Local Weather Person)*; Emma Stock *(Snake Screamer)*; Stephen Caywood *(Body Double)*; Audra Wilks *(Waitress)*; Brett Zebrowski *(Secret Service Agent #2)*; Jacqueline Chernov *(Teacher #2)*

If Richie Rich had been adopted by the President of the United States, you might end up with a movie like FIRST KID, which focuses on the antics of the lonely only child of the commander in chief. The only surprise in this movie, however, is that no one ever thought of it before.

FIRST KID is set, of course, in Washington, DC, where Luke (Brock Pierce), the son of President Davenport (James Naughton) and Linda Davenport (Lisa Eichhorn), creates mischief for his personal Secret Service agent, Woods (Timothy Busfield). When Woods loses his temper with Luke in front of Linda, he also loses his job. Meanwhile, a flamboyant Secret Service agent, Sam Simms (Sinbad), lobbies to secure the job protecting the President, but gets saddled with replacing Woods instead.

At first, Luke gives Sam a difficult time, but soon the wise agent realizes that the boy is merely lonely, always attending official functions instead of normal children's activities. Sam helps Luke by sneaking him out of the White House to teach him how to fight against the school bully. Sam even plays Cyrano to help Luke win a date with a pretty student. But when Sam spirits Luke away to the school dance (when Luke is supposed to stay at home), Sam gets fired. Nevertheless, Sam feels obligated to protect his former ward. When he realizes that Luke is meeting an Internet pal who secretly plans to kidnap him, Sam traces the First Kid to a mall where he foils the evil plan of the villain, his disgraced predecessor Woods. As a reward for his heroism, Sam is offered the job of protecting the President, but he prefers to stay by Luke's side.

FIRST KID follows GUARDING TESS, THE AMERICAN PRESIDENT, and MY FELLOW AMERICANS as a comedy about American's Royal Family. Like these other films (and older Hollywood efforts like KISSES FOR MY PRESIDENT), FIRST KID mixes sentiment and silliness to only minor effect. The only political satire is juvenile—a teleclip "cameo" by Bill Clinton giving advice to the new president and a forgettable walk-on by Sonny Bono. Sinbad's innocuous streetwise humor perks up a few scenes (teaching the boy to dance, for example), but his turn as the snotty child's guardian becomes tiresome. Sinbad's worst moment comes when he dresses up as Coca-Cola mascot at a skating rink (one of several product-placement ads in the film). Also, Sinbad's romance with Fawn Reed (as Luke's teacher) is pallid. It's hard to imagine children enjoying the adult scenes or the tacked-on, surprisingly violent ending, but some might identify with Brock Pierce's lonely, rebellious youth. For most adults, FIRST KID will do little to restore faith in government or in the Hollywood comedy. *(Violence, nudity.)* — E.M.

d, David Mickey Evans; p, Roger Birnbaum, Riley Kathryn Ellis; exec p, Sinbad, Dale De La Torre, Tim Kelleher; assoc p, Dorothea Adkiins; co-p, Jeffrey Chernov; w, Tim Kelleher; ph, Anthony B. Richmond; ed, Harry Keramidas; m, Richard Gibbs; prod d, Chester Kaczenski; art d, Marc Dabe; set d, Judi Giovanni; sound, Garry Cunningham (mixer); fx, Bob Vazquez, Kevin Koneval, Buena Vista Special Effects; casting, Shari Rhodes, Joseph Middleton; cos, Grania Preston; makeup, Jeannee Josefczyk; stunts, Rusty McClennon, Tony Brubaker

Children's/Comedy (PR: A MPAA: PG)

FIRST WIVES CLUB, THE ★★

(U.S.) 105m Scott Rudin Productions; Paramount ~ Paramount c

Bette Midler *(Brenda Morelli Cushman)*; Goldie Hawn *(Elise Elliot Atchison)*; Diane Keaton *(Annie MacDuggan Paradise)*; Maggie Smith *(Gunilla Garson Goldberg)*; Sarah Jessica Parker *(Shelly)*; Dan Hedaya *(Morty Cushman)*; Bronson Pinchot *(Duarto Feliz)*; Jennifer Dundas *(Chris Paradise)*; Eileen Heckart *(Catherine MacDuggan)*; Stephen Collins *(Aaron Paradise)*; Victor Garber *(Bill Atchison)*; Elizabeth Berkley *(Phoebe LaVelle)*; Stockard Channing *(Cynthia Swann Griffin—uncredited)*; Marcia Gay Harden *(Dr. Leslie Rosen)*; Philip Bosco *(Uncle Carmine)*; Rob Reiner *(Dr. Morris Packman)*; James Naughton *(Gil Griffin)*; Ari Greenberg *(Jason Cushman)*; Aida Linares *(Teresa)*; Ivana Trump *(Herself)*; Gloria Steinem *(Herself)*; Edward I. Koch *(Himself)*; Kathie Lee Gifford *(Herself)*; Christopher Burge *(Auctioneer)*; Stephen Pearlman *(Mr. Christian)*; J. Smith-Cameron *(Ms. Sullivan)*; Walter Bobbie *(Man in Bed)*; Kate Burton *(Woman in Bed)*; Gregg Edelman *(Mark Loest)*; Mark Nelson *(Eric Loest)*; Harsh Nayyar *(Mohammed)*; Sue Simmons *(Newscaster)*; Timothy Olyphant *(Brett Artounian)*; Edward Hibbert *(Maurice)*; Teresa DePriest *(Hostess)*; Johnny Sanchez *(Busboy)*; J.K. Simmons *(Federal Marshall)*; Stephen Mendillo *(Federal Marshall)*; Robin Morse *(Karen)*; Peter Frechette *(Broadway Director)*; Mark Perman *(The Cantor)*; George Vlachos *(Waiter)*; Armand Dahan *(Contractor)*; Lea De Laria *(Elise's Fan)*; Debra Monk *(Jilted Lover)*; Jennifer Lam *(Chris's Friend)*; Michele Brilliant *(Young Brenda)*; Dina Spybey *(Young Elise)*; Adria Tennor *(Young Annie)*; Juliehera DeStefano *(Young Cynthia)*; Paul Hecht; Anne Shropshire; Chelsea Altman; Eric Martin Brown *("A Certain Age" Cast)*; Nancy Ticotin *(Dancer)*; Roxane Barlow *(Dancer)*; Amy Heggins *(Dancer)*

THE FIRST WIVES' CLUB drearily proves that a sound comic premise and a dream cast do not guarantee a heavenly farce.

When Cynthia Griffin (Stockard Channing) commits suicide over being deserted by her husband for a younger woman, her three best school chums feel her pain all too well. Soundly middle-class Brenda (Bette Midler) is going through the same thing, having been dumped by Morty (Dan Hedaya) for a vulgar, albeit beautiful bimbo (Sarah Jessica Parker). Rich Upper East Side matron Annie (Diane Keaton) has been in therapy with an esteemed pop shrink (Marcia Gay Harden) to deal with her repressed anger and lifeless marriage to an advertising executive (Stephen Collins). The sessions come to a screeching halt, however, when she discovers that the two of them have been carrying on behind her back. Elise (Goldie Hawn), a fading, desperate movie star, has also been given the heave-ho by her producer-husband (Victor Garber), who looks to fresher, more nubile talent (Elizabeth Berkley), to fill her part on- and offscreen.

The three ladies meet up at Cynthia's funeral, get hysterically drunk, and plot revenge on their no-good husbands. They cook up an elaborate scheme to ruin the men financially, calling upon sources as varied as a wacky British interior decorator (Bronson Pinchot), a doyenne of New York high society (Maggie Smith), and even the Mafia to help them. They officially form The First Wives' Club to bring them to terms. But while Brenda's troubled, alienated son (Ari Greenberg) and Annie's lesbian daughter (Jennifer Dunning) look on in astonishment at their mothers' transformation, the three women begin turning on one another.

A painful rift ensues between them, but they are shaken back to a higher purpose and decide to use the funds they have extorted from their begrudging husbands to form a women's support group and shelter. At the splashy grand opening of the shelter, everything seems to be coming up roses, and Brenda and Morty look to be dancing their way to a full reconciliation.

As was the case with another popular battle-of-the-sexes film, 9 TO 5 (1980) the fun here is all in the set-up; after the first half hour or so, the film bogs down cartoonishly in petty bitchery and unrelenting vengefulness. The women scream and sneer and slap so much that your sympathy very nearly goes out to their beleaguered victims. Even in a hard-bitten farce like this, a little humanity would go a long way. If a husband had shown even a tiny bit of remorse, or a wife had responded with something besides self-pitying rage, it would have leavened matters considerably.

Director Hugh Wilson throws pace, nuance, and logic to the wind, giving the impression that he was so awestruck by his trove of divas that he left them largely to their own devices. Even so, the actresses don't bring anything fresh or exciting to their flatly drawn roles. Midler, as a struggling single mom wistfully pining over her wandering hubby, seems totally out of her element; when she breaks out with a catty line or pops up in an outlandish disguise, it's a welcome relief, but also out of character. Hawn seems to be enjoying herself as the collagened epitome of an aerobicized, mindlessly determined West Coast careerist. But we've seen her do the funny-shallow-vain bit already, and Robert (STEEL MAGNOLIAS) Harling's script (adapted from a best-selling novel by Olivia Goldsmith) doesn't allow for her to do much more than have copious drunken breakdowns which become decreasingly amusing as the film wears on. Keaton, unfortunately, is the real embarrassment here. WASP-y repression and spinster-like nervousness have sadly become her stock-in-trade, and she falls too easily back on these, veering from uncontrollable giggles to rampaging hysteria and back again. She's memorable when she hisses *"lesbian"* at her recalcitrant daughter; one wishes to have seen more of this harder edge. On the plus side, Smith gives her few scenes the benefit of her majestic comic style; Parker is fitfully amusing, as is Harden. But the men, even the usually gritty Hedaya, are total ciphers; they're blustering hot-air balloons begging to be deflated, much like the film itself. *(Sexual situations, adult situations, substance abuse, profanity.)* — D.N.

d, Hugh Wilson; p, Scott Rudin; exec p, Ezra Swerdlow, Adam Schroeder; assoc p, Craig Perry, Heather Neely, Noah Ackerman; co-p, Thomas Imperato; w, Robert Harling (based on the novel by Olivia Goldsmith); ph, Donald Thorin; ed, John Bloom; m, Marc Shaiman; prod d, Peter Larkin; art d, Charles Beal; set d, Leslie E. Rollins; sound, Peter Kurland (mixer); fx, Matt Vogel, VIFX; casting, Ilene Starger; cos, Theoni V. Aldredge; makeup, Bernadette Mazur; stunts, Jack Gill

AAN Best Original Musical or Comedy Score: Marc Shaiman

Comedy **(PR: C MPAA: PG)**

FIST OF THE NORTH STAR ★

(U.S.) 90m Zeta Entertainment; Toei Company ~ BMG Video c

Gary Daniels *(Kenshiro (Ken))*; Costas Mandylor *(Lord Shin)*; Chris Penn *(Jackal)*; Malcolm McDowell *(Ryuken)*; Melvin Van Peebles *(Asher)*; Dante Brasco *(Bat)*; Nalona Herron *(Lynn)*; Bill Nagel *(Miner)*; Clint Howard *(Stalin)*; Andre Rosey Brown *(Sandman)*; Paolo Tocha *(Stone)*; Tracey Walter *(Paul)*; Rowena Guinness *(Jill)*; Isako Washio *(Julia)*; Michael Charles Friedman *(Neuter)*; Tony Halme *(Zeed)*

Based on a wildly popular Japanese comic book, this neo-Fascist meditation on the divine right of martial artists is unyieldingly boring.

Wandering warrior Kenshiro "Ken" (Gary Daniels), coached by his dead but still-psychic father Ryuken (Malcolm McDowell), eschews mere vengeance. He would much rather eradicate post-apocalyptic dissension between the Northern Star and Southern Star factions of the kingdom.

Flashbacks reveal that Ken was literally ripped apart by ruthless Southern Star warlord Shin (Costas Mandylor), who has unbalanced the cosmic order by pitting the Northern and Southern contingents against each other. Having healed his seven wounds, Ken initially resists his savior-destiny, even though Shin has locked Ken's Princess-babe Julia (Isako Washio) in a golden cage. Moved by the human misery at a resistance camp, Ken battles Shin's stormtroopers under the leadership of Jackal (Chris Penn).

After trekking away from the rag-tag underdogs, Ken and Northern Star guerrilla Bat (Dante Brasco) return to find the residents of the wasteland outpost massacred and Bat's sister Lynn (Nalona Herron) endangered due to her psychic knowledge of Ken's game plan. As Ken marches to unseat the supernaturally empowered Lord Shin, Jackal terrorizes Julia. By the time resourceful Julia destroys the headgear that keeps Jackal's head from exploding, Ken gains the upper hand over Lord Shin, whose flesh-tearing power deserts him. In slaying Shin, Ken restores the Northern-Southern Star balance which his late father devoutly championed to maintain peace.

Although action buffs may enjoy the martial arts expertise of studly star Gary Daniels and a team of masterful stuntmen, viewers also may feel cheated, as if this gruesome downer were punishing them for any pleasure they garner. Might makes right in most superhero spectacles, but this film has no inherent nobility, no milk of human kindness, and no tongue-in-cheek humor to leaven its oppressive hero worship.

Presumably there's a market for futuristic adventures about master races, but do fans want their he-man wish fulfillment filmed in washed-out sepia and laced with lip-smacking brutality? If the answer is yes, then they are welcome to this action pic where dismemberment seems to be a hobby. FIST OF THE NORTH STAR is as much action-jammed fun as attending a vivisection demonstration. *(Graphic violence, profanity.)* — R.P.

d, Tony Randel; p, Mark Yellen, Aki Komine; exec p, Taka Ichise, Zane W. Levitt; assoc p, Roy McAree; co-p, Joel Soisson; w, Tony Randel, Peter Atkins (based on the comic book *Fist of the North Star* by Tetsuo Hara and Buronson Hara); ph, Jacques Haitkin; ed, Sonny Baskin; m, Christopher L. Stone; prod d, Clark Hunter; art d, Wendy Guidery; set d, Traci Kirshbaum; sound, Dan Monahan (mixer); fx, Clark Schaffer, Sota FX; casting, Linda Francis; cos, Merrie Lawson; makeup, Becky Cotton, Roy Knyrim, Jerry Macaluso; stunts, Rocky Capella, Winston Omega

Martial Arts **(PR: O MPAA: R)**

FLAMING EARS

(Austria) 84m Hamburger Filmburo ~ Water Bearer Home Video c

(ROTE OHREN SETZEN DURCH AFCHE)

Susana Helmayr *(Spy)*; Ursula Purrer *(Volley)*; Angela Hans Sheirl *(Nun)*; Margarete Neumann *(M)*; Gabriele Szekatsch *(Blood)*; Anthony Escott *(Man with Cactus)*; Luise Kubelka *(Little Girl)*; Dietmar Schipek *(Undertaker)*; Heiderose Hildebrand *(Tailor)*; Sabine Perthold *(Tolisa)*; Norbert Gmeindl *(Ex-*

plosive Dealer #1); Billa Gmeindl *(Explosive Dealer #2)*; Karin Melton *(Club Bouncer #1)*; Birge Krondofer *(Vampire)*; Arleen Schloss *(Passerby)*; Julia Kordina *(Narrator)*

This vexingly confusing shocker proudly palms itself off as a "cyber-dyke" experience; its combination of same-sex shenanigans and sci-fi doesn't herald a happy aesthetic future for either gays-in-space films or homo-apocalyptic adventures. This mishmash out of Austria needs more than better subtitles to make its intentions clear, e.g., an auteur's lucid purview, sharply drawn characters, or a guiding cinematic intelligence with a grasp of basic screen direction.

In the bleak futureworld of 2700 AD, where lesbians rule the roost, fascist power brokers don't appreciate the political cartoons created by Spy (Susana Heilmayr). Meanwhile, through a labyrinth of after-hours sex clubs, brutal performance artist Volley (Ursula Purrer) manhandles opponents of the sex-obsessed status quo and dabbles in arson. Amusing herself with multiple lovers, Volley lives with an androgyne named Nun (Angela Hans Scheirl), who subsists on a diet of roadkill and represents a nurturing counterpart to Volley's sadism. Having been terrorized in her apartment and notified of the destruction of her printing press, Spy leaves her ivory tower to crusade against her shadowy persecutor, Volley.

Risking her own neck, Nun rescues wounded Spy, whose revolutionary zeal garnered her a beating outside one of Volley's night spots. Nun hides the fallen, failed hit lady in their apartment, right under Volley's nose. In the surreal climax, a revitalized Spy succeeds in ending Volley's reign of terror.

On several occasions throughout this dismal miasma of butch posturing, characters presumed dead are inexplicably alive and well and shooting. What does it mean? That death is a tenuous concept in futuristic homosexual metropolises? If the film has so zany a disregard for the integrity of its own plot, then what is the viewer expected to do? Simply throw reality out the window and enjoy the proceedings as a sapphic floor show?

Droning on and on, FLAMING EARS, a festival of ugliness, has but one asset: a potent use of pop art graphics and mini-models that pokes fun at its own shoestring budget. The talentless actresses strut as if treading a fashion runway at a Ken Russell madhouse that's presenting a spring line of retro '60s outfits. Sadly, this morose film won't even please hard-core gay cinephiles who prefer that a cult film provide a camp sensibility to accompany its grotesqueries. *(Graphic violence, extensive nudity, substance abuse, sexual situations.)* — R.P.

d, Angela Hans Scheirl, Ursula Purrer, Dietmar Schipek; p, Angela Hans Scheirl, Ursula Purrer, Dietmar Schipek; assoc p, Ulrike Zimmerman; w, Angela Hans Scheirl, Ursula Purrer, Dietmar Schipek; ph, Margarete Neumann, Manfred Neuwirth, Herman Leweth, Gurd Duca; ed, Angela Hans Scheirl; m, Dietmar Schipek, Gurd Duca; fx, Anthony Escott, Andrea Witzmann; makeup, Elfi Mueller

Science Fiction **(PR: O MPAA: NR)**

FLATTERED ★★½

(U.S.) 107m Silent H Films c

Mark Haas *(Jack Roberts)*; Ann Richards *(Chelsea Welles)*; Ron Link *(Ray)*; Andy Kiss; Eric Coble

A slight but likable romantic comedy shot on 16mm by local Cleveland talent, FLATTERED checks in as Woody Allen lite.

College guy Jack Roberts (Mark Haas) is a nebbish around women. When he sights coed Chelsea (Ann Richards), smitten Jack can't even speak to her or maintain bowel control.

Learning that Chelsea has an estranged boyfriend, Jack confers with various male cohorts on how to make all the right moves to win over his dream girl. Two self-styled mentors (Andy Kiss, Eric Coble) urge poetry, flowers and patience, while Ray (Ron Link), Jack's sexist boss at a video store, holds the sanguine view that "Women want the same thing that men want—power." Jack rejects Ray's aggressive approach and plies Chelsea with sweet platitudes, chaste dates, and a surprise delivery of a single perfect rose that makes Chelsea break down in tears.

Although Jack's choreographed performance was perfect, instead of falling into his arms, Chelsea reunites with her old boyfriend. Jack's pragmatic pals comfort the heartbroken swain with the certainty that Chelsea will forever remember him as the romantic ideal; he should feel "flattered" that he touched her heart. Jack brightens as another girl makes her entrance.

The pic's feature length stretches anecdotal plot material terribly thin, but writer-director John Hlavin has a knack for snappy, amusing guytalk—maybe even too much so, since his script grinds to a halt when he gives compensatory time to the ladies, and token interludes with Chelsea and her friends are static and stilted. The no-name cast acquit themselves well, and filming (around the Case Western Reserve University campus and the filmmakers' homes) is uncluttered and to the point. *(Sexual situations, profanity, nudity, substance abuse.)* — C.C.

d, John Hlavin; p, Kirk Zehnder; w, John Hlavin; ph, Jeff Barklage; ed, Vagn L. Steen; m, Mike Petrone, John Cesario

Comedy/Romance **(PR: C MPAA: NR)**

FLED ★

(U.S.) 105m MGM ~ MGM/UA c

Laurence Fishburne *(Piper)*; Stephen Baldwin *(Dodge)*; Will Patton *(Gibson)*; Robert John Burke *(Pat Schiller)*; Robert Hooks *(Lieutenant Clark)*; Victor Rivers *(Santiago)*; David Dukes *(Chris Paine)*; Ken Jenkins *(Warden Nichols)*; Salma Hayek *(Cora)*; Michael Nader *(Mantajano)*; Brittney Powell *(Faith/Cindy)*; Steve Carlisle *(Herb Foster)*; Brett Rice *(Officer Thornhill)*; J. Don Ferguson *(Chairman)*; Kathy Payne *(Margaret Parks)*; Bob Apisa *(Jose Marti)*; Gary Yates *(Sergeant Bailey)*; Jon Huffman *(Milliner)*; Anderson Martin *(Officer Kevin)*; Bob Hannah *(Mason)*; Margo Moorer *(Waitress)*; Angela Mills *(Jocelyn)*; Michael Hooks *(Vonte)*; Joe Torry *(Bo Grant)*; Bill Bellamy *(Ray)*; RuPaul *(Himself)*; Robby Preddy *(Zestos Waitress)*; Taurean Blacque *(Les)*; K. Addison Young *(Puffy)*; Libby Whittemore *(Sandra)*; Meredith Gordon *(Officer)*; David Dwyer *(Sergeant Leonard)*; Michael H. Moss *(Dispatcher)*; James Michael Hill *(Man in the Bathroom)*; Tom Turbiville *(Security Guard)*; Charles Gershon; Molli D. Gershon; Brannon Bates; Katie Glendinning; Phonz Bass; Karl D. Gardner *(Gondola Passenger)*; Mark Gardiner *(Police Pilot)*; William Lyle McMillan *(Government Pilot)*; Matt Wallace *(Schiller Pilot)*

Definitely not THE DEFIANT ONES (1958). Salt-and-pepper fugitives fight in flight in this absolutely inane buddy-actioner, which features some of the most egregious grammar-mangling in recent memory, evident even in the movie's title.

Convicts Luke Dodge (Stephen Baldwin) and Charles Piper (Laurence Fishburne) are chained together while working on a Georgia road crew. They escape, but on their trail is a local sheriff, Matt Gibson (Will Patton), and a federal marshal, Pat Schiller (Robert John Burke).

Dodge is a computer hacker whose crime was stealing $25 million from an off-shore corporation that, unbeknownst to him, is really a front for the Cuban mafia. Schiller wants the computer disk onto which Dodge copied the accounting records of the corporation. The mob sends a hitman, Santiago (Victor Rivers), to kill Dodge.

In Atlanta, the fugitives kidnap Cora (Salma Hayek), a beautiful and very helpful woman who breaks the tie that binds them, feeds and clothes them, and quickly becomes a love interest for Piper. Dodge sets off to retrieve the disk, proceeds to get his girlfriend and his best friend killed, and then himself captured by Santiago. Piper comes to the rescue and reveals he's really a cop who was assigned by Schiller to tag along with Dodge on the engineered jailbreak, and lead the Feds to the disk. Schiller turns out to be working for the mob, though, and when Piper and Dodge find the disk, he tries to kill them. Luckily, Gibson has figured all this out, and he arrives in time to save them. After a high speed chase, both Santiago and Schiller "pay the piper" in a final showdown.

With all due respect to the work of Adam Sandler, Tom Arnold, Chris Farley, David Spade, and (of course) Pauly Shore, FLED was the flat-out stupidest Hollywood release of 1996. One cliched scene of completely ridiculous dialogue follows another. (They stop after a shoot-out, during a high-speed chase, to offer exposition. "We gotta fled!") The characters' actions go beyond illogical and dive headlong into imbecilic. (Why would Piper, who has to keep Dodge safe and on the run, stop and beat the hell out of him? Why would Cora be so eager to help her abductors?) And FLED can't even justify any of this with the "it's just a comedy" defense. It doesn't have the good sense to let the stars act like they're in on a joke (*a la* BULLETPROOF, another 1996 buddy-actioner). Director Kevin Hooks (PASSENGER 57) seems to think he can distract the audience from the canyons in the plot by never having a shot where the camera isn't moving, or is at least set up at a 30-degree angle, and pumping up the bass on the soundtrack to thunderous levels. *(Profanity, violence, nudity.)* — P.R.

d, Kevin Hooks; p, Frank Mancuso Jr.; exec p, Preston A. Whitmore II; assoc p, Vikki Williams; w, Preston A. Whitmore II; ph, Matthew F. Leonetti; ed, Richard Nord, Joseph Gutowski; m, Graeme Revell; prod d, Charles Bennett; art d, Charles Breen; set d, Mary Stacy, Katie Pinholster; sound, Mary H. Ellis (recordist); fx, Bob Shelley, Gary Bentley, Peter Montgomery; casting, Amanda Mackey Johnson, Cathy Sandrich; cos, Jennifer Bryan; makeup, Lynn Barber, Bill "Splat" Johnson; stunts, John Meier

Action/Crime/Drama (PR: C MPAA: R)

FLIPPER ★★

(U.S.) 96m Bubble Factory; American Film Productions; Perry Katz Productions; Universal ~ Universal c

Elijah Wood *(Sandy)*; Paul Hogan *(Porter)*; Jonathan Banks *(Dirk Moran)*; Chelsea Field *(Cathy)*; Jessica Wesson *(Kim)*; Isaac Hayes *(Sheriff Buck Cowan)*; Bill Kelley *(Tommy)*; Jason Fuchs *(Marvin)*; Mary Jo Faraci *(Sandy's Mom)*; Allison Bertolino *(Sandy's Sister)*; Mal Jones *(Russ)*; Louis Seeger Crume *(Mr. Dunnahy)*; Robert Deacon *(Bounty Fisherman #1)*; Ann Carey *(Fisherman's Wife)*; Mark Casella *(Bounty Fisherman #2)*; Luke Halpin *(Bounty Fisherman #3)*; Lindsay Treco *(Little Girl)*; Bill Nolan *(Bartender)*

Yet another attempt to update a beloved Baby Boomer TV series for the movies, the stale dolphin tale of FLIPPER combines a formulaic coming-of-age plot with far more talk than animal action.

Surly teen Sandy Ricks (Elijah Wood) has been shipped off by his divorced mom to spend the summer with his Uncle Porter (Paul Hogan) in Florida. Happy-go-lucky Porter, a commercial fisherman, is a charming eccentric who lives in a ramshackle beach house. In addition to a beer-drinking pelican, Porter has a long-suffering girlfriend, Cathy (Chelsea Field), who gave up being a marine biologist in Boston to run a bait shop and has been waiting for Porter to decide to marry her.

A complicated story ensues having primarily to do with Captain Moran (Jonathan Banks) of the symbolically named "Bounty Hunter" boat, who is responsible for dumping toxic waste. Along the way, Sandy finds the dolphin who becomes his summer friend. When Sandy later uses his saltwater chum to impress Kim (Jessica Wesson)—using the line, "Like my dolphin?"—he has to hurriedly devise a name. The dolphin hints by frantically flapping a flipper. Seeing that Flipper is keen to do tricks. Sandy and Kim begin charging kids to watch Flipper perform.

Uncle Porter soon puts a stop to this sideshow, then turns home into boot camp and tells Sandy if he's going to keep a dolphin as a pet, he has to care for it. Moran isn't pleased to have a local-celebrity dolphin scaring away the fish, and after trying unsuccessfully to capture Flipper, turns Porter in to Sheriff Buck Cowan (Isaac Hayes). Alas, Flipper must be put back out to sea, and the gang reluctantly takes him. When Sandy and Kim later return to look for Flipper, they spy Moran dumping toxic-waste barrels. Sometime afterward, Flipper washes up on the beach, poisoned. Cathy nurses him back to health, after which Sandy and friends teach Flipper how to find the toxic-waste site. There is a scary interlude where Sandy is left at the mercy of Moran, but Flipper saves the day. In the end, the toxic dumper is arrested, a newly mature Sandy returns home, and Porter finally brings Cathy roses.

Miraculously, Hogan, Banks and Field each give their cardboard characters a smart, engaging presence—Banks in particular is a malevolent hoot—and Wood makes an assured transition from child to teen roles. Flipper—a combination of real, animatronic, and computer-animated dolphins—looks admirably real except in the final shot. Yet the story, though padded and talky, leaves out much pertinent information (the least of which is why Floridian Uncle Porter has an Australian accent while his sister, Sandy's mom, doesn't). Although the film at first tries to keep things plausible, FLIPPER soon succumbs to the Lassie Syndrome: "TREEEP TREEEP!" "What's that, Flipper? You've found the toxic-waste barrels?" Additionally, the endless parade of product placements are among the most blatant ever seen.

Of note for Baby Boomer trivia buffs: Luke Halpin, in the nameless role of Bounty Fisherman #3, played 15-year-old Sandy Ricks, son of widowed Coral Key Park Ranger Porter Ricks, on the 1964-68 TV show "Flipper."— F.L.

d, Alan Shapiro; p, James J. McNamara, Perry Katz; exec p, Lance Hool; assoc p, Doug Merrifield; co-p, Conrad Hool, Darlene Spezzi; w, Alan Shapiro (based on the 1963 screenplay by Arthur Weiss, from a story by Ricou Browning and Jack Cowden); ph, Bill Butler; ed, Peck Prior; m, Joel McNeely; prod d, Thomas A. Walsh; art d, Kim Hix; set d, David Schlesinger; sound, Steve Aaron (mixer), Harry E. Snodgrass (design); fx, Peter Knowlton, Brad Kuehn, Karen Murphy; casting, Julie Ashton-Barson; cos, Matthew Jacobsen; makeup, Kris Evans; stunts, Doug Coleman

Adventure/Children's (PR: A MPAA: PG)

FLIRT ★★½

(U.S./Germany/Japan) 85m True Fiction Pictures; Pandora Films; NDF; Filmboard Berlin-Brandenburg GmbH ~ CFP Distribution c

Bill Sage *(Bill)*; Martin Donovan *(Walter)*; Parker Posey *(Emily, Bill's Girlfriend)*; Dwight Ewell *(Dwight)*; Geno Lechner *(Greta, Werner's Wife)*; Miho Nikaidoh *(Miho)*; Kumiko

Ishizuka *(Naomi, Miho's Friend)*; Chikako Hara *(Yuki, Ozu's Wife)*; Michael Imperioli *(Michael, Bill's Friend)*; Holt McCallany *(Bartender)*; Karen Sillas *(Dr. Clint)*; Erica Gimpel *(Nurse)*; Lianna Pai *(Woman at Phone Booth)*; Hannah Sullivan *(Trish the Waitress)*; Harold Perrineau *(Men's Room Man #1)*; Robert John Burke *(Men's Room Man #2)*; Paul Austin *(Men's Room Man #3)*; Jose Zuniga *(Cab Driver)*; Patricia Scanlon *(Woman at Bar)*; Peter Fitz *(Doctor)*; Dominik Bender *(Johan, Dwight's Boyfriend)*; Susanna Simon *(Elisabeth, Dwight's Friend)*; Boris Aljinovic *(Simon(e), Fashion Stylist)*; Maria Schrader *(Woman at Phone Booth)*; Elina Lowensohn *(Nurse)*; Nils Bruck *(Tom)*; Sebastian Koch *(Dick)*; Frank Schendler *(Harry)*; Hans Martin Stier *(Boris, Laborer #1)*; Lars Rudolph *(Peter, Laborer #2)*; Jorg Biester *(Mike, Laborer #3)*; Gerhard Severin *(Mac the Bartender)*; Sabine Svoboda *(Barkeeper)*; Susie Bick *(Model)*; Amina Gusner *(Photographer)*; Stefan Kolosko *(Assistant)*; Jakob Klaffke *(Werner)*; Joy Kraft *(Greta's Daughter)*; Bano Dost *(Neighbor)*; Hasan Ali Mete *(Man)*; Toshizo Fujiwara *(Mr. Ozu)*; Meikyoh Yamada *(Mochi the Policeman)*; Mansaku Ikeuchi *(Tomo the Younger Policeman)*; Yutaka Matsushige *(Doctor)*; Tomoko Fujita *(Nurse)*; Eri Yu *(Kazuko, Jailbird #1)*; Yuri Aso *(Shoko, Jailbird #2)*; Natsumi Mizuno *(Narumi, Jailbird #3)*; Hal Hartley *(Hal, Miho's Boyfriend)*; Masatoshi Nagase *(Hal's Assistant)*; Tetsuya Tabata; Hirofumi Nakagawa; Morito Ikeda; Kenji Yamaguchi; Junji Iijima; Tetsushi Yamazaki *(Dancers)*

Despite the cleverness of the narrative experiment and a terrific international cast, Hal Hartley's FLIRT falls flat.

The film opens in New York City in 1993 when Emily (Parker Posey), about to leave to Paris, demands that Bill (Bill Sage) either commit or end their relationship. Bill, meanwhile, is sorting out his feelings about Margaret, his other lover. Margaret's husband, Walter (Martin Donovan), catches up with Bill in a bar and threatens to shoot himself over the affair. Bill tries to save him, but is accidentally shot instead. After Bill is released from the hospital, he rushes after Emily, who has flown to Paris.

A year later in Berlin, Johan (Dominik Bender), a German art dealer, demands that his lover Dwight (Dwight Ewell), a young African-American, end his relationship with Werner (Jakob Klaffke), a married German man. When Dwight visits Werner to discuss the matter, Werner's wife, Greta (Geno Lechner), threatens to shoot herself over the affair. Dwight tries to take her gun away and is accidentally shot. By the time Dwight is released from the hospital, Johan is gone.

In 1995 Tokyo, an American filmmaker, Hal (Hal Hartley), asks Miho (Miho Nikaidoh), his girlfriend, to travel back to the US with him, but Miho needs time to assess her feelings about her dance instructor, Mr. Ozu (Toshizo Fujiwara). While visiting her school, Miho confronts Yuki (Chikako Hara), Ozu's wife, who plans to shoot herself over the *perceived* affair between Miho and Mr. Ozu. Miho is accidentally shot while keeping Yuki from committing suicide, but recovers in time to leave the country with Hal.

In previous short and feature-length work (SURVIVING DESIRE, TRUST), Hal Hartley ingeniously used Brechtian techniques to explore relationship issues. But later films like SIMPLE MEN (1992), AMATEUR (1994), and now FLIRT, continue this stylistic venture in a much more heavy-handed way. It seems he has allowed the comparisons critics have made between him and Jean-Luc Godard to go to his head. FLIRT poses interesting what-if questions about the plot's romantic scenarios, but Hartley dashes the opportunity to comment on critical social issues by leaving only two constants: dull stories and implausible dialogues. Of course, the unlikely and the artificial are a major part of Hartley's style, but much of a great cast—including Parker Posey, Michael Imperioli, Karen Sillas, and Maria Schrader—are wasted in bit parts that require them to deliver lines in a mannered, amateurish way. *(Violence, nudity, sexual situations, adult situations, profanity.)* — E.M.

d, Hal Hartley; p, Ted Hope; exec p, Reinhard Brundig, Satoru Iseki, Jerome Brownstein; assoc p, Hisami Kuroiwa, Carleen L. Hsu; w, Hal Hartley; ph, Michael Spiller; ed, Hal Hartley; m, Ned Rifle, Jeffrey Taylor; prod d, Steven Rosenzweig; art d, Karin Wiesel; set d, Amy Tapper; sound, Jeff Pullman (mixer); casting, Billy Hopkins, Suzanne Smith; cos, Alexandra Welker; makeup, Judy Chin

Comedy/Drama (PR: C MPAA: NR)

FLIRTING WITH DISASTER ★★½

(U.S.) 487m Flirting With Disaster Films; Miramax ~ Miramax c

Ben Stiller *(Mel Coplin)*; Patricia Arquette *(Nancy Coplin)*; Tea Leoni *(Tina Kalb)*; Mary Tyler Moore *(Mrs. Coplin)*; George Segal *(Mr. Coplin)*; Alan Alda *(Richard Schlicting)*; Lily Tomlin *(Mary Schlicting)*; Richard Jenkins *(Paul)*; Josh Brolin *(Tony)*; Celia Weston *(Valerie Swaney)*; Glenn Fitzgerald *(Lonnie Schlicting)*; Beth Ostrosky *(Jane)*; Cynthia Lamontagne *(Sandra)*; David Patrick Kelly *(Fritz Boudreau)*; John Ford Noonan *(Mitch)*; Charlet Oberly *(B&B Lady)*

Everything's relative where FLIRTING WITH DISASTER is concerned. To some, the sight of Mary Tyler Moore (yes, *our* Mary) demonstrating the firmness of her breasts was a shocking, big laugh-getter. To those familiar with writer-director David O. Russell's first feature, SPANKING THE MONKEY (1994) about consensual incest, his second is a rather timid affair.

Since his son's birth, neurotic New Yorker Mel Coplin (Ben Stiller) has been afflicted with debilitating impotence. He can't have sex with his lovely wife, Nancy (Patricia Arquette), and he can't settle on a name for their baby. Both problems frustrate Nancy; the latter consternates Mel's ever-bickering, adoptive parents (Mary Tyler Moore and George Segal) to no end. Mel believes he's found the solution to his troubles in Tina (Tea Leoni), a very leggy psychologist who wants to lead Mel to his biological parents so she can document the reunion.

Tina's information isn't 100 percent certain, though, and she takes Mel and Nancy on a couple of wild goose chases. In San Diego, the "reunion" with Valerie Swaney (Celia Weston), a fading Southern belle with a glass menagerie, gets Mel excited about the name Beauregard. In Michigan, Mel's "reunion" with Fritz Boudreau (David Patrick Kelly), a crazy truck driver, ends in the destruction of a post office. This brings FBI agents Paul and Tony (Richard Jenkins and Josh Brolin), who happen to be gay lovers, into the picture. Tony is an old school friend of Nancy's, and the two Feds decide to tag along to New Mexico.

In the desert town of Antelope Wells, Tina finally reunites Mel with his birth parents, the Schlictings (Lily Tomlin and Alan Alda), a pair of '60s dropouts who still throw bad pottery and cook up LSD in the basement. While Nancy and Tony, and Mel and Tina, attempt respective affairs—and fail, Paul accidentally drops acid and trips out. When Paul reveals he's an FBI agent, the Schlictings take it on the lam to Mexico, as the elder Coplins show up to lay claim to their family. The younger Coplins re-consummate their union, and name the baby "Jerry" after the late lead singer of the Grateful Dead.

A subversive take on the children's book *Are You My Mother?* laced with not quite bawdy humor, FLIRTING WITH DISASTER displays a comedic sensibility best described as post-modern Woody Allen. Russell joins the generation of film and sitcom makers who came of age on the "funny" Woodman of the 70s.

They emulate the neurotic bemusement and insecurity, but lack Allen's intellectual curiosity and his way of looking at the world, leaving only Nick-at-Nite and themselves as areas of interest for their comedy. Russell's characters trade witty barbs and throw out intelligent asides, but the targets are bland: bed-and-breakfasts and rent-a-cars (thankfully, no airline food jokes).

The movie is loaded with great, screwball portent, but the laughs come in fits and starts. Rather than building to explosive climaxes, or probing his characters' depths, Russell diffuses sequences prematurely with pratfalls. (One can only imagine what Allen would have done with the scene of Jewish Mel meeting the very Nordic Swaney sisters.) Things really start cooking when veteran scene-stealers Tomlin and Alda come on. Russell has the viewer set up to expect fireworks when both of Mel's mothers meet, but that confrontation is literally just a bump in the night.

FLIRTING WITH DISASTER is a rare, decidedly adult comedy designed to elicit actual laughs. And it has more on its mind than most current cinematic fare—movies falling over each other to be dumber and dumbest. But DISASTER ultimately will have to do its competing on the small screen; and frankly, it doesn't pack many more laughs into its 90 minutes than a good, 30-minute episode of "Seinfeld." *(Profanity, violence, sexual situations.)* — P.R.

d, David O. Russell; p, Dean Silvers; exec p, Bob Weinstein, Harvey Weinstein; assoc p, Christopher Goode; co-p, Kerry Orent; w, David O. Russell; ph, Eric Edwards; ed, Christopher Tellefsen; m, Stephen Endelman; prod d, Kevin Thompson; art d, Judy Rhee; set d, Ford Wheeler; sound, Rolf Pardula (mixer), Wendy Hedin (design); casting, Ellen Parks, Risa Bramon Garcia; cos, Ellen Lutter

Comedy **(PR: C MPAA: R)**

FLOWER OF MY SECRET, THE ★★★½
(Spain/France) 107m CiBy 2000; El Deseo SA ~ Sony Pictures Classics c
(LA FLOR DE MI SECRETO)

Marisa Paredes *(Leo Macias)*; Juan Echanove *(Angel)*; Imanol Arias *(Paco)*; Carmen Elias *(Betty)*; Rossy de Palma *(Rosa)*; Chus Lampreave *(Mother)*; Joaquin Cortes *(Antonio)*; Manuela Vargas *(Blanca)*; Kiti Manver; Gloria Munoz; Juan Jose Otegui; Nancho Novo; Jordi Molla; Alicia Agut; Marisol Muriel; Teresa Ibanez; Jose Palau; Abraham Garcia

The films of Spanish maverick Pedro Almodovar serve up a heady blend of soap opera and campiness. In THE FLOWER OF MY SECRET, however, melodrama clearly overshadows farce as a romance novelist reels from the pitfalls of conducting her personal life as if she were one of her own compulsive heroines.

A best-selling author under the pen name "Amanda Gris," Leo Macios (Marisa Paredes) faces a tumultuous turning point in her life. At the same time that she is trying to write a more realistic novel, she is attempting to resuscitate her already-dead marriage to Paco (Imanol Arias), a NATO officer who is often away from home. Although unable to extricate herself from her unrequited love, she jump-starts her professional life by taking a critic's post at *El Pais,* a newspaper run by the portly Angel (Juan Echanove), who unwittingly assigns her the task of reviewing her latest pseudonymous book. Absorbed in heartache, Leo doesn't realize that Angel has more than an editorial interest in her.

Leo angers her book publisher by submitting a seedy crime novel instead of the contracted potboiler. She tosses the rejected manuscript into her trash can. It is found by her maid's son, Antonio (Joaquin Cortes), who sells it in his own name to a film producer to raise funds for his upcoming dance concert.

When the unresponsive Paco returns for a brief visit, Leo's emotional neediness soon drives him away again. Despondent, Leo halfheartedly attempts suicide, but a phone message from her mother (Chus Lampreave) rouses her from her barbiturate stupor. Accompanying her mother back to her childhood village, Leo recuperates in the company of the local widows. Once again, Angel proves to be a godsend by ghostwriting the Amanda Gris books Leo is contractually obligated to submit.

Returning to Madrid to start a new life without Paco, a psychologically frail Leo nearly breaks down in the midst of a chaotic student protest, but Angel comes to the rescue. In Angel's company, Leo attends Antonio's successful flamenco recital starring Leo's maid. When Antonio admits to having plagiarized her discarded manuscript, Leo calmly forgives him—she no longer feels any attachment to that uncharacteristically pessimistic work, nor to the inner turmoil it represented. Leo embraces her loyal suitor Angel, and initiates a more mature, less passion-crazed relationship with him.

Fluidly directed, this wittily conceived exploration of loving well but unwisely parallels serious scenes and pastel parodies. For example, the competitive arguments between Leo's widowed mother and her unhappily married daughter Rosa (Rossy de Palma) are not only among the funniest scenes of domestic discord ever recorded, they also shed light on the terrible cost that a self-image as "wife" extracts from women.

Questioning the notion of undying, idealized love, THE FLOWER OF MY SECRET shifts from tragedy to comedy, signaling Leo's healing process after fate severs her ties to the disdainful Paco. In coming to terms with his heroine's unhealthy obsession, Almodovar deliberately has Leo's neuroses collide and then regroup in a saner, more centered personality. Moreover, Almodovar views Leo's identity crisis as a necessary condition of her artistic growth. Stifled by her pop fiction, she rushes into bitter, fact-based territory, only to discover that there are valuable qualities in the crowd-pleasing escapism for which she is famous. Perhaps this clever film signifies Almodovar's own acceptance of his unique gifts as soap opera jester. But there's nothing more serious than the aspects of love he deals with, and comedy is not a diminishing factor in expressing emotional wounds.

Although one admires THE FLOWER OF MY SECRET for its richly symbolic odyssey, Almodovar fans will miss the blissful highs of LAW OF DESIRE (1987) or WOMEN ON THE VERGE OF A NERVOUS BREAKDOWN (1988)—essentially black comedy entertainments where laughter held dominant sway. Paredes is a superb dramatic actress, who meshes beautifully with the melancholy of this Almodovar offering. Through this vibrant actress, Almodovar counsels inveterate sufferers that, by working through their pain, they can reach a future that flowers more sublimely than any unfulfilled romantic past. This bracing comedy-drama holds out a hand to anyone who has ever despaired of finding love a second or third time around. *(Extreme profanity, sexual situations, substance abuse, adult situations.)* — R.P.

d, Pedro Almodovar; p, Esther Garcia; exec p, Agustin Almodovar; w, Pedro Almodovar; ph, Affonso Beato; ed, Jose Salcedo; m, Alberto Iglesias; art d, Wolfgang Burmann; set d, Miguel Lopez Pelegrin; sound, Bernardo Menz, Graham V. Haststone (mixer); fx, Molina; cos, Hugo Mezcua, Marisa Paredes, Juan Echanove; makeup, Juan Pedro Hernandez

Drama/Romance **(PR: C MPAA: R)**

FLY AWAY HOME ★★★½
(U.S.) 110m Branti Film Productions; Sandollar Productions ~ Columbia c

Jeff Daniels *(Thomas Alden)*; Anna Paquin *(Amy Alden)*; Dana Delany *(Susan Barnes)*; Terry Kinney *(David Alden)*; Holter Graham *(Barry Stickland)*; Jeremy Ratchford *(Glen Seifert)*; Deborah Verginella *(Amy's Mother)*; Michael J. Reynolds *(General)*; David Hemblen *(Dr. Killian)*; Ken James *(Developer)*; Nora Ballard *(Jackie)*; Sarena Paton *(Laura)*; Carmen Lishman *(Older Girl)*; Christi Hill *(Older Girl)*; Judith Orban *(Teacher)*; Jeff Braunstein *(Chairman)*; John Friesen *(Smalltown Businessman)*; Chris Benson *(Farmer)*; Kevin Jubinville *(Military Police)*; Philip Akin *(Air Force Reporter)*; Gladys O'Connor *(Farm Woman)*; Geoff McBride *(Clerk)*; Dick Callahan *(Customs Inspector)*; Cheryl MacInnis; Mark Wilson; J. Craig Sandy *(Reporters)*; Wendy Walsh; Larry McCormick; Richard Saxton; Linden Chiles *(Television Anchors)*; Timm Zemanek *(Husband)*; Diane Douglass *(Wife)*; Azura Bates *(Bratty Sister)*; Jonathan Bates *(Bratty Borther)*; Michael Vollans *(Bratty Brother)*; Michael Copeman *(Gun Shop Owner)*; John E. Nelles *(Tower Supervisor)*; Jeffrey W. Poulis *(Tower Operator)*; Christopher Lorenz *(Tower Operator)*; Melissa Tanti *(Dune Woman)*

An incredible journey in the air becomes a voyage of self-discovery for a young girl in this touching tale directed by Carroll Ballard (THE BLACK STALLION). One of the best "family films" of 1996, FLY AWAY HOME was not produced by Disney, and so was overlooked by audiences who claim to clamor for such offerings from Hollywood.

After her mother's death in an auto accident, 13-year-old Amy Alden (Anna Paquin, THE PIANO) is uprooted from her New Zealand home and sent to live with a father she doesn't remember in Ontario, Canada. Tom Alden (Jeff Daniels) is an eccentric artist, inventor, and flying enthusiast, who lives in a ramshackle farmhouse. He hasn't a clue about how to reach out to Amy, who's stewing in her isolation.

When a nearby woods are clear-cut by developers, Amy discovers an abandoned nest of goose eggs amid the fallen timber. She secretly adopts them, nestling them in her mother's old scarves, and when the goslings hatch, they imprint on Amy as their mother goose. As the birds mature, the Aldens face a dilemma: by law, domesticated geese must be pinioned, a procedure Amy refuses to allow, but her flock doesn't know how to migrate. That's when Tom hatches a crazy scheme. He will fly the migration route with Amy following him in her own plane, and the geese following behind her.

With only a few days to make the journey, the Aldens take off for a wetlands preserve in North Carolina that's being threatened by developers. After a forced landing at an Air Force base and an accidental detour through downtown Baltimore, the flight becomes a *cause celebre* for the media. Near the end, Tom's plane crashes and Amy refuses to go on alone. An inspirational speech about how she's strong—"just like her mother"—gets Amy back in the air. Just as the bulldozers are about to roll, Amy and her geese land at the preserve amidst a cheering throng.

Be assured, though a reading of FLY AWAY HOME's plot rings like a knock-off of FREE WILLY, the film is a resonant and affecting work. Based on the true incident of a man who led geese south in a plane, everything about Amy's character is pure invention by the screenwriters; so, yes, the story does take a few too many hokey turns in the final act, and the "greenie," anti-developer polemics are a bit much. However, this only makes Ballard's, and cinematographer Caleb Deschanel's, achievement—turning a potentially banal duckling into a swan—so special.

Ballard relies on visuals to tell the story and effectively reign in the melodrama. For example, the fatal accident that opens the movie is presented in powerful, preternatural silence with light strobing through the rain-soaked windshield. Throughout the film, the imagery is beautiful and poetic. One shot of Paquin laying in a field quotes the Andrew Wyeth painting "Christina's World," and it's not just a conceit on Ballard's part. Wyeth's aesthetic informs the entire film. Ballard fuses Amy's emotional state to the landscape she inhabits, so that nature becomes an expressive, dramatic device.

Thus, Paquin, who gives a nicely modulated performance, need not overplay. Amy's desolation in the beginning is conveyed by the overcast sky that dwarfs her; and later, her conquering of the clear, blue sky signals her transformation. Understatement allows viewers to invest their own identification in Amy. And so, in the end, when she soars through the clouds over the Carolina coast with the white ocean shoals below, Ballard has correctly calculated that the viewer's spirit will soar as well.— P.R.

d, Carroll Ballard; p, John Veitch, Carol Baum; exec p, Sandy Gallin; assoc p, John M. Eckert; w, Robert Rodat, Vince McKewin (based on the autobiography by Bill Lishman); ph, Caleb Deschanel; ed, Nicholas C. Smith; m, Mark Isham; prod d, Seamus Flannery; set d, Dan Conley; sound, Douglas Ganton (mixer); fx, Martin Malivoire, John Mariella, C.O.R.E. Digital Pictures; casting, Reuben Cannon, Deirdre Bowen; cos, Marie-Sylvie Deveau; makeup, Donald J. Mowat

AAN Best Cinematography: Caleb Deschanel

Children's/Drama **(PR: AA MPAA: PG)**

FOR BETTER OR WORSE ★

(U.S.) 95m Castle Rock Entertainment ~ Columbia Pictures/Turner Home Entertainment c

(AKA: STRANGER THINGS)

Jason Alexander *(Michael Makeshift)*; Lolita Davidovich *(Valerie)*; James Woods *(Reggie)*; Joe Mantegna *(Stone)*; Jay Mohr *(Dwayne)*; Beatrice Arthur *(Beverly)*; Robert Constanzo *(Landlord)*; Rip Torn; Ben Stiller; Rob Reiner; Steven Wright; John Amos

Woody Allen's movies inevitably make audience members cuddle up to the nebbish protagonist; FOR BETTER OR WORSE, on the other hand, makes the viewer willingly accept its central figure's self-pity. In the final anaylsis, the question remains: why should viewers subject themselves to this putz's unfunny melancholia?

Michael Makeshift (Jason Alexander) is a loser, unlike his colorful petty criminal brother, Reggie (James Woods). Nerdy Michael can't get a life after being unceremoniously dumped by his girlfriend. He also is having trouble paying his overdue rent, demanded by his slob of a landlord (Robert Costanzo).

Reggie pays Michael to baby-sit his new bride, Valerie (Lolita Davidovich), while he pursues a pie-in-the-sky heist of the credit union where his mom, Beverly (Beatrice Arthur), works. Michael tries to placate Valerie, who is unaware that her new husband is a thief. In the meantime, Reggie is outsmarted by potential partners Stone (Joe Mantegna) and Dwayne (Jay Mohr), who try to exclude him from his own scam by beating the necessary security codes out of him. Leaving Reggie tied up, the thug duo chases after Valerie, who unknowingly carries the info in her suitcase. On the lam with her, Michael tips off Valerie about Reggie's bad habits; the two become amorous.

Not only do Stone and Dwayne acquire the codes, but they also force Reggie and Valerie to participate in the daylight robbery. The caper reaches a chaotic pitch when Michael decides to single-handedly thwart the theft, which turns into a hostage crisis. After Michael and Reggie's errant father picks this moment to return to reclaim his wife and family bliss, the bungling crooks discover their pistols aren't even loaded.

Although the tense situation ends happily, Valerie frets that she's a jinx to the men she loves. After Reggie steps aside, Michael lovingly persuades her otherwise.

As a second banana on TV's "Seinfeld," Alexander easily scored laughs as a neurotic underdog character. As a leading man here, he proves to be nothing more than a glorified character actor. To make matters worse, he chose to direct this excruciatingly unfunny vehicle; his comic pacing as a filmmaker is way off, and he consistently choses to milk each and every set-up. Although the curly wig he sports here may make him look like a shorter, roly-poly version of Albert Brooks, he has none of the latter's talent.

Also unfortunately cast are sledgehammer talent Woods, not known for his feathery comic finesse, and the cloying Davidovich.

It may be unfair to harp on bad acting when the script is so remarkably unencumbered by comic sparkle. As the film gasps from terminal cuteness, director Alexander eschews charm and sophistication for imbecilic slapstick. This corpse of a comedy is embalmed with a doo-wop soundtrack that sounds like the Manhattan Transfer scoring a specialty number for Captain Kangaroo's Dancing Bear. *(Profanity, adult situations, violence.)*—R.P.

d, Jason Alexander; p, David Rotman; w, Jeff Nathanson; ph, Wayne Kennan; ed, Michael Jablow; prod d, Bill Elliot; art d, Kenneth A. Hardy; set d, Bruce Gibeson; sound, Bob Eber; fx, Danny Gill; casting, Artz & Cohen; cos, Charmaine Simmons

Comedy/Romance (PR: C MPAA: PG-13)

FOR THE MOMENT ★★

(Canada) 120m John Aaron Features II; National Film Board of Canada; Telefilm Canada; Manitoba Cultural Industries Development Office; Rogers Telefund ~ John Aaron Releasing c

Russell Crowe *(Lachlan)*; Christianne Hirt *(Lill)*; Wanda Cannon *(Betsy)*; Scott Kraft *(Zeek)*; Peter Outerbridge *(Johnny)*; Sara McMillan *(Kate)*; Bruce Boa *(Mr. Anderson)*; Katelynd Johnston *(Marion)*; Tyler Woods *(Charlie)*; John Bekavac *(Dipper)*; Robert G. Slade *(Scotty)*; Kelly Proctor *(Dennis)*; Roxanne Boulianne *(Anne)*; David Warburton *(Commander Levin)*; Ari Cohen *(Cecil)*; Glen Thompson *(Nigel)*; Guy Stewart *(Richard)*; Grant Dilworth *(Navigation Instructor)*; Curtis Sali *(Dipper's Cronie #1)*; Sean Bowie *(Dipper's Cronie #2)*; Alistair Abell *(Airman #1)*; Riel Langlois *(Frenchie)*; Clement Nelson *(Black Dancer)*; David Cowie *(Controller)*; Steve James Young *(New Zealander)*

FOR THE MOMENT starts off aloft with a striking title sequence, but quickly plummets into a cliched and slow-moving WWII romantic drama. Even fans of star Russell Crowe (ROMPER STOMPER) will be disappointed by the use of the up-and-coming actor in this botched creation.

In Manitoba, Canada, during the summer of 1942, a group of fighter pilots, members of the British Commonwealth Air Training Plan, prepare for war on the farm community's air training base. One pilot, an Australian volunteer named Lachlan (Crowe), meets Lill (Christianne Hirt), a spunky prairie woman whose husband has been away at war for two years. The two strangers are immediately attracted. Lill tries to discourage a romantic relationship, but eventually submits to temptation.

While they carry on their secret affair, another romance between Lachlan's friend Zeek (Scott Kraft), a flight instructor from Chicago, and Betsy (Wanda Cannon), single mother of two, stirs the normally quiet hamlet. Matters come to a head the night a group of unruly aviators threaten Betsy sexually, but Betsy single-handedly takes care of herself and her children.

Zeek dies in a training routine, and Lachlan comforts Betsy in her grief. Lill discovers Lachlan in bed with Betsy and breaks off their romance. Later, when Lill finds out that her husband has died in battle, she decides to forgive Lachlan for his weakness. During the funeral, one of the villagers sees Lill kissing Lachlan and tells her family. Despite the pain the news causes them, Lill's friends and relatives accept her back into the fold, and she bids a fond adieu to Lachlan, who joins his comrades in a high-flying mission across the ocean.

Writer-director Aaron Kim Johnston aims FOR THE MOMENT at audiences who enjoyed such modern-day military love stories as a TOP GUN (1986) and AN OFFICER AND A GENTLEMAN (1982). But FOR THE MOMENT owes even more to such Hollywood classics as TEST PILOT (1938), SINCE YOU WENT AWAY (1944), and UNTIL THEY SAIL (1957). By remaking this sort of "homefront" war film, FOR THE MOMENT promises to look at the WWII period with new insight. But except for a brief, simplistic episode about racism, the new film covers the same old ground—just technically not as well.

After the aerial opener (scored to Pachelbel's "Canon"), most of FOR THE MOMENT is set in a dry Manitoba farm community and shot with minimal visual imagination. The dialogue sounds as if it would have been trite even in 1942. Crowe, looking jowly and morose, tries to breath life into his role, but he gets no help from a barely passable supporting cast that acts anachronistically modern in demeanor. Viewers looking for a four-hankie cry over heroic love and loss during wartime would do better by sifting through their local video store bins than by spending money on this would-be heart-tugger. *(Violence, nudity, sexual situations, adult situations, substance abuse, profanity.)* — E.M.

d, Aaron Kim Johnston; p, Jack Clements, Aaron Kim Johnston; co-p, Joe MacDonald, Ches Yetman; w, Aaron Kim Johnston; ph, Ian Elkin; ed, Rita Roy; m, Victor Davies; prod d, Andrew Deskin; art d, Jim Phillips; set d, Mark Andrew Webb; ch, Ian Elkin; sound, David Husby (mixer); fx, Ted Ross; casting, Anne Tait; makeup, Pamela Athayde

Romance/War/Drama (PR: A MPAA: PG-13)

FORBIDDEN ZONE: ALIEN ABDUCTION ★

(U.S./Romania) 70m Twilight Entertainment; Section 8 Productions ~ Amazing Fantasy Video/Cult Video c

Meredyth Holmes *(Veronica)*; Darcy DeMoss *(Sheri)*; Pia Reyes *(Tedra)*; Dumitru Bogomaz *(The Alien)*; Horin Chiriac *(Josh)*; Carmen Lacatus *(Red-headed Friend)*; Alina Chivulescu *(Brunette Friend)*

At the heart of a mystery surrounding the best and weirdest sex they've ever had, three women discover they were victims of an alien abduction in this direct-to-video release. Aiming to be high-minded erotica, FORBIDDEN ZONE: ALIEN ABDUCTION is just silly and pretentious soft-core porn.

Virginal Veronica (Meredyth Holmes) and her friends Sheri (Darcy DeMoss) and Tedra (Pia Reyes) meet in a sauna to discuss—and piece together through flashbacks—what happened to them one strange night during a recent trip.

Travelling through a deserted wood, they observe some strange lights, then their car breaks down. Seeking help, Sheri is picked up by a thin, pale veterinarian. First, they stop at an Old West saloon, then he takes her on a stable-call, but the patient isn't a horse, it's a nymphomaniac wearing a saddle. Sheri and the girl run off, and have a torrid affair in a 19th-century mansion. Tedra, who's previous sexual experiences have all been drunken and degrading one-night stands, has fulfilling sex with a thin, pale jogger, then finds herself battling him in a futuristic arena. Though Tedra and Sheri claim their stories are true, both admit they seem less like reality than a surreal collage of dreams, fantasies, and distant memories.

Veronica explains, to her friends' disbelief, what really happened. They were taken aboard a UFO by a thin, pale alien (Dumitru Bogomaz), who explored their minds searching for one woman to carry his dying species' progeny. He chose Veronica because her sexual fantasy was this very situation. In the end, it's confirmed that Veronica is pregnant with the alien's baby.

FORBIDDEN ZONE: ALIEN ABDUCTION features unusually high production values—grand sets and costumes, some ideas about its characters, and lots of very "European" (i.e., artsy-fartsy) touches; it *is* interesting to look at. But for all the earnest acting by its suitably beautiful, towel-clad cast, the movie can't overcome the fact that it's just a coy and overly talky come-on that never pays off in a satisfying or surprising way. *(Extensive nudity, sexual situations.)* — P.R.

d, Lucian S. Diamonde; exec p, Alan B. Bursteen; w, Vernon Lumley; ph, Adolfo Bartoli; ed, Steve Nielson; prod d, Valentin Calinescu

Science Fiction/Erotic/Mystery (PR: O MPAA: R)

FOREST WARRIOR ★

(U.S.) 98m Lot Productions ~ Turner Home Entertainment c

Chuck Norris *(McKenna/Forest Warrior)*; Terry Kiser *(Travis Thorne)*; Max Gail *(Sheriff Ramsey)*; Roscoe Lee Browne *(Clovis)*; Trenton Knight *(Justin)*; Megan Paul *(Austene)*; Josh Wolford *(Logan)*; Michael Friedman *(Lewis)*; William Sanderson *(Paul Carpio)*; Dennis Paladino *(Mark)*; John Dennis Johnston *(Williams)*; Elya Baskin *(Buster)*; Loretta Swit *(Shirley)*; Michael Beck *(Arlen)*; Wyl Shriner *(Jack)*; Barbara Niven *(Stacy)*; Carly Scott *(Thomas Jorgenson)*; Chris Doyle *(Holly)*; Jimmy Ortega *(Surveyor)*; Adam Berg; Jolene Kay; F. A. J. Howard *(Thorne Persons)*; George Buck Flower *(Barney)*

This is a folksy, self-righteous, coming-of-age tract with a heavy pro-conservation angle that features Chuck Norris personifying Nature by morphing into a range of animals, from a grizzly bear to a frisky raccoon.

When not hiking through the forest, Logan (Josh Wolford), Austene (Megan Paul), Justin (Trenton Knight), and their pals enjoy the tall tales of Pacific Northwest storyteller Clovis (Roscoe Lee Browne). One such legend relates the saga of the Forest Warrior (Chuck Norris). Hunted down for his valuable land and slain while seeking medicinal herbs to save his wife, the Forest Warrior lives on as a specter protecting the interests of Mother Nature.

While the kids hang out at a magnificent tree house, land developer Travis Thorne (Terry Kiser) rushes through a massive timber-clearing before a town ordinance can come into effect. Thorne's men endanger the children with demolition charges, but are outmatched by the Forest Warrior, who can change himself into a soaring hawk at will, or simply kickbox Thorne's thugs. Not only does this magic spirit of the glade heal Austene after the tree house explodes, but he actively backs up the kids's sabotage against Thorne's clear-cutting operation. Eventually, Thorne's personal encounter with the Forest Warrior rattles him sufficiently to quash further crimes against the trees. After Thorne and his men are arrested, the townspeople rebuild the children's tree house. The Forest Warrior continues to keep a vigilant eye on preserving the wilderness.

Looking ridiculous in a scruffy hippie hairdo, Norris embodies the stoic spirit with a pitiful lack of verve. The characters he played in SIDEKICKS or FOREST WARRIOR will never be as impressive as the Norris of SILENT RAGE. In these kid-video surroundings, his kickboxing energy is diminished not due to any slackening of skill, but by the namby-pamby Disney-esque blandness.

It's possible that youngsters will respond to the trained animals representing the various transformations of the Forest Warrior, but grown-ups will be less enthused. They'll be shaking their heads in disbelief at the slapstick *reductio ad absurdum* of the kung-fu matches, at Norris's comatose benevolence, and at the criminal waste of such fine character actors as Browne, Kiser, and Max Gail. *(Violence, adult situations.)* — R.P.

d, Aaron Norris; p, Andy Howard; exec p, Avi Lerner, Danny Dimbort, Seth Willenson; assoc p, Rebecca Norris, Leonard Zisman, Marcus Manton; co-p, Sanford Hampton; w, Ron Swanson, Donald Thompson; ph, Joao Fernandes; ed, Marcus Manton; m, Bill Elliot; prod d, Gene Abel; set d, Ann Job; sound, Doug Arnold (mixer); fx, Michael Lambert; casting, Iris Hampton; cos, Dorothy Amos; makeup, Myke Michaels; stunts, Hank Baumert

Action/Adventure/Martial Arts (PR: AA MPAA: PG)

4 TALES OF 2 CITIES ★★½

(U.S.) 93m Homegrown Pictures ("Urban Legend"); Sudden Picture ("Urban Legend"); J.D.I. Productions ("Phinehas"); The Independent Film Channel ("Boy Crazy Girl Crazier"); Chanticleer Films ("The Duke of Groove"); Ma & Pa Pictures ("The Duke of Groove") c

"Urban Legend" Jan Leslie Harding *(Homeless Woman)*; Julia Mueller *(Annie)*; David Hamilton Simonds *(Basketball Guy)*; Melinda Wade Kaufman *(Norma the Waitress)*; "Phinehas" Patrick Breen *(Billy)*; Preston Foerder *(Voice of Phinehas)*; "Boy Crazy Girl Crazier" Illeana Douglas *(Celena)*; Kevin Breznahan *(Charlie)*; "The Duke of Groove": Kate Capshaw *(Rebecka)*; Carey Lowell *(Shannon)*; Elliott Gould *(Dennis)*; Tobey Maguire *(Rich)*; Kiefer Sutherland *(Hugo, The Host)*; Uma Thurman *(Maya)*; Tim Guinee *(Let It Go Guy)*; Udo Kier *(Earl)*; Jennifer Lloyd *(Janis Joplin)*

4 TALES OF 2 CITIES groups together four short films set in New York and Los Angeles and directed by performers taking a turn behind the camera. The results are mildly interesting, but none of the four shorts makes a great impact.

The first of the four tales, "Urban Legend," takes place in downtown Manhattan, where a troubled young woman, Annie (Julia Mueller), sits on a park bench and receives unexpected comfort from a homeless woman (Jan Leslie Harding) who claims to be a psychoanalyst. Through their unusual encounter session, Annie gains a new perspective on her despair, after which the odd woman moves on to coach a basketball player nearby.

The second story, "Phinehas," also takes place in Manhattan, inside the basement of a man named Billy (Patrick Breen). Billy has kidnapped a children's television show puppet named Phinehas (the voice of Preston Foerder) in the futile hope that the popular "Phinehas" show will educate the public on AIDS. He also makes demands on the puppet that are unrealistic at best. In the end, Phinehas comforts Billy while he dies of AIDS.

Set in LA, "Boy Crazy Girl Crazier," focuses on an aspiring actress (Illeana Douglas) who gets dumped by her actor-boyfriend (Kevin Breznahan) after they return from a Hollywood party. The actress' sadness turns to rage, however, when she learns that a top director picked the young man for a movie role she had wanted—he obtained it by pretending he was gay, and recounting his girlfriend's stormy life story, claiming it as his own. She takes revenge on her caddish ex-lover by threatening him physically and forcing him to call the director and confess that he is not worthy of the role. In the end, the actress gets the part.

The last story, "The Duke of Groove," is set in 1970, also in LA. On the night of a big Hollywood party, Rebecka (Kate Capshaw) invites her 15-year-old son, Rich (Tobey Maguire), to escort her while her husband is away. Rich is excited at the prospect of meeting celebrities at the party, and gladly accepts the invitation. At the wild shindig, Rebecka gets stoned, while Rich looks on in awe at the arrival of Janis Joplin (Jennifer Lloyd) and other celebrities. He also receives his first kiss from a beautiful hippie named Maya (Uma Thurman). After the party, Rebecka tells Rich the truth about her marriage: it's over. Later in his bedroom, Rich is comforted by a vision of Janis Joplin.

Like GIRLFRIENDS (1996), 4 TALES OF 2 CITIES shrewdly links several disparate short subjects by a single theme and packages the bunch as a feature. GIRLFRIENDS centers around contemporary lesbian issues; 4 TALES deals with urban angst, but the results of the latter are somewhat more mixed.

It's difficult to pick a "best tale" from the four, since the most technically polished, "Boy Crazy Girl Crazier" (nicely photographed in widescreen by Kent Wakeford), is also the least interesting narratively. Star-director-writer Ileanna Douglas goes over the top with her performance, and belabors the dog-eat-dog spoof aspects of the Hollywood "scene."

The longest tale, the Oscar-nominated "The Duke of Groove," is an ambitious (albeit unconvincing) effort to recreate another era. Co-written by Griffin Dunne (who directed) and Adam Brooks, it features the biggest stars (Kiefer Sutherland and Elliot Gould make cameos). Unfortunately, it sours as it progresses due to the writers' reactionary attitude toward hippie culture and women. The final shot involving the vision of Joplin also rankles because of its pretentiousness and the inexplicable use of a Bob Dylan (not a Joplin) song on the soundtrack.

By default, the New York tales, while highly theatrical, are much more successful. Adrienne Shelly's "Urban Legend" captures city "craziness" without being condescending to its characters, and Fisher Stevens's "Phinehas" (written by its star, Patrick Breen), while somewhat drab, is surprisingly touching. *(Violence, adult situations, substance abuse, profanity.)* — E.M.

d, Adrienne Shelly ("Urban Legend"), Fisher Stevens ("Phinehas"), Illeana Douglas ("Boy Crazy Girl Crazier"), Griffin Dunne ("The Duke of Groove"); p, Jonna Mattingly ("Urban Legend"), Hilary Gilford ("Phinehas"), Dan Etheridge ("Boy Crazy Girl Crazier"), Martin Yu ("Boy Crazy Girl Crazier"), Thom Colwell ("The Duke of Groove"); exec p, Adrienne Shelly ("Urban Legend"), Jana Sue Memel ("The Duke of Groove"), Jonathan Sehring, Caroline Kaplan; assoc p, Hillary Anne Ripps ("The Duke of Groove"); w, Adrienne Shelly ("Urban Legend"), Patrick Breen ("Phinehas"), Illeana Douglas ("Boy Crazy Girl Crazier"), Adam Brooks ("The Duke of Groove"), Griffin Dunne ("The Duke of Groove"); ph, Tami Reiker ("Urban Legend"), Michael Spiller ("Phinehas"), Kent Wakeford ("Boy Crazy Girl Crazier"), John J. Campbell ("The Duke of Groove"); ed, Doug Abel ("Urban Legend"), Gary Winick ("Phinehas") , James Kwei ("Boy Crazy Girl Crazier"), Michelle Gorchow ("The Duke of Groove"); m, Evan Lurie ("Phineh; makeup, Gina Monaci ("The Duke of Groove"), Todd Kleitsch

Drama/Comedy **(PR: C MPAA: NR)**

FOXFIRE ★½

(U.S.) 102m Rysher Entertainment; Chestnut Hill Productions; Red Mullet Productions ~ Samuel Goldwyn Company c

Hedy Burress *(Maddy Wirtz)*; Angelina Jolie *(Legs Sadovsky)*; Jenny Lewis *(Rita Faldes)*; Jenny Shimizu *(Goldie Goldman)*; Sarah Rosenberg *(Violet Kahn)*; Peter Facinelli *(Ethan Bixby)*; Dash Mihok *(Dana Taylor)*; Michelle Brookhurst *(Cindy)*; Elden Ratliff *(Bobby)*; Cathy Moriarty *(Martha Wirtz)*; Richard Beymer *(Mr. Parks)*; Fran Bennett *(Judge Holifield)*; John Diehl *(Mr. Buttinger)*; Chris Mulkey *(Dan Goldman)*; Jay Acovone *(Chuck)*; Arwen Carter *(Leaflet Girl)*; Ever Carradine *(Girl in Printshop)*; Maria Celedonio *(Zoe)*; Raissa Fleming *(Rita's Mom)*; T.J. Galash *(Teenage Boy)*; Scott Gallegos *(Jock Friend)*; Jason Wilhite *(Jock Friend)*; Kaci Garcia *(Rita's Younger Sister)*; Wesley Johnson *(Tom)*; Rick Jones *(Security Guard)*; Joel Moore *(First Geek)*; Betty Moyer *(Violet's Mother)*; Barbara Niven *(Goldie's Stepmother)*; Steven Clark Pachoso *(Cop)*; Stuart Regen *(Art Teacher)*; Lori Rogers *(First Year Girl)*; Burl Ross *(Mr. Penn)*; Shiloh Strong *(Steve)*; Rasa Yurchis *(Street Junkie)*

Based on Joyce Carol Oates's novel, this unoriginal depiction of female adolescence strains for sensitivity, but bland performances and dreary writing effectively sink its good intentions.

Into the relatively uneventful lives of a group of Portland, Oregon, high-school girls—Maddy (Hedy Burress), Rita (Jenny Lewis), Goldie (Jenny Shimizu), and Violet (Sarah Rosenberg)—walks Legs (Angelina Jolie), a charismatic drifter. One rainy afternoon, Legs comes strutting into Mr. Buttinger's (John Diehl) biology class, just in time to rescue the squeamish Rita from being forced to dissect a live frog. Legs quickly splits, but returns after school with Maddy, Violet, and Goldie to save Rita once again, this time from Mr. Buttinger's lecherous advances. They beat him up and are suspended for the assault. All of the girls, particularly Maddy, are taken with Legs' street-smart ways and smoldering beauty, and together they find refuge away from their unsympathetic families in an abandoned house. There, the girls form a gang, dubbed "Foxfire," and tattoo one another with the image of a flame.

As the friendship between Legs and Maddy grows in intensity, the girls spend much of their time hanging out at the house, exhilarated by their new found freedom and power. But the idea of a gang of independent young women rubs a few of the local boys the wrong way, particularly a group of high school jocks led by Dana (Dash Mihok). One afternoon, Dana's girlfriend Cindy (Michelle Brookhurst) comes to the Foxfire house and tells her that Dana has been beating her. She asks Maddy to escort her home, but it's a set-up: as soon as they reach the road, Dana and his buddies grab Maddy and drag her into their truck, threatening to rape her. But before they can drive off, Legs appears with a knife and forces Dana to release Maddy and turn over the truck. Maddy and Legs drive off on a wild joyride, picking up Goldie, Rita, and Violet along the way. Speeding through town, the girls are pursued by the police, and in an attempt to elude them, Legs swerves and crashes the truck.

The girls are unhurt, but are charged with car-jacking, and, thanks to Cindy's bogus testimony, Legs is sent away for six months. The girls are lost without her, particularly Goldie, whose heroin addiction has spun out of control. Meanwhile, Cindy, guilt-ridden over having lied in court, admits that the girls acted in self-defense, and Legs is released. Returning to the Foxfire house, Legs finds the girls caring for Goldie, and decides to confront Goldie's abusive father, Mr. Goldman (Chris Mulkey). Walking into his house, Legs demands he fork over the $10,000 needed for Goldie's detox, but he refuses. Legs pulls out a gun and orders Mr. Goldman into his car. Back at the Foxfire house, with Mr. Goldman tied to a chair, Legs suggests they call Mrs. Goldman (Barbara Niven) and demand the money as ransom. At this point, Maddy and the others balk: things are getting out of control. As the girls argue, Rita accidentally fires the gun and wounds Mr. Goldman. In a panic, they drive him to the hospital, leaving Maddy and Legs behind. Legs realizes it's time she moved on. Standing on the bridge leading out of town, she asks Maddy to go with her, but Maddy knows she can't. When a truck stops to pick up Legs, she bids her goodbye.

We're in Gus Van Sant territory here: anguished youth in the wet, drug-susceptible American Northwest. Sadly, director Annette Haywood-Carter has none of his biting, insightful humor. The film is basically unmoving, pussyfooting around any lesbian implications, although Legs is adoringly photographed. The cinematography is otherwise dark and rainwashed, to match the film's general mood. Unfortunately, a single mood spun out to the length of a feature film can easily engender a trance-like state in the viewer or, even more accurately, a nap.

None of the characters are compelling. Jolie, the daughter of actor Jon Voight, is fetching with her androgynous look and endless limbs, but is weak and unconvincing in a key role. Japanese-American Calvin Klein model Shimizu also has an intriguing appearance, and much more might have been made of her ethnicity. Unfortunately, Haywood-Carter focuses on the drably spiritual Burress, who's sort of the Everygirl here. All the males, meanwhile, are basically unruly, dumb beasts, unable to appreciate even a *soupcon* of these girls' supposedly extraordinary qualities. *(Nudity, substance abuse, violence, profanity, adult situations.)* — D.N.

d, Annette Haywood-Carter; p, Jeffrey Lurie, John Bard Manulis, John P. Marsh; exec p, Paige Simpson, Mike Figgis, Laura Friedman; co-p, Marc S. Fischer; w, Elizabeth White (based on the novel *Foxfire: Confessions of a Girl Gang* by Joyce Carol Oates); ph, Newton Thomas Sigel; ed, Louise Innes; m, Michel Colombier; prod d, John Myhre; art d, Alan Locke; set d, Marthe Pineau; sound, Jim Hawkins (mixer); fx, I.J. Van Perre Jr.; casting, Emily Schweber; cos, Laura Goldsmith; makeup, Eileen Kastner-Delago; stunts, Russell Towery

Drama **(PR: C MPAA: R)**

FRAME BY FRAME ★★½

(Canada/U.S.) 97m All Media Inc. ~ Republic Pictures Home Video c
(AKA: CONUNDRUM)

Marg Helgenberger *(Rose Ekberg)*; Michael Biehn *(Stash Horak)*; Ron White *(Gordan Mulvaney)*; Harvey Chao *("Tony" Tam)*; Dan Lett *(Jimmy)*; Von Flores *(Linh Say Chou)*; Karen Wadell *(Julie Horak)*; Russell Yuen *(Dennis Kye)*; Arthur Eng *(Joey Tam)*; Alan Van Sprang *(Ted)*; Peter MacNeill *(Hershel Kirkland)*

Though ill-designed to shoulder weighty issues like gender politics, this Showtime cable thriller makes a dismal case for the role of women in law enforcement.

No-nonsense lady detective Rose Ekberg (Marg Helgenberger) already had one lustful co-worker keel-hauled on sexual-harassment charges. She enjoys a warmer working relationship with her partner, Stash Horak (Michael Biehn). After his pregnant wife is savagely raped and murdered, eyebrows go up all over the department when Rose and the grieving Stash become lovers. But the stakes rise much higher once their main informant inside the Minneapolis Asian mob turns up battered to death; his fingerprints were found on the dead woman.

Rose believes local godfather Tam (Harvey Chao) is the real culprit behind the killings, and she covers for an increasingly unstable Stash when Internal Affairs starts snooping around. Then, planted evidence points the finger of suspicion at Rose herself.

Now a fugitive, the policewoman realizes that Stash is guilty after all. Motivated by both his wife's infidelity—the fetus wasn't his—and a blackmail plot by Tam, Stash paid the informant to slay his spouse, then killed the assassin in turn, and finally framed Rose. Rose confronts her estranged partner during a raid on Tam's. Stash shoots Tam, and then blows his brains out with Rose's gun.

Taken at face value, this grim potboiler suggests that sex rules the station house, whether it's Stash being cuckolded, divorcee Rose sleeping with the enemy, or one of the few friendly males in the precinct cautioning the heroine with, "Just do what I've been doing for years—watch your ass." Though she's somehow exonerated in Stash's portentous suicide at the end, Rose will never fit in with the boys's club.

While most Hollywood policewomen seem to be recruited fresh out of modeling school, the hard-edged Helgenberger brings verisimilitude to a difficult part. Biehn gets little chance to develop beyond a rogue cop—and, sure enough, Vietnam vet—who goes nuts in the last reel. *(Sexual situations, nudity, violence, adult situations.)* — C.C.

d, Douglas Barr; p, Thomas Baer; w, Douglas Barr; ph, Rodney Charters; ed, Raul Davalos; m, Mark Snow; prod d, James McAteer; art d, Gordon Lebredt; set d, Bruce Mailing; casting, Beth Klein; cos, Kei Yano; stunts, Steve Lucescu

Crime/Thriller **(PR: O MPAA: R)**

FRANCOIS TRUFFAUT: STOLEN PORTRAITS ★★★½

(France) 93m Chrysalide Films; France 2 Cinema; INA; Maecenas Films; Premiere ~ AAA/Myriad Pictures c/bw

Gerard Depardieu; Fanny Ardant; Marie-France Pisier; Nathalie Baye; Marcel Ophuls; Alexandre Astruc; Bertrand Tavernier; Claude Miller; Eric Rohmer; Olivier Assayas; Jean-Louis Richard; Claude DeGivray; Jean Aurel; Jean Gruault; Annette Insdorf; Albert Duchesne; Janine Bazin; Lilian Siegel; Marcel Bernert; Yann Dedet; Monique Lucas; Madeleine Morgenstern; Laura Truffaut; Ewa Truffaut; Claude Chabrol; Robert Lachenay

This exemplary documentary about an icon of international cinema boldly makes the statement that filmmaker Francois Truffaut reinvented himself on film. Through clips from his challenging body of work and exhaustive interviews, this fascinating remembrance of various "Truffauts" past proves its point about a director using his movies as selective autobiography.

Rather than adopting a purely chronological approach, Truffaut's biographers, Serge Toubiana and Michel Pascal, trace the director's life like a detective story with evidence gleaned from an array of French film industry celebrities plus family and friends. Unsurprisingly, they say Truffaut's personality shines through his signature film THE 400 BLOWS (1959), a sort of payback for a loveless childhood. In fact, the young hero is a composite of Truffaut and lifelong friend Robert Lachanay, whose bravado the shy Truffaut so admired that he borrowed it for his onscreen persona, Antoine Doinel.

The documentary reveals that Truffaut was the illegitimate son of a Jewish dentist; his free-spirited mother married his stepfather to give Truffaut a name. Interviewees say this outcast status and the uncertainty of his mother's love shaped Truffaut's character. Movies became his refuge. Perhaps the clearest indication of his resolve to live through cinema isn't his marriage to Madeleine Morgenstern, whose father financed his first feature, but his opportunistic print campaign for the auteur theory. Truffaut launches his *Cahiers du Cinema* attack on sacred cows of the French film industry to make a name for himself. While he generously restores the pre-eminence of the director, he shatters several reputations. So intent was he to make feature films, and to exorcise his childhood demons, that he relives his adult life onscreen with the assistance of actor-surrogate, Jean-Pierre Leaud. Eventually, his brand of personal cinema demands that he act in his own movies, as in THE WILD CHILD (1970) and THE GREEN ROOM (1978). Immortalized through vivid classics like JULES AND JIM (1962) and STOLEN KISSES (1968), Truffaut cheats death without ever coming to terms with the little boy he created in THE 400 BLOWS, an aggrieved child he carries with him throughout his life and in all his films.

Not only is this celebratory documentary absorbing movie history and expert biography, but it also offers cinephiles an invaluable opportunity to become acquainted with director Claude Chabrol and writer-director Alexandre Astruc, whose interviews are often as reflective of themselves as they are of Truffaut. More importantly, this documentary explores Truffaut's versatile legacy from progenitor of the New Wave to the traditionalist of movies like THE LAST METRO (1980), a classic that the young turk Truffaut might have disparaged in his *Cahiers* days. Wisely reinforcing its theme of reinvention with clips from Truffaut's oeuvre, FRANCOIS TRUFFAUT: STOLEN PORTRAITS transcends the talking-heads genre by letting movies like THE SOFT SKIN (1964) and TWO ENGLISH GIRLS (1972) speak for Truffaut.

As a probing examination of what makes a genius tick, this documentary about myth-making is remarkable, not because it gives us all the right answers, but because it forces us to ask the right questions. Although one wonders why no clips were included from STORY OF ADELE H. (1975), whose intense central romance mirrors Truffaut's obsessive love of cinema, the other great films are interwoven adroitly into the texture of Toubiana and Pascal's suppositions about Truffaut.

By closing with the comments of actress Fanny Ardant (with whom Truffaut had a daughter), STOLEN PORTRAITS refocuses our attention on the reciprocated affection so many actors felt for this director. Yet, even with the obvious adoration of his compatriots and family, Truffaut's principal love was filmmaking, which provided him with the kind of unconditional love whose absence haunted his childhood and shaped his destiny. *(Profanity, adult situations, sexual situations, nudity.)* — R.P.

d, Serge Toubiana, Michel Pascal; p, Monique Annaud; exec p, Bertrand Van Effenterre, Catherine Siriez; w, Serge Toubiana, Michel Pascal; ph, Maurice Fellous, Jean Yves LeMener, Michel Sourioux; ed, Dominique Martin; sound, Vincent Arnardi

Documentary **(PR: C MPAA: NR)**

FREEWAY ★★★½

(U.S.) 102m Republic Pictures; Kushner-Locke; Samuel Hadida; August Entertainment; Davis Films; Illusion Entertainment Group; Muse/Wyman ~ Roxie Releasing c

Kiefer Sutherland *(Bob Wolverton)*; Reese Witherspoon *(Vanessa)*; Brooke Shields *(Mimi Wolverton)*; Wolfgang Bodison *(Detective Breer)*; Dan Hedaya *(Detective Wallace)*; Amanda Plummer *(Ramona—Vanessa's Mother)*; Michael T. Weiss *(Larry—Vanessa's Stepdad)*; Bokeem Woodbine *(Chopper)*; Brittany Murphy *(Rhonda)*; Sidney Lassick *(Norman)*; Kitty Fox *(Grandma)*

Propelled by Reese Witherspoon's fierce and funny performance, FREEWAY merges a black comic excursion through LA's underbelly with a feminist update of "Little Red Riding Hood."

Witherspoon plays 15-year-old Vanessa Lutz, daughter of a crack whore (Amanda Plummer) and stepdaughter of Larry (Michael T. Weiss), an ex-con who molests her. Vanessa, herself, has a rap sheet and is illiterate. After Mom and Larry are dragged off to jail, Vanessa, clad in crimson and toting a picnic basket, heads for her grandmother's house.

Stranded on the freeway, Vanessa is picked up by Bob Wolverton (Kiefer Sutherland), a psychologist who specializes in treating juvenile delinquents. Bob probes Vanessa about her tragic life—her father's murder, abuse in foster care—but when his queries turn perverse and sexual, she realizes he is the notorious "I-5 serial killer." Bob has a straight-razor, but Vanessa has a gun. She shoots him several times, and leaves him for dead in a ditch.

Miraculously, Bob survives, and Vanessa is arrested—no one believes her story about Bob trying to kill and rape her. The detectives on the I-5 killer case, Wallace and Breer (Dan Hedaya and Wolfgang Bodison), decide to investigate Vanessa's claims. They discover evidence incriminating Bob—in response to which, his wife (Brooke Shields) blows her head off. Vanessa, having escaped from prison, heads for grandma's trailer. In granny's bed, Bob is waiting for her, but again Vanessa gets the upper hand and kills him. When Wallace and Breer arrive at the macabre scene, they and Vanessa just laugh.

In FREEWAY, Reese Witherspoon, often relegated to "sweet little girl" roles (S.F.W., FEAR), uses that innocent look as an ironic, comic layer for Vanessa. Witherspoon portrays the uneducated Vanessa as a guileless survivor, unknowingly—but no less determinedly—making a journey of empowerment. As one of the disposable people on the last rung of the social ladder, she is forced to take unusual steps, acquiescing to sex and resorting to violence as a matter of course, necessary when people won't "let her be." Society won't even recognize Bob as a monster, even after Vanessa disfigures him so he appears monstrous. Such discrimination leaves her no choice but to pursue justice on her own.

Imbedded in "Little Red Riding Hood" is a cautionary fable about the dangerous power of female sexuality and the need for society to repress it. Vanessa's innocence may be lost, but she is yet pure—pure survival instinct. Turning traditional hegemony on its ear, she refuses to let any detour deter her progress on the road to freedom—or, what one might call her "freeway." *(Graphic violence, extreme profanity, sexual situations, adult situations.)* — P.R.

d, Matthew Bright; p, Brad Wyman, Chris Hanley; exec p, Oliver Stone, Dan Halsted, Richard Rutowski; co-p, Marc Ezralow, Adam J. Merims; w, Matthew Bright; ph, John Thomas; ed, Maysie Hoy; m, Danny Elfman; prod d, Pam Warner; sound, Ed White; casting, Mary Vernieu; cos, Merrie Lawson; makeup, Elisabeth Fry, John Buechler; stunts, Troy Gilbert

Crime/Thriller **(PR: O MPAA: R)**

FRENCH TWIST ★★½

(France) 100m Renn Productions; TF1 Films; Les Films Flam; Canal Plus ~ Miramax Zoe Films c

(GAZON MAUDIT)

Victoria Abril *(Loli)*; Josiane Balasko *(Marijo)*; Alain Chabat *(Laurent)*; Ticky Holgado *(Antoine)*; Miguel Bose *(Diego, the Young Man)*; Catherine Hiegel *(Dany)*; Catherine Samie *(The Prostitute)*; Catherine Lachens *(Sopha, the Boss)*; Michele Bernier *(Solange)*; Telshe Boorman *(Dorothy Crumble)*; Veronique Barrault *(Emily Crumble/Vero)*; Sylvie Audcoeur *(Ingrid)*; Maureen Diot *(Cristelle)*

FRENCH TWIST tries to update classic French farce with a brazen new sexual awareness, but this love triangle involving a unhappily married couple and the lesbian who comes between them seems more forced than funny.

In Avignon, France, Loli (Victoria Abril) and Laurent (Alain Chabat) live a seemingly peaceful and happy existence with their two young sons. The only problem is that Laurent spends many evenings away from home with his realty "clients," who are in fact his many mistresses. Laurent justifies his cheating to his friends and himself but remains discreet, while Loli does not suspect a thing.

Marijo (Josiane Balasko), a heavyset but attractive lesbian, enters Loli and Laurent's home and life when her truck breaks down and Loli invites her in. Loli is attracted to Marijo and when she discovers that Laurent has betrayed his wedding vows, she asks Marijo to stay with her. A furious Laurent retaliates by inviting Marijo's old girlfriend, Dany (Catherine Hiegel), whom he has met by happenstance, to stay with them too.

Although Dany's visit gets cut short, Loli becomes jealous and leaves home. That night, in order to get pregnant, Marijo requests that Laurent make love to her. Nine months later, Loli finds out about the night of mechanical sex and visits Marijo in the Paris nightclub where she is a DJ to confront her. Laurent steps in during the showdown, but the encounter changes nature when Marijo goes into labor. Some time later, Loli and Marijo are seen raising their new child under the same roof as Laurent, who now considers dating male clients.

FRENCH TWIST generates humor out of situations that grow increasingly absurd. Director, star, and co-screenwriter Balasko fully explores the various possibilities of the love triangle, while commenting on gender roles by mixing up romantic traditions. To its credit, this modern-day screwball farce possesses the pace and look of a subdued Pedro Almodovar picture (Abril is often the lead in Almodovar's films, although her character here is somewhat less silly). Balasko even uses a Spanish-style score (by Manuel Malou) in key parts, which brightens the mood. Best of all, the actors carry off the difficult task of alternating emotions constantly and making inane moments believable (for example, when Marijo and Laurent go to bed together).

Potentially, FRENCH TWIST should appeal to any audience—male, female, gay, straight—but moral prudes may not be the only ones to have trouble with it. Despite the high level of energy and talent, FRENCH TWIST quickly becomes unsettling because none of the characters show basic respect for one another. All the revenge and counter-revenge is supposed to be funny but is merely unpleasant, and Balasko glosses over how these "adults" are affecting their children with their behavior (the two little boys glimpsed early on in the story mysteriously disappear as the story progresses). It is hard to enjoy a film that tries to be different and funny at the expense of everyone—including the viewer. *(Violence, nudity, sexual situations, substance abuse, extreme profanity.)* — E.M.

d, Josiane Balasko; p, Claude Berri; exec p, Pierre Grunstein; w, Josiane Balasko, Telsche Boorman; ph, Gerard De Battista; ed, Claudine Merlin; m, Manuel Malou; prod d, Claude Parnet, Bernard Prim; sound, Dominique Hennequin (mixer); cos, Fabienne Katany; makeup, Didier Lavergne

Comedy/Drama/Romance **(PR: O MPAA: R)**

FRIEND OF THE FAMILY 2 ★

(U.S.) 90m Royal Oaks Entertainment ~ Orion Home Video c

Shauna O'Brien *(Linda)*; Paul Michael Robins *(Alex Madison)*; Jenna Bodnar *(Maddy)*; Jeff Rector *(Mark)*; Don Scribner *(Simon)*; Emmett Grennan *(Marcel)*; Arthur Roberts *(Mr. Gates)*; Sid Farley *(Byron)*; Sam Hiona *(Mr. Tashima)*; Claire Pollan *(Potential Nanny)*; Steve Scionti *(Waiter)*

In the first entry in the FRIEND OF THE FAMILY franchise, our self-sacrificing heroine was a sexual healer guaranteeing erotic bliss to the orgasmically deprived. In this feverish follow-up (a FATAL ATTRACTION clone), the female protagonist is now a vengeful harpy, intent on using her hard-body and soft soap to destroy a happy home.

When tightly-wound Linda (Shauna O'Brien) publicly breaks off her engagement to Marcel (Emmett Grennan) in a fancy restaurant, married man Alex Madison (Paul Michael Robinson) pays her tab, beds her until she forgets all about Marcel, and promises her undying love. Unfortunately, this New Orleans roll-in-the-hay can't realistically go on, because businessman Alex has a wife, Maddy (Jenna Bodnar), and infant son waiting for him on the West Coast. Trouble in Alex's paradise brews after Maddy decides to return to work and begs Alex to house her layabout brother, Byron (Sid Farley), temporarily. Guess whom Maddy hires as her au pair girl? Why, Linda, of course!

Furious with persistent homewrecker Linda, Alex is nonetheless forced to accede to her dominatrix wishes in bed and right under his wife's nose. To consolidate her power, Linda beds Byron and turns him against his brother-in-law. Already worn out by sexual blackmail, Alex hits the roof when his boss dumps dinner with an important client in his already crowded lap. Poisoning Maddy, Linda pulls off the social event in high style. By the time clueless Alex goes to the hospital to retrieve Maddy, Linda is busy accommodating Alex's business associate Mark (Jeff Rector). When Mark realizes Linda is actually Alex's former out-of-town pickup, he makes the mistake of calling her crazy; to prove he's right, Linda shoots him dead.

Determined to come clean to Maddy, Alex discovers he has no car brakes. Battered by a car wreck, riled-up Alex confesses his infidelity and decks Byron, who admits to brake-tampering. When the cops arrive at the domestic disturbance, Linda wounds Alex, but the police blast her away. Unfortunately, Maddy discovers her baby is missing.

FRIEND OF THE FAMILY 2 deserves credit for that last-minute shocker. We never do find out what happened to the infant. Otherwise, this film is the predictable soft-core schlock you'd expect. Even the sex scenes aren't arousing because the actors portray their roles so woodenly. The new line of boudoir vamps like O'Brien toil at their sex appeal like Girl Scouts trying to get a merit badge for playing Delilah in a jamboree. For a hotter homewrecker fantasy, rent SCORNED (1994) with Shannon Tweed. *(Violence, extensive nudity, extreme profanity, sexual situations, adult situations.)* — R.P.

d, Nicholas Medina; p, Noble Henry; exec p, Alan Burstein; w, Henry Krinkle; ph, Gary Graver; ed, Ronald Basswood; m, Adam Berry; prod d, David Blass; sound, David Waelder (mixer); cos, Gwen Lavery; makeup, Marjolein Moore

Erotic/Drama **(PR: O MPAA: NR)**

FRIGHTENERS, THE ★★★½

(U.S.) 106m Wingnut Films ~ Universal c

Michael J. Fox *(Frank Bannister)*; Trini Alvarado *(Lucy Lynskey)*; Peter Dobson *(Roy Lynskey)*; John Astin *(The Judge)*; Jeffrey Combs *(Milton Dammers)*; Dee Wallace Stone *(Patricia Bradley)*; Jake Busey *(Johnny Bartlett)*; Chi McBride *(Cyrus)*; Jim Fyfe *(Stuart)*; Troy Evans *(Sheriff Perry)*; Julianna McCarthy *(Old Lady Bradley)*; R. Lee Ermey *(Hiles)*; Elizabeth Hawthorne *(Magda Rees-Jones)*; Angela Bloomfield *(Debra Bannister)*; Desmond Kelly *(Harry Sinclair)*; Jonathan Blick

(Steve Bayliss); Todd Rippon; John Sumner; Michael Robinson; Jim McLarty; Anthony Ray Parker; Paul Yates; Melanie Lynskey *(Deputies)*; John Leigh *(Bryce Campbell)*; Nicola Cliff *(Young Patricia)*; Ken Blackburn *(Dr. Kamins)*; Stuart Devenie *(Museum Curator)*; Genevieve Westcott *(TV Presenter)*; KC Kelly *(Doctor)*; Leslie Wing *(Mrs. Waterhouse)*; Leslie Klein *(Maid)*; Frank Edwards *(Resuscitating Man)*; Alan O'Leary *(The Waiter)*; Danny Lineham *(Barry)*; Charlie McClellan *(Reporter)*; William Pomeroy *(Jacob Platz)*; George Port *(Orderly)*; Billy Jackson *(Baby in Bouncer)*; Sophie Watkins; Taea Hartwell; Max Grover; George Grover *(Nursery Babies)*; Tony Hopkins; Lewis Martin *(Hospital Patients)*; Clay Nelson; Robert McNeill; Matthew Chamberlain *(Passersby)*; Vivienne Kaplan; Liz Mullane *(Nuns)*

After winning widespread acclaim with his dark, fact-based drama HEAVENLY CREATURES (1994), director Peter Jackson returns to over-the-top horror with this energetic ghost story.

In the town of Fairwater, Frank Bannister (Michael J. Fox) practices paranormal scams with the help of three friendly ghosts only he can see. After "cleansing" the home of Dr. Lucy Lynskey (Trini Alvarado), however, her husband (Peter Dobson) is killed by a real, Grim Reaper-like spirit, in one of many recent deaths that have been classified as heart attacks. When people begin to expire in Frank's presence (after he sees spectral numbers on their foreheads), he becomes a prime suspect, and is investigated and jailed by unbalanced FBI agent Milton Dammers (Jeffrey Combs).

Lucy helps Frank to escape and together they put him into a deathlike state so he can combat the evil spirit on its own terms. He learns that the phantom is the ghost of Johnny Bartlett (Jake Busey), who years ago went on a murderous rampage at a local hospital with his girlfriend, Patricia Bradley (Dee Wallace Stone). Patricia got off easily and now lives with her overbearing mother (Julianna McCarthy), but Johnny was executed. As a ghost, he's been vengefully claiming new victims ever since—including Frank's wife, who was killed in the incident that gave Frank his powers of paranormal perception. Frank returns to his corporeal state and rescues Lucy from the now-crazed Patricia and the ghostly Johnny at the Bradley home, where the murderous couple have also killed Patricia's mother. Capturing Johnny's spirit in the urn containing his ashes, Frank and Lucy hope to lay him to rest at the old hospital, but they are interrupted by Dammers, who frees Johnny's ghost before Patricia shoots him. The madwoman then chokes Frank to death, and his spirit grabs her and carries her up toward heaven. Johnny pursues them and catches up to Patricia—but having left the earthly plane, they are both sucked down to hell. Informed that it is "not his time," Frank is returned to life and a happy future with Lucy.

Those who first discovered Jackson upon the release of HEAVENLY CREATURES expressed surprise that this outrageous spectacle was its follow-up. THE FRIGHTENERS, however, is very much in the spirit of his previous anything-goes horror outings like BAD TASTE (1988) and DEAD ALIVE (1993), but packed with visual effects and spirits both funny and fearsome. Those who expect another GHOSTBUSTERS-style romp miss the point; this isn't a supernatural comedy so much as an occult thriller with a comic edge. The film's only flaw is that humor and horror aren't as seamlessly integrated as in Jackson's previous genre outings. The first half hour or so goes for straight chuckles but isn't as funny as it could be, despite fun performances by veterans John Astin and R. Lee Ermey as two of the spirits. The farther the movie ventures into the macabre, however, the tighter its hold becomes. Jackson and co-scripter Fran Walsh expertly handle the revelation of backstory, gradually tying all the plot threads together into a cohesive, scary whole. The final half hour, when Johnny and Patricia really get down to murderous business, is a tour de force of haunted-house horror.

None of this would work without the right performances or special effects, and both are right on the money in THE FRIGHTENERS. The Grim Reaper effects are striking; like all the computer-generated visuals, they were created by WETA FX. Fox, though at first seemingly miscast, gives Frank unexpected shadings, and Alvarado's plucky heroine complements him nicely. Horror veteran Combs is marvelously unbalanced, while Stone and Busey carry off their malevolent roles with scary panache. *(Graphic violence, adult situations, profanity.)* — M.G.

d, Peter Jackson; p, Jamie Selkirk, Peter Jackson; exec p, Robert Zemeckis; assoc p, Fran Walsh; co-p, Tim Sanders; w, Fran Walsh, Peter Jackson; ph, Alun Bollinger, John Blick; ed, Jamie Selkirk; m, Danny Elfman; prod d, Grant Major; art d, Dan Hennah; sound, Hammond Peek (recordist); fx, Charlie McClellan, Steve Ingram; casting, Victoria Burrows; cos, Barbara Darragh; makeup, Marjory Hamlin; stunts, Bruce Brown

Horror/Comedy **(PR: C MPAA: R)**

FRISK ★

(U.S.) 83m Industrial Eye ~ Strand Releasing c

Michael Gunther *(Dennis)*; Jaie Laplante *(Julian)*; Craig Chester *(Henry)*; Raoul O'Connell *(Kevin)*; Michael Stock *(Uhrs)*; Parker Posey *(Ferguson)*; James Lyons *(Gypsy Pete/Pete)*; Alyssa Wendt *(Susan)*; Alexis Arquette *(Punk—Victim #3)*; Michael Waite *(Gary)*; Mark Ewert *(Young Dennis/Jan—Victim #1/Young Boy in Park—Victim #4)*; Eric Sapp *(Sampson)*; Timothy Innes *(Warren)*; David Webb *(Married John)*; Peter Searls *(Finn)*; Daniel Boyle *(Boy on Train)*; Michael Now *(Shopkeeper)*; Eric Dekker *(John—Victim #2)*; Joan Jett Black *(Silver)*; Mark Finch *(Newscaster)*; Todd Verow *(Blond Man in Bathroom)*; Bonnie Dickenson *(Blond Party Girl)*; Roberto Friedman *(Bartender)*; Dustin Schell *(Snuff Photographer)*; Dennis Cooper *(Man in Hall)*; Frankie Payne *(Uhrs' Porn Co-Star)*; Damian Roberts *(Porn Crew Member)*; Mark Miller; B.J. Calnor; Howard Pope; Terry S. Seiler; Kevin Masters; Robin Gurney *(Porn Actors)*; Nathan Melendres; Jason Rail; Tonia Kohl; Bill Zindel; Lea Rude *(Bar Flies)*; Michael Wilson; Paul B. Riley; Donald Mosner; James Mackay; Brook Dillon; Kimberly MacInnis; Edward Zold; Sean Bumgarner; Kari Birmingham; Joseph Smith *(Party Goers)*; Joshua Tager; Tyler Ingolin; Martin E. Helton; Jim Davis; Flynn Hastings; John Waxel; Laurel Waco; Matthew Landis; Andrew M. Bourn; Glenn Golz *(Bar Extras)*

In their quest for something "edgy," the makers of FRISK have gone completely off the deep end with a work that could very well be the most offensive film in recent memory. Sadomasochism, murder, and an amoral absence of human feeling are all celebrated here; a sophomorically nihilistic desire to turn you *off* is its basic aim.

Dennis (Michael Gunther) is a gay man obsessed with the most violent types of sex. In a series of letters written to ex-boyfriend Julian (Jaie Laplante), he describes his evolution from sexually curious teenager to full-time fantasist. His singular interests first take root in a bookstore when a helpful clerk shows him some snuff shots of young men in body bags, their faces and torsos grotesquely contorted. Years later, he meets sub-human Henry (Craig Chester), the masochist who modelled for some of these photographs. Their encounter leaves both of their twisted needs satisfied, but when Dennis later hears of Henry's murder, he can't help but imagine it taking place in some sadist's dungeon. Later, he takes up with a German hustler (Michael Stock). Dennis's obsessions intensify to the point where he fantasizes committing three different sex murders. The final one is the most elaborate and stomach-turning. With the aid of a couple of collaborators (James Lyons, Parker Posey), he shoots up a hapless party boy (Alexis Arquette), has group sex with him, and then kills him. The apotheosis of his mania is reached when he finally envisions enslaving and murdering Julian's younger and devoted innocent of a brother Kevin (Raoul O'Connor).

This debut feature by Todd Verow is an insistently provocative, utterly worthless piece of trash. In a tired equation, he approaches the inflammatory, repulsive material with determinedly post-modern cool. He favors dialogue of the dryest, flattest type delivered by his willing cast in like fashion: "It takes a lot longer to strangle someone than you might think. It's hardly worth the effort." The actors uniformly give deadpan performances that one presumes are meant to be the height of sexy diffidence. Cast primarily for their pectorals and haircuts, they're annoyingly indistinguishable. "I shoved one hand down his throat and one in his ass and shook hands with myself," one character relates for your edification. Homophobes and the religious right will doubtlessly have a field day with it. Gays may just reject the self-hating sexual preoccupation that permeates both it and the inane Dennis Cooper novel on which it's based. Despite all the nudity and coupling, it's completely unerotic. This is no doubt exactly what Verow intended: a guaranteed bad time for the audience. In all, FRISK can only be recommended to the most committed sexual and cinematic masochists. *(Sexual situations, adult situations, nudity, extreme violence, substance abuse, profanity.)* — D.N.

d, Todd Verow; p, Marcus Hu, Jon Gerrans; exec p, George La Voo; assoc p, Mark Jan Wlodarkiewicz; co-p, Richard Huggard; w, Jim Dwyer, George La Voo, Todd Verow (based on the novel by Dennis Cooper); ph, Greg Watkins; ed, Todd Verow; m, Coil, Lee Ranaldo; prod d, Jennifer Graber; art d, Deborah A. Hohenberg; sound, Art Lopez (recordist), Mark Jan Wlodarkiewicz (design); fx, CWI; makeup, Jason Rail, Stephan Dupuis

Drama **(PR: O MPAA: NR)**

FROM DUSK TILL DAWN ★★

(U.S.) 108m A Band Apart Productions; Les Hooligans Productions; Miramax ~ Dimension c

Harvey Keitel *(Jacob Fuller)*; George Clooney *(Seth Gecko)*; Quentin Tarantino *(Richard Gecko)*; Juliette Lewis *(Kate Fuller)*; Cheech Marin *(Border Guard/Chet Pussy/Carlos)*; Fred Williamson *(Frost)*; Salma Hayek *(Santanico Pandemonium)*; Marc Lawrence *(Old Timer)*; Michael Parks *(Texas Ranger Earl McGraw)*; Kelly Preston *(Newcaster Kelly Houge)*; Tom Savini *(Sex Machine)*; John Saxon *(FBI Agent Stanley Chase)*; Danny Trejo *(Razor Charlie)*; Ernest Liu *(Scott Fuller)*; John Hawkes *(Pete Bottoms)*; Heidi McNeal *(Red-Headed Hostage)*; Aimee Graham *(Blonde Hostage)*; Brenda Hillhouse *(Hostage Gloria)*; Tito Larriva *(Titty Twister Guitarist & Vocalist)*; Pete Atasanoff *(Titty Twister Saxophonist)*; Johnny Vatos Hernandez *(Titty Twister Drummer)*; Gino Crognale *(Mouth Bitch Victim)*; Cristos *(Danny)*; Mike Moroff *(Manny)*; Ernest Garcia *(Big Emilio)*; Michelle Berube; Neena Bidasha; Veena Bidasha; Ungela Brockman; Madison Clark; Maria Daiz; Rosalia Hayakawa; Janine Jordae; Jacque Lawson; Houston Leigh; Janie Liszewski; Tia Texada *(Bar Dancers)*; Jon Fidele; Michael McKay; Walter Phelan; Henrik Von Ryzin; Jake McKinnon; Josh Patton; Wayne Toth *(Monsters)*

Two of the more promising creative talents in contemporary genre filmmaking, some marquee-value, and several pop cult icons conspired to produce the prodigious waste of time that is FROM DUSK TILL DAWN. Though not without some entertainment value, the film is an aggressively mindless addition to an already heavily populated sub-genre of the horror film.

The criminal Gecko brothers are on the lam after a string of violent armed bank robberies in the American Southwest. The elder, Seth (George Clooney), is a smooth but volatile professional thief, while the younger, Richard (Quentin Tarantino), is a nerdy-looking psycho. Richie's delusions and hallucinations contribute to the growing body count they leave behind them. Bound for Mexico, where an associate offers sanctuary, the Geckos take a female hostage to a cheap motel, where they cross paths with the Fuller family. Jacob Fuller (Harvey Keitel) is a former pastor who has suffered a crisis of faith after the tragic death of his wife in a car accident. His teen-aged children, Kate (Juliette Lewis) and Scott (Ernest Liu), are accompanying him on a cross-country vacation in their mobile home.

Much to Seth's consternation, Richie rapes and murders their hostage. Needing new hostages, the Geckos kidnap the Fullers and commandeer their vehicle, demanding that Jacob drive them to Mexico. Fearing that they will soon be killed, Scott urges Jacob to ask for help at the border checkpoint, but he refuses even when a suspicious border guard (Cheech Marin) boards the vehicle. In Mexico, the group arrives at the Titty Twister, a rollicking roadhouse bar where the Geckos are scheduled to meet their friend. A colorful pitch man (Cheech Marin) lewdly advertises the fleshly pleasures for sale within.

Inside the bar, Richie is enchanted by the charms of exotic dancer Satanico Pandemonium (Salma Hayek), but as she turns into a vampire, his lust becomes horror. Bedlam erupts as the Geckos, the Fullers, and several human customers join forces to battle the vampiric management and clientele. Richie is the first casualty. Seth, Jacob and the kids make a last stand during which Scott and his father are lost. As dawn approaches, Seth and Kate battle hordes of vampires. When Seth's associate, Carlos (Cheech Marin), arrives in the morning, sunlight destroys the remaining vampires. Kate asks to join Seth and Carlos, who plan to travel deeper into Mexico, but Seth demurs, tossing her a wad of cash. She drives away in the mobile home.

This film's more than respectable theatrical performance and a vibrant life on video would seem to suggest that there is an audience hungry for this kind of light fare. But FROM DUSK TILL DAWN offers excess and allusion, and pitifully few new wrinkles in the vampire's cape. The filmmakers also trot out some second-string 70s genre figures as if their mere presence might elevate the tiresome proceedings. Admittedly, it *is* nice to see blaxploitation vet Fred Williamson, special makeup effects maestro Tom Savini, low-rent leading man John Saxon, and TV's "Then Came Bronson" star Michael Parks, all alive and working, but such treats should be appetizers rather than the main course.

Once the slick but repetitious gore effects of the final half hour are stripped away, what's left is a half-baked crime movie with some good performances. Clooney quickly establishes himself as a credible action anti-hero, and even Tarantino is surprisingly restrained and inoffensive. Keitel, however, seems to have wandered in from another movie.

The basic problem in FROM DUSK TILL DAWN is that the film never finds a consistent tone. The fugitives-on-the-run aspect is promising but too quickly discarded. The American family imperiled by degenerate outsiders is another popular theme but it's impossible to fathom the filmmakers' attitude toward the Fullers. Worse yet, Tarantino's vaunted skill with dialogue seems to have abandoned him on this project. And while his editing remains as deft as ever, Rodriguez fails to stage any truly inspired action set-pieces. The most memorable sequence is the musical number performed by the stunning Hayek with a huge snake. One expects a bit more from the creators of PULP FICTION

(1994) and EL MARIACHI (1993). *(Graphic violence, extreme profanity, adult situations.)* — K.G.

d, Robert Rodriguez; p, Gianni Nunnari, Meir Teper; exec p, Lawrence Bender, Robert Rodriguez, Quentin Tarantino; co-p, Paul Hellerman, Elizabeth Avellan, Robert Kurtzman, Jon Esposito; w, Quentin Tarantino (from a story by Robert Kurtzman); ph, Guillermo Navarro; ed, Robert Rodriguez; m, Graeme Revell; prod d, Cecilia Montiel; art d, Mayne Schuyler Berke; set d, Felipe Fernandez del Paso; sound, Mark Ulano (mixer); fx, Daniel A. Fort, Diana Dru Botsford, T. "Brooklyn" Belissimo, Charles Belardinelli, Bellisimo/Belardinelli Effects Inc.; casting, Johanna Ray, Elaine J. Huzzar; cos, Graciela Mazon; makeup, Ermahn Ospina, Robert Kurtzman, Greg Nicotero, Howard Berger, K.N.B. EFX Group, Kamar Bitar; stunts, Steve Davison

Horror/Crime/Comedy (PR: O MPAA: R)

FROM THE JOURNALS OF JEAN SEBERG ★★★
(U.S.) 97m Couch Potato Productions ~ International Film Circuit c/bw

Mary Beth Hurt *(Jean Seberg)*

FROM THE JOURNALS OF JEAN SEBERG inventively reconsiders the work of actress Jean Seberg. Director Mark Rappaport's tribute extends beyond the traditional documentary format, looking at a life, and an era, in a lively, original way.

Despite the fact that Seberg died 16 years ago at the age of 40, Mary Beth Hurt plays Jean Seberg as she might appear in 1995 (that is, older but still sporting her trademark blond prepunk hairstyle). Looking back on her life with ironic detachment (and addressing the viewer directly), Seberg begins in 1957, when the 17-year-old Iowan was selected out of a nationwide talent hunt to play Joan of Arc in Otto Preminger's SAINT JOAN. Despite Preminger's insistence on (mis)casting the teenager, the critical and commercial failure of the film were clearly laid at Seberg's feet. Still, Preminger used her again, far more effectively, in the 1958 melodrama, BONJOUR TRISTESSE.

BONJOUR TRISTESSE also failed at the box office, but it caught the attention of director Jean-Luc Godard, who cast Seberg as an American student in Paris in BREATHLESS (1959), the groundbreaking French New Wave gangster film. Seberg revived her career and continued working in France, until Hollywood offered her the title role in LILITH (1964), the study of an emotionally imbalanced woman. Seberg fondly recalls her work in BONJOUR TRISTESSE, BREATHLESS and LILITH, despite the sexist filmic conventions and social attitudes that undercut even her best, most challenging roles.

Reflecting on the politically tumultuous 1960s, Seberg compares herself to fellow activists, Jane Fonda and Vanessa Redgrave. All three women were vilified for their causes (Fonda was a Vietnam war protester, Redgrave supported the PLO, and Seberg helped the Black Panther movement), yet, as Seberg points out, her cinematic "sisters" were protected from lasting professional damage by their star status and family pedigrees. Seberg, on the other hand, was hounded for years by both J. Edgar Hoover's FBI surveillance and vicious press gossip.

Her Hollywood career faltered once again with the musical, PAINT YOUR WAGON, in 1968. She then returned to making European coproductions, including two films directed by her second husband, French novelist Romain Gary, who cast her in tawdry, unflattering roles. Finally, Seberg, who had been battling drug use, alcoholism and clinical depression for many years, committed suicide in 1979. Apparently, her exploitation at the hands of so many was complete.

FROM THE JOURNALS OF JEAN SEBERG defies several documentary conventions. First, there are no real "Journals". Filmmaker Mark Rappaport freely invented the Seberg observations and judgments for his film essay. Second, Mary Beth Hurt's ghostly role as a talking corpse represents an outlandish conceit more common in fiction films than documentaries. And third, Rappaport uses his subject at times to theorize about major cultural and sociological issues, including the relationship of the spectator to the film medium.

Rappaport, who tackled gay themes and concerns in ROCK HUDSON'S HOME MOVIES (1992), generally succeeds with his larger mission: making bold, feminist arguments about women's role in the history of cinema, and the inequities of gender representation in film.

Rappaport's film is more a treatise than a conventional documentary. Viewers expecting a solid biography of Jean Seberg will probably be disappointed by the scant attention given to many aspects of her life (the FBI years and mysteries surrounding her death, for example) and her work (some underrated films, including THE FIVE DAY LOVER (1961) and MOMENT TO MOMENT (1966), receive no attention). Yet, despite its lack of thoroughness, FROM THE JOURNALS OF JEAN SEBERG deserves acclaim for the iconoclastic approach it takes toward its iconoclastic subject. *(Sexual situations, adult situations.)* — E.M.

d, Mark Rappaport; assoc p, Coleen Fitzgibbon; w, Mark Rappaport; ph, Mark Daniels; ed, Mark Rappaport; sound, Tony Volonte; cos, Janet Cassady

Docudrama/Documentary/Biography (PR: A MPAA: NR)

FUGITIVE RAGE ★
(U.S.) 90m Royal Oaks Entertainment; Roxie/Rosie Ruby Productions ~ A-Pix Entertainment c

Wendy Schumacher *(Tara McCormick)*; Jay Richardson *(Tommy Stompanato)*; Tim Abell *(James O'Keefe)*; Ross Hagen *(Ryker)*; Shauna O'Brien *(Josie Williams)*; Toni Naples *(Helga)*; Katherine Victor *(Miss Prince)*; Johnny Vincent *(Farino)*; Rick Montana *(Deluca)*; Calista Carradine *(Sharrisse)*; Nikki Fritz *(Nurse Wendy)*; Beth Ulrich *(Spider)*; Carroll Schumacher *(Quarter Master)*; Robert Connel *(Judge)*; Claire Hagen *(D.A.)*; Vikki Skinner *(Gabe Danning)*; Richard Abraham *(Jury Foreman)*; Daniel Rodrigo *(Bailiff)*; G. Gordon Baer *(Hillbilly Thug)*; Dan Golden *(Hillbilly Thug)*; Kimberly Read *(Tough Girl #1)*; Kristin Jadrnicek *(Tough Girl #2)*; Cathy Cathcart *(Guard #1)*; Kristin Loris *(Guard #2)*; Fred Olen Ray *(Mob Attorney)*; J. Longfellow *(Stompanato Trial Lawyer)*; Bobby Bragg *(Goon #1)*; John Michael Vaughn *(Goon #2)*; Stefano Scionti *(Goon #3)*; Andre Fortin *(Goon #4)*; John Greene *(Goon #5)*; Dani Michaeli *(Goon #6)*

The story of a convict released from prison in order to wipe out a mob boss, FUGITIVE RAGE is glaringly implausible.

Mob leader Tommy Stompanato (Jay Richardson) is acquitted of the murder of the sister of ex-cop Tara McCormick (Wendy Schumacher); she shoots him in the courtroom and is subsequently arrested. Soon after her arrival in prison, federal agent O'Keefe (Tim Abell) offers her early release in return for joining a Stompanato investigation. Tara refuses, but when she and her cellmate Jessie (Shauna O'Brien) are attacked in hit ordered by Stompanato, she decides to join in the scheme, demanding a full pardon for Jessie, too. Discovering that Tara has been freed, Stompanato and his lieutenant Frank Ryker (Ross Hagen) decide to go after Jessie. Ryker kidnaps her out of solitary confinement and the mob boss tortures her, trying to discover what Tara and the Feds are up to. Soon after Tara's cover is blown, she decides to attack. She kills nine mobsters, including Stompanato, and frees Jessie. But as they make their exit, O'Keefe pulls a gun and reveals that he and Ryker are renegade agents who have used

Tara to help them take over the mob. After a struggle, Tara leaves Jessie to finish off O Keefe while she goes and kills Ryker. When Jessie asks what they'll do now, Tara smiles and asks if she's ever seen the movie THELMA AND LOUISE.

FUGITIVE RAGE is an utter fantasy, and a bad one at that. Never mind that it's difficult to smuggle guns into a courtroom, that federal agents don't normally liberate incarcerated ex-cops for help in racketeering investigations, or that the Feds would then give their recruit license to kill at will: *Everything* about this film is ridiculous. Schumacher's flat acting and Richardson's over-acting are painful. The big culprits here, however, are scripters Dani Michaeli and Sean O'Bannon—who have fashioned a confused affair filled with horrible attempts at humor—and whoever greenlighted the film in the first place. *(Nudity, violence, profanity.)* — S.K.

d, Fred Olen Ray; p, Fred Olen Ray, Noble Henry; w, Dani Michaeli, Sean O'Bannon; ph, James Spencer; ed, Peter Miller; m, Adam Berry; prod d, Helen Harwell; art d, Lori Kussin; sound, David Waelder (mixer); fx, Kevin McCarthy; cos, Ricardo Delgato; makeup, Megan Johnson; stunts, Bobby Bragg

Action/Thriller **(PR: O MPAA: R)**

FULL BODY MASSAGE ★★½

(U.S.) 93m Full Body Productions; Showtime ~ Paramount Home Video c

Mimi Rogers *(Nina)*; Bryan Brown *(Fitch)*; Christopher Burgard *(Douglas)*; Elizabeth Barondes *(Alice)*; Gareth Williams *(Harry Willis)*; Patrick Neil Quinn *(Andy)*; Heather Gunn *(Dee Dee)*; Laura Saldivar *(Young Nina)*; Brian McLane *(Young Fitch)*; William Fuller *(Fitch's Dad)*; Lynette Bennett *(Fitch's Mom)*; Rachel Nolin *(Fitch's Sister)*; Michael Edmonds *(Hopi Medicine Man)*; Ross McKerras *(Rancher)*

Despite the unassailable asset of a half-naked Mimi Rogers sprawled on a massage table, this story of soul-searching approaches worthlessness.

Self-made entrepreneur Nina (Mimi Rogers) triumphs over her compartmentalized emotional past and pours her energies into running art galleries. A worldly success, Nina ends up so relationship-challenged that she settles for the sensual intimacy of massage with a flirtatious masseur, Douglas (Christopher Burgard). One day, charm-boy Douglas cancels and sends a brusque replacement, Fitch (Bryan Brown), who rocks cynical Nina's complacency. While Fitch waxes philosophical during her rubdown, Nina recalls her affairs with past lovers. Fitch questions Nina's value system and reminisces about his Hopi Indian amour Alice (Elizabeth Barondes), who taught him the healing arts and helped him come to terms with his past. Before the session ends, Fitch confronts his grief about Alice, who died in a car accident. Nina experiences revelations about her shallow insularity and schedules another appointment with Fitch, who apparently is better for more than her back.

Not since Lily Tomlin and John Travolta in 1978's MOMENT BY MOMENT has there been such a vacuous examination of spiritual longing. FULL BODY MASSAGE resembles a terrible two-character play that has been prepped for the movies with flashy intercut flashbacks. Shallow victims of the tumults of modern relationships, Nina and Fitch pine nostalgically for every emotional grievance they've ever suffered. Time becomes a sticky taffy-pull to the audience as unfolding events are stretched out of shape by the characters' confessional chatter.

Can director Nicolas Roeg (HEART OF DARKNESS) still be considered a major talent based on the evidence of his impersonal facility here? The psychological posturing of the leading actors rubs viewers the wrong way; it seems the jaded rich who can afford the quick fixes of the 90s don't deserve them. *(Extensive nudity, profanity, adult situations.)* — R.P.

d, Nicolas Roeg; p, Michael Nolin, Julie Ahlberg; exec p, Robert Littman; w, Dan Gurskis; ph, Anthony B. Richmond; ed, Louise Rubacky; m, Harry Gregson-Williams; prod d, Jeffrey T. Schell; set d, Patricia Elias; sound, Michael Moore (mixer); fx, Frank Ceglia; casting, Justine Jacoby, Tammara Blick; cos, Deena Appel; makeup, Suzanne Willett

Drama **(PR: C MPAA: R)**

FUNERAL, THE ★★½

(U.S.) 99m J.J. Pix; C & P Capitol; October Films ~ October Films c

Christopher Walken *(Ray)*; Chris Penn *(Chez)*; Annabella Sciorra *(Jean)*; Isabella Rossellini *(Clara)*; Vincent Gallo *(Johnny)*; Benicio Del Toro *(Gaspare)*; Gretchen Mol *(Helen)*; John Ventimiglia *(Sali)*; Paul Hipp *(Ghouly)*; Victor Argo *(Julius)*; Gian Di Donna *(Ray Tempio, Sr.)*; Demitri Pryeres *(Sentieri)*; Paul Perri *(Young Ray)*; Gregory Pirelli *(Young Chez)*; Joey Hannon *(Middle Chez)*; Robert Miano *(Enrico)*; Frank John Hughes *(Bracco)*; Andrew Fiscella *(Murder Witness)*; Anthony Alessandro *(Doctor)*; Robert Castle *(Priest)*; Santo Fazio *(Undertaker)*; Daniel Scarpa *(Crying Kid)*; Nicholas Decegli *(Victor)*; Amber Smith *(Bridgette)*; Edie Falco *(Union Speaker)*; David Patrick Kelly *(Michael Stein)*; Carrie Slaza *(Fox)*; Phil Neilson *(Billy)*; Patrick McGaw *(The Mechanic)*; Lance Guerria *(Flashback Victim)*; Doug Crosby *(The Florist)*; Ida Bernadini *(Aunt Rosa)*; John Hoyt *(Big John)*; John "ChaCha" Ciarcia *(Cha Cha)*; Heather Bracken *(Liz)*; Frank Cee *(Bartender Frank)*; Chuck Zito *(Zito)*; Mia Babalis *(Mia)*

Abel Ferrara's latest film, THE FUNERAL, seems like Coppola redux. There are some rewards to this Depression-era story of Italian- American gangster clans, but much of it looks like THE GODFATHER II on a shoe-string budget.

In New York in the mid-1930s, the two surviving Tempio brothers, Ray (Christopher Walken) and Chez (Chris Penn), mourn the death of their youngest sibling, Johnny (Vincent Gallo). During the funeral, through flashbacks, more is revealed about the family tragedy.

The three racketeering brothers run a business that provides protection for the unions. When a rival gangster, Gaspare Spoglia (Benicio Del Toro), asks the brothers to lighten up on a businessman forced to lay off union workers, Johnny, unlike his brothers, sees it as a moral affront against the common working man. The fact that he is sleeping with Gaspare's wife does not improve the Tempio family's relationship with Gaspare.

While walking home from the movies, Johnny is gunned down by an unseen assailant. His murder forces Ray to track down the killer. While Ray immediately suspects Gaspare, he eventually learns that Johnny's killer was a young man who sought to even an old score. Ray struggles with whether to kill the man in revenge, his late father's method, or, in an act of forgiveness, let him live, something his wife, Jeanette (Annabella Sciorra) implores him to do. Ray finally decides to kill the man, but the violence only leads to more violence, as the unstable Chez becomes completely unhinged and engages Ray in a tragic bloodbath.

Abel Ferrara is a director who can be masterful with some material (THE BAD LIEUTENANT) and mediocre with other material (THE BODY SNATCHERS). THE FUNERAL, written by Nicholas St. John, falls somewhere in between.

It's a frustrating effort, filled with an equal measure of dull and intriguing moments. True to Ferrara's usual form, violence and sex punctuate the action in THE FUNERAL, but the livelier scenes aren't necessarily the better ones. In fact, Ray's quiet, internal struggle about whether to seek vengeance for the death of his brother proves much more riveting than Chez's over-the-top psychodramatics.

Also, the peripheral character stories are poorly developed, making THE FUNERAL resemble the bowdlerized version of Sergio Leone's period gangster epic, ONCE UPON A TIME IN AMERICA. Not surprisingly, the two-dimensional female characters get the least to do, although Sciorra, in the hand-wringing wife role, scores in her one big scene.

While it does not romanticize the Mafia as much as the GODFATHER saga did, THE FUNERAL never attains the artistry of the Coppola films. This new film represents an offer one could refuse. *(Violence, nudity, sexual situations, adult situations, substance abuse, extreme profanity.)* — E.M.

d, Abel Ferrara; p, Mary Kane; exec p, Michael Chambers, Patrick Panzarella; assoc p, Russell Simmons, Jay Cannold, Annabella Sciorra; co-p, Randy Sabusawa; w, Nicholas St. John; ph, Ken Kelsch; ed, Bill Pankow, Mayin Lo; m, Joe Delia; prod d, Charles Lagola; art d, Beth Curtis; set d, Diane Lederman; sound, Rosa Howell-Thornhill (mixer); casting, Ann Goulder; cos, Mindy Eshelman; makeup, Patricia Regan

Crime/Drama **(PR: C MPAA: R)**

FUNNYMAN, THE ★

(U.K.) 89m Nomad Pictures ~ Arrow Video c

Tim James *(The Funnyman)*; Christopher Lee *(Callum Chance)*; Benny Young *(Max Taylor)*; Ingrid Lacey *(Tina Taylor)*; Pauline Black *(The Psychic Commando)*; Matthew Devitt *(Johnny Taylor)*; Chris Walker *(The Hard Man)*; Rhona Cameron *(Thelma Fudd)*; George Morton *(The Crap Puppeteer)*; Jamie Heard *(Jamie Taylor)*; Harry Heard *(Harry Taylor)*; Ed Bishop; Bob Sessions; John Chancer *(Cardplayers)*; Jana Sheldon *(The Nurse)*; Barnaby North *(The Waiter)*; Steve Wright *(Radio DJ)*

THE FUNNYMAN is a wholly pointless exercise in special effects and self-indulgent humor along the lines of the NIGHTMARE ON ELM STREET films. How many times must filmmakers conjure up evil entities in spooky old houses? The superior production design is all that keeps THE FUNNYMAN from earning the lowest possible rating.

At a high-stakes poker game, record producer Max Taylor (Benny Young) wins the ancestral mansion of mysterious Callum Chance (Christopher Lee). Visiting England with his wife and two children, he decides to have a look at his new acquisition. Following in a van with some of Max's belongings is his brother Johnny (Matthew Devitt), a former rock guitarist now reduced to doing errands for his successful sibling.

In the house's game room, Max spins a dial whose needle lands on "Lose." He and his family separate to explore the rest of the house, not knowing that the dial has revived a supernatural creature with the costume and appearance of a grotesque harlequin. The Funnyman kills Max's wife, son, and daughter before incapacitating Max by use of a hypnotic cassette tape.

Johnny arrives at the house along with four hitchhikers he has picked up on the way. One by one, they are lured into imaginary scenarios by the Funnyman and killed. Chance, who has been glimpsed peering at the audience throughout these events, is shown building houses of cards in an insane asylum.

If nothing else, THE FUNNYMAN is extremely British. It's hard enough to follow the film given a cast of characters who mutter in indecipherable accents. But the situations in which the titular bogeyman engages his victims are so particularly British that it seems a bit unfair to judge it by American standards.

This effort offers neither enough gruesome special effects to satisfy the *Fangoria* crowd, nor a minimum of story and characterizations to hold the attention of more discerning viewers. It also must be noted that the top-billed Christopher Lee makes little more than a guest appearance. *(Graphic violence, nudity, sexual situations, adult situations, substance abuse, profanity.)* — M.F.

d, Simon Sprackling; p, Nigel Odell; exec p, Gareth Wiley, Steve Parsons; co-p, Tim James, David Redman; w, Simon Sprackling; ph, Tom Ingle Jr.; ed, Ryan L. Driscoll; m, Parsons/Haines; prod d, David Endley; art d, Catriona Maclean; fx, Neill Gorton, Jim Francis; cos, Alex Westover; makeup, Robert Frampton, Bettina Graham

Horror/Comedy **(PR: O MPAA: R)**

G

GALAXIES ARE COLLIDING ★
(U.S.) 97m SC Entertainment ~ Paramount Home Video c

Dwier Brown *(Adam)*; Kelsey Grammer *(Peter)*; Susan Walters *(Beth)*; Karen Medak *(Margo)*; James K. Ward *(Psycho)*; Rudy Hornish *(Mr. Toast)*; Rick Overton *(Rex)*; Mary Quigley *(Wanda)*; Chuck Riley *(Narrator)*; Steve Ruggles *(Gas Station Guy)*; Rick Livingston *(Paul)*; Nicholas Ladizinsky *(Buffhead)*; Sharon Barr *(Waitress)*; Nick Scarduzio *(Trucker)*; David Sage *(Reverend)*; Patricia Thornton *(Adam's Mom)*; Myron Natwick *(Adam's Dad)*

GALAXIES ARE COLLIDING concludes that love is a quick-fix for the philosophical quandaries mystifying great minds for eons. Congratulations, you don't have to watch the movie now.

On his wedding day, deep thinker Adam (Dwier Brown) disappears into the desert. At a memorial service, his parents, cloying bride Beth (Susan Walters), and assorted wedding/funeral guests comment on the late Adam's depressed reactions to natural catastrophes, astronomy, quantum physics, and approaching nuptials. Flashing back and forth from Adam's trance-like wanderings, as he encounters numerous loonies, to his wake, the narrative demonstrates the hero's gradual withdrawal from society, so overwhelmed is he by world hunger, strife, faith, God, and nothingness. When Beth purposely allows him to catch her in apparent infidelity with a stud, she can't ignite the slightest spark. Only a street evangelist rouses Adam, to a duel of contradictory Bible quotes. As his survivors mourn, Adam ends up at a diner with Margo (Karen Medak), free spirit and would-be actress who manipulates men for a hitch to L.A. Though Adam fled the prospect of connubial bliss, or even sex, with Beth, he comes back to life dancing in an empty church with vapid chatterbox Margo. Final scenes put the pieces together: En route to the wedding Adam abandoned his car at a weapons-testing ground where it was immediately fired upon; his loved ones have presumed him dead. Freed from the stasis of past commitments, Adam finds a universe of possibilities with Margo.

Documentaries have long been disparaged as talking-heads films; GALAXIES ARE COLLIDING is a romantic comedy to answer to this charge. On and on, in a most contrived manner, Adam's friends toast and roast his need to comprehend human suffering and existence to the point of leaving him psychologically immobile. But one man's burning theoretical musing is another's kvetching, and this tedious talkfest spotlights a zonked-out protagonist whose catatonia seems less a charming eccentricity than psychosis, and parasitic Margo makes a pitiful candidate for anyone's cosmological epiphany and redemption. Squeaking laughs out of peripheral characters, like an escaped mental patient played by James K. Ward doing marathon celebrity impressions, the ghastly GALAXIES ARE COLLIDING unfolds in a void. Its central dilemma of a man too bright and caring to function in the real world crystallizes the Meaning of Life in the adage: All he needs is love. Made in 1992, this unreleasable indulgence emerged in 1996 on Paramount's home-video label, as did the unnervingly similar space-brained romances WAVELENGTH (1996) and PONTIAC MOON (1994). *(Sexual situations, profanity, adult situations.)* — R.P.

d, John Ryman; p, Syd Cappe, Nicolas Stiliades; exec p, Robert H. Straight; assoc p, Jenny Manriquez; co-p, John Ryman, Stanley Wilson; w, John Ryman; ph, Philip Lee; ed, Ivan Ladizinsky;

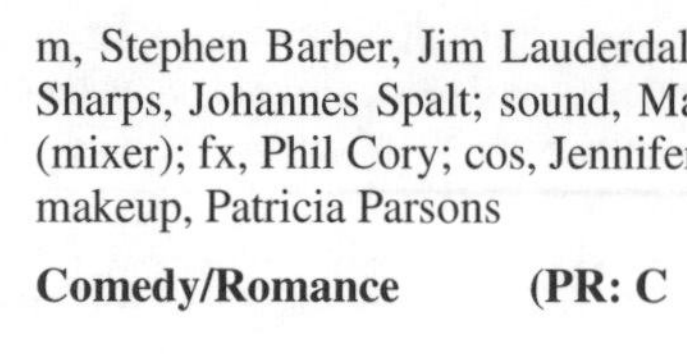

m, Stephen Barber, Jim Lauderdale; art d, Ted Sharps, Johannes Spalt; sound, Margaret Duke (mixer); fx, Phil Cory; cos, Jennifer McManus; makeup, Patricia Parsons

Comedy/Romance **(PR: C MPAA: R)**

GAMES OF LOVE, THE
(SEE: LA COMEDIE-FRANCAISE OU L'AMOUR JOUE)

GAZON MAUDIT
(SEE: FRENCH TWIST)

GET ON THE BUS ★★★
(U.S.) 122m 40 Acres and a Mule Filmworks ~ Columbia TriStar c

Richard Belzer *(Rick)*; DeAundre Bonds *(Junior)*; Andre Braugher *(Flip)*; Thomas Jefferson Byrd *(Evan Thomas, Sr.)*; Gabriel Casseus *(Jamal)*; Albert Hall *(Craig)*; Hill Harper *(Xavier)*; Harry Lennix *(Randall)*; Bernie Mac *(Jay)*; Wendell Pierce *(Wendell)*; Roger Guenveur Smith *(Gary)*; Isaiah Washington *(Kyle)*; Steve White *(Mike)*; Ossie Davis *(Jeremiah)*; Charles S. Dutton *(George)*; Joie Lee *(Jindal)*; Kristin Wilson *(Shelly)*; Frank Clem *(Jefferson)*; Bob Orwig *(Rodney)*; Gary Lowery *(Mitch)*; Debra Rogers *(Sandy)*; William B. Barillaro *(Officer Mike)*; Susan Baston *(Dr. Cook)*; Paula Jai Parker *(Jamilia)*; Gina Ravera *(Gina)*; Jadi McCurdy *(Ja-Dee)*; Dr. Hosea Brown III *(Doc)*; Guy Margo *(Khalid)*

Designed as a small-scale, low-budget commemoration of the October 16, 1995, Million Man March in Washington, DC, and released theatrically on the march's first anniversary, GET ON THE BUS is essentially a thumbnail encapsulation of many of the issues that informed the march, as well as a pointed celebration of black male camaraderie.

George (Charles S. Dutton), a Los Angeles bus driver, has arranged for a cross-country bus to take paying customers from South Central LA to the Million Man March called by Nation of Islam leader Minister Louis Farrakhan. The 15 black male passengers cover a diverse range of socioeconomic and cultural types, including Flip (Andre Braugher), an attention-seeking aspiring actor; Gary (Roger Guenveur Smith), a biracial son of a murdered black cop and a white woman; Jamal (Gabriel Casseus), a gangbanger turned Muslim; Xavier (Hill Harper), a film student videotaping the ride; Randall (Harry Lennix) and Kyle (Isaiah Washington), a gay couple on the verge of breaking up; Evan Thomas (Thomas Jefferson Byrd) and his son Junior (DeAundre Bonds), who are chained together by a court order; and Jeremiah (Ossie Davis), the group elder, a laid-off factory worker with heart trouble, who launches the trip with a stirring benediction and plays an African drum to keep up the men's spirits.

The ride suffers a setback when an accident leaves the bus disabled. A replacement bus arrives with a white driver, Rick (Richard Belzer), who, as a Jew, takes issue with Farrakhan's anti-Semitism and expresses great discomfort at participating in such a venture. He later leaves the bus mid-trip, forcing George to handle the driving chores.

In the course of the ride, the men discuss family relationships, treatment of women, infidelity, economic troubles, sexual preference, and racial identity. They engage in spirited sessions of male camaraderie, including several impromptu songs and a clapping-and-chanting routine, in which each member of the group gets to introduce himself with a rhyming quatrain.

Travel through the south includes a search of the bus for drugs by a white Tennessee state trooper (an unbilled Randy Quaid) and the pickup of a new passenger, an affluent black car dealer (Wendell Pierce) and avowed Republican, whose verbal attacks on "niggers" who blame all their troubles on the white man so inflame the other passengers that they forcibly evict him from the bus.

They finally get to DC, but their elation is tempered by Jeremiah's heart attack and subsequent coma. Half the group attend the march, while the others stay at the hospital. Jeremiah dies and George leads the men in a ceremony at night at the Lincoln Memorial in which he reads to the men, gathered in a circle, the poem Jeremiah had written for them.

The mixed blessings of a low budget ($2.4 million), a cramped setting, and an ensemble cast enable director Lee to streamline his usual grandiose cinematic strategies in order to make his most focused film yet. This time around, handheld camera work and changes in film stock constitute Lee's only concessions to style. The film is no less compelling or consistently stimulating than Lee's previous films, thanks to a handful of well-etched characters, a concise, tightly packed script by Reggie Rock Bythewood, and a strong cast. Lee's persistent tendency to preach is no less evident either, as characters make speeches and launch into intimate personal discussions on a wide range of issues.

If there is any glaring flaw, it is in the narrow scope of black viewpoints represented and the script's insistence on political correctness. The one black character to voice conservative points of view is such a crude, insensitive boor that his character is unfairly used to dismiss all black conservatives and Republicans. While the film stops short of endorsing Minister Louis Farrakhan, it explicitly credits him as the catalyzing force behind the march, while paying lip service to oft-cited criticism of Farrakhan's anti-Semitism, albeit through Richard Belzer's labored cameo as a patronizing, white, Jewish pseudo-liberal.

For all its proselytizing, the film remains a joyous, moving, energetic, and highly cinematic celebration of black male camaraderie, at a time when such images are rare in mainstream films. Perhaps this should not be considered a mainstream film; director Lee received no studio financing, but funded it through the donations of 15 black men, including actors Danny Glover, Wesley Snipes, Robert Guillaume, and Will Smith; lawyer Johnnie L. Cochran Jr.; and Lee himself. *(Profanity.)* — B.C.

d, Spike Lee; p, Reuben Cannon, Bill Borden, Barry Rosenbush; exec p, Spike Lee; w, Reggie Rock Bythewood; ph, Elliot Davis; ed, Leander T. Sales; m, Terence Blanchard; prod d, Ina Mayhew; sound, Oliver Moss (mixer); casting, Reuben Cannon; cos, Sandra Hernandez; makeup, Judy Murdock; stunts, Jeff Ward

Drama **(PR: C MPAA: R)**

GETTING AWAY WITH MURDER ★½

(U.S./Canada) 90m Price Entertainment; Parkway Productions; Savoy Pictures ~ Savoy Pictures c

Dan Aykroyd *(Jack Lambert)*; Lily Tomlin *(Inga Mueller)*; Jack Lemmon *(Mueller/Luger)*; Bonnie Hunt *(Gail Holland)*; Brian Kerwin *(Marty Lambert)*; Jerry Adler *(Judge)*; Andy Romano *(Psychiatrist)*; Robert Fields *(Sgt. Roarke)*; J.C. Quinn *(Detective Stanley)*; Susan Forristal *(Waitress Patti)*; Marissa Chibas *(Liz Lambert)*; Jon Korkes *(Chemistry Lab Professor)*; Kathleen Marshall; Jacqueline Klein; Alex Appel; Jillian Hirasawa; Rino Romano *(Students)*; Jack Jessup *(Old Man)*; Judy Sinclair *(Old Woman)*; David Nichols *(Lawyer Brownell)*; Damon D'Oliveira *(Electronic Salesman)*; Wayne Robson *(Bartender)*; Richard Blackburn *(Nazi Sympathizer)*; Thomas Mitchell *(Nazi Sympathizer)*; Richard Liss; Kevin Frank; Ann Marie MacDonald; Caroline Yeager *(Marty's Party Guests)*; Bernard Shaw; Bobbie Battista; John McLaughlin; Morton Kondracke; Fred Barnes; Eleanor Clift; Roy Hobbs; Heather Kahn *(Themselves)*; Brett Moon; Ryan Moon *(Inga's Twins)*; Victor Chan *(Waiter)*; Dick Callahan *(Mueller's Neighbor)*; Diane Douglass *(Mueller's Neighbor)*; Mary Ann Coles *(Mueller's Neighbor)*; Howard Glassman *(Radio Talk Show Host)*; Jamie Harrold *(Jack's Stepson)*; Camille James Adams *(Postal Clerk)*; Gabriel Regev *(Israeli Defense Minister)*; Colleen Reynolds *(Ferry Woman #1)*; Janet Land *(Ferry Woman #2)*; Johnnie Chase *(Detective)*; Luke Costello *(Halloween Kid)*; Kerry MacDonald *(Halloween Kid)*; Ron Hartman *(Cemetery Minister)*; Brian Kennington *(Court Clerk)*; Herb Lovelle *(Blind Man)*; Robert Morgenroth *(Newscaster)*; Doug O'Keefe *(Gail's Date)*; Jerry Savoy *(Cab Driver)*; Helen Taylor *(Veterinarian)*; Nicholas Pasco *(Cop in Jail)*

It's hard to know what to make of GETTING AWAY WITH MURDER, a farce so low-key and muddled it practically disappears before one's eyes. The filmmakers seem scared of the implications in their own material.

Ethics professor Jack Lambert (Dan Aykroyd) lives in a Boston neighborhood next to Max Mueller (Jack Lemmon), an elderly German. One day reporters accuse Max of being a notorious Nazi death camp commandant nicknamed the Beast of Berkau. Jack initially doubts the stories, but after visiting Mueller, his Teutonic daughter Inga (Lily Tomlin), and his anti-semitic friends, the professor begins believing the worst. Jack decides to make justice prevail by killing Mueller. To spare his patient girlfriend Gail (Bonnie Hunt) any involvement in the murder, Jack breaks off his romance, much to her confusion. After Jack fatally poisons Mueller, new evidence suggests he was innocent. A troubled conscience compels Jack to marry the bereaved Inga, but during the honeymoon Jack discovers Max may have been guilty after all. Feeling vindicated about his crime, Jack quickly ends his marriage to Inga to return to his true love Gail. Finally, Jack quits his job as a professor and enrolls as a full-time law student.

GETTING AWAY WITH MURDER isn't so much bad as peculiarly unfunny. The premise of a milquetoast discovering that the nice old guy next door could be a monster seems comedically promising, but despite the film's cheery tone there are very few attempts at humor per se, even macabre ones. It's not the potentially tasteless subject matter that ruins GETTING AWAY WITH MURDER; it's timidity in dealing with it (the word "Jew" is used only once). Aykroyd and Lemmon play their parts nearly straight, leaving Tomlin and Hunt to supply what few yocks there are. And both women deserve better than having to play love interest to Aykroyd. Particularly tasteless is Tomlin's sex scene with Aykroyd, which climaxes with a visual joke about the volume of his ejaculation.

Briefly slipped into theaters in 1996 after years on the release slate of the ill-fated Savoy Pictures, GETTING AWAY WITH MURDER had the bad luck of arriving soon after the brief Broadway run of Stephen Sondheim's critically-panned whodunit of the same title. In terms of bad luck alone, this strange movie may hold some morbid interest even as it fails on so many basic levels. *(Violence, sexual situations, adult situations, profanity.)* — E.M.

d, Harvey Miller; p, Frank Price, Penny Marshall; exec p, Frederic W. Brost, Elliot Abbott; assoc p, Gail Sicilia; w, Harvey Miller; ph, Frank Tidy; ed, Richard Nord; prod d, Jay Moore; art d, Jeff Ginn; set d, Tracey Doyle; sound, Douglas Ganton (mixer), David Lee (mixer); fx, Martin Malivoire, Kaz Kobielski; casting, Walken/Jaffe; cos, Aleida MacDonald, Judy Gellman; makeup, Irene Kent; stunts, Branko Racki

Comedy **(PR: C MPAA: R)**

GHOST AND THE DARKNESS, THE ★★★
(U.S.) 103m Douglas/Reuther Productions; Constellation Films; Paramount ~ Paramount c

Michael Douglas *(Remington)*; Val Kilmer *(John Patterson)*; Bernard Hill *(Dr. Hawthorne)*; John Kani *(Samuel)*; Tom Wilkinson *(Beaumont)*; Brian McCardie *(Starling)*; Henry Cele *(Mahina)*; Om Puri *(Abdullah)*; Emily Mortimer *(Helena Patterson)*; Kurt Egelhof *(Indian Victim)*; Satchu Annamalai *(Worker #1)*; Teddy Reddy *(Worker #2)*; Rakeem Kahn *(Worker #3)*; Jack Devnarain *(Nervous Sikh Orderly)*; Glen Gabela *(Orderly #1)*; Richard Nwamba *(Orderly #2)*; Nick Lorentz *(Photographer)*; Alex Ferns *(Stockton)*; Kaycey Padayachee *(Beaumont's Valet)*; Giles Masters *(Beaumont's Clerk)*; Patrick Gifford; Justin Gifford *(Patterson's Son)*; George Middlekoop *(Station Master)*

Based on actual events in the late 1800s, this JAWS-in-the-jungle flick pits an Irish bridge builder and a Confederate bounty hunter against two man-eating lions in the heart of Africa.

When Irish engineer John Patterson (Val Kilmer) is hired by an English trade company to lead the effort to build a railway bridge through a particularly hazardous part of Africa, he is delighted to finally visit the land of his dreams. Even the squabbling workers and malaria epidemics cannot quell his excitement—that is, until his workers fall prey to a series of vicious and frequent lion attacks. Initially, Patterson and his foreman, Samuel (John Kani), attempt to deal with the lion themselves, but they are astonished to discover not one but two lions stalking their camp—an unprecedented discovery, since man-eaters are famously solitary. The native workers, already spooked, dub these beasts "the ghost and the darkness," incarnations of pure evil placed on earth to rid Africa of white men and their railroad.

As the workers, first in a trickle and then a flood, begin to leave the camp, Patterson makes several vain attempts to trap or kill the lions. Frustrated and tired, he is finally aided by Charles Remington (Michael Douglas), a Confederate soldier turned hunter of uncanny skill who fled the re-unified United States for the wilds of Africa. Together, Patterson and Remington track the lions to their den, a mountain cave piled with the bones of more than a hundred men—revealing the lions to be not man-eaters but man-killers, slaughtering humans for the sheer sport of it. The two men succeed in killing one of the lions, but Remington is taken by the other during the night. Now enraged, Patterson burns the plains in order to flush out the last lion, forcing a final epic confrontation in which Patterson dispatches the beast.

There are many reasons to like THE GHOST AND THE DARKNESS, beginning with the sheer look of the film. Shot by veteran cinematographer Vilmos Zsigmond, the plains of Africa convey both aching beauty and bloodcurdling menace. The lions, too, are filmed expertly, moving in and out of the high grass like smoke before exploding into the camp to pounce on one or a dozen helpless workers in some of the most viscerally exciting attack sequences since JAWS (1975). (To be fair, THE GHOST AND THE DARKNESS takes more than a few pages from JAWS's playbook, but, in this case, it seems a truly sincere form of flattery.) In the character of John Patterson, legendary screenwriter William Goldman transcends the man-versus-nature cliche admirably, and Val Kilmer's trademark stiff performance actually works to the film's advantage—particularly when director Stephen Hopkins (JUDGMENT NIGHT, BLOWN AWAY) allows Michael Douglas to snack on the scenery a bit. All told, though, it is the undiluted menace of the lions that makes the film. When the narrator warns us that, if you look into the eyes of the lions, now on display at the Chicago Field Museum, "you will be afraid," we believe him. *(Violence, profanity.)* — B.T.

d, Stephen Hopkins; p, Gale Anne Hurd, Paul Radin, Kitman Ho; exec p, Michael Douglas, Steven Reuther; co-p, Grant Hill; w, William Goldman; ph, Vilmos Zsigmond; ed, Robert Brown, Steve Mirkovich; m, Jerry Goldsmith; prod d, Stuart Wurtzel; art d, Giles Masters, Malcolm Stone; set d, Hilton Rosemarin; sound, Simon Kaye (mixer), Bruce Stambler; fx, Chris Corbould, John Rosengrant, Stan Winston Studios; casting, Mary Selway, Sarah Trevis; cos, Ellen Mirojnick; makeup, Paul Engelen; stunts, Danny Baldwin

AAN Best Sound Effects Editing: Bruce Stambler

Historical/Adventure/Drama **(PR: C MPAA: R)**

GHOST IN THE SHELL ★★★
(Japan/U.K.) 83m Kodansha; Bandai Visual; Manga Entertainment ~ Manga Entertainment c
(KOKAKU KIDOTAI)

VOICES OF: Richard George *(Bateau)*; Mimi Woods *(Kusanagi)*; William Frederick *(Aramaki)*; Abe Lasser *(Puppet Master)*; Christopher Joyce *(Togusa)*; Mike Sorich *(Ishikawa)*; Ben Isaacson *(Nakamura)*; Hank Smith *(Minister)*; Steve Davis *(Diplomat)*; Phil Williams *(Willis)*; David Conrad *("Bad Guy")*; Tom Carlton *(Garbage Collector A)*; Doug Stone *(Garbage Collector B)*

A Japanese animated tale of cyborg cops in search of an elusive computer hacker, GHOST IN THE SHELL takes viewers through a slow, eerie, and often complicated ride through a visually stunning 21st century cityscape.

In 2029 Japan, a time when most humans habitually acquire electronic parts, Major Kusanagi and her male partner, Bateau, cyborg cops from Section 9, follow the trail of the mysterious "puppet master," a master hacker who taps into the "ghosts"—the cyber-brains—of cyborgs. When an unprogrammed female cyborg "shell" (body) is mysteriously activated and escapes the Mega Tech factory, it is caught and brought into Section 9 for examination.

Battles between different government factions erupt over the cyborg, leading to a violent confrontation in an abandoned museum during which Major Kusanagi taps into the female cyborg's "ghost," which reveals itself to be the sought-after Puppet Master. A government-created computer entity, the Puppet Master has escaped its creators and seeks a host body and an independent life of its own. It asks to merge with the sympathetic Kusanagi.

Government copters attack and destroy the two female cyborgs. However, Bateau is able to save Kusanagi's brain and transfer it to a young girl's body that he'd picked up on the black market. Kusanagi and the Puppet Master had succeeded in their merge and formed a new entity, calling itself a "Newborn," which goes out to start a new life.

Reportedly beating out both WINGS OF HONNEAMISE (1987) and AKIRA (1989) as the most expensive animated film yet made in Japan, GHOST IN THE SHELL does, in fact, boast extraordinary visual effects, imaginative camera angles, and breathtaking, incredibly detailed vistas of a 21st century cityscape. American fans were impressed enough to make this one of the best-selling home videos of 1996.

The overall mood of the piece is quiet, dark and dreamlike, with occasional bursts of violence, pursuit and gun battles. There are long passages where characters travel through the gleaming cityscape, giving viewers the ability to enjoy the abundant detail while listening to a haunting, vocal score by Kenji Kawai.

The story posits a future of cybernetic bodies and electronic brains and asks if entities that are part machine or even entirely machine-created can lay claim to being living things. Unfortunately, the plot takes so long to get moving that by the time it formulates that question, the film quickly grinds to a halt. Furthermore, the mechanized nature of the protagonists serves only to distance the viewer from the action. In contrast, the *manga* (comic book) by Masamune Shirow on which the film is based, features cyborg characters who behave in recognizably human fashion, complete with the semi-slapstick and shrillness familiar to fans of Shirow's *Dominion Tank Police,* which was also adapted for anime. With its attention to urban cityscapes and the class contrasts contained therein, GHOST IN THE SHELL has more in common thematically and stylistically with other works by its director Mamoru Oshii, including DALLOS (1983) and PATLABOR: MOBILE POLICE FORCE (1989). *(Violence, nudity, profanity.)* — B.C.

d, Mamoru Oshii; p, Yoshimasa Mizuo, Ken Matsumoto, Ken Iyadomi, Mitsuhisa Ishikawa; exec p, Teruo Miyahara, Shigeru Watanabe, Andy Frain; assoc p, Hiroshi Yamazaki, Yasushi Sukeof, Laurence Guinness, Makoto Ibuki; w, Kazunori Ito (based on the graphic novel by Shirow); ph, Hisao Shirai; ed, Shuichi Kakesu; m, Kenji Kawai, Passengers; prod d, Takashi Watabe; art d, Hiromasa Ogura; anim, Toshihiko Nishikubo, Kazuchika Kise, Hiroyuki Okiura; sound, Kazuhiro Wakabayashi (design); fx, Mutsu Murakami, "Matrix" Yutaka, Hoshiba, Toshio Hasegawa, Noriyuki Ota

Animated/Science Fiction/Crime (PR: C MPAA: NR)

GHOSTS OF MISSISSIPPI ★★½
(U.S.) 123m Frederick Zollo; Castle Rock Entertainment ~ Columbia c

Alec Baldwin *(Bobby DeLaughter)*; Whoopi Goldberg *(Myrlie Evers)*; James Woods *(Byron De La Beckwith)*; Craig T. Nelson *(Ed Peters)*; Wayne Rogers *(Morris Dees)*; William H. Macy *(Charlie Crisco)*; Susanna Thompson *(Peggy Lloyd)*; Lucas Black *(Burt DeLaughter)*; Joseph Tello *(Drew DeLaughter)*; Alexa Vega *(Claire DeLaughter)*; Lloyd "Benny" Bennett *(Himself)*; Darrell Evers *(Himself)*; Yolanda King *(Reena Evers)*; James Van Evers *(Himself)*; Jerry Levine *(Jerry Mitchell)*; Sky Rumph *(Jared Lloyd)*; Margo Martindale *(Clara Mayfield)*; Zoaunne Leroy *(Thelma De La Beckwith)*; Michael O'Keefe *(Merrida Coxwell)*; Bill Smitrovich *(Jim Kitchens)*; James Pickens Jr. *(Medgar Evers)*; Virginia Madsen *(Dixie DeLaughter)*; G. Ja'ron Henderson *(Darrell—Age 11)*; Rae'ven Larrymore Kelly *(Reena—Age 10)*; Curtis Tyler Haynes *(Van—Age 3)*; Richard Riehle *(Tommy Mayfield)*; Jim Harley *(Delamar Dennis)*; Bonnie Bartlett *(Billie DeLaughter)*; Brock Peters *(Walter Williams)*; Finn Carter *(Cynthia Speetgens)*; William Howard *(Fred Sanders)*; Diane Ladd *(Caroline Moore)*; Andy Romano *(Hardy Lott)*; Richard Stahl *(Judge Hendrick)*; David Carpenter *(Bill Waller)*; Bill Cobbs *(Charlie Evers)*; Jordan Lund *(Deputy)*; Jerry Hardin *(Barney DeLaughter)*; Ramon Bieri *(James Holley)*; C. R. Doan *(Bob Patterson)*; Katherine Wood *(Young Barbara Holder)*; L. D. Bass Sr. *(Black Man)*; Monty Thomas *(Security Guard)*; Eliott Keener *(Sheriff McMillan)*; Brandon McKennah *(Roy Wilkins)*; William L. Donald *(Waiter at Country Club)*; Jim Stallings *(Hollis Cresswell)*; Michael Strasser *(Bomb Squad Man)*; Diana Bellamy *(Barbara Holder)*; Rance Howard *(Ralph Hargrove)*; Thomas Kopache *(Thorn McIntyre)*; Frank Hoyt Taylor *(Dan Prince)*; Sarah Hunley *(Peggy Morgan)*; Marilynn Lovell; Jill Andre; Leigh French *(Bridge Ladies)*; James Marshall Wolchok *(Press Reporter)*; John A. Horhn *(CNN Reporter)*; Spencer Garrett; Fenton Lawless; David Armstrong; Michael Hewes; James Homer Best *(Reporters)*; Thomas Barry *(Bennie Thompson)*; Louis E. Armstrong *(Louis Armstrong)*; Ed Bryson *(Himself)*; Maggie Wade *(Herself)*; J. J. Chaback *(Assistant D.A.)*; Keanan K. Evers *(Daniel Evers-Everette)*; Nicole Evers-Everette *(Cambi Evers-Everette)*; Dijon S. Williams *(Keanan Evers)*; Tracey Costello *(Assistant D.A.)*

Rob Reiner's GHOSTS OF MISSISSIPPI is a well-meaning drama focusing on the decades-long struggle to bring the killer of civil rights activist Medgar Evers to justice.

In the early morning hours of June 12, 1963, Evers (James Pickens Jr.) is gunned down in the driveway of his Jackson, MS, home and left to die in full view of his wife Myrlie (Whoopi Goldberg) and children. His killer, Byron De La Beckwith (James Woods), a dyed-in-the-wool racist, is arrested and brought to trial, but in spite of the overwhelming evidence against him, he's acquitted by two all-white hung juries.

Twenty-five years later, Myrlie Evers approaches the Hinds County District Attorney's office in an effort to have the case against Beckwith re-opened. The case is handed to up-and-coming Assistant DA Bobby DeLaughter (Alec Baldwin), who is at first leery of opening old wounds, particularly when his own career is at stake. But after a little digging, he discovers that a number of crucial items from the previous trials have conveniently gone missing, including De La Beckwith's shotgun and the original trial manuscript. Sensing an unconscionable miscarriage of justice, DeLaughter rises to the challenge, but is met with opposition: his Southern-belle wife Dixie (Virginia Madsen), daughter of a prominent conservative Mississippi judge, fears he's risking his reputation, dwelling on old troubles that might win him some powerful enemies, while black activists are wary of the crusading white man, as is Myrlie herself.

Determined to see justice done, DeLaughter and his aides (William H. Macy and Lloyd Bennett) set about reconstructing the thirty-year-old case against the now elderly De La Beckwith, who arrogantly flaunts his infamy to the press without the slightest pretense of maintaining his innocence. Despite the dearth of hard evidence and the fact that many of the original witnesses are either dead or now unwilling to testify, DeLaughter manages to build a case, but not without paying a personal price: Bobby's children are routinely beaten up—their father's a "nigger-lover"— and a disgusted Dixie eventually leaves him. Finally, DeLaughter contacts a witness who heard De La Beckwith brag about the Evers murder at a white supremacist gathering. Armed with this testimony, the now-recovered murder weapon, the original trial transcripts (which, it turns out, Myrlie had in her possession all along), and the trust and support of Evers's widow, DeLaughter is ready to go to trial. Thirty years after the murder of Medgar Evers, his murderer is finally brought to justice: De La Beckwith is found guilty.

GHOSTS OF MISSISSIPPI is not without a certain integrity and Lewis Colick deserves credit for distilling a complex judicial case into a workable and, at times, poetic screenplay. Unfortunately, like Alan Parker's 1988 film, MISSISSIPPI BURNING, Reiner attempts to tell what is essentially a black story from the point of view of a white man—in this case, DeLaughter, played vigorously by Alec Baldwin—and the number of black characters who appear in the film is disturbingly low. That De La Beckwith is ultimately convicted is something of a foregone conclusion, even for viewers unfamiliar with the case, but that it takes more than two solemn hours of film time to do it suggests the filmmakers may have been too caught up in the nobility of their cause without realizing the serious errors they were committing.

Woods walks off with virtually every scene he appears in—a problem when a most despicable character turns out to be most charismatic. Macy delivers another of his cleanly crafted, slightly quirky performances, and Margo Martindale is a delight as Clara Mayfield, DeLaughter's wise-cracking secretary. Goldberg works hard at combining Myrlie Evers' combativeness and humanity, but one can almost see her acting gears turning and the character never really takes wing. Reiner's direction is competent, if unspectacular, telling the story faithfully, almost to an artistic fault. *(Violence, profanity.)* — E.K.

d, Rob Reiner; p, Frederick Zollo, Nicholas Paleologos, Andrew Scheinman; exec p, Jeffrey Scott, Charles Newirth; co-p, Frank Capra III; w, Lewis Colick; ph, John Seale; ed, Robert Leighton; m, Marc Shaiman; prod d, Lilly Kilvert; art d, Christopher Burian-Mohr; set d, Karen A. O'Hara; sound, Robert Eber; fx, David Blitstein, Gary Schaedler; casting, Jane Jenkins, Janet Hirshenson; cos, Gloria Gresham; makeup, Hallie D'Amore, Matthew W. Mungle, Deborah La Mia Denaver; stunts, Greg Wayne Elam

AAN Best Supporting Actor: James Woods; *AAN Best Makeup:* Matthew W. Mungle, Deborah La Mia Denaver

Docudrama **(PR: C MPAA: PG-13)**

GIRL FROM MARS, THE ★★

(Canada) 91m Northstar Entertainment; South Pacific Pictures; CanWest Broadcasting ~ Atlantic Releasing/Live Home Video c

Edward Albert *(Dan)*; Eddie Albert *(Charles)*; Sarah Sawatsky *(Dee Dee)*; Gwynyth Walsh *(Stacey)*; Christianne Hirt *(Liane)*; Gary Day *(Virgil)*; Leslie Carlson *(Mr. Sharbut)*; Kaj-Eric Erikson *(Ricky)*; Lochlyn Monro *(Earl West)*; Jeremy Radick *(Wayne West)*; John Cassini *(Stumpy)*; Todd Duckworth *(Kevin)*; Suzi Kaiser *(Winnie)*; Richard Newman *(Bobby Holliday)*; Walter Marsh *(Doc Gilliwig)*; Helen Honeywell *(Mrs. Parker)*; Ernie Prentice *(Mr. North)*

Smacking of the same sappiness that pervades an "Afterschool Special," THE GIRL FROM MARS fudges its simple premise: could a mixed-up teen actually be an interplanetary visitor?

Troubled by the death of her mom, intense 13-year-old Dee Dee Putnam (Sarah Sawatsky) gets a reputation as a high-school weirdo due to her obsession with extra-terrestrial life. When not visiting her scientist pal Charles (Eddie Albert) at the observatory, she attempts to electronically communicate with Mars.

Neglected by her loving father Dan (Edward Albert), who's running for local office on an ecological platform, Dee Dee disrupts the school study period with a homemade flying saucer accidentally launched in the library. In trying to prevent school bullies Earl (Lochlyn Monro) and Wayne (Jeremy Radick) from interrupting her dad's press conference, she causes a worse hubbub as mice get loose in full view of out-of-town media. Then, Charles fails to support, with his research findings, Dan's crusade to save the endangered white owl. Now Dee Dee truly feels as if she doesn't belong on Earth. Branded a misfit, she shaves her head. As hostility toward her builds, Dee Dee's heretofore untapped telekinetic powers emerge. It seems to fellow students that she really could be from outer space.

Misunderstood, Dee Dee rigs the screen at the local drive-in so she can appear and condemn the startled townspeople in full space drag before flying away in a flimsy spaceship. Although she insists she's a Martian, earthbound Dee Dee only travels far enough to locate the last remaining white owls. Armed with this information, Dee Dee can save her dad's campaign. Validated by proving her usefulness to the community, she rethinks her identity as "the girl from Mars."

Brimming with touching moments, THE GIRL FROM MARS isn't artful enough in playing its guessing game about Dee Dee's possibly alien homeland. This tale of alien-ation expects patient viewers to admire Dee Dee's ingenuity and spunk, even while the script mines her increasingly bizarre antics for comic effect.

Losing credibility, the film escalates Dee Dee's reliance on space lingo and Martian regalia without coming to terms with the neuroses behind these episodes. Although it fails to fully appreciate its protagonist's hurtful dilemma, this coming-of-age film is adeptly acted by Sawatsky, who sensitively explores the downside of teenage fantasy life. What we remember from the movie isn't the adolescent's ultimate resignation to normalcy, but this ugly duckling's defiant pain at never connecting with others. *(Violence.)* — R.P.

d, Neill Fearnley; p, Mary Kahn; exec p, Michael McMillan, Terry Botwick, Harry Young, Don Reynolds; assoc p, Larry Raskin, Daphne Ballon; w, Brian Allen Lane; ph, Warrick Attewell; ed, George Appleby; m, Louis Natale; art d, Phil Schmidt; set d, Dave Birdsall; sound, Tim Richardson (mixer); casting, Stuart Aikins; cos, Maureen Hiscox; makeup, Imelda Bain-Partin; stunts, Danny Virtue

Drama **(PR: AA MPAA: NR)**

GIRL 6 ★★★½

(U.S.) 109m 40 Acres and a Mule Filmworks; Fox Searchlight ~ Fox Searchlight c

Theresa Randle *(Girl 6)*; Isaiah Washington *(Shoplifter)*; Spike Lee *(Jimmy)*; Jenifer Lewis *(Boss #1—Lil)*; Debi Mazar *(Girl #39)*; Peter Berg *(Caller #1—Bob)*; Michael Imperioli *(Scary Caller #30)*; Madonna *(Boss #3)*; Dina Pearlman *(Girl #19)*; Maggie Rush *(Girl #42)*; Desi Moreno *(Girl #4)*; Kristen Wilson *(Salesgirl #1)*; k funk *(Salesgirl #2)*; Debra Wilson *(Salesgirl #3)*; Quentin Tarantino *(Director #1—NY)*; Ron Silver *(Director #2—LA)*; Naomi Campbell *(Girl #75)*; Gretchen Mol *(Girl #12)*; Shari Freels *(Girl #29—Punkster)*; Richard Belzer *(Caller #4—Beach)*; Larry Pine *(Caller #33—Wall Street)*; Coati Mundi *(Caller #8—Martin)*; Delilah Cotto *(Caller #8—Christine)*; Anthony Nocerino *(Caller #6)*; Tom Byrd III *(Caller #18)*; Bray Poor *(Caller #14)*; Joseph Lyle Taylor *(Caller #3/Caller #16)*; Arthur Nascarella *(Boss #2—Male in Office)*; John Turturro *(Murray the Agent)*; Mica Hughes *(Director's Assistant)*; Leonard Thomas *(Co-Agent)*; Joie Susannah Lee *(Switchboard Operator)*; Rolonda Watts *(Reporter Nita)*; Carol Jenkins *(Newscaster Carol)*; Jim Jensen *(Newscaster Jim)*; Halle Berry *(Herself)*; Jacqueline McAllister *(Angela)*; Novella Nelson *(Angela's Aunt)*; Billie Neal *(Angela's Mother)*; Susan Batson *(Acting Coach)*; Ranjit Chowdhry *(Indian Shopkeeper)*; Rita Wolf *(Wife of Indian Shopkeeper)*; Andrea Navedo *(Phone Girl)*; Lesley-Camille Troy *(Phone Girl)*; Michele Kelly *(Phone Girl)*; Yohan Lim *(Korean Deli Owner)*; Anne Ok *(Wife of Korean Deli Owner)*; John Cameron Mitchell *(Rob)*; Keith Smith *(2nd A.D.)*; Nelson Vasquez *(Ronnie the Guard)*; Al Palagonia *(Man Mistaken for Bob Regular)*; Jeff Ward *(Bad Guy #1)*; Chuck Jeffreys; Andy Duppin; Jalil Lynch; David Lomax *(Bad Guys)*; Carlo Vogel *(Male Assistant)*; Brian Konowal *(Male Assistant)*; Jennifer Ramos; Jennifer Lee; Tomoko Hagane; Genevieve Yrola; Jennifer Ceballos *(Topless Dancers)*

Spike Lee's first commercial film, SHE'S GOTTA HAVE IT (1986), was a comedy with a female lead. He returns to that formula with GIRL 6, a tale of a would-be actress who takes a job as a phone sex operator. Despite its many good qualities, the film did not do well at the box office, perhaps because its mix of comedy, drama, reality, and fantasy makes it a hard film to characterize and advertise.

Girl 6 (Theresa Randle)—whose name, Judy, isn't used until the very end of the film—hopes to be an actress, but when asked to undress one too many times, she walks out on a big audition.

She is dumped by both her agent and her acting coach. Needing to pay rent and faced with the alternative of handing out flyers on busy sidewalks, she takes a job as a phone sex operator.

She works for a small, family-like company. Her boss (Jenifer Lewis) and the other operators look out for her, and most of the callers are silly and fun. Even though she still has fantasies about acting, she enjoys her job. In fact, she enjoys it a little too much and arranges to meet one of her callers. After he doesn't show up for the date, her disillusionment turns into obsession, and her boss asks her to take a leave of absence to refresh herself. Instead, she takes a job with a less reputable company, working out of her own home.

One night, she gets death threats from a caller who claims to know her address. She decides to quit her job and move to Los Angeles. In her first audition there, she's again asked to take off her shirt. She is strong and confident in her decision not to do so. She still has no acting career, but she does have her self-respect.

GIRL 6 turns a potentially heavy subject into a light film. Lee's decision to show the male phone callers leads to hilarious scenes, such as when one man, clad only in a jock strap, engages Judy in a baseball fantasy. Equally entertaining are her acting fantasies, in which Lee recreates scenes from the likes of CARMEN JONES (1954), FOXY BROWN (1974), and the TV show "The Jeffersons."

One of Lee's strengths as a filmmaker is his ability to smoothly steer a film in several directions. Here, subplots about Judy's relationships with next-door neighbor Jimmy (Lee) and her ex-husband (Isaiah Washington IV) strengthen her character and add to the film's appeal.

Unfortunately, a less well-defined subplot, about a little girl and an elevator accident, is confusing. The girl's accident parallels Judy's fears and anxiety, and her response to the mishap shows her emotional side. But the scenes seem forced, as does Lee's use of distorted lenses to show Judy's moods and feelings.

Nonetheless, Lee's willingness to experiment is admirable, and there are as many successes (such as the fantasy sequences and the use of jump cuts) as failures.

GIRL 6's negative critical response may be partially due to the fact that more substance was expected of Lee. Perhaps GIRL 6 is a fluffy film, but few films are made about African-American women, and so it is especially disappointing that GIRL 6 didn't receive better press. Randle's performance is outstanding. She is fresh, smart and sexy. Lee and Washington are also excellent as the men in her life. GIRL 6 includes several cameos, some amusing, others perfunctory.

While not one of Lee's best films, GIRL 6 still shows why he's one of America's most daring and interesting filmmakers. *(Sexual situations, nudity, extreme profanity.)* — A.M.

d, Spike Lee; p, Spike Lee; exec p, Jon Kilik; assoc p, Cirri Nottage; w, Suzan-Lori Parks; ph, Malik Hassan Sayeed; ed, Sam Pollard; m, Prince; prod d, Ina Mayhew; set d, Paul R. Weathered; sound, Allan Byer (mixer); fx, Steve Kirshoff, Randall Balsmeyer; casting, Aisha Coley; cos, Sandra Hernandez; makeup, Anita Gibson, Diane Hammond; stunts, Jeff Ward

Comedy/Drama **(PR: O MPAA: R)**

GIRLFRIENDS ★★½

(U.S./Australia/U.K./New Zealand) 102m Little Women in Transit Productions; Australian Film, Television & Radio School; ITVS; Dancing Girl Productions; Good Machine Productions; Australian Film Commission; New South Wales Film & Television Office; Oceania Parker Films; Short Film Fund of the New Zealand Film Commission ~ First Run Features c/bw

"Little Women in Transit" Magdalena Gross *(Jenny)*; Cara Jedell *(Dana)*; Danielle Shuman *(Lisa)*; David Little *(Father)*; Sally Heller *(Mother)*; "Jumping the Gun" Jenny Vuletic *(The Host)*; Georgia-Troy Barnes *(The Guest)*; "Carmelita Tropicana: Your Kunst is Your Waffen" Carmelita Tropicana; Sophia Ramos; Anne Lobst; Livia Daza Paris; "Greetings from Africa" Nora Breen *(L)*; Cheryl Dunye *(Herself)*; Jocelyn Taylor *(Dee)*; Jackie Woodson *(The Girlfriend)*; "Excursion to the Bridge of Friendship" Andrea Moor *(Maria)*; Karin Mainwaring *(Nadezhda)*; Genevieve Lemon *(Grace)*; Mary Regan; John E. Hughes *(Keith)*; Alex Menglet *(Stoyan)*; John Samaha *(Father)*; Cathren Michalak *(Grandma)*; Lucky Starr *(Club Manager)*; Alan Parry *(Young Maria)*; Bianca Roussos *(Young Stephanie)*; Elyse Tabone *(Young Nicola)*; Stefan Kozuharov *(Bulgarian Dancer)*; Misho Petrov *(Bulgarian Dancer)*; Trevor Fiarbairn *(Bulgarian Dancer)*; David Field; Maria Mazzorana; Eva Choc; Kim Sanders *(Bulgarian Musicians)*; Eshref Eyiam *(Customs Officer)*; Alexandra Souvlis *(Air Hostess)*; "Peach" Tania Simon *(Sal)*; Joel Tobeck *(Mog)*; Lucy Lawless *(The Tow Truck Driver)*

GIRLFRIENDS, an anthology of short films made by and about lesbians, serves up an uneven—but generally satisfying—100 minutes of entertainment.

First Run Features distributed this eight-film package in 1996 in a feature format. While the films come from different directors from all over the world, with some more technically polished than others, they are all more humorous than erotic.

Barbara Rose Michels' "Watching Her Sleep" (one of the shortest and most ingenious of the bunch) mixes humor with pathos as the heroine fantasizes an entire relationship with a stranger she sees in a supermarket check-out line. Jane Schneider's "Jumping the Gun" also uses comic fantasy to depict the paranoid vision of a woman who thinks that her new lover has strayed. It's a clever piece that is marred by an abrupt resolution. Christina Andreef's "Excursion to the Bridge of Friendship," on the other hand, only gets going at the end, but still comments wryly on ethnic and cultural differences (and looks good in widescreen black and white).

Cheryl Dunye's "Greeting from Africa" finishes on the perfect ironic note, summing up the difficulties of the lesbian dating scene, while "Little Women in Transit" (directed by Barbara Hellen), about a family car trip, employs sarcastic humor and ends more gruesomely. Both Ela Troyano's "Your Kunst Is Your Waffen" ("Your Art Is Your Weapon") and Monica Pellizzari's "Just Desserts" possess a quirkier sensibility, and are, therefore, less accessible. But at least "Kunst" performance artist Carmelita Tropicana (a Carmen Miranda for the '90's), delights as a political activist who gets thrown into jail, while "Desserts," which is about a young woman who associates sex with her mother's cooking, features another splendid use of widescreen. Christine Parker's "Peach," the last film on the program, employs a familiar coming-out plot, and is notable for an appearance by Lucy Lawless (television's "Xena") playing a truck driver who comes between an unhappily married couple.

While some of the films work better than others, all are spirited and accomplished. GIRLFRIENDS also makes a fun way to catch up on a variety of short subjects. . . other distributors should take note. *(Violence, nudity, sexual situations, adult situations, profanity.)* — E.M.

d, Barbara Heller, Jane Schneider, Ela Troyano, Cheryl Dunye, Christina Andreef, Barbara Rose Michels, Monica Pellizzari, Christine Parker; p, Barbara Heller, Murray Fahey, Cheryl Dunye, Mary Jane Skalski, Karen Yaeger, Helen Bowden, Christopher Borden, Barbara Rose Michels, Caterina De Nave; exec p, Ela Troyano, Ted Hope, James Schamus; assoc p, Marcella Ferreri, Sara Rychtarik, Jessica Hobbs; w, Milly Heller (based on her short story "Little Women in Transit"), Hilary Beaton, Carmelita Tropicana, Ela Troyano, Cheryl Dunye, Christina Andreef, Barbara Rose Michels, Christine Parker; ph, Tami Reiker, Chantal Abouchar, Sarah Cawley, Garry Phillips, Stuart Dryburgh; ed, Anne McCabe, Linda Gahan, Freddie Rodriquez, Joan Caplin, Heidi Kenessey, Christine Jeffs; m, Cheryl Flint, Fernando Rivas, Glorified Magnified, David Bridgman; prod d, Jo Weatherby, Janet Patterson, Grant Major; art d, Shawn Atkins, Janet Merewether; sound, Kenji Tanaka, Rick Dior (mixer), Greg Hodge (design), A; makeup, Luciana Moreira, Veronica Williams

Drama/Comedy **(PR: C MPAA: NR)**

GIRLS TOWN ★★★

(U.S.) 109m C-Hundred Film Corp.; Boomer Pictures ~ October Films c

Lili Taylor *(Patti)*; Bruklin Harris *(Angela)*; Anna Grace *(Emma)*; Aunjanue Ellis *(Nikki)*; Guillermo Diaz *(Dylan)*; Michael Imperioli *(Anthony)*; Ramya Pratt *(Tomy)*; Asia Minor *(Marlys)*; Nathaniel Freeman *(Cam)*; John Ventimiglia *(Eddie)*; Tom Gilroy *(Richard Helms)*; Stephanie Berry *(Angela's Mom)*; Ernestine Jackson *(Nikki's Mom)*; Mary Joy *(Cora)*; Tara Carnes *(Heather)*; Yassira *(Benita)*; Shondalon *(Teacher)*; Andrew Vandusen *(Helms's Co-worker)*; Carl Kwaku Ford *(Jessie—Boom Box Guy)*

Lili Taylor heads the trio of actresses whose excellent performances are the reason to visit GIRLS TOWN, an experiment in improvisational filmmaking gone right. GIRLS TOWN won two awards at the 1996 Sundance Film Festival—the Filmmakers Trophy for Best Drama, and a Special Recognition for Artistic Collaboration.

Taylor plays single mother Patti Lucci, a high school senior finally set to graduate after having been held back a few times. But what does Patti, who's poor and still dealing with her abusive ex-boyfriend Eddie (John Ventimiglia), have to look forward to? "This ain't no 90210," she observes as she surveys her life's landscape in Hackensack, NJ, just across the George Washington Bridge from the Bronx. Patti's best friends, Emma (Anna Grace) and Angela (Bruklin Harris), have concrete post-graduation plans to attend college. A fourth friend, Nikki (Aunjanue Ellis), who seems to have the brightest future, having been accepted to Princeton, surprisingly commits suicide.

When they discover that Nikki killed herself because she had been raped by a co-worker at the magazine where she interned, the bonds of the remaining trio's friendship grow deeper. Realizing that the personal is political, they get angry and they get busy. Their first action is trashing the car of a football player who date-raped Emma. Second is a bathroom wall campaign to "out" sexually abusive students and teachers. Then, they burglarize Eddie's apartment and hock the goods to buy clothes and food for Patti's child. Finally, they confront Nikki's rapist, and beat him up on the street.

Warned by the school principal—who is named "Clinton"—that she's throwing her future away, Angela replies that the future means nothing. Still, at the movie's end, as they watch a passing train, all three girls express hope that the immediate future will be better.

No one would ever confuse this GIRLS TOWN with the 1959 Mamie Van Doren vehicle of the same name, but a comparison is apt, as those responsible for this movie are too savvy to have chosen the title unadvisedly. In that camp classic, Van Doren plays a teen-age "bad girl" who gets straightened out by the tough nuns at a detention home. Back then, authority figures presumably had the cure for the teen ills of necking, smoking, contrariness, gum-snapping, and fast driving.

Here, we're presented with a portrait of contemporary reality in which young women face very different concerns, pressures, and dangers—most notably, physical and sexual abuse. Further, these girls have no one to turn to but each other—and, tragically, Nikki can't even do that. Institutions like church, school, police, and family are uncaring, absent, or ineffective. For good or bad, Patti, Emma, and Angela take their empowerment where they can find it. GIRLS TOWN isn't a message movie per se (the filmmakers certainly aren't advocating violence); it's more like a sociological snapshot, leaving viewers to make their own judgements.

Shot in less than two weeks on a shoestring budget, the characters and story for GIRLS TOWN developed wholly out of an improvisational process. Stars Taylor, Harris, and Grace, along with director Jim McKay and Denise Casano, are co-credited with the screenplay. Without mimicking the faux verite of KIDS (1995), or disguising reportage as narrative like 1994's MI VIDA LOCA, GIRLS TOWN achieves its verisimilitude with dialogue that rings true and organic characterizations. *(Profanity, violence.)* — P.R.

d, Jim McKay; p, Lauren Zalaznick; co-p, Sarah Vogel, Kelley Forsyth; w, Jim McKay, Denise Casano, Anna Grace, Bruklin Harris, Lili Taylor; ph, Russell Fine; ed, Jim McKay, Alex Hall; m, Guru; prod d, David Doernberg; art d, Melissa P. Lohman; sound, Charles R. Hunt (mixer), Rob Larrea (mixer), Irin Strauss (mixer), Gus Koven (mixer), Noah Timan (mixer); casting, Adrienne Stern; cos, Carolyn Grifel

Drama **(PR: C MPAA: R)**

GLASS CAGE, THE ★

(U.S.) 95m Playboy Films; Motion Picture Corporation of America ~ Orion Home Video c

Charlotte Lewis *(Jaqueline)*; Richard Tyson *(Paul Yaeger)*; Eric Roberts *(Detective Montrachet)*; Stephen Nicholas *(Renzi)*; Joseph Campanella *(LeBeque)*; Richard Moll *(Ian Dexter)*; Horacio Anthony *(Marko)*; Anthony Curtis *(Anton)*; Maria Ford *(Dianne)*; Lisa Marie Scott *(Kika)*; Carlos Carrasco *(Homer)*; Richard Paul *(Silkerman)*

Some people will rent just about any video with half-naked women on the box. Even so, it's unlikely too many people suckered by THE GLASS CAGE will stay awake through it. It's a silly, ugly story about the crooked owners of an upscale strip club and the ex-CIA agent who brings them down. The film is so stylistically unctuous and vacant that even the naked bodies become boring.

A drifter named Paul Yaeger (Richard Tyson) walks into a fancy New Orleans strip club owned by two French brothers, Marko and Anton (Horacio Anthony and Anthony Curtis). Paul, who apparently has a history with Marko's lover Jacqueline (Charlotte Lewis), immediately gets a job as a bartender.

Marko and Anton are smuggling everything from diamonds to heroin to Cuban refugees. They are assisted by Detective Montrachet (Eric Roberts), who plays both sides of the fence, and rich patron Tobias Silkerman (Richard Paul). Montrachet discovers that Paul was once a CIA agent, now on the trail of other CIA agents who betrayed him in Africa. Paul had left Jacqueline in Africa, the only way to save his own skin.

Marko cheats on Jacqueline with her friend Dianne (Maria Ford), and Jacqueline returns to Paul. Marko uses her as bait and cons Paul into joining the business.

Marko and Silkerman plan a huge diamond heist behind Anton's back. Although Paul is set up, he exposes Marko with the help of Montrachet. He plans to escape with Jacqueline, but this time *she* leaves *him* behind. Paul has the last laugh; she thinks he gave her the diamonds, but as she leaves the country, she discovers he's lied to her and she has nothing.

THE GLASS CAGE is exploitation, but takes itself seriously anyway. As the naked bodies writhe in the background, the foreground contains a surprisingly complicated plot, one that's sure to lose most viewers. For example, we learn that Paul is still seeking the mysterious LeBeque (Joseph Campanella), who sold him out in Africa. When some of Paul's CIA acquaintances show up (and pin a murder on Paul), it's never made clear that LeBeque is there in New Orleans and behind much of Marko and Anton's work. We also never figure out who the other CIA men are. The filmmakers should have known better than to try to be clever with this plot.

The strip bar and blues soundtrack could have created a wonderfully seedy atmosphere for this story of double-crossing, love gone wrong, and revenge. However, with its slick lighting and remarkably clean sets, THE GLASS CAGE loses its own identity. The ludicrous sex scenes, cheap special effects, and lame attempts at humor don't help.

The acting isn't much better. Richard Tyson, as Paul, shows emotion only by a distrustful snarl or a flex of his biceps. Charlotte Lewis, as Jacqueline, is given top billing, probably because her naked body is bathed in the most complimentary light. What the extremely talented Eric Roberts is doing in the throwaway role of Montrachet is anybody's guess. *(Graphic violence, extreme profanity, extensive nudity, sexual situations, substance abuse.)* — A.M.

d, Michael Schroeder; p, Brad Krevoy, Steve Stabler; exec p, Tony Lynn, Richard P. Rosetti; co-p, Jeremy Kramer, Cathy Gesualdo, Simon Tse; w, Peter Yurksaitis, David Keith Miller; ph, John Aronson; ed, John Lafferty; m, Marcus Barone; prod d, Elisabeth A. Scott; sound, Patrick M. Griffith; fx, Lou Carlucci; casting, Donald Paul Pemrick; cos, Kristen Anacker; makeup, Michael Hunt

Crime/Drama/Erotic **(PR: O MPAA: R)**

GLIMMER MAN, THE ★★★

(U.S.) 91m Seagal/Nasso Productions; Warner Bros. ~ Warner Bros. c

Steven Seagal *(Detective Jack Cole)*; Keenen Ivory Wayans *(Detective Jim Campbell)*; Bob Gunton *(Frank Deverell)*; Brian Cox *(Mr. Smith)*; Michelle Johnson *(Jessica Cole)*; John M. Jackson *(Donald Cunningham)*; Stephen Tobolowsky *(Christopher Maynard)*; Peter Jason *(Millie's Father)*; Ryan Cutrona *(Captain Harris)*; Richard Gant *(Detective Roden)*; Johnny Strong *(Johnny Deverell)*; Robert Mailhouse *(Smith's Bodyguard)*; Jesse Stock *(Cole's Son)*; Alexa Vega *(Cole's Daughter)*; Nikki Cox *(Millie)*; Wendy Robie *(Melanie Sardes)*; Harris Laskawy *(Coroner)*; Dennis Cockrum *(Detective Tom Farrell)*; Blake Lindsley *(School Teacher)*; John Bluto *(Hotel Desk Clerk)*; Sid Conrad *(Cemetery Priest)*; George Fisher *(Misha)*; Michael Bryan French; Victor Ivanov *(Russian Detectives)*; Stephen Mills *(Hostage Priest)*; Bibi Osterwald *(Woman in Ovington Arms)*; George Couts *(Ghetto Kid)*; Susan Reno *(Mrs. Roslov)*; Freda Foh Shen *(Polygraph Technician)*; Richard Tanner *(Lento's Maitre D')*; Paul Raci; Kevin White *(Internal Affairs Agents)*; Ellis E. Williams *(Brother Gaglio)*; Mireille Fournier *(Sister Rose)*; Patricia Carraway *(Female Detective)*; Paige Rowland *(Hostess)*; Fritz Coleman *(Himself)*; Albert Wong *(Mr. Lee)*; Nancy Yee *(Mae Lee)*; John P. Gulino *(Task Force Lawyer)*; Stacy Studen *(NY Detective)*; Michael Tamburro *(Helicopter Pilot)*

Love them or hate them, Steven Seagal's films are remarkably consistent, and THE GLIMMER MAN is his best since UNDER SIEGE (1992).

Los Angeles is being terrorized by "the family man," a serial killer who crucifies the bodies of his victims, all Catholics. Investigating homicide detective Jim Campbell (Keenen Ivory Wayans) is assigned a partner for this high-profile case. Recently relocated to LA from New York City, Jack Cole (Steven Seagal), to Campbell's general irritation, dresses in Hindu clothing and makes frequent references to Eastern philosophies.

When another couple is murdered, Cole's fingerprint turns up at the murder scene. The victims are identified as Cole's ex-wife and her new husband. Campbell quietly does a background check on his mysterious partner, but finds almost no information. Meanwhile, Cole pays a visit to "Mr. Smith" (Brian Cox), his contact when he was a special operative for the CIA. Cole suspects Smith or someone else is trying to frame him.

A murder suspect is positively identified and apprehended. But a check into his movements proves what Cole has come to suspect, that several of the murders were committed by a professional assassin using the serial killer's MO to cover his tracks. Cole and Campbell discover a scheme involving Mr. Smith and powerful businessman Frank Deverell (Bob Gunton) to sell chemical weapons imported from Russia to Serbian terrorists. Prior to a meeting where the deal is to be finalized, Cole and Campbell trick Deverell's "security officer" Donald Cunningham (John Jackson) into believing that he is to be killed after the deal. Cunningham, the real killer of Cole's ex-wife, kills Deverell before being killed himself in a fight with Cole.

The plot of THE GLIMMER MAN (the title refers to Jack Cole's code name when he worked as a government assassin in the jungles of the Third World) is fairly preposterous if one stops to think about it. But thinking during an action movie is something one does only if the movie isn't doing its job. It's a compliment to the makers of this one to say that almost no viewer will spend much time thinking about it.

Unlike most action stars, former martial arts instructor and international security specialist Steven Seagal has maintained tight control over his own career since his first film, ABOVE THE LAW (1988). Seagal generally co-writes and produces his films, investing them with his personal concerns, particularly Eastern philosophies, environmentalism, and a deep outrage at covert government activities in Third World nations. And if films like THE GLIMMER MAN seem unlikely vehicles to raise political consciousness, well, maybe that makes them all the more effective.

Although he has undeniable physical presence, Seagal speaks in a monotonous whisper and has an unvarying facial expression that can render him dull. So it was inevitable that he would end up in a "buddy-cop" film, paired with a more lighthearted actor. For that role, Keenen Ivory Wayans was not an inspired choice. Like his brother Damon, this Wayans has of late foresaken comedy in an attempt to become a straight action star, and as such adds little to the film.

But THE GLIMMER MAN is first and foremost an action film, and it does contain lots of action, all rather impressively designed and photographed. Director of photography Rick Bota has a penchant for showy tracking shots as well.

Production designer William Sandell (ROBOCOP) does the near impossible in finding a different look for Los Angeles, evoking a rainy atmosphere. The final third of the film features two big explosions that probably cost obscene amounts of money, but look impressive as hell (literally). *(Graphic violence, nudity, sexual situations, adult situations, substance abuse, profanity.)* — M.F.

d, John Gray; p, Steven Seagal, Julius R. Nasso; exec p, Michael Rachmil; co-p, Ed McDonnell; w, Kevin Brodbin; ph, Rick Bota; ed, Donn Cambern; m, Trevor Rabin; prod d, William Sandell; art d, Nancy Patton; set d, Ernie Bishop; sound, Edward Tise (mixer), Robert Alan Wald (mixer); fx, Ken Pepiot; casting, Debbie Manwiller Associates; cos, Luke Reichle; makeup, Jef Simons; stunts, Dick Ziker

Action/Thriller **(PR: C MPAA: R)**

GRACE OF MY HEART ★★½

(U.S.) 115m Cappa Productions ~ Gramercy Pictures c

Illeana Douglas *(Denise Waverly/Edna Buxton)*; John Turturro *(Joel Millner)*; Matt Dillon *(Jay Phillips)*; Eric Stoltz *(Howard Caszatt)*; Bruce Davison *(John Murray)*; Patsy Kensit *(Cheryl Steed)*; Jennifer Leigh Warren *(Doris Shelley)*; Bridget Fonda *(Kelly Porter)*; Chris Isaak *(Matthew Lewis)*; Christina Pickles *(Mrs. Buxton)*; Richard Schiff *(Audition Record Producer)*; Sissy Boyd *(Dress Saleswoman)*; Jill Sobule *(Talent Show Contestant)*; Tegan West *(M.C. at Talent Show)*; Natalie Venetia Belcon *(Betty)*; Kathy Barbour *(Sha Sha)*; Diane Robin *(Waitress in Diner)*; Portrait; Eric Jerome Kirkland; Irving Eugene Washington III; Kurt Jackson; Michael Saulsberry *(The Stylettes)*; Drena De Niro *(Receptionist #1)*; Jade Gordon *(Girl in Coffee Shop)*; Tracy Vilar *(Annie)*; Amanda De Cadenet *(Receptionist #2)*; Martin Valinsky *(Brill Building Songwriter)*; Lita Stevens *(Radio Station Receptionist)*; For Real *(Brill Building Hallway Singers)*; Larry Klein *(Record Producer)*; The Williams Brothers *(Click Brothers)*; Lucinda Jenney *(Marion)*; Deidre Lewis *(Girl in Howard's Bed)*; Buster *(Baby Luma)*; John Nacco *(Cab Driver)*; Lynne Adams *(Kindly Nurse)*; Brittany English Stevens *(Luma)*; Johnny Thomas III *(Annie's Son)*; Harry Victor *(Journalist)*; Jeffrey McDonald; Steven McDonald; Brian Reitzell *(The Riptides)*; Christina Ehrlich *(The Riptides' Dancing Girl)*; Melanie A. Gage *(The Riptides' Dancing Girl)*; Albert Macklin *(TV Interviewer)*; J. Mascis *(The Riptides' Engineer)*; Eric A. Stromer *(Doris' LA Boyfriend)*; Robert Brunner *(Theremin Player)*; Chris Shearer *(Security Expert)*; China Kantner; Paige Dylan; Alicia Jaffee *(Singers on Beach)*; Alice Cohen; Lita Hernandez; Delia Gonzalez *(Singers in Tree)*; David Clennon *(Dr. Jones—"Jonesy")*; Precious Chong *(Crying Woman at Funeral)*; Peter Fonda *(Voice of Guru Dave)*; Shawn Colvin *(Commune Guitarist)*

GRACE OF MY HEART, Allison Anders' most ambitious film to date, is a well-intentioned but fitful look back at the early days of rock 'n' roll. Likeable on its slim surface, Anders' episodic tale of a 1960s female songwriter achieves its best moments almost glancingly, while failing to deliver on its larger theme of a woman's odyssey to find herself personally and aristically.

Edna Buxton (Illeana Douglas) is a singer-turned-songwriter from Philadelphia's Main Line, who longs for success in the pre-Beatles world of pop music. Save for her social background, Edna could almost be Carole King as she enters the fabled world of New York's Brill Building, where Tin Pan Alley and rock composers alike turn out three-minute pop classics practically round-the-clock. There, the fledgling songwriter is taken under the wing of frenetic Joel Milner (John Turturro), a Phil Spector-like wunderkind, who changes Edna's name to Denise Waverly and puts her to work writing songs. Soon, Denise teams up with Howard (Eric Stoltz), a seasoned Brill Building writer, whom she marries and later divorces. Hits come and go during the heady '60s, and Denise finishes the decade in California, where she falls in love with Jay (Matt Dillon), a West Coast musical "genius" not unlike the Beach Boys' Brian Wilson. Convinced of Jay's artistry, Denise tries earnestly to win him over from his self-destructive ways, but the ocean beckons. Jay's suicide represents an epiphany for Denise, who re-invents herself as a singer-songwriter and embarks on a new career.

GRACE OF MY HEART's narrative is nothing if not lumbering and, at nearly two hours running time, the film's elliptical structure is taxing. Moreover, its lead character is far from compelling. Anders, who wrote the screenplay, seems bent on celebrating a smart, personable woman's journey to emotional and creative fulfillment, but, oddly enough, given the feminism of the filmmaker's GAS FOOD LODGING (1992) and MI VIDA LOCA (1994), Edna/Denise is something of a cipher, and a rather passive one at that. Douglas gives a winning performance, but seems restricted by the reactive role she's saddled with. Turturro tries hard to make Joel a New York eccentric, but winds up overwhelming his co-star. Stoltz captures Howard's brash and charming nature, but is less convincing during his later, more caddish scenes. Dillon looks the part of the tortured artist, but can't get past the role's archetypal boundaries. It remains for Bridget Fonda to pump up the movie wickedly as a Lesley Gore-like singer with sapphic electricity.

GRACE OF MY HEART re-creates the innocence and enthusiasm of rock 'n' roll during its halcyon days, not just in Francois Seguin's production design, but in Susan Bertram's often witty costumes. Also on the plus side is an original music score, featuring the likes of Joni Mitchell, Lesley Gore and, in something of a coup, the songwriting team of Elvis Costello and Burt Bacharach. *(Sexual situations, substance abuse, profanity.)* — E.K.

d, Allison Anders; p, Ruth Charny, Daniel Hassid; exec p, Martin Scorsese; w, Allison Anders; ph, Jean-Yves Escoffier; ed, Thelma Schoonmaker, James Kwei, Harvey Rosenstock; m, Larry Klein; prod d, Francois Seguin; art d, Mayne Berke; set d, Sara Andrews; sound, Stephen Halbert (mixer); fx, John Hartigan; casting, Russell Gray; cos, Susan Bertram; makeup, Christine M. Steele; stunts, Michael T. Brady

Drama/Musical **(PR: C MPAA: R)**

GRASS HARP, THE ★★

(U.S.) 107m Davis Entertainment; Matthau Company; Paribas Entertainment ~ Fine Line c

Piper Laurie *(Dolly Talbo)*; Walter Matthau *(Judge Charlie Cool)*; Sissy Spacek *(Verena Talbo)*; Jack Lemmon *(Morris Ritz)*; Mary Steenburgen *(Sister Ida)*; Edward Furlong *(Collin Fenwick—as a teen)*; Grayson Fricke *(Collin Fenwick—child)*; Roddy McDowall *(Amos Legrand)*; Nell Carter *(Catherine Creek)*; Charles Durning *(Reverend Buster)*; Sean Patrick Flanery *(Riley)*; Joe Don Baker *(Sheriff)*; Mia Kirshner *(Maude)*

THE GRASS HARP is a tasteful, but exceedingly slow and talky, adaptation of Truman Capote's semi-autobiographical 1951 novel about a young Southern boy in the 1930s and '40s.

After the death of his mother, 11-year-old Collin Fenwick (Grayson Fricke) goes to live with his father's spinster cousins, Verena Talbo (Sissy Spacek), a strong-willed businesswoman, and her sister, Dolly (Piper Laurie), a sweet and simple eccentric. Collin grows close to Dolly, and he joins her and their housekeeper, Catherine (Nell Carter) on expeditions into the woods to Dolly's secret treehouse, and to collect herbs, which she uses to concoct a homemade elixir for dropsy.

A few years later, Collin (Edward Furlong) starts to date and gets a job at the local pharmacy. Verena discovers that Dolly's dropsy cure is making a lot of money, and she tries to horn in on her business. She and her gentleman friend, a slick "Doctor" from Chicago named Morris Ritz (Jack Lemmon), tell Dolly that they want to patent her medicine and turn it into a big business, but Dolly refuses to allow it, and they have a fight. Dolly runs away to her treehouse and is joined by Collin and Catherine. The town's sheriff (Joe Don Baker) tries to bring Dolly back, but retired Judge Charlie Cool (Walter Matthau) intercedes and stops him. The judge begins to pay frequent visits to the treehouse, and eventually proposes to Dolly. Meanwhile, Verena discovers that Morris has been swindling her out of her money.

A group of evangelists, led by Sister Ida (Mary Steenburgen) and her 15 children, meet Dolly in the woods and ask for her help after being thrown out of town by the sheriff. Dolly feeds them, and Judge Cool gives them some money. But the sheriff and his men show up to force them to leave, and in the ensuing scuffle, Collin is shot in the shoulder. He recovers, the judge continues to see Dolly, and all seems well, until one day, Dolly suffers a stroke and dies.

The next fall, Collin tells Verena that he's going to New York to become a writer. He says goodbye to everyone and returns to the treehouse with Verena, Catherine and Judge Cool to listen to "the grass harp"—the windswept fields that Dolly said carry the voices of the dead.

When a movie with an all-star cast featuring Walter Matthau and Jack Lemmon sits on the shelf for over a year, and then only receives a token theatrical release, that's a sure sign that something is wrong. THE GRASS HARP certainly proves that theory. It's not bad, but there's no real reason for its existence, either, apart from having Walter Matthau gather together a group of his friends to enable his son, Charles, to direct a movie.

THE GRASS HARP probably should have been made as a TV movie, where its literary pedigree, torpid pace, conventionally pretty visuals and amber-tinted nostalgia would have seemed comparatively classy. On the big screen, it comes off as a wan and episodic coming-of-age tale whose tone wavers uncomfortably from caricatured parody of lovable Southern eccentrics to reverent earnestness.

Charles Matthau's direction is competent, but unimaginative and uninspired. Mostly, he simply plunks the camera down and lets his impressive cast do their thing. The performances are all fine, although it's a little strange to see Sissy Spacek, who was Piper Laurie's daughter in CARRIE (1976), now playing her sister. *(Profanity, adult situations.)* — M.S.

d, Charles Matthau; p, Charles Matthau, Jerry Tokofsky, John Davis; exec p, John Winfield; co-p, Stirling Silliphant, Kirk Ellis; w, Stirling Silliphant, Kirk Ellis (based on the novel by Truman Capote); ph, John A. Alonzo; ed, Sidney Levin, Tim O'Meara; m, Patrick Williams; prod d, Paul Sylbert; cos, Albert Wolsky

Drama **(PR: C MPAA: PG)**

GRAVE, THE ★★

(U.S.) 96m Kushner-Locke; HBO Pictures ~ Republic Pictures Home Video c

Anthony Michael Hall *(Travis)*; Craig Sheffer *(King)*; Josh Charles *(Tyn)*; John Diehl *(J. C. Cole)*; Gabrielle Anwar *(Jordan)*; Donal Logue *(Cletus)*; Max Perlich *(Boo)*

Occasionally entertaining and featuring a worthwhile performance from Mr. Whatever-happened-to, Anthony Michael Hall, THE GRAVE is essentially a hillbilly heist flick that is way too complicated for its own good.

The eponymous grave belongs to Mr. Matheson Hoke, the backwoods' answer to Donald Trump, who—legend has it—was buried with the key to a vault containing his immense wealth. So compelling is the legend that it prompts convicts King (Craig Sheffer) and Tyn (Josh Charles) to break out of prison in search of the buried booty. Though they escape without incident by bribing a guard, J. C. Cole (John Diehl), they are caught stealing clothes off a laundry line and Tyn takes a belly full of buckshot. Panicked, King takes his friend to the nearest thing to a doctor he can find: Travis (Anthony Michael Hall), who works at a funeral home. Travis' contributions are negligible, of course, and Tyn soon dies—but not before telling Travis about the grave.

While King seeks out an old girlfriend, Jordan (Gabrielle Anwar), Travis and his hillbilly buddies, Cletus and Boo (Donal Logue and Max Perlich), load the pickup with shovels and head for Hoke's final resting place. What they find there, not surprisingly, is a badly decomposed corpse wearing an ornate gold ring, but no sign of treasure. Travis and Cletus take the ring to Jordan, who informs them that there must be a second ring that, when combined with this one, reveals the secret location of Hoke's stash. She also tells them the story of Hoke's young wife, Ophelia, who, unable to bear children, allegedly bought a black-market baby girl before dying under mysterious and violent circumstances.

Meanwhile, Boo has been captured by Cole, the prison guard, who is looking for his share of the take. Travis and Cletus once again exhume Hoke's carcass and retrieve the second ring, which points to the grave of Ophelia Hoke as the entrance to the famed vault. Joined by King (who had been bashed over the head with a shovel by Boo, mistaken for dead, buried, and unearthed), they eagerly desecrate Ophelia's tomb, revealing a passageway to old Hoke's treasure trove. Blinded by gold, they hardly notice as Jordan—Ophelia's "daughter" and the true heir to the Hoke fortune—seals the grave behind them, burying them alive.

We can almost hear the pitch: RESERVOIR DOGS (1992) meets THE USUAL SUSPECTS (1995) meets DELIVERANCE (1972). Rife with Tarantino-esque dialogue, following the quirky-cast formula that has proliferated over the last few years, and told via a jail cell interrogation-confession, THE GRAVE offers a few interesting scenes but ultimately collapses under the ponderous weight of its too-complex plot. The premise—what if a bunch of backwoods rednecks tried to pull a heist—is not a bad starting point, but writer-director Jonas Pate's decision to weave in the tale of the dysfunctional Hoke family makes the story far too cumbersome to carry and telegraphs the "twist" ending almost an hour in. The one standout in the cast is Anthony Michael Hall (yes—the same Anthony Michael Hall), who conveys both cunning and stupidity in an almost animal fashion; with THE GRAVE's straight-to-cable release, though, it probably won't get him many jobs. *(Graphic violence, sexual situations, profanity.)* — B.T.

d, Jonas Pate; p, Peter Glatzer; exec p, Peter Locke, Donald Kushner, Lawrence Mortorff; assoc p, Michael Wexler, Alex Byrne; co-p, Scott Kalmbach; w, Jonas Pate, Josh Pate (based on a story by Jonas Pate, Josh Pate, Michael Wexler, and Peter Glatzer); ph, Frank Prinzi; ed, Paul Trejo; m, Alex Wurman; prod d, John Kretschmer; art d, Chuck Potter; casting, Annette Horning, Robin Carol; cos, Gloria Glynn

Crime/Mystery **(PR: C MPAA: R)**

GREAT WHITE HYPE, THE ★★½

(U.S.) 109m Atman Entertainment; Fred Berner Films; 20th Century Fox ~ 20th Century Fox c

Samuel L. Jackson *(Reverend Fred Sultan)*; Jeff Goldblum *(Mitchell Kane)*; Peter Berg *(Terry Conklin)*; Damon Wayans *(James "The Grim Reaper" Roper)*; Jon Lovitz *(Sol)*; Corbin Bernsen *(Peter Prince)*; Cheech Marin *(Julio Escobar)*; John Rhys-Davies *(Johnny Windsor)*; Salli Richardson *(Bambi)*; Jamie Foxx *(Hassan El Ruk'n)*; Rocky Carroll *(Artemus St. John Saint)*; Albert Hall *(Roper's Manager)*; Susan Gibney *(Vivian)*; Michael Jace *(Marvin Shabazz)*; Duane Davis *(Palace Guard*

#1); Lamont Johnson *(Palace Guard #2)*; Sam Whipple *(Artie)*; Lydell M. Cheshier *(Palace Guard #3)*; Stu Nahan *(Fight Announcer #1)*; Ferdie Pacheco M.D. *(Fight Announcer #2)*; Al Rodrigo *(Press Member #1)*; Phil Buckman *(Lee the Drummer)*; Renee Ammann *(Angel)*; Bert Randolph Sugar *(Himself)*; Walter Addison *(Michael Katz)*; Jonathan P. Hicks *(Sports Writer)*; Craig Modderno *(Sports Writer)*; Tim Kawakami *(Himself)*; Michael Fairman *(Chairman Jerry Schwartz)*; Brad Blaisdell *(Press Corps #1)*; James Hardie *(Press Corps #2)*; Nedra Volz *(Old Lady)*; Rick Scarry *(White Middle American)*; Elizabeth LaRou *(Pretty Young Woman #1)*; Alyson Croft *(Pretty Young Woman #2)*; Christal L. House *(Pretty Young Woman #3)*; Richard Steele *(Referee)*; Anthony "A.J." Johnson *(Sultan's Valet)*; Brian Setzer *(Himself)*; Method Man *(Himself)*; Irv L. Dotten *(Roper's Crony #1)*; Deezer D. *(Roper's Crony #2)*; Reno Wilson *(Roper's Crony #3)*; Art Evans *(Minister)*; Randy "Roughhouse" Harris *(Palace Guard #4)*; G. John Slagle *(Kane's Cameraman)*; Leon Frederick *(Roper Cornerman #1)*; James H. Hayes *(Roper Cornerman #2)*

This send-up of the world of professional boxing also means to take some jabs at such recent American verities as race, success, and political correctness. Unfortunately, the screenwriters and director allow the crudeness of their characters to dictate the level of the film's humor. Whereas an approach more suited to adults might have sustained interest, the film is too puerile and primitive to reveal anything more about the sport than a typical pre-bout press conference.

"The Reverend" Fred Sultan (Samuel L. Jackson) is a major boxing promoter and con artist. Concerned about the decline in pay-per-view revenue generated by heavyweight champ James "The Grim Reaper" Roper (Damon Wayans), Sultan has an inspired idea: to manufacture a "Great White Hope," match him up against Roper, and rake in the proceeds from a newly fascinated white public. He finds a willing patsy in Terry Conklin (Peter Berg), a one-time Golden Gloves champ who beat Roper as an amateur, but never made the jump to professional. Lately, Conklin has been doing most of his fighting not in the ring, but in the mosh pit at a Cleveland punk rock club.

Conklin steals the hearts of female fans by promising his share of the proceeds to eradicating homelessness "in America, and in the United States too." Sultan cynically sells his boy's not-so-guileless altruism, packaging him as a plucky Irishman from Middle America (although the fighter insists he is not Irish). Charged as a fraud by the outraged boxing press, Sultan countercharges the press with racism, anti-Semitism, and anything else he can think of. Roper, meanwhile, watches disgustedly from a distance, his pride wounded by the sudden turn in his fans' loyalty. In the end, he works out his frustrations in the ring by pulverizing the uppity challenger. Roper retains his title, and Conklin decides to go back to safer pursuits like slam dancing.

There are a few good satirical barbs here—especially in the spectacle of both white and black con-men working together to bilk the racist public of its disposable dollars. Both Wayans, as the increasingly portly champ, and Berg, as a worse punk rocker than he is a boxer, do good comedic turns. The be-turbaned, fright-wigged Samuel L. Jackson remains the bemused, manipulating ringmaster. Though they do rip off the basic premise of ROCKY (1976), the screenwriters deserve to be commended for resisting the temptation to rip off that film's unlikely climax.

But too much is left undeveloped. The screenwriters never do quite figure out whether Conklin is stupidly dishonest or honestly stupid. The subplot featuring reporter-*cum*-promoter Mitchell Kane (Jeff Goldblum) seems only incidentally related to the rest of the film. The antics of such toadying hangers-on as Sol (Jon Lovitz) are unfunny at best, and verge on the genuinely annoying. The same might be said of many of the pratfalls, gutter insults, and other gags in the film. To be fair, it's difficult to satirize a sport like boxing, which regularly satirizes itself. Aggressively "dumbed down" films like this simply don't have a prayer of going the distance. *(Extreme profanity, violence, sexual situations.)* — N.N.

d, Reginald Hudlin; p, Fred Berner, Joshua Donen; co-p, Barry Berg, Neil Leifer; w, Tony Hendra, Ron Shelton; ph, Ron Garcia; ed, Earl Watson; m, Marcus Miller; prod d, Charles Rosen; art d, Scott Ritenour; set d, Mary McIntosh; sound, David Chornow (mixer); fx, Ronald Nary, Mike Thompson; casting, Eileen Mack Knight; cos, Ruth Carter; makeup, Marietta Carter-Narcisse; stunts, Eddie L. Watkins

Comedy/Sports **(PR: C MPAA: R)**

GRIM ★½

(U.S.) 89m Peakviewing Productions ~ A-Pix Entertainment c

Peter Tregloan *(Grim)*; Emmanuel Xuereb *(Rob)*; Tres Hanley *(Penny)*; Kadamba *(Katie)*; John Chancer *(Steve)*; Jules DeJongh *(Sarah)*; Louise Hickson *(Wendy)*; Michael Fitzpatrick *(Ken)*; Nesba Crenshaw *(Trish)*; Nadia De Lemeny *(Mary)*; Adam Tury *(Wendy's Boyfriend)*; David Kennedy *(Mary's Husband)*

Ladling on gore instead of legitimately scaring viewers with character-driven suspense, GRIM is defeated by haphazard scripting, derivative directing, and overly theatrical acting.

In a prologue, partying young adults conjure up a cavern-dwelling carnivore, Grim (Peter Tregloan), who seizes Wendy (Louise Hickson) and takes her back to his subterranean home. Katie (Kadamba) and Katie's lover Steve (John Chancer) get away but remain psychically connected with the supernatural creature. When concerned locals plan a scouting party, Steve and Katie accompany mining engineer Rob (Emmanuel Xuereb), his ex-girlfriend Penny (Tres Hanley), Ken the mayor (Michael Fitzpatrick), Ken's wife Trish (Nesba Crenshaw), and Katie's tag-along sister Sarah (Jules DeJongh) on a journey through the caves beneath their suburban community. What these spelunkers don't realize is that Grim has been raiding local residences for his food supply—and these seven cave explorers are just people-tartare waiting to happen. After chomping off a portion of Trish's face, playful Grim seals off the humans' potential escape route. Their spirits aren't buoyed by mercurial Steve's bouts of possession by Grim, or by the caging of Ken and Sarah who await their turn on the fiend's butcher block. Protected by a pentagram circle after Katie and Steve reveal their history with the monster, the survivors temporarily escape. After Steve sets off explosions to slow down the insatiable beast, he, Penny, and Katie learn that Grim is vulnerable to bright lights. They lure the monster into a cave that is gradually filling with daylight. Rob and Penny survive, but the light melds Grim and Katie together into a rock formation.

Admittedly, sadistic movie-going sport can be had by genre buffs. Aside from offering the satisfaction of sneering as foolhardy explorers get polished off one by one, GRIM wears out the patience of horror fans with: (a) wearisome crosscutting between the squealing humans and Grim as he brings home more human bacon; (b) a failure to exploit the supernatural link between Steve, Katie, and the gluttonous fiend; and (c) an over-reliance on splatter effects. As with most fast-buck horror enterprises, the characters are not fleshed out as individuals but only exist as flesh to entice the monster. Since the protagonists register as interchangeable snacks, it's difficult to root for the fortunates who don't wind up chomped. In one sense, fright films have never recovered from the impact of the FRIDAY THE

13TH series in which young audiences demanded bloodletting rather than logic, sympathy for characters, or narrative payoffs. Accepting the audience for a pack of nondiscriminating Roman arena descendants, films like GRIM settle for making us passive spectators in a slaughter festival. *(Graphic violence, extreme profanity, adult situations.)* — R.P.

d, Paul Matthews; p, Elizabeth Matthews; exec p, Robert Baruc; assoc p, Amy Moore; w, Paul Matthews; ph, Alan Trow; ed, Peter Matthews; m, Dennis Michael Tenney; prod d, David Endley; sound, Michael J. White (design), Malcolm Davies (mixer); fx, Jim Francis, Neal Champion; makeup, Joanne Frye, Janine Schneider, Neil Gorton

Horror/Action/Science Fiction (PR: O MPAA: R)

GUIMBA THE TYRANT ★★

(Mali/Burkina Faso/Germany/France) 93m Les Films de la Plaine; Kora Films; Mali National Center for Film Production; Direction of Film Production of Burkina Faso; Westdeutscher Rundfunk ~ Kino International c
(GUIMBA, UN TYRAN, UNE EPOQUE)

Falaba Issa Traore *(Guimba)*; Lamine Diallo *(Janguine)*; Mouneissa Maiga *(Kani)*; Helene Diarra *(Meya)*; Bala Moussa Keita *(Mambi)*; Habib Dembele *(Sambou, the Griot)*; Fatoumata Coulibaly *(Sadio)*; Cheick Oumar Meiga *(Siriman)*

Among the many African films that have been showcased on the film festival circuit and released theatrically in the US, GUIMBA THE TYRANT is a major disappointment. Perhaps festival judges were bewitched by GUIMBA's pretty sets and costumes, but most western audiences will be more likely bothered and bewildered by the film's troubling, mixed message about an oppressive pre-Colonial African dictator.

GUIMBA THE TYRANT opens with a *griot*, or storyteller (Habib Dembele), narrating the tale of Guimba (Falaba Issa Traore) and his downfall at the hands of his own people.

Guimba rules the African kingdom of Sitikali in the Sahara. He kills or banishes his opponents and coddles his favorites, including his son, Janguine (Lamine Diallo), a nasty dwarf who'd rather bed—or rape—women than get involved in politics.

Since her birth, Kani Coulibaly (Mouneissa Maiga), has been promised to Janguine. But during a courtship visit to Kani, Janguine becomes obsessed with Kani's mother, Meya (Helene Diarra), and decides to marry her instead. Guimba agrees to the new arrangement and banishes Meya's husband, Mambi (Bala Moussa Keita), after he refuses to divorce his wife. Now Janguine will have Meya, and Guimba will take Kani for himself.

The citizens of Sitikali are furious at Guimba's actions, and Mambi finds help among other banished hunters who organize a revolt against the tyrant. Siriman Keita (Cheick Oumar Meiga), the hunter who chooses to battle with Guimba, captures Sitikali and holds it under siege. Using sorcery, cunning and violence, the two men combat each other from the north and south ends of the village. After the battle, Guimba is humiliated and left for dead as the *griot* ends the story.

It is hard to know exactly what the motivation was behind GUIMBA THE TYRANT. At times, writer-director Cheick Oumar Sissoko suggests a morbid comedy on the order of Barbet Shroeder's IDI AMIN DADA (1974), but more often Sissoko presents a straightforward account about the despot and his people.

There are at least two bothersome consequences of Sissoko's ambivalent approach. First, in the story itself, it makes no sense that Siriman and the other village outcasts would have been waiting some 20 years to rise up against Guimba and his son. And second, many scenes of Guimba and his son's tyranny are treated too lightheartedly (e.g. from Guimba's appearance in his silly headdress to Janguine's raping of the village women, which is viewed as an expression of his uncontrollable lust). Thus, GUIMBA THE TYRANT suffers from what might be called "The 'Hogan's Heroes' Syndrome," as evil characters are presented as comic buffoons and, thus, they become less threatening.

Granted, GUIMBA THE TYRANT presents a colorful view of a rarely depicted culture. But as a political or social document, the film probably would have been far more pungent and accessible (at least to most western viewers) had it been helmed by the great Ousmane Sembene. *(Violence, sexual situations, adult situations.)* — E.M.

d, Cheick Oumar Sissoko; exec p, Idrissa Ouedraogo, Sophie Salbot; w, Cheick Oumar Sissoko; ph, Lionel Cousin; ed, Kahena Attia, Joelle Dufour; m, Pierre Sauvageot, Michel Risse; prod d, Baba Keita, Boubacar Doumbia; sound, Martin Boisseau, Joel Rangon; cos, Kandjoura Coulibaly

Fantasy/Comedy/Drama (PR: C MPAA: NR)

GUIMBA, UN TYRAN, UNE EPOQUE

(SEE: GUIMBA THE TYRANT)

HALBMOND
(SEE: HALFMOON)

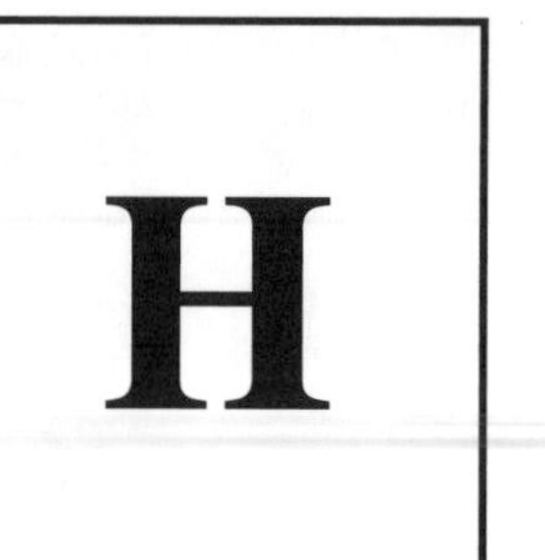

HALFBACK OF NOTRE DAME, THE ★½
(U.S.) 97m Showtime Network; Sugar Entertainment ~ Hallmark Home Entertainment c

Gabriel Hogan *("Crazy" Modeau)*; Emmanuelle Vaugier *(Esmeralda)*; Allen Cutler *(Archie)*; Scott Hylands *(Coach Modeau)*; Sandra Nelson *(Miss Martin)*; Nicole Parker *(Darla)*; Laura Harris *(Jill)*; Don McKay *(Father O'Malley)*; Gillian Barber *(Sister Mary Catherine)*; Betty Linde *(Sister O'Hara)*; Howard Dell *(Coach Dell)*; Scott Swanson *(Mr. Shaughnessy)*; Jason Alisharan *(Victor)*; Doron Bell *(Hugo)*

Amiable, but unremarkable. That best describes this teen love story, which relies on sports movie cliches and allusions to Victor Hugo's classic tale in its effort to be interesting. The movie premiered on the Showtime cable network and later was released to home video.

Halfback Craig "Crazy" Modeau (Gabriel Hogan)—a sweet lug—is the unheralded MVP of the Notre Dame High School football team. Popular quarterback Archie (Allen Cutler)—a rich brat—thinks he's the reason for the team's success. Their coach (Scott Hylands) is Craig's father, who only cares about the city championship and getting his son to the pros. Beautiful Esmeralda (Emmanuelle Vaugier), a French exchange student and classical pianist, comes between the winning combination. At first she dates Archie, but dumps him when he uses her to do his schoolwork. Then she befriends Craig and starts giving him piano lessons. Coach Modeau, who wants Craig to focus on football, forbids him to play the piano or see Esmeralda.

Right before the championship game, Craig quits the team. Archie frames Esmeralda for cheating on an exam, and she's expelled. Unaware that Esmeralda is being packed off to Paris, Craig watches the team struggle without him, suits up and comes to the rescue. With time running out, he recovers a fumble and scores the winning touchdown. Then he climbs the school's bell tower and rings the big bell signaling to Esmeralda. She returns, and Craig "convinces" Archie to confess about his wrongdoing. Finally, the elder Modeau offers his approval of his son's piano playing, and gives his blessing to Craig and Esmeralda.

HALFBACK's "triumph of the outsider" teen romance and sports story is straightforward, and the cast is pleasant. As a result, the movie isn't particularly charming, but neither is it grating. Children who have seen Disney's THE HUNCHBACK OF NOTRE DAME (1996) may get a kick out of the movie's references (two of the football players are named Victor and Hugo). Otherwise, the movie has little else to recommend it.—P.R.

d, Rene Bonniere; p, Larry Sugar; w, Mark Trafficante, Richard Clark; ph, Maris Jansons; ed, Bill Goddard; m, George Blondheim; prod d, Andrew Wilson; art d, Catherine Quinn; casting, Stuart Aikins

Children's/Romance/Sports **(PR: AA MPAA: G)**

HALFMOON ★★½
(Germany) 93m Filmgalerie 451; Filmforderung Baden-Wurttemberg; Hamburger Filmburo; Nordrhein-Westphalen Filmburo ~ First Run Features c
(AKA: PAUL BOWLES: HALFMOON; HALBMOND)

Paul Bowles *(Narrator)*; "Merkala Beach": Samir Guesmi *(Lahcen)*; Khaled Ksouri *(Idir)*; Sondos Belhassan *(Girl from Meknes)*; "Call at Corazon": Veronica Quilligan *(Woman)*; Sam Cox *(Man)*; "Allal": Said Zakir *(Allal)*; Mohammed Belfquih *(Old Man)*; Abderrahim Etaadili; Zaid Bassadouk

HALFMOON presents three short stories written and narrated by expatriate author Paul Bowles, but unlike Bernardo Bertolucci's 1990 adaptation of Bowles' *The Sheltering Sky,* this new film omnibus package is a modest, unambitious effort.

The first story, "Merkala Beach," concerns two young Moroccans who are close friends but very different from one another. When Lahcen (Samir Guesmi) drinks, he becomes loud and angry, but when Idir (Khaled Ksouri) smokes *kif* (marijuana), he gets mellow. After Lahcen begins a relationship with a beautiful but shy girl (Sondos Belhassan), he puts both his friendship and his romance to the test by leaving Idir alone with his new girlfriend. As Lahcen expected, Idir and the girl sleep together. Lahcen and Idir have their inevitable confrontation on Merkala Beach. Punching and kicking, Idir makes quick work of Lahcen, leaving him lying on the sand.

The second story, "Call at Corazon," follows a British couple's strained honeymoon aboard an old steamboat taking them up the Amazon. The newlyweds (Veronica Quilligan and Sam Cox) argue so much during the difficult journey that they finally separate on the boat one night. The next morning, the husband discovers that his wife has slept with a crew member. At the very next port, the husband abandons his bride, leaving her to fend for herself.

The last story, "Allal," tells how a lonely outcast Arab boy named Allal (Said Zakir) becomes so entranced with a snake that he steals it from an elderly snake charmer (Mohammed Belfquih). While playing with the poisonous snake, however, the two magically trade bodies. Unaware of the transformation, the townspeople hunt down the snake inhabited by Allal. One of them is bitten before they can kill it. When they find Allal, he behaves wildly (presumably because *his* body is possessed by the snake). They assume he must have gone insane, and they lock him up.

Except for a few moments in HALFMOON, Irene von Alberti and Frieder Schlaich's adaptations of Bowles' short stories seem somewhat hampered by the German filmmakers' obvious reverence for the author. (Bertolucci, on the other hand, was castigated by Bowles for freely changing *The Sheltering Sky.*) Fortunately, Bowles' introductions to the three stories in HALFMOON give wry, much-needed counterweight to the earnestness of the enterprise.

The first and weakest story, "Merkala Beach," shows, according to Bowles, the "superior effects of smoking cannabis over those of alcohol," but the "twist" ending barely makes this point, while the preceding half-hour slowly and routinely documents some rather bad behavior.

"Call at Corazon" tells a far more interesting story (it's like *The Sheltering Sky* in miniature) and provides a closer pictorial equivalent to the author's sensibility. Volker Tittel's camerawork is moodier and more fluid here as well. The only drawback to "Corazon" is that, again, the ending is somewhat disappointing, although it certainly fulfills Bowles' promise to depict "revenge and counter-revenge."

The last and best story, "Allal," begins too slowly and doesn't end where it should, but offers the most provocative and observant drama, starting with the boy's enthrallment with the poisonous snake. The suspenseful climax includes nifty shots from the snake's point of view and a psychedelic dream sequence that utilizes superimposed footage.

Overall, HALFMOON seems only half-successful, but Bowles' fans will probably find that this film makes an adequate companion piece to the documentary profile, PAUL BOWLES: THE COMPLETE OUTSIDER (1994). *(Violence, sexual situations, adult situations, substance abuse, profanity.)* — E.M.

d, Frieder Schlaich, Irene von Alberti; p, Frieder Schlaich, Irene von Alberti; w, Irene von Alberti, Frieder Schlaich (based on short stories by Paul Bowles); ph, Volker Tittel; ed, Magdolna Rokob, Margarete Rose; m, Roman Bunka, El Houssaine Kiti; prod d, Harald Turzer; sound, Peter Henrici ("Merkala Beach" and "Call at Corazon"), Volker Zeigermann ("Allal"), Stephan Konken (mixer); fx, Lutz Garmsen; cos, Anne Schlaich, ChoAhnne Anderson; makeup, ChoAhnne Anderson, Sergio da Paz

Drama **(PR: C MPAA: NR)**

HAMLET ★★½

(U.S.) 242m Castle Rock Entertainment; Fishmonger Films Ltd. ~ Columbia c

Kenneth Branagh *(Hamlet)*; Derek Jacobi *(Claudius)*; Julie Christie *(Gertrude)*; Richard Briers *(Polonius)*; Kate Winslet *(Ophelia)*; Nicholas Farrell *(Horatio)*; Michael Maloney *(Laertes)*; Gerard Depardieu *(Reynaldo)*; Billy Crystal *(First Gravedigger—uncredited)*; Robin Williams *(Osric—uncredited)*; Jack Lemmon *(Marcellus)*; Charlton Heston *(Player King)*; Rufus Sewell *(Fortinbras)*; Richard Attenborough *(English Ambassador)*; Brian Blessed *(Ghost)*; Timothy Spall *(Rosencrantz)*; Reece Dinsdale *(Guildenstern)*; John Gielgud *(Priam)*; Judi Dench *(Hecuba)*; Ken Dodd *(Yorick)*; Ray Fearon *(Francisco)*; Rosemary Harris *(Player Queen)*; Ian McElhinney *(Bernardo)*; John Mills *(Old Norway)*; Simon Russell Beale *(Second Gravedigger)*; Michael Bryant *(Priest)*; Thomas Szekeres *(Young Hamlet)*; Ben Thom *(Player 1)*; Perdita Weeks *(Player 2)*; Riz Abassi *(Attendant to Claudius)*; David Blair *(Attendant to Claudius/Servant)*; Peter Bygott *(Attendant to Claudius)*; Charles Daish *(Stage Manager)*; Angela Douglas *(Attendant to Gertrude)*; Rob Edwards *(Lucianus)*; Jimmy Ellis *(Old Fortinbras)*; Yvonne Gidden *(Doctor)*; Jeffrey Kissoon *(Fortinbras' Captain)*; Sarah Lam *(Attendant to Gertrude)*; Jimi Mistry *(Sailor 2)*; Frank Morgan *(Pyrrus)*; Sian Radinger *(Prologue)*; Melanie Ramsey *(Prostitute)*; Orlando Seale *(Boatman)*; Don Warrington *(Valtemand)*

Kenneth Branagh stars in and directs HAMLET, an opulent, if uninspired, four-hour adaptation that's notable for being in 70mm and presenting the play's entire text on film for the first time.

Shortly after the death of the king in 19th Century Denmark, his widow, Gertrude (Julie Christie), marries the king's brother, Claudius (Derek Jacobi), who becomes the new king. Gertrude's son, Hamlet (Kenneth Branagh), who's still grieving over his father's death, is appalled by his mother's new marriage. The ghost of Hamlet's father appears and tells Hamlet that Claudius murdered him by pouring poison in his ear. Unsure of how to exact his revenge, Hamlet starts to behave strangely and a courtier named Polonius (Richard Briers) thinks that Hamlet is going mad because he's in love with his daughter, Ophelia (Kate Winslet).

A troupe of traveling players arrive at the court and Hamlet has them perform a play about a king who's murdered by poison. Outraged, Claudius walks out and goes to the confessional, where he admits that he killed his brother. Hamlet overhears this but can't bring himself to stab Claudius. Hamlet goes to his mother's room, and Polonius hides behind the curtains to eavesdrop. Hamlet hears him stirring, and thinking it's Claudius, pulls out a dagger and repeatedly stabs the curtains. Polonius is killed, and Hamlet hides his body. But Gertrude tells Claudius about it, and he sends Hamlet away to England. While traveling, Hamlet learns about a plot by Prince Fortinbras of Norway (Rufus Sewell) to conquer Denmark.

After learning of her father's death, Ophelia goes mad and drowns herself. Her brother, Laertes (Michael Maloney), plots with Claudius to kill Hamlet. Hamlet returns from England during Ophelia's burial, and Laertes challenges him to a duel. During the duel, Claudius tries to get Hamlet to drink from a poisoned cup, but Hamlet refuses. Gertrude inadvertently drinks the poison, and Laertes cuts Hamlet with a poisoned sword. Hamlet mortally wounds Laertes, but before he dies, he admits to Hamlet that he had conspired with Claudius. Hamlet makes Claudius drink the poison, then succumbs to it himself. Fortinbras, whose troops have been storming the castle during the duel, walks into the court and finds the corpses of Hamlet, Laertes, Gertrude and Claudius, and declares himself the new king. Hamlet is given a state funeral, and a statue of Hamlet's father at the castle's front gate is torn down.

As a director, Kenneth Branagh falls squarely into that category in which Orson Welles placed William Wyler—that of a great producer. Branagh is, at heart, a showman, not a true filmmaker. His previous Shakespeare films as a director impart a modern sensibility and rollicking energy, if not incisiveness or subtlety. He knows how to put together commercial packages of potentially difficult fare, and here, the package consists of a complete, four-hour version of a classic, "stunt" casting featuring British, American, and French actors, and a prodigious 70mm production. It's impossible not to be impressed, although the overall impression is one of being bludgeoned into respect, rather than being overwhelmed by any great artistry or insight.

Branagh employs hyperactive Steadicam, slow-motion flashbacks, and high-tech digital effects to appeal to contemporary audiences, while the bombastic music and sound mix frequently drown out the poetry being spoken. The use of 70mm, while admirable, is debatable, since most of the play takes place indoors and one is left with little to look at except the extraordinary clarity and sharpness of the threads on costumes, or the imperfections of the actors's complexions. Branagh's performance is technically proficient, but it's all surface mechanics. He rushes through speeches with breathless speed, as if he needed to finish quickly in order to relieve himself. Derek Jacobi is brilliant as Claudius, giving the finest performance in the film, and the rest of the British cast is typically polished. Gerard Depardieu merely has one scene, muttering "Yes, my Lord" over and over, while the gimmicky casting of Billy Crystal, Robin Williams and Jack Lemmon is jarringly anachronistic, illustrating Branagh's attempt to appeal to the widest possible audience at the expense of the material's integrity. Charlton Heston, however, is excellent as the Player King.

The presentation of the complete text doesn't really make all that much of a difference, but it does give a better sense of the play's immense proportions and brilliant psychological detail. If the play's the thing, then "Hamlet" is indestructible, even in a flawed production. It's just a shame that Branagh didn't heed Hamlet's own advice to the traveling players when he admonishes them not to overact, or Shakespeare's dictum that "Brevity is the soul of wit." *(Violence, sexual situations.)* — M.S.

d, Kenneth Branagh; p, David Barron; w, Kenneth Branagh (based on the play *The Tragedy of Hamlet, Prince of Denmark* by William Shakespeare); ph, Alex Thomson; ed, Neil Farrell; m, Patrick Doyle; prod d, Tim Harvey; art d, Desmond Crowe; sound, Peter Glossop; fx, Josh Williams; casting, Vanessa

Pereira, Simone Ireland; cos, Alexandra Byrne; makeup, Tina Earnshaw; stunts, Simon Crane

AAN Best Art Direction: Tim Harvey; *AAN Best Costume Design:* Alexandra Byrne; *AAN Best Original Dramatic Score:* Patrick Doyle; *AAN Best Adapted Screenplay:* Kenneth Branagh

Drama **(PR: C MPAA: PG-13)**

HAPPY GILMORE ★½

(U.S.) 92m Brillstein-Grey Entertainment; The Robert Simonds Company; Universal ~ Universal c

Adam Sandler *(Happy Gilmore)*; Christopher McDonald *(Shooter)*; Julie Bowen *(Virginia)*; Frances Bay *(Grandma)*; Carl Weathers *(Chubbs)*; Alan Covert *(Otto)*; Robert Smigel *(IRS Agent)*; Bob Barker *(Himself)*; Richard Kiel *(Mr. Larson)*; Dennis Dugan *(Doug Thompson)*; Joe Flaherty *(Jeering Fan)*; Lee Trevino *(Himself)*; Kevin Nealon *(Potter)*; Ben Stiller *(uncredited)*; Verne Lundquist *(Announcer)*; Jared Van Snellenberg *(Happy's Waterbury Caddy)*; Ken Camroux *(Coach)*; Rich Elwood *(Assistant Coach)*; Nancy McClure *(Terry)*; Helena Yea *(Chinese Lady)*; William Sasso *(Mover)*; Dee Jay Jackson *(Mover)*; Ellie Harvey *(Registrar)*; Ian Boothby *(Guy on Green)*; Andrew Johnston *(Crowd Guy—Waterbury)*; Kimberly Restell *(Crowd Girl—Waterbury)*; Fred Perron *(Waterbury Heckler)*; Helen Honeywell *(Crazy Old Lady)*; Paul Raskin *(Starter #1—Waterbury)*; William Samples *(Starter #2—AT&T)*; John Shaw *(Daniel Lafferty)*; Ted Deekin *(Auctioneer)*; John Destrey *(Zamboni Driver)*; Jim Crescenzo *(Shooters AT&T Caddy)*; Brett Armstrong *(Shooters Tournament Caddy)*; Stephen Tibbetts *(Pro Golfer)*; Edward Lieberman *(Pro Golfer)*; Donald MacMillan *(Young Happy)*; Louis O'Donoghue *(Happy's Dad)*; Lisanne Collett *(Happy's Mom)*; Stephen Dimopoulos *(Italian Guy)*; Douglas Newell *(Starter #4—Pro-Am)*; Frank L. Frazier *(Blue Collar Fan)*; David Kaye *(Reporter)*; Zachary Webb *(Batting Kid)*; Simon Webb *(Doctor)*; Mark Lye *(Himself)*; Betty Linde *(Elderly Woman)*; Dave Cameron *(Reporter #2)*; Lou Kliman *(Reporter #3)*; Brent Chapman *(Official)*; Jessica Gunn *(Signed Chest Woman)*; Phillip Beer *(Cowboy Joe)*; Fat Jack *(Jack Beard)*; Michelle Holdsworth *(Babe on Green)*; Charles L. Brame *(Abe Lincoln)*

Adam Sandler takes another swing at big-screen stardom in HAPPY GILMORE, but he ends up in the rough with this sorry excuse for a comedy about an unusually talented golfer.

Sandler plays Happy Gilmore, a suburban youth who grows up with dreams of hockey stardom. Yet, while Happy possesses the hair-trigger temperament for the game, he lacks talent. On the same day Happy finds out that his grandmother (Frances Bay) is being evicted from her home for not paying taxes, he also discovers by chance that his wildly inaccurate hockey shooting style can be converted into an incredibly powerful golf swing.

While making some quick cash on driving range bets to stall the IRS from seizing his grandmother's house, Happy meets and teams up with Chubbs (Carl Weathers), a golf coach. Encouraged by Chubbs, Happy enters a local tournament to raise even more money for his grandmother. His surprising success inspires him to turn professional. Unfortunately, before Happy embarks on his pro tour, he is forced to place his homeless grandmother in a nightmarish nursing facility.

Happy begins winning cash on the tour right away, despite his poor putting ability and volatile disposition. With Chubbs' help, however, Happy improves his overall game, and prepares to face off against the favored pro, Shooter (Christopher McDonald), in the upcoming championship contest. Tragically, Chubbs dies before the game, but Happy is consoled by the tournament publicist, Virginia (Julie Bowen). During the final competition, Shooter tries to sabotage Happy's game, but Happy ultimately wins and saves his grandmother's house.

HAPPY GILMORE is inspired as much by the tradition of the goofy sports comedy—from SAFETY LAST (1923) to MAJOR LEAGUE (1989)—as by the recent phenomenon of young upstarts like Tiger Woods entering the sport of the elite. In fact, the subtext of the violent humor throughout HAPPY GILMORE suggests class-warfare comedy at its most vicious. Yet, while one might expect CADDYSHACK-type digs at the expense of the rich, there is no reason for Sandler and co-writer Tim Herlihy to joke about the abuse of the elderly in nursing homes or to include a mean-spirited alligator-wrestling scene.

Perhaps the angry humor might have worked better with ACE VENTURA's nuttier Jim Carrey, but HAPPY GILMORE is built around a performer who is limited both as an actor and a comic. Sandler's serious moments are dramatically deadly, while a little of his comedy goes a long way. At least he doesn't sing in this outing, and Weathers and Kevin Nealon aid him in some of the flakier routines. By default, Christopher McDonald gives the most rounded performance as Happy's jock-nemesis.

The worst moments occur as famous anti-vivisectionist Bob Barker fights with Happy during a match following the nasty alligator-wrestling bit.

It is not saying much that this film is slightly better than BILLY MADISON (1995), Sandler's debut feature.

Not since Jerry Lewis's HARDLY WORKING (1981), have there been so many plugs in a film, including spots for AT&T, Budweiser, Pepsi, Visa and the commercial-within-the-film for Subway restaurants. *(Violence, adult situations, extreme profanity.)* — E.M.

d, Dennis Dugan; p, Robert Simonds; exec p, Brad Grey, Bernie Brillstein, Sandy Wernick; co-p, Warren Carr, Jack Giarraputo; w, Tim Herlihy, Adam Sandler; ph, Arthur Albert; ed, Jeff Gourson; m, Mark Mothersbaugh; prod d, Perry Andelin Blake, William Heslup; art d, Richard Harrison; set d, Mark Lane; sound, Rick Patton (mixer); fx, Bill Orr, Clayton Scheirer, Keith Wardlow; casting, Joanna Colbert; cos, Tish Monoghan; makeup, Lisa Roberts; stunts, Brent Woolsey

Comedy **(PR: C MPAA: PG-13)**

HARD JUSTICE ★★

(U.S.) 95m Nu Image/TM Entertainment ~ New Line Home Video c

David Bradley *(Nick Adams)*; Charles Napier *(Pike)*; Yuji Okumoto *(Jimmy Wong)*; Clabe Hartley *(Larry Dickerson)*; Benita Andre *(Hannah)*; Jim Maniaci *(Mr. Clean)*; Adam Clark *(Squid)*; Alon Stivi *(Riggs)*; William Wong *(Lee)*; Johnny Koyama *(Chow)*; Vernon Wells *(Galaxy 500)*; Patrick Francis Bishop *(Webster)*; Mali Hofesh *(Girl)*; Doug Kruse *(Mani)*; Arthur Roberts *(Dr. Ellis)*

With a furrowed brow passing for a performance, high-kicking David Bradley stars in this busy piece of deja-vacuity.

Maverick federal agent Nick Adams (Bradley) literally swings into the middle of an illegal arms deal in a garage and barely escapes a conflagration ignited by gangster Jimmy Wong (Yuji Okumoto). Nick gets his man, but at the cost of the life of an innocent hostage. Wracked by self-doubt, Nick takes an undercover assignment that has already killed one buddy agent, in a penitentiary known for links to the underworld. Incarcerated Nick quickly sniffs out corruption emanating from deranged Warden Pike (Charles Napier) and barely survives day-to-day torment by gangsters who are using the jail as a clearinghouse for firearms. With fellow agent Hannah (Benita Andre) his liaison to the outside, Nick's cover is jeopardized finds himself in jeopardy when Wong is transferred to his cellblock. After surviving a stabbing by Wong, Nick fails in a breakout bid. Hannah learns that their government boss Dickerson (Clabe Hartley) is the mastermind behind the prison rackets. Unlocking all the cells, Nick starts a riot that gives him the chance to fight a half-dozen or so showdowns. He shoots Pike, divests himself of Dickerson during a helicopter wrestling match, and rescues Hannah in a final battle with Wong.

HARD JUSTICE may set a record for the number of ancillary incidents squeezed into one pea-brained action flick, clearly aspiring to the manic high style of John Woo (THE KILLER, HARD BOILED) in a plot recycled from equal parts Woo and the Jean-Claude Van Damme prison thriller DEATH WARRANT (1990). In aping his Hong Kong betters, 24-year-old director Gregory Yaitanes piles on pyrotechnic special effects and carnage, but so many beautifully timed near-misses and creative homicides dampen the film's energy rather than stoking it. "Never a dull moment" may be the credo of the action pic, but beneath the growling and brawling we have to care for the characters, or at least for the mighty hero. But everything here is lost in an avalanche of stunts, explosions and subplots about colorfully-nicknamed jailhouse fixers and allies. Bradley always seems like a beefcake poster boy perplexedly trying to recall the whisperings of an acting coach. Like the film he toplines, he lacks persuasiveness, a quality that allows bad actors like Schwarzenegger to get by on charm in between stunts. *(Graphic violence, extreme profanity.)* — R.P.

d, Gregory Yaitanes; p, Boaz Davison, Tzury Mimon; exec p, Avi Lerner, Danny Dimbort, Trevor Short; assoc p, Aria Ben Yishay; co-p, Gregory Dix, Alex Hazan; w, Chris Bold, Nicholas Amendolare, Dennis Dimster-Denk; ph, Moshe Levin; ed, Omer Tal; m, Don Peake; prod d, Aria Ben Yishay; art d, Manuel Ramon; set d, Jennifer Nejman; sound, Joe Zappala (design), Pat Toma (mixer); fx, Kevin McCarthy; casting, Leeza Davidson, Jacov Bresler; cos, Betty Fenner; stunts, Michael John Serna, Eric Mansker, Alon Stivi

Action/Crime/Martial Arts (PR: C MPAA: R)

HARD WAY OUT: BLOODFIST VIII ★

(U.S./Ireland) 78m New Concorde Productions; Transpacific Corporation ~ New Horizons Home Video c
(AKA: BLOODFIST VIII)

Don "The Dragon" Wilson *(Rick Cowan/George Macready)*; Chris Cowan *(John Patrick White)*; Jillian McWhirter *(Danielle Mendelsohn)*; Richard Farrell *(The Major)*; Warren Burton *(Michael Powell)*; Donny Hair *(Emeric Pressburger)*; Conor Nolan *(Carlo Gianini)*; John McHugh *(Det. Terry O'Leary)*; Mike Mahoney *(McGrath)*; Liam Silke; Brendan Murray; Margaret Mangan; Bebihinn Kelly; Shawn Brewster

This misconceived blarney, loaded with plot cliches and hokey combat, bodes ill for the Irish kickboxer-espionage genre.

Widower Rick Cowan (Don "The Dragon" Wilson) is a high school teacher and a pretty dull guy, at least to his rebellious teen, Chris (John Patrick White)—until assassins try to kill them. It turns out the reason for dad's long absences during the boy's childhood was his secret work as overseas CIA operative "George Macready." One of Cowan/Macready's missions led to the JFK-style murder of an Italian politician, and now it appears Rome is striking back.

Cowan and son flee to Ireland, home of the Major (Richard Farrell), a retired spy Cowan can still trust. Too late, the Major learns that the Italians are just hirelings, employed by Cowan's old Company boss, Michael Powell (Warren Burton), to eliminate witnesses to his own involvement in dirty tricks. Powell and his flunkies seize Chris—repeatedly—and the kid gains a new appreciation for his old man as Cowan shoots, kicks, and chops down the baddies in their shipboard hideaway.

The BLOODFIST series consists of several martial-arts features from Roger Corman, linked only by action-hero Wilson in the main roles. Except for the realistic prison drama BLOODFIST III: FORCED TO FIGHT (1992), all are forgettable, and by the time the eighth installment rolled around, the filmmakers evidently felt behooved to acknowledge Wilson's younger fans with the hackneyed father-son bonding. Too bad both Wilson and "juvenile" lead White could pass for being in their mid-to-late 20s. Though he sometimes plays conflicted Asian-Americans, Wilson is actually of Japanese-Irish descent, which perhaps explains the odd sortie to the Emerald Isle—with its nonstop lute and uilleann pipe melodies on the soundtrack—and a fight in a cramped village pub that replaces the customary biker bar-strip club brawl.

Even the combat is substandard: The punch-outs are framed much too tightly, and the edits confound coherency. The plot is all predictable double-crosses and cartoon cynicism about a CIA that resembles the Mafia, but with less honor. Viewers smart enough to get in-jokes in character names like Michael Powell, Emeric Pressburger, and George Macready deserve better. *(Violence, profanity.)* — C.C.

d, Barry Samson; p, Mary Ann Fisher; exec p, Roger Corman; w, Alex Simon; ph, John Aronson; ed, John Gilbert; m, John Faulkner; prod d, Sinead Nie Fhlanncha; set d, Nicola Moroney; casting, Jan Glaser; stunts, Carl Milinac

Action/Thriller/Martial Arts (PR: C MPAA: R)

HARRIET THE SPY ★★½

(U.S.) 101m Rastar Productions; Nickelodeon Movies; Paramount ~ Paramount c

Michelle Trachtenberg *(Harriet)*; Gregory Smith *(Sport)*; Vanessa Lee Chester *(Janie)*; Rosie O'Donnell *(Ole Golly)*; J. Smith-Cameron *(Mrs. Welsch)*; Robert Joy *(Mr. Welsch)*; Eartha Kitt *(Agatha K. Plummer)*; Charlotte Sullivan *(Marion Hawthorne)*; Teisha Kim *(Rachel Hennessy)*; Cecilley Carroll *(Beth Ellen Hansen)*; Dov Tiefenbach *(Boy With Purple Socks)*; Nina Shock *(Carrie Andrews)*; Conor Devitt *(Pinky Whitehead)*; Alisha Morrison *(Laura Peters)*; Nancy Beatty *(Miss Elson)*; Don Francks *(Harrison Withers)*; Eugene Lipinski *(George Waldenstein)*; Gerry Quigley *(Sport's Dad)*; Jackie Richardson *(Janie's Mother)*; Mercedes Enriquez *(Windchime Lady)*; Mung-Ling Tsui *(Mrs. Hong Fat)*; Ho Chow *(Mr. Hong Fat)*; Byron Wong *(Frankie Hong Fat)*; Paul Lee *(Bruno Hong Fat)*; Kim Lieu *(Paige Hong Fat)*; Kwok-Wing Leung *(Grandpa Hong Fat)*; Sally Cahill *(Maid)*; Roger Clown *(Dr. Wagner)*; Jamie Jones *(Pickpocket)*; Bob Windsor *(Dog Delivery Guy)*; Gladys O'Connor *(Woman With Purse)*; Vic Ho *(Acupuncturist)*; Roland Kirouac Jr. *(Choreographer)*

Though packed with sensitivity and smarts, this is a botched screen version of a magical book. Still, it can be recommended as infinitely superior to most movies made for young viewers.

Eleven-year-old Harriet (Michelle Trachtenberg) is the only child of well-to-do but neglectful parents. Harriet, a budding writer, polishes her talent by spying on her friends and neighbors and jotting her pitilessly honest observations down in a cherished notebook.

Harriet's confidante is her beloved nanny, Ole Golly (Rosie O'Donnell). Golly's suitor, a kindly store clerk (Eugene Lipinski), takes them both out to a movie one night. They have a ball but stay out too late, to the distress of Harriet's parents, who fire Golly.

Further disaster befalls Harriet when her dreaded rival, the school's Miss Perfect, Marion Hawthorne (Charlotte Sullivan), steals the book and reveals the contents to everyone she's ever scribbled about, including Harriet's best friends, Janie (Vanessa Lee Chester) and Sport (Gregory Smith).

Harriet is ostracized by everyone, even Janie and Sport, and Marion organizes other kids against her. Harriet resorts to acts of revenge, but Golly eventually persuades her that her notebooks contained only surface truths about people, and that she needs to look more closely at them. Mending her ways, she decides to put her talents to better use by editing the school newspaper.

Louise Fitzhugh's 1964 novel *Harriet the Spy* is one of those works that can be truly called a classic. Perhaps the most sophisticated children's book ever written, it presupposes a level of intelligence, urbanity and nonconformity in its young readers. The filmmakers have unfortunately made rather a hash of the book, but, somehow, its essential spirit pokes through. The film's first big mistake was changing the locale from brittle Upper East Side Manhattan to bland suburban Toronto. In the interests of flavor, the original time period of the early '60s also should have been retained, with its distinctive slang and martini-swilling, Kennedy-era ethos ("fink" instead of "dork," roller-skates instead of blades).

A bespectacled, nonconforming, scruffy tomboy, Harriet has been made distressingly generic and movie-attractive in the person of the angelically blonde Trachtenberg. To her credit, however, she's quite charming and evinces real intelligence.

For the politically correct, some of the characters in Fitzhugh's all-white world have been ethnicized. All well and good, although the sight of a shrieking family of squabbling Chinese (replete with acupuncture needles like porcupine quills) would seem to undermine these worthy intentions.

The filmmakers did well, at least, to cast O'Donnell as Ole Golly. In her prim-and-proper overcoat and bonnet, she's affectingly timeless, a modernized, cut-the-crap Mary Poppins. Unfortunately, O'Donnell's distinctive raw humor barely has a chance to glimmer through all the complacent platitudes and advice she is given to dole out.

Many of the supporting players make strong impressions. Sullivan is wonderfully imperious as gimlet-eyed Marion Hawthorne, commanding, "Harriet, you go and sit over there while we decide what to do with you." Gregory Smith as Sport has a fresh, androgynous appeal as a boy who is caretaker to his struggling writer dad. Lipinski has a low-keyed sweetness as Golly's beau.

And, as two of Harriet's spy subjects, a couple of musical stars of the past get to show their stuff. Don Francks, who crooned "That Old Devil Moon" in Francis Ford Coppola's FINIAN'S RAINBOW (1968), does some jazz scatting as Mr. Withers, a man obsessed by cats and birdcages. A pink-haired Eartha Kitt scarily lunges for her closeups with Norma Desmond intensity and, of course, guffaws hysterically, to one of her old Middle-Eastern-flavored records. — D.N.

d, Bronwen Hughes; p, Marykay Powell; exec p, Debby Beece; assoc p, Julie Pistor; co-p, Nava Levin; w, Douglas Petrie, Theresa Rebeck (based on Greg Taylor and Julie Talen's adaptation of the novel by Louise Fitzhugh); ph, Francis Kenny; ed, Debra Chiate; m, Jamshied Sharifi; prod d, Lester Cohen; art d, Paul Austerberry; set d, Gordon Sim; sound, Glen Gauthier (mixer), Cameron Frankley (design), David F. Van Slyke (design); fx, Bob Hall, Jason Board, Tim Lidstone, Arthur Langevin, Doug Bell; casting, Jill Greenberg Sands; cos, Donna Zakowska; makeup, Donald J. Mowat; stunts, Alison Reid, Ken Quinn

Children's/Comedy **(PR: A MPAA: PG)**

HARVEST OF FIRE ★★

(U.S.) 99m Sofronski Productions; Hallmark Hall of Fame Productions ~ Hallmark Home Entertainment c

Patty Duke *(Annie Beiler)*; Lolita Davidovich *(Sally Russell)*; J. A. Preston *(Sheriff Garrison)*; Jean Louisa Kelly *(Rachel)*; Tom Aldredge *(Jacob Hostetler)*; James Read *(Scot)*; Craig Wasson *(Philip Dixon)*; Gabriel Mick *(John Beiler)*; Eric Mabius *(Sam Hostetler)*; Wesley Addy *(Bishop Levi Lapp)*; Bette Henritze *(Mary Lapp)*; Gary Bisig *(Amos Zook)*; Madeleine Potter *(Miriam Zook)*; Pamela Sam *(Irene Yoder)*; Marta Kristen *(Martha Troyer)*; Peter McRobbie *(Reuben Troyer)*; Jennifer Garner *(Sarah Troyer)*; Sam Trammel *(Simon Troyer)*; Millie Perkins *(Ruth)*; Isa Thomas *(Barbara)*; Catherine Kellner *(Nancy)*; Justin Chambers *(George)*; Jeff Kizer *(Lester)*; Joel De Somber *(David Beiler)*; Sam Huntington *(Nathan Hostetler)*

Inspired by true incidents, HARVEST OF FIRE is generally well staged, insufferably well-intentioned, and ultimately uninteresting. Trying to embody the pure-in-spirit Amish, the cast becomes unintentionally condescending, as if their research into unworldliness had gotten mixed up with a study of village idiocy. When young Turk critics slam Hallmark Hall of Fame presentations, it's this species of lofty TV special they're lamenting.

Stung by relationship crises with her live-in boyfriend, Scot (James Read), self-centered career Fed Sally Russell (Lolita Davidovich) is reluctant to take a charter plane to a case in the boondocks of Iowa, where age-old tranquility has been disrupted by barn fires plaguing the Amish.

Uncomfortable with the homespun ways of the simple folk, FBI gal Sally is unable to penetrate the Amish wall of silence at first. But, after breaking bread with charitable widow Annie Beiler (Patty Duke), hardened Sally revises her estimate of the villagers.

Misled by her own hate crime theory, Sally targets some young heathens who are ticked off at an Amish teen, Annie's son John (Gabriel Mick), for romancing a town girl named Nancy (Catherine Kellner). Although Sally's self-absorption melts through her exposure to Amish traditions, she also learns this religious community is not immune to all the seven deadly sins. When an otherwise upright Amish man, Jacob (Tom Aldredge), is shunned for pride in not complying with barn-design restrictions, his son, Sam (Eric Mabius), is no longer regarded by Annie as suitable marriage material for her daughter, Rachel (Jean Louisa Kelly). In his confused anger, Sam set the fires devastating his own community.

After Sally is reunited with her estranged beau, Scot, she has the unenviable task of arresting Sam, following his public confession. At the court proceedings, the Amish rally round their lost sheep, Sam.

Penetrating another culture may be a matter best left to anthropologists. This superficial TV movie registers like the Amish segment of an "It's a Small World" TV special direct from Disneyworld.

Because the screenplay only scratches the surface of the Amish people's fallibility, the characters seem oversimplified and unbelievable. More taxing to the viewer is the synthetic manner in which the big-city protagonist's Me-Generation attitude is contrasted with the Amish villagers' selflessness. The juxtaposition of her brittle sophistication with their pie-baking folksiness is much too facile. Thus, this film creaks with the dramatically familiar and expected. Despite the compelling subject matter, one grows irritated by Davidovich's telegraphing of her cynicism and by Duke's turning the other cheek like an Amish Bobbin-head doll.

Skimming the surface of a heartbreaking tragedy, HARVEST OF FIRE diminishes the pain of the misunderstood Amish by having them express themselves in platitudes instead of dialogue from the heart. *(Violence, adult situations.)* — R.P.

d, Arthur Allan Seidelman; exec p, Richard Welsh, Bernard Sofronski; co-p, Brent Shields; w, Richard Alfieri, Susan Nanus; ph, Neil Roach; ed, Bert Glatstein; m, Lee Holdridge; prod d, Jan Scott; art d, Paul Steffensen; sound, Richard Birnbaum (mixer); fx, Jack D. Bennett; casting, Phyllis Huffman, Olivia Harris; cos, Vicki Sanchez; makeup, Jennifer Walder

Drama **(PR: A MPAA: PG)**

HATE ★★½

(France) 98m Les Productions Lazennec; Le Studio Canal+; La Sept Cinema; Kaso Inc. Productions ~ Gramercy Pictures bw
(LA HAINE)

Vincent Cassel *(Vinz)*; Hubert Kounde *(Hubert)*; Said Taghmaoui *(Said)*; Karim Belkhadra *(Samir)*; Edouard Montoute *(Darty)*; Francois Levantal *(Asterix)*; Solo Dicko *(Santo)*; Marc Duret *(Inspector "Notre Dame")*; Heloise Rauth *(Sarah)*; Rywka Wajsbrot *(Vinz's Grandmother)*; Tadek Lokcinski *(Monsieur Toilettes)*; Choukri Gabteni *(Nordine)*; Nabil Ben Mhamed *(Boy Blague)*; Felicite Wouassi *(Hubert's Mother)*; Fatou Thioune *(Hubert's Sister)*; Zinedine Soualem *(Plainclothes Policeman)*; Bernie Bonvoisin *(Plainclothes Policeman)*; Cyril Ancelin *(Plainclothes Policeman)*; Patrick Medioni *(CRS Cave)*; Karin Viard *(Gallery Girl)*; Julie Mauduech *(Gallery Girl)*; Benoit Magimel *(Benoit)*; Medard Niang *(Medard)*; Arash Mansour *(Arash)*; Abdel-Moulah Boujdouni *(Young Businessman)*; Mathilde Vitry *(Journalist)*; Christian Moro *(CRS TV Journalist)*; JiBi *(Fat Youth)*; Thang Long *(Grocer)*; Cut Killer *(DJ)*; Sabrina Houicha *(Said's Sister)*; Sandor Weltmann *(Vinz Lookalike)*; Peter Kassovitz *(Gallery Patron)*; Vincent Lindon *(Really Drunk Man)*; Mathieu Kassovitz *(Young Skinhead)*; Anthony Souter; Florent Lavandeira; Teddy Marques; Samir Khelif *(Skins)*; Virginie Montel *(SDF Metro)*; Abdel Ahmed Ghili *(Abdel)*; Joseph Momo *(Ordinary Guy)*; Olga Abrego *(Vinz's Aunt)*; Laurent Labasse *(Cook)*; Andree Damant *(Concierge)*; Marcel Marondo *(Bouncer)*; Eric Pujol *(Assistant Policeman)*; Philippe Nahon *(Police Chief)*; Sebastien Tavel *(Hospital Policeman)*; Francois Toumarkine *(Hospital Policeman)*; Jose-Philippe Dalmat *(Hospital Policeman)*; Christophe Rossignon *(Taxi Driver)*

Mathieu Kassovitz's overly self-conscious film HATE focuses specifically on 24 hours in the lives of three disaffected young men of the neighborhood.

The residents of a multiracial housing project in a suburb of Paris are rioting. They have stormed the police station and torched cars in protest over the arrest and beating of a young Arab, Abdel.

Said (Said Taghmaoui), an Arab, is deeply affected by the racial strife but takes his cues on how to react from his friends, Vinz and Hubert. Vinz (Vincent Cassel) is a violence-prone Jew who has a fanatical hatred of cops. He has pocketed a policeman's gun lost during the riot and vows to kill a cop if Abdel should die from his injuries. The Smith & Wesson .44 concealed in Vinz's pocket becomes a ticking time bomb waiting to go off during the merest altercation.

Hubert (Hubert Kounde), an African, is a part-time drug dealer who wants to quit running the streets and become a boxer. In the aftermath of the riots, the three friends discover that Hubert's gym has been wrecked.

The three young men go into town to collect money owed them by Asterix (Francois Levantal), a wealthy drug lord. In a typical display of bravado, Vinz flashes the gun, sending Said and Hubert running—into the hands of the police, who subject the two young men to an abusive interrogation. A particularly menacing and racist inspector (Marc Duret), significantly dressed in a Notre Dame jacket, takes the lead as a rookie looks on helplessly. Said and Hubert run into Vinz, who had escaped, at the train station, where the three of them discover that they have missed the last train to their neighborhood. They roam the streets, encountering a parade of eccentric people.

They try unsuccessfully to steal a car and end up sleeping in a shopping mall. They learn from a television news broadcast that Abdel has died. Said and Hubert grow angry with Vinz when they are forced to restrain him from attacking a traffic cop. They leave Vinz behind, only to be jumped by skinheads. Vinz arrives in the nick of time, again brandishing the gun, and scares off all but one of the skinheads. He intends to shoot this last skinhead, but doesn't pull the trigger.

They catch the morning train back home, where Vinz hands the gun over to Hubert, asking him to dispose of it. Suddenly, a police car pulls up and a cop jumps out. Vinz struggles with him, but in the melee, the cop's gun fires, shooting Vinz in the head. In the heat of the moment, Hubert pulls the Smith & Wesson out and faces off against the cop in an inevitable, final showdown. Said watches in horror as the sounds of gunfire resound off-screen.

Kassovitz, 27, seems desperate to occupy the cinematic cutting edge. Though undeniably powerful, his film is overly manipulative and extremely derivative. It's a blowhard movie, full of posturing attitude, just like his main characters. His technique is gritty, with grainy, in-your-face black-and-white imagery in the place of realism. The viewer perceives that Kassovitz is trying to demonstrate how hollow life in these suburban projects is, but the ugliness becomes emptily oppressive. Youth may account for the confusion of unsmiling seriousness with real depth. In comparison, Spike Lee (a clear influence) seems subtle. On the surface, HATE looks like the work of an outsider (a guerrilla filmmaker), when in reality, Kassovitz is the offspring of film professionals. In this light, his affinity for the less privileged, more "colorful" classes is all too predictable. Ultimately, the rebel veneer cannot disguise the cliches.

For all its seeming objectivity of presentation, the film simply would not exist without its pointed fascination with Vinz, a lens-grabbing psychopath from the De Niro-Pacino mold. Naturally, the only sympathetic character is the sensitive black man. And for humor, Vinz delivers the umpteenth version of the "You talkin' to me?" speech from TAXI DRIVER (1976). There is even a surreal, Fellini-esque image of a cow wandering through the streets. Kassovitz has undeniable confidence as a filmmaker—a dizzying, hand-held chase is the best, most exciting sequence in the film—but what he accomplishes already has been done better by others. *(Extreme violence, profanity, adult situations, substance abuse.)* — D.N.

d, Mathieu Kassovitz; p, Christophe Rossignon; assoc p, Adeline Lecallier, Alain Rocca; w, Mathieu Kassovitz; ph, Pierre Aim; ed, Mathieu Kassovitz, Scott Stevenson; art d, Giuseppe Ponturo; sound, Vincent Tulli (design), Dominique Dalmasso (mixer), Bruno Cottance (recordist), Valerie Trouette (recordist); fx, Pierre Foury; casting, Jean-Claude Flamand; cos, Virginie Montel; makeup, Sophie Benaiche; stunts, Philippe Guegan

Drama **(PR: O MPAA: NR)**

HAUNTED ★★½

(U.K./U.S.) 108m Double "A" Pictures; American Zoetrope; Lumiere Pictures ~ Evergreen Entertainment c

Aidan Quinn *(David Ash)*; John Gielgud *(Dr. Henry Doyle)*; Kate Beckinsale *(Christina Mariell)*; Alex Lowe *(Simon Mariell)*;

Anthony Andrews *(Robert Mariell)*; Anna Massey *(Nanny Tess Webb)*; Victoria Shalet *(Juliet)*; Geraldine Somerville *(Kate)*; Linda Bassett *(Madame Brontski)*; Liz Smith *(Old Gypsy Woman)*; Hilary Mason *(Elderly Lady)*; Peter England *(Young David)*; Alice Douglas *(Clare)*; Edmund Moriarty *(Liam)*; Emily Hamilton *(Mary)*

An oddly wistful attempt at a classic English ghost story (think 1961's THE INNOCENTS) *sans* gore or special-effects indulgence, HAUNTED is handsome but short-lived.

David Ash (Aidan Quinn), American-born psychic researcher and debunker in 1920s England, is invited to pack his skepticism and weekend at Edbrook mansion, a country estate supposedly wracked by spooks. There David finds curiously immature adult heirs Robert and Simon Mariell (Anthony Andrews, Alex Lowe) and sister Christina (Kate Beckinsale). Only terrified, elderly Nanny Tess (Anna Massey) hints at ghosts-at-large. David is more bewitched by flirt Christina, but at night he experiences guilty visions of his sister Juliet (Victoria Shalet), who drowned within his reach when they were children. David's love for Christina sours with a revelation of her long-term incest with Robert, but David doesn't appreciate how long it's gone on until phantom Juliet shows him the Mariell tombstones. Christina, Robert, and Simon—sadists and psychotics—perished years ago in a fire set by an outraged Tess. Their vengeful spirits have kept the nanny prisoner in the charred ruins of Edbrook, preservation of which is just a supernatural mirage. Ruse ended, the ghosts kill Tess, while David is led to safety by Juliet—though affectionate Christina follows close behind.

Glorious cinematography and production design evoke the between-the-wars period of the 1920s and 1930s so favored in British drama. Alas, the sunny croquet grounds and ponds of Edbrook would better suit Bertie Wooster and Jeeves than the gothic presence of unquiet dead. Even at their most malevolent, HAUNTED's specters seem little more threatening than Mary Poppins as they slay Nanny Tess with a high-speed game of ring-around-the-rosy. Novelist James Herbert reportedly conceived the book *Haunted* as a BBC-TV series pilot, but much menace washed out in the transmutation from script to prose and back (like Herbert's payoff that Juliet is the most wrathful of the wraiths). The noble cast seems straight out of *Brideshead Revisited*—and in fact Andrews and John Gielgud teamed for 1981's TV miniseries based on Evelyn Waugh's saga of a not-dissimilarly dysfunctional household of aristocrats. Director Lewis Gilbert, whose career encompasses ALFIE (1966), THE SPY WHO LOVED ME (1977), EDUCATING RITA (1983), and more, renders HAUNTED with refinement, but it needs a jolt of Hammer horror. Despite Francis Ford Coppola as executive producer, the film went straight to home video in the US after 1995 theatrical release in England and overseas. *(Nudity, sexual situations, adult situations, violence.)* — C.C.

d, Lewis Gilbert; p, Lewis Gilbert, Anthony Andrews; exec p, Francis Ford Coppola, Fred Fuchs, Jeff Kleeman, Ralph Kemp; co-p, William F. Cartlidge; w, Tim Prager, Robert Kellett, Lewis Gilbert (based on the novel by James Herbert); ph, Tony Pierce-Roberts; ed, John Jympson; m, Debbie Wiseman; prod d, John Fenner, Brian Auckland-Snow; art d, Gary Tomkins; set d, Marc Boyle, Sy Hollands; sound, Ken Weston (recordist); fx, Peter Hutchinson; casting, Joyce Nettles; cos, Candy Paterson, Jane Robinson; makeup, Christine Beveridge; stunts, Marc Boyle, Sy Hollands

Horror **(PR: O MPAA: R)**

HEAD OF THE FAMILY ★

(U.S.) 82m Pulp Fantasy Productions ~ Amazing Fantasy Entertainment c

Blake Bailey *(Lance)*; Jacqueline Lovell *(Loretta)*; Bob Schott *(Otis)*; James Jones *(Wheeler)*; Dianne Colazzo *(Ernestine)*; Gordon Jennison *(Howard)*; J. W. Perra *(Myron)*; Vickie Lynn *(Susie)*; Robert J. Ferrelli *(Weasel)*; Bruce Adel *(Ticket Agent)*; Gary Anello *(Arthur Raskow)*; Dyer McHenry *(Truck Driver)*; Rob Roeser *(Justice)*; Steve Novak *(Cauchon)*; Van Epperson *(Chorus)*; Ruth Townsend *(Receptionist)*; Suzie Chidley *(Pretty Girl)*; Tamarah Talbot; Rick Phares; Garvy McNab; Loray Quain; Samara; Russ Herpich; Christopher Bergschneider *(Freaks)*

Peculiar instead of amusing, this is a misfired attempt to combine horror and black humor.

In the town of Nob Hollow, young schemer Lance (Blake Bailey) has been having a torrid affair with Loretta (Jacqueline Lovell), and both would love to get rid of her biker husband, Howard (Gordon Jennison). Lance gets an idea when he witnesses a trucker being waylaid by the strange Stackpool siblings: Otis (Bob Schott), Wheeler (James Jones), and Ernestine (Dianne Colazzo). The three have been procuring unwilling subjects for human experiments being performed by their huge-headed, small-bodied brother Myron (J.W. Perra), who controls his siblings psychically. Soon Lance has manipulated Howard into becoming their next victim.

But Lance gets greedy and tries to blackmail the wealthy Stackpools, who promptly abduct both Lance and Loretta to the family's mansion. There, Lance is to be Myron's next experiment while Myron's lobotomized subjects prepare to burn Loretta at the stake. Simple-minded Otis has become attracted to Loretta, however, and rescues her as the house burns down on top of everyone else. Realizing that Otis is now the sole heir to the Stackpool fortune, Loretta marries him.

This entry from the low-budget film factory of Charles Band (who takes the pseudonym "Robert Talbot" here) was clearly intended to follow in the ghoulishly comic footsteps of Band and Stuart Gordon's RE-ANIMATOR (1984), complete with a villain whose head is his most prominent feature. The new movie, however, has a weak, uninspired sense of both horror and humor, with Band-Talbot apparently thinking that the simple presentation of bizarre events and characters is enough on its own.

The trifling attempts to frighten the viewer become downright misogynist by the end when Loretta is gratuitously stripped naked before the attempt to burn her, and the script is so desperate that the big-domed Myron is actually made to describe himself as "the head of the family," in case anyone didn't get the joke in the title.

While it's fairly well-produced, and at least appears to be trying for some originality, the whole movie reeks of a lack of inspiration, seeming to have been churned out as a piece of product and nothing more. *(Graphic violence, extensive nudity, sexual situations, extreme profanity.)* — M.G.

d, Robert Talbot; p, Robert Talbot; co-p, Kirk Edward Hansen; w, Benjamin Carr (based on a story by Robert Talbot); ph, Adolfo Bartoli; ed, Steve Nielson, Poppy Das, Lazar Djokic; m, Richard Band, Steven Morell; prod d, AnnMarie Roberts; art d, Margarette Epstein; sound, Patrick M. Griffith; fx, Mark A. Rappaport; casting, Robert MacDonald, Perry Bullington; cos, Heather Priest; makeup, Palah Sandling

Horror/Comedy **(PR: O MPAA: R)**

HEADLESS BODY IN TOPLESS BAR ★★

(U.S.) 110m Green Tea Productions ~ Northern Arts Entertainment c

Raymond J. Barry *(The Man)*; Rustam Branaman *(Vic Palmieri)*; April Grace *(Letitia Jackson)*; Jennifer MacDonald *(Candy)*; Taylor Nichols *(Danny)*; David Selby *(Bradford Lumpkin)*; Paul Williams *(Carl Levin)*; Biff Yeager *(Joe)*; Tom Breznahan *(Drunk)*

Inspired by an infamous *New York Post* headline, this potboiler fleshes out the true-life story in a gritty but extremely predictable manner. Despite the circumstances, some of the actors manage to come through with strong performances.

The Man (Raymond J. Barry) bursts into a topless bar in New York City one night and, in a botched robbery attempt, kills the bartender, Joe (Biff Yeager). He then proceeds to hold the bar's patrons at gunpoint. Bradford Lumpkin (David Selby) is a strait-laced corporate lawyer from Stamford. Vic Palmieri (Rustam Branaman) and Danny (Taylor Nichols) are a pair of Long Island hockey fans out on the town. Carl Levin (Paul Williams) is a lonely, friendless strip-club regular. Candy (Jennifer MacDonald), the club's topless dancer, is a hard-bitten woman who's seen it all. When her friend, Letitia (April Grace), comes to pick her up, she haplessly becomes another hostage.

To while away the time, The Man decides to play a game of "Nazi Truth" with his victims. At gunpoint, each is forced to bear his or her respective soul. In the process, a pair of handcuffs and some rubber briefs are found in Lumpkin's briefcase; Carl is discovered to have multiple sclerosis; Danny's swaggering machismo is undermined after he is forced to perform a striptease which humiliates both him and his pal Vic; Candy and Letitia are revealed to be lovers. After The Man discovers that Letitia works as a mortician's assistant, he demands she saw the head off Joe's corpse in order to dispose of the incriminating bullet in his skull. Shrinking in horror, she performs the deed. The Man takes off with his gory trophy, leaving the others behind in the bar.

Director James Bruce and scriptwriter Peter Koper, veterans of the television series "America's Most Wanted," have concocted a seamy stew awash in dramatic cliches, from the stereotypically "unlikely" mix of characters to the predictably dirty little secrets they devulge. Shot in "real time," it's more excruciating than immediate, and the one-set premise adds to the general sense of claustrophobia.

Barry is the best thing about the film, instilling his pivotal character with a whiplash shrewdness and dark humor that ironically makes him the most sympathetic character in the film. MacDonald is good, too, in her cynical urban way, despite the fact that she's half-naked throughout most of the proceedings. Selby is as predictable as his part, and actor-songwriter Williams turns in a bathetic performance. Nichols's role is something of a stretch from the nerdy yuppies he's familiar for playing (METROPOLITAN), but he doesn't do much more than display a rather buff torso while disrobing. *(Violence, nudity, sexual situations, adult situations, profanity.)* — D.N.

d, James Bruce; p, Charles Weinberger, Rustam Branaman, Steven Falick; exec p, Tom Breznahan, Sean Gavigan, Boyd Willat; co-p, Peter Koper; w, Peter Koper; ph, Kevin Morrisey; ed, Robert Barrere; m, Karyn Rachtman; prod d, Gustav Alsina; sound, Charles Barnett; casting, Joseph Middleton; cos, Natasha Landau

Drama **(PR: O MPAA: NR)**

HEAVEN'S PRISONERS ★★½

(U.S.) 104m Rank Film Distributors; PVM Entertainment; Savoy Pictures; New Line ~ New Line c

Alec Baldwin *(Dave Robicheaux)*; Kelly Lynch *(Annie Robicheaux)*; Mary Stuart Masterson *(Robin Gaddis)*; Eric Roberts *(Bubba Rocque)*; Teri Hatcher *(Claudette Rocque)*; Vondie Curtis Hall *(Minos P. Dautrieve)*; Badja Djola *(Batist)*; Samantha Lagpacan *(Alafair)*; Joe Viterelli *(Did Giancano)*; Tuck Milligan *(Jerry Falgout)*; Hawthorne James *(Victor Romero)*; Don Stark *(Eddie Keats)*; Carl A. McGee *(Toot)*; Paul Guilfoyle *(Detective Magelli)*; Chris Krisea *(Priest)*; Saul Stein *(Dom)*; Chuck Zito *(Tony)*; Socorro Santiago *(Spanish Nun)*; Patricia Huston *(Nun)*; Don Yesso *(Jungle Room Bartender)*; Anne Schedeen *(Jungle Room Patron)*; Joe Hess *(Johnny Dartez)*; Gray Frederickson *(Sheriff Len Whitley)*; Lenore Banks *(Woman Driver)*; Don Brady *(Apartment Man)*; Marion Zinser *(Apartment Woman)*; Glenn Gomez *(Piano Mover)*; James "Hooks" Reynolds *(Truck Driver)*; Tom Burgess *(Prison Guard)*; Herman Myles Sr. *(Clarence)*; Jerry Procanik *(Patron)*; Connie Whittemore *(Stripper)*

Alec Baldwin and company chew up the scenery in this New Orleans-based thriller. But HEAVEN'S PRISONERS, with its basic "a man's gotta do what a man's gotta do" premise and its none-too-original script, actually works just fine, largely thanks to sure-handed direction and a snappy soundtrack.

Recovering alcoholic Dave Robicheaux (Alec Baldwin) has retired from the force to pursue a more peaceful existence, running a bait shop with his wife, Annie (Kelly Lynch), in Louisiana's bayou country. But Dave becomes embroiled in a nest of New Orleans vipers when a small plane crashes into the bay where he and Annie are fishing. Dave dives to the rescue, but the only survivor is a little girl (Samantha Lagpacan), the youngest of a group of illegal Central American immigrants. The couple surreptitiously adopts the child and names her Alafair.

Dave knows something is afoot when official reports of the crash fail to mention the large man with a snake tattoo whom he clearly saw among the bodies. Suspecting the crash wasn't an accident, he enlists the help of an erstwhile lover, Robin (Mary Stuart Masterson), a French Quarter stripper who still carries a torch for Dave. Robin tips him off to the mystery man's identity: Johnny Dartez, a drug runner for Dave's old high school buddy, Bubba Rocque (Eric Roberts), who has become a powerful local crime boss. Bubba lives in high style on a plantation, attended to by his restless wife, Claudette (Teri Hatcher), who whiles away the days in a gin-rickey haze. For her trouble, Robin has her fingers broken by two of Bubba's thugs, who also pay Dave a brutal visit. Dave ships Robin off to Key West for safety. Dave learns that Dartez was not only working for Bubba, but for the DEA as well, which would help explain the crash and the disappearance of the body.

Dave's curiosity abruptly turns into a thirst for revenge when Annie is murdered one night. Three hired guns open fire in the Robicheaux's bedroom after a sleepless Dave has luckily stepped outside for air. Bubba denies having ordered the hit, and matters are complicated when the grieving Dave falls off the wagon and Robin returns from Key West to care for him. As Dave battles demons both without and within, he hunts down Annie's murderers through every back alley and over every rooftop in New Orleans. Dave exacts his revenge, but still doesn't know who gave the orders until, in the third killer's hideout, he spots the telltale water ring left by one of Claudette's gin rickeys. Dave confronts a drunken Claudette at Bubba's mansion and she admits to everything, including her plan to muscle Bubba out of the operation and run the whole thing herself. Dave calls the police, but before they arrive, Bubba, who has overheard the whole confession, guns Claudette down. Dave returns home to find a good-bye note from Robin and Alafair asleep in her bed.

The performances may be caricatures, ranging from gruesomely stereotyped villains to a black custodian who serves as a sort of modern Mammy, rocking a terrified child to sleep, but the film does carry the compulsive fascination of the most lurid dime novel. Phil Joanou's direction is steeped in the steamy, dilapidated glory that is New Orleans, and Harris Savides' extraordinary photography weaves a humid, yet icy, spell. Sinuous editing and crisp sound make the most of the hair-raising plane crash, and a couple of extended, outrageous chase scenes are both appalling and funny. George Fenton again proves himself one of the best composers in the business with a drivingly dramatic score. And, happily, the movie is filled with enough colorful characters, including three vividly drawn women, to help camouflage any expository lulls.

Baldwin, who also acted as executive producer, casts himself as the ultimate beleaguered guy in need of salvation. He is frequently overwrought, but his sheer presence manages to carry the day. Matching Baldwin for sleazy fervor is the uniquely slimy Roberts, mush-mouthed, corn-rowed, and utterly contemptible. As a drug enforcer, Vondie Curtis Hall has some really lame lines to deliver but retains his comic grit. Lynch brings her attractive strength as the doomed wife, while Masterson, as always, works hard as the supportive stripper. But it's Teri Hatcher who's the real wild card here. As a Cajun vamp, she's no great shakes acting-wise, but her smoky charisma recalls the young Natalie Wood—exactly the kind of juice that pulp like this needs. *(Nudity, profanity, violence, substance abuse, sexual situations.)* — D.N.

d, Phil Joanou; p, Albert S. Ruddy, Andre E. Morgan, Leslie Greif; exec p, Hildy Gottlieb, Alec Baldwin; assoc p, Michael Alan Khan; co-p, Gray Frederickson; w, Harley Peyton, Scott Frank (based on the novel by James Lee Burke); ph, Harris Savides; ed, William Steinkamp; m, George Fenton; prod d, John Stoddart; art d, Monroe Kelly; set d, Dorree Cooper; sound, Kim Ornitz (mixer); fx, Dennis Dion, Mike Shea; casting, Linda Phillips-Palo; cos, Aude Bronson-Howard; makeup, Stacy Stewart Kelly; stunts, Glen Wilder

Drama/Crime/Mystery (PR: C MPAA: R)

HEAVY ★★★½

(U.S.) 105m Available Light, Inc. ~ CFP Distribution c

Pruitt Taylor Vince *(Victor)*; Liv Tyler *(Callie)*; Shelley Winters *(Dolly)*; Deborah Harry *(Delores)*; Joe Grifasi *(Leo)*; Evan Dando *(Jeff)*; David Patrick Kelly *(Grey Man in Hospital)*; Marian Quinn *(Darlene)*; Meg Hartig *(Donna)*; Zandy Hartig *(Jean)*; Peter Ortel *(Tony)*; George Alvarez *(Orderly)*; Cordis Heard *(Nurse)*; J.C. Mackenzie *(Gas Man)*; Allan D'Arcangelo *(Sonny)*

The slow-moving but memorable story of a heavy-set pizza chef and his obsession with a beautiful waitress, HEAVY takes an unusual and sympathetic look at working-class America.

The story takes place in a sleepy, rural town in upstate New York. Victor (Pruitt Taylor Vince), an introverted and unhappy cook, works for his mother, Dolly (Shelly Winters), the owner of "Pete and Dolly's" Tavern. Life changes for Victor when Dolly hires a new waitress, Callie (Liv Tyler), a college drop-out. Victor becomes mesmerized by the young woman's beauty, but remains silent because of his weight. Callie's arrival is resented by both Delores (Deborah Harry), the tavern's long-time waitress, and Leo (Joe Grifasi), a regular customer. Away from the diner, Callie fights with her boyfriend, Jeff (Evan Dando), a part-time musician, part-time mechanic, who wants her to quit her dead-end job and move in with him.

One day, Dolly collapses and is rushed to the hospital. Callie delays her decision to leave the tavern, but after two weeks, she insists Victor bring her to visit Dolly. Instead of taking Callie to the hospital, however, he brings her to a graveyard. Callie then realizes that Dolly has been dead for several days and that Victor withheld telling anyone so that she would stay on at the diner. She forgives Victor for his poor judgement and decides to return to college. Victor begins to lose weight and feel better about himself, even striking up a friendship outside the diner that invites the possibilities of new romance.

Writer-director James Mangold makes an accomplished debut with HEAVY, an independent feature. He concentrates more on character than plot, yet this deliberately-paced narrative is oddly compelling: one becomes caught up in the lives of the characters even though very little occurs in those lives. The natural, unaffected work of Vince, Tyler, Harry, and a surprisingly restrained Winters make this "family" seem all the more genuine. As a director, Mangold refrains from flashy techniques; in fact, HEAVY is composed primarily of still shots that focus intensely on seemingly minor details and close-ups of faces. Mangold also uses an interesting balance of juke-box standards like "Moonlight in Vermont" and a haunting original score by Sonic Youth's Thurston Moore.

Some might argue that HEAVY tells its story well but has nothing new to say. It does, however, effectively depict lives that are too often made into jokes on screen. *(Profanity.)* — E.M.

d, James Mangold; p, Richard Miller; exec p, Herbert Beigel; assoc p, Scott Ferguson, Jane Wright; w, James Mangold; ph, Michael Barrow; ed, Meg Reticker; m, Thurston Moore; prod d, Michael Shaw; art d, Daniel Goldfield; set d, Kara Chessman; sound, Jan McLaughlin (mixer); casting, Todd Thaler; cos, Sara Jane Slotnik; makeup, Tracy Warbin

Drama (PR: C MPAA: NR)

HECK'S WAY HOME ★★½

(Canada) 92m Atlantis Films; Credo Entertainment; Family Channel; CTV Television Network; Super Ecran; Television Quatre Saisons; Manitoba Television Network; Showtime ~ Hallmark Home Entertainment c

B.C. *(Hector)*; Don Francks *(Red)*; Chad Krowchuk *(Luke Newfield)*; Michael Riley *(Rick Newfield)*; Gabe Khouth *(Mickey)*; Alan Arkin *(The Dogcatcher)*; Shannon Lawson *(Sheila Newfield)*; Cecilley Carroll *(Casey)*; Tim Jackson; Peter Jordan; Tannis Kowalchuk; Nancy Drake

Odorless, colorless, flavorless, inoffensive movies like HECK'S WAY HOME will always find a place in the hearts of harried parents looking for treats for their youngsters. Maybe it's because they can forget it so easily

Inventor Rick Newfield (Michael Riley) accepts an offer to move his whole family on short notice from Winnipeg, Canada, to Australia, to supervise the mining rig he developed. In his rush, Mr. Newfield has no time to find Hector, the household's shepherd-border collie mix, who was cast adrift on a raft by local bullies. By the time Hector gets back to the house, the Newfields are on their way to the port of Vancouver. The dog begins an INCREDIBLE JOURNEY-style overland hike, including a stint riding the rails with hobo Red (Don Francks).

Meanwhile, various snafus keep the Newfields holed up in their Vancouver hotel, delaying their departure for Down Under by boat. Homesick and Heck-less son Luke (Chad Krowchuk) is able to get the word out seeking his pet's return, and Red sends a response that Hector is on the way. Late complications include a meanie hotel manager who tries to prevent a nice bellboy from helping Luke, and Heck's old nemesis, a Winnipeg dog catcher (Alan Arkin), who was ready to set sail for his retirement but reverts to the Ahab-Moby pursuit when he glimpses Hector on the loose in Vancouver. Hector leaves him locked in a crate bound for a distant port, and happily reunites with Luke.

When "Come back, you mangy mutt!" represents a typical specimen of dialogue, it's best not to get one's hopes up. There's a canned theme about how the annoying Mr. Newfield finally realizes that his single-minded careerism prevents him from being a Better Father, but the major achievement of HECK'S WAY HOME is refreshing acknowledgment, right up front, that this picture takes place in Canada. Many Canadian features, driven by perceived market pressures and something of a native inferiority complex, warily keep their geography as bland and generic as possible in an attempt to pass themselves off as a product of Hollywood.— C.C.

d, Michael Scott; p, Derek Mazur, Valerie Gray; exec p, Bill Gray; w, Chris Haddock; ph, Maris Jansons; ed, Lara Mazur; m, Randolph Peters; prod d, Bill Fleming; art d, Kim Forrest; casting, Bette Chadwick

Children's/Comedy/Adventure (PR: AA MPAA: NR)

HEDD WYNN ★★★

(Wales) 123m Pendefig for S4C ~ S4C International/Northern Arts Entertainment c

Huw Garmon *(Ellis Evans/Hedd Wynn)*; Catrin Fychan *(Magi Evans)*; Ceri Cunnington *(Bob Evans)*; Lilio Silyn *(Mary Evans)*; Grey Evans *(Evan Evans)*; Gwen Ellis *(Mary Evans)*; Emma Kelly *(Evid Evans)*; Sioned Jones Williams *(Cati Evans)*; Lilyr Joshua *(Ifan Evans)*; Geraint Roberts *(R. Williams Parry)*; Anghaard Roberts *(Ann Evans)*; Emlyn Gomer *(Morris Davies)*; Guto Roberts *(Esiteddfod Leader)*; Gruffuld Aled *(Griff Jones)*; Derec Brown *(Reverend Richards)*; Arwel Gruffyd *(William Morris)*; Sue Roderick *(Lizzie Roberts)*; Manon Prysor *(Girl)*; Lydia Griffiths *(Organist)*; J. O. Jones; Judith Humphreys *(Jini Owen)*; Sian Summers *(Gwen Williams)*; Nia Dryhurst *(Mary Catherine Hughes)*; Phil Reid *(Fred Hainges)*; Doc O'Brien *(Mr. Kirby)*; Roger McKern *(Sergeant)*; Jack James *(Censoring Officer)*; Gwyn Vaughn *(Owen Hughes)*; Dylan Jones Roberts *(Bob Morris)*

Sumptuously photographed and infused with snippets of fiercely beautiful Welsh poetry, HEDD WYNN is the true story of a country bard who gave his life in WWI as he was on the verge of national prominence. Oscar-nominated for best foreign film (a first for the country of Wales), this breathtaking movie draws reserves of strength and nostalgia from its use of language. Like John Huston's THE DEAD (1987), it's an elegy to a past that lives again through a writer's enduring words.

Tilling the soil of his family farm and keeping marriage-minded lasses like Lizzie (Sue Roderick) at arm's length, Ellis Evans (Huw Garmon) dreams of winning the poetry prize at the National Eisteddfod. He uses the pen name of Hedd Wynn.

Fun-loving Ellis leads an idyllic existence with his large family and good pals Griff (Gruffuld Aled) and Morris Davies (Emlyn Gomer). Unlike his teenage brother, Bob (Ceri Cunnington), Ellis opposes the Great War as British conscriptors descend on the Welsh countryside.

Dismissed by Lizzie, who brands him a coward, Ellis keeps company with the serious-minded Jini Owen (Judith Humphreys) and forges a platonic bond with the local schoolmarm, who encourages his career as his confidence erodes. Despite his parents' hardship pleas, Ellis is drafted. Thrust into the service, he shucks off his callowness and sets his tortured feelings down on paper. Although his superior officer puts up roadblocks, Ellis submits his most ambitious ode to the National Poetry Committee.

Like Griff and hundreds of fellow countrymen, Ellis doesn't survive the front lines of battle. Ironically, after receiving notification of their son's death, the Evanses also learn that Ellis has posthumously won the National Poetry Competition, a glittering prize that eluded him in his lifetime. His final ode synthesizes arguments against war and immortalizes the dead poet's talent.

Leisurely paced and photographed as if each shot were the cinematographer's last, HEDD WYNN is a surpassingly eye-filling biography. It is both a tribute to this poet-soldier's indomitability and an immaculate reproduction of a vanished pastoral way of life, a world whose innocence was destroyed by WWI. Structured artfully around shots of the fallen-in-battle Ellis nursing wounds and memories, HEDD WYNN moves effortlessly between his unfettered past and Ellis's final rites of wartime passage.

But the movie's abiding passion and strongest asset stems from the waves of Hedd Wynn's rapturous poetry, unforgettable because the poet had a facility for capturing human experience in sensuous, illuminating ways. It's also depressing, because that gift was snuffed out prematurely. However, the film suggests that, in some way, Ellis Evans' war experience liberated a facet of his expressive power and transformed him from neophyte to mature talent in a short time. Thus, HEDD WYNN is a pacifist tract whose most crucial diatribe against war concerns the gift of poetry sacrificed in the trenches.

A bit overlong, HEDD WYNN repeats expository material that impedes the inevitable march to the battlefield-graveyard. Aiming for moody *tristesse,* the film weakens its melancholy by not being selective enough about events from Ellis's past. Some are not vital to this necessarily compressed narrative.

The biggest bonus of this splendidly acted saga is the glorious Welsh language, in which transcendent poetry seems but a small remove from everyday discourse. The true hero of the movie is this writer's legacy of language molded into art. *(Violence, extreme profanity, extensive nudity, sexual situations, adult situations, substance abuse.)* — R.P.

d, Paul Turner; p, Shan Davies; w, Alan Llwyd, Paul Turner; ph, Ray Orton; ed, Chris Lawrence; m, John E. R. Hardy; prod d, Martin Morley; set d, Jane Roberts; sound, Jeff Matthews; fx, Steve Breheny, Evan Green Hughes, David Williams; cos, Celia Pye; makeup, Cherry West, Barbara Southcoutt

War/Historical/Biography (PR: C MPAA: NR)

HEIDI CHRONICLES, THE ★★★

(U.S.) 94m Amblin Entertainment; Michael Brandman Productions ~ Turner Home Entertainment c

Jamie Lee Curtis *(Heidi)*; Tom Hulce *(Peter)*; Kim Cattrall *(Susan)*; Peter Frechette *(Scoop)*; Eve Gordon *(Lisa)*; Sharon Lawrence *(Denise)*; Roma Maffia *(Andrea)*; Shari Belafonte *(April)*; John St. Ryan *(Nick)*; Nicki Vannice *(Becky)*

At first, this production of the play *The Heidi Chronicles* seems to furnish another example of a theatrical blockbuster's untranslatable magic. As the piece's shorter, more gimmicky scenes give way to longer, less superficial speeches, this serio-comic play's appeal takes hold and builds to a nostalgic trajectory of recklessly abandoned youthful optimism.

In the 1960s, high school activist Heidi (Jamie Lee Curtis) seeks her voice in a male-dominated world. She maintains special bonds with a gay schoolmate, Peter (Tom Hulce); her energetic but shallow pal, Susan (Kim Cattrall); and her first lover, firebrand reporter Scoop Rosenbaum (Peter Frechette). Through the years, Heidi's goal of rewriting art history to embrace neglected female artists remains constant, but her feminism ebbs and flows through such events as the war in Vietnam, Nixon's resignation, and the assassination of John Lennon. Heidi's journey through cultural upheaval isn't nearly as painful as absorbing the shock of Scoop's marriage to a woman willing to make this attractive chauvinist her number one priority. Feeling betrayed by her own inability to compromise and drifting through less significant love affairs, Heidi ends up wondering whatever happened to the Women's Movement, particularly after her childhood girlfriend, Susan (now a successful TV executive), can barely make time for a visiting Heidi in between power lunches. Fulfilled by her career but increasingly self-absorbed, Heidi takes best pal Peter for granted until he shakes her out of her routine assumptions by pointing out the reality of the AIDS plague in his life. Still in love with Scoop and conflicted about her crusading past, Heidi adopts a child and looks forward to an emancipated future in which her daughter will be able to balance her own life's work and personal happiness.

Wendy Wasserstein's Pulitzer Prize winner may strike some as the fortunate beneficiary of perfect timing. Striking all the right chords about Baby Boomer disillusionment, this trendy feminist play made a splash on Broadway. Addressing too many political flash points and balancing an exhaustive number of perspectives, *The Heidi Chronicles* facilely saves itself the trouble of exploring any single issue in depth. While compelling, this screen version often shies away from the basic gravity of Wasserstein's fast-food cynicism and settles for a more conventional laughter-through-tears melodrama. If one can forgive this shallow screen treatment's tendency to dwell on the play's sitcom essence in its establishing scenes, the movie gets better as it goes along.

As the college-girl humor recedes, Wasserstein's contemplation of waylaid dreams achieves a universal significance deeper than push-button social satire. In three climactic sequences, THE HEIDI CHRONICLES evokes tragic recognition from the audience: (1) Scoop's realization of what he lost by undervaluing Heidi's self-determination; (2) Peter's bitter evaluation of a relationship that's become Heidi's friendship-of-convenience; and (3) Heidi's denunciation of her own destructive pigeonholing of other women during an innocuous guest lecture that turns into a biting confessional soliloquy. In astonishingly powerful yet understated acting, Jamie Lee Curtis ties together Wasserstein's themes as Heidi's self-reproach sounds a temporary death knell for sisterhood. Before its ambiguously happy ending, this movie muses provocatively about the betrayal of idealism in a world geared to expect second best. Ultimately, the movie audiences understand what theater audiences responded to so passionately. *(Profanity, adult situations, sexual situations, substance abuse.)* — R.P.

d, Paul Bogart; p, Leanne Moore; exec p, Michael Brandman; co-p, Steven J. Brandman; w, Wendy Wasserstein (based on her play); ph, Isidore Mankofsky; ed, Stan Cole; m, David Shire; prod d, Dins Danielsen; art d, Easton Michael Smith; set d, Susan Benjamin; sound, William Fiege (mixer); casting, Juel Bestrop; cos, Betty Pecha Madden; makeup, Tania McComas

Drama **(PR: C MPAA: NR)**

HEIDI FLEISS HOLLYWOOD MADAM ★★★½

(U.S./U.K./Canada/Germany) 107m Cinemax; Lafayette Film ~ In Pictures c

Heidi Fleiss; Ivan Nagy; Madame Alex; Victoria Sellers; "Cookie"; Daryl Gates; L'Hua Reid; Ron Jeremy; Vicky Deger; Corinne Bohrer; Nick Hamm; Jim Butcher; Julianna Reese

Producer-director Nick Broomfield doggedly teases out a portrait of high-priced prostitution in this BBC-backed documentary. Heidi Fleiss, who ran a multimillion-dollar call-girl ring catering to the wealthy, famous, and powerful, rose to the top of her profession and took a fall for it, convicted of pandering and tax evasion, all by the age of 28.

Broomfield's first interview with the recently arrested Fleiss was canceled when she was ordered into drug rehab. With his subject mostly unavailable, he pieces together a picture of the sordid inner workings of her business via interviews with a crew of motley, paranoid, and backstabbing friends and associates who record each other's phone conversations and will do anything for a buck.

Porn directors and actresses lead Broomfield to two women who claim to have worked for Heidi. From there, he tracks down Victoria Sellers, daughter of Peter Sellers and Britt Ekland, who was Fleiss's roommate and best friend until a falling out prior to Fleiss's legal problems. Broomfield then secures interviews with Madam Alex, once Hollywood's most powerful madam, who claims that Fleiss worked for her for 18 months and stole her business, and Ivan Nagy, Fleiss's sometime lover, a former television director and convicted bookmaker. Once a partner (and later a bitter adversary) of Madam Alex, Nagy desperately tries to prove his deep and abiding love for Fleiss (and hers for him). But he also sells to Broomfield a home video showing Fleiss nude, and shows him footage for an adult CD-ROM he is making called "Heidi's Girls" and an exploitation film he has produced about a man who tortures prostitutes, in which the main character is named Heidi.

Broomfield is obviously as fascinated by the system that places societal and economic constraints on women as by the women who transgress these boundaries. He gathers evidence suggesting that Hollywood madams have been permitted to operate if they also act as police informants; Fleiss may have been prosecuted so heavily because of her refusal to cooperate with the police. Nagy looms menacingly in Broomfield's sympathetic view of Fleiss; there is evidence that he not only introduced her to prostitution but also provided information to the police that led to her arrest. Near the film's end, as he is about to interview Fleiss herself, Broomfield increasingly focuses on whether Fleiss and Nagy are still romantically involved. Unabashed about offering his own opinions, he treads on dangerous ground, apparently trying to intervene in their obviously unhealthy relationship at the inopportune moment when Fleiss is about to enter prison.

But then objectivity has never been a strong point with Broomfield, who has produced a string of probing documentaries and seems to be making a specialty of subjects who cannot or will not be interviewed, a la Margaret Thatcher in his TRACKING DOWN MAGGIE. His native curiosity, satisfied not by collecting facts but by delving for a deeper understanding of his subject, prevents even his most lurid investigations from becoming simple tabloidism. He lays bare the mechanics of his work, sometimes filming the moment when he pays interviewees for their time (in Madam Alex's case, $2,500; former LA police chief Daryl Gates accepts a handful of bills for his comments on his brother's rumored liaisons with prostitutes). Despite the inherent difficulties of making such a film, Broomfield has produced a fascinating look not only at his subject matter, but also at documentary practice itself. *(Extensive nudity, sexual situations, extreme profanity.)* — C.Ch.

d, Nick Broomfield; p, Nick Broomfield; assoc p, Riete Oord; co-p, Jamie Ader-Brown, Kahane Corn; ph, Paul Kloss; ed, S.J.

Bloom; m, David Bergeaud; sound, Dirk Farner, Mark Rozett (mixer)

Documentary **(PR: C MPAA: NR)**

HELLRAISER IV
(SEE: HELLRAISER: BLOODLINE)

HELLRAISER: BLOODLINE ★★
(U.S.) 85m Elysium Entertainment; Trans Atlantic Entertainment ~ Dimension c
(AKA: HELLRAISER IV)

Bruce Ramsay *(Phillip/John/Paul)*; Valentina Vargas *(Angelique)*; Doug Bradley *(Pinhead)*; Charlotte Chatton *(Genevieve)*; Adam Scott *(Jacques)*; Kim Myers *(Bobbi)*; Mickey Cottrell *(Duc de L'Isle)*; Louis Turenne *(Auguste)*; Courtland Mead *(Jack)*; Louis Mustillo *(Sharpe)*; Jody St. Michael *(The Beast)*; Paul Perri *(Edwards)*; Pat Skipper *(Carducci)*; Christine Harnos *(Rimmer)*; Wren Brown *(Parker)*; Tom Dugan *(Chamberlain)*; Michael Polish *(Twin 1)*; Mark Polish *(Twin 2)*; Jimmy Schuelke *(Security Guard 1)*; David Schuelke *(Security Guard 2)*

Though it may be ambitious, this fourth entry in the HELLRAISER saga is easily the least of the film series inspired by author/filmmaker Clive Barker's dark imagination.

In the year 2127 soldiers board Space Station Minos and discover lone scientist Paul Merchant (Bruce Ramsay) experimenting with an antique puzzlebox. He tells one of the group, Rimmer (Christine Harnos), his tale: In 18th-century France, his ancestor Phillip Lemarchand (Ramsay again) invents the box—named in studio publicity material, but not in the dialogue, as the Lament Configuration—for the Duc de L'Isle (Mickey Cottrell). To his horror, Phillip discovers the nobleman using the box in a ritual to raise demons, creating the satanic seductress Angelique (Valentina Vargas). Phillip is killed trying to counteract his key to hell, but the rest of the Lamarchand family escapes.

In 1996, descendant John Merchant (Ramsay once more) is a Los Angeles architect whose latest building design follows subconscious memories of the Lament Configuration. Ageless Angelique arrives from Paris with the puzzle box, with which she summons the sadomasochist "Cenobite" demon known as Pinhead (Doug Bradley). They threaten John's family to coerce him into activating his new atrium as a diabolical gateway. But John has been working on the Elysium Configuration, a cube of reflected light which negates the portal of hell. He dies winning a temporary victory against the fiends.

Back on the space station Pinhead and his minions are afoot, having been conjured by Paul for a showdown. They decimate the disbelieving soldiers, but Paul's own hologram of himself distracts Pinhead while Merchant and Rimmer flee in a shuttlecraft. By remote control Paul activates a modified Elysium Configuration that transforms Minos itself into one huge puzzlebox that engulfs and vanquishes the Cenobites forever.

HELLRAISER: BLOODLINE became notorious among horror fans for its troubled production history. Original director Kevin Yagher (a veteran makeup-effects artist who took the helm on several episodes of TV's "Tales from the Crypt") was replaced by the studio with Joe Chappelle (HALLOWEEN: THE CURSE OF MICHAEL MYERS) for reshoots. The completed film was credited with the infamous industry pseudonym "Alan Smithee." At first, the movie belies its troubles, as opening scenes efficiently set up the story. The first segment's heavy gothic atmosphere and squirm-inducing climax also work well. But the 1996 chapter sends everything down the tubes. None of the Merchant/Lamerchand protagonists are especially interesting or sympathetic, and here they take center stage. Worse, development of Cenobite mythology, including Pinhead's rivalry with "Princess" Angelique (reportedly the heart of Yagher's original concept about power struggles for dominance in hell) is scuttled in favor of dumb supporting characters eliminated like teens in a slasher pic. Returning to the space station only devolves the material into an ALIEN clone, as hapless troops wander claustrophobic corridors for no other reason than to be picked off.

Bradley is still in good form as the commanding Pinhead, but despite postproduction tinkering to give him more screen time he doesn't make much of an impression. Remaining cast range from just acceptable to distractingly poor, and the whole production has an underbudgeted feel, with out-of-focus cinematography in several scenes. Science-fiction hardware and effects employed for Pinhead's ultimate fate are impressive, though, and the finale represents a fitting end for the character. At least one hopes it's the end. *(Graphic violence, nudity, sexual situations, extreme profanity.)* — M.G.

d, Kevin Yagher; p, Nancy Rae Stone; exec p, Clive Barker, Paul Rich, C. Casey Bennett; assoc p, Anna C. Miller; w, Peter Atkins; ph, Gary Lively; ed, Rod Dean, Randolph K. Bricker, Jim Prior; m, Daniel Licht; prod d, Ivo Cristante; art d, Ken Larson; set d, Tim Colohan; sound, Ed White (mixer); fx, John Hartigan, Richard Kerrigan; casting, Anrea Stone, Laurel Smith; cos, Eileen Kennedy; makeup, Anne Hyeronimus, Gary Tunnicliffe, Kevin Yagher; stunts, Tom Deweir

Horror **(PR: O MPAA: R)**

HIDDEN ASSASSIN ★★
(U.S.) 88m Rohmwest Ltd.; Ricochet Productions; Transatlantique Films ~ Buena Vista/Dimension c

Dolph Lundgren *(Michael Dane)*; Maruschka Detmers *(Simone)*; Assumpta Serna *(Marta)*; Gavan O'Herlihy *(Dick Powell)*; John Ashton *(Alex Reed)*; Simon Andreu *(Alberto Turena)*; Paulo Scola *(Delgado)*; Miroslav Walter *(Police Captain)*; Michael Rogers *(Henchman 1)*; Pavel Vokolin *(Henchman 2)*; Martin Hus *(Henchman 3)*; Robert Thomas *(Bodyguard)*; Alexandra Kotcheff *(Child)*; Thomas Kotcheff *(Child)*; Peter Drozda *(Marcus)*; Jana Althanova *(Screaming Woman)*; Jim Krauss *(Cab Driver)*; Enid Rose *(Mistress)*

HIDDEN ASSASSIN is a series of chase sequences cobbled together into a screenplay. Proficient martial arts matchups, pungent European local color, and the de rigeur lethal target practice invest HIDDEN ASSASSIN with enough noisy thrills to satisfy action buffs and espionage groupies.

Having wiped out the Cuban ambassador to the US, a right-wing US government splinter group huddles with Cuban traitors to cripple an upcoming US-Cuban peace summit in Europe. Told half-truths, US Marshal Michael Dane (Dolph Lundgren) is summoned by his foster father, Agent Alex Reed (John Ashton), in an effort to arrest suspected assassin Simone (Maruschka Detmers). Outsmarting Dane and Reed in the wine cellar of a Prague restaurant, ex-hit lady Simone proves a political embarrassment to Dane and Reed's boss, attache Dick Powell (Gavan O'Herlihy), who soothes the ruffled feathers of Cuban diplomat Alberto Turena (Simon Andreu) about the US agents' failure to intercept Simone.

Eluding Dane during a high-speed train chase to Vienna, Simone claims to be a retired mercenary when she's finally captured, a claim Dane believes after secret agents seeking to kill her cut them off. Forging a relationship in adversity, Dane and Simone rush back to Prague to prevent the next planned assassination. By the time Simone is gunned down at Reed's apartment, Dane has concluded that Reed is the conspiracy's triggerman.

Trailing Alex to a sewer where he's positioned to kill, Dane futilely reasons with Reed, who's revealed to be a rogue hit man for Turena's planned coup d'etat. After Dane thwarts Reed's mission, Reed sacrifices himself when double-crossing Cubans toss a grenade in the sewer. Bloodied but unbowed, Dane storms the hotel peace conference site, publicly arrests Turena during a shoot-out, and blasts him away up on the hotel roof. Cynically, big-shot Powell plants Simone's fingerprints on the assassin's rifle so that Reed's heroic reputation remains sacrosanct.

In peak condition, Dolph Lundgren leaps trains, kicks the crap out of assailants, and handles a rifle like a pro. He's still a terrific athlete, but shows signs of histrionic mobility here. Perhaps it's the sleek production values in this movie, but his love scenes with sex bomb Detmers seem assured and committed to the romantic situation.

Aside from Dolph's improved acting and the gorgeous scenery, the film is a run-of-the-mill catch-me-if-you-can thriller, because Reed's complicity can be so easily spotted. Top-level government hits, Cold War political ploys, and professional betrayals are dug up from the espionage thriller graveyard without even shaking off the dust. Because the movie shows no interest in exploring morality and ethics, it's best to enjoy HIDDEN ASSASSIN as a long celebrity commercial for running shoes. *(Graphic violence, extreme profanity, nudity, adult situations, substance abuse.)* — R.P.

d, Ted Kotcheff; p, Paul Pompian, Silvio Muraglia; exec p, Craig Baumgartner, Gary Adelson, Daniel Jakub Sladek; assoc p, Jan Bilek; w, Yves Andre Martin, Billy Ray, Meg Thayer; ph, Fernando Arguelles; ed, Ralph Brunjes; m, Stefano Mainetti; prod d, Brian Eatwell; art d, Martin Maly; sound, John Midgley; fx, Gary Cohen; casting, Melissa Skoff; cos, Winkie McPherson; makeup, Ramon Diego Dominguez; stunts, Jeff Jensen

Spy/Action/Martial Arts **(PR: C MPAA: R)**

HIE SHAN LU

(SEE: BLACK MOUNTAIN)

HIGH SCHOOL HIGH ★

(U.S.) 86m Homeroom Pictures; Zucker Brothers Productions; TriStar Pictures ~ Columbia TriStar c

Jon Lovitz *(Richard Clark)*; Tia Carrere *(Victoria Chappell)*; Louise Fletcher *(Evelyn Doyle)*; Mekhi Phifer *(Griff McReynolds)*; Malinda Williams *(Natalie)*; Guillermo Diaz *(Paco)*; Lexie Bigham *(Two Bags)*; Gil Espinoza *(Alonzo)*; John Neville *(Thaddeus Clark)*; Brian Hooks *(Anferny)*; Natasha Gregson Wagner *(Julie)*; Marco Rodriguez *(DeMarco)*; Nicholas Worth *(Rhino)*; Eric Allen Kramer *(Hulk)*; Lu Elrod *(Ms. Wells)*; Eve Sigall *(Miss Foley)*; Michael Nye *(Mr. Arnott)*; Joan Ruedelstein *(Griff's Mom)*; McNally Sagal *(Female Teacher)*; Mallory Sandler *(Operator)*; Carlos Flores-Recinos *(Blind Student)*; Sonya Eddy *(Nurse)*; Adam Otokiti *(African Translator)*; Seami Nakamura *(Viet Translator)*; Marabina Jaimes *(Central American Translator)*; Baoan Coleman *(Mou Mou/Bartender)*; Michelle Jones *(Maitre d')*; Vernon P. Burton *(Cop)*; Pat Harvey *(Anchorwoman)*; Christian Dyer Mills *(Student)*; Susan Breslau *(Thaddeus's Secretary)*; John Ducey *(Student With Paper)*; Ricky Harris *(DJ)*; Steven Kent *(Panhandler)*; Christopher J. Keene *(Faculty Member)*; Thom Barry *(Teacher)*; Abdul Goznobi *(Tourette's Kid)*; Drew O'Connell *(Rookie Cop)*; Jeff Wright *(Security Officer)*; Shauna Robertson *(Little Slut)*; Kotoko Kawamura *(Asian Woman)*; Ali Hojat *(Drama Coach)*; Charlotte Zucker *(Woman Smoking Pipe)*; Jeremy Breslau; Ben Breslau; Isaac Ardolino *(Wellington Students)*; Io Perry *(Moaning Woman)*; Allen J. Smith *(Watch Salesman)*; Michael W. Williams *(Kid in Hallway)*; Nicole Ann Cohen *(Girl in Class)*; Mina Nims; Rachelle Roderick *(Strippers)*; Mark Swenson *(Pizza Guy)*; Colleen Fitzpatrick *(Singer)*; Stephen Cilurzo *(Flowbee Announcer)*

Ostensibly a parody of DANGEROUS MINDS (1995) and LEAN ON ME (1989), HIGH SCHOOL HIGH comes from the writing team of THE NAKED GUN 33-1/3 (1004), and marks a new low for those invoking the Zucker-Abrahams-Zucker legacy.

Nebbish and dedicated teacher Richard Clark (Jon Lovitz) arrives at urban nightmare Marion Barry High School with high hopes of making a difference. His idealism earns Clark the admiration of sexy colleague Victoria Chappell (Tia Carrere) and the animosity of bat-wielding Principal Doyle (Louise Fletcher), who sees her role as warden, not educator. Barry students are being terrorized by drug dealer Paco (Guillermo Diaz) and, when Clark foils his attempt to rape Chappell, the new teacher becomes the thug's enemy.

Clark convinces Griff (Mekhi Phifer), a reformed gang leader, to help him turn Barry High around by preparing the students for an academic proficiency test. They succeed, but Paco, eager to keep his clientele in despair and on drugs, doctors the exams so everyone fails. Feeling betrayed, the students turn on Clark, and Doyle fires him.

Seeking to expose the deception, Clark and Chappell go undercover as drug dealers and reveal Doyle as the drug kingpin behind the nefarious goings-on. When Griff and the other students rally to Clark's aid, the bad guys get their due, and Clark is venerated.

A movie that stars voice-over specialist Lovitz (formerly of "Saturday Night Live") and bosomy prop Carrere (WAYNE'S WORLD) faces an uphill battle, but HIGH SCHOOL HIGH isn't so much a jarringly bad comedy as it is a stunningly lazy and timid one.

In THE NAKED GUN series, writer-director David Zucker's comedic forte was the outrageous treatment of sacred cows (The World Series, the President, the Oscars). HIGH SCHOOL HIGH's target was inevitably the culture of inner city African-Americans, and outrageous jokes certainly would have run the risk of being offensive and potentially racist. It's a risk HIGH SCHOOL HIGH was afraid to take.

As it is, HIGH SCHOOL HIGH has a good share of gags, but it always feels like it's backing off; and when it gets serious in the final act, it feels interminable. *(Profanity, violence, adult situations.)* — P.R.

d, Hart Bochner; p, David Zucker, Robert LoCash, Gil Netter; exec p, Sasha Harari; assoc p, Jeff Wright, Bill Johnson; co-p, Patricia Whitcher; w, David Zucker, Robert LoCash, Pat Proft; ph, Vernon Layton; ed, James R. Symons; m, Ira Newborn; prod d, Dennis Washington; art d, Tom Targownik; set d, Kathryn Peters; sound, Hank Garfield (mixer); fx, Thomas L. Fisher, Scott R. Fisher, T.R.I.X. Unlimited Special Effects, Syd Dutton, Bill Taylor, Illusion Arts; casting, Elisabeth Leustig; cos, Mona May; makeup, Peter Montagna, Tony Gardner, Alterian Studios; stunts, Jeff Ward

Comedy **(PR: C MPAA: PG-13)**

HOLLOW POINT ★★½

(U.S./Canada) 102m Nu Image; Trimark Pictures; Daewoo; Sergio Leone Productions ~ Vidmark c

Donald Sutherland *(Garrett Lawton)*; John Lithgow *(Thomas Livingston)*; Tia Carrere *(Diane Norwood)*; Thomas Ian Griffith *(Max Perish)*; David Hemblen *(Oleg Krezinsky)*; Carl Alacchi *(Alberto Capucci)*; Robert Ito *(Shin Chan)*; Andreas Apergis *(Ivan Krezinsky)*; Lisa Bronwyn Moore *(Vicky)*; Kliment

Denchev *(Patriarch)*; Vlasta Vrana *(FBI Agent)*; Richard Zeman *(Police Officer)*; Richard Jutras *(Russian Hearse Driver)*; Vikram Sahay *(Livingston's Assistant)*; Penny Mancuso *(Sequin)*; Richard Zeppieri *(Precinct Officer)*; Emidio Michetti *(Italian Bodyguard)*; Russell Yuen *(Chinese Bodyguard)*; Sheena Larkin *(Lacie)*; David Francis *(Charity President)*; Matthew Boylan *(Train Yard Policeman)*; Kimberly Madden *(Dancer)*; Jason Blicker *(Train Yard Hood)*; Claude Genest *(Killer Doctor)*

This jaunty crime thriller aims for the black comedy of PRIZZI'S HONOR as well as the fizzy tang of the best caper films, but an overly dense script and lackluster direction bog it down.

Posing as the intended bride of a Russian Mafioso's son, FBI agent Diane Norwood (Tia Carrere) almost arrests her groom's kingpin father, Oleg Krezinsky (David Hemblen), during her nuptials. Unfortunately, her clever sting is compromised by desk-bound DEA agent Max Perish (Thomas Ian Griffith), who wants to nab Krezinsky as proof that he can still excel in the field. While the two feds clash, Krezinsky and his silent partner, Thomas Livingston (John Lithgow), decide to teach meddling Norwood a lesson by hiring an assassin, Garret Lawton (Donald Sutherland), to poison Norwood's best friend, Vicky (Lisa Bronwyn Moore). Meanwhile, Livingston's syndicate prepares to pull off one final mega-million dollar money transfer, even though his associates, Krezinsky, Capucci (Carl Alacchi), and Chan (Robert Ito) nurse doubts about Livingston's good intentions. Despite being at war with each other, Norwood and Perish capture Lawton, who has learned that Livingston plans to eliminate him as a loose end. After the assassin escapes, the feds recapture Lawton from a Russian hit squad. Norwood and Perish are then forced to trust Lawton, who advises the feds to pit Livingston against his partners.

Perish, Norwood, and Lawton stir up sentiments against Livingston at the docks, until Norwood becomes seduced by the fortunes changing hands. Eventually returning to her senses, Norwood crushes Livingston to death with a transport-loader. Driving off with a truckload of cash, Lawton leaves behind enough loot for Perish and Norwood to emerge as heroes at their respective agencies for busting the syndicate.

Despite their personal attractiveness, leads Griffith and Carrere have no flair for tongue-in-cheek effervescence. That's why HOLLOW POINT is fortunate to have the demented duo of Lithgow and Sutherland, who know how to camp up their villainy with star-power gusto.

HOLLOW POINT is jam-packed with careening plot twists and double-crosses, but suffice it to say, this white-collar crime fable is about the life expectancy of betrayal. Norwood and Perish learn that trust is a crapshoot at the hands of their homicidal mentor, Lawton.

The problems plaguing the cynical HOLLOW POINT stem from the screenplay's tendency to revisit the same ground. Lacking subtle direction, the film can't move past its over-plotted back-stabbings. At times the nasty comic edge becomes oppressive, as if the director felt the need to oversell the punch line. But thanks to clever one-liners and Lithgow's and Sutherland's puckish performances, HOLLOW POINT entertains as often as it exasperates. *(Extreme profanity, violence, substance abuse, adult situations.)* — R.P.

d, Sidney J. Furie; p, Nicolas Clermont; exec p, Elie Samaha, Avi Lerner; w, James H. Stewart, Robert Geoffrion; ph, David Franco; ed, Yves Langlois; m, Brahm Wenger; prod d, Gilles Aird; art d, Helene LaMarre; set d, Paul Hotte; sound, Patrick Rousseau (mixer); fx, Louis Craig; casting, Vera Miller, Rosina Bucci, Nadia Rona; cos, Nicoletta Massone; makeup, Nicole Lapierre; stunts, Shane Cardwell

Crime/Thriller/Comedy **(PR: C MPAA: R)**

HOMAGE ★★½

(U.S.) 100m Skyline Entertainment ~ Arrow Releasing c

Blythe Danner *(Katherine Samuel)*; Frank Whaley *(Archie Landrum)*; Sheryl Lee *(Lucy Samuel)*; Bruce Davison *(Joseph)*; Danny Nucci *(Gilbert)*

HOMAGE takes a simple story of star obsession and turns it into a treatise on the ills of society. Consequently, some parts of this off-beat film work better than others.

Through flashbacks and present-day scenes, HOMAGE tells the story of Archie (Frank Whaley), a genius mathematician who, in a detour from the world of academia, finds a job as the caretaker of a country home in New Mexico. The owner of the estate, Katherine (Blythe Danner), immediately establishes a close relationship with Archie, but their friendship is soon tested by an unexpected visit from Katherine's daughter, Lucy (Sheryl Lee), a popular television star, who is on hiatus from her show.

While Katherine and Lucy attempt to resolve old family conflicts, Archie alternately helps and hinders the process. His obsession with Lucy quickly intensifies from romantic bumbling to sociopathic pursuit, and her constant rejections of his affections causes him to grow delusional, completely unable to distinguish Lucy from the character she plays on TV. At the same time, Katherine and Lucy confront their past problems, but, in order to make peace with one another, they realize Archie must leave the premises. When Katherine orders him to go, he responds by killing Lucy.

Archie is soon taken into custody by the police. While in prison, he taunts a guard, Gilbert (Danny Nucci), a former friend of Lucy's, who responds by killing Archie. Later, Archie's attorney, Joseph (Bruce Davison), a friend of Katherine's, readily defends Gilbert for the act of vengeance.

In HOMAGE, his directorial debut, Ross Marks goes out of his way with flashback structuring and visual pyrotechnics to distance himself from Mark Medoff's theater piece, THE HOMAGE THAT FOLLOWS. Some of the film still feels theatrical, particularly the polemical debates about the responsibility of parents and the media in society. These moments (and the revelation of the climactic event at the *start* of the film) drain HOMAGE of tension, but there are some curious and intriguing fragments left over, thanks primarily to the work of the cast—Blythe Danner, Frank Whaley, Bruce Davison (as the family lawyer and friend) and Sheryl Lee (in a role not unlike her Laura Palmer of "Twin Peaks").

Otherwise, HOMAGE lacks the distinctive point-of-view techniques of 1995's schizophrenia case study, CLEAN, SHAVEN, the trashy fun of the 1981 obsessed-fan thriller, THE FAN, and the dark humor of Robert De Niro's 1983 cult classic, THE KING OF COMEDY. But what makes HOMAGE better than a TV movie of the week is the meditative, unsensational way that it tries to explore and understand the various dynamics of tragic and seemingly irrational events. HOMAGE is far from a total success, but it deserves appreciation for not suggesting easy answers to perplexing questions. *(Violence, nudity, sexual situations, adult situations, profanity.)* — E.M.

d, Ross Kagan Marks; p, Elan Sassoon, Mark Medoff; exec p, Ross Kagan Marks; assoc p, Frank Whaley; co-p, Raimond Reynolds; w, Mark Medoff; ph, Tom Richmond; ed, Kevin Tent;

m, W.G. Snuffy Walden; prod d, Amy Ancona; casting, Shari Rhodes, Joseph Middleton; cos, Vicki Graef

Drama **(PR: C MPAA: R)**

HOMECOMING ★★½

(U.S.) 100m Showtime; Hallmark Entertainment; USA Network ~ Evergreen Entertainment c

Anne Bancroft *(Abigail "Ab" Tillerman)*; Bonnie Bedelia *(Aunt Eunice)*; Kimberlee Peterson *(Dicey Tillerman)*; Trevor O'Brien *(James Tillerman)*; Hanna Hall *(Maybeth Tillerman)*; William Greenblatt *(Sammy Tillerman)*; Anna Louise Richardson *(Liza Tillerman)*; Scott Michael Campbell *(Windy)*; Jacque Lynn Colton *(Millie)*; R. D. Reid *(Guard)*; Kenner Ames *(Gas Station Attendant)*; Roger Dunn *(Father Joseph)*; Richard Fitzpatrick *(Detective Gordo)*

What could have been another unremarkable addition to the "feisty old lady" TV-movie genre is saved by Anne Bancroft, who paints a corrosive portrait of a resentful, solitary soul furious at being interrupted by visitors.

Dicey Tillerman (Kimberlee Petersen) is a teenager in trouble. She and her siblings have been abandoned in the family car by their mentally ill mother. But Dicey resolves to visit their Aunt Cilla in Bridgeport, Connecticut. She pushes younger siblings James (Trevor O'Brien), Maybeth (Hanna Hall), and Sammy (William Greenblatt) on a grueling pilgrimage. Penniless and starving, the brood is befriended by a Yale University student, Windy (Scott Michael Campbell), who drives them to Aunt Cilla's place.

Although Aunt Cilla is deceased, her daughter, Eunice (Bonnie Bedelia), takes temporary custody of the children. But her refusal to care for the boys on a long-term basis forces Dicey to seek their only other living relative, Grandma Ab (Anne Bancroft). Pocketing money awarded them for their impounded family car, the Tillerman kids board the bus for reclusive Ab's ramshackle farm in Crisfield, Maryland.

Inhospitable Grandma Ab allows Dicey to prolong the children's visit, but insists that she's too old and miserable to raise kids again. Carving out a niche through hard chores, the Tillermans are devastated to learn that their mother has turned up in a mental hospital, in a catatonic state. Just as Ab is shipping her downtrodden grandchildren back to Eunice, she has a change of heart at the bus stop and determines to accept responsibility for them after all.

For much of its running time, HOMECOMING is predictably full of the ragamuffin pluckiness and widder-woman grousing that are associated with Hallmark Hall of Fame family-friendly TV presentations. Having premiered on the prestige-hungry USA Channel, HOMECOMING expends too much energy on the inspirational aspects of these quasi-orphans trudging along America's highways.

When the children arrive to an unwelcoming reception at Granny's, however, the film becomes a touching reconciliatory yarn. Bancroft bravely lays Granny's cards on the table. Ab is a truculent woman honest enough to admit her relief at the death of her esteem-sucking husband. In one scene that can be called an acting epiphany, Bancroft redefines her coldness toward Dicey as a cultivated fear of rearing more traumatized children like her institutionalized daughter.

Vibrating with enough melodramatics to reward those so inclined, HOMECOMING is worth watching, particularly for Bancroft's translucent performance. *(Profanity, adult situations.)* — R.P.

d, Mark Jean; p, Jack Baran; exec p, Shiro Sasaki; w, Christopher Carlson, Mark Jean (based on the novel by Cynthia Voigt); ph, Toyomichi Kurita; ed, Nancy Richardson; m, W. G. Snuffy Walden; prod d, James McAteer, Ed Hanna; art d, Gordon Lebredt; set d, Liz Calderhead; sound, Thomas Hidderley (mixer); casting, Joy Todd, Tina Gerussi; cos, Mary Partridge Raynor; makeup, Linda McCormack; stunts, Alison Reid

Drama **(PR: A MPAA: PG)**

HOMEWARD BOUND II: LOST IN SAN FRANCISCO ★★

(U.S.) 89m Walt Disney Pictures ~ Buena Vista c

Michael J. Fox *(Voice of Chance)*; Sally Field *(Voice of Sassy)*; Ralph Waite *(Voice of Shadow)*; Al Michaels *(Voice of Sparky Michaels)*; Tommy LaSorda *(Voice of Lucky LaSorda)*; Bob Uecker *(Voice of Trixie Uecker)*; Tress MacNeille *(Voice of French Poodle)*; Jon Polito *(Voice of Ashcan)*; Adam Goldberg *(Voice of Pete)*; Sinbad *(Voice of Riley)*; Carla Gugino *(Voice of Delilah)*; Tisha Campbell *(Voice of Sledge)*; Stephen Tobolowsky *(Voice of Bando)*; Ross Malinger *(Voice of Spike)*; Michael Bell *(Voice of Stokey)*; Robert Hays *(Bob)*; Kim Greist *(Laura)*; Veronica Lauren *(Hope)*; Kevin Chevalia *(Jamie)*; Benj Thall *(Peter)*; Michael Rispoli *(Jack)*; Max Perlich *(Ralph)*; Kristina Lewis *(Stacey)*; Adrienne Carter *(Tough Girl)*; Deryl Hayes *(Skycap)*; Gary Jones *(Baggage Handler)*; Jeff Chivers *(Baggage Handler)*; Robin Douglas *(Airport Worker)*; Ernie Prentice *(Poodle Owner)*; Ed Hong-Louie *(Fish Seller)*; Keegan MacIntosh *(Tucker)*; Sandra Ferens *(Tucker's Mom)*; Hrothgar Mathews *(Animal Control Officer)*; Andrew Airlie *(Tucker's Dad)*; Rhys Huber *(Boy)*; Nathaniel De Veaux *(Fire Captain)*; William Sasso *(Pizza Boy)*; Tom Wagner *(Truck Driver)*

HOMEWARD BOUND II: LOST IN SAN FRANCISCO continues the adventures of a trouble-prone talking animal trio, with the same mixture of comedy, action and family sentiment as 1993's HOMEWARD BOUND.

The Seavers, a suburban California family, board a plane for a Canadian vacation with their pets, mischievous bulldog Chance (voiced by Michael J. Fox), Himalayan cat Sassy (Sally Field) and the older, wiser retriever Shadow (Ralph Waite). Chance panics, certain the uniformed baggage-handlers are dogcatchers, and escapes from his pet-carrier on the tarmac. The other two follow as the Seavers' flight takes off. Chance and Sassy bicker while Shadow referees during an attempt to navigate their way back home, but without a sure sense of direction they enter San Francisco and intrude upon street curs guarding their turf, gangland-style.

The tired and hungry threesome get unexpected help from other strays who live in an abandoned warehouse. Their top dog Riley (Sinbad) tries to teach his new friends to distrust all humans, while Delilah (Carla Gugino) falls in love with Chance. Meanwhile, Chance, Shadow and the others narrowly escape the clutches of two cruel but foolish dognappers (Michael Rispoli, Max Perlich), who sell dogs for medical experiments. Finally, Chance sniffs out a way back home. He encourages Delilah to follow, but she decides to run wild with her pack. Chance joins Sassy and Shadow as they scurry to the suburbs. Simultaneously, the Seavers return from their vacation to look for the errant pets. With perfect timing, the animals and their owners meet in a near-collision on the road back to the house, and joyously reunite.

With much the same cast in place as the initial HOMEWARD BOUND (except for the late Don Ameche, replaced by Waite) HOMEWARD BOUND II severely pushes the limits of the talking-animal gambit. In its predecessor only the three animal leads shared verbal repartee (via voiceovers *a la* LOOK WHO'S TALKING). Rare here is the critter who *doesn't* speak, and the dialogue makes the ripostes from LOOK WHO'S TALKING NOW seem bright and sophisticated by comparison. "That's so funny I forgot to bark," and (to a butterfly), "You butterfly away" are samples. Fox (who is more a mutt than a bulldog type, anyway) emphasizes his voiceovers in cocky, grating style, while Field overplays the adjective that gives Sassy her name. The supporting oral cast leans regrettably towards facile ethnic stereotypes: a poodle sputters in a Looney Toons French accent, while Riley and his mangy, feral, ever-mistrustful pack suggest an uncomfortable parallel to urban Black culture.

While the first film focused straightforwardly on an incredible journey, LOST IN SAN FRANCISCO is just, well, lost. Lacking a clear narrative drive, the filmmakers fall back on such hackneyed bits as Chance and Sassy saving youngsters from a blazing house.

Tot viewers may enjoy this stuff, but it's worth noting for parents and kids alike that neither HOMEWARD BOUND measures up to its source, 1963's THE INCREDIBLE JOURNEY, a Disney adventure in which animals expressed themselves without uttering a word.— E.M.

d, David R. Ellis; p, Barry Jossen; assoc p, Gena Desclos, Angel Pine; co-p, James Pentecost, Justis Greene; w, Chris Hauty (from a story by Chris Hauty and Julie Hickson, based on characters from the novel *The Incredible Journey* by Sheila Burnford); ph, Jack Conroy; ed, Michael A. Stevenson, Peter E. Berger; m, Bruce Broughton; prod d, Michael Bolton; art d, Eric Fraser; set d, Lin MacDonald; sound, Robert L. Sephton, Fred Judkins, Rob Young (mixer); fx, Bill Orr; casting, Megan McConnell; cos, Stephanie Nolin; makeup, Sandy Cooper; stunts, Annie Ellis, Ernie Jackson

Adventure/Children's (PR: AA MPAA: G)

HONG FEN
(SEE: BLUSH)

HORSEMAN ON THE ROOF, THE ★★½
(France) 136m Hachette Premiere et Cie; France 2 Cinema; C.E.C. Rhone-Alpes ~ Miramax c
(LE HUSSARD SUR LE TOIT)

Juliette Binoche *(Pauline de Theus)*; Olivier Martinez *(Angelo)*; Laura Marioni *(Carla)*; Paul Chevillard *(Giacomo)*; Patrick Medioni *(Austrian Agent)*; Philippe Guegan *(Austrian Agent)*; Jean-Francois Pages *(Austrian Agent)*; Richard Sammel *(Franz)*; Claudio Amendola *(Maggionari)*; Elizabeth Margoni *(The Farmer's Wife)*; Carlos Moreno *(Harvester)*; Jean-Claude Dumas *(Harvester)*; Jean-Paul Journot *(Harvester)*; Georges Neri *(The Old Harvester)*; Virginie Matheron *(The Sick Servant)*; Christophe le Masne *(Martial, the Valet)*; Gerard Lacombe *(The Inn Owner)*; Francois Cluzet *(The Doctor)*; Didier Bourguignon *(The Cholera Sufferer)*; Isabelle Carre *(The Tutor)*; Antonin Lebas-Joly *(Edmond, the Little Boy)*; Azur Guillier *(Camille, the Little Girl)*; Rene-Andre Fernandez *(Militiaman)*; Jacques Pater *(Militiaman)*; Robert Lucibello *(The Man in the Apron)*; Jacques Sereys *(The Old Man)*; Viviane Cayol *(The Sick Lady)*; Claire Massabo *(Madame Terrasson)*; Celita Villar *(The Lady at the Window)*; Bruno Cecillon *(The Bourgeois)*; Frederique Ruchaud *(Madame Marguerite)*; Jocelyne Carmichael *(The Harpy)*; Gerard Bayle *(The Owner of the Forge)*; Desire Saorin *(Blacksmith)*; Gerard Dubouche *(Blacksmith)*; Alexis Nitzer *(The Hysterical Man)*; Lionel Robert *(The Excited Man)*; Serge Pauthe *(Police Station Employee)*; Gerard Depardieu *(Police Commissioner)*; Michel Carliez *(Man With the Sabre)*; Carlo Cecchi *(Guiseppe)*; Herve Pierre *(Brigadier Maugin)*; Michel Cordes *(The Sergeant)*; Eric Debrosse *(Soldier)*; Pascal Rozand *(Young Man on the Farm)*; Jean Yanne *(Door to Door Salesman)*; Daniel Russo *(Rigoard)*; Christiane Cohendy *(Madame Peyrolle)*; Yolande Moreau *(Madame Rigoard)*; Christophe Odent *(Monsieur Barthelemy)*; Nathalie Krebbs *(Madame Barthelemy)*; Yvonne Gamy *(Grandmother)*; Francoise Blanc *(Lucienne)*; Brigitte Canaan *(Denise)*; Tony Lemiere *(Adrien)*; Jacob Reymond *(Doctor Arnoux)*; Pierre Arditi *(Monsieur Peyrolle)*; Joelle Sevilla *(Religious Woman)*; Joelle Cattino *(Religious Woman)*; Jean-Marie Winling *(Alexandre Petit)*; Fany Watier; Michel Bellier; Dany Castaing; Norbert Sammut; Henriette Palazzi *(Fugitives)*; Alain Bauguil *(The Peasant in the Trap)*; Paul Freeman *(Laurent de Theus)*

Jean Giono's 1951 novel, *The Horseman on the Roof,* gets appropriately lavish screen treatment, but even connoisseurs of Hugo and Stendhal may be overwhelmed by the romanticism of this art-house release.

In 1835 Europe, as a cholera epidemic rages and the Austrian Empire crushes revolutionary forces throughout the land, Angelo (Olivier Martinez), a member of Carbonari, a secret society of Italian freedom fighters, travels to France to escape the Austrian spies on his trail. Angelo flees to the city of Manosque, where he takes refuge in a mansion inhabited by the noblewoman, Pauline (Juliette Binoche). Pauline aids the young man, and, in gratitude, Angelo changes his plans to return to Italy and takes her to her hometown of Theus, where she hopes to rejoin her husband.

During their travels through France, Angelo and Pauline discover the epidemic has grown more serious. While trying to avoid the disease, they also fight off or hide from French soldiers who are enforcing the quarantine. In the meantime, they also fall in love. Finally, as they reach Theus, Pauline discovers her husband has been a traitor to the revolution. She decides then to consummate her love for Angelo, but soon after she contracts cholera. Angelo tries to save his lover with a medicinal potion, but it's too late: Pauline dies, and Angelo pledges to fight on.

Director Jean-Paul Rappeneau mounts the classic tale of love and chivalry in 1830s France with sweep, color and pageantry. In the promising opening, Rappeneau pays homage to Millet's "peasant" paintings, but the rest of HORSEMAN is more reminiscent of costume pictures from Hollywood's Golden Age.

But also like those spectacles of yore (and the French Romanticism of its source material), THE HORSEMAN ON THE ROOF glosses over its own political attitude against conformity and classicism with a stodgy and, yes, *classical* filmmaking style. Co-screenwriters Nina Companeez and Jean-Claude Carriere try to create an AIDS allegory out of the cholera epidemic, but Rappeneau misdirects his actors to behave like silent screen characters, thus ruining the effect. Some of the heroics even border on parody, such as when Angelo saves Pauline from a menacing crow. Imagine what Luis Bunuel would have done with this scene.

As Angelo, Olivier Martinez looks handsome but lacks star quality, while, as Pauline, Juliette Binoche gets to wear some attractive dresses, but otherwise suggests an actress biding her time between great roles. Also in the tradition of an old Hollywood movie, Gerard Depardieu pops up for a hammy star turn as a police superintendent. Extravagance aside, THE HORSEMAN ON THE ROOF is an empty affair. *(Violence, nudity, adult situations, profanity.)* — E.M.

d, Jean-Paul Rappeneau; p, Rene Cleitman; exec p, Bernard Bouix; w, Jean-Paul Rappeneau, Nina Companeez, Jean-Claude Carriere (based on the novel by Jean Giono); ph, Thierry Arbogast; ed, Noelle Boisson; m, Jean-Claude Petit; art d, Francois Hamel; set d, Christian Marti, Jacques Rouxel; sound, Pierre Gamet, Eric Chevallier (recordist), Alain Primot (recordist); fx, Georges Demetrau, Frederic Moreau; casting, Frederique Moidon; cos, Franca Squarciapino; makeup, Joel Lavau, Daniel Parker, Kuno Schlegelmich; stunts, Michel Carliez

Drama/Historical **(PR: C MPAA: R)**

HOSTILE INTENTIONS ★

(U.S.) 86m Libra Pictures ~ WarnerVision c

Tia Carrere *(Nora)*; Tricia Leigh Fisher *(Maureen)*; Lisa Dean Ryan *(Caroline)*; Carlos Gomez *(Juan)*; Roman Cisneros *(Captain Rivera)*; Luis Antonio Ramos *(Officer Sergito)*; Ramon Franco *(Officer Alonso)*; Geoffrey Rivas *(Manuel)*; Christina Solis *(Maria)*; Oscar Peralta *(Juanito)*; Romeo Rene Fabian *(Carlito)*

A Tijuana getaway turns into terror for three photogenic actresses in this unpleasant, direct-to-video mishmash.

Three girlfriends drive to Tijuana for a bachelorette weekend. Nora (Tia Carrere) is oldest and leader of the group. Maureen (Tricia Leigh Fisher) is the wildest, and naive Caroline (Lisa Dean Ryan) is the one getting married. Invited to a party by two guys they meet at a bar, Caroline samples some bad cocaine and gets sick, but the sleazebag hosts won't let the ladies leave. They manage to escape only to be stopped and arrested by Mexican police. Two officers try to rape Maureen in the jailhouse, but Nora grabs one assailant's gun and kills them both. The women go on the lam with another prisoner, Juan Delgado (Carlos Gomez), who says a man named "Coyote" can get them across the border for $300, but all their money is back at the house where the fateful party took place. After a shootout with its occupants, Juan and Nora get the cash, but, upon returning to Juan's *casa*, discover some of his family and friends massacred by the treacherous "Coyote." With Maureen and Caroline they try to hop the border anyway—and run into a border patrol. Juan is killed, but the heroines and Juan's son successfully make it into the USA.

HOSTILE INTENTIONS doesn't know if it intends to be a feminist action movie, expose of illegal aliens and Mexican police corruption, or pandering rape-and-revenge exploitation. It ends up a pretentious mess that won't satisfy any demographic. The message seems to be that men are pigs, especially Mexican men with badges. The depiction of Mexican society looks like something out of a wartime propaganda film, while the feminist angle might be a little more convincing if the female characters were given any depth or substance beyond an unlikely transformation from Valley Girl bimbettes to pistol-packing dynamos with a social conscience. Even after rape and murder, the script still finds time for an insipid jealousy scene where Caroline accuses Maureen of sleeping with her fiance. That it was written and directed by a woman only makes the caricatures and stereotypes more egregious. *(Graphic violence, nudity, sexual situations, substance abuse, profanity.)* — M.S.

d, Catherine Cyran; p, Ronnie Hadar; exec p, Lance H. Robbins; w, Catherine Cyran; ph, Azusa Ohno; ed, Glenn Garland; m, Marcos Loya; prod d, Michael Pearce; art d, Tom Capaletti; sound, Dan Monahan; fx, Ron W. Trost; casting, Laura Schiff; cos, Elizabeth Jett; makeup, Corey Jeen

Action/Crime **(PR: O MPAA: R)**

HOURGLASS ★

(U.S.) 91m LIVE Entertainment ~ Crystal Sky Communications/LIVE Home Video c

C. Thomas Howell *(Michael Jardine)*; Ed Begley Jr. *(Detective Dish)*; Timothy Bottoms *(Jurgen Brauner)*; Sofia Shinas *(Dara Jensen)*; Colette O'Connell *(Kami)*; Anthony Clark *(Jimmy Jardine)*; Terry Kiser *(Henry Jardine)*; Johnny Venokur *(David)*; Y. Hiro Abe *(Juzo Narita)*; Toshi Toda *(Tak Narita)*; Donnie Most *(Andre)*; Chris Devlin *(Tommy)*; Teresa Wells Jones *(Harriet)*; Joanne Baron *(Desk Nurse)*; Patrick Wright *(Guard)*; Eric Simon *(Detective)*; Theya Sbrocca *(Janice)*; Kiefer Sutherland *(cameo)*; Lou Diamond Phillips *(cameo)*

Fashion, murder, sex, and revenge are tucked into the sands of HOURGLASS. But even those elements don't enliven this tale of a selfish playboy who meets his downfall at the hands of a vengeful lesbian.

Buying up the stock of outclassed rivals like Jurgen Brauner (Timothy Bottoms), fashion house scion Michael Jardine (C. Thomas Howell) overextends his company in order to steamroll a sweet deal with Japanese backers.

Stamping himself in the mold of his stroke-ridden father, Henry (Terry Kiser), and entrusting too much flexibility to his alcoholic brother, Jimmy (Anthony Clark), Michael sinks into a sex-mad vortex after spotting Dara Jensen (Sofia Shinas), who has been provocatively placed in his path by his assistant, Kami (Colette O'Connell).

Distracted by sex games, Michael becomes the prime suspect in the slaying of his ex-wife, Nancy. Although Michael's also implicated in the throat-slashing murder of his gay associate, David (Johnny Venokur), he tunes out reality even after he blows his Japanese deal by pursuing Dara.

After Dara drugs him so she and her playmates can disgrace him in his sick father's bedroom, Michael discovers that Jimmy has jeopardized company stock put up for collateral. With his empire collapsed, his dad hospitalized, and Jimmy slain, Michael now learns he has been set up for a fall. Dara is a lesbian whose father killed himself after being squeezed out of business by Henry Jardine. Managing to toss Kami out the window, beleaguered Michael takes the fall for several murders, all of which have been committed by Dara, but survives his ordeal by spending his jail time plotting revenge.

HOURGLASS is like a home movie by survivors of the Hollywood Brat Pack, with a musical score that pierces the eardrums and showy cameos by the likes of Kiefer Sutherland. Director-star Howell is a perpetual teen sent to do a leading man's work, and would-be vamp Sofia Shinas has a face that wouldn't launch a leaky canoe, let alone a thousand ships. Rounding out the egregious ensemble is eye-popping Bottoms, who seems to eschew acting in favor of having nervous breakdowns onscreen. *(Graphic violence, extreme profanity, extensive nudity, sexual situations, substance abuse.)* — R.P.

d, C. Thomas Howell; p, Steven Paul; assoc p, Frank Strick; w, C. Thomas Howell, Darren Dalton; ph, John Lambert; ed, Frank Sacco; m, Chris Saranec; prod d, Jacques Hebert; art d, Dean Timoner; sound, Arnold Braun (mixer); casting, Dorothy Koster; cos, Julie Silverman; makeup, Samantha Weaver; stunts, Chris Howell

Crime/Drama **(PR: O MPAA: R)**

HOUSE ARREST ★½

(U.S.) 108m Polone/Winer Company; Rysher Entertainment ~ MGM/UA c

Kyle Howard *(Grover Beindorf)*; Russel Harper *(T.J. Krupp)*; Jamie Lee Curtis *(Janet Beindorf)*; Kevin Pollak *(Ned Beindorf)*; Amy Sakasitz *(Stacy Beindorf)*; Mooky Arizona *(Matt Finley)*; Caroline Aaron *(Louise Finley)*; Alex Seitz *(Jimmy)*; Josh Wolford *(Teddy)*; Wallace Shawn *(Vic Finley)*; Jennifer Love Hewitt *(Brooke Figler)*; Patrika Darbo *(Cafeteria Cashier)*; Ray Walston *(Chief Rocco)*; Christopher McDonald *(Donald Krupp)*; Colleen Camp *(Mrs. Burtis)*; Sheila McCarthy *(Gwenna Krupp)*;

Jennifer Tilly *(Cindy Figler)*; K. Todd Freeman *(Officer Davis)*; Daniel Roebuck *(Officer Brickowski)*; Ben Stein *(Ralph Doyle)*; Michael Hitchcock *(Cop)*; Rosie Winer *(Flower Girl)*; Jessica Frank *(Jr. Bridesmaid)*

"Parents seeking divorce" is the subject of this dismal and misguided attempt at children's comedy. That the cardboard-stock parents are played by such talented performers as Jamie Lee Curtis, Kevin Pollack, Wallace Shawn, and Jennifer Tilly only proves that actors in Hollywood have mortgage payments, too.

When Janet and Ned Beindorf (Curtis and Pollack) announce to their kids that they're getting a divorce, son Grover (Kyle Howard) doesn't take it well. Convinced his parents just need to spend some time together, Grover locks them in the basement. His best friend Matt (Mooky Arizona) thinks this is a great idea, so he brings over his bickering parents (Shawn and Caroline Aaron) to add to the mix. When he finds out about the "parent prison," class bully T.J. (Russel Harper) develops new respect for Grover, and decides to dump his dysfunctional folks (Christopher McDonald and Sheila McCarthy) in the Beindorf basement, too. Finally, Brooke (Jennifer Love Hewitt)—the object of Grover's major league crush—adds her ditsy mom (Jennifer Tilly) to the cellar.

With their parents gone, the first thing the kids do is throw a party. But afterwards, they start acting a lot more grown up than their parents below, who are constantly at each others' throats. Grover tries to engage the adults in some group therapy, but after several days with no progress, he is ready to give up. Eventually, a nosy neighbor (Ray Walston) smells something fishy and calls the cops. Upon release, Janet and Ned do reconcile, and Grover not only has his family back, but has a girlfriend and is a hero to his classmates, to boot.

Rather than a clever revenge fantasy, HOUSE ARREST offers 90 minutes of curdled new age homilies and parents hurling sordid accusations at each other. ("You're never home!" "You're too controlling!" "Shut up!!") Given the kind of real-life marital troubles that today's kids live with, it's hard to imagine that they would want to see this in a movie.

Besides annoyance, the predominant reaction this film will provoke in adults is sorrow for Defiance, Ohio. You see, HOUSE ARREST aggressively seizes every opportunity to identify screenwriter Michael Hitchcock's hometown as its setting, and now the good people of Defiance are left with this awful movie as their collective claim to fame. Maybe they can file a class action slander suit. *(Violence.)* — P.R.

d, Harry Winer; p, Judith A. Polone, Harry Winer; exec p, Keith Samples; assoc p, Laura Friedman; co-p, Carroll Newman; w, Michael Hitchcock; ph, Ueli Steiger; ed, Ronald Roose; m, Bruce Broughton; prod d, Peter Jamison; art d, Chris Cornwell; set d, Linda Spheeris; sound, David MacMillan (mixer), David Kirschner (mixer); fx, Dennis Dion; casting, Wendy Kurtzman; cos, Hope Hanafin; makeup, Melanie Hughes; stunts, Chris Howell

Comedy/Children's (PR: A MPAA: PG)

HOW THE WEST WAS FUN ★½

(U.S.) 93m Dualstar Productions; Kicking Horse Productions; Warner Bros. TV ~ MGM/UA Home Video c

Mary Kate Olsen *(Susie)*; Ashley Olsen *(Jessica)*; Patrick Cassidy *(Stephen)*; Michele Greene *(Laura)*; Martin Mull *(Bart)*; Peg Phillips *(Natty)*; Ben Cardinal *(George)*; Leon Pownall *(McGrugger)*; Wes Tritter *(Cookie)*; Heather McCallum *(Leona)*; Shaun Johnston *(Phil)*; Dan Libman *(Roger)*; Lizzie Olsen *(Girl in Car)*; Jacqueline Robbins *(Twin 1)*; Joyce Robbins *(Twin 2)*; George Collins *(Mrs. Plaskett)*; Bartley Bard *(Mr. Sulton)*

Sweet enough to rot the teeth and distort one's perspective on children, the Olsen moppets are back in a snappy binge of wholesomeness. This propaganda for family values is recommended only for parents armed with Prozac and for kids whose self-esteem is so low that the Olsens are their role models.

After receiving a missive announcing the imminent sale of their late mother's childhood vacation spot, sisters Susie (Mary Kate Olsen) and Jessica (Ashley Olsen) are determined that their father Stephen (Patrick Cassidy) save Mom's dude ranch pronto. Freeing up Daddy's schedule by getting him fired (without his knowledge) from a dead-end job, the girls accompany him out West to bail out godmother Natty (Peg Phillips), whose property is being bartered for quick profit by her underhanded son Bart (Martin Mull).

Working on instinct, the twins learn that the ranch could become a crowd-pleasing draw, but Bart shortchanges that potential to realize his dream of creating a plasticized Western theme park. Susie and Jessica storm the corporate barricade of Bart's buyer, Mr. McGregger (Leon Pownall) and persuade him to sample a free weekend at Natty's old-fashioned resort. Although Bart's repertoire of sabotage tricks hit their mark, McGregger enjoys himself enough to tout the outdoorsy experience as a retreat for harried executives. Although Bart kidnaps the meddlers on a raft, he fails to navigate the rapids as the twins escape onto a hanging tree branch. All wet, Bart survives to see the resurgence in popularity of Natty's dude ranch.

You'll have plenty of time to reflect on the Olsen phenomenon since it takes the smart-alecky duo forever to bring this film to its sappy conclusion. The Olsens's other films benefited from the presence of hammy termagants like Rhea Perlman and Cloris Leachman; here, there's no vinegar to counteract the ultra-sweet stars. Saddled with a script that suggests a labor of love slaved over by drips who never wanted to leave summer camp, this family fare extols the praises of the great outdoors, while shoving two tiny living-room sophisticates down our throats.— R.P.

d, Stuart Margolin; p, Mark Bacino, Adria Later; exec p, Allen Epstein, Jim Green; w, Jurgen Wolff; ph, Richard Leiterman; ed, David Blangsted; m, Richard Bellis; prod d, Rick Roberts; set d, Jim Murray; sound, Daryl Powell (mixer); fx, Lee Routly; casting, Victoria Burrows; cos, Wendy Partridge; makeup, Gail Kennedy; stunts, Tom Eirikson

Children's/Comedy (PR: AA MPAA: NR)

H.P. LOVECRAFT'S NECRONOMICON: BOOK OF THE DEAD

(SEE: NECRONOMICON: BOOK OF THE DEAD)

HUNCHBACK OF NOTRE DAME, THE ★★★

(U.S.) 95m Walt Disney Pictures ~ Buena Vista c

VOICES OF: Tom Hulce *(Quasimodo)*; Demi Moore *(Esmeralda)*; Tony Jay *(Frollo)*; Kevin Kline *(Phoebus)*; Paul Kandel *(Clopin)*; Jason Alexander *(Hugo)*; Charles Kimbrough *(Victor)*; Mary Wickes *(Laverne)*; David Ogden Stiers *(Archdeacon)*; Mary Kay Bergman *(Quasimodo's Mother)*; Corey Burton *(Brutish Guard)*; Bill Fagerbakke *(Oafish Guard)*; Frank Welker *(Baby Bird)*; Gary Trousdale *(The Old Heretic)*; Jim Cummings *(Guards and Gypsies)*; Patrick Pinney *(Guards and Gypsies)*; Heidi Mollenhauer *(Singing Voice of Esmeralda)*; Jane Withers *(Additional Laverne Dialogue)*

Disney's ambitious, animated adaptation of Victor Hugo's classic 1831 novel reduces a complex tale of 15th century Paris to a formulaic, emotionally thin story overwhelmed by visual splendor.

A deformed infant is orphaned when sanctimonious, gypsy-hating Judge Claude Frollo's (voice of Tony Jay) horse accidentally runs down its fleeing gypsy mother outside Notre Dame cathedral. Frollo is about to murder the baby but, excoriated by the Archdeacon (voice of David Ogden Stiers), he agrees to raise the child on the condition that the boy, now named Quasimodo, stays hidden inside the cathedral forever.

"Quasi" (voice of Tom Hulce) grows into a young man who, despite his twisted shape, is able to clamber acrobatically about the cathedral. His only friends are three gargoyles: prim, proper Victor (voice of Charles Kimbrough); fat, funny Hugo (voice of Jason Alexander); and the cantankerous yet wise Laverne (voices of Mary Wickes and Jane Withers, who stepped in after Wickes's death).

During the annual Festival of Fools, Quasi sneaks out and joins the throng. A beautiful gypsy dancer, Esmeralda (voice of Demi Moore, singing voice of Heidi Mollenhauer), thinking that Quasi is in costume, pulls him onstage where contestants in ugly masks are competing to be crowned King of Fools. Quasi wins easily, but when the crowd discovers he isn't wearing a mask, they tie him up and pelt him with garbage. Esmeralda rushes to his rescue, but Frollo, angry at Quasi's disobedience, forbids her to untie him. She does so anyway, and Frollo orders her arrest. Esmeralda and Quasi escape into the cathedral with the help of the good-hearted Phoebus (voice of Kevin Kline), the captain of the guard. When Frollo finds them, Esmeralda claims sanctuary in the cathedral, from which a now love-struck Quasi then helps her to escape undetected. As a token of her thanks, she gives Quasi an inscribed medallion which, unbeknownst to him, is actually a miniature map to the gypsies' secret enclave, the Court of Miracles.

Frollo, to his horror, also has become infatuated with Esmeralda, and he orders Phoebus and his troops to find her. When Phoebus disobeys, Frollo orders his execution. Esmeralda saves the wounded Phoebus, takes him to the cathedral, and places him in the care of Quasi, whose heart is broken when he sees Esmeralda and Phoebus kiss.

Later, Frollo tells Quasi of his plan to storm the Court of Miracles, hoping that Quasi, in an effort to warn the gypsies, will lead him to the hideout. Quasi and Phoebus, discovering the true meaning of the medallion, rush to the Court. But before the gypsies can escape, Frollo and his troops arrive, imprisoning everyone save Quasi, who's taken back to Notre Dame and chained. When he sees Esmeralda about to be burned at the stake in the square below, Quasi breaks his bonds, frees her, and carries her back to the cathedral. Frollo orders his men to storm Notre Dame, but Phoebus incites the citizens to revolt. Frollo still manages to slip inside, but after a struggle with Quasi on a balcony, Frollo falls to his death. Phoebus and Esmeralda are united, and the lovelorn Quasi is hailed as a hero.

HUNCHBACK is distinct from other animated Disney films in that for the first time, the source material is an adult melodrama. While it serves up a plethora of gorgeous vistas and good gags, the overall tone is dark and cynical—all of which show Disney's admirable willingness to stretch. Unfortunately, these daring efforts are overlaid with new Disney animation cliches—primarily the strong-willed heroine whose entire personality can be summed up as "feisty." Even more problematic, Quasimodo has been made into a hero with no vice other than unfailing virtue, and the film's lackluster, downbeat songs only serve to illuminate the characters overall lack of dimension.

Visually, however, HUNCHBACK is one of Disney's most well-realized films. The layered Parisian locales are exquisitely textured, and the computer-generated longshots of the crowds seem three-dimensional. But given the rich internal lives and complex emotional webs of such recent Disney masterpieces as THE LION KING (1994) and BEAUTY AND THE BEAST (1991), the beautiful but by-the-numbers HUNCHBACK OF NOTRE DAME is a big step forward in animation but a step backward in storytelling. Unlike the bells of Notre Dame, it lacks resonance. *(Adult situations, violence.)* — F.L.

d, Gary Trousdale, Kirk Wise; p, Don Hahn; assoc p, Phil Lofaro; co-p, Roy Conli; w, Tab Murphy, Irene Mecchi, Bob Tzudiker, Noni White, Jonathan Roberts (from a story by Tab Murphy, based on the novel *Notre Dame de Paris* by Victor Hugo); ed, Ellen Keneshea; m, Alan Menken; art d, David Goetz; anim, James Baxter, Tony Fucile, Kathy Zielinski, Russ Edmonds, Danny Galieote, David Pruiksma, Will Finn, Ron Husband, Dave Burgess, Gregory Griffith, Mike "Moe" Merell; fx, Christopher Jenkins; casting, Ruth Lambert

AAN Best Musical or Comedy Score: Alan Menken (music, orchestral score), Stephen Schwartz (lyrics)

Animated/Romance/Musical (PR: A MPAA: G)

HUNG FAN KUI

(SEE: RUMBLE IN THE BRONX)

HYPE! ★★★

(U.S.) 85m Cinepix Film Properties ~ CFP Distribution c

Ledge Morrisette; Dave Crider; John Mortenson; Aaron Roeder; The Mono Men; Charles Peterson; Art Chantry; Jack Endino; Chris Eckman; Carla Torgerson; The Walkabouts; Nils Bernstein; Steve Fisk; Dawn Anderson; Matt Cameron; Kim Thayil; Soundgarden; Kim Warnick; Kurt Block; Lulu Gargiulo; The Fastbacks; Calvin Johnson; Van Conner; Barrett Martin; Screaming Trees; Buzz Osborne; Dale Crover; Melvins; Don Blackstone; Matt Wright; Tom Price; Joe Newton; Gas Huffer; Mark Arm; Steve Turner; Mudhoney; Jim Sangster; Tad Hutchison; Scott MacCaughey; The Young Fresh Fellows; Leighton Beezer; Martin Rushent; Conrad Uno; Ron Heathman; Eddie Spaghetti; Dan Siegal; The Supersuckers; Daniel House; Kurt Danielson; Tad Doyle; Tad; Jonathan Poneman; Bruce Pavitt; Megan Jasper; Susan Silver; Susie Tennant; Eddie Vedder; Pearl Jam; Blake Wright; Rob Skinner; Peter Litwin; David Brooks; Jeff Lorien; Coffin Break; Selene Vigil; Elizabeth Davis; Valerie Agnew; 7 Year Bitch; Mike Varney; John Atkins; Wade Neal; Seaweed; Frank Harlan; Blood Circus; Crackerbash; Dead Moon; Flop; Girl Trouble; The Gits; Hammerbox; Love Battery; Nirvana; Some Velvet Sidewalk; Zipgun

Doug Pray's HYPE! is a lively, often humorous, documentary about the rise and decline of the Seattle rock music scene during the late 1980s and early 1990s. Shot over a span of nearly four years, Pray's film explores the origins of grunge rock, its steady rise to prominence, its media flowering as personified by bands like Nirvana, Pearl Jam, Soundgarden and Alice in Chains, and the inevitable "morning after" once the bloom was off the rose and Seattle achieved a post-phenomenon splashdown. The grunge explosion in the Pacific Northwest had its antecedents in punk rock of the late '70s and the ongoing popularity of heavy metal. Seattle was full of "fake Ramones," according to Leighton Beezer, HYPE!'s resident historian, who displays for the filmmakers a self-designed "family tree" of Northwest bands, with his own 1970s group, The Blunt Objects, among the progenitors.

Pray's movie, though it makes a serious attempt to chronicle the grunge scene, is never so earnest that it can't satirize its own objectives. In straight-faced fashion, the film offers the theory that the region's cold, rainy weather drove teenagers indoors where they inevitably began playing musical instruments. "We were just trying to keep warm," one rocker notes, explaining away the grunge fad for flannel shirts. Pray also turns his cameras on some self-absorbed promoters who used the rock explosion to make a handsome profit.

Both a dedicated musicologist and a cynical observer would likely respond to the movie's comprehensive look at this cultural phenomenon. For however limited a time, it put Seattle, like Liverpool and San Francisco in earlier days, at the temporary "ground zero" point of the pop music universe. HYPE!'s inclusion of collector's item footage of Nirvana's first-ever performance of "Smells Like Teen Spirit" gives this documentary a special cachet. Unquestionably, the "spirit" of Nirvana, however dispersed by the death of Kurt Cobain, hangs over HYPE! like an uneasy cloud.

Not to be upstaged, however, Eddie Vedder of Pearl Jam weighs in with some lofty observations and publicist Megan Jasper (who puckishly invented a glossary of "grunge slang terms" that was dutifully reprinted in The New York Times) provides a few laughs.

Regardless of how one feels about grunge rock, Seattle was, for a time, a legitimate cultural capital, and HYPE! gives us a thoughtful, entertaining overview of how that happened. *(Profanity.)* — E.K.

d, Doug Pray; p, Steven Helvey; co-p, Lisa Dutton, Pete Vogt; w, Brian Levy; ph, Robert Bennett; ed, Earl Ghaffari, Doug Pray, Joan Zapata

Documentary **(PR: C MPAA: NR)**

I SHOT ANDY WARHOL ★★★

(U.S.) 103m Playhouse International Pictures; BBC Arena; Orion ~ Samuel Goldwyn Company c

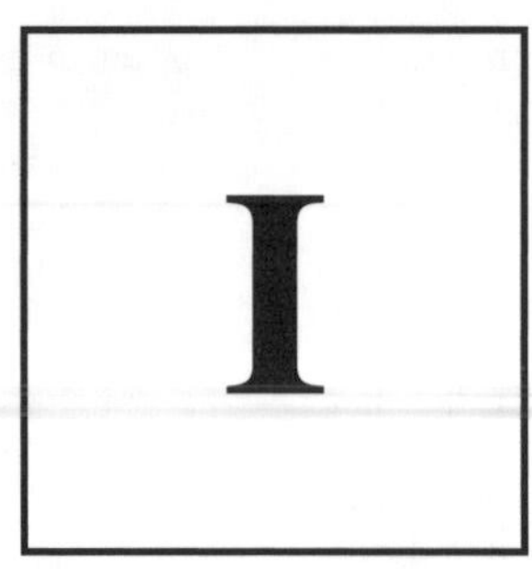

Lili Taylor *(Valerie Solanas)*; Jared Harris *(Andy Warhol)*; Stephen Dorff *(Candy Darling)*; Martha Plimpton *(Stevie)*; Danny Morgenstern *(Jeremiah)*; Lothaire Bluteau *(Maurice Girodias)*; Michael Imperioli *(Ondine)*; Reg Rogers *(Paul Morrissey)*; Coco McPherson *(Brigid Berlin)*; Donovan Leitch *(Gerard Malanga)*; Tahnee Welch *(Viva)*; Craig Chester *(Fred Hughes)*; James Lyons *(Billy Name)*; Anna Thomson *(Iris)*; Jamie Harrold *(Jackie Curtis)*; Myriam Cyr *(Ultra Violet)*; Bill Sage *(Tom Baker)*; Lorraine Farris *(Susan)*; Victor Browne *(Danny)*; Billy Erb *(Rotten Rita)*; Jill Hennessy *(Laura)*; Kevin Rendon *(Amphetamine Head)*; Caroline Benezet-Brown *(Isabelle De Courcy)*; Anh Duong *(Comtesse De Courcy)*; Massimo Audiello *(Mario Amaya)*; Christina McKay *(Warhol Superstar 1)*; Eugenie Vincent *(Warhol Superstar 2)*; Georgia Hubley; Ira Kaplan; James McNew; Tara Key *(The Party Band)*; Mark Margolis *(Louis Solanas)*; Dawn Didawick *(Waitress)*; Faith Geer *(Mrs. Warhola)*; Jeff Webster *(Assistant D.A. Lanklar)*; Lola Pashalinski *(Psychiatrist)*; Henry Cabot Beck *(Reporter 1)*; Christopher Cook *(Reporter 2)*; Edoardo Ballerini *(Editor of School Paper)*; Gabriel Mick *(Clean Cut Boy)*; Mariah Quinn *(Jean)*; Fenton Lawless *(John Who Likes Golf Shoes)*; Laura Ekstrand *(Marilyn)*; Michelle Hurst *(Nedick's Manager)*; Michael Stumm *(Chelsea Manager)*; Justin Theroux *(Mark the Revolutionary)*; Eric Mabius *(Revolutionary No. 2)*; Peter Friedman *(Alan Burke)*; Isabel Gillies *(Alison)*; Davis Hall *(Alan Burke Show Director)*; Paco Juanas *(Flamenco Guitarist)*; Steve Itkin *(Police Chief on TV)*; Bill Lin *(Passerby Man)*; Debbon Ayer *(Passerby Girl)*; Anna Grace *(Passerby Girl 2)*; Daniel Haughey *(The Pornographer)*; Lynn Cohen *(Hotel Concierge)*

Propelled by an ensemble of manic and mannered performances, I SHOT ANDY WARHOL follows quintessential outsider Valerie Solanas from obscure feminist writer to Warhol Factory wannabe and would-be assassin. Writer-director Mary Harron's debut feature offers a slickly verite tour through the Factory and its margins, never lacking in style, if often short on real insight into her characters and their motivations.

The film is framed by sequences in which Solanas (Lili Taylor) reads passages from her best-known piece of writing, an essay titled "The SCUM Manifesto" ("SCUM" being an acronym for "Society for Cutting Up Men"). Solanas pulls no punches about her passionately held theory that the male is a chromosomal accident, and the world would be a better place if left to females, the male population culled to the bare minimum required to sustain human life. A few incidents from her student life in the late 1950s—a lesbian flirtation, her dedicated study of biology—provide some background.

In the 1960s, she moves New York City, where she, despite her ostensible separatism, works as a prostitute who is as adept at engaging clients in conversation as in sex.

Solanas also writes plays based on her radical sexual politics, and one day stumbles upon a film crew shooting a scene for one of Warhol's films. Fascinated, she becomes determined to meet the pop artist (Jared Harris) and eventually does, but her pleas that he produce one of her plays go unanswered. Eventually, Warhol does take an interest in her—pity or affection, it's hard to tell. Oblivious to Warhol's disinterest in theater and the disdain aimed at her by his entourage, Solanas persists with pathetic verve in pursuing his support.

As Valerie's friend, Candy Darling (Stephen Dorff), a whispery-voiced transvestite, rises in popularity among the Factory denizens, her modicum of acceptance fades. She also is unable to begin writing a novel commissioned by Maurice Girodias (Lothaire Bluteau) for his Olympia Press, and she is fitfully paranoid over the book contract she has signed. These failures exacerbate her feelings of rejection.

Finally, Solanas's rage boils over, and she steals a gun from a revolutionary street-theater troupe member. On June 3, 1968, she goes to the new Factory office and shoots Warhol at point-blank range.

In the late 1970s, Warhol, still haunted by the event, imagines that he sees Solanas staring at him as he enters Studio 54.

While Harron has neatly constructed a fictionalized biographical film about a woman about whom little is actually known, I SHOT ANDY WARHOL fails to tell us much more than the facts. Despite an astute eye for detail and astounding production design by Therese Deprez, the film remains as cynical and detached as the Factory crowd itself. The people around Warhol, including Ondine (Michael Imperioli), Brigid Berlin (Coco McPherson), and Fred Hughes (Craig Chester) are colorfully portrayed as a band of arrogant and paranoid posers, each with their own peculiar magnetism that offsets their less-than-attractive sides. One can easily fault I SHOT ANDY WARHOL for skimming the surface of a violent story of brilliance and tragedy in the personas of both Warhol and Solanas. Whether or not this one-dimensionality simply reflects its subject matter, it certainly portrays enough of the spirit—if not the innermost emotions—of the milieu explored to warrant a serious look. *(Violence, sexual situations, substance abuse, profanity.)* — C.Ch.

d, Mary Harron; p, Tom Kalin, Christine Vachon; exec p, Lindsay Law, Anthony Wall; w, Mary Harron, Daniel Minahan; ph, Ellen Kuras; ed, Keith Reamer; m, John Cale; prod d, Therese Deprez; art d, John Bruce; set d, Diane Lederman; sound, Robert Taz Larrea (mixer); casting, Billy Hopkins, Suzanne Smith, Kerry Barden; cos, David Robinson; makeup, Judy Chin, Rob Benevides

Docudrama/Biography/Drama (PR: O MPAA: R)

IF LUCY FELL ★½

(U.S.) 93m Motion Picture Corporation of America ~ TriStar c

Sarah Jessica Parker *(Lucy Ackerman)*; Eric Schaeffer *(Joe MacGonaughgill)*; Ben Stiller *(Bwick Elias)*; Elle Macpherson *(Jane Lindquist)*; James Rebhorn *(Simon Ackerman)*; Robert John Burke *(Handsome Man)*; David Thornton *(Ted)*; Bill Sage *(Dick)*; Dominic Chianese *(Al)*; Scarlett Johansson *(Emily)*; Michael Storms *(Sam)*; Jason Myers *(Billy)*; Emily Hart *(Eddy)*; Paul Greco *(Rene)*; Mujibur Rahman *(Counterman)*; Sirajul Islam *(Counterman)*; Ben Lin *(Chinese Messenger)*; Alice Spivak *(Elegant Middle-Aged Woman)*; Lisa Gerstein *(Saleswoman)*; Molly Schulman *(Kid)*; Peter Walker *(Bag Man)*; Brad Jenkel *(Neighbor)*; Brian Keane *(Man in Gallery)*

Eric Schaeffer showed promise coming off the block with 1994's MY LIFE'S IN TURNAROUND, but stumbled with a failed Fox sitcom and this no-brain romance with a bad case of the cutes.

Lucy (Sarah Jessica Parker), a Manhattan psychologist, could probably use a little therapy herself. She has "commitment issues"—the story opens with her dumping a longtime lover because he brought up marriage. Lucy shares her enormous apartment with Joe (Schaeffer), a struggling painter who teaches art to precocious children.

The two have been best friends since college, but have never considered each other romantically. Back in college, Lucy and Joe made a suicide pact: if they hadn't found their respective Mr. and Miss Right by the time Lucy turned 30, they would jump off the Brooklyn Bridge. Lucy's deadline is a month away, and she insists they honor the pact. This lights a fire under Joe, who invites Jane (Elle Macpherson), a gorgeous neighbor he's been obsessed with for years, to his first gallery opening. Jane likes Joe's work—it's all paintings of her—and they begin dating. At the same time, Lucy starts dating Bwick (Ben Stiller), a weird, flavor-of-the-month artist. He paints with his feet and can't utter a coherent sentence. Neither relationship works out, as both Lucy and Joe realize that what they've been searching for has been (surprise!) right under their noses all along. On Death-Pact Day, they meet on the bridge and pledge undying love.

IF LUCY FELL certainly has its (mostly second-hand) Woody Allen pedigree in order. There's Parker, who starred in the Allen-esque MIAMI RHAPSODY, Stiller, who played the Allen-ish "Mel" in FLIRTING WITH DISASTER, and Macpherson, who appeared in Allen's ALICE. What the film doesn't have, with its familiar presentation of neurotic New Yorkers dancing around love, are interesting people saying interesting things, unless one counts Lucy asking why exchanging saliva during a kiss is romantic, but just spitting into someone's mouth is considered gross. Writer-director-star Schaeffer wastes his talented cast (only Stiller is moderately amusing), failing to provide even himself with characterization of note beyond wearing goofy hats. All IF LUCY FELL has to offer are bored, impatient, self-absorbed, adorable Generation X-ers wondering why their dreams haven't come true. Ticket sales for this 1996 theatrical release were, understandably, weak. *(Sexual situations, profanity.)* — P.R.

d, Eric Schaeffer; p, Brad Krevoy, Steve Stabler, Brad Jenkel; co-p, Terence Michael, Deborah Ridpath, Eric Schaeffer; w, Eric Schaeffer (from a story by Eric Schaeffer and Tony Spiridakis); ph, Ron Fortunato; ed, Susan Graef; m, Charlton Pettus, Amanda Kravat; prod d, Ginger Tougas; set d, Betsy Alton; sound, Pawel Wdowczak (mixer); fx, John Stifanich; casting, Sheila Jaffe, Georgianne Walken; cos, Ane Crabtree; makeup, Tracy Warbin

Comedy/Romance **(PR: C MPAA: R)**

IL MOSTRO

(SEE: MONSTER, THE)

I'M NOT RAPPAPORT ★★★½

(U.S.) 136m Madcap Film Company; Under Ten; Universal ~ Gramercy Pictures c

Walter Matthau *(Nat)*; Ossie Davis *(Midge)*; Amy Irving *(Clara)*; Craig T. Nelson *(The Cowboy)*; Boyd Gaines *(Danforth)*; Martha Plimpton *(Laurie)*; Guillermo Diaz *(J. C.)*; Elina Lowensohn *(Clara Lemlich)*; Ron Rifkin *(Feigenbaum)*; Marin Hinkle *(Hannah)*; Nancy Giles *(Ella Mae Tilden)*; Ranjit Chowdhry *(Kamir)*; Irwin Corey *(Sol)*; Mina Bern *(Rifka)*; Salem Ludwig *(Walter)*; Fanni Green *(July Carbonelle)*; Richard Council *(Butcher)*; Shirl Bernheim *(Russian Lady)*; Steve Ryan *(Harry)*; Alan North; Sidney Armus; Tony Gillan *(Gristedes Customers)*; York Bergin *(Boy at Gristedes)*; Richard Korthaze *(Tango Dancer and Partner)*; William Preston *(Jake)*; Becky Ann Baker *(Nurse)*; Arthur Anderson *(Mr. Gunther)*; Michael Angarano *(3-Yr. Old Cowboy)*; Jennie Moreau *(Mother of 3-Yr. Old Cowboy)*; Jake Gardner *(Bat Kid)*; Adam Lamberg *(Spiderman Kid)*; Josh Pais *(Rodney)*; Vincent Laresca *(Renaldo)*; Elvis Nolasco *(Driver)*; Bobby Cannavale *(Parking Lot Customer)*; Peter Friedman *(Young Nat's Father)*; Alexander Goodwin *(5-Yr. Old Nat)*; Cheryl Giannini *(Italian Woman)*; Donna Hooper; Diana Agostini; Katherine Hiler; Tessa Auberjonois; Heather Goldenhersh *(Strike Women)*; Edoardo Ballerini *(Man at Rally)*; Jonathan Teague Cook; Richard Spore; Ray Anthony Thomas; Marion Killinger *(Homeless Men)*; Adger Cowans *(The Saxophonist)*; Phillip Parnes *(The Violinist)*; Arturo Millan *(Drummer)*; Arkan V. LaCharles *(Drummer)*; Sammy Garruba *(Doorman)*

Herb Gardner produced, directed, and wrote this adaptation of his 1986 Tony Award-winning stage play. Witty dialogue and winning performances overshadow the film's main fault—a staginess that seems unnatural on film.

Octogenarians Nat (Walter Matthau) and Midge (Ossie Davis) forge a grudging friendship while passing time on a park bench in New York's Central Park. Nat is an incorrigible liar, or as Midge puts it, he "ain't even friendly with the truth." While Midge would rather shrink from conflict, Nat takes on all comers, especially those who take advantage of older people. Nat effortlessly adopts any persona, from Cuban spy to mafioso, to score his point. Unfortunately, his efforts are largely unsuccessful.

After 40 years of service, Midge is being forced out of his job as superintendent of an apartment building. When Danforth (Boyd Gaines), the head of the tenants' committee, delivers the bad news to Midge, Nat intervenes. He claims to be an attorney with a human rights association, and his gruff manner and threats of arbitration frighten Danforth into backing off—for a time. Eventually, Danforth learns that Nat is a fraud, and Midge loses his apartment, his job and his severance pay.

Nat's daughter, Clara (Amy Irving), worries that Nat's shenanigans will get him into trouble and tries to force him to move into a retirement home. To escape that fate, Nat invents a story of a long-ago affair which produced a child, now a grown woman, who has offered to take care of Nat. Next, Nat pulls Midge into another scheme, involving a drug dealer named The Cowboy (Craig T. Nelson) who has been threatening a young artist (Martha Plimpton) in the park. Nat's plan to scare The Cowboy off backfires and lands Midge in the hospital. After his convalescence, Midge returns to the park bench, where he finds Nat has given in to Clara's wishes and claims to have turned over a new leaf. But before long, Nat is once again spinning tales for Midge, who prefers the lies to the boring old truth.

Matthau and Davis are a delightful team, playing off each other marvelously. Matthau is known for playing grumpy old men, but this is not a one-note performance. Nat's gruff exterior and vaudevillian shtick (the film's title refers to an old vaudeville routine Nat is fond of repeating) do not conceal his character's compassion and frailty. Davis (who replaced the originally cast Louis Gossett Jr.) was one of the actors who played Midge in the Broadway production. He is not only Nat's straight man and foil, but a fully developed character, and one who commands respect.

Like many successful stage plays adapted for the big screen, I'M NOT RAPPAPORT retains a theatricality that detracts from its realism. Though it was filmed on location in New York, it's hard to escape the feeling that the story is being played out on a stage rather than the gritty streets of Manhattan. Also hindering the film's sense of realism is the improbable drug operation, in which Nat takes on The Cowboy on behalf of a pretty stranger.

The film's theme of ageism is hard to ignore and strikes a universal chord. At film's end, Nat and Midge remain what they were at its opening—gray, unhealthy men who each day matter a little less to the world outside than they did the day before. But the audience knows they won't give up without a fight, and therein lies hope. *(Violence, profanity, substance abuse.)* — B.R.

d, Herb Gardner; p, John Penotti, John Starke; exec p, David Sameth; w, Herb Gardner (based on his play); ph, Adam Holender; ed, Wendey Stanzler, Emily Paine; m, Gerry Mulligan; prod d, Mark Friedberg; art d, Ginger Tougas; set d, Stephanie Carroll; sound, James Sabat; fx, John Ottesen, Ron Ottesen; casting, Lynn Kressel; cos, Jennifer Von Mayrhauser; makeup, Naomi Donne

Comedy/Drama **(PR: C MPAA: PG-13)**

IMMORTALS, THE ★

(U.S.) 92m Nu Image; Phoenician Films Entertainment ~ Evergreen Entertainment c

Eric Roberts *(Jack)*; Tia Carrere *(Gina)*; Tony Curtis *(Dominic)*; Joe Pantoliano *(Pete)*; Chris Rock *(Duke)*; Kevin Bernhardt *(Billy)*; Brian Finney *(George)*; Kieran Mulroney *(Kerry)*; Clarence Williams III *(Benny)*; William Forsythe *(Tim)*; Michael Paul Chan *(Mifune)*; Alex Meneses *(Cleopatra)*; Alisa Christensen *(Stripper Shooter)*; Brian Grant *(Chef)*

THE IMMORTALS is a Hollywood exploitation product designed to help fill the vast wasteland of cable, and/or to sucker unwary renters. It's remarkable only for its overall poor quality and Tia Carrere's visual appeal.

Jack (Eric Roberts) owns a strip bar and has underworld connections. He contacts a group of previously unacquainted criminals whose mission is to steal four suitcases of cash from mob drop points. Their reward is a cut of what they bring back.

Each crook is assigned a partner (producing predictable squabbles) and the teams leave for destinations contained in sealed envelopes. They all complete their tasks sloppily, alerting the mob, and the cops, who converge on the club with guns blazing. Inside, Jack tries to double-cross them all, but survival dictates that they all fight the cops and goons together.

During the ensuing shootfest, the team discovers what they all have in common: cancer, AIDS, or some other terminal condition. Each has a sob story; apparently medical bills and social pressures have driven each of them to a life of crime. They were chosen because they were going to die anyway, although the rationale for this is unclear. George (Brian Finney) is the lone exception: he's retarded but otherwise healthy.

Dominic (Tony Curtis), Pete (Joe Pantoliano), Duke (Chris Rock), Billy (Kevin Bernhardt), Benny (Clarence Williams III), Tim (William Forsythe), and Kerry (Kieran Mulroney) are all killed, learning to love each other in the long, noisy process. Gina (Tia Carrere) escapes, posing as a hostage. Jack and George confront and kill Mifune (Michael Paul Chan), the evil Japanese mastermind behind it all, and walk off together into the LA darkness.

The sophomoric screenplay (by Kevin Bernhardt) is the root cause of THE IMMORTALS' singular lack of coherence. Various shopworn but serviceable plot devices are introduced, then left to die the same slow, unlovely deaths as the main characters. Jack's briefing and the preparations for the heist resemble a staff meeting in a failing office. The antagonistic partners subplot is a total flop. Reasons why the partners hate, and later love, each other are predictable but unconvincing, i.e., a gay new-ager (Bernhardt) with a macho wiseguy, or a black stud (Chris Rock!) with feminist tough cookie Carrere.

THE IMMORTALS is filled with gratuitous violence, bad language, and obnoxious racial slurs and stereotypes. All this offensiveness is uneasily contradicted by the warm, fuzzy, everybody-dies-together theme (they don't). Money spent on the destruction of lavish sets is wasted. If the film is meant as an industry in-joke, it isn't funny. Visually clumsy, badly edited, poorly acted, and cluttered, THE IMMORTALS may aim at parody, but achieves only myopic Hollywood excess. *(Graphic violence, extensive nudity, extreme profanity, adult situations.)* — C.M.

d, Brian Grant; p, Elie Samantha; exec p, Avi Lerner, Danny Dimbort, Trevor Short; assoc p, Joe Pantoliano, Tia Carrere, Tom Wright Jr.; co-p, Kevin Bernhardt; w, Kevin Bernhardt (based on a story by Elie Samantha); ph, Anthony B. Richmond; ed, Richard Trevor; m, Claude Gaudette; art d, Fanee Aaron; sound, Kim Ornitz; fx, Frank Ceglia, Paul Haines; casting, Geno Havens; cos, Roseanne Fielder; makeup, Peggy Hannaman

Action/Crime **(PR: O MPAA: R)**

IN LOVE AND WAR ★★

(U.S.) 115m Dimitri Villard Productions; New Line ~ New Line c

Sandra Bullock *(Agnes von Kurowsky)*; Chris O'Donnell *(Ernest Hemingway)*; Mackenzie Astin *(Henry Villard)*; Emilio Bonucci *(Domenico Caracciolo)*; Ingrid Lacey *(Elsie "Mac" MacDonald)*; Margot Steinberg *(Mabel "Rosie" Rose)*; Tara Hugo *(Katherine "Gumshoe" De Long)*; Colin Stinton *(Tom Burnside)*; Ian Kelly *(Jimmy McBride)*; Rocco Quarzell *(Roberto Zardini)*; Vincenzo Nicoli *(Enrico Biscaglia)*; Alan Bennett *(Porter)*; Terence Sach *(Porter)*; Carlo Croccolo *(Town Mayor)*; Gigi Vivan *(Italian Child)*; Giuseppe Bonato *(Grandfather)*; Allegra Di Carpegna *(Loretta Cavanaugh)*; Diane Witter *(Adele Brown)*; Mindy Lee Raskin *(Charlotte Anne Miller)*; Tracy Hostmyer *(Ruth Harper)*; Kaethe Cherney *(Veta Markley)*; Lauren Booth *(Anna Scanlon)*; Rebecca Craig *(Elena Crouch)*; Frances Riddelle *(Katherine Smith)*; Wendi Peters *(Emily Rahn)*; Laura Nardi *(Teresa)*; Maria Petrucci *(Sonia)*; Valeria Fabbri *(Anna Maria)*; Quinto Rolman *(Italian Man)*; Raph Taylor *(Francesco)*; George Rossi *(Triage Medic)*; Todd Curran *(Skip Talbot)*; Matthew Sharp *(Joseph Larkin)*; Nick Brooks *(Louis Burton)*; Tom Goodman-Hill *(Houston Kenyon)*; Doreen Mantle *(Emilia)*; Tim McDonell *(Adjutant)*; Vincenzo Ricotta *(Italian Officer)*; Reno Porcaro *(Italian Photographer)*; Bruno Majean *(Alberto Zardini)*; Joseph Long *(Italian Doctor)*; Bruce Lidington *(American Surgeon)*; Colin Fox *(Dr. Hemingway)*; Kay Hawtrey *(Grace Hemingway)*; Roseline Garland *(Carol Hemingway)*; Evan Smirnow *(Leicester Hemingway)*; Avery Saltzman *(Oak Leaves Reporter)*; Rodger Barton *(Sun Times Reporter)*; Richard Blackburn *(Tribune Reporter)*; Gil Filar *(Boy)*; Noah Reid *(Boy)*; Richard Fitzpatrick *(Mailman)*; Philippe Leroy *(Count Sergio Caracciolo)*; Laura Martelli *(Isabella Caracciolo)*; Cyril Taylor *(Maitre D')*; Milan Rosandic *(Waiter)*

Richard Attenborough's IN LOVE AND WAR is a lackluster account of the bittersweet romance between young Ernest Hemingway and a Red Cross nurse in 1918 Italy.

Northern Italy, 1918: American soldiers and Red Cross nurses volunteer to help morale and assist the Italians during WWI. Among them are 19-year-old "Ernie" Hemingway (Chris O'Donnell), who gets shot in the leg. At the hospital, he's cared for by 26-year-old nurse Agnes von Kurowsky (Sandra Bullock), who fights to save his leg from being amputated. As Ernie recovers, he becomes infatuated with Agnes, but she dismisses him as a "kid." Dr. Caracciolo (Emilio Bonucci), an Italian surgeon, also takes an interest in Agnes, as does another wounded American at the hospital, Ernie's friend Henry Villard (Mackenzie Astin).

During a picnic with Agnes, Henry and Ernie fight over her. When Ernie lies to his friend that he and Agnes have slept together, she slaps him and leaves. Later, Ernie apologizes and confesses his love for her. She receives orders to go to the front. Ernie's request to join her is denied because of his leg, but he goes anyway. The two go to a hotel and have a passionate night of love. When Ernie's orders to return to the US come through, and he asks Agnes to marry him. She agrees and tells him she loves him.

Ernie returns home while Agnes remains in Italy. Soon, Dr. Caracciolo invites her to his villa in Venice. Back in the States, Ernie writes Agnes every day, but she stops sending him letters. At the war's end, Caracciolo asks Agnes to marry him: she feels torn, but finally agrees, and writes to Ernie. When he receives the news, he smashes his room to pieces with a bat and sinks into bitterness and despair. Eight months later in New York, Agnes meets Henry at a restaurant and tells him that she didn't marry Caracciolo after all. He tells her that Ernie, still angry, has retreated to a fishing lodge in Michigan. Agnes visits him to apologize, but he can't forgive her, replying, "The kid's grown up, thanks to you." Agnes tells him she'll love him forever and walks away.

IN LOVE AND WAR is earnest, handsome, and respectable. It's also deadly dull and inexplicably passionless, bringing to mind director Alex Cox's comment that Attenborough's heart is always in the right place, but his camera rarely is. The actors speak in hushed, whispered tones, underplaying their roles to the point of somnolence, while the camera curiously shoots them from behind, or from a long distance, withholding any spark of emotion from the audience. All the big scenes (Agnes and Ernie's love scene, Ernie lashing out after receiving Agnes's "Dear John" letter) lose their dramatic impact due to the overly restrained direction. It's as if Attenborough was afraid of being swept away by the characters' mad passion. The ending, which should be heartbreaking, simply isn't. The two stars are both capable, even if O'Donnell is too callow to suggest Hemingway's dark side, but Attenborough's old-fashioned British virtues of taste and decorum are fatal to a story of this type, and the result is cold and unmoving. *(Violence, sexual situations, profanity.)* — M.S.

d, Richard Attenborough; p, Dimitri Villard, Richard Attenborough; exec p, Sara Risher; co-p, Diana Hawkins; w, Allan Scott, Clancy Sigal, Anna Hamilton Phelan (based on the memoir *Hemingway in Love and War: The Lost Diary of Agnes von Kurowsky* by Henry S. Villard and James Nagel); ph, Roger Pratt; ed, Lesley Walker; m, George Fenton; prod d, Stuart Craig; art d, John King, Michael Lamont; set d, Stephenie McMillan; sound, Simon Kaye, Jonathan Bates, Gerry Humphreys; fx, Richard Conway; casting, Jeremy Zimmerman, Rene Haynes, Clare Walker; cos, Penny Rose; makeup, Daniel Parker; stunts, Eddie Stacey

Biography/Romance/War **(PR: C MPAA: PG-13)**

IN THE BLEAK MIDWINTER
(SEE: MIDWINTER'S TALE, A)

IN THE LINE OF DUTY: SIEGE AT MARION
(SEE: CHILDREN OF FURY)

INDEPENDENCE DAY ★★½
(U.S.) 146m Centropolis Entertainment; 20th Century Fox ~ 20th Century Fox c

Will Smith *(Captain Steve Hiller)*; Bill Pullman *(President Thomas J. Whitmore)*; Jeff Goldblum *(David Levinson)*; Mary McDonnell *(Marilyn Whitmore)*; Judd Hirsch *(Julius Levinson)*; Robert Loggia *(General William Grey)*; Randy Quaid *(Russell Casse)*; Margaret Colin *(Constance Spano)*; James Rebhorn *(Albert Nimziki)*; Harvey Fierstein *(Marty Gilbert)*; Adam Baldwin *(Major Mitchell)*; Brent Spiner *(Dr. Brakish Okun)*; James Duval *(Miguel)*; Vivica A. Fox *(Jasmine Dubrow)*; Lisa Jakub *(Alicia)*; Ross Bagley *(Dylan)*; Mae Whitman *(Patricia Whitmore)*; Bill Smitrovich *(Captain Watson)*; Kiersten Warren *(Tiffany)*; Harry Connick Jr. *(Jimmy)*; Guiseppe Andrews *(Troy)*; John Storey *(Dr. Isaacs)*; Frank Novak *(Teddy)*; Devon Gummersall *(Philip)*; Leland Orser *(Tech/Med. Asst. #1)*; Mirron E. Willis *(Aide)*; Ross Lacy *(Aide)*; David Pressman *(Whitmore's Aide)*; Vivian Palermo *(Tech/Med. Asst. #2)*; Raphael Sbarge *(Commander/Tech)*; Bobby Hosea *(Commanding Officer)*; Dan Lauria *(Commanding Officer)*; Steve Giannell *(Radar Tech)*; Eric Paskel *(Radar Tech)*; Carlos LaCamara *(Radar Operator)*; John Bennett Perry *(Secret Serviceman)*; Troy Willis *(Secret Serviceman)*; Tim Kelleher *(Technician)*; Wayne Wilderson *(Area 51 Technician)*; Jay Acovone *(Area 51 Guard)*; James Wong *(SETI Tech One)*; Thom Barry *(SETI Tech Two)*; Jana Marie Hupp *(SETI Tech Three)*; Matt Pashkow *(Second Officer)*; Robert Pine *(Chief of Staff)*; Marisa Morell *(Co-Worker #2)*; Michael Winther *(Co-Worker #3)*; Dexter Warren *(Co-Worker #4)*; Paul LeClair *(Co-Worker #5)*; Capt. Michael "Chewy" Vacca *(Lt. Peterson)*; David Chanel *(Secret Service Agent)*; John Capodice *(Mario)*; Greg Collins *(Military Aide)*; Derek Webster *(Sky Crane Pilot)*; Mark Fite *(Pilot)*; Eric Neal Newman *(Pilot)*; Levani *(Russian Pilot)*; Kristof Konrad *(Russian Pilot)*; Kevin Sifuentes *(Tank Commander)*; Elston Ridgle *(Soldier)*; Randy Oglesby *(Mechanic)*; Jack Moore *(Mechanic)*; Barry Del Sherman *(Street Preacher)*; Lyman Ward *(Secret Service Guy)*; Anthony Crivello *(Lincoln)*; Richard Speight Jr. *(Ed)*; Barbara Beck *(Monica Soloway)*; Joe Fowler *(Reporter)*; Andrew Warne *(Reporter)*; Sharon Tay *(Reporter)*; Peter Jozef Lucas *(Russian Reporter)*; Yelena Danova *(Russian Newscaster)*; Derek Kim *(Korean Newscaster)*; Vanessa J. Wells *(Newscaster)*; Jessika Cardinahl *(German Video Newscaster)*; Gary W. Cruz; Ron Pitts; Wendy L. Walsh; Christine Devine; Mark Thompson; Jack Germond; Morton Kondracke *(Video Newscasters)*; Ernie Anastos *(Rex Black/NY Newscaster)*; Cinckevin Cooney *(Atlantic Air)*; Rance Howard *(Chaplain)*; Nelson Mashita *(Japanese Tech)*; Jeff Phillips *(B-2 Pilot)*; Sayed Badreya *(Arab Pilot)*; Adam Tomei *(Sailor)*; John Bradley *(Lucas)*; Kimberly Beck *(Housewife)*; Thomas F. Duffy *(Lieutenant)*; Andrew Keegan *(Older Boy)*; Jon Matthews *(Thomson)*; Jim Piddock *(Reginald)*; Fred Barnes; Eleanor Clift; Jerry Dunphy; John McLaughlin; Barry Nolan; George Putnam *(Themselves)*; Eric Michael Zee *(Northridge Field Reporter)*; Pat Skipper *(Redneck)*; Carlos Lara *(Farmer Kid)*; Mike Monteleone *(Butler)*; Lee Strauss *(Elvis Fanatic)*; Lisa Star *(Woman on Roof)*; Malcolm Danare *(Intellectual on Roof)*; Arthur Brooks *(Trucker on Roof)*; Michael G. Moertl *(Thief)*; James J. Joyce *(Master C.P.O.)*; Joyce Cohen *(Kim Peters—Reporter)*; Julie Moran *(Entertainment Tonight Reporter)*; Robin Groth *(Flagstaff News Anchor)*; Richard Pachorek *(LAPD Helicopter Pilot)*; Dakota *(Boomer)*

One of the highest grossing films in history, INDEPENDENCE DAY is a triumph for special-effects designers and art directors. In technical terms, it's a masterpiece. As sci-fi, this blockbuster is rather standard; as entertainment, it's effective in a bustling, bullying way but sorely lacking in wonder, surprise, and eccentricity.

US President Whitmore (Bill Pullman) tackles an apocalyptic crisis that no other world leader has ever faced—invasion from outer space. In spaceships so huge they engulf entire cities, the mysterious visitors make their intentions deadly obvious by unleashing global destruction. Barely escaping a White House blitz with his daughter, press secretary Constance Spano (Margaret Colin), and a skeleton staff, President Whitmore frets about his wife, Marilyn (Mary McDonnell), who's been injured in the alien devastation of Los Angeles. Throughout the USA, pockets of resourceful humans nurse fading hopes while making a mass exodus from major cities. In the country's heartland, Russell (Randy Quaid), the alcoholic survivor of a close encounter many years before, awakens his self-discipline and restores his family's faith in him by volunteering for a special flight force. Separated from his live-in love Jasmine (Vivica A. Fox), pilot Steve Hiller (Will Smith) not only lands safely after an extraterrestrial attack but captures a space creature, which he drags along to his Air Force base. Meanwhile, Jasmine and her son outrun a fireball in a tunnel and come to the aid of injured victims, including First Lady Whitmore. Accompanied by his curmudgeonly dad, Julius (Judd Hirsch), New York physicist David Levinson (Jeff Goldblum), former husband of presidential aide Spano, fervidly rushes to contact President Whitmore with his anti-alien theorizing.

All the principals converge at the Air Force Base, where Hiller's captured monster proves lethally lively during an autopsy, luckily performed in a sealed lab. Ascertaining that the invaders don't desire rapprochement, President Whitmore hedges about nuking Houston to blow up the Mother Ship; when he accedes to the atomic attack, it has no impact on the flying fortress. Soon, Hiller is reunited with Jasmine, and the President takes time for a final goodbye with his mortally injured wife. Having exhausted all other possibilities, Whitmore ignores military advisors and agrees to Dr. Levinson's far-out plan to plant a computer virus in the Mother Ship that would lower the defense shields of all the spacecrafts. Hiller, Russell, and an airsick Levinson challenge the technically advanced invaders with all-American chutzpah. Although the computer virus gets planted, the aliens don't take this counter-offensive lying down. With human casualties mounting, Russell seizes his chance and sacrifices himself in a kamikaze attack that blasts the Mother Ship to smithereens. With the aliens suddenly made vulnerable, the war of the worlds ends with a resounding victory for the Earthlings.

In STARGATE (1994), their previous major-studio science fiction outing, director Roland Emmerich and screenwriter Dean Devlin successfully leavened the cliffhanging serial riffs with humor that didn't vitiate genre directives. In INDEPENDENCE DAY, the moviemaking team invents a state-of-the-art weapon that shoots satiric holes in sci-fi formulas, while at the same time asking viewers to surrender to the film's dramatic weight. At hairpin turns of the narrative, viewers are expected to be moved by events that the filmmakers themselves take lightly. INDEPENDENCE DAY features one-dimensional characters that are defined only by ethnic shtick. No fully realized characters and no emotional stakes mar the perfect course of annihilation that the film maps out. Crowd-pleasers are always populated with stock characters, but Quaid, Fierstein, and Hirsch are playing stereotypes of stereotypes.

INDEPENDENCE DAY is almost never frightening, save for that messy autopsy scene. Perhaps it's unfair to blame this movie for not being streamlined, scary sci-fi like THE THING (1951) or THEM! (1954), because basically it more closely resembles a 1950s war movie such as BATTLEGROUND (1949). The faceless space invaders could just as easily be Nazis or "Commies" following a makeover by H. R. Geiger. Viewed as a gung-ho flick extolling xenophobia, INDEPENDENCE DAY acquires some snap, crackle, and pop; the science fiction is just a sideshow to the main carnival celebrating Uncle Sam's destructive know-how.

Zapping the spectators on a thrill-ride of inventive effects, INDEPENDENCE DAY is often rousing fun if one does not look beyond its sleek, impersonal surface. Intermittently exciting, as Air Force top guns scramble through the invaders' gauntlet, and suspenseful, as scientist Goldblum races through his anti-alien repertoire while mankind's fate hangs in the balance, INDEPENDENCE DAY can be enjoyed as a feel-good, Earthman's pep rally. Sadly, it is also the most benign movie ever made about the end of our universe. *(Violence, profanity, adult situations, substance abuse.)* — R.P.

d, Roland Emmerich; p, Dean Devlin; exec p, Ute Emmerich, Roland Emmerich, William Fay; assoc p, Peter Winther; w, Dean Devlin, Roland Emmerich; ph, Karl Walter Lindenlaub; ed, David Brenner; m, David Arnold; prod d, Patrick Tatopoulos, Oliver Scholl; art d, Jim Teegarden; set d, Jim Erickson; sound, Jeff Wexler (mixer), Chris Carpenter, Bill W. Benton, Bob Beemer; fx, Clay Pinney, Volker Engel, Douglas Smith, Joseph Viskocil; casting, Wendy Kurtzman; cos, Joseph Porro; stunts, Dan Bradley

AA Best Visual Effects: Volker Engel, Douglas Smith, Clay Pinney, Joseph Viskocil; *AAN Best Sound:* Chris Carpenter, Bill W. Benton, Bob Beemer, Jeff Wexler

Science Fiction/Thriller/Action (PR: C MPAA: PG-13)

INDIAN IN PARIS, AN

(SEE: LITTLE INDIAN, BIG CITY)

INFINITY ★★

(U.S.) 119m First Look Pictures ~ First Look Pictures c

Matthew Broderick *(Richard Feynman)*; Patricia Arquette *(Arline Greenbaum)*; Peter Riegert *(Mel Feynman)*; Dori Brenner *(Tutti Feynman)*; Peter Michael Goetz *(Dr. Hellman)*; Zeljko Ivanek *(Bill Price)*; Matt Mulhern *(Gate Guard)*; Joyce Van Patten *(Aunt Ruth)*; James LeGros *(John Wheeler)*; Jeffrey Force *(Young Richard)*; David Drew Gallagher *(Harold)*; Raffi Diblasio *(Robert)*; Joshua Wiener *(David)*; James Hong *(Abacus Adder)*; Emerson Tran *(Kid)*; Melissa Delizia *(Young Joan)*; John Hammil *(Country Doctor #1)*; Jack Lindine *(Mr. Greenbaum)*; Helene Moore *(Country Nurse #1)*; Mary Pat Gleason *(Country Doctor #2)*; Horton Foote Jr. *(Neighborhood Doctor)*; Mary Kay Wulf *(Aunt Rose)*; Laurence Haddon *(Family Doctor)*; Tom Kurlander *(Driver)*; Mark Burnham *(Passenger #1)*; Googie Gress *(Passenger #2)*; Joshua Goldin *(Passenger #3)*; Erich Anderson *(Gil)*; Matt Mulhern *(Gate Guard)*; Drew Ebersole *(Calculator Kid #1)*; John Patterson *(Stan Ivanek)*; Damion Scheller *(Calculator Kid #2)*; Joshua Malina *(Calculator Kid #3)*; Demetrius Navarro *(Calculator Kid #4)*; Cosimo Sherman *(Garo)*; Geoffrey Nauffts *(Rob)*; David Barrera *(Chepa)*; Kelly Wolf *(Nurse Kate)*; Patrick James Clark *(Strong Fellow)*; Kirk Fox *(Mechanic)*; Marianne Muellerleile *(Nurse Gracie)*; Michelle Feynman *(Sewing Girl on Train)*; Kristin Dattilo Hayward *(Joan Feynman)*; Bill Bolender *(Isadore Rabi)*; Corbitt Smith *(Henry)*

The early life of Nobel Prize-winning nuclear physicist Richard P. Feynman is really no more than a pretext for a plain, uncomplicated romantic drama.

Mel Feynman (Peter Riegert) demonstrates basic physics to his son Richard using a ball in a red wagon. Richard (Matthew Broderick) is raised in a loving Long Island Jewish household and grows into the very model of the scientist-next-door. He excels scholastically and has his choice of colleges. At a party, he meets Arline Greenbaum (Patricia Arquette), a lively neighborhood girl, and is instantly smitten. They date, and she listens attentively as he rattles on about the theory of relativity, while she points out to him the finer, more immediate things in life, such as a pretty red dress in a shop window. To her regret, he is busy with his graduate studies in math and science and thinks he doesn't earn enough to marry her. More angst comes their way when she is diagnosed with a mysterious fatal illness that could be either tuberculosis or Hodgkin's disease. Richard tries to keep the truth from her, but she inevitably finds out. Over the opposition of his anxious parents, he marries her when he is offered work on the Manhattan Project. They move from New York, he to the facilities at Los Alamos, she to a hospital in Albuquerque where he can visit her on weekend leaves. As Richard's work on the bomb proceeds, Arline's condition worsens. She dies, leaving Richard with a lifelong memory of love, just as the first tests triumphantly emit their mushroom clouds.

In his first feature behind the camera, Broderick's direction is much like his acting: antiseptic, unemotional, inoffensive, pleasantly bland. The film is so low-key as to be nearly nonexistent. Richard and Arline meet nice, stay nice, and then she dies. That's really about it, apart from some pleasant period flavor. Broderick collaborates with his mother Patricia, who scripted with the film, to create a perfect apple-pie, small-town American world in which these two quirky kids can roam. When the action moves to the desert, he barely takes notice of the surrounding physical splendors. Feynman may have been working on one of the world-changing projects of our century, but it never really figures in the movie, save for some trouble it affords him trying to get leave to see Arline. Direly underpopulated, the film is overly dominated by these two, while talented actors like Peter Riegert, Dori Brenner, Joyce Van Patten, and James LeGros are largely wasted.

Broderick's Richard is his same old cutie pie-nerd schtick. It's a lightweight charmer's turn, but too inconsequential to truly carry a movie, unless the film is an out-and-out comedy a la FERRIS BUELLER'S DAY OFF. If anything, he presents the most milk-fed, well-adjusted portrait of a scientific genius ever.

If the film remains at all watchable, it's largely due to Arquette. Arline is an earthy, radiantly normal woman, and Arquette, armed with a charmingly untutored Long Island accent, pumps her full of life. When Richard first sees her pounding out boogie-woogie on an upright piano, his immediate attraction to her is fully understandable. She and Broderick get a lulling comic rhythm going in some of the scenes wherein he attempts to explain his work to her unblinking, curious gaze. Arquette achieves true pathos and terror in the dying scenes; her very straightforwardness in the role constitutes her considerable allure here. *(Adult situations.)* — D.N.

d, Matthew Broderick; p, Joel Soisson, Michael Leahy, Matthew Broderick, Patricia Broderick; assoc p, Philip Euling; co-p, Don Phillips; w, Patricia Broderick (based on the memoirs *Surely You're Joking, Mr. Feynman!* and *What Do You Care What Other People Think?* by Richard Feynman); ph, Toyomichi Kurita; ed, Elena Maganini, Bill Johnson, Amy Young; m, Bruce Broughton; prod d, Bernt Capra; art d, Jeffrey "Tex" Schell; casting, Lisa Bankert; cos, Mary Jane Fort; makeup, Angela Margolis Moos

Romance/Drama (PR: A MPAA: PG)

INSTITUTE BENJAMENTA ★★★

(U.K.) 105m Film Four International; British Screen; Koninck Studios; Image Forum; Pandora Film ~ Zeitgeist Films bw

Mark Rylance *(Jakob von Gunten)*; Alice Krige *(Lisa Benjamenta)*; Gottfried John *(Johannes Benjamenta)*; Daniel Smith *(Kraus)*; Joseph Alessi *(Pepino)*; Jonathan Stone *(Hebling)*; Cesar Sarachu *(Inigo)*; Peter Lovstrom *(Jorgenson)*; Uri Roodner; Peter Whitfield *(Null)*

The first live-action feature from the brothers Quay, twin siblings renowned for dark and cryptic short animated pieces, INSTITUTE BENJAMENTA highlights the Quays' superb visual techniques and their abilities to transform modernist ideas into dream-like images, but, as a feature-length film, it is tedious, remote, and monotonous.

Jakob (Mark Rylance) arrives at the Institute Benjamenta, a school for servants and butlers, aspiring to become someone who will one day be of service to someone else. After undergoing a physical exam by headmaster Herr Benjamenta (Gottfried John) that includes prodding, a study of the oral cavity, and measuring of the skull, Jakob joins his fellow pupils, a gangly group of imbeciles and nobodies, all of whom aspire to be—like the top student, Kraus (Daniel Smith)—the perfect zero. Each day the students perform the exact same lesson, a repetitive series of meaningless tasks resembling a macabre dance, under the guidance of headmistress Lisa Benjamenta (Alice Krige). Lisa manages the Institute's daily functions while her brother the headmaster sits dreamily in his office, longing for escape.

Jakob learns that the school is no longer taking in students and that he was the last to be admitted. Entropy and stagnation gradually turn toward decline and ruin as Jakob is pulled reluctantly into the unhappy inner worlds of his masters, who may or may not be having an incestuous relationship. Both Herr Benjamenta and Lisa separately begin to make sexual advances and to share confidences with Jakob, who responds with silence and fear.

Herr Benjamenta encourages Jakob to forget the school and run off with him. But Jakob desires Lisa and feels only disgust for her brother. Lisa's growing desire for Jakob drives her away from her lessons and into dreams and longing. When Lisa mysteriously dies of despair, Jakob is unhappily forced to follow his joyous and liberated master out of the Institute.

INSTITUTE BENJAMENTA displays the Quay brothers' fascination with dreams and the brooding, surrealistic corners of European modernism. It is based loosely on the novella, *Jakob von Gunten,* by Swiss author Robert Walser, whose writings were a major influence on Franz Kafka.

Filmed in black and white, it is set almost entirely within the decrepit, crumbling walls of the Institute. The final shots are the first images seen of the outside world, and serve to reflect back on the pervading metaphor of the Institute as the oppressive parameters within which human life is confined.

The previous, animated works of the Quays, such as THE COMB and THE STREET OF CROCODILES, relied on fabricated miniature sets and puppets. As a result, the Quays have refined a sophisticated use of light and space, but made character secondary. The greatest accomplishment of the film is its dense, dusty, and trance-like atmosphere, heavy with diffused nocturnal light and intricate spatial distortions. The camera moves around as if in a fishbowl, gazing through rounded lenses and enlarging and examining details and body parts. Unfortunately, this stunning, cob-webbed atmosphere also swallows the narrative, which becomes inconsequential and hopelessly remote. *(Adult situations.)* — R.C.

d, The Brothers Quay; p, Keith Griffiths, Janine Marmot; co-p, Karl Baumgartner, Katsue Tomiyama; w, Alan Passes, The Brothers Quay (based on the novella *Jakob von Gunten* and other texts by Robert Walser); ph, Nic Knowland; ed, Larry Sider; m, Lech Jankowski; prod d, Jennifer Kernke; art d, Alison Riva; anim, The Brothers Quay; sound, Peter Glossop (recordist); fx, 1st Effects, Snow Business; casting, Irene Lamb; cos, Nikky Gillibrand; makeup, Suzie Zamit, Caroline Clements

Fantasy/Drama (PR: A MPAA: NR)

IRON EAGLE IV ★

(Canada) 96m Norstar Entertainment ~ Vidmark Entertainment c

Louis Gossett Jr. *(Chappy Sinclair)*; Jason Cadieux *(Doug "Bucky" Masters)*; Al Waxman *(General Kettle)*; Joanne Vannicola *(Wheeler)*; Max Piersig *(Peter Kane)*; Karen Gayle *(Dana Osborne)*; Ross Hull *(Malcolm Porter)*; Rachel Blanchard *(Kitty Shane)*; Dominic Zamprogna *(Rudy Marlowe)*; Sean McCann *(Wilcox)*; Victoria Snow *(Amanda)*; Jason Blicker *(Sgt. Osgood)*; Jack Nicholsen *(Luther Penrose)*; Aidan Devine *(Corporal Fincher)*; Dean McDermott *(Major Pierce)*; Matt Cooke *(Capt. McQuade)*; Jeff Pustil *(Airman)*; Chas Lawther *(Colonel Birkett)*; Marilyn Lighthouse *(Dr. Francis Gully)*; Ron Lea *(Snyder)*

The IRON EAGLE series, like TOP GUN (1986) which inspired it, had always been pitched at the youth crowd. Now, an entire squadron of streetwise urchins soar to the rescue. If Louis B. Mayer had been this shameless, there would have been anti-Luftwaffe classes at BOYS TOWN.

The setup rewrites IRON EAGLE II (1988), in which Doug Masters, co-hero of the first in the series, was blown up over Soviet airspace. It turns out Masters (Jason Cadieux, replacing Jason Gedrick) survived to spend years in a gulag. Released, he resentfully resists joining his mentor, retired USAF Gen. Chappy Sinclair (Lou Gossett Jr.), who rehabs youthful incorrigibles from a nearby correctional facility by teaching them flight skills. Among the car thieves, phone phreaks and hackers in the pilot program is unrepentant drug courier Catherine Wheeler (Joanne Vannicola), who takes a plane to rip off former associates. Doug follows, and when they land at an abandoned airbase, their lives are threatened by mystery commandoes unearthing cannisters. They escape to report the skullduggery. Placing his trust in old buddy General Kettle (Al Waxman) to protect the kids, Sinclair exposes the right-wing Operation Pandora, an unauthorized drop of lethal biological agents on Castro's Cuba. When a sheriff arrives to shut down the flight program, the adolescents revolt and fortify Sinclair's lone-wolf mission to stop the toxic convoy, even as Kettle turns out to be Operation Pandora's secret mastermind. The trainees distinguish themselves by outmaneuvering Air Force vets, supporting Masters in mortal combat, and infiltrating the germ-carrier plane, from which one teen dumps the deadly canisters in the ocean. General Kettle commits suicide in a plague-filled lab, and Wheeler is offered work at the relaunched flight school alongside Masters and Sinclair.

Yep, viewers will be cheering as troubled teens save America's reputation in the free world, and further repay their teacher's faith by choosing to be instructors at his unorthodox school. That Chappy Sinclair must be some teacher! Guaranteed to win howls of derision from the same cynical young viewers to which it panders, this franchise left over from the Reagan '80s demonstrates how B-movie hacks must invent wars where none exist. Here, inbred paranoia about covert military operations makes a strange bedfellow for the second-chance optimism of juvenile delinquent flicks. It's the Scared Straight Kids vs. the Special Forces, and damned if the flying teenagers don't make those Pentagon renegades cry Uncle Sam!

In this gung-ho milieu, nothing makes realistic sense; still, there's no defense for a scene in which Masters psychologically tortures a captive bad guy with a bottle of wasps while explaining how the insects sting worse than bees. (Closeups show the 'wasps' are common honeybees after all.) As for other winged things, flight sequences and explosions are good enough to make one wish the opportunistic producers hadn't gambled on teen toughlove for a refueling. Maybe rebel James Dean could have saved Sal Mineo had they a cause like the Iron Eagle high school dropouts. *(Violence, profanity.)* — R.P.

d, Sidney J. Furie; p, Peter R. Simpson; exec p, Joseph Cohen, Mark Amin, Joseph Newton; w, Michael Stokes; ph, Curtis Petersen; ed, Jeff Warren; m, Paul Zaza; art d, Michael Parks; set d, Dominic Parker; sound, Ao Loo; fx, Ron Craig; casting, Rosina Bucci; cos, Joyce Schure; makeup, Liz Gruzka; stunts, Shane Cardwell

Action/War **(PR: C MPAA: PG-13)**

ISLAND OF DR. MOREAU, THE ★★½

(U.S.) 90m Moreau Productions; Edward R. Pressman Film Corp.; New Line ~ New Line c

Marlon Brando *(Dr. Moreau)*; Val Kilmer *(Montgomery)*; David Thewlis *(Edward Douglas)*; Fairuza Balk *(Aissa)*; Daniel Rigney *(Hyena-Swine)*; Temuera Morrison *(Azazello)*; Nelson De La Rosa *(Majai)*; Peter Elliott *(Assassimon)*; Mark Dacascos *(Lo-Mai)*; Ron Perlman *(Sayer of the Law)*; Marco Hofschneider *(M'Ling)*; Miguel Lopez *(Waggdi)*; Neil Young *(Boar Man)*; David Hudson *(Bison Man)*; Clare Grant *(Fox Lady)*; Kitty Silver *(Sow Lady #1)*; Fiona Mahl *(Sow Lady #2)*; William Hootkins *(Kiril)*; Agoes Soedjarvo *(Captain)*; Ron Vreeken *(Soldier #1)*; Lou Horvath *(Soldier #2)*

THE ISLAND OF DR. MOREAU is yet another update of H. G. Wells's creepy yarn about a mysterious scientist in the tropics who conducts experiments on animals and men. It's a glossy, blustery, and ultimately silly movie starring a plump Marlon Brando and, from all accounts, a cranky Val Kilmer.

Montgomery (Kilmer) rescues a stranded United Nations peace negotiator named Edward Douglas (David Thewlis) and brings him to the South Pacific island where his employer, Dr. Moreau (Brando), said to be a Nobel laureate, carries out genetic engineering experiments. At first, Douglas is grateful, but when he is locked into his quarters in the compound, he grows suspicious.

Douglas meets Aissa (Fairuza Balk), the doctor's exotic daughter, who offers to guide him off the island. She takes Douglas through the jungle to seek assistance from the "local inhabitants," who turn out to be human-animal hybrids produced by Moreau's unconventional work. One of the creatures, the Sayer of the Law (Ron Perlman), explains the rules Moreau has established to govern his society of beastmen: they may not kill or eat meat.

Before Douglas can escape, Montgomery, Moreau, and a large entourage of creatures catch up with him. Moreau persuades Douglas to suspend judgment of his work and return to the compound. There, he introduces his other "children," M'Ling (Marco Hofschneider), Azazello (Temuera Morrison), Kiril (William Hootkins), and Majai (Nelson De la Rosa). All of them, as well as Aissa, are products of his experiments.

Moreau gives an impassioned account of his life's work: to create a more perfect version of the human species by mixing animal and human DNA. Douglas finds this disgusting and insane, and he learns that Moreau uses surgically implanted pain-inducing devices to control his creations.

Some of the hybrids witness Montgomery killing a rabbit. This initiates a reversion to natural animal behavior, abandonment of the Law, and, ultimately, an uprising against Moreau. Hyena-Swine (Daniel Rigney) removes his pain device and leads a band of reverting beastmen against the compound, killing Moreau.

Montgomery tries to take Moreau's place as the leader of the island, but he destroys the serum he and Moreau used to administer to the hybrids to prevent reversion. Without it, even Aissa is destined to revert to her animal self.

The increasingly wild creatures end up killing Montgomery and Aissa. Douglas narrowly escapes the island in a boat.

Moreau is presented here as an archetypal mad scientist. Brando, who gives an idiosyncratic performance akin to his work in THE MISSOURI BREAKS (1976) and APOCALYPSE NOW (1979), downplays the doctor's idealism (which Wells had suggested in the book) in favor of extravagant, if oddly entertaining, antics. Looking a bit like the late Divine in roomy robes and colorful headgear, and sounding a bit like the late Truman Capote, Brando dominates every scene he's in.

John Frankenheimer, who replaced screenwriter Richard Stanley as director, knows his way around the horror/sci-fi genre (SECONDS) and is comfortable with absurdist irony (THE MANCHURIAN CANDIDATE), but this has the look of a troubled movie. Thewlis tries to craft a complex performance, but the script, credited to Stanley and Ron Hutchinson, gives him little with which to work. Kilmer gives the impression that he would rather be somewhere else. Brando, for all his campy histrionics ("I think I'm simply going to perish from this heat," he laments from beneath a curious sun bonnet), is out of the movie within an hour, leaving a voluminous void.

Frankenheimer may have inherited something of a sinking ship in this project, but he does give the film a vigorous widescreen style one can admire. The same can be said for Stan Winston's creatures, which occasionally recall the critters in PLANET OF THE APES (1968), but prove diverting anyway. *(Violence, substance abuse, profanity.)* — E.K.

d, John Frankenheimer; p, Edward R. Pressman; exec p, Tim Zinnemann, Claire Rudnick-Polstein; w, Richard Stanley, Ron Hutchinson (based on novel by H.G. Wells); ph, William A. Fraker; ed, Paul Rubell; m, Gary Chang; prod d, Graham "Grace" Walker; art d, Ian Gracie; set d, Beverley Dunn, Lesley Crawford; sound, David Lee (recordist); fx, Brian Cox, Michael Z. Hanan, J. Alan Scott, Kevin Mack, Digital Domain; casting, Valerie McCaffrey; cos, Norma Moriceau; makeup, Lance Anderson, Stan Winston, Shane Patrick Mahan; stunts, Glenn Boswell

Science Fiction/Horror **(PR: C MPAA: R)**

IT CAME FROM OUTER SPACE II ★

(U.S.) 85m Duchowny/Dow Films; Finnegan/Pinchuk Company ~ MCA/Universal Home Video c

Brian Kerwin *(Jack Putnam)*; Elizabeth Pena *(Ellen Fields)*; Jonathan Carrasco *(Stevie Fields)*; Bill McKinney *(Roy Minter)*; Adrian Sparks *(Alan Paxson)*; Howard Morris *(Ben Cully)*; Mickey Jones *(Chance Madison)*; Lauren Tewes *(Carolee Minter)*; Dean Norris *(Dave Grant)*; Dawn Zeek *(Linda Grant)*; I'ilana B'tiste *(Kathy Paxson)*; Jerry Giles *(Zack)*; Michael Ray Miller *(1st Desert Rat)*; Clement Blake *(2nd Desert Rat)*; Thomas Adcox *(Hughy)*; Connie Sawyer *(Mrs. Otis)*; Bonnie Helman *(Mrs. Hughy)*; Richard Stay *(Onlooker)*; Lauren Dow *(Zack's Wife)*

This Sci-Fi Channel presentation tries to cash in on the success of a tidy 1950s B movie with a bigger budget and smaller imagination. The lack of suspense is matched only by the shoddiness of its interplanetary set design and its cheapjack makeup effects.

Ace photographer Jack Putnam (Brian Kerwin) fails to find respite when he returns home to his desert community turned ghost town. Pestered by a fatherless youngster, Stevie Fields (Jonathan Carrasco), Jack grudgingly makes Stevie an apprentice on a desert shoot that's interrupted by a bizarre space storm. Pausing only to notice Stevie's concerned mom, Ellen (Elizabeth Pena), Jack resists accepting a mind-boggling explanation for the meteorological phenomenon he witnessed: alien invasion.

Pieces of rock from the invaders' life-form prove deadly for a prospector, Ben Cully (Howard Morris), who explodes one. Subsequently, Roy Minter (Bill McKinney) is not only sucked into the rock-like blob but is replaced by a body-snatcher who murders Roy's wife, Carolee (Lauren Tewes). Panic spreads as the cosmic force sucks up the water supply and raises the temperature to 140 degrees. While Jack tries to placate vigilantes, the Roy-like alien slays Jack's buddy, Alan Paxson (Adrian Sparks); then both Stevie and his mom become victims of the human duplicators. After communicating with the extraterrestrials through Ellen's body-inhabitant, Jack realizes that the space visitors are more curious than hostile. Although Jack is unable to prevent the town rabble from trying to blow up the alien's space rock, the departing vanguard releases the entrapped human beings and leaves Earth with a low opinion of mankind's threshold for violence.

So much running time is wasted establishing paper-thin characters that the film's build-up to the E.T.'s mischief-making never acquires momentum. Under the guidance of a hack director, the actors shriek at each other about desert exoduses while the camouflaged aliens infiltrate the neighborhood—it's about as scary as nursery school trick-or-treaters saluting George Romero. Without thrills and without narrative tension, this spineless chiller also crucifies itself with tacky production values; the space rock's interior is festooned with white fluff that resembles a drag queen's closet of boas. An insult to the taut original, this update of 1953's IT CAME FROM OUTER SPACE is notable only for the genuine acting of Pena and Carrasco; the other performers are as lively and interesting as granite lumps. *(Profanity, violence, adult situations.)* — R.P.

d, Roger Duchowny; p, Tony Dow, Roger Duchowny; exec p, Sheldon Pinchuk; w, Jim Wheat, Ken Wheat (from a screeplay by Harry Essex, based on a short story by Ray Bradbury); ph, Robert C. New; ed, Michael S. McLean; m, Shirley Walker; prod d, Anthony Tremblay; art d, Claire Christine Walker; sound, Chuck Buch (mixer); fx, John Hartigan; casting, Caro Jones; cos, Sharon Rosenberg; makeup, Roy Mansano, Myrav Levy; stunts, Charlie Croughwell

Science Fiction **(PR: A MPAA: PG-13)**

IT'S MY PARTY ★★

(U.S.) 109m Opala Productions; United Artists ~ MGM/UA c

Eric Roberts *(Nick Stark)*; Gregory Harrison *(Brandon Theis)*; Margaret Cho *(Charlene Lee)*; Marlee Matlin *(Daphne Stark)*; Lee Grant *(Amalia Stark)*; Bronson Pinchot *(Monty Tipton)*; George Segal *(Paul Stark)*; Bruce Davison *(Rodney Bingham)*; Paul Regina *(Tony Zamara)*; Devon Gummersall *(Andrew Bingham)*; Olivia Newton-John *(Lina Bingham)*; Roddy McDowall *(Damian Knowles)*; Steve Antin *(Zack Phillips)*; Christopher Atkins *(Jack Allen)*; Dimitra Arlys *(Fanny Kondos)*; Ron Glass *(Dr. David Wahl)*; Lou Liberatore *(Joel Ferris)*; Victor Love *(Matt Paulson)*; Peter Murnik *(Greg King)*; Felix A. Pire *(Soli Real)*; Joel Polis *(Tim Bergen)*; Jon David Weigand *(Joe Lovett)*; Sally Kellerman *(Sara Hart)*; Greg Louganis *(Dan Zuma)*; Nina Foch *(Brandon's Mother)*; Dennis Christopher *(Douglas Reedy)*; Robert Fitzpatrick *(Bill Hart)*; Talia Paul *(Pat Bergen)*; Eugene Robert Glazer *(Jim Bixby)*; David Knapp *(Carl Fertig)*; Jim Kline *(Cowboy)*; Raul Seymour *(Gym Rat)*; Mike Pointer *(Alex)*; David Medina *(Juan)*; Rhapsody *(Miss Texas-At-Large)*; Brian To *(Boy in Pool)*; David Holladay *(Gene)*; Michael Kearns *(Party Guest)*; Matthew Rickard *(Young Andrew)*; Steve Kmetko *(Newscaster)*

This fact-based soap opera seems to have been made up haphazardly as it went along, but is redeemed by some honest, moving performances.

Hollywood insider Nick (Eric Roberts) is diagnosed with AIDS and with the CMV virus, an infection causing blindness. Not wanting to undergo a slow, painful and disfiguring death, he throws himself a two-day party, at the end of which he plans to swallow enough Seconal to make a quicker, more graceful exit.

Invited friends and relatives show up, each with varying attachments and memories. There's Nick's uncomprehending Greek mother (Lee Grant) and sister (Marlee Matlin); his estranged, equally clueless father (George Segal); and a large number of supportive friends (Margaret Cho, Bronson Pinchot, Olivia Newton-John, Roddy McDowell), whose ranks have been thinned by the AIDS virus. The one uninvited guest is Brandon, his ex-lover (Gregory Harrison), who couldn't deal with Nick's illness and walked out on him.

In a tumultuous 48 hours of drinking and commiserating, tears are shed, enmities aired and wounds healed. Eventually, Nick and Brandon have a timely rapprochement, and he is able to slough off his mortal coil with relative peace.

Gallows humor in the face of the AIDS scourge is always tricky, however admirable the wish to lighten grief's load. The fact that this is based on an actual story makes the film's scattered approach even more problematic. It's a tall order for any filmmaker, and Randal Kleiser lacks the sensitivity to carry it off. His directorial style is all over the place: spontaneous home movies, soap opera-ish duologues, idyllic flashbacks and turgid dream sequences follow each other with a complete lack of logic. (You *can* predict, however, that it won't be long before the cast breaks out into a tired chorus of "It's my party and I'll *die* if I want to.") What should have been an hysterical, kaleidoscopic blow-out (as, indeed, some memorial services are) seems but one long, morose wake with a live corpse in attendance.

That the film somehow manages to be affecting is a tribute to the acting of Roberts and Harrison. Archetypically Southern Californian, they make a super-attractive, wholly convincing gay couple, far more complex and passionate than the antiseptic heroes of PHILADELPHIA. Roberts, in particular, is better than he's been in years. Saddled with a shoddy script, he shows a devil-may-care attitude and a commitment to truth that skirts bathos and portrays real valor. Harrison, admirably, doesn't soften his character's basic callousness. This makes his determination to make amends in the face of the universal opprobrium of Nick's friends all the more courageous. The devastating soul-kiss they share at the film's climax should relieve any reservations one might feel about the casting of these heterosexual actors. A quiet shot of an AIDS memorial Nick has set up for departed real-life movie figures, like Colin Higgins and James Bridges, is the film's most touching moment.

Grant's role is sheer cliche, but she brings to it raw strength and a cannily gauged Greek accent. Cho plays the "understanding friend in terminal circumstances" part. Barely allowing for the wicked wit she's shown in her stand-up act, the role relegates her to making a lot of fat jokes about herself. She emerges as eminently likable nonetheless.

Pinchot delivers mostly lame wisecracks at a machine-gun pace as the kind of relentlessly bitchy, movie-quoting gay one might have thought Mart Crowley's THE BOYS IN THE BAND had finally put an end to. In assorted cameos, Segal, Newton-John and Paul Regina don't embarrass themselves. Unfortunately, Matlin, McDowell and Bruce Davison (reprising his oh-so-sympathetic turn in LONGTIME COMPANION) do. *(Profanity, adult situations, sexual situations, substance abuse)* — D.N.

d, Randal Kleiser; p, Joel Thurm, Randal Kleiser; exec p, Gregory Hinton, Robert Fitzpatrick; assoc p, Dessie Markovsky; w, Randal Kleiser; ph, Bernd Heinl; ed, Ila Von Hasperg; m, Basil Poledouris; prod d, Clark Hunter; set d, Traci Kirshbaum; sound, Emile Razpopov (design), Randall Johnson (mixer); casting, Joel Thurm, Steven Fertig; cos, Daniele King; makeup, Zoe

Drama/Comedy **(PR: C MPAA: R)**

JACK ★★

(U.S.) 104m American Zoetrope; Hollywood Pictures ~ Buena Vista c

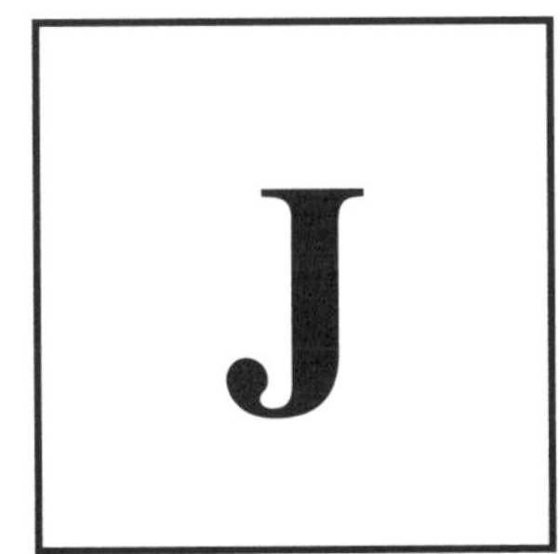

Robin Williams *(Jack Powell)*; Diane Lane *(Karen Powell)*; Brian Kerwin *(Brian Powell)*; Jennifer Lopez *(Miss Marquez)*; Bill Cosby *(Lawrence Woodruff)*; Fran Drescher *(Dolores Durante)*; Adam Zolotin *(Louis Durante)*; Todd Bosley *(Edward)*; Seth Smith *(John-John)*; Mario Yedidia *(George)*; Jeremy Lelliott *(Johnny Duffer)*; Jurnee Smollett *(Phoebe)*; Dani Faith *(Jane)*; Hugo Hernandez *(Victor)*; Rickey D'Shon Collins *(Eric)*; Michael McKean *(Paulie)*; Edward Lynch *(Angry Man)*; Don Novello *(Bartender)*; Allan Rich *(Dr. Benfante)*; Keone Young *(Dr. Lin)*; Irwin Corey *(Poppy)*; Al Nalbandian *(Principal McGee)*; Dwight Hicks *(High School Principal)*; Allison Whitbeck *(Lucy)*; Sam Ritzenberg *(Boy in Classroom)*; Terry Ricardo Jefferson II *(Eric's Brother)*; Studio Gutierrez *(Mario)*; Joe Akins *(Big Joe)*; Kendra Sutherland *(Kendra)*; Ashlee Lauren *(Allison)*; Wilma Bonet; Abigail Van Alyn; Rainer Judd; Marcella Pabros; Jennifer Garces *(Nurses)*; Marc Coppolo *(Radio Personality)*; Terry McGovern *(Radio Personality)*; Kim Wonderly *(Radio Personality)*; Bria Neuenschwander *(Drugstore Clerk)*; Steven Anthony Jones *(Officer at Jail)*; Jeanette Etheredge *(Cat)*; Jacqui De La Fontaine *(Cat)*; Josh Kornbluth *(Pack of Cigarettes)*; Helen Shumaker *(Martini)*; Pete Escovedo with the New Morty Show *(Conga Band)*; Michael Madland *(Louis at 18)*; Matt Kroot *(Edward at 18)*; Ryan Kennedy *(George at 18)*; Tyler Smith *(John-John at 18)*; Jesse James Chisholm *(Johnny Duffer at 18)*; Jonathan A. Turner *(Eric at 18)*; Kamela Peart *(Phoebe at 18)*; Jennifer Hagan *(Jane at 16)*

JACK offers a twist on the premise of BIG, with Robin Williams as a boy in a man's body trying to fit in with the lunchbox, instead of the briefcase, set. But director Francis Ford Coppola strives a little too earnestly to be bittersweet, and crosses the line into melancholia.

Due to a mysterious medical condition that causes his body to age at four times the normal rate, Jack (Williams), at age ten, has the appearance of a forty-year-old man. With the best intentions of protecting him, Jack's parents (Diane Lane and Brian Kerwin) have kept him secluded at home, bringing in a tutor, Mr. Woodruff (Bill Cosby), for his schooling. But Jack longs to be around other children, so he enters the fifth grade. At first, the other kids avoid him and call him "freak." Things turn around when Jack helps Louie (Adam Zolotin) and his friends beat some playground bullies in a game of basketball. When they discover that Jack can buy porno magazines, the gang eagerly accepts him as one of their own, inviting Jack to their treehouse for sleep-overs and fart-lighting contests.

An assignment to write an essay on what he wants to be when he grows up forces Jack to realize that he never will—if he's lucky, he'll live into his early twenties. He takes a stab at living like an adult by meeting Louie's mom (Fran Drescher) for an ill-fated date, but discovers he has no place in that world. Despondent, Jack quits school and refuses to see his friends. Mr. Woodruff convinces him to return by telling Jack that he's a "shooting star," and that he shouldn't give up on living just because his life will be short. In an epilogue scene set seven years later, an elderly-looking but happy Jack is shown graduating from high school alongside his friends.

The concept of Williams as a ten-year-old is a pitchman's dream, and JACK was sold easily to audiences with advertising that emphasized its star's special appeal to children. The film's first half provides some genuinely touching and funny moments with Williams cavorting amidst his young co-stars. But the story runs into the proverbial wall of death (the logical consequence of its own premise), and once Jack has his own end in his sights, JACK becomes a fairly maudlin affair. Not that the inevitable need be denied (a *deus ex machina* cure would have been really lame), but the back end of JACK plays like it's determined to milk every sob and wring every tear out of the audience. Instead, the film might better have explored the fulfillment that fatherless Louie finds with Jack, and the loss that Jack's mother (Lane is woefully underused) feels when her best friend runs off to school.

Known for directing decidedly adult dramas like THE GODFATHER and APOCALYPSE NOW, Coppola was drawn to this Disney project because his own "shooting star," his son Giancarlo (to whom he dedicates the film), died at the age of 22. And while no one would question the heartfelt sincerity with which Coppola means to deliver JACK's "carpe diem" message, one might view it as unintentionally ironic. Ten years ago, when Coppola trafficked in a similar sort of sentimental fantasy-land with PEGGY SUE GOT MARRIED, Kathleen Turner boldly decried the value of learning algebra. Despite the film's admonition to the contrary, young viewers of JACK might be just as skeptical that enduring junior high is indeed living life to its fullest. *(Profanity.)* — P.R.

d, Francis Ford Coppola; p, Richard Mestres, Fred Fuchs, Francis Ford Coppola; exec p, Doug Claybourne; w, James DeMonaco, Gary Nadeau; ph, John Toll; ed, Barry Malkin; m, Michael Kamen; prod d, Dean Tavoularis; art d, Angelo Graham; set d, Armin Ganz, Barbara Munch; sound, Agamemnon Andrianos; fx, John McLeod, Gary Gutierrez; casting, Fred Roos, Linda Phillips Palo, Rosalie Joseph; cos, Aggie Guerard Rodgers; makeup, Ken Diaz; stunts, Michael Ruyard, Jack Gill

Comedy **(PR: A MPAA: PG-13)**

JACK & SARAH ★★

(U.K./France) 110m PFE; British Screen; Canal Plus; Granada TV Prods.; Mainstream ~ Gramercy Pictures c

Richard E. Grant *(Jack)*; Samantha Mathis *(Amy)*; Judi Dench *(Margaret)*; Ian McKellen *(William)*; Cherie Lunghi *(Anna)*; Eileen Atkins *(Phil)*; Imogen Stubbs *(Sarah)*; David Swift *(Michael)*; Laurent Grevill *(Alain)*; Kate Hardie *(Pamela)*; Bianca Lee; Sophia Lee *(Sarah as a Baby)*; Sophia Sullivan *(Sarah as a Toddler)*; Niven Boyd *(Nathaniel)*; Tracy Thorne *(Susan)*; Lorraine Ashbourne *(Jackie)*; Deborah Findlay *(Miss Cartwright)*; Claire Toeman *(Health Visitor)*; Geff Francis *(Rob)*; Matyelok Gibbs *(Physiotherapist)*; Michael McStay *(Security Man)*; James Bannon *(City Boy)*; David J. Nicholas *(Delivery Man)*; Susie McKenna *(Paramedic)*; Keith Bartlett *(Taxi Driver)*; John Grillo *(Landlord)*; Richard Leaf *(Stoned Man)*; Andrew Read *(Office Boy)*; Raymond Brodie *(Office Party Guest)*

JACK & SARAH begins so promisingly and deteriorates so inexorably that one has to wonder what writer-director Tim Sullivan was trying to do in this ambitious but hollow first feature.

Jack (Richard E. Grant) is an Englishman who has everything he could want—a successful law career, a loving wife (Imogen Stubbs), and a baby on the way. But Jack's wife dies giving birth to baby Sarah and he is thrown into a tailspin of drinking and despair. Worse, he hasn't a clue about being a single father. Enter Amy (Samantha Mathis), an American airhead abroad, who agrees to be Sarah's nanny, since she's just gotten fired from her waitressing job. Amy isn't a particularly competent nanny, as Jack's mother (Judi Dench) points out, but she hangs in there and

Jack eventually falls in love with her, and she with him. End of movie.

The first 15 minutes of JACK & SARAH raise viewer expectations that this will be an original dark comedy about the cruelty of fate and the absurdity of grief. Instead, Sullivan's screenplay makes a sharp, puzzling turn from its intriguing premise and veers into a lane marked: "Warning: Imitation of FOUR WEDDINGS AND A FUNERAL Ahead." (JACK & SARAH was made soon after that hit British comedy and, very likely, the producers were hoping to duplicate its success.) It's only a coincidence that both movies star an actor named Grant, but Richard E. has a harder edge than Hugh, an edge that was effectively displayed in the 1986 cult movie, WITHNAIL AND I. Here, though, he just seems uncomfortable, perhaps because his leading lady Mathis is miscast—wooden and uninspired as a character, it's impossible to believe that she could make Jack forget his dead spouse.

JACK & SARAH is the cinematic equivalent of a shoplifter, pocketing elements from other movies at every turn (i.e., the romantic comedy formula, the slapstick, and the idiosyncratic supporting characters seem awfully familiar). Ian McKellen turns up as an alcoholic homeless man who, somewhat improbably, becomes Jack's butler; moreover, Eileen Atkins lends her pedigree to the proceedings, but to no avail. Even these splendid actors can't rescue this plodding comedy which, despite Simon Boswell's relentlessly chirpy musical score (or partly because of it), never takes wing after its initial, brief flight. *(Adult situations, sexual situations.)* — E.K.

d, Tim Sullivan; p, Pippa Cross, Simon Channing-Williams, Janette Day; w, Tim Sullivan; ph, Jean-Yves Escoffier; ed, Lesley Walker; m, Simon Boswell; prod d, Christopher J. Bradshaw; art d, Humphrey Bangham; sound, Ken Weston (mixer); casting, Simone Reynolds; cos, Dany Everett; makeup, Christine Beveridge; stunts, Nick Powell

Comedy/Drama/Romance (PR: C MPAA: R)

JAG ★★½

(U.S.) 94m Belisarius Productions; NBC; Paramount Pictures ~ Paramount Home Video c

David James Elliott *(Lt. Harmon Rabb Jr.)*; Andrea Parker *(Lt. Kate Pike)*; Terry O'Quinn *(Capt. Thomas "Cag" Boone)*; Raye Hollitt *(Lt. Cassie Puller)*; John Roselius *(Admiral Drake)*; Scott Jaeck *(Commander Dooley)*; Katie Rich *(Lt. Angela Arutti)*; Steve Fitzpatrick *(Lt. Zane Lubin)*; Cliff De Young; Kevin Dunn; Patrick Labyorteaux; W. K. Stratton; Joe Sabatino; Gregory McKinney; Kane Picoy; Glenn Morshower

This is the feature pilot for a TV series notable for merging two pop-culture fads: high-tech service dramas (TOP GUN and quick-cancelled network fare like "Call to Glory" and "Supercarrier") and the legal-thriller genre, present since the days of "Perry Mason," but exceptionally hot in the 1990s.

On the aircraft carrier *Seahawk* in the Adriatic, Lt. Angela Arutti (Katie Rich) touches down a national hero after a victorious dogfight with Serbian MIGs over Bosnia. But in fact the enemy planes were shot down by her commanding officer, Capt. Thomas Cag Boone (Terry O'Quinn), who wants Arutti to get the credit in order to improve attitudes toward women in the armed forces. Arutti, wracked by doubts over her courage under fire, types her resignation, trysts that night with a mystery lover on the flight deck, and is deliberately shoved off the ship by a shadowy assailant. To investigate whether her disappearance is suicide or foul play, Washington sends two J.A.G. (Judge Advocate General) Navy lawyers, Lt. Harmon Rabb Jr. (David James Elliott) and Lt. Kate Pike (Andrea Parker) to the *Seahawk*. Lt. Rabb's presence carries plenty of baggage; he had to leave active service because his impaired vision led to a crash landing that killed his co-pilot, and "Cag" was his MIA father's wing man in Vietnam. When fishermen find Arutti's body, the evidence points to murder. Ultimately, Lt. Rabb is able to pull off the considerable feat of redeeming himself in battle (landing a wounded Cag safely after a nocturnal strafing run on the Serbs) while *simultaneously* cracking the Arutti case—she was killed by a grudge-holding male officer who mistook her in the dark for another female flyer.

JAG does not open promisingly. If the thick soldierly jargon doesn't get to you (only one term—"stay on my six"—is defined), then the aggressive posturing of the *Seahawk's co-ed crew will, recalling the macho stereotypes of TOP GUN at their most juvenile. But the Arutti murder comes as a real shock; that the affair turns out to be a far simpler crime than the shipwide conspiracy first suspected is also a surprise, and makes an effective launch for all the melodrama. Too bad that what the characters are talking about is often much more intelligent than the way they say it; the dialogue overflows with double-entendres to reflect the growing attraction between Rabb and Pike. References to the Balkan civil war and real-life Navy sex scandals strive to endow JAG with verisimilitude, but Lt. Rabb's contrived personal problems and tormented flashbacks are exactly the sort of service-drama cliches burlesqued in the popular satire HOT SHOTS! (1991) and it's all hard to take despite yeoman work by the cast. Aficianados of the action game show "American Gladiators" should recognize body builder Raye Hollitt as Arutti's weightlifter roommate. She's a special effect equal to the cool computer graphics in the aerial scenes, but the climactic mission is marred by what sounds like a high school marching band fanfare on the soundtrack.*

JAG also had a rough flight as a network series, with Lt. Rabb investigating military-related mysteries around the world on a weekly basis. The expensive program, from the creators of "Magnum P.I." and "Quantum Leap," started out on NBC but ran into low-ratings turbulence. Dropped from the network's lineup, the show was later picked up by CBS, concurrent with the pilot movie's debut on home video in 1996. *(Violence, adult situations.)* — C.C.

d, Donald P. Bellisario; p, Howard Kazanjian; exec p, Donald P. Bellisario; w, Donald P. Bellisario; ph, Thomas Del Ruth; ed, John Koslowsky; m, Bruce Broughton; prod d, Mayling Cheng; art d, George Becket; set d, Peg Cummings; fx, Larry Fuentes, Tim Landry; casting, Nan Dutton, Clare Walker; cos, Robert Turturice; stunts, Diamond Farnsworth

War/Crime/Drama (PR: C MPAA: NR)

JAMES AND THE GIANT PEACH ★★★½

(U.S.) 80m Skellington Productions; Allied Filmmakers; Walt Disney Pictures ~ Buena Vista c

Paul Terry *(James/Voice of James)*; Simon Callow *(Voice of Grasshopper)*; Richard Dreyfuss *(Voice of Centipede)*; Susan Sarandon *(Voice of Spider)*; Jane Leeves *(Voice of Ladybug)*; David Thewlis *(Voice of Earthworm)*; Joanna Lumley *(Aunt Spiker)*; Miriam Margolyes *(Aunt Sponge/Voice of Glowworm)*; Pete Postlethwaite *(Old Man)*; Steven Culp *(James' Father)*; Susan Turner-Cray *(James' Mother)*; Mike Starr *(Beat Cop)*; Cirocco Dunlap *(Girl With Telescope)*; Chae Kirby *(Newsboy)*; Michael Girardin *(Reporter #1)*; J. Stephen Coyle *(Reporter #2)*; Tony Haney *(Reporter #3)*; Katherine Howell *(Woman in Bathrobe)*; Jeff Mosely *(Hard Hat Man)*; Mario Yedidia *(Street Kid)*; Emily Rosen *(Innocent Girl)*; Al Nalbandian *(Cabby)*

Disney brings to life the wonderful story of a young boy's adventures on an airborne peach in JAMES AND THE GIANT PEACH. The story is based on the tale by Roald Dahl, an English writer notorious for giving children the dark, bizarre horrors they actually enjoy, in which children set off on their own and wicked adults are ruthlessly punished. Filmed in both live-action and stop-action puppet animation, this film benefits from the technology and talents of THE NIGHTMARE BEFORE CHRISTMAS (1993) crew, including director Henry Selick and coproducers Tim Burton and Denise Di Novi.

Young James Trotter (Paul Terry) is enjoying an idyllic day with his loving parents on the British seashore, where the three take pleasure in planning a trip to New York City. Life is perfect until one day a giant rhinoceros descends from the sky and devours his parents. James is then delivered into the care of his two wicked and ghastly aunts, Sponge (Miriam Margolyes) and Spiker (Joanna Lumley), who proceed to make him their indentured slave.

One day, a mysterious man (Pete Postlethwaite) finds the miniature hot air balloon James has made out of a New York travel brochure and returns it to James filled with tiny, neon-green crocodile tongues. The tongues escape and burrow into the soil causing a barren tree to yield a single vibrant peach that quickly grows to enormous proportions.

James climbs inside the peach and turns into an animated puppet character. Inside, he finds companionship in the form of a cast of large, animated puppet bugs, including a dignified caterpillar (voice of Simon Callow), a sexy spider (voice of Susan Sarandon), a doting ladybug (voice of Jane Leeves), a brash centipede (voice of Richard Dreyfuss), and a sluggish earthworm (voice of David Thewlis).

The peach rolls down the hill and into the sea and the group sets off, determined to reach Manhattan. When the ocean proves too dangerous, James captures a flock of seagulls and binds them with the spider's web, and the peach takes to the sky. The group endures both hardship and delights on their travels. They are exuberant when they finally see the lights of Manhattan below, but suddenly the giant rhinoceros of James' darkest fears gallops out of the clouds and attacks the vulnerable peach. It plunges from the sky but lands miraculously atop the Empire State Building.

During the crash, James returns to his live-action form. He is rescued and brought down to a crowd of onlookers. Suddenly, Spiker and Sponge appear out of nowhere, insisting that James be returned to their care. James has trouble convincing the crowd of his implausible story until his animated bug friends arrive. The wicked aunts are bound up like spider's prey and shipped away, and James and the bugs set up residence in the city and enjoy a lifetime of fame and good fortune.

This is an interesting and innovative film with fantastic visuals designed by children's book illustrator Lane Smith. There are stark, high-contrast images of unforgettable beauty, such as the bright and voluptuous peach against the dark, foreboding, crooked sea-cliff home, and the image of the peach carried through the dark sky by white bird puppets. But the film's narrative often fails to measure up to the surrealist logic of Dahl's writing, and, at times, the story seems absurd. Nevertheless, this is a wonderful Disney creation that pushes the borders of the genre while at the same time depicting traditional childhood fears and secret desires: loss of the parents, long voyages, unconquerable monsters, and the rewards of friendship.— R.C.

d, Henry Selick; p, Denise Di Novi, Tim Burton; exec p, Jake Eberts; co-p, Brian Rosen, Henry Selick; w, Karey Kirkpatrick, Jonathan Roberts, Steve Bloom (based on the book by Roald Dahl); ph, Pete Kozachik, Hiro Narita; ed, Stan Webb; m, Randy Newman; prod d, Harley Jessup; art d, Bill Boes, Kendal Cronkhite; set d, Kris Boxell; anim, Paul Berry; sound, Agamemnon Andrianos (mixer), Gary Rydstrom; fx, Steven Riley, Craig Mohagen, Thomas F. Sindicich, Pete Kozachik, Amy Hollywood Wixson, Mickey McGovern, Sony Pictures Imageworks, Lynda Lemon, Buena Vista Visual Effects; casting, Robin Gurland, Brian Chavanne, Ros Hubbard, John Hubbard; cos, Julie Slinger; makeup, Richard Snell; stunts, Rocky Capella

AAN Original Musical or Comedy Score: Randy Newman

Animated/Children's/Fantasy (PR: A MPAA: PG)

JANE EYRE ★★½

(France/Italy/U.S./U.K.) 112m Rochester Films Ltd.; Cinertimo S.R.L.; Flach Film; Mediaset; R.C.S. Editori S.P.A.; Fininvest; Miramax ~ Miramax c

Charlotte Gainsbourg *(Jane Eyre)*; William Hurt *(Rochester)*; Anna Paquin *(Young Jane Eyre)*; Joan Plowright *(Mrs. Fairfax)*; John Wood *(Mr. Brocklehurst)*; Geraldine Chaplin *(Miss Scatcherd)*; Billie Whitelaw *(Grace Pool)*; Elle Macpherson *(Blanche Ingram)*; Fiona Shaw *(Mrs. Reed)*; Samuel West *(St. John Rivers)*; Edward De Souza *(Mason)*; Amanda Root *(Miss Temple)*; Maria Schneider *(Bertha)*; Charlotte Attenborough *(Mary Rivers)*; Nic Knight *(John Reed)*; Nicola Howard *(Eliza Reed)*; Sasha Graff *(Georgiana Reed)*; Leanne Rowe *(Helen Burns)*; Richard Warwick *(John)*; Judith Parker *(Leah)*; Josephine Serre *(Adele)*; Simon Beresford *(Henry Eshton)*; Chris Larkin *(Frederick Lynn)*; Miranda Forbes *(Lady Ingram)*; Ann Queensberry *(Lady Lynn)*; Sheila Burrell *(Lady Eshton)*; Sara Stevens *(Amy Eshton)*; Orina Messina *(Louisa Eshton)*; Marissa Dunlop *(Mary Ingram)*; Julian Fellowes *(Colonel Dent)*; Barry Martin *(Sir George Lynn)*; Walter Sparrow *(Lord Eshton)*; Steffan Boje *(Party Guest)*; Golda Broderick *(Mrs. Bennett)*; John Tranter *(Dr. Carter)*; Ralph Nossek *(Reverend Wood)*; Peter Woodthorpe *(Briggs)*

Franco Zeffirelli's JANE EYRE adds little more than previous film versions of Charlotte Bronte's novel, but the story of the headstrong governess gets respectable treatment that might appeal to less-than-discriminating romantics.

JANE EYRE begins with the childhood of the orphaned Jane (Anna Paquin) in 1834 England. Jane yearns to leave the household of her reserved, self-centered aunt, Mrs. Reed (Fiona Shaw), but her eventual escape is short-lived. Jane is placed in a charity school called Lowood, where she is subjected to strict handling by the headmaster, Mr. Brocklehurst (John Wood), and his assistant, Miss Scatcherd (Geraldine Chaplin). Jane spends the rest of her childhood and much of her adolescence confined to this cold environment. Her only allies include a sympathetic teacher, Miss Temple (Amanda Root), and a sickly schoolmate.

After Jane's childhood friend dies, Jane braces herself for more misery until the day she is able to leave the institution.

As a young woman, Jane (Charlotte Gainsbourg) finally leaves Lowood and takes a position as a governess at the estate of the wealthy but enigmatic Rochester (William Hurt). Jane begins caring for Rochester's daughter, Adele (Josephine Serre), before ever meeting her employer. When she finally encounters Rochester, Jane is infatuated, and the feelings become mutual. Eventually, the two decide to marry, despite the fact that Rochester seems to be hiding something from Jane.

The housekeeper, Mrs. Fairfax (Joan Plowright), tries to protect Jane from Rochester's dark secret, but the town's judge forces Rochester to tell Jane the truth on their wedding day. Rochester explains how his first wife became mentally ill, but out of loyalty to her, he has kept her in the attic of his home. As Rochester tells the sad tale, his first wife sets fire to their estate.

He rushes back to the mansion to save Adele, but when he fails to return, he is presumed dead.

Jane moves on to other governess jobs, but finally returns to the destroyed mansion. She is surprised to find Rochester alive, but blind, and living in the ruins. She promises to stay by him through all his days. Miraculously, his eyesight returns.

This new JANE EYRE looks and sounds like a lot of other movies, despite the fact that it is based on a specific, well-known literary source. There always has been something Dickensian about the story itself, so it's not surprising that there is a resemblance to the 1970 British version of DAVID COPPERFIELD as well as the 1970 WUTHERING HEIGHTS.

Zeffirelli's moody but measured style here looks more like the better BBC-TV versions of the classics than his own florid book-to-film works. In many ways, this JANE EYRE accomplishes what 1995's very similar LITTLE PRINCESS tried but failed to do in terms of recreating a lavish costume epic of yore. And this film also fits into the recent spate of Jane Austen adaptations like SENSE AND SENSIBILITY (1995) and PERSUASION (1995), which have been inappropriately romanticized. Finally, the presence of Paquin deliberately conjures visions of THE PIANO, although the 1993 Jane Campion period piece was more feminist and ambiguous in meaning.

Ultimately, however, this JANE EYRE does not surpass the last two film renditions of Bronte's story, the 1944 Hollywood classic starring Joan Fontaine and Orson Welles, and the 1971 British TV version starring Susannah York and George C. Scott.

Granted, this remake is much better than the stiff, low-budget 1934 Hollywood version—with a miscast Virginia Bruce as Jane—but now as then, an American actor—in this case, Hurt—struggles with a British accent. Hurt tries admirably to make Rochester a strapping yet sensitive figure, but fails to erase memories of Welles and Scott.

Also, the 1944 version's judicious cutting kept the story moving without compromising Bronte. The black & white production design also made more out of the Gothic horror elements; Zeffirelli's inspiration seems to be Vermeer. Most of all, Fontaine provided a spirited yet tremulous star turn that outshines the pleasant but uncharismatic Gainsbourg. In other words, JANE EYRE needs a star, but Gainsbourg isn't one—not yet, and not here, anyway. *(Adult situations, profanity.)* — E.M.

d, Franco Zeffirelli; p, Dyson Lovell; co-p, Giovannella Zannoni, Jean Francois Lepetit; w, Hugh Whitemore, Franco Zeffirelli (based on the novel by Charlotte Bronte); ph, David Watkin; ed, Richard Marden; m, Alessio Vlad, Claudio Capponi; prod d, Roger Hall; art d, Dennis Bosher, Caroline Cobbold; sound, David Stephenson (recordist); fx, Geoff Clifford; casting, Noel Davis; cos, Jenny Beavan; makeup, Sara Monzani; stunts, Graham Crowther

Drama/Romance **(PR: A MPAA: PG)**

JERRY MAGUIRE ★★★½

(U.S.) 135m Gracie Films ~ Columbia Tristar c

Tom Cruise *(Jerry Maguire)*; Cuba Gooding Jr. *(Rod Tidwell)*; Renee Zellweger *(Dorothy Boyd)*; Kelly Preston *(Avery Bishop)*; Bonnie Hunt *(Laurel Boyd)*; Jerry O'Connell *(Frank Cushman)*; Jay Mohr *(Bob Sugar)*; Regina King *(Marcee Tidwell)*; Jonathan Lipnicki *(Ray Boyd)*; Todd Louiso *(Chad the Nanny)*; Mark Pellington *(Bill Dooler)*; Jeremy Suarez *(Tyson Tidwell)*; Jared Jussim *(Dicky Fox)*; Benjamin Kimball Smith *(Keith Cushman)*; Ingrid Beer *(Anne-Louise)*; Jann Wenner *(Scully)*; Nada Despotovich *(Wendy)*; Alexandra Wentworth *(Bobbi Fallon)*; Aries Spears *(Tee Pee)*; Kelly Coffield *(Jan)*; Alice Crowe *(Alice)*; Larina Adamson; Winnie Holzman; Diana Jordan; Susan Norfleet; Susan Pingleton; Cha-Cha Sandoval; Hynden Walch *(Women's Group)*; Glenn Frey *(Dennis Wilburn)*; Donal Logue *(Rick (Junior Agent))*; Tom Gallop *(Ben)*; Beaumont Bacon *(Cleo)*; Lisa Amsterdam *(Patricia Logan)*; Angela Goethals *(Kathy Sanders)*; Leslie Upson *(Flight Attendant)*; Rick Johnson *(John Swenson)*; Lightfield Lewis *(Room Service Waiter)*; Jerry Cantrell *(Jesus of CopyMat)*; Toby Huss *(Steve Remo)*; Drake Bell *(Jesse Remo)*; Christina Cavanaugh *(Mrs. Remo)*; Russel Lunday *(Doctor)*; Eric Stoltz *(Ethan Valhere)*; Lamont Johnson *(Weepy Athlete)*; Brent Barry *(Calvin Nack)*; Rod Tate *("Baja" Brunard)*; Charlie Cronin *(Hootie Fan)*; Theo Greenly *(Hootie Fan)*; Danny Rimmer *(Sad Autograph Boy)*; Michael James Johnson *(Clark Hodd)*; Jordan Ross *(Art Stallings)*; Brandon Christianson *(Young Golfer)*; Jerry Ziesmer *(Trainer)*; Kirsten Krueger *(Draft Reporter)*; Shannon Thornton *(Pressbox Columnist)*; Luis Damian; Jesus Alberto Guzman; Juan Arnoldo Morales; Alberto Alfavo *(Mariachi Band)*; Andrea Ferrell; Anthony Natale *(Elevator Couple)*; David Ursin *(General Manager)*; Thomas J. Reilly *(Reverend)*; Reagan Gomez-Preston *(Tidwell's Cousin)*; Jim Moffatt; Leo Zick; Klair Bybee *(NFL Guests)*; Stanley Sessoms *(Shower Man)*; Gale Hilman *(Locker Room Athlete)*; Heather Cheney *(Idealized Kissing Wife)*; Dennis Fitzgerald *(Idealized Kissing Husband)*; Lucy Alexis Liu; Stephanie Furst; Justina Vail; Sam Smith; Ivana Marina; Lisa Rotondi; Lisa Stahl; Emily Procter; Amaryllis Borrego; Stacey Williams; Lauren Parker; Lisa Ann Hadley; Kymberly Kalil; Alison Armitage; Rebecca Rigg; Golde Starger *(Former Girlfriends)*; Roy Firestone; Al Michaels; Dan Dierdorf; Frank Gifford; Mel Kiper; Jeff Lurie; Drew Rosenhaus; Richie Kotite; Tim McDonald; Mike Tirico; Wayne Fontes; Evelyn Fontes; Mike White; Johnnie Morton; Rick Mirer; Drew Bledsoe; Rob Moore; Ki-Jana Carter; Herman Moore; Art Monk; Troy Aikman; Katarina Witt; Dean Biasucci; Warren Moon; Kerry Collins; Erica Sorgi; Tom Friend; Dallas Malloy; Jim Irsay; Meg Irsay *(Themselves)*

A romantic comedy by one of the best in the business, writer-director Cameron Crowe, JERRY MAGUIRE features standout performances by Tom Cruise and Oscar winner Cuba Gooding Jr., as well as impressive turns by Renee Zellweger and Jonathan Lipnicki.

Jerry Maguire (Tom Cruise) is a sports agent who wins his clients salaries and endorsements so overinflated that they repel fans.

But something is happening to Jerry. During a fit of guilt, he experiences an epiphany about the amorality of his trade. Riding the righteous wave, Jerry drafts a "mission statement" outlining his views on how sports agencies ought to work: less about money and clients, and more about personal attention.

Though the memo earns Jerry the admiration of his fellow agents (who are also suffering some ethical queasiness), his agency, of course, cannot tolerate such heresy, and he is fired; in a last-ditch effort to stay in the game, he convinces one of his clients—Rod Tidwell (Cuba Gooding Jr.), a receiver for the Arizona Cardinals who still sees in Jerry his ticket to the big money—to stick with him as he builds a solo career. As Jerry packs up his desk and leaves, he implores his co-workers to follow him. The only one who agrees is Dorothy Boyd (Renee Zellweger), an accountant who has secretly been attracted to Jerry for some time.

As Jerry busily hypes Rod, a sputtering romance begins between him and Dorothy, fueled largely by Jerry's love for Dorothy's young son, Ray (Jonathan Lipnicki). But the money isn't rolling in like the old days, so Dorothy plans to accept an out-of-town job until things pick up. Struggling to keep her, Jerry proposes to Dorothy and the two are quickly married, even though Jerry is clearly uncomfortable with the role of husband.

Also struggling is Rod's career, which lingers just below the marquee-player status enjoyed by such athletes as Troy Aikman and Barry Sanders. Those players, Jerry explains, play with passion—the kind of passion Rod shows in his marriage but can't seem to transfer to his game. Conversely, Rod tells Jerry that he needs to take the kind of passion he shows in his work and apply it to his own marriage, or he's liable to lose Dorothy.

Each man strives desperately to attain that next level, transformations that occur simultaneously during "Monday Night Football": Rod risks injury to make a big play, while Jerry risks rejection to win back his wife's love. In the end, Rod is offered the contract of a lifetime, and Jerry is finally able to give his heart to Dorothy.

Like SAY ANYTHING (1989) and, to a lesser degree, SINGLES (1992), JERRY MAGUIRE displays Cameron Crowe's ability to create romantic relationships that ring true. His characters are the kind of people we all know, falling into bad relationships and fumbling good ones, stumbling around in defiant ignorance of their best interests. Crowe also nimbly avoids the stereotype traps that characters like Jerry Maguire and Rod Tidwell often place in a writer's path. Though JERRY MAGUIRE's happy ending is a bit too neat, the overall package is well worth the price of admission.

JERRY MAGUIRE also gives audiences a rare look at Cruise's underappreciated comic side. After TOP GUN (1986), Cruise's performances became increasingly intense, with only flashes of his charming wit. Not since RISKY BUSINESS (1983) has Cruise allowed himself to once again exercise his comedic muscles as he does in JERRY MAGUIRE, displaying deft comic timing and a surprising aptitude for physical humor.

The film's other pleasant surprise is the performance of Gooding, who easily holds his own against Cruise. He even manages to steal a few scenes from the star, and scored himself an Oscar in the process. *(Violence, nudity, sexual situations, profanity.)* — B.T.

d, Cameron Crowe; p, James L. Brooks, Laurence Mark, Richard Sakai, Cameron Crowe; assoc p, Lisa Steward, J. Michael Mendel; co-p, Bruce S. Pustin, John D. Schofield; w, Cameron Crowe; ph, Janusz Kaminski; ed, Joe Hutshing; m, Nancy Wilson; prod d, Stephen Lineweaver; art d, Virginia Randolph, Clayton Hartley; set d, Clay A. Griffith; sound, Jeff Wexler; fx, Paul Haines Jr.; casting, Gail Levin; cos, Betsy Heimann; makeup, Michele Burke-Winter; tech, Leigh Steinberg, Jeffrey Moorad

AA Best Supporting Actor: Cuba Gooding Jr.; *AAN Best Picture; AAN Best Actor:* Tom Cruise; *AAN Best Film Editing:* Joe Hutshing; *AAN Best Original Screenplay:* Cameron Crowe

Comedy/Drama **(PR: C MPAA: R)**

JINGLE ALL THE WAY ★½

(U.S.) 80m 1492 Films; 20th Century Fox ~ 20th Century Fox c

Arnold Schwarzenegger *(Howard Langston)*; Sinbad *(Myron Larabee)*; Phil Hartman *(Ted Maltin)*; Rita Wilson *(Liz Langston)*; Robert Conrad *(Officer Hummell)*; Martin Mull *(DJ)*; Jake Lloyd *(Jamie Langston)*; James Belushi *(Mall Santa)*; E J De La Pena *(Johnny)*; Lorraine Newman *(First Lady)*; Justin Chapman *(Billy)*; Harvey Korman *(President)*; Richard Moll *(Dementor)*; Daniel Riordan *(Turbo Man)*

JINGLE ALL THE WAY is a seldom amusing holiday tale that presents another version of the kinder, gentler Arnold Schwarzenegger.

Howard Langston (Schwarzenegger) is a skilled salesman. His grip on family life, however, is not so sure. Working late, Howard has missed his son Jamie's (Jake Lloyd) karate-school graduation. By way of apology, Howard promises a trip to the Christmas holiday parade, which will feature action hero Turboman. Later, his wife, Liz (Rita Wilson), reminds him of the Turboman talking action figure he was to get for Jamie but that Howard forgot. Now, at the last minute, he must find the season's hottest toy.

Howard's quest begins outside a toy store, where a crowd of anxious parents have gathered. There he meets Myron (Sinbad), an edgy postman who is also hoping to acquire Turboman. After trampling the store to pieces, the toy hunters come up empty-handed. Howard races from store to store, nearly attaining his goal at a mall, but he is thwarted by the manic Myron. He later encounters a ring of black market Santas who are trafficking in hard-to-find items; unfortunately, the Turboman they have speaks Spanish. Howard and Myron then storm a radio station that is giving away a Turboman, but their irrational behavior draws the police. Myron distracts the officers by pretending to have a mail bomb, and the two escape.

Howard returns home, Turboman-less, to discover that his neighbor Ted (Phil Hartman), an unctuous, divorced superdad, has been horning in on Howard's fatherly Christmas duties as well as putting the moves on Howard's wife. Liz and Jamie, angered by Howard's neglectful behavior, accept Ted's invitation to the parade, leaving Howard behind. Disgusted with himself, Howard goes to the parade to make amends to his wife and son; while searching them out, however, he is spotted by a police officer from the radio station, who pursues him into the warehouse that serves as a staging area for the Turboman float. Mistaking Howard for the actor who is to play Turboman, organizers quickly dress the confused father in the action hero costume and place him on the float. As part of the show, Turboman is to select a youngster and award him a special edition Turboman. Naturally, Howard selects his own son. Myron has other plans, however, and, dressed in the costume of Turboman's arch enemy, swings down and steals the toy from Jamie. To the crowd's delight, Howard and Myron fight it out over the doll. Myron chases Jamie to a rooftop, and Howard uses Turboman's jetpack to save his son. Jamie is delighted to discover his father is Turboman, and Myron is captured by police—before they take him away, though, Jamie gives the postman his Turboman doll, explaining that he doesn't need the doll because he has the real Turboman at home.

Hoping to trade on the warm, huggable image Schwarzenegger has cultivated with such popular films as TWINS (1988) and KINDERGARTEN COP (1990), the makers of JINGLE ALL THE WAY have instead delivered an empty, joyless film that confuses mayhem and physical violence with comedy. Numerous sets are trashed in hamfisted attempts at slapstick, including a painfully unfunny sequence in which Schwarzenegger chases a child through a mall playground. JINGLE ALL THE WAY's physical comedy makes Chris Columbus's similar orchestrations in 1990's HOME ALONE appear Chaplinesque by comparison. Also unpleasant is the palpable sense of desperation conveyed by the shopping parents; it is uncomfortable watching the hapless fathers flounder to make their kids happy. The film's most truthful moment comes in a monologue by Myron on the mania that merchandisers create for children's toys and their intimation that parents who fail to give their children these toys are inadequate. The script flirts with satirizing this topic but ultimately favors noise over nuance. Perhaps fearful of attention-challenged youngsters, director Brian Levant (whose style is best described as Ivan Reitman-lite) feels compelled to stack the film with cacaphonous set pieces that garner few laughs.

Of the stars, Hartman fares the best, yet he's done this character before, *ad nauseum.* Schwarzenegger's comedic skills rely heavily on his Teutonic mangling of dialogue and good-natured awkwardness, but his efforts here seem strained and insincere. Ah-nuld's shortcomings are negligible, however, in comparison to Sinbad's strident mailman (how original, a crazed postal worker!). In a career-threatening performance, the comedian shamelessly mugs for attention, ranting his lines at unintelligible speeds. Cartoonish Myron lacks the humanity that provokes audience sympathy; and it is this overall lack of real emotion that ultimately scuttles the entire film. Scenes that should resonate with warm holiday feeling come off plastic and over-merchandised—like Turboman himself. *(Violence, profanity.)* — D.G.

d, Brian Levant; p, Chris Columbus, Mark Radcliffe, Michael Barnathan; exec p, Richard Vane; assoc p, Paula DuPre', Warren Zide; co-p, Jennifer Blum, James Mulay; w, Randy Kornfield; ph, Victor J. Kemper; ed, Kent Beyda, Wilton Henderson; m, David Newman; prod d, Leslie McDonald; fx, Gregory L. McMurray; casting, Judy Taylor; cos, Jay Hurley

Comedy/Action **(PR: A MPAA: PG)**

JOE'S APARTMENT ★

(U.S.) 80m Roachco, Inc.; MTV Films; Geffen Pictures ~ Warner Bros. c

Jerry O'Connell *(Joe)*; Megan Ward *(Lily)*; Robert Vaughn *(Senator)*; Sheik Mahmud-Bey *(Vlad)*; Don Ho *(Alberto Bianco)*; Jim Sterling *(Jesus)*; Jim Turner *(Walter)*; David Huddleston *(P.I. Smith)*

Quick, get the Raid! MTV's first foray into feature filmmaking, JOE'S APARTMENT, comes full of bugs. This comedy about a bunch of singing and dancing cockroaches wants to be a modern-day GULLIVER'S TRAVELS, but winds up being a cinematic pest.

Joe (Jerry O'Connell) is a young man from Iowa who arrives in New York to start a life in the Big City. Joe gets an immediate taste of things to come when he is mugged the moment he steps off the bus that brought him to Manhattan. His luck seems to turn around when he stumbles upon a run-down but affordable apartment on Manhattan's Lower East Side. But Joe does not at first realize that the vicious landlord, Alberto Bianco (Don Ho), has hired two henchmen to chase out—or kill—all the tenants of the building so that the city can build a maximum-security prison on the site.

Fortunately, Joe acquires new friends in the forms of thousands of cockroaches who live in his apartment. Two of the insects, Ralph (the voice of Billy West) and Rodney (the voice of Reginald Hudlin) lead the others in preventing the hoodlums from taking over the apartment. Initially, Joe has qualms about sharing his space with the singing and dancing six-legged creatures, but he changes his tune after they help him win over Lily (Megan Ward), a city worker who dreams of converting a lot in Joe's slum neighborhood into a beautiful garden.

Unbeknownst to Joe and Lily, her father, Senator Dougherty (Robert Vaughn), is in cahoots with Bianco. Finally, however, with the help the roaches, Joe defeats the nasty landlord, and Lily gets her lush nursery.

Based on the short film of the same name, JOE'S APARTMENT might have worked as a dark comedy had the filmmakers used the roaches in a similar way to either the creepy CREEPSHOW (1982) episode starring E.G. Marshall or the infamous roach-assault sequence in PACIFIC HEIGHTS (1990). But instead, writer-director John Payson has chosen a style that crosses BEN, the execrable 1972 movie about a sickly boy and his trained rats, with the crude humor of a Troma flick (e.g. THE TOXIC AVENGER). Thus, a typical "gag" in this film finds Joe (the vacuous O'Connell) trying to impress Lily (the bland Ward) by collecting animal excrement for her garden. Other "highlights" include the roach's high-pitched singing of Kevin Wiest's "roach" tunes; plugs for MTV's "Beavis and Butt-head"; and a dated, unimaginative spoof of RAMBO (FIRST BLOOD, 1982). Youngsters are advised to check out the more charming animation-live action mix, TWILIGHT OF THE COCKROACHES (1990).

In the underwhelming supporting cast, Vaughn plays a senator who likes to wear women's undergarments, and Ho gets to wear Hawaiian shirts. It remains baffling why talented African-American director Hudlin signed up to dub the voice of one of the cockroaches, particularly since the film makes an unseemly and racist association between the insects and black culture (they sing a gospel number at one point).

Granted, a few of the computer-animated roaches are convincingly formed, and the film's running time is mercifully short at about 80 minutes. Still, JOE'S APARTMENT does nothing more than worsen the reputation of some much-maligned critters. *(Violence, profanity, sexual situations.)* — E.M.

d, John Payson; p, Diana Phillips, Bonni Lee; exec p, Abby Terkuhle, Judith McGrath, Griffin Dunne; w, John Payson; ph, Peter Deming; ed, Peter Frank; m, Carter Burwell; prod d, Carol Spier; art d, Ed Check; set d, Karin Wiesel; sound, Rosa Howell-Thornhill (mixer); fx, Michael Turoff, Chris Wedge, Blue Sky Productions; casting, Meg Simon; cos, Stephanie Maslansky

Comedy **(PR: C MPAA: PG-13)**

JOHN CARPENTER'S ESCAPE FROM L.A. ★★½

(U.S.) 102m Debra Hill Productions; Rysher Entertainment; Paramount ~ Paramount c

Kurt Russell *(Snake Plissken)*; A.J. Langer *(Utopia)*; Steve Buscemi *(Map to the Stars Eddie)*; George Corraface *(Cuervo Jones)*; Stacy Keach *(Malloy)*; Michelle Forbes *(Brazen)*; Pam Grier *(Hershe)*; Jeff Imada *(Saigon Shadow)*; Cliff Robertson *(President)*; Valeria Golino *(Taslima)*; Peter Fonda *(Pipeline)*; Ina Romeo *(Blonde Hooker)*; Peter Jason *(Duty Sergeant)*; Jordan Baker *(Police Anchor)*; Caroleen Feeney *(Woman on Freeway)*; Paul Bartel *(Congressman)*; Tom McNulty *(Com Officer)*; Bruce Campbell *(Surgeon General of Beverly Hills)*; Breckin Meyer *(Surfer)*; Robert Carradine *(Skinhead)*; Shelly Desai *(Cloaked Figure)*; Leland Orser *(Test Tube)*; Kathleen Blanchard *(Female Narrator)*; William Luduena *(Mescalito)*; Gabriel Castillo *(Mescalito)*; William Pena *(Jacket Mescalito)*; David Perrone *(U.S. Cleric Justice)*

After 15 years, Kurt Russell reprises his role of S. D. "Call me 'Snake'" Plissken in JOHN CARPENTER'S ESCAPE FROM L.A.. The film is called a sequel, but in reality it's a big-budget remake of John Carpenter's cult hit ESCAPE FROM NEW YORK (1981).

The year is 2013. The United States is a theocratic police state run by a "President for Life" (Cliff Robertson)—a cross between Pats Buchanan and Robertson. All "moral aberrants" are deported to the prison island of Los Angeles, separated from the mainland by an earthquake. War-hero-turned-outlaw Snake Plissken, who 16 years ago rescued a president from the Manhattan Island Penitentiary, gets an offer he can't refuse: LA's rebel chieftain, Cuervo Jones (George Corraface), has the controls to the US's Satellite Defense System, and Snake's been given just eight hours to retrieve those controls. His life and the future of the nation depend on his success.

Roaming rubble-strewn Santa Monica and Sunset Boulevards, Snake meets *uber*-surfer dude Pipeline (Peter Fonda) and weaselly Map to the Stars Eddie (Steve Buscemi), who want to be Snake's agents. In Beverly Hills, Snake and the beautiful Taslima (Valeria Golino) are captured by the deformed victims of repeated cosmetic surgeries who want to harvest the duo's body parts. Snake eventually falls into Cuervo's hands, and the Emperor Jones puts him on display in the LA Coliseum. With the help of an old partner in crime, transsexual Hershe Las Palmas (Pam Grier), Snake defeats Cuervo, and returns to the mainland just in the nick of time. As he did with the vital audio cassette after his escape from New York, Snake switches the CD in the SDS control with a fake; and after plunging the world into crisis again, he disappears into darkness.

ESCAPE FROM L.A. isn't just a remake with a change of locale; it's a complete refit and upgrade. ESCAPE FROM NEW YORK's wimpy, synth-pop score has been replaced with hard-driving rock by flavor-of-the-month bands. Gone are the cheesy, pre-ILM special effects. Every explosion—and there are lots of them—is pointlessly huge!

The problem is that, having seen the "ESCAPE FROM. . . " formula reworked over and over in films from RAMBO: FIRST BLOOD, PART 2 (1985) to DIE HARD (1988) to THE ROCK (1996), Carpenter, Russell, and producer Debra Hill, the trio who wrote the screenplay, couldn't resist placing their tongues squarely in their cheeks. By the time Snake surfs a tsunami down Wilshire and leaps from his board to catch Eddie's speeding convertible, ESCAPE FROM L.A. has gone so far over the top one can't take the stakes involved very seriously.

Some of what ESCAPE FROM L.A. aimed for was achieved better in DEMOLITION MAN (1993), where the humor meshed with a sunnier vision of LA's future. Here, the right black-comic tone is never struck to balance the lighthearted air with the bleakness of the film's atmosphere. *(Violence, profanity.)* — P.R.

d, John Carpenter; p, Debra Hill, Kurt Russell; w, John Carpenter, Debra Hill, Kurt Russell (based on characters created by John Carpenter and Nick Castle); ph, Gary B. Kibbe; ed, Edward A. Warschilka; m, Shirley Walker, John Carpenter; prod d, Lawrence G. Paull; art d, Bruce Crone; set d, Kathe Klopp; sound, Thomas Causey (mixer), John Pospisil (design); fx, Kimberly K. Nelson, Marty Bresin, Dale Ettema, Michael Lessa, Juliette Yager, Buena Vista Visual Effects; casting, Carrie Frazier; cos, Robin Michel Bush; makeup, Kandace Westmore, Rick Baker; stunts, Jeff Imada

Action/Science Fiction (PR: C MPAA: R)

JOHNNY CIEN PESOS

(SEE: JOHNNY 100 PESOS)

JOHNNY 100 PESOS ★★★★

(Chile/Mexico) 90m Catalina Cinema; Arauco Films; Vision Comunicaciones ~ August Entertainment/PWI/Patagonia Pictures c/bw
(JOHNNY CIEN PESOS)

Armando Araiza *(Johnny Garcia)*; Patricia Rivera *(Gloria)*; Willy Semler *(Freddy)*; Luis Gnecco *(Don Alfonso)*; Aldo Parodi *(Loco)*; Rodolfo Bravo *(Washington)*; Eugenio Morales *(Leo)*; Sergio Hernandez *(Mena Mendoza)*; Boris Quercia *(Parker)*; Paulina Urrutia *(Paty)*; Luis Alarcon *(Judge)*; Patricia Guzman *(Johnny's Mother)*; Cristian Campos *(Beaucheff)*; Jose Manuel Salcedo *(Baby)*; Aldo Bernales *(Rebolledo)*; Hugo Medina *(Professor)*; Gabriela Hernandez *(Custodian)*; Patricio Bunster *(Old Man)*; Claudio Viancos *(Carlos)*; Valeria Chignoli *(TV Announcer)*; Roberto Sancho *(Police Chief)*; Alfredo Ahumada *(Pilot)*; Agustin Iglesias *(Mobile TV Unit Driver)*; Max Marino *(Mobile TV Unit Technician)*; Helena Ahumada *(Judge's Secretary)*; Amaya Forch *(Ministry Secretary)*; Victor Mix *(Young Man in Ministry)*; Vittorio Yaconi *(Security Guard)*; Gabriel Aldunate *(Junior)*; Cesar Arredondo; Muriel Cornejo; Mares Gonzalez; Mario Bustos; Roberto Chignoli

Based on a true story of a bungled video-store heist in Santiago, this was Chile's entry for the 1994 Foreign Film Academy Award. It's not a perfect film, but it is a taut, powerful crime drama as well as a thought-provoking, tightly scripted view of how one media event can have a huge effect on a society. It's a better and more honest film than most of the fluffier European films that usually get notice from our Academy.

Under the cover of a video store, Don Alfonso runs an illegal money-exchange business. A gang of criminals breaks into the store. They don't know that Alfonso and the money are locked in a back room, so by the time they find it, the police and media have been alerted and surround the building. The criminals' only recourse, since they choose not to give up, is to take hostages.

Of all the criminals, the novice, 17-year-old schoolboy Johnny Garcia, gets the most attention. A TV crew interviews his mother, his teachers and his ex-girlfriend. The one female hostage, Glorita, takes a liking to him. He gives her some of the money and asks her to wait for him to finish his inevitable prison term.

Although Chile's newly elected democratic government wants the incident to be stopped, they tread lightly so as to prevent deaths of either hostages or criminals. Responding to continued pressure from the police, the criminals demand to be safely exiled to Cuba. Johnny's mother discovers that he's been a thief for a long time. A TV crew films her as she speaks to Johnny on the phone. She tells him that he deserves to go to jail. In anger and frustration, he shoots the television.

Knowing that their time is running out, the criminals begin to swallow the hostages' jewelry and coins. Breaking an earlier promise, Glorita tells Johnny she won't visit him in prison. The criminals free the hostages and allow themselves to be captured, but Johnny stays behind. Deathly afraid of prison, he shoots himself. He survives, and wakes up in an ambulance. The ambulance's window slats look like prison bars. He covers his face with a sheet to block out the light.

JOHNNY 100 PESOS starts out like a simple crime thriller, but develops in unexpected directions. It's a political allegory, an exploration of the media's role in Chile's society, and a tale of troubled youth. The depth of the writing is impressive, as are the writers' abilities to veer into several subplots without becoming confused or losing focus.

Johnny is a great protagonist—inexperienced and naive, with an innocent face, but also brash and energetic. Refreshingly, no psychological explanations are offered for his behavior. He simply became a criminal, and, due to his inexperience, his emotions get the better of him.

The video store and office (on the 8th floor of a downtown building) create a powerfully claustrophobic atmosphere, as does the camera work. As the other men taunt Johnny with tales of the realities of prison life, the camera closes in on his horror-stricken face. The suffocating presence of the media and police, constantly on the office TV, shouting up into the building, and milling about in the halls, builds suspense and contributes to the feeling of doom that surrounds Johnny.

JOHNNY 100 PESOS could have taken the easy way out and ended with a barrage of gunshots. Though the ending lacks action, its straightforward authenticity gives a stronger message:

life goes on, and we have to deal with the consequences of our actions. With the inclusion of the subplots about the media, the government, and Johnny's school, JOHNNY 100 PESOS shows that Chilean society is not much different from ours. In both places, much of what we do is driven by outside influences.

It's rare for a Chilean film to receive theatrical or video release in the US, and JOHNNY 100 PESOS did not attract much attention here. Nonetheless, it shows a universal theme in a unique circumstance and is an extremely welcome import. *(Extreme profanity, sexual situations, extensive nudity, violence.)* — A.M.

d, Gustavo Graef-Marino; p, Patricia Navarrete, Ignacio Prieto; exec p, Abdullah Ommidvar; w, Gustavo Graef-Marino, Gerardo Caceres; ph, Jose Luis Arredondo; ed, Danielle Fillios; m, Andres Pollak; art d, Juan Carlos Castillo; sound, Marcos De Aguirre (design, mixer), Gloria Loyola (mixer), Maria Teresa Bacigalupe, Nadine Boullieme, Roberto Espinoza, Freddy Gonzalez; fx, Roberto Sancho; casting, Blanca Esthela Limon; cos, Loreto Vuskovic; makeup, Constanza Racz

Crime/Drama/Thriller (PR: O MPAA: NR)

JOHNNY SHORTWAVE ★★½
(Canada) 92m Bockner-Boboras Productions bw

Emmanuel Mark *(Johnny Shortwave—John Howard Clayton)*; John Tench *(The Photographer)*; Mona Matteo *(Wilma Clayton)*; Dougie Richardson *(Cosmo Unitas)*; Jim Feather *(Vernon King)*; Rebecca Maynard *(Lotte the Pollster)*; Valerie Buhagiar *(Photographer's Wife)*; Doug O'Keeffe *(Interrogator #1)*; Robert Cotie *(Interrogator #2)*; Andy Dan *(Electrician)*; Gillian Stevie *(Hannah Clayton)*; Bernie Leon *(Deputy Minister)*; Paul Amato *(Recording Secretary)*; Peter Read *(Deputy Minister's Adjutant)*; Siria Jarvel *(Adjutant's Assistant)*; Allen Roy *(Arms Keeper)*; Lois Harrison *(Border Guide)*; Martin Bockner *(Pool Player)*; Peter Boboras *(Face of the Industrial Party)*

A spare and simple black–and–white film with some original visual style, JOHNNY SHORTWAVE attempts to be a futuristic parable in the vein of *1984* by addressing the threat of military-industrial domination. But its script isn't inventive enough to sustain interest.

In 1998, a corsortium of military and industrial leaders known as the Industrial Alliance has taken over Canada. The Industrial Alliance's economic and social policies have resulted in mass unemployment and homelessness. The government, having abolished the social safety net, disregards the needs of the populace and exploits the natural resources of Canada to increase its wealth. To help fight the power, mysterious rebel mouthpiece Johnny Shortwave (Emmanuel Mark) broadcasts inspirational radio messages to the Resistance Underground.

John Howard Clayton, aka Johnny Shortwave, is a be-stubbled, be-spectacled, handsome fanatic who composes his tracts on a manual typewriter and broadcasts on an old transmitter from an abandoned factory in the City-State of Toronto. After the Industrial Alliance discovers his hideout, they bug it. The Alliance hears everything when Shortwave is visited by his estranged wife Wilma (Mona Matteo). Wilma informs Shortwave that she has sent their daughter to the Freelands, where Resistance Underground members are fleeing to escape the increasingly repressive policies of the government. She implores Shortwave to join them there, but he refuses.

Shortwave discovers and destroys the bugs. As a result, an Industrial Alliance agent comes to his hideout and gives Shortwave the opportunity to save his own life by renouncing his messages on the air. Shortwave complies, but when he deviates from the prepared script, the agent shoots him. After the murder, a radio broadcast informs the public that both Canada and Mexico are becoming part of the United States.

JOHNNY SHORTWAVE uses an unusual mix of glamorous noir imagery (Shortwave's gadgets appealingly recall the 1940s) and gritty urban realism to create a menacing view of the near future. The film's political message is unsophisticated, but nonetheless hits close enough to home to be disturbing. Unfortunately, the power of that message is dampened by a one-note and predictable script. The performances are decent, but unmemorable. *(Violence.)* — N.Z.

d, Michael Bockner; p, Michael Bockner, Peter Boboras; exec p, Peter Boboras; assoc p, Audrey Colville-Reeves, Frank Caruso; w, Michael Bockner, Peter Boboras; ph, Rick Fester, Andreas Trauttmansdorff; ed, Michael Bockner; m, Joel Rosenbaum; set d, Wendy Robbins, Lesley Ann MacFadyen; sound, Max Sartor (recordist); fx, Peter Ferri; cos, Gudrun Heinze; makeup, Pra

Drama/Political/Fantasy (PR: C MPAA: NR)

JOSEPH CONRAD'S THE SECRET AGENT ★★
(U.K.) 94m Heyman/Hoskins Productions ~
Fox Searchlight c
(AKA: SECRET AGENT, THE)

Bob Hoskins *(Verloc)*; Patricia Arquette *(Winnie)*; Gerard Depardieu *(Ossipon)*; Robin Williams *(The Professor)*; Jim Broadbent *(Chief Inspector Heat)*; Christian Bale *(Stevie)*; Eddie Izzard *(Vladimir)*; Elizabeth Spriggs *(Winnie's Mother)*; Peter Vaughan *(The Driver)*; Julian Wadham *(The Assistant Commissioner)*; Roger Hammond *(Michaelis)*; Ralph Nossek *(Yundt)*; Neville Phillips *(Ticket Clerk)*

JOSEPH CONRAD'S THE SECRET AGENT is a dreary and pretentious adaptation of Conrad's 1907 novel about terrorism and anarchists in 1880s London.

Adolph Verloc (Bob Hoskins), a British shopkeeper who sells pornography on the side, lives with his young wife Winnie (Patricia Arquette) and her mentally retarded brother, Stevie (Christian Bale). Verloc holds meetings at his house for a group of political refugees and anarchists, including a Frenchman named Ossipon (Gerard Depardieu), but is secretly working as an agent provocateur for the Russians, reporting to them on the activities of the anarchists, as well as serving as an informant for the British police. Verloc's new contact at the Russian embassy orders him to instigate a series of incidents that will be blamed on terrorists, beginning with a bomb attack on the Greenwich Observatory. Verloc buys a bomb from a deranged bombmaker known as The Professor (Robin Williams), who keeps explosives wired to his body and a detonator in his pocket at all times. Verloc has Stevie unwittingly take the bomb to Greenwich Park, but Stevie trips and the bomb goes off, killing him.

A police detective discovers Stevie's name tag with Verloc's address on it at the crime scene, and goes to Verloc's home. Verloc admits what happened to Stevie, and Winnie overhears it. He tries to apologize to her, but she's horrified and packs her bags. As she's leaving, she picks up a carving knife and stabs him to death, then goes to Ossipon, and asks him to help her leave the country. They get all of Verloc's savings, and Ossipon buys Winnie a railroad ticket. He gets on the train with her, but as it pulls out of the station, he jumps off with all of her money. Later, while having drinks with The Professor, a remorseful Ossipon reads about the mysterious suicide of a woman matching Winnie's description who jumped off a ferry. The Professor leaves and walks through a crowded street, then puts his hand in his pocket and pulls out his bomb detonator.

Alfred Hitchcock's adaptation of Conrad's THE SECRET AGENT, filmed in 1936 as SABOTAGE (not to be confused with his later SABOTEUR, or his earlier film called THE SECRET AGENT, which was based on Somerset Maugham's "Ashenden"), updated the story to the 1930s, and made Verloc the proprietor of a movie house, as well as making Stevie a much younger boy. All of these changes increased the suspense and tension of the story, two qualities that writer-director Christopher Hampton seems to have studiously avoided. Faithfulness to the letter of a classic novel is not always enough, and neither is an authentically gloomy recreation of Victorian London, as Hampton proves in this drab and plodding adaptation. His solemnly reverent attitude to the novel drains the film of thrills and excitement. His attempt to treat the story as an existential meditation on the human cost of terrorism rings hollow because the characters are never more than one-dimensional figures.

The decision not to show Stevie's death but to reveal it through a series of fragmented flashbacks is a key tactical error, robbing the incident of shock and horror. While Hitchcock later told Francois Truffaut that he regretted showing the bombing because it angered the audience, the scene in SABOTAGE is a masterpiece of sweat-inducing tension, and is truly radical in its shattering of accepted dramatic norms. Hampton's approach may feel less exploitive, yet it ends up being much more manipulative and dishonest, culminating in an absurd shot of the boy's severed head resting in a tree. The ending, which intercuts Winnie on the ferry, Ossipon and the Professor in the bar, and Ossipon and Winnie on the train, also employs this self-defeating, elliptical technique, jumping back and forth in time until audience confusion turns to apathy.

Hampton simply doesn't have the cinematic finesse to pull off such a complicated style, and though he often borrows Hitchcock's trademark subjective point-of-view camera movements, he lacks the master's visual flair or sense of story construction. Hoskins gives a convincingly dour performance, but Arquette's British accent comes and goes, and an uncredited Williams (who's becoming the king of unbilled cameos), supposedly quietly chilling, comes off as self-conscious and campy. *(Violence, sexual situations.)* — M.S.

d, Christopher Hampton; p, Norma Heyman; exec p, Bob Hoskins; co-p, Christopher Hampton; w, Christopher Hampton (based on the novel by Joseph Conrad); ph, Denis Lenoir; ed, George Akers; m, Philip Glass; prod d, Caroline Amies; art d, Frank Walsh; sound, Peter Lindsay (mixer); casting, Janey Fothergil; cos, Anushia Nieradzik

Spy/Thriller **(PR: C MPAA: R)**

JOSH KIRBY ... TIME WARRIOR!: EGGS FROM 70,000,000 B.C. ★½

(U.S.) 93m Kushner-Locke; Moonbeam Entertainment ~ Paramount Home Video c

Corbin Allred *(Josh Kirby)*; Jennifer Burns *(Azabeth)*; Barrie Ingham *(Professor Irwin 1138)*; Derek Webster *(Zoetrope)*; Steve Wilder *(Akira Storm)*; Ilinca Goya *(Professor Goya)*; Gary Kasper *(Drednought)*; Carmen Lacatus *(Female Technician)*; Claudiu Trandifar *(Male Technician)*

Of all the entries in the home-video serial, this space-scramble bears the strongest resemblance to the series' model, STAR WARS (1977). For that derivative reason, this adventure may have marginally more appeal to the target audience of pre-teen sci-fi fans. Yet, like all JOSH KIRBY exploits, this film lacks the blissful ignorance of 1940s continued-next-week escapism. Instead, it's more like that dweeby Spielbergian wannabe, EXPLORERS (1985).

Racing against time while crisscrossing the constellations, Josh Kirby (Corbin Allred), Princess Azabeth (Jennifer Burns), Professor Irwin 1138 (Barrie Ingham), and their pet fuzzball, Prism, continue their search for missing pieces of the Nullifier device. Their mission to beat grasping Zoetrope (Derek Webster) in the Nullifier scavenger hunt is complicated by the onboard hatching of alien eggs from 70 million B.C.

Cuddly at first, the prehistoric gluttons soon take over the timepod, eating everything in sight. Crash-landing their disabled vehicle lets Azabeth rejoin her countrymen, led by Akira Storm (Steve Wilder). He has been scouring the universe for her while warding off the space enslaver Drednought (Gary Kasper). Splitting the ranks of her people, headstrong Azabeth takes the side of her Earthling companions after Akira imprisons them for safe-keeping.

With Drednought bombarding them mercilessly, Josh hits on a plot to rid them of the gobbling egg beasts and defeat Drednought. Pied-pipering the munching mini-monsters onto a space vehicle, Josh launches them toward Drednought, who believes he's capturing Akira. Unprepared for the hungry eggsters, Drednought beams down for a final duel, which he loses to Akira. Refusing to abandon her comrades in their mission to control mankind's destiny with the Nullifier, Azabeth resumes aiding Josh Kirby's time control spree.

THE NULLIFIER might be a good alternate title for this series, since it cancels out most forms of audience enjoyment—big–budget thrills, outrageous camp, thought-provoking sci-fi. But even if one can overlook the seams showing through the mise-en-scene and even if one can turn the other way as each JOSH KIRBY installment bears a cheesy similarity to its predecessor, one cannot make excuses for all those dialogue-laden scenes. They jam on the brakes for action buffs with speechifying about the commandments of Azabeth's Kang religion, Josh's time-bending contortions, and the twisted motivations of Nullifier-Bwana, Zoetrope. Talk, talk, talk.

Grownups who can shut out the sci-fi spacespeak will still suffer under the heavy combined hand of Irwin Allen and Sid and Marty Kroft, who seem to be the true inspiration for this series, a sort of Saturday morning live-action freak show at heart.— R.P.

d, Mark Manos; p, Vlad Paunescu, Oana Paunescu; exec p, Charles Band, Debra Dion; w, Patrick Clifton; ph, Viorel Sergovici; ed, Gregory Sanders; m, Reginald Powell, Richard Band; prod d, Colin De Rouin, Vali Calinascu; sound, Camil Silviu, Tiberiu Borcoman; fx, Boyd Lacrosse, Mark Rappaport; casting, Perry Bullington, Robert MacDonald; cos, Oana Paunescu, Michael Roche; makeup, Dana Busoiu; stunts, Ioan Albu

Children's/Fantasy/Science Fiction/Adventure **(PR: AA MPAA: PG)**

JOSH KIRBY ... TIME WARRIOR!: JOURNEY TO THE MAGIC CAVERN ★½

(U.S.) 93m Kushner-Locke; Moonbeam Entertainment ~ Paramount Home Video c

Corbin Allred *(Josh Kirby)*; Jennifer Burns *(Azabeth)*; Barrie Ingham *(Professor Irwin 1138)*; Derek Webster *(Zoetrope)*; Matt Winston *(Colonel Beauregard Damon)*; Nick De Gruccio *(Porcini)*; Cindy L. Sorenson *(Ding Dong)*; Michael Hagiwara *(Dr. Shitake)*; Lomax Study *(Lord Truffle)*; Mihai Niculescu *(Puff Ball)*

Part five of Charles Band's straight-to-video serial JOSH KIRBY. . . TIME WARRIOR! This has one neat plot twist near the end. But is reaching it worth the seven-and-a-half hours of tedious viewing?

Having lost their time machine in the last episode (JOSH KIRBY. . . TIME WARRIOR!: EGGS FROM 70,000,000 B.C.), the title teen (Corbin Allred) and his allies, Irwin 1138 (Barrie

Ingham) and Azabeth Siege (Jennifer Burns), still lack one component of the Nullifier, a powerful weapon scattered through time and space.

By using the nearly-complete Nullifier as a means of homing in on the absent piece, Josh and the gang teleport to a network of caves filled with a benign kingdom of whimsical mushroom people. Azabeth rashly takes a bite out of one and immediately falls ill. The antidote to the poison lies with a mushroom who was taken by a much-feared creature known as the Muncher.

Accompanied by a few brave 'shroom guides, the heroes embark on a quest through the network of caverns in search of the Muncher. It turns out to be a giant rodent-shaped machine controlled by Col. Beauregard Damon (Matt Winston), an impresario who has been rounding up 'shrooms and other oddities for his intergalactic circus. Irwin is able to turn the Colonel's own hypnotic ray against him, the captive 'shrooms recover from their trance, and Azabeth is cured.

But it doesn't end there, of course. This entry in the series, all shot in Romania, is simultaneously underplotted and overplotted, with the Magic Cavern and its campy 'shrooms—think the dancing fungi from FANTASIA (1940) doing schtick. One 'shroom is a William Shatner impressionist. There is also an aggravating detour in the main narrative about rival time-traveler Dr. Zoetrope (Derek Webster) trying to gain the Nullifier himself. When Zoetrope finally intervenes, he saves Josh's life, uncharacteristic behavior for such a villain. Then Zoetrope is ambushed, and the last Nullifier component is taken from him by a triumphant Irwin. The episode ends on the question of whether genial Irwin was the *real* bad guy all along, answered in the final chapter JOSH KIRBY. . . TIME WARRIOR!: LAST BATTLE FOR THE UNIVERSE.

The real problem throughout this saga is the 90-minute length of each installment. Each chapter is top-heavy with padding, pointless digressions, and loads of morale-building dialogue for the youngsters who are the intended viewers. This costs the filmmakers the forward momentum of their overarching story line.

Irwin's treachery is a real surprise, if a bit of a sour note for viewers who might have been rooting for him all along. But it comes too late to rescue this series from terminal, temporal anomie.— C.C.

d, Ernest Farino; p, Vlad Paunescu, Oana Paunescu; exec p, Charles Band, Debra Dion; w, Ethan Reiff, Cyrus Voris; ph, Viorel Sergovici; ed, Kate MacDonald; m, Reginald Powell, Richard Band; prod d, Colin De Rouin, Vali Calinascu; art d, Robert E. Lee; sound, Tiberiu Borcoman (mixer), Camil Silviu (mixer); fx, Boyd Lacrosse, Mark Rappaport; casting, Perry Bullington, Robert MacDonald; cos, Oana Paunescu; makeup, Dana Busoiu; stunts, Ioan Albu

Children's/Science Fiction/Fantasy/Adventure **(PR: AA MPAA: PG)**

JOSH KIRBY ... TIME WARRIOR!: LAST BATTLE FOR THE UNIVERSE ★½

(U.S./Romania) 90m Kushner-Locke; Moonbeam Entertainment ~ Paramount Home Video c

Corbin Allred *(Josh Kirby)*; Barrie Ingham *(Irwin 1138)*; Jennifer Burns *(Azabeth Siege)*; Derek Webster *(Dr. Zoetrope)*; Michael Mahon *(Mr. Kirby)*; Stacy Sullivan *(Mrs. Kirby)*; Charisma Carpenter *(Beth Sullivan)*; Johnny Green *(Duke)*; Helen Siff; Jonathan Charles Kaplan

This is the finale of a tiresome effort by low-budget producer Charles Band to revive the old-fashioned movie serial in the modern form of direct-to-video installments. But compared to its quicksilver ancestors of the 1930s and '40s (which wisely confined themselves to half-hour chapters or less), the JOSH KIRBY series is a bore—a real "serial" killer.

In the first five episodes, it was assumed that ordinary teenager Josh (Corbin Allred) had been swept up in adventures through time and space by 25th-century good-guy scientist Irwin 1138 (Barrie Ingham), in pursuit of the evil Dr. Zoetrope (Derek Webster), who was supposedly bent on destroying the universe once he assembled an alien device called the Nullifier. But, in truth, Zoetrope is a freedom fighter who invented the Nullifier to counter the Decimator, the actual doomsday gadget that allows a far-future dictator to rule Earth. Irwin is the tyrant's stooge, collecting Nullifier components from throughout time so he can scatter them again but do a better job of it. The tyrant goes back to his lab, leaving his duped allies marooned with Zoetrope.

But Josh has a rare genetic ability to manipulate time, and he, Zoetrope, alien creature Prism, and warrior girl Azabeth Siege (Jennifer Burns) try leaping to Josh's original hometown of Green Oaks just before he initially encountered Irwin. They land in the neighborhood 14 years too early, when Josh is just an infant.

Two Joshes in one place cancels out the teenage Josh's superpowers, so Zoetrope, Azabeth and Prism sacrifice themselves to propel Josh forward to 2420 to face Irwin. The boy induces Irwin's armor and weapons to rapidly age and decay, leaving the villain helpless when the heavily-fortified Zoetrope makes his entrance, but to save humanity, not threaten it.

When Josh awakens in his own bed, he treats everything that happened as a dream. But, at school, he meets Azabeth, incarnated in a tough new student who chases away the bullies tormenting him.

To quote from the previous episode, JOSH KIRBY. . . TIME WARRIOR!: JOURNEY TO THE MAGIC CAVERN: "Have courage Josh. The ordeal is almost over." There's a slight sense of BACK TO THE FUTURE (1985) and its sequels in Josh revisiting events from prior movies and seeing them in a whole new light. But there's even more useless padding of the story line to distend what should have been a brisk 40 minutes into a dull 90-minute feature.

The main extraneous subplot puts Josh in 1980, conveniently invisible, to muse mournfully over the ill-fated young mother he never knew. Meanwhile, Irwin 1138's flight through clips from the previous Josh Kirby chapters chews up additional screen time at no extra cost. The hero's confrontation with Irwin, despite grandiose billing as the "last battle for the universe," also is impressive only in its chintziness.

History may not remember the JOSH KIRBY. . . TIME WARRIOR! series along with such other noble, monumental follies as Erich Von Stroheim's seven-hour GREED (1924), David Lynch's five-hour original cut of DUNE (1984) or Abel Gance's never-filmed continuations of NAPOLEON. But an attempt was made to do something a little different, even if the filmmakers' approach doomed it from the start. *(Violence.)* — C.C.

d, Frank Arnold; p, Vlad Paunescu, Oana Paunescu; exec p, Charles Band, Debra Dion; w, Ethan Reiff, Cyrus Voris; ph, Vivi Dragan Vasile; ed, Bert Glatstein, Mary Ann Smith; m, Richard Band, Reginald Powell; prod d, Colin de Rouin, Vali Calinascu; fx, Mark Rappaport; casting, Robert MacDonald, Perry Bullington; cos, Oana Paunescu, Michael Roche

Children's/Science Fiction/Fantasy/Adventure **(PR: A MPAA: PG)**

JOSH KIRBY ... TIME WARRIOR!: TRAPPED ON TOY WORLD ★
(U.S.) 90m Kushner-Locke; Moonbeam Entertainment; ~ Paramount Home Video c

Corbin Allred *(Josh Kirby)*; Jennifer Burns *(Azabeth)*; Barrie Ingham *(Professor Irwin 1138)*; Derek Webster *(Zoetrope)*; Sharon Lee Jones *(Annie)*; Buck Kartalian *(Gepetto)*; J. P. Hubbell *(Action Jack)*; Lucian Cojocaru *(Theodore the Bear)*; Bogdan Voda *(Troll)*

This entry in producer Charles Band's six-episode made-for-home-video series is a gob of cotton candy that plays like the films featured in no-budget kiddie matinees from the '50s and '60s.

Time traveller Josh Kirby (Corbin Allred) searches once more for the Nullifier device but gets sidetracked by an unexpected descent into Toyworld. In this toy graveyard, the residents evince little interest in Josh's quest to beat Zoetrope (Derek Webster) to the Nullifier. While companions Azabeth (Jennifer Burns) and Professor Irwin 1138 desperately seek contact from their spaceship, Josh tries to marshal the cooperation of dancing bear Theodore (Lucian Cojocaru), human toymaker Gepetto (Buck Kartalian), and Rag Doll Annie (Sharon Lee Jones), who has a crush on Josh. Diametrically opposed to the saccharine tranquility of Toyworld, military play-figure Action Jack (J.P. Hubbell) eagerly paves the way for Zoetrope's aggressive demands.

After journeying with Josh through Nightmare Forest, Gepetto launches a full-scale (but non-lethal) counter-offensive against Zoetrope. Improvising with some radio parts, Josh communicates with his time travel cohorts while Action Jack tries to storm the Toy Bastille with reluctant troops. After Gepetto rescues Annie from Zoetrope, Josh reboards his just-landed space vehicle and flies off on another perilous time-jaunt.

In other JOSH KIRBY adventures, the helpless viewer merely had to fend off cheapjack special effects, drippy performances, and recycled story lines. But here, one is barraged by a meteor storm of cuteness, horrific production numbers, and moralistic gibberish, all proffered in the name of good clean family fun. But for whose family? One that could exist on a diet of jelly beans, Fruit Loops, and homemade jams put up by the Waltons? As the toy people sing their tuneless drivel, the viewer gets a sugar high that soars to toxic levels.

TRAPPED ON TOYWORLD, in short, is the sort of movie that militant family-values proponents deserve. *(Violence.)* — R.P.

d, Frank Arnold; p, Vlad Paunescu, Oana Paunescu; exec p, Charles Band, Debra Dion; w, Nick Paine; ph, Viorel Sergovici; ed, Gregory Sanders; m, Reginald Powell, Richard Band; prod d, Colin De Rouin, Vali Calinascu; art d, Robert E. Lee; sound, Tiberiu Borcoman; fx, Wendy Grossberg, Mark Rappaport; casting, Robert MacDonald, Perry Bullington; cos, Oana Paunescu, Michael Roche; makeup, Dana Busoiu; stunts, Dogu Doumitrescu

Children's/Science Fiction/Fantasy/Adventure **(PR: AA MPAA: PG)**

JOSHUA TREE
(SEE: WOMAN UNDONE, A)

JUDE ★★★
(U.K.) 123m Revolution Films ~ Gramercy Pictures c

Christopher Eccleston *(Jude Fawley)*; Kate Winslet *(Sue Bridehead)*; Liam Cunningham *(Richard Phillotson)*; Rachel Griffiths *(Arabella)*; June Whitfield *(Aunt Drusilla)*; Ross Colvin Turnbull *(Little Jude)*; James Daley *(Jude as a Boy)*; Berwick Kaler *(Farmer Troutham)*; Sean McKenzie *(1st Stonemason)*; Richard Albrecht *(2nd Stonemason)*; Caitlin Bossley *(Anny)*; Emma Turner *(Sarah)*; Lorraine Hilton *(Shopkeeper)*; James Nesbitt *(Uncle Joe)*; Mark Lambert *(Tinker Taylor)*; Paul Bown *(Uncle Jim)*; Amanda Ryan *(Gypsy Saleswoman)*; Vernon Dobtcheff *(Curator)*; David Tennant *(Drunken Undergraduate)*; Darren Tighe *(Punter)*; Paul Copley *(Mr. Willis)*; Ken Jones *(Mr. Biles)*; Roger Ashton Griffiths *(Auctioneer)*; Raymond Ross *(Old Man)*; Freda Dowie *(Elderly Landlady)*; Dexter Fletcher *(Priest)*; Moray Hunter *(Politician)*; Adrian Bower *(Blacksmith)*; Kerry Shale *(Showman)*; Billie Dee Roberts *(Little Sister)*; Chantel Neary *(Baby)*; James Scanlon *(Newborn Baby)*

Faithful *and* engaging as a film, JUDE is an adaptation of Thomas Hardy's classic novel, *Jude the Obscure.* Powerful performances, a rich atmosphere, and good writing make the film well worth the harrowing ordeal of this resilient story of love struggling against poverty and social injustice.

Young Jude Fawley (Ross Colvin Turnbull) dreams of escaping his impoverished country life through education. His schoolmaster, Phillotson (Liam Cunningham), advises him that the way out of his hometown of Marygreen begins at the university in nearby Christminster. Jude dutifully and diligently studies into his young adulthood.

As he matures, however, Jude (Christopher Eccleston) develops other interests. The most distracting is Arabella (Rachel Griffiths), the daughter of a local pig farmer. Arabella seduces the unsophisticated Jude in the squalid barn. Jude's Aunt Drusilla (June Whitfield)—his only family—warns him that the Fawleys aren't cut out for marriage, but Jude plows ahead anyway. No sooner has he married Arabella than she runs off to Australia.

Jude moves to Christminster, utterly dominated by the gothic university, and finds work as a stonemason, while continuing his studies. He locates his cousin, Sue Bridehead (Kate Winslet), and follows her without introducing himself. Previously, he has only seen her in a photograph in Aunt Drusilla's house. Later, she comes to visit him, and Jude is struck by her beauty and sophistication. He quickly falls in love with her.

When Sue loses her job, Jude tries to help her find a way to stay in Christminster. He takes her to meet his old schoolmaster, hoping that he will take her on as a teaching assistant. Phillotson has failed to get admitted to the university and is still only a schoolteacher. He finds work for Sue at his school, gradually falling in love with her as well. When Jude is rejected by the university despite his demonstrated learning, he moves back to Marygreen.

His obsessive love for Sue grows during their separation. When Sue writes to tell him that she and Phillotson have moved to Melchester and that she longs to see him, Jude packs immediately and moves there too. Reunited, they convey their feelings to each other openly, but when Jude tells Sue about his previous marriage to Arabella, she withdraws, hurt, and consents to marry Phillotson. Fresh from this disappointment, Jude unexpectedly runs into Arabella and winds up sleeping with her.

Jude returns to Marygreen to take care of his dying Aunt Drusilla. Sue arrives for the funeral and tells Jude that she is terribly unhappy with Phillotson. She later writes to Jude, who again rushes off to Melchester. Phillotson invites him to spend the night. He recognizes the bond of love between Sue and Jude, and he agrees to let Sue go.

Jude and Sue struggle to survive in several towns where they are repeatedly shunned, fired, and put out on the street because of their sinful union. One night, Jude runs into Arabella again. She informs Jude that she had a son by him, whom she can no longer care for. The boy, young Jude, arrives alone by ship from

Australia, and Sue and Jude agree to take him in. Soon they also have two children of their own.

The family returns to Christminster, where Jude finds work as a stonemason again. The struggle to survive takes its toll on the family, but at least Jude and Sue are together. Then one day, they return home to find that young Jude has smothered the babies and hanged himself, in a misguided effort to alleviate the family's poverty and hardship.

Sue withdraws from Jude again, screaming at him, "Your baby killed my babies!" Jude tries to sustain their love, but this final tragedy proves too much for them to bear.

From the opening shots in Marygreen, JUDE is bathed in the bleak light of an overcast sky, reminiscent of a hand-tinted black-and-white photograph, pale and washed out except for occasional blushes of muted color. The subtly modulated production design underscores Jude and Sue's ultimate inability to transcend the constraints that their society has placed upon them and their class. JUDE feels more contemporary than many of the films in the recent spate of period adaptations. This is partly due to the language (though in fact much of Hardy's dialogue is preserved in the script), and partly to the style of the camerawork and editing, which is more "athletic" than one expects. But the credit goes mostly to the direction and the performances from Eccleston, Winslet, Cunningham, and Griffiths, who "own" their dialogue and characters deeply and convincingly.

Any adaptation of a novel such as *Jude the Obscure* is likely to elicit accusations of infidelity and butchery from some corner, and no doubt JUDE falls short of the interior psychological complexity of Hardy. But JUDE ultimately adheres to the paramount virtues of the novel: its themes of social injustice and the collision of hope with destiny and reality. *(Adult situations, extensive nudity, sexual situations, graphic violence.)* — A.J.

d, Michael Winterbottom; p, Andrew Eaton; exec p, Stewart Till, Mark Shivas; assoc p, Sheila Fraser Milne; w, Hossein Amini (based on the novel *Jude the Obscure* by Thomas Hardy); ph, Eduardo Serra; ed, Trevor Waite; m, Adrian Johnston; prod d, Joseph Bennett; art d, Andrew Rothschild; set d, Judy Farr; sound, Martin Trevis (recordist); fx, John Markwell; casting, Simone Ireland, Vanessa Pereira; cos, Janty Yates; makeup, Amanda Warburton; stunts, Roy Alon

Drama **(PR: C MPAA: R)**

JUROR, THE ★★

(U.S.) 120m Winkler Films ~ Columbia c

Demi Moore *(Annie)*; Alec Baldwin *(Teacher)*; Joseph Gordon-Levitt *(Oliver)*; Anne Heche *(Juliet)*; James Gandolfini *(Eddie)*; Lindsay Crouse *(Tallow)*; Tony Lo Bianco *(Louie Boffano)*; Michael Constantine *(Judge Weitzel)*; Matt Craven *(Boone)*; Todd Susman *(Bozeman)*; Michael Rispoli *(Joseph Boffano)*; Julie Halston *(Inez)*; Frank Adonis *(DeCicco)*; Matthew Cowles *(Rodney)*; Polly Adams *(Forewoman)*; Jack Gilpin *(Accountant)*; Chuck Cooper *(Stockbroker)*; Charle Landry *(Musician)*; Tom Signorelli *(Locksmith)*; Frances Foster *(Housewife)*; Robin Moseley *(Matron)*; Rosemary De Angelis *(Mrs. Riggio)*; Joseph Perrino *(Thomas Riggio)*; James Michael McCauley *(Carew)*; William Hill *(Walters)*; Randy Jurgensen *(Court Clerk)*; Chuck Zito *(Frankie)*; Steve Santususso *(Dom)*; Peter Rini *(Archangelo)*; Gayle Scott *(Party Singer)*; Gary R. Wordham *(Flirting Intern)*; Anne Bobby *(Ticket Agent)*; Fiona Gallagher *(Ticket Agent)*; Luisa Huertas *(Car Rental Agent)*; Daniel Martinez *(Jeep Guy)*; Melissa Murray *(Lainie)*; Brett Barsky *(Jesse)*; Denise Burse *(Secretary)*; Jose Senteno *(Gold Tooth)*; Kalani Queypo *(Deer Dancer)*; Alejandro Garcia *(Deer Dancer)*; Rauol Morales *(Shooter)*; Marco Quezaza *(Shooter)*; Jose Jara *(Gunman)*; Al Cerullo Jr. *(Helicopter Pilot)*

THE JUROR jumbles the standard elements of the courtroom melodrama into a dissatisfying star vehicle for Demi Moore and Alec Baldwin. What might have been an eye-opening look into the systemic corruption of the American legal system turns into a stodgy "lady-in-distress" thriller.

The placid life of upstate New York artist and single mother, Annie Laird (Demi Moore), becomes a nightmare after she is selected for jury duty on the Boffano mob trial. "The Teacher" (Alec Baldwin), a mysterious mob figure, chooses Annie to ensure a hung jury by insisting on a not-guilty verdict for the accused mobster. Before the trial gets under way, the Teacher gets close to Annie by pretending to be an art collector, but soon she discovers his real purpose in meeting her: the Teacher tells her that her son, Oliver (Joseph Gordon-Levitt), will be harmed if she casts a guilty ballot.

During the trial, the Teacher surveys Annie and Oliver's every move, and threatens them whenever he suspects they are seeking help. He even romances Annie's best friend, Juliet (Anne Heche), a doctor, in order to maintain control of the situation. Meanwhile, Annie's fear for Oliver's life outweighs her concern for justice. When the Teacher realizes that Boffano (Tony Lo Bianco), his boss, would prefer an acquittal rather than a hung jury, he forces Annie to convince the other jurors to vote not guilty with her.

The eventual acquittal, however, does not end the Teacher's menace. Boffano's fear that Annie will work with Federal agents against the Family leads the Teacher to continue his threats against Oliver. Spurred on by the shocking murder of Juliet, Annie finally strikes back at the Teacher by reporting to Boffano on the Teacher's plans to take over the Family. As Boffano tries to "take out" the Teacher, however, the Teacher kills Boffano and his lead henchmen. As revenge on Annie for the betrayal, the Teacher then tracks down Oliver in Guatemala, where federal agents have hidden the boy. But the Teacher gets a deadly surprise visit from Annie during the cat-and-mouse hunt, leaving mother and son to finally get on with their lives.

In recent years, Moore has appeared in a series of morally offensive melodramas, including INDECENT PROPOSAL (1993) and DISCLOSURE (1994). Playing "strong" women has been Moore's sop to feminism, but, for the most part, these films have been outrageously sexist when not downright laughable, like THE SCARLET LETTER (1995). THE JUROR, an odious drama, gives Moore the chance to play Hollywood's favorite oxymoron—the feminist woman-in-jeopardy.

In the tradition of both THE SILENCE OF THE LAMBS (1991)—which Ted Tally also wrote—and WHAT'S LOVE GOT TO DO WITH IT? (1993)—which Brian Gibson also directed—THE JUROR puts a feisty, smart and strong-willed woman in a physically and mentally debilitating situation. There is no real difference between the high-pitched melodrama of THE JUROR and Pearl White being tied to the railroad tracks in those old silent pictures, except that White was a bit more subtle an actress than Moore, and the new film rationalizes the plight inflicted on our heroine through gimmicky plot twists. In the tradition of nearly all Hollywood films, THE JUROR even finds a way to execute the obligatory stars-kiss scene, although, thankfully, Annie and the Teacher never sleep together.

As if the film's embedded misogyny wasn't enough, THE JUROR also makes a mockery of the racially tense post-O.J. Simpson trial atmosphere by attributing the inflammatory line, "I don't understand the evidence. . . I don't need evidence, I know," to an elderly African-American woman juror. Such moments would not stand out so glaringly if THE JUROR offered any kind of fun—even Sidney Lumet's flawed but similar GUILTY AS SIN (1993) had an air of this-is-only-a-movie amusement. But THE JUROR is as grim and strident as its leading lady. At least Baldwin suggests a more complex characterization in his seductive psychopath, but he is left too often in the shadows—literally.

As a powerhouse actress-producer in Hollywood, Moore's art cannot disguise—or transcend—her questionable ideology. *(Violence, nudity, sexual situations, adult situations, substance abuse, extreme profanity.)* — E.M.

d, Brian Gibson; p, Irwin Winkler, Rob Cowan; exec p, Patrick McCormick; w, Ted Tally (based on the novel by George Dawes Green); ph, Jamie Anderson; ed, Robert Reitano; m, James Newton Howard; prod d, Jan Roelfs; art d, Charley Beal; set d, Leslie A. Pope; sound, Les Lazarowitz; fx, John Ottesen, Daniel Ottesen; casting, Louis DiGiaimo; cos, Colleen Atwood; makeup, Leslie Fuller; stunts, Phil Neilson

Thriller **(PR: C MPAA: R)**

JUST YOUR LUCK ★★½

(U.S.) 88m Propaganda; Global Entertainment Network ~ PolyGram Video c

Sean Patrick Flanery *(Ray)*; Virginia Madsen *(Kim)*; Ernie Hudson *(Willie)*; Alanna Ubach *(Angela)*; Vince Vaughn *(Barry)*; Jon Favreau *(Straker)*; Jon Polito *(Nick)*; Mike Starr *(Carl)*; Carroll Baker *(Mamie)*; John Lurie *(Coker)*; Flea *(Johnny)*; Bill Erwin *(Pops)*; Lee Weaver *(Wino)*

Despite an able cast and a promising premise, JUST YOUR LUCK is a Tarantino wannabe with all of the moves and none of the inspiration.

Late at night in a Manhattan diner, old Pops (Bill Erwin) bums a newspaper, discovers that he has won $6 million in the lottery—and dies of a heart attack. While the patrons and staff argue about what to do with the ticket, Straker (Jon Favreau), a horse player in debt to the mob, pulls a gun and demands the ticket. A scuffle ensues, and Straker is accidentally killed when he backs into a knife held by yuppie lawyer Ray (Sean Patrick Flanery). Ray and Nick (Jon Polito), the diner's owner, take the body away to dispose of it. After a few failed attempts, they decide to return to the diner and leave it in the dumpster.

Back in the diner, everything seems to be all right until Pops groans and they realize that he isn't dead yet. Lawyer Kim (Virginia Madsen), who sees her share of the money as a way out of the New York rat race, puts a plastic bag over Pops' head and suffocates him. They put the body in the dumpster.

Hoods Coker (John Lurie) and Johnny (Flea) arrive to collect money Straker owes their boss. Sensing tension, they learn what has happened and cut themselves in on the deal. Cops Carl (Mike Starr) and Barry (Vince Vaughn) also sense trouble when they stop in, and find Straker's body in the dumpster. As everyone is arrested, the lottery ticket winds up with crazy bag lady Mamie (Carroll Baker), who tears it up and eats it.

It's a testament to Quentin Tarantino's abilities as a director and (especially) a screenwriter that so many indie filmmakers have tried to imitate him and so few have pulled it off. These Tarantino manques usually feature an ensemble cast, hip music, and a cynical attitude, but the defining factor is the dialogue. Plot and characterization are an excuse for the writer to indulge in quirky exchanges of dialogue, whether or not they have anything to do with the ostensible story.

Tarantino himself does this kind of thing with great panache, which is why viewers let him get away with it: the dialogue is good enough to be an end in itself. Director Gary Auerbach and his co–scripter Todd Alcott, on the other hand, aren't quite as talented. Their characters are constantly starting promising exchanges, like cop Carl's theory that the city of New York, having been built in a single fifty-year period, will also crumble in a fifty-year period, but failing to spin them out.

JUST YOUR LUCK has an interesting story, but no real ending: everything erupts into chaos as the soundtrack is given over to an operatic aria, which not only obscures the dialogue but makes the film seem awfully pompous. The strong cast is all fine, and the viewer is left longing for the much better film this could have been. *(Violence, profanity.)* — M.F.

d, Gary Auerbach; p, Greg Cundiff; exec p, Stephen Gelber; assoc p, William Gilmore, Stan Bernstein, Melanie Luciano, Brian Lutz; w, Todd Alcott, Gary Auerbach (based on a story by Gary Auerbach); ph, Roberto Schaefer; ed, Larry Bock; m, Mark Sandman; prod d, Chuck Conner; art d, Chase Harlan; sound, Richard Davis; casting, Pamela Basker; cos, Nina Canter; makeup, Brigette Myre, Michael Tomasino

Crime/Thriller **(PR: C MPAA: R)**

JUSTICE WOMEN

(SEE: MIDNIGHT ANGEL)

KAMIKAZE TAXI ★★½
(Japan) 170m Pony Canyon Inc.; Right Vision Entertainment ~ Pony Canyon Inc. c

Takahashi Kazuya *(Tatsuo Minami)*; Koji Yakusho *(Tama)*; Kenishi Yajima *(Ishida)*; Mickey Curtis *(Animura)*; Keji Yakusho *(Kazumasa)*; Caesar Takeshi; Chika Nakagami; Miyako Takagi; Isako Saneyoshi

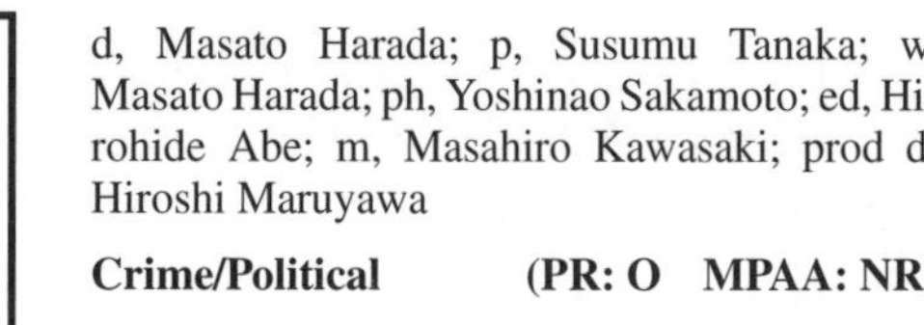

Overheard at a screening of KAMIKAZE TAXI: one audience member remarked to his date, "Now you know why editors win Oscars." Flabby extraneous scenes make this expose on Japanese society as ungainly as a 500-lb. sumo wrestler in a hammock.

Tatsuo (Takahashi Kazuya) is a rising hoodlum in a Tokyo *yakuza* mob, but he's disgusted by the corruption he sees when the syndicate introduces him to their political patron Ishida (Kenishi Yajima), a member of the Diet and a former kamikaze pilot who whitewashes Japanese war atrocities, and in private sadistically beats the high-class prostitutes Tatsuo delivers. When one girl is murdered, Tatsuo and friends impulsively decide to get even by stealing $2 million in mob money from Ishida's safe. The *yakuza* old guard are outraged by the betrayal and pitilessly hunt down and execute the novice thieves. Only Tatsuo escapes, thanks mainly to hulking, illiterate, but serenely wise cab driver Kazumasa (Keji Yakusho), one of many recent arrivals from the Japanese-descended peasant community in Peru. Evolving from hostage to chauffeur to true pal, Kazumasa helps Tatsuo evade pursuit, then takes his wounded fare to a secluded self-improvement resort to recover. Although it's suicide, Tatsuo insists on going back to kill Animaru (Mickey Curtis), his erstwhile boss. Sure enough, he's gunned down immediately. Kazumasa, instead of taking the $2 million and walking away, completes Tatsuo's mission. With jungle stealth, he sweeps through Ishida's compound, slaying the politician and all his *yakuza* lackeys.

A documentary-style opening explains that KAMIKAZE TAXI was filmed from April to May 1994 and underscores the scandals that rocked Japan in that period, from corruption in the Diet to racism against foreign-born citizens (Peruvian immigrants in particular) to the apocalyptic "Supreme Truth" religious cult that released poison gas in the Tokyo subway. Writer-director Masato Harada, a US-educated former film critic and journalist, explores a catalogue of Japanese social ills, but doesn't know when to quit. After a frenetic start (Tatsuo and his cohorts romp around, literally, like a pack of frisky puppies), KAMIKAZE TAXI idles for an unbearably tedious stopover at the self-improvement spa. In sequences that seem to go on forever, Tatsuo, Kazumasa, assorted salarymen, and a Charlie Chaplin mime (!) perform confidence-building exercises, hold pillow fights, and bond all around. The sessions build to Kazumasa's emotional monologue about his home village back in Peru laid waste by fanatical Maoist guerillas—a history that shames the self-absorbed sophisticates listening in. Vital as that payoff is, it doesn't justify the full hour's worth of footage that precedes it. As Animaru lies dying at the end, he asks who Kazumasa is and why he's done this. The big guy begins politely retelling his life story, and for a moment the viewer fears that indeed Harada will keep his camera running and recap the whole yarn all over again. He doesn't. Whew! KAMIKAZE TAXI should be memorable for its righteous anger, cross-cultural tapestry, and well-acted characters, but the massive cinematic indulgence obscures more passionate concerns. *(Violence, sexual situations, adult situations, substance abuse, profanity, nudity.)* — C.C.

d, Masato Harada; p, Susumu Tanaka; w, Masato Harada; ph, Yoshinao Sakamoto; ed, Hirohide Abe; m, Masahiro Kawasaki; prod d, Hiroshi Maruyawa

Crime/Political **(PR: O MPAA: NR)**

KANSAS CITY ★★★½
(U.S.) 110m Sandcastle 5; CiBy 2000 ~ Fine Line c

Jennifer Jason Leigh *(Blondie O'Hara)*; Miranda Richardson *(Carolyn Stilton)*; Harry Belafonte *(Seldom Seen)*; Michael Murphy *(Henry Stilton)*; Dermot Mulroney *(Johnny O'Hara)*; Steve Buscemi *(Johnny Flynn)*; Brooke Smith *(Babe Flynn)*; Jane Adams *(Nettie Bolt)*; Jeff Feringa *(Addie Parker)*; A.C. Smith *(Sheepshan Red)*; Martin Martin *("Blue" Green)*; Albert J. Burnes *(Charlie Parker)*; Ajia Mignon Johnson *(Pearl Cummings)*; James Carter; Craig Handy; David Murray; Joshua Redman; Jesse Davis; David "Fathead" Newman Jr.; Don Byron; Olu Dara; Nicholas Payton; James Zollar; Curtis Fowlkes; Clark Gayton; Victor Lewis; Geri Allen; Cyrus Chestnut; Ron Carter; Christian McBride; Tyrone Clark; Russell Malone; Mark Whitfield; Kevin Mahogany *(Hey Hey Club Musicians)*

Robert Altman's hometown of Kansas City, MO is the setting for this atmospheric period piece about a hopelessly misconceived kidnapping. As always with Altman, the milieu is richly textured, and the characters' weaknesses inform the story line.

Expecting her manicurist for a home appointment, Carolyn Stilton (Miranda Richardson) is surprised by a substitute—a tough-talking brunette who calls herself Blondie (Jennifer Jason Leigh) and has come to kidnap her. Blondie has chosen to abduct "Carol" (as she is known) in order to force Carol's husband, presidential advisor Henry Stilton (Michael Murphy), to help her out of a jam. Blondie's hoodlum husband, Johnny O'Hara (Dermot Mulroney), has foolishly robbed Sheepshan (A.C. Smith), a high-rolling gambler who had come to town to visit the Hey Hey Club, run by ruthless gangster Seldom Seen (Harry Belafonte). Infuriated by the robbery, Seldom holds Johnny and his accomplice, cabbie "Blue" Green (Martin Martin), hostage, intending to kill them. Blondie brings the laudanum-addicted Carol to the local train station, where Blondie works at the Western Union office. Blondie sends Stilton a wire notifying him of the kidnapping and demanding that he intercede with Seldom and have Johnny freed. Stilton calls the governor to request his help. In the meantime, Seldom has Blue stabbed to death.

The next morning, Election Day, Blondie takes Carol to a bar owned by her brother-in-law, Johnny (Steve Buscemi), who is rounding up men to vote illegally. Blondie next drags Carol to the home of the train station cleaning woman, Addie Parker (Jeff Feringa). There, the two women encounter a pregnant teen whom they drop off at a halfway house. The final stop on their itinerary is Blondie's house, where she plans to wait for Johnny to be delivered by Stilton. As time ticks away, Johnny makes an earnest pitch to Seldom, saying that he's eager to work for him.

With Carol's assistance, Blondie dyes her hair blonde to resemble her heroine, Jean Harlow. Johnny finally arrives, but quickly dies; his belly has been cut open. Blondie panics, screaming for Carol to help her. Carol puts her out of her misery by shooting her in the head. Carol walks out of the house and joins Stilton, who is waiting outside in a car.

After a trio of densely-populated "tapestry" films that placed him back in the Hollywood mainstream (THE PLAYER, SHORT CUTS, READY TO WEAR), Altman reaffirms his status as a master storyteller with this small, dark character study.

While keeping the focus on two closely related plot strands—Blondie's abduction of Carol, and Seldom's intimidation of Johnny—Altman and co-scripter Frank Barhydt (SHORT CUTS) supply vivid period detail spotlighting various early 1930s phenomena: the consolidation of jazz styles; the corrupt political "machines" that ran certain cities; and rabid movie fandom. But the film's central theme is one that Altman has explored in most of his major works from MCCABE AND MRS. MILLER (1971) to SHORT CUTS (1993): the instability of love relationships. Blondie would clearly do anything for Johnny, whom Altman and Barhydt depict as a self-centered creep. Carol, on the other hand, clearly recognizes that her relationship with Henry is a loveless one and seems genuinely perplexed by the lengths Blondie has gone to in order to free her man. Blondie's self-delusion blinds her to the danger that her acts could produce; Carol's clarity of vision forces her to seek an escape through drugs (much like Julie Christie's Mrs. Miller did in MCCABE).

Altman labeled the film a "jazz memory" and made sure to set the action against an all-night jam session at Seldom's club. The participants are real figures from the period (Lester Young, Count Basie), interpreted by noted musicians of the 1990s. Surprisingly, given its central placement in the film, the music is only a backdrop—a fact that infuriated jazz purists, but seems understandable in light of the dreamlike progression of the story line and the fact that Altman has used musical performances as counterpoint in his past work (CALIFORNIA SPLIT, SHORT CUTS, NASHVILLE).

Altman's strong point is his direction of actors, and KANSAS CITY offers three excellent lead performances. Jennifer Jason Leigh delivers another extraordinarily nuanced turn as the hard-boiled Blondie. Celebrated for her chameleon-like ability to disappear into a role, Leigh extracts qualities from the character that make her final fate all the more touching. Richardson supplies a nice balance as the socially proper but very stoned Carol. And offering the film a strong backbone, Belafonte is superlative as the ominously verbose Seldom. The singer does such an incredible job here that one wishes he had devoted himself more fully to acting in the period since his brilliant work in such 1950s films as ODDS AGAINST TOMORROW. *(Violence, substance abuse, profanity.)* — E.G.

d, Robert Altman; p, Robert Altman; exec p, Scott Bushnell; assoc p, James McLindon; co-p, Matthew Seig, David C. Thomas; w, Robert Altman, Frank Barhydt; ph, Oliver Stapleton; ed, Geraldine Peroni; m, Hal Willner; prod d, Stephen Altman; art d, Richard L. Johnson; set d, Susan J. Emschwiller; sound, John Pritchett; casting, Elisabeth Leustig; cos, Dona Granata

Crime/Drama **(PR: C MPAA: R)**

KASPAR HAUSER ★★★

(Germany) 137m Multimedia Munchen; Bayerischer Rundfunk; Westdeutscher Rundfunk; Osterreichischer Rundfunk Fernsehen; Sveriges TV; ARTE; Telepool; Bayerischen Filmforderung der Landesanstadtafar Aufbaufarderung ~ Leisure Time Features C (VERBRECHEN AM SEELENLEBEN EINES MENSCHENS)

Andre Eisermann *(Kaspar Hauser)*; Udo Samel *(Tutor Daumer)*; Jeremy Clyde *(Lord Stanhope)*; Katharina Thalbach *(Grafin Hochberg)*; Cecile Paoli *(Stefanie von Baden)*; Hansa Czypionka *(Hennenhofer)*; Hermann Beyer *(Anselm Ritter von Feuerbach)*; Dieter Mann *(Baron Wedel)*; Johannes Silberschneider *(Tutor Meyer)*; Peter Lohmeyer *(Leopold von Baden)*; Tilo Nest *(Karl von Baden)*; Dieter Laser *(Ludwig I. von Bayern)*; Uwe Ochsenknecht *(Ludwig von Baden)*; Anja Schiller *(Sophie von Baden)*; Gerd Lohmeyer *(Blochmann)*; Franz Baumgartner *("Mann")*; Valerie Vail *(Dalbonne)*; Jan Skvar *(Kaspar as a boy)*; Oldrich Vlach *(Burgermeister Binder)*; Jennifer Chamberlain *(Eleonore)*; Ladislav Kreemer *(Zentner)*; Oldrich Slavik *(Medizinalrat)*; Eva Zabelicka *(Mother Daumer)*; Jiff Schmitzer *(Anton)*; Jan Kehar *(Polizeisoldat)*; Milan Vagner *(Vorstecher Appellationsgericht)*; Barbara Lukesov *(Josephine)*; Vaclav Mares *(Von Beerstett)*; Oldrich Bartik; Dana Bartunkova; Katerina Brozova; Milan Charvat; Jaroslav Durek; Alice Dvorakova; Milan Findejs; Karel Habl; Stanislav Hajek; Karel Hlusicka; Karel Huraib; Gabriela Jeskova; Josef Jurasek; Lubomir Kostelka; Vaclav Kozibraska; Jan Kucera; Vaclav Legner; Jiri Lir

Peter Sehr's KASPAR HAUSER is a powerful and absorbing, if overlong and complicated, account of the life of one of Europe's most mysterious legends, the "wild child" who was born into royalty but kept locked in a dungeon for 12 years.

1812 Germany. Stefanie von Baden (Cecile Paoli), the wife of Karl von Baden (Tilo Nest), head of the Royal House of Baden, gives birth to Kaspar, who will become the new Crown Prince. However, scheming Countess Hochberg (Katharina Thalbach) kidnaps the baby and substitutes a servant's sickly baby who soon dies. Hochberg spirits Kaspar away to use as a pawn to advance her own political ambitions. Karl is poisoned by his brother Ludwig von Baden (Uwe Ochsenknecht) so he can assume the throne. Kaspar is kept in South Baden, then moved to Hungary until the age of four, then sold to the Bavarians, archrivals of the House of Baden, who want a part of Baden returned to them. For 12 years, Kaspar is kept chained in a dungeon while the Bavarians use him as a pawn to try to get their land back.

In 1828, Kaspar is freed from captivity and released by the Bavarians in Nuremberg, barely able to walk or talk. He's taken into custody and becomes a cause celebre, going to live with Professor Daumer (Udo Samel), who becomes his tutor and mentor, and tries to piece together his past, based on dreams and foggy memories. News of Kaspar's reappearance reaches Ludwig, and he sends an officer to kill him, but the assassination attempt fails.

A decadent English aristocrat named Lord Stanhope (Jeremy Clyde) befriends Kaspar and becomes his father figure, providing him with luxuries as well as physical affection. But he's actually working for Countess Hochberg, and abandons Kaspar after promising to take him to England. Meanwhile, Kaspar's mother learns of his existence, but refuses to acknowledge him, fearing it would create a family scandal. In 1883, a man who promises to tell Kaspar who his real parents are lures him into the countryside and stabs him to death. Kaspar is buried at the age of 21, with an epithet on his tombstone reading: "Here lies Kaspar Hauser, enigma of his age, of undiscovered origin, mysterious his death."

The legend of Kaspar Hauser has inspired more than 2,000 books in Europe, and of course, Werner Herzog's visionary 1974 classic, EVERY MAN FOR HIMSELF AND GOD AGAINST ALL (aka: THE MYSTERY OF KASPAR HAUSER), which focused on the existential clash between Hauser's primitive innocence and the harsh reality of "civilization." In KASPAR HAUSER, director Sehr takes a conspiracy theory approach to the story, positing as fact that Hauser did indeed have royal lineage and was kidnapped as part of an elaborate Machiavellian plot. (An addendum to the credits states that even in 1993, the House of Baden still keeps all records regarding the case under lock and key.) The film is also much more of an opulent, historical epic than Herzog's film, detailing the internecine court intrigue, which while occasionally confusing is always fascinating.

The sadistic cruelty of Kaspar's enemies is often heartbreaking and quite difficult to watch, as when 4-year-old Kaspar is locked up in the darkened dungeon with only a toy horse to play with. In a particularly notorious scene, a cold-blooded officer with a Hitler-mustache insures that the substituted servant's infant will die by holding him upside down and brutally whacking him in the head. Sehr claimed that his intention was to draw analogies to Auschwitz and "demonstrate to the German people something in themselves that they know is there, and they don't want to see."

Despite the controversy caused by this scene, the film won the German Film Prize (an equivalent to the Oscars) for Best Film, Director and Actor (Andre Eisermann). Eisermann, the son of circus performers, is quite effective as Kaspar, both physically and emotionally. Sehr's direction is straightforward and uncluttered, allowing the incredible "facts" of the story to speak for themselves. Made in 1993, the film was shown in Europe in a 178–minute version. *(Violence, sexual situations, adult situations.)* — M.S.

d, Peter Sehr; p, Andreas Meyer; w, Peter Sehr; ph, Gernot Roll; ed, Heidi Handorf, Susanne Hartmann; art d, O. Jochen Schmidt, Karel Vacek; sound, Hamo Hayder, Rainer Carben (mixer); fx, Heinz Ludwig; casting, Sabine Schroth; cos, Diemut Remy; makeup, Helga Sander, Mia Schopke

Drama/Biography/Historical (PR: O MPAA: NR)

KAZAAM ★½

(U.S.) 93m Polygram; Interscope Communications; Touchstone Pictures ~ Buena Vista c

Shaquille O'Neal *(Kazaam)*; Francis Capra *(Max)*; Ally Walker *(Alice)*; Marshall Manesh *(Malik)*; James Acheson *(Nick)*; Fawn Reed *(Asia Moon)*; John Costelloe *(Travis)*; Joanne Hart *(Mrs. Duke)*; Brandon Durand *(Vasquez)*; Wade J. Robson *(Elito)*; Jake Glaser *(Jake)*; Efren Ramirez *(Carlos)*; Jonathan Carrasco *(Z-Dog)*; Jesse Perez *(Vasquez's Sidekick)*; Todd Sible *(Engineer Ed)*; Juan "Rambo" Reynoso *(Hassem)*; Anthony Ferar *(El-Baz)*; Randall Bosley *(Foad)*; Steve Barr *(Spam)*; Deidra "Spin" Roper *(Spinderella)*; Kashi Barrett; Eboni Parson; Iris Burruss; Shawntae Harris *(Da Brat)*; Nicole Jackson *(Da Brat's Assistant)*; Altameza Reeves; Sandra Chriss; Shana Renee *(The Kazettes)*; Davidson King *(Rasta Singer)*; Deborah Rennard *(Malik's Dinner Mate)*; Kelly Duncan *(Cindi)*; Bob Clendenin *(Stage Manager)*; Eugene McCarthy *(Kitchen Worker #1)*; Jeffrey Paul Johnson *(Kitchen Worker #2)*; Brad Wilson *(Club Curmudgeon)*; Miguel Escobar *(Additional Gang Kid)*; Hector Jimenez *(Additional Gang Kid)*; Michael Wajacs *(Truck Driver)*; Rory Leidelmeyer *(Bouncer)*; Charles E. Bennett *(Roadie)*; Larry Clardy *(Fireman)*

Arguably a magician on the basketball court, Shaquille O'Neal (who has appeared in 1994's BLUE CHIPS and has occasionally turned his attention to playing in the NBA) is supposed to be a jovial genie in this overproduced, under-written comedy. Perhaps O'Neal should not give up his day job just yet.

Max (Francis Capra) is a bright but alienated 12-year-old deep in the adolescent blues. Not only is he regularly beaten up in school, but his divorcee mom Alice (Ally Walker) is contemplating marriage with the unacceptable Travis (John Costelloe). His luck turns, of course, when he accidentally frees the 7'2" genie Kazaam (O'Neal) from inside an old boom box.

Wise to the ways of the streets, Max at first doesn't believe Kazaam when the genie offers him the requisite three wishes. Unfortunately, Kazaam's miracle-making skills are rusty after his long confinement; he only gets back on track when he makes a cloudburst of french fries, jelly beans, and candy bars.

What the boy needs most, naturally, is a friend. Max, therefore, delays making his last two wishes, and enlists Kazaam in helping him track down his father (James Acheson), who turns out to be a crook in the service of unscrupulous record pirate Malik (Marshall Manesh). Observing Max and Kazaam around the studio, Malik figures out that Kazaam is a genie and attempts to steal the magic boom box. Max is killed, and in a rage, Kazaam disposes of Malik and brings the boy back to life—despite the fact that he is a purely materialistic genie, and "doesn't do ethereal stuff." Kazaam is at last freed from his bondage in the boom box and Max learns to respect his mother and accept his future stepfather.

The screenplay by Christian Ford and Roger Soffer is not much more interesting than an "Afterschool Special," padded with several million dollars' worth of special effects. Though KAZAAM is supposed to be fantastical, director Paul Michael Glaser proved more creative with his action satire THE RUNNING MAN (1987). Nor was there much chance the brooding, pubescent character of Max was going to give the film much of a lift.

The lift, of course, was supposed to be supplied by O'Neal. To his credit, he doesn't embarrass himself here: he knows that his bulk can be a comedic asset (though he doesn't quite know how to use it yet), and he just may possess more natural acting talent than some other more successful athletes-turned-movie stars (Arnold Schwarzenegger, for one). The film is sunk anyway by Ford and Soffer's threadbare story line, combined with Shaquille's penchant for truly miserable rap riffs, including the gem: "I experienced my academia / In Upper Mesopotamia / But nothing is more major / Than my studies in Asia." Shaq may have the skills to pay the bills, but no dunk will save this skunk. *(Violence.)* — N.N.

d, Paul Michael Glaser; p, Scott Kroopf, Paul Michael Glaser, Bob Engelman; exec p, Ted Field, Robert W. Cort, Leonard Armato, Shaquille O'Neal; w, Christian Ford, Roger Soffer (from a story by Paul Michael Glaser); ph, Charles Minsky; ed, Michael E. Polakow; m, Christopher Tyng; prod d, Donald Burt; art d, Mick Strawn; set d, Kate Sullivan; sound, Robert Janiger (mixer), Lance Brown (design), Victor Iorillo (design); fx, Charles Gibson, Ron Trost, Class A Special Effects, Ed Lee, Rhythm & Hues Studios, Jacquie Barnbrook, Chad Merriam; casting, Dianne Crittenden; cos, Hope Hanafin; makeup, Michael "Mic" Tomasino; stunts, Jeff Imada

Children's/Fantasy/Comedy (PR: AA MPAA: PG)

KIDS IN THE HALL: BRAIN CANDY ★★½

(U.S.) 89m Lakeshore Entertainment; Paramount ~ Paramount c

David Foley *(Marv/Psychiatrist/New Guy/Raymond)*; Bruce McCulloch *(Alice/Cisco/Grivo/Worm Pill Scientist/Cop #2/Cancer Boy/White Trash Man)*; Kevin McDonald *(Chris/Chris' Dad/Doreen/Lacey)*; Mark McKinney *(Simon/Don Roritor/Cabbie/Gunter/Cop #1/Nina Bedford/Melanie/Drill Sergeant/White Trash Woman)*; Scott Thompson *(Baxter/Mrs. Hurdicure/Wally/Malek/The Queen/Scientist Phil/Raj/Clemptor)*; Kathryn Greenwood *(Ginny)*; Amy Smith *(Raymond's Kid)*; Lachlan Murdoch *(Raymond's Kid)*; Nicole deBoer *(Groupie)*; Krista Bridges *(Groupie)*; Christopher Redman *(Wally's Son)*; Erica Lancaster *(Wally's Daughter)*; Jackie Harris *(Natalie)*; Jonathan Wilson *(Panicky Assistant)*; Tony Ning *(Mai Tai Waiter)*; Jason Barr *(Young Chris)*; Jack Jessop *(Old Man in Audience)*; Sharon Dyer *(Woman in Audience)*; Diane Flacks *(Tom Jones Girl)*; Barbara Lynn Redpath; Jason D'Addario; Carrie Betker; Elijah R. Brown; Trenton Howe; Pat Patterson;

Kay Hawtrey *(Wally's Neighbors)*; Luciano Casimiri *(Doorman)*; Janeane Garofalo *(Woman at Party)*; Adam Reid *(Scarred Teenager)*; Larry Mannell; Donald Tripe; Kirsten Johnson; Lindsay Leese *(Scientists)*; Andy Jones *(Monkey Scientist)*; Thom Bell *(Old Man in Pie)*; Eric Tunney *(Wally's Lover)*; Ann Holloway *(Disco Woman)*; Amanda Payton Stewart *(Young Disco Woman)*; Sherry Hilliard *(Coma Queen)*; Jenni Soosar *(Runner-up)*; Ingrid Hart *(Runner-up)*; Jared Wall *(Miguel)*; Paul Bellini *(Himself)*

When the Canadian comedy troupe Kids in the Hall—David Foley, Bruce McCullough, Kevin McDonald, Mark McKinney, and Scott Thompson—ended their TV show in 1994, it was partly to move into movies. Unfortunately, like many talented sketch comedians, the Kids' talents don't work as well in a feature format, though BRAIN CANDY is not without its high points.

Don Roritor (McKinney), CEO of Roritori Pharmaceuticals, is desperate for a new top-selling drug. When he questions research scientist Dr. Chris Cooper (McDonald) about his work, Cooper reports that his team has had some success with a new drug to treat chronic depression. The drug works by locating a patient's happiest memory and then mimicking the sensations it produced. Afraid of losing his funding, Cooper tells the board of directors what they want to hear, that the drug is ready to be sold, even though it needs more testing.

"Gleemonex," as it is named by marketing genius Cisco (McCullough), is a huge hit, outselling even penicillin in its first month. Crime and tourism plummet. Among those helped by Gleemonex are rock star Grivo (McCullough), who forsakes his gloomy metal tirades for a folky hit, "Happiness Pie"; Mrs. Hurdicure (Thompson), a lonely old lady who finds a new career as a nude figure model; and Wally (Thompson), a gay man in denial deeper than the Cayman Trough. The only unhappy person is Dr. Cooper, and even he learns to lighten up when Cisco's marketing makes him a media celebrity.

Sales are so great that Don applies for, and gets, non-prescription status for Gleemonex. But a downside appears when the drug's users start going into comas. Dr. Cooper calls a press conference to alert the world, but Don and his minion Marv (Foley) pre-empt him by turning it into a PR event to promote the comas as a desirable benefit of Gleemonex use. The few journalists listening to Dr. Cooper are lured away when Marv offers them free food. Dr. Cooper tricks both Don and Marv into taking the drug, then goes underground with his research team to work on a cure. In the meantime, millions of people refuse to give up the drug—instead, they hold parades to celebrate the comatose.

During their five-year run on television, the Kids were often compared to Britain's legendary sketch comedy troupe, Monty Python's Flying Circus. The Kids clearly hoped to repeat the Pythons' successful transition into movies; the tactic of using a simple plot upon which to hang a series of sketches (featuring each of the Kids in multiple roles) is similar to MONTY PYTHON AND THE HOLY GRAIL (1975) and MONTY PYTHON'S THE MEANING OF LIFE (1983). Unfortunately, BRAIN CANDY gets too caught up advancing the rather dull plot, leaving precious little time for more re-form comedy. Combine this with the choice of McDonald (arguably the least charismatic Kid) as the film's central character and the result is pretty forgettable, despite sporadic glimpses of the dark humor of the TV shows.

Longtime fans of the Kids may notice a lack of chemistry between the stars when Foley is on screen. Having begun work on the NBC series "News Radio," Foley was reportedly reluctant to work on the film. His screen time is minimal, and his name absent from the writing credits. To retain a link to the series, BRAIN CANDY features all of the Kids (except Foley) in female roles; there are also such familiar characters as McKinney's crabby Croatian cabbie, Thompson's Queen Elizabeth, and the towel-clad Bellini. Unfortunately, they serve mostly to remind us of past glories. *(Nudity, sexual situations, profanity.)* — B.T.

d, Kelly Makin; p, Lorne Michaels; exec p, Tom Rosenberg, Sigurjon Sighvatsson, David Steinberg; co-p, Barnaby Thompson, Richard S. Wright; w, Norm Hiscock, Bruce McCullogh, Kevin McDonald, Mark McKinney, Scott Thompson; ph, David A. Makin; ed, Christopher Cooper; m, Craig Northey; prod d, Gregory P. Keen; art d, Paul Denham Austerberry; set d, Mike Harris; sound, Bruce D. Carwardine (mixer); fx, Performance Solutions, Film Effects, Inc., John Gejdecki, Ltd., Jon Campfens; casting, Ross Clydesdale; cos, Delphine White; makeup, Geralyn Wraith; stunts, Ted Hanlan

Comedy **(PR: C MPAA: R)**

KINGPIN ★★★

(U.S.) 113m Rysher Entertainment; Motion Picture Corporation of America ~ MGM/UA c

Woody Harrelson *(Roy Munson)*; Randy Quaid *(Ishmael)*; Vanessa Angel *(Claudia)*; Bill Murray *(Ernie McCracken)*; Chris Elliott *(The Gambler)*; William Jordan *(Mr. Boorg)*; Richard Tyson *(Owner of Stiffy's)*; Lin Shaye *(Landlady)*; Zen Gesner *(Thomas)*; Prudence Wright Holmes *(Mrs. Boorg)*; Rob Moran *(Stanley Osmanski)*; Danny Green *(Calvert Munson)*; Will Rothhaar *(Young Roy)*; Mark Charpentier; Brad Faxon; Billy Andrade; Paul DeWolf *(1979 Bowling Buddies)*; Jill Lytle *(Odor Eater Babe)*; Willie Beauchene *(Bunion Boy)*; Sayed Badreya *(Fatima)*; Linda Carola *(1979 Waitress)*; Monica Shay *(1979 Diner Floozy)*; Danny Murphy *(Beaver Valley Bowl Manager)*; David Shackelford *(Red Neck Stutterer)*; Mike Cerone; Mike Cavallo; Rick Barker; Paul Pelletier; Tom Leasca; Tom Lupo *(Beaver Bowl Hustlers)*; Jimmy Shay *(Invisible Hustler)*; Hank Brandt *(Bowling Priest)*; Suzan Hughes *(Cocktail Waitress)*; Michael Corrente *(Scranton Wino)*; Herbie Flynn *(Scranton Wino)*; Joe "Smokey" Krawlicky *(Pennsylvania Hall O' Fame Bowler)*; Googy Gress *(Lancaster Bowl Manager)*; Hillary Matthews *(Mother with Carriage)*; Ryan Heggs; William Heggs *(Baby in Carriage)*; Willie Garson *(Purse Snatcher)*; Nancy Frey-Jarecki *(Sarah Boorg)*; Robby Thibeau *(Lucas Boorg)*; Helen Manfull *(Grandma Boorg)*; Terry Mullany *(Amish Saw Guy)*; Brian Stube *(Amish Saw Guy)*; Chris Spain *(Amish Saw Guy)*; Rose Smith-Lotenero *(Amish Babe)*; Michelle Matheson *(Rebecca)*; Nicholas Greenbury *(Amish Kid)*; Andrew Greenbury *(Amish Kid)*; Pucky Lippincott *(Amish Bellringer)*; Mark "Chief" Wasler *(Make-Out King)*; Gretchen Treser *(Make-Out Queen)*; Patrick Healy *(Urinal Boy)*; Sean P. Gildea *(McKnight Bowl Bartender)*; Jackie Flynn *(Dog Boy)*; Jonathan Richman *(Tavern Band Member)*; Tommy Larkins *(Tavern Band Member)*; Bob Weeks *(Waiter)*; Roger Clemens *(Skidmark)*; Libby Langdon *(Skidmark's Squirrel)*; Liza; Wallace Lester; Mark Pauperas; Sid Greenbud; Kipp Stroden; Sidney J. Barrymore Jr. *(Tavern Drunks)*; Rosey Brown *(Skidmark's Friend)*; John Jordan *(Skidmark's Friend)*; Mark Miosky *(Skidmark's Friend)*; John Woodin; Gordie Merrick; Steven R. Gehrke; Clem "Mandingo" Franek *(Bowling Steelworkers)*; Kathy Farrelly *(Bowling Biker Babe)*; Stacy Lundin *(Bowling Biker Babe)*; Jonathan "Earl" Stein *(Bowling Farmer)*; Alex Stohn *(Bowling Farmer)*; Lori Bagley *(Beautiful Dancer)*; Jo Marcus *(Sexy Senior Bowler)*; Cecile Krevoy *(Sexy Senior Bowler)*; Mary Stohn *(Sexy Senior Bowler)*; Docky *(Uncle Willy)*; The Artist Formerly Known as Docky *(Uncle Willy)*; Louis Charles Consolo *(Stiffy's Goon)*; Joanne Wolfe *(Silver Legacy Waitress)*; Danielle Parsons

(Silver Legacy Waitress); Jane Pratt *(TV Interviewer)*; Steve Stabler *(TV Cameraman)*; Elizabeth Jordan *(Silver Legacy Maid)*; Cynthia Farrelly Gesner *(Silver Legacy Maid)*; Brian Mone *(Psycho Guy)*; Taryn Chilivis *(Cute Mother)*; Lisa Stothard; Melinda Kocsis; Rachel Wagner; Victoria Scott *(Unified Fund Moms)*; Kevin O'Brien *(Pizza Guy)*; Nancy Farrelly *(Nouchi's Gal)*; Mariann Farrelly *(Tournament Sign-up Lady)*; Aggie Byers *(Tournament Sign-up Lady)*; John Popper *(Bowling Tournament Announcer)*; Don Julio; Kevin Civale; Brian Voss; Mark Roth; Justin Hromek; Ron Palumbi Jr.; Parker Bohn III; Randy Pederson *(Pro Bowlers)*; John Cioffoletti *(Philips Head Bowler)*; Jon Dennis *(Himself)*; Chris Schenkel *(Himself)*; Clint Allen *(Store Clerk)*; Urge Overkill *(National Anthem Band)*; Jessica Byers *(Big Ern's Valet)*; Julie Byers *(Big Ern's Valet)*; Preston Thomas *(Tournament Liaison)*; Jeff Thomas *(Tournament Liaison)*; Jim Ahern *(Sport)*; John Neary *(Mission Priest)*; Kenny Griswold *(Barfly)*; George Bedard *(Barfly)*; Joe Lewis *(Barfly)*; Andy Taylor *(Custodian)*; Brad Norton *(MIA Guy)*; Blues Traveler *(Amish Band)*; Elliott Morris *(Mr. Harrelson's Bowling Double)*

The bowling comedy KINGPIN comes "from the idiots what brung you DUMB AND DUMBER" (so the ad catchphrase went). But rather than recycle the gags from an earlier hit it scores in its own right—if not a strike at least a solid spare.

Roy Munson (Woody Harrelson) is a regional bowler who defeats Ernie "Big Ern" McCracken (Bill Murray) at the 1979 Odor Eaters Championship. Ernie takes revenge on Roy by tricking him into hustling some fellow bowlers, then leaving him to the furious losers. They destroy Roy's bowling arm in a ball return machine, and the appendage must be replaced by a wooden replica. 17 years later, broke, alcoholic, bottomed-out Roy works as a bowling supplier in Pittsburgh. At the bowling lanes he spots Ishmael (Randy Quaid), a natural talent he thinks he can train for the winner-take-all tournament in Reno, and thus be Roy's ticket out of Palookaville. Ishmael belongs to the strict, insular Amish community of Pennsylvania Dutch Country, but he also needs money to halt the foreclosure of his family's farm. On their trip together Roy and Ishmael unsuccessfully try to hustle gangster Stanley (Rob Moran) and must make a desperate getaway. Mob moll Claudia (Vanessa Angel) escapes with them, and helps her new partners in scamming en route to Reno. Once they arrive in the glittering city, the trio's luck turns bad; Ishmael hurts his hand in a confrontation with Big Ern, Stanley returns to take revenge, and Claudia suddenly leaves with Stanley and all the cash she made on the road. Undaunted, Roy takes Ishmael's place in the tournament. Despite his handicap—a prosthetic bowling hand—he becomes a finalist against old nemesis Big Ern. Roy loses the match, but is comforted by Claudia, who returns with money in tow. He also gets a sizable check from a condom company to endorse their product, enabling Ishmael to save his farm.

DUMB AND DUMBER (1994) clearly provided a model for KINGPIN, and Woody Harrelson and Randy Quaid seem to enjoy themselves filling in for Jim Carrey and Jeff Daniels. Surprisingly, KINGPIN contains a genuine sweetness beneath the expected crude bathroom humor and outrageous sex jokes. By right, the film should offend women, the Amish, Native Americans, animal-rights activists and other sensitive types, but the misanthropy is so evenhanded, it's hard to complain.

Numerous, funny send-ups include Harrelson's entrance (set to the Trammps's "Disco Inferno") quoting John Travolta's intro in SATURDAY NIGHT FEVER (1977); Roy and Claudia brutally fight to the strains of the theme from LOVE STORY (1970); and Ishmael strips to make extra cash a la Demi Moore in STRIPTEASE (1996), released to theaters simultaneously with KINGPIN. And just like STRIPTEASE, this zany spoof was not a great box-office success. Notably, an earlier 1996 release, HAPPY GILMORE, the golf comedy vehicle for Adam Sandler, had similar plot-points, including a character with a prosthetic arm.

What makes KINGPIN work especially well is that, unlike the Adam Sandlers and Chris Farleys of fast-forgotten farces, Harrelson and Quaid play real, empathetic characters—and stay in character. The rest of the cast is also in good form. Vanessa Angel transcends the sexist trappings of her role by giving an appealing performance, and Bill Murray, as the villainous strike artist, nearly steals the film with his brand of understated irony. There are a few sluggish spots, but credit the filmmakers with concocting a low-brow comedy about a group of losers that actually comes out a winner. *(Violence, sexual situations, adult situations, substance abuse, profanity.)* — E.M.

d, Peter Farrelly, Bobby Farrelly; p, Brad Krevoy, Steve Stabler, Bradley Thomas; exec p, Keith Samples; assoc p, James B. Rogers; co-p, Jim Burke, John Bertolli; w, Barry Fanaro, Mort Nathan; ph, Mark Irwin; ed, Christopher Greenbury; m, Freedy Johnston; prod d, Sidney Jackson Bartholomew Jr.; art d, Jay Vetter; set d, Bradford Johnson; sound, Jonathan "Earl" Stein (mixer), Jon Johnson (design), Michael Chandler (design); fx, David Kelsey; casting, Rick Montgomery, Dan Parada; cos, Mary Zophres; makeup, Kimberly Greene, K.N.B. Effects Group; stunts, Rick Barker, Tim Trella

Comedy/Sports **(PR: O MPAA: PG-13)**

KISSINGER AND NIXON ★★½

(U.S.) 93m Paragon Entertainment Corp. ~ Turner Home Entertainment c

Ron Silver *(Henry Kissinger)*; Beau Bridges *(Richard Nixon)*; Matt Frewer *(Alexander Haig)*; Ron White *(H. R. Haldeman)*; George Takei *(Le Duc Tho)*; Kenneth Walsh *(James Reston)*; Tony Rosato *(Charles Colson)*; Henry Chan *(Nguyen Van Thieu)*

Relying too heavily on impersonations rather than character development, this made-for-TV docudrama deifies controversial US Secretary of State Henry Kissinger while condemning Richard Nixon.

North Vietnamese leader Le Duc Tho (George Takei) decides to deal directly with Kissinger (Ron Silver), then National Security Advisor, in the upcoming peace talks, thus superseding the State Department. President Nixon (Beau Bridges), jealous of Kissinger's growing importance, asks Deputy Security Advisor Alexander Haig (Matt Frewer) to leak any information on the peace talks. Nixon does not want to appear weak to the public while seeking reelection. Although President Thieu (Henry Chan) of South Vietnam has rejected past proposals for peace, Kissinger and Tho reach an agreement that addresses all issues except one: the North insists on keeping troops in South Vietnam. On the eve of Tho's deadline Thieu rejects this plan as well. Despite a press conference in which Kissinger pressures Thieu to accept, the proposal falls apart after the 1972 election. Nixon resumes bombing North Vietnam, choosing civilian targets. International outrage and the domestic political damage caused by the Watergate break-in compels Nixon to hold new talks. This time Kissinger succeeds in bringing all sides to an accord, ending US involvement in Vietnam.

While painting both title subjects in one-dimensional terms, KISSINGER AND NIXON is very flattering to Kissinger. Rather than attempting a mighty saga on the scale of Oliver Stone's NIXON (in theaters the same year this premiered on smaller screens) the teleplay views two complex men through the limited prism of essentially only one incident. By starting after Kissinger has begun the peace process, the audience never sees the Kissinger who advised Nixon on earlier bombings; instead, Saint Henry sacrifices himself for peace. Nixon, meanwhile, is little more than a buffoon with lines like "Where's my Jewboy?" and "I plan to leave office a hero."

Of the actors, Frewer stands out as Haig, honestly torn between Kissinger, his boss, and Nixon, his commander-in-chief. Silver gets lost in his accent while Bridges tries too hard to impersonate Nixon, unfortunately sounding more like Jimmy Stewart. The script also repeats itself *ad nauseum* about diplomatic and political issues, as if the living-room audience would never understand anything stated only once. *(Profanity.)* — K.Fr.

d, Daniel Petrie; p, Richard Borchiver; exec p, Jon Slan, Judith James, Daniel H. Blatt, Lionel Chetwynd; w, Lionel Chetwynd (based on *Kissinger: A Biography* by Walter Isaacson); ph, Rene Ohashi; ed, Stephen Lawrence; m, Jonathan Goldsmith; prod d, Karen Bromley; sound, David Lee; casting, Deirdre Bowen; cos, Lynda Kemp; makeup, Kevin Haney

Docudrama/Political **(PR: A MPAA: NR)**

KOKAKU KIDOTAI

(SEE: GHOST IN THE SHELL)

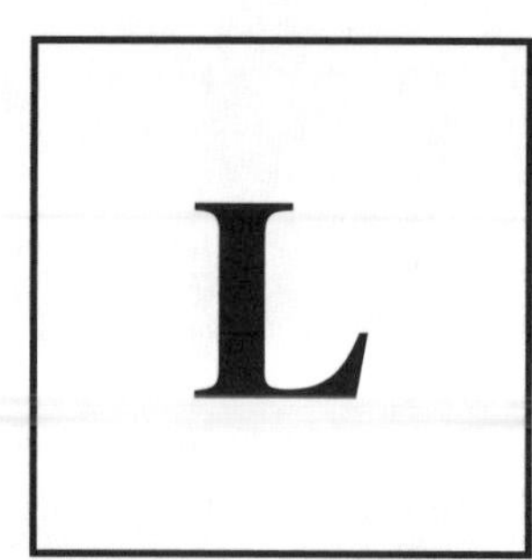

LA CEREMONIE ★★★★

(France/Germany) 111m MK2; France 3 Cinema; Prokino Filmproduktion; OLGA; Zweites Deutsches Fernsehen ~ New Yorker Films c

Isabelle Huppert *(Jeanne)*; Sandrine Bonnaire *(Sophie)*; Jacqueline Bisset *(Catherine)*; Jean-Pierre Cassel *(Georges)*; Virginie Ledoyen *(Melinda)*; Valentin Merlet *(Gilles)*; Julien Rochefort; Dominique Frot; Jean-Francois Perrier

Claude Chabrol ratchets up the suspense while making keen political points in LA CEREMONIE, a deftly turned thriller about a quiet maid who forms a deadly alliance with a postal worker while working for a middle-class French family.

LA CEREMONIE is set in an upscale suburb of contemporary France. Sophie (Sandrine Bonnaire), a shy young woman, comes to work for the Lelievres, including Catherine (Jacqueline Bisset), Georges (Jean-Pierre Cassel), their teenage son, Gilles (Valentin Merlet), and Melinda (Virginie Ledoyen), Georges' 19-year-old-daughter from a previous marriage. Sophie seems passively tolerant of the family's haughty manner, while she keeps a major secret from them: she is unable to read or count change.

Sophie finds a friend in Jeanne (Isabelle Huppert), an outspoken postal clerk who resents the upper classes and particularly despises Georges. She and Sophie quickly form a bond that threatens the family's security. With Jeanne's encouragement, Sophie grows bolder in her manner and even runs off early from serving at Melinda's engagement party in order to celebrate her own birthday. When Melinda discovers that Sophie is illiterate and threatens to tell the family, Sophie pre-empts her by revealing that Melinda has recently had a abortion. The news upsets the family enough to prompt Georges to fire Sophie and give her one week to find a new place to live.

One night, later in the week, Sophie and Jeanne sneak back into the house to get Sophie's belongings. Once inside, they create mischief and "trash" the house, while the family—oblivious to the rampage—watches a Mozart concert on television in the living room. Eventually, Catherine hears a noise in the kitchen and Georges investigates. When the patriarch enters the kitchen, Sophie shoots him in cold blood. The women brutally execute the rest of the family, then leave the house.

On her way out of the driveway, Jeanne's car stalls, and she is killed in a collision with another car. Sophie awaits her fate as the police arrive and discover an audio tape recording of the murders inadvertently made during the TV broadcast.

First released in France in 1995, LA CEREMONIE marks a triumph for all those involved. Chabrol returns to the suspense form he used in such classics as LA FEMME INFIDELE (1969) and LE BOUCHER (1969). Huppert, who gave some of her best performances in Chabrol's VIOLETTE (1978) and THE STORY OF WOMEN (1988), delivers another razor-sharp portrait. Bisset has her best role in years and the rest of the cast rise to the occasion, too.

Although adapted from British mystery writer Ruth Rendell's *A Judgement in Stone,* LA CEREMONIE takes on a distinctly Gallic tone (the new title refers to the French ritual before an execution). As in his best work, Chabrol skewers the French bourgeoisie with subtle yet indelible details: the family referring to Sophie in the third person in her presence; asking Sophie to serve a party on her birthday; dressing in evening clothes to watch "Don Giovanni" on television. The feeling of dread created here as a result of the arrogance and resentment sparked by class differences is palpable.

While the flaws of LA CEREMONIE are minor, they keep it from being a masterpiece. The relationship between Sophie and Jeanne suggests lesbianism in a coy way that seems old-fashioned. The conclusion (after a literally explosive climax) is a little disappointing, too: perhaps Chabrol was reaching for a "crime does not pay" ironic twist, but both Jeanne's sudden demise and the contrivance of the murders having been recorded fall flat.

Still, LA CEREMONIE generates tremendous suspense from issues too often ignored in both art and life. *(Graphic violence, adult situations, substance abuse, extreme profanity.)* — E.M.

d, Claude Chabrol; p, Marin Karmitz; co-p, Ira Von Ganaith; w, Claude Chabrol, Caroline Eliacheff (based on the novel *A Judgement in Stone* by Ruth Rendell); ph, Bernard Zitzermann, Michel Thiriet; ed, Monique Fardoulis; m, Matthieu Chabrol; art d, Daniel Mercier; set d, Catherine Pierrat; sound, Jean-Bernard Thomasson; cos, Corinne Jorry; makeup, Thi Loan Nguyen

Thriller/Drama/Crime **(PR: C MPAA: NR)**

LA COMEDIE-FRANCAISE OU L'AMOUR JOUE ★★★★

(France/U.S.) 223m Zipporah Films ~ Zipporah Films (U.S.)/Ideale Audience (French) c
(AKA: GAMES OF LOVE, THE)

"La Double Inconstance" Jean-Pierre Miquel *(Director)*; Claire Vernet *(Flaminia)*; Philippe Torreton *(Arlequin)*; Coraly Zahonero *(Silvia)*; Michel Robin *(Trivelin)*; "Occupe-toi d'Amelie" Roger Planchon *(Director)*; Nicolas Silberg *(Prince)*; Catherine Sauval *(Irene)*; Thierry Hancisse *(Marcel)*; Celine Samie *(Charlotte)*; Florence Viala *(Amelie)*; "Dom Juan" Jacques Lassalle *(Director)*; Jacques Sereys *(Dom Louis)*; Roland Bertin *(Soaharelle)*; Catherine Sauval *(Charlotte)*; Jean Dautremay *(Monsieur Dimanche)*; Isabelle Gardien *(Mathurine)*; Andrzej Seweryn *(Dom Juan)*; "La Thebaide" Yannis Kokkos *(Director)*; Catherine Samie *(Jocaste)*; Anne Kessler *(Antigone)*

Frederick Wiseman continues his unexpected but fascinating meditation on high-art culture with LA COMEDIE-FRANCAISE OU L'AMOUR JOUE (THE GAMES OF LOVE), the documentarian's 29th film, and his first made about a non-American subject.

Over the winter months of December 1994 and January 1995, Wiseman peeks into the preparations of La Comedie-Francaise, the 300-year-old theatrical company of France. First, the actors are seen rehearsing a scene on stage from Marivaux's "La Double Inconstance" ("The Inconstant Lovers"). Off-stage, the costume cutters go to work while one of the company directors guides a young actress through a difficult scene from the same play. More rehearsals occur as eager theater patrons fight with a cashier at the box-office over the advance seating. At a business meeting about the company's finances, an older actress argues for better care for retired members. Finally, the performance of the Marivaux play goes on for the public.

Later in the season, as the set designers put the finishing touches on the props in a nearby warehouse, several actors argue over modernizing another of the company's standard works, Moliere's "Don Juan." After agreeing to disagree over the matter, another business meeting takes place where the top administrator lays out the paradox of the federally-financed company: La Comedie-Francaise can only receive government subsidies as long as it runs a deficit! Next, a reporter engages one of the directors in a discussion about gender politics in Marivaux and the relevance of the playwright's work today. Backstage, several actors put on their make-up and get ready for another performance of "La Double Inconstance." After the show, the company enjoys a cast party, but the threat of a strike by the electricians and other stagehands the next day puts a damper on the festivities. Finally, the actors and administrators join each other and the local mayor at the Artist Mutual Benefit Society, a retirement home for La Comedie-Francaise, where the company doyenne celebrates her 100th birthday.

Frederick Wiseman may be best known for films that have revealed the problems within national social institutions (HIGH SCHOOL, HOSPITAL, WELFARE, et al.), but LA COMEDIE-FRANCAISE, like 1995's BALLET (about the American Ballet Theater), looks closely at a venerable arts organization. Nevertheless, through his subtle but deliberate editing of the many hours of rehearsals, performances, stage crew preparations, and behind-the-scenes business meetings, Wiseman makes important statements about the politics of gender, race, class, and the role of art in the culture.

Yes, the excerpts from Moliere and Marivaux are entertaining, but the real strength of this documentary comes from the contrasts between the actions onstage and off (and how they sometimes mirror each other). Despite what may seem to some like an excessive running time (3 hours, 40 minutes), every scene—every movement and gesture, really—says volumes about a variety of issues.

Notwithstanding the touching finale set in the government-sponsored actor's home, LA COMEDIE-FRANCAISE refuses to opt for easy answers to its probing questions; instead, it makes a consistently incisive and thoughtful critique. *(Profanity.)*— E.M.

d, Frederick Wiseman; p, Jean Labib, T. Celal, Pierre-Olivier Bardet, Dominique Bourgois, Frederick Wiseman; ph, John Davey; ed, Frederick Wiseman; sound, Frederick Wiseman

Documentary **(PR: A MPAA: NR)**

LA FILLE SEULE
(SEE: SINGLE GIRL, A)

LA FLOR DE MI SECRETO
(SEE: FLOWER OF MY SECRET, THE)

LA GUERRE DES BOUTONS, CA RECOMMENCE
(SEE: WAR OF THE BUTTONS, THE)

LA HAINE
(SEE: HATE)

LA MACHINE
(SEE: MACHINE, THE)

LA PROPRIETAIRE
(SEE: PROPRIETOR, THE)

L'AMERIQUE DES AUTRES
(SEE: SOMEONE ELSE'S AMERICA)

LAND AND FREEDOM ★★★½

(U.K./Spain/Germany) 110m Parallax Pictures; Messidor Films; Road Movies Dritte Produktion; British Screen; The European Co-production Fund; Television Espanola; Canal Plus; BBC Films; ARD; Filmstiftung Nordrhein-Westfalen ~ Gramercy Pictures c
(AKA: LAND AND LIBERTY)

Ian Hart *(David Carne)*; Rosana Pastor *(Blanca)*; Iciar Bollain *(Maite)*; Tom Gilroy *(Gene Lawrence)*; Marc Martinez *(Vidal)*; Frederic Pierrot *(Bernard)*; Andres Aladren; Sergi Calleja; Raffaele Cantatore; Pascal Demolon; Paul Laverty; Josep Magem; Eoin McCarthy; Jurgen Muller; Roca; Emilia Samper *(The Militia)*; Suzanne Maddock *(Kim)*; Mandy Walsh *(Dot)*; Miguel Cabrillana *(Speaker at Meeting)*; Angela Clarke *(Kitty)*; Rafael Diaz *(Barracks Officer)*; Felicio Pellicer *(Nationalist Officer)*; Ricard Arilla *(Priest)*; Jordi Dauder *(Salas)*; Pep Molina *(Pepe)*; Enriqueta Ferre *(Concierge)*; Asuncion Royo *(Old Woman)*; Francesc Orella *(Casado)*; Phil O'Brien *(Ambulance Man)*; Dave Seddon *(Ambulance Man)*; Xavier Amatller; Jaime Prats; Jose Luis Prats; Carles Vilarrasa *(People on the Train)*; Fina Alcaniz; Claudio Dominguez; Ernesto Grau; Maria Folch; Maites Lucas; Sebastia Marmana; Lola Olives; Ma Eugenia Palatsi; Pepa Palatsi; Miguel Quintana; Aniceto Rallo; Paco Rangel; Jose Antonio Ripolles; Consol Segura; Manolo Vicent *(Townspeople)*; David Allen; Manel Anoro; Lali Cambra; Cristobal Estudillo; Adoni Gonzalez; Jose Luis ; Marius Lou; Pep Navarro; Antonio Pellicer; Pepe Valenzuela *(People on the Roof)*; Joan Pau Romani; Santi Celaya; Josep Galindo; Sergio Garcia; Daniel Munoz *(People in the Cafe)*; Neus Agullo; Pep Cortes *(Blanca's Parents)*

Winner of the 1995 Felix Award for Best European Film and the Critics Prize at Cannes, LAND AND FREEDOM is a heartfelt film about an epochal 20th century struggle that most Americans know far too little about.

In 1936, Liverpudlian David Carne (Ian Hart) decides to join the fight against the fascist forces of General Franco that are trying to overthrow the newly elected democratic government of Spain. Making his way illegally across the border, David joins a militia unit of POUM (the Spanish acronym for the Workers' Marxist Unity Party), a ragtag but democratically organized force of men and women from many countries. Conditions are extremely difficult, but all are united by a strong sense of common purpose.

David becomes friendly with some of his fellow militia fighters including Blanca (Rosana Pastor). The POUM attacks and captures a town which had been held by the fascists. A meeting is held during which POUM members and local residents argue passionately over whether to unify the farmlands into communes.

David is injured in a training exercise when a decrepit rifle explodes in his face. While recuperating, he is visited by Blanca. She tells him she wants to feel human for a night, and they make love. But they part on a sour note when David tells her that he has decided to join the International Brigades, the group that is backed by the Communist Party even though it is felt by many (including POUM) not to have Spain's best interests at heart.

The groups opposed to the fascists are at war with each other as much as with Franco, and David quickly becomes disheartened by the amount of infighting. Realizing that Stalin is more interested in manipulating the Spanish struggle to his own ends, David renounces his Communist Party membership and rejoins the POUM. Shortly after, they are visited by a former comrade, now an officer in the International Brigades. He informs them that the POUM has been outlawed for the patently absurd charge of collaborating with the fascists. In the fracas that breaks out, Blanca is shot to death. At her funeral, David scoops up a handful of Spanish soil and leaves to return to England.

It's hardly surprising that LAND AND FREEDOM didn't do much business during its brief run in American theaters. Viewers don't necessarily have to sympathize with European socialism to watch the film, but they do need a little understanding of its history, and that's something on which few American history texts spend much time.

For director Ken Loach and his regular scriptwriter, Jim Allen, as for many committed leftists, the Spanish Civil War is the great socialist myth, a time when people rose up as one to fight a particularly egregious instance of fascism as represented by Franco. The bitter downside, most famously reported by George Orwell in his *Homage to Catalonia*, is that this was a revolution betrayed by its own allies.

But even for those coming to these events for the first time, LAND AND FREEDOM is filled with a compellingly cleared-eyed view of the real world. As rigid a believer in the proper use of film as Mike Leigh (though their differences are as great as their similarities), Loach goes to his own lengths to gain the most natural performances possible, including shooting on location, never giving his performers more than the current day's script, and shooting strictly in sequence. He also dares to take risks, most notably with a long scene in which villagers and members of the militia argue over the merits of collectivization. Even though his point is to show that politics is something grounded in reality, it's the kind of scene that has been parodied too often and too cruelly for him to overcome the prejudices against it. Still, Loach's refusal to give in to cynicism has always been his greatest strength. (Violence, sexual situations, profanity.) — M.F.

d, Ken Loach; p, Rebecca O'Brien; exec p, Sally Hibbin, Gerardo Herrero, Ulrich Felsberg; assoc p, Marta Esteban; w, Jim Allen; ph, Barry Ackroyd; ed, Jonathan Morris; m, George Fenton; prod d, Martin Johnson; sound, Ray Beckett (recordist); fx, Reyes Abades; casting, Marta Valsecchi, Richard Rousseau, Wendy Ettinger, Susie Figgis; cos, Ana Alvargonzalez; makeup, Anne McEwan

Historical/War/Drama (PR: C MPAA: NR)

LAND BEFORE TIME IV: JOURNEY THROUGH THE MISTS ★★

(U.S.) 74m Universal Cartoon Studios; Akom Productions Co. Ltd. ~ MCA/Universal Home Video c

VOICES OF: Jeff Bennett *(Petrie/Ichy)*; Linda Gray *(Grandma)*; John Ingle *(Narrator/Cera's Father)*; Heather Hogan *(Ducky)*; Candace Hutson *(Cera)*; Scott McAfee *(Littlefoot)*; Rob Paulsen *(Spike)*; Kenneth Mars *(Grandpa)*; Tress MacNeille *(Dil)*; Carol Bruce *(Old One)*; Juliana Hansen *(Ali)*; Charles Durning *(Archie)*; Frank Whelker *(Tickles)*

Memories of Don Bluth's engaging original THE LAND BEFORE TIME continue to grow dimmer with this indifferent sequel to the animated dinosaur saga.

When a herd of migrating "longnecks" enter the Great Valley where he lives, Littlefoot meets Ali, a young female of his own species. They become fast friends, though Littlefoot's old friends are jealous of Ali. She fears them in turn because they're of different species from her own. Littlefoot's aging grandfather falls ill, and all that can save him is a flower that grows in the dangerous "land of mists." Ali tells Littlefoot she can take him there, as long as he doesn't bring his other friends. Reluctantly, he agrees, and the two begin their journey.

Along the way, an earthquake traps Littlefoot in a cave. While Ali goes back to the valley for his friends, Littlefoot escapes the deadly team of Dil (a near-blind crocodile) and Ichy (her seeing-eye bird) with the aid of toothless old turtle Archie. Littlefoot's friends arrive and set him free, and Ali and Cera overcome their differences and become friends. The group reaches the land of mists, meet new creatures (including a rat that Duckie names "Tickles"), find the night flowers, and, after evading more attacks from Dil and Ichy, return home to the Great Valley. Littlefoot's grandfather recovers and Ali moves on with her tribe, though the narrator assures us that they will all meet again someday.

Having turned into an indifferent franchise that continues to make money simply because children always want to see more of the same, this latest LAND BEFORE TIME offers little to distinguish it from Saturday morning television fare. Littlefoot and his long-necked grandparents remain appealing and lively characters, but the backgrounds are murky and the animation overall is bland and colorless. Messages about cooperation between races are simply repeated from the earlier entries, the songs are eminently forgettable, and whoever thought up the idea of a cute, cuddlesome rat obviously doesn't have children. *(Violence.)* — M.F.

d, Roy Allen Smith; p, Roy Allen Smith; co-p, Zahra Dowlatabadi; w, Dev Ross (based on characters created by Judy Freudberg and Tony Geiss); ed, Warren Taylor; m, Michael Tavera, James Horner, Leslie Bricusse; art d, Anthony B. Christov; anim, Claude Chiasson, Patrick Gleeson; fx, Jeff Howard, Jung Kim

Animated/Children's (PR: AA MPAA: G)

LARGER THAN LIFE ★½

(U.S./Italy/Japan) 93m TRM Pictures International; United Artists ~ MGM/UA c

Bill Murray *(Jack Corcoran)*; Janeane Garofalo *(Mo)*; Linda Fiorentino *(Terry Bonera)*; Keith David *(Hurst)*; Pat Hingle *(Vernon)*; Matthew McConaughey *(Tip)*; Jeremy Piven *(Walter)*; Lois Smith *(Luluna)*; Anita Gillette *(Mom)*; Maureen Mueller *(Celeste)*; Harve Presnell *(Trowbridge Bowers)*; Tracey Walter *(Wee St. Francis)*

Bill Murray has to go cross-country with an uncooperative elephant in LARGER THAN LIFE, a comedy that tries to split the difference between grown-up and kiddie appeal, only to end up without much of either.

Jack Corcoran (Murray), a jaded motivational speaker, suddenly receives word that his father, whom he never knew and always thought was dead, has only recently passed away and left him a *huge* inheritance. It turns out Jack's father was a circus clown, and he left his son an elephant named Vera. Looking to turn a quick buck, Jack makes a deal to sell Vera to Mo (Janeane Garofalo) at the San Diego Zoo. Then he turns around and accepts a better offer from Terry Bonera (Linda Fiorentino), an animal show operator in LA. Still, to collect, Jack has to get Vera from Baltimore to California.

By train, they get to Kansas City, where Jack meets Vernon the Human Blockhead (Pat Hingle), one of his father's old circus cronies. Then, Jack cons a nutty trucker named Tip Tucker (Matthew McConaughey, A TIME TO KILL), who drives Jack crazy with his conspiracy theories about how the government poisons our food, into hauling him and the pachyderm as far as the Continental Divide. From there, Jack and Vera hoof it, so to speak. In New Mexico, Vera saves a church threatened by flood waters—by propping up the wall—and she is provided a heroine's escort to LA. When Jack discovers that sexy Terry uses electric prods on her animals, he decides to go with stalwart Mo, despite the fact that she can no longer pay him any money. As he bids Vera farewell, Jack acknowledges that he's a better person for having known the special elephant.

The last few years, Bill Murray has been more likely found on ESPN, chatting about his golf handicap and Michael Jordan, than starring in a movie, and his hardcore fans from the CADDYSHACK (1980) days are now more likely to be found at the videostore with the kids than at the cineplex with the guys. Thus, LARGER THAN LIFE with the large costar—after all, kids do love elephant jokes. But really, this is 90 minutes of Murray, the smarmy wise guy, firing a volley of droll one-liners; and frankly, a little of that goes a long way. This is a lot of it.

Murray needs a partner who can fire back. (Weren't "SNL" nerds Todd DiLaMuca and Lisa Loopner way funnier than Nick the lounge singer?) Here, he's serving lobs to an empty court. The movie has some funny sequences: Murray learning to drive a truck, and those with McConaughey. In their one scene together, Murray and Garofalo (THE TRUTH ABOUT CATS AND DOGS) show some spark, suggesting they could rally if matched. Mostly though, LARGER THAN LIFE suggests that Murray's star has set, and he might be better off in the supporting roles (as in this year's KINGPIN and SPACEJAM) that have been his recent wont.— P.R.

d, Howard Franklin; p, Pen Densham, John Watson, Richard B. Lewis; exec p, Wolfgang Glattes, Guy East; co-p, Sue Baden-Powell; w, Roy Blount Jr, Garry Williams (from a story by Pen Densham); ph, Elliot Davis; ed, Sidney Levin; m, Miles Goodman; prod d, Marcia Hinds; art d, Bo Johnson; set d, John Dwyer; sound, Thomas Causey (mixer); fx, Alan E. Lorimer; casting, Gail Levin; cos, Jane Robinson

Comedy **(PR: A MPAA: PG)**

LARRY MCMURTRY'S STREETS OF LAREDO ★★½

(U.S.) 300m DePasse Entertainment; Larry Levinson Productions; RHI Entertainment ~ Cabin Fever Entertainment c
(AKA: STREETS OF LAREDO)

James Garner *(Captain Woodrow F. Call)*; Sissy Spacek *(Lorena Parker)*; Sam Shepard *(Pea Eye Parker)*; Ned Beatty *(Judge Roy Bean)*; Randy Quaid *(John Wesley Hardin)*; Sonia Braga *(Maria Garza)*; George Carlin *(Billy Williams)*; Wes Studi *(Famous Shoes)*; James Gammon *(Charles Goodnight)*; Miriam Colon *(Estrella)*; Charles Martin Smith *(Mr. Brookshire)*; Kevin Conway *(Mox Mox)*; Alexis Cruz *(Joey Garza)*; Tristan Tait *(Deputy Ted Plunkert)*; Anjanette Comer *(Beulah)*; David S. Cass Sr. *(Sheriff Doniphan)*; James Victor *(Gordo)*; Doran Atherton *(Bobby Fant)*; Stephen W. Bridgewater *(Redfoot)*; Julio Carreon-Reyes *(Rafael Garza)*; Helen Cates *(Susanna Slack)*; Ashley Coe *(Claire Parker)*; Carlos Compean *(Vaquero No. 1)*; Emily Courtney *(Doobie Plunkert)*; Rutherford Cravens *(Lordy)*; Hank Crowell *(Texas Ranger No. 1)*; David Denney *(Young Cowboy)*; Bunk Duncan *(Hergardt)*; Cameron Finley *(Ben Parker)*; Weasel Forshaw *(Olin Roy)*; Tony Frank *(Sheriff Bob Jekyll)*; Jack Garner *(Old Waiter)*; Raquel Gavia *(Maria's Grandmother)*; Bill Gribble *(Blue Duck)*; Kirk Griffith *(Deputy Jerry Brown)*; Nik Hagler *(Tinkersley)*; William Hardy *(Lichtenstein)*; Joaquin Jackson *(Cowboy No. 2)*; Karen Jones *(Cherie)*; Fredrick Lopez *(Quick Jimmy)*; Larry Mahan *(Texas Ranger No. 2)*; John L. Martin *(Presidio Doctor)*; Vanessa Martinez *(Teresa Garza)*; Jeffrey Meyer *(Cowboy No. 3)*; Richard Nance *(Patrick O'Brien)*; Robert Norseworthy *(Fort Stockton Sheriff)*; Renee Olstead *(Marice Fant)*; Peyton Park *(Ben Lily)*; Jill Parker-Jones *(Maggie)*; Lanell Pena *(Negra)*; Lidia Porto *(Marieta)*; Steven Chester Prince *(Cowboy No. 1)*; Lori Ripper *(Young Maria)*; Roland Rodriguez *(Jorge)*; Joanna Sanchez *(Gabriela)*; Joe Stevens *(Deputy Tom Johnson)*; Billy Tolson *(August Parker)*; Angelina Calderon Torres *(Naiche)*; Manuel Valdez *(Vaquero No. 2)*; Christopher Wagner *(Georgie Parker)*; Wally Welch *(Deputy Joe Means)*

A sprawling, star-studded horse opera, LARRY MCMURTRY'S STREETS OF LAREDO, the sequel to LONESOME DOVE (1989), has more to do with the reality of 1990s TV than with the myth of the American West.

Pea Parker (Sam Shepard), a homesteader, gets word from Captain Woodrow Call (James Garner), a bounty hunter and former Texas Ranger; Call wants Parker's help tracking a sadistic young bandit, Joey Garza (Alexis Cruz), responsible for a string of bloody train robberies. Parker, loath to leave his wife Lorena (Sissy Spacek), an ex-hooker turned schoolmarm, and family, sets out with misgivings.

Call rides with Ted Plunkert (Tristan Tait), a young deputy, and Ben Brookshire (Charles Martin Smith), a railroad clerk from back east, the quintessential tenderfoot. Parker is supposed to catch up with them. Another robbery leads Call to believe that Mox Mox (Kevin Conway), a bandit he'd thought dead, is on the warpath also.

Maria Garza (Sonia Braga), Joey's mother, a healer, midwife, and earth mother personified, hears about Call's plans and rides to warn her wayward son. Arriving in Crow Town, a bandit hangout, she confronts John Wesley Hardin (Randy Quaid), proving her grit. She warns Joey, who goes off to hunt Call and company.

Pea, riding to catch up with Call, meets Famous Shoes (Wes Studi), an Indian, who agrees to help track Joey if Lorena will teach him to "follow tracks in books." In Fort Stockton, Pea and Famous Shoes are arrested by evil Sheriff Doniphan (David S. Cass Sr.), who plans to hang Famous Shoes on a trumped-up charge. Call shows up and springs them.

Back home, Lorena hears about Mox Mox's reappearance (he tried to burn her in LONESOME DOVE). She sends the kids up north, and rides off to find Pea and warn him. In Laredo she meets Call, who has left his posse to track Mox Mox, and persuades him to let her go back with him. Call fatally wounds Mox Mox, but later Joey wounds Call badly, and Lorena has to amputate his leg in the desert.

Joey harasses the posse, kills Ben, and wounds Pea, who wounds him back. Joey seeks shelter at his mother's, where he finds Lorena and Call. He drowns his half-brother and tries to drown his blind sister in the river; Maria manages to stop him but he stabs her fatally before dying. With her last breath, Maria asks Lorena to care for her remaining children.

Famous Shoes leads Lori to Pea, and he, Call, Lori, and Maria's kids head north to pick up the other children, and they all end up back home—even Famous Shoes. As we leave the happy extended family, Call is reading fairy tales to the enraptured blind girl, whose education he has arranged for.

If this all sounds like a string of cliches, it is. STREETS is a miniseries *and* a sequel, and neither category is strong on originality. It manages to be both slick and earnest: a formula for melodrama. There's a lot of killing in STREETS, but there's no moral reason for it, no sense of loss, and no vengeful satisfaction. Sex and romance are barely present—the closest we get is when Lorena cuts off Call's leg after mutual demonstrations of selflessness: Sissy Spacek bounces around, sawing away, with a look of agony easily mistaken for ecstasy.

The acting, for the most part, is uninspired. This is due to a screenplay which tries to have a little something for everyone, and ends up lacking direction. Randy Quaid plays the character John Wesley Hardin with a demonic intensity which outshines the rest of the cast. Ben Brookshire, a sympathetic character, dies stupidly, never fulfilling the expectation of quiet heroism his role generates. Mox Mox is barely present, but leeringly evil and craven in his one big scene.

Sets, costumes, and direction are workmanlike. Wounds heal remarkably fast, and folks stay clean and well-groomed despite trying circumstances. The score beats the *Streets of Laredo* theme into the ground (Laredo is of minor significance otherwise).

Almost gripping and somewhat entertaining, LARRY MCMURTRY'S STREETS OF LAREDO, like too much TV fare, is best watched while doing something else. LONESOME DOVE fans will, no doubt, disagree. *(Violence.)* — C.M.

d, Joseph Sargent; exec p, Suzanne DePasse, Robert Halmi Jr., Larry McMurtry, Diana Ossana, Larry Levinson; assoc p, Joe Lunne, Ted Nelson; co-p, Frank Q. Dobbs; w, Larry McMurtry, Diana Ossana (based on the novel *Streets of Laredo* by Larry McMurtry); ph, Edward Pei; ed, Debra Karen; m, David Shire; prod d, Jerry Wanek; art d, John Bucklin; set d, Carla Curry; sound, Ken Willingham; fx, Lyn Caudle; casting, Lynn Kressel; cos, Jim Echerd; makeup, David Atherton, Selina Jayne; stunts, David S. Cass Cass

Western **(PR: C MPAA: NR)**

LAST DANCE ★½

(U.S.) 103m Touchstone ~ Buena Vista c

Sharon Stone *(Cindy Liggett)*; Rob Morrow *(Rick Hayes)*; Randy Quaid *(Sam Burns)*; Peter Gallagher *(John Hayes)*; Jack Thompson *(The Governor)*; Jayne Brooke *(Jill)*; Pamala Tyson *(Legal Aid Attorney)*; Skeet Ulrich *(Billy)*; Don Harvey *(Doug)*; Diane Sellers *(Reggie)*; Patricia French *(Frances)*; Jeffery Ford *(Rusk)*; Dave Hager *(Detective Vollo)*; Christine Cattell *(Louise)*; Peg Allen *(Helen)*; Peggy Walton Walker *(Governor's Wife)*; Deena Dill *(Carolyn)*; Diana Taylor *(Etta)*; Mimi Craven *(Stripper in Bar)*; John Cunningham *(McGuire)*; Randy Hresko *(Betty)*; Charlotte Hackman *(Grace)*; Ralph Wilcox *(Warden Rice)*; Ken Jenkins *(Warden Laverty)*; Joe Inscoe *(Reverend Cummins)*; Elizabeth Omilami *(Officer Mulkey)*; Sandra Thigpen *(Governor's Receptionist)*; Michael Montgomery *(Governor's Aide)*; Rachel Glass *(Debbie)*; Kyle Hester *(Matt)*; Ginny Parker *(Sue Hunt)*; Kaitlyn Kenney *(Tiffany Hunt)*; Kenneth Schulz *(Paul Faring)*; Dennis Ferrier; Demetria Kalodimos; Jeff McAtee; Cynthia Williams; Ava P. Philson; Carlene Moore *(Reporters)*; Ted Manson *(Judge Gorman)*; William Thorp *(Motorboat Pilot)*; Richard Cowl *(Judge Butler)*; Dionne Gardner *(Dress Shop Sales Girl)*; Asha J. King *(Linda's Daughter)*; B.J. Brown *(Drill Instructor)*; Thomas "Kirk" Hawkins *(Sea Plane Pilot)*; Susan Jeffrey *(Party Clown)*; Trilby Beresford *(Title Sequence Girl)*; Dottie Snow *(Cindy's Aunt)*; Kuldeep Narain *(Tour Guide)*

LAST DANCE, dubbed "Dead Woman Walking" by some wags, was the second of three major death-row films in less than a year, and it covers much of the same territory as the earlier DEAD MAN WALKING (1995). The ground it covers has been well-trod by a long list of much better films.

Rick Hayes (Rob Morrow) gets a job in a state clemency office, thanks to his brother, John (Peter Gallagher), chief of staff to the governor (Jack Thompson). Rick's first assignment is to review the case of convicted double-murderer Cindy Liggett (Sharon Stone).

Rick visits Cindy in prison, finding her much mellowed and possibly rehabilitated after 12 years of incarceration. Determined to convince the notoriously unforgiving governor to commute her death sentence, Rick dives into a full-blown investigation of Cindy's case, re-interviewing the people surrounding her case. Instead, the governor grants clemency to a high-profile black prisoner (Charles S. Dutton) who, while incarcerated, has become a celebrity. Furious, Rick confronts the governor at a party—a stunt that gets him fired.

No longer in a position to plead for Cindy's clemency, Rick discovers a flaw in the state's original case against her and convinces her lawyer to appeal the ruling. Time is ticking away for Cindy, though, and she spends her last night with Rick and her newly-reconciled brother (Skeet Ulrich).

She is taken to the chamber, and an IV is placed in her arm. But moments before the lethal poison can be administered, there is a call from the governor ordering a stay of execution while Rick's appeal is reviewed. The reprieve is short-lived, though. The Supreme Court quickly dismisses the appeal, and Cindy is hauled again to the chamber, where she is finally executed.

Everything bad about LAST DANCE—and there's plenty—stems from the film's terrible script. Characters appear and disappear arbitrarily, no attempt is made to provide motivation for the characters' actions (including Cindy's crime), and unforgivable liberties are taken with reality. For example, the night before Cindy's execution, when she has been transferred to a men's maximum-security prison and placed on "death watch," guards allow both Rick and Cindy's brother—who is also a convict—to sleep in the cell with her. In the seemingly interminable execution scenes, every hoary death-row cliche is trucked out not once, but twice.

Stone's unrelenting scowl is broken only by self-serving tears, a combination that alienates the audience and makes one question why anybody would want to grant her clemency in the first place. Even with LAST DANCE's terrible script, a better actress could have made the audience care whether she lives or dies, instead of inspiring cheers for the executioner, if only to get it over with already.

LAST DANCE was written by Ron Koslow (writer of FIRST BORN, INTO THE NIGHT, TOM AND HUCK), with co-story credit by Steven Haft (producer of DEAD POETS SOCIETY and EMMA). Sharing the blame is director Bruce Beresford (DRIVING MISS DAISY, BREAKER MORANT), whose normally light touch fails him here. *(Violence, profanity, adult situations.)* — B.T.

d, Bruce Beresford; p, Steven Haft; exec p, Richard Luke Rothschild; co-p, Chuck Binder; w, Ron Koslow (based on a story by Steven Haft and Ron Koslow); ph, Peter James; ed, John Bloom; m, Mark Isham; prod d, John Stoddart; art d, Monroe Kelly; set d, John Anderson; sound, Hank Garfield (mixer); fx, Gary D'Amico; casting, Shari Rhodes, Joseph Middleton; cos, Colleen Kelsall; makeup, Susan Cabral; stunts, Randy Fife

Drama **(PR: C MPAA: R)**

LAST MAN STANDING ★★

(U.S.) 102m Lone Wolf Films; Arthur Sarkissian Productions; New Line ~ New Line c

Bruce Willis *(John Smith)*; Bruce Dern *(Sheriff Ed Galt)*; William Sanderson *(Joe Monday)*; Christopher Walken *(Hickey)*; David Patrick Kelly *(Doyle)*; Karina Lombard *(Felina)*; Ned Eisenberg *(Fredo Strozzi)*; Alexandra Powers *(Lucy Kolinski)*; Michael Imperioli *(Giorgio Carmonte)*; Ken Jenkins *(Captain Tom Pickett)*; R.D. Call *(Jack McCool)*; Ted Markland *(Deputy Bob)*; Leslie Mann *(Wanda)*; Patrick Kilpatrick *(Finn)*; Luis Contreras *(Comandante Ramirez)*; Raynor Scheine *(Gas Station Attendant)*; Tiny Ron *(Jacko the Giant)*; John Paxton *(The Undertaker)*; Michael Cavalieri *(Berto)*; Hannes Fritsch *(Santo)*; Michael Strasser *(Docker)*; Matt O'Toole *(Burke)*; Lin Shaye *(The Madam)*; Larry Holt *(Border Patrolman)*; Allan Graf *(Convoy Driver)*; Cassandra Gava *(Barmaid)*; Randy Hall *(Doyle Thug)*; Jimmy Ortega *(Ramirez Bodyguard)*; Tom Rosales *(Ramirez Bodyguard)*; Dean Rader-Duval *(Donnie)*; Michael Prozzo *(Roca)*; Chris Doyle *(Brothel Thug)*; Jim Palmer *(Brothel*

Thug); Kerry Lynch; Paul Lyons; Rick Merring; Michael McBride; Scott Pierce; Ed Rote; Scott Strand; Jim Wilkey *(Doyle Gang Members)*; Andrew Alden; Arnie Alpert; Dana Bambo; Philip Ciano; Robert Coffee; Michael Cordeiro; Sonny D'Angelo; Carmine Grippo; Timothy Gallegos; Michael Lerner; Ken Medlock; Bill Rochon; Joe Kay; Rocky Reyna Galiente *(Strozzi Gang Members)*

LAST MAN STANDING is action director Walter Hill's attempt to join the ranks of masters Akira Kurosawa and Sergio Leone by refashioning the former's samurai film YOJIMBO (1961), as well as Leone's Italian western remake A FISTFUL OF DOLLARS (1967).

Prohibition-era hired gun John Smith (Bruce Willis), en route to a hideout in Mexico, stops for gas in Jericho, Texas, and finds a dusty, near-ghost town populated almost exclusively by members of two rival bootlegging gangs, an Irish group headed by Doyle (David Patrick Kelly), and an Italian one headed by Strozzi (Ned Eisenberg). Smith outguns and kills a Doyle man in an early confrontation and goes to work for the Strozzis, helping them hijack a liquor shipment from Mexico intended for Doyle.

Seeking to play both ends against the middle, Smith develops a small group of allies and pumps them for information. They include Lucy (Alexandra Powers), a moll connected with the Strozzis; Joe Monday (William Sanderson), the town's lone bartender; and Sheriff Galt (Bruce Dern), who tries to keep out of the conflict, but winds up helping Smith when the Texas Rangers pressure him to restore order to the town.

After supplying info that helps Doyle get revenge on the Strozzis for hijacking the liquor, Smith goes to work for Doyle, but his intent is to locate Felina, a Mexican girl being held by the infatuated Doyle against her will. She wants to return to Mexico to her husband and child. Smith, sent to check up on Felina's guards, kills them all and frees Felina, sending her by car to Mexico and telling the Doyles that the Strozzis did it. While Doyle and his top killer, Hickey (Christopher Walken), go off to search for Felina, Doyle's lieutenant McCool (R.D. Call) discovers Smith's deception and has him beaten and held captive. Seriously injured, Smith manages to outwit his captors and escapes to hide out in an abandoned church on the outskirts of town, where he is aided by Joe and Galt.

After a raid on the Strozzis' stronghold, which results in their complete destruction, Doyle's gang continues to search for Smith, torturing Joe Monday and holding him hostage until Smith sends a message demanding a face-off with Doyle and Hickey. In a final shoot-out, Smith kills the remaining Doyles and prepares to move on to Mexico.

Although the prohibition-era setting harks back to Dashiell Hammett's 1929 novel *Red Harvest* (the source for Kurosawa's YOJIMBO), there is no trace of Hammett's carefully etched picture of a western mining town beset by labor troubles and subsequent conflicts between rival groups of power-hungry goons. Hill draws more closely for inspiration on A FISTFUL OF DOLLARS (although only Kurosawa gets a credit here), even down to specific shots and aspects of production design. In the staging of the shoot-outs, Hill actually borrows more from Hong Kong director John Woo, particularly in the way star Willis enters a room with outstretched dual automatics, blasting away nonstop.

In the earlier films, both Toshiro Mifune and even the young Clint Eastwood projected an innate sense of justice that allowed the audience to sanction their violent responses to the deeply corrupt characters they encountered. Willis is effective in the kind of proactive action roles he's had in the past, such as in the DIE HARD series, where he's simply required to run, leap, shoot, and crack jokes. Here, however, he lacks the moral weight the character requires; his deadpan countenance and voice-over monotone fail to convey any deeper sense of world-weariness or inner anguish. He is not particularly distinguishable from his opponents, who are neither brutal nor decadent enough to justify the kind of violence exacted upon them. They never look like anything but boys playacting. *(Violence, sexual situations, profanity.)* — B.C.

d, Walter Hill; p, Walter Hill, Arthur Sarkissian; exec p, Sara Risher, Michael De Luca; assoc p, Paula Heller; co-p, Ralph Singleton; w, Walter Hill (based on the story by Ryuzo Kikushima and Akira Kurosawa); ph, Lloyd Ahern; ed, Freeman Davies; m, Ry Cooder; prod d, Gary Wissner; art d, Barry Chusid; set d, Gary Fettis; sound, Lee Orloff (mixer); fx, Lawrence James Cavanaugh, R. Bruce Steinheimer; casting, Mary Gail Artz, Barbara Cohen; cos, Dan Moore; makeup, Gary Liddiard

Action/Crime/Western (PR: O MPAA: R)

LAST SUPPER, THE ★½

(U.S.) 94m Vault, Inc.; Sony Pictures Entertainment ~ Sony Pictures Entertainment c

Cameron Diaz *(Jude)*; Ron Eldard *(Pete)*; Annabeth Gish *(Paulie)*; Jonathan Penner *(Marc)*; Courtney B. Vance *(Luke)*; Jason Alexander *(Anti-Environmentalist)*; Nora Dunn *(Sheriff Stanley)*; Charles Durning *(Reverend Hutchens)*; Bryn Erin *(Heather)*; Mark Harmon *(Dominant Male)*; Bill Paxton *(Zack)*; Ron Perlman *(Norman Arbuthnot)*; Nick Sadler *(Homeless Basher)*; Dan Rosen *(Deputy Hartford)*; Warren Hutcherson *(Nation Man)*; Pamela Gien *(Illiterate Librarian)*; Rachel Chagall *(Abortion Activist)*; Amber Taylor *(Girl in Coffee Shop)*; Matt Cooper *(Jerk in Coffee Shop)*; Gil Segel *(Iowa Resident at Door)*

An unpleasant little comedy of murders, THE LAST SUPPER is the story of a group of smug, liberal grad students who systematically slay a succession of local right-wing crackpots.

After his Mercedes-Benz breaks down, Pete (Ron Eldard) is brought home by Zack (Bill Paxton) in his pickup. Pete and his housemates, Paulie (Annabeth Gish), Jude (Cameron Diaz), Marc (Jonathan Penner), and Luke (Courtney B. Vance), invite the young trucker to stay for dinner. When Zack reveals himself to be a violent bigot, a fight breaks out and he is killed. After burying their victim in the backyard, the five graduate students decide to perform a series of righteous executions. An anti-homosexual priest (Charles Durning), a male chauvinist (Mark Harmon), an anti-abortion zealot (Rachel Chagall)—one by one they and others of their ilk are invited to dinner, poisoned, and buried outside.

Meanwhile, the local sheriff (Nora Dunn) is tracking Zack, who turns out to have been a brutal sex criminal. One day, her investigation leads her to the students' house where Luke, afraid she will discover the murder victims' graves, kills her.

The gang of five's last guest of honor is Norman Arbuthnot (Ron Perlman), a reactionary TV talk show host. When Arbuthnot's after-dinner conversation proves to be surprisingly moderate and reasonable, the confused students retreat to the kitchen to debate his fate. After returning to the dining room, they drink a toast, unaware that their guest, who has surmised their secret, has poisoned their wine.

Making murder funny isn't easy, despite the success of ARSENIC AND OLD LACE (1944) and a couple of Ealing comedies. Even Hitchcock wasn't able to salvage THE TROUBLE WITH HARRY (1955). The trouble with THE LAST SUPPER is its hosts. Only similarly brainwashed viewers will be able to identify with or warm up to the movie's liberal lynching party—a sanctimonious gang of "politically correct" vigilantes with barely an ounce of charisma among them. Effective comedies crave the presence of at least one sympathetic character, but you won't find him or her here. The difficulty surfaces right in the first reel when the students start patronizing Zack even *before* they discover he is a vicious bigot.

Director Stacy Title may have been aware of the sympathy problem confronting her here, in her first feature film, but she was unable to solve it. As the movie is rather good-looking despite a low budget, and since Title's only previous film (a short called "Down on the Waterfront") was adept and amusing, one has to assume that most of THE LAST SUPPER's unattractive and alienating qualities can be blamed on scriptwriter Dan Rosen. *(Violence, sexual situations, extreme profanity.)* — D.T.

d, Stacy Title; p, Matt Cooper, Larry Weinberg; exec p, David Cooper; assoc p, Luis Colina; co-p, Lori Miller, Dan Rosen; w, Dan Rosen; ph, Paul Cameron; ed, Luis Colina; m, Mark Mothersbaugh; prod d, Linda Burton; set d, Dea Jensen; sound, Don H. Matthews (mixer); fx, Performance World; casting, Debra Zane, Bonnie Zane; cos, Leesa Evans; makeup, Desne Holland; stunts, Bjorn Johnson

Comedy/Political **(PR: C MPAA: R)**

LATE SHIFT, THE ★★

(U.S.) 95m HBO Pictures; Northern Lights ~ HBO Home Video c

Kathy Bates *(Helen Kushnick)*; John Michael Higgins *(David Letterman)*; Daniel Roebuck *(Jay Leno)*; Treat Williams *(Mike Ovitz)*; Rich Little *(Johnny Carson)*; Bob Balaban *(Warren Littlefield)*; Reni Santoni *(John Agoglian)*; Peter Jurasik *(Howard Stringer)*; Ed Begley Jr. *(Rod Perth)*; John Kapelos *(Robert Morton)*; Steven Gilhorn *(Peter Lassally)*; John Getz *(Brandon Tartikoff)*; Lawrence Pressman *(Robert Wright)*; Paul Elder *(Rupert Murdoch)*; Nicholas Guest *(Robert Iger)*; Edmund L. Shaff *(Jack Welch)*; Kevin Scannell *(Dick Ebersol)*; David Brisbin *(Alan Levine)*; Michael Fairman *(Michael Gartner)*; Arthur Taxier *(Lee Gabler)*; Michael C. McCarthy *(Jimmy Brogan)*; Penny Peyser *(Susan Binford)*; Lucinda Jenney *(Debbie Vickers)*; Ann Ryerson *(Betty Hudson)*; Aaron Lustig *(Paul Shaffer)*; Ken Kragen *(Himself)*; Little Richard *(Himself)*; Sandra Bernhard *(Herself)*

This chronicle of the machinations behind the high-profile battle for control of "The Tonight Show" puts heavy emphasis on the wheeling and dealing behind the scenes of late-night television. The movie premiered on HBO in February of 1996, and was later released to home video.

Late night programming is a $70 million profit machine for the NBC television network. Johnny Carson (Rich Little) is the host of "The Tonight Show" and the undisputed king of the late shift. Jay Leno (Daniel Roebuck), the popular "permanent guest host" of Carson's show, and David Letterman (John Michael Higgins), a self-contained institution in the hour after Carson, both stand as heirs presumptive to Johnny's throne. When Carson announces his retirement, NBC executives, who've been bullied by Leno's acerbic manager Helen Kushnick (Kathy Bates), make the strategic decision to maintain the status quo, and name Kushnick's client as Carson's replacement. In response to this, Letterman signs with powerful Hollywood *uber*-agent Mike Ovitz (Treat Williams) and seeks release from his "indentured servitude" to NBC.

With Kushnick installed as "The Tonight Show"'s executive producer, the outset of Leno's stint as host is a stormy affair. Kushnick delights in playing a zero-sum game of hardball with guests, their managers, NBC colleagues, and her bosses. Eventually, fed-up NBC executives fire her, and make it clear to Leno that if he walks off the show out of loyalty, they'll replace him with Letterman. Meanwhile, Ovitz has engineered a bidding war for his client's services, and the NBC brass start second guessing their choice. Desperate to keep Letterman, they finally offer him "The Tonight Show." After seeking counsel from Carson, his Yoda, Letterman decides the job he covets is now damaged goods, and he defects to rival network CBS.

THE LATE SHIFT is spiritual kin to another made-for-HBO movie, 1993's BARBARIANS AT THE GATE, wherein the behind-the-scenes chronicle of a corporate takeover became a pointed satire of '80s greed culture. THE LATE SHIFT makes its point in the scene where NBC President Warren Littlefield (played by Bob Balaban) takes a phone call, while on the toilet, from Leno. Littlefield is caught, literally, with his pants down as Leno reveals his knowledge of the merciless remarks made about him by NBC execs at a (supposedly) secret meeting. This tone—"Look at how stupid these NBC bigwigs are!"—is the movie's major flaw.

Adapted from Bill Carter's book, which was published in 1994, THE LATE SHIFT reflects the conventional wisdom of that time: NBC made a big mistake choosing Leno and letting Letterman get away. Then, it appeared CBS and Letterman had scored a resounding victory with the new "Late Show," as Leno continued to struggle. As fortunes have since turned, that attitude appears misguided and the movie feels dated. (Imagine, a two-year-old period piece.)

Given the public's current, seemingly insatiable appetite for entertainment "news," THE LATE SHIFT's premiere generated immense media attention. It received acclaim primarily for the performances of Williams and Bates. Helen Kushnick, who died in the fall of 1996, sued over how she was portrayed. Leno generally avoided commenting on the movie or its unflattering portrait of him. Letterman offered hilarious parodies on his show and, perhaps, the best assessment of THE LATE SHIFT as much ado about "a job interview." *(Extreme profanity.)* — P.R.

d, Betty Thomas; p, Don Carmody; exec p, Ivan Reitman; co-p, Joe Medjuck, Daniel Goldberg; w, Bill Carter, George Armitage (based on the book by Bill Carter); ph, Mac Ahlberg; ed, Peter Teschner; m, Ira Newborn; prod d, Garreth Stover; art d, Linda Berger; casting, Nancy Foy; makeup, June Westmore

Docudrama/Comedy **(PR: C MPAA: R)**

LAWNMOWER MAN 2: JOBE'S WAR

(SEE: LAWNMOWER MAN 2: BEYOND CYBERSPACE)

LAWNMOWER MAN 2: BEYOND CYBERSPACE ★½

(U.S./U.K.) 95m Lane/Pringle Productions; Allied Vision ~ New Line c
(AKA: LAWNMOWER MAN 2: JOBE'S WAR)

Patrick Bergin *(Dr. Benjamin Trace)*; Matt Frewer *(Jobe)*; Austin O'Brien *(Peter)*; Ely Pouget *(Cori)*; Camille Cooper *(Jennifer)*; Patrick La Brecque *(Shawn)*; Crystal Celeste Grant *(Jade)*; Sean Parhm *(Travis)*; Mathew Valencia *(Homeless Kid)*; Kevin Conway *(Walker)*; Trevor O'Brien *(Young Peter)*; Richard Fancy *(Senator Greenspan)*; Ellis Williams *(Chief of Security)*; Castulo Guerra *(Guillermo)*; Molly Shannon *(Homeless Lady)*; Ralph Ahn *(Doctor)*; David Byrd *(Judge)*; Stephanie Menuez *(Female Lawyer)*; Nancy Chen *(Cashier)*; Amanda Hillwood *(News Anchor)*; Patricia Belcher *(Impatient Customer)*; Gregg Daniel *(Trace's Lawyer)*; Arthur Mendoza *(Technician)*; Dale E. House *(Helicopter Pilot)*; John Benjamin Martin *(Henry the Guard)*; Ayo Adejugbe *(Nigerian Businessman)*; Yoshio Be *(Japanese Businessman)*; Carl Carlsson-Wollbruck *(German Business-*

man); David Gibbs *(Male Pilot)*; Pamela West *(Female Co-pilot)*; Dan Lipe *(Securtiy Guard)*; Kenny Endoso *(Train ConductorCashier)*

Contrary to what viewers saw at the end of 1992's surprise box-office hit THE LAWNMOWER MAN, Jobe, a retarded gardener turned into a godlike entity via computer science, did physically survive a lab explosion—only to star in this thoroughly routine sequel.

Jonathan Walker (Kevin Conway), ruthless president of the Virtual Light Institute, forces Jobe (Matt Frewer), crippled and helpless when he's not plugged into virtual reality, to create a global network linking all computers. Jobe, still power-mad, exploits a friendship from his low-IQ days with Peter (Austin O'Brien), a teenage hacker. Peter helps Jobe locate the reclusive Dr. Benjamin Trace (Patrick Bergin) whose breakthrough "kyron" chip will help Walker achieve his goals.

Jobe's agenda, however, is to misuse worldwide computer systems and make reality so miserable that people everywhere will be happy to don virtual-reality headsets and dwell forever in cyberspace under Jobe's absolute domination. Realizing how they've all been duped, Trace, Peter, and other plucky pals race against time and various perils to prevent the takeover scheme, but are unable to halt the "Global Interface." Jobe turns against Walker, but a fail-safe in the kyron chip induces an overload that regresses the lawnmower man back to his harmless self. Jobe even lends a feeble hand aiding Trace and the good guys in their showdown with the maniacal Walker.

Replacing Jeff Fahey in the title role—reconstructive plastic surgery offered by way of explanation—Matt Frewer plays Jobe with a flip manner similar to his computerized TV character "Max Headroom" over a decade ago (LAWNMOWER 2 is directed by Headroom's creator, Farhad Mann). If Frewer often acts like a tired Jim Carrey clone, blame a hackneyed plot partially pirated from Carrey's "Riddler" plotline in BATMAN FOREVER.

For a high-tech adventure, both the action scenes and the computer animation special effects have a ho-hum quality even inferior to the first film. Like many mainstream sci-fi thrillers, this reveals a cowardly ambivalence about high technology. Production design of the near future is unimaginative, signified by the presence of ATMs and credit cards. Still, with the fact that CNN is the only TV channel mentioned in the story, film distributor New Line (owned by CNN's Ted Turner) has added an oppressive Orwellian element that was probably unintended.

For a movie that should have been a CD-ROM to begin with, LAWNMOWER MAN 2 proves that acting, direction and writing can be as mechanical as any computer program. *(Violence, profanity.)* — E.M.

d, Farhad Mann; p, Keith Fox, Edward Simons; exec p, Steve Lane, Bob Pringle, Peter McRae, Clive Turner, Avaram Butch Kaplan; assoc p, Masao Takiyama; w, Farhad Mann, Michael Miner (from a story by Farhad Mann); ph, Ward Russell; ed, James D. Mitchell, Joel Goodman; m, Robert Folk; prod d, Ernest H. Roth; art d, Vincent Reynaud, John Michael Kelly; set d, Alexander Carle; sound, Richard Schexnayder (mixer); fx, Mike Meinardus, Cinesite; casting, Glenn Daniels; cos, Deborah Everton; makeup, Natalie Wood, Dianne O.; stunts, Spiro Razatos, Ken Bates

Science Fiction/Action/Fantasy (PR: C MPAA: PG-13)

LAZARUS MAN, THE ★★½

(U.S.) 90m Castle Rock Entertainment ~ Turner Home Video c

Robert Urich *(Lazarus Man)*; John Diehl *(Nat Patchett)*; David Marshall Grant *(General Sherman)*; Elizabeth Dennehy *(Elizabeth Patchett)*; John Christian Graas *(Davey Patchett)*; Wayne Grace *(Derby Hat Man)*; Brion James *(Tom Holleran)*; John Furlong *(Barkeep)*; Natalija Nogulich *(Joie)*; Terry Gardner *(Big Yank)*; Forrie Smith *(Blood Knight)*; Jake Walker *(Broussard)*; Bill Pearlman *(Doctor)*; Fritz Sperberg *(Carney)*; Bill Allen *(Lieutenant 1)*; J. D. Garfield *(Lieutenant 2)*; Bret Davidson *(Blood Knight 2)*; Marc Miles *(Little Man)*; Blake Conway *(Man)*; Boots Southerland *(Sergeant)*; Robert Harvey *(Soldier)*; Nicholas Anthony *(Provost Marshall)*; Isabelle Townsend *(Dark-Haired Woman)*

This pilot film for a promising western series features a to-be-continued gimmick (the amnesiac hero's search for his identity) that would have ensured the show a decent run. Panicked by their star Robert Urich's cancer diagnosis, the producers scuttled the series, which combined "The Fugitive" and "Branded" into adult western escapism with deeper psychological underpinnings than most hard-riding frontier adventures.

Buried alive, the Lazarus Man (Robert Urich) is found near death by young Davey Patchett (John Christian Graas) and his circumspect father, Nat Patchett (John Diehl), on All Hallow's Eve, 1865.

Nursed back to health by Nat's wife, Elizabeth (Elizabeth Dennehy), the confused stranger awakens weeks later, sans memory, in San Sebastian, Texas, where rancor about the Civil War persists. Unsure of his own sympathies, the Lazarus Man witnesses the slaying of a bluejacket soldier by an outlaw Rebel vigilante group, the Blood Knights, headed by Tom Holleran (Brion James). After kidnapping the Lazarus Man, Holleran releases him because he believes he is actually Jack Broussard, a desperado the Blood Knights have hired to assassinate visiting President Ulysses S. Grant.

Down at the military settlement, suspicious Yankee General Sherman (David Marshall Grant) keeps a watchful eye on the Lazarus Man; flashbacks suggest that the man with no memory also might have been a secret serviceman. The Lazarus Man becomes further sidetracked when he has to save his benefactor, Nat Patchett, from the paranoid Blood Knights.

One possibility about the Lazarus Man's identity clears up when the real Jack Broussard (Jake Walker) turns up to kill President Grant. After escaping a lynching at the hands of Holleran, the Lazarus Man thwarts the assassination attempt by lobbing a baseball at Broussard's firing arm. General Sherman guns down the rabid Holleran; Nat gets wounded while preventing Broussard from retaliating against the Lazarus Man; and the Blood Knights are wiped out by the US Cavalry.

Star-powered by TV veteran Urich, this gritty western sets up an intriguing premise: from a living death, a frontier Galahad is reborn as a blank slate that both the Yanks and the Rebs want to write on. Nailing the rancorous historical period following the Civil War, this morality tale registers more authentically than other standardized frontier sagas; in this movie, one can feel the characters shaking off the prairie dust.

If the protagonist's desperate detective work lacks variety and if the film's echoes of SHANE (1953) are too pronounced, THE LAZARUS MAN still maintains a brisk canter past most western cliches. With several standout set-pieces, such as the graveyard resurrection that opens the film and the water tower contretemps between Broussard and the Lazarus Man during the assassination attempt, this dark fable engrosses even when it drops the suspense ball, and intrigues even when the other cast members don't measure up to Urich's vigorous portrayal of the hero. *(Graphic violence, profanity, adult situations.)* — R.P.

d, Johnny E. Jensen; p, Harvey Frand, John Binder; exec p, Michael Ogiens, Norman S. Powell; assoc p, Bruce Margolis, Tony Palermo; co-p, Colleen O'Dwyer, Marc Zicree; w, Dick

Beebe; ph, Gary Holt; ed, Christopher Nelson; m, John Debney, Charles Sydnor; prod d, William Sandell; set d, Robert Gould; sound, Andre Perreault (mixer); fx, Andre Ellingson; casting, Sharon Bialy, Susan Booker; makeup, Rod Wilson; stunts, Justin Lundin

Western **(PR: C MPAA: NR)**

LE HUSSARD SUR LE TOIT
(SEE: HORSEMAN ON THE ROOF)

LE RIDICULE
(SEE: RIDICULE)

LEGEND OF GATOR FACE, THE ★★½
(U.S./Canada) 100m Showtime Networks, Inc.; Ministry of Film; Alan Mruvka/Marilyn Vance Productions ~ Hallmark Home Entertainment c

John White *(Danny)*; Dan Warry-Smith *(Phil)*; Paul Winfield *(Bob)*; C. David Johnson *(Sheriff)*; Charlotte Sullivan *(Angel)*; Gordon Michael Woolvet *(Chip)*; Kathleen Laskey *(Danny's Mom)*; Pam Hyatt *(Mayor's Wife)*; Roger Dunn *(Mayor)*; Matt Evans *(Gator Face)*

THE LEGEND OF GATOR FACE is a derivative and innocuous, but quite watchable, children's fantasy-adventure about a mythical half-man, half-gator creature that lives in the swamps of a small southern town.

Danny (John White) and Phil (Dan Warry-Smith), two mischievous friends, are on summer vacation and looking for some pranks to pull. An old hermit named Bob (Paul Winfield), who lives in a shack on the swamp, tells them about the legend of Gator Face, a half-man, half-alligator creature that supposedly has been haunting the area for 50 years. As a joke, Danny and Phil make an alligator costume which Phil wears to terrorize the town. The sheriff (C. David Johnson), who is Danny's dad, forms a posse after the boys scare three campers in the woods, and the story makes the news. Phil goes out by himself one night and Danny runs after him, but when he trips and is about to be bitten by a rattlesnake, the real Gator Face (Matt Evans) appears and saves Danny's life. Danny tells Phil about the real Gator Face, but he doesn't believe him. After Phil scares the mayor's wife (Pam Hyatt) in his costume, the mayor (Roger Dunn) calls in the National Guard.

Danny takes Phil back into the swamp to look for Gator Face; they find him trapped in a net. Danny cuts him loose, and Danny, Phil, and another friend, devise a plan to rescue Gator Face. Danny dresses in the fake costume and lures the National Guard to an old barn, where he has painted the words: "I tricked you. I was a joke—Gator Face" on the wall, but when he runs inside the barn, the townsfolk set the barn on fire, trapping Danny inside. Phil tells Danny's dad that Danny's inside and he tries to rescue him, but the fire is too strong. Suddenly, Gator Face shows up and carries Danny to safety. One of the soldiers shoots the creature and he dies. A strange noise is heard in the swamp and the skies start to swirl. The bullet hole in Gator Face closes up and he is revived. Danny and his friends form a human shield around Gator Face and urge the National Guard to let the creature go. They do.

THE LEGEND OF GATOR FACE is a blatant E.T. rip-off (even down to a shot where Danny and the creature touch fingers), but it's a surprisingly effective children's movie nevertheless. With its blue eyes, benign expressions, and magical connection with children, the creature looks like a cross between E.T. and a gentle, baby Godzilla. The story has the usual cliched lessons about tolerance for those who are different (i.e., Bob, the black hermit, and the Gator Face), but it's not too preachy or heavy-handed (until the protracted finale) and the emphasis is on lighthearted adventure from a child's point-of-view. The creature looks like a leftover from the 1959 schlock classic THE ALLIGATOR PEOPLE, and is only marginally more convincing than the costume that Danny and Phil make. At 100 minutes, the film is at least 10 minutes too long, but the direction is competent and the cast is likable. The atmosphere of kids looking for some summer fun and excitement in a sleepy rural town is captured fairly well.*(Violence.)* — M.S.

d, Vic Sarin; p, Marilyn Vance, Alan Mruvka; co-p, Patrick Whitley; w, David Covell, Alan Mruvka, Sahara Riley; ph, John Tarver; ed, David Goard; m, Joseph Williams; prod d, Marian Wihak; art d, Lisa Lev; sound, Thomas Hidderley; fx, Brock Jolliffe, Paul L. Jones, Image Animation Canada; casting, Tina Gerusi; cos, Melanie Jennings; makeup, Jordan Samuel

Fantasy/Adventure **(PR: A MPAA: PG)**

LES RENDEZ-VOUS DE PARIS
(SEE: RENDEZVOUS IN PARIS)

LES SILENCES DU PALAIS
(SEE: SILENCES OF THE PALACE, THE)

LES VISITEURS
(SEE: VISITORS, THE)

LES VISITEURS: ILS NE SONT PAS NES D'HIER!
(SEE: VISITORS, THE)

LES VOLEURS ★★½
(France) 117m Les Films Alain Sarde ~ Sony Pictures Classics c
(AKA: THIEVES)

Catherine Deneuve *(Marie)*; Daniel Auteuil *(Alex)*; Laurence Cote *(Juliette)*; Benoit Magimel *(Jimmy)*; Fabienne Babe *(Mireille)*; Didier Bezace *(Ivan)*; Julien Riviere *(Justin)*; Ivan Desny *(Victor)*; Pierre Perez *(Fred)*; Regis Betoule *(Regis)*; Naguime Bendidi *(Nabil)*; Didier Raymond *(Lucien)*

Andre Techine gets Tarantino-itis in LES VOLEURS, a dense, intricately-plotted mystery about the death of a mob figure. The convergence of characters and events in the film should be explosive, but it's only confusing in the end.

A mobster, Ivan (Didier Bezace), who had been running a car-smuggling ring, dies, leaving a 10-year-old son, Justin (Julien Riviere). The detective on the case, Alex (Daniel Auteuil), who happens to be Ivan's brother, investigates several people connected to Ivan in Lyon. He starts with Juliette (Laurence Cote), a headstrong young woman who had worked for Ivan in his nightclub. As he gets to know her better, Alex falls for Juliette, unaware at first that she is also involved with Marie (Catherine Deneuve), a whiskey-drinking grandmother and college philosophy teacher.

When Alex discovers that he has a romantic rival, he meets with Marie and they quarrel over Juliette. Both seasoned lovers are becoming overly infatuated with the young woman, but are reluctant to admit it. Alex discovers that Ivan was killed by a security guard while stealing cars. Juliette breaks off her affairs with both Alex and Marie. Marie, in turn, kills herself after a bout of depression.

LES VOLEURS represents a step forward for French director Andre Techine in terms of re-configuring narrative. The screenplay by Techine, Gilles Taurand, Michel Alexandre, and Pascal Bonitzer tells an already involved tale from four points of view (echoing RASHOMON), while it also incorporates flashbacks without clear denotations and withholds crucial information for long periods of time. Techine had worked in the mystery-romance-thriller genre before (notably with SCENE OF THE CRIME, 1986, also with Deneuve), but LES VOLEURS, possibly influenced by the international success of PULP FICTION, is a more daring storytelling experiment.

Ironically, the qualities that had made Techine's most recent films (WILD REEDS and MA SAISON PREFEREE) so touching are almost completely absent here. In these other films, the director used a simpler narrative frame to explore the psychological dimensions of the characters' lives. The almost impressionistic use of character point of view made MA SAISON PREFEREE (1993) particularly haunting. Auteuil and Deneuve of the latter film are reteamed in LES VOLEURS in a far less evocative way, as if their characters now are mere pawns in the overly tricky plot.

Actually, the most memorable performer in LES VOLEURS is newcomer Cote. Her tomboyish Juliette may not seem quite worth all the fuss the other characters raise, but Cote's sharp performance provides a ballast to the story. Some other fine attributes of the film include the handsome production design (by Ze Branco), appropriately dark cinematography (by Jeanne Lapoirie), and a charmingly staged fragment from Mozart's "The Magic Flute." LES VOLEURS is not without merit, but by the end, the puzzle pieces hardly seem worth putting together. *(Violence, nudity, sexual situations, adult situations, substance abuse, extreme profanity.)* — E.M.

d, Andre Techine; p, Alain Sarde; w, Andre Techine, Gilles Taurand, Michel Alexandre, Pascal Bonitzer; ph, Jeanne Lapoirie; ed, Martine Giordano; m, Philippe Sarde; prod d, Ze Branco; sound, Jean-Paul Mugel, Jean-Pierre Laforce; casting, Michel Nasri; cos, Elisabeth Tavernier; makeup, Michel Deruelle, Cedric Gerard

Thriller/Drama (PR: C MPAA: NR)

LET'S GET BIZZEE ★★½

(U.S.) 90m Spectrum Clay Productions ~ Xenon Entertainment c

Doug E. Fresh *(Sam Baker)*; Anthony Chisholm *(Tony Dillon)*; Lisa Carson *(Cheryl Parker)*; Starletta Dupois *(Helen Baker)*; Marie Victoria Garcia *(Betty)*; Ernest Rayford *(Cecil Jiggs)*; Robert McKenna *(Meade)*; Ademeyi E. Nixon *(Bill McCoy)*; Janice Cornelius *(Mrs. Sargent)*; Giovanni Gudluvin *(Nunsie)*; Kim Burrell; Steven Flum; Fulton Hodges; Augustin Rodriguez; Gil Finch; Lamar Hill; Antar Jones

LET'S GET BIZZEE showcases actor Doug E. Fresh in a novel mix of hip-hop and civics.

Graduating from all-black Al Jolson High School, 18-year-old Sam Baker (Doug E. Fresh) dimly contemplates a career in fast food until political awareness strikes in the form of a former family friend, Queens assemblyman Tony Dillon (Anthony Chisholm), now rightfully regarded as a sellout to corrupt white interests. While placating the African-American community with shiny new basketball courts, Dillon takes kickbacks to support a luxury condo development that would bulldoze housing projects and displace the 'hood's low-income residents.

Attempting to ride to the rescue is Bill McCoy (Adeyemi E. Nixon), a former basketball star who is running against Dillon in the imminent election. Sam jumps aboard his campaign, but Dillon's camp arranges McCoy's demise in a traffic accident. The incumbent's victory seems assured until Sam volunteers to replace McCoy on the ticket. His rapping talents appeal to disaffected black youths, despite violence among rowdies at his concert-style rally.

Dillon counters with various dirty tricks, including a botched blackmail scheme concerning Sam's illegitimate son. Finally, he tries to bribe Sam to get him to concede. Despite some rough moments, Sam hangs in, while Dillon's own campaign collapses under the scrutiny of a criminal investigation. Finally, the assemblyman flees the country.

The upbeat finale sidesteps the facts that Sam is a novice, his platform includes such questionable planks as vigilante justice against pushers, and his candidacy is largely inspired by lust for a pretty McCoy campaign manager (Lisa Carson), who, sure enough, winds up as Sam's docile bedmate. Filmmaker Carl Clay allows a public debate between the rivals to degenerate into "Yo' mama!" obscenities on both sides. There is also a tasteless anti-Dillon commercial (sponsored by "Homeboys to Elect Sam Baker") that even evokes some sympathy for the villain.

There are ingredients here for a minority takeoff on Michael Ritchies' grand political farce THE CANDIDATE (1972), but LET'S GET BIZZEE settles for empowerment comedy that compares Sam Baker, rather unpersuasively, to Martin Luther King and Malcolm X. *(Profanity, substance abuse, sexual situations)* — C.C.

d, Carl Clay; p, Carl Clay; w, Carl Clay, Andy K. Gill, Eugene Jordon III; ph, Bill Dill; ed, Joseph Burton; m, Derek Galloway, Robert Meeks; prod d, Charles Rice; casting, Linda Anderson

Political/Comedy (PR: C MPAA: NR)

LETTER TO MY KILLER ★★½

(U.S.) 92m Sanford Pillsbury Productions ~ MCA Universal c

Mare Winningham *(Judy Parma)*; Nick Chinlund *(Nick Parma)*; Rip Torn *(Russell Vanyk)*; Josef Sommer *(Martin Prescott)*; Eddie Jones *(Wilson Hartwick)*; James Murtaugh *(Darryl)*; Dey Young *(Helen Maris)*; Todd Louiso *(Bradley)*; Earl Theroux *(George Maris)*; James Keane *(Ray)*; Linda Hoy *(Maureen)*; Miriam Flynn *(Personnel Director)*; Kenneth Schmidt *(Bobby)*; Will Rothaar *(Danny)*; Aixa Clement *(Diane)*; Lois Hall *(Librarian)*; Sarah Ann Morris *(Leona)*; Beverly Neufeld *(Bank Employee)*; Don Pugsley *(Hunter 1)*; Carl Gabriel Yorke *(Hunter 2)*; Joyce McNeal *(Bag Lady)*; Lisa Lord *(Bill Collector)*; Larry Nash *(Construction Foreman)*; Mark Chaet *(Angry Man at Bank)*; Stacey Evans *(Young Vanyk)*; Jock MacDonald *(Young Prescott)*; Steven Mainz *(Young Hartwick)*

Though this suspense film's mystery is transparent, and its protagonists are oblivious, it still is mildly diverting. Produced by the socially conscious team of Sarah Pillsbury and Midge Sanford (AND THE BAND PLAYED ON), the movie sandwiches in an earnest message about the callousness of Big Business. But the do-gooder story content is at odds with the manufacture of thrills.

In 1965, a pharmaceutical company secretary, Helen Maris (Dey Young), is murdered for attempting to reveal the criminal negligence of her Unidek Company bosses, Russell Vanyk (Rip Torn), Martin Prescott (Josef Sommer), and Wilson Hartwick (Eddie Jones).

Thirty years later, Helen's evidence surfaces at a building site where down-on-his-luck construction worker Nick Parma (Nick Chinlund) works. Nick's wife, Judy (Mare Winningham), hatches a blackmail plot against the Unidek triumvirate. But, at an arranged info-for-money exchange, a bag lady gets blown up by a bomb meant for Judy.

Tricked out of their hard evidence, Nick and Judy decide that the only way they can stay alive is to prove Helen's conspiracy theory about Unidek withholding reports about the side effects of their chemical fertilizer, Compound K. Working from Helen's old steno tapes and questioning Helen's brother, George Maris (Earl Theroux), the Parmas underestimate the ruthlessness of Vanyk. The villain drowns vacillating partner Hartwick and hires a hit man, who murders Helen's brother George before tracking down Nick and Judy.

Determined to rock Vanyk's world for destroying so many innocent lives with harmful Compound K, Nick meets with Vanyk and Prescott. From a distance, Judy tapes their admissions of guilt, but the assassin pursues her through the woods. After a brain-damaged guard, Bradley (Todd Louiso), one of the fertilizer's victims, rescues Judy by shooting her assailant, the Parmas wait for the police to arrest a defeated Prescott and an unrepentant Vanyk for their crimes against the community.

The basic problem with LETTER TO MY KILLER is its failure to reconcile its social-problem dramatic concerns with its identity as an amateur detective potboiler. Fortunately, the screenplay convincingly etches the Parmas' change of motive as they're redeemed by a Ralph Nader-ish zeal to bait the corporate monsters.

One would expect this thriller to juice up its voltage as the Parmas lose their early rounds against the big boys. Instead, the movie works better as a soap opera in which the married couple's mettle is tested not by hysterical blindness, amnesia, or infidelity, but by a pharmaceutical company's corrupt game plan; the Parmas' crusade saves their marriage from dissension caused by money worries. Intrigued by the Parmas' scattered efforts at justice, the audience is even more moved as they react to the human ramifications of Unidek's betrayal.

LETTER TO MY KILLER is AN ENEMY OF THE PEOPLE adapted not by Arthur Miller, but by Barbara Taylor Bradford.*(Violence, profanity, adult situations.)* — R.P.

d, Janet Meyers; p, Vicky Herman; exec p, Sarah Pillsbury, Midge Sanford; w, Norman Strum; ph, Stephen Katz; ed, Anita Brandt-Burgoyne; m, Mason Daring; prod d, Nicholas T. Preovolos; art d, Lori Yvonne Mazuer; set d, Beau Petersen; sound, Geoffrey Lucius Patterson; fx, Martin Becker; casting, Mary Gail Artz, Barbara Cohen; cos, Enid Harris; makeup, Cheryl Ann Markowitz; stunts, Bob Minor

Thriller/Crime/Drama (PR: C MPAA: PG-13)

LIFEFORM ★★

(U.S.) 90m Stargate Entertainment; Alterian Studios ~ Showcase Entertainment/Live Home Video c

Cotter Smith *(Case Montgomery)*; Deirdre O'Connell *(Dr. Gracia Scott)*; Robert Wisdom *(Col. Jesse Pratt)*; Ryan Phillippe *(Private Ryan)*; Raoul O'Connell *(Private Jeffers)*; Carlos Carrasco *(Sgt. Lopez)*; Leland Orser *(Michael Perkett)*; Kevin Cooney *(General McClintoch)*; Joseph Romanov *(Private Hawkins)*; Damon Saleem *(Private Talbert)*; Ivan Gueron *(Lt. Angstrom)*; Timothy Charles *(Ian Ochs)*; Gregory Webb *(Recovery Team Member)*; Peter McKernan *(Chopper Co-pilot)*; Dirk Vahle *(Chopper Pilot)*; Burke Roberts *(Check Point Guard)*; Kim Collins *(Sgt. Reynolds)*; Jeff Gardner *(Private Zebrasky)*; Andrew Endsley *(Decontamination Technician)*; Leif Tilden *(The Invader)*; Andrew Alden; Michael Bailous; Dennis Chamberlain; Mike Derey; John Dewey; Ryan Dunn; Dwight Dyer; Tommy Heisler; Chuck Lynn; Angus McLellan *(Army Privates)*

Though slightly more ambitious than the usual alien-on-Earth exercise, this low-budgeter is generally content just to go through the motions.

A Viking II rocket returns from a trip to Mars and touches down near an Army base in the southwest. The craft is taken inside, where a foreign object is discovered on it; the pod proves to be the incubator for an alien creature. The extraterrestrial soon breaks out and escapes into the base, which is sealed up and put on quarantine. Case Montgomery (Cotter Smith) and Dr. Gracia Scott (Deirdre O'Connell) lead a team of soldiers and scientists in tracking down both the lifeform—which feeds on electricity—and Jeffers (Raoul O'Connell), a private believed to be infected by it. After claiming a few victims, the alien is killed and autopsied, and an unhatched egg is removed from the remains.

Jeffers proves actually to be suffering from appendicitis, and while Dr. Scott begins to operate on him, two other soldiers discover the egg has hatched. The new alien, after quickly growing to maturity, breaches one of the base's walls. With quarantine broken, the entire base is nuked. Soon thereafter, it is discovered that another Viking lander is approaching Earth.

"You just let a potentially dangerous exobiological lifeform out of quarantine, and now the whole building is contaminated!" From that snippet of dialogue, it's pretty easy to tell how the story of LIFEFORM will proceed: Dr. Scott spouts plenty of techno-jargon and questions like "What is the point of exploring space if we're going to kill everything we meet?" while the colonel in charge (Robert Wisdom) simply wants the invader killed. There are a few minor variations on the standardized story, but it's telling that the most dramatic plot development involves not the alien but Jeffers' appendicitis.

The acting is generally competent or better (aside from the unconvincing Raoul O'Connell); Alterian Studios' alien effects are well-crafted (particularly the final, centaur-like incarnation); and the plot never slides into silliness or tedium. But the movie is so cut-and-dried, it's difficult to work up any real enthusiasm for it. The only unpredictable element is the surprisingly downbeat ending, which suggests a harder edge that might have benefited LIFEFORM had it been applied throughout.*(Graphic violence, profanity.)* — M.G.

d, Mark H. Baker; p, Mark H. Baker, Madelyn Curtis, Rick Baer; assoc p, James Glennon; co-p, Tony Gardner, Cynthia Gardner; w, Mark H. Baker; ph, James Glennon; ed, Jan Northrop; m, Kevin Kiner; prod d, Villamor Cruz; art d, Scott Malchus; sound, Tommy Lockett, Paul Ratajczak; casting, Laurel Smith; cos, Nazhat Hester; makeup, Beate Eisele

Science Fiction/Horror (PR: O MPAA: R)

LILY DALE ★★

(U.S.) 98m Producers Entertainment Group ~ Showtime/Hallmark Entertainment c

Mary Stuart Masterson *(Lily Dale)*; Sam Shepard *(Pete Davenport)*; Stockard Channing *(Corella)*; Tim Guinee *(Horace Robedeaux)*; John Slattery *(Will Kidder)*; Jean Stapleton *(Mrs. Coons)*; Sean Hennigan *(Card Player)*; Chamblee Ferguson *(Drummer)*; Elbert Lewis *(Vegetable Vendor)*; Jonathan Bren; Brent Anderson *(Trio Singers)*; Mark Walters *(Uncle Albert)*; Angee Hughes *(Mrs. Westheimer)*; John Hussey *(Mr. Westheimer)*; Horton Foote *(Voice of Old Horace)*

To call a Horton Foote drama low-key may be redundant, but it's particularly true in the case of this adaptation of one of his plays, set (as usual) in the turn-of-the-century Texas of his own upbringing.

Horace Robedeaux (Tim Guinee) has lived alone since his widowed mother Corella (Stockard Channing) remarried Pete Davenport (Sam Shepard). Davenport took Corella and Horace's younger sister Lily Dale (Mary Stuart Masterson) back with him to Houston, but felt that 12-year-old Horace was best left to make his own living. Now 19, Horace receives an invitation to visit from his mother.

Horace arrives in Houston to an indifferent welcome from his self-absorbed sister. His mother invited Horace at this time only because her husband was to be away on business for several weeks. When Davenport returns early, he is openly unhappy to find Horace in his house. But the young man becomes ill and spends several weeks feverish and unconscious on the living room sofa.

Angered by Davenport's intimations that he is faking his illness to get free room and board, Horace tries to leave on several occasions but is still too weak. Lily Dale and Horace argue; she accuses him of living in the past and he states how much he despises Davenport. Considering marriage, Lily Dale asks Corella how babies are made. Corella tells her only that she'll find out when she's married, but that childbirth is so painful that she should avoid it. Horace returns home to take a new job.

Aside from his Oscar-winning script for TO KILL A MOCKINGBIRD (1962), which was adapted from Harper Lee's novel, plot has never been a strong point of the screenplays of Horton Foote (TENDER MERCIES; 1918; THE TRIP TO BOUNTIFUL, the most notable film from LILY DALE director Peter Masterson). But even by Foote's standard, LILY DALE is exceptionally vague. Why does Davenport hate Horace so much, a hatred which apparently began when this apparently inoffensive youth was a boy of 12? Does he regard him as the heir of his father, a scholarly lawyer who succumbed to alcoholism? Davenport is stodgily anti-alcohol and anti-intellectual, boasting of the fact that he's never read a book; but there's no evidence that he even knew his wife's first husband. And why is this drama, which centers on this battle between these two men, named for Horace's sister? (The part gets top billing for Masterson, who is at least 10 years too old for the role of this teenaged flibbertigibbet.) Are we supposed to presume that there are sexual tensions in the Davenport household? Davenport never speaks his mind; Corella is largely afraid to; and what's on Lily Dale's mind generally isn't worth hearing.

Foote's usual strength is characterization, but this adaptation fails there as well. Sam Shepard is stolid at best, Masterson merely dislikable (and uninterestingly so). As a mother and son unable to resume a relationship that was taken away from them, Stockard Channing and Tim Guinee are appealing and able; the script's failure to tell us more about them is its chief failing. *(Adult situations.)* — M.F.

d, Peter Masterson; p, John Thomas Lenox; exec p, Hallie Foote, Irwin Meyer, Peter Crane, Linda Curran Wexelblatt; assoc p, Joe Pope, Alison Meyer; w, Horton Foote (based on his play); ph, Don E. Fauntleroy; ed, Michael N. Knue; m, Peter Rodgers Melnick; prod d, Barbara Haberecht; art d, Jack Marty, Chris Henry; casting, Jeanne McCarthy, Rody Kent; cos, Jean-Pierre Dorleac; makeup, Robert Harper, Patty York

Drama **(PR: A MPAA: PG)**

LINE KING: THE AL HIRSCHFELD STORY, THE ★★½

(U.S.) 87m Times History ~ Castle Hill c

Al Hirschfeld; Carol Channing; Colleen Dewhurst; Margo Feiden; Jules Feiffer; Arthur Gelb; Brendan Gill; Eric Goldberg; Adam Gopnik; Philip Hamburger; Katharine Hepburn; Kitty Carlisle Hart; Dolly Hass Hirschfeld; Nina Hirschfeld; Stefan Kanfer; Louise Kerz; Paula Laurence; Dr. Calvin F. Nodine; Joseph Papp; Maria Riva; Jason Robards; Florence Rome; Clara Rotter; Daniel Mayer Selznick; Lauren Bacall; Cy Coleman; Joan Collins; Robert Goulet; Geoffrey Holder; Robert Loggia; Barbara Walters

Perhaps as much a promotional piece as documentary, THE LINE KING surveys the career of 93-year-old master caricaturist Al Hirschfeld. Directed by the *New York Times* in-house documentarian Susan W. Dryfoos (who, at the time of filming, had held the title of "Director of Times History Productions" for more than a decade), this likable puff piece garnered an Academy Award nomination for Best Feature Documentary.

From the very beginning, THE LINE KING genuflects at the altar of Hirschfeld, opening with a montage of celebrities mooning over his artistry. Liza Minnelli gushes that "one of the highest honors a member of our profession can achieve is to be immortalized with a stroke of a pen by this master of portraiture." Hepburn, Bacall, Channing, the tributes continue and the film rarely gets off its knees.

After this hagiographic barrage, the white-bearded Methuselah recounts his childhood; family photographs and early century stock footage complement his tale. Raised in St. Louis by a working mother and a stay-at-home father (who supposedly coined the term "senior citizen"), the young Hirschfeld loved to draw, and his talent encouraged the family to move to New York. Mesmerized by the stage, the prodigy became art director at Selznick Pictures while still a teenager. But the apotheosis—the fateful moment that led to his ascension as the Line King (or, more accurately, led to his seven-decade career as a caricaturist)—hadn't arrived yet.

After a brief fling with sculpture, Hirschfeld joined the Lost Generation in Paris and dabbled in painting. Then, back in Manhattan, it happened: one evening at the theater in 1926, a publicity agent peered over Hirschfeld's shoulder as the artist sketched the French actor Sacha Guitry on his program. The agent sold the drawing to the *Herald Tribune,* and it wasn't long before the *Times* bought Hirschfeld's services for life.

Decade by decade, the film flashes through an entertaining evocation of the performing arts as captured in Hirschfeld's beloved swirling lines. Images of his graphically inspired, sometimes mischievous drawings are accompanied by show tunes from the appropriate era. These pictures are followed by Hirschfeld's own anecdotes from the corresponding decades. For example, Hirschfeld once tried to convince Moss Hart not to pen "My Fair Lady" because it would be folly to tamper with Shaw's "Pygmalion." On another occasion, he drew the loathsome producer David Merrick as "vicious[ly]" as he could, as an evil, snaggletoothed Santa Claus. Merrick bought the picture and put it on his Christmas cards.

Unfortunately, although THE LINE KING covers a lengthy period of time, it often lacks substance. Filmmaker Dryfoos fails to ask Hirschfeld any follow-up questions in her interviews. Her portrayal shies away from conflict. What did the other children think when the Hirschfelds moved to New York for twelve-year-old Al? Where is the criticism of his drawings? What of Hirschfeld's troubled romantic life, which Dryfoos presents in a surprisingly cursory fashion? Her emphasis on the happy details of Hirschfeld's life only serves to underscore these omissions.

Probably the best-known element of Hirschfeld's work is his inclusion of the name "Nina" in every drawing, hidden in the swirls of beards and the folds of gowns. Originally conceived to celebrate the birth of his daughter Nina, Hirschfeld feels that without this signature device, people would take his work more seriously, but he fears the deluge of letters that would swamp him if he stopped. His daughter is troubled by a celebrity status that she didn't earn herself. As expected, the film sidesteps this potential point of interest.

Editor Angelo Corrao follows the two-second rule: never leave any drawing on screen for more than two seconds. Thus, the audience never has the chance to look for a "Nina"—or, more importantly, to appreciate Hirschfeld's drawings of the endless neck of Lynn Fontanne, the many images of Fred Astaire defying gravity, or the "pile of dirty laundry" that captures Zero Mostel. On the whole, THE LINE KING sacrifices depth for breadth: it's an enjoyable repast, but it's not terribly filling.— T.Y.

d, Susan W. Dryfoos; assoc p, Angelo Corrao; w, Susan W. Dryfoos; ph, Richard Blofson, Jeffrey Grunther; ed, Angelo Corrao; sound, Sam Russell, Scott Nielsen, John Tipton, John Andres

AAN Best Documentary Feature

Documentary **(PR: A MPAA: NR)**

LITTLE DEATH, THE ★★

(U.S.) 91m Island Pictures ~ PolyGram c

Dwight Yoakam *(Bobby Lomax)*; J. T. Walsh *(Ted Hannon)*; Pamela Gidley *(Kelly Hannon)*; Brent Fraser *(Nick Hannon)*; D. W. Moffett *(Paul Hannon)*; Troy Beyer *(Defense Attorney)*; Richard Beymer *(Prosecutor)*; Amy Stock-Poynton *(Meredith Hannon)*; Philip Baker-Hall *(Detective Snyder)*

Using every cliche in the erotic-thriller book, THE LITTLE DEATH is almost instantly forgettable, despite a cast and production design that are slightly above average.

Nick Hannon (Brent Fraser), a struggling young musician, takes a job with his domineering, wealthy father, Ted (J.T. Walsh). Ted is married to Kelly (Pamela Gidley), a much younger woman who is being stalked by an apparent psychopath named Bobby (Dwight Yoakam). Since Bobby persists even after several unpleasant encounters, Ted goes to Bobby's apartment in a rage, where Bobby calmly shoots him.

Kelly begins an affair with Nick shortly after Ted's death, while Bobby continues to pursue her. During his trial, Bobby claims self-defense and is found not guilty. We learn that Kelly planned the whole thing with Bobby to get Ted's money. Kelly then turns on Bobby and kills him after setting it up to look as if he raped her. Nick begins to suspect and finds evidence linking Kelly and Bobby. He confronts her and she kills herself rather than face prison.

THE LITTLE DEATH has a very polished, professional look to it. Also, Walsh, Fraser—brother of actor Brendan Fraser—and country-music star Yoakam all have screen presence. But the positive points end there. The lion's share of screen time is given to Gidley, who overacts throughout and is not nearly as attractive as she thinks she is. An actress would need a lot more talent to pull off the unbelievable part of Kelly.

The film is also weighed down by occasionally cheesy editing, which reaches its nadir in some very obvious body-double shots during the sex scenes. The script is the biggest problem, though. The audience is expected to believe, for example, that Bobby could legitimately claim self-defense after shooting an unarmed man from across the room with a sawed-off shotgun. Of course, any other outcome to the trial would have detracted from the utter predictability that plagues this entire movie. *(Violence, profanity, nudity, sexual situations)* — K.Fr.

d, Jan Verheyen; p, Chris Zarpas, Ann Dubinet; exec p, Mark Burg, Dan Genetti; co-p, Carrie Morrow; w, Nicholas Bogner, Michael Holden; ph, David Phillips; ed, Joseph Gutowski; m, Christopher Tyng; prod d, Armin Ganz; sound, Stephen A. Tibbo; fx, Mark DiSarro; casting, Mali Finn; cos, Mimi Melgaard; makeup, Samantha Weaver

Erotic/Thriller **(PR: O MPAA: NR)**

LITTLE INDIAN, BIG CITY ★★★

(France) 87m Ice Films; TF1 Films Productions; Canal Plus; Procirep ~ Buena Vista c
(AKA: INDIAN IN PARIS, AN; UN INDIEN DANS LA VILLE)

Thierry Lhermitte *(Stephan Marchado)*; Patrick Timsit *(Richard)*; Ludwig Briand *(Mimi-Siku)*; Miou-Miou *(Patricia)*; Arielle Dombasle *(Charlotte)*; Sonia Vollereaux *(Marie)*; Tolsty *(Pavel)*; Jackie Berroyer *(Jonavisky)*; Marc de Jonge *(Rossberg)*; Louba Guertchikoff *(Mrs. Godette)*; Philippe Bruneau *(Mr. Marshal)*; Dominique Besnehard *(Master Dong)*; Cheik Doukoure *(Mr. Bonaventure)*; Marie-Charlotte LeClaire *(Rossberg's Secretary)*; Olga Jirouskova *(Sonia Koutchnoukov)*; Chick Ortega *(Russian)*; Paco Portero *(The Snake Man)*; Sonia Lezinska *(Stewardess)*; Marc Brunet *(Policeman)*; Olivier Hemon *(Policeman)*; Thierry Desroses *(Customs Officer)*; Katia Weitzenbock *(Miss Van Hodden)*; Feliciano Tello Rossi *(Chief Mouloukou)*; Maurice Illouz *(Man in Airplane)*; Suzy Marquis *(Woman in Building)*; Carlos Reyes *(Mailman in the Amazon)*; Richard Holzle *(Man with Canoe)*; Christian Roy *(Missile Technician)*; Jean-Pierre Richette *(Man at the Red Light)*; Pauline Pinsolle *(Sophie)*; Stanley Zana *(Jonathan)*; Gaston Dolle *(Benjamin)*

This was a major hit in its native France in 1994, and when Disney bought remake rights they went an extra step in the deal made with the French distributors; a dubbed edition of the original UN INDIEN DANS LA VILLE received an unusual wide release in the United States. Most American reviewers lambasted it for the dubbing, and box-office returns were regrettably meager for a cute and thought-provoking mix of children's adventure and broad anthropological farce.

Stephan (Thierry Lhermitte) is a workaholic businessman whose wife Patricia (Miou-Miou) left him 13 years ago. In order to marry his beautiful but dippy new love he travels to Patricia's new home, a remote Amazon island, to finalize the divorce. She agrees to the divorce, but reveals that when she left him she was pregnant. She introduces Stephan to his son, Mimi-Siku (Ludwig Briand), raised as a member of the island Indian tribe. To get to know the boy better, Stephan takes Mimi-Siku to Paris. Retaining his jungle instincts, Mimi-Siku kills a pigeon that is resting on a neighbor's porch, climbs the Eiffel Tower, eats pet fish, and his pet tarantula scares the fiancee of Stephen's partner into spending her day locked in the bathroom.

In Stephan's absence, partner Richard neglected to sell their company's soybean stock, and its value plummeted. To rectify matters, Richard arranges to sell it to some Russian mobsters. Stephan sends Mimi-Siku off for a day with Richard's family, and the boy charms their 14-year-old daughter. Meanwhile, the Russians find out the stock is worthless and the threatened partners must back the issue, whose value unexpectedly skyrockets, making them rich. But Stephan's experience with Mimi-Siku changes him, despite his newfound wealth. He leaves Paris to be with the boy and Patricia, who is still legally his wife. Richard and his family join them.

On one level, LITTLE INDIAN, BIG CITY is a silly comedy about a savage adapting to unfamiliar surroundings, often hilariously as when Mimi-Siku goes on a carnival ride and attacks the "scary" fake animals. On another level, LITTLE INDIAN, BIG CITY is a soft slap in the face to those who prize money, power, and status over family and friends. Mimi-Siku is charming, and though his primitivism is a source of humor, the screenplay never condescends, and in fact shows the "civilized" city people to be the true fools (not unlike THE GODS MUST BE CRAZY, another hit comedy initially scorned by American reviewers). His love of nature, ability to fend for himself, and naive charm win over his Parisian relations and the audience.

Despite its slapstick, the film has many subtleties, its criticism of the fast pace and inhumanity of modern society cleverly presented. Mimi-Siku's pet spider only becomes dangerous when humans are angry and noisy, the boy finds nature (fish, pigeons) in the middle of an urban environment, and running gags lampoon white-collar dependence on computers and cellphones. Although the subplot about vicious Russian thugs is unnecessarily alarming, the film respects the intelligence of its target audience of children. Perhaps the American public and pundits didn't expect a live-action Disney release that dared to show kids as they often are in reality: bratty and undisciplined.

Lhermitte and Briand are gifted comic actors, and both city and jungle get a spectacular treatment by the camera. The dubbing *is* atrocious, but that's a minor drawback for something warmer and more sophisticated than most American children's films.*(Sexual situations, profanity.)* — A.M.

d, Herve Palud; p, Louis Becker, Thierry Lhermitte; w, Herve Palud, Igor Aptekman, Thierry Lhermitte, Philippe Bruneau; ph, Fabio Conversi; ed, Roland Baubeau; m, Manu Katche, Geoffrey Oryema, Tonton David; prod d, Ivan Maussion; sound, Pierre Lorrain, Vincent Arnardi; fx, Jean-Francois Lemaire, Jean-Louis Trinquier; casting, Mamade, Carlos Reyes; cos, Martine Rapin; makeup, Eric Pierre, Muriel Baurens, Gil Robillard

Children's/Comedy **(PR: A MPAA: PG)**

LITTLE WITCHES ★½

(U.S.) 91m Le Monde Entertainment ~ A-Pix Entertainment c

Mimi Reichmeister *(Faith)*; Sheeri Rappaport *(Jamie)*; Jennifer Rubin *(Sherilyn)*; Jack Nance *(Father Michael)*; Zelda Rubinstein *(Mother Clodah)*; Zoe Alexander *(Nicole)*; Clea Duvall *(Kelsey)*; Tommy Stork *(Daniel)*; Melissa Taub *(Erica)*; Eric Pierpoint *(Sheriff Gordon)*; Landon Hall *(Masked Girl)*; Lalaneya Hamilton *(Gina)*; Sister Napolitano *(Herself)*; Constance Crossea; Erica Doering; Valerie Roberts; Cheri Rae Russell; Robin South *(Illuminati Girls)*

Obviously intended to cash in on the theatrical release THE CRAFT (1996), this tacky direct-to-video item especially suffers from the comparison.

While most of the girls at the Catholic Santa Clarita Academy go home for Easter break, a small group stays behind, including sweet, troubled Faith (Mimi Reichmeister) and bad girl Jamie (Sheeri Rappaport). Workers repairing earthquake damage uncover a secret chamber behind the church, and the girls learn that a group of female students calling themselves the Illuminati Society held rituals there 100 years before. Jamie leads the other girls in re-enacting those rites, and employs Faith to translate a Latin book of incantations they find in the crypt. They discover that the rituals are intended to raise a being known as "He Who Comes"; meanwhile, Faith becomes friendly with hunky workman Daniel (Tommy Stork).

Increasingly overcome by the evil she's invoking, Jamie attempts to seduce Daniel and contrives the deaths of aged Mother Clodah (Zelda Rubinstein) and Father Michael (Jack Nance), believing each may be the "Lord's guardian" who can stop her. Instead, friendly teacher Sherilyn (Jennifer Rubin) proves to be the guardian, and Jamie stabs her. It falls to Faith to stop the girls' final sacrifice of Daniel; "He Who Comes" rises in the form of a horrible demon that drags Jamie down to hell, and the book falls after them.

Even divorced from comparisons to THE CRAFT, LITTLE WITCHES is a most unconvincing tale of teenage sorcery. Despite being directed by a woman (Jane Simpson), the film has no real empathy for its female characters or any suggestion that their occult dabblings stem from their life problems; they simply start indulging in witchcraft because it's, like, kinda cool. And the closest the script comes to dramatizing ancient Earth magic is a moment when Jamie tells the girls, "We have to get rid of anything modern," which means, of course, that they must immediately remove all their clothes.

The characterizations are strictly surface-level—Faith's a good girl, Jamie's a bad one, and that's about it, with some of their fellow junior witches barely even introduced by name. Simpson's direction incorporates several awkward camera moves and insert shots, and by the end, when the action lurches from one location to another without rhyme or reason, sticking with the movie has become more toil and trouble than it's worth. *(Graphic violence, extensive nudity, sexual situations, profanity.)* — M.G.

d, Jane Simpson; p, Donald P. Borchers; exec p, John Fremes, Robert Baruc; w, Brian DiMuccio, Dino Vindeni; ph, Ron Turowski; ed, Kristina Trirogoff; m, Nicholas Rivera; prod d, Jodi Ginnever; sound, Patrick M. Griffith; fx, Gabe Bartalos, John Hartigan; cos, Vincent Lapper; makeup, Cristina Patterson

Horror **(PR: O MPAA: R)**

LIVE NUDE GIRLS ★★★½

(U.S.) 93m Spelling Entertainment; Steve White Properties ~ Republic Pictures Home Video c

Dana Delany *(Jill)*; Kim Cattrall *(Jamie)*; Laila Robins *(Rachel)*; Lora Zane *(Georgina)*; Olivia d'Abo *(Chris)*; Cynthia Stevenson *(Marcy)*; Glenn Quinn *(Randy)*; Tim Choate *(Jerome)*; V.C. Davis *(Pool Man)*

The misleadingly titled LIVE NUDE GIRLS offers thoughtful conversation and intense personality conflicts as six 30-ish women discuss their sexuality at a bachelorette party. The talky but consistently surprising and often hilarious film has a strong ensemble cast and is cleverly scripted by first-time writer-director Julianna Lavin.

Jamie (Kim Cattrall) is a flighty B-movie actress who's about to enter into her third marriage. A party for her is hosted by Georgina (Lora Zane), a bisexual whose rocky relationship with her live-in partner Chris (Olivia d'Abo) is threatened by Georgina's attraction to a male co-worker.

Jamie and Georgina are joined at the party by lifelong friends Marcy (Cynthia Stevenson), a seemingly prim accountant who is being stalked by a house painter with whom she had a fling; Jill (Dana Delany), a racy, gossipy married woman who's ambivalent about her second pregnancy; and Jill's older sister, Rachel (Laila Robins), whose wealth and upper-class tastes don't make her feel better about being single and childless.

Jamie arrives at the party, ready to call off her wedding because her fiance Jerome's friends hired a stripper for his bachelor party. Her distress is one-upped by the antipathy between the sisters, whose petty jealousies erupt into rage and tears when Rachel discovers Jill's unwanted pregnancy. Meanwhile, Marcy gets drunk and befriends Chris, and Georgina ponders her future.

In between the arguments and disclosures, the five friends tell stories about their sex lives. The stories range from Jamie seducing a young Greenpeace canvasser, to Jill's fantasy of being spanked by a mob boss, to Marcy's fantasy of herself as Barbie, being spied on as she visits a public restroom. The torn relationships between Jill and Rachel, and Georgina and Chris, aren't patched up during the evening. But Jamie does decide to carry on with her upcoming marriage when she discovers that her doting fiance has canceled the stripper, and all six women wake the next morning with a better understanding of themselves and each other.

Perhaps the film's title is a joke at the expense of men who would flock to see "live nude girls" and then be shocked to discover women talking frankly about sex. Such female bonding hasn't been filmed often and may make men uncomfortable. LIVE NUDE GIRLS flawlessly uses dialogue to develop the women's personalities and unveil their personal crises. Though the film is mostly conversation, it is fast-paced and creatively presented, especially the hilarious flashbacks, including dead-on depictions of the 1970s, and the melodramatic sequence where Jamie pleads with her ex-husband to return and winds up seducing the Greenpeace teenager.

Even better are the scenes where the women wonder what kind of crazy antics Jerome and his pals are up to, and the film cuts to the geeky men making bets on things like how much money it would take for them to put their hands into toilets.

The ensemble cast is outstanding, especially d'Abo and Stevenson. Sharply written peripheral characters and a few in-jokes spice up the film. The frank dialogue never seems forced or unrealistic, which allows the women's personalities to resonate beyond their somewhat stereotypical basic natures.

The ending wisely leaves a few loose ends, and despite the use of flashbacks and several fantasy sequences, LIVE NUDE GIRLS is a realistic and authentic film that doesn't take itself too seriously. *(Extensive nudity, sexual situations, profanity.)* — A.M.

d, Julianna Lavin; p, Cara Tapper, Steve White, Barry Bernardi; exec p, Heather Bernt, Mel Layton; w, Julianna Lavin; ph, Christopher Taylor; ed, Kathryn Himoff; m, Anton Sanko; prod d, Jerry Fleming; sound, Jim Dehr; casting, Gary Zuckerbrod, Marcia Ross; cos, Israel Segal

Comedy **(PR: O MPAA: R)**

LIVE WIRE: HUMAN TIMEBOMB ★★½
(U.S.) 98m Nu World Inc. ~ New Line c

Bryan Genesse *(Parker)*; Joe Lara *(Price)*; J. Cynthia Brooks *(Gina)*; Anthony Fridjohn *(Gen. Arnaz)*; Frantz Dobrowsky *(Pablo)*; Leslie Fong *(Ernesto)*; Lionel Hunter *(Bost)*; Robert Whitehead *(Julio)*; Gideon Emery *(Cell Guard)*; Bill Flynn *(Juarez)*; Thorsten Wedekind *(Treasury Agent 1)*; Larry Shakinovsky *(Treasury Agent 2)*; James Whyle *(Gang Leader)*; Chris Buchanan *(FBI Leader)*; Trevor Kass *(Beefy Guard)*; Crispen De Nys *(Surgeon)*; Pamela Nomvete *(FBI Boss)*; Kryska Witkowska *(Juanita)*; Mike Joyce *(Gen. Atwater)*; Clive Scott *(Crocker)*; Roberto Perez *(Mendoza)*; Kurt Egelhof *(Chopper Pilot)*; Bruce Millar *(Newscaster)*; Lisa De Villiers *(Bride)*; Gary Wright *(Groom)*; Jo Da Silva *(Sonya)*; Gavin Hood *(Mike)*; Isaac Mavimbela *(Malinga)*; Barbara Rubin *(Julio's Woman)*

LIVE WIRE: HUMAN TIMEBOMB is a lightning-paced thrill-ride that suffers from an addiction to stunts and a nose-thumbing attitude toward plot.

Having busted druglord Pablo Arnaz (Frantz Dobrowsky), maverick FBI officer Parker (Bryan Genesse) gets ticked off when he's employed in a prisoner-swap for Arnaz in Cuba. While the US government preps Parker for retrieving military biochips that could transform ordinary soldiers into incredible hulks, his temporary superior, Treasury Agent Gina (J. Cynthia Brooks) accepts the Cuban mission, so she can free her POW brother Mike (Gavin Hood). Outsmarted by Pablo's uncle, General Arnaz (Anthony Fridjohn), Parker and Gina—who are hiding a biochip—become the guests of Arnaz and US traitor Price (Joe Lara) at Arnaz's scientific/military compound. Scrambling to build a super army, Arnaz has the chip implanted in Parker. Arnaz then unleashes his ultra-warriors at a wedding feast, where Parker kills a weak-willed government minister and Price slaughters the minister's daughter. During a subsequent fracas, Parker's chip is knocked loose and he's freed from the control device. Therefore, Price replaces Parker with Mike for use as a human time bomb to sabotage a peace summit.

Duped into believing Price is the kamikaze messenger, Parker breaks loose, pursues Price, navigates his way through unfriendly US agents, and ultimately uses Price as a human shield until Price is gunned down. As they battle their way out onto a window ledge, Parker can't prevent Mike from falling and exploding on the street below. After Gen. Arnaz is arrested, the peace conference proceeds without further interruption.

First the biochip is in one man, then it's transplanted into another; first Gina blames Parker for her brother's original capture, then she gets lovey-dovey. Yet, for a movie that seems to improvise its story line as it goes along, LIVE WIRE is surprisingly entertaining—implausible and hard to follow, but fun. A lot of its devil-may-care attitude can be attributed to Genesse, who proves to be a self-deprecating comic in addition to being a good actor. What makes Genesse's comic savoir-faire so essential here is that his love interest is a real wet blanket and the high-tech surgical scheme is a tiresome sci-fi retread. The real live wire here is the star, who performs acrobatic, athletic self-defense moves with killer instincts. *(Graphic violence, extreme profanity, adult situations, substance abuse.)* — R.P.

d, Mark Roper; p, Danny Lerner; exec p, Avi Lerner, Danny Dimbort, Trevor Short; assoc p, Brigid Olen; w, Jeff Albert; ph, Rod Stewart; ed, Daniel Lowenthal; m, Itai Haber; prod d, Raymond Wilson; art d, Janet Lombard; set d, Lisa Hart; sound, Nico Louw (mixer); fx, Rick Cresswell; casting, Christa Schamberger; cos, Ruy Filipe; makeup, Daphne Williams; stunts, Roly Jansen, Bryan Genesse

Martial Arts/Thriller/Political **(PR: C MPAA: R)**

LO BALLO DA SOLA
(SEE: STEALING BEAUTY)

LOADED ★★
(U.K./New Zealand) 108m Movie Partners; New Zealand Film Commission; Strawberry Vale; BFI Production; Channel Four Films; Geissendorfer Film; British Screen ~ Miramax c
(AKA: BLOODY WEEKEND)

Oliver Milburn *(Neil)*; Nick Patrick *(Giles)*; Catherine McCormick *(Rose)*; Thandie Newton *(Zita)*; Mathew Eggleton *(Lionel)*; Danny Cunningham *(Lance)*; Biddy Hodson *(Charlotte)*; Dearbhla Molloy *(Ava)*; Caleb Lloyd *(Young Neil)*; Joe Gecks *(Brother on Bike)*; Bridget Brammall *(Shop Assistant)*; Tom Welsh *(Skinhead)*

Anna Campion makes her directorial debut with LOADED, a slow, talky thriller about a group of teenagers who experience a tragedy while making a horror film. Although LOADED shares the pretensions of RIVER'S EDGE (1986), it lacks the suspense required of the better films of the genre.

In the present-day English countryside, seven teenage friends gather together one weekend to film a horror movie on an eerie estate. They include the disturbed Neil (Oliver Milburn), the beautiful but virginal Rose (Catherine McCormick), the arrogant Lance (Danny Cunningham), the intellectual Giles (Nick Patrick), the wealthy but weary Charlotte (Biddy Hodson), the sensitive, shy Zita (Thandie Newton), and the spiritual Lionel (Mathew Eggleton).

The filming of the Celtic fantasy story becomes periodically interrupted by both personal and artistic arguments within the group. Rose is particularly upset that her character seems to be based on her real-life situation. One night, in order to ease the tensions on the set, Lance gives everyone a new designer drug to take. Unfortunately, the drug works like a truth serum, causing the rifts to widen even further.

During the night, Neil and Lance try to clear their heads by taking a drive in their van. Lionel leads their way in the dark on his motorcycle, but Neil and Lance, who are still "loaded," accidentally kill him by running into his bike. When Neil and Lance return to the mansion with Lionel's body, the group decides to hide the corpse in the woods rather than call the police. The next morning, it seems as if Lionel's body has disappeared, which frightens the remaining friends as they try to understand the significance of the events from the night before.

LOADED distinguishes itself immediately from THE OLD DARK HOUSE (1932), THE HAUNTING (1963), and countless other haunted-house movies by interjecting extended philosophical pronouncements by the characters. The tortured British teen rebels-without-causes argue about such topics as religion and psychopathology—but while these people might be interesting to listen to on MTV's "The Real World," they emerge as merely tedious wet blankets in this thriller.

Anna Campion, like her sister Jane Campion (THE PIANO), has a talent for creating an atmospheric mise-en-scene. The dark lighting (even in daytime) and the moody, sometimes discordant music add to the ambiance. The director also gets good performances from her young cast. Yet Campion's script (whose skeletal plot suffers from predictability) lacks both suspense and surprise, which is itself a surprise since the old haunted-house gambit is a time-worn goose-bump producer for a good reason: it usually works!

LOADED means to be an art-horror film, but viewers looking for fun and thrills should stick to William Castle's 1958 cult classic, HOUSE ON HAUNTED HILL. *(Violence, nudity, sexual situations, adult situations, substance abuse, profanity.)* — E.M.

d, Anna Campion; p, David Hazlett, Caroline Hewitt, Bridget Ikin, John Maynard; exec p, Ben Gibson; w, Anna Campion; ph, Alan Almond; ed, John Gilbert; m, Simon Fisher Turner; prod d, Alistair Kay; art d, James Hambidge; sound, Peter Lindsay (recordist), Gethin Creagh (mixer), Michael Hedges (mixer); casting, John Hubbard, Ros Hubbard; cos, Stewart Meachem; makeup, Fae Hammond; stunts, Jim Dowdall

Drama/Thriller/Horror **(PR: C MPAA: R)**

L'OEIL DE VICHY

(SEE: EYE OF VICHY, THE)

LONE JUSTICE: SHOWDOWN AT PLUM CREEK ★★½

(U.S.) 95m CBS Entertainment Productions ~ Orion/Triboro Entertainment Group c

Brad Johnson *(Ned Blessing)*; Luis Alvalos *(Crocenio)*; Brenda Bakke *(Wren)*; Wes Studi *(One Horse)*; Rusty Schwimmer *(Big Emma)*; Stephen Frye *(Oscar Wilde)*; Richard Riehle; Rob Campbell; Bill McKinney; Tim Scott; William Sanderson

LONE JUSTICE: SHOWDOWN AT PLUM CREEK is the third full-length home-video release to be culled from the CBS miniseries NED BLESSING. Since this is a compilation of three episodes, each directed and written by different people, quality and style vary, and if one isn't already familiar with the series it takes a while to figure the territory. Unlike earlier compilations, SHOWDOWN AT PLUM CREEK has a clear, definite ending.

Plum Creek's sheriff Ned Blessing (Brad Johnson) discovers that the body of his predecessor, Sheriff Larsen, has disappeared from its grave. Larsen's preserved head is similarly AWOL from Blessing's office. Blessing's Indian friend One Horse (Wes Studi) had seen a headless man walking through town the previous evening. That night, Blessing and his friend Crocenio are trapped in a cave by Big Emma (Rusty Schwimmer), who takes the opportunity to take over the town saloon. Blessing discovers Larsen's head in the cave, and a boulder serendipitously dislodges, freeing the duo. Blessing returns to the saloon to confront Emma. Her cohort fights Blessing, only to be attacked by a ghost who turns him into an emotionless, mute zombie. Townspeople find Larsen, head back on his body, in his grave.

An effeminate but charming Englishman, Oscar Wilde (Stephen Frye), shows up in Plum Creek. Ridiculed by local roughnecks, he stands up for himself and breaks the nose of Silas, one of the town's biggest bullies. Wren (Brenda Bakke), Blessing's girlfriend, finds Wilde charming and goes riding with him. Wilde tells her that he was sent to Plum Creek by Blessing's lost childhood love, Jilly Blue. Saddened by Blessing's devotion to Jilly, Wren considers going to Europe with Wilde. Silas captures Wilde and attempts to hang him, and Blessing comes to the rescue. Blessing is also captured, and Wilde heroically risks his life to save Blessing. Wilde, now respected by all, returns to Europe. Wren stays in Plum Creek.

Big Emma hires the thuggish Sminck brothers to kill Blessing, but the intended victim arrests them first for an unrelated crime. Blessing invites County Sheriff John Mason Albright to Plum Creek to hang the varmints. On the road into town, Emma murders Albright, and the Smincks break out of jail. Blessing shoots down one, and the other is about to confess but Emma nails him first. Blessing never learns that she was behind the assassination plot. Blessing finally professes his love for Wren, who stood by him during the shootout.

The three stories combined in LONE JUSTICE: SHOWDOWN AT PLUM CREEK form an intricately plotted western with enough bizarre and surreal moments to make the story fresh. Not many westerns would bring Oscar Wilde to the middle of a one-horse Texas town. Even more amusing is the coma-zombie who sits around the saloon, gets fed by Emma, and basically blends into the townspeople like there's nothing wrong. The Wilde episode is by far the best of the three stories, with romance and humor, and Frye's flashy performance among a sedate cast is a breath of fresh air. Johnson's Blessing is an uncharismatic lead; it's a wonder Wren doesn't leave him for Wilde and Europe after all.

The problem with any TV serial repackaged as a stand-alone feature film is the absence of exposition and characterization established at the outset. At least the writing here is crisp, the stories easy to follow. Except for Wilde's wild west, the energy level is low for a sagebrusher, but a lighthearted spirit compensates.*(Violence.)* — A.M.

d, Jack Bender, Dan Lerner, David Hemmings; exec p, Bill Witliff; assoc p, Lee Haxall; w, Bill Witliff, Stephen Harrigan; ph, Neil Roach; ed, Terry Blythe, Jim McElroy, Keith Reamer; m, David Bell; prod d, Cary White; sound, John Pritchett; casting, Robert J. Ulrich, Eric Dawson; cos, Van Broughton Ramsey, Jim Echerd; makeup, Carla Palmer

Western **(PR: A MPAA: PG)**

LONE STAR ★★★★
(U.S.) 138m Rio Dulce, Inc.; Castle Rock Entertainment ~ Columbia Pictures c

Chris Cooper *(Sam Deeds)*; Elizabeth Pena *(Pilar Cruz)*; Joe Morton *(Delmore Payne)*; Miriam Colon *(Mercedes Cruz)*; Clifton James *(Mayor Hollis Pogue)*; Kris Kristofferson *(Sheriff Charley Wade)*; Ron Canada *(Otis Payne)*; Matthew McConaughey *(Buddy Deeds)*; Frances McDormand *(Bunny)*; Eddie Robinson *(Chet Payne)*; Stephen Mendillo *(Cliff)*; Stephen J. Lang *(Mikey)*; LaTanya Richardson *(Priscilla Worth)*; Chandra Wilson *(Athena Johnson)*; Damon Guy *(Shadow)*; Eleese Lester *(Molly)*; Gonzalo Castillo *(Amado)*; Carina Martinez *(Paloma)*; Gilbert R. Cuellar Jr. *(Eladio Cruz)*; Richard Coca *(Enrique)*; Maricela Gonzalez *(Anselma)*; Eduardo Martinez *(Jamie)*; Oni Faida Lampley *(Celie)*; Carmen de Lavallade *(Carolyn)*; Tony Frank *(Fenton)*; Jesse Borrego *(Danny)*; Richard A. Jones *(Ben Wetzel)*; Richard Reyes *(Jorge)*; Joe Stevens *(Deputy Travis)*; Tony Plana *(Ray)*; Randy Stripling *(Roderick Bledsoe)*; Beatrice Winde *(Minnie Bledsoe)*; Leo Burmester *(Cody)*; Tony Amendola *(Chucho Montoya)*; Gordon Tootoosis *(Wesley Birdsong)*; Sam Vlahos *(Pete)*; Jeff Monahan *(Young Hollis)*; Dee Macaluso *(Anglo Mother)*; Luis Cobo *(Mexican-American Father)*; Marco Perella *(Anglo Father)*; Don Phillips *(Principal)*; Mary Jane R. Hernandez *(Mexican-American Mother)*; Gabriel Casseus *(Young Otis)*; Olga Luna *(Waitress)*; Juan Vega III *(Cook)*; Lizzie Curry Martinez *(Girl)*; Vanessa Martinez *(Young Pilar)*; Tay Strathairn *(Young Sam)*; James Borrego *(Young Chucho)*; Lisa Suarez *(Marisol)*; Jesus Ramirez *(Driver)*; John Griesemer *(Voice of Football Announcer)*; Azalea Mendez *(Young Mercedes)*

John Sayles is at the peak of his form with LONE STAR, a revisionist western that weaves together many narrative threads across time and place. As usual, Sayles makes wise observations about race and gender, but this time he also tells a good story in an artful way.

In the dusty Texas town of Frontera, two off-duty sergeants (Stephen Mendillo and Stephen J. Lang) find skeletal remains and a rusty sheriff's badge on a deserted rifle range. Frontera's current sheriff, Sam Deeds (Chris Cooper), son of the late legendary lawman Buddy Deeds (Matthew McConaughey), opens up an investigation. Sam quickly learns that the bones are those of the corrupt sheriff his father was reputed to have run out of town, Charley Wade (Kris Kristofferson).

Sam's hostile relationship with his father also drove him out of Frontera until after Buddy's death. Now that Mayor Hollis Pogue (Clifton James) and the city council plan to name the new courthouse after Buddy Deeds, Sam's old feelings about his father resurface. Sam's memories of growing up in this border town include a teen-age romance with a Mexican-American girl, Pilar Cruz (Elizabeth Pena), which was broken up by his father. The recently widowed Pilar is the daughter of a successful restaurateur, Mercedes Cruz (Miriam Colon), a woman ashamed of her people and her past.

Pilar is a high school teacher, one of many embroiled in a fight with the minority Anglo community over how regional history should be taught. Among her students is the son of the Army post commander, Colonel Delmore Payne (Joe Morton). Payne accepted the command at this outpost despite the fact that his own estranged father, Otis (Ron Canada), lives in Frontera.

By re-establishing his ties to Pilar and the others in the community, Sam learns how his father avenged the death of the innocent Eladio Cruz, Mercedes' husband, by killing Charley Wade. He also learns that his father, not Eladio Cruz, was Pilar's father. Despite the revelation that they are half-brother and sister, Sam and Pilar decide to make a go of their now adult romance.

With its Mexican border-town setting, racially-charged incidents, and corrupt sheriff character, LONE STAR could pass as a modern-day version of TOUCH OF EVIL. The shocking denouement, on the other hand, seems like an homage to CHINATOWN. And while LONE STAR never quite reaches the stylistic heights of Welles or Polanski, it nonetheless artfully combines genre revisionism with progressive ideology and a fairly intriguing mystery story.

Without too much preaching (as in some of Sayles' earlier work), LONE STAR touches on topics like the contemporary immigration "problem," multi-culturalism in classroom teaching, interracial romance, and the legacy of racism. LONE STAR lacks humor—save Frances McDormand's cameo as Sam's manic-depressive ex-wife—but crackles with intelligence and authorial control. Technically, Sayles has rarely been better, as he shows in Sam's poetic, nocturnal driving sequence and in his off-beat choice of American and Mexican songs on the soundtrack.

A fine ensemble brings the diverse characters and stories to life. Cooper is especially effective as the doleful hero forced to confront the past. In the much smaller role of the film's main villain, Kristofferson gives his best performance to date. All the others follow suit, including Colon, who carries off a difficult about-face in Mercedes Cruz's tough-cookie character. LONE STAR brings back the western in a way that satisfies much more than the neo-classical designs of either LONESOME DOVE or UNFORGIVEN. *(Violence, nudity, sexual situations, adult situations, substance abuse, profanity.)* — E.M.

d, John Sayles; p, R. Paul Miller, Maggie Renzi; exec p, John Sloss; assoc p, Jan Foster; w, John Sayles; ph, Stuart Dryburgh; ed, John Sayles; m, Mason Daring; prod d, Dan Bishop; art d, Kyler Black; set d, Dianna Freas; sound, Clive Winter (mixer); fx, Jack Bennett; casting, Avy Kaufman; cos, Shay Cunliffe; makeup, Lori Hicks

AAN Best Original Screenplay: John Sayles

Drama **(PR: C MPAA: R)**

LONG KISS GOODNIGHT, THE ★★½
(U.S.) 103m Juno Pix, Inc.; Forge Productions; LKG Production Services Limited Partnership ~ New Line c

Geena Davis *(Samantha Caine/Charly Baltimore)*; Samuel L. Jackson *(Mitch Henessey)*; Yvonne Zima *(Caitlin)*; Craig Bierko *(Timothy)*; Tom Amandes *(Hal)*; Brian Cox *(Nathan)*; Patrick Malahide *(Perkins)*; David Morse *(Luke/Daedalus)*; Joseph McKenna *(One-Eyed Jack)*; Melina Kanakaredes *(Trin)*; Dan Warry-Smith *(Raymond)*; Kristen Bone *(Girl #1)*; Jennifer Pisana *(Girl #2)*; Rex Linn *(Man on Bed)*; Alan North *(Earl)*; Edwin Hodge *(Todd Henessey)*; Bill MacDonald *(Hostage Agent)*; Gladys O'Connor *(Alice)*; Frank Moore *(Surveillance Man)*; G.D. Spradlin *(President)*; Graham McPherson *(CIA Director)*; Sharon Washington *(Fran Henessey)*; Judah Katz *(Harry—Perkins' Aide)*; Robert Thomas *(Alley Agent)*; John Stead *(Deer Lick Sentry)*; Marc Cohen *(Teenage Burnout #1)*; Chad Donella *(Teenage Burnout #2)*; Debra Kirshenbaum *(Operator)*; Shawn Doyle *(Donlevy Bum Cop)*; Michael K. Jones *(Bum Cop #2)*; Ken Ryan *(News Anchor)*; Craig Eldridge *(Crime Scene Reporter)*; Susan Henley *(Church Mother)*; Reginald Doresa *(Bar Patron)*; Chuck Tamburro *(Helicopter Pilot)*; Larry King *(Himself)*

After the fiasco of 1995's CUTTHROAT ISLAND, director Renny Harlin and wife-star Geena Davis re-team for THE LONG KISS GOODNIGHT, a ludicrously implausible—but enjoyably trashy—piece of pulp about a sweet mom with amnesia who discovers that she used to be a highly-trained assassin for the CIA.

A narrator (Geena Davis) informs us her name is Samantha Caine, and that she has had amnesia for the past eight years. She lives in a quaint New England town with her young daughter, Caitlin (Yvonne Zima), though she isn't sure if the man she lives with is the father. While driving home after a Christmas party, her car hits a deer and crashes into a tree. Recovering in the hospital, she begins to get memory flashes of her past, including a bloodied image of herself holding a knife. Mitch Henessy (Samuel L. Jackson), a sleazy private investigator she has hired to find out who she used to be, calls to tell her he thinks he has found her uncle. Meanwhile, someone breaks into her house and tries to kill her, but he ends up dead instead.

Samantha goes off with Henessy to meet her "uncle," but a gang of hit men are waiting for them and a wild shootout ensues. Samantha and Henessy escape and meet her uncle, who claims that he's not her uncle, but actually her former boss. He informs her that she was a hit woman named Charly Baltimore for a covert government group, and that her life is in danger because she was supposed to have been eliminated eight years ago. The three of them are then abducted by a vicious killer named Timothy (Craig Bierko), who works for Perkins (Patrick Malahide), the corrupt government intelligence chief. Timothy kills Samantha's old boss and tortures her, but the shock of this fully jars her memory and she reverts to her Charly persona and escapes with Henessy.

Timothy kidnaps Caitlin and arranges a meeting with Charly near Niagara Falls. When she and Henessy get there, she manages to rescue Caitlin, but they're captured again by Timothy and Perkins, who inform her they plan to set off a truck-bomb and blame it on terrorists so that they can get more funding from Congress. Charly again escapes, but Caitlin accidentally hides inside the truck-bomb, so Charly has to commandeer the truck, rescue Caitlin, kill Timothy and about 100 other agents, and prevent the bomb from killing innocent civilians.

Mission accomplished, she remembers that a key she has opens a locker that contains loads of cash. Finally, Henessy appears on TV as a hero, and Charly receives a thank-you call from the President, then returns to her family with the money.

Despite a title that intentionally recalls classic film noirs such as THE LONG GOODBYE (1973) and KISS TOMORROW GOODBYE (1950)—this movie even throws in a clip of the former—THE LONG KISS GOODNIGHT is little more than a gender-switch variation of writer Shane Black's own LETHAL WEAPON (1987) script—black and white buddy cops, obscene wisecracks, wholesale slaughter—crossed with the LA FEMME NIKITA (1990) formula—in which Susie Homemaker is transformed into Susie Super Spy. There is also an intriguing subtext about the search for identity and the dual nature of good and evil, but director Harlin is content to stage the same old proficient, slow-motion, bullet-sprayed, pyrotechnic set–pieces in which everybody but the two leads are killed, and everything gets "blowed up real good."

Compensating somewhat for the mind-numbing massacre and total disregard for logic is the comic chemistry between Davis and Jackson and some amazing stunts, while Black's script cleverly integrates virtually every prop into later use in the plot.

Even though the film delights in referring to every female character as a "bitch," it purports to offer the feminist message that the only way women can survive is by having bigger balls than men. There are also numerous phallic references and penis jokes.

THE LONG KISS GOODNIGHT is the kind of nihilistic, cynical "fun" wherein the viewer is never bored, but can't remember one darn thing about it two seconds after leaving the theater. *(Graphic violence, extreme profanity.)* — M.S.

d, Renny Harlin; p, Renny Harlin, Stephanie Austin, Shane Black; exec p, Steve Tisch, Richard Saperstein, Michael De Luca; co-p, Carla Fry; w, Shane Black; ph, Guillermo Navarro; ed, William Goldenberg; m, Alan Silvestri; prod d, Howard Cummings; art d, Steve Arnold, Dennis Davenport; set d, Michael Taylor; sound, Doug Ganton (mixer); fx, Allen L. Hall, Jeffrey A. Okun, Estee Chandler, Special Effects Unlimited; casting, Mary Vernieu, Ronnie Yeskel; cos, Michael Kaplan; makeup, Christine Hart; stunts, Steve M. Davidson

Action/Thriller **(PR: C MPAA: R)**

LONG ROAD HOME, THE ★★

(U.S.) 88m Rosemont Productions ~ New Horizons Home Video c

Mark Harmon *(Ertie Robertson)*; Lee Purcell *(Bessie Robertson)*; Morgan Weisser *(Jake Robertson)*; Leon Russom *(Titus Wardlow)*

A Texas family who lost everything during the Great Depression seeks to have a home of their own once again in this predictable drama.

The Robertsons go from farm camp to farm camp, picking crops for a nickel per basket. Dad Ertie (Mark Harmon) is a former rodeo star, clearly degraded by migrant life, and unable to provide for his brood of eight. At El Adobe the family is paid in brass coins, which they can only use at the camp. Ertie demands cash and is promptly fired. "They ain't lettin' me work nor be a man," he laments. He is unable to save the life of the youngest Robertson girl, who dies of diphtheria.

The Robertsons' suffering contrasts with the greedy pleasure that Depression entrepreneur Titus Wardlow (Leon Russom) enjoys as he keeps the unorganized farm workers down. Hope for the family seems embodied by Bessie (Lee Purcell), Ertie's wife, determined to finding a permanent home. They find a place that's little more than a shack, and is still more than the Robertsons can afford. At a union-friendly farm camp, Ertie's target-shooting wins a little money to put towards the house.

Meanwhile, union activists rise up in protest when one of their men is shot in the back by Wardlow. Ertie's teenaged son Jake (Morgan Weisser) wants to join the union, against his cowed father's wishes. To thwart the labor movement, Titus arrives with a doctor and nurse to uncover health violations as an excuse to torch the workers' tents. The experts judge the camp up to code, but Titus sets fire to it anyway. This sends Ertie over the edge. He fights with Titus who nearly kills him. Jake saves his father's life by shooting Titus dead. Ultimately, the Robertsons move into their own home and finally sit down under one roof to eat a real dinner together.

Though based on a book by Ronald B. Taylor, this comes across like a Cliff's Notes version of John Ford's adaptation of Steinbeck's *The Grapes of Wrath.* It fails to provide any characters real enough to care about, just morsels about Ertie's bronc-bustin' days and his attachment to his gun—but no meat, nothing of depth. Mark Harmon gives a whiny performance that only engages when he is suddenly motivated enough to take action. THE LONG ROAD HOME was made for cable TV in 1991 and was released on video in 1996. *(Violence.)* — J.D.

d, John Korty; p, Ira Marvin; exec p, David A. Rosemont; w, Jane Howard-Hammerstein (based on the book by Ronald B. Taylor); ph, Kees Van Oostrum; ed, James Oliver; m, Craig Saffon; prod d, David Ensley

Drama/Western **(PR: C MPAA: NR)**

LOOKING FOR RICHARD ★★½
(U.S.) 109m Jam Productions ~ Fox Searchlight c

Al Pacino *(Richard III)*; Estelle Parsons *(Queen Margaret)*; Alec Baldwin *(Clarence)*; Kevin Spacey *(Buckingham)*; Winona Ryder *(Lady Anne)*; Aidan Quinn *(Richmond)*; Penelope Allen *(Queen Elizabeth)*; Gordon MacDonald *(Dorset)*; Madison Arnold *(Rivers)*; Vincent Angell *(Grey)*; Harris Yulin *(King Edward)*; Timmy Prairie *(Prince Edward)*; Kevin Conway *(Hastings)*; Larry Bryggman *(Lord Stanley)*; Phil Parolisi *(Halberd/Messenger)*; Bruce MacVittie *(1st Murderer)*; Paul Guilfoyle *(2nd Murderer)*; Richard Cox *(Catesby)*; Julie Moret *(Mistress Shore)*; Frederic Kimball *(Bishop of Ely)*; Dan Von Bargen *(Ratcliffe)*; James Colby *(Lovel)*; Ira Lewis *(Tyrell)*; Neal Jones *(Messenger)*; Luke Toma *(Messenger)*; Andre Sogliuzzo *(Messenger)*; Marlon Pollick *(Soldier)*; Kenneth Branagh *(Himself)*; Kevin Kline *(Himself)*; James Earl Jones *(Himself)*; Rosemary Harris *(Himself)*; Emrys Jones *(Himself)*; Peter Brook *(Himself)*; Barbara Everett *(Himself)*; Derek Jacobi *(Himself)*; John Gielgud *(Himself)*; Vanessa Redgrave *(Himself)*

As films-about-films go, LOOKING FOR RICHARD lacks the qualities that made DAY FOR NIGHT (1973) and 8 1/2 (1963) alternately wondrous and incisive. Al Pacino's passion for Shakespeare's *Richard III* is clearly evident, but the actor-director looks foolish trying to analyze the play while mounting an all-star production of it within this new documentary.

LOOKING FOR RICHARD jumps back and forth between Pacino's off-stage ruminations about the historical drama to scenes from a film adaptation in which he stars. First, Pacino asks many people to help him understand the relevancy of this 16th-century play about England's 15th-century king. He talks to pedestrians on the streets of New York and London; scholars Emrys Jones and Barbara Everett; British actors Kenneth Branagh, John Gielgud, Derek Jacobi and Vanessa Redgrave; and American actors Kevin Kline and James Earl Jones.

During rehearsals, Pacino and his all-star performing troupe grapple with the familiar characterizations of Richard (Pacino), Queen Margaret (Estelle Parsons), Clarence (Alec Baldwin), Buckingham (Kevin Spacey), Lady Anne (Winona Ryder), and Richmond (Aidan Quinn). Pacino even stages several scenes in the restructured Globe Theater in London to achieve a sort of intimate authenticity.

Finally, several key scenes from the play are reproduced for the cameras, including Richard's seduction of Lady Anne; Clarence's death at the hands of Richard's henchmen; Richard's betrayal of Buckingham as he ascends the throne; and Richard's demise during his battle with Richmond.

LOOKING FOR RICHARD sounds like a documentary about the recent surprise rediscovery of James Keane's 1912 RICHARD III film. But Pacino's film is about a different sort of search: the search for meaning. Unfortunately, with its MTV-style cutting, LOOKING FOR RICHARD blends the approaches of a Mel Brooks blooper reel with a "legitimate" but conventional reading of Shakespeare's work. The results stay closer to Kenneth Branagh's cutesy 1995 A MIDWINTER'S TALE (about the staging of A WINTER'S TALE) than to Orson Welles's multi-layered FILMING OTHELLO (1977).

Pacino proves that Americans can play British roles, but elitist Anglophilia tends to overcome Pacino's gruff populism. Pacino's use of big-name stars is more distracting than enchanting, and his claims of creating something purely artistic are dashed by the commercial pandering of the enterprise. Pacino himself plugs his 1994 Oscar winner by wearing a SCENT OF A WOMAN baseball cap during rehearsals.

And whatever happened to the RICHARD III film Pacino takes years to shoot within this production? Perhaps it has fallen by the wayside like Pacino's first, unreleased directorial effort, THE LOCAL STIGMATIC (1989). Or perhaps this is another unstated "mockumentary" a la Fellini's INTERVISTA (1987) and the more recent DADETOWN (1995). In either case, LOOKING FOR RICHARD quickly becomes a vanity effort that appears vapid next to Ian McKellen's boldly revisionist RICHARD III (1995). *(Violence, profanity.)* — E.M.

d, Al Pacino; p, Michael Hadge, Al Pacino; exec p, William Teitler; w, Al Pacino, Frederic Kimball; ph, Robert Leacock; ed, Pasquale Buba, William A. Anderson, Ned Bastille; m, Howard Shore

Drama **(PR: C MPAA: PG-13)**

LOOKING FOR TROUBLE ★
(U.S.) 73m Pacific Trust; Aubrey Tors Entertainment ~ Califilm/New Horizons Home Video c

Holly Butler *(Jamie Miller)*; Shawn McAllister *(Harry)*; Susan Gallagher *(Susan Miller)*; Gerry Russell *(Ben)*; J. Kelly Dennehy *(Madame Primrose)*; Art Turk *(Alexander Eyestone)*; Fred Peterson *(Sheriff Peckler)*; Fred Tamparo; Aaron Menom; David Spates; Jason Brown

Even with a short running time, this entry from Roger Corman's "family entertainment" phase overstays its welcome.

Petless due to her new stepfather's allergy, little Jamie (Holly Bulter) befriends a trained baby elephant that briefly escapes a circus touring Florida. Trouble—as Jamie nicknames the animal—is summarily returned to its abusive owner, fright-wigged impresario Alexander Eyestone (Art Turk).

Jamie runs away from home to trail Trouble to Gainesville, stowing away in the van of alcoholic ex-magician Harry (Shawn McAllister). Jamie frees Trouble from Eyestone's infernal cackling and electric cattle prods, but police capture Harry and force him to divulge the duo's junkyard hideout.

A $10,000 reward for Jamie's safe return enables the now-sober Harry to buy Trouble and start his own fledgling circus, with Eyestone's defecting performers in the ranks and Jamie as the official elephant trainer.

This movie was the result of an alliance between Corman's company and the Miami-based family-film dynasty founded by the late producer-writer-director Ivan Tors, whose management of menageries led to the TV shows "Flipper," "Gentle Ben," and films like ZEBRA IN THE KITCHEN (1965). Indeed, LOOKING FOR TROUBLE could have ambled in straight from the mid-1960s, with its muddy photography, cookie-cutter music, and supporting performances by thespians who apparently learned their craft at the hot end of an electric cattle prod. Pachyderm fans may be disappointed that the elephant star remains largely off-screen, with the spotlight instead on cute leading lady Butler and her therapeutic pairing with down-and-out Harry.

Aside from a disgruntled clown's line, "The circus ain't no place for kids," it's all quite bland. *(Substance abuse.)* — C.C.

d, Jay Aubrey, Peter Tors; p, Jay Aubrey; exec p, Mike Elliott; w, Jay Aubrey, Peter Tors, Jeffrey Dowdy, Christopher Wooden; ph, Robert Reed Altman; ed, Patricia Harrington; m, David Wurst, Eric Wurst; prod d, Russell Durham; casting, Marty Lewis; cos, Barbara Altman, Juslene Aubrey

Children's/Comedy **(PR: A MPAA: PG)**

LOSING CHASE ★★★½
(U.S.) 92m Showtime Networks ~ CFP Distribution c

Helen Mirren *(Chase Philips)*; Kyra Sedgwick *(Elizabeth Cole)*; Beau Bridges *(Richard Philips)*; Michael Yarmush *(Little Richard)*; Lucas Denton *(Jason Philips)*; Elva Mai Hoover *(Margaret Thompson)*; Nancy Beatty *(Cynthia Porter)*; Rino Romano *(Bartender)*; Simon Reynolds *(Instructor)*; B.J. McLellan *(Winston)*; Bunty Webb *(Housekeeper)*; Kate Hennig *(Katherine)*; Cheryl Swarts *(Nurse)*; Ron Gabriel *(Jack)*

Kevin Bacon makes an impressive feature film directorial debut with LOSING CHASE, a lyrical character study celebrating the emotional bond between two women. Helen Mirren and Kyra Sedgwick turn in dynamic performances in this simple but eloquent film, which was produced for Showtime and had a brief theatrical run.

Upon her release from a hospital, Chase Philips (Mirren), a middle-aged mother of two recovering from a nervous breakdown, returns to her home on Martha's Vineyard with her husband, Richard (Beau Bridges), and their sons, "little" Richard (Michael Yarmush) and Jason (Lucas Denton). Alternately sarcastic and moody, Chase spends her days resting and smoking on the front porch. Little Richard is enraged by her eccentricity, which he views as insanity, while her superficial husband is mortified and tries to keep her isolated.

To get Chase back on her feet, Richard hires Elizabeth Cole (Kyra Sedgwick), an amiable college grad whom he hopes will smooth out Chase's hard edges. But strong-willed Chase immediately cuts Elizabeth to the quick by barking orders at her and taunting her. This treatment continues until Elizabeth lashes out with a startling ferocity. In her distress, Elizabeth has mistaken Chase for her mother, whom she reveals also suffered from mental illness and subsequently committed suicide. Chase is touched by Elizabeth's candor and reaches out to comfort her. The next day, Elizabeth immediately apologizes to Chase, but Chase's spirits are too lifted to be anything but content.

Richard returns to work in Boston, leaving Elizabeth in charge of the house. The women spend the next few weeks entertaining the children, opening up to each other about their pasts, and taking drives in the sports car Chase has kept hidden. In an unguarded moment on the beach, Chase uncorks her simmering sexual feelings by grabbing Elizabeth and kissing her tenderly—a scene little Richard witnesses. The panic-stricken boy reports this to his father, who admonishes Chase for her indiscretions. Chase confesses she's in love with Elizabeth. The next morning, while Chase is sleeping, Richard hastens Elizabeth's departure. But Chase tracks them down at the ferry and gives Elizabeth a blatant final embrace, along with the keys to her sports car. Later, Chase and Richard part ways; Chase doesn't see Elizabeth again, but she's found the courage to make positive choices for her future.

Lushly photographed by cinematographer Dick Quinlan, LOSING CHASE basks in the glow of the gorgeous Martha's Vineyard location. Screenwriter Anne Meredith deals credibly with Chase's coming out as a lesbian, but also finds the subtle dynamics of a blossoming relationship: shared confidences after midnight; subtle but meaningful glances; quiet reflection in each other's company. Bacon's sensitive direction, while neither flashy nor intrusive, does have its share of awkward moments. He shoots some of the scenes between Chase and Elizabeth in such darkness that any intimacy he might have been trying to achieve is diminished. Still, there's evident chemistry between the actresses, and it's not exploited for cheap titillation.

The film's strongest assets are the performances. Mirren's richly textured and sympathetic portrayal of an initially disagreeable woman earned her a Golden Globe award for Best Actress in a mini-series or telefilm. Sedgwick (Bacon's real-life wife and the film's executive producer) is also compelling, striking an appealing balance between vulnerability and strength. Yarmush and Denton give unpretentious performances as Chase's sons. Unfortunately, Bridges fares the worst. His Richard is much too self-consciously mannered; when he shouts "perversion!" at his wife, it's not only a ludicrously dated insult, but it also justifies Chase's desire to make a quick getaway. *(Adult situations, profanity.)* — D.O.

d, Kevin Bacon; p, Milton Justice; exec p, Kyra Sedgwick; w, Anne Meredith (based on her novella *A Wonderful Story*); ph, Dick Quinlan; ed, Alan Baumgarten; m, Michael Bacon; prod d, Lindsey Hermer-Bell; art d, Dean A. O'Dell; set d, Megan Less; sound, Urmas Rosin; casting, Tina Gerussi; cos, Jocelyn F. Wright; makeup, Kathleen Graham

Drama **(PR: C MPAA: R)**

LOTTO LAND ★★★

(U.S.) 87m IN Pictures ~ CFP Distribution c

Larry Gilliard Jr. *(Hank)*; Wendell Holmes *(Milt)*; Barbara Gonzalez *(Joy)*; Suzanne Costallos *(Florence)*; Jaime Tirelli *(Popi)*; Luis Guzman *(Reinaldo)*; Paul Calderon *(Ricky)*

All you need is a dollar and a dream, or so the old New York Lotto slogan goes. For the working-poor denizens of LOTTO LAND, it's the dreams that are the hardest to come by, as illustrated in this sensitive and moving story about courage and hope in difficult surroundings.

A $27 million Lotto jackpot has people in an economically marginalized section of Brooklyn buzzing—especially Hank (Larry Gilliard Jr.), who bought $100 worth of tickets. About to graduate from high school, Hank has had to put his plans for the future on hold. He didn't receive the college basketball scholarship he pinned his hopes on, and now he's shunned by his peers, who have entered the lucrative local drug trade, because he works for "chump change" at a liquor store.

At the liquor store (which serves as the neighborhood's lottery outlet), Hank's boss is Flo (Suzanne Costallos), a practical-minded widow. She is also the legal guardian of Hank's girlfriend, Joy (Barbara Gonzalez), who is estranged from her father, Popi (Jaime Tirelli), a homeless drunk and occasional crack dealer. Joy and Flo live next door to Hank and his divorced father, Milt (Wendell Holmes), a sage street musician, in a tenement apartment building, of which Milt is the de facto super.

The winning Lotto ticket is purchased in Flo's store, but no one claims the prize. Popi, after spending a week in jail, sees the winning numbers and excitedly runs into the street where he is hit by a truck and killed. That night, Hank and Joy attend the prom, after which they make love, both for the first time. Meanwhile, Flo and Milt, who are melancholy about their kids growing up, begin a tentative romance.

Eventually, Hank realizes that Popi hit the numbers, and a frantic search begins for the missing ticket—to no avail. If Hank is to realize his dreams, the price will be hard work and patience, not one dollar—and, as Milt observes, that might be for the best.

Like the great documentary HOOP DREAMS (1994), LOTTO LAND is unusual cinema because it offers a sympathetic portrait of members of the American underclass (black and Hispanic), a segment of our society that too often is ignored and scapegoated, but rarely treated gently on film. There is little plot and no conventional movie heroism, only the heroism of parents performing the small miracle of raising their children under difficult circumstances and instilling in them values and moral rectitude.

Writer-director John Rubino chronicles common moments—rites of passage, really—in American life: Joy, nervous and excited, dresses for the prom with Flo's help; Hank gets a lesson in plumbing repair from Milt. The movie is warm and tender, never overly sentimental, owing greatly to the charming naturalism of Holmes and Costallos.

The mystery of the winning Lotto ticket is just a red herring. A viewer may remain convinced to the end that Flo or Hank is going to find it. Only after it is confirmed that the ticket is lost forever does the viewer fully appreciate how such an occurrence of "movie luck" would have completely undercut the true message of hope and optimism that LOTTO LAND conveys. *(Profanity, sexual situations, violence.)* — P.R.

d, John Rubino; p, John Rubino, Michael J. Rubino; exec p, Carlos Hernandez; co-p, Jeffrey Beer; w, John Rubino; ph, Rufus Standefer; ed, Jack Haigis; m, The Holmes Brothers; prod d, Paola Ridolfi; sound, Matthew Price; cos, Carolyn Grifel

Drama/Romance **(PR: C MPAA: NR)**

LOVE IS ALL THERE IS ★★★

(U.S.) 98m Cinema Seven Productions ~ Samuel Goldwyn Company c

Lainie Kazan *(Sadie)*; Paul Sorvino *(Piero)*; Barbara Carrera *(Maria)*; Joseph Bologna *(Mike)*; Angelina Jolie *(Gina)*; Nathaniel Marston *(Rosario)*; Renee Taylor *(Mona)*; William Hickey *(Monsignor)*; Dick Van Patten *(Dr. Rondino)*; Abe Vigoda *(Rudy)*; Connie Stevens *(Miss DeLuca)*; Blessed Roscoe *(Himself)*; Vera Lockwood *(Donna)*; Joy Behar *(Mary)*; Irma St. Paul *(Mrs. Rondino)*; Andy Shreeman *(Mima)*; Annie Meisels *(Dottie)*; Windland Smith *(Carmella)*; Alanna Ubach *(Niccolina)*; Celeste Russi *(Isabel)*; Tighe Swanson *(Francis)*; Gabriel Bolongna *(Tony)*; Bobby Alto *(Joe Fasuli)*; Sal Richards *(Emcee)*; Edith Fields *(Mrs. Frederico)*; Ron Macone *(Mr. Frederico)*; Catherine Cosenza *(Bea)*; Mark Wasserman *(Malacici Driver)*; Jennifer Daniels *(Woman Singer)*; Paul Greco *(Nunzio)*; Chuck Bergansky *(Rocco)*; Larry Romano *(Waiter #1)*; Mitch Poulas *(Waiter #2)*; Jery Hewitt *(Waiter #4)*; Dominic Chianese *(Italian Council)*

This Renee Taylor-Joseph Bologna riff on *Romeo and Juliet* is not only more entertaining than the irreverent 1996 Baz Luhrmann update, but it's also more poignant, and oddly enough, truer to the Shakespearean essence. Resetting the notorious rivalry of the Montagues and Capulets against the background of Italian food catering allows for plenty of genial satire, earthy humor, and star-crossed lust in this laugh-out-loud funny film.

Deep in the Bronx, Sicilian-Americans Sadie Capamezza (Lainie Kazan) and her husband Mike (Joseph Bologna) corner the market for overproduced wedding receptions until their catering reputation is threatened by the arrival of the snooty Piero Malachichi (Paul Sorvino) and his wife Maria (Barbara Carrera), who specialize in upscale Northern Italian dishes. While the Capamezzas and Malachichis belittle each other's contrasting styles, teenager Rosario Capamezza (Nathaniel Marston) plays Romeo to Gina Malachichi's (Angelina Jolie) Juliet in a production staged for a church benefit. Alarmed by her batty psychic, Mona (Renee Taylor), Sadie tries to head off Rosario and Gina's predicted romance. Sure enough, Gina plans to defy her folks and stay with Rosario instead of beginning her studies with the Ballet Russe in Paris; Rosario and Gina consummate their love at the Capamezzas' house while Sadie and Mike look for them at the local passion-pit motel.

Shocked by their daughter's socially disastrous love match, the Malachichis hurl insults at the Capamezzas and temporarily disown Gina. Then, during the Capamezzas' catering event of the year—the wedding reception of Isabel Fasuli (Celeste Russi)—the Malachichis lure their daughter home, separate her from Rosario, and wreak havoc at Isabel's nuptial celebration. In turn, Rosario and his pals create a diversion by sabotaging a Malachichi banquet so Rosario can reclaim the heavily guarded Gina. During the lovers' flight, Rosario and Gina get locked in a smokehouse that is tipped over by Isabel's rampaging relatives.

Panicking over a letter misinterpreted as a double suicide note, Sadie revs up her latent psychic powers, allowing the Capamezzas and Malachichis to rescue the fugitive teens before a broken gas line in the smokehouse suffocates them. With their children safe, the feuding families bury the cleaver, treat Rosario and Gina to a lavish wedding, and permit them to attend college together in Paris.

Resourceful scriptwriters Taylor and Bologna turn Shakespeare's gloomy play inside out and transform it into a daffy comedy reminiscent of *A Midsummer Night's Dream.* Not only do they emphasize the lunacy of the diametrically opposed parents, but they also poke fun at the smugness of the enamored adolescents. Here, only well-prepared food is more important than erotic satisfaction; the Capamezzas and Malachichis regard catered affairs as performance art.

Unfortunately, Taylor and Bologna's directorial skills aren't in league with their writing gifts. They allow their farcical ending to sprawl a bit; snappier editing could have shaved a few minutes off the finale to good effect. Luckily, the zany concept and flavorful one-liners are so rich that stale camera compositions don't spoil the fun. The film abounds in clever running gags, such as Rosario's Grandma spotting the onstage bulge in her grandson's tights during his tumescent interpretation of the crypt scene in *Romeo and Juliet,* or a fog-out at Isabel's wedding feast when the atmospheric smoke machine goes haywire and turns the hall into a scene worthy of the Wolfman.

Whereas the romantic leads are merely serviceable, the older cast members savor their roles with a relish the audience will share. Compare Sorvino's unintelligible pomposity in the same role of Juliet's father in WILLIAM SHAKESPEARE'S ROMEO + JULIET (1996) with his funny, blustering double takes in this film. Best of all are Taylor as a New Age channeler and the magnificently vulgar Kazan, who is hilarious and touching as an overprotective mother learning to let go of her son. It's depressing that this poorly marketed movie wasn't a mainstream hit; it contains more genuine laughs and ribald spirit than the less polished, more crass comedies the moviegoing public usually embraces. *(Violence, sexual situations, extreme profanity.)* — R.P.

d, Rene Taylor, Joseph Bologna; p, Elliott Kastner; exec p, George Pappas; co-p, Andrew A. Kosove, Broderick Johnson, Tim Kelly, Chantal Ribeiro; w, Renee Taylor, Joseph Bologna; ph, Alan Jones; ed, Nicholas Eliopoulos, Dennis M. O'Connor; m, Jeff Beal; prod d, Ron Norsworthy; art d, Ellee Wynn Brisco; set d, Regina Graves; sound, Joe Romano (mixer); casting, Robyn Knoll; cos, Dona Granata; makeup, Gina G. Ricci; stunts, Jery Hewitt

Comedy/Romance/Drama **(PR: C MPAA: R)**

LOVER'S KNOT ★★½

(U.S.) 85m Lover's Knot L. P. ~ Cabin Fever Entertainment c

Bill Campbell *(Steve Hunter)*; Jennifer Grey *(Megan Forrester)*; Tim Curry *(Cupid Caseworker)*; Adam Baldwin *(John Read)*; Mark Sheppard *(Nigel Bowles)*; Tom McTigue *(Doug Meyers)*; Holly Fulger *(Gwen Meyers)*; Kristin Minter *(Cheryl)*; Elaine Hendrix *(Robin)*; Adam Ant *(Marvell)*; Dr. Joyce Brothers *(Herself)*; Ann Francis *(Marian Hunter)*; Harold Gould *(Alan Smithee)*; Byrne Piven *(William Shakespeare)*; Sheryl Lee Ralph *(Charlotte)*; Zelda Rubinstein *(Woman in AIDS Clinic)*; Dawn

Wells *(Mary Ann)*; Julie Caitlin Brown *(Monique)*; John E. Goetz *(Todd)*; Tiffany Salerno *(Juliet)*; Marla Sucharetza *(Erin)*

Romance always has been a favorite subject of movies, so there's nothing terribly new or unusual about LOVER'S KNOT. Still, writer-director Pete Shaner has a penchant for whimsical invention that makes the film at least agreeable, if hardly necessary, viewing.

Cupid sends a caseworker (Tim Curry) to earth to help foster a romance between two souls who are meant to be together. Steve Hunter (Bill Campbell) is a graduate student teaching poetry at a Los Angeles university while he works on his dissertation, "How To Make Love Last: Lessons From the Renaissance Poets." Megan Forrester (Jennifer Grey) is a pediatrician, on the rebound from a failed affair with shallow cosmetic surgeon John Read (Adam Baldwin).

The Caseworker, who is allowed only the most limited intervention in human affairs, ensures that Steve and Megan meet at a costume party. While they are attracted to each other, romance is not immediately forthcoming due to a combination of misunderstandings, misreadings, and personal agendas. After a few ups and downs, they declare their love for each other and Megan invites Steve to move in with her.

Things are blissful for a few months, but passion starts to fade in the face of daily life and job pressures. Megan accuses Steve of being unwilling to put in the work that is required to make love last, and they break up. He has an affair with a ditzy student, while she goes back to John. At the same annual party at which they first met, Steve makes an impassioned plea to Megan and she declares her love for him. Prompted by the Caseworker, Steve punches John in the nose.

Campbell and Grey ignite few sparks onscreen as characters whose relationship merely regurgitates standard cliches about men and women. Of the supporting cast, only Mark Sheppard as Steve's randy friend Nigel makes much of an impression. As a heavenly emissary, Curry is invisible, unable to interact with the rest of the cast, and therefore largely wasted.

Although it somewhat echoes the style of ANNIE HALL, LOVER'S KNOT thankfully doesn't try too hard to delve into the mysteries of modern romance. The best moments in this film are on the sidelines, such as a flashback to a teenage Steve, playing the lead in a high school production of *Romeo and Juliet* and deciding to improvise a new, happy ending.

Shaner also adds a parade of witnesses who address the camera on the subject of love. Film buffs will get a chuckle out of an explanation of romantic movie cliches delivered by Harold Gould as "Alan Smithee, famous movie director"—Smithee is the fictitious name used when a director wants his name taken off the credits of a film. Adam Ant pops up as the Renaissance poet Marvell to admit that his most famous lines were written only to con a young virgin into bed. And Shakespeare reveals that he gave *Romeo and Juliet* a largely arbitrary ending to appeal to the audience's bloodlust, that being the secret of box-office success. Perhaps that explains Steve bopping his vanquished rival on the nose at the conclusion of this film? *(Nudity, sexual situations, adult situations, profanity.)* — M.F.

d, Pete Shaner; p, Paul A. Kaufman, Paul Rauch; exec p, Randy Simon; co-p, Kevin Hamburger; w, Pete Shaner; ph, Garrett Griffin; ed, Tatiana S. Riegel; m, Laura Karpman; prod d, David Huang; casting, Victoria Burrows; cos, Cathryn Wagner; makeup, Judy Kaye Yonemoto

Comedy/Drama **(PR: C MPAA: R)**

LOW LIFE, THE ★★½

(U.S.) 98m Man Way, Inc.; Autumn Pictures ~ CFP Distribution c

Rory Cochrane *(John)*; Sean Astin *(Andrew)*; Kyra Sedgwick *(Bevan)*; Ron Livingston *(Chad)*; Christian Meoli *(Leonard)*; Sara Melson *(Suzie)*; James LeGros *(Mike, Jr.)*; J.T. Walsh *(Mike, Sr.)*; Shawnee Smith *("Little Tramp" Woman)*; Jefferson Mays *(Hollywood Mogul)*; Brent J. Williams *(Uncle Darr)*; Antoni Cornoe *(Louis)*; Angel Aviles *(Latina Girlfriend)*; Mark Blum *(Matthew Greenberg)*; Channon Roe *(Craig)*; Michael Massee *(Bartender)*; Patrick Ladislav *(Patrick)*; Renee Zellweger *(Poet)*; Matthew Warren *(Hat Guy)*; Otto Coelho *(Chuck)*; Timothy Gallaher *(Performance Artist/UFO)*; Jan Boyer *(Waitress)*; Donald Zuckerman *(Married Attorney)*; Jon Beatty *(Office Supervisor)*; F. Joseph Schulte *(Temp Office Manager)*; Marianne Meullerleile *(Temp Dispatcher)*; Rommel Hyacinth *(Haitan Man)*; Kristina Loggia *(Andy's Sister)*; Bernie Lane *(Andy's Father)*; George Hickenlooper Sr. *(Priest)*; Mark Moran *(Jorge)*; Harold Jose Martinez *(Julio's Friend)*; Esther Scott *(Mrs. Raymond)*; James Katsuki Taenaka *(Wineshop Clerk)*; Michael Beugg; James Blevins; Tobin Heminway; Mark Anthony Little *(Police Officers)*

Director George Hickenlooper dives into the Generation X movie pool and promptly drowns. Despite a fine ensemble cast and some sporadically engaging writing, THE LOW LIFE is as listless and mundane as its self-torturing characters.

Fresh out of Yale, John (Rory Cochrane) moves to Los Angeles with dreams of becoming a fiction writer. To pay the rent, he takes on a series of mindless temp jobs, as do his similarly waiting-for-a-break buddies Chad (Ron Livingston) and Leonard (Christian Meoli). The three spend most of their time at Kavanaugh's Bar cadging food and drinks from waitress Suzie (Sara Melson). The well-meaning but impossibly needy Andrew (Sean Astin) becomes John's roommate and struggles to gain his friendship, but John remains aloof. Meanwhile, his pals take advantage of Andrew as a source of free booze.

John takes on a new job at Schroeder's Properties, which is owned by Mike Sr. (J.T. Walsh) and sleazily run by Mike Jr. (James Le Gros). Mike Jr. is barely one step ahead of the law and talks John into doing some of his dirty work. In the process, John meets Bevan (Kyra Sedgwick), a flirty man-eater, and sleeps with her. When his Uncle Darr (Brent J. Williams) dies, John is unmoved. He has always followed his uncle's advice: "Don't feel anything for anyone." But that advice becomes difficult for John to follow when Leonard has a near-breakdown, Mike Jr. is arrested for arson, Bevan refuses to commit to a relationship, and Andrew is killed in a traffic accident. After John hitches to Andrew's sparse funeral in Modesto, he cries for the first time in his life at the gravesite.

Director George Hickenlooper (who co-wrote THE LOW LIFE with John Enbom) has imbued his characters with every possible "slacker" cliche: They're overeducated and under-motivated, detached and jaded, wondering when the rest of their lives will begin. Early on in the film, Hickenlooper brings some welcome visual irony into play—his images are elegantly composed, with almost no camera movement. But as the movie wears on and the thin plot (and putative humor) wears out, he makes the mistake of taking his characters ultra-seriously, and the audience is forced to do the same. John's crying signals either the end of his life or the beginning—your choice.

Some fine talent is wasted here. Rory Cochrane, who was terrific in LOVE AND A .45 (1994) and DAZED AND CONFUSED (1993), wanders through the film as if he just woke up and is waiting for someone to bring him coffee. Kyra Sedgwick and her "Tobacco Road"-company Southern accent are truly awful. Some outre moments are provided by Shawnee Smith as a slutty partygoer and the director's father as a priest. Sean Astin, as the ill-fated nerd, gives the brightest performance. The film is clearly autobiographical for ex-Yalie Hickenlooper, who directed 1993's fictional short film SOME FOLKS CALL IT A SLING BLADE (which Billy Bob Thornton expanded into the feature SLING BLADE) and the cult horror western GHOST BRIGADE (1993), and co-directed the documentary HEARTS OF DARKNESS (1991). *(Sexual situations, profanity.)* — D.B.

d, George Hickenlooper; p, Donald Zuckerman, Tobin Heminway; exec p, Mark Blum, George Hickenlooper, Gary Siegler, Leslie Zuckerman; assoc p, Michael Beugg, H. Ben Morgenthau; co-p, Dan Etheridge, Martin Yu; w, John Enbom, George Hickenlooper (from a story by John Enbom); ph, Richard Crudo; ed, Yaffa Lerea, Jim Makiej; m, Bill Boll; prod d, Deborah Smith; set d, Gregory Arnett; sound, Peter Meiselmann (recordist); casting, Heidi Levitt, Rick Montgomery, Dan Parada; cos, Alexandra Welker; makeup, Sandy Beatty

Comedy/Drama **(PR: C MPAA: R)**

L'UOMO DELLE STELLE

(SEE: STAR MAKER, THE)

M

MADAME BUTTERFLY ★★★

(France) 129m ZDF; S4C; BBC; Canal Plus; Centre National de la Cinematographie ~ Sony Classical c

Ying Huang *(Cio-Cio-San)*; Ning Liang *(Suzuki)*; Richard Troxell *(Pinkerton)*; Richard Cowan *(Sharpless)*; Jing-Ma Fan *(Goro)*; Constance Hauman *(Kate Pinkerton)*; Christopheren Nomura *(Prince Yamadori)*; Yo Kuskabe *(Uncle)*; Miki-Lou Pinard; Nabil Agoun; Lotfi Bahri; Salem Zahrouni; Yoshi Oida; Therese Nguyen Ba Hau; Wen-Juan Zhao; Midori Mornet; Kamel Touati; Santy Norasingh; Abdelazziz Aslen; Wahid Touihiri

Frederic Mitterand's faithful adaptation of Puccini's glorious *Madama Butterfly* ranks as one of cinema's best opera films, comparable to Ingmar Bergman's THE MAGIC FLUTE and Franco Zeffirelli's LA TRAVIATA.

At the turn of the century, Lieutenant Pinkerton (Richard Troxell), an American naval officer, becomes engaged to Cio-Cio-San, or Madame Butterfly (Ying Huang), a sensitive, kind-hearted young woman in the Japanese harbor town of Nagasaki. What the bride fails to comprehend is that Pinkerton doesn't take the wedding seriously and longs for the day when he can "really" be married back in the United States. Though the married couple sings a wonderful love duet following the ceremony, Pinkerton returns to the US, leaving his Japanese wife behind with her faithful maid Suzuki (Ning Liang).

Three years later, Butterfly sings her ecstatic aria "Un Bel Di," in which she pictures Pinkerton one day sailing into the harbor to rejoin her. Instead, she is visited by Sharpless (Richard Cowan), the American consul, who, knowing that Pinkerton has married an American woman back home, urges Butterfly to forget him and find a new man. But Butterfly has a son, fathered by Pinkerton, and she dreams of a reunion. When Pinkerton finally arrives, he is accompanied by Kate (Constance Hauman), his American wife. Overcome with grief, Butterfly takes her own life.

The story of MADAME BUTTERFLY remains as poignant today as when it was first performed in 1904. Mitterand's film treats Puccini's classic opera with the respect it deserves, resisting the temptation to go for close-ups in favor of a mid-distance camera approach. As photographed by Philippe Welt, the result is cinema that retains theatricality in keeping with the grand sweep of Puccini's music, which is conducted with majesty by James Conlon. Twenty-three-year-old soprano Ying Huang has a lovely, formidable voice and acting ability to match; she delivers a touching, powerful performance. Sporting an agreeable tenor voice, Troxell is handsome and persuasive as Pinkerton, while baritone Cowan is an assured, memorable Sharpless. For the record, old Nagasaki was re-created on a hill outside Tunisia, but the beauty and scope of Puccini's masterpiece are as timeless as ever. — E.K.

d, Frederic Mitterrand; p, Daniel Toscan du Plantier, Pierre-Olivier Bardet; assoc p, Samsung Nices, Ahmed Baha Eddine Attia; w, Giuseppe Giacosa, Luigi Illica (based on the book by John L. Long and the drama by David Belasco); ph, Philippe Welt; ed, Luc Barnier; m, Giacomo Puccini; prod d, Michele Abbe-Vannier; art d, Michel Glotz, Daniel Zalay; sound, Didier Gervais, Guy Level, Stephanie Granel, William Flageollet; casting, Isabelle Partiot; cos, Christian Gasc; makeup, Thi Loan Nguyen

Opera/Drama/Romance **(PR: A MPAA: NR)**

MA SAISON PREFEREE ★★★½

(France) 124m Les Films Alain Sarde; TF1 Films Production; D.A. Films ~ Filmopolis Pictures c
(AKA: MY FAVORITE SEASON)

Catherine Deneuve *(Emilie)*; Daniel Auteuil *(Antoine)*; Marthe Villalonga *(Berthe)*; Jean-Pierre Bouvier *(Bruno)*; Chiara Mastroianni *(Anne)*; Carmen Chaplin *(Khadija)*; Anthony Prada *(Lucien)*; Michele Moretti *(Manager of Home)*; Jacques Nolot *(Man at Cemetery)*; Bruno Todeschini *(Man at Hospital)*; Jean Bousquet *(Emilie's Father)*; Roschdy Zem *(Medhi)*; Ingrid Caven *(Woman in Bar)*

Troubled family relationships are explored in this pensive, moving character study. MA SAISON PREFEREE (MY FAVORITE SEASON) takes its time telling its story, but when it focuses on the three main characters, it rings true.

The relationship between lawyer Emilie (Catherine Deneuve) and her brother, Antoine (Daniel Auteuil), a research scientist, is strained when their mother's health begins to fail. Berthe (Marthe Villalonga), the mother, moves from her home to stay with Emilie; her husband, Bruno (Jean-Pierre Bouvier), who is also Emilie's law partner, and their teenage children, Anne (Chiara Mastroianni, the real-life daughter of Deneuve and Marcello Mastroianni) and Lucien (Anthony Prada). But Berthe dislikes Emilie's family and requests that Antoine take her in. When he refuses, Berthe goes back to her own home in the country.

Meanwhile, Emilie and Bruno decide to separate, while Anne forms a close friendship with Khadija (Carmen Chaplin), a young Moroccan woman with whom she feels closer than to her own family.

After Berthe collapses in her garden one day, Emilie and Antoine move her into a nursing home against her will. Seemingly overnight, Berthe loses her powers of reason, while both Emilie and Antoine begin fantasizing about past regrets and present challenges. When they finally realize that Berthe has suffered a cerebral hemorrhage, Emilie and Antoine move her out of the nursing home and into a hospital, where she soon dies. The family members mourn Berthe's death but achieve a new level of awareness about themselves.

Brother-and-sister relationships are, according to Joseph Campbell, the most mythopoetically charged, yet the least often explored on screen. Of course, there are such exceptions as the classic ghost story, THE UNINVITED (1944), and John Cassavetes' underrated LOVE STREAMS (1984). But most male-female sibling depictions on screen are clouded with acts or implications of incest, as in BUNNY LAKE IS MISSING (1965), BROTHERLY LOVE (1970), and LAST SUMMER IN THE HAMPTONS (1995). MA SAISON PREFEREE at least takes a less sensational approach, and looks at how family problems can produce restless spirits later in life.

Some might argue that a little sensation would do the film good. Granted, it is slow-moving and deliberately paced, using the four seasons as guideposts to story and character development. Also, Anne's relationship with Khadija and Emilie's relationship with Bruno deserve separate film treatments of their own.

Yet, MA SAISON PREFEREE skillfully plays against the expectations of most family melodramas. Director and co-writer Andre Techine (BAROCCO, WILD REEDS) depicts an aging and ailing mother, for example, who is neither Marmee of LITTLE WOMEN nor the wicked, morbid Tatie Daniel, but something (more realistically) in between. Likewise, Berthe's deterioration and her children's realizations about the past (particularly, their dislike of their mother) occur gradually, not in over-the-top dramatic scenes. These low-key moments are memorable nevertheless, particularly Berthe's bitter, deglamorized deathbed speech.

The association of character epiphanies with natural surroundings are made through a superb, impressionistic use of pictorial backdrops, and the actors give expert, well-modulated performances, particularly the three leads, whose nervous, uneasy, sometimes funny interactions seem spontaneous and real.

The film may be too quiet to be considered a breakthrough achievement, but it does show an alternative way of depicting family relationships honestly. *(Nudity, sexual situations, extreme profanity.)* — E.M.

d, Andre Techine; p, Alain Sarde; w, Andre Techine, Pascal Bonitzer; ph, Thierry Arbogast; ed, Martine Giordano; m, Philippe Sarde; prod d, Carlos Conti; set d, Alain Pitrel; sound, Remy Attal, Jean-Paul Mugel; fx, Philippe Hubin; cos, Claire Fraisse; makeup, Cedric Gerard

Drama **(PR: C MPAA: NR)**

MABOROSI ★★★

(Japan) 110m TV Man Union ~ Milestone Films c
(MABOROSI NO HIKARI)

Makiko Esumi *(Yumiko)*; Takashi Naito *(Tamio—Yumiko's Second Husband)*; Tadanobu Asano *(Ikuo—Yumiko's First Husband)*; Gohki Kashiyama *(Yuichi—Yumiko's Son)*; Naomi Watanabe *(Tomoko—Tamio's Daughter)*; Midori Kiuchi *(Michiko—Yumiko's Mother)*; Akira Emoto *(Yoshihiro—Tamio's Father)*; Matsuko Sakura *(Tomeno)*; Hidekazu Akai *(Master)*; Hiromi Ichida *(Hatsuko)*; Minori Terada *(Detective)*; Ren Ohsugi *(Hiroshi—Yumiko's Father)*; Kikuko Hashimoto *(Kiyo—Yumiko's Grandmother)*; Shuichi Harada *(Cop)*; Takashi Inoue *(Driver)*; Sayaka Yoshino *(Yumiko as a Young Girl)*

MABOROSI is the Japanese word for a phantom or illusion, a fleeting mirage-vision that disappears the moment it is seen. This is a film built from just such fleeting characters and images, connected as much by atmosphere as narrative. Like the *maborosi* of the title, the film's haunting, austere beauty lingers in the viewer's mind long after the house lights go up.

The protagonist, Yumiko (Makiko Esumi), appears first as a 12-year-old child. In a dream, she runs after her grandmother (Kikuko Hashimoto), who has disappeared from the family apartment in Osaka. That evening, Yumiko finds her walking across a bridge. Her grandmother explains that she wants to return to her hometown to die. She crosses the bridge and disappears, never to be seen again. It happens that a little boy, Ikuo, is riding by on a bicycle just at this moment. When she wakes from the dream, Yumiko is an adult. She has married Ikuo (Tadanobu Asano), now a factory worker, and they have a young son, Yuichi. One day, when the baby is three months old, the police arrive to tell Yumiko that Ikuo has apparently killed himself, walking on the nearby train tracks in front of an oncoming train. There is no explanation for his suicide other than a sense that it is connected to the disappearance of Yumiko's grandmother—by fate and by Yumiko's feelings of culpability.

Several years later, Yumiko remarries, through the arrangement of her neighbor, Mrs. Ono, to a handsome man named Tamio (Takashi Naito), who is himself a widower and the father of a little girl, Tomoko (Naomi Watanabe). Yumiko moves to his remote, coastal village of Noto, at once beautiful and bleak. At first, Yumiko is able to stave off her feelings of grief and guilt by concentrating on settling into her new life. When the Noto villagers come to pay their respects and celebrate the wedding, she tries—unsuccessfully—to join into the spirit of things. Tomoko takes Yuichi on a walk that leads them into a dark tunnel. It seems that they, too, will disappear, but they are soon found and brought home.

Later, Yumiko takes the two children back to Osaka to attend her brother's wedding. She drops in on Mrs. Ono, visits her old apartment, and a coffee shop which she and Ikuo frequented. Back in Noto, Yumiko is changed; the trip has rekindled memories of Ikuo's death—and all the disappearances of her past. Tamio tries in vain to draw her out.

Yumiko sees an old fishing woman, Tomeno (Matsuko Sakura), heading out to sea to catch crabs. Tomeno promises to bring her three crabs. That night, a storm has gathered and Tomeno has not returned. Yumiko worries that Tomeno will disappear, too, despite reassurances from Tamio's father, Yoshihiro (Akira Emoto). Sure enough, Tomeno returns with the three crabs.

One night, when Tamio returns home, drunk and late, Yumiko blows up, clearly fearing yet another disappearance. Later, Tamio finds Yuichi playing by himself and asks after Yumiko, who has gone missing. Searching frantically, Tamio finally finds her in the funeral procession of a complete stranger, which culminates with a cremation on the beach. When Yumiko explains that she is still haunted by the mystery of Ikuo's death, Tamio tells her of the illusory light that lures sailors far out to sea, the *maborosi no hikari.* "It can happen to anyone," he says. The new family has reached some form of harmonious balance with the phantoms of the past, as Tamio and Tomoko teach Yuichi to ride a bicycle, watched by Yumiko and Tamio's father.

Director Hirokazu Kore-eda has a documentarian's sense of the immanent power of images, sounds, faces, moments. But the style of the film is anything but naturalistic or realistic. The camera nearly always lingers, motionless, to capture the passing of real time in a fixed frame, without the interference or emphasis of fancy montage. Kore-eda shows a special fondness for graphic, symmetrical compositions, which are usually considered static and decorative. The result is frequently alienating and dissatisfying, but occasionally succeeds in penetrating into the characters. The style flows naturally from Yoshihisa Ogita's script, which eschews psychological motivation and shrouds plot in unexplained, unresolved mysteries. *(Adult situations, nudity.)* — A.J.

d, Hirokazu Kore-eda; p, Naoe Gozu; exec p, Yutaka Shigenobu; w, Yoshihisa Ogita (based on the short story "Maborosi no Hikari/Illusory Light" by Teru Miyamoto); ph, Masao Nakabori; ed, Tomoyo Ohshima; m, Chen Ming-Chang; art d, Kyoko Heya; set d, Keiji Akatsuka; sound, Masatoshi Yokomizo (recordist); fx, Minoru Nakano; cos, Michiko Kitamura; makeup, Yukiko Nishio

Drama **(PR: C MPAA: NR)**

MABOROSI NO HIKARI

(SEE: MABOROSI)

MACHINE, THE ★★½

(France/Germany) 96m Hachette Premiere et Cie; D. D. Productions; Prima; M6 Films; France 2 Cinema; Studio Babelsberg GmbH; Canal Plus ~ Hachette Premiere et Cie c
(LA MACHINE)

Gerard Depardieu *(Dr. Marc Lacroix)*; Nathalie Baye *(Marie Lacroix)*; Didier Bourdon *(Michel Zyto)*; Natalia Woerner *(Marianne)*; Erwan Baynaud *(Leonard Lacroix)*; Marc Andreoni; Alain Azerot; Wilfred Benaiche; Christian Bujeau; Julie Depardieu; Patty Hannock; Arsene Jiroyan; Alexis Nitzer; Christian Pereira; Christian Ruche; Pascal Ternisiern; Aude Thirion

Just because most foreign films that are imported to the US are of superior quality (that being, after all, the reason they are imported) doesn't mean that other countries don't make their share of formulaic movies. The most surprising thing about THE MACHINE is the oversupply of talent that went into this wholly routine thriller.

Dr. Marc Lacroix (Gerard Depardieu), a psychiatrist specializing in treatment of the criminally insane, has invented a machine to examine the inner workings of the brain. His chosen test subject is Michel Zyto (Didier Bourdon), an impotent psychopath who has stabbed four women to death. But the machine has an unforeseen result: it transfers Zyto's mind into Lacroix's body and vice versa. Zyto overpowers Lacroix and returns him (in Zyto's body) to his cell.

Zyto takes his place in Lacroix's family. He discovers that he is able to have normal sexual relations with Lacroix's wife, Marie (Nathalie Baye), although he is still troubled by murderous impulses. Lacroix (in Zyto's body) escapes to the apartment of his mistress Marianne (Natalia Woerner), the only person who knows about the machine. Marianne tries to warn Marie, who doesn't believe her and passes her story on to Zyto. Zyto goes to Marianne's apartment and stabs her to death.

Zyto brings Lacroix's son, Leonard (Erwan Baynaud), to the lab and tricks him into changing minds, leaving Zyto's mind in Leonard's body and Leonard's mind in his father's body. Lacroix and Leonard escape, but are too late to prevent Zyto from killing Marie. After overpowering Zyto, Lacroix puts everyone's minds back in their proper bodies, kills Zyto, and destroys the machine. He confesses his actions to the police, and hopes that his mind is still entirely his own.

All that separates THE MACHINE from dozens of hokey mad scientist movies dating back to the glory days of Universal Studios are subtitles and an explicit interest in sex, although the psychosexual babble offered in the script is strictly Psych 101: Zyto murders women to whom he is attracted with a knife out of frustration at his own impotence.

One is left to wonder why top stars like Depardieu and Baye would agree to appear in something like this. Perhaps the original novel, prominently mentioned in the credits, was more substantial. Or perhaps Depardieu was attracted to the chance to play three different characters in the same body, though none of them is developed enough to make it worth his (or the viewer's) while. *(Graphic violence, nudity, sexual situations, adult situations, profanity.)* — M.F.

d, Francois Dupeyron; p, Patrick Bordier; exec p, Bernard Bouix, Ingrid Windisch; w, Francois Dupeyron (based on a story by Rene Belletto); ph, Dietrich Lohmann; ed, Noelle Boisson; m, Michel Portal; prod d, Rene Cleitman; set d, Carlos Conti; sound, Pierre Gamet, Gerard Lamps; fx, Georges Demetrau; casting, Jeanne Biras; cos, Elisabeth Tavernier

Science Fiction/Thriller **(PR: O MPAA: NR)**

MACHINE GUN BLUES

(SEE: BLACK ROSE OF HARLEM)

MAD DOG TIME ★★

(U.S.) 93m Dreyfuss/James Productions; Skylight Films ~ MGM/UA c

(AKA: TRIGGER HAPPY)

Ellen Barkin *(Rita Everly)*; Gabriel Byrne *(Ben London)*; Richard Dreyfuss *(Vic)*; Jeff Goldblum *(Mickey Holliday)*; Diane Lane *(Grace)*; Gregory Hines *(Jules Flamingo)*; Kyle MacLachlan *(Jake Parker)*; Burt Reynolds *("Wacky" Jacky Jackson)*; Billy Idol *(Lee Turner)*; Rob Reiner *(Albert the Chauffeur)*; Joey Bishop *(Mr. Gottlieb)*; Paul Anka *(Danny Marks)*; Larry Bishop *(Nick)*; Richard Pryor *(Jimmy the Gravedigger)*; Juan Fernandez *(Davis)*; Christopher Jones *("Nicholas Falco")*; Michael J. Pollard *(Red Nash)*; Billy Drago *(Wells)*; Real Andrews *(Clarke)*; Jon Ingrassia *(Young)*; Angie Everhart *(Gabriella)*; Henry Silva *(Sleepy Joe Carlisle)*

Ostensibly a black comedy, MAD DOG TIME is a cameo-laden gangster film that is certainly dark but not particularly funny.

Ever since local godfather Vic (Richard Dreyfuss) was sent to the mental hospital, the balance of power at Vic's Rough House lounge has swung wildly between right-hand-man Ben London (Gabriel Byrne), hired gun Mickey Holliday (Jeff Goldblum), and rival thug Jake Parker (Kyle MacLachlan). When Vic returns, rested but by his own admission still looney, the principals do their best to play the others against Vic. Of the three, Mickey holds the advantage, as he alone knows the whereabouts of Vic's love interest, Grace (Diane Lane). One by one, Vic's friends and rivals eliminate each other, until all that remain are Vic, Mickey, Grace, her sister Rita (Ellen Barkin) with whom Mickey has recently hooked up, and Vic's new trigger-man, the ultra-smooth Nick Falco (Larry Bishop). Secrets are revealed, shots are fired, and the balance of power finally comes to rest again, with Vic and Grace reconciled and Mickey exonerated.

Writer-director Larry Bishop's script, originally called "Trigger Happy," generated so much buzz that stars from all over lined up to appear in cameos, including Gregory Hines, Burt Reynolds, Billy Idol, Rob Reiner, Joey Bishop (Larry's dad), Paul Anka, and Richard Pryor. But after seeing MAD DOG TIME, one can't help but wonder why. Essentially a two-hour premise (what happens when a mob guy goes crazy?), the film is long on actors but short on characters—or story, for that matter. Bishop creates a nice mood, a world where the booze and bullets are plentiful and the Rat Pack is always singing in the background, but the screen is filled with too many characters who apparently exist only to get shot. Particularly disappointing is Dreyfuss (whose excitement over the script reportedly drew many of the cameo actors to the project): coming off his Oscar-nominated performance in MR. HOLLAND'S OPUS (1995), Dreyfuss smirks his way through MAD DOG TIME, conveying neither madness nor menace as the supposedly looney Vic. Goldblum and Barkin turn in their standard performances, whereas Byrne might be more tolerable if his character were not so inexplicably annoying. Of all the characters, the only plum role is uber-assassin Nick Falco, which writer-director Bishop keeps for himself. *(Violence, profanity.)* — B.T.

d, Larry Bishop; p, Judith Rutherford James; exec p, Stephan Manpearl, Len Shapiro; co-p, Larry Bishop; w, Larry Bishop; ph, Frank Byers; ed, Norman Hollyn; m, Earl Rose; prod d, Dina Lipton; art d, Michael Atwell; set d, Kathy Lucas; sound, Rick Waddell (mixer), Stephen Hunter Flick (design); fx, Charlie Belardinelli, Bellissimo/Belardinelli Effects, Inc.; casting, Amy Lieberman; cos, Ileane Meltzer; makeup, Ron Berkeley, Kathleen Berkeley; stunts, Gary Jensen

Crime/Comedy/Drama **(PR: C MPAA: R)**

MADAGASCAR SKIN ★★½

(U.K.) 93m Dan Films Production; British Film Institute; Channel Four Films ~ International Film Circuit c

Bernard Hill *(Flint)*; John Hannah *(Harry)*; Mark Anthony *(Adonis)*; Mark Pettit; Danny Earl *(Lovers)*; Robin Neath *(Thug)*; Simon Bennett *(Thug)*; Matthew Davies *(Thug)*; Alex Hooper

(Sailor); Alex Symons-Sutcliffe *(Little Girl)*; Virginia Davies *(Little Girl)*; Susan Harries *(Black Bikini Woman)*; George Thomas *(Crab Hunter)*; Sarah Thomas *(Crab Hunter)*; William Burke *(Old Man)*

The story of an evolving romance between two seemingly mismatched men, MADAGASCAR SKIN starts out rather *avant-garde* but seems to slip into a more conventional mode as it ends.

Harry (John Hannah) visits a gay bar. The Madagascar-shaped birthmark that covers most of the left side of his face prevents this painfully self-conscious young man from participating in the erotic activities of the bar's other customers. Unbearable loneliness and sexual deprivation launch the virginal Harry on a desperate trip to the seashore, where he spends the night in his car. The next morning, he discovers a bucket on the beach; under the bucket is the head of Flint (Bernard Hill) who, neck-deep in sand, has been left by enemies to die. Harry frees Flint and together they discover an abandoned cottage in which they set up housekeeping.

The fiftyish Flint, who claims to be a scaffolder, is somewhat loutish but amiable. He amuses his new housemate with his mischievous wit and audacious eating habits: he likes insects, mice, and broken glass. Harry quickly falls for the older man, but Flint, an apparent heterosexual, rejects his love at first. Eventually, Flint reconsiders and the two begin a sexual relationship. Meanwhile, Harry becomes distressed when he discovers that Flint is a kleptomaniac who has been burglarizing a neighborhood house. When their hideaway is reclaimed by its rightful owners, Harry (who has apparently become reconciled to his lover's dishonest tendencies) and Flint hit the road. At the end of the story, they are without a home, family, friends, professions, or incomes, but it is clear that they are fully, mutually, joyfully in love.

Chris Newby had directed a series of offbeat shorts and one well-received feature, ANCHORESS (1993), prior to MADAGASCAR SKIN. Shot along the picturesque coastline of South Wales, the film, virtually a two-character piece, is quite convincingly played by John Hannah and Bernard Hill—though it's a little hard to believe that Flint, whom the picture's distributors and some of its reviewers describe as "a rampant heterosexual" and "thumpingly heterosexual," would turn gay in mid-life. A series of interesting still lives provide the supporting cast: an abandoned pair of shoes on a desolate beach, a starfish resting on a matchbox, etc.

Though a very sketchy story, the film, like young Harry himself, succeeds by steadfastly refusing to beg for affection. But it lacks the kind of substance that might—with the help of a bigger budget and more narrative ambition—have made it exceptional. *(Sexual situations, extreme profanity.)* — D.T.

d, Chris Newby; p, Julie Baines; exec p, Ben Gibson; assoc p, Sarah Daniel; w, Chris Newby; ph, Oliver Curtis; ed, Chris Newby, Annabel Ware; prod d, Paul Cross; art d, Rachael Robertson; sound, Mark Holding (recordist); casting, Simone Ireland; cos, Annie Symons; makeup, Christine Allsop

Romance/Drama **(PR: C MPAA: NR)**

MADAME WANG'S ★★★½

(U.S.) 95m c

Patrick Schoene *(Lutz)*; Christina Indri *(Girl in Temple)*; William Edgar *(Billy/Door Knob Collector)*; Susan Blond *(Long Beach Party Giver)*; Virginia Bruce *(Madame Wang)*; Paul Ambrose *(Madame Wang's Manager)*; Jimmy Madaus

MADAME WANG'S represents another over-the-top, fiercely funny attack on social mores and cinematic forms from the underappreciated "underground" director, Paul Morrissey. This 1981 curiosity makes most of the other films of the past year seem tame by comparison.

MADAME WANG'S takes place in Long Beach in the early 1980s, when the Cold War between the East and West got even colder. Lutz (Patrick Schoene), an East German undercover KGB agent, comes to America to plot a Communist invasion by connecting with Western leftist sympathizers like Jane Fonda. Lutz first meets a prostitute (Christina Indri), who introduces him to her over-stimulated pimp, Billy (William Edgar), her transvestite father (Jimmy Madaus), and her father's bunch of untalented transvestite friends. Without any other place to live, Lutz moves in with the transvestites in the basement of the Long Island Masonic Temple, while the group of men in drag rehearse for their big audition at Madame Wang's, a trendy nightclub in the city.

While planning his overthrow of the government, Lutz realizes he needs money to live in America. The prostitute, who has grown fond of Lutz, teaches him to be her new pimp, but Lutz fails miserably in the role. Later, Lutz is mistaken for a prostitute himself as he, his prostitute friend, Billy, and the transvestites are all invited to a posh house party thrown by a suburban matron (Susan Blond). The hostess of the party takes a particular liking to Lutz, but instead of having sex with him, she asks him to kill her abusive husband. Lutz fails as badly as a paid assassin as he did as a pimp.

Next, Lutz visits a local Jane Fonda Workout Center in the hopes of meeting her in person, but he is disappointed to find out that she does not work at the site. Finally, feeling desperate for work, Lutz auditions as a punk rock singer at Madame Wang's, but during his routine he slashes himself with a knife rather than perform the primitive gyrations he is taught by a fellow rocker. Madame Wang (Virginia Bruce) likes Lutz's original, if bloody, act, but Lutz himself feels disgusted by his experiences in America and decides to return to East Germany.

Inept acting. Bad eye-line matches. Microphones visible in the camera lens. Even the earliest work (FLESH, TRASH) of Morrissey, the ex-Warhol Factory auteur, was more technically polished than MADAME WANG'S. Yet, if this later film seems ostensibly like the work of an amateur, Morrissey's "bad" technique perfectly complements his sly genre deconstructions. The director cleverly assaults everything from punk rock to DOUBLE INDEMNITY melodramas to Cold War spy thrillers to PYGMALION comedies. He even finds odd pathos amidst all the transvestite characters' lusting and desperation.

Best of all, Morrissey critiques Western capitalism through his sharp-eyed mise-en-scene. Lutz's pursuit of Fonda at her exercise club hilariously juxtaposes the star's Vietnam War-protester past and her wealthy fitness-queen persona of 1981, while the prostitutes' search for clients in front of a savings bank simultaneously contrasts and conflates two supposedly disparate business institutions.

Fifteen years after it was made, MADAME WANG'S' cryptically campy take on the American Dream looks funnier and more relevant than ever. *(Violence, nudity, sexual situations, adult situations, profanity.)* — E.M.

d, Paul Morrissey; exec p, Jack Simmons; assoc p, Dan Woodruff; w, Paul Morrissey (based on his story); ph, Juan Drago, Jim Tynes; ed, George Wagner, Michael Nallin; m, Leroy and the Lifters, Phranque, The Mentors, Butch, The Boneheads

Comedy/Drama **(PR: C MPAA: NR)**

MADDENING, THE ★★

(U.S.) 94m Greif Company; Charles Finch Productions; Trimark Pictures ~ Vidmark Entertainment c

Burt Reynolds *(Roy Scudder)*; Angie Dickinson *(Georgina Scudder)*; Mia Sara *(Cassie Osborne)*; Brian Wimmer *(David Osborne)*; Josh Mostel *(Detective Chickie Ross)*; William Hickey *("Daddy")*; Kayla Buglewicz *(Samantha)*; Candace Huston *(Jill)*

The director-son of John Huston lured Burt Reynolds and Angie Dickinson into starring in this forgettable psychothriller.

Suburban Florida yuppie David Osborne (Brian Wimmer) has to hit the road again for his high-pressure job, leaving behind five-year-old daughter Samantha (Kayla Buglewicz) and wife Cassie (Mia Sara). Cassie decides to take Samantha for an impromptu road trip to her sister in Tampa, just to spite her husband.

When Cassie stops for gas, she meets the intense station owner, Roy Scudder (Burt Reynolds), who rigs her car to break down conveniently near his house. Scudder takes them home, where they meet his delusional wife Georgina (Angie Dickinson) and belligerent offspring Jill (Candace Huston), who are both convinced that the Osbornes are long-lost relatives. The hospitable Scudders proceed to lock Cassie in her predecessor's old room and Jill acts as Samantha's abusive guardian, tying the younger girl to her with a rope to ensure this "playmate" won't run away.

Warden-like Roy encourages the domestic prisoners to answer to the names of the ominously-vanished kinfolk, but he cannot control the taunting hallucination of his dead father (William Hickey), the personification of a guilty conscience over his violent temper, lust for Cassie, and most of all how he killed his own sickly young son and buried the boy in secret.

David, meanwhile, is the cops' prime suspect in his spouse and child's disappearances. The fugitive trails his missing family down to the Scudder farm, but Roy knocks out the intruder and throws him down a well. David manages to recover, climb out, and reunite with Cassie. In a delusional fit, Roy mistakes Georgina for his disapproving daddy and shoots her. Then, while he's grappling with David, Cassie grabs the gun and blasts the madman out a second-floor window. At daybreak, only Jill remains, angry and alone, on the Scudder homestead.

Burt Reynolds' best dramatic roles, like DELIVERANCE (1972) and THE LONGEST YARD (1974), hinted at darker, dangerous things lurking behind his virile charm and good-old-boy smile, and here, as in 1996's STRIPTEASE, the onetime top box-office attraction seeks to reinvent himself. Reynolds and Dickinson (reunited for the first time since 1969's SAM WHISKEY), manage to maintain a degree of dignity and wit throughout this inferior suspense tale, whose artless script alternates stupid comic relief (two Bill-and-Ted buttheads at the gas station) with waiflike Mia Sara's agony in tearing off a fingernail trying to pry up a door's hinge. THE MADDENING received overseas theatrical release, but in the US mainly maddened viewers on home video. *(Adult situations, profanity, violence.) — J.D.*

d, Danny Huston; p, Leslie Greif; exec p, Mark Amin, Charles Finch; w, Henry Sleizer, Leslie Greif (based on the novel *Playmates* by Andrew Neiderman); ph, Nicky McLean; ed, Roberto Silvi, Eric L. Beason; m, Peter Manning Robinson; prod d, Bobby Amor; sound, Joe Foglia, L. Mo Weber; cos, Howard Sussman

Horror/Mystery/Thriller **(PR: C MPAA: NR)**

MAGIC HUNTER ★★

(Hungary/France/Switzerland/Canada) 106m Accent Productions; Gargantuan Motion Pictures; Budapest Filmstudio; UGC Images; Vega Film; Studio Babelsberg; WDR Fernsehen; Union Generale du Cinematographique ~ Shadow Distribution c
(BUVOS VADASZ; DER FREISCHUTZ)

Gary Kemp *(Max)*; Sadie Frost *(Eva)*; Alexander Kaidanovsky *(Maxim)*; Peter Vallai *(Kaspar)*; Mathias Gnadinger *(Police Chief)*; Alexandra Wasscher *(Lili)*; Ildiko Toth *(Lina)*; Natalie Conde *(The Virgin Mary)*; Zoltan Gera *(Shoemaker)*; Philippe Duclos *(Monk)*; Andor Lukats *(One-Eyed Monk)*; Gyorgy Bardy *(Theologian)*; Eszter Csakanyi *(Nanny)*; Tibor Bitskey *(Surgeon)*

A disappointingly self-indulgent sophomore effort by the director of the acclaimed MY 2OTH CENTURY (1989), this loose adaptation of the same European folktale that inspired Carl Maria von Weber's opera *Der Freischutz* is over-laden with confusingly shifting perspectives, heavy-handed transition devices, and obliquely related parallel narratives.

In what appears to be the bomb shelter of a Hungarian opera house, Eva (Sadie Frost) tries to reassure her young daughter, Lili (Alexandra Wasscher), with a story as bombs explode outside. The story concerns a hunter named Max who sold his soul to the Devil for seven magic bullets that could unerringly hit any target. Unbeknownst to Max, the final target would be chosen by the Devil himself. Eva's pearl necklace breaks, and the point of view shifts to that of a single pearl as it rolls out to a forest where Eva's husband, police sniper Max (Gary Kemp), is trying to take down a man with a hostage (Ildiko Toth). Max shoots the hostage by accident, badly wounding her; guilt consumes him.

The scene shifts to medieval Hungary, where Christian monks prepare to chop down a tree in order to prove the pagan Norse god Thor doesn't live there. A rabbit startles them and hurries down a hole; the rabbit's point of view segues to a hospital suite in the present, where Kaspar (Peter Vallai), a creepy cop, is told that the wounded woman will pull through. But Kaspar tells Max it's iffy, and convinces him to use three "magic" bullets at the firing range to help get his nerve back. Later, Max is assigned to surreptitiously guard a visiting Russian chess master, Maxim (Alexander Kaidanovsky), who's in danger of assassination by unknown forces yet shuns police protection. Meanwhile, back in medieval times, Kaspar, as the Devil, tempts Max, here a hunter, to cross a bridge that leads to a magical portrait of the Virgin Mary. The townsfolk say the Devil will steal the first soul that crosses the bridge, and the hunter is saved by an unwitting snail, inching its way across. The Virgin Mary (Natalie Conde) comes to life and saves a rabbit from a pack dogs.

In the present, Max begs Kaspar for four more bullets, but wastes two on target practice. He shoots himself in the head with the third, but the bullet is magically deflected. While tailing Maxim, Max sees him getting cozy with Eva and Lili at the park. Later, after Max catches Maxim and Eva chatting intimately at his apartment-house gate, he invites Maxim in and confesses that he's been following him for his own protection, and Maxim expresses his gratitude. While Max and Maxim are at dinner the following evening, Kaspar calls Eva and convinces her to join them. She arrives just as Max notices a sniper; Max pushes Maxim out of harm's way and fires his final bullet at the assassin, not knowing that the target of the last magic bullet is to be chosen by the Devil. The bullet heads for Eva in slow motion. Meanwhile, the Virgin Mary of the medieval portrait comes to life in the present and rushes through crowded streets. Suddenly Max, Eva, and Lili are in an opera house, getting up from their seats as the opera ends; Eva is seen back in the opera house bomb shelter finishing her story; then back to the restaurant, where the running Virgin Mary turns into Lili, who safely catches the bullet before it hits her mother.

Folktales generally have a solid, illustrative point to make or moral to teach, but the moral which MAGIC HUNTER purports to address—that it costs dearly to sell one's soul—becomes lost in the mess of parallel narratives and is finally obliterated by the film's bewildering conclusion. Is the viewer meant to believe that the power of God is stronger than that of the Devil, but we must first have faith? That only the past holds the key to our salvation? Or is it that, simply, love conquers all? In the end, it's hard to say, and the sparse subtitles, which leave many untranslated spans of dialogue, do little to help the viewer reach a coherent conclusion. *(Violence.)* — F.L.

d, Ildiko Enyedi; p, Andras Hamori, Wieland Schulz-Keil; exec p, Susan Cavan, David Bowie, Robert D. Goodale; assoc p, Peter Koltai, Lacia Kornylo; co-p, Ferenc Kardos, Yves Marmion, Ruth Waldburger; w, Ildiko Enyedi, Laszlo Laszlo Revesz; ph, Tibor Mathe; ed, Maria Rigo; m, Gregorio Paniagua; prod d, Attila Ferenczfy-Kovacs; sound, Istvan Sipos (mixer); fx, Peter Szilagyi, Gyula Zsalek, Yves Pupulin, Excalibur; cos, Gyorgyi Szakacs; makeup, Erzsebet Forgacs, Ivan Poharnok, Imre Orosz

Fantasy/Drama (PR: C MPAA: NR)

MAGIC IN THE MIRROR ★

(U.S./Romania) 82m Bibi Productions; Moonbeam Entertainment ~ Paramount c

Jamie Renee Smith *(Mary Margaret "Daisy")*; Kevin Wixted *(Tansy)*; Saxon Trainor *(Sylvia/Queen Hyssop)*; David Brooks *(Bloom)*; Godfrey James *(Mellilot)*; Christian Motriuc *(Swanson/Dr. Schmidt)*; Eileen T'Kaye *(Dragora)*; Ion Haiduc *(Dabble)*; Ilana Sandulescu *(Bella)*; Daniela Marzavan *(Donna)*; Rodica Lupu *(Teacher 1)*; Luana Stoica *(Teacher 2)*; Julia Boros *(Teacher 3)*; Constantin Cotamanis *(Teacher 4)*; Stelian Nistor *(Teacher 5)*; Constantin Radoaca *(Mover 1)*; Dan Astilean *(Mover 2)*

Spare kids and grownups alike this preachy fantasy that's good for their souls! Baldly ripping off *The Wizard of Oz* and *Alice in Wonderland,* MAGIC IN THE MIRROR deals with a looking glass that opens onto another world. That world is rife with second-rate optimism, third-rate actors, and fourth-rate art direction.

The plot revolves around inquisitive misfit Mary Margaret "Daisy" (Jamie Renee Smith), who is constantly irking her perfectionist mother, Sylvia (Saxon Trainor), with her typical-kid behavior. Descended from a line of botanists, Mary Margaret prizes an intricately carved full-length mirror, bequeathed to her by her grandmother, and an heirloom book containing plants and berries with magical properties.

After a dinner party at which Sylvia subtly disparages Mary Margaret's dad, the little girl is primed for a wondrous, unexpected journey through her looking glass to a parallel dimension. At the portals to this strange, new world, she causes pandemonium for two mirror guardians, Tansy (Kevin Wixted) and Mellilot (Godfrey James), and tries to figure out a way back home. Meanwhile, Dragora (Eileen T'Kaye), the Queen of Ducks who is notorious for turning humans into aromatic teas, wants the "entrance berries" Mary Margaret has taken with her from home. Wriggling out of Dragora's grasp several times with the help of Pixies Bella (Ilana Sandulescu) and Donna (Daniela Marzavan), the human child reaches the court of true Queen Hyssop (Saxon Trainor).

The queen informs Mary Margaret that the lives of unwatchful scouts Tansy and Mellilot will be spared only if the little girl thwarts Dragora's search for the berries. Downplaying her scientific, pragmatic side, Sylvia bravely takes an intra-mirror trip to rescue her daughter. Thanks to mother love and Mary Margaret's pluck, the Earth and Mirror kingdoms are safeguarded from invasion hereafter.

Stridently overplayed as if viewers had need of ear trumpets, this whimsy sports a straight-from-a-costume-shop appearance and a literal-minded approach to fantasy. Though one can appreciate the neatness of plot payoffs, such as having Mary Margaret's invisible pals on Earth turn out to be real-live Pixies in the reflecting world, most of MAGIC IN THE MIRROR isn't so clever and can be Windexed away quickly. The script explores the dark fabric of mother-daughter hostility with all the finesse of a shrink solving emotional problems with lobotomies. And what is one to make of a subplot about trapping little girls in tea bags and steeping them into beverages? What the movie itself boils down to is a makeshift parenting guide filtered through a cavalcade of kiddie-literature borrowings. *(Violence.)* — R.P.

d, Ted Nicolaou; p, Kevin Hyman, Vlad Paunescu; exec p, Charles Band; w, Ken Carter Jr., Frank Dietz; ph, Adolfo Bartoli; ed, Gregory Sanders; m, Richard Kosinski; prod d, Cristian Niculescu; art d, Viorel Ghenea; set d, Alexandru Constantinescu; sound, Tiberiu Borcoman (mixer); fx, Mark Rappaport; casting, Ed Mitchell, Robin Ray; cos, Oana Paunescu, Viorica Petrovici; makeup, Dana Roseanu

Children's/Fantasy (PR: AA MPAA: G)

MAHJONG ★★½

(Taiwan) 121m Atom Films c
(MAJIANG)

Virginie Ledoyen *(Marthe)*; Tang Tsung-sheng *(Red Fish)*; Ko Yu-lun *(Lun-lun)*; Chang Chen *(Hong Kong)*; Wang Chi-tsan *(Little Buddha)*; Nick Erickson *(Markus)*; Chao Te *(Jay)*; Ivy Chen *(Alison)*; Andrew Tsao *(David)*; Diana Dupuis *(Ginger)*; Carrie Ng *(Angela)*; Wu Nien-jen *(Older Mobster)*; Wang Po-sen *(Younger Mobster)*; Chang Kuo-chu *(Winston Chen)*; Elaine Jin *(Chen's Wife)*

MAHJONG tells a tale set in Taipei, "the city of the 21st century," involving European expatriates and a Taiwanese gang. Director Edward Yang's film is remarkably uneven, where the good and bad moments exist side by side.

MAHJONG looks at the high and low societies of modern Taipei and shows how the two intersect. The story begins when the tycoon, Winston Chen (Chang Kuo-chu), owing money to the Taipei underworld, goes into hiding. Two hoods (Wu Nien-jen, Wang Po-sen) sent to find Chen begin looking for the missing millionaire by tailing his son, Red Fish (Tang Tsung-sheng), the leader of a young gang that also includes hairdresser-hustler "Hong Kong" (Chang Chen); retiring Lun-lun (Ko Yu-lun), the group's chauffeur and translator; and the fortune-telling oddball "Little Buddha" (Wang Chi-tsan).

While the hoods keep tabs on Red Fish and the gang commits petty extortion schemes, several foreigners enter the picture. At the Hard Rock Cafe, where the gang hangs out, Marthe (Virginie Ledoyen), a young woman from France, seeks out Markus (Nick Erickson), a British interior designer with whom she had an affair in Paris. Marthe is hurt when she finds Markus together with Alison (Ivy Chen), his new Chinese girlfriend, so she goes with Lun-lun and the gang back to their apartment for some sexual mischief.

At the club, Ginger (Diana Dupuis), an American with an escort service, hopes to recruit Marthe, but Lun-lun, who is slowly growing fond of Marthe, protects her against Ginger's designs. Red Fish, meanwhile, seeks revenge on Angela (Carrie Ng), a wealthy Hong Kong woman who had betrayed his father many years earlier. When he tracks down his father to tell him, Red Fish finds Chen has been murdered. Angrily, Red Fish then plots to kill those responsible. Finally, Marthe decides to ditch

Markus for Lun-lun, and the gang begins to break up in light of the new circumstances.

MAHJONG mixes genres, styles, and even languages with much more abandon than most American independent films (e.g., the work of Jarmusch, Hartley, and Demme). It's screwball comedy crossed with crime melodrama, art film crossed with exploitation pic, and English crossed with Taiwanese (and some Mandarin). However, the odd jumble seems more like two or three films patched together than a postmodern critique of mainstream film practices.

Perhaps if director Yang (THE TERRORIZER, A CONFUCIAN CONFUSION) had asserted stronger control of the various elements and used fewer stereotypical characters, MAHJONG might have worked as the forward-looking mural it probably was meant to be. As it is, the scenes involving Marthe and Markus's romance weigh the film down due to weak writing and Nick Erickson's amateurishly affected performance. (Virginie Ledoyen is adequate, but she can be seen to expert advantage in A SINGLE GIRL and LA CEREMONIE, both also in 1996.) Similarly, the subplot involving Ginger's escort service—however titillating—collapses under Diana Dupuis's unconvincing portrayal.

And yet, most of the scenes involving the gang and the hoodlums are well acted, well written, and—for whatever reason—better directed (perhaps Yang is more comfortable with non-English speaking actors). In any case, the scenes of blackmail and revenge across generational and economic lines are both funny and scary. MAHJONG needs some major pruning, but there's a good film in it waiting to get out. *(Graphic violence, nudity, sexual situations, substance abuse, extreme profanity.)* — E.M.

d, Edward Yang; p, Yu Wei-yen; exec p, David Sun; w, Edward Yang; ph, Li Yi-hsu, Li Lung-yu; ed, Chen Powen; art d, Yu Wei-yen; sound, Tu Tu-chih, Phil Heywood, Martin Oswin

Comedy/Romance/Mystery (PR: O MPAA: NR)

MAJIANG
(SEE: MAHJONG)

MAKING THE CASE FOR MURDER: THE HOWARD BEACH STORY
(SEE: SKIN)

MAN BY THE SHORE, THE ★★★
(Haiti/France/Canada) 106m Les Productions du Regard; Froma Films International ~ KJM3 Entertainment c

Jennifer Zubar *(Sarah)*; Toto Bissainthe *(Grand-mere Desrouillere)*; Jean-Michel Martial *(Janvier)*; Patrick Rameau *(Gracieux/Sorel)*; Mireille Metellus *(Tante Elide)*; Francois Latour *(Francois Jansson)*; Albert Delpy *(Assad)*; Magaly Berdy *(Mirabelle)*; Michele Marcelin *(Madame Janvier)*; Ailo Auguste *(Gisele Jansson)*; Johanne Degand *(Jeanne)*; Douveline Saint-Louis *(Sabine)*

Set in Papa Doc Duvalier's Haiti, this grim tale of one family's struggle with petty tyranny is told through the eyes of a young girl whose spirit is not broken by the atrocities that surround her.

A young Haitian girl, Sarah (Jennifer Zubar), sneaks a peek through the blinds of her grandmother's (Toto Bissainthe) attic and what she sees makes her cry out in horror. A narrator explains that this is in the past and that the little girl has survived and escaped.

She watches as Sorel (Patrick Rameau), her godfather, is tortured by the village *tonton macoute* (secret police), Janvier (Jean-Michel Martial), for speaking against the government. After Sorel's public disgrace and subsequent arrest, her own father, ostensibly the top military man in town, chooses to flee the island. He knows that Janvier wants to obliterate him and his contentious family.

Sarah and her two older sisters are forced to stay behind and hide in a convent. When Janvier storms in and bullies the nuns for harboring "subversives," the girls take refuge in their defiant grandmother's attic. Grandmother Desrouillere struggles gamely to smuggle the girls out of the country, enlisting her friend, Lebanese merchant Assad (Albert Delpy), to buy counterfeit passports and visas for the girls. But Janvier outsmarts him and sets up a roadblock where he summarily shoots Assad.

Meanwhile, Sorel is released and lives in a small shack by the shore, when he is not wandering aimlessly through the village. Transformed into a walking mental and physical ruin, Sorel is unrecognizable, and Sarah cannot believe her benevolent godfather is now the village idiot. When Duvalier declares amnesty for political dissidents, Sarah goes bike riding with her friend, Sabine (Douveline Saint-Louis). They are accosted by the brutal Janvier, and while Sabine gets away, Janvier mercilessly pins Sarah down and attempts to rape her. In the struggle, Sarah gets Janvier's pistol. When a shot rings out, the camera pans to Sorel who is also holding a pistol. Did Sorel kill Janvier or did Sarah?

Filmed with a deliberate, controlled, classical pace and a beautiful eye for detail and color, the film rarely lags. The performances of Zubar, Bissainthe, and Rameau are top notch. Blatantly political and humanistic in an age when very few films tackle such concerns, THE MAN BY THE SHORE is especially pertinent because it illuminates conditions in Haiti, a country that usually only merits notice when there is a political coup.

The film received a limited release and generally positive critical reaction. But the best intentions of critics could not save this film from the indifference of the public to harsh political and moral stories. *(Graphic violence, adult situations.)* — S.C.

d, Raoul Peck; p, Pascal Verroust; assoc p, Jean-Roche Marcotte, Raymond Blumenthal; w, Raoul Peck, Andre Grall; ph, Armand Marco; ed, Jacques Comets; m, Amos Coulanges, Dominique Dejean; prod d, Gilles Aird; sound, Eric Devulder; cos, Chantal Bourbigot; makeup, Michele Dion

Drama/Political (PR: C MPAA: NR)

MAN IN THE ATTIC, THE ★½
(U.S./Canada) 104m Atlantis Films; Donald March Productions; CBS Entertainment Productions; Showtime Original Pictures ~ Paramount Home Video c

Neil Patrick Harris *(Edward Broder)*; Anne Archer *(Krista Heldman)*; Len Cariou *(Joe Heldman)*; Alex Carter *(Gary)*; Deborah Drakeford *(Amy)*; Rick Roberts *(Reporter)*; Toby Proctor *(Karl Heldman)*; Nahanni Johnstone *(Leslie)*; Judith Orban *(Mrs. Meyer)*; Bruce Vavrina *(Detective)*; Richard Liss *(Waiter)*; James Mainprize *(Mayor)*; Pixie Bigelow *(Mayor's Wife)*; Tedde Moore *(Another Wife)*; Sam Malkin *(Guard)*; Christopher Marren *(Charles)*; James Binkley *(Officer)*

Based on a case history from the book, *Sex and the Criminal Mind,* this film is an exceedingly tame slice of erotica. Bodices pop open, hungry lips seek to be fed, and flaming passions burn with all the ardor of a Hardy Boy getting pecked on the cheek by Mrs. Cleaver.

Dedicated to bettering his lot in 1910 Milwaukee, honorable orphan Edward Broder (Neil Patrick Harris) becomes a family fixture at the home of sewing machine magnate Joe Heldman (Len Cariou). When best buddy and heir apparent Karl Heldman (Toby Proctor) dies in an influenza epidemic, romantically quixotic Mrs. Krista Heldman (Anne Archer) regards Edward not so much as a second son but as a surrogate husband.

Although the sexually-predatory Krista persuades her teen lover to run away with her, proprietary Joe finds them, forgives his spouse, and banishes feckless Edward forever. Hypocritically professing fidelity, Krista installs Edward in her attic. When possible detection by outsiders threatens, she cajoles Joe into relocating to Los Angeles.

Content to have Joe bring home the bacon while Edward serves other practical purposes, the years pass happily, until Krista demands that pliable Edward allow her the luxury of other bedmates. One day, the unthinkable happens after Joe and Krista argue vociferously. Scurrying from his hiding place, selfless Edward shoots down an astonished Joe. The scandalous crime of passion does not result in convictions for either Krista or Edward.

Certainly this movie will provide realtors with a whole new selling angle for three-story houses. Unlike THE BLISS OF MRS. BLOSSOM (1968), which played a similar prisoner-of-love story line for laughs, this asthmatic heavy-breather treats its obsessive material seriously, with no flair for showcasing the tale's inherent suspense or shocking abnormal psychology. Instead, THE MAN IN THE ATTIC is a well-appointed soap opera, sort of like "Days of Our Lives" detouring through a flashback to 1910.

Although rich in prurient interest, this manicured period romance is a too-tasteful glimpse into the consequences of sexual greed. As the principals undress, there's never a sense of muss or fuss or of ecstatic exclamations that might give away the game. Are they extolling some form of Zen sex that's been purified of pleasure? Prissy Archer tackles her seductress role as if she were playing Miss Jean Brodie at a sex education class; Harris plays the love machine as if he were a grocery boy and Archer's body were just something he had to shelve for quick sale.

Attaining neither the giddy excess of director Zalman King nor the campy delirium of DESPERATE REMEDIES (1994), THE MAN IN THE ATTIC is a sex film with no interest in getting down and dirty. *(Sexual situations, violence.)* — R.P.

d, Graeme Campbell; p, Brian Parker; exec p, Peter Sussman, Donald March; co-p, James Nadler; w, Duane Poole, Tom Swale (from a story by Norman Winski); ph, Dick Bush; ed, Ralph Brunjes; m, Lou Natale; prod d, Susan Longmire; art d, Alta Louise Doyle; set d, Christine MacLean; sound, Jack Buchanan; casting, Darlene Kaplan, Deirdre Bowen, Tina Gerussi; cos, Trysha Bakker; makeup, Ava Stone; stunts, Bryan Renfro

Erotic/Drama **(PR: C MPAA: R)**

MAN OF THE YEAR ★

(U.S.) 85m Artisan Productions ~ Seventh Art Releasing c

Dirk Shafer *(Himself)*; Claudette Sutherland *(Tammy Shafer)*; Michael Ornstein *(Mike Miller)*; Cal Bartlett *(Ken Shafer)*; Mary Stein *(Angela Lucassey)*; Beth Broderick *(Kelly Bound)*; Cynthia Szigeti *(Betty Levy)*; Dennis Bailey *(Howie Diadone)*; Charles Sloane *(Ed, the Photographer)*; Patricia Domiano *(Ballroom Dancer)*; Dawn Christie *(Woman Exercising)*; Phyllis Franklin *(Dr. Marsha Demarky)*; Bill Brochtrup *(Pledge Cartwright)*; Lu Leonard *(Dee Dee Sweatman)*; Rhonda Dotson *(Lady La Flame)*; Thom Collins *(Himself)*; Deidra Shafer *(Herself)*; Paul Fow *(Rex Chandler)*; Fort Atkinson *(Buck Hallren)*; Felix Montano *(Jimmy Morgan)*; Michael Mueller *(ACT OUT #1)*; Kevin Bandy *(ACT OUT #2)*; Brett Sylver *(ACT OUT #3)*; Fabio *(Himself)*; Vivian Paxton *(Chris)*; Joe Fusco *(ACT OUT Stage Manager)*; Merri Biechler *(Leslie Dameron)*; Mindy Sterling *(Cindee)*

This inane faux documentary must have provided a lot of fun for its creators. That same amusement is, unfortunately, one that is completely unshared by the viewer.

This film outlines the based-on-true-life experiences of Dirk Shafer, *Playgirl* magazine's 1992 Man of the Year. Shafer's posing for a seemingly innocuous photo shoot results in a spread in *Playgirl* magazine. The magazine's editors and readers evidently like what they see and he is crowned the year's most popular centerfold. His duties entail numerous appearances on national television and radio talk shows in which he is required to show off his physique and talk about his dream woman. There's a catch, however—Shafer is gay. Nonetheless committed to the job, he decides to play it "straight," and achieves a certain notoriety appearing on daytime talk shows, making personal appearances, and hosting a romance phone line.

Conflict arises for Dirk in the varying forms of an obsessed fan, the Lady La Flame (Rhonda Dotson), who vows to be his "friend till the end"; Act Out, a militant gay group bent on publicly "outing" him; and, most importantly, his lover, Mike (Michael Ornstein), who balks at being forced back in the closet for the duration of Dirk's reign. Particularly stressful is the "Win-a-Date" contest, in which Angela (Mary Stein), a fan from Reno, wins a dream-date with *Playgirl*'s Man of the Year. Angela and Dirk are flown to Manhattan where, accompanied by *Playgirl's* pushy publicist (Cynthia Szigeti) and her macho boyfriend (Dennis Bailey), they spend a night out on the town. Since it's Valentine's Day, however, Dirk has Mike stashed away back at the hotel. Angela gets drunk and throws herself at Dirk. When he resists and tries to explain, Angela cuts him off: she admits she spotted Mike hiding in Dirk's hotel room before the date even started, and she figured then that he was gay. Ultimately, Dirk realizes that his stint as Man of the Year is not only threatening to destroy his relationship with Mike, but also his sense of well-being. After his close friend Pledge (Bill Brochtrup) dies of AIDS, Dirk rethinks his priorities and decides to go public with his sexuality.

This film absolutely defines the term "vanity production," as it happens to be about, stars, and is written and directed by none other than Shafer himself. It is, in a word, tired. Devoid of wit or charm, it's awash in a peculiarly clueless and bland sort of tackiness. Worst of all, Shafer's film is based on some very tired assumptions about female desire and, consequently, most of the women in the film come off as rather stupid. The innocent viewer, who would watch this in the hope that it might deliver some of the same goods for which *Playgirl* itself is famous, is ripped off: the nudity is strictly of the teasingly coy variety. As for personality, he projects a patented boy-next-door quality that wears thin after the first minute. The other actors all weigh in, desperate for their respective 15 minutes. Particularly embarassing are Szigeti, who does a wearisome strident-Jewish caricature; Beth Broderick, who plays a glossy *Playgirl* editor who's strictly a bad hetero male fantasy; and Ornstein, who is a smarmily perfect mate for Shafer. The one exception to this is club comedian Vivian Paxton who, as Shafer's best friend, has a wacky, natural appeal. Despite Shafer's Academy Award nomination for his short film "Lace Ladies," there's little filmmaking talent in evidence here. *(Nudity, adult situations, profanity.)* — D.N.

d, Dirk Shafer; p, Matt Keener; exec p, Christian Moey Aert; assoc p, Jeff Collins, Jeff Marcus; co-p, Simon Bowler; w, Dirk Shafer; ph, Stephen Timberlake; ed, Barry Silver, Ken Solomon; m, Peitor Angell; prod d, Michael Meuller; sound, Jack Lindauer (recordist), Giovanni DeSimone (recordist), Arnold Anderson (recordist); cos, Michael Mueller; makeup, Vivian Paxton, Yvonne DePatis Kupko, Lisa Mayer, Mi Yeoun Lee

Docudrama **(PR: A MPAA: NR)**

MAN WITH A PLAN ★★★½

(U.S.) 89m Bellwether Films; Bodine & Herzog ~ Bellwether Films c

Fred Tuttle; Bill Blachly; Joe Tuttle; Bryan Pfeiffer; Bruce Lyndes; Jim Wallace; Tom Blachly; Kermit Glines; Euclid Farnham; Priscilla Farnham; Edgar Dodge; William Sloane Coffin; Barbara Kohn

MAN WITH A PLAN is the second film (after VERMONT IS FOR LOVERS) in writer-director John O'Brien's Vermont trilogy. It's the story of Fred Tuttle, an elderly farmer with a 10th grade education and no money who runs for Congress. Although the script is fiction, Tuttle and most of the other characters in the film play themselves, and their natural spirit and ingenuous personalities combine with O'Brien's sharp, witty script to make MAN WITH A PLAN unique, top-notch entertainment.

Fred Tuttle is 73 years old and flat broke. He's recently sold his farm, and his father needs money for an operation. Deciding that no other job is appropriate for a man of his age, education, and lack of experience, Fred decides to run for Congress. Fred's opponent, incumbent Bill Blachly, doesn't take him seriously, but Fred's homey personality, honesty, and lack of political guile slowly but surely attract voters. Fred's campaign (whose slogan asks "Why vote for Fred? Why not?") swings into gear at the well-attended county fair, where Fred kisses lots of babies and meets hundreds of Vermont voters.

Fred is coached by a diction expert, and attracts attention by appearing in a demolition derby and by putting a huge hand-painted "Fred" sign on top of his car. Blachly, realizing that Fred is becoming a threat, sends out a gossip columnist to dig up some dirt, but Fred outwits the man and leaves him in the back yard, holding up a collapsing barn. Blachly's anti-Fred TV commercials and speeches have no effect on Fred's growing popularity.

The two men debate, and Blachly's experience and knowledge are overwhelmingly defeated by Fred's charm. In a last ditch effort, Blachly tries to get compromising pictures of Fred at a hillside "orgy," but a curious passing dog plays with the camera and exposes the film. The election is very close. As the night goes on and the results get counted, Fred gradually closes the gap between himself and Blachly. He wins by one vote and heads for Washington.

Fred Tuttle is an unforgettable, instantly lovable character. Whether he's learning to pronounce his name so it doesn't sound like "furry turtle," making campaign promises to send all of Vermont's garbage into space, or just walking around in his overalls and "Fred" hat, he has the makings of a true cult hero. Most of his dialogue is improvised, and though he's intended to be simple, he's treated with dignity and respect by the people in his life and by writer-director O'Brien.

MAN WITH A PLAN is filled with comic highlights. Sight gags, such as Fred continually closing one door of his car, only to have the other open, exist side-by-side with clever political satire and the narration's dry wit. The setting is perfect; in the context of this film, it never seems unlikely that Fred could become so popular in a small state like Vermont.

O'Brien's filmmaking style is distinctive and satisfying. As in VERMONT IS FOR LOVERS, Vermonters play themselves, and O'Brien expertly combines the real characters and genuine dialogue with his own script. He has an obvious love of his home state, and uses the authentic settings to great advantage. The cinematography is simple and unpretentious. O'Brien doesn't attempt anything more complicated than close-ups of people and animals (especially cows and sheep) and spacious shots of gorgeous Vermont scenery.

MAN WITH A PLAN is one of the most popular films in Vermont history, and set a record for video sales in the state. In the 1996 national election, Fred Tuttle actually received several hundred write-in votes for various offices. Its success is deserved; Hollywood comedies often spend MAN WITH A PLAN's $10,000 budget on coffee and don't produce as many genuine laughs as this film's first five minutes. *(Profanity.)* —A.M.

d, John O'Brien; p, John O'Brien; assoc p, Richard Morse, Molly O'Brien, Jack Rowell; w, John O'Brien; ph, Richard Morse, John O'Brien; ed, John O'Brien; sound, Richard Morse, Jack Rowell; stunts, Baxter Doty

Comedy **(PR: A MPAA: NR)**

MAN WITH THE PERFECT SWING, THE ★★

(U.S.) 93m Perfect Swing Productions ~ Monarch c

James Black *(Anthony Babe Lombardo)*; Suzanne Savoy *(Susan Lombardo)*; Marco Perella *(Chuck Carter)*; James Belcher *(Lou Gallo)*; Richard Bradshaw *(Bonelli)*; William Hardy *(Albert Scardino)*; Harold Suggs *(Father Mac)*; Blue Deckert *(Coach)*; Werner Richmond *(Squeaky)*; Doyle Carter *(Ben Hogan)*; Bettye Fitzgerald *(Mrs. Gillespie)*; Harlow Blackmon *(Hap)*; Terry Brennan *(Skip)*; Randy Salazar *(Harold's Salesman)*; John Biondi *(Harold)*; Bill Dando *(Tony Scardino)*; Gerry Katsuyama *(Nick Makita)*; Thi Pham *(Ho)*; Matt Yoeman *(Valet)*; Steven Owsley *(Pro Golfer)*; Linden Hudson *(Golf Course Starter)*; Anthony Babe Navarro *(Greg Norman Fan)*

This low-budget inspirational tale never supplies key incidents from its real-life antihero's biography with any psychological acuity, leaving viewers with a glorified home movie about someone you don't know and don't care to.

Having blossomed early as a college football hero and fancy restaurateur, middle-aged Babe Lombardo (James Black) scrounges to make a living. Financially and emotionally supported by his wife, Susan (Suzanne Savoy), Babe fights depression as he hustles a few bucks with amateur golfing bets. Robbing Peter to pay Paul, he talks trusting clients into prepayment of late shipments and forever promises admiring backer Lou Gallo (James Belcher) profits from his latest pie-in-the-sky sports equipment invention.

Recalling how his dad cheated Babe's father out of a grocery business, mobster Bonelli (Richard Bradshaw) takes a dim view of Babe's welching on golf wagers and becomes apoplectic when Babe finally outplays him one day. When not risking his meager earnings on bets, Babe develops what he feels is the perfect golf swing, adaptable to any player. With the IRS breathing down his neck, Babe tries to package his discovery as a video through old pal Chuck (Marco Perella). Protecting his last chance at the big time, Babe goes for broke on marketing his perfect swing video through the endorsement of an up-and-coming champ, Tony Scardino (Bill Dando). Backed into a corner after spokesperson Scardino proves a liability due to an undiagnosed eye problem, Babe decides to try to qualify for the Pro Tour at La Quinta. Exceeding beyond expectations, he still doesn't make the final cut. Finally, one of his golf merchandise inventions sells with enough profit to keep Babe out of the red.

If the self-deceived producers of THE MAN WITH THE PERFECT SWING hoped to cash in on the success of TIN CUP (1996), they should have guessed again. In opting for deglamorized realism, they deprive the audience of the uplift they expect from these neo-Frank Capra exercises. Despite all negative feedback to the contrary, the filmmakers present this material as a sports fairy tale about a little guy beating the odds. Does Babe's never-say-die attitude really signal success or delusion? Even for the viewer who's conditioned by his own share of evanescent pipe dreams and dwindling career options after 40, this film is a downer. All that registers is the daunting perspective of never-ending financial losses. More damagingly, it may be difficult for the viewer to indulge this professional backslapper and his last chance at the brass ring.

Because Babe occasionally lives off his wife, takes loyal friends to the cleaners, and never considers working at something practical to bankroll his goals, the audience is asked to identify with a loser. We're supposed to admire his determination; what we end up feeling is turned off by his chutzpah. *(Extreme profanity, adult situations.)* — R.P.

d, Michael Hovis; p, Michael Hovis, Angela Sembera Hovis; assoc p, Todd McCord; w, Michael Hovis; ph, Jim Barham; ed, Michael Hovis; m, Paul English; art d, Jeanette Scott; set d, Christopher Stull; sound, Linden Hudson (mixer); cos, Angela Sembera Hovis

Drama/Comedy/Sports **(PR: C MPAA: NR)**

MANNY & LO ★★★½

(U.S.) 89m Pope Entertainment Group ~ Sony Pictures Classics c

Mary Kay Place *(Elaine)*; Scarlett Johansson *(Amanda—Manny)*; Aleska Palladino *(Laurel—Lo)*; Paul Guilfoyle *(Mr. Humphreys, Country House Owner)*; Glenn Fitzgerald *(Joey)*; Cameron Boyd *(Chuck)*; Novella Nelson *(Georgine)*; Angie Phillips *(Connie)*; Monica Smith *(Chuck's Mom)*; Dean Silvers; Marlen Hecht; Forrest Silvers; Tyler Silvers *(Suburban Family)*; Lisa Campion *(Convenience Store Clerk)*; Susan Decker *(Baby Store Customer #1)*; Marla Zuk *(Baby Store Customer #2)*; Bonnie Johnson *(Baby Store Customer #3)*; Melissa Johnson *(Child)*; Melanie Johansson; Karsten Johansson; Hunter Johansson; Vanessa Johansson *(Golf Course Family)*; David DeStaebler *(Golf Course Cop)*; Mark Palmieri *(Golf Course Cop)*; Tony Arnaud *(Sheriff)*; Nicholas Lent *(Lo's Baby)*

Virulently non-traditional family values are celebrated in this engagingly original indie delight. A completely uncondescending view of adolescence is just one of the film's unexpected pleasures.

Two sisters, 16-year-old Laurel, nicknamed Lo (Aleksa Palladino), and 11-year-old Manny (Scarlett Johansson) run away from their separate foster homes. Living out of a station wagon, they rob convenience stores and squat in unoccupied model homes. Manny dreams of finding a real family and gazes longingly at fake family photos arranged over pre-fab fireplaces. Lo aspires to be an airline stewardess, using Manny's back to perfect her balance during "turbulence." A wrench in their freestyle life occurs when Lo realizes she has become pregnant. It's too late for an abortion, so they decide to wait things out in a deserted vacation home in the mountains. Both are natally clueless, so when they see Elaine (Mary Kay Place), a clerk in a baby-item store proffering all sorts of child-rearing wisdom, they kidnap her. Elaine at first resists, but becomes very protective when she realizes Lo's state. The three form a very odd little family unit, as preternaturally calm Manny warms to Elaine while Lo remains an emotional holdout. It turns out the hostage is far from what she seems. On top of everything else, the real owner of the house turns up—an escapee from his own family. The trio is faced with the dilemma of what to do about him as well as the upcoming blessed event.

Lisa Krueger's debut feature is quirky to a fault. The synopsis would seem to promise a sticky surfeit of whimsy, but Krueger has happily charged it with leavening amounts of heart and humor. ("But I'm the *coffee chairperson*!" wails an abducted Elaine in one of the many sideways-funny lines). Krueger also knows her film craft well: the whole thing has the kind of technical smoothness which greatly helps off-kilter comedy. Tom Krueger (the director's brother) photographs with a keen awareness of farcical contrasts; the early model-home scenes have a plastic, sitcom feel to them, while the later rustic episodes are verdantly frontier, apt for the outlaw/pioneer triad. John Lurie contributes a typically sensitive, eclectic music score, from moodily evocative to all-out head-banging.

Best of all are the charming performances. Palladino has the toughest role; it would be easy to hate the abrasive, alienated Lo, but Palladino shows you the panic behind her hard, skeptical eyes without once stooping to sentiment. Johansson is a spunky but sweet delight, reminiscent of young Linda Manz in DAYS OF HEAVEN (1978). Krueger's achievement here is an absolutely realistic portrayal of childhood and adolescence, even given a wildly improbable premise. The girls have individualism and delicate moments of sensitivity, and Mary Kay Place gives a juicily suggestive performance as she hops about the house in ankle chains, doling out comfort and advice in a tone that seems, in context, downright suspicious. Place's career has been so sketchy that it would be easy to overlook that she has managed to be herself over three decades, from the TV soap-opera spoof "Mary Hartman, Mary Hartman" to the Alcott & Andrews besuited yuppie in THE BIG CHILL (1983), to this character, whose mysterious, scattered psyche and infobyte-gleaned assurance are the perfect, damaged *zeitgeist* for the 1990s. *(Adult situations, profanity, sexual situations.) — D.N.*

d, Lisa Krueger; p, Dean Silvers, Marlen Hecht; exec p, Klaus Volkenborn; assoc p, Gary Kauffman; w, Lisa Krueger; ph, Tom Krueger; ed, Colleen Sharp; m, John Lurie; prod d, Sharon Lomofsky; set d, Dina Goldman; sound, Irin Strauss (mixer); casting, Ellen Parks; cos, Jennifer Parker; makeup, Frances Sorenson

Comedy/Drama **(PR: C MPAA: R)**

MARK DACASCOS REDEMPTION: KICKBOXER 5

(SEE: REDEMPTION: KICKBOXER 5)

MARS ATTACKS! ★★★

(U.S.) 105m Warner Bros. ~ Warner Bros. c

Jack Nicholson *(President James Dale/Art Land)*; Glenn Close *(First Lady Marsha Dale)*; Annette Bening *(Mrs. Barbara Land)*; Pierce Brosnan *(Professor Donald Kessler)*; Danny DeVito *(Rude Gambler)*; Martin Short *(Press Secretary Jerry Ross)*; Sarah Jessica Parker *(Nathalie Lake)*; Michael J. Fox *(Jason Stone)*; Rod Steiger *(General Decker)*; Tom Jones *(Himself)*; Lukas Haas *(Richie Norris)*; Natalie Portman *(Taffy Dale)*; Jim Brown *(Byron Williams)*; Lisa Marie *(Martian Girl)*; Sylvia Sidney *(Grandma Norris)*; Paul Winfield *(General Casey)*; Pam Grier *(Louise Williams)*; Jack Black *(Billy Glenn Norris)*; Janice Rivera *(Cindy)*; Ray J. *(Cedric)*; Brandon Hammond *(Neville)*; Joe Don Baker *(Glenn Norris)*; O-Lan Jones *(Sue Ann Norris)*; Christina Applegate *(Sharona)*; Brian Haley *(Mitch)*; Jerzy Skolimowski *(Doctor Zeigler)*; Timi Prulhiere *(Tour Guide)*; Barbet Schroeder *(French President)*; Chi Hoang Cai *(Mr. Lee)*; Tommy Bush *(Hillbilly)*; Joseph Maher *(Decorator)*; Gloria M. Malgarini; Betty Bunch; Gloria Hoffmann *(Nuns)*; Willie Garson *(Corporate Guy)*; John Roselius *(GNN Boss)*; Michael Reilly Burke; Valerie Wildman; Richard Irving *(GNN Reporters)*;

Jonathan Emerson *(Newscaster)*; Tamara Curry; Rebecca Broussard *(Hookers)*; Vinny Argiro *(Casino Manager)*; Steve Valentine *(TV Director)*; Coco Leigh *(Female Journalist)*; Jeffrey King *(NASA Technician)*; Enrique Castillo *(Hispanic Colonel)*; Don Lamoth *(2nd Colonel)*; C. Wayne Owens; Joseph Patrick Moynihan *(Strangers)*; Roger Peterson *(Colonel)*; John Finnegan *(Speaker of the House)*; Ed Lambert *(Morose Old Guy)*; John Gray *(Incredibly Old Guy)*; Gregg Daniel *(Lab Technician)*; J. Kenneth Campbell; Jeanne Mori *(Doctors)*; Rance Howard *(Texan Investor)*; Richard Assad *(Saudi Investor)*; Velletta Carlson *(Elderly Slots Woman)*; Kevin Mangan *(Trailer Lover)*; Rebeca Silva *(Hispanic Woman)*; Josh Weinstein *(Hippie)*; Juian Barnes *(White House Waiter)*; Ken Thomas *(White House Photographer)*; Darelle Porter Holden; Christi Black; Sharon Hendrix *(Tom Jones Backup Singers)*; Poppy *(Poppy)*

A childlike sense of malicious fun pervades MARS ATTACKS!, a film which proves that Tim Burton is one of the few directors working within the Hollywood mainstream who can combine a big budget, "name" performers, and special effects from the soulless ILM shop to produce a movie true to his own singularly bent vision.

As spaceships approach Earth, life continues as usual for unsuspecting Americans like dedicated Washington, DC mom Louise Williams (Pam Grier); her ex-husband, Byron (Jim Brown), a former heavyweight champion now working as a "greeter" in a Las Vegas casino; alienated Kansas teen Richie Norris (Lukas Haas); Las Vegas entrepreneur Art Land (Jack Nicholson); his enlightenment-seeking wife, Barbara (Annette Bening); and rival New York news anchors Natalie Lake (Sarah Jessica Parker) and Jason Stone (Michael J. Fox), who live together while competing for plum assignments.

After a televised message from the Martian Ambassador is interpreted to have a friendly tone, the shallow but telegenic President of the United States (also played by Nicholson) schedules an event to welcome them. Unfortunately, the Martian soldiers open fire and kill dozens, including Earth's goodwill ambassador General Casey (Paul Winfield) and Jason, and kidnap Natalie and her pet chihuahua. The Martian Ambassador sends a formal apology to the President, who schedules a second meeting in Congress against the advice of gung-ho General Decker (Rod Steiger). The Martians again kill dozens of the assembled and kidnap key Presidential advisor Donald Kessler (Pierce Brosnan). In the ensuing attack, Art and Richie's parents (Joe Don Baker and O-Lan Jones) are among the casualties. Meanwhile, romance blossoms aboard a spaceship between Natalie, whose head has been transplanted onto the body of her chihuahua, and the disembodied head of Kessler. (The destruction of the spaceship later on ends their brief affair.) The Martians soon dispose of Decker and the President in the Presidential War Room.

In Las Vegas, Barbara, Byron, singer Tom Jones (playing himself), and a waitress, Cindy (Janice Rivera), escape to a small plane. Martians surround them before they can take off; Byron stays to take on the Martians while the other three fly away to safety. In Kansas, Richie rushes to save his grandmother (Sylvia Sydney); when she plays a Slim Whitman record, the singer's high-pitched yodelling makes the Martians' heads explode. Trucks blaring Whitman's music are deployed all over the country, and the Martians are destroyed. Triumphant Byron returns home to Louise and their sons (Brandon Hammond and Ray J.), and Richie is commended by the only remaining member of the First Family, the President's daughter, Taffy (Natalie Portman).

Inspired by an infamous set of Topps trading cards so graphically violent for their era (1962) that protests from parents caused them to be withdrawn, MARS ATTACKS! stands as one of the better contemporary evocations of the low-budget alien invasion movies of the 1950s. Burton's affection for those films—and their later television ("The Outer Limits") and trading-card equivalents—is apparent as the film bounces quickly and energetically from location to location. Despite its many narrative strands, the film still clocks in at only 105 minutes, so it never wears out its welcome; Burton clearly felt no need to extend the running time simply to justify his special-effects budget.

Burton's casting of "name" performers in the lead roles could be perceived as an attempt to attract audience attention, but the nasty way in which most of the same names are incinerated only serves to reinforce the sense of vicious glee with which Burton seems to have approached the project. Several of the disposed-of give wonderful performances, including Nicholson as the preening, simpering President, and Lisa Marie, who gives a brief but memorable turn as a Martian disguised as a slinky hooker. Others—like Danny De Vito, playing a gambler, and Nicholson, in his goofy turn as Art Land—seem to be on hand merely to be killed. The film's conclusion sees the most effective performers survive, including Grier and Brown, who manage to render their characters nicely three-dimensional; Bening, who makes the most of kooky Barbara; and gawky Haas, who functions well as Burton's ever-present misfit-protagonist.

But despite the notable cast, it's the Martians who steal the show. These small, computer-generated creatures provoke laughs as they chatter and waddle along, but any time the film seems in danger of becoming irretrievably cute, Burton returns to the element that made the "Mars Attacks" cards so controversial (and attractive to youngsters)—gore and violence with no apologies. *(Violence, adult situations.)* — E.G.

d, Tim Burton; p, Tim Burton, Larry Franco; w, Jonathan Gems (from his story, based on the Topps trading-card series); ph, Peter Suschitzky; ed, Christopher Lebenzon; m, Danny Elfman; prod d, Wynn Thomas; art d, John Dexter; set d, Nancy Haigh; sound, Dennis Maitland; fx, Michael Lantieri, James Mitchell, Industrial Light & Magic, Warner Digital Studios; casting, Victoria Thomas, Jeanne McCarthy, Matthew Barry; cos, Colleen Atwood; makeup, Valli O'Reilly; stunts, Joe Donne

Science Fiction/Comedy **(PR: C MPAA: PG-13)**

MARVIN'S ROOM ★★★

(U.S.) 95m Scott Rudin/Tribeca ~ Miramax c

Meryl Streep *(Lee)*; Diane Keaton *(Bessie)*; Leonardo DiCaprio *(Hank)*; Gwen Verdon *(Ruth)*; Robert De Niro *(Dr. Wally)*; Hume Cronyn *(Marvin)*; Hal Scardino *(Charlie)*; Dan Hedaya *(Bob)*; Margo Martindale *(Dr. Charlotte)*; Cynthia Nixon *(Retirement Home Director)*; Kelly Ripa *(Amber/Coral)*; John Callahan *(Lance)*; Olga Merediz *(Beauty Shop Lady)*; Joe Lisi *(Bruno)*; Steve Dumouchel *(Gas Station Guy)*; Bitty Schramm *(Janine)*; Victor Garber *(Minister)*; Lizbeth MacKay *(Novice)*; Helen Stenborg *(Nun on Phone)*; Sally Parrish *(Nun #3)*

Adapted from a 1990 play, MARVIN'S ROOM teams two superb actresses—Diane Keaton and Meryl Streep—in an emotional drama about family illness, estrangement, and love.

Bessie (Diane Keaton) is a 50-ish woman who has devoted her life to caring for her totally incapacitated father, Marvin (Hume Cronyn), and eccentric aunt, Ruth (Gwen Verdon). For 20 years, she has been out of touch with her younger sister, Lee (Meryl Streep), a hairdresser and single mother with two sons, Hank (Leonardo DiCaprio) and Charlie (Hal Scardino). When Hank, a troubled 17-year-old, deliberately burns down their home, he is placed in a mental institution.

Bessie is diagnosed with leukemia, and Lee and her two boys are summoned from Ohio to Florida as potential bone marrow donors. After they arrive, Bessie exhorts her sister to be ready to step in as family caregiver if necessary. Lee refuses—her freedom is more important to her—and the sisters exchange bitter words. Meanwhile, Bessie and Hank establish a friendly relationship with each other. The sisters quickly reconcile and become close for the first time in their lives. Then Bessie's doctor (Robert De Niro) reports that her bone marrow doesn't match up with that of her sister or either of her nephews.

Having been given the medical equivalent of a death sentence, Bessie philosophizes that the opportunity to devote herself to looking after her father and aunt has made her life a rich and full one. As the story ends, it appears that Lee is seriously considering remaining in Florida and assuming her selfless sister's family role.

In the original theatrical production, Marvin is never seen. He does, however, appear prominently in the movie, although he is given no dialogue. Except for this revision—plus the additions of a trip to Disney World and a cliched scene in which Hank and Bessie take a joyride in the family car through the surf—MARVIN'S ROOM remains quite close to its source. The film, which appears to contain less dialogue than the play, is rendered fairly briskly in reasonably short scenes, and is generally well acted. The sobriety of the theme is relieved by frequent comic touches, some of them successful (the droll performances of De Niro as the physician and Dan Hedaya as his totally clueless brother-assistant), some of them less so (the occasional cheap laugh induced by Aunt Ruth, who at one point advises Bessie, "You don't make stinky often enough.").

Like all screen adaptations of plays, MARVIN'S ROOM loses something in translation; but it remains admirable for its honest examination of a potentially depressing subject matter and for limning the joys of caring for others without sidestepping the accompanying pain and sacrifice. The drama might have been more effective if the estrangement between the sisters ran a bit deeper and their battles with each other were a little less theatrically direct.

The author of MARVIN'S ROOM, Scott McPherson, died of AIDS at the age of 33, shortly after his play's New York premiere. *(Profanity.)* — D.T.

d, Jerry Zaks; p, Scott Rudin, Jane Rosenthal, Robert De Niro; exec p, Tod Scott Brody, Lori Steinberg; assoc p, Craig Gering, John Guare; co-p, David Wisnievitz, Bonnie Palef, Adam Schroeder; w, Scott McPherson (based on his play); ph, Piotr Sobocinski; ed, Jim Clark; m, Rachel Portman; prod d, David Gropman; art d, Peter Rogness; set d, Tracey Doyle; sound, Danny Michael; casting, Ilene Starger; cos, Julie Weiss; makeup, Allen Weisinger; stunts, Frank Ferrara; tech, Dr. Tony Costanzo

AAN Best Actress: Diane Keaton

Drama **(PR: C MPAA: PG-13)**

MARY REILLY ★½

(U.S.) 118m Hyde Films Ltd.; Channel Productions; TriStar ~ TriStar c

Julia Roberts *(Mary Reilly)*; John Malkovich *(Dr. Jekyll/Mr. Hyde)*; Glenn Close *(Mrs. Farraday)*; George Cole *(Mr. Poole)*; Michael Gambon *(Mary's Father)*; Kathy Staff *(Mrs. Kent)*; Michael Sheen *(Bradshaw)*; Bronagh Gallagher *(Annie)*; Linda Bassett *(Mary's Mother)*; Henry Goodman *(Haffinger)*; Ciaran Hinds *(Sir Danvers Carew)*; Sasha Hanau *(Young Mary)*; Moya Brady *(Young Woman)*; Emma Griffiths Malin *(Young Whore)*; David Ross *(Doctor)*; Tim Barlow *(Vicar)*; Isabella Marsh *(Screaming Girl)*; Wendy Nottingham *(Screaming Girl's Mother)*; Richard Leaf *(Screaming Girl's Father)*; Stephen Boxer *(Inspector)*; Bob Mason *(Policeman)*; Ellie Crockett; Robbi Stevens; Kadamba; Evelyn Doggart; Piu Fan Lee; Mimi Potworowska; Samantha Hones; Julia Hagen *(Farraday Girls)*

In MARY REILLY, Dr. Jekyll turns himself into the most dreaded movie monster of them all . . . a thudding bore! This UPSTAIRS/DOWNSTAIRS approach to the Jekyll-Hyde legend (told from the maid's point of view) is by turns tedious and laughable.

In 19th-century London, the Irish-born Mary Reilly (Julia Roberts) lives in the house of Dr. Henry Jekyll (John Malkovich), a distinguished scientist. Mary is one of several devoted servants to Dr. Jekyll, but her vulnerable, innocent nature makes her his favorite. Mary's trust is a blessing to the doctor as he embarks on a new experiment, which requires understanding and secrecy. During her private duties for the doctor, Mary meets his elusive new assistant, Mr. Hyde (John Malkovich), a lascivious and quick-witted character.

Mary finds herself drawn to the seductive Mr. Hyde, but she grows uncomfortable about relaying messages for him to a local brothel owner, Mrs. Farraday (Glenn Close). Mary also begins to suspect that Mr. Hyde is involved in some terrible secrets. As Hyde grows stronger, the doctor grows weaker, and Mary finally confronts the demons in her own dark past. During the burial of her mother (Linda Bassett), Mary defies her father (Michael Gambon) for his years of abuse and neglect. Back at the Jekyll household, she figures out that Jekyll and Hyde are one in the same person. Despite her fondness for both men, Mary decides to pack up and leave the sinister estate.

There is a germ of a valid idea behind Valerie Martin's source novel (based, of course, on Robert Louis Stevenson's "The Strange Case of Dr. Jekyll and Mr. Hyde"), but director Stephen Frears and screenwriter Christopher Hampton (the team who gave us DANGEROUS LIAISONS) create a stodgy, slow-moving adaptation with several dialogue howlers. Hyde, for example, describes his relationship with Jekyll to Mary by saying, "I am the bandit. He is merely the cave which I shelter." No silly lines, however, can top the final scene in which Jekyll literally gets in touch with his inner child, and Mary loses her romantic interest in the schizoid doctor.

Aided immeasurably by cinematographer Philippe Rousselot and production designer Stuart Craig, Stephen Frears at least creates the right look for a horror movie, and there are many elegant, fog-enshrouded shots. But there is no suspense in a story where the audience is always several steps ahead of the characters, and Frears too often resorts to music and sound effects to jolt the audience.

The woeful leads further sink this "prestige" enterprise. Struggling with her Irish accent (and contending with an awful coiffure), the usually gutsy Roberts seems hampered playing the nervous, wide-eyed, and sexually repressed heroine. Malkovich, who drops *his* accent after his first scene, brings to mind Somerset Maugham's quip about Spencer Tracy's 1941 portrayal, "Which one is he now, Jekyll or Hyde?" Malkovich's DANGEROUS LIAISONS (1988) co-star, Close, pops up for a cameo as the bizarrely-accented madam, who looks like a cross between Norma Desmond and Cloris Leachman's Nurse Diesel from HIGH ANXIETY (1977).

Unintended chuckles aside, MARY REILLY is soporific and dull. "I think we've had enough excitement for one evening," Hyde tells Mary. Hardly! *(Graphic violence, sexual situations, profanity.)* — E.M.

d, Stephen Frears; p, Ned Tanen, Nancy Graham Tanen, Norma Heyman; exec p, Lynn Pleshette; co-p, Iain Smith; w, Christopher Hampton (based on the novel by Valerie Martin); ph,

Philippe Rousselot; ed, Lesley Walker; m, George Fenton; prod d, Stuart Craig; art d, John King, Michael Lamont, Jim Morahan; set d, Stephenie McMillan; sound, Clive Winter (recordist); fx, Richard Conway, Kent Houston, Mark Nelmes; casting, Leo Davis, Juliet Taylor; cos, Consolata Boyle; makeup, Jenny Shircore; stunts, Jim Dowdall

Horror/Drama **(PR: C MPAA: R)**

MATERNAL INSTINCTS ★★

(U.S.) 92m Shooting Star Entertainment; Wilshire Court Productions ~ Paramount Pictures Home Video c

Delta Burke *(Tracy Patterson)*; Beth Broderick *(Dr. Eva Warden)*; Garwin Sanford *(Gary Warden)*; Sandra Nelson *(Sabrina Crane)*; Tom Mason *(Stan Patterson)*; Gillian Barber *(Julie Taft)*; Kevin McNulty *(Joe Reilly)*; Tom Butler *(Dr. Milton Shaw)*; Malcolm Stewart *(Sidney Gordon)*; Maria Herrera *(Martha)*; Suzy Joachim *(Linda)*; Chilton Lane *(Sue)*; Lorena Gale *(Anita)*; Jerry Wasserman *(Detective Kramer)*; Tashia Simms *(Real Estate Agent)*; Peter Hanlon *(Bailey)*; Doug Cameron *(Hotel Clerk)*; Don McKay *(Doctor)*; Gloria Macarenko *(TV Host)*

Instead of maximizing its tacky, over-the-top potential, MATERNAL INSTINCTS mistakenly insists that viewers be touched by the plight of its vengeful, infertile heroine.

Unhealthily obsessed with conceiving her own child, Tracy Patterson (Delta Burke) intends to compensate for the enduring emotional bankruptcy she feels as an orphan. When a top gynecologist, Dr. Eva Warden (Beth Broderick), prepares to surgically implant Tracy with eggs, she discovers a cancer-ridden ovary. Without consulting Tracy, who is under anesthesia, Tracy's husband Stan (Tom Mason) and her best friend Sabrina (Sandra Nelson) coax the doctor to perform a hysterectomy. Already unstable and now barren, Tracy accidentally kills Stan by pushing him headfirst into a woodpile.

To get revenge on Dr. Warden, Tracy tampers with the pregnant, miscarriage-prone doctor's hormone injection; uses deception to land a job at the lab where Dr. Warden sends client specimens; and switches pregnancy results so that Dr. Warden and her partner face malpractice suits. Tracy then wheedles a real estate position out of Sabrina in order to lure Dr. Warden's architect husband Gary (Garwin Sanford) out of town. After pitching an interfering Sabrina down a skyscraper shaft, Tracy fails to seduce Gary at a hotel, but does succeed in hitting him with her car and depositing his near-lifeless body on Dr. Warden's doorstep. While Gary recuperates, Dr. Warden gives birth to a healthy baby. Tracy steals Dr. Warden's newborn and wheels the groggy doctor to the hospital basement, where she attacks a nosy mechanic and falls down some stairs while trying to kill her *bete noire*. In a coda, psychotic Tracy vows to go baby-snatching again.

MATERNAL INSTINCTS does deliver one inviolable moment of camp greatness: the sight of Delta Burke busting up a cradle like a shopaholic who didn't find a bargain at a Macy's sale. Aside from this scene and other scattered, unintentionally comic violence ("See Burke smack a mechanic in the snout with the world's biggest monkey wrench!"), MATERNAL INSTINCTS doesn't ooze with the cheap kicks suggested by its high concept.

Thrill-seekers tuning in for the promise of watching Burke voraciously chew the scenery will find their desires precluded by TV-movie stereotyping and hack direction that vacuums out suspense. They'll have to settle for yet another USA Network movie about a pampered woman settling a sterility score; the only difference is how its serious, core issues of fertility and motherhood are shredded by the definition of its heroine as a deranged, mascara-smudged, spoiled brat who hurls ice cream at television screens when miffed and murders friends and family when contradicted. *(Violence, adult situations, profanity.)* — R.P.

d, George Kaczender; p, Mary Eilts; exec p, Lisa Friedman Block, Delta Burke; co-p, Kathy Kirtland Silverman; w, Lisa Friedman Block, Kathy Kirtland Silverman; ph, Lazlo Gyuriko George; ed, Stephen Michael; m, Lawrence Shragge; prod d, Guy Lalande; set d, Katterina Keith; sound, William Butler (mixer); fx, Rae Reedyk; casting, Dan Shaner, Sid Kozak; cos, Cynthia Summers, Delta Burke Design; makeup, Aliki Demetriades; stunts, Bill Ferguson

Thriller/Drama **(PR: C MPAA: PG-13)**

MATILDA ★★½

(U.S.) 93m Jersey Films ~ TriStar c
(GB: ROALD DAHL'S MATILDA)

Mara Wilson *(Matilda)*; Danny DeVito *(Mr. Wormwood)*; Rhea Perlman *(Mrs. Wormwood)*; Embeth Davidtz *(Miss Honey)*; Pam Ferris *(Trunchbull)*; Paul Reubens *(FBI Agent)*; Tracey Walter *(FBI Agent)*; Brian Levinson *(Michael)*; Jean Speegle Howard *(Miss Phelps)*; Sara Magdalin *(Matilda, 4 years)*; R.D. Robb *(Roy)*; Goliath Gregory *(Luther)*; Fred Parnes *(Waiter)*; Kiami Davael *(Lavender)*; Leor Livneh Hackel *(Julius Rottwinkle)*; Jacqueline Steiger *(Amanda Thripp)*; Jimmy Karz *(Bruce Bogtrotter)*; Michael Valentine *(Nigel Hicks)*; Liam Kearns *(Charles)*; Mark Watson *(Magnus)*; Kira Spencer Hesser *(Hortensia)*; J.C. Alexander *(Nearby Boy)*; Malone Brinton *(Older Boy)*; Marion Dugan *(Cookie)*; Joshua Alvarez; Max E. Blum; Erin M. Gray; Misty L. Oppenheim; Christopher Shepard Hughes; Rachel Snow *(Children at Assembly)*; Craig Lamar Traylor; Jennifer Key; Marty Bautista; Anthony Hernandez; Raina Cease; Jonathan Cease; Vinnie Buffolino; Marcella Sassano; Johnny Thomas III; Shannon Hughes; Christel Khalil; Cassie Colaw; Justin Stout; Cindy Tran; Jonathan Feyer *(Children in Classroom)*; Alissa Graham; Amanda Graham; Trevor Gallagher; James Gallagher *(Newborn Matilda)*; Kayla Fredericks; Kelsey Fredericks *(Matilda, 9 Months)*; Amanda Fein; Caitlin Fein *(Matilda, Toddler)*; Nicholas Cox *(Michael, 6 years)*; Amanda Summers; Kristin Summers *(Miss Honey, 2 years)*; Phoebe Pearl *(Miss Honey, 5 years)*; Kathy Lynn Barbour *(Million $ Sticky Showgirl)*; Donna Spangler *(Million $ Sticky Showgirl)*; Marianne Curan *(Million $ Sticky Contestant)*; Penny Holland *(Million $ Sticky Contestant)*; Richard E. Coe *(Million $ Sticky Contestant)*

Danny DeVito's adaptation of a Roald Dahl children's tale bludgeons every simplistic plot point home to the point of giving viewers a senselessly brutal workout.

Matilda (Mara Wilson) is the unloved genius daughter of the crass Wormwoods (Danny DeVito and Rhea Perlman). As an infant, she was able to write her name in spilled baby food. Now, she is able to read books far beyond her years, but this is nothing to her boorish used-car salesman of a dad who can barely be bothered to remember her name or correct age. Mom is just as bad, more concerned with her makeup than her daughter's education. Factor in a fat, nasty, favored brother and it's a wonder poor Matilda manages to be as bright and hopeful as she is. At the age of six, she convinces her wayward parents that it's time for her to go school. Reluctantly, they acquiesce, sending her to a scary establishment called Crunchem Hall. There, she encounters her biggest nemesis of all, the headmistress of her school, Miss Trunchbull (Pam Ferriss), a Third Reich-type who thinks nothing of tossing disobedient charges clear across campus, or locking them in a terrifying closet filled with glass shards. She is especially averse to Matilda, since Trunchbull has stupidly bought one of Wormwood's defective jalopies.

One day, Matilda discovers that she has the ability to transport inert objects without so much as touching them. With the help of this special talent and her beloved teacher, Miss Honey (Embeth Davidtz), she makes sure all the meanies get their comeuppance. Trunchbull suffers a humiliating expulsion from the school, to the gleeful delight of the liberated kids. The Wormwoods are forced to flee when their shady business (buying stolen car parts) is uncovered by a couple of clumsy FBI agents spying on them. It would seem that Matilda will be an orphan, but Miss Honey, who reveals that Trunchbull is indeed her evil sister, provides a special doll and a loving haven for the grateful girl.

The film abounds in the comedy of sadistic cruelty. Student torture chambers, graphic child abuse and an endless scene of Trunchbull's humiliation are relished with unholy glee. DeVito has Ferriss give an over-the-top villainous turn that calls to mind the late Anne Ramsey in his THROW MOMMA FROM THE TRAIN (1987).

Wilson, so obnoxiously cute in MRS. DOUBTFIRE (1993), remains resolutely unappealing. As Matilda's little friend, Lavendar, Kiami Davael has a charming presence—she's an oasis of naturalism amid all the racket. Davidtz's wan sweetness fits in all too neatly with the Dahl/DeVito idea of female as saint or monster. There's also that idiotically extraneous subplot involving the two bumbling FBI agents, one played by the erstwhile Pee-Wee Herman, Paul Reubens. *(Graphic violence, adult situations)* — D.N.

d, Danny DeVito; p, Danny DeVito, Michael Shamberg, Stacey Sher, Liccy Dahl; exec p, Michael Peyser, Martin Bregman; assoc p, Joshua Levinson; co-p, Robin Swicord, Nicholas Kazan; w, Nicholas Kazan, Robin Swicord (based on the book by Roald Dahl); ph, Stefan Czapsky; ed, Lynzee Klingman, Brent White; m, David Newman; prod d, Bill Brezeski; art d, Philip Toolin; set d, Jennifer Polito-Gaulke; sound, David Kelson (mixer); fx, Michael Lantieri, Chris Watts; casting, David Rubin, Renee Rousselot; cos, Jane Ruhm; makeup, Ve Neill; stunts, R.A. Rondel

Children's/Comedy/Fantasy (PR: A MPAA: PG)

MAXIMUM RISK ★★

(U.S.) 126m Roger Birnbaum Productions; Moshe Diamant Productions ~ Columbia c

Jean-Claude Van Damme *(Alain/Mikhail)*; Natasha Henstridge *(Alex)*; Jean-Hugues Anglade *(Sebastien)*; Zach Grenier *(Ivan)*; Paul Ben-Victor *(Pellman)*; Frank Senger *(Loomis)*; Stefanos Miltsakakis *(Red Face)*; Frank Van Keeken *(Davis)*; David Hemblen *(Kirov)*; Stephanie Audran *(Chantal)*; Dan Moran *(Yuri)*; Donald Burda *(Nicholas)*; Rob Kaman *(Morris)*; Herb Lovelle *(Martin)*; Denis Costanzo *(Innkeeper)*; Mark Estrada Tournie *(Inspector)*; Carlo Rota *(Bohemia Bartender)*; Joe Pingue *(Bohemia Doorman)*; Hugh Thompson *(Bohemia Doorman)*; Gloria Slade *(Airline Steward)*; Jackie Richardson *(Large Woman)*; Ed Sahely *(Desk Clerk)*; Martine Pujol *(Cleaning Lady)*; Albert Schultz *(Anderson)*; Dan Duran *(Reporter)*; Raymond Accolas *(Bank Manager)*; Kedar Brown *(Tough Teen)*; Claire Cellucci *(Yuri's Girlfriend)*; John Bayliss *(Kirov's Butler)*; Henry Gomez *(Cab Driver)*; Louise Naubert *(Secretary)*; Phillip Wotton *(Sebastien's Driver)*; Jean-Pierre Galleri *(Paris Police Detective)*; Stephan Muller *(Paris Fireman)*; John Nelles *(Nervous Passenger)*; John Pearson *(Guard Sargeant)*; Kevin Rushton *(Guard)*; Sharon Bernbaum *(Assistant Bank Manager)*; David Christoffel *(Bank Security Guard)*; Branko Racki *(Vladmir)*; Kamel Krifa *(Boris)*; Brian Jagersky *(Tim)*; Irene Pauzer; Peter Messaline; Jim Millington *(FBI Boss)*; George Kash *(Man in Private Room)*; David Turner *(Inspector #2)*; Veronique Diehl *(Mother (Villefranche Apt.))*; Alain Phillip *(Morgue Attendant)*; Christine Manning *(Woman in Vault)*; Jaques Authier *(Priest)*; Charles Drummond *(Officer at Bank)*; Bruno Magnes *(Innocent Driver)*; Danny Lima *(Guard #3)*; Lon E. Katzman *(Bodyguard)*; Ed Queffelec *(Bodyguard)*; Ron Van Hart *(Ivan's Bodyguard)*; Brian Kaulback *(Ivan's Bodyguard)*; Eugene Allin *(Val)*; Armin Konn *(Petrie)*; Sveltlana Medianik *(Club Bohemia Singer)*; Andrei Smal; Alexander Kanewsky; Mikhael Ziskine; Andrei Denga; Arkadij Kaplan *(Club Bohemia Band)*

The second Jean-Claude Van Damme vehicle to feature the martial arts star as twins, MAXIMUM RISK also marks the Hollywood directorial debut of celebrated Hong Kong action director Ringo Lam. This convoluted tale offers continuous movement, frequent action scenes, and the gritty urban textures of a '70s-era crime thriller.

When Mikhail Suverov, a Russian mobster, is found dead in Nice after a high-speed chase, French cop Alain Moreau (Jean-Claude Van Damme) is shocked to discover the dead man is his twin brother, who was given up for adoption as an infant. Seeking to uncover the mystery of his brother's life and violent death, Alain takes on his brother's identity and goes to New York, where he visits Little Odessa, the Russian emigre neighborhood in Brooklyn. Alain's presence at a nightclub precipitates a brawl with a gang of thugs working for local mobster Ivan Dzasokhov (Zach Grenier).

Mikhail's girl, Alex (Natasha Henstridge), comes to Alain's aid and the two elude pursuit by Ivan and his gang. From a pair of duplicitous FBI agents (Paul Ben-Victor, Frank Senger), Alain learns of a list of Russian mobsters and corrupt agents that Mikhail had stowed in a safe-deposit box in Nice.

Fearful of being exposed as corrupt, the two feds hold Alex hostage until Alain gains access to the safe-deposit box. All travel to Nice, where Ivan and his gang ensure Alain's cooperation by holding his French partner, Sebastian (Jean-Hugues Anglade), hostage.

Alain retrieves the incriminating evidence, as well as a cache of American money and a tape-recorded message from Mikhail, warning Alain not to trust anyone. He sets off a fire alarm as a diversion and, with the help of local police, rescues Sebastian from Ivan and then pursues the FBI men who are holding Alex. After a shoot-out and confrontation in a slaughterhouse, Alain rescues Alex, and the French police apprehend the two feds. Alain then takes Alex to meet his mother (Stephane Audran).

Hong Kong director Lam is best known for such high-octane thrillers as FULL CONTACT, PRISON ON FIRE and, of course, CITY ON FIRE (1979)—the caper film which partly inspired Quentin Tarantino's RESERVOIR DOGS (1993). He brings to Hollywood a keen sense of pace and an eye for the more dramatic corners of modern urban space—the back alleys, rooftops, sleazy clubs, and bathhouses of New York and Nice, even though the New York scenes were largely shot in Toronto and Philadelphia.

With the proper script, this could have been a crack B-crime thriller, recalling Lam's other films. Instead, the arbitrary plot twists leave the viewer little sense of where it's going or what the point is. For much of the film, it's not only unclear what the bad guys want, but unclear who the bad guys are. The perfunctory action scenes—mostly chases and very brief martial arts turns by the star—never deliver the action goods that Hong Kong films usually do. Van Damme actually does more running away than fighting.

This is the second Van Damme vehicle to serve as the American directorial debut for a Hong Kong director. The first was John Woo's HARD TARGET (1993), and the third was the 1997 release DOUBLE TEAM, which was the American debut of legendary producer/director Tsui Hark (ONCE UPON A TIME IN CHINA). This is fortunate for Van Damme, who has been used quite well in these films, where he has been notably grim, laconic, and resolute.

Unlike DOUBLE IMPACT (1991), his earlier dual-role-as-twins opus, Van Damme doesn't have to compete with himself here since his mobster twin is killed off in the opening scene. Van Damme and his leading lady, Henstridge, play vigorous, tough, compassionate characters, although the rest of the cast—largely French and French-Canadian—lacks color. It is a rare pleasure, however, to see Audran in a cameo as Van Damme's mother. Henstridge, coming off her auspicious debut in SPECIES (1995), is alternately sultry and energetic, demonstrating a talent for playing spunky heroines or slinky femmes fatales. *(Sex, violence, profanity)* — B.C.

d, Ringo Lam; p, Moshe Diamant; exec p, Roger Birnbaum; assoc p, Limor Diamant, Richard G. Murphy, Eugene Van Varenberg; co-p, Jason Clark; w, Larry Ferguson; ph, Alexander Gruszynski; ed, Bill Pankow; m, Robert Folk; prod d, Steven Spence; art d, Leslie Thompkins, Damien Lanfranchi; set d, Christian Calivera; sound, Glen Gauthier (mixer), Bruce Litecky (mixer); fx, Henry Kline II, Martin Malivoire, Jeff Jarvis; casting, Deborah Brown; cos, Joseph Porro; makeup, Zoltan; stunts, Charles Picerni

Action/Crime **(PR: C MPAA: R)**

MAYBE ... MAYBE NOT ★★½

(Germany) 93m Neue Constantin Film Produktion; Olga Film ~ Orion Classics c
(DER BEWEGTE MANN)

Til Schweiger *(Axel)*; Katja Riemann *(Doro)*; Joachim Krol *(Norbert)*; Rufus Beck *(Waltraud)*; Antoina Lang *(Elke)*; Armin Rohde *(Horst)*

German cinema is not renown for sophisticated comedy. It would be if there were more like DER BEWEGTE MANN, released in the US as MAYBE. . . MAYBE NOT.

Axel (Til Schweiger), a handsome ne'er-do-well Berliner, two-times too often on his girlfriend, Doro (Katja Riemann). She kicks him out, and he goes over to a friend's place where a male discussion group is taking place. There, he meets dumpy vegetarian, Norbert (Joachim Krol), a homosexual instantly smitten by the visitor, and Axel moves in with him purely out of convenience. To Norbert's frustration, Axel is an incorrigible womanizer with no other inclinations, and nothing carnal ensues, but a definite comradeship forms between the roommates from opposite sides of the sexual fence. Axel becomes quite relaxed in the gay milieu. Norbert, for his part, must deal with a range of experiences quite outside his ken, like disgruntled brides and even childbirth—when Doro reappears on the scene to inform Axel of her pregnancy and catches the two in a compromising, though basically innocent situation. Doro assumes that her blowup traumatized Axel into homosexuality, a feeling she can't shake even after they marry. She suspects evasive Axel is still dallying on the side with Norbert; in fact, her husband is cheating on her yet again with an old girlfriend. Everything culminates in a frenzied scene at Norbert's, involving bull hormones, a stark naked Axel, and Doro going into labor as the truth hits her.

This bright comedy was a top-grosser in its native Germany, prompting interest in a Hollywood remake (just as the popular French transvestite farce LA CAGE AUX FOLLES was co-opted for Mike Nichols' BIRDCAGE). It's not hard to see why. Despite the contemporary queer aesthete, the mistaken-gender-identity premise is as corny as Kansas and accessible to mainstream audiences. A lot of heart, observation, and apt melancholy (via Norbert's unrealized passion for the friendly but unattainable Axel) make it a superior crowd-pleaser. Director Sonke Wortman keeps the pace brisk and throws in a lot of sharp observation amidst the expected camp. It's based on a popular Ralf Konig comic book series (though considerably "straightened" up) and serves as a kind of blithe Cook's tour of gay Berlin. There's a good moment after the guys have had a stormy cafe encounter: Axel flounces away in a huff, leaving Norbert holding the check, a small detail that does not go unmarked by him. Then there's Norbert's new boyfriend Horst (Armin Rohde), referred to as the straightest-acting gay man ever; with his unapologetic carnivorous appetite and very capable way with gay-bashers, he's anything but a stereotype, and embodies a definite type of man many gays often settle with. The film's comic highlight is a disastrous visit to an arthouse showing of DEATH IN VENICE. Beleaguered cinephiles the world over should be able to relate.

Wortman culls strong performances from the cast: Krol makes a very empathetic gay Everyman, nebbishy in his eternal romantic-loser style, but possessed of a steely strong spine and survivor's sensibility and humor; however hopeless his choice of love object, he is nobody's fool. Schweiger, a top draw in Germany, is a charmer, with his Calvin Klein-ad looks and irrepressible horniness. Riemann has a thankless, homophobic role, but manages to invest even this rather misogynistic cartoon with some juicy verve. Gernot Roll's excellent photography fluently abets the comedy and there's a snappy, eclectic score, liberally dosed with that piquant *sprechesang* which has enlivened Teutonic entertainment since the days of Dietrich. *(Sexual situations, adult situations, nudity, substance abuse, profanity.)* — D.N.

d, Sonke Wortmann; p, Bernd Eichinger; exec p, Martin Moszkowicz, Molly Von Furstenberg, Harry Kugler, Elvira Senft; w, Sonke Wortmann (based on the comic books by Ralf Konig); ph, Gernot Roll; ed, Ueli Christen; m, Torsten Breuer; prod d, Monika Bauert; sound, Simon Happ; cos, Katharina Von Martius

Comedy **(PR: O MPAA: R)**

MERCY ★★½

(U.S.) 85m Injosho Films; Elevator Pictures ~ Unapix Films c

John Rubinstein *(Frank Kramer)*; Amber Kain *(Ruby)*; Sam Rockwell *(Matty)*; Jane Lanier *(Carol)*; Novella Nelson *(Angela)*; Phil Brock *(Phil Kline)*; Rhea Silver-Smith *(Nicole)*; Christopher J. Quinn *(Joey)*; Kevin Joseph *(Livingston)*; Maura Tierney *(Simonett)*; Mark Mullin *(Mr. Funbags the Clown)*; Flotilla DeBarge *(Transvestite Hooker)*; Rick Gomez *(Peter)*; Robert Shepard *(Bartender)*; Ajay Mehta *(Cab Driver)*; Dan Atkins *(Wendell)*; Judy Goldschmidt; Joe Donahue; Billy Lux

John Rubinstein proves himself a forceful actor in MERCY, a mediocre melodrama about a wealthy father put through a cat-and-mouse game by his daughter's kidnappers. It has been seen before, but Rubinstein carries the load.

Frank Kramer (John Rubinstein) is a New York society lawyer whose world is turned upside down when his young daughter, Nicole (Rhea Silver-Smith), is kidnapped. Unbeknownst to Kramer, the abductor is Ruby (Amber Kain), the daughter of the family housekeeper, Angela (Novella Nelson), and once Nicole's best friend. During the cold, winter night, Ruby and her partner, Matty (Sam Rockwell), send Frank on a wild goose chase from phone booth to phone booth all over the city. With each phone call, Frank is forced to meet a new set of demands.

In the morning, Frank returns to his apartment where his ex-wife, Carol (Jane Lanier), and the FBI are waiting for him. Frank arrogantly circumvents the efforts of the head agent, Phil

Kline (Phil Brock), and continues acting unilaterally to save his daughter's life. When Frank's plan fails, it becomes apparent to both Frank and the agents that the kidnappers are out for more than money.

With the help of the housekeeper, they realize that one of the kidnappers is Ruby, and Frank finally understands that his seduction and abandonment of Ruby as a teenager three years earlier had prompted her abrupt departure and her present vendetta. Frank gets Nicole back, but not without learning a lesson in humility and compassion.

MERCY combines the plots of several kidnapping pictures and adds a racial twist that gives extra weight to the basic narrative. Just cross ONE FALSE MOVE (1992) with DIE HARD WITH A VENGEANCE (1995), RANSOM (1996), and older fare like NIGHT OF THE JUGGLER (1980). Of course, there is built-in suspense to the kidnapping formula, which keeps MERCY watchable, but some of writer-director Richard Shepard's lack of technical polish and weak dialogue detract from the story. Annoying little details—how the FBI inexplicably ignores Frank after his harrowing night, how it takes so long for Ruby's own mother to recognize her daughter's voice, etc.—also put MERCY at cable-TV movie level.

Shepard's attempt to send a message about race and class inequity probably is meant to put the movie in the same category as the great films of this type (Hitchcock's THE MAN WHO KNEW TOO MUCH, Kurosawa's HIGH AND LOW), but here it looks like an obvious device (rendered silly in the "family values" ending).

Still, MERCY does contain a fine lead performance by veteran character actor Rubinstein (the other performers are just passable). From his earliest appearance jogging up the steps of his building and telling his assistant, "I'm about six seconds too fat," Rubinstein craftily conveys the type of egotistical, insensitive man he is playing without resorting to stereotype. The actor's reactions to his crisis are so realistic at times that he actually makes his character more sympathetic than some of the other characters—particularly his bitter ex-wife—would lead one to believe. Viewers may even find themselves rooting for Frank when he finally scares an inquisitive child away from the ransom drop site by maliciously cooing, "Hey, little boy, you want some candy?"

Just like Frank, Rubinstein is very persuasive, and MERCY would mean little without him. *(Violence, nudity, sexual situations, adult situations, extreme profanity.)* — E.M.

d, Richard Shepard; p, Rolfe Kent, Rocky Collins, Richard Shepard; exec p, Jennifer L. Pearlman; assoc p, D.J. Atkins, Adam Lichtenstein, Thom Powers; w, Richard Shepard; ph, Sarah Cawley; ed, Adam Lichtenstein; m, Rolfe Kent; prod d, Anne Ross; art d, Leanne Sharpton; sound, Irin Strauss; casting, Julie Hughes, Barry Moss; cos, Leonardo Iturregui

Crime/Drama **(PR: C MPAA: R)**

MERLIN'S SHOP OF MAGICAL WONDERS ★

(U.S.) 92m ~ Monarch Home Video c

Ernest Borgnine *(Grandfather)*; Mark Hurtado *(Grandson)*; George Milan *(Merlin)*; John Terrance *(Jonathan Cooper III)*; Patricia Sansone *(Madeline Cooper)*; Bunny Summers *(Zurella)*; Ben Mendelsohn *(David Andrews)*; Struan Robertson *(Michael Andrews)*; Bruce Perry *(Pete)*; J. Renee Gilbert *(Marie Andrews)*; Madelon Phillips *(Adrienne)*; Ben Sussman *(Jay Cosgrove)*

An easy way for novices to break into features is to string together various short subjects, shot on the cheap at different times, into a crazy-quilt anthology picture. That seems a likely explanation for this straight-to-video hodgepodge.

A retired scriptwriter (Ernest Borgnine) tells his grandson bedtime stories about legendary wizard Merlin (George Milan) materializing in the present day to spread magic and wonder. How? By opening a grotto-like store in a northern California town.

First, Merlin gives a book of spells to skeptical newspaper columnist Jonathan Cooper III (John Terrence). The arrogant scribe is delighted that its dangerous incantations are genuine, but he rapidly ages every time he works sorcery. The book contains a rejuvenation formula, but it turns Cooper into an infant, granting the wish of his barren wife to have a baby.

Next, a mechanical monkey stolen from Merlin's shop is resold as a birthday gift for a little boy. His father, David (Ben Mendelsohn), notices that the monkey sometimes clashes its cymbals of its own volition, and a succession of housepets perish under mysterious circumstances. David tries to get rid of the infernal plaything before it can strike again and kill a person. But the monkey keeps reappearing, until Merlin finally retrieves it.

The Merlin footage in this second episode was clearly shot much later and inserted into an existing production. The quality of the film stock changes every time the old magician and his polyester-white fake beard enter the frame, and he never interacts with the principal cast.

That's not the only supernatural transformation wrought in MERLIN'S SHOP OF MAGICAL WONDERS. With occasional deaths, attempted shock endings, and mild gore effects, the tales come across as straightforward horror. Somewhere along the line, writer-producer-director Kenneth J. Burton reworked the material as kiddie fantasy, thanks to bookend scenes with guest star Borgnine.

MERLIN'S SHOP OF MAGICAL WONDERS isn't wholly unsuitable for youngsters, but it clearly isn't what it started out to be. *(Violence, profanity.)* — C.C.

d, Kenneth J. Burton; p, Kenneth J. Burton; exec p, Rose Ciolino, Grace Beretta; w, Kenneth J. Burton; ph, Michael Gfelner, Tony Martin; m, Todd Hayen, Frank Macchia; prod d, Lee Sjostrum, Melodie Ennist; art d, Laura Chariton; makeup, Doug White, Howard Tsuruba

Children's/Horror/Fantasy **(PR: C MPAA: NR)**

MESSAGE TO LOVE: THE ISLE OF WIGHT FESTIVAL ★★★½

(U.S./U.K.) 128m Castle Music Pictures; Initial Film and Television; BBC ~ Strand Releasing c

Jimi Hendrix; Jim Morrison; The Doors; The Who; Joan Baez; Leonard Cohen; Donovan; Miles Davis; Joni Mitchell; Jethro Tull; Kris Kristofferson; Free; The Moody Blues; Tiny Tim; Ten Years After; John Sebastian; Taste; Emerson, Lake & Palmer

As rock festivals go, the 1970 Isle of Wight Festival was perhaps not as mythic as Woodstock, but it occupies a unique niche in pop-culture history. The five-day, end-of-summer gathering on the normally sedate island off England's south coast drew upwards of 600,000 people (200,000 more than Woodstock) who came to hear Jimi Hendrix, The Doors, The Who, and other top rock attractions. The crowd also created an ad hoc community which, as fans continued to arrive—many of them on drugs and some without tickets—began to resemble a microcosm of society itself. MESSAGE TO LOVE: THE ISLE OF WIGHT FESTIVAL, a documentary directed by Murray Lerner, chronicles the event from both a musical and a social perspective, capturing some remarkable performances and some bizarre offstage wrangling. This is a film that arrives a quarter of a century too late (it apparently took Lerner that long to secure post-shoot funding), but despite its period-piece flavor, it has a strange, timeless relevance.

Money and music appear to have been the twin hallmarks of the 1970 festival, which was essentially the brainchild of Rikki Farr, a somewhat manic promoter who doubled as onstage emcee. A recurring visual amid the backstage chaos is money—dollars, pounds, francs, marks—being frantically counted, while agents and managers hover nearby, often demanding cash up front before their performers will go onstage. Tiny Tim's ukulele "doesn't even tune up without the money," growls the agent for that curious '60s icon. But the show does go on, and some of it is electrifying. The Who, then at the peak of their careers, do a frisky version of "Young Man Blues." Leonard Cohen offers a haunting "Suzanne," which brings a hush to the vast nighttime crowd. And Hendrix astonishes with four songs, playing guitar like he would live forever. Twelve days later, he was dead.

If there is a certain bittersweet tone to the festival, there is also an ongoing tension generated by hundreds of disgruntled fans unable or unwilling to pay their way in. Gathered outside the festival grounds in a makeshift bivouac christened "Desolation Row," this band of bitter and often wickedly funny malcontents stage periodic assaults on the festival fence—it eventually will be torn down—and philosophize to the camera about capitalism and revolution. "I think they're gonna shoot us," mutters a cranky Kris Kristofferson, who has a tantrum and stalks off in mid-set. "I believe this is *my* festival," proclaims a stoned Desolation Row denizen who gets inside the fence and actually makes it to the stage, creating some anxious moments for Joni Mitchell, who is trying to sing "Woodstock," with its plea to "get ourselves back to the garden." At moments like this, MESSAGE TO LOVE exhibits a welcome sense of irony.

The movie, reportedly culled from 200 hours of film shot by nine crews, captures the gradual unraveling of the festival, which could almost serve as a metaphor for the fading of '60s idealism. Before the event had run its five-day course, Farr, who spent more than a year organizing it, had lost everything. "We're not really pigs and capitalists," he moans. "We just wanted to break even." It remains for Jim Morrison, only months prior to his death, to sum things up in his chilling "The End," intoning the prophetic "I'll never look into your eyes again." *(Profanity, substance abuse, adult situations.)* — E.K.

d, Murray Lerner; p, Murray Lerner; exec p, Geoff Kempin, Rocky Oldham, Malcolm Gerrie, Avril MacRory; ph, Andy Carchrae, Jack Hazan, Nic Knowland, Norman Langley, Murray Lerner, Richard Stanley, Charles Stewart, Mike Whittaker; ed, Einar Westerlund, Stan Warnow, Greg Sheldon, Howard Alk; sound, Greg Bailey, Ron Geesin, Gareth Haywood, Mike Lax, Mike McDuffie, Colin Richards, Ivan Sharrock, Rick Dior

Musical/Documentary **(PR: A MPAA: NR)**

MICHAEL ★★½

(U.S.) 105m Alphaville Productions; Turner Pictures ~ New Line c

John Travolta *(Michael)*; William Hurt *(Frank Quinlan)*; Andie MacDowell *(Dorothy Winters)*; Robert Pastorelli *(Huey Driscoll)*; Jean Stapleton *(Pansy Milbank)*; Bob Hoskins *(Vartan Malt)*; Teri Garr *(Judge Esther Newberg)*; Wallace Langham *(Bruce Craddock)*; Joey Lauren Adams *(Anita)*; Carla Gugino *(Bride)*; Tom Hodges *(Groom)*; Catherine Lloyd Burns *(Evie)*; Richard Schiff *(Italian Waiter)*; Calvin Trillin *(Sheriff)*; Don Lee *(Court Bailiff)*; Joann Jansen *(Tammy)*; David Harrod *(Mal)*; Jane Lanier *(Suzanne)*; John Hussey *(Minister)*; Margaret Travolta *(Reporter No. 1)*; David Bernstein *(Reporter No. 2)*; Betsy Sokolow *(Reporter No. 3)*; Tracey Doyle *(Reporter No. 4)*; Blue Deckert *(Joe)*; Debrah Nunez *(Woman No. 1)*; Dell Aldrich *(Woman No. 2)*; Kay Colvin *(Woman No. 3)*; James Harrell *(Old Geezer No. 1)*; Peyton Park *(Old Geezer No. 2)*; Dianne Dreyer *(Jennifer)*; Tim Harrison *(Slacker No. 1)*; Daniel Mimura *(Slacker No. 2)*; Mark Nutter *(Counterman)*

John Travolta's charms carry MICHAEL, a comedy-fantasy about a naughty angel and the three jaded humans he helps during a Midwestern road trip. This New Age WIZARD OF OZ fable contains some pleasant moments, but also many awkward ones.

Michael (Travolta) is a heaven-sent angel whose miraculous assistance to an Iowa motel owner, Pansy (Jean Stapleton), inspires the elderly woman to write to Frank Quinlan (William Hurt), the lead reporter at Chicago's *National Mirror* tabloid. Sensing a scoop for his paper, Frank asks his hard-nosed boss, Vartan Malt (Bob Hoskins), if he may travel to Iowa and bring the supposed angel to Chicago in time for Christmas. Malt allows Frank to go, on the condition he take along an angel "expert," Dorothy Winters (Andie MacDowell), and Huey Driscoll (Robert Pastorelli), another reporter. Sparky, the paper's canine mascot, comes along for the ride.

As the trio travels to Iowa, each believes that the angel story is phoney—that is, until they arrive at the motel and meet Michael. The reporters remain skeptical, but are shocked nonetheless by his huge wings and slovenly appearance.

When Pansy dies suddenly, Michael agrees to go back to Chicago. During the trip, Frank, Dorothy, and Huey try not to believe in Michael, but are dumbstruck by his apparent ability to produce minor miracles. They are also confounded by his playboy lifestyle, which leads to a barroom incident that lands them in jail. But Michael's seductive way with a local judge (Teri Garr) gets them out of trouble as quickly as he got them into it.

By the time they approach Chicago, Frank and Dorothy grow closer to each other. After a night of passion, Frank admits that he was once a respected journalist whose alcoholism got him fired from a major paper. That same morning, Dorothy confesses that she is not an angel expert, but a dog trainer and aspiring singer-songwriter whom Vartan hired to take over Huey's job.

Then, suddenly, Sparky is killed in an auto accident. Frank insists that Michael bring the dog back to life, which he does, but at great cost to his own "mortality." By the time they reach Chicago, the rapidly molting Michael dies and returns to heaven. Frank tells Vartan, then, that the angel story was a hoax, and both he and Dorothy walk out on the paper, leaving Huey comfortably in his old job. Frank and Dorothy then go their separate ways, until, through Michael and Pansy's heavenly guidance, they are brought back together, realizing that their love is a miracle, too.

After THE PREACHER'S WIFE, MICHAEL was the second major angel movie of the 1996 Christmas season. Of course, the genre goes way back to such classics as ANGEL ON MY SHOULDER (1946), IT'S A WONDERFUL LIFE (1946), and THE BISHOP'S WIFE (1947; the source for THE PREACHER'S WIFE). What makes MICHAEL unique, however, is the appearance of a "good" angel that is "not a saint" (as the ads wink), and Travolta makes the perfect raunchy angel.

But those who made MICHAEL seem more interested in creating funny or touching bits than in making sense of their own story, and that keeps MICHAEL from achieving great heights. For example, one might wonder why Michael craves such earthly delights as sex and Frosted Flakes if he is, indeed, heaven-sent. It is also never explained why Michael can achieve some miracles but not others, and the introduction of his limited time on earth comes too late for viewers to start worrying about his fate.

Director Nora Ephron makes some of the same mistakes that kept SLEEPLESS IN SEATTLE (1993) uncomfortably calculated. There are too many cute moments, and there are too many pop standards on the soundtrack, bridging the scenes and montages of the bumpy plot. But how can anyone be too unkind to a movie about angels and the power of believing? So accept MICHAEL, the movie, like Michael, the character, flaws and all. *(Violence, sexual situations, profanity.)* — E.M.

d, Nora Ephron; p, Sean Daniel, Nora Ephron, James Jacks; exec p, Delia Ephron, Jonathan D. Krane; assoc p, Donald J. Lee Jr, Alan Curtiss; co-p, G. Mac Brown; w, Nora Ephron, Delia Ephron, Pete Dexter, Jim Quinlan; ph, John Lindley; ed, Geraldine Peroni; m, Randy Newman; prod d, Dan Davis; art d, James Tocci; set d, Tracey Doyle; sound, Geoffrey Lucius Patterson; fx, David Blitstein; casting, Mary Goldberg; cos, Elizabeth McBride; makeup, Deborah Larsen; stunts, Charlie Croughwell

Fantasy/Comedy/Drama (PR: C MPAA: PG)

MICHAEL COLLINS ★★★½

(U.S./U.K.) 117m Evergreen Entertainment; Geffen Pictures ~ Warner Bros. c

Liam Neeson *(Michael Collins)*; Aidan Quinn *(Harry Boland)*; Stephen Rea *(Ned Broy)*; Alan Rickman *(Eamon De Valera)*; Julia Roberts *(Kitty Kiernan)*; Charles Dance *(Soames)*; Ian Hart *(Joe O'Reilly)*; Richard Ingram *(British Officer)*; John Kenny *(Patrick Pearse)*; Roman McCairbe *(Thomas McDonagh)*; Ger O'Leary *(Thomas Clarke)*; Michael Dwyer *(James Connolly)*; Martin Murphy *(Captain Lee-Wilson)*; Sean McGinley *(Smith)*; Gary Whelan *(Hoey)*; Frank O'Sullivan *(Kavanagh)*; Frank Laverty *(Sean McKeoin)*; Owen O'Neill *(Rory O'Connor)*; Stuart Graham *(Tom Cullen)*; Brendan Gleeson *(Liam Tobin)*; Gerard McSorley *(Cathal Brugha)*; Liam d'Staic *(Austin Stack)*; Owen Roe *(Arthur Griffith)*; Paul Bennett *(Cosgrave)*; Claude Clancy *(Vaughan's Hotel Clerk)*; Paul Hickey *(Dublin Castle Soldier)*; Tom Murphy *(Vinny Byrne)*; David Gorry *(Charlie Dalton)*; Gary Lydon *(Squad Youth #1)*; David Wilmot *(Squad Youth #2)*; Joe Hanley *(Squad Man #1)*; Colm Coogan *(Squad Man #2)*; Aiden Grennell *(Chaplain at Lincoln Jail)*; Dave Seymour *(Lincoln Taxi Driver)*; Ian McElhinney *(Belfast Detective)*; Tony Clarkin *(Soldier on Station)*; Luke Hayden *(McCrae)*; Gary Powell *(Black and Tan on Larry)*; Max Hafler *(Black and Tan on Larry)*; Laura Brennan *(Rosie)*; Aidan Kelly *(Gresham Hotel Bellboy)*; Jim Isherwood *(Man Following Broy)*; Michael James Ford *(Black and Tan)*; Mal Whyte *(Officer in Bath)*; Martin Phillips *(Officer in Bed)*; Aisling O'Sullivan *(Girl in Bed)*; Malcolm Douglas *(Officer in Park)*; Brians "Joker" Mulvey *(Croke Park Hurler)*; Frank Patterson *(Tenor in Restaurant)*; Peter O'Brien *(Pianist in Restaurant)*; Cafe Orchestra *(Orchestra in Restaurant)*; Mike McCabe *(Journalist)*; Vinnie McCabe *(Speaker in the Dail)*; Alan Stanford *(Vice-Consul McCready)*; Gary Paul Mullen *(Young Gunman)*; Barry Barnes *(Free State Soldier)*; Denis Conway *(Republican #1)*; Don Wycherley *(Republican #2)*; Paraic Breathnach *(Santry the Blacksmith)*; Jonathan Rhys Myers *(Collins' Assassin)*

In bringing his biography of Irish revolutionary Michael Collins to the screen, writer-director Neil Jordan tells us only part of the story. We learn about Collins, but are left in the dark about some of the history through which he moved.

The 1916 Easter Rising. Irishmen seize the General Post Office in Dublin and fight off British troops for a week. After the surrender, Irish fighters are arrested, among them Michael Collins (Liam Neeson), Harry Boland (Aidan Quinn), and Eamon De Valera (Alan Rickman). The rebellion's leaders are executed, but two years later, Collins, Boland, and De Valera are free.

Collins goes about rousing his countrymen against the British, and succeeds in converting Ned Broy (Stephen Rea), an Irishman working for the British, who allows Collins to view the British files. Learning of an attempt to arrest the Irish leaders, Collins warns De Valera, who prefers to be arrested to draw attention to their cause.

Left virtually alone to run the war in Ireland, Collins and Boland form an assassination squad dubbed "the 12 apostles." These are men trained to kill British agents in cold blood to force an end to England's rule. Collins, meanwhile, becomes intrigued with Boland's girlfriend, Kitty Kiernan (Julia Roberts). Collins and Boland break De Valera out of prison. Once free, "Dev" decides to go to America to build support for the Republic of Ireland, taking Boland with him.

After De Valera's departure, the Irish are further besieged by the Black and Tans, a group of brutal Scottish servicemen. Though Collins is able to have some of their leaders killed, the Black and Tans capture Broy and torture him, then raid a football match and massacre civilians on what came to be known as "Bloody Sunday." In Boland's absence, Collins and Kitty grow closer.

Once De Valera and Boland return, "Dev" proposes a more conventional attack on the British Customs house; this fails, but the British finally agree to negotiate a peace settlement. "Dev" decides to send Collins to represent the Irish. Collins returns with a treaty establishing the Irish Free State, an independent government but still answerable to the King. "Dev" is furious over the loss of complete independence and vows to fight Collins. This brings civil war to Ireland, as Collins is forced to fire upon De Valera's men. Boland joins De Valera's forces, further splitting with Collins, who has now asked Kitty to marry him. During the fighting, Boland tries to flee from Collins's troops and is killed. "Dev" agrees to talk with Collins but only in Collins's home county of Cork. On his way there, Collins is ambushed and killed.

MICHAEL COLLINS looks beautiful. Jordan and cinematographer Chris Menges do an excellent job of evoking the Dublin of 80 years ago and the grandeur of the story. Several of the performances are outstanding: Rickman has rarely been better than in his portrayal of De Valera; his every act seems to be politically considered, and he brings the perfect amount of detachment to the role. Likewise, Rea inhabits Broy with the proper reserve of a man torn between his position and what he believes is right. Neeson, of course, is the center of the film, and he holds it through a good part of the action. A decade too old for the role (Collins was 31 when he was killed), Neeson has the strength and character needed to portray such a larger-than-life figure. Neither Quinn nor Roberts are given roles with as much depth as these three, though both are certainly adequate. Wisely, neither overdoes the Irish brogue.

Where the film stumbles is in its portrayal of history. We learn Collins's story, but are left in the dark about much Irish history. Little background is provided and no follow up is given. By failing to do this, Jordan runs the risk that audiences will not identify with a hero who orders cold-blooded executions. Several scenes stray from the real story; Boland's death is embellished and Broy's beating is invented. Since the true story is quite engaging, such changes are pointless.

Michael Collins is obviously a hero to Jordan, and this film, a labor of love. With a little more care and attention to detail, MICHAEL COLLINS could have been one of the better biographical films of recent years. That it comes close and fails is a real disappointment. *(Graphic violence, profanity.)* — K.Fr.

d, Neil Jordan; p, Stephen Woolley; co-p, Redmond Morris; w, Neil Jordan; ph, Chris Menges; ed, J. Patrick Duffner, Tony Lawson; m, Elliot Goldenthal; prod d, Anthony Pratt; art d, Arden Gantly, Jonathan McKinstry, Cliff Robinson; set d, Josie

MacAvin; sound, Kieran Horgan (recordist); fx, Yves De Bono, Gerry Johnston; casting, Susie Figgis; cos, Sandy Powell; makeup, Lynda Armstrong; stunts, Greg Powell

AAN Best Cinematography: Chris Menges; *AAN Best Original Dramatic Score:* Elliot Goldenthal

Biography **(PR: C MPAA: R)**

MICROCOSMOS ★★
(France/Switzerland/Italy) 77m Galatee Films ~ Miramax Zoe c

Kristin Scott Thomas *(Narrator)*

MICROCOSMOS is an insufferably clever nature documentary with art-film pretensions that seeks to graft personalities onto an assortment of insects rather than let nature take its course.

In the course of 24 (time-lapsed) hours in the grassy meadows and swampy ponds of Aveyron, France, nature's wonders abound. Starting in the air, several bees collect pollen by flying from flower to flower. On plants, ants protect aphids from hungry ladybugs and a spider catches a grasshopper in its web. On the ground, two snails court each other and mate, some caterpillars emerge from cracks in the earth, a dung beetle rolls a ball of manure across a road, and a pheasant feasts on an ant colony.

In the water, a waterstrider eats a dragonfly, but a sea creature eats the waterstrider. A rain storm sends the insects and other animals underwater. After the rain, two stag beetles battle. At night, a frog and a mole beetle make brief appearances. Finally, in the morning mist, a mosquito emerges from its larval sac and flies away.

Like other French nature films such as THE CLAW AND THE TOOTH and ATLANTIS, MICROCOSMOS deserves credit for its superb photography. The two years of equipment design and three years of shooting pay off in a series of impressive close-up images of the animal (mostly minute insect) world. But co-writers-directors Claude Nuridsany and Marie Perennou (who both also operated the cameras with Hughes Ryffel and Thierry Machado) turn their great pictures and "15 years of research" into a silly semi-narrative that personifies the creatures more heavy-handedly than a Disney TV special. Much of this unnecessary anthropomorphizing is achieved through the soundtrack. Thus, the Burgundy snails mate to opera music, the caterpillars form a circle to horror movie music, and the dung beetle rolls its ball to a light comic theme.

What is more disturbing about the film is how it sacrifices education for formalist thrills. Almost nothing is learned about the insects or other animals, making the score and amplified sound effects far less satisfying than a good, old-fashioned narrator—Marlon Perkins, we miss you! Worse still, it appears that Nuridsany and Perennou have "cheated" between some shots to increase the drama. For example, did their cameras miraculously happen to catch the dung beetle tripping over a twig in extreme close-up, or was this a cruel set-up by the filmmakers? Earlier, the grasshopper seems to be thrown into the spider's web as opposed to hopping freely into it.

Nuridsany and Perennou may want us to behold the wonders of nature, but perceptive viewers may only see the manipulative tricks of human beings behind the scenes. Such observers will be far better served by a "Nova" or Discovery Channel special. This is a case where traditional is better. — E.M.

d, Claude Nuridsany, Marie Perennou; p, Jacques Perrin, Christophe Barratier, Yvette Mallet; exec p, Michel Faure, Philippe Gautier, Andre Lazare, Patrick Lancelot; w, Claude Nuridsany, Marie Perennou; ph, Claude Nuridsany, Marie Perennou, Hughes Ryffel, Thierry Machado; ed, Marie-Josephe Yoyotte, Florence Ricard; m, Bruno Coulais; sound, Philippe Barbeau, Bernard Leroux, Laurent Quaglio

Documentary **(PR: A MPAA: G)**

MIDNIGHT ANGEL ★★
(Hong Kong) 90m New Treasurer Films Co. ~ Arena Home Video c
(AKA: JUSTICE WOMEN)

May Law *(Rabbit)*; Yukari Oshima *(Ying)*; Angile Leung *(Cherry—the Middle Sister)*; Miu Kiu-Wai *(Chief Yau)*; Mark Cheng *(Tak)*; Shih Kien *(Grandpa)*; Melvin Wong *(Bull)*; Ng Man Tat *(Commissioner)*; Cho Tat-Wah; Lily Chung; Kam Seung-Yuk; Yim Chau-Wah; Hon Chun; Yu Ming; Christine Duhler; Lok Ying-Kwan

A contemporary superhero yarn released on video in the US, MIDNIGHT ANGEL follows the exploits of a female avenger who puts on a mask and costume to battle criminals in modern Hong Kong. Lacking the polish and high–octane thrills of other Hong Kong fare, it nonetheless boasts some impressive, high-kicking kung fu action.

A small group of police, that has connections to three adopted sisters and their retired grandfather (Shih Kien), is confronted by a crime wave led by gang boss Bull (Melvin Wong), who is responsible for several guns-for-drugs deals. When a raid on Bull results in the death of Detective Tak (Mark Cheng), the fiance of oldest sister Ying (Yukari Oshima), the group is determined to capture Bull.

In response to growing crime, Rabbit (May Law), the youngest sister, puts on a mask and black costume and becomes the "Cotton Flower," so called because she leaves tiny cotton flowers with the crime victims she rescues. Rabbit ultimately directs her efforts against Bull and his gang. One of the police, Chief Yau (Miu Kiu-Wai), seeks the identity of Cotton Flower, with help from old Inspector Chao.

Rabbit discovers that Tak is alive and working undercover and tells Ying. When Rabbit tries to break up one of Bull's drug deals, she is joined by a second Cotton Flower, who turns out to be Ying. Back home, Rabbit and Ying are joined by Tak, who warns them of the impending arrival of Bull's assassins. A major battle is halted only by the arrival of more police.

Bull sets a trap for Cotton Flower, but is met at his dockside hideout by all three sisters dressed in masks and black costumes. They engage Bull and his gang in a furious battle. Bull is killed and dressed up as Cotton Flower to fool the persistent Inspector Chao.

Like so many Hong Kong action films, MIDNIGHT ANGEL takes a good premise and dilutes it with unnecessary farcical elements. While the scenes of the masked female avengers in action generate some excitement, the film's bumbling male cops continually undercut any suspense or tension.

However, fans will welcome the escalating fight scenes in which the three fighting females take on the bad guys with displays of kung fu and acrobatics, dominated by Oshima, whose high-kicking skills made her a cult favorite. Also on hand is Shih Kien, remembered by kung fu fans as the villainous Master Han in Bruce Lee's ENTER THE DRAGON (1973). *(Violence.)* — B.C.

d, Chik Ki Yee; p, Ng Ming Toi; w, Kwong Man-Wai; stunts, Tsui Chung-Sun

Action/Crime/Martial Arts **(PR: C MPAA: NR)**

MIDNIGHT DANCERS ★★
(Philippines) 115m Tangent Films ~ First Run Features c

(SIBAK)

Alex Del Rosario *(Joel)*; Gandong Cervantes *(Dennis)*; Lawrence David *(Sonny)*; Perla Bautista *(Mother)*; Nonie Buencamino *(Dave)*; Soxy Topacio *(Dominic)*; R.S. Francisco *(Michelle)*; Luis Cortez; Richard Cassity; Danny Ramos; Leonard Manalanson

This mildly entertaining Filipino exploitation flick introduces a seamy, singular world that is rather fascinating until the film turns to didactic melodrama.

Sonny (Lawrence David) lives with his family in the Philippines. His brothers Joel (Alex Del Rosario) and Dennis (Gandong Cervantes) convince him to get a job at the gay bar where they work as dancers. The real money to be made, however, is from private clients willing to pay for more intimate sessions with the young men. Sonny makes his debut and is a big hit with the customers. His mother Lita (Perla Bautista) worries about her sons' wild lives but is grateful for the money they bring home. Also appreciative is Joel's wife Zenny, who turns an obligingly blind eye on her husband's lover, Dave (Nonie Buencamino), who helps to support them all.

The dark side of this existence begins to threaten the family. Dennis is constantly in trouble with crime gangs to whom he owes money, and an adopted brother, Bogart, also has a long history of misdeeds trailing behind him. On top of everything else, Gregorio, the boys' father, has been seeing another woman. When Lita angrily confronts her, a scandalous public fight ensues. The family's home is invaded by hoodlums looking for Bogart, who beat up Lita. Dennis is killed in a shoot-out, and Sonny kills the gang member responsible for his death. Sonny and Joel must now go into hiding to escape both prosecution and gang retaliation. An anguished Lita weeps over her destroyed family.

Mel Chionglo's film is both a tribute to and something of a ripoff of Lino Brocka's 1988 MACHO DANCER. It's a gritty tale of poverty, and where it can lead a young man in the Philippines. Dramatically, it's as crude as can be, and somewhat overlong. Lita cries to the heavens at the end, "We always get trampled on! We need to stand up for our rights!" Chionglo appears to want to have it both ways: his film purports to be a diatribe against the vulturine nature of prostitution, while at the same time licentiously lingering over the boys' young bodies. The plot line is confusing to follow as many of the characters seem almost indistinguishable. The choreography is of the same, monotonous type featured in MACHO DANCER: a sensual writhing in tiny bikinis in time to some execrable Muzak. There's a funny male madam, "Mommy," who watches over the boys and congratulates the ones who quit to seek another life or go back to their studies. The gay bar scenes capture the fetid, darkly humorous atmosphere of such pay-for-play places.

MIDNIGHT DANCER is better when it stays in the bar or Sonny's home. The scenes of street violence are clumsily staged, as in a Grade-Z kung fu movie. The film's saving graces are the convincing, touching performances of the cast and its earthy moments of humor, sometimes unintentional. At one point, the boys teach their father some of their onstage moves—a long way from pitching ball in the backyard. The club stages an Independence Day Special entitled "Clash of the Macho Dancers" just before being raided by the police. "This is a cultural event, a tribal dance!" cries Mommy. "It's a fund-raiser!"

Del Rosario is cherubically attractive and charming as Sonny. He's good delivering the big speech that summarizes his plight, "They say we lose nothing because we are men. That's not true. Every night we go to bed with different men. We don't even know them. We do things against our wishes. They pay for our bodies but we lose something. I don't know what, but something's lost." *(Nudity, adult situations, sexual situations, profanity, violence.)* — D.N.

d, Mel Chionglo; p, Richard Wong Tang; w, Ricardo Lee; ph, George Tutanes; ed, Jess Navarro; m, Nonog Buenoamino; prod d, Edgar Martin Littaua; sound, Ramon Reyes

Drama (PR: O MPAA: NR)

MIDWINTER'S TALE, A ★★½

(U.K.) 98m Midwinter Films; Kenneth Branagh Limited ~ Sony Pictures Classics bw

(GB: IN THE BLEAK MIDWINTER)

Richard Briers *(Henry Wakefield)*; Hetta Charnley *(Molly)*; Joan Collins *(Margaretta D'Arcy)*; Nicholas Farrell *(Tom Newman)*; Mark Hadfield *(Vernon Spatch)*; Gerard Horan *(Carnforth Greville)*; Celia Imrie *(Fadge)*; Michael Maloney *(Joe Harper)*; Jennifer Saunders *(Nancy Crawford)*; Julia Sawalha *(Nina)*; John Sessions *(Terry Du Bois)*; Ann Davies *(Mrs. Branch)*; James D. White *(Tim)*; Robert Hines *(Mortimer)*; Allie Byrne *(Tap Dancer)*; Adrian Scarborough *(Young Actor)*; Brian Petifer *(Ventriloquist)*; Patrick Doyle *(Scotsman)*; Shaun Prendergast *(Mule Train Man)*; Carol Starks *(Audience Member)*; Edward Jewesbury *(Nina's Father)*; Katy Carmichael *(Mad Puppet Woman)*

Kenneth Branagh has written and directed but chosen not to star in this cozily old-fashioned theatrical romp. There's nothing really new or inordinately hilarious in the cartoonish black-and-white proceedings. It's the old "Brotherhood of Actors/Thespian Happy Families" scheme, but Branagh directs it at a whiz-bang pace that keeps it bumping along over the many weak spots, clunky punchlines, and cliches.

Struggling actor Joe Harper (Michael Maloney) is determined to direct and star in a production of *Hamlet.* With the reluctant help of his more commercially minded agent, Margaretta D'Arcy (Joan Collins), he puts together the most motley crew imaginable. Air-headed Nina (Julia Sawalha) is to be his Ophelia; veteran hack Henry (Richard Briers) is Claudius; intense Method monster Tom (Nicholas Farrel) essays a myriad of roles, including Laertes and Fortinbras; drunken, lovable Carnforth (Gerard Horan) is Rosencranz *and* Guildenstern; and campy homosexual Terry du Bois (John Sessions) will do Gertrude. . . in drag. With a shoestring budget, they descend upon a small English village and begin rehearsals in the local church. The characters, of course, bring their own considerable personal agendas with them, and the rehearsal process is marked by all manner of fits, starts, and stormy blow-ups.

Things are made additionally worse by Joe's production designer, whimsical Fadge (Celia Imrie), who has yet to come up with a single sketch or concrete idea. Things somehow begin to come together on the eve of the performance, with a hint of romance in the offing between Joe and Nina, to boot. A last-minute call from Margaretta with the news that Joe has been cast in a big-budget Hollywood thriller sends everything into a tailspin, however. But Joe's finer instincts prevail, and he does indeed impersonate the Melancholy Dane. The happy ending is compounded by Margaretta's arrival with Nancy Crawford (Jennifer Saunders), a big-time Hollywood producer, who is duly impressed by what she sees.

Branagh's way with comedic direction could best be described as unsubtle. His love for the profession of acting is, however, always evident as the performers are given every opportunity to shine, some more so than others. Briers is a funny old curmudgeon, insisting on "huge shoulderpads: Claudius must be butch." His character Henry is full of hard-gained showbiz know-how, like what to do when one forgets a Shakespearean line: "Just say, 'Crouch we here and lurk awhile.'" In the stereotypical gay role essential to British theatre, Sessions scores his laughs and gets up some nice teamwork with Briers. He even dilutes some of the inherent sentimentality of his reunion with a heretofore recalcitrant son. Maloney is adequate, but lacks the charisma Branagh would have brought to the part, had he deigned to play it.

Collins is cheekily assured as a hustling ten-percenter, yakking numbers on a cell phone while keeping that figure toned on an exercise machine. Sawalha appears a bit slovenly and is saddled with a lot of idiotic, nearsighted business, having to bump into walls and take endless pratfalls. Her acting is too unnuanced, showing nothing of the killer smarts and timing of her "Saffron" character on the British sitcom "Absolutely Fabulous." Another "AbFab" alumnus pops up in the form of Saunders who, likewise, overdoes it with a Texas accent from hell. And Imrie takes twee wackiness about as far as it can go. Judging from these performances, Branagh is no George Cukor when it comes to directing women. But he gives the cast their moments, whether funny, eccentric, or infuriating. — D.N.

d, Kenneth Branagh; p, David Barron; assoc p, Iona Price, Tamar Thomas; w, Kenneth Branagh; ph, Roger Lanser; ed, Neil Farrell; m, Jimmy Yuill; prod d, Tim Harvey; sound, Peter Glossop (mixer); cos, Caroline Harris; makeup, Jenny Shircore

Comedy **(PR: C MPAA: R)**

MILLE BOLLE BLU ★★★★

(Italy) 83m Penta Film; Sorpasso Film ~ New Yorker Video c

Paolo Bonacelli *(Mario Gora)*; Stefania Montorsi *(Elvira Caliciotti)*; Stefano Dionisi *(Antonio)*; Nicoletta Boris *(Tecla Rossi)*; Claudio Bigagli *(Guido)*; Evelina Gori *(Guido's Mother)*; Clelia Rondinella *(Caligiuri)*; Matteo Fadda *(Sandrino)*; Roberto Stocchi*(Vittorio Gora)*; Stefano Masciarelli *(Mr. DiBlasi)*; Carla Benedetti *(Mrs. DiBlasi)*; Vittorio Viviani *(Murena)*; Grazio Stracuzzi *(Gino)*; Cesare Gelli *(Decio Rossi)*; Manuele Pompili *(Sara's Son)*; Enza Aliseo *(Elena Caliciotti)*; Franco Mescollini *(Mr. Caliciotti)*; Lydia Biondi *(Mrs. Caliciotti)*; Mario de Candia *(Giovanni)*; Vera Furlan *(Aunt Lola)*; Maria D'Ayala *(Aunt Delia)*; Giovanna Mori *(Gina)*; Mario Bianco *(Papalla)*; Maurizio Mattioli *(Quintillo)*; Gigi Proietti *(Narrator)*

Confined to 24 hours in the lives of residents of an Italian apartment building, MILLE BOLLE BLU is a solid and satisfying debut effort from Italian filmmaker Leone Pompucci.

On a summer day in 1961, the residents of an apartment block carry on their lives while anticipating the total eclipse of the sun that will occur the next day. Children play games in the courtyard and on the rooftop, spying on their elders as they do. While her family prepares for her wedding to the son of a prominent engineer, Elvira Coliciotti (Stefania Montorsi) is unable to forget her true love, Antonio (Stefano Dionisi). Meanwhile, members of the Rossi family gather at the apartment of their just-deceased father, eager to claim their inheritances. The only one who mourns the dead man is his housekeeper, Sara (Gina Rovere), whose Down's syndrome son was always treated with kindness by Mr. Rossi.

Caligiuri (Clelia Rondinella), an inept criminal, breaks out of prison to pay a conjugal visit to his wife, while in another apartment, blind trumpeter Guido (Claudio Bigagli) anxiously awaits the moment when he can remove his bandages to find out whether a sight-restoring operation has succeeded. Guido's mother (Evelina Gori) dreads equally two possible outcomes of the operation: that it has failed, or that it has succeeded, and her only child will choose to leave her.

The next day, Sara reveals to Rossi's children that they will receive no inheritance: Rossi, the father of her son, secretly married her a year ago. As the eclipse begins, everyone in the building rushes out to see it. In the courtyard, Elvira meets Antonio. He tells her what she already knows—that life with her husband will never be as good as what they had together. When he asks her to come away with him, she tells him that she can't because she is pregnant. Hearing the sound of applause at the end of the eclipse, Guido removes his bandages and is able to see. A narrator tells us what has happened to all these people in the years since this day.

The extraordinary thing about MILLE BOLLE BLU (the title refers to a popular song to which Caligiuri and his wife dance comically) isn't that Pompucci packs so much life into it—it's that he does so with such economy. In a mere 83 minutes, the film has no trouble painting an indelible portrait of the lives of several dozen people. It could probably have lasted longer, but it doesn't need to.

A key element in the film's success is the cinematography of Massimo Pau, who uses large but graceful movements to link different areas of the apartment building and its environs. It's similar to what Richard Linklater does in SLACKER, giving the viewer a dream-like feeling of eavesdropping on a varied group of people. While all of the performances are strong, few (by design) stand out from the ensemble, though special mention should be made of Clelia Rondinella's comic work as the preposterously but sincerely lovestruck husband Caligiuri and Claudio Bigagli as blind Guido, who has a beautiful moment when he removes his bandages and we can't quite tell if he can see or not. MILLE BOLLE BLU is a small but perfectly wonderful film in the best tradition of Italian cinema. *(Profanity.)* — M.F.

d, Leone Pompucci; p, Marco Risi, Maurizio Tedesco; w, Filippo Pichi, Leone Pompucci, Paolo Rossi; ph, Massimino Pau; ed, Mauro Bonanni; m, Franco Piersanti; art d, Maurizio Marchitelli; cos, Catia Dottori

Comedy/Drama **(PR: C MPAA: NR)**

MIND RIPPER ★½

(U.S.) 96m WarnerVision; Kushner-Locke Company ~ WarnerVision Films c

Lance Henriksen *(James Stockton)*; Claire Stansfield *(Joanne)*; Natasha Wagner *(Wendy)*; Giovanni Ribisi *(Scott)*; John Diehl *(Alex)*; Gregory Sporleder *(Rob)*; Dan Blom *(Thor)*; Adam Solomon *(Mark)*; John Apicella *(Larry)*; Peter Shepherd *(Frank)*

Presented by horrormeister Wes Craven, this exercise in chills almost completely lacks the imagination and distinctiveness of its sponsor's best work.

In the underground GenTec biological lab, a nearly dead human test subject, injected with a regenerative virus, has begun having seizures. Team leader Alex Hunter (John Diehl), who has secretly been giving the subject overdoses of the virus, seeks the help of James Stockton (Lance Henriksen), the former head of the project who quit after discovering that the Army wanted to use his research to create a super-soldier. By the time Stockton arrives with his son Scott (Giovanni Ribisi), daughter Wendy (Natasha Wagner), and her boyfriend Mark (Adam Solomon) in tow, the human guinea pig, known as Thor (Dan Blom), has awakened and killed everyone in the lab save Joanne (Claire Stansfield) and Rob (Gregory Sporleder).

Thor kills Rob and abducts Stockton. Joanne and the youngsters are able to trap Thor and rescue Stockton, though Mark dies in the process. Thor escapes and kidnaps Wendy, but the others subdue him, reclaim Wendy, and flee to the surface. There, Thor attacks the van and then the plane the group escapes in; they push him from the side of the plane, but later he shows signs of having survived the fall.

MIND RIPPER began life as a second sequel to Craven's cult classic THE HILLS HAVE EYES (1978). Produced and co-written by Craven's son Jonathan, the film ultimately emerges as a very uneasy mix of family bonding drama and ALIEN (1979) knockoff, complete with music that apes James Horner's score from ALIENS (1986). The trite conflicts between Stockton and his teenage children are awkward, played out in frequently moronic dialogue against a cliched horrific backdrop. Occasionally, a well-judged scene does occur, such as an escape attempt through a room filled with nuclear waste drums.

Dependable genre veteran Henriksen is the best resource the movie has to offer, lending a sense of gravity to otherwise schizophrenic material. By the end, though, with its ludicrous series of multiple climaxes, the movie has lost any hope of being taken seriously. Intended for theaters, MIND RIPPER made its debut on cable before hitting video. *(Graphic violence, nudity, extreme profanity.)* — M.G.

d, Joe Gayton; p, Jonathan Craven; exec p, Wes Craven; co-p, Peter Shepherd; w, Jonathan Craven, Phil Mittleman; ph, Fernando Arguelles; ed, Harry Hitner; m, J. Peter Robinson; prod d, Jeremy Levine; art d, Prolet Spasova Georgieva; sound, Roberto Alberghini, Jacqueline Cristianini; fx, Paul Jones; cos, Elizabeth Jett; makeup, Anastasia "Sia" Sotirova, Kristo Naidenov

Horror/Science Fiction (PR: O MPAA: R)

MIRROR HAS TWO FACES, THE ★★½

(U.S.) 126m Phoenix Pictures; New Regency Productions; Barwood Films; Columbia TriStar ~ Columbia TriStar c

Barbra Streisand *(Rose Morgan)*; Jeff Bridges *(Gregory Larkin)*; Lauren Bacall *(Hannah Morgan)*; George Segal *(Henry Fine)*; Mimi Rogers *(Claire)*; Pierce Brosnan *(Alex)*; Brenda Vaccaro *(Doris)*; Austin Pendleton *(Barry)*; Elle Macpherson *(Candy)*; Ali Marsh *(First Girl Student)*; Leslie Stefanson *(Sara Myers)*; Taina Elg *(Female Professor)*; Lucy Avery Brooks *(Felicia)*; Amber Smith *(Felicia)*; David Kinzie *(Claire's Masseur)*; Rabbi Howard S. Herman *(Rabbi)*; Thomas Hartman *(Reverend)*; Trevor Ristow *(Trevor)*; Brian Schwary *(Mike—Student)*; Jill Tara Kushner *(Jill—Student)*; Randy Pearlstein *(Randy—Student)*; Stacie Sumter *(Stacie—Student)*; Cindy Guyer *(Taxi Stealer)*; Thomas Saccio *(Taxi Driver)*; Andrew Parks *(Waiter)*; Jimmy Baio *(Jimmy the Waiter)*; Emma Fann *(Henry's First Date)*; Laura Bailey *(Henry's Second Date)*; Mike Hodge *(Justice of Peace)*; Anne O'Sullivan *(Gloria)*; Sandi Schroeder *(Female Student)*; Kiyoko M Hairston *(Female Student)*; Ben Weber *(Male Student)*; Christopher Keys *(Male Student)*; Lisa Wheeler *(Female Aerobic Instructor)*; Kirk Moore *(Male Aeorbic Instructor)*; Regina Viotto *(Make-up Artist)*; Paul LaBreque *(Hair Colorist)*; Ruggero Comploj *(Waiter)*; William Cain *(Mr. Jenkins)*; Adam LeFevre *(Doorman)*; JoAn Mollison *(Irate Woman)*; Carlo Scibelli *(Opera Man)*

THE MIRROR HAS TWO FACES tells the classic tale of an ugly duckling who emerges a swan. But Barbra Streisand's modern romantic-comedy version seems at odds with itself in tone, message, and quality. Ultimately, this movie has two faces!

The plain but passionate Rose Morgan (Barbra Streisand) teaches Romantic Literature at Manhattan's Columbia University, but fails to find romance in her own life, while the sexy but stuffy Gregory Larkin (Jeff Bridges), a published author and mathematics teacher also working at Columbia, longs for a sexless union that will not distract him from his work.

Gregory's personal ad for "a woman interested in common goals and companionship," attracts the attention of Rose's beautiful sister, Claire (Mimi Rogers), who has just married Rose's unrequited love, Alex (Pierce Brosnan). Claire sets Rose up with Gregory, and, despite their differences, the two enjoy each other's company. Despite the skepticism of their friends and families, Rose and Gregory's platonic friendship leads to an unusual marital arrangement in which intellectual passion replaces sexual heat.

After a few months, Rose tires of her celibate life. She asks Gregory to consummate their marriage, but Gregory resists, and Rose, thinking—mistakenly—that he has rejected her because of her looks, moves back with her domineering mother, Hannah (Lauren Bacall), a glamorous beautician.

While Gregory is on a European sabbatical, Rose decides to win him back by changing her "ugly duckling" image. With diet, exercise, and beauty tips from her mother, Rose emerges as a sexy, exciting blonde. Upon his return, Gregory is stunned by the "new" Rose. But Rose leaves him again because she still feels underappreciated. During a night out with Alex, who has just separated from Claire, Rose finally realizes that she doesn't need a man to love her for her appearance, and that Gregory loves her for herself. She and Gregory later reunite, dancing in the streets of Manhattan.

Gay activist Larry Kramer ranted when Barbara Streisand chose to direct the "fluffy" THE MIRROR HAS TWO FACES rather than the AIDS-drama, THE NORMAL HEART. But one can see why Streisand was attracted to this piece: it is the star-director's first film to address directly the issue of her famous looks. For a romantic comedy, THE MIRROR HAS TWO FACES includes some surprisingly touching moments concerning the heroine's feelings about looking plain. In the tradition of THE ENCHANTED COTTAGE (1945) and the more recent MURIEL'S WEDDING (1994), MIRROR sometimes sharply examines the difficulties of being an outcast because of one's appearance.

Yet, Barbara's ultimate "makeover" movie blinks several times. The screenplay by Richard LaGravenese appears feminist on the surface—paraphrasing every writer from Naomi Wolf to Nancy Friday—but ultimately reinforces the most basic assumptions about feminine beauty and male-female relationships (at least Streisand co-wrote her superior first directing job, YENTL). LaGravenese and director Streisand also make fun of sexy vamps throughout the film, but they see nothing contradictory about turning second-hand Rose into the same thing. And it seems odd that Streisand approved Gregory's final line ("You're a very sexy girl!"), unless she cared more about her star appearance than the "beauty is only skin deep" message.

With Streisand crowding out everyone, the all-star cast never stood a chance. Jeff Bridges gets almost as much screen time (and soft-focus) as his co-star, but struggles valiantly with the cartoon role of a man who cannot control his lust. Lauren Bacall delivers some sharp one-liners, but seems wrongly cast as Streisand's mother. Despite her Jewish heritage, Bacall has always represented a WASP beauty ideal—an issue only skirted around here. Mimi Rogers is better cast as the beautiful sister, but is underused, as are Pierce Brosnan and Brenda Vaccaro.

THE MIRROR HAS TWO FACES wants to be a charming update on the sort of old movies Rose watches throughout the story. But compared to these classics, THE MIRROR is flawed. *(Sexual situations, profanity.)* — E.M.

d, Barbra Streisand; p, Barbara Streisand, Arnon Milchan; exec p, Cis Corman; w, Richard LaGravenese (from a story by Richard LaGravenese based on the screenplay "Le Miroir a Deux Faces" by Andre Cayatte and Gerard Oury); ph, Dante Spinotti,

Andrzej Bartkowiak; ed, Jeff Werner; m, Marvin Hamlisch; prod d, Tom John; art d, Teresa Carriker-Thayer; set d, John Alan Hicks, Pamela Turk; sound, Thomas Nelson (mixer), Julia Patsos (recordist); casting, Bonnie Finnegan, Todd Thaler; cos, Theoni V. Aldredge; makeup, Ed Henriques, Randy Houston Mercer, Lynn Campbell; stunts, Vince Deadrick Deadrick

AAN Best Actress: Lauren Bacall; *AAN Best Original Song:* Barbra Streisand, Marvin Hamlisch, Bryan Adams, Robert "Mutt" Lange

Comedy **(PR: C MPAA: PG-13)**

MIRROR, MIRROR III: THE VOYEUR ★

(U.S.) 91m MTI-Miranda Entertainment ~ MTI Home Video c

Billy Drago *(Anthony)*; Monique Parent *(Cassandra)*; David Naughton *(Det. Kobeck)*; Mark Ruffalo *(Joey)*; Elizabeth Baldwin *(Carolyn)*; Richard Cansino *(Julio)*; Rudolf Weber *(Ramone)*; Brandon Scott Peterson *(1st Mobster on Bridge)*; Matthew J. Chontos *(2nd Mobster on Bridge)*; James Ian Lifton *(Thug with Rifle)*; Derrick J. Costa *(Thug on Stairs)*; Brandy Payne *(Carlotta)*; Ingrid Hyross *(Girlfriend)*; Florence Smith *(Old Cassandra)*

The subtitle on the third entry in the MIRROR MIRROR series amounts to wishful thinking, as it's hard to imagine anyone but the most desperate horror/sex fans wanting to watch it.

Two months after drug kingpin Julio (Richard Cansino) is killed in a police raid and his wife Cassandra (Monique Parent) disappears, Anthony (Billy Drago), an artist who was having an affair with Cassandra, moves into her expansive house. He soon finds that the spirit of Cassandra, an occult practitioner, resides in an antique mirror, and she emerges to have sex with him. At the same time, Detective Kobeck (David Naughton) has been casing the house, in search of money Julio had hidden there.

After witnessing Anthony making love to gallery owner Carolyn (Elizabeth Baldwin), an angry Cassandra warns Anthony not to bring her back into the house. While Anthony is out, his brother Joey (Mark Ruffalo) brings Carolyn over for a tryst, and Cassandra kills her. Kobeck sneaks into the house in search of the cash stash, and Cassandra dispatches him as well. She then confronts Anthony and attempts to stab him fatally so he can join her on the other side. Joey intervenes and is killed, and Cassandra's spirit evaporates as Anthony takes her place, trapped in the mirror's netherworld.

The only surprise to be had in MIRROR, MIRROR III is that it took two credited directors to pilot this melange of listless acting, perfunctory horror elements, lengthy but ineffective sex scenes, and amateurish action setpieces. Possessed of so much exposition that there are nearly 20 minutes of setup before the opening credits even appear, the story never builds an ounce of tension, sexual or otherwise, and the sound recording is so bad that a good deal of the uninspired dialogue is practically inaudible. The actors, meanwhile, behave as though they're in it for the paycheck and nothing more, and only his associate producer credit explains why Drago, who usually plays villains and is few people's idea of a hunky hero, receives so many sex scenes with the gorgeous leading ladies. *(Violence, extensive nudity, sexual situations, profanity.)* — M.G.

d, Rachel Gordon, Virginia Perfili; p, Jimmy Lifton; exec p, Armen Boladian, Virginia Perfili; co-p, Billy Drago, Mark Headley; w, Steve Tymon; ph, Nils Erickson; ed, Paulette Renee Victor; m, Peter Waldman, Marc Mann, Jimmy Lifton; art d, Rachel Martinet; sound, Nick Kitinski, Gabriel Kitinski, Marcus Dawson; fx, Virginia Perfili, Bob Stone, Sam Cicchirillo; casting, Gerald I. Wolff; cos, Celestine Hickman; makeup, Sandy Williams

Horror/Erotic **(PR: O MPAA: NR)**

MISSING PIECES ★

(U.S.) 92m Aaron Russo Entertainment ~ Orion Pictures/HBO Home Video c

(AKA: AUF DER SONNENSEITE DES LEBENS)

Robert Wuhl *(Lou Wimpole)*; Eric Idle *(Wendell Dickens)*; Lauren Hutton *(Jennifer)*; Bob Gunton *(Gabor)*; Richard Belzer *(Baldisari)*; Bernie Koppel *(Dr. Gutman)*; Kim Lankford *(Sally)*; Donald Gibb *(Hurrodnik)*; Leslie Jordan *(Krauss)*; Louis Zorich *(Ochenko)*; Don Hewitt *(Scarface)*; John De Lancie *(Paul/Walter Thackeray)*; James Hong *(Chang)*; Janice Lynde *(Marion)*; Mary Fogarty *(Mrs. Callahan)*; Bruce Kronenberg *(Chauffeur)*; Stacey Ann Logan *(Elisa)*; Derek Meader *(Joseph)*; Kate Stern *(Myra Gluckman)*; Paul Keith *(Father of Bride)*; Sharon Brown *(Bernice)*; Andrea Garfield *(Nurse)*; Darryl Chan *(Young Chinese Man)*; Louise Troy *(Mrs. Waldham)*; Leonard Stern *(Man at Concert)*; Gloria Stroock *(Woman at Concert)*; Richard Kwong *(Chinese Man)*; Kellie Jo Tackett *(Receptionist)*

Dated and frenetic, MISSING PIECES might have been written by a pool of Bob Hope's former writers at a geriatric home. The result is a road picture that goes all over the place without getting anywhere.

Wendell (Eric Idle) is an orphaned greeting card writer with a plan. He wants to catapult his cellist pal, Lou (Robert Wuhl), to philharmonic fame. But Wendell's good intentions are compromised by an unexpected inheritance.

Mr. Chen Who, one of Wendell's many foster fathers, has left the financially strapped Wendell nothing more than a perplexing riddle. In the course of solving Who's paradox, Wendell squirrels away clues garnered from two sources. The first, a private eye named Baldisari (Richard Belzer), winds up planted in the trunk of Wendell's car. The other, photographer Paul Thackeray (John De Lancie), dies with a photo of an LA antique shop clutched in his hand. Can Wendell discover the mastermind who ordered these murders, committed by an assassin named Scarface (Don Hewitt)?

Meanwhile, Mr. Who's attorney, Krauss (Leslie Jordan), and a one-armed antique dealer, Gabor (Bob Gunton), are up to no good. Seeking a priceless object identified in Who's riddle, they wheedle their way into Wendell's confidence. Wendell and Lou deduce that the riddle's object is a rare dagger, But that knowledge leaves Wendell and Lou vulnerable to attack when they travel to LA and stay with Lou's ex-wife and her girlfriend.

At the Melrose Avenue antique store pictured in the photograph, Wendell meets Paul's twin, Walter (John De Lancie), who informs him that a client is holding a clock sold by Chen Who. The homicide suspects multiply to include psychiatrist-coroner Gutman (Bernie Koppel) and Chen Who's cousin, Chang (James Hong).

Lou and Wendell locate the priceless dagger in the clock. 'Twas greedy Gutman who organized the murder conspiracy to get his mitts on the dagger. While Lou battles Scarface, Wendell grapples with Gutman on a rooftop from which he drops the ancient weapon. Gutman then sails over the roof to his death, and the falling dagger lodges itself in Scarface's back.

Jacked up with enough plot twists for a dozen mysteries, MISSING PIECES aspires to be as diverting as a game of "Clue." But this ramshackle farce mistakes energy for panache. Imagine the Keystone Kops too drunk to master their timing: that's how badly the sight gags are fumbled by the director and stars.

Primarily a verbal comic, Wuhl sputters dialogue with gusto. But even his good lines are drowned in the noisy chaos. Monty Pythonite Eric Idle is no stranger to physical comedy, but he seems ill at ease, as if the pratfalls are beneath him.

Where it needs comic precision, MISSING PIECES shoots itself in the foot by resorting to frantic cavorting and mugging. Ultimately, the proceedings crawl to a standstill in a mystery-burlesque that is too desperate to be funny. *(Violence, profanity, adult situations.)* — R.P.

d, Leonard Stern; p, Aaron Russo; exec p, William Carraro; w, Leonard Stern; ph, Peter Stein; ed, Evan Lottman; m, Marvin Hamlisch; prod d, Michael Hanan; art d, Mark Zuelske; set d, Doug Mowat; sound, Bill Daly (mixer); fx, Cliff Wenger; casting, Jennifer Hughes, Barry Moss; cos, Mary Ellen Winston, Bobbie Read; makeup, Marilyn Carbone; stunts, Joe Dunne

Comedy **(PR: C MPAA: PG)**

MISSION: IMPOSSIBLE ★★★

(U.S.) 110m CW Productions; Paramount British Pictures ~ Paramount c

Tom Cruise *(Ethan Hunt)*; Jon Voight *(Jim Phelps)*; Emmanuelle Beart *(Claire)*; Henry Czerny *(Kittridge)*; Jean Reno *(Krieger)*; Ving Rhames *(Luther)*; Kristin Scott Thomas *(Sarah Davies)*; Vanessa Redgrave *(Max)*; Emilio Estevez *(Jack Harmon—uncredited)*; Dale Dye *(Frank Barnes)*; Marcel Iures *(Golitsyn)*; Ion Caramitru *(Zozimov)*; Ingeborga Dapkunaite *(Hannah)*; Valentina Yakunina *(Drunken Female IMF Agent)*; Marek Vasut *(Druken Male IMF Agent)*; Nathan Osgood *(Kittridge Technician)*; John McLaughlin *(TV Interviewer)*; Rolf Saxon *(CIA Analyst William Donloe)*; Karel Dobry *(Matthias)*; Andreas Wisniewski *(Max's Companion)*; David Shaeffer *(Dipolmat Rand Housman)*; Rudolf Pechan *(Mayor Brandl)*; Gaston Subert *(Jaroslav Reid)*; Ricco Ross *(Denied Area Security Guard)*; Mark Houghton *(Denied Area Security Guard)*; Bob Friend *(Sky News Man)*; Annabel Mullion *(Flight Attendant)*; Garrick Hagon *(CNN Reporter)*; Jirina Trebicka *(Cleaning Woman)*; Andrzei Borkowski; Maya Dokic; Sam Douglas; Oleg Fedorov; Carmela Marner; Mimi Potworowska *(Kiev Room Agents)*; David Schneider *(Train Engineer)*; Helen Lindsay *(Female Executive in Train)*; Pat Starr *(CIA Agent)*; Richard D. Sharp *(CIA Lobby Guard)*; Randall Paul *(CIA Escort Guard)*; Suzanne Doucette *(CIA Agent)*; Graydon Gould *(Public Official)*; Tony Vogel *(M15 Agent)*; Michael Rogers *(Large Man)*; Laura Brook *(Margaret Hunt)*; Morgan Deare *(Donald Hunt)*; David Phelan *(Steward on Train)*; Melissa Knatchbull *(Air Stewdardess)*

The Impossible Missions Force returns, having traded its walkie-talkies for high-speed modems, in Brian De Palma's big-screen upgrade of the TV show "Mission: Impossible." The movie features fast-paced action, brilliant special effects, lots of miniaturized spy equipment, and a product placement coup by Apple Computers, whose laptops get as much screen time as star Tom Cruise.

A stewardess on an international flight hands Jim Phelps (Jon Voight) a set of headphones and some music for relaxation. When Phelps inserts the disk, however, instead of Mantovani he hears a familiar voice: "Good morning, Mr. Phelps."

The mission, should Phelps choose to accept it, is to retrieve a stolen list of undercover agents' real names and identifying information before it is used to find and eliminate US operatives throughout the world.

The audiovisual recording concludes with the ominous warning, "As always, should you or any member of your IM Force be caught or killed, the secretary will disavow any knowledge of your actions." Following tradition, the disk self-destructs, producing a trail of smoke.

In Prague, Phelps assembles his team—a small group of wisecracking, thirtysomething daredevils that includes team leader Ethan Hunt (Tom Cruise), techno-whiz Jack Harmon (Emilio Estevez), and Phelps's wife Claire (Emanuelle Beart)—and outlines their task. They will infiltrate an embassy ball, where the list is to be passed to an enemy agent; they will photograph the transaction, then intercept the list.

At first, the mission appears to be proceeding smoothly, but things start to go terribly wrong. One by one, the IM agents, including Phelps, are killed. Ethan is the only survivor, and the list has disappeared.

Ethan's first instinct is to contact his superior, Kittridge (Henry Czerny), but, to his dismay, he discovers that he has been tagged a double agent and "disavowed."

To prove his innocence, Ethan must find the missing list. He is joined by IM teammate Claire, Phelps's widow, who appears at the safe house explaining that she wasn't blown up after all.

Soon Ethan realizes he needs a larger team, and he recruits two more agents from a roster of ex-IMF members who have, like Ethan, been disavowed by the secretary.

To retrieve the stolen list, Ethan's team must hack a mainframe computer which, for reasons of security, is not connected to any network. Furthermore, the computer is protected by multiple sensors and alarms. But this is a small matter for Ethan, who simply downloads the list while suspended in mid-air.

An enemy agent, Max (Vanessa Redgrave), wants to purchase the list, and Ethan has set up a bogus sale. The transaction takes place on a high-speed train, where Ethan himself, it seems, is walking into a setup. There are a number of surprises and a dramatic struggle on top of the train, but the team prevails and Ethan is vindicated.

MISSION: IMPOSSIBLE, with its spectacular effects and a complex plot that defies you to look away, is a thrilling and satisfying motion picture. But the film does have a few deficiencies, notably Cruise. He can be an extremely good actor when he wants to (RISKY BUSINESS, RAIN MAN), but during much of MISSION: IMPOSSIBLE, he recites his lines without conviction, as if he's not quite sure what the words mean. Annoyingly, throughout the movie, he punctuates his sloppy performance with lengthy and entirely unnecessary displays of his teeth.

The IMF apparently has a female membership, but from what we see here, the girls are pretty darn useless. Two of the women are picked off immediately, but even Claire, who returns and has a large co-starring role, does nothing that would suggest the talent and training of a serious IM operative. Claire's entire function, in fact, seems to be standing around looking fetching and disheveled.

Unlike the bloodless TV series, the motion picture version features several deaths, including Estevez's early and unlikely impalement while operating a computer inside an elevator shaft. The deaths are not gratuitous, however; in the real-world spy trade, some loss of life is expected. Moreover, given De Palma's presence in the director's chair, the total amount of gore is actually quite moderate, almost tasteful.

Overall, MISSION: IMPOSSIBLE is a supercharged piece of entertainment, with extraordinary effects, terrific gadgets, a fast-moving story full of genuine surprises, and, of course, the legendary theme music. It is a worthy successor to a television classic. *(Violence, sexual situations.)* — J.W.

d, Brian De Palma; p, Tom Cruise, Paula Wagner; exec p, Paul Hitchcock; w, David Koepp, Robert Towne (from a story by David Koepp and Steven Zaillian, based on the television series created by Bruce Geller); ph, Stephen H. Burum; ed, Paul Hirsch; m, Danny Elfman, Lalo Schifrin; prod d, Norman

Reynolds; art d, Frederick Hole; set d, Peter Howitt; sound, David Crozier (mixer); fx, John Knoll, Richard Yuricich, Lyn Nicholson, Industrial Light & Magic; casting, Mali Finn, Patsy Pollock; cos, Penny Rose; makeup, Lois Burwell, Amanda Knight, Rob Bottin; stunts, Greg Powell

Thriller/Spy/Action **(PR: C MPAA: PG-13)**

MR. HOLLAND'S OPUS ★★

(U.S.) 142m Interscope Communications; The Charlie Mopic Company ~ Buena Vista c

Richard Dreyfuss *(Glenn Holland)*; Glenne Headly *(Iris Holland)*; Jay Thomas *(Bill Meister)*; Olympia Dukakis *(Principal Jacobs)*; William H. Macy *(Vice Principal Wolters)*; Alicia Witt *(Gertrude Lang)*; Terrence Howard *(Louis Russ)*; Damon Whitaker *(Bobby Tidd)*; Jean Louisa Kelly *(Rowena Morgan)*; Alexandra Boyd *(Sarah Olmstead)*; Nicholas John Renner *(Cole at 6 Years Old)*; Joseph Anderson *(Cole at 15 Years Old)*; Anthony Natale *(Cole at 28 Years Old)*; Joanna Gleason *(Adult Gertrude)*; Beth Maitland *(Deaf School Principal)*; Patrick Fong *(Study Hall Student)*; Benjamin J. Dixon *(Mr. Mims)*; Kathryn Arnett *(Ms. Swedlin)*; Freeman O. Corbin *(Mr. Sullivan)*; Moira Feeney *(Ms. Godfrey)*; Joshua Minnick *(Mr. Shapiro)*; Ashley Hamrick *(Miss Reeves)*; Janine Shouse *(Miss Schumaker)*; Spencer Riviera *(Mr. Hosta)*; Daniel J. Vhay *(Mr. Malone)*; Sean Bevington *(Mr. McMartin)*; John Henry Redwood *(Mr. Russ)*; Ted Roisum *(Dr. Sorenson)*; Mark Daniels *(Ralph)*; Kaili Carlton *(Ms. Wayne)*; Adam Fitzhugh *(Mr. McKenzie)*; Eric Michael Cole *(Boy 2)*; Joe Campbell *(Boy 3)*; Tomiko Peirano *(Girl 2)*; Kasey Nelson *(Girl 3)*; Zoe McLellan *(Girl 4)*; Kelly M. Casey *(Deaf School Teacher)*; Michael Mendelson *(Chaplain)*; Alex Dudgeon *(Auditoner 1)*; Rachel Wooley *(Auditioner 2)*; Jordan Carlton *(Auditioner 3)*; Aurora J. Miller *(Auditioner 4)*; Paul Bernard *(Auditioner 5)*; Mary Kay O'Mealy *(Auditioner 6)*; Dieffyd Gilman-Frederick *(Auditioner 7)*; Tara Eng *(Auditioner 8)*; Jay Frank *(Auditioner 9)*; Conan Doherty *(Toby Klein)*; Stacey Siegel *(Diner Waitress)*; Nicolas Sirianni *(Football Player 1)*; Jacob Adams *(Football Player 2)*; Chris Marth *(Football Player 3)*; Brent Archie *(Football Player 4)*; Kevin Calaba *(Football Player 5)*; Keith Swift *(Football Player 6)*; John Boyer *(Billy Faraday)*; Linda Williams Janke *(Secretary)*; David Clegg *(Superintendent)*; Don Burns *(City Official)*; Dennis Biasi *(Adult Stadler)*

MR. HOLLAND'S OPUS wants desperately to be the baby boomer IT'S A WONDERFUL LIFE (1946). It's too bad that position is already held by FORREST GUMP (1994).

The film opens in 1964 as Glenn Holland (Richard Dreyfuss) becomes the music teacher at the newly renamed John F. Kennedy High School in Portland, Oregon. He intends the job to be temporary, just something to pay the bills until his "real" career as a composer takes off. Helping an inept but determined clarinetist (Alicia Witt), Mr. Holland discovers his gift for teaching and the positive impact the act of learning has on a child's self-esteem. His newfound dedication to teaching earns him the admiration of the principal (Olympia Dukakis), but his use of rock-and-roll music in the classroom raises eyebrows. Pretty soon, Mr. Holland is organizing a marching band, and his wife Iris (Glenne Headly) is pregnant. In a tragic twist, their son, Cole, is born deaf.

Suddenly, it's 1980 and Mr. Holland is staging a Gershwin revue at JFK. He and the show's beautiful ingenue, Rowena Morgan (Jean Louisa Kelly), develop a deep affection. She has dreams of singing on Broadway, and he encourages her to pursue them. When Rowena asks him to leave his wife and go with her to New York, Mr. Holland considers the offer, but declines. The consideration, though, is indicative of problems in his marriage: for years, he and Iris have been at odds over Cole. Unable to share his love of music with his son, Mr. Holland has ignored him; he's never even learned sign language. After the shooting of John Lennon, Cole confronts his father. Mr. Holland sees the light and stages a concert at Cole's school, the finale of which is Mr. Holland singing and *hand signing* Lennon's "Beautiful Boy."

In the present, due to budget cuts, all arts education at JFK is being eliminated, and Mr. Holland is being terminated. Iris and Cole, now a teacher, join him on his last day. They direct Mr. Holland to the auditorium where hundreds of students, past and present, including Gertrude Lang (Joanna Gleason), the inept clarinetist who is now Governor of Oregon, have gathered to pay him tribute. The film's finale is the performance of one of Mr. Holland's emotionally stirring compositions.

MR. HOLLAND'S OPUS is a real tearjerker, but when the tears come, you feel like a jerk. Patrick Sheane Duncan's script is a formula of connect-the-dots cloying moments, and Stephen Herek directs it with all the push-button manipulation and ham-fisted subtlety he brought to THE MIGHTY DUCKS (1992). They should at least be ashamed of the mawkish use of John Lennon's music and memory. Dreyfuss gives a very able performance as the earnest Every-ham, for which he received a Best Actor Oscar nomination.

The crisis in public education is like the weather—everyone complains about it, but no one does anything about it—and MR. HOLLAND'S OPUS certainly won't motivate anyone to action. It gives audiences a chance to feel warm and fuzzy about underpaid teachers whose efforts they claim to value but whose salaries they refuse to pay. The movie even trots out the line about Mr. Holland really being "a rich man" a la IT'S A WONDERFUL LIFE's George Bailey. However, in its climax, the film is absurdly ironic. This isn't Mr. Holland's retirement party—he's been fired. It's hard to believe he wouldn't seize the opportunity (what with all those taxpayers and the *Governor* there) to point the finger of blame. By the film's illogic, the people cheering Mr. Holland aren't the same ones handing him his pink slip. We needn't worry about Mr. Holland, though. Based on the evidence of his "American Symphony" (by Michael Kamen)—an untextured hodgepodge of bombast without nuance—there's a job waiting for him in Hollywood, scoring bad movies like. . . well, need it be said?— P.R.

d, Stephen Herek; p, Ted Field, Michael Nolin, Robert W. Cort; exec p, Scott Kroopf, Patrick Sheane Duncan; co-p, William Teitler, Judith James; w, Patrick Sheane Duncan; ph, Oliver Wood; ed, Trudy Ship; m, Michael Kamen; prod d, David Nichols; art d, Dina Lipton; set d, Jan Bergstrom; ch, Bruce McDonald; sound, Kirk Francis; fx, Bob Riggs; casting, Sharon Bialy; cos, Aggie Guerard Rodgers; makeup, Gerald Quist, Martin "Vinnie" Hagood; stunts, Steve Boyum

AAN Best Actor: Richard Dreyfuss

Drama **(PR: A MPAA: PG)**

MR. ICE CREAM MAN ★★½

(U.S.) 66m Hail/Mills Productions; New Breed Productions ~ Dead Alive Home Video c

Henry Weckesser *(Joey Cole)*; Jim Mills *(Detective Jeff Hailey)*; Cindy Reed *(Samantha Cole)*; Mack Hail *(Ice Cream Man)*; DeVonn Carral *(Roland Pirtle)*; Alisha Lobato *(Emily Harper)*; Alicia Schossig *(Nikki)*; Kim Bruno *(Lisa)*; Joe McCourt *(Lt. Gale Gibbs)*; Ron Kusiak *(Det. Callegan)*; Alan Jones *(Ditcher)*; James Brooks *(Roland's Dad)*; Dan R. Davis *(Motor Officer)*; Nathan Lobato *(Party Boy #1)*; Philip Sterbling *(Party Boy #2)*; Cheriesa Lobato *(Party Girl #1)*; Francia Luna *(Party Girl #2)*;

Katherine Greene *(Teacher)*; Audrey Keller *(Babysitter)*; Mindy Oliver *(Crime Photo)*; Jeremy Settles *(K9 Officer)*; Mike Baker *(Uniformed Officer)*; Eric Beilstein *(Detective #1)*; Kevin Price *(Detective #2)*; Jessica Oliver *(Little Girl)*; Cheryl Lowe *(Waitress)*; Tiffany Keller *(Franky's Mother)*; Ryan Keller *(Little Franky)*

Despite being made on a much lower budget than the Clint Howard vehicle ICE CREAM MAN (1995), this is a more successful combination of black humor and chills.

Joey (Henry Weckesser), Roland (DeVonn Carral), and Emily (Alisha Lobato) are grade-school friends who receive a lecture on safety from young detective Jeff Hailey (Jim Mills) after the disappearance of one of their classmates. Though no one suspects him at first, the culprit is the new ice cream man in town (Mack Hail), who unnerves Joey when he drives past the boy's window at night. While Hailey is striking up a relationship with Joey's single mother, Samantha (Cindy Reed), the ice cream man kills another local boy and a female jogger who's taunted him, and just misses luring Emily into his clutches.

Soon thereafter, the killer chases down Roland, crashing his truck in the process, and adds the boy to the body count. He then invades Joey's birthday party, terrorizing Samantha and the young guests and revealing to Joey that he's actually his father. Hailey, however, has discovered the disabled truck and Roland's body, and arrives in time to rescue Samantha and the kids and send the ice cream man into a fatal fall down a staircase.

The makers of MR. ICE CREAM MAN maintained that it was too uncomfortable a coincidence when, shortly after they got underway on their project, the announcement was made about the similarly themed Howard vehicle. And although produced for much less money (the feature was shot on video) and given a lower-profile release, this version is more accomplished on a creative level. Eschewing cheap humor and daring to have its villain actually knock off his young targets, MR. ICE CREAM MAN proves to be a confident and creditable low-budget effort.

Ordinarily, a director casting himself in the lead of an independent feature is a sign of either budgetary constraints or ego, but Hail proves himself in both areas here. His visuals are occasionally quite imaginative and evocative, and he brings an amusingly creepy aura to his film's villain, resisting the easy approach of camping it up. (He should have maintained the same control over Carral, whose outspoken performance as Roland is the movie's most grating element.) The script by Hail and Jim Mills, who also steps before the camera as the steadfast hero, is rather insubstantial—the movie is barely feature length—but unlike so many other indie horror flicks, this one doesn't have a chance to wear out its welcome. *(Graphic violence, adult situations, profanity.)* — M.G.

d, Mack Hail; p, Jeremy A. Settles; exec p, Yvette Hoffman; w, Mack Hail, Jim Mills; ph, Lynn Nicholson; ed, Larry Uelmen; m, Jeff Day, Rob Pottorf; sound, Tony Kremer; fx, Jeremy Settles

Horror **(PR: O MPAA: NR)**

MR. STITCH ★★½

(U.S./France) 98m Studio Megaboom; Rysher Entertainment ~ WarnerVision c

Rutger Hauer *(Dr. Rue Wakeman)*; Wil Wheaton *(Lazarus)*; Nia Peeples *(Dr. Elizabeth English)*; Ron Perlman *(Dr. Frederick Texarian)*; Taylor Negron *(Dr. Al Jacobs)*; Michael Harris *(Gen. Hardcastle)*; Ron Jeremy Hyatt *(Lt. Periwinkle)*; Stevo Polyi *(Stevo)*; Rowland Wafford *(Rowland)*; Richard Louderback *(Red-haired Skull Soldier)*; Kevin White *(Overzealous Soldier)*; Luke Straite-McClure *(Thorn Gardener)*; Al Sapienza *(Clay Gardener)*; Valerie Trapp *(Sandy Gardener)*; Philip Wotton *(Frank)*; Kario Salem *(Ornery Policeman)*; Salvator Xuereb *(Deputy Dog)*; Tom Savini *(Chemical Weapons Engineer)*

An imaginative variation on the Frankenstein story, MR. STITCH stretches its low budget with commendable facility.

In a secret underground lab, a team of scientists led by Dr. Rue Wakeman (Rutger Hauer) has created a patchwork man (Wil Wheaton) out of body parts from 88 different individuals. Psychiatrist Dr. Elizabeth English (Nia Peeples) is brought in to orient this creation, who, after reading the Bible, chooses to call himself Lazarus. Lazarus begins to bond with Dr. English, but also becomes tormented by visions—memories, it turns out, from his many "donors." When Dr. Wakeman decides that Dr. English has gotten too close to Lazarus, she is removed from the project, inspiring Lazarus to escape from the lab.

Eluding armed pursuers, Lazarus visits a woman whose husband and son—two of his donors—were killed in a car accident, to tell her that her husband and son still love her. He then finds his way to Dr. English's apartment, where he reveals that another of his donors was her former lover Dr. Frederick Texarian (Ron Perlman), a scientist colleague who was killed when he tried to stop Wakeman's project. Lazarus, it turns out, was intended to be a supersoldier, and he realizes that there's only one way to end the experiments. Returning to the lab, he confronts General Hardcastle (Michael Harris), the project's military backer, and kills both the general and himself.

MR. STITCH signals a new direction for writer-director Roger Avary, who co-wrote PULP FICTION (1994) and helmed the similarly themed KILLING ZOE (1994). By eschewing the in-your-face violence and camerawork of his previous movies, Avary has crafted a spare, frequently almost surreal film. A good deal of the story takes place in the sterile, white, dimensionless lab space, empty save for Lazarus, his occasional visitors, some simple furniture, and a large, floating eyeball that watches over him (a nifty computer-generated effect). Yet the film never becomes monotonous; Avary keeps the drama building as Lazarus discovers truths about himself and develops genuine feelings for Dr. English.

While the performances are uneven, the central emotions ring true, anchored by the empathetic performance of Wheaton (even under his very convincing, multi-colored skin makeup by Tom Savini). And when the action moves outside the lab, Avary serves up a genuinely exciting car chase. The fact that some of the soldiers pursue Lazarus in what look like souped-up go-carts is all of a piece with Avary's off-kilter visual style, which succeeds through the confidence and coherence he has applied to it.

Originally developed as a pilot for a television series, MR. STITCH had a troubled production history (evidenced by its lack of a producer credit), culminating with Hauer walking off the film midshoot. The result is that Lazarus confronts General Hardcastle instead of Dr. Wakeman at the climax, and this incongruity—coupled with Harris's overacting—makes the ending something of a letdown after the compelling 90 minutes preceding it. *(Violence, sexual situations, profanity.)* — M.G.

d, Roger Avary; exec p, Rutger Hauer, Roger Avary, Morgan Mason; w, Roger Avary; ph, Tom Richmond; ed, Sloane Klevin; m, tomandandy; prod d, Damien LaFranche; art d, Kevin White, Richard Louderback; sound, Daniel Brisseau, Jeff Wannberg, Tim Bindel; fx, Jan Bird, John Wake; casting, Rick Montgomery; cos, Jaleh; makeup, Tom Savini, Richard Luzy

Science Fiction/Thriller **(PR: O MPAA: R)**

MR. WRONG ★★½

(U.S.) 92m Mandeville Films; Touchstone ~ Buena Vista c

Ellen DeGeneres *(Martha Alston)*; Bill Pullman *(Whitman Crawford)*; Joan Cusack *(Inga)*; Dean Stockwell *(Jack Tramonte)*; Joan Plowright *(Mrs. Crawford)*; John Livingston *(Walter)*; Robert Goulet *(Dick Braxton)*; Ellen Cleghorne *(Jane)*; Hope Davis *(Annie)*; Brad Henke *(Bob)*; Christine Cattell *(Nancy Culpepper)*; Peter White *(Mr. Alston)*; Polly Holliday *(Mrs. Alston)*; Briant Wells *(Stuart)*; Camille Saviola *(Consuela)*; Maddie Corman *(Missy)*; Jonathan Hernandez *(Cody)*; Victoria Flores *(Nicole)*; Louie Anderson *(Himself)*; Casey Kasem *(Himself)*; Jean Kasem *(Herself)*; Hector Elias *(Mexican Detective)*; Frank Roman *(Mexican Lieutenant)*; Shea Farrell *(James)*; Frank Lugo *(Priest)*; Johnny Miller *(Old Man)*; John Cothran Jr. *(Owner)*; Wayne Alexander *(Man at Opera)*; Jamie McGurk *(Waitress)*; Christopher Kriesa *(Cop #1)*; Frederick Dawson *(Cop #2)*; Gil Combs *(Flower Truck Delivery Man)*; Charlene Castle *(Woman at Wedding)*; Bob Harvey *(Bartender)*; Mickey Harrison *(Elder Neighbor)*; Jenny Turnham *(Aunt Belinda)*; Ivor Shier *(Helicopter Pilot)*

Comic Ellen DeGeneres gained prominence in a network TV sitcom initially called "These Friends of Mine" that soon dubbed itself "Ellen" after its strongest feature. The big screen beckoned, and in this showcase, DeGeneres and her strong supporting cast brighten a comedy that starts out cute but gets ugly before one's eyes.

Martha Alston (Ellen DeGeneres), a 31-year-old producer for San Diego television, enjoys her job and circle of friends but feels lonely without a significant other, especially after her kid sister's marriage. One night in a bar, Martha meets Whitman Crawford (Bill Pullman), a sexy, charming, and wealthy unpublished poet. Martha's passionate, whirlwind affair with Whitman cools quickly when he takes her to meet his dotty mother (Joan Plowright). Martha is appalled by their behavior and later, in an effort to be more "himself," Whitman forces Martha to shoplift beer. Martha also finds herself terrorized by Whitman's spurned ex-girlfriend, Inga (Joan Cusack).

Martha tries to break up with Whitman, but he showers her with flowers, gifts, and unwelcome attention. Getting no aid from police, Martha hires a private detective, Jack Tramonte (Dean Stockwell), to fend off the psychotic suitor, but Whitman—who is indeed wealthy, if no longer charming—buys his loyalty and continues the courtship. Hit by a car (while attempting to flee) and hospitalized, Martha is kidnapped first by vengeful Inga, then by Whitman, who conveys a drugged Martha to a dusty Mexican village where he has arranged a lavish marriage ceremony. At the last moment, Martha's assistant from work, Walter (John Livingston), who's adored her from afar all along, attempts a rescue, but it's a sniper's bullet from Inga that stops the nuptials.

The best parts of MR. WRONG are the early ones portraying an aging, single career woman under pressure to find a life mate; DeGeneres's sly sarcastic responses to the absurdities and unpleasantness of dating make some genuinely funny moments and set the stage for Pullman's ideal "Mr. Right" to slowly reveal his actual, deranged personality. But somewhere between Martha losing her job and Inga's torture/ritual-murder scheme, the comedy turns sadistic, and DeGeneres' efforts to maintain a light comedic touch in the darker, frenzied second half give her character a wan, spineless quality that the scriptwriters (three men) and director Nick Castle should have considered more carefully. When a defeated Martha stands at the altar, almost ready to accept the inevitable, there's a sense of Kafkaesque doom ("All men are horrible in their own way," advises a gal pal early on. "You're just going to have to accept that.") that would have hit home had not the actors been mugging like clowns and the filmmakers intent on wrapping things up in a silly, mock-violent finale owing quite a bit to the work of director Robert Rodriguez. What is most unfortunate is that a good idea (and a good cast) gets lost in the haywire action, which isn't funny and wasn't necessary. The film turned off critics and public alike during its Spring 1996 release and presaged the disappointed reception of Jim Carrey's much-touted THE CABLE GUY, another laugh riot about a crazed stalker. *(Violence, sexual situations, adult situations, substance abuse, profanity.)* — E.M.

d, Nick Castle; p, Marty Katz; exec p, David Hoberman; assoc p, Mark Sherman, Mark Indig; co-p, Ira Shuman; w, Kerry Ehrin, Chris Matheson, Craig Munson; ph, John Schwartzman; ed, Patrick Kennedy; m, Craig Safan; prod d, Doug Kraner; art d, Nancy Patton; set d, Cloudia; sound, Mark Hopkins McNabb (mixer); fx, James M. Hart, Michael Lessa; casting, Jane Jenkins, Janet Hirshenson; cos, Ingrid Ferrin; makeup, Ben Nye Jr.; stunts, Gil Combs

Comedy **(PR: C MPAA: PG-13)**

MODERN AFFAIR, A ★★½

(U.S.) 91m Nick of Time Productions; Tribe Productions; In Pictures ~ Tara Releasing c
(AKA: #247)

Lisa Eichhorn *(Grace Rhodes)*; Stanley Tucci *(Peter Kessler)*; Caroline Aaron *(Elaine)*; Mary Jo Salerno *(Lindsay)*; Tammy Grimes *(Dr. Gresham)*; Wesley Addy *(Ed Rhodes)*; Robert Joy *(Ernest Pohlsab)*; Cynthia Martells *(Ellen)*; Robert LuPone *(Ben)*; J. Smith-Cameron *(Diane)*; Vincent Young *(Tony)*; Len Stanger *(Older Executive)*; Jon Huberth *(Suit #1)*; Jim Lavin *(Suit #2)*; Claywood Sempliner *(Suit #3)*; Gary Lahti *(Jerry)*; Vern Oakley *(Man with Baby)*

A MODERN AFFAIR is not without its mild charms, but the operative word here is "mild."

Grace Rhodes (Lisa Eichhorn) is a Manhattan advertising executive whose professional life is more successful than her emotional one. Tired of waiting for Mr. Right, she decides to have a baby through artificial insemination.

Peter Kessler (Stanley Tucci) is a photographer with a gallery in upstate New York. A contented bachelor with a married lover, Lindsay (Mary Jo Salerno), he makes weekly donations to a sperm bank, and his anonymous sample finds its way to Grace. Once pregnant, Grace wonders about her child's biological father. She persuades friend Elaine (Caroline Aaron) to pose as an office temp at the sperm bank to access their confidential donor records.

After finding Peter's name, Grace visits his studio pretending to be a customer. They have lunch, then a few dates. Though she tells Elaine that her curiosity is satisfied and each date will be the last, she realizes she is falling in love with Peter. When she reveals that she is carrying his child, Peter reacts badly and ends the relationship. But after Lindsay tells Peter that she herself recently had an abortion because she wasn't sure the baby was his or her husband's, Peter has a change of heart and reunites with Grace in Manhattan.

Aside from the title, there's nothing particularly modern about A MODERN AFFAIR, which is essentially just another variation on girl meets boy, girl loses boy, girl gets boy back. Eichhorn and Tucci are likeable—by far the most important thing in the romantic-comedy genre. They provide their characters with just a bit of an edge: she's picky and nervous; he's a mild misanthrope who refuses to photograph people because they "mess up the composition." Likewise, the script has just enough quirky moments to hold your interest over an undemanding length. If that seems like faint praise, it's even fainter considering that the script was written by Paul Zimmerman, who did Martin Scorsese's THE KING OF COMEDY. *(Sexual situations, profanity.)* — M.F.

d, Vern Oakley; p, Vern Oakley, Melanie Webber, Jennifer Wilkinson; exec p, Marc Bailin; assoc p, Elliot Sears, Mark Garland, Ernest Kalman; w, Paul Zimmerman (from a story by Vern Oakley and Paul Zimmerman); ph, Rex Nicholson; ed, Suzanne Pillsbury; m, Jan Hammer; prod d, Cathy T. Marshall; set d, Janna Fournier; sound, William Kozy (recordist); casting, Bernard Telsey; cos, Gayle Alden Robbins; makeup, Kara Crean

Romance/Comedy/Drama **(PR: C MPAA: R)**

MOLL FLANDERS ★★

(U.S.) 123m Spelling Films; Trilogy Entertainment Group; MGM ~ MGM/UA c

Robin Wright *(Moll Flanders)*; Morgan Freeman *(Hibble)*; Stockard Channing *(Mrs. Allworthy)*; Brenda Fricker *(Mrs. Mazzawatti)*; John Lynch *(Jonathan)*; Geraldine James *(Edna)*; Aisling Corcoran *(Flora)*; Jim Sheridan *(Priest)*; Jeremy Brett *(Jonathan's Father)*; Britta Smith *(Artist's Mother)*; Cathy Murphy *(Polly)*; Emma McIvor *(Mary)*; Maria Doyle Kennedy *(Alice)*; Ger Ryan *(Orphanage Woman)*; Harry Towb *(Magistrate)*; Alan Stanford *(Mr. Mazzawatti)*; Eileen McCloskey *(Mazzawatti Daughter)*; Nicola Teehan *(Mazzawatti Daughter)*; Chris Curran *(Mazzawatti Butler)*; Rynagh O'Grady *(Kindly Sister)*; Maria Hayden *(Disciplinary Nun)*; Janet Moran *(Allworthy Maid)*; Kieran Hurley *(Physician)*; Mary McEvoy *(Mother Superior)*; Brendan Conroy *(Delivery Man)*; Rita Hamill *(Moll's Mother)*; Birdy Sweeney *(Doctor of Sorts)*; Brendan Cauldwell *(Mr. 100 Guineas)*; Mal Whyte *(Bald Cleric)*; Barry Barnes *(Older Brother)*; Paul Hickey *(Younger Brother)*; Tom Jordan *(Greying Father)*; Charlotte Bradley *(Artist's Sister)*; Brian de Salvo *(Artist's Butler)*; Brian Munn *(Carriage Driver)*; Gina Moxley *(Girl at Confessional)*; Jonathan Ryan *(Goldsmith)*; Pat Leavy *(Widow)*; Stanley Townsend *(Gambler)*; Tom Lawlor *(Shop Owner)*; Gerry Walsh *(Man with Blunderbuss)*; Joe Savino *(Threatening Man)*; Gary Whelan *(Prison Guard)*; Helene Montague *(Woman with Baby)*; Eileen Reid *(Smallpox Woman)*; Brendan Dempsey *(Lord with Dog)*; Ardal O'Hanlon *(Gentleman from East Chiswick)*; Conor Lovett *(Footman)*; Teacel Hines *(Young Footman)*; Des Braiden *(Gatekeeper)*; Elizabeth McKnight *(Maid)*; E'Dena Hines *(Maid)*; Audrey Tom *(Red Dress Prostitute)*; Magael McLaughlin *(Allworthy Girl)*; Courtney King *(Allworthy Girl)*; Carol Jahme *(Allworthy Girl)*

In a time with precious few good roles for actresses, an adaptation of Daniel Dafoe's 1722 classic *Moll Flanders* promises a healthy exception. Unfortunately, a *good* adaptation requires a sense of humor and nuance that seems quite beyond the abilities of screenwriter–director Pen Densham.

Actually, Densham's MOLL FLANDERS is only "based on the character from the novel." This much is obvious from the framing device he has contrived for the story: cantankerous nine-year-old Flora (Aisling Corcoran) is languishing in a church orphanage when a stranger named Hibble (Morgan Freeman) comes to take her off to America. His price: that she listen attentively to his recitation of her mother's diary.

This "diary," presented in flashback, takes up some (but not all) of the themes of Dafoe's novel. Flora's mother Moll (Robin Wright) was born just before her own mother, a convicted thief, was hanged in prison. Raised in a nunnery, Moll flees the lascivious pawings of her father confessor and finds herself adopted by a bourgeois family, the Mazzawattis.

Though outwardly ennobled by the Christian spirit of Mrs. Mazzawatti (Brenda Fricker), this family has deep mortal flaws, most especially the jealousy of the Mazzawatti daughters (Eileen McCloskey and Nicola Teehan) for their adopted sister. The self-confidence and goodness of Moll humiliate the better-bred girls, but when they attempt to match her virtue, they only manage to get themselves violated in an ill-advised alms-giving trip to a rough neighborhood.

Moll is compelled to ramble again, and lands in the employ of an unscrupulous madam, Mrs. Allworthy (Stockard Channing). Though only a kitchen maid, she decides her best chance for a comfortable life is to meet a fine gentleman by entering Mrs. Allworthy's "service." Meanwhile, she befriends her procuress's servant, Hibble—a former thief Mrs. Allworthy holds in her power on the threat of exposing him to the authorities.

After entertaining hundreds of customers, Moll begins to despair of her plans for a decent marriage. Gin-soaked, her looks fading, she chances to meet Jonathan (John Lynch), a young artist who becomes obsessed with rendering her spirit on canvas. At first reluctantly, then totally, Moll falls in love with him and conceives a child, Flora. Her happiness ends when Jonathan dies of smallpox and she is forced to feed herself and her child by selling off his precious paintings.

Desperate, Moll resorts to petty theft and is immediately arrested. She is once again "rescued" by Mrs. Allworthy, who is anxious to have her best girl back in her employ. But as Mrs. Allworthy, Moll, and Hibble are about to relocate to America, Flora disappears in a tenement fire. They are forced to sail without the child, and Moll is heartbroken. Fortunately, Mrs. Allworthy drowns when their ship goes down, and Moll cleverly takes on her identity (and her assets). She later sends Hibble back to England to find her daughter. The diary completed, Moll introduces herself to Flora again, and the unlikely family commences a happy life on their Caribbean plantation.

The problems with this film largely begin and end with Densham's script. Any adaptation of this novel must be alive to the deliberately delicious moral ironies of Dafoe's story, but Densham seems to prefer an inert seriousness. (This failure is particularly evident in reversals such as when Moll, the orphan of a thief, shows herself more worthy than the Mazzawatti sisters, yet finds that her good example only leads to disaster.) Equally fatal are the voice-over narration, whose disposability is only matched by its clunky straining for eloquence, and Densham's dialogue, which includes such gems as "Strangely, I find her mystery intriguing. . . ."

With the wealth of talent to chose from, the casting of Robin Wright as Moll is the real mystery. While her physical appeal is never in doubt, Wright never commands the screen in the way the role demands. On the bright side, the production is well-designed, and Morgan Freeman does lend his particular gravity to the film, mostly by not trying to do too much. Both he and Dafoe deserved better support. *(Violence, nudity, profanity, adult situations.)* — N.N.

d, Pen Densham; p, John Watson, Richard B. Lewis, Pen Densham; exec p, Morgan O'Sullivan; assoc p, Terri Clark; co-p, Tim Harbert; w, Pen Densham (from a story by Pen Densham, based on the character from the novel by Daniel Defoe); ph, David Tattersall; ed, Neil Travis, James R. Symons; m, Mark Mancina; prod d, Caroline Hanania; art d, Steve Simmonds; set d, Fiona Daly; sound, Kieran Horgan (mixer); fx, Maurice Foley; casting, Ros Hubbard, John Hubbard; cos, Consolata Boyle; makeup, Michele Burke; stunts, Fiona McLoughlin, Ray Nicholas, Alan Walsh

Drama/Adventure/Historical **(PR: C MPAA: PG-13)**

MONSTER, THE ★★★
(Italy/France) 111m UGC Images; Melampro; Iris Film ~ CFP Distribution c
(IL MOSTRO)

Roberto Benigni *(Loris)*; Nicoletta Braschi *(Detective Jessica Rosetti)*; Michel Blanc *(Taccone — the Psychiatrist)*; Jean-Claude Brialy *(Roccarotta — Loris's Landlord)*; Dominique Lavanant *(Jolanda — Taccone's Wife)*; Franco Mescollini *(Chinese Teacher)*; Ivano Marescotti *(Pascucci)*; Laurent Spielvogel *(Frustaluppi — Chief of Police)*; Massimo Girotti *(Loris's Neighbor)*

Roberto Benigni is the star, co-writer, and director of THE MONSTER, an amusing black comedy that became the biggest box-office hit in Italian history when it was released.

A sex maniac in Italy has attacked and dismembered 18 women and eluded police for 12 years. Police chief Frustaluppi (Laurent Spielvogel) dubs the killer "The Monster" and vows to catch him.

Sexually frustrated Loris (Roberto Benigni) is installing a mannequin display at a party when a friend tells him that one of the guests is a nymphomaniac. Misunderstanding who he meant, Loris crudely tries to pick up the wrong woman and is rebuffed. A few minutes later, she sees him holding a chainsaw that he can't turn off and stuffing what appear to be dead bodies (actually mannequins) into a van. Coming to the wrong conclusion, she describes him to the police as The Monster.

Having no evidence with which to arrest and try him, the police decide to use a female officer, Detective Jessica Rosetti (Nicoletta Braschi), as a decoy to draw him out. Learning that Loris is looking for a roommate, she pays him a cash advance and moves in. Her attempts to lure The Monster by being sexually provocative, however, only put Loris off. Police psychiatrist Taccone (Michel Blanc) becomes increasingly fascinated with the (wholly erroneous) pathology he has built up for Loris, and wants to study him at close range, so he and his wife pose as friends of Jessica and come over for dinner. Through no fault of Loris's, Taccone's wife becomes persuaded that his every move is meant to kill her, and the evening is a disaster.

Jessica finally concludes that Loris is not The Monster. But as she is making her report to her superiors, another murder occurs, and Taccone is convinced that Loris went berserk as soon as Jessica left. An uncomprehending Loris is chased by police and everyone who sees him. He hides out at the apartment of his friend, a language teacher (Franco Mescollini), whom Jessica has just discovered is the real killer. Loris makes the same discovery, and is saved from becoming The Monster's next victim in the nick of time by Jessica.

Benigni has often been described as the "Italian Jim Carrey" despite the fact that he's been around a lot longer than Carrey. Although they both rely heavily on physical contortions and wild-eyed hysterics, Carrey's persona is that of an adult who acts like an idiotic child, while Benigni's comedy is based on the impossibility of trying to suppress the "perverse" adult impulses of a childlike innocent. A more apt comparison would be to call him a maniacal version of Jacques Tati.

The funniest gags in THE MONSTER are the long, dialogue-free sequences, such as when Loris goes shoplifiting, or when he has a cigarette dropped down his pants. These rely on split-second timing and physical slapstick, and they're very effective, if not exactly subtle. Benigni's cinematic technique is similar to Tati's, with the camera often just a distant, objective observer of the scene, allowing the audience to take in a whole gag without interruption or stylistic commentary.

Unlike his American "counterpart," Benigni surrounds himself with equally excellent *farceurs*, such as his real-life wife Braschi and the always superb Blanc. With a plot revolving around rape and murder, THE MONSTER could be accused of tastelessness, but it's in the grand tradition of earthy Italian farces. The story is a pretext for the elaborately constructed scenes of mistaken intentions and misunderstandings. In its own strange way, it's rather sweet and charming. *(Profanity, adult situations, sexual situations.)* — M.S.

d, Roberto Benigni; p, Roberto Benigni, Yves Attal; exec p, Elda Ferri; assoc p, Gianluigi Braschi; w, Roberto Benigni, Vincenzo Cerami, Michel Blanc (from a story by Vincenzo Cerami); ph, Carlo Di Palma; ed, Nino Baragli; m, Evan Lurie; prod d, Giantito Burchiellaro; sound, Jean-Paul Mugel; fx, Germano Natali, Giovanni Corridori; cos, Danilo Donati

Comedy **(PR: C MPAA: NR)**

MONSTERSHOW ★★★
(U.S.) 90m bw

Paul Shuster *(Master of Ceremonies)*; Alan Benson *(Narrator)*; Mary Blatnik; Eric Lucas; John Jackson; Judy Tompkins; Connie Kramer; Marjory Myers

Experimental filmmaker Richard Myers took seven years to construct this amalgam of familiar horror stories and personal dreams. Its unusual style is both exciting and confusing. The depth of the symbolism and imagery combines well with haunting visuals, but the constant barrage of ideas is overwhelming. Myers' theme, that the horror stories are ingrained in each of us, is undercut by use of dreams that reflect only his own viewpoint.

MONSTERSHOW has no plot. A traveling show consisting of a narrator (Alan Benson) and an actor (Paul Shuster) act out, in the Grand Guignol style, the stories of Frankenstein, Dracula, and Jekyll and Hyde. Myers presents the show as a montage of action and spoken words, with the addition of images from previous film versions of the stories. Different sequences are woven together by mobile painted sets, scenes of the performers traveling from spot to spot, and shots of the audience's response to the show.

The film is divided into twelve segments, each roughly seven and a half minutes long. Six segments are readings from the original texts of *Frankenstein*, *Dracula*, and *The Strange Case of Dr. Jekyll And Mr. Hyde* overlaid with the monstershow itself. The other six segments are dream sequences, including subtitles and narration, which occasionally overlap. The dream sequences make use of blurred still images and surreal monologues.

One of the film's strongest scenes is one of those dream sequences showing a contortionist being put into a suitcase in a room while a man is being tossed up and down outside of the room's window.

The stories are acted out, then the show travels to a new location. One of the film's pleasures comes from understanding that the viewer is meant to take the information however he or she chooses, that sequence and continuity don't matter. Myers expects that different viewers will respond to different dreams and will also respond differently to the three main stories. His own preference for *Frankenstein* is shown partially by the inclusion of an unfinished Frankenstein film he made when he was only 12.

The black–and–white photography adds to the eeriness of the Monstershow and the surreality of the dreams. The layering of subtitles over narration allows the viewer to enter his or her own dream state as two separate stories drift in and out of consciousness.

The wealth of material in the film is impressive, but also one of MONSTERSHOW's main flaws. The steady pace is overwhelming, and the film would have been stronger if an occasional break, such as a silent image or more deliberately paced shot of the show's action, gave the viewer time to assimilate some of the images before the next ones appear. After a while, it is easy for the viewer to tune out completely.

Myers' dreams and images are fascinating and his method of connecting them to the well-known tales is powerful. Nonetheless, it is difficult for the tales to take on the universal meaning he ascribes to them when the film's other images are all specifically his. MONSTERSHOW would have been stronger and more involving if he had included other people's dreams or more universal narratives. *(Adult situations, profanity.)* — A.M.

d, Richard Myers; p, Richard Myers; w, Richard Myers; ph, Richard Myers; ed, Richard Myers; prod d, Richard Myers, Paul Shuster, John Jackson; art d, Richard Myers, Paul Shuster, John Jackson; sound, Marlowe Taylor

Fantasy/Drama (PR: C MPAA: NR)

MOON VALLEY
(SEE: WEEKEND IN THE COUNTRY, A)

MOONSHINE HIGHWAY ★★½
(U.S./Canada) 96m Showtime Networks ~ Paramount Home Video c

Kyle MacLachlan *(Jed Muldoon)*; Maria Del Mar *(Ethyl Miller)*; Randy Quaid *(Wendell Miller)*; Gary Farmer *(Hooch Wilson)*; Jeremy Ratchford *(Dwayne Dayton)*; Alex Carter *(Bill Rickman)*; Lori Hallier *(Rose)*; Dennis Fitzgerald *(Clancy Clayton)*; Raleigh Wilson *(Claude Clayton)*; Les Carlson *(Pappy)*; Jody Racicot *(Heywood Possum)*; David Cronenberg *(Clem Clayton)*; Beau Starr; Michael Copeman; Eleanor Joy Lind; Rick Roberts; Dick Callahan

In a market saturated by "erotic thrillers" and cheapo alien spectacles, Showtime Networks revisits hillbilly moonshine B-features of yesteryear.

It's the 1950s, and despite his distinguished war record, Tennessee-bred Jed Muldoon (Kyle MacLachlan) is back to what he does best: smuggling illegal corn liquor in his souped-up Lincoln down treacherous mountain roads by night. Mechanic Hooch (Gary Farmer) urges Muldoon to apply his talents instead to stock-car races while his lover, Ethyl (Maria Del Mar), wants Muldoon to take her away from town and her abusive husband, local sheriff Wendell Miller (Randy Quaid). Though Sheriff Miller has long accepted bribes from moonshiners to look the other way, he's under pressure from federal agent Rickman (Alex Carter) to stop the alcohol pipeline and wants to put an end to Muldoon anyway. Distrusting Miller, Rickman visits the speedway and recruits hotshot racer Dwayne Dayton (Jeremy Ratchord), a former moonshine runner, to be his specialty driver in catching the high-speed hillbillies. Things boil over when Miller murders Muldoon's pa and attempts to pin the crime on a pair of clodhoppers feuding with Muldoon. It ends with a multi-car chase that leaves Rickman and Dayton in the dust, and Miller exploded in a head-on crash. Muldoon, Ethyl, and Hooch depart for a successful future on the racetrack circuit.

The film is flawed on many levels. The car-chase scenes are more like ritualized jousts than anything else, hindered by unconvincing day-for-night photography. The story stalls in its easygoing, low-gear narrative that idles way too long with Muldoon's indecision. Wooded Ontario, Canada tries to pass for Tennessee hill country, the noble attempt aided by a soundtrack selection of Johnny Cash, Elvis Presley, and Billy Riley.

An Elvis-coiffed MacLachlan is surprisingly good in the rural milieu, and may have studied Robert Mitchum in THUNDER ROAD (1958) a few times. The reliable Quaid does what he can with his underwritten villain, and other roles are nicely cast right down to filmmaker David Cronenberg (SCANNERS, NAKED LUNCH, CRASH) as a somewhat creepy good ol' boy. Writer-director Andy Armstrong puts a straight face on material too often milked for "Li'l Abner"-style camp, and there's an interesting cultural sidelight about how moonshine fueled the emerging sport of stock-car racing. *(Violence, sexual situations, substance abuse.)* — C.C.

d, Andy Armstrong; p, Andy Armstrong, Becky Arntzen; w, Andy Armstrong; ph, Dick Quinlan; ed, Pat McMahon; m, Steve Dorff; prod d, Ed Hanna; fx, Michael Kavanagh; casting, Beth Klein, Clare Walker; cos, Luis Sequeira; stunts, Andy Armstrong

Historical/Crime/Drama (PR: C MPAA: PG-13)

MOTHER ★★★½
(U.S.) 104m Scott Rudin Productions ~ Paramount c

Albert Brooks *(John Henderson)*; Debbie Reynolds *(Beatrice Henderson)*; Rob Morrow *(Jeff Henderson)*; Lisa Kudrow *(Linda)*; Isabel Glasser *(Cheryl Henderson)*; Peter White *(Charles)*; Paul Collins *(Lawyer)*; Laura Weekes *(Karen Henderson)*; John C. McGinley *(Carl)*; Richard Assad *(TV Installer)*; Joey Naber *(TV Installer)*; Vanessa Williams *(Donna)*; Danielle Quinn *(Jill Henderson)*; Spencer Klein *(Josh Henderson)*; Ernie Brown *(Man at Rest Stop)*; Anne Haney *(Helen)*; Billye Ree Wallace *(Alice)*; James Gleason *(Waiter)*; Matt Nolan *(Gap Salesman)*; Harry Hutchinson *(Pet Store Salesman)*; Kimiko Gelman *(Lingerie Saleslady)*; Rosalind Allen *(Woman at Gas Station)*

MOTHER, Albert Brooks's first film as a director since 1991's DEFENDING YOUR LIFE, is a low-key gem that's both hilarious and warmhearted, featuring a smashing comeback performance by Debbie Reynolds as the mother from hell who turns out to be a real human being after all.

After his second divorce, 40-year-old blocked science-fiction writer John Henderson (Albert Brooks) meets a buddy at a bar and tries to figure out why his relationships with women keep failing. Following a disastrous date with a vapid woman he met at a supermarket and a humiliating dinner with his brother's family, John decides to move from LA and return to his mother's house in Sausalito in order to get to the root of his problems.

John's disapproving mother Beatrice (Debbie Reynolds) is skeptical and reluctant to participate in "The Experiment," as John calls it, but he moves back into his old room, restoring it to how it was in the late 1960s. John is convinced that his bad relationship with his mother is the cause of his problems, so he decides to spend all of his time with her until they can work things out. They go to the supermarket, then to a mall, and have dinner at a fancy restaurant, but always end up arguing. John is constantly embarrassed by his mother's need to tell strangers every detail of his life, and he also feels that she favors his younger brother Jeff (Rob Morrow) because he's a successful sports agent. When Beatrice cancels a visit to Jeff's house for the weekend so she can stay with John, Jeff unexpectedly shows up and tries to guilt her into leaving with him, but she refuses, leading to a big fight between Jeff and John.

One night, when Beatrice is on a date, John accidentally discovers some short stories that she had written years ago. When she comes home and discovers he's read them, she gets very angry, but then tells him about her thwarted desires to be a writer. John believes this is the breakthrough he's been looking for, that he finally knows why she hates him, and that now he can get on with his life. Driving home, John stops at a gas station and meets a woman who tells him he's her favorite author. He asks her to follow him back to LA and she agrees. Meanwhile,

Beatrice starts to write a story about "The Experiment" on the computer that John had left in his room.

MOTHER is that rarest of modern comedies that is not only funny, but wise and compassionate as well. Albert Brooks has never been that interested in jokes, per se, and MOTHER excels in the kind of humor that derives from behaviorial observation of "normal" neuroses and the embarrassing emotional dynamics of all family relationships. There are, of course, the usual Brooksian putdowns and one-liners, and some moments that are absolutely hysterical, but the film's true concerns are serious psychological ones and it deals with them in an honest and therapeutic way. All of the characters could easily have been made into foolish caricatures, particularly the mother, but Brooks and longtime co-writer Monica Johnson have created a script that exposes people's flaws in a humorous way, yet subscribes to Jean Renoir's philosophy that "everyone has their reasons." Just when the basic premise of a grown son moving back home begins to lose its comic steam, the film turns into a perceptive and poignant study of an elderly woman's inner life, revealing her to be a flesh and blood person with real feelings, hopes, and dreams. As John finally comes to forgive and understand her, he happily exclaims, "I no longer think of you as just a mother. I can now think of you as a failure."

Debbie Reynolds is nothing less than a revelation in her first leading role since 1971's WHAT'S THE MATTER WITH HELEN? Giving a performance of perfect timing and subtle understatement, she's so good that one is tempted to think (uncharitably) that she's not acting at all, but is merely playing herself. Brooks reportedly offered the role first to Nancy Reagan, then considered Doris Day and Esther Williams, but Reynolds brilliantly captures every emotional nuance and brings just the right mix of flakiness and sarcasm to the role. Rob Morrow is also excellent as the mama's-boy son.

All of Brooks's movies have been about a gnawing dissatisfaction with modern life and relationships resulting in a spiritual quest for a kind of unattainable happiness and harmony; in MOTHER, he attempts nothing less than to discover the reason why we act, think, feel, and love the way we do. *(Sexual situations, profanity.)* — M.S.

d, Albert Brooks; p, Scott Rudin, Herb Nanas; co-p, Barry Berg, Adam Schroeder; w, Albert Brooks, Monica Johnson; ph, Lajos Koltai; ed, Harvey Rosenstock; m, Marc Shaiman; prod d, Charles Rosen; art d, Charles Butcher; set d, Anne D. McCulley; sound, Kim Ornitz; casting, Deborah Aquila, Jane Shannon Smith; cos, Judy L. Ruskin; makeup, Bob Ryan

Comedy **(PR: C MPAA: PG-13)**

MOTHER ★★½

(U.S.) 90m Kings Road Productions ~ Triboro c

Diane Ladd *(Olivia Hendrix)*; Olympia Dukakis *(Mrs. Jay)*; Morgan Weisser *(Tom Hendrix)*; Ele Keats *(Audrey)*; Matt Clark *(Ben Wilson)*; Scott Wilson *(Dr. Chase)*; Lucy Lee Flippin *(Chloe)*; Steven Anderson *(Dr. Baeden)*; Andy Garrison *(Grave Digger 1)*; Jason Adams *(Grave Digger 2)*; Janna Robbins *(Flower Lady)*; Rick Grove *(Bartender)*; Jake Schmittler *(Little Cowboy (Tom's Brother))*; Noelle McGrath *(Receptionist)*; Phyllis Applegate *(Nurse)*; Mell Wells *(Mr. Brimley)*; Bette Rae *(Mrs. Stallings)*; Jack Andreozzi *(Sgt. Nick Ross)*; Flo Du Re *(Shop Owner)*; Russ Fega *(Photographer)*

Maverick filmmaker Frank Laloggia is a director whose facility for stylistic flourishes is more pronounced than his ability to structure a coherent thriller. MOTHER, like previous Laloggia mixed blessings (FEAR NO EVIL, LADY IN WHITE), is more intriguing in parts than as a whole, but it does demonstrate that Laloggia is a rarity: a contemporary horror director with a psycho-sexual agenda rather than a hack mowing down his casts like a Grim Reaper working on commission.

Maintaining a stranglehold on her doting son Tom Hendrix (Morgan Weisser), Olivia Hendrix (Diana Ladd) lacks the normal maternal instinct to back off in the face of her teenager's sexual maturity. Bolstering her possessiveness is the warped Mrs. Jay (Olympia Dukakis), whose friendship masks a chickenhawkish desire to bed young Tom. Egged on by Mrs. Jay, Olivia confiscates letters of college acceptance and scholarship offers and embarrasses Tom in public when he sneaks off for a date with Audrey (Ele Keats).

While Tom's plans to design greeting cards remain tangled in Mama's apron strings, a mystery man, Ben Wilson (Matt Clark) searches for him. It is revealed that Olivia kidnapped Tom from Ben, his father, after a tragic accident; on the day she and Ben brought newborn Tom home from the hospital, his older sibling fell out the window.

Clutching at Tom through a drug overdose and hospitalization, Olivia will stop at nothing to pry him from Audrey; she even bashes in the skull of her psychiatrist Dr. Chase (Scott Wilson) when he attempts to tell Tom that his father is alive.

When frustrated Mrs. Jay is spurned by Tom, she blabs to Olivia that Tom has consummated his relationship with Audrey. As Ben zeros in on his absentee family, crazed Olivia learns about Mrs. Jay's ulterior motive from Audrey, who she electrocutes in a bathtub. Then Olivia knifes Mrs. Jay. Freaked out by the frying of his beloved, Tom almost shoots Olivia. Ben intervenes, but the gun goes off anyway. Wounded, Olivia clings to a fire escape landing, and plunges to her death when it pulls loose from the wall.

Bubbling with repressed sexuality, MOTHER concentrates on heady atmosphere and fleshed-out characterizations—the elements most mainstream horror flicks dispense with altogether. A serious stab at reviving the BABY JANE geriatric-freak shows, MOTHER doesn't exercise enough finesse in integrating its flashbacks to escalate tension. Instead of imploding from its Oedipal taboos at the climax, the film loses power with mini-explosions throughout.

Although the screenwriter is sharp enough to ground Olivia with a MILDRED PIERCE-ian motivation, the director doesn't exploit a fear-and-pity dichotomy in his presentation of this character; instead, this Mommie Dearest becomes FRIDAY THE 13TH's Jason Vorhees in a housedress, despite Ladd's subtle efforts to humanize her maniacal role. Worse off is Dukakis who preens in an ill- conceived part. Her jealousy should register as poisonously intrusive, but Dukakis seems to be playing Auntie Mame fighting her menstrual cycle.

Having laid the groundwork for a truly malevolent chiller, this unusually bleak movie doesn't go deep enough in its Mother-bashing. Because Laloggia chooses not to force our faces down into the darkest reflections of family dysfunction, we remain detached. He plays superficially with abnormal psychology before letting his protagonist go on a typical slasher spree. *(Graphic violence, extreme profanity, adult situations.)* — R.P.

d, Frank Laloggia; p, Patrick Peach; exec p, Stephen Friedman, Sidney Kimmel; co-p, Diane Ladd; w, Michael Angelella; ph, Gerry Lively; ed, Bette Jane Cohen; m, Peter Bernstein; prod d, Jonathan Carlson; art d, Jeremy Cassells; set d, Susan Degas; sound, Itzhail "Ike" Magal (mixer); fx, Larry Fioritto; casting, Elisa Garver; cos, Nadine Reimers; makeup, Francis Kolar; stunts, Rawn Hutchinson

Horror/Thriller **(PR: C MPAA: NR)**

MOTHER NIGHT ★★

(U.S.) 113m Kings Gate Productions; Whyaduck Productions; Fine Line ~ Fine Line c

Nick Nolte *(Howard Campbell)*; Sheryl Lee *(Helga Noth)*; Alan Arkin *(George Kraft)*; John Goodman *(Frank Wirtanen—uncredited)*; Kirsten Dunst *(Resi Noth)*; Arye Gross *(Abraham Epstein)*; Frankie Faison *(Black Fuehrer of Harlem)*; David Strathairn *(Bernard B. O'Hare)*; Bernard Behrens *(Dr. Lionel Jones)*; Norman Rodway *(Werner Noth)*; Anna Berger *(Epstein's Mother)*; Henry Gibson *(Adolph Eichmann's Voice)*; Anthony J. Robinow *(Prison Warden)*; Michael McGill *(Prison Official)*; Shimon Aviel *(Guard Bernard Liebman)*; Bill Corday *(Campbell's Father)*; Brownen Mantel *(Campbell's Mother)*; Brawley Nolte *(Young Howard Campbell)*; Louis Strauss *(Old Jewish Man)*; Zach Grenier *(Joseph Goebbels)*; Richard Zeman *(Rudolph Hess)*; Thomas Hauff *(SS Officer)*; Jeff Pufah *(Young German Soldier)*; Vlasta Vrana *(August Krapptauer)*; Gerard Parkes *(Father Keeley)*; Michael Moran *(Violent Man)*; William Haughland *(TV Reporter)*; Joel Miller *(Israeli Vice-Consul)*; Kurt Vonnegut *(Sad Man on Street)*; Richard Jutras *(G-Man)*; Don Jordan *(Cop)*

The cinematic potential of Kurt Vonnegut's 1961 novel is left frustratingly untapped in this adaptation by Keith Gordon, whose directorial style comes across as an absence of style in which ennui holds sway over drama.

In 1961, American playwright Howard W. Campbell (Nick Nolte) sits in an Israeli jail awaiting trial as a Nazi war criminal. A typewriter, paper, and ribbon are brought to him so he can write his memoirs.

In a series of flashbacks, Campbell is revealed to be the son of an American businessman who had emigrated to Germany after WWI. Campbell became a star in the theatre and the darling of the German literati through his highly moralistic plays and his marriage to the beautiful actress Helga Noth (Sheryl Lee).

One day, he meets a mysterious American, Frank Wirtanen (John Goodman), who offers him the tantalizing opportunity to become a spy for the US government. Campbell does this through the writing and delivering of inflammatory radio broadcast speeches in which America, President Roosevelt, and the Jews are denounced. Hidden within this rhetoric of hatred are secretly encoded messages in the form of coughs, stammers, and snorts. He becomes a hero to the Germans but is reviled by all Americans except the two who are in on the plan—President Roosevelt and Wirtanen. Campbell's considerable ego is stoked by the attention, but his world begins to crumble with the fall of the Reich and Helga's death while entertaining troops at the front.

With Wirtanen's help, Campbell manages to escape to America and live quietly and anonymously in New York's Greenwich Village, where his only friend is a neighboring Jewish artist, George Kraft (Alan Arkin). His life turns around when he learns of a woman trying to escape from East Germany who claims to be Helga. In fact, she is Resi (also played by Lee), Helga's sister, who has long adored Campbell. Wirtanen informs Campbell that Resi and Kraft are Soviet spies hoping to lure Campbell over to their side. After this is revealed, Resi commits suicide and Kraft leaves New York. Suddenly struck by the fact that he has never been in control of his own destiny, Campbell surrenders himself to his neighbor Abraham Epstein (Arye Gross), a survivor of a concentration camp.

After Campbell is arrested, Wirtanen assures him that he will speak at his trial and reveal the truth. Campbell, however, decides to forego the trial and hangs himself instead.

Like Gordon's gruelling THE CHOCOLATE WAR (1988) and A MIDNIGHT CLEAR (1992), this film has a profoundly soporific effect on the viewer. Wars come and go, virulent racism is perpetuated, history marches on, and it's all rendered completely uninvolving at Gordon's weighty hand. Viewers may feel every bit as imprisoned as Campbell in his jail cell, longing for reprieve.

Nolte's performance lacks the passion and depth needed to convey the many layers of Campbell's puffed-up ego, survivor's instinct, and furtive intelligence. He's as wooden as the direction, miring the film even deeper in listlessness. Lee, well-known for her embodiment of the dead Laura Palmer character in the television series "Twin Peaks," seems no more lively here. Most of the other performances are already familiar; Arkin's portrayal of a shifty urbanite with something to hide is dully predictable, and Goodman appears to be reprising the same menacingly jovial role he played in BARTON FINK (1991). Vonnegut himself pops up in a silent cameo, which sums up the lackadaisical feeling of the entire enterprise. *(Violence, sexual situations, adult situations, substance abuse, profanity.)* — D.N.

d, Keith Gordon; p, Keith Gordon, Robert B. Weide; exec p, Ruth Vitale, Mark Ordesky, Linda Reisman; w, Robert B. Weide (based on the novel by Kurt Vonnegut); ph, Tom Richmond; ed, Jay Rabinowitz; m, Michael Convertino; prod d, Francois Seguin; art d, Zoe Sakellaropoulo; set d, Simon LaHaye; sound, Claude Hazanavicius; casting, Valerie McCaffrey; cos, Renee April

Drama/Spy **(PR: C MPAA: R)**

MOTHER OF KINGS ★★★½

(Poland) 120m Film Polski "X" and "Rondo" ~ Polart bw

Henryk Bista *(Gregory)*; Michal Juszczakiewicz *(Stas)*; Adam Ferency *(Zenon)*; Jerzy Stuhr *(Interior Ministry Official)*; Magda Teresa Wojcik *(Lucia)*; Franciszek Pieczka *(Cyga)*; Zbigniew Zapasiewicz *(Victor Lewen)*; Boguslav Lina *(Clement)*

Based on a Kasimierz Brandys novel, *Sons and Comrades*, that appeared after the 1956 reforms, this is one of ten films that the government of communist Poland shelved in 1983 after only one look—and with good reason, since it depicts the destruction of idealist hopes at which Stalin's supporters were so adept, even before WWII. Beginning in 1933, the film covers more than 20 years of Poland's tragic modern history, focusing on a poor Warsaw family.

The father of the Krol family is killed in a streetcar accident, leaving behind his young widow, Lucia (Magda Teresa Wojcik), with three young sons and a fourth on the way. A practical woman, Lucia rather easily resists the sexual blandishments of the carter, Cyga (Franciszek Pieczka), who nevertheless helps out at crucial points in Lucia's life. She is apparently less indifferent to Victor Lewen (Zbigniew Zapasiewicz), a local lawyer, Communist, and Jew, whose office and apartment she cleans. She is sympathetic to his cause and tells him of police interest in his activities. She is, however, unaware of the can of worms represented by his more doctrinaire and senior comrades. Eventually, Lewen is arrested by the Polish police. While in prison he learns that the Polish Communist Party has been officially disbanded on Stalin's express order. One comrade shrugs in disgust and goes to sleep, leaving Lewen to contend with another who launches into a session of self-criticism, figuring that Stalin must have had good reasons for his decision.

The German invasion and the arrival of war cause constant hardship and peril. Lucia has to dodge a Gestapo roundup, all the while caring for her family and Lewen, released and living in her basement. When a drunk German soldier barges in looking for the local whorehouse, a fight with Lewen ensues, leaving the soldier dead. Cyga helps Lucia dispose of the body.

Later, Lucia's favorite son, Clement (Boguslav Lina), is captured by the Gestapo and subsequently sent to Auschwitz. At the end of the war, he returns an idealistic Communist. In one of the film's ironically cheery episodes, he waves to Lewen, up on the podium, from his place among the ranks of happy workers.

Soon, however, Lewen's pre-war political error (his membership in the old, dissolved Communist Party) catches up with him. Clement is arrested, and it becomes clear that he is to be the key witness against Lewen. He refuses to betray his mentor and suffers interrogations and torture for his defiance. Lewen at first promises Lucia his help, but soon realizes the vulnerability of his own position. He does nothing while the police try to extract a confession from Clement. Cyga correctly tells Lucia that the worst treatment in the prisons of the People's Poland is reserved for "heretical" Communists.

One of Lucia's other sons does everything expected of him, becoming a pampered official. The eldest ends up a drunkard, while the youngest becomes a petty criminal. Lucia petitions the new president for help.

MOTHER OF KINGS reveals in explicit detail the nasty inner workings of the Communist Party that help to explain why it collapsed in Poland. The Party had alienated many potential supporters, not to mention the vast majority of ordinary citizens. Using brief documentary film clips, the film is shot in high contrast black-and-white that mirrors the melodrama but can make it difficult to read the subtitles. Many of the principal characters are familiar Polish types, including the martyred Clement; the long-suffering mother, Lucia; and the weary, wise Cyga. Zapasiewicz frequently has played troubled intellectuals, and in this film he is doubly threatened as a member of the old, dissolved Party and as a Jew. Moreover, the lenient pre-war treatment of Lewen, like the far harsher punishment of Clement, is partially contrasted by recitation of the bare facts by the same official voice. With a final irony, the film closes with film clips of the crowds shouting their approval of the 1956 reforms, one of the many false dawns in Polish history. *(Violence, adult situations, sexual situations, nudity.)* — L.R.

d, Janusz Zaorski; p, Andrzej Smulski; w, Janusz Zaorski (based on the novel *Sons and Comrades* by Kasimierz Brandys); ph, Edward Klosinski, Witold Adamek; ed, Jozef Bartczak; m, Przemyslaw Gintrowski; prod d, Teresa Barkska; fx, Zygmunt Nowak; cos, Gabriela Stat-Tyskiewicz; makeup, Aurelia Lopatorska

Political/Historical/Drama **(PR: C MPAA: NR)**

MOTHER'S PRAYER, A ★★

(U.S.) 94m MTE/USA Pictures ~ MCA Universal Home Video c

Linda Hamilton *(Rosemary Holstrom)*; Noah Fleiss *(T. J. Holstrom)*; Bruce Dern *(John Walker)*; Kate Nelligan *(Sheila Walker)*; RuPaul *(Dede)*; S. Epatha Merkerson *(Ruby)*; Corey Parker *(Spence Walker)*; Jenny O'Hara *(Val)*; Gail Strickland *(Ruth)*; McNally Sagal *(Dr. Kahn)*; Aaron Lustig *(Dr. Shapiro)*; Jane Whitney *(Herself)*; Nancy Cassaro *(Sophia)*; Alex Kapp *(Martha)*; James Arone *(Man at Social Services)*; Claire Malis Callaway *(Mrs. Ford)*; Julie Garfield *(JoAnne Wasserman)*; Greg Trock *(Billy)*; Ryan J. O'Neill *(Freddie)*; Barney McFadden *(Mr. Evans)*; Elizabeth Davidson *(Little Girl in Audience)*; Trish Doolan *(A. D.)*; Michael Kearns *(Buddy)*

How terminal illness affects families is often a subject of cinematic scrutiny, but the AIDS epidemic warrants less shallow treatment than A MOTHER'S PRAYER provides.

Without warning, low-risk widow Rosemary Holstrom (Linda Hamilton) is diagnosed HIV-positive at a clinic supervised by Nurse Ruby (S. Epatha Merkerson). Initially disbelieving his mother, then angrily ignoring reality, Rosemary's eight-year-old son T. J. (Noah Fleiss) clings to hopes of her recovery. Increasingly ill, Rosemary storms a bureaucratic Bastille as she personally endeavors to select a new home for her child, even taking her struggle to the media for fast results—an act which aggravates T. J. after his schoolmates see her adoption request plastered on page one of the *New York Daily News*.

With the support of New York's Gay Men's Health Center and the encouragement of fellow AIDS sufferer, Dede (RuPaul), Rosemary enrolls T. J. and herself in psychological counseling. Battling the ravages of the disease, Rosemary accepts the offer of T. J.'s shrink Spence Walker (Corey Parker) to meet his folks John (Bruce Dern) and Sheila (Kate Nelligan), who tentatively offer to raise T. J. Barely able to let go of her son, Rosemary finally consents to the adoption. Coming to terms with his mother's prognosis, estranged T. J. embraces his new family without pulling away from his dying mother.

It's the hem of an old Hollywood Fatal Disease Soap with a few pertinent facts about AIDS sewn in. But chin-quivering nobility doesn't make AIDS a glamorous illness; Linda Hamilton is definitely not Bette Davis, Kay Francis, or even Debra Winger. Each mini-crisis is dragged out interminably and every climax rings with overheard echoes of superior melodrama.

Dying motherhood was better served in the Ann-Margret TV film WHO WILL LOVE MY CHILDREN? (1983). This film's trite treatment of a potentially rich drama will leave audiences painfully disappointed. *(Adult situations, profanity.)* — R.P.

d, Larry Elikann; p, Sally Young; exec p, Lee Rose; w, Lee Rose; ph, Eric Van Haren Noman; ed, Peter White; m, Tom Scott; prod d, James Allen; art d, Leon Ranch; set d, Susan Cordova; sound, Mark Hopkins McNabb; casting, Marsha Kleinman; cos, Dorothy Amos; makeup, Pamela Peitzman; stunts, Chuck Waters

Drama **(PR: C MPAA: PG-13)**

MOUTH TO MOUTH ★½

(Spain) 110m Sogetel; Bocaboca Producciones; Star Line Productions ~ Miramax c

(BOCA A BOCA)

Javier Bardem *(Victor)*; Josep Maria Flotats *(Ricardo)*; Aitana Sanchez-Gijon *(Amanda)*; Maria Barranco *(Angela)*; Myriam Mezieres *(Shiela)*; Jordi Bosch *(Thug)*; Sam Makenzie *(Oswaldo)*; Fernando Guillen-Cuervo *(Raul)*; Amparo Baro *(Margot)*; Candela Pena *(Tanya)*

MOUTH TO MOUTH, a manic Spanish farce, is as charmless as its repugnant hero, a boorish and no-talent hustler who wants to be a movie star. What was clearly intended as an exhilarating fiesta in the tradition of Pedro Almodovar, palls due to an overall lack of wit and talent.

In Madrid, struggling actor Victor (Javier Bardem) is reduced to taking a job as an operator with the Hot Line phone-sex company, run by sleazy Raul (Fernando Guillen-Cuervo). With a movie still of his idol, Robert DeNiro, above his work spot to inspire him, he becomes adept at hustling gay customers, particularly a closeted plastic surgeon named Ricardo (Josep Maria Flotats). Meanwhile, his long-suffering agent Angela (Maria Barranco) is trying to land him a role in an expensive American feature. One night, Victor meets up with the sexy Amanda (Aitana Sanchez-Gijon), another satisfied customer of his who claims to be Ricardo's wife. Completely besotted by this vamp, he agrees to help her get a divorce by setting Ricardo up in an incriminating gay love-nest situation. To their surprise, a hit man arrives on the scene, and Ricardo and Victor narrowly escape being gunned down. They figure out that they were actually set up by Ricardo's real wife Margot (Amparo Baro) and her lover, David (Emilio Guttierez Caba), Ricardo's double-dealing business partner. Sleazy Raul helped arrange the whole thing, implicating Amanda, the wife he abuses between her go-go gigs at the racy nightclub, *Boca a Boca*. With the hit man still hot on his trail, Victor struggles to make sense of his love for Amanda while keeping appointments with the upcoming film's director (Sam Makenzie) and sexpot star Tanya Reynolds (Candela Pena). In the end, Victor not only averts getting killed, but ends up landing the film job.

This belabored farce, chock full of misogyny and homophobia, is a miss in almost every way. Striving for the outrageous ebullience of Almodovar or Bigas Luna, Manuel Gomez Pereira has taken a complicated story and staged it frenetically—but only to a weary, desperate effect. Pereira might have at least injected some sensuality into his film but, for all its piquant phone trysts and slithery seduction scenes, MOUTH TO MOUTH is as sexless as a rubber chicken.

The actors don't help the situation any. As Victor, Bardem has the overripe good looks of a young Anthony Quinn, but much of Quinn's overbearing quality, as well. (Even sadder, Bardem does what must be the millionth bad impersonation of DeNiro in TAXI DRIVER, to boot.) As Ricardo, Flotat's performance is almost as annoying—it's the kind of limp-wrist, asexual portrait of a repressed homosexual that should have gone out with the Hays Code. If possible, though, the women are even more caricatured. As Amanda, Sanchez-Gijon is fetching indeed, but what a clueless bimbo she's called upon to play! Baro is a conniving shrew, played without any self-dramatizing humor. Barranco tries to drum up some of the blithe charm she's evinced for Almodovar, but utterly is defeated. And as for the dragon-ish Pena, well, she's just scary. Some have called Pena's character a takeoff on Sharon Stone. Unfortunately, satire demands both keen observation and wit to carry it off. Here, the filmmakers have none.*(Nudity, adult situations, sexual situations, substance abuse, violence, profanity.)* — D.N.

d, Manuel Gomez Pereira; p, Cesar Benitez, Joaquin Oristrell, Manuel Gomez Pereira; exec p, Cesar Benitez, Fernando Garcillan; assoc p, Juan Alexander; w, Joaquin Oristrell, Juan Luis Iborra, Naomi Wise, Manuel Gomez Pereira; ph, Juan Amoros; ed, Guillermo Represa; m, Bernardo Bonezzi; art d, Luis Valle; sound, Carlos Faruolo; cos, Nereida Bonmati; makeup, Karmele Soler

Comedy **(PR: O MPAA: R)**

MRS. MUNCK ★★½

(U.S.) 99m All Media Inc.; Showtime ~ Republic Pictures Home Video c

Diane Ladd *(Mrs. Rose Munck)*; Bruce Dern *(Patrick Leary)*; Kelly Preston *(Young Rose Munck)*; Shelley Winters *(Aunt Monica)*; Scott Fisher *(Felix)*; Jim Walton *(Harley)*; Vincent Sciullo *(Marine)*; Seymour Cassell *(Gem)*; Michael Rhodes *(Glass Man)*; Darryl Palmer *(Man in Restaurant)*; Mickie Moore *(Woman in Restaurant)*; Bernard Irene *(Maitre D')*; Phallon Carpino *(2 Year-Old Daughter)*; Travis Kyle Davis *(Boy)*; Chris Leavens *(Steve)*

Diane Ladd is star, director, and screenwriter of MRS. MUNCK, a nostalgia binge about an embittered woman victimized by her memories and nearly driven mad by her inability to bend the past to her own will.

At the funeral of her ineffectual but loving spouse, Harley (Jim Walton), Rose Munck (Diane Ladd) explains in a voice-over how she's going to bear widowhood by becoming the caregiver to unloved ex-business magnate Patrick Leary (Bruce Dern). Nursing deep resentment toward this grumpy old man, the redoubtable Mrs. Munck puts him on a health regimen that borders on cruel and unusual punishment.

It seems that, years before, married community pillar Patrick seduced and abandoned country bumpkin Rose Munck (Kelly Preston). After young Rose refused an abortion and bore his child, Patrick threatened to sue for custody of the girl. During an altercation between the warring couple, their daughter was accidentally killed by a falling steam iron.

Now in control of the man who ruined her life, Mrs. Munck refuses to let ailing Patrick indulge in self-pity, and bamboozles his relatives, who don't want to reclaim the old coot anyway. Despite the remorseful strides Patrick makes, simmering anger over their shared tragedy makes rapprochement impossible. Having restored the decrepit ingrate to a dignified, vital state, a saddened but relieved Mrs. Munck realizes their karmic bond is broken, and she can let go of Patrick and her past.

Superbly performed by Ladd and ex-husband Dern, MRS. MUNCK is a delicate character study marred by Ladd's frivolous meddling with the story's tone. Jumping all over the genre map, MRS. MUNCK is alternately a black comedy, nostalgia workout, MISERY-type horror-thriller, and twisted love story. Nor does the wide range of moods seem intentional; this actors' duel doesn't have its feet planted on terra firma. Fortunately, as Mrs. Munck bakes up a lifetime of gripes into a humble pie for her captive ward, the two stars have ample opportunity to scintillate.

Ladd opts for a different perspective on the theme of revenge. There are, after all, positive side effects to the enforced rejuvenation of her old flame. Ladd tries to embroider her film with filigrees of irony, but she is constantly thwarted by flashbacks which needlessly throw ice water on the piping-hot exchanges between the aged Mrs. Munck and her decaying beau.

Ladd stretches her considerable talents a wee bit thin here. Flexing more directorial muscle than screenwriting savvy, she elicits smooth performances in the service of a fatally flawed concept.*(Extreme profanity, nudity, violence, adult situations.)* — R.P.

d, Diane Ladd; p, Barbara Boyle, Michael Taylor; exec p, Diane Ladd; assoc p, Scott Alsop, Christopher Cuddihy; co-p, Stephanie Durkos; w, Diane Ladd (from the novel by Ella Lefflang); ph, James Glennon; ed, Maysie Hoy; m, Leonard Rosenman; prod d, James Allen; art d, Peter Grundy; set d, James Ferrell Jr.; sound, Bryan Day (mixer); fx, Laird McMurray; casting, Beth Klein, Clare Walker; cos, Linda Matheson; makeup, Frances McMurray; stunts, Shane Cardwell

Comedy/Drama **(PR: C MPAA: R)**

MRS. WINTERBOURNE ★½

(U.S.) 104m A & M Films; TriStar ~ TriStar c

Shirley MacLaine *(Grace Winterbourne)*; Ricki Lake *(Connie Doyle)*; Brendan Fraser *(Bill/Hugh Winterbourne)*; Miguel Sandoval *(Paco)*; Loren Dean *(Steve DeCunzo)*; Peter Gerety *(Father Brian)*; Jane Krakowski *(Christine)*; Debra Monk *(Lieutenant Ambrose)*; Cathryn de Prume *(Renee)*; Kate Hennig *(Sophie)*; Susan Haskell *(Patricia Winterbourne)*; Justin Van Lieshout; Alec Thomlison *(Baby Hughie)*; Jennifer Irwin *(Susan)*; Victor Young *(Dr. Hopley)*; Tony Munch *(Steve's Pal)*; Nesbitt Blaisdell *(Homeless Man)*; David Lipman *(Conductor)*; Jim Feather *(Conductor)*; Irene Pauzer *(Woman on Train)*; Bertha Leverone *(Vera)*; Johnie Chase *(Detective at Steve's)*; Craig Eldridge *(Ambrose's Assistant)*; Jack Mosshammer *(Scuzzy Friend)*; Santino Buda *(Scuzzy Friend)*; Marco Kyris *(Scuzzy Friend)*; Thomas Joyce *(Jeweler)*; Tom Harvey *(Ty Winthrop)*;

Caroline Yli-Loumi *(Florist)*; Peter Fleming *(Wedding Planner)*; Joa Gamelin *(Wedding Gown Designer)*; Colin Fox *(Wedding Guest)*; Joan Luchak *(Wedding Guest)*; Melanie Zuber *(Wedding Guest)*; Bob McAlpine; Rob Gusevs; Shawn Eisenberg; Glyn Stephens *(Music Combo)*

Though it's actually a remake of the 1950 Barbara Stanwyck drama NO MAN OF HER OWN, audiences can be excused for mistaking this flat romance for an instant remake the 1996 hit WHILE YOU WERE SLEEPING.

Connie Doyle (Rickie Lake) is a very pregnant young woman with no money, no family—no *nothing*. She ends up on a train where she meets Hugh Winterbourne (Brendan Fraser), a Boston blue blood who's bringing his pregnant wife home to meet his family for the first time. The train wrecks, the newlyweds are killed, and when Connie wakes up a week later in a hospital, she has a baby boy and a new identity.

Having been mistaken for the new Mrs. Winterbourne, Connie is taken in by Hugh's fabulously wealthy family. She wants to be honest, but because she also wants the best for her son, she goes along with the charade. Though matriarch Grace Winterbourne (Shirley MacLaine) takes a shine to her, snobby Bill (Brendan Fraser) suspects something amiss when he meets his late twin brother's decidedly lower class widow. However, after a kiss and a tango in the night, Bill falls under Connie's spell. They fall in love and plan to marry.

The day before the wedding, Steve DeCunzo (Loren Dean)—the man who impregnated Connie and threw her out—shows up with blackmail on his mind. Connie wants to kill him, but someone else beats her to it. When the police come around, Grace confesses to protect Connie. No need—the cops have the culprit; Steve's latest girlfriend had grown to detest him as much as Connie had. Connie comes clean about her true identity and, with Grace's blessing, Connie Doyle finally becomes the real Mrs. Winterbourne.

MRS. WINTERBOURNE is based on the Cornell Woolrich mystery *I Married a Dead Man*, which has been adapted for the screen twice before, in NO MAN OF HER OWN (1950) and I MARRIED A SHADOW (1982), both of which were dramas. This attempt to put a "romantic comedy spin" on the material yields miserable results. The movie starts out depressing and only improves to bland. It might have helped if more had been made of the "fish out of water" class collision, but even that probably wouldn't have been enough.

Ricki Lake gained select fame in John Waters' comedies (HAIRSPRAY, for one), and then got really famous hosting a daytime talk show. That stint seems to have deteriorated her acting skills. She never finds a consistent tone for her character—one moment she's scared and overwhelmed, the next she's droll and self-satisfied. Mostly, Lake just displays the "roll with the punches" demeanor she's developed refereeing verbal wrestling matches on TV. *(Profanity.)* — P.R.

d, Richard Benjamin; p, Dale Pollock, Ross Canter, Oren Koules; exec p, Patrick Palmer; w, Phoef Sutton, Lisa-Maria Radano (based on the novel *I Married a Dead Man* by Cornell Woolrich); ph, Alex Nepomniaschy; ed, Jacqueline Cambas, William Fletcher; m, Patrick Doyle; prod d, Evelyn Sakash; art d, Dennis Davenport; set d, Casey Hallenbeck; sound, Richard Lightstone (mixer); fx, Michael Kavanagh; casting, Nancy Foy; cos, Theoni V. Aldredge; makeup, Christine Hart; stunts, Larry McLean

Comedy/Romance/Drama (PR: C MPAA: PG-13)

MULHOLLAND FALLS ★★½

(U.S.) 107m Largo Entertainment; The Zanuck Company; MGM ~ MGM/UA c

Nick Nolte *(Hoover)*; Melanie Griffith *(Katherine)*; Chazz Palminteri *(Coolidge)*; Michael Madsen *(Eddie Hall)*; Chris Penn *(Relyea)*; Treat Williams *(Fitzgerald)*; Jennifer Connelly *(Allison Pond)*; Daniel Baldwin *(McCafferty)*; Andrew McCarthy *(Jimmy Fields)*; John Malkovich *(Timms)*; Kyle Chandler *(Captain)*; Ed Lauter *(Earl)*; Larry Garrison *(Perino's Maitre d')*; Chelsea Harrington *(Lolita)*; Johna Johnson *(Bar Woman)*; Rick Johnson *(Staff Car Sergeant)*; Britt Burr *(Staff Car Driver)*; Melinda Clarke *(Cigarette Girl)*; Ernie Livley *(Foreman)*; Richard Sylbert *(Coroner)*; Michael Krawic *(Assistant Coroner)*; Titus Welliver *(Kenny Kamins)*; Robert Peters *(Cop #1)*; Father William M. Thigpen *(Priest)*; Drew Pillsbury *(Chief'sAssistant)*; Brad Hunt *(Guard)*; Aaron Neville *(Nite Spot Singer)*; Buddy Joe Hooker *(DC-3 Pilot)*; Eddie Caicedo *(Gasping Patient)*; Price Carson *(Honor Guard)*; Azalea Davila *(Perino's Girl)*; Sky Solari *(Perino's Girl)*; Alisa Christensen *(Spaghetti Girl)*; William Petersen *(uncredited)*; Rob Lowe *(uncredited)*; Bruce Dern *(uncredited)*; Louise Fletcher *(uncredited)*

MULHOLLAND FALLS, Lee Tamahori's flashy, 1950s cop melodrama, takes its title from a remote Los Angeles palisade that offers a long trip down for anyone unlucky enough to be thrown from it. This movie celebrates a rascally band of LA cops and their derivative hard-boiled swagger.

Max Hoover (Nick Nolte) is the hard-drinking, volatile leader of the husky quartet, high on testosterone and short on benevolence towards the crooks and lowlifes who cross their path. Coolidge (Chazz Palminteri) is the most amiable of the foursome, while Eddie (Michael Madsen) is the most debonair, and Relyea (Chris Penn), the heaviest. Hoover gets a surprise when called on to investigate the death of Allison Pond (Jennifer Connelly), a voluptuous "party girl" whose broken body is found embedded in the ground of remote construction site. Hoover is shaken: some time back and unbeknownst to his wife, Katherine (Melanie Griffith), he had an affair with Allison. When a steamy home movie of Allison and an unidentified older man is sent to his office, Hoover goes looking for answers, as much to save his own skin as to find the killer. The film was sent by Allison's best friend, Jimmy Fields (Andrew McCarthy), an amateur filmmaker with a penchant for secretly filming Allison and her "dates"—Hoover among them. Fields identifies the older man as General Thomas Timms (John Malkovich), head the Atomic Energy Commission. Shortly after, Fields is found murdered. Hoover and his cohorts sneak into the restricted desert army base near the A-bomb test site but are halted by the hard-nosed Colonel Fitzgerald (Treat Williams), who takes Hoover to see General Timms. Timms admits to having spent part of the weekend in question with Allison, but naturally insists that when he left her, she was still alive.

Meanwhile, Katherine is sent a copy of one of Fields's films, this one starring Allison and her own husband, and she threatens to leave. Hoover receives a phone call from Fitzgerald, who is ready to bargain. He'll swap the original film of Hoover and Allison for the one with Timms. Hoover studies the Timms film one last time, this time taking special notice of inexplicable opening shots of an army barracks and a bandaged soldier that precede the sex play. He and Coolidge drive out to the base, and while waiting for Fitzgerald, Hoover recognizes the barracks from the film. Breaking in, he discovers a ward full of dying soldiers, each covered with tumors and radiation burns. Hoover realizes that Allison also had made this discovery, and that's why she was killed. Hoover and Coolidge drive to Timms's house, where they find the general also dying of cancer. Timms admits to the human radiation experiments, but still denies killing Allison, and orders Fitzgerald to fly the cops back to LA. Midflight, it dawns on Hoover that Allison's body had been thrown from a plane, and that he and Coolidge are about to meet the same fate at the hands of Allison's killer: Colonel Fitzgerald. A gunfight breaks out, and Hoover and Coolidge toss the colonel and his flunky out the open jump door. The seriously wounded pilot crash-lands the plane in the desert, but Coolidge, who also had been shot, soon dies in Hoover's arms. At the funeral, Katherine tells Hoover that she can't forget his infidelity and that their marriage is over. With Coolidge dead, Hoover breaks up the squad.

Nick Nolte, whose sheer physical presence has driven and/or rescued many a film, works mightily to give Hoover the rugged, complex individuality required, but it's an uphill struggle. Pete Dexter's script, though peppered with some suitably hard-boiled dialogue, doesn't leave much room for audience empathy, and the miscasting of Griffith as Hoover's domestic, '50s-style "little woman" pushes the movie into an unintentionally comedic no-man's land. The script, based on a story by Floyd Mutrux, borrows unabashedly from Roman Polanski's CHINATOWN (1974), with its elaborate film noir plot twists involving lurid sex, betrayal and corruption in high places, but the whole thing suffers from the inevitable comparison. Richard Sylbert's admirably detailed production design looks flat next to his work in Polanski's film, while David Grusin's Goldsmith-style musical score is completely forgettable. And aside from some breathtaking desert vistas, even Haskell Wexler's cinematography is a disappointment. This is a movie made by people who appreciate and, in some cases, have been connected with excellent films from the past. Still, MULHOLLAND FALLS, for all its style and cleverness, wears thin after its first half-hour, perhaps because while imitation may be the sincerest form of flattery, it can also be the most tiresome. *(Violence, profanity, nudity, sexual situations.)* — E.K.

d, Lee Tamahori; p, Richard D. Zanuck, Lili Fini Zanuck; exec p, Mario Iscovich; w, Pete Dexter (from a story by Floyd Mutrux and Pete Dexter); ph, Haskell Wexler; ed, Sally Menke; m, Dave Grusin; prod d, Richard Sylbert; art d, Gregory William Bolton; set d, Claire Jenora Bowin; sound, James E. Webb Jr. (mixer), Gary Ritchie (recordist), Kathleen McCart (recordist); fx, Thomas R. Ward; casting, Shari Rhodes, Joseph Middleton; cos, Ellen Mirojnick; makeup, Mike Hancock, Matthew W. Mungle, John E. Jackson; stunts, Buddy Joe Hooker

Crime/Mystery/Drama **(PR: O MPAA: R)**

MULTIPLICITY ★

(U.S.) 110m Columbia ~ Columbia c

Michael Keaton *(Doug Kinney)*; Andie MacDowell *(Laura Kinney)*; Zack Duhame *(Zack Kinney)*; Katie Schlossberg *(Jennifer Kinney)*; Harris Yulin *(Dr. Leeds)*; Richard Masur *(Del King)*; Eugene Levy *(Vic)*; Ann Cusack *(Noreen)*; John DeLance *(Ted)*; Judith Kahan *(Franny)*; Obba Babatunde *(Paul)*; Brian Doyle-Murray *(Walt)*; Julie Bowen *(Robin)*; Dawn Maxey *(Beth)*; Kari Coleman *(Patti)*; Steven Kampmann *(Coach Jack)*; Michael Milhoan *(Irate Football Parent)*; Skip Stellrecht *(Irate Football Parent)*; James Piddock *(Maitre d')*; Robin Duke *(Ballet School Receptionist)*; Suzanne Herrington *(Den Mother)*; Robert Ridgely *(Laura's Father)*; Glenn Shadix *(Building Inspector)*; Dennis R. Lyell *(Construction Worker)*; Richard Plon *(Lab Technician Twin)*; Harold Plon *(Lab Technician Twin)*; George D. Wallace *(Man in Restaurant)*; Justine A. Johnston *(Woman in Restaurant)*

This is an utterly awful movie, to the nth degree, from a very talented pair of comedians who, one has to assume, were busy elsewhere while their doubles made it.

Doug Kinney (Michael Keaton) is an architect whose demands at home and at work are tearing him apart. In danger of losing his job to vicious backstabbing rival Ted (John DeLancie) if he doesn't put in triple overtime, and in danger of losing his wife, Laura (Andie McDowell) and two kids if he does, Doug discovers a solution when he works on a job for a Malibu institute. There, he encounters Dr. Leeds (Harris Yulin), a mysterious scientist. Dr. Leeds has discovered a way to clone a fully grown, completely functional copy of anyone, and offers Doug the opportunity to be in two places at once.

At first, a bit put out with a second body to care for and secretly house, Doug sends the clone to work in order to spend more time at home. The results are so satisfactory for Doug that he soon opts for a third copy of himself to have around the house so he can make a little time for himself and learn how to sail. The clones begin to splinter into (entirely predictable) personalities: the testosterone-laden #1 kicks ass and takes names at the construction site where Doug works, firing perpetual goof-up Vic (Eugene Levy); the more effete #2 lectures Laura on food wrapping and storage procedures and even speaks with a slight lisp. Behind Doug's back, they make yet another clone to clean up their dorm and order pizza. This one suffers a bit from the degradation of repeated copying and has no social or physical graces.

Doug eventually loses his job when the clones switch roles. The plot gets hung up on the queasy subject of the multiples bedding Laura, who eventually gets to have sex with all three clones in one night (while the original Doug is off boating). When the truth inevitably comes out, Laura packs up the kids and, not surprisingly, makes tracks. Pulling his clones into a combination of pseudo-family and serf-like laborers, Doug finally attempts to woo Laura back by rebuilding the house that has been under construction forever. And, of course, since this is supposed to be a comedy, it works, and the clones drive off into the sunset to find themselves—in Las Vegas.

This is a shockingly dull film to come from Harold Ramis, veteran of Second City and the creator of GROUNDHOG DAY (1993), a funny and wise film with a similarly fantastic premise. Directed with a banality worthy of a sub-par sitcom, Ramis slugs along from one poorly conceived bit to the next, neither building toward some kind of climax nor providing anything entertaining enough to fill the time.

But it's not entirely Ramis's fault; he didn't actually write this mess. The moment the names Lowell Ganz and Babaloo Mandel appear on the screen, abandon all hope. There are no actual jokes in the script, and the desperation with which Keaton grasps for amusing readings and funny expressions is too depressing to describe. With the possible exception of one exchange with his clone, culminating in macho chest-butting, there isn't even a semblence of the exuberant, sardonic mania that is Keaton's sole comedic strength. Opposite the lovely but bland MacDowell, whom he spends most of the film avoiding, there are no opportunities for snappy dialogue or sexual banter beyond a few moments of frat-boy innuendo.

This film is best forgotten, lest it sully the reputations of Keaton and Ramis, who have done, and doubtless will do, better. (One last sad footnote: Keaton's character is named for one of Ramis's personal friends and co-founder of *The National Lampoon,* the late Doug Kenney, a brilliant, original clown who deserves a better memorial than this dumb movie.) *(Adult situations, profanity.)* — R.S.

d, Harold Ramis; p, Trevor Albert, Harold Ramis; exec p, Lee R. Mayes; assoc p, Suzanne Herrington; co-p, Whitney White; w, Chris Miller, Mary Hale, Lowell Ganz, Babaloo Mandel (based on the short story by Chris Miller); ph, Laszlo Kovacs; ed, Pam

Herring, Craig Herring; m, George Fenton; prod d, Jackson DeGovia; art d, Geoff Hubbard; set d, K.C. Fox; sound, Dennis L. Maitland Sr. (mixer), Sandy Berman (design); fx, Richard Edlund, Tom Ryba, Brian Samuels, Boss Film Studios; casting, Howard Feuer; cos, Shay Cunliffe; makeup, Cheri Minns, Matthew W. Mungle, John E. Jackson; stunts, Mike Cassidy

Comedy/Fantasy **(PR: C MPAA: PG-13)**

MUPPET TREASURE ISLAND ★★½

(U.S.) 99m Jim Henson Productions; Walt Disney Pictures ~ Buena Vista c

Tim Curry *(Long John Silver)*; Kevin Bishop *(Jim Hawkins)*; Billy Connolly *(Billy Bones)*; Jennifer Saunders *(Mrs. Bluveridge)*; Frederick Warder *(Calico Jerry)*; Peter Greeves *(Black Eyed Pea)*; Danny Blackner *(Short Stack Stevens)*; Harry Jones *(Easy Pete)*

This adaptation of Robert Louis Stevenson's classic adventure novel features plenty of not-too-menacing pirates, and exactly the sort of schtick one expects from the Muppets. It will provide an entertaining diversion for children and adults.

Orphan Jim Hawkins (Kevin Bishop) and his friends Rizzo the Rat and The Great Gonzo toil in a tavern, fantasizing about adventure on the high seas. When patron Billy Bones (Billy Connolly) dies and leaves the infamous Captain Flint's treasure map in Jim's hands, those dreams become reality faster than you can say, "Yo, ho, ho and a bottle of rum."

The threesome find themselves aboard the *Hispainiola*, an unusual ship with a frog (Kermit as Captain Smollett) at the helm, rats booked as tourists, and hecklers Statler and Waldorf on the bow as figureheads. Jim is befriended by Long John Silver (Tim Curry), the ship's peg-legged cook, who has a talking lobster named Polly. Silver has secretly stocked the crew with pirates, and plans to mutiny once they reach Skeleton Island. The voyage is long and hard, and includes some production numbers.

When they reach the island, Silver and his men overtake the ship and put ashore, with Jim as their hostage, to find Flint's buried treasure. Attempting a rescue, Smollett, Rizzo, and Gonzo are captured by the native swine. The pigs' queen is none other than (you guessed it) Miss Piggy, an old girlfriend of Smollett's, who had been stranded on the island by Flint. She has the treasure now, and when Silver comes after it, he and Smollett cross swords. In the end, the good guys make it back to the *Hispainiola* safely and set sail for England. The mutineering pirates are left behind on the island. Silver manages to escape with a chest of gold. . . in a very leaky rowboat.

The second Muppet movie produced since the death of creator Jim Henson, MUPPET TREASURE ISLAND suggests that the Muppets (now under the direction of Henson's son, Brian) are charting a new course—literary adaptations. 1992's THE MUPPET CHRISTMAS CAROL was a fine effort, mixing the Muppets in Dickens's tale without detracting from the drama. MUPPET TREASURE ISLAND is, frankly, not as good, but it's hard to harbor too much ill will towards a movie so eager to entertain.

At the movie's outset, Stevenson's sense of adventure and the Muppet brand of humor (a mix of wit, slapstick, self-reflexive references, and anachronisms) are blended well. Once the story goes to sea, though, the mix is less successful with too much emphasis on human actors. Curry, who's usually over the top with relish, seems restrained alongside the Muppet scene-stealers, and young Bishop simply doesn't stand a chance. Adding to their handicap are the songs provided by Barry Mann and Cynthia Weil, none of which are particularly catchy or memorable.

Faithful Muppet fans can rest assured all of their favorite characters (Fozzie Bear, Sam Eagle, Bunsen Honeydew, Beaker, the Swedish Chef, Sweet-ums the Monster, and Animal) have roles or make cameos. As with the 1992 film, the two Muppet superstars, Kermit and Miss Piggy, are relegated to supporting, almost minor, roles. This, and the spotlight he chooses to place on his human stars, hints that Brian Henson doesn't have his father's confidence in the "humanity" and appeal of the felt menagerie.— P.R.

d, Brian Henson; p, Brian Henson, Martin G. Baker; assoc p, Michael Jablow; w, Jerry Juhljim Hart, Kirk Thatcher; ph, John Fenner; ed, Michael Jablow; m, Hans Zimmer; prod d, Val Strazovec; art d, Alan Cassie; set d, Simon Wakefield; sound, Peter Lindsay (recordist); fx, Nick Allder, Tom Smith; casting, Mike Fenton, Suzanne Crowley, Gilly Poole; cos, Polly Smith; makeup, Linda Armstrong; stunts, Nick Powell

Children's/Comedy/Musical **(PR: AA MPAA: G)**

MURDERED INNOCENCE ★★

(U.S.) 88m The Rayfield Co. ~ Columbia TriStar Home Video c

Jason Miller *(Detective Rollins)*; Fred Carpenter *(Scott)*; Jacqueline Macario *(Lauren)*; Gary Aumiller *(William "Teach" Spencer)*; Ellen Greene *(Mrs. Baron)*; Bob Shlesinger *(Detective Walters)*; Donna Bostany *(Detective Leone)*; Craig Morris Weintraub *(Young Scott)*; Bryant Holt *(Bateman)*; Victor Campos *(Warden)*; Deborah Mayo *(Desk Clerk)*; John Lee *(Cop Outside Deli)*; Thom Sciacca *(Gas Station Attendant)*; Jeff Edelman *(Guard Driving Van)*; Theresa Vagliardo *(Woman on Bus)*; Frank Coraci *(Wacko on Bus)*; Michael Nolan *(Reporter)*; Eileen Shanahan *(TV Reporter)*; Aloysius Wilson; Doug Hurst; Donald Graham; John Petti; Eddie Freeman; Matt Farago *(Attica Cons)*; Brett Albanese *(Bus Driver)*; Stan Kromfeld *(Scott's Dad)*; Daniel Goldfarb *(Prison Guard Who's Shot)*

MURDERED INNOCENCE throws an inexhaustible supply of sophisticated film technique at the audience. But all its fancy camouflage doesn't distract viewers from deducing the solution of a decades-old murder mystery. Robbed of that central surprise, this jazzed-up thriller merely forestalls the obvious.

Twenty years ago, as a youngster, Scott Baron (Craig Morris Weintraub) stood by helplessly at the stabbing of his mother (Ellen Greene), witnessed the subsequent shooting of his father by police officer Rollins (Jason Miller), and later identified his mother's lover, William Spencer (Gary Aumiller), as his mom's assailant.

Now, after serving time for petty crime in Atlanta, adult Scott (Fred Carpenter) heads for his tragic Long Island home. Meanwhile, hard-drinking Rollins faces a full house in his jurisdiction when parole-denied Spencer busts out of Attica with a gang of loyal inmates and revenge in his heart.

A chance encounter with a sexy hitchhiker nets big trouble for ex-con Scott after his passenger, Lauren (Jacqueline Macario), shoots a masher named Bateman (Bryant Holt), who menaces them on the highway. Already freaked out about learning of Spencer's jailbreak, Scott vacillates about facing the music in his former home, the scene of the 20-year-old crime. Haunted by the Baron case, Detective Rollins isn't forthcoming with his new partner (Donna Bostany) when Scott's name surfaces on the police blotter after the Bateman homicide. Meanwhile, loyal Lauren refuses to abandon Scott.

In a strange turn of events, Scott shoots two of the Attica fugitives while they are robbing a convenience store before heading for his face-off with Spencer. (A flashback now reveals that Spencer accidentally backed Mrs. Baron into scissors wielded by young Scott himself.) After Scott dispatches several Attica escapees, Spencer holds a gun to Lauren's head, forces Scott to disarm, and pistol-whips him. Arriving in the nick of time, Rollins guns down Spencer and then places the Bateman murder weapon in dead Spencer's hand. Feeling guilty about shooting Scott's innocent father, Rollins allows Scott and Lauren to exit without fear of prosecution.

The intriguing MURDERED INNOCENCE raises troubling questions about the aftershocks of a heinous crime and lifts the lid on a Pandora's box of official cover-ups. What it fails to exploit properly is the irony of unjustly jailed Spencer's predicament. In stressing Scott's trial by fire, the film soft-pedals Spencer's fury at being locked up for murder in what was, at best, a third-degree manslaughter case. The director is so busy fidgeting with showy flashbacks that he can't get a grip on the zigzagging screenplay about the different ways guilt manifests itself.

Although neither Aumiller nor Carpenter seems up to the challenge, this thriller should have explored the weird karmic bond between traumatized child-eyewitness and vindictive interloper; there's a suggestion that young Scott wanted to punish Spencer for messing up his happy home life with mom and dad. Compellingly conceived but weakly acted and superficially directed, MURDERED INNOCENCE plays out like an extended episode of "Unsolved Mysteries." *(Graphic violence, extreme profanity, sexual situations, adult situations, substance abuse.)* — R.P.

d, Frank Coraci; p, Phyllis Alia, Fred Carpenter; exec p, Sid Farber, Leonard Weintraub; w, Steven Peros, Frank Coraci, Fred Carpenter; ph, William Francesco; ed, Thomas Lewis, Suzanne Pillsbury ; m, Alan Pasqua; art d, Jack Parente; set d, Jack Parente; sound, Craig Gabor (mixer); casting, John Cameron; cos, Loyce Arthur; makeup, Angela Blumberg

Crime/Drama (PR: C MPAA: R)

MUTANT MAN ★

(U.S.) 73m DeLaurentis & Jim Haas III Productions ~ Dead Alive Home Video c

Yvonne Buchanan *(Charlotte)*; Sula von Woltor *(Fruit Stand Lady)*; Billy Villegas *(Jimmy)*; John Battaglia *(Twitch)*; Carol Furphy *(Vivian)*; Kelley Harkins *(Helen)*; Kate Skwire *(Sandy)*; Amy Wicki *(Maureen)*; Charlie Patiro *(Charlie)*; Christian Monroe *(Eugene)*; Jim Baldi *(Mutant Man/Leroy)*; Joe Giordano *(Jeff)*; Gene Bozzi *(Butch)*; Susan Levin *(Pregnant Woman)*; Jonathan Nurkiewicz *(Young Charlie)*; Gabriella Nurkiewicz *(Young Charlotte)*; Joseph Mazzeo *(Motorcycle Cop)*; Elena Louise Acri *(Farm Girl)*; Jimmy DeLaurentis *(Cop 1)*; R. J. Burns *(Cop 2)*; Joe Wiessner *(Biker 1)*; Wayne Archison *(Biker 2)*; Byran Sorrentino *(Farm Worker 1)*; Byran Knight *(Farm Worker 2)*

As blatant and graceless as its title, MUTANT MAN is bottom-of-the-barrel low-budget horror.

Young, recently widowed Helen (Kelley Harkins) is taking a motor home trip with her sister-in-law Vivian (Carol Furphy), brother Jimmy (Billy Villegas), and sister Sandy (Kate Skwire), along with Jimmy's pal Twitch (John Battaglia) and Sandy's friend Maureen (Amy Wicki). They get lost and come across a fruit stand run by an older woman (Sula von Woltor) and her grown children, Charlotte (Yvonne Buchanan), Charlie (Charlie Patiro), and Eugene (Christian Monroe). One of the "boys" sabotages the motor home, and after it breaks down, the group accepts an invitation to the family's isolated house. They are joined along the way by a couple of cops (Joe Giordano and Gene Bozzi), one of whom is an old college friend of Helen's.

Once at the house, Vivian is lured into the cellar, where she is set upon by huge, deformed son Leroy (Jim Baldi). The whole family proves to be homicidally insane, and as night falls they pick off their visitors one by one. Two more arriving cops are also killed, and Jimmy takes off in their car as the demented brood moves in on Sandy, the only other survivor.

MUTANT MAN is the kind of depressingly opportunistic project made by people who have an idea of what horror films traditionally contain, but no clue about how to craft one. Piling on the cliches without any apparent awareness that they *are* cliches, the movie pillages the likes of THE TEXAS CHAINSAW MASSACRE (1974) and THE HILLS HAVE EYES (1977) without an ounce of their tension or atmosphere. The characters are all one-dimensional and largely caricatures, their dialogue is simple-minded, and despite the overacted dementia of the farm family, none of their guests seems to catch on that hanging around them might be a bad idea.

It's a measure of the movie's storytelling ineptitude that despite the supposed remoteness of the farmhouse, two of the killers chase an early victim right to a crowded football game. The chase-capture-and-kill scenes proceed without a hint of escalating fear, and the ending is abrupt and arbitrary. *(Graphic violence, extensive nudity, sexual situations, substance abuse, profanity.)* — M.G.

d, Suzanne DeLaurentis; p, Suzanne DeLaurentis; exec p, Jim Haas III; assoc p, John T. Wiessner; w, Suzanne DeLaurentis; ph, Dwight Lay; ed, Pietro Cecchini; m, Allen Ett, James Lay; art d, Damon L. Bartraw; sound, Ye Zhang, James Lay; fx, Paul "Cowboy" Swanger; cos, Tonya Lee; makeup, Janice Buck

Horror (PR: O MPAA: NR)

MY FAVORITE SEASON

(SEE: MA SAISON PREFEREE)

MY FELLOW AMERICANS ★★

(U.S.) 101m Peters Entertainment; Storyline Productions; Warner Bros. ~ Warner Bros. c

Jack Lemmon *(Russell P. Kramer)*; James Garner *(Matt Douglas)*; John Heard *(Ted Matthews)*; Dan Aykroyd *(William Haney)*; Sela Ward *(Kaye Griffin)*; Wilford Brimley *(Joe Hollis)*; Everett McGill *(Col. Paul Tanner)*; Bradley Whitford *(Carl Witnaur)*; Lauren Bacall *(Margaret Kramer)*; James Rebhorn *(Charlie Reynolds)*; Esther Rolle *(Rita)*; Conchata Ferrell *(Woman Truck Driver)*; Jack Kehler *(Wayne)*; Connie Ray *(Genny)*; Tom Everett *(Wilkerson)*; Mark Lowenthal *(Caldwell)*; Jeff Yagher *(Dorothy)*; Edwin Newman *(Himself)*; Lynn Clark *(Chrissy Kramer)*; Leigh Rose *(Katherine Douglas)*; Mihoko Tokoro *(Japanese Singer)*; Ken Enomoto *(Hiroshi Ashino)*; Gunnar Peterson *(Bruce)*; Scott Burkholder *(Greg)*; Wayne Duvall *(Chet)*; Jack Garner *(President Haney's Caddy)*; Gene Bolande *(Injured Golf Spectator)*; Francesca Rollins *(Reporter #1)*; Paul Feig *(Reporter #2)*; Cathy Ladman *(Reynolds' Secretary)*; Tom Wright *(Jim)*; Dana Gould *(Sandwich Guy at Book Convention)*; Scott Hoxby *(Man with Subpoena)*; Jonathan Osser *(Kramer's Grandson)*; Mitch Braswell *(Marine One Pilot)*; Art Booth *(Marine One Co-Pilot)*; Steve Carlisle *(Man in Train Station Bathroom)*; Todd McDurmont *(Elvis)*; Madison Wellington *(Tina)*; David "Skippy" Malloy *(Will)*; Jennifer L. Jones *(Fran)*; Bobby Bass *(NSA Hit Man #1)*; Steve Chambers *(NSA Hit Man #2)*; Jimmy Nickerson *(NSA Hit Man #3)*; Cara Gooden *(Truck Stop Girl)*; Matt Zboyovski *(Truck Stop Boy)*; Michael Pena *(Ernesto)*; Alex Joganic *(Kevin)*; Ocie Pouncie *(Man in Diner)*; Neva Howell *(Charlene - Budget Agent)*; Sheri Mann Stewart *(Sandy - Budget Agent)*; Pete Penuel *(Man in Parade)*; John

O'Leary *(Caretaker Ben)*; Leighanne Wallace *(Witnaur's Girlfriend)*; Rick Hall *(White House Guard)*; Eric Siegel *(President Haney's Aide)*; Ann Cusack *(White House Tour Guide)*; Jean Speegle Howard *(Asthmatic Woman on Tour)*; Dorothy Lucey *(News Anchor)*; Jeff Mandon; James Bissell; Shawn D. Woodyard *(Secret Service Agents)*; Stephen Wedan *(Mounted Police #1)*; Tom Sean Foley *(Mounted Police #2)*; Michael Russo *(White House Sharpshooter)*; Chris Kriesa *(Agent Kopeck)*; William Kerr *(V. P. Matthews' Make-Up Man)*; Peter Segal *(TV Technician)*

MY FELLOW AMERICANS is a highly contrived, sitcom-ish tale of two feuding ex-Presidents thrown together to expose a kickback scandal at the Executive level.

Money-grubbing former Republican president Russell P. Kramer (Jack Lemmon) and womanizing former Democratic president Matt Douglas (James Garner), old enemies, are forced to travel together to attend a state funeral. Meanwhile, when White House chief-of-staff Witnaur (Bradley Whitford) informs current President William Haney (Dan Aykroyd) that a defense contract kickback Haney received is about to be exposed, they decide to frame Kramer for the job.

When a bomb explosion on their helicopter nearly kills Kramer and Douglas, the two set out for Kramer's Presidential library in Ohio to get the documents which would clear him. Several cross-country adventures later, they befriend a marcher in a gay pride parade, who gives Kramer a bracelet and arranges for them to ride to Ohio with a lesbian biker gang. At the library, they find that the documents have been tampered with, so they drive to Witnaur's house, kidnap him, and force him to confess to the frame-up. Kramer and Douglas then sneak into the White House and are chased by a rogue agent named Tanner (Everett McGill), who orders his men to shoot them. One of the agents, however, is the man from the gay pride parade; he recognizes Kramer's bracelet and shoots Tanner instead. After hearing Witnaur's taped confession, Haney resigns. Kramer and Douglas realize that Tanner was actually working for Vice-President Matthews (John Heard) who would, of course, be named President when Haney resigned. Douglas gets Matthews to confess to the scheme on tape, Matthews is arrested, and Kramer and Douglas decide to run for re-election together.

As numerous critics have pointed out, MY FELLOW AMERICANS should have been called GRUMPY OLD PRESIDENTS, since it so shamelessly copies the Jack Lemmon-Walter Matthau GRUMPY OLD MEN formula of casting veteran stars as crotchety enemies who insult each other with crude wisecracks for two hours. The busy plot of MY FELLOW AMERICANS is absurdly contrived and implausible, even for a silly mainstream comedy such as this, while the alleged political satire is both toothless and perfunctory. The script's last-minute attempt to insert homilies about learning valuable lessons from the simple folk and showing tolerance and compassion for minorities and gays is insulting and disingenuous, since virtually all of the characters Russell and Douglas meet in the "heartland" are grotesquely stereotyped "wetbacks," hicks, or trailer trash.

Lemmon and Garner are both game; the film's few laughs are due solely to their charisma and comic timing. But the whole production is puposely aimed at the lowest common demoninator, from the cliched script to the heavy-handed direction and bland, TV-style visuals. Hollywood's idea of life in the U.S. in between the two coasts is frightening: all fast-food restaurants, truck stops and dumb working stiffs. As the closing credits roll, John Mellencamp sings "Ain't That America." God, let's hope not.*(Profanity, violence, sexual situations.)* — M.S.

d, Peter Segal; p, Jon Peters; exec p, Craig Zadan, Neil Meron, Tracy Barone; co-p, Jean Higgins, Michael Ewing; w, E. Jack Kaplan, Richard Chapman, Peter Tolan; ph, Julio Macat; ed, William Kerr; m, William Ross; prod d, James Bissell; art d, Gae Buckley; set d, Gary Fettis; sound, Hank Garfield; fx, Alan E. Lorimer; casting, Karen Rea; cos, Betsy Cox; makeup, Steve LaPorte; stunts, Freddie Hice; tech, Robert Snow

Comedy **(PR: C MPAA: PG-13)**

MYSTERY SCIENCE THEATER 3000: THE MOVIE ★★½

(U.S.) 74m Best Brains, Inc. ~ Gramercy Pictures c

Trace Beaulieu *(Dr. Clayton Forrester/Voice of Crow T. Robot)*; Michael J. Nelson *(Mike Nelson)*; Jim Mallon *(Voice of Gypsy)*; Kevin Murphy *(Voice of Tom Servo)*; John Brady *(Benkitnorf)*

MYSTERY SCIENCE THEATRE 3000: THE MOVIE is the big-screen version of the cult cable TV show about a man in outer space and his two robot pals who make sarcastic remarks as they're being subjected to some of the worst movies ever made.

A mad scientist named Dr. Clayton Forrester (Trace Beaulieu) tells us that he is engaged in a diabolical experiment which will enable him to take over the world. He has sent a man named Mike Nelson (Michael J. Nelson) into space and is forcing him, along with his robot assistants Crow and Tom, to watch an unending series of horrible movies in order to drive them insane.

The movie they're viewing today is a 1955 Technicolor sci-fi epic from Universal-International called THIS ISLAND EARTH. The plot concerns the adventures of stalwart scientist Cal Meachum (Rex Reason), who's working on atomic energy. He's invited to a research center along with a group of other experts, where he meets, and romances, the attractive Dr. Ruth Adams (Faith Domergue). Cal and Ruth learn that their hosts are actually aliens who want plutonium so that they can conquer the earth. While trying to escape in a plane, Cal and Ruth are sucked up into a spaceship which takes them to the planet Metaluna. After tangling with a giant, mutant bug-like creature, they manage to destroy the planet and return safely to earth. The screening of the film is interrupted twice for some "comical" vignettes aboard the spacecraft, involving Mike and the robots, and Dr. Forrester returns after the film is over to wrap things up.

MYSTERY SCIENCE THEATER 3000, the TV show, is the kind of thing one comes across while channel surfing at two in the morning. Watching it is a bit like eating junk food: at first you resist, then you're sucked in and get giddy while overindulging, then you feel a sense of guilt and a finally, a hollow, empty void. The concept of ridiculing and laughing at old movies is probably the apotheosis of smug, smart-aleck post-modernism, but at its best, the show can inspire uncontrollable laughter. With its relentless, scattershot stream of esoteric showbiz in-jokes, hip pop-culture references and schoolboy wisecracks, it can be hysterical when its targets are straight-faced educational films or bottom-of-the-barrel exploitation pics.

The problem with MYSTERY SCIENCE THEATER 3000: THE MOVIE is that it's not nearly as funny as the TV series on which it's based, because the film which has been chosen to be spoofed is not that bad. In fact, in terms of writing, direction, production design and overall imagination, it's clearly superior to the spoofer. There are a few good laughs, but the only thing that distinguishes this from a TV episode is the use of some mild profanity and a surprisingly inordinate number of gay jokes. Although the running time is even shorter than a typical TV episode, this is actually a good thing, since the whole concept wears out its welcome pretty quickly.

However, THIS ISLAND EARTH ends up being cut by almost a half-hour, which hardly seems fair given that it's set up as a dead duck to begin with. The probable reason it was chosen is simply because Universal owns the rights to it, it's in garish Technicolor, and it features some risible alien makeup effects. If the makers of MSTK3: THE MOVIE really wanted to rip into a bad 1950s Universal sci-fi pic, they should have chosen THE MOLE PEOPLE (1956) or THE LEECH WOMAN (1960), but of course, those are in "dull" black-and-white, which we know nobody will pay to see. THIS ISLAND EARTH is certainly no classic, with its wooden acting and the usual dated technology, but it did have a fairly large budget and features some striking sets, decent effects (for its era), and an oddly compelling plot.

As for the lame new segments featuring Dr. Forrester, Mike and the crew of the spaceship, suffice it to say that they are what the fast-forward button was invented for. In the end, the whole MSTK3 phenomenon merely represents the epitome of self-conscious passivity: we are sitting at home, or in a theater, watching a movie and laughing at others who are watching a movie and making fun of it. Television ultimately has the reductive effect of grinding everything it touches to the same mundane level of utter banality, and even the cinematic experience is not safe from its clutches. *(Profanity.)* — M.S.

d, Jim Mallon; p, Jim Mallon; assoc p, Trace Beaulieu, Kevin Murphy; w, Michael J. Nelson, Trace Beaulieu, Jim Mallon, Kevin Murphy, Mary Jo Pehl, Paul Chaplin, Bridget Jones (based on the TV show "Mystery Science Theater 3000" created by Joel Hodgson); ph, Jeff Stonehouse; ed, Bill Johnson; m, Billy Barber; prod d, Jef Maynard; set d, Blakesley Clapp; sound, Thomas A. Naunas (mixer); fx, Paul Murphy, Eric Howell, PM Effects; cos, Linda Froiland; makeup, Andrea Jackson DuCane, Robert I. Phillips, Glen Griffin

Comedy **(PR: C MPAA: PG-13)**

NAKED SOULS ★★

(U.S.) 90m Vanguard Entertainment ~ WarnerVision c

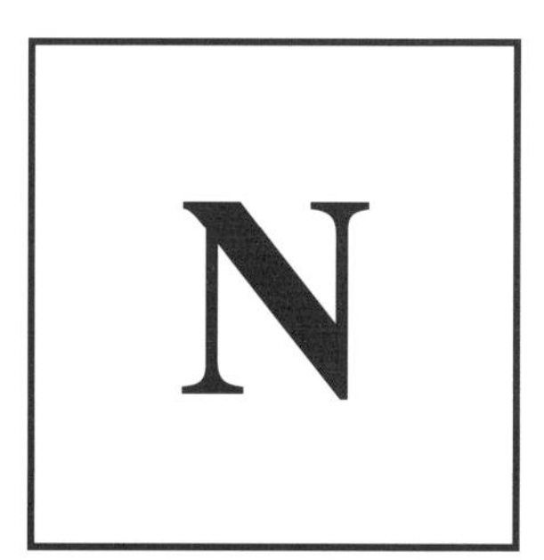

Pamela Anderson *(Britanny "Brit" Clark)*; Brian Krause *(Edward Adams)*; David Warner *(Everett Longstreet)*; Clayton Rohner *(Jerry)*; Justina Vail *(Amelia)*; Dean Stockwell *(Duncan Ellis)*; Victor Talmadge *(Travis)*; Elizabeth Low *(Model)*; Deryl Carroll *(Clinic Doctor)*; Pat Malicano *(1st Paramedic)*; Alex Manette *(2nd Paramedic)*; Yonda Davis *(Nurse)*; Jennifer Collins *(Hospital Doctor)*; Michael Papajohn *(Driver)*; Thomas Milan *(Homeless Man)*; Chris Holder *(Cop)*; Chantel King *(Woman in Bath)*; Jackie Brune *(Woman in Car)*; Seana Ryan *(Woman in Pool)*; Keita *(Woman in Doorway)*

NAKED SOULS has little going for it beyond the pneumatic talents of Pamela Anderson. The "Baywatch" star's presence lends elevated hype to this otherwise forgettable story of body-switching.

Artist Brit Clark (Anderson) is having her first gallery show. Her mood is dampened, however, by the late arrival of her scientist boyfriend, Edward (Brian Krause). Edward's experiments have brought him very close to "digitizing the chemical components of memory," which will allow him to record memories on a computer. Brit is angry that Edward's work leaves little time for her. Leaving the gallery, Edward meets a mysterious man in a wheelchair.

The next day Edward learns that his grant was not approved, despite his success in recording the memories of a deceased serial killer. Fatefully, Edward again encounters the mysterious man, who identifies himself as Everett Longstreet (David Warner), a brilliant, dying scientist. Wishing for some kind of immortality, Longstreet offers his estate to Edward provided that the young man legally assume Longstreet's identity. Longstreet shows Edward mystical techniques that allow him access to collective memory. This inspires Edward, and his work progresses quickly. Despite this success, Edward is plagued by strange, violent dreams. This problem is forgotten, however, when Brit arrives to rekindle their romance. While Brit and Edward make love, Longstreet tampers with Edward's computer programs. Later, Edward begins his experiment, entering a chamber that will record his memories.

Longstreet has other plans, however, and when Edward exits the chamber, he finds that Longstreet has switched bodies with him and, even worse, poisoned him; he manages to call for help before collapsing.

In Edward's body, Longstreet attempts to impress Brit with money. Sensing something odd, Brit is scornful of him. Angered by this rejection, Longstreet-as-Edward storms out and is overcome by violent imagery and impulses. He realizes that Edward's brain is corrupted with the serial killer's memories. He goes to Edward-as-Longstreet in the hospital, telling him that he has kidnapped Brit and will kill her if Edward does not help him. Back at the lab, Edward resets the computers to eradicate the killer's presence. As the process begins, Longstreet shoots Edward. Brit finds a CD-ROM containing Edward's memory patterns. She reverses the procedure, restoring Edward's memory to his body. With his original body dead, Longstreet's consciousness evaporates.

Appropriating themes from such superior films as BRAINSTORM (1983), BODY PARTS (1991), and the Steve Martin comedy ALL OF ME (1984), NAKED SOULS offers an unsatisfying mishmash of science fiction body-switching and B-movie erotic thrills. While the production values are above average, the film is hampered by predictable plot devices and overworked themes. Capitalizing on her starring role in the successful "Baywatch" series, Anderson's artificial beauty and featherweight dramatic skills provide campy pleasures. Unfortunately—and despite her top billing—Anderson has little screen time, leaving the focus on Krause. Krause, who brings to mind a milquetoast Jon Bon Jovi, lacks the charisma to carry the film, and he gets little help from a sleepwalking Warner.

From the images of beautiful naked women (including Anderson) that recur throughout NAKED SOULS, it's clear that the filmmakers were not out to break new cinematic ground, but rather to supply the viewer with titillating images ensconced in a comfortably familiar thriller package. In that much, at least, they succeed. *(Violence, extensive nudity, sexual situations, profanity.)* — D.G.

d, Lyndon Chubbuck; p, Lyndon Chubbuck, Ivana Chubbuck; exec p, William Talmadge; co-p, Randolf Turrow; w, Frank Dietz; ph, Eric J. Goldstein; ed, Rebecca Ross; m, Nigel Holton; prod d, Elisabeth Scott; casting, Liane Dietz; cos, Kristen Anacker; makeup, Barbara Wilder, Alexis Vogel

Science Fiction/Erotic/Thriller (PR: O MPAA: R)

NATIONAL LAMPOON'S FAVORITE DEADLY SINS ★★½

(U.S.) 90m Imagination Productions ~ Republic Pictures Home Video c

Joe Mantegna *(Frank Musso)*; Cassidy Rae *(Norma Jean Hazelrig)*; William Ragsdale *(Todd Ferrett)*; Brian Keith *(Noble Hart)*; Lois Foraker *(Charlotte)*; Caroline Key Johnson *(Freda)*; Lee Everett *(Imogene)*; Allan Rich *(Siggy Brillman)*; Thomas Bellin *(Priest)*; Christopher Carroll *(Cellblock Guard)*; Dale Raoul *(Allison Shoop)*; Max Barrie *(Barry Brillman)*; Kristopher Logan *(Reporter 1)*; Steven M. Porter *(Reporter 2)*; Patricia Belcher *(Modesto Judge)*; Chip Heller *(Guard 1)*; Andrew Clay *(Dick)*; Farrah Forke *(Dick's Girlfriend)*; Kenneth Randle *(Kid)*; Bee-Be Smith *(Mom)*; Ted Davis *(Store Manager)*; Susan Barnes *(Cat Food Lady)*; Clyde Kusatsu *(Saint Peter)*; Gerrit Graham *(Lucifer)*; Robert LaSardo *(Gangbanger 1)*; David Harris *(Gangbanger 2)*; Denis Leary *(Jake)*; Tanya Pohlkotte *(Sara)*; Annabella Sciorra *(Brenda)*; David Butler *(Sara's Husband)*; Emma Thaler *(Amy)*; Saverio Guerra *(Eddie)*; Gabriela May-Ladd *(Nancy)*

Two out of three ain't bad for any omnibus. Edited down from the original Showtime film series, this satiric contemporization of the seven deadliest transgressions does justice to Greed and Anger, but sins against Lust.

In the "Greed" episode, Hollywood huckster Frank Musso (Joe Mantegna) tries to get the jump on oily agent Todd Ferrett (William Ragsdale) in the exploitative purchase of true-life crime tales. In the rush to turn trailer-trash lives into marketable TV-movie commodities, Musso involves himself in the commission of a felony: the Cinderella Killings. Egging on curvaceous Norma Jean Hazelrig (Cassidy Rae), Musso stands by when Norma Jean torches her stepmother and stepsisters, then masterminds her defense by telegenic attorney Noble Hart (Brian Keith). When agent Ferrett points out Musso's profitable double crossing, Norma Jean cheats the gas chamber by blaming the arson murders on Musso, who goes out with a ratings bang by televising his own execution as a variety special.

In Episode Two, "Anger," Dick (Andrew Clay) unleashes an obscene invective against his girlfriend (Farrah Forke) who has run out of tampons. Blowing his top at a convenience store clerk, startled customers, robbers who shoot Dick during a hold-up, and ultimately against Satan himself, foul-mouthed Dick is returned to Earth where we discover that his girlfriend has an even nastier temper.

In the "Lust" segment, a married milquetoast, Jake (Denis Leary), peers out his apartment window and dreams of the luscious babe, Sarah (Tanya Pohlkotte), across the courtyard. However, his shrewish wife Brenda (Annabella Sciorra) becomes a lot more desirable after Jake realizes that Sarah is a dedicated lesbian.

Although a lot of inside jokes may zip past viewers of "Greed" who aren't addicted to Entertainment Channel updates, enough accessible caustic wit remains to ensure merriment. A bit overplayed by Mantegna, "Greed" is an unremittingly sarcastic send-up of the Made-for-TV mentality, a mindset in which people are tempted to kill for 15 minutes of fame, capped off by making the cover of *People* magazine. The comic high attained by "Greed" continues with "Anger," which may delight even those normally offended by Andrew "Dice" Clay's trademark sexism. On an adrenaline rush of anti-social soapboxing, Clay baits everyone he meets. Structured ingeniously to build to a sidesplitting payoff, "Anger" never relents as the Big Mouth spews hatred so volcanically that even Hell has no place for him.

More pretentious than the episodes preceding it, "Lust" is weak-kneed Walter Mittydom for Leary, whose sexist shtick has never registered so impotently. His bitter musing about how the grass in the other man's bedroom always seems greener is lazily written and handicapped with insane fantasy sequences. It leaves a sour aftertaste without garnering even one belly laugh. For a good time, unrepentant sinners are advised to succumb to "Greed" and vent their "Anger," but not to give into "Lust." *(Violence, nudity, extreme profanity, sexual situations, substance abuse.)* — R.P.

d, David Jablin, Denis Leary; p, Peter Manoogian; exec p, David Jablin; assoc p, Kira Cartensen; co-p, James Jimirro; w, Ann Lembeck, Jim Mulholland, Michael Barrie, Lee Biondi; ph, Jamie Thompson, Tony Jannelli; ed, Michelle Gorshow; m, Christopher Tyng, Adam Roth; prod d, John Iacovelli, Jefferson Sage, Ruth Ammon; set d, Roland Rosenkranz, Paul Cheponis, Jacqueline Jacobson; sound, Judy Karp, Craig Woods; casting, Meg Liberman, Marc Hirschfield, Patrick Rush, Todd Thaler; cos, Mary Kay Stolz, Tanya Seeman; makeup, Chris Laurence, Cinzia Zanetti; stunts, Joe Stone

Comedy **(PR: C MPAA: R)**

NECRONOMICON: BOOK OF THE DEAD ★★★

(U.S.) 97m August Entertainment; Davis Film ~ New Line Home Video/Turner Home Entertainment c
(AKA: H.P. LOVECRAFT'S NECRONOMICON: BOOK OF THE DEAD)

"The Library:" Jeffrey Combs *(H. P. Lovecraft)*; Tony Azito *(Librarian)*; Juan Fernandez *(Assistant)*; Brian Yuzna *(Cabbie)*; "The Drowned:" Bruce Payne *(Edward DeLapoer)*; Richard Lynch *(Jethro DeLapoer)*; Belinda Bauer *(Nancy Callmore)*; Maria Ford *(Clara)*; Vladimir Kulich *(Villager)*; William Jess Russell *(Doctor)*; Denice D. Lewis *(Emma DeLapoer)*; Vincent Hammond *(Darkman)*; Peter Jasienski *(Jethro's Son)*; "The Cold:" David Warner *(Dr. Madden)*; Bess Meyer *(Emily/Ann Osterman)*; Millie Perkins *(Lena)*; Dennis Christopher *(Dale)*; Gary Graham *(Sam)*; Curt Lowens *(Al)*; James Paradise *(Policeman)*; Sebastian White *(Policeman #2)*; "Whispers:" Signy Coleman *(Sarah)*; Don Calfa *(Mr. Benedict)*; Judith Drake *(Mrs. Benedict)*; Obba Babatunde *(Paul)*

Inspired by the work of H.P. Lovecraft, this horror anthology contains a high percentage of successful stories.

In 1932, Lovecraft (Jeffrey Combs) sneaks into the cellar of a religious library to get a look at the *Necronomicon*, the book of the dead. He reads three stories—from the past, the present, and the future. . .

In "The Drowned," Edward DeLapoer (Bruce Payne) takes possession of an inherited mansion where his great-uncle Jethro (Richard Lynch) once indulged in satanic rituals to bring his drowned wife and son back to life. Edward duplicates Jethro's rites to revive his deceased fiancee, Clara (Maria Ford), but she returns as a zombie in thrall to a huge sea monster, and Edward is forced to dispatch the creature, losing Clara once more.

In "The Cold," reporter Dale (Dennis Christopher) interviews Amy Osterman (Bess Meyer), believing her mother, Emily, to be in league with a doctor who may be a serial killer. Emily was indeed involved with Dr. Madden (David Warner), who murdered for the spinal fluid he needed to prolong his own life. The doctor is now dead, and Amy is in fact Emily, who now needs Dale's spinal fluid.

In "Whispers," cops Sarah (Signy Coleman) and Paul (Obba Babatunde) crash their car during a chase. Paul is dragged off. Following him into the bowels of a strange building, Sarah discovers a race of winged creatures that usurp human bodies, and she becomes their next victim. Back in the library, a horrible monster attacks Lovecraft, who escapes with the *Necronomicon* as the librarian (Tony Azito) falls victim in his place.

Unlike many multi-story chillers, NECRONOMICON presents its most effective segment first. Following the fun introduction directed by Brian Yuzna (who previously produced the Lovecraft-inspired RE-ANIMATOR and FROM BEYOND, also starring Combs), Christophe Gans' "The Drowned" is a frightening, fast-paced piece, drenched with eerie atmosphere. After this strong start, "The Cold" is a tepid letdown, especially disappointing as it was directed by Shusuke Kaneko, who brought real energy to the newfangled Japanese monster film GAMERA: THE GUARDIAN OF THE UNIVERSE. Yuzna's "Whispers," though thin on the story level, gets things back up to speed and rates high on the shock meter.

Lovecraft purists may object to the liberties taken with the author's stories, and certainly the emphasis on showy makeup effects is a far cry from the ambiguity and suggestiveness of Lovecraft's written horrors. But the parade of gruesome creations has been very well-executed by a large team of artists, and for the most part, the directors orchestrate them for maximum effectiveness. (One of the most startling effects is one of the simplest: a squidlike mass suddenly bursting from the mouth of Jethro's son.) Although the whole film is technically top-notch, it sat on the shelf following its 1993 production while producer Samuel Hadida rejected US deals he found financially unsatisfactory; after playing theatrically overseas, the movie finally debuted on video three years after its completion. *(Graphic violence, nudity, sexual situations, profanity.)* — M.G.

d, Brian Yuzna, Christophe Gans, Shusuke Kaneko; p, Samuel Hadida, Brian Yuzna; exec p, Taka Ichise; co-p, Aki Komine; w, Brent V. Friedman ("The Library," "The Drowned," "The Cold," and "Whispers"), Christophe Gans ("The Drowned"), Kazunori Ito ("The Cold"), (Based on short stories by H. P. Lovecraft); ph, Gerry Lively, Russ Brandt; ed, Christopher Roth, Keith Sauter; m, Joseph LoDuca, Daniel Licht; prod d, Anthony Tremblay; art d, Aram Allen; sound, Geoffrey Lucius Patterson, David Lewis Yewdall; fx, Thomas C. Rainone; casting, Jeffery Passero; cos, Ida Gearon; makeup, Lisa Buono, John Vulich

Horror **(PR: O MPAA: R)**

NELLY AND MONSIEUR ARNAUD ★★★
(France/Italy/Germany) 106m Les Films Alain Sarde; TF1 Films Production; Cecchi Gori Tiger Group Cinematografica S.R.L.; Prokino Filmproduktion GmbH ~ Artificial Eye c
(NELLY ET M. ARNAUD)

Emmanuelle Beart *(Nelly)*; Michel Serrault *(Monsieur Arnaud)*; Jean-Hugues Anglade *(Vincent)*; Claire Nadeau *(Jacqueline)*; Francoise Brion *(Lucie)*; Michele Laroque *(Isabelle)*; Michael Lonsdale *(Dollabella)*; Charles Berling *(Jerome)*; Jean-Pierre Lorit *(Christophe)*; Michel Albertini *(Taieb)*; Coraly Zahonero *(Marianne)*; Graziella Delerm *(Laurence)*; Olivier Pajot *(Jean-Marc)*; Alexandre Chappuis *(Luc)*; Karine Foviau *(Sandrine)*; Laure Chamay *(Girl in the Bistro)*; Sylvie Jobert *(Valerie)*; Janine Souchon *(Maria)*; Judith Vittet *(Benedicte)*; Mathilde Vitry *(The Judge)*; Angelin *(Monsieur Toux)*; Thierry Heckendorn *(Director P.A.O.)*; Abel Jefry *(Ami Taieb)*; Philippe Lelievre *(Manager of the Printers)*; Suzy Marquis *(Madame Toux)*

A gentle and old-fashioned Gallic comedy, NELLY AND MONSIEUR ARNAUD tells the story a beautiful young woman and an elderly gentleman who help each other through transitions in both their lives. With his latest film, veteran director Claude Sautet creates a pleasant character study that is enjoyable if undemanding.

Nelly (Emmanuelle Beart), a young Parisian woman, tires of supporting her lazy husband, Jerome (Charles Berling), by working odd jobs. Then she meets Monsieur Arnaud (Michel Serrault), an ex-Magistrate and the former lover of her best friend, Jacqueline (Claire Nadeau). Arnaud offers Nelly a job as his typist with money up front. Nelly takes the position, divorces Jerome, and moves into a small studio near her new employer. As Nelly records his life story, Arnaud attempts to seduce his attractive assistant with his charm, but Nelly instead becomes infatuated with Arnaud's publisher, Vincent (Jean-Hugues Anglade).

Arnaud grows jealous of the new romance, especially after learning that Vincent has told Nelly unflattering things about him. Arnaud retaliates by angrily venting his feelings to Nelly, who then leaves Arnaud. She later meets him at Jacqueline's apartment and they reconcile. Vincent then pressures Nelly to live with him. When she refuses, he breaks off their romance. Now that she feels closer to Arnaud, Nelly is surprised to hear that he is leaving on a trip to the U.S. with his estranged wife (Francoise Brion) to see their son. Arnaud entrusts Nelly with the final sections of his manuscript and, after he is gone, she hands in the completed story to Vincent, while reflecting on her odd relationship with Arnaud.

Claude Sautet (CESAR AND ROSALIE, UN COEUR EN HIVER) has always been more neo-bourgeoisie than *nouvelle vague*, but NELLY AND MONSIEUR ARNAUD is a lovely film of its kind. Not so superficially, Sautet's film evokes the narrative and thematic concerns of Krzysztof Kieslowski's THREE COLORS: RED (1994), which was set in nearby Geneva and also charted the growing friendship between a beautiful young woman experiencing man troubles and a mysterious older man who was once a former judge. While Kieslowski's final film sent its message about healing psychic wounds with humanitas through a dark and stylish mise-en-scene, NELLY takes a generally bright and light-hearted approach. There are even moments in NELLY that owe something to the sunny Hollywood comedies of yore.

Fortunately, the charming performances of Emmanuelle Beart (UN COEUR EN HIVER, L'ENFER) and Michel Serrault (LA CAGE AUX FOLLES) enrich the often thin material, making their climactic encounter particularly moving. Audiences looking for a simple story with delicate humor and only a touch of melancholy could not do much better than to acquaint themselves with NELLY AND MONSIEUR ARNAUD. *(Sexual situations, Profanity.)* — E.M.

d, Claude Sautet; p, Alain Sarde; assoc p, Antoine Gannage; w, Claude Sautet, Jacques Fieschi, Yves Ulmann; ph, Jean-Francois Robin; ed, Jacqueline Thiedot; m, Philippe Sarde; prod d, Carlos Conti; art d, Alain Pitrel, Maya Wendling; sound, Pierre Lenoir, Jean-Paul Loublier (mixer); casting, Gerard Moulevrier, Alberte Garo; cos, Corinne Jorry; makeup, Marie Lastennet Fournier

Drama/Romance **(PR: C MPAA: NR)**

NELLY ET M. ARNAUD
(SEE: NELLY AND MONSIEUR ARNAUD)

NEMESIS III: PREY HARDER ★
(U.S.) 90m Imperial Entertainment; Filmwerks ~ WarnerVision c
(AKA: NEMESIS 3: TIME LAPSE)

Sue Price *(Alex Rain)*; Xavier DeClie *(Johnny)*; Tim Thomerson *(Farnsworth 2)*; Norbert Weisser *(Edson)*; Ursula Sarcev *(Rane)*; Sharon Bruneau *(Lock)*; Debbie Muggli *(Ditko)*; Earl White; Karen Studer; Jon Epstein

B-filmmaker Albert Pyun styles the third in his NEMESIS series like a comic book but with half the pages missing.

Musclegirl Alex Rain (Sue Price) awakens on the East African plain with no memory, having been shot clean through the head. That she's otherwise in fine shape is attributable to her ill-defined superpowers as a "DNA mutant" bred to combat the evil cyborgs who have usurped mankind in the future. Alex was sent back in time to war-torn, 20th-century Africa for safekeeping, but cyborgs pursue. (In NEMESIS 2 she battled the monstrous "Nebula" model.)

Bit by bit, her memory returns as she is examined by Farnsworth 2 (Tim Thomerson), lead cyborg disguised as a friendly soldier of fortune in the local civil war. Alex shoots him, then flashes back to the past 24 hours, when she was contacted by fellow DNA mutant Rane (Ursula Sarcev), hooked up with treacherous flesh-and-blood mercenary Edson (Norbert Weisser), and met FORREST GUMP-ish, brain-damaged guerilla hero Johnny (Xavier DeClie), whose combat skills and machismo return as he helps Alex defend herself against Farnsworth 2's posse of time-warping cyborgs. Even the sundered Nebula is reanimated and hunts Alex again, while slippery Edson changes loyalties to save his own skin. So what exactly happened to him, Johnny and Rane, and how did Alex get brainshot? She can't recall. The viewer must wait for the next sequel—NEMESIS 4.

The cheat non-ending caps an installment that doesn't advance this cycle in any useful manner. The original NEMESIS (1993) was a men-vs-cyborgs actioner with the trappings of a crime flick. NEMESIS 2: NEBULA dropped such pretensions to be an outright TERMINATOR (1984) ripoff, with the gimmick of champion bodybuilder Sue Price blending both the Arnold Schwarzenegger and Linda Hamilton personas (with the acting talent of neither). Part three shotgun-marries the other two. Farnsworth 2 and his mob squabble over rank and rewards in a way that blunts the edge of their supposed inhuman menace. After the armored horror in NEBULA, the machine-creatures are back to looking like mere people with an occasional overlay of computer graphics, the best of which is a translucent, refractive bubble vehicle driven by two female cyborgs. These cybersirens (Sharon Brunea, Debbie Muggli), possibly inspired by the "cat sisters" from the Japanese *anime* DOMINION TANK POLICE, invariably look at each other and laugh inanely before firing at victims; this *always* gives Alex and friends the chance to escape. It's hard to believe that director Albert Pyun once interned with Kurosawa. Arizona substitutes for the "African" veldt and resembles the post-apocalyptic terrain of past "Pyun-ishments," such as CYBORG (1989) and RADIOACTIVE DREAMS (1986). *(Violence, profanity.)* — C.C.

d, Albert Pyun; p, Gary Schmoeller, Tom Karnowski; exec p, Paul Rosenblum; w, Albert Pyun; ph, George Mooradian; ed, Ken Morrisey; m, Tony Riparetti; fx, David Barton, Maurine Schlenz; casting, J. Budin, Kenneth Kassel; cos, Shelly Boies; makeup, K.C. Marks

Science Fiction/Action (PR: C MPAA: R)

NEMESIS 3: TIME LAPSE
(SEE: NEMESIS III: PREY HARDER)

NEON BIBLE, THE ★★½
(U.K./U.S.) 88m Scala Productions; Channel Four Films; Miramax International ~ Strand Releasing c

Gena Rowlands *(Aunt Mae)*; Diana Scarwid *(Sarah)*; Denis Leary *(Frank)*; Jacob Tierney *(David—Age 15)*; Leo Burmester *(Bobbie Lee Taylor)*; Frances Conroy *(Miss Scover)*; Peter McRobbie *(Reverend Watkins)*; Joan Glover *(Flora)*; Bob Hannah *(George)*; Tom Turbiville *(Clyde)*; Drake Bell *(David—Age 10)*; Dana Atwood *(Jo Lynne)*; Virgil Graham Hopkins *(Mr. Williams)*; Aaron Frisch *(Bruce)*; Sharon Blackwood *(Schoolmistress)*; Charlie Franzen *(Tannoy)*; Sherry Velvet *(Testifier No. 1)*; Stephanie Astalos Jones *(Testifier No. 2)*; Ian Shearer *(Billy Sunday Thompson)*; Duncan Stewart *(Head Boy)*

A sad but stubbornly unaffecting story about a boy and his family struggling through the FDR years is told in THE NEON BIBLE. Although never less than a treat to look at, this film is an important director's honorable failure.

Ten-year-old David (Drake Bell) lives with his mother, Sarah (Diana Scarwid), his father, Frank (Denis Leary), and his aunt, Mae (Gena Rowlands), a small-time vocalist. David is shy and sensitive, Sarah is repressed and apprehensive, Frank is temperamental and periodically brutal, and Mae is warmhearted but frustrated. Both of them lonely and starved for affection, David and Mae become buddies of sorts.

After Frank is killed serving in WWII, Sarah begins to lose her mind. Now 15, David (Jacob Tierney), who has landed a job as a salesclerk, meets Jo Lynne (Dana Atwood) and takes her out on a date. Mae moves to Nashville to join her boyfriend (Tom Turbiville), who has assured her he can find her lucrative work singing on the radio and records. Before leaving, she promises David that she will send for him and Sarah within a week or two.

In order to look after his insane mother, David is forced to quit his job. Before doing so, he frightens Jo Lynne by impulsively proposing to her. The girl slaps his face and runs.

Sarah kills herself, and David hides her body in the yard. When the local minister (Peter McRobbie) appears at the house with the intention of taking Sarah to the insane asylum, the boy shoots him dead.

David spends his entire savings on a train ticket. Aside from a few vague notions of getting a job and eventually proceeding to Nashville to find Aunt Mae, he hasn't a clue as to where he is going or what he will do when he gets there.

In THE NEON BIBLE, director Terence Davies, a Liverpudlian, is not very successful in capturing the essence of the American rural South. Although the film is nearly as technically accomplished and aesthetically idiosyncratic as Davies' remarkable first feature, DISTANT VOICES, STILL LIVES (1988), and reprises several of its themes, the inborn intimacy required by regional filmmaking is missing.

THE NEON BIBLE parades several familiar and largely welcome peculiarities of its director—the hypnotic traveling shots with which he transports his audiences, not toward action, but toward dreamy memory; the pungent but unsentimental nostalgia for the days of youth; the immersion in the world of a sensitive boy growing up amidst doting females and a tyrannical father. But Davies in Dixie is a fish out of water.

THE NEON BIBLE is based on a book written at the age of 16 by John Kennedy Toole, the author of *A Confederacy of Dunces.* Davies' adaptation of the Toole novel is rather anemic. Especially flatfooted are David's voice-over critique of small-town conformity and Mae's speeches on loneliness and aging—themes that frequently have been explored more cleverly and articulately elsewhere.

The film's satirical attacks on fly-by-night Christian evangelism and backwoods Puritanism also are largely unsuccessful, these targets having been riddled beyond repair by artists far more familiar with the territory. Furthermore, Davies is much too gifted to be stooping to satire, however muted. Satirists are a dime a dozen, but genuine cinema poets and innovators like Davies are precious.*(Violence, profanity.)* — D.T.

d, Terence Davies; p, Elizabeth Karlsen, Olivia Stewart; exec p, Nik Powell, Stephen Woolley; w, Terence Davies (based on the novel by John Kennedy Toole); ph, Mick Coulter; ed, Charles Rees; m, Robert Lockhart; prod d, Christopher Hobbs; art d, Phil Messina; set d, Kristin Messina; sound, Thomas Varga (mixer); fx, Lisa Reynolds; casting, Laura Rosenthal; cos, Monica Howe; makeup, Sarah Mays; stunts, Lonnie Smith

Drama (PR: C MPAA: NR)

NEUROSIA: 50 YEARS OF PERVERSITY ★★★½
(Germany) 87m Rosa von Praunheim Produktion ~ First Run Features c
(NEUROSIA: FUNFZIG JAHRE PERVERS)

Desiree Nick *(Gesine Ganzman-Seipel)*; Rosa von Praunheim; Lotti Huber; Evelyn Kunneke; Luzi Kryn; Eva Ebner; Friedrich Steinhauer; Gertrud Mischwitzky; Ichgola Androgyn; Carsten Hadler; Tima die Gottliche; Volker Eschke; Rainer Kranich; Ovo Maltine; Vardis Marinakis; Valentin Passoni; Ursula Rollwage; Mike Shephard; Frank Schafer; Bev Stroganov; Wesley Greenbaum; Taylor Mead; Fernando Cavelhosa; Brandon Judell; Mae Sackeroff; Lindzee Smith; Ingrid Scheib

NEUROSIA: 50 YEARS OF PERVERSITY is German director Rosa von Praunheim's hilariously subversive, sexually explicit poke in the ribs to self-indulgent filmmakers who make themselves the subject of their own movies. Ironically, by making *himself* the lighthearted subject of his movie, von Praunheim has a blast making fun of his own radical politics, ribald sex life, and career as Germany's most daring and controversial underground filmmaker.

TV tabloid reporter Gesina Ganzmann-Seipel (Desiree Nick) is assigned to do a multi-part series on the murder of director Rosa von Praunheim, who was shot while introducing one of his latest movies to a hostile and bored audience. When his body mysteriously vanishes, Gesina's curiosity is piqued and she begins digging for dirt on the director's sex life and his work as an AIDS activist.

To her surprise, she discovers that he was despised for his gay politics, "amateurish" filmmaking, and hunger for publicity. It seems that the very name Rosa von Praunheim provokes outrage from associates, friends, and lovers—that is, those who consent even to speak to her.

Gesina's first stop takes her to von Praunheim's apartment, where people seem to come and go without much concern for the locks on the door. Rosa's mother, an affable woman who lives with her son, befriends Gesina and allows her to look around the place. What she finds disgusts her: condoms, lubricant, and videotapes containing lovemaking sessions with his various lovers.

Gesina's invitation to a "symbolic" funeral for Rosa (which nobody attends) brings her in contact with an actress who praises the director for his sensitivity. But Gesina wants scandal, so a former lover, who broke off their affair because Rosa's lovemaking caused too much pain, suggests that Gesina might have better luck at Rosa's cruising spots in the park and public toilet. Gesina tries to question one amorous couple, who dismiss von Praunheim as a lousy director who loves attention. Other men simply refuse to speak about him at all.

Gesina's research then takes her to New York, where Rosa frequently showed his films. In disguise, she infiltrates a men-only dark room (where she thinks she spots Rosa) and the Gay Pride parade—both to no avail.

Discouraged, she goes back to Berlin, where she receives an anonymous tip from a radical gay group called the Pink Army Faction, which has information about Rosa's whereabouts. Gesina turns detective and eventually finds Rosa. He has been kidnapped by the Pink Army Faction, tortured and ordered to stop making gay films. When Rosa finally is released to Gesina, it's too late. Her network suddenly pulls the plug on her series, because only three people were watching.

Episodic in structure, NEUROSIA: 50 YEARS OF PERVERSITY unfolds like an elliptical entry in a giant diary. Although he appears only briefly in the movie, von Praunheim and his dramatic life are captured vividly through a collage of home movie footage and newsreels featuring a Who's Who of gay icons: Harvey Milk, Divine, Andy Warhol, and even the homophobic Anita Bryant. Von Praunheim wants to shock and annoy his audience and does so by taking boyish delight in showing frank sexual acts between men or having the cast break into song for no particular reason.

The film's true pleasure comes from Nick's wonderfully sly and deadpan performance as Gesina, a straight woman caught up in the forbidden excitement of a gay man's world. Watching her casually approach a male couple in the throes of passion—and then asking them for an interview—is truly priceless. Who knew that the politically-minded director of A VIRUS KNOWS NO MORALS (1986) and IT IS NOT THE HOMOSEXUAL WHO IS PERVERSE, BUT THE SITUATION IN WHICH HE LIVES (1970) could make such a witty and lighthearted comedy?*(Violence, sexual situations, adult situations.)* — D.O.

d, Rosa von Praunheim; w, Valentin Passoni; ph, Lorenz Haarmann; ed, Mike Shepard; m, Alexander Kraut; art d, Volker Marz; sound, Mike Shepard; cos, Desiree Nick, Daniela Bimek, M.T. Schrader

Comedy **(PR: O MPAA: NR)**

NEUROSIA: FUNFZIG JAHRE PERVERS
(SEE: NEUROSIA: FIFTY YEARS OF PERVERSITY)

NEW LIFE, A ★★★
(France) 122m Arena Films ~ Pyramide c
(UNE NOUVELLE VIE)

Sophie Aubry *(Tina)*; Judith Godreche *(Lise)*; Bernard Giraudeau *(Constantin)*; Christine Boisson *(Laurence)*; Philippe Torreton *(Fred)*; Bernard Verley *(Ludovic)*; Nelly Borgeaud *(Nadine)*; Antoine Basler *(Kleber)*; Roger Dumas *(Martin)*; Nathalie Boutefeu *(Brigitte)*; Richard Bean *(Gerard)*; Maite Maille *(France)*

A French woman meets the half-sister she never knew in A NEW LIFE, a rewarding yet unnecessarily convoluted art film by Olivier Assayas.

Set in contemporary Paris, A NEW LIFE first centers around Tina (Sophie Aubry), an embittered young woman who operates a forklift in a supermarket stockroom. After work one day, Tina argues with both her hotheaded boyfriend, Fred (Philippe Torreton), and her dysfunctional mother, Nadine (Nelly Borgeaud). Later, mysteriously, she is awakened by a man named Constantin (Bernard Giraudeau), and finds herself in a plush apartment where she has passed out from a pill overdose.

Tina soon realizes that the apartment is owned by her father, whom she has never known, and is shared by Lise (Judith Godreche), a half-sister she did not realize even existed. Constantin, her father's lawyer and Lise's boss-lover, has arranged for the sisters to meet. When they do, the women tentatively get to know each other, and Lise invites Tina to stay with her. Tina finally meets her father, Ludovic (Bernard Verley), but reacts negatively to his selfish ways. Meanwhile, Lise finds Tina's presence more intrusive than welcome, as Tina tries to heal her psychic wounds.

Part of Tina's "new life" includes taking up with the demanding and brutish Constantin (without telling Lise), then breaking up with Fred. Later, Constantin's neglected wife tells Tina that she shouldn't be optimistic about her clandestine relationship with her husband. Finally, after more traumatic events, Tina breaks up with Constantin, and reconciles with Lise.

The "Cahiers du Cinema" critic-turned-filmmaker, Olivier Assayas, has a small but devoted following that appreciates his ambiguous stories, complex characters, and fluid camerawork. There is no doubt that Assayas is an accomplished filmmaker, and that A NEW LIFE, his fourth feature, contains all the characteristics of his best work, as well as an adroit use of Panavision widescreen (Denis Lenoir is the cinematographer). Through subtle techniques, Assayas inverts the family melodrama to the point that the viewer must work hard to understand the literal narrative level of action. The brief fades-to-black, for example, make many scenes only comprehensible in reflection (in this way, Assayas takes after his mentor, director Andre Techine, for whom he wrote RENDEZVOUS and SCENE OF THE CRIME).

The downside to Assayas's method in A NEW LIFE is that the most dramatic scenes lack passion because they are difficult to completely grasp. Tina's growth from suicidal youth to searching adult, while never forced, loses some of its power, since major developments (including her affair with the repellent Constantin) require extraordinary viewer empathy and projection. Tina's journey of discovery bears some similarity to Julie's in BLUE (1993), but that Kieslowski film, while also humorless and inscrutable, retained all the right pieces of its cinematic puzzle so that the viewer feels it is worth putting together. A NEW LIFE, alas, lacks that special something that makes beautiful art great art. *(Nudity, sexual situations, profanity.)* — E.M.

d, Olivier Assayas; w, Olivier Assayas; ph, Denis Lenoir; ed, Luc Barnier; sound, Francois Musu

Drama **(PR: C MPAA: PG-13)**

NICO ICON ★★★
(Germany) 75m CIAK-Filmproduktion ~ Roxie Releasing c/bw

John Cale; Paul Morrissey; Jackson Browne; Billy Name; Viva; Tina Aumont; Ari Boulogne; Jonas Mekas; Sterling Morrison;

Danny Fields; Edith Boulogne; Nico Papatakis; Lutz Ulbrich; Carlos de Maldonado-Bostock; Alan Wise; Helma Wolff; James Young

Fame flirted with Nico throughout her life, rather than the other way around. Best known as the "chanteuse" who appeared on the Velvet Underground's 1967 debut album, she seems to have floated through her life, indifferent to what others wanted to make of her. Although this documentary compiles an astonishing amount of footage of Nico, it never breaks through to the woman beneath the image—assuming that there actually was a woman there.

Filmmaker Susanne Ofteringer mixes archival footage with interviews with people who knew and worked with Nico. Although much of what she is told is contradictory (especially regarding Nico's days as part of the Andy Warhol entourage), a story of her life emerges.

Born Christa Paffgren in 1938, Nico was raised in Germany during WWII. Her father was a German soldier who apparently was killed by the Nazis after a head injury left him mentally unfit for duty. Like many children of her generation, she hated Germany and left as a teenager to embark on a successful modeling career. She made a brief but memorable appearance in LA DOLCE VITA (1960), and Fellini apparently was interested in making her a protege, but despaired of her laziness.

Although Nico is remembered as asexual at best, she had an affair with French actor Alain Delon, who refused to recognize the son, Ari, she bore him. Delon's mother, Edith Boulogne, says that when she decided to raise the boy, her son disowned her and never again spoke to her.

After recording a forgettable pop single, Nico moved to Manhattan and fell in with Andy Warhol and his "Factory." He made a place for her in the Velvet Underground, much to the frustration of the band members—although Lou Reed and especially John Cale guided much of her solo career. Around this time, she began to become openly disdainful of her beauty as she sought to develop her own voice as a musician. She met Jim Morrison, who considered her a soulmate, and Jackson Browne, who at the age of 18 became her lover and wrote songs for her.

In the 1970s, Nico returned to Europe. She lived with Philippe Garrel and appeared in his experimental films. She also found the great love of her life: heroin. When her son, Ari, came to live with her, she introduced him to heroin as well.

As her own music and that of the Velvet Underground was rediscovered in the post-punk '70s and '80s, Nico was able to support herself and her habit by touring and occasionally recording, performing gloomy songs in her deep Teutonic voice, accompanied by her droning harmonium.

Nico died after a bicycle fall on the island of Ibiza in 1988. Her son says he believes she died of exposure to the sun.

While many of the people who were intimate with Nico declined to be interviewed for this film, including Reed, Delon and Garrel, there are enough interviewees to make the point that no one truly knew Nico. Those who claim they did obviously are projecting their own desires and images onto her. She can be an icon to suit whatever purpose the viewer desires because there was no real Nico to get in the way. Early in NICO ICON, Ofteringer cuts from a shot of Nico in an early 60s commercial, all picture-perfect beauty, to a similar pose of her near the end of her life, gray-haired, face lined and worn, looking at the world with eyes that seem to see straight into hell. The accomplishment of this generally straightforward documentary is that the viewer comes away from it feeling, with Nico, a certain grim satisfaction at her "deterioration" as the ultimate rejection of a shallow world. *(Adult situations, substance abuse, profanity.)* — M.F.

d, Susanne Ofteringer; p, Annette Pisacane, Thomas Mertens; w, Susanne Ofteringer; ph, Judith Kaufmann, Katarzyna Remin, Sibylle Sturme; ed, Elfe Brandenburger, Guido Krajewski; sound, Lothar Segeler (mixer), Jens Tukiendorf, Charles Blackwell

Documentary **(PR: C MPAA: NR)**

NIGHT OF THE SCARECROW ★★½

(U.S.) 85m Steve White Entertainment ~ Republic Pictures Home Video c

Elizabeth Barondes *(Claire Goodman)*; John Mese *(Dillon Hale)*; Stephen Root *(Frank)*; Bruce Glover *(Thaddeus)*; Dirk Blocker *(George)*; Howard Swain *(Scarecrow)*; Gary Lockwood *(William)*; John Hawkes *(Danny Thompson)*; William Joseph Barker *(Kyle)*; Martine Beswick *(Barbara)*; Cristi Harris *(Stephanie)*; Cynthia Merrill *(Lorraine)*; Bob Harvey *(Ben)*; Robin Bernardi *(Fountain Girl)*; Duane Whitaker *(Deputy #1)*; Joe Unger *(Deputy #2)*; Harri James *(Lucinda)*; John LaZar *(Warlock)*

A healthy dose of directorial style and energy makes this prosaic low-budget chiller a tense, entertaining diversion.

Claire Goodman (Elizabeth Barondes) returns to her prosperous farming hometown, where her father William (Gary Lockwood) is mayor. She soon becomes friendly with construction foreman Dillon Hale (John Mese). Good-for-nothing Danny Thompson (John Hawkes) goes on a drunken joyride with a tractor and cracks open a stone tomb in a field; an evil spirit escapes and possesses a scarecrow (Howard Swain) that kills Claire's uncle George (Dirk Blocker). Claire discovers the body and briefly spots the scarecrow, yet the rest of her family insists the death was an accident. Subsequently, the scarecrow assaults Claire's minister uncle Thaddeus (Bruce Glover) and kills his rebellious daughter Stephanie (Cristi Harris) and Danny.

Claire and Dillon discover the wounded Thaddeus, who reveals that the spirit animating the scarecrow belongs to a warlock who bestowed prosperity on the town many decades ago, only to be betrayed and entombed by the Goodmans' ancestors. The scarecrow kills William, Thaddeus, and the latter's wife; accused of the murders, Dillon sets out with Claire to stop the monster. Sheriff Frank (Stephen Root), another of Claire's uncles, and his deputies are also slaughtered by the scarecrow. Finally, Claire and Dillon dig up and destroy the warlock's bones, ending the creature's rampage.

While there's nothing truly groundbreaking or original about NIGHT OF THE SCARECROW, it has been crafted with a professionalism that prevents it from ever becoming tiresome. The conventional elements (the possessed monster, the guilty town secret it avenges, the plucky young couple pitted against the creature) are convincing, and performed by a cast that mixes likable newcomers (Barondes and Mese) with welcome veterans (Glover, 2001's Lockwood, Martine Beswicke). Most importantly, director Jeff Burr, finally escaping from the realm of direct-to-video sequels (STEPFATHER II, PUMPKINHEAD II, and several others), gives the movie a snappy pace and a slick look.

The film may hold no real surprises, but it does contain some memorably gruesome setpieces, like the scarecrow painfully stitching Thaddeus's mouth closed and vines bursting from Stephanie's body. And while the movie incorporates some of the inevitable cliches of the modern monster genre—occasional one-liners from the scarecrow, a sequel-ready ending—it never falls into the campy self-consciousness that marrs many recent low-budget genre films. *(Graphic violence, nudity, sexual situations, profanity.)* — M.G.

d, Jeff Burr; p, Barry Bernardi, Steve White; assoc p, Steve Tyler Sahlein; w, Reed Steiner, Dan Mazur; ph, Tom Calloway; ed, Bob Murawski; m, Jim Manzie; prod d, Mick Strawn; art d, Brad Johnson; sound, Peter Meiselmann, Phillip Raves; fx, David Miller, Tom Rainone; casting, Abra Edelman, Elisa Goodman; cos, Mark Bridges; makeup, Judy Mathai

Horror **(PR: O MPAA: R)**

NIGHT OF THE TWISTERS ★★½
(U.S.) 91m Atlantis Films; MTM Enterprises; Family Channel; Porchlight Entertainment ~ GoodTimes Entertainment c

Devon Sawa *(Dan Hatch)*; John Schneider *(Jack Hatch)*; Lori Hallier *(Laura Hatch)*; Amos Crawley *(Arthur Darlington)*; Laura Bertram *(Stacy Darlington)*; Jhene Erwin *(Jenny)*; Helen Hughes *(Grandma Belle)*; David Ferry *(Bob Iverson)*; Alex Lastewka *(Baby Ryan)*; Thomas Lastewka *(Baby Ryan)*; Megan Kitchen *(Ronnie Vae)*; Graham McPherson *(Calvert)*; Don Allison *(Phil Roth)*

A moderately suspenseful tale of a midwestern family coping with an outbreak of tornadoes, NIGHT OF THE TWISTERS offers low-budget thrills, a competent no-name cast, and a simple morality piece about father-son relations.

Rogue weather patterns cause an unprecedented array of twisters to converge on Blainsworth, Nebraska, and the Hatch family finds its various members scattered across town. When the storm hits, teenaged Dan (Devon Sawa) and his friend Arthur (Amos Crawley) get baby Ryan and head for the basement. The boys climb out after the tornadoes subside, only to find the house destroyed. Soon joined by Arthur's sisters, Stacey and Ronnie Vae (Laura Bertram and Megan Kitchen), the kids find the town's banker dead on the road and decide to use his car to seek out Dan's parents. Dan and Stacey eventually leave the others at a roadblock; taking the car, they locate and rescue Grandma Belle (Helen Hughes) from the wreck of an animal shed and help free their stepfather, Jack (John Schneider), from an overturned truck.

Jack and Dan, heretofore struggling through a difficult relationship, now work together to find Dan's mom, Laura (Lori Hallier). When they finally reach the community shelter, they learn that Laura and Jenny (Jhene Erwin) have gone with meteorologist Bob Iverson (David Ferry) to the Hatch home. Everyone is soon reunited at the remains of the house. On the way back to the shelter, another twister hits and literally chases them up the highway and through the ruins of the town. The family finds shelter in an underpass and stay there until the twister passes. In the morning, they all resolve to stay and rebuild the town.

NIGHT OF THE TWISTERS combines made-for-TV disaster thrills with a Middle American coming-of-age family drama as son-and-stepfather tensions get resolved in the heat of crisis. While there is nothing here to match the flying cows and spinning gas trucks of 1996's TWISTER—NIGHT's biggest effect is a refrigerator being sucked clear across a kitchen floor and out the door—imaginative direction and clever production design vividly recreate the effects of a vicious storm on a midwestern community. The scenes of the ruined town at night are particularly evocative as the protagonists frantically search for each other.

The only names in the cast being erstwhile teen idol Devon Sawa (LITTLE GIANTS, NOW AND THEN) and former Duke of Hazzard John Schneider, the film works at creating a portrait of ordinary people, rather than Hollywood stars, caught in a crisis situation.— B.C.

d, Timothy Bond; p, Sean Ryerson, Stephen Roloff; exec p, Anne Marie La Travese, Wayne M. Robers, William F. Burns; w, Sam Graham, Chris Hubbell (based on the novel by Ivy Ruckman); ph, Peter Benison; ed, Gary L. Smith; m, Lawrence Shragge; prod d, Stephen Roloff

Children's/Disaster/Drama **(PR: A MPAA: NR)**

NIGHT ON THE GALACTIC RAILROAD ★★½
(Japan) 108m Asahi Group; Herald Group/TAC ~ Central Park Media c

Based on a celebrated 1927 Japanese children's story, *Milky Way Railroad,* NIGHT ON THE GALACTIC RAILROAD is a feature-length animated fable set in a Mediterranean-style town with the characters drawn as anthropomorphic cats. This tale of a child who rides through the galaxy on a heavenly passenger train takes Japanese animation in a different direction with its deliberate pace, storybook art, and reliance on symbolism.

Schoolboy Giovanni must work to provide for his ailing mother while waiting for the return of his fisherman father. Something of an outcast at school, he finds a sympathetic classmate in the equally quiet and studious Campanella. One night, after being taunted by his schoolmates at the Festival of Stars, Giovanni runs off to the outskirts of town. He finds refuge in a meadow, and looks up at the Milky Way, the "heavenly river" described by his astronomy teacher.

He is startled by the sudden arrival of a massive locomotive in the field. He boards it and is overjoyed to find Campanella already a passenger. Together they experience an unusual journey through time and space, past different stations and distinct landscapes, some recalling places on earth, others quite heavenly in appearance.

They meet all sorts of peculiar characters including an archaeologist studying prehistoric bones and million-year-old walnuts, an old bird catcher who has sacks of dead herons that taste like candy, and the train's blind wireless operator, who keeps picking up snatches of a Christian hymn. At one point, they are joined by three human children who died at sea when their passenger ship (presumably the *Titanic*) was struck by an iceberg.

Eventually Giovanni and Campanella are the only passengers remaining and Giovanni takes comfort in the fact that he and Campanella will ride together to the end of the universe. But soon Campanella must leave and Giovanni cannot follow him. As the train heads into a black hole, Giovanni wakes up in the meadow, apparently having dreamed the whole adventure.

Back in town he learns from a classmate that less than an hour earlier Campanella had rescued a boy from the river but had disappeared underwater, and had never resurfaced. Strangely becalmed, Giovanni looks up at the night sky and declares, "Campanella is at the edge of the universe. We explored it together."

NIGHT ON THE GALACTIC RAILROAD tells its allegorical tale of childhood and death in a finely-wrought picture book style that seeks to be more descriptive than action-oriented. It presents a child's eye view of the world, with the buildings and streets of town looming large and overpowering, the open fields and night sky offering freedom, and the massive locomotive appearing dark and mysterious.

While the film is beautiful to watch, the filmmakers carefully maintain an emotional distance. The revelation that Giovanni had accompanied his friend's soul to heaven satisfies one's curiosity but registers little of the emotional impact that Americans normally seek from such a story. This approach may, however, more closely reflect the way children actually experience such events.

Director Gisaburo Sugii went on to animate another Japanese literary work, *The Tale of Genji,* which has a similarly slow, careful, intricate style. The influence of the book *Milky Way Railroad,* can also be seen in the 1970s animated Japanese TV series, "Galaxy Express," and its subsequent feature film adaptation, GALAXY EXPRESS 999. — B.C.

d, Gisaburo Sugii; p, Masato Hara, Atsumi Tashiro; exec p, John O'Donnell; w, Minoru Betsuyaku (based on the 1927 novel *Milky Way Railroad* by Kenji Miyazawa), Jay Parks (english rewrite); ph, Yasuo Maeda; m, Haruomi Hosono; art d, Mihoko Magoori; anim, Takao Kodama, Marisuke Eguchi

Animated **(PR: AA MPAA: NR)**

NIKI DE SAINT PHALLE: WHO IS THE MONSTER — YOU OR ME? ★★★

(Germany/France/Switzerland) 93m ~ Artistic License Films c

Niki de Saint Phalle

Aficionados of the avant garde will enjoy NIKI DE SAINT PHALLE: WHO IS THE MONSTER—YOU OR ME?, a tribute to the eponymous feminist artist. Despite some omissions, it more than adequately illuminates its subject.

Film clips, stills and narration by de Saint Phalle guides the viewer from her unhappy childhood in France to participation in the 1960s art scene, where she responded creatively to her father's sexual abuse through experimental film and gestural abstract art. Both de Saint Phalle's "Shooting Paintings" and her giant, voluptuous female sculptures of this period brought her notoriety as a modern feminist artist. NIKI DE SAINT PHALLE also shows aspects of her professional and private love affair with Swiss artist Jean Tinguely, who died in 1991, her herculean efforts to build a sculptured home in Tuscany, and her current-day struggles with bad health. The film ends on a positive note as de Saint Phalle (now in her 60s) maintains an edge in new works.

For someone best known for fine-art works (paintings and sculptures in Paris, Central Park and the Pompidou Center), Niki de Saint Phalle has a surprising amount of film archive material about her life. Writer-director-producer Peter Schamoni chose the perfect subject for his documentary, since the artist is also a dynamic, photogenic creature (a "double Scorpio") with an interesting history. It's particulary fun to watch the young de Saint Phalle blasting bags of paint with a rifle shots, splattering blank canvas. Extended clips from the artist's short films, DADDY and DREAM—LONGER THAN THE NIGHT, also exemplify her iconoclastic humor even as their creator remains offscreen.

Schamoni skims over some biographical details like his subject's first marriage and children, who are referred to late in the film, while overemphasizing the relationship with Jean Tinguely (television news coverage of his funeral is excessive). Likewise, Schamoni gives surprisingly short shrift to the tumultuous period in which de Saint Phalle emerged as an artist—her painter friends, Jasper Johns and Robert Rauschenberg, are barely mentioned. It may be argued that de Saint Phalle as herself is more interesting than much of her art. Conceptually radical and visionary, but aesthetically crude (her statue colors are often bright and garish), de Saint Phalle may be best remembered as the woman who inspired more sophisticated later talents like Matthew Barney and Theo Sable. Of course, this is not a fault of the documentary itself, which nicely captures an original artist in a favorable light. — E.M.

d, Peter Schamoni; p, Peter Schamoni; w, Peter Schamoni; ph, Michael Bartlett, Rodger Hinricks, Ernst Hirsch, Bernard Zitzermann, Francois de Menil, Peter Whitehead; ed, Thomas Kratenmacher

Documentary **(PR: C MPAA: NR)**

NORMA JEAN AND MARILYN ★★★

(U.S.) 132m HBO Pictures; Caravel Entertainment ~ HBO Home Video c

Ashley Judd *(Norma Jean Dougherty)*; Mira Sorvino *(Marilyn Monroe)*; Josh Charles *(Eddie Jordan)*; Ron Rifkin *(Johnny Hyde)*; David Dukes *(Arthur Miller)*; Peter Dobson *(Joe DiMaggio)*; Taylor Nichols *(Fred Karger)*; John Rubenstein *(Darryl Zanuck)*; Allan Corduner *(Billy Wilder)*; Dana Goldstone *(Lee Strasberg)*; Micole Mercurio *(Mozelle Hyde)*; Lindsay Crouse *(Natasha Lytess)*; John Apicella *(Milton Krasner)*; Robert Alan Beuth *(Commissary Photographer)*; Frank Irney *(Preacher)*; Earl Boen *(Studio Physician)*; Kevin Bourland *(David March)*; Dennis Bowen *(Tom Kelly)*; Ardie Bryant *(Tap Dancer)*; Nancy Linehan Charles *(Bette Davis)*; Jeffrey Combs *(Montgomery Clift)*; Steven Culp *(Robert Kennedy)*; Lou Cuttel *(Henry Weinstein)*; Artur Cybulski *(Camera Assistant)*; Joe D'Angerio *(Whitey Snyder)*; Marianne Davis *(Young Norma Jean)*; Bebe Drake *(Shampoo Lady)*; Ellerinei *(Ella Fitzgerald)*; Edith Fields *(Nana Karger)*; Yvette Freeman *(Hazel Washington)*; David Drew Gallagher *(Danny Greenton)*; Jimm Giannini *(Reporter No. 1)*; Kevin Goetz *(Studio Flack)*; Beth Grant *(Grace Goddard)*; Ian Gregory *(Truck Driver)*; Alex Henteloff *(Dr. Gurdin)*; Lise Hillboldt *(Sylvia March)*; Neil Hunt *(George Sanders)*; Ivan Kane *(Lefty O'Doul)*; Sandra Ellis Lafferty *(Inez Melson)*; Michael Laskin *(Sidney Skolsky)*; Floyd Levine *(Spiros Skouras)*; Marc Lynn *(Photo Assistant)*; Keith MacKechnie *(Unit Photographer)*; Scott Menville *("Misfits" A. D.)*; Herb Mitchell *(Ben Lyon)*; Virginia Morris *(Dr. Marianne Kris)*; Marianne Muellerleile *(Mrs. Dewey)*; Kelsey Mulrooney *(Child Norma Jean)*; Christopher Murray *(Doc Goddard)*; Erika Nann *(Jane Russell)*; Audrie Neenan *(Sylvia Barnhart)*; Terrence O'Connor *(Gladys Baker)*; Michael O'Neill *(Mr. Kimmel)*; Adam Paul *(Junior Reporter)*; Howard Platt *(Howard Hawks)*; Eric Poppick *(Producer)*; Mary Porster *(Adrian Wallingford)*; Allyson Reed *(Natalie Kelly)*; John Roselius *(Earl Moran)*; Peter Sands *(Peter Lawford)*; Sam Shamshak *(Ted Lewis)*; Perry Stephens *(John F. Kennedy)*; Carol Swarbrick *(Emeline Snively)*; Warren Sweeney *(Reporter No. 2)*; Rosie Taravella *(Electrologist)*; Wendy Worthington *(Mrs. Gifford)*

Monroe cultists will undoubtedly have a field day with NORMA JEAN AND MARILYN, alternately being titillated by and disputing the facts presented here. A good example of fuel for the first is the fact that the film shows Marilyn dying chastely dressed, in contradiction to what is perhaps the most commonly-known "fact" about her, that her corpse was found nude.

At a church service, 18-year-old Norma Jean Dougherty (Ashley Judd) stands naked and unembarrassed among the other churchgoers. It is a dream she is recounting to her new friend Eddie Jordan (Josh Charles), who is smitten with Norma Jean and her open sexuality. Norma Jean makes no secret of the fact that she will do whatever is necessary to become a Hollywood star, including sleeping with anyone who can further her career.

As she pursues this path, flashbacks show her early life, spent in a succession of abusive foster homes after her mentally ill mother was institutionalized.

In the style of the times, Norma Jean submits to various cosmetic "adjustments" to her image. After plastic surgery, she emerges as Marilyn Monroe (Mira Sorvino). Norma Jean remains as a presence who advises Marilyn on her career, beating back her confused emotions, and encouraging her to be hard-headed and practical.

As her career skyrockets, Marilyn continues to be torn between these two poles. Unable to deal with her own insecurities, the pressures of stardom, a series of failed romances, and her fears of succumbing to the same mental illness that cursed her mother and grandmother, she commits suicide in 1962.

Like the Kennedy assassination (to which it is inevitably linked), the life and death of Marilyn Monroe, nee Norma Jean Mortenson Baker Dougherty, continues to fascinate those with a yen for popular myths in which an unknown "true" story beckons seductively from behind a cloud of cover-ups, disputed facts, and whispered innuendo.

For non-Monroe cultists, NORMA JEAN AND MARILYN is less a Hollywood expose than a grim psychological portrait of an emotionally disturbed woman. The strategy of having Norma Jean and Marilyn portrayed by two different actresses, who appear on screen together to verbalize her inner turmoil, has some basis in fact: Monroe did complain of hearing voices in her head telling her what to do. If Judd turns in the better performance, it must be said that she has more to work with. Not only is Sorvino constrained by the need to impersonate the Monroe we remember, but her part is much more reactive than that of the hard-bitten Norma Jean. *(Violence, extensive nudity, sexual situations, adult situations, substance abuse, profanity.)* — M.F.

d, Tim Fywell; p, Guy Riedel; exec p, Marvin Worth; assoc p, Udi Nedivi; w, Jill Isaacs; ph, John Thomas; ed, Glenn Farr; m, Christopher Young; prod d, Cynthia Charette; art d, Troy Sizemore; casting, Nancy Foy; cos, Ha Nguyen; makeup, Deborah Larsen

Biography/Drama **(PR: O MPAA: R)**

NORMAL LIFE ★★★½

(U.S.) 102m McNaughton/Jones Motion Pictures; Normal Life Productions ~ Fine Line c

Ashley Judd *(Pam Anderson)*; Luke Perry *(Chris Anderson)*; Bruce Young *(Agent Parker)*; Jim True *(Mike Anderson)*; Dawn Maxey *(Eva)*; Tom Towles *(Frank Anderson)*; Penelope Milford *(Adele Anderson)*; Kate Walsh *(Cindy Anderson)*; Scott Cummins *(Hank Chilton)*; Edmund Wyson *(Darren)*; Michael Skewes *(Swift)*; Kevin Mukherji *(Homeowner)*; Brian McCann *(Justice of the Peace)*; Kevin Hurley *(Norman)*; Brian Blondell *(Toy Store Clerk)*; Grady Hutt *(Jeremy Anderson)*; Jonathan Lavan *(Funeral Director)*; Diane Dorsey *(Head Teller)*; Jennifer Chada *(FBI Technician)*; Tony Fitzpatrick *(New House Neighbor)*; Tony Mockus Jr. *(FBI Agent)*; Letitia Hicks *(Woman Customer)*; Eric Young *(Chris's Lawyer)*; Carlton Miller *(Prosecutor)*; Fred Stone *(Judge)*; Rich Wilkie *(Markey)*; Linda Perlin *(Rivas)*; Stacy Logan *(Becker)*

Based on the true tale of husband-and-wife bank robbers Jeffrey and Jill Erickson, this character study follows a loving but mismatched couple from first encounter to tragic downfall.

We first see Chris (Luke Perry) and Pam (Ashley Judd) armed and in disguise. While hot-wiring a car, Chris is arrested and Pam takes off, the police in hot pursuit. The story then flashes back two years earlier, to their first barroom encounter. Chris is a straight-arrow rookie patrolman; Pam's a pot-smoking, hard-drinking beauty. Despite her volatile moments, Chris marries her. Pam deteriorates further once she's trapped in his world of everyday responsibilities. She trashes their home, alienates Chris from his family, and maxes out their credit cards; after an argument over money, she slices up her torso in a fit of depression.

Fired from his job, Chris becomes so desperate that, unbeknownst to Pam, he parlays his police/security guard skills into a successful career in bank robbery. He's soon able to afford the quaint little suburban house of his dreams. But when Pam accidentally spots him in the middle of one of his hold-ups, she's so turned on that she later experiences her first orgasm and asks to come along on his next job. After Chris is forced to shoot a policeman, he ditches the criminal career and buys a used bookstore. But Pam, disappointed with their return to a "normal life," leaves him until he resumes the robberies. By now, though, the cops are onto them. The film returns to the opening sequence; Chris is arrested and Pam kills herself when the police trap her in a suburban cul-de-sac. Chris is put on trial; still obsessed with Pam, however, he steals a cop's gun, tries to escape, and kills himself.

The combination of crime and doomed romance is nothing new, but this film is a bleak and compelling new addition to that roster. Instead of using its characters' lawless ways as an excuse for cheap melodrama, director John McNaughton (HENRY: PORTRAIT OF A SERIAL KILLER) downplays the more sensationalistic aspects of the story. Playing chilly voyeur to the Andersons' day-to-day lives and downward spiral, he lays out the facts with little judgment or sledgehammer psychology. The result is akin to a modern update of BADLANDS (1973). At its core lies a brilliant, open-wound performance by Judd as the compellingly screwed-up Pam. Putting his "Beverly Hills 90210" persona behind him, Perry is also surprisingly effective as an average guy suddenly overwhelmed by his emotions. Middle-class Illinois locales prove an effective backdrop for the characters' overwhelming desperation. It's an unflinching love story that gives new meaning to the term dysfunctional. *(Violence, nudity, sexual situations, substance abuse, profanity.)* — S.P.

d, John McNaughton; p, Richard Maynard; exec p, John Saviano; co-p, Steven A. Jones; w, Peg Haller, Bob Schneider; ph, Jean DeSegonzac; ed, Elena Maganini; m, Robert McNaughton, Ken Hale; prod d, Rick Paul; set d, Nancy Fallace; sound, Curt Frisk (mixer); fx, Guy Clayton; casting, Richard S. Kordos, Nan Charbonneau; cos, Jacqueline Saint Anne; makeup, Jamie Sue Weiss

Crime/Romance/Drama **(PR: C MPAA: R)**

NOT BAD FOR A GIRL ★★

(U.S.) 88m Spitshine Productions; Lisa Rose Apramian ~ Horizon Unlimited c

Joan Jett; Courtney Love; Donita Sparks; Kat Bjelland; Becky Wreck; L7; Hole; Babes in Toyland; Lunachicks; Mudwimin; Silverfish; Bobsled; Bulimia Banquet; Calamity Jane; Rock 'n' Roll High School

Subtitled "An analytic approach to the functions of music and gender deconstruction," this video documentary about contemporary female rockers and "riot grrrls" isn't as pompous as it sounds. It just doesn't have much to say that hasn't been said a thousand times before.

Documentarian Lisa Rose Apramian, Ph.D., is seen explaining her interviewing methodology to Donita Sparks of the band L7. She will ask questions in two areas. The first will be about the musicians' relationships to their music, or "How you channel your experience into sound, how your music mimics the kinetic energy of your emotional state, what sounds appeal to you and why, and how writing and playing and performing work for you." The second half of the interviews will focus on gender issues. Dr. Apramian is seen only briefly for the remainder of the video.

Joan Jett speaks about the negative reactions to her 1970s band the Runaways. Otherwise, those interviewed are all members of current bands with small followings. The video was completed in 1994 but features footage compiled over several years, before bands like Hole and L7 began to reach wide audiences.

For the most part, the interviewees talk about performing music in the same terms that rockers always have, emphasizing the music's viscerality and their desire to be onstage and lose themselves in their performance. Like most "alternative"" musicians, they also scorn the artificiality of pop stardom, preferring to present themselves as plainly or unattractively as possible.

Footage taped at a 1992 "riot grrrl" convention in Washington, DC, shows women demonstrating self-defense techniques and giving spoken-word performances. In a segment taped at the "Rock and Roll High School" in Australia, the school's founder notes that her pre-teen and teenage students show a preference for atonal noise music over pop or ballads, and almost never produce love songs.

Every bit as smart, well-spoken, and clear-thinking as their male counterparts, the interviewees talk about frustration with female stereotypes, but they seldom draw any connection between such stereotypes and their music. If anything, NOT BAD FOR A GIRL simply proves a negative: that despite various reasons that keep larger numbers of them from doing so, women can make the same kind of music men do. Dr. Apramian would have done better to have kept the interview segments to a minimum and show some of her subjects in uninterrupted performances. By keeping the musical clips to short bits, she de-emphasizes the value of their music, reducing it to a level of simple kinetic therapy. To thus imply that these women are doing nothing but, as one puts it, "getting their ya-yas out," demeans them. *(Extensive nudity, adult situations, substance abuse, extreme profanity.)* — M.F.

d, Lisa Rose Apramian; p, Lisa Rose Apramian, Kyle C. Kyle; exec p, Tina Silvey; w, Lisa Rose Apramian, Kyle C. Kyle; ph, Kyle C. Kyle; ed, Kyle C. Kyle

Documentary **(PR: C MPAA: NR)**

NOT OF THIS EARTH ★★½

(U.S.) 88m Concorde/New Horizons ~ New Horizons Home Video c

Michael York *(Paul Johnson)*; Parker Stevenson *(Jack Sherbourne)*; Richard Belzer *(Jeremy Pallin)*; Elizabeth Barondes *(Amanda Sayles)*; Ted Davis *(Rodman Felder)*; Mason Adams *(Dr. Rochelle)*; Julia Mueller *(Alien Woman)*; Bob McFarland *(Detective Mark Willows)*; Wendy Buckner *(Cheryl)*; Joshua D. Cohen *(Danny)*; Jennifer Coolidge *(Nurse)*; Eddie Driscoll *(John)*; Mary Scheer *(Saleswoman)*; Arthur Roberts *(Cheryl's Father)*; Diana Miranda *(Luisa)*; Chuck Martinez *(Hector)*; Athena Stensland *(Nurse)*; Ellen Statham *(Parking Attendant)*; John Buechler *(The Other)*

Perhaps dissatisfied with director Jim Wynorski's lackluster 1988 remake, schlock king Roger Corman has overseen a new production of his 1957 camp classic NOT OF THIS EARTH. Aside from a few technical, sexual, and thematic elements unattainable in 1957, this new version remains faithful to the tone of the original.

Paul Johnson (Michael York), while appearing human, is an alien from a distant planet, sent to Earth in search of a cure for the rare blood disease threatening his homeland. Johnson discovers that human blood temporarily ameliorates his illness; he attacks people by burning their eyes and draining them dry. Seeking a better solution, Johnson uses mind control to force blood specialist Dr. Rochelle to search for a cure. He also brainwashes the doctor into hiring out his nurse, Amanda Sayles (Elizabeth Barondes), who moves into Johnson's house to administer daily blood infusions.

Amanda notices that Johnson moves and talks in odd ways and never removes his sunglasses. Initially, she dismisses it, but she grows suspicious when Johnson's twitchy butler, Jeremy (Richard Belzer), tells her about disappearing visitors and the house's creepy basement. Amanda's cop boyfriend, Jack (Parker Stevenson), is also suspicious. Johnson, meanwhile, has learned from his superiors that civil war has left his planet in chaos. He encounters a female refugee from his world, and, using Rochelle's newfound cure, the pair plan to breed a new lineage and return to claim control of their planet. The female dies, however, when Johnson mistakenly infuses her with rabid blood. By now, Amanda and Jeremy have found considerable evidence that Johnson is an alien and they confront him. Jeremy is burnt to a crisp by Johnson's eye-rays and Amanda flees. Amanda manages to call Jack, who arrives on his motorcycle. After a chase, Jack forces Johnson's car over a cliff; the alien dies. At Johnson's grave site, Jack and Amanda ponder the alien's horrific and sad fate. A man with odd mannerisms and dark glasses approaches the grave as they walk away.

Corman's producing presence on this remake insures that nothing is taken too seriously. The space vampire plot is strictly B-movie fodder and the filmmakers openly acknowledge this and use it to their advantage. York clearly enjoys himself here, and his twitchy, semantically-challenged alien is the best thing about the film, a goofball version of Jeff Bridges's character from STARMAN (1984). Barondes, Belzer, and Stevenson are also quite good, with Barondes standing out as the sharp-tongued nurse Amanda (a role essayed by ex-porn star Traci Lords in the 1988 remake). Screenwriter Charles Philip Moore also deserves credit for smart, funny dialogue and timely references to AIDS as it relates to the alien's blood ailment. While such contemporary themes, as well as some suitably slimy special effects, have updated this NOT OF THIS EARTH, it is its faith to the Corman ideals of fun-loving camp that ultimately redeem the film and make it an enjoyable experience. *(Violence, nudity, profanity.)* — D.G.

d, Terence H. Winkless; p, Mike Elliott; exec p, Roger Corman, Lance H. Robbins; assoc p, Jan Kikumoto; co-p, Mike Upton; w, Charles Philip Moore (based on a screenplay by Charles B. Griffith and Mark Hanna); ph, Philip Holahan; ed, James Stellar Jr.; m, Jeff Winkless; prod d, Nava; art d, Aaron Mays; fx, Digital Drama; casting, Naomi Yoelin; cos, Elizabeth Ennis; makeup, Magical Media Industries, John Carl Buechler, John Foster, Lynn Buechler, Brad Hardin, Dave Barrett, Scott Phillips

Science Fiction **(PR: C MPAA: R)**

#247

(SEE: MODERN AFFAIR, A)

NUTTY PROFESSOR, THE ★★½

(U.S.) 95m Imagine Entertainment ~ Universal c

Eddie Murphy *(Sherman Klump/Buddy Love/Lance Perkins/Papa Klump/Mama Klump/Grandma Klump/Ernie Klump)*; Jada Pinkett *(Carla Purty)*; James Coburn *(Harlan Hartley)*; Larry Miller *(Dean Richmond)*; Dave Chappelle *(Reggie Warrington)*; John Ales *(Jason)*; Patricia Wilson *(Dean's Secretary)*; Jamal Mixon *(Ernie Clump, Jr.)*; Nichole McAuley *(Fit Woman)*; Hamilton Von Watts *(Health Instructor)*; Chao-Li Chi *(Asian Man)*; Tony Carlin *(Host)*; Quinn Duffy *(Bartender)*; Doug Williams *(Band Leader)*; David Ramsey *(Student)*; Chaz Lamar Shepherd *(Student)*; Lisa Halpern *(Sad Fat Girl)*; Mark McPherson *(Doctor)*; John Prosky *(Doctor)*; Michael Rothhaar *(Doctor)*; Sara Ballantine *(Nurse)*; Greg Natale *(Cop)*; Roy Werner *(Guy in Crowd)*; Retha Jones *(Woman in Crowd)*; Steve Monroe *(Student)*; Joe Greco *(Security Guard)*; Nick Kokotakis

(Waiter); Stanley D. Petter III *(Fireman)*; Mohammad Mohsen *(Bodybuilder)*; Michael D. Starks *(Boxing Trainer)*; Julianne Christie *(Sporting Goods Clerk)*; Christie Blanchard-Power *(Woman Dignitary)*; Alexia Robinson *(Sexy Girl)*; Lisa Boyle *(Sexy Girl)*; Athena Massey *(Sexy Girl)*; Judith Woodbury *(Wellman College Alumna)*

Eddie Murphy devised a comeback for himself using a remake of Jerry Lewis's biggest hit, THE NUTTY PROFESSOR, as a vehicle, but he fails to make the classic comedy his own in any entertaining way.

Sherman Klump (Eddie Murphy) is a kindly if absent-minded science teacher with a weight problem. At the midwestern university where he works, Sherman conducts extra-curricular weight-loss experiments on lab hamsters—to the consternation of the dean, Mr. Richmond (Larry Miller). Carla (Jada Pinkett), an attractive new grad student at the school, takes a liking to the misunderstood professor in spite of his girth, and accepts a date from him.

Sherman tries to lose weight the traditional way for his date, but his efforts are futile, and his night out with Carla begins uneasily as his family (including Mama, Papa, Grandma and Ernie Klump—all played by Murphy) trade insults over dinner. Then disaster strikes at a nightclub when a young comic, Reggie (David Chappelle) makes fun of Sherman in front of Carla and the crowd.

Wounded by the "fat" jokes and blinded by love, Sherman decides to test his hamster formula on himself. Late one night, he drinks the potion and, sure enough, transforms into a leaner, more dashing figure. Calling himself "Buddy Love" (Murphy again), Sherman ingratiates himself into Carla's life as a new man she does not recognize. Carla finds Buddy attractive, but is put off by his mean streak. Apparently, the testosterone in the serum makes Buddy not only cruel—he takes revenge on the young nightclub comic both verbally and physically—but also extra libidinous. The change is only temporary, and Buddy becomes Sherman once again.

The same night that Sherman must present his scientific discoveries to wealthy college donor Harlan Hartley (James Coburn), Buddy emerges, and fights to take over Sherman's mind and body. At the ritzy party for Hartley, Sherman and his alter ego reveal themselves at the same time, astonishing the crowd. Sherman thinks that his days as a scientist and teacher are numbered, but Hartley is so impressed by the experiment, that he insists Sherman continue his work for the school. Sherman (sans Buddy) also finds Carla proudly waiting for him on the dance floor.

This remake falters not only because Jim Carrey had already reworked the 1963 NUTTY PROFESSOR as THE MASK in 1994, but because Murphy's tired spin on the material strains for laughs by adding special effects in the excessive, grotesque manner of DEATH BECOMES HER. By retaining Jerry Lewis as an executive producer, at least Murphy cannot be accused of outright theft. But neither Murphy nor director Tom Shadyac (of Carrey's ACE VENTURA: PET DETECTIVE) succeed in duplicating the brilliant way the Lewis film played with the two sides of Lewis's public persona—introverted nerd and extroverted lounge lizard. Murphy simply cannot pull off the sensitive scenes convincingly, because his characters have always been based on his jovial, devilish personality. It is especially hypocritical business every time Murphy/Sherman seeks sympathy for his weight problems, since Murphy/Buddy enjoys plenty of "fat" jokes at Sherman's expense. Murphy's other characterizations as Sherman's low-class family members rely on flatulence jokes and racist stereotypes for humor.

Murphy briefly shows signs of his old comic skill as Buddy becomes increasingly deranged, but, otherwise, this NUTTY PROFESSOR is mean-spirited and depressing—not a good way for Murphy to win back the audience he has lost. *(Violence, sexual situations, extreme profanity.)* — E.M.

d, Tom Shadyac; p, Brian Grazer, Russell Simmons; exec p, Jerry Lewis, Karen Kehela, Mark Lipsky; co-p, James D. Brubaker; w, David Sheffield, Barry W. Blaustein, Tom Shadyac, Steve Oedekerk (based on the motion picture written by Jerry Lewis and Bill Richmond); ph, Julio Macat; ed, Don Zimmerman; m, David Newman; prod d, William Elliott; art d, Greg Papalia; set d, Kathryn Peters; sound, Jose Antonio Garcia (mixer); fx, Jon Farhat, Burt Dalton; casting, Aleta Chappelle; cos, Ha Nguyen; makeup, Geri B. Oppenheim, Rick Baker, David Leroy Anderson; stunts, Mickey Gilbert

AA Best Makeup: Rick Baker, David Leroy Anderson

Comedy **(PR: C MPAA: PG-13)**

OBLIVION 2
(SEE: BACKLASH: OBLIVION 2)

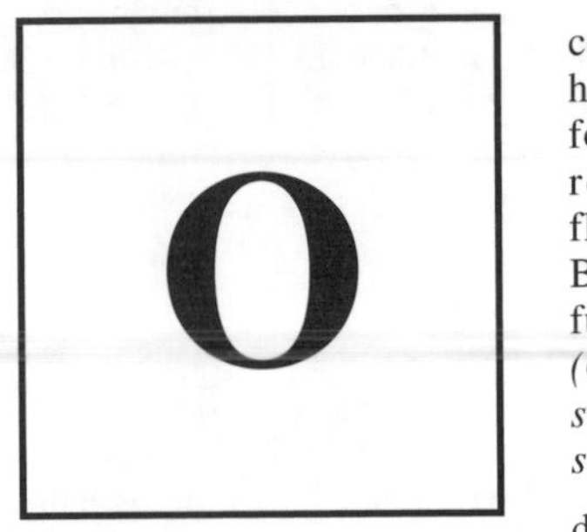

OF LOVE AND SHADOWS ★★
(Spain/Argentina) 104m Aleph Productions; Betka Film Ltd.; Tesauro ~ Miramax c
(DE AMOR Y DE SOMBRA)

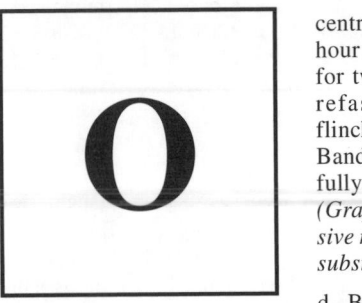

Jennifer Connelly *(Irene Beltran)*; Antonio Banderas *(Francisco Leal)*; Stefania Sandrelli *(Beatriz)*; Diego Wallraff *(Jose)*; Camillo Gallardo *(Gustavo)*; Patricio Contreras *(Mario)*; Jorge Rivera Lopez *(Professor Leal)*; Angela Ragno *(Hilda Leal)*; Alejandro Toccalinos *(Roadblock Guard)*; Alfredo Martin *(Surgeon)*; Anita Lesa *(Evangelina)*; Carmen Renard *(Rich Widow)*; Cesar Parlani *(Reverend)*; Claudio Ciacci *(Comandant Ramirez)*; Daniel Alvaredo *(Freedom Fighter)*; Dario Fernandez *(Ministry Employee)*; Dennis Dann *(Ministerial Official)*; Diego Leske *(Firing Squad Captain)*; Enrique Bustos *(Guide)*; Eva Cabral *(Mama Encarnacion)*; Ignacio Lopez *(Jacinto)*; Jacques Arndt *(General)*; Jean Pierre Reguerraz *(Cardinal)*; Jorge Ochoa *(Padre Cirilo)*; Jose Bonafoux *(Death in Person)*; Juanita Alzenberg *(Leal Child 1)*; Gonzalo Allende *(Leal Child 2)*

On the basis of this potboiler and the ludicrous THE HOUSE OF THE SPIRITS (1993), one can make the assumption that the novels of Isabel Allende do not translate well to the screen. Instead of being swept away by a tide of passion, audiences are dragged down by posturing crusaders and their caricatured military foes.

In 1973, a military junta ruled Chile with the power of martial law. Cocked in a see-no-evil environment of privilege, sheltered magazine editor Irene Beltran (Jennifer Connelly) enjoys the courtship of her dashing cousin-finance Gustavo (Camillo Gallardo), a career officer in the army. Irene's insularity shatters after she hires a photographer, Francisco (Antonio Banderas), whose priestly brother Father Jose (Diego Wallraff) works for the human-rights underground.

Irene's magazine covers the story of a local living saint who disappears after meeting Francisco and Irene. Commanding officer Ramirez (Claudio Ciacci) scuttles rumors of miracles by killing the woman's brother. Irene's search for the vanished holy woman leads her to a disgruntled soldier, who slips her a notebook cataloging the military's campaign of terror against the populace.

Francisco and Irene discover and publicly reveal a mass grave of government victims. Their rebel activities don't go unnoticed by spies tapping the residence of Father Jose's cardinal. To maintain the official policy of suppression, soldiers try to gun Irene down. When this assassination attempt on his betrothed opens his eyes, Gustavo prepares a coup, but is apprehended, tortured, and executed before a firing squad. Gustavo dies without revealing Francisco's scheme to smuggle a disguised Irene out of her hospital, across the border, to exile in Spain. Fifteen years later, Francisco and Irene return to a democratized Chile.

Although you can feel the filmmakers' desire to raise viewers' hackles about this dictatorship, OF LOVE AND SHADOWS is nothing but a lump of good intentions, full of breast-beating nobility and hollow-sounding dubbing. The dialogue, in thick Spanish accents to foster an ersatz South American flavor, is delivered as if the cast were being fed their lines through hidden ear-mikes.

Even a masterful director would be hard-pressed to visualize Allende's supernatural-tinged material. How do you present mysticism in conventional melodrama without provoking the audience's sense of the absurd or distancing viewers from the central romance? Eventually, Chile's saddest hour becomes nothing more than a plot-hook for two box office stars; it's political torture refashioned as colorful backdrop. One flinches as the lush music swells so pretty Banderas and prettier Connelly can kiss soulfully as totalitarians crush Chile underfoot. *(Graphic violence, extreme profanity, extensive nudity, sexual situations, adult situations, substance abuse.)* — R.P.

d, Betty Kaplan; p, Richard Goodwin, Paul Mayersohn, Betty Kaplan; exec p, Ernst Goldschmidt, Isidro Miguel, Herve Machuel; assoc p, Paula Franchini; w, Donald Freed (based on the novel by Isabel Allende); ph, Felix Monti; ed, Kathryn Himoff, Bill Butler; m, Jose Nieto; prod d, Abel Faccello; art d, Graciela Oderigo; sound, Jose Luis Diaz (recordist); fx, Tom Cundom; casting, Pamela Rack, Alejandro Maci; cos, Beatriz De Benedetto; makeup, Maria Laura Lopez

Drama/Political/Romance **(PR: C MPAA: R)**

OF UNKNOWN ORIGINS
(SEE: BLACK SCORPION)

OFF AND RUNNING ★
(U.S.) 90m Paved Productions; Aaron Russo Entertainment ~ HBO Video c

Cyndi Lauper *(Cyd)*; David Keith *(Jack Cornett)*; Johnny Pinto *(Pompey)*; Richard Belzer *(Milt)*; David Thornton *(Reese)*; Jose Perez *(Woody)*; Anita Morris *(Florence)*; Hazen G. F. Ford *(John Sasser)*; Linda Hart *(Gina Pompeii)*; Tracy Roberts *(Patti)*; Dana Mark *(April)*; Heather Davis *(Loree)*; Sy Bondy *(Norman)*; Tony Jones *(Curtis Valentine)*; George Richards *(Auctioneer)*; Steven Reibel *(Bid Spotter)*; Mark Harris *(Shriner)*; E. Duke Vincent *(Vincent)*; Gary Snow *(Yuppie Dad)*; Nancy Duerr *(Yuppie Mom)*; Sydney Sanders *(Desk Clerk)*

After glowing with star power in the kooky misfire VIBES (1988), Cyndi Lauper sabotages her film career with this road picture.

Flapping her fins as a singing mermaid at a Florida tourist bar, Cyd (Cyndi Lauper) faces a submerged future until an unlikely Prince Charming—horse trainer Woody Villa (Jose Perez)—surfaces in her life. After proposing marriage, Woody introduces Cyd to his pride and joy, champion horse Molnir. To increase Molnir's worth as a stud, John Sasser (Hazen G. F. Ford) destroys the steed and orders his enforcer Reese (David Thornton) to beat uncooperative Woody to death. Before Woody expires, he passes Cyd the key to a fortune (we later learn that the fortune is a canister containing Molnir's sperm samples) and draws a heart-shaped clue in his own blood.

Fleeing with the key after Reese spots her, Cyd steals a hooker's car, wrecks it in a pond, and gets rescued by small-time motel entrepreneur, Jack (David Keith). Unfortunately, her cover story about a child-custody battle backfires when Jack retrieves the hooker's neglected son, Pompey (Johnny Pinto), and the foul-mouthed boy insists on tagging along on Cyd's journey. After taking temporary refuge with her mother (Anita Morris), Cyd allows Pompey to steal train tickets from a tourist family. Cyd realizes the heart-shaped clue refers to Wood's Belmont pal, Curtis "Valentine" (Tony Jones). At Belmont Race Track, Cyd discovers Valentine's corpse and a merciless Reese lying in wait. Fortunately, after Pompey swallows the coveted key, a jittery horse fatally kicks Reese in the head. At Valentine's pad, Cyd stops Sasser from killing her friends by tossing the vials of

Molnir's sperm at him. Later, she shares her good fortune as racehorse owner with Jack, Pompey, and Pompey's mom.

OFF AND RUNNING never makes it out of the starting gate. Shimmeringly photographed by gifted cinematographer Andrzej Bartkowiak, this SOMETHING WILD-wannabe can't transcend a script that's a congealed mess of lame comedy, desperate road-movie cliches, and pre-fab heartwarming drama. As if that horse-sperm scramble wasn't a tricky enough proposition to pull off, this mangled screenplay saddles itself with a bonding between Cyd and an adorable, streetwise kid. This ragamuffin is one piece of dramatic baggage too many.

Featuring two brief musical interludes in which Lauper shines, OFF AND RUNNING is otherwise unremittingly dreary, a black-comedy travel nightmare smeared with too much graphic brutality. Although a good time is had by none, Lauper fans in particular will be reaching for handfuls of anti-depressants. *(Graphic violence, nudity, extreme profanity, adult situations, substance abuse.)* — R.P.

d, Edward Bianchi; p, Aaron Russo; co-p, Bill Carraro; w, Mitch Glazer; ph, Andrzej Bartkowiak; ed, Rick Shaine; m, Mason Daring; prod d, Maher Ahmad, Nina Ramsey; sound, Michael Tromer (mixer); fx, J. B. Jones; casting, Hughes-Moss Ltd.; cos, Bobbie Read; makeup, Jay Cannistraci, Marie Del Russo; stunts, Artie Malesci

Thriller/Comedy/Adventure (PR: C MPAA: R)

ONCE UPON A TIME ... WHEN WE WERE COLORED ★★★

(U.S.) 113m Black Entertainment Television Pictures; United Image Entertainment ~ IRS Releasing c

Al Freeman Jr. *(Poppa)*; Phylicia Rashad *(Ma Ponk)*; Leon Robinson *(Uncle Melvin)*; Paula Kelly *(Mama Pearl)*; Salli Richardson *(Miss Alice)*; Anna Maria Horsford *(Miss Annie)*; Bernie Casey *(Mr. Walter)*; Isaac Hayes *(Preacher Hurn)*; Richard Roundtree *(Cleve)*; Polly Bergin *(Miss Maybry)*; Karen Malina White *(Mary)*; Willie Norwood Jr. *(Cliff—age 10/11)*; Damon Hines *(Cliff—age 17)*; Charles Earl "Spud" Taylor Jr. *(Cliff—age 5)*; Phill Lewis *(Sammy—age 19)*; Taj Mahal *(Mr. Will)*; Iona Morris *(Nila)*; Phill Lewis *(Narrator)*

Based on Clifton Taulbert's memoirs, ONCE UPON A TIME . . . WHEN WE WERE COLORED documents the first 16 years in the life of an African-American boy from the South. The story spans 1946-62, a turbulent period, but the hopeful outlook easily makes the viewer forget the prejudices and inequities the characters fight. ONCE UPON A TIME . . . WHEN WE WERE COLORED is a feel-good movie, and is enjoyable even though its rosy depiction of difficult living situations doesn't quite ring true.

In 1946, in the Mississippi Delta, newborn Willie's young mother is not capable of caring for him, so he is sent to live with his grandparents. As he grows, he bonds with the older family members, especially his great-grandfather (Al Freeman Jr.), whom he calls "Poppa." The family lives in the racially segregated town Glen Allen, where most of the townspeople pick cotton for a living. People look out for one another and have a strong sense of community and loyalty. One day, Poppa takes Willie across the tracks into the white part of town, and teaches Willie his first two letters of the alphabet, "W" and "C." Willie doesn't yet know the difference between "white" and "colored," but learns the letters and is able to "follow the rules."

As Willie gets a little older, he moves in with his great aunt, Ma Ponk (Phylicia Rashad). The school-aged boy is befriended by his slightly older Uncle Sammy, who is strong and independent, and is determined not to pick cotton when he grows up. Ma Ponk's son, Melvin (Leon Robinson), who had moved north to Detroit, comes for a visit. He is full of stories about the good jobs and racial equality in the North, and tells Sammy "change is coming; don't let anybody beat you down."

When Willie turns 12, he begins to do yard work for a wealthy white woman, Miss Maybry (Polly Bergen), who listens to him as he shares his family's feelings about racial inequity and allows him to borrow great books from her. The circus comes to town, and a dancing girl stays with Willie and Ma Ponk. She charms them with her tales of the big city and the North, but she also learns from Ma Ponk, who convinces the girl to seek out her long-lost mother. Sammy is beaten for trying to rally the cotton-pickers. He runs away to the North.

A few years later, when a white-owned ice company puts pressure on the townspeople to do business with them, Glen Allen's residents side with Cleve (Richard Roundtree), the local black ice dealer. They all quit their cotton-picking jobs, leaving the white plantation owner with no workers. Change is about to come.

ONCE UPON A TIME . . . WHEN WE WERE COLORED's lesson is that if people stand strong and struggle to survive, they will. It is an uplifting film, showing the strength of family and human will through the eyes of a young boy. Director Tim Reid's choice of approaching the subject matter with joy and wit rather than tragedy and despair suits his strengths as a director. The best scenes are those in good humor and those that depict family bonding, the value of education, and the characters' small pleasures, such as the circus.

The film's dramatic moments are less subtle and often overdone. The care Reid puts into keeping the drama from being too disturbing keeps the film light, but unchallenging. As enjoyable as ONCE UPON A TIME . . . WHEN WE WERE COLORED is, it leaves an impression that life was happier for African-Americans during this time of great oppression than it is many years later, in a time of relative freedom.

The performances are first-rate, especially Freeman as Poppa. Reid's use of slow motion and handheld cameras add personality to the film, though the corny narration is an annoyance. For a first-time director, Reid shows great promise, leaving the viewer to hope that his next film will be one that takes a few more risks. *(Violence, adult situations.)* — A.M.

d, Tim Reid; p, Tim Reid, Michael Bennett; exec p, Butch Lewis; assoc p, Freddye Chapman; co-p, Clifton Taubert, Paulette Millichap; w, Paul W. Cooper (based on the book by Clifton Taulbert); ph, John Simmons; ed, David Pincus; m, Steve Tyrell; prod d, Michael Clausen; art d, Geoffrey S. Grimsman; set d, Kristen McGary; sound, Mike Patillo; casting, Jackie Brown-Karman; cos, Winnie D. Brown

Biography/Drama (PR: A MPAA: PG)

ONE FINE DAY ★★★

(U.S.) 108m Lynda Obst; Fox 2000 ~ 20th Century Fox c

Michelle Pfeiffer *(Melanie Parker)*; George Clooney *(Jack Taylor)*; Mae Whitman *(Maggie)*; Alex D. Linz *(Sammy)*; Charles Durning *(Lew)*; Holland Taylor *(Rita)*; Jon Robin Baitz *(Yates Jr.)*; Ellen Greene *(Elaine Lieberman)*; Joe Grifasi *(Manny Feldstein)*; Pete Hamill *(Frank Burroughs)*; Anna Maria Horsford *(Evelyn)*; Gregory Jbara *(Metro Reporter)*; Sheila Kelley *(Kristen)*; Barry Kivel *(Yates Sr.)*; Robert Klein *(Dr. Martin)*; George Martin *(Smith Leland)*; Michael Massee *(Eddie)*; Amanda Peet *(Celia)*; Bitty Schram *(Marla)*; Rachel York *(Liza)*

It's no IT HAPPENED ONE NIGHT (1934), but ONE FINE DAY wrings enough humor and charm out of the charismatic coupling of its very fine-looking stars to be an entertaining entry in the screwball-romance genre that had its heyday 60 years ago.

Meet architect Melanie Parker (Michelle Pfeiffer) and reporter Jack Taylor (George Clooney). She's one of "those American women" who thinks she can "do it all" on her own, and so has written men off. He's an overgrown little boy, who has written women off because they're all like Parker. Both are divorced, single parents—Parker has a son, Sammy (Alex D. Linz); Taylor has a daughter, Maggie (Mae Whitman)—and both miss the boat, literally, when they meet after arriving too late to send off their classmate kids on an all-day, nautical field trip. Neither has anyone they can turn to for help; so, although they both have very hectic days ahead (she's making the most important presentation of her life; he's sniffing out a City Hall garbage scandal), they take their tots in tow for better or for worse.

It's worse, of course. The kids are impossible—Sammy is accident prone; Maggie is prone to wander off. Parker and Taylor meet up again with a plan. He takes both kids while she makes her presentation, which goes great—she even stands up to her boss. She takes them while he tracks down a witness that can confirm his charges linking the mayor to the mob and graft. By the end of the day, their tough exteriors have softened. She learns it's okay to ask for a man's help; he starts behaving more responsibly. That night, he shows up on her doorstep, and they confess their feelings for each other. The two decide to pursue romance, but fall asleep on the couch before the chase can begin.

The design of this romantic comedy—antagonistic meeting, love at first sight, denial, flirtatious bickering for nine reels, admission of what the audience has known all along—is certainly one with which moviegoers will be familiar, even those who think Meg Ryan is the genre's foremost leading lady. But ONE FINE DAY also contains many story elements that refer back to classic screwball comedies from IT HAPPENED ONE NIGHT to WOMAN OF THE YEAR (1942).

Most obvious is Jack Taylor, the jaded reporter with a nose for sensationalism hounded by a gruff, but malleable, editor (here, Charles Durning). The political scandal and the device of Parker and Taylor exchanging their snappy dialogue over (cell) phones echoes HIS GIRL FRIDAY (1940). Parker comes from wealth (the delightful Holland Taylor plays her socialite mother) but has distanced herself from that world. Consequently, ONE FINE DAY avoids addressing class, a central theme of the earlier screwball comedies. Here, more thematic emphasis is placed on "the battle of the sexes," reminiscent of the Tracy-Hepburn films, but with the modern twist of emphasizing the woman's strength and the male protagonist's vulnerability.

George Clooney and Michelle Pfeiffer possess real on-screen chemistry, something that can't be produced by design and that all directors just have to hope and pray for. They sparkle together, and the comedy crackles. Clooney brings to this, his first romantic, leading film role, the same "yumminess" that has made him a TV heartthrob. Pfeiffer marvelously mixes her allure with wit, as she did in THE FABULOUS BAKER BOYS (1989). (Did someone say Carole Lombard?) Both the next Batman and the former Catwoman work well with the kids, Whitman and Linz, who are too adorable for words, but whose antics will have many viewers rethinking their plans for reproduction. *(Adult situations, profanity.)* — P.R.

d, Michael Hoffman; p, Lynda Obst; exec p, Kate Guinzburg, Michelle Pfeiffer; co-p, Mary McLaglen; w, Terrel Seltzer, Ellen Simon; ph, Oliver Stapleton; ed, Garth Craven; m, James Newton Howard; prod d, David Gropman; art d, John Warnke; set d, Anne Kuljian; sound, Petur Hliddal; casting, Lora Kennedy; cos, Susie DeSanto

AAN Best Original Song: James Newton Howard, Jud J. Friedman, Allan Dennis Rich

Romance/Comedy **(PR: A MPAA: PG)**

ONE GOOD TURN ★★

(U.S.) 90m Zeta Entertainment Ltd.; Overseas Film Group; First Look Pictures ~ BMG Video c

James Remar *(Simon)*; Suzy Amis *(Laura)*; Lenny Von Dohlen *(Matt)*; John Savage *(Santapietro)*; Richard Minchenberg *(John)*; Audie England *(Kristen)*; Rowena Guinness *(Kim)*; Andre Rosey Brown *(Salako)*; Michael Kopelow *(Brent)*; Elizabeth Alvarez *(Panamanian Girl)*; Melanie Good *(Newton)*; Rebecca Riley *(Woman at Wreck)*; Andrew Murphy *(Man at Wreck)*

A thriller about a twisted acquaintance who wreaks vengeance on his good Samaritan pal, ONE GOOD TURN is a psycho drama as cliched as its title.

On an LA street, Matt (Lenny Von Dohlen) briefly spots Simon (James Remar), who pulled him from a bombed car in Panama City years ago. After private eye Santapietro (John Savage) locates Simon, a down-and-out drifter, Matt gives him a job and keys to his pool house. After Matt confesses that a hooker died in his car when the bomb went off, his relationship deteriorates with his wife, Laura (Suzy Amis), who gets plenty of Simon's attention.

Santapietro discovers Simon has lied about his past, but the shifty drifter changes his story to avert Matt's suspicions. When his parole papers are accidentally delivered to the kid next door, Simon slyly engineers his death, inducing him to play a game of chicken with an oncoming train.

Aware that Matt's company is about to sell a new video game, Simon fiddles with a computer and renames the game's master file. Matt and Laura go on a romantic getaway, but Matt rushes back to LA, recovers the missing file, and discovers that it was Simon who tinkered with his terminal.

Meanwhile, Simon shows up at the vacation house, offering to cook Laura dinner. At the same time, Santapietro discovers that Simon was convicted of manslaughter. He calls the vacation house, and when Simon answers, he rushes to protect Laura. Just as he tells Laura about her murderous guest, Simon kills him. Crazed, Simon tells Laura that Matt tried to buy his girlfriend, the woman who died in the car bombing.

When Matt returns, Simon shoots at the couple and tries to run them over. His car crashes, and Matt, returning a favor of long ago, tries to rescue his nemesis, but Simon locks the door and blows up.

A classic of straight-to-video suspense, ONE GOOD TURN has a few real moments of horror and tension, all provided by James Remar's creepy character. Unfortunately, this evil character has no depth. One minute he's an aimless drifter; the next he's a thoroughly calculating psycho hell bent on vengeance. The finale, though marred by confusing editing, is fun, if only because this see-through story ends with a bang, not a whimper. *(Violence, nudity, adult situations.)* — S.K.

d, Tony Randel; p, Zane W. Levitt, Mark Yellen; co-p, Don Phillips; w, Jim Piddock; ph, Jacques Haitkin; ed, Kevin Tent; m, Joel Goldsmith; prod d, Carol Strober; set d, Traci Kirshbaum; sound, Ed White (mixer); fx, Larry Roberts; casting, Linda Francis; cos, Wendy Benbrook; makeup, Kenneth Michael Beck; stunts, Gary Paul

Thriller **(PR: O MPAA: R)**

101 DALMATIANS ★★

(U.S.) 103m Great Oaks Entertainment; Walt Disney Pictures ~ Beuna Vista c

Glenn Close *(Cruella DeVil)*; Jeff Daniels *(Roger)*; Joely Richardson *(Anita)*; Joan Plowright *(Nanny)*; Hugh Laurie *(Jasper)*; Mark Williams *(Horace)*; John Shrapnel *(Skinner)*; Tim McInnerny *(Alonzo)*; Hugh Fraser *(Frederick)*; Zohren Weiss *(Herbert)*; Mark Haddigan *(Alan)*; Michael Percival *(Police Inspector)*; Neville Phillips *(Minister)*; John Evans *(Pensioner with Bulldog)*; Hilda Braid *(Woman on Park Bench)*; Margery Mason *(Woman on Park Bench)*; John Benfield *(Doorman)*; Andrew Readman *(Police Officer #1)*; John Peters *(Police Officer #2)*; Bill Stewart *(Arresting Officer)*; Gerald Paris *(Doctor)*; Joe Lacey *(Veterinarian)*; Brian Capron *(Television News Reporter)*

This live reenactment of one of Disney's best, most commercially successful animated features is long and loud, but short on real wit or charm. In time-honored "family entertainment" fashion, it confuses cutesiness with true enchantment and is oppressively dominated by Glenn Close's leeringly overdone lead performance.

Anita (Joely Richardson) is a put-upon fashion designer working for Queen Bitch of London, Cruella DeVil (Glenn Close). She suffers the insults of her boss-from-hell as well as her very un-p.c. fashion ideas involving the use of furs from various endangered species. One day in the park, she meets Roger (Jeff Daniels), a video game designer. Actually, it's their pet dalmatians, Pongo and Perdy, who begin the introductions, by falling instantly in love. The human owners immediately follow suit and are married. It is not long before the patter of little feet is heard, belonging to the amazing litter of 15 puppies which Perdy bestows on them. Cruella unfortunately learns of this blessed event and becomes obsessed with turning them all into the coat of her dreams. She hires two bumbling goons, Jasper (Hugh Laurie) and Horace (Mark Williams), who steal the pups and spirit them away to a deserted country mansion, already occupied by some 86 stolen dalmatians. The parents are desolated, but soon seemingly every animal in the UK rallies to their aid. A helpful assortment of birds, raccoons, horses, pigs and mice lead Pongo and Perdy to their brood and aid in their escape. Goodness prevails and crime is punished when Cruella, Horace, and Jasper are all hauled off to the hoosegow. Meanwhile, Roger turns this adventure into a successful video game that enables him and Anita to retire to a huge estate capable of housing their newfound 101 pets.

The dogs Pongo and Perdy give by far the best performances in the film. Hack Disney house director Stephen Herek (THE MIGHTY DUCKS, MR. HOLLAND'S OPUS) leaves no antic stone unturned, lavishing them with closeups in which they run the gamut of emotions from the elation of first love to blissful parenthood to childless sorrow. The dalmatian lends itself beautifully to such emotive wringing. An army of dog trainers was on hand to help effect this; theirs is possibly the only honest work apparent on the screen. We can accept the dogs' instant infatuation as being natural; it's the humans' love-at-first-sight that strains belief. If John Hughes, who phoned in this shameless nothing of a script, had bothered to provide even one scene in which Roger and Anita had a normal conversation, we might have let ourselves be charmed by them. Instead, we're given a hugely lavish double wedding ceremony, attended by an entire congregation of dogowners and their pets.

As staged, the climactic birth scene is both idiotic and chauvinistic, with Roger and Pongo awaiting the results, with everything but cigars sticking out of their mouths, while the women busy themselves offscreen. This regressive tone is echoed in the offensive scene during which a tiresome Nanny (Joan Plowright) extolls the virtues of motherhood, while Anita listens raptly, physically aping her every uttered, inane cliche of an observation. 101 DALMATIANS appears to have taken a long, hard look at 1995's pig flick BABE: many of the various highjinks of the farmyard animals, many of whom are puppets, seem lifted whole from that overbaked epic of adorableness. The conspiratorial escape hatched by the beasts is a completely rote thing, devoid of suspense or real ingenuity. Most insultingly, Disney appears to have skimped on the dalmatians. Without deft animation, at most, you see maybe twenty. Ah, the limitations of live reenactments!

The humans fare decidedly less well than the dogs. Their role here is strictly supportive: big on concerned looks and helpless shruggings of shoulders over the animals. Daniels could have given this performance in his sleep. Richardson manages to give a slight impression of charm in her seriously undeveloped role. As that infernal Nanny, Plowright is the perfect Disney idea of a human English tea cozy; she has no life whatsoever, apart from her employers and their pets. Laurie and Williams, wicked in that patentedly comic HOME ALONE way, are able to evoke an occasional viewer smirk. And Close, of course, has a field day emulating the villainous excess of Jack Nicholson's Joker. In her chiaroscuro hair and gaudy-baroque Anthony Powell ensembles, she's a visual joke that wears progressively thinner with her every hooting, cackling, snorting scene. "Woof! Woof!" she screams derisively, before dissolving into the hysterical laughter that ends each of her onscreen appearances. *(Mild violence.)* — D.N.

d, Stephen Herek; p, John Hughes, Ricardo Mestres; exec p, Edward S. Feldman; assoc p, Rebekah Rudd; w, John Hughes (based on the novel *The One Hundred and One Dalmatians* by Dodie Smith); ph, Adrian Biddle; ed, Trudy Ship; m, Michael Kamen; prod d, Assheton Gorton; art d, Alan Tomkins, John Ralph; set d, Joanne Woollard; sound, Clive Winter; fx, Michael Owens, Chrissie England, George Gibbs, Industrial Light & Magic, Jim Henson's Creature Shop; casting, Celestia Fox, Marcia Ross; cos, Anthony Powell, Rosemary Burrows; makeup, Lynda Armstrong; stunts, Simon Crane

Children's/Comedy **(PR: AA MPAA: G)**

ONE LESS EGG TO FRY ★★★

(U.S.) 80m J. M. Pictures ~ J. M. Pictures c/bw

Joe Marzano *(Hapless Hugo)*; Ann Marie Marino *(Lara, the Waitress)*; Nathan Schiff *(Spider)*; Dennis Cianni *(Bebert)*; Chris Crawford *(The Singer)*

Director Joe Marzano pays tribute to the hard-boiled film noirs of yore with ONE LESS EGG TO FRY, a super-low-budget feature that displays more guts than Hollywood's cynical neo-noirs.

Male customers at Nick's, the greasy spoon highway diner in Lynbrook, NJ, are more interested in ogling Lana the lunch wagon woman (Ann Marie Marino) than eating the lousy food. Hapless Hugo (Joe Marzano), a grocery store stock clerk, has been particularly fascinated with Lana, and finally gets the nerve to ask her out. Surprisingly, the buxom, wisecracking waitress agrees to go on a date with the shy, portly Hugo, but during their night out she tells him that she is in love with The Bear (Dennis Cianni), a local hoodlum. Later, when Bear throws Lana out during an argument, Hugo lets her move into his small apartment.

Hugo tries to satisfy Lana, telling her that he is the manager of the grocery store where he works, but Lana demands that Hugo support her in a luxurious lifestyle. As a result, Hugo teams up with another gangster, Spider (Nathan Schiff), to try stealing money from Hugo's Uncle Carlo's pizza place. What Hugo does not know, however, is that Lana has secretly reunited with Bear and plans to leave Hugo after he gets the money for her. Hugo and Spider pull off the heist, but Bear throws Lana out again when he discovers that Hugo only stole some cheese from Uncle Carlo. Hugo finally realizes how foolish he has been over Lana and tries to go on without her.

Marzano is a director who continues to revamp and revise generic conventions on the slimmest of budgets. Beginning with his seven-minute version of THE DANGEROUS GAME (1953) and right up to his three-minute Busby Berkeley-style music video, ANGEL (1995), Marzano plays wittily but thoughtfully with old movie conventions. ONE LESS EGG TO FRY, his most ambitious feature to date, reproduces 1940s and '50s noir with the sort of ironic plot twists, despairing characters, shadowy black-and-white photography, bleak settings, overstated dialogue and violent action set pieces that marked so many "B" classics. Marzano also updates the noir style with an extra dose of kinky sex and a bit of color—Hugo and Lana's first date is turned into a music video set to Johnny Green's classic, "Out of Nowhere." Throughout the movie, Marzano's music choices are excellent—the title of the film, of course, comes from the Fifth Dimension's classic, "One Less Bell To Answer."

Despite its many riches, Marzano makes some errors. He waits too long before cutting between shots—it's okay for him to be cheap, not sloppy—and the overall film feels too long. More importantly, Marzano invests ONE LESS EGG TO FRY with more feeling than most noir parodies—such as Carl Reiner's DEAD MEN DON'T WEAR PLAID (1982) and FATAL INSTINCT (1993)—but fails to modernize the femme fatale. Lana looks like a joke next to the more sympathetic Hugo. On the other hand, Marzano may be on to something by being overly faithful to convention—Marino goes over the top tossing off nonsense '40s-style lines. In any case, ONE LESS EGG TO FRY works much better than many big-budget glosses on noir-movie cliches. *(Violence, nudity, sexual situations, adult situations, substance abuse, extreme profanity.)* — E.M.

d, Joe Marzano; p, Joe Marzano; assoc p, Joseph Parda, Nathan Schiff; w, Joe Marzano; ph, Joe Marzano; ed, Joe Marzano

Drama/Crime/Romance **(PR: C MPAA: NR)**

ONE MAN'S JUSTICE ★★

(U.S.) 100m Westwind Productions ~ LIVE Entertainment c
(AKA: ONE TOUGH BASTARD)

Brian Bosworth *(John North)*; Bruce Payne *(Karl Savak)*; Jeff Kober *(Marcus)*; Dejuan Guy *(Mikey)*; M. C. Hammer *(Dexter Kane)*; Neal McDonough *(Agent Ward)*; Robert Kotecki *(Agent Klark)*; Deborah Worthing *(Darlene)*; Rachel Duncan *(Marianne)*; Cyrus Farmer *(Chocolate)*; M. C. Gainey *(Hank)*; Robert La Sardo *(Tatooist)*; Leo Lee *(Agent Tan)*; Christopher Brown *(Jake)*; R. B. Bowens *(Mustapha)*; Angelle Brooks *(India Adams)*; Nick Richert *(Dred #1)*; Lawrence Lowe *(Luther Kane)*; Bruno Marcotulli *(Col. Comstead)*; Clifton Gonzalez-Gonzalez *(Jarhead)*; Christopher Kriesa *(Quartermaster Lane)*; James Harper *(Senior FBI Agent)*; Jamaal Carter *(Black Youth)*; Brady Chin *(Baseball Cop)*; Ryan Tomlinson *(Bobby)*; Michael Mishaud *(Doctor)*; Michael Stone *(Wexler)*; James Short *(Pyke)*; Irene Nettles *(Aunt Irene)*; Johnny Rogers *(Elevator Boy)*; Humberto Ortiz *(Stevie)*; Scott Pulman *(Transient)*; Darryl Alan Reed *(Army Chaplain)*

In an action pic bogged down with a domestic conscience, monolithic Brian Bosworth is wrenched from his loved ones only to gain a streetwise foster child.

Master Sergeant John North (Bosworth) is one tough Marine. When wife and daughter become crime statistics in a hostage fiasco following an illegal arms deal, North walks into the impasse, taking a few bullets while bringing the perps to justice. After recovering, North is unhappy to learn that rogue FBI agent Karl Savak (Bruce Payne) has enrolled Marcus (Jeff Kober), the killer of his family, in a witness protection program. North goes vigilante to bring down a conspiracy that embraces Marcus, drug dealer Dexter King (M. C. Hammer) and a stolen-military-weapons mastermind, who turns out to be Savak. Concurrent with this lawlessness epidemic, ghetto youngster Mikey (Dejuan Guy) steels himself to avenge the death of a schoolmate. Since North has a nodding acquaintance with Mikey's mom, he plays surrogate father figure while using the boy to penetrate the city's underbelly of drug couriers. But when North finally gets scurvy Marcus in his gunsights, he can't bring himself to kill with Mikey looking on. Later Savak liquidates Marcus himself, and wipes out Dexter and his gang in a complex web of betrayals and reprisals. Before Savak can remove loose-end Mikey, North fights him on a rooftop. Savak dies in a headlong plunge. Mikey adopts North as a role model of restraint.

ONE MAN'S JUSTICE plays like an infomercial for a militant wing of Big Brothers of America. The assorted double-crosses in triplicate are so clumsily scripted that viewers need a hand-out to explain the family tree of druggies, artillery thieves, and bent feds. Required to act bereaved, Bosworth strains to appear tearful, as if his trainer had just added one barbell plate too many to his bench press.

In this condescending civics lesson Man and Boy reach out to each other and learn that dozens of wrongs don't make a right (or a good film). Never mind that Bosworth's many self-defense moves send the message that if we were all as fit as drill sergeants we could thrash our enemies with impunity. That's a moral lesson genre buffs can dig; they don't want the pious frou-frou of a troubled African-American lad lectured by a self-righteous Caucasian super hero. *(Graphic violence, extreme profanity, adult situations, substance abuse.)* — R.P.

d, Kurt Wimmer; p, William Webb; exec p, Gary Wichard; assoc p, Thomas Schuler, Carol Schuler, Deborah Brock; co-p, Kurt Anderson; w, Steven Selling; ph, Jurgen Baum, John Huneck; ed, Michael Thibault; m, Anthony Marinelli; prod d, Terri Schaetzle; art d, Lece Edwards-Bonilla; set d, Courtney Jackson; sound, Dan Monahan (mixer); fx, Beverly Hartigan; casting, Mary Margiotta, Karen Margiotta; cos, Pennie Fien, Merrie Lawson; makeup, Deborah McNulty, Ted Haines; stunts, Kurt Bryant

Crime/Action **(PR: C MPAA: R)**

ONE NIGHT STAND ★★

(U.S.) 88m Concorde Films; New Horizons; Jack Schwartzman Productions; New World Entertainment ~ New Horizons Home Video c

Ally Sheedy *(Michelle Sanderson)*; Frederic Forrest *(Michael Joslyn)*; A Martinez *(Jack Gillman)*; Diane Salinger *(Barbara Joslyn)*; Gina Hecht *(Cy Watson)*; Don Novello *(Warren Miller)*; Elsa Raven; Millie Slavin

Who would have thought Talia Shire, mousy heroine of ROCKY (1976), had a steamy, erotic thriller up her sleeve? Completed in 1994 but released (barely) in 1996, ONE NIGHT STAND typifies the sort of late-night thriller fare that has proliferated on pay-TV cable: a hollow affair.

Michelle "Micky" Sanderson (Ally Sheedy) is a pretty but lonely young divorcee and designer for a small Los Angeles ad agency. At a baby shower Micky meets a handsome stranger (A

Martinez) and goes back to his pad. They make love all night, but Micky wakes to find him gone. Later in the day, Micky returns to the man's apartment, where she finds the actual owner, Michael Joslyn (Frederic Forrest), an odd character who says he knows nothing about her mystery lover. Later Micky's one-night stand calls her for a date. He says his name is Jack Gillman, he owns a building firm, and his first wife, Ellen, died in an accident. Micky becomes increasingly suspicious about that late wife after witnessing Jack's violent, jealous nature. She visits Joslyn and his wife (Diane Salinger) and learns Jack is their son-in-law. Mrs. Joslyn insists Jack murdered Ellen while Michael counters that an intruder killed their daughter. When Micky eventually confronts Jack with her misgivings, Jack now claims to have just discovered Michael Joslyn himself slew Ellen when, following an abortion, she threatened to reveal their incestuous relationship. Exposed, Michael tries to kill Jack and Micky, but Jack subdues his father-in-law. Mystery solved, Micky resumes her romance with Jack.

Shire made her debut here as director (and took over the reins after the death of her husband, producer Jack Schwartzman). Initially she shows particular insight in the woman's point of view, mixing feminism and formal dynamics in scenes of Micky resisting her boss' sexual overtures on the job, followed by an idyllic night of passion. For a while ONE NIGHT STAND appears promising in the manner of Shire's 1979 gender-reversal vehicle OLD BOYFRIENDS. But Marty Casella's screenplay devolves quickly and predictably into a cheap retread of sexist lady-in-distress thrillers like 1941's SUSPICION and 1944's GASLIGHT (and 1995's NEVER TALK TO STRANGERS, which also featured a Latino lothario who may or may not be terrorizing his lover, though the race issue is never addressed in either film). The normally-fine Frederic Forrest goes over the top and throws the film off balance. It hardly matters, however; despite the interesting early scenes, ONE NIGHT STAND isn't much to throw. *(Violence, nudity, sexual situations, adult situations, profanity.)* — E.M.

d, Talia Shire; p, Alida Camp; exec p, Jack Schwartzman, Roger Corman; co-p, Mike Elliot; w, Marty Casella; ph, Arthur Albert; ed, Jim Prior; m, David Shire; prod d, Rusty Smith; sound, Cameron Hamza; casting, Laura Schiff; cos, Louise Mingenbach

Romance/Mystery/Thriller (PR: O MPAA: R)

ONE TOUGH BASTARD

(SEE: ONE MAN'S JUSTICE)

OPEN SEASON ★½

(U.S.) 97m Frozen Rope Productions ~ Legacy Releasing/Republic Pictures Home Video c

Robert Wuhl *(Stuart Sain)*; Rod Taylor *(Billy Patrick)*; Gailard Sartain *(George Plunkett)*; Helen Shaver *(Rachel Rowen)*; Maggie Han *(Cary Sain)*; Steve White *(Leon)*; Timothy Arrington *(Herbert Goodfellow)*; Colin Fox *(Jackson Carp)*; Javanni Sy *(Gossage)*; Marvin Ishmael *(Rawley)*; Dina Merrill *(Doris Hays-Britton)*; Saul Rubinek *(Eric Schlockmeister)*; Joe Piscopo; Tom Selleck; Bob Costas; Regis Philbin; Larry King; Roger Dunne; Barry Flatman; Hadley Sandiford; Alan Thicke; Jimmy Walker; Darlene Cooke; George Buza; Alexe Duncan; Tony Guida

Subtitled "A Fable by Robert Wuhl," this poor man's NETWORK flails away ineffectively at easy targets like bad TV and corporate greed, in a plot so filled with holes as to seem nearly surreal.

Scrupulously honest Stuart Sain (Robert Wuhl) feels unfulfilled in his position with Fielding, a company that uses computerized boxes to monitor which television programs American families are watching. Up for a promotion, he is asked to represent the company on a TV talk show. But when he accidentally discovers just before taping that he has been passed over in favor of a junior employee, he crankily agrees on the air with a TV critic's claim that ratings do nothing but guarantee low-quality TV programming. This earns him the admiration of the program's other guest, Rachel Rowen (Helen Shaver), president of Public Broadcasting Television, and she offers him a vaguely defined PR job.

Meanwhile, the latest batch of Fielding boxes malfunction, erroneously crediting last-place PBT with an enormous rise in viewers. While media pundits enthuse over America's new infatuation with "culture," the competition panics, especially at first-place network GPN, whose tycoon owner George Plunkett (Gailard Sartain) believes in winning at all costs. GPN frantically counter-programs, going so far as to broadcast uncensored pornography and Iraqi executions; yet PBT remains number one. One of Sain's former colleagues at Fielding discovers the error and tells him about it on the same night that he and Rowen are due to receive Peabody Awards. Rather than cover up the error, Sain blurts out the facts before the assembed media. Plunkett then hires Sain as GPN's new program director.

His mischievous features seemingly set in a permanent wiseguy smirk, Wuhl is miscast in his own film (and underwritten in his own script) as the guileless, upstanding hero who cares more about the office softball team than the bottom line. With no clear target, the film takes potshots at movie multiplexes, women's fashions, Bible-thumpers, trailer park residents, and whatever may have seemed like a good idea at the time. "Wuhl's World" might be a more apt title for this grab bag of indignant satire, less a cohesive narrative (*much* less) than a dribble of smarmy vignettes bashing an industry without which a vanity project like OPEN SEASON wouldn't exist in the first place. There must be a moral in there somewhere. *(Extreme profanity, sexual situations, substance abuse, nudity.)* — C.C.

d, Robert Wuhl; p, Daniel Raskov; exec p, Ron Shelton; assoc p, Lori Miller; co-p, Karen Koch; w, Robert Wuhl; ph, Stephen Lighthill; ed, Seth Flaum; m, Marvin Hamlisch; prod d, Linda Burton; art d, Jacques Bradette; set d, Cal Loucks; sound, Ao Loo, Michael Sanchez; casting, Ed Johnston; cos, Marie-Sylvie Deveau

Comedy (PR: C MPAA: R)

ORGANIZED CRIME & TRIAD BUREAU ★★

(Hong Kong) 91m Magnum Films ~ Tai Seng Video c
(ZHONG AN SHI LU LING JI)

Danny Lee *(Lee)*; Anthony Wong *(Tung)*; Cecilia Yip *(Cindy)*; Roy Cheung *(Fan Tsi-Tsing)*; Elizabeth Lee *(Female Cop)*; Parkman Wong; Yi Fan-Wai; Fan Siu-Wong; Lee Fai

ORGANIZED CRIME & TRIAD BUREAU offers a trio of interesting leads and lots of location action to dress up a strictly routine cops-and-robbers chase thriller. The second in a trilogy of Hong Kong crime films by Kirk Wong, it was preceded by CRIME STORY (1993), with Jackie Chan, and followed by ROCK 'N' ROLL COP (1994), with Anthony Wong—both of which were far superior.

Inspector Lee (Danny Lee) of the Organized Crime and Triad Bureau (OCTB) sets his sights on armed robber Tung (Anthony Wong), who has eluded capture by holing up with his volatile mistress, Cindy (Cecilia Yip), and three henchmen on Cheung Chau Island off Hong Kong. After roughing up other suspects in order to learn Tung's whereabouts, OCTB is faced with brutality complaints from CAPO, the Hong Kong Police Department's Internal Affairs Division.

By tapping the phone of Tung's wife, the police manage to piece together enough clues to determine Tung's location. They raid Cheung Chau Island and conduct an all-out search, failing to turn up either Tung or Cindy, until a local funeral party arouses suspicion. Tung is found inside the coffin and apprehended.

Still at large, Cindy works with Tung's confederates and a pair of corrupt cops to engineer Tung's escape from jail. Finally, a failed escape attempt in court serves as a ruse which enables Cindy and a henchman to hijack the police van taking Tung back to jail. In hot pursuit, Lee orders the traffic signals turned off, causing a massive tie-up which forces the fugitives to flee on foot.

After a lengthy chase and shoot-out, the three fugitives take a store owner hostage, leading to a tense standoff. Lee, who has already earned Tung's respect from their previous encounters, enters the store alone and unarmed and finds all three criminals seriously wounded. Tung gets Lee to promise lenient treatment for Cindy. Tung then takes Cindy's hidden gun and shoots himself.

As Lee walks away, officers from CAPO demand an explanation for Tung's death, but are beaten up by Lee's men as the press corps deliberately look the other way.

For fans of Hong Kong crime films, Kirk Wong's work ranks third after that of directors John Woo (HARD-BOILED) and Ringo Lam (CITY ON FIRE). Unlike Wong's earlier films, OCTB never quite pulls its narrative strands together to make a dramatic point.

The characters are all weakly drawn and give us no reason to care about them. Tung never strikes us as a formidable villain because we never see him commit any crimes other than a jewelry store robbery seen briefly in flashback. Yip's tortured gang moll is the most compelling character, while both Lee (CITY ON FIRE) and Anthony Wong (HARD-BOILED) have played far more interesting characters in similar fare.

Despite the poor script, this film is extremely lively and well-directed, boasting the gritty feel for location action shooting that distinguishes the best Hong Kong crime films. Ultimately, however, the frenetic proceedings add up to little more than one long chase, with no point other than an occasional dig at Hong Kong's Internal Affairs division. *(Violence, sexual situations, profanity.)* — B.C.

d, Kirk Wong; exec p, Danny Lee; w, Winky Wong, Lou Bing; ph, Wong Wing-hang, Chan Kwong-hung; ed, Choi Hung; m, Tsung Ding-yat; art d, Hsu Wing-choi

Crime/Thriller **(PR: C MPAA: NR)**

ORIGINAL GANGSTAS ★★½

(U.S.) 99m Po'Boy Productions; Hammertime Productions; Management Company Entertainment Group; Orion ~ Orion c

Fred Williamson *(John Bookman)*; Jim Brown *(Jake Trevor)*; Pam Grier *(Laurie Thompson)*; Paul Winfield *(Reverend Dorsey)*; Isabel Sanford *(Gracie Bookman)*; Oscar Brown Jr. *(Marvin Bookman)*; Richard Roundtree *(Slick)*; Ron O'Neal *(Bubba)*; Christopher B. Duncan *(Spyro)*; Eddie Bo Smith Jr. *(Damien)*; Dru Down *(Kayo)*; Shyheim Franklin *(Dink)*; Robert Forster *(Detective Slatten)*; Charles Napier *(Mayor)*; Wings Hauser *(Michael Casey)*; Frank Pesce *(Detective Watts)*; Godfrey C. Danchimah *(Marcus)*; Tim Rhoze *(Blood)*; Seraiah Carol *(Thelma/Mrs. Jones)*; Dawn Stern *(Princess)*; Timothy Lewis *(Kenny Thompson)*; Linda Marie Bright *(Lisa Bookman)*; Kevin Watson *(Bobby)*; Anthony Snowden *(Doctor)*; Nick Edenetti *(TV Announcer)*; Jacqueline Swike *(TV News Reporter)*; Kimberly Shufford *(Lady in Gym)*; Idella Haywood *(2nd Lady in Gym)*; 1st Baptist Church Choir *(Christian Chapel Choir)*; Raymond Taylor *(Boy Left in Street)*; Scarface *(Rebel Guard at Party)*; Bushwick Bill *(Party Cigar Smoker)*; Dani Girl *(Dancer at Party)*; Luniz *(Customers at Thelma's Cafe)*; The Chi-Lites *(Themselves)*

More a revisiting of 1970s blaxploitation standards than a revisionist update, ORIGINAL GANGSTAS is a lean little B-movie that gets a boost from a cast of the genre's stars.

In Gary, Indiana, young basketball hustler Kenny Thompson (Timothy Lewis) scams members of the ruthless Rebels street gang and is gunned down in retribution. Shopkeeper Marvin Bookman (Oscar Brown Jr.) witnesses the attack and, despite the protests of his wife, Gracie (Isabel Sanford), tells the police what he saw. He, too, is assaulted by the Rebels, landing him in the hospital and inspiring his son, John (Fred Williamson), to return to town. John was once a member of the Rebels, as was Kenny's father, Jake (Jim Brown). Jake abandoned Kenny's mother, Laurie (Pam Grier), years before but also has returned to Gary in the wake of the shootings. Disgusted by their old gang's descent into wanton, random violence, John and Jake resolve to put a stop to its reign of terror, assisted by old friends Slick (Richard Roundtree) and Bubba (Ron O'Neal).

Gary's mayor (Charles Napier) hopes to achieve peace through mediation with the gang, with the help of the Rev. Marshall Dorsey (Paul Winfield), but their efforts come to naught. John and his friends conspire to precipitate a war between the Rebels and a rival gang, the Diablos, but the Rebels discover their trickery and lay waste to a section of the city. The result is a pitched battle between the young punks and the original gangstas, with John and his old friends emerging triumphant.

ORIGINAL GANGSTAS was directed by Larry Cohen, a B-movie veteran whose credits include some of the original blaxploitation movies, such as the Williamson vehicles BLACK CAESAR (1973) and HELL UP IN HARLEM (1973). Given that his work has often been distinguished by a quirky sense of satire, the general lack of a subversive approach in this film is something of a surprise. The idea of older tough guys showing a younger, out-of-control gang who's boss held possibilities for both social comment and dark comedy, but for the most part, the stars teach the gangbangers about respect by—well, killing them all. And while the movie is progressive in some aspects (the white characters aren't so much villainous as ineffective), it's more retrograde than its predecessors in others. In particular, Grier, who was more than capable of holding her own in the 1970s films, is largely reduced to the sidelines of the action while the men have all the fun.

That said, it's a real kick to see this crew back together, proving they can still be taken seriously as action heroes even after the spoof I'M GONNA GET YOU SUCKA comically deflated the genre. Williamson (who also produced), Brown, and Grier give solid performances, while O'Neal and Roundtree provide good backup in smaller roles. The casting of the white supporting parts with veterans like Napier, Robert Forster, and Wings Hauser further accentuates the B-nostalgia feeling. Even the occasionally ragged editing (an unintentional Cohen trademark) serves to transport the viewer back to the days when movies like this were being churned out on a regular basis. *(Graphic violence, substance abuse, extreme profanity.)* — M.G.

d, Larry Cohen; p, Fred Williamson; exec p, David Chackler, Eric Brooks; w, Aubrey Rattan; ph, Carlos Gonzalez; ed, David Kern, Peter B. Ellis; m, Valdimir Horunzhy; prod d, Elayne Barbara Ceder; sound, J. Byron Smith (mixer); fx, Bob Shelley;

casting, Craig Campobasso; cos, Lisa Moffie; makeup, Connie Kallos; stunts, Bob Minor

Action/Crime/Drama **(PR: C MPAA: R)**

ORIGINAL SINS ★★½

(U.S.) 108m Seven Pillars Productions ~ Something Weird Video c

Cheryl Clifford *(Diedra)*; Angelique de Rochambeau *(Kierstan)*; Faustina *(Mary Catherine)*; D. Cur *(Lila)*; Ivo Ing *(Father Sean)*; Scooter McCrae *(Kaps)*; Kevin Marr *(Rramnivek)*; Garry Novikoff *(Clark)*; Laura Bronte *(Coma Girl)*; Lionel Johnson *(Ken)*; John Weiner *(Dani)*; Arthur Jolly *(Tim)*; Stephen Rajkumar *(Stripe)*; Robert Wells *(Dr. Smith)*; Dani Michaeli *(Creep in Cellar)*; C. A. Fryharski *(Mrs. Mulrooney)*; Debra Joy Berger *(Mother)*

Deeply sacrilegious but wickedly inspired, this bizarre shocker has enough craft to make up for its indulgence.

Three passionately committed Catholic schoolgirls, Diedra (Cheryl Clifford), Kierstan (Angelique de Rochambeau), and Mary Catherine (Faustina), are overcome by a mysterious force that ravishes them simultaneously. Believing the presence to be Jesus Christ himself, the girls devote themselves to serving him, which includes further sexual submission as well as the bloody sacrificing of innocent fund-raiser Ken (Lionel Johnson). When Mary Catherine starts to dissent, the other two strangle her.

Kierstan's sister Lila (D. Cur) offers to dispose of the body, and delivers it to a heavy metal band who need a dead virgin for a ritual to invoke Satan. Instead, they raise a cranky demon named Kaps (Scooter McCrae), who kills them all. Mary Catherine revives, and the three girls meet their "Lord"—who proves to be the alien Rramnivek (Kevin Marr). He attempts to take Kierstan away, but Diedra stabs her to prevent him from doing so, and she is in turn swept down to Hell by Kaps as Rramnivek departs, leaving Mary Catherine the only survivor of the three.

There's more—a lot more—going on in this movie than the synopsis suggests, and if ORIGINAL SINS has a key flaw, it's that for ali their twisted creativity, writer-director-producers Matthew Howe and Howard Berger don't know when to quit. There are about 20 minutes of scenes and subplots that could easily be jettisoned—not for questions of taste, but for narrative expedience. As it stands, ORIGINAL SINS is an overlong but bracingly outrageous work that, while in the worst possible taste, has been made with undeniable conviction. The central story proceeds with compellingly warped logic, and Howe and Berger wring their jet-black humor from the characters and situations instead of poking fun at the genre.

While this shot-on-video production has a low-budget look, it possesses a much stronger visual sense than one usually finds in this kind of project. The acting is also far better than one might expect, with the three leads quite convincing throughout their debauchery and McCrae a devilish delight as the unconventional hell-spawn Kaps. Had the movie tightened its focus, it might have been a small winner, but there's still plenty here to entertain adventurous viewers. *(Graphic violence, extensive nudity, sexual situations, adult situations, extreme profanity.)* — M.G.

d, Matthew Howe, Howard Berger; p, Matthew Howe, Howard Berger; exec p, David Siegel; w, Matthew Howe, Howard Berger; ph, Matthew Howe; ed, Matthew Howe, Howard Berger; m, David Siegel; sound, Lamont Cranston, Jeff Kushner, Matthew Howe; fx, Josh Turi, Kevin Marr; cos, Renaissance Goddess Unlimited; makeup, Josh Turi

Horror/Comedy **(PR: O MPAA: NR)**

ORSON WELLES: THE ONE-MAN BAND ★★½

(Germany/France/Switzerland) 87m Medias Res; Mediterranee; BOA c/bw

Oja Kodar; Orson Welles

ORSON WELLES: THE ONE-MAN BAND offers the rare opportunity to see excerpts from several of the great filmmaker's legendary uncompleted and unreleased projects, including features, shorts, and television programs. Unfortunately, the clips shown represent only a small percentage of the available material, and they're presented in a frustratingly haphazard manner, resulting in a film that is as disappointing as it is tantalizing.

Welles' live-in companion the last 20 years of his life, Oja Kodar, shows clips from a number of projects, intercut with excerpts from a Q & A session with Welles and a college audience. Among the clips shown: John Huston playing a veteran director holding a press conference, with Peter Bogdanovich and Susan Strasberg, in THE OTHER SIDE OF THE WIND, which was shot between 1970 and 1976 and is virtually complete but may never be released due to legal problems, since it was financed by the Iranian government under the late Shah; a lengthy trailer for F FOR FAKE (1975) starring Welles and Kodar; MOBY DICK, consisting entirely of close-ups of Welles performing dramatic readings from the book; TAILORS, a comical sketch in which Welles is ridiculed for his girth by British tailors who are measuring him for a suit; THE DEEP, a thriller starring Welles, Jeanne Moreau, and Laurence Harvey, which was abandoned after Harvey's death; THE MERCHANT OF VENICE, with Welles portraying Shylock, never completed due to some of its negative being stolen; ONE-MAN BAND, featuring Welles playing several characters during a satirical tour of "swinging London;" THE MAGIC SHOW, a television special about one of Welles' favorite hobbies; THE ORSON WELLES SHOW, an unsold pilot for a TV talk-show, in which Welles interviews the Muppets; THE DREAMERS, an adaptation of a Tania Blixen story; and another, highly erotic, scene from THE OTHER SIDE OF THE WIND.

ORSON WELLES: THE ONE-MAN BAND is more notable for what it has to present than for how it's presented. The huge amount of material (over two tons of film cans) cries out for a simple, straighforward compilation, with each clip clearly identified and put into context. But, instead, this is a pseudo-artsy presentation featuring a portentous, philosophizing narrator, who rarely tells the title of what is being shown, whether it was intended as a feature or shot for TV, nor are any dates given for the footage. The clips are not shown in chronological order, often cutting back and forth between different projects in a confusing manner, making it virtually impossible to evaluate Welles' evolving style. Worst of all, the clips are really just fragments, lasting no longer than a few minutes each. Near the beginning of the film, Kodar states that she didn't want to reveal any of this material to the public after Welles died in 1985, but after 10 years has reluctantly decided that it should be seen. She says she wants to show that Welles was not idle during the last 20 years of his life. But the approach she and the filmmakers take is self-defeating, since hundreds of film cans are shown in her warehouse, yet only a miniscule amount of it is seen in the movie. Also, there is no footage at all from Welles' most personal (and infamous) unfinished project, DON QUIXOTE, which barely rates a passing mention.

As for the material itself, the scenes from THE OTHER SIDE OF THE WIND are somewhat startling in their frenetic use of a handheld camera, yet still demonstrate Welles' hallmark of expertly moving performers in and out of the frame and speaking on top of one another, while the rapid-fire editing is similar to the style employed in F FOR FAKE. THE MERCHANT OF

VENICE and THE DREAMERS display Welles' mastery of composition, and the short scene from THE DEEP evokes a sinister atmosphere which recalls TOUCH OF EVIL (1958). The various sketches (apparently intended for British TV), while amusing, are no more than clever little vignettes, while the TV magic show and the Muppets interview are depressing reminders of what the great man was reduced to in his final years. The notion that the genius who directed CITIZEN KANE (1941), let alone THE MAGNIFICENT AMBERSONS (1942), TOUCH OF EVIL and others, needs to have his reputation rehabilitated is spurious and absurd. But as long as there remains a wealth of unreleased material out there, it demands a proper, scholarly presentation, perhaps as a multi-part video project, which would enable serious students to critically appraise it. *(Nudity.)* — M.S.

d, Vassili Silovic; p, Dominique Antoine, Fredy Messmer, Roland Zag; exec p, Pit Riethmuller; w, Vassili Silovic, Roland Zag; ph, Thomas Mauch; ed, Marie-Josephe Yoyotte; m, Simon Cloquet

Documentary **(PR: C MPAA: NR)**

OUT THERE ★★

(U.S.) 98m Retrofit Co.; IRS Media ~ Paramount Home Video c

Bill Campbell *(Mosley)*; Wendy Schaal *(Paige Davis)*; Rod Steiger *(Col. Buck Gunner)*; Jill St. John *(Bunny Wells)*; Leslie Bevis *(Deputy Nicole Savage)*; Paul Dooley *(Emmett Davis)*; David Rasche *(Polson)*; Julie Brown *(Joleen)*; Bobcat Goldthwait *(Cobb)*; Billy Bob Thornton *(Biker)*; Carel Struycken *(Mr. Burke)*; Tom Kenny *(Man)*; P. J. Soles *(Young Woman)*; Cindy Morgan *(Judith Daws)*; Michael Mahon *(Guard)*; June Lockhart *(Donna)*; Michael Talbott *(Roussell)*; Karl Bury *(Young Emmett)*; Abraham Benrubi *(Roy)*; Gailyn Addis *(Marilyn)*; Richard Speight Jr. *(Taves)*; Robert Picardo *(Walter Danverstein)*

This goofy comedy might have been a MELVIN AND HOWARD for the alien abductee set. Instead, it settles for patronizing the ET fan clubbers, while constantly refocusing its energy on heroic skirmishes against the busybodies from beyond. OUT THERE throws in a redemptive romance for good measure.

Pulitzer Prize-winning photographer Mosley (Bill Campbell) purchases a 25-year-old camera, containing an undeveloped film roll, at a house sale. When he develops the film, he sees that it documents a welcome party for interplanetary visitors. The photos are dismissed by the Pentagon but snapped up by tabloid publisher Polson (David Rasche), who claims to be an editor for Omni magazine.

Mosley finds himself lumped together with tabloid wackos like former alien pick-up Joleen (Julie Brown), and so he hesitates to help Paige Davis (Wendy Schaal), whose missing father, Emmett (Paul Dooley), is immortalized in the alien visitor photos. Researching the vanishing act of Emmett and his hunting partner, Mosley and Paige stumble upon a cover-up concerning a grade Z alien movie hoax. Beneath the convenient theory that the aliens were only acting in a space flick lies the truth: The Earth is being conquered through global marketing, masterminded by slick extraterrestrials on Madison Avenue.

Mankind's bad taste enables otherworldly merchandising geniuses to hoodwink humanity until Mosley, Paige, and Joleen escape from an underground brainwashing facility. They link up with Emmett, who has been undermining the conspiracy for decades. Playing dreaded accordion music which obliterates the aliens, the heroes free the human race from full-scale invasion and lowered standards of consumerism.

Savoring its zestier moments, the audience wants to like OUT THERE in all its loopy splendor. But its inspired flights of fancy (mainly provided by the divine Julie Brown) are undercut by draggy direction and editing of an episodically tailored screenplay. Even more of a fun-retardant is the film's dogged charting of Mosley's self-actualization. Treated as serious uplift material, the shutterbug's spiritual rebirth through his embrace of the anti-alien crusaders takes too long to develop.

But despite its pokiness and fuzzy focus, OUT THERE bubbles with fitful inventiveness as Hollywood veterans have a high time camping it up. Such delights include Rasche's portrayal of a Carl Sagan-ish figure, June Lockhart crying a river in a demonstration of Earth-like bereavement, and a chipper Jill St. John misrepresenting facts like a Home Shopping Network representative from Venus. *(Violence, extreme profanity.)* — R.P.

d, Sam Irvin; p, Larry Estes; exec p, Paul Colichman, Miles Copeland III; assoc p, Jonas Thaler, Cindy Morgan; w, Thomas Strelich, Alison Nigh; ph, Gary Tieche; ed, Stephen Myers; m, Frankie Blue, Deborah Holland; prod d, M. Nord Haggerty; art d, Adam Olszewski; set d, Dawn Ferry; sound, D. J. Ritchie; fx, Mark Rappaport; casting, Donald Paul Pemrick; makeup, Jennifer Montgomery; stunts, J. Suzanne Rampe

Science Fiction/Comedy **(PR: C MPAA: NR)**

OUTER LIMITS: SANDKINGS, THE ★½

(Canada) 92m Trilogy Entertainment Group; Atlantis Films Ltd. ~ MGM/UA Home Video c

Beau Bridges *(Dr. Simon Kress)*; Helen Shaver *(Kathy Kress)*; Dylan Bridges *(Josh Kress)*; Lloyd Bridges *(Simon's Father)*; Kim Coates *(Dave Stockley)*

THE SANDKINGS was the pilot episode for a revival of "The Outer Limits" TV series, which ran in the mid-60s and still has a cult following. While the feature is long on moody atmospherics and morality, it's decidedly short on the thrills modern horror audiences have come to expect.

For nine years, scientist Simon Kress (Beau Bridges) has worked in a top-secret government lab, analyzing and evolving a microscopic species of Martian insects that he has dubbed "the Sandkings." Kress is certain his work will eventually be made public, and he will be awarded the Nobel Prize. But the project is unceremoniously terminated, as is he. Seeking glory, Kress swipes some of the Sandkings, builds a giant terrarium in his barn, and continues his work. Free of restrictions, he quickly develops the Sandkings into intelligent, scorpion-like creatures which seem to revere him as a god.

Kress's obsession with his secret work alienates, and finally drives away, his family. After one of the Sandkings bites him, he slowly begins to lose his sanity. Kress invites his former supervisor (Kim Coates) over, and throws him into the terrarium to be devoured by the Sandkings. His struggle breaks the glass and the Sandkings escape. In the end, Kress has no choice but to blow up his house, and himself with it, to destroy the alien invaders.

On the positive side, THE SANDKINGS is well-acted and well-made. It continues "The Outer Limits" tradition of emphasizing moody visuals and intense atmospherics over scenes of explicit horror. On the negative side, it languishes over its characterization and plot to the point where the movie becomes very dull in its final third. "The Outer Limits" always offers a moral—here, a caution about delusions of grandeur—but THE SANDKINGS is so determined to drive its point home, it leaves interesting story points unexamined. For example: how *exactly* does the bite affect Kress, and were the Sandkings just conning Kress with their worship to gain their freedom?

THE SANDKINGS was broadcast in 1995, and released to home video in 1996. With its decided lack of graphic shocks, THE SANDKINGS might be a choice for parents searching for "sanitized" entertainment for their children. Conversely, kids acquainted with Freddy Krueger will probably find THE SANDKINGS tame, and be put off by its platitudes. *(Adult situations, violence.)* — P.R.

d, Stuart Gillard; p, Justis Greene; exec p, Pen Densham, Richard B. Lewis, John Watson; w, Melinda Snodgrass (based on the novella by George R. R. Martin); ph, Philip Linzey; ed, Michael Robison; prod d, Brent Thomas; fx, John Gajdecki, Paul Boyington

Horror/Science Fiction **(PR: A MPAA: NR)**

OUTPOST, THE ★★★

(Hungary/Romania) 84m Hunnia Filmstudio Ltd.; Domino Film Bucharest; Neuropa KFT; MTV Dramai Studioja ~ Cinemagyar Hungarofilm Export Ltd. c

(AKA: THE SECTION; A RESZLEG; DERNIERE FRONTIERE; POSTE AVANCE)

Mari Nagy *(Gizella Weiss)*; Jozsef Szarvas; Valentin Teodosiu; Misu Dimvale; Andrei Finti; Geza Toth; Alexandra Bindea

Form follows function in THE OUTPOST, a spare allegory for the fates of many a dissident or victim of political purges.

Gizella (Mari Nagy), a middle-aged engineer, is informed by superiors that she has been promoted to oversee a field site. The divorced woman bids a bittersweet goodbye to friends and coworkers and embarks for the company outpost. Her train terminates at a filthy mining settlement, where the male handlers treat the newcomer with scorn and barely-suppressed lust, as Gizella is stripped and her books confiscated. Sullen men pumping a railway handcart convey her far into the snowy mountains. On the way, she glimpses another expedition dragging back what's left of the previous supervisor. Once a respected scholar, he has sunken into a catatonic stupor. Gizella is given over to a peasant guide who openly pities her during the last stage of the journey. He assures her that he will bring onions every Wednesday, so she won't lose track of what day it is. The outpost turns out to be a desolate, weasel-infested shack. One man, a remote acquaintance of Gizella, already resides within, half-crazed. Their job is to spend months, perhaps years, pounding pegs into the ground at intervals. The man stays sane by bitterly vowing to outlive the bureaucrats who sent him. Gizella maintains a positive outlook.

The nation depicted is never named, but could easily pass for Ceaucescu's Romania—or for that matter, any East European dictatorship that shipped innocent citizens to languish in prison camps located in stark hinterlands. With THE OUTPOST, director Peter Gothar distills the essence of internal exile in a socialist dictatorship—the faceless "company" for whom everyone works. It's a feature-length escort to a bleak limbo, with only the slightest embroidery of Kafkaesque metaphor. What keeps it from utter despair is the quietly determined heroine who, enigmatically, holds onto hope when none seems present. Leading lady Mari Nagy, one of Hungary's foremost stage actresses, is on screen for the entire film, but must contend with the severe script, which keeps the heroine's background and personality as vague as possible. *(Substance abuse, nudity, adult situations)* — C.C.

d, Peter Gothar; p, Andras Ozarai; exec p, Sandor Simo, Sandor Szonyi; co-p, Cristian Comeaga, Mihail Cociasu; w, Adam Bodar, Peter Gothar (based on the short story by Adam Bodar); ph, Vivi Dragan Vasile; ed, Peter Timar, Eszter Majoros; m, Gyorgy Selmeczy, Gyorgy Orban; prod d, Zsolt Khell, Cristian Niculescu; sound, Janos Reti; cos, Janos Breckl

Political/Drama **(PR: C MPAA: NR)**

OUTRAGE ★★★

(Spain/Italy) 108m Arco Films; Metrofilms ~ A-Pix Entertainment c

(DISPARA)

Antonio Banderas *(Marco Vallez)*; Francesca Neri *(Ana)*; Walter Vidarte *(Manuel)*; Eulalia Ramon *(Mother)*; Chema Manzo *(Father)*; Archero Manas *(Mario)*; Rodrigo Valverde *(Paco)*; Coque Malla *(Juan)*; Concha Leza *(Doctor)*; Alessandro Grassini; Corrado Bonora; Danilo Macaggi; Noel Sansom; Gonzalo Duran; Ignacio Carremo; Natalin Menendez; Sara Matute; Rosario Santesmases; Elena Ferreira; Tania Salas

A well-acted revenge drama, OUTRAGE seems rather anomalous to the career of acclaimed director Carlos Saura (CRIA, BLOOD WEDDING). It's not that his skills—potent compositions, an affinity for eroticism—aren't in evidence, but that they service a merely workmanlike screenplay.

Cynical newshound Marco Vallez (Antonio Banderas) discovers his latent romantic instincts stirred at the circus by Italian-born sharpshooter Ana (Francesca Neri). They commence an affair, but while Marco toils out of town on assignment Ana is brutally raped by three itinerant laborers. Badly injured and still in shock, Ana tracks down the trio to a garage and cold-bloodedly guns them down. Hunted by police and pilloried in the tabloids, Ana nearly runs down a child, then takes the boy's family hostage in their home. Pressured by his editor to put a personal spin on the now-notorious Ana's standoff, reporter Marco refuses and races to save his lover's life. Trading places with the terrified family, Marco cradles Ana, but his intervention is too late. By daybreak, she dies from internal bleeding.

Eloquently capturing the trauma of rape without sensationalizing the crime, Saura delivers a vivid exploration of how violence begets violence. Although Ana's downward spiral isn't that suspenseful, Saura lets the audience fall in love with volatile heroine Ana along with Marco, thus making her degradation all the more hideous. Without excusing her actions, Saura sets up the payback tragedy in fatalistic terms; in more ways than one, the rape is a death sentence not just for the perpetrators but for Ana, whose violation destroys her spirit before it breaks her body.

What Saura can't do is transcend the limits of the material's straightforward presentation. Even if we're not in Charles Bronson-DEATH WISH territory, the film lacks the quirkiness and depth of melodramas like 1988's THE ACCUSED or 1987's SHAME. OUTRAGE piques viewer involvement without ever suggesting that this well-crafted outcry is a project close to the director's heart. The film bears the stamp of a master, not a sense of the director's personality or burning desire to make this particular movie. *(Extreme profanity, graphic violence, extensive nudity, sexual situations, substance abuse.)* — R.P.

d, Carlos Saura; p, Galliano Juso, Jaime Comas Gil; w, Enzo Monteleone, Carlos Saura (based the story "Spara Che Ti Pasa" by Giorgio Scerbanenco); ph, Javier Aguirresarobe; ed, Juan Ignacio San Mateo; m, Alberto Iglesias; prod d, Rafael Palermo; art d, Rafael Palermo; set d, Gonzalo Thovar Del Solar; sound, Riccardo Palmieri; fx, Reyes Abades; cos, Maria Jose Iglesias, Maria Carulli; makeup, Alfredo Marazzi

Thriller/Drama **(PR: O MPAA: R)**

OVER THE WIRE ★★

(U.S.) 90m SC Productions ~ Playboy Entertainment/Royal Oak Entertainment c

Landon Hall *(Susan)*; David Christensen *(Bruce)*; Shauna O'Brien *(Rachel)*; Keith Lewis *(Roy Walker)*; Tim Abell *(Mark)*; Ross Hagen *(Detective Jackson)*; C. B. Stevens *(Jenny)*; Lisa Pratt *(Hostess)*; Bob Dole *(Phone Sex Guy)*; Kimberly Blair *(Sascha)*; John LaZar *(Assassin)*

As an erotic aid, OVER THE WIRE has its batteries fully charged. But as a conventional made-for-Playboy-cable whodunit, this heavy-breathing thriller is a few stiletto-heeled paces ahead of the competition.

When telephone repairman (and ex-cop) Bruce (David Christensen) overhears a potentially deadly business conversation over crossed wires, he dutifully reports his concern to his police-detective pal, Roy Walker (Keith Lewis). Bruce believes that one of two sisters—realtor Susan Sternam (Landon Hall) and exotic dancer Rachel Sternam (Shauna O'Brien)—has hired a hit man to eliminate the other. Playing the good citizen against Roy's advice, Bruce confronts both women, immediately suspecting overtly bitchy Susan (whom he nonetheless beds) and shielding troubled Rachel, who presents herself as the victim of her controlling older sister. Meanwhile, Susan's unfaithful boyfriend Mark (Tim Abell) tangles with Roy, who mistakes him for the hit man.

The only thing Bruce's snooping reveals is that a deceased aunt's will stipulates the Sternam sisters must live together for five years in order to inherit—unless one dies first. Assuming that greed is the motive, Bruce succumbs to Rachel in a hot tub. Meanwhile, the hit man (John LaZar) shoots meddling Mark and prepares for his killing *du jour*. After Rachel lets a piece of incriminating information slip, Bruce suddenly realizes that Rachel is actually the murderess-to-be, motivated by simple jealousy. After shooting at Bruce, Rachel grazes Roy in the head when he arrives to save his buddy. In a hail of bullets, Bruce kills Rachel before heading to the Sternam house, where he interrupts the hit man as he's about to perform his assignment. The hit man wounds Bruce, and Susan—innocent all along—kills the hit man with the gun Bruce dropped.

Viewers of "erotic thrillers" are by now accustomed to how often steamy scenes pointlessly jam up the narrative flow. But when OVER THE WIRE pauses to slip a condom over its plot, it always manages to return to its exposition without a feeling of "plot-us interruptus." While the blue interludes may be a few too many, OVER THE WIRE is marred more by mediocre dialogue and performances. Still, the amateurish quality doesn't extend to the ingenious scenario in which two sisters are pitted against each other not by financial one-upmanship, but by endemic sibling rivalry. Delivering both suspenseful chills and bedroom thrills, OVER THE WIRE offers those who regard crime-solving as an alternative aphrodisiac two distinct avenues of satisfaction. *(Violence, extensive nudity, sexual situations, extreme profanity.)* — R.P.

d, Nicholas Medina; p, Don Key Jr.; w, Pete Slate; ph, Howard Walker; ed, Jay Gottlieb, Martin Del Mar; prod d, Helen Harwell; art d, Cynthia Palormo; sound, Matt Rauchsberg (mixer); cos, Mandana Yamin; makeup, Marjolein Moore; stunts, Bob Bragg

Erotic/Mystery/Thriller (PR: O MPAA: R)

PAINTED HERO ★★

(U.S.) 105m Sound Shore Productions; Americana Images Inc. ~ Cabin Fever Entertainment c

Dwight Yoakam *(Virgil Kidder)*; Michelle Joyner *(Katelin)*; Kiersten Warren *(Teresa)*; Cindy Pickett *(Sadie)*; John Getz *(Sheriff Acuff)*; Bo Hopkins *(Brownie)*; Walton Goggins *(Roddy)*; Terry McIlvain *(Gus)*; Peter Fonda *(Ray the Cook)*; Brent Anderson *(Clay)*; Toby Metcalf *(Luke)*; Bill Thurman *(Old Man Bolen)*; Boyd Polhamus *(Rodeo Announcer Night)*; Justin McKee *(Rodeo Announcer Day)*; Jonathan Ross *(Deputy Joe Nathan)*; Brad Leland *(Deputy Roy)*; Jake Clifton *(Old Cowboy)*; Art Watson *(Cowboy in Chute)*; Lisa Cawthorn *(April)*; Dana Jackson *(May)*; Elizabeth Anderson *(Lilly)*; John Davies *(Coroner)*; Chase Gallatin *(Chance)*; Chase Benedict *(Boy at Carnival)*; Hunter Tharp *(Boy with Gun)*

Whatever magnetic appeal Dwight Yoakam might have in the country music arena doesn't translate to his dramatic turn in PAINTED HERO. Low charisma is just one of the strikes against this stroll through William Inge country—it also suffers from a poorly structured screenplay, soap-opera dialogue, and matter-of-fact direction fiercely at odds with the script's melodramatic revelations.

Content with his aimless life as a rodeo clown, former buckaroo star Virgil Kidder (Dwight Yoakam) grudgingly gives in to the pleading of rodeo impresario, Brownie (Bo Hopkins) to book Virgil into a hometown appearance. As Virgil suspects, his reception there is frosty. Former main squeeze Katelin (Michelle Joyner) is still annoyed over Virgil's neglect of their now-deceased illegitimate son; the town's corrupt Sheriff Acuff (John Getz) resentfully lives for the opportunity to bust Virgil on any pretext; and Virgil's one-time rival, Roddy (Walton Goggins), doesn't cotton to Virgil's interest in Roddy's Lolita-like sister, Teresa (Kiersten Warren).

Fancying herself a seductress, the wired and disturbed Teresa begs bedmate Virgil to lock her in his car trunk. When obliging Virgil finds her the following morning, Teresa has been lethally staked; the only suspect is Virgil.

The politically ambitious sheriff, who is Teresa's uncle, orders his gung-ho deputy to gun down Virgil, but Virgil manages to escape long enough to lobby for Katelin's help. Disguising himself in the makeup of a different rodeo clown, Virgil stalls for time as the sheriff plans to arrest him in the arena. Instead, the sheriff's long-suffering sister, Sadie (Cindy Pickett), comes forward with shocking accusations: Sadie is not Teresa's mother but her aunt; Sheriff Acuff is really the father of Roddy and Teresa. Having killed their mother years before, Acuff murdered his daughter, Teresa, to stop the old scandal from resurfacing. His reputation ruined, the sheriff is trampled by a bull let loose by his infuriated son, Roddy. Cleared of the charges, Virgil blows town with Katelin.

Whew! That last-minute outburst may remind the audience of the climax of a classic tragedy, but the film lacks the Greeks' ability to build their dramas to a crescendo; this corn-pone opera doesn't prepare us for its overwrought finale. PAINTED HERO repeats its protagonists' psychological war stories *ad infinitum* and bores the audience so thoroughly that the viewer becomes inured to the film's whopper of a *deus ex machina*.

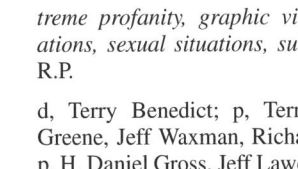

Because the conclusion's emotional extravagance contrasts so sharply with the laid-back presentation preceding it, the response is nervous laughter. Padded with rodeo footage and lacking respect for the viewer's ability to grasp plot points quickly, PAINTED HERO is little more than a feeble melodrama. *(Extreme profanity, graphic violence, adult situations, sexual situations, substance abuse.)* — R.P.

d, Terry Benedict; p, Terry Benedict, Peter Greene, Jeff Waxman, Richard Weinman; exec p, H. Daniel Gross, Jeff Lawenda; assoc p, Tony Grazia; co-p, Tom Molito; w, Terry Benedict, Stan Bertheaud; ph, David Bridges; ed, Gary McLaughlin; m, Rick Marotta; prod d, Elayne Barbara Ceder; set d, Cindy Downes; sound, Paul Ratajczak (mixer), David O. Daniel (mixer); fx, Randy Moore; casting, Judith Pope, Melissa Skoff, Mike Perkins; cos, Sandy B.; makeup, Donna Kaigler, Beau Wilson; stunts, Mike Watson

Drama **(PR: C MPAA: R)**

PALLBEARER, THE ★½

(U.S.) 104m Abrams/Katims/Webster Productions ~ Miramax c

David Schwimmer *(Tom Thompson)*; Gwyneth Paltrow *(Julie DeMarco)*; Michael Rappaport *(Brad)*; Toni Collette *(Cynthia)*; Carol Kane *(Tom's Mom)*; Bitty Schram *(Lauren)*; Barbara Hershey *(Ruth Abernathy)*; Michael Vartan *(Scott)*; Matthew Faber *(Jared)*; Robin Morse *(Sylvie)*; Edoardo Ballerini *(The Job Interviewer)*; Tony Machine *(The Undertaker)*; Robert Katims *(Minister)*; Greg Grunberg *(Abernathy Cousin)*; David Vadim *(Abernathy Cousin)*; Zak Orth *(Abernathy Cousin)*; Kevin Corrigan; Joseph D'Onofrio; John Mudd; Eric Morace *(The Pallbearers)*; Elizabeth Franz *(Aunt Lucille)*; Marnie Pomerantz *(Roller Coaster Rider)*; Mark Margolis *(Philip DeMarco)*; Jean DeBaer *(Suzanne DeMarco)*; George Masters *(Maitre d')*; Todd Schrenk *(The Other Tom)*; Rabbi Joel Zion *(Rabbi)*; Sal Maneri *(Wedding Guest)*; Gwen Goldsmith *(Wedding Guest)*

A vehicle for sitcom star David Schwimmer, THE PALLBEARER is a dark comedy filled with neurotic, romantically-challenged, twentysomething characters and no worthwhile lessons.

Tom Thompson (Schwimmer) is just about the biggest loser you can imagine: he is unable to find a job, land a girlfriend, move out of his mom's house, or even comb his hair neatly. He is shocked to discover that he has been asked to serve as pallbearer and eulogist at the funeral of Bill Abernathy, a man he's never heard of. Too wimpy to admit to Bill's grieving mother, Ruth (Barbara Hershey), that he doesn't remember her son, Tom does his funereal duties—all the while swooning for one Julie DeMarco (Gwyneth Paltrow), a beautiful young girl for whom Tom has carried a Statue of Liberty-sized torch since high school. On a lark, Julie joins Tom's friends in attendance at Bill's funeral—primarily to watch Tom squirm his way through a sloppily improvised eulogy. Determined not to let this second chance pass him by, Tom puts his first-date-style moves on Julie; though she initially rebuffs his faltering advances, having returned to her home town to recover from a bad breakup, Julie soon begins to fall for Tom. At the same time, Tom becomes enmeshed in a weird Oedipal relationship with Ruth that includes both sex and attending family picnics in her dead son's swimsuit. Finally, Tom is forced to come clean to Julie about his relationship with Ruth, and to Ruth about his non-relationship with the late Bill. At first everybody hates Tom, but eventually decide they love the big lug after all.

On paper, THE PALLBEARER must have looked like a good idea to somebody, but the final product is a perplexing attempt at black romantic comedy that misses the mark by miles. Screenwriters Matt Reeves (UNDER SIEGE 2: DARK TERRITORY)

and Jason Katims mistakenly center the film around a pathetic character who is just too much of a two-faced loser to evoke sympathy, let alone make his romance with Julie believable. Tom's character flaws are compounded by the casting of Schwimmer, whose simpering, stuttering delivery may work well in small, television-sized doses, but in a feature film only further irritates the already suffering audience. Its main character a lost cause, THE PALLBEARER's script spins out of control, particularly when Tom and Ruth begin their rather unsettling sexual relationship. Nor does it help that Tom's mean-spirited, petty friends are just as annoying and unlikeable as he is. Only Paltrow (SEVEN, EMMA) turns in a satisfying performance as the love interest, but it's hard to believe that she would fall for a schmuck like Tom—and harder to believe she'd take him back at the film's end. *(Profanity, sexual situations.)* — B.T.

d, Matt Reeves; p, Jeffrey Abrams, Paul Webster; exec p, Bob Weinstein, Harvey Weinstein, Meryl Poster; co-p, Jason Katims; w, Jason Katims, Matt Reeves; ph, Robert Elswit; ed, Stan Salfas; m, Stewart Copeland; prod d, Robin Standefer; art d, Stephen Alesch; set d, Kate Yatsko; sound, Michael Barosky (mixer); casting, Billy Hopkins, Suzanne Smith, Kerry Barden; cos, Donna Zakowska; makeup, Allen Weisinger; stunts, George Augustus Aguilar

Comedy/Romance **(PR: C MPAA: PG-13)**

PALOOKAVILLE ★★½

(U.S.) 92m Playhouse International Pictures; Redwave Films; Samuel Goldwyn Company ~ Orion c

Adam Trese *(Jerry)*; Vincent Gallo *(Russ)*; William Forsythe *(Sid)*; Gareth Williams *(Ed)*; Lisa Gay Hamilton *(Betty)*; Bridgit Ryan *(Enid)*; Kim Dickens *(Laurie)*; Frances McDormand *(June)*; Suzanne Shepherd *(Mother)*; Nicole Burdette *(Chris)*; Robert LuPone *(Ralph)*; Walter Bryant *(Money Truck Driver)*; Douglas Seale *(Old Man)*; William Riker *(Old Arthur)*; Nesbitt Blaisdell *(Old Fritz)*; Leonard Jackson *(Bus Driver)*; William Duell *(Money Truck Guard)*; Peter McRobbie *(Chief of Police)*; Stan Tracy *(Barney)*; Gerry Robert *(Cop)*; Mario Todisco *(Gangster)*; Paul Austin *(Sergeant)*; Sam Coppola *(Mr. Kott)*; Jerome LePage *(Walt)*; Skylar Lewis *(Ricky)*

Call it Scorsese-lite. PALOOKAVILLE tells the story of three Italian-American men who bumble their way through a life of crime only to become heroes for preventing a crime. While hardly substantial, the film at least provides an hour-and-a-half of easy-going entertainment.

Set in contemporary Jersey City, PALOOKAVILLE begins with the three friends—Sid (William Forsythe), Russ (Vincent Gallo), and Jerry (Adam Trese)—attempting a jewelry store robbery. Although their theft goes awry, the men decide to continue their criminal ways, at least until they find well-paying jobs. Meanwhile, Russ lives at home with his domineering mother, sister, and brother-in-law (who is a cop), and divides his non-domestic time between a teenage girl next door (Kim Dickens) and a prostitute (Frances McDormand). Sid, who lives alone with his pet dog, attempts to make money by creating an illegal taxi service for the elderly, while Jerry depends on his wife, Betty (Lisa Gay Hamilton), for financial support from her supermarket job.

One day the friends save the life of the driver of an armored car that regularly stops at Betty's supermarket. After the incident, they hatch a plan to rob the cash receipts from the same car. As homework, they watch the 1950 movie, ARMORED CAR ROBBERY; later, they adjust the vehicle's radiator to make it overheat at a specific location, at which point they plan to hold up the driver using toy guns. But once in action, the scheme fails, in part because Russ's brother-in-law follows the men during their suspicious trek after the armored car. Finally, just when the men think they are being arrested for attempted robbery, the police bring them into a news conference, where they are celebrated as heroes for saving the life of the driver some days earlier.

PALOOKAVILLE will surprise audiences with its well-drawn characters, pleasing score (by Rachel Portman), enjoyable performances, and quiet, quirky tone. However, PALOOKAVILLE suffers somewhat from its too-cute approach to the amateur-crime theme. Despite an admirable attempt to show the causal relationship between poverty and criminal behavior, David Epstein's screenplay (an adaptation of an Italo Calvino story) emphasizes the humor over the pathos.

But even when it becomes overly endearing, PALOOKAVILLE sustains itself, thanks mainly to the cast: Vincent Gallo sharply defines the frustrations of Russ, the film's most tragicomic character (also, his extemporaneous version of Mimi Ripperton's "Lovin' You" steals the film); Adam Trese (LAWS OF GRAVITY) makes the naive Jerry believable; and William Forsythe (VIRTUOSITY) nicely underplays the typical, bespeckled nerd of the bunch. The supporting players also contribute winning moments, although the biggest name in the cast, Frances McDormand, plays the least well-defined character, making one wonder just what is she doing in this movie anyway.

Those looking for an alternative to the violence of modern-day gangster pictures will probably enjoy PALOOKAVILLE, while those looking for blood, guns, and shock effects may consider this one too much like the pastries that figure in the story: sweet and airy. *(Violence, sexual situations, adult situations, profanity.)* — E.M.

d, Alan Taylor; p, Uberto Pasolini; exec p, Lindsay Law; co-p, Scott Ferguson; w, David Epstein; ph, John Thomas; ed, David Leonard; m, Rachel Portman; prod d, Anne Stuhler; art d, Roswell Hamrick; sound, Peter Schneider (mixer); fx, Drew Jiritano; casting, Billy Hopkins, Kerry Barden, Suzanne Smith; cos, Katherine Jane Bryant; makeup, Nicki Ledermann; stunts, Peter Bucossi

Comedy/Crime **(PR: C MPAA: R)**

PARADISE LOST: THE CHILD MURDERS AT ROBIN HOOD HILLS ★★★★

(U.S.) 150m Hand-to-Mouth Productions; HBO ~ HBO c

Jessie Lloyd Misskelley; Damien Wayne Echols; Charles Jason Baldwin; Pan Hobbs; Terry Hobbs; Melissa Byers; John Mark Byers; Todd Moore; Diane Moore; Shelby Misskelley; Jessie Lloyd Misskelley; Lee Rush; Gail Grinnell; Pan Echols; Joe Hutchison; Domini Teer; John N. Fogleman; Brent David; Chief Inspector Gary Gitchell; Daniel T. Stidham; Gregory L. Crow; Paul N. Ford; Dr. James Rasicot; Scott Davidson; Judge David Burnett; Val P. Price

PARADISE LOST: THE CHILD MURDERS AT ROBIN HOOD HILLS documents the true story of the most infamous murder case in Arkansas history. At the beginning of this disturbing film, three children are found mutilated and killed, while three teenagers are held responsible for the crime. But PARADISE LOST keenly probes the facts and ultimately questions the guilt of the defendants. Not surprisingly, the outcome is haunting.

PARADISE LOST: THE CHILD MURDERS AT ROBIN HOOD HILLS begins with the murders of three eight-year-old boys, whose disfigured remains were found in a shallow creek in West Memphis, Arkansas. The community calls for justice, and one month later, the police bring in three local teenagers accused of killing the boys as part of a satanic ritual. According to the police, Jessie Misskelley, 17, voluntarily confesses to playing a role in the murders. His statement implicates Jason Baldwin, 16, and Damien Echols, 18, two self-described devil-worshippers. News reports about the teens' alleged blood-drinking and sexual deviance influences public opinion before the trial even begins.

Despite the public anger towards them, the three defendants maintain their innocence. During the first trial, Jessie, with an IQ of only 72, reveals that he had been coerced into confessing because of police pressure. In the later, separate trial of the other two, Damien tells the court how his "different" ways of dressing and interest in the occult had made him a scapegoat long before this incident; and Jason protests that his close friendship with Damien is his only "crime." Meanwhile, the Bible-spouting father of one of the victims, Mark Buyer, seems to have more to hide than any of the three accused. Nonetheless, despite the lack of physical evidence connecting the teens to the crime, the jury finds all three guilty. Today, Damien awaits execution by lethal injection and Jason and Jessie plan to spend the rest of their lives in jail.

In PARADISE LOST, filmmakers Joe Berlinger and Bruce Sinofsky do not hide their empathy for the accused. Just as in their startling first documentary, BROTHER'S KEEPER (1992), Berlinger and Sinofsky present evidence no less crucial for a retrial than the facts brought to light in Errol Morris's THIN BLUE LINE (the 1988 documentary that helped free a falsely accused man from jail). Not only do the filmmakers spot the weaknesses of the case against the teens, they even seem to find the actual culprit in a shocking trial sequence that ends up a mere digression from the ultimate convictions. (Unlike the Morris film, PARADISE LOST does not try to recreate the crime, but with the revealing interview footage, it hardly needs to.)

In addition, through their careful selection of material and skillful editing, Berlinger and Sinofsky make a powerful statement about how class and religion play a role in the hysteria surrounding the case, and how the media fosters this hysteria; the film is similar in many ways to David Van Taylor's DREAM DECEIVERS, in which the rock group Judas Priest is tried for instigating teenage suicide. If you missed PARADISE LOST on HBO, where it first aired, it would be well worth seeing on video. *(Graphic violence, nudity, adult situations, extreme profanity.)* — E.M.

d, Joe Berlinger, Bruce Sinofsky; p, Joe Berlinger, Bruce Sinofsky; exec p, Sheila Nevins, Loren Eiferman; w, Joe Berlinger, Bruce Sinofsky; ph, Robert Richman; ed, Joe Berlinger, Bruce Sinofsky, M. Watanabe Milmore; m, Metallica; sound, Michael Karas

Documentary **(PR: O MPAA: NR)**

PARIS WAS A WOMAN ★★½

(U.S./Germany) 77m Jezebel Productions; Cicada Film ~ Zeitgeist Films c/bw

Gisele Freund; Sam Steward; Berthe Cleyrergue; Catharine R. Stimpson; Shari Benstock; Juliet Stevenson *(Narrator)*

Literary legends, lesbian sex, betrayal, alcohol abuse, war—all the ingredients are here for a fascinating voyage to avant-garde, early 20th-century Paris in this detailed look at the women of the Left Bank by acclaimed documentarists Greta Schiller and Andrea Weiss. Given the wealth of talent and the sheer size of the pool being examined (see below), it's hard to imagine how producer-writer Weiss and director-editor Schiller could go—if not wrong—then at least skewed to the bludgeoningly bland in this informative yet overearnest and solemn film.

It's certainly not for lack of interesting subject matter. The "women of the Left Bank" comprised an illustrious list, including: writers Djuna Barnes, Colette, and Gertrude Stein; Stein's lover and small-press publisher, Alice B. Toklas; Rue de l'Odeon bookstore owners and literary supporters Sylvia Beach and Adrienne Monnier; poet and salon-hostess Natalie Clifford Barney; *New Yorker* diarist Janet Flanner, a.k.a. "Genet"; and photographer Gisele Freund, among others. Contemporary interviewees include Freund herself; Shari Benstock, author of *Women of the Left Bank: Paris 1900-1940*; and the delightful eyewitness Berthe Cleyrergue, Barney's longtime housekeeper. Sylvia Beach and the hilariously acerbic Janet Flanner are among those seen in vintage interviews; it's Flanner who chides rule-breaking artist Picasso for taking the same unvarying route home every night, and it's also Flanner who says of the portly Stein, "She never finished [anything]. Except at the table, of course."

With such a literary dream team, it's difficult to pinpoint where this documentary acquires it sluggish pace. Part of the problem comes from the filmmakers placing their subjects on pedestals—which is doubly troubling since many of the artists already place themselves there! Even more disturbing is the fact that even though most of women studied in the film were lesbian, the filmmakers do not attempt place this information in a broader sociological context—for instance, Weiss and Schiller do not theorize that their subjects' orientation not only helped give them the freedom to travel to Paris (i.e., unencumbered by children or husbands) to find themselves, but also a large impetus to do so, since they could more freely live as lesbians abroad.

Regardless of the filmmakers neglect to contextualize much of the story, many of the anecdotes themselves, of course, are priceless. Beach—who speaks in a whispery, high-pitched voice—relates how she met Hemingway when he "rambled in" to her shop, Shakespeare and Company, and "showed me his scars." Freund recalls how Monnier had to keep an audience of writers away from the bookshelves when Freund showed her groundbreaking color photo-portraits, since the writers had a tendency to filch the tomes. More tragic is the story of James Joyce's abandoning of Beach, who risked all her meager capital to publish *Ulysses* when no one else would, and then was left bankrupt when Joyce found fame and left her for Random House (though some insight into Joyce's side of the story would have been welcome).

A significant technical problem throughout the documentary is its sound quality: The oldest interviewees (many sporting difficult accents) often needed subtitling, as did some of the vintage recorded interviews. Surely this was a budgetary limitation—one that PBS, The History Channel, or some other TV outlet would surely have sprung to fix had it been presented to them. *(Adult situations.)* — F.L.

d, Greta Schiller; p, Frances Berrigan, Greta Schiller, Andrea Weiss; exec p, Frances Berrigan; assoc p, Jennifer Romine, Melissa Cahill Tonelli; co-p, Bjoern Koll; w, Adrea Weiss; ph, Nurith Aviv, Greta Schiller, Renato Tonelli, Fawn Yacker; ed, Greta Schiller; m, Janette Mason; sound, Ronald Bailey, Al Livecchi, Barbara Zahm

Documentary **(PR: A MPAA: NR)**

PARISIAN ENCOUNTERS

(SEE: RENDEZVOUS IN PARIS)

PASOLINI, AN ITALIAN CRIME

(SEE: WHO KILLED PASOLINI?)

PASOLINI, UN DELITTO ITALIANO

(SEE: WHO KILLED PASOLINI?)

PASSION OF DARKLY NOON, THE ★★★
(U.K./Germany/Belgium) 101m Fugitive Features; Die Hauskunst; Keytsman ~ Entertainment Film Distributors/New Capital Group c

Brendan Fraser *(Darkly Noon)*; Ashley Judd *(Callie)*; Viggo Mortensen *(Clay)*; Loren Dean *(Jude)*; Grace Zabriskie *(Roxie)*; Lou Meyers *(Quincey)*; Kate Harper *(Ma)*; Mel Cobb *(Pa)*; Josse de Pauw *(Ringmaster)*; Gabi Binder; Maximillian Paul *(Ringmaster's Family Member)*; Knut Samel *(Ringmaster's Family Member)*

In this, his second feature film, writer-director Philip Ridley revisits much of the same territory as his debut, the mesmerizing cult film, THE REFLECTING SKIN (1990), but to lesser effect. A similar message is watered down by weaker imagery and simpler execution that seem to indicate a filmmaker afraid to give his vision full rein.

When he finds an unconscious young man in the woods, delivery man Jude (Loren Dean) takes him to a secluded house where Callie (Ashley Judd) agrees to care for him. His name, taken from the Bible, is Darkly Noon (Brendan Fraser), and he is the only survivor of a fundamentalist sect that was massacred by villagers. Callie invites Darkly to stay and become part of a family with her and her mute lover, Clay (Viggo Mortenson).

Darkly becomes sexually attracted to the uninhibited Callie. Unable to express feelings he has been taught to repress, he vents his frustration by scourging himself with barbed wire.

In the woods, Darkly meets Roxie (Grace Zabriskie), an older woman who considers Callie an evil witch. She claims Callie bewitched her husband and her son—Clay. Callie says that Roxie has been unhinged since her husband died trying to rape her. But because he believes in witches, Darkly considers this a possible explanation for the frustrations he feels. Upset by Darkly's increasingly bizarre behavior, Callie tells him to leave.

Roxie commits suicide, and Darkly discovers her body. He prays to his parents, who were killed in the massacre, for guidance. They appear and tell him that Callie is a witch who must be killed. At night, Darkly paints his body red, returns to the house and attacks Callie and Clay. With Darkly on the verge of killing Callie, she screams, "I love you." Darkly hesitates, and is shot to death by Jude.

THE PASSION OF DARKLY NOON has much in common with THE REFLECTING SKIN: an isolated rural setting bathed in blinding sunlight; ubiquitous religious imagery; and a view of human sexuality as a mystifying, frightening possibility for an immature soul who has not yet experienced it. But while THE REFLECTING SKIN was ominously suggestive about the nature of evil in the human spirit—imagine "The Turn of the Screw" mixed with THE WIZARD OF OZ (1939), with substantial debts to David Lynch and Peter Greenaway—THE PASSION OF DARKLY NOON is a relatively simplistic tract about the anti-human nature of religion. The same general criticism applies to the entire production: every element seems a blander retread. The rural scenery—shot, surprisingly, in Germany—is lovely, but not so striking; Nick Bacat's score, which includes two eerie songs, sung by PJ Harvey and Gavin Friday, is evocative, but not so spellbinding.

Of course, it's unfair to judge a work entirely in relation to another by the same filmmaker. On its own, THE PASSION OF DARKLY NOON would seem an intriguing but overwrought effort by a talented filmmaker who needs to focus on his goals. Viewed in tandem with THE REFLECTING SKIN, it seems more likely that Ridley is mistakenly going in the opposite direction: He needs to give his imagination freer, rather than tighter, rein. *(Graphic violence, nudity, sexual situations.)* —M.F.

d, Philip Ridley; p, Dominic Anciano, Frank Henschke, Alan Keytsman; exec p, Jim Beach, Ray Burdis, Shelly Bancroft; w, Philip Ridley; ph, John de Borman; ed, Leslie Healey; m, Nick Bicat; prod d, Hubert Pouille; art d, Willem Klewais, Vera Dobroschke; sound, Nigel Galt; fx, Uli Nefzer; casting, Victoria Thomas; cos, Gabi Binder, Anne Verhoeven; makeup, Eddy van den Abbeele

Drama **(PR: C MPAA: R)**

PATLABOR 2: MOBILE POLICE ★★½
(Japan) 108m Bandai Visual; Tohokushinsha Film Corp. ~ Manga Entertainment c

(English Version) VOICES OF: Peter Marinker *(Gotoh)*; Sharon Holm *(Shinobu)*; Edward Glen *(Shige)*; Bill Roberts *(Sakaki)*; Blair Fairman *(Arikawa)*; David Jarvis *(Asuma)*; Briony Glassco *(Noa)*; Alan Marsh *(Matsui)*; Martin McDougall *(Ohta)*

Based on a popular animated Japanese made-for-video series, PATLABOR 2 tells of a plot to foment civil war in Japan in the year 2002. Stunning animation helps viewers negotiate a frequently confusing and talky story line.

When an unidentified military jet fires a missile that blows a hole in the massive Yokohama Bay Bridge, the incident sparks fears of rogue elements within the Japan Self-Defense Forces. A military intelligence investigator, Arikawa, approaches Captain Shinobu Nagumo and Captain Gotoh, commanders of the Police Labor Force, a division employing one-man construction vehicles modified for law enforcement purposes (called Patrol Labors).

Arikawa identifies the man behind the attack as Yukihito Tsuge, a leading proponent of military applications of Labors, who had disappeared after a disastrous test of Labors on a United Nations peacekeeping mission in Southeast Asia in 1999.

Increased tension results when three F16-J fighter jets make an unauthorized flight over Tokyo. Soon the local police begin surrounding military bases. The military responds by sending tanks, troops, and helicopters to occupy the streets of Tokyo. Fears of a military takeover and the collapse of civilian rule abound. Military helicopters attack key communications centers, including the phone company headquarters, as well as the hangars storing the police Labors.

Arikawa reveals to Gotoh that a landfill known as Lot 18 is the site from which Tsuge is manipulating the entire operation. Gotoh and Nagumo round up their Labor crew and refurbish some of the damaged Labors in time to launch a raid on Lot 18 by way of an abandoned construction tunnel. After a fight with robot guards, Nagumo and the men emerge on the surface of Lot 18 only to find Tsuge sitting alone amidst thousands of sea gulls. Before he is handcuffed by Nagumo, Tsuge tells her his goal was simply to "make people aware that all their certainties, their illusions, can disappear suddenly, completely, leaving no trace."

Alternately mesmerizing and infuriating, PATLABOR 2 has scenes of great beauty and power that represent Japanese animation at its most artistic and technically adept. Yet it suffers from long bouts of talkiness, a confusing plot line, an anticlimactic ending, a paucity of action, and several strains of thought that are never fully explored. Gotoh and Arikawa engage in several lengthy philosophical discussions that would register better in subtitled form. The English dubbers try to imitate the monotones of Japanese voice artists, without capturing any of the subtle inflections that make those monotones so multi-layered and effective in the Japanese originals.

Directed by Mamoru Oshii, whose GHOST IN THE SHELL was a 1996 breakout hit for Japanese animation in the US, this 1993 film has the director's characteristic flair for urban flavor, mixing sleek modern surfaces and technology with the textures of older, rundown industrial spaces, a contrast emphasized in both GHOST and his previous PATLABOR film as well. The film includes an evocative score by Oshii's regular composer, Kenji Kawai. Also, the film adopts a design strategy truly radical for anime, making all the characters look recognizably Japanese. *(Profanity)* — B.C.

d, Mamoru Oshii; p, Shin Unozawa, Tsuyoshi Hamawatari, Mitsuhisa Ishikawa; exec p, Makoto Yamashina, Tetsu Uemura, Laurence Guinness; w, Kazunori Itoh (based on the original story "Headgear"), George Roubicek (English script adaptation); ph, Akihiko Takahashi; ed, Shuichi Kakesu; m, Kenji Kawai; art d, Hiromasa Ogura; anim, Akemi Takada, Masami Yuuki, Toshihiko Nishikubo, Kazuchika Kise

Animated/Science Fiction (PR: A MPAA: NR)

PAUL BOWLES: HALFMOON
(SEE: HALFMOON)

PEOPLE VS. LARRY FLYNT, THE ★★★½
(U.S.) 130m Phoenix Pictures; Ixtlan Productions ~ Columbia c

Woody Harrelson *(Larry Flynt)*; Courtney Love *(Althea Leasure)*; Edward Norton *(Isaacman)*; Brett Harrelson *(Jimmy Flynt)*; Miles Chapin *(Miles)*; Donna Hanover *(Ruth Carter Stapleton)*; James Cromwell *(Charles Keating)*; Crispin Glover *(Arlo)*; Vincent Schiavelli *(Chester)*; James Carville *(Simon Leis)*; Richard Paul *(Jerry Falwell)*; Burt Neuborne *(Roy Grutman)*; Jan Triska *(The Assassin)*; Cody Block *(10 Year Old Larry)*; Ryan Post *(8 Year Old Jimmy)*; Robert Davis *(Old Hillbilly)*; Kacky Walton *(Young Ma Flynt)*; John Ryan *(Young Pa Flynt)*; Kathleen Kane *(1st Stripper)*; Greg Roberson *(Disc Jockey)*; Jim Peck *(Old Printer)*; Mike Pniewski *(Trucker)*; Tim Parati; Rick Rogers; Dan Lenzini; David Compton; Gary Lowery *(Staffers)*; Stephen Dupree *(Stills Photographer)*; Rainbeau Mars *(Tovah)*; Tam Drummond *(News Dealer)*; Nancy Lea Owen *(Ma Flynt)*; John Fergus Ryan *(Pa Flynt)*; Oliver Reed *(Governor Rhodes)*; Meresa T. Ferguson *(Jacuzzi Girl)*; Andrena Fisher *(Jacuzzi Girl)*; Ken Kidd *(Police Detective)*; Larry Flynt *(Judge Morrissey—Cincinatti Court)*; Janie Paris *(Jury Forewoman—Cincinatti Court)*; Carol Russell-Woloshin *(Court Clerk—Cincinatti Court)*; Miss Ruby Wilson *(Rally Singer)*; Eddie Davis *(Announcer at Rally)*; Blaine Pickett *(Ad Sales Guy)*; Kerry White *(Georgia Cop)*; Joey Hadley *(Georgia Cop)*; Chris Schadrack *(Robert Stapleton)*; Mac Pirkle *(Georgia Prosecutor)*; Mark W. Johnson *(Georgia Doctor)*; Doug Bauer *(Flynt's Personal Bodyguard)*; Roberto Roman Ramirez *(Bodyguard)*; Blaine Nashold MD *(Dr. Bob)*; Aurelia Thierree *(Cute Receptionist)*; Scott Winters *(Blow Dried Jerk)*; D'Army Bailey *(Judge Thomas Mantke—LA Court)*; Mike McLaren *(Lawyer—LA Court)*; Andrew Stahl *(Network Lawyer)*; Michael Detroit *(Delorean Attorney)*; Jaime Jackson *(Keating's Secretary)*; David Dwyer *(Federal Marshall)*; Richard Birdsong *(Deputy Marshall)*; James A. White *(Deputy Marshall)*; Gerry Robert Byrne *(Butler)*; Benjamin Greene Jr. *(Bailiff—LA Court)*; Mary Neal Naylor *(Mantke Clerk)*; Tina M. Bates *(Springfield Prison Guard)*; Evans Donnell *(Divinity Student)*; Jay Adams *(Divinity Student)*; Bennett Wood *(Dean of Liberty College)*; Janice Holder *(Judge Kirk—Roanoke Court)*; A. V. McDowell *(Jury Foreman—Roanoke Court)*; Jim Grimshaw *(Chief Justice Rehnquist)*; James Smith *(Justice Marshall)*; Rand Hopkins *(Justice Scalia)*; Charles M. Crump *(Justice Stevens)*; Pierre Secher *(Supreme Court Marshall)*; Linn Sitler *(Svelte Reporter)*; Mary M. Norman; Jack Shea; Lisa Lax *(Reporters)*; Susan Howe; Michael Davis; Dennis Turner; Patti Hatchett; Ann Marie Hall; Nate Bynum; Paula Haddock; Gary Kraen *(Georgia Reporters)*; Norm MacDonald *(Network Reporter)*; Jeff Johnston *(LA Reporter)*; Joey Sulipeck *(Falwell Reporter)*; Jim Palmer *(Falwell Reporter)*; Gene Lyons; Saida Pagan; Jim Hild; Michael Klastorin *(DC Reporters)*; Michelle Robinson *(TV Reporter at Supreme Court)*

A warm fuzzy movie for armchair liberals, THE PEOPLE VS. LARRY FLYNT whitewashes the life of the infamous pornographer for the benefit of viewers who are all for the First Amendment—so long as it doesn't protect anything too unpleasant.

In 1972 Larry Flynt (Woody Harrelson), a grade-school dropout from the backwoods of Kentucky, runs a string of Cincinnati strip clubs. He hits on the idea of publishing a newsletter featuring nude photographs of strippers who appear in the clubs. The idea is a big success, largely because the photographs are substantially more explicit that those found in mainstream men's magazines like *Playboy* and *Penthouse*. Expanded to magazine format, *Hustler* becomes a huge hit after Flynt publishes nude paparazzi photos of Jacqueline Onassis.

Aided by his wife and business partner Althea (Courtney Love), a former stripper, Flynt becomes a wealthy man by testing the limits of obscenity and good taste. As the national mood of the late 1970s grows more conservative, Flynt becomes the object of numerous obscenity lawsuits—some of which he openly provokes.

To the surprise of everyone who knows him, and the disgust of Althea, Flynt becomes a born-again Christian under the tutelage of evangelist Ruth Carter Stapleton (Donna Hanover). It is a faith he abandons when a sniper's bullet leaves him paralyzed from the waist down. Flynt becomes addicted to pain killers, while Althea, attempting to retain contact with her husband, becomes addicted to heroin. An operation eventually removes Flynt's pain and his need for drugs, but Althea's addiction remains. In 1984 she dies of complications related to AIDS.

To the dismay of his lawyer Alan Isaacman (Edward Norton), Flynt continues to provoke lawsuits. Such outrageous behavior as pelting judges with oranges and appearing in court wearing a diaper made from an American flag, along with his refusal to reveal how he obtained a videotape of the FBI entrapping John Delorean in a cocaine sale, lead to his incarceration for fifteen months in a federal psychiatric center.

Flynt is sued for libel by "Moral Majority" leader Jerry Falwell (Richard Paul) for publishing a parody in which Falwell "admits" to having had sex with his mother in an outhouse. The case goes all the way to the U.S. Supreme Court, which unanimously rules that the right to make fun of public figures, no matter how scabrously, is protected by the First Amendment.

You'd have to go back to NIGHT AND DAY (1946), starring Cary Grant as a happily hetero Cole Porter, to find a biopic that whitewashes its subject so thoroughly as THE PEOPLE VS. LARRY FLYNT. At least that musical got Porter's work, his songs, right. But the impression you get from this film by Milos Foreman (who admits to never having seen an issue of *Hustler*) is that Flynt's magazine was simply a more down-to-earth variation on *Playboy*. In truth, *Hustler* is a catalogue of scatological vulgarities, racism, sexism, and anything else that might be construed as offensive. It extends the notion of pornography beyond the merely sexual by tweaking its blue-collar readership's desire to see forbidden sights, staying just the other side of the line that defines hard-core pornography (i.e., erect penises and genital penetration).

Of course, we expect controversial subjects to be watered down in mass-market films. It's not surprising that this film neglects to mention that Flynt was married three times before Althea (and once after), or that he fathered a number of children whom he chose never to live with. And if likeable Woody Harrelson bears little resemblance to the piggish Flynt (who can be seen in a cameo as a trial judge), well, that's Hollywood. But in a film whose professed purpose is to salute our Constitutional guarantee of free speech, the shocking contents of *Hustler* properly are an issue: the filmmakers' support of the First Amendment is seriously compromised by their failure to trust their audience with the knowledge of what kind of material that right protects.

Despite lacking the courage of its convictions, THE PEOPLE VS. LARRY FLYNT is generally an intelligent and entertaining film. Harrelson's good-ol'-boy raunchiness is amusing, and singer Courtney Love gives an astonishingly good performance in her first substantial film role. Foreman continues his predilection for casting non-actors with the use of political consultant James Carville as an anti-obscenity prosecutor, NYU law professor Burt Neuborne as Falwell's attorney, and Donna Hanover, the wife of New York Mayor Rudolph Guiuliani, as Ruth Carter Stapleton. (Less well known is Flynt's back surgeon, who plays himself.) *(Extensive nudity, sexual situations, adult situations, substance abuse, extreme profanity.)* — M.F.

d, Milos Forman; p, Oliver Stone, Janet Yang, Michael Hausman; assoc p, Scott Ferguson, George Linardos; w, Scott Alexander, Larry Karaszewski; ph, Philippe Rousselot; ed, Christopher Tellefsen; m, Thomas Newman; prod d, Patrizia Von Brandenstein; art d, James Nezda, Shawn Hausman; set d, Maria A. Nay, Amy Wells; sound, Chris Newman; fx, Rodman Kiser; casting, Francine Maisler; cos, Theodor Pistek, Arianne Phillips; makeup, Ben Nye, Bron Roylance; stunts, Tim Trella

AAN Best Actor: Woody Harrelson; *AAN Best Director:* Milos Forman

Biography **(PR: O MPAA: R)**

PERFECT CANDIDATE, A ★★★

(U.S.) 105m Arpie Films ~ Seventh Arts Distribution c

Oliver North; Charles Robb; Mark Goodin; Don Baker

A PERFECT CANDIDATE confirms some of the worst suspicions regarding the politics behind the political process. This documentary, subtitled "Inside the Oliver North-Chuck Robb Campaign," entertains while it sheds light on a rarely-seen aspect of American democracy-in-action.

A PERFECT CANDIDATE contrasts TV news clips from the contentious 1994 Virginia Senate race with behind-the-scenes footage of the two candidates and their staffs. The film begins with career sketches of the opponents. Oliver North becomes a celebrity in the 1980s as the "point man" behind Iran-Contra, the Reagan Administration's arms-for-hostages imbroglio. The Lt. Colonel challenges the Senate during its 1987 investigations with a self-righteous, gung-ho attitude toward his clandestine activities. North then develops a Right-wing populist following that eventually drives his bid for the Republican nomination for the Senate. Chuck Robb is viewed as the privileged incumbent, a conservative Democrat married to LBJ's daughter, whose association with drugs and extra-marital sex taints his public image prior to the 1994 campaign.

A PERFECT CANDIDATE thereafter focuses on two peripheral figures, North's campaign manager, Mark Goodin, and WASHINGTON POST reporter Don Baker. Goodin attempts to portray North's political scandal as a boon to the public, showing him as a patriot and maverick who tried to free the hostages in Iran. In speeches, radio appearances and interviews with the media, North and Goodin also appeal heavily to the ultra-conservative issues and concerns of the religious Right.

Meanwhile, Don Baker comments on the foundering Robb campaign, noting that the Democrat-turned-Independent politician, former Governor Douglas Wilder, is siphoning votes away from Robb. When Robb bumbles his way through a crucial debate with both North and Wilder, North gains in popularity. But Baker sees three events that save Robb's campaign: Wilder's sudden withdrawal from the race and pledge of support to Robb; Robb's belated but effective offensive attack on North's record (linking North to the Ku Klux Klan and other extremists); and (with President Bill Clinton's help) Robb's successful appeal to the African-American vote throughout the State. Robb eventually wins the close race, but Mark Goodin bitterly announces that the next time around he "will cut the guy's balls off."

Comparisons to THE WAR ROOM, the inside story of Bill Clinton's 1992 campaign, are inevitable: A PERFECT CANDIDATE, which shows the egregiously flawed North and Robb compete for attention and votes along the campaign trail, while their operatives reveal jaded insights about the world of politics, is more dramatically interesting than the upbeat WAR ROOM, because North's manager, Mark Goodin, so often exposes his smoldering resentment in personal terms (the considerable access A PERFECT CANDIDATE has to the North team should make network TV documentarians drool, and it is never less than astonishing how frank the interviewees are in front of the camera).

The only major flaw here is that directors R.J. Cutler (producer of THE WAR ROOM) and David Van Taylor (director of DREAM DECEIVERS) insist on constructing a protagonist out of WASHINGTON POST reporter Don Baker. Not only are Baker's views superfluous, but his excessive presence diminishes the film's all-too-limited analysis of the media itself (a few disparaging words from a Republican about "liberal bias" hardly constitutes informed critique). Had the filmmakers trusted their raw material more, they might have made an even stronger statement (a la the work of Frederick Wiseman).

Some other problems with the film include the imbalanced attention toward the North campaign (clearly, the filmmakers were given less access to Robb and his staff) and the sparse treatment of the highly dramatic Robb-Douglas Wilder feud before and during the Democratic Primary. Still, A PERFECT CANDIDATE is an insightful document about elections—both past and future. *(Profanity.)* — E.M.

d, R.J. Cutler, David Van Taylor; p, R.J. Cutler, David Van Taylor; co-p, Ted Skillman, Dan Partland; ph, Nicolas Doob; ed, Mona Davis; sound, David Van Taylor

Docudrama/Political **(PR: A MPAA: NR)**

PERSONAL JOURNEY WITH MARTIN SCORSESE THROUGH AMERICAN MOVIES, A ★★★★

(U.K./U.S.) 226m British Film Institute; Channel Four ~ Mirimax c/bw

Martin Scorsese *(Host/Narrator)*; Gregory Peck; Billy Wilder; Clint Eastwood; George Lucas; Francis Ford Coppola; Brian De Palma; Fritz Lang; Howard Hawks; John Ford; Nicholas Ray; Andre De Toth; Douglas Sirk; Sam Fuller; Orson Welles; Elia Kazan; Arthur Penn; John Cassavetes

This is Martin Scorsese's scholarly, yet highly idiosyncratic, contribution to the British Film Institute's "Century of Cinema" series. Illustrious filmmakers from around the world were commissioned by the series to create documentaries about the history of their country's cinema. Scorsese concentrates on the esoteric and the obscure, purposely omitting the standard Hollywood classics in order to focus on lesser known films and directors.

In "The Director's Dilemma," Scorsese ruminates on the eternal struggle between art and commerce, with clips from THE

BAD AND THE BEAUTIFUL (1952), and explains how some directors circumvented the studio system by adopting the philosophy of "making one for them and one for yourself." The producer's omnipotent role in the old Hollywood is examined by focusing on David O. Selznick. In "The Director as Storyteller," Scorsese looks at three classic American genres: westerns, gangster films, and musicals. Westerns are covered with the films of John Ford, Anthony Mann, and others, while gangster films are represented by a variety of titles, including SCARFACE (1932) and FORCE OF EVIL (1948). Musicals are discussed in terms of having dark subtexts, as shown with clips from Busby Berkeley's depression-era production numbers and MEET ME IN ST. LOUIS (1944).

"The Director as Illusionist" deals with film technology and cinematic grammar as it was developed in silent films by such pioneers as D.W. Griffith, King Vidor, Raoul Walsh, Cecil B. De Mille, F.W. Murnau, and Frank Borzage. Other subjects covered include the talkie revolution, mobile camerawork, three-strip Technicolor, CinemaScope, epic films, special effects, and modern computer technology.

"The Director as Smuggler" is devoted to the makers of mostly B-movies who managed to find cracks in the system and smuggle in radical ideas of a political, social, or personal nature. Directors discussed include Jacques Tourneur, Joseph H. Lewis, Andre De Toth, Ida Lupino, Edgar G. Ulmer, Anthony Mann, Robert Aldrich, Allan Dwan, Douglas Sirk, Nicholas Ray, and Samuel Fuller.

"The Director as Iconoclast" focuses on Erich Von Stroheim, Orson Welles and other mavericks who clashed with the system and invariably lost. Post-WWII directors who fought the production code by dealing with adult material are also examined, including Elia Kazan, Otto Preminger, and Billy Wilder, whose battles led to the breakthrough work of such 1960s directors as Arthur Penn, Stanley Kubrick and John Cassavetes.

This documentary is a thoroughly enjoyable and entertaining compilation of pristine film clips and candid interviews, which reminds the viewer just how rich and varied the history of American film really is, once one digs beneath the surface of the accepted list of classics. The assertion that B-movies were sometmes more stylish and interesting than A-movies, or that cult directors like Fuller, Ray, Sirk, Ulmer, et al. deserve the same recognition and praise as some of the more famous names, is not exactly a new idea, but the film brilliantly demonstrates just why that assertion is true.

By letting the clips run long, Scorsese allows the audience to get a real feel of each director's style and themes. For instance, one segment shows how John Ford's view of the west changed and matured, with examples from the '30s, '40s, and '50s.

As one would expect from Scorsese's own movies, his tastes generally run to dark themes, and it's clear that he's drawn to feverish, overwrought melodramas like DUEL IN THE SUN (1946) and LEAVE HER TO HEAVEN (1946), while even his choice of musicals dwell on the dark side, such as A STAR IS BORN (1937, 1954), or MY DREAM IS YOURS (1949), a seemingly escapist Doris Day movie, which he acknowledges as a major inspiration for NEW YORK, NEW YORK (1977).

At the beginning of the film, Scorsese quotes Frank Capra as saying that "film is a disease," and at the end he talks about viewing films as an eternal search for a "shared common experience."

Scorsese, whose reputation as the ultimate film buff is starting to overshadow his reputation as a great director, is an admitted movie junkie. A 1996 *New York* magazine profile depicted him as an agoraphobic loner who has very little human contact and spends all of his time making, watching, and cataloguing films. One can picture him alone late at night running 16-millimeter prints of Cinecolor westerns, trying to recapture that innocent moment of childhood wonder when the curtains parted in a darkened theater and a bright light projected dreams upon a giant screen. *(Violence, profanity.)* — M.S.

d, Martin Scorsese, Michael Henry Wilson; p, Florence Dauman; exec p, Colin McCabe, Bob Last; assoc p, Raffaele Donato; w, Martin Scorsese, Michael Henry Wilson; ph, Nancy Schreiber, Francis Reid, William G. Webb, Jean-Yves Escoffier; ed, Thelma Schoonmaker; m, Elmer Bernstein; sound, Beau Baker, Raoul A. Bruce, Sarah Chin, Linda Coffey, William Flick, Tom Paul

Documentary **(PR: AA MPAA: NR)**

PHANTOM 2040: THE GHOST WHO WALKS ★★

(U.S./France) 97m Minos SA; France 3; ITN ~ LIVE Entertainment c

VOICES OF: Scott Valentine *(Kit Walker/Phantom)*; Margot Kidder *(Rebecca Madison)*; Ron Perlman *(Graft)*; J.D. Hall *(Guran)*; Jeff Bennett *(Maxwell Madison)*; Carrie Snodgress *(Aunt Heloise)*; Deborah Harry *(Vaingloria)*; Paul Williams *(Mr. Cairo)*; Kath Soucie; Allan Oppenheimer; Leah Remini; Pamela Segall; Bibi Osterwald; Rob Poulsen; Mark Hamill

What an oddball enterprise—an incredibly long animated flick targeted for kids but written in an adult sensibility! On the heels of a lackluster live-action THE PHANTOM (1996) film, this dark cartoon is recommended for adult connoisseurs who haunt collectors comic book dens and for sophisticated children hooked on superhero sagas instead of classic literature.

In Metropia City in 2040, an ecological engineering student, Kit Walker (voice of Scott Valentine), discovers he has a dormant life purpose: to assume the identity of the environmentally-minded hero, the Phantom, once inhabited by Kit's late father. After an attack by Artificials on Kit's Aunt Heloise (voice of Carrie Snodgress) and his father's old crony, Guran (voice of J.D. Hall), Kit stalls accepting his destiny—until two pals need rescuing from a video arcade where the customers are brainwashed to riot. This civil disobedience is the tactic of Rebecca Madison (voice of Margot Kidder), a control freak. She is seeking city council sanctions for an inner city biodome dominated by her, her diabolical inventor son, Maxwell (voice of Jeff Bennett), and her humanoid enforcer, Graft (Ron Perlman). While Kit perfects his invisibility powers as riots proliferate, Maxwell hinders the Phantom's peacekeeping by creating a criminal doppelganger of the superhero. Circumventing Rebecca's plot to smuggle in nano-chips to build a robot army, the Phantom teams up with a young computer hacker, eludes capture by police who regard him as a subversive, foils a mass hypnosis scheme involving a rock star named Vaingloria (Deborah Harry), and accelerates the battle against mad Rebecca's plot to assume control of Metropia from her power base.

The cartoon is loaded with subplots, including sidelights about a sympathetic female cop and a double-crossing internet surfer. Well-drawn within its familiar bleakly futuristic designs, PHANTOM 2040 has a built-in audience of serious youngsters weaned on Saturday morning cartoons about masked men flexing extraordinary powers under their crime fighting costumes. For those who get off on a volcanic spewing of crypto-scientific jargon and who thrill to the sight of android junk heaps crumbling like the losing participants at a monster truck rally, PHANTOM 2040 delivers sci-fi action. But its violence is unsatisfyingly smothered, like leftovers covered by plastic wrap.

Most puzzling, the film presents (for a part-kiddie audience) a dominating mother relying on her effete son's destructive input. Instead of zapping these two with his stun gun, the Phantom should have come armed with the collected works of Freud. *(Violence.)* — R.P.

d, Michel Lyman, Gwen Sandiff-Wetzler; exec p, William E. Miller, Jeffrey Schon, David J. Corbett; assoc p, Mary Katherine Moore; w, Judith Reeves-Stevens, Garfield Reeves-Stevens (based on the comic strip by Lee Falk); m, Gerald O'Brien; art d, Thom Schillinger; anim, Osamu Tsuruyama

Animated **(PR: A MPAA: NR)**

PHANTOM, THE ★★
(U.S.) 96m Ladd Company; Village Roadshow Pictures ~ Paramount C

Billy Zane *(Phantom/Kit Walker)*; Kristy Swanson *(Diana Palmer)*; Treat Williams *(Xander Drax)*; Catherine Zeta Jones *(Sala)*; James Remar *(Quill)*; Cary-Hiroyuki Tagawa *(Kabai Sengh)*; Bill Smitrovich *(Uncle Dave)*; Casey Siemaszko *(Morgan)*; David Proval *(Charlie Zephro)*; Joseph Ragno *(Ray Zephro)*; Samantha Eggar *(Lilly Palmer)*; Jon Tenney *(Jimmy Wells)*; Patrick McGoohan *(Phantom's Dad)*; Robert Coleby *(Captain Horton)*; Al Ruscio *(Police Commissioner Farley)*; Leon Russom *(Mayor Krebs)*; Bernard Kates *(Falkmoore)*; John Capodice *(Al the Cabby)*; Bob Kane *(Mounted Cop)*; William Jones *(Cycle Cop)*; John Prosky *(Cycle Cop)*; Alan Zitner *(Dr. Fleming)*; Dane Carson *(Corporal Weeks)*; Chatpong "Jim" Petchlor *(Zak)*; Dane Farwell *(Breen)*; Jared Chandler *(Styles)*; Radmar Agana Jao *(Guran)*; William Zappa *(Ugly Pirate)*; Agoes Widjaya Soedjarwo *(Pirate #1)*; Clint Lilley *(Gangster #1)*; Jo Phillips *(Female Pilot)*; Austin Peters *(Boy Phantom)*; Victor Madrona *(Shaman)*; Valerie Flueger *(Receptionist)*; Rod Dailey *(Short Order Cook)*

The fuchsia-clad hero of Lee Falk's comic strip is brought to the big screen. His mission: to squash injustice—and launch a PHANTOM franchise. The first task is, of course, a never-ending battle, and the movie's poor reception at the box office quelled hopes for a franchise.

"The Phantom" is a moniker and mantle that has passed from father to son for 400 years and made the seemingly immortal crimefighter a legend. Now, in 1938, Kit Walker (a totally buff Billy Zane) dons the Phantom's tight, purple suit and combats evil in general, and the pirates of the Sengh Brotherhood in particular.

The film begins when one of the pirates, Quill (James Remar), invades the remote jungle island of Bengalla (the Phantom's home base) and steals one of the fabled Skulls of Tooghanda. It's said when the three skulls are brought together, they will summon a force more powerful than all the armies of the world.

Walker is visited by his father's ghost (Patrick McGoohan), who reveals that it was Quill who killed him. He implores his son to recover the skull, avenge his death, and find a nice girl to marry.

Quill is in the employ of industrialist and bad egg Xander Drax (Treat Williams), whose newfound interest in archaeology and mysticism piques the curiosity of adventuress-socialite Diana Palmer (the always spunky Kristy Swanson). When Diana heads for Bengalla to investigate, Drax has her kidnapped, but the Phantom rescues her. (Coincidentally, Diana was Kit's college love.)

In New York, where the second skull is in a museum, the Phantom attempts to thwart Drax's plans, but fails. All involved end up back in the South Pacific, at the Sengh hideout, home of the third skull. Drax summons the forces of Evil, but the Phantom uses the Power of Good to repel them, destroying Drax, Quill, and the Sengh. Finally, Kit reveals his secret to Diana and proposes, but she'll only give him a definite "maybe."

Remember the opening of RAIDERS OF THE LOST ARK (1981) when Indy enters the jungle cave to swipe a golden idol and is almost crushed by a giant boulder? A viewer of THE PHANTOM will be reminded of that and many, many, *many* other scenes from the Indiana Jones movies, including the rope bridge and plane crash from INDIANA JONES AND THE TEMPLE OF DOOM (1984) to name but two. (Surprise! PHANTOM's screenwriter also wrote THE LAST CRUSADE.) THE PHANTOM'S problem is that, literally and metaphorically, the giant boulder never drops.

Not only is director Simon Wincer (FREE WILLY, OPERATION DUMBO DROP) unable to match the elaborate inventiveness of Spielberg's action set pieces, but his understanding of the anatomy of a successful action sequence is hopelessly out of date. A good stunt, like someone jumping out of a plane onto a horse, isn't an action sequence in itself; it's only *part* of it. Criticism of the action wouldn't be so pertinent, except the narrative has only a perfunctory arc, never suggesting the attendant drama of someone saving the world.

Recreating the old-fashioned innocence of cliffhanger serials is, like the Phantom's nifty trick of shooting the guns out of the bad guys' hands, both moral imperative and gimmick. THE PHANTOM eschews the "mindlessly destructive violence" that is the current standard in actioners and offers itself as an alternative for younger moviegoers. But one might question this business judgment, considering movies like BATMAN FOREVER (1995) get rated PG-13, and count on those same moviegoers for their massive repeat ticket sales. *(Violence.)* — P.R.

d, Simon Wincer; p, Robert Evans, Alan Ladd Jr.; exec p, Dick Vane, Joe Dante, Graham Burke, Greg Coote, Peter Sjoquist, Bruce Sherlock; assoc p, Bonnie Abaunza; co-p, Jeffrey Boam; w, Jeffrey Boam (based on the Phantom characters created by Lee Falk); ph, David Burr; ed, O. Nicholas Brown, Bryan H. Carroll; m, David Newman; prod d, Paul Peters; art d, Lisette Thomas; set d, Amy Wells; sound, Ben Osmo; fx, Alan E. Lorimer, Wally Schaab, Buena Vista Visual Effects; casting, Deborah Aquila, Jane Shannon Smith; cos, Bruce Hogard, Lisa Lovaas; makeup, Judy Lovell; stunts, Billy Burton

Adventure/Action **(PR: A MPAA: PG)**

PHARAOH'S ARMY ★★★
(U.S.) 90m TMF-Metro; Cicada Films; Sinkhole Productions ~ Cinepix Film Properties, Inc. c

Chris Cooper *(Captain John Hull Abston)*; Patricia Clarkson *(Sarah Anders)*; Kris Kristofferson *(Preacher)*; Richard Tyson *(Rodie)*; Robert Joy *(Chicago)*; Frank Clem *(Neely)*; Huckleberry Fox *(Newt)*; Will Lucas *(Boy)*

PHAROAH'S ARMY, based on a supposedly true Kentucky legend, is a war movie without the war. For those who don't fight the battles but still have to take sides, the inner struggles can be as heartbreaking as the war itself. Director Robby Henson's stark, unsentimental telling of the story has a powerful emotional impact.

Looking for enemies, a group of five Union soldiers, led by Captain John Abston (Chris Cooper), search a farm owned by Sarah Anders (Patricia Clarkson). As they're about to leave, one unlucky soldier, Newt (Huckleberry Fox), falls off a ladder onto a pitchfork. The men decide to stay at Sarah's home until Newt heals.

Sarah's husband is away, fighting for the Confederacy, and she and her son, known only as Boy (Will Lucas), tend the farm. Sarah has a deep hatred for Yankees, who dug up the grave of her daughter, forcing Sarah to rebury her on the farm. Nonetheless, she has no choice but to house the soldiers.

Abston, who joined the army to free the slaves, helps with farming chores. Sarah takes a liking to him, but after Rodie (Richard Tyson), a troublesome soldier, claims Abston's generosity is an attempt at seduction, she reminds herself that Abston is the enemy and sends her boy into town to tell the preacher (Kris Kristofferson) that the soldiers are there.

After another argument, Rodie deserts the squad and Abston is forced to shoot him. In the confusion that follows, the preacher's slave is shot.

When Newt recovers, the soldiers go on their way. Abston leaves Sarah a rifle, which she points at him but can not shoot. As the soldiers leave, the boy runs after them with a pistol and shoots Newt. Abston goes back to the farm to confront Sarah and the boy. He fires two shots in the air and returns to his men, who believe he shot the two for revenge. Sarah's husband never returns from the war.

In a deceptively simple way, PHAROAH'S ARMY depicts the random pointlessness of war. Everything happens by circumstance. If Newt hadn't been injured, the men would not have stayed at the farm. If Rodie hadn't run away, the preacher's slave wouldn't have been killed, and the boy would have had no reason for revenge. Ultimately, we see that war is pointless. The slave, whose freedom is being fought for so passionately, is killed by accident. The time the soldiers spend on the farm proves worthless, since Newt also dies in the end. Henson seems to be saying that in times of war, normality and rationality don't exist, and even people who mean well end up unable to communicate. Under other circumstances, Abston and Sarah may have fallen in love. As it is, her only emotion is hatred for an enemy she doesn't understand.

The simple acoustic guitar score and scenic photography suit the film well. The peacefulness of the backdrop and the film's mild pace belie its dark emotional core. In this topsy-turvy world at war, action is presented in a peaceful way, and the near-romantic scenes are full of tension.

The acting is outstanding, and the dialogue tight. Though the characterizations are strong and the emotions palpable, the action scenes are somewhat confusing. When Sarah attempts to shoot Abston, it is not entirely clear why the rifle won't fire.

With a bit more clarity, PHAROAH'S ARMY could have been a great film and made a clearer statement about the futility of war. *(Violence, adult situations, profanity.)* — A.M.

d, Robby Henson; p, Doug Lodato, Robby Henson; assoc p, Elizabeth Rodgers, Tracy Kristofferson; w, Robby Henson; ph, Doron Schlair; ed, Robby Henson; m, Vince Emmett, Charles Ellis, Michael Stamper, Robert Friedman; prod d, Jana Rosenblatt; sound, Yehuda Maayan; cos, Jana Rosenblatt

Drama/War **(PR: C MPAA: NR)**

PHAT BEACH ★

(U.S.) 99m LIVE Entertainment; Connection III Entertainment ~ Orion c

Jermaine "Huggy" Hopkins *(Benny King)*; Brian Hooks *(Durrel Jackson)*; Coolio *(Himself)*; Tiny Lister Jr. *(Tiny)*; Nic-Nam; Sonshine; Vayne; Yesz *(Y?N-Vee)*; Gregg D. Vance *(Mikey Z.)*; Claudia Kaleem *(Candace Williams)*; Sabrina De Pina *(Tanya Watkins)*; Jennifer Lucienne *(Denise Marie)*; Eric Fleeks *(Carl N. King)*; Alma Collins *(Janet R. King)*; Tre Black *(DJ)*; Lawrence J. Lejohn *(Hamburger Joint Manager)*; Candice Merideth *(Tasha King)*; Devin De Ray *(Durrel's Stripper/Cheek Slapper)*; Glenise Brathwaite *(Benny's Stripper/Catholic Girl)*; Tamara Nicole Bennett *(Stripper on Pole)*; Sean Welton *(Strip Club Bouncer)*; Nicole Amaral *(Inga)*; Tanya Reid *(Ulga)*; Laura L. Weber *(Swedish Twin)*; Debora Ann *(Volleyball Sign-Up Girl)*; Dotan Bental *(Geek)*; Corey Ann Chang *(Stacey)*; Domonique Garcia *(Army Girl)*; Glori Gold *(Amy)*; Kate Ann Haney *(Fat Woman in Hamburger Joint)*; Chad Edward McDaniel *(Volleyball Kid)*; Bud Montgomery *(1st Cop)*; Panthere *(Dana)*; Paul Tranghese *(2nd Cop)*; Scott Vener *(Volleyball Dude)*; Anelique Perrin *(Aquanetta)*; Tiara English *(Girl on Beach)*; Natalie Duvernay *(Girl on Beach)*

How hard can it be to make a low-budget beach movie that's at the very least a trashy good time? That's one of the many questions begged by this raunch comedy, which is a true chore to sit through.

Benny King (Jermaine "Huggy" Hopkins) is an overweight, aspiring teen poet whose artistic aspirations are belittled by his father Carl (Eric Fleeks), who insists that Benny take a summer job at a fast-food joint. Benny's fast-talking friend Durrel (Brian Hooks), however, is pushing him to take a road trip to the nearby Southern California beaches, where he schemes to make money selling cheap sunglasses and score with as many women as possible. When Benny's family goes away on vacation, Durrel convinces Benny to take Carl's prized Mercedes and hit the road.

Once they arrive at the beach, things go from bad to worse: Benny spends all their money at a strip club; Durrel's sunglasses are stolen; the girls won't give the guys the time of day. On top of that, the pair get into a running battle with white homeboy-wannabe Mikey Z. (Gregg D. Vance), who ends up stealing the Mercedes shortly before Benny's family turns up at the same hotel where Benny and Durrel are staying. But Benny's skill in a volleyball contest puts an end to their money woes, and he connects with a good-hearted girl named Tanya (Sabrina De Pina). The car is reclaimed, and Carl decides to allow Benny to pursue his literary dreams.

From all appearances, PHAT BEACH would seem to be cut from the same cloth as the hip, energetic HOUSE PARTY (1990), or at least the lowbrow-but-fun PARTY sequels and FRIDAY (1995). But a witless, disorganized script and Doug Ellin's flat-footed direction (not to mention the fact that most of the scenes were shot on overcast days) drain out all the fun. It lacks even the crude enthusiasm of the youth-oriented comedies Crown International used to churn out for the drive-in trade, and it's even sloppier technically; during the volleyball scenes, one can easily see a wire attached to the ball.

The movie proves to be even more sexist than the average T&A comedy. Hopkins's searching-for-true-love character was evidently supposed to sweeten the latent misogyny, yet he's given just as many bimbos-in-heat fantasies as the randy schemer played by Hooks. And of course, the "nice girl" Benny winds up with is the only one in the movie who wears jeans and sneakers on the beach and doesn't look like a model. Even the extensive rap soundtrack consists of uninspired, unexciting tunes that fail to add the intended energy. *(Extensive nudity, sexual situations, substance abuse, extreme profanity.)* — M.G.

d, Doug Ellin; p, Cleveland O'Neal; assoc p, Donna Shirazi; co-p, Brian E. O'Neal; w, Brian E. O'Neal, Ben Morris, Doug Ellin (from a story by Brian E. O'Neal and Cleveland O'Neal); ph, Jim Lebovitz, Jurgen Baum; ed, Richard Nord; prod d, Terri Schaetzle, Colleen Devine; art d, Le'ce Edwards-Bonilla, Suzan A. Muszynski0; sound, Paul Bacca (mixer); fx, Josh Hakian; casting, Alphy Hoffman, Donna Shirazi, Connection III/In House; cos, Mona Thalheimer; makeup, Beverly Jo Pryor, Dominique Bram, Stacye Branche

Comedy **(PR: O MPAA: R)**

PHENOMENON ★★
(U.S.) 117m Boyle/Taylor Productions; Touchstone Pictures ~ Buena Vista c

John Travolta *(George Malley)*; Kyra Sedgwick *(Lace Pennamin)*; Forest Whitaker *(Nate Pope)*; Robert Duvall *(Doc)*; David Gallagher *(Al)*; Ashley Buccille *(Glory)*; Tony Genaro *(Tito)*; Sean O'Bryan *(Banes)*; Bruce Young *(Jack Hatch)*; Michael Milhoan *(Jimmy)*; Vyto Ruginis *(Ted Rhome)*; Elisabeth Nunziato *(Ella)*; Jeffrey DeMunn *(Professor Ringold)*; Richard Kiley *(Dr. Wellin)*; Mark Valim *(Alberto)*; Troy Evans *(Roger)*; Ellen Geer *(Bonnie)*; James Keane *(Pete)*; Susan Merson *(Marge)*; James Cotton *(Cal)*; Brent Spiner *(Niedorf)*; Tony A. Mattos *(Ella's Father)*; Anni Long *(Major Benz)*; Mark Soper *(Reporter)*; Daniel Zacapa *(Sick Boy's Father)*; Justin DiPego *(Intense Man at Library Fair)*; Cab Covay *(Taunting Man at Library Fair)*; Jewel Benedict *(May)*; Carl Parker *(Man in Orchard)*; Tom Fridley *(Agent)*; Richard Gross *(Customer at Malley's)*; Beth Kennedy *(Celia)*; Mariann V. Carothers *(Furniture Store Owner)*; Isaac Reiswig *(Man in Crowd)*; Claudia Crespin *(Woman in Crowd)*; Michael Forner *(Man at Bar #1)*; Joseph A. Nicosia *(Man at Bar #2)*; Dan Partain *(Man at Bar #3)*; Betsy Berryhill *(Woman at Bar)*; Jack Chouchanian *(Technician #1)*; Sage Callaway *(Female Officer)*; Eric G. Tignini *(Agent #2)*; Will Prater *(Helicopter Pilot)*

Intelligently exploiting his newfound market value, John Travolta has sought out films that will enhance his reputation and roles that will both target his core audience and still allow him to stretch a little. On that level, PHENOMENON was a tremendous success; otherwise, it's pretty mundane.

George Malley (Travolta) is an ordinary guy who fixes cars, tries lamely to teach himself Spanish, and raises his own rabbit-nibbled tomatoes in a rural Northern California town. On the night of his 37th birthday, he is struck by a mysterious flash of light and begins to develop extraordinary powers of perception. He can't sleep; instead he stays up all night reading or tinkering with solar panels, fertilizer, and car parts. He learns languages in mere hours, reads three or four books a day, and is able to decipher high-speed Morse code signals heard over a ham radio. His friends begin to regard him suspiciously, except for his best friend Nate (Forrest Whitaker), who is alternately dismayed and amused by him. The town's crusty old MD (Robert Duvall) brings George in for some tests, at which point George demonstrates his newly found telekinetic powers.

Meanwhile, George has been pursuing divorced mom Lace (Kyra Sedgwick), buying up all her handmade willow chairs and inviting himself to dinner. Lace finds George simultaneously attractive and threatening, but in her backyard, George feels weird vibrations, and calls the tectonics lab at Berkeley to report an imminent earthquake. He stays for supper and ingratiates himself with the children; after he leaves, the promised earthquake comes. Professor Ringold (Jeffrey DeMunn) drives up from Berkeley to meet George, just in time to witness him learn Portuguese in 20 minutes and, using telepathy and telekinesis, rescue a sick boy hiding in an orchard. Just as George is ready to head off to the University to discuss his experiments on photosynthesis, the FBI arrives, angry over George's interference in the government's Morse code exercise.

George is interviewed by an easily impressed scientist (Brent Spiner); a nameless government agency tries to compel him to work for them. He resolutely refuses; he wants to go home and help people improve their farms and their lives. Back home, he finds fear and confusion. He becomes increasingly dissociated and shows signs of deterioration. Lace finally succumbs to his charm, helping him clean up and prepare for a public talk, which goes radically awry when people incessantly question him about aliens and beg for healings. He is tussled by the crowd and, after falling over a table, is struck by another bolt of light.

In the hospital, he learns he has a web-like tumor spreading through his brain, stimulating the nerve cells while eventually strangling them. He is visited by a calculating researcher (Richard Kiley), who wishes to perform "open brain surgery" in order to learn about higher brain function while in effect killing him. George declines, but the researcher has him declared incompetent and places him in a restricted ward. George escapes, returning to Lace's home to spend his last few days with her and complete his notes. He dies peacefully the night before the professor gets there. A year later, the people of George's town gather, happily married or pregnant, raising thick fields of corn, and celebrating his memory.

PHENOMENON has many moments of genuine originality and insight, but each time it flirts with being profound, it settles for "heart-warming" instead. The lead performances are solidly on target when the script allows the actors to behave like human beings. Whitaker in particular is winning as a lonely framer with a Diana Ross obsession. Duvall is always a pleasure to watch, especially when giggling with childish glee at the telekinesis demo. But the film hangs on Travolta, who is remarkably breezy, affectless, and, in the first hour, totally convincing. He only bogs down later when forced to preach a bit too earnestly about the power of the human mind, spewing a facile evolutionary optimism owing more to Travolta's Scientology than to any coherent philosophy. Sedgwick is the weak link; she and Travolta lack chemistry; she has a minimally conceived role that ultimately disintegrates into cheap tear-jerker cliche.

A workmanlike production with a highly bankable star, PHENOMENON was a minor box office hit, but it is about as memorable as a diet soda and not quite as substantial. *(Mild profanity, adult themes.)* — R.S.

d, Jon Turteltaub; p, Barbara Boyle, Michael Taylor; exec p, Charles Newirth, Jonathan D. Krane; w, Gerald DiPego; ph, Phedon Papamichael; ed, Bruce Green; m, Thomas Newman; prod d, Garreth Stover; art d, Bruce Alan Miller; set d, Jay Hart; sound, Ronald Judkins (mixer); fx, David Blitstein, Ken Ralston, Mageara Cameron, Sony Pictures Imageworks; casting, Renee Rousselot; cos, Betsy Cox; makeup, Hallie D'Amore; stunts, Jeff Cadiente

Drama **(PR: C MPAA: PG)**

PHOENIX ★
(U.S.) 94m Triad Studios ~ Monarch Home Video c

Stephen Nichols *(McClain)*; Brad Dourif *(Reiger)*; Billy Drago *(Kilgore)*; Denice Duff *(Seline)*; Peter Murnik *(Dillon)*; William Sanderson *(Miro)*; Robert Gossett *(Barker)*; Betsy Soo *(Chin)*; Jeremy Roberts *(Tanner)*; Leland Orser *(Dr. Riley)*; Robert Clotworthy *(Man No. 1)*; Dan Kern *(Man No. 2)*; Forbes Riley *(Controller)*; John Allee *(Android)*

Stillborn in conception and moribund in execution, this dismal android odyssey fails to live up to its title by rising from the ashes of its own cliches.

Reports of insurrectionist behavior among replicants on the mining colony Titus 4 alarm the Rydel Corporation's Board of Directors. Employed to mine the precious ore Diridium, these artificials have been acquiring such human characteristics as pig-headedness, and go on strike. Rydel CEO Kilgore (Billy Drago) compels his second-in-command, Reiger (Brad Dourif), to take care of the situation.

Reiger hires a jailed former crony, Tyler McClain (Stephen Nichols), and his unconventional crew: Dillon (Peter Murnik), Barker (Robert Gossett), and Chin (Betsy Soo). Soon after they arrive at Titus 4, the clean-up quartet learns from rebel android Miro (William Sanderson) that Kilgore plans to sabotage his own replicants and replace them with a more violent brand. His goal is to corner the world's Diridium market after forcing his own associates out of the competitive loop.

Reiger rigs the mining perimeters with enough explosives to wipe out evidence of Kilgore's plot. Snooping around a Rydel lab while recovering from a gunshot wound, Tyler discovers sadistic experimentation techniques that would give Kilgore an unstoppable army of killer androids.

Teaming up with Miro's forces, Tyler not only learns that he has been betrayed by Seline (Denice Duff), the woman he loves, but that he, too, is a replicant. The ranks of human and artificial life-forms are thinned as Barker, Reiger, and Miro take direct hits. After Seline's last-ditch act of decency costs her her life, Tyler shoots Kilgore, and his mad plan for a super army dies with him. Surviving humans and robots now coexist peacefully.

Substandard from start to finish, PHOENIX unreels like a textbook example of uncommitted movie-making. It's as if cast and crew were under threat of death not to veer from formula: one can practically feel them towing the mark just to collect their paychecks. Despite an adequate budget for its purposes, the professionalism is stifling, and a good time is had by none. The subject of revolt-bound robots has grown hoary in the direct-to-video marketplace; philosophical musings about mankind and copycat android-people were more succinctly and lucidly handled on 1960s "Twilight Zone" episodes. Never actively terrible, and painless to sit through, PHOENIX simply doesn't provide enough of anything to make it worth a genre buff's time. *(Graphic violence, nudity, adult situations.)* — R.P.

d, Troy Cook; p, Jimmy Lifton, Dan Bates, Troy Cook; exec p, Morton Salkind; co-p, Billy Drago; w, Jimmy Lifton, Troy Cook; ph, Alexander Melville, Mark Melville; ed, Paulette Renee Victor; m, Ridgeback Studios; prod d, James Scanlon; art d, Rosslyn Johanna; set d, Rosslyn Johanna; sound, James Einolf (mixer); fx, Dale Newkirk, Phil Cook; casting, Kathy A. Smith; cos, Susan Wachsler; makeup, Lori Baker, Martin Mercer; stunts, Chuck Borden

Science Fiction/Action (PR: C MPAA: NR)

PIE IN THE SKY ★★

(U.S.) 94m New Line Cinema; Fine Line Features ~ New Line Home Video c

Josh Charles *(Charlie Dunlap)*; John Goodman *(Alan Davenport)*; Christine Lahti *(Ruby)*; Anne Heche *(Amy Morgan)*; Peter Reigert *(Mr. Dunlap)*; Christine Ebersole *(Mrs. Dunlap)*; Wil Wheaton *(Jack)*; Bob Balaban *(Mr. Enamen)*; Dey Young *(Mrs. Tarnover)*; David Rasche; Kathryn Brody; Brent Spiner; The Bridge Dance Theater

The arcane art of radio traffic reporting provides an unconventional route to low-gear romantic comedy.

Being conceived in his bickering parents' front seat during a traffic jam has permanently skewed Charlie Dunlap's (Josh Charles) notions of love and career. While his folks want him to become a middle manager, Charlie desires to work as an airborne commentator monitoring the highways, like his idol, mellifluous Los Angeles drive-time voice Alan Davenport (John Goodman).

Charlie also desires Amy Morgan (Anne Heche), the kid next door who matures into a flaky but alluring would-be dancer. They share an intimate idyll before Amy goes to LA and joins a troupe of performance artists. Charlie follows, with thoughts of hooking up with Alan Davenport.

Though stuffy station executives doubt the earnest traffic groupie, Davenport is happy to make Charlie his personal assistant-acolyte. Things go less well in winning Amy away from her engagement to a plastic surgeon. She decides to move to Paris and dance, and Charlie must choose between his avocation and pursuing her. When Davenport shows up too drunk to fly (his marriage has broken up), Charlie takes the great man's place behind the cockpit microphone for a flawless day of drive-time reporting. He's fired, because egomaniac Davenport now considers him a threat.

After some soul-searching, Charlie races the rush hour to catch Amy's plane to Paris. Since France also has cars, he's last seen as a helicopter traffic reporter, hovering over the Champs d'Elysees.

This oddball tale should have worn a bumper sticker reading "I brake for subplots," as the easygoing narrative detours up many a blind alley and humor cul-de-sac, like Amy's cheerfully dysfunctional family and Charlie's fling with his lusty LA landlady (Christine Lahti, gone to waste).

Along the way are gentle pokes at West Coast attitudes, none of much import or impact, and when the fresh young leads play out a nice romantic interlude on an overpass, it turns into a downright embarrassing music-video sequence.

Things perk up considerably whenever the terrific John Goodman illuminates the screen with his high-beams of charisma.

This is the first feature film from writer-director Bryan Gordon, winner of a Best Live Action Short Film Oscar in 1987 for RAY'S MALE HETEROSEXUAL DANCE HALL. But PIE IN THE SKY barely saw theatrical release, adding to a number of duds in 1996 that dulled the luster of New Line Cinema after their smash hits THE MASK (1994), SEVEN (1995), and DUMB AND DUMBER (1994). *(Substance abuse, sexual situations, profanity.)* — C.C.

d, Bryan Gordon; p, Denise Shaw, Allan Mindel; w, Bryan Gordon; ph, Bernd Heinl; ed, Colleen Halsey; m, Michael Convertino; prod d, Linda Pearl; art d, Michael Atwell; set d, Klaus Hasmann, Gail Bennett; casting, Rik Pagano, Debi Manwiller; cos, Louise Frogley

Comedy/Romance (PR: C MPAA: R)

PIG'S TALE, A ★

(U.S.) 94m DDF Films ~ PolyGram Video c
(AKA: SUMMER CAMP)

Joe Flaherty *(Milt)*; Poppy Cee Jay Monroe *(Grady Lake Girl)*; Jon Gudmundson *(Delivery Guy)*; Olumiji Aina Olawumi *(Rodman)*; Patrick O'Neill *(Hertz)*; Graham Sack *(Andy)*; Chaz Shepherd *(Royce)*; Jimmy Zepeda *(Cruz)*; Kimberly Anders *(Paige)*; Whitney Anderson *(Jenna)*; Sean Babb *(Boner)*; Christopher Daniel Barnes *(Barry)*; Samantha Becker *(Stacy)*; Jake Beecham *(Swackback)*; Ned Bellamy *(Scrappy)*; Greg Crane *(Sanders)*; Mike Damus *(Frank)*; Jonathan Hilario *(Griff)*; Lisa Jakub *(Tiffany)*; Andrew Harrison Leeds *(Troy Beckerwood)*; Erin Dean *(Heather)*; Jackie Hoffman *(Cora)*; Alex Greenwald *(Von Hofferman)*; Marin May *(Ellen)*; Anne McEnroe *(Mrs. Lipman)*; Rebecca Bacon *(Kid 1)*; Hunter Garner *(Wolf 2)*; Andrew Keegan *(Wolf 1)*

This reprehensible miniaturization of MEATBALLS (1979) is a junior league celebration of belching, breakin' wind, and breast-ogling. In other words, it's an opportunity for sexist dads to prepare their sons to be piggish grownups. Oink! Oink!

At Camp Kipperman, so-called losers like Andy (Graham Sack), nerdy Rodman (Olumiji Aina Olawumi), and smart-aleck Frank (Mike Damus), et al., are relegated to the most revolting cabin. While Andy and his Pig pals languish here, the stuck-up Wolves, led by wealthy brat Troy Beckerwood (Andrew Harrison Leeds), rate comfy digs and preferential treatment from camp counselors. Initially, the Pigs tolerate abuse from their well-heeled rivals; Andy even steps aside when Troy puts the moves on camp beauty, Tiffany (Lisa Jakub).

One day, despite the Wolves' sabotage, Andy's unexpected expertise on water skis proves a turning point in the self-esteem of all Pigs. Fighting back, the camp pariahs revamp their sty, outdo the Wolves at the yearly panty raid, and become underdog figureheads. Unable to win fairly, Troy spray paints his quarters with graffiti so that the falsely accused Pigs are booted out. Undaunted, the disgraced Pigs buck up their courage, return unofficially, and beat the Wolves in the summer's major Flag-Tag game. Due to Tiffany's finger-pointing at a paint-spattered, mendacious Troy, the Pigs prove their innocence as well as their superiority to the deceptive Wolves.

What can the video spectator do, sitting there all lethargic and miserable as dirty tricks bombard the Camp Kipperman factions? First, the Pigs get latrine duty; then the Wolves get pelted with ice cream all over their pristine cabin, etc., etc. As if the ebb and flow of pre-teen revenge isn't tedious enough, A PIG'S TALE throws in a ludicrous subplot involving wiseacre Frank's crush on a sexy teenage ghost who haunts the nearby woods! Yep, it's tumescence time for all rapidly developing boys who are presumably the target audience for this kind of offensive fare.

What's most appalling about this flick's feel-good air is the attitude that the schlemiels are justified in resorting to the same disgusting antics as the spoiled jocks. Do parents really want their kids brainwashed with this turnabout-is-fair-play garbage? Youngsters learn from this movie that good manners are for sissies, that women are prizes in some never-ending male competition, that beating the other guy through subterfuge is okay if you're poor and he's privileged. Instead of worrying about installing V-chips to screen out soft-core porn, parents should be vigilant about this sort of drivel that indoctrinates kids into the joys of adult competitive cruelty. *(Profanity, violence.)* — R.P.

d, Paul Tassie; p, Gregory Goodman, Matthew Loze; exec p, Steve Golin, Sigurjon Sighvatsson; co-p, Lynn Weimer; w, Todd Richardson, Scott Sandorf, Charles Ransom; ph, Ron Garcia; ed, Lou Angelo; m, Anthony Marinelli; prod d, Nicholas Preovolos; art d, Andrea Dopaso; set d, Beau Petersen; sound, Paul Trautman (mixer); fx, Lou Carlucci; casting, Linda Kohn; cos, Terry Dresbach; makeup, Cynthia Bachman; stunts, Jeffrey Dashnaw

Comedy **(PR: A MPAA: PG)**

PINOCCHIO'S REVENGE ★★½

(U.S.) 94m Trimark Pictures; Blue Rider ~ Vidmark c

Rosalind Allen *(Jennifer Garrick)*; Brittany Alyse Smith *(Zoe Garrick)*; Todd Allen *(David Kaminsky)*; Aaron Lustig *(Dr. Edwards)*; Candace McKenzie *(Sophia)*; Ron Canada *(Barry)*; Lewis Van Bergen *(Vincent Gotto)*; Larry Cedar *(District Attorney)*; Tara Hartman *(Beth)*; Michael Connors *(Young Priest)*; Ivan Gueron *(Rookie Patrolman)*; Thomas Wagner *(Homicide Detective)*; Janis Chow *(Newscaster)*; Janet MacLachlan *(Judge Allen)*; Sarah Kaite Coughlan *(Schoolteacher)*; Danielle Weiner *(Beth's Friend)*; Carianne Goldsmith *(Beth's Friend)*; Jose Rey *(Prison Guard)*; Ian Gregory *(Prison Chaplain)*; Dani Blair *(Mother at Party)*; Larry Ziegelmeyer *(Principal)*; Robert Winley *(Biker)*; Shelley Robertson *(Nurse)*; James W. Quinn *(Paramedic)*; Sal Viscuso *(Jail Guard)*; Ed Bernard *(Jail Guard)*

With the simple, on-screen title PINOCCHIO, this is an ambitious if not entirely successful attempt to transcend the '90s trend for mini-monsters.

Public defender Jennifer Garrick (Rosalind Allen) has taken the case of Vincent Gotto (Lewis Van Bergen), who five years earlier was discovered burying his young son's body next to a large Pinocchio puppet and who was also convicted of several other child murders. Though Gotto says he wants to die, Jennifer is not entirely convinced of his guilt. Circumstances land the puppet in the possession of Jennifer's young daughter Zoe (Brittany Alyse Smith), who has been sullen and resentful ever since her father left her and Jennifer. Zoe becomes instantly attached to Pinocchio, who seems to speak to her—and to contrive "accidents" in which Zoe's school rival Beth (Tara Hartman) and Jennifer's boyfriend David (Todd Allen) are badly injured.

Pinocchio appears to come to life; Zoe follows him to the hospital, where David is killed. Zoe's doctor (Aaron Lustig) tells Jennifer that the troubled girl should be committed, while Jennifer comes to believe that Gotto's son, under Pinocchio's influence, was responsible for the child murders. Jennifer's housekeeper Sophia (Candace McKenzie) is murdered, apparently by Pinocchio, who then assaults Jennifer; but when their struggle ends, her attacker proves to be Zoe. The girl is put away, but Jennifer remains unconvinced of her guilt, still believing that Pinocchio was responsible.

Commissioned by Trimark to create a film about a diminutive demon similar to the star of its successful LEPRECHAUN series, writer-director Kevin S. Tenney came up with something a little more challenging—a film in which it's not clear, even by the end, whether the ostensible villain is truly alive and responsible for the ensuing mayhem. Tenney carries off this conceit well for the most part, but the approach is compromised somewhat by the producers' insistence that the audience see the puppet running about on its own, talking and pursuing its victims. And the suggestion that Pinocchio carries a malefic influence even if he's not truly "alive" forgoes the disturbing possibility that Zoe is committing the violence entirely of her own will.

Tenney stages his action and horror scenes well, even if it's fairly clear who will fall victim and when, and the movie as a whole has been put together with slick professionalism. The acting is also generally good, with young Smith ably keeping the viewer guessing as to just how disturbed she is. But this is a case where even a little more ambiguity might have helped; as it stands, PINOCCHIO'S REVENGE is better than expected—enough to make one wish it was even better than it is. *(Graphic violence, extensive nudity, adult situations, profanity.)* — M.G.

d, Kevin S. Tenney; p, Jeff Geoffray, Walter Josten; exec p, Mark Amin; co-p, Jonathon Komack Martin; w, Kevin S. Tenney; ph, Eric Anderson; ed, Daniel Duncan; m, Dennis Michael Tenney; prod d, Candi Gutteres; sound, Tony Smyles, Joel E. Smith; fx, Gabe Bartalos; casting, Tedra Gabriel; cos, Judi Jensen; makeup, Judy Yonemoto

Horror **(PR: O MPAA: R)**

PIRANHA ★★

(U.S.) 81m Concorde-New Horizons ~ New Horizons Home Video c

William Katt *(Paul Grogan)*; Alexandra Paul *(Maggie MacNamara)*; Mila Kunis *(Susie Grogan)*; Soleil Moon Frye *(Laura)*; Kehli O'Byrne *(Gina)*; Monte Markham *(J. R. Randolph)*; Darleen Carr *(Dr. Leticia Baines)*; Leland Orser *(Terry Wechsler)*; Lorissa McComas *(Barbara Randolph)*; Billy Whorley *(Whitney)*; James Karen *(Governor)*

In the 1990s the Showtime cable network began airing all-new Roger Corman remakes of his past exploitation cheapies like WASP WOMAN (1959) and NOT OF THIS EARTH (1957). Some were better and others, but in any case the ever-resourceful

Corman managed to make money off the same material twice, which, for PIRANHA, is where inspiration evidently ended.

To hunt a missing hiker, investigator Maggie MacNamara (Alexandra Paul) teams with environmental lawyer Paul Grogan (William Katt), resident of the mountain area where the boy disappeared. They search a seemingly-abandoned government research site in the hills, and Maggie incautiously drains a large pool, figuring there may be a body at the bottom. In fact, the kid and his large-breasted girlfriend were chewed to pieces by the pool's mutated piranha, capable of spawning and thriving anywhere. Developed by military geneticists as a biological weapon, the whole species has now been accidentally flushed into the community river system. Maggie and Paul race to warn the public but are frustrated by Paul's old eco-nemesis, J. R. Randolph (Monte Markham), a developer opening a waterfront resort that day. Lawmen on his payroll lock the heroes in jail, and Maggie and Paul break out too late to prevent a bloodbath at Randolph's gaudy fete. Paul endures piranha bites to swim to a sunken toxic waste tank and release the poison before the fish escape downstream.

This copies the John-Sayles-scripted 1978 original, saluted by Steven Spielberg as the cleverest of the many JAWS (1975) imitations—virtually scene-for-scene. But everybody knows how seafood smells when it's no longer fresh. The best that can be said for this 1996 helping is that it's utterly flavorless. High-tech special effects make no notable improvement; in fact, the genius of the piranha concept was how it avoided the need to show a costly creature in the first place. More so than the first film, this fish dish serves up heavy-handed environmental platitudes, with Markham stereotyped as the Evil Businessman who ultimately blows his brains out in an office walled with hunting trophies. At least Alexandra Paul's no-nonsense performance ranks well above the bimbo heroine from last time. After airing on Showtime, the feature flopped onto videocassette via Corman's own home-video distribution company. *(Violence, nudity)* — C.C.

d, Scott Levy; p, Chako Van Leeuwen, Mike Elliott; exec p, Roger Corman; w, Alex Simon (based on a screenplay by John Sayles); ph, Christopher Baffa; ed, John Gilbert; m, Christopher Lennertz; prod d, Roger Cowan; fx, Greg C. Landerer; casting, Jan Glaser; cos, Tami Moore, Rina Ramon Fiddler; makeup, John Buechler, Brad Hardin

Horror/Science Fiction **(PR: C MPAA: R)**

PLAYBACK ★½

(U.S.) 91m Playboy Entertainment Films; Precious Films ~ Paramount Home Video c

Charles Grant *(David Burgess)*; Tawny Kitaen *(Sara Burgess)*; Shannon Whirry *(Karen Stone)*; George Hamilton *(Gil Braman)*; Harry Dean Stanton *(Ernie Fontonot)*; Jodi Thelen *(Mary)*; Quinn Duffy *(Robert Miller)*; Scott Williamson; Daryl Roach; Hitoe Otaki; Candy Sherwin; Traci Adell; Kareen Germain

Is it languid business intrigue seasoned with sex or languid sex seasoned with business intrigue? Either way, PLAYBACK just lies there, faking it.

Brainstorming a satellite-communications merger, corporate vice president David Burgess (Charles Grant) is too busy to pay attention to spouse Sara (Tawny Kitaen). Realizing their marriage is on the verge of bankruptcy, they both loosen up and experiment with erotic videos as sexual aids. Back in the boardroom, conniving exec Karen Stone (Shannon Whirry) sees David's recharged libido as leverage for her own career. She arranges a liaison between Sara and company CEO Gil Braman (George Hamilton), and has a seedy PI (Harry Dean Stanton) snap pictures of the pair in a compromising position and mail them to David. Whether she seduces David or takes his place at Gil's side, Karen seems destined for success when a jealous David punches out Gil. But David realizes the truth and secretly reconciles with Sara. Sara tricks Gil into a videotaped S&M session, inserted into the multimedia presentation shown to the amused partners in the merger. Meanwhile David and some upstart allies put together a better merger deal on their own.

With COVER ME (1995) and TEMPTRESS (1995), this makes a trio of spicy narrative features produced by the Playboy empire for the 1990s straight-to-video market and distributed via Paramount. Writer-director Francis "Oley" Sassone once did a half-decent steamy suspense film, FINAL EMBRACE (1992), for Roger Corman, but by the time Playboy got his services, the erotic-thriller genre, once boosted by the 1992 blockbuster BASIC INSTINCT, was basically stale. And so is PLAYBACK.

Between torpid, torrid encounters, it strives for redeeming social value with a speech by Harry Dean Station scolding men like David for ruining countless lives in corporate streamlinings and restructurings; David's subsequent mega-deal is admired as an enlightened masterpiece of humane and fair management. Executive ethics and explicit eros are strange bedfellows indeed, and if PLAYBACK is any indication, a dull coupling. Tellingly, Playboy's later forays into B-filmmaking were not carried by Paramount; they later moved to Orion Home Video. *(Adult situations, nudity, sexual situations, profanity)* — C.C.

d, Oley Sassone; p, Joseph Sassone; exec p, Richard P. Rosetti, Tony Lynn; w, Oley Sassone, David DuBos; ph, Russ Brandt; ed, Matt Eberlein; m, Emilio Kauderer; prod d, Gary Randall; art d, Gregory Wolfson; casting, Harriet Greenspan, Rhonda Young, Clare Walker; cos, Jillian Ann Kreiner

Erotic/Drama **(PR: O MPAA: R)**

POISON IVY 2: LILY ★½

(U.S.) 112m Turner Home Entertainment ~ New Line Home Video c

Alyssa Milano *(Lily)*; Johnathon Schaech *(Gredin)*; Xander Berkeley *(Donald Falk)*; Belinda Bauer *(Angela Falk)*; Camilla Belle *(Daphne Falk)*; Katherine Dora Brown *(Tanya)*; Walter Kim *(Robert)*; Victoria Haas *(Bridgette)*; Tara Ellison *(Catherine)*; Mychal Wilson *(Spin)*; Joey Krebs *(Peter)*; Kate Rodger *(Isabel)*; Howard Brown *(Rocco)*; Johnny Rabbit *(Himself)*

This sequel's producers would have been well-advised to hire Drew Barrymore for its flashbacks. Without her tawdry brand of hedonism, this film is a follow-up without a frame of reference.

Impressionable Lily Leonetti (Alyssa Milano) comes to study at a trendy LA art institute. A devoted family gal, Lily clings to her Midwestern ethics in the student house she shares with attentive lesbian Tanya (Katherine Dora Brown), bitchy slut Bridgette (Victoria Haas), shy violist Robert (Walter Kim), and Beverly Hills rebel/sculptor Gredin (Johnathon Schaech). After reading the sexually-oriented diary of Ivy, a former house occupant, Lily's good-girl moral resolve weakens. She brightens up her staid look, gives gives big-man-on-campus Gredin a tumble, and accepts a baby-sitting gig for her tumescent professor Donald Falk (Xander Berkeley).

Lily poses nude for Falk and drives a coquettish wedge in his marriage to Angela (Belinda Bauer) before opting for true *amour* with simpatico Gredin. At a Thanksgiving dinner, Falk attempts to rape her. Viewing Viewing this assault causes Falk's daughter to rush out into the street where she's knocked senseless by a car. At the communal house, Falk knocks ,out Gredin, pushes an interfering Robert down the stairs and drags Lily onto the roof.

When Gredin rescues her, the besotted Falk loses his grip and falls to the pavement below.

Trying desperately to cash in on the mega-rental success of POISON IVY, this insipid rip-off makes its predecessor seem like a classic of erotic stimulation. Written in the sketchy psychological profiling perfected by TV shrinks, POISON IVY 2 fails to impress because we neither connect with its underdeveloped characters nor care about their overdeveloped urges. At no point does this film give a sense of Lily being possessed by Ivy, the voice of unzippable pleasure in the diary. If the invasiveness of Ivy's personality isn't palpable, the film has no point.

Milano lacks the acting resources to pull off a character transformation that goes from Sleeping Beauty to Snow White Who Drifted. Berkeley and Bauer effectively illustrate the debilitating effects of 7-year itch, but POISON IVY 2 gets no help from its younger cast members. Watchable only as a soap opera about what every parent fears about dorm life, the film fails at its arousal mission. One gets the feeling Lily isn't reading a red-hot personal journal but a fashion spread in *Seventeen* magazine about what coeds are wearing to beer blasts this season. *(Violence, extreme profanity, extensive nudity, sexual situations, substance abuse.)* — R.P.

d, Anne Goursaud; p, Paul Hertzberg, Catalaine Knell; exec p, Peter Morgan, Steve Einhorn; co-p, Amy Labowitz, Melissa Goddard; w, Chloe King; ph, Suki Mendencevic; ed, Terilyn A. Shropshire; m, Joseph Williams; prod d, Robert DeVico; set d, Sue L. Steinberg; sound, Craig Woods; casting, Jeffrey Passero; cos, Paki Wolfe; makeup, Martina Kohl; stunts, Gary Paul

Thriller/Erotic (PR: C MPAA: R)

POLYMORPH ★★★

(U.S.) 86m Suburban Tempe Co. ~ Tempe Video/E.I. Independent Cinema c

James L. Edwards *(Ted)*; Ariauna Albright *(Donna)*; Tom Hoover *(Carlos)*; Sasha Graham *(Tarper)*; Joseph A. Daw *(Bill)*; Jennifer Huss *(Alice)*; Pam Zitelli *(Regine)*; Leo Anastasio *(Franco)*; Pete Jacelone *(Dr. Lester Clark)*; Michael L. Raso *(Womeldorf)*

Though formulaic at its core, POLYMORPH is a snappy science fiction thriller that represents regional genre filmmaker J. R. Bookwalter's best work to date.

While investigating a meteor crash in the woods, Dr. Lester Clark (Pete Jacelone) and security guard Womeldorf (Michael L. Raso) are shot dead by Tarper (Sasha Graham), who has been guarding a drug stash in a nearby cabin. An organism from the meteor infects Tarper, and her body is discovered in the cabin by Clark's students Bill (Joseph A. Daw) and Ted (James L. Edwards), Bill's girlfriend Alice (Jennifer Huss), and Ted's blind date Donna (Ariauna Albright). Tarper's cohorts Carlos (Tom Hoover), Regine (Pam Zitelli), and Franco (Leo Anastasio) show up, and after a standoff, the youths lock them in a room and flee.

Tarper revives and frees her partners, but soon proves to be possessed by an alien. Once Tarper is killed for good, the creature takes over the body of Alice, who has been shot by Regine. After Bill and Franco also fall victim, Ted, Donna, and Carlos realize they must join forces. The three are eventually able to destroy the alien, but not before Ted is mortally wounded. Carlos and Donna drive off together, but Carlos, who wants no witnesses to his criminal activities, shoots Donna dead.

After taking a significant step up with THE SANDMAN, Bookwalter has crafted one of the best of the new breed of shot-on-video genre movies. He maximizes his low budget by keeping the locations simple and the cast small, compensating with a fast pace and creative camerawork. The plot may be strictly comic-book, but Bookwalter acknowledges this with frequent comic-panel-styled subtitles that add to the fun. POLYMORPH is also the sharpest of his movies visually, with a film-like quality that avoids the murkiness of his previous work and some striking low-budget opticals to configure the alien's possession of its victims.

Edwards' tongue-in-cheek script rarely slips over the line into outright parody or unintentional humor, and allows the characters (especially Albright's and his own, of course) a few nicely timed human moments in the midst of the action. While none of the characters are especially deep, the cast is energetic down the line, and the unexpectedly downbeat ending gives the movie an extra touch of resonance. POLYMORPH may not have too much on its mind, but it puts many higher-budgeted projects to shame for pure entertainment value. *(Graphic violence, substance abuse, extreme profanity.)* — M.G.

d, J.R. Bookwalter; p, J.R. Bookwalter, David A. Wagner; assoc p, Ariauna Albright, Doug Snauffer; w, James L. Edwards (based on a story by J.R. Bookwalter); ph, J.R. Bookwalter; ed, J.R. Bookwalter; m, Matthew Jason Walsh; art d, Lonnie Love; sound, David A. Wagner, Jeffrey W. "Spud" Scaduto; fx, Frank Terranova, Digital Armageddon; casting, Xavier Bronkowitz, Ariauna Albright; makeup, David Lange

Science Fiction/Horror/Action (PR: O MPAA: NR)

POMPATUS OF LOVE, THE ★½

(U.S.) 99m In Pictures; BMG Independents ~ CFP Distribution c

Jon Cryer *(Mark)*; Adrian Pasdar *(Josh)*; Tim Guinee *(Runyon)*; Adam Oliensis *(Phil)*; Mia Sara *(Cynthia)*; Kristin Scott Thomas *(Caroline)*; Arabella Field *(Lori)*; Paige Turco *(Gina)*; Dana Wheeler-Nicholson *(Kathryn)*; Kristen Wilson *(Tasha)*; Charlie Murphy *(Saxaphone Man)*; Liana Pai *(Ting)*; Jim Turner *(Dick Spellman)*; Rene Props *(Flynn)*; Michael McKean *(Sitcom Star)*; Fisher Stevens *(Sitcom Star)*; Jennifer Tilly *(Tarzaan)*; Roscoe Lee Browne *(Leonard Folder)*

Jon Cryer wrote, co-produced, and stars in THE POMPATUS OF LOVE, a romantic comedy that is, sadly, short on both romance and comedy. Cryer was obviously aiming to make something more "profound," but this uneven and sometimes irritating film is best when its at its simplest.

THE POMPATUS OF LOVE takes its odd title from the lyrics of the Steve Miller song, "The Joker." In the story, four male friends—Mark (Jon Cryer), Runyon (Tim Guinee), Phil (Adam Oliensis), and Josh (Adrian Pasdar)—argue over a period of four days about life, love, and the meaning of that old pop tune.

First, Mark, a therapist and writer, describes how his relationship with Tasha (Kristen Wilson), a fashion designer, has hit a snag ever since they agreed to move in together. Mark has been comfortable living in his West Side apartment, but the thought of moving into a loft space in Soho—and committing to Tasha—brings out his insecurities. He spends his days arguing with Tasha and his nights drinking with his buddies.

Runyon, an up-and-coming playwright, mopes about Kathyrn (Dana Wheeler-Nicolson), the woman who left him to start a new life in California. When Runyon gets a chance to pitch his latest project to a sitcom producer in Los Angeles, his friends warn him against looking up Kathyrn. Nevertheless, Runyon tries and fails to win her back.

Unlike the others, Phil is married with children, but when Caroline (Kristin Scott Thomas), a beautiful interior designer, drops into his plumbing store one day and seems to suggest starting an affair, the family man begins questioning his life choices. After much agonizing, Phil decides to remain faithful to his wife, only to find out that Caroline had never intended to have a romance—at least so she says!

Josh is the playboy of the bunch, but his womanizing catches up with him when the one woman he cares about, Gina (Paige Turco), an abused wife, turns to him for help. Josh decides that it is time for him to take more responsibility in life. At the end of four tumultuous days, all four friends finally agree that "the pompatus of love" describes the chasm between the sexes.

First-time director Richard Schenkman infuses THE POMPATUS OF LOVE with pseudo-reflexive bursts of fast-paced editing that camouflage Jon Cryer's theatrically stagnant pronouncements on love, sex, and dating in the 1990s. The many scenes of the men talking about the women in their lives are punctuated by short, direct-address "essays" that merely repeat the tired ideas of the story's dialogue. It is unfortunate that neither writer nor director gives equal time to the women's riffs on the men, especially since the female characters and the stars who play them are far more appealing. Moreover, all the characters—male and female—sound alike reciting Cryer's wordy, Dennis Miller-style one-liners.

But THE POMPATUS OF LOVE does contain a few worthwhile moments, including a very funny spoof of a Hollywood "pitch" session and multiple covers of Steve Miller's classic title song (the last—and surprisingly the best—comes from Sheryl Crow). Also, Kristin Scott Thomas is entrancing throughout, but it is all too typical of the film that a microphone slips into frame during the actress's big seduction scene. In the end, it is hard to imagine anyone apart from an undemanding and immature 30-year-old male enjoying this indulgent mess of a movie. *(Nudity, sexual situations, substance abuse, extreme profanity.)* — E.M.

d, Richard Schenkman; p, D.J. Paul, Jon Resnik; co-p, Jon Cryer, Adam Oliensis, Richard Schenkman; w, Jon Cryer, Adam Oliensis, Richard Schenkman; ph, Russell Lee Fine; ed, Dan Rosen; m, John Hill; prod d, Michael Krantz; casting, Judy Henderson; cos, Carolyn Grifel

Comedy/Drama/Romance (PR: C MPAA: NR)

PORTRAIT OF A LADY, THE ★★★½

(New Zealand/U.K./U.S.) 144m Propaganda Films ~ Gramercy c

Nicole Kidman *(Isabel Archer)*; John Malkovich *(Gilbert Osmond)*; Barbara Hershey *(Madame Serena Merle)*; Mary-Louise Parker *(Henrietta Stackpole)*; Martin Donovan *(Ralph Touchett)*; Shelley Winters *(Mrs. Touchett)*; Richard E. Grant *(Lord Warburton)*; Shelley Duvall *(Countess Gemini)*; Christian Bale *(Edward Rosier)*; Viggo Mortensen *(Caspar Goodwood)*; Valentina Cervi *(Pansy Osmond)*; John Gielgud *(Mr. Touchett)*; Roger Ashton-Griffiths *(Bob Bantling)*; Catherine Zago *(Mother Superior)*; Alessandra Vanzi *(Nun No. 2)*; Katie Campbell *(Miss Molyneux No. 1)*; Katherine Anne Porter *(Miss Molyneux No. 2)*; Eddy Seager *(Strongman's Spruiker)*; Pat Roach *(Strongman)*; Emanuelle Carucci Viterbi *(Roccanera Butler)*; Francesca Bartellini *(Isabel's Maid)*; Achille Brugnini *(Footman at Ballroom)*

Director Jane Campion's feminist intentions come through in her cinematic interpretation of Henry James's classic novel. While it does not command the power, originality, and subtlety of Campion's previous films, there is still much to be admired.

An assortment of contemporary women are seen before an abrupt segue to the 19th century, where Isabel Archer (Nicole Kidman), an American woman in her early twenties, refuses a marriage proposal from Lord Warburton (Richard E. Grant). Recently orphaned, Isabel has come to live at Gardencourt, the English home of her wealthy aunt and uncle, Mr. and Mrs. Touchett (John Gielgud and Shelley Winters), and their consumptive son, Ralph (Martin Donovan). An independently minded young woman whose bold plans for the future don't include marriage, Isabel soon declines a second lucrative offer, this time from Caspar Goodwood (Viggo Mortensen), a rich American industrialist.

Isabel finds inspiration in the mysterious widow, Madame Merle (Barbara Hershey), who arrives at Gardencourt after Mr. Touchett falls seriously ill. Isabel admires Madame Merle's worldly independence, and the two become fast friends. After her uncle dies, Isabel is surprised to learn that he has left her a large fortune, a move secretly orchestrated by Ralph, who adores Isabel and is curious to see what a headstrong young woman can accomplish with the kind of freedom only money can buy.

Isabel travels to Italy, where Madame Merle introduces her to Gilbert Osmond (John Malkovich), an American expatriate with exquisite taste but little money. Prompted by the scheming Madame Merle, Osmond seduces Isabel with his sophistication and rarefied sense of beauty. Isabel agrees to marry him, despite Ralph's obvious displeasure. Osmond soon reveals himself to be a sadistic and opportunistic dilettante, who only cares for his objets d'art and finding a rich husband for his teenage daughter, Pansy (Valentina Cervi). He asks Isabel to help bring about a union with Lord Warburton, who has recently arrived in Rome and has expressed some interest in the girl. But Isabel, who by now is too familiar with the torment of an oppressive, loveless marriage, knows Pansy is in love with the younger but poorer Edward Rosier (Christian Bale), and she subtly discourages Warburton. When he leaves Italy without making a proposal, Osmond, and, to Isabel's consternation, Madame Merle, accuse Isabel of sabotage.

Isabel's growing suspicions of Madame Merle's duplicity are confirmed after Osmond cruelly denies Isabel permission to return to England to visit Ralph, who is now dying. Isabel is consoled by her sister-in-law, the Countess Gemini (Shelly Duvall), who tells Isabel that not only were Madame Merle and Osmond once lovers, but Pansy is really Madame Merle's daughter. Emboldened by the knowledge of their deceit, Isabel disobeys her husband and leaves for England, arriving in time to bid Ralph a tearful goodbye. At the funeral, Isabel again encounters Caspar Goodwood, who begs her to make a total break with Osmond and return with him to America. After a brief, passionate embrace, Isabel tears herself away and runs back to the now empty Gardencourt.

Campion takes the title of James's novel fully to heart, offering up an enticing visual portrait of a woman constrained by the limits of a patriarchal society. As such, there are perhaps too many obvious cinematic metaphors to be found, such as a gate casting its prison-bar-like shadow over Isabel. Yet Campion spices up what could have been another pretty period piece by taking some commendable visual risks, such as unconventional framing and camera angles, fantasy scenes, and changes in film speed.

Malkovich masterfully brings forth the complicated, cruel villain lurking underneath Osmond's innocuous exterior, but this territory has become so firmly associated with Malkovich that his performance seems entirely familiar. Kidman's thoughtful portrayal of Isabel has depth, but all too often she comes off as timid and meek, unable to measure up to the unusual strength, determination, and intelligence found in the novel and screenplay. Hershey, however, is a revelation. Her complex portrayal of a ruthless woman torn between the need to provide for herself—and, as it turns out, her child—and a genuine horror at her own manipulations is both chilling and heartbreaking.

Despite its faults, this is a film that has obviously been made with considerable effort, care, and risk. It is not Campion's best work, but it is certainly an adequate follow-up, critically if not commercially, to the success of her Academy Award-winner THE PIANO (1993). By reinterpreting the 19th century from a contemporary feminist viewpoint, Campion exposes herself to the possibilities of absurdity and incongruence; she escapes these dangers through intelligence and sincerity, pointing out the reality that even today there are certain social structures and hierarchies which generate an insurmountable loss of freedom for women—and that these structures sometimes define the frame within which a portrait of femininity must be set. *(Adult situations, nudity.)* — R.C.

d, Jane Campion; p, Monty Montgomery, Steve Golin; assoc p, Ute Leonhardt, Heidrun Reshoeft, Mark Turnbull; co-p, Ann Wingate; w, Laura Jones (based on the novel by Henry James); ph, Stuart Dryburgh; ed, Veronika Jenet; m, Wojiech Kilar; prod d, Janet Patterson; art d, Martin Childs; set d, Jill Quertier; sound, Lee Smith, Peter Glossop; casting, Beth Charkham; cos, Janet Patterson; makeup, Peter Owen, Magdalen Gaffney

AAN Best Supporting Actress: Barbara Hershey; *AAN Best Costume Design:* Janet Patterson

Drama **(PR: C MPAA: PG-13)**

PORTRAITS OF A KILLER ★½

(U.S./Canada) 93m Illusions Entertainment ~ LIVE Entertainment c

(AKA: PORTRAITS OF INNOCENCE)

Jennifer Grey *(Elaine Taylor)*; Costas Mandylor *(George Kendell)*; Patricia Charbonneau *(Carolyn Price)*; M. Emmett Walsh *(Raymond Garrison)*; Michael Ironside *(Sgt. Ernie Hansen)*; Roxanne Kraemer *(Sandy)*; Currie Graham *(Wade Simms)*; Paul Coeur *(Roy Brown)*; Meaghan Ball *(Lisa Parker)*; Kenneth Welsh *(Jim Miller)*; Brian Dooley *(Lieutenant)*; Daryl Shuttelworth *(Mark)*; Mary Hennigan *(Shelly)*; David McNally *(Dan Goldberg)*; Andy Maton *(Reporter)*; Esther Purves-Smith *(Darla)*; Carrie Schiffler *(Beckie)*; Val Planche *(Joan)*; Danielle Evans; Sherry Sonnleitner; Tracy Hemeyer; Aisha Freeman *(Models)*

Costas Mandylor woodenly essays an enigmatic murder suspect, a professional photographer of prostitutes who has sex with all his models.

"Portraits of Innocence" is the latest published portfolio from controversial street shooter George Kendell (Costas Mandylor). It's expected to sell briskly since four of the teenage hookers Kendell photographed are now dead, victims of an unknown serial slayer. Hard-driving prosecutor Carolyn Price (Patricia Charbonneau), who happens to run a halfway-house for wayward women, has Kendell arrested on suspicion of committing the murders in a sick bid for publicity.

Kendell's legal advisors secure novice attorney Elaine Taylor (Jennifer Grey) for the defense. Taylor even surprises herself by getting Kendell released pending an indictment. The tainted shutterbug sweeps his rookie lawyer off her feet and into bed. She even provides an alibi for him when another "Portraits of Innocence" girl is killed. But Kendell's evasive manner and hidden stash of victim's jewelry convinces Elaine that she's made a terrible mistake, and she runs to Carolyn Price for help.

Carolyn insists that Elaine go on defending her client. In fact, the prosecutor has a guilty secret as well; she killed one of the whores during an argument, and now someone is mailing her pictures of the foul deed.

Carolyn comes to Elaine's office to confront her with proof of guilt. A struggle ensues. Kendell is exonerated, even though Elaine knows he's the primary perpetrator.

It's hard to discern a point to this murky jurisprudence noir—except that for the umpteenth time a lawyer's libido leads to danger (as in JAGGED EDGE, BASIC INSTINCT, or LEGAL EAGLES). Somehow, Elaine makes partner in her firm, despite perjured testimony and evidence tampering, suggesting that none of the scriptwriters have had any acquaintance with courtrooms apart from tacky suspense thrillers.

Despite the high hooker count, this movie shies away from explicit erotica, but the cynical, winking attitude of police characters toward the flesh-peddling underworld is offensive enough on its own terms. It's an indication of how times change that in Martin Scorsese's TAXI DRIVER (1976), one abused, underaged streetwalker was a moral outrage. Here, a whole gallery of them are just wallpaper. The cast deserves better, as does Curtis Petersen's moody cinematography. *(Violence, adult situations, sexual situations.)* — C.C.

d, Bill Corcoran; p, Bruce Harvey, Shauna Shapiro-Jackson; exec p, David A. Jackson, Stefano Dammico; w, Bruce Harvey, Nancy Laing, Scott McPherson; ph, Curtis Petersen; ed, Doug Forbes; m, Graeme Coleman; prod d, Michael Nemirsky; set d, Melodi McGill; sound, Kevin Sands; fx, Jim Cammaert; casting, Dori Zuckerman, Leslie Swan; cos, Tania Morris; makeup, Pearl Louie; stunts, John Scott

Crime/Thriller **(PR: O MPAA: R)**

PORTRAITS OF INNOCENCE

(SEE: PORTRAITS OF A KILLER)

POSTE AVANCE

(SEE: OUTPOST, THE)

PREACHER'S WIFE, THE ★★½

(U.S.) 124m Touchstone; Samuel Goldwyn; Parkway Productions; Mundy Lane Entertainment ~ Buena Vista c

Denzel Washington *(Dudley)*; Whitney Houston *(Julia Biggs)*; Courtney B. Vance *(Henry Biggs)*; Gregory Hines *(Joe Hamilton)*; Jenifer Lewis *(Marguerite Coleman)*; Loretta Devine *(Beverly)*; Justin Pierre Edmund *(Jeremiah Biggs)*; Lionel Richie *(Britsloe)*; Paul Bates *(Saul Jeffreys)*; Lex Monson *(Osbert)*; Darvel Davis Jr. *(Hakim)*; Willie James Stiggers Jr. *(Billy Eldrigde)*; Marcella Lowery *(Anna Eldridge)*; Cissy Houston *(Mrs. Havergal)*; Aaron A. McConnaughey; Shyheim Franklin; Taral Hicks; Kennan Scott *(Teens)*; Jernard B. Burks *(Pizza Man)*; Michael Alexander Jackson *(Robber)*; Jaime Tirelli *(Liquor Store Owner)*; Shari Headley *(Arlene Chattan)*; Lizan Mitchell *(Judge)*; Robert Colston *(Bailiff)*; Victor Williams *(Robbie)*; Juliehera DeStefano *(Receptionist)*; Charlotte d'Amboise *(Deborah Paige)*; Delores Mitchell *(Mary Halford)*; David Langston Smyrl *(Hanley's Waiter)*; Harsh Nayyar *(Christmas Tree Man)*; Mervyn Warren; Roy Haynes; George Coleman; Ted Dunbar; Jamil Nasser *(Jazz Quintet)*; Helmar Augustus Cooper *(Johnson Keeley)*; St. Cecilia Choir *(Hamilton's Carolers)*; Mary Bond Davis *(Bernita)*; Toukie Smith *(Teleprompter Operator)*; Georgia Mass Choir & Band *(St. Matthew's Choir & Band)*; Mozelle Hawkins Allen; Eloise Beasley; Yolanda Beasley-Prime; Cassondra M. Breedlove; Dirk Chaney; Brenda J. Childs; Anthony Dean Copeland; Hayward Cromartie; Betty Cromartie Davis; Valerie Inez Edwards; Kimberley M. Garrett; Rutha Harris; Carolyn Henry; Gary Nuckles-Holt; Teretha G. Houston; Angela L. Jones; Morris Vernon Jones; Rose Merry Jordan; Jacqueline Martin; Betty Matthews; Naguanda Miller; Sharon A. Mitchell; Rev. Corey McGee; Beverly S. Nixon; Krishna Presha; Jacqulyn V. Saunders; Constance Small; Troy L. Sneed Sr.; Rev. Lawrence K. Thomas; Ulisa A. Thomas; V. Ranaldo Welcome;

Berta J. Williams; Kimberly L. Wright *(St. Matthew's Choir & Band)*; Steven Brown *(Drummer)*; Rick Carter *(Bass Player)*; Sterling Holloman II *(Lead Guitar Player)*; Rev. Kenneth Paden *(Pianist)*; Dwain L. White *(Organist)*; Aaron Jordan *(Eldridge Kid)*; Yakin Manassah Jordan *(Eldridge Kid)*; Joshua Jordan *(Donkey - Nativity Choir)*; Tiffany Joseph *(Shepherd - Nativity Choir)*; Jessica Malloy *(Mary - Nativity Choir)*; Amia Hart *(Beverly's Child)*; Brittany Anderson *(Sheep - Nativity Choir)*; Christopher Malloy *(Angel - Nativity Choir)*; Andal Fequiere *(Joseph - Nativity Choir)*; Mark Gilbert *(Wise Man - Nativity Choir)*; Michael Marshall *(Wise Man - Nativity Choir)*; Shaun Purefoy *(Wise Man - Nativity Choir)*; Tiffiny Money Graham *(Angel - Nativity Choir)*; Khalia Hamilton-Montoute *(Angel - Nativity Choir)*; Marquis Bowen-Wallace *(Shepherd - Nativity Choir)*; Lakeya Enos *(Shepherd - Nativity Choir)*; Christine Lameisha Koon *(Camel - Nativity Choir)*; Anthony Biggham *(Lamb - Nativity Choir)*; Taleah Enos *(Ox - Nativity Choir)*; Soul Tempo; Jerry Brunsin; Anthony Burnett; Kevin Mitchell; Phillip Mitchell *(Painting Singers - Nativity Choir)*

THE PREACHER'S WIFE tells the story of an angel who helps a minister and his family during a crisis. This African-American musical remake of THE BISHOP'S WIFE respectably retains some of what worked well in 1947, but also adds new elements that only work on and off.

With its story updated to an Eastern US inner-city, THE PREACHER'S WIFE now concerns the family troubles of Henry Biggs (Courtney B. Vance), a minister whose church faces bankruptcy and possible demolition. Meanwhile, Julia (Whitney Houston), Henry's faithful wife and lead singer in the church choir, feels some alienation from her husband when he considers offers of help from greedy developer Joe Hamilton (Gregory Hines). Meanwhile, Henry and Julia's child, Jeremiah (Justin Pierre Edmund), loses his best friend to a foster home. Into this strife comes Dudley (Denzel Washington), a charismatic angel set on aiding Henry and his family.

Dudley tells only Henry his real mission, but the supposedly religious man doubts his word. Still, Dudley secures his new position as Henry's assistant by charming everyone else in the Biggs household, including Julia; Jeremiah; Julia's sassy mother, Marguerite (Jenifer Lewis); and Henry's blubbering secretary, Beverly (Loretta Devine). Unfortunately, Dudley's presence only creates more friction between Henry and Julia, especially after Henry forgets to take Julia out on a date and leaves Dudley to do the job.

Despite the setback, circumstances finally turn around when Henry refuses to accept Joe Hamilton's grand redevelopment plans for the church. Instead, Henry plans a major TV event in the church to rouse his dwindling congregation. Dudley helps by bringing Henry and Julia closer together during rehearsals, and by causing Joe to realize the error of his ways. After Joe attends the Christmas Eve telecast, he backs off from his plans to take over the church. Dudley also reunites Jeremiah with his best friend, who returns to the neighborhood. With his work done, Dudley then vanishes, leaving only little Jeremiah with the ability to remember him.

The initial plans for this remake of THE BISHOP'S WIFE (1947) included casting Laurence Fishburne in the role of the preacher. Although Courtney B. Vance does well by the role (originally played by David Niven), Fishburne might have added a bit of grit and tension that is missing from this slick, sweet fairy tale. The plot involving the developer and a subplot about a wayward teenager Henry tries to help are clunky attempts by the new screenwriters (Nat Mauldin and Allan Scott) to make the original script by Robert E. Sherwood and Leonardo Bercovici more "real" and up-to-date.

Some of the other changes are more welcome. The character of Dudley has been turned into a slightly bumbling, comic angel (unlike the ultra-professional one played by Cary Grant in '47) and Denzel Washington shows a new, pleasant side in the lightweight role. The character of Julia (originally played by Loretta Young) hasn't changed much, however, and Whitney Houston's acting has not improved since THE BODYGUARD (1992), but Houston's singing enlivens both her part and the film on several occasions. The acerbic professor played by Monty Wooley in the original is thankfully replaced by the acerbic mother-in-law acted winningly by Jenifer Lewis. Even the famous skating scene from the original is improved upon here (mainly because this time they don't use stunt doubles).

But director Penny Marshall misses her chance to make a new classic. For whatever reason, there is actually less sexual chemistry between Washington and Houston than there was between Grant and Young. Also, the songs include one too many gospel numbers and no Christmas classics (which would have helped make this at least a three-hankie melodrama). Some scenes (especially toward the end) run too long; the film could use a good edit. And like MICHAEL, the other 1996 Christmas season angel movie, THE PREACHER'S WIFE is completely artless, although Marshall's direction is not really any worse than Henry Koster's (in 1947). Since Marshall is a woman, it is ironic that the new film validates patriarchy even more forcefully than before. Considering that Hollywood is still so male-dominated, any other message from such a film surely would have been miraculous. *(Profanity.)* — E.M.

d, Penny Marshall; p, Samuel Goldwyn Jr.; exec p, Robert Greenhut, Elliot Abbott; assoc p, Bonnie Hlinomaz; co-p, Debra Martin Chase, Amy Lemisch, Timothy M. Bourne; w, Nat Mauldin, Allan Scott (based on the 1947 screenplay *The Bishop's Wife* by Robert E. Sherwood and Leonardo Bercovici, based on the novel by Robert Nathan); ph, Miroslav Ondricek; ed, Stephen A. Rotter, George Bowers; m, Hans Zimmer; prod d, Bill Groom; art d, Dennis Bradford; set d, George Detitta; sound, Les Lazarowitz; fx, Connie Brink; casting, Paula Herold; cos, Cynthia Flynt; makeup, Edna Sheen

AAN Best Original Musical or Comedy Score: Hans Zimmer

Drama/Fantasy **(PR: A MPAA: PG)**

PREDICTIONS OF FIRE ★★½
(U.S./Yugoslavia) 85m TV Slovenia Arts Programs; Kinetikon Pictures ~ Artistic License Films c/bw

Matej Russ

PREDICTIONS OF FIRE locates the point where art, history and politics are clashing in the former Yugoslavia, but while this new film offers important information in an original way, it also becomes heavy-going and off-putting.

PREDICTIONS OF FIRE charts the history of Laibach, an industrial rock band formed in the Yugoslav republic of Slovenia during the early 1980s. The film also pauses to document the history of Slovenian culture in the twentieth century, including the impact of WWII and the Cold War on different art forms. PREDICTIONS OF FIRE then shows how Laibach inspired the painting group Irwin and the theater group Red Pilot. Patterned after a socialist state bureaucracy, and calling themselves NSK (New Slovenian Arts), these three groups have used totalitarian aesthetics to expose fascist ideology and have grown in political power within Slovenia. The leaders of NSK are currently challenging the republic's official government by issuing NSK passports.

Producer-writer-director Michael Benson scores some points using a mixture of traditional and avant-garde techniques to document the evolution of NSK. By quoting Bertolt Brecht and Walter Benjamin, Benson also grounds his study of image-making in central Europe with keen intelligence. The combination of voice-overs, newsreel footage, interviews, and newly created collages of sounds and images only works for a while, however; by midpoint, the film has become repetitious and uninvolving. PREDICTIONS OF FIRE mentions that the cinematic medium is NSK's most powerful weapon, but this documentary never packs the punch of Dusan Makavejev's WR: MYSTERIES OF THE ORGANISM (1971), with its wild take on Eastern bloc art through history, or Marcel Ophuls's THE TROUBLES WE'VE SEEN (1995), with its multi-faceted portrait of the break-up of Yugoslavia. While some of the critics interviewed complain about the obliquely ironic, crypto-fascist elements of the NSK art movement, the problem with this film is that it lacks its own sense of distance and irony in handling the controversial subject matter. PREDICTIONS OF FIRE means well but lacks fire. — E.M.

d, Michael Benson; p, Michael Benson, Milan Blazin; exec p, Stephen Gallagher; w, Michael Benson; ph, Teodoro Maniaci; ed, Nika Lah; m, Laibach, Srecko Bajda; prod d, New Collectivism, Kinetikon Pictures; sound, Damjan Kunej (mixer), Boris Pavlin (recordist)

Documentary **(PR: C MPAA: NR)**

PRE-MADONNAS ★★

(U.S.) 98m The Star/Matovich/Pegasus Investment Group ~ WarnerVision Entertainment c
(AKA: SOCIAL SUICIDE)

Bobbie Bresee *(Ava Sterling)*; Shannon Sturges *(Kim Sterling)*; Peter Anthony Elliott *(Tom Garcia)*; Margaret Silbar *(Mildred Sterling)*; Dan Cashman *(Bob Sterling)*; Pamela S. Neill *(Constance)*; Kenn Cooper *(Scott Robertson)*; Jack Carter *(Senator Robertson)*; Trini Lopez *(Himself)*; C. J. Bau *(Dean Webster)*; Kelly Nelson *(Peter)*; Louise DeMangus *(John)*; Leslie Horan *(Maggie)*; Friday the Dog *(Colonel)*

PRE-MADONNAS, shot in 1991 under the title SOCIAL SUICIDE, is a harmless satire about California debutantes and what happens when one of them wants to attend a coming-out ball with a Hispanic boy instead of the rich WASP approved by her mother.

Snobby Beverly Hills matron Ava Sterling (Bobbie Bresee) wants her daughter, Kim (Shannon Sturges), to go to the Las Madonnas debutante ball with Scott Robertson (Kenn Cooper). Scott is the son of Senator Robertson (Jack Carter), who could help Ava's husband in a lucrative land development deal.

But Kim stuns her mother by saying she wants to attend the ball with a Mexican classmate, Tom Garcia (Peter Anthony Elliott). Kim goes to see Tom at his job at a melon-packing factory and convinces him to take her to the ball.

Kim's parents try to talk her out of it, offering her a Porsche, but she refuses. Ava offers Tom $100 and a one-way ticket to Mexico, but he turns her down because, unbeknownst to Kim, he lives in Bel Air and his family owns the fruit-packing company.

Kim is impressed with Tom because he's in competition for a prestigious university award, so Ava schemes to make Scott a nominee as well. During a school presentation, Scott sabotages Tom's speech, and the dean tells Tom the only chance he has to win the award is to perform a special community service assignment—the same night as Kim's ball. When Tom tells Kim he can't go to the ball, she's so mad at him that she agrees to go with Scott.

Tom changes his mind, but Ava purposely tells him the wrong time to pick Kim up. By the time Tom arrives at the house, Scott and Kim are already gone, but Kim's sympathetic grandmother drives Tom to the dance.

Kim shocks everyone at the ball by appearing in a garish, flamenco-style dress. Tom sneaks inside and dances with Kim, but Scott arranges for a stripper to pop out of a cake and say that Tom hired her. Tom responds by calling all his Hispanic friends, who turn the ball into a wild party. Scott lures Kim into a back room and starts to molest her, but Tom beats him up, wins Kim's heart, and is awarded the college prize.

PRE-MADONNAS was made five years before its direct-to-video release. That might explain its dated sensibility, which is a mixture of John Hughes's 1980s teen satires and the slew of slobs vs. snobs comedies inspired by ANIMAL HOUSE. The humor is typically crude, although largely innocuous.

The cast is amiable, with B-movie horror star Bobbie Bresee quite amusing as the snooty mother. As Kim, Shannon Sturges has little to do except pout and be cute, and she performs that task adequately enough. But one wonders what her grandfather, the legendary writer-director Preston Sturges, would make of her Valley Girl dialect, let alone the whole film. *(Sexual situations, profanity).* — M.S.

d, Lawrence D. Foldes; p, Victoria Paige Myerink; exec p, Frank D. Rowe; assoc p, Larry Chambers, Yelena Guzman; co-p, Mitchel J. Matovich Jr., Aaron Speiser; w, Elisa J. Charouhas, Lawrence D. Foldes, Melanie Anne Phillips, Mark Buntzman, Adam Slater (based on a story by Elisa J. Charouhas); ph, Stuart Kiehl, Geza Sinkovics; ed, Melanie Anne Phillips, Jon Yamaoka; m, Roger Bellon; prod d, Peter Kanter; art d, Elizabeth Simakis; sound, Roberta Doheny; fx, Lisa Romanoff; cos, Patte Dee

Comedy **(PR: C MPAA: PG-13)**

PRIMAL FEAR ★★★

(U.S.) 130m Rysher Entertainment ~ Paramount c

Richard Gere *(Martin Vail)*; Laura Linney *(Janet Venable)*; John Mahoney *(Shaughnessy)*; Alfre Woodard *(Shoat)*; Frances McDormand *(Molly)*; Edward Norton *(Aaron/Roy)*; Terry O'Quinn *(Yancy)*; Andre Braugher *(Goodman)*; Steven Bauer *(Pinero)*; Joe Spano *(Stenner)*; Tony Plana *(Martinez)*; Stanley Anderson *(Rushman)*; Maura Tierney *(Naomi)*; Jon Seda *(Alex)*; Reg Rogers *(Connerman)*; Kenneth Tigar *(Weil)*; Brian Reddy *(Woodside)*; Christopher Carroll *(M.C.)*; Wendy Cutler *(Lou)*; Ron O.J. Parson *(Turner)*; Sigrid K. Zahner *(Vail's Secretary)*; Diann Burns *(WLS Anchor)*; Linda Yu *(WLS Anchor)*; Andy Shaw *(WLS Location Reporter)*; Mary Ann Childers *(WBBM Anchor)*; Lester D. Holt *(WBBM Anchor)*; Sylvia Gomez *(WBBM Location Reporter)*; Jon Duncanson *(WBBM Location Reporter)*; David Eckert *(WGN Anchor)*; Robert Jordan *(WGN Anchor)*; Joanie Lum *(WGN Location Reporter)*; Randy Salerno *(WGN Location Reporter)*; Kyle Colerider-Krugh *(Postman)*; Joseph Luis Caballero *(Joe)*; Randall Slavin *(Young Boy)*; Mike Bacarella *(Sergeant)*; Turk Muller *(Precinct Jailer)*; Joe Kosala *(Cop)*; Lenny Wilson *(Bartender)*; Peter Schreiner *(Bailiff)*; Joseph R. Ryan *(Old Man)*; Azalea Davila *(Linda)*; Wayne Wright *(Court Clerk)*; Tony Fitzpatrick *(Duty Officer)*; Clarence Williams Jr. *(Arresting Cop)*; Rosalie V. Lewis *(Stenographer)*; Dwight Brad Dyer *(Prison Guard)*; Larry Cook *(Pilot)*; Bob Kenney *(Pilot)*

With its painfully generic title, it is not surprising that PRIMAL FEAR is just another in a long list of nearly indistinguishable courtroom dramas, offering up the standard flashy lawyer and maybe-innocent, maybe-guilty defendant and culminating in an artlessly contrived twist.

When a Chicago archbishop is brutally murdered in his bedroom, glorified ambulance chaser and self-proclaimed "hotshot lawyer" Martin Vail (Richard Gere) sees defending the alleged killer, Aaron (Edward Norton), as the self-promotion opportunity of a lifetime. Though Aaron cannot remember the events leading up to his being found covered with the archbishop's blood, Vail, a true product of the modern legal system, is less concerned with his client's guilt or innocence than with how convincingly ingenuous he can appear on the stand.

As the flashy Vail and his ex-lover, Janet Venable (Laura Linney), go head-to-head in the courtroom, a psychologist specializing in amnesia (Frances MacDormand) begins to suspect that Aaron may be possessed of multiple personalities—specifically, a short-fused redneck named Roy who appears easily capable of murder. Knowing that it is too late to change to an insanity plea, Vail orchestrates a chaotic courtroom scene in which Aaron becomes Roy and attacks Janet, necessitating a mistrial and setting up the big revelation: Aaron, not Roy, is the false personality, a pitiful hayseed concocted by the murderous but perfectly sane Roy to garner Vail's sympathies. Realizing he was played like a violin by a true master of manipulation, Vail storms out of the courthouse more cynical than ever.

Director Gregory Hoblit earned his stripes in prime time, directing episodes of such television series as "Hill Street Blues," "LA Law," and "NYPD Blue," and ultimately garnering an Emmy. It is not surprising, then, that PRIMAL FEAR comes across as a particularly long episode of "LA Law" or "Law and Order"—though not nearly as good as the best of either series. To be fair, Hoblit is hobbled by a spare and unambitious script, full of silly side plots and abandoned story threads, so that the end result is slick-looking but fairly empty.

Much was made of Gere's performance by critics and moviegoers alike. And rightly so: where Gere's pretty-boy shallowness has so often hindered his performances, in PRIMAL FEAR it works to his advantage like nowhere else; but for a jarringly out-of-character scene in which Vail expounds on his belief in the goodness of mankind, PRIMAL FEAR represents Gere's best role since 1990's INTERNAL AFFAIRS. Unfortunately, this star vehicle is a one-seater: the excellent supporting cast—including MacDormand, John Mahoney, Alfre Woodard, Andre Braugher, Terry O'Quinn, and Maura Tierney—is wasted, almost completely ignored by both the director and the screenwriters. Only newcomer Edward Norton's memorable portrayal of Aaron-Roy is given enough screen time to compete with Gere. *(Violence, nudity, sexual situations, profanity.)* — B.T.

d, Gregory Hoblit; p, Gary Lucchesi; exec p, Howard W. Koch Jr.; assoc p, Arnold Rudnick, Patricia Graf; co-p, Robert McMinn; w, Steve Shagan, Ann Biderman (based on the novel by William Diehl); ph, Michael Chapman; ed, David Rosenbloom; m, James Newton Howard; prod d, Jeannine Oppewall; art d, William Arnold; set d, Cindy Carr; sound, Steve Cantamessa (mixer); fx, Thomas P. Ryba, Rob Burton, Dream Quest Images; casting, Deborah Aquila, Jane Shannon; cos, Betsy Cox; makeup, Hallie D'Amore, Matthew Mungle; stunts, Ernie Orsatti

AAN Best Supporting Actor: Edward Norton

Drama/Crime/Thriller **(PR: C MPAA: R)**

PROPRIETOR, THE ★★

(France/Turkey/U.S.) 105m Merchant-Ivory Productions; Largo Entertainment; Ognan Pictures; Fez Productions Ltd. ~ Warner Bros. c
(LA PROPRIETAIRE)

Jeanne Moreau *(Adrienne Mark)*; Josh Hamilton *(William O'Hara)*; Austin Pendleton *(Willy Kunst)*; Nell Carter *(Milly)*; Marc Tissot *(Patrice Legendre)*; Sean Young *(Virginia Kelly)*; Christopher Cazenove *(Elliot Spencer)*; Sam Waterston *(Harry Bancroft)*; Jean-Pierre Aumont *(Franz Legendre)*; Pierre Vaneck *(Raymond T.K.)*; Charlotte de Turckheim *(Judith Mark)*; Michael Bergin *(Bobby)*; Joanna Adler *(F. Freemder)*; James Naughton *(Texan)*; J. Smith-Cameron *(Texan)*; Michael Bergin *(Bobby)*; John Dalton *(Emilio)*; Jack Koenig *(Apartment Doorman)*; Panther; Bull; Kim Gilmore; Falcon *(Guardian Angels)*; Joan Audiberti *(French Lady)*; Katherine Argo *(French Lady)*; Judy Alanna *(Woman in Park)*; Hubert St. Macary *(Taxi Driver)*; Diane Nignan *(Pedestrian)*; Guillemette Grobon *(Suzanne T.K.)*; Cherif Ezzeldin; Valerie Toledano *(French Couple)*; Jorg Schnass; Paula Kein *(German Couple)*; Suzanna Pattoni *(Concierge)*; Alain Rimoux *(Notaire)*; Humbert Balsan *(Maitre Vicks)*; Donald Rosenfeld *(Maitre Ertaud)*; Frank De La Personne *(TV Moderator)*; Gilles Arbona *(Politician)*; Henri Garcia *(Interviewer)*; Jeanne-Marie Darblay *(Journalist)*; Catherine Kinley *(Entertainment Tonight Presenter)*; Marjolaine de Graeve *(Young Adrienne)*; Carole Franck *(Shop Assistant)*; Azmine Jaffer *(Shop Assistant)*; Brigitte Catillon *(Aristocratic Lady)*; Jean-Yves Dubois *(Fan-Fan)*; Herve Briaux *(Aristocratic Man)*; Sophie Camus *(Girl in Nightmare)*; Eric Ruf *(Theodore)*; Elodie Bouchez *(Young Girl)*; Judith Remy *(Nadine)*; Wade Childress *(Ben)*; Thomas Tomazewski *(Franck)*

A picture with no interesting characters and a plot virtually invisible to the naked eye, THE PROPRIETOR might have made an intriguing novel. As a movie, about all it has to offer is Jeanne Moreau's incandescent smile.

Adrienne Mark (Jeanne Moreau), a 60-something French writer living well in New York City, is plagued by recurring dreams and memories. When she was a child growing up in Paris, her mother (Charlotte de Turckheim), a successful Jewish dressmaker, was arrested by the Nazis. She never came home.

After learning that the Mark family apartment is up for sale, Adrienne, haunted by remorse, sells nearly all of her possessions and returns to Paris in the hope of buying and moving back into the vacant flat. In Paris, she is greeted by old friends and her ex-husband, Elliot (Christopher Cazenove), and learns of plans to produce a third film version of her most popular book.

When Patrice (Marc Tissot), the son of the original film's director, meets with Virginia (Sean Young), the producer of the new version, he is disappointed to learn that she prefers "Call Me French," the tawdry Hollywood adaptation of Adrienne's book, to "My Name Is France," the '60s New Wave version. Patrice converts Virginia by screening the original for her, and a romance develops between the two.

Adrienne is unable to match the top bid for her childhood apartment. Hearing of this back in New York, her longtime housekeeper and friend, Milly (Nell Carter), sells a painting Adrienne had given her and sends the money to Paris. With this $250,000, Adrienne is able to purchase the family flat she covets.

Later, at the Cannes Film Festival, Adrienne is being honored. After announcing that she and Elliot plan to remarry, Adrienne, now at peace with her past, imagines herself happily dancing with her mother.

The problem with filming an interior drama like this is finding something to photograph. Director Ismail Merchant's somewhat desperate response to this challenge is to inject a series of rather extraneous street disturbances into his movie along with a pair of incongruous musical numbers: an impromptu song by Milly and a scene in which Patrice courts Virginia by singing "If I Didn't Care," a la Bill Kenny of The Ink Spots, as she cavorts through a fountain. This truly odd interlude recalls A WOMAN IS A WOMAN (1960), in which Jean-Luc Godard elicited, more successfully than Merchant, a modicum of charm from his players' amateurish excursions into musical comedy.

This is not the only cinema reference bogging down THE PROPRIETOR. An unseen character is called Chris Marker, the name of the filmmaker who created the mini-masterpiece LA JETEE (1964). The movie in pre-production is to be called LOLA, the title of memorable films by Demy and Fassbinder. An excerpt from "My Name Is France" evokes Godard again but lurches into absurdity when an interview degenerates into softcore shenanigans closer to Radley Metzger than the rather puritanical Jean-Luc. Indeed, the clips from "My Name Is France," which is supposed to be a good movie, are even sillier than those we see from "Call Me French," which is supposed to be trash. And the presence in THE PROPRIETOR's cast of Jean-Pierre Aumont recalls Francois Truffaut's DAY FOR NIGHT (1973), a far better movie about making a film. *(Sexual situations, adult situations, profanity.)* — D.T.

d, Ismail Merchant; p, Donald Rosenfeld, Humbert Balsan; exec p, Paul Bradley, Osman Eralp; assoc p, Richard Hawley; w, Jean-Marie Besset, George Trow (from a story by Ismail Merchant); ph, Larry Pizer; ed, William Webb; m, Richard Robbins; prod d, Bruno Santini, Kevin Thompson; art d, Bernadette Saint-Loubert; set d, Patrick Colpaert, C. Ford Wheeler; sound, Didier Sain (mixer); casting, Frederique Moidon; cos, Anne de Laugardiere, Abigail Murray; makeup, Nicolas Degennes

Drama/Romance (PR: C MPAA: R)

PROTEUS ★★½

(U.K.) 97m Victor Film Corp.; Metrodome Films; Wonderful Films ~ Vidmark Entertainment c

Craig Fairbass *(Alex)*; Toni Barry *(Linda)*; William Marsh *(Mark)*; Jennifer Calvert *(Rachel)*; Robert Firth *(Paul)*; Margot Steinberg *(Christina)*; Ricco Ross *(Buckley)*; Jordan Page *(Dr. Soames)*; Nigel Pegram *(Dr. Shelley)*; Doug Bradley *(Leonard Brinkstone)*; John Chase *(Chinese Guard)*; Jerry Grayson *(Pilot)*; Neil Finnegan; Tom Lucy; Billy Davey; Lance Peters *(Armed Guards)*; Duncan Jarman *(Himself)*

Like its titular shape-changing monster, this British production mutates from something pokey and derivative into a tense and exciting (if still derivative) creature feature.

A trio of drug-smuggling couples—Alex (Craig Fairbrass) and Rachel (Jennifer Calvert), Mark (William Marsh) and Christina (Margot Steinberg), and Paul (Robert Firth) and Linda (Toni Barry)—wind up adrift at sea in a life raft after their yacht catches fire. They come upon and board an oil rig, where they discover a genetics laboratory and only a few hostile occupants. After a slimy parasite jumps down the throat of the injured Rachel, Alex discovers that a creature created in the lab has consumed everyone on board, and can imitate anyone it has killed.

Now an alter ego of the monster, Rachel recovers and attacks Mark and Christina. Alex reveals to Linda that he and Rachel are actually a cop and federal agent who have infiltrated the gang. They then encounter Paul, who also proves to be the creature in disguise: Alex blows him up with a grenade. Paul's remains recombine just as Brinkstone (Doug Bradley), the head of the DNA project, arrives with an armed detachment. Enlarging to towering size, the monster kills Brinkstone and his men, and Alex and Linda escape in his helicopter as a bomb activated by Brinkstone destroys the rig and the creature. But the pilot also appears to be possessed.

Director Bob Keen, a makeup effects veteran whose Image Animation company created PROTEUS's monsters, is clearly more at ease directing creatures than people, and the script by John Brosnan (adapting a novel he wrote under the pseudonym Harry Adam Knight) doesn't offer much in the way of human interest. The characters have little to do in the first half except bicker and curse incessantly, and Alex and Rachel's undercover identities aren't exploited for the potential tension that might have made the proceedings more intriguing. Once the excessive hallway-creeping ends and the protagonists finally realize what they're up against, however, Keen's hand becomes surer, and he stages the subsequent gruesomeness with skill.

The basics of PROTEUS certainly won't surprise anyone who's seen ALIEN or John Carpenter's remake of THE THING, but the actors are good enough to sustain tension in the latter reels, and the makeup effects are grotesquely well-crafted. If the climatic monster isn't completely convincing, it is certainly impressive for the scale of its construction, and Keen shoots and edits its rampage for maximum effect. There's also fun to be had with the appearance of Bradley (Pinhead in the HELLRAISER films), and with some of the dialogue; when the creature in human form proclaims its superiority, Fairbrass responds, "Superior? You're a fucking fish with a drug habit!" *(Graphic violence, sexual situations, substance abuse, extreme profanity.)* — M.G.

d, Bob Keen; p, Paul Brooks; exec p, Barry Barnholtz, Alan Martin, Alasdair Waddell; assoc p, Simon Brooks; w, John Brosnan (based on the novel *Slimer* by Harry Adam Knight (aka John Brosnan)); ph, Adam Rodgers; ed, Liz Webber; m, David A. Hughes, John Murphy; prod d, Mike Grant; art d, James Ridpath, Moving Jim; sound, Andy Kennedy, Ian Wilson; fx, Duncan Jarman, Tom Harris, Image Animation; casting, Carl Proctor; cos, John Krausa; makeup, Tori Wright

Science Fiction/Horror (PR: O MPAA: R)

PUBLIC ACCESS ★★

(U.S.) 89m Cinemabeam ~ Triboro c

Ron Marquette *(Whiley Pritcher)*; Burt Williams *(Bob Hodges)*; Leigh Hunt *(Intersect Host)*; John Renshaw *(Jock Talk Host)*; Jessie *(Jock)*; Jennifer McManus *(Receptionist)*; Brandon Boyce *(Kevin Havey)*; Dina Brooks *(Rachel)*; Craig Stovall *(Cameraman 1)*; Bruce Germaine *(Cameraman 2)*; Margaret Kerry *(Marge)*; Elizabeth Ince *(Tatting Tales Hostess)*; Charles Kavanaugh *(Mayor Breyer)*; Randall Slavin *(Pudd)*; Liz Dilts *(Lisa)*; Heidi Van Lier *(Heather)*; John Ellis *(Russ)*; Shawn Ellis *(Drug Dealer)*; Ross Collins *(Man With Baby)*; Virginia Perry *(Mayor's Daughter)*; Mark Norling *(Lyle)*; Larry Maxwell *(Jeff Abernathy)*; Jason Vallance *(Tray)*

The writer-director team who gave us THE USUAL SUSPECTS (1995) first collaborated in 1993 on this deliberately obscure thriller, which didn't see a widespread release until after SUSPECTS' success.

The sleepy vale of Brewster is shaken up by the arrival of Whiley Pritcher (Ron Marquette), who kicks off his public access cable TV show with the question: "What's wrong with Brewster?"

With the town's oral history provided by Whiley's landlord, Bob Hodges (Burt Williams), Whiley dredges up grievances only to squash them. Rankling the populace, Whiley distracts the citizenry from their real problems while supporting the conservative line handed out by Mayor Breyer (Charles Kavanaugh).

Dating the town librarian, Rachel (Dina Brooks), Whiley ostensibly sympathizes with her sob story about her favorite teacher, Jeff Abernathy (Larry Maxwell), who has been fired by the school board. Opposed to the Mayor's policies, educator Abernathy has dug up damning evidence that Breyer has sold Brewster down the river for personal profit.

Whiley's modus operandi turns lethal when he befriends, then vilifies and murders Abernathy in a hanging arranged to look like a suicide. Preserving Mayor Breyer's squeaky clean image, Whiley also kills Rachel so that no proof can surface that will open the eyes of the gullible villagers. With the status quo spin securely in place, Whiley's work is done. Walking past shuttered establishments and bankrupt businesses, Whiley travels to his next site of despoilment.

As hard to see through as obsidian, PUBLIC ACCESS is one of those visually adroit think pieces that irritates the audience with overweening glibness. (Forget the time-splintering flashbacks and flashforwards. Why didn't the filmmakers do something about the stasis in the screenplay?)

What exactly does Whiley represent? Is he a mythical anti-humanist figure like the Keyzer Soze character in THE USUAL SUSPECTS, or just a small-town version of Rush Limbaugh, warming up for TV stardom? Since he partakes of no financial gain, can we assume that Whiley just gets his kicks ensuring fat cats stay in office? Wouldn't the screenplay have been better off delving into Whiley's psychotic dislike of Norman Rockwell's America? As it stands, liberals will feel like the butt of a politically incorrect joke, and conservatives will refuse to recognize Whiley as a kindred spirit. The apolitical will be put off by the director's arty footwork in the service of shadow-satire.

The soulless PUBLIC ACCESS suggests that economic devastation is the price "yokels" pay for their sheep-like behavior. Proud of their own stylistic flourishes, the makers of this bleak film don't realize that there are worse things than the blind faith of middle-class average Joes—for example, the artistic smugness of a smart-alecky, blackhearted thriller. *(Extreme profanity, violence, nudity, adult situations.)* — R.P.

d, Bryan Singer; p, Kenneth Kokin; exec p, Bryan Singer; co-p, Adam Ripp; w, Christopher McQuarrie, Bryan Singer, Michael Feit Dugan; ph, Bruce Douglas Johnson; ed, John Ottman; m, John Ottman; prod d, Jan Sessler; art d, Bruce Sulzberg; set d, Martin Dammaschk; sound, Adam Joseph (mixer), Mark A. Lanza (design); fx, Jake the Snake McKinnon; casting, Dean Jacobson; cos, Jennifer McManus; makeup, Stacy Minkin

Drama/Mystery/Thriller **(PR: C MPAA: NR)**

PUBLIC ENEMIES ★★

(U.S.) 95m Trimark Pictures ~ Vidmark c

Theresa Russell *(Ma Barker)*; Alyssa Milano *(Amaryllis)*; Eric Roberts *(Arthur Dunlop)*; Leah Best *(Young Kate Clarke)*; Chip Heller *(Mr. Clarke)*; Richard Eden *(George Barker)*; Tom Ward *(Paymaster)*; Brent O'Plotnik *(Herman at 11)*; Trevor Meeks *(Lloyd at 10)*; Joseph Lindsey *(Herman)*; Joseph Dain *(Lloyd)*; James Marsden *(Arthur "Doc")*; Gavin Harrison *(Freddie)*; Terry Seago *(Tall Sheriff)*; Brian Peck *(J. Edgar Hoover)*; Dan Cortese *(Melvin Purvis)*; Grant Cramer *(Sam Cowley)*; Frank Stallone *(Alvin Karpis)*; Rex Linn *(Al Spencer)*; Robert Griffis *(Desk Clerk)*; Paul Newsom *(Mr. Beltran)*; Castagna Rasmussen *(Hotel Guest)*; Brenda Williams *(Ms. Racine)*; Ed Dollson *(Mr. Harris)*; Allena Brackin *(Mrs. Harris)*; Gary Sievers *(Doctor)*; Michael Stadvec *(Man in Honky-tonk)*

This synthetic retelling of the Ma Barker legend vibrates with lip-smacking sex and blood pellet-spattering violence, but to little avail. Featuring a large cast of actors who seem uncomfortable in their period costumes, PUBLIC ENEMIES is far inferior to Roger Corman's BLOODY MAMA, which delved into the Barker clan's psychosexual dynamics much more credibly.

Sexually abused by her father and brothers, little Kate Clarke (Leah Best) runs off and becomes a succeessful moonshiner in a male-dominated crimescape. The grown Kate (Theresa Russell) catches the eye of decent drudge George Barker (Richard Eden), and they marry. After raising four headstrong sons, she tires of getting nowhere fast and instructs her boys in fast pay-offs, culminating in the robbery-shooting of a venal paymaster (Tom Ward). The Barkers' callous disregard for human life garners headlines and attracts the attention of J. Edgar Hoover (Brian Peck), who orders G-man Melvin Purvis (Dan Cortese) to nail Ma and her brood: sharpshooting Herman (Joseph Lindsey), oversexed Arthur—nicknamed "Doc" (James Marsden), heroin-addicted getaway driver Lloyd (Joseph Dain), and crime tyro Freddie (Gavin Harrison). But the Barkers cut a huge crime swath and prove difficult to nab.

Using one of Doc's fancy women as a decoy at a posh hotel, the Feds ambush the elusive Barkers but fail even to scratch them. Big-timer Alvin Karpis (Frank Stallone) teams up with Ma Barker, but challenges her authority with a robbery that culminates in Herman's death and Freddie's arrest. After facilitating Freddie's escape, a bent jail guard, Arthur Dunlop (Eric Roberts), is welcomed into the Barker fold and Ma's bed.

Branching out, the Barkers adopt Dunlop's scheme to kidnap a millionaire for $100,000. Due to Dunlop's drunken bragging, however, the ransom pick-up nearly proves fatal for the Barkers. Having gotten back in Ma's good graces by strangling Doc's traitorous girlfriend, Amaryllis (Alyssa Milano), Karpis bids his co-conspirators adieu and heads for Canada. The Barkers murder Dunlop in retaliation for his drunken slip, and then slay a plastic surgeon who disfigured Doc instead of disguising him. In Chicago, the G-men finally apprehend Lloyd and Doc. Down South, Ma and Freddie Barker go down in a hail of bullets.

This noisy crime spree has several strikes against it. Revisiting such a familiar tale without a fresh approach to the material seems somewhat pointless. The lame-brain script doesn't position the family's escalating violence in a compelling narrative fashion—one robbery trips on the heels of another without any rise in tension. More damaging than this generic gangster flick's impersonality and monotonous brutality, though, is the contrived performance by Russell, who begins by impersonating Ma Joad before ending up as Mae West with a twist of Dixie. In addition to her total failure to build a credible characterization, the other cast members appear to be drama students gussied up for a gangster sitcom audition. With this lightweight cast, the Barker saga's story value plummets to zero.

For fans of mindless shoot-'em-ups and devotees of populist criminals, PUBLIC ENEMIES goes rat-a-tat with sufficient energy. But anyone expecting a revisionist FBI fable, an entertainingly lurid biopic, or a smashingly directed crime thriller should look elsewhere. *(Graphic violence, extreme profanity, nudity, substance abuse, adult situations, sexual situations.)* — R.P.

d, Mark Lester; p, Mark Lester, Dana Dubovsky; exec p, Barry Barnholtz; assoc p, David Berlatsky; co-p, Phillip Goldfine, Daniel Zelik Berk; w, Courtney Joyner; ph, Misha Suslov; ed, David Berlatsky; m, Christopher Franke; prod d, Trae King; art d, Brian Massey; set d, Troy Myers; sound, Peter Halbert (mixer); fx, Larry Fioritto; casting, Gerald Wolff; cos, Karen Keech-Swerling; makeup, James Ryder, Kelly Raye Gore; stunts, Michael Sarna, Bobby J. Foxworth

Action/Crime **(PR: C MPAA: R)**

PURE DANGER ★

(U.S.) 99m PM Entertainment Group, Inc. ~ PM Entertainment c

C. Thomas Howell *(Johnny Dean)*; Teri Ann Linn *(Becky)*; Michael Russo *(DePalma)*; Marcus Chong *(Freethrow)*; Leon *(Felix)*; Rick Shapiro *(Dice)*; Ray Laska *(Miccelli)*; Bill Rutkoski

(Tony); Elisa Leonetti *(Stella)*; Lou Casal *(Farmentero)*; Mark Holman *(Tick)*; Max Holman *(Tock)*; Mitch Parnes *(Jimmy)*; Rosey Brown *(Shyboy)*; Irwin Keyes *(Killjoy)*; Bob Baker *(Frederick)*; Christopher Mathew Devlin *(Thug #1)*; Frank Strick *(Clerk)*; Patricia Scanlon *(Receptionist)*; Carrot Top *(Morgue Truck Driver)*; Nania Reeves *(Waitress)*; Darren Dalton *(Cook)*

C. Thomas Howell directed and stars in this direct-to-video action film, a convoluted crime caper centered around some stolen diamonds.

Johnny Dean (Howell) is a cook at a lonely desert diner where nothing ever happens—until a gangster carrying a satchel of stolen diamonds dies at a table. When two rival groups of thugs arrive looking for the jewels, Johnny takes off with the loot and waitress Becky (Teri Ann Linn). Johnny, who has served time for petty juvenile crimes, has grown tired of flipping burgers for a living and sees the diamonds as his ticket to the good life. He looks up an old crony, Dice (Rick Shapiro), who agrees to help him fence the diamonds. Dice unwittingly leads Johnny into an ambush by the two groups who are after the diamonds—one led by Italian mob boss DePalma (Michael Russo), and the other by black gangster Felix (Leon). Dice is killed in the crossfire, but Johnny and Becky manage to escape with the diamonds, which they hide on Dice's body and later try to reclaim at the morgue. The body is cremated before anyone can get to the diamonds, and both Johnny and Felix chase after the morgue truck in an attempt to get Dice's diamond-studded ashes. Johnny and Becky, both badly wounded, discover that the real diamonds have been hidden in their trunk all along—they had unknowingly planted phonies on Dice's body. They make it to a desolate cafe and die at the table. The waitress and cook discover the diamonds and take off on their own adventure.

It's never quite clear whether PURE DANGER is intended as comedy or drama. The video box art and copy suggest a straight action-adventure, but the dialogue is jokey, and Howell mugs his way through the film. Then there's comedian Carrot Top as a reckless truck driver, further evidence of the film's comic aspirations. Trouble is, the film is never actually funny, unless hiding the loot in a corpse's anal cavity constitutes hilarity. The script by Joseph John Barmettler and William Applegate, Jr. borders on the truly tasteless, and features too many criminals to keep track of.

Among the players, only Linn stands out as a credible performer. Howell must have been too preoccupied with his directing duties to take the time to craft a three-dimensional character. Leon is suitably sinister as the seemingly indestructible Felix. Patricia Scanlon, as the morgue receptionist, makes her minor scene the film's best.

The film features several violent car-chase scenes filmed in the mountains and canyons of Los Angeles County. Viewers familiar with the area will wonder how the thugs can leave a Vegas casino, hop into their cars and chase each other through L.A.'s Laurel Canyon. *(Graphic violence, extensive nudity, sexual situations, adult situations, extreme profanity)* — B.R.

d, C. Thomas Howell; p, Richard Pepin, Joseph Merhi; assoc p, Frank Strick; co-p, Scott McAboy; w, Joseph John Barmettler, William Applegate Jr.; ph, Ken Blakey; ed, Scott Riddle; m, K. Alexander Wilkinson; prod d, Steve Ramos; art d, Thomas Salvitti; casting, Mark Sikes; cos, Lisa Dyehouse; makeup, Jori Jenae; stunts, Spiro Razatos

Action/Comedy/Drama **(PR: O MPAA: R)**

QUEST, THE ★★

(U.S.) 95m MDP Worldwide; Universal ~ Universal c

Jean-Claude Van Damme *(Chris Dubois)*; Roger Moore *(Dobbs)*; James Remar *(Maxie)*; Janet Gunn *(Carrie)*; Jack McGee *(Harry)*; Aki Aleong *(Khao)*; Abdel Qissi *(Khan)*; Louis Mandylor *(Riggi)*; Chang Ching Peng Chaplin *(Master Tchi)*; Ryan Cutrona *(Officer O'Keefe)*; Shane Meier *(Red)*; Matt Lyon *(Billy)*; Jen Sung Outerbridge *(Phang)*; Peter Wong *(Chinese Fighter)*; Kitao *(Sumo Fighter)*; Habby Heske *(German Fighter)*; Cesar Carneiro *(Brazilian Fighter)*; Takis Triggelis *(French Fighter)*; Azdine Nouri *(Turkish Fighter)*; Stefanos Miltsakakis *(Greek Fighter)*; Peter Malota *(Spanish Fighter)*; Ellis Winston *(African Fighter)*; Ong Soo Han *(Okinawan Fighter)*; Brick Bronsky *(Russian Fighter)*; Ip Choi Nam *(Korean Fighter)*; Michael Ian Lambert *(Scottish Fighter)*; Gordon Masten *(Bartender)*; Zev Revach *(Turk Captain)*; Manon Marcoux *(Nanny)*; Kristopher Van Varenberg *(Young Chris)*; Cherdpong Laoyant *(Dining Salon Bangkok Waiter)*; Vichai Indtrasathit *(Tibetan Monk in New York)*; Chai Chapanond *(Lama—Announcer)*; H. Rudy Gontha *(Innkeeper)*; Jodie Charattanawet *(Annan)*; Tara Nichelle Biberstein *(Little Girl)*; Jason Cavalier *(Youth #1)*; Rik Kiviaho *(Youth #2)*; Anderson C. Bradshaw *(Youth #3)*; Michael Caloz *(Child #1)*; Camelia Lightbourne *(Child #2)*; Emilio Migliozzi *(Riggi's Mug)*; Brauno Belfiore; Michael Davila; Magnus Ljungberg; Joseph Dykes; Martin Gerber; Lindsay Sargeant; Scott Wilson; Paul Moses *(Fighters' Entourage)*

Jean-Claude Van Damme makes a passable directorial debut in THE QUEST, an extremely derivative and hokey martial arts adventure about the ultimate secret fighting competition.

An elderly man named Chris Dubois (Jean-Claude Van Damme) goes into a New York City bar and has to beat up some punks who try to rob it. The bartender asks Chris how he learned to fight, and there is a flashback to 1925, where Chris is the leader of a group of street urchins. After stealing some mob money, Chris flees and stows away on a cargo ship bound for the Far East. The crew is smuggling guns, and Chris is put in chains. When the ship is attacked by pirates, Chris is rescued by the charming scoundrel Lord Dobbs (Roger Moore), who then sells him to a kickboxing master named Khao (Aki Aleong) on the remote island of Muay Thai.

Khao turns Chris into a fighting expert and six months later, he runs into Lord Dobbs and his sidekick, Harry (Jack McGee). Chris tells Dobbs about the secret Gang-gheng fighting competition in the Lost City of Tibet, and they plot to steal the prized Golden Dragon award. Chris, Dobbs, and Harry are joined in their quest by the US boxing champion Maxie Devine (James Remar) and a pretty, blonde journalist named Carrie Newton (Janet Gunn). After an arduous trip through the jungle and desert by horse, elephant, and bus, the group arrives in Tibet and observes a series of brutal qualifying matches featuring champions from around the world. Maxie realizes he has no chance of winning, and after a fight with Chris, he gives his title to him and lets Chris take his place.

Dobbs tries to convince Chris to take a dive, but Chris refuses. Dobbs and Harry try to steal the Golden Dragon, but they get caught. Chris makes a deal to save their lives by offering to give up his prize if he wins. He takes on the Mongolian champion in an epic battle that spills out of the ring and onto the street. Chris finally emerges victorious, and he returns to New York to save his street kids. Back to the present, Chris finishes telling the bartender his tale, and closes a book called "The Quest," written by Carrie Newton.

Van Damme has stated that THE QUEST is his tribute to the action movies of his boyhood, and the script certainly plays like a computer printout of every adventure yarn ever made, evoking ideas and images from OLIVER TWIST (1948) to ANGELS WITH DIRTY FACES (1938) to KING SOLOMON'S MINES (1985), as well as myriad Hong Kong kung-fu movies. Yet Van Damme the director treats the formulaic, simple-minded plot as if it were some sort of personal statement, even inserting ponderous slow-motion flashbacks to show his character as a child as he learns he's being abandoned by his mother. Additionally, the framing story showing Chris as an old man seems to be aiming for a kind of epic Sergio Leone-esque melancholy, but only comes off as a ludicrous display of bad makeup and Van Damme's limited acting skills. The fight scenes are competently staged, but Van Damme presents them in a series of quick cuts, slow motion, and tilted camera angles, negating the athleticism of the performers. Roger Moore adds a touch of dry wit as the amoral Dobbs, but he's mostly there as a reminder of another action hero—James Bond—shamelessly introducing himself as "Dobbs. . . Lord Dobbs." THE QUEST is mindlessly watchable, and not particularly bad, but there is nothing really inspired or distinguished about it, either. *(Violence, profanity.)* — M.S.

d, Jean-Claude Van Damme; p, Moshe Diamant; exec p, Peter MacDonald; assoc p, Jack Frost Sanders, Eugene Van Varenberg, Richard G. Murphy; w, Steven Klein, Paul Mones (from a story by Frank Dux and Jean-Claude Van Damme); ph, David Gribble; ed, John F. Link, William J. Meshover; m, Randy Edelman; prod d, Steve Spence; art d, Chaiyan "Lek" Chunsuttiwat; set d, Kuladee "Gai" Suchatanont; sound, David Stephenson (mixer); fx, David Watkins; casting, James F. Tarzia; cos, Joseph Porro; makeup, Zoltan Elek; stunts, Mark Stefanich, Seng Kawee Strikhanerut

Martial Arts/Adventure/Action (PR: C MPAA: PG-13)

RACE THE SUN ★½

(U.S.) 105m Morrow/Heus Productions ~ TriStar c

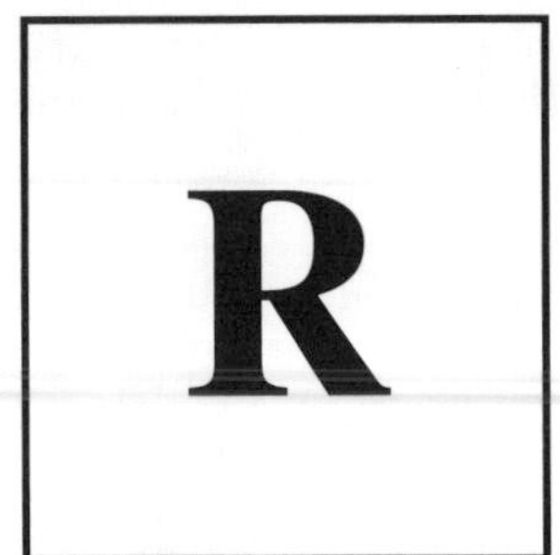

Halle Berry *(Sandra Beecher)*; James Belushi *(Frank Machi)*; Bill Hunter *(Commissioner Hawkes)*; Casey Affleck *(Daniel Webster)*; Eliza Dushku *(Cindy Johnson)*; Kevin Tighe *(Jack Fryman)*; Anthony Ruivivar *(Eduardo Braz)*; J. Moki Cho *(Gilbert Tutu)*; Dion Basco *(Marco Quito)*; Sara Tanaka *(Uni Kakamura)*; Nadja Pionilla *(Oni Nagano)*; Adriane Napualani Uganiza *(Luana Kanahele)*; Steve Zahn *(Hans Kooiman)*; Robert Hughes *(Judd Potter)*; Jeff Truman *(Ed Webster)*; Joel Edgerton *(Steve Fryman)*; Tyler Coppin *(Bob Radford)*; Marshall Napier *(Mr. Cronin)*; Gabrielle Hammond *(Barb Webster)*; Robyn Moore *(Mrs. Chang)*; Michael Burgess *(Guy)*; John Alan Su *(Another Teacher)*; John Negro Ponte *(Detention Teacher)*; Marc Gray *(Academy Student)*; Jo-Anne Cahill *(Weigh-in Judge)*; Rick Adams *(Stanford University Guy)*; Rostislav Orel *(Pavel)*; Archer Lyttle *(Tom Foote)*; Piero von Arnim *(Gautier)*; Amanda Wenban *(Alice Springs Reporter)*; Jimmy Sadeli *(Hawaiian Reporter)*; Clarence Dahy *(Reporter)*; Harry Pavlidis *(Reporter)*; Franko Milostnik *(Reporter)*; Tim Aris *(Scrutineer)*; Monroe Reimers *(Football Coach)*; Jeamin Lee; Kuni Hashimoto *(Oni's Parents)*; Vera Hong *(Detention Student)*; Prasitt Clifton *(Basket Maker)*

This solar-driven youth adventure goes for the corn at every turn. Excruciatingly predictable and awash with stereotypes, it even manages to demean its premise of ethnic acceptance.

Led by their teachers, Sandra Beecher (Halle Berry) and Frank Machi (James Belushi), a group of academically challenged Hawaiian kids—"lolos" in local parlance—tackle a very big science project: they are determined to build a solar-powered race car and enter it in a cross-continental competition against the big boys in Australia. Horrendous weather and turf conditions, rickety equipment, evil rival big-business interests and, of course, their own inner fears stand in their way to glory.

Along the very bumpy road, fights break out among the kids and they are brutally beset by their more high-tech rivals. These "lolos" are nothing if not determined, however, and with guts to rival Stallone *and* Schwarzenegger, they defeat the considerable odds and make it across the finish line in first place.

RACE THE SUN could be described as a junior GRAND PRIX (1966) meets DANGEROUS MINDS (1995), and it nearly outdoes both films for pure puerility. Despite the ethnically diverse casting, teachers and students alike are utter stereotypes.

Charles T. Kanganis directs with a brutally obvious hand, favoring lingering close-ups that hammer home both pathos and attempted humor. His hamfisted style is matched by Barry Morrow's script. It scores easy points off dysfunctional families, teenage drinking, obesity and racial tension. The epithet "haole" (the Hawaiian equivalent of "honky") is tossed around liberally by the kids, as is the lesser-known "mahu" (gay). Their chief racing nemesis is, of course, a perfect Nazi of a German driver, and there's a Southern cracker of a mean old industrialist, to boot.

Graeme Revell's score is an uneasy melting pot of bright Hawaiian contemporary and the reggae which traditionally is misused to represent the 50th state.

As a supposedly committed pedagogue, Berry wears an unseemly series of skintight ensembles which are as unconvincing as her chirruping milquetoast performance. At regular intervals, she remembers to correct her students's usage of "ain't." Belushi is his usual unappetizing wiseacre, blowhard self. "They're *lolos*, lady. They don't need another lesson in failing. You're setting them up to have their hearts stomped!" he says. To express enthusiasm, both actors overuse the thumbs-up sign accompanied by a fervent "Yes!"

As a teenage surfer-turned-solar wiz, Casey Affleck is somewhat appealing. The other kids include a fat doofus of a Hawaiian boy, a typically brainy Japanese nerd, the requisite hot-tempered bully, and a little Filipina sexpot. Their performances are under-directed and subsequently clumsy. Their pidgin accents, essential to the locale and an unmined lode of potential ethnic humor, come and go like the Hawaiian trade winds.

Youngsters may be the only ones entertained by this pubescent "triumph of the human spirit." *(Profanity.)* — D.N.

d, Charles T. Kanganis; p, Richard Heus, Barry Morrow; exec p, David Nichols; assoc p, Beau St. Clair; co-p, Herb Squires, Summer Ku'ulei Kirn; w, Barry Morrow; ph, David Burr; ed, Wendy Greene Bricmont; m, Graeme Revell; prod d, Owen Paterson; art d, Richard Hobbs, Michelle McGahey; set d, Lea Worth; sound, David Lee (recordist); fx, David Roberts, Tad Pride, Norman McGeoch; casting, Sharon Bialy; cos, Margot Wilson; makeup, Nikki Gooley; stunts, Glenn Boswell

Comedy **(PR: A MPAA: PG)**

RAGE ★★½

(U.S.) 94m PM Entertainment Group ~ PM Entertainment Group c

Gary Daniels *(Alex Gainer)*; Kenneth Tigar *(Harry)*; Fiona Hutchinson *(Mary)*; Jillian McWhirter *(Bobby T)*; Peter Jason *(Griggs)*; Mark Metcalf *(Lt. Governor Dalquist)*; Tim Colceri *(Parrish)*; Dave Powledge *(Kelly)*; Doren Fein *(Kathy Kay)*; Judith Marie-Bergan *(Gladys)*; Chuck Butto *(Tenny)*; Rod Britt *(Fred)*; Emilio Rivera *(Javier)*; Dave Aranda-Richards *(Governor)*; Barry Nolan *(Himself)*

RAGE is a routine direct-to-video action film featuring solid performances and some exciting, if overdone, chase sequences.

When Alex Gainer (Gary Daniels), a law-abiding schoolteacher and family man, is car-jacked by a man trying to elude police, his life is forever changed. Rather than rescuing Alex, the cops beat him into unconsciousness and take him to Westech Labs, where he is used as a guinea pig for chemical experiments. Alex is injected with chemicals that induce uncontrollable rage.

Alex manages to escape from the lab, killing several people in the process. Desperate to conceal their secret, the police use all their resources to recapture Alex, but Alex continues to elude his pursuers, killing more people with each encounter.

Alex is soon a media celebrity, with all reports branding him a guilty man. Only one journalist, Harry Johansen (Kenneth Tigar), believes in Alex's innocence, and he gives Alex a chance to tell his story on television. When the interview airs and the governor learns the truth about Westech, he calls off the police. Alex is given the antidote to the rage-inducing chemicals and returns to his family.

Gary Daniels is a fine action hero, though the script never explains how this mild-mannered Brit became so skilled at martial arts and gunplay. Fiona Hutchinson is convincing as his agonized wife, Mary. The fact that Alex and Mary have British accents, but their daughter and Mary's brother sound as American as apple pie, is either a casting faux pas or yet another unexplained script element. Tigar delivers a memorable characterization as an unlikely defender of justice, but the bad guys are strictly stereotypes.

The film is technically proficient in every department, with special mention going to stunt coordinator Spiro Razatos for choreographing imaginative action sequences involving cars, trucks, helicopters, and even a merry-go-round. *(Violence, sexual situations, profanity)* — B.R.

d, Joseph Merhi; p, Joseph Merhi, Richard Pepin; assoc p, Marta Merrifield, Gary Daniels; co-p, Scott McAboy; w, Joseph John Barmettler, Jacobsen Hart; ph, Ken Blakey; ed, Chris Worland; m, Louis Febre; prod d, Gregory Martin; art d, Jared Fleury, Mark Richardson; casting, Mark Sikes; cos, Lisa Dyehouse; stunts, Spiro Razatos

Action **(PR: C MPAA: R)**

RANSOM ★★★

(U.S.) 121m Ransom Productions; Segue Productions; Imagine Entertainment; Touchstone Pictures; Scott Rudin Productions ~ Buena Vista c

Mel Gibson *(Tom Mullen)*; Gary Sinise *(Jimmy Shaker)*; Rene Russo *(Kate Mullen)*; Delroy Lindo *(Agent Lonnie Hawkins)*; Lili Taylor *(Maris Connor)*; Brawley Nolte *(Sean Mullen)*; Liev Schreiber *(Clark Barnes)*; Donnie Wahlberg *(Cubby Barnes)*; Evan Handler *(Miles Roberts)*; Nancy Ticotin *(Agent Kimba Welch)*; Michael Gaston *(Agent Jack Sickler)*; Kevin Neil McCready *(Agent Paul Rhodes)*; Paul Guilfoyle *(Wallace)*; Allen Bernstein *(Bob Stone)*; Jose Zuniga *(David Torres)*; Dan Hedaya *(Jackie Brown)*; Iraida Polanco *(Fatima)*; John Ortiz *(Roberto)*; Mike Hodge *(Man at Party)*; Paul Geier *(Mayor Barresi)*; Louisa Marie *(Woman at Party)*; Edward Francis Joseph *(Guest at Party)*; A.J. Benza *(Reporter Guest)*; Peter Anthony Tambakis *(Nelson)*; Tony Hoty *(Doorman)*; Daniel May Wong *(Agent Sam)*; John Short *(Agent Dewey)*; Ed Jupp *(Technician)*; Stephen Oates *(NYPD/SWAT)*; Gene Harrison *(FBI/SWAT Leader)*; Mick O'Rourke *(FBI/SWAT)*; Henry Kingi Jr. *(FBI/SWAT)*; Roy Farfel *(FBI/SWAT)*; Lex D. Geddings *(FBI/SWAT Sniper)*; Donna Hanover *(News Reporter)*; Rosanna Scotto *(News Anchor)*; Tony Potts *(News Anchor)*; John "Spike" Finnerty *(Newshound)*; Todd Hallowell *(Don Campbell)*; Joe Bacino *(Cop #1)*; Carl S. Redding *(Cop #2)*; James Georgiades *(Cop #3)*; Christian Maelen *(Cop #4)*; David Vadim *(Cop #5)*; Addie O'Donnell; Judy Hudson; Mitzie Pratt; Lynne Redding *(Reporters)*; Michael Countryman *(Bank Manager)*; Chris Lopata *(Agent Levin)*; John Richard Hartmann *(Agent Lambert)*; Anton Evangelista *(FBI Agent)*; Richard Price *(Detective #1)*; Joe Badalucco Jr. *(Liquor Store Cop)*; Dell Maara *(Liquor Store Perp)*; Tommy Allen *(Detective at Kidnap House)*; John Dorish *(Paramedic)*; Vincent Burns *(Detective Doran)*; Brad Brewer; Darren Brown; Marvin Brown; Glenn King *(The Crowtations)*; Cheryl Howard *(Science Fair Coordinator)*; James Ritz *(Science Fair Judge)*; Anna Marie Wieder *(Woman at Science Fair)*; Joan D. Lowry *(Mayor's Wife)*; Craig Castaldo *(Radioman)*; Teodorina Bello *(Woman on Street #1)*; J.J. Chaback *(Woman on Street #2)*; Lori Tan Chinn *(Woman on Street #3)*; Carl Don *(Man on Street #1)*; Nathaniel Freeman *(Man on Street #2)*; Phil Parolisi *(Man on Street #3)*; Rafael Osorio *(Man on Street #4)*; Leslie Devlin *(Newscaster)*; Lewis Dodley *(Newscaster)*; John Brian Rogers *(ND Cop #1)*; Jeffrey Kaufman *(ND Cop #2)*; Mark Smith *(Undercover Cop)*; Jim Whalen *(Detective)*; Kim Snyder *(Kate's Friend)*; Panicker Upendran *(Store Owner)*

The men behind two of 1995's most successful movies, BRAVEHEART star Mel Gibson and APOLLO 13 director Ron Howard, teamed up the following year for the kidnap thriller RANSOM, a film that displays the best strengths and also the worst limitations of a big-budget Hollywood production.

Gibson plays Tom Mullen, a self-promoting entrepreneur who built a world-class airline from scratch. He and his beautiful wife Kate (Rene Russo) have it all; that is, until their young son Sean (Brawley Nolte, Nick's son) is kidnapped. The abductors, led by lovers Maris Connor (Lili Taylor) and Jimmy Shaker (Gary Sinise), demand a $2 million ransom. Confident in his agency's ability to handle the case, FBI agent Lonnie Hawkins (Delroy Lindo) recommends paying up. What he doesn't know is that Shaker is a police detective who knows the FBI's procedures and tricks inside out.

After a disasterous first drop attempt, Tom refuses to make a second. Convinced the kidnappers plan to take the money and kill Sean anyway, Tom goes on TV and offers the $2 million as a bounty on their heads. Kate accuses Tom of putting his own hubris before their son's welfare, but he stands firm. Determined to get the money at any cost, Shaker puts on his badge, shoots his compatriots (including Maris) and steps forward to be heralded as the hero cop who saved Sean Mullen. Weeks later, Shaker shows up to collect the reward, but Sean's terrified reaction to his voice tips Tom off to the man's true role in the kidnapping. Backed up by Hawkins, Tom ends up killing Shaker in a shootout on the street.

At its core, RANSOM wants to be a game of psychological "chicken" between the father and the kidnapper. On the surface lies a plot full of generic brand action which should be all too familiar to moviegoers. It's what fills the space in between the grafting of image-friendly heroics onto hard-to-sell suspense that makes RANSOM the apotheosis of what passes for a thriller in Hollywood today. Aiming for a box-office blowout on its opening weekend, RANSOM's producers used the "big twist" of Mullen's refusal to pay the ransom as the film's selling point; basically, assuring audiences that Gibson would take matters into his own hands in his own car-leaping, window-busting fashion.

That said, RANSOM remains surprisingly effective. Owing to the multiple script rewrites by Richard Price (CLOCKERS), the movie contains many compelling scenes. The byzantine course of the first drop is terrific: Price has Shaker commit the kidnapping as an act of class warfare against rich people like Mullen who buy justice; Mullen, in turn, is a compromised hero, who has very dirty hands from illegal business dealings.

Across the board, the cast gives excellent performances. They believe in their characters and invest in the story, so we do as well. The movie is on Gibson's shoulders, though; no other male lead of his box office caliber can take a character to the emotional edge and remain sympathetic like Mad Mel. RANSOM probably wouldn't be worth seeing if Gibson weren't in it. *(Adult situations, graphic violence, profanity.)* — P.R.

d, Ron Howard; p, Scott Rudin, Brian Grazer, B. Kipling Hagopian; exec p, Todd Hallowell; assoc p, Aldric La'auli Porter, Louisa Velis; co-p, Adam Schroeder, Susan Merzbach; w, Richard Price, Alexander Ignon (from a story by Cyril Hume and Richard Maibaum); ph, Piotr Sobocinski; ed, Dan Hanley, Mike Hill; m, James Horner; prod d, Michael Corenblith; art d, John Kasarda; set d, Susan Bode; sound, Danny Michael (mixer); casting, Jane Jenkins, Janet Hirshenson; cos, Rita Ryack; makeup, Allen Weisinger; stunts, Jeff Ward; tech, Bob Shea, Jerry Savnik

Thriller/Action **(PR: C MPAA: R)**

RASPUTIN ★★½

(U.S.) 104m Rysher/Citadel Entertainment; HBO Pictures ~ HBO Home Video c

Alan Rickman *(Rasputin)*; Greta Scacchi *(Alexandra)*; Ian McKellen *(Nicholas)*; David Warner *(Doctor Botkin)*; John

Wood *(Stolypin)*; James Frain *(Prince Yussoupov)*; Ian Hogg *(Purishkevich)*; Sheila Ruskin *(Princess Marisa)*; Peter Jeffrey *(Bishop Hermogones)*; Freddy Findlay *(Alexei)*; Julian Curry *(Doctor Lazovert)*; Laszlo Aron *(Imperial Chauffeur)*; Janos Buta *(Detective #1)*; Istvan Bicskei *(Derevenko)*; Istvan Bubik *(Landowner's Son)*; John Cater *(Efim)*; Laszlo Csurka *(Man in Sable Coat)*; Constantine Frolov *(Bolshevik Soldier #1)*; Eugine Gamelin *(Bolshevik Soldier #2)*; Nikolett Gallusz *(Lady #5)*; Nick Gillot *(Geologist #2)*; Kiril Gorov *(Cossack Captain)*; Janos Gosztonyi *(1st Minister)*; Barbara Horvath *(Lady #2)*; Istvan Hunyudkurti *(Yegorov)*; Zsofia Ivony *(Grand Duchess Maria)*; Victor Khozianov *(Bolshevik Soldier #3)*; Tibor Kenderesi *(Maitre D')*; Ferenc David Kiss *(Siberian Peasant)*; Agi Kokenyessy *(Prostitute)*; Andras Komlos *(Old Man)*; Gabor Koncz *(Yurovsky)*; Patricia Kovacs *(Grand Duchess Anastasia)*; Robert Lang *(Protopopov)*; Alexander Lykov *(Revolutionary)*; Elena A. Malashevskaya *(Grand Duchess Olga)*; Zsuzsa Malnai *(Tsar's Maid)*; Iren Markus *(Lady #3)*; Michael Mehlman *(Priest)*; Ferenc Nemethy *(2nd Minister)*; Anna Crosz *(Lady #4)*; Fanni Peto *(Princess Sophia)*; Alexander Plovtsev *(Bolshevik Soldier #4)*; Diana Quick *(Grand Duchess Ella)*; Adrienne Rajczi *(Lady #1)*; Natasha Roshetnikova *(Grand Duchess Tatiana)*; Laszlo Sinko *(General Russky)*; Anatoly Slivnikov *(Palace Guard)*; Miklos B. Szekely *(Siberian Man)*; Peter Szokol *(Geologist #1)*; Tamas Toth *(Young Rasputin)*; John Turner *(Grand Duke Serge)*; Bela Unger *(Overseer)*; Andras Varkonyi *(Detective #2)*; Nandor Wampetich *(Tsar's Butler)*

An HBO-produced movie with big-screen ambitions, RASPUTIN is an extravagantly produced biopic depicting the life of the debauched mystic who was assassinated on the eve of the Russian Revolution. A wild-eyed Alan Rickman won the Best Actor Emmy with his appropriately maniacal performance.

In 1883 Siberia, a young Rasputin exhibits his mind-reading talents for his fellow peasants. Twenty years later, the mystic is beaten for failing to live up to his psychic reputation. He lies bleeding on the open tundra when his gaze up at the sun is met with a divine vision. Imbued with the spirit of the Virgin Mary, Rasputin heads to St. Petersburg, the seat of Imperial Russia.

Via hypnosis, this slovenly creature convinces a Bishop (Peter Jeffrey) of his powers and soon after, he's summoned by Czarina Alexandra (Greta Scacchi). Her hemophiliac son, Alexei (Freddy Findlay), heir to the throne, is dying, and Rasputin is her last hope. The Mad Monk eases the boy into a trance and assumes his pain with mystical rants. Then, miraculously, Alexei can walk! But Czar Nicholas (Ian McKellen) doesn't believe in Rasputin's powers and, repulsed by his crude behavior, Nicholas overrides his wife and kicks the charlatan out.

Once again, Alexei gets sick, and Rasputin is called away from his whoring to work his magic. Triumphant and apparently in the good graces of Nicholas, Rasputin reels around the palace, seducing the blue bloods and announcing: "Although the soul may belong to God, the flesh belongs to us." Embarrassed, Nicholas expels Rasputin, but his son becomes ill again. Once more, Rasputin proves his touch, and finally Nicholas agrees to grant Rasputin a permanent place in his court.

As revolutionaries riot in the streets, WWI explodes and the corpses mount. Nicholas goes to the front, leaving domestic affairs to Alexandra, the Mad Monk at her side. A royalist faction is sickened by Rasputin's growing power and plot his death. The drunken mystic is fed cyanide-laced cakes by the plotters. The consumption of only one is supposed to be lethal, but he eats three with no effect. The plotters then ply him with poisoned wine. Nothing. They shoot him in the chest and though he's at first declared dead, he leaps up and runs away. Finally, he's tracked down and shot to death.

Earlier, Rasputin had foretold the deaths of the Romanovs within two years of his own assassination. The prophecy comes true when Nicholas, Alexandra, and their children are executed by the Bolsheviks.

With his intense stares, Rickman's Rasputin is a hypnotic character who mixes religious fervor with mischievous abandon. The movie is at its best when it lets Rickman revel in his character's irreverence. It's irresistible fun to watch him sit at the dinner table with the perfectly mannered royal family, eating with his hands and telling stories of sodomizing monks. Or to watch him convince a noblewoman that the only way to regain her faith is to sleep with him.

Unfortunately, lost in its finely rendered period decor, RASPUTIN is often too demure for its own good. It conveys the impression that this is an important period film that must have a certain air of propriety, even though it's about one of the world's great hedonists. Perhaps director Uli Edel should have stolen a page or two from Fellini.

But with all its historical import, the script fails to show the extent of Rasputin's power over Russian policy. Inaccuracies abound. Writer Peter Pruce has Stolypin (John Wood), the Czar's prime minister, taking part in the plot to kill Rasputin. This despite the fact that the real-life Stolypin met his end in 1911, five years before Rasputin was poisoned and shot. If history is wanted, read a good book; but for a bravura performance, see RASPUTIN. *(Violence, sexual situations.)* — T.Y.

d, Uli Edel; p, Nick Gillott; exec p, David Kirkpatrick, David R. Ginsburg; co-p, Galina Tuchinsky; w, Peter Pruce; ph, Elemer Ragalyi; ed, Seth Flaum, Dan Rae; m, Brad Fiedel; prod d, Miljen Kreku Kljakovic; art d, Branimir Babic; sound, David Allen (recordist); fx, Alan Whibley; casting, Joyce Nettles; cos, Natasha Landau; makeup, Jenny Shircone

Biography/Historical **(PR: C MPAA: R)**

RATTLED ★★½

(U.S.) 90m Great Falls Productions ~ MCA/Universal Home Video c

William Katt *(Paul Donahue)*; Shanna Reed *(Krista Donahue)*; Ed Lauter *(Murray Hendershot)*; Bibi Besch *(Gail Hendershot)*; Monica Creel *(Michelle)*; Ian Abercrombie *(Dr. Remsen)*; Michael Galeota *(Adam)*; Zack Eginton *(Ricky)*; Diane Delano *(Ronnie)*; Clint Howard *(Andy Parsons)*; Richard Minchenberg *(Dr. Crittenden)*; C. C. Pulitzer *(Patient)*; Susan Beaubian *(Emergency Room Nurse)*; Mimi Savage *(Young Nurse)*; Michael Leopard *(Technician)*; Joe Minjares *(Foreman)*; Willie C. Carpenter *(Contractor)*; Nancy Sullivan *(Toddler's Mom)*; Benjamin Tshudy; Michael Tshudy *(Toddler)*; Barry Livingston *(Supervisor)*; Kate Murtagh *(Nursery Worker)*; Bernard Hocke *(Worker)*; Frank R. Lugo *(Groundsman)*

RATTLED has a built-in advantage over many horror flicks since most moviegoers cringe at the very mention of the word "snake." Even if this film slithers down the most obvious of fright trails, there are plenty of indisputable screams in store to drown out the sound of rattling cliches.

As a relatively new hubby and stepfather, environmentally sensitive construction consultant Paul Donahue (William Katt) tries to care for his ready-made family while protecting their neighborhood from damage from site blasting. At a time when his biggest concern is placating his resentful stepson, Adam (Michael Galeota), Paul doesn't realize that his employer's demolition charges have unearthed a community of subterranean rattlesnakes.

Hungry and homeless, the serpents are in a foul mood. Because the fanged cause of a foreman's demise is overlooked when he is subsequently flattened by a truck, the adaptive snakes seize the chance to resettle in Adam's play-fort. In their new neighborhood, they snack on the pet birds of Gail Hendershot (Bibi Besch), the wife of Paul's impatient boss, Murray Hendershot (Ed Lauter), and put the bite on a landscaper. But when Murray is found dead of a snakebite, Paul seeks advice from a snake specialist, Dr. Remsen (Ian Abercrombie).

Paul and Doc Remsen head for a power station, the rattlers' new housing project. Despite warnings, headstrong Adam disobediently bikes right into the rattlers' den. Paul overcomes his fear of snakes to rescue his stepchild and carries him to safety.

While the individual scare scenes in RATTLED are real grabbers, the build-up between them is often slack. The screenplay construction isn't tight or ingenious enough to create true momentum. But, never bored, the audience gets its money's worth every time the little darlings show up. If we're not constantly on the edge of our seats, then isolated jolts, such as a curious toddler's continually reaching out for a snake as if it were a toy, will have the susceptible viewer reaching for Valium.

In fact, RATTLED is a whiz at false alarms; the spectator grips his chair every time an unsuspecting hand dips into a clothes hamper or searches under a bed. This air of uncertainty keeps horror buffs nicely jittery even when the film's subtext about family divisiveness sets them groaning. (Spiteful little Adam is as good a candidate for a rattler's dinner as one could envision.) Milking its frights within genre conventions, RATTLED is blessed with a likable cast that keeps us rooting for their characters. *(Violence, adult situations.)* — R.P.

d, Tony Randel; p, Gary L. Messenger, John V. Stuckmeyer; exec p, Howard Kazanjian; w, Ken Wheat, Jim Wheat (based on the book *Rattlers* by Joseph Gilmore); ph, Jacques Haitkin; ed, Claudia Finkle, Gina Mittelman; m, Joel Goldsmith; prod d, Phillip Vasels; art d, Chris Miller; set d, Cindy Coburn; sound, Ed White (mixer), Richard Schexnayder (mixer); fx, Larry Fioritto, Bruce Mettox, Virgil Sanchez; makeup, Susan Reiner; stunts, Cole McKay

Horror/Thriller (PR: C MPAA: PG-13)

RAVENHAWK ★★

(U.S.) 88m Ravenhawk Productions ~ Columbia Tristar Home Video c

Rachel McLish *(Rhyia Shadowfeather)*; John Enos *(Marshall Del Wilkes)*; William Atherton *(Philip Thorne)*; Ed Lauter *(Sheriff Daggert)*; Matt Clark *(Ed Hudson)*; Michael Champion *(Gordon Fowler)*; Mitch Pileggi *(Carl Rikker)*; Mitchell Ryan *(White)*; Nicholas Guest *(Larsen)*; John DeLancie *(Stansfield)*; Bill Bird *(Houser)*; Virginia Harris *(Dr. Helen Harris)*; John Fleck *(Ed Kaplin)*; Jerry Garcia *(Old Indian)*; Randy Hall *(Garfield)*; Pato Hoffman *(Rhyia's Father)*; Kimberly Norris *(Rhyia's Mother)*; Vincent Klyn *(Tracker)*; Michelle Marsh *(Mrs. Wilkes)*; Thom Mathews *(Stiles)*; Lee McLaughlin *(Dunbar)*; Beau Michaels *(Security Guard)*; Jan Nahtanaba *(Hudson's Wife)*; Alan Oliney *(Wilson)*; Charlie Skeen *(Ranch Hand)*; Adrien Sparks *(Paul Soffit)*; James Tarwater *(Sven)*; Dick Warlock *(Dole Rice)*; Karina Yharra *(Young Rhyia)*

The avenging Native-American heroine of RAVENHAWK is ably embodied by bodybuilding queen Rachel McLish, who is stunning when she kicks and stupefying when she speaks.

In order to build a super factory on sacred ground, a venal consortium headed by tycoon Philip Thorne (William Atherton) slays a tribal chief and his wife and frames their young daughter for this "ritual" murder. As a result, Rhyia Shadowfeather (Rachel McLish) is raised in a mental institution and a juvenile detention center. But then an accident during a prison transfer enables her to escape, while the authorities presume that she is dead.

While Indian Affairs agent Marshall Wilkes (John Enos) investigates the Rhyia Shadowfeather case and the unsolved murder of an EPA agent, Rhyia polishes off one of her parents' killers with a boating "accident." After Rhyia drops another yellow-bellied conspirator off a bridge, a nervous Thorne quells his surviving associates' fears by hiring professional assassins.

After the thugs torture Rhyia's only tribal friends to death, she knifes hit man #1. Dragged by killer #2 behind his horse, Rhyia climbs up the rope and chokes Thorne's assassin to death. After Thorne loyalist Rikker (Mitch Pileggi) wounds her on an escarpment, Rhyia sends him sailing over the mountainside. Although Wilkes stops vengeance-driven Rhyia from delivering a coup de grace to master crook Thorne, he provokes Thorne into drawing a gun on him, then arranges Thorne's death to look like a suicide. Allowing the officially dead Rhyia to escape, Wilkes feels vindicated by the closing of Thorne's toxin-belching plant and by restitution made to the tribesmen of Rhyia and her late parents.

Not since Custer's Last Stand have so many Caucasians bit the dust at the hands of any Native American. Exceptionally violent, RAVENHAWK should satisfy ambidextrous action buffs who can applaud McLish's kickboxing skill with one hand while wolf-whistling her form-fitting vengeance silhouette with the other. In a few bold strokes, RAVENHAWK sets up its simple premise and adheres to the brutal slaughter at hand. The subplot about peacekeeper Wilkes just interrupts the main events.

Limited only by a colorless speaking voice, alluring McLish has enough fighting flourish to ensure a long martial arts movie career as long as her gifted legs hold out. *(Graphic violence, extreme profanity, adult situations.)* — R.P.

d, Albert Pyun; p, Ron Samuels; exec p, Jim Davis, Gail Davis, Kevin Elders; assoc p, Nora Gaye; co-p, James Alsobrook; w, Kevin Elders; ph, George Mooradian; ed, Dennis M. O'Connor; m, Johnny Harris; prod d, E. Colleen Saro; art d, Teddi Rice; sound, Rick Waddell (mixer), Kim Ornitz (mixer); fx, Linus Huffman; casting, Vickie Huff; cos, Shelly Busalacchi; makeup, Maurine Wirgler; stunts, Bobby Brown

Action/Martial Arts/Crime (PR: C MPAA: R)

RAW TARGET ★

(U.S.) 85m Davian Productions ~ Vidmark c

Dale "Apollo" Cook *(Johnny Rider)*; Mychelle Charters *(Susan)*; Nick Hill *(Rod Sparks)*; Ron Hall *(Det. Bill Williams)*; Robert Marius *(Mike)*; Steve Rogers *(Larry)*; Paul Strahan *(Bernard)*; Ned Hourani *(Nick)*; John Barwise *(Tripe)*; Pinky Roces; Nick Nicholson; Henry Strzalkwoski; Renee Steward

Saddled with a by-the-numbers revenge plot, poor acting and muddy cinematography, this direct-to-video release is sure to leave plenty of raw feelings among its target audience of martial-arts fans.

Pro kickboxer Johnny Rider (Dale "Apollo" Cook) accidentally kills an opponent in the ring and mopes around as a homeless penitent until his police-informant brother is slain by sadistic kung-fu drug kingpin Rod Sparks (Nick Hill). Seeking revenge, Johnny masquerades as a freelance thug and gets hired in Sparks's organization. Johnny's payback plans are disrupted by Det. Bill Williams (Ron Hall), Sparks's prime nemesis on the force. This martial-arts cop is also the brother of the kickboxer Johnny killed, and Williams has sworn to take lethal revenge on Johnny. Sparks gives Johnny orders to assassinate the troublesome lawman. After Johnny saves the intended target's life a few times, Williams voids his vow. The new pals converge on Sparks in his gymnasium lair. After a brutal one-on-one, Johnny makes Sparks fly off a railing to his doom.

Hill seems to be having a grand time as the cackling Sparks, apparently clad in a leftover MORTAL KOMBAT (1995) uniform; but all his scenery chewing doesn't excuse the fact that he's a lousy actor. Heroine-love interest Mychelle Charteris—as the lady officer who sent Johnny's brother to his death—is so evasive and sketchy a character that one expects her to be a traitor on Sparks's payroll, but that never happens.

The film comes with a pair of Vegas-style songs, "Raw Target" and "Never Say Die," meant to underscore Johnny's soul-searching.

RAW TARGET, like many of its breed, seems to occur in some parallel universe where nine out of 10 extras at any given setting are karate brawlers who erupt into violence at the least excuse. If the cinematography weren't so dim, you might be able to see it. The budget of RAW TARGET evidently did not cover electric bills. *(Violence, substance abuse, profanity, nudity, sexual situations)* — C.C.

d, Tim Spring; p, David Hunt; exec p, Anjanantre Hunt; assoc p, Vivian Villahermosa; w, Larry Maddox, Steve Rogers; ph, Bruce Dorfman; ed, Dave Bestman; m, Jun Lupito; art d, Jun Peregrino

Martial Arts/Crime/Action **(PR: O MPAA: R)**

RED LINE ★½

(U.S.) 99m Caroli Pictures ~ Triboro Entertainment/Orion Home Video c
(AKA: THE SQUANDERERS)

Chad McQueen *(Jim)*; Roxana Zal *(Gem)*; Jan-Michael Vincent *(Keller)*; Michael Madsen *(Larry)*; Corey Feldman *(Tony)*; Dom DeLuise *(Jerry)*; Julie Strain *(Crystal)*; Tawnya Faskett *(Jo)*; Chuck Zito *(Dick)*; Robert Z'Dar; Ron Jeremy; Joe Estevez; William Buzick III; Ben Marley

All men are crooks, all women abused sluts in this amoral B movie.

Champion stock-car racer Jim (Chad McQueen) works ostensibly as a mechanic under Jerry (Dom DeLuise), a repairman-customizer for LA mobsters. But grand theft auto is Jim's true calling, and that draws the attention of Jerry's longtime client Keller (Jan-Michael Vincent). Keller orders Jim to grab a Ferrari belonging to rival hood Larry (Michael Madsen). Jim carries out the job, and takes on car-wash tramp Gem (Roxana Zal) as a passenger after he stands up to her violent boyfriend. The well-matched pair decide that if Keller wants the Ferrari so much he'll pay extra for it. Knowing Keller will kill him anyway, Jim also offers to ransom the precious car back to Larry. Keller thinks he's finally got Jim under control when his thugs kidnap the car-wash girl, but they've got the wrong car-wash girl. The Ferrari turns out to be filled with diamonds. It's smashed in a chase with Larry's lackeys, but Jim and Gem escape with a fortune in gems. Jim has the wreck towed right into a Larry-Keller armed standoff, leaving the gangsters to slay each other over the supposed loot.

Jan-Michael Vincent appears throughout this stuff like a sight out of David Cronenberg's CRASH (1996), with his face a discolored knot of fresh stitches, attributed in the dialogue to an attempted mob hit. Cold comfort though it may be, Vincent's gruff, blunt line readings count as RED LINE's most convincing performance. McQueen (son of Steve McQueen) and Madsen both breeze through their parts with a minimum of expression, while Zal jettisons any viewer sympathy when she casually abandons her best girlfriend to an uncertain fate at Keller's hands. She and McQueen are nonetheless heroes-by-default in the pointless script. *(Violence, substance abuse, extreme profanity, sex, nudity)* — C.C.

d, John Sjogren; p, Scott Ziehl, Chad McQueen; assoc p, Pat Sjogren, Jan-Michael Vincent, Robert Z'Dar; w, John Sjogren, Scott Ziehl, Rolf Kanefsky; ph, Kevin McKay; ed, John Sjogren, Scott Ziehl; m, Jim Walker, Craig Carothers; art d, Steven Halter; cos, Allison Roth

Thriller/Crime **(PR: O MPAA: R)**

RED SCORPION 2 ★★

(U.S.) 94m Northwood Productions ~ MCA Universal c

Matt McColm *(Nick Stone)*; John Savage *(Andrew Kendrick)*; Jennifer Rubin *(Sam Guiness)*; Michael Ironside *(Colonel West)*; Paul Ben-Victor *(Vince D'Angelo)*; Michael Covert *(Billy Ryan)*; Real Andrews *(Winston Powell)*; Duncan Fraser *(Mr. Benjamin)*; George Touliatos *(Gregori)*; Vladimir Kulich *(Hans)*; Suki Kaiser *(Donna)*; Jerry Wasserman *(Steinberg)*; Tony Lung *(Joe)*; Anthony Staubdulieh *(Abdu)*; Samantha Schubert *(Renee)*; Wren Robertz *(Club Attack Leader)*; Andrew Binks *(Man in Club)*; Dean McKenzie *(Man in Club)*; Patrick Stevenson *(Bartender)*

With state-of-the-art demolition, expertly choreographed battle scenes, and enough weaponry for a military garage sale, this special-forces flick feeds hunger for action but suffers a story line that's hard to swallow.

The National Security Commission assembles a crack team to undermine the white supremacist empire of Andrew Kendrick (John Savage). Despondent about losing a partner on his last mission, Agent Nick Stone (Matt McColm) reluctantly heeds the call of his mentor Colonel West (Michael Ironside) to work on the case. Stone soldiers up with, among others, Sam Guiness (Jennifer Rubin), computer expert Vince D'Angelo (Paul Ben-Victor), and Billy Ryan (Michael Covert).

Initially, the agents play tag with Kendrick's Citadel Organization as it carries out hate crimes nationwide. After journalist Steinberg (Jerry Wasserman) is kidnapped for liberalism and an elusive computer file makes Kendrick's deadly targeting obvious, Stone and his comrades decide to infiltrate Citadel headquarters. Posing as right-wing backers, Stone and Guiness snoop around while Billy Ryan palms himself off as a bigoted redneck. Although Kendrick knows of the charade, West stations other squad members at the Citadel's periphery to support the advance team inside. After slaying Steinberg and separating the now-captured government spies, Kendrick begins his plot to assassinate liberal politicians. Fortunately, Guiness breaks loose, D'Angelo blows up power transformers, and Stone eventually gets free and rescues Billy Ryan. While Kendrick holds a recaptured Guiness as bait, Stone eliminates Kendrick's right-hand man Hans (Vladimir Kulich) before demolishing Kendrick's computer. With the Citadel stronghold and his plans destroyed, Kendrick waits for flames in an escape tunnel to consume him. The surviving agents are left to dismantle the racist network.

Once the Red Scorpion super soldiers storm the Citadel, the action swings into thrilling overdrive. Unfortunately, the build-up to this assault is marred by sequences that distract the audience with high action before properly introducing the participants. The movie's unsubtle caricature of neo-Nazism is equally sloppy. In a role similar to one he had on the TV series "Walker, Texas Ranger," Savage's overplaying exceeds the worst of Brion James, Richard Lynch, and Trevor Goddard combined. The combination of blatant rancor and unfocused energy will leave escapist moviegoers eyeing the exit sign. *(Graphic violence, profanity, nudity, adult situations.)* — R.P.

d, Michael Kennedy; p, Robert MacLean; exec p, Jack Abramoff, Robert Abramoff, Dale Andrews; assoc p, Michelle White; co-p, Mary Eilts; w, Troy Bolotnick, Barry Victor (based on characters created by Arne Olsen); ph, Curtis Petersen; ed, Gary Zubeck;

m, George Blondheim; prod d, Brent Thomas; art d, Randy Chodak; set d, Lesley Beale; sound, Frank Griffiths (mixer); fx, Rory Cutler; casting, Stuart Aikens, Fern Orenstein; cos, Lyn Kelly; makeup, Pearl Louie; stunts, Mohammed Tabatabai

Action/Martial Arts (PR: C MPAA: R)

REDEMPTION: KICKBOXER 5 ★

(U.S.) 87m Kings Road Entertainment ~ Vidmark c
(AKA: MARK DACASCOS REDEMPTION: KICKBOXER 5)

Mark Dacascos *(Matt Reeves)*; James Ryan *(Negaal)*; Geoff Mead *(Paul Croft)*; Tony Caprari *(Moon)*; Greg Latter *(Bollen)*; Duane Porter *(Bull)*; George Moolman *(Pinto)*; Rulan Booth *(Angie)*; Robert Whitehead *(Tito)*; Denney Pierce *(Johnny)*; John Hussey *(Chalky)*; Dale Cutts *(Trainer)*; Frank Notaro *(Maxwell)*; Matthew Stewardson *(Valet)*; Burton Richardson *(Jack)*; Robin Smith *(Chauffeur)*; Dean Fourie *(1st Inmate)*; Waddy Jones *(2nd Inmate)*; Patrick Emerson *(French Champ)*; Thembi Nyandeni *(Shopkeeper)*; Eric Miyeni *(Mabiza)*; Thomas Witt *(Trustee)*; Gavin Hood *(German Champ)*; Cecil Carter *(Croupier)*; Victor Melleny *(US Prison Clerk)*; Vrenika Prather *(Negaal's Date)*; Herbie Vermuellen *(Referee)*; Vernon Herbert *(Johnny's Opponent)*

REDEMPTION: KICKBOXER 5 is a film where no cliche is left unexplored and everything is worked out according to formula, amidst completely pointless violence.

Matt Reeves (Mark Dacascos) is a former kickboxing champ now working as an instructor. His friend Johnny (Denney Pierce) wins the American championship, but Matt advises him against joining the Negaal Kickboxing Federation, based in South Africa. Johnny's refusal to join results in his death. We learn that Negaal (James Ryan) is a psychopath who relentlessly kills those who oppose his revenge against the kickboxing authorities who have banned him from the sport.

Negaal arranges to have Paul Croft (Geoff Meed) released from prison to kill Matt. Paul refuses and joins Matt in his fight against Negaal. The two escape from Negaal's goons at the Johannesburg airport, but are soon imprisoned on trumped-up charges. Their cellmate agrees to help them escape, after which they are aided by Paul's sister Angie (Rulan Booth). The three crash a party that Negaal is throwing, where Matt beats Negaal at roulette and insults him. The stage is set for their confrontation, where Matt kills Negaal with a blow to the throat, then takes back Johnny's championship belt.

REDEMPTION: KICKBOXER 5 is hardly a movie that keeps you guessing. The good guys win every fight scene; Matt decides to fight again after having given it up; and, of course, the bad guy gets it in the end. This might be excusable if the script were well written or the acting were good. Unfortunately, neither is the case. When Matt finally meets the evil Negaal, for example, he calls him "butt-face." And except for Dacascos, who has some charisma as Matt, the rest of the cast are caricatures at best. Half of them can't seem to remember if they have South African accents.

Additionally, though much of the action was filmed in South Africa itself, it may as well have been a Hollywood backlot. We get no sense of local color—not the case in the original KICKBOXER (1989). In the end, the movie is just an excuse for several scenes of brutal violence. *(Graphic violence, profanity.)* — K.Fr.

d, Kristine Peterson; p, Michael S. Murphey; w, Rick Filon; ph, Paul Michelson; ed, Kert Vandermeulen; m, John Massari; prod d, Robert Van De Coolwijk; set d, Emelia Roux; sound, Alan Gerhardt (mixer); casting, Marina Von Tonder, Karen Lawson, Cathy Henderson, Tom McSweeney; cos, Jo Katsaras; makeup, Anni Bartels, Eckart Artus; stunts, Gavin Mey, Burton Richardson, Mark Dacascos

Martial Arts/Action/Sports (PR: C MPAA: R)

RENDEZVOUS IN PARIS ★★★★

(France) 100m La Compagnie Eric Rohmer; Canal Plus ~ Artificial Eye c
(AKA: PARISIAN ENCOUNTERS; LES RENDEZ-VOUS DE PARIS)

THE SEVEN O'CLOCK RENDEZVOUS/LE RENDEZ-VOUS DE 7 HEURES Clara Bellar *(Esther)*; Antoine Basler *(Horace)*; Mathias Megard *(The Flirt)*; Judith Chancel *(Aricie)*; Malcolm Conrath *(Felix)*; Cecile Pares *(Hermione)*; Olivier Poujol *(The Waiter)*; THE BENCHES OF PARIS/LES BANCS DE PARIS Aurore Rauscher *(The Woman)*; Serge Renko *(The Man)*; MOTHER AND CHILD/MERE ET ENFANT Michael Kraft *(The Painter)*; Benedicte Loyen *(The Young Woman)*; Veronika Johansson *(The Swedish Woman)*

Eric Rohmer continues the interruption of his TALES OF FOUR SEASONS series to offer a charming, if less rigorous, omnibus package, RENDEZVOUS IN PARIS. RENDEZVOUS's three separate tales of love represent a minor achievement in the director's canon, but provide pleasing entertainment nonetheless.

The first story, "The Seven O'Clock Rendezvous," concerns a young woman, Esther (Clara Bellar), who is told by a friend, Felix (Malcolm Conrath), that her boyfriend, Horace (Antoine Basler), has been seen with another woman. Felix suggests to the distraught Esther that she make Horace jealous by finding a guy of her own. The next day, in a Montmartre market, she meets a young man (Mathias Megard) who asks her to meet him at the Beaubourg cafe that evening for a date. When she gets home, Esther realizes her wallet has been stolen and suspects the young man of the theft. Luckily, a stranger, Aricie (Judith Chancel), arrives to return the wallet. Since Aricie also is going to the Beaubourg to meet a man, the two women travel together. When they arrive, Esther discovers that Aricie's boyfriend is none other than Horace. Esther leaves immediately and misses out on her date with the young man from Montmartre, who was clearly innocent of wallet-snatching.

The second story, "The Benches of Paris," depicts the prelude to an affair between a young woman (Aurore Rauscher) and a young man, a college professor (Serge Renko). As they meet clandestinely in the parks of Paris, the woman discusses her feelings about leaving her fiance, while the man begs her to move into his Paris apartment. Finally, they decide to spend three days together in a Montmartre hotel while her fiance is away. But, on the day they arrive at the romantic hideaway, the woman sees her fiance with another woman at the same hotel. Enraged at being deceived, she decides to end her affairs with both men.

In the third and final story, "Mother and Child," a painter suffering from a creative block (Michael Kraft) takes an acquaintance, a Swedish visitor (Veronika Johansson), on a date to the Picasso Museum. Although the Swede demonstrates some knowledge about the paintings, the painter fails to connect romantically with her. Instead, he becomes much more interested in another young woman (Benedicte Loyen), who admires the 1907 work, "Mother and Child." Leaving the Swede behind, the painter follows the other woman out of the museum and through the streets. After they talk awhile, the woman invites herself up to his studio to see his work, despite the fact she is engaged to be married. Finally, once they arrive, they talk about art and love, but despite their attraction for one another, the woman decides to leave him on a philosophical note. The painter, now alone, breaks through his block and begins painting a new canvas.

RENDEZVOUS IN PARIS (a.k.a. LES RENDEZVOUS DE PARIS) is catnip for Rohmer fans, and a quaint, wispy primer to the director's style for everyone else. Certainly the film neither looks nor sounds like Rohmer's best work. The production is less well composed visually and the slightness of the tales (with the possible exception of the first) has less resonance than the Chinese box approach of his denser narratives (particularly TALE OF FOUR SEASONS and his 1993 film, THE TREE, THE MAYOR AND THE MEDIATHEQUE).

And yet, the artless cinema verite approach to the shots of Paris serves to de-romanticize the city in much the same way the bittersweet tales themselves question the vagaries of love. (Here, Rohmer harkens back not only to the 1960s nouvelle vague, but also to the deliberately awkward photography of Eugene Atget.) As is more his custom, Rohmer allows the dialogue to soar with both wit and suspense, particularly in the first and third stories. It helps that the actors in these two vignettes are charming newcomers. (Clara Bellar is particularly delightful.)

Unfortunately, the second story is problematic not only for its stubborn simplicity, but for the annoying way the female character leads on her lover, then unceremoniously dumps him. She also makes unchecked racist remarks. If Rohmer had depicted this foolish woman with a trace of irony, he might have had one of his most winning portrayals; as it is, he produces one of his rare mistakes. At least, the rest of the film makes up for it with intelligence and humor. *(Profanity.)* — E.M.

d, Eric Rohmer; p, Francoise Etchegaray; w, Eric Rohmer; ph, Diane Baratier; ed, Mary Stephen; m, Sebastien Erms; sound, Pascal Ribier

Romance/Drama/Comedy (PR: C MPAA: NR)

RETURN OF THE TEXAS CHAINSAW MASSACRE, THE

(SEE: TEXAS CHAINSAW MASSACRE: THE NEXT GENERATION)

RICH MAN'S WIFE, THE ★★

(U.S.) 95m Caravan Pictures ~ Buena Vista c

Halle Berry *(Josie Potenza)*; Christopher McDonald *(Tony Potenza)*; Clive Owen *(Jake Golden)*; Peter Greene *(Cole)*; Charles Hallahan *(Dan Fredericks)*; Frankie Faison *(Ron Lewis)*; Clea Lewis *(Nora Golden)*; Loyda Ramos *(Grace)*; William Crossett *(Cab Driver)*; Eddie Francis *(Bartender)*; Lou DiMaggio *(Party Guest)*; Alexandra Hedison *(Party Guest)*; John Paragon *(Maitre d')*; Marc Shelton *(Instateller Man)*; Kelly Jo Minter *(Cursing Hooker)*; Allan Rich *(Bill Adolphe)*; Marc Lynn *(Police Photographer)*; Zoaunne LeRoy *(Gray-Haired Waitress)*; Greg Serano *(Gangbanger)*; Michelle Bonilla *(Gangbanger)*; Rolando Molina *(Gangbanger)*; Valente Rodriguez *(Freeway Driver)*; Michael Marich *(Williams)*; Suzanne Michaels *(Newscaster)*; Bruce Wright *(Newscaster)*; Angela Nogaro *(Receptionist)*

THE RICH MAN'S WIFE is an alternately laughable and pedestrian update of the wife-in-distress thriller, a staple of classical Hollywood cinema. Anyone who has ever seen SUSPICION (1941), MIDNIGHT LACE (1960), SLEEPING WITH THE ENEMY (1991), or any of the countless others in this insidiously sexist film cycle will know the scenario by heart.

Josie Potenza (Halle Berry) sits in an LA police station and explains to two detectives the events leading up to a murder she has just committed. Josie tells the men how, just a few months earlier, she had it all: a fabulous home, a life of privilege, and Tony (Christopher McDonald), her rich, older husband. But in the extended flashback, not all is as wonderful for Josie as it seems, for Tony drinks heavily, and Josie is having a secret affair. In an attempt to save their marriage and reconnect to happier times, Josie and Tony spend a weekend in the mountains at their private cabin. But Tony leaves Josie in the middle of their stay to take care of an emergency at the television network where he works.

While Josie stays on her own in the mountains, a stranger, Cole (Peter Greene), helps her when her vehicle gets stuck. Feeling grateful, Josie joins Cole for a drink in a nearby bar, but pulls back from starting a romance when Cole mentions the idea of bumping off Tony for his money. After Cole drives Josie back to her cabin, he tries to attack her, but Josie fends him off.

Back in the city, Josie and Tony again attempt to make their marriage work, but Cole appears on the scene and kills Tony during his trip from work to his house one night. Cole then convinces Josie that she will be a prime suspect in the murder if she does not cooperate with his blackmail threats. Apparently, Cole has been working in tandem with Josie's lover, Jake Golden (Clive Owen), a once-wealthy, now destitute restaurateur.

Josie indeed becomes the prime suspect in Tony's death, since she has the most to gain from his demise. But the detectives (Frankie Faison, Charles Hallahan) keep an open mind after talking to Nora Golden (Clea Lewis), Jake's gossipy ex-wife.

Finally, the unhinged Cole kills Jake for trying to protect Josie, then stalks Josie throughout her home. Josie, however, beats and kills Cole, and then is taken into custody by the detectives. After telling her story, Josie is released, but it is revealed to the audience that she has lied and is responsible for Tony's murder after all.

THE RICH MAN'S WIFE is an old-hat thriller about the nouveau riche. Granted, this time there are two new elements: the wife is black and the end has a twist. But the twist melds the flashback "cheating" of Hitchcock's STAGE FRIGHT (1950) and the gimmicky windup of Brian G. Hutton's NIGHT WATCH (1973), and so THE RICH MAN'S WIFE's biggest surprise turns out to be not that original.

Everything else is woefully familiar, with lots of scenes of Berry walking into dangerous situations and being terrorized. Josie's apparently foolish actions force the talented Berry (LOSING ISAIAH) to look silly, and, likewise, the usually interesting Peter Greene (CLEAN, SHAVEN) is pushed to overplay his psychotic villain role.

Writer-director Amy Holden Jones shows some flair for the glossy marital soap opera that underlies the drama, and, thankfully, the film is never as manipulative as Jones's sexist script for INDECENT PROPOSAL (1993). Yet, even with the aforementioned twist ending, Jones allows the gender roles to remain firmly traditional. Also, she plays the race card a bit, and, as a director, her handling of the noir-ish suspense scenes is titter-inducing. *(Violence, sexual situations, adult situations, substance abuse, extreme profanity.)* — E.M.

d, Amy Holden Jones; p, Roger Birnbaum, Julie Bergman Sender; exec p, Jennifer Ogden; w, Amy Holden Jones; ph, Haskell Wexler; ed, Wendy Greene Bricmont; m, John Frizzell; prod d, Jeannine Oppewall; art d, William Arnold; set d, Cindy Carr; sound, Ed Novick (mixer); fx, Eric Rylander; casting, Nancy Klopper; cos, Colleen Kelsall; makeup, Angela Nogaro, Scott Tebeau, Todd Masters; stunts, Jeffrey J. Dashnaw

Thriller/Drama (PR: C MPAA: R)

RIDERS OF THE PURPLE SAGE ★★★

(U.S.) 90m Rosemont Productions; Zeke Productions; Amer Productions ~ Turner Home Entertainment c

Ed Harris *(Lassiter)*; Amy Madigan *(Jane Withersteen)*; Henry Thomas *(Bern Venters)*; Robin Tunney *(Bess)*; Norbert Weisser *(Deacon Tull)*; G. D. Spradlin *(Pastor Dyer)*; Lynn Wanlass *(Hester Brandt)*; Bob L. Harris *(Collier Brandt)*; Jerry Wills *(Oldring)*; Rusty Musselman *(Matthew Blake)*

A labor of love for the husband-and-wife team of Ed Harris and Amy Madigan, RIDERS OF THE PURPLE SAGE took ten years to produce. The completed frontier parable shows every ounce of nurturing artistry that went into it.

Hectored by self-righteous church elder Pastor Dyer (G. D. Spradlin), Cottonwoods rancher Jane Withersteen (Amy Madigan) defies the religious dictates of the late 19th Century by refusing the hand of her suitor, Deacon Tull (Norbert Weisser). Dyer's congregation intensifies the war of attrition by trying to run Jane's ranch-hand, Bern Venters (Henry Thomas), out of town. Intervening for no readily apparent motive is roving gunslinger Lassiter (Ed Harris), who rescues Bern and stands by Jane as Pastor Dyer cooperates with cattle thief Oldring (Jerry Willis) in the rustling of Jane's herd.

Bern is forced to kill Oldring in self-defense. He regretfully wounds Bess (Robin Tunney), one of Oldring's riders, and nurses her back to health. Jane learns that Lassiter is avenging a dead woman named Millie who had been kidnapped to Cottonwoods by three hired guns in league with Dyer. Unfortunately, Lassiter's mission of vengeance is complicated by his growing love for Jane.

After Dyer's disciples kill one of Jane's crew and arrest Bern, Lassiter reveals that Millie was his sister, that he has already slain three of her abductors, and that he's trying to find her abandoned child. Jane confesses that her late father ordered Dyer to kidnap Millie in order to gratify Mr. Withersteen's sexual desires. Millie ultimately committed suicide after killing Jane's father to avoid being raped by him.

During a climactic gun battle, Lassiter kills Dyer. Tull escapes and regroups with a posse. With Bern and Bess serving as decoys to draw the posse away, Tull closes in on Jane and Lassiter, but they crush him with a rock slide. His vengeance complete, Lassiter is finally, happily reunited with his long-lost niece, Millie's daughter Bess.

Evocatively filmed in scenic Moab, Utah, this classically designed Western not only outshines made-for-television Westerns like LARRY MCMURTRY'S STREETS OF LAREDO (1995) and CHILDREN OF THE DUST (1995) but also compares favorably to plangent theatrical releases like THE UNFORGIVEN (1960). Although unusually plot-heavy for a Western, RIDERS OF THE PURPLE SAGE maintains a full gallop by humanizing its genre-ready characters. If RIDERS is flawed, it's due to the expository glitches in the retelling of Millie's complicated history and the screenplay's failure to give the Bern-Bess subplot the same weight applied to the redemptive love story between Jane and Lassiter. And even if the film errs by soft-pedaling the identity of Jane's tormentors (Zane Grey made it clear in his novel that they were Mormons), the nameless church's evil is incisively rooted in a power-money base determined to maintain its status quo by marrying off independent women such as Jane.

Fiercely acted sans showy histrionics by Madigan and Harris, the Jane-Lassiter relationship is one of the most complex to be found in the genre; one doesn't encounter this kind of equal partnership in a John Ford Western. Actor-turned-director Charles Haid exhibits a freewheeling cinematic brio not seen in his previous lackluster efforts (IRON WILL). Impassioned and provocative, RIDERS presents characters whose life-and-death revelations are accessible to contemporary audiences without having to rely on an anachronistic veneer of modern psychology. *(Violence, adult situations, profanity.)* — R.P.

d, Charles Haid; p, Thomas Kane; exec p, Ed Harris, Amy Madigan, David A. Rosemont; assoc p, Stella Theodoulou; w, Gill Dennis (based on the novel by Zane Grey); ph, William Wages; ed, David Holden; m, Arthur Kempel; prod d, Michael Baugh; art d, Page Holland; set d, Bill Vail; sound, Jonathan Stein (mixer), Ike Magall (mixer); fx, Matt Vogel; casting, Susan Bluestein; cos, Durina Wood; makeup, Richard Arias; stunts, Monty Stuart

Western **(PR: C MPAA: NR)**

RIDICULE ★★★½

(France) 102m Epithete; Cinea; France 3 Cinema; Investimage 4; Procirep; Gras Savoye ~ Miramax c
(LE RIDICULE)

Charles Berling *(Ponceludon de Malavoy)*; Jean Rochefort *(Marquis de Bellegarde)*; Fanny Ardant *(Madame de Blayac)*; Judith Godreche *(Mathilde de Bellegarde)*; Bernard Giraudeau *(Abbot de Vilecourt)*; Bernard Dheran *(Monsieur de Montalieri)*; Carlo Brandt *(Knight de Milletail)*; Jacques Mathou *(Abbot de l'Epee)*; Urbain Cancelier *(Louis XVI)*; Albert Delpy *(Baron de Gueret)*; Bruno Zanardi *(Paul)*; Marie Pillet *(Charlotte)*; Jacques Roman *(Colonel de Chevernoy)*; Philippe Magnan *(Baron de Malenval)*; Maurice Chevit *(The Notary)*; Jacques-Francois Zeller *(Maurepas)*; Gerard Hardy *(Victor)*; Marc Berman *(Duke de Guines)*; Philippe du Jannerand *(The Genealogist)*; Claude Dereppe *(Monsignor d'Artimont)*; Isabelle Spade *(Baroness de Boisjoli)*; Isabelle Petit-Jacques *(Baroness d'Oberkirchner)*; Nathalie Mann *(Countess de Blancfagot)*; Etienne Draber *(Viscount du Closlabbe)*; Fabrice Eberhard *(Knight de St. Tronchain)*; Stephane Fourmond *(Marquis de Carmes)*; Jean-Jacques Le Vessier; Lucien Pascal *(Monsieur de Blayac)*; Nicolas Chagrin *(Lord Bolingbroke)*; Fabien Behar *(Secretary to the King)*; Mirabelle Kirkland *(Marie-Antoinette)*; Marie Llano *(Leonard's Mother)*; Antonin Lebas Joly *(Leonard)*; Didier Abot *(The Priest)*; Julien Bukowski *(Gentleman)*; Jose Fumanal *(Officer in Duel)*; Sylvie Herbert *(Ponceludon's Mother)*; Alain Hocine *(Le Player)*; Clementine Buxtorf *(The Sister)*; Boris Napes *(The Painter)*; Gerard Sergue *(The Thief)*; Laurent Valo *(Simon)*; Claire Garguier *(Therese)*; Marine Guez *(The Singer)*

Thanks largely to a wonderfully literate script, RIDICULE is a flavorful *divertissement* which recalls the great French films of yore. Somewhere, Guitry and Duvivier are smiling.

In the Versailles of Louis XVI, a country engineer, Ponceludon de Malavoy (Charles Berling), comes to court to plead the cause of his disease-ridden people; he hopes to dredge his land's mosquito-ridden swamps. He was selected due to his natural wit, which is seen as a way of gaining access to the King (Urbain Cancelier) in a palace that worships a well-turned phrase.

Rescued by the Marquis de Bellegarde (Jean Rochefort) after being set upon by a highwayman, Malavoy is taken under the Marquis' wing. The Marquis is supportive of Malavoy's cause and agrees to coach him in the Byzantine ways of court etiquette: dressing, dancing, and above all, language.

The young man is a hit at Versailles when he effectively takes on some of the court's most feverishly ambitious minds. He is quickly seduced by the formidable Madame de Blayac (Fanny Ardant), a widow who is a courtesan of the King, among others. However, Malavoy really loves the Marquis' independent daughter, Mathilde (Judith Godreche). Theirs is not an easy courtship, however, as Mathilde is put off by Malavoy's ever-growing infatuation with the artifice of Versailles. Through his new popularity at court and the aid of the Countess, Malavoy seems to draw ever nearer to an actual meeting with the King. Each day, with a multitude of other hopeful petitioners, he waits to be called into the royal chambers and watches the downfall and disgrace of many who presume too much or commit fatal gaffes. However, when Malavoy makes his intention to marry Mathilde public, the humiliated Countess sets about to avenge herself: she arranges to have him tripped at a masked ball. Ridiculed by the other guests, Malavoy picks himself up off the floor and indignantly declares, "Children will die tomorrow because you ridiculed me today," then takes his leave. He and Mathilde happily return to his homeland with the first rumblings of the French Revolution sounding around them.

Remi Waterhouse's lovingly crafted script is a deceptively fragile, highly inventive bauble that still manages to provide a steely foundation for the film. The barbed repartee flows like wine, and the matching of wits in salons is as absorbing and gripping as any sports match. Patrice Leconte's direction follows suit and is far more animated than seen in his previous works (MONSIEUR HIRE [1989], THE HAIRDRESSER'S HUSBAND [1992]). Shot on the dream location of the gardens of Versailles, the production is handsome and, best of all, looks *lived* in. (Anyone expecting a lavish spectacle on the order of MARIE ANTOINETTE [1938] or even DANGEROUS LIAISONS [1988] will be disappointed by the relatively low-key but historically evocative decor here.) Antoine Duhamel's score is both original and apt, particularly in the autumnal ball scene.

The bright, brainy cast revels in the rococo garb and effervescent dialogue. Rochefort gives a magnificently winning performance, and Berling is at once fresh, intelligent, and dashing. Ardant is perfect, and Godreche makes a strong impression in the refreshingly uninsipid ingenue role. Her experiments with deep sea equipage are a welcome antidote to the stiflingly arch peregrinations of Versailles. Bernard Giraudeau is superbly contemptible as one court wit who goes too far. *(Nudity, sexual situations, adult situations.)* — D.N.

d, Patrice Leconte; p, Gilles Legrand, Frederic Brillion, Philippe Carcassonne; w, Remi Waterhouse, Michel Fessler, Eric Vicaut; ph, Thierry Arbogast; ed, Joelle Hache; m, Antoine Duhamel; prod d, Ivan Maussion; sound, Paul Laine, Dominique Hennequin (mixer); cos, Christian Gasc; makeup, Judith Gayo

AAN Best Foreign Language Film

Historical/Drama **(PR: C MPAA: R)**

ROAD HOME, THE ★★

(U.S.) 90m Libra Films; Astral Films ~ Republic Pictures Home Video c

Kris Kristofferson *(Davis)*; Danny Aiello *(Duke)*; Rick Aiello *(Yale Preacher)*; Don Dorza *(Train Cop)*; Alex Doduk *(Martin)*; Robin Dunne *(Clay Berry)*; Will Ester *(Michael)*; Daniella Evengelista *(Pretty Girl)*; Peter Fleming *(Dr. Hale)*; Tyler Jay *(Jimmy)*; Keegan McIntosh *(John)*; Don McKay *(Henry)*; John Novak *(Daniel Murphy)*; Sheila Patterson *(Sister Elizabeth)*; Robert Prosky *(Father Tierney)*; Alan Robertson *(Geoffrey)*; Mickey Rooney *(Father Flanagan)*; Stellina Rusich *(Eleanor)*; Vincent Schiavelli *(Davinport)*; Charles Martin Smith *(Merrimam)*; Dee Wallace Stone *(Mrs. Bastian)*; Jim Townsend *(Train Clerk)*

This treacly Depression-era period piece nonetheless tugs the heartstrings and is recommended for enthusiasts of The Family Channel. In its favor is a steel story-spine concerning the subjects of parental loss and the helplessness of orphans in determining their own fates.

Impoverished but proud, the Murphy family deals together with life's vicissitudes until the day a freak fire caused by a gas jet wipes out the parents. Due to a death-bed promise to his pa, older Murphy brother Michael (Will Ester) assumes responsibility for younger sibling John (Keegan MacIntosh) even as they come to grips with orphanage regulations. Despite assurances from parish priest Father Tierney (Robert Prosky) and foundling home manager Sister Elizabeth (Sheila Patterson), John is removed without Michael's knowledge and adopted by a high-strung society woman, Mrs. Bastian (Dee Wallace Stone).

Unable to dismiss his late father's final request, Michael engineers John's kidnapping with the aid of fellow orphan Clay Berry (Robin Dunne), who gets caught during a railyard escape. As if guided by Providence, Michael and John wriggle out of a police dragnet and elude gung-ho detective Merrimam (Charles Martin Smith) hired by Mrs. Bastian. Shown the ropes of the open road by sympathetic hobos led by The Duke (Danny Aiello), the brothers embark on an impossible scheme Michael has been hatching since Clay Berry put the bug in his ear: to reach Father Flanagan (Mickey Rooney) cross-country at Boy's Town. En route to Omaha, the Murphy boys follow a circuitous route mapped out by the tramps to fool the police. Hidden by a boatsman, Mr. Davis (Kris Kristofferson), who ferries them across the Des Moines River, the fugitives are betrayed by a farmer after John comes down with a fever. With the timely interference of the train bums who've crisscrossed the USA, the boys near their goal; their grit finally convinces Mrs. Bastian to call off her child-hunt. Carrying his ill sibling into Boy's Town, Michael informs Father Flanagan, "He ain't heavy, he's my brother."

A feel-good flick with that certain Hallmark Hall of Fame aura, THE ROAD HOME celebrates the human spirit as it travels long stretches of highway and miles of familiar plotting. With a regrettably soupy musical score, this minor film could leave cynics gagging for a burst of genuine pessimism. The Robin Hood-ish band of merry rail-hoppers is just too cute for words. Although the screenplay and direction draw sufficient nail-biting gusto out of a quest we assume will end happily, the picture's real strength lies not in its ability to keep its storyline from flagging but in its bleak portrait of some 1930s realities. Without overdoing the Dickensian aspects, the movie doesn't sugarcoat the predicament in which the parentless kids find themselves; the nun's decision to deny them a farewell seems a particularly cruel example of "doing what's best for a child."

Nostalgists will get misty-eyed over the astute casting of Mickey Rooney, who played a troubled lad in the 1938 BOY'S TOWN; his larger-than-life presence anchors the film. Also of note is the movie's portrayal of the wealthy villainess who appears initially to be a pampered bloodsucker purchasing a child as a prop for a crumbling social facade—in this film, no one with money or power is perceived positively. However, for those predisposed to surrender to this domestic tearjerker's puppy-doggish charms, one question remains: Couldn't Father Flanagan and all his residents have sashayed into town and given bedraggled Michael a hand carrying his brother? The entrance requirements for Boy's Town are tough indeed! *(Violence, adult situations.)* — R.P.

d, Dean Hamilton; p, Dean Hamilton; exec p, Randolf Turrow, James Shavick; assoc p, Jim Townsend, Ermanno Barone, Donald Borza II; w, Keith O'Leary; ph, Robert Fresco; ed, Frank Faugno; m, Michael Conway Baker; prod d, Andrew Wilson; casting, Russell Gray, Tom McSweeney; stunts, Marc Akerstream

Children's/Drama **(PR: AA MPAA: PG)**

ROAD TO GALVESTON, THE ★★½
(U.S.) 93m CNM Entertainment ~ Paramount Home Video c

Cicely Tyson *(Jordan)*; Tess Harper *(Julia Archer)*; Salle Ellis *(Gayle)*; James Daniels *(Marcus Roosevelt)*; Penny Johnson *(Laney Roosevelt)*; Brandon Hammond *(Marcus Roosevelt, Jr.)*; Stephen Root *(Ed Kirkman)*; Piper Laurie *(Wanda Kirkman)*; Clarence Williams III *(Christopher)*; Starletta Dupois *(Shirley)*; Dennis Letts *(Roland)*; Patti Yasutake *(Nurse Dickerson)*; Tony Frank *(Leroy)*; Dee Hennigan *(Linda Archer)*; Haskel Craver *(Bubba)*; Alex Morris *(Teddy Roosevelt)*; Akin Babatunde *(Rev. Vernon)*; John S. Davies *(Mr. Evans)*; Kory Washington *(Shopping Teen 1)*; Alfred Smith *(Shopping Teen 2)*; Ptosha Storey *(Motel Clerk)*

Based on a touching true story but handled with a simplistic TV-movie approach, this soap opera jerks tears by treating Alzheimer's victims as lovable, loony stereotypes.

When Teddy Roosevelt (Alex Morris) dies, he leaves his widow Jordan (Cicely Tyson) destitute, and bequeaths his only asset—the heavily mortgaged homestead—to their son Marcus (James Daniels). Marcus, who plans to unload the property, invites Jordan to come live with his family. Encouraged by her blind friend Sally (Starletta Dupois), the feisty Jordan defies her son, stalls the property's sale and starts training as a caregiver for Alzheimer's patients. Merely scraping by with payment from her first live-in patient Gayle (Sally Ellis), resolute Jordan takes on more than she can handle with Julia Archer (Tess Harper), an embittered alcoholic in the disease's early stages, and Wanda Kirkman (Piper Laurie) a prejudiced, motor-mouthed grande dame whose son can no longer care for her.

Alternating tough love with tender loving care, Jordan can't make her managed-care facility a going concern. Wanda steals Julia's journal, and Julia drunkenly trashes the premises to locate it. She also starts a costly fire on a neighbor's property.

Faced with ruin, Jordan decides to drive with her boarders to Galveston, a dream trip she never got to take with her spouse. Despite alarming everyone's relatives with the impromptu journey, Jordan revives the women's spirits; Wanda is even reunited with former beau Christopher (Clarence Williams Jr.). Proud of his mother's spunk, Marcus changes his mind about supporting her bid for independence. With his assistance, Jordan hangs onto her farm as an Alzheimer's care facility.

Aiming for some of the geriatric-brotherhood elan of the classic DRIVING MISS DAISY (1989), THE ROAD TO GALVESTON is above-average melodrama. The problem with such tearjerkers is predictability and the inadvertent dishonesty that requires calamities that might have given pause to Job to be worked out triumphantly. This is a contradiction in terms for any serious treatment of Alzheimer's Disease. In order to tie a shiny ribbon around the movie's ending, the illness displayed must be written shallowly and played eccentrically.

Movies this formula-driven rise and fall on their performances; this ROAD TO GALVESTON is not without its bumps in that regard. Tyson and Dupois are believably proud and gutsy, so that the racial harmony aspect of the script works best. At the other end of the spectrum, Harper chews up the scenery as if it were impossible to convey anguish with underplaying. The usually splendid Laurie tackles the most challenging role, but her prattling reveries don't acquire pathos; the actress's built-in directness goes against the grain of this genteel lost soul's floundering state. Good intentions smoothly pave THE ROAD TO GALVESTON, however, and it provides ample crying jags for those predisposed to victory-over-adversity tearjerkers. *(Adult situations, substance abuse.)* — R.P.

d, Michael Toshiyuki Uno; p, Bob Roe; assoc p, Howard Griffith; w, Tony Lee; ph, Joao Fernandes; ed, Cari Coughlin; m, Stanley Clarke; prod d, Pam Warner; set d, Nancy Arnold; sound, Shirley Libby (mixer); casting, Dan Shaner; cos, Van Broughton Ramsey; makeup, Sharin Helgestad

Drama **(PR: C MPAA: PG-13)**

ROALD DAHL'S MATILDA
(SEE: MATILDA)

ROBIN OF LOCKSLEY ★★½
(Canada) 97m All Media Inc. ~ Hallmark Home Entertainment c

Devon Sawa *(Robin McAllister)*; Sarah Chalke *(Marian)*; Billy O'Sullivan *(Will Scarlett)*; Tyler Labine *(John Little)*; Annie Charles *(Rosie)*; Josh Jackson *(John Prince Jr.)*; Tom Butler *(John Prince Sr.)*; Colin Cunningham *(Agent Walter Nottingham)*; James Bell *(Father Tuck)*; Robert Fox *(Tommy Tarla)*; Robert Thurston *(Bryan Harvey)*; Alfred E. Humphreys *(Grant McAllister)*; Elizabeth Carol Savenkoff *(Janet McAllister)*; Chad Todhunter *(Warner)*; Kevin Hanson *(Gibson)*; Michael St. John *(Smith)*; Sheri-D Wilson; Julie Bond; Sean Milliken; Fred Henderson; L. Harvey Gold; Donald Morin

First aired on the Showtime cable TV network, this fair family feature reinvents the Robin Hood legend in a modern-day, prep-school setting.

Robin McAllister (Devon Sawa) is a bright 16-year-old whose parents have turned into jet-setting scatterbrains since winning millions in a lottery. Robin, left on his own most of the time, attends an exclusive private school called Locksley. There, bully John Prince Jr. (Josh Jackson) and his posse terrorize new arrivals and run the student archery club like their own personal fiefdom. The spineless principal and teachers do nothing because John's father (Tom Butler) heads a multi-billion-dollar corporation. Barred from the Locksley target range, Robin soon gathers his own small band of merry boys, like slingshot marksman Will Scarlett (Billy O'Sullivan) and beefy John Little (Tyler Labine), plus the obligatory girl-next-door Marian (Sarah Chalke). When a child is injured in a fire and needs a series of operations, Robin uses his computer-hacking skills to rob from the rich (the Prince corporate treasury) and give to the poor (a church-based fund for the hospitalized boy, run by a certain Father Tuck). Robin transfers $30,000 to the obscure charity. Miserly Mr. Prince notices, and his alert brings a visit from supercilious FBI Agent Walter Nottingham (Colin Cunningham), who suspects everyone from John Prince Jr. to Robin McAllister's parents. At Locksley's traditional medieval festival, swarms of Feds prepare to make an arrest. A costumed Robin first bests John Prince Jr. in an archery tournament, then confesses all. Sensing a public-relations mess, Mr. Prince declines to press charges and commits to further charitable donations.

To paraphrase a famous vice-presidential debate, we know Robin Hood. We like Robin Hood. And thou, ROBIN OF LOCKSLEY, art no Robin Hood. It is admittedly a clever concept that misses no opportunity to evoke the celebrated bandit of Sherwood Forest, right down to some awful puns, but it lacks the enduring appeal of the historical Robin Hood arising from romance and high adventure. ROBIN OF LOCKSLEY instead concentrates on voice-pattern software and how to manipulate dummy bank accounts via modem. There's little chance for swashbuckling in a milieu in which the worst that could happen is being sent to the principal's office. The all-is-forgiven finale particularly falls flat.

Sawa is a likable hero and, though no substitute for Errol Flynn, a cut above many teen protagonists in movies. The young thespians play their parts relatively straight, while most of the adult actors overdo it. — C.C.

d, Michael Kennedy; p, Larry Sugar; w, Larry Sugar; ph, Mark Irwin; ed, Bill Goddard; m, John Welsman; prod d, Andrew Wilson; art d, Catherine Quinn; set d, Kat Keith; cos, Karen Nosella

Children's **(PR: AA MPAA: NR)**

ROCK, THE ★★

(U.S.) 136m Simpson-Bruckheimer Productions; Hollywood Pictures ~ Buena Vista c

Sean Connery *(John Patrick Mason)*; Nicolas Cage *(Stanley Goodspeed)*; Ed Harris *(General Francis X. Hummel)*; John Spencer *(FBI Director Womack)*; David Morse *(Major Tom Baxter)*; William Forsythe *(Ernest Paxton)*; Michael Biehn *(Commander Anderson)*; Vanessa Marcil *(Carla Pestalozzi)*; John C. McGinley *(Marine Captain Hendrix)*; Gregory Sporleder *(Captain Frye)*; Tony Todd *(Captain Darrow)*; Bokeem Woodbine *(Sergeant Crisp)*; Jim Maniaci *(Private Scarpetti)*; Greg Collins *(Private Gamble)*; Brendan Kelly *(Private Cox)*; Steve Harris *(Private McCoy)*; Danny Nucci *(Lieutenant Shepard)*; Claire Forlani *(Jade Angelou)*; Celeste Weaver *(Stacy Richards)*; Todd Louiso *(Marvin Isherwood)*; David Bowe *(Dr. Ling)*; Raquel Krelle *(Agent Margie Wood)*; Dennis Chalker *(Seal Boyer)*; Marshall Teague *(Seal Reigert)*; Duffy Gaver *(Seal Dando)*; Steve Decker; Joseph Hawes; Carlos Sandoval; Mike Mahrer; Rick Toms; Billy Devlin *(Navy Seals)*; Jack Yates *(Hummel Marine "A")*; Juan A. Riojas *(Hummel Marine "B")*; Joseph Patrick Kelly *(Hummel Marine "C")*; Ingo Neuhaus *(Marine that Dies)*; Harry Humphries *(Navy Admiral)*; Howard Platt *(Louis Lindstrom)*; Willie Garson *(Francis Reynolds)*; John Nathan *(FBI Radar Technician)*; Robert M. Anselmo *(FBI Radar Technician)*; Jack Ford *(Military Official)*; T.J. Hageboeck *(FBI Agent Cord)*; Dwight Hicks *(FBI Agent Star)*; Ralph Peduto *(FBI Agent Hunt)*; Anthony Clark *(Paul the Hotel Bartender)*; Andy Ryan *(Lab Technician)*; Hans Georg Struhar *(Valet)*; Robert C. Besgrove *(FBI Agent)*; Sean Skelton *(Kid on Motorcycle)*; Raymond O'Connor *(Park Ranger Bob)*; Jane Sanguinetti *(Female Tourist)*; Luenell *(Female Tourist)*; John W. Love Jr. *(Male Tourist)*; Sam Whipple *(Larry Henderson)*; Tom Towles *(Alcatraz Park Ranger)*; Robert Ben Rajab *(Alcatraz Park Ranger)*; Ronald Simmons *(Alcatraz Park Ranger)*; Leonard McMahan *(Cable Car Conductor)*; Anthony Guidera *(Lead F-18 Pilot)*; James Caviezel *(Rear F-18 Pilot)*; John Enos III *(Sea Stallion Pilot)*; Ken Kells *(Spotter)*; Fred Salvallon *(Chef)*; Buck Kartalian *(Reverend)*

Although Sean Connery's crafty character quotes Oscar Wilde, don't expect much intelligence from THE ROCK. This last film from the team of Don Simpson and Jerry Bruckheimer (Simpson died early in 1996) allows the TOP GUN producers to go out with a bang—and then some.

THE ROCK stars Nicolas Cage as Stanley Goodspeed, a biochemist, whose sometimes explosive lab experiments are nothing compared to the adventure into which he is reluctantly pulled. Deranged Gen. Francis X. Hummel (Ed Harris) leads a group of renegade Marines in a takeover of Alcatraz, the defunct prison off the coast of San Francisco. Hummel threatens to kill the visitor-hostages on the island and release a batch of deadly chemical weapons unless the U.S. government makes reparations to the families of 80-odd soldiers who died in covert military operations.

Goodspeed is recruited by the government to defuse the chemical bombs Hummel plans to release. But, in order to get to Alcatraz, he is forced to work with John Patrick Mason (Sean Connery), a wily, angry prisoner who has been released prematurely to help with this dangerous mission.

With Goodspeed's scientific expertise and Mason's keen knowledge of the Alcatraz layout, the men should make a good team, but they argue constantly. When Hummel assassinates their Navy Seal back-up team, Goodspeed and Mason only have each other. So, to maximize their efforts, Mason plays decoy to Hummel's men while Goodspeed defuses the bombs.

Finally, Mason and Goodspeed usurp Hummel's position and free the hostages. Mason is allowed to reunite with his daughter, while Goodspeed flies to Kansas, where he marries his fiancee and—thanks to a tip from Mason—uncovers a national secret: microfilm that reveals the identity of JFK's true killer!

THE ROCK borrows not only from the Simpson-Bruckheimer canon, but from several other pictures, too, including FAIL SAFE (1964), CLEAR AND PRESENT DANGER (1994), DIE HARD (1988), BROKEN ARROW (1964), the last several Sean Connery buddy-buddy movies, and even the syringe-in-the-heart bit from PULP FICTION (1994). In fact, THE ROCK becomes a virtual index of action-adventure shtick, despite a clunkily-structured buildup to the central operation on Alcatraz.

And, while THE ROCK shifts moods more frequently than Frank Tashlin's THE DISORDERLY ORDERLY (1964), at least it avoids dwelling on the frightened but foolish hostages or making the bad guys Middle Eastern. Still, the completely fictitious THE ROCK is never as satisfying as Don Siegel's 1979 ESCAPE FROM ALCATRAZ, which was based on a true story. THE ROCK has many flaws—from laborious subplots involving Mason's daughter and Goodspeed's girlfriend to bad dialogue that saddles the film's best actor, Ed Harris, with the worst lines. There are also disturbing moments, such as when Cage's science-nerd-hero becomes a vengeful and unremorseful killer on the island (shades of LORD OF THE FLIES and STRAW DOGS, but without the social commentary).

Action fans will appreciate the fact that THE ROCK solves Hollywood's biggest post-Cold War dilemma: finding new ways to depict heroic bloodletting in peacetime. No doubt, John Milius would approve. *(Graphic violence, nudity, sexual situations, adult situations, extreme profanity.)* — E.M.

d, Michael Bay; p, Don Simpson, Jerry Bruckheimer; exec p, William Stuart, Sean Connery, Louis A. Stroller; assoc p, Barry Waldman, Kenny Bates; w, David Weisberg, Mark Rosner, Douglas S. Cook (from a story by David Weisberg and Douglas S. Cook); ph, John Schwartzman; ed, Richard Francis-Bruce; m, Nick Glennie-Smith, Hans Zimmer; prod d, Michael White; art d, Mark Mansbridge, Ed McAvoy; set d, Rosemary Brandenburg; sound, Keith A. Wester (mixer), Christopher Boyes (design), Kevin O'Connell, Greg P. Russell; fx, Hoyt Yeatman, Michael Meinardus, Dream Quest Images; casting, Heidi Levitt, Billy Hopkins; cos, Bobbie Read; makeup, Pat Gerhardt, Tony Gardner, Alterian Studios, Inc.; stunts, Kenny Bates

AAN Best Sound: Kevin O'Connell, Greg P. Russell, Keith A. Wester

Action/Prison/Adventure **(PR: O MPAA: R)**

ROLLING STONES ROCK-AND-ROLL CIRCUS, THE ★★★½

(U.K.) 65m ABKCO Films ~ ABKCO Films c

The Rolling Stones; The Who; Jethro Tull; Taj Mahal; The Dirty Mac; The Nurses; Mick Jagger; Keith Richards; Brian Jones; Bill Wyman; Charlie Watts; Nicky Hopkins; Rocky Dijon; John Lennon; Eric Clapton; Yoko Ono; Marianne Faithfull; Pete Townshend; Roger Daltrey; Keith Moon; John Entwhistle; Ian

Anderson; Glenn Cornick; Clive Bunker; Tony Iommi; Jesse Ed Davis; Gary Gilmore; Chuck Blackwell; Mitch Mitchell; Ivry Gitlis; Sir Robert Fossett's Circus

Filmed in 1968 but not seen until 1996, THE ROLLING STONES ROCK-AND-ROLL CIRCUS transforms several major rock acts from the 1960s into circus routines. This lively concert film could not have possibly lived up to its "holy grail" legend, but the plotless, music-jammed hour (plus) features a fascinating, heretofore unseen glimpse into the rock-pop culture of yesteryear.

In THE ROLLING STONE ROCK-AND-ROLL CIRCUS, Mick Jagger introduces a series of circus and music acts within a circus tent filled with rock fan spectators. Jethro Tull performs "Song for Jeffrey" with his band. The Who follow him with "A Quick One (While He's Away)." An elderly couple from Sir Robert Fossett's Circus then perform an act. Taj Mahal belts "Ain't That A Lot of Love." Marianne Faithfull croons "Something Better." An African circus team performs an exotic routine. John Lennon and Mick Jagger share a "babbitt and bromide" moment off-stage. The Dirty Mac, an impromptu all-star band featuring Lennon, Eric Clapton, Keith Richard and Mitch Mitchell, jam to "Yer Blues." Yoko Ono joins the Dirty Mac for "Whole Lotta Yoko." Jagger and the Rolling Stones execute a set of five numbers, including, "Jumpin' Jack Flash," "Parachute Woman," "No Expectations," "You Can't Always Get What You Want" and "Sympathy for the Devil." Finally, the Stones and the entire cast and audience sing and sway to "Salt of the Earth," the grand finale.

In the pre-music video era of the rock concert and rock documentary film (GIMME SHELTER, WOODSTOCK, LET IT BE), THE ROLLING STONES ROCK-AND-ROLL CIRCUS might have been overlooked as a short, relatively lightweight cycle entry without the proper social significance—i.e. overt references to the Vietnam War, the drug culture and '60s angst. Yet, CIRCUS never saw the light of day in '68 because the film's creator, Mick Jagger, reportedly felt that The Who stole the film from the Stones with their one powerhouse number, "A Quick One (While He's Away)." (This sequence was later used as an excerpt in The Who's 1979 film, THE KIDS ARE ALRIGHT). Today, the reconstructed CIRCUS film—once thought lost—is enjoyable to watch as a time capsule of the era: admittedly, CIRCUS is more HULLABALOO than Maysles brothers, but Mick really has nothing to worry about, performance-wise.

The highlights of CIRCUS include not only the Who and Stones segments (Jagger is particularly good on "Sympathy for the Devil"), but also Taj Mahal's one number. Marianne Faithful, then Jagger's girlfriend, shines during her torch song, but she is given less screen time than any of the other stars. The sexism continues at the end when Jagger blocks Faithfull's face during the finale. The only other female star, Yoko Ono, supplies the low point of the picture—an ear-shattering wail to her own composition, "Whole Lotta Yoko." The biggest disappointment of CIRCUS is that then-and-now legends, Jagger and Lennon, banter amusingly, but make no music together—a prime opportunity lost. They do both appear in the finale, but this campy, humanitarian-themed song (with lines like "say a prayer for the common foot soldier") is at odds with the sexy, hard-rock business that has preceded it. By the end, THE ROLLING STONES ROCK-AND-ROLL CIRCUS serves its purpose as a satisfying film record of some talented individuals—and some tacky circus acts—although to declare the film itself as great is probably overstating the case. — E.M.

d, Michael Lindsay-Hogg; p, Robin Klein; exec p, Sandy Leiberson; assoc p, Mitch Gochanour; ph, Anthony B. Richmond; ed, Ruth Foster, Robin Klein; sound, David Ashley Smith, John Hales (recordist), Fred Hughesdon (recordist); makeup, Linda Devetta, Norma Camara, Leslie Smallhorn

Documentary/Musical **(PR: A MPAA: NR)**

ROMEO AND JULIET
(SEE: WILLIAM SHAKESPEARE'S ROMEO + JULIET)

ROTE OHREN SETZEN DURCH AFCHE
(SEE: FLAMING EARS)

ROUJIN-Z ★★½

(Japan) 84m Tokyo Theaters Co.; The Television Inc.; Movie Co.; TV Asahi; Sony Music Entertainment ~ Kit Parker Films c

VOICES OF: Allan Wenger *(Terada)*; Toni Barry *(Haruko)*; Barbara Barnes *(Nobuko)*; Adam Henderson *(Maeda)*; Jana Carpenter *(Norie)*; Ian Thompson *(Kijuro Takazawa)*; John Jay Fitzgerald *(Hasegawa)*; Graydon Gould *(Minagawa)*; Nicolette McKenzie *(Haru)*; Sean Barrett *(ACHE)*; Blain Fairman *(ACHE)*; Nigel Anthony *(ACHE)*

From the creator of the anime sci-fi thriller AKIRA (1988) comes ROUJIN-Z, a contemporary fable combining the theme of technology gone awry with a statement about the treatment of the aged in Japanese society. While lacking the sheer scope and raw energy of the futuristic, post-apocalyptic AKIRA, it nonetheless offers charm and imagination, and an optimistic take on intergenerational relations.

In present-day Tokyo, the Department of Health demonstrates a new device—a robotic bed called Z-001—which can care for a bed-ridden elderly patient without the need for human intervention. The test subject is an old man named Kijuro Takazawa who is taken from his home to a hospital and placed in the new computerized bed. Disoriented by the unfamiliar setting, Takazawa somehow manages to place a call for help through the hospital's computer network to Haruko, the student nurse who's been caring for him.

Haruko and three fellow students try to rescue Takazawa but are caught by Terada, the project director, Hasegawa, the bed's inventor, and hospital security officers. With the help of an aged computer hacker in the hospital's senior citizens ward, Haruko manages to communicate with Takazawa and even finds a way for the computer to simulate the voice of Haru, Takazawa's late, beloved wife. They also find they are able to direct the movements of Z-001 to enable Takazawa to move it himself. Miraculously, however, the bed takes on a life of its own and escapes the hospital, traveling on its own power at high speeds through the streets. As it travels, the bed picks up signs, lampposts, and other metal objects and incorporates them into its structure.

Takazawa, in a brief moment of consciousness, asks to go to Kamakura Beach and Z-001 endeavors to take him there, precipitating a wild and spectacular chase through the city. The machine trashes numerous police and public vehicles and adds them to its form, creating an ever-expanding Z-001.

Finally, Haruko is recruited to try and knock out the machine's "core chip," as identified by the old hacker. When she does so, the original Z-001 bed pops out of the mechanical mountain it has created. Terada, in a burst of compassion, carries Takazawa down to the beach himself.

Puzzled by Z-001's awesome capabilities, Terada is shocked to learn it was secretly designed by Hasegawa for military purposes for the U.S. government. Terada publicly brands the inventor the scapegoat for the failure of the project and the millions of dollars of damage.

Written by Katsuhiro Otomo, ROUJIN-Z echoes themes from Otomo's dystopian AKIRA, particularly its concern about secret government projects and the visual motif of an ever-expanding metamorphosing entity. Otherwise it lacks the sharp visuals and violent, apocalyptic tone of the earlier film. More family entertainment, ROUJIN-Z offers generally pleasant characters, with even the sinister project director, Terada, becoming an ally of the good guys, while the true villain turns out to be the U.S. military/intelligence apparatus. The film succeeds as yet another Japanese animated comment on man's steadily-declining ability to retain humanity in the face of an increasingly sophisticated technology.— B.C.

d, Hiroyuki Kitakubo; p, Kazufumi Nomura, Yasuhisa Kazawa, Yoshiaki Motoya; exec p, Laurence Guinness; w, Katsuhiro Otomo, George Roubicek (from a story by Katsuhiro Otomo); ph, Hideo Okazaki; ed, Eiko Nishiide; m, Fumi Itakura, Michio Ogawa; prod d, Fumio Iida; art d, Hiroshi Sasaki; anim, Toshio Ikeuchi, Yuji Matsuhara, Mitsumochi Nakasaki, Wombat, Boomerang, Poem Cinema; sound, Yasunori Honda (sound direction), Clive Mitchison (recordist, English soundtrack); fx, Ken'ichi Abe; casting, Jill Wilmot

Science Fiction/Animated **(PR: A MPAA: PG-13)**

RUDE ★★½

(Canada) 88m Conquering Lion; Telefilm Canada; Ontario Film Development Corp.; CRB Foundation; KJM 3 Entertainment Group ~ Alliance International c

Maurice Dean Witt *(General)*; Rachael Crawford *(Maxine)*; Clark Johnson *(Reece)*; Richard Chevolleau *(Jordan)*; Sharon M. Lewis *(Rude)*; Melanie Nicholls-King *(Jessica)*; Stephen Shellen *(Yankee)*; Gordon Michael Wolvett *(Ricky)*; Dayo Ade *(Mike)*; Dean Marshall *(Joe)*; Ashley Brown *(Johnny)*; Andy Marshall *(Addict)*; Falconer Abraham *(Austin)*; Junior Williams *(Curtis)*; Andrew Moodie *(Andre)*; Nicole Parker *(Niki)*; Michael Greyeyes *(Spirit Dancer)*; Ramiah Hylton *(Spirit Girl)*; Xuan Fraser *(Junior)*; Thomas Mitchell *(Cop)*; Joel Gordon *(Youth at Wall)*; Danny Ho *(Ice Cream Vendor)*; Randy Hughson; Conrad Coates; Clifton Joseph; Karen Robinson; Alison Sealy-Smith *(Rude Callers)*

Eschewing the gritty treatment typical of film portraits of inner-city life, this stylized Canadian drama is eye-opening on a formal level, but eye-closing on a narrative one.

While radio DJ Rude (Sharon M. Lewis) spews a cryptically carnal rant that ends with a woman wondering whether if she's pregnant, unrelated characters in an unnamed city are introduced. A girl named Maxine (Rachael Crawford) gets videotaped in bed by her unseen boyfriend. A hoodlum named Reece (Clark Johnson) tries to collect on a drug debt and ends up pulling a gun on his brother, General (Maurice Dean Witt), who has just gotten out of prison. Jordan (Richard Chevolleau), a young boxer, remains silent in the shower while his pals discuss plans to beat up a gay man.

General visits his cop girlfriend, Jessica (Melanie Nicholls-King), and their son, Johnny (Ashley Brown), and she asks General if he intends to go back to dealing drugs. Jordan fails to stop the gay bashing and reluctantly joins in, hurting his hand with a thunderous punch. In her apartment, Maxine copes with the breakup with her boyfriend, and remembers conversations about an abortion.

Drug dealer Yankee (Stephen Shellen) entreats General to come back to work for him, and General eventually agrees, to the chagrin of Reece, who also works for Yankee and feels he should have been given General's job. He confronts Yankee, who launches into a racist rant and calls Reece a "worthless nigger." Reece quits and begins using drugs himself. Meanwhile Jordan shows his injured hand to his sparring partner; he expresses concern, and the two kiss.

When General sees his brother on drugs, he changes his mind about working for Yankee and tells him so. Enraged, Yankee holds General's son Johnny at gunpoint, threatening to kill the boy. General pulls a gun on Yankee; the standoff is broken by Jessica, who shoots Yankee dead.

RUDE's unrelated stories are held together with slick, artful editing that makes the vignettes slip into each other. There are touches—particularly a little girl who seems to haunt Maxine—that lend a surreal quality to the film. That said, the theatrical sets, the acting, and, especially, DJ Rude's poetic narration often feel overwrought.

Writer-director Clement Virgo displays directorial ambition and talent. Judging by the thin and uninspiring morality plays at the center of RUDE, however, narrative drama is not yet his forte. *(Substance abuse, violence, adult situations, profanity.)* — S.K.

d, Clement Virgo; p, Damon D'Oliveira, Karen A. King; exec p, Colin Brunton; co-p, Clement Virgo; w, Clement Virgo; ph, Barry Stone; ed, Susan Maggi; m, Aaron Davis; prod d, Bill Fleming; sound, John Lang (design), Jane Tattersall (design)

Drama **(PR: C MPAA: R)**

RUMBLE IN THE BRONX ★★

(Hong Kong/U.S.) 87m Maple Ridge Films; Golden Harvest Films Ltd. ~ New Line c
(HUNG FAN KUI)

Jackie Chan *(Keung)*; Anita Mui *(Elaine)*; Francoise Yip *(Nancy)*; Bill Tung *(Uncle Bill)*; Marc Akerstream *(Tony)*; Garvin Cros *(Angelo)*; Morgan Lam *(Danny)*; Alien Sit; Chan Man Ching; Fred Andrucci; Mark Antoniuk; Lauro Chartrand; Chris Franco; Lance Gibson; David Hooper; Kathy Hubble; Terrance Leigh; Dean McKenzie; Kimani Ray Smith; Lisa Stevens *(Tony's Gang)*; Kris Lord *(White Tiger)*; Richard Faraci; Mark Fielding; Terry Howsen; Jordan Lennox; Gabriel Ostevic; John Sampson; Owen Walstrom *(White Tiger's Gang)*; Carrie Cain Sparks *(Whitney)*; Guyle Frazier *(Police Officer)*; David Fredericks *(Police Officer)*; Gary Wong *(Police Officer)*

The first of Hong Kong action star Jackie Chan's homegrown films to win nationwide US release, RUMBLE IN THE BRONX was a success at the box office, winning Chan a new legion of fans. It's unfortunate, though, that an even better film couldn't have served as his American breakthrough.

Chan plays Keung, who arrives in the Bronx from Hong Kong to visit his uncle Bill (Bill Tung) on the eve of the latter's wedding. Before going on honeymoon, Bill sells his grocery store to Elaine (Anita Mui), and when Keung thrashes some local bikers who try to shoplift, he and the store earn the gang's wrath. Their attacks grow increasingly vicious, and after a particularly violent assault, the wounded Keung seeks help at the home of a wheelchair-bound neighbor boy, Danny (Morgan Lam). He ends up befriending the kid's older sister, Nancy (Francoise Yip)—who turns out to be the girlfriend of biker leader Tony (Marc Akerstream), leading to further altercations.

When a group of local mobsters working for crime boss White Tiger (Chris Lord) crash their car during a diamond heist, one of the bikers steals the gems and hides them in the seat of Danny's wheelchair. Attempting to reclaim the stones, the mobsters wage a violent campaign against both Keung and the gang (who have settled their differences after a lengthy brawl), and tear down Elaine's store.

They then kidnap several of Keung's new friends, holding them hostage on a huge hovercraft. Keung sets out after them, leading to a lengthy chase through the city's streets. After much destruction, Keung rescues the hostages and puts a stop to White Tiger and his thugs.

Despite the title, this Chan vehicle wasn't originally tailored to introduce the Asian action star to a US audience, and indeed, anyone with even a passing familiarity with the Bronx will find the location fakery laughable. The film was shot largely in Vancouver, with mountains and lakes that are hardly extant in the Bronx. New Line Cinema picked up the film following its successful run in Hong Kong, chopped 18 minutes from the original 105-minute running time, and gave the movie a dubbing job just a step above the imported kung-fu programmers of the 1970s (aside from Chan's redubbing of his own dialogue). RUMBLE IN THE BRONX serves as a good introduction to the Chan style of action filmmaking, even though it's one of his weaker movies overall.

In addition to the bogus locales, the movie suffers from not having a clearly defined antagonist throughout, and as usual in the Chan films directed by Stanley Tong, the story sometimes bogs down in between action sequences. But those scenes are first-rate, demonstrating both the star's over-the-top, often overtly comic approach and his daredevil risk-taking. As Keung, Chan leaps between buildings, jumps onto and dangles from the side of the speeding hovercraft and engages in breathtaking martial arts matches with the bad guys. He's a cinematic force of nature, a joy to behold, and an ingratiating presence to boot, never coming off like the egomaniacal supermen who dominate so much of the American action trade. It's a shame that SUPERCOP, the next Chan film to see wide US release, was not as successful financially, even though it was both a superior film initially and was better dubbed and recut. *(Violence, adult situations, profanity.)* — M.G.

d, Tong Kwei Lai; p, Barbie Tung; exec p, Leonard Ho; co-p, Roberta Chow; w, Edward Tang (from a story by Stanley Tong and Ma Mei-ping); ph, Jingle Ma; ed, Chan Kar-fei, Peter Cheung; art d, Oliver Wong; sound, Mark Schroeder (mixer), Roger Stafeckis (mixer); fx, Al Benjamin, David Paller; casting, Ann Forry; makeup, Pauline Tso; stunts, Marc Akerstream, Jackie Chan, Stanley Tong

Martial Arts/Action/Crime **(PR: C MPAA: R)**

RUMPELSTILTSKIN ★½

(U.S.) 91m Transnational Entertainment; Trimark Pictures ~ Legacy/Republic Pictures Home Video/Vidmark c

Kim Johnston Ulrich *(Shelly Stewart)*; Tommy Blaze *(Max Bergman)*; Allyce Beasley *(Hildy)*; Max Grodenchik *(Rumpelstiltskin)*; Vera Lockwood *(Matilda)*; Jay Pickett *(Russell Stewart)*; Sherman Augustus *(John McCabe)*; Valerie Wildman *(Nedda)*; Jack McGee *(Detective Ben Smith)*; Mark Holton *(Huge Man)*; Donna Barnes *(Mother at Stream)*; Marsha Dietlein *(Young Mother)*; Ben Marley *(Deputy Joe)*; Elmarie Wendel *(Gypsy Woman)*; Rachel Duncan *(Little Girl at Stream)*; Robert Harvey *(Dr. Anzinger)*; Eric Lawson *(Sheriff)*; Judith Drake *(Woman Deputy)*; Madalyn Carol *(Village Mother)*; Ted Haler *(Biker)*; Don Dowe *(Deputy Barnes)*; Ousaun Elam *(Carjacker)*; John Ducey *(Deputy Kalish)*; Caren Caty *(Village Woman)*; Lisa Simmons *(Village Woman)*; Stephanie Jones *(Little Girl)*; Rick Barker *(Tanker Driver)*; Patrick Massett *(Deputy Marley)*; Brianna Ferraro; Brittani Ferraro

Briefly released to theaters before reaching its natural habitat on video, RUMPELSTILTSKIN is no improvement on director Mark Jones' previous fairy-tale monster flick, LEPRECHAUN (1993).

In the 1300s, deformed baby-snatcher Rumpelstiltskin (Max Grodenchik) is transformed into a stone icon and tossed into the sea. In the present, the rock is purchased from an antique store by young widow Shelly Stewart (Kim Johnston Ulrich), whose policeman husband, Russell (Jay Pickett), was shot by a carjacker. Her wish to see Russell again soon comes true when he appears in her apartment, and they spend the night making love. Come morning, Russell is gone, and Rumpelstiltskin appears; having granted her wish, he demands her baby as payment. She flees to the house of her friend, Hildy (Allyce Beasley), but Rumpelstiltskin follows and kills Hildy as Shelly escapes.

After her car breaks down, Shelly is picked up by obnoxious talk show host Max Bergman (Tommy Blaze). Commandeering a tanker truck, Rumpelstiltskin pursues them, but Max lures him into a fiery crash.

Once Shelly and Max have left the scene, Rumpelstiltskin comes back to life and kills a couple of cops. Shelly and Max are arrested for the murders, allowing Rumpelstiltskin to steal the baby. Escaping from jail, Shelly and Max track the fiend to a graveyard, where they use fire, straw, and an incantation to turn him back into stone, and Shelly reclaims her baby.

An inevitable coda shows the Rumpel rock being found by a couple of kids, but unlike LEPRECHAUN, this movie is unlikely to spawn any sequels. The legend of Rumpelstiltskin certainly provides the basis for a potentially scary film, but Jones and co-scripter Joe Ruby take only the crassest, most obvious approach, seeming to make up the supernatural rules as they go along. Instead of a genuinely scary character, this Rumpelstiltskin is clearly intended to be a franchise monster *a la* Freddy Krueger, given to lame, tension-destroying wisecracks and much unmotivated evil laughter.

Given that the film was shot by Doug Milsome (whose credits include FULL METAL JACKET), the video release looks remarkably washed-out and grainy, and the low budget shows in other areas: when the Rumpel rock lands on "the ocean floor," it's clearly coming to rest at the bottom of a fish tank. Despite good makeup effects by Kevin Yagher, RUMPELSTILTSKIN will unnerve no one except those who might be worried about an infant being placed in the midst of horrific situations. But they will be placated by a closing credit: "No babies or children were placed in dangerous or traumatic situations. . . audible cries were added with imitation sound effects." *(Graphic violence, nudity, sexual situations, extreme profanity.)* — M.G.

d, Mark Jones; p, Joe Ruby, Ken Spears, Michael Prescott; w, Mark Jones, Joe Ruby (inspired by the fairy tale recounted by the Brothers Grimm); ph, Doug Milsome; ed, Christopher Holmes; m, Charles Bernstein; prod d, Ivo Cristante; art d, Ken Larson; set d, Tim Colohan; sound, James Thornton; fx, Kevin Yagher, Ron Trost; casting, Victoria Burrows; cos, Holly Davis; makeup, Kevin Yagher, Lisa Buono

Horror **(PR: O MPAA: R)**

SABRINA, THE TEENAGE WITCH ★★
(U.S.) 91m Viacom; Once and Future Films; Hartbreak Films ~ Showtime Networks/Hallmark Home Video c

Melissa Joan Hart *(Sabrina Sawyer)*; Sherry Miller *(Aunt Hilda)*; Charlene Fernetz *(Aunt Zelda)*; Michelle Beaudoin *(Marny)*; Ryan Reynolds *(Seth)*; Tobias Mehler *(Harvey)*; Lalaina Lindbjerg *(Katy)*; Laura Karris *(Freddie)*; Jim Swansburg *(Mr. Dingle)*; Paul Feig *(Lyle Pool)*; Noel Geer *(Jeff)*; Kea Wong *(Fran)*; Joe Bates *(Coach)*; Janine Cox *(Sales Clerk)*; Biski Gugushe *(Larry)*; Tyler Labine *(Mark)*; Volton *(DJ)*

Based on a character who first appeared in "Archie" comics in 1962, this quite literal wish-fulfillment comedy premiered on the Showtime cable network, and was then developed into a series for ABC.

Pretty Sabrina Sawyer (Melissa Joan Hart), newly arrived in Riverdale from her native Massachusetts, seems like a typical teen. Her eccentric aunts, caring for Sabrina while her parents travel, know better. Just as they did, Sabrina will inherit magical abilities upon the first full moon after her imminent 16th birthday.

When Sabrina prematurely opens her gift, an ancient book of spells, she unknowingly gets a foretaste of the powers. In school, Sabrina achieves perfect test scores, performs superhuman athletic feats, and generally outshines snotty class queen Katy (Lalaina Lindbjerg).

Finally, she learns her true heritage as a witch, and tries not to rely too much on magic for easy solutions. In fact, the sorcery has prescribed limits. She cannot effectively cast a love spell, and an early attempt on high-school lothario Seth (Ryan Reynolds) has left her vulnerable to being turned into an animal if they kiss. It's not an issue, however, as Sabrina realizes that best buddy Harvey (Tobias Mehler) is the one who truly adores her. Resentful Katy opens Sabrina's locker and finds the book of spells, but a brief transformation into a poodle scares her silent.

SABRINA, THE TEENAGE WITCH goes to extremes to be mild, with a portrayal of witchcraft inoffensive to all but the most hysterical fundamentalist. "When you feel good about who you are, being true to yourself, then nothing can keep you down," counsel the aunts, teaching the girl to fly. The loose, suspense-free plot line won't send any pulses racing, and Sabrina's romantic dilemma, going after the Flashy Jock and overlooking the Nice Guy who deserves her, was a predictable cliche even when John Hughes used it for trendy teen dramas like PRETTY IN PINK (1986).

Melissa Joan Hart, late of the Nickelodeon cable show "Clarissa Explains It All," is a winning personality. She and other performers actually look and sound somewhat like contemporary teenagers, a rare virtue considering the hopelessly square source material. Archie, Jughead, and other Riverdale High alumni never appear, although director Tibor Takacs uses a page-turning screen "wipe" for transition scenes as a nod to Sabrina's comic-book origin.

Producer Paula Hart acquired rights to the Sabrina character as a vehicle for her actress daughter, and it paid off when "Sabrina, The Teenage Witch" the TV series materialized, with Melissa Joan Hart and Michelle Beaudoin the only carryovers from this feature. The program was ABC's sole solid ratings hit among newcomers in the 1996-97 broadcast season, and it upstaged a highly-touted prime-time show based on the popular theatrical teen comedy, CLUELESS (1995). — C.C.

d, Tibor Takacs; p, Richard Davis, Alana H. Lambros; exec p, Paula Hart, Barney Cohen, Kathryn Wallack; assoc p, Brian Irving; w, Barney Cohen, Kathryn Wallack, Nicholas Factor (based on characters created in Archie Comics); ph, Bernard Salzman; ed, Daria Ellerman; m, Greg DeBelles; prod d, John Kavelin; set d, Ian Nothnagel; sound, Roger Stafeckis; fx, Eric Alba, Rae Reedyk; casting, Carol Kelsay; cos, Vicky Mulholland; makeup, Lili Marchenski; stunts, Ben Derrick

Children's/Fantasy/Comedy (PR: A MPAA: PG)

SAIMT EL QUSUR
(SEE: SILENCES OF THE PALACE, THE)

SAINTS AND SINNERS ★★★
(U.S.) 99m Sinners Inc.; Signature Productions; The Farm ~ Live Home Video c

Damian Chapa *(Dave "Pooch" Puccia)*; Jennifer Rubin *(Eva)*; Scott Plank *(Big Boy Baynes)*; William Atherton *(McCone)*; Damon Whitaker *(Rockitt)*; Charles Guardino *(Tommy the Cow)*; Bob Larkin *(Tony)*; Panchito Gomez *(Juanito)*; Dejuan Guy *(Arthur)*; Sal Landi *(Director)*; Bob Delegall *(Capt. Reneke)*; Eugene Bondurant *(Mel Tayback)*; Phillip Casnoff *(Det. Battaglia)*; Jeff Cadiente *(Bartender)*; Billy Bastiani *(Waiter)*; Gianin Loffler *(Rico)*; Ricco Chapa *(Little Boy)*; Roy Matlen *(Dacey)*; Juan Fernandez *(Priest)*

Many direct-to-vids are less like recognizable old friends than crashing bores who grab your lapels at a party. The flavorful SAINTS AND SINNERS introduces a brand new acquaintance to the jaded viewer. Although the film's criminal testing ground is familiar terrain, these saints and sinners shout down their demons of guilt in freshly conceived and exhilaratingly authentic ways.

Having run afoul of the power hierarchy at his previous precinct, former street tough turned idealistic cop Dave "Pooch" Puccia (Damian Chapa) is reassigned to the rough neighborhood where he grew up. Unbeknownst to his life-long pal, Big Boy Baynes (Scott Plank), Pooch is working undercover to bring down Big Boy's drug trafficking operation. As an accomplice to Big Boy and the suspicious Juanito (Panchito Gomez), Pooch provides muscle for their ongoing efforts to consolidate Big Boy's influence with uptown mobsters Tony (Bob Larkin) and Tommy the Cow (Charles Guardino). What Pooch doesn't know is that his superior officer McCone (William Atherton) is a crooked cop prepared to sacrifice Pooch and the other small-timers at the behest of the Mafiosi. With his life and career on the line, Pooch complicates the betrayal equation by falling for goodtime gal Eva (Jennifer Rubin), who comes between Pooch and Big Boy via a menage a trois. Too late, Pooch realizes that Eva is working for Tony and Tommy. Smelling a rat, Pooch feeds false info to McCone in order to save Big Boy from a mob ambush disguised as McCone's police sting. In a barrage of bullets, Pooch is wounded, but the other mobsters are killed. After McCone's duplicity is uncovered, a redeemed-by-love Eva encourages Pooch to turn himself in, so they can enroll in a witness protection program.

Viewers who have endured countless stuck-in-the-mud action pics will be pleasantly suprised by SAINTS AND SINNERS. Its greatest strength (besides gritty direction) is dialogue that realistically approximates street vernacular while maintaining an artful, exaggerated quality uniquely its own. Thanks to the screenwriter's loving care, the audience is alert to stylized poetic resonances of the kind most crime flicks don't bother with. If the screenplay's undercurrents about crooked cops allied with mobsters are interwoven into the central story line rather perfunctorily, the scenes involving drug trade have a jagged immediacy (particularly one in which a grade school drug runner dies planting a bomb at Juanito's and another in which Juanito shoots a quivering messenger to demonstrate his authority).

However, realism is only one of this startlingly intense film's assets. It magnetizes the audience by evoking the affection between Big Boy and Pooch, a love that circumstance will soon compromise and destroy. Equally mesmerizing is Pooch's passion for opportunist Eva, so afraid of this emotional upheaval that she tries to diminish its magic by including Big Boy in the relationship. For once in the macho-dominated action arena, a female protagonist is neither Victoria's Secret window-dressing nor a one-note Jezebel. Although she's self-destructive, Eva's expediency, unlike Pooch's survival scheme, does not involve the betrayal of a friend. Yet even Pooch's department-sanctioned back-stabbing makes dramatic sense in this movie's bleak universe, where everybody is someone else's patsy. In SAINTS AND SINNERS, saving one's neck becomes an art form. *(Graphic violence, extreme profanity, extensive nudity, sexual situations, substance abuse.)* — R.P.

d, Paul Mones; p, Paul Mones; exec p, Jon Kilik, Guy Rydell; assoc p, Marcia Shulman; co-p, Michele Weisler; w, Paul Mones; ph, Michael Bonvillain; ed, Leo Trombetta; m, Tom Varner, Steve Miller; prod d, Vincent Jefferds; art d, Vincent Jefferds; set d, Natalie Cohen; sound, Stephen A. Tibbo (mixer); fx, Larry Roberts; casting, Marcia Shulman; cos, Melinda Eshelman; makeup, Suzanne Diaz; stunts, Jeff Cadiente

Crime/Drama/Erotic **(PR: O MPAA: R)**

SALEM'S GHOST
(SEE: WITCHCRAFT: SALEM'S GHOST)

SAM & PHYLLIS
(SEE: SUGARTIME)

SANCTUARY: THE MOVIE ★★½
(Japan) 70m Sho Fumimura; Ryoichi Ikegami; Shogakukan; OB Planning; Toho; VAP ~ Viz Video c

VOICES OF: Sho Hayami *(Hojo)*; Kazuhiro Nakada *(Asami)*; Hiromi Tsuru *(Ishihara)*; Takaya Haji *(Tokai)*; Tomokazu Seki *(Tashiro)*; Masaharu Sato *(Murata)*; Shigezo Sasagawa *(Sagara)*; Takeshi Watabe *(Isaoka)*

An animated adaptation of a popular *manga* (comic book) series, SANCTUARY tells a complex tale of shifting loyalties, deception, and betrayal among gangsters and politicians in modern Japan. Simple but powerful graphics, modeled closely on the original artwork by Ryoichi Ikegami ("Crying Freeman"), replace flashy effects and excessive violence to bring a new dimension to anime.

Friends since their school days, Akira Hojo, an ambitious young yakuza, and Chiaki Asami, private secretary to Sakura, a parliamentary member of the Diet, have forged an alliance designed to put Asami on the fast track to a political career as part of their plan to bring young men into the ruling bureaucracy. Hojo and his assistant, Tashiro, attempt to blackmail Sakura with photos of him taken during a tryst with a prostitute, but Sakura calls their bluff and throws them out of his office. Secretary General Isaoka of the ruling Liberal Democratic Party (LDP) receives copies of the incriminating photos and suggests that Sakura not run for reelection. Sakura insists to Asami that his constituency remains solid, but Asami turns against him and declares his own candidacy for the parliament seat.

Deputy Police Chief Kyoko Ishihara and Detective Ozaki observe and monitor Hojo's activities, hoping to get enough evidence to put him behind bars. Hojo's aging syndicate boss, Don Sagara, warns Hojo to leave politicians alone.

Newly released from prison, Tokai, a reckless gangster who was Hojo's mentor, comes into conflict with the more polished Hojo. Asami initially gets the Secretary General's approval to run for Sakura's seat, but is betrayed when Isaoka suddenly backs another old party member in the race.

Don Sagara doesn't trust Hojo's ambitions and manipulates tensions within his group to get Tokai to eliminate Hojo. In a showdown for control of their syndicate, Hojo shoots and wounds Don Sagara, leaving him permanently disabled, and assumes the position of Don himself, with Tokai confirmed as his ally. Asami joins an opposition party and begins a new campaign. Police Chief Ishihara learns of Hojo's and Asami's school ties and resolves to watch their rising careers with interest.

One of the few anime productions to deal with modern Japan in a realistic style, SANCTUARY tells a compelling story of two young men seeking to force a change in the nation's political structure by bringing in new blood. The theme of youthful dissatisfaction with the aging ruling elite is rare in Japanese entertainment and may signal a social upheaval in the making.

One of many animated productions based on Japanese *manga,* this one is notable for sticking closely to the sharp, detailed style of the original, a popular series which is also available in an English edition. This is the first in a continuing series. Oriented to character rather than action, the animation emphasizes the faces and overall look of the characters and their places in the varied urban settings. Scenes of misogynist sex between the unsavory male antagonists and various prostitutes serve to illustrate the characters' depravity. Lacking a woman protagonist to balance these portrayals—other than the ineffectual Chief Ishihara—these scenes may put off some viewers while, of course, titillating others. *(Violence, nudity, sexual situations, profanity.)* — B.C.

d, Takashi Watanabe; p, Masamichi Fujiwara, Umeo Ito, Koichiro Inomata, Toshifumi Yoshida; exec p, Ken Usami, Seiji Horibuchi; co-p, Haruo Sai, Haruo Okamoto, Ayao Ueda, Kayo Fukuda; w, Kenshi Terada (based on the *manga^ series byR Sho Fumimura and Ryoichi Ikegami), Trish Ledoux (English script editor); ph, Kazushi Torigoe; md, Masafumi Mima; art d, Hiroshi Kato; anim, Hidemi Kubo*

Animated/Crime **(PR: O MPAA: NR)**

SANDMAN, THE ★★½
(U.S.) 90m The Suburban Tempe Co. ~ Tempe Video c

A. J. Richards *(Gary)*; Rita Gutowski *(Maris)*; Terry J. Lipko *(Bud)*; James Viront *(Zachariah)*; Barbara Katz-Norrod *(Mrs. Martinak)*; Stan Fitzgerald *(Sandman)*; Matthew Jason Walsh *(Ozzy)*; Mary Wilkerson *(Bizarre)*; Jennifer Barrett *(Bimbo Model)*; Lisa Neeld *(Bedelia)*; Nicholas Cleland *(Pugsley)*; James L. Edwards *(Gerald Rivers)*; Lawrence Latsko *(Joyner)*; George Abrams *(Hershberger)*; Hal Vandersall *(Hooper)*; Douglas Bouslough *(Merle)*; Jennifer Mullen *(Slutty Metal Chick)*; Jack Jordan; Tom Hoover *(Male Paramedics)*; Barbara Hazlett; Sandy Parise *(Female Paramedics)*; Jamey Kraft; Matt Reese; Corrie Lynn; Brian Vivich; Donna Goodhart; Danielle Cowgill; Bo Gutierrez; D'Urville Edwards *(Ozzy's Friends)*; Steve Jasecko; Tina Malizia; R. Bruce Trittschuh; Chris Kupel; Lori Pesci *(Police Officers)*; Joe Cabot *(TV Sandman)*; Jerry Wilkerson *(TV Kid)*; Michael Munsen *(Jeremy the Dead Kid)*;

Bill Morrison; Ron Bonk *(TV Technicians)*; Linda Weaver; Cecelia Bouslough; Amanda Ruby *(Waitresses)*

Though produced on a tiny budget, THE SANDMAN demonstrates a commendable amount of imagination—and restraint—for a movie of its nature.

Gary (A.J. Richards), a young man living in a trailer park, aspires to be a novelist and has a tempestuous relationship with his girlfriend Maris (Rita Gutowski). Soon he has something else to concern him: people in the area have been mysteriously dying in their sleep, and Gary thinks he sees a strange, shadowy figure lurking in the neighborhood. Neither Maris nor Gary's friend Bud (Terry J. Lipko) believe his stories, but one night, Gary sees the creature, a hooded phantom known as the Sandman (Stan Fitzgerald), looming over Maris as she sleeps and barely manages to save her.

Gary soon learns from his Vietnam-veteran neighbor Zachariah (James Viront) that the Sandman steals people's souls while they sleep. Bud becomes the next victim, and when Maris can no longer stay awake, Gary goes to guard her. With Zachariah's help, Gary takes on the Sandman when it arrives, ultimately sending it into the netherworld where the souls of its victims reside, and they destroy the creature. Gary wakes up in an ambulance with Maris—but as they're driven away, they see the Sandman's glowing eyes in every nearby window.

After being responsible for a few low-budget films, notable largely for their gore content, and a string of no-budget video productions, director-cowriter J.R. Bookwalter takes a step up with THE SANDMAN. While the look is still cheap (video run through a rather murky film-looking process), Bookwalter has a much better story to work with here, one that emphasizes mood and suspense rather than exploitation elements. He also demonstrates a facility with camerawork and editing that gives the movie an air of professionalism lacking in many projects of its ilk.

While most of the supporting characters are caricatures who detract from the seriousness of the basic story, leads Richards and Gutowski are believable enough, and the tall, cloaked Fitzgerald cuts an imposing figure as the Sandman. The phantom's attacks are more moody than scary, but that seems to have been Bookwalter's aim, and he keeps a minor but palpable tension going for most of the running time. Evidently aiming to create an unpretentious, old-fashioned creature feature, Bookwalter has by and large succeeded; his immediate follow-up, POLYMORPH (1996), was even better. *(Violence, sexual situations, profanity.)* — M.G.

d, J. R. Bookwalter; p, James L. Edwards, Linda Weaver, J. R. Bookwalter; assoc p, Ariauna Albright, Barbara Katz-Norrod; w, Matthew Jason Walsh, J. R. Bookwalter (based on a story by J. R. Bookwalter, David Lange, and Matthew Jason Walsh); ph, Ron Bonk; ed, J. R. Bookwalter; m, Matthew Jason Walsh; prod d, Lonnie Love; sound, Richard Dolenz, David Wagner; fx, Steve Kalman; casting, LeModeln, Ltd.; makeup, Bill Morrison, Linda Weaver

Horror **(PR: O MPAA: NR)**

SANTA CLAWS ★

(U.S.) 83m Market Square Productions; New Age Pictures ~ American Home Entertainment c

Debbie Rochon *(Raven Quinn)*; Grant Kramer *(Wayne)*; John Mowod *(Eric Quinn)*; Karl Hardman *(Bruce Brunswick)*; Marilyn Eastman *(Mrs. Quinn)*; Julie Wallace *(Peggy Quinn)*; Savannah Calhoun *(Savannah Quinn)*; Dawn Michelucci *(Angela Quinn)*; Christine Cavalier *(Laura Britton)*; Terri Lewandowski *(Wayne's Mother)*; Ed Lewandowski *(Uncle Joe)*; Christopher Boyle *(Young Wayne)*; Lisa Delien *(Mary Jane Austin)*; Susan Ellen White *(Debbie Darwin)*; Bill Hinzman *(Director)*; Mary Beth Boyle *(Diane Heller)*; Bob Michelucci *(Cop)*; John A. Russo *(Detective)*; Terry Weston *(Santa/Crew Person)*; Don Crotsley *(Crew Person)*; Jack Smith *(Crew Person)*; Diana Michelucci *(Production Assistant)*; Bobby Michelucci; Mary Lou Russo; Julia Ann Russo *(Santa Contributors)*

A cheap and opportunistic project, SANTA CLAWS adds little to the "killer Kringle" subgenre or to the world of horror films in general.

Young Wayne (Christopher Boyle) finds his very recently widowed mother (Terri Lewandowski) and Uncle Joe (Ed Lewandowski) in bed together and shoots them. Years later, he lives next door to horror film star Raven Quinn (Debbie Rochon), on whom he has a psychopathic fixation. Believing model Laura Britton (Christine Cavalier) to be a threat to Raven's "stardom," Wayne kills her at a photo studio.

Unaware of Wayne's dementia, Raven takes him up on his offer to baby-sit her daughters Savannah (Savannah Calhoun) and Angela (Dawn Michelucci), as her photographer husband Eric (John Mowod) is out of town (and, unbeknownst to her, having an affair with one of his models). Wayne drugs the kids, dresses in a Santa Claus suit, and commits more murders. Eric calls off his affair and returns home—just in time to confront Wayne, who has painted his Santa suit black and is threatening Raven. A fight ensues, and Raven kills Wayne with his own weapon.

In the 1990s, NIGHT OF THE LIVING DEAD (1968) coauthor John A. Russo has devoted most of his time to the softcore "horror" magazine *Scream Queens Illustrated*, for which his SANTA CLAWS depressingly amounts to a barely disguised 83-minute product plug. Many of the mag's models and workers have acting roles, a good deal of the movie was shot at its offices, and there's much functional dialogue revolving around the dubious "scream queen" phenomenon.

Needless to say, there's not much room for interesting or original horror here. The plot is cliched from the "source of the psycho's madness" opening on down; Russo's direction is clumsy (particularly in the murder scenes), and the technical credits are barely passable, with often overmodulated sound and a host of lousy songs on the soundtrack. The only positive thing one can say is that unlike so many cheesy "scream queen" movies, this one was at least shot on film instead of video. Horror fans will recognize Karl Hardman, Marilyn Eastman, and Bill Hinzman, who appear briefly, from the cast of the original NIGHT OF THE LIVING DEAD. *(Graphic violence, extensive nudity, sexual situations, profanity.)* — M.G.

d, John A. Russo; p, Bob Michelucci, Jack Smith; exec p, Bob Michelucci, John A. Russo, Jack Smith; assoc p, Mike Smith, Tara Alexander; w, John A. Russo; ph, Bill Hinzman; ed, Tara Alexander; m, Paul McCullough; prod d, Bob Michelucci; sound, Tara Alexander; fx, Bob Michelucci; casting, Marquette SPI; cos, Mike Lucci; makeup, Gray Dawn

Horror/Erotic **(PR: O MPAA: NR)**

SANTA WITH MUSCLES ★★

(U.S.) 98m Hit Entertainment; Cabin Fever Entertainment ~ Legacy Releasing c

Hulk Hogan *(Blake Thorn)*; Ed Begley Jr. *(Ebner Frost)*; Don Stack *(Lenny)*; Robin Curtis *(Leslie Morgan)*; Kevin West *(Dr. Blight)*; Garrett Morris *(Clayton)*; Clint Howard *(Policeman)*

Though highly unlikely to become a Christmas classic, SANTA WITH MUSCLES is pretty much everything Hulk Hogan's fans might expect—at least, all of his fans under the age of 12.

Blake Thorn (Hulk Hogan) is the wealthy owner of a health food company who follows a code of behavior that emphasizes putting yourself first. But when he loses his memory in an accident after donning a Santa Claus disguise, he is persuaded that he really is Santa by Lenny (Don Stack), a hustler who swiped Thorn's wallet while he was unconscious. Thorn fills in for an absent Santa at a shopping mall, and foils a robbery of money intended to save a local orphanage. Although he doesn't know why, he feels compelled to help the orphanage in its fight against Mr. Frost (Ed Begley Jr.) and his evil henchmen.

At the orphanage, "Santa" soon wins the adoration of the three remaining orphans, as well as the gratitude of caretakers Leslie (Robin Curtis) and Clayton (Garrett Morris). They discover that Mr. Frost wants the orphanage in order to gain access to valuable energy-bearing crystals located in a cavern underneath the building. Thorn regains his memory in time to help fight off the final assault of Frost; he also learns from Clayton that he and Frost were childhood friends who at one time lived at this same orphanage. Although Thorn and the orphans manage to overcome Frost, the battle causes the crystals to explode and the orphanage is destroyed. Cured of his selfish old ways, Thorn relocates the orphanage to his palatial estate.

While most of professional wrestling star Hulk Hogan's movies have been made for family audiences, SANTA WITH MUSCLES is primarily aimed at children; adults may get a few chuckles out of it, but unless you're sharing it with viewers whose age is in the single digits you probably won't want to bother. The plot and characterizations are as silly (if not quite so loud) as what you'd encounter in professional wrestling, particularly Mr. Frost's bizarre henchmen: a doctor, a chemist, an electrician, and a geologist.

Hogan himself continues to show a flair for self-deprecating comedy that, if ever put in the service of a real movie, might be quite engaging. Being surrounded by mugging second bananas and abnormally cute children in vehicles like this, however, doesn't exactly bring out the best in him. To call him the best thing in SANTA WITH MUSCLES is faint praise, given this film's general low level of acting, indifferent plotting, and nonexistent production values; check out the less than spectacular orphanage collapse at the film's conclusion. *(Violence.)* — M.F.

d, John Murlowski; p, Brian Shuster; exec p, Harry Shuster, Jordan Belfort, Danny Porush; co-p, David Silberg, James R. Rosenthal, M. Charles Cuddy; w, Jonathan Bond, Fred Mata, Dorrie Krum Raymond; ph, Michael Gfelner; ed, William D. Marrinson, Stephen Myers; m, James Covell; prod d, Chuck Conner; art d, Chase Harlan; fx, Albert Zannotti; casting, Tom McSweeney; cos, Cathryn Wagner; makeup, Pamela Phillips

Children's/Comedy (PR: AA MPAA: PG)

SAWBONES ★★

(U.S.) 86m Concorde-New Horizons ~ New Horizons Home Video c

Adam Baldwin *(Burt Miller)*; Nina Siemaszko *(Jennie Sloan)*; Barbara Carrera *(Rita Baldwin)*; Don Stroud *(Capt. Mowbray)*; Don Harvey *(Willy Knapp)*; Nicholas Sadler *(Brad Fraser)*; Luis Antonio Ramos *(Hank)*; Brian Finney *(Dr. Wilfred Knapp)*; Phil LaMarr *(Stanley Johnson)*; Roman Cisneros *(Harry)*; James Gleason *(Coroner)*; Lillian Lehman *(Lt. Heineman)*; Karen Maruyama *(Polito)*; Joey Aresco *(Blue Collar Victim)*; Jack Verell *(Hobby Store Clerk)*; Michael James McDonald *(Prostitute)*; Avner Garbi *(Tow Truck Driver)*; Cheryl Bartel *(Beautiful Woman)*; Ralph Meyering Jr. *(John Pratt)*; Clint Howard *(Sephus McCoy)*; Jacob Witkin *(Dr. Zorn)*; Giles Hunt *(Doctor)*; Hillary Matthews *(Jocelyn)*; Nathalia Momtchilova *(Vicki)*; Geoffrey Rivas *(Crime Scene Patrolman)*; Gladys Jimenez *(Nurse)*; John Vasey *(Neighbor)*; Nickolai Stoilob *(Philip Conrad)*

The intriguing premise of this grisly slasher pic about a surgical serial killer is riddled with too many coincidences to generate scares. However, because the film's cop hero and amateur detective heroine are sensibly written with recognizable human flaws, SAWBONES commands attention even at its most ridiculous.

Constantly put down by her medical student boyfriend, Brad (Nicholas Sadler), hospital admissions secretary Jennie Sloan (Nina Siemaszko) marshals her unfocused energies into crimesolving after she discovers a mutilated corpse in an alley. The deceased woman is one of a string of victims slain by Willy Knapp (Don Harvey), a rejected med school candidate. Unable to match the brilliance of his late surgeon father, psychotic Willy makes barbaric surgery his hobby. Pressured to capture elusive Willy (who uses a muscle tranquilizer but no anesthetic on his captive patients), police detective Burt Miller (Adam Baldwin) prevails upon Jennie to provide hospital and med school info denied him by admissions director Rita Baldwin (Barbara Carrera). While Burt is chastised for interrogating a prominent citizen's son and Jennie gets fired for raiding her institution's files, Willy continues his deadly surgery on a tow truck driver, a blue-collar worker, and a beautiful young woman.

Serendipitously locating Knapp's misplaced file, Jennie provokes Willy with a nasty official rejection letter to flush him out. Meanwhile, Burt is able to narrow the suspect field due to an obsolete surgical tool Knapp leaves embedded in a discarded corpse.

Jennie walks in on Brad and Rita having sex. Distraught, she leaves. To avenge his medical-school rejection, the deranged Willy kidnaps the cheating lovers to prepare Rita for a Hoover-powered liposuction and Brad for the relocation of his testicles. Posing as an assistant physician, brave Jennie gains entry into Willy's home operating room after leaving a message for Burt to meet her there. Jennie survives a life-and-death struggle with suspicious Willy, and when Burt arrives, Willy attacks him with a surgical saw. Jennie shoots Willy with the gun Burt drops. Frustrated Sawbones Willy faces life in a madhouse. Dropping her beau Brad, Jennie bonds with simpatico Burt.

Aside from irking the audience with the foolhardy risks its heroine takes, the major problem with SAWBONES is its wavering treatment of the villain, Willy Knapp. Poised on the verge of camp, actor Don Harvey doesn't quite get all he can out of his one-liners. Conversely, he doesn't register as diabolically terrifying either; the handling of the film's titular figure is perfunctory. Because the movie indecisively shifts from over-the-top Grand Guignol to straightforward suspense, sickie surgeon Willy never rattles the audience's bones. Although gore groupies get their money's worth with the sadistic operation scenes, horror film traditionalists will prefer the relationship developed between hard-pressed cop Burt Miller and perpetual doormat Jennie Sloan, whose self-esteem is elevated by cracking this murder case. If the parallel story of Willy's tragic keeping-up-with-Daddy complex exhibited a pathos that complemented Jennie's psychological struggle, SAWBONES might have been a complex genre piece instead of just another passable nail-biter. *(Graphic violence, extensive nudity, extreme profanity, sexual situations, adult situations.)* — R.P.

d, Catherine Cyran; p, Mike Elliott; exec p, Roger Corman, Lance H. Robbins; co-p, Mike Upton; w, Sam Montgomery; ph, Christopher Baffa; ed, Norman Buckley; m, Don Preston; prod d, Michael Pearce; art d, Danielle Berman; set d, Dan Sherrill, Kelly Eddleman; sound, Thomas Boyle (mixer); fx, Jerry

Whitcher; casting, Jan Glaser; cos, Bonnie Ann Stauch; makeup, Yolanda Porter; stunts, Brett Davidson

Horror/Thriller **(PR: O MPAA: R)**

SCHATTEN DER ENGEL
(SEE: SHADOW OF ANGELS)

SCHLAFES BRUDER
(SEE: BROTHER OF SLEEP)

SCREAM ★★★½
(U.S.) 100m Wes Craven Films; Woods Entertainment; Dimension Films ~ Dimension Films c

Drew Barrymore *(Casey)*; Courteney Cox *(Gale Weathers)*; David Arquette *(Dewey)*; Roger Jackson *(Phone Voice)*; Kevin Patrick Walls *(Casey's Father)*; Carla Hatley *(Casey's Mother)*; Neve Campbell *(Sidney)*; Skeet Ulrich *(Billy)*; Lawrence Hecht *(Mr. Prescott)*; Linda Blair *(Obnoxious Reporter)*; W. Earl Brown *(Kenny)*; Rose McGowan *(Tatum)*; Lois Saunders *(Mrs. Tate)*; Henry Winkler *(Principal Himbry)*; Joseph Whipp *(Sheriff Burke)*; Matthew Lillard *(Stuart)*; Jamie Kennedy *(Randy)*; Lisa Beach *(Reporter #1)*; Tony Kilbert *(Reporter #2)*; C. W. Morgan *(Hank Loomis)*; Frances Lee McCain *(Mrs. Riley)*; Liev Schreiber *(Cotton Weary)*; Troy Bishop *(Ghost Teen #1)*; Ryan Kennedy *(Ghost Teen #2)*; Leonora Scelfo *(Cheerleader in Bathroom)*; Nancy Ann Ridder *(Girl in Bathroom)*; Lisa Canning *(Mask Reporter)*; Bonnie Wood *(Young Girl)*; Lucille Bliss *(Check-out Lady)*; Aurora Draper *(Party Teen #1)*; Kenny Kwong *(Party Teen #2)*; Justin Sullivan *(Teen on Couch)*; Kurtis Bedford *(Bored Teen)*; Angela Miller *(Girl on Couch)*

Director Wes Craven continues his reign as one of horror's kingpins with this self-reflexive twist on "dead-teen" movies—which hit their peak in the late 1970s with HALLOWEEN (1978), only to give birth to a plethora of cut-rate offspring. Reinventing the genre for the 90s, the film mixes sly humor and grisly demises into a tale that both updates and satirizes the slasher genre.

The terror begins as teenaged Casey Becker (Drew Barrymore) is home alone, preparing to watch a "scary movie," when she's terrorized by repeated calls from a stranger on a cellular phone, who says he's watching her. To prove his threats, he murders her boyfriend before her eyes and chases her throughout her house. Casey is finally gutted by the fright-masked intruder, who leaves her hanging from a tree for her parents to discover.

While the police interrogate at the high school, we meet Sidney (Neve Campbell), who, a year after her mother's brutal rape-murder, is still traumatized by the event. These new killings only make her edgier, especially with the reappearance of TV tabloid reporter Gail Weathers (Courteney Cox), who covered her mom's murder and still thinks the man they convicted was innocent. Sidney is the next person to get a visit from the killer, but she's able to fend him off, just as boyfriend Billy (Skeet Ulrich) arrives—only to briefly find himself a suspect. We also meet Sidney's friends, including girlfriend Tatum (Rose McGowan), her wiseass boyfriend Stu (Matthew Lillard), and horror-movie-obsessed video clerk Randy (Jamie Kennedy). Meanwhile, Weathers tries to charm info out of Tatum's deputy-brother Dewey (David Arquette), while Sidney's missing father becomes the next suspect.

In the wake of these attacks, the local teens get together for a night of drinking and horror movies, with Weathers sneaking a compact video camera into their party. And despite Randy's explanation of "How to Survive a Scary Movie" (no drugs, no sex, and don't ever leave the group), the kids immediately flout these rules. The killer arrives, murdering anyone left behind, including Tatum (with the aid of an electric garage door) and Billy (after he had sex with Sidney). With much of the cast dispatched, Sidney is confronted by Stu and the surprisingly alive Billy, who confess to the recent murders, as well as to that of Sidney's mom. Their plan is to pin the crimes on Sidney's father, whom they kidnapped days before, and the two go so far as to shoot themselves to make their scenario more believable to the police. Sidney turns the tables on the wounded pair, and kills both with the aid of Weathers, who pops up at the precise moment to save the day.

Unlike most modern horror movies, which are little more than exploitation cash cows, director Craven and scriptwriter Kevin Williamson have created a surprisingly clever thriller, which embraces the genre, even as they subvert it for their own ends. It's fast-paced and complex enough to keep viewers guessing, and though never aiming for outright comedy, the in-jokes will get laughs from knowing viewers.

Better still, in a change from the teen horror films of the 80s, the cast actually has an opportunity to act! And moviegoers tired of the misogynist overtones of most fright flicks will be glad to see that the females are the most resourceful of the bunch, while the males are either crazy or dead. Campbell is sympathetic as the emotionally abused (but strong-willed) heroine; McGowan is full of attitude and sex appeal, and Drew Barrymore's small but pivotal role sets the edgy tone for the entire film. In the adult roles, Henry Winkler ditches his Fonzie stereotype to play the definitely *uncool* principal, and Linda Blair can be seen briefly as a reporter. But above all, this is Craven's show. He knows how to ladle on the thrills, get an audience to jump, or pull back for a laugh. It's a tightrope act that succeeds, thanks to a deft script, a solid cast, and a refreshing respect for the subject matter. *(Graphic violence, sexual situations, profanity.)* — S.P.

d, Wes Craven; p, Cary Woods, Cathy Konrad; exec p, Bob Weinstein, Harvey Weinstein, Marianne Maddalena; assoc p, Nicholas C. Mastandrea; co-p, Dixie J. Capp; w, Kevin Williamson; ph, Mark Irwin; ed, Patrick Lussier; m, Marco Beltrami; prod d, Bruce Alan Miller; art d, David Lubin; set d, Michele Poulik; sound, Richard Goodman; fx, Frank Ceglia, Kamar Bitar; cos, Mathew Clayton Hooey, Gary J. Saldutti; makeup, Carol Schwartz; stunts, Tony Cecere

Horror **(PR: C MPAA: R)**

SCREAMERS ★★
(Canada) 107m Allegro Films ~ Triumph Releasing c

Peter Weller *(Hendricksson)*; Roy Dupuis *(Becker)*; Jennifer Rubin *(Jessica)*; Andy Lauer *(Ace)*; Charles Powell *(Ross)*; Ron White *(Elbarak)*; Michael Caloz *(David)*; Liliana Komorowska *(Landowska)*; Jason Cavalier *(Leone)*; Leni Parker *(Corporal McDonald)*; Sylvain Masse *(NEB Soldier)*; Bruce Boa *(Secretary Green)*; Tom Berry *(Technician)*; Henry Ramer *(Narration)*

Though the title of this Canadian-made science-fiction shocker accurately refers to both its human and non-human characters, it's not likely to describe anyone watching it.

In the late 21st century, a war is raging between rebel Alliance forces and the New Economic Bloc (NEB). On the desolate mining planet Sirius 4B, a messenger is killed outside an Alliance bunker by screamers—man-made, underground burrowing, robotic weapons that have become autonomous and self-replicating. Alliance commander Joseph Hendricksson (Peter Weller) discovers that the messenger was carrying an NEB invitation for peace negotiations; soon thereafter, a troop transport ship crashes nearby, with only soldier, Ace (Andy Lauer), left alive. He joins Hendricksson in setting out for a nearby NEB base.

Along the way, they encounter an orphaned young boy, David (Michael Caloz), and allow him to tag along.

At the NEB base, Hendricksson and Ace discover only a few survivors: soldiers Becker (Roy Dupuis) and Ross (Charles Powell) and black marketeer Jessica (Jennifer Rubin). David proves to be one of the screamers, which are now able to take human form, and must be destroyed. Tension develops among the group when they realize that any one of them might be a screamer in disguise. When they make it back to the Alliance bunker, they find it overrun with screamer-children. A firefight ensues, and only Hendricksson and Jessica survive; when they make it to a hidden escape craft, Jessica also turns out to be a screamer. Hendricksson destroys her and heads for Earth, not noticing that a teddy bear stowed on board is moving. . .

With a title like SCREAMERS, one might expect that the film would devote a good deal to the conflict between its human characters and the titular creatures. But too much running time is devoted to pat human conflict centered around the usual struggle against callous big business (the NEB here), and the "who-do-you-trust?" tension surrounding the fact that anyone could be a screamer. Both of these elements will be all too familiar to anyone who has seen ALIEN (1979) and the remake of THE THING (1982); indeed, like its monsters, the film seems to have developed the ability to mimic any other movie it needs to in order to keep the plot moving.

Director Christian Duguay does whip up a couple of good action and shock sequences (especially the opening attack scene), and the makeup and physical effects are first-rate. But the movie takes entirely too long to tell its essentially simple story, seeming to end at least two or three times before it really reaches its conclusion (complete with a groan-inducing final shot). The cast is solid, but the characters are all familiar types without the necessary shading, and the plausibility of the screamers themselves is somewhat lacking. It's never explained how they became able to replicate themselves and mutate into human form; having a character simply *say* they can, and act puzzled about it himself, doesn't wash. *(Graphic violence, profanity.)* — M.G.

d, Christian Duguay; p, Tom Berry, Franco Battista; exec p, Charles W. Fries; assoc p, Stefan Wodoslawsky; w, Dan O'Bannon, Miguel Tejada-Flores (based on the short story "Second Variety" by Philip K. Dick); ph, Rodney Gibbons; ed, Yves Langlois; m, Normand Corbeil; prod d, Perri Gorrara; art d, Michael Devine; set d, David Jaquest; sound, Richard Nichol (recordist); fx, Ernest Farino, Richard Ostiguy, Ryal Cosgrove, Cineffects Productions Inc.; casting, Mary Margiotta, Karen Margiotta, Lucie Robitaille; makeup, Roxy D'Alonzo, Adrien Morot, Karl Gosselin, Benoit Tisseur, Ronny Gosselin; stunts, Michael Scherer

Science Fiction **(PR: C MPAA: R)**

SEARCH FOR ONE-EYE JIMMY, THE ★½

(U.S.) 82m Orenda Films; Cabin Fever Entertainment ~ Northern Arts Entertainment c

Nick Turturro *(Junior)*; Steve Buscemi *(Ed Hoyt)*; Michael Baldalucco *(Joe Head)*; Ray "Boom Boom" Mancini *(Lefty)*; Holt McCallany *(Les)*; Anne Meara *(Holly Hoyt)*; John Turturro *(Disco Bean)*; Samuel L. Jackson *(Colonel Ron)*; Jennifer Beals *(Ellen)*; Tony Sirico *(The Snake)*; Aida Turturro *(Madame Esther)*; Wayne Maugans *(Tommy Hoyt)*; Pat McNamara *(Harold Hoyt)*; Joe Siravo *(Father Julio)*; Adam LeFevre *(Detective)*; Lodge Kerrigan *(Cameraman)*; Louis Coletta *(Anthony)*; Sam Rockwell *(One-Eye Jimmy)*; Judson Camp *(One-Arm Jimmy)*

A would-be "gritty," "authentic" comedy about colorful Brooklyn street guys, THE SEARCH FOR ONE-EYE JIMMY is a gruesome auto accident of a film, crumpling and crashing in excruciating slow motion. Muddled and befuddled, it lurches between naturalistic comedy of manners and broadly surreal Benny Hill farce.

Les (Holt McCallany) is an expatriate from the seedy Brooklyn neighborhood of Red Hook. He's returned from film school to shoot a documentary about the neighborhood. Hearing that local loser One-Eye Jimmy Hoyt has gone missing, he decides to film Jimmy's chronically unemployed friends, Junior (Nick Turturro), Joe Head (Michael Badalucco) and Lefty (Ray "Boom Boom" Mancini) as they haphazardly search for him. Along the way, Les encounters such zanies as 1970s throwback Disco Bean (John Turturro), 'Nam-vet wacko Colonel Ron (Samuel L. Jackson), and a loan-shark (Tony Sirico) who used to be called The Whale but lost 200 pounds and wants to be called The Snake.

Les brings the missing-persons case to the police, who dutifully make note of it. Jimmy s devastated mother (Anne Meara) prefers putting up signs around the neighborhood and consulting a psychic (Aida Turturro). Junior, a zoot-suited Dominican in an Irish-Italian neighborhood, occasionally steals cars from people he knows, doing it several times to Lefty and once to Les. He also sends a fake ransom note to try and collect $10,000, even though he's a friend of Jimmy's family and knows they'd have to go to a loan shark. For some reason, no one ever presses charges. A haggard Jimmy finally comes home, with the grand revelation he got locked in the basement when the elevator broke down five days ago. The fire door was locked and the super was on vacation. Les, having hoped for something more dramatic, declares his film career over. Sometime later, however, two Hollywood execs love the finished film—which now belongs to Junior and Joe Head, who used some loophole to sue Les.

A vanity production by first-time director-screenwriter Sam Henry Kass—a former playwright and "Seinfeld" sitcom scripter, who stated that he and Nick Turturro put up the $150,000 budget themselves—ONE-EYE JIMMY was shot in Red Hook in about 20 days. The film was copyrighted 1993. Kass has said he based the film on his own real-life neighborhood and events, yet most of the characters are less fondly remembered eccentrics than broad and largely unsympathetic cliches. Mostly, they're either stupid without innocent charm or else arrogant, lying hustlers.

Kass buries a few promising, brief moments of funny dialogue within overlong scenes as plot-point repetitive as the worst TV detective shows. Worst of all, the film's astonishingly inconsistent tone sets one level of relative-reality, then switches blithely to another for the sake of a (usually unfunny) gag, regardless of context. The anticlimactic final scene is so discordant, it might as well be from another movie.

Kass somehow enticed several recognizable names into his effort, including Anne Meara, Jennifer Beals and Steve Buscemi. Photographically, the film looks great. McCallany is magnetic, though he's doing what seems like a Christopher Walken impression throughout, and Badalucco is eerily dead-on as a certain type of fat slacker who still lives with his family. And poor Anne Meara, playing Jimmy's devastated mother, seems caught in the net of an indecisive director who couldn't tell her whether she was to play her part straight or as a broad Edith Bunker type.*(Profanity, adult situations.)* — F.L.

d, Sam Henry Kass; p, Robert Nickson, Lisa Bruce; w, Sam Henry Kass; ph, Chuck Levey, Lodge Kerrigan; ed, Mark Juergens; m, Bill Bloom; prod d, Ray Recht; art d, Mario R. Ventenilla; set d, Mario R. Ventenilla; sound, Rob Taz (mixer), Jay Kessel (design); casting, Marcia Shulman; cos, Joan Fedyszyn; makeup, Jane Dipersio

Comedy **(PR: C MPAA: NR)**

SECRET AGENT, THE
(SEE: JOSEPH CONRAD'S THE SECRET AGENT)

SECRETS & LIES ★★★★½
(U.K.) 142m CiBy 2000; Thin Man Films ~ October Films c

Timothy Spall *(Maurice)*; Phyllis Logan *(Monica)*; Brenda Blethyn *(Cynthia)*; Claire Rushbrook *(Roxanne)*; Marianne Jean-Baptiste *(Hortense)*; Elizabeth Berrington *(Jane)*; Michele Austin *(Dionne)*; Lee Ross *(Paul)*; Lesley Manville *(Social Worker)*; Ron Cook *(Stuart)*; Emma Amos *(Girl with Scar)*; Brian Boyell *(Hortense's Brother)*; Trevor Laird *(Hortense's Brother)*; Clare Perkins *(Hortense's Sister-in-Law)*; Elias Perkins McCook *(Hortense's Nephew)*; June Mitchell *(Senior Optometrist)*; Janice Acquah *(Junior Optician)*; Keeley Flanders *(Girl in Optician's)*; Hannah Davis *(First Bride)*; Terrence Harvey *(First Bride's Father)*; Kate O'Malley *(Second Bride)*; Joe Tucker *(Groom)*; Richard Syms *(Vicar)*; Grant Master *(Best Man)*; Annie Hayes *(Mother in Family Group)*; Jean Ainslie *(Grandmother)*; Daniel Smith *(Teenage Son)*; Lucy Sheen *(Nurse)*; Frances Ruffelle *(Young Mother)*; Felix Manley *(Baby)*; Nitin Chandra Ganatra *(Potential Husband)*; Metin Marlow *(Conjuror)*; Amanda Crossley *(Raunchy Woman)*; Su Eliot *(Raunchy Woman)*; Di Sherlock *(Raunchy Woman)*; Alex Squires *(Triplet)*; Lauren Squires *(Triplet)*; Sade Squires *(Triplet)*; Dominic Curran *(Little Boy)*; Stephen Churchett; David Neilson; Peter Stockbridge; Peter Waddington *(Men in Suits)*; Rachel Lewis *(Graduate)*; Paul Trussell *(Grinning Husband)*; Denise Orita *(Uneasy Woman)*; Margery Withers *(Elderly Lady)*; Theresa Watson *(Daughter)*; Gordon Winter *(Laughing Man)*; Jonathan Coyne *(Fiance)*; Peter Wight *(Father in Family Group)*; Gary McDonald *(Boxer)*; Alison Steadman *(Dog Owner)*; Liz Smith *(Cat Owner)*; Sheila Kelley *(Fertile Mother)*; Angela Curran *(Little Boy's Mother)*; Linda Beckett *(Pinup Housewife)*; Philip Davis *(Man in Suit)*; Wendy Nottingham *(Glum Wife)*; Anthony O'Donnell *(Uneasy Man)*; Ruth Sheen *(Laughing Woman)*; Mia Soteriou *(Fiance)*

Winner of the Palme d'Or at Cannes, Mike Leigh's fascinating slice-of-life drama may seem like a change of pace to those familiar only with NAKED, his best-known film in the US, but it is quite typical of his unique oeuvre.

Maurice (Timothy Spall), a successful commercial photographer, lives in a tastefully decorated suburban house with his slightly snobbish wife, Monica (Phyllis Logan). Though childless, they are fond of Maurice's niece, Roxanne (Claire Rushbrook). Relations are strained between them and Maurice's sister, Cynthia (Brenda Blethyn). Cynthia raised Maurice from a young age after their parents died and feels somewhat resentful of his success. A middle-aged single mother, she works in a factory and lives with Roxanne in a cramped rental house. She feels she has nothing to show for her life, and all of her emotionally desperate efforts to pull people closer to her (particularly the sullen Roxanne) only drive them away.

Maurice visits Cynthia, and they reminisce about their childhoods. Cynthia breaks down in tears, adding to Maurice's discomfort. He tells her that he and Monica would like to have a party for Roxanne's upcoming 21st birthday, and Cynthia agrees to come.

After the death of her adoptive mother, Hortense (Marianne Jean-Baptiste), a young black woman living in London, learns that Cynthia is her birth mother and telephones her. Initially shocked, Cynthia agrees to meet her at a coffeeshop. When they see each other, Cynthia assumes there has been a mistake, until she remembers having had a one-night stand with a black man. As they talk, they begin to develop a rapport, and they part on good terms, agreeing to meet again.

Several weeks later, Cynthia, Roxanne and her boyfriend, Paul (Lee Ross), arrive at Maurice's house for Roxanne's party. Having been invited by Cynthia, who asked her brother if she could invite "a friend from work" to the party, Hortense arrives a little later. Upset when Maurice and Monica give Roxanne an extravagant check as a gift, Cynthia reveals that Hortense is her daughter. This revelation leads everyone in the family to discuss the matters that have been troubling them, including Monica's inability to have children. The family becomes closer as a result of airing their problems, and Roxanne and Hortense agree to accept each other as sisters.

On paper, the plot of a Mike Leigh film often sounds like the stuff of TV soap opera, and that's especially true in the case of SECRETS AND LIES. But where soaps breed familiarity over time, Leigh and his actors hone characters so sharply that viewers become as familiar with them over the running time of a film as they would with people they have known for years.

This has everything to do with Leigh's manner of working. Contrary to what is often reported, his actors do not improvise their parts on camera. Leigh begins with a general notion of issues he wants to address. Assembling the actors, he discusses with each a list of people the actor knows in real life. From those discussions, they choose a person who will be the basis for a character the actor will develop. Several months of improvisations follow, in which Leigh sends the actors out into the city and instructs them to act as their character would. He arranges for actors to intersect but doesn't provide information about the other. From observing these improvisations, Leigh creates a tight script that is as true as possible to his characters, because those "characters" have had a hand in their own creation.

It helps to understand Leigh's method, because it illustrates how deceptive the low-key nature of his films can be. Leigh's films are staged so simply, not because of laziness or indifference, but because he has in every case found the single best point from which to view the proceedings. And, of course, he has perfect faith that his performers know what they're doing. SECRETS AND LIES contains several long scenes shot in single takes that would be impossible for actors working under standard filming conditions: the long take of Cynthia and Hortense at their first meeting is particularly astonishing. This scene alone is enough to merit the Best Actress Award Blethyn received at Cannes, as well as the Oscar nominations for both her and Jean-Baptiste. SECRETS AND LIES may be a trifle long, but there isn't a moment in it that needs to be cut. *(Adult situations, profanity.)* — M.F.

d, Mike Leigh; p, Simon Channing-Williams; w, Mike Leigh; ph, Dick Pope; ed, John Gregory; m, Andrew Dickson; prod d, Alison Chitty, Georgina Lowe; sound, George Richards (recordist); casting, Stern and Parriss; cos, Maria Price; makeup, Christine Blundeli

AAN Best Picture; AAN Best Actress: Brenda Blethyn; *AAN Best Supporting Actress:* Marianne Jean-Baptiste; *AAN Best Director:* Mike Leigh; *AAN Best Original Screenplay:* Mike Leigh

Drama **(PR: C MPAA: R)**

SECTION, THE
(SEE: OUTPOST, THE)

SGT. BILKO ★½
(U.S.) 94m Imagine Films Entertainment ~ Universal c

Steve Martin *(Master Sgt. Ernest G. Bilko)*; Dan Aykroyd *(Colonel Hall)*; Phil Hartman *(Major Thorn)*; Glenne Headly *(Rita Robbins)*; Daryl Mitchell *(Wally Holbrook)*; Max Casella *(Dino Paparelli)*; Eric Edwards *(Duane Doberman)*; Dan Ferro *(Tony Morales)*; John Marshall Jones *(Sgt. Henshaw)*; Brian Leckner *(Sam Fender)*; John Ortiz *(Luis Clemente)*; Pamela Segall *(Sgt. Raquel Barbella)*; Mitchell Whitfield *(Mickey Zimmerman)*; Austin Pendleton *(Major Ebersole)*; Chris Rock *(Lt. Oster)*; Catherine Silvers *(Lt. Monday)*; Steve Park *(Captain Moon)*; Debra Jo Rupp *(Mrs. Hall)*; Richard Herd *(General Tennyson)*; Steve Kehela *(Master Sergeant Sowicki)*; Dale Dye *(First Engineer)*; Charles Stevenson *(Minister)*; Rance Howard *(Mr. Robbins)*; Christopher Paul Hart *(Nelson)*; Steph Benseman *(Bartender)*; Sammy Micco *(Blackjack Dealer)*; Ursula Burton *(Assistant Casino Manager)*; Carol Rosenthal *(G.H.Q. Corporal)*; Henry Hayashi *(First Technician)*; Anthony Monroy-Marquez *(Schoolboy Actor)*; Lauren Kate Weinger *(Schoolgirl Actress)*; Tami-Adrian George *(Janet)*; Travis Tritt *(Himself)*; Reno Wilson *(Radio Disc Jockey)*; Sally Ann Brooks *(Second Technician)*; Derek Basco *(Soldier)*; Carmela Rappazo *(Telephone Operator)*; Dwayne Chattman *(1st Soldier)*; Clifton Gonzalez *(2nd Soldier)*; Andrea Robinson *(First Vegas Woman)*; Lynn Tulaine *(Second Vegas Woman)*; Cheryl Francis Harrington *(Corporal #2)*; Michael D. Starks *(Boxing Trainer)*; David E. Cousin *(Craps Dealer)*; Allan Bragg *(D.O.D. Dignitary)*; Frank Romano *(Pit Boss)*; Russell Bobbitt *(Valet Parker)*

The American service comedy is alive—but not very well—in SGT. BILKO, a pointless update of the classic 1950s Phil Silvers sitcom about a conniving sergeant and his various money-making schemes.

Master Sgt. Ernie Bilko (Steve Martin) runs the motor pool at Fort Baxter in Kansas. He also runs a gambling house on the premises and has numerous other enterprises designed to separate the soldiers from their money. His superior, Colonel Hall (Dan Aykroyd), is an affable buffoon who's oblivious to Bilko's chicanery.

Bilko stands up his long-suffering fiancee Rita (Glenne Headly) at the altar for the umpteenth time, and tells his platoon a story about how he was responsible years before for framing a lieutenant named Thorn and getting him transferred to Greenland. The Pentagon sends (now) Major Thorn (Phil Hartman) to Fort Baxter to observe a demonstration of a new, experimental $70 million hover-tank. The demonstration is a disaster, and Thorn tells Hall the base may have to be closed. As he's about to leave, Thorn learns that Bilko is assigned to the base and decides to stay so he can get his revenge.

Thorn brings in auditors to check the books for pilfering, but they can't find anything to pin on Bilko, so he decides to try and woo Rita away from the sergeant. While Bilko and his platoon are away on maneuvers for the weekend, Thorn breaks into Bilko's computer and enters fake entries about diverting funds from the hover-tank project. He takes the "evidence" to Col. Hall who authorizes that Bilko be transferred to Greenland. Bilko convinces Hall to let him stay if he can get the hover-tank to work properly and put on a big show for the army brass. Thorn sabotages the tank to ensure it won't function, but Bilko rigs a phony demonstration and it fools everyone. An enraged Thorn tells the Pentagon officials that he knows the demo was a fake, since he personally sabotaged the tank. Naturally, he's transferred back to Greenland. Bilko finally shows up for his wedding with Rita, but this time, she's an hour late.

Although the Phil Silvers TV series is generally known as "Sgt. Bilko," that is only what it was titled for syndicated reruns. Its first title was "You'll Never Get Rich," which was changed after a few weeks to "The Phil Silvers Show." These two original titles clearly illustrate the major problems of this movie: firstly, Phil Silvers's Bilko was basically a miserable, if eternally hopeful, loser, and his schemes almost always fell apart. Steve Martin's Bilko, however, is a feel-good kind of guy, constantly rolling in money, and having a non-stop party. And secondly, Phil Silvers wasn't just playing Ernie Bilko, he *was* Ernie Bilko, and vice-versa. As funny as he sometimes is, Martin is just doing shtick, just a comic actor playing another character. It's like having Tom Arnold play Ralph Kramden (and as ridiculous as that may sound, it was being planned before the twin bombs of CARPOOL and THE STUPIDS). The point is that Silvers and Bilko are inseparable, just as Charlie Chaplin and the Tramp character were one and the same.

Even with all these problems, the film would still be somewhat tolerable if only the script were funnier or had some originality, but unfortunately it is merely a celebration of cowardice, incompetence, and stupidity. Most of the jokes are scatological, albeit in an inoffensive PG-way, and there's even a feeble "don't-ask-don't-tell" gay impersonation gag. Martin manages to coax some laughs by reverting to his wild-and-crazy-guy persona, but when he tries to imitate Silvers's trademark of incoherently barking orders to his troops, he only conjures up memories of the original. Among the rest of the cast, only Headly and Hartman give real performances, while Aykroyd does an embarrassing imitation of Paul Ford, although at least he's now portly enough to resemble him physically. Jonathan Lynn's direction is flat and uninspired, with bright colors and wall-to-wall pop songs in lieu of any real sense of fun or good humor. *(Profanity.)* — M.S.

d, Jonathan Lynn; p, Brian Grazer; co-p, Mary McLaglen; w, Andy Breckman (based on the TV series created by Nat Hiken); ph, Peter Sova; ed, Tony Lombardo; m, Alan Silvestri; prod d, Lawrence G. Paull; art d, Bruce Crone; set d, Rick Simpson; sound, Robert Anderson Jr.; fx, Steve Galich, Patrick McClung, Digital Domain; casting, Jane Jenkins, Janet Hirshenson; cos, Susan Becker; makeup, Gerald Quist; stunts, Ernie Orsatti

Comedy **(PR: C MPAA: PG)**

SGT. KABUKIMAN N.Y.P.D. ★

(U.S./Japan) 104m K-M Productions; Gaga Communications; Namco Ltd.; Troma, Inc. ~ Troma, Inc. c

Rick Gianasi *(Harry Griswold/Sgt. Kabukiman)*; Susan Byun *(Lotus)*; Bill Weeden *(Reginald Stuart)*; Thomas Crnkovich *(Rembrandt)*; Larry Robinson *(Reverend Snipes)*; Noble Lee Lester *(Captain Bender)*; Brick Bronsky *(Jughead)*; Pamela Alster *(Connie LaRosa)*; Shaler McClure *(Felicia)*; Jeff Wineshmutz *(Hernandez)*; Joe Fleishaker *(Josephs)*; Fumio Furuya *(Sato)*; Masahiro Yamaguchi *(Ichiro)*; Traci Mann *(Ichiro's Wife)*; The Blonde Fox *(Waitress)*; Herbert Becker *(Mr. Goldberg)*; Andrew Osborne *(Ford)*; Rick Collins *(Interviewer)*; Michael Deeg; David Floyd; Marcelo Giscome; Paul Hiatt; Danny Provenzano II; Joseph Scerri *(Snipe's Gang)*; Brian Bilcher; Richard DeMaree; John Graziano; Todd Kimmell; William Mann; Nick Palmer; Richard Slater *(Stuart's Evil Men)*; Andrew Michael Wolk *(Arthur)*; Bruce Barney *(Yuppie)*; John Nathan *(Lawyer #1)*; Michael Artura *(Lawyer #2)*; Susu Dopman *(Mona)*; Ann-Mari Jacobsen *(Amanda)*; Patricia Kaufman *(Birthday Mom)*; Sarah Uffelman *(Mom #2)*; Lily Hayes Kaufman *(Party Kid)*; Sean O'Neill *(Stuart's Male Secretary)*; Jane Kober *(Prissy Lady in Theater)*; Robert Pemberton *(Man in Big Red Hat)*; James Van Vladricken *(Kid on Tricycle)*; Anthony Falco *(Truck Driver)*; Phil Rivo *(Drunk)*; Fred Fredrickson *(Homeless Man)*; Madelin Correa *(Woman in Car)*; Jerry Meko *(Large Woman in Precinct)*; Burt Wright *(Gentleman in Pre-*

cinct); Tony Messina *(Plainclothesman)*; Mary Linn Miller *(Detective)*; Charlotte Kaufman *(Ichiro's Child)*; Lisbeth Kaufman *(Ichiro's Child)*; Jeffrey W. Sass *(Doctor)*; Nevada Belle *(Hospital Administrator)*; Judy Prianti *(Nurse #1)*; Diane Fischetti *(Nurse #2)*; Ann Phuvan *(Sato's Assistant)*; Maria Shibaji *(Sato's Assistant)*; Steve Ferguson *(Car Thief)*; Alan Rhea *(Purse Snatcher)*; Joy Palevsky *(Female Reporter)*; Gordon Bryan *(Pimp)*; Andrea "Andi" Giordano *(Pimp's Woman)*; Pattie Meyer *(Pimp's Woman)*; Stanley L. Kaufman Sr. *(Distinguished Man in Park)*; Robert Volpe II *(Big Man Holding Little Boy)*; Zachary Daniel Sass *(Toddler in Arms)*; Paul McCarthy *(Hairdresser)*; Maria Fridmanovich *(Kabuki Cut Woman)*; Mario Joyner *(Hole in the Head Thug)*; Michael O'Pelka *(Acid Faced Thug)*; Judy Fuhrer *(Beautiful Woman in Times Square)*; Aubu *(Himself)*; Mac Sutherland *(Dog Walker)*; Daniel Boone *(Toyota)*

SGT. KABUKIMAN NYPD is a political film. Yes, the latest offering from the Troma Team (THE TOXIC AVENGER) cinematically mirrors the philosophy of right-wing radio talk-show hosts. Hence, only fans of venom-spewing Rush Limbaugh will find humor in this sad "creation."

SGT. KABUKIMAN NYPD begins when Police Capt. Dick Bender (Noble Lee Lester) assigns Sgt. Harry Griswold (Rick Gianasi) to investigate the brutal slaying of a famous Japanese Kabuki actor. Bender questions Griswold's skill, but Griswold tries to make up in tenacity and hard work what he lacks in finesse. Through a bizarre accident during his hunt for the killer, Griswold is transformed into Sergeant Kabukiman, a Japanese hero possessing many great magical powers.

As Kabukiman, Griswold wields a strange array of weapons against local criminals, including projectile parasols, suffocating sushi rolls, fatal flying footwear, and lethal chopsticks. Kabukiman can also fly, but Griswold lacks a confident understanding of his new abilities. Lotus (Susan Byun), a young Japanese woman, volunteers to train Kabukiman so that he can properly fight against Reginald Stuart (Bill Weeden), a wealthy industrialist who plots to take over the city with a fearsome crime wave.

According to Lotus, Kabukiman has only a limited amount of time to conquer Stuart. Meanwhile, Bender and the other precinct officers look skeptically at Griswold's Kabukiman caper. But with Lotus's help and growing love, Kabukiman triumphs over Stuart and his thugs and solves the murder of the Kabuki actor.

In recent years, Troma founder and KABUKIMAN cowriter-producer-director Lloyd Kaufman has been bidding for artistic respectability. By maneuvering his low-budget exploitation pictures into such prestige outfits as the British Film Institute, the American Film Institute, and (with KABUKIMAN) New York's Film Forum, Kaufman has been craftily laying the groundwork for a re-interpretation of his work. Presumably, he would like to be known as a postmodern auteur who mixes high and low art forms and genres, explores multiple (multicultural) points of view, and comments on the film form itself.

But if these are Kaufman's aims, he is an auteur manque: despite many opportunities in KABUKIMAN, there is little reflexive humor (one wink into the camera by our hero) and very few direct references to the works the film is supposedly spoofing (e.g., "NYPD Blue," samurai movies, "Madame Butterfly"). Instead of turning stereotypes on their heads, KABUKIMAN intensifies negative perceptions about Asians and blacks, and an episode involving the gang rape of the female officer is an unpleasant addition to a film that purports to be a comedy.

Thus, SGT. KABUKIMAN NYPD not only produces an all-around assault on the senses, but is so filled with bad karma, one may well worry about the fate of Lloyd Kaufman and his Troma empire. *(Violence, nudity, sexual situations, adult situations, substance abuse, extreme profanity.)* — E.M.

d, Lloyd Kaufman, Michael Herz; p, Lloyd Kaufman, Michael Herz; exec p, Masaya Nakamura, Tetsu Fujimura; assoc p, David Greenspan, Andrew Wolk; w, Lloyd Kaufman, Andrew Osborne, Jeffrey W. Sass; ph, Bob Williams; ed, Ian Slater, Peter Novak; stunts, Edgard Mourino

Comedy/Crime/Fantasy (PR: O MPAA: NR)

SERIAL KILLER ★★

(Canada) 91m Image Organization; Inferno Productions ~ Republic Pictures Home Video c

Kim Delaney *(Selby Younger)*; Gary Hudson *(Cole Grayson)*; Tobin Bell *(William Lucian Morrano)*; Pam Grier *(Capt. Maggie Davis)*; Marco Rodriguez *(Manny Ramirez)*; Joel Polis *(Jack Blund)*; Lyman Ward *(Dr. Harvard Jankowitz)*; Cyndi Pass *(Marianne Capriato)*; Andrew Prine *(Perry Jones)*; Leonard Termo *(Loft Manager)*; Kimberly Faith Jones *(Lisa)*; Anne Bellamy *(Nana Younger)*; Jean Pflieger *(Selby's Neighbor)*; Jodi Karger *(Jenny Woods)*; Gaby Nimier *(Female Victim)*; Michael Briggs *(SWAT Commander)*

SERIAL KILLER is a mechanical, barely competent thriller from Canadian director Pierre David (SCANNER COP) that is saved by an effectively repulsive performance by Tobin Bell as a psycho who plays a cat-and-mouse game with an FBI psychologist.

A serial killer is stalking Los Angeles. FBI Special Agent Selby Younger (Kim Delaney), who is part of the "Mindwalker" unit, is able to deduce that the killer is a taxidermist named William Lucian Morrano (Tobin Bell). Morrano goes to Younger's apartment and is about to kill her when he is shot by her detective-boyfriend, Cole Grayson (Gary Hudson).

Two years later, Morrano is taking part in an experimental cancer treatment in jail, and is able to escape from the hospital. He starts to taunt Younger and Grayson with phone calls, leaving a trail of corpses for them to discover, including a woman whose eyeballs he cut out. Morrano also finds a tabloid TV reporter who did a negative story about him and severs his vocal chords.

After he shoots a police colleague of Younger's and kidnaps a young girl she knows, Younger agrees to meet Morrano to get him to stop. He tells her that he's dying and wants her to have his child so that his legacy will live on. He tries to force her into a car, but she manages to drive away. The cops chase him, but he escapes.

Younger and Grayson then conceive an elaborate plan to trap Morrano by having Younger fake her own suicide, then letting him see that she's actually alive in order to lure him back to the house to kill her. The plan works and Morrano breaks into her house, but Grayson is waiting and kills him.

Set in L.A., but shot mostly in Canada, SERIAL KILLER has the flat, sterile look of a TV-movie and is made with no more imagination or originality than absolutely necessary. It's also a surprisingly tame entry in the "cop-catches-psycho-killer-by-thinking-like-him" genre, with most of the violence taking place off-screen. Instead, the overly talky script is rife with facile psychology and perfunctory allusions to PSYCHO (1960)—Morrano kills his abusive mother and loves to stuff animals.

The one saving grace is the albino-like Bell, who is truly creepy as Morrano—possibly the most convincing screen sicko since Andy Robinson in DIRTY HARRY (1971)—but the rest of the cast sleepwalks through their parts. And Pam Grier is wasted in a brief bit as the standard gruff police captain. *(Violence, profanity.)* — M.S.

d, Pierre David; p, Pierre David; assoc p, Lawrence Goebel, Meyer Shwarzstein; co-p, Noel A. Zantisch, Martin Kitrosser; w, Mark Sevi; ph, Thomas Jewett; ed, Julian Semilian; m, Louis Febre; prod d, W. Brooke Wheeler; sound, Daniel D. Monahan; fx, Ted Coplan, Ultimate Effects; casting, Cathy Henderson; cos, Damita J. Roldan; makeup, Becky Cotton

Thriller **(PR: O MPAA: R)**

SERPENT'S LAIR ★
(U.S.) 92m Castel Films ~ Republic Pictures Home Video c

Jeff Fahey *(Tom Bennett)*; Lisa B. *(Lillith)*; Heather Medway *(Alex Bennett)*; Patrick Bauchau *(Sam)*; Anthony Palermo *(Mario)*; Kathleen Noone *(Betty)*; Jack Kehler *(Occult Expert)*; Taylor Nichols *(Paul Douglas)*; Stuart Blatt *(Cop)*; Valentin Popescu *(Bob, the Complaining Neighbor)*

The Romanian crew of SERPENT'S LAIR might have gotten a thrill out of filming this bad variation on Roman Polanski's ROSEMARY'S BABY, but viewers of the film won't reciprocate.

Tom Burnett (Jeff Fahey) and his wife Alex (Heather Medway), move into a new apartment. They are heartily welcomed by their neighbor Sam (Patrick Bauchau), an effete and suspiciously cheery gentleman. The couple adopts—or, rather, are adopted by—a black cat that is *very* affectionate with Tom but seems to have it in for Alex. The cat sends Alex on an "accidental" trip down the stairs. While Alex is in the hospital, Lillith (Lisa B.), the sexpot sister of the previous tenant (who had committed suicide), arrives to pack up her brother's library of the occult. Lillith begins a campaign of seduction that Tom initially resists. When Tom finally succumbs, he and Lillith embark on a passionate and relentless affair. By Lillith's arrangement, Alex finds out and leaves her husband. Lillith reveals herself to be an ancient Egyptian cat goddess and legendary Scottish witch who drives men to madness with her insatiable lust, saps their souls, and uses them to seed her demon spawn. Sam, to whom Alex has turned for consolation, is actually Satan. When Tom gets a breather from his wild relations with Lillith, he does some reading and discovers the truth. He has sex with Lillith, and when she gets distracted, he sets her on fire.

For everyone who associates the name "Lillith" with the pale, icy, de-sexed Dr. Sternin-Crane from the television series "Cheers," SERPENT'S LAIR might change that view. Otherwise, this tepid witch's brew—a mixture of Gothic trappings, brain-dead suspense, and cable-ready eroticism—serves no purpose. To its slim credit, SERPENT'S LAIR does feature fluid direction by Jeffrey Reiner and good production values by direct-to-video standards. *(Violence, nudity, sexual situations, profanity.)* — P.R.

d, Jeffrey Reiner; p, Vlad Paunescu; assoc p, Marc Rosenberg; co-p, Harriet Brown; w, Marc Rosenberg; ph, Feliks Parnell; ed, Virginia Katz; m, Vinny Golia; prod d, Stuart Blatt

Horror/Thriller **(PR: C MPAA: R)**

SET IT OFF ★★½
(U.S.) 126m Peak Production; New Line ~ New Line c

Jada Pinkett *(Stony)*; Queen Latifah *(Cleo)*; Vivica A. Fox *(Frankie)*; Kimberly Elise *(Tisean)*; John C. McGinley *(Detective Strode)*; Blair Underwood *(Keith)*; Vincent Baum; Van Baum *(Jajuan)*; Chaz Lamar Shepard *(Stevie)*; Thom Byrd *(Luther)*; Charlie Robinson *(Nate)*; Ella Joyce *(Detective Waller)*; Anna Maria Horsford *(Ms. Wells)*; Samantha MacLachlan *(Ursuala)*; WC *(Lorenz)*; Lawrence Calhoun Jr. *(Darnell)*; Edmond Schaff *(Mr. Zachery)*; Natalie Desselle *(Tanika)*; Dr. Dre *(Black Sam)*; Bruce Williams *(Bruce)*; Gordon Embry *(Doctor)*; Charles Walker *(Captain Fredricks)*; Geoff Callan *(Nigel)*; Roseanna Iversen *(Patrice)*; Jeris Poindexter *(Pete Rodney)*; Tamara Clatterbuck *(Luther's Girlfriend)*; Tonia Rowe *(Waitress)*; Big Daddy Wayne *(B.B.)*; Mark Thompson *(TV Anchor)*; Darryl Gibson *(Bundy)*; Twain Tyler *(Detective)*; Walter Robles *(Homeless Man)*; George Fisher *(Cop)*; Brantley Bush *(Bank Customer)*

A formula caper film, SET IT OFF offers the novelty of a quartet of young black working-class girls from South Central L.A. who turn to bank robbing when times get tough. Although the characters are well played, their contrived motivations for turning to crime and the overly flamboyant action scenes make for an uneven mix of social drama and exploitation film.

Bank teller Frankie Scott (Vivica A. Fox) is fired from her job and joins three friends in working for a late-night cleaning service. Complaining about the work, she suggests in jest that they rob a bank. Cleo (Queen Latifah), a hard-drinking, tough-talking lesbian and the only one in the group with a criminal record, is seriously interested. Both Stony (Jada Pinkett), a young woman trying to put her brother through college, and Tisean (Kimberly Elise), a single mother, dismiss the notion out of hand.

Events take a turn for the worse when Stony's brother, Stevie (Chaz Lamar Shepard), is killed by police in a case of mistaken identity, and Tisean's son is taken from her by Child Protective Services after he accidentally swallows cleaning fluid at the girls' workplace.

Frankie insists that, with her knowledge of banks, they can plan a foolproof job, and she and Cleo convince the other two that they can get out of South Central for good with enough cash. Stony is sent to case Downtown Federal, where she catches the eye of Keith (Blair Underwood), a handsome, well-educated bank manager who gives her his phone number. They soon begin dating.

The four girls execute their first bank job wearing wigs and sunglasses and make off with $12,000. A second robbery nets them $300,000, enough for them to leave L.A. They hide the loot inside an air vent in the cleaning office. They decide to wait three days before leaving town, until after Tisean's court date to get her child back. Meanwhile, Detective Strode (John C. McGinley) and his female partner (Ella Joyce) doggedly pursue all leads and identify Stony, Frankie and Cleo as suspects.

Learning that their boss, Luther (Thom Byrd), has fled with the stolen money, the girls enlist the aid of Black Sam (Dr. Dre), a local gang leader, to track Luther down to a seedy motel. When Luther pulls a gun on Cleo, Tisean shoots and kills him. But they are unable to find the money.

The girls plan one last bank job—at Downtown Federal, where Keith works. In order to get Keith out of the bank during the robbery, Stony calls him and tells him to meet her. Strode and his partner interrupt the robbery and get the drop on all four girls. In the ensuing confrontation, a bank guard fires and wounds Tisean and is then shot by Stony. The girls flee with the money and manage to elude the police for several hours. Before the night is over, Tisean dies from her wounds, and Cleo and Frankie are both killed by police bullets in separate incidents. Stony manages to get on a bus to Mexico and freedom. She calls Keith and thanks him.

SET IT OFF offers four intriguing young black female characters, a rare grouping in any Hollywood movie (and the first of its type to appear since the success of 1995's WAITING TO EXHALE). Three of the group constitute the hottest young black female actresses of the day, Jada Pinkett (THE NUTTY PROFESSOR), Vivica A. Fox (INDEPENDENCE DAY), and rapper-sitcom star Queen Latifah ("Living Single"). Unfortunately, the only way Hollywood knows how to bring such characters to the screen is to make them gun-toting, foul-mouthed criminals.

But the film is fast-paced and well-acted. The director, F. Gary Gray, who previously directed the rap comedy FRIDAY (1995), makes imaginative use of the familiar, sprawling L.A. metropolis, setting the city's black ghetto firmly in the economically depressed post-industrial landscape.

Still, the film leaves a foul taste and is simply an exploitation film dressed up with an expedient social conscience. It touches on the issue of black women's rage and then only exploits it to make another violent melodrama. *(Violence, sexual situations, profanity.)* — B.C.

d, F. Gary Gray; p, Dale Pollock, Oren Koules; exec p, Mary Parent, F. Gary Gray; assoc p, Robert J. Degus; co-p, Takashi Bufford, Allen Alsobrook; w, Kate Lanier, Takashi Bufford (from a story by Takashi Bufford); ph, Marc Reshovsky; ed, John Carter; m, Christopher Young; prod d, Robb Wilson King; set d, Lance Lombardo; sound, Richard Lightstone (mixer), Ann Scibelli (designer); fx, Tom Bellissimo; casting, Robi Reed-Humes; cos, Sylvia Vega-Vasquez; makeup, Rea Ann Silva, Thomas E. Surprenant, Blake Shepard; stunts, Bob Minor

Crime/Action/Thriller **(PR: C MPAA: R)**

SHADOW OF ANGELS ★★★

(Switzerland) 103m Albatros Produktion ~ Water Bearer Films c
(SCHATTEN DER ENGEL)

Ingrid Caven *(Lily Brest)*; Rainer Werner Fassbinder *(Raoul)*; Klaus Loewitsch *(The Broker)*; Annemarie Duringer *(Mrs. Muller)*; Adrian Hoven *(Mr. Muller)*; Boy Gobert *(Chief of Police)*; Ulli Lommel *(Little Lord)*; Jean-Claude Dreyfus *(Dwarf (Zwerg))*; Irm Hermann *(Emma)*; Debria Kalpatru *(Marie-Antoinette)*; Hans Gratzer *(Oscar)*; Peter Chatel *(Thomas)*; Ila Von Hasperg *(Violet)*; Christine Jirku *(Tau)*; Alexander Allerson *(Jim)*; Harry Baer *(Hellfritz)*

Daniel Schmid's elegantly directed stroll through the lower depths is indelibly stamped by the personality of his co-screenwriter, Rainer Werner Fassbinder (who adapted his own controversial play, *Garbage, the City, and Death*). SHADOW OF ANGELS has clear connections to Fassbinder's earlier, more theatrically-stylized, films.

Warmed in Germany's chilly night air only by the companionship of other whores, consumptive streetwalker Lily Brest (Ingrid Caven) fails to catch the eye of most of the lustful johns passing her by. Primed by beatings from her kept lover Raoul (Rainer Werner Fassbinder), Lily seems headed for an early grave. One evening, the disenchanted hooker captures the fancy of The Broker (Klaus Loewitsch), a powerful real estate developer who trusts no one except his bodyguard associates Little Lord (Ulli Lommel) and Dwarf (Jean-Claude Dreyfuss). Finding Lily's self-destructiveness alluring, The Broker transforms her into his glamorous nightclub accessory.

Lily's upward mobility challenges Raoul's concept of his manhood and ruins their relationship. Simultaneously, The Broker spitefully throws Lily before her father, Herr Muller (Adrian Hoven), a drag performer who was once Lily's incestuous lover. Pining for Raoul, whose latent bisexuality surfaces and nets him a vicious beating, Lily convinces The Broker to end her misery by strangling her to death. This mercy killing by the town's wealthiest benefactor is overlooked by police until power-hungry Little Lord snitches on his employer. Intent on allowing the town's money-greased machinery to continue grinding, the police toss Little Lord out the window and pin Lily's murder on expendable Raoul instead.

It may be an exercise in futility to try to determine whose authorship SHADOW OF ANGELS bears more strongly—that of director Schmid or his co-screenwriter Fassbinder. Together, they flesh out a bleak universe of human commodities whose destinies are predetermined by money, an asset viewed as the 20th century equivalent of fate. But the obvious symbols Fassbinder and Schmid brandish in this polemic against post-WWII Germany can't undercut the searing intensity of the underlying melodrama. While the film picks at the scabs of social diseases left over from WWII (such as anti-Semitism), it succeeds as a redemptive tragedy rather than as an overly schematized diatribe. Although some literary flights of fancy taken in the dialogue come off as bad poetry, other stilted turns of phrase work eloquently and contribute to the film's stylized air. If Lily emerges tellingly as a symbol of Germany's post-WWII malaise, it's not entirely clear what the other characters represent. No matter; the downward spiral of Lily's life holds the viewer rapt even when Fassbinder and Schmid's heavy-handed social criticism weighs a ton.

Flagrantly disregarding Cinema School 101 rules, director Schmid poses his actors in theatrical tableaux (reminiscent of such Fassbinder films as THE BITTER TEARS OF PETRA VON KANT). By creating an environment of entrapment within the frame (through moving the characters from foreground to background and vice versa), Schmid manipulates his mise-en-scene without relying on cinematic movement through editing. Using theater-derived visual techniques on screen as formally as the traditions of Greek tragedy recycled by Sophocles, he creates a fiercely hopeless landscape of the soul. This striking film views pity as a luxury in Germany, where paying for the sins of the father parallels the damnation of Lily Brest, set in motion by childhood sexual abuse.

In SHADOW OF ANGELS, Germany's history repeats itself so cruelly that no punishment in any afterlife could begin to compare with it. *(Graphic violence, sexual situations, adult situations, substance abuse, extreme profanity.)* — R.P.

d, Daniel Schmid; p, Michael Fengler, Jordan Bojilov, Eric Franck; w, Rainer Werner Fassbinder, Daniel Schmid (based on the play *Der Mull die Stadt und der Tod oder Frankenstein am Main* by Rainer Werner Fassbinder); ph, Renato Berta; ed, Ila Von Hasperg; m, Peer Raben, Gottfried Huensberg; prod d, Raul Giminez; sound, Gunther Kortwich

Drama/Political **(PR: O MPAA: NR)**

SHADOW WARRIORS ★★

(U.S.) 80m S.A.K. Entertainment ~ New Horizons Home Video c

Terry O'Quinn *(Dr. Connors)*; Evan Lurie *(TS4)*; Russ Tertyask *(TS3)*; Timothy Patrick Cavanaugh *(Barkeley)*; Ashley Anne Graham *(Natalie)*

SHADOW WARRIORS is a poor man's TERMINATOR. The premise sparks interest: high-tech bodyguards are created from human remains. But in spite of this offbeat starting-point and relatively high production values, the film tells its story with about as much passion and insight as a cheap computer program.

Dr. Connors (Terry O'Quinn), a greedy personal security expert, sells computerized bodyguards who are created from the corpses of humans. Although Security Council Head Barkeley (Timothy Patrick Cavanaugh) keeps a watchful eye on the clearly self-serving doctor, Connors is still able to build two high-tech "technosapiens," called TS3 and TS4.

TS4, formerly known as Mikhail, was programmed by a computer savvy doctor named Natalie (Ashley Anne Graham) and resides in the Ukraine. Natalie discovers that TS3 is flawed by Dr. Connor's standards. He maintains traces of human memory, and has begun maniacally stalking and killing brawny human men who appear to be good specimens for future models. Barkeley and Natalie fly to the Ukraine to reprogram him, and for help and protection bring along TS4, formerly known as John Taylor (Evan Lurie), a less savage Technosapien. Barkeley and Natalie soon realize that TS3 has been programmed to kill. . . by Dr. Connors. TS4 tries desperately to stop TS3 from his killing spree.

Throughout his rampages, TS3 shows signs of human kindness. He is protective of old people and children, and keeps having flashbacks to a woman (whose face is unseen) and children playing on a beach. Barkeley starts to realize that Natalie's connection to TS3 is more than mechanical. She finally confesses that she was married to TS3/Mikhail and brought him back in this form to save him. In TS3's final flashback we see that it was Natalie and their children on the beach.

A confused and still violent TS3 kidnaps Natalie. TS3 and TS4 have a knock-down-drag-out fight on a speedboat. The fight ends with TS4 allowing both of them to be blown up by a Security Bomber.

In the epilogue of SHADOW WARRIORS, we find Barkeley and Natalie back in the states programming a new Technosapien ... Dr. Connors.

SHADOW WARRIORS has more potential than true substance. Dr. Connors isn't given much dimension, which is too bad, because O'Quinn makes an attempt to give a rousing and eccentric performance, just as he did in THE STEPFATHER (1987). TS3's flashback sequences are predictable but nonetheless haunting, and probably the best part of the film. Director Lamar Card was clearly influenced by BLADE RUNNER (1983) and the TERMINATOR movies, but does an injustice to the grain of inspiration within the story, and makes a slick predictable action flick instead.— J.D.

d, Lamar Card; p, Nicolas T. Kimaz; exec p, Rachel Assouma; w, Steve A. Finly; ph, M. David Mullen; ed, Daniel Loewenthal; m, Christopher Tyng; prod d, Sal Caplan

Action/Science Fiction/Thriller (PR: C MPAA: R)

SHADOW YOU SOON WILL BE, A ★★

(Argentina) 105m Instituto Nacional de Cinematografia; Tercer Milenio ~ New Yorker Home Video c
(UNA SOMBRA YA PRONTO SERAS)

Miguel Angel Sola *(Engineer Zarate)*; Pepe Soriano *(Coluccini)*; Luis Brandoni *(Barrante)*; Diego Torres *(Boris)*; Gloria Carra *(Rita)*; Eusebio Poncela *(Lem)*; Roberto Carnaghi *(Father Salinas)*; Hernan Gimenez *(Rubio)*; Pedro Segni *(Petiso)*; Alfonzo De Grazia *(Maldonado)*; Marita Ballesteros *(Alicia)*; Juan Jose Ghisalberti *(Hotel Concierge)*; Leandro Regunaga *(Motel Employee)*; Susan Cabrera *(Julia)*; Mario Lozano *(Bar Patron)*; Horacio Nittalo *(Comisario)*; Augusto Larreta *(Captain of Navy)*; Alicia Bruzzo *(Nadia)*

Heavily symbolic and sometimes amazingly precious, A SHADOW YOU SOON WILL BE is a picaresque Fellini-wannabee by eclectic Argentine filmmaker Hector Olivera, whose work embraces everything from A FUNNY, DIRTY LITTLE WAR (1983) to BARBARIAN QUEEN (1985). Talk about versatile! In a playful metaphysical mood here, Olivera explores fate with ponderous whimsy.

Once a successful computer programmer in Italy, penniless Zarate (Miguel Angel Sola) returns to his Argentina homeland, but is unable to assuage his guilt about abandoning his daughter overseas. Hitchhiking, down-on-his-luck Zarate gets a lift from a dissembling circus performer, Coluccini (Pepe Soriano), who claims to be waiting for a partner to accompany him to greener pastures in Bolivia. Next, Zarate makes the acquaintance of mystery man Lem (Eusebio Poncela), an adventurer who solicits his computer expertise at breaking the bank at casinos. After Lem takes off without explanation, Zarate accepts a ride from an oversexed tarot reader, Nadia (Alicia Bruzzo), but Zarate leaves her when Lem reappears. At a rundown motel, Zarate strikes up a friendship with a hippie couple and meets an itinerant laborer claiming to be Coluccini's missing partner.

Incredibly, the distraught motel owner shoots the itinerant laborer during an unrelated lover's spat. When Coluccini arrives, he grieves briefly, before appropriating a map belonging to crooked priest Father Salinas (Robert Carnaghi), who has buried the collection money he has been skimming for years. At an abandoned building, Coluccini faces off against Salinas and his clerical gang, but enterprising Nadia grabs the map and the loot at gunpoint. Hoping to recoup with cardsharking, Zarate and Coluccini botch a gambling scam and narrowly escape from their patsies. After discovering that Lem has killed himself, Zarate bids Coluccini adieu and decides to forge a long-distance relationship with his daughter. The meaning of life, it would seem, lies in taking responsibility for someone else.

Nominated for an Oscar for best foreign film in 1994, A SHADOW YOU SOON WILL BE tweaks the noses of those cruel gods who toy with us mortals. For the most part, Olivera leavens his philosophical ramble with comic touches, but the humor itself isn't exactly featherweight. Initially, the viewer eagerly accompanies forlorn Zarate on his bizarre travels, because one wonders what kind of oddball he'll meet next and if he will actually engineer Lem's casino hoax. Unfortunately, Olivera isn't interested in anything as linear as a casino rip-off, and one gets weary of the traffic jam of eccentrics piling up during the protagonist's journey to self-awareness. Apparently, the normal people in Argentina don't take to the roads. Despite the plethora of Zarate's free-spirited soulmates, Olivera's musings don't carry much dramatic force. In a film that could be called "Waiting for Godot in South America," the hero is redeemed of selfishness by his exposure to raffish vagabonds. By the time Zarate reaches the conclusion of his pilgrimage, viewers may be resentful that Olivera conned them into taking a cinematic head-trip that feels like one long, ever-encircling detour. *(Violence, extreme profanity, sexual situations, adult situations.)* — R.P.

d, Hector Olivera; p, Hector Olivera; exec p, Fernando Ayala; w, Hector Olivera, Osvaldo Soriano (based on the novel by Osvaldo Soriano); ph, Felix Monti; ed, Eduardo Lopez; m, Osvaldo Montes; art d, Emilio Basaldua; sound, Jorge Stavropulos; cos, Margarita Jusid

Drama (PR: C MPAA: NR)

SHAMELESS ★★

(U.K.) 99m Overseas Filmgroup; Moviescreen Entertainment; Moor Street Films ~ BMG c

Elizabeth Hurley *(Antonia Dyer)*; C. Thomas Howell *(Mike Stone)*; Joss Ackland *(Sam Stringer)*; Frederick Treves *(Sir Harry Dyer)*; Andrew Connolly *(Clive Nathan)*; Jeremy Brett *(Tony Vernon-Smith)*; Claire Bloom *(Liz Stringer)*; Chris Adamson *(Max Quinlan)*; Brett Forrest *(Spider)*; David Harewood *(Jessop)*; Louise Delamere *(Sandy)*; Paula Hamilton *(Charlie)*; Marcus Bentley *(Photographer's Assistant)*; Russ Cane *(Flying Eye Reporter)*; Cheryl Doll *(Young Antonia)*; Nicola Duffert *(Diane)*; Alan "Fluff" Freeman *(DJ)*; Ian Henderson *(Surveil-*

lance Detective); Kate Howard *(Melissa Dyer)*; Howard Hughes *(Newsreader)*; Daniel Jenkins *(Junkie)*; Glenn Marks *(Junkie)*; Jason Lake *(Natty)*; Patrick Lichfield *(Himself)*; Julie Nicholson *(Ad Agency Receptionist)*; Hugh Sachs *(Brooks)*; Peter Stockbridge *(Gent #1)*; Herbert Leslie Wright *(Herbie)*

Dedicated to a group of people who apparently died of drug abuse, SHAMELESS is a mixed bag that doesn't have much impact in any area.

The daughter of a rich industrialist, Antonia (Elizabeth Hurley) has taken to heroin in the year since her mother died of a drug overdose. While she makes a token effort at holding down a job, she spends most of her time partying at the house of Tony Vernon-Smith (Jeremy Brett), drug dealer to the "in" crowd.

Another regular at Tony's is Sandy Stringer (Louise Delamere), who fancies herself Tony's girlfriend. She is also having a casual affair with her stepfather, veteran police detective Sam Stringer (Joss Ackland). Stringer is horrified to learn that he is actually Sandy's real father.

Stringer and Antonia meet each other outside Tony's house. Not knowing who he is, Antonia casually admits to having given drugs to Sandy. Stringer attacks Antonia and dumps her into a river in an attempt to make it look like she committed suicide. Recovering, but with no memory of the incident, she and her boyfriend Mike (C. Thomas Howell) go to her family estate in the country.

Afraid that Antonia will identify him, Stringer arranges to have her killed. When the murderers botch the assignment, Stringer tracks Antonia back to London and Tony's house. He finds Tony watching a pornographic film featuring Sandy. He shoots Tony and a woman behind the screen he assumes to be Antonia. But when the screen is removed, the dead woman is Sandy.

The depiction of drug use in the mysteriously named SHAMELESS is rather less horrifying than the average Hollywood film's portrayal of beer use. The worst effect of heroin use on these characters, aside from exacerbating the indolence to which they all seem prone anyway (oh, the travails of being rich and good-looking) is that it brings them in contact with characters not normally found in better social circles. Its social conscience can be measured by a scene in which bike messenger Mike delivers a fix to Antonia, and they follow it with great sex. Any sympathy we might be expected to have for this spoiled little rich girl is lost in Elizabeth Hurley's flat performance.

The plot line involving cop Sam Stringer's efforts to battle drug lords seems to belong to a totally different movie. And even that one doesn't know which way it wants to go, veering between tragic melodrama and Quentin Tarantino-ish excess (both the opening sequence and several scenes of criminal brutality refer clearly but pointlessly to RESERVOIR DOGS). *(Graphic violence, nudity, sexual situations, adult situations, substance abuse, extreme profanity.)* — M.F.

d, Henry Cole; p, Peter Watson-Wood, Nigel Thomas; exec p, Ashley Levett; assoc p, David Marlow; w, Tim Sewell (from a story by Henry Cole); ph, John Peters; ed, Simon Hilton, Lionel Selwyn; m, Barrie Guard; prod d, Tony Stringer; art d, Sonja Klaus; casting, Ros Hubbard, John Hubbard; cos, Lisa Johnson; makeup, Trefor Proud, Tracy Lee

Drama/Thriller **(PR: O MPAA: R)**

SHARON'S SECRET ★★

(U.S.) 91m USA Pictures; Seabourn Productions; MCA Television Entertainment ~ MCA/Universal Home Video c

Mel Harris *(Dr. Laurel O'Connor)*; Alex McArthur *(Frank Bodin)*; Candace Cameron *(Sharon)*; Paul Regina *(Dr. Gordon Davies)*; Gregg Henry *(Detective Thomas McGregor)*; James Pickens Jr. *(District Attorney Julius Ashmore)*; Elaine Kagan *(Dr. Patricia Raines)*; John Chandler *(Stan)*; Al Fann *(Old Sergeant)*; Mark Conlon *(Dr. Chandler)*; Judson Morgan *(Dr. Ainsworth)*; Kevin Dash *(Orderly)*; Tim Bohn *(Officer)*; Jennifer MacWilliams *(Supervising Nurse)*; Patty Toy *(Duty Nurse)*; Adilah Barnes *(Head Nurse)*; Henry Hayashi *(Resident)*; Bill Handy *(Reporter No. 1)*; Juli Donald *(Reporter No. 2)*; Joseph Whipp *(Sergeant)*; James Kirayama-Lem *(Policeman)*; Greg Collins *(Officer No. 1)*; Steven R. Barnett *(Officer No. 2)*; Beau Dremann *(Young Cop)*; Benita Andre *(Waitress)*; Thomas J. Hamilton *(Danny Fisk)*

This mildly engrossing mystery works better as a crime melodrama than as a psychological suspense drama. SHARON'S SECRET maintains suspense by expertly disguising the true identity and motives of the culprit.

During a crime scene investigation of the double homicide of a millionaire couple, their unbalanced daughter, Sharon Hartly (Candace Cameron), viciously attacks a police officer. This makes her the number one suspect.

Laurel O'Connor (Mel Harris), the psychiatrist assigned to her case, feels that there's something too neat about the case. This pits her against those who believe Sharon is guilty, including her superior, Dr. Raines (Elaine Kagan), DA Ashmore (James Pickens Jr.), persuasive police detective Thomas McGregor (Gregg Henry), and Frank Bodin (Alex McArthur), the silky lawyer who handled the Hartly finances and now begins wooing Dr. O'Connor.

Despite the efforts of a shadowy figure to frighten both her and Sharon, the psychiatrist digs deep enough to learn that the late Mrs. Hartly once had an out-of-town abortion. Other clues seem to point to Bodin and then to the the Hartly family handyman who is killed before he can be interrogated.

When Sharon is released from the mental institution, her concerned psychiatrist follows her to the Hartly mansion—and into a raging basement fire. Escaping through a window, Dr. O'Connor sees Sharon shooting the real killer— Detective McGregor. Having helped the Hartlys during a financial impropriety probe, McGregor became Mrs. Hartly's lover. Dismissed when he was no longer of any use, McGregor turned to murderous revenge. He is about to finish off the family when Sharon, though wounded, knocks him into the midst of the burning house.

Mystery fans willing to settle for an attractive placement of red herrings in a suspense buffet may find their appetite satisfied by SHARON'S SECRET. Even though Henry has played two-faced criminals before (BODY DOUBLE), he is so good at appearing wholesomely macho that he fools less discerning armchair detectives again.

Despite solidly professional acting, this cornered-woman thriller lacks visual dexterity, sparkling dialogue, and any semblance of originality.

The titular character is so catatonic (a clever way to get around Cameron's lack of acting skill?) that one never cares about her dilemma. And Harris, a likable but lightweight actress, isn't quite up to the shadings required by the role of the emotionally panicked headshrinker, who bears most of the film's weight.

Artificially sweetened with lots of surprises, this empty calorie diversion eventually sours, due to the deficiencies of its female stars and the transparency of its mystery formulas. *(Violence, profanity, adult situations, substance abuse.)* — R.P.

d, Michael Scott; p, Barry Greenfield; exec p, Melissa Goddard, Peter Morgan; co-p, Ed Lahti; w, Mark Homer; ph, Stephen Katz; ed, Scott Smith; m, Philip Giffin; prod d, Timothy S. Stepeck; art d, Matthew Carey; set d, Ronaldo V. Franco; sound,

Mick E. Fowler (mixer); fx, J. D. Street IV; casting, Mary Jo Slater, Steve Brooksbank; cos, Greg LaVoi; makeup, Mary Kay Morse; stunts, Jeff Jensen

Thriller/Mystery **(PR: C MPAA: R)**

SHE'S THE ONE ★★½

(U.S.) 96m Good Machine; Marlboro Road Gang Productions; South Fork Pictures ~ Fox Searchlight c

Jennifer Aniston *(Renee)*; Maxine Bahns *(Hope)*; Edward Burns *(Mickey Fitzpatrick)*; Cameron Diaz *(Heather Davis)*; John Mahoney *(Mr. Fitzpatrick)*; Mike McGlone *(Francis Fitzpatrick)*; Anita Gillette *(Carol)*; Frank Vincent *(Ron)*; Malachy McCourt *(Tom)*; Leslie Mann *(Connie)*; Tom Tammi *(Father John)*; Amanda Peet *(Molly)*; Robert Weil *(Mr. De Lucca)*

For the follow-up to his debut, the surprise art-house hit THE BROTHERS MCMULLEN (1995), writer-director Edward Burns sticks with the subjects of troubled families and romances. While the title, SHE'S THE ONE, is cribbed from a Springsteen rocker about dark, driving passions, Sonny and Cher's lightweight pop hit "I Got You Babe" might have been a better choice.

Burns and his MCMULLEN brother Mike McGlone star as Mickey and Francis Fitzpatrick, who along with their father (John Mahoney) comprise "The Fighting Fitzpatricks," a middle-class New York family. (Mom never appears, but gets discussed a lot.) Most of the fighting is about what wusses the old man thinks his "daughters" are, especially where the opposite sex is concerned. During the last few years, Mickey literally has been spinning his wheels, driving a taxi, ever since he caught his fiancee with another man. Francis, a Wall Street stockbroker, is married to Renee (Jennifer Aniston), but they haven't had sex in months. At first Renee blames herself; then she starts thinking Francis might be gay. Actually, Francis has been having an affair with Mickey's ex, Heather (Cameron Diaz), a Wall Street yuppie who put herself through college by working as a call girl.

One day, Hope (Maxine Bahns) hops into Mickey's cab on the way to the airport. They hit it off, and she asks him to drive her to New Orleans. Within 24 hours, they are married. Things are initially rosy between Mickey and Hope, but hit a snag when she reveals that she will be going to France to study at the Sorbonne. Mickey doesn't want to go, and she doesn't see what reason he has to stay.

Francis announces that he will leave his wife to marry Heather, which infuriates Mickey. Their father decides they should settle their differences in a boxing match, which Mickey wins with a single punch. Unhappy with her husband's behavior, Hope decides to go to Paris alone.

Mickey tells Francis about Heather's past as a prostitute. While he is storming over this information, Heather gets married to another, older man—one of her former clients. Mr. Fitzpatrick learns that his wife, who was supposedly spending all of her time at church, is really having an affair. The Fitzpatrick men reunite for their final fishing trip of the season, and Dad apologizes for the bad advice he has given his sons. On the boat, Mickey discovers that his father has invited one more guest: Hope, the first woman ever to set foot aboard.

SHE'S THE ONE is a likable enough little romantic comedy. Made for only $3 million (more than 100 times the cost of THE BROTHERS MCMULLEN, but still low budget by Hollywood standards) and Burns' first studio work, it bodes well for the auteur's future. Still, SHE'S THE ONE sorely lacks what MCMULLEN had in spades—a fresh and charming realism. Watching the McMullens was like peeking in on real lives, and the importance of religion in those lives provided depth. In place of moral dilemmas, SHE'S THE ONE offers cheap shots at yuppies and musings on whether love can pay the rent. One can almost hear a producer telling Burns, "We like your work kid, just lose all that Catholic stuff."

With its comic riffs on vibrators and "down cycles" in marital relations, and that cute cab courtship, SHE'S THE ONE has an odd alchemy of observational humor and farce that makes it play more like a TV sitcom pilot than a feature film. (That's not much of a criticism if you compare the quality of writing on "Friends" and "Frasier" with that of recent movie comedies.) Part of the problem is that Burns is repaying favors by casting McGlone and Bahns in pivotal roles. They are simply, and frankly, out of their depth. This weakness is especially glaring in Bahns' case, since both Diaz and Aniston (despite their top billing) are provided with so little to do. *(Profanity, sexual situations.)* — P.R.

d, Edward Burns; p, Ted Hope, James Schamus, Edward Burns; exec p, Robert Redford, Michael Nozik; w, Edward Burns; ph, Frank Prinzi; ed, Susan Graef; m, Tom Petty; prod d, William Barclay; art d, Caty Maxey; set d, Harriet Zucker; sound, T.J. O'Mara (mixer); casting, Laura Rosenthal; cos, Susan Lyall

Romance/Comedy **(PR: C MPAA: R)**

SHINE ★★★½

(Australia) 105m Momentum Films ~ Fine Line c

Geoffrey Rush *(David as an Adult)*; Armin Mueller-Stahl *(Peter)*; Lynn Redgrave *(Gillian)*; Noah Taylor *(David as a Young Man)*; John Gielgud *(Cecil Parkes)*; Alex Rafalowicz *(David as a Child)*; Googie Withers *(Katharine Susannah Prichard)*; Sonia Todd *(Sylvia)*; Nicholas Bell *(Ben Rosen)*

SHINE tells the true story of David Helfgott, a gifted pianist whose troubled private life cut short a brilliant career. Scott Hicks's film is neither exploitative nor excessively sentimental, managing the difficult task of relating familiar screen biography material in a fresh way. Geoffrey Rush won a deserved Best Actor Oscar for his portrayal of Helfgott.

Australia in the early 1980s. David (Rush), an apparently disoriented, giggling man in his forties, enters a bar on a rainy night and charms the owner, Sylvia (Sonia Todd), with his odd, loquacious demeanor and delightful piano-playing. Sylvia gives David a job without realizing that he was once a famous musical prodigy.

As a little boy, David (Alex Rafalowicz) is forced to play piano by his domineering father, Peter (Armin Mueller-Stahl), a Holocaust survivor who was denied the opportunity to play music during his own upbringing. David shows great promise as a pianist and tours on the local competition circuit. Eventually, the teen David (Noah Taylor) wins national acclaim which leads to a scholarship to study in America with Isaac Stern. But Peter resents David's success and forbids him to leave home. Later, through the encouragement of an elderly writer, Katherine Susannah Prichard (Googie Withers), David defies his father and leaves to study in London's Royal College of Music. Under the guidance of professor Cecil Parkes (John Gielgud), David grows as a musician to even greater heights. But news of Katherine's death, estrangement from his family, and the stress of rehearsing an extremely difficult piece cause David to break down in the middle of a performance.

David returns to Australia where his father permits him to receive electro-shock therapy. As a mental patient of an institution, David is prohibited to play the piano for fear that it might excite him too much. Many years go by for David with little human contact until the night he wanders into Sylvia's bar and begins playing again. Despite his pronounced but harmless oddities, David makes friends with Gillian (Lynn Redgrave), an astrologer and friend of Sylvia's who takes a liking to the eccentric man. Slowly, David finds an inner peace and, with Gillian at his side, learns to accept his dying father. Finally, David becomes ready for a comeback as a great pianist.

SHINE succeeds better than many stories about artists overcoming ailments and adversity because it does not condescend to the characters or the audience. Although David's jabbering adult self is annoying to listen to at first, Rush makes him a fully-rounded character. Likewise, the father-son melodrama at the heart of the film resists becoming a simplistic power struggle. Hick's frequent cutting between past and present gives an impressionistic causality to the narrative pieces in a similar manner to Karel Reisz's ISADORA (1968).

Rush is well-supported by the entire cast, including Noah as the young David, Mueller-Stahl as the psychotic stage "dad" (one of his best performances), and Redgrave as the nurturing Gillian (a part too small for its importance to Helfgott's life). Gielgud and Withers give welcome old-time zip to their roles, although some of Gielgud's lines (e.g. "Don't you love those big, fat chords?") sound suspiciously like Lee Remick's overripe epigrams in THE COMPETITION (1980), another piano teacher-student drama. Otherwise, SHINE's production is well-mounted in a classical way that befits the enterprise (the musical warhorses include selections by Liszt, Chopin and Rachmaninoff, mostly played by the real Helfgott on the soundtrack). This emotionally forceful film will be appreciated by all audiences, not just classical-music lovers. *(Violence, adult situations, nudity, profanity.)* — E.M.

d, Scott Hicks; p, Jane Scott; w, Jan Sardi (from a story by Scott Hicks); ph, Geoffrey Simpson; ed, Pip Karmel; m, David Hirschfelder; prod d, Vicki Niehus; cos, Louise Wakefield

AA Best Actor: Geoffrey Rush; *AAN Best Picture; AAN Best Supporting Actor:* Armin Mueller-Stahl; *AAN Best Director:* Scott Hicks; *AAN Best Film Editing:* Pip Karmel; *AAN Best Original Dramatic Score:* David Hirschfelder; *AAN Best Original Screenplay:* Jan Sardi, Scott Hicks (story)

Drama **(PR: C MPAA: PG-13)**

SHOOTFIGHTER 2: KILL OR BE KILLED! ★★

(U.S.) 90m ANA ~ Columbia TriStar Home Video c

Bolo Yeung *(Shingo)*; William Zabka *(Ruben)*; Michael Bernardo *(Nick)*; Chase Randolph *(Lew Rawlins)*; Brett Clark *(Shark)*; Kristy K. Eisenberg *(Sheri)*; Joe Son *(Lance Stuart)*; Jorge Gil *(Eddie)*; Marc Macaulay *(Malo)*; W. Paul Bodie *(Lt. Jamison)*; John Paul Smith *(Tony)*; Bill Shaw *(Lt. Jamison's Asst.)*; Raul San *(Latino Owner)*; Bob Kranz *(Hal Jansen)*; Vince Cecere *(Karl)*; Joseph Cox *(Joe Rawlins)*; Cesar Carniero *(Brazilian Fighter)*; Tony Deleron *(Sargon)*; Nelson Garcia *(Chico)*; Armando Ramos *(Anatoli)*; Mike Dore *(Bruce)*; Klodi Lemoine *(Grunner)*; James Lee *(Kahn)*; Dexter Fletcher *(Luzan)*; Alan Jordan *(Moon)*; Mike Nunn *(Pascal)*; Sang Kang *(Saki)*; Ruddy Ester *(Tovar)*; Lisa Gaylord *(Buffy)*

You've already seen this rumble before; the stars may have been different, but the recycled plot about the gladiatorial thumbs-down boxing biz remains unchanged. All the world's an arena, and everyone in it is a fighter with a short life expectancy.

When his son Joe (Joseph Cox) dies while trying to quit the mortal combat rackets, San Francisco Police Chief Lew Rawlins (Chase Randolph) squeezes his snitch Eddie (Jorge Gil) for profiles on shootfighters (freelance warriors). Because Miami is the newest hotbed of illegal kickboxing exhibitions, Rawlins decides to pool resources with Lt. Jamison (W. Paul Bodie) to bust up the death games in the Sunbelt. Reluctant at first, four retired vets of the lethal sport agree to go undercover for Rawlins with Eddie posing as their manager. Backed up by Jamison's force, Rawlins sets up a sting involving Ruben (William Zabka), Nick (Michael Bernardo), Shark (Brett Clark), and Shingo (Bolo Yeung) in an effort to put jackal Lance Stuart (Joe Son) out of business. Expecting to pull out of the operation safely, the quartet is shocked when Lance strong-arms Eddie into betraying them; they're forced to lay their lives on the line for Lance's profit. Separated from the protective buffer of the police, the shootfighters are thrust into fatal skirmishes and eventually pitted against one another. Nothing evil is beyond Lance, who's Shingo's long-lost brother; he even throws Rawlins in the ring when he comes snooping. Cheered by a bloodthirsty crowd, Shingo challenges pistol-packing Lance to combat. Already stripped of his gambling fortune by the heroic shootfighters' victories, a disgraced Lance loses to Shingo and commits harakiri. Another pugilistic scourge is vanquished.

As expected, the hand-to-hand combat is choreographed with pugnacious panache and plenty of high energy. Those adjectives do not apply to any other department of SHOOTFIGHTER 2, a drably shot assembly-line sausage. Sluggishly directed, tepidly acted, and annoyingly written with no boxing cliche left unturned, the film plays out like one of those early all-star revues (e.g., 1930's PARAMOUNT ON PARADE), where the contract stars strutted their stuff in specialty spots—just replace the time steps with flying kicks, and you get the idea. Aficionados are advised to fast forward to the mini-spurts of violence and to treat SHOOTFIGHTER 2 as if its expository scenes were boring ring announcements in between world championship karate events at Madison Square Garden. *(Graphic violence, extreme profanity, extensive nudity, sexual situations.)* — R.P.

d, Paul Ziller; p, Alan Amiel; assoc p, Bolo Yeung, Jim Bigham; w, Greg Mellott, Pete Shaner; ph, Hanania Baer; ed, Omer Tal; m, K. Alexander Wilkinson; prod d, Robert Butcher; sound, Tony Cannella (design), Carl Carden (mixer); casting, Yonit Duchman, Ed Arenas; cos, Ellen Falguiere; makeup, Carol Raskin-Smaling; stunts, John Paul Salvitti, Alan Amiel

Martial Arts/Crime **(PR: C MPAA: R)**

SHOPPING ★★½

(U.K.) 86m Impact Productions; Channel Four Films ~ Concorde Pictures c

Sadie Frost *(Jo)*; Jude Law *(Billy)*; Sean Pertwee *(Tommy)*; Fraser James *(Be Bop)*; Sean Bean *(Venning)*; Marianne Faithfull *(Bev)*; Jonathan Pryce *(Conway)*; Danny Newman *(Monkey)*; Lee Whitlock *(Pony)*; Ralph Ineson *(Dix)*; Eammon Walker *(Peters)*; Jason Isaacs *(Market Trader)*; Chris Constantinou *(Yuppie)*; Tilly Vosburgh *(Mrs. Taylor)*; Melanie Hill *(Sarah)*; Grant Russell *(Store Owner)*; James Hill *(Lippy Kid)*; Clint Dyer *(Car Thief)*; Brian Croucher *(Billy's Dad)*; Simon Bateso; Polly Moore; Vinny Mann; Julian Sandell *(Tommy's Gang)*; Sarah Phillips *(Reporter's Voice)*; DJ Tim *(Himself)*; Kate Lauren *(Policewoman)*; Paul McNeilly; Dave Roberts; Simon Austin; Sidney Cole; Chris Armstrong *(Policemen)*; Paul Wong *(Venning's Member)*; Shion Abdillah *(Local Kid)*; Francis Pope *(Kid)*; Leon Black *(Kid)*; Anthony Lee *(Kid)*; Becky van der Post; Clio Gould; Monica Scott; Philip Bagenal *(String Quartet)*

SHOPPING is a strictly standard youth-angst vehicle that's all posturing and no substance. Roger Corman's New Horizons company brought this British work to the US, then mysteriously cut some of the movie's contents, making the superficial story line even more confusing and full of plot holes.

Local punk hero Billy (Jude Law) meets up with his ready-for-anything girlfriend, Jo (Sadie Frost), after serving a three-month sentence for "shopping" (driving a stolen car through a storefront and stealing the goods). Billy and Jo immediately steal a BMW and head out for some kicks. The police are soon on their trail, and the thrill-seeking Billy engages them in a high-speed chase, until he and Jo easily elude them.

Though he rarely steals any goods, Billy's fearlessness on the streets is legendary and has won him legions of admirers—and a few enemies. Billy's rival is Tommy (Sean Pertwee), a fellow shopper who is in it strictly for business and doesn't appreciate Billy's intrusion on his turf. At the same time, Billy's parole officer, Conway (Jonathan Pryce), trails his every move.

To get Billy off his back, Tommy suggests that they become partners, but Billy's pride stands in the way, and he refuses. Tommy then tries to recruit Jo, who also declines. Out of frustration, Tommy and his lads go on a rampage, smashing police cars and increasing their looting.

Conway approaches Billy about this rash of thefts and demands a confession, but Billy remains unmoved and continues to increase his hits. The next target of Billy and Jo is an exclusive store that Tommy had earmarked for a big deal. Tommy, blind with rage, proceeds to vandalize the caravan where Billy lives. Unfazed as always, Billy simply moves into an abandoned subway car.

The escalating violence frightens Jo, who tries to persuade Billy to leave town with her. But Billy wants to commit the ultimate heist to prove that he is the king. He and his mates Be Bop and Monkey (Fraser James, Danny Newman) target the town's huge mall. Tommy gets wind of the plan and demands that Billy team up with him or suffer the consequences. Billy promises an answer by the next night, but instead plans to follow through with the hit behind Tommy's back.

Later that night, Billy, Jo, Be Bop, and Monkey head for the mall. However, Conway and his back-ups are there waiting, thanks to an anonymous tip by Tommy. Be Bop and Monkey lose control of their car and die instantly, while Billy and Jo manage to escape to a garage. Thinking they have escaped, Billy speeds out of the garage and unwittingly crashes head-on into a phalanx of police cars. Jo dies, but Billy remains alive long enough to look into the eyes of a store mannequin peering at him through the window.

Writer-director Paul Anderson, who tasted Hollywood success with MORTAL KOMBAT (1995), belongs to a group of British filmmakers known as the "multiplex generation" because of their love of commercial and high-action cinema. SHOPPING really bears the stamp of that youthful glee: the movie's opening credits, for example, feature a spectacular overhead pan across a bleak industrial landscape over the sounds of a pulsating industrial rock soundtrack. He also is very adept at staging action sequences and employing snazzy visual flourishes, but unfortunately, has no idea how to direct actors. Law's matinee-idol good looks serve him well, but one never gets any sense of why he is so angry and aimless. Frost fares better, and she manages to bring some electricity to her scenes with Law. Pertwee is effectively sleazy, and an almost unrecognizable Marianne Faithfull has an all-too-brief cameo appearance.

During the lulls in action, however, SHOPPING is one dull movie. As in all movies about misunderstood youth, the police are dunderheads and the ill-mannered kids are the heroes. *(Violence, profanity, adult situations.)* — D.O.

d, Paul Anderson; p, Jeremy Bolt; w, Paul Anderson; ph, Tony Imi; ed, David Stiven; m, Barrington Pheloung; prod d, Max Gottlieb; art d, Chris Townsend; sound, Colin Nicolson (recordist); fx, Vendetta FX; casting, Jane Frisby; cos, Howard Burden; makeup, Pebbles; stunts, Jim Dowdall

Drama/Crime **(PR: C MPAA: NR)**

SHOT, THE ★★½

(U.S.) 86m Bread & Water Productions ~ Bread & Water Productions c

Dan Bell *(Dern Reel)*; Michael Rivkin *(Patrick St. Patrick)*; Jude Horowitz *(Anna)*; Vincent Ward *(Smith)*; Mo Gaffney *(Sheila Ricks)*; Michael DeLuise *(Bob Mann)*; Jack Kehler *(Det. Martinson)*; Ted Raimi *(Officer Corelli)*; Tracy Arnold; Dana Carvey; Paul Provenza; Natalija Nogulich

Packed with wry (if familiar) actors' laments lensed on 16mm, THE SHOT is Hollywood satire by insiders who know whereof they grumble.

Dern Reel (Dan Bell) is a serious-minded "Method" thespian who turns down movie or TV jobs he feels aren't Brando material even though he's broke. Reel and parasitic roommate Patrick St. Patrick (Michael Rivkin) are disgusted by an untalented colleague (Michael DeLuise) landing the lead in "Burnt Sienna Sunset," a blockbuster by hot director David Egoman. To get even the duo sneak into Egoman's mansion during a private screening of the film and steal the final cut. But a mystery attacker shoots, stabs, and bludgeons the much-despised Egoman.

With the great man comatose, St. Patrick realizes the snatched celluloid is their "shot" at success. He and Reel try to ransom it to studio honcho Sheila Ricks (Mo Gaffney), unaware she has already re-edited the film to suit her own agenda and plans to set them up.

A confrontation between the gun-toting exec and the protagonists is interrupted by the timely arrival of the police and Sheila's arrest for the assault on Egoman, who, incredibly, recovers from his multiple traumas. Hailed as heroes, Reel and St. Patrick star in a glamorized reenactment of their own story—but Reel quits when he accidentally discovers who *really* knifed Egoman. Egoman was wounded by just about every other major suspect—except Durn Reel—in a spontaneous outburst of vengeance. Wanting no part of his roommate's self-serving whitewash, Reel goes back to doing florid Tennessee Williams productions with his actress girlfriend.

While THE SHOT finds easy targets in well-worn La-La Land complaints like tyrant moguls, health nuts, parking tickets, violence-obsessed LAPD and miscellaneous weirdoes, the solid foundation of the comedy is the team of Bell and Rivkin as well-matched losers. Reel may be a lunkhead, but he's principled, while the sponging St. Patrick eagerly joins the studio system he scorns. Their byplay is consistently amusing, whether the subject is murder or a missing 20 bucks.

THE SHOT calls to mind JIMMY HOLLYWOOD (1994), but predates Barry Levinson's portrait of Tinseltown fringies. Actor-playwright Bell, an alumnus of the Lee Strasberg Institute with a recurring part in the WAYNE'S WORLD comedies, concocted the farce years earlier as an L.A. theater piece and reworked it as his filmmaking debut. Using his earnings from WAYNE'S WORLD (1992) and its sequel, private investors, volunteers and support from the Sam Raimi and DeLuise clans, Bell completed the handsome-looking feature for a remarkable $40,000—in 1995 terms, less than the cost of many short subjects—though Bell and his producer eventually had to undertake distributing the comedy themselves.

Bell reprises his stage character based on himself in younger days. Another cast notable, New Zealand auteur Vincent Ward (MAP OF THE HUMAN HEART), hams it up as a crazed scriptwriter. Dana Carvey heard Bell discuss THE SHOT on the set of WAYNE'S WORLD 2 and talked his way into a cameo: with only an hour before leaving to do THE ROAD TO WELLVILLE (1994), Carvey dropped by to play himself, a star who awes Reel and St. Patrick in a sidewalk encounter. *(Violence, profanity, alcohol use)* — C.C.

d, Dan Bell; p, Jude Horowitz, Sherrie Rose; w, Dan Bell (based on his play); ph, Alan Candillo; ed, Kevin Greutert; m, Dan Sonis; prod d, Diamond Jim Braverman; cos, Mari-An Ceo

Comedy **(PR: C MPAA: R)**

SHOWGIRL MURDERS, THE ★★½
(U.S.) 85m Califilm ~ New Horizons Home Video c

Maria Ford *(Jessica)*; Matt Preston *(Mitch)*; D. S. Case *(Carolyn)*; Bob McFarland *(Ridley)*; Kevin Alber *(Joey)*; Jeff Douglas *(Crank)*; C. B. Baldwin *(Regular #1)*; Floyd Baldwin *(Regular #2)*; Nikki Fritz *(Dancer)*; Jane Stowe *(Dancer)*; Crescendo *(Dancer)*

Maria Ford delivers the sleazy goods in SHOWGIRL MURDERS, an above-average, soft-core THE POSTMAN ALWAYS RINGS TWICE (1981)/DOUBLE INDEMNITY (1944) ripoff from Roger Corman's direct-to-video exploitation factory.

A sultry blonde named Jessica (Maria Ford) gets a job as a cocktail waitress at a rundown bar owned by Mitch (Matt Preston), and his wife Carolyn (D.S. Case), who has turned into a drunk to assuage her guilt over having killed a little boy in a car accident. Jessica turns the bar into a strip club called "Pandora's Boxxx," bringing in $2,000 per night with her X-rated dances. One night, a man named Joey (Kevin Alber), whom Jessica recognizes, tries to molest her, and he gets into a fistfight with Mitch. Jessica gets him to leave, but doesn't tell Mitch she knows him. A DEA agent named Ridley (Bob McFarland) shows up at the club and tells Mitch that Joey is a drug dealer out on parole. Ridley asks Mitch to sign a warrant for his arrest so Ridley can get him for violating his parole, but Jessica tells Mitch not to sign it, so he refuses.

Afterwards, Jessica seduces Mitch and while they're having sex, talks him into killing his wife. Mitch tries to stab Carolyn while they're dancing, but can't go through with it, so Jessica hires Joey to do it, telling him that Carolyn is going to sign his arrest warrant. Joey stabs Carolyn outside the club, but Ridley witnesses it and calls the cops. A high-speed car chase leaves Joey dead, and an ambulence takes Carolyn to the hospital. Ridley tells Mitch that Jessica stole $100,000 from Joey's brother, an ex-boyfriend named Crank (Jeff Douglas) who doublecrossed the Feds on a sting operation and kept the money. Jessica convinces Mitch that she's changed her evil ways, and while his wife is recovering in the hospital, she turns the club into an even bigger success. When Carolyn returns, she tells Mitch she's going to stay sober and wants to sell the club. Jessica tells Mitch that she'll kill Carolyn herself this time if he can't do it. They manage to get Carolyn drunk, and slip some rat poison in her drink. Carolyn starts to dance and passes out, and Jessica bashes her brains in with a lamp while Carolyn is writhing on the floor.

The cops can't prove Carolyn's death wasn't an accident, but Ridley continues to hound Mitch and Jessica, and gets snapshots of them having sex while disposing of Carolyn's ashes after her funeral. Mitch and Jessica get married, but Ridley blackmails them with the photos, and Jessica agrees to pay him $150,000 from Carolyn's insurance. Then, Crank shows up and demands his cash back, but Jessica convinces him that she took the money so she could launder it at the club, and informs him that she's the sole beneficiary of Mitch's will. Jessica then tells Mitch about Crank and suggests they get rid of him by burning down the club for the insurance, while Crank is inside. While Crank is watching Jessica rehearse her act, Mitch cuts a gas line and sneaks up behind Crank with a metal pipe, but as he's about to hit him, Jessica alerts Crank, who grabs the pipe away from Mitch and kills him with it, then sets the club on fire. Jessica collects the insurance money and she and Crank go on a vacation. In Mexico, Jessica pulls a gun on Crank and shoots him, then goes to sun herself on a beach.

SHOWGIRL MURDERS is an utterly trashy, semi-pornographic film noir that surprisingly works better than most direct-to-video "erotic thrillers," thanks to competent direction, understated acting, and a reasonably engaging story. Although the specifics of the plot are laughable in terms of plausibility, the cast brings conviction to their roles. The numerous no-holds-barred S & M dance sequences, staged and performed by the redoubtable Ms. Ford, are certain to please fans of the genre, particularly a Garden of Eden lesbian number, replete with apple, snake, and Fred Olen Ray fave Nikki Fritz. Ford throws herself into her amoral part with reckless abandon, and there are also some unusual touches, such as Carolyn's nightmare-flashback sequences. These are imaginatively shot and edited, although the ending, lifted directly from BODY HEAT, comes as no surprise. SHOWGIRL MURDERS may be a totally depraved concoction, but at least it's a lot more honest, not to mention entertaining, about its lowly intentions, than the phony, big-budget tease of SHOWGIRLS (1995). *(Extensive nudity, sexual situations, graphic violence, extreme profanity.)* — M.S.

d, Gene Hertel; p, Darin Spillman; w, Christopher Wooden; ph, Harry Box; ed, J. J. Jackson; m, David Wurst, Eric Wurst; prod d, Nava; art d, Louis Moulinet; sound, Joel E. Smith; casting, J. L. Whitworth; cos, Esther Lee; makeup, Tania Wanstall

Erotic/Thriller **(PR: O MPAA: R)**

SIBAK
(SEE: MIDNIGHT DANCERS)

SILENCE OF NETO, THE ★★★½
(Guatemala/U.S.) 110m Morningside Movies; Buenos Dias ~ Forefront Films c
(EL SILENCIO DE NETO)

Oscar Javier Almengor *(Antonio "Neto" Ypes)*; Herbert Meneses *(Ernesto Ypes)*; Julio Diaz *(Eduardo Ypes)*; Eva Tamargo Lemus *(Elena Ypes)*; Pablo Arenales *(Rodrigo)*; Indira Chinchilla *(Nidia)*; Mildred Chavez *(Rosa)*; Ingrid Hernandezo *(Ani)*; Patricia Orantes *(Tia Cristy)*; Sergio Paz *(Alberto)*; Diego Peralta *(Mario)*; Eduardo Jose Guerrero *(German)*; Frida Henry *(Abuela Mercedes)*; Ricardo Mendizabal *(Arzobispo)*; Zoila Portillo *(Matilde)*

Luis Argueta's first feature film is also the first major feature to come out of Guatemala. In it, he uses one of the most traumatic eras in his country's history as a backdrop for a fairly universal coming-of-age tale.

It is 1954, and adolescent Antonio "Neto" Ypes (Oscar Javier Almengor) is visited by the ghost of his Uncle Ernesto (Herbert Meneses), who counsels, "The worst thing you can do is not say what you feel." A flashback to six months earlier shows Neto, a privileged kid in the nation's capital, troubled by an uncomfortable relationship with his domineering, emotionally remote father Eduardo (Julio Diaz), a judge. Uncle Ernesto is Neto's favorite, a footloose dandy compelled by ill health to return to the household he once abandoned. Neto's 14th birthday crystallizes the contrast between the grown-ups: Ernesto gives Neto a paper balloon to release in a traditional celebration, but Eduardo takes charge and launches it himself, rather than accord his son the privilege.

Meanwhile, the elected leftist president of Guatemala has offended US commercial interests, particularly those of the United Fruit Company, and Washington-directed leaflets drift down from the heavens naming public servants, including Neto's father, as Communists. Soon aerial bombardment of a more explosive sort forces the Ypes's temporary evacuation to Ernesto's earlier residence on Antigua. When they return to bullet-pocked Guatemala City, a Yankee-friendly regime is in power, some neighbors have permanently "disappeared," a few corpses still lie unburied, new schoolteachers are rabidly pro-USA, and Senor Ypes has lost his job to a *junta* appointee. During the tumult, the truth gradually emerges that Ernesto once loved Neto's mother Elena (Eva Tamargo Lemus). When Ernesto dies, the Ypes family's children and remaining servants honor him with another paper balloon, this time launched by Neto.

The young, endearingly ungainly Neto is mainly a passive observer of events and something of an enigma to the viewers. Though clearly cognizant of the adult crises and insanity around him, the boy drifts casually through them, recalling Truffaut's dictum about childhood being a "state of grace." When he and his friends find a loaded machine gun in the underbrush and near-tragedy results, they all just laugh it off and continue with their pretend adventures as radio heroes "The Three Villalobos." Even in a state of emergency, argues the filmmaker, kids the world over have their own inner lives and concerns upon which not even the United Fruit Company may intrude. *(Adult situations.)* — C.C.

d, Luis Argueta; p, Luis Argueta; assoc p, Abigail Hunt; w, Justo Chang, Luis Argueta; ph, Ramon Suarez; ed, Gloria Pinyero, David Tedeschi; m, Jose Gallegos, Maurice Gallegos; prod d, Justo Chang; art d, Ana Solares; sound, Antonio Arroyo (mixer); cos, Gloria Wurmser

Drama/Political **(PR: C MPAA: NR)**

SILENCES OF THE PALACE, THE ★★★★
(France/Tunisia) 116m Mat Films; Cinetelefilms; Magfilm ~ Capitol Entertainment c
(SAIMT EL QUSUR; LES SILENCES DU PALAIS)

Amel Hedhili *(Khedija)*; Hend Sabri *(Young Alia)*; Najia Ouerghi *(Khalti Hadda)*; Ghalia Lacroix *(Adult Alia)*; Sami Bouajila *(Lotfi)*; Kamel Fazaa *(Sidi Ali)*; Hichem Rostom *(Si Bechir)*; Helene Catzaras *(Fella)*; Sonia Meddeb *(La Jneina)*; Mechket Krifa *(La Memia)*; Kamel Touati *(Houssine)*; Fatma Ben Saidane *(Mroubia)*; Zahira Ben Ammar *(Habiba)*; Sabah Bouzouita *(Schema)*; Bechir Feni *(Bey)*; Khedija Ben Othman *(Sarra)*; Taoufic Bahri; Abdellatif Kheireddine; Naoufel Zaghbib; Noureddine Annabi; Med Iamine Cherif; Med Chedly Sfar; Rafaeil Mastier; Alberto Canova; Cristian Chartian; Jalel Ben Saad; Abdelaziz Belgaeid; Rachida Ben Rabiaa; Saima Hafsi; Ichraf Azzouz; Asmna Zouheir; Karima Ajimi; Khaoula Mezzi; Ramia Ayari; Zohra Rafraf; Abdelkerim Toumi; Beya Fazzani; Paula Craft

Moufida Tlatli, a veteran film editor, makes her directorial debut with THE SILENCES OF THE PALACE, a remarkable film about subjugation, alienation, and the bumpy path to knowledge and independence.

The unhappy face of Alia (Ghalia Lacroix) fills the frame as she sings unenthusiastically for a wedding party, sometime in 1960s Tunisia, after the overthrow of the beys. She returns to the drab apartment she shares with her boyfriend, Lotfi (Sami Bouajila), where he encourages her to endure yet another abortion, scheduled for the following day. Before her appointment, she learns of the death of Prince Sidi Ali (Kamel Fazaa), her former master and the man she believes was her father.

She returns to the palace and wanders the dark and dusty rooms, asking questions of the remaining servant women and recollecting the scenes of her youth, particularly the relationship between the young Alia (Hend Sabri) and her servant mother Khedija (Amel Hedheli).

Khedija gives birth to Alia the same night that the wife of Sidi Ali's brother, Si Bechir (Hichem Rostom), gives birth to Sarra (Khedija Ben Othman). Sidi Ali's own wife, La Jneina (Sonia Meddeb), is infertile. Alia and Sarra grow up as close friends, and Alia is allowed to exist on the fringes of the family, though she is despised by Jneina and the truth of her paternity is shrouded in silence.

Alia's curiosity grows as she develops into a young women and learns that her mother's domestic servitude is coupled with sexual servitude. She eavesdrops on the beys as they enjoy their pleasures with the servants, and she watches her mother being forced to dance provocatively at social gatherings much to the discomfort of the wives. Alia's confusion takes the form of illnesses, headaches, and silence.

Alia's beauty and her rich soulful singing voice bring her to the attention of the men of the palace, and when she is asked to sing at their parties, and then summoned by Si Bechir for sexual service, her mother lashes out at her with fearful reproaches. Only as an adult is Alia able to understand and forgive her mother's silences—her constant refusal to name her father, her inability to express her knowledge that the palace will rob Alia of her soul and her voice, and her sad attempt to abort a pregnancy that eventually leads to her death.

After her mother's death, Alia escapes the oppression of the palace with her lover, but the freedom she pursues still eludes her. Only in revisiting the palace is Alia able to begin to gather strength and combat her pain. She leaves committed to bearing her child, to whom she will give her mother's name.

Director Moufida Tlatli reveals with painstaking realism how the patriarchal lifestyle of this ruling class imprisons Muslim women. The family strives to maintain respectability by veiling the indiscretions of the patriarch; and both wives and servants are bred to guard this honor with silence. Behind these silences lies the torment of the loss of both self and will. When her lover assures her that she will feel fine after the abortion, she retorts that every abortion is a painful loss, "a part of me that abandons me," and when Sidi Ali dies she describes him as taking a part of her history with him.

Alia reflects back on a critical moment in both her personal and social history. Her emancipation from childhood actually mirrors the overthrow of an era.

Tlatli won the Satyajit Ray Award, honoring a filmmaker of exceptional promise, and the film was awarded Special Mention at the 1994 Cannes Film Festival. *(Adult situations)* — R.C.

d, Moufida Tlatli; p, Ahmed Baha Eddine Attia, Richard Magnien; w, Moufida Tlatli; ph, Youssef Ben Youssef; ed, Moufida Tlatli, Camille Cotte, Kerim Hammouda; m, Anouar Brahem; set d, Rachid Basti, Khaled Ben Massaoud; sound, Faouzi Thabet (recordist); casting, Adel Koudhaei; cos, Magdalena Garcia; makeup, Fatma Jaziri

Drama **(PR: C MPAA: NR)**

SINGLE GIRL, A ★★★★
(France) 90m Cinea; La Sept Cinema ~ Strand Releasing c
(LA FILLE SEULE)

Virginie Ledoyen *(Valerie)*; Benoit Magimel *(Remi)*; Dominique Valadie *(Mother)*; Vera Briole *(Sabine)*; Virginie Emane *(Fatiah)*; Michel Bompoil *(Jean-Marc)*; Jean-Chretien Sibertin-Blanc *(Patrice)*; Long Nguyen Khac *(Mr. Tranh)*; Aladin Reibel *(Mr. Sarre)*; Guillemette Grobon *(Mme. Charles)*; Guila Urso; Antonio Cecchinato; Jean-Claude Frissung; Catherine Guittonneau; Herve Gamelin; Alain Rolan; Jean-Claude Masson; Mateo Blanc

A top performance mixes beautifully with an engrossing film technique in A SINGLE GIRL, Benoit Jacquot's charming French film about a young woman's first day on the job as a hotel waitress.

In a Parisian cafe, Valerie (Virginie Ledoyen) meets her boyfriend, Remi (Benoit Magimel), to tell him over morning coffee that she is pregnant. His cold reaction prompts her to doubt whether to continue their relationship. In any case, she is late for her first day working at the Concord, a nearby four-star hotel. Valerie leaves the cafe, walks over to the Concord, and immediately begins her apprenticeship delivering breakfast trays to the guests' suites.

During the busy morning, Valerie gets acquainted with her fellow employees, including the frosty Sabine (Vera Briole); the offensive Jean-Marc (Michel Bompoil), a sexual harasser; the bright Fatiah (Virginie Emane); and the silly Patrice (Jean-Chretien Sibertin-Blanc). She also finally meets her boss, Mme. Charles (Guillemette Groben), a stern woman who cross-examines her about her previous employment and warns her that her good looks may encourage sexual harassment. After a disturbing episode in which she brings a tray to a couple having sex, Valerie takes a coffee break. She returns to the cafe to again meet with Remi and tells him she wants to break off the relationship. She has decided to have her baby on her own.

In the epilogue, Valerie and her mother (Dominique Valadie) walk in a park and discuss their latest romantic attachments while caring for Valerie's young baby.

A SINGLE GIRL applies the cinema verite technique of "real time" to a fictional story. Director Jacquot succeeds with this stunt by carefully and skillfully maintaining the illusion of reality over 80 minutes. He and cowriter Jerome Beaujour also focus on a rarely explored subject—the everyday work of room service personnel. Best of all, A SINGLE GIRL is blessed with the presence of Ledoyen, a young actress who deserves the many accolades she has received for this film. (She already had shown great promise in Olivier Assayas's COLD WATER, but her smaller roles in Claude Chabrol's recent LA CEREMONIE and Edward Yang's MAHJONG hardly tapped the surface). Ledoyen's fresh, engaging presence makes every minute worth watching, no matter how boring or routine the tasks her character performs.

On a thematic level, A SINGLE GIRL echoes Ingmar Bergman's early work, including MONIKA (1952), and the more carefree French New Wave films of the 1960s, which also showcased independent female characters and occasionally addressed issues of sexism and sexual harassment. The experiment with compressed time recalls Agnes Varda's classic from that period, CLEO FROM 5 TO 7 (1962). The only major miscalculation in A SINGLE GIRL is the way the film ends—with an expendable epilogue set some time later. Overall, though, this is a film and a star to watch. *(Nudity, sexual situations, adult situations, extreme profanity.)* — E.M.

d, Benoit Jacquot; p, Philippe Carcassonne; exec p, Brigitte Faure; w, Benoit Jacquot, Jerome Beaujour; ph, Caroline Champetier; ed, Pascale Chavance; m, Kvarteto Mesta Prahi; sound, Michel Vionnet; casting, Frederique Moidon; makeup, Evelyne Byot

Drama **(PR: C MPAA: NR)**

SKIN ★★★½

(U.S.) 95m Patchett-Kaufman Entertainment ~ New Horizons Home Video c
(AKA: MAKING THE CASE FOR MURDER: THE HOWARD BEACH STORY)

Daniel J. Travanti *(Joe Hynes)*; Joe Morton *(Cedric Sandiford)*; William Daniels *(Slaney)*; Cliff Gorman *(Dick Bernstein)*; Dan Lauria *(Doug)*; Kurt Naebig *(Robert Riley)*; Anthony Russell Jr. *(Timothy Grimes)*; Ernest Perry Jr. *(Clayton Barry)*; Julianne Buescher *(Teresa Fisher)*

With fast-paced editing and a sharp script, the made-for-TV SKIN makes an interesting drama of New York's infamous Howard Beach case.

The film begins in late 1986, when three black men, whose car has broken down, wander into a pizzeria in the Howard Beach section of Queens. No sooner have they left the restaurant than they are taunted and threatened by a group of white youths. One of the black men, Michael Griffith, is chased onto a highway and killed by a passing car, and another, Cedric Sandiford (Joe Morton), is savagely beaten.

After the white boys are arrested, Joe Hynes (Daniel J. Travanti) is asked to prosecute them for the city. Hynes' first order of business is to pressure one of them, Robert Riley (Kurt Naebig), to turn evidence against the others. Riley's version of the story holds up, and Hynes decides to prosecute for murder. But as the trial begins, things start to go wrong for Hynes. Sandiford has trouble remembering details, while the other victim, Timothy Grimes (Anthony Russell Jr.), admits to pulling a knife on the white group. Eventually, however, Hynes is able to locate an eyewitness to Sandiford's beating and Griffith's death, and the jury finds three of the four defendants guilty of second-degree manslaughter.

SKIN was originally aired on TV in 1989 under the title HOWARD BEACH: MAKING THE CASE FOR MURDER. Despite the weaker title, SKIN hums along by keeping fairly close to the facts of the case and rarely becoming bogged down in details. Except for several slow scenes showing Hynes's domestic life, there are few wasted moments. The often complex legal points are well described. Also, though the filmmakers are obviously on the side of Hynes, neither he nor the victims are shown to be completely faultless.

Credit for this above-average TV movie should go to director Dick Lowry and especially editor Byron Brandt, whose wham-bam style keeps what could be a slow legal drama moving like an action film. Travanti is sharp in his portrayal of Hynes, as is the always-interesting Morton as Sandiford. Some might quibble over the few amalgam characters used, but SKIN gets closer to the heart of the matter than do most docudramas. *(Violence.)* — K.Fr.

d, Dick Lowry; p, J. Boyce Harman Jr.; exec p, Tom Patchett, Kenneth Kaufman; w, Steve Bello; ph, Ron Fortunato; ed, Byron "Buzz" Brandt; m, Jonathan Elias; art d, Michael Merritt; sound, J. Paul Oddo; fx, Sam Barkan; casting, Jane Alderman, Shelly Andreas; cos, Jay Hurley; makeup, Lillian Toth

Docudrama **(PR: C MPAA: NR)**

SKYSCRAPER ★★

(U.S.) 96m PM Entertainment Group, Inc. ~ PM Entertainment Group, Inc. c

Anna Nicole Smith *(Carrie Wink)*; Richard Steinmetz *(Gordon Wink)*; Branko Cikatic *(Zarkor)*; Charles Huber *(Fairfax)*; Calvin Levels *(Hakim)*; Jonathan Fuller *(Jacques)*; Lee de Broux *(Capt. Wood)*; Deidre Imershein *(Natasha)*; Deron McBee *(Led-*

ermeier); Vince DePalma *(Johnny)*; Alan Brooks *(Booker)*; Gary Imhoff *(Dudley)*; Bob McCracken *(William)*

Imagine a Z-grade rip-off of DIE HARD (1988), fleshed-out with soft-core sex interludes and starring Amazonian Playboy model Anna Nicole Smith in the Bruce Willis role, and you get an idea of what SKYSCRAPER has to offer. Connoisseurs of ludicrous plotting, laughable dialogue and poor acting will have a field day with this one.

A Shakespeare-spouting terrorist named Fairfax (Charles Huber) is on a killing spree in his quest to obtain four separate suitcases containing components of a satellite weapons system. He manages to get three of them, but must break into the Zi-Tex building to get the last.

He hires helicopter charter pilot Carrie Wink (Anna Nicole Smith) to land him on the roof of the skyscraper. A little upset, Carrie has just come from a big fight with her detective husband, Gordon (Richard Steinmetz), over Carrie's desire to have a baby.

Carrie lands Fairfax on the roof of the building, while his gang kills the guards and takes over the high-tech security system. Fairfax meets the man who has the fourth component case, but the man manages to escape with it after Fairfax shoots him. The wounded man runs into Carrie and gives her the case. Eventually captured by Fairfax, Carrie takes him to the case, only to discover it's been picked up by a janitor. Fairfax goes to look for it, and leaves Carrie with one of his thugs.

A swat team shows up and unsuccessfully tries to get into the building. The thug tries to rape Carrie, but she shoots him to death. Fairfax finds the case, then heads for the chopper on the roof, grabbing an office worker's kid as a hostage and forcing Carrie to go with him. Gordon is waiting for them on the roof and tries to shoot Fairfax; Carrie knocks Fairfax's gun away and throws him off the roof. As Carrie and Gordon get into an ambulance, he tells her he's now ready to have a baby.

SKYSCRAPER may be hysterically bad, replete with muscle-bound terrorists delivering laughable lines in really bad German accents, but it's also mindlessly entertaining as long as it sticks to the PM Entertainment Group formula of daredevil stunts, slow-motion gunfights, car crashes, and fiery explosions. It also has the added attraction of the wondrous Ms. Smith.

Her performance consists of pouting and moaning, as she delivers supposedly life-and-death lines in a thick Texas twang. Her delivery conveys all the emotion of having discovered she just broke a nail. ("Oh, I've been taken hostage by terrorists! Why tonight?") Those nails, incidentally, are razor-sharp and bright red, as we're continually shown in hilarious inserts of her hand wrapped around the helicopter joystick.

Smith is hardly modest about exposing her body: a gratuitous shower scene is staged like a centerfold shoot, and the filmmakers earn bonus points for the ingenious way they manage to work in a nude scene during the skyscraper siege—to show that she's a good shot, Carrie has a flashback in which Gordon gives her a shooting lesson, which segues into a sex-on-the-grass frolic.

And of course, before she kills the terrorist who tries to rape her, she "plays along" with him for a few minutes. Yet despite, or perhaps because of, Smith's ineptitude, there's something oddly likable about her. Here is a woman who was born too late. In the 1950s, she could have been a femme fatale for Howard Hughes or Hugo Haas; Russ Meyer would have turned her into a goddess in the '60s; and in the '70s and '80s, she could have starred in a string of Andy Sidaris's action epics. Now, she's forced to toil in the direct-to-video factory. *(Graphic violence, extreme profanity, extensive nudity, sexual situations.)* — M.S.

d, Raymond Martino; p, Richard Pepin, Joseph Merhi; assoc p, Anna Nicole Smith, Charles Huber, Branko Cikatic; co-p, Scott McAboy; w, John Larrabee, William Applegate Jr.; ph, Frank Harris; ed, Kevin Mock; m, Jim Halfpenny; prod d, Steve Ramos; art d, Thomas Salvitti; sound, Raymond E. Spiess; fx, Larry Roberts; casting, Mark Sikes; cos, Lisa Dyehouse; makeup, Jori Jenae; stunts, Cole McKay

Action/Thriller (PR: O MPAA: R)

SLEEPERS ★★

(U.S.) 140m Propaganda Films; Baltimore Pictures; PolyGram Filmed Entertainment ~ Warner Bros. c

Jason Patric *(Lorenzo/"Shakes")*; Brad Pitt *(Michael)*; Billy Crudup *(Tommy)*; Ron Eldard *(John)*; Robert De Niro *(Father Bobby)*; Dustin Hoffman *(Danny Snyder)*; Kevin Bacon *(Sean Nokes)*; Vittorio Gassman *(King Benny)*; Minnie Driver *(Carol Martinez)*; Terry Kinney *(Ferguson)*; Jeffrey Donovan *(Addison)*; Lennie Loftin *(Styler)*; Joe Perrino *(Young "Shakes")*; Brad Renfro *(Young Michael)*; Jonathan Tucker *(Young Tommy)*; Geoff Wigdor *(Young John)*; Bruno Kirby *(Lorenzo's Father)*; Sean Reilly *(Young King Benny)*; Joe Urla *(Carson)*; Wendell Pierce *(Little Caesar)*; Frank Medrano *(Fat Mancho)*; John Slattery *(Fred Carlson)*; Aida Turturro *(Mrs. Salinas)*; Ben Hammer *(Judge Weisman)*; James Pickens Jr. *(Marlboro)*; Peter Gerety *(Juvenile Lawyer)*; Michael Moran *(Juvenile Judge)*; Peter Appel *(Boyfriend)*; Tom Signorelli *(Confession Man)*; Gayle Scott *(Confession Woman)*; Eugene Byrd *(Rizzo)*; William Butler *(Juanito)*; Dash Mihok *(K.C.)*; Zach Ansley *(Burly Man)*; Daniel Mastrogiorgio *(Nick Davenport)*; Peter Rini *(Frank)*; Larry Romano *(1st Man)*; Saverio Guerra *(2nd Man)*; Henry Stram *(Prison Doctor)*; Mary McCann *(Sister Carolyn)*; John DiBenedetto *(Tony)*; Monica Polito *(Young Carol)*; John Stevens Jones *(Black Kid)*; Sean Hatosy *(1st Inmate)*; Conrad Meertens *(2nd Inmate)*; Pat McNamara *(Wilkinson Guard)*; Patrick Tull *(Jerry)*; Marco Greco *(Waiter)*; Paul Herman *(Bailiff)*; Gina Menza *(Foreman)*; Joseph Attanasio *(Male Juror)*; Don Hewitt *(James Caldwell)*; Debra Watkins *(Miss Pippin)*; Bruce Smolanoff *(Man in Tub)*; Jenique Torres *(Davy's Sister)*; Ruth Maleczech *(Subway Woman)*; Salvatore Piro *(Pizza Guy)*; Pasquale Cajano *(Super)*; Mario Bosco *(Joey)*

A new film from Oscar-winning director Barry Levinson, with a script based on a controversial best-seller, and a cast led by acting titans Robert De Niro and Dustin Hoffman, and featuring screen idol Brad Pitt. It sounds unsinkable, but somehow SLEEPERS can't steer clear of a proverbial iceberg: utter lack of drama.

1966. "Shakes," Michael, John, and Tommy (Joe Perrino, Brad Renfro, Geoff Wigdor, and Jonathan Tucker) are best friends growing up on the mean streets of New York's Hell's Kitchen. Under the watchful eyes of Father Bobby (Robert De Niro), the streetwise and sympathetic parish priest, and King Benny (Vittorio Gassman), neighborhood mafioso, the boys torment local merchants with endless mischief. When one prank goes too far (they push a hot dog cart down a flight of steps and injure a man), they're sent off to the Wilkerson Home for Boys. There, sadistic guards Nokes (Kevin Bacon) and Ferguson (Terry Kinney) beat and rape the boys with savage regularity.

1981. John and Tommy (Ron Eldard and Billy Crudup), hardened criminals, spot Nokes in a bar and gun him down. Their trial becomes the opportunity for revenge that Michael (Brad Pitt) has been waiting for most of his life. Now a prosecuting attorney, he takes on the seemingly unlosable case. He enlists Shakes (Jason Patric), now an aspiring writer, their childhood friend Carol (Minnie Driver), and King Benny to aid him in his plan to expose the truth about Nokes and the Wilkerson Home. Working from a script prepared by Michael, drunken defense attorney Danny Snyder (Dustin Hoffman) gets Ferguson to admit on the stand that he and Nokes were pedophilic rapists. Then, in the coup de grace, Father Bobby falsely testifies that he was with John and Tommy the night of the murder. They are acquitted, Michael has his revenge, and Shakes has a good idea for a book.

The first half of SLEEPERS is very good. The scenes in Hell's Kitchen combine the humane observation of DEAD END (1937) with the melodrama of ANGELS WITH DIRTY FACES (1938) in an engaging update. The scenes at Wilkerson effectively convey a dark, harrowing atmosphere.

Then, in a move that defies basic Screenwriting 101, Levinson kills off his villain, and in a misguided nod to realism, makes his hero (an underused Pitt) inaccessible. As a direct result, SLEEPERS fails as a vigilante justice potboiler—Nokes never has to really suffer for his crimes and wastes the opportunity to characterize how the trauma of abuse still effects its adult survivors, as was done so well in the Canadian film, THE BOYS OF ST. VINCENT (1993).

Since there's never a moment's doubt Father Bobby will provide an alibi for his boys (though how he reconciles this ethically—three wrongs make a right?—is never touched upon), SLEEPERS's overlong second half is undramatic and unengaging; Hoffman's performance is the only interesting thing happening. Meanwhile, Jason Patric's blandness in the lead suggests he can only be "promising" for so long. *(Graphic violence, profanity, adult situations.)* — P.R.

d, Barry Levinson; p, Steve Golin; exec p, Peter Giuliano; assoc p, Gerrit Van Der Meer; w, Barry Levinson (based on the novel by Lorenzo Carcaterra); ph, Michael Ballhaus; ed, Stu Linder; m, John Williams; prod d, Kristi Zea; art d, Tim Galvin; set d, Beth Rubino; sound, Tod Maitland (mixer); casting, Louis DiGiaimo, Ellen Chenoweth; cos, Gloria Gresham

AAN Original Dramatic Score: John Williams

Drama **(PR: C MPAA: R)**

SLING BLADE ★★★½

(U.S.) 135m Shooting Gallery ~ Miramax c

Billy Bob Thornton *(Karl Childers)*; Dwight Yoakam *(Doyle Hargraves)*; J.T. Walsh *(Charles Bushman)*; John Ritter *(Vaughan Cunningham)*; Lucas Black *(Frank Wheatley)*; Natalie Canerday *(Linda Wheatley)*; James Hampton *(Jerry Woolridge)*; Robert Duvall *(Karl's Father)*; Rick Dial *(Bill Cox)*; Brent Briscoe *(Scooter Hodges)*; Christy Ward *(Melinda)*; Sarah Boss *(Marsha Dwiggins)*; Kathy Sue Brown *(Theresa Evans)*; Wendell Rafferty *(Melvin)*; Colonel Bruce Hampton *(Morris)*; Vic Chesnutt *(Terence)*; Mickey Jones *(Monty Johnson)*; Ian Moore *(Randy Horsefeathers)*; Judy Pryor Trice *(Mrs. Woolridge)*; Scott Stewart *(Bubba Woolridge)*; Betty Lynn Hall *(Sister)*; Jim Jarmusch *(Fostee Cream)*; Gary Don Fletcher *(Preacher)*; Tim Holder *(Albert)*; Tom Kagy *(Freddy)*; Stacy Barrow *(Woolridge Secretary)*; Jackie Stewart *(Walter)*; Jamie Stewart; D.J. Royston *(Housekeeper)*; Lacy Bailey *(Karen)*; Raymond Lewallen *(Ticket Agent)*

In a long, unusual, and compelling film written and directed by its star, Billy Bob Thornton portrays a mentally retarded man who experiences love and moral awakening despite his handicaps and memories of a horrifying childhood. Thornton's script garned him a Best Adapted Screenplay Oscar.

In an Alabama mental institution, a young reporter interviews Karl Childers (Thornton), who is about to be released after having served a 25-year sentence. Although wary of strange people, he tells her his story: Because his parents considered his mental disabilities shameful, they kept him in a shack outside the house where he slept in a hole in the dirt. He was generally made fun of by the other children for his strange appearance and voice. One day when he was 12, he saw a young man who was especially fond of bullying him having sex with his mother. Confused and infuriated, Karl killed him with a scythe ("sling blade"); when he discovered that his mother was enjoying what they had been doing, he killed her too. During his 25 years of confinement, he has read the Bible. Asked if he will kill again, Karl answers that he doesn't feel he has any need to kill anyone.

With nowhere to go, Karl returns to his hometown. Having a knack for mechanical repair, he is able to get a job as a mechanic. He befriends a young boy, Frank (Lucas Black), whose widowed mother, Linda (Natalie Canerday), lets Karl stay with them. He is treated kindly by both Linda and her longtime friend Vaughan (John Ritter), a gay man. A fish out of water in this area, Vaughan would leave but stays because of a romantic attachment and because he is worried about Linda's boyfriend, Doyle (Dwight Yoakam), an abusive bully and a mean drunk.

Karl begins to feel at home in his surroundings, though he is still haunted by his past. He tells Frank that his parents had another child, but because they didn't want the baby made Karl bury it alive. Karl visits the house where he was raised to find his father (Robert Duvall) still living there, alone and in squalor. Unable to make contact, he leaves the old man.

Doyle continues to abuse Linda, and though she throws him out of her house, she takes him back when he promises to mend his ways. But he demands that Karl leave, and makes it clear to Frank (whom he considers a weakling) that he will be the new boss. Realizing that Linda is unable to rid herself of Doyle, and that the well-meaning but cowardly Vaughan can be of no help, Karl has himself baptized, waits until Doyle is in the house alone, and kills him with a sharpened lawnmower blade. He turns himself into the police and is returned to the mental hospital.

Thornton introduced his character Karl Childers in a performance piece, then brought him to the screen in a short called SOME FOLKS CALL IT A SLING BLADE (1993) directed by George Hickenlooper. SLING BLADE, the feature-length account of Karl's moral odyssey, received, in addition to Thornton's scripting Oscar, a special jury prize at the Chicago International Film Festival.

A mental defective one step below Forrest Gump in brainpower and social skills, Karl looks and sounds like a cartoon character. Thornton invests him with the underslung jaw of the Tasmanian devil, the bow-armed posture of a Monty Python moron, and some of the vulnerability and gentle dignity of Boris Karloff's Frankenstein monster. His wardrobe is limited to a single gray sport shirt (top button unstylishly buttoned, of course), one pair of gray pants, and a pair of clunky black shoes. He speaks in a gravelly monotone—in a voice one character likens to "a race car motor." Increasingly endearing are the raspy "um-hum"'s that end most of his sentences and the "alright then" that serves as his stock response to virtually every request and suggestion. Thornton's inspired and humane performance earns his character great sympathy and respect, beginning with the movie's most powerful set piece: a long monologue in which Karl relates the key events of his traumatic childhood, his recitation underscored and enhanced by the slow, sad, portentous music of Daniel Lanois.

SLING BLADE's somber plot is frequently undercut by humor. At one point Vaughan takes Karl to lunch and attempts to communicate with him in the half-baked psychological terms of the times. Karl doesn't have a clue what Vaughan is talking about, but what makes the scene so memorably funny is that Karl has no clue he has no clue. Another hilarious moment arises when Karl tries to tell Linda a dirty joke he doesn't really understand.

Superbly photographed by Barry Markowitz in small-town Arkansas, SLING BLADE affords respect to both its characters and its viewers by telling its story in long, straightforward, and subtly absorbing takes—an admirable stylistic approach that ought to have been tempered with a few more close-ups (we never get a really good look at Karl's father or Linda). Despite a very minor slackening and softening of the plot in the last act, SLING BLADE is a moving, thought-provoking, and accomplished piece of filmmaking. *(Violence, extreme profanity.)* — D.T.

d, Billy Bob Thornton; p, Brandon Rosser, David L. Bushell; exec p, Larry Meistrich; w, Billy Bob Thornton (from his screenplay "Some Folks Call It a Sling Blade"); ph, Barry Markowitz; ed, Hughes Winborne; m, Daniel Lanois; prod d, Clark Hunter; set d, Traci Kirshbaum; sound, Jeff Kushner (design), Paul Ledford; casting, Sarah Tackett; cos, Douglas Hall

AA Best Adapted Screenplay: Billy Bob Thornton; *AAN Best Actor:* Billy Bob Thornton

Drama **(PR: C MPAA: R)**

SMALL FACES ★★★

(U.K.) 109m Skyline Easterhouse; BBC Scotland; BBC Films ~ October Films c

Iain Robertson *(Lex MacLean)*; Joseph McFadden *(Alan MacLean)*; J. S. Duffy *(Bobby MacLean)*; Laura Fraser *(Joanne MacGowan)*; Garry Sweeney *(Charlie Sloan)*; Clare Higgins *(Lorna MacLean)*; Kevin McKidd *(Malky Johnson)*; Mark McConnochie *(Gorbals)*; Steven Singleton *(Welch)*; David Walker *(Fabio)*; Ian McElhinney *(Uncle Andrew)*; Paul Doonan *(Jake)*; Colin Semple *(Dowd)*; Colin McCredie *(Doug)*; Debbie Welch *(Rebecca)*; Eilidh McCormack *(Alice)*; Monica Brady *(Aunt)*; Elizabeth McGregor *(Mrs. MacGowan)*; Andy Gray *(Tactless Man)*; Louise O'Kane *(Polly)*; Lisa McIntosh *(Patty)*; Kirsty Mitchell *(Maggie)*; Sheila Greer Smith *(Assistant)*; Karen McColl *(Helen)*; Karen Murphy *(Maria)*; Carmen Pieraccini *(Jeannie)*; Rab Christie *(Talker)*; Allan Atkins *(Boy with Scar)*; Tom Gallacher *(Davie)*; Joanne Reilly *(Barbara)*; Matt Costello *(Shuggy)*; Liz Lochhead *(Librarian)*; John Murtagh *(Teacher)*; Tom Logan *(Tutor)*

Gillies and Billy MacKinnon set and shot their semiautobiographical film SMALL FACES in the scruffy Govanhill section of Glasgow where they grew up. Penetrating and very competently made, SMALL FACES won the Michael Powell Award for Best New British Film at the Edinburgh Film Festival.

Glasgow, 1968. Thirteen-year-old Lex MacLean (Iain Robertson) lives in a small apartment with his widowed mother (Clare Higgins) and his two older brothers, Bobby and Alan. Bobby (J. S. Duffy) is a mercurial boy who hangs with a local street gang called the Glen, while Alan (Joseph McFadden) is a budding artist of talent. Alan has recently begun seeing Joanne (Laura Fraser), a girl who is coveted by both Charlie Sloan (Garry Sweeney), the leader of the Glen, and Malky Johnson (Kevin McKidd), the leader of the Tongs, a rival gang from another neighborhood.

Tensions are growing between the Glen and the Tongs. During a rumble between the two rival gangs, Bobby smashes Malky's nose with a brick. Lex, possibly to divert Malky's attention from Bobby, ventures onto Tong turf and tells Malky where Charlie goes ice-skating on Saturdays. But Malky is not pleased when he learns that Lex is reponsible for earlier shooting him (by accident) with an air gun. He's even less pleased to learn that it was one of Lex's brothers who bashed his nose, and that his other brother is dating Joanne.

That Saturday at the skating rink, Bobby is fatally stabbed by one of the Tongs. Feeling responsible for his brother's death, Lex confronts Malky with a knife, but is scared off. Malky's bullied stepbrother, Gorbals (Mark McConnochie), surreptitiously turns on the gas jets in their apartment and Malky blows himself up lighting a cigarette. Now safe from Malky and his vendetta, Lex dreams that Bobby is alive and happy, that Alan moves out and enrolls in art school, and that he himself has turned into a terrible creature: a grown man. "Luckily," he says, "when I woke up I was still a boy."

Expertly photographed by the talented John de Borman, SMALL FACES is a familiar story set in a place that is unfamiliar to most moviegoers: low-rent Glasgow, 1968, where we meet three teenaged brothers trying to survive at one or two socioeconomic levels below that of the luckier Scottish youngsters introduced to us by Bill Forsyth in THAT SINKING FEELING (1979) and GREGORY'S GIRL (1980). Like Forsyth's adolescents, the MacKinnon brothers' kids have an openness and charm that is surprising given the traditional stereotyping of Scots as a dour people and of teenagers as an inscrutable species.

Particularly endearing are the very expressive Iain Robertson, as the intelligent and sensitive yet unspoiled and valiant Lex, and J. S. Duffy, whose poignant portrayal of the troubled Bobby—a lad who alternates seemingly arbitrary bouts of destructiveness and desperation with moments of childlike sweetness and ingenuousness—almost makes you want to adopt him. Also quite good are the rival gang leaders: Kevin McKidd as the loutish Malky and Garry Sweeney as the mock-elegant Charlie.

Standout scenes are many, among them the one in which the MacLean family, adults and children alike, enjoy an informal house party, complete with a trombone solo (Lex), a ballad (Mrs. MacLean), and drunken high jinks (Uncle Andrew). This scene reminds us how infrequently intergenerational partying is depicted in American movies, which have so long been preoccupied with exploring the generation gap, they've become committed to promoting and expanding it. Near the end of SMALL FACES occurs a less successful scene in which Lex, tormented by his problems, finds a moment of respite at a kids movie matinee—a conceit that is closer to a writer's idea of a cinematic epiphany than to an actual one.

A commendable film, SMALL FACES might have been a classic (though probably more difficult to finance and promote) if the MacKinnon brothers had de-emphasized the somewhat tired gang war plot and diverted their considerable insight and creative talent to a more episodic, less narratively charged survey of the Glasgow scene they know so well. *(Violence, nudity, profanity.)* — D.T.

d, Gillies MacKinnon; p, Billy MacKinnon, Steve Clark-Hall; exec p, Mark Shivas, Andrea Calderwood; w, Gillies MacKinnon, Billy MacKinnon; ph, John de Borman; ed, Scott Thomas; m, John Zeane; prod d, Zoe MacLeod; art d, Pat Campbell; sound, Louis Kramer (recordist); casting, Hayley Murt, Pat Harkins; cos, Kate Carin; makeup, Robert McCann

Drama **(PR: C MPAA: R)**

SMALL WONDERS ★★

(U.S.) 77m Four Oaks Foundation ~ Miramax c
(AKA: FIDDLEFEST: ROBERTA GUASPARI-TZAVARAS AND HER EAST HARLEM VIOLIN PROGRAM)

Roberta Guaspari-Tzavaras; Karen Briggs; John Blake Jr.; Ani Kavafian; Ida Kavafian; Midori Diane Monroe; Mark O'Connor; Itzhak Perlman; Arnold Steinhardt; Isaac Stern; Billy Taylor; Michael Tree; Nicholas Tzavaras; Diana Wan; Charlene Bishop; Jacob Blitz; Marisa Guttman Bushman; Sara Carrero; Erika Castaneda; Wendy Castaneda; Robyn Creswell; Melia Crumbley; Michael Brian Cruz; Allison Joy During; Molly Gia Foresta; Nora Friedman; Cristina Gomez; Omar Grant; Jeffery Horton; Stefanie-Erin Horton; Kendra Mack; Fabian Marcano; Emilia Maynard; Aida Morales; Aurora Nonas-Barnes; Krystal Perez; Christian Rios; Emma Sacks; Aaliyan Sharif; Jason Stanger-Ortiz; Matthew Stanger-Ortiz; Evin Steed; Jairus Steed; Anaar Stephens; Joshua Stephens; Shantha Susman; Anika Tam; Andres Tavarez-Terrero; Omari Toomer; Susanna Gabriela Traverzo; Sarah Walter

SMALL WONDERS tells the true and supposedly inspirational story of a teacher who transforms her East Harlem students into maestro violinists. Unfortunately, the tone of the film is inadvertently patronizing and ultimately off-putting.

SMALL WONDERS (formerly titled FIDDLEFEST) follows the teacher, Roberta Guaspari-Tzavaras, through her day-to-day efforts to mold the bright, young students of three East Harlem public schools into violinists. Along the way, Roberta remembers how she started her non-profit violin program after budget cuts forced the Board of Education to eliminate her position as a violin teacher in 1990. The popularity of her program over the following years then required Roberta to establish a lottery that would impartially select 150 students annually for instruction.

During practice, Roberta shows a tough, no-nonsense approach to her craft, dismissing students who either have scheduling conflicts or forget to bring their violins to class. She works hard to train the youngsters to play "The National Anthem" for an appearance in Madison Square Garden before a Knicks basketball game, which goes successfully. She also rehearses her group for a climactic performance at Carnegie Hall, which is capped by a Bach concerto, featuring several international violin stars playing along side Roberta's students. After the concert, Roberta proudly tells the children's parents, "I knew they'd be wonderful, but couldn't tell them 'til it was over."

To be sure, there will be many admirers of this ragged-looking, small-scale effort (it was nominated for the Best Documentary Feature Oscar in 1995). After all, who could dislike the many adorable children on-screen? The problem with SMALL WONDERS, as one can tell from the title, is that director Allan Miller (FROM MAO TO MOZART—ISAAC STERN IN CHINA) has adopted the point of view of the domineering teacher, Roberta Guaspari-Tzavaras, to the exclusion of everyone else on screen (she refers to the students as puppets and typically bellows at them, "Whatever I do, you do!").

Thus, like a Hollywood movie of the 1930s (e.g. THEY SHALL HAVE MUSIC, 1939), the film's disturbing subtext is that the liberal elite feels obligated to give the ethnic "ghetto" children a dose of "class" by championing the artform of violin music. Itzhak Perlman's cameo here is little different from Jascha Heifetz's God-like role in the aforementioned Depression-era movie. Most distressing of all is the scene in which a working-class mother barely recognizes her son while dressing him for the Carnegie Hall concert finale (she even asks him if he's her son!).

In 1994, Frederick Wiseman also praised Harlem's Central Park East's High School in his documentary, HIGH SCHOOL 2, yet managed to convey the perspectives of the students, teachers, administrators and parents. It's too bad that more people will probably see SMALL WONDERS, but then facile romanticism often does prevail over careful, weighty deliberation. — E.M.

d, Allan Miller; p, Susan Kaplan, Walter Scheuer; exec p, Walter Scheuer; ph, Kramer Morgenthau; ed, Allan Miller, Donald Klocek; sound, Gautam K. Choudhury

Documentary **(PR: A MPAA: G)**

SOCIAL SUICIDE

(SEE: PRE-MADONNAS)

SOLITAIRE FOR TWO ★

(U.K.) 105m Dove International; Cavalier Features ~ Paramount Home Movies c

Mark Frankel *(Daniel Becker)*; Amanda Pays *(Katie Burrill)*; Roshan Seth *(Sandip Tamar)*; Jason Isaacs *(Harry)*; Maryam d'Abo *(Caroline)*; Helen Lederer *(Cop)*; Malcolm Cooper *(Cop)*; Annette Crosbie *(Mrs. Dwyer)*; Neil Mullarkey *(Parris)*; Liza Walker *(Lucy)*; Kelly Salmon *(Young Katie)*; Ricky Jones *(Young Boy)*; Diana Eskell *(Squeegee Girl)*; Robert Harley *(Barman)*; Colin Wakefield *(Businessman)*; Phil Fox *(Businessman)*; Michael Shaw *(Scientist)*; Alister Cameron *(Scientist)*; Carli Harris *(Clare)*; Rosalind Knight *(Receptionist)*; Michael Schneider *(Vincenzo)*; Paul Simpkin *(Waiter)*; Norman Caro *(Joe the Florist)*; John Levitt *(Sharples)*; Catherine Russell *(Julie Parrish)*; Otto Jarman *(Neighbor)*; Stefan Schwartz *(Neighbor)*

Would you green-light this unpromising script pitch? An assertiveness-training professor with a minor in body language falls for a psychic paleontologist who responds to men's impure thoughts with compulsive violence. Sabotaging its minimal screwball potential with two exceedingly charmless leads, SOLITAIRE FOR TWO makes DUMB AND DUMBER and TOMMY BOY seem like triumphs of gossamer sophistication.

Philandering Non-Verbal Communications professor Daniel Becker (Mark Frankel) finds lasting love when he meets no-nonsense paleontologist Katie Burrill (Amanda Pays), who responds with a roundhouse punch. Dedicated to fossil research and hoping to finalize a dream project in India, spinster Katie is able to psychically read men's thoughts—or at least the lewd ones. During her first date with smitten Daniel, mindreader Katie KOs the waiter for nursing sexual desires about her. Daniel's unrelenting passion initially drives Katie deeper into prehistoric prehistoric studies with her associate Sandip Tamar (Roshan Seth), whom she believes to be asexual. Sending out mixed signals to each other, the couple argue heatedly and often. On the eve of her departure for India, Katie causes friction between Daniel and his married friends with her unsolicited psychic pronouncements. But when she realizes that Tamar also also has sexual designs on her, Katie shelves her dream project and opts for married life with Daniel, who's sworn off playing the field forever.

SOLITAIRE FOR TWO is one of those creaky romantic fabrications full of pathetic running gags (Katie's pugilistic responses) and few payoffs (Daniel's mildest-mannered pupil takes his assertiveness training so well that he pulls a pistol on his nasty boss). These slight synthetic comic bits mesh perfectly with a story line so billowy it seems to have been written on thistles.

Not only does the film's direction have all the pull of an infomercial, but the tacky dialogue appears to have been penned by "Dating Game" staffers trying to recycle double entendres into a full-length screenplay. There's something especially disheartening about a smutty romantic comedy; it's as if one awakens after a one-night stand to find one's bedmate and one's wallet gone. Violated by this dysfunctional bedroom farce, the audience finds nothing humorous in this valentine to violence. *(Extreme profanity, nudity, sexual situations, violence.)* — R.P.

d, Gary Sinyor; p, Gary Sinyor, Richard Holmes; exec p, Nigel Savage; assoc p, Nick O'Hagan; co-p, Andrew Cohen, Stephen Alexander; w, Gary Sinyor; ph, Henry Braham; ed, Ewa J. Ling; m, David A. Hughes; prod d, Carmel Collins; art d, Tim Ellis; set d, John Hand; sound, Stuart Wilson (recordist); fx, Any Effects;

casting, Emma Style; cos, Rodger Parker; makeup, Jacquetta; stunts, Rod Woodruff

Comedy/Romance **(PR: C MPAA: R)**

SOLO ★★

(U.S./Mexico) 93m Triumph Pictures; Orpheus Films; John Flock Productions ~ Triumph Releasing c

Mario Van Peebles *(Solo)*; Barry Corbin *(General Clyde Haynes)*; William Sadler *(Colonel Madden)*; Jaime Gomez *(Lorenzo)*; Damian Bechir *(Rio)*; Seidy Lopez *(Agela)*; Abraham Verduzco *(Miguel)*; Joaquin Garrido *(Vasquez)*; William Wallace *(Mr. Thompson)*; Adrien Brody *(Bill Stewart)*; Brent Schaefer *(Communications Officer)*; Lucas Dudley *(Heimsman)*; Christopher Michael *(Flight Deck Officer)*; Rafael Velasco *(Justos)*; Abel Woolrich *(Lazaro)*; Fernecio de Bernal *(Father Cerna)*; Socorro Avelar *(Abuelita)*; Alvaro Carcano *(Elder #1)*; Carlos Quintero *(Elder #2)*; William Ungerman *(Bayne)*; Greg Collins *(Scanion)*; Randy Reyes *(Locke)*; Sid Belk *(Pierson)*; Kevin Cole *(Hawkins)*; Charlie Tuitavuki *(Stone)*; Norberto Barba *(Rebel Soldier)*; John Flock *(Lab Tech)*; Julian Buccio *(Rebel in Church)*

As a slick little "B"-movie vehicle for Mario Van Peebles, SOLO should please the actor-director's less demanding fans. But, while the star has some fun playing the robotic title hero, there is little else to recommend here.

"Solo" (Van Peebles) looks like flesh and blood, but is actually a $2 billion fighting machine of the future, made out of chips and polymers. Gen. Haynes (Barry Corbin), the top US military advisor in charge of Project Solo, sends the covert killer weapon on a top secret mission against rebel forces in Latin America. During his assignment, however, Solo refuses a command that would result in the deaths of innocent noncombatants. The mission goes awry, Solo is damaged, and his military superiors, who see his refusal as a clear defect in his software, order his creator, computer whiz Bill Stewart (Adrien Brody), to reprogram him.

Realizing that reprogramming would wipe out his memory and his burgeoning "human" qualities, Solo escapes to the jungles of Latin America, still damaged and quickly losing power. He collapses inside an ancient Mayan temple, where he is found by a young boy, Miguel (Abraham Verduzco), who takes him to his village, which is under attack by the ruthless rebels.

Determined not to lose Solo, Gen. Haynes sends Madden (William Sadler), a troubleshooting colonel, and a team of trained killers to retrieve the robot. But Solo resists the intruding soldiers, and forces Haynes to send a robotic version of Madden to fight Solo to the death. Solo wins the hearts of the villagers by trouncing the US military team, the new robot and the band of local rebels.

Mario Van Peebles has developed a habit of appearing in silly action movies when not directing more serious films with "black" themes and concerns (i.e. NEW JACK CITY, POSSE, PANTHER). Norberto Barba, not Van Peebles, directed SOLO from a screenplay by David L. Corley, which contains a more than passing resemblance to ROBOCOP (1987), TERMINATOR 2: JUDGMENT DAY (1991), and TV's "The Six Million Dollar Man," VIRTUOSITY (1995), and PREDATOR (1987), likewise filmed in the jungles of Puerto Vallarta, Mexico. Even the final fight scene looks conspicuously like the climax of THE JUROR (another 1996 Columbia picture). The comic-book heroics enliven a few scenes like the final fight between the robots, but most of the story, direction and acting is as mechanical as the lead character. The fact that Solo chooses to be "like Mike" Jordan (i.e. a "black" robot), could have given SOLO an undercurrent of humor or even social commentary, but most of the laughs here seem unintentional (the film is no better informed about Central American politics). It should be noted, however, that like other recent action pictures, but in a less qualified way, the film implicitly criticizes the US military. And, while Van Peebles gives new meaning to the expression, "one-note performance," his front-right-and-center derring-do holds together this tenuous formula picture. *(Violence, profanity.)* — E.M.

d, Norberto Barba; p, John Flock, Joseph Newton Cohen; co-p, Jose Ludlow, Gina Resnick; w, David Corley (based on the novel *Weapon* by Robert Mason); ph, Christopher Walling; ed, Scott Conrad; m, Christopher Franke; prod d, Markus Canter; art d, Jose Luis Aguilar; set d, Jorge Lara Sanchez; sound, Salvador de la Fuente (recorder); fx, Federico Farfan; casting, Karen Rea; cos, Estella Fernandez; makeup, Alfredo Mora, Gary Tunnicliffe, Image Animation; stunts, Tom Muzila

Action/Adventure **(PR: C MPAA: PG-13)**

SOME FOLKS CALL IT A SLING BLADE ★★★

(U.S.) 38m ~ Kino-Eye American/videos.com Inc. bw

Molly Ringwald *(Teresa Tatum)*; J. T. Walsh *(Psycho)*; Suzanne Cryer *(Frances Mormon)*; Jefferson Mays *(Jerry Woolrich)*; Billy Bob Thornton *(Karl)*; Abby Abernathy; Brent Briscoe; Otto Coecho; Abe Dalool; Ron Livingston; Aaron Wheeler; Bill Boll; Chester Dent; Bill Spargue; Joey Blow; Mark Gimbrere; Michael D. Beugg; Linda Beugg; Trevor A. Tarr; Mike Herman; Glennon Schneider; Kevin Hell; Rob Beaumont; Carlos Sanchez; Anthony Guneratne; Nikywa Prevost; Beth Ruggiero; Rosalie Barron; DeWitte Briggs; Jude Barron; Kevin Hudnell; Mark Sellors; Lincoln Schlei; Joel Milner; Brent Williams

SOME FOLKS CALL IT A SLING BLADE is a crisp, dark, stylized short about mental illness, combining cinema verite and film noir influences. The film's length and format mean you probably won't find it at your local theater, but it's well worth checking out on video.

Karl (Billy Bob Thornton) has spent the last 25 years in a mental institution for, as a 13-year-old boy, he brutally murdered his mother and her lover. Now he is scheduled for release. Teresa (Molly Ringwald) is a young, nervous, newspaper reporter sent to interview Karl for a feature on his release. She convinces administrator Jerry Woolrich (Jefferson Mays), a bureaucratic sycophant, to permit the interview, despite his numerous objections. Karl supposedly won't talk to women or permit photos, but will "tell his story" (no questions) in a darkened room, with only Teresa and Woolrich present. Terrified and minus her photographer, Frances (Suzanne Cryer), Teresa heads for the interview, expecting the worst.

Karl is obviously disturbed, but not violent. He speaks in a halting Texas drawl, telling Teresa how his parents (who believed Karl's ugliness was their punishment for having sex) made him sleep in a hole under a shed and fed him "pretty regular." He explains that he found his mother having extramarital sex and dispatched first her lover, then her, with a "kaiser blade" ("Some folks call it a sling blade. . . ," he explains), a scythe-like agricultural implement. Teresa asks if he would do it again in the same circumstances. He says yes. Will he kill again? He says he has no reason to.

At a later time, Karl prepares to enter the world outside. As he exits, Karl tells an attendant, "I reckon I'm gonna have to get used to looking at pretty people. I reckon I'm gonna have to get used to them looking at me too." The attendant silently removes a tag from Karl's new shirt. His "free" future is as bleak as his past.

As the film progresses, our sympathy shifts from Teresa to Karl (this is subtly aided by the fact that no flashbacks are included to illustrated his story). Shot in black and white, its frequent slow tracking shots and claustrophobic framing create a mood of antiseptic menace, reminiscent of Frederick Wiseman's mental-illness documentary, TITICUT FOLLIES (1967). Amplified ambient sound (footsteps, etc.) intensifies this mood. In the first minutes of SOME FOLKS, we watch through safety-glass windows as a psychotic (J.T. Walsh) moves across the dayroom and delivers a twisted monologue to Karl. Only later do we discover that Walsh is not the main character.

Billy Bob Thornton wrote the part of Karl for himself and invited George Hickenlooper to direct his screenplay; they work well together. Both admitted (in the video found on the same tape, "The Making of SOME FOLKS CALL IT A SLING BLADE") that their goal is to collaborate on feature films. When the time came to transform this short film into a feature, however, Thornton chose to direct the resulting film, simply titled SLING BLADE, himself, and didn't do too bad for his efforts, earning a Best Adapted Screenplay Oscar for it. *(Adult situations, profanity.)* — C.M.

d, George Hickenlooper; p, Adam Lindemann, George Hickenlooper, Kevin Hudnell; exec p, Brad Schlei, Mike Herman, Kevin Hell; co-p, Michael Beugg; w, Billy Bob Thornton; ph, Kent Wakeford; ed, Henni Bouwmeester, George Hickenlooper; m, Bill Boll; art d, Deborah Smith; sound, Peter V. Meiselmann, Gary Shepherd, Mike Gitman; cos, Matthew Jacobsen; makeup, Elena Arroy

Drama/Crime **(PR: C MPAA: NR)**

SOME MOTHER'S SON ★★★

(Ireland/U.S./U.K.) 112m Hell's Kitchen; Castle Rock Entertainment ~ Columbia c

Helen Mirren *(Kathleen Quigley)*; Aidan Gillen *(Gerald Quigley)*; Fionnula Flanagan *(Annie Higgins)*; David O'Hara *(Frank Higgins)*; John Lynch *(Bobby Sands)*; Tim Woodward *(Harrington)*; Tom Hollander *(Farnsworth)*; Ciaran Hinds *(Danny Boyle)*; Gerard McSorley *(Father Daly)*; Geraldine O'Rawe *(Alice Quigley)*; Dan Gordon *(Inspector McPeake)*; Grainne Delany *(Theresa Higgins)*; Ciaran Fitzgerald *(Liam Quigley)*; Robert Lang *(Government Minister)*; Stephen Hogan *(Young Turk)*; Peter Howitt *(SAS Leader)*; Bosco Hogan *(British Captain)*; Jimmy Keogh *(Jimmy Higgins)*; John Kavanagh *(Cardinal)*; Oliver Maguire *(Frank Maguire)*; Doreen Keogh *(Mother Superior)*; Anna Megan *(Rosie Quigley)*; Hugh O'Donnell *(Paddy)*; John Higgins *(John Deegan)*; Joan Sheehy *(1st Woman Searcher)*; Mal Whyte *(Barrister)*; Alan Barry *(Judge)*; Barry Cassin *(Prosecutor)*; Brian Mallon *(Prison Office Jones)*; Sean Lawlor *(Platoon Leader)*; Michael Sherrie *(Assistant Governor)*; James Hickey *(Young Son)*; Karen Carlisle *(Prisoner's Girlfriend)*; Fiona Higgins *(Prisoner's Sister)*; Jer O'Leary *(Hunger Striker)*; Tim McDonnell *(Hunger Striker)*; Tony Flynn *(Cyclist)*; Liam Byrne *(Prisoner Murphy)*; Pat Mulryan *(1st IRA Man)*; Valerie Roe *(Girl in Farnsworth's Office)*; Deirdre McAliskey *(Woman in Court)*; Michael S. O'Sullivan *(Prison Office David)*; Jennifer Gibney *(2nd Woman Searcher)*; Robert Taylor *(Election Agent)*; Kate Perry *(Prison Officer's Widow)*; Anthony Brophy *(Prisoner's Leader)*; Mickey McEneaney; Paddy McEneaney; Gene Berrills *(Merry Mac Members)*; Ronan O'Donoghue *(Radio Announcer)*; Richard Neilson *(Radio Announcer)*

This tale of two mothers puts a human face on the struggle for Irish independence. SOME MOTHER'S SON is set during the 217-day hunger strike of 1981 in which 10 men, including IRA leader Bobby Sands, died for their political beliefs.

Kathleen (Helen Mirren) is a middle-class, apolitical schoolteacher and mother of three in a small village in Northern Ireland. Annie (Fionnula Flanagan) is a farmer and staunch supporter of the republican cause. Annie's son, Frank (David O'Hara), and Kathleen's son, Gerard (Aiden Gillen), have been arrested after a shootout with the British Army. Sent to the Maze Prison, they decide to take part in a hunger strike designed to gain hard-won and often unsatisfactory concessions from the British. The protesters want to wear civilian clothes to show that they are not criminals but prisoners of war. Denied this right, they reject their uniforms and take to wearing nothing but blankets, letting themselves go unkempt and unshaven. Denied the use of bathrooms, they smear their own excrement on the walls. Britain, under the iron claw of Margaret Thatcher, is implacable.

Kathleen is slowly shaken out of her non-involvement and joins forces with Annie in protesting for their sons: she suffers the disapprobation of her school superiors and is spat upon in the street. These two women, worlds apart, begin a wary, mutually respectful friendship. On the positive side, Sands is elected to the British Parliament, but he soon dies. People take to the streets in a huge demonstration of affection for their fallen leader.

As the prisoners' conditions worsen, the women are faced with a dire choice. They must either watch their children die for their convictions or go against their express wishes and save their lives. When Frank dies and Gerard lapses into a coma, Kathleen decides that enough is enough and signs the documents enabling him to receive a doctor's aid.

For pure emotional power, this is one of 1996's strongest releases. It's admirably even-handed in its treatment of the opposing sides. Terry George, who directed and co-wrote with Jim Sheridan, cannily lets viewers come to know the characters' differing lives. It's a far simpler and superior work to this same team's IN THE NAME OF THE FATHER (1993), which suffered from histrionic grandstanding and flamboyant and suspiciously MTV-ish photography of its prison scenes. George avoids political rhetoric in the interests of getting at the raw, contentious passions of the story. The razor-sharp photography and moody, melancholy music serve his intent beautifully. The sudden, terrifying infiltration of ferreting British Army forces into a quiet family celebration is thrillingly staged. The massed funeral scene for Sands is impressively big and stirring, suddenly throwing the deeply personalized conflict into higher relief.

Mirren triumphs in her beautifully economic, dramatic way, again proving herself one of the screen's finest actresses. Her Kathleen is the most normal of women thrown into the most challenging of circumstances. It's an admirably controlled performance, kept strictly in check until a climactic scene in a hospital room. Flanagan is no less impressive: tough as nails, unquestioning in beliefs held from birth, she is the no-nonsense soul of Eire. One would think twice before tangling with this skeptical daughter of the sod. The pub scene in which the two women come to know each other, Queen Elizabeth's portrait humorously hanging just above their sozzled heads, is a brief and welcome respite from the "troubles."

The film does have one minor problem: the men are too undifferentiated. They're politically passionate, of course, but they lack individuality, interchangeable in personality as well as in shaggy Christ-like appearance. For all the brutalization of their imprisonment, one doesn't feel half as strongly for them as for the women. *(Violence, adult situations, profanity.)* — D.N.

d, Terry George; p, Jim Sheridan, Arthur Lappin, Ed Burke; assoc p, Helen Mirren; w, Terry George, Jim Sheridan; ph, Geoffrey Simpson; ed, Craig McKay; m, Bill Whelan; prod d, David Wilson; art d, Conor Devlin; set d, Carolyn Scott; sound, Brian Simmons; casting, Nuala Moiselle; cos, Joan Bergin

Drama **(PR: C MPAA: R)**

SOMEONE ELSE'S AMERICA ★★★½
(France/U.K./U.S.) 96m MACT Productions; Intrinsica Films; Lichtblick Filmproduktion; Stefi 2; Pandora Cinema ~ October Films c
(L'AMERIQUE DES AUTRES)

Tom Conti *(Alonso)*; Miki Manojlovic *(Bayo)*; Maria Casares *(Alonso's Mother)*; Zorka Manojlovic *(Bayo's Mother)*; Sergej Trifunovic *(Luka)*; Jose Ramon Rosario *(Panchito)*; Lanny Flaherty *(Guide)*; Michalis Yannatos *(Greek Agent)*; Michael Willis *(Foreman)*; Predrag Ejdus *(Doctor)*; Chia-Ching Niu *(Chinese Girl)*; Andjela Stojkovic *(Savka)*; Lazar Kalmic *(Pepo)*; Ananda Ellis *(Afisi)*; John Norman Thomas *(Afisi's Brother)*; Jonathon Peck *(Sam)*; Yan Shi *(Chou)*; Miou *(Japanese Girl)*; Anibal Lleras *(Philipino)*; Ai Ya *(Chinese Grandma)*; Shuain Hui *(Chinese Grandpa)*; Loi Gao Li *(Chinese Musician)*; Dominique Lasaki; Robert Franz; Juan Rodriguez Vila *(Flamenco Group)*

A heartfelt, melancholic tale about European immigrants, SOMEONE ELSE'S AMERICA presents a strange, foreign conception of America, an America that always will be the land of opportunity. This often humorous character study won the audience prize at Cannes in 1995.

The film centers on the friendship of two shaggy survivors: Alonso (Tom Conti), a legal immigrant from Spain, and the not-so-legal Bayo (Miki Manojlovic) from Montenegro. Alonso owns a rundown cantina where he lives and cares for his blind, elderly mother, Mrs. Victoria (Maria Casares). In exchange for custodial services, Alonso lets a room to Bayo and his pet rooster. But Bayo is more than a boarder. When Alonso becomes infatuated with a Syrian beauty, Bayo acts as his romantic advocate, only to suffer a brutal beating on behalf of his friend.

In order to support himself and send money to his mother, Anja (Zorka Manojlovic), who takes care of his three children in Montenegro, Bayo takes jobs that only an illegal alien would be offered, like cleaning up toxic waste. Unknown to Bayo, his letters and money never reach Anja, and she struggles to support her grandchildren. Bayo's little daughter, Savka (Andjela Stojkovic), misses her father so much that she has become gravely ill, and the eldest, Luka (Sergej Trifunovic), has gotten himself into trouble with the authorities. Only Bayo's favorite, Pepo (Lazar Kalmic), maintains his high spirits.

Anja decides to uproot her grandchildren and find their father in America. The circuitous journey takes them through Mexico, where they confront the Rio Grande. Crossing the river, Pepo is swept away by the powerful current. Upon hearing the news, Bayo travels to Texas, Alonso at his side, refusing to believe that the angelic Pepo is dead. He obsessively conducts a long, fruitless search for his child.

Back in Brooklyn, Bayo irrationally blames Luka for the loss. A wily hustler, Luka is hurt but far from devastated by his father's rebukes. Luka is infected with the American dream—succeed at any cost. With his eyes on a green card, he seduces, then marries, a Chinese-American neighbor. He also gets his grandmother, a fine cook, to help him turn Alonso's bar into a successful restaurant.

Eventually, Luka and his Chinese wife move to San Francisco, accompanied by Anja and Savka. Now Bayo is left with no one but Alonso, whose mother is now dead. The final shot shows the two immigrants as they literally rise out of their dismal surroundings and float above the New York skyline.

At times too episodic for its own good, SOMEONE ELSE'S AMERICA is held together by engaging performances, particularly that of Manojlovic as the volatile Montenegrin. Manojlovic invests the sad, clownish Bayo with a depth and pathos that counterbalances his comic bullheadedness and helps ground the sprawling story.

Written and directed by Serbs, produced by a Franco-British-German troika, shot by a Greek, and starring another Serb (Manojlovic), this thoroughly European production creates a New York that one would be hard-pressed to find anywhere near the island of Manhattan. Brooklyn is seen as an idyllic melting pot where immigrants of all backgrounds share the struggle. Even the look of director Goran Paskaljevic's Brooklyn, with its flat emptiness, takes one far away from any of the five boroughs. This is not surprising since most of the film was shot on a soundstage in Germany. *(Profanity, adult situations.)* — T.Y.

d, Goran Paskaljevic; p, Antoine de Clermont-Tonnerre, David Rose, Helga Bahr; co-p, Gabrielle Tana, Johanna Baldwin; w, Gordan Mihic; ph, Yorgos Arvanitis; ed, William Diver; m, Andrew Dickson; prod d, Miljen Kljakovic; art d, Wolf Seesselberg; sound, Aad Wirtz, Christian Wangler, Francois Groult; fx, Conrad Brink, Jeff Brink; casting, Robi Reed; cos, Charlotte Holdich; makeup, Francoise Chapuis-Asselin; stunts, Manny Siverio

Comedy/Drama **(PR: C MPAA: R)**

SOMETIMES THEY COME BACK ... AGAIN ★★
(U.S.) 98m Trimark Pictures ~ Vidmark c

Michael Gross *(Jon Porter)*; Alexis Arquette *(Tony Reno)*; Hilary Swank *(Michelle Porter)*; Jennifer Elise Cox *(Jules Martin)*; W. Morgan Sheppard *(Father Archer Roberts)*; Bojesse Christopher *(Vinnie Ritacco)*; Jennifer Aspen *(Maria Moore)*; Glen Beaudin *(Sean Patrick)*; Michael Malota *(Young Jon)*; Gabriel Dell Jr. *(Steve Pagel)*; Patrick Renna *(Young Alan)*; Leslie Danon *(Lisa Porter)*; Ingrid Sthare *(Jennifer Hadley)*; Michael Stadvec *(Jim Thorn)*; Andree Gibbs *(Page Porter)*; Molly Hagen *(Officer Violet Searcey)*

Stephen King fans trying to keep up with the slew of mediocre direct adaptations of his work will also have to contend with a growing brood of lackluster, "unofficial" sequels like this one.

Jon Porter (Michael Gross) returns to his small hometown with his daughter Michelle (Hilary Swank) following the death of his mother. As a boy, Jon interrupted—and inadvertently caused the deaths of—a group of demonic youths led by Tony Reno (Alexis Arquette) as they were preparing to sacrifice his sister Lisa (Leslie Danon).

Through supernatural means, Tony returns to life, and the evil greaser begins putting the moves on Michelle. He also begins claiming more victims to bring his cohorts Vinnie (Bojesse Christopher) and Sean (Glen Beaudin) back from the dead. Retarded groundskeeper Steve (Gabriel Dell Jr.) and Michelle's friend Maria (Jennifer Aspen) are murdered, as is Jules (Jennifer Elise Cox), a psychic girl who has become suspicious of Tony.

Unnerved by Tony's reappearance and the string of deaths, Jon seeks help from Father Archer Roberts (W. Morgan Sheppard) before the latter is also killed. Michelle is kidnapped by Tony, and the three demons prepare her as their final sacrifice before Jon intervenes and, in a re-enactment of his boyhood encounter, dispatches the evil trio once and for all.

Billed as a sequel to a 1991 TV movie based on a King short story, this direct-to-video project actually just rehashes the author's plot with different characters and a bushel of supernatural cliches.

Director/co-writer Adam Grossman is stronger with individual setpieces than the big picture. The resurrection of the naked, demonic Vinnie from a pool of blood has true eerie power, and Jon has a relatively scary nightmare involving his daughter and Tony indulging in satanic sex. But the movie as a whole has no honest tension, because everything that happens is a foregone conclusion, from the deaths of the obvious victims-to-be to the climax where history violently repeats itself.

Casting "Family Ties"'s Gross as a dad who has *real* problems with his family is a nice touch, but the younger performers are unpersuasive, including Arquette (who was much better in the New Zealand-made chiller JACK BE NIMBLE) and Cox (Jan from the BRADY BUNCH movies)—though the latter's death by flying Tarot cards is admittedly novel. Still, it's clear that aside from the opportunity to further exploit King's name, there was no real reason for this particular story to "come back." *(Graphic violence, nudity, sexual situations, profanity.)* — M.G.

d, Adam Grossman; p, Michael Meltzer; exec p, Mark Amin, Barry Barnholtz; co-p, Phillip B. Goldfine, Milton Subotsky; w, Guy Riedel, Adam Grossman (based on characters created by Stephen King); ph, Christopher Baffa; ed, Michael E. Polakow, Stephen Myers; m, Peter Manning Robinson; prod d, Aaron Osborne; sound, Cameron Hamza, John Brasher, Marty Hutcherson, L. Mo Weber; fx, Evan Jacobs, Jon Warren, Douglas Miller, Vision Crew Unlimited; casting, Ed Mitchell, Robyn Ray; cos, Bonnie Ann Stauch; makeup, Bart J. Mixon, Earl Ellis, Elisabeth Fry, ME*FX

Horror **(PR: O MPAA: R)**

SONG SPINNER, THE ★★★

(Canada) 96m Pin Drop Productions ~ Distribution La Fete/Hallmark Home Entertainment c

Patti Lupone *(Zantalalia)*; Meredith Henderson *(Aurora)*; David Hemblen *(Captain Nizzle)*; Wendel Meldrum *(Mona)*; John Neville *(Frelo the Magnificent)*; Matthew Lerigny *(Tibo)*; Paul Couer *(Larch)*; Leslie Carlson *(Lorio)*; Julian Richings *(Calio)*; Brent Carver; Kathy Laird; Ross Campbell; The Ukranian Shumka Dancers

Set in a mythical realm, this made-for-TV feature cloaks an anti-censorship allegory in austere fantasy.

The medievalesque kingdom of Shandrilan has been cold and quiet ever since its poltroon of a monarch, Frelo the Magnificent (John Neville), proclaimed the "Hush Law" banning music and regulating sound itself. Enforcing the order is power-hungry Captain Nizzle (David Hemblen), whose Noise Police seize unlicensed musicians, balladeers, or anyone who accidentally makes a racket. Then a Shandrilan exile returns, a melodious "witch" named Zantalalia (Patty Lupone), who defiantly hums and carries an empty birdcage. Aurora (Meredith Henderson) is the daughter-apprentice of the Court Whisperer, trained to make announcements in the most muted tones. Yet she hears music in her dreams; her late grandfather, a friend of Zantalalia's, was a horn player. Zantalalia shows the girl a song spinner, a sort of choral music box left over from pre-Hush Law days. Nizzle arrests Zantalalia and orders the song spinner to be burned in public. A contrite Frelo visits the prisoner; it seems he had once loved Zantalalia, and passed the Hush Law in a jealous pique to focus her attentions on him, instead of on her passion for singing. The crucial "Sunwatch" ritual, in which all Shandrilan must raise their voices to serenade the changing seasons, is about to take place. If they perform only the silent dance now allowed, winter will persist. Using the song spinner and her own vocals, Aurora reintroduces music to the citizens, causing a bloodless revolt that overthrows Nizzle, as Frelo repudiates the Hush Laws and tentatively renews his relationship with Zantalalia.

Fairy tales are one of mankind's oldest narrative forms. Yet rarely do filmmakers try to weave a wholly original fantasy without falling back on hoary cliches of unicorns, dragons, swordsmen and, lately, a heavy STAR WARS (1977) influence. THE SONG SPINNER is a modest wonder, a dramatic parable that doesn't indulge in special-effects glitz or childish whimsy. The uncommonly somber atmosphere is a shock at first, as is the sight of famed Broadway diva Lupone, shorn of glamour and mascara, heading a cast right out of a peasant canvas by Pieter Brueghel the Elder. The forbidden music itself is a strange harmonic chant, rather than Disney show tunes. The moody treatment respects the serious subject matter of tyranny and artistic suppression, even if the sense of danger is low (the worst the Noise Police can ever do is send people into exile) and the metaphors a bit obvious. THE SONG SPINNER was filmed in Alberta and Nova Scotia, making good use of an icy climate and colonial fortifications.— C.C.

d, Randy Bradshaw; p, Douglas MacLeod, Randy Bradshaw; exec p, Meyer Shwarztenn, Kevin Tierney; w, Pauline Le Bel; ph, Francois Protat; ed, Doug Forbes; m, Lawrence Shragge; prod d, John Blackie; art d, Louise Middleton; ch, John Pichlyk, Victor Litvinov; casting, Leslie Swan

Children's/Political/Fantasy **(PR: AA MPAA: NR)**

SONIC OUTLAWS ★★½

(U.S.) 87m Other Cinema c

Negativland; The Tape-beatles; John Oswald; Emergency Broadcast Network; Douglas Kahn; The Barbie Liberation Organization; Alan Korn

With the motto "copyright infringement is your best entertainment value," Craig Baldwin's documentary SONIC OUTLAWS celebrates the creative and often subversive work of a number of musicians and conceptual artists. The concepts in SONIC OUTLAWS are fascinating and often side-splittingly funny, but a myopic point of view and Baldwin's confusing attempt to make the film a "collage" make the film difficult and, at times, overwhelming.

In 1990, Negativland, a band whose music consists of found noises and various other sound effects, released a single called "U2." The song contained samples from U2's music and from DJ Casey Kasem outtakes, and the record cover was designed to look like that of a new U2 album. Negativland was sued, and their career was almost ruined as a result. Much of SONIC OUTLAWS examines the various ramifications of this case, and another Negativland publicity stunt that went awry: they created a press release which erroneously linked their song "Christianity Is Stupid" to a Minnesota murderer, mostly to prove that journalists don't check their sources.

In addition to Negativland, SONIC OUTLAWS profiles people who illegally listen to others' cellular phone calls, people who take over live radio waves to broadcast their messages, The Barbie Liberation Organization (who switch voice boxes from Barbie Dolls to GI Joe dolls), Mark Pauline, who alters billboards to create subversive messages, and The Tape-beatles, who actually copyrighted the term "plagiarism" for their work.

Interviews with the artists are combined with clips from old science fiction films, various other film footage, and high paced barrages of images. The resulting collage effect is a good visual representation of Negativland's music, but does not work well in the context of the film as a whole. Some of the best material is obscured. For example, the billboards are flashed on the screen quickly, to mimic the way someone driving down the highway would see them. The effect is accurate, but leaves on wishing that one could have deciphered more of the messages. After about an hour of interviews combined with massive quantities of MTV-style images, it's easy to lose focus, especially when much of the audio is from poorly recorded tapes and phone calls. Baldwin is so busy proselytizing that he forgets that his subject matter is entertaining.

SONIC OUTLAWS preaches to the converted. The material is presented under the assumption that the audience either knows about Negativland's U2 record, or can figure out what's going on without a detailed explanation. The statements in favor of appropriating imagery are convincing, especially when modern music is compared to art, literature, and footnoted articles. However, Baldwin and Negativland make their case as if they're right and those who disagree are greedy and evil. A less biased approach may have allowed the viewer to come to the same conclusion, but without feeling manipulated.

Some of the found images (used without permission, of course) are cleverly integrated into the context of the film, notably a film of a young boy using Silly Putty to pick up a cartoon image from a newspaper. The artists are consistently intelligent and in good humor; they're great subjects for the film. Real news clips about many of the artists are hilarious, but also show that their hard work has not gone unnoticed. It's too bad that the film isn't a more straightforward documentary. An unbiased approach would have been less spiteful and more constructive. As it is, SONIC OUTLAWS is an entertaining but frustrating in-joke. *(Extreme profanity.)* — A.M.

d, Craig Baldwin; p, Craig Baldwin; w, Craig Baldwin; ph, Bill Daniel; ed, Bill Daniel; sound, Gibbs Chapman

Documentary **(PR: A MPAA: NR)**

SONS OF TRINITY ★★

(Italy/U.S.) 90m Trinidad Films ~ Triboro c

Heath Kizzier *(Trinity)*; Keith Neubert *(Bambino)*; Yvonne De-Bark *(Benita)*; Renata Scarpa *(Pablo)*; Ronald Nitschke *(Sheriff)*; Siegfried Rauch *(Parker)*; Renato D'Amore *(Ramirez Primero)*; Eduardo MacGregor *(Judge)*; Blaki *(Doctor)*; Jorge Oscar Bosso *(1st Gunslinger)*; Riccardo Pizzuti *(2nd Gunslinger)*; Jose Lifante Ruiz *(Hangman)*; Ana Sorlano Perez *(Katherine)*; Luis De Otezza Ortiz *(Pedro)*; Juan Ruiz Garcia *(Paco)*; Varona Martin *(Deputy)*

Yet another Spaghetti western farce with the dubbing aura of a Steve Reeves movie and the artistic soul of "Hee-Haw." Pratfalls, earthy jokes, and galumphing galoots vie for our attention in a foreign-lensed prairie parody that does for the moribund comic Western genre what a beautician does for a corpse.

Just like their forefathers, Trinity (Heath Kizzier) and Bambino (Keith Neubert) maintain a friendly rivalry. One day, Trinity discovers that burly Bambino has been falsely imprisoned for cattle rustling from Rancher Parker (Siegfried Rauch). Deceiving an itinerant hangman (Jose Lifante Ruiz), Trinity rescues truculent Bambino while ostensibly taking his measurements for the gallows. Unaware that the Sheriff (Ronald Nitschke) ordered Bambino's hanging in order to deflect attention from his thieving partnership with Mexican banditos, the newly minted heroic duo secures its freedom, outwits some gamblers for horses, and rides off to rundown San Clementino.

In this outlaw-oppressed village, Bambino and Trinity accept the posts of sheriff and deputy and restore the law and order which had been vitiated by the Ramirez Brothers. Locating Parker's misbranded cattle at the Ramirez camp, Trinity and Bambino cagily spring a trap for the Sheriff and the Ramirez ruffians. During a hay maker free-for-all (complete with mass handcuffings), the Sheriff's rustling sideline is exposed and the desperadoes lose their cattle brand-forging franchise. When Parker rewards Bambino and Trinity for locating his longhorns, they bestow their dough on the poor people of San Clementino.

If you bust a gut watching "Dukes of Hazzard" reruns or simply enjoy balmy physical comedy framed by an imitation Knotts Berry Farm backdrop, then SONS OF TRINITY could be your cup of frontier ale. Inoffensively high-spirited and dead from the neck up, this slackly edited ramble pokes fun at Western cliches in a manner that could be described as tranquilized slapstick. Overpopulated by European goofballs and gadflies playing cowboy dress-up, SONS OF TRINITY never aspires to outright hilarity; since it only aims for and musters non-threatening amusement, the film has no edge—and therefore, no belly laughs. Stale of wit, narrow in scope, and as authentically of the frontier as one of Dr. Quinn, Medicine Woman's smiles, SONS OF TRINITY is a hard-to-dislike, easy-to-forget, grabbag of CAT BALLOU (1965) gag-recycling. *(Violence, profanity.)* — R.P.

d, E. B. Clucher; p, Italo Zingarelli; exec p, Ezio Palaggi; assoc p, Marisa Palaggi; w, Marcotullio Barboni (based on his story); ph, Juan Amoros; ed, Antonio Siciliano; m, Stefano Mainetti; prod d, Enzo Bulgarelli; sound, Alberto Doni (mixer); fx, Midro Ruano Rogriguez; casting, Louis DiGiaimo; makeup, Jose Quatolas Rubio

Western/Comedy **(PR: A MPAA: NR)**

SOUTH BEACH ACADEMY ★

(U.S.) 91m Future Films ~ LIVE Home Video c

Keith Colouris *(Harry Spencer)*; Elizabeth Kaitan *(Shannon)*; Corey Feldman *(Billy Spencer)*; Al Lewis *(Uncle Gene)*; James Hong *(Johnny Staccato)*; Lorelei Leslie *(Harley)*; Julie Lynn Cialini *(Phyllis)*; Marcus Mueller *(Pigiron)*; Amy Lynn Rosenthal *(Erika)*; Ute Weigel *(Solitaire)*; Tiffany Cara *(Ginger)*; Christine Bauerle *(Dominique)*; Ron Hyatt *(Weed Wacker)*; Kristina Rodriguez *(Pina Kollata)*; Mindy Feldman *(Francesca)*; Gary Bristow *(Drill Sgt.)*; Maria McLendon *(Gene's Girlfriend)*; Gil Gesualdi *(Frankie)*; Jennifer Cole *(Tracy)*

If a shark attacked the female cast of SOUTH BEACH ACADEMY, would they survive with only puncture marks to their breast implants? This is the kind of thought inspired by this girl-watchers extravaganza about beach volleyball, perfect tans, and making whoopie.

Volleyball coach Harry Spencer (Keith Colouris) is trying to save his main squeeze, Shannon (Elizabeth Kaitan), from Asian gangster Johnny Staccato (James Hong). The film then backtracks to reveal how Harry got into this predicament.

Unable to turn down a bet, Harry's impulsive Uncle Gene (Al Lewis) accepts Staccato's challenge to pit his nephew's volleyball team against Staccato's competitive recruits. The prize is ownership of Uncle Gene's lucrative South Beach Academy.

Frustrated in his attempts to round up a winning all-girl team, Harry is cheered by the arrival of his party dude brother, Billy (Corey Feldman). Meanwhile, Harry's new Valentine Shannon reveals Staccato wrecked her Olympic chances and framed her brother for his own fraud.

After refusing to represent Uncle Gene's sun-and-fun school, Shannon signs up her former teammates, then dashes Harry's hopes by defecting to Staccato's side. Well aware of Staccato's hold on Shannon's brother, Harry persuades her to rejoin his volleybabes in exchange for a tape-recording of Staccato's confession of the crime for which her brother's serving time.

Harry's beach bunnies save South Beach Academy in the winner-take-all match.

What red-blooded heterosexual male would call for a lifeguard when he's drowning in breasts? That's the real question posed by SOUTH BEACH ACADEMY, which is only ostensibly about volleyball tourneys, gangster film send-ups, and the tawdry residue of WHERE THE BOYS ARE (1960).

The movie is actually about breast fixation. How else does one account for the numerous bikini fantasy scenes, or all those camera angles aimed ever upward and bra-ward for maximum jiggle? Full of dorky repartee, off-color smarminess, and beer blast Muzak, the film is acted by Olympic hopefuls who seem to have just failed a steroid abuse test. Although one isn't surprised to spot Corey Feldman cavorting in these sordid surroundings, it's jarring to observe the former Grandpa Munster up to his fangs in bouncing protuberances. Al Lewis brings shame to his Bermuda shorts. *(Extensive nudity, profanity, sexual situations, substance abuse.)* — R.P.

d, Joe Esposito; p, Bob Gallagher, Suzanne Migdall, Grant Saidiner; exec p, Mara Saidiner, Harvey Leonard, Mark Kreloff; assoc p, Gary Sax; co-p, Jerry Garfinkle; w, William R. Milling; ph, Wes Llewellyn; ed, Matt Eberlein; m, Grant Saidiner; art d, Martin Druda; sound, Brent Winter (recordist); makeup, Cindy Jordan

Comedy/Sports **(PR: C MPAA: R)**

SPACE JAM ★★

(U.S.) 87m Northern Lights Entertainment; Courtside Seats Productions; Warner Bros. ~ Warner Bros. c

Michael Jordan *(Himself)*; Theresa Randle *(Juanita Jordan)*; Danny DeVito *(Voice of Swackhammer)*; Billy West *(Voices of Bugs Bunny/Elmer Fudd)*; Wayne Knight *(Stan Podolak)*; Bradley Baker *(Voices of Daffy Duck/Tasmanian Devil/Bull)*; Bob Bergen *(Voices of Bertie/Hubie/Marvin the Martian/Porky Pig/Speedy Gonzales/Tweety)*; Bill Farmer *(Voices of Sylvester/Foghorn Leghorn/Yosemite Sam)*; Kath Soucie *(Voice of Lola Bunny)*; Charles Barkley *(Himself)*; Bill Murray *(Himself)*; Patrick Ewing *(Himself)*; Larry Johnson *(Himself)*; Muggsy Bogues *(Himself)*; Shawn Bradley *(Himself)*; Larry Bird *(Himself)*

A high-powered marketing ploy designed to keep the Warner Bros. cartoon franchise alive for a new generation, SPACE JAM combines Bugs Bunny and company with live-action basketball star Michael Jordan in a hastily concocted story. Designed more for children than for those who grew up on Looney Tunes, it is devoid of the wit, imagination, and the vocal talent that distinguished the originals.

Playing himself, Michael Jordan announces his retirement from basketball to try his hand at baseball. Meanwhile, in outer space, the alien race of Nerdlucks seeks new attractions for its Galactic Amusement Park. Park owner Swackhammer (voiced by Danny DeVito) orders five diminutive Nerdlucks to earth to abduct the cast of the Looney Tunes cartoons for his park.

Bugs Bunny strikes a bargain with the aliens, getting them to agree to a basketball game and promising they will all go with the aliens if the Looney Tunes lose the game. The Nerdlucks attend NBA games and use their powers to steal the ball-playing talents of Charles Barkley, Patrick Ewing, Muggsy Bogues, Larry Johnson and Shawn Bradley. While the pro players are confused over the loss of their skills, the aliens return to Looney Tunes land and transform into the "Monstars," titans of the court. Bugs and company prepare to kidnap a ringer of their own. While Jordan is golfing with friends, he is sucked down a golf hole and spirited to the cartoon world.

On the night of the big game, all the Looney Tunes characters turn out to watch, as does the alien Swackhammer. Jordan and Bugs lead a team that includes Lola Bunny, Daffy Duck, Porky Pig, Elmer Fudd, Yosemite Sam, Sylvester, and Foghorn Leghorn. After taking a beating from the Nerdlucks in the first half, Jordan gives the Looney Tunes a half-time pep talk and the team drinks "Michael's Secret Stuff," which energizes them to go out and begin scoring.

The Looney Tunes win, only to discover that the "secret stuff" was just water. At Jordan's exhortation, the Nerdlucks strap Swackhammer to a rocket and blast him into space. Jordan also gets them to return their stolen basketball talents back to their original owners. Jordan then decides to return to basketball.

A corporate product designed to sell Jordan, the Warner Bros. cartoon characters, and a pop soundtrack, SPACE JAM plays like a 90-minute TV commercial. The plot is simply an excuse to showcase Jordan's talents and position him as a film star, while capitalizing on the fame of the WB cartoon stars. David Falk, Jordan's sports agent and manager, came up with the idea after Jordan's appearance with Bugs Bunny in a Nike commercial several years ago and is said to have persuaded Warner Bros. to make the reported $90 million investment in the film.

This is no relative of WHO FRAMED ROGER RABBIT?, which at least boasted a message about corporate corruption and a genuinely witty and imaginative intermingling of live-action and cartoon worlds. There is no clear strategy for this in SPACE JAM; one minute we're in a live-action setting and the next we're in the Looney Tunes world, with no attempt to bridge the two.

Since the cartoon characters act as a team here, they are never allowed to be their old combative Looney Tune selves. They exist solely as celebrities, useful because they are familiar to the audience. Bugs Bunny is particularly emasculated. Having once waged war on the federal government ("Rebel Rabbit," 1949), here he caves in to the aliens without so much as a cry.

The new vocal actors never capture the varied inflections that voice artist Mel Blanc gave the characters during his 50-year career. The new animators clutter up the character designs with intrusive shading, and dispense with the individual expressions and gestures that gave the characters such a vivid emotional life so many years ago.

The only real interest for cartoon buffs is in spotting the dozens of minor characters who graced one or more of the old cartoons, including Pete Puma, Claude Cat, Hubie and Bertie, and gangsters Rocky and Muggsy, all of whom appear too briefly.— B.C.

d, Joe Pytka; p, Ivan Reitman, Joe Medjuck, Daniel Goldberg; exec p, David Falk, Ken Ross; co-p, Gordon Webb, Sheldon Kahn, Curtis Polk; w, Leo Benvenuti, Steve Rudnick, Timothy Harris, Herschel Weingrod (based on characters created by Chuck Jones and Tex Avery and Friz Freleng); ph, Michael Chapman; ed, Sheldon Kahn; m, James Newton Howard; prod d, Geoffrey Kirkland; art d, David Klassen; anim, Bruce Smith, Tony Cervone, Ron Tippe, Bill Perkins; sound, Roger Daniell; fx, Darrell Pritchett, Helen Elswit, Ed Jones, Cinesite; casting, Jane Jenkins, Janet Hirshenson; cos, Marlene Stewart

Comedy/Adventure/Animated **(PR: AA MPAA: PG)**

SPELLBREAKER: SECRET OF THE LEPRECHAUNS ★★

(U.S.) 84m Moonbeam Entertainment ~ Paramount Home Video c

Gregory Edward Smith *(Mikey Dennehy)*; John Bluthal *(Michael Dennehy)*; Godfrey James *(King Kevin)*; Madeleine Potter *(Morgan de la Fey/Nula)*; Sylvester McCoy *(Flynn)*; James Ellis *(Patrick)*; Tina Martin *(Maeve)*; Ion Haiduc *(Wizard)*; Mike Higgins *(Casey)*

This sequel to the direct-to-video LEAPIN' LEPRECHAUNS! (1995) indicates the major difference the least bit of freshness makes. Same cast, same producers, same director; but in a second go-round, the bloom is off the clover.

American boy Mikey Dennehy (Gregory Edward Smith) visits his grandfather Michael (John Bluthal) in rural Ireland, where the elder Dennehy has long consorted with the mischievous local leprechauns. If you capture a leprechaun you can have three wishes, and when the wee King Kevin (Godfrey James) spies pretty lass Morgan de la Fey (Madeleine Potter) in the woods, he is not displeased at all to be hoisted up in her pouch and obliged to grant her desires. But Morgan is really Nula, Queen of the Dead. She bewitches King Kevin into leaving his leprechaun realm unguarded and open to conquest by the skull-faced King of the Underworld. Mikey, however, is owed a leprechaun wish himself. Yolked and forced to tow a box of imprisoned wee folk into Underworld, he tricks Nula into poisoning herself, then wishes everyone back home safely.

Grandfather Michael, however, has been shrunk to leprechaun size, and that particular spell cannot be broken. But he doesn't mind too much as the freed leprechauns welcome him as a guest, in what looks like the setup for yet another sequel.

While the first LEAPIN' LEPRECHAUNS! brought the title figures to the US for a cute twist on the fish-out-of-water formula, this stays less rewardingly on home sod (Ireland here is actually verdant Romania, where both movies were done) and leaves imported British actors to carry most of the action with frantic hamming. White-bearded James seems King Lear-y indeed, gamboling about in the throes of enchantment, and there are double entendres on the word "fairy" that should safely elude young viewers. But even kids may be disappointed by the cheap special effects, with a crude illusion of miniaturization attempted merely by posing "leprechauns" as far away from the camera as possible, with magnified objects in the foreground. On the other hand, ornate costumes and interiors (even a properly spooky, fiery Underworld) are quite impressive, and most likely creditable to the opera and theater craftspeople of Bucharest. — C.C.

d, Ted Nicolaou; p, Vlad Paunescu, Oana Paunescu; exec p, Charles Band, Debra Dion; w, Patrick Clifton, Ted Nicolaou (based on characters created by Michael McGann); ph, Adolfo Bartoli; ed, Gregory Sanders; m, Richard Kosinski, William Levine, John Zeretzke; prod d, Radu Corciova; art d, Ioana Corciova; fx, Mark Rappaport; casting, Robert MacDonald, Perry Bullington, Clare Walker; cos, Oana Paunescu, Michael Roche; makeup, Michael S. Deak

Children's/Fantasy **(PR: AA MPAA: G)**

SPIDER & ROSE ★★★½

(Australia) 94m Dendy Films ~ Southern Star c

Simon Bossell *(Spider McCall)*; Ruth Cracknell *(Rose Dougherty)*; Max Cullen *(Jack)*; Henry Bennett *(Miles)*; Nallie Bennett *(Sarah)*; Tina Bursill *(Sister Abbott)*; Beth Champion *(Nurse Price)*; Jennifer Cluff *(Helen Dougherty)*; Lewis Fitzgerald *(Robert Dougherty)*; Harry Tritton *(Paddy)*; Brian Vriends *(Spider's Mate)*; Bob Baines *(Ambulance Driver)*; Emily Dawe *(Ambulance Officer)*; Marshall Napier *(Ambulance Dispatcher)*; David Cockburn *(Dying Boy)*; Helen O'Connor *(Distressed Mother)*; Judith Stratford *(Hospital Sister)*; Bruce Venables *(Truck Driver)*

SPIDER & ROSE, released in Australia in 1994 and in the US in 1996, is a road movie about a feisty 70-year-old woman paired with a impudent, punky 21-year-old guy. The story of vastly different people developing a friendship when forced to spend time together has been told countless times. But writer-director Bill Bennett has injected this particular version with witty dialogue, unique characters, stylish camerawork and some stunning surprises.

One year after a car accident that killed her husband and put her in the hospital, Rose (Ruth Cracknell) plans to return from Sydney to her son's country farmhouse. Spider (Simon Bossell), in his last day as an ambulance driver, is employed to take her on the six-hour drive. More concerned with returning in time for a party that evening than with Rose's well-being, he treats her with little respect. She is no pushover, though, and ditches him for a ride with a kind, quirky beekeeper named Jack (Max Cullen).

Spider, now assured of missing his party, finds Rose and insists upon finishing his job. Just as the two start to become friendly, a kangaroo jumps in front of the ambulance, and they crash, breaking Spider's leg. While they wait for help, they discover that they're both free spirits, and slowly they become friends.

Eventually, they bump into Jack again and make their way to the home of Rose's son. They're just in time for Rose's 70th birthday party, but she loses her good cheer when she discovers that her son wants to put her in a nursing home. Jack asks her to go away with him, but his plans are not exciting enough for her. At the party, Rose collapses, the victim of an apparent heart attack. Spider starts to drive her towards the hospital, but then stops the car. Rose has faked the heart attack. He lets her take the car, and she drives away in search of more excitement and adventure.

Bennett made SPIDER & ROSE to explore his belief that people must learn to coexist. The two characters learn from each other through conversation and crisis. In one day, they progress from Rose throwing Spider's favorite tape out the window to the two sharing a bathtub (platonically).

Even more impressive than the script is the startling and daring use of the camera. Close-ups, spiraling camera shots, unusual angles and quick zooms are used effectively to characterize people and situations, and to keep the story fresh and unpredictable. The two car accidents are shocking and exciting, and the film switches abruptly from comedy to drama without seeming choppy or haphazard. As the film progresses, the framing, dialogue, and combination of comedy and drama combine to tell a powerful story.

Given Bennett's love of precision, however, a scene in which Rose contemplates suicide is unnecessarily melodramatic, and the focus on insects, though it adds atmosphere, does not have enough connection to the story to warrant as much attention as it receives.

Cracknell and Boswell, both popular television personalities in Australia, are outstanding, making Spider and Rose multidimensional characters who will give the viewers much to relate to. Ultimately, their friendship shows that any two people can get along if given the time and opportunity. *(Violence, adult situations, nudity, mild profanity.)* — A.M.

d, Bill Bennett; p, Lyn McCarthy, Graeme Tubbenhauer; w, Bill Bennett; ph, Andrew Lesnie; ed, Henry Dangar; m, Cruel Sea; prod d, Ross Major; sound, Syd Butterworth, Andrew Plain; cos, Ross Major

Comedy/Thriller **(PR: C MPAA: NR)**

SPITFIRE GRILL, THE ★★

(U.S.) 90m Gregory Productions; Mendecino Productions ~ Columbia c

Alison Elliott *(Percy Talbott)*; Ellen Burstyn *(Hannah Ferguson)*; Marcia Gay Harden *(Shelby Goddard)*; Will Patton *(Nahum Goddard)*; Kieran Mulroney *(Joe Sperling)*; Gailard Sartain *(Sheriff Gary Walsh)*; John M. Jackson *(Johnny B./Eli)*; Louise De Cormier *(Effy Katshaw)*; Ida Griesemer *(Rebecca Goddard)*; Lincoln Grow; Louise Grow *(Molly Goddard)*; Sam Lloyd Sr.

(Meeshack Boggs); Lisa Louise Langford *(Jolene)*; Forrest Murray *(Stuart)*; Patty Smith *(Customer #1)*; Faith Caitlin *(Neighbor)*; Janet St. Onge *(Town Member #2)*; Jim Hogue *(Deputy)*; Stacy Becker *(Clare)*; Cliff Levering *(Aaron Sperling)*; Dennis Mientka *(Customer #2)*; Stuart Jackson *(Customer #3)*; Monica Callan *(Woman at Bar)*; Richard Addis *(Man at Bar)*

Competent but dull, THE SPITFIRE GRILL includes all the right ingredients for an old-fashioned tearjerker, but ends up coming off like a Sam Shepard play re-written by Pat Robertson.

THE SPITFIRE GRILL begins when Percy (Alison Elliott), a young woman, is released from a Maine prison. Rather than return to her native Ohio, Percy decides to find a place to live in the small town of Gilead, Maine. The residents of the town, however, are uneasy about Percy and her mysterious criminal past. Nevertheless, Sheriff Gary Walsh (Gailard Sartain) asks Hannah Ferguson (Ellen Burstyn), the owner of the popular Spitfire Grill, to let Percy take a room above the restaurant in exchange for her services as a waitress. After a tense, bumpy start, Percy becomes a genuine help to Hannah. Slowly, the customers too begin to accept the town's newcomer.

One day, when Hannah injures her leg, Percy offers to take over running the restaurant. Hannah's nephew, the suspicious Nahum Goddard (Will Patton), disapproves of the new arrangement and suggests that his wife, the meek Shelby Goddard (Marcia Gay Harden), become manager. Hannah nixes the idea, but allows Shelby to cook for the establishment, since Percy lacks that ability. Soon, Percy and Shelby have the Spitfire functioning better than ever, and Hannah's leg heals sufficiently for her to supervise the operation.

As the three women become friends, they tell each other their deepest secrets. Shelby reveals the extent of her abusive marriage to Nahum. Percy talks about the incident that led to her arrest and imprisonment. And Hannah divulges the reason she has wanted to sell the Spitfire Grill for several years, although she does not betray the identity of the mysterious stranger who picks up a bag of canned goods from the back porch every night.

Over time, the women confront their past and present problems. Shelby's work in the restaurant strengthens her resolve to do something about her troubled marriage, and both she and Percy help Hannah sell the Spitfire by devising a nationwide contest, where $100 and the best essay about the restaurant wins the writer complete ownership. Just as the contest gets underway, however, both Hannah's money and Percy disappear. Nahum and many townspeople immediately suspect that the ex-convict stole the money, when in fact Percy left the Spitfire merely to spend time alone in church. During a massive hunt for Percy throughout Gilead, Nahum and the police find the mysterious stranger in the woods. As Percy enters the scene to protect the stranger, she is accidentally shot and killed. Later, when the misplaced money is found and the town learns the truth about Percy, a group mourning takes place. The stranger, meanwhile, emerges from the woods and reunites with Hannah, who we learn is his mother.

THE SPITFIRE GRILL (originally titled CARE OF THE SPITFIRE GRILL) attracted controversy at the 1996 Sundance Film Festival (where it won the Audience Award), because it was discovered that the small, "independent" film had been made with money from a Mississippi-based Catholic group, the Sacred Heart League. Despite protests by the filmmakers that their film had not been ideologically tainted during production, SPITFIRE GRILL tells a parable filled with themes of Christian love, charity, acceptance, and redemption, and almost all the establishing shots of the Vermont setting include the church that later becomes the setting for not one but *two* climactic confessionals.

Quite apart from the obviousness of the religious motifs, THE SPITFIRE GRILL never comes alive as a drama. Despite the presence of a fine cast, almost everyone, including a shamelessly hammy Ellen Burstyn, use a New England accent that makes the folks on "Murder, She Wrote" sound subtle and convincing. Newcomer Alison Elliott also employs a phoney accent (her character is from Ohio), but otherwise gives the best performance.

Likewise, the technical values of the film are above-average, but lack any sort of visual appeal (SPITFIRE marks the feature debut of writer-director Lee David Zlotoff, the creator of the TV action series, "MacGuyver"). So if you enjoy that other sort of made-for-tv fare, the wholesome pap on Pat Robertson's Family Channel, then you will probably appreciate this formulaic soap opera. Those looking for a better treatment of similar themes should try HEAVY, the other new-waitress-in-town drama released in 1996. *(Profanity.)* — E.M.

d, Lee David Zlotoff; p, Forrest Murray; exec p, Warren G. Stitt; assoc p, Linda H. Miller, Deborah Stitt; co-p, Edward E. Vaughn, Marci Liroff; w, Lee David Zlotoff; ph, Rob Draper; ed, Margie Goodspeed; m, James Horner; prod d, Howard Cummings; art d, Peter Borck; set d, Larry Dias; sound, Steuart Pearce (mixer); casting, Marci Liroff; cos, Louise Mingenbach; makeup, Lynne Eagan; stunts, Danny Aiello Aiello

Drama (PR: A MPAA: PG-13)

SPY HARD ★½

(U.S.) 81m Friedberg/Draizin/Konvitz Productions; Hollywood Pictures ~ Buena Vista c

Leslie Nielsen *(Dick Steele—Agent WD-40)*; Nicollete Sheridan *(Veronique Ukrinsky— Agent 3.14)*; Charles Durning *(The Director)*; Marcia Gay Harden *(Miss Cheevus)*; Barry Bostwick *(Norman Coleman)*; John Ales *(Kabul)*; Andy Griffith *(General Rancor)*; Elya Baskin *(Professor Ukrinsky)*; Mason Gamble *(McCluckey)*; Carlos Lauchu *(Slice)*; Stephanie Romanov *(Victoria/Barbara Dahl)*; Dr. Joyce Brothers *(Steele's Tag Team Member)*; Ray Charles *(Bus Driver)*; Roger Clinton *(Agent Clinton)*; Robert Culp *(Businessman)*; Fabio *(Himself)*; Robert Guillaume *(Agent Steve Bishop)*; Hulk Hogan *(Steele's Tag Team Member)*; Pat Morita *(Brian the Waiter)*; Alexandra Paul *(Woman in Murphy Bed)*; Mr. T. *(Agency Helicopter Driver)*; Alex Trebek *(Agency Tape Recorder Voice Over)*; Curtis Armstrong *(Pastry Chef)*; Tina Arning *(Dancer #1)*; Bruce Paul Barbour *(Stunt Double for Leslie Nielsen)*; William Barillaro *(Blind Driver)*; Michael Berryman *(Bus Patron with Oxygen Mask)*; Julie Brown *(Cigarette Girl)*; Stephen Burrows *(Agent Burrows)*; Keith Campbell *(Thug #2)*; Carl Ciarfalio *(Thug #1)*; Johnny Cocktails *(Postal Worker)*; Wayne Cotter *(Male Dancer)*; Rick Cramer *(Rancor Terrorist—Helmlich)*; Eddie Deezen *(Rancor Guard Who Gets Spit On)*; Joey Dente *(Dead Wise Guy—Goombah)*; Paul Eliopoulos *(Agent #1)*; Andrew Christian English *(Paratrooper)*; Brad Garrett *(Voice for Short Rancor Guard)*; Michael Lee Gogin *(Short Rancor Guard)*; Bruce Gray *(The President)*; Hollis Hill *(Agent #2)*; Brian Howe *(Clubhouse Bartender)*; Nia James *(Rancor Terrorist)*; Valentino Johnson *(Michael Jackson Look-alike)*; Elizabeth Kaitan *(Helicopter Ticket Agent)*; John Kassir *(Rancor Guard at Intercom)*; Diane Klimaszewski *(Twin #1)*; Elaine Klimaszewski *(Twin #2)*; Austin Kottke *(Boy with Balloons)*; Clyde Kusatsu *(Noggin)*; Kelly Lange *(Herself)*; Michael Leahs *(Jogger)*; Tara Leon *(Manicurist)*; Bruno Marcotulli *(Sad Mime)*; Esau McKnight *(Skippy—Warrior on Cell Phone)*; Katherine Moffat *(Agent Moffat)*; Fran Montano *(Carny at Weapons Lab)*; Desiree More *(Herself)*; Ron Morgan *(Weapons Lab Worker)*; Joanne Nerlino *(Machine Gun Packing Nun Leader)*; Mil Nicholson *(English Countdown Lady)*; Gayle Obodzinski *(Dancer #2)*; Gary Owens

(M.C. for Rancor Extortion Video); Tyler Patton *(Punk Leader)*; Julie Payne *(Mother Superior)*; Pee Wee Piamonti *(Fighting Rancor Guard)*; Jeff Sanders *(Bird-Calling Rancor Guard)*; Thom Sharp *(Agent Sharp)*; Shari Shattuck *(Stewardess)*; Pat Tanzillo *(Agent Tanzillo)*; Thuy Trang *(Masseuse)*; Angela Visser *(Georgeous Blonde)*; Reid Worthington *(Balloon Popping Boy)*; Maxi Anderson; Billie Barnun; Maria Del Rey; Linda Harmon; Darlene Koldenhoven; Carol Lombard; Jeanie Long; Sally Stevens; Tata Vega; Jeannine Wagner; Julia Waters; Maxine Waters *(Singing Nuns)*

Leslie Nielsen mugs his way through another tired genre spoof in SPY HARD, an innocuous addition to the endless list of AIRPLANE!/NAKED GUN-style parodies.

Secret agent Dick Steele, aka: WD-40 (Leslie Nielsen), foils a plot by the nefarious General Rancor (Andy Griffith) by blowing up his helicopter. But Steele's girlfriend, agent Barbara Dahl, apparently dies during the incident.

Fifteen years later, Rancor resurfaces, his arms replaced by prosthetics, and sends a tape to Steele's boss, the Director, showing Dahl's daughter Victoria strapped to a missile which he plans to use to take over the world. He says that he'll kill Victoria unless he gets a microchip for the weapon. The Director assigns Steele to go to Los Angeles to locate Professor Ukrinsky, the scientist who invented the microchip.

Steele meets up with Ukrinsky's sultry daughter Veronique (Nicolette Sheridan), and the two try to find her father, but Veronique is abducted by Rancor's goons. Steele finds the professor and hides him with agent McCluckey, who's a young boy. After being chased by some of Rancor's henchmen, Steele hides out in a convent and poses as a nun, then manages to rescue Veronique. Some goons go to McCluckey's house and beat him up, then kidnap the professor and take him to Rancor's secluded jungle hideout, where he gives them the microchip. Steele and Veronique follow them to the island and rescue Barbara, then overpower Rancor, strap him to the missile and launch it into space. Rancor smashes into the Apollo capsule and his severed legs fall to the Earth.

Despite its title, SPY HARD is mostly a spoof of the James Bond films, and though it doesn't have a DIE HARD parody, its repertoire does include CLIFFHANGER, MISSION: IMPOSSIBLE, TRUE LIES, PULP FICTION, SPEED, SISTER ACT, HOME ALONE, IN THE LINE OF FIRE, JURASSIC PARK, and even BUTCH CASSIDY AND THE SUNDANCE KID.

The combination of bad puns, double-entendres, non-sequiters, scenes from other movies, and "celebrity" cameos which the Zucker Bros. originated and perfected has been copied and imitated so many times that normal criticism is useless. The basic premise of such films, which are predicated upon puncturing the pretensions of self-serious action-hero movies, is funny in itself, but the jokes and sight gags have deteriorated to such a degree that the films now consist solely of restaging whole sequences from other movies, without feeling the need to add any humor of their own. SPY HARD fully subscribes to this notion, and while its unrestrained silliness does produce a few giggles, it never approaches the level of its obvious inspiration—TV's "Get Smart." The level of wit is indicated by characters identified by such titles as: "Rancor Guard Who Gets Spit on" and "Machine Gun Packing Nun Leader," while its cameos include the less-than-stellar likes of Hulk Hogan, Dr. Joyce Brothers, Pat Morita, Fabio, Mr. T, and the voice of Alex Trebek.

SPY HARD does have a few amusing bits, such as a parody of the requisite Bond "weapons lab demonstration" scene, and a nastily funny gag involving the Macaulay Culkin-like child agent, who tries to battle the thugs a la HOME ALONE, and ends up being beaten senseless and thrown through a window as they yell, "That's for GETTING EVEN WITH DAD, that's for MY GIRL" etc. Indeed, most of the original humor relies heavily on physical cruelty, such as Rancor's loss of limbs and Steele's accidental bludgeoning of virtually everyone who crosses his path.

You know a movie's in trouble when the best thing in it is a Weird Al Yankovic opening-credits song sequence that parodies Maurice Binder's floating-female silhouette titles for the James Bond series. Weird Al directed this sequence as well, and perhaps should have done so for the entire movie, since he's clearly more talented at this sort of thing than director Rick Friedberg, who previously collaborated with Leslie Nielsen on some comedy golf videos.

Nielsen, of course, has created a second career for himself and plays it straight as a deadpan reminder of all those bland, square-jawed authority figures he played in bad movies since the 1950s, practically wink at the audience during every scene.*(Sexual situations, violence.)* — M.S.

d, Rick Friedberg; p, Rick Friedberg, Doug Draizin, Jeffrey Konvitz; exec p, Robert L. Rosen, Leslie Nielsen; w, Dick Chudnow, Rick Friedberg, Jason Friedberg, Aaron Seltzer (from a story by Jason Friedberg and Aaron Seltzer); ph, John R. Leonetti; ed, Eric Sears; m, Bill Conti; prod d, William Creber; art d, William J. Durrell Jr.; set d, Ernie Bishop; sound, David Ronne (mixer); fx, Chuck Stewart, SPFX Unlimited, Steven R. Benson, International Creative Effects; casting, Fern Champion, Mark Paladini; cos, Tom Bronson; makeup, Ken Chase; stunts, Fred Waugh; tech, Steven R. Benson

Comedy/Spy **(PR: O MPAA: PG-13)**

SQUANDERERS, THE
(SEE: RED LINE)

STAND OFF, THE ★★

(Canada) 92m April One Productions; Telefilm Canada ~ Monarch Home Video c

Stephen Shellen *(David Maltby)*; Djanet Sears *(Jane Briscoe)*; Gordon Clapp *(Gordon Davies)*; David Strathairn *(Don McCowan)*; Wayne Robson *(Wayne Brock)*; Pierre Curzi *(Jean Leduc)*; Martin Julien *(Tom Ennis)*; Jain Dickson *(Justine)*; Shannon Lawson *(Sally)*; Lyne Tremblay *(Lucie)*; Thomas Hauff *(Jerry Brownstein)*; Elizabeth Harpur *(Gina Tyrell)*; Steve Mousseau *(RCMP Interrogator)*; Geza Kovacs *(RCMP Interrogator)*; Ed Clements *(Audio Cop)*; Christian Laurin *(Larose)*; Calvin Butler *(Terrence Briscoe)*; Diana Pemberton *(Secretary)*; Alec Stockwell *(Father Spencer)*; Bob Windsor *(Janitor)*; David Harvey *(Commissionaire)*; Steve Lucas *(Reporter)*; Matt Cooke *(SWAT Commander)*; Kevin Wash *(Technician)*; Andrew Lewarne *(Dispatcher)*; Zack Vierra *(Boy)*; Jon Comerford *(Stan Olivero)*

Saddled with stodgy direction and a lackluster screenplay, THE STAND OFF takes volatile material about a hostage crisis and dulls it down. The entire film seems to be one unending establishing shot for a drama that never really begins.

Disguised as a priest, ex-convict David Maltby (Stephen Shellen) seizes control of the Bahamian Consul's office. He has a dual purpose: to ensure the release of his former cellmate Tom Ennis (Martin Julien); and to shame his city into opening a homeless shelter.

As the media and police descend on the building's perimeter, levelheaded Consul Jane Briscoe (Djanet Sears) dickers with her troubled captor, whose desperate act is the culmination of frustrations stemming from life within the penal system. Defusing the tense situation, Chief Don McCowan (David Strathairn) rejects the gung ho approach proposed by SWAT team leader Captain Jean Leduc (Pierre Curzi).

Given 14 hours to talk Maltby into surrender, McCowan negotiates with the prison, assuages Maltby's fears, and arranges a phone call for Maltby to Ennis. With Leduc priming his men for deadly force, Briscoe initially refuses to leave when Maltby agrees to free her. Jettisoning his grand scheme, Maltby addresses the plague of reporters; Briscoe finally walks to safety. A coda states that Maltby served six years for this crime, and was later arrested with an accomplice on kidnapping and murder charges.

Rich in irony, STAND OFF cries out for the kind of heated sensibility Sidney Lumet brought to DOG DAY AFTERNOON (1975). Instead of resembling a media circus, the film plays more like a talky press conference. Only the suspense inherent in the hostage dilemma and capable performances save this mundane plea for tolerance. If ever a movie needed an infusion of outrageousness, it's this somber melodrama. Thrills are put on the back burner in favor of routine soul-searching.

To the actors' credit, the movie is able to forge a Stockholm Syndrome relationship between Briscoe and Maltby; their instant rapport seems genuine. But STAND OFF also trumps up a rivalry between the unflappable police chief and the trigger-happy SWAT leader; their antagonism rings hollow and doesn't build any excitement. For a thriller about risking one's life for principles and a pal, STAND OFF is oddly becalmed. *(Violence, extreme profanity, adult situations.)* — R.P.

d, Murray Battle; p, Julia Sereny; exec p, W. Paterson Ferns, Annette Cohen; w, Murray Battle; ph, Mark Irwin; ed, Roger Mattiussi; m, Jonathan Goldsmith; prod d, Ian Brock; art d, Ian Brock; set d, Doug McCullough; sound, Leon Johnson (mixer); casting, Jon Comerford; cos, Jill Aslin; makeup, Marie Nardella; stunts, Marco Bianco

Drama/Crime **(PR: C MPAA: NR)**

STAR MAKER, THE ★★★

(Italy) 117m CG Group Tiger Cinematografica ~ Miramax C

(L'UOMO DELLE STELLE)

Sergio Castellitto *(Joe Morelli)*; Tiziana Lodato *(Beata)*; Franco Scaldati *(Brigadiere Mastropaolo)*; Leopoldo Trieste *(Mute)*; Clelia Rondinella *(Anna's Mother)*; Tano Cimarosa; Nicola Di Pinto *(Communal Functionary)*; Costantino Carrozza *(The Collector)*; Jane Alexander *(Princess)*; Tony Sperandeo *(1st Baldalamenti)*; Leo Gullotta *(Vito)*; Luigi Maria Burruano *(Flirtatious Client)*; Carmelo Di Mazzarelli *(Old Man in Wheelchair)*; Marzio Onorato *(Architect Panebianco)*; Antonella Attili *(Nurse)*; Domenico Dolce *(Peasant on Bus)*; Stefano Gabana *(Photographer on Bus)*; Maria Rosa Parrello *(Santina)*; Rita Lia *(Pinuccia)*; Vincent Navarra *(Shepherd)*; Alessandro Guarrera *(Clapboard Kid)*; Spiro Scimone *(1st Nasca Brother)*; Francesco Sframeli *(2nd Nasca Brother)*; Tony Palazzo *(Pio Li Fusi)*; Mimmo Gennaro *(1st Mafioso)*; Emilio Scimone *(2nd Mafioso)*; Massimo Pupella *(Bordonaro Jr.)*; Giorgio Guerrieri *(Cinema Cashier)*; Salvatore Billa *(Prince)*; Peppino Tornatore *(Dottore Mistretta)*; Filippo Tarantino *(2nd Badalamenti)*; Onofrio Ducato *(Mafia Boss Realzisa)*; Paolo Noto *(Zu' Leonardo)*; Turi Killer *(Boy with Garabaldino)*; Pino Calabrese *(1st Carabiniere)*; Antonio Miceli *(Cosima Millelire)*; Rori Quatrocchi *(Prostitute)*; Elia Nicosia *(Barber)*; Simona Merito *(Anna)*; Giuseppe Zardo *(1st Friend)*; Sandro Piro *(2nd Friend)*; Vincenzo Fiorenza *(3rd Friend)*; Filippo Spitale *(1st Man in Club)*; Pino Pellegrino *(2nd Man in Club)*; Rosario Lanzafame *(3rd Man in Club)*; Pippo Provvidenti *(Don Lucio)*; Giorgio Li Bassi *(Innkeeper)*; Pasquale Palumbo *(Mayor)*; Angelo Colajemma *("Vitti Na Crozza")*; Antonello Pugliesi *(Man Quoting Mussolini)*; Daniele Ferretti *(Village Idiot)*; Filippo Alesi *(Young Farm Laborer)*; Emilio Adrisani *(Peasant by the River)*; Francesco Guzzo *(Tavern Boy)*; Giuseppe Funari *(Armless Man)*; Bruno Torrisi *(Carwash Man)*; Umberto Terranove *(Band Master)*; Rosolino Cottone *(Partisan)*; Giovanni Alamia *(1st Warehouse Man)*; Corrado Solari *(2nd Warehouse Man)*

Director Guiseppe Tornatore is fascinated by film as a medium, as a process, and most of all, as a catalyst for change in people's lives. His international hit CINEMA PARADISO (1988) beautifully portrayed the profound cultural impact of movie-going. With the entertaining but flawed THE STAR MAKER, he explores how being in front of the camera, even momentarily, has an equally profound effect.

In the early 1950s, Joe Morelli (Sergio Castellitto) travels throughout Sicily's small towns conning gullible country folk. He claims to be a talent scout from Rome's Universal Studios, and offers screen tests for a small sum of money. Even the poorest people take him up on his offer, and it soon becomes clear that his screen tests stand for more than just the possibility of fame and fortune. Being in front of Joe's camera is a form of therapy. His words of encouragement make people feel good about themselves, and the tests allow them to express feelings and emotions they've previously kept dormant. When people forget their lines, Joe tells them to simply be themselves, and he is witness to tears, confessions, political rantings, and wild stories. One man speaks for the first time in years. Joe even uses screen tests to stop a policeman from ticketing him and to keep thugs from robbing him.

On one trip, a teenager named Beata (Tiziana Lodato) takes a fancy to him and follows him to his next town. Because of her age and his unwillingness to be tied to anyone, he resists her, but after he is swindled and robbed, her continued devotion wears him down and they become lovers.

After succeeding at his ruse in several towns, Joe is caught and arrested, then beaten up. After two years in jail, he is set free to begin a new life. He looks for Beata. He learns that she waited for him for six months, but now resides in an asylum. He visits her there, and she insists that Joe is dead. He pretends to be Joe's best friend and tells her that she's the only woman Joe ever loved. He drives away, sadly remembering the people he had filmed.

The first half of THE STAR MAKER is virtually plotless, simply chronicling the screen tests and Joe's journey from town to town. The film shines in these scenes. The wonderful cinematography and beautiful use of light, color, and shadow portray the beauty of film as an art form, while the screen tests themselves reveal the beauty of film as a medium for people's hopes and dreams. The script is extremely sharp, teaching us more about these people in a one-minute soliloquy than many films do in an hour of characterization.

Unfortunately, once Beata is introduced and the film becomes plot-driven, it loses its charm. While the early scenes are concise and emotionally powerful, the later, more drawn-out scenes are overly sentimental and tedious. Beata is one of the most pathetic female characters of the 1990s. She has no mind of her own, humiliates herself to gain Joe's attention, gives her innocence to him, and then goes mad when she loses him. The film's other female characters are either desperate schemers or innocent, starry-eyed fools. Also, Joe's hostile manner during the sex scenes is disturbing and incongruous in what otherwise is a light film. *(Sexual situations, violence, extreme profanity, extensive nudity.)* — A.M.

d, Giuseppe Tornatore; p, Vittorio Cecchi Gori, Rita Cecchi Gori; exec p, Mario Cotone; w, Giuseppe Tornatore, Fabio Rinaudo (from a story by Giuseppe Tornatore); ph, Dante Spinotti; ed, Massimo Quaglia; m, Ennio Morricone; prod d, Francesco Bronzi; sound, Massimo Loffredi (mixer); cos, Beatrice Bordone

AAN Best Foreign Language Film

Drama **(PR: C MPAA: R)**

STAR TREK: FIRST CONTACT ★★★
(U.S.) 105m Rick Berman ~ Paramount c

Patrick Stewart *(Captain Jean-Luc Picard)*; Jonathan Frakes *(Commander William Riker)*; Brent Spiner *(Lieutenant Commander Data)*; LeVar Burton *(Lieutenant Commander Geordi La Forge)*; Michael Dorn *(Lieutenant Commander Worf)*; Gates McFadden *(Dr. Beverly Crusher)*; Marina Sirtis *(Counselor Deanna Troi)*; Alfre Woodard *(Lily Sloane)*; James Cromwell *(Zefram Cochrane)*; Alice Krige *(Borg Queen)*; Michael Horton *(Security Officer)*; Neal McDonough *(Lt. Hawk)*; Marnie McPhail *(Eiger)*; Robert Picardo *(Holographic Doctor)*; Dwight Schultz *(Lt. Barclay)*; Adam Scott *(Defiant Conn Officer)*; Jack Shearer *(Admiral Hayes)*; Eric Steinberg *(Porter)*; Scott Strozier *(Security Officer)*; Patti Yasutake *(Nurse Ogawa)*; Victor Bevine; David Cowgill; Scott Have; Annette Helde *(Guards)*; C.J. Bau *(Bartender)*; Hillary Hayes *(Ruby)*; Julie Morgan *(Singer in Nightclub)*; Ronald R. Rondell *(Henchman)*; Don Stark *(Nicky the Noose)*; Cully Fredricksen *(Vulcan)*; Tamara Lee Krinsky *(Townsperson)*; Don Fischer; Andrew Palmer; Robert L. Zachar; J.R. Horsting; Jon David Weigand; Heinrich James; Dan Woren *(The Borg)*

FIRST CONTACT is the eighth film in the STAR TREK movie series, and continues the tradition of the even-numbered entries' superiority. It's the second STAR TREK movie to feature the cast of TV's "The Next Generation," and the first with no members of the original show's cast.

In the 24th century, Captain Jean-Luc Picard (Patrick Stewart) is shaking down a new Starship Enterprise when the Borg, a heinous race of cyborgs bent on human annihilation, attack. Rather than fight fair, the Borg time travel to the 21st century to assimilate humanity without resistance; it's up to Picard and crew to stop them.

In the year 2063, humanity is struggling to pick up the pieces after the devastation of WWIII. According to the (23rd-century) history books, the man who will singlehandedly elevate mankind out of the ashes is Zephram Cochrane (James Cromwell), the scientist who captains the planet's first warp-driven spaceflight; that achievement will be noticed by extraterrestrials—friendly members of the Federation—who establish "first contact" with humans, ushering in an era of universal brotherhood. The Enterprise crew surmise that the Borg plan to attack before Cochrane's historic flight, preventing first contact and dooming humanity to a future of assimilated slavery. An away team including Commander William Riker (Jonathan Frakes), Lieutenant Commander Geordi La Forge (LeVar Burton), and Counselor Deanna Troi (Marina Sirtis) is dispatched to Earth to ensure Cochrane's success. To the team's surprise, however, Cochrane is not the storybook hero of yore, but a cynical, money-grubbing boozehound—albeit a rather clever one.

Meanwhile, out in space, Picard leads the battle for control of the Enterprise. The Borg Queen (Alice Krige) captures the android Data (Brent Spiner) and starts grooming him to share her throne. In a Melvillian twist, Picard s past dealings with the Borg both fuel his fighting furor and cloud his command judgment; finally, however, he's convinced to blow up the ship and all the Borg with it. Still, he insists on risking his life to purge his personal demons and save Data. It looks like Picard is outmatched by the Queen, until Data double-crosses her. The Borg are destroyed, and the Enterprise is saved. Meanwhile, with Riker along, Cochrane makes his flight and first contact, setting history back on its proper course.

Saving the universe is small potatoes compared to the real mission assigned Frakes (who also directed), Stewart, and company. This casts' prime directive: Save the Franchise! Previously, movies featuring the original show's cast were increasingly sluggish and the franchise was held hostage by the popularity of James Kirk and the rest of the crew. Now, free of the demands of pop culture, Trek flicks can actually be good films. Like the new Enterprise introduced at its beginning, FIRST CONTACT is sleek and ready for action.

The storyline follows up on "The Next Generation's" most popular episode, in which Picard was captured and assimilated by the Borg. The film is action-heavy; a far cry from the ponderous philosophizing of the recent TREK movies, FIRST CONTACT is closer to the kicking-ass spirit of INDEPENDENCE DAY. The script is smart, putting Alfre Woodard in Stewart's tow to pull exposition out of him, and weeding out the ensemble, leaving the most popular characters —Picard, Data, and Worf the Klingon (Michael Dorn)—to handle the action. And in a big departure from TREK tradition, this film features camp-free acting. Stewart and Krige, specifically, give performances of depth as their characters battle over a soul torn between being man or machine. Action *and* thoughtfulness. Maybe the franchise is in good hands after all. *(Violence.)* — P.R.

d, Jonathan Frakes; p, Rick Berman; exec p, Marty Hornstein; co-p, Peter Lauritson; w, Rick Berman, Brannon Braga, Ronald D. Moore (from a story by Rick Berman, Brannon Braga and Ronald D. Moore); ph, Matthew F. Leonetti; ed, John W. Wheeler; m, Jerry Goldsmith; prod d, Herman Zimmerman; art d, Ron Wilkinson; set d, John M. Dwyer; sound, Thomas Causey (mixer); fx, Terry D. Frazee, Jeff Olson, Scott Rader, Adam Howard, Industrial Light & Magic; casting, Junie Lowry-Johnson, Ron Surma; cos, Deborah Everton; makeup, Michael Westmore, Scott Wheeler, Jake Garber; stunts, Ronald R. Rondell

AAN Best Makeup: Michael Westmore, Scott Wheeler, Jake Garber

Science Fiction/Adventure **(PR: C MPAA: PG-13)**

STEALING BEAUTY ★★½
(Italy/U.K./France) 119m Fiction Cinematografica; Recorded Picture Company; UGC Images ~ Fox Searchlight c
(LO BALLO DA SOLA; BEAUTE VOLEE)

Liv Tyler *(Lucy Harmon)*; Jeremy Irons *(Alex Parrish)*; Sinead Cusack *(Diana Grayson)*; Carlo Cecchi *(Carlo Lisca)*; Jean Marais *(M. Guillaume)*; Donal McCann *(Ian Grayson)*; D.W. Moffett *(Richard Reed)*; Stefania Sandrelli *(Noemi)*; Rachel Weisz *(Miranda Fox)*; Joseph Fiennes *(Christopher Fox)*; Jason Flemyng *(Gregory)*; Anna Maria Gherardi *(Chiarella Donati)*; Ignazio Oliva *(Osvaldo Donati)*; Francesco Siciliano *(Michele Lisca)*; Leonardo Treviglio *(Lieutenant)*; Rebecca Valpy *(Daisy Grayson)*; Alessandra Vanzi *(Marta)*; Roberto Zibetti *(Niccolo Donati)*

It is refreshing to see director Bernardo Bertolucci return to a smaller-scale film following years of making overblown epics, but STEALING BEAUTY lacks the artistic and political passion of his early work. The story of a young woman's sexual awakening is turned into a pretty but dramatically vapid travelogue.

Liv Tyler plays the young woman, Lucy Harmon, an American who travels to Tuscany for the summer following her mother's suicide. Lucy plans to stay with Ian and Diana Grayson (Donal McCann, Sinead Cusack), who were friends of her poet-model mother. The purpose of Lucy's vacation is ostensibly to have her portrait painted by Ian, but Lucy's secret plan is to reunite with Grayson's young, handsome neighbor, Niccolo (Roberto Zibetti), with whom she once shared a kiss. On her trip, Lucy also spends her time reading her mother's diaries, trying to figure out the identity of her biological father, a man she has never known.

Once she settles in at the Graysons' picturesque villa, Lucy discovers that Niccolo is away. Disappointed, she spends her time posing for Ian and getting to know the other houseguests: Alex (Jeremy Irons), a playwright with a terminal illness; Guillaume (Jean Marais), an elderly French art dealer; Miranda (Rachel Weisz), a snooty jewelry designer who is Diana's daughter from a previous marriage; Richard (D.W. Moffett), Diana's entertainment lawyer boyfriend; and Noemi (Stefania Sandrelli), an advice columnist. The assorted expatriates take an interest in Lucy's many dilemmas, with the fey Alex most curious about the teenager's desire to lose her virginity.

When Niccolo returns home, Lucy gets a new look at her former sweetheart, who suddenly appears callow and unromantic. Lucy shifts her romantic attention to the other available men, including the slick, philandering Richard, but eventually she settles on Carlo (Carlo Cecchi), a shy native of the village. Following a spirited bacchanal in a nearby palace one night, Lucy and Carlo spend a day together alone to make love—both for the first time. When Lucy returns to the villa, Ian finishes her portrait and reveals that he is her real father. With the mystery solved, Lucy bids a poignant adieu to the other houseguests and her new love, Carlo.

STEALING BEAUTY's main problem is its screenplay, written by Bertolucci and novelist Susan Minot. The setting and structure of the drama invoke Chekhov, but the dialogue sounds hollow and pretentious.

As director, Bertolucci keeps the images looking good throughout, but the continuous celebration of art, life, love, music, food, and the beauty of nature eventually becomes wearisome. The characters are so insulated in their paradise, one yearns for some of the fervor that sparked such Bertolucci films as BEFORE THE REVOLUTION (1964), THE SPIDER'S STRATAGEM (1970), and LAST TANGO IN PARIS (1972).

The talented cast struggles with poorly written roles. Tyler (daughter of rock star Steven Tyler) makes her Henry James-style heroine more appealing than she might have been, but this actress may be seen to better advantage in 1996's HEAVY. Cusack is given little to work with as Diana but hints at a great untold story behind her character. McCann lends solidity to the role of Ian, and the supporting players flesh out the smaller parts. Unfortunately, the best-known actors, Irons and Marais, overplay the two potentially most moving parts.

It is hard to totally dismiss any film by Bertolucci, who stages the nocturnal bacchanal with a flourish. It's too bad, then, that so much of the film seems like an advertisement for bottled wine and Armani suits. *(Nudity, sexual situations, substance abuse, profanity.)* — E.M.

d, Bernardo Bertolucci; p, Jeremy Thomas; assoc p, Chris Auty; w, Susan Minot (from a story by Bernardo Bertolucci); ph, Darius Khondji; ed, Pietro Scalia; m, Richard Hartley; prod d, Gianni Silvestri; art d, Domenico Sica; set d, Cinzia Sleiter; sound, Ivan Sharrock (mixer); casting, Howard Feuer, Celestia Fox; cos, Louise Stjernsward, Giorgio Armani; makeup, Nilo Iacoponi

Romance/Drama **(PR: O MPAA: R)**

STEPHEN KING'S THINNER ★★½

(U.S.) 92m Thinner Productions; Spelling Entertainment ~ Paramount c

Robert John Burke *(Billy Halleck)*; Joe Mantegna *(Richie Ginelli)*; Kari Wuhrer *(Gina Lempke)*; Lucinda Jenney *(Heidi Halleck)*; Michael Constantine *(Tadzu Lempke)*; Joy Lenz *(Linda Halleck)*; Daniel Von Bargen *(Duncan Hopley)*; John Horton *(Judge Rossington)*; Sam Freed *(Mike Houston)*; Elizabeth Franz; Howard Erskine

This entry in the unending stream of Stephen King films is ironically titled: it has the bare bones of what made King's novel work, but lacks much of the flesh.

Overweight defense lawyer Billy Halleck (Robert John Burke) celebrates the acquittal of his mobster client, Ginelli (Joe Mantegna). While he's driving home, his wife, Heidi (Lucinda Jenney), gets frisky and distracts him, and he accidentally runs down the daughter of an aged gypsy, Tadzu Lempke (Michael Constantine), whose caravan is being run out of town by police chief Duncan Hopley (Daniel Von Bargen).

After the chief and Judge Rossington (John Horton) conspire to clear Billy of wrongdoing in the woman's death, Lempke places a gypsy curse on Billy, causing him to lose weight inexorably, no matter how much he eats. Hopley and Rossington are also subjected to disfiguring spells.

Tracking down the gypsy caravan, Billy confronts Lempke, who refuses to lift the curse. Billy is forced to seek Ginelli's help. The mobster threatens Lempke's daughter, Gina (Kari Wuhrer), and shoots up their camp, whereupon Lempke finally relents. Presenting Billy with a magical pie, the old gypsy has him drip some blood in, then tells Billy it must be eaten by someone else so that the curse can be transferred.

Returning home, Billy feeds some to Heidi, whom he suspects of cheating on him with their doctor, Mike Houston (Sam Freed), during his ordeal. The next morning, he awakens next to her corpse, but is horrified to find that his teenage daughter, Linda (Joy Lentz), has also eaten some of the pie. Mike arrives at the door, and Billy invites him in for a bite.

King's novel *Thinner* first came out in 1984. One of the acknowledged stumbling blocks in its trip to the screen was the makeup effects technology required to present a lead character who begins at nearly 300 pounds and wastes away to a near-skeletal state.

But an equal, more subtle challenge also existed. As presented by King, Billy Halleck is an unsympathetic protagonist in many ways, and it was the author's writing skill that kept readers caught up in his plight. Creating that empathy on screen is a trickier proposition, one that actor Burke and director Tom Holland haven't entirely achieved.

While Greg Cannom's makeup effects are generally realistic, Burke's performance is less convincing. He never really disappears into the makeup, seeming less like a genuinely fat man than an actor of normal build *acting* overweight. In addition, his mannered approach to the character negates some of the empathy Billy requires. More successful are Mantegna as the sympathetic hood and Constantine as the vengeful gypsy: both make their characters more believable—and thus, their own destructive actions more understandable—than Burke's. Holland, who scripted with Michael McDowell, retains some of the book's basic power, and a couple of sequences in the gypsy camp generate true tension.

Unfortunately, test-audience reactions led Paramount to order changes in the original ending—one of the most chilling in all King's work, in which Halleck discovers that he has doomed his daughter as well as his wife, and sits down to eat the gypsy pie himself. Though its downbeat tone remains unchanged, the conclusion has been expanded in a manner that doesn't make sense. If Heidi and Linda ate the pie at the same time, why is Heidi a desiccated corpse and Linda, at least for the moment, still healthy? *(Graphic violence, sexual situations, extreme profanity.)* — M.G.

d, Tom Holland; p, Richard P. Rubenstein; exec p, Stephen F. Kesten; assoc p, Welch Lambeth; co-p, Mitchell Galin; w, Michael McDowell (based on the novel *Thinner* by Stephen King); ph, Kees Van Oostrum; ed, Marc Laub; prod d, Laurence Bennett; art d, Chuck Parker; set d, Nina Bradford; sound, Jay Meagher (mixer); fx, Ken Estes; casting, Leonard Finger; cos, Ha Nguyen; makeup, Bob Laden, Greg Cannom

Horror **(PR: C MPAA: R)**

STONEWALL ★★½

(U.S.) 93m BBC ~ Strand Releasing c

Guillermo Diaz *(LaMiranda)*; Frederick Weller *(Matty Dean)*; Brendan Corbalis *(Ethan)*; Duane Boutte *(Bostonia)*; Bruce MacVittie *(Skinny Vinnie)*; Matthew Faber *(Mizz Moxie)*; Dwight Ewell *(Helen Wheels)*

Although riddled with cliches, sentimentality, and simplifications, this film is a strangely stirring account of an event that could be likened to a gay Boston Tea Party. Searingly vivid performances and a very apt sense of the time are to be credited for this film's making it to safe harbor.

On a late June night in 1969, a group of gay patrons of the Mafia-owned Stonewall bar in Greenwich Village held a violent protest against the police, who were conducting one of their regular raids on gay bars. The uprising officially ushered in the beginning of gay liberation, and Nigel Finch's film purports to recreate that night and certain events leading up to it. Loosely based on a book by Martin Duberman, it starts off in classic movie fashion with Matty Dean (Frederick Weller), a fresh, idealistic Midwestern boy arriving in New York in search of a gay urban oasis. He quickly meets up with LaMiranda (Guillermo Diaz), a flamboyant Puerto Rican drag queen. Attracted to his complete openness in a very repressed time, Matty becomes LaMiranda's lover. Ever the explorer, however, he also becomes involved with Ethan (Brendan Corbalis), a teacher who is active in the Homophile Society (read Mattachine Society), a conservative group given to demure picketing, dressed in business suits in an effort to look "normal." There is a telling encounter between the drags, led by the imperious Bostonia (Duane Boutte), and the besuited Homophiles. Matty's intro to New York includes an excursion he takes with Ethan to Fire Island, where he witnesses more examples of police and societal repression of gays. Back in the city, the corrupt Sixth Precinct goes about its business of shakedowns and brutal intimidation. Matty is placed in the difficult position of having to choose between LaMiranda and Ethan, who abhors "ditsy" drag queens and is determined to change the system from within. In a subplot, the mobster Skinny Vinnie (Bruce MacVittie), the manager of a gay bar, is carrying on a turbulent destined-to-be-tragic affair with the willful Bostonia. He wants Bostonia to have a sex change operation so the two of them can settle down to domestic bliss.

LaMiranda's suicide attempt and a desire to bring about change through more radical means than those advocated by the Homophiles cause Matty to return to the Village on the fateful night of Judy Garland's funeral. The Stonewall uprising finally occurs, with windows smashed and heads knocked about, to the accompaniment of shouts of "Gay Power!" and an informal chorus line of drag queens singing an anthem to the tune of the "Howdy Doody" theme. LaMiranda gets the last word in a disclaimer for whatever historical inaccuracies may have been perpetrated: "I'm a drag queen. And we don't always deal in reality. We deal in dreams. We're as American as apple pie."

Director Nigel Finch (who died before the film's release) makes emblematic work of these real-life events. The movie pays effective homage to both the time and the various icons which influenced it. One smiles in recognition at the first scenes of Matty's arrival in Manhattan; they're incredibly similar to Joe Buck s arrival at the beginning of MIDNIGHT COWBOY (1969). Drag queens lip-synching to various boy-crazy anthems of the '60s is fun and apotheosizes the bright veneer of the era, which masked the oppression gays were actually forced to endure. Finch holds your interest as he explores the diverse worlds of the drags, the Homophiles, the police and the Mafia, investigating the less than six degrees that separates each group. Not since Fassbinder's FOX AND HIS FRIENDS (1975) has a film so thoroughly explored the ways in which gays oppress each other. Finch stages the Stonewall Uprising very effectively, miraculously one could say, on a shoestring budget, cannily gauging the dilemmas of the separate characters as they converge on that one incendiary night. LaMiranda tearfully watching footage of Judy Garland's funeral on TV is the chord-striking image that kicks off the whole shebang.

Diaz's performance dominates the film. LaMiranda is no little cupcake out of TO WONG FOO. . . (1995) or THE BIRDCAGE (1996), but rather a character of unconquerable sassy survivalism and acid-tongued anger. As fierce as he is, Boutte nearly goes him one further in terms of pure "diva-fied" regality. Weller manages to charm as an idealized romantic and hunky revolutionary, even when singing corny gay liberation songs to the tune of "The Battle Hymn of the Republic." *(Profanity, nudity, sexual situations, violence, substance abuse, adult situations.)* — D.N.

d, Nigel Finch; p, Christine Vachon, Ruth Caleb; exec p, George Faber, Anthony Wall; assoc p, Matthew Hamilton; w, Rikki Beadle Blair (based on the book by Martin Duberman); ph, Chris Seager; ed, John Richards; m, Michael Kamen; prod d, Therese Deprez; casting, Billy Hopkins, Suzanne Smith, Kerry Barden; cos, Michael Clancy

Historical/Drama **(PR: C MPAA: NR)**

STORY OF XINGHUA, THE ★★★½

(China) 93m Beijing Film Academy Youth Film School ~ Evergreen Entertainment c

Zhang Guoli *(Fulin)*; Jiang Wenli *(Xinghua)*; Tian Shaojun *(Wanglai)*

A beautifully understated tale of love and ambition, THE STORY OF XINGHUA addresses universal human themes with a feminist twist.

Wanglai (Tian Shaojun) is a brutal, greedy, egotistical peasant, the boss of a work crew that steals and sells stones from the Great Wall. Wanglai's younger brother, Fulin (Zhang Guoli), is his antithesis, a gentle, handsome tree farmer. Xinghua (Jiang Wenli), Wanglai's beautiful young wife, is submissive but obviously unhappy: she doesn't love her husband and finds him physically repulsive. Wanglai wants an heir to his growing fortune, but, unsurprisingly, his wife remains barren.

Wanglai gets Fulin to help Xinghua plow Wanglai's field; Xinghua and Fulin become lovers and she gets pregnant. Unaware of this, Wanglai becomes obsessed with rumors of a treasure buried beneath an ancient watchtower and shrine. He convinces his gang to dig for it, despite the dangers of structural collapse, government intervention, and supernatural displeasure. At the same time, his mistress tells him about Xinghua and Fulin. He beats Fulin while his gang destroys Fulin's beloved trees; later, Fulin tearfully admits to Xinghua that he too wanted an heir. When Xinghua tells Wanglai that she is carrying Fulin's child, he is first angry, then overjoyed by the prospect of an heir, however begotten. Trying to placate her, he goes to dig up the treasure and is killed when the tower collapses on him. Xinghua leaves the village, and Fulin, without saying goodbye. Her future is uncertain, but she is no longer a pawn to male ambitions.

THE STORY OF XINGHUA is a wonderful piece of visual storytelling. Dialogue is sparse and simple, so subtitles inform without distracting the viewer. Wanglai, Xinghua, and Fulin are believable stereotypes, so their acting transcends linguistic and cultural barriers, recalling the best silent films. The film relies on mise-en-scene and intimate tracking shots, usually alternating between interior and exterior, day and night, ending each scene with a simple fade to black. The film's rhythm mirrors that of village life, leaving tensions to build as the result of character interactions, and eschewing visual pyrotechnics in favour of symbolism. When Xinghau and Fulin first make love, we hear her cries, but see a field drenched with rain. In XINGHUA, cliches are transformed into archetypes.

The story's simplicity is deceptive. We expect either tragedy or a happy ending, but, like the heroine, we are left hanging. XINGHUA's minor flaws, ambivalence about religion and government, are due to fear of censorship. On almost every level, XINGHUA quietly affirms film's unique capacity to convey the universality of human experience. *(Sexual situations, violence.)* — C.M.

d, Yin Li; p, Ming Liu; ph, Jiaguo Li; ed, Yihua Zhao; m, Weigong Liu; art d, Junde Cui; sound, Guoqiang Yao

Romance/Drama (PR: C MPAA: NR)

STRANGER THINGS

(SEE: FOR BETTER OR WORSE)

STREET FIGHTER II: THE ANIMATED MOVIE ★★½

(Japan) 99m Capcom; Sony Music Video; Manga Entertainment ~ Sony Music Video c

VOICES OF: Hank Smith *(Ryu)*; Ted Richards *(Ken)*; Mary Briscoe *(Chun Li)*; Phil Matthews *(Bison)*; Donald Lee *(Guile)*; William Johnson *(Zangief)*; John Hammond *(DJ)*; Patrick Gilbert *(E. Honda)*; Steve Davis *(Vega)*; David Conrad *(Sagat)*; S. J. Charvin *(Cammy)*; George Celik *(Master)*; Tom Carlton *(Blanka)*; Don Carey *(Dhalsim)*; Richard Cardona *(T-Hawk)*; Joe Michaels *(Balrog)*; Toni Burke *(Eliza)*; Phil Williams *(Fei Long)*

STREET FIGHTER II: THE ANIMATED MOVIE is the English-dubbed version of a Japanese animated theatrical film based on the popular martial-arts video game. It offers plenty of action, spectacular animation, and an engaging story for youthful fans of the game.

Young Japanese martial artist Ryu travels the Far East seeking to perfect his martial arts skills in competition with other "street fighters," freelance martial artists who fight in illegal matches for money. He attracts the notice of M. Bison, leader of the terrorist organization Shadowlaw, who seeks to recruit the best street fighters to serve as assassins for him. Bison abducts young American fighter Ken Masters, Ryu's blood brother, and brainwashes him in the hopes of using him to lure Ryu into the organization.

The assassination of a London diplomat by a brainwashed British agent, Cammy White, draws Interpol into the case. Agent Chun Li works with US military liaison Capt. Guile to track down known street fighters in order to intercept Bison's thugs.

Guile's investigation leads him to a Himalayan mountain retreat, where he finds Ryu in training with sumo wrestler E. Honda. Having tailed Guile, Bison arrives in a powerful airplane and brings out a brainwashed Ken to fight Ryu. While Guile fights Bison, Ken and Ryu battle each other, until Ryu's efforts manage to jog Ken's memory. They then join their powers to defeat Bison.

One of several recent Japanese animated features based on video games, STREET FIGHTER II brings the characters to life in a compelling and dramatic manner, succeeding where its live-action American counterpart, STREET FIGHTER (1994), failed. While the American film sought to give prominence to all 16 characters from the Street Fighter II video game, the Japanese version focuses primarily on the two youthful characters, Ryu and Ken, presenting them as aspiring martial arts champions on a journey of discovery. As a result, the story is made more coherent and engaging.

The filmmaker, Gisaburo Sugii (THE TALE OF GENJI, NIGHT ON THE GALACTIC RAILROAD), is a veteran director of Japanese animation and his sure, skillful touch is evident throughout the film, particularly in the starkly realistic production and character design. The film offers a nod to the video game in its frequent battles, opening up the characters' skirmishes in a way not available to the game's creators. If there is any single problem with the film, it's in the rather abrupt resolution. The final battles come too soon and end too quickly.

The film was followed in Japan by a 29-episode TV series entitled "Street Fighter II V," which offered greater character development, an epic narrative, and a cliffhanger structure. The 1996 US video release version comes with a grafted-on hard rock score and some cuts of violence and nudity. *(Violence, Nudity.)* — B.C.

d, Gisaburo Sugii; p, Kenichi Imai; exec p, Hiroshi Inagaki, Akio Sakai; assoc p, Takeshi Sekiguchi, Megumu Sugiyama, Mitsuhisa Hida; w, Kenichi Imai, Gisaburo Sugii; ph, Hiroaki Edamitsu; m, Cory Lerios, John D'Andrea; art d, Hajime Matsuoka; anim, Minoru Maeda, Marishuke Eguchi, Shuko Murase

Adventure/Animated/Martial Arts (PR: C MPAA: PG-13)

STREETCAR NAMED DESIRE, A ★★½

(U.S.) 156m CBS Entertainment Productions ~ CBS Video c

Jessica Lange *(Blanche DuBois)*; Alec Baldwin *(Stanley Kowalski)*; Diane Lane *(Stella)*; John Goodman *(Mitch)*; Rondi Reed *(Eunice Hubbell)*; Fred Coffin *(Steve Hubbell)*; Carlos Gomez *(Pablo)*; Matt Keeslar *(The Collector)*; Jerry Hardin *(The Doctor)*; Carmen Zapata *(The Flower Seller)*; Tina Lifford *(Neighbor)*; Patricia Herd *(The Matron)*

This made-for-TV version of Tennessee Williams' classic play is little more than a photographed recording of the Broadway revival starring Jessica Lange.

On a leave of absence from the school where she teaches, Blanche DuBois (Jessica Lange), arrives in the French quarter of New Orleans for a visit with her pregnant sister, Stella (Diane Lane), and her husband, Stanley (Alec Baldwin). Stella is shocked to learn that their family estate has been lost to creditors. Blanche's reluctance to provide details and her expensive wardrobe arouse Stanley's suspicions.

Blanche meets and flirts with Stanley's friend Mitch (John Goodman), a courtly middle-aged bachelor. Stanley learns that

Blanche had a reputation in her home town for promiscuity and unstable behavior, and was in fact fired from her job for seducing a teenaged boy. Stella refuses to believe these stories, defending her sister as emotionally delicate. Stanley also tells this to Mitch, who had been considering proposing to Blanche.

Stella goes into labor. While she and Stanley are at the hospital, Mitch confronts Blanche. After forcing her to show herself in the lights she has always avoided because they give away her true age, he leaves, disgusted at the way she has manipulated him. Stanley returns home, jubilant at his impending fatherhood. He tries to be conciliatory toward Blanche, but they fight again, and he rapes her.

With her sister unwilling to believe her version of what happened, Blanche loses her precarious hold on reality and is sent to a mental institution, believing that the doctor who comes for her is a gentleman admirer.

The sole advantage of this STREETCAR over its 1951 predecessor is its use of the complete text of Tennessee Williams' play. Most notably, it restores the speech in which Blanche discusses the homosexuality of her dead husband and the ending in which Stella stays with Stanley, choosing not to believe Blanche's accusation of rape. That Blanche is indeed raped is also more clearly (though tastefully) shown.

But in every other respect, this is a prime example of the dangers of remaking a classic. Perhaps it was wise for director Glenn Jordan to choose not to compete with Elia Kazan: rather than make the play into a film, as did Kazan, Jordan treats this as a "You Are There" look at the Broadway revival he is adapting. However, the production would have had to be much stronger for that strategy to succeed. Of the cast's quartet of leading players, only John Goodman succeeds in escaping the shadow of the famous film: as Mitch, he isn't better than Karl Malden, but he is different and performs respectably. Diane Lane makes little impression as a surprisingly sultry Stella. Alec Baldwin is quite miscast—he isn't nearly brutish enough to play Stanley (though who is?), and too often seems to be imitating Marlon Brando's performance. Jessica Lange doesn't seem to have watched Vivien Leigh's Blanche at all, but perhaps she should have. Lange and Blanche bring out the worst in each other, as the actress utterly fails to evoke any of the sympathy the character needs. It's Acting with a capital "A," as if she were playing Norma Desmond playing Blanche DuBois. *(Violence, sexual situations, adult situations.)* — M.F.

d, Glenn Jordan; p, Glenn Jordan; exec p, Robert Gros; co-p, Robert Bennett Steinhauer; w, (From the play by Tennessee Williams); ph, Ralf Bode; ed, David Simmons; m, David Mansfield; prod d, Fred Harpman; art d, Janet Stokes; sound, Michael Moore; fx, Albert Marangoni; casting, Marsha Kleinman; cos, Theoni V. Aldredge; makeup, Alan Friedman

Drama **(PR: C MPAA: NR)**

STREETS OF LAREDO

(SEE: LARRY MCMURTRY'S STREETS OF LAREDO)

STRIPTEASE ★★

(U.S.) 115m Castle Rock Entertainment; Lobell/Bergman Productions ~ Columbia c

Demi Moore *(Erin Grant)*; Armand Assante *(Al Garcia)*; Ving Rhames *(Shad)*; Burt Reynolds *(Congressman David L. Dilbeck)*; Robert Patrick *(Darrell Grant)*; Paul Guilfoyle *(Malcom Moldovsky)*; Jerry Grayson *(Orly)*; Rumer Willis *(Angela Grant)*; Robert Stanton *(Erb Crandal)*; William Hill *(Jerry Killian)*; Stuart Pankin *(Alan Mordecai)*; Dina Spybey *(Monique Jr.)*; Pasean Wilson *(Sabrina Hepburn)*; Pandora Peaks *(Urbana Sprawl)*; Barbara Alyn Woods *(Lorelei)*; Kimberly Flynn *(Ariel Sharon)*; Rena Riffel *(Tiffany Glass)*; Siobhan Fallon *(Rita)*; Gary Basaraba *(Alberto)*; Matthew Baron *(Paul Guber)*; Gianni Russo *(Willie Rojo)*; Jose Zuniga *(Chris Rojo)*; Anthony Jones *(Pierre)*; Eduardo Yanez *(Chico)*; Antoni Corone *(Nico)*; Frances Fisher *(Donna Garcia)*; Teddy Bergman *(Andy)*; Louis Seeger Crume *(Judge Fingerhut)*; Aymee Garcia *(Temp)*; Deborah Magdalena *(Secretary)*; Keone Young *(Ling)*; Johnny Cocktails *(DJ)*; Anthony Giaimo *(Medical Examiner)*; Jerry Pacific *(Parking Valet)*; Anna Lobell *(Video Clerk)*; Diane Adams *(Hospital Volunteer)*; Chad Ayers *(Young Christian)*; April Sharpe *(Seaquarium Guide)*; Maria Gennaro *(TV Reporter)*; Keith Blaney *(Bachelor No. 1)*; Marc Chaykin *(Bachelor No. 2)*; Edward Goldstein *(Bartender)*; Christi Bauerle *(Cocktail Waitress)*; Yoshi Obata *(Business Man in Club)*; Tony Toyoda *(Business Man in Club)*; Scott Oughterson *(Business Man in Club)*; Ted Niarchos Jr. *(Patron in Club)*; Darreck Crane *(Patron in Club)*; Marco Assante *(Patron in Club)*

Based on Carl Hiaasen's 1993 novel *Strip Tease* (note the inexplicable title change), Andrew Bergman's film wants to replicate the palm tree-potboiler style of novelists like Hiaasen and Elmore Leonard. STRIPTEASE is less successful in this regard than the hipper, funnier GET SHORTY.

Erin Grant (Demi Moore) is a physically attractive ex-secretary for the FBI. After losing a bitter custody fight with her ex-husband Darrell (Robert Patrick), she proves her parental responsibility by taking a job at the Eager Beaver, a local strip bar. Her choreographic stylings are popular with the customers—especially Jerry Killian (William Hill), a socially graceless loner who worships the ground she walks on, and the chronically dissipated US Congressman David L. Dilbeck (Burt Reynolds).

When Dilbeck staggers into a drunken brawl onstage, Jerry recognizes him and sees a way to help his favorite stripper with her court fight. Later, Erin is surprised to learn that Jerry has washed up, drowned near the vacation home of Miami police detective Al Garcia (Armand Assante) soon after he confronted Dilbeck and his conniving assistant Erb Crandal (Robert Stanton). When yet another potential blackmailer approaches Dilbeck with pictures of the brawl, Crandal and Dilbeck's sugar industry sponsors begin to wonder how much Erin herself knows about Dilbeck's sexual foibles. The congressman, meanwhile, insists he will reform himself before the next election if he can spend one hour alone with Miss Grant. The offer is made.

Seeing this as a way to finance her escape with her daughter from the felonious Darrell, Erin accepts. Crandal, however, sees this as an opportunity to rid the congressman of the stripper, whom he notes "is not dumb enough." He does not figure on the arrival of Darrell, stoned on morphine, who sneaks onto Dilbeck's party yacht and beats Crandal senseless. Erin steals away with the drunken congressman, and gets him to admit his complicity to Jerry's murder on tape. Crandal soon shows up with his goons, but Erin is saved thanks to the timely arrival of Detective Garcia, Shad (Ving Rhames), the tart-tongued bouncer from the Eager Beaver, and the CNN video crew Erin was prescient enough to summon before meeting with the congressman.

One doesn't need to be a believer of the 104th Congress or an apologist for Big Sugar to recognize that STRIPTEASE is a grossly preposterous tale. It's not so much that the viewer is asked to believe that in a booming Florida economy the only job an experienced secretary—one with her child's custody on the line, no less—is in a strip joint. After all, it's dubious a major studio would be interested in the travails of a single mother on the extreme edge of southern Appalachia if she didn't look like Demi Moore and dance in a strip club. Where the novel got by with mordant wit and sharply sketched detail, writer-director Bergman can find no visual equivalent for Hiaasen's style.

Literary conceits aside, the point of STRIPTEASE is the stripteasing. There's plenty of that here, almost to the point of seeming as unmotivated as the "dancing" in SHOWGIRLS (1995). The atmosphere is lightened by some witty dialogue, delivered mostly by Rhames. Some of the routines of the other dancers are also amusing—but not Moore's, which seem as hyped and self-serious as Moore herself. And though this faded stardom earned him little attention in the film's promotion, Burt Reynolds is quite good in a buffoon's role. His comeback deserves a better vehicle. *(Extensive nudity, sexual situations, profanity.)* — N.N.

d, Andrew Bergman; p, Mike Lobell; exec p, Joseph Hartwick; assoc p, Daneen Lagrone Conroy; w, Andrew Bergman (based on the novel by Carl Hiaasen); ph, Stephen Goldblatt; ed, Anne V. Coates; m, Howard Shore; prod d, Mel Bourne; art d, Elizabeth Lapp; set d, Leslie Bloom; ch, Marguerite Pomerhn Derricks; sound, James J. Sabat (mixer); casting, John Lyons; cos, Albert Wolsky; makeup, Sharon Ilson; stunts, Phil Neilson

Crime/Comedy **(PR: C MPAA: R)**

STUPIDS, THE ★★

(U.S.) 93m Savoy Pictures; Imagine Entertainment ~ New Line c

Tom Arnold *(Stanley Stupid)*; Jessica Lundy *(Joan Stupid)*; Bug Hall *(Buster Stupid)*; Alex McKenna *(Petunia Stupid)*; Scott Kraft *(Policeman)*; Victor Ertmanis *(Garbageman #1)*; Earl Williams *(Garbageman #2)*; George Chiang *(Chinese Waiter #1)*; Max Landis *(Graffiti Artist)*; Carol Ng *(Jade Palace Hostess)*; Arthur Eng *(Chinese Waiter #2)*; Jennifer Dean *(Meter Maid)*; Mark Metcalf *(Colonel)*; Mark Keeslar *(Lieutenant)*; Garry Robbins *(Extremely Tall Guy)*; Nicu Branzea *(Arms Buyer #1)*; Richard Crook *(Arms Buyer #2)*; Gurinder Chadha *(Reporter #1)*; Mick Garris *(Reporter #2)*; Jeremey Ratchford *(Soldier)*; John Stoneham Jr. *(Green Alien)*; Ken Quinn *(Orange Alien)*; Gillian Vanderbugh *(Alien Stewardess)*; Harvey Atkin *(Deli Guy)*; David Cronenberg *(Postal Supervisor)*; Markus Parilo *(Special Forces Guy)*; Constantin Costa Gavras *(Gas Station Guy)*; Mif *(Explosive Guy)*; Walter Alza *(Taxi Driver)*; Robert Wise *(Stanley's Neighbor)*; Christopher Lee *(Evil Sender)*; Frankie Faison *(The Lloyd)*; Mo Kelso *(Airbag Woman)*; Sherry Miller *(Anchorwoman)*; Bob Keeshan *(Charles Sender)*; Jeff Clarke *(Delivery Guy)*; Atom Egoyan *(TV Studio Guard)*; Wendy Hopkins *(TV Assistant Director)*; Jacqueline McLeod *(Make-Up Woman)*; Jenny McCarthy *(Glamorous Actress)*; David Ferry *(Late Night Show Host)*; Norman Jewison *(TV Director)*; Frederic Devancker *(French Chef)*; Rolanda Watts *(Talk Show Hostess)*; Gillo Pontecorvo *(Talk Show Guest #1)*; Nicholas Rice *(Talk Show Guest #2)*; Julie Champnella *(Talk Show Guest #3)*; Philip Akin *(Henchman #1)*; Kevin Conway *(Henchman #2)*; Carol Anderson *(Checkpoint Guard)*; Rick Avery *(Bad Guy)*; Fiona Highet *(Cop #1)*; Phillip Jarrett *(Cop #2)*; Jim Amross *(Cop #3)*; Wayne Ward *(Cop #4)*

Based on a series of popular children's books, THE STUPIDS is a title that intends no irony. Mildly succeeding at being no more than silly fun, the movie at least deserves some credit for countering the assumption that all children's entertainment must be heartwarming.

Stanley Q. Stupid (Tom Arnold) is the stupid head of the world's stupidest family. As a group, the Stupids are a cross between "The Beverly Hillbillies" and Oliver Stone—they always leap to the wrong conclusion and see conspiracies everywhere. On the trail of "the thieves" that come in a big truck every week and steal the trash, Stanley crosses paths with the traitorous Colonel Niedermeyer (Mark Metcalf). Meanwhile, searching for Stanley, Joan Stupid (Jessica Lundy) and the two Stupid children, Petunia and Buster (Alex McKenna and Bug Hall), go to the local newspaper where their antics result in a banner headline about nose-picking space aliens. When reunited, the Stupids conclude that the garbage stealing is part of a world domination plot masterminded by one "Mr. Sender" (as in "Return to. . . ") (played by a diabolical Christopher Lee), who they believe also steals mail. Following a *real* Mr. Sender (Bob "Captain Kangaroo" Keeshan), the Stupids first visit a museum, and then a TV station where Stanley goes on a daytime talk show and performs the nonsense song "I'm My Own Grandpa." Eventually, the family ends up in a warehouse where Col. Niedermeyer is selling arms to terrorists. Oblivious to what's happening, the Stupids manage to save the day, but before they can celebrate their victory over trash thieves, Stanley will have to deal with some insulted extra-terrestrials.

There's a distinction to be made between family entertainment and children's entertainment; the former becoming so accepted as a euphemism for the latter, the terms seem synonymous. Usually, the fortunes of true family fare suffer from this (e.g., adults avoid THE LITTLE PRINCESS because it's perceived as a "children's" movie). THE STUPIDS, however, provides a good example of the reverse situation: this movie is not for "families," and particularly not for adults; it is strictly for kids only. (In fact, THE STUPIDS should have a special NB-10 rating: nobody over 10 admitted). By adult standards, THE STUPIDS unabashedly lives up to its name, but kids will like it because it is goofy, wide-eyed, and unbelievable amusement.

As SPINAL TAP's David St. Hubbins once observed, "It's such a thin line between stupid and clever." Where that line is drawn often depends on one's age. Kids should be allowed to enjoy this movie—but just as long as they don't expect any adults to stay in the room and watch. *(Violence.)* — P.R.

d, John Landis; p, Ron Howard, Brian Grazer, Leslie Belzberg; w, Brent Forrester (based on characters created by James Marshall and Harry Allard); ph, Manfred Guthe; ed, Dale Beldin; m, Christopher Stone; prod d, Phil Dagort; art d, Rocco Matteo; set d, Carol Lavoie; sound, Owen Langevin (mixer); fx, Ted Ross, Walter Hart; casting, Amy Lippens; cos, Deborah Nadoolman; makeup, Dorothy Smith; stunts, Rick Avery

Comedy/Children's **(PR: A MPAA: PG)**

SUBSTANCE OF FIRE, THE ★★½

(U.S.) 101m Goldheart Films ~ Miramax c

Benjamin Ungar *(Young Isaac Geldhart)*; Ron Rifkin *(Isaac Geldhart)*; Tom McDermott *(Old Printer)*; George Morfogen *(Otto the Printer)*; Lee Grant *(Cora Cahn)*; Tony Goldwyn *(Aaron Geldhart)*; Andrew Pang *(Mr. Otani Junior)*; Edmund Ikeda *(Mr. Otani Senior)*; Elizabeth Franz *(Miss Barzakian)*; Gil Bellows *(Val Chenard)*; Eric Bogosian *(Gene Byck)*; Ronny Graham *(Louis Foukold)*; Timothy Hutton *(Martin Geldhart)*; John Sullivan *(Stewart)*; Sophia Salguero *(Rachel)*; Sarah Jessica Parker *(Sarah Geldhart)*; John Patrick Walker *(Peter)*; Roger Rees *(Max)*; Viola Davis *(Nurse)*; David S. Howard *(Dr. Bernard Kramer)*; Gregory Burke *(Young Martin)*; Adolph Green *(Mr. Musselblatt)*; William Cain *(Mr. Cox)*; Alec Mapa *(New Receptionist)*; Edgar Martinez *(Miguel)*; John Christopher Jones *(Book Binder)*; Dick Latessa *(Mr. McCormack Senior)*; Patrick Page *(Mr. McCormack Junior)*; Kate Forbes *(Rizzoli Book Buyer)*; Gloria Irizarry *(Esme)*; Barbara Eda-Young *(Reena Geldhart)*; Matt McGrath *(Young Book Clerk)*; Jose Ramon Rosario *(Dennis the Tailor)*; William Meisle *(Customer with*

Shoes); Gina Torres *(Maitre D')*; Debra Monk *(Martha Hackett)*; Rabbi Marc Schneider *(Rabbi)*

A good cast struggles with heavyweight material in THE SUBSTANCE OF FIRE, a stagy adaptation of Jon Robin Baitz's Broadway hit. The story of a book publisher facing a family crisis has much to say but fails to say it well.

In the New York book-publishing world, distinguished academic tomes win praise but not profits. Isaac Geldhart (Ron Rifkin), a childhood survivor of the Holocaust, would rather risk bankruptcy by printing a four-volume history of Nazi medical experiments than anything commercial. When his son and partner, Aaron (Tony Goldwyn), tries to convince him to publish a potential best-seller, written by Val (Gil Bellows), Aaron's gay lover, Isaac dismisses the book as trash.

In retaliation against his father and in order to save the business, Aaron enlists the help of his siblings—his sister, Sarah (Sarah Jessica Parker), a children's TV show host, and his brother, Martin (Timothy Hutton), a sickly professor at Vassar. As co-owners of Geldhart Publishing, the children gang up on Isaac, who responds by leaving the company and starting a new publishing house. While Aaron succeeds with Val's novel, however, Isaac destroys his career by insisting on publishing the costly Holocaust volumes.

Having clearly become mentally unstable, Isaac shuts out the world—especially his children—and fantasizes about his deceased wife. Martin, however, makes an attempt to reconcile with the difficult man by moving into his apartment and taking care of him. Unfortunately, Martin, who has Hodgkin's disease, experiences a heart attack before he is able to reach a *rapprochement.* After Martin's funeral, Isaac learns that his family's love is something he cannot afford to lose.

Jon Robin Baitz's play, *The Substance of Fire,* took Broadway by storm by touching on a variety of themes: the Holocaust, homosexuality, family honor, the mentally ill, western materialism, and much, much more. The film version of *Substance* is no less portentous in that it, too, addresses these topics. But something has clearly gone wrong in the translation.

Daniel Sullivan, a theater veteran *(I'm Not Rappaport, The Sisters Rosensweig)* but a first-time film director, preserves too much of the theatricality of the play and, thus, undermines the more subtle, psychological aspects of the drama. Even the fine actors appear as if they are playing to the rafters in scenes that are set up like theater set pieces and filmed in conventional ways. (Surprisingly, the gifted Ron Rifkin is unpersuasive in his role.) Moreover, the abundance of issues that emerge from the basically simple narrative clutter the overriding humanist message (although this might have been a problem with Baitz's original text). THE SUBSTANCE OF FIRE is all substance and no fire. *(Adult situations, extreme profanity.)* — E.M.

d, Daniel Sullivan; p, Jon Robin Baitz, Randy Finch, Ron Kastner; co-p, Lemore Syvan; w, Jon Robin Baitz (based on his play); ph, Robert Yeoman; ed, Pamela Martin; m, Joseph Vitarelli; prod d, John Lee Beatty; art d, Mark Ricker; set d, Shelley Barclay; sound, Pawel Wdowczak; fx, Drew Jiritano; casting, Meg Simon; cos, Jess Goldstein; makeup, Todd Thomas, Tracy Warbin

Drama **(PR: C MPAA: R)**

SUBSTITUTE, THE ★★½

(U.S.) 114m Dinamo/H2 Productions; LIVE Entertainment ~ Orion c

Tom Berenger *(Shale)*; Diane Venora *(Jane Hetzko)*; Ernie Hudson *(Rolle)*; Marc Anthony *(Juan Lucas)*; Glenn Plummer *(Mr. Sherman)*; Maria Celedonio *(Lisa)*; Sharron Corley *(Jerome)*; Raymond Cruz *(Joey Six)*; Luis Guzman *(Rem)*; Richard Brooks *(Wellman)*; William Forsythe *(Hollan)*; Willis Sparks *(John Janus)*; Rodney A. Grant *(Johnny Glades)*; Maurice Compte *(Tay)*; Vincent Laresca *(Rodriguez)*; Ian Marioles *(KOD Punk)*; David Spates *(Michael)*; David Hayes *(Frank)*; Peggy Pope *(Anna Dillon)*; Cliff DeYoung *(Wolfson)*; Steve Zurk *(PE Coach)*; Mike Benitez *(Chemistry Teacher)*; Jody Wilson *(Mrs. Andrewson)*; Steve Dumochel *(Buyer)*; Noelle Beck *(Deidre)*; Mercedes Eriquel *(High School Nurse)*

Sometimes, an action film is designed to be a camped-up assault on the senses, like SAVAGE STREETS (1984) or CLASS OF 1984 (1982). Unfortunately, THE SUBSTITUTE tries to have its intentional laughs and eat them, too. Directed with a hard-driving edge but written with sugary sincerity, the movie is sometimes funny when it wants to be—and sometimes, when it does not.

After he has been put out of business by his CIA connections, former mercenary Shale (Tom Berenger) must find a new line of work. When his long-time lover Jane Hetzko (Diane Venora) gets beaten for interfering in drug activities at the high school where she teaches, Shale secretly poses as her substitute replacement and persuades his cronies to keep the school under high-tech surveillance.

Juan Lucas (Marc Anthony) is the leader of KOD, the school's primo drug gang. Shale zeroes in on him and soon discovers that the school's unctuous principal, Mr. Rolle (Ernie Hudson), doubles the learning facility as a clearing house for the drug network of Johnny Glades (Rodney A. Grant). Tackling his teaching duties like a commando mission, Shale begins to influence his surly students positively while battling KOD toughs.

Rolle is unhappy when he is unable to fire Shales due to a technicality. Shale also busts up a Glades-backed powder conclave. Dumping the drugs in the bay, Shale uses the dealer's trading cash to buy school equipment. Complications arise when a fellow teacher, Mr. Sherman (Glenn Plummer), makes Jane aware of Shale's double life. While Shale is engaged in a car chase with Glades's thugs, Sherman and a pupil, Lisa (Maria Celedonio), stumble upon Rolle's operations in the school basement.

After Sherman is killed in the gymnasium, Lisa and another student, Jerome (Sharron Corley), seek out Shale at Jane's apartment, where all three are held captive by Juan's boys.

Upon Shale's arrival, Juan threatens to kill Jane, but Jerome shoots him first. Back at the school, a full-scale shootout between Shale's and Glades' men leaves Glades dead, Rolle in the hands of the police, and Shale presiding over a newly drug-free school.

Pulse-racing thrills and satisfying vigilante turnabouts propel THE SUBSTITUTE. However, its outlandish plot transforms it into something out of the mainstream. The problem is the film's schizophrenic nature, an entertainment that takes its anti-substance abuse message seriously, yet kids its own crusade at inopportune moments. It's best to view THE SUBSTITUTE as a mega-hardware war movie where the battleground just happens to be a schoolyard. Since Hollywood already has squeezed maximum juice out of Nazis, commies, skinheads, and extra-terrestrials, why not give in-school drug pushers a place in the Villain Hall of Infamy?

If THE SUBSTITUTE persuasively portrays how Shale trusts his survival instincts in unfamiliar turf, it's less assured when the super soldier starts flashing his war wounds to personalize a history lesson on Viet Nam. The classroom discussion scenes provide the off-the-wall film with its most unintentionally amusing moments.

THE SUBSTITUTE won't disappoint die-hard action buffs, but it may confuse them. They take their thrills seriously. THE SUBSTITUTE takes its kicks any way it can. *(Substance abuse, extensive nudity, adult situations, extreme profanity, graphic violence.)* — R.P.

d, Robert Mandel; p, Morrie Eisenman, Jim Steele; exec p, Devora Cutler, Steven Bakalar; w, Roy Frumkes, Rocco Simonelli, Alan Ormsby; ph, Bruce Surtees; ed, Alex Mackie; m, Gary Chang; prod d, Ron Foreman; art d, Richard Fojo; set d, Barbara Peterson; sound, Joe Foglia (mixer); fx, Rick Jones; casting, Carol Lewis; cos, Patricia Field; makeup, Jay Cannistraci, Cheryl Voss; stunts, Glenn Randall

Action/Action **(PR: C MPAA: R)**

SUGARTIME ★★★

(U.S.) 110m Pacific Western Productions; HBO Pictures ~ HBO Home Video c
(AKA: SAM & PHYLLIS)

John Turturro *(Sam Giancana)*; Mary-Louise Parker *(Phyllis McGuire)*; Elias Koteas *(Butch Blasi)*; Maury Chaykin *(Tony Accardo)*; Louis Del Grande *(Chuckie English)*; Deborah Duchene *(Christine McGuire)*; Larissa Lapchinski *(Dorothy McGuire)*; Cristopher Barry *(Photographer)*; Richard Blackburn *(Police Captain)*; Amanda Blitz *(Annette Giancana)*; Renessa Blitz *(Francine Giancana)*; Kelly Bodanis *(Doris)*; Valerie Boyce *(Showgirl)*; Bob Clout *(Mr. McGuire)*; Stuart Clow *(Vince Inserra)*; Bill Cross *(Maheu)*; Reg Dreger *(Wadden)*; Todd Duckworth *(2nd Reporter)*; Gregg Ellwand *(William Roemer)*; Neil Foster *(Reporter)*; Ron Gabriel *(Frederick Jones)*; Carole Galloway *(Mrs. McGuire)*; Yamit Gieger *(Bonnie Giancana)*; Sam Grana *(Johnny Rosselli)*; Graham Harley *(Introducer)*; Howard Jerome *(Russian Louie)*; Nahanni Johnstone *(Carlene Delfano)*; Patrick Jude *(Frank Sinatra)*; Brian Kaulback *(US Marshall)*; David Keeley *(Ralph Hill)*; Debra Kirshenbaum *(Marie Perno)*; John Kozak *(Eddie Vogel)*; Peter Krantz *(Bobby Kennedy)*; Corinne Langston *(Queen Mother)*; Adam Large *(Fanning)*; Shawn Lawrence *(Pit Boss)*; Tim Lee *(Assistant)*; John Lefebvre *(Bennett Williams)*; Dan Lett *(Maitre D')*; Vincent Marino; Joe Matheson *(Emcee)*; Robin McCulloch *(Dick Martin)*; Gerry Mendecino *(Libonati)*; Valerie Moore *(Choreographer)*; Tony Munch *(Moretti)*; Scott Nichol *(Dealer)*; Michael Polley *(Security)*; Miles Potter *(Grand Jury Foreman)*; Michael Rhoades *(Schippers)*; Nicholas Rice *(Judge Campbell)*; Bill Roemer *(CIA Agent)*; Rino Romano *(Phil Aldresio)*; Tony Rosato *(Frank Ferraro)*; Chuck Shamata *(Michael Delfano)*; Kent Sheridan *(Man)*; Ralph Small *(John Bassett)*; Danny Smith *(Stagehand)*; Dylan Smith *(Prison Guard)*; Peter Snider *(Other Man)*; Andrew Stelmack *(Gondolier)*; Kristina Watson *(Maid)*; Jonathan Whittaker *(Dan Rowan)*; Jonathan Wilson *(Delivery Man)*; Timm Zemanek *(3rd Reporter)*

A workmanlike "true story" about the affair between mobster Sam Giancana and singer Phyllis McGuire, SUGARTIME (which was first shown on HBO in 1995) pushes all the gangster-movie buttons, but lacks zest.

1960. Testifying before the US Senate Subcommittee on Organized Crime, Chicago crime boss Sam Giancana (John Turturro) takes the Fifth, refusing to answer Attorney General Bobby Kennedy's questions. Afterwards, in Las Vegas, he spots Phyllis McGuire (Mary-Louise Parker), lead singer of the McGuire Sisters trio. The act is cute and wholesome, in a calculated way. Sam is smitten with Phyllis, and the "class" she apparently represents. He begins a boorish wooing process, filling her dressing room with flowers and cajoling the reluctant Phyllis on a date, supposedly to meet Frank Sinatra.

They end up in a Nevada motel, where Phyllis plays hard to get. A local cowgirl, Doris (Kelly Bodanis), explains the uses of men with money, and when Sam gives Phyllis a new Thunderbird, she relents.

Despite Sam's high-level connections (he supposedly helped finance JFK's campaign, the CIA wants him to eliminate Castro), his affair with Phyllis causes headaches for both. Printed rumors poison her career: His associates don't appreciate the publicity. Time spent with Phyllis makes him neglect his "business" (an excuse for several nasty executions). When he builds her the "Villa Venice" club in Chicago, complete with artificial lake and singing gondolier, only his sterling gangster credentials prevent mob retribution.

Phyllis is subpoenaed to testify against the mob, but she stonewalls. Sam is granted full immunity, but when he refuses to testify, he is jailed for contempt and extradited to Mexico.

Seven years later, Sam returns to testify at Congressional hearings, a broken man. Butch Blasi (Elias Koteas), his one-time lieutenant, greets him at the airport, feeds him a sumptuous meal, and, after Sam refuses to drop Phyllis, kills him.

Titles state no one was convicted of the murder, and Phyllis continues to live alone in a Las Vegas mansion.

SUGARTIME (the name of a McGuire Sisters tune) is based on ex-federal agent William F. Roemer, Jr.'s book *Man Against The Mob* (Roemer has a cameo role as a CIA agent.) In what is ostensibly a love story, Sam and Phyllis lack chemistry as lovers, and Parker's Phyllis is too passive to be a convincing golddigger. Turturro is believable as Sam the weasel, not as a lovestruck wiseguy. The leads' failure to strike sparks makes SUGARTIME's lavish production numbers, gangster talk, and Tarantino-style violence almost superfluous.

The script frequently refers to Sam's jealousy, but he never acts on it. Apparently, Phyllis reduces Sam the tough guy to a little boy begging for candy. In one scene, he dangles jewelry in her face as they make love. Phyllis seems incapable of passion even then.

Like many docudramas, SUGARTIME is caught on the horns of a dilemma. It's not convincing enough for "real life" and not exciting enough for fiction. But, despite its shortcomings, SUGARTIME's detailed period recreations, campy showtunes, and the occasional mob "hit" make for entertaining viewing. *(Violence, profanity, sexual situations)* — C.M.

d, John N. Smith; p, David Coatsworth; exec p, Gale Ann Hurd, Martyn Burke; co-p, David Gale; w, Martyn Burke (suggested by the book *Roemer: Man Against the Mob* by William F. Roemer, Jr.); ph, Pierre Letarte; ed, Ralph Brunjes; m, Sidney James; prod d, Barbara Dunphy; art d, Lucinda Zak; set d, Charles Dunlop, Tom Doherty; ch, Valerie Moore; sound, Tom Mather, Oliver Moss; fx, Martin Malivoire; casting, Claire Hewitt, Diane Kerbel; cos, Denise Cronenberg; makeup, Shonagh Jabour; stunts, Marco Bianco

Crime/Drama **(PR: C MPAA: R)**

SUITE 16 ★★½

(U.K./Belgium) 110m Corsan Productions; Theorema Films ~ A-Pix Entertainment c

Pete Postlethwaite *(Glover)*; Antonie Kamerling *(Chris)*; Geraldine Pailhas *(Helen)*; Tom Jansen *(Paul)*; Bart Slegers *(Rudy)*; Suzanne Colin *(Woman with Dog)*; Viviane de Muynck *(Woman Scene 1)*; Dirk Roofthooft *(Marc)*; Corinne Rivierre *(Shop Manageress)*; Henri Masini *(Cashier)*; Stephane Leveque *(Room Service Manager)*; Jean-Paul Ferrari *(Male Prostitute)*; Stephanie Jacquinot *(S&M Woman)*; Isabelle Maman *(Receptionist)*; Jean Yves Bordet *(Receptionist)*; Simone Helme *(Frightened Woman)*; Vic Deruddere *(Child in Bus)*; Valerie van Nitsen; Marielle van Sauers; Francoise Le Bihan; Florence Risler; Latifa Abdelmoujoud; Magali Cordelier; Veronique Levy; Lysiane Lahier-Bertrand; Ines Jourdan; Nathalie Lions; Laurence Rabattidevalle; Claire Mercier; Sarah Kunstlich; Sylvie Jourdan; Sylvie Beme *(Prostitutes)*

A homoerotic drama filled with heterosexual sex, SUITE 16 examines a twisted relationship between two very crippled but manipulative characters. The story of love and control is, like a train wreck, at once unwatchable and morbidly fascinating.

Chris (Antoinie Kamerling), a hustler, smashes a bottle over his friend's head after some nasty words. He drives to a hotel, picks up a woman and then tries to rob her after sex. A fight ensues and he bolts from the room, bleeding, in full sight of a bellboy. Unable to leave the hotel, he stumbles into Suite 16, where the wheelchair-bound Glover (Pete Postelwaite) helps him stop the bleeding. Glover says the woman Chris robbed is dead and suggests his "guest" hide in the suite.

Chris tells Glover of his dream—opening a club in the Caribbean—and Glover in turn gets a hooker for Chris and asks him about the sex. Later, Glover muses about being "killed by someone who loves you." Chris discovers Glover spying on his trysts, but calms down when Glover offers to pay him for his time. Endless sessions of cocaine-aided sex follow. Eventually, Chris threatens to leave yet again, but remains when Glover offers him a double-or-nothing deal which calls for Chris to narrate, via radio, the seduction and murder a shop girl named Helen (Geraldine Pailhas). He fails, but while outside, he sees the woman who cut his face.

Furious, Chris leaves Glover and runs into one of his old pals. They get drunk and the friend reveals that Chris's earlier bottle-smashing incident proved fatal, and he tries to kill Chris. Surviving another fight, Chris runs back to Suite 16, where he finds Glover now dining with Helen. Helen quickly realizes her companions are disturbed, but after rebuffing Glover's advances, she sleeps with Chris.

The next morning, as the young lovers prepare to leave, Glover hugs Helen and injects her with poison. Chris smashes Glover's head against the floor, killing him—but not before Glover says, "Thank you." Downstairs, the concierge offers Chris money, which he refuses. Chris boards a bus and smiles at a child; behind him, a man approaches from the back of the bus.

Flemish director Dominique Deruddere's prurient film is not for the faint of heart, and it does manage to draw the viewer in with its shocking scenario based on an unholy trinity of money, sex and power. Postlethwaithe creates an intriguing portrait of an impotent man with brutal psychological powers. Pailhas's Helen is the coquette that gives the movie a burst of much-needed charm, hope, and heroism. Deruddere's biggest problem here is trying to transform Kamerling's Chris from a menacing thug to a heroic victim. Based on his previous antics, it's hard to rehabilitate his image in the eyes of even the most generous viewer. In the end, that's a blessing. With no emotional stake in the characters, SUITE 16 becomes easier to watch. *(Violence, sexual situations, adult situations, substance abuse, profanity.)* — S.K.

d, Dominique Deruddere; p, Paul Breuls; assoc p, Catherine Vandeleene, Bernard Mazauric, San Fu Maltha; co-p, Frank Bak; w, Charles Higson, Lise Mayer; ph, Jean-Francois Robin; ed, Kant Pan; m, Walter Hus; prod d, Niek Kortekaas; set d, Maurice Zisswiller; sound, Dirk Bombey (recordist), Daniel Brisseau (recordist); casting, Peter Breuls, Hans Kemma Casting, Nicole Octobon, Caroline Mazauric; cos, Loret Meus; makeup, Brigitte Pleijzier, Marly van de Wardt; stunts, Pierre Rosso

Erotic/Thriller **(PR: O MPAA: NR)**

SUMMER CAMP

(SEE: PIG'S TALE, A)

SUNCHASER ★½

(U.S.) 121m New Regency Productions; Vecchio-Appledown ~ Warner Bros. c

Woody Harrelson *(Dr. Michael Reynolds)*; Jon Seda *(Brandon "Blue" Monroe)*; Anne Bancroft *(Dr. Renata Baumbauer)*; Alexandra Tydings *(Victoria Reynolds)*; Matt Mulhern *(Dr. Chip Byrnes)*; Talisa Soto *(Navajo Woman)*; Richard Bauer *(Dr. Bradford)*; Victor Aaron *(Webster Skyhorse)*; Lawrence Pressman *(AIC Collier)*; Michael O'Neill *(Agent Moreland)*; Harry Carey Jr. *(Cashier)*; Mickey Jones *(Biker)*; Gregory Scott Cummins *(Biker)*

Souped-up but sluggish, Michael Cimino's soppy male weepie is a misguided attempt at interbreeding genres and sub-genres (road movie, terminal illness soap, crime drama, buddy film) to manufacture a surefire box office hit. Contrary to its concept-heavy intentions, the ploy fails.

Hotshot LA oncologist Michael Reynolds (Woody Harrelson) is a man who has everything but emotional stability; he's never recovered from a childhood incident in which he pulled the plug on the life support of his 11-year-old older brother, who was suffering from inoperable cancer. As part of his staff duties, Reynolds is now forced to treat a callous 16-year-old convict, Brandon "Blue" Monroe (John Seda), who's regularly shipped from his prison cell to Reynolds's hospital for abdominal cancer care.

En route to another facility's experimental program, Blue, who was previously slipped a gun by a visiting pal, pulls his piece on his guard and coerces Reynolds to drive him on a pilgrimage to the Sacred Healing Mountain of his Navajo people. Reynolds warns that Blue is only hastening his disease's progress, but the sullen convict feels he has nothing to lose. When Reynolds makes an escape attempt at a Country & Western hangout, Blue vengefully accuses Reynolds of molesting him in front of Hell's Angels, who beat the living daylights out of the doctor. Rescuing Reynolds so he can continue on as captive chauffeur, Blue regains the upper hand—even after Reynolds tosses away his cash and credit cards—by stealing gas and cowing Reynolds with threatening gunshots.

After their stolen car expires in the desert, Reynolds is bitten by a rattler; Blue saves his life by using jumper cables to extract the venom. The fugitive pair hitch a ride with new-age practitioner Renata Bambauer (Anne Bancroft), who applauds Blue's initiative in seeking alternative medicine. Reynolds re-evaluates his Hippocratic hypocrisy and tarnishes his reputation by stealing drugs from a hospital in order to stabilize Blue's failing condition. After reaching the Navajo holy ground, a shaman leads Blue to his destiny; Blue becomes one with the mystical lake below Sacred Mountain. A police helicopter picks up the career-damaged but spirit-enriched Reynolds.

Even the most farfetched adventures require inherent logic or a sharp sense of spacing out the story's cliffhangers, not to mention deft direction and robust performances that sweep all disbelief aside. But SUNCHASER has none of these qualities; chase scenes are distended, histrionic confrontations are staged haphazardly, and the editing rhythm is lackadaisical.

An anti-materialism, anti-medical establishment diatribe, SUNCHASER somehow equates spiritual enlightenment with intolerance of the upper middle class. Barrio pride born of poverty and childhood abuse gives Blue the right to have a chip on his shoulder. Despite all its philosophical hooey, SUNCHASER is basically a test of the viewer's endurance as he or she watches Blue (physically) and Reynolds (spiritually) bleed all over each other. The smug doctor accepts the young punk's street wisdom; the oppressed adolescent learns to trust a WASP whose humanity has been on hold since a boyhood mercy killing. The moral is "death be not proud," just schematized enough for screenwriter Charles Leavitt to over-elaborate on Native American pieties and for Cimino to put on a bleeding-heart floor show.

Over two hours in length, SUNCHASER plays out like a maudlin disease-of-the-week TV movie which legitimized a big-screen venue through swank production values and trendy posturing. This movie's grasp of the social divide is so shallow that it isn't content to simply show Reynolds driving in a panic through a graffiti-covered, inner-city slum; it drives him right into the aftermath of a gang shoot-out and a convenience store robbery. In fact, everything about SUNCHASER is annoyingly blatant, beginning with a one-note performance by Harrelson and ending with a pseudo-mystical claptrap finale. *(Violence, adult situations, substance abuse, extreme profanity.)* — R.P.

d, Michael Cimino; p, Arnon Milchan, Michael Cimino, Larry Spiegel, Judy Goldstein, Joseph M. Vecchio; exec p, Michael Nathanson, Joseph M. Caracciolo; w, Charles Leavitt; ph, Doug Milsome; ed, Joe D'Augustine; m, Maurice Jarre; prod d, Victoria Paul; art d, Lee Mayman, Edward L. Rubin; set d, Jackie Carr; sound, Douglas Axtell; casting, Terry Liebling; cos, Ruth Carter

Adventure/Drama/Crime (PR: C MPAA: R)

SUNSET PARK ★★

(U.S.) 100m Jersey Films; Daniel L. Paulson Productions; TriStar ~ TriStar c

Rhea Perlman *(Phyllis Saroka)*; Fredro Starr *(Shorty)*; Carol Kane *(Mona)*; Terrence DaShon Howard *(Spaceman)*; Camille Saviola *(Barbara)*; De'Aundre Bonds *(Busy-Bee)*; James Harris *(Butter)*; Anthony Hall *(Andre)*; Antwon Tanner *(Drano)*; Shawn Michael Howard *(Kurt)*; Guy Torry *(Boo Men)*; Scott Burkholder *(Morris Bernstein)*; John Aprea *(Dominic)*; John Vargas *(Mr. Santiago)*; Rhonda Stubbins White *(Carla)*; Steffen Foster *(Washington Heights Coach)*; Hattie Winston *(Judge Meyer)*; Tim Hutchinson *(Referee)*; Charles E. Thompson *(Referee)*; Curtis McGee *(Referee)*; Paul Johnson *(East Flatbush Player)*; Tracy Vilar *(Shirley)*; Michael Mack *(Sal the Janitor)*; Lucien Lewis *(Kid Gloc)*; Eric George *(Coney Island Player)*; Gary Dourdan *(Dreadlock Guy)*; Silk Willie Dunn *(School Bus Driver)*; Melissa Berger *(Cop at Apartment)*; Trula Marcus *(Marisa)*; Vincent Pastore *(Charlie the Super)*; A. Doran Reed *(Carlton Palmer)*; Bee-Be Smith *(Regina)*; Malinda Williams *(Cheryl)*; Jay Della *(Bar Customer)*; Christopher *(McHale)*

"You guys were fantabulous!" exclaims Rhea Perlman's inner city high school basketball coach after her team wins a game in SUNSET PARK, yet another inspirational teacher-and-troubled-students movie with a sugar-coated message.

Rhea Perlman plays Phyllis Saroka, a Brooklyn High School teacher who dreams of opening her own restaurant on the island of St. Croix. After Phyllis's boyfriend leaves her—taking most of her possessions with him—Phyllis realizes she needs some extra money, and signs up for a second job coaching the school's all-African-American male basketball team. Despite her lack of knowledge about the sport, Phyllis gets the position. The team, however, remains unconvinced that this untrained Caucasian woman will be able to learn the ropes fast enough to be any good.

Realizing that the students on the team are ignoring her instructions during practice, Phyllis sets out to learn the game inside-out and to win over the most skeptical player, Shorty (Fredro Starr). Phyllis secures Shorty's trust by advising him on matters of romance. Thereafter, the team begins playing better and finds itself heading toward a championship tournament.

On the eve of the big game, Phyllis reveals to Shorty her dream of leaving the school and opening the restaurant. This upsets the troubled young man, who, after being spurned by his girlfriend, shoots his romantic rival. Phyllis gets Shorty a lawyer and bails him out of jail, but he remains angry at her. It is only after Phyllis changes her mind about leaving that Shorty rejoins his friends to play in the championship game, taking the team to victory.

In SUNSET PARK, Rhea Perlman makes a bid for the kind of big screen stardom enjoyed by her husband, Danny DeVito (an executive producer on this film and the star of 1994's similar RENAISSANCE MAN). But Perlman's Phyllis reveals the kind of humanity and sensitivity that the actor's wittier "Cheers" character, Carla, would have teased mercilessly. (Soon after the release of SUNSET PARK, Perlman returned to the small screen playing "Pearl," a parent returning to college.)

Predictably for this sort of film, a boring anti-drug/pro-higher education message emerges from the superficially "cool" screenplay (filled with street lingo) by Seth Zvi Rosenfeld and Kathleen McGhee-Anderson. Director Steve Gomer gets solid work from the cast of young actors that comprise the team (especially Fredro Starr as Shorty), but the faux-HOOP DREAMS approach devalues African-American culture. Worst of all, this has been done before: in DANGEROUS MINDS (1995), THE AIR UP THERE (1994), WILDCATS (1086), et al.

Admittedly, the film could have been much *more* patronizing, and there are a few entertaining moments along the way, but SUNSET PARK is certainly no "White Shadow" for the '90s. *(Violence, extreme profanity.)* — E.M.

d, Steve Gomer; p, Danny DeVito, Michael Shamberg, Dan Paulson; exec p, Elizabeth Cantillon; co-p, Mary Kane, Cara Buonincontri; w, Seth Zvi Rosenfeld, Kathleen McGhee-Anderson; ph, Robbie Greenberg; ed, Arthur Coburn; m, Miles Goodman, Kay Gee; prod d, Victoria Paul; art d, Lee Mayman; set d, Brian Kasch; sound, Felipe Borrero (mixer), Tim Gomillion (recordist); casting, Robi Reed-Humes; cos, Carol Ramsey; makeup, Bonita DeHaven; stunts, Shane Dixon

Drama/Comedy/Sports (PR: C MPAA: R)

SURGEON, THE ★½

(U.S./Germany) 100m Connexion Film; Capella International ~ A-Pix Entertainment c
(AKA: EXQUISITE TENDERNESS)

Isabel Glasser *(Dr. Theresa McCann)*; James Remar *(Dr. Benjamin Hendricks)*; Sean Haberle *(Dr. Julian Matar)*; Charles Dance *(Dr. Ed Mittlesbay)*; Peter Boyle *(Lt. Daryl McEllwaine)*; Malcolm McDowell *(Dr. Roger Stein)*; Charles Bailey-Gates *(Sgt. Ross)*; Beverly Todd *(Nurse Barnes)*; Walter Olkewicz *(Dr. Meade)*; Mother Love *(Milly Putnam)*; Gregory West *(Tommy Beaton)*; Juliette Jeffers *(Lisa Wilson)*; Nancy Banks *(Loreen Ridgeway)*; Kim Robillard *(Dr. Eugene Kaiser)*; Teryl Rothery *(Officer Pierson)*; Joe-Norman Shaw *(Detective Edwards)*; Don Thompson *(Father — 1958)*; Marilyn Norry *(Mother — 1958)*; Codie Lucas Wilbee *(Older Boy — 1958)*; Jarrett Lennon *(Young Matar — 1958)*; Tom Heaton *(Doctor — 1958)*; Walter Marsh *(Parking Security)*; Rosanne Hopkins *(Mrs. Rodriguez)*; Debbie Podowski *(Dr. Melissa Kyle)*; Larry Musser *(Anesthesiologist)*; Michael Tiernan *(Anesthesiologist)*; C. Dale Best *(Doctor in Operating Theater)*; Daniel Rubin *(Doctor in Operating Theater)*; Akiko Morison *(Operating Nurse)*; Rebecca Toolan *(Mittlesbay's Secretary)*; Robin Kelly *(ICU Nurse)*; Sandra P. Grant *(ICU Nurse)*; Bernie Coulsen *(Flower Delivery Boy)*; Veena

Sood *(Doctor in Dialysis)*; Frank Cassini *(Intern in Dialysis)*; Curt Willinton *(Pizza Delivery Boy)*; Alex Diakun *(County General Doctor)*; Ken Roberts *(County General Guard)*; Zoltan Buday *(County General Patrol Guard)*; Sheelah Megill *(Nurse Worley)*; Dee Jay Jackson *(Hospital Orderly)*; John Destrey *(Hospital Superintendent)*; Andrew Wheeler *(Cop in Tunnel)*; Matt Bennett *(Young Cop)*; Richard Newman *(Cop in O.R.)*; Sydney Mentiply *(Doorman)*; Christy Lynne *(Officer White)*; Walker Bonshor *(Soap Opera Television Doctor)*; Kendra Tucker *(Soap Opera Television Nurse)*

Though this would-be chiller was shot in Canada in 1994 as EXQUISITE TENDERNESS, its ultimate U.S. video title proves much more reflective of both its subject matter and its banal bluntness.

Dr. Theresa McCann (Isabel Glasser) goes to work at a hospital where Dr. Roger Stein (Malcolm McDowell) is working on an abdominal implant intended to render dialysis obsolete. When a test ape dies and one of Stein's patients goes into renal failure, McCann has the patient moved into dialysis, where she's poisoned by a mysterious doctor. Suspended as a result of this incident, McCann investigates with the help of Dr. Benjamin Hendricks (James Remar), and discovers that the killer is Dr. Julian Matar (Sean Haberle), who was himself suspended three years before when McCann uncovered his unorthodox experiments.

After killing Stein and threatening McCann, Matar is badly injured during his arrest and taken to another hospital. But a serum he has concocted from pituitary fluid allows him to heal any wound almost instantaneously. He escapes and returns to McCann's hospital, where he kills several patients and administrator Dr. Ed Mittlesbay (Charles Dance). Apparently shot dead while threatening McCann, Matar revives himself once more and murders Hendricks at McCann's apartment before she kills him once and for all.

During this movie's production, its makers insisted on representing it as a psychological medical thriller, which was no doubt how they were able to lure its high-profile cast. But despite the actors' best efforts, this remains little more than a slasher schlocker with delusions of grandeur. Just because the script offers a scientific rationale for its killer's unstoppability doesn't make it any less of a cliche. The film wallows in numerous other exploitation standards, including graphic gore, an over-insistent musical score, and a laughably gratuitous (and surprisingly explicit) love scene between Glasser and Remar.

The plotting is lopsided, the dialogue in Patrick Cirillo's script is awkward, and director Carl Schenkel's attempts to class things up (like setting one of the movie's many unconvincing expository dialogue scenes in a restaurant where white whales swim behind glass walls) seem misguided, particularly given the crass manner in which he stages the horrific setpieces. *(Graphic violence, extensive nudity, sexual situations, extreme profanity.)* — M.G.

d, Carl Schenkel; p, Alan Beattie, Chris Chesser, Willi Baer; exec p, Rolf Deyhle, David Korda; co-p, Dennis E. Jones; w, Patrick Cirillo (based on a screenplay by Bernard Sloane); ph, Thomas Burstyn; ed, Jimmy B. Frazier; m, Christopher Franke; prod d, Douglas Higgins; art d, Randy Chodak; sound, Eric Batut, John Fasal; fx, Steve Johnson, Gary Paller, XFX; casting, Hank McCann; cos, Ushi Zech, Debbie Geaghan; makeup, Jan Newman

Horror **(PR: O MPAA: R)**

SURVIVING PICASSO ★★½

(U.S.) 100m Merchant Ivory/Wolper ~ Warner Bros. c

Anthony Hopkins *(Pablo Picasso)*; Natascha McElhone *(Francoise)*; Julianne Moore *(Dora Maar)*; Joss Ackland *(Henri Matisse)*; Peter Eyre *(Sabartes)*; Jane Lapotaire *(Olga Picasso)*; Joseph Maher *(Kahnweiler)*; Bob Peck *(Francoise's Father)*; Diane Venora *(Jacqueline Roque)*; Joan Plowright *(Francoise's Grandmother)*; Susannah Harker *(Marie-Therese Walter)*; Dennis Boutsikaris *(American Art Dealer)*; Peter Gerety *(Picasso's Driver)*; Dominic West *(Paulo Picasso)*

The preeminent painter of the 20th century, Pablo Picasso, gets the Merchant-Ivory treatment in a low-key drama told from the point of view of the artist's young mistress during the years 1943-1953. But while Anthony Hopkins convincingly displays both the charming and malicious sides of the painter's mercurial personality, a stronger actress is needed to convey his mistress's considerable triumph of the spirit.

In Nazi-occupied Paris, young aspiring painter Francoise Gilot (Natascha McElhone) meets the famed Picasso (Hopkins) and quickly falls under his tutelage, attracted by his charm, attentiveness, and raw energy. Despite the presence in Picasso's life of a prior mistress, Dora Maar (Julianne Moore), as well as Marie-Therese (Susannah Harker), the mother of his daughter, Maya, Francoise soon moves in with Picasso and becomes his lover and devoted assistant, although she insists on pursuing her own painting. In doing so, Francoise leaves an angry father (Bob Peck), who wanted her to follow his own footsteps and go to law school, and a doting grandmother (Joan Plowright), who disapproves of Picasso because of his well-known mistreatment of women.

During the course of a decade with Picasso, Francoise gives birth to two children, Claude and Paloma, travels with him to his country homes, watches him play cat-and-mouse with dealers, listens to him pontificate on art and life, meets his mentor, Henri Matisse (Joss Ackland), and continues to paint on her own. She sees Picasso at his best, in the throes of inspiration and artistic activity, and at his worst, throwing childish temper tantrums and abusing those closest to him, including his oldest son, Paulo (Dominic West), and his first wife, Olga (Jane Lapotaire). Picasso thrives on Francoise's attentions and devotion, but eventually his affections are diverted to another young artist, Jacqueline Roque (Diane Venora), whom he meets at a pottery works when he takes up ceramics.

When her grandmother is felled by a stroke, Francoise leaves the country home for Paris, accompanied by the two children. Upon learning her grandmother is dead, she decides to stay in Paris, but not with Picasso. Despite his attempts to instill guilt in her, she makes up her mind to leave him and does so with the assistance of her father and her longtime friend, Genevieve, her companion on the fateful trip to Picasso's studio when she first met him back in 1943. When the press learns of this, it becomes big news because of Picasso's notorious hold on the women in his life.

During the summer, Francoise takes the children to visit Picasso and is asked by him to lead the procession in his honor at a local bullfight. Secure enough in herself to acknowledge the role he has played in her life, she agrees, as a way of honoring both him and her own newfound freedom.

As the one woman to escape Picasso's psychological stranglehold, Gilot remains the most intriguing figure in Picasso's life—after the artist himself—and the one who speaks most to modern audiences. However, the real Gilot's refusal to sell the rights to her own book led Merchant-Ivory to purchase Arianna Stassinopoulos Huffington's *Picasso: Creator and Destroyer,* which relied heavily on Gilot's book. As a result, the filmmakers managed to tell Gilot's story.

Picasso's estate refused to sell the rights to any genuine Picasso paintings for use in the production, so only stylistic imitations are used.

The story of Gilot's submission to the charismatic, abusive painter and ultimate escape remains of great importance in this post-feminist age, so the actress playing the part needs to convey the emotional ups and downs, artistic aspirations, devotion to Picasso, and ultimate urge for freedom that are part of Gilot's 10-year odyssey from naive schoolgirl to autonomous artist in her own right. Unfortunately, McElhone, making her film debut, is not well-formed enough to make the character stand out from Hopkins's Picasso. Too often, she substitutes a silly grin for genuine feeling, even during the grimmest of circumstances. A more seasoned actress, perhaps even a French one, would have been far more effective.

Hopkins, however, is very good, capturing all sides of Picasso's personality. While one jeers him when he lapses into juvenile behavior, one soars with him when he embraces his art. The supporting parts are all rather small, if well-played, with spectacular turns by Plowright as Francoise's loving, if disapproving, grandmother, and Ackland as the nonagenarian, ever-magisterial Matisse.

Overall, the production is well-mounted without being showy, with the emphasis on the characters rather than the period setting. *(Adult situations.)* — B.C.

d, James Ivory; p, Ismail Merchant, David L. Wolper; exec p, Donald Rosenfeld, Paul Bradley; co-p, Humbert Balsan; w, Ruth Prawer Jhabvala; ph, Tony Pierce-Roberts; ed, Andrew Marcus; m, Richard Robbins; prod d, Luciana Arrighi; cos, Carol Ramsey

Biography/Drama **(PR: C MPAA: R)**

SWEEPER, THE ★★

(U.S.) 101m PM Entertainment Group, Inc. ~ PM Entertainment Group, Inc. c

C. Thomas Howell *(Mark Goddard)*; Ed Lauter *(Molls)*; Kristen Dalton *(Rachel)*; Janet Gunn *(Melissa)*; Felton Perry *(Foster)*; Max Slade *(Young Mark)*; Cynda Williams *(Diane)*; Kathrin Lautner *(Amy)*; Mark Knudsen *(Mall Stepfather)*; John Saint Ryan *(Richman)*; Jim O'Malley *(Sean)*; Jon Ingrassia *(Marsh)*; Christopher Allport *(Grubb)*; Shannon Welles *(Grandmother)*; Steve Eastin *(Richard)*; Tim Colceri *(Mathews)*; Jeff Fahey *(Dale)*

THE SWEEPER, an undistinguished action flick about a secret police society, provides nothing more substantial than another entry on C. Thomas Howell's increasing direct-to-video resume.

When Mark Goddard (Howell) was a young boy, he witnessed the execution of his family, including his father, Dale (Jeff Fahey), an honest cop who wanted his son to follow in his footsteps. Fifteen years later, Mark is a police officer whose bitterness over his past has cost him his marriage and jeopardized his job. He is censured for his violent methods after killing nine of his suspects.

Mark is recruited by Justice Incorporated, an underground organization of former police officers who take justice into their own hands by killing criminals. After completing several assignments for JI, Mark begins to question the organization's methods and motives, and learns that there is a connection between the organization and his own past, eventually discovering that his father was killed by the organization because he refused to join. Mark goes to JI headquarters to seek answers and revenge. A climactic car-to-airplane chase ends in the death of JI's leader, Molls (Ed Lauter). Mark reconciles with his ex-wife and puts his past behind him.

There is little to distinguish THE SWEEPER from the other action video product put out by its distributor, PM Entertainment Group. They generally include a bounty of drawn-out car chases, one gratuitous sex scene, and loads of gunplay. THE SWEEPER is no exception. The action sequences, which obscure the thin plot, are abundant but not spectacular. Howell is saddled with a character which holds little appeal, and isn't helped by his grungy appearance. When Mark isn't fighting off bad guys, he is brooding and petulant. Fahey (who also received Associate Producer credit) provides the film's most compelling performance, and after his character is killed off, the film loses steam. *(Violence, nudity, sexual situations, profanity.)* — B.R.

d, Joseph Merhi; p, Joseph Merhi, Richard Pepin; assoc p, Jeff Fahey; co-p, Marta Merrifield; w, William Applegate Jr., Karen McCoy (based on a story by Jacobsen Hart); ph, Ken Blakey; ed, Paul G. Volk; m, K. Alexander Wilkinson; prod d, Robert Cowan; art d, David Sandefur; casting, Mark Sikes; cos, Lisa Dyehouse; stunts, Spiro Razatos

Action **(PR: C MPAA: R)**

SWEET NOTHING ★★★

(U.S.) 90m Acme Company; Concrete Films ~ Warner Bros. c

Michael Imperioli *(Angel)*; Mira Sorvino *(Monika)*; Paul Calderon *(Raymond)*; Patrick Breen *(Greg)*; Richard Bright *(Jack the Cop)*; Billie Neal *(Rio)*; Brian Tarantina *(Dee Dee)*; Maria Tucci *(Monika's Mother)*; Christopher Marquette *(Richie)*; Michele Casey *(Annie)*; John O'Keefe *(Howard)*; Lisa Langford *(Edna)*; William Rothlein *(Rodriquez)*; Jean LeMarre *(Beany)*; Bruce Smolanoff *(Mal)*; Anibal O. Lleras *(Georgy)*

Hard-edged yet compassionate, SWEET NOTHING looks at a family destroyed by one man's crack addiction. This low-budget feature tells its sordid tale from the addict's point of view without glamorizing its subject.

On the night of his daughter's birth, Angelo "Angel" Gazetta (Michael Imperioli) is introduced to crack by his best friend, Raymond (Paul Calderon). Soon after, Angel resists the temptation to buy more drugs, choosing instead to remain devoted to his wife, Monika (Mira Sorvino) and their two children. In the course of a month, however, the lure of crack overwhelms the family man.

Angel decides to join Raymond drug dealing as a way to better his family financially. Angel is immediately successful but Monika worries about the source of their new-found wealth. Angel placates Monika's fears by buying her expensive gifts and by promising his new line of work will be only temporary. However, Angel only gets more caught up in both his deals and his own drug use, forcing Raymond to confront him. The one-time friends end their partnership after a fight and go their separate ways over the next few years.

Without Raymond's steady hand behind the operation, Angel's business suffers and he becomes more and more addicted. During a harrowing three-day period, Angel verbally and physically abuses Monika and threatens to hurt his children. Monika finally finds the strength to throw Angel out of their apartment, only to take him back in later.

Angel finally resolves to clean up his act, but must first pay off two past debts. He uses Monika's jewelry as collateral to buy more drugs, then successfully repays one debt. When Angel finds himself unable to pay off the second debt, Raymond intervenes and strikes a deal: If Angel will chop off the fingers of a suspected thief, the debt will be repaid; if not, Angel will be ruthlessly beaten. Angel refuses and the latter occurs. But Angel sees his survival after the incident as a second chance. He enters a rehabilitation program and hopes that his family will take him back.

Bleakly realistic, SWEET NOTHING resembles the sort of social-problem film that was made more often in the 1970s, such as PANIC IN NEEDLE PARK (1975). It is also far more subtle than the classic Hollywood depictions of drug abuse like THE MAN WITH THE GOLDEN ARM (1955) or A HATFUL OF RAIN (1957). Without reaching one way or the other, director Gary Winick skillfully draws the viewer into Angel's world: as the character's addiction worsens, Winick uses jump cuts and discordant music to mirror his fractured existence. Except for the Tarantino-style torture scene involving the threatened finger-chopping, SWEET NOTHING compliments its themes with understated images—a garbage barge floating by symbolizes Angel's life at one point.

Best of all, Imperioli makes this anti-hero's downfall sad and entirely convincing. Sorvino has less to work with in the traditional hand-wringing wife role, but she plays her part well. (SWEET NOTHING was filmed prior to her Oscar-winning role in 1995's MIGHTY APHRODITE.)

SWEET NOTHING avoids major gaffes, but is damaged slightly by the excessive narration, which seems too poetic at times for Angel's character. There are also some awkward time shifts in the early part of the film: "Three years later" is followed by "Three weeks later." But these problems in Lee Drysdale's screenplay rarely get in the way of the sobering and uncompromising account.

Re-released by Warner Bros. after its initial 1996 run, SWEET NOTHING is a bitter something. *(Graphic Violence, adult situations, substance abuse, extreme profanity.)* — E.M.

d, Gary Winick; p, Rick Bowman, Gary Winick; exec p, Mark Ross; w, Lee Drysdale; ph, Makoto Watanabe; ed, Niels Mueller; m, Steven M. Stern; prod d, Amy Tapper; art d, Amy Silver; set d, Chad Jacobson; sound, Steve Rogers (mixer); casting, Brett Goldstein; cos, Franne Lee

Drama **(PR: O MPAA: NR)**

SWINGERS ★★★

(U.S.) 96m Independent Pictures ~ Miramax c

Jon Favreau *(Mike)*; Vince Vaughn *(Trent)*; Ron Livingston *(Rob)*; Patrick Van Horn *(Sue)*; Alex Desert *(Charles)*; Heather Graham *(Lorraine)*; Deena Martin *(Christy)*; Katherine Kendall *(Lisa)*; Brooke Langton *(Nikki)*; Blake Lindsley *(Girl with Cigar)*; Kevin James Kelly *(Vegas Dealer)*; Stephanie Ittleson *(Vegas Waitress)*; Vernon Vaughn *($100 Gambler)*; Joan Favreau *($5 Winner)*; Maddie Corman *(Peek-a-Boo Girl)*; Jan Dykstra *(Girl at Party)*; Rio Hackford *(Skully)*; Marty & Elayne *(Dresden Lounge Act)*; Big Bad Voodoo Daddy *(Derby Band)*; Stasea Rosenblum *($100 Gambler)*; Sheri Rosenblum *($100 Gambler)*; Pamela Shaw *($5 Gambler)*; Tom Alley *(Pit Boss)*; Reverend Phil Dixon *(Lounge Lizard)*; Ashley M. Rogers *(Bartender)*; Jay Diola; Nicholas Gagliarducci; David Gould; Bill Phillips *(Skully's Crew)*; Mensur Hamud *(Pink Dot Guy)*; Ahmed Ahmed *(Party Mystery Guy)*; Eufemia Plimpton *(Derby Lady)*; Melinda Starr *(Derby Lady)*; Samantha Lemole *(Dresden Lady)*; Jessica Buchman *(Dresden Lady)*; Caroline O'Meara *(Diner Waitress)*; Gary Aurbach *(Derby Doorman)*; Brad Halvorson *(Derby Doorman)*; Christopher A. Joyce; Edward Rissien; Jenna Rissien; Mark Smith *(Diner Patrons)*

Short, cute and slyly appealing, SWINGERS peeks into the lives of two lovable losers. Written, coproduced and starring Jon Favreau, this light comedy stands apart from other recent attempts to depict modern man's problems with life and love on the screen.

In the less well-known nightspots of Hollywood, where Mike (Favreau), a hapless aspiring comic from New York obsesses about his ex-girlfriend, Michelle, with whom he broke up six months before. All over town, Mike talks about Michelle with his best friend, Trent (Vince Vaughn), an aspiring producer. Trent and Mike's other buddies, Rob (Ron Livingston), Sue (Patrick Van Horn), and Charles (Alex Desert), encourage Mike to join them for a night of bar-hopping to forget his troubles, but his encounter with a beautiful woman in one bar ends in disaster.

Later, Trent whisks Mike off to Las Vegas for fun and excitement. While in the gambling town, Mike and Vince meet two waitresses who take a liking to them. That same night, the men join the women back at a trailer home. Unfortunately, Mike ruins the double date by again moping about Michelle.

Finally, back in Hollywood, Mike becomes seriously depressed. Trent gets him out of his apartment one more time and takes him to the Derby, where couples dance to retro-swing music. At the club, Mike meets Lorraine (Heather Graham), a young woman who is not put off by his kvetching. Slowly, a romance develops and Mike even forgets about his former girlfriend—that is, until she calls one day. But Mike has an easy time choosing between the past and present: Lorraine is the woman he wants.

SWINGERS became a sleeper hit in late 1996 thanks to some smart promotion by Miramax, but this lively low-budget feature happens to merit the attention it got. Unlike previous small-scale films about the professional and personal plight of contemporary urban males (KICKING AND SCREAMING, THE POMPATUS OF LOVE), SWINGERS never tries to make an important statement and eschews flashy, pretentious cinematic techniques. Instead, SWINGERS' minimally plotted narrative spends much more time with developing funny but real character comedy—and the results pay off, particularly in scenes with Mike humiliating himself in front of potential dates. The highlight of the film finds him leaving a series of pathetic messages on the answering machine of women he has just met.

Jon Favreau creates Mike perfectly through perceptive acting and writing. One of the drawbacks to SWINGERS, however, is that Favreau does not always create enough authorial distance from his two male lead characters to encourage viewer criticism of their sometimes sexist remarks. Director Doug Liman inventively mixes the comic set pieces with tributes to Scorsese and Tarantino, vintage swing music and stale club acts, including the hilariously campy Marty and Elayne, but Liman lacks sure handling of some technical elements. In any case, SWINGERS' rough edges rarely hurt the overall piece since the characters are a bit dog-eared from the start. Neuroses haven't been this charming since the early days of Woody Allen. *(Violence, sexual situations, substance abuse, extreme profanity.)* — E.M.

d, Doug Liman; p, Victor Simpkins, Nicole Shay LaLoggia; exec p, Cary Woods; assoc p, Bradford L. Schlei, Avram Ludwig; co-p, Jon Favreau; w, Jon Favreau; ph, Doug Liman; ed, Stephen Mirrione; m, Justin Reinhardt; prod d, Brad Halvorson; art d, David Gould, Diana Pederson; sound, Alan B. Samuels (mixer); cos, Genevieve Tyrrell; makeup, Eric A. Polita, Molly R. Stern

Comedy/Drama **(PR: C MPAA: R)**

SYNTHETIC PLEASURES ★½

(U.S.) 82m Caipirinha Productions ~ Samba Entertainment c

John Perry Barlow; Jeffrey Baxter; Scott Bukatman; Robert Ettinger; Scott Frazier; Robert Gurland; Michio Kaku; Jaron Lanier; Timothy Leary; Max Moore; Orlan; Lisa Palac; Ed Regis; Howard Rheingold; Steve Roberts; R.U. Sirius

What do cryogenics, robots, e-mail, genetic engineering and the drug Ecstasy have in common? Nothing—but that doesn't stop the makers of SYNTHETIC PLEASURES from lumping them together in this mishmash of a documentary, a MONDO CANE for the cyber age.

The filmmakers claim that SYNTHETIC PLEASURES is about "new technologies." But the science of cryogenics has been at its current level for two or three decades. At any rate, SYNTHETIC PLEASURES makes pointless predictions about what may happen in 100 years. Despite interviews with such authorities as Timothy Leary, '70s rock discard Jeffrey "Skunk" Baxter, and an editor at *Future Sex* magazine, SYNTHETIC PLEASURES nonetheless is brimming with blue-sky predictions anyone could make. And wait till you get to the alternative culture Beavis & Butt-Heads ruining their own case for "smart drinks."

Yet even those two don't corner the market on embarrassingly sophomoric remarks. Someone else praises "hyperreal environments." "Hyperreal?" Cute. What does it mean? Realer than real? Not judging from the film's supposedly cutting-edge graphics; the film's computer-screen blowups are so liney and low-resolution, they're practically unwatchable. When one interviewee claims you can't tell anymore what's real and not TV, his statement is accompanied by glaringly fake and unrealistic-looking examples. And ironically, for a film purporting to be about high-tech, it's incredibly grainy. Some gruesome plastic-surgery footage just raises this film's ugliness level that much higher.

Working against itself on so many levels, the narrator-less SYNTHETIC PLEASURES has all the surface-thought pop-prescience of those 1930s science magazines predicting flying cars and moon colonies by the brave new 1990s. Lacking even one iota of naive, gosh-wow charm, SYNTHETIC PLEASURES is an organic pain.— F.L.

d, Iara Lee; p, George Gund III; ph, Marcus Hahn, Kramer Morgenthau, Toshifumi Furusawa; ed, Adreas Troeger, Stacia Thompson; sound, Antonio Arroyo (recordist), Matthew Sigal (recordist), Yoshiteru Takahashi (recordist)

Science Fiction/Documentary (PR: C MPAA: NR)

T

TAILS YOU LIVE, HEADS YOU'RE DEAD ★★
(U.S.) 91m Wilshire Court Productions ~ Paramount Home Video c

Corbin Bernsen *(Neil Jones)*; Tim Matheson *(McKinley)*; Ted McGinley *(Jeff Quint)*; Jeff Pustil *(Phil Wiseman)*; Maria Del Mar *(Melanie)*; John White *(Kevin)*; David Fraser *(Brad)*; Christopher Britton *(Tony)*; Sibongile Nene *(Secretary)*; David Blacker *(Security Guard)*; James Binkley *(Airline Clerk)*; Harold Burke *(Handyman)*; Jackie Harris *(Angie)*; Dave Nichols *(Detective Kessel)*; Melissa Bell *(Janice Wiseman)*

Another variation on THE MOST DANGEROUS GAME (1932), TAILS YOU LIVE. . . is long on coarsely-manufactured excitement and short on logic or integral suspense.

Businessman Jeff Quint (Ted McGinley) drops by his favorite watering hole, where he is sidetracked by competitive bar patron Neil Jones (Corbin Bernsen) into a card game. Jeff soon discovers that Neil is a serial killer who likes to toy with his victims. After being nearly run over on the street and tormented at home and office by weird phone calls, Jeff takes the advice of friend Phil Wiseman (Jeff Pustil) and hires a private eye and former Marine, McKinley (Tim Matheson).

Neil poses as a security system repairman and disturbs Jeff's wife, Melanie (Maria Del Mar), after gaining her confidence and entry in the house. Luring his main quarry to an underground garage, Neil shoots at Jeff; later he infests his home with scorpions. McKinley persuades Jeff to lull Neil into a false sense of security by faking his own death. Distracting the stalker with a fake client, Wiseman, McKinley, and Jeff invade Neil's fortress-like domicile, where they find find photos of his homicides. Wised up to the trick, Neil shoots McKinley to death before the detective can bring his evidence to the police.

After getting the drop on Wiseman, whom he chains in a rapidly filling bathtub, Neil tangles with the one easy mark that got away. In a hail of bullets, Jeff wounds Neil and then ends the executive slayer's killing hobby by shooting him fatally. Rescuing Wiseman, Jeff nonetheless remains haunted by dreams of bogeyman Neil garroting him.

Failing to exploit the implications of a murder spree by a company president, TAILS YOU LIVE. . . misses the opportunity to send up the cutthroat world of corporate gamesmanship. Instead, this average made-for-cable chiller foolishly salivates over its villain's run-of-the-mill sadism, aimed at a rather colorless adversary. Although the pacing's a bit off, director Matheson invests the stalker set pieces with ample frissons and allows his actors grace notes in their performances, although McGinley is too lightweight for even accidental hero status.

Fueled by Matheson's wry minor turn and Bernsen's delicious portrayal of a mover-and-shaker chafing under a white collar of normal behavior, TAILS YOU LIVE. . . engrosses in a professional, impersonal manner. Holding back the film are instances of the "idiot plot," where characters do something unbelievable only because it is needed to move the plot along. *(Violence, profanity, adult situations.)* — R.P.

d, Tim Matheson; p, Julian Marks; exec p, Ruben Preuss; co-p, Miguel Tejada-Flores; w, Miguel Tejada-Flores (based on the short story "Liar's Dice" by Bill Pronzini); ph, Francois Protat; ed, Christopher Rouse; m, David Michael Frank; prod d, William Beeton; art d, David Ferguson; set d, Peter Razmofsky; sound, Brian Day (mixer); fx, Michael

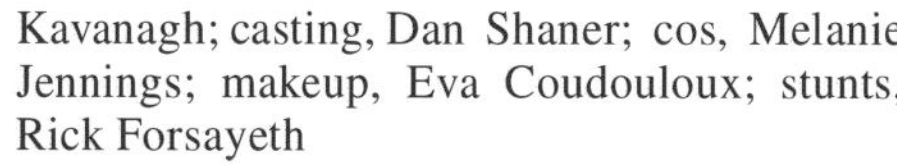

Kavanagh; casting, Dan Shaner; cos, Melanie Jennings; makeup, Eva Coudouloux; stunts, Rick Forsayeth

Action/Crime/Thriller (PR: C MPAA: R)

TAKEOVER, THE ★
(U.S.) 91m Takeover Productions ~ LIVE Entertainment c

Billy Drago *(Danny Stein)*; John Savage *(Greg)*; Nick Mancuso *(Tony Vilachi)*; David Amos *(Jonathan Fitzsimmons)*; Gene Mitchell *(Mickey Lane)*; Cali Timmins *(Kathy)*; Anita Barone *(Cindy Lane)*; Tony Longo *(Waldo)*; Manu Tupou *(Manu)*; Greg Lewis *(Vic)*; Sam Scarber *(Moore)*; James Donzell *(Stein's Associate)*; Arlene Rodriguez *(Brandi)*; Eric DaRe *(Vilachi Henchman)*

Of all the unkind fates that can befall a trashy movie, a congealed tone is the toughest one for an audience to tolerate. Alternating the gratuitously violent with the grimacingly campy, THE TAKEOVER is full of sound effects and fury signifying nothing.

Popping his eyes, apoplectic gangster Tony Vilachi (Nick Mancuso) is not willing to fold his tent when big-time muscle from Chicago, Danny Stein (Billy Drago), decides to move in on his LA turf. Stein's every move is suported by his primary partner, Greg (John Savage). While Tony plans counterattacks to protect his exotic club, Bare Elegance, as well as an impending mega drug-deal on the docks, Stein uses dirty tricks to reawaken the loyalty of jailed patsy Jonathan Fitzsimmons (David Amos). Jonathan's restaurant was nabbed and coarsened by Vilachi into a strip joint. Warning his cellmate Mickey Lane (Gene Mitchell) that Stein will extract a high cost for any favor granted them, Jonathan and Mickey nonetheless allow Stein to spring them from jail after Mickey shivs one of Stein's enemies in the prison shower. Like a yo-yo, wharf boss Manu (Manu Tupou) swings between Stein and Vilachi. The war turns uglier as Stein insists that Jonathan undermine Vilachi's make-or-break drug deal by kidnapping club hostess Kathy (Cali Timmins), Vilachi's main squeeze and formerly Jonathan's close associate. After an ambush at Bare Elegance leaves Vilachi's nephew dead, Jonathan and Mickey double-cross Stein by rescuing Kathy. Stein's men inadvertently pounce on Mickey's sister Cindy (Anita Barone) by mistake. During a pow-wow in which Manu's men bounce back to Vilachi's camp, Stein and Vilachi wind up in a Mexican stand-off. Casualties mount. After Vilachi wounds Kathy for not reciprocating his twisted adoration, Jonathan pops Vilachi. Stein wounds Mickey who blasts him right back, and Jonathan finishes off slimy Stein. Jonathan, Mickey, Cindy, and Kathy step over assorted Mafia corpses and nurse their various injuries in a future, where dons can't keep calling in favors and where Bare Elegance is once again a posh eatery.

Despite a bevy of B-movie star-powered names, THE TAKEOVER is a numbingly routine crime-stopper in which the three pairs of protagonists (Stein and Greg, Jonathan and Mickey, Vilachi and Kathy) seem to be coming from separate films, all unconvincingly pasted together. One can't shake the sense that this cast never really acted opposite each other; perhaps their performances were spliced together and matched through matting and post-production optical effects. Irritatingly, THE TAKEOVER slobbers after a blackly comic tone, treating its caricatures of chintzy mobsters as highly satirical. Aiming for PULP FICTION (1994), but only giving us the pulp, the film's coarse humor magnifies its cartoonish aspects to the detriment of suspense. Fashioned in that 10-ton tongue-in-cheek style popularized by Stallone and Schwarzenegger, the witless quipping could best be described as Noel Coward on steroids. There's plenty of muscle on display, but most of it is in the actors' thick tongues.

Besides the crushing rib-tickling that turns this film into THE GODFATHER (1972) redone as a Fox sitcom, THE TAKEOVER handles all its reversals of fortune with a cloddish eagerness. The car chases hog too much screen time; the prison scenes are sanitized; the hopscotching with the dock boss is a tiresome game of shifting priorities. More galling is the movie's premise that a career crook like Vilachi would screw up the score of a lifetime over a woman who loathes him. Add up all these debits, and one is left with a gangland spree that neither stimulates nor amuses. Redeeming itself somewhat with a bullet-ballet of a climax, THE TAKEOVER confuses busyness with eclat and fails to answer one essential question: Why do patrons keep frequenting Vilachi's establishment when it seems to be the best place in town to get shot at in between highballs? These ecdysiasts must put on some show! *(Graphic violence, extreme profanity, extensive nudity, sexual situations, adult situations, substance abuse.)* — R.P.

d, Troy Cook; p, Cheryl Cook; exec p, Michael Woods; w, Gene Mitchell; ph, T. Alexander; ed, Bruce Cook; m, Jimmy Lifton; prod d, James Scanlon; art d, Jamie McCrae; sound, James Einolf (mixer); fx, Paul Kocar; casting, Kathy A. Smith; cos, Dana Loats; makeup, Lori Ann Baker, Bill Myrick; stunts, Phil O'Dell

Crime/Action **(PR: C MPAA: R)**

TALES FROM THE CRYPT PRESENTS BORDELLO OF BLOOD ★½

(U.S.) 87m Tales From the Crypt Productions; Donner/Schuler-Donner Productions; Silver Pictures ~ Universal c

John Kassir *(Voice of the Crypt Keeper)*; Dennis Miller *(Rafe Guttman)*; Erika Eleniak *(Katherine Verdoux)*; Angie Everhart *(Lilith)*; Chris Sarandon *(Reverend Current)*; Corey Feldman *(Caleb Verdoux)*; Aubrey Morris *(McCutcheon)*; Phil Fondacaro *(Vincent Prather)*; William Sadler *(Mummy)*; Ciara Hunter *(Tamara)*; Leslie Ann Phillips *(Patrice)*; Juliet Reagh *(Tallulah)*; Eli Gabay *(Miguel)*; Matt Hill *(Reggie)*; Eric Keenleyside *(Noonan)*; Kim Kondrashoff *(Jenkins)*; Robert Paul Munic *(Zeke)*; Gary Starr *(Jed)*; Robin Douglas *(Louise)*; Dorian "Joe" Clark *(Jonas)*; Ravinder Toor *(Bartender)*; Robert Rozen *(Rabbi Goldman)*; Jen Jasey *(Woman)*; Heather Hanson *(Babe)*; Sibel Thrasher; Tom Pickett; Topaz Hasfal; Lovie Eli *(Gospel Singers)*; Korrine St. Onge; Claire Marie Harvey; Lyne Hachey; Sheena Galloway; Kikka Ferguson; Melody Cherpaw *(Bordello Vampires)*; Sheila Mills *(Bride of Frankenstein)*; Natalie Ross *(Dancer)*; Angela Nesbitt-Dufort *(Dancer)*; Gloria Roy *(Waitress)*; Maria Marhoffer-Bains *(Waitress)*; Whoopi Goldberg *(uncredited)*

A cheesy, sleazy melange of sex and gore, BORDELLO OF BLOOD is a sad comedown from the energetic first TALES FROM THE CRYPT movie, DEMON KNIGHT (1995).

Down-on-his-luck private detective Rafe Guttman (Dennis Miller) is hired by the lovely Katherine Verdoux (Erika Eleniak) to find her missing brother, Caleb (Corey Feldman). Unbeknownst to them at first, Caleb's last stop was a brothel run by Lilith (Angie Everhart), an ancient vampire whose bloodsucking working girls made short work of Caleb. Lilith is in league with showy televangelist Rev. Jimmy Current (Chris Sarandon), who controls her with an ancient talisman and uses her to dispose of sinners while selling off the victims' personal effects for his own gain.

Guttman follows Caleb's trail to the bordello, where Lilith unsuccessfully attempts to seduce him. He begins to realize what's going on, but Katherine (who is working for Current) doesn't believe him at first. Eventually, she is captured by Lilith, who also rebels against Current, and the preacher teams with Guttman to assault the brothel. Armed with water guns filled with holy water, they destroy the vampire hookers, rescue Katherine and pursue Lilith to the set of Current's TV show. Current is killed, and Guttman and Katherine then dispatch Lilith with a cross-shaped laser beam. But, out in Guttman's car, Katherine proves to have been vampirized herself.

There's nothing worse than a horror movie made by people with no true feeling for the genre, and a subtle contempt for both the material and the audience runs through almost all of this hack job. As in many of their televised "Crypt" shows, the team of Gilbert Adler and A.L. Katz demonstrate no true affinity for horror, showering the screen with gimmickry and treating the genre as a big joke. There is some fun to be had with Miller's wisecracks (a number of them almost certainly improvised) in the first half, but the movie completely falls apart the moment the audience is supposed to take him seriously as the hero. And when his character says the line "I feel like I'm in a bad 'Tales from the Crypt' episode" at one point, that contempt practically leaps off the screen, as if the filmmakers were spitting in the viewer's face.

The plot is for the birds, the film is never the least bit scary, the ending is predictable, and when Miller and Sarandon take on the vampire hookers with their holy-water guns, the spectacle of the screaming naked women being burned to death is played as good clean fun, complete with an upbeat pop song in the background. But with absolutely nothing underlying the scene except its makers' misguided ideas of how to appeal to the youth crowd, it becomes one of 1996's most offensive movie sequences. Even the framing scenes featuring the Crypt Keeper are lackluster, with the character delivering gag lines that wouldn't pass muster on the TV series. *(Graphic violence, extensive nudity, sexual situations, substance abuse, extreme profanity.)* — M.G.

d, Gilbert Adler; p, Gilbert Adler; exec p, Richard Donner, David Giler, Walter Hill, Joel Silver, Robert Zemeckis; assoc p, Dan Cracchiolo, Richard Mirisch, Scott Nimerfro; co-p, Al Katz, Alexander Collett; w, Al Katz, Gilbert Adler (from a story by Bob Gale and Robert Zemeckis, based on the *Tales From the Crypt* comic books originally published by William M. Gaines); ph, Tom Priestley; ed, Stephen Lovejoy; m, Chris Boardman, Danny Elfman; prod d, Gregory Melton; art d, Sheila Haley; set d, Rose Marie McSherry, Annemarie Corbett; sound, Larry Sutton (mixer); fx, Tim Storvick, Terry Sonderhoff, John T. Van Vliet, Available Light Ltd.; casting, Victoria Burrows; cos, Trish Keating; makeup, Victoria Down, Christopher Nelson, Chris Nelson, Kevin Yagher Productions; stunts, Shane Dixon, Tim Davison, David Jacox, G. Scott Wilder

Horror/Comedy **(PR: O MPAA: R)**

TALES OF EROTICA ★★½

(U.S./U.K./Germany) 104m Westdeutscher Rundfunk; Regina Ziegler Filmproduktion ~ Vidmark Entertainment c (DIE EROTISCHE GESCHICHTEN)

THE DUTCH MASTER: Mira Sorvino *(Teresa)*; Aida Turturro *(Kim)*; Rick Pasqualone *(Joey)*; Charles Gerbel *(Dr. Rosenman)*; Sharon Angela *(Dorothy)*; Salsh Veldman; Emanuel Xuereb; Rudolph Martin; Ruth Maleczen; THE INSATIABLE MRS. KIRSCH: Simon Shepherd *(Narrator)*; Hetty Baynes *(Mrs. Kirsch)*; Ken Russell *(Mr. Kirsch)*; VROOM VROOM VROOOOM: Richard Barboza *(Leroy)*; Laura Lane; Dewar Zazee; Willie "Spaceman" Patterson; Kim Smith; WET: Arliss Howard *(Bruce Lomann)*; Cynda Williams *(Davida Urked)*; Kathleen Wilhoite *(Jolene Wolff)*; John Toles-Bey *(William)*

Released on home video in 1996, this is an ersatz anthology feature culled from a high-profile 1993 series of short subjects done for German television, in which assorted guest filmmakers expounded upon sex. Despite the exploitable title, the overall effect is more ribald than erotic.

In "The Dutch Master," young New Yorkers discuss the strange case of their pal Teresa (Mira Sorvino). Three weeks before her marriage she becomes enamored with a Vermeer-style painting in an art museum. She believes she can see randy Netherlanders and their serving wenches within the canvas coming to life and reacting, invitingly, to her presence. Teresa begins wearing clogs and bonnets to her dental-assistant job, with sexier things on her mind than teeth. Ultimately, she steps into the painting and becomes part of the action just out of the frame. Her friends and fiance search for her in vain.

In "The Insatiable Mrs. Kirsch," an unnamed narrator (Simon Shepherd) holidays in Dorset, his work on a novel distracted by fellow guest Mrs. Kirsch (Hetty Baynes), a seemingly ordinary middle-aged woman whose husband is absent. He is fascinated by the lady's frequent exits, followed by the buzzing of a vibrator in her room. Pressed by the storyteller into a luncheon date, Mrs. Kirsch still can't help leaving for another round with the apparatus. Ultimately the innocent truth emerges: she recently gave birth to a sickly child, and those suggestive noises are really portable breast pumps, storing mother's milk for when the baby is well enough to leave the hospital.

In "Vroom Vroom Vroooom," Leroy (Richard Barboza) is a kid in the deep south who has no luck with girls. He asks a voodoo witch doctor to give him what he most desires. And in a lightning-streaked churchyard he finds her—a sleek, new motorcycle. This is no ordinary machine; as he accelerates, its chassis morphs into a beautiful woman between Leroy's legs, and their joyride becomes a sex act. Local girls now notice Leroy for his hot wheels, and one of them talks her way into a ride. The jealous motorcycle pitches them off, and when the girl mounts it solo to get help, the bike transforms between her legs—into a handsome and welcoming young man.

In "Wet," bathroom-fixtures salesman Bruce (Arliss Howard) is closing up for the night when he gets an enticing and insistent customer, Davida (Cynda Williams). She will buy a hot tub, she says, but only if she can try it out first. She strips down and insists Bruce join her in the showroom floor model, to try out the fit. This is all being videotaped by a female accomplice outside the store window. She and Davida run numerous scams like this, and their apartment residence is filled with luxuries purchased through blackmail.

While none of the individual segments in TALES OF EROTICA are completely successful, and they hang much better together than separately. Seidelman's "The Dutch Master" (nominated for an Academy Award for Best Live-Action Short Subject) ends on a creepy note of multiple voyeurism, as its colorless heroine placidly submits to being a sort of painting within the painting; with a slight adjustment in tone this could have gone very easily from bachelorette raunchy to "Twilight Zone" eerie. Ken Russell's extended anecdote is a masterful build-up of lewd innuendo, with a grand sight gag involving a English tourist attraction—a naked caveman-type painting on an English hillside, on which Mrs. Kirsch dances with delight. Melvin Van Peebles is in fine stylistic form with his funky tall tale of a rebel and his bike (enhanced by nice computer graphics) but there's not quite enough plot to fill out its proscribed 26-minute length—and seven minutes of padding and repetition can seem like an eternity in the short-subject format. Rafelson's closing sketch, though more character-driven than the others, winds up serving a rather pointless O. Henry trick ending.

As a whole, TALES OF EROTICA is a far better omnibus than such lamentable exercises as ARIA and FOUR ROOMS. Though Russell and Van Peebles are clearly the flamboyant and provocative auteurs in the bunch, its quartet of directors each put a distinctive stamp on their entries. The viewer comes away with a sense of having sampled a diverse assortment of cinematic appetizers, if not a whole buffet. *(Nudity, adult situations, sexual situations, substance abuse, profanity.)* — C.C.

d, Susan Seidelman, Ken Russell, Melvin Van Peebles, Bob Rafelson; p, Jonathan Brett, Ronaldo Vasconcellos, Melvin Van Peebles, Noah Golden; exec p, Regina Ziegler; w, Susan Seidelman ("The Dutch Master"), Jonathan Brett ("The Dutch Master), Melvin Van Peebles ("Vroom Vroom Vroooom"), Bob Rafelson ("Wet"); ph, Maryse Alberti, Hong Manley, Igor Sunara; ed, Mona Davis, Xavier Russell, Melvin Van Peebles, Michael Elliot; m, Wendy Blackstone, Melvin Van Peebles, David McHugh; prod d, Lester Cohen, Brian Eatwell; art d, James Sherman; ch, Louis Johnson; fx, Randall Balsmeyer; casting, Jakki Fink, Jori Weitz; cos, Julie Rae Engelsman

Comedy/Erotic **(PR: O MPAA: R)**

TALKING ABOUT SEX ★★
(U.S.) 87m Pegasus Productions ~ Leo c

Kim Wayans *(Andie White)*; Daniel Beer *(Doug Penn)*; Daria Lynn *(Joan Morgan)*; Randy Powell *(Carl Morgan)*; Kerry Ruff *(Michael Columbus)*; Marcy Walker *(Rachel Parsons)*; Michael Columbo *(Matthew Jacobs)*; Joe Richards *(Lou Jacobs)*; Mark Cuban *(Macho Mark)*; Charles Stransky *(Larry Lepke)*; Jules Mandel *(Norman)*; Sylvia Saxon *(Emma)*; Selma Benjamin *(Lou's Girlfriend)*; Gary M. Bettman; Charlene Blaine; Vito Bonaza; Lois Bostwick; Kahlena Cooper; Ken Cooper; Vna Zen Frater; Doug Glen; Luann Gold; Catherine Grace; Donna Harazim; Michael Henderson; Casey Lee; Carol Maitland; Cara Miller; Ed Miller; Charles Mitri; Michael Mizgalski; Rene Mujica; Patti Neill; Gaby Nimier; David Pecchia; Bronwyn Queen; Kim Reader; Delores Scozzesi; Deborah Selby; Albert Siedman; Liza Siegel; Harry Weinberger; Camie Young

There's much more talking then sex in this gabfest that bears more than a passing resemblance to any given film by Henry Jaglom.

Andie (Kim Wayans) is a freelance editor who has collaborated on a book with Michael Columbus (Kerry Ruff), a slightly stodgy sex therapist. Having produced a vanity printing of the book and a prototype of a videotape to accompany it (both financed by her boyfriend Doug [Daniel Beer]), Andie plans a party at which she hopes to interest Carl Morgan (Randy Powell) in publishing them. Carl is having sexual problems with his wife Joan (Daria Lynn), who is unable to tell him her wants and is also seeing Michael for therapy.

At the party, sexual undercurrents among the guests rise to the surface. Doug and Andie fight over his refusal to get married. Michael shows his disdain for Andie's friend Rachel (Marcy Walker), an alternative therapist. After failing to seduce Doug, Rachel has her first-ever orgasm with the aid of Andie's shower head. Andie's neighbor tries to set her up with his grandson, whom he doesn't realize is gay. Carl accuses Joan of having an affair with Michael, but he learns more about her when he watches Andie's revealing videotape. At the end of the night, Rachel leads the remaining people at the party in a "rebirthing session," at which the skeptical Michael gets in touch with his true feelings about his father. Everyone ends the night with more knowledge about themselves and their partners.

TALKING ABOUT SEX could hardly have been more suitably titled. Its purpose, like that of the fictional book that sparks the plot, seems to be to encourage viewers to talk out their sexual desires and problems. While it isn't as unbearably didactic as it sounds, neither is it particularly interesting dramatically; the film simply tries to pack too much into its running time, with a spectrum of relationship problems ticked off as regularly as could be seen in any given month of a daytime soap opera. Those having trouble communicating with their sexual partners may well find this movie useful, but that's less a recommendation than a prescription. *(Nudity, sexual situations, adult situations, profanity.)* — M.F.

d, Aaron Speiser; p, Gary M. Bettman; exec p, Aaron Speiser; assoc p, Heath Slane; co-p, Morgan Higby; w, Aaron Speiser, Carl Nelson; ph, Thomas Jewett; ed, Wayne Schmidt; m, Tim Landers; art d, Lauree S. James; casting, Peter Fitzpatrick; cos, Tammy Stevenson; makeup, Shauna G.

Drama/Comedy **(PR: O MPAA: NR)**

TARGET ★★★

(India) 104m Creative Entertainment Group ~ Filmopolis Pictures c

Om Puri *(Bharosa Ram)*; Mohan Agashe *(Vindhyachai Singh)*; Anian Srivastava; Baroon Chakravarty; Champa Islam *(Bijari)*

Sandip Ray, son of legendary Indian filmmaker Satyajit Ray, brings one of his father's last scripts to the screen in TARGET. Like THE BROKEN JOURNEY (1992), also written by Satyajit and directed by Sandip, this film casts a scornful glare at the injustices and human suffering caused by the Indian caste system. In this story, the good Bharosa Ram (Om Puri), a member of the lowest caste, is pitted against the decadent and arrogant landowner Vindhyachai Singh (Mohan Agashe).

Wealthy landlord Singh, once a great hunter, has lost his shooting ability as a result of a life of alcohol and debauchery. Unwilling to give up the hunt, he is reduced to hiring a *shikari,* a rifleman. Bharosa, a humble untouchable, is brought in and proves his skill with stunning accuracy. Being an untouchable, he is not permitted to stay in the house and accommodations are secured for him with workers from his own caste.

The untouchable camp is teeming with political unrest over low wages and is planning to abandon the landowner for a competitor. Bharosa, who has no qualms about his wage, tries to maintain his distance. He is given a hut and provided with meals and cleaning by a young woman named Bijari (Champa Islam). Having no experience with women, Bharosa is nervous and intrigued by her presence. Bijari, on the other hand, has had three failed marriages and is bitter and cynical. Gradually they fall in love.

Bharosa enjoys his accommodations and his role in the master's household, but gradually his foothold in polite society begins to disintegrate. On his first hunting expedition he kills a leopard, but when the photographer summons him to stand by his kill, Singh intervenes and takes the credit. Singh resents the skill and strength of Bharosa, and his jealousy is further exacerbated when he summons his men to abduct Bijari, who refuses his desire and flees to Bharosa. The following day, Bharosa approaches Bijari's assailants but is put in his place and then brutally assaulted in the woods on his way home. He survives the attack but returns to his camp with his shooting arm permanently disabled.

Stripped of his dignity and his means of livelihood, Bharosa despairs. He obsessively practices his aim but misses the target repeatedly. His dedication and single-mindedness is finally rewarded when he learns how to use his body to steady the gun. He returns to the camp exhilarated but finds it on the brink of siege. After getting word from an informant about the villagers' plans, Singh and his men come to torch the village by night. When Bharosa approaches the men alone, Singh laughs and dismisses the cripple. Bharosa raises his gun, aims at his target, and Singh falls from his horse. When Bharosa cocks the gun again, Singh's men flee, and the villagers rush onward to victory. Bharosa embraces Bijari and proposes marriage.

The satisfying charm of this political melodrama about injustice and the dignity of the human spirit makes it easy to overlook the overly simplistic plot and the sentimental ending. The good guys are unassuming, kind, and humble, but behind their lowliness lies a great strength and perserverance. The bad guys are decadent, weakened by privilege, and too arrogant to even notice that they are outnumbered and have grown soft. Ultimately this film has very little of the style or complexity of the works of Satyajit Ray, but if one can get over looking for the father in the son, it has its pleasures.— R.C.

d, Sandip Ray; w, Satyajit Ray (based on the novel by Prafulla Roy); ph, Barun Raha; ed, Dulal Dutta; m, Satyajit Ray; prod d, Ashoke Bose

Drama **(PR: A MPAA: NR)**

TATTOO BOY ★★½

(U.S.) 72m Oregon Pictures ~ Gotham Entertainment c

C. J. Barkus *(Sam)*; Amandda Tirey *(Arizona)*; Matthew James *(Shane)*; Howard Shook *(Fagin)*; Joel Spencer *(Nerve)*; John Bowling *(Steve)*; Arron Lewis *(Tim)*; Tonya Turner; Trisha Turner; Shirley Williams; Pamela Byrd; Dan Davis; Todd McNeeley

Properly free of Hollywood gloss, this independent 16mm feature sympathetically portrays sexually-exploited runaway teens fending for themselves in an unspecified Midwest city.

Bisexual hustler Sam (C. J. Barkus) never got over seeing his brother die in an accident caused by their mother's alcoholism. Now, too mature to appeal to most johns, Sam reluctantly pimps younger runaways while watching out for their welfare. His headstrong 17-year-old girlfriend Arizona (Amandda Tirey) urges Sam to leave town with her for a better life.

A recent arrival on the streets is the naive, possibly schizoid, Shane (Matthew James), 14 and appealing meat for paying perverts. Sam, Arizona and Shane's quasi-family unit is disrupted by Sam's old cohort Fagin (Howard Shook), now working for an East Coast underground network that supplies children to molesters. Despite the money offered, Sam refuses any deal. But Fagin indoctrinates Shane anyway, marking him like cattle with the syndicate's tattoo symbol. Sam catches up with Fagin, beats him and steals his bankroll. Shane, sought for vehicular assault on his parents, is caught by police before he can rendezvous with Sam and Arizona at their departing bus. Fagin revives to find his face vengefully tattooed by Sam.

Filmed in the Dayton, Ohio area, this debut feature from 22-year-old Larry Smith (allegedly a filmmaker from the age of seven) tackles its harrowing subject with an uneasy mixture of realism and awkward melodrama. It's no coincidence the bad guy is named Fagin, and his fisticuffs with Sam are punctuated by silly bam! pow! chords on the overemphatic musical score. Comparisons with Larry Clark's looser, much-hyped KIDS, released that same year, are inevitable, especially in recurring images of an even-younger lost generation. This includes a scene that shows Arizona's tot siblings methodically vandalizing a vacant suburban home. (Their out-of-it mom somehow thinks they're at school on a Saturday).

While TATTOO BOY may not have gained a high profile, it did win First Prize at the 1995 New York Underground Film Festival. *(Adult situations, substance abuse, sexual situations, profanity, violence.)* — C.C.

d, Larry Turner; p, Shelly Sinclair; w, Larry Turner; ph, David Litz; ed, Jon Menell; m, Darron Bell

Drama **(PR: O MPAA: NR)**

TEMECULA
(SEE: WEEKEND IN THE COUNTRY, A)

TERMINAL IMPACT ★★
(U.S.) 94m Nu World ~ New Line Home Video c

Frank Zagarino *(Saint)*; Bryan Genesse *(Max)*; Jennifer Miller *(Evelyn)*; Ian Roberts *(Sheen)*; Justin Illusion *(Adam)*; Michael Brunner *(Dr. Phelps)*; Hal Orlandini *(Cooper)*; Ian Yule *(Harvey)*; Jurgen Hellberg *(Derrick)*; Tony Caprari *(Seth)*; Martin Le Maitre *(Lennie)*; Tyrone Stevenson *(Oscar)*; Douglas Bristow *(TV Anchor)*; Hendrick Crawford *(Senior Lab Technician)*; Brian Lucas *(Gate Guard)*; Steven Rymer *(Truck Driver)*; Kevin Fitzpatrick *(Gas Station Attendant)*; J. D. Du Plessis *(TV Cameraman)*; Darryl Wenner *(Cooper Security #1)*; Graham Press *(Cooper Security #2)*; Ernest Meinze *(Cooper Security #3)*

Here's a scenario you don't bump into every day: geneticists implant insect DNA into human test subjects so that they can develop a cyborg with a cockroach-like resistance to atomic fallout! Unfortunately, this movie's weird but original sci-fi premise gets mired in genre stereotypes, flaccid direction, and plot reiteration.

Bounty hunters Saint (Frank Zagarino) and Max (Bryan Genesse) tire of small gigs like tagging tax-evading crop dusters. When their skinflint boss, Harv (Ian Yule), offers them a big-bucks assignment at Delta Tech Labs, they ask no questions.

Altogether more inquisitive, TV reporter Evelyn Reid (Jennifer Miller) plans to produce an expose on Delta Tech chairman Sheen (Ian Roberts). Armed with info provided by laboratory snitch Derrick (Jurgen Hellberg), Evelyn garners evidence of Sheen's mad scheme involving insect-to-human DNA bending and the construction of indestructible cyborgs equipped with this DNA. Sheen wants Saint and Max to locate the snooping newswoman and retrieve a voice-control module that activates the cyborgs. What Saint and Max don't realize is that unlucky Evelyn was surgically altered with the cyborg implant before she fled Delta Tech.

While Sheen's prized cyborg, Adam (Justin Illusion), demonstrates his destructive capacity for Sheen's edification, whistleblower Derrick is killed on Sheen's orders. Suspicious of Sheen's motives, Saint and Max back out of their deal and aid Evelyn. After Sheen also eliminates Harv, Saint and Max head to an auto junkyard to retrieve the coveted cyborg control device, which is hidden in Max's wrecked car. Although Saint and Max finally level the unstoppable Adam with an auto-flattener, they are also forced to execute Evelyn after Sheen activates her killer-android capacity. Dedicated to finishing what Evelyn began, Max sprays a flammable substance all over Delta Tech from a crop duster's plane; Saint then ignites the premises. Sheen and his insane dreams of building a cyborg master race perish in the flames that incinerate the labs.

In a more deftly constructed screenplay, the science-fiction aspects of this wild scenario would bracket and sustain the film's showy action set-pieces, lending the *de rigueur* demolition and boxing bouts variety and substance. Instead, this sloppily written adventure treats the cyborg shtick like an afterthought. Although the film has plenty of flash, it contains many sequences which are simply replays of earlier moments. If its clumsy exposition had been removed, the movie would probably run half an hour.

As for the cast, stars Zagarino and Genesse adopt a jokey tone throughout the proceedings. Is the director so insecure about how to present this fantastic material that he has to resort to half-hearted self-parody that clearly constricts his cast? The creative personnel seem to have no faith in the preposterous—but viable—plot on which razzle-dazzle stuntwork and special effects are wasted. *(Graphic violence, profanity, adult situations.)* —R.P.

d, Yossi Wein; p, Danny Lerner; exec p, Avi Werner, Danny Dimbort, Trevor Short; assoc p, Brigid Olen; w, Jeff Albert, Dennis Dimster Denk; ph, Rod Stewart; ed, Mac Errington; m, Sam Sklair; prod d, Leith Ridley; art d, Ray Wilson; set d, Lisa Hart; sound, Nico Louw (mixer); fx, Rick Cresswell, Heather Oosthuizen; casting, Christa Schamberger; cos, Yvonne De Nekker; makeup, Anni Taylor; stunts, Roly Jansen

Action/Martial Arts **(PR: C MPAA: R)**

TEXAS CHAINSAW MASSACRE: THE NEXT GENERATION ★★★
(U.S.) 102m Return Productions ~ Columbia TriStar Home Video c
(AKA: RETURN OF THE TEXAS CHAINSAW MASSACRE, THE)

Renee Zellweger *(Jenny)*; Matthew McConaughey *(Vilmer)*; Robert Jacks *(Leatherface)*; Tony Perenski *(Darla)*; Joe Stevens *(W.E.)*; Lisa Newmeyer *(Heather)*; John Harrison *(Sean)*; Tyler Cone *(Barry)*; Vince Brock *(Eric)*; Susan Loughran *(Amanda)*; David Laurence *(Jack)*; James Gale *(Rothman)*

TEXAS CHAINSAW MASSACRE: THE NEXT GENERATION is an earnest attempt to recreate the atmosphere and sheer terror of the original TEXAS CHAINSAW MASSACRE. While not completely successful, it has moments of brilliance, and its audacity and reverence for its source make it superior to the two unrelated previous sequels.

Twenty years on, the deranged cannibalistic family from THE TEXAS CHAINSAW MASSACRE still lives in a dilapidated home in rural Texas. Four teenagers are riding home from their prom in a nearby town. On a back road, they discover a boy who collapses when he gets out of his car. Three of the kids go for help, while one, Sean (John Harrison), stays. A man in a truck arrives, and instead of helping, he breaks the injured boy's neck and runs Sean over with the truck.

Meanwhile, two of the other three kids stumble upon an old house. While looking for occupants, they are attacked. One is clubbed; the other is put in a freezer, then on a meathook. The remaining teenager, Jenny (Renee Zellweger), is picked up by the truck driver. When she discovers what happened to Sean, she dives out of the truck and is chased through the house. She jumps through a closed window and escapes.

Jenny runs to another house, where she meets Darla (Tony Perenski), a beautiful young woman who at first seems sympathetic, but then turns out to be part of the savage gang. Jenny is thrown in a car trunk and brought back to the gang's house. Once there, Jenny fights for survival, stealing the car and jumping through more windows, but she is captured again and again.

The gang is headed by Vilmer (Matthew Conaughey), who scares everyone else into obedience. His brother, W.E. (Joe Stevens), is Darla's lover, and treats her as violently as Vilmer treats them both. While Jenny is being held captive, Vilmer's "boss" Rothman (James Gale) arrives. It turns out that Vilmer works for a secret and extremely powerful corporation.

The next morning, Jenny escapes. As she runs away, a low-flying plane kills Vilmer. Jenny is picked up by a limousine, which is owned by Rothman. She goes to the police, safe at last.

TEXAS CHAINSAW MASSACRE: THE NEXT GENERATION was written and directed by Kim Henkel, who wrote the original TEXAS CHAINSAW MASSACRE. His command of the creepy scenes in and around the family's home is stunning, with enough suspense, horror, and bizarre black humor (in one scene, the cannibals order a vegetarian pizza) to rival any horror film of the 90s. He's equally good at creating atmosphere, using heavy fog and lighting night scenes with car headlights, flashlights, and the moon. Almost all of the action takes place at night, and even the indoor scenes are dimly lit. Henkel clearly learned some lessons from the success of the first CHAINSAW movie, and while he offers nothing new, his version of the familiar story is stylish enough to make the viewer forgive its lack of originality. As in the first film, violent acts are portrayed without screen gore, demonstrating that the imagination is more frightening than big special effects.

Unfortunately, the rest of the film is pedestrian and confusing. Rothman's role is never clearly defined; we don't know if he's a good guy or a bad guy. We never learn what the corporation does or how Vilmer fits in. The stupid subplots about the bickering teenagers are only partially redeemed by the ultimate disclosure of Jenny's brains and inner strength. She's a great heroine, but her companions are uninteresting stereotypes. The chainsaw-wielding family doesn't match the all-out psychosis of their counterparts from the first film, but have their share of memorable idiosyncrasies (one quotes classic literature as he attacks, another has an electric false leg).

TEXAS CHAINSAW MASSACRE: THE NEXT GENERATION is an independent production, and was first released to film festivals, then to small test markets, where it failed and was shelved. While it's only partially successful, it shows great promise and is better than almost any Hollywood horror film of its era. It's a shame that it didn't receive a decent theatrical run and the only available video version as of this writing is shortened by twenty minutes. *(Violence, adult situations, nudity, extreme profanity.)* — A.M.

d, Kim Henkel; p, Robert Kuhn; assoc p, Cevin Cathell; w, Ken Henkel; ph, Levie Isaacks; ed, Sandra Adair; prod d, Debbie Pastor; sound, Scott Szabo; cos, Kari Perkins

Horror **(PR: O MPAA: R)**

TEXAS PAYBACK ★★

(U.S.) 95m Century Film Partners ~ New City Releasing/Cabin Fever Entertainment c

Sam Jones *(Louis Gentry)*; Gary Hudson *(Cody Giles)*; Patrick St. Espirit *(Jimmy)*; Angelo Tiffe *(Frank)*; Kathleen Kinmont *(Angla)*; Bo Hopkins *(Sheriff Bishop)*; Nick Oleson *(Billy)*; Joe Wheeler *(Dawson)*; Craig Vincent *(Miller)*; Mike Riordan *(Maxwell)*; Danny Holguin *(Dejeseus)*; Milissa Griffus *(Sally)*

TEXAS PAYBACK is a competently made, by-the-numbers revenge actioner starring direct-to-video stalwart Sam Jones, but it plays like a dated throwback to another, less-jaded era.

Ruthless killer Cody Giles (Gary Hudson) escapes from prison with help from his brother and immediately concocts a plan to get revenge on Louis Gentry (Sam Jones), the ex-Texas Ranger who put him away. Gentry is now working security for a Las Vegas casino and is engaged to a singer there named Angela (Kathleen Kinmont). Sheriff Bishop (Bo Hopkins) informs Gentry about Giles's escape, and Giles kills another former Texas Ranger named Maxwell after finding out where Gentry lives.

Giles assembles a gang, including another brother, to stage a raid on Bishop's house. Gentry and Bishop are ready for the attack and kill two of the gang members, but the raid was just a decoy, and the three brothers go to the casino to abduct Angela. They take her back to the ranch Gentry is building and attack her, then set it on fire. Gentry shows up to save Angela and take her to the hospital, and finds a note from Giles that says "Del Rio."

Gentry then chases the brothers down to the Mexican border and manages to kill two of them, leading to a final mano-a-mano showdown between Giles and Gentry. After a brutal fistfight, Giles pulls out a gun, but Gentry throws a knife and hits Giles right in the heart. Then Gentry rides off into the sunset.

TEXAS PAYBACK has the kind of old-fashioned crime drama plot that might have been made into a better-than-average 70-minute B-movie back in the 1950s by Don Siegel or Phil Karlson, but in today's market of computerized mayhem and pyrotechnics, it comes off as fairly lackluster entertainment. There is some good location photography of Las Vegas and the surrounding desert, nicely capturing the dusty ambiance, but the stunts and explosions all seem pretty tame, and the gunshots sound like cap pistols.

Jones—who once upon a time starred in FLASH GORDON—has all the charisma of a two-by-four, and Kinmont provides some unintentional laughs performing a couple of country & western songs that pad out the running time unnecessarily. And while it's always fun to watch veteran character actor Bo Hopkins, it's a bit depressing to see him as aging and paunchy in such a routine time-killer. *(Violence, nudity, profanity.)* — M.S.

d, Richard W. Munchkin; p, Aron Schifman, Richard W. Munchkin; assoc p, Mike Riordan, Ron Wielochowski; w, Brian Page; ph, Mark Morris; ed, John David Dagnen; m, Jim Halfpenny; prod d, David Huang; sound, Jim Slinguff; casting, Jean Levine; cos, Julia Schclair; makeup, Kristin Lamar

Action/Crime **(PR: O MPAA: R)**

THAT THING YOU DO! ★★½

(U.S.) 110m Clinica Estetico; Clavius Base ~ 20th Century Fox c

Tom Everett Scott *(Guy Patterson)*; Liv Tyler *(Faye Dolan)*; Johnathon Schaech *(Jimmy Mattingly)*; Steve Zahn *(Lenny)*; Ethan Embry *(The Bass Player)*; Tom Hanks *(Mr. White)*; Charlize Theron *(Tina)*; Obba Babatunde *(Lamarr)*; Giovanni Ribisi *(Chad)*; Chris Ellis *(Horace)*; Alex Rocco *(Sol Siler)*; Bill Cobbs *(Del Paxton)*; Peter Scolari *(Troy Chesterfield)*; Rita Wilson *(Margueritte)*; Chris Isaak *(Uncle Bob)*; Kevin Pollak *(Boss Vic Koss)*; Robert Torti *(Freddy Fredrickson)*; Chaille Percival *(Diane Dane)*; Holmes Osborne Jr. *(Mr. Patterson)*; Claudia Stedelin *(Mrs. Patterson)*; Dawn Maxey *(Darlene Patterson)*; Jack Milo *(Villapiano)*; Keith Neubert *(Dentist)*; Lee Everett *(Kitty)*; Sean Whalen *(Heckler)*; Clint Howard *(KJZZ Disc Jockey)*; Sarah Koskoff *(Chrissy Thompkins)*; Mark Brettschneider *(Talent Show M.C.)*; Kathleen Kinmont *(Koss's Secretary)*; Warren Berlinger *(Polaroid T.V. Host)*; Clive Rosengren *(Wisconsin Cop)*; Brittney Powell *(Shades Fan)*; Jonathan Demme *(Major Motion Picture Director)*; Erika Greene *(Major Motion Picture A.D.)*; Dave Oliver *(Rick)*; Tracy Reiner *(Anita)*; Barry Sobel *(Goofball)*; Paul Feig *(KMPC D.J.)*; Gedde Watanabe *(Play-Tone Photographer)*; Michael P. Byrne; Dick Corman; Diane McGee *(Play-Tone Reporters)*; Randy Fechter *(Play-Tone Tour Manager)*; Mars Callahan *(Disc Master Engineer)*; Benjamin John Parrillo *(Marine Sergeant)*; Robert Ridgely *(Hollywood Showcase Announcer)*; Marc McClure *(Hollywood Showcase Director)*; Karen Praxel *(Hollywood Showcase Script Supervisor)*; Paulie DiCocco *(Hollywood Showcase Floor Manager)*; Bryan Cranston *(Virgil "Gus" Grissom)*; Charlie Frye *(Plate Spinner)*; Colin Hanks *(Male Page)*; Elizabeth Hanks *(Bored Girl in Dress Shop)*; Bill Wiley; Cheryl L. Bruton *(Pageant Helpers)*; Heather Hewitt *(Sales Lady)*; Renee Lippin *(Beauti-*

cian); Carol Androsky *(Diner Waitress)*; Ginger Slaughter *(Ambassador Waitress)*; Robert Wisdom *(Bobby Washington)*; Larry Antoinio *(Scott "Wolfman" Pell)*; Kennya J. Ramsey; Julie L. Harkness; Darlene Dillinger *(Chantrellines)*; Jennifer York; Bethany Hartf; Kathy Stuber; Cathryne Senescu *(Folk Girls)*; Steve Billington; Andy Duncan; Dave Ryan; Todd Simon; Mike Uhler; Marco Villanova *(Legends of Brass)*; Rick Elias; Ted Kramer; Howard Locke; Don Markese; Paula Nichols; Scott Rogness; Angel Sheppard; Wade Short; Scott Strecker; Jimmy Willis *(Play-Tone Band)*; Thomas Cleo; Ken Empie; Ron Jeffrey; Mike Piccirillo; Chris Wilson *(Saturn 5)*; Barth Beasley; James Leary; Alphonse Mouzon *(Blue Spot Trio)*; Kristie J. Canavan ; Bethany Chesser; Tara Schwartz; Melissa Hurley; Cherie Hill; Robin Lindsley Allen *(Wisconsin Dancers)*

The brainchild of Tom Hanks, THAT THING YOU DO! chronicles the quick rise and quicker demise of a fictional, 1960s pop band. Fluff by design, the movie is undemandingly pleasant, but no more than that, owing to Hanks' apparent belief in the mutual exclusivity of innocence and drama.

In 1964, Guy Patterson (Tom Everett Scott) toils by day in his father's appliance store in Erie, Pa., and after work, he steals away to the basement to play the drums. When a local garage band called the Oneders—a misbegotten pun that gets mispronounced, "Oh-need-ders," at every turn—needs a fill-in drummer for a college talent show, Guy answers the call. Set to perform an original ballad by lead singer Jimmy Mattingly (Johnathon Schaech), Guy spontaneously decides to speed up the tempo, transforming "That Thing You Do!" into a pop gem suitable for the frug. Pretty soon, all of Erie's youths have Onedermania, and the group is signed to a recording contract by Mr. White (Tom Hanks).

The renamed Wonders—Guy, Jimmy, guitarist Lenny (Steve Zahn), and the unnamed bass player (Ethan Embry)—along with Jimmy's devoted girlfriend, Faye (Liv Tyler), set off on a summer tour of state fairs. While they criss-cross the country by bus with a mixture of up-and-coming acts and has-been stars, "That Thing You Do!" climbs the charts. When it hits the Top Ten, the Wonders head for Hollywood, where they appear in a beach party movie, and Guy meets his idol, jazz legend Del Paxton (Bill Cobbs).

The "One Hit Wonders" make their historic appearance on national television, and immediately afterward disband. Lenny runs off to Vegas with a Playboy bunny, and the bass player goes AWOL. His ego inflated, Jimmy unceremoniously dumps Faye, then he clashes with Mr. White and quits the band. Encouraged by Paxton, Guy decides to remain in LA and keep drumming. And before she can return to Erie, Guy asks Faye to stay with him.

THAT THING YOU DO! is Hanks's breezy manifesto on the nature of fame and how to handle it. His prime directive is that stars should keep their egos in check, and, tellingly, he gives himself a small role. Ever the sunny realist, Hanks believes fame comes with an eventual downward slide, but not necessarily a downside. His philosophy appears to be: Enjoy the ride, but never take it seriously.

But Hanks's general niceness also is the major weakness of THAT THING YOU DO! There are no villains or conflict. Everybody gets a happy ending, even Jimmy, who at his worst moment just takes himself too seriously (believing he's an "artist"). No devil, Mr. White is just able and pragmatic about the business of show. There's really no rivalry between Jimmy and Guy. In fact, until the end, only Mr. White recognizes that Faye, not fame, is the real prize.

Also problematic is Hanks's decision to totally fictionalize the story, and to use no actual period music or real-life reference points. So, the Wonders tour with a Supremes-like group, and appear on an Ed Sullivan-like TV show. As a result, THAT THING YOU DO! isn't so much nostalgic as a series of allusions to nostalgia. The movie is meant to be a joyous look back at a time of innocence and exuberance. But anyone seeking such entertainment will be better off renting a double feature of AMERICAN GRAFFITI (1973) and I WANNA HOLD YOUR HAND (1978). *(Profanity, adult situations.)* — P.R.

d, Tom Hanks; p, Gary Goetzman, Jonathan Demme, Edward Saxon; assoc p, Terry Odem; w, Tom Hanks; ph, Tak Fujimoto; ed, Richard Chew; m, Howard Shore; prod d, Victor Kempster; art d, Dan Webster; set d, Merideth Boswell; ch, Toni Basil; sound, John Patrick Pritchett (mixer); fx, Thomas R. Ward, Steve Rundell; casting, Howard Feuer; cos, Colleen Atwood; makeup, Daniel C. Striepeke, Frank H. Griffin Jr.

AAN Best Original Song: Adam Schlesinger

Musical/Comedy/Drama (PR: A MPAA: PG)

THEODORE REX ★★

(U.S.) 92m Shooting Star Entertainment;
J & M Entertainment ~ New Line c

Whoopi Goldberg *(Katie Coltrane)*; Armin Mueller-Stahl *(Dr. Edgar Kane)*; Juliet Landau *(Dr. Shade)*; Bud Cort *(Spinner)*; Stephen McHattie *(Edge)*; Richard Roundtree *(Commissioner Lynch)*; Peter Mackenzie *(Alex Summers)*; Peter Kwong *(Toymaker)*; VOICES OF: George Newbern *(Theodore Rex)*; Carol Kane *(Molly Rex)*

THEODORE REX blends children's picture and cop drama styles to odd but unsuccessful effect. The story of a space-age cop who teams up with a dinosaur on a case is far less interesting than the behind-the-scenes saga of this straight-to-video production.

Futuristic inner-city law enforcer Katie Coltrane (Whoopi Goldberg) is paired reluctantly with Theodore "Teddy" Rex (the voice of George Newbern), an English-speaking, human-sized T. Rex. Teddy, who desperately wants to become a detective, gets his chance to show his abilities as Katie's partner after a suspicious "dino-cide" occurs. Police Commissioner Lynch (Richard Roundtree) sees hiring the bumbling dinosaur during the investigation as a way to smooth over human-animal relations in the community.

Katie and Teddy get few leads in their case until the son of Katie's friend, Sebastian, is kidnapped by the notorious Dr. Edgar Kane (Armin Mueller-Stahl). Katie and Teddy force a toymaker in cahoots with Kane to tell them where to find him. Meanwhile, Kane also kidnaps Molly Rex (the voice of Carol Kane), Teddy's girlfriend, as part of his plot to create a new ice age by freezing a selected group of animals and sending them into orbit.

Finally, Katie and Teddy track Kane and his assistant, Dr. Shade (Juliet Landau), to their headquarters. Although they are taken prisoner at first, they break free and battle with Kane's henchmen. Kane attempts to put his plan into action by detonating his missile, but Teddy foils the scheme by sending the evil doctor himself into orbit. For his bravery, Teddy is made a detective first-class, and he chooses Katie as his partner for all his future cases.

New Line's THEODORE REX probably never had a chance. The curious mix—BLADE RUNNER (1983) meets TV dino "Barney"—stumbles conceptually; yet, what might have been a cute kiddie movie in spite of itself also got damaged by the troubles on the set of the wildly expensive ($35 million) production. Whoopi Goldberg's reluctance to undertake the film (she was forced to perform via legal action) was one of several reported backstage fiascos.

Goldberg seems stiff and uncomfortable in her one outfit—a black leather number that looks like a cast-off from Angela Bassett in STRANGE DAYS (1995). Yet, even at her least spirited, Goldberg gives more to the screenplay (written and directed by Jonathan Betuel, who directed MY SCIENCE PROJECT) than it deserves, whether she is sparring with her rubbery costar or shooting at hairy assassins. (Considering the money spent on the production, it is somewhat surprising how low-budget the dinosaurs appear.)

Thematically, THEODORE REX has to do with following your dreams and not discriminating against fellow creatures. Unfortunately, the unlikely and superficially "color-blind" attitudes of the story muddles the message. Adult viewers may note, in a mix of bad choices, that Whoopi is treated as an asexual "other," her character partakes in a police brutality episode that reverses the Rodney King racial dynamics in disturbing ways, and Richard Roundtree's African-American commissioner has the unfortunate surname of "Lynch." *(Violence.)* — E.M.

d, Jonathan Betuel; p, Richard Abramson, Sue Baden-Powell; exec p, Stefano Ferrari; w, Jonathan Betuel; ph, David Tattersall; ed, Rick Shaine, Steve Mirkovich; m, Robert Folk; prod d, Walter Martishius; art d, Bo Johnson; fx, Robert Habros, Criswell Productions; cos, Mary Vogt

Children's/Comedy/Fantasy (PR: A MPAA: PG)

THEREMIN: AN ELECTRONIC ODYSSEY ★★★★

(U.S.) 85m Kaga Bay Productions ~ Orion c

Leon Theremin; Clara Rockmore; Todd Rundgren; Brian Wilson; Robert Moog; Nicolas Slonimsky; Paul Shure; Henry Solomonoff

THEREMIN is a well-done documentary on the life of a unique man and the fascinating, but obscure, electronic instrument he created. Weaving together interviews with friends and admirers and old newsreel and concert clips, and covering the 1920s to the 1990s, this film manages to subtly bind the life of this unusual man and instrument with the strange course of the twentieth century, its technological transformations, and its movement from high culture to a dominant popular culture.

Professor Lev (Leon) Sergeivich Theremin, a Russian refugee, came to New York City in 1928 and soon established a reputation as a gifted inventor and musician. He became known for his invention of a strange classical instrument, resembling a wood lectern and played entirely by moving one's hands in the air above the instrument's electromagnetic field. The device, dubbed the theremin, seemed to capture the ethereal quality of music, merging the body and music together in a single expression. Theremin even tried to adapt his instrument for dancers, positioning its components under the floorboards. A forerunner of the modern synthesizer, the theremin combined in its high-pitched, haunting sound, the dreams of a space age future, and the somber melancholy of a fading classical age.

Theremin's protege, the beautiful Clara Rockmore, took the instrument to classical heights, and still reigns today as the world's theremin virtuoso. Some of the best moments in the film are her emotional performances and the quiet truth that emerges about her life-long love and devotion for her mentor Theremin, who on her 18th birthday made her a cake that began to revolve automatically as she approached it. He also imagined such other outrageous and dreamlike inventions as an invisible bridge that used electronic fields to sustain the weight of cars voyaging over water.

Theremin's creative life in New York was tragically cut short in 1938 when he was abducted from his studio by the Soviet KGB and forcibly returned to Russia. His wife and friends launched desperate attempts to find and retrieve him, but after a number of years without success he was assumed dead. The highlight of the film is the moment, taking place a half a century later, when he reemerges and is brought back to Manhattan in order to appear in this documentary. In a voice not only heavy with age and accent, but that also seems to express an English of his own invention, he tells with the aid of subtitles his tragic story of life in Russian prison camps and of years of his talents being put to use devising electronic surveillance tools during the war and various utilitarian city projects in the postwar years.

Despite the classical origins of his instrument, the theremin is ironically best known for the popular exposure it received in his absence, most notably its use in the eerie background music used during depictions of psychological trauma or alien invasion in sci-fi films of the 1950s such as THE DAY THE EARTH STOOD STILL (1951), THE THING (1951), and IT CAME FROM OUTER SPACE (1953), and for its prominent part in the Beach Boys hit song "Good Vibrations." Clara Rockmore frowned upon this popular use of her beloved instrument and even refused to endorse a proposal by electronic music pioneer Robert Moog to mass produce an inferior version of the theremin that he had developed.

At the film's end, Leon Theremin is finally reunited with the now aged Clara Rockmore. The reunion of these two would-be lovers grown hopelessly antique and seeming like specimens of another age in a Manhattan grown high-tech, is much like the film itself: poignant, melancholy, and satisfying. Leon Theremin died in 1993 at the age of 97. — R.C.

d, Steven M. Martin; p, Steven M. Martin; assoc p, Kate Carty, Frank De Marco, Brian Kelly, Amy Smith, Robert Stone; w, Steven M. Martin; ph, Frank DeMarco, Robert Stone, Cris Lombardi, Ed Lachman; ed, David Greenwald; m, Hal Willner; sound, Andy Green (mixer), Kim Aubry (mixer)

Documentary (PR: A MPAA: NR)

THEY BITE ★★½

(U.S.) 98m Trio Entertainment ~ MTI Home Video c

Donna Frotscher *(Melody Duncan)*; Nick Baldasare *(Mel Duncan)*; Christina Veronica *(Tammy)*; Charlie Barnett *(Larry)*; Ron Jeremy *(Darryl)*; George Mazzone *(Sam Nicholhoff)*; Alex Pirnie *(Rev. Rex Stoner)*; Patrick Williams *(Biff)*; Susie Owens *(Katie)*; Roy A. Peddie *(Brannigan)*; Blake Pickett *(Model)*; Thomas Cavanno *(Photographer)*; Ludy Goodson *(Mother)*; Joe Belitzky *(Father)*; Jeremy Steele *(Boy at Beach)*; Rebecca Moss; Haylie Moss *(Girls at Beach)*; Fred Smith *(Sheriff)*; Matthew Z. Cunningham *(Deputy)*; Travis McMillan *(Mike)*; Margarette McLellan *(Cashier)*; Jay May *(Dave)*; Tom Meserve *(Ron)*; Kathy Donnelly *(Leigh)*; Becky Harris *(Susan)*; Ben Gunter *(Hotel Desk Clerk)*; Alexander Zubatov *(Delivery Boy)*; James Noble *(Scientist #1)*; Jane Pitts *(Parishioner)*; John Vail *(Bartender)*; Vince Campiti *(Boyfriend)*; Julie Smith *(Wet T-Shirt Winner)*; Ty Wold *(Scientist #2)*; Steve Williams *(Van Driver)*; Cathy Craig *(Cashier)*; Pam Parker *(Debbie)*; Bruce Duncan *(Nightclub MC)*; Victoria Horton *(Waitress)*; Jeyer Brock *(Spritzer Sprayer)*; Chris King *(Bar Patron)*

Though it parodies exploitation cinema just as much as it honors it, THEY BITE is a highly entertaining horror/comedy that never condescends to the genre or its fans.

After a model (Blake Pickett) is killed by a humanoid sea monster during a Florida photo shoot, the photographer (Thomas

Cavanno) sends the pictures to the local sheriff, who in turn mails them to visiting ichthyologist Melody Duncan (Donna Frotscher). A mixup at her hotel lands the photos in the hands of porno filmmaker Mel Duncan (Nick Baldasare), and when his producer, Sam Nicholhoff (George Mazzone), sees them, he decides to turn their movie into a fish monster porn flick. After resolving the confusion over the photos, Melody and Mel agree to split the rights to the story of the real creatures, which are continuing to terrorize the area.

Soon, the group comes across the body of a creature that has been run down on the road and puts it in the back of a truck, figuring they're onto a gold mine. When they stop at a beachside bar to make a phone call, the place is attacked by more monsters. Right behind them, however, is another group of strangely suited figures, which vaporize the creatures and their victims and abscond with the unconscious Larry (Charlie Barnett), a member of the crew. He is spirited to the underwater spaceship of what prove to be aliens; when he is revived, he is jettisoned from the craft, and joins the others on the beach as the craft rises from the water and shoots off into the sky.

At one point in THEY BITE, someone remarks that fish monster movies never lose money: it is ironic, then, that this one, which was completed in 1992, took four years to be released, and then only on a minor video label. Director-writer Brett Piper is a veteran of Troma films, but THEY BITE bears few traces of the self-conscious smart-asser humor that mars so many low-budget horror satires. While it's immensely knowing about its B-movie forebears, it establishes its own sense of humor, and is marked by clever writing and some very witty dialogue.

Nor does Piper play his monster scenes for intentional cheesiness. Though the sea creature suits—designed by Piper himself, without credit—aren't quite state of the art, the sea creatures' attacks are handled with an effectively straight face. The sort of movie that might well have become a summer perennial during the drive-in era, THEY BITE is a treat for B-movie fans. *(Graphic violence, extensive nudity, sexual situations, extreme profanity.)* — M.G.

d, Brett Piper; p, William J. Links; exec p, James E. Links; w, Brett Piper; ph, Brett Tromie; m, Stephen Melillo; sound, David Molinari; fx, Cheap Tricks, Atlanta Film Effects; casting, Cavanno Productions; cos, Eastern Costume Rental

Horror/Comedy/Science Fiction (PR: O MPAA: NR)

THIEVES

(SEE: LES VOLEURS)

THIN LINE BETWEEN LOVE AND HATE, A ★★½

(U.S.) 107m Jackson-McHenry Productions; You Go Boy! Productions; Savoy Pictures ~ New Line c

Martin Lawrence *(Darnell)*; Lynn Whitfield *(Brandi)*; Regina King *(Mia)*; Bobby Brown *(Tee)*; Della Reese *(Ma Wright)*; Malinda Williams *(Erica)*; Daryl Mitchell *(Earl)*; Roger E. Mosley *(Smitty)*; Simbi Khali *(Adrienne)*; Tangie Ambrose *(Nikki)*; Wendy Robinson *(Gwen)*; Stacii Jae Johnson *(Peaches)*; Miguel A. Nunez Jr. *(Reggie)*; Faizon Love *(Manny)*; Michael Bell *(Marvis)*; Dartanyan Edmunds *(Rodney)*; Greer Bohanon *(Parking Attendant)*; Michael Taliferro *(Club Security #1)*; Tiny Lister *(Tyrone)*; Tracy Morgan *(Bartender)*; Tom Stillman *(Officer #1)*; Arkay Stevens *(Officer #2)*; Charles Walker *(Officer Evans)*

A THIN LINE BETWEEN LOVE AND HATE straddles the apparently thin line between a social realist 'hood melodrama and a light, romantic Eddie Murphy comedy. Despite some engaging moments, this oddball genre blend never comes together.

Martin Lawrence plays Darnell Martin, a ladies' man with a cocky attitude, who lives in Los Angeles. While working in a downtown club, Chocolate City, Darnell and his best friend, Tee (Bobby Brown), convince their boss, Smitty (Roger E. Mosley), that they could improve business if they had a stake in the hip nightspot themselves. That same day, Darnell runs into the wealthy, elegant realtor Brandi Webb (Lynn Whitfield), who ignores his sexual advances. Undaunted, Darnell pursues Brandi, despite his renewed interest in a childhood friend, Mia (Regina King), who has just returned from the Air Force and lives near his mother (Della Reese).

One night, Brandi accepts Darnell's open invitation to tour Chocolate City, only to slight him again. But Darnell refuses to give up on his latest conquest, boasting to Tee that he can bed Brandi without uttering the forbidden "L" word (love). Finally, through persistence and clever maneuvering, Darnell wins over Brandi, but, in the course of his love-making, he accidentally utters the "L" word. Darnell soon discovers that he prefers "hanging" in the 'hood with Mia to attending cocktail parties with Brandi, but it's too late.

Brandi refuses to be abandoned, just as she had been in her traumatic first marriage. When Darnell misses her birthday party, Brandi exacts revenge by vandalizing Darnell's car, his apartment, and the Chocolate City club. She even injures herself to get Darnell into trouble. Darnell tries to end the affair peaceably, but Brandi's delusions turn deadly. She plots to kill Darnell and almost succeeds with her plans, but Tee and Mia intervene in time to save their friend. Darnell settles down with Mia after the hair-raising experience.

Martin Lawrence, the director, co-writer, producer, and star of A THIN LINE BETWEEN LOVE AND HATE, patterns the lothario-gets-his-comeuppance plot after Eddie Murphy's BOOMERANG (1992), in which Lawrence played the best-friend role. (Perhaps inadvertently, A THIN LINE also resembles a hip, urban remake of PAL JOEY, with R&B replacing Rodgers and Hart.) On the plus side, Lawrence creates a loose, fun HOUSE PARTY-type atmosphere, and generously gives his talented co-stars well-scripted dialogue with which to work.

Surprisingly, Lawrence is less generous to himself: the deft and funny comic (on the TV show, "Martin" and in the concert film, YOU SO CRAZY) shortchanges himself by cutting off his comedy bits too soon and shooting them at too great a distance. Also, Lawrence cannot seem to decide whether he is making a serious FATAL ATTRACTION (IN THE 'HOOD) or a parody of that film in the manner of SO I MARRIED AN AX MURDERER (1993). To confuse matters even further, New Line Cinema marketed A THIN LINE BETWEEN LOVE AND HATE as a male answer to 1995's WAITING TO EXHALE, although that doesn't excuse Lawrence's sometimes immature and paranoid projections of female sexuality.

One expects better from this film if only because Lawrence has the potential to make a great vehicle for himself. Maybe next time he will draw more from his own unique resources and less from the bottomless well of commercial hit formulas. *(Violence, sexual situations, extreme profanity.)* — E.M.

d, Martin Lawrence; p, Douglas McHenry, George Jackson; exec p, Martin Lawrence; assoc p, Peaches Davis; co-p, David Raynr, Suzanne Broderick, William C. Carraro; w, Martin Lawrence, Bentley Kyle Evans, Kenny Buford, Kim Bass (from a story by Martin Lawrence); ph, Francis Kenny; ed, John Carter; m, Roger Troutman; prod d, Simon Dobbin; art d, David Lazan; set d, Tessa Posnansky; sound, David Barr Yaffe (mixer), Robert Alan Wald (mixer); fx, Beverly Hartigan, Ultimate Effects; casting,

Mary Gail Artz, Barbara Cohen; cos, Eduardo Castro; makeup, Stacye P. Branche; stunts, Kurt Bryant

Comedy **(PR: C MPAA: R)**

THREE IFS AND A MAYBE
(SEE: BIG SQUEEZE, THE)

THREE LIVES AND ONLY ONE DEATH ★★★½
(France/Chile) 123m Gemini Films; La Sept Cinema; Madragoa Filmes ~ New Yorker Films c

Marcello Mastroianni *(Mateo Strano/George Vickers/The Butler/Luc Allamand)*; Anna Galiena *(Tania)*; Marisa Paredes *(Maria)*; Melvil Poupaud *(Martin)*; Chiara Mastroianni *(Cecile)*; Arielle Dombasle *(Helene)*; Feodor Atkine *(Andre)*; Jean-Yves Gautier *(Mario)*; Jacques Pieiller *(Tania's Husband)*; Pierre Bellemare *(The Narrator)*; Smain *(Luca)*; Lou Castel *(First Beggar)*; Roland Topor *(Second Beggar)*; Jacques Delpi *(Third Beggar)*; Jean Badin *(Antoine Jose)*; Monique Melinand *(Mrs. Vickers)*; Bastien Vincent *(Carlito)*

Marcello Mastroianni buoyantly plays four roles in four tales in THREE LIVES AND ONLY ONE DEATH, a clever, intricate exercise in avant-garde storytelling. Critiquing various aspects of art, psychology and philosophy, Raul Ruiz's first film since 1990's THE GOLDEN BOAT is slightly more reserved than usual.

THREE LIVES AND ONLY ONE DEATH tells four tales, all set in Paris, that seem disparate at first, but in fact are related. In the first, Mastroianni plays Mateo Strano, a traveling salesman who returns to his wife Maria (Marisa Paredes) after a 20-year absence to change places with her new husband, Andre (Feodor Atkine). After their encounter in a bar, Mateo lures Andre to his apartment, where he kills him when Andre refuses to make the switch.

In the second story, Mastroianni plays George Vickers, a professor of "negative anthropology" at the Sorbonne, who, one day, leaves the home of his invalid mother and becomes a homeless beggar. On the street he meets Tania (Anna Galiena), a prostitute who also has a double life—as the president of a huge corporation. When Tania goes to jail for trying to murder her menacing ex-husband (Jacques Pieiller), George bails her out and the two get married.

In the third tale, Mastroianni plays a butler to a penniless couple, Cecile and Martin (Chiara Mastroianni and Melvil Poupaud) who inherit a mysterious mansion. However, eerie events at the estate drive the young lovers back into poverty.

In the fourth and final story, Mastroianni plays Luc Allamand, a wealthy businessman who nervously awaits a visit from his estranged family. The problem for Luc is that his family had always been imaginary—until now! A famous psychiatrist sorts out the confusion in Luc's life by explaining that he has a split personality. Thus, as Mateo, George, and the butler, Luc has been living separate lives.

THREE LIVES AND ONLY ONE DEATH functions best as a warped fairy tale that questions the notion of storytelling. While some of the stories are loosely based on works by Nathaniel Hawthorne, Ruiz and co-writer Pascal Bonitzer also pay tribute to Honore de Balzac and Jorge Luis Borges by collapsing all the stories into one in the final quarter and allowing the characters to discover their relationships to one another.

Aesthetically, THREE LIVES AND ONLY ONE DEATH shares much with the surrealist art of the 1920s: the images are irrational, funny and darkly unsettling. Ruiz also sprinkles in references to radical culture icons like Karl Marx and Jean-Luc Godard, and uses carefully controlled camerawork, production design and special effects to create a realistic urban world with fun-house mirror distortions.

Adding to the mix, composer Jorge Ariagada toys with Bernard Herrmann's themes from Alfred Hitchcock's late-period work, and the cast plays along perfectly with the director's games. Naturally, Mastroianni stands out in his four roles, but his daughter, Chiara, makes a surprisingly plain ingenue.

What's missing from THREE LIVES is that burst of creative energy that made the films of Luis Bunuel (L'AGE D'OR, BELLE DE JOUR) so distinct from other surrealist work. Ironically, both Bunuel and Ruiz were iconoclasts exiled from their native countries, but it is Ruiz who—in this film, at least—has softened his socio-political criticism. THREE LIVES AND ONLY DEATH is engaging entertainment, but it will hardly shock the sensibilities of the bourgeoisie. *(Violence, sexual situations, adult situations, substance abuse, profanity.)* — E.M.

d, Raul Ruiz; p, Paulo Branco; w, Raul Ruiz, Pascal Bonitzer; ph, Laurent Machuel; ed, Rodolfo Wedeles; m, Jorge Arriagada; prod d, Luc Chalon; sound, Gerard Rousseau, Laurent Poirier

Fantasy/Drama **(PR: C MPAA: NR)**

TIGER HEART ★
(U.S.) 87m PM Entertainment Group Inc. ~ PM Entertainment Group Inc. c

T. J. Roberts *(Eric)*; Jennifer Lyons *(Stephanie)*; Robert LaSardo *(Paulo)*; Rance Howard *(Mr. Johnson)*; Timothy Williams *(Brad)*; Carol Potter *(Cynthia)*; David Michael *(Bobby)*; Brian Gross *(Steve)*; Vincent DePalma *(Manny)*; Christopher Kriesa *(Nat)*; Gene Armor *(Randolph)*; Elena Sahagun *(Chi-Chi)*; Diane Klimaszewski *(Amy)*; Elaine Klimaszewski *(Amanda)*; Lorissa McComas *(Jill)*; Art Camacho *(Sensei)*; George Calil *(Jack)*; Gary Bullock *(Brad's Father)*

TIGER HEART is a juvenile, direct-to-video knockoff of RUMBLE IN THE BRONX, designed for the *Tiger Beat* set, starring pint-sized teen T.J. Roberts as a martial-arts expert who takes on a gang of thugs.

Eric (T.J. Roberts) and his buddy Brad (Timothy Williams) are looking for some summer fun before they start college. They go to a party but get kicked out by a rich kid named Steve (Brian Gross) who's in Eric's martial-arts class.

Meanwhile, a greasy hood named Paulo (Robert LaSardo), meets with a corrupt developer who orders him to scare a group of restaurant and store owners on a block where he wants to build a property. Paulo and his gang go to a convenience store where a pretty girl named Stephanie (Jennifer Lyons) works. Paulo tries to scare her uncle into selling his store, but he refuses. Eric just happens to be at the store buying some soda, so he comes to the rescue and beats up the gang.

Eric and Stephanie start to date and one night while they're out, Paulo and the gang go back to the store and threaten Stephanie's uncle, who has a heart attack. While he's recovering in the hospital, the developer convinces Stephanie to sell the store, but Eric shows up at the last minute and starts to fight the gang. Paulo escapes and takes Stephanie with him. Eric and his whole martial-arts class track the gang to a nightclub where a giant fight ensues. Eric saves Stephanie, and Paulo and the developer are arrested.

TIGER HEART is a thoroughly routine release from schlock-video purveyors PM Entertainment, whose films are notable for their explosions and huge fireballs, and little else.

Roberts, who used to be known as Ted Jan in his previous movies, is apparently trying to cultivate a hipper, tougher image, so he is billed as T.J. here. Unfortunately, with his skinny build and high voice, he's downright laughable as a wannabe teen martial-arts master, single-handedly defeating gangs of huge, leather-clad bad guys with tattoos and Hispanic accents.

The script is simply a formulaic RUMBLE rip-off, with little except teen fantasies, bad rock music, and puerile humor to fill in the time between the requisite fight scenes, which occur like clockwork about every 10 minutes. Like most of its ilk, there is an abundance of offensive ethnic and gay stereotyping and the acting is embarrassingly amateurish. *(Violence.)* — M.S.

d, Georges Chamchoum; p, Joseph Merhi, Richard Pepin; assoc p, T. J. Roberts, Bob Roberts; co-p, Marta Merrifield; w, William Applegate Jr.; ph, Maurice McGuire; ed, Kevin Mock, Ron Shaw; m, John Gonzalez; prod d, Jared Fleury; casting, Mark Sikes; cos, Lisa Dyehouse; makeup, Jori Jenae

Action/Martial Arts **(PR: C MPAA: PG-13)**

TIME TO KILL, A ★½

(U.S.) 128m Regency Enterprises; Arnon Milchan ~ Warner Bros. c

Matthew McConaughey *(Jake Brigance)*; Sandra Bullock *(Ellen Roark)*; Samuel L. Jackson *(Carl Lee Hailey)*; Kevin Spacey *(Rufus Buckley)*; Oliver Platt *(Harry Rex Vonner)*; Charles S. Dutton *(Sheriff Ozzie Walls)*; Brenda Ficker *(Ethel Twitty)*; Donald Sutherland *(Lucien Wilbanks)*; Kiefer Sutherland *(Freddie Cobb)*; Patrick McGoohan *(Judge Omar Noose)*; Ashley Judd *(Carla Brigance)*; Tonea Stewart *(Gwen Hailey)*; Rae'ven Larrymore Kelly *(Tonya Hailey)*; Darrin Mitchell *(Skip Hailey)*; LaConte McGrew *(Slim Hailey)*; Devin Lloyd *(Willie Hailey)*; John Diehl *(Tim Nunley)*; Chris Cooper *(Deputy Looney)*; Nicky Katt *(Billy Ray Cobb)*; Doug Hutchison *(Pete Willard)*; Kurtwood Smith *(Stup Sisson)*; Tim Parati *(Winston)*; Mark Whitman Johnson *(Deputy Hastings)*; Beth Grant *(Cora Cobb)*; Joe Seneca *(Reverend Isaiah Street)*; Anthony Heald *(Dr. Rodeheaver)*; Thomas Merdis *(Reverend Ollie Agee)*; Alexandra Kyle *(Hannah Brigance)*; Terry Loughlin *(Jury Foreman)*; Andy Stahl *(Reluctant Male Juror)*; Joe Bullen *(Joe Frank Perryman)*; Lorraine Middleton *(Blonde Woman Juror)*; Graham Timbes *(Male Juror)*; Jonathan Hadary *(Norman Reinfield)*; Benjamin Mouton *(Klan Bomber)*; Byron Jennings *(Brent Musgrove)*; Patrick Sutton *(Militant Teenager)*; Greg Lauren *(Taylor)*; Danny Nelson *(Bud Twitty)*; Mike Pniewski *(Deputy Tatum)*; Elizabeth Omilami *(Woman Angry at Klan)*; Lukas Cain *(Looney's Son)*; Stacy Rae Toyon *(Looney's Wife)*; Wayne DeHart *(Claude)*; Helen E. Floyd *(Waitress at Claude's)*; David Brian Williams *(Customer at Claude's)*; Octavia Spencer *(Roark's Nurse)*; Rebecca Koon *(Dell)*; James M. Crumley Jr. *(Guardsman Mackenvale)*; Jim Ritchie *(Tom Hardy)*; Perry Ritchie *(Sarah Hardy)*; Mike McLaren *(Administrator at Whitfield)*; Timothy F. Monich *(Reverend Fink)*; Leonard Thomas *(Man in Lumberyard)*; Brance H. Beamon *(Noose's Butler)*; Mildred J. Gilbreath *(Noose's Housekeeper)*; Will Crapps *(Minister)*; David U. Hodges *(Bailiff)*; Maggie Wade Dixon *(T.V. Anchor)*; Russell Hambline *(Old Man Bates)*; Robert Chapman *(Young Fisherman)*; Robert R. Bell Jr. *(Fisherman)*; Tommy McCullough *(Old Fisherman)*; Ryk St. Vincent *(Deputy)*; Bettina Rose *(Buckley's Secretary)*; Linda Calvin Johnson *(Sugar)*; Terrance Freeman *(Court Deputy)*; Alice Julius-Scott *(NAACP Woman)*; Dr. William Truly Jr. *(NAACP Man #1)*; Walter L. Hutchins *(NAACP Man #2)*; Jerry Hunt *(Electrical Company Worker)*; Howard Ballou *(Reporter #1 with Hastings)*; Todd Demers *(Reporter #1 with Jake)*; Stephanie Strickland *(Reporter #1 with Buckley)*; Kim Hendrix *(Reporter #2 with Buckley)*; Rob Jay *(Reporter #3 with Buckley)*; Sherri Hilton *(Reporter #2 with Jake)*; Steve Coulter *(Klansman)*; Jackie Stewart *(Fire Chief)*; Rosebud Dixon-Green *(Woman at Rally)*; M. Emmet Walsh (Dr. Willard Tyrell Bass—uncredited)

This over-hyped adaptation of John Grisham's freshman novel glorifies anti-law and uncivilized behavior. It doesn't even stick to a consistent argument, making it even more of a muddled misfire than it appears at first glance.

In Madison County, Mississippi, in and around the town of Canton, a pair of evil rednecks (Doug Hutchison and Nicky Katt) rape and leave for dead a ten-year-old African-American girl, Tonya Hailey (Rae'ven Larrymore Kelly). Sheriff Ozzie Walls (Charles S. Dutton) and his deputies arrest the men with a witness and clear-cut evidence. Nonetheless, Tonya's father, Carl Lee Hailey (Samuel L. Jackson) kills the men with automatic-weapons fire as they're marching to arraignment. He also maims Deputy Looney (Chris Cooper) in the process.

Hailey turns to struggling young lawyer Jake Brigance (Matthew McConaughey). Brigance, with few clients beating on his door, takes the case, with plans to plead Hailey temporarily insane. He soon realizes the case is a media bonanza, as questions arise about a fair trial for an African-American in a predominantly Caucasian town. Upping the stakes is arrogant District Attorney Rufus Buckley (Kevin Spacey), who has political ambitions tied to winning this case.

Soon, at the behest of Freddie Cobb (Kiefer Sutherland), the brother of one of the dead men, the Ku Klux Klan gets involved. Threats, explosives and burning crosses abound. Brigance's wife, Carla (Ashley Judd) and young daughter, Hannah (Alexandra Kyle), go visit her parents till things blow over.

Enter Bostonian scion Ellen Roark (Sandra Bullock), a top law student at nearby Ole Miss. The daughter of a famous lawyer herself, she repeatedly volunteers her help—which Brigance keeps refusing until she pulls his fat from the fire a couple of times.

As threats and racial tensions mount, Brigance huddles with his disbarred, idealistic mentor, Lucien Wilbanks (Donald Sutherland); his divorce-lawyer buddy, Harry Rex Vonner (Oliver Platt), and Roark, with whom he almost sleeps.

The day before the trial, Roark is kidnapped by the KKK, and Brigance's house is burned to the ground. Roark is eventually rescued by Tim Nunley (John Diehl), an FBI undercover agent who's been infiltrating the white-supremacist community.

Various obstacles arise, including Hailey's own admission on the stand that the rapists deserved to be killed and the revelation that Brigance's psychiatrist witness has served time for statutory rape. In spite of these troubles, Brigance's eloquence before the jury results in a not guilty verdict for Hailey.

A potboiler despite pretensions to Important Issues, the supremely glossy A TIME TO KILL is shockingly simple-minded. Brigance, suddenly ignoring the insanity plea in his summation, argues to the all-Caucasian jury that Hailey acted reasonably: What would *you* do if someone raped your daughter?

Even as summer popcorn fare, it's cheesy. The Perry Mason histrionics and Jake's wildly unethical courtroom behavior are beyond the pale. Director Joel Schumacher, best known for such pulp-fiction fare as BATMAN FOREVER (1995) and THE LOST BOYS (1987), likewise turns Cobb's audience with local KKK Grand Wizard Stump Sisson (Kurtwood Smith) into some Republic Serial/Fu Manchu bit of camp. And is there some unstated reason that Roark, who wants to be taken seriously, dresses sleazily in stretch tops with her lace bra showing through?

The smartest cast member is M. Emmet Walsh, playing defense witness Dr. Willard Tyrell: his appearance is unbilled. *(Graphic violence, sexual situations, profanity, adult situations.)* — F.L.

d, Joel Schumacher; p, Arnon Milchan, Michael Nathanson, Hunt Lowry, John Grisham; assoc p, William M. Elvin; w, Akiva Goldsman (based on the novel by John Grisham); ph, Peter

Menzies Jr.; ed, William Steinkamp; m, Elliot Goldenthal; prod d, Larry Fulton; art d, Richard Toyon; set d, Dorree Cooper; sound, Petur Hliddal (mixer), Roland Thai (designer); fx, Steve Galich, Andrew Adamson; casting, Mali Finn; cos, Ingrid Ferrin; makeup, Marietta Carter-Narcisse; stunts, Mickey Gilbert

Drama **(PR: C MPAA: R)**

TIMELESS ★★½

(U.S.) 84m TGOM Productions ~ Phaedra Cinema c

Peter Byrne *(Terry)*; Melissa Duge *(Lyrica)*; Joe Hart *(Flood)*; Michael Griffiths *(Tommy)*; Jim Cronin *(Dix)*; Larry Robinson *(Max)*; Tony Kruk *(Manny Gould)*; Marilise Tronto *(Grace)*; Thomas Grube; Marta Bukowski

In his low-budget first feature, filmmaker Chris Hart shows tremendous passion for the moving image. Similar care for the written word, however, would have helped.

Trying to raise enough money to flee an unhappy home run by an alcoholic father, in the absence of his mentally-ill mother, New York City youth Terry (Peter Byrne) reluctantly assists in theft, drugs, and gun-running. Racketeer Tommy (Michael Griffiths), Terry's regular employer, keeps moll Lyrica (Melissa Duge) on a tight leash as both personal concubine and star prostitute. Appointed her chaperone, Terry falls for Lyrica. The pair plot to escape together, Terry rightly assuming that Tommy won't care enough to take action. Unfortunately, the boy doesn't know that Lyrica has augmented their nest egg by ripping off Tommy's capital from a gun deal. Tommy and his hoods jump the fugitive lovers at a motel, and only Terry survives the shootout.

"How do you feel?" asks Terry during a brief beachfront idyll. "Timeless," responds Lyrica—one of the few haunting lines in a thin script. Hart focuses his attention on creative visuals: A poetic melange of tight closeups and images of waves lapping over sand; coarse-grained monochromatic imagery; and whole sequences between Terry and Lyrica that unfold in still photos (a technique recalling "mod" '60s cinema a la TOM JONES). Limpid romance permeates TIMELESS; a spare subplot has Terry's father staggering out on a successful quest to reunite with his own beloved spouse. Documentary-raw NYC settings and unglamorized performers temper the sentiment. When filmmakers throw every technique they know at the screen it's often an act of desperation, but Hart's debut sincerely justifies the arty approach. There wouldn't be much film without one. *(Violence, profanity, adult situations, sexual situations, substance abuse.)* — C.C.

d, Chris Hart; p, Chris Hart, Patricia Bice; co-p, Joe Hart; w, Chris Hart; ph, Chris Norr; ed, Chris Hart; m, Joseph V. Hart; art d, Beth Curtis

Crime/Drama/Romance **(PR: C MPAA: NR)**

TIN CUP ★★★

(U.S.) 133m New Regency Productions; Warner Bros. ~ Warner Bros. c

Kevin Costner *(Roy "Tin Cup" McAvoy)*; Rene Russo *(Dr. Molly Griswold)*; Cheech Marin *(Romeo Posar)*; Don Johnson; Linda Hart *(Doreen)*; Dennis Burkley *(Earl)*; Lou Myers *(Clint)*; Rex Linn *(Dewey)*; Richard Lineback *(Curt)*; Mickey Jones *(Turk)*; Michael Milhoan *(Boone)*; George Perez *(Jose)*; Gary McCord *(Himself)*; Craig Stadler *(Himself)*; Peter Jacobsen *(Himself)*; Jim Nantz *(CBS Announcer)*; Ken Venturi *(CBS Announcer)*; Ben Wright *(CBS Announcer)*; Frank Chirkinian *(CBS Coordinating Producer)*; Lance Barrow *(CBS Director)*; Brian Hammons *(1st Golf Channel Announcer)*; Mike Ritz *(2nd Golf Channel Announcer)*; Peter Kostis *(Golf Channel Reporter)*; Jimmy Roberts *(ESPN Reporter)*; George Michael *(Sports Machine Host)*

If golf on the small screen often sparks little more than yawns, is there any hope for golf on the big screen? Writer-director Ron Shelton, who has built films around baseball (BULL DURHAM, COBB) and basketball (WHITE MEN CAN'T JUMP), makes a credible attempt with TIN CUP. While the film is not exactly a "birdie," it is a respectable par on a tough hole.

Roy "Tin Cup" McAvoy (Kevin Costner) is a former college gold star (whatever that is), part-time alcoholic, and full-time golf pro at a ramshackle driving range in West Texas. ("Last chance to hit golf balls for 520 miles," the sign reads.) One day, two visitors rouse him from his underachieving torpor. First, the town's newest and only psychotherapist, Dr. Molly Griswold (Rene Russo), shows up for a golf lesson with a short skirt and a discerning eye for Tin Cup's many charming character flaws; second, his former college rival, now big-time golf pro David Simms (Don Johnson) drops by with an offer for Tin Cup to join him at a prestigious local tournament—as his caddie. Already ducking the IRS and deeply in hock to a former girlfriend, McAvoy takes the job.

Their partnership is cut short when Tin Cup openly criticizes his boss for his conservative play. Simms fires him. Insult is added to injury as Simms turns out to be Molly's boyfriend. His ardor immediately stoked, McAvoy vows to impress Molly by qualifying for the U.S. Open and whipping Simms. Qualify he does, but not without a struggle with the "inner demons" which Molly diagnoses as a juvenile fixation on doing everything his way.

Things go no differently at the U.S. Open. After setting a course record and putting himself in a position to win, Tin Cup insists on going for a gloriously impossible drive over a water hazard on the last hole of the last round. He misses—and insists on trying again. And again. After multiple failures, he finally does make the shot. With Molly at his side, Tin Cup becomes the most celebrated also-ran in Open history.

Shelton (with co-writer John Norville) has basically resurrected the formula of his biggest success here: like BULL DURHAM (1988), TIN CUP is a combination of sports, poetry, femmes and trash talk that mostly works well. Unlike his work in BULL DURHAM, though, Costner brings a winning boyishness to this character, at one point mining real pathos out of a case of "the shanks" in his golf swing. Essentially, he has taken the role played by Tim Robbins in the other picture but retained an air of ill-deserved hard luck. Costner also gets good comic support from a suitably neurotic Russo (though she is no Susan Sarandon) and Cheech Marin (in a refreshingly restrained turn).

In TIN CUP, as before, Shelton uses sports as a stage for dramatizing his own notions of character-as-destiny. While the theme that one can lose the game and still be a winner is hardly new, it looks veritably Sophoclean next to the "just win baby" sensibility behind other Hollywood sports movies, such as the ROCKY II-V series.

Shelton's biggest obstacle, however, is the nature of this particular game: for many viewers, the stakes in a sport where one barely ever breaks a sweat just aren't high enough. Those who can't appreciate the many cameos by professional golfers (Greg Stadler, et al.) may not get the rest, either. *(Sexual situations, profanity.)* — N.N.

d, Ron Shelton; p, Gary Foster, David Lester; exec p, Arnon Milchan; assoc p, Karin Freud, Kellie Davis; w, Ron Shelton, John Norville; ph, Russell Boyd; ed, Paul Seydor, Kimberly Ray; m, William Ross; prod d, James Bissell; art d, Gae Buckley, Chris

Burian-Mohr; set d, Ric McElvin; sound, Kirk Francis; casting, Victoria Thomas, Ed Johnston; cos, Carol Oditz

Romance/Comedy/Sports (PR: C MPAA: R)

TO GILLIAN ON HER 37TH BIRTHDAY ★★★

(U.S.) 93m Rastar/David E. Kelley ~ Triumph c

Peter Gallagher *(David Lewis)*; Michelle Pfeiffer *(Gillian Lewis)*; Claire Danes *(Rachel Lewis)*; Laurie Fortier *(Cindy Bayles)*; Wendy Crewson *(Kevin Dollof)*; Bruce Altman *(Paul Wheeler)*; Kathy Baker *(Esther Wheeler)*; Freddie Prinze Jr. *(Joey Bost)*; Rachel Seidman-Lockamy *(Megan Weeks)*; Lori New *(Blonde on the Beach)*; Danny Crook *(Lifeguard)*; Seth Green *(Danny)*; Todd Haven *(Paramedic)*

Acclaimed television producer David E. Kelley ("Chicago Hope", "Picket Fences") makes a foray into the realm of feature films with this wispy drama about a husband so in love with his wife's ghost he risks losing his daughter. Michelle Pfeiffer, *Mrs.* David Kelley, adds her star-shine to the movie, playing the departed.

Two years ago, David Lewis (Peter Gallagher) lost his beloved wife in a boating accident; since then, he's immersed himself in behavior that runs the gamut from eccentric to downright crazy. He's left his Harvard professorship to hole up in a beachhouse on Nantucket; and at night, he takes to the sand and hallucinates that Gillian (Pfeiffer) joins him for walks, talks, and moonlight swims.

Over Labor Day weekend, David and his teenage daughter, Rachel (Claire Danes), are joined by his in-laws: Gillian's sister, Esther (Kathy Baker), and her quip-happy husband, Paul (Bruce Altman). Also in the house is Rachel's best friend, Cindy (Laurie Fortier), who's *really* blossomed over the summer. Paul and Esther have mistakenly brought along a date for David, a woman named Kevin (Wendy Crewson). How bad an idea that is becomes apparent when David reminds Esther that the weekend coincides with both the anniversary of Gillian's death and what would have been her 37th birthday. What was supposed to be a fun, getaway weekend of karaoke sing-alongs and sand castle building becomes, at Esther's behest, a referendum on David's sanity. His midnight rendezvous with Gillian, and the revelation of a suicide attempt, confirm her worst fears. She announces plans to petition a court for custody of Rachel.

David accuses Esther of trying to take Rachel from him in an effort to grab some of the love Gillian and he shared—and which he still clings to—but which she and Paul lack. It's not such a far-fetched charge since Paul seems to be considering an affair with Cindy. The pressure builds until Rachel, who seems well-adjusted, explodes, and it becomes apparent that she has put off dealing with her grief to protect her father. David agrees to let Esther take Rachel, but after a talk with Gillian, he realizes he has to let go of his wife and hold on to his daughter.

Kelley adapted the screenplay for TO GILLIAN from Michael Brady's play, and fans of Kelley's TV work will immediately recognize what attracted him to it. On "Picket Fences," he loved to bring the show's extended family of characters together for a special occasion, and then have them hash out their issues. With respect to "how they hash," TO GILLIAN displays weaknesses borne of its theatrical origins: scenes are staged with deliberately showy fronts. The dialogue is too often glib and unctuous.

Pfeiffer's presence serves to draw attention to what otherwise would be a low profile production, but she also serves to upset the drama's balance. When she appears, always in luminous moonlight, she's so amazingly gorgeous you can't blame David for still being desperately in love with her. Esther's insensitivity (a sister wouldn't remember such significant anniversaries?) casts her not just as the heavy, but as a bitch. This positions Gallagher with the opportunity to play victim, open wide his blue eyes, gaze wistfully, and provoke tears from female audience members, but such obvious calculation wraps the first two-thirds of TO GILLIAN in an air of artificiality.

Then comes a scene in which Danes must play charming, sick, embarrassed, and angry—all the while playing drunk; doing so, she never hits a false note. After that, Rachel dreams of seeing her mother, and Danes is so believable and affecting, and Rachel's grief emerges as so authentic and poignant, David's treacle is pushed aside and Rachel becomes the focal point of the story. At this point, TO GILLIAN becomes her movie, and she manages to single-handedly redeem it. *(Profanity.)* — P.R.

d, Michael Pressman; p, Marykay Powell, David E. Kelley; co-p, Terry Morse; w, David E. Kelley (based on the play by Michael Brady); ph, Tim Suhrstedt; ed, William Scharf; m, James Horner; prod d, Linda Pearl; art d, Michael Atwell; set d, Linda Pearl; sound, David Kirschner (mixer), Dessie Markovsky (design), Emile Razpopov (design); fx, Shirley Montefusco, Vincent Montefusco; casting, Lynn Stalmaster; cos, Deborah L. Scott; makeup, John R. Bayless; stunts, Ernie Orsatti

Drama/Romance (PR: C MPAA: PG-13)

TOLLBOOTH ★★

(U.S.) 108m Roadkill Films; Sneak Preview Productions ~ New Line Home Video c

Fairuza Balk *(Doris)*; Lenny Van Dohlen *(Jack)*; Will Patton *(Dash Pepper)*; Louise Fletcher *(Lillian)*; Seymour Cassel *(Larry Borders/Leon Borders)*; James Wilder *(Vic)*; William Katt *(Waggy)*; Kathryn Klvana *(Young Lillian)*; Roberta Hanley *(TV Reporter Twyla)*; Ed Amatrudo *(Cop #1)*; Robert Deacon *(Vice Cop Jim)*; Mark Macaulay *(Cop #2)*; Dan Fitzgerald *(Head Cop)*; Violet Carpenter *(Mrs. Drake)*; Rene Lavan *(Julio)*; Mal Jones *(Frank)*; Jody Wilson *(Taxi Dispatcher)*; Xavier Coronel *(Money Delivery Guy #1)*; David Arisco *(Money Delivery Guy #2)*; Georgia Cranford *(Boy)*; Alexandra Nunez *(Young Doris)*; Laird Stuart *(Desk Sergeant)*; Kevin Bailey *(Barfly)*

A would-be romantic comedy with a video-box cover designed to say "erotic drama," this determinedly quirky tale of little guys with little dreams in the quaint and oddball Florida Keys is patronizing, forced, and worst of all, unfunny.

Jack (Lenny Von Dohlen) works a quiet tollbooth on a two-lane road in the Keys. He dreams of becoming a Miami vice cop. Jack dates Doris (Fairuza Balk), a solemn yet professionally flirty young gas-station attendant. Doris believes that her long-ago runaway father, Leon Borders (Seymour Cassel), will return someday and have to stop for gas or to pay the toll. She loves Jack, but is "saving" herself—except for athletic trysts with Jack's friend, bait-shop owner and novelist-wannabe Dash Pepper (Will Patton).

Jack, anxious to get his life moving, searches for Leon—who shows up on his own, driving a Checker cab. He s a belligerent, roadkill-eating, knife-wielding creep. He tries to kill Jack for his nosiness, but gets accidentally electrocuted on a bug zapper. To avoid telling Doris he killed her father, panicky Jack has Dash get rid of Leon's body. He abruptly also decides to take Leon's taxi and become a cab driver. Concurrently, Lillian snaps to, and Doris accepts that her dad's not coming back. Dash grinds Leon's body into "secret recipe" bait. Jack and Doris get married, and Dash publishes a novel based on the events.

Filmed in 1993 and shown the following year in festivals, TOLLBOOTH weaves from genre to genre—psychodrama, black comedy, symbolist fable—like a drunken driver. The only genre this feature really belongs to, however, is "pretentious first film." The main actors acquit themselves remarkably well, given the material; William Katt, perhaps through last-minute editing, has only about two lines as the gas-station manager. Writer-director Salome Breziner uses alarmingly trite symbolism, such as a moth flying too close to the light. Further muddying the pointless and perplexing screenplay are undistinguished direction, a couple of non-sequitur jump cuts, and a squawking soundtrack of bad musical choices. *(Violence, sexual situations, adult situations, profanity.)* — F.L.

d, Salome Breziner; p, Steven J. Wolfe; exec p, Herschel Weingrod, Robert M. Bennett, Paul Rich, Rena Ronson; assoc p, David Goodman; w, Salome Breziner; ph, Henry Vargas; ed, Peter Teschner; m, Adam Gorgoni; prod d, Brenden Barry; sound, Carl Carden; casting, Linda Francis, Cheryl Louden, Beth Sale, Paul Tannenbaum; cos, Kelly Zitrick; makeup, Kelcey Fry

Drama/Comedy/Crime **(PR: O MPAA: R)**

TOO FAST, TOO YOUNG ★

(U.S.) 92m Mid Metro Productions ~ Monarch Home Video c

Michael Ironside *(Capt. Floyd Anderson)*; Kasia Figura *(Kaddy Havel)*; James Wellington *(Chase Parrish)*; Patrick Tiller *(Dalton Parrish)*; Marshall Bell *(Detective Quentin Thompson)*; Richard Riehle *(Sergeant)*; Randy Crowder *(Officer Bullock)*; Charlie Dierkop *(Businessman)*; David Darmstaedter *(Desk Officer)*; Jon Chardiet *(Gang Leader)*; Beverly Graham *(Bank Teller)*; Robert Gentili *(Gypsy Joe)*

In this woozy caper film about how easy it is for adolescents to fall in with the wrong crowd—in this case, a criminal relative—the gravest danger for the young is close proximity to a robbery.

Raised by his antisocial cousin Dalton (Patrick Tiller), loyal Chase Parrish (James Wellington) can't muster a polite "no" when Dalton insists that he help in an armored car robbery. A petty thief appalled by violence, Chase is an easy mark for wild man Dalton, who left a slew of dead cops in his path when he recently broke out of prison. Standing between Chase and Dalton is Chase's main squeeze Kaddy (Kasia Figura), who declares that she'll leave him if Chase drives the getaway car. Local official Capt. Floyd Anderson (Michael Ironside) knows that fugitive con Dalton is planning a robbery, but doesn't know how to prevent it.

The heist is on. Dalton casually kills van guards, flees with his cut of the caper, and slyly informs the police about Chase's planned rendezvous with the duo's fence, Gypsy Joe (Robert Gentili). While Chase and Gypsy Joe shoot it out with Capt. Anderson's men, Dalton attempts to rape Kaddy, who stabs him in self-defense. Gunfire kills Gypsy Joe, but Chase, only wounded, escapes. Capt. Anderson spots Dalton attacking Kaddy and shoots him—but allows Chase and Kaddy to escape.

Beyond the eternal lesson that crime doesn't pay, all this film has to offer is a bombastic screenplay full of cheesy one-liners, a love-purifies-all crime film formula that glamorizes lawbreaking as a pastime of mixed-up, misunderstood adolescents, and comically bad acting by Tiller, who threatens to implode from his own histrionics, and by the zoftig Figura, about whom it can kindly be said that, as an actress, she cuts quite a "figura." The rest is standard mad-dog-killer/corruption-of-innocence pap with Ironside edited into the violent brouhaha like a judgmental cigar store Indian. *(Graphic violence, extreme profanity, nudity, sexual situations.)* — R.P.

d, Tim Everitt; p, Verna Mitchell, Tom Gamble; exec p, Cico Dammico, Stefano Dammico, Robert Nau, Kimberly McClain; w, Tim Everitt; ed, Ron Cabreros; m, Robert O. Ragland; sound, Tom Boyle; fx, Tassilo Burr; makeup, Geoff Leavitt; stunts, Spiro Rozato

Crime/Action **(PR: C MPAA: R)**

TRACKS OF A KILLER ★★½

(U.S./Canada) 100m James Shavick Film Co.; Libra Pictures ~ LIVE Entertainment c

James Brolin *(David Hawkner)*; Wolf Larsen *(Patrick Hausman)*; Howard Storey *(Executive)*; Akiko Morison *(Sally)*; Kelly LeBrock *(Claire Hawkner)*; Courtney Taylor *(Bella)*; George Touliatos *(McCready)*; Ken Camroux *(Sheriff)*

If a direct-to-video movie can't be good, it can at least be campily entertaining. At an early juncture, this schizophrenic enterprise abandons the pretense of being a spiky thriller about an imperiled lady and correctly chooses to become a crude black comedy about a resourceful dame turning the tables on a psychotic.

Self-made, pompous tycoon David Hawkner (James Brolin) toys with retirement from the company he built. Before turning over the reigns, however, he invites a corporate ladder-climber, Patrick Hausman (Wolf Larsen), and his diabetic wife, Bella (Courtney Taylor), to accompany him and his wife, Claire (Kelly LeBrock), on a wilderness weekend to test the upstart's mettle. Impatient with David's macho posturing, devious Patrick takes matters into his own hands by hacksawing David's snowmobile. Unfortunately, the women choose to cruise the mountainside in the sabotaged vehicle, and Bella is accidentally killed. Doctoring David's spare tank with water before David takes the snowbike to get aid 100 miles away, Patrick also dismantles the distress radio so bruised Claire can't signal for help.

Barely strong enough to foil Patrick's plan to inject her with Bella's insulin, Claire wounds Patrick with a pen, escapes his clutches, and later sticks him with the insulin needle. Although she neatly trusses Patrick up, a neighbor, Mr. McCready (George Touliatos), innocently unties her tormentor. After blasting McCready and his snowmobile into flames, Patrick shoots a recaptured Claire, finishes off the badly burned McCready, and corners the wounded Claire in a shed. When David and mountain troops show up, Claire tosses Patrick a pistol smeared with superglue which sticks to his hand. When the police spot Patrick brandishing a weapon at them, they shoot him down, no questions asked.

Can it be this thriller's intention that Brolin's tycoon Hawkner is such an arrogant control freak, you can't entirely blame Patrick for wanting to murder him out of the company ownership? Fortunately for the film and for viewers, Brolin absents himself for much of the film, leaving a hard-working LeBrock to play hide-and-seek with her husband's nemesis.

Baiting each other like a secret society of S&M weekenders, snarling LeBrock and eye-popping Larsen seem invigorated by vocational cruelty. Why doesn't the unhinged yuppie just toss Claire off the nearest crevice? Because the audience is having too much fun watching them duel with hot tongs or industrial-size sewing hooks. Jolted suspensefully by Claire's survival antics, the film is aesthetically sloppy but schlockily diverting. LeBrock and Larsen slamdance each other with exuberantly lunatic over-acting, recalling the heyday of such past ham masters as Jack Palance, Robert Newton, Susan Tyrell, and Shelley Winters. *(Graphic violence, extreme profanity, extensive nudity.)* — R.P.

d, Harvey Frost; p, James Shavick; exec p, Lance H. Robbins; w, Michael Cooney; ph, Bruce Worrall; ed, Stein Myhrstad; m, Barron Abramovitch; art d, Lana Kozack; set d, Margaux MacKenzie; sound, John Megill (mixer); fx, Rae Reedyk; casting,

Laura Schiff, Rosanne Laurence; cos, Morgan Montgomery; makeup, Diana Davison; stunts, Scott Ateah, Marc Akerstream

Thriller/Horror/Comedy **(PR: C MPAA: R)**

TRAINSPOTTING ★★★½

(U.K.) 93m Figment Films; Noel Gay Motion Picture Company; Channel Four Films ~ Miramax c

Ewan McGregor *(Mark Renton)*; Ewen Bremner *(Spud)*; Jonny Lee Miller *(Sick Boy)*; Kevin McKidd *(Tommy)*; Robert Carlyle *(Begbie)*; Kelly Macdonald *(Diane)*; Peter Mullan *(Swanney)*; James Cosmo *(Mr. Renton)*; Eileen Nicholas *(Mrs. Renton)*; Susan Vidler *(Allison)*; Pauline Lynch *(Lizzy)*; Shriley Henderson *(Gail)*; Stuart McQuarrie *(Gavin/US Tourist)*; Irvine Welsh *(Mikey)*; Dale Winton *(Game Show Host)*; Keith Allen *(Dealer)*; Kevin Allen *(Andreas)*; Annie Louise Ross *(Gail's Mother)*; Billy Riddoch *(Gail's Father)*; Fiona Bell *(Diane's Mother)*; Vincent Friel *(Diane's Father)*; Hugh Ross *(Man 1)*; Victor Eadie *(Man 2)*; Kate Donnelly *(Woman)*; Finlay Welsh *(Sheriff)*; Eddie Nestor *(Estate Agent)*

TRAINSPOTTING. 1: British hobby of wasting long periods of time loitering near train tracks watching trains approach, pass, and disappear. 2: an unforgettably gritty, blackly funny, offensive, remarkable British film from the writer-director-producer team that gave us 1994's SHALLOW GRAVE.

Our tour guide on this strange ride is Mark Renton (Ewan MacGregor), the film's on-again, off-again heroin addict narrator. Speaking for both himself and the disenfranchised youth of Britain in general, he asks: "Choose life. Choose a job. . . . Choose your future. . . . Why would anybody want to do a thing like that?" Disheartened by life in Scotland—a place worse even than England, Renton explains, since the English are merely "wankers," while Scotland was "colonized by wankers" and drawn to the easy camaraderie that binds addicts—he and his friends wander aimlessly through life, getting drunk, mugging tourists, deliberately screwing up job interviews in order to maintain their place on the dole, and generally looking for ways to kill the time between highs. Along for the ride are fellow heroin junkies Spud (Ewan Bremner) and Sick Boy (Jonny Lee Miller), as well as the hot-tempered Francis Begbie (Robert Carlyle).

After Renton comes dangerously close to overdosing, his parents intervene, locking him in his bedroom until he sweats it out of his system. Determined to stay off drugs, Renton heads to London to get a real job as a real estate agent. Just when it looks like he's broken free from his old life, Begbie and Sick Boy show up with dreams of scoring on a big drug deal: seems they've come across a generous amount of heroin—all they need is 2,000 pounds from Renton and someone (i.e., Renton) to "test" it (i.e., shoot up). With Renton slipping again into his old ways, they successfully unload the drugs for the sum of 16,000 pounds—not enough to make them rich, but easy money just the same. Before a split can be made, though, Renton takes the money for himself, and as he disappears into the London streets, he warns us: "I'm buying the house in the suburbs. I'm buying the big TV. I'm choosing life. I'm gonna be just like you."

British Gen-Xers, hungry for their own pop-culture-meets-highbrow-cinema hit a la PULP FICTION, eagerly embraced TRAINSPOTTING, making it a hit of phenomenal stature long before it crossed the Atlantic to the United States. Indeed, there is much to recommend TRAINSPOTTING: screenwriter John Hodge's flawless adaptation of Irvine Welsh's controversial novel gracefully conveys the characters' slacker-esque ennui, as well as the reluctant joy they feel when indulging their addictions, eliciting from the audience a seemingly impossible degree of sympathy toward these directionless dregs. Add the singular vision of director Danny Boyle, who populates the film with a host of indelible images—Renton's headlong dive into Scotland's filthiest commode in search of a heroin suppository, his hallucination of a demonic baby crawling across the ceiling, an addict sinking slowly into a carpeted grave—and the result is an audacious, inventive, fearless romp through some pretty awful terrain.

Credit must also be extended to MacGregor, whose portrayal is equal parts heroic and pathetic particularly during his ridiculously awkward attempts at integrating into mainstream society, halfheartedly hawking real estate in an ill-fitting suit that barely covers his addict-thin limbs. Noteworthy, too, is Carlyle as Begbie, whom Renton and the others seem to keep as a friend simply because it's safer than being his enemy—but only slightly.

Much of the controversy surrounding TRAINSPOTTING came from its stance on drug use and addiction. The way Renton and his buddies unapologetically embrace their lifestyle of drugs, violence, squalor, and death led many critics to identify its position as somewhat ambivalent, neither glorifying nor demonizing the characters or their drug of choice. However, on closer inspection some less-than-ambivalent anti-heroin themes become apparent. Heroin is responsible for the deaths of two (relative) innocents: Sick Boy's infant son, who succumbs to crib death while the others are off on a nod, and Tommy, the group's only sober friend, who contracts AIDS from his first experimental hit. Larceny to pay for heroin lands Spud in jail, while the promise of a heroin sale lures the maniacal Begbie to London in search of the briefly-rehabilitated Renton. Even when Renton ultimately abandons his emulation of mainstream life, he does not return to the heroin flop houses he and his friends once haunted.

For its American release, Boyle agreed to re-record much of the dialogue, which was reportedly almost impenetrably authentic in its use of Scottish brogues and slang; in extreme cases, particularly indistinguishable lines were subtitled—a practice that seems slightly condescending, as the characters *are* speaking English, after all. *(Graphic violence, extensive nudity, sexual situations, substance abuse, extreme profanity.)* — B.T.

d, Danny Boyle; p, Andrew Macdonald; w, John Hodge (based on the novel by Irvine Welsh); ph, Brian Tufano; ed, Masahiro Hirakubo; prod d, Kave Quinn; art d, Tracey Gallacher; sound, Colin Nicolson (recordist); fx, Grant Mason, Tony Steers; casting, Gail Stevens, Andy Pryor; cos, Rachael Fleming; makeup, Graham Johnston; stunts, Terry Forrestal

AAN Best Adapted Screenplay: John Hodge

Drama **(PR: O MPAA: R)**

TREES LOUNGE ★★★

(U.S.) 94m LIVE Entertainment; Addis/Wechsler; Hanley-Wyman; Seneca Falls Productions ~ Orion Pictures c

Steve Buscemi *(Tommy Basilio)*; Mark Boone Jr. *(Mike)*; Chloe Sevigny *(Debbie)*; Michael Buscemi *(Raymond)*; Anthony LaPaglia *(Rob)*; Elizabeth Bracco *(Theresa)*; Daniel Baldwin *(Jerry)*; Carol Kane *(Connie)*; Bronson Dudley *(Bill)*; Eszter Balint *(Marie)*; Kevin Corrigan *(Matthew)*; Debi Mazar *(Crystal)*; Annette Arnold *(Sandy)*; Steven Randazzo *(Vic)*; Suzanne Shepherd *(Jackie)*; Rockets Redglare *(Stan)*; Michael Imperioli *(George)*; Samuel L. Jackson *(Wendell)*; Seymour Cassel *(Uncle Al)*; Mimi Rogers *(Patty)*; Victor Arnold *(Tony Basilio)*; John Ventimiglia *(Johnny)*; Joe Lisi *(Harry)*; Richard Boes *(Freddie)*; Brooke Smith *(Tina)*; Carina Finn *(Anna)*; Michael Storms *(Little Boy)*; Irma St. Paule *(Grandma)*; Daniella Rich *(Samantha)*;

Marilyn Chris *(Josie Basilio)*; Christina Gildea *(Marie's Mother)*; Marissa Lanzello *(Lisa)*; Roberta Hanley *(Roberta)*; Larry Guillard Jr. *(James)*; Io Tillett Wright *(Little Girl)*; Lucian Buscemi *(Crystal's Son)*; Bianca Bakija *(Kelly)*; Charles Newmark *(Puck)*

Character actor Steve Buscemi's debut as a writer-director, TREES LOUNGE is a lightly likable film about a nice-guy loser. Budgeted at a thrifty $1,500,000, the film wears its "worthy indie" credentials like a badge of honor though there really isn't much here that we haven't seen before—and better. Buscemi fans will doubtlessly enjoy it more than the casual viewer.

Tommy Basilio (Steve Buscemi) is a 31-year-old barfly killing time in suburban Valley Stream, a white working-class community in Long Island, NY. His favorite haunt is the Trees Lounge, the bar over which he lives. An unemployed auto mechanic, Tommy can't get his own car-or his life—to run properly. His pregnant former girlfriend, Theresa (Elizabeth Bracco) has taken up with his best friend/former employer Rob (Anthony LaPaglia), who fired Tommy after discovering that he had embezzled money from the garage.

Hanging out at "the Trees," Tommy tries new tricks and scams to pick up women and to extend his shaky line of credit. Other regulars include Mike (Mark Boone Jr.), a scruffy newcomer; Bill (Bronson Dudley), a stonily quiet alcoholic senior; and bleary-eyed barmaid Connie (Carol Kane). Tommy learns that Mike owns a fleet of five ice-cream trucks, including one driven by the black elder-youth team of Wendell (Samuel L. Jackson) and James (Larry Guillard Jr.), but there are no openings. He finally lands a job after one of the drivers, his ribald but beloved Uncle Al (Seymour Cassel), suffers a fatal heart attack while on his route. Tommy takes over the route but has little success until he informally teams up with Theresa's niece Debbie (Chloe Sevigny).

While ostensibly sleeping over at a friend's place, Debbie and her friend go out to Trees Lounge late one night armed with fake IDs. Hooking up with Tommy and Mike, the girls end up at Mike's house where they add marijuana and cocaine to their party favors. The evening breaks up when Mike's estranged wife Marie (Eszter Balint) calls home. Finding Debbie too stoned to go home, Tommy takes her to his apartment where they end up making out. The next day, Debbie is "busted" by her brutish father Jerry (Daniel Baldwin), who learns that she was not where she claimed to be. She refuses to tell the truth even after a beating but, seeing that there is no future with Tommy, leaves to live in NYC with a friend. Learning from Connie that Tommy and Debbie had left the bar together, Jerry tracks him down, beats him with a baseball bat and trashes the ice cream truck. Tommy returns to the bar where he learns that Bill had been hospitalized after experiencing an attack. Sitting on Bill's stool, he nurses his drink.

Clearly a personal project, TREES LOUNGE is set in Buscemi's hometown, incorporates much of his autobiographical data, and overflows with his family and friends. Some fairly big names flit by, ennobled by their lack of makeup. Even the inelegant compositions, drab colors, and rudimentary camerawork add to the subtle air of self-congratulation. All this "integrity" may impress youngsters who are unfamiliar with the works of actor-writer-director John Cassavetes. Buscemi's script was inspired by his attendance of a Cassavetes retrospective at NYC's Museum of Modern Art. Like his muse, Buscemi aspires to create a somewhat improvisatory actor-oriented cinema that is sensitive to the nuances of suburban living. This first effort is, however, at best, "Cassavetes Light," far less mad, risky, and thoughtful than the illustrious originals.

Despite its ragged edges, TREES LOUNGE is ultimately too neat and heavy-handed. Characters are presented in an obvious manner and no one, especially the protagonist, is allowed to come off too badly. This may be less indicative of a tolerant sensibility than a hesitance to make the audience too uncomfortable. A case in point is the handling of the fateful nocturnal encounter between Tommy and Debbie. Do they or don't they? Tommy claims they did not but Jerry won't listen. Such a momentous plot element is rendered unnecessarily ambiguous. Such reticence appears calculated to allow Buscemi's character to complete the story with his likability intact. TREES LOUNGE is a pleasant diversion that offers strong performances (especially by Sevigny) and a convincing sense of place. *(Profanity, substance abuse, adult situations, violence.)* — K.G.

d, Steve Buscemi; p, Brad Wyman, Chris Hanley; exec p, Julie Silverman Yorn, Nick Wechsler; assoc p, Christina Larsson; co-p, Kelley Forsyth, Sarah Vogel; w, Steve Buscemi; ph, Lisa Rinzler; ed, Kate Williams; m, Evan Lurie; prod d, Steve Rosenzweig; art d, Jennifer Alex; casting, Walken/Jaffe; cos, Mari-An Ceo; makeup, Joanne M. Ottaviano; stunts, Arthur M. Jolly

Comedy/Drama **(PR: C MPAA: R)**

TREMORS 2: AFTERSHOCKS ★★½
(U.S.) 99m Stampede Entertainment ~ MCA/Universal Home Video c

Fred Ward *(Earl Bassett)*; Christopher Gartin *(Grady Hoover)*; Helen Shaver *(Kate)*; Michael Gross *(Burt Gummer)*; Marcelo Tubert *(Senor Ortega)*; Marco Hernandez *(Julio)*; Jose Rosario *(Pedro)*; Thomas Rosales *(Oil Worker)*

This movie is a rarity among direct-to-video sequels, one that's not only worthy of its theatrical predecessor but suggests that it, too, belongs on the big screen.

When "graboids"—giant, carnivorous underground worms—threaten the Mexican Petromaya oil refinery, its owners call on Earl Bassett (Fred Ward), who once helped defeat a quartet of the creatures. Having squandered his resulting celebrity status, Earl is convinced by the $50,000-a-head bounty offered, as well as the enthusiasm of young admirer Grady (Christopher Gartin), who becomes his partner. At Petromaya, the duo meets geologist Kate (Helen Shaver) and begin worm hunting, tricking the creatures into swallowing bomb-rigged, remote-controlled cars. When they find they're facing more monsters than expected, Earl calls on his old friend Burt Gummer (Michael Gross), a survivalist who arrives well-stocked with armaments.

It's not long, however, before Earl and Grady discover a dead, hollowed-out graboid and find that it has birthed human-sized, two-legged offspring that chase their prey on land. A swarm of these monsters soon has Earl, Grady, Burt and Kate trapped in the refinery, thwarting all of their efforts to escape. Ultimately, they succeed in confining the horde to one of the buildings, and using Burt's explosives, they blow the creatures to kingdom come.

One of the nice things about TREMORS II is the way it knowingly and logically follows up on the first movie's events. Acknowledging the media attention that would no doubt follow a real-life creature encounter, the sequel finds Earl sharing his trailer with a "Graboid" video game and having done a Reebok commercial with fellow monster-killer Val (absent here, as actor Kevin Bacon declined to return). And when he returns to worm-hunting duty, Earl learns from prior events and employs the much safer remote-controlled-car ploy. Given this, it's all the more fun when he and his cohorts are confronted with a new, even more lethal menace, with the last half of the movie finding the humans and the newfangled monsters taking turns outwitting each other.

First-time director S.S. Wilson (who wrote both the original TREMORS and this sequel with Brent Maddock) ably replicates the tense-funny tone of the first film, and indeed, only the familiarity of the basic story and approach takes some of the edge off this follow-up. As before, however, the actors are most engaging, with Ward taking full advantage of the opportunity to take center stage. Despite the significantly lower budget, the monsters remain entirely convincing, with the two-legged creatures represented by a mix of effective full-scale props and computer-generated images (supervised by JURASSIC PARK's Phil Tippett) that are easily the equal of work seen in much bigger theatrical features. *(Violence, profanity.)* — M.G.

d, S. S. Wilson; p, Nancy Roberts, Christopher DeFaria; exec p, Brent Maddock, Ron Underwood; w, Brent Maddock, S. S. Wilson; ph, Virgil Harper; ed, Bob Ducsay; m, Jay Ferguson; prod d, Ivo Cristante; art d, Ken Larson; sound, Rick Waddell, Joe Zappala; fx, Alec Gillis, Tom Woodruff Jr., Tippett Studio; casting, Meryl O'Loughlin; cos, Rudy Dillon; makeup, Camille Henderson

Science Fiction/Horror/Comedy (PR: C MPAA: PG-13)

TRIGGER EFFECT, THE ★★

(U.S.) 93m Amblin Entertainment; Universal ~ Gramercy Pictures c

Kyle MacLachlan *(Matthew)*; Elisabeth Shue *(Annie)*; Dermot Mulroney *(Joe)*; Richard T. Jones *(Raymond)*; Bill Smitrovich *(Steph)*; Michael Rooker *(Gary)*; Tori Kristiansen; Tyra Kristiansen *(Sarah)*; Rick Worthy *(Johnny)*; Edhem Barker *(Trendy German Guy)*; Tyrone Tann *(Tripping Guy)*; David O'Donnell *(Hand Holding Guy)*; Monica Torres *(Hand Holding Girl)*; Greg Grunberg *(Double Date Guy)*; Kerri Vickers *(Double Date Girl)*; Christina Alvarado *(Counter Girl #1)*; Victoria Fleming *(Counter Girl #2)*; Molly Morgan *(Babysitter)*; Philip Bruns *(Mr. Shaefer)*; Kirk Fox *(Drugstore Announcer)*; William Lucking *(Pharmacist)*; Rosanna Huffman *(Arguing Customer)*; Andy Walker *(Ball Bouncer)*; Carl Ciarfalio *(Security Guard)*; Wanda-Lee Evans *(Admitting Nurse)*; Richard Schiff *(Gun Shop Clerk)*; Jack Noseworthy *(Prowler)*; Shishir Kurup *(Raji)*; Gary Bayer *(Middle Aged Neighbor)*; Conor O'Farrell *(Police Officer #1)*; Eugene Collier *(Police Officer #2)*; Devoy White *(Waiter)*; Amanda Grillo *(Girl at Ice Cream Truck)*; Parker Swanson *(Medic)*; Jonathan Mumm *(Man at Table)*; Elizabeth Gandy *(Cafe Waitress)*; Dorian Dunbar *(Kari)*

If Hitchcock had been a Laputan, he might have conjured up a thriller as high-minded and ultimately ineffective as THE TRIGGER EFFECT; one so concerned with its mood and philosophical questions that it never gets around to the work of developing characters or narrative.

After a massive power failure leaves the entire West Coast with no electricity or phones, Matt and Annie Kay (Kyle MacLachlan and Elisabeth Shue) find their world coming apart. In a realization of the classic ethical dilemma, Matt can't buy some needed baby medicine and feels that he is left no choice but to steal it—an act that recharges his previously flagging libido. In response to rumors of widespread looting, Matt's friend, Joey (Dermot Mulroney), convinces him to buy a shotgun for protection. That night, when someone does break into the Kays' home, Joey and Matt chase the intruder out into the street where a neighbor (Bill Smitrovich) shoots and kills the fleeing thief. The act earns Joey's praise, but Matt's contempt.

The next day, the Kays and Joey leave the city and head for Colorado. Out on the highway, a stranded motorist (Michael Rooker) shoots Joey and steals their car. Unable to flag down help, Matt, armed with the shotgun, heads for an isolated farmhouse to acquire transportation. He ends up in a stand-off with a man (Richard T. Jones) and has to decide if he's willing to kill for the car he needs. Instead, Matt lays down his weapon and asks the man to trust him. He does, and Joey is saved. Eventually, the power comes back on, returning things to "normal."

THE TRIGGER EFFECT opens with a long, searching shot that observes typical behavior in a mall on a Friday night. People shove and bump into each other with no regard for the people they're pushing around. It's a world in which it's sensible and safer to change seats in a movie theater rather than risk provoking the talkers behind you. The point: it's a thin line (here, a power line) between the everyday rudeness society has come to accept grudgingly and a world where everyone is shooting each other for gasoline. The film poses the question: Can civilization survive the death of civility? And, when all the rules are off, what will mankind establish among itself to maintain the social contract?

If this parable sounds familiar, that's because the premise comes from a classic "Twilight Zone" episode (1960's "The Monsters are Due on Maple Street"), a debt acknowledged within the film (check out where the Kays live). Besides lacking Rod Serling's famous, ironic twist ending, THE TRIGGER EFFECT suffers from having to stretch what worked so well for less than 30 minutes to over 90. Writer and first-time director David Koepp was scribe on some big, Hollywood hits (MISSION: IMPOSSIBLE and JURASSIC PARK) and, surprisingly, he seems to have put more thought into his camera set-ups than his narrative.

A triangle of tension and resentment is established among the three leads, but it never climaxes, nor is any side developed to satisfaction. In particular, there's a hot flirtation scene between sexy Shue and hunky Mulroney that seems to exist solely for the sake of appearing in the film's promotional trailer. All the *sturm und drang* amounts to little, blurring the focus of the film. After a while, a viewer starts pondering the questions left unanswered by the plot, rather than the big questions raised by the story. *(Violence, profanity, adult situations.)* — P.R.

d, David Koepp; p, Michael Grillo; exec p, Walter Parkes, Laurie MacDonald, Gerald R. Molen; assoc p, Fernando Altschul, Michele Weisler; w, David Koepp (inspired by the BBC Television series "Connections"); ph, Newton Thomas Sigel; ed, Jill Savitt; m, James Newton Howard; prod d, Howard Cummings; art d, Jeff Knipp; set d, Larry Dias; sound, John Pritchett (mixer); fx, Larry Roberts; casting, Nancy Nayor; cos, Dana Allyson; makeup, Desne Holland; stunts, Merritt Yohnka

Thriller/Drama (PR: C MPAA: R)

TRIGGER HAPPY

(SEE: MAD DOG TIME)

TRUMAN ★★★

(U.S.) 130m Spring Creek Productions ~ HBO Pictures/HBO Video c

Gary Sinise *(Harry Truman)*; Diana Scarwid *(Bess Wallace Truman)*; Richard Dysart *(Henry Stimson)*; Colm Feore *(Charlie Ross)*; James Gammon *(Sam Rayburn)*; Tony Goldwyn *(Clark Clifford)*; Pat Hingle *(Thomas Joseph Pendergast)*; Harris Yulin *(George Marshall)*; Leo Burmester *(Frank Vassar)*; Amelia Campbell *(Margaret Truman)*; Virginia Capers *(Elizabeth Moore)*; John Finn *(Bob Hannagan)*; Lee Richardson *(Franklin Roosevelt)*; Zeljko Ivanek *(Eddie Jacobsen)*; Remak Ramsey *(Dean Acheson)*; Marian Seldes *(Eleanor Roosevelt)*; Lois Smith

(Madge Wallace); Richard Venture *(J. Lester Perry)*; Daniel Von Bargen *(Douglas MacArthur)*; Craig Benton *(Marine)*; Jim Birdsall *(Engineer)*; Freeman Bosley Sr. *(Alonzo)*; Walter Coppage *(Black Delegate)*; Nora Denney *(Mama Truman)*; Jessica Drake *(Woman Reporter)*; John Durbin *(Producer)*; Joe Erker *(Lazy Worker)*; Peggy Friessen *(Newswoman)*; David Fritts *(MacArthur Reporter)*; Harry Gibbs *(Garner)*; David Lansbury *(James Pendergast)*; Tim Gillin *(MacArthur's Officer)*; Larry Greer *(Ike Aide)*; Wiley Harker *(Senator 1)*; Marlon Hoffman *(Convention Reporter 1)*; Harold Herd *(First Politician)*; Gary Holcombe *(Senator 2)*; Hollis Houston *(Sgt. O'Hare)*; Jerry Longe *(Judge Vrooman)*; Joseph Moynihan *(Fred Wallace)*; Holmes Osborne *(Dixicrat)*; Jerel Taylor *(Barnett)*

Over-applauded by many critics, TRUMAN is sturdy, standardized biographical moviemaking elevated by incontestably brilliant acting. Unfortunately, this cavalcade of facts and figures is conceived and executed impersonally like a docent delivering a speech in front of the waxworks at a Presidential museum.

Late bloomer Harry S. Truman (Gary Sinise) marries Bess Wallace (Diana Scarwid) and serves proudly in WWI before opening a haberdashery with partner, Eddie Jacobsen (Zeljko Ivanek). Nothing in his farmland background indicated later entry in the political arena. When the Depression nearly bankrupts him, Harry becomes amenable to the career change offered by corrupt ward-healer Thomas Pendergast (Pat Hingle).

Intransigently honest, Truman isn't the pliable figurehead Pendergast expected. Truman realizes he can't pass sweeping road improvements for his poor constituents without turning his back on small-time graft. His ascent from the Senate to the vice-presidency is remarkable considering his penchant for deflating special interest groups. When FDR (Lee Richardson) dies in office, patriotic Truman plunges into the thankless job, even as Bess repeatedly absents herself from the Washington, DC social whirl.

In the greatest campaign upset of all time, whistle-stopping Truman defeats the favored Republican, Thomas Dewey, and wins a term of office on his own. However, Truman's presidency is fraught with international crises that he confronts without apology; the historical verdict is still out on some Truman decisions such as dropping atomic bombs on Japan, choosing not to blackmail Senator Joe McCarthy into dropping the Red Witch Hunts, and firing the power-hungry but popular General Douglas McArthur (Daniel Von Bargen). Deciding not to run again, Truman backs off from controversy and thus ushers in the Eisenhower era. Dismissed and even reviled when he retired from public office, Truman is now placed by historical revisionists in the forefront of American leaders, perhaps our last great US president.

History groupies will have a field day with this docudrama that dredges up every key and trivial event in Truman's colorful heyday. Perhaps this film will pack even more punch for those unfamiliar with the finer points of the rise and fall—and rise again—of Truman's reputation. What is sorely lacking here is a stronger guiding hand; the audience doesn't require a heavily biased approach to Truman, but it needs—and does not receive—a sense that Truman's travails have been shaped on screen by a filmmaker's passion. What we get is a checklist of Truman's greatest hits.

In its principal players, this HBO production could not be improved upon. Without submerging himself in mere impersonation, Gary Sinise captures Truman's granite resilience and just-plain-folks demeanor *sans* condescension. Matching him is idiosyncratic actress Diana Scarwid, who ages gracefully into her interpretation of matronly Bess by giving indications of Mrs. Truman's tartness in her scenes as the young, indomitable Bess. Magnificently supported by a galaxy of familiar and unfamiliar character actors and shrink-wrapped in documentary footage, TRUMAN offers the satisfaction of textual thoroughness and seamless storytelling, but few flashes of inspiration or imagination. *(Profanity, violence, adult situations.)* — R.P.

d, Frank Pierson; p, Doro Bachrach; exec p, Paula Weinstein, Anthea Sylbert; w, Tom Rickman (based on the book by David McCullough); ph, Paul Elliott; ed, Lisa Fruchtman; m, David Mansfield; prod d, Stephen Marsh; art d, Gary Kosko; set d, Joyce Anne Gilstrap; sound, Reinhart Stergar; casting, Mary Colquhoun; cos, Jill Channeson; makeup, Russell Cate, Gordon J. Smith; stunts, Andy Armstrong

Docudrama/Biography/Historical (PR: A MPAA: PG)

TRUTH ABOUT CATS AND DOGS, THE ★★

(U.S.) 97m Noon Attack Productions; 20th Century Fox ~ 20th Century Fox c

Uma Thurman *(Noelle)*; Janeane Garofalo *(Abby)*; Ben Chaplin *(Brian)*; Jamie Foxx *(Ed)*; James McCaffrey *(Roy)*; Richard Coca *(Eric)*; Stanley DeSantis *(Mario)*; Antoinette Valente *(Susan)*; Mitch Rouse *(Bee Man)*; La Tanya M. Fisher *(Emily)*; Faryn Einhorn *(Child Model)*; David Cross *(Male Radio Caller/Bookstore Man)*; Mary Lynn Rajskub *(Female Radio Caller)*; Bob Odenkirk *(Bookstore Man)*; Dechen Thurman *(Bookstore Cashier)*; Victoria Edwards *(Mother)*; Lisa Marie Russell *(Saleswoman)*; Robert Brinkmann *(Irate Director)*; Josiah Polhemus; Nigel Gibbs; David Phelps; Linda Porter; Michael Burke; Vanessa J. Wells *(Newscast Auditioners)*

Janeane Garofalo's well-timed wisecracks save THE TRUTH ABOUT CATS AND DOGS from utter disaster. Otherwise, this high-tech screwball farce starts out on the wrong paw and never recovers.

Abby (Janeane Garofalo) is a single woman living in Santa Monica who hosts a popular radio talkshow for pet owners. One day, Abby takes a call from Brian (Ben Chaplin), a handsome photographer who needs help with an uncooperative dog he is using on a shoot. After Abby solves Brian's problem, he asks her out on a blind date. Abby is flattered, but feels so inferior about her plain looks that she describes herself as tall blonde and tries to keep Brian interested in a phone-call-only relationship.

Meanwhile, Abby befriends her apartment-house neighbor, Noelle (Uma Thurman), who is tall and blonde and a model, to boot. When Brian shows up unexpectedly at the radio station one day while Noelle is also visiting, Abby asks her new pal to pretend to be her. Noelle plays along with the deception and agrees to go on a date with Brian as a favor, but quickly discovers that she, too, likes the young man. Abby finds herself torn between helping Noelle realize her dream of becoming a newscaster and feeling a twinge of jealousy over her friend's romantic interest in Brian.

After more complications ensue, Brian finally figures out that Abby is really two people—the cynical but appealing voice on the phone and the silly but beautiful blonde he has been dating. Brian feels hurt by the ruse and leaves both women, indicating that he would have loved Abby for herself had she been honest. After some time has passed, however, Abby bumps into Brian on the street and re-ignites the spark to their relationship.

Neither the gender-reversed *Cyrano de Bergerac* plot nor the related phone-sex subplot (with its shades of DENISE CALLS UP and the better 1-900) generates any laughs in THE TRUTH ABOUT CATS AND DOGS because writer-producer Audrey Wells' premise degenerates into a contrived and "misogynist cliche" (as Abby herself puts it). The blossoming friendship between Abby and Noelle also fails to be convincing, perhaps because of the residue tension from the reported off-screen "catfighting" between the mismatched female leads. (To be fair to the actresses, however, Brian's friendship with his African-American assistant, Ed, seems just as forced and phony.) There are indirect references to all sorts of movies, from PILLOW TALK (1959) and BELLS ARE RINGING (1960) to even PERSONA (1966), but nothing here freshens the mistaken-identity plots of yore.

Director Michael Lehmann, who has not made a satisfying film since HEATHERS (1989), stages the physical comedy (much of it involving cute animals) poorly. Thankfully, none of the visual animal jokes are as crude as the one in Lehmann's HUDSON HAWK (1991)—about the dog who takes a liking to Bruce Willis's genitals—but it seems cruel to have forced Hank (the dog here) into casters that send him sailing around the set during an early passage. The director also makes odd choices on story emphasis (the scene representing the crucial test of Brian's love is turned into a sappy music video, while Noelle's falling-in-love moment is extended into a cake-feeding montage reminiscent of NINE 1/2 WEEKS). Fortunately, Garofalo's tough, funny spirit shines through the mess (one wonders if she wrote her own dialogue), but it's not enough to prevent THE TRUTH ABOUT CATS AND DOGS from becoming cinematic roadkill. *(Sexual situations, profanity.)* — E.M.

d, Michael Lehmann; p, Cari-Esta Albert; exec p, Richard Hashimoto, Audrey Wells; w, Audrey Wells; ph, Robert Brinkmann; ed, Stephen Semel; m, Howard Shore; prod d, Sharon Seymour; art d, Jeff Knipp; set d, Maggie Martin; sound, Douglas Axtell (mixer); fx, Scott Forbes; casting, Debra Zane; cos, Bridget Kelly; stunts, Ernie Orsatti

Comedy/Romance (PR: C MPAA: PG-13)

TUNNEL VISION ★★★

(Australia) 100m Avalon Productions ~ Triboro Entertainment c

Patsy Kensit *(Kelly Wheatstone)*; Robert Reynolds *(Frank Yanovitch)*; Rebecca Rigg *(Helena M. Yanovitch)*; Gary Day *(Steve Doherty)*; Shane Briant *(Kevin Bosey)*; Justin Monjo *(Craig Breslin)*; David Woodley *(David DeSalvo)*; Vanessa Steele *(Rachel Kossinger)*; Craig Ashley *(Karl Knowles)*; Dean Nottle *(Dr. Samuels)*; Anthony Phelan *(Martin Chalmers)*; Liz Burch *(Mrs. Leyton)*; Jonathan Hardy *(Henry Adams)*; Nathan McGregor *(Danny)*; Paul Denny *(Driver)*; Brad Buckley *(Youth)*; Puven Panther *(Youth)*; Stephen Davis *(Pelegrini)*; Bob Reynolds *(Barman)*; Malcolm Cork *(Bouncer)*; Peter Power *(Detective)*; Gennie Nevinson *(Club Owner)*; Catherine Jones *(Bunny)*; Christophe Broadway *(Gorilla)*; Greg Arthur *(Policeman)*; Andrew Booth *(Policeman)*; Ray Marsh *(Director)*

For those who are too often disappointed by direct-to-video releases, a sneakily structured serial killer spree like TUNNEL VISION can seem like manna from heaven.

Bolstered by the apparent support of partner Kelly Wheatstone (Patsy Kensit), Detective Frank Yanovitch (Robert Reynolds) faces a rocky road in marriage and career. His pencil-pushing boss, Chief Kevin Bosey (Shane Briant), detests Frank's Dirty Harry style; Frank blindly suspects his newlywed bride Helena (Rebecca Rigg) of dallying with her coworker, David DeSalvo (David Woodley); and Frank's task force can't solve a string of slayings in which a madman poses his victims like models. As the investigation reaches a dead end with alibied gallery owner Craig Breslin (Justin Monjo), the homicides, linked to an S&M club, continue.

Unable to stem his jealousy, Frank becomes the prime suspect after his wife's associate David turns up dead—right after Frank goes ballistic over planted love letters from David that Helena denies ever seeing. On the lam to prove his innocence, Frank outmaneuvers Chief Bosey when he tries to apprehend fugitive Frank single-handedly. Kelly is, however, more than a born crime-solver who eventually cracks the serial killer case; surreptitiously, she has undermined Frank and Helena's relationship with incriminating traces of adultery and has killed David, not out of jilted passion for Frank, but out of unrequited love for Helena. After knocking out Frank at her home, Kelly grapples with Breslin. Although fatally wounding Kelly and garroting Frank, murderer Breslin falls prey to a bullet from the dying Kelly. With Kelly out of the way and the artistic killer slain, Frank can rejoin the force and reconcile with Helena.

What makes this gritty whodunit so bracing is its sophisticated ability to juggle two tenuously related plot threads. Armchair private eyes are in the enviable position of mulling over the wherefores of two unsolved mysteries. Whereas the denouement of the serial slaying case might have wound down with a fuller array of suspects, one can't lodge any niggling criticism against Kelly's campaign of malice against her patsy Frank. The deft screenplay pulls the wool over our eyes, as sweet-faced, oh-so-concerned Kelly practices domestic terrorism.

Adroitly planting red herrings to cause the viewer to stumble away from quick solutions, TUNNEL VISION prolongs its wrap-up suspensefully. Instead of edge-of-seat thrills, this startlingly acrid examination of criminal behavior on both sides of the law creates an environment where the innocent behave guiltily and the culpable hide their cunning. The "tunnel vision" of the title is actually the audience's. *(Graphic violence, extreme profanity, extensive nudity, adult situations.)* — R.P.

d, Clive Fleury; p, Phil Avalon; w, Clive Fleury; ph, Paul Murphy; ed, John Scott; m, David Hirschfelder, Ric Formosa; prod d, Phil Warner; sound, John Schiefelbein (recordist); casting, Liz Mullinar; cos, Rosalea Hood; makeup, Sally Gordon; stunts, Chris Anderson

Thriller/Crime/Mystery (PR: C MPAA: NR)

TUSKEGEE AIRMEN, THE ★★★

(U.S.) 107m Price Entertainment; HBO Pictures ~ HBO Home Video c

Laurence Fishburne *(Hannibal Lee)*; John Lithgow *(Sen. Conyers)*; Allan Payne *(Walter Peoples)*; Malcolm Jamal Warner *(Leroi Cappy)*; Courtney B. Vance *(Lt. Glenn)*; Andre Braugher *(Benjamin O. Davis)*; Chris Mcdonald *(Major Joy)*; Daniel Hugh Kelly *(Col. Rogers)*; Cuba Gooding Jr. *(Billy Roberts)*; Mekhi Phifer *(Lewis Johns)*; Christopher Bevins *(Young Hannibal)*; Eddie Braun *(Tail Gunner)*; Max Daniels *(Left Waist Gunner)*; Jack Dwyer *(Operations Officer)*; James Field *(Conductor)*; Vivica Fox *(Charlene)*; Bennet Guillory *(Hannibal's Father)*; David Harrod *(White Pilot #1)*; Johnny Judkins *(White Pilot #2)*; Tim Kellehen *(Lt. Wesley (B-17))*; Doug Krouse *(Walter's Instructor)*; Ed Lauter *(Gen. Stevenson)*; Barry Lehman *(German Prisoner)*; Janet MacLachlan *(Hannibal's Mother)*; Allan McCormick *(Lewis's Instructor)*; Willie Minor *(Black Prisoner)*; Perry Moore *(Reggie Newton)*; Rosemary Murphy *(Eleanor Roosevelt)*; Marco Perella *(Col. Sirca)*; David Pickens *(Gang Boss)*; William Earl Ray *(Tank)*; Rick Snyder *(Chairman Cassidy)*; Allan R. Stokes *(Drill Sgt.)*; Ned Vaughn *(Capt. Butler (B-17))*

A made-for-cable historical drama about the first all-black fighter squadron in the US army air corps, THE TUSKEGEE AIRMEN is polished, inspiring, and well acted.

On a train bound for Tuskegee Air Base in Alabama, Hannibal Lee (Laurence Fishburne) meets black fellow passengers Walter

Peoples (Allen Payne), and Leroi Cappy (Malcolm Jamal Warner). All are flight cadets, going to join the 99th Fighter Squadron, a newly created unit. But the conductor makes them vacate their compartment for German prisoners; Jim Crow still rules in 1942.

At Tuskegee they meet Lieutenant Glenn (Courtney B. Vance) and his white superiors: Major Joy (Chris Mcdonald), a bigot; and Colonel Rogers (Daniel Hugh Kelly), tough but color-blind. Their squadmates are black, middle-class, and educated: a minority elite.

Flight training is dangerous. Lewis Johns (Mekhi Phifer) crashes and dies. Walter is expelled and takes a suicide flight. Other cadets wash out. Eleanor Roosevelt (Rosemary Murphy) visits Tuskegee and flies with Hannibal. As the men get to know their machines and each other, *esprit de corps* grows. Meanwhile in Washington, Senator Conyers (John Lithgow) attempts to kill the Tuskegee program on racial grounds. He delays the 99th's deployment for a year.

The squadron is sent to Morocco, to strafe railyards, but sees little air action. Its commander, Lt. Colonel Davis (Andre Braugher), testifies against Conyers' allegations that his unit is unfit, proving it was deliberately sandbagged by racist bureaucrats. The 99th is transferred to Italy, flying escort for bombers as far as Berlin. Its record is outstanding: no bombers lost to enemy action. Bomber formations begin to request the 99th as escorts. Billy and Leroi are killed; Hannibal sinks a destroyer, earning a medal and promotion the day after Leroi's death. The film ends with old footage and photos. Titles supply the 99th's combat record.

THE TUSKEGEE AIRMEN's theme is the struggle for equal rights. It addresses racism directly, but not shrilly. Various incidents portray segregation as an ingrained system of laws and beliefs. White bigots are not demonized but portrayed as victims of ignorance and rigid thinking (a white pilot "explains" that the black pilots who saved his life can't be black). The airmen often discuss lynching and their personal experiences with bigotry. Walter's suicide symbolizes the rage they feel after the myriad petty humiliations in civilian and military life.

America in the 1940s is fighting a just war and undergoing progressive social change, and AIRMEN shows how racist attitudes contradict both American ideology and the national mood. Black pilots, aware of their unique situation, display dignity despite provocation; sometimes this dignity appears exaggerated, but the superb teleplay compensates with numerous humanizing details.

AIRMEN is a superbly crafted production featuring outstanding aerial sequences. If the heroes of AIRMEN are somewhat idealized, the villians they fight, on the ground and in the air, are real. Their victory, as black Americans, is also real. In an age lacking believable heroes, AIRMEN is a breath of fresh air. *(Violence, adult situations, profanity.)* — C.M.

d, Robert Markowitz; p, Bill Carraro; exec p, Frank Price, Robert Williams; co-p, Carol Bahoric; w, Paris Qualles, Trey Ellis, Ron Hutchinson (from a story by Robert Williams and T. S. Cook); ph, Ronald Orieux; ed, David Beatty; m, Lee Holdridge; prod d, Christiaan Wagener; art d, Russell Smith; set d, Sue Savage; cos, Ileane Meltzer; stunts, Tony Brubaker, Kevin LeRosa

Docudrama/Historical **(PR: C MPAA: PG-13)**

TWELFTH NIGHT ★★

(U.K./U.S.) 125m Circus Films; Renaissance Films ~ Fine Line c

Helena Bonham Carter *(Olivia)*; Richard E. Grant *(Sir Andrew Aguecheek)*; Nigel Hawthorne *(Malvolio)*; Ben Kingsley *(Feste)*; Mel Smith *(Sir Toby Belch)*; Imelda Staunton *(Maria)*; Toby Stephens *(Orsino)*; Imogen Stubbs *(Viola/Cesario)*; Steven Mackintosh *(Sebastian)*; Nicholas Farrell *(Antonio)*

William Shakespeare's romantic rondelay, *Twelfth Night*, gets opulent screen treatment here. Yet, despite the presence of a top name cast and colorful location photography, this popular comedy has been turned into a squatty bore. All the plot twists, mistaken identities, and misdirected passions have been retained from the 1601 play for this cinematic rendering, though the events now take place in the 1890s.

The story starts as a ship, carrying the identical twin performers, Viola (Imogen Stubbs) and Sebastian (Steven Mackintosh), is wrecked off the coast of Illyria, which is at war with the twins country. Viola is washed ashore on this alien coast and becomes convinced that her beloved brother is dead. She learns that she is near the home of Olivia (Helena Bonham Carter), a young countess who is also in mourning, for her recently dead father and brother. Accordingly, Olivia has sworn to have no contact with men for seven years, and in particular she rejects the amorous advances of the young Duke Orsino (Toby Stephens).

Desperate to know how to survive, and to keep the spirit of her twin brother alive, Viola decides to disguise herself as a boy. She transforms herself into "Cesario," enters into the service of Orsino, and is soon sent to woo Olivia on the Duke's behalf. Olivia remains unmoved by Orsino's attentions but finds herself instead attracted to young "Cesario," who in turn begins to fall in love with Orsino. When Viola's twin, Sebastian, suddenly emerges, alive and well, this hopeless triangle gets even more complicated.

While Orsino, Viola, Olivia, and Sebastian are preoccupied with their romantic destinies, Olivia's household is equally engrossed in a power struggle between the ill-tempered steward, Malvolio (Nigel Hawthorne), and Olivia's vociferous uncle, Sir Toby Belch (Mel Smith), accompanied by his oddball friend, Sir Andrew Aguecheek (Richard E. Grant), and Olivia's maid, Maria (Imelda Staunton). For his own financial ends, Sir Toby encourages Sir Andrew to woo Olivia, while plotting Malvolio's humiliation. Throughout, Feste (Ben Kingsley), an enigmatic entertainer, comes and goes between the two households, chiding all the players for their follies. After many misunderstandings, the true identities of Viola and Sebastian are revealed, leading them to unite with their destined loves—Viola with Orsino and Sebastian with Olivia.

The fault with TWELFTH NIGHT, dear viewer, lies not in the stars but in Trevor Nunn, the former Royal Shakespeare Company director whose previous forays into film (HEDDA, LADY JANE) also exposed his stage roots. Nunn, who adapted the play, tries to "open up" the text by staging most of the scenes in exterior settings. But, like the overrated work of Kenneth Branagh, Nunn's direction of both the action and the actors remains resolutely theatrical.

In the cast, only the charming Helena Bonham Carter escapes Nunn's affected devices, while such actors as Richard E. Grant, Mel Smith and Nigel Hawthorne (repeating his MADNESS OF KING GEORGE shtick) mug shamelessly. Of this low-comedy crowd, Ben Kingsley is especially grating as Feste, the ubiquitous singing narrator. As the twins, whose separation propels the mistaken identity plots, Imogen Stubbs (Nunn's real-life wife) and Stephen Mackintosh appear nothing alike and also perform in Royal Shakespeare Company-style. Stubbs likewise has the bad fortune of looking about as much like a man as Julie Andrews does in her VICTOR/VICTORIA drag, thus watering down the already tentative lesbian subtext.

Shakespeare purists may approve of this TWELFTH NIGHT, but fans of gender-bending classics like SYLVIA SCARLET

(1936) and the more inventive displays of the Bard on film, such as RICHARD III (1995) and ROMEO AND JULIET (1996), will find little to like here. *(Adult situations.)* — E.M.

d, Trevor Nunn; p, Stephen Evans, David Parfitt; exec p, Greg Smith; w, Trevor Nunn (based on the play by William Shakespeare); ph, Clive Tickner; ed, Peter Boyle; m, Shaun Davey; prod d, Sophie Becher; art d, Ricky Eyres; set d, Marianne Ford; sound, David Crozier (recordist); cos, John Bright; makeup, Christine Beveridge

Comedy/Drama/Romance **(PR: A MPAA: PG)**

TWISTER ★★★

(U.S.) 117m Amblin Entertainment; Universal; Warner Bros. ~ Warner Bros. c

Bill Paxton *(Bill Harding)*; Helen Hunt *(Jo Harding)*; Cary Elwes *(Dr. Jonas Miller)*; Jami Gertz *(Melissa)*; Lois Smith *(Aunt Meg)*; Alan Ruck *(Dusty)*; Philip Seymour Hoffman *(Rabbit)*; Abraham Benrubi *(Bubba)*; Nicholas Sadler *(Kubrick)*; Sean Whalen *(Sanders)*; Wendel Josepher *(Haynes)*; Joseph Slotnick *(Joey)*; Ben Weber *(Stanley)*; Jeremy Davies *(Laurence)*; Eric Laray Harvey *(Eric)*; Scott Thomson *(Preacher)*; Todd Field *(Beltzer)*; Gregory Sporleder *(Willie)*; Patrick Fischler *(The Communicator)*; Anthony Rapp *(Tony)*; Jake Busey *(Mobile Lab Technician)*; Melanie Hoopes *(Patty)*; J. Dean Lindsay *(Dean)*; Dan Kelpine *(Diner Mechanic)*; Sharonlyn Morrow *(Waitress)*; Richard Lineback *(Father)*; Rusty Schwimmer *(Mother)*; Alexa Vega *(Five Year Old Jo)*; Taylor Gilbert *(NSSL Scientist Bryce)*; Bruce Wright *(NSSL Scientist Murphy)*; Gary England *(TV Meteorologist No. 1)*; Jeff Lazalier *(TV Meteorologist No. 2)*; Rick Mitchell *(TV Meteorologist No. 3)*; John Thomas Rhyne *(Paramedic)*; Paul Douglas *(Bodger)*; Samantha McDonald *(Drive-In Girl)*; Anneke De Bont *(Farm Girl)*

As Sears has its yearly catalogue, Hollywood brings out one film every summer, designed to show off the latest in special effects technology. TWISTER was the 1996 model, and it makes no more sense to complain about its cliched characters and situations than it does to bemoan the lack of literary merit offered by the Sears people. What this movie was designed to do, it does spectacularly well.

Meteorologist Jo Harding (Helen Hunt) has been obsessed with tornadoes ever since the age of five, when she saw her father carried away by one. She and her estranged husband, Bill (Bill Paxton), have invented a device, nicknamed "Dorothy," which is capable of studying the inner workings of a tornado. The drawback is that it has to be planted in the center of one, and twisters by nature cannot be predicted more than a few minutes in advance. Stressed out by the demands of his job and Jo's obsession, Bill has left both for more placid work as a TV weatherman.

On a summer day when tornadoes seem likely, Jo and her team assemble to test Dorothy. They are in competition with the unscrupulous Dr. Jonas Miller (Cary Elwes), who has stolen Dorothy's design and is working with the financial backing of a large corporation.

While assembling her equipment and crew, Jo is visited by Bill and his fiancee, Melissa (Jami Gertz), a prim therapist, who need Jo to sign divorce papers. Before she gets the chance to sign, Jo and her team are off on a storm sighting. Bill tags along, unable to restrain his curiosity about the machine he designed.

For the remainder of the day, Jo and her team risk their lives in attempts to place Dorothy properly within a tornado. Bill finds it increasingly hard to deny the passions he has been trying to leave behind, and Melissa breaks off their engagement.

Bill and Jo concoct a method to get Dorothy into the midst of a particularly fierce tornado, one that kills Miller when he fails to heed their warnings. Putting the device in position leaves them without enough time to escape the storm, but they survive by chaining themselves to an iron post secured into a farm field. Returning to base, they find that their experiment has been a success.

For all the awe-inspiring power of this particular natural phenomenon, tornadoes have peculiar drawbacks as movie menaces. They strike with almost no warning, they last only a few minutes, and nothing can be done to stop or deter them. On the other hand, their ability to pick up and relocate anything less mobile than a mountain make them a natural for a movie. Director Jan De Bont (SPEED) and his crew have responded to that opportunity with such gusto and apparent glee that the uninvolving story line hardly matters.

Still, TWISTER's dramaturgy could have been better. While Michael Crichton is credited as co-writer (with his wife), the script offers none of the pop-science lectures that lent plausibility to films like COMA (1978), THE ANDROMEDA STRAIN (1971), and JURASSIC PARK (1993).

Hunt may have been cast primarily on the basis of hair length (just long enough to blow about fetchingly in the near-perpetual winds), but she's so inherently likable that she makes this character interesting. Co-stars Paxton, Gertz, and Elwes, on the other hand, are respectively Heroic, Bitchy and Evil, period.

But the actors are there only to mark time between the effects scenes, all of which are first rate, and all of which are greatly enhanced by the sound effects designed by Steve Flick. *(Violence, adult situations, profanity.)* — M.F.

d, Jan De Bont; p, Kathleen Kennedy, Ian Bryce, Michael Crichton; exec p, Steven Spielberg, Walter Parkes, Laurie MacDonald, Gerald R. Molen; w, Michael Crichton, Anne-Marie Martin; ph, Jack N. Green; ed, Michael Khan; m, Mark Mancina; prod d, Joseph Nemec III; art d, Dan Olexiewicz; set d, Ron Reiss; sound, Geoffrey Patterson, Steve Maslow, Gregg Landaker, Kevin O'Connell; fx, Stefen Fangmeier, John Frazier, Habib Zargarpour, Henry La Bounta, Industrial Light & Magic; casting, Risa Bramon Garcia; cos, Ellen Mirojnick; makeup, Brad Wilder; stunts, Mic Rogers

AAN Best Visual Effects: Stefen Fangmeier, John Frazier, Habib Zargarpour, Henry La Bounta; *AAN Best Sound:* Steve Maslow, Gregg Landaker, Kevin O'Connell, Geoffrey Patterson

Thriller **(PR: C MPAA: PG-13)**

TWO-BITS & PEPPER ★

(U.S.) 89m PM Entertainment Group ~ Republic Pictures Home Video c

Joe Piscopo *(Spider/Zike)*; Lauren Eckstrom *(Tyler)*; Rachel Crane *(Katie)*; Perry Stephens *(Roger)*; Kathrin Lautner *(Carla)*; Dennis Weaver *(Sheriff Pratt)*; Shannon Gallant *(Monica)*; Ethan Erickson *(Boyfriend)*; George Fisher *(Deputy Daniels)*; Tim Redwine *(Justin)*

From PM Entertainment, proud purveyors of direct-to-video crash-and-burn action movies, comes TWO-BITS & PEPPER, a demented "family" film for those who consider kidnapping, animal abuse, and undertones of child molestation to be good, clean fun.

A pony named Two-Bits and an older horse named Pepper, who talk to each other when nobody's around, are owned by a young girl named Tyler (Lauren Eckstrom). When she and her best friend Katie (Rachel Crane) ride the horses into town after being warned not to by Tyler's parents, Tyler and her mother have a big fight, and Tyler runs away from home and goes to Katie's house. Meanwhile, leather-jacketed, chain-smoking, tatooed kidnapper Spider (Joe Piscopo) and his nerdy, lisping brother Zike (Piscopo) cruise around town, hanging out at playgrounds and schoolyards, trying to lure little boys and girls into their car. Tyler's parents go to the police to report her missing, and Two-Bits and Pepper leave their barn to look for her.

Spider and Zike are pulled over by a suspicious cop, but they escape and wind up at Katie's house. They break in and cut off the electricity and telephone. Zike accidentally sets fire to the house and Katie and Tyler run away. Katie's sister comes home from a date and sees the house burning, then calls Tyler's parents, who notify the cops. Spider and Zike track down Katie and Tyler who are hiding out in an abandoned shack and hold them captive. Katie manages to wriggle out of her ropes, run outside, and flag down a police helicopter, but Spider and Zike escape in a truck with Tyler. Two-Bits and Pepper chase down the truck and stop it by blocking its path. Spider gets out and shoots Two-Bits, then tries to drive away, but the cops rescue Tyler and capture Spider and Zike. Two-Bits is rushed to the vet, where surgery is successfully performed, and a while later is almost fully recovered, as the girls ride away on Pepper.

TWO-BITS & PEPPER is a prurient, mind-boggling concoction that mixes HOME ALONE (1990), talking horses, children and animals in jeopardy, and last, but not least, an unbelievably embarrassing performance by Joe Piscopo in a dual role. It's also probably the only film ever made to depict a flashback from a horse's point-of-view: a scene where a drunk driver runs over Two-Bits's mother is revealed to be the pony's recurring nightmare! Pretending to be a children's film, its most likely appeal will be to dirty old men and child molesters, featuring two nubile pre-teens being tied up and slobbered over by a pair of leering, repulsive kidnappers. Although, Spider and Zike are supposed to be comically inept bumblers, the only "comedy" is offered by Zike's chronic flatulence, while Spider viciously threatens to break the girls' legs with a metal pipe and actually tries to lure kids into his car by offering them candy. To prove how versatile he is, Piscopo lays on the menace extra thick as Spider, and acts retarded as Zike; it's truly a disturbing sight to behold. As for the fantasy elements, the talking horses are accomplished simply by inserting voice-overs, with the voice of Pepper being a blatant "Mr. Ed" rip-off, and neither of the animals even moving their mouths while talking. Writer-director Corey Michael Eubanks, a former direct-to-video action performer, and producers Richard Pepin and Joseph Merhi should stick to the formula of exploding cars and slow-mo shoot-outs, because this surprisingly PG-rated attempt to crack the lucrative family-video market is an atrocity that only the Manson family could love. *(Violence, profanity.)* — M.S.

d, Corey Michael Eubanks; p, Richard Pepin, Joseph Merhi; co-p, Scott McAboy, Gil Wadsworth; w, Corey Michael Eubanks; ph, Jacques Haitkin; ed, Howard Flaer; m, Louis Febre; prod d, Zeev Tankus; sound, Mike Hall, Mark Allen; fx, Ron Bawden; casting, Dennis Gallegos; cos, Claudia Portillo; makeup, Victoria Sazani

Crime/Comedy/Fantasy (PR: C MPAA: PG)

2 DAYS IN THE VALLEY ★★★

(U.S.) 105m Rysher Entertainment; Redemption; MGM ~ MGM/UA c

Danny Aiello *(Dosmo Pizzo)*; Greg Cruttwell *(Allan Hopper)*; Jeff Daniels *(Alvin Strayer)*; Teri Hatcher *(Becky Foxx)*; Glenne Headly *(Susan Parish)*; Peter Horton *(Roy Foxx)*; Marsha Mason *(Audrey Hopper)*; Paul Mazursky *(Teddy Peppers)*; James Spader *(Lee Woods)*; Eric Stoltz *(Wes Taylor)*; Charlize Theron *(Helga Svelgen)*; Keith Carradine *(Detective Creighton)*; Louise Fletcher *(Evelyn)*; Austin Pendleton *(Ralph Crupi)*; Kathleen Luong *(Midori)*; Michael Jai White *(Buck)*; Cress Williams *(Golfer)*; Lawrence Tierney *(Older Man)*; Micole Mercurio *(Older Woman)*; William Stanton *(Man at Bar)*; Deborah Benson-Wald *(Driver's Friend)*; Ada Maris *(Detective Valenzuela)*

Misleadingly promoted at the time of its release as a Quentin Tarantino-style thriller, 2 DAYS IN THE VALLEY is actually more reminiscent of the films of Alan Rudolph, detailing the interactions of a large, seemingly unconnected group of characters. What links these residents of southern California's San Fernando Valley (sneered at by many in Los Angeles as the home of losers and wanna-bes) is that most of them are in desperate need of a second chance in life.

Hired to take part in a contract killing, has-been hitman Dosmo Pizzo (Danny Aiello) finds he's really the fall guy in a complicated plot engineered by manipulative sociopath Lee Woods (James Spader). After Lee murders his target, he shoots Dosmo and leaves him for dead. Lee and his sexy partner, Helga (Charlize Theron), plan to leave town as soon as they collect their payment from Becky Foxx (Teri Hatcher), the dead man's ex-wife.

Saved by a bulletproof vest, Dosmo escapes and hides out in the isolated house of art dealer Allan Hopper (Greg Cruttwell). While biding his time, Cosmo takes a liking to Allan's abused assistant, Susan Parish (Glenne Headly). Two visitors also are taken hostage: Allan's half-sister, Audrey (Marsha Mason), and her new friend, Teddy Peppers (Paul Mazursky), a suicidal film director.

The murdered man is discovered by undercover vice cops Wes Taylor (Eric Stoltz) and Alvin Strayer (Jeff Daniels). Against the advice of his burned-out partner, ambitious Wes decides to poke into the case himself. Returning to the house that evening, he runs into Lee, who has come to collect his money. Lee catches Wes off-guard and knocks him unconscious but is forced to flee before he can kill him.

Lee returns to Helga, who has been injured after a fight with Becky. Certain she is dying, he decides to finish the job. But before he can do so, Helga escapes. Staggering into the street, she is almost struck by a car containing the fleeing Dosmo and his hostages. A gunfight breaks out among Lee, Dosmo, and Wes, in which Lee is killed. Dosmo and Susan head for New York, where they plan to use Lee's blood money to open a pizzeria.

Despite the busy plot, John Herzfeld (the award-winning director of such TV movies as THE RYAN WHITE STORY and A FATHER'S REVENGE) is more interested in characters than story. So it's fitting that 2 DAYS works best as a showcase for its ensemble cast. While Herzfeld wrote the script in a burst of frustration after another project fell apart, his most engaging characters aren't the sympathetic losers but the unrepentant bad guys. James Spader steals the film in a role that could have been tailor-made for his talents, as the ice-cool killer with a macabre sense of humor. British actor Greg Cruttwell is only slightly less odious than the monstrous yuppie he played in Mike Leigh's NAKED (1993). And Charlize Theron makes a memorable debut as Spader's spandex-wearing Nordic consort, particularly in a knock-down brawl with Teri Hatcher. The weak link is Dosmo (Danny Aiello in a part that ironically was written for him). Although he's supposed to emerge as the film's hero, he never gains our sympathy. It's to Herzfeld's credit that he wanted to give his characters plausibly human faults, but Dosmo has just too many of them—cowardly, vain, a bully, a failure at his chosen profession (but arrogant about it anyway), and terrified of dogs to boot. While this weakness eventually keeps 2 DAYS from achieving all it hopes for, it still has enough small virtues to make for entertaining, if not wholly satisfying, viewing. *(Violence, nudity, sexual situations, adult situations, profanity.)* — M.F.

d, John Herzfeld; p, Jeff Wald, Herb Nanas; exec p, Keith Samples, Tony Amatullo; assoc p, Mindy Marin, Terry Miller, David Gaines; co-p, Jim Burke; w, John Herzfeld; ph, Oliver Wood; ed, Jim Miller, Wayne Wahrman; m, Anthony Marinelli; prod d, Catherine Hardwicke; art d, Kevin Constant; set d, Gene Serdena; sound, Kim H. Ornitz (mixer); fx, Larry Fioritto; casting, Mindy Marin, John Papsidera; cos, Betsy Heimann; makeup, Deborah La Mia Denaver, Debbie Zoller; stunts, Charles Picerni Picerni

Crime/Thriller/Comedy **(PR: C MPAA: R)**

TWO DEATHS ★★½

(U.K.) 102m BBC Films ~ Castle Hill c

Michael Gambon *(Daniel Pavenic)*; Sonia Braga *(Ana Puscasu)*; Patrick Malahide *(George Bucsan)*; Ion Caramitru *(Carl Dalakiss)*; Nickolas Grace *(Marius Vernescu)*; John Shrapnel *(Cinca)*; Ravil Isyanov *(Lieutenant)*; Sevilla Delofski *(Elena)*; Matthew Terdre *(Leon)*; Lisa Orgolini *(Young Ana)*; Niall Refoy *(Young Pavenic)*; Amanda Royle *(Cora Bucsan)*; Karl Tessler *(Roberto Constantin)*; Andrew Tiernan *(Captain Jorgu)*; Rade Serbedzija *(Colonel George Lapadus)*; Laura Davenport *(Marta)*

Michael Gambon and Sonia Braga give compelling performances in Nicolas Roeg's TWO DEATHS, an ambitious allegorical drama about sexual obsession and twisted desire, set against the violent backdrop of a revolution.

In an eastern European country, wealthy Dr. Daniel Pavenic (Michael Gambon) receives three old school friends, George, Carl, and Marius (Patrick Malahide, Ion Caramitru, Nickolas Grace), at his house for a lavish dinner party as part of their annual reunion.

The guests arrive as government troops battle students in the streets. Conversation turns to an old photo of the host's beautiful housekeeper, Ana (Sonia Braga). Pavenic boasts to his guests that he destroyed her life and tells how they met many years before, when he became obsessed with her but she rejected him because of her engagement to a man named Roberto.

Pavenic's story is interrupted by news that his blind cook has been killed by troops after she violated the curfew. Pavenic forces Ana to strip nude to prove to his guests that his story is true, then takes them to the attic and shows them the bed-ridden Roberto (Karl Tessler), explaining that he was paralyzed from the neck down after his motorcycle was rammed by a car.

After a visit from another school friend, who's now a military torturer, Pavenic treats some wounded soldiers and continues his story, explaining how he made a deal with Ana to care for Roberto, and in exchange she would give him her body and submit to his desires. The other men are appalled by this, but Pavenic's candor inspires them to reveal secrets of their own. Pavenic tells the men about how Ana forced him to perform an abortion on her, killing his own son, since having children was not part of their bargain.

Ana goes to the attic and shoots Roberto, then fires shots at some soldiers from the roof to draw them to the house. When they come to search for weapons, she embraces Pavenic and brandishes her gun. A soldier kills them both. The next morning, as the city continues to be destroyed, Ana and Pavenic are buried next to each other.

TWO DEATHS is very well-acted and sharply made, but its characters are vile, resulting in a film that's simultaneously fascinating and repellent. Though unidentified, the setting is clearly meant to be Romania during the fall of the Ceausescu regime in 1989. Roeg uses actual news footage, along with his own stylistic techniques, to tell a metaphorical tale of sexual and political fascism.

Memories of THE COOK, THE THIEF, HIS WIFE AND HER LOVER (1989), summoned by the casting of Gambon as the brutal Pavenic, are reinforced by Roeg's elliptical editing, which equates food and eating with violence. The symbolism can get pretty heavy-handed, however, such as the use of grotesque close-ups of dinner guests swallowing oysters, while death and destruction rage in the streets.

Roeg imposes a rigorous visual structure by filming all scenes set in the present in a dark, grainy and claustrophobic style, while the flashbacks are filled with sweeping camera movements and have a sunny elegance about them, despite the horrendous events being depicted.

TWO DEATHS is unpleasant and highly flawed, and not as good as Roeg's best films, such as WALKABOUT (1971) or DON'T LOOK NOW (1973). But it is still quite interesting and at least tries to do something different from the usual cookie-cutter Hollywood films. *(Graphic violence, graphic nudity, sexual situations, profanity.)* — M.S.

d, Nicolas Roeg; p, Carolyn Montagu, Luc Roeg; exec p, Allan Scott, Jonathon Olsberg, Mark Shivas; w, Allan Scott; ph, Witold Stok; ed, Tony Lawson; m, Hans Zimmer; prod d, Don Taylor; art d, Charmian Adams; sound, Jim Greenhorn (mixer); fx, Stuart Brisdon; casting, Celestia Fox; cos, Elizabeth Waller; makeup, Ann Buchanan

Drama **(PR: O MPAA: R)**

TWO FRIENDS ★★★½

(Australia) 76m Australian Broadcasting Corporation ~ Milestone Films c

Emma Coles *(Louise)*; Kris Bidenko *(Kelly)*; Kris McQuade *(Janet)*; Stephen Leeder *(Jim)*; Debra May *(Chris)*; Peter Hehir *(Malcolm)*; Tony Barry *(Charlie)*; Kerry Dwyer *(Alison)*; Arthur Faynes *(Chemist)*; Kim Antonios *(Cleaner Girl)*; Denise Roberts *(Cleaner Woman)*; Jim Madias *(Con)*; John Sheerin *(Dead Girl's Father)*; Jim Waites *(Dinner Party Guest)*; Mario Monti *(Italian Janitor)*; Peter Griffiths *(Jason)*; Ken Porter *(Jason's Father)*; Amanda Frederickson *(Kate)*; Steve Bisley *(Kevin)*; Georgia Anderson *(Kisser)*; Murat Bayari *(Kisser)*; Lisa Rogers *(Little Helen)*; Sean Travers *(Matthew)*; Carolyn Devlin *(Mother)*; Elizabeth Gentle *(Mother)*; Peter Bowden *(Panky)*; Martin Armiger *(Phillip)*; Giovanni Marangoni *(Renato)*; Steven Walton *(Renato's Friend)*; Benny Ulizzi *(Sam)*; Lynne Murphy *(School Prinicpal)*; Lorna King *(Shop Assistant)*; Kirsty Gowans *(Sick Girl)*; Emily Stocker *(Soula)*; Neil Campbell *(Teacher)*; Sher Guhl *(Teacher)*; Rory Delaney *(Wally)*; Jane Ahlquist *(Woman Friend)*

Director Jane Campion made her feature debut with TWO FRIENDS, a trenchant and moving study of a dissolving friendship. Despite some technical rough edges, this restored 1986 film is well worth a look.

TWO FRIENDS tells its story backward, opening in the midst of an involved situation. In a New Zealand suburb in July 1985, Kelly (Kris Bidenko), a homeless teenager, visits her family during a birthday party for her mother, Chris (Debra May). But she leaves when Malcolm (Peter Hehir), her stepfather, criticizes her punk style of dress. Kelly sends a letter to Louise (Emma Coles), a prep school student, who used to be her best friend. Louise reads sadly of how Kelly is fending for herself in the world.

Five months earlier, Louise learns that Kelly is quitting high school, leaving her home to live with her real father. But on her first night at her father's apartment, Kelly is sexually harassed by one of her father's friends; Kelly then winds up on Louise's doorstep. Janet (Kris McQuade), Louise's mother, disapproves of Kelly, but takes her in briefly.

One month earlier, Kelly chides Louise for buying an expensive uniform to wear at her new school, City Girls' High. She then angers Janet by drinking and carousing with a young man in their home. Kelly later apologizes for her behavior, but the girls' friendship is clearly changing. One month earlier, during an orientation party for incoming City Girls' High students, Malcolm tells Kelly that he will not permit her to attend the school because he thinks it's elitist.

Two months earlier, Kelly and Louise wait and worry about passing their entrance exams to City Girls' High. After they promise never to live without one another, they learn that they have both passed the exam. The future for these best friends looks bright and exciting.

While her 1993 international breakthrough hit, THE PIANO, displayed a filmmaker's eye for startling imagery, Campion's lesser-known earlier works, including SWEETIE (1988), AN ANGEL AT MY TABLE (1990) and this first film, actually were bolder in criticizing socio-economic conditions of the director's native New Zealand. In fact, it could be argued that TWO FRIENDS represents Campion's most experimental and progressive film thanks to Helen Garner's screenplay, which tells its story backwards (a la Harold Pinter's BETRAYAL), and thereby forces immediate reflection upon the chain of events. TWO FRIENDS may be less cinematically stylish than either THE PIANO or Peter Jackson's HEAVENLY CREATURES (1994), another New Zealand film about an intense friendship between two teenagers fighting social and parental pressures. But TWO FRIENDS triumphs nonetheless with biting observations about class, gender, and generational issues.

Despite reportedly extensive repair work, TWO FRIENDS's success is diminished by technical problems that often are found in first-time independent films. The sound quality is poor, and audiences outside of New Zealand may be bothered by the thick accents of the actors. Also, the editing is not always clean. In any case, viewers willing to put up with the glitches will be rewarded with an probing drama. *(Sexual situations, adult situations, substance abuse, profanity.)* — E.M.

d, Jane Campion; exec p, Jan Chapman; w, Helen Garner; ph, Julian Penney; ed, Bill Russo; md, Martin Armiger; prod d, Janet Patterson; sound, Chris Alderton (recordist); fx, Laurie Faen; casting, Jennifer Allen; makeup, Sandie Bushell

Drama **(PR: C MPAA: NR)**

TWO GUYS TALKIN' ABOUT GIRLS

(SEE: . . . AT FIRST SIGHT)

TWO IF BY SEA ★

(U.S.) 97m Morgan Creek ~ Warner Bros. c

Denis Leary *(Frank)*; Sandra Bullock *(Roz)*; Stephen Dillane *(Evan Marsh)*; Yaphet Kotto *(O'Malley)*; Mike Starr *(Fitzie)*; Jonathan Tucker *(Todd)*; Wayne Robson *(Beano)*; Michael Badalucco *(Quinn)*; Lenny Clarke *(Kelly)*; Jonny Fido *(Burke)*; Don Gavin *(Sully)*; Shaun R. Clark *(Sweeney)*; Markus Parilo *(Peters)*; John Friesen *(Sheriff Horn)*; Ian White *(Jim Kellerher)*; Jane Moffat *(Marcy Kellerher)*; Geoffrey McLean *(Crew Member)*; Sean Runnette *(Marty)*; Richard Fitzpatrick *(FBI Chief)*; Ferne Downey *(Mercedes Owner)*; Philip Williams *(Man with Phones)*; Katya Ladan *(Older Woman)*; Lorne Cossette *(Older Man)*; John Fulton *(Driver)*; Angela Moore *(Nanny)*; Kay Hawtrey *(Lady with Dog)*; Claire Rankin *(Reporter #1)*; Michael Risley *(Reporter #2)*; Martha Irving *(Duty Manager)*; Leslie Boyd *(Video Woman)*; Dennis O'Connor *(Cop on Scene)*; Joseph Di Mambro *(Cop #1)*; Tracy Jones *(Cop #2)*; Sandi Ross *(Conductor)*; Chris Benson *(Local Cop)*; Julia Montgomery Brown *(Beautiful Woman)*; Gary Vermeir *(Buyer)*

Warner Bros. must have known they had a real dud on their hands when they dumped TWO IF BY SEA into theaters during the first weeks of 1996. This awkward "romantic comedy" wastes Sandra Bullock at the peak of her popularity.

Roz (Bullock) is the gum-snapping, "Noo-Joizey" girlfriend of Frank O'Brien (Denis Leary), a dim-witted, small-time thief from "Bah-ston." They've stolen a Matisse painting worth $4 million (though neither realizes quite how valuable it is) and they have to sit on it for a few days while they wait for Frank's fence.

The theft draws the attention of FBI agent O'Malley (Yaphet Kotto), who has been chasing an art thief called "Phil the Shill" for years. On the lam, and leaving a trail of clues behind them like bread crumbs, Frank and Roz end up in a small town on Cape Cod, where they hole up in a conveniently empty and accessible mansion. Roz catches the eye of local rake Evan Marsh (Stephen Dillane), the local rake, and while he shows her the swank life—sailing, horseback riding, painting—Frank stews with jealousy.

Though they've always quarreled, the ocean view gives Frank and Roz a new perspective on their relationship. He resents her ability to assimilate, and she resents his lack of ambition and direction. They decide to go their separate ways after they sell the painting.

When Beano the fence (Wayne Robson) shows up to take Frank to the anonymous buyer, they end up leading the Feds right to "Phil," who turns out to be Marsh. The revelation sends Roz right back into Frank's arms.

While Bullock's surprise hit WHILE YOU WERE SLEEPING (1995) was in theaters, she was tucked away in Nova Scotia filming TWO IF BY SEA. For Bullock, far from the madding crowds and show business weasels, the shoot was like a welcome vacation. But fans won't enjoy themselves nearly as much watching this dreary comedy. After its opening with Frank and Roz, seemingly oblivious to the police chasing them, bickering about the cultural merits of "Cats" versus BATMAN RETURNS (1992), the movie's moments of amusement are few and far between—and feature Beano and his lunkhead henchmen, not the stars.

TWO IF BY SEA is really a vehicle for top-billed Leary. The darkly caustic comic gained widespread recognition on MTV. TWO IF BY SEA, which Leary co-wrote, is meant to change his image; unfortunately, he tries to soften his edge by softening his brain, and he is too smart to wear dumbing-down well. *(Profanity.)* — P.R.

d, Bill Bennett; p, James G. Robinson; exec p, Gary Barber, Bill Todman Jr.; co-p, Michael MacDonald; w, Denis Leary, Mike Armstrong (from a story by Denis Leary, Mike Armstrong, and Ann Lembeck); ph, Andrew Lesnie; ed, Bruce Green; m, Nick Glennie-Smith, Paddy Moloney; prod d, David Chapman; art d, Mark Haack; set d, Steven Shewchuk; sound, Glen Gauthier (mixer); fx, Laird McMurray; casting, Todd Thaler; cos, Olga Dimitrov; makeup, Julie Houle; stunts, Branko Racki

Comedy/Romance **(PR: C MPAA: R)**

TWO MUCH ★½

(Spain/U.S.) 118m Sogetel; Lola Films; Occidental Media Inc.; Fernando Trueba P.C.; Interscope Communications; Polygram; Touchstone ~ Buena Vista c

Antonio Banderas *(Art/Bart)*; Melanie Griffith *(Betty Kerner)*; Daryl Hannah *(Liz Kerner)*; Danny Aiello *(Gene Paletto)*; Joan Cusack *(Gloria)*; Eli Wallach *(Sheldon)*; Gabino Diego *(Manny)*; Austin Pendleton *(Dr. Huffeyer)*; Allan Rich *(Reverend Larrabee)*; Vincent Schiavelli *(Sommelier)*; Phil Leeds *(Member of Lincoln Brigade)*; Sid Raymond *(Member of Lincoln Brigade)*; Louis Seeger Crume *(Member of Lincoln Brigade)*; Jeff Moldovan *(Goon)*; Joe Hess *(Goon)*; Theodora Castellanos *(Conchita)*; Genevieve Chase *(Mrs. Doyle)*; Marcella Vitalainai Aitken *(Mrs. Paletto)*; Ellen Jacoby *(Waitress)*; Santiago Segura *(Paparazzi)*; Gabriel Traversari *(Paparazzi)*; Rosa Jimenez *(Maria)*; Katrina Flett *(University Student)*; George Kapetan *(Tailor)*; Don McArt *(Funeral Priest)*; Levis Mora-Arriaga *(Mariachi)*; Jose Mora-Arriaga *(Mariachi)*; David Mora-Arriaga *(Mariachi)*

As bland as a Doublemint gum commercial, this farce about faking twinship proves that pleasantly pepperminty performers can't inject flavor into chewed-over screenplays.

Nearly bankrupt gallery owner Art Dodge (Antonio Banderas) is so cash-poor, he scams recent widows for purchases. When he tries bilking the widowed mother of Mafia bigwig Gene Paletto (Danny Aiello), Art goes from the frying pan and into the fire. He's rescued by Gene's scatterbrained ex-wife Betty (Melanie Griffith); an inveterate romantic, Betty hears wedding bells, whereas her cupid-shy sister Liz (Daryl Hannah) regards Art as a conniving gigolo. Although engaged to Betty, Art falls head over heels for Liz. With the occasional complicity of his girl Friday Gloria (Joan Cusack), altar-bound Art embarks on a no-win scheme: the impersonation of a fictitious twin brother named Bart. While Art sexually satisfies Betty, "Bart" romances Liz. Slipping out of the clutches of Gene's goon squad, Art can't control his multiplying mistaken-identity crises. By the time Liz catches onto the ruse, Betty has realized that diamond-in-the-rough Gene is the only guy for her. Chastened by the collapse of his charade, Art re-dabbles in painting while Gloria takes over running the gallery. After Liz forgives Art for pretending to be Bart, the lovers are reunited.

Photographed with the kind of sunny sheen that will make viewers feel as if they're sipping a pina colada, TWO MUCH offers a pretty picture of pretty people doing some ugly things for laughs. The twin-thin plot has been a fixture of romantic comedies for eons, and it's only made more tedious by the strenuously overwritten screenplay and asleep-at-the-wheel direction. With comic potential muffled, TWO MUCH only comes to life in the bittersweet alliance of hustler Art and world-weary Liz. The entire cast tries hard (maybe too hard) to spark laughter: Aiello is like Sheldon Leonard sans the self-parody; Griffith is like Judy Holliday without the submerged intelligence; and Banderas is like Victor Mature dubbed into Spanish. While it may not be fair to cursorily dismiss stars forced to push elephantine material up a steep mountain (or turn in two equally strained performances), Banderas cannot escape censure as the film's prime stumbling block. Whatever elan he displayed as an un-obscure object of desire in the films of Pedro Almodovar (MATADOR, TIE ME UP! TIE ME DOWN!) will vanish completely if he continues to appear in films such as this on these shores. *(Violence, sexual situations, substance abuse, profanity.)*— R.P.

d, Fernando Trueba; p, Cristina Huete; exec p, Ted Field, Adam Leipzig, Robert W. Cort; assoc p, Fernando Garcillan, Paul Diamond; w, Fernando Trueba, David Trueba (based on the novel by Donald E. Westlake); ph, Jose Luis Alcaine ; ed, Nena Bernard; m, Michel Camilo; prod d, Juan Botella; art d, Carlos Arditti; set d, Barbara Peterson; sound, Pierre Gamet (recordist); fx, Richard Jones; casting, Johanna Ray, Elaine J. Huzzar; cos, Lala Huete; makeup, John Sobeck; stunts, Thom Bahr

Comedy/Romance **(PR: C MPAA: PG-13)**

UV

UN INDIEN DAN LA VILLE
(SEE: LITTLE INDIAN, BIG CITY)

UNA SOMBRA YA PRONTO SERAS
(SEE: SHADOW YOU SOON WILL BE, A)

UNDER THE DOMIM TREE ★★★
(Israel) 102m H.S.A. Ltd.; Under the Domim Tree Ltd. ~ Strand Releasing c
(ETZ HADOMIM TAFUS)

Kaipo Cohen *(Aviya)*; Juliano Mer *(Teacher)*; Gila Almagor *(Aviya's Mother)*; Riki Blich *(Mira)*; Orli Perl *(Yola)*; Ohad Knoller *(Yurek)*; Jeniya Catzan *(Ze'evik)*; Aya Stiffel *(Sara B.)*

Based on an autobiography by Gila Almagor, this coming-of-age story revolves around a group of youths in the 1950s who live in an Israeli camp for children whose parents were Holocaust victims. It has been made with care and is well-acted, but suffers from an overdose of sensitivity.

Aviya (Kaipo Cohen) has a mother, Gila (Almagor), who is confined to a hospital because she mentally relives concentration camp experiences, even though she was never actually in one. Aviya is wooed by Yurek (Ohad Knoller). A normal, sunny youth by day, at night, Yurek and Ze'evik (Jeniya Catzan) become haunted, pathetic creatures trying to run away from their nightmarish past. Yola (Orli Perl) is excited to hear that her father, presumed dead in the war, is still alive, but her hopes are dashed when it turns out to be a case of mistaken identity.

Wim, a Dutchman who sheltered Jews during the war, receives a fervently sung welcome upon his arrival at the camp, and he promptly sets about getting the kids to grow a tulip garden.

One day, a couple comes to the village seeking Mira (Riki Blich), whom they claim is their daughter. She denies this and runs away, remembering all too well the beatings she suffered at this same couple's hands. Their claim winds up in court. Miraculously, the girl has a sudden memory breakthrough and is able to recall her actual family in full detail for the court. She wins the case to the cheers of her campmates, assembled to lend moral support. The would-be parents are revealed as impostors, greedy for the money which would have accompanied Mira's return to them. Upon their return, Wim greets them excitedly. The tulips have bloomed.

This is a sensitive story sensitively handled for the most part by director Eli Cohen. It is beautifully photographed and alert to the emotional nuances of its characters. Cohen has gotten some wonderfully natural, humorous performances from his young cast. The characters seem, on the surface, like normal teenagers, with their bickering and bonding and first discovery of love. However, they are all marked by the horror and tragedy of what they have endured.

What keeps the film from being really memorable is a surfeit of tact, along with a contradictory tendency towards heavy-handedness. It becomes dramatically predictable, in a "Hallmark Hall of Fame" way. It is best when it shows the kids's normal interactions—the sniping and discontent which crops up among any group of individuals thrown into close contact. There are a few too many artfully arranged tableaux of hand-holding.

It would have been enlightening to see more of the adult instructors and their dealings with the various challenges that arise. They're presented as rather blank, albeit kindly, authority figures, shaking their heads and asking, "Where did we go wrong?" when things go awry. Also, Mira's false parents seem like stock villains. *(Adult situations, sexual situations.)* — D.N.

d, Eli Cohen; p, Gila Almagor, Eitan Evan; w, Gila Almagor, Eyal Sher, Eli Cohen (based on the book by Gila Almagor); ph, David

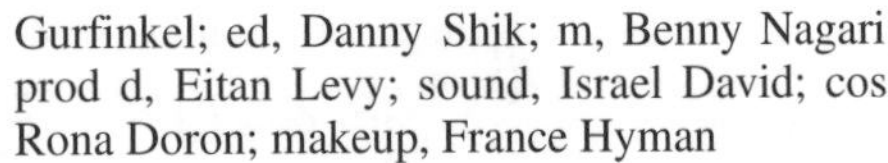

Gurfinkel; ed, Danny Shik; m, Benny Nagari; prod d, Eitan Levy; sound, Israel David; cos, Rona Doron; makeup, France Hyman

Drama/Romance (PR: C MPAA: NR)

UNDER THE HULA MOON ★
(U.S.) 96m Periscope Pictures; Jersey Born Pictures ~ Turner Home Video c

Stephen Baldwin *(Buzz)*; Emily Lloyd *(Betty)*; Chris Penn *(Turk)*; Musetta Vander *(Maya Gundinger)*; Pruitt Taylor Vince *(Bob)*; Robert Marid *(Juan)*; Edie McClurg *(Dotty)*; James Staskel *(Trucker)*; Carel Struyken *(Clyde)*; Ray Bumatai *(King Kamehameha)*; Tina Naughton *(Reporter)*; Debra Christofferson *(Kim Jones)*; Bill Campbell *(Marvin)*; Molly McClure *(Grandmother)*; Deep Roy *(Bus Driver)*; Eric Welch *(Young Man)*; Bobby McGee *(Leon)*; Willard Pugh *(Duane)*; Gary Cervantes *(Bandito)*; Luis Contreras *(Bandito)*; Patrick Dollaghan *(Agent Kepner)*; Gregory Webb *(Military Man)*; R. Lee Ermey *(Colonel McIntire)*

When Jonathan Demme concocted SOMETHING WILD, he opened up the floodgates to dozens of derivatives that miss the point of juxtaposing violence and comedy. One is UNDER THE HULA MOON, a SMOKEY AND THE BANDIT movie with delusions of social satire.

Betty (Emily Lloyd) and Buzz (Stephen Baldwin) share a trailer in the Cactus Gulch area of the Arizona Desert. Their dream is to move to Hawaii. Betty seeks this goal by entering sweepstakes, while Buzz tries to market his invention, a potent sunscreen called Cammo. Unbeknownst to the wishful thinkers, Buzz's psychotic brother Turk (Chris Penn) has just busted out of prison and murdered a motorist for his car.

After learning that Betty has won a $10,000 prize, Turk assaults his brother and kidnaps Betty. While Turk heads for Mexico with Betty and her prize, Buzz is counseled by a Hawaiian god to find his inner courage. Accompanied by ex-girlfriend/local reporter Maya Gundinger (Musetta Vander), who smells a career-making scoop, Buzz test-runs his bravery by rescuing a car accident victim, then closes in on Turk and Betty at a sleazy cantina. Let down by the resident criminal element, Buzz is forced to combat his brother single-handedly. After nearly killing Turk, Buzz falls with his sibling through the bar-room floor and into the covert headquarters of the Department of Justice, which just happens to be located under the bar.

Betty gives her prize winnings to the family of a prison guard slain by Turk, and Buzz receives an offer from the military to market his revolutionary sunblock as camouflage for the armed forces. Millionaires, the couple goes to Hawaii.

This unwieldy congealing of low humor and sadomasochism leaves the audience in a hostile mood because of the way it patronizes its just-plain-folks protagonists. Instead of propelling the narrative forward by using Turk's anti-social behavior as a commentary on the underside of the American Dream, this coarsely conceived road picture seems to revel in the bad guy's cruelty. For example, the sequence in which mad-dog Turk shoots off the ear of a decent driver begging for his life is sick and pointless; this grotesque comedy never recovers from that literal overkill.

The movie doesn't present recognizable human beings, just punching bags for the the writer and director to maneuver around. Although Penn has some facility for limning pea-brained, slap-around heavies, Lloyd is too talented to be playing a variation on Elly Mae Clampett. As for the boyishly handsome Baldwin, his dramatic skills can take him as high as his flashy turn in FALL TIME or as low as his wholesome heroism in NEW

EDEN, but he is a hopelessly bogus comic actor. Still, his lack of finesse could not find a better home than in this fatuous slam at country bumpkinism. *(Graphic violence, extreme profanity, sexual situations.)* — R.P.

d, Jeff Celantano; p, Stacy Codikow; exec p, Jim B. Hodge; assoc p, Gregory Webb; w, Jeff Celantano, Gregory Webb; ph, Phil Parmet; ed, Donald Likovich; m, Hidden Faces; prod d, Randal Earnest; art d, David Fitzpatrick; set d, Brent Bye; sound, Mary Jo Devenney (mixer); fx, Bruno Stempel; casting, Elizabeth Leustig; cos, Susana Puisto; makeup, Nancy Montgomery; stunts, Keii Johnston

Comedy/Action/Crime **(PR: C MPAA: R)**

UNDERSTUDY: GRAVEYARD SHIFT 2, THE ★★
(Canada) 90m Cinema Ventures Inc. ~ Virgin Video c

Wendy Gazelle *(Camilla Turner/Patti Venus)*; Silvio Olivierio *(Baisez)*; Mark Soper *(Matthew)*; Ilse von Glatz *(Ash)*; Lesley Kelly *(Martina)*; Timothy Kelleher *(Duke/Lenny)*; Carl Alacchi *(Ramon/Apache)*; Paul Amato; John Tench; John Copping; Agi Gallus

Filmmaker Gerard Ciccoritti's febrile follow-up to his previous vampire tale, GRAVEYARD SHIFT (1990), is a wildly recursive chiller set against a filmmaking backdrop—DAY FOR NIGHT (1973) with night creatures.

Rising actress Camilla Turner (Wendy Gazelle) portrays the heroine in an arty, low-budget horror production about a legendary pool hustler vampire. Camilla has visions of Baisez (Silvio Olivierio), a seductive, spectral vampire in search of a body to possess. To gain immortality, Camilla tricks him into using hers. Sometimes Camilla is herself, sometimes she's physically transformed into Baisez, and the shooting schedule suffers accordingly with the leading lady's mysterious illnesses and absences.

After Camilla-Baisez kills off the actor who plays the vampire snooker champ, Baisez successfully auditions to play the part. Camilla's fiance, film editor Matthew (Mark Soper), figures out what's happening, and challenges Baisez to a winner-take-all billiards match on the soundstage, mirroring one in the script. Baisez, no longer incarnated in Camilla, tries to kill Matthew, but the editor destroys the fiend with sunlight. Then Matthew slashes his own wrists, and forces vampire Camilla to conjoin with him just as she had done with Baisez. Taking the name of her screen character, Camilla haunts city poolrooms by night.

The outright shocks in THE UNDERSTUDY, like a decapitation and assorted impalings, aren't very scary and almost seem beside the post-modern point, made by one character's soliloquy: "The vampire is the perfect movie star. . . . The shape changes, it lives forever in the dark, it feeds on us, and vanishes in the light." Creepier than all the plastic fangs is how eagerly Camilla accepts vampirism as an embodiment of the immortality and power that cinema can only pretend to convey. Ciccoritti knows his lore, treats the dubious premise seriously, and pays tribute to Dreyer's 1932 classic, VAMPYR (which Matthew complains has just been computer "colorized" for TV). Still, it's hard to swallow the film-within-a-film-that-becomes-reality premise, a vampiric version of THE HUSTLER (1961), with billiard balls resounding like gunfire thanks to the living dead's supernatural pool-cue prowess. Olivierio is convincing as both sexual stud and ghoulish predator, and may or may not be the cab-driving urban blood drinker slain at the end of GRAVEYARD SHIFT. Either way, this quasi-sequel stands up on its own, although traditional horror-and-gore fans might find its self-referential puzzles not their cup of tea. *(Violence, profanity, sexual situations, nudity, substance abuse.)* — C.C.

d, Gerard Cicoritti; p, Stephen R. Flacks, Arnold H. Bruck; w, Gerard Cicoritti; ph, Barry Stone; ed, Neil Grieve; m, Philip Stern; art d, Nicholas White; makeup, Andrea Sicova, Adrianna Sicova; stunts, Ken Quinn

Horror **(PR: C MPAA: R)**

UNDERTOW ★★
(U.S.) 92m Weintraub/Kuhn Productions ~ Republic Pictures Home Video c

Lou Diamond Phillips *(Jack Ketchum)*; Charles Dance *(Lyle Yates)*; Mia Sara *(Willie)*

A thriller pared to the absolute basics, UNDERTOW is an insignificant affair, despite the participation filmmaker Kathryn Bigelow (NEAR DARK, STRANGE DAYS) as co-writer.

Drifter Jack Ketchum (Lou Diamond Phillips) runs off the road in a forest during a thunderstorm. He awakens at gunpoint in the secluded cabin lair of violent recluse Lyle Yates (Charles Dance), who resides with his abused young bride Willie (Mia Sara), acquired at age 13 to pay her father's debts. Despite a hurricane evacuation in progress, paranoid Lyle refuses to leave. Instead, he and Jack play games of macho one-upsmanship, utilizing the cabin's supply of bladed weapons and beartraps. Willie is attracted to the prisoner/houseguest, and Jack tries to persuade her to flee with him in Lyle's truck. Lyle grows more unstable as the storm rages, and Jack mashes him with the truck. But Willie chooses her crazy husband over her new lover, and Jack can only spin his wheels in frustration in the muddy road. By daybreak the sky clears, but Jack knows a showdown is nigh. He and Lyle maul each other until the dying mountain man shows some mercy and lets Willie and the interloper escape, as a giant moonshine boiler in the cellar explodes.

UNDERTOW, which premiered on cable TV, seems like a troglodytic cousin of Roman Polanski's KNIFE IN THE WATER (1962), another sinister three-character piece that explored tricky power-plays of personal relationships and dangerous passions in a confined space (in that case, a sailboat). There the resemblance ends (although, despite its American setting, UNDERTOW was also shot in Eastern Europe). Unsubtle and unappealing, UNDERTOW opens on a dark and stormy night and stays at that pitch throughout. It may be intentional that Ketchum, in his own callow way, is little better than lunatic Lyle; the youth's opening voice-over indicates he's on the run from a bad situation involving a sheriff's daughter, and watching Willie torn between these two possessive men is more depressing than anything else, lyrical sex scenes notwithstanding. Eric Red's direction emphasizes Wellesian low angles, too much slow-motion, and archival lightning footage. The pieces come together only late in the action, in stock shock scenes when Lyle, supposedly killed, keeps coming back; such is Dance's primal force that one could well believe Lyle has that much raw meanness in him. *(Violence, substance abuse, profanity, sexual situations, nudity, adult situations)* — C.C.

d, Eric Red; p, Tom Kuhn, Fred Weintraub; exec p, Lewis B. Chesler, David M. Perlmutter; assoc p, David Baird; w, Eric Red, Kathryn Bigelow; ph, Geza Sitkovics; ed, Claudia Finkle; m, John Frizzell; prod d, Bill Brodie; art d, Galius Klicius; set d, Bronius Galvydius; sound, Kip Gynn; casting, Karen Rea; cos, Rita Riggs; makeup, Kelly Phillips; stunts, Giedrius Nagys

Thriller **(PR: O MPAA: R)**

UNE NOUVELLE VIE
(SEE: NEW LIFE, A)

UNFORGETTABLE ★★

(U.S.) 111m Dino De Laurentiis Communications; MGM ~ MGM/UA c

Ray Liotta *(David Krane)*; Linda Fiorentino *(Martha Briggs)*; Peter Coyote *(Don Bresler)*; Christopher McDonald *(Stewart Gleick)*; David Paymer *(Curtis Avery)*; Duncan Fraser *(Michael Stratton)*; Caroline Elliot *(Cara Krane)*; Colleen Rennison *(Lindy Krane)*; Kim Cattrall *(Kelly)*; Stellina Rusich *(Mary Krane)*; Kim Coates *(Eddie Dutton)*; Suzy Joachim *(Sheila Wills)*; Garwin Sanford *(Joseph Bodner)*; Jenafor Ryane *(Donna Berman)*; Jimmy Broyden *(Boyfriend)*; Dean Choe *(Assistant Pharmacist)*; Mike Crestjo *(Pharmacist)*; Joanna Piros *(Media)*; Kevin Hayes *(Media #2)*; Cheryl Wilson *(Female Colleague)*; Nathaniel Deveaux *(George Guard #1)*; Dwight McFee *(Andy Guard #1)*; Claudio de Victor *(Building Manager)*; Arlen Jones *(Priest)*; Sidonie Boll *(Mother)*; Eric Pospisil *(Small Son)*; Rondel Reynoldson *(Nurse Karen)*; Brock Chapman *(Young Eddie Dutton)*; Bob Wilde *(Eddie's Dad)*; Cory Dagg *(Lawyer)*; Robert Metcalfe *(District Attorney)*; Henry Watson *(Judge)*; William B. Davis *(Dr. Smoot)*; Tong Lung *(Police Sketch Artist)*; Robin Douglas *(Receptionist)*; Callum Keith Rennie *(Drug Dealer)*; Roland Corkum *(Priest at Wedding)*; Leslie Graham *(Nurse)*; David Sobolov *(Paramedic)*; Kate Lancaster *(Female Nude Corpse)*; Tom Davies *(Male Nude Corpse)*; Dave St. Pierre *(Sexy Guy)*; Isabel Price *(Sexy Girl)*; Dale Villeneuve *(Sexy Girl)*; Azalea Davila *(Eddie's Girlfriend)*

Ray Liotta and Linda Fiorentino are two fine actors who seem right together, but UNFORGETTABLE, a sloppy noir pastiche, defeats its charismatic stars with weak plotting and direction.

Dr. David Krane (Ray Liotta) is a forensic pathologist who works closely with the Seattle Police Department. David has lived under a cloud of suspicion since the brutal murder of his wife, Mary. Accused of the crime, he was released on a technicality, but many, including Mary's sister, Kelly (Kim Cattrall), who has temporary custody of David's children, still believe he is a murderer.

To clear his name and figure out who really killed his wife, David becomes acquainted with Dr. Martha Briggs (Linda Fiorentino), a pioneering neurobiologist who has been experimenting with memory transfer in rats. Linda has discovered that profound memories are stored in the cerebral spinal fluid, and has developed a formula that can retrieve these events. David volunteers to be Linda's human guinea pig for this potentially dangerous experiment, but Linda refuses for fear of damaging David's heart.

Nevertheless, David steals the formula and injects himself with Mary's memories. By reliving her slaying, David thinks he has discovered her killer, a street thug named Michael Stratton (Duncan Fraser), but later he realizes that the story of his wife's murder is much more complicated. Feeling increasingly sympathetic, Linda helps David by monitoring her "patient" as he activates more sordid memories.

Finally, together, David and Linda narrow down the list of suspects to one of David's colleagues on the police force who was having an affair with Mary—either Detective Stewart Gleick (Christopher McDonald), the coroner Curtis Avery (David Paymer), or David's boss, Detective Don Bresler (Peter Coyote). By returning to the scene of the crime in his old house, David figures out that Mary was having an affair with his corrupt boss, Det. Bresler, who killed her to cover up their clandestine activities. When Bresler arrives at the house to kill David as well, the men engage in a fierce battle. Ultimately, David loses the fight, but his death allows him to be reunited with his wife in the hereafter.

The chief trouble with UNFORGETTABLE lies with Bill Geddie's hole-ridden screenplay, which jumbles together bits and pieces from several old and new noir thrillers, including the doctor-patient mystery melodrama from SPELLBOUND (1945), and the falsely-accused-doctor-clearing-his-name-in-his-wife's-murder scenario from THE FUGITIVE (1993). Even the "flashback" gimmick (which seems farfetched in this realistic milieu) puts a pharmacological twist on the virtual reality device in STRANGE DAYS. Over-hyped 'B' director John Dahl (RED ROCK WEST, THE LAST SEDUCTION) tries distracting viewers from the familiar plot and characters with these quickly-cut, sometimes confusing flashbacks, but they become annoying and repetitious after a while (technically, the film isn't very accomplished, either).

The only reasons to watch UNFORGETTABLE are Liotta and Fiorentino. Liotta makes his doomed hero's obsessive quest almost believable, while Fiorentino does as much as she can with the underwritten role of the scientist sidekick. Fiorentino even gives the film its very few moments of humor, although her character is a weak sister next to her LAST SEDUCTION femme fatale, and, of course, Dahl still finds a way to photograph Fiorentino in underwear and high heels. Nevertheless, UNFORGETTABLE depends too much upon its stars to carry it off. Hollywood should realize by now that Liotta and Fiorentino deserve better than a rehash of old movie cliches. *(Violence, adult situations, substance abuse, profanity.)* — E.M.

d, John Dahl; p, Dino De Laurentiis, Martha De Laurentiis; exec p, Andrew Lazar, Rick Dahl, William Teitler; w, Bill Geddie; ph, Jeffrey Jur; ed, Eric L. Beason, Scott Chestnut; m, Christopher Young; prod d, Rob Pearson; art d, Doug Byggdin; set d, Elizabeth Wilcox; sound, Eric J. Batut (mixer); fx, Gary Paller, David Cowan; casting, Carol Lewis; cos, Terry Dresbach, Glenne Campbell; makeup, Linda A. Brown; stunts, Bill Ferguson

Mystery/Horror/Drama (PR: C MPAA: R)

UNHOOK THE STARS ★★★½

(U.S.) 105m Hachette Premiere; Miramax ~ Miramax c

Gena Rowlands *(Mildred)*; Marisa Tomei *(Monica)*; Gerard Depardieu *(Big Tommy)*; Jake Lloyd *(J.J.)*; Moira Kelly *(Ann Mary Margaret)*; David Sherrill *(Ethan)*; David Thornton *(Frankie)*; Bridgette Wilson *(Jeannie)*; Bobby Cooper *(Bernt)*; Clint Howard *(Gus)*; Dave Rowlands *(George)*; James Bozian *(Jason)*; Christy Lenk *(Miss Manis)*; Brittney Lewis *(Hospital Receptionist)*; Vinny Curto *(Danny)*; D. Chance Williams *(Bartender)*; Gerard L'Heureux *(Mover)*; Tom Proctor *(Duncan)*; Dru Homer *(Bar Patron)*

UNHOOK THE STARS, Nick Cassavetes' feature directing debut, is a funny, perceptive slice-of-life movie with a knockout performance by Gena Rowlands, who happens to be the director's mother.

Mildred (Gena Rowlands) is a bright, sixtyish widow living in a comfortable, but now a little too empty, suburban house. Her son Ethan (David Sherrill) left the nest some time ago and is now a successful, married career man in San Francisco. Mildred's daughter (Moira Kelly) is a rebellious teenager who comes home mostly to crash and can't even hold down a paper-route job. After a particularly vivid blowup between mother and daughter, the latter takes off, seemingly for good, and Mildred finds herself completely alone. Companionship arrives via the unlikely persona of Monica (Marisa Tomei), a brash blue-collar neighbor who turns up on Mildred's doorstep in search of a last-minute baby-sitter for her six-year-old son J. J. (Jake Lloyd). Although Monica is a complete stranger, Mildred agrees to look after the boy for the day, and she and J. J. form a strong bond. The youngster is charmed by Mildred's patient, instructive manner and Mildred finds in J. J. a bright, receptive child who makes her feel valuable. Soon, the two are practically inseparable. Monica can't believe her luck, since Mildred doesn't charge for baby-sitting, and she too warms up to the older woman. Mildred's simple, generous decision winds up changing a number of lives, not least of all her own.

By the time she has become a concerned observer in Monica's volatile relationship with estranged husband Frankie (David Thornton), Mildred herself meets a French-Canadian truck driver named Big Tommy (Gerard Depardieu). A hard-drinking, rather bashful gentleman, Big Tommy is quickly smitten, a development which Mildred initially finds perplexing, but which soon intrigues her. Eventually, the two become so close that Tommy asks her to go with him to Florida, but Mildred declines the invite, choosing instead to stay and look after J. J.

On a certain level, the narrative and, indeed, Cassavetes' directorial approach, might be considered naturalistic, but hardly in the gritty, even exploitative vein that a story involving an absent father (although a contrite Frankie does resurface) and a temporarily neglected child might generally invite. This is a movie that recognizes sentiment but elects to refrain from it in favor of something more poetic. Tomei gives a spirited performance as the working-class mom who sometimes feels she's at the end of her rope. Kelly brings a fierceness to Mildred's daughter which explains a lot about their relationship. Mildred is far from perfect, even if Gena Rowlands' performance is perfection itself. Long distinguished for her emotionally-charged performances in husband John Cassavetes' movies, Rowlands here is called on to convey some very subtle changes in the life of a woman who appears "ordinary," but longs for a deeper meaning to her life.

The scenes involving Mildred and Big Tommy, shot in a boisterous tavern and the cab of his huge rig, are totally charming. That neither Cassavetes' direction nor his screenplay, written with Helen Caldwell, condescends to this tentative romance is emblematic of UNHOOK THE STARS' thoughtful view of the changeable relationships which provide the film's dynamics. It's nice, too that the ending doesn't suggest for Mildred a "happy-ever-after" life in Florida with Big Tommy, but an independent existence closer to home. *(Adult situations, profanity).* — E.K.

d, Nick Cassavetes; p, Rene Cleitman; exec p, Bernard Bouix; co-p, Panos C. Nicolaou; w, Nick Cassavetes, Helen Caldwell; ph, Phedon Papamichael; ed, Petra Von Oelffen; m, Steven Hufsteter; prod d, Phedon Papamichael Sr.; set d, Barbard Ward; sound, Jonathan "Earl" Stein (mixer); fx, Peter Daniels, Rolf Larsen, Marc Arcolio; casting, Matthew Barry; cos, Tessa Stephensen; makeup, Christina Smith; stunts, Terri Sue Judkins

Drama/Comedy **(PR: C MPAA: R)**

UNKNOWN ORIGIN ★★

(U.S.) 76m Pacific Trust ~ New Horizons Home Video c

Roddy McDowall *(Dr. Lazarus)*; Alex Hyde-White *(Jedediah Pickett)*; Melanie Shatner *(Catherine Hardy)*; Don Stroud *(Louis)*; Rodger Halston *(Wyatt)*; Emile Levisetti *(Brill)*; Richard Briggs *(Hawkes)*; Sha-ri Pendleton *(Fife)*; Miro Polo *(Russian Officer)*; Tim Trevan *(Russian Man)*

UNKNOWN ORIGIN is a B-movie chiller that steals from ALIEN (1979) so shamelessly that it's like watching a page-by-page remake. Set in the ocean depths, UNKNOWN ORIGIN is a submerged road-show approximation of the original classic tale of parasitic invasion.

On the ocean floor in 2020, scientists and technicians for Mobicom Industries receive a distress call from an underwater Russian mining community. Clashing over the crisis are Capt. Jedediah Pickett (Alex Hyde-White), who urges caution, and Dr. Lazarus (Roddy McDowall), who wants to get his hands on a two-million-year-old creature just awakening from suspended animation. Having mortally dehydrated most of the Russian crew, the intelligent creature is a beast that is capable of multiplying and must seek out fresh human hosts every few days. His new food supply is composed of Pickett's crew.

Although company executive Catherine Hardy (Melanie Shatner) sides with Pickett, Lazarus reprograms his android, Brill (Emile Levisetti), to keep the beast alive at all costs.

In rapid order, crewman Louis (Don Stroud) becomes infected, and a dying Russian survivor passes his intrusive organism on to Fife (Sha-ri Pendleton). Paranoia sweeps the underwater mission so totally that Capt. Pickett decides to force the lifeforms out of hiding by subjecting each of his co-workers to oxygen deprivation. Quickly, the oceanic invader deserts crewmember Hawkes (Richard Briggs) for the healthier insides of a startled Dr. Lazarus.

Although the inhabited Louis is blasted to death, Dr. Lazarus prevails with android assistance and summons a topside rescue team to dive downward. The as-yet uninfected trio of Pickett, Hardy, and Wyatt (Rodger Halston) eventually outwits the inhabited Lazarus, who is subsequently torched by Wyatt and Hardy. Unfortunately, Wyatt succumbs to a parasite during a solo cavern reconnaissance, so his associates eliminate him. Safely tucked inside an escape pod, Pickett and Hardy await salvation. What their rescuers don't realize is that Pickett and Hardy also house the life-sucking creatures.

The team behind UNKNOWN ORIGIN copies ALIEN so thoroughly that this sci-fi cheapie is practically a homage, despite the fact that UNKNOWN ORIGIN is not set in outer space. An alien fiend inspired by H.R. Giggler doesn't lose its basic identity in salt water. Here is a short list of what the two movies have in common: (1) a secretive android, (2) the process of human-inhabitation by the original creature, (3) the use of human hosts to incubate future eggs, and (4) an embittered crew employed by a venal corporation unconcerned with its workers' safety.

This film does mount an escalating atmosphere of paranoia. It remains watchable despite routine direction and wooden acting.

In space, no one can hear you scream; on the ocean floor, however, everyone can easily identify the sounds of an influential film being ripped off. *(Graphic violence, nudity, substance abuse, adult situations, profanity.)* — R.P.

d, Scott Levy; p, Mike Elliott; exec p, Roger Corman; co-p, Bill Bromley Jr.; w, Alex Simon; ph, Mike Mickens; ed, John Bergstresser; m, Christopher Lennertz; prod d, Doug Meerdink; art d, Michelle Fort; set d, Ron Durant; sound, Christopher Taylor (mixer); fx, Lou Carlucci, Robert Skotak, Dennis Skotak; casting, Jan Glaser; cos, Tami Mor Wyman, Rina Ramon Fiddler; makeup, Tania Wanstall, Fionaugh Cush; stunts, Patrick Statham

Science Fiction/Adventure/Horror **(PR: C MPAA: R)**

UP CLOSE AND PERSONAL ★★

(U.S.) 124m Cinergi Productions; UCP Productions; Scott Rudin Productions; The Avnet/Kerner Company; Touchstone ~ Buena Vista c

Robert Redford *(Warren Justice)*; Michelle Pfeiffer *(Tally Atwater)*; Stockard Channing *(Marcia McGrath)*; Joe Mantegna *(Bucky Terranova)*; Kate Nelligan *(Joanna Kennelly)*; Glenn Plummer *(Ned Jackson)*; James Rebhorn *(John Merino)*; Scott Bryce *(Rob Sullivan)*; Raymond Cruz *(Fernando Buttanda)*; Dedee Pfeiffer *(Luanne Atwater)*; Miguel Sandoval *(Dan Duarte)*; Nobel Willingham *(Buford Sells)*; James Karen *(Tom Orr)*; Brian Markinson *(Vic Nash)*; Michael Laskin *(IBS Director)*; Robert Keith Watson *(IBS Makeup Man)*; Lily Nicksay

(Star Atwater); Joanna Sanchez *(Ileana)*; Daniel Zacapa *(Harvey Harris)*; Heidi Swedberg *(Sheila)*; Fern Buchner *(WMIA Makeup Woman)*; Miguel Perez *(WMIA Floor Manager)*; Nicholas Cascone *(WMIA Director)*; Kenneth Fuchs *(WMIA Assistant Director)*; Julie Foreman *(WMIA Producer)*; Edwina Moore *(WMIA Co-Anchor)*; Patti Davis Suarez *(WMIA Reporter)*; Marc Macaulay *(Police Spokesman)*; Ed Amatrudo; Ana Azcuy; Peter D'Oench; Dave Game; Michelle Gillen; Eliott Rodriguez; Jennifer Valoppi *(Miami Reporters)*; Yareli Arizmendi *(Inez Cifuentes)*; Salvador Levy *(Congressman Diaz)*; Manny Suarez *(Diaz Aide)*; Neil Giuntoli *(Trailer Park Manager)*; Jason Sanford *(Photographer)*; Michael Villani *(Doug Dunning)*; Elizabeth Ruscio *(Lulu Delano)*; Michael Shamus Wiles *(WFIL Cameraman)*; Nigel Gibbs *(WFIL Floor Manager)*; Mary Elizabeth Sheridan *(98-year-old Twin)*; Marian Lamb Bechtelheimer *(98-year-old Twin)*; Natalie Barish; Wanda Lee Evans; Charles Noland; Charles Martiniz; Charles C. Stevenson Jr.; Cynthia Szigeti *(Focus Group)*; Guillermo Gentile *(Chess Player)*; Fabian *(Himself)*; Richard Alliger *(Right to Life Protester)*; Ginny Graham *(Homeless Woman)*; Frederick Strother *(City Councilman)*; Larry John Meyers *(Murray Gordon)*; Andy Prosky *(Cord Otavio)*; Bruce Gray *(Gabe Lawrence)*; Norman Parker *(Mark Lindner)*; Lori New *(Merino's Secretary)*; Charlie Holliday *(Priest)*; Leontine Guilliard *(Guard Shay)*; Johnnie Hobbs Jr. *(Warden)*; Tom McCarthy *(Negotiator)*; Roger Rathburn *(Gary Logan)*; Dennis Dun *(Satellite Van Technician)*; Rhonda Overby *(WFIL Reporter)*; Lexie Bigham *(Convict)*; Jack Shearer *(Prison Expert)*; Andrew Glassman *(Shouting Questioner)*; Rick Warner *(Spokesman)*; Joe B. Shapiro *(Waiter)*; Rosie Malek-Yonan *(Boarding Agent)*; Chris Stone *(Backstage Floor Manager)*

Imagine TO DIE FOR without the satire and you have UP CLOSE AND PERSONAL, a deliberately veiled version of the Jessica Savitch story.

Sallyanne Atwater (Michelle Pfeiffer) is an eager and talented local reporter and former beauty contest winner from Reno, Nevada. Thanks to her appealing demo reel, Sallyanne lands a job as a newsroom assistant at a Miami station presided over by Warren Justice (Robert Redford), a much-married former White House correspondent. In a short span of time, Sallyanne impresses Warren enough to audition as the station's weather girl, but just before the broadcast, she gets stage fright, so Warren helps out by changing her name to Tally, which is easier for her to pronounce.

With her new name and a new stylish image, Tally presses Warren for more challenging assignments. He allows her to interview a local politician about a police investigation, during which she displays cool professionalism despite her lack of familiarity with the case. Warren's growing respect for Tally turns into concern when she leaves the station to help her destitute sister pay off a debt. Tally is angered, however, when Warren follows her to Reno and pays off the debt himself.

Back in Miami, Tally convinces Warren to make her co-anchor despite the objections of Rob Sullivan (Scott Bryce), the current solo anchor. Tally is an immediate hit as an anchor and gets a job offer in Philadelphia to be a reporter with a major station. Before Tally leaves for Philadelphia, she and Warren acknowledge their love for one another and decide to get married.

At the new station, Tally feels intimidated by the resident anchor, Marcia McGrath (Stockard Channing), and struggles with her reporting duties. Visiting from Miami, Warren helps Tally to overcome her fears and become a star in local TV news. Eventually, Tally replaces Marcia as the show's anchor, and her new popularity attracts the network brass at IBS in Washington, DC. Tally clinches a major anchoring deal with IBS by reporting live from a prison during a dangerous riot, after which Warren tells Tally that he wants to go back to reporting, too. But soon after Warren heads down to Panama to uncover a top secret story, Tally learns that Warren has been killed in a shootout. Tally is devastated by the news, but recovers in time to pay tribute to Warren during an IBS ceremony in his honor.

According the recent, juicier made-for-cable TV movie, ALMOST GOLDEN: THE JESSICA SAVITCH STORY (1995), the late Jessica Savitch symbolized the news industry's pursuit of personality (and profit) over true talent. That point also is made superficially in UP CLOSE AND PERSONAL, except that glamorous neophyte reporter Tally Atwater represents the opposite of Savitch: she's supposedly full of talent and just *happens* to be unbelievably gorgeous. Yet, while Tally adopts Warren's credo that news is "not about lipstick," director and coproducer Jon Avnet's entire production *is* about lipstick—and haircuts and clothes—that never get mussed. Forget the whitewashing of the Savitch story (Tally's strongest bit of substance abuse involves a banana daiquiri); UP CLOSE AND PERSONAL lectures about journalistic integrity while hypocritically reveling in glossy close-ups of its two vanilla-bean stars (Tally's last line to Warren says it all: "You look so good"). To paraphrase Marshall McLuhan, "The makeup is the message."

A more pernicious form of sexism emerges quickly in the A STAR IS BORN-styled script by novelists Joan Didion and John Gregory Dunne. Tally never once proves her worth as a reporter or anchor without the help of her Svengali, Warren. Even during the prison riot, Warren is on the scene feeding her lines. This is curious since the film, like James Brooks's BROADCAST NEWS (1987), elsewhere criticizes "dumb" anchors for getting their lines fed by smarter writer-producers. Tally's tribute to the godlike, literally larger-than-life image of Warren at the end provides fitting closure for a film about a woman reporter that gives top billing to its male star.

What's left to like in this draggy two-hour-plus epic are a few sharp moments from Stockard Channing and Kate Nelligan, both playing tough, older rival anchors. The viewer won't notice them for long, however: these two actors are passed over in the film in the same way their two characters are passed over in the story. This oversight is unfortunate since Channing and Nelligan give something genuine to a drama that is otherwise cosmetic. *(Violence, sexual situations, adult situations, profanity.)* — E.M.

d, Jon Avnet; p, Jon Avnet, Dick Nicksay, Jordan Kerner; exec p, Ed Hookstratten, John Foreman; co-p, Lisa Lindstrom, Martin Huberty; w, Joan Didion, John Gregory Dunne (suggested by the book *Golden Girl* by Alanna Nash); ph, Karl Walter Lindenlaub; ed, Debra Neil-Fisher; m, Thomas Newman; prod d, Jeremy Conway; art d, Mark W. Mansbridge, Bruce Alan Miller; set d, Dorree Cooper; sound, Charles Wilborn (mixer); fx, Chuck Stewart; casting, David Rubin; cos, Albert Wolsky; makeup, Fern Buchner; stunts, Jery Hewitt, Doug Coleman

AAN Best Original Song: Diane Warren

Romance/Drama **(PR: A MPAA: PG)**

VENUS RISING ★

(U.S.) 91m IRS Media; Lumiere Pictures; Cyberfilms, Inc. ~ Columbia TriStar Home Video c

Audie England *(Eve)*; Costas Mandylor *(Vegas)*; Billy Wirth *(Nick)*; John Kerry *(Man in Lifeboat)*; Richard Vidan *(Lujan)*; Ivory Ocean *(Wyndham)*; Mark Schneider *(Tourist on Beach)*; Meredith Salenger *(Maria)*; Jessica Marie Alba *(Young Eve)*; Greg Wrangler *(Cop under Pier)*; Sean Rolf *(Conductor)*; Joel Grey *(Jimmie)*; Dennis Dun *(Eddie)*; Henry Bean *(Customer in Bar)*; Morgan Fairchild *(Peyton)*; Adrian Vitoria *(Bodyguard)*

Set in one of those not-so-distant futures that look surprisingly like an already-here present, this ineffably dull virtual-reality bomb makes feeble use of its sci-fi subtext.

After skipping out of a near-impregnable prison island, K314, where the powerful Pacifica Corporation banishes felons, Evie (Audie England), who's been raised in captivity, gets separated from her fugitive beau, Vegas (Costas Mandylor), and tries to enter polite society on the Pacifica mainland. Fearful of tarnishing his "foolproof" method of convict-containment, Warden Wyndham (Ivory Ocean) convinces lifer Nick (Billy Wirth) to help him recapture the island escapees in exchange for freedom.

Before the manhunt kicks in, Evie kills an insistent man who has paid her for sex. Serendipitously, Evie is befriended by a manic-depressive bisexual, Maria (Meredith Salenger), whose suicidal cliffside plunge paves the way for Evie to assume her identity. Sharing Maria's penchant for virtual reality trips, Evie is also taught the ropes of non-penitentiary lifestyles by Maria's neighbor Jimmie (Joel Grey).

While Nick noses around for clues, Evie takes a job waitressing at a trendy club owned by the Warden's business partner, Peyton (Morgan Fairchild). Balancing her dwindling loyalty to Vegas, whom she temporarily aids, with her growing affection for Nick, Evie tries to submerge painful memories of childhood sexual abuse at the prison colony.

After Vegas jealously kills Jimmie, he viciously assaults Nick, who is as yet unaware that the Warden plans to terminate him after he leads the Warden to the escapees. During a stand-off at Evie's pad, Nick slays Vegas in self-defense and also kills Wyndham. Evie leaves the wounded Nick. Years later, Evie, now the owner of Peyton's place, and Nick, now the Crime Commissioner, are reunited by their love of virtual reality.

After STRANGE DAYS, VIRTUOSITY, CYBER BANDITS, BLUE FLAME, etc. shouldn't Hollywood producers declare a moratorium on virtual reality-themed action opuses? Perhaps they should just insist that their screenwriters brain-travel through the scripts of better movies. With paper-thin characters acted by stars who seem to have just awakened, this torpid crime-and-punishment flick never once quickens the pulse of spectators. Scripted in a vacuous fashion and directed in a desultory mood, no connection exists between the characters and no momentum builds between potentially cathartic events. This movie is a fugue state for souls like Evie, who have been reborn yesterday.

A minor misfire, VENUS RISING shoots itself in the foot instead of fashioning suspense out of Nick tracking a suspect who bewitches him, and fails to juice any voltage out of Evie being torn between two lovers.

In the leading roles, England, Wirth, and Mandylor merely pose their way through the story line like a trio of fashion-model zombies. *(Graphic violence, extreme profanity, extensive nudity, sexual situations, substance abuse.)* — R.P.

d, Leora Barish, Edgar Bravo; p, Thomas Small, Johnna Levine, Albert Dickerson III; exec p, Lila Cazes, Miles A. Copeland III, Paul Colichman; w, Leora Barish (based on a story by Leora Barish and Henry Bean); ph, John Thomas; ed, James Fletcher, Edgar Bravo; m, Deborah Holland; prod d, Kathleen McKernin; set d, Katie Lipsitt; sound, Bill Robbins (mixer); fx, Mike Goedecke; casting, Donald Paul Pemrick; cos, Kathleen De Toro; makeup, Lori Depp, Josh Brezner, Mike Brezner; stunts, Patrick Statham

Action/Science Fiction/Crime (PR: C MPAA: R)

VERBRECHEN AM SEELENLEBEN EINES MENSCHENS

(SEE: KASPAR HAUSER)

VERY BRADY SEQUEL, A ★★★

(U.S.) 90m Ladd Company; Paramount ~ Paramount c

Shelley Long *(Carol Brady)*; Gary Cole *(Mike Brady)*; Christopher Daniel Barnes *(Greg Brady)*; Christine Taylor *(Marcia Brady)*; Paul Sutera *(Peter Brady)*; Jennifer Elise Cox *(Jan Brady)*; Jesse Lee *(Bobby Brady)*; Olivia Hack *(Cindy Brady)*; Henriette Mantel *(Alice)*; Tim Matheson *(Roy Martin/Trevor Thomas)*; Whip Hubley *(Explorer/Dead Husband)*; Whitney Rydbeck *(Auctioneer)*; Sue Casey *(Art Patron #1)*; Gregory White *(Art Patron #2)*; RuPaul *(Ms. Cummings)*; Diana Theodore *(Ms. Cummings's Daughter)*; David Ramsey *(Brent the Lifeguard)*; Phil Buckman *(Jason the Lifeguard)*; Steven Gilborn *(Mr. Phillips)*; Michael Weatherred *(Flower Delivery Guy)*; Yvonne Farrow *(Charity Chairperson)*; Zsa Zsa Gabor *(Herself)*; Skip O'Brien *(Construction Worker)*; Jennifer Aspen *(Kathy Lawrence)*; Ian M. Galespie *(Coffee Shop Guy)*; Brian Van Holt *(Warren Mulaney)*; Bodhi Pine Elfman *(Coffee Customer)*; Richard Belzer *(Detective)*; Connie Ray *(Flight Attendant)*; Don Nahaku *(Car Rental Guy)*; Anthony J. Silva Jr. *(Hotel Concierge)*; Laura Weekes *(George Glass's Mother)*; Bill Applebaum *(George Glass's Father)*; Michael Lundberg *(George Glass)*; Sidney Liufau *(Security Guard)*; John Hillerman *(Dr. Whitehead)*

That rare follow-up film that's at least as entertaining as the original, A VERY BRADY SEQUEL is a savvy romp through our pop-culture consciousness. As in THE BRADY BUNCH MOVIE (1995), the blended Brady family of six step-siblings remains blithely and evidently unknowingly entrenched in the 1970s, while modern '90s life goes on about them. Ironically, SEQUEL isn't even particularly much of a sequel; there's little if anything here that depends on continuity from the first film. But then, irony is what the BRADY films are all about.

The plot is essentially a string—macrame, no doubt—on which to hang parody set-pieces. As in the series, oldest step-sibs Greg (Christopher Daniel Barnes) and Marcia (Christine Taylor) fight over who gets to move into the newly available attic room; unlike the series, they compromise by sharing it, with a sheet between the beds. Young Cindy (Olivia Hack) has lost her Kitty Karry-All doll; equally young Bobby (Jesse Lee) helps her look for it with his junior detective kit. Middle boy Peter (Paul Sutera) is reluctant to intern for dad Mike (Gary Cole) at his architectural firm; middle daughter Jan (Jennifer Elise Cox) has invented an imaginary boyfriend. Housekeeper Alice (Henriette Mantel) mugs and makes wise cracks. And mom Carol (Shelley Long) provides the central conflict.

It seems that Carol's long-presumed-dead adventurer husband, Roy Martin (Tim Matheson), has shown up at the Brady home. He insists he's making no claim for Carol, and Mike, of course, is as gracious and welcoming as any Brady male should be. Carol, however, finds herself increasingly plagued by guilt, and as nervous about making the right choice as any Brady female should be.

But "Roy" is really a con man and thief who apparently inflicted harm on the real Roy, a professor. (A short prologue involves an Indiana Jones-like quest for a priceless artifact, and treachery on a storm-tossed sea.) He's after the cheesy, and by now iconic, horse statue sitting on the credenza by the stairs in the Brady living room. Roy can't steal it yet, since Carol has taken it in to be cleaned. But this being the Brady home, he's more than welcome to be their guest. Roy's efforts to pilfer the horse are again temporarily thwarted when Carol donates it to a charity auction. In between, he's shanghaied by the always eerily cheerful kids for a musical set-piece sojourn to a mall, and has an inadvertent acid trip when Alice thoughtfully puts a whole bunch of his "gourmet mushrooms" into his spaghetti. His trip involves an animated musical sequence (based on the Saturday-morning cartoon series "The Brady Kids," complete with silent cameos by Moptop the dog, Marlon the mynah bird, and pandas Ping and Pong).

Detective Bobby eventually discovers that Roy's a fraud. Roy, however, absconds with the statue of the horse after he unsuccessfully tried to buy it at the auction, where Zsa Zsa Gabor and friend Rosie O'Donnell (in an uncredited cameo) bid for it. Carol winds up as his hostage as he jets to Hawaii to deliver the purloined goods. Mike and the kids follow, of course, and they all have a showdown at the mansion of millionaire art collector Dr. Whitehead (John Hillerman). Though good triumphs in the end, there is sadness, too—Dr. Whitehead's son, Gilligan, was on that sabotaged boat, the *Minnow.*

This hilarious sequel is best summed up by the fake Professor Roy Martin who, after ingesting a whole lotta 'shrooms, disbelievingly realizes, "I'm tripping with the Bradys." This is, indeed, a trip of bountiful gags, laser-precise parodies, and music Quentin Tarantino would love. A VERY BRADY SEQUEL also carefully and very shrewdly extends the mythos: With the game approval of series creator Sherwood Schwartz (briefly appearing in the final scene when Mike and Carol renew their vows), we even get to see a physical moment of what we always *thought* was happening between Greg and Marcia!

Gary Cole is the standout performer, again eerily channeling his TV-series predecessor, Robert Reed. David Spade has an uncredited cameo as a hairdresser, Sergio; Barbara Eden is likewise uncredited at the end as Jeannie from TV's "I Dream of Jeannie." *(Adult situations.)* — F.L.

d, Arlene Sanford; p, Sherwood Schwartz, Lloyd J. Schwartz, Alan Ladd Jr.; co-p, Michael Fottrell, Kelliann Ladd; w, Harry Elfont, Deborah Kaplan, James Berg, Stan Zimmerman (from a story by Harry Elfont and Deborah Kaplan, based on characters created by Sherwood Schwartz); ph, Mac Ahlberg; ed, Anita Brandt-Burgoyne; m, Guy Moon; prod d, Cynthia Charette; art d, Troy Sizemore; set d, Bob Kensinger; sound, Jim Tanenbaum (mixer); fx, Richard Stutsman, Tom Mertz; casting, Deborah Aquila, Jane Shannon Smith; cos, Rosanna Norton; makeup, Todd McIntosh; stunts, John Robotham

Comedy **(PR: C MPAA: PG-13)**

VIKING SAGAS, THE ★

(Iceland/U.S.) 83m Gurian Productions ~ New Line Home Video c

Ralf Moeller *(Kjartan)*; Ingibjorg Stefansdottir *(Gudrun)*; Sven-Ole Thorsen *(Gunnar)*; Thorir Waagfjord *(Bolli)*; Hinrik Olafson *(Ketil)*; Raimund Harmstorf *(Valgaurd)*; Magnus Jonsson *(Eirik)*; Magnus Olafsson *(Bjorn)*; David Kristjansson *(Ketil's Lieutenant)*; Rurik Haraldson *(Magnus)*; Bryndis Petursdottir *(Helga)*; Valgerdur Runarsdottir *(Loyal Servant)*; Johonna Jonas *(Kristin)*; Egill Olafsson *(Hrut)*; Porstein Bachman *(Drunken Viking)*; Hans-Martin Stier *(Mord)*; Bjorn Floberg *(Sighvat)*; Margret Helga Johannsdottir *(Sighvat's Mother)*; Gudmundur Thrainsson *(Ulf)*; Gunter Ziegler *(Viking on Roof)*; Gudrandur Sigurdsson *(Ghost)*; Gunnar Eyjolfsson *(Eirik the White)*; Margret Olafsdottir *(Hildegard)*; Jon Baldvinsson *(Thord the Strong)*; Theodor Juliusson *(Onund)*

As director of this clanging historical spectacle, Michael Chapman—cinematographer of RAGING BULL (1980)—ineptly stages action scenes and incompetently handles actors, thus demonstrating the wisdom of sticking to what one does best.

Due to the sagacity of dying Icelandic ruler Valgaurd (Raimund Harmstorf), his heir apparent Kjartan (Ralf Moeller) eludes slaughter at the hands of the throne-usurper Ketil (Hinrik Olafson). Escaping with the Ghost Sword that Ketil covets (and will later recapture), Kjartan wanders into the land of Lawgiver Magnus (Rurik Haraldson), just in time to prevent physically the marriage of Magnus's daughter Gudrun (Ingibjorg Stefansdottir) to Ketil's brutal ally, Mord (Hans-Martin Stier). Afterward, in the icy wasteland, Kjartan trains in warriordom with disgraced clansman, Gunnar (Sven-Ole Thorsen), who prepares Kjartan for his destiny, although he lusts after Kjartan's new love, Gudrun. In a loyalty conundrum, unhinged Gunnar breaks tribal law by slaying two of Ketil's scouts from the same family. Meanwhile, ever conscious of fulfilling a prophecy regarding Kjartan and Gudrun's reign over Iceland, Magnus and his family sacrifice their lives so Kjartan and Gudrun can ride further out of Ketil's clutches.

Although Gunnar cracks under pressure and begins killing innocent Vikings, Kjartan and Gudrun are able to extend their life spans due to the interference of a benevolent ghost who wipes out an entire Ketil contingent. Intent on wedding Gudrun to consolidate his power, Ketil agrees to a tribal powwow, but Gudrun tricks him; instead of conceding to a betrothal, she declares herself the new Lawgiver. When Kjartan arrives, he beats Ketil fairly in combat and reclaims his family's Ghost Sword; Gudrun and Kjartan establish a new era of Viking peace and prosperity.

Primitive rather than primal, this celluloid comic strip isn't nearly as much fun as Richard Fleischer's THE VIKINGS (1958). Despite gorgeous on-location shooting, THE VIKING SAGAS is an ancient superhero dud that confuses spilled gore with invigorating action. Bogged down by pompous narration, this flick is essential viewing only for the non-discriminating who prefer their violence fantasies cloaked in legendary dress-up. The most perplexing question revolves around director Chapman's technique: why does he continually cut away to close-ups of lopped-off limbs during battle scenes? Blood-drenched nonsense, the film fails on a visceral level and doesn't come close to engaging the audience emotionally with its clumsy approach to myth-making. *(Graphic violence, extensive nudity, adult situations, sexual situations.)* — R.P.

d, Michael Chapman; p, Paul Gurian; exec p, Tim Van Relim; w, Paul Gurian, Dale Herd; ph, Dean Lent; ed, Lawrence Jordan; m, George S. Clinton; prod d, Bryce Perrin; set d, Arni Pall Johannsson; sound, Sigurdur Sigurdsson (mixer); fx, John Hartigan, Paul White; casting, Pennie Dupont; cos, Pamela Tait; makeup, Ragna Fossberg; stunts, Paul Weston

Adventure/Historical **(PR: C MPAA: R)**

VIRTUAL COMBAT ★★

(U.S.) 97m Amritraj/Stevens Entertainment ~ A-Pix Entertainment c

Don "The Dragon" Wilson *(David Quarry)*; Athena Massey *(Lana)*; Michael Bernardo *(Dante)*; Michael Dorn *(Voice of Dante)*; Ken McLeod *(John)*; Dawn Ann Billings *(Greta)*; Carrie Mitchum *(Cathy)*; Larry Poindexter *(Employee)*; Johnny Williams *(Fred)*; Ron Barker *(Burroughs)*; Turhan Bey *(Dr. Cameron)*; Loren Avedon *(Parness)*; Tim Baker *(Thug)*; Dave Sinnott *(Ken)*; Peggy Trentino *(Debbie)*; Stella Stevens *(Mary)*; Rip Taylor *(Cyber-Sex Pitchman)*; Gilbert Lewis *(A. C. Doyle)*

VIRTUAL COMBAT treads familiar ground with a gimmicky plot line about fantasy figures from virtual reality games coming to life.

For Nevada border cops Dave Quarry (Don "The Dragon" Wilson) and his pal John (Ken McLeod), virtual reality combat is a challenging way to hone kickboxing skills. Meanwhile, Dr. Lawrence Cameron (Turhan Bey) has perfected his astounding "cyberplasmic" theory for greedy mogul Mr. Burroughs (Ron Barker) and DNA-ed two VR sexmates into existence through the company computer. While Burroughs prepares Lana (Athena Massey) and Greta (Dawn Ann Billings) for an out-of-town marketing kickoff, VR game figure Dante (Michael Bernardo) frees himself from the game. Planning to liberate his equally vicious combat cronies from the company's mainframe, Dante celebrates his new life-state by annihilating several peace officers, including John.

Lana and Greta break free of Burroughs but fall under Dante's telepathic command, while Dave resolves to avenge John's death despite a manhunt launched against him by Burroughs. Betrayed by his own superior officer, Dave pursues arch-foe Dante, deactivates Greta, and teams up with Lana before she's recaptured. Making short work of Burroughs' thugs, the cop blows up Burroughs with his own enslaver necklace and then squares off against Dante, who destroys Lana for aiding the human hero. Replaying their rivalry from the VR game, Dave and Dante fight to the death. The cop neutralizes Dante and obliterates his cyberplasmic playmates before they're brought into existence via a computer.

Action-packed but over-plotted, VIRTUAL COMBAT loses intensity and suspense because of its emphasis on martial arts fight sequences. Wilson isn't actor enough to tame all this film's wilder storylines; with so many double-crosses and public enemies, the movie meanders anticlimactically during its final segments. The film fortunately does have one imaginative element—a "Frankenstein"-like take on virtual reality.

Not as spiffy and high-energy as other Don "The Dragon" vehicles, VIRTUAL COMBAT suffers from Andrew Stevens' incohesive direction. Still, if the star's flying feet can't compensate for unfocused direction and cluttered writing, they perform one vital function: distracting viewers from the desire to glance at their wristwatches. *(Graphic violence, extensive nudity, profanity.)* — R.P.

d, Andrew Stevens; p, Ashok Amritraj; assoc p, James Holt; w, William C. Martell; ph, David Miller; ed, Mark Speer, Wayne Schmidt, Tony Mark; m, Claude Gaudette; prod d, Roger Nall; art d, Helen Harwell; sound, James Einolf (mixer), Arnold Braun (mixer); fx, Neil Smith; cos, Suzanne Schwarzer; makeup, Kathleen Karridene, Anthony Ferrante, Sam Greenmum; stunts, Art Camacho

Action/Science Fiction/Martial Arts (PR: C MPAA: R)

VIRTUAL ENCOUNTERS ★

(U.S.) 86m Surrender Cinema ~ Surrender Cinema/Amazing Fantasy Entertainment c

Elizabeth Kaitan *(Amy)*; Taylore St. Claire *(Maggie)*; Rob Lee *(Michael)*; Mickey Ray *(Guard/Patron)*; Lori Morrisey *(Candle Girl)*; Jim Caciola *(Candle Boy/Cyber Boy)*; Jacqueline Lovell *(Kika)*; Tricia Yen *(Miko)*; Michelle Barry *(Ginger/Dierdre)*; Jill Kelly *(Cave Girl)*; Vince Vouyer *(Cave Boy)*; Ashley Yates *(Erica)*; Noelle *(Brandy)*; Everett Rodd *(Water Boy/Cyber Boy)*; Sheron Drew; T. J. Hansen *(Go-Go Girls)*

It's a good thing science and technology continue to progress, given the endless need of low-budget filmmakers for new excuses to put naked, writhing women onscreen.

Amy (Elizabeth Kaitan) has been avoiding having sex with her new boyfriend Michael (Rob Lee), even though she loves him. Before leaving on a business trip, Michael gives her a birthday gift—a series of visits to Virtual Encounters. They offer the ultimate in virtual reality experiences: sexual encounters geared to the personality particulars of the client.

In a skin-tight suit and special headset, Amy views a series of sexual encounters with a couple in a jungle setting and on a bed, and between two women. When her unseen guide decides it is time for her to become a participant, she vicariously enjoys the feelings of a dancer who seduces a patron.

Leaving work early the next day, Amy returns for more encounters in which she "virtually" makes love to her secretary, experiences sex as a man, and finally makes love as her own, newly uninhibited self. When Michael returns from his business trip, he is delighted at what Amy has learned.

As soft-core porn goes, VIRTUAL ENCOUNTERS is relatively unambitious, offering a parade of not-too-explicit sex scenes interrupted by only the barest semblance of a plot. But, aside from timid couples just rescued from a forty-year stay on a desert island, it's hard to imagine who could get terribly excited about this. The cinematographer and editors cram as many angles, positions, cuts and pans as possible into each act, as if that would somehow lessen the charge of prurience. VIRTUAL ENCOUNTERS is unobjectionable by the standards of the genre—but erotica that wouldn't offend anyone isn't likely to interest anyone else, either. *(Extensive nudity, sexual situations.)* — M.F.

d, Cybil Richards; p, Pat Siciliano; w, Lucas Riley; ph, Lester Wisbred; ed, Lowell Danner, Peregrine Beckman, Dan Lowenthal; m, Ollie Wood; prod d, John Zachery; casting, Pat Siciliano, Keely Rene; makeup, Ronda Rae

Erotic (PR: O MPAA: NR)

VIRUS ★★

(U.S.) 90m Spill Productions ~ Vidmark c

Brian Bosworth *(Ken Fairchild)*; Leah Pinsent *(Larraine Keller)*; David Fox *(George Skanz)*; Daniel Kash *(Ripley)*; Eric Peterson *(Eric Black)*; Stephen Markle *(President John L. Wheeler)*; Patrick Galligan *(Alex Bur)*; Janet Lund *(Natalie)*; Chuck Shamata *(Leo Burns)*; Rhea Akler *(First Scientist)*; Bill Copeland *(Chet Keller)*; Phillip Jarrett *(Isaac Smith)*; Ronn Sarosiak *(Norton)*; Jeffrey Akomah *(Kid)*; Eric Murphy *(Birk)*; Allan Goldstein *(Bobby)*; Kyle Schmid *(Sick Boy)*; Anthony Tullo *(Technician)*; Matt Birman *(Suspicious Man)*; Kate Greenhouse *(Reporter)*; Chris Gillette *(Doc)*; Kevin Riordan *(Park Officer)*

Yet another entry in the never-ending cycle of man-made laboratory catastrophes, this bio-thriller is a routine frightfest jump-started by spectacular stunt work. As an action hero, however, ex-football player Brian Bosworth acts as if he were sitting out the game on the bench.

Patriotic Secret Serviceman Ken Fairchild (Brian Bosworth) diligently guards President J. L. Wheeler (Stephen Markle) as he prepares for a World Eco-Conference at Thermal Wells National Park, Oregon. Meanwhile, all hell breaks loose at Prodichem Military Lab after an accident involving a bio-warfare virus results in a deadly cover-up by facility director, George Skanz (David Fox). Without presidential authority, Wheeler's right-wing aide, Eric Black (Eric Peterson), has already established a viral strike force program without sufficient safeguards. Tracked down by Skanz and Black's operatives, Prodichem scientist Alex Bur (Patrick Galligan) plans to disrupt the World Eco-Conference with damaging evidence of the bio-program's instability. Although Alex pays a drugged-up trucker, Ripley (Daniel Kash), to deliver a shipload of the dangerous bio-warfare material to the conference, Skanz murders Alex before he can enlighten the liberal press about Prodichem Lab. Meanwhile, substance-abuser Ripley crashes his deadly cargo with devastating results for Oregon and the world.

Thrust into the spill's aftermath, Fairchild convinces Ripley and local doctor Larraine Keller (Leah Pinsent) to try to stem the contagion, even as Skanz attempts to protect the president's reputation by eliminating any witnesses. Made immune by the common cold, Fairchild, Ripley, and Keller don't join the wave of casualties felled by the plague. Tipped off by Alex before he was killed, Fairchild's reporter-buddy, Leo (Chuck Shamata), travels to the conference site, but gets killed by Skanz; fortunately, he leaves behind Alex's incriminating data for Fairchild. Prior to the conference kick-off, Fairchild blasts Skanz away in a geyser valley and prevents Skanz's plan to extend the range of the virus. Disillusioned upon learning that the president did nothing to put a lid on Black's viral experimentation folly, Fairchild blows the whistle to the media and dismantles the power base of the president and his xenophobic advisor, Black.

Conspiracy thrillers have a long, honorable tradition in American movies, but flicks like this one that proceed on the assumption that our government hierarchy is staffed by trigger-happy fascists fall apart quickly. Silken deception and quick-wittedness are requisites for high office; bungling eager beavers like Skanz and Black couldn't possibly ascend past the crooked alderman stage.

Basically, VIRUS is about a big, strapping lummox who saves the world while assaulted by the triple plague of malaise-inducing plot-padding, debilitating deja vu, and feverish overplaying by supporting players and extras hoping to get noticed. Fans of muscular action will enjoy Bosworth's athleticism even if the script talks his anti-viral strategy to death. Viewers may feel as if the infected plague survivors have come down with a case of boring dialogue that could prove fatal to the audience. *(Extreme profanity, graphic violence, substance abuse.)* — R.P.

d, Allan A. Goldstein; p, Damian Lee; exec p, Gary Wichard, Ashok Amritraj; assoc p, John Gillespie; co-p, Helder Goncalves; w, Les Standiford (based on his novel, *Spill*); ph, Nicolas Von Sternberg; ed, Evan Landis; m, Larry Cohen; prod d, Tim Boyd; art d, Barry Isenor; set d, Mary Wilkinson; sound, Robert Woolfson (mixer); fx, Ron Craig; casting, Marjorie Lecker; cos, Marie Duplaga; makeup, Traci Loader; stunts, John Stoneham Stoneham

Action/Thriller **(PR: C MPAA: PG-13)**

VISITORS, THE ★★

(France) 107m Gaumont; France 3 Cinema; Alpilles Productions; Amigo Productions; Canal+ ~ Miramax Zoe c (LES VISITEURS; LES VISITEURS: ILS NE SONT PAS NES D'HIER!)

Christian Clavier *(Jacquouille/Jacquart)*; Jean Reno *(Godefroy)*; Valerie Lemercier *(Frenegonde/Beatrice)*; Marie-Anne Chazal *(Ginette)*; Christian Bujeau *(Jean-Pierre)*; Isabelle Nanty *(Fabienne Morlot)*; Gerard Sefty *(Edgar Bernay)*; Didier Pain *(Louis VI)*; Jean-Paul Muel *(Marechal des Logis Gibon)*; Ariel Semenoff *(Jacqueline)*; Michel Peyrelon *(Edouard Bernay)*; Pierre Vial *(Wizard Eusebius/Dr. Eusebe)*; Francois Lalande *(Priest)*; Didier Benureau *(Boarder)*; Frederic Baptiste *(Freddy)*; Pierre Aussedat *(Sergent-Chef Morlet)*; Tara Gano *(Witch)*; Stephanie Marie; Jean-Luc Caron; Anna Gaylor; Claire Magnin; Eric Averlant; Jean-Pierre Clami; Thierry Liagre; David Gabison; Patrick Burgel; Paul L Bandey ; Jerome Berthoud; Amandine Boyadjian; Yohan Boyadjian; Katia Delagarde; Eric Denize; Bela Gruschka; Dominique Hulin; Jean-Guillaume Le Dantec

Jean Reno and Christian Clavier star as a 12th-Century knight and his squire who are transported to modern-day France in THE VISITORS, a crude time-travel farce that became France's highest-grossing movie of all-time ($90 million) when it was released there in 1993. After numerous delays, it was released in America in 1996, and not surprisingly, was much less successful.

In the year 1122, French knight Godefroy (Jean Reno), is en route to marry Frenegonde (Valerie Lemercier), the Duchess of Pouille, but stops to capture a sorceress, who drugs him and causes him to shoot to death Frenegonde's father. Godefroy goes to see a wizard named Eusebius, who concocts a magic potion that will take him back in time so he can prevent this mishap, but instead, the potion sends Godefroy and his loyal servant Jacquouille (Christian Clavier) centuries into the future to the 1990s. After a series of culture-shock experiences, they are taken in by a local countess named Beatrice, who resembles Frenegonde, and who is a distant descendant of Godefroy's. She believes that Godefroy is her crazy, long-lost cousin Hubert, and has him examined by a psychiatrist when he insists he's really a knight from the 12th Century.

Godefroy is shocked to learn that the family palace has been turned into a hotel, which is managed by a prissy Jacquouille-lookalike named Jacquart, and he and Jacquouille go there to find the wizard's magic spell book, which will enable them to return to the past. The hotel's master bedroom has a secret passage to the dungeon, but the spell book has been destroyed. However, Godefroy finds a telephone number of a Dr. Eusebe, and the doctor is able to give him the magic potion. Jacquouille refuses to go back, having discovered the joys of modern-day society in which he no longer has to be a servant. Godefroy insists, so Jacquouille manages to get Jacquert to drink the potion, and he's unwittingly transported back in time along with Godefroy. In the 12th century, Godefroy kills the witch and successfully changes the path of the bullet that would have killed Frenegonde's father.

The incredible European success of the low-brow THE VISITORS indicates that it's not really necessary to protect France from the corruption of American cultural imperialism, something which the French are always complaining about. Perhaps we should question who is going to protect us from movies such as this, and other insipid hits such as 1995's UN INDIEN DANS LA VILLE (released here as LITTLE INDIAN, BIG CITY and remade as 1996's JUNGLE 2 JUNGLE). In an era when new films by such distinguished French directors as Bertrand Blier, Eric Rohmer, and Bertrand Tavernier don't get released in the US, Disney, and its subsidiary Miramax, are obsessed with importing and/or remaking bad French comedies.

At first, THE VISITORS was scheduled to be released in America in a dubbed version which was supervised by Mel Brooks. However, after years of delays, that version was deemed unreleasable after some disastrous test-screenings, so Miramax finally put out the original subtitled version with little fanfare, barely causing a ripple.

The most shocking thing about the film, beyond its general paucity of laughs and overall stupidity, is its relentlessly scatological tone, with blood, excrement, vomit, and other grotesque bodily functions dominating virtually every scene. Much of the humor relies on French slang and puns, but the basic fish-out-of-water premise is simple-minded and obvious, and the juxtaposition of the medieval primitives who encounter 20th-Century society lacks wit and originality.

Under the circumstances, the acting is quite good, with Christian Clavier (who also co-wrote it) outstanding in the dual-role of the moronic squire Jacquouille and his modern-day descendant, the fey Jacquart. The production is also quite handsome, with sweeping widescreen lensing, impressive sets, and good special effects providing a classy look. It's just too bad that all this effort was put to use in the service of a script that would have seemed dumb as a sketch on "The Benny Hill Show." *(Profanity, violence, adult situations.)* — M.S.

d, Jean-Marie Poire; p, Alain Terzian; w, Christian Clavier, Jean-Marie Poire, Chantal Pernecker, Celine Migeon, Caroline Emery, Rachel Corlet; ph, Jean-Yves Le Mener; ed, Catherine Kelber; m, Eric Levi; art d, Hugues Tissandier; set d, Betrand Seitz; sound, Claude Villand, Bernard Leroux, Jerome Levy, Jean-Charles Rualt; fx, Jean-Marc Mouligne, Excalibur, Duboi; casting, Francoise Menidrey, Celina Blanc; cos, Catherine Leterrier; makeup, Muriel Baurens, Jacques Gastineau

Comedy **(PR: C MPAA: R)**

VIVE L'AMOUR ★★½

(Taiwan) 118m Sunny Overseas; Shiung Fa Corporation; Central Motion Pictures Corporation ~ Strand Releasing c

Yang Kuei-mei *(May)*; Chen Chao-jung *(Ah-jung)*; Lee Kang-sheng *(Hsiao-kang)*

Formally elegant, the Taiwanese film VIVE L'AMOUR meticulously maps out an emotional state of modern alienation. This movie's detached aura and coolly distant use of long shots encapsulate its artistic message about contemporary lives that intersect but never really touch. Winner of the best film prize at the Venice Film Festival, VIVE L'AMOUR pigeonholes its purpose so completely that the end effect is admirable but airless.

In rootless, urban Taiwanese society, yuppies connect with their occupations more easily than with each other. Although swimming with the other real-estate sharks, career woman May Lin (Yang Kuei-mei) doesn't have her heart in hustling high-priced properties. She distractedly leaves the key in the door of an unsold high-rise apartment. Seizing the opportunity, a suddenly homeless, suicidal gay man named Hsiao-kang (Lee Kang-sheng) becomes a squatter, living phantom-like in this expensive, vacant room. May Lin shuffles living quarters for people on the move, and Hsiao-kang also sells space to customers—but his properties are crematorium containers for those at the end of life's journey.

Walking the evening streets alone, as usual, May Lin picks up a handsome street vendor, Ah-jung (Chen Chao-jung), who lives out of his suitcases. She escorts him back to the empty, sterile apartment. As May Lin and Ah-jung have sex, secret tenant Hsiao-kang vicariously enjoys their lovemaking without revealing his presence. Without May Lin's knowledge, Ah-jung lifts her keys and decides to crash at this showplace, too. After playing hide-and-seek, Ah-jung and Hsiao-kang discover that they are roommates. While Ah-jung drives Hsiao-kang to Taipei's main mausoleum, May Lin revisits the flat and luxuriates in the post-coital scent of the bed; but she can't break out of the rut of avoiding committed contact with anyone. Platonically, Ah-jung grows closer to Hsiao-kang than to May Lin, but Hsiao-kang daydreams of a physical rapport. When Ah-jung goes out on business, Hsiao-kang models a woman's outfit.

When May Lin and Ah-jung have their next tryst, Hsiao-kang lies under their bed and masturbates to the rhythm of their passion. The next morning, he stealthily slips into the bed and steals a kiss from the sleeping Ah-jung. Wandering in despair through the city's outskirts, May Lin breaks down in an outcry against her own inability to connect meaningfully with another human being. The trio of city-dwellers never conquers the overwhelming sense of isolation.

Director Tsai Ming-liang boxes his unhappy characters, and the audience, into an evocative serio-comedy about isolation—not as a choice but as the inescapable destination of modern life. If Tsai succeeds in conveying this bleak vision of a social structure that precludes emotional harmony, it is by distancing the viewers from feeling anything about his three troubled characters. Tsai has been compared to Michelangelo Antonioni, and cinephiles will pick up a dash of Robert Bresson as well, but Tsai's directorial flourishes seem to be cleverly applied touches rather than the inherent expression of an auteur's vision. It's not that he doesn't have something to say, or that he doesn't know how to say it. It's that he keeps saying something that's already been said, in ways that call celebrated filmmakers to mind.

Reservations aside, Tsai demonstrates a talent for framing images that can be haunting; he also has an almost musical gift for intercutting. For example, the way he juxtaposes the dual solitude of unable-to-love May Lin with unloved Hsiao-kang heightens their torment. It's as if we are eavesdropping simultaneously on the soliloquies of their souls. When May Lin raids her ice box and Hsiao-kang conducts his futile fashion show—as if willing himself to be what his heterosexual acquaintance desires—we realize that no subliminal substitution will ever satisfy these characters's loneliness. Short shrift, however, is given to love-object Ah-jung. Perhaps if the director didn't allow so many scenes to transpire in real time, he could have devoted more footage to fleshing out this catalytic character's personality.

In a movie devoted to ironies, May Lin sleeps with the dreamboat, Ah-jung, but uses him as a palliative to stave off panic; Hsiao-kang must content himself with being an erotic spy existing on the perimeter of other people's lust. Everyone loses. Everyone pines away in this fable where the villain is contemporary life. In the director's purview, his protagonists are casualties of an existential epidemic—and there is no cure for what ails them. *(Adult situations, nudity, sexual situations.)* — R.P.

d, Tsai Ming-liang; p, Chung Hu-pin, Hsu Li-kong; exec p, Jiang Feng-chyi; w, Tsai Ming-liang, Yang Pi-ying, Tsai Yi-chun; ph, Liao Pen-jung; ed, Sung Shin-cheng; art d, Lee Pao-ling; set d, Chen Chien-hsun; sound, Yang Jing-an, Hsin Chiang-sheng (design), Yang Ching-an, Hu Ding-yi; cos, Luo Chung-hung

Drama **(PR: C MPAA: NR)**

VUKOVAR ★★½

(Yugoslavia) 94m Dan Films Productions ~
Tara Releasing c
(VUKOVAR POSTE RESTANTE)

Mirjana Jokovic *(Anna)*; Boris Isakovic *(Toma)*; Monica Romic *(Ratka)*; Nebojsa Glogovac *(Fadil)*; Svetlana Bojkovic *(Vilma)*; Predrag Ejdus *(Stjepan)*; Dusica Zegarac *(Vera)*; Mihajlo Janketic *(Dusan)*

VUKOVAR places a Serb Romeo and a Croatian Juliet directly in the line of fire between warring factions in the former Yugoslavia. Yet, what should be heart- and gut-wrenching material suffers from the political slant of the filmmakers and some ordinary storytelling.

In 1989, the citizens of Vukovar, a Croatian town on the Danube, celebrate the fall of Communism as they watch on television the razing of the Berlin Wall. Particularly delighted by events are Anna (Mirjana Jokovic), a Croatian woman, and her Serb fiance, Toma (Boris Isakovic). Because of the good will in the air, the lovers' families give their blessings to the marriage despite the ethnic differences.

On their wedding day, however, hostilities break out between Serbs and Croatians in the town, and Toma is drafted into the Serb army. Anna, who is pregnant, moves in with her parents. One day, Anna leaves the house briefly to trade gold for bread. When she returns, she finds her parents have been killed by shelling. Soon after, Anna and a friend, Ratka (Monica Romic) are raped by Serb soldiers while Ratka's young daughter is forced to watch.

Toma finds his way back to Anna, but barely spends any time with her before he ends up fighting with Croatian soldiers. While

Toma is injured and gets separated from Anna again, Anna and Ratka take revenge on one of their rapists. Anna gives birth to her baby without anyone around to help.

Anna and Toma see each other again while sitting on buses leaving the city, headed in different directions.

Despite the many opportunities, writer-director Boro Draskovic and co-writer Maja Draskovic clarify neither the historical-political events leading up to the Bosnian conflict—as detailed in Marcel Ophuls's THE TROUBLES WE'VE SEEN—nor the social nuances that have impacted the situation, as detailed in Emir Kusturica's UNDERGROUND. But like UNDERGROUND, VUKOVAR has been criticized for favoring the Serb point of view despite the overwhelming evidence that the Serbs have been the primary aggressors in this horrific civil war.

Still, there are some strong moments in the drama, including the gang-rape scene; Toma's nearly surreal encounter with three women who resemble the witches from "Macbeth"; and the final shot of the film—an aerial view of what's left of the bombed-out city. It's too bad that so many other scenes resemble a Serb propaganda piece, the gang-rape notwithstanding. *(Graphic Violence, nudity, sexual situations, adult situations, profanity.)* — E.M.

d, Boro Draskovic; p, Danka Muzdeka Mandzuka; exec p, Steve North; assoc p, Zlatko Mandzuka, Dante Palladino; w, Maja Draskovic, Boro Draskovic; ph, Aleksandar Petkovic; ed, Snezana Ivanovic; art d, Miodrag Maric

War/Drama **(PR: C MPAA: NR)**

VUKOVAR POSTE RESTANTE

(SEE: VUKOVAR)

WALKING AND TALKING ★★★

(U.S.) 83m Good Machine Productions; Zenith Productions; Channel Four Films; TEAM; Pandora; Mikado; Electric ~ Miramax c

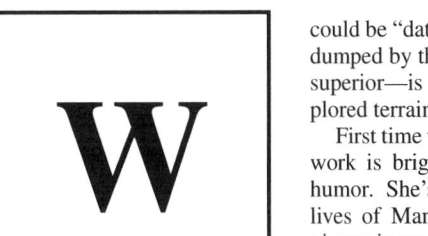

Catherine Keener *(Amelia)*; Anne Heche *(Laura)*; Liev Schreiber *(Andrew)*; Todd Field *(Frank)*; Kevin Corrigan *(Bill)*; Randall Batinkoff *(Peter)*; Joseph Siravo *(Amelia's Therapist)*; Vincent Pastore *(Laura's Devil-Seeing Patient)*; Lynn Cohen *(Andrew's Mom)*; Lawrence Holofcener *(Andrew's Dad)*; Amy Braverman *(Young Amelia)*; Miranda Stuart Rhyne *(Young Laura)*; Brenda Thomas *(Denmark)*; Rafael Alvarez *(Laura's Sexy Patient)*; Ritamarie *(Kelly)*; Steve Cohen *(Actor in Play)*; Jordan Levinson *(Peter's Friend)*; Heather Gottlieb *(Amelia's Co-Worker)*; Nitza Wilon *(Cat Sympathizer)*; Allison Janney *(Amelia's Neighbor—Gum Puller)*; Alice Drummond *(Amelia's Neighbor—Betsy)*; Louise Yanofsky *(Virginia)*; Michael Kroll *(Rick)*; Isa Thomas *(Aunt Cynthia)*

Although it has moments of maddening preciousness, the charm and insight of this comedy about friendship are enough to carry it off. It's blessed with a raft of delightful performances from a fresh cast of newcomers.

Laura (Anne Heche) and Amelia (Catherine Keener) have been best friends since childhood, sharing everything. Their happy pact is somewhat shattered when Laura decides to take the plunge and marry her live-in, jewelry designer boyfriend, Frank (Todd Field). Amelia has made a drastic decision of her own: she's quitting therapy. As the wedding day approaches, Laura finds that certain of Frank's traits—calling waitresses by their first names, a worrisome mole he neglects to have checked out—really annoy her. She begins to fantasize about a patient at the psychiatric clinic where she works.

Amelia, meanwhile, is going through her own traumas. Plagued by abandonment issues, she feels deserted by the soon-to-be-wed Laura, but her therapist won't take her back. Her cat has been diagnosed with cancer and is undergoing expensive chemotherapy. She and her ex-boyfriend, Andrew (Liev Schreiber), remain locked in a unhealthy codependent relationship. Moreover, she has become involved with Bill (Kevin Corrigan), a weird, homely clerk at her video store, whose idea of fun is watching slasher films and going dwarf-tossing.

After a round of passionate sex with Amelia, poor Bill overhears a bitchy phone message from Laura in which makes a reference to his unfortunate appearance. Bill promptly dumps Amelia, who realizes too late that he just might have been the one. Frank, Laura, and Amelia plan a weekend at Amelia's country house to plan the wedding. There, Frank and Laura have a blow-out, ostensibly over Frank's mole, and Frank storms back to New York. That night, Andrew arrives to protect the women from a pesky obscene phone caller, and he and Amelia talk honestly about what went wrong with their relationship. Back in New York, Frank makes a weird attempt at a reconciliation by presenting the now excised mole to Laura in a jewelry box. Laura is initially horrified, but they soon get back together. After a heated spat over the ways in which the one feels abandoned by the other, Amelia and Laura also reconcile. On the morning of the wedding, the two friends discuss the ways in which their friendship has changed over the years and, as the ceremony is about to begin, they reaffirm their commitment to one another.

This is a sweet little notion with a piquant theme. The subject of how a marriage can tear people apart as well as join them has been addressed before in films like LITTLE WOMEN (1933, 1949, 1994) and, especially THE MEMBER OF THE WEDDING (1952). However, another theme—the idea that someone could be "dating down" and then unaccountably dumped by the very person to whom one felt so superior—is particularly provocative and unexplored terrain for the big screen.

First time writer-director Nicole Holofcener's work is brightly observant, filled with quirky humor. She's wonderfully accurate about the lives of Manhattan singles but, just when the viewer is ready to succumb to her quirky vision, she goes ultra-cutesy with some nonsense about cat chemotherapy. And then, just as suddenly, she recaptures one's affection with some irresistibly real, smile-provoking fillip.

To its credit, WALKING AND TALKING is never formulaic. It shows casual, sprightly charm and has a poignant ending that adroitly wraps things up. It's deftly photographed, capturing the hallucinatory heat of New York streets in summertime, and Billy Bragg's wistfully engaging music adds to the effect.

Luckily, both Keener and Heche are skillful comediennes. The first is acidly pretty, the very type of self-centered miss it might well be hard to become friends with. Heche retains the appealingly raw, embattled humanity she evinced in LIVING IN OBLIVION (1995) in a much less glamorous role. She's the quintessential female urbanite, fiercely protective of her own privacy and desperately needy as well. Corrigan is perfect as the nerdy Bill; his scenes with Keener are small classics of the modern-day mating game. Schreiber is the typical kind of slacker with whom a lot of women fall into bed. Field, however, is a bit too fey as Frank, making Amelia's pre-nup jitters all too understandable. *(Sexual situations, adult situations, profanity.)* — D.N.

d, Nicole Holofcener; p, Ted Hope, James Schamus; exec p, Dorothy Berwin, Scott Meek; w, Nicole Holofcener; ph, Michael Spiller; ed, Alisa Lepselter; m, Billy Bragg; prod d, Anne Stuhler; art d, Roswell Hamrick; sound, David Powers (mixer); casting, Avy Kaufman; cos, Edi Giguere; makeup, Nicki Jasny Ledermann

Comedy/Romance **(PR: C MPAA: R)**

WALLACE AND GROMIT: THE BEST OF AARDMAN ANIMATION ★★★

(U.K.) 77m Aardman Animation ~ Nothern Arts Entertainment c

The short subject, "A Close Shave," may have won a 1995 Oscar, but there are many other highlights to WALLACE AND GROMIT: THE BEST OF AARDMAN ANIMATION, a spirited compilation of darkly humorous claymation cartoons.

Released in the US in 1996, WALLACE AND GROMIT showcases several shorts from Britain's Aardman studio. The feature includes "Early Bird," about a DJ waking up to a series of on-air mishaps; "My Baby Just Cares for Me," a nightclub scene with a singing cat dubbed by vocalist Nina Simone; "Electric Stuff," an appliance commercial spoof; "Rex the Runt," a morning TV show spoof in two parts; "Creature Comforts," a series of interviews with disgruntled zoo animals; "Pib and Pog," a children's TV show spoof with two destructive hosts; "Wat's Pig," a medieval "Prince and the Pauper" tale; "Ident," a futuristic bit set in a labyrinth; and "A Close Shave," a satiric mystery about an inventor, Wallace, and his faithful dog assistant, Gromit, who together uncover a nefarious sheep-rustling plot in their quiet neighborhood.

WALLACE AND GROMIT deserves its considerable following, despite the fact that the claymation work of the Aardman studio is really no more dynamic or innovative than the 1960s Saturday morning TV show, "Davey and Goliath." Also, Disney's JAMES AND THE GIANT PEACH (1996) and its predecessor, TIM BURTON'S THE NIGHTMARE BEFORE CHRISTMAS (1993), have stolen some of the thunder from Britain's premiere animators by popularizing a similar, dark tone. On the other end of the satire spectrum, WALLACE's humor looks fairly tame next to the Quay Brothers s more grotesque and ingenious work.

WALLACE AND GROMIT still delivers the goods, despite outside competition and its own internal unevenness. The best of the bunch includes Peter Peake's six-minute "Pib and Pog," with its razor-sharp references to Gumby, Mr. Bill, Bert and Ernie, Kukla, Fran & Ollie and—in the sugary theme song—Barney the dinosaur. Richard Goleszowski's two entries, "Rex the Runt" and "Ident," come the closest to matching the Quay Brothers' creepiness and stand out creatively from the other sequences. Nick Park's "Creature Comforts" is amusing, and comparatively more suitable for the children, but Park's celebrated "A Close Shave" runs too long at 30 minutes, and contains a few overly precious excesses. The only real dud in the bunch, curiously, is "Wat's Pig," which is also the most elaborate. Peter Lord's use of animation, widescreen and split-screen is visually stunning, but the story of royal twins who are separated at birth but later swap identities does not contain a single laugh. Except for this last short, most of WALLACE AND GROMIT offers enough off-beat entertainment to engage both children and their parents. — E.M.

d, Luis Cook, Dave Alex Riddett, Richard Goleszowski, Nick Park, Peter Lord, David Sproxton, Peter Peake; p, David Mazor, John Lawrence Re; exec p, Peter Lord, David Sproxton; w, Lius Cook, Dave Alex Riddett, Richard Goleszowski, Nick Park, Peter Lord, David Sproxton, Peter Peake; anim, Nick Park

Animated/Comedy **(PR: A MPAA: NR)**

WAR AT HOME, THE ★★★½

(U.S.) 124m Touchstone Pictures; Avatar Entertainment ~ Buena Vista c

Emilio Estevez *(Jeremy Collier)*; Kathy Bates *(Maurine Collier)*; Martin Sheen *(Bob Collier)*; Kimberly Williams *(Karen Collier)*; Corin Nemec *(Donald)*; Ann Hearn *(Music Teacher)*; Carla Gugino *(Melissa)*; Marcus H. Nelson *(Private Poe)*; Michael Wiseman *(Lieutenant)*; Jena Kraus *(Coffee House Singer)*; Chad Morgan *(Bus Station Clerk)*; Penny Allen *(Marjoree)*; Lane Smith *(Hal)*; Geoffrey Blake *(David)*; Renee Estevez *(Brenda)*; Tuan Tran *(Viet Cong)*; Paloma Estevez *(Little Girl)*; Effrain Briones Jr.; Tyler Shea Cone; Harvey L. Cyphers; Christopher Dahlberg; Chris Drewy; Reed Frerichs; Anthony D-Wayne Kitchen; Enoch Lawrence; Joe Lowry; Le'roy Nellis Jr.; Lee Andrew Pachicano; Jeff D. Richey; Yogi Rise; Octavio O. Sanchez; Derrick Sanders; William Carvell Townsel; Paul A. Watkins *(Jeremy's Squad)*

A surprisingly mature film from actor-director Emilio Estevez, THE WAR AT HOME focuses on a family's failure to come to terms with a son who has returned from Vietnam a stranger.

Jeremy Collier (Emilio Estevez), home from the war in Vietnam for nearly a year, still can't readjust. His father, Bob (Martin Sheen), suspects he's just feeling sorry for himself, while Jeremy's mother, Maurine (Kathy Bates), a narcissistic control freak, takes her son's anti-social behavior as a personal insult. Denying any real problem, she fusses over the details of the family's Thanksgiving dinner.

Sister Karen (Kimberly Williams) thinks she understands what her brother is going through, and tries to explain how many veterans are experiencing readjustment problems, but Bob is only concerned that she not air the family's dirty laundry. What the Colliers don't realize is that Jeremy has brought the war back home with him and routinely experiences frightening battle flashbacks that leave him sweating and exhausted.

A rare amicable moment between Jeremy and Bob soon turns ugly when Bob reminds his son that it's time to move on and forget about the war. Thanksgiving morning, Maurine is particularly edgy. Aunt Marjoree and her family are due later that afternoon, and Maurine accuses Jeremy of eating some peanut brittle she has been saving for the guests. He flies into a rage, and a tense breakfast follows.

Jeremy later dresses for dinner in his army fatigues, which precipitates another crisis. He locks himself in his room, and Bob threatens to throw him out of the house if he doesn't change his clothes and come down for dinner. Maurine is nearly hysterical by the time the doorbell rings.

The Colliers sit down to dinner with Aunt Marjoree (Penny Allen), Uncle Hal (Land Smith), and their family. But tempers rise and Bob storms out of the house, driving to his office, where he is later met by Jeremy. Bob hands his son a wad of cash and tells him to move out.

Back home, Jeremy is about to leave for the bus station when he notices that Maurine has put his childhood prayer plaque with his luggage. The sight of it sets Jeremy off. He smashes the plaque and pulls out a gun. Jeremy reminds his father that when he asked him for the money to move to Canada and avoid the draft, Bob refused. With the gun to his head, Bob admits that it was a point of honor—his honor—that his son should risk his life and sanity in Vietnam and not embarrass his family. Somewhat placated by this confession, Jeremy leaves home for good.

Based on James Duff's 1985 Broadway play *Home Front*, THE WAR AT HOME deals very little with the war itself. Estevez and Duff, who adapted his play for the screen, treat it as a catalyst that pushes an already dysfunctional family to the breaking point. There are a few Vietnam flashbacks, and they're well done. The shots of a quiet suburban evening that pan to reveal Jeremy's horrific hallucinations effectively convey the terrible immediacy of his past.

Estevez maintains a tight, intimate focus throughout, and while his occasionally heavy-handed direction exacerbates a few of Duff's more florid moments, he does allow much of the script's humor to come through.

What really makes it all work, however, is the film's fine ensemble cast. Bates is outstanding, bringing her particular brand of pathos to a character that could very easily come off as ridiculous. But while the real-life father-son chemistry between Estevez and Sheen here leads to some of Sheen's best work in years, Estevez would have done better to cast a stronger acting talent than himself in the crucial lead role. *(Violence, profanity.)* — K.F.

d, Emilio Estevez; p, Emilio Estevez, Brad Krevoy, Steve Stabler, James Duff; exec p, Tracie Graham Rice; assoc p, Jeff Ivers, Peter Richards; co-p, Mickey McDermott, Jonathan Brandstein; w, James Duff (based on his play *Home Front*); ph, Peter Levy; ed, Craig Bassett; m, Basil Poledouris; prod d, Eve Cauley; set d, Jeanette Scott; sound, Jennifer Murphy (mixer); fx, Lou Carlucci; casting, Judy Taylor; cos, Grania Preston; makeup, Jaquline Nealy-Dobbie; stunts, Bernie Pock

Drama **(PR: C MPAA: R)**

WAR OF THE BUTTONS, THE ★★½

(U.K./France) 90m Enigma Productions; Productions de la Geuville; Hugo Films ~ Warner Bros. c

(LA GUERRE DES BOUTONS, CA RECOMMENCE)

Gregg Fitzgerald *(Fergus (The Ballys))*; Gerard Kearney *(Big Con (The Ballys))*; Daragh Naughton *(Boffin (The Ballys))*; Brenda McNamara *(Tim (The Ballys))*; Kevin O'Malley *(Fishy (The Ballys))*; John Cleere *(Peter (The Ballys))*; Anthony Cunningham *(Little Con (The Ballys))*; Thomas Kavanagh *(Riley (The Ballys))*; Eveanna Ryan *(Marie (The Ballys))*; John Crowley *(Pat (The Ballys))*; Stuart Dannell-Foran *(Tich (The Ballys))*; Danielle Tuite *(Fionnuala (The Ballys))*; Helen O'Leary *(Helen (The Ballys))*; Yvonne McNamara *(Maeve (The Ballys))*; John Coffey *(Geronimo (The Carricks))*; Paul Batt *(Gorilla (The Carricks))*; Karl Byrne *(Mickey Moon (The Carricks))*; Barry Walsh *(Willie (The Carricks))*; Niall Collins *(Chick (The Carricks))*; Derek O'Leary *(Brendan (The Carricks))*; Rory White *(Bernard (The Carricks))*; Liam Cunningham *(The Master)*; Johnny Murphy *(Jonjo)*; Colm Meaney *(Geronimo's Dad)*; Bairbre Dowling *(Geronimo's Mum)*; Alan Devlin *(Mr. Riley)*; Brid McCarthy *(Mrs. Riley)*; Pat Laffan *(Mr. Connor)*; Ruth Hegarty *(Mrs. Connor)*; Jim Bartley *(Fergus's Dad)*; Ger Ryan *(Fergus's Mum)*; John Olohan *(Fat Pat's Dad)*; Frank Kelly *(Gorilla's Dad)*; Martin Dunne *(Willie's Dad)*; Andrew Goyvaerts *(Gerard)*; Frank Grimes *(Christian Brother)*; Donncha Crowley *(Police Sergeant No. 1)*; Maurice O'Donoghue *(Police Sergeant No. 2)*; Frank O'Sullivan *(Fisherman No. 1)*; Eamonn Hunt *(Fisherman No. 2)*; Jack Lynch *(Mr. Riley's Friend)*; Declan Mulholland *(Priest)*; Maureen Bennett *(Master's Wife)*; Helene Montague *(Tich's Mum)*; Brendan Caldwell *(Carrickdowse Priest)*; Dervla Kirwan *(Voice of Marie)*

Following in the tradition of English-language remakes of French films, this pleasant but innocuous rendition of LA GUERRE DES BOUTONS (1962) concerns two warring gangs of Irish boys.

In the semi-rural north of Ireland, the Carricks, led by Geronimo (John Coffey), and the Ballys, led by Fergus (Gregg Fitzgerald) dispute each other over territorial rights to sell hospital charity bazaar tickets. The first skirmish between the gangs leads to the claiming of buttons as war trophies.

After a series of battles, Fergus denounces Riley (Thomas Kavanagh) as a traitor to the cause. The final showdown has the Ballys attacking an abandoned castle defended by the Carricks; the Carricks lose, and, taken prisoner, Geronimo himself cuts off his buttons and gives them to Fergus. While the Ballys celebrate in their headquarters, Geronimo, driving Riley's father's tractor like a tank, levels the Bally clubhouse. Finally fed up, the towns' adults, including Geronimo's father (Colm Meaney) and Fergus's abusive stepfather (Jim Bartley), reclaim their children. Geronimo and Fergus flee. They are hunted down by the parents and police, and Fergus saves Geronimo's life when the pair attempt to climb a sheer mountain cliff to escape. Some time later, Geronimo and Fergus meet again in a reformatory where they've been sent for punishment, and they resume their fighting, this time playfully, with pillows.

Yves Robert's 1962 film, based on the classic 1911 novel by Louis Pergaud (which was also filmed in 1938 as GENERALS WITHOUT BUTTONS in France), was a minor, sincere low-budget effort which received some cultish art-house success in the US. This new edition is a concise, mirror-image remake, although the screenplay by Colin Welland (YANKS, CHARIOTS OF FIRE) pretty much eradicates the first film's quietly effective anti-war stance, as well some of its charming innocence.

Though it is carefully grounded in reality (circa 1970s), the rugged Irish country side and ruined buildings of North Cork give the film an aura of fairy tale timelessness. The uninflected performances by the boys, as well as by Eveanna Ryan as Marie, are unselfconscious and effective, and in smaller roles Liam Cunningham as the supportive schoolmaster and Meaney (THE SNAPPER, THE COMMITMENTS) as Geronimo's father are excellent. John Roberts has directed straightforwardly, although he pretty much flubs the Ballys' nude attack sequence, so startling in Robert's film. This remake is interesting but never intriguing or surprising; it's well made but pointless. The British-French co-production, produced by the British veteran David Puttnam (THE KILLING FIELDS, THE MISSION), was released in Europe in October 1994. Warner Bros. briefly opened it in Los Angeles in 1995 before sending it off to video and pay-cable TV. *(Violence, profanity.)* — D.B.

d, John Roberts; p, David Puttnam; exec p, Xavier Gelin, Stephane Marsil, David Nichols; assoc p, Steve Norris; co-p, Yves Robert, David Nichols; w, Colin Welland (based on the novel *La Guerre des Boutons* by Louis Pergaud); ph, Bruno DeKeyzer; ed, David Freeman; m, Rachel Portman; prod d, Jim Clay; art d, Chris Seagers; sound, David John (mixer), Paul Cridlin (recordist); fx, Peter Hutchinson; casting, Ros Hubbard, John Hubbard; cos, Louise Frogley; makeup, Dominique Henri-Perez, Patricia Kirkman; stunts, Greg Powell

Adventure/Drama/Children's (PR: C MPAA: PG)

WARHEAD ★★

(U.S./South Africa) 97m Nu World ~ Vidmark c

Frank Zagarino *(Tannen)*; Joe Lara *(Kraft)*; Elizabeth Giordano *(Jessica)*; Brian O'Shaughnessy *(Edwards)*; Todd Jensen *(Lansdale)*; Michael McCabe *(Dr. Evans)*; Ian Yule *(Colonel)*; Ross Preler *(P. J.)*; Alan T. Marks *(Spotter)*; Jamie Bartlett *(Wilson)*; Jo Da Silva *(Joyce)*; Grethe Fox *(Victoria)*; Greg Poustie *(Corporal Whitey Jackson)*; Ricardo Coen *(Lee)*; Keith Van Hoven *(Allen)*; Justin Illusion *(Garcia)*; Lee Ann Liebenberg *(Jones)*; David Webb *(Parks)*; Doug Parker *(Penn)*; Cordell McQueen *(Larry)*; Daniel Van Rensberg *(Karl)*; Darryl Werner *(Shemp)*; Nick Smit *(Bunker Guard)*; Chris Buchanan *(Colonel Liddy)*; Terry Loftus *(Haig)*; Andre Marrero *(Haldeman)*; Quinton Voges *(North)*; Mark McKenzie *(Dole)*; Bryan De Klerk *(Marine MP)*; Frank Notaro *(Senator)*

In the direct-to-video marketplace, 1996 was a banner year for man-made virus outbreaks and anti-government, ex-military terrorists. In WARHEAD, a former Pentagon agent heads the UPN, a rabid militia bent on forcing the US president's resignation.

Although ace operative Tannen (Frank Zagarino) stages a Waco-like raid on the stockpiled fortress of messianic General Kraft (Joe Lara), Tannen's commando mission doesn't put a dent in Kraft's master plan. With the cooperation of turncoat scientist Dr. Evans (Michael McCabe), who is kidnapped from protective custody on an army plane, Kraft can access missile codes triggering warheads at two farm-belt silos.

Due to the forked tongue of presidential advisor Lansdale (Todd Jensen), Tannen feels he cannot derail Kraft's scheme to extort millions and force the president to step down. Lansdale tips off Kraft, who ambushes Tannen's search-and-destroy mission in Haiti. What Lansdale fails to realize is that madman Kraft places a higher priority on his political goal than on the monetary one. Kraft wants to control the Commander-in-Chief.

Disgusted with the casualties in Haiti and with the shilly-shallying of his mentor, General Edwards (Brian O'Shaughnessy), Tannen resigns, only to be coaxed into an active anti-Kraft role by electronics whiz Jessica Evans (Elizabeth Giordano), daughter of Dr. Evans.

Showing he means business, Kraft launches one missile into the desert before aiming the second at Washington, DC. Infiltrating Kraft's headquarters, Tannen battles UPN forces while Jessica circumvents her father's warhead code control. After Dr.

Evans stops a bullet meant for his daughter, Tannen breaks Kraft's neck.

Aborting the warhead's instructions, Jessica and Tannen barely escape the missile mini-base as the nuclear weapon self-destructs and obliterates the surrounding area. Set up to die twice by the conniving Lansdale, Tannen finds him in Switzerland and traps him in a car rigged with explosives.

WARHEAD would be typical boys-will-be-boys escapism were it not for the screenplay's murmurs of vigilantism. The filmmakers express a grudging respect not for terrorism but for the basic soundness of General Kraft's distaste for a liberal government.

Ignoring these super-patriotic tinges, audiences are stuck with the usual action formulas, slack patches of verbiage, and buddy-buddy camaraderie interspersed with deafening explosions and bone-crunching kickboxing. Those who expect intelligence or elan in their nuclear countdown thrillers will be annoyed by the flick's static direction, repetitive exposition, and egregiously bad acting. *(Graphic violence, extreme profanity, adult situations.)* — R.P.

d, Mark Roper; p, Danny Lerner; exec p, Avi Lerner, Danny Dimbort, Trevor Short; assoc p, Brigid Olen; w, Jeff Albert; ph, Rod Stewart; ed, Alain Jakubowicz; m, Robert O. Ragland; prod d, David Varod; set d, Barry Nash; sound, Henry Prentice (mixer); fx, Rick Cresswell; casting, Jane Warren; makeup, Debra Fouche, Pia Cornelius; stunts, Roly Jansen

Action/Martial Arts/War (PR: C MPAA: R)

WATCH ME ★

(U.S.) 90m Cameo Films ~ Triboro Entertainment c

Jennifer Burton *(Samantha)*; Robert Medford *(Paul)*; Kelly Burns *(Elise)*; Steven Sherwin *(Alex)*; Alex Demir *(Armen)*; Marvy Mayer *(Grace)*; Sheila Redgate *(Sherry)*; Chris Winfield *(Lovett)*; John V. Fisher *(Bartender)*; John R. F. Halaby *(Painter 1)*; Marc Jason Robinson *(Painter 2)*; John Fraser Brown *(Painter 3)*; Lynn Wolf *(Nadia)*

WATCH ME is a dull sex farrago with about as much plot as a grade school primer: See Dick fall for buxom Jane! See Jane masturbate! See everybody get off! Recommended only for the erotically challenged.

Although his artistic genius is blocked, hot-shot photographer Paul (Robert Medford) feels his inspiration unclogging when mystery woman Elise (Kelly Burns) moves in across the way. Stifled by his relationship with Samantha (Jennifer Burton), who chides Paul about commitment while sleeping with his best buddy, apartment handyman Alex (Steven Sherwin), Paul reassures backers that his first solo exhibit will be ready in time. Elise handles her break-up with control-freak Armen (Alex Demire) by spying on Samantha and Alex at S&M play. Unzipping into action, Paul joins the onanistic daisy chain while snapping telephoto candids of Elise—guaranteed to make him a big name in NY art circles. After he entices Elise into becoming an active photo model, Paul reaches an crossroads when he learns of Samantha's hypocritical cheating. Firing bedhopping Alex, Paul coaxes Elise away from her window and into his boudoir. Critically acclaimed for his one-man show, Paul can enjoy intercourse with Elise and save his old reliable hand for changing f-stops.

Less a movie than a video manual about the ultimate in safe sex, WATCH ME avoids the first cardinal sin of Porn-Lite by throughly integrating the Kama Sutra into its central plot line. Voyeurs will applaud Paul's shutterbug shenanigans for allowing ample opportunities for full female frontal nudity. Unfortunately, this skinflick trips into pitfall number two in the arousal genre: too much of a good thing is, well, too much. After viewing what seems like decades of male butts rising and falling atop babes like muscular bellows stoking fireplaces, the spectator's interest waxes, wanes, and disappears. Even the chronically horny may end up searching in vain for a morsel of pithy dialogue or a surprising plot twist to sustain them. *(Extreme profanity, extensive nudity.)* — R.P.

d, Lipo Ching; p, Samantha Kash; w, Beth Salmon (based on a story by Beth Salmon and Lipo Ching); ph, Andreas Kossak; ed, Carol Oblath; m, Yoav Goren; prod d, Marc Robinson; art d, Warren Alan Young; sound, John R. F. Halaby (mixer); casting, Lori Cobe; cos, Nena Jones; makeup, L.M.C.

Erotic (PR: O MPAA: R)

WAVELENGTH ★★

(U.K./U.S.) 94m Dove International ~ Paramount/Dove Entertainment c

Jeremy Piven *(Paul Higgins)*; Kelli Williams *(Claire Higgins)*; Liza Walker *(Lucy Amore)*; James Villiers *(James Mallinson)*; James Faulkner *(Eric Amore)*; Byrne Piven *(President)*; Nicholas Marcq *(Leo)*; Dominic West *(Spike)*; Richard Attenborough *(The Visitor)*; Tabitha Wady *(Leo's Girl)*; Michael Keating *(Reporter)*; Benjamin Fry *(Waiter)*

WAVELENGTH is the first cinematic drama about Einstein's theory of wave-particle duality. Non-physicists, beware.

Brilliant theoretical scientist Paul Higgins (Jeremy Piven), an American resident at Oxford University, is up against the wall. His marriage with Claire (Kelli Williams) is in trouble, and the funding for his program is in jeopardy when department chairman James Mallinson (James Villiers) leaves for MIT. Dedicated to wrapping up Einstein's unfinished work in the field of wave-particle duality, Paul and his colleagues Spike (Dominic West), Leo (Nicholas Marcq), and Paul's lover Lucy Amore (Liza Walker) knock themselves out despite the disapproval of new chairperson, Dr. Eric Amore (James Faulkner). He begrudges Paul's unconventional genius and despises Paul's dalliance with his daughter, Lucy.

Paul's slim chances for university funding diminish when Lucy, jealous of his marriage, feeds Paul's notes to her father in advance. Aided by a backer (Byrne Piven) from the field of psychic phenomena, Paul scandalizes the Oxford establishment by going over Dr. Amore's head and invoking the dusty privilege of confronting the school's Visitor (Richard Attenborough) with his petition. Shocked when Claire threatens divorce after discovering her husband's affair, Paul rebounds and successfully secures research moneys from the sympathetic Visitor. Placating Claire, Paul returns to his dream of explaining how matter can exist both as a wave and as a manifested particle.

Brain matter gets a real workout from the scientific theories, but emotions will remain unengaged by the surprisingly ordinary soap opera shenanigans haloing the scientific arguments. If the director had invested Paul's race to save his project with minimal suspense or if he had captured the research team's devotion to their work, WAVELENGTH might have reached more than a coterie of physicist-moviegoers. Antagonizing the audience with the self-centeredness of protagonist Paul Higgins, the movie needlessly dissipates tension in the central scientific quest-for-knowledge with dull tearjerking setbacks. How can viewers care about the hero's earth-shattering mandate when it keeps retreating to his mundane heartaches? This film is closer in spirit to Dr. Ruth than to Dr. Einstein. *(Extreme profanity, sexual situations, nudity, adult situations.)* — R.P.

d, Benjamin Fry; p, Andre Burgess, Benjamin Fry; assoc p, Miles Millar; w, Benjamin Fry; ph, Chris Middleton; ed, Clive Barrett; m, Michael Storey; prod d, Caroline Greville-Morris; art d, Rebecca Gillies, Steve Hudson; sound, Steve Taylor (mixer); casting, Celestia Fox, Meredith Kaplan; cos, Caroline Harris; makeup, Victoria Wright; stunts, Rod Woodbury

Drama **(PR: C MPAA: R)**

WEEKEND IN THE COUNTRY, A ★½

(U.S.) 94m Rysher Entertainment; 3 Arts Entertainment ~ Evergreen Entertainment c
(AKA: TEMECULA; MOON VALLEY)

Richard Lewis *(Bobby Stein)*; Christine Lahti *(Ruth Oakley)*; Rita Rudner *(Sally Shelton)*; Jack Lemmon *(Bud Bailey)*; Dudley Moore *(Simon Farrell)*; Faith Ford *(Susan Kaye)*; John Shea *(Michael)*; Dan Cortese *(Thunder)*; James Shanta *(Fan at Airport)*; Ernie Dingo *(Rupert)*; Jennifer Cox *(Arista)*; Betty White; The Roches

The stars of WEEKEND IN THE COUNTRY can be thankful that this dismal romantic comedy went straight to commercial cable and then was banished to the bottom shelves of most video stores after a very limited release.

Artificially inseminated Sally (Rita Rudner) flies from New York to California and poses as a magazine interviewer to meet wine magnate Simon Farrell (Dudley Moore), the father of her unborn baby. Though Sally is seven months pregnant, Simon, not knowing he's the father, seduces Sally, then dumps her. She commiserates with Ruth (Christine Lahti), an eccentric bed-and-breakfast owner, who gives her the lowdown on Simon's sleazy history.

Comedian Bobby Stein (Richard Lewis) is another New Yorker staying at Ruth's bed-and-breakfast. Ostensibly in wine country to perform, Bobby arrives to continue his affair with the married Susan (Faith Ford). Although they don't know the first thing about grapes, Susan and her new husband Michael (John Shea) recently bought a winery. Unfortunately for Bobby, Susan falls back in love with her husband once more and ends the extramarital romance. Bobby is left to deal with Bud Bailey (Jack Lemmon), a failed comedian who ineptly promotes Bobby's show.

Bobby and Sally, both depressed, bond at the local fair. The next night, during Bobby's act, Sally goes into labor and Bobby leaves the stage to accompany her to the hospital. Bud assumes the empty stage and resurrects his stand-up career.

Also in the hospital is heart attack victim Simon Farrell. The medical scare teaches Simon to be less self-absorbed and appreciate his daughter Arista (Jennifer Cox) and her new Australian boyfriend Rupert (Ernie Dingo). At the same time, love blooms in the delivery room where Sally gives birth and Bobby plays surrogate father. They drive back to New York with a new baby girl.

After their very modest success with PETER'S FRIENDS (1992), the conjugal writing team of Rita Rudner and Martin Bergman inflict this unfunny mess on the public. They attempt to juggle too many story lines, eventually dropping them all. Ultimately, one hardly cares about Bobby and Sally's romance, let alone the even flimsier relationships of Susan and Michael, Arista and Rupert, et al.—an endless list of couples without a single spark among them. Get past its middlebrow tone and this film is nothing more than a landlocked "Love Boat" episode (a collection of second-rate and has-been actors playing cardboard types who all find love in the end).

It's a shame to see an actress of Christine Lahti's caliber playing a modern comedy cliche, the "New Age" flake. The flatly drawn, unappealing characters bring out the worst in each of the actors. Jack Lemmon's tendency to overact becomes painfully clear in his portrayal of the grating, phony Bud. (Could this be the same man who displayed such brilliant comic timing in THE APARTMENT and THE ODD COUPLE?) Richard Lewis comes off almost as poorly as Lemmon. Director Bergman fails to utilize Lewis's greatest asset—his boundless neurotic energy. In any event, the actors should have known that when Dudley Moore is cast in a movie, one should run—not walk—in the opposite direction. *(Sexual situations, profanity.)* — T.Y.

d, Martin Bergman; p, Martin Bergman, Nancy Paloian, John Bard Manulis; exec p, Larry Estes, Michael Rotenberg, Jack Lemmon, Rob Kenneally; w, Rita Rudner, Martin Bergman; ph, Roger Lanser; ed, Francoise Bonnot; m, Patrick Williams; set d, Don Ferry; sound, Giovanni DiSimone; cos, Warden Neil

Comedy/Romance **(PR: C MPAA: R)**

WELCOME TO THE DOLLHOUSE ★★★½

(U.S.) 87m Suburban Pictures ~ Sony Pictures Classics c

Heather Matarazzo *(Dawn Wiener)*; Brendan Sexton Jr. *(Brandon McCarthy)*; Daria Kalinina *(Missy Wiener)*; Matthew Faber *(Mark Wiener)*; Angela Pietropinto *(Mrs. Wiener)*; Eric Mabius *(Steve Rodgers)*; Bill Buell *(Mr. Wiener)*; Victoria Davis *(Lolita)*; Christina Brucato *(Cookie)*; Christina Vidal *(Cynthia)*; Siri Howard *(Chrissy)*; Telly Pontidis *(Jed)*; Herbie Duarte *(Lance)*; Scott Coogan *(Troy)*; Josiah Trager *(Kenny)*; Ken Leung *(Barry)*; Dimitri Iervolino *(Ralphy)*; Rica Martens *(Mrs. Grissom)*; Stacey Moseley *(Mary Ellen Moriarty)*; Will Lyman *(Mr. Edwards)*; Elizabeth Martin *(Mrs. Iannone)*; Zsanne Pitta *(Ginger Friedman)*; Richard Gould *(Mr. Kasdan)*; Beverly Hecht *(Steve's Girlfriend)*; Teddy Coluca *(Police Sergeant)*; Tommy Fager *(Tommy McCarthy)*; James O'Donoghue *(Mr. McCarthy)*

The big hit of the 1996 Sundance Film Festival was WELCOME TO THE DOLL HOUSE, an engaging black comedy about an 11-year-old girl suffering through the seventh grade and junior high school.

Somewhere in suburban New Jersey, young, plain Dawn Wiener (Heather Matarazzo) lives with her self-centered parents (Angela Pietropinto, Bill Buell), her computer-nerd older brother Mark (Matthew Faber), and her comely, spoiled younger sister Missy (Daria Kalinina). Dawn fights constantly with her siblings, but her mother often sides against her and her father remains passive and remote.

At school, life isn't much easier. Dawn gets picked on by bullies, and her teacher, Miss Grissom (Rica Martens), is unsympathetic to her plight. When one bully, Brandon McCarthy (Brendan Sexton Jr.), threatens Dawn for not letting him cheat off her test paper, Dawn prepares herself for the worst. But Brandon surprises Dawn by not attacking her after school as promised, becoming friends with her instead.

Meanwhile, back at home, Dawn falls for Steve Rodgers (Eric Mabius), a handsome—though vapid—teenage singer in her brother's school band. Whenever Steve comes to the Wiener household, Dawn tries to get close to him. Her crush, however, ends her friendship with Brandon, who gets jealous. Dawn is then devastated when Steve gets mad at Mark and the band breaks up. Life gets even worse when Dawn's mother punishes her for not destroying her backyard clubhouse in order to make room for an upcoming anniversary party. Meanwhile, Dawn visits Brandon to make up with him, but she finds that he is planning to run away from home to avoid being sent to a reform school.

Feeling miserable, Dawn's only satisfaction comes when her sister, Missy, gets kidnapped one afternoon. But after watching her family suffer from the loss, Dawn travels to New York City to try to find Missy herself. Dawn is unsuccessful in her search, but Missy is found alive and well in the basement of a neighbor's house. Dawn then returns home, too, ending her eventful first year in junior high school with the expectation that the following year will not be much better.

WELCOME TO THE DOLLHOUSE fits in somewhere between the caustic, distance of Todd Haynes (DOTTIE GETS SPANKED, POISON, SAFE) and the quirkier tactics of David Russell (SPANKING THE MONKEY). Like Haynes and Russell, director Todd Solondz shows a flair for recreating the painful yet curious experience of growing up in suburban America. Solondz's film (his second feature) is possibly the most original conceptually of this youth-film trend in that it centers around a 11-year-old (pre-adolescent) *girl*, never shying away from the unpleasant details of her life, and yet never losing itself (until the last reel) in unlikely dramatic scenarios.

The best characteristic of WELCOME TO THE DOLLHOUSE is the courage it exhibits to be honest about everything, including a leading protagonist who is nerd-like but not always innocent or sympathetic. It is astonishing how unselfconscious newcomer Heather Matarazzo remains throughout the demanding role (she's in every scene), and she is followed closely behind by Angela Pietropinto, who gives an understated but chilling performance as Dawn's toxic mother.

Technically, DOLLHOUSE lacks the aesthetic rigor of Todd Haynes's recent work, but it more than sufficiently replicates the suffocating qualities of working-class suburbia, from the garish backyard parties to the cacophonous school band jam sessions to the school lunchroom-seating intricacies. Solondz's dialogue is especially good at capturing nuclear family dysfunction without pushing the characters too far. Solondz is less successful with the plot itself, particularly at the point where Missy is kidnapped. Borrowing the premise from Gus Van Sant's overrated TO DIE FOR (1995), Solondz reaches for a ripped-from-the-headlines bit of melodramatic satire that gets too broad and cartoon-like for such an otherwise precise and insightful comedy about the big little things in life. In general, however, Solondz's dark, funny sensibility makes WELCOME TO THE DOLLHOUSE most welcome. *(Violence, extreme profanity.)* — E.M.

d, Todd Solondz; p, Todd Solondz; exec p, Donna Bascom; assoc p, Jason Kliot, Joana Vicente; co-p, Dan Partland, Ted Skillman; w, Todd Solondz; ph, Randy Drummond; ed, Alan Oxman; m, Jill Wisoff; prod d, Susan Block; art d, Lori Solondz; sound, Alex Wolfe; casting, Ann Goulder; cos, Melissa Toth; makeup, Heidi Kulow

Comedy/Drama **(PR: C MPAA: R)**

WHARF RAT, THE ★

(U.S.) 88m All Media, Inc.; Showtime Entertainment Group ~ Paramount Home Video c

Lou Diamond Phillips *(Petey Martin)*; Rachel Ticotin *(Dexter Ireland)*; Judge Reinhold *(Doc)*; Scott Cohen *(Matt Martin)*; Rita Moreno *(Mom)*; William Dunlop *(Bucko)*; Alan Vint *(Eli)*; Paul Willson *(Sloopy)*; Peter Radon *(Mario)*; Loren Farmer *(Max Cowan)*; Wilfred Bray *(Customs Agent)*; Steven Randazzo *(Seafood Foreman)*; Beau Starr *(Joey the Fist)*; Thoywell Hemmings *(Basketball Kid)*; Judy Coffey *(Meter Maid)*; Rusty Ryan *(Drag Queen)*; Stephen Jackson *(Officer—Funeral)*; Jank Azman *(Funeral Director)*; Desmond Campbell *(Jail Officer)*; Jean Luke Cote *(Showgirl)*; Scott Wickware *(Guard at Armored Yard)*; Nicole Farmer *(Natalie)*; Don DeFina *(Ship's Captain)*; Richard Blackburn *(Sergeant)*; Jeff Christensen *(Freighter Captain)*; Shawn Lawrence *(Armored Car Guard)*; Ray Paisley *(Armored Car Driver)*; Chris Peterson *(Dancer No. 1)*; J. J. Murray *(Dancer No. 2)*; Danny White *(Dancer No. 3)*

Many poor action movies exist *only* to pump up an audience and give little regard to narrative sense. Still, their lack of clarity is usually redeemed by flashy camerawork, succulent villains, or dramatic staging of fight sequences. With this in mind, THE WHARF RAT would be totally worthless if not for the fact that it brings two under-utilized actresses to the screen.

Two brothers, Matt Martin (Scott Cohen), a cop, and Petey Martin (Lou Diamond Phillips), a wharf thief, are in constant conflict, even though Petey once served time for his brother on a youthful offense. When Matt and his crooked partner, Doc (Judge Reinhold), apprehend Petey in a computer-chip robbery, Doc offers a deal: if Matt looks the other way concerning Doc's illegal activities, Doc will let Petey off the hook. The transaction is witnessed by roving reporter Dexter Ireland (Rachel Ticotin), who snaps photos of this cover-up without realizing how deeply corrupt the police force really is.

During a drug bust, Doc cold-bloodedly ices the drug vendors and also kills Matt. Now aware that the crooked cops will sooner or later figure out she's spied on them, Dexter teams up with Petey. Confiding in a friendly cop, Mario (Peter Radon), Petey sets out to ensnare Doc and the officials who sanctioned Matt's assassination. Doc forces inside information about Petey's next move out of Petey's ex-prisonmate, Bucko (William Dunlop). But Bucko remains on Petey's side; he and Petey subsequently heist an armored car. When Mario surprisingly tries to betray Petey, Petey foils Mario's plans. Mario, in turn, is killed by Doc so that he can't cut himself in on the take. Petey paves the way for honest department heads to nab Doc.

By the time this action flick reaches its puff-of-steam climax, viewers will have tuned out completely. It aims to involve the viewer in a Chinese puzzle of complexities, but instead it's a shell game designed by a screenwriter who jettisons logic on whim. This lame enterprise doesn't even attempt to seize upon any of its campier opportunities, such as Petey's use of a drag bar as a hangout in which Ticotin performs the dreariest Victor/Victoria gambit on record. The film's lowest point is the sequence in which the cops hold a disrespectful funeral for Matt, complete with booze and a coffin-side stripper; the film's biggest crime is the manner in which it wastes the talents of Ticotin and, in the small role of the protagonists' mother, the always watchable Rita Moreno. *(Graphic violence, sexual situations, adult situations, substance abuse, extreme profanity.)* — R.P.

d, Jimmy Huston; p, Paul Kimatian; w, Jimmy Huston (based on a story by Jimmy Huston and Paul Kimatian); ph, Levie Isaacks; ed, Christopher Rouse; m, Mervyn Warren; art d, Terry Wareham; sound, Bryan Day; casting, Beth Klein

Action/Crime **(PR: C MPAA: R)**

WHEN THE BULLET HITS THE BONE ★

(Canada) 83m Terror Zone Productions ~ New Horizons Home Video c

Jeff Wincott *(Jack Davies)*; Michelle Johnson *(Lisa)*; Doug O'Keefe *(Nick Turner)*; Torri Higginson *(Allison)*; Roy Lewis *(Daemon)*; Phillip Jarrett *(Trevor)*; Jennifer Pisano *(Marie)*; Jack Jessop *(Jack Davies, Sr.)*; Richard Fitzpatrick *(Sgt. Striker)*; Howard Jerome *(Senator Rollins)*; Yanira Contreres *(Maid)*

A controversial, globe-hopping conspiracy theory that links the US government to the drug trade combines with a simplistic script, an almost non-existent budget and laughable execution to make WHEN THE BULLET HITS THE BONE a shambles of a straight-to-video action flick.

Physician Jack Davis (Jeff Wincott) sees daily horrors in the emergency room, the result of drugs saturating the streets. When he interrupts a situation between high-class hooker Lisa (Michelle Johnson) and pimp-pusher Trevor (Phillip Jarrett), Jack is gravely wounded. Reviving in his hospital bed, Jack erases his whole identity by simply discarding his wallet, and strides forth as a relentless, vengeful vigilante.

But assassination squads are already hunting him. It seems Lisa and Trevor were no common skid-row slime: She's the abused, heroin-addicted wife of Nick Turner (Doug O'Keefe), the nation's biggest drug kingpin, with allies in Congress and the CIA; Trevor is a key player in pouring crack into the American ghetto. Trevor is slain in a Company power struggle. Any witnesses must be eliminated, but through sheer force of will and a pistol that never seems to need reloading, Jack survives attacks by drug gangs, and sadistic torture by government goons.

He steals incriminating computer files that prove Washington controls the crack racket, saves Lisa and her little daughter, and puts an end to Turner by playing the rogue agents and mob thugs against each other. Jack drives off with Lisa after blackmailing CIA honchos into temporarily halting coke shipments to give the suffering citizens some much-needed relief—for a short time, anyway.

In 1995-96, *The San Jose Mercury-News* newspaper ran a controversial series of articles tying America's cocaine epidemic to an alleged Reagan-era CIA policy of importing drugs to finance Nicaraguan Contra "freedom fighters." That conspiracy seems to the basis of this movie. Another conspiracy theory could be that the CIA financed WHEN THE BULLET HITS THE BONE to make speculation on their involvement in narco-terrorism look laughable by association. Few sights are as embarrassing as a Grade-Z genre flick preaching Big Ideas. And prolific cheapjack Canadian producer-director Damian Lee, whose wide-ranging output—DEATH WISH 5, SKI SCHOOL, BABY ON BOARD, FUN—aspires to camp at best, trips over his soapbox in trying to depict a United States rotten with violent crime, greed, political corruption, mongrel gangs, South American generals, loathsome liberals and a cabal of right-wing Anglo masterminds who monitor the carnage approvingly. And all of them apparently operate within the same few slum districts and an adjoining suburb, to judge by the production's low-budget scope.

The nondescript Wincott, turbo-charged by his bullet wound from angst-ridden sawbones to angry white superman, is just a joke as he single-handedly exposes the evil CIA shadow-government network by bursting through a few doors and shooting. Whatever truth lay behind the *Mercury-News* allegations, one word aptly sums this hysterical anti-drug flick: crackpot. *(Violence, extreme profanity, substance abuse)* — C.C.

d, Damian Lee; p, Damian Lee, Helder Goncalves, Julian Grant; exec p, Ashok Amritraj, Jeff Sackman; assoc p, Jeff Wincott; co-p, John Gillespie; w, Damian Lee; ph, Gerald R. Goozee; ed, David Ransley; m, Ken Greer; art d, Tim Boyd; cos, Judith England; makeup, A. Scott Hamilton; stunts, Andy Townsend

Political/Action/Thriller (PR: O MPAA: R)

WHEN WE WERE KINGS ★★★½

(U.S.) 88m Das Films ~ Gramercy Pictures c

Muhammad Ali; George Foreman; Don King; President Mobuto Sese Seko; James Brown; B.B. King; The Spinners; Miriam Makeba; George Plimpton; Malik Bowens; The Crusaders; The Fugees; Brian McKnight; Diana King; Spike Lee *(Narrator)*; Norman Mailer *(Narrator)*; Thomas Hauser *(Narrator)*; Lloyd Price *(Narrator)*

WHEN WE WERE KINGS, directed by Leon Gast, is a fast-paced documentary about the "Rumble in the Jungle," the 1974 heavyweight championship bout between Muhammad Ali and George Foreman. Comprised of period footage and recent updates, this is an informative and entertaining movie that goes beyond sports to touch, however lightly, on political and cultural issues.

If it seems like only yesterday that Muhammad Ali and George Foreman went to Zaire for their celebrated showdown, a viewing of WHEN WE WERE KINGS might change one's perception. In 1974, Ali was a brash, righteous challenger at the peak of physical health, while Foreman was a surly, menacing champ, light years away from the cuddly TV-pitchman he would become. Gast's lively, engaging movie reminds one of an earlier time that was paradoxically more volatile and more innocent than what came later.

WHEN WE WERE KINGS chronicles the $10 million-purse championship fight from its initial promotion in the U.S. through a six-week postponement (Foreman had suffered an injury during a sparring match) that left the fighters, their entourages and the world's sports press waiting with varying degrees of impatience in Kinshasa, the capital city of an impoverished African nation. Foreman broods in his hotel over the delay, but Ali ventures out daily to interact with the locals, especially the children, who are charmed by his animated personality and playful sense of humor. "Ali, bomaye!" ("Ali, kill him!") they take to chanting, a cry that Ali later encourages during the fight itself to boost his determination. More than a 3-1 underdog, Ali becomes the people's favorite, in contrast to the obdurate Foreman, who arrived in Zaire with a German shepherd, once the symbol of that country's Belgian colonialists, who had used them as police dogs.

Director Gast doesn't camouflage his admiration for the charismatic Ali, whose good-natured antics provide the film's most enjoyable moments. Waxing poetic on TV broadcaster Howard Cosell's toupee, Ali declaims: "That thing you got on your head is a phony, and it comes from the tail of a pony." In a prophetic mood, Ali offers the couplet: "You think the world was surprised when Nixon resigned? Wait till I kick Foreman's behind." But more important than Ali's doggerel humor was his connection to Zaire's people and, by extension, to blacks around the world, a connection which, the film suggests, enabled Ali to conquer his fear of Foreman and lift himself to a higher, even spiritual, level of courage.

During its first hour, the film captures the fighters in preparation for the bout, augmenting that with Taylor Hackford's subsequently shot footage of boxing enthusiasts George Plimpton, Norman Mailer and Spike Lee, among others, commenting on the fight's significance. Looking startled at his own recollections, Plimpton tells of meeting "a woman with trembling hands," who assured him, before the fight, that a succubus would get to George Foreman. "That impressed me enormously," Plimpton admits. Mailer, true to form, muses about Zaire leader Mobutu's women and analyzes the title fight, which, he points out, was won not just by Ali's celebrated "rope-a-dope" technique, but by his throwing of a daring "right lead" punch that the champion hadn't anticipated. Lee, less caught up in macho posturing, sees the fight in larger terms, as a pivotal event in black history.

Gast reportedly shot some 250 hours of footage related to the fight, but much of it was tied up for years due to the disappearance and death of several African backers. In the finished product, a good portion of the actual bout is shown, as are performance segments featuring James Brown, B.B. King, Miriam Makeba and others from an international music festival that was a sidebar to the main event. WHEN WE WERE KINGS is an enjoyable, instructive look back at a fascinating event in which boxing, politics and pop culture intersected. *(Violence, nudity, profanity.)* — E.K.

d, Leon Gast; p, Leon Gast, David Sonenberg, Taylor Hackford; exec p, David Sonenberg; co-p, Keith Robinson, Vikram Jayanti; ph, Albert Maysles, Kevin Keating, Paul Goldsmith, Roderick Young, Maryse Alberti; ed, Leon Gast, Taylor Hackford, Jeffrey Levy-Hinte, Keith Robinson; sound, Gene Defever (recordist), Peter Hliddal (recordist), Ed Lockman (recordist), Tony Miller (recordist), Mark Paturet (recordist), Randal Shepard (recordist), Richard Wells (recordist), Shane Zarantash (recordist)

AA Best Documentary Feature:

Documentary **(PR: C MPAA: PG)**

WHERE'S THE MONEY, NOREEN? ★
(U.S.) 92m Power Pictures; Wilshire Court Productions ~ Paramount Home Video c

Julianne Phillips *(Noreen Rafferty)*; A Martinez *(Lou Gardella)*; Nigel Bennett *(Briscoe)*; Nancy Warren *(Cheryl Benet)*; Simon Reynolds *(Teddy)*; Jeremy Ratchford *(Satterfield)*; Stuart Clow *(Craig Benet)*; Gerry Quigley *(Donald Olmsted)*; Anna Louise Richardson *(Marilyn Olmsted)*; Colm Feore *(Kevin Hanover)*; Paul Lee *(Gene Kajikawa)*; Billy Otis *(Harlan Dietz)*; Sarah Goodwill *(Pamela Olmsted)*; Steven Hill *(Brian Olmsted)*; Maggie Huculak *(Discharge Officer)*; Howard Hoover *(Male Reporter)*; Catherine Swing *(Female Reporter)*; Michael Copemen *(Personnel Director)*; Sandra Caldwell *(Insurance Adjuster)*; Don Allison *(TV Host)*; Aaron Tager *(Manager)*; Steve W. Smith *(Wino)*; Robert Racki *(Armored Driver)*; Dwayne McLean *(Armored Guard)*; Roy T. Anderson *(DaCosta)*; Katherine Trowell *(Public Defender)*; Bill Lake *(District Attorney)*

Isn't it a mistake to encapsulate your entire plot line into your title? You'll be wondering where the mystery is in this low-octane crime melodrama about a botched armored-car robbery that leaves participants dead, money missing, and the audience confused as to why they should care about either.

Flashbacks rehash the tale of ex-con Noreen Rafferty (Julianne Phillips), who drove the getaway car for an armored car heist facilitated by her brother, Teddy (Simon Reynolds). The prospect of fast money is betrayed when gang leader Satterfield (Jeremy Ratchford) mows down the guards and "apparently" vanishes with the dough (actually Noreen has hidden the money), after Teddy is slain by a rookie cop. After paying her debt to society, Noreen can't relax due to the persistence of the original arresting officer, Briscoe (Nigel Bennett). Although Satterfield has been killed in prison, he blabbed info to his cellmate Harlan Dietz (Billy Otis), who begins threatening Noreen about the missing moolah.

Determined to figure out the identity of the insider at the security firm who masterminded the robbery, Noreen can't decide whether the crime instigator who ruined her life is her solicitous bakery co-worker Gardella (A Martinez), an overly romantic customer named Kevin Hanover (Colm Feore), or the late father of an insurance claims clerk, Gene Kajikawa (Paul Lee), who works for the firm that originally investigated this case. While Gene cooperates with Noreen to clear his dad of suspicion and make a name for himself, Noreen is menaced by Dietz who gets tossed off a roof by Gardella. Tipped off by her ongoing research that Hanover is the inside man responsible for her brother's death, Noreen confronts Hanover at one of his salvage-operation sites, and pushes him to his death. Learning that Gardella is an undercover cop, and satisfied that the man responsible for leading her brother astray has been punished, Noreen retrieves the money that she stashed in a church. Giving some of her ill-gotten gain to a homeless family that befriended her, patient Noreen, who has outwitted authorities and crooks alike, begins a new life with the coveted blood money.

If only one gasped with surprise when innocent-looking Noreen lays her mitts on the filthy lucre! Instead, one's response is: doesn't the church pay anyone to dust its alcoves? Aside from the 12-1/2 years of plot dust settled on Noreen's quest, the viewer has little of interest to ponder; the suspense ploys are transparent, and there are enough flashbacks for these sequences to secede from the proceedings and form a separate movie. Foolishly, the lazy screenwriter feels that merely by zeroing in on Noreen's justice-search for the inside man, we won't harbor suspicions about her hidden agenda.

As the bored viewer seeks solace in repeating the film's title (each time emphasizing a different word: *Where's* the Money, Noreen? Where's the *Money,* Noreen? Where's the Money, *Noreen?*), the spectator chants a mantra of viewer dissatisfaction. As the lame subterfuges aimed at pressuring Noreen to divulge the location of the money pass by indifferently, the audience doesn't care where Noreen stashed that booty. What they want to know is "Where's the *Excitement,* Noreen?" It isn't to be found in a tiny suspect pool, rotting red herrings, or underestimating the ability of armchair detectives to spot this movie's surprises a mile away. *(Violence, profanity, adult situations.)* — R.P.

d, Artie Mandelberg; p, Julian Marks; co-p, Jonathan Goodwill; w, Carla Jean Wagner; ph, Brenton Spencer; ed, Neil Mandelberg; m, Richard Bellis; prod d, David Moe, Terry Wareham; set d, Doug McCullough; sound, John J. Thomson (mixer), Michael Lacroix (mixer); fx, Michael Kavanagh; casting, Dan Shaner; cos, Laurie Drew; makeup, Lesley Haynes; stunts, Branko Racki

Mystery/Crime **(PR: C MPAA: PG-13)**

WHISPERING, THE ★★
(U.S.) 88m Crystal Sky Int'l.; Prodigee Films ~ A-Pix Home Video c

Cedrick Terrel *(Boy)*; Mette Holt *(The Woman)*; Tracey Abbott *(Demon)*; Scott Johnson *(Chris)*; Leslie Danon *(Lisa Smyths)*; Maxwell Rutherford *(Professor Bettman)*; L. B. Bogdanovich *(Shawnee)*; Josh Brezner *(Paul)*; Stuart Hama *(Lansing)*; Tiffany Salerno *(Jenna)*; Leif Garrett *(Peter Ransket)*; Henry Nemo *(Neighbor)*; Dirk Dahl *(Cop with Goatee)*; Carroll Oden *(Mike Greene)*; Damian Gil *(Jackson)*; Tonya Fogerty *(Brenda)*; Christopher Russell *(Pruitt)*; Brandon Meyer *(Kramer)*; Jan Patrick Schwieterman *(Sean)*; Patrick Ewald *(Lame D. J.)*; Tom Patton *(Dr. Jake Meyers)*; Morris Ruskin *(Stiff Student)*; Ross Worthly *(Punk)*; Ramin Ackert *(Cashier)*; Mary Boucher *(Jenna's Mother)*; Mark Breit *(Jenna's Brother)*; Skyler *(Ghost Girl)*; Cynthia Denzler *(Sara)*

Despite the usual shortcomings built into a low-budget presentation, THE WHISPERING is suprising because of its reasonably sober approach. Mercifully, it's not a gory spectacle awash in blood, rudely interrupted by sexual couplings, and loaded with special effects. If only the screenplay's liabilities didn't leave so much room for improvement.

A community is plagued by a series of suspicious suicides. Bounced off the police force, rebellious insurance claims agent Peter Ransket (Leif Garrett) defies superiors by probing the mysterious Lansing case instead of closing inquiries quickly and profitably for his firm. Drawn to the dead man's ex-girlfriend, Lisa (Leslie Danon), Peter witnesses Lansing's fate firsthand when he can't prevent the shooting of his own pal, Mike (Carroll Oden), at an outdoor Christmas tree lot. There, a supernatural figure (Mette Holt) whispers to the wounded Mike to surrender his soul to her.

Spooked by this spectral visitation, Peter seeks the counsel of a theological shrink, Jake Myers (Tom Patton), while pushing aside guilt feelings about his younger sister's childhood suicide. Under hypnosis, Peter relives a previous life as a Mr. Hank Petrie, a man who mentions being softly persuaded into relinquishing his life in 1944. After Peter's ex-lover ends her life because of his involvement with Lisa, Peter becomes more sensitive to the Whisperer's presence but barely saves an inebriated Lisa from vehicular homicide. Jake, Peter, and Lisa perform a New Age exorcism as poltergeists scurry about, and Jake's house is nearly blown apart due to a detached gas hose.

Smack dab against the soul-sucking Angel of Death who preys on the most psychologically vulnerable, Peter and Lisa jointly disengage the powerful Spirit's grip on them. Sending the Whisperer to from whence it came, they succeed where weaker souls have failed because they confronted their fears directly and, unlike their loved ones, didn't succumb to the soothing siren call of this creature.

Rather than capitalize on a nifty rewiring of the basic tenets of vampirism, THE WHISPERING stretches its narrative into increasingly far-fetched flights of fancy. Unfortunately, the film doesn't concentrate on the seductive intelligence of the monster, who has a powerful arsenal of psychological weapons at her disposal. Instead, she is depicted as being devoid of any individualized evil. The film also regrettably doesn't personalize any of her victims, except for Peter. Further trouble lies with the movie's poor expository skill; it wastes screen time dispensing facts that have already been noted. Shouldn't Peter and Lisa be racing against time to save a series of lost souls, while still dealing with their own susceptibility?

Instead of developing meaty possibilities for dramatic terror, THE WHISPERING sidesteps psychology and winds up a haunted house sideshow flick. One feels as if the cleverest writing student in class had been forced to turn over an assignment to a drop-out, who raced to finish it before being booted out of school. What might have been a fresh glimpse into creative soul-snatching ends up instead a power-of-positive-thinking saga about getting quickly out of the path of ambulatory furniture. *(Violence, extreme profanity, extensive nudity, sexual situations, substance abuse.)* — R.P.

d, Gregory Gieras; p, Leslie Danon, Gregory Gieras, Stuart Hanna; exec p, Steven Paul; w, Leslie Danon, Austin Reid (based on the story by Leslie Danon); ph, Samuel Ameen; ed, Tracy Curtis; m, Marco Beltrami; prod d, Katy Jenkins; art d, Katy Jenkins; set d, Katy Jenkins; sound, Sergei Popovic (mixer), Bob Sheridan (mixer); fx, Scott Johnson; cos, Katy Jenkins; makeup, Soo Y. Kang

Horror **(PR: C MPAA: R)**

WHITE BALLOON, THE ★★★

(Iran) 85m IRIB Channel Two; Farabi Cinema Foundation ~ October Films c
(BADKONAK-E SEFID)

Aida Mohammakhani *(Razieh)*; Mohsen Kalifi *(Ali)*; Fereshteh Sadr Orfani *(Mother)*; Anna Bourkowska *(Old Woman)*; Mohammad Shahani *(Soldier)*; Mohammad Bahktiari *(Tailor)*

Emerging from what appears to be a popular new wave of Iranian filmmaking, THE WHITE BALLOON tells a charming tale about a little girl who loses her mother's money while shopping for a pet goldfish. This award-winner at the 1995 Cannes Film Festival is an engaging, bittersweet comedy.

THE WHITE BALLOON takes place on New Year's Day in modern day Tehran, where seven-year-old Razieh (Aida Mohammadkhani) wishes to purchase a large white goldfish for her family's holiday celebration. Along with her older brother, Ali (Mohsen Kalifi), Razieh convinces her reluctant mother (Fereshteh Sadr Orfani) to give her the money needed to buy the fish before the stores close that evening.

On her way to the pet store, Razieh's money is taken by two wily snake charmers. Although she eventually gets it back, Razieh soon loses it again while continuing her walk to the store. Upon her arrival, Razieh asks the uncaring shopkeeper to reserve the special goldfish while she looks for her money. With the help of an elderly woman (Anna Bourkowska), Razieh retraces her steps and finds the valuable note, which has fallen through a sidewalk grate in front of a closed store.

Some time later, Ali happens upon Razieh and joins her in trying to get the attention of a busy tailor (Mohammad Bahktiari) to help them. Unfortunately, they are unsuccessful. In desperation, Ali looks for the owner of the closed store, while a kind soldier (Mohammad Shahani) keeps Razieh company, but Ali's search through the neighborhood is fruitless. Finally, Ali borrows a stick from a balloon salesman so that he can poke it through the grate and lift the note. At first, the salesman fights with Ali over the stick, but, eventually, he helps him extract the money. Razieh and Ali then happily run off to buy the goldfish.

THE WHITE BALLOON was written by Abbas Kiarostami, the director of THROUGH THE OLIVE TREES (1984), and like that Iranian film, THE WHITE BALLOON is carefully made, lightly intriguing and not much more. Still, both films are better than the bulk of family fare coming out of Hollywood today. The idea behind THE WHITE BALLOON seems to be inspired by the French children's book and award-winning short subject film, THE RED BALLOON, about a balloon that follows and watches over a little boy all over Paris. THE WHITE BALLOON tells a different tale in a different setting, but also focuses on a small child and involves a balloon that becomes a *deus ex machina* of sorts. (The film also quotes from THE BICYCLE THIEF (1948) in the neo-Neo- Realist approach to the material, and in one particular shot of the two children sitting on the sidewalk.)

First-time feature film director Jafar Panahi (who served both as an actor in and as an assistant on THROUGH THE OLIVE TREES) succeeds in limiting his narrative to its basic elements, but the story might have had even greater impact had he filmed more shots at Razieh's literal point-of-view level and not brought in her brother in the last third to share her experience. In fact, by the climax, when the money is recaptured, the audience loses much of its connection to the girl, whose best moments come earlier, such as when her money is first taken by the snake charmers. In that scene, the girl's tears seem genuine and her fear nearly palpable as the camera stealthily tracks her approach to the snake, which holds her money.

It is too bad Panahi (who also edited the film and designed the sets) does not maintain his affinity for the child's point of view throughout, since he so meticulously constructs it at the beginning. But this lapse does not take anything away from Aida Mohammadkhani, whose fine, natural performance as the strong-willed Razieh contributes greatly to the overall pleasure of the piece. Even when this child actor nearly flubs a line, the audience roots for her!

If THE WHITE BALLOON has something to say, it seems to be about the lack of humanitas in the world today, and how a small act of kindness can make a difference. Most audiences will probably enjoy this little film whether they get the message or not. — E.M.

d, Jafar Panahi; p, Kurosh Mazkouri; w, Abbas Kiarostami (based on an idea by Jafar Panahi and Parviz Shahbazi); ph, Farzad Jowdat; ed, Jafar Panahi; art d, Jafar Panahi; sound, Mojtaba Mortazavi (engineer), Said Ahmadi (engineer), Mehdi Dejbodi (mixing engineer)

Drama/Comedy/Children's (PR: AA MPAA: NR)

WHITE SQUALL ★★½

(U.S.) 128m Scott Free; Largo Entertainment; Hollywood Pictures ~ Buena Vista c

Jeff Bridges *(Christopher Sheldon)*; Caroline Goodall *(Dr. Alice Sheldon)*; John Savage *(McCrea)*; Scott Wolf *(Chuck Gieg)*; Jeremy Sisto *(Frank Beaumont)*; Ryan Phillippe *(Gil Martin)*; David Lascher *(Robert March)*; Eric Michael Cole *(Dean Preston)*; Jason Marsden *(Shay Jennings)*; David Selby *(Francis Beaumont)*; Julio Mechoso *(Girard Pascal)*; Zeljko Ivanek *(Sanders)*; Balthazar Getty *(Tod Johnstone)*; Ethan Embry *(Tracy Lapchick)*; Jordan Clarke *(Charles Gieg)*; Lizbeth MacKay *(Middy Gieg)*; Jill Larson *(Peggy Beaumont)*; James Medina *(Cuban Commander)*; James Rebhorn *(Tyler)*; Nicole Ann Samuel *(Girl in Brothel)*; Becky Ann Baker *(Ms. Boyde)*; Camilla Overbye Roos *(Bregitta)*; Nathaniel Ives *(Relief Bo'sun)*; Chris Condon *(Crew Member)*; Andrew Hartley *(Crew Member)*; Peyton Thomas *(Crew Member)*; Jordan Scott; Nynne Christiansen; Charlotte Anderson; Lene Kristensen; Anja Clausen; Anita Weider; Emily Chittell; Mette Hocke *(Danish Schoolgirls)*

Based on the true story of the 1961 wreck of the Ocean Academy brigantine, the Albatross, in which four students and two crew members were killed, WHITE SQUALL is an ill-structured high seas adventure.

In the fall of 1960, thirteen teenaged boys set sail for a year as the crew of the Albatross, a floating prep school. Their skipper, Christopher Sheldon (Jeff Bridges) runs a tight ship, and the boys learn right away that this character-building trip isn't going to be easy. The crew bonds as they face the rigors of the sea and bridge the gap between adolescence and manhood. Chuck Gieg (Scott Wolf, who also narrates) soon emerges as the leader of the young recruits. He befriends Gil (Ryan Phillippe), a timid youth, and reforms Dean (Eric Michael Cole), a tough-acting rebel.

On the homeward leg of its 12,000 mile journey, the Albatross is hit by a freak weather condition known as a white squall. The storm destroys the ship and claims six lives, including Sheldon's wife Alice (Caroline Goodall) and Gil. The survivors are rescued after two days adrift, but their ordeal is not over once they reach dry ground. The crew attends the Coast Guard tribunal of Sheldon, who is charged with neglect in the incident. Sheldon offers to turn in his license, but Chuck challenges him to stand up to the charges. Finally, the shipmates stand together and Sheldon is vindicated.

Judged solely as a high seas adventure, WHITE SQUALL could have been a contender. As staged by Ridley Scott (THELMA AND LOUISE, ALIEN), the film boasts some of the most thrilling sea footage in recent years. The storm of the film's title is a long time coming, but when it hits, it explodes onto the screen with staggering force. Filmed in a giant water tank off the coast of Malta, the squall roars with a terrifying white-knuckled realism. Unfortunately, it encompasses only a small amount of screen time, the rest devoted to a tired coming of age theme which offers no new insights and mostly bogs down the picture in banalities.

Bridges plays a skipper equally crusty and compassionate, but it's a tough sell; his motivations remain unclear. The only crew member who stands out from the pack is Geig, thanks to Wolf's earnest performance. Goodall, John Savage and David Selby make strong impressions in lesser roles. But the real star of WHITE SQUALL is the storm itself, and one wishes it had demanded more screen time. *(Violence, nudity, sexual situations, profanity.)* — B.R.

d, Ridley Scott; p, Mimi Polk Gitlin, Rocky Lang; exec p, Ridley Scott; co-p, Nigel Wooll, Todd Robinson; w, Todd Robinson; ph, Hugh Johnson; ed, Gerry Hambling; m, Jeff Rona; prod d, Peter J. Hampton, Leslie Tomkins; sound, Ken Weston (mixer); fx, Joss Williams; casting, Louis DiGiaimo; cos, Judianna Makovsky; makeup, Sarah Monzani; stunts, Eddie Stacey

Drama/Adventure (PR: C MPAA: PG-13)

WHITE TIGER ★

(U.S.) 94m Gail Force Films Inc.; Evergreen Entertainment ~ Keystone Pictures c

Gary Daniels *(Mike Ryan)*; Matt Craven *(John Grogan)*; Cary Hiroyuki-Tagawa *(Victor Chow)*; Julia Nickson *(Jade)*; Lisa Langlois *(Joanne Grogan)*; Ron Winston Yuan *(Severin)*; Dana Lee *(Zhou)*; George Cheung *(Fong)*; Philip Granger *(Capt. McGuire)*; Max Kirishima *(Tang)*; John Kirkconnell *(Josh Grogan)*

Aussie kickboxer Gary Daniels stars in WHITE TIGER, a low-grade addition to the swelling ranks of the genre that calls for a cop to take revenge on the drug lord who killed his partner.

DEA agents Mike Ryan (Gary Daniels) and John Grogan (Matt Craven) are on a camping trip in New York with Grogan's wife and son when they get a call to fly to Seattle to bust ruthless drug dealer Victor Chow (Cary Hiroyuki-Tagawa).

Chow meets with another dealer named Tang (Max Kirishima) to convince him to buy an addictive new drug he has invented, but Tang refuses and a gunfight erupts. Ryan and Grogan are caught in the crossfire, and Chow manages to escape by abducting Grogan and using him as a shield. Chow shoots and kills Grogan and jumps on a boat as Ryan watches helplessly.

After the funeral, Ryan is told to lay off the case by his superiors and sent home, but he decides to go after Chow anyway. Meanwhile, crime lords in Hong Kong decide that Chow's violent behavior and his new drug will put them out of business, so they put out a hit on him.

At a nightclub Chow owns, Ryan meets a mysterious woman named Jade (Julia Nickson), and as he's leaving the club, a gang of hoods attack Ryan, but he beats them all up. After following some of Chow's men to a pier where Chow keeps his drug lab on a freighter ship, a cop named Fong (George Cheung) comes to escort Ryan out of town, but he's actually on Chow's payroll. Fong tries to kill Ryan, but Ryan strikes first, then goes to Jade's house, where the two make love.

Jade tells Ryan where Chow lives, and Ryan manages to break into his house, kill dozens of bodyguards and confront Chow. He tries to arrest him, but Jade shows up and claims she's been hired by the Chinese mob to kill Chow. A bodyguard comes in and knocks out Ryan, and Chow forces Jade to get on his ship. Ryan escapes and sneaks onto the ship, kills a dozen more men, then fights Chow. The drug lab catches fire, and Ryan jumps into the water as the ship explodes, killing Chow. Jade is reunited with her daughter and Ryan finishes the camping trip with Grogan's son.

WHITE TIGER is a strictly routine direct-to-video revenge actioner that brings nothing new to the genre and is tediously stretched out with endless slow-motion shots of shootouts and explosions. Daniels may be capable in the martial arts, but with his bland personality, shaggy blond hair and somnambulistic acting, he's about as threatening as a California surfer dude.

Hiroyuki-Tagawa does his usual odious Asian bit. In fact, all of the Asians in the cast play nefarious criminals. As with most films of this type, more imagination has gone into the stunts than the script, which is filled with laughable tough-guy dialogue and pathetic wisecracks. *(Graphic violence, profanity, nudity, sexual situations.)* — M.S.

d, Richard Martin; p, Robert Vince, William Vince; exec p, Roy McAree, Michael Strange; w, Don Woodman, Gordon Melbourne, Roy Sallows (based on a story by Bey Logan); ph, Gregory Middleton; ed, Kerry Uchida; m, Graeme Coleman; art d, Don MacAulay; sound, Marc Benoit; fx, Andrew Chamberlayne; casting, Abra Edelman, Elisa Goodman; cos, Barb Nixon; makeup, Gina Hole

Action/Martial Arts (PR: O MPAA: R)

WHITE WOLVES II: LEGEND OF THE WILD ★

(U.S.) 95m Tessa Trust ~ New Horizons Home Video c

Elizabeth Berkley *(Crystal)*; Ele Keats *(Beri)*; Jeremy London *(Mason)*; Corin Nemec *(Ben)*; Ernie Reyes Jr. *(Steve)*; Justin Whalin *(Jeff)*

Dumbfounded, the hapless viewer sits through this run-of-the-mill outdoor adventure and wonders for whom this wilderness ramble was intended. Although it's designed as a kiddy adventure, it's stocked with cliched, adolescent-troublemaker characters played by young adult stars too old for these jejune activities.

Animal activist Ben Harris (Corin Nemec) annually employs delinquent teens in his ongoing crusade to take wolves off the endangered species list. This summer, his crew is composed of graffiti renegade Steve (Ernie Reyes Jr.), sneak thief Crystal (Elizabeth Berkley), and violent-tempered nihilist Beri (Ele Keats), who has a bigger chip on her shoulder than any found on the nearby mountains. En route to retrieving a hidden camera, which has been charting wolves in their natural habitat, Ben's fledgling staff shoots the rapids, hones survival skills, and learns to put personal differences aside.

During the course of their on-the-job training, the wildlife recordists meet two paragliding brothers, braggart Mason (Jeremy London) and his passive-aggressive sibling Jeff (Justin Whalin). Ben saves two orphaned cubs, but Steve, Crystal, and Beri endanger the baby wolves when they decide to hang out with Jeff and Mason. After show-off Mason wipes out in a crash-landing, Ben decides to accompany him to a first-aid station and to entrust his lupine studies to his anxious crew. While rafting to civilization, Ben and Mason are both seriously injured in a capsizing accident. Initially panicking, Ben's summer crew persuades chicken-hearted Jeff to paraglide for emergency help. After Mason and Ben are airlifted to safety and they recuperate, Beri, Crystal, Steve, and Jeff remain behind to complete Ben's cataloguing work with the unearthed camera.

My, my, my, how quickly those long-in-the-tooth teens brave adversity, swallow their pride, and pitch in to conserve the wolf population. With the flimsiest of screenwriting barriers blocking their way, the city slickers acquire respect for Mother Nature and for themselves in record time. Mesmerized by the splendid scenery, the audience may be lulled into enjoying WHITE WOLVES II as a "National Geographic" special interrupted by bouts of unfulfilling drama. What's so preposterous about this travelogue adventure is that it appears to have been written with problem children in mind, but then it was filmed with older delinquent characters instead. The screenwriter has little understanding of kids or teens. Too tame for young adults, who will require a lot more violence than this movie's Smokey the Bear attack on a pup-tent, WHITE WOLVES II will conversely tick off youngsters who will wonder what these mature adolescents are doing usurping their own Outward Bound fantasies. As a result, this Save-the-Wolves odyssey plays to an empty house. *(Violence, profanity.)* — R.P.

d, Terence H. Winkless; p, Julie Corman; w, Dylan Kelsey Hadley; ph, John Aronson; ed, John Gilbert; m, Gene Ober; art d, Barry Schroeder; sound, Brian Crain (mixer); casting, Jan Glaser; cos, Tamara Thomson; makeup, Christina Criswell; stunts, Gary Morgan

Adventure (PR: A MPAA: PG)

WHO KILLED PASOLINI? ★★½

(Italy) 101m Cecchi Gori Group Tiger Cinematographica; Cecchi Gori Group Leopard; Numero Cinque; Flach Film ~ Roxie Releasing c/bw

(AKA: PASOLINI, AN ITALIAN CRIME; PASOLINI, UN DELITTO ITALIANO)

Carlo De Filippi *(Pino Pelosi)*; Nicoletta Braschi *(Graziella Chiarcossi)*; Tony Bertorelli *(Inspector Pigna)*; Andrea Occhipinti *(Furio Columbo)*; Victor Cavallo *(Antonio Pelosi)*; Rosa Pianeta *(Maria Pelosi)*; Giulio Scarpati *(Nino Marazzita)*; Francesco Siciliano *(Apprentice)*; Biagio Pelligra *(Police Official)*; Umberto Orsini *(High Ranking Judge)*; Krum De Nicola *(Adolfo De Santis)*; Claudio Amendola *(Trepalle)*; Enzo Marcelli *("Braciola")*; Antonio Petrocelli *(Tommaso Spaltro)*; Vittorio De Bisogno *(Vincenzo Spaltro)*; Ivano Marescotti *(Law Firm Client)*; Claudio Bisagli *(Guido Calvi)*; Antonello Fassari *(Rocco Mangia)*; Massimo De Francovich *(Faustino Durante)*; Ennio Coltorti *(Juvenile Court Judge)*; Adriana Asti *(Teacher)*; Paolo Graziosi *(Luigi Cancrini)*; Giacomo Piperno *(Alfredo Carlo Moro)*; Maurizio Di Carmine *(Giuseppe Salame)*; Claudia Pozzi *(Journalist)*; Lello Serao *(Police Officer Cuzzupe)*; Eduardo Cuomo *(Guglielmi)*; Mimmo Mignemi *(Brigadiere)*; Giorgio Crisafi *(Carabinieri Officer)*; Alessandro Carlone *(Cellmate)*; Maria Grandi *(Maria Teresa Lollobrigida)*; Romano Jannelli *(Ennio Slavitti)*; Renato Campese *(Judge Tranfo)*; Vanni Fois *(Carabinieri Colonel)*; Gaetano Sersale; Dino Gentili; Simona Ferraro; Emilia Marra; Paolo Bonanni; Marco Caporali *(Reporters)*; Claudio Alfonsi *(TG1 Commentator)*; Claudio Parise *(TG2 Commentator)*; Walter Da Pozza *(Citta Futura Commentator)*; Elisa Lancione *(Susanna Pasolini)*; Franco Mescollini *(Agency Director)*; Walter Piretti *(Agency Editor)*; Giovanni Marsala *(Claudio Seminara)*; Massimiliano Petrucci *(Salvatore Deidda)*; Riccardo Calvani *(Barman)*; Augusto Vacca *("Riccio")*; Fabrizio Vitale *("Stecco")*; Daniele Taffone *("Farfalla")*; Simone Melis *("Bracioletta")*; Franca Scagnetti *(Woman)*; Vito Passeri *(Tall Man)*; Valentino Simeoni *(Short Man)*; Mattia Osti *(Durante's Assistant)*; Antonio Ferrante *(Chief of Police)*; Costantino Meloni *(Casal del Marmo Kid)*; Paolo De Giorgio *("Il Pugliese")*; Roberto Accornero *(Juvenile Court Judge)*; Clarizio Di Ciaula *(Court Clerk)*; Maurizio Greco *(Public Attorney)*; Giorgio Colangeli *(Honorary Judge Guarino)*; Alessandra Vanzi *(Honorary Judge Milone)*; Antonio Falvo *(Court Usher)*

A reenactment of the events following the killing of the prominent Italian filmmaker and poet, Pier Paolo Pasolini, this docudrama strongly suggests that he was the victim not of a lone perpetrator, as widely believed, but of a group of thugs quite possibly commissioned by right-wing terrorists.

In the early morning hours of November 2, 1975, 17-year-old Pino Pelosi (Carlo De Filippi) is pulled over by Rome highway police. The Alpha Romeo he is driving belongs to Pier Paolo Pasolini, whose mangled corpse is soon discovered in one of the city's slums. In an off-the-record statement, a resident of the area maintains that he had witnessed four or five men beating up Pasolini. In jail, a cell mate (Alessandro Carlone) advises Pelosi to claim sole responsibility for the slaying and thus avoid being tried as an adult, receiving a heavy sentence, and being marked as an informer. Pelosi comes up with the following story: Pasolini picked him up, took him to dinner, and later, after the pair had engaged in fellatio, tried to force him to submit to anal sex. A fight ensued, which ended with Pelosi beating Pasolini unconscious with a board. The boy then got into Pasolini's car and fled.

Largely as a result of widespread anti-homosexual sentiment, those in charge of the police and journalistic investigations are essentially unwilling to probe more deeply into the matter. After an autopsy reveals that Pasolini's body had been run over by his car, an attorney (Giulio Scarpati) representing the dead man's family begins to suspect that Pasolini, an outspoken Marxist, was the victim of a contract killing commissioned by fascists and carried out by a gang of teenage hoodlums.

The Pasolini family lawyers persuasively argue this position in juvenile court, while the defendant, although he revises his original story somewhat, continues to claim that he acted alone. Inspired by the spirit of Pasolini's social idealism, his family requests that Pelosi be tried as a juvenile and drops their civil case against him. Nevertheless, the court declares him an adult, finds him guilty of voluntary manslaughter, and sentences him to a stiff term of nearly ten years in prison. Although the lower court has been convinced that Pelosi acted "with unknown accomplices," a court of appeals deems this finding improbable and the case is officially closed.

WHO KILLED PASOLINI? is an ably directed and accessible presentation of the Pasolini case. If one can assume that its creators have stated their point of view without deliberate distortion of the facts or undue bias, the film makes its case persuasively and does not appear to be the product of left-wing paranoia. It appears to be generally free of righteous rigging, despite a scene in which Pelosi's somewhat devious and bombastic attorney is shown practicing his opening statement in front of a mirror—as if honest, idealistic lawyers do not rehearse their courtroom presentations.

The movie might have benefited from a deeper probing into the complexity of Pasolini's personality and character. It largely ducks, for instance, the implicit irony of a Marxist of comfortable means habitually purchasing sexual favors from the same sort of downtrodden adolescents whom he champions in his art and social criticism.

Without having made a mountain out of a molehill, the producers may have made a movie-of-the-week out of material better suited to treatment in a long article or a 30-minute TV documentary. In part because the story is (necessarily) unresolved, few but avid Pasolini fans will find the film worthy of the effort involved in making it. Furthermore, despite the good intentions of everyone involved, history is never well served when several screenwriters and dozens of actors are recruited to tell a true story. *(Violence, adult situations, extreme profanity.)*
— D.T.

d, Marco Tullio Giordana; p, Vittorio Cecchi Gori, Rita Cecchi Gori, Claudio Bonivento; co-p, Jean-Francois Lepetit; w, Marco Tullio Giordana, Stefano Rulli, Sandro Petraglia (from a story by Marco Tullio Giordana, Stefano Rulli, and Sandro Petraglia, inspired by the books *Pasolini, Un Delitto Italiano* by Marco Tullio Giordana and *Vita Di Pasolini* by Enzo Siciliano); ph, Franco Lecca; ed, Cecilia Zanuso; m, Ennio Morricone; prod d, Elisabetta Montaldo; sound, Gianni Zampagni; cos, Elisabetta Montaldo

Docudrama/Biography/Mystery (PR: O MPAA: NR)

WHOLE WIDE WORLD, THE ★★★

(U.S.) 105m Cineville Inc; Eventide Productions; Kushner-Locke ~ Sony Pictures Classics c

Renee Zellweger *(Novalyne Price)*; Vincent D'Onofrio *(Robert E. Howard)*; Ann Wedgeworth *(Mrs. Howard)*; Harve Presnell *(Dr. Howard)*; Benjamin Mouton *(Clyde Smith)*; Michael Corbett *(Booth Adams)*; Helen Cates *(Enid)*; Marion Eaton *(Woman on Bus)*; Leslie Berger *(Ethel)*; Chris Shearer *(Truett)*; Sandy Walper *(Mammy)*; Dell F. Aldrich *(Mrs. Hemphill)*; Libby Villari *(Etna Reed Price)*; Antonia Bogdanovich *(Teacher)*; Elizabeth D'Onofrio *(Mrs. Smith)*; Stephen Marshall *(Director)*

An honest, grown-up, and deeply felt docudrama about a young couple who love each other but are unable to connect, THE WHOLE WIDE WORLD, based on a memoir by an elderly schoolteacher, will primarily appeal to romance fans; others may find it a little too talky, repetitious, and, ultimately, downbeat.

In rural Texas in the early 1930s, an old boyfriend introduces Novalyne Price (Renee Zellweger), a high school teacher, to Bob Howard (Vincent D'Onofrio), a pulp writer who has achieved enormous success with his character Conan the Barbarian. A year-and-a-half later she calls him up on an impulse but is unable to reach him. Suspecting that his mother is not relaying her messages, Novalyne decides to make a personal appearance at the Howard home, where after some difficulty she is able to penetrate the protective shell erected around Bob by his parents (Harve Presnell and Ann Wedgeworth). An aspiring writer, Novalyne asks Bob's advice on how to get published. He drives her home and asks her for a date.

Novalyne is peeved when Bob shows up for their first date minus tie and jacket. They spend the evening discussing their radically different approaches to fiction: he specializes in fantastic, atavistic "yarns"; she wants to write stories about everyday reality.

Novalyne falls in love with Bob but is increasingly disturbed by his antisocial attitudes and his exaggerated devotion to his sickly mother. The more the couple see of each other, the more apparent their incompatibility.

Realizing this, Novalyne begins to go out with an old friend of Bob's. His mother very ill, Bob desperately turns to Novalyne for love, but it is too late. She leaves for LSU to study for her master's degree in education. His mother now at death's door, Bob kills himself.

As the story ends, a series of cards tells us that Novalyne Price spent her next 44 years as a teacher, married in 1947, and, at the age of 76, wrote the book on which THE WHOLE WIDE WORLD is based.

If this movie belongs in any category, it's the *Men Are From Mars, Women Are From Venus* genre. THE WHOLE WIDE WORLD, however, has little in common with other films of this genre, being less allegorical than CRAZY QUILT (1966), for example, and less sociologically inquisitive than BABY IT'S YOU (1983). Indeed, one of the film's most distinctive qualities is its downplaying of social determinism, its grounding of the couple's incompatibility in their conflicting temperaments and worldviews rather than in family disapproval or class differences. Bob and Novalyne are neither Romeo and Juliet nor Minnie and Moskowitz.

The decision to proffer this story as essentially a two-character piece with minimal interplay from contiguous characters is both a measure of the film's audacity and one of the sources of its occasional tedium. (Another is redundancy: Novalyne and Bob seem to be having the same argument over and over and over.) An additional mark of the film's integrity, rare in contemporary cinema, is its presentation of a couple who fail to jump immediately into each other's arms and beds. In fact, it is an hour into the movie and over a year into their on-again, off-again relationship when Novalyne and Bob share their first kiss, which turns out to be nearly their last.

D'Onofrio is good as the psychologically disturbed Bob, and Zellweger, a very appealing hybrid of Miriam Hopkins and Molly Ringwald, is even better as Novalyne. It takes an above average actress to play an "average" woman so insightfully and arrestingly. Blessed with muted and modest wide-screen cinematography that evocatively captures the wistful lonesomeness of the Texas terrain, THE WHOLE WIDE WORLD is an admirable and affecting work that is to be applauded for courageously and unostentatiously assuming a bundle of commercial risks—not the least of which is daring to be sad. *(Profanity.)* — D.T.

d, Dan Ireland; p, Carl-Jan Colpaert, Kevin Reidy, Dan Ireland, Vincent D'Onofrio; exec p, Donald Kushner, Peter Locke, Gregory Cascante; assoc p, Luis Colina; co-p, Benjamin Mouton, Michael Scott Myers; w, Michael Scott Myers (based on the novel *One Who Walked Alone* by Novalyne Price Ellis); ph, Claudio Rocha; ed, Luis Colina; m, Hans Zimmer, Harry Gregson-Williams; prod d, John Allen Frick; set d, Terri L. Wright; sound, Lance Brown; casting, Laurel Smith; cos, Gail McMullen; makeup, Tammy Lema

Romance/Biography **(PR: A MPAA: PG)**

WICKED CITY, THE ★★★

(Hong Kong) 88m Golden Princess Film Production Ltd.; Film Workshop ~ Fox Lorber Home Video c

Leon Lai *(Lung/Taki)*; Jacky Cheung *(Ying/Ken)*; Michelle Reis *(Gaye/Genki May/Windy)*; Tatsuya Nakadai *(Yuen Tai Chung/Gen. Daisaw/Daishu)*; Roy Cheung *(Gwei/Shudo)*; Carman Lee *(Loh/Shira/Orchid)*; Yuen Woo Ping *(Squad Chief)*

A live-action adaptation of a Japanese animated film of the same title, THE WICKED CITY offers an imaginative, unmistakably Hong Kong approach to a tale of conflict between humans and alien counterparts with a blend of horror, science fiction, crimefighting, and romantic melodrama unthinkable in any other cinema.

In the near future in Hong Kong, a new drug fad, centering on the high-energy "Happiness," is linked to increased activity by super-powered, other-dimensional beings known as "Rapters" who disguise themselves as humans and infiltrate human society. The Anti-Rapter Bureau assigns top agent Lung (Leon Lai) to monitor Yuen Tai Chung (Tatsuya Nakadai), a wealthy Asian industrialist who is suspected of being a Rapter. Lung asks for Ying (Jacky Cheung) to be his partner but the squad chief, Yuen (Woo Ping), refuses out of distrust of Ying, whose mother was a Rapter.

Yuen works with other powerful businessmen, Rapters in human guise, to try to engineer peaceful relations with humans, but he's consistently undermined by his reckless son, Gwei (Roy Cheung), who wants to take over his father's enterprises and lead a Rapter conquest of the human world. Yuen's mistress is Gaye (Michelle Reis), a Rapter with whom Lung once had an affair and whom he still loves.

Ying is suspected of leaking information to the Rapters, but the traitor in the Bureau turns out to be Loh (Carman Lee), the girl Ying loves, who is spotted engineering a major drug deal with Gwei. After the Bureau apprehends Yuen, Gwei kidnaps Gaye and manages to break the magnetic defense shield erected by the Bureau, causing time to begin running backwards. Lung and Ying free Yuen and proceed to engage in battle with Gwei, who has reverted to his scaly, reptilian Rapter form. Yuen and Gwei fight atop jumbo jets over the Hong Kong skyline, as Yuen begins reverting to Rapter form as well. Lung and Gaye seek to stop Ying from turning into a Rapter himself. Finally, with Gwei destroyed, Lung allows Yuen and Gaye to escape, hoping that Gaye will one day return to him.

WICKED CITY offers the most extravagant special effects yet seen in Hong Kong cinema. A female Rapter turns into a liquid monster, a pinball machine writhing in ecstasy as the villain plays her, and finally a motorcycle ridden by her opponent, Yuen. In a scene borrowed directly from the Japanese animated version, another female Rapter turns into a bony, multi-legged, spider-like creature in the throes of a sexual liaison with the hero. During the final battle, the Rapter characters change into their hidden reptilian selves, replete with claws, scales, and long tails.

Produced by the prolific Tsui Hark (ONCE UPON A TIME IN CHINA), the film is easily one of the most bizarre and delirious of Hong Kong creations, but also one of the most consistent in its stark, deadly serious depiction of a future world where interdimensional trickery can rend the fabric of time and space as humans know it. A romantic undercurrent devoted to the thwarted love between Lung and Gaye anchors the often surrealistic proceedings in a more familiar emotional drama.

The character names and names for the Rapters vary in different versions of this film. The main character is addressed as Lung on the Cantonese soundtrack and is so named in the subtitles of the American version, but is referred to as Taki (the character's name in the Japanese version) in the original subtitled Hong Kong print and the American dubbed version. The Rapters are so named only in the Hong Kong subtitled print, and are referred to as "Reptoids" in the English dubbed version and "monsters" in the American subtitled version. *(Violence, sexual situations.)* — B.C.

d, Mak Tai Kit; p, Raymond Lee, Mak Chi Sin; exec p, Tsui Hark; w, Tsui Hark, Roy Szeto (based on the comic strip by Hideyuki Kikuchi); ph, Andrew Lau, Joe Chan

Science Fiction/Fantasy/Action **(PR: C MPAA: NR)**

WIDOW'S KISS ★★

(U.S.) 103m Smokescreen Productions ~ HBO Home Video c

Mackenzie Astin *(Sean Sager)*; Beverly D'Angelo *(Vivian Fairchild)*; Dennis Haysbert *(Eddie Costello)*; Bruce Davison *(Justin Sager)*; Anna Maria Horsford *(Capt. Lavonda Harrison)*; Michael Woolson *(Paul)*; Barbara Rush *(Edith Fitzpatrick)*; Leslie Horan *(Kelly)*; Brad Joseph Dubin *(Chris)*; Pat Thomas *(Sgt. Burnette)*; Leonard Salazar *(Carlos Fuentes)*; Margarette Silverstein *(Claudette Nevins)*; Michael Des Barres *(Steven Rose)*; James Harper *(Dr. Isaacs)*

A proven cast marks time in this languid, rather depressing suspense-drama that makes use of numerous red herrings to flesh out a routine erotic-thriller on its way to late-night cable.

Relations between young Sean Sager (Mackenzie Astin) and his millionaire attorney father, Justin (Bruce Davison), have been strained ever since the death of Mrs. Sager in a car wreck. The boy is hardly enchanted when his dad brings home a new paramour, glamorous widow Vivian Fairchild (Beverly D'Angelo), who arrives complete with a grown-up son of her own, the vaguely menacing Paul (Michael Woolson).

Abruptly, Justin Sager drops dead, and Vivian and Paul take over the household. Sean knows the gold-digging newcomers are responsible, and to help prove murder he turns to Eddie Costello (Dennis Haysbert), a cop his father occasionally employed. Meanwhile, Vivian learns she will inherit the entire $10 million fortune only if Sean perishes. Paul—actually Vivian's lover, not her offspring—schemes to do the job during a college fraternity hazing, but Sean comes prepared and shoots the assassin dead.

When Sean confronts Vivian with this news, she tries to recruit him as her latest partner in crime, revealing that poisoning Justin wasn't even her idea, but rather a hired hit commissioned by Sean's grandmother (Barbara Rush), who is vengeful over her daughter's death. Leaving Costello to arrest Vivian, Sean visits his grandmother, gets a confession out of her, then gives her a revolver with which she commits suicide as the police close in.

Astin makes a callow and surly young hero, and for a moment the script implies he might have killed his father after all—the deed takes place off-screen, muddying things considerably. Numerous red herrings are dropped along the sordid story line in half-hearted fashion—from Vivian's apparent incest with Paul to her possible drug addiction—but only the grandmother's complicity comes as any surprise, and one finds precious little entertainment value in the old lady's unmasking and destruction.

There's really not much point to WIDOW'S KISS, except to fill time in late-night slots on cable TV—and to keep a number of good actors with scant marquee value employed between prestige jobs. D'Angelo in particular handles her seductive, sinister role as well as one could ask, given the material. She goes back and forth between movies like this to doing Sam Shepard plays on-stage. Haysbert also brings an edge to what would otherwise be a marginal character. *(Violence, adult situations, sexual situations, nudity, substance abuse, profanity)* — C.C.

d, Peter Foldy; p, Bruce Cohn Curtis; exec p, Keith Samples; w, Peter Foldy, Mark Donnelly; ph, Doyle Smith; ed, Doug H. Lloyd; m, Robert Sprayberry; prod d, Alfred Sole; set d, Antoinette A. Ensley; fx, Lou Carlucci; casting, Denise Chamion; cos, Barbara Palmer; makeup, Suzanne Diaz; stunts, Gary Wayton

Thriller **(PR: O MPAA: R)**

WIFE, THE ★★★

(U.S.) 101m Genre Film; CiBy 2000 ~
Artistic License c

Julie Haggerty *(Rita)*; Tom Noonan *(Jack)*; Wallace Shawn *(Cosmo)*; Karen Young *(Arlie)*

Tom Noonan's second directorial feature, THE WIFE, features four great performances—including his own—but the film rambles and sputters before collapsing altogether.

THE WIFE takes place in a single night at the elegant but remote suburban farmhouse of two New Age analysts, Jack (Noonan) and Rita (Julie Hagerty). Cosmo (Wallace Shawn) makes an unannounced visit to see Jack and Rita for some additional counseling and to introduce them to his wife, Arlie (Karen Young), whom he feels is the source of all his problems. When the aggressive Arlie invites herself and Cosmo for dinner, Jack sees an opportunity to work therapeutically with the couple. Rita, on the other hand, feels her privacy has been invaded.

At dinner, Arlie drinks heavily and describes her dark view of the world, while Cosmo tries—with Jack's prodding—to reveal his pent-up feelings. Rita sees Jack manipulating their guests and gets upset whenever he tries to undercut her statements. Finally, Cosmo tells Arlie that he no longer wants to be married, and Arlie responds with an angry account of her background as a topless dancer, then leaves the house. Jack follows Arlie into the cold night, and Rita, fearing Jack is attracted to Arlie, takes some quaaludes to calm down.

Outside, Arlie kisses Jack and tells him about the baby she recently miscarried. Jack tries seduce Arlie in her rare state of vulnerability, but she rebuffs him. Inside, Cosmo and Rita carry on a strange tango, until she rejects his sexual advances. Finally, as the night comes to an end, Cosmo reconciles with Arlie and they drive away, while Jack sadly carries the sedated Rita to bed.

THE WIFE seems like a natural: an examination of two deeply flawed marriages, incorporating and updating ideas from WHO'S AFRAID OF VIRGINIA WOOLF? (1966), SCENES FROM A MARRIAGE (1973), THE EXTERMINATING ANGEL (1962), NO EXIT (1930 and 1962), and even THE MAN WHO CAME TO DINNER (1942) and WHAT ABOUT BOB? (1991). As in his powerful debut film, WHAT HAPPENED WAS. . . (1994), writer-director-star-composer-editor Noonan observes Sartre's notion of "nothingness"—the awkward silences and gestures between people—with a caustic but realistic eye. Noonan's ensemble here also deftly realizes Sartre's maxim that "hell is other people." The cast—particularly Noonan as the controlling Jack and Hagerty as the high-strung Rita—brilliantly gets under the skin of these difficult, repulsive characters.

While the story of two couples dredging up the ugly truths about their marriages should be just as provocative, THE WIFE never takes off and soars like WHAT HAPPENED WAS. . . . The main problem is that its roots as a play called *Wifey* are all too apparent, and the elaborate set-up to throw these characters together seems contrived and unnecessary. Also, it seems at times as if the cast is fighting stereotypes about domineering wives, child-like husbands and nutty psychiatrists. It might have worked better, for instance, if Jack and Rita had been portrayed as competent analysts, and, thus, all the *more* destructive. The "shrink" jokes and modern marriage travails were handled better, quite frankly, on the old "Bob Newhart Show."

THE WIFE presents a tired battle between the sexes, and audiences might concur when Shawn's character says, "This is not going well." *(Nudity, sexual situations, substance abuse, extreme profanity.)* — E.M.

d, Tom Noonan; p, Scott Macaulay, Robin O'Hara; exec p, Michael D. Aglion, Pierre Edelman; assoc p, Jonathan Cordish, Scott Ramsey; w, Tom Noonan (based on his play); ph, Joe DeSalvo; ed, Richmond Arrley; m, Ludovico Sorret; prod d, Dan Ouellette; art d, Sarah Lavery; sound, Tom Paul (mixer), Juan Carlos Martinez (design); cos, Kathryn Nixon; makeup, Jennifer Baker

Drama/Comedy **(PR: C MPAA: R)**

WILD SIDE ★★★

(U.S.) 96m John Langley Productions; Nu Image ~
Evergreen Entertainment c

Christopher Walken *(Bruno Buckingham)*; Joan Chen *(Virginia Chow)*; Steven Bauer *(Tony)*; Anne Heche *(Alex Lee)*; Allen Garfield *(Dan Rackman)*; Adam Novack *(Lyle Litvak)*; Zion *(Hiro Sakamoto)*; Richard Palmer *(Cop Driver)*; Randy Crowder *(Federal Agent)*; Marcus Aurelius *(James Reed)*; Michael Rose *(Agent Morse Jaeger)*; Lewis Arquette *(The Chief)*; Rolando De La Maza *(Steward)*; Candace Camille Bender *(Lotus Ita)*; Ian Johnson II *(Philip Hamlyn)*; Gena Kim *(Massage Girl)*; Robert Mazzola *(Gilberto)*

Some surprising twists make WILD SIDE, which first appeared on the HBO cable network, is an engaging, if gratuitously sleazy, modern film noir.

After she rejects the advances of a client, California banker Alex Lee (Anne Heche) is warned by her boss that principles have no place in the world of high finance. Although Alex won't prostitute herself for her firm, she decides to pick up some work as an expensive freelance call girl, with some kinky specialties. By doing this, she figures that she can pay off the hefty mortgage on her beach house.

Her first client, Bruno Buckingham (Christopher Walken), is a rich and powerful crook in the business of money laundering. Bruno is smitten with smart Alex but is paranoid about federal agents watching him, so he sends his chauffeur, Tony (Steven Bauer), to make sure she is not a cop. As it turns out, Tony himself is an undercover fed who is looking to sting his rich boss. Tony rapes Alex and then blackmails her into working undercover with him as the bait he needs to catch Bruno.

Tony sends Virginia Chow (Joan Chen), a Chinese businesswoman, to see Alex and set up a bank account with Bruno's money. The two women take an instant liking to each other and, after an intense and tipsy lunch, they enjoy a torrid sexual encounter in the executive powder room. Alex, who quickly realizes that Virginia is actually Bruno's wife, still can't help falling in love. Alex reveals her feelings to Virginia and confesses to the mess she's in. Although Virginia at first seems typically possessive of her man, and harshly judges Alex as a whore, she can't help but be swept away by Alex's bold, romantic invitation to elope with her to Mexico.

Before they can take off, complications set in. Alex warns Virginia that she may be the fall guy in Tony's sting because Bruno's money is in her name. Alex makes sure that Bruno finds out just how disloyal Tony is. Cracking under pressure, Virginia attempts suicide but survives. Bruno walks in on Tony trying again to rape Alex. Bruno turns the tables on the vicious undercover cop, and comes dangerously close to raping him.

In the end, Alex saves Bruno from getting caught by the cops and Bruno kills Tony in retaliation for his betrayal. Bruno leaves town, strangely alone and vulnerable, and the two women head off together into the Guadalajara sunset with plenty of Bruno's money to live on.

WILD SIDE, though incredibly violent, is a flawed but imaginative spin on some classic noir themes. It frequently borders on exploitation, but never crosses the line. Most surprising is the fact that the lesbian relationship is seen as complete, sexy and emotional, and totally separate from any connection to the two men. Another welcome, modern angle is the exploration of the homoerotic relationship between the two tough guys, reaching a peak of sorts in the unconventional scene in which Bruno nearly rapes Tony.

Walken galvanizes the proceedings with his trademark borderline-psycho/philosophisizing-hood characterization. Heche acquits herself nicely in the lead, making Alex's choices seem natural despite the odd obstacles thrown in her path, while Chen (who also served as the film's associate producer) proves enticing as her character lures Alex into Walken s corrupt circle. Bauer strikes several false notes as the fed-gone-wrong (his Cuban accent is horribly overdone), but his crudely-drawn performance at points seems perfectly in keeping with the film's over-the-top style. The movie crosses a lot of boundaries by portraying an essentially feminist tale. Alex, who claims not to believe in love, only in using sex as power in a man's world, manages to end up with both the money and the girl.

Soon after the film was recut without his consent (and credited to the pseudonym "Franklin Brauner"), director Donald Cammell (PERFORMANCE) commited suicide at the age of 62. *(Violence, sexual situations, nudity, profanity.)* — J.D.

d, Donald Cammell; p, Elie Cohn, John Langley; exec p, Trevor Short, Avi Lerner, Andrew Pfeffer, Danny Dimbort; assoc p, Joan Chen; co-p, Boaz Davidson, Joanna Lancaster; w, Donald Cammell, China Kong; ph, Sead Mutarevic; ed, Frank Mazzola; m, Jon Hassell; prod d, Claire Bowin; art d, Kaki Wall; set d, Shana Sigmond; sound, Benjamin Patrick (mixer); fx, Eric Rylander; casting, Pamela Rack; cos, Alison Hirsch; makeup, Ashley Scott; stunts, Spike Silver

Drama/Thriller **(PR: O MPAA: R)**

WILLIAM SHAKESPEARE'S ROMEO + JULIET ★½
(U.S./Australia/Canada) 113m Bazmark Productions ~ 20th Century Fox c
(AKA: ROMEO AND JULIET)

Leonardo DiCaprio *(Romeo)*; Claire Danes *(Juliet)*; John Leguizamo *(Tybalt)*; Paul Rudd *(Dave Paris)*; Jesse Bradford *(Balthasar)*; Harold Perrineau *(Mercutio)*; Dash Mihok *(Benvolio)*; Diane Venora *(Gloria Capulet)*; Paul Sorvino *(Fulgencio Capulet)*; Brian Dennehey *(Ted Montague)*; Christina Pickles *(Mrs. Montague)*; Miriam Margoyles *(The Nurse)*; Zak Orth *(Gregory)*; Jaime Kennedy *(Sampson)*; Vincent Laresca *(Abra)*; Carlos Martin Manzo *(Petruchio)*; Vondie Curtis Hall *(Captain Prince)*; M. Emmet Walsh *(The Apothecary)*; Pete Postlethwaite *(Father Laurence)*

Baz Luhrmann's boldly conceived adaptation of *Romeo and Juliet* doesn't so much pump up a classic for easily bored teens as use the play as a pretext for directorial handsprings and back flips. Recklessly energetic, it spirals out of control after a clever credit sequence and power walks right past Shakespeare's prose while the winded cast struggles to catch up.

In the smoggy, crime-filled Verona metropolis of 1996, two corporate dynasties, the Montagues, headed by Mr. Montague (Brian Dennehy), and the Capulets, presided over by Mr. Capulet (Paul Sorvino), compete so viciously that succeeding generations are poisoned by their rivalry. Brewing hostility between Montagues—like Benvolio (Dash Mihok) and Mercutio (Harold Perrineau)—and Capulets—like Tybalt (John Leguizamo)—threaten Verona's peace on the eve of the betrothal of Juliet Capulet (Claire Danes) to eligible bachelor Dave Paris (Paul Rudd). At a Capulet party, Juliet becomes smitten by Romeo Montague (Leonardo DiCaprio), and the lovers prevail upon Juliet's maid (Miriam Margolyes) and Romeo's priest, Father Laurence (Pete Postlethwaite), to facilitate their secret wedding. Happiness proves short-lived after impulsive Tybalt stabs Benvolio, a crime that leads to Romeo's assassination of Tybalt and subsequent banishment. In exile at a trailer park, Romeo doesn't receive Father Laurence's missive about a plan to fake Juliet's death. After defying police, Romeo discovers Juliet's seemingly lifeless body in a crypt and poisons himself. Awakening from her drug-induced coma, grief-shocked Juliet spots dead Romeo and shoots herself with his gun. The tragedy moves the surviving Montagues and Capulets to abandon their seasoned hatred.

To their credit, director Baz Luhrmann and co-screenwriter Craig Pearce foster a sense of urgency in their retelling of this centuries-old play by investing the characters with a state of adrenaline overdrive; everyone seems to be hurtling toward premature death. However, Luhrmann doesn't bother to support or dramatize Shakespeare's tragedy-laden text; his startling imagery pushes all the pesky dialogue into the wings where it's left to fend for itself. Unlike the magically revamped RICHARD III (1995), which positioned that upstart's treachery in a 20th century fascist environment, this febrile adaptation is pointlessly updated with pop-culture references and a hip sensibility. Whereas WEST SIDE STORY (1961) rethought the Montague-Capulet enmity in terms of street gang prejudices, this ROMEO AND JULIET offers no explanation for its multicultural families' murderous competitiveness. If Luhrmann's lurid imagination had induced him to portray his contemporary Montagues and Capulets as warring Mafiosi, the film might have had a dramatic center, but Luhrmann and Pearce seem to care as little for bolstering dramatic motivations as they do for illuminating Shakespeare's language.

Whether he's whimsically speeding up the camera or overrelying on extreme close-ups, Luhrmann presents a careening visual cacaphony that winds up boring the viewer through overkill. At points one would swear the director was treating the material as a parody (such as when Mercurio dresses in drag), but his ineptnitude for staging dysfunctional confrontation scenes suggests that the lampooning is often unintentional, thereby resulting in an apparent, underlying contempt for Shakespeare's text. The cinematic assault also leaves the story bereft of sensuality; Franco Zeffirelli's ROMEO AND JULIET (1968), while superficially erotic, still makes a far more satisfying date movie.

Box-office returns indicate that Luhrmann bullied his way into a hit with his target audience. But he was mistaken in the belief that his exaggerated filmmaking mannerisms, which helped propel the romantic musical fantasy of his STRICTLY BALLROOM (1995), could also stimulate a romantic tragedy. Moreover, his abuse of Shakespeare runs a close second to his thrashing of a talented cast. Gloriously photogenic Leonardo DiCaprio gives a moving performance only when he isn't required to speak; Claire Danes summons up the mournfulness of a cheerleader who's been stood up on prom night. Only Margolyes and Postlethwaite acquit themselves with dignity. The others wrestle with histrionic mediocrity, except for three astonishing offenders: John Leguizamo snarls throughout like Snidely Whiplash; Paul Sorvino mistakes apoplexy for scene-stealing; and Diane Venora seems hell-bent on duplicating Jessica Lange's performance as Blanche Dubois in A STREETCAR NAMED DESIRE (1996). Expressing no feeling for the lush words they garble, the cast rushes through the dialogue as if it were their enemy. Revamping Shakespeare for jaded teens makes commercial sense, but why not update the language? The only answer seems to be so that teenagers can feel superior to a genius they resent having to read. *(Graphic violence, nudity, sexual situations, adult situations, substance abuse, profanity.)* — R.P.

d, Baz Luhrmann; p, Gabriella Martinelli, Baz Luhrmann; co-p, Martin Brown; w, Baz Luhrmann, Craig Pearce (based on the play by William Shakespeare); ph, Don McAlpine; ed, Jill Bilcock; prod d, Catherine Martin; art d, Doug Hardwick; set d, Brigitte Broch; sound, Rob Young (mixer); fx, Laurnecio "Chov" Cordero; casting, David Rubin; cos, Kym Barett; makeup, Maurizio Silvi; stunts, Brent Woolsey

AAN Best Art Direction: Catherine Martin, Brigitte Broch

Romance/Drama **(PR: C MPAA: PG-13)**

WIND IN THE WILLOWS, THE ★★½

(U.K.) 72m TVC ~ Goodtimes Home Video c

Vanessa Redgrave *(Narrator)*; VOICES OF: Alan Bennett *(Mole)*; Michael Palin *(Ratty)*; Rik Mayall *(Toad)*; Michael Gambon *(Badger)*; James Villiers; Emma Chambers; Judy Cornwell

Despite the occasional ANIMAL FARM (1955) and WATERSHIP DOWN (1978), British feature animation did not thrive on any scale approaching the Disney, Hanna-Barbara or Warner Brothers cartoon factories in Hollywood. Perhaps the best-established UK equivalent is London's TVC Animation Studio, which inked YELLOW SUBMARINE (1968), parts of HEAVY METAL (1981), and in 1996 offered this faithful but flat rendering of Kenneth Grahame's classic 1908 novel.

An Edwardian-era mother (Vanessa Redgrave) reads *The Wind in the Willows* to her children in a boat. Tired of spring-cleaning chores, the normally timid Mole (voice of Alan Bennett) forsakes his underground den and seeks adventure on the Great River. He encounters Ratty (voice of Michael Palin), a friendly rodent who introduces him to other animal characters in the adjoining Wild Wood: the imposing but good-natured Badger (voice of Michael Gambon) and the recklessly impulsive Toad (voice of Rik Mayall). Thanks to inherited wealth, Toad indulges every passing whim and mania. His obsession with the newly-invented motorcar leads him far astray into the world of men, and into jail. Escaping back to the Wild Wood, Toad returns to his neglected Toad Hall to find it now a squatter's camp for a gang of weasels. Mole, Ratty, and Badger help a (briefly) repentant Toad clear out the verminous intruders. In a subplot, Mole and Ratty search for a lost otter child and are rewarded with a glimpse of Great Pan, spirit of the forest.

Detailed artwork looks splendid enough to be illustrations on the pages of a color printing of *The Wind and the Willows,* and there's the rub; this static feature feels more like an inert storybook or CD-ROM, slavishly following the author's dense verbiage with insufficient vigor or life of its own. When Walt Disney distilled this material down to a half-hour (released to theaters in 1949 doubled with his LEGEND OF SLEEPY HOLLOW under the umbrella title THE ADVENTURES OF ICHABOD AND MR. TOAD), he deleted Grahame's romantic mysticism to focus on the frolicsome Toad. It wasn't the book—but it was fun, a quality in short supply here despite the vocal cast of fine British character actors. Palin had the unusual distinction of playing in two *Wind in the Willows* features in succession. After this film, he reunited with fellow members of the Monty Python comedy team for a strange, updated, live-action revision by Terry Jones, in which Eric Idle played Rat while Palin smiled down from on high as the Sun. Other animators in England and the US have yielded their own versions over the years, and even TVC encored with a cartoon of William Horwood's lesser-known literary sequel *The Willows in Winter.*— C.C.

d, Dave Unwin, Dennis Abey; p, John Coates, Dennis Abey; exec p, Jonathan Peel; w, Ted Walker (based on the novel by Kenneth Grahame); ed, Andy Kemp; m, Colin Towns; art d, Loraine Marshall; sound, Mark Edwards; cos, Julia Radakovic

Animated/Children's **(PR: AA MPAA: NR)**

WING CHUN ★★½

(Hong Kong) 95m Taiwan Film Culture Co.; Wo Ping Films ~ Tai Seng Video c

Michelle Yeoh *(Wing Chun)*; Donnie Yen *(Leung Pok To)*; Tsui Siu Keung *(Flying Chimpanzee)*; Waise Lee *(Scholar Wong)*; Catherine Hung; Yuen King Tan

This costume comedy-adventure about a female martial artist who protects a young widow from lustful bandits in a provincial Chinese town is a fine showcase for Hong Kong action star Michelle Yeoh (SUPERCOP).

An ailing traveler dies in a remote river town. His widow, Charmy, finds sanctuary and a job with Yim Wing Chun (Michelle Yeoh) and her aunt, Abacus "Stinky" Fong, who together manage a shop serving soybean cube. One night, bandit leader Flying Monkey leads a raid to kidnap Charmy, but Wing Chun, disguised as a man, fights off the attack with her superior kung fu. Scholar Wong (Waise Lee) seeks to marry Wing Chun in the hope that she will go back to his village with him to protect it from bandits, but he soon falls for Charmy.

Leung Pok To (Donnie Yen) has returned home after a ten year absence seeking his childhood sweetheart Wing Chun. Seeing Charmy in the attractive Miss Soybean Cube costume once worn by Wing Chun, he believes it is she. Wing Chun recognizes Pok To, but won't reveal herself because she doesn't want to interfere with his true feelings. The leader of the bandits, Flying Chimpanzee (Tsui Siu Keung), leads a second raid to kidnap Charmy.

After a battle with Wing Chun, he succeeds in taking Charmy and challenges Wing Chun to a duel.

Wing Chun journeys to the bandits' fortress with Pok To, after informing him of her true identity. She fights Flying Chimpanzee, narrowly beating him, and is allowed to leave with Charmy. She leaves Charmy and Pok To together and goes off to visit her master, Ng Mui (Cheng Pei Pei), who tells Wing Chun she should settle down.

Pok To realizes he loves Wing Chun, not Charmy, and is happy to receive a message from her, prompting him to return to the bandits' fortress to join Wing Chun who confronts Flying Chimpanzee one more time for a knock-down, dragout battle which ends with the defeated Chimpanzee and his men humbly agreeing to call Wing Chun "Mommy" and vowing to give up thievery. Wing Chun and Pok To get married. Scholar Wong winds up marrying Aunt Fong and Charmy remains alone, running the soybean shop.

Although based on the true story of the only female disciple at the famed Shaolin Temple, the film prefers to avoid historical details altogether in favor of light comedy and clever stunts. Director Yuen Woo Ping previously teamed with Michelle Yeoh for TAI CHI MASTER (1993) and with Donnie Yen for IRON MONKEY (1993), both of which boasted spectacular battles with all sorts of exaggerated feats of strength, fanciful props, and elaborate settings. The fights here are equally imaginative, but favor acrobatics and comedy with no blood or lethal tactics. All of the fight scenes feature the graceful dancer-turned-fighting star Yeoh, while the skilled and agile Yen plays second fiddle. Some of the secondary characters, such as Aunt Fong and Scholar Wong, are amusing, but their comic antics might irritate the fight fans in the audience. *(Sexual situations.)* — B.C.

d, Yuen Woo Ping; p, Yuen Woo Ping, Wang Po Ming; exec p, Jim Jao; w, Anthony Wong, Elsa Tang; ph, Mark Lee

Action/Martial Arts/Historical (PR: A MPAA: NR)

WITCHCRAFT: SALEM'S GHOST ★

(U.S.) 90m Vista Street Entertainment; Marketing Media Corp. ~ A-Pix Entertainment c

(AKA: WITCHCRAFT VIII; SALEM'S GHOST)

Lee Grober *(Sonny Dunaway)*; Kim Kopf *(Mary Ann Dunaway)*; Tom Overmyer *(McArthur)*; David Weills *(Mitch Baker)*; Anthoni Stewart *(Gayle Baker)*; Jack Van Landingham *(Simon Winfrough)*; Mai-Lis Holmes *(Cathy)*; William Knight *(Dean Simpson)*; John E. Holiday *(Fred Victor)*; David Jean Thomas *(Scully)*; Angela Tassoni *(School Girl No. 1)*; Brandi Pearson *(School Girl No. 2)*; Roddy Arnold *(Cop No. 1)*; B. Allen *(Cop No. 2)*

Sophisticated special effects have so devalued horror movies that an actual appearance of Satan via hologram would probably do little to stir jaded fright freaks. Direct-to-video schlockmeisters opt instead for techno-trickery and easy laughs in the eighth film in the seemingly endless WITCHCRAFT series, SALEM'S GHOST.

In a prologue set in 1692, Satanist Simon Winfrough (Jack Van Landingham) is burned at the stake and sealed in a crypt with a Christian sword. Flashforward to 1996: Hoping to iron out the wrinkles in his troubled marriage, college prof Sonny Dunaway (Lee Grober) takes his wife Mary Ann (Kim Kopf) to their new dream house in Salem, MA. The couple's reconciliation is jeopardized by the still-slumbering spirit of Simon, whose crypt is in the house's basement, as well as the designs of nubile student Cathy Williams (Mai-Lis Holmes). Welcomed by nosy neighbors, Mitch the plumber (David Weills) and his wife Gayle (Anthoni Stewart), the Dunaways agree to let Mitch survey pipe damage, not suspecting he will greedily remove the ancient weapon that traps the Satanist's spirit behind a wall. As nastiness seeps into Mitch's personality, the house's dormant evil infects Sonny and Mary Ann with phantasmagoric visions of blood-filled bathtubs and a devil-man having his way with Mary Ann.

After a few other eerie occurrences, the Dunaways seek the help of Clarence McArthur (Tom Overmyer), a Protestant witchcraft specialist. Warning Sonny that the over-sexed warlock will prey on his fears, McArthur prepares for his first exorcism. After the police arrest the now-deranged Mitch, the Dunaways retrieve the magic sword. Simon zaps McArthur with hell-sent lightning, but Sonny vanquishes the brimstone spell caster with the holy weapon.

Video stores are increasingly overcrowded with fright night escapist tales that could be dubbed, "Things that Go Hump in the Night." Besides relying on special effects interludes, movies like WITCHCRAFT: SALEM'S GHOST push their narrative aside to drool over sex between hero and heroine, fiend and heroine, and subsidiary players often dispensable to the plot. This film doesn't even have a glimmer of intelligent scripting, completely ignoring the opportunity to use the Dunaways' sexual dysfunction as a pretext for the warlock's invasion of their bedtime. In addition to jettisoning spine-tinglers, this lazy chiller affirms its innate stupidity by dragging in comic relief less subtle than the humorous sideshows found in hard-core porn pics. *(Graphic violence, extreme profanity, extensive nudity, sexual situations.)* — R.P.

d, J. J. Barmettler Jr.; p, Michael Feifer; exec p, Jerry Feifer; assoc p, Robyn Mellin; w, Joseph John Barmettler Jr. (based on a story by Jerry Feifer); ph, Denis Maloney; ed, Keith Markinson; m, Miriam Cutler; prod d, Helmut Dusek; sound, Arthur Joe Lopez; cos, Marcelle McKay; makeup, Alan Tuskes, Seamus Walsh, Bart Mixon's Monster Fixins; stunts, Dan Speaker, Dave Speaker

Horror/Erotic (PR: O MPAA: NR)

WITCHCRAFT VIII

(SEE: SALEM'S GHOST)

WITHIN THE ROCK ★★

(U.S.) 88m 360 Entertainment; Le Monde; Prism Pictures ~ A-Pix Entertainment c

Xander Berkeley *(Ryan)*; Caroline Barclay *(Dr. Dana Shaw)*; Bradford Tatum *(Cody Harrison)*; Brian Krause *(Luke Harrison)*; Barbara Patrick *(Samantha "Nuke-em" Rogers)*; Michael Zelniker *(Archer)*; Duane Whitaker *(Potter)*; Calvin Levels *(Benton)*; Earl Boen *(Michael Isaacs)*; Dale Dye *(General Hurst)*

Although professionally done on every level, this entry in the endless string of ALIEN (1979) knockoffs contains little to set itself apart.

In the year 2017, a renegade moon called Galileo's Child threatens to impact with the Earth. Scientist Dana Shaw (Caroline Barclay) develops a plan to tunnel into the moon and plant explosives that will redirect its course. While drilling through the rock, her group of deep space miners comes across a platinum chamber and a strange fossil. Team leader Ryan (Xander Berkeley) threatens the already delayed schedule by insisting on recovering all the platinum. Meanwhile, the fossil comes to life as a humanoid monster that starts slaughtering the workers. The only survivors, Dr. Shaw, Cody (Bradford Tatum) and Archer (Michael Zelniker), attempt to destroy the monster. Ryan, thought to have been killed by the creature, reappears and tries to stop them, but is killed by the monster himself. The others then drill the monster to death, plant what explosives they can, and flee Galileo's Child; from an escape craft, they see that their efforts have successfully altered its course.

By this point, there is little to say about WITHIN THE ROCK that can't be said of the dozens of other low-budget ALIEN imitations, except that it's slightly better than some of them and has a personable cast of potential victims. First-time writer-director Gary J. Tunnicliffe, a makeup effects veteran (the HELLRAISER films, among others), clearly devoted as much attention to his characters as to his monster, and works in some diverting details. But the general story development is all too predictable, and the action and horror setpieces have a perfunctory feel. Given the movie's cable-friendly restraint, it's not surprising that this production debuted on the Sci-Fi Channel. *(Graphic violence, profanity.)* — M.G.

d, Gary J. Tunnicliffe; p, Stanley Isaacs, Scott McGinnis, Robert Patrick; exec p, John Fremes, Barry Collier, Barbara Javitz; assoc p, Thomas Carl McGuinness; w, Gary J. Tunnicliffe; ph, Adam Kane; ed, Roderick Davis; m, Rod Gammons, Tony Fennell; prod d, Dorian Vernacchio, Deborah Raymond; sound, John Brasher, Marty Hutcherson, Ezra Dweck, L. Mo Weber; fx, Gary J. Tunnicliffe, Image Animation; casting, Linda Francis; cos, Kristin M. Burke; makeup, Elizabeth Fry

Science Fiction/Horror **(PR: O MPAA: R)**

WITHOUT MERCY ★★

(U.S.) 88m Rapi Films ~ LIVE Entertainment c

Frank Zagarino *(John Carter)*; Martin Kove *(Wolf Larsen)*; Ayu Azhari *(Tanya)*; Frans Tumbuan *(Captain Karno)*; Advent Bangun *(Tomo)*; Joseph Hungan *(Chin)*; Him Damsyik *(Old Man)*; Anna M. Tarigan *(Anna)*; Eddy Hansudi *(Omar)*; John Honeyben *(Doc)*; Rony S. *(Waiter)*; Silva Sandiarin *(Little Girl)*; Diaz Tangkilisan *(African Boy)*; Titi Suwarino *(Tanya's Mother)*; Arta *(Tomo's Girl)*; Lisa Santi *(Sushi Girl)*; Meity *(Teenage Girl)*; Jurex Kline *(Larsen's Bodyguard)*

WITHOUT MERCY offers yet another saga of a damaged protagonist, spooked by memories of the war in Vietnam.

Marine officer John Carter (Frank Zagarino) travels the globe for Uncle Sam, until a peacekeeping stint in Somalia ends with the slaughter of his men and his own imprisonment.

Three years later, the shattered former POW explores Asia's lower depths, a crime turf battled over by Tomo (Advent Bangun) and ex-US soldier Wolf Larsen (Martin Kove). The nefarious Larsen sets up Carter with a hooker, Tanya (Ayu Azhari), with whom Tomo is in love. When Tomo attacks Carter, he is forced to kill him in self-defense. As the cops investigate Carter's possible link to Larsen's flesh-peddling and dope rackets, Carter vows revenge for being set up by Larsen.

Playing the angles, drug-addicted Tanya also snitches for the police. Larsen's physician, Doc (John Honeyben), discovers her treason and tells Larsen. At the docks, after unloading a shipment of illegal aliens and rubbing out Doc for being a tattletale, Larsen sends a cargo-lifter to snatch Tanya and Carter. But they both later escape. When Carter is unjustly arrested, Larsen arranges an ambush and jail-break for him, because he wants the slippery Carter out of the country for good.

As maniacal Larsen motorboats away with Tanya as security, the cops recognize Carter's innocence and land him via helicopter on Larsen's boat. Tanya escapes, and Carter grapples with Larsen; when the boat sails across a dam, the men hang on to an overpass. Carter can't prevent a dangling Larsen from slipping out of his grip.

Martial arts fans can do worse than Zagarino's brand of self-defense, but the story line isn't as lithe as the athletics. WITHOUT MERCY is set apart from the usual kickboxing slogging by its fixation on the physical and psychological aftershocks of torture. Flashing back to Carter's POW days or dwelling on Larsen's morphine treatment of war injuries, the film seems obsessed with pain as a tool to mold character.

But aside from a pervasive sense of cruelty, WITHOUT MERCY is the expected crime-world plunge into Oriental intrigue, complete with visual exotica and wretched performances by the suppporting cast. *(Graphic violence, profanity, nudity, adult situations, substance abuse.)* — R.P.

d, Robert Anthony; p, Gope T. Samtani; exec p, Sam S.; co-p, Raju Wadhwan; w, Robert Anthony; ph, Gerry Lively; ed, Rob Kobrin, David Hewitt; m, Steve Edwards; prod d, Hendro Tangkilisan; set d, Ujang Padli; sound, Kang Rizal Zaini; fx, Hendro Tangkilisan; cos, Harry Hendrawan; makeup, Any Umar Bani, Rosita; stunts, Gatot & Group, Frank Zagarino

Action/Crime **(PR: O MPAA: R)**

WOLVES, THE ★★

(U.S./Germany/Russia) 87m CCC Filmkunst Berlin; Mosfilm Inc.; Courier Film Studios ~ Vidmark c

Darren Dalton *(Blackie)*; Kristen Hocking *(Barbara)*; Raimund Harmstorf *(King)*; John Furey *(Connors)*; Ben Cardinal *(Chilkoot)*

The animals out-act the humans cast in this mediocre environmental thriller about the advantages of being pals with wolves.

Abandoning a financially unsatisfying career as a Miami paramedic, Blackie (Darren Dalton) flies to the icy Alaskan lands inherited by his family under a Russian land grant. His sister Barbara (Kristen Hocking) has become romantically involved with forest ranger Connors (John Furey), a henchman of greedy entrepreneur King (Raimund Harmstorf). Barbara is willing to sell the family land, but Blackie won't comply.

King has been using the heirs' land as a lucrative toxic dump. Not counting on tenderfoot Blackie making waves like previous troublemakers, the greedy developer saddles him with an Indian guide, Chilkoot (Ben Cardinal), to keep Blackie far from environmentally unfriendly secrets.

While Connors tries to coax Barbara into signing away her inheritance for a quick pay-off, Blackie bonds with alcoholic Chilkoot and re-evaluates his feeling toward his new Alaskan property. Transformed by the land's beauty, Blackie helps an injured wolf, who returns the favor by pointing out the location of King's dumpsite. An attack on the toxic chemical haulers launches a full-scale war in which Blackie is hurt, but saved by the wolves.

A take-charge Chilkoot orders Connors to fly Barbara to safety in Fairbanks, but the ranger is killed by King's men. Recovered from his wound, Blackie rescues his sister while Chilkoot eliminates the despoiler's henchmen before succumbing to King's rifle blast. Before King can hunt down Blackie and Barbara, Blackie's wolf pal rips the wicked hunter's throat to shreds right after King's bulletry sets fire to the chemical waste. Blackie decides to manage the family inheritance as a wildlife preserve.

THE WOLVES offers many portentious themes, including modern man's selling out the environment and the absolute necessity of respecting the rights of wildlife. Dramatic tension, however, is low. Additionally, the film's battle scenes are second-rate, and the path of Blackie's self-realization appears too smooth and easy. Reassuringly running its course, the film's predictability isn't as big a drawback as its amateurish performances. Adequate in their quieter moments, Dalton and Hocking shout their sibling rivalry with childish zeal. But at least their noisy "acting" alerts the viewer to successive mini-climaxes, keeping spectators in a scrappy frame of mind. *(Graphic violence, adult situations, substance abuse.)* — R.P.

d, Steve Carver; p, Wolf Brauner; w, Steven Peters, Art Bernd (based on a story by Kurt Wimmer and Charles Osburn); ph, Eugene Shugleit; ed, Ludwig Labik; m, Rolf Bauer, Alexander Kraut; art d, Leonid Platow, Andrej Platow; sound, Richard Kazarian; fx, Nickolai Nejaglov, Sergei Zaharov; cos, Marina Tarasova, Nina Martynova; makeup, Zinaida Egorova, Roman Darensky

Action/Thriller (PR: C MPAA: PG-13)

WOMAN UNDONE, A ★★

(U.S.) 91m Neufeld/Rehme Productions; David Lancaster Productions ~ Republic Pictures Home Video c

(AKA: JOSHUA TREE)

Mary McDonnell *(Teri Hansen)*; Randy Quaid *(Allen Hansen)*; Sam Elliott *(Ross Bishop)*; Benjamin Bratt *(Jim Mercer)*; Charles Noland *(Trim)*; Cheryl Anderson *(Nina)*; Troy Evans *(Mac)*; Tara Hartman *(Miranda)*; Scanlon Gail *(Gun Salesman)*; Georgann Johnson *(Enid)*; Kevin Cooney *(Chuck)*; Michael Chieffo *(Roy)*; Trishalee Hardy *(Eileen)*; Alex McKenna *(Jennifer)*; Peta Wilson *(Receptionist)*; Carl Thibault *(Workman)*; Patricia Belcher *(Televangelist)*; Douglas Roberts *(Redman)*; Jim McClure *(Jury Foreman)*; Esther Scott *(Matron)*

Once upon a happier, more escapist time, the damsel-in-distress thriller afforded glitzy film stars the opportunity to scream photogenically at the top of their lungs. Unfortunately, the creative personnel behind A WOMAN UNDONE are more interested in a brand of realism which the "imperiled lady" subgenre is too shallow to support.

A distraught woman, Teri Hansen (Mary McDonnell), is found cowering in a dry gulch after her husband, Allen (Randy Quaid), has been burned to death in the family car. As sketchy details crystallize, Teri is arrested for murder and defended by attorney Ross Bishop (Sam Elliott). Flashbacks highlight the Hansens' incompatible marriage, particularly Allen's paranoid jealousy and Teri's attempt to soothe her sexual dissatisfaction with an affair Allen refuses to forgive. History repeats itself in Teri's steamy relationship with pleasure-seeking Jim (Benjamin Bratt), and marital tensions are exacerbated when Teri becomes pregnant but tells Allen that she wants an abortion.

In the present, Bishop can't explain the six bullets the coroner found in Allen's charred corpse. A final memory of past arguments prompts Teri's desert journey, in which she foolishly baits her spouse by revealing that she's already terminated her pregnancy. She jumps out of the car. When Allen follows on foot, a frightened Teri hits him with a rock and grabs his gun. Pursuing her by car, Allen crashes and gets trapped inside the flaming wreckage. In what amounts to euthanasia, Teri shoots her burning hubby with his gun. Teri is found guilty in a verdict that hinges on damaging facts rather than an interpretation of Teri's humane motives. Gulping and accepting her prison stretch, Teri bravely carries on in the knowledge that her attorney will be waiting for her.

A WOMAN UNDONE is like a reduction of Bergman's SCENES FROM A MARRIAGE (1973) with all the angst moved outdoors to a series of desert showdowns. As flashbacks reveal the Hansens' unsuitability for each other, one sympathizes with Teri up to the point when her appalling judgment turns the audience against her. Romping in a heated pool with a hunk is understandable, if immoral, but failing to gauge her unbalanced husband's sore points is stupid. Blabbing about an aborted child to a macho sexist during a trek into the wilderness ranks as a classic of suicidally bad timing. At the climax one feels nothing for Teri but the urge to say, "I could have told you this would happen."

A botch as a fast-paced psychological thriller and a flop as a marital problem flashback drama, A WOMAN UNDONE wastes some fine acting, particularly from Quaid as a family man enamored of weapons and unable to comprehend the inner needs of a wife whom he treats like a possession. *(Extreme profanity, graphic violence, adult situations, sexual situations.)* — R.P.

d, Evelyn Purcell; p, David Lancaster; exec p, Mace Neufeld, Robert Rehne; assoc p, Amy Krell; co-p, William Mickleberry, Evelyn Purcell; w, William Mickleberry; ph, Toyomichi Kurita; ed, Stan Salfas, Quincy Gunderson; m, Dan Licht; prod d, Steven Legler; art d, Nanci B. Roberts; set d, Barbara Cassel; sound, L. Mo Weber (design), Stephen Halbert (mixer); fx, Frank Ceglia; cos, Eduardo Castro; makeup, Tony G., David Barton; stunts, Debby Lynn Ross

Erotic/Thriller/Drama (PR: C MPAA: R)

YANKEE ZULU ★

(South Africa) 89m Toron Screen Corp.; Koukos Troika Production ~ Columbia TriStar Home Video c

Leon Schuster *(Rhino)*; John Matshikiza *(Zulu)*; Wilson Dunster *(Die Hard)*; Terri Treas *(Rowena)*; Michelle Bowes *(Tienkie)*; Skye Svornic *(Prince William)*; Ruan Mandelstam *(Young Rhino)*; Bob Seritsani *(Young Zulu)*; Marie Van Deventer *(Young Rowena)*; Mbali Dlada *(Thiandi)*; Tolla Van Der Merwe *(Uncle Bok)*; Chris Biko *(Shadrack)*; Christine Le Brocq *(Nanny)*; Peter Hugo *(Prince Charles)*; Tessa Ziegler *(Ashley)*; Nick Barklem *(Aide de Camp)*; Russell Savadier *(Makeup Artist)*; Lilian Dube *(Rosie)*; David Webb *(Warden)*; Karl Johnson *(Chief Warden)*; Tony Caprari *(Poacher)*; Julie Strudom *(Ma)*; Julius Van Zyl *(Mean Boy)*; Ted LePlat *(Scratch 'N' Win President)*

YANKEE ZULU is one of the highest-grossing film in the box-office history of South Africa; this fact offers daunting evidence that no innovative cinema has been developing in that country. Alternately an anti-apartheid lampoon, a HOME ALONE (1990) rip-off, and a potpourri of slapstick techniques, this vulgar family fare is boundlessly energetic and stupefyingly crass.

As lads in the veldt, young Rhino (Ryan Mandelstam) and his native pal Zulu (Bobo Seritsani) play innocently until a racist Afrikaaner teen-ager, Rowena (Marie Van Deventer), captures Rhino's pubescent interest. Years later, Zulu (John Matshikiza), a petty criminal guest of the US penal system, gets deported to his South African homeland. Meanwhile, Rhino (Leon Schuster), who has adopted Tienkie (Michelle Bowes), a child actually fathered by a clueless Zulu, struggles to protect his animal preserve from his ex-wife Rowena (Terri Treas) and her equally bigoted lover, Die Hard (Wilson Dunster).

As founder of an apartheid organization, Die Hard is delighted when he wins an opportunity for a televised $500,000-prize drawing with a scratch-and-win lotto ticket. Unfortunately, he transports new deportee-prisoner Zulu to jail and the wily Zulu pockets the ticket, escaping in a stolen cop car. Zulu is reunited with buddy Rhino whose financial hardship induces him to abet Zulu in gaining the lotto jackpot. Eluding Rowena and Die Hard, with the occasional interference of Tienkie and her new playmate Prince William of England (Skye Svornic), Rhino wins the prize on TV, but an argumentative Zulu tears off half of the check for safekeeping. Disguising themselves as members of the opposite race, a white-faced Zulu and black-faced Rhino crash a neo-Nazi party. Because Tienkie now has Rhino's check fragment, Die Hard and Rowena pilfer Zulu's half, then leave Zulu and Rhino dangling over a precipice. Taunting the prejudicial pair, Tienkie and Prince William pelt greedy Rowena with ostrich eggs and trick her onto a runaway mining car; Die Hard ends up in an alligator pit, a porcupine den, and a bathtub full of flammable material, which gets ignited. With the $500,000 payoff wrenched from defeated Rowena and Die Hard, Zulu reunites with daughter Tienkie, and Rhino saves his beloved wildlife habitat.

Inanely written and directed with the kind of overkill in which the energy level is pitched too high to be enjoyable, YANKEE ZULU takes swipes at racism in a cartoonish manner. While celebrating the prankish dexterity of children, the film plays like a Road Runner cartoon with a political subtext. Despite the nastiness of the villains, this comedy seems genuinely sadistic; the lavish sight gags (and the logistics involved in executing them) don't make this escaspist fare.

Pawns in the director's physical comedy set-pieces, the actors ham it up as if they'd been injected with essence of Jim Carrey. Their strenuous efforts and the movie's laboriously detailed slapstick is more likely to evoke audience murmurs of "That looks like it hurts!" than peals of spontaneous laughter. *(Violence, profanity.)* — R.P.

d, Gray Hofmeyr; p, Andre Scholtz; exec p, Edgar Bold; co-p, Carl Fischer, Leon Schuster; w, Leon Schuster, Gray Hofmeyr; ph, James Robert Sass; ed, Johan Lategen, Tiny Laubscher, Gerrie Van Wyck, Alastair Henderson; m, Stanislas Syrewicz, Zane Pronje; prod d, Jon-Jon Lambon, Robert Van De Coolwijk; set d, Eva Strack; sound, Mark Phillips (mixer); fx, Rick Cresswell; casting, Pat Melton; makeup, Marie Roney; stunts, Roly Jansen

Comedy/Action **(PR: A MPAA: PG)**

YESTERDAY'S TARGET ★★

(U.S.) 80m I.R.S. Media ~ Showtime/Republic Pictures Home Video c

Daniel Baldwin *(Paul Harper)*; Stacey Haiduk *(Jessica Harper)*; T. K. Carter *(Carter)*; LeVar Burton *(Winstrom)*; Richard Herd *(Aaron Winfield)*; David Netter *(Roland)*; Malcolm McDowell *(Holden)*; J. C. Wendel *(Brenda Holden)*; Page Mosely *(Ricky)*; Trevor Goddard; Tom Poster; Mary Kathleen Gordon

Even by the elastic standards of science fiction, this derivative time-travel tale, which premiered on the Showtime cable network, ties logic into loops on its way to retreading familiar ground and calling attention to its flaws.

Three visitors from 2025 arrive in the 1990s, plagued by amnesia. A few years later, Paul (Daniel Baldwin) works oblivously as a mechanic, until mysterious dandy Aaron Winfield (Richard Herd) prods him toward a destiny foretold by Paul's latent but powerful telekinesis.

A government hit team, headed by cold-blooded Holden (Malcolm McDowell) is already on Paul's trail, and the hero barely stays one step ahead as he reunites with his former companions, Jessica (Stacey Haiduk), a crooked gambler able to foresee imminent events, and Carter (T.K. Carter), a cook who ignites fires with his mind.

At Winfield's safe house, most of the blanks are filled in: The gifted trio, whose mothers all underwent 11-month pregnancies, represent a leap in human evolution. Such superior mutants are suffering genocide in 2025, because of the threat the 11-monthers pose to ruling authorities. Paul, Jessica and Carter went back in time to stop Holden's incipient extermination campaign and to preserve Winfield's underground superhuman-rights movement.

In a confrontation with Holden, Paul disarms the foe with news that Holden's own wife will soon have an 11-month pregnancy—and Holden's son will be Paul. No longer threatened, Paul, Jessica and Carter drive off together.

This movie evokes the famous paradox of the time-traveler who kills his own father in violation of laws of cause-and-effect, which is frequently cited as why such journeys are quite impossible. While THE TERMINATOR (1984), STAR TREK IV: THE VOYAGE HOME (1986) and others kept the viewer entertained enough to avoid asking sensible questions about time travel, YESTERDAY'S TARGET painfully emphasizes inherent contradictions, with repeat assurances that Paul and his pals are following pre-determined paths to a foregone conclusion. Even a traitorous telepath (LeVar Burton) claims that he's just following orders. So why was a mission necessary in the first place?

Though the filmmakers try to wring maximum wonder from the plot through an oblique narrative structure, science-fiction fans should be able to spot rampant plundering of TWELVE MONKEYS (1995). While the ruthless anti-mutant death squad—strongly reminiscent of characters in stories by Philip K. Dick—is a neat conceit, a cheap special-effects budget precludes showing too much of the heroes's paranormal powers in action, and the performances all strike a monotone note of grim resolve. *(Violence, substance abuse.)* — C.C.

d, Barry Samson; p, Larry Estes, Albert T. Dickerson; exec p, Miles A. Copeland III, Melanie Ray; w, David Bourla; ph, Brian Capener; ed, Michael Bloecher; m, Todd Hayen; prod d, William V. Ryder; art d, Robyn Bushmann; set d, Kyra Cunningham; fx, Mike Goedecke; casting, Donald Paul Pemrick; cos, Elena Baranova

Science Fiction **(PR: C MPAA: R)**

YOU'LL NEVER MAKE LOVE IN THIS TOWN AGAIN ★½

(U.S.) 90m Dove International ~ Dove International c

Robin; Liza; Linda; Tiffany; Peter Bart

YOU'LL NEVER MAKE LOVE IN THIS TOWN AGAIN is a gossip-fest that's all talk and no action, a "talking heads" documentary about sex and sleaze in Hollywood.

The film consists of separate interviews with Robin, Liza, Linda and Tiffany, the four "authors" of the best-selling book of the same name. In segments titled "The First Time," "The First Time For Money," "Pimps and Madams," et al., the women discuss their personal experiences either as dates or prostitutes to the stars and executives that run tinseltown. Occasionally, VARIETY editor Peter Bart also comments on sex in the industry.

Clearly tied in to its concurrent paperback publication, YOU'LL NEVER MAKE LOVE IN THIS TOWN AGAIN seems more like a lengthy infomercial than a film. The sets look cheap, the music sounds electronic, and the graphics are fuzzy. One can only pity the four subjects—not for their sometimes sad exploits, but for having to "tell all" in such a tacky, overlit setting.

What disappoints most about YOU'LL NEVER MAKE LOVE IN THIS TOWN AGAIN is the way the name-dropping becomes so monotonous. During the film's most promising segment, "Sleeping with Celebrities," the four women recount the sexual exploits of stars like James Caan, Timothy Hutton and Jack Nicholson. But without docudrama re-enactments or tough questioning, most of the stories merely serve to titillate (while probably boosting the egos of the stars mentioned).

Occasionally, the women make thoughtful comments about the drug scene, AIDS, or women's role in the industry, but these issues aren't given nearly as much attention as they could have been. Fans of either tabloid-TV shows or incisive documentaries on the same topic will be left high and dry. *(Adult situations, extreme profanity.)* — E.M.

d, Michael Viner; p, Michael Viner; w, Michael Viner (based on the book by Robin, Liza, Linda, and Tiffany, as told to Joanne Parrent); ph, Eric Bakke, Chip Goebert; ed, Tony Nassour; sound, Matthew Dewan (mixer), Michael Guske (mixer); makeup, Beverley Ashley-Collins

Documentary **(PR: O MPAA: NR)**

YOUNG POISONER'S HANDBOOK, THE ★★★

(U.K./Germany/France) 99m Mass Productions; Kinowelt; Haut et Court; British Screen ~ CFP Distribution c

Hugh O'Conor *(Graham)*; Antony Sher *(Dr. Zeigler)*; Ruth Sheen *(Molly)*; Roger Lloyd Pack *(Fred)*; Charlotte Coleman *(Winnie)*; Paul Stacey *(Dennis)*; Samantha Edmonds *(Sue)*; Vilma Hollingbery *(Aunt Panty)*; Frank Mills *(Uncle Jack)*; Charlie Creed-Miles *(Berridge)*; Arthur Cox *(Ray)*; John Thomson *(Nathan)*; Jean Warren *(Debra)*; Simon Kunz *(John)*; Frank Coda *(Billy)*; Tim Potter *(Simon)*; Hazel Douglas *(Edna)*; Roger Frost *(Geoff)*; Norman Caro *(Mr. Goez)*; Dorothea Alexander *(Mrs. Goez)*; Robert Demeger *(Mr. Dexter)*; Jack Deam *(Mick)*; Peter Pacey *(Dickie Boone)*; Rupert Farley *(Nurse Trent)*; Malcolm Sinclair *(Dr. Triefus)*; John Abbott *(Chairman)*; Cate Fowler *(Social Services Lady)*; Frank Baker *(Placement Officer)*; David Saville *(Chief Medical Officer)*; Mark Gordon *(Vicar)*; Tobias Arnold *(Young Graham)*; Joost Siedhoff *(Dr. Scott)*; Anna Kollenda *(Chairman)*; Katja Kollenda *(Baby Donna)*

Based on the real-life exploits of Graham Young, the notorious English poisoner, THE YOUNG POISONER'S HANDBOOK is a startlingly strong debut for director Benjamin Ross.

14-year-old Graham Young (Hugh O'Conor) is a precocious, 1960s London schoolboy with a unhealthy preoccupation with toxic substances. When he's not at the chemist's or holed up in medical section of the library, Graham spends most of his time in his room, trying to reproduce Isaac Newton's experiment in which he was able to transform antimony, a lethal poison, into a synthetic diamond. Graham's attempt literally blows up in his face, but he soon finds another use for his surplus of antimony. After he learns his friend Mick (Jack Deam) plans on taking out Sue (Samantha Edmonds), a young librarian who had also caught Graham's eye, Graham mixes the poison with a little mustard, then feeds Mick a very dangerous ham sandwich. Mick becomes violently ill, and the ecstatic Graham finds a new guinea pig: his hated step-mother (Ruth Sheen), whom he slowy poisons with thallium. After her grueling death, and amid mounting suspicion, Graham then turns his attention towards his abusive father (Roger Lloyd Pack), but before he can properly finish him off, Graham's plot is uncovered and he's sentenced to Harshhurst Prison for the criminally insane.

At Harshhurst, Graham encounters Dr. Zeigler (Antony Sher), a doctor specializing the rehabilitation of psychopaths through dream analysis. Dr. Ziegler takes a special interest in this warped genius, and Graham's anxious to take part in a program he hopes will lead to his eventual release from Harshhurst. But Graham is unable to provide the dreams Dr. Ziegler's work demands, so he turns to another inmate, Berridge (Charlie Creed-Miles), for his dream supply. Graham wakes him once every hour to record his horrifying dreams, a regimen that soon drives the already deeply disturbed Berridge to suicide. But his work with Dr. Ziegler is considered a resounding success, and, eight years after his arrest, Graham Young is judged fit to return to society.

But old habits die hard. Graham finds work at a photographic equipment lab, where, to his delight, he finds a plentiful stock of his beloved thallium. Fortuitously appointed tea-boy, Graham once again takes up his nihilistic program, putting measured amounts of the poison into the tea of those coworkers who have earned his enmity. Graham keeps careful records: he knows exactly which distinctively patterned tea mug belongs to whom, and who is getting how large a dosage. Two deaths later, and as a third coworker lies dying in the hospital, Graham's ambition to become the world's greatest toxicologist comes to an unexpected end. One afternoon at tea-time, Graham finds that all the mugs have been replaced with ones bearing identical Union Jack insignias, and his ensuing panic gives him away. In prison, Graham shaves down a synthetic diamond ring that once belonged to his mother—in effect reversing Newton's experiment—and poisons himself with the toxic dust.

With a suitably grotesque situation at his film's core, Ross works in a stylistically baroque mode that owes a considerable debt to David Lynch. But while his confidence may be impressive, Ross's limited, obsessive vision belies his relative youth. He tells his story solely from the viewpoint of the killer, with numerous scenes of Graham being batted about by his parents and so-called friends. The huge-eyed, androgynous O'Conor gives an opaque, almost catatonic performance that amusingly recalls a more robotic version of Bud Cort in HAROLD AND MAUDE (1971). Pack, Sheen, and Charlotte Coleman (as Graham's sister, Winnie) go the opposite route, playing the other members of the Young family with so much nerve-wracking hysteria one can hardly blame the boy. Sher, as the well-meaning psychiatrist, is surprisingly subdued in a role that could have used more eccentric color, though perhaps not quite as much as he exhibited in the unforgettably warped SHADEY (1985).

Production designer Maria Djurkovic contributes to the film's impressive look with her careful recreations of the most hideous style-notions of the 1960s and '70s. (Those personalized employee coffee cups and coronation plates hanging on the walls are particularly heinous emblems of Graham's detested suburbia.) The many lab scenes, with their bubbling, rainbow-hued flasks, are as photogenic as anything in James Whale's *oeuvre,* and the soundtrack's fine selection of prime period bubblegum pop adds an amusing counterpoint to the grisly goings-on. One does wish, however, that the script went for a little more character than schema, as it becomes rather thin and O'Conor's acting too monotonous.*(Graphic violence, adult situations, profanity.)* — D.N.

d, Benjamin Ross; p, Sam Taylor; exec p, Caroline Hewitt, Eric Stonestrom, Cameron McCracken; assoc p, David Redman; co-p, Carole Scotta, Rainer Kolmel; w, Jeff Rawle, Benjamin Ross; ph, Hubert Taczanowski; ed, Anne Sopel; m, Robert Lane, Frank Strobel; prod d, Maria Djurkovic; art d, Mark Stevenson; sound, Eckhard Kuchenbecker; fx, Stuart Drisden; casting, Michelle Guish; cos, Stewart Meachem; makeup, Lindy Shaw; stunts, Andy Bradford

Crime/Comedy/Drama (PR: C MPAA: NR)

ZARKORR! THE INVADER ★

(U.S.) 79m Monster Island Entertainment ~ Amazing Fantasy Entertainment c

Rhys Pugh *(Tommy Ward)*; De'Prise Grossman *(Stephanie Martin)*; Mark Hamilton *(George Ray)*; Charles Schneider *(Arthur)*; Eileen Wesson *(Debby Dalverson)*; Torie Lynch *(Proctor)*; Franklin Vallette *(Horrace)*; Don Yanan *(Dunk)*; Peter Loovey *(Billy)*; Dyer McHenry *(Al)*; Stan Chambers *(Stan)*; Robert Craighead *(Marty Karlson)*; Mary Ostow *(Reporter)*; Jim Glassman *(Stage Manager)*; Emmett Grennan *(Crew Member)*; Mike Turner *(Guard No. 1)*; Robert J. Ferrelli *(Guard No. 2)*; Ron Barnes *(Larry Bates)*; Bob Van Dusen *(Winston Bergmann)*; Christopher Boyer *(John Blake)*; William Knight *(Sheriff Rocker)*; Dave Richards *(Welles)*; Ben "Killa" Ramsey *(Quincy)*; Steven Novak *(State Trooper)*; R. Allan Bexton *(Doctor)*; Elizabeth Anderson

Anyone who ever criticized a Godzilla movie will be forced to bite their tongues when they see ZARKORR! THE INVADER, which looks cheaper than the worst of its Japanese forebears and isn't the least bit of fun.

In Aurora, CA, the towering monster Zarkorr bursts from a mountainside and begins a rampage of destruction. In New Jersey, postal clerk Tommy (Rhys Pugh) is visited by a diminutive holographic girl, Proctor (Torie Lynch), who informs him that aliens have unleashed the beast as a test of mankind, and that he, having been judged dead average in terms of human worth, has been assigned to stop it.

Desperate, Tommy races to a TV station to seek help from scientist Stephanie Martin (De'Prise Grossman). A hostage situation develops, but a sympathetic cop (Mark Hamilton) intervenes on Tommy's behalf. The trio visit Stephanie's computer hacker friend, Arthur (Charles Schneider), who deduces that the monster's emergence must have been accompanied by a concurrent event that can provide the key to its destruction. Sure enough, in Utah, the group discovers that a shield-like object fell from space at the time Zarkorr arrived. Wielding it against the beast, Tommy reflects its death rays back and destroys Zarkorr, becoming a national hero.

During an early scene between Tommy and Proctor, the tiny teen informs him that she can't be tape-recorded, since she's a visual projection that exists only inside his head; this occurs just after she has picked up a pencil and tossed it onto his desk. The rest of ZARKORR! THE INVADER pays just as much attention to narrative consistency, and even less to narrative energy, proceeding as a series of static, one-set scenes that drag on forever and are never interrupted by anything as ambitious as a subplot.

As if remembering only sporadically that this is supposed to be a monster movie, the filmmakers cut back every so often to a bit of Zarkorr's rubber-suited mayhem, but since our heroes are never directly threatened until the very end, no tension ever develops.

Though cheap-looking, the monster set-pieces at least reflect a slight amount of ambition, which is more than can be said about the rest of the film. Inspiration clearly ended with the idea to create *something* to fill in the gaps between creature scenes. *(Violence, profanity.)* — M.G.

d, Aaron Osborne; p, Sally Clarke, Kirk Edward Hansen; exec p, Albert Band; co-p, Steve Sechrest, Rob Martin; w, Benjamin Carr; ph, Joe Caramico Maxwell; ed, Felix Chamberlain; m, Richard Band; prod d, Danielle Berman; art d, Jessie Vint IV; sound, Patrick M. Griffith; fx, Michael S. Deak; casting, Robert MacDonald, Perry Bullington; cos, Jodi Zimelman; makeup, Ronda Rae

Science Fiction (PR: C MPAA: PG-13)

ZHONG AN SHI LU LING JI

(SEE: ORGANIZED CRIME & TRIAD BUREAU)

ACADEMY AWARDS

69th AWARDS OF THE ACADEMY OF MOTION PICTURE ARTS AND SCIENCES
(Listings in italics indicate winners)

Best Picture
Saul Zaentz, THE ENGLISH PATIENT
Ethan Coen, FARGO
James L. Brooks, Laurence Mark, Richard Sakai, Cameron Crowe, JERRY MAGUIRE
Simon Channing-Williams, SECRETS & LIES
Jane Scott, SHINE

Best Performance by an Actor in a Leading Role
Geoffrey Rush, SHINE
Tom Cruise, JERRY MAGUIRE
Ralph Fiennes, THE ENGLISH PATIENT
Woody Harrelson, THE PEOPLE vs. LARRY FLYNT
Billy Bob Thornton, SLING BLADE

Best Performance by an Actress in a Leading Role
Frances McDormand, FARGO
Brenda Blethyn, SECRETS & LIES
Diane Keaton, MARVIN'S ROOM
Kristin Scott Thomas, THE ENGLISH PATIENT
Emily Watson, BREAKING THE WAVES

Best Performance by an Actor in a Supporting Role
Cuba Gooding Jr., JERRY MAGUIRE
William H. Macy, FARGO
Armin Mueller-Stahl, SHINE
Edward Norton, PRIMAL FEAR
James Woods, GHOSTS OF MISSISSIPPI

Best Performance by an Actress in a Supporting Role
Juliette Binoche, THE ENGLISH PATIENT
Joan Allen, THE CRUCIBLE
Lauren Bacall, THE MIRROR HAS TWO FACES
Barbara Hershey, THE PORTRAIT OF A LADY
Marianne Jean-Baptiste, SECRETS & LIES

Best Achievement in Directing
Anthony Minghella, THE ENGLISH PATIENT
Joel Coen, FARGO
Milos Forman, THE PEOPLE vs. LARRY FLYNT
Mike Leigh, SECRETS & LIES
Scott Hicks, SHINE

Best Screenplay Written Directly for the Screen
Ethan Coen, Joel Coen, FARGO
Cameron Crowe, JERRY MAGUIRE
John Sayles, LONE STAR
Mike Leigh, SECRETS & LIES
Jan Sardi, Scott Hicks, SHINE

Best Screenplay Based on Material Previously Produced or Published
Billy Bob Thornton, SLING BLADE
Arthur Miller, THE CRUCIBLE
Anthony Minghella, THE ENGLISH PATIENT
Kenneth Branagh, HAMLET
John Hodge, TRAINSPOTTING

Best Foreign Language Film
KOLYA (Czech Republic)
A CHEF IN LOVE (Georgia)
THE OTHER SIDE OF SUNDAY (Norway)
PRISONER OF THE MOUNTAINS (Russia)
RIDICULE (France)

Best Achievement in Art Direction
Stuart Craig, Stephenie McMillan, THE ENGLISH PATIENT
Bo Welch, Cheryl Carasik, THE BIRDCAGE
Brian Morris, Philippe Turlure, EVITA
Tim Harvey, HAMLET
Catherine Martin, Brigitte Broch, WILLIAM SHAKESPEARE'S ROMEO & JULIET

Best Achievement in Cinematography
John Seale, THE ENGLISH PATIENT
Darius Khondji, EVITA
Roger Deakins, FARGO
Caleb Deschanel, FLY AWAY HOME
Chris Menges, MICHAEL COLLINS

Best Achievement in Costume Design
Ann Roth, THE ENGLISH PATIENT
Paul Brown, ANGELS AND INSECTS
Ruth Meyers, EMMA
Alex Byrne, HAMLET
Janet Patterson, THE PORTRAIT OF A LADY

Best Achievement in Documentary Features
Leon Gast, David Sonenberg, WHEN WE WERE KINGS
Susan W. Dryfoos, THE LINE KING: THE AL HIRSCHFELD STORY
Jo Menell, Angus Gibson, MANDELA
Anne Belle, Deborah Dickson, SUZANNE FARRELL: ELUSIVE MUSE
Rick Goldsmith, TELL THE TRUTH AND RUN: GEORGE SELDES AND THE AMERICAN PRESS

Best Achievement in Documentary Short Subjects
Jessica Yu, BREATHING LESSONS: THE LIFE AND WORK OF MARK O'BRIEN
Jeffrey Marvin, Bayley Silleck, COSMIC VOYAGE
Perry Wolff, AN ESSAY ON MATISSE
Susanne Simpson, Ben Burtt, SPECIAL EFFECTS
Paul Seydor, Nick Redman, THE WILD BUNCH: AN ALBUM IN MONTAGE

Best Achievement in Film Editing
Walter Murch, THE ENGLISH PATIENT
Gerry Hambling, EVITA
Roderick Jaynes, FARGO

Joe Hutshing, JERRY MAGUIRE
Pip Karmel, SHINE

Best Achievement in Makeup
Rick Baker, David Leroy Anderson, THE NUTTY PROFESSOR
Matthew W. Mungle, Deborah La Mia Denaver, GHOSTS OF MISSISSIPPI
Michael Westmore, Scott Wheeler, Jake Garber, STAR TREK: FIRST CONTACT

Best Achievement in Music (Original Dramatic Score)
Gabriel Yard, THE ENGLISH PATIENT
Patrick Doyle, HAMLET
Elliot Goldenthal, MICHAELCOLLINS
David Hrischfelder, SHINE
John Williams, SLEEPERS

Best Achievement in Music (Original Musical or Comedy Score)
Rachel Portman, EMMA
Marc Shaiman, THE FIRST WIVES CLUB
Alan Menken, Stephen Schwartz, THE HUNCHBACK OF NOTRE DAME
Randy Newman, JAMES AND THE GIANT PEACH
Hans Zimmer, THE PREACHER'S WIFE

Best Achievement in Music (Original Song)
Andrew Lloyd Webber, Tim Rice, "You Must Love Me" (EVITA)
Diane Warren, "Because You Loved Me" (UP CLOSE AND PERSONAL)
James Newton Howard, Jud J. Friedman, Allan Dennis Rich, "For the First Time" (ONE FINE DAY)
Barbra Streisand, Marvin Hamlisch, Bryan Adams, Robert "Mutt" Lange, "I Finally Found Someone" (THE MIRROR HAS TWO FACES)
Adam Schlesinger, "That Thing You Do!" (THAT THING YOU DO!)

Best Achievement in Animated Short Films
Tyron Montgomery, Thomas Stellmach, QUEST
Timothy Little, Chris Peterson, CANHEAD
Richard Condie, LA SALLA Peter Lord, WAT'S PIG

Best Achievement in Live Action Short Films
David Frankel, Barry Jossen, DEAR DIARY
Antonio Urrutia, DE TRIPAS, CORAZON
Kim Magnusson, Anders Thomas Jensen, ERNST & LYSET
Juan Carlos Fresnadillo, ESPOSADOS
Bernadette Carranza, Antonello De Leo, WORDLESS

Best Achievement in Sound
Walter Murch, Mark Berger, David Parker, Chris Newman, THE ENGLISH PATIENT
Andy Nelson, Anna Behlmer, Ken Weston, EVITA
Chris Carpenter, Bill W. Benton, Bob Beemer, Jeff Wexler, INDEPENDENCE DAY
Kevin O'Connell, Greg P. Russell, Keith A. Wester, THE ROCK
Steve Maslow, Gregg Landaker, Kevin O'Connell, Geoffrey Patterson, TWISTER

Best Achievement in Sound Effects Editing
Bruce Stambler, THE GHOST AND THE DARKNESS
Richard L. Anderson, David A. Whittaker, DAYLIGHT
Alan Robert Murray, Bub Asman, ERASER

Best Achievement in Visual Effects
Volker Engel, Douglas Smith, Clay Pinney, Joseph Viskocil, INDEPENDENCE DAY
Scott Squires, Phil Tippett, James Straus, Kit West, DRAGONHEART
Stefen Fangmeier, John Frazier, Habib Zargarpour, Henry La Bounta, TWISTER

Honorary Award
Michael Kidd, choreographer

Irving G. Thalberg Memorial Award
Saul Zaentz, producer

Scientific and Technical Oscar
Imax Corporation

OBITUARIES

(January 1 to December 31, 1996)

by Frank Lovece and Joe Frazzetta

Abbott, John

born: June 5, 1905, London, England
died: May 24, 1996, Los Angeles, CA, age 90

British character actor, mostly in American films.

John Abbott began appearing in London amateur productions in 1930, and four years later joined the Old Vic Company. He made his Broadway debut in *He Who Gets Slapped* (1946). Abbott made his film debut in MADEMOISELLE DOCTEUR (UK 1937) and went on to appear in between 70 and 100 movies, including MRS. MINIVER (1942), MISSION TO MOSCOW (1943), JANE EYRE (1944), ANNA AND THE KING OF SIAM and HUMORESQUE (1946), MADAME BOVARY (1949), THE MERRY WIDOW (1952), GIGI (1958), THE GREATEST STORY EVER TOLD (1965), THE BLACK BIRD (1978), and FOUR WEDDINGS AND A FUNERAL (1994).

Abbott's countless television appearances began with the BBC's seminal broadcasts prior to WWII. On American television, he guested on such series as "Alfred Hitchcock Presents," "The Beverly Hillbillies," "Bewitched," "Flipper, " "Get Smart," "Gunsmoke," "The Man from UNCLE," "McMillan and Wife," "77 Sunset Strip," and "Star Trek."

No cause of death was reported.

Adair, Peter

born: c. 1943
died: June 27, 1996, San Francisco, CA, age 53
educ: Antioch College

Documentary filmmaker, primarily covering gay themes.

Given a movie camera as a high-school graduation present, Peter Adair completed his first major documentary while still in college, the 53-minute HOLY GHOST PEOPLE (1967 or 1968). After several years of working for hire, including serving as a cinematographer on GIMME SHELTER (1971), he became an independent filmmaker. Adair produced and co-directed WORD IS OUT: STORIES OF SOME OF OUR LIVES (1978), a series of 26 direct-to-camera discourses by gay men and women that was five years in the making.

Adair's other films include STOPPING HISTORY (1984), about anti-nuclear activism; THE AIDS SHOW: ARTISTS INVOLVED WITH DEATH AND SURVIVAL (1986); and ABSOLUTELY POSITIVE (1990; co-director), focusing on how 11 men and women, including Adair, adjusted to being HIV positive. Adair also provided additional photography for THE TIMES OF HARVEY MILK (1984), and played a role in the fiction film THE DOLLAR BOTTOM (1981).

Adair died of complications from AIDS.

Addy, Wesley

born: Aug. 4, 1913, Omaha, NE
died: Dec. 31, 1996, Danbury, CT, age 83
educ: UCLA

Character actor and husband of actress Celeste Holm.

Wesley Addy, a longtime stage and film actor, made his Broadway debut in *Panic* (1935). After WWII, he entered films with THE FIRST LEGION (1951). He became a favorite supporting player of director Robert Aldrich, appearing in his THE BIG KNIFE and KISS ME DEADLY (1955), TEN SECONDS TO HELL (1959), WHAT EVER HAPPENED TO BABY JANE? (1962), FOUR FOR TEXAS (1963) and HUSH . . . HUSH, SWEET CHARLOTTE (1964).

Some of Addy's other films include MY SIX CONVICTS (1952), TIMETABLE(1956), THE GARMENT JUNGLE (1957), MISTER BUDDWING and SECONDS (1966), TORA!TORA! TORA! (1970), THE GRISSOM GANG (1971), NETWORK (1976), THE EUROPEANS(1979), THE VERDICT (1982), THE BOSTONIANS (1984), and A MODERN AFFAIR and BEFORE AND AFTER (1996). Addy became Holm's fourth husband in 1966.

No cause of death was reported.

Alea, Tomas Gutierrez

SEE Gutierrez Alea, Tomas

Alton, John

born: Oct. 5, 1901, Sopron, Hungary
died: June 2, 1996, Santa Monica, CA, age 94

Academy Award-winning cinematographer of more than 80 films.

John Alton, whose work helped establish the visual language of film noir, immigrated to America in 1919. In the late 1920s, after four years as an MGM lab technician, he became a cameraman at Paramount. Alton went to Europe to shoot backgrounds for director Ernst Lubitsch's THE STUDENT PRINCE IN OLD HEIDELBERG (1927), and stayed in Paris to head the camera department of the Joinville Studios. In 1932, Alton moved to Argentina to help design that country's first sound-film studio. He remained for seven years, shooting more than a dozen films and directing EL HIJO DEPAPA/PAPA'S BOY (1932).

Returning to the US in 1939, Alton was hired by RKO, where he worked primarily on second features. After WWII, he returned to work on such B-pictures as BURY ME DEAD(1947) and HOLLOW TRIUMPH aka THE SCAR (1948), as well as a series of films with director Anthony Mann that included T-MEN (1947), RAW DEAL (1948), and BORDER INCIDENT (1949). In the process, Alton developed the low-lit, high-contrast pattern-lighting that has come to define the look of film noir.

His fortunes took a more prestigious turn upon shooting director Vincente Minnelli's FATHER OF THE BRIDE (1950) and AN AMERICAN IN PARIS (1951), for which he and Alfred Gilks shared the Academy Award for best color cinematography. Other notable Alton films include FATHER'S LITTLE DIVIDEND (1951), I, THE JURY (1953), CATTLE QUEEN OF MONTANA (1954), THE BIG COMBO (1955), TEA AND SYMPATHY and THE TEAHOUSE OF THE AUGUST MOON (1956), DESIGNING WOMAN (1957), THE BROTHERS KARAMAZOV (1958), and ELMER GANTRY (1960), his last completed film. Alton and his Argentine wife spent most of the succeeding decades in relative seclusion in Europe and South America, until film scholars discovered he had returned to the US. He then became the subject of tributes at the Telluride Film Festival and the American Museum of the Moving Image, and received the Lifetime Career Achievement Award from the Los Angeles Film Critics Association. Alton's books on cinematography include *Painting With Light* (1949).

Alton died of natural causes, after undergoing hip-replacement surgery two weeks prior to his death.

Amsterdam, Morey

born: Dec. 14, 1908 (some sources say 1912 or 1914), Chicago, IL (some sources say San Francisco, CA)
died: Oct. 27, 1996, Los Angeles, CA, age 87
educ: University of California at Berkeley

Film and television comedian best known for his role on "The Dick Van Dyke Show," and considered a father of modern standup comedy.

Trained as a cellist, Morey Amsterdam used the instrument as a prop in vaudeville, nightclub, and radio routines. Known as the "Human Joke Machine," Amsterdam wrote gags for the likes of Will Rogers, Fanny Brice, Jack Benny, Henny Youngman, and Milton Berle. Amsterdam entered film in the 1930s as an apparently uncredited MGM gag–writer, and wrote or co-wrote the scripts to THE GHOST AND THE GUEST and KID DYNAMITE (both 1943). A major radio and television star of the 1940s and 1950s, he played wisecracking comedy writer Maurice "Buddy" Sorrell on "The Dick Van Dyke Show" (CBS 1961-66).

Amsterdam, who made his movie acting debut with IT CAME FROM OUTER SPACE (1953), also appeared in MURDER, INC. (1960), MACHINE GUN KELLY (1958), BEACH PARTY (1963), MUSCLE BEACH PARTY (1964), THE HORSE IN THE GRAY FLANNEL SUIT (1968), and WON TON TON, THE DOG WHO SAVED HOLLYWOOD

(1976). He produced and co-wrote the farce DON'T WORRY, WE'LL THINK OF A TITLE (1966).

Amsterdam died of a heart attack.

Anders, Luana

aka: Lu Anders
born: 1940 or 1942, CA
died: July 21 1996, Mar Vista, CA, age c. 56

Leading lady of low-budget 1960s independent films, a favorite of producer/director Roger Corman.

Luana Anders began in films while in her teens, often playing sexy juvenile delinquents in such pictures as REFORM SCHOOL GIRL (1957), her debut, and LIFE BEGINS AT 17 (1958). She later went on to play groovy hippies and other libidinous chicks in films like SEX AND THE COLLEGE GIRL(1964), before aging into mainstream films and TV movies. Her best-known roles are as the swimmer killed by an ax in Coppola's DEMENTIA 13 (1963) and the commune dweller who digs Peter Fonda in EASY RIDER (1969). She was also notable in Corman's THE PIT AND THE PENDULUM(1961), THE YOUNG RACERS (1963), and THE TRIP (1967), as well as in THE LAST DETAIL (1973) and MOVERS AND SHAKERS (1985). Anders also appeared in NIGHT TIDE (1963), GAMES (1967), THAT COLD DAY IN THE PARK (1969), GREASER'S PALACE (1972), SHAMPOO (1975), THE MISSOURI BREAKS(1976), GOIN' SOUTH (1978), PERSONAL BEST(1982), ONE FROM THE HEART (1983), IRRECONCILABLE DIFFERENCES (1984), THE TWO JAKES (1990), and WILD BILL (1995). She co-wrote and appeared in LIMIT UP(1989). Her final film was AMERICAN STRAYS (1996).

Anders died of cancer.

Annabella

born: Suzanne Georgette Charpentier, July 14, 1909, LaVarenne-Saint-Hilaire, France
died: Sept. 18, 1996, Neuilly-sur-Seine, France, age 86.

Popular French "gamine" actress of the 1930s.

A publisher's daughter and teenage dancer who made her first film appearance with a minor role in Abel Gance's NAPOLEON (France 1927), Annabella went on to additional small roles until plucked by director Rene Clair to star in the classic LE MILLION/THE MILLION (France 1931) and QUATORZE JUILLET/JULY 14TH (France 1933). For five years she appeared in films in France and Britain before moving to the US , where she starred in a half-dozen features. Among them was SUEZ (1938), in which she co-starred with Tyrone Power; the following year she divorced her husband, French actor Jean Murat, and married Power. Annabella became an US citizen in 1942, but, after a minor American film success, she returned to France after divorcing Power in 1948. Unable to reclaim her past glory, she retired to her Pyrenean farm.

Annabella died of a heart attack

Ayres, Lew

born: Lewis Frederick Ayres III, Dec. 28, 1908, Minneapolis, MN; raised Minneapolis and San Diego, CA
died: Dec. 30, 1996, Los Angeles, CA, age 88
educ: University of Arizona (medicine)

Popular and well-regarded leading man of ALL QUIET ON THE WESTERN FRONT(1930) and the "Dr. Kildare" movie series, who was blackballed by the major studios and exhibitors for his conscientious objection to WWII, despite later earning three battle stars serving in combat with the Army Medical Corps.

A musician who was discovered by an agent while performing at a Hollywood night club. Lew Ayres appeared in bit parts before gaining notice as Greta Garbo's lover in THE KISS (1929). The following year, he reaped stardom and critical acclaim as the pacifist German soldier in ALL QUIET ON THE WESTERN FRONT (1930).

Among Ayres's more than 60 films are George Cukor's HOLIDAY (1938), JOHNNY BELINDA (1948), for which he garnered a Best Actor Academy Award nomination; and nine"Dr. Kildare" films, bookended by YOUNG DR. KILDARE (1938) and DR. KILDARE'SVICTORY (1942). The end of that series coincided with Ayres's declaration of conscientious objection. Ostracized by the film industry, he spent three months in a labor camp before distinguishing himself as a Medical Corps noncombatant. Regardless, roles remained few and far between, and except for JOHNNY BELINDA, Ayres found work only at small studios such as RKO. After playing a fiendish scientist in DONOVAN'S BRAIN (1953), Ayres wrote, produced, and narrated the five-part documentary, ALTARS OF THE EAST (1955), based on his book. He later directed, produced, photographed, and edited a 150-minute follow-up, the Golden Globe-winning documentary ALTARS OF THE WORLD (1976). (He also directed the 1936 Civil War drama HEARTS IN BONDAGE, in which he did not appear.)

After working primarily in television in the 1950s, Ayres returned to movies at the urging of Otto Preminger, who directed him in ADVISE AND CONSENT (1962). He appeared in a half-dozen more movies through 1978, including BATTLE FOR THE PLANET OF THE APES (1973), and his final film, DAMIEN—OMEN II (1978).

Ayres, who served on the US National Committee for UNESCO, a United Nations relief organization, married and divorced the actresses Lola Lane (1931-33) and Ginger Rogers (1934-41). In 1964, he married flight attendant Diana Hall.

No cause of death was reported.

Atsumi, Kiyoshi

born: c. 1928, Tokyo, Japan
died: Aug. 4, 1996, Tokyo, Japan, age 68

Japanese movie star in the Charlie Chaplin/Jacques Tati Everyman mold.

Kiyoshi Atsumi—Japan's most famous actor, though little-known outside his country—played the beloved Torajiro "Tora-san" Kuruma in the 48 "Otokowa Tsurai Yo/It's Tough Being a Man" film series, from OTOKO WA TSURAIYO (Japan 1969; the spelling transliterates variously from the Japanese characters) to TORA-SAN TO THE RESCUE (Japan 1995). After beginning on stage in the 1950s, Atsumi collaborated with director friend Yoji Yamada and developed the Tora-san character for television in 1968. The TV series was adapted to a feature in 1969, and went on to become a blockbuster series of movies—reportedly the world's second-longest-running feature-film series, after James Bond, and the largest in number of features produced. Two Tora-san movies were released in the US: ZOKU OTOKOWA TSURAIYO/TORA-SAN'SCHERISHED MOTHER/TORA-SAN PART 2 (Japan 1970) and OTOKOWA TSURAIYOOTORAIJIRO KOKORO NO TABIJI/TORA-SAN GOES TO VIENNA (Japan 1989).

Atsmui's other films include the non-Tora-san dramas KINEMA NO TENCHI/FINAL TAKE: THE GOLDEN AGE OF MOVIES (1986), DAUNTAUN HIROZU (1988), GAKKO (Japan 1993), and CLASS TO REMEMBER (1994).

Atsumi died of lung cancer.

Balsam, Martin

born: Nov. 4, 1919, New York, NY
died: Feb. 13, 1996, Rome, Italy, age 76
educ: DeWitt Clinton High School and Actors Studio, New York, NY

Venerable dean of character actors, who won a Supporting Actor Academy Award for A THOUSAND CLOWNS (1965) and a Tony for Broadway's *You Know I Can't Hear You When the Water's Running* (1967).

Balsam began in show business playing with the wedding/bar-mitzvah band "Murray Levine and His Syncopated Five." Balsam emceed at a vacation resort and acted in summer stock before making his stage debut in 1941. After WWII, he returned in 1947 to be chosen one of the original members of the Actors Studio, appearing in the legendary acting school's first public production, director Elia Kazan's *Sundown Beach* .

Balsam made his film debut playing an investigator in ON THE WATERFRONT (1954), and distinguished himself in such major features as TWELVE ANGRY MEN (1957), PSYCHO (1960), BREAKFAST AT TIFFANY'S (1961), SEVEN DAYS IN MAY (1964), CATCH-22 and LITTLE BIG MAN (1970), THE TAKING OF PELHAM ONE TWO THREE (1974), ALL THE PRESIDENT'S MEN (1976), and both the 1962 original and 1991 remake of CAPE FEAR. A tireless working actor who shunned the thought of retirement, Balsam worked regularly on television from the 1950s, as well as in many minor European films in the 1970s.

The second of his three marriages was to actress Joyce Van Patten, with whom he had actress daughter Talia Balsam.

Balsam, who lived on Manhattan's Upper West Side, died of a stroke at the Ripetta Residence hotel in Rome while on vacation.

Bass, Saul

born: May 8, 1920, New York, NY
died: April 25, 1996, Los Angeles, CA, age 75
educ: Art Students League, New York, NY; Brooklyn College

Graphic designer who revolutionized motion-picture title sequences.

After studying on scholarship at the Art Students League and later with Gyorgy Kepes at Brooklyn College, Saul Bass began his career with Manhattan design firms. Moving to Los Angeles in the early 1950s to open his own studio, he hired Elaine Makatura as his first employee; in 1961 she became his second wife, and later co-director of Bass's own independent short films.

Bass's innovative title sequence for Otto Preminger's heroin-addiction drama THE MAN WITH THE GOLDEN ARM (1955)—a jagged animated arm scurrying desperately in the manner of a junkie seeking a fix—helped to establish movie titles as a creative entity in their own right. Bass, who also designed trademarks, corporate logos and even airplane graphics, went on to design roughly 50 film titles, including those of Alfred Hitchcock's VERTIGO (1958), NORTH BY NORTHWEST (1959,) and PSYCHO (1960); Preminger's ANATOMY OF A MURDER (1959), EXODUS (1960), and ADVISE AND CONSENT (1962); and Martin Scorsese's GOODFELLAS (1990), CAPE FEAR (1991), THE AGE OF INNOCENCE (1993), and CASINO (1995). Other titles include AROUND THE WORLD IN 80 DAYS (1956; also poster), SAINT JOAN (1957; also poster), WEST SIDE STORY (1961; also "visual consultant" and poster), SECONDS (1966), BROADCAST NEWS (1987), BIG (1988), THE WAR OF THE ROSES (1989), DOC HOLLYWOOD (1991), and MR. SATURDAY NIGHT (1992). Bass is also credited as "pictorial consultant" on PSYCHO. In Donald Spoto's *The Dark Side of Genius: The Art of Alfred Hitchcock*, Joseph Stefano, PSYCHO's screenwriter, relates that Hitchcock engaged Bass to storyboard the legendary shower sequence, though Hitchcock devised the two key shots of the knife to the abdomen and the blood in the drain. Bass also helped Stanley Kubrick design the final battle scene in SPARTACUS (1960), for which he was credited as "design consultant."

Bass himself co-directed with Elaine Bass a series of well-received shorts, including the Academy Award-winning Documentary Short "Why Man Creates" (1968). His others include Eastman Kodak's "The Searching Eye" (1964), United Airlines' "From Here to There (1964), and Warner Bros. '"Notes on the Popular Arts" (1977) and "The Solar Film" (1981). Bass also directed the science-fiction feature PHASE IV (US-UK 1973).

Bass, whose work is part of the permanent collections of the Museum of Modern Art, the Smithsonian Institution, the Library of Congress, the Prague Museum, the Stedelijk Museum in Amsterdam, and the Israel Museum in Jerusalem, died of non-Hodgkins lymphoma.

Baxter, Jane

born: Feodora Forde, c. 1909, Bremen, Germany
died: Sept. 13, 1996, London, England, age 87

British actress.

Jane Baxter appeared in dozens of plays and nearly 30 films, mostly in the UK. Hating Hollywood, where she played small film roles in the 1930s, she gave up a long-term relationship with Ronald Colman in order to return to England. She played the recurring role of a mischievous viscountess in the 1970s British series "Upstairs, Downstairs," seen in the US on PBS. Baxter's films include KNOCK ON ANY DOOR (1949).

No cause of death was reported.

Baxter, Les

born: 1922
died: Jan. 15, 1996, Newport Beach, CA, age 73

Prolific film music composer.

Les Baxter began as a jazz musician, backing such luminaries as Billie Holiday and Mel Torme, and arranging for Nat King Cole and others. He provided music for more than 70 films, and countless TV shows—among them, the mournful whistling theme of "Lassie." Many of his scores were for the production companies Bel-Air in the 1950s and AIP in the 1960s. Baxter also wrote songs and produced albums for Yma Sumac and others.

Baxter entered film composition in the 1950s with such films as TANGA-TIKA (1953) and THE YELLOW TOMAHAWK (1954). He went on to score such popular films as THE PIT AND THE PENDULUM (1961), PANIC IN YEAR ZERO! (1962), BEACH PARTY, THE RAVEN, and "X"—THE MAN WITH THE X-RAY EYES (1963), MUSCLE BEACH PARTY (1964), DR. GOLDFOOT AND THE BIKINI MACHINE, and HOW TO STUFF A WILD BIKINI (1965), WILD IN THE STREETS (1968), and FROGS (1972; also co-music director). His last film score was for THE BEAST WITHIN (1982).

Baxter composed scores for the American editions of Mario Bava's LA MASCHERA DEL DEMONIO/BLACK SUNDAY (Italy; US release 1960), replacing Roberto Nicolosi's existing score, and I TRE VOLTI DELLA PAURA/BLACK SABBATH (US-Italy-France 1963).

Baxter lived in Mexica, TX. No cause of death was given.

Beckerman, Barry

born: c. 1943
died: July 30, 1996, Los Angeles, CA, age 53

Studio executive turned film writer-producer.

Barry Beckerman joined the Warner Bros. creative affairs department in 1969, helping to acquire and develop such films as DIRTY HARRY and KLUTE (1971) and THE EXORCIST (1973). Ten years later, he joined Peter Guber at PolyGram, where he was involved in the initial development of BATMAN (1989). Beckerman wrote the Burt Reynolds film SHAMUS (1973), as well as the telefilm RAID ON ENTEBBE (1977), for which he garnered an Emmy nomination and a Golden Globe award; he also produced RED DAWN (1984). In later years, he worked as a consultant to Warner Bros. and Sony.

Beckerman died of cancer.

Beich, Albert

born: June 25, 1918 or 1919, Bloomington, IL; raised Laguna Beach, CA
died: March 30, 1996, Scottsdale, AZ, age 76 or 77
educ: McGill University (bachelor's degree)

Screenwriter and playwright.

Albert Beich began writing for radio while still a teenager, and after college worked as a screenwriter for Republic Pictures. He scripted CAMPUS RHYTHM, Edgar G. Ulmer's GIRLS IN CHAINS and WEST SIDE KID (1943) before serving in WWII. His films include: GANGS OF THE WATERFRONT (1945), based on a story by Sam Fuller, GAY BLADES (1946), THE BRIDE GOES WILD (1948), THE YELLOW CAB MAN (1950), THE LIEUTENANT WORE SKIRTS (1956), DEAD RINGER (1964), and THE PERILS OF PAULINE (1967).

Beich died of an embolism.

Belli, Melvin

born: Melvin Mouron Belli, July 29, 1907, Sonora, CA
died: July 9, 1996, San Francisco, CA, age 88
educ: Stockton High School (valedictorian), University of California at Berkeley

Flamboyant and controversial attorney who occasionally appeared in films.

Melvin Belli, nicknamed "The King of Torts" by *Life* magazine, was defense attorney for Lee Harvey Oswald's killer, Jack Ruby; actors Errol Flynn, Mae West, and Mickey Rooney; and boxer Muhammed Ali. Belli made cameos appearances, generally as himself, in WILD IN THE STREETS (1968); the concert film GIMME SHELTER (1970), featuring clients The Rolling Stones; and GROUND ZERO (1973). He played the mayor of San Francisco in the telefilm LADY OF THE HOUSE (1978), and appeared as an alien on "Star Trek."

Belli, who was diagnosed with pancreatic cancer in April, suffered a stroke two weeks before his death from pneumonia.

Bentine, Michael

born: Jan. 26, 1922, Watford, Hertfordshire, England
died: Nov. 26, 1996
educ: Eton College

Comedian and scriptwriter.

Graduating from the comedy stage, Michael Bentine worked with the celebrated 1950s British radio-comedy troupe, The Goons (Harry Secombe, Spike Milligan, and Peter Sellers), and made his film debut in the Goons' film DOWN AMONG THE Z MEN aka STAND EASY (UK 1952). He co-wrote and co-starred in his next film, FORCES' SWEETHEART (UK 1953). A noted television performer, Bentine also appeared in the films RAISING A RIOT (UK 1957), I ONLY ARSKED! (UK

1958), THE SANDWICH MAN (UK 1966; also co-writer), THAT SWINGING CITY (UK 1966), and the John Cleese and Graham Chapman-penned RENTADICK (UK 1972).

No cause of death was reported.

Beradino, John

born: John Berardino, May 1, 1917, Los Angeles, CA
died: May 19, 1996, Los Angeles, CA, age 79
educ: University of Southern California

Actor best known for his 33-year run as Dr. Steve Hardy on the soap opera "General Hospital."

As a child, John Beradino had bit parts in the earliest silent "Our Gang" comedy shorts. A professional baseball player until a 1953 leg injury ended his career, Berardino began acting in sports movies such as THE WINNER'S CIRCLE (1948), THE KID FROM CLEVELAND (1949), and THE KID FROM LEFT FIELD (1953). Upon retiring, he returned to acting with bits in the movies SUDDENLY and THEM! (1954). Though guesting on a number of television series, Beradino appeared as Dr. Hardy on "General Hospital," from its April 1, 1963 debut to just a week before his death. He received three Emmy nominations and a 1993 star on the Hollywood Walk of Fame. Along with other soap stars, he did a cameo in the soap-satire feature YOUNG DOCTORS IN LOVE (1982). Other films include THE KILLER IS LOOSE and SEVEN MEN FROM NOW (1956), THE NAKED AND THE DEAD and THE WORLD WAS HIS JURY (1958), NORTH BY NORTHWEST (1959), SEVEN THIEVES (1960), and THE SCARFACE MOB (1962).

Beradino died of cancer.

Berman, Pandro S.

born: March 28, 1905, Pittsburgh, PA
died: July 13, 1996, Beverly Hills, CA, age 91

Respected producer of more than 100 films, including a large number of classics.

Pandro S. Berman, the son of a Universal Pictures general manager, began his film career at 18, working in various capacities before becoming an RKO producer in 1931 (moving to MGM in 1940).

Among the highlights of Berman's nearly 40-year career are all but the first of the RKO Fred Astaire-Ginger Rogers musicals: THE GAY DIVORCEE (1934), ROBERTA and TOP HAT (1935), FOLLOW THE FLEET and SWING TIME (1936), SHALL WE DANCE (1937), CAREFREE (1938), and THE STORY OF VERNON AND IRENE CASTLE (1939); the Elizabeth Taylor films NATIONAL VELVET (1944), FATHER OF THE BRIDE (1950), and BUTTERFIELD 8 (1960); Katharine Hepburn's CHRISTOPHER STRONG and MORNING GLORY (1933); the Marx Brothers' ROOM SERVICE (1938); Elvis Presley's JAILHOUSE ROCK (1957); and such films as OF HUMAN BONDAGE (1934), SYLVIA SCARLETT and MARY OF SCOTLAND (1936), STAGE DOOR (1937), THE HUNCHBACK OF NOTRE DAME (1939), THE THREE MUSKETEERS (1948), MADAME BOVARY (1949), IVANHOE and THE PRISONER OF ZENDA (1952), BLACKBOARD JUNGLE (1955), TEA AND SYMPATHY (1956), and A PATCH OF BLUE (1965). His final film was MOVE (1970). Berman received the Motion Picture Academy's Irving G. Thalberg Memorial Award in 1977 and the Producers Guild's David O. Selznick lifetime achievement honor in 1992.

Berman died of congestive heart failure.

Bernard, Jason

born: May 17, 1938, Chicago, IL
died: Oct. 18, 1996, Burbank, CA, age 58

Well-regarded African-American character actor who specialized in stuffy yet avuncular roles.

Chicago-reared Jason Bernard made his film debut in THOMASINE AND BUSHROD (1974) and CAR WASH (1976), gaining his first major exposure in the telefilm WILMA (1977). Other telefilms include A WOMAN CALLED MOSES (1978), THE NIGHT THE CITY SCREAMED (1980), PRAY TV (1981), and V—THE FINAL BATTLE (1984). Employed steadily in television, Bernard had regular roles on "Cagney and Lacey" (CBS 1982-88), "High Performance" (ABC 1983), "Herman's Head" (Fox 1991-94), and "The Flash" (CBS 1990-91). He was acclaimed for his performance as Dr. Martin Luther King Jr. in THE MEETING (1991), an "American Playhouse" adaptation of the 1987 one-act play about a fictional meeting between King and Malcolm X.

Bernard's films include UNCLE JOE SHANNON (1978), BLUE THUNDER, THE STAR CHAMBER, and WARGAMES (1983), ALL OF ME (1984), NO WAY OUT (1987), BIRD (1988), WHILE YOU WERE SLEEPING (1995), and LIAR LIAR (1997, released posthumously)

Bernard died of a heart attack suffered during a car accident while driving in Hollywood, CA.

Bertino, Albert

born: c. 1912
died: Aug. 25, 1996, Los Angeles, age 84

Movie animator and Disneyland ride-creator.

Albert Bertino joined the Walt Disney studio in 1939 after working as a cartoonist and illustrator. He worked on Disney animated shorts, was involved with the animated features FANTASIA and PINOCCHIO (1940), and was an animator on the feature MAKE MINE MUSIC (1946). Bertino also later wrote for the TV series "Walt Disney's Wonderful World of Color" (NBC 1961-81). He is credited with creating the Disneyland theme-park attractions "Pirates of the Caribbean, " "Mr. Toad's Wild Ride," "Haunted Mansion, " and "Country Bear Jamboree," a stage show featuring an animatronic bear named "Big Al," which Bertino said was modeled on himself.

No cause of death was reported.

Besch, Bibi

born: Feb. 1, 1940, Vienna, Austria; raised Mount Kisco and Chappaqua, NY
died: Sept. 7, 1996, Los Angeles, CA, age 56
educ: Connecticut College

Prolific actress and a board member of the Screen Actors Guild.

Bibi Besch made her film debut with DISTANCE (1975), and went on to appear in at least a dozen more features and several dozen TV episodes and telefilms. Her Broadway plays include *Fame* , The Chinese Prime Minister , *Here Lies Jeremy Troy* , and *Once for the Asking* . Telefilms include VICTORY AT ENTEBBE (1976) and THE DAY AFTER (1983). Besch earned a 1992 Supporting Actress Emmy nomination for the Fox telefilm DOING TIME ON MAPLE DRIVE, and a 1993 Guest Actress nomination for her recurring role on "Northern Exposure."

A director of the Screen Actors Guild from 1990 until her death, Besch appeared in films including THE PACK (1977), HARDCORE (1979), THE BEAST WITHIN and STAR TREK II: THE WRATH OF KHAN (1982), THE LONELY LADY (1983), WHO'S THAT GIRL (1987), STEEL MAGNOLIAS (1989), BETSY'S WEDDING and TREMORS (1990), LONELY HEARTS (1992) and MY FAMILY, MI FAMILIA (1995).

Besch died of cancer. Her daughter is actress Samantha Mathis.

Bessell, Ted

born: March 20, 1935, New York (Flushing), NY
died: Oct. 6, 1996, Los Angeles, CA, age 61
educ: Georgetown University; University of Colorado

Popular actor best known as Marlo Thomas' patient beau on the sitcom "That Girl."

A piano prodigy who performed a Carnegie Hall recital at age 12, Ted Bessell returned to New York after college to work and study at the Neighborhood Playhouse. He made his film debut as the elevator operator in LOVER COME BACK (1961). Bessell broke into television in 1962 with regular and guest roles in various sitcoms before going on to "That Girl" (ABC 1966-71). Bessell starred or co-starred in the series "Me and the Chimp" (CBS 1972), "Good Time Harry" (NBC 1980), and "Hail to the Chief" (ABC 1985). He later become a well-regarded TV producer-director, sharing a 1989 Emmy Award as a producer of Best Variety or Comedy Program for "The Tracey Ullman Show" (Fox). Bessell's films include THE OUTSIDER (1962), CAPTAIN NEWMAN, MD (1963), McHALE'S NAVY JOINS THE AIR FORCE (1965), and DON'T DRINK THE WATER (1969).

He died of an aortic aneurysm.

Bissell, Whit

born: Whitner Bissell, Oct. 25, 1909. New York, NY
died: March 5, 1996, Woodland Hills, CA, age 86
educ: University of North Carolina (BA)

Highly prolific character actor of at least 93 films.

Whit Bissell began as a child actor onstage in his native New York before going to Hollywood in the 1940s. He made his film debut in HOLY MATRIMONY (1943), and in his long career often played no-nonsense professionals, sometimes exaggerated into fussbudgets. He also appeared on a huge number of TV shows and telefilms, and played General Heywood Kirk in the cast of "The Time Tunnel" (ABC 1966-67).

Bissell's films included both mainstream dramas and film noirs, among them DESTINATION TOKYO (1944), BRUTE FORCE (1947), HE WALKED BY NIGHT and RAW DEAL (1948), THE RED BADGE OF COURAGE (1951), THE CAINE MUTINY and RIOT IN CELL BLOCK 11 (1954), THE BIG COMBO, THE DESPERATE HOURS, and SHACK OUT ON 101 (1955), GUNFIGHT AT THE O. K. CORRAL (1957), THE DEFIANT ONES (1958), THE MAGNIFICENT SEVEN (1960), THE MANCHURIAN CANDIDATE (1962), HUD and SPENCER'S MOUNTAIN (1963), SEVEN DAYS IN MAY (1964), FIVE CARD STUD (1968), AIRPORT (1970), and THE LINCOLN CONSPIRACY (1977). He was particularly known for his roles in several classic science fiction and horror movies, including LOST CONTINENT (1951), CREATURE FROM THE BLACK LAGOON and TARGET EARTH (1954), INVASION OF THE BODY SNATCHERS (1956), MONSTER ON THE CAMPUS (1958), THE TIME MACHINE (1960), and SOYLENT GREEN (1973). His performances as scientists-playing-God in I WAS A TEENAGE WEREWOLF (1957) and I WAS A TEEN-AGE FRANKENSTEIN (1958) helped net him the life career award from the Academy of Science Fiction, Fantasy and Horror Films in 1994.

Bissell, who served on the Screen Actors Guild board of directors for 18 years, died of undisclosed causes.

Blau, Raphael

born: Raphael David Blau, c. 1913; raised New York, NY, and London, England
died: March 31, 1996, New York (Brooklyn), NY, age 83
educ: Columbia University

Screenwriter who co-wrote the story basis for BEDTIME FOR BONZO.

Raphael Blau wrote radio mysteries in the mid-1940s before turning to screenwriting, Blau provided the story basis for the comedy MOTHER IS A FRESHMAN (1949). Drawing on his academic background in psychology, he and his journalist brother-in-law, Ted Berkman wrote the story for BEDTIME FOR BONZO (1951), which eventually became a cult hit. Blau and Berkman collaborated on a series of scripts, many with psychological themes, most notably FEAR STRIKES OUT (1957). Other films included SHORT CUT TO HELL (1957) and GIRL OF THE NIGHT (1960). In the early 1960s, Blau moved to Yarmouth, Nova Scotia, and wrote occasional television scripts.

He died of heart failure.

Bonner, Priscilla

born: c. 1898, Adrian, MI
died: Feb. 21, 1996, Los Angeles, CA, age 97

Silent film star.

Priscilla Bonner, who was raised in Washington state, appeared in more than two dozen silent movies, starring opposite Lon Chaney Sr. in SHADOWS (1922), Harry Langdon in Frank Capra's THE STRONG MAN (1926), and Clara Bow in IT (1927). She married and retired circa 1928. Her sister, Marjorie, was also a silent film actress. Bonner's films include HONEST HUTCH (1920), with Will Rogers, HOME STUFF (1921), THE SON OF WALLING FORD (1921), APRIL SHOWERS (1923), CHARLEY'S AUNT, PROUD FLESH, and THE RED KI-MONO (1925), THREE BAD MEN (1926), LONG PANTS (1927), and GIRLS WHO DARE (1929).

No cause of death was reported.

Bowen, Roger

born: May 25, 1932, Attleboro, MS; raised Providence, RI
died: Feb. 16, 1996, Florida, age 63
educ: University of Chicago

Versatile actor-writer who co-founded the Second City improvisational-comedy troupe, and played Col. Henry Blake in the movie M*A*S*H (1970).

Former law student Roger Bowen was among the seven performers comprising the first cast of Chicago's newly established Second City in 1959. He made his film debut with FUNNYMAN (1967), and his telefilm debut with DEADLOCK (1969). The bespectacled, middle-manager-type Bowen was seen in a number of TV series including "Arnie" (CBS 1970-72), "The Brian Keith Show" (NBC 1972-74; second season only), and "House Calls" (CBS 1979-82). Films include PETULIA (US-UK 1968), MOVE (1970), STEELYARD BLUES (1973), TUNNELVISION (1976), HEAVEN CAN WAIT (1978), THE MAIN EVENT (1979), FOXES (1980), ZAPPED! (1982), MORGAN STEWART'S COMING HOME (1987) and WHAT ABOUT BOB? (1991). He also appeared in the telefilms PLAYMATES (1972), HUNTER (1973), IT COULDN'T HAPPEN TO A NICER GUY (1974), THE MONEYCHANGERS (1976), THE BASTARD (1978) and THE MURDER THAT WOULDN'T DIE (1980).

Bowen, who also wrote novels and satirical sketches for theater and TV, died of a heart attack.

Bremer, Lucille

born: Feb. 21, 1917, Amsterdam, NY; raised Philadelphia, PA
died: April 16, 1996, La Jolla, CA, age 79

Actress-dancer who partnered with Fred Astaire in two films.

At age 12, Lucille Bremer danced with the Philadelphia Opera Company ballet. Later, while a Rockette at Radio City Music Hall, she was discovered by MGM producer Arthur Freed. After making her film debut in MEET ME IN ST. LOUIS (1944), she played opposite Astaire in YOLANDA AND THE THIEF and was Astaire's principal dance partner in ZIEGFELD FOLLIES (both 1945). Bremer retired from film in 1948, upon marrying Abelardo Rodriguez, a former Mexican president's son, whom she met while filming ADVENTURES OF CASANOVA (1947) in Mexico City. They divorced in 1971, and Bremer later owned a children's dress shop in La Jolla. She lived there and in Las Cruces, Baja California, Mexico. Her other films include TILL THE CLOUDS ROLL BY (1946), DARK DELUSION aka CYNTHIA'S SECRET (1947), and BEHIND LOCKED DOORS aka THE HUMAN GORILLA and RUTH-LESS (1948).

Bremer died of complications after suffering a heart attack.

Broccoli, Albert R. (Cubby)

born: Albert Romolo Broccoli, April 5, 1909, New York, NY
died: June 27, 1996, Beverly Hills, CA, age 87

Producer best known for launching the James Bond movie series.

The son of immigrants from the Calabria region of Italy, Albert R. Broccoli worked in the family vegetable and coffin businesses until 1938 when, while visiting a Hollywood-agent cousin, Broccoli met and befriended Cary Grant (years later the best man at Broccoli's wedding), and decided to try the movie business. Working his way up starting with a mail-room job at 20th Century-Fox, became a producer with PARA-TROOPER aka THE RED BERET (UK 1954).

Broccoli and new partner Harry Saltzman obtained the rights to spy-turned-novelist Ian Fleming's "James Bond" stories and books. United Artists gambled a modest $1 million to distribute the first James Bond film, DR. NO (UK 1962). Saltzman, who died in September 1994, left the partnership in 1976, with Broccoli retaining the Bond film rights. With the exceptions of CASINO ROYALE (1967) and NEVER SAY NEVER AGAIN (UK 1983), all of the Bond films were co-produced or produced by Broccoli; GOLDENEYE (UK 1995) was produced by Broccoli's daughter, Barbara, and his stepson, Michael G. Wilson. Broccoli received the Motion Picture Academy's Irving G. Thalberg Memorial Award in 1982 and the Order of the British Empire in 1987.

Broccoli's other films as producer include HELL BELOW ZERO (UK 1954), A PRIZE OF GOLD (UK 1955), ZARAK (UK 1956), FIRE DOWN BELOW (US-UK 1957), THE MAN INSIDE (UK 1958), CALL

ME BWANA (UK 1963), and CHITTY CHITTY BANG BANG (UK 1968).

Broccoli, who had been in declining health, died as a result of heart trouble.

Brownrigg, S. F.

born: no date reported
died: September 20, 1996, Dallas, Texas

Horror movie producer-director whose DON'T LOOK IN THE BASEMENT (1973) was a seminal example of the "don't [verb] in the [noun]" school of splatter.

S. F. Brownrigg, a transplanted Arkansan who spent most of his career in Texas, learned filmmaking while in the Army. Afterward, he teamed with prolific, low-budget Texan filmmaker Larry Buchanan, serving in sound-production capacities on such Buchanan films as THE NAKED WITCH (1961) and ZONTAR! THE THING FROM VENUS and MARS NEEDS WOMEN (1966), as well as for Irvin Berwick's STRANGE COMPULSION (1964). His third film as a director, SCUM OF THE EARTH (1976; also producer), was retitled POOR WHITE TRASH PART 2 to be marketed as the sequel to a 1957 hillbilly sleaze picture. In the 1990s, Brownrigg was president of the Dallas production facility Century Studios. He was married to NAKED WITCH star Libby Hall. His son Stacy works in film and telefilm sound-production, and worked with his father on THINKIN' BIG (1986), Brownrigg's last movie.

Brownrigg's other films include DON'T OPEN THE DOOR! aka SEASONS FOR MURDER (1974) and KEEP MY GRAVE OPEN aka THE HOUSE WHERE HELL FROZE OVER (1980; also producer).

Brownrigg died of cancer.

Buchman, Herman

born: c. 1920
died: Jan. 27 1996, Santa Fe, NM, age 75

Makeup artist.

Herman Buchman, who wrote two books on his craft, worked on films including 12 ANGRY MEN (1957), HAPPY ANNIVERSARY (1959), GONE ARE THE DAYS (1963), LONG DAY'S JOURNEY INTO NIGHT and THE MIRACLE WORKER (1962), THE INCIDENT (1967), and THE PANIC IN NEEDLE PARK (1971), as well as in theater, opera, and television. He was an associate professor of theater arts at the State University of New York at Purchase, and taught makeup at the Julliard School and at the original Theater Wing. He later served as director of makeup for the New York City Opera.

Buchman died of cancer.

Burns, George

born: Nathan Birnbaum, Jan. 20, 1896, New York (Lower East Side), NY
died: March 9, 1996, Beverly Hills, CA, age 100

Beloved comedian, producer, and actor, whose remarkable career spanned vaudeville, radio, film, television, books, recordings, and nightclubs.

George Burns was one of 12 children of a a part-time cantor who died when Burns was seven. Leaving school to sing on street corners for pennies, he formed the Pee Wee Quartet and sang in taverns and on the Staten Island ferry. In his teens, he worked as a trick roller skater and dance teacher, and paired with several partners in unsuccessful vaudeville acts. In 1923 he met Gracie Allen, a struggling 17-year-old actress from San Francisco with whom he teamed as a comedy act. They were married from 1926 until her death from a heart attack in 1964. Under contract to the prestigious Keith vaudeville circuit, Burns and Allen performed nationwide and in Europe. In 1930, CBS gave the popular comics their own radio show, which became a blockbuster lasting 18 years. In 1931, Burns signed with Paramount Pictures to write and appear in a series of 10-minute shorts. Burns and Allen made their feature debut in the all-star extravaganza THE BIG BROADCAST (1932), and their films together included COLLEGE (1933), MANY HAPPY RETURNS (1934), THE BIG BROADCAST OF 1936 and LOVE IN BLOOM (1935), THE BIG BROADCAST OF 1937 (1936), A DAMSEL IN DISTRESS (1937), and HONOLULU (1939).

In 1950, Burns and Allen conquered the young television medium with a groundbreaking series, "The George Burns and Gracie Allen Show" (CBS 1950-58), a self-referential, mildly surreal domestic sitcom in which Burns would routinely break the fourth wall and address the audience, or occasionally turn on a television to "watch the show" and see what Gracie and the other cast-members were up to. The series lasted until 1958, when Allen retired due to a chronic heart condition.

Burns continued solo from October 1958 to April 1959 with "The George Burns Show" (NBC), and later tried to revive the format opposite Connie Stevens on "Wendy and Me" (ABC 1964-65). He also produced the series "The People's Choice" (NBC 1955-58), "The Bob Cummings Show" aka "Love That Bob" (CBS/NBC 1955-59), and "Mr. Ed" (syndicated/CBS 1961-65).

Following Allen's death in 1964, Burns retreated from the spotlight after "Wendy and Me" ended the following year. Ten years of relative seclusion ended in 1975 when his friend Jack Benny died shortly before he was to co-star with Walter Matthau in THE SUNSHINE BOYS (1975). Burns filled in—just six weeks after triple-bypass surgery—and his performance won him an Academy Award for Best Supporting Actor. His career revived at the age of 81, Burns went on to star in the films OH, GOD! (1977)—which spawned two sequels with Burns in 1980 and 1984—JUST YOU AND ME KID (1979), GOING IN STYLE (1980), and 18 AGAIN! (1988). In 1988, Burns was inducted into the Television Academy Hall of Fame, and in 1994 he was given the Screen Actors Guild Lifetime Achievement Award. At the age of 95, Burns became the oldest-ever Grammy award nominee with his spoken-word record *Gracie—A Love Story* , based on his 1988 book.

Burns, whose health had deteriorated since falling in a Las Vegas shower in July 1994, died in his sleep one hour after a doctor pronounced his heart "extremely weak."

Byers, Billy

aka: Bill Byers
born: May 1, 1927
died: May 1, 1996, Malibu, CA, age 69

Musical arranger for film, TV, and Broadway.

A musical prodigy who took up the piano at age six, Billy Byers was playing professionally at eight. He began his television career in the 1950s scoring Sid Caesar's "Your Show of Shows." A regular visitor to Paris, Byers wrote for radio orchestras there and taught Paul Newman to play the trombone for the movie PARIS BLUES (1961). Byers performed with and provided arrangements for Count Basie, Duke Ellington, Quincy Jones, Tony Bennett, Bing Crosby, Diana Ross, Frank Sinatra, Barbra Streisand, and Sarah Vaughn. He did orchestrations for Broadway musicals including *A Chorus Line* and *City of Angels* , and worked on TV shows and specials, winning nine Emmy Awards.

Byers served as composer or musical director on a variety of films including MOONCHILD aka FULL MOON (1972), THE STING and THE WAY WE WERE (1973), MAME (1974), WHITE LINE FEVER (1975), SAME TIME, NEXT YEAR (1978), SOPHIE'S CHOICE (1982), and JOSHUA THEN AND NOW (Canada 1985).

Byers died of cancer.

Caesar, Irving

born: July 4, 1895, New York (Lower East Side), NY
died: Dec. 17, 1996, New York, NY, age 101

Lyricist whose reported 2, 200 songs include "Swanee" (with composer George Gershwin) and "I Want to Be Happy" and "Tea for Two" (with Vincent Youmans).

Irving Caesar's venerable songs have appeared in many films, from the George Jessel musical LUCKY BOY (1929) to the drama ORPHANS (1987). Among his best-known compositions are "It's All So New to Me" (with Ted Koehler and Ray Henderson), from CURLY TOP (1935); "That's What I Want for Christmas" (with Gerald Marks), sung by Shirley Temple in STOWAWAY (1936); "Crazy Rhythm" (with Roger Wolfe Kahn and Joseph Meyer), from YOU WERE MEANT FOR ME (1948); and "I Want to Be Happy" and the title song from TEA FOR TWO (1950). Caesar owned his own publishing company in New York's Brill Building and gave breaks to many aspiring songwriters.

His cause of death was undisclosed.

Cain, Mary

born: July 4, 1916, Corpus Christi, TX; raised Hollywood, CA
died: March 30, 1996, Los Angeles, CA, age 79
educ: Hollywood High

Animation artist and pioneering proprietor of one of the industry's first independent paint-and-ink companies.

Mary Cain worked on the "Krazy Kat" cartoon series in the paint-and-ink department at Charles Mintz Studio, staying on as department supervisor after the studio was purchased by Columbia Pictures and renamed Screen Gems. While working there full-time, she also worked nights at UPA Studios, supervising their first project, "Hell Bent for Election" (1944), a United Auto Workers-sponsored campaign short promoting President Franklin Roosevelt. She began working full-time for UPA's paint-and-ink department, supervising the Academy Award-winning short "Gerald McBoing-Boing" and the "Mr. Magoo" series. She left in 1952 to open Mary Cain Ink and Paint, contracting with UPA and other animation studios. She closed shop in 1962 to supervise paint-and-ink at Playhouse Pictures, where she stayed until semi-retiring in 1991, after which she worked as an animation checker at her home until her death.

Cain died of cancer.

Cammell, Donald

born: c. 1934, Edinburgh, Scotland
died: April 24, 1996, Hollywood, CA, age 62
educ: Westminster School, London; Byam Shaw School of Art, London; Royal Academy School of Art, London

Screenwriter-director best known for co-directing the film PERFORMANCE (1970).

After graduating from the Royal Academy School of Art, Donald Cammell became a London "celebutante," painting portraits and presiding over glittery salons. He moved to Paris in 1961 to paint, but was drawn to film instead. After appearing as the "Boy at St. Tropez" in Eric Rohmer's LA COLLECTIONNEUSE (France 1967), he co-wrote the story and script for DUFFY (UK 1968). Cammell then secured a co-directorial slot alongside cinematographer-director Nicolas Roeg for PERFORMANCE by getting his friend Mick Jagger to agree to star; Cammell also wrote the script for the influential film of decadent 1960s counterculture.

Though the stylish film's immediate cult success led to Hollywood's beckon, Cammell was beset with aborted projects. He stayed busy writing screenplays, doctoring scripts, and directing music videos. Cammell directed DEMON SEED (1977); co-scripted TILT (1979); directed and co-scripted (with second wife China Kong Cammell) the novel adaptation WHITE OF THE EYE (UK 1987); and directed and co-scripted (with China Kong Cammell) WILD SIDE, a feature so reedited by production company NuImage that Cammell changed his director's credit to "Franklin Brauner."

He died of a self-inflicted bullet wound.

Campbell, Bruce Post

born: c. 1932
died: Nov. 3, 1996, La Crosse, WI, age 64

Producer of independent films and TV specials.

As a founding member of the production company Campbell-Silver-Cosby, Bruce Post Campbell produced Bill Cosby specials in the 1960s. His films included THE PICASSO SUMMER (1969) and JOHNNY GOT HIS GUN (1971), which won the Palme d'Or Peace Prize at the Cannes Film Festival.

Campbell died of a cerebral hemorrhage.

Carfagno, Edward C.

born: c. 1907, Los Angeles, CA
died: Dec. 28, 1996, Woodland Hills, CA, age 89
educ: University of Southern California

Three-time Academy Award-winning art director.

In a film career spanning five decades, Edward C. Carfagno garnered 13 Oscar nominations and worked on more than 70 films, including some of Hollywood's biggest spectacles. He and various collaborators shared Art Direction-Set Decoration Academy Awards for THE BAD AND THE BEAUTIFUL (1952), JULIUS CAESAR (1953) and BEN-HUR (1959). Carfagno, who spent 46 years at MGM, also worked on such films as THE BARKLEYS OF BROADWAY (1949), QUO VADIS (1951), THE LONG, LONG TRAILER (1954), TEA AND SYMPATHY (1956), THE WONDERFUL WORLD OF THE BROTHERS GRIMM (1962), VIVA LAS VEGAS (1964), THE CINCINNATI KID (1965), THE MAN WHO LOVED CAT DANCING and SOYLENT GREEN (1973), THE HINDENBURG (1975), DEMON SEED and LOOKING FOR MR. GOODBAR (1977), TIME AFTER TIME (1979), and ALL OF ME (1984). He worked with Clint Eastwood on eight films, including HONKYTONK MAN (1982), SUDDEN IMPACT (1983), PALE RIDER (1985), and HEARTBREAK RIDGE (1986).

No cause of death was reported.

Carlin, Edward

born: c. 1932, New York (The Bronx), NY
died: Oct. 24, 1996, Los Angeles, CA, age 64
educ: UCLA

International film marketer and producer, mostly of genre films.

After graduating from college, Edward Carlin worked as an art director under Millie Braverman. He later produced such pictures as BLOOD AND LACE (1971), MAMA'S DIRTY GIRLS (1974), THE NIGHT GOD SCREAMED aka SCREAM (1975), THE SWINGING BARMAIDS aka EAGER BEAVERS (1976), THE EVIL (1978), SUPERSTITION aka THE WITCH (filmed 1981, released 1985), and FAST FUN (1993). He was a founding member of the American Film Marketing Association and headed international sales for Roger Corman's Concorde-New Horizons and later for InterOcean, while continuing to work as a producer.

Carlin died of complications following a stroke.

Carne, Marcel

born: Aug. 18, 1906, Paris, France
died: Oct. 31, 1996, Paris, France, age 90

French director who embodied "poetic realism" in such films as LE JOUR SE LEVE (France 1939) and LES ENFANTS DU PARADIS (France 1945).

The son of an often absent cabinetmaker and a mother who died when he was five, Carne was raised largely by his grandmother and an aunt. He worked briefly as an insurance clerk while studying film at a technical school at night. Writing film criticism during his 20s, Carne became editor of the weekly periodical *Film-Hebdo* . Carne found work as assistant cameraman on Jacques Feyder's LES NOUVEAUX MESSIEURS (France 1928). He continued to work with Feyder on LE GRAND JEU (France 1933), PENSION MIMOSA (France 1934), and LA KERMESSE HEROIQUE (France 1935), and also served as Rene Clair's assistant director on SOUS LES TOITS DE PARIS/UNDER THE ROOFS OF PARIS (France 1930). During this period, Carne co-wrote and co-directed the short amateur documentary "Nogent—Eldorado du Dimanche" (France 1929; with Michel Sanvoisin), made several two-minute commercials for movie theaters, and wrote about film for French magazines. With Feyder's assistance, Carne directed his first feature, JENNY (France 1936), starring Feyder's wife, Francoise Rosay.

The following year, Carne teamed with poet and screenwriter Jacques Prevert on DROLE DE DRAME/BIZARRE BIZARRE (France 1937). The two would partner frequently, creating such well-regarded hits as QUAI DES BRUMES/PORT OF SHADOWS (France 1938), LE JOUR SE LEVE/DAYBREAK, LES VISITEURS DU SOIR/THE DEVIL'S ENVOYS (France 1942), LES ENFANTS DU PARADIS/CHILDREN OF PARADISE—one of the world's best-loved films—and LES PORTES DE LA NUIT/GATES OF THE NIGHT (France 1946; US release 1950). LES ENFANTS DU PARADIS, the most expensive French film at that time, was begun in 1943 and filmed under extremely difficult conditions during the German occupation. In 1948, Carne and Prevert went their separate ways after their film LA FLEUR DE L'AGE collapsed in mid-production.

Despite the success of Carne's LES TRICHEURS/THE CHEATERS (France 1958), the director found his lush studio style going out of fashion, a trend cemented in the late 1950s by the arrival of the French New Wave. His last fictional film was LA MERVEILLEUSE VISITE (France 1974; also co-script), and his last feature the documentary LA BIBLE (France 1976). In 1992, Carne found backing for an adaptation of Guy de Maupassant's short story "Mouche." Ten days into shooting, per various reports, either the director fell ill and backing was withdrawn, or funding problems forced a halt and the production company later went bankrupt.

Carne's other directing credits include the classic HOTEL DU NORD (France 1938) and LES JEUNES LOUPS/THE YOUNG WOLVES (France 1968); as director and co-writer, LA MARIE DU PORT (France 1950), JULIETTE OU LA CLE DES SONGES (France 1951), THERESE RAQUIN/THE ADULTERESS (France 1953), L'AIR DE PARIS (France 1954), LE PAYS D'OU JE VIENS (France 1956), TERRAIN VAGUE (France 1960), DU MOURON POUR LES PETITS OISEAUX (France 1963), TROIS CHAMBRES A MANHATTAN (France 1965), and LES ASSASSINS DE L'ORDRE (France 1971)

No cause of death was reported.

Casares, Maria

born: Maria Casares Quiroga, Nov. 21, 1922, Spain
died: Nov. 22, 1996, La Vergne, Charente region, France, age 74

Beautiful and acclaimed French theater and film actress, named "the last great tragedienne" by *Le Monde* magazine.

Maria Casares was the daughter of a Spanish lawyer turned senior official of the 1930s Spanish Republican government. She was 14 when General Francisco Franco crushed the Republic and Casares' father moved the family to France. By 20, she had become an acclaimed actress in her second language. From the 1950s to the '80s, she was a major figure in theater. She won France's National Theater Prize at age 68, and in 1993 played the title role in *King Lear* .

Casares debuted onscreen in Marcel Carne's legendary LES ENFANTS DU PARADIS/CHILDREN OF PARADISE (France 1945), playing Natalie, the neglected wife of the mime Baptiste. She also played the Princess in Jean Cocteau's films OPRHEE/ORPHEUS (France 1949) and LE TESTAMENT D'ORPHEE/THE TESTAMENT OF ORPHEUS (France 1959). Other films, all French, include the Cocteau-Robert Bresson collaboration LES DAMES DU BOIS DE BOULOGNE/LADIES OF THE PARK (1945); Christian-Jaques's LA CHARTREUSE DE PARME/THE CHARTERHOUSE OF PARMA (1948); L'ADIEU NU (1975); BLANCHE ET MARIE (1984); LA LECTRICE (1988); and DE SABLE ET DE SANG/SAND AND BLOOD (1989).

No cause of death was reported.

Chao Lei

born: Wang Yu-Min, c. 1928
died: June 24, 1996, Hong Kong, age 68

Popular 1950s and '60s Hong Kong star.

Within a few years after joining the Shaw Bros. studio in 1953, Chao Lei was a major box-office star both in Hong Kong and Taiwan. Leaving Shaw Bros. in 1963, the "Little Emperor" (so dubbed for his specialty playing imperial roles in period dramas) joined the Cathay studio. By the 1970s, however, he had reduced his film output in order to concentrate on a restaurant business in Taipei. Chao made a dozen films with director Li Han-Hsiang, among them the costume dramas THE KINGDOM and THE BEAUTY (Hong Kong 1958) and HSI SHIH (Hong Kong 1965). Among his reported 100-plus films, his US releases include: PAI-SHE CHUAN/MADAME WHITE SNAKE (Hong Kong; US release 1963), WU-HOU/EMPRESS WU (Hong Kong; US release 1965), and Li Han-Hsiang's YANG KWEI FEI/THE MAGNIFICENT CONCUBINE (Hong Kong; US release 1964) and CHIN NU YU HUN/THE ENCHANTING SHADOW (Hong Kong; US release 1965).

Chao, who was married to actress Shih Ying, died of pneumonia after a long history of lung problems.

Cherrill, Virginia

aka: Virginia Cherrill Martini
born: Apr. 12, 1908, near Carthage, IL
died: Nov. 14, 1996 Santa Barbara, CA, age 88

The blind flower girl of Chaplin's classic CITY LIGHTS (1931).

Although midwestern society girl Virginia Cherrill had no previous acting experience when Chaplin had her audition for the silent CITY LIGHTS, the legendary filmmaker found her portrayal of blindness convincing. Indeed, critics who praised the movie singled out her heartbreaking performance. Cherrill, who considered herself "no great shakes as an actress," was married to Cary Grant from 1933-35, and retired in 1937 upon marrying the ninth Earl of Jersey. As the Countess of Jersey, she did charity work in Britain during WWII. Later, she married war flying ace Florian Martini.

Cherrill's other films include THE BRAT, DELICIOUS, and GIRLS DEMAND EXCITEMENT (1931), CHARLIE CHAN'S GREATEST CASE, FAST WORKERS, LADIES MUST LOVE, and THE NUISANCE (1933), HE COULDN'T TAKE IT, MONEY MAD, and WHITE HEAT (1934), WHAT PRICE CRIME? (1935), LATE EXTRA (UK 1935), and TROUBLED WATERS (UK 1936).

No cause of death was reported.

Christine, Virginia

born: Virginia Kraft, March 5, 1920, Stanton, Iowa
died: July 24, 1996, Los Angeles (Brentwood), CA, age 76
educ: UCLA

Character actress of at least 50 films, who gained fame playing the Swedish-accented "Mrs. Olson" in Folger's coffee commercials.

At age 17, Virginia Christine moved to Los Angeles to study drama. In 1940, she married actor Fritz Feld (1900-93). Christine made her film debut in the Errol Flynn picture EDGE OF DARKNESS (1943), ironically as a Norwegian girl named Miss Olson. Along with other television work, she spent roughly 15 years (c. 1970-85) in the series of commercials as wise next-door neighbor Mrs. Olson, who could resolve any crisis with warm advice and hot coffee. Christine's hometown converted its water tower into the shape of a coffeepot in her honor.

Christine appeared in several prominent films, including MISSION TO MOSCOW (1943), THE KILLERS (1946), CYRANO DE BERGERAC (1950), HIGH NOON (1952), NOT AS A STRANGER (1955), INVASION OF THE BODY SNATCHERS (1956), THE SPIRIT OF ST. LOUIS (1957), JUDGMENT AT NUREMBERG (1961), 4 FOR TEXAS (1963), THE KILLERS (1964), BILLY THE KID VS. DRACULA (1966), and GUESS WHO'S COMING TO DINNER (1967), in which she played Katharine Hepburn's bigoted business partner.

Christine died of a heart ailment.

Clement, Rene

born: March 18, 1913, Bordeaux, France
died: March 17, 1996, Monte Carlo, age 82

France's leading director of the post-war period, whose movies twice took Oscars for Best Foreign Language Film.

Forced to abandon architectural studies at age 20 because of his father's death, Rene Clement, directed the animated short "Cesar chez les Gaulois" (1931) before going on to work as a cameraperson and assistant director in 1934. In 1936, he directed the short "Soigne ton Gauche" (1936), written by and starring future screen-comedy legend Jacques Tati, for whom Clement had worked as a gag writer. Clement spent several years (including 1939-40 with the French Army's film division) making documentary shorts. His first feature was the semidocumentary LA BATAILLE DU RAIL/BATTLE OF THE RAILS (1946).

After serving as a technical consultant on Jean Cocteau's LA BELLE ET LA BETE/BEAUTY AND THE BEAST (1946), Clement went on to direct and often write films noted for their keen naturalism and understanding of the human ability to survive and adapt. His neo-realistic AU-DELA DES GRILLES/LE MURA DI MALAPAGA/THE WALLS OF MALAPAGA (France-Italy 1949) and children-in-wartime drama LES JEUX INTERDITS/FORBIDDEN GAMES (1952; also co-script adaptation) won Academy Awards for Best Foreign Language Film. His later output was mixed, combining such successes as the historical drama GERVAISE (1956) and the scintillating crime thrillers PLEIN SOLEIL/LUST FOR EVIL/PURPLE NOON (France-Italy 1959; also co-script adaptation) and LE PASSAGER DE LA PLUIE/RIDER ON THE RAIN (France-Italy 1970) with bloated international coproductions like PARIS BRULE-T-IL?/IS PARIS BURNING? (France-US 1966), which included Gore Vidal and Francis Ford Coppola among its seven writers. His last film was LA BABY-SITTER (Italy-France-West Germany 1975; also co-script).

Clement, a member of the French Academy of Fine Arts since 1986, won top awards at Cannes, Venice, and many other film festivals, and received a 1984 French Cesar for lifetime achievement. His films, several of which he co-wrote or co-adapted, include LE PERE TRANQUILLE/MR. ORCHID (1946), LES MAUDITS/THE DAMNED (1947), LE CHATEAU DE VERRE (France-Italy 1950), MONSIEUR RIPOIS/KNAVE OF HEARTS/LOVERS HAPPY LOVERS/LOVER BOY (France-UK 1954), LA DIGA SUL PACIFICO/THIS ANGRY AGE/THE SEA WALL (France-Italy-US 1958), QUELLE JOIE DE VIVRE/CHE GIOIA VIVERE (France-Italy 1961), LE JOUR ET

L'HEURE/TODAY WE LIVE/THE DAY AND THE HOUR (France-Italy 1963), LES FELINS/THE LOVE CAGE/JOY HOUSE (1964), LA MAISON SOUS LES ARBRES/THE DEADLY TRAP (France-Italy-US 1971), and LA COURSE DU LIEVRE A TRAVERS LES CHAMPS/AND HOPE TO DIE (France-US 1972).

Clement died following heart trouble.

Cohn, Joan Perry

SEE Perry, Joan

Cohn, Joseph Judson aka J. J. Cohn

born: 1895
died: Jan. 12, 1996, Beverly Hills, CA, age 100

Producer, film executive, and a founding member of the Academy of Motion Pictures Arts and Sciences.

Joseph Judson Cohn joined New York City's Fox Film Company in 1915, working in the scenario and editing departments. Three years later, he joined the nascent Samuel Goldwyn Company as a cashier and purchasing agent. With Goldwyn's 1919 purchase of the Triangle Studio in Culver City, CA, Cohn headed west to serve as the company's business manager and later production manager—a post he continued to hold for 19 years after the 1924 merger that formed Metro-Goldwyn-Mayer. Cohn was promoted to MGM executive producer in 1937, and became the studio's vice president in 1948. Cohn joined the newly formed Academy in 1927. Among the films he personally produced are THE LAST GANGSTER and THE THIRTEENTH CHAIR (1937) and OUT WEST WITH THE HARDYS (1938).

No cause of death was reported.

Cohn, Robert

born: Sept. 6, 1920, Avon, NJ
died: May 27, 1996, Los Angeles, CA, age 75
educ: University of Michigan (BA)

Producer scion of the Columbia Pictures Cohn clan.

Robert Cohn—whose father Jack Cohn (1889-1956) and uncle Harry Cohn (1891-1958) co-founded Columbia Pictures—joined the family studio in 1938 as an assistant director. He later began as a producer with such Columbia films as ADVENTURES IN SILVERADO aka ABOVE ALL LAWS, BLACK EAGLE, and RUSTY LEADS THE WAY (1948), and KAZAN (1949). After MISSION OVER KOREA (1953), Cohn became a studio and production executive. He returned to producing with THE INTERNS (1962) and its sequel, THE NEW INTERNS (1964). Cohn's Columbia-produced documentary YOUNG AMERICANS was forced to forfeit its 1968 Academy Award for documentary after the Academy discovered Columbia had released the film briefly the year before.

Cohn died of heart failure.

Colbert, Claudette

born: Claudette Lily Chauchoin, Sept. 13, 1903, Paris, France; raised New York, NY
died: July 30, 1996, Barbados, age 92
educ: Washington Irving High School and the Art Students League, New York, NY

Legendary star of the 1930s and '40s, and the Oscar-winning leading lady of the classic comedy IT HAPPENED ONE NIGHT (1934).

Claudette Colbert immigrated to New York City at age six and, after graduation from high school, took classes at the Art Students League with the thought of becoming a dress designer. She became an actress when a meeting with playwright Anne Morrison at a party led to an invitation to a bit part in Morrison's *The Wild Wescotts* (1923), and worked steadily on Broadway throughout the 1920s. Colbert left the theater in 1929 to become a contract player for Paramount Pictures, then located in Astoria, Queens, NY. After a series of undistinguished films, she gained public attention in Ernst Lubitsch's THE SMILING LIEUTENANT (1931) and Cecil B. DeMille's THE SIGN OF THE CROSS (1932). In 1934, after Colbert balked at several studio assignments, Paramount "punished" her by loaning her out to then minor-player Columbia for the role of the spoiled, madcap heiress in IT HAPPENED ONE NIGHT. Though she had little hope for the film, the movie became a screwball comedy classic that swept the Academy Awards, winning five Oscars including Best Actress and Best Picture.

The film's great success turned Colbert from ingenue to star; she played the title role in DeMille's CLEOPATRA (1934) and was well-regarded in Universal's IMITATION OF LIFE (1934). She went on to acclaim in such films as THE GILDED LILY (1935), TOVARICH (1937), BLUEBEARD'S EIGHTH WIFE (1938), DRUMS ALONG THE MOHAWK (1939), BOOM TOWN (1940) THE PALM BEACH STORY (1942), SO PROUDLY WE HAIL (1943), and TOMORROW IS FOREVER (1946). She took Oscar nominations for the dramas PRIVATE WORLDS (1935) and SINCE YOU WENT AWAY (1944). By 1938, under the guidance of her manager-brother, Charles, Colbert was Hollywood's highest-paid star, reportedly earning more than $400,000 a year. When her Paramount contract expired, she went freelance at $150,000 a picture. Her last hit was the popular comedy THE EGG AND I (1947).

Colbert's film career waned in the 1950s, and she went overseas to film THE PLANTER'S WIFE/OUTPOST IN MALAYA (UK 1952), and DAUGHTERS OF DESTINY (France 1953). Colbert returned to theater in 1956, appearing in several plays up until 1985. The last of Colbert's more than 60 films was PARRISH (1961); her final screen appearance was in her only TV-movie, THE TWO MRS. GRENVILLES (NBC 1987). In 1984, Colbert received a lifetime achievement honor from the Film Society of Lincoln Center, and in 1989, she was honored at the Kennedy Center's annual Awards ceremony.

In 1928, she married Norman Foster, but they divorced in 1935. In December of that same year, she married Dr. Joel Pressman, who died in 1968.

Three years prior to her death, Colbert, who divided her time between her Manhattan apartment and her estate in Barbados, settled permanently in Barbados after suffering a stroke. Colbert died as a result of lingering ill health.

Condon, Richard

born: Richard Thomas Condon, March 18, 1915, New York, NY
died: April 9, 1996, Dallas, TX, age 81
educ: De Witt Clinton High School, New York, NY

Versatile novelist and scriptwriter who earned an Oscar nomination co-adapting his book *Prizzi's Honor* .

Richard Condon spent 22 years in movie publicity for nearly every major Hollywood studio before returning to New York and writing *The Oldest Confession* (1958), the first of his 26 novels. It was made into the Rita Hayworth-Rex Harrison picture THE HAPPY THIEVES (1962). The success of that book and his second, *The Manchurian Candidate* (1959)—the basis for the acclaimed 1962 John Frankenheimer film—allowed Condon to travel and write worldwide. He and his family lived in Mexico, Switzerland, and Ireland before Condon settled in Dallas in 1980. His 1974 novel *Winter Kills* was made into a 1979 movie. Condon and Janet Roach co-adapted his well-received 1982 mobster novel *Prizzi's Honor* , into the critical- and commercial-hit 1985 movie.

Condon died after having suffered a long illness that included kidney failure.

Cronenweth, Jordan

aka: Jordan S. Cronenweth
born: Feb. 20, 1935, Los Angeles, CA
died: Nov. 29, 1996, Los Angeles, CA, age 61
educ: North Hollywood High School; Los Angeles City College

Groundbreaking, highly respected cinematographer of BLADE RUNNER (1982).

Having previously acted onscreen in a juvenile role in CARBINE WILLIAMS (1952), Jordan Cronenweth briefly worked as a cameraman in Oklahoma before leaving college to pursue a film career. After serving as one of four cinematographers on Frank Perry's TRUMAN CAPOTE'S TRILOGY (1969), he served as co-cinematographer on Robert Altman's BREWSTER McCLOUD (1970). Cronenweth's first solo credits were on the Western COUNT YOUR BULLETS aka CRY FOR ME BILLY and PLAY IT AS IT LAYS (1972). He quickly came into his own with such films as ZANDY'S BRIDE and THE FRONT PAGE (1974). Though diagnosed with Parkinson's disease in 1978, Cronenweth went on to shoot ALTERED STATES (1980) and CUTTER'S WAY (1981), establishing a reputation as a director of photography who helped to redefine the language of cinematography. Although his work on the future-noir BLADE RUNNER helped make it a science-fiction classic and won him a British Academy Award, Cronenweth was never nominated for an Oscar. Other films include ROLLING THUNDER (1977), CITIZENS BAND (1977), BEST FRIENDS (1982), JUST BETWEEN FRIENDS (1986), PEGGY SUE GOT MARRIED (1986), GARDENS OF STONE (1987), RATTLE AND HUM (1988), STATE OF GRACE (1990), and FINAL ANALYSIS (1992)

Cronenweth died of Parkinson's disease.

Culhane, Shamus

born: James H. "Jimmy" Culhane, Nov. 12 1908, Ware, MA
died: Feb. 2, 1996, New York (Manhattan), NY, age 87
educ: P. S. 82 and Boy's High School, New York (Brooklyn), NY

Animator and animation director.

Determined to be an artist, James (Shamus) Culhane won medals for his drawings while still in elementary school. At 16 he took an office-boy job with Walter Lantz, who was then the head of animation for cartoon producer J. R. Bray. Culhane also worked for the Mintz and Fleischer Studios. His first full cartoon as an animator was "Swing, You Sinners" (1930). After stints with Ub Iwerks's Celebrity Productions, and the Van Beuren Studio, Culhane took a cut in pay and a demotion to do in-betweener work at Walt Disney Productions.

Following an apprenticeship with Bill Roberts and Ben Sharpsteen at Disney, Culhane was promoted to animator. Among his most notable work for Disney is the "Heigh Ho" musical sequence in SNOW WHITE AND THE SEVEN DWARFS (1937). While animating major character sequences in PINOCCHIO (1940), ill health prompted a move to Miami, FL, where Fleischer had relocated; there Culhane headed a unit that animated sections of the features GULLIVER'S TRAVELS (1939) and MR. BUG GOES TO TOWN (1941). He returned to Hollywood, where he worked a few months at Warner Bros. on Chuck Jones's "Inki" cartoons. He went on to the Walter Lantz studio to direct several "Silly Symphonies" shorts as well as some of the Woody Woodpecker cartoons.

He then formed Shamus Culhane Productions, which became a major player in TV-commercial animation. After the studio collapsed circa 1960, Culhane worked on TV animation. In November 1965, he was named head of Paramount's animation studio. Departing in 1967, Culhane went on to work on children's educational films and animated ABC specials. His first wife, Maxine Marx, was the daughter of Chico Marx.

No cause of death was reported.

Cummings Jr. , Irving

born: c. 1918
died: March 26, 1996, Van Nuys, CA, age 77

Writer-director-producer son of prolific actor-director Irving Cummings (1888-1959).

Irving Cummings Jr. co-wrote, with partner William Conselman Jr. , YESTERDAY'S HEROES (1940), THE LAST OF THE DUANES and RIDE, KELLY, RIDE (1941), LONE STAR RANGER (1942), and HE HIRED THE BOSS (1943), and went on to write or co-write with others DANGEROUS MILLIONS and DEADLINE FOR MURDER (1946) and JEWELS OF BRANDENBURG (1947). Turning to production, Cummings produced John Sturges's THE SIGN OF THE RAM (1948), WHERE DANGER LIVES (1950), and A GIRL IN EVERY PORT (1952). He both produced and directed DOUBLE DYNAMITE aka IT'S ONLY MONEY (1951), starring Frank Sinatra and Jane Russell. He went on to become a producer of the long-running boy-and-his-horse TV series "Fury" (NBC 1955-66).

Cummings died of cancer.

Dallas, Paul

born: c. 1962
died: August 3, 1996, Los Angeles, CA, age 34

Stuntperson.

Paul Dallas, whose credits include such major productions as STARGATE (1994) and BLOWN AWAY (1994), was fatally injured performing a stunt for the television series "L. A. Heat." Playing a character falling over a three-foot railing, Dallas hit the corner rather than the center of an airbag 50 feet below, deflecting him into a metal railing where he hit his head. His other movies include SISTER ACT 2: BACK IN THE HABIT (1993) and MAJOR PAYNE (1995), and the cable TV remake of NOT OF THIS EARTH (1995).

D'Arcy, Alex

aka: : Alexander Sarruf, Alexander Sarruf Efflatoun
born: 1908, Cairo, Egypt
died: April 20, 1996, West Hollywood, CA, age 87

Handsome veteran actor whose career spanned 15 countries and six decades.

Alex D'Arcy—whose best-known roles include Marilyn Monroe's "dream husband" in HOW TO MARRY A MILLIONAIRE (1953) and the amorous music teacher beaten up by Irene Dunne's jealous husband, Cary Grant, in the comedy THE AWFUL TRUTH (1937)—made his film debut in actor-director Rex Ingram's overseas-made silent, THE GARDEN OF ALLAH (1928). He went on to appear or star in a string of European films, including Alfred Hitchcock's silent CHAMPAGNE (UK 1928), A NOUS LA LIBERTE (France 1931), LA KERMESSE HEROIQUE/CARNIVAL IN FLANDERS (France 1935), and the historically interesting A ROMANCE OF SEVILLE (UK 1929), a very rare example of pre-1930's color photography. D'Arcy made his US film debut in STOLEN HOLIDAY (1937), and appeared prominently that same year in THE AWFUL TRUTH and THE PRISONER OF ZENDA. He went on to such films as ANOTHER THIN MAN, IRENE (1940), VICKI (1953), and LES CLANDESTINES/VICE DOLLS (France 1954; US release 1961), but then found himself relegated to lesser films. He played a spider monster in the horror film EIN TOTER HING IM NETZ/IT'S HOT IN PARADISE a. k. a. HOT IN PARADISE (Yugosalvia-West Germany; US release 1959) and a suburban Dracula in Al Adamson's BLOOD OF DRACULA'S CASTLE (1967). D'Arcy also appeared in Russ Meyer's FANNY HILL: MEMOIRS OF A WOMAN OF PLEASURE (US-West Germany 1965) and THE SEVEN MINUTES (1971) and Roger Corman's THE ST. VALENTINE'S DAY MASSACRE (1967). His final film was Samuel Fuller's DEAD PIGEON ON BEETHOVEN STREET (1972). He also guested on such TV series as "Batman" and "Voyage to the Bottom of the Sea." One of D'Arcy's many wives was 1930s leading lady Arleen Whelan.

D'Arcy, who remained active in cabaret, revues and theater, died of natural causes.

David, Saul

born: 1921, Springfield, MA
died: June 7, 1996, Culver City, CA, age 74
educ: Rhode Island School of Design

Producer and film executive.

Saul David, who attended college on an art scholarship and helped create a mural chosen for an exhibition at the 1939 New York World's Fair, worked for the military newspaper *Stars and Stripes* during WWII, and saw service in North Africa and Europe. In Cairo, he met future boss Oscar Dystel, who would later promote him to the editorship of Bantam Books. David went on to Hollywood in 1960, holding executive slots at Columbia, Warner Bros. , and 20th Century-Fox. During the 1970s, he worked at Universal, Rastar and MGM. David, who was instrumental in the careers of Burt Reynolds, Raquel Welch, and James Coburn, produced VON RYAN'S EXPRESS (1965), OUR MAN FLINT (1966) and its sequel , IN LIKE FLINT (1967), as well as FANTASTIC VOYAGE (1966), SKULLDUGGERY (1970), in which he also appeared in the bit part of Berle Tanen, and LOGAN'S RUN (1976). He also served as executive producer of RAVAGERS (1979). More recently, David taught in the Peter Stark Producing Program at USC while developing screenplays for Touchstone and Interscope.

David died of complications from congestive heart failure.

Dawson, Billy

born: William S. Dawson, c. 1926
died: April 1, 1996, age 69

American juvenile actor.

Billy Dawson played Knute Rockne at age 12 in KNUTE ROCKNE—ALL AMERICAN (1940), and starred in the remake of FATHER'S SON (1941), as a boy who fakes his own kidnapping to bring together his parents, who've separated because of his pranks. His films include HERE COMES MR. JORDAN and REMEMBER THE DAY (1941), THE MAJOR AND THE MINOR (1942), and LADY IN THE DARK (1944), LADIES MUST LIVE (1940), NOTHING BUT THE TRUTH (1941), and SWEET AND LOWDOWN (1944).

No cause of death was reported.

DeSantis, Pasqualino

aka: . Pasquale De Santis
born: April 24, 1927, Fondi, Italy
died: June 23, 1996, Lvov, Ukraine, age 69
educ: Center for Experimental Cinematography, Rome

Academy Award-winning cinematographer of Franco Zeffirelli's ROMEO AND JULIET (UK-Italy 1968).

Pasquale De Santis, known by the diminutive Pasqualino, began his film career in postwar Italy as an apprentice camera operator under Gianni Di Venanzo, a favored cinematographer of such directors as Fellini and De Sica. While De Santis did photograph the film UNDER THE OLIVE TREE (Italy 1950), in collaboration with his older brother, director Giuseppe De Santis, his first major work as cinematographer came when Di Venanzo took ill during the shooting of Francesco Rosi's MOMENT OF TRUTH (Italy 1965); De Santis succeeded him as director of photography. He went on to bring his expressionistic camerawork to most of Italy's major directors, on such films as Lucchino Visconti's LA CADUTA DEGLI EI/GOTTERDAMMERUNG/THE DAMNED (Italy-West Germany 1969; co-cinematographer) and MORTE A VENEZIA/DEATH IN VENICE (Italy 1971), Vittorio De Sica's ill-received GLI AMANTI/A PLACE FOR LOVERS (Italy-France 1968), Ettore Scola's UNA GIORNATA SPECIALE/A SPECIAL DAY (Italy-Canada 1977) and, with longtime friend and collaborator Rosi, C'ERA UNA VOLTA/MORE THAN A MIRACLE (Italy-France 1967), LUCKY LUCIANO (Italy-France-US 1974), CRISTO SI E FERMATO A EBOLI/CHRIST STOPPED AT EBOLI/EBOLI (Italy 1979), and TRE FRATELLI/THREE BROTHERS (Italy-France 1981). His American films include MISUNDERSTOOD (filmed 1982, released 1984) and SHEENA (1984).

De Santis, in recent years, also worked in television and in the theater, where he designed acclaimed sets for the 1992 stage version of the novel *La Signorina Papillon* . His last film was A MONTH BY THE LAKE (1995).

He died after suffering a heart attack while working on location with Rosi on a film with John Turturro, based on Primo Levi's autobiographical novel, *The Truce* .

Dibbs, Kem

born: c. 1917
died: March 28, 1996, Rancho Mirage, CA, age 78.

Actor who played TV's first Buck Rogers.

Stockbroker-turned-actor Kem Dibbs had small roles in major films and was the first of two men to play the title role of the seminal TV sci-fi series "Buck Rogers" (1950-51; succeeded by Robert Pastene). He made his movie debut in THE BIGAMIST (1953), and went on to roles in such films as SUDDENLY (1954), UNTAMED, HIGH SOCIETY, and ABBOTT AND COSTELLO MEET THE MUMMY (1955), THE TEN COMMANDMENTS and TERROR AT MIDNIGHT (1956), PATHS OF GLORY and THE LIFE, LOVES AND ADVENTURES OF OMAR KHAYYAM (1957), PARTY GIRL (1958), and FATE IS THE HUNTER (1964), his last film. He also guested on such TV fare as "Studio One," "Playhouse 90," and the series version of "Hallmark Hall of Fame."

No cause of death was reported.

Dilian, Irasema

born: c. 1924, Brazil
died: April 16, 1996, Ceprano, Italy, age 71

Leading lady of postwar Italian films.

Irasema Dilian was discovered by actor-director Vittorio De Sica and cast opposite him in his romantic comedy MADDALENA. . . ZERO IN CONDOTTA/MADDALENA, ZERO FOR CONDUCT (Italy 1940). She teamed with De Sica again in TERESA VENERDI aka. DOCTOR BEWARE (Italy 1941), playing one of three women with whom doctor De Sica is involved. Dilian was best-known for director Mario Mattoli's drama ORE 9: LEZIONE DI CHIMICA/SCHOOLGIRL DIARY (Italy 1941, US release 1947), Mario Soldati's MALOMBRA (Italy 1942), and Mario Camerini's LA FIGLIA DEL CAPITANO/THE CAPTAIN'S DAUGHTER (Italy 1947). She also played swashbuckling Rossano Brazzi's love interest in AQUILA NERA/RETURN OF THE BLACK EAGLE (Italy 1946, US release 1949), and starred in Luis Bunuel's ABISMOS DE PASION/CUMBRES ORRASCOSAS/WUTHERING HEIGHTS (Mexico 1953).

Dilian died of a heart attack.

Doleman, Guy

born: 1923, Australia or New Zealand (sources vary)
died: Jan. 30, 1996, Los Angeles, CA, age 72

Character actor with a 50-year career in radio, theater, TV, and film.

Guy Doleman worked in radio and appeared onstage in New Zealand before expanding to Australia, the UK and the US. He broke into film with such Aussie fare as ALWAYS ANOTHER DAWN (1948), THE KANGAROO KID (1950), and THE PHANTOM STOCKMAN (1953). He went on to work in mid-50s British films, a pair of American films—ON THE BEACH (1959) and CAPTAIN SINBAD (1963)—and a long run again in the UK. He played Major Ross in the three Michael Caine spy films based on Len Deighton's "Harry Palmer" novels, THE IPCRESS FILE (UK 1965), FUNERAL IN BERLIN (UK 1966), and BILLION DOLLAR BRAIN (UK 1967). Doleman had a small role as Colonel Lippe in the James Bond movie THUNDERBALL (UK 1965) and played the beekeeper in the horror film THE DEADLY BEES (UK 1967).

After staking his claim to cult immortality playing the role of "Number Two" in the first episode of the acclaimed TV series "The Prisoner" in 1968, Doleman concentrated on the small screen, guesting on such series as "Murder, She Wrote," "The Six Million Dollar Man," and the soap opera "General Hospital. " He also appeared in such telefilms as TAGGET (UK 1991), and in miniseries such as the "The Shiralee" (Australia 1988). His final films include A DANGEROUS SUMMER a. k. a. BURNING MAN (1981) and GOODBYE PARADISE (Australia 1983).

Doleman died of lung cancer.

Donovan, Terence

born: c. 1936
died: Nov. 22, 1996, London, England, age 60

Leading British fashion and society photographer, who also made music videos, TV commercials, and at least one feature film.

Terence Donovan was found hanged in his London studio; his family attributed the suicide to "a severe reaction to medication." In his career, he had photographed the world's top fashion models as well as such royals as Princess Diana. His work was a staple of major publications. Donovan produced and directed the spy drama YELLOW DOG (UK 1973).

Dostal, Zero

born: 1934, Czechoslovakia
died: Jan. 27, 1996, Prague, Czech Republic, age 62

Czech director and writer.

Zeno Dostal entered filmmaking in 1960 at Barrandov Film Studios in what was then Czechoslovakia. Prevented by the ruling Communist Party from making his own films, he served as an assistant director on reportedly 60 or so films, while also writing screenplays and novels. He directed his first film, KRAL KOLONAD/KING OF THE COLONNADE, in 1990, followed by the Czech telefilm VAHY/THE BALANCES. His third and final film was GOLET/THE GOLET IN THE VALLEY (Czech 1995). He had planned a sequel to it as his fourth film.

Dostal died of cancer.

Dru, Joanne

born: Joanne Letitia LaCock, Jan. 31, 1923, Logan, WV
died: Sept. 10, 1996, Beverly Hills, CA, age 73

Popular leading lady of the 1940s and '50s, best known as the co-star of classic John Ford and Howard Hawks westerns.

Joanne Dru had changed her last name to Marshall while a teen model in New York, where she and her mother had moved after the death of Dru's pharmacist father. She danced in the chorus of *Hold Onto Your Hats,* Al Jolson's last Broadway show, before marrying singer Dick Haymes in 1941. (They divorced in 1949.) Haymes brought her to Hollywood, where she was spotted by Hawks; she changed her name to Dru at the director's behest.

After making her film debut playing Rosemary Murphy in the critically reviled ABIE'S IRISH ROSE (1946), Dru made an auspicious second-chance breakthrough with her second film, co-starring with John Wayne and Montgomery Clift in Hawks's RED RIVER (1948). There, she met her second husband, actor John Ireland, whom she married in 1949.

Dru went on in quick succession to Ford's SHE WORE A YELLOW RIBBON (1949) and WAGONMASTER (1950), and to a plum role as the respectable girl turned Governor Willie Stark's mistress in Robert

Rossen's Academy Award-winning Best Picture ALL THE KING'S MEN (1949). Ireland, from whom Dru was divorced in 1956, also appeared in that film.

Dru starred in a string of lesser films through the 1950s, including MR. BELVEDERE RINGS THE BELL (1951), THE PRIDE OF ST. LOUIS (1952), the 3D western HANNAH LEE a. k. a. OUTLAW TERRITORY (directed by Ireland) (1953), THREE RING CIRCUS (1954), SINCERELY YOURS (1955), HELL ON FRISCO BAY (1956), THE LIGHT IN THE FOREST (1958), and the 3D romance SEPTEMBER STORM (1960).

Dru had appeared in many live TV-drama anthologies as "Playhouse 90" and"Studio 57" through the '50s. She went on to star in the dude-ranch sitcom "Guestward Ho!" (ABC 1960-61) and occasionally appeared afterward in such series as "The Green Hornet," "The Smith Family," and, in 1975, "Marcus Welby, M. D." her TV finale. Her last two films were SYLVIA (1965) and SUPER FUZZ a.k.a. SUPERSNOOPER (US-Italy 1981).

Dru, whose brother is TV game-show host Peter Marshall and whose nephew is baseball major-leaguer Pete LaCock, died of a respiratory illness.

Duckworth, Dortha

born: c. 1905, Newton, KS
died: Nov. 14, 1996, Camp Hill, PA, age 91

Veteran actress who came late to movies.

Dortha Duckworth, whose most prominent role may have been as Shirley Stoler's mother in the cult classic THE HONEYMOON KILLERS (1969), moved to New York to study acting in the 1920s. She made her Broadway debut in the farce *Goodbye Again* (1932), and appeared in many other Broadway shows as well as in Broadway road shows. She went on to appear in TV commercials, and in movies, including RACHEL, RACHEL (1968), PROTOCOL and NOTHING LASTS FOREVER (1984), MURPHY'S ROMANCE, THE MAN WITH ONE RED SHOE and THE ULTIMATE SOLUTION OF GRACE QUIGLEY a. k. a. GRACE QUIGLEY (1985), and STANLEY AND IRIS (1990).

Duckworth died at a nursing home after being in declining health for years.

Duras, Marguerite

born: April 4, 1914, Gia Dinh, French Indochina
died: March 4, 1996, Paris, France, age 81

Renowned playwright, filmmaker, and novelist.

Marguerite Duras was one of the consummate women of letters, a major figure in French and feminist culture, the writer of the Alain Resnais classic HIROSHIMA, MON AMOUR (France-Japan 1959), and the author of the best-selling, semiautobiographical novel *L'Amant/The Lover*. The daughter of teachers Henri and Marie Donnadieu, of France's colonial service, she changed her name to Duras in the 1930s. Raised in economic hardship after her father died when she was a child, Duras attended school in Saigon, then moved to France at age 18 to study law and political science.

Upon graduation, she worked as a secretary in the French Ministry of the Colonies until 1941 and Nazi occupation. Two years later, she joined the French Resistance in a group that included future French president Francois Mitterrand, who became a lifelong friend. Duras had married the writer Robert Antelme in 1939, but he was later arrested and deported to Dachau. When he returned in 1945, Duras was involved with Dionys Mascolo, who became her second husband and the father of her son, Jean.

Duras published her first book, *Les Impudents,* in 1943 and thereafter wrote professionally for more than 50 years, examining the mysteries of unsentimental love, sex and desire in more than 70 novels, plays, and screenplays. Her novels include *Sea Wall,* adapted by Irwin Shaw and Rene Clement for Clement's LA DIGA SUL PACIFICO/THIS ANGRY AGE (US-Italy-France 1958); *Moderato Cantabile,* which she co-adapted with Gerard Jarlot and Peter Brook for Brook's same-name, 1960 French-Italian film; *Le Marin de Gibraltar,* adapted by Tony Richardson, Christopher Isherwood, and Don Magner for Richardson's THE SAILOR FROM GIBRALTAR (UK 1967); and *L'Amant,* adapted by Gerard Brach and Jean-Jacques Annaud for Annaud's THE LOVER (France-UK 1992). She and Jules Dassin adapted one of her novellas for 10:30 P. M. SUMMER (US-Spain 1966), and with Jarlot, a short story for UNE AUSSI LONGUE ABSENCE/THE LONG ABSENCE (France-Italy; US release 1962).

After co-directing (with Paul Saban) the 1967 film adaptation of her play *La Musica,* Duras directed DETRUIRE, DIT-ELLE/DESTROY, SHE SAID (France 1969), based on her novel. She also wrote and directed LA FEMME DU GRANGE/WOMAN OF THE GRANGES (France 1964) and INDIA SONG (France 1975), which reworked events and characters from three of her novels. Her more experimental films include NATHALIE GRANGER (France 1972; also music composer), SON NOM DE VENISE DANS CALCUTTA DESERT (France 1976), which matched new images to the soundtrack of INDIA SONG, and LE CAMION (France 1977).

Duras, who for years struggled with emphysema, died at her home on the Left Bank's Rue St.-Benoit. No cause of death was reported.

Edelman, Herb

born: Nov. 5, 1930 or 1933 (sources vary), New York City (Brooklyn), NY
died: July 21, 1996, Woodland Hills, CA, age 62 or 65
educ: Brooklyn College (BA)

Tall, bald, New York character actor prolific in TV, film, and theater.

Herb Edelman studied acting at Brooklyn College, and through stints as a bellhop, cab driver, and NBC page, made his professional stage debut in 1961 with a touring company of *The Threepenny Opera.* A favorite of Neil Simon's, he appeared in both the 1963 Broadway production and the 1967 film version of *Barefoot in the Park,* as the wheezing telephone installer, and likewise did double duty with *The Odd Couple* (1965 play, 1968 film), playing Murray the Cop; he also appeared in Simon's film CALIFORNIA SUITE (1978).

After breaking into TV with a 1964 episode of "The Reporter, " he went on to make countless guest appearances in sitcoms and dramas. He was Emmy-nominated for his recurring guest role on "The Golden Girls," where he played Dorothy's (Beatrice Arthur) ex-husband Stan Zbornak. Edelman starred with Bob Denver in "The Good Guys" (1968-70), and also had recurring roles on several series including "Knots Landing" (during 1990-91 season).

Edelman's films include IN LIKE FLINT (1967), I LOVE YOU, ALICE B. TOKLAS! (1968), THE WAR BETWEEN MEN AND WOMEN (1972), THE WAY WE WERE (1973), THE FRONT PAGE (1974), THE YAKUZA (1975), and Jerry Lewis's CRACKING UP aka SMORGASBORD (1983). Telefilms include IN NAME ONLY (1969), THE NEON CEILING and BANYON (1971), CROSSFIRE (1975), and MARATHON (1980). One of his wives was "Days of Our Lives" star Louise Sorel, from 1964-70, and his companion at the time of his death was "St. Elsewhere" cast member Christina Pickles.

Edelman, who lived in Oxnard, CA, died of emphysema.

Edwards, Percy

born: June 1, 1908
died: June 8, 1996, age 88

British dean of vocal artists.

Percy Edwards spoke for the animals in countless films, TV shows, and commercials, vocalizing whales in ORCA (1977), dogs in THE PLAGUE DOGS (1982), reindeer in SANTA CLAUS (1985)—and the insectoid Alien in ALIEN (1979). Though his specialty was animal impersonation, Edwards also voiced made-up beasties in such animatronic and puppet films as THE DARK CRYSTAL (UK 1983), as the voice of Fizzgig, LABYRINTH (1986), as well as in the animated feature VALHALLA (1986). Edwards, who had a reported 600 voices in his repertoire, also appeared onscreen in the Peter Cook political comedy THE RISE AND RISE OF MICHAEL RIMMER (UK 1970)—playing a bird impersonator.

Edwards died in his sleep of unspecified causes.

Edwards, Vince

born: Vincent Edward Zoino (or Zoin; sources differ), July 9, 1928, New York City (Brooklyn), NY
died: March 11, 1996, Los Angeles, CA, age 67
educ: Ohio State University; University of Hawaii; American Academy of Dramatic Arts, New York, NY

TV's Ben Casey, and a featured actor in films ranging from Stanley Kubrick's THE KILLING (1956) to Roger Corman's SPACE RAIDERS (1983).

After college and acting school, Vince Edwards made his Broadway debut in the musical *High Button Shoes* (1947). He broke into movies with MR. UNIVERSE and SAILOR BEWARE (1951), and into television with such anthology dramas as the "Ford Theater" production "Garrity's Sons" (3/24/55). His dark, brooding, square-jawed good looks landed him leading-man roles in such features as HIAWATHA (1952), MURDER BY CONTRACT (1958), THE SCAVENGERS aka CITY OF SIN (US-Philippines 1959), and CITY OF FEAR (1959).

Edwards played the title role in the gritty, humanistic TV hospital drama "Ben Casey" (1961-66), directing a dozen episodes. At the height of his TV stardom, Edwards recorded six albums, and headlined in Las Vegas, Reno, New York City, and Los Angeles. He went on to the series "Matt Lincoln" (1970-71), about a hip young psychiatrist, then appeared mostly in telefilms—beginning with SOLE SURVIVOR (1970) and including EVENING IN BYZANTIUM (1978) and THE DIRTY DOZEN: THE DEADLY MISSION (1987), as well as the miniseries "The Rhinemann Exchange."(1977). He became an established TV director, helming episodes of such series as "Police Story, " "Fantasy Island," "Medical Story," and "The Fall Guy." Edwards once again played Ben Casey in the telefilm THE RETURN OF BEN CASEY (1988).

Edwards's later film work includes such marginal films such as RETURN TO HORROR HIGH (1987), CELLAR DWELLER (1988), and INVASION OF THE SPACE PREACHERS (1992).

Edwards died of pancreatic cancer.

Elder III, Lonnie

born: c. 1926 or Dec. 31, 1931 (sources vary), Americus, GA
died: June 11, 1996, Woodland Hills, CA, age 64 or 69
educ: Yale (filmmaking)

Acclaimed African-American playwright and screenwriter.

Lonne Elder III moved during childhood to Jersey City, NJ, to live with an aunt and uncle after the death of his parents. At age 19, living in Harlem, he entered the theater as an actor, appearing on Broadway in the original production of Lorraine Hansberry's *A Raisin in the Sun.*

Writing poems and stories led to his first and most prominent play, which began its production life in 1965 as a workshop reading at the New Dramatists Committee. When the Negro Ensemble Company was founded in 1967, Elder was named head of the playwrights' unit. *Ceremonies in Dark Old Men* In 1969, the play moved from its NEC production to an extended off-Broadway run. In 1969 also, Elder married actress Judyann Johnson; the following year they moved to Los Angeles.

There, Elder began his film career with Martin Ritt's SOUNDER (1972), a drama of sharecroppers during the Depression. Elder received an Academy Award nomination for Adapted Screenplay. He also wrote the script adaptation for the crime drama MELINDA (1972), in which he and his wife also played small acting roles, and SOUNDER, PART 2 (1976). Elder and Richard Pryor provided the story basis for the Pryor vehicle BUSTIN' LOOSE (1981). His TV work includes adapting the Marcy Hardish novel *A Woman Called Moses* into the acclaimed 1978 telefilm, and scripting for TV series including "McCloud. " In 1988, Elder returned to off-Broadway with the monodrama *Splendid Mummer,* starring Charles S. Dutton. In 1990, Elder was brought in to rewrite the book for *King,* a musical about Martin Luther King Jr. , produced in London.

Elder died after what former wife Johnson described as "a chronic illness."

Endo, Shusaku

born: c. 1923, Tokyo; raised China
died: Sept. 29, 1996, Tokyo, age 73
educ: Keio University, Tokyo (French literature); University of Lyon, France

Japanese author.

Novelist Shusaku Endo, who won virtually every major Japanese literary award, was an internationally known writer of literary novels, religious-themed plays, and humor. Raised in China but returning to Japan in 1933 with his mother after his parents were divorced, Endo was kept from WWII military service due to ill health. In 1950, he became one of the first Japanese to study abroad after the war. Returning to Japan, he published the Akutagawa Prize-winning novel *Shiroi Hito/White Man* (1955). Other novels include *Umi to Dokuyaku* (1957), published in English as *The Sea and Poison* (1972), and *Chimmoku* (1966), published in English as *Silence* (1969). He wrote the story for, and made a cameo appearance in, WATASHI GA SUTETA ONNA/THE GIRL I ABANDONED (Japan; US release 1970).

Endo died of respiratory complications caused by hepatitis.

Everson, William K.

born: April 8, 1929, Yeovil, Somerset, UK
died: April 14, 1996, New York City (Manhattan), NY, age 67

Renowned film historian, teacher, author, and preservationist.

In the era before home video, film scholar William K. Everson amassed a collection of more than 4,000 often lost or neglected feature films—many of them, particularly from the 1920s and '30s, literally rescued from the trash bin—and held important salon screenings for cineastes that included such fledgling filmmakers and critics as Stanley Kubrick, Lindsay Anderson, Bertrand Tavernier, Leonard Maltin, Andrew Sarris, Molly Haskell, and Peter Bogdanovich. Hundreds of his films are unavailable in any other archive. His nearly 20 books include *American Silent Film, The American Movie, The Films of Laurel and Hardy, The Western: From Silents to Cinerama* (with George N. Fenin), *The Bad Guys,* and *The Art of W. C. Fields.*

While still a teen in his native England, Everson began as a publicist for Renown Pictures, a distributor of old British films. He also ran film societies, wrote criticism, and helped found the London Regional Group of the Federation of Film Societies. After immigrating to the US in 1950, he became a publicist for independent film distributors for five years. Around that time, he helped organize the Theodore Huff Society, which presented public screenings of classic films, and from 1958 to 1995 continued to do so at Greenwich Village's New School for Social Research. Everson wrote, edited, and did research for the local New York TV series "Movie Museum" and for the Ernie Kovacs-hosted "Silents, Please" (1960-62). He also was involved with such TV specials as "Hollywood, the Golden Years," "The Legend of Valentino," and "The Great Director," a documentary about D. W. Griffith. Everson presented screenings at New York City's School of Visual Arts from the mid-1960s to 1984, and in 1968 was given a tenured position as professor of cinema studies at New York University. From 1977 to 1987, he was a co-director of the Telluride Film Festival in Colorado.

Everson died of prostate cancer.

Fabregas, Manolo

born: Manuel Sanchez Navarro, c. 1920
died: Feb. 4, 1996, Mexico City, Mexico, age 75

Actor, producer, and director.

Manolo Fabregas, who appeared in more than 60 mostly Spanish-language films, was a third-generation member of well-known theatrical family. He founded his own acting company in 1948, adopting the surname of his grandmother, Virginia Fabregas, a famous actress in Mexico and Spain. His films as actor include AVENTURERA (1950; US release 1995), CAPTAIN SCARLETT (1953), THE CANDY MAN (1969), TWO MULES FOR SISTER SARA (1970), and such Mexican films as ARRABALERA, LAGUNILLA MI BARRIO, LA MUJER LEGITIMA, and BANDERA ROTA, HISTORIA DE UN CRIMEN.

Fabregas died of a heart attack.

Factor Jr. , Max

born: 1908, St. Louis, MO
died: June 7, 1996, West Los Angeles, CA, age 87 or 88

Makeup mogul whose products were a staple of stars and movies.

Max Factor Jr. , scion of a father who had been the personal cosmetician to Russia's royal family, collaborated with his father to create brands of makeup that were first used in the film industry and later adopted by regular consumers. As a young chemist, Factor Jr. began in the cosmetics business with his father during the silent film era. After his father's death in 1938, Factor Jr. ran the established Max Factor Company, and is credited with inventing Tru-Color lipstick, a landmark in the cosmetics trade because it did not smear. Lana Turner, Rita Hayworth, and Marlene Dietrich were among the actresses who used Max Factor cosmetics both on and off the screen.

No cause of death was reported.

Fielding, Lisabeth

aka: Lisabeth Fielding Field
born: c. 1923
died: April 13, 1996, Hollywood Hills, CA, age 72
Actress in film, TV and theater.

Field guested on numerous TV series, from "The Loretta Young Show," "77 Sunset Strip," "Maverick," and "The Invaders" in the 1960s to "Mannix," "Longstreet," and "Police Woman" in the '70s. Her stage work includes *Springtime for Henry* with Edward Everett Horton, *The Rainmaker,* and *Pygmalion.* Her handful of feature films include FOX-FIRE (1955).

Fielding died of heart disease.

Finn, Lila

born: Lila Shanley, Nov. 28, 1909, Los Angeles, CA
died: Nov. 15, 1996, Santa Monica, CA, age 86
Pioneering cinema stuntwoman.

Lila Shanley Finn, the founding president of the Stunt Woman's Association and a founding member of the Screen Actors Guild (SAG), was a member of the US women's volleyball team from 1959-60, winning a silver medal in the Pan-American Games in Chicago—at age 50. She doubled in reportedly more than 100 films over six decades, including such landmark work as stunt doubling for Vivien Leigh in GONE WITH THE WIND (1939), Donna Reed in IT'S A WONDERFUL LIFE (1946), and Dorothy Lamour in THE HURRICANE (1937). She appeared in onscreen bit parts in such films as SCARLET ANGEL (1952), INCIDENT IN AN ALLEY aka LINE OF DUTY (1962), DRUM (1976), ROBOCOP 2 (1990), and THE ROCKETEER (1991). Finn, remarkably, continued to do stunts through the 1980s and '90s in such films as PREDATOR (1987), the NAKED GUN trio (1988-94), and TRUE LIES (1994). She was recognized with a lifetime achievement award from Women in Film in 1993.

Finn died of heart failure.

Fitch, Louise

aka: Louise Lewis
born: c. 1915
died: Sept. 11, 1996, Venice, CA, age 81
Veteran actress blacklisted during the McCarthy era.

Louise Fitch performed in Chicago radio in the 1930s before moving to New York City to act in early live-TV dramas. She was blacklisted as a purported Communist in 1953, and worked only sporadically the next 10 years. As Louise Lewis, her married name, she starred in the horror film BLOOD OF DRACULA (1957), and played supporting roles in that same year's I WAS A TEENAGE WEREWOLF and THE VAMPIRE aka MARK OF THE VAMPIRE. She also guested on several TV series. As Louise Fitch, she appeared in the John Cassavetes film OPENING NIGHT (1977), as well as in TRUE CONFESSIONS (1981) and the direct-to-video feature THE SOFT KILL (1994).

Fitch died of natural causes.

Fitzgerald, Ella

born: April 25, 1917, Newport News, VA
died: June 15, 1996, Beverly Hills, CA, age 79
America's legendary "First Lady of Jazz," who appeared in a handful of films.

Ella Fitzgerald's common-law parents, William and Temperance Williams Fitzgerald, were separated within a year of her birth. (Most sources list 1918 as her birth year, but her birth certificate and school records both give 1917.) When her mother died suddenly in 1932, Fitzgerald went to live with an aunt in Harlem. After winning the $25 first prize at the Apollo Theater amateur-night contest on Nov. 21, 1934, Fitzgerald soon went on to sing with the band of drummer-bandleader Chick Webb, who became her legal guardian. She and Webb shortly thereafter starred in the NBC radio show "The Good Time Society," and Webb's music group broke a color barrier by becoming the first African-American band to play at major venues and hotel ballrooms in Boston and New York City. After making her first recording in 1935 ("Love and Kisses," with Webb), Fitzgerald scored a million-selling record and world fame with "A-Tisket, a-Tasket" (1938), which she helped write and which became one of her standards. When Webb died the following year, she took over the band and renamed it Ella Fitzgerald and Her Famous Orchestra. Her singing career continued as a major critical and commercial force in music through more than 250 albums, over a dozen Grammy Awards, and accolades including a 1979 Kennedy Center honor and a 1987 National Medal of Arts. She performed regularly on TV variety shows, and appeared in two specials with Frank Sinatra and one with Duke Ellington.

In the Abbott and Costello comedy RIDE 'EM, COWBOY (1942), Fitzgerald, as singer Ruby, performs numbers including "A-Tisket, a-Tasket. " As Maggie Jackson in PETE KELLY'S BLUES (1955), she sings the title song and "Hard-Hearted Hannah," and does a small supporting turn. Fitzgerald played herself in the W. C. Handy biopic ST. LOUIS BLUES (1958), and essayed a straight dramatic supporting role in the drama LET NO MAN WRITE MY EPITAPH (1960). Most unusually, perhaps, she provided the "Voice of Ella Fitzgerald" in the French-Italian-Yugoslavian-West German coproduction ONKEL TOMS HUTTE/UNCLE TOM'S CABIN (1969).

Fitzgerald had cataract surgery in 1971, open-heart surgery in 1968, and—continually plagued thereafter by illnesses including diabetes and related eyesight and circulatory-system complications—had her legs amputated below the knees in 1993.

No specific cause of death was reported.

Forbes, Brenda

born: Jan. 14, 1909, London, England
died: Sept. 11, 1996, New York City (Manhattan), NY, age 87
Film and stage character actress.

Brenda Forbes's mother, Mary Forbes, was an actress and her brother, Ralph Forbes, an actor; Brenda joined the family business onstage at the Old Vic in 1927. She left England as a teen to join her mother in Hollywood, where Brenda performed onstage at the Vine Street Theater before being spotted for the Broadway play *The Barretts of Wimpole Street* (1931). She made the part of Wilson, Elizabeth Barrett's loyal maid, her signature role, going on to tour in the play and to return in the 1945 revival. Her Broadway plays include *Pride and Prejudice* , *Storm Over Patsy* , *Heartbreak House* , *Ring Around the Moon* and *Quadrille* (with the Lunts). Forbes also appeared in such plays as *The Reluctant Debutante* , *The Loves of Cass McGuire* (with Ruth Gordon) and *The Constant Wife* (with Ingrid Bergman), and played Mrs. Higgins in the 1976 Broadway revival of *My Fair Lady* . As a performer in revues—such as three Nancy Hamilton works she did on Broadway, including *Three to Make Ready* —Forbes was compared to Beatrice Lillie and Fanny Brice.

Forbes's films include THE PERFECT GENTLEMAN aka THE IMPERFECT LADY (1935), VIGIL IN THE NIGHT (1940), THIS ABOVE ALL, and Academy Award-winning Best Picture MRS. MINIVER (1942), playing Gladys, the Housemaid, and THE WHITE CLIFFS OF DOVER (1944). She also appeared in three telefilms with Katharine Hepburn: MRS. DELAFIELD WANTS TO MARRY (1986), LAURA LANSING SLEPT HERE (1988), and THE MAN UPSTAIRS (1992).

Forbes died of cancer.

Fox, Michael

born: c. 1921, Yonkers, NY
died: June 8, 1996, Los Angeles, CA, age 75
Prolific TV and film actor, and the reason actor Michael J. Fox added the middle initial to his official Screen Actors Guild name.

Michael Fox—who had an eight-year stint as Saul Feinberg on the CBS soap opera "The Bold and the Beautiful"—appeared on Broadway in *The Story of Mary Surratt* (1947), opposite Dorothy Gish. He became a contract player with Columbia and Warner Bros. , and made his film debut in 1952, with LAST TRAIN FROM BOMBAY and VOODOO TIGER. Fox played support in such movies as MACHINE GUN KELLY (1958), THE INTERNS and WHATEVER HAPPENED TO BABY JANE? (1962), BILLIE (1965), THE DUNWICH HORROR (1970), BLOODY MAMA (1970), QUICKSILVER (1986), OVER THE TOP (1987), and SKINHEADS—THE SECOND COMING OF HATE (1990), his last film. Fox's extensive TV credits range from the 1960s "Perry Mason" to "Cagney & Lacey," "E. R. ," and "N. Y. P. D. Blue." His at least three dozen films include several horror and sci-fi movies, in which he often played prominent roles as scientists and authorities. Among them: THE MAGNETIC MONSTER and THE BEAST FROM 20,000 FATHOMS (1953), GOG and RIDERS TO THE STARS (1954), CONQUEST OF SPACE (1955), and WAR OF THE SATELLITES (1958). Fox also was the founder of the actors organization, Theater East.

Fox died of complications from pneumonia.

Frankel, Mark

born: June 13, 1962, London, England
died: Sept. 24, 1996, London, England, age 34

Up-and-coming leading man who died of injuries from a motorcycle accident.

Mark Frankel played professional tennis during his college years, then landed his first professional stage role in *Days of Cavafy.* Spotted by TV director Jerry London, Frankel was cast as the title star of the six-hour miniseries MICHELANGELO—A SEASON OF GIANTS (TNT 1991). He co-starred opposite Julia Ormond and Vanessa Redgrave in the historical-drama telefilm YOUNG CATHERINE (TNT 1991), and appeared in several BBC productions including "Vanity Dies Hard" and "Maigret." Frankel made his film debut in the comedy LEON THE PIG FARMER (UK 1992), and went on to the British feature SOLITAIRE FOR TWO (1994). Frankel also co-starred in the short-lived Fox TV series "Kindred: The Embraced."

Friedman, Stephen

aka: Stephen J. Friedman
born: March 15, 1937, New York City (Brooklyn), NY
died: Oct. 4, 1996, Brentwood, CA, age 59
educ: Midwood High School, Brooklyn; Wharton School at the University of Pennsylvania; Harvard University (law)

Producer.

Stephen Friedman, whose debut film as a producer was Peter Bogdanovich's acclaimed THE LAST PICTURE SHOW (1971), was an entertainment lawyer for the Paramount and Columbia studios and the Ashley Famous talent agency, the precursor of International Creative Management (ICM). Intent on producing, he acquired the rights to the Larry McMurtry novel *The Last Picture Show,* the movie of which went on to earn eight Academy Award nominations, including best picture. He stumbled with his next film, both writing and producing the Sidney Lumet-directed LOVIN' MOLLY aka THE WILD AND THE SWEET (1974), an adaptation of McMurtry's *Leaving Cheyenne* ; the novelist disavowed the film. Friedman went on to produce such notable films as SLAP SHOT (1977), LITTLE DARLINGS (1980), EYE OF THE NEEDLE (1981), ALL OF ME (1984), ENEMY MINE (1985), and THE BIG EASY (1987). From 1984, most were under his Kings Road Entertainment banner. He served as executive producer of THE INCUBUS (Canada 1982), as Stephen J. Friedman; as a producer, he used his middle initial only once, on the direct-to-video KICKBOXER 4: THE AGGRESSOR (1994).

Friedman died of multiple myeloma.

Fulci, Lucio

aka: Louis Fulci
born: 1927
died: March 13, 1996, Rome, Italy, age 68
educ: Centro Sperimentale di Cinematografia, Rome, Italy

Influential, cult-favorite Italian exploitation director best-known as the helmer of some of his country's most flamboyantly gory films.

After fighting with the partisans in WWII, then studying at film school, Lucio Fulci made documentaries and worked on scripts before directing his first feature, THE THIEVES (Italy 1959), starring the popular comedian Toto. Through the 1960s, Fulci went on to make such comedies as AGENTI SEGRETISSIMI/OH THOSE MOST SECRET AGENTS aka 00-2 MOST SECRET AGENTS (Italy; US release 1965; also co-script), DOS COSMONAUTAS A LA FUERZA (Spain-Italy; US release 1967), OPERAZIONE SAN PIETRO/OPERATION ST. PETER'S (Italy 1968; also co-script), starring Edward G. Robinson; and a musical, URLATORI ALLA SBARRA (Italy 1960). A genre director who followed the trends, Fulci directed the spaghetti westerns TEMPO DI MASSACRO (Italy 1967), THE BRUTE AND THE BEAST (Italy 1968; co-director with Terry Vantell), and SILVER SADDLE (1978), and such hardboiled *gialli* as UNA LUCERTOLA CON LA PELLE DI DONNA/A LIZARD IN A WOMAN'S SKIN (Italy 1971).

Such Fulci thrillers as UNA SULL'ALTRA/ONE ON TOP OF THE OTHER (Italy 1969) and NON SI SEVIZIA UN PAPERINO/DON'T TORTURE A DUCKLING (Italy 1972) led to the first of his seminal Italian gorefests—among the first to break certain boundaries in the highly stylized Italian horror/thriller arena. Though a mediocre director at best, Fulci became highly influential worldwide due to his stunningly stylish and trailblazingly graphic moments in such works as the parodic IL CAV. COSTANTE NICOSIA DEMONIACO OVVERO: DRACULA IN BRIANZA (Italy 1975) and SETTE NOTE IN NERO/THE PSYCHIC (Italy 1977; US release 1979; also co-script), with American actress Jennifer O'Neill.

His breakthrough came with ZOMBI 2/ZOMBIE 2 aka ZOMBIE FLESH EATERS

(Italy 1979; US release 1980), which was shadily distributed in Italy as a purported sequel to George Romero's DAWN OF THE DEAD (1978), which had played in that country as ZOMBI. Fulci followed up with three more zombiefests: PAURA NELLA CITTA DEI MORTI VIVENTI/THE GATES OF HELL aka TWILIGHT OF THE DEAD aka CITY OF THE DEAD (US-Italy 1980; US release 1983; also co-writer); L'ALDILA/THE BEYOND (Italy 1981), considered his high-watermark; and QUELLA VILLA ACCANTO AL CIMITERO/THE HOUSE BY THE CEMETERY (Italy 1981; US release 1984; also co-script).

Fulci continued to work in genres as diverse and as blended as sword-and-sorcery, science fiction, and *gialli* -meets-FLASHDANCE. His films include the Poe adaptation THE BLACK CAT (Italy-UK 1981; US release 1984; also co-script), MANHATTAN BABY aka POSSESSED (Italy 1982; US release 1986), LO SQUARTATORE DI NEW YORK/THE NEW YORK RIPPER (Italy 1982), CONQUEST (Italy-Spain-Mexico 1983; US release 1984), and IL MIELE DE DIAVOLO/THE DEVIL'S HONEY (Italy 1986). Fulci played himself in the post-modern, self-critique horror-fiction UN GATTO NEL CERVELLO/NIGHTMARE CONCERT (Italy 1990). As Louis Fulci, he served as an associate producer on American actor David Keith's directorial debut, THE CURSE aka THE FARM (1987).

With his health failing due to a long battle with severe diabetes, Fulci's planned return to zombiedom with ZOMBI 3 (Italy 1988) was compromised by the need to replace him (with Bruno Mattei) during production. In 1995, Fulci began work on LA MASCHERA DI CERA/WAX MASK, a remake of MYSTERY OF THE WAX MUSEUM (1933) and HOUSE OF WAX (1953), but he died days before principal photography was to begin.

Gale, June

SEE Levant, June

Garson, Greer

born: Sept. 29, 1903, County Down, Ireland; raised London, England
died: April 6, 1996, Dallas, TX, age 92
educ: University of London; University of Grenoble (France)

Nobly beautiful, Oscar-winning star of MRS. MINIVER.

Greer Garson won the Academy Award for best actress for the wartime family drama MRS. MINIVER (1942), and earned six other Oscar nominations, including supporting-actress for her first film, GOODBYE, MR. CHIPS (US-UK 1939).

After her father died when she was a year old, Garson was raised in London. She graduated from university there, then studied abroad, intending to become a teacher. Instead, she worked at an advertising agency and performed in amateur dramatics before making her professional debut at the Birmingham Repertory Theatre in *Street Scene* (1932). She made her London debut during the 1934 season, and was subsequently commissioned by Laurence Olivier to understudy for and later play the lead in *Golden Arrow.* This led to starring roles in West End productions. Visiting MGM studio head Louis B. Mayer spotted her in a production and signed her to a contract.

Immediately popular with her 1939 debut feature GOODBYE MR. CHIPS (for which she was nominated for a Best Actress Oscar), Garson headlined several films, before etching her signature in the title role of MRS. MINIVER (1942). That year's Oscar-winning picture, MRS. MINIVER won seven Academy Awards in all, and is credited as having contributed much to American wartime morale. Garson went on to appear in several other films opposite MINIVER husband Walter Pidgeon, including the dud sequel THE MINIVER STORY (1950). In 1943, the fortyish Garson (who had divorced first husband Abbot Slenson, a British civil servant, in 1937) married her MRS. MINIVER son, 26-year-old Richard Ney; they divorced in 1947.

With the retirement of Greta Garbo and Norma Shearer, Garson landed most of MGM's plum women's roles. A string of hit films followed: RANDOM HARVEST (1942), MADAME CURIE (1943), MRS. PARK-

INGTON (1944), THE VALLEY OF DECISION (1945); she received Oscar nominations for the last three. ADVENTURE (1946), Clark Gable's first film after returning from the service, is chiefly remembered for the famous promo line "Gable's back and Garson's got him."

After a succession of flops, MGM dropped her contract in 1954. By then, however, Garson had been married for five years to Texas oil and real-estate magnate Elijah E. (Buddy) Fogelson (d. 1987), and Garson happily went into semi-retirement. However, she earned one last Oscar nomination with her "return" film SUNRISE AT CAMPOBELLO (1960), in which she played Eleanor Roosevelt. But after small roles in PEPE (1960), THE SINGING NUN (1966), and the Disney vehicle THE HAPPIEST MILLIONAIRE (1967), Garson left the big screen for good.

Her television career began with the "Producers Showcase" production of "Reunion in Vienna" (NBC 4/4/55) and included appearances in other dramatic anthology series. By chance, she guest-starred in one episodic series per decade: "Father Knows Best" in 1960, "The Men from Shiloh" in 1970, and "The Love Boat" in 1982. Garson hosted the PBS series "The Pallisers" (1977), narrated the animated specials "The Little Drummer Boy" (1971) and "The Little Drummer Boy, Book II" (1976), and played Kathryn March in LITTLE WOMEN (1978), her only telefilm. Onstage, she succeeded Rosalind Russell in Broadway's *Auntie Mame* in 1958. Her other films include THAT FORSYTE WOMAN (1949) and JULIUS CAESAR and SCANDAL AT SCOURIE (1953).

Garson, who had a long history of heart trouble, suffering a heart attack in 1980 and undergoing quadruple-bypass surgery in 1988, died of heart failure.

Gates, Larry

born: Sept. 24, 1915, St. Paul, MN
died: Dec. 12, 1996, Sharon, CT, age 81
educ: University of Minnesota (chemical engineering)

Five-decade stage and screen character actor.

Larry Gates, whose work in TV's "The Guiding Light" won the 1984/85 Daytime Emmy Award for supporting actor, was considered an "actor's actor," admired by his peers and theatergoers for his versatility. After appearing in college productions, he came to New York in 1938 and made his Broadway debut a year later in *Speak of the Devil*. After WWII Army service, he returned to tour with the Margaret Webster Shakespeare Company. In 1951, he appeared in Broadway's *Bell, Book and Candle* opposite Rex Harrison and Lilli Palmer, and acted with them again two years later in Peter Ustinov's *Love of Four Colonels.* Other Broadway productions include *Teahouse of the August Moon* and *A Case of Libel* (1963 Tony Award nomination for supporting actor), and *First Monday in October* (1978). A veteran Shakespearean, he portrayed Falstaff and other great comic roles, and also starred twice in *King Lear.* Gates often played real-life personages, such as Bernard Baruch in FUNNY LADY (1975), Dean Rusk in the TV dramatic special "The Missiles of October" (ABC 1974), and Herbert Hoover in the miniseries BACKSTAIRS AT THE WHITE HOUSE (NBC 1979).

Gates entered film in 1952, with GLORY ALLEY and HAS ANYBODY SEEN MY GAL?, and played prominent support in such movies as INVASION OF THE BODY SNATCHERS (1956), THE BROTHERS RICO (1957), CAT ON A HOT TIN ROOF (1958), and IN THE HEAT OF THE NIGHT (1967). Active on television from the 1950s heyday of live anthologies, Gates also appeared in such telefilms as ALOHA MEANS GOODBYE (1974), KATE MCSHANE (1975), and FDR—THE LAST YEAR (1980). He also was an outspoken council member of Actors Equity.

Gates, who died of unspecified causes, lived in Cornwall, CT.

Glenville, Peter

born: Oct. 28, 1913, London, England
died: June 3, 1996, New York, NY, age 82
educ: Oxford (law)

Esteemed director, producer, screenwriter, and actor.

Peter Glenville, the son of theatrical performers Shaun Glenville and Dorothy Ward, left Oxford to become an actor as well; his earliest roles included Puck in Max Reinhardt's famed staging of *A Midsummer Night's Dream.* After spending time in repertory in Stratford and Manchester, Glenville made his stage directing debut at the Old Vic in 1944, but did not direct his first film, THE PRISONER (UK 1955), starring Alec Guinness, until after he himself had played everything from support to romantic leading men in such films as HIS BROTHER'S KEEPER (UK 1939), RETURN TO YESTERDAY and TWO FOR DANGER (UK 1940), HEAVEN IS ROUND THE CORNER and UNCENSORED (UK 1944), MADONNA OF THE SEVEN MOONS (UK 1945), and GOOD TIME GIRL (UK 1950). Glenville went on to direct several mostly well-regarded and faithful screen adaptations of acclaimed works he had produced and directed on the London and Broadway stages, including Danny Kaye's ME AND THE COLONEL (1958; based on *Jacobowsky and the Colonel*); the Tennessee Williams adaptation SUMMER AND SMOKE (1961); the highly acclaimed BECKET (UK 1964; based on the Jean Anouilh play), for which Glenville earned one of the film's 12 Academy Award nominations; and the Feydeau adaptation HOTEL PARADISO (UK 1966; also producer, co-script adaptation), in which Glenville had a small role as Feydeau himself. His other films, both novel-based, were TERM OF TRIAL (UK 1962; also screenwriter) and THE COMEDIANS (US-France 1967; also producer).

No cause of death was reported.

Goldfarb, Howard

born: c. 1941
died: Oct. 5, 1996, Los Angeles, CA, age 55

Film distributor and occasional producer.

A pioneer of independent film distribution and a founding member of the American Film Marketing Association, Goldfarb established his own company in 1978 after working for several of the studios. In 1991, he was convicted on charges stemming from a legal dispute over a film sale. Goldfarb served as executive producer on the films THE UNSEEN (1981) and MISSION KILL (1987).

He died of heart failure following open-heart surgery.

Goodman, Miles

born: 1949, Los Angeles, CA
died: Aug. 16, 1996, Santa Monica, CA, age 47
educ: Antioch College, Yellow Springs, OH (theater)

Movie composer/orchestrator and record producer.

Through the help and influence of his cousin, Oscar-winning film composer Johnny Mandel, Miles Goodman became interested in film scoring. Upon starting out professionally, he met and teamed with Oscar Castro-Neves, who became his friend and musical collaborator for 30 years. Goodman studied with Albert Harris in the early 1970s, and in his early career did music for the films SLUMBER PARTY '57 (1976) and LAST CRY FOR HELP and SKATETOWN, USA (1979), and orchestrated several of Mandel's film scores, including those for BEING THERE (1979) and THE VERDICT (1982). With the TV drama series "James at 15/James at 16" (NBC 1977-78), Goodman established what would become his professional signature—combining original music with a song score, as he would do on such films as FOOTLOOSE (1984) and LA BAMBA (1987).

Goodman additionally became a record producer in 1990, producing items such as "The Billie Holiday Songbook." Other films for which he supplied music include: JINXED (1982), TABLE FOR FIVE (1983), TEEN WOLF (1985), LITTLE SHOP OF HORRORS (1986), WHAT ABOUT BOB? (1991), SISTER ACT 2: BACK IN THE HABIT (1993), DUNSTON CHECKS IN, and SUNSET PARK (1996), with LARGER THAN LIFE and 'TIL THERE WAS YOU (both 1996), unreleased at the time of his death.

Goodman died of an apparent heart attack.

Gould, Morton

born: Dec. 10, 1913, Richmond Hill, NY
died: Feb. 21, 1996, Orlando, FL, age 82

Pulitzer Prize-winning composer who dabbled in film.

Morton Gould was a child prodigy who wrote his first composition at age 6; at age 19, hired as staff pianist at New York's Radio City Music Hall, he played at its Dec. 27, 1932 opening night. Gould recorded dozens of classical albums and composed more than 1,000 works, from his early advertising jingles to his *Fall River Legend* ballet for Agnes de Mille and the 1995 Pulitzer-winning *Stringmusic* . The much-honored Gould, who served as president of ASCAP for eight years, received a Kennedy Center honor in 1994. In film, Morton Gould and His Orchestra appeared as themselves in Arthur Lubin's DELIGHTFULLY DANGEROUS (1945), with Gould providing the film's music. Gould also wrote the score for the movies CINERAMA HOLIDAY (1955) and WINDJAMMER (1958), and the network miniseries "Holocaust" (1978).

Gould, who lived in Great Neck, NY, died while visiting the Disney Institute adult education center, where he was to conduct a program of his works. No cause of death was reported.

Grangier, Gilles

born: May 5, 1911, Paris, France
died: April 28, 1996, Paris, France, age 84

French director of more than 40, mostly routine commercial productions, including several Jean Gabin "quickies."

After a brief business career destroyed by the European Depression, Gilles Grangier was hired by Paramount at Joinville Studios in 1933 as an actor. By the decade's end, he had become an assistant director, working on such films as Sacha Guitry's DESIREE (France 1938). After WWII military service from 1939-42, in which he escaped as a prisoner of war, Grangier directed his first feature, ADEMAI, BANDIT D'HONNEUR; made in 1942, it was not released until the war's end.

Grangier's films released in the US include JUPITER (France 1952), LE VIEUX DE LA VIEILLE (1960; also script), LE DESORDRE ET LA NUIT/NIGHT AFFAIR (France 1961; also co-script), LE CAVE SE REBIFFE/THE COUNTERFEITERS OF PARIS aka MONEY, MONEY, MONEY (France-Italy 1961; also co-script), ARCHIMEDE, LE CLOCHARD/THE MAGNIFICENT TRAMP (France-Italy 1959; also co-script; US release 1962), and LA CUISINE AU BEURRE/MY WIFE'S HUSBAND (France-Italy 1963; US release 1965). Grangier, who also directed for TV, was decorated a Chevalier of the Legion of Honor in 1994.

No cause of death was reported.

Green, Joseph

born: Joseph Greenberg, April 23, 1900, Lodz, Poland
died: June 20, 1996, Great Neck, Long Island, NY, age 96

Major Yiddish filmmaker, whose four films as producer-director are considered among the zenith of the form.

Joseph Green studied drama in German-occupied Warsaw during WWI, then moved to Berlin, where as an actor he joined an offshoot of the Yiddish acting company the Vilna Troupe; he came to America with them in 1924. As half of the father-and-son acting team of Rudolph and Joseph Schildkraut, Green went to Hollywood in 1927. There, he landed a bit part in the historic film THE JAZZ SINGER (1927). Back in New York, he acted with several Yiddish theater groups, including Maurice Schwartz's Yiddish Art Theatre. In 1932, Green was hired to dub Yiddish dialogue into a silent Italian feature, JOSEPH IN THE LAND OF EGYPT. As payment, he received a print of the movie and spent the next two years touring Poland with the film, which enabled him to finance his own filmmaking career. Signing American Yiddish-theater star Molly Picon for her first starring screen role, Green turned a script called "The Wandering Musicians" into the gender-bending musical comedy YIDL MITN FIDL/YIDDLE WITH A FIDDLE aka CASTLE IN THE SKY (Poland 1935) ("yidl" loosely translates as "young Jewish lass"). The film became the first international hit in Yiddish cinema, which dates to 1911.

Green followed with DER PURIMSHPILER/THE JESTER (Poland 1937), MAMELE/LITTLE MOTHER (Poland 1938), with Picon, and A BRIEVELE DER MAMEN/A LITTLE LETTER TO MOTHER (Poland 1938). Made in the shadow of war, they document what all involved knew to be a disappearing way of European life. Green returned to New York in 1939, and during the war briefly returned to the stage, leasing the Yiddish Art Theater on Second Avenue to produce the plays *The Miracle of the Warsaw Ghetto* by H. Lalvick and *We Will Live* by David Bergelson. He became a film distributor, releasing YIDL MITN FIDL in an English version.

Green died of emphysema.

Grey, Denise

born: c. 1896
died: Sunday, Jan. 13, 1996, age 99

Doyenne of the French stage.

Denise Grey particularly excelled at playing feisty grandmothers—after starting her career with the Follies Bergeres review in 1915. She long played the lead role in the French theater version of *Harold and Maude.* An indefatigable actress in film and TV as well, she appeared in at least eight films released in the US: LE DIABLE AU CORPS/THE DEVIL IN THE FLESH (France 1946), JULIETTA (France 1957), FRANCAISE ET L'AMOUR/LOVE AND THE FRENCHWOMAN (France; US release 1961), LA BONNE SOUPE/THE GOOD SOUP (Italy-France 1964), HELLO—GOODBYE (UK 1970), and LA BOUM/READY FOR LOVE (France 1981). Other films include PAS DE CAVIAR POUR TANTE OLGA (France 1965), LA BOUM 2 (France 1982), SAISONS DU PLAISIR (France 1988), and TCHIN-TCHIN (Italy 1991). Grey retired in 1991.

No cause of death was reported.

Guess, Alvaleta

aka: Alvaletah Guess
born: c. 1960
died: Sept. 2, 1996, New York City (Manhattan), NY, age 36

New York theater and film actress.

Alvaleta Guess appeared in the plays *Avenue X* and *Nunsense* , and the musical *Swinging On A Star;* she also toured nationally in *Once on This Island* and *Ain't Misbehavin'.* She appeared in small roles in MONEY TRAIN (1995), as Alvaletah Guess in DEAD PRESIDENTS (1995), and in BIG NIGHT (1996).

Guess died of breast cancer.

Gutierrez Alea, Tomas

born: Dec. 11, 1926 or 1928 (sources differ), Havana, Cuba
died: April 16, 1996, Havana, Cuba, age 67 or 69
educ: Centro Sperimentale di Cinematografia, Rome, Italy

The leading director-screenwriter of Cuba and the venerable dean of Latin American cinema.

Tomas Gutierrez Alea, whose surname is a compound in the manner of many Spanish names, consistently tackled political or culturally sensitive topics in his tightly controlled native land with little, if any, compromising of his craft. His international success, FRESA Y CHOCOLATE/STRAWBERRY AND CHOCOLATE (Cuba-Mexico-Spain 1994), was the first Cuban film with an openly gay main character. In satirical works such as MUERTE DE UN BUROCRATA/DEATH OF A BUREAUCRAT (Cuba 1966), Gutierrez Alea criticized the government while being himself a government insider; he was a founder of the Instituto del Arte y Industria Cinematograficos (ICAIC), established in 1959 as a collective designed to make Marxist revolutionary films.

The son of a wealthy family, Gutierrez Alea started out to be a lawyer, studying law at the same time and at the same Havana school as a young Fidel Castro. Veering into filmmaking in 1952, Gutierrez Alea studied in Rome, where he was influenced by the neorealist movement. Upon returning to Cuba, he joined the radical cultural society "Nuestro Tiempo." With fellow filmmaker Julio Garcia Espinosa, he co-directed the controversial documentary short "El Megano" (1955); it was considered subversive by the Batista government and was confiscated by police. After the Castro revolution and the founding of ICAIC, Gutierrez Alea made his directorial feature debut with the tri-part HISTORIAS DE LA REVOLUCION/STORIES OF THE REVOLUTION (Cuba 1960), a documentary-like look at the Cuban Revolution. He established his international reputation with MEMORIAS DEL SUBDESAROLLO/MEMORIES OF UNDERDEVELOPMENT (Cuba 1968), about a dispassionate, dissolute, upper-class intellectual choosing to remain in Cuba after the Revolution despite himself and the crumbling economy and culture.

Gutierrez Alea's films—some of which star his actress wife, Mirta Ibarra—cover a range of genres and themes. LAS DOCE SILLAS/THE TWELVE CHAIRS (Cuba 1962) was a knockabout comedy. LA ULTIMA CENA/THE LAST SUPPER (Cuba 1976; director-actor only) was a fact-based historical drama about a major 18th-century slave uprising. The exquisite CARTAS DEL PARQUE/LETTERS FROM THE PARK (director only), made as a 1988 telefilm for Spain and released in the US direct-to-video, was a romantic period seriocomedy. His other films include DE CIERTA MANERA (Cuba 1977), LOS SOBREVIVIENTES/THE SURVIVORS (Cuba 1978), and his last, GUANTANAMERA (Cuba-Spain-Germany 1995). Both it and STRAWBERRY AND CHOCOLATE, made when Gutierrez Alea's health was deteriorating, were co-directed with his colleague Juan Carlos Tabio. STRAWBERRY AND CHOCOLATE was shown at the 1994 New York Film Festival, and was nominated for a 1995 Academy Award for foreign-language film.

Gutierrez Alea died of cancer.

Halliday, Bryant

born: c. 1928
died: July 28, 1996, Paris, France, age 68

Co-founder of the film distributor Janus Films, who also starred in a handful of horror movies.

Bryant Halliday spent his early years at a Benedictine monastery in preparation for the priesthood. At 21, he left to pursue acting, joining the Brattle Theatre Company in Cambridge, MA, where he performed in more than 50 repertory productions. He and associate Cyrus Harvey founded Janus in 1950, using New York City's 55th Street Playhouse Cinema as a first-run venue for foreign-language and art films. Years later, he sold Janus, but remained active as a producer, writer, and actor in the Paris theater and on French television. As an actor, he starred as the ventriloquist the Great Vorelli, in DEVIL DOLL (UK 1964), and went on to headline CURSE OF THE VOODOO aka CURSE OF SIMBA aka LION MAN (UK 1965), THE PROJECTED MAN (UK 1967), and TOWER OF EVIL aka BEYOND THE FOG aka HORROR OF SNAPE ISLAND (UK 1972).

Halliday died of a stroke.

Hannah, Bob

born: c. 1942
died: Aug. 14, 1996, age 54

Atlanta-based character actor specializing in Southerner roles.

Bob Hannah entered film in 1979 with NORMA RAE, and appeared in prominent supporting roles in a number of major films—among them, Patsy Cline's husband in COAL MINER'S DAUGHTER (1980), car dealer Red Mitchell in DRIVING MISS DAISY (1989), and Mary Stuart Masterson's defense attorney in FRIED GREEN TOMATOES (1991). He guested on such TV series as "Matlock," "In the Heat of the Night, " and "Savannah," and appeared in such telefilms as ANGEL CITY(1980), THE RYAN WHITE STORY (1988), MOTHER'S RIGHT: THE ELIZABETH MORGAN STORY (1992), and TO DANCE WITH THE WHTIE DOG (1994).

Other films include JAWS OF SATAN aka KING COBRA (filmed 1979, released 1981), CARNY (1980), THE LOVELESS (1982), TANK (1984), INVASION U. S. A. (1985), CHATTAHOOCHEE (1990), THE PRINCE OF TIDES (1991), LOVE CRIMES (1992), NEON BIBLE (UK 1995), and FLED (1996).

Hannah died of a heart attack.

Hargreaves, John

born: 1945, Australia
died: Jan. 8, 1996, Sydney, Australia, age 50
educ: National Institute of Dramatic Art, Australia (grad. 1970)

Distinguished Australian actor and leading man.

John Hargreaves, the only actor to be awarded his nation's Byron Kennedy Award, given to individuals for "pursuit of excellence, " also won three Australian Film Institute awards in his career: as actor, for MY FIRST WIFE (Australia 1984), and as supporting actor for CAREFUL, HE MIGHT HEAR YOU (Australia 1983) and MALCOLM (Australia 1986).

Hargreaves played the lead in his first film, the play adaptation THE REMOVALISTS (Australia 1974; US release 1975), and shortly thereafter played the title character in Bruce Beresford's popular comedy DON'S PARTY (Australia 1976). Other films include MAD DOG MORGAN (Australia 1976), BEYOND REASONABLE DOUBT (New Zealand 1980), CRY FREEDOM (UK 1987), COUNTRY LIFE (Australia 1994), and HOTEL SORRENTO aka SORRENTO BEACH (Australia 1995), in his last leading role; he appeared posthumously in a cameo in Paul Cox's LUST AND REVENGE (Australia 1996).

Hargreaves died after what was reported as a long illness.

Helm, Brigitte

born: Gisele Eve Schittenhelm or Eva Gisela Schittenhelm, March 17, 1906 or 1908 (sources vary), Berlin, Germany
died: June 11, 1996, Ascona, Switzerland, age 88 or 90

The robotic Maria—an immortal cinematic icon—of Fritz Lang's legendary METROPOLIS (Germany 1926).

Brigitte Helm, the beautiful, most immensely sought-after female star of Germany's golden age of filmmaking, died amid the same aura of mystery in which she lived, in the Swiss home where she had resided in seclusion for three decades. She had become a film star immediately upon her debut in Lang's masterpiece of futuristic class warfare—starring in 22 sound and silent films in nine years, eschewing Hollywood, turning down the lead in THE BLUE ANGEL, and retiring from film in her 20s in disgust at the Nazi takeover of the industry.

The daughter of a Prussian Army officer who died when she was a toddler, Helm was a studious boarding-school pupil who appeared willingly in school plays but regarded film acting with aristocratic disdain as a frivolous if not immoral profession. Helm's mother sent her teenaged daughter's photograph to Lang's wife, screenwriter Thea von Harbou; Helm was reportedly then "tricked" into taking a screen test, and was cast as the idealistic worker Maria in METROPOLIS (Germany 1926). Perfectionist Lang worked Helm so hard over the course of the 18-month production that Helm refused to ever work with him again.

Helm successfully segued to sound, beginning with her role as the cold and morally corrupt daughter midwifed by a scientist experimenting in the then science-fiction realm of artificial insemination in ALRAUNE/UNHOLY LOVE aka DAUGHTER OF EVIL (Germany 1930). She also appeared in the musical BLUE DANUBE (UK 1932), in which she played a countess; G. W. Pabst's mythical DIE HERRIN VON ATLANTIS/THE MISTRESS OF ATLANTIS aka LOST ATLANTIS (Germany 1932), essaying the island's sexually voracious queen; and GOLD (Germany 1934), her second-to-last film, in which she played the lab-assistant lover to a modern-day alchemist. Helm appeared in both the 1930 German film DIE SINGENDE STADT and the 1931 UK version, THE CITY OF SONG, as well as in both the German and French versions of GLORIA (1931).

In 1935, with the Nazis in control of the film industry, Helm abruptly retired to marry anti-Nazi industrialist Hugo von Kunheim. They left Germany for Italy in 1942, returning after the war. Helm made no further films, and declined to be interviewed for the remainder of her life.

No cause of death was reported.

Hemingway, Margaux

born: Feb. 19, 1955, Portland, OR
died: June 30, 1996, Santa Monica, CA, age 41

Actress-model granddaughter of Ernest Hemingway, and sister of actress Mariel Hemingway.

The second of the three daughters of John Hadley Hemingway (Ernest's oldest son) and Byra "Puck" Whitlock Hemingway, Margaux—named after her parents' favorite Chateau Margaux wine—moved variously with her family to Ernest's farm in Cuba, to San Francisco, and finally, in 1967, to Ketchum, ID, where Ernest had also lived. At 19, working for a Ketchum public-relations firm and tagging along on a New York business trip, the six-foot-tall beauty was swept off her feet by 33-year-old hamburger-chain heir Errol Wetson. Four months later, she moved to Manhattan to marry Wetson (in 1975; they divorced 1978). He introduced her to officials at Faberge, and she soon became one of the country's highest-paid models, signing a then-record $1 million contract to be Faberge's "Fabulous Babe." Soon a club-scene "celebutante," she was rushed to star in the revenge thriller LIPSTICK (1976); it also featured younger sister Mariel, who would go on to a solid career in film and television. LIPSTICK's critical and commercial drubbing essentially ended Hemingway's film career—though she did go on to appear in at least 10 more small or direct-to-video movies through 1994.

Hemingway—who spent many years battling dyslexia, epilepsy, bulimia, and depression while abusing alcohol and drugs—married Venezuelan film director Bernard Foucher in 1979. They moved to Paris, but Hemingway experienced more career and substance-abuse setbacks and divorced him in 1985. After filming LOVE IN C MINOR (France 1990) and posing nude in 1990 for "Playboy," she landed such direct-to-video fare as INNER SANCTUM (1991), DEADLY RIVALS and FRAME-UP 2: THE COVER-UP (1993), and DOUBLE OBSESSION and INNER SANCTUM 2 (1994).

Hemingway's severely decomposed body was found on July 1. She had died two days before. An autopsy fixed the cause of death as suicide by acute phenobarbital intoxication.

Heppenstall, John Staunton

born: c. 1958
died: June 11, 1996, Bryn Mawr, PA, age 38
educ: Boston University (cum laude, BFA acting program)

Tom Hanks's stand-in on PUNCHLINE (1988) and THE BONFIRE OF THE VANITIES (1990). Heppenstall also worked in many stage productions off-Broadway and at the Southampton Playhouse on Long Island. He died of complications from AIDS.

Heyman, Barton

born: Jan. 24, 1937, Washington, DC
died: May 15, 1996, New York City (Manhattan), NY, age 59
educ: UCLA (theater)

Prolific actor who gained his most prominent notice as the prison-guard captain who uttered the title words in DEAD MAN WALKING (1995).

Barton Heyman, a working actor in films since 1968, was also a versatile staple of the New York stage. He appeared in several New York Shakespeare Festival productions. His Broadway credits include *Indians* , *Sleep* , and *The Enclave* , as well as originating the role of the bartender in *The Night Hank Williams Died* . His last theater role was in the Elvis Presley fantasy-drama *Him* (1995). Barton made his film debut in NAKED FLAME (1968), and went on to such diverse movies as the dramas THE TRIAL OF THE CATONSVILLE NINE (1972), BANG THE DRUM SLOWLY (1973), CRUISING (1980), AWAKENINGS, and THE BASKETBALL DIARIES (1995); the comedies THE HAPPY HOOKER (1975), QUICK CHANGE (1990), and JEFFREY (1995); the horror films and thrillers THE EXORCIST (1973), and RAISING CAIN (1992); and the western VALDEZ IS COMING (1971). His final film was RESCUING DESIRE (1996).

Heyman died of heart failure at his home.

Hill, Dana

aka: Dana Hill Goetz
born: May 6, 1964, Van Nuys, CA
died: July 15, 1996, Burbank, CA, age 32

Actress and vocal performer.

Dana Hill, the daughter of Theodore and Sandra Goetz, went from juvenile to young-adult parts in a career that gained attention early with her role as a 12-year-old enticed into child pornography in the telefilm FALLEN ANGEL (1981). She was perhaps best known for her teen-daughter roles in her big-screen debut, SHOOT THE MOON (1982), and in NATIONAL LAMPOON'S EUROPEAN VACATION (1985).

Hill appeared in two aired but unsold 1979 TV pilots before making her miniseries debut with "The French-Atlantic Affair" (1979) and her telefilm debut with THE $5. 20 AN HOUR DREAM (CBS 1980). The following year, she was cast in the Peter Cook sitcom "The Two of Us" (CBS 1981-82). Hill appeared in Martin Ritt's CROSS CREEK (1983), and went on to provide vocals in the animated films THE JETSONS: THE MOVIE (1990), ROVER DANGERFIELD (1991), and TOM AND JERRY—THE MOVIE (1993), as the famous mouse Jerry. Hill guested frequently on TV series and provided vocals on several cartoon shows. Other work included "Afterschool Specials," the live dramatic special "NBC Live Theater: A Member of the Wedding" (1982), and telefilms, including SILENCE OF THE HEART (1984) and WHERE ARE MY CHILDREN (1994). Onstage, Hill won an LA Drama Critics Circle Award for *Picnic* , in a production later televised on Showtime, and appeared in *Steel Magnolias* at Pasadena Playhouse.

Hill died of diabetes complications.

Hill, Ralston

born: c. 1927, Cleveland, OH
died: Oct. 19, 1996, New Jersey, age 69

Veteran actor.

Ralston Hill died with his boots on, while rehearsing for a Paper Mill Playhouse production of *Gigi* . The New York City-based actor appeared in several stage and TV productions, and originated the role of Secretary Charles Thomson in the Broadway musical *1776* , which he reprised for the 1972 film.

Hill died of natural causes.

Horn, Camilla

born: April 25, 1903, Frankfurt-am-Main, Germany
died: Aug. 14, 1996, Gilching, Germany, age 93

One of the last stars of the German golden age of silent film.

A dancer and seamstress with no formal acting training other than appearing as a film extra and substituting for Lil Dagover in F. W. Murnau's TARTUFFE (Germany 1926), Camilla Horn was nonetheless chosen by Murnau to star as Gretchen in his classic FAUST (Germany 1926) after Lillian Gish pulled out. Projecting a femme-fatale image of intelligence and sex appeal, Horn became a star in Germany. Though signing a four-year contract with the leading studio, UFA, and making such films as JUGENDRAUSCH/EVA AND THE GRASSHOPPER and DER FROLICHE WEINBERG (Germany 1927), she was wooed by Hollywood (literally, as the girlfriend of United Artists executive Joseph M. Schenck). There, billed as "the blond vamp," she made TEMPEST (1928) and ETERNAL LOVE (1929), two silents both directed by Ernst Lubitsch, and Warner Bros. ' German-language THE ROYAL BOX (1929), reportedly the first foreign-language film made in the US.

With the emergence of sound, Horn returned home, where her popularity was so great that one of her next films was her own biography, DIE GROSSE SEHNSUCHT/THE GREAT YEARNING (Germany 1930), in which she starred. Horn went on to reportedly make more than 60 films in all. Horn fell out of favor with the Nazis, and her career faltered after WWII; she continued to make middlingly successful appearances onstage and on TV. After a long span off the big screen, Horn returned to movies in the 1980s with such films as FRANKIES BRAUT (W. Germany 1982), and DER UNISCHTBARE/THE INVISIBLE MAN and SCHLOSS KONIGSWALD aka DIE LETZTE GESCHICHTE VON SCHLOSS KONIGSWALD/THE LAST STORY OF KONIGSWALD CASTLE (W. Germany 1987), for which she won the Bavarian Film Prize. Horn was married four times.

No cause of death was reported.

Hunter, Ross

born: Martin Fuss, May 6, 1916, Cleveland, OH
died: March 10, 1996, Los Angeles, CA, age 80
educ: Western Reserve University (MA)

Actor-turned-producer, whose lavish films in the latter capacity in the 1950s and '60s helped change Universal's image from that of a B-movie studio.

As Martin Fuss, Ross Hunter taught school until WWII, when he served for two years with US Army intelligence. He returned to teaching, but his good looks led to a Paramount screen test; ironically, it was a New York radio assignment that caught the attention of a Columbia Picture talent scout, which brought a contract and, per Columbia casting director Max Arnow, his new "nom de cinema". He became a teen idol in such six-day productions and B-films as LOUISIANA HAYRIDE (his debut), HIT THE HAY (1945), and THE BANDIT OF SHERWOOD FOREST (1946). With his contract ending and an allergic reaction on the set of THE DUCHESS OF IDAHO (1950) putting him out of work for a year, Hunter briefly resumed acting before returning to teaching. He became an instructor at the Ben Bard Dramatic School, but, having decided to become a producer, mounted such stage fare as a San Fernando Valley production of *Dream Girl* , starring his friends Virginia Grey and Lucille Ball.

Hunter successfully trimmed costs on the film FLAME OF ARABY (1951), on which Universal executive Leonard Goldstein had given him a two-week associate-producer assignment, and he served as a $75-a-week associate producer on such films as THE BATTLE AT APACHE PASS, THE SON OF ALI BABA and STEEL TOWN (1952). He turned producer with such films as the hit TAKE ME TO TOWN (1953), before finding his fortune-making niche by persuading Universal to let him make "women's pictures"—old-fashioned love stories and soap-opera dramas. His first, ALL I DESIRE (1953), starring Barbara Stanwyck, embodied his philosophy of name performers—usually older actresses—at moderate prices, and opulent costumes and sets. His breakthrough came the next year with his hit remake of MAGNIFICENT OBSESSION, starring Jane Wyman. His coyly teasing romantic comedies with Doris Day and Rock Hudson, such as PILLOW TALK (1959) and THE THRILL OF IT ALL (1963), helped turn Hudson into a major star and re-establish former hot-tomato chanteuse Day into her successful "professional virgin" persona. A teenage twist on that formula resulted in the successful "Tammy" films, including TAMMY AND THE BACHELOR (1957). Hunter's formula also, however, produced such unremarkable films as the remake of the classic MY MAN GODFREY (1957).

Through the mid-1950s to '60s, Hunter continued to churn out such moneymakers as ALL THAT HEAVEN ALLOWS (1955), the remake of IMITATION OF LIFE (1959), PORTRAIT IN BLACK (1960), FLOWER DRUM SONG (1961), and the play adaptation THE CHALK GARDEN (1964). Hunter's last two films were, respectively, his biggest hit and a legendarily huge flop that threatened to sink Columbia: AIRPORT (1970) and the musical remake LOST HORIZON (1973). Hunter, who from 1961-71 ran Ross Hunter Productions in partnership with Universal, then briefly headed Brut Productions and afterward briefly joined Paramount. Turning to TV, Hunter produced such telefilms as THE LIVES OF JENNY DOLAN (1975) and A FAMILY UPSIDE DOWN (1978), as well as series pilots.

Hunter died after a long battle with lymphoma.

Hyson, Dorothy

born: Dec 24, 1914, Chicago, IL; raised London, England
died: May 23, 1996, London, England, age 81

Stage and screen beauty of the 1930s and '40s, often said to have inspired the 1935 Rodgers and Hart hit song "The Most Beautiful Girl in the World."

As a child, Dorothy Hyson moved to London with her parents, one of whom was the musical-comedy star Dorothy Dickson, who died in 1995 at the age of 102. As a juvenile actress, she made her film debut in MONEY MAD, starring Dickson, and her stage debut in London in J. M. Barrie's *Quality Street* (1927). Her films (all British) include THAT'S A GOOD GIRL (1933), A CUP OF KINDNESS, THE GHOUL, and THE WOMAN IN COMMAND (1934), SPARE A COPPER (1940), and YOU WILL REMEMBER (1941). Hyson's marriage to actor Robert Douglas ended in divorce; she later married actor-director Sir Anthony Quayle, who died in 1989.

Hyson had been in declining health following a stroke.

Johnson, Ben

born: June 13, 1918, Foraker or Foreacre (sources vary), OK
died: April 8, 1996, Mesa, AZ, age 77

Authentically weathered rodeo champion and western supporting star, who won an Oscar and a New York Film Critics Award playing aging pool-hall manager Sam the Lion in THE LAST PICTURE SHOW (1971).

Ben Johnson grew up a cowboy on the Chapman-Bernard Ranch. Hired as a groom on location shoots for Howard Hughes's THE OUTLAW (1939), Johnson accompanied the production back to Hollywood. Several actors including former Montana ranchhand Gary Cooper sponsored his membership in the Screen Actors Guild so that he could double and do equestrian stunts in films. After doing so for the likes of John Wayne and Henry Fonda, Johnson was noticed by director John Ford, who called him "the most photogenic, natural actor in town" and cast him in 3 GODFATHERS (1948), SHE WORE A YELLOW RIBBON (1949), and RIO GRANDE and WAGON MASTER (both 1950). His authenticity never in question, Johnson returned periodically to the rodeo circuit, winning a World Champion Cowboy title in 1953. In 1985 he established the Ben Johnson Celebrity Rodeo in Guthrie, OK, raising money to benefit Children's Medical Research Inc. Johnson also established a $1 million Research Chair in Pediatric Cancer Research at the University of Oklahoma. He received a star on the Hollywood Walk of Fame in 1994.

Johnson appeared in at least 56 films (reportedly more than 300 counting uncredited double and stunt work), including MIGHTY JOE YOUNG (1949), SHANE (1953), OKLAHOMA! (1955), ONE-EYED JACKS (1961), THE WILD BUNCH (1969), JUNIOR BONNER (1972), DILLINGER (1973), THE SUGARLAND EXPRESS (1974), TERROR TRAIN (Canada 1980), TEX (1982), ANGELS IN THE OUTFIELD (1994) and THE EVENING STAR (1996). Television work included the recurring role of Sleeve on "The Monroes" (ABC 1966-67) as well as such telefilms as BONANZA—THE RETURN (1994).

Johnson died of an apparent heart attack while visiting his mother at Leisure World, a suburban Phoenix retirement community where they both lived.

Johnston, Johnnie

aka: Johnny Johnston
born: c. 1914, St. Louis, MO
died: Jan. 6, 1996, Cape Coral, FL, age 81

Singer, actor, and sports color-commentator.

Johnny Johnston, who recorded hit versions of the standards "That Old Black Magic" and "Laura," won pocket billiards championships while a teenager until his smooth baritone landed him singing jobs in Chicago clubs in the 1930s. In the 1940s he signed first with Paramount Pictures and later with MGM, appearing in such films as STAR SPANGLED RHYTHM (1942), SWEATER GIRL (1942), YOU CAN'T RATION LOVE (1944), TILL THE CLOUDS ROLL BY (1946) and THIS TIME FOR KEEPS (1947), before ending his movie career with ROCK AROUND THE CLOCK (1956).

Johnston was married to Kathryn Grayson from 1947-51, with whom he had a daughter. He died of heart failure.

Katzman, Leonard

born: Sept. 2, 1927, New York City, NY
died: Sept. 5, 1996, Malibu, CA, age 69
educ: Fairfax High School, Los Angeles, CA

Writing-producing-directing force behind TV's "Dallas."

Leonard Katzman got his start in film working for his uncle, exploitation mogul Sam Katzman, who put him to work on movie serials. He served as assistant director on IT CAME FROM BENEATH THE SEA (1955), THE GIANT CLAW (1957), FACE OF A FUGITIVE (1959), and ANGEL BABY (1961), and both wrote and directed SPACE MONSTER aka FIRST WOMAN INTO SPACE aka VOYAGE BEYOND THE SUN (1965). Katzman became a successful TV producer on such series as "Hawaii Five-O," "Petrocelli," "Gunsmoke," "The Fantastic Journey" and "Logan's Run."

Katzman died of an apparent heart attack not long after finishing writing, producing, and directing a "Dallas" reunion telefilm.

Keith, Byron

born: c. 1917
died: Jan. 19, 1996, Burbank, CA, age 78

Character actor.

Byron Keith started in radio in Boise, Idaho. He entered film with Orson Welles's THE STRANGER (1946), and bounced between film and TV roles through the 1960s. He co-starred in "77 Sunset Strip" (ABC 1958-64) as LAPD Lt. Gilmore, and played the recurring role of Mayor Linseed in "Batman" (ABC 1966-68). He also guested on series including "Playhouse 90," "GE Theatre," and "Mission: Impossible." Keith's films include DALLAS (1950), JOURNEY INTO LIGHT and QUEEN FOR A DAY (both 1951), THE BLACK LASH (1952), ABBOTT AND COSTELLO MEET THE KEYSTONE KOPS (1955), CHICAGO CONFIDENTIAL and UNDER FIRE (both 1957), SPEED CRAZY (1959), and THE GREAT BANK ROBBERY (1969).

He died of cancer.

Kelly, Gene

born: Eugene Curran Kelly, Aug. 23, 1912, Pittsburgh, PA
died: Feb. 2, 1996, Beverly Hills, CA, age 83
educ: Pennsylvania State College; University of Pittsburgh (economics degree, 1933)

Legendary dancer, actor, director and choreographer who helped make the image of dance in popular films as athletic and all-American as it was artful.

Before and behind the camera, Gene Kelly helped create such well-loved classics as ON THE TOWN (1949), perhaps the first musical shot on-location; AN AMERICAN IN PARIS (1951), winner of the Oscar for Best Picture; and SINGIN' IN THE RAIN (1952). The son of a sales executive and a former stage actress who insisted that all five of her children study music and dance, Kelly also played on his high-school football and hockey teams; when college was interrupted by the Depression, he taught gymnastics at a summer camp. After a brief stint in law school, Kelly worked for a dancing school partly owned by his mother; two years later, it was renamed the Gene Kelly Studio of the Dance. Kelly also directed local plays, formed a dance act with his brother Fred, with whom he performed in a children's theater at the Chicago World's Fair in 1934, and worked with passing vaudeville acts.

Moving to New York in 1938, Kelly landed a Broadway chorus job in *Leave It to Me,* starring Mary Martin. He was soon hired as dance director for Billy Rose's *Diamond Horseshoe Revue* (1940), where he met his first wife, actress Betsy Blair. (They divorced in 1957.) Kelly had by this time won critical kudos in *The Time of Your Life* (1939), and *Pal Joey* (1940). Signed by David O. Selznick to a Hollywood contract even though Selznick's studio had no musicals for him, Kelly was loaned out to MGM. There he made his film debut (opposite Judy Garland) in FOR ME AND MY GAL (1942), the success of which prompted MGM to buy out his contract. His pleasant musical voice and cheerfully casual screen presence blended with a masculine dancing style that contrasted with the elegant, uptown approach of Fred Astaire.

Kelly's career took off with COVER GIRL (1944; also chor.), his first film with frequent collaborator Stanley Donen. It was here that Kelly began experimenting with purely cinematic uses for dance, in a scene in which he dances with his own superimposed image. Similarly, in ANCHORS AWEIGH (1945; also chor.), for which he received a Best Actor Academy Award nomination, Kelly danced a duet with the animated character Jerry the mouse. Kelly also starred in such musicals as LIVING IN A BIG WAY (1947; also chor.), THE PIRATE (1948; also co-chor.), TAKE ME OUT TO THE BALL GAME (1949; also co-story, co-chor.), SUMMER STOCK (1950), BRIGADOON (1954; also chor.), IT'S ALWAYS FAIR WEATHER (1955; also co-dir.), LES GIRLS (1957) and the unfortunate, late-in-life lark XANADU (1980). Other appearances included ZIEGFELD FOLLIES (1946), THE THREE MUSKETEERS and WORDS AND MUSIC (both 1948), IT'S A BIG COUNTRY and THE DEVIL MAKES THREE (both 1952), MARJORIE MORNINGSTAR (1954), INHERIT THE WIND (1960), WHAT A WAY TO GO (1964), LES DEMOISELLES DE ROCHEFORT/THE YOUNG GIRLS OF ROCHEFORT (France 1973), 40 CARATS (1973), and VIVA KNIEVEL! (1977). He danced once onscreen with his brother Fred, in a cameo appearance in DEEP IN MY HEART (1954). He made his solo directing debut with the experimental, no-dialogue musical INVITATION TO THE DANCE (1956; also star, script, chor.). Though received ambivalently by audiences and critics, it won the Grand Prize at the West Berlin Film Festival.

Not limited to musicals, Kelly also directed films like THE HAPPY ROAD (1957; also prod. , co-star), TUNNEL OF LOVE (1958), GIGOT (1962), A GUIDE FOR THE MARRIED MAN (1967), HELLO DOLLY! (1969), and THE CHEYENNE SOCIAL CLUB (1970; also prod.). His career as a leading man faded with the demise of the Hollywood musical, but Kelly remained vibrant in many media. In 1960, he wrote and choreographed for the Paris Opera ballet troupe a modern jazz ballet set to Gershwin's "Concerto in F," and punningly titled *Pas de Dieux* ; partly for this, he was awarded the Chevalier of the Legion of Honor by the French government. He also acted and directed for Broadway and television. Bridging generations, Kelly was asked by Madonna in 1993 for professional input into the stage-tour choreography of an homage to SINGIN' IN THE RAIN, and his last film credit was as a consultant for the dance sequences in the animated feature CATS DON'T DANCE (1997).

Kelly married former dancing assistant Jean Coyne in 1960; she died in 1973. In 1990 he married Patricia Ward, a young writer he had hired to collaborate on his memoirs. His awards include a Special Academy Award (1951), life achievement honors from the Kennedy Center (1982) and the American Film Institute (1985), and the National Medal of Arts, awarded by President Clinton at a White House ceremony in 1994.

Kelly died following complications of strokes suffered in 1994 and 1995.

Kieslowski, Krzysztof

born: June 27, 1941, Warsaw, Poland
died: March 13, 1996, Warsaw, Poland, age 54
educ: Lodz School of Cinema and Theatre (Poland)

Internationally acclaimed, Oscar-nominated writer-director best known in the US for his "Three Colors" trilogy.

Greatly influenced by fellow countryman Andrzej Wajda, Krzysztof Kieslowski spent the early years of his career as a documentarist making films about Poland's acute social and political problems. After his feature directing debut, PICTURE (Poland 1969), he made a series of fictional and documentary shorts and features that were often banned by government censors or else preemptively shelved, though some won awards at international film festivals. His breakthrough film, AMATOR/CAMERA BUFF (1979), a satiric look at a corrupt provincial factory, earned him international attention. However, his 1982 film PRZYPADEK/BLIND CHANCE was banned until 1987.

Kieslowski, who taught in the radio and television department of the University of Silesia, also made films for television, and in 1988, he co-wrote and directed "The Decalogue," an ambitious series of 10 hour-long films inspired by the Ten Commandments. Set in modern-day Poland, with each installment themed to a biblical commandment while commenting on the drab reality of Polish life, it caused an international sensation. He remade two of the segments as feature films, KROTKI FILM O MILOSCI/A SHORT FILM ABOUT LOVE and KROTKI FILM O ZABIJANIU/A SHORT FILM ABOUT KILLING (both 1988); they won, respectively, the Felix Award for best European film of the year and the Cannes Festival Jury Prize.

Kieslowski followed with the critical and commercial hit PODWOJNE ZYCIE WERONIKI/LA DOUBLE VIE DE VERONIQUE/THE DOUBLE LIFE OF VERONIQUE (France-Poland 1991). He then launched into the "Three Colors" trilogy, named for the colors of the French flag and exploring their symbolic themes of liberty (blue), equality (white), and fraternity (red). TRZY KOLORY: NIEBIESKI/TROIS COULEURS: BLEU/BLUE (France-Poland-Switzerland-UK 1993) shared the Golden Lion at the 1993 Venice Film Festival, and star Juliette Binoche was named best actress. TRZY KOLORY: BIALY/TROIS COULEURS: BLANC/WHITE (France-Poland-Switzerland 1994) won Kieslowski the Berlin Film Festival's award for director. TRZY KOLORY: CZERWONY/TROIS COULEURS: ROUGE/RED (France-Poland-Switzerland 1994), considered the strongest of the three, won numerous prizes, including best foreign film from the NY and LA Film Critics groups, and a best-director Academy Award nomination.

While Kieslowski announced his retirement from filmmaking in 1994, by the time of his death he had apparently reconsidered and was working with his usual co-scripter Krzysztof Piesiewicz on scripts for a new trilogy, "Heaven," "Hell," and "Purgatory. " Not long before his death, he appeared in a documentary with a deceptively modest self-assessment: KRZYSZTOF KIESLOWSKI: I'M SO-SO. . . (1996).

Hospitalized in August 1995 after a heart attack, Kieslowski underwent a bypass operation but never fully recovered.

Kimbrough, Clint

aka: Clinton Kimbrough
born: c. 1932, Oklahoma City, OK
died: April 9, 1996, Ada, OK, age 63
educ: University of Oklahoma; American Academy of Dramatic Arts; Actors Studio

Actor.

Clint Kimbrough reportedly gave up a creative-writing scholarship to Princeton University to try for a New York acting career. Under contract to producer Hal Wallis, he appeared in director Daniel Mann's HOT SPELL (1958), then came to Broadway in 1961 with fellow young actor Burt Reynolds in *Look: We've Come Through.* Kimbrough was a regular in films directed by Roger Corman or made for Corman's New World Pictures, including BLOODY MAMA and VON RICHTHOFEN AND BROWN (both 1970), NIGHT CALL NURSES (1974), and CRAZY MAMA (1975). He also appeared in Dennis Hopper's THE LAST MOVIE (1975).

Kimbrough died of pneumonia.

Kindle, Tom

born: c. 1949
died: Feb. 12, 1997, Los Angeles, CA, age 47
educ: University of North Carolina

Character actor.

Tom Kindle served in the military in Vietnam, and by 1975, after college, was performing in off-Broadway plays. After the 1977 feature SUPER VAN and the 1979 telefilm WHEN HELL WAS IN SESSION, Kindle worked primarily in television. Along with appearances on such series as "M*A*S*H," "Remington Steele," "Newhart, " "Cheers," and "Evening Shade," he appeared in telefilms including BADGE OF THE ASSASSIN (1985), DEAD SILENCE (1991), and the satiric miniseries "Fresno" (1986). His movies include ALLIGATOR (1980), BUDDY BUDDY (1981), and THE ROCKETEER (1991).

Kindle died of AIDS complications.

King, Paul

aka: Paul Donaldson King
born: Los Angeles, CA
died: July 10, 1996, Newport Beach, CA, age 69
educ: Loyola High School, Loyola University, University of Southern California (master's degree English, 1950)

Oscar-nominated screenwriter.

After college and a hitch in the Navy, Paul King and partner Joseph Stone wrote the script for WILD HERITAGE (1958) and the story for the Cary Grant-Tony Curtis comedy OPERATION PETTICOAT (1959), sharing Academy Award and Writers Guild of America nominations with scripters Stanley Shapiro and Maurice Richlin. King worked as a writer/producer on more than 30 TV series, including "Bat Masterson," "Bonanza, " "Rawhide" and "Wagon Train." King was a television executive for most of his career.

King died of cancer.

Kobayashi, Masaki

born: Feb. 14, 1916, Otaru, Hokkaido, Japan
died: c. early October, 1996, Tokyo, Japan, age 81
educ: Waseda University (Tokyo)

Acclaimed Japanese director.

Masaki Kobayashi studied philosophy and oriental art in college and briefly worked in film before being drafted in 1941. Courageously and defiantly refusing to be promoted above the rank of private, he spent the last year of WWII as a POW in an Allied camp. He resumed his movie career in 1946 as an assistant to Keisuke Kinoshita at the Shochiku studio, and directed his first film, MY SON'S YOUTH, in 1952. In 1953, Kobayashi directed the semiautobiographical KABE ATSUKI HEYA/ROOM WITH THICK WALLS aka THE THICK-WALLED ROOM, about captured junior officers scapegoated as war criminals; its touchy subject matter kept it unreleased until 1956.

Not long afterward, Kobayashi embarked on his anti-war epic NINGEN NO JOKEN/THE HUMAN CONDITION (1959-61), a three-film, nine-and-a-half-hour cycle about a conscientious man trapped in the Japanese Army's brutal 1930s Manchurian War campaign in China, who dies trying to flee a Soviet concentration camp. Part I, NO GREATER LOVE (1959; also scr.), won the San Giorgio Prize at the 1960 Venice Film Festival; it was followed by ROAD TO ETERNITY (1959) and A SOLDIER'S PRAYER (1961), both of which Kobayashi also scripted and produced. Kobayashi's damning and disapproving Samurai drama SEPUKKU aka HARAKIRI (1962), won the 1963 International Jury Prize at Cannes, as did his KAIDAN aka KWAIDAN (1964), a ghost-story anthology.

Kobayashi's films include THE YOUTH OF JAPAN aka HYMN TO A TIRED MAN (1968), a 213-minute version of his eight-hour telefilm, MOERU AKI/GLOWING AUTUMN (1979), and SHOKUTAKU NO NAI IE/THE EMPTY TABLE (1985). He also produced Akira Kurosawa's DODES'KA-DEN (1970).

Kobayashi died of cardiac arrest at his home.

Kressyn, Miriam

born: c. 1912, Bialystock, Poland
died: Oct. 28, 1996, New York City, NY, age 84

"The First Lady of the Yiddish Theater."

Miriam Kressyn acted, wrote, sang, translated, and taught drama in a career spanning more than 60 years. She performed in the US and abroad, winning numerous awards including two Yiddish organization "Goldies" for acting and for lifetime achievement. She was a star of Joseph Green's classic Yiddish-language film DER PURIMSHPILER/THE JESTER (Poland 1937). Active into her eighties, Kressyn was a professor of drama at Queens College (New York City) for 10 years prior to her death.

Kuenstler, Frank

born: c. 1928
died: Aug. 11, 1996, New York, NY, age 68

Poet and filmmaker.

Frank Kuenstler's poems first appeared in the 1960s in the quarterly journal "The Eventorium Muse"; he published several books of poetry and was also a sculptor. In the late 1960s, he made three alternative/experimental films, "Color Idioms," "Two Plays by Serge Gavronsky" and "Our Magazine No. 1," and appeared in Jonas Mekas's underground feature GUNS OF THE TREES (1964).

Kuenstler died of esophageal cancer.

Kumar, Raj

aka: Raaj Kumar
born: Kulbhushan Pandit, Oct. 8, 1927, Loralai (formerly India, now Pakistan)
died: July 3, 1996, Bombay, India, age 68

Veteran Hindi-cinema actor, leading man in more than 60 films.

Raj Kumar grew up in a middle-class family, the son of an Army officer. Kumar was a policeman until 1952 when his rich, baritone voice helped him land his first movie role in RANGEELI/MERRY WOMAN. His breakthrough was MOTHER INDIA (1957), an international hit still considered one of the finest films of India's "Bollywood." In another of his signature roles, Kumar turned in a sublime performance as the wealthy young man in love with a Muslim courtesan in the luxurious classic of Indian melodrama PAKEEZAH/THE PURE ONE (1971).

Kumar died of blood cancer.

Kwan Tak-hing

born: 1905, Guangzhou (Canton), China
died: June 28, 1996, Hong Kong, age 91

Legendary Cantonese actor, action star, and opera performer.

After becoming an opera star, Kwan Tak-hing toured China during World War II, entertaining the troops, and visited the US for fund-raising efforts. He played the role of martial arts hero Huang Fei-hung in 59 movies from 1949 through the late 1960s. A martial artist himself, Kwan also ran a dojo in Hong Kong, and in the early 1980s was awarded Britain's MBE.

Kwan died of cancer.

La Plante, Laura

born: Laura La Plant, Nov. 1, 1904, St. Louis, MO
died: Oct. 14, 1996, Woodland Hills, CA, age 91

Silent screen star who made the transition to sound as the first woman to sing on film (as Magnolia in 1929's SHOW BOAT).

Laura La Plante was the movies' archetypal damsel-in-distress, but also played many comedic roles in a career of at least 81 features, serials and shorts. After coming to Hollywood with her divorced schoolteacher mother, La Plante entered film at 15 as an extra, appeared in the serial THE GREAT GAMBLE aka THE BIG PLUNGE (1919), and played bit parts in two-reel comedies by producer-director Al Christie, including two based on the popular "Bringing Up Father" comic strip. In 1921 she won a contract with Universal, and became one of the studio's top female star. Initially cast in Hoot Gibson westerns, La Plante graduated to bigger films after director William Seiter persuaded her to bob and bleach her hair. She married Seiter in 1926. They divorced in 1932, and she remarried Irving Asher, a producer who had been running the Warner Brothers studio in London.

A "girl-next-door" type, La Plante's best-known role, besides that of Magnolia, is that of heroine Annabelle West of the silent classic THE CAT AND THE CANARY (1927). La Plante retired in the mid-1930s and became a highly regarded Hollywood hostess. She came out of retirement twice to play character roles, in LITTLE MISTER JIM (1946) and SPRING REUNION (1957). Other films include PERILS OF THE YUKON (1922 serial), THE KING OF JAZZ (1930; playing herself), and GOD'S GIFT TO WOMEN aka TOO MANY WOMEN (both 1931), and CHURCH MOUSE, MAN OF THE MOMENT and WIDOW'S MIGHT (all 1935).

No cause of death was given.

LaCentra, Peg

born: Margherita LaCentra, Boston, MA, c. 1910
died: June 1, 1996, Los Angeles, CA, age 86

Singer and occasional actress.

The singer with Artie Shaw's first band in 1936, Peg LaCentra made records both with Shaw and solo, and in 1939 starred in her own NBC radio program. LaCentra appeared in musical film shorts and dubbed the singing voices of Ida Lupino in THE MAN I LOVE (1946) and Susan Hayward in SMASH-UP, THE STORY OF A WOMAN aka A WOMAN DESTROYED (1947). She played a nightclub singer in HUMORESQUE and sang in COWBOY BLUES (both 1946) before moving to character roles in films such as EMERGENCY HOSPITAL (1956), CRIME OF PASSION (1957), and THE DARK AT THE TOP OF THE STAIRS (1960).

LaCentra, who was married to radio actor Paul Stewart from 1939 until his death in 1986, died of a heart attack.

Lamour, Dorothy

born: Mary Leta Dorothy Slaton or Mary Leta Dorothy Kaumeyer (sources differ), Dec. 10, 1914, New Orleans, LA
died: Sept. 22, 1996, Los Angeles, CA, age 81

Dark, vaguely exotic beauty who brought the word "sarong" into the American lexicon, most memorably in the popular Bing Crosby-Bob Hope "Road" movies.

Raised in tight circumstances by her divorced mother during the Depression, Dorothy Lamour forged her mother's signature in order to leave high school at 15 and attend secretarial school. A year later, she won the 1931 Miss New Orleans beauty contest and moved to Chicago. While working as a department store elevator operator, the young beauty won an audition as a vocalist with bandleader Herbie Kaye, despite a lack of musical training. (She and Kaye were married from 1935 to 1939.) Lamour made her film debut in THE JUNGLE PRINCESS (1936), and appeared in 15 more movies before the first of her Hope and Crosby pictures, ROAD TO SINGAPORE (1940). Her standard role in these was as the exotic but modest straight-girl wooed and won by suave crooner Crosby at the expense of comic patsy Hope. The highly popular and well-paid Lamour appeared in all of the "Road" films—ROAD TO ZANZIBAR (1941), ROAD TO MOROCCO (1942), ROAD TO UTOPIA (1946), ROAD TO RIO (1948), and ROAD TO BALI (1953). Although she retired from movies after BALI, she returned for ROAD TO HONG KONG (1962), a failed attempt to revive the series; her role was planned as a cameo, but grew in size during filming. Her only film appearances after that were guest or character parts in DONOVAN'S REEF (1963), PAJAMA PARTY (1964), THE PHYNX (1970), and CREEPSHOW 2 (1987).

Offscreen, Lamour starred in the 1968 national roadshow production of "Hello, Dolly!," and performed in cabaret through the 1980s. During WWII she was dubbed the "Bond Bombshell" for helping raise some $300 million in War Bonds. During one bond drive, Lamour met advertising and frozen-food executive William Ross Howard III, whom she married in 1943; he died in 1978.

Lamour died a few hours after being admitted to St. Vincent Medical Center with stomach pains; the exact cause of death was unreported.

Lang, Jennings

born: May 28, 1915, New York City, NY
died: May 29, 1996, Palm Desert, CA, age 81
educ: St. John's University, New York City (Queens), NY (BS, JD)

Producer and studio executive credited with helping develop Sensurround.

Attorney and talent agent executive Jennings Lang endured a major scandal in 1951 when producer Walter Wanger, husband of Lang client Joan Bennett, accused Lang of philandering with his wife and shot him in the groin. Lang (who denied the accusation, as did Bennett) recovered, and Wanger plea-bargained a 100-day minimum-security sentence. After spending the 1950s and 1960s as a television executive, Lang moved into feature films in the late 1960s as producer or executive producer of many noteworthy films, including WINNING (1969), PLAY MISTY FOR ME (1971), SLAUGHTERHOUSE-FIVE (1972), HIGH PLAINS DRIFTER and CHARLEY VARRICK (1973), EARTHQUAKE (1974), and ROLLERCOASTER (1977), the last two of which both utilized Sensurround. Lang also provided the voice of a hot-tempered studio executive in Albert Brooks' REAL LIFE (1979). Lang's wife was actress-singer Monica Lewis, who appeared in at least eight of his films; their son Rocky is a director.

Lang died of pneumonia.

Larsen, William

born: Lake Charles, LA; raised Houston, TX
died: Jan. 21, 1996, Friendswood, TX, age 68
educ: University of Texas

Veteran stage character-actor who appeared in films and telefilms.

A founding member of the New York repertory company APA, William Larsen was in the original cast of the off-Broadway landmark *The Fantasticks.* His Broadway plays and musicals include *Half a Sixpence, Funny Girl* and the 1974 revival of *Cat on a Hot Tin Roof.* Larsen began his career as a resident actor in Nina Vance's Alley Theater in Houston, and in the 1980s was a member of Dallas Theater Center's acting company. He appeared in telefilms including THE INCREDIBLE HULK and DELTA COUNTY USA (1977), and GO WEST, YOUNG GIRL (1978). Other feature films included HEAVEN CAN WAIT (1978), FIVE DAYS FROM HOME (1979), FULL MOON IN BLUE WATER (1988), and JFK (1991).

Larsen died of a heart attack.

LaRue, Lash

born: Alfred LaRue, June 15, 1917, Michigan or Gretna, LA (sources vary)
died: May 24, 1996, Burbank, CA, age 79
educ: College of the Pacific

Bullwhip-cracking cowboy star who led a highly troubled, if colorful, life.

Variously a real-estate agent and a hairdresser who acted on the side, Alfred LaRue earned the nickname "Lash" for his maneuvers with his trademark 15-foot bullwhip in low-budget westerns (the evident inspiration for the title character in Steven Spielberg's INDIANA JONES series). Because his resemblance to Humphrey Bogart reportedly kept him from finding major-studio film roles, LaRue started in films as villains in Poverty Row productions. His breakthrough came with SONG OF OLD WYOMING (1945), in which, as the Cheyenne Kid, he turned Hollywood cowboy convention on its head by wearing black, riding a black horse (named Rush), and besting the bad guys less through courage and goodness than through simply being meaner and tougher. LaRue starred in at least two dozen such low-budget oaters. For television, he hosted the 15-minute film-excerpt series "Lash of the West" (syndication beginning 1951; ABC Jan. -May 1953), assisted by his movie sidekick Al "Fuzzy" St. John. LaRue hit the rodeo and carnival circuit in the early 1950s, but was dogged by a combination of numerous failed marriages (he claimed 10, by the end of his life), tax troubles, and several well-publicized arrests (among them drunkenness, public brawling, receiving stolen property, marijuana possession, and vagrancy). In the mid-1960s, LaRue became an evangelist working with alcoholics in St. Petersburg, FL. He returned to film briefly in the mid-1980s with a few low-budget films and the telefilm remake of STAGECOACH (1986). The secretive and tall-tale-spinning LaRue apparently lived in Gaffney, SC, where his last wife resided. LaRue had recently undergone triple-bypass surgery and suffered from emphysema.

No specific cause of death was reported.

Laye, Evelyn

born: Elsie Evelyn Lay, July 10, 1900, Bloomsbury, London, England
died: Feb. 17, 1996, London, England

Last great survivor of the golden age of British musical, who also conquered Broadway, appeared in films, and defied Louis B. Mayer.

Evelyn Laye made her stage debut at 15, and by 1923 was the most popular musical and operetta star in London. She married fellow musical star Sonnie Hale a few years later, divorcing him when he ran off with actress-singer Jessie Matthews in a highly publicized 1929 scandal. Laye made a smash Broadway debut in Noel Coward's *Bitter Sweet* (1930), and for several years worked regularly in films and on stage in both the US and London. Laye lost her chance at an MGM contract when she married her second husband, actor Frank Lawton, in 1934 over the specific objections of MGM chief Mayer; the marriage lasted until Lawton's death in 1969. She remained a Broadway and West End star until after WWII. In the 1950s, she retooled her career to play elegant dowagers in stage comedies. Laye's films include MAKE MINE A MILLION (UK 1959), THEATRE OF DEATH aka BLOOD FIELD (UK 1957), SAY HELLO TO YESTERDAY (1971), and NEVER NEVER LAND (UK 1980). She was appointed CBE in 1973.

No specific cause of death was reported.

Leary, Timothy

born: Oct. 22, 1920, Springfield, MA
died: May 31, 1996, Beverly Hills, CA
educ: West Point, University of Alabama, Washington State University, University of California at Berkeley

Psychologist, teacher, author, lecturer, computer-game inventor, occasional actor.

As a psychologist, Dr. Timothy Leary was discouraged by conventional means of probing the psyche and sought chemical methods of inquiry that he believed offered more profound insights. After experimenting with psychedelic drugs, Leary's well-respected academic career at Harvard ended in the early 1960s. Much of his life thereafter revolved around drugs. Possession of two marijuana cigarettes landed him in jail, but he escaped. By the time the busted-out fugitive was recaptured, served his time, and was back in society, he had attained counter-culture fame. Leary capitalized on his unique celebrity by doing stand-up comedy, lecturing, writing books, and taking small parts in minor theatrical features and TV movies, often with drug-related themes.

Leary's work on film was generally on the order of "guest star," with his presence intended as something of an inside joke: as an icon of the 1960s drug culture, he lent "credibility" to comedies like CHEECH AND CHONG'S NICE DREAMS (1981) and RUDE AWAKENING (1989). In Wes Craven's horror flick, SHOCKER (1989), Leary was a TV Evangelist. He also had bit parts in TED AND VENUS (1991), ROADSIDE PROPHETS (1992), HOLD ME, THRILL ME, KISS ME (1993), and CULTIVATING CHARLIE (1994). As an authentic 60s survivor, he contributed an array of pithy sound bites to the documentaries IT WAS 20 YEARS AGO TODAY (1987), THE LIFE AND TIMES OF ALLEN GINSBERG (1994), and SYNTHETIC PLEASURES (1996).

Leary died of prostate cancer.

Leder, Paul

born: 1925, Springfield, MA; raised New York City (Brooklyn), NY
died: April 8, 1996, Los Angeles, CA, age 70

Independent filmmaker of horror films and thrillers, including the memorably titled I DISMEMBER MAMA aka POOR ALBERT AND LITTLE ANNIE (1972).

Initially a singer on Molly Goldberg's radio show, Leder served as an Army medic in WWII, treating the survivors at Buchenwald. After the war, he worked as a truck driver and as a singer/dancer on Broadway before moving into film in the 1960s. He both starred in and produced THE GRASS EATER (1961), and starred in THE ROTTEN APPLE aka 5 MINUTES TO LOVE (1963), both starring Rue McClanahan. Leder's films from the late 1980s on were primarily for the direct-to-video market; his GOIN' TO CHICAGO (1989) was honored at the 1990 Santa Barbara Film Festival. His films as director, many of which he also produced, wrote and edited, included MARIGOLD MAN (1970), A*P*E (1976), SKETCHES OF A STRANGLER (1978), I'M GOING TO BE FAMOUS (1981), 11th COMMANDMENT (1987), MURDER BY NUMBERS (1990), EXILED IN AMERICA (1992), MOLLY AND GINA (1993), THE BABY DOLL MURDERS (1993), and KILLING OBSESSION (1994).

Leder died of lung cancer.

Leeds, Peter

born: May 30, 1917, Bayonne, NJ
died: Nov. 12, 1996, age 79

Highly prolific actor and comedian in film, TV, and theater.

A longtime straight man for Bob Hope and others, who worked with Hope on TV specials from 1954-91 and through 14 Vietnam War tours to entertain troops, Peter Leeds claimed to have made 8,000 TV and 3,000 radio appearances. Leeds began in film in 1941 with PUBLIC ENEMIES and made nearly three dozen movies through WITH SIX YOU GET EGGROLL (1968). Leeds was president of the Los Angeles AFTRA local for five years during the 1970s, and received the group's highest honor, the Gold Card, in 1992. He was also on the board of Governors for the Academy of Television Arts and Sciences. Leeds's films include REUNION IN FRANCE (1942), MA AND PA KETTLE BACK ON THE FARM (1951), STALAG 17 (1953), THE LAST TIME I SAW PARIS and THE LONG, LONG TRAILER (both 1954), I'LL CRY TOMORROW, IT'S ALWAYS FAIR WEATHER and LOVE ME OR LEAVE ME (1955), TEA AND SYMPATHY (1956), GIRLS' TOWN (1959), PLEASE DON'T EAT THE DAISIES (1960), and THE OSCAR (1966).

Leeds died of cancer.

Leigh, Norman

born: c. 1930
died: Sept. 11, 1996, New York City, NY, age 66

Cinematographer.

Norman Leigh served as director of photography on the satiric sitcom "Sledge Hammer!" (ABC 1986-88) and on telefilms including THIN ICE (1981). His films include THE BRINK'S JOB (1978), SCHIZOID (1980), LOVE (Canada 1982; co-dp), and DEADLY FORCE (1983; co-dp).

Leigh died of cancer.

Leiser, Erwin

born: c. 1923, Berlin, Germany
died: Aug. 22, 1996, Zurich, Switzerland, age 73
educ: University of Lund, Sweden

Documentary filmmaker.

Erwin Leiser, a German-born Jew, fled Hitler's Germany as a child. After living in a Jewish children's home in rural Sweden and later attending college, Leiser became a journalist in Stockholm. After working in TV news, he made the documentary feature MEIN KAMPF (1960), a history of Germany under Hitler, using newsreel clips and film obtained from both Allied and German sources. It proved a box-office hit even in West Germany. Leiser made two other documentaries about the Nazi era: EICHMANN AND THE THIRD REICH (1961) and FOLLOWING THE FUHRER (1986), the latter mixing documentary and fictional footage. Leiser made more than 50 documentaries on such WWII-related subjects as the Holocaust and the atomic bombing of Japan, as well as on contemporary artists and writers including Willem de Kooning and Isaac Bashevis Singer.

Leiser died of heart failure.

Lenard, Mark

born: 1924 or 1928 (sources vary), Chicago, IL
died: Nov. 22, 1996, New York City (Manhattan), NY, age 68 or 72

Accomplished stage actor best known as Spock's Vulcan father in the "Star Trek" TV series and movies.

After off-Broadway work in the mid-1950s, Mark Lenard made his Broadway debut in Carson McCullers' *Square Root of Wonderful* (1957), and went on to further Broadway work and the New York Shakespeare Festival. He appeared in different roles on the original "Star Trek" TV series, the animated series, STAR TREK: THE MOTION PICTURE (1979), STAR TREK III: THE SEARCH FOR SPOCK (1984), STAR TREK IV: THE VOYAGE HOME (1986), STAR TREK VI: THE UNDISCOVERED COUNTRY (1991), and episodes of "Star Trek: The Next Generation." Other films include THE GREATEST STORY EVER TOLD (1965), HANG 'EM HIGH (1968), and, in a bit part as a naval officer, ANNIE HALL (1977).

Lenard died of multiple myeloma and pneumonia following cancer surgery.

Lenox, John Thomas

born: July 23, 1946, Fort Worth, TX
died: July 23, 1996, Los Angeles, CA, age 50
educ: Southern Methodist University (BFA cinematography)

Executive producer of SPLASH (1983).

John Thomas Lenox moved to Hollywood in 1970 to enter the Directors Guild of America Apprenticeship Program, and then worked as assistant director on such TV series as "The Odd Couple," "Happy Days" and "Love American Style"; he made his directorial debut with "Laverne and Shirley" in 1975. He produced the CBS sitcom "Busting Loose" (1976) and co-executive-produced the two-part telefilm THE LONG HOT SUMMER (1985). In 1989, Lenox co-founded UCLA Extension's "Making the Short Film" program for new filmmakers. Lenox's final production was the Showtime telefilm LILY DALE (1996).

Lenox died on his fiftieth birthday; no specific cause of death was reported.

Levant, June

aka: June Gale, June Gilmartin Levant
born: June Gale, c. 1919
died: Nov. 13, 1996, Los Angeles, CA

Fox contract player, TV personality and the widow of actor-pianist Oscar Levant.

As part of vaudeville's popular dancing Gale Quadruplets (actually two sets of young twins), June Gale played the Palace and appeared on Broadway. At 19, she became a contract player for 20th Century-Fox, appearing in at least two dozen films, including MELODY IN SPRING (1934), ONE IN A MILLION (1936), SING AND BE HAPPY (1937), CHARLIE CHAN AT TREASURE ISLAND (1939), and CITY OF CHANCE (1940). She retired from film to marry Oscar Levant, well-known as a witty panelist on the radio quiz show "Information, Please." As June Levant, she became known as a paragon of devotion after Oscar became addicted to prescription drugs. Following his recovery they worked, together and separately, on local KCOP/Los Angeles TV programs. After Oscar died in 1972, June was briefly married to screenwriter Henry Ephron.

She died of complications of pneumonia.

Levin, Irving H.

born: Sept. 8, 1921, Chicago, IL
died: March 20, 1996, Los Angeles (Brentwood), CA, age 74
educ: University of Illinois

Independent producer and film executive instrumental in financing movies ranging from the grade-Z THE BEGINNING OF THE END (1957) to such respected fare as DINER and POLTERGEIST (both 1982).

After highly decorated service in WWII, Irving H. Levin entered the film industry in 1948 as a partner in Kranz-Levin Pictures and Realart Pictures. He held various producer, executive producer and executive posts at Mutual Productions, Filmmakers Releasing Organization, AB-PT Picture Corp. , Atlas Enterprises and Atlantic Pictures. In the early 1960s, he formed National General with Gene Klein, and in 1969 helped form First Artists, which produced such films as THE GETAWAY and UP THE SANDBOX (both 1972) and STRAIGHT TIME (1978). His later company SLM financed numerous Fox and MGM films including ROMANCING THE STONE (1984). In the late 1980s, Levin formed New Century Productions, with merged with Taylor Hackford's New Visions. He personally produced two films, HELL TO ETERNITY (1960) and TO LIVE AND DIE IN LA (1985).

Levin died of cancer.

Lewin, Albert E.

born: July 29, 1916, Chicago, IL
died: April 23, 1996, Los Angeles, CA, age 79
educ: Art Institute of Chicago; Los Angeles Valley College

Screenwriter.

After his WWII Army service, Albert E. Lewin wrote for various popular radio series. He was a contract scriptwriter for 20th Century-Fox from 1948-51 and 1959-61, and often co-wrote with Norman Panama or Burt Styler. During the 1960s, he scripted for more than 20 TV series, mostly sitcoms. He also wrote the plays *The Gift Horse* (with Styler) and *The Will.* His films include CALL ME MISTER (1951), DOWN AMONG THE SHELTERING PALMS (1953), BOY, DID I GET A WRONG NUMBER! (1966), EIGHT ON THE LAM (1967), THE WICKED DREAMS OF PAULA SCHULTZ (1968), and I WILL, I WILL . . . FOR NOW (1976).

Lewin died of heart failure.

Li Han-hsiang

born: March 7, 1926, Jinxi, Liaoning province, China
died: Dec. 17, 1996, Beijing, China, age 70
educ: National Arts Institute, Beijing (painting)

Seminal figure of Hong Kong's postwar Mandarin film industry and director of more than 70 features.

Expelled from college for political reasons, Li Han-hsiang settled in Hong Kong in 1948. After stints in advertising and as an art director, scriptwriter and assistant director, Li made his directing debut in 1952. Three years later, he signed with the Shaw Bros. studio, setting the standard for opulent costume epics with THE KINGDOM AND THE BEAUTY, THE MAGNIFICENT CONCUBINE, and WU-HOU/EMPRESS WU (the latter released in the US in 1965). Following a dispute with the Shaws Li moved to Taiwan in 1963, and there made some of his most prominent features, including HSI SHIH/BEAUTY OF BEAUTIES, THE WINTER, THE STORY OF TI YING and FOUR MOODS. Nonetheless, his production firm, the Grand Motion Picture Company, collapsed, and he returned to Hong Kong and Shaw Bros. in 1972. He directed lavish costume dramas and sex comedies, including THE WARLORD, GOLDEN LOTUS, THE LAST TEMPEST, and THE DREAM OF THE RED CHAMBER. He left the Shaws again in the early 1980s to make further costume epics in mainland China, including BURNING OF THE SUMMER PALACE, REIGN BEHIND A CURTAIN, and THE EMPRESS DOWAGER. Li, who published a four-volume set of memoirs in 1983-84, was married in 1953 to former actress Chang Tsui-ying.

Li fell ill with heart pains at CCTV's Beijing studio while directing the 40-part serial THE BURNING OF AH-FANG'S PALACE.

Lo Wei

born: 1918, Jiangsu Province, China
died: Jan. 20, 1996, Hong Kong, age 76

Hong Kong actor and director-producer who gave early career breaks to such stars as Bruce Lee, Jackie Chan, and Jet Li.

After acting in films in Chongquig during WWII, Lo Wei became a matinee idol after moving to Shanghai in 1948. He began directing in 1957. In 1965, he joined the Shaw Bros. studio, for which he helmed 17 films, including such martial-arts films as DRAGON SWAMP and THE GOLDEN SWORD. Signing with Shaw rivals Golden Harvest in 1970, Lo fortuitously took the reins when the original director was fired from FISTS OF FURY aka THE BIG BOSS (Hong Kong 1972; also scr.), the film that made Bruce Lee a world-wide star. Lo subsequently directed Lee in THE CHINESE CONNECTION aka FISTS OF FURY (Hong Kong 1972). Lo left Golden Harvest in 1975 to establish his own company, signing then little-known Jackie Chan to a multipicture contract. Ironically, Chan was out on loan for SNAKE IN THE EAGLE'S SHADOW (Hong Kong 1978), his own breakthrough film. Never a critics' darling, Lo made a series of commercial flops; that, combined with contractual disputes with Chan, led to his retirement in the early 1980s. As an actor, he appeared in at least two films released in America, WU-HOU/EMPRESS WU (Hong Kong; US release 1965) and CALL HIM MR. SHATTER aka SHATTER (UK-Hong Kong; US release 1976). Lo's first wife, whom he divorced in the 1970s, was actress Liu Liang-hua.

Lo died of heart failure.

Lynn, Rita

born: c. 1921
died: Jan. 21, 1996, Santa Monica, CA, age 74

Actress, activist and humanitarian.

Rita Lynn was born into a showbiz family, the daughter of an actress and MGM's first casting director and head of talent. After early stage and film work including CODE OF THE WEST (1947) and EAST SIDE, WEST SIDE (1949), Lynn concentrated on TV, appearing in many dramatic series. Later films included JOE DAKOTA and THE WAYWARD GIRL (both 1957), CAST A LONG SHADOW (1959), and MADIGAN (1968). Lynn was a member of the National Board of Directors of the Association of Film, Television and Recording Artists, and was active in civil rights and mental health organizations.

Lynn died after a long bout with cancer, and is survived by her husband, actor Frank Maxwell.

Madison, Guy

born: Robert Ozell Moseley, Jan. 19, 1922, Pumpkin Center, CA; raised Bakersfield, CA
died: Feb. 6, 1996, Palm Springs, CA, age 74
educ: Bakersfield Junior College (animal husbandry)

Film and TV actor best-known to a generation of 1950s kids as the star of "Wild Bill Hickok."

The son of a railroad machinist, strikingly handsome Guy Madison joined the Coast Guard in 1942. While in Hollywood on a pass he was spotted by a talent scout and brought to Paramount Pictures chief David O. Selznick, who had the sailor written into SINCE YOU WENT AWAY (1944). His three-minute scene as a lonely sailor generated much fan mail, and after his discharge Madison was cast in leading-man roles in TILL THE END OF TIME (1946) and HONEYMOON (1947). His inabilities as an actor threatened to cut his career short until he was cast in the hit TV series "Wild Bill Hickok" (113 episodes syndicated 1951-54; ABC/CBS daytime 1955-58). Typecast as a tight-lipped western hero, Madison became a poor man's Clint Eastwood in such spaghetti westerns as [all dates of US release] SEIDA A RIO BRAVO/GUNMEN OF THE RIO GRANDE (France-Italy-Spain 1965), I CINQUE DELLA VENDETTA/FIVE GIANTS FROM TEXAS (Italy-Spain 1966), and THE BANG BANG KID (US-Spain-Italy 1968). His final film role was a guest bit in WON TON TON, THE DOG WHO SAVED HOLLYWOOD (1976). Madison lived in Morongo Valley, CA, and was married to and divorced from actresses Gail Russell and Sheilah Connolly.

He died of emphysema.

Marks, Alfred

born: Alfred Edward Touchinsky, Jan. 28, 1921, Holborn, London, England
died: July 1, 1996, age 75
educ: Jewish Free School, London

British actor-comedian.

Primarily a stage performer in musical comedies, Alfred Marks worked steadily in radio and British television with occasional forays into film after 1951's PENNY POINTS TO PARADISE. His role as a nightclub owner in THE FRIGHTENED CITY (UK 1961) led stage and film director Lindsay Anderson to cast Marks in the Royal Court play *The Fire Raisers* ; his success in that drama led to further serious roles. He was awarded an OBE in 1976. Marks' British films include DESERT MICE (1959), JOHNNY, YOU'RE WANTED (1956) THERE WAS A CROOKED MAN and SHE'LL HAVE TO GO aka MAID FOR MURDER (1962), SCREAM AND SCREAM AGAIN (1970), VALENTINO (1977), FANNY HILL (1984), and ANTONIA & JANE (1991; orig. for UK TV).

Marks died of cancer.

Mason, Pamela

born: Pamela Helen Ostrer, March 10, 1916, London or Southend-on-Sea (sources vary), England
died: June 29, 1996, Beverly Hills, CA, age 80

Author, actress, talk-show host, socialite, and one-time wife of actor James Mason.

Pamela Ostrer left school at age nine and married cinematographer Roy Kellino at 16. In 1939 they pooled their resources with housemate James Mason to make an independent film (released theatrically in the US in 1953 as CHARADE). Mason and Pamela fell in love and, after her amicable divorce from Kellino, they were married in 1941. They moved to the US in the early 40s, performing together on Broadway and with their friend Richard Burton in the dramatic-reading TV series "The James Mason Show" (syndicated 1956). She published several novels including *This Little Hand* (1942) and *The Blinds are Down* (1946). The Masons were divorced in 1964, with Pamela very successfully represented by attorney Marvin Mitchelson. She hosted several syndicated talk shows and wrote a newspaper column about Hollywood and advice books. Mason appeared in several low-budget films, including FIVE MINUTES TO LIVE aka DOOR-TO-DOOR MANIAC (1961), SEX KITTENS GO TO COLLEGE aka BEAUTY AND THE ROBOT (1960), WILD IN THE STREETS (1968, as herself), and the telefilm MY WICKED WAYS: THE LEGEND OF ERROL FLYNN (1985).

Mason died of heart failure.

Mastroianni, Marcello

born: Marcelo Vincenzo Domenico Mastroianni, Sept. 28, 1923 or 1924 (sources vary), Fontana Liri, Italy; raised Turin and Rome
died: Dec. 19, 1996, Paris, France, age 72 or 73
educ: Centro Teatro, Rome University

Internationally beloved dramatic actor, romantic charmer, self-deprecating comic performer, and European icon.

Marcello Mastroianni was the son of poor peasants living 50 miles south of Rome. His father, a cabinetmaker, went blind from diabetes, but lived long enough to hear his son's voice onscreen. Mastroianni worked as a surveyor/draftsman, hoping to become an architect, but during WWII was assigned to draw maps for Mussolini's retreating armies. He later was drafted into digging ditches in the Alps (or working in a German labor camp; accounts differ). He escaped and hid in Venice until the Italian Armistice in 1944. Afterward, he worked as a clerk in the accounting department of the British film studio Eagle-Lion's Rome office, while taking theater classes at a city university. There he joined a college theatrical company where he met both Federico Fellini and his wife, actress Giulietta Masina. Mastroianni made his screen debut with a small role in I MISERABILI/LES MISERABLES (Italy 1947). He married fellow student Flora Carabella in 1948, the same year he joined Luchino Visconti's stage stock company. In his early films, Mastroianni gradually built a home-country reputation onstage and onscreen. He became a star in CRONACHE DI POVERI AMANTI/CHRONICLE OF POOR LOVERS (Italy 1954), his first film opposite frequent co-star Sophia Loren. His international reputation grew with Visconti's LE NOTTI BIANCHE/WHITE NIGHTS (Italy 1957) and the caper classic I SOLTI IGNOTI/BIG DEAL ON MADONNA STREET (Italy 1958).

The first of Mastroianni's half-dozen films with Fellini was LA DOLCE VITA(Italy-France 1960). Its images of black-suit-and-tie nightclubbers splashed against a deadening, hollow glamour remain iconic to this day, anchored by Mastroianni as a dashing yet spiritually empty celebrity journalist who yearns to write of "important things" but lacks the will do to so. The duo's next pairing was OTTO E MEZZO/8 1/2 (Italy 1963), a phantasmagoria in which Mastroianni played a Fellini-like director. Their subsequent collaborations were ROMA aka FELLINI'S ROMA (Italy-France 1972), LA CITTA' DELLE DONNE/CITY OF WOMEN (Italy-France 1980), the sweet, poignant GINGER E FRED/GINGER AND FRED (Italy-France-West Germany 1986), in which Mastroianni co-starred with Masina, and INTERVISTA aka FEDERICO FELLINI'S INTERVISTA (Italy 1987), in which both the filmmaker and the actor loosely play themselves.

At the other end of the spectrum were Mastroianni's 13 films with Loren. They include a trio of classic comedies: director Vittorio De Sica's IERI OGGI DOMANI/YESTERDAY, TODAY, AND TOMORROW (Italy, 1963) and MATRIMONIO ALL'ITALIANA/MARRIAGE ITALIAN STYLE (Italy, 1964); and Dino Risi's LA MOGLIE DEL PRETE/THE PRIEST'S WIFE (Italy-France 1971).

Truly an international star, Mastroianni, who spoke French and English as well as Italian, was thrice nominated for a Best Actor Academy Award, for DIVORZIO ALL'ITALIANA/DIVORCE, ITALIAN STYLE (Italy 1961), A SPECIAL DAY (Italy-Canada 1977); and OCI CIORNIE/DARK EYES (Italy 1987). He was named Best Foreign Actor by the British Film Academy for DIVORCE, ITALIAN STYLE and YESTERDAY, TODAY, AND TOMORROW, and won the Best Actor Prize at Cannes for Ettore Scola's DRAMA DELLA GELOSIA/THE PIZZA TRIANGLE (Italy 1970) and for DARK EYES. He received a Golden Lion for lifetime achievement at the 1990 Venice Film Festival.

Other notable roles from his more than 120 films include John Boorman's LEO THE LAST (UK 1970), Yves Robert's SALUT L'ARTISTE (France 1974), Ettore Scola's LA NUIT DE VARENNES (France-Italy 1982), Theo Angelopoulos's THE SUSPENDED STEP OF THE STORK (Greece-France-Switz. -Italy 1991), USED PEOPLE (US 1992), A FINE ROMANCE (US-Italy 1992), and DO ESO NO SE HABLA/I DON'T WANT TO TALK ABOUT IT (Argentina-Italy 1993). Though married for decades, Mastroianni, who had a way of remaining friends with ex-lovers and his long-suffering wife Carabella, shared a long romance in the 1970s with actress Catherine Deneuve, with whom he had a daughter, Chiara Mastroianni, born in 1972. Mastroianni and Carabella also had a daughter, Barbara, born in 1950. He had highly publicized romances of varying degrees with actresses Faye Dunaway (for three years in the 1960s), Jacqueline Bisset, and Jeanne Moreau. His younger brother, film editor Ruggero Mastroianni, died three months before Marcello.

Mastroianni, who had homes in Paris and Rome, suffered from pancreatic cancer, though no official cause of death was reported.

Mastroianni, Ruggero

born: Nov. 7, 1929
died: Sept. 9, 1996, Tor Vaianica, Italy, age 66

Major Italian film editor for more than three decades, and the younger brother of actor Marcello Mastroianni.

Ruggero Mastroianni began his career of at least 70 features with Enzo Provenzale's VENTO DEL SUD (Italy 1959). Like his brother Marcello, Ruggero enjoyed a close working relationship with Federico Fellini, and beginning with GIULIETTA DEGLI SPIRITI/JULIET OF THE SPIRITS (France-Italy-West Germany 1965) edited all of the director's major films. He also edited all of Francesco Rosi's features from UOMINI CONTROL (Italy 1970) on, including CRISTO SI E FERMATO A EBOLI/CHRIST STOPPED AT EBOLI (Italy-France 1979), TRE FRATELLI/THREE BROTHERS (Italy 1980), and BIZET'S CARMEN aka CARMEN (France-Italy 1984). Other major films include Luchino Visconti's LA CADUTA DEGLI DEI/THE DAMNED (Italy-West Germany 1969) and MORTE A VENEZIA/DEATH IN VENICE (Italy-France 1971), and Elio Petri's INDAGINE SU UN CITTADINO AL DI SOPRA DI OGNI SOSPETTO/INVESTIGATION OF A CITIZEN ABOVE SUSPICION (Italy 1970). At the time of his death, Mastroianni was editing Rosi's adaptation of Primo Levi's WWII memoir, *The Truce.*

Mastroianni died of a heart attack at his beach-resort home near Rome, three months before his brother's death.

Matas, Alfredo

born: c. 1920
died: July 22, 1996, Barcelona, Spain, age 76

Spanish theater executive and film producer.

Alfredo Matas founded the exhibition company Cinesa in 1958 to popularize the Cinerama system in Spain; by the early 1990s it was the country's largest theater chain. Matas, whose various companies produced 37 films including Luis Berlanga's PLACIDO, LIFE SIZE, and THE HEIFER and Luis Bunuel's last movie, THAT OBSCURE OBJECT OF DESIRE (Spain-France 1977), fought famously against censorship. He personally screened a copy of PLACIDO for dictator Francisco Franco, who banned the film from being shown at the Venice Film Festival. Pilar Miro's second film, THE CUENCA CRIME, which Matas produced, resulted in Miro's court-martial. Matas was awarded a lifetime achievement Gold Medal by Spain's Academy of Cinematographic Arts and Sciences in 1994.

He died of lung cancer.

Mateos, Julian

born: c. 1939
died: Dec. 27, 1996, Madrid, Spain, age 57

Spanish actor-turned-acclaimed-producer.

As an actor in the early 1960s, Julian Mateos appeared in films including JUVENTUD A LA INTEMPERIE/THE UNSATISFIED (Spain 1961, US release 1964), RETURN OF THE SEVEN and Jules Dassin's 10:30 PM SUMMER (both US-Spain 1966), I CRUDELI/THE HELLBENDERS (US-Italy-Spain 1967), SHALAKO (UK 1968), FOUR RODE OUT (US-Spain 1969), CATLOW (Spain 1971), and DEMON WITCH CHILD (Spain 1974). He produced LOS SANTOS INOCENTES/THE HOLY INNOCENTS (Spain 1984), which was shown at the New York Film Festival; cast members Alfredo Landa and Francisco Rabal shared an award for best actor at the 1984 Cannes International Film Festival. Other films as producer include EL VIAJE A NINGUNA PARTE/TRIP TO NOWHERE (Spain 1986) and EL NINO DE LA LUNA/THE MOON'S CHILD (Spain 1988).

Mateos died of lung cancer.

McKay, Wanda

born: Dorothy McKay, c. 1916, Portland, OR
died: April 11, 1996, Los Angeles, CA, age 80

Actress in low-budget features.

Shortly after winning the title of "Miss American Aviation" in 1938, Wanda McKay was signed to a contract by Paramount. In 1939, the former TWA stewardess appeared in her first film, the low-budget feature $1,000 A TOUCHDOWN, and during her 13-year movie career, she was cast in small parts in mostly minor movies. She occasionally appeared in an "A"-budget production like THE LADY EVE (1941) and THE MERRY WIDOW (1952), but most of McKay's more than 35 films included the likes of THE ROYAL MOUNTED PATROL (1941), TWILIGHT ON THE TRAIL (1941), BELLE OF THE YUKON (1944), KILROY WAS HERE (1947), and JIGGS AND MAGGIE IN SOCIETY (1948). In the 1950s, McKay guested on the television series "The Lone Ranger" and "The Cisco Kid."

McKay was married to the late composer and performer Hoagy Carmichael. She died of cancer.

McDermott, Tom

born: c. 1912; raised Chicago
died: March 6, 1996, New York City, NY, age 83

Veteran actor who worked to help minority colleagues in the theater.

Tom McDermott began acting while a high-school student in Chicago, and in a career spanning 64 years appearead in numerous Broadway and off-Broadway productions. McDermott served on the Actor's Equity Council from 1974-85 and was a founder of the organization's Paul Robeson Award; he also served on the Committee for Racial Equality and on the League of Regional Theaters Committee. His films include OVER THE BROOKLYN BRIDGE (1984), PLAYING FOR KEEPS and JUMPIN' JACK FLASH (both 1986), LIEBESTRAUM (UK 1991) and THE CRUCIBLE (1996).

Married for 61 years to actress Mary Hayden, McDermott died of complications of prostate cancer.

Meadows, Audrey

born: Audrey Cotter, Feb. 8, 1924, Wu Chang, China
died: Feb. 3, 1996, Los Angeles, CA, age 71

Actress best remembered as Alice Kramden on TV's "The Honeymooners."

Audrey Meadows and her actress sister Jayne were born in China to parents who were Episcopal missionaries. When the family came to New York City in the 1930s, both sisters took up acting and singing. Audrey debuted at Carnegie Hall as a coloratura soprano at age 16, and sang with civic light opera companies. Popular both on stage and television, she debuted on Broadway in the hit *Top Banana* (1951), opposite Phil Silvers, while concurrently appearing as a TV regular on a number of shows, including "The Jackie Gleason Show" (CBS 1952-55, 1956-57, 1958-61). That show incorporated the regular sketch "The Honeymooners," later spun off into a separate, filmed series (CBS 1955-56). (She was the second Alice Kramden: Pert Kelton preceded her, and Sheila MacRae followed her in the 1960s "Honeymooners" sketches.) She won the 1954 Emmy Award for Supporting Actress in a Series (for "The Jackie Gleason Show"). She co-starred in three movies: THAT TOUCH OF MINK (1962), TAKE HER, SHE'S MINE (1963), and ROSIE! (1967). She published her memoirs, *Love, Alice: My Life as a Honeymooner,* in 1994. Tough yet feminine and delightfully smart-mouthed, Meadows was married a quarter-century to second husband Bob Six, a Continental Airlines executive, who died in 1986. She herself served on banking and other business boards.

Meadows died of cancer.

McLean, Barbara

born: Barbara Pollut, c. 1905; raised Palisades Park, NJ
died: March 28 1996, Newport Beach, CA, age 92

Academy Award-winning film editor—one of the movie's first women in that field—and an advisor to Fox studio chief Darryl F. Zanuck.

Barbara McLean, who edited some of Hollywood's biggest films, began cutting and splicing film while a teenager working in her fathers' New Jersey film lab. She moved to Hollywood in 1924 with her husband, projectionist Gordon McLean. There she found work as a film technician, later becoming an assistant editor for a number of studios. In the early 1930s, she began her long association as Zanuck's unofficial right hand; the fearsome studio head inevitably selected her to edit his personal productions at Fox. These included two of her first films, THE MIGHTY BARNUM and THE HOUSE OF ROTHSCHILD (both 1934, co-ed with Allen McNeil). She earned her first Academy Award nomination for LLOYDS OF LONDON (1936), and was also nominated for ALEXANDER'S RAGTIME BAND (1938), THE RAINS CAME (1939), THE SONG OF BERNADETTE (1943), WILSON (1944, for which she won the Oscar), and ALL ABOUT EVE (1950). In all she edited roughly 50 films, including SUEZ (1938), JESSE JAMES (1939), LITTLE OLD NEW YORK (1940), A YANK IN THE RAF and TOBACCO ROAD (both 1941), WINGED VICTORY (1944), A BELL FOR ADANO (1945), TWELVE O'CLOCK HIGH (1949), NO WAY OUT (1950), THE SNOWS OF KILIMANJARO and VIVA ZAPATA! (both 1952), NIAGARA (1953), THE EGYPTIAN (1954), and UNTAMED (1955). She retired in 1969 after 20 years as the head of Fox's editing division. McLean, whose first marriage ended in divorce, married director Robert Webb in 1951 after working with him on DAVID AND BATHSHEBA (1951).

No cause of death was reported.

Morris, Greg

born: Sept. 27, 1934, Cleveland, OH
died: Aug. 27, 1996, Las Vegas, NV
educ: Ohio State University, University of Iowa

Actor best known for a starring role on TV's "Mission: Impossible" (1966-73).

After serving in the Army for three years, Greg Morris went to Hollywood in the early 1960s seeking a career in movies and television. He had small parts in a few TV sitcoms and series, such as "Twilight Zone," "The Dick Van Dyke Show," "Ben Casey, " and "I Spy," while also making a handful of movies. His film roles at that time included THE NEW INTERNS (1964), THE LIVELY SET (1964), and THE SWORD OF ALI BABA (1965).

Fame came to Morris in 1966 when, because of his athletic ability, he was cast as Barney Collier, the hi-tech expert of the Impossible Missions Force, in the popular TV series, "Mission: Impossible. " (Morris became the second African-American to star in an action series; Bill Cosby was the first in 1965's "I Spy"). Morris more than held his own in an ensemble cast of versatile and first-rate actors. After a run of seven seasons with the series, Morris made several TV movies and acted in the mini-series "Roots: The Next Generations." He appeared in the 1976 adventure film S. T. A. B. (1976) and was one of the leads in the Nigerian-made COUNTDOWN AT KUSINI (1976).

While costarring in the 1978 TV series, "Vegas," Morris settled in Las Vegas, where he died of cancer.

Morris, Richard

born: c. 1924 Burlingame, CA
died: April 27, 1996, Encino-Tarzana Regional Medical Center, CA, age 72
educ: Chouinard Art Institute, Los Angeles, CA; Neighborhood Playhouse, New York, NY

Screenwriter.

Richard Morris served with the special services division of the Army during WWII; afterward, he studied acting under Sanford Meisner in Manhattan, while also writing sketch comedy for young performers like Kaye Ballard. Brought to Los Angeles by a Universal Pictures talent scout, Morris wrote or co-wrote the scripts to such films as FINDERS KEEPERS (1951), MA AND PA KETTLE AT THE FAIR (1952), and TAKE ME TO TOWN (1953). Though he wrote primarily for television, he wrote the book (music and lyrics by Meredith Willson) for the hit Broadway musical *The Unsinkable Molly Brown,* and did the screenplay adaptation for the 1964 movie version. He had another hit with the musical THOROUGHLY MODERN MILLIE (1967); his script won the Writers Guild Award for best American musical.

Morris, who lived in Sherman Oaks, CA, died of cancer.

Muir, Jean

born: Jean Muir Fullarton, Feb. 13, 1911, Suffern, NY
died: July 23, 1996, Mesa, AZ, age 85
educ: The Sorbonne, Paris, France

Actress and organizer whose 1950 blacklisting from television highlighted the insidious practice in that medium.

Signed to a Warner Bros. contract by a talent scout who spotted her on Broadway in 1933, Jean Muir appeared in some two dozen movies, often as a feisty ingenue. Her films include SON OF A SAILOR (1933), AS THE EARTH TURNS, BEDSIDE, DESIRABLE, DOCTOR MONICA, and A MODERN HERO (all 1934), A MIDSUMMER NIGHT'S DREAM (1935), WHITE FANG (1936), and HER HUSBAND'S SECRETARY, THE OUTCASTS OF POKER FLAT and WHITE BONDAGE (all 1937). She remained active in small theater companies and productions, and in 1939 helped organize the American Guild of Variety Artists (AGVA). Muir made three more films—AND ONE WAS BEAUTIFUL and THE LONE WOLF MEETS A LADY (both 1940), and THE CONSTANT NYMPH (1943)—before devoting herself to stage and later television work. Because her name was listed in the "Red Channels" pamphlet that branded performers as Communists or sympathizers, right-wing groups protested her being cast in 1950 as the second Mrs. Aldrich (succeeding Lois Wilson) on the TV version of "The Aldrich Family." Though Muir denied any Communist leaning, General Foods, the shows sponsor, stated that no matter the truth, she was being fired as "a controversial personality." The emotional toll of the blacklisting eventually led Muir to alcoholism, and she didn't work in TV again until 1958; she retired from television for good in 1962. Muir, who received a star on the Hollywood Walk of Fame in 1960, appeared in one more film, STRIP TEASE MURDER (UK 1961), and spent the remainder of her career teaching drama at several colleges and universities.

No cause of death was reported.

Mulligan, Gerry

born: April 6, 1927, New York City, NY; raised Philadelphia, PA
died: Jan. 20, 1996, Darien, CN, age 68

Jazz great and one-time husband of Judy Holliday, who appeared in and did music for a number of films.

Baritone saxophonist Gerry Mulligan, who helped create the "cool jazz" movement of the 1940s and worked with Dave Brubeck, Miles Davis and Duke Ellington, wrote arrangements for Johnny Warrington's radio band while still a teenager, and wrote for Gene Krupa's band after returning to New York in 1946. Performing and recording, he won his first major acclaim in 1952 after forming a piano-less jazz quartet with Chet Baker on trumpet. Mulligan played a musician in I WANT TO LIVE! (1958) and appeared in similar roles in THE SUBTERRANEANS, THE RAT RACE and Holliday's last film, BELLS ARE RINGING (all 1960). He composed music for films including A THOUSAND CLOWNS (1963), LUV (1967), and I'M NOT RAPPAPORT (1996), and appears in the concert film JAZZ ON A SUMMER'S DAY (1959) and the feature documentaries JAZZ IN AMERICA (1981) and A GREAT DAY IN HARLEM (1995).

Mulligan reportedly died of complications from a knee infection.

Nadia

aka: : "Fearless" Nadia
born: Mary Evans, Jan. 8, 1908, Perth, Australia
died: Jan. 9, 1996, Bombay, India, age 88

Unique, enormously popular figure in Indian cinema.

Mary Evans, the daughter of an Australian mother and an English father who was transferred to India when she was five, starred in more than 50 films as the blonde, blue-eyed, Amazonian swashbuckler who became an Indian Robin Hood/Zorro figure. After learning horseback riding and ballet, she joined the Zarko Circus in 1930; a fortune teller reportedly convinced her to change her name to Nadia. After breaking into film with two 1934 Hindi movies, DESH DEEPAK and NOOR-E-YAMAN, she quickly became a star with HUNTERWALI/THE LADY HUNTER, launching "Fearless" Nadia as national icon.

When producer-director Homi Wadia cast her in THE DAUGHTER OF HUNTERWALI (India 1943), it revived the genre of Indian stunt films, such as Nadia's own TIGRESS, STUNT QUEEN and LADY ROBIN HOOD. In 35 of her films, she co-starred with bodybuilder John Cawas. Fearless Nadia largely retired from acting in 1961 to marry Wadia and breed racing thoroughbreds, but returned at least once, in 1968, with the Wadia-directed KHILARI/THE PLAYER. Her films include DIAMOND QUEEN (1940), MISS FRONTIER MAIL, HURRICANE HANSA, JUNGLE PRINCESS, and BAGDAD KA JADOO/THE MAGIC OF BAGDAD.

No cause of death was reported.

Nance, Jack

aka: John Nance
born: Marvin John Nance, 1943; raised Dallas, TX
died: Dec. 30, 1996, South Pasadena, CA, age 53

Star of David Lynch's ERASERHEAD (1978), and a supporting-actor fixture in Lynch's oeuvre.

Jack Nance studied with Paul Baker, founder of the Dallas Theater Center, before moving to California in the 1960s and working at the Pasadena Playhouse and at the Circus Theater Company in San Francisco. After appearing in an early movie, FOOLS (1970), he starred eight years later (billed as John Nance) in Lynch's surreal debut feature, the midnight-movie classic ERASERHEAD. The black-and-white film's key image of Nance's character—a Jacques Tati innocent in a surreally menacing nightmare world, his shock of hair standing like wild grass—is one of the movies' most recognizable. Nance went on to appear in small parts in Lynch's DUNE (1984), BLUE VELVET (1986), WILD AT HEART (1990), the TV series "Twin Peaks" (ABC 1990-91) as Pete Martell, a character he recreated in TWIN PEAKS: FIRE WALK WITH ME (1992), and LOST HIGHWAY (1997). He also appeared in Lynch's 22-minute French short "Le Cowboy et le Frenchman" (1988).

Nance appeared in small roles in many films as well, including BREAKER! BREAKER! (1977), HAMMETT (1983), BARFLY (1987), COLORS and THE BLOB (1988), THE HOT SPOT (1990), WHORE (1991), MOTORAMA (1992), LOVE AND A . 45 (1994), and LITTLE WITCHES (1996). He often portrayed priests, doctors, Good Samaritans, and other helpful souls who nonetheless may have seen too much of life.

Nance—who at one time was married to another Lynch regular, actress Catherine E. Coulson (the Log Lady of "Twin Peaks")—was found dead at his home by a friend on Dec. 30. The day before, he had had an argument with two men while at a doughnut shop across the street; at least one of the men hit Nance in the head with his fist. Homicide detectives have determined Nance had suffered blunt-force trauma to his head, although no cause of death was initially announced.

Neise, George

born: George N. Neise, c. 1917, Chicago, IL
died: April 14, 1996, Hollywood, CA, age 79

Longtime character actor.

George Neise, who served as a colonel in the Army Air Force during WWII, entered films as a Republic Pictures player, appearing in the likes of the "Three Mesquiteers" installment VALLEY OF HUNTED MEN (1942). Neise appeared in film through 1971's THE BAREFOOT EXECUTIVE (playing a TV exec), and gave pungent character moments to such films as NO TIME FOR SERGEANTS (1958), as a baker, and ON A CLEAR DAY YOU CAN SEE FOREVER (1970). He appeared on numerous TV programs.

Neise died of natural causes.

Nelson, Gene

born: Eugene Leander Berg, March 24, 1920, Seattle, WA
died: Sept. 16, 1996, Calabasas, CA, age 76

Dancer-choreographer turned actor-director who played the boyish blonde lasso dancer in OKLAHOMA! (1955) and did similarly athletic turns in other films before turning to dramatic roles and directing.

A high-school gymnast and ice skater, Gene Nelson appeared regularly on Broadway and won a Tony Award for *Follies* (1971). During WWII, Nelson entertained American troops in Europe. Upon returning to Los Angeles, Nelson won a two-year contract with 20th Century-Fox and appeared in I WONDER WHO'S KISSING HER NOW (1947), and THE WALLS OF JERICHO and APARTMENT FOR PEGGY (1948). A three-year contract with Warner Bros. followed, leading to a string of musicals for that studio and others, including THE DAUGHTER OF ROSIE O'GRADY (1950), TEA FOR TWO and THE WEST POINT STORY (1950), SHE'S WORKING HER WAY THROUGH COLLEGE (1952), THREE SAILORS AND A GIRL (1953), and SO THIS IS PARIS (1954; also choreography).

Nelson turned to dramatic roles as his dancing years ended, starring in CRIME WAVE (1954), THE ATOMIC MAN (1955), and THE PURPLE HILLS (1961), as well as a family drama, THUNDER ISLAND (1963). As his acting career cooled down, Nelson began directing, mostly for producer Sam Katzman. He directed HAND OF DEATH (1962), HOOTENANNY HOOT (1963), YOUR CHEATIN' HEART aka THE HANK WILLIAMS STORY (1964), and HARUM SCARUM (1965); he both wrote and directed THE COOL ONES (1967) and KISSIN' COUSINS (1964). He directed numerous television episodes and telefilms. Nelson's last film as an actor was S. O. B. (1981).

Nelson, who lived in Los Angeles, died of cancer.

Ngor, Haing S.

born: March 22, 1940, Samrong Young, Cambodia
died: Feb. 25, 1996, Los Angeles, CA, age 55

Cambodian-refugee doctor whose portrayal of a Cambodian journalist imprisoned by the Khmer Rouge in THE KILLING FIELDS (UK 1984) earned him an Academy Award.

Haing S. Ngor was trained as a medical doctor in his native land. After the bloody 1975 takeover of Cambodia by the Khmer Rouge rebels, who overthrew the country's US-backed government, he and countless other doctors, teachers, professionals, and other examples of Western influence were captured and tortured. When a Vietnamese invasion ousted the rebels four years later, Ngor escaped to Thailand. In 1980, he settled in the US, where he worked various jobs before resuming his medical career. He was cast, out of hundreds of auditioning Cambodian actors and non-actors, to play Dith Pran, the associate of *New York Times* foreign correspondent Sydney Schanberg, whose magazine article "The Death and Life of Dith Pran" formed the basis for THE KILLING FIELDS. Ngor's performance won him the Oscar for best supporting actor, making him the first non-professional to receive an Academy Award since Harold Russell in THE BEST YEARS OF OUR LIVES (1946). He went on to act regularly in movies and on television, and in his later years devoted considerable time and money to organizing Cambodian-refugee charities. Ngor's films include EASTERN CONDORS (1986), THE IRON TRIANGLE (1989), VIETNAM, TEXAS (1990), AMBITION (1991), MY LIFE and HEAVEN AND EARTH (1993), and FORTUNES OF WAR (1994). His autobiography was published in 1988.

Ngor was found shot to death beside his car outside his home in the Chinatown section of Los Angeles. In April 1996, three suspects, reportedly members of an Asian street gang, were charged with murder committed during a robbery.

Nicholas, George

born: 1911, Vermilion, OH
died: Nov. 23, 1996, Edinboro PA, age 85

Animator.

George Nicholas worked on such animated features as Disney's CINDERELLA (1950) and SLEEPING BEAUTY (1959), and THE PHANTOM TOLLBOOTH (1969), adapted from the book illustrated by Jules Feiffer.

Niver, Kemp R.

born: c. 1912, Los Angeles, CA
died: Oct. 15, 1996, Los Angeles, CA, age 84

Film historian.

Kemp R. Niver wrote books and articles about film history, and was instrumental in a 15-year preservation project saving some 3,000 turn-of-the-century films, some dating to 1894, in the collection of the Library of Congress. He designed a printer to transfer the library's perishable paper prints onto conventional 16-millimeter film stock. Niver won an honorary Oscar in 1954 for his efforts. He also had a small role in the comedy THE GROOM WORE SPURS (1951).

No cause of death was reported.

O'Brien, Liam

born: c. 1912, New York City, NY
died: March 24, 1996, Los Angeles, CA, age 83
educ: Fordham University, Manhattan College, New York City, NY

Academy Award-nominated screenwriter, TV producer, occasional actor, and brother of actor Edmond O'Brien (1910-85).

Liam O'Brien was a poet, cartoonist, labor organizer and WWII Army Signal Corps soldier before becoming a playwright. His breakthrough came with Broadway's *The Remarkable Mr. Pennypacker.* He and Robert Riskin shared an Oscar nomination for Best Story for HERE COMES THE GROOM (1951). Other films O'Brien wrote or co-wrote include CHAIN LIGHTNING and THE REDHEAD AND THE COWBOY (1950), YOUNG AT HEART (1955), TRAPEZE (1956), THE GREAT IMPOSTOR (1960), and THE DEVIL AT 4 O'CLOCK (1961).

In later years, O'Brien turned largely to television scripting, and was a producer on "Police Story" and "Miami Vice. " O'Brien played a Supreme Court Justice in the telefilm GIDEON'S TRUMPET (1980), and appeared in THE SPIRIT OF '76 (1990).

He died of heart failure.

O'Connell, David J.

born: c. 1916, Brightwaters, NY
died: Jan. 16, 1996, Santa Monica, CA, age 79
educ: Brooklyn Prep, Fordham University, New York City, NY

TV producer who made theatrical feature-film versions of two series.

David J. O'Connell—who as producer of "Marcus Welby, MD" shared a 1969/70 Emmy Award for Best Dramatic Series—worked in various production and post-production capacities at Republic Pictures in the 1950s. In 1953, he began a long stint at Revue Productions (later Universal Studios Television), before becoming a producer in 1965. During the 1960s and '70s, his series and pilots included "Ironside," "The Name of the Game," and "Operation Petticoat." O'Donnell produced the well-regarded BACKTRACK (1969), a crossover episode of "The Virginian" and "Laredo, " and the less-well-received MISSION GALACTICA:THE CYLON ATTACK (1979), edited from two episodes of that series.

O'Connell, who retired in 1981, died of chronic lung disease.

O'Donnell, Lynn

born: c. 1952, Berkeley, CA
died: April 17, 1996, San Francisco, CA, age 43
educ: San Francisco State U. (filmmaking degree)

Documentary filmmaker who produced the acclaimed CRUMB (1995).

Lynn O'Donnell's works include VOICES OF THE TANGO, a PBS documentary about Carlos Gardel, as well as a portrait of the 1980 Nobel Laureate for literature, CZESLAW MILOSZ: THE POET REMEMBERS, directed by Jane Nemec. O'Donnell also produced Steven Okazaki's first feature film, the independent comedy LIVING ON TOKYO TIME (1987). CRUMB, directed by Terry Zwigoff, won the Grand Prix at the Sundance Film Festival.

O'Donnell died of ovarian cancer.

O'Neal, Charles

aka: "Blackie" O'Neal
born: 1904, Raeford, NC; raised Atlanta, GA
died: Aug. 29, 1996, Beverly Hills, CA, age 92
educ: Georgia Tech; University of Iowa (literature)

Film and TV screenwriter, the father of actor Ryan O'Neal and screenwriter Kevin O'Neal, and the grandfather of actors Tatum, Griffin, and Patrick O'Neal.

Charles O'Neal acted onstage in New York, southern California, and Chicago, eventually becoming a leading member of the Old Globe Shakespearean Repertory in San Diego. Among the films he wrote or co-wrote are THE SEVENTH VICTIM (1943), CRY OF THE WEREWOLF (1944), I LOVE A MYSTERY (1945), JOHNNY TROUBLE (1957), and THE ALLIGATOR PEOPLE (1959). He also wrote for television and the stage, including the Broadway musical *Three Wishes for Jamie* (1952), adapted from his novel *The Three Wishes of Jamie McRuin* (1949).

No cause of death was reported.

Opatoshu, David

born: Jan. 30, 1918, New York City, NY
died: April 30, 1996, Los Angeles, CA, age 78

Emmy Award-winning character actor best known for his role as Akiva Ben-Canaan, the scholarly Jewish resistance leader in EXODUS (1960).

The son of Yiddish novelist Joseph Opatoshu, David Opatoshu began his acting career in the Yiddish theater. He kept close ties to those roots throughout his career, debuting in film as the youthful star of the Yiddish-language feature FISHKE DER KRUMER aka DIE KLATSCHE/THE LIGHT AHEAD (1939); in 1985, he narrated ALMONDS AND RAISINS, a documentary on the Yiddish theater in America.

Opatoshu made his Broadway debut in 1938. After his Hollywood feature debut with THE NAKED CITY (1948), he played villains, thoughtful heroic men, and complex authority figures in such films as THE BROTHERS KARAMAZOV (1958), CIMARRON (1960), TORN CURTAIN (1966), ENTER LAUGHING (1967), THE FIXER (1968), DEATH OF A GUNFIGHTER (1969), and WHO'LL STOP THE RAIN? (1978). On television he appeared in such telefilms as RAID ON ENTEBBE (1977) and CONSPIRACY: THE TRIAL OF THE CHICAGO 8 (1987).

Opatoshu wrote the screenplay for, and also appeared in, ROMANCE OF A HORSE THIEF (1971), based on a novella by his father. His films include THIEVES' HIGHWAY (1949), THE GOLDBERGS (1950), PARTY GIRL (1958), TARZAN AND THE VALLEY OF GOLD (1966), AMERICATHON (1979), FORTY DAYS OF MUSA DAGH (Turkey 1986), and BEYOND EVIL (1980).

Opatoshu died after a long illness.

Pascal, Christine

born: Nov. 29, 1953 Lyons, France
died: Aug. 30, 1996, Paris, France, age 42

Popular, doe-eyed French actress with a raspy-yet-girlish voice, who made her acting debut at 20 and directed her first film at 25.

After appearances on French TV, Christine Pascal made her film debut with a small role in Bertrand Tavernier's L'HORLOGER DE SAINT-PAUL/THE CLOCKMAKER (France 1973). She went on to appear in four other Tavernier movies: QUE LA FETE COMMENCE/LET JOY REIGN SUPREME (France 1975; US release 1977); DES ENFANTS GATES/THE SPOILED CHILDREN (France 1977), which she co-wrote; JUGE ET L'ASSASSIN/THE JUDGE AND THE ASSASSIN (France 1979); and 'ROUND MIDNIGHT (US-France 1986). Her breakthrough came with LES GUICHETS DU LOUVRE/BLACK THURSDAY (France 1973).

Pascal began writing-directing with FELICITIE (France 1979), in which she starred, and went on to write and direct films, including LA GARCE/THE BITCH (France 1984; also actor), ZANZIBAR (France 1988), LE PETIT PRINCE A DIT/AND THE LITTLE PRINCE SAID (France 1992), which won the Prix Louis-Delluc at Cannes, and her final feature, ADULTHRE, MODE D'EMPLOI/ADULTERY, A USER'S MANUAL (1995).

Pascal's films as actress include Andrzej Wajda's THE YOUNG GIRLS OF WILKO (Poland-France 1979), COUP DE FOUDRE/ENTRE NOUS (France 1983), SIGNI CHARLOTTE/SINCERELY CHARLOTTE (France 1986), LE GRAND CHEMIN/THE GRAND HIGHWAY (France 1987), REGARDE LES HOMMES TOMBER/SEE HOW THEY FALL (France 1994), and LES PATRIOTES/THE PATRIOTS (France 1994).

Pascal committed suicide by throwing herself out the window of a clinic on the outskirts of Paris, where she had apparently been battling depression.

Patten, Luana

born: July 6, 1938, Long Beach, CA
died: May 1, 1996, Long Beach, CA, age 57

Popular Disney child star of the 1940s.

Luana Patten made her movie debut at age eight, with the films LITTLE MISTER JIM and Disney's SONG OF THE SOUTH (both 1946). As one of the studio's first contract players, she made three other Disney features: FUN AND FANCY FREE (1947), MELODY TIME (1948; voice only), and SO DEAR TO MY HEART (1949), before taking a hiatus for school. Patten later returned to Disney for JOHNNY TREMAIN (1957) and FOLLOW ME, BOYS! (1966). Under contract with Universal and MGM, she made such films as ROCK, PRETTY BABY (1956), JOE DAKOTA (1957), THE RESTLESS YEARS (1958), HOME FROM THE HILL (1960), and GO NAKED IN THE WORLD (1961). She retired from acting in 1968. She married actor John Smith in 1960, divorcing after four years.

Patten died of respiratory failure.

Perepelkin, Keith

born: c. 1964
died: Oct. 31, 1996, Squamish, BC, Canada, age 32

Stuntman.

Keith Perepelkin, of Vancouver, was killed while working on the movie FIRESTORM. During a second-unit shoot 65 miles north of Vancouver, at a remote, 2,000-foot high, granite rock-climbing site called Stawmus Chief, Perepelkin, clutching a dummy, jumped from a helicopter. His parachute failed to open, and though a backup chute did, it was not in time to adequately slow his descent.

Perry, Joan

aka: Joan Perry Cohn
born: Betty Miller, c. 1911, Pensacola, FL
died: Sept. 15, 1996, Montecito, CA, age 85

Starlet who became the longtime wife of Columbia Pictures co-founder Harry Cohn.

Joan Perry was put under contract with Columbia in 1935, at about the same time as Rita Hayworth. Per Hollywood lore, Cohn told Perry, "Hayworth will become a star, and you'll become my wife. " They were married in 1941, after she had done a number of pictures for Columbia and Warner Bros. including GALLANT DEFENDER (1935), DANGEROUS INTRIGUE, MEET NERO WOLFE, MYSTERIOUS AVENGER (1936), COUNTERFEIT LADY (1937), START CHEERING (1938), THE LONE WOLF STRIKES (1940), and MAISIE WAS A LADY, BULLETS FOR O'HARA, and STRANGE ALIBI (1941).

After her husband's death in 1958, Cohn married shoe tycoon Harry Karl, a longtime family friend. The marriage made headlines after lasting only 21 days, with Cohn receiving a $100,000 settlement. She married actor Laurence Harvey in 1968, divorcing after four years.

Perry died of emphysema.

Pertwee, Jon

born: John Devon Roland Pertwee, July 7. 1919
died: May 20, 1996, New York, NY, age 76
educ: Sherborne; Royal Academy of Dramatic Art (RADA), London, England

Actor best known as the third star to portray the lead role in the TV cult-classic "Dr. Who."

Jon Pertwee came from a theatrical background. During the 1930s, while doing repertory theater and odd jobs, Pertwee began to make a name for himself on commercial radio with his chameleon-like ability to hop from one accent and dialect to another at great speed. Pertwee began his film career in the late 1930s and continued through the 1960s with a gaggle of TV, radio, film, and summer theatrical revues, taking small parts in a host of the long-running "Carry On" films, including CARRY ON CLEO (1964), and CARRY ON COWBOY and CARRY ON SCREAMING (1966).

In 1970, with the show in its seventh season, Pertwee took over the lead in the long-running sci-fi series, "Dr. Who" (BBC 1963-present). Of the eight actors to date to portray the role of the time-traveling doctor, Pertwee and immediate successor Tom Baker are considered the definitive interpreters. Pertwee remained for four seasons.

Pertwee's many films (all UK) include A YANK AT OXFORD (1938), THE SECRET FOUR (1940), HELTER SKELTER (1949), MISS PILGRIM'S PROGRESS (1950), MR. DRAKE'S DUCK (1951), A YANK IN ERMINE (1955), THE UGLY DUCKLING (1959), NEARLY A NASTY ACCIDENT (1962), YOU MUST BE JOKING! (1965), and THE HOUSE THAT DRIPPED BLOOD (1971).

Pertwee's 1955 marriage to actress Jean Marsh ended in divorce. His second wife, Ingeborg, is a novelist. He died under unreported circumstances while vacationing in the US.

Peterson, Arthur

born: Nov. 18, 1912, Mandan, ND
died: Oct. 31, 1996, Pasadena, CA, age 83
educ: University of Minnesota (theater degree)

Character actor best known as The Major on the satiric sitcom "Soap" (1977-81).

Arthur Peterson began his acting career in Chicago, as a company member of the first Depression-era Federal Theater Project. He made his film debut in CALL NORTHSIDE 777 (1948). Prominent in theater, radio, and television, his other films include RETURN TO PEYTON PLACE (1961), THE CHILDREN'S HOUR (1962), INVITATION TO A GUNFIGHTER (1964), BORN WILD, TARGETS, and YOURS, MINE AND OURS (1968), THE GREAT NORTHFIELD, MINNESOTA RAID (1972), and ROLLERCOASTER (1977). In 1971, he founded the Actors Alley Repertory Theater, a local institution that continues to operate in North Hollywood.

Peterson died of complications of Alzheimer's disease.

Pistilli, Luigi

born: c. 1929, Italy
died: April 21, 1996, Milan, Italy, age 66
educ: acting school of the Piccolo Teatro, Milan, Italy (1955)

Italian film, theater, and TV actor.

Luigi Pistilli was considered one of Italy's foremost interpreters of Bertolt Brecht. A noted stage actor, he also appeared in such films as (all Italian or Italian co-productions) DARK PASSAGE (1947), PER QUALCHE DOLLARO IN PIU/FOR A FEW DOLLARS MORE (1965), IL BUONO, IL BRUTTO, IL CATTIVO/THE GOOD, THE BAD AND THE UGLY, and TEXAS, ADDIO (1966), A CIASCUNO IL SUO/WE STILL KILL THE OLD WAY (1967), DA UOMO A UOMO/DEATH RIDES A HORSE, IL DOLCE CORPO DI DEBORAH/THE BODY aka THE SWEET BODY OF DEBORAH (1969), GLI INTOCCABILI aka MACHINE GUN McCAIN (1970), REAZIONE A CATENA/LAST HOUSE ON THE LEFT, PART II aka TWITCH OF THE DEATH NERVE (1971), CADAVERI ECCELLENTI/ILLUSTRIOUS CORPSES (1976), and TOTTERING LIVES aka THE EERIE MIDNIGHT HORROR SHOW (1976).

Pistilii committed suicide at his home shortly before he was due to go onstage.

Popplewell, Jack

born: c. 1909
died: Nov. 16, 1996, Bath, England, age 87

Hit songwriter and playwright.

Jack Popplewell wrote the standards "If I Should Fall in Love Again," recorded by Gracie Fields and others, and "My Girl's an Irish Girl," popularized by Bing Crosby. His first produced play, *Blind Alley* (1953), was adapted as the film TREAD SOFTLY, STRANGER (1958). Other plays include *Dead on Nine, Dear Delinquent, Hocus-Pocus, High Infidelity,* and *The Queen's Favorites.*

No cause of death was reported.

Prince, William

born: Jan. 26, 1913, Nichols, NY
died: Oct. 8, 1996, Tarrytown, NY, age 83
educ: Cornell University

Veteran Broadway, film, and television actor.

William Prince worked in regional, touring, and Broadway theater productions before being signed to a Hollywood contract. He appeared in such films as DESTINATION TOKYO (1943), HOLLYWOOD CANTEEN (1944), OBJECTIVE, BURMA! (1945), SHADOW OF A WOMAN (1946), DEAD RECKONING (1947), LUST FOR GOLD (1949), and CYRANO DE BERGERAC (1950), in one of his most notable roles, as the handsome but inarticulate Christian. For most of the 1950s and '60s, he worked primarily in theater and television, including many daytime serials. Aging into a character actor, Prince also appeared in THE HEARTBREAK KID (1972), THE STEPFORD WIVES (1975), FAMILY PLOT and NETWORK (1976), ROLLERCOASTER and THE GAUNTLET (1977), SPIES LIKE US (1985), NUTS (1987), VICE VERSA (1988), and THE TAKING OF BEVERLY HILLS (1991). His final film role was as Michael Keaton's father in THE PAPER (1994; his wife Augusta Dabney, whom he married in the mid-1960s, played Keaton's mother).

Prince, who lived in Dobbs Ferry, NY, died of undisclosed causes.

Prouse, Derek

born: July 10, 1922
died: Dec. 25, 1996, age 74

British film writer, translator, and film festival professional.

Among other accomplishments, Derek Prowse translated Eugene Ionesco's classic play *Rhinoceros,* scripted Claude Chabrol's THE CHAMPAGNE MURDERS (1967), and served on the jury of the 15th International Cannes Film Festival (1962).

No cause of death was reported.

Prowse, Juliet

born: Sept. 25, 1936, Bombay, India; raised South Africa
died: Sept. 14, 1996, Los Angeles (Holmby Hills), CA, age 59
educ: Royal Academy of Dance, South Africa

Popular actress-dancer and celebrity fixture.

Juliet Prowse was known for her comedic good nature and leggy, athletic dance style. Born to British parents, she lived in India until she was three, when her father died. After studying ballet for some years, she became too tall to continue and switched to modern dance. Prowse performed in European nightclubs and in musicals, where Hollywood choreographer Hermes Pan saw her and cast her in the musical CAN-CAN (1960). Though the era of Hollywood musicals was in its twilight, limiting her career, Prowse became an overnight sensation. She went on to act and/or dance in such movies as G. I. BLUES (1960), THE FIERCEST HEART, THE RIGHT APPROACH, and THE SECOND TIME AROUND (1961), WHO KILLED TEDDY BEAR? (1965), DINGAKA (South Africa 1965), and SPREE aka LAS VEGAS BY NIGHT (1967). Along with a comically rubbery face, Prowse was hailed as having the best legs in Hollywood since Betty Grable. After largely ending her brief film career, she remained successful with TV specials, theatrical productions, and nightclub acts.

Romantically linked to Elvis Presley and her CAN-CAN co-star Frank Sinatra (to whom she was engaged for six weeks), Prowse had a brief, early marriage which she rarely discussed. She married actor John McCook in 1980, shortly after giving birth to their son; the couple later divorced.

Prowse died of pancreatic cancer.

Rama Rao, N. T.

aka: Nandamuri Taraka Rama Rao
born: c. 1922
died: Jan. 11, 1996, Hyderabad, India, age 73

Indian film star turned political leader.

The actor N. T. Rama Rao appeared in what the Reuters news agency characterized as "hundreds" of Indian films. He was the titular leader of the left-wing National Front alliance between his regionally-based Telugu Desam Party and the Janata Dal. Though the Telugu Desam party had swept to power in its home state of Andhra Pradesh in the December 1994 elections, Rama Rao was nonetheless ousted not long afterward by son-in-law Chandrababu Naidu. His films—few if any of which came to general commercial release in the US—include PATALA BHAIRAVI aka PATAAL BHAIRAVI / THE GODDESS FROM BELOW THE EARTH (1951).

Rama Rao died of a heart attack.

Randall, Dick

born: c. 1925
died: May 14, 1996, London, England, age 70

Exploitation film producer with a remarkably diverse, worldwide career.

Dick Randall, who founded the independent production and distribution company Spectacular Trading, produced a colorful array of movies through four decades. He produced and directed the comedy SHANGRI-LA (1961), one of the comedic "nudie-cutie" pictures of its era, and he himself starred in director-producer Jose Benazeraf's innocently naughty PARIS EROTIKA/PARIS OOH-LA-LA! (US-France 1963). Randall was a producer of Jayne Mansfield's L'AMORE PRIMITIVO/PRIMITIVE LOVE (Italy; US release 1966) and of the horror/sci-fi films CROCODILE (Thailand-Hong Kong; US release 1979), SUPERSONIC MAN (Spain; US release 1979), DON'T OPEN TILL CHRISTMAS (UK 1984), SLAUGHTER HIGH (1987; also bit actor), and Paramount Pictures' attempt at an indie-style slasher flick, APRIL FOOL'S DAY (1986). He adapted the Bill Warren comic-magazine story "For the Love of Frankenstein" into the story basis of the cult-classic T&A horror film LA FIGLIA DI FRANKENSTEIN/THE DAUGHTER OF FRANKENSTEIN aka LADY FRANKENSTEIN (Italy 1971). His final feature was LIVING DOLL (1990), with Eartha Kitt.

Randall died of heart failure following a series of strokes.

Rapp, Philip

born: c. 1911
died: Jan. 23, 1996, Beverly Hills, CA, age 85

Veteran comedy writer and screenwriter who created the classic radio series "The Bickersons."

Philip Rapp, who besides creating that hilarious Don Ameche-Frances Langford husband-and-wife fight-fest, also was a writer for Eddie Cantor's long-running network radio show, and wrote two of Fanny Brice's shows, "Good News Series" and "Maxwell House Coffee Time," which featured Brice's signature character, Baby Snooks. As a screenwriter, Rapp collaborated on such films as STRIKE ME PINK (1936), START CHEERING (1938), ZIEGFELD FOLLIES (1945), and AIN'T MISBEHAVIN' (1955). Rapp, along with Joel Sayre and Morrie Ryskind, were uncredited gag writers on THERE'S ALWAYS A WOMAN (1938), Columbia's failed attempt to launch Joan Blondell and Melvyn Douglas as the studio's own THIN MAN-type series. Rapp also co-wrote the Danny Kaye films WONDER MAN (1945) and THE INSPECTOR GENERAL (1949); some sources also list Kaye's THE SECRET LIFE OF WALTER MITTY (1947), though Rapp is uncredited onscreen. For television, Rapp wrote and directed for the sitcom "Topper" (CBS 1953-55) and wrote for the Wally Cox series "The Adventures of Hiram Holliday" (NBC 1956-57).

Rapp, whose son, Paul, is a producer and son Joel, a writer, died of natural causes.

Regan, Phil

born: Philip Joseph Christopher Aloysios Regan, May 28, 1906, New York City (Brooklyn), NY
died: Feb. 11, 1996, Santa Barbara, CA, age 89

"The Singing Cop" of nearly two dozen films of the 1930s and '40s.

Phil Regan, the youngest of five children of Irish immigrants, was a New York City police officer whose entertainment career began, as Hollywood lore has it, during an assignment that posted him at a vaudeville producer's party. He drifted to a piano, began singing in his tenor voice, a radio producer heard him, and a star was born. He began appearing on radio with George Burns and Gracie Allen, and was put under a film contract with Warner Bros. He appeared in such musicals (and the occasional drama, playing a crooner) as DAMES, THE PERSONALITY KID, STUDENT TOUR, and the Bette Davis drama HOUSEWIFE (1934). In SHE MARRIED A COP (1939), he co-starred with Jean Parker as a singing cop who's hired to do movie vocals, not realizing it's for cartoon character Paddy the Pig. He also played himself in Bing Crosby's THREE LITTLE WORDS (1950).

After performing on "The Ed Sullivan Show" and hosting radio's "The Phil Regan Armed Forces Show" (1951), Regan retired from show business to work in public relations, eventually expanding from showbiz clients to the likes of Anheuser-Busch and the steelworkers union. He grew wealthy through investments in Texas oil.

No cause of death was reported.

Reid, Beryl

born: June 17, 1920, Hereford, England
died: Oct. 13, 1996, age 76

Film character actress and Tony Award-winning stage performer who was among the most popular stars of British theater and TV.

Beryl Reid left school at 16 to become an entertainer, making her debut in 1936 as a music hall performer at the Floral Hall, Bridlington, England. Through the 1930s and '40s, as a stand-up comic and a comedian, she performed in variety shows. As something of an earlier generation's Tracey Ullman, she created and played both a schoolgirl in love with a ventriloquist's dummy, and an earthier teenage girl with airs, on the BBC radio series "Educating Archie." After making her London stage debut in "After the Show" (1951), she starred in a series of musical revues in which, chameleon-like, she played 16 to 18 characters a night. Reid would eventually make a transition to dramatic acting, performing in plays by Joe Orton, Edward Albee, and Peter Nichols, as well as in classics for the Royal Shakespeare Company and England's National Theater.

Reid's sly, powerful performance in Frank Marcus's play *The Killing of Sister George* (1965)—as a lusty, cigar-smoking, radio soap star being excised from her show, just as her real-life lesbian relationship is deteriorating—was a hit in Bristol and London, and her Broadway recreation won her a Tony Award in 1967. Reid reprised her role in Robert Aldrich's 1968 film version.

Reid's films (all UK except as noted) include THE BELLES OF ST. TRINIAN'S (1954), THE EXTRA DAY (1956), TWO-WAY STRETCH (1960; US release 1961), THE DOCK BRIEF aka TRIAL AND ERROR (1962), INSPECTOR CLOUSEAU (1968), STAR! (US 1968), THE ASSASSINATION BUREAU (1969), ENTERTAINING MR. SLOANE (1970), the film version of the Joe Orton play (reprising her role as the seductive landlady, a part she later recreated for the 1975 Royal Court Theater production), THE BEAST IN THE CELLAR (1970); DR. PHIBES RISES AGAIN (1972), PSYCHOMANIA aka THE DEATH WHEELERS (1973; US release 1974), opposite George Sanders, JOSEPH ANDREWS (1977), CARRY ON EMMANUELLE (1978), NO SEX PLEASE—WE'RE BRITISH (1979), YELLOWBEARD (1983), and THE DOCTOR AND THE DEVILS (1985).

Among her most popular TV roles was George Smiley's (Alec Guiness) former research aide, Connie Sachs, in the John le Carre adaptations TINKER, TAILOR, SOLDIER, SPY (1980) and SMILEY'S PEOPLE (1982). Reid was awarded the Order of the British Empire (OBE) in 1986.

Reid, who lived in Wraysbury, outside London, died after developing pneumonia following a knee operation.

Rene, Norman

born: c. 1951, Bristol, RI
died: May 24, 1996, New York City (Manhattan), NY, age 45

Theater and film producer-director.

Norman Rene, who originally intended to become a psychologist, left Johns Hopkins University after a year to study acting, later switching to directing, at Carnegie Mellon. During summers, he helped run Pittsburgh's repertory Red Barn Theater, and after graduating, moved to New York City. In 1977, with three fellow alumni, he founded the off-off-Broadway theater troupe, The Production Company, which produced works by such playwrights as Craig Lucas—including *Missing Persons* (1981), *Blue Window* (1984), *Three Postcards* (1987), *reckless* (1988) and the Obie Award-winning *Prelude to a Kiss* (1990)—and Nicholas Kazan, including *Blood Moon.* Rene also worked with resident theater companies, and directed productions both on Broadway and off, including Beth Henley's *Debutante Ball,* George Furth's Broadway play *Precious Sons,* Timothy Mason's play *Fiery Furnace,* and Karen Trott's one-woman show, *Springhill Singing Disaster.*

Rene directed the "American Playhouse" film LONGTIME COMPANION (1990), from an original screenplay by Lucas and one of the first films to deal with AIDS. It won the Audience Award at the Sundance Festival. He also directed and was a producer of the film adaptation of PRELUDE TO A KISS (1992). The Rene-Lucas play *reckless* was made into a 1995 film independent of them.

Rene died of complications from AIDS.

Rettig, Tommy

born: Thomas Noel Rettig, Dec. 10, 1941, New York City (Jackson Heights), NY
died: Feb. 15, 1996, Marina Del Rey, CA, age 54

Child actor best known as the first human companion of TV's "Lassie."

Rettig, who played Jeff Wilson with the famous collie character from 1954-57, was already a well-established actor when chosen for "Lassie" (CBS/syndicated 1954-74). He had begun acting at six, making his debut opposite Mary Martin in a touring company of *Annie Get Your Gun* and broke into movies in 1950 with four films—FOR HEAVEN'S SAKE, THE JACKPOT, PANIC IN THE STREETS, and TWO WEEKS WITH LOVE—all released the same year. He was the juvenile lead in the cult hit, live-action, musical-fantasy THE 5,000 FINGERS OF DR. T (1953), co-written by Ted Geisel (Dr. Seuss). Rettig's pre-"Lassie" credits also include TV going back to 1949, with series including "Kraft Television Theater," "Studio One" ("Mary Poppins"), "Four Star Playhouse," "Your Play Time," "Ford Theater," and "Omnibus." After his run on "Lassie" (aka in syndication "Jeff's Collie"), Rettig did no more films but guested frequently on such series as "Wagon Train, " "Sugarfoot," "Peter Gunn," "Death Valley Days," "Mr. Novak," "The Fugitive," and the dog series "The Littlest Hobo." Rettig was also a star of the youth-oriented soap-opera "Never Too Young" (1965-66).

His career faded in the mid-1960s, and Rettig, in his mid-20s, worked at a series of jobs including photographer, tool salesperson, and health-club manager. There were drug-related arrests, among them for growing marijuana at his farm near San Luis Obispo, CA, in 1972, and for conspiring to smuggle cocaine from Peru, in 1975. A public defender helped him successfully appeal the 5 1/2-year prison sentence for the latter. He was arrested at a cocaine lab at Lake Arrowhead, CA, in 1980, but his complicity in any crime could not be proven, and charges were dropped. Rettig, a vocal advocate of recreational marijuana use, helped back a 1983 California initiative to legalize it. In later years, Rettig became a computer programmer and ran a drug-counseling service in Los Angeles that sought to help drug-users manage, rather than quit, their addiction.

Rettig's films include ELOPEMENT, THE STRIP, and WEEKEND WITH FATHER (1951), GOBS AND GALS and PAULA (1952), THE LADY WANTS MINK and SO BIG (1953), THE EGYPTIAN, THE RAID, and Otto Preminger's RIVER OF NO RETURN (1954), starring Marilyn Monroe, AT GUNPOINT and THE COBWEB (1955), and THE LAST WAGON (1956).

Rettig was found dead in his home, reportedly of natural causes.

Revueltas, Rosaura

born: c. 1909, Durango, Mexico
died: Apr. 30, 1996, Cuernavaca, Mexico, age 86

Mexican actress blacklisted after starring in the landmark workers-rights drama SALT OF THE EARTH (1954).

Raised in an artistic family based in the northern-Mexico state of Durango, Rosaura Revueltas was an author and dancer in addition to an actress. Her films in her native Mexico include ISLAS MARIAS and MUCHACHAS DE UNIFORME/GIRLS IN UNIFORM (1950), and she appeared in the American musical SOMBRERO (1953). The classic drama SALT OF THE EARTH concerned a strike by poor Mexican-American miners and was considered such a controversial "anti-business" subject during the Communist-witch-hunt era that many who worked on it were blacklisted. Revueltas herself, as a result of industry and political harassment, was arrested by immigration officials for a technical passport violation and deported. Some of her scenes were shot with a double, others with her in Mexico—where, with McCarthyism having spread, Revueltas was doubly blacklisted and filming had to be done secretly. Revueltas would go on to work with playwright-composer Bertolt Brecht in Germany from 1957-60. She wrote her memoirs, *The Revueltas* (1979), and later taught dance and yoga.

Revueltas died after a long illness.

Roarke, Adam

born: Richard Jordan Gerler, c. 1937, New York City (Brooklyn), NY.
died: Apr. 27, 1996, Euless, TX, age 58

Film and TV actor, often in biker movies, who later taught acting.

Adam Roarke, the son of a chorus-line dancer and a vaudeville comedian, began in film as a short-lived contract player with Universal Pictures. His first credited role was in the Tony Randall-Shirley Jones children's movie FLUFFY (1965). Roarke then found himself doing a world of such low-budget sci-fi pictures as CYBORG 2087 and WOMEN OF THE PREHISTORIC PLANET aka PREHISTORIC PLANET WOMEN (1966), and such exploitation fare as several motorcycle-gang movies, including HELL'S ANGELS ON WHEELS (1967), opposite Jack Nicholson, as well as Richard Rush's THE SAVAGE SEVEN (1968), HELL'S BELLES (1969), and THE LOSERS (1970). He also made the occasional art film, such as PLAY IT AS IT LAYS (1972) and THE STUNT MAN (1980), in which he plays the actor for whom Steve Railsback doubles. Roarke guested in such TV series as "The Mod Squad," "The Man From U. N. C. L. E. , " and "Star Trek."

In the early 1980s, while visiting a friend in Dallas, Roarke met a group of young actors, including a fledgling Lou Diamond Phillips, at a Halloween party. Noting the burgeoning Dallas film community, he opened an acting school, the Film Actors Lab, in nearly Las Colinas, TX, in 1982. The following year, Roarke acted in and co-directed TRESPASSES, eventually released in 1987. Roarke also played small roles in the Phillips-directed SIOUX CITY and Phillips written-and-directed DANGEROUS TOUCH (both 1994). Roarke's films include EL DORADO (1967), with John Wayne, PSYCH-OUT (1968), A BULLET FOR PRETTY BOY (1970), FROGS (1972), DIRTY MARY, CRAZY LARRY (1974), THE FOUR DEUCES (1976), BEACH GIRLS (1982), and SLIPPING INTO DARKNESS (1989).

Roarke died of a heart attack.

Roerick, William

born: Dec. 17, 1912, Hoboken, NJ
died: Nov. 28, 1995, Monterey, MA, age 82
educ: Hamilton College; Berkshire Playhouse School (Stockbridge, MA)

Actor, TV scriptwriter, and playwright, who continued in his role as businessperson Henry Chamberlain in "The Guiding Light" up until his death.

William Roerick, who began on that CBS soap opera in June 1980, appeared on Broadway for decades in such productions as *Dear Charlie* with Tallulah Bankhead, *The Heiress* with Basil Rathbone, *The Importance of Being Earnest* with Estelle Winwood and Clifton Webb, *Saint Joan* with Katherine Cornell and Maurice Evans, and *Romeo and Juliet* with Cornell. He co-authored the Broadway play *The Happiest Years* Other stage works include John Gielgud's *Hamlet, The Homecoming, The Trials of Oz,* and *A Passage to E. M. Forster.* English novelist Forster dedicated his last book of essays to Roerick.

Roerick wrote scripts for such early TV series as "Crime Photographer" (CBS 1951-52) and "Climax!" (CBS 1954-58). In 1991, he received a Daytime Emmy nomination for supporting actor.

Roerick, known to genre buffs for the Roger Corman films NOT OF THIS EARTH (1957) and THE WASP WOMAN (1959), appeared in such films as THE HARDER THEY FALL (1956), THE LOVE MACHINE (1971), A SEPARATE PEACE (1972), THE DAY OF THE DOLPHIN (1973), 92 IN THE SHADE and THE OTHER SIDE OF THE MOUNTAIN aka A WINDOW TO THE SKY (1975), GOD TOLD ME TO aka DEMON (1976), and THE BETSY (1978).

No cause of death was reported.

Rollins, Howard

aka: Howard E. Rollins Jr.
born: Oct. 17, 1950, Baltimore, MD
died: Dec. 8, 1996, New York City (Manhattan), NY, age 46
educ: Towson State College, Maryland

Academy Award-nominated actor and TV-series star haunted by drug abuse.

Howard Rollins became interested in acting while in college. He moved to New York, eventually appearing, often to acclaim, in a host of plays, including *G. R. Point, The Mighty Gents, We Interrupt This Program, Medal of Honor Rag,* and *Fathers and Sons.* He also appeared in *I'm Not Rappaport* in London and in a Canadian production of *Othello.*

In 1979, he appeared in THE HOUSE OF GOD, which went unreleased until 1984, when some of its young stars, including Rollins, Tim Matheson, Charles Haid, and Bess Armstrong, became well-known. His breakthrough came with RAGTIME (1981), in which he played a young African-American man seeking justice in the turn-of-century mosaic of New York City. His performance brought him an Oscar nomination as best supporting actor. Rollins also starred as the investigating Army captain in the acclaimed A SOLDIER'S STORY (1984). Other films include ON THE BLOCK (1991) and DRUNKS, which premiered on the cable service Showtime and then played theaters in 1997.

Rollins's television work includes the telefilms HE'S FIRED SHE'S FIRED (1984), THE JOHNNIE GIBSON STORY (1986), and CHILDREN OF TIMES SQUARE (1986). He was nominated for a Supporting Actor Daytime Emmy in 1982 for the soap opera "Another World." He co-starred in the series "Wildside" (ABC 1985), and in the hit series "In the Heat of the Night" (NBC/CBS 1988-94), in which, opposite Carroll O'Connor, he played the Virgil Tibbs role created by Sidney Poitier in the 1967 film. Rollins's drug problems caused him to be written out of the latter series, and in its final season, with Tibbs having "gone back to law school," he very infrequently guested.

Rollins pleaded guilty to cocaine possession in Louisiana in 1988; pleaded guilty to driving under the influence of a tranquilizer in 1992, for which he was sentenced to two days in jail, fined $1,000 and lost his driver's license; and spent a month in jail for reckless driving in 1993.

Rollins, whose health had badly deteriorated, died of a bacterial infection caused by complications from lymphoma.

Rosatti, Greg

aka: Gregory Joseph Rosatti
born: c. 1952
died: Mar. 31, 1996, Sherman Oaks, CA, age 43

Dancer-choreographer.

On film, Greg Rosatti appeared as a dancer in GREASE (1978), ZOOT SUIT (1981), and NORTH (1994; also asst. choreographer). He was nominated for the Bob Fosse Award in 1995 for his choreography of Jessica Lange in her Academy Award-winning performance in BLUE SKY (1994).

Rosatti died of complications from AIDS.

Rovere, Luigi

born: c. 1908
died: Oct. 20, 1996, Rome, Italy, age 88

Italian producer whose films include Federico Fellini's first solo feature.

Luigi Rovere entered the film industry by chance, just before WWII, when his carpentry company was contracted by Turin's Fert Studios to build sets for a feature. Rovere soon segued into producing films, eventually co-founding RDL (Rovere-De Laurentiis) with fellow producer Dino De Laurentiis. Early RDL films include Alberto Lattuada's THE BANDIT (1946) with Anna Magnani, Duilio Coletti's IL PASSATORE (1947) with Rossano Brazzi, and Carlo Borghesio's war satire COME PERSI LA GUERRA, which while a domestic hit so infuriated Italian authorities with its irreverent portrayal of wartime Fascist officials that it was banned for export.

Moving to Rome, Rovere joined Lux Film, a major post-war Italian film company also home to De Laurentiis and Carlo Ponti, where films under his auspices included Pietro Germi's early features, IL NOME DELLA LEGGE aka MAFIA 1949/IN THE NAME OF THE LAW (Italy 1949), and IL BRIGANTE DI TACCA DEL LUPO/THE BRIGAND OF TACCA DEL LUPO (1952), and Mario Camerini's LA FIGLIA DEL CAPITANO/THE CAPTAIN'S DAUGHTER (1947).

Rovere produced Fellini's LO SCEICCO BIANCO/THE WHITE SHEIK (1952), the director's first solo effort after having co-directed VARIETY LIGHTS with Lattuada. Rovere's various companies produced more than 30 films from the 1950s to '70s, with Rovere personally producing films (virtually all Italian or Italian co-productions) including PERSIANE CHIUSE/BEHIND CLOSED SHUTTERS (1950), ACCOUNT RENDERED (UK 1957), ROMMEL'S TREASURE (1959; US release 1962), and the spaghetti Western UCCIDI O MUORI/KILL OR BE KILLED aka RINGO AGAINST JOHNNY COLT (1967).

Rovere died of a heart attack.

Schneider, Magda

born: May 17, 1909, Augsburg, Bavaria, Germany
died: July 30, 1996, Schoenau, Germany, age 87

Highly popular, light romantic lead of German and Austrian films of the 1930s, and the mother of actress Romy Schneider.

Magna Schneider was trained as a singer and dancer, and began her career in operetta. She entered film with a flourish of 1932 releases, including SEHNSUCHT 202, MARION DAS GEHORT SICH NICHT, ZWEI IN EINEM AUTO (the German-language version of the French film PARIS-MEDITERRANEE), and DAS LIED EINER NACHT (plus the English-language version TELL ME TONIGHT aka BE MINE TONIGHT). Among her most best-known leading roles was Christine Weyring in Max Ophuls's LIEBELEI (1933).

Daughter Romy (nee Rosemarie), whose father was actor Wolf Albach-Retty, made her film debut in WENN DER WEISSE FLIEDER WIEDER BLUEHT (Germany 1953), playing her real-life mother's screen daughter. The two went on to appear together in Romy's highly popular (though critically disdained) Austrian "Sissi" trilogy, about a romanticized Empress Elizabeth, SISSI (1955), SISSI—DIE JUNGE KAISERIN (1956) and SISSI—SCHICKSALSJAHRE EINER KAISERIN (1957). They also appeared together in ROBINSON SOLL NICHT STERBEN/THE GIRL AND THE LEGEND aka THE LEGEND OF ROBINSON CRUSOE (Germany 1957). Schneider left film after MORGEN BEGINNT DAS LEBEN (Austria 1961).

Schneider's films include RENDEZVOUS IN WIEN (Austria 1936), MUSIK FUR DICH (Austria 1937), MADCHEN IM VORZIMMER (Germany 1940), DIE HEIMLICHEN BRAUTE (Germany 1944), MADCHENJAHRE EINER KONIGIN/THE STORY OF VICKIE (Germany 1954), and DAS DREIMADERLHAUS/THE HOUSE OF THE THREE GIRLS (Austria 1958).

Scott, Synda

aka: Synda Scott Thor
born: Synda Scott MacFetridge, June 12, 1914 or 1923, Evanston, IL
died: June 23, 1996, Los Angeles, CA, age 82
educ: Goodman Theatre School

Film, stage, radio, and television actress.

Synda Scott started her acting career on the Broadway stage while still a teenager, most impressively in the Orson Welles-directed *Native Son.* She was quite active in radio and later did small parts in several films, but her major successes were on television. With her husband, the late Jerome Thor—a Brooklyn-born, stage-trained actor—she starred in the TV series "Foreign Intrigue" between 1951 and 1953. The very successful show was set in Stockholm with episodes filmed throughout Europe. The trenchcoat Scott used in the series is housed in the Smithsonian Institute. Additionally, Scott appeared in over 100 TV anthology shows.

Scott's films include CRACK IN THE WORLD (1965), MR. SYCAMORE (1975), 10 TO MIDNIGHT (1983), MESSENGER OF DEATH (1988), and SCROOGED (1988).

Known as Scotty, Scott died of cancer, and at that time her age was given as 82, which conflicts with her "official" birth year of 1923.

Scotti, Vito

born: Jan. 26, 1918, San Francisco, CA
died: June 5, 1996, Woodland Hills, CA, age 78

Extremely prolific character actor, mostly in film and TV comedies, whose diminutive frame, mustache, and jaunty demeanor made him instantly recognizable from "Gilligan's Island" to GET SHORTY.

Vito Scotti, whose theatrical-family background included a vaudeville-impresario father and a mother he described as "the Dinah Shore of the popular Italian songs," appeared in nearly four dozen movies and countless TV episodes. In the pre-WWII Italian theater circuit, he joined a New York City commedia dell'arte troupe, and later developed a nightclub act. He made his film debut as Julio the newsboy in the film noir CRY OF THE CITY (1948), and appeared in ILLEGAL ENTRY, EAST SIDE, WEST SIDE, and (uncredited, as a truck usher) CRISS CROSS (1959) before going on to star in the short-lived sitcom "Mama Rosa" (May 21-June 11, 1950), one of the few produced live in Hollywood. Scotti would go on to cast or recurring roles on "Life with Luigi" (1952-53), replacing J. Carrol Naish as Luigi Basco in the retooled spring 1953 version; the children's series "Andy's Gang" (1955-60); "The Flying Nun" (1968-69); "To Rome with Love" (1969-71); and "Barefoot in the Park" (1970-71).

Scotti's best-remembered film roles include the restaurateurs in THE GODFATHER (1972) and GET SHORTY (1995), the chef in HOW SWEET IT IS (1968), and the POW-camp officer who cooks gourmet meals for the prisoners in THE SECRET WAR OF HARRY FRIGG (1968). He appeared in several Disney films, including NAPOLEON AND SAMANTHA (1972). Other films include WHERE THE BOYS ARE (1960), HEAD (1968) and NATIONAL LAMPOON'S LOADED WEAPON 1 (1993).

Scotti guest-starred on numerous sitcoms, including "The Dick Van Dyke Show," Tony Danza's Uncle Aldo Micelli on "Who's the Boss?," and in one of his final roles, a brusque Italian tailor on "Mad About You." His telefilms include TWICE IN A LIFETIME (1974), and COLUMBO: MURDER—A SELF PORTRAIT (1989).

Scotti died of lung cancer.

Seneca, Joe

born: c. 1914, Cleveland, OH
died: Aug. 15, 1996, New York City (Manhattan), NY, age 82

Character actor and musician who often played bluesmen and figures of authority and quiet dignity.

Joe Seneca began in show business as a singer with a group called The Three Riffs. He wrote or co-wrote several popular songs, including "Break It to Me Gently," "Talk to Me," and "Here We Go Again," then switched to acting in the early 1970s. Seneca worked in regional theater and at the Eugene O'Neill National Playwrights Conference in Waterford, CT. He made both his Broadway and movie debuts in 1974, with *Of Mice and Men* (starring James Earl Jones), and THE TAKING OF PELHAM ONE TWO THREE, as a police sergeant. He performed on Broadway in *The Little Foxes* (1981) before making his breakthrough as blues trombonist Cutler in *Ma Rainey's Black Bottom* (1984), August Wilson's first Broadway play.

After his film debut, Seneca went on to the telefilms WILMA (1977) and THE TENTH MONTH (1979), and a bit part in KRAMER VS. KRAMER (1979), before gaining notice as a witness in THE VERDICT (1982). His films include CROSSROADS (1986), THE BLOB (1988), MO' BETTER BLUES (1990), MISSISSIPPI MASALA (1991), MALCOLM X (1992), and his final feature, A TIME TO KILL (1996).

He appeared on television in such series as "Law & Order," "China Beach," and "The Equalizer," and in telefilms including SAMARITAN: THE MITCH SNYDER STORY (1986), A GATHERING OF OLD MEN aka MURDER ON THE BAYOU (1987), and the British telefilm THE LONGEST MEMORY, in which he starred just before his death.

Seneca, who lived on Roosevelt Island in Manhattan's East River, died of coronary arrest after an asthma attack.

Shaftel, Josef

born: Mar. 14, 1919, Cleveland, OH
died: Mar. 9, 1996, London, England, age 76

UK-based American producer-writer-director.

Josef Shaftel was a child violin prodigy who performed in concerts until he was 16. Switching to photojournalism, he worked in Italy and later covered the Israeli War of Independence in 1948; his experiences formed the basis for Robert Nathan's bestseller *A Star in the Wind* (1962). Shaftel turned to producing with THE MAN WHO WATCHED TRAINS GO BY aka THE PARIS EXPRESS (UK 1953), and both produced and directed NO PLACE TO HIDE (1956) and THE NAKED HILLS (1956; also scripted) He also both wrote and produced THE BIGGEST BUNDLE OF THEM ALL (1968), filmed in Italy and France.

Films produced by Shaftel—all British or US-UK co-productions—include THE BLISS OF MRS. BLOSSOM (1968), SAY HELLO TO YESTERDAY, THE TROJAN WOMEN, and the David Niven oddity THE STATUE (1971), THE ASSASSINATION OF TROTSKY, WHERE DOES IT HURT?, and the all-star ALICE'S ADVENTURES IN WONDERLAND (1972), THE SELL OUT (1975), and the live-action/animated GULLIVER'S TRAVELS (1976).

Upon being diagnosed with what became terminal multiple myeloma, Shaftel devoted the last three years of his life to raising money for the Yehudi Menuhin School for gifted young musicians.

Shakur, Tupac

aka: 2Pac
born: Tupac Amaru Shakur, June 16, 1971, New York City, NY
died: Sept. 13, 1996, Las Vegas, NV, age 25
educ: High School of the Performing Arts, Baltimore, MD

Rap artist and actor.

Tupac Shakur was the son of ostensible Black Panther Afeni Shakur, who was in jail on bombing charges (and later acquitted) while pregnant with him. After moving with his mother to Baltimore, he studied acting at that city's High School of the Performing Arts. He wrote and began performing his first rap song, about gun control, after a friend was shot while playing with guns. He dropped out of high school and moved to Marin City, CA, later earning a general equivalency diploma (GED).

After auditioning for the rap group Digital Underground, he was hired for the road crew and eventually performed and recorded with the band. He also performed with the band in the film NOTHING BUT TROUBLE (1991). Shakur went on to appear in the co-starring role of the violent Bishop in director Ernest Dickerson's JUICE (1992) before beginning his solo recording career with the hit album "2Pacalypse Now." After another top seller, "Strictly for my N. I. G. G. A. Z. . . ." (1993), his 1995 album "Me Against the World" debuted at number-one on the *Billboard* pop chart. The "Me Against the World" 1996 double album—the first in rap/hip-hop—proved his biggest seller.

Among the news-making incidents in his career: In November 1993, Shakur was indicted on charges that he and associates sodomized a 20-year-old woman in a Manhattan hotel suite; he was sentenced to 1 1/2 to 4 1/2 years in prison for sexual assault. Before the trial, he was arrested in Atlanta and charged with shooting two off-duty cops; the charges were later dropped. During the trial, he was shot twice as he entered a Manhattan recording studio. On April 29, 1995, while in prison, he married longtime girlfriend Keisha Morris, but the marriage was annulled. He was released from prison after eight months in October 1995, pending appeal. Shakur played opposite Janet Jackson in John Singleton's POETIC JUSTICE (1993), followed by a supporting role in ABOVE THE RIM (1994), in which the hit single "Pour a Little Liquor" appeared on the soundtrack. Shakur also starred in the posthumous direct-to-video release BULLET (1996) and the theatrical release GRIDLOCK'D (1997).

Shakur was shot on Sept. 7, 1996 as he was leaving the Mike Tyson-Bruce Seldon prizefight in Las Vegas. He lapsed into a coma and died six days later.

Shipman, David

born: c. 1934, Norwich, England
died: Apr. 22, 1996, Hampshire, England, age 63
educ: Merton College of Oxford University

Film writer and historian.

David Shipman compiled and wrote the encyclopedic three-volume *The Great Movie Stars: The Golden Years* (1970), whose exhaustive research and personable style also characterized his subsequent film encyclopedias, subtitled *The International Years* (1972) and *The Independent Years* (1991), all of which remain in print to date. Other books included biographies of Marlon Brando and Judy Garland; a history of sex in cinema; *Movie Talk: Who Said What About Whom* , and *Cinema: the First 100 Years*. His work often led to related duties, such as curating film programs at the National Film Theatre in London. He was working on a biography of Fred Astaire at the time of his death.

Shipman, who lived in the Chelsea section of London with his companion and editor of 30 years, Felix Brenner, died in his country home of a heart attack.

Silliphant, Stirling

born: Jan. 16, 1918, Detroit, MI
died: April 26, 1996, Bangkok, Thailand, age 78
educ: University of Southern California

Prolific, Academy Award-winning screenwriter and producer of IN THE HEAT OF THE NIGHT (1967), whose notable successes extended to both film and TV.

In 1938, following college, Stirling Silliphant worked as a publicist for Walt Disney Productions, moving to 20th Century-Fox in 1942 to work for Fox president Spyros Skouras; after WWII service, he returned to Fox as New York publicity director. Silliphant left to produce THE JOE LOUIS STORY (1953), and to write novels (including the acclaimed *Maracaibo* , which was made into a 1958 movie), short stories, and screenplays. He next produced 5 AGAINST THE HOUSE (1955), co-adapting the screenplay from the Jack Finney novel. Silliphant went on to write or co-wrote scripts for NIGHTFALL and HUK aka HUK! (1956), THE LINEUP and DAMN CITIZEN (1958), VILLAGE OF THE DAMNED (1960), and THE SLENDER THREAD (1965), and for TV series including "Alcoa Theatre," "Alfred Hitchcock Presents," "General Electric Theater, " "Naked City," "Perry Mason," and the series with which he is most identified, "Route 66."

After IN THE HEAT OF THE NIGHT won five Academy Awards, including those for picture and adapted script, the prolific Silliphant became a star screenwriter. The poignant CHARLEY (1968), based on Daniel Keyes' classic story "Flowers for Algernon," won Silliphant the Golden Globe (as did IN THE HEAT OF THE NIGHT). Turning 180 degrees from intimate human drama, he wrote the archetypal disaster films THE POSEIDON ADVENTURE (1972) and THE TOWERING INFERNO (1974). Other screenplays include MARLOWE (1969), A WALK IN THE SPRING RAIN (1970; also producer), SHAFT IN AFRICA (1973), director Sam Peckinpah's THE KILLER ELITE (1975), Clint Eastwood's THE ENFORCER (1976), , and his final film, THE GRASS HARP (1996; co-producer, co-writer). He continued to produce and write for TV series through the 1970s, and wrote the teleplays for the miniseries "James A. Michener's Space" (1985), and "Pearl" aka "Pearl Harbor. "

Silliphant, who moved to Thailand in 1988 with his Vietnamese actress-filmmaker wife Tiana Du Long (nee Thi Thanh Nga), died of cancer.

Simpson, Don

born: Oct. 29, 1943, Seattle, WA; raised Anchorage, AK
died: Jan. 19, 1996, Los Angeles (Bel-Air), CA, age 52
educ: University of Oregon (Phi Beta Kappa)

Producer, with partner Jerry Bruckheimer, of archetypal 1980s Hollywood blockbusters.

After joining the Jack Woodell advertising agency in San Francisco in 1969, working with their client Warner Bros. , Simpson joined the studio as a marketing executive in 1971, working first on MEDICINE BALL CARAVAN. He befriended producer Steve Tisch, who encouraged and supported Simpson in the film business, and eventually introduced him to Bruckheimer; Tisch also introduced him to Paramount's Vice President of Production, Richard Sylbert, who hired Simpson as a production executive in 1975. At Paramount, the cannily youth-attuned Simpson rose to become president of worldwide production in 1981. Two years later, he co-founded Simpson-Bruckheimer Productions. The partners, in association with Paramount, produced the blockbusters FLASHDANCE (1983), BEVERLY HILLS COP (1984), and TOP GUN (1986)—all of which spun off hit soundtrack albums, garnering 18 Grammy Award nominations in all. During this time, they also produced the interesting if commercially unsuccessful THIEF OF HEARTS (1984) and BEVERLY HILLS COP 2 (1987).

The duo signed a self-described "dream deal" with Paramount in February 1990, but the failure of Tom Cruise's DAYS OF THUNDER (1990; also bit-part actor) and disagreements over the increasingly hubristic pair's spending patterns led to the contract's dissolution nine months later. Simpson and Bruckheimer went to Disney in 1991, where after years of fruitless project development and such disappointing films as THE REF (1994; executive producer only), they scored three-in-a-row hits with BAD BOYS, CRIMSON TIDE and DANGEROUS MINDS (1995). By this time, most of the day-to-day duties were reportedly Bruckheimer's alone as Simpson, plagued by personal demons and longstanding drug addictions, rarely ventured from his home. Bruckheimer announced the partnership's breakup in December 1996. Simpson appeared as himself in the non-fiction James Toback film THE BIG BANG 1989), and as a Pinkerton Man in YOUNG GUNS II (1990).

Simpson died of an apparent heart attack. The Los Angeles coroner's office asserted no drugs were found at his mansion and no evidence drugs were involved in his death.

Sinden, Jeremy

born: June 14, 1950
died: May 29, 1996, age 45

British actor.

Jeremy Sinden, who often played comically starchy English types or broad yet endearing parts in children's works, was best known in the US for the Great Performances telecast of "Brideshead Revisited" (1982). The son of veteran actor Donald Sinden, he left prep school to establish an acting career, and though lacking leading-man looks, built a niche in theater as both a supporting player and a character lead. After repertory theater, two seasons with the Royal Shakespeare Company at Stratford (where he worked as an assistant stage manager, and understudied 45 parts), he made his West End debut as Private Broughton in a revival of R. C. Sherriff's *Journey's End* (1972). He then made the unusual step of going back to school for formal training on a three-year course at the London Academy of Music and Dramatic Art (LAMDA).

Sinden appeared in STAR WARS (1977), in the final battle sequence as X-wing pilot Pops (Gold 2). He went on to do much multi-part British TV through the 1980s, including "Danger UXB" (1979), shown on "Masterpiece Theater" in the 1980-81 season; including "The Far Pavillions" (1984). The British telefilm VIRTUOSO (1989) premiered here on A&E. Sinden appeared in CHARIOTS OF FIRE (UK 1981) as the president of the Gilbert and Sullivan Society, and in films including ASCENDANCY (UK 1982), MADAME SOUSATZKA (1988), THE OBJECT OF BEAUTY and LET HIM HAVE IT (UK 1991), and THE INNOCENT (1993). He and actress wife Delia Lindsay, whom he married in 1978, toured in *An Ideal Husband* in 1989. Sinden had recently enjoyed his biggest critical kudos, however, playing Mr. Toad in a revival of *Wind in the Willows* at the Old Vic in London.

In November 1995, shortly after taking the role, Sinden was diagnosed with cancer. He continued as Mr. Toad until spring 1996.

Smitha, Silk

born: Vijayalakshmi Smitha, c. 1963
died: c. Sept. 23, 1996, Madras, India, age 33

Famed Indian actress.

Silk Smitha, who became famous in her assumed name after her first movie, in which she was nicknamed "Silk," acted in reportedly about 300 movies in the Tamil, Telugu, and Hindi languages. She became famous for her gyrating dances in scanty costumes, yet suffered financial difficulties after producing three commercially unsuccessful movies.

Smitha was found dead, hanging from a ceiling fan with a sari around her neck, with a suicide note near her body. Police made the announcement Sept. 23, 1996, without specifying the date of death.

Stanley, Alvah W. Jr.

born: c. 1940, Iowa
died: Aug. 6, 1996, Los Angeles, CA, age 56
educ: Grinnell College (bachelor's degree), U. of South Dakota (master's degree), University of Minnesota (doctoral studies)

Stage actor who appeared in two films.

Alvah W. Stanley Jr. came to the University of Missouri-Kansas City in 1965 as an assistant professor of theater arts, and became artist in residence of the affiliated Missouri Rep. He also served as artistic director of the Resident Theater of the Jewish Community Center. He moved to Los Angeles in 1975, and did film, TV, and theater there. Stanley had just completed a year in the lead role of the Euro Disney production of *Buffalo Bill's Wild West Show.* Stanley, whose wife, Vivien, is an actress, appeared in the films THE SWORD AND THE SORCERER (1982) and THE TRAGEDY OF ROMEO AND JULIET (1989), directed by William Woodman.

Stanley died of a heart attack.

Stevenson, McLean

born: Nov. 14, 1929, Normal, IL
died: Feb. 15, 1996, Tarzana, CA, age 66
educ: Northwestern University (theater arts)

The much-liked Lt. Col. Henry Blake of TV's "M*A*S*H. "

McLean Stevenson, the son of a cardiologist, went into acting at age 31, after having attended college, serving in the Navy, and taking on various jobs. Venturing to New York in the 1960s, he won a scholarship to a dramatic academy, and while studying under Sanford Meisner and Lee Strasberg, wrote comedy material and performed at such nightclubs as Upstairs at the Downstairs, in summer stock (making his acting debut in *The Music Man* in 1962), and in TV commercials and series, including "Naked City," and "Car 54, Where Are You?" He moved to Hollywood and worked as a comedy writer and sketch performer for both "The Smothers Brothers Comedy Hour" and "That Was the Week That Was"—the latter with future "M*A*S*H" star Alan Alda.

After breaking into movies with a part in director Floyd Mutrux' fast-lane, riches-to-rags story THE CHRISTIAN LICORICE STORE (1971), Stevenson went on to co-star on the acclaimed movie-spinoff series "M*A*S*H" (CBS 1972-83), appearing in the first three seasons. Beginning in fall 1973, Stevenson, a popular guest on "The Tonight Show," began a long-running second career as a guest host there. His attempt at a sitcom career, however, led to a string of disappointments, including "The McLean Stevenson Show" (1976-77), and "Hello, Larry" (1979-80). He continued to guest on the occasional sitcom, and appeared in telefilms including SHIRTS/SKINS (1973) and CLASS CRUISE (1989). His films include WIN, PLACE, OR STEAL aka THREE FOR THE MONEY (1975) and THE CAT FROM OUTER SPACE (1978).

Stevenson, who won a 1973 Golden Globe Award and garnered a 1973-74 Emmy nomination, died of a heart attack after a bladder operation.

Sullivan, Fred

born: c. 1945, Glens Falls, NY
died: Apr. 18, 1996, Saranac Lake, NY, age 50
educ: Fordham University, New York, NY (bachelor's degree, history); Boston University (master's degree, filmmaking, 1973)

Unabashedly independent filmmaker based in New York State's Adirondack Mountains.

Fred Sullivan, who worked as director of development at Paul Smith's College in Franklin County, NY, wrote, produced, and directed COLD RIVER (1981), a drama of two children surviving in the wilderness after their father had died. Following SULLIVAN'S PAVILION (1987), which Sullivan wrote, produced, directed, edited, and appeared in, the filmmaker reaped good notices for his quirky THE BEER DRINKER'S GUIDE TO FITNESS AND FILMMAKING (1988), a montage of the life of the struggling filmmaker, his wife, and their four children, all stuffed into a small home. The wry, self-deprecating film won warm attention at the 1987 Sundance Film Festival, and at his death, Sullivan was working on a sequel.

Sullivan collapsed while playing a weekly pickup basketball game at Paul Smith's College. He was pronounced dead of heart failure at the Adirondack Medical Center in Saranac Lake.

Sweeney, Kester

born: 1910, California
died: Jan. 1, 1996, Lake Forrest, CA, age 85
educ: UCLA

Famed MGM makeup artist.

Kester Sweeney, who worked on a host of Oscar-winning performers and countless features and TV series, started at MGM while still a college art student. He worked with such major stars as Greta Garbo, Jean Harlow, Lana Turner, Elizabeth Taylor, Fred Astaire, Clark Gable, Frank Sinatra, and James Stewart—as well as MGM's mascot, Leo the Lion, whose nose needed makeup for the filming of MGM's famous logo. In the late 1950s, Sweeney moved on to projects outside the MGM studio, working on films including SUNRISE AT CAMPOBELLO (1960), A MAN CALLED HORSE (1970), and THE GREATEST STORY EVER TOLD (1965). Sweeney ended his career as head makeup artist on the TV series "He and She," "Gilligan's Island," and "Hawaii Five-0."

Sweeney died of natural causes.

Takemitsu, Toru

born: Oct. 8, 1930, Tokyo, Japan
died: Feb. 20, 1996, Tokyo, Japan, age 65

Composer of film scores and screenwriter.

While Toru Takemitsu is perhaps most widely known as a composer of film music, he was also a well-respected concert musician and composer, very much in the forefront of the contemporary Japanese New Wave. His distinctive style blended traditional western and classical Japanese instrumentations. Takemitsu worked extensively in the concert world, as well as on the soundstage.

Takemitsu started scoring films early in his career, but it was not until the success of Hiroshi Teshigahara's masterful, Oscar-nominated (foreign language film) WOMAN IN THE DUNES, aka WOMAN OF THE DUNES (1964), that Takemitsu gained attention as an important film composer. He later scored Teshigahara's SUMMER SOLDIER (1972). Takemitsu worked twice with Akira Kurosawa: DODES'KA-DEN (1970) and RAN (1985). Among the movies he scored are HARAKIRI (1962), KWAIDAN (1964), the Japanese BLACK RAIN (1989), and RISING SUN (1993). In 1969, Takemitsu co-wrote the screenplay, as well as the score, for DOUBLE SUICIDE. The composer himself was the subject of the documentary MUSIC FOR THE MOVIES: TORU TAKEMITSU (1994).

Takemitsu, who was undergoing cancer treatments, died of pneumonia.

Talbot, Lyle

born: Lysle Henderson, Feb. 8, 1902, Pittsburgh, PA
died: March 3, 1996, San Francisco, CA, age 94

Burly actor who, with his rather ordinary features, didn't quite fit Hollywood's standard leading-man mold and early on became a well-known and respected character actor.

Lyle Talbot was born into a theatrical family and even had his own theater company, The Talbot Players. Like so many stage performers, he could speak well and had a solid acting technique—just the type of actor Hollywood was looking for at the start of the sound era. In 1932, he appeared in nine movies, the most memorable being THREE ON A MATCH, in which he played an underworld character, romancing both Joan Blondell and Ann Dvorak. Because of his strong, menacing appearance, he often played gangsters. The first of his 10 releases in 1933 was as a mobster opposite Spencer Tracy in 20,000 YEARS IN SING SING. Occasionally, Talbot was given a heroic part, such as "Three Star" Halsey, ace pilot, in the minor melodrama MURDER IN THE CLOUDS (1934). But for most of his over 150 theatrical features (he took pride in the fact that he was never out of work for more than a few weeks), he was often an unlikable or only marginally likable character, cast in supporting roles. Talbot was also in Ed Wood Jr. 's camp classic, PLAN 9 FROM OUTER SPACE (1959).

Talbot was active in helping organize the Screen Actors Guild, which came into existence in 1933. Talbot's image mellowed as he got older, and his television work in several popular sitcoms revealed that he was very comfortable with comedy. Some of his TV work included the recurring roles of neighbor Joe Randolph in "The Adventures of Ozzie and Harriet," and Paul Fonda in "Love That Bob, " and several guest appearances in such popular shows as "Burns and Allen," "The Danny Thomas Show," "The Lucy Show," "Green Acres," and more recently, "Who's the Boss?"

No cause of death was reported.

Tesich, Steve

born: Stoyan Tesich, Sept. 29, 1942, Titovo Utice, Yugoslavia
died: July 1, 1996, Sydney, Nova Scotia, Canada, age 53
educ: Indiana University, Columbia University

Screenwriter, playwright, short story writer, and novelist who often used his immigrant-view of America in his works.

Steve Tesich's father, a career soldier, fled Marshall Tito's communist Yugoslavia shortly after WWII, settling in East Chicago, IN. Working as a machinist, he was able, in 1957, to send for his wife, son, and daughter. Tesich was a teenager and spoke no English. Even though the dingy, industrial town he was brought to was unlike his native country, he quickly adapted and came to love the US (Tesich became a naturalized citizen in 1961), eventually excelling in school and developing his English-language skills with the sensibilities of a born writer.

After attending Indiana University (graduating in 1965) on a wrestling scholarship, Tesich worked on his Ph. D at New York's Columbia University. It was shortly after he left Columbia that he started his career as a playwright. He wrote several plays that were produced at the American Place Theater.

Just before he started writing movies, Tesich's play *Nourish the Beast* was the basis for the TV sitcom "Apple Pie" (1978), which was not successful. Tesich's interest in the sport of bicycling and fascination with small-town America led him to write *The Eagle of Naptown* and *The Cutters,* both of which became the genesis for his Academy Award-winning script (written directly for the screen), BREAKING AWAY (1979). It took Tesich and director Peter Yates eight years to get the property filmed. Tesich also worked with Yates on EYEWITNESS (1981), providing an original screenplay, and ELENI (1985), adapting Nicholas Gage's book. The main character in the Arthur Penn-directed FOUR FRIENDS (1981) is a young Yugoslavian immigrant dealing with a changing America in the 1960s, not unlike Tesich himself. He wrote the screenplay for THE WORLD ACCORDING TO GARP (1982), adapting John Irving's best-selling novel. (Tesich, like the Garp character, was a formidable competitive wrestler in school, as had been author Irving.) In AMERICAN FLYERS (1985), Tesich again used the bicycling theme, but far less successfully than in BREAKING AWAY.

Tesich's play, *Division Street,* (1980), was not a success on Broadway; however, during the last years of his life, he continued to write plays.

Tesich, who married Rebecca Fletcher in 1971, died of a heart attack while vacationing with his family in Canada.

Tiny Tim

born: Herbert Khaury, April 12, 19??, New York, NY
died: Nov. 30, 1996, Minneapolis, MN

Whimsical novelty singer, ukulele player, and sometime actor.

Herbert Khaury couldn't make any headway as an ordinary, wavy-haired crooner, so to add a bit of novelty to his image, his manager renamed him Sir Timothy Thames. That didn't help, so the singer's name was finally shortened to Tiny Tim. The complete transformation and fame came rather late; he was in his mid-40s when he caused a minor sensation singing a 1926 ditty, "Tip Toe Thru the Tulips With Me." He sang the perky song in a high-pitch, nasal, quivering voice while strumming a ukulele; and with his stringy hair, dark features, and pale complexion (enhanced by white makeup), his persona seemed at odds with the song's innocent lyrics. He remained popular for almost 30 years, forging a career by singing his signature song as the highlight of his act almost anywhere anyone would pay money to see him. During his latter years, he would often appear at music festivals and obscure clubs, as part of nostalgia tours.

While Tiny Tim's television appearances were primarily on musical variety and talk shows, he did the 1967 TV movie IRONSIDES, which served as the pilot for the series. Tiny Tim was also a character thought to be a Vampire in a 1971 segment of "Love American Style, " called "Love and the Vampire." He even managed, during his long career, to make a few theatrical films. He played himself in four movies: YOU ARE WHAT YOU EAT (1968), ONE TRICK PONY (1980), MESSAGE TO LOVE: THE ISLE OF WIGHT FESTIVAL (1996), and doing a walk-on in the MTV Awards scene in PRIVATE PARTS (1997). He had a character part, that of a weird clown who's a murder suspect, in the creepy BLOOD HARVEST (1987).

His much-publicized wedding to Miss Vicki on the "Tonight Show" was one of 1969's most highly rated shows. The marriage didn't last, and neither did his second to Miss Jan. His third wife, Susan, was with him when he died.

It was while performing "Tip Toe Thru the Tulips With Me" onstage at a benefit in Minneapolis that he collapsed, and later died, from a heart attack. Tiny Tim was coy about revealing his age or the year of his birth; several different birth years have been reported. He was thought to be between 65 and 72 years old.

Toumanova, Tamara

born: March 2, 1919, Toumen, Russia
died: May 29, 1996, Santa Monica, CA, age 77

Ballerina, stage performer, and film actress.

Tamara Toumanova, the daughter of a czarist army colonel, was born en route to France, in a boxcar, while her parents were escaping the Bolshevik Revolution. Studying ballet in Paris and making her dancing debut with the Paris Opera at the age of 9, she attained international acclaim by the time she was 13 as one of the principal dancers with Col. W. de Basil's Ballets Russes. Her career as a dancer spanned 40 years, during which time she also acted in movies and appeared on Broadway. Taking time out from dancing with the new Ballet Russe de Monte Carlo in 1939, Toumanova was prominently featured, along with stars Ethel Merman and Jimmy Durante, in the lavish Broadway musical *Stars in Your Eyes.* After its modest run, Toumanova returned to ballet, touring the world. Between engagements, she appeared in several movies.

Her first screen appearance was as a dancer in an early 1940s ballet film, SPANISH FIESTA, which she made with the Ballet Russe. Her acting debut was in the lead role of Nina, a ballerina turned Soviet freedom fighter defending the homeland against the Nazis in DAYS OF GLORY (1944). (Shortly after completion of the movie, Toumanova wed the film's producer, Casey Robinson. They later divorced.) She did a guest stint as famed ballerina Anna Pavlova in TONIGHT WE SING (1953); appeared in MGM's all-star biopic of composer Sigmund Romberg, DEEP IN MY HEART (1954); danced with Gene Kelly in the "Ring Around the Rosy" segment in INVITATION TO THE DANCE (1957, but filmed in 1952); played a ballerina again, this time a spy as well, in Hitchcock's TORN CURTAIN (1966); and was a Russian ballerina in Billy Wilder's THE PRIVATE LIFE OF SHERLOCK HOLMES (1970), her last film.

Toumanova became a United States citizen in 1944 and lived her later years in Beverly Hills.

No cause of death was reported.

Tramont, Jean-Claude

born: c. 1930, Brussels, Belgium
died: Dec. 27, 1996, Los Angeles, CA, age 66

Director, screenwriter.

Jean-Claude Tramont, who was raised and educated in Paris, had a small film output. This is perhaps attributable to the failure of his first produced screenplay, ASH WEDNESDAY (1973). The Elizabeth Taylor vehicle, about a desperate woman who undergoes plastic surgery in an attempt to save her marriage, was poorly received. It was not until 1977 that another Tramont script would be produced: LE POINT DE MIRE (FOCAL POINT), which he also directed.

His only American-financed film as a director, ALL NIGHT LONG (1981), is a delightful, if unexceptional, comedy about an all-night drugstore manager (Gene Hackman) in full-blown mid-life crisis. But early in the film's production, controversy erupted when Barbra Streisand joined the cast as a last-minute replacement for Lisa Eichhorn. Some Hollywood insiders cried foul, because Streisand, who exclusively worked with established directors, was a client of Tramont's wife, the powerful superagent Sue Mengers.

Tramont's next directed the 1986 HBO-movie, "As Summers Die," an ambitious and well-cast, but unsuccessful, drama about southern racial prejudice and chicanery.

Tramont died of cancer.

Travers, P. L.

born: Helen Lyndon Goff, Aug. 9, 1899, Maryborough, Australia
died: April 26, 1996, age 96

Creator, in 1934, of the practically perfect Mary Poppins.

P. L. (Pamela Lyndon) Travers, author of one of the most successful series of books on a single character, didn't like Walt Disney's MARY POPPINS (1964). Travers's Edwardian nanny, unlike the movie Mary, is more mature and less physically attractive, with not a hint of sweetness or sentimentality. But Disney wanted to go younger, prettier, and just a bit sweeter. He proved to be correct—the movie has so far grossed over $102 million, and it received five Academy Award nominations, including a Best Actress Oscar for Julie Andrews.

Because of Travers's dissatisfaction with Disney's movie, she wouldn't allow a sequel to be made by Hollywood. However, in 1983, the English nanny turned up in a Soviet TV children's musical, "Merri Poppins, Do Svidanya (Mary Poppins, Goodbye)."

No cause of death was reported.

Uys, Jamie

born: Jacobus Johannes Uys, May 30, 1921, Boksburg, South Africa
died: Jan. 29, 1996, Pretoria, South Africa, age 74
educ: Pretoria University

South African-based screenwriter, producer, director, actor.

Jamie Uys (pronounced ACE), like his parents before him, was a teacher; both he and his wife taught high school mathematics for several years. He was also a farmer and a trader when, in 1949, he borrowed a camera and started a one-man film-making enterprise: producing, directing, writing, filming, and acting. He eventually formed a company, making several documentaries for the State Information Services. After more than 30 years in the business and dozens of films, Uys's satirical and original THE GODS MUST BE CRAZY (1981, US release 1984) was an unexpected international hit. Uys couldn't account for its broad appeal and even tried to duplicate its success with a sequel, THE GODS MUST BE CRAZY II (1989), which was generally well received but considerably less successful at the box office.

As an actor, he appeared in THE HELLIONS (1962), his own (as writer-producer-director) AFTER YOU, COMRADE (1967), and the first GODS movie. His comedic documentary, ANIMALS ARE BEAUTIFUL PEOPLE (1974), won a Golden Globe award. Other films include DINGAKA (1965), FUNNY PEOPLE (1977), a candid-camera style comedy, and its follow-up FUNNY PEOPLE II (1983).

Uys has been described as the father of the South African movie industry and its only cineaste to have been acclaimed internationally. Shortly after jogging, he died of a heart attack in his wife's arms.

Vacio, Natividad

born: c. 1912, El Paso, TX
died: May 30, 1996, age 84, Burbank, CA

Actor, singer, guitarist.

While growing up in Pasadena, California, Natividad Vacio joined the Pasadena Community Playhouse where he acted and performed as a musician in several plays. He turned to teaching shortly after serving in WWII, but eventually chose a career in show business. Vacio acted in movies and TV shows, performed in concerts as a singer/guitarist, appeared in plays, and made recordings.

Vacio appeared in a number of films, most often playing Hispanic characters. These included BRANDED (1950), THE HITCH-HIKER (1953), GREEN FIRE (1954), GIANT (1956), ESCAPE FROM RED ROCK (1958), CASTLE OF EVIL (1967), THE MAN WITH TWO BRAINS (1983) and THE MILAGRO BEANFIELD WAR (1988). Of his many TV roles, his most prominent was "Frank the Gardener" on "Father Knows Best"; he also made guest appearances on "The Adventures of Superman" and "Mission: Impossible."

Vacio died of cancer.

Van Fleet, Jo

born: Dec. 30, 1914, Oakland, CA
died: June 10, 1996, New York City (Jamaica), NY, age 81
educ: University of the Pacific; Neighborhood Playhouse, NY

Stage, film, and television actress.

Elia Kazan directed Jo Van Fleet on Broadway in *Flight Into Egypt* (1952) and *Camino Real* (1953), and he knew her work as a member of the famed Actors Studio. When he was ready to cast the important role of Kate in his screen version of EAST OF EDEN (1955), he chose Van Fleet to portray the outwardly tough brothel madam, whom her son, Cal (James Dean), discovers to be more insecure and frightened than her demeanor and profession would suggest. For it, she won an Academy Award as the year's best supporting actress. That same year, 1955, Van Fleet had a small part in THE ROSE TATTOO and a more important one as the ambitious, monomaniacal stage mother of Lillian Roth (Susan Hayward) in I'LL CRY TOMORROW. Van Fleet worked with Kazan again, in WILD RIVER (1960), as the proud and determined Ella Garth, an octogenarian who defies the government and nature by refusing to leave her flood-imperiled home. She also appeared in Raoul Walsh's western, THE KING AND FOUR QUEENS (1956), GUNFIGHT AT THE O. K. CORRAL (1957), and COOL HAND LUKE (1967).

Between films, of which Van Fleet made several well into the late 1980s, she returned to the stage. Some of her successes include *The Trip to Bountiful* (1954), for which she won a Tony Award as best supporting actress, *Look Homeward, Angel* (1957) and *The Glass Menagerie* (1965 revival). Van Fleet appeared in many television roles, including the stepmother in Rodgers and Hammerstein's "Cinderella" (1964 version). Van Fleet was married to dancer and choreographer William Bales, who died in 1990.

No cause of death was reported.

Varno, Roland

born: Jacob Frederik Vuerhard, 1908, Utrecht, Netherlands
died: May 24, 1996, Lancaster, CA, age 88

Film, stage and radio actor.

Roland Varno came to the US from the Netherlands, with a stopover in Berlin where he started his film career, most significantly by supporting Emil Jennings and Marlene Dietrich in THE BLUE ANGEL (1931). Because Varno was fluent in several languages and adept at accents and dialects, he was in demand in Hollywood, especially for propaganda and war movies, and radio dramas. He worked steadily in films, radio, and on the stage, taking time out to serve in the Office of Strategic Services during WWII. Varno's many films include QUALITY STREET (1937), CONQUEST (1937), GUNGA DIN (1939), TO BE OR NOT TO BE (1942), HITLER'S CHILDREN (1943), BATTLEGROUND (1949), and ISTANBUL (1957).

Varno died of a heart attack.

Vernon, Harvey

born: Chester Smith, c. 1927
died: Oct. 9, 1996, Sun Valley, CA, age 69
educ: University of Michigan

Film, television, and stage actor.

Harvey Vernon, a name not generally familiar to the average moviegoer or television watcher, was an actor who worked fairly constantly in the industry for over 40 years, ever since he was discharged from the Coast Guard after serving in WWII. Following some New York stage and television work, his first feature film was MACARTHUR (1977), in which he played Admiral Sherman. In between television parts in several movies, sitcoms, and dramas, some of his other theatrical movies include ALL OF ME (1984), TEEN WOLF (1985), STOOGEMANIA (1986), SOMEONE TO WATCH OVER ME (1987), MONKEY TROUBLE (1994), and LOVE IS A GUN (1994).

Vernon was a regular on the 1977-79 TV series "Carter Country," and guested on almost all the top TV sitcoms and dramas. Some of the shows in which he appeared are "The Mary Tyler Moore Show," "Cybill," "The Cosby Show," "The Golden Girls," "Moonlighting," "Dallas," and "Charlie's Angels."

The cause of death was heart failure.

Vernon, Howard

born: Mario Lipert, July 15, 1914, Baden, Switzerland
died: July 24, 1996

International film actor.

Born to a Swiss father and an American mother, Howard Vernon was raised in the United States and returned to Europe as a young adult to complete his studies in France and Switzerland. He eventually worked in the hotel trade, but gave that up to become an actor in Paris. Vernon studied drama and supported himself by tap dancing in Parisian stage revues. Much of his time abroad was spent in Nazi-occupied France during WWII. Shortly after the liberation of Paris, he made his film debut in the resistance drama UN AMI VIENDRA CE SOIR (1945), in the same part he had played on stage.

With his austere, autocratic demeanor, cold Prussian-blue eyes, grim countenance, and raspy, authoritative voice, Vernon was often seen on screen as a Nazi. His break came when director Jean-Pierre Melville cast him as a sensitive German officer in LE SILENCE DE LA MER/THE SILENCE OF THE SEA (1949). Before Melville used him again in BOB LE FLAMBEUR (1955) and LEON MORIN, PRETRE (1961), Vernon appeared in several international productions, such as Britain's THE FIGHTING PIMPERNEL (1950), America's THE ADVENTURES OF CAPTAIN FABIAN (1951), and France's AFFAIRS IN VERSAILLES (1954/US 1957, as ROYAL AFFAIRS IN VERSAILLES). After being cast as a killer for hire in Fritz Lang's last feature, THE THOUSAND EYES OF DR. MABUSE (1960), Vernon became inescapably identified as a macabre villain in low-budget horror thrillers. He was the AWFUL DR. ORLOFF (1961), a character he essayed through a series of films for Spanish filmmaker Jesús Franco (aka Jess Franco, Clifford Brown, and a multitude of pseudonyms). Vernon also made several other films for Franco over a 25-year period, including NECROMONICON, aka SUCCUBUS (1967), DRACULA VS. FRANKENSTEIN (1970), VIRGIN AMONG THE LIVING DEAD (1971), LES EXPÉRIENCES ÉROTIQUES DE FRANKENSTEIN (1972) and LE JOURNAL INTIME D'UNE NYMPHOMANE (1973).

Vernon's career was a bit more distinguished than some of his exploitation films might suggest. He was well-cast and memorable in John Frankenheimer's THE TRAIN (1964), Jean-Luc Godard's ALPHAVILLE (1965), Woody Allen's LOVE AND DEATH (1975), and the Jean-Pierre Jeunet/Marc Caro DELICATESSEN (1991).

No cause of death was reported.

Villard, Henry

born: c. 1901, New York, NY
died: Jan. 21, 1996, Los Angeles, CA, age 95
educ: Harvard University, Oxford University

Author and silent movie bit player.

For a brief time in his youth, Henry Villard was in silent movies as a bit player. He preferred writing, taking jobs as a reporter in Los Angeles and Miami; he was also interested in international politics, eventually working for the State Department and forging a successful diplomatic career. After retirement, Villard wrote several books, one being *Hemingway in Love and War: The Lost Diary of Agnes von Kurowsky,* about the love affair between Ernest Hemingway and his nurse in an Italian hospital during WWI. Villard knew Hemingway, having shared a hospital room with him after both had been wounded. Villard's book was one of the sources for Sir Richard Attenborough's movie IN LOVE AND WAR (1997), which stars Sandra Bullock as the nurse and Chris O'Donnell as the young Hemingway.

Villard died of pneumonia.

Vouyouklaki, Aliki

born: July 20, 1933
died: July 23, 1996, Athens, Greece, age 63

Greek film and stage actress.

Aliki Vouyouklaki was a well-known star in Greece for over 50 years, adored by her public. She came to acting through modeling, having had only a few acting lessons soon after finishing school. Her striking good looks were made more unique when a studio executive in Athens suggested that she bleach her dark hair blonde. She was then publicized as Greece's answer to Marilyn Monroe and Brigitte Bardot. Her first film was THE LITTLE MOUSE (1954) and her first big hit was ALIKI IN THE NAVY (1960). Even though she made about 40 movies, few have been seen outside of Greece. America saw two of her more popular ones, ASTRO (1960) and MADALENA (1965), which also played at the 1961 Cannes Film Festival.

She stopped making movies about 15 years ago and concentrated on the stage. Vouyouklaki was performing in *The Sound of Music* when she was diagnosed with the cancer which eventually claimed her life.

Walker, Keith

born: c. 1935
died: Dec. 30, 1996, Franklin, TN, age 61

Author, actor, radio and TV personality.

Keith Walker started in show business producing radio shows and later hosted his own talk show, as well as a TV show. He became a TV series actor, appearing in such shows as "The Rookies," "Mannix, " and "Mission Impossible." As a writer, he wrote TV scripts for "Emergency" and "Quincy," among others.

He wrote the story and co-wrote the screenplay for the movie FREE WILLY (1993), a surprise box-office hit that spawned two sequels, neither of which involved Walker.

Walker died of cancer.

Warshawsky, Ruth

born: c. 1915, Philadelphia, PA
died: Feb. 1, 1996, Los Angeles, CA, age 80

Character actress.

Before Ruth Warshawsky became a professional actress, she was very active in community theater. Her love of theater brought her to Hollywood, where she launched a 30-year career appearing mostly on stage and in many television shows. Among her few films are THE SINGING NUN (1966), BORN LOSERS (1967), THE STUDENT TEACHERS (1973), DEATH GAME (1977), RETURN FROM WITCH MOUNTAIN (1978), and ALMOST AN ANGEL (1990).

No cause of death was reported.

Weeks, Clair

born: c. 1912, India
died: August 26, 1996, Los Angeles, CA, age 84

Cartoonist, animation ambassador.

Clair Weeks was born and raised in India, the son of missionary parents. After graduating from high school, he came to the US and got a job as an assistant animator at the Disney studios. Weeks worked on such classic animated features as SNOW WHITE AND THE SEVEN DWARFS (1937), BAMBI (1942), CINDERELLA (1950), and PETER PAN (1953).

For many years, Weeks served as an animation ambassador to India and several countries in Southeast Asia, where he helped develop the animation industry.

Weeks died of cancer.

Weston, Jack

born: Jack Weinstein, Aug. 21, 1924, Cleveland, OH
died: May 3, 1996, New York, NY, age 71

Rotund character actor usually cast in comedic roles but equally effective in serious parts.

As a child, Jack Weston was encouraged by his shoemaker father to become a performer. When his teachers tagged him as the class clown, Weston was enrolled, at age 10, for stage training at the Cleveland Playhouse. After a stint in the Army as a machine-gunner in Italy and a USO performer in the Pacific, Weston headed for New York.

He worked at a lot of odd and menial jobs, but did manage to get some acting experience, including a tour in the musical *Anything Goes* and a part in the radio soap opera "The Right to Happiness." He also played Ranger Wormser on TV's "Rod Brown of the Rocket Rangers," a Saturday morning children's show. In 1958, both he and his wife at the time, Marge Redmond, were appearing in small roles in the hit Broadway musical *Bells Are Ringing* when they decided to quit and drive to Los Angeles to try their luck in the movies.

As a young, quirky urban character actor with a style that was not too unlike the man himself, Weston was cast in many movies, including I WANT TO LIVE (1958), IMITATION OF LIFE (1959), PLEASE DON'T EAT THE DAISIES (1960), ALL IN A NIGHT'S WORK (1961), IT'S ONLY MONEY (1962), and MIRAGE (1965). A big break came with the thriller WAIT UNTIL DARK (1967). In it, Weston had one of his best roles: an evil drug dealer who is part of the trio terrorizing a blind woman (Audrey Hepburn).

He was in two early TV sitcoms that were not successful, "My Sister Eileen" (1960-61) and "The Hathaways"(1961-62). He had no better luck in sitcomland when he recreated his neurotic dentist character in a television version of his hit movie, Alan Alda's THE FOUR SEASONS (1981).

Although there were a lot of films, Weston still found time to go back to Broadway, and struck success with Terence McNally's *The Ritz*. When it came time to film the farce, Weston repeated his stage role. THE RITZ (1976) was filmed in England by director Richard Lester, and while not too well received at the time of its release, it now has a cult following.

Some other Weston films are the musical MARCO (1973), ISHTAR (1987), DIRTY DANCING (1987), and SHORT CIRCUIT 2 (1988).

Weston succumbed to lymphoma.

White, Eddie R.

aka: Edward R. White
born: born 1919, New York City (Bronx,) NY
died: Oct. 22, 1996, NJ, age 77

Stage producer, songwriter, and actor.

Eddie R. White wore many show business hats. He produced shows on and off Broadway, wrote songs for many pop singers of the 1950s, arranged pop-artist concert tours, and acted in movies.

White's roles in several of his movies are so small that he often told people that one would have to look for him very fast, or you could miss him. Two of those films are Woody Allen's ANNIE HALL (1977) and MANHATTAN (1979). He was also briefly seen in Sam Peckinpah's THE KILLER ELITE (1975), with Robert Duvall, and in the Duvall-directed ANGELO, MY LOVE (1983). He had a bit of screen time in the New Jersey-filmed LOU, PAT & JOE D (1988) and the 1996 Alaska-filmed TV movie OUT AND ABOUT.

White died of heart failure.

Wood, Forrest

aka: Forrest Benjamin Wood
born: c. 1920, Ticonderoga, NY
died: July 22, 1996, Los Angeles, CA, age 76

Singer, songwriter, and actor.

Forrest Wood started out as a musician, songwriter, and recording artist, performing with his group the Forrest Wood Trio, but he was always interested in acting. He was in his friend Charlton Heston's movie THE PIGEON THAT TOOK ROME (1962). Then Wood's hit song, "Laura Lee," was used as the theme for Heston's MAJOR DUNDEE (1965). Although Wood did not appear in this Heston film, the two had a long and lasting friendship, and Wood subsequently acted in several other Heston movies, including THE WAR LORD (1965), NUMBER ONE (1969), OMEGA MAN (1971), SKYJACKED (1972), SOYLENT GREEN (1973), AIRPORT 1975 (1974), and TWO-MINUTE WARNING (1976). Wood also had small parts in THE BOSTON STRANGLER (1962) and THE HAWAIIANS (1970).

No cause of death was reported.

Young, Faron

born: Feb. 25, 1932, Shreveport, LA
died: Dec. 10, 1996, Nashville, TN, age 64

Actor, country singer, and song writer.

Faron Young, a farm boy, started singing country music while still a teenager, and within a year of performing on a radio show, he graduated to the Grand Ole Opry. He had a number one country song with "Live Fast, Love Hard, Die Young" and provided Willie Nelson with his first big hit, "Hello, Walls."

When Young entered films in 1956 with HIDDEN GUNS, it was in a series of low-budget westerns and country-music quickies. His movies include RAIDERS OF OLD CALIFORNIA, DANIEL BOONE, and TRAIL BLAZER (all 1957). In his last three films, SECOND FIDDLE TO A STEEL GUITAR (1965), NASHVILLE REBEL (1966), and WHAT AM I BID? (1967), he played himself.

Young was also a successful businessman. At one time, he owned *Music City News* , a country-music publication, and his other holdings have included a booking agency, a race track, and real estate.

Young, who suffered from emphysema and had undergone prostate surgery, died from an apparently self-inflicted gunshot wound.

Youngquist, Robert W.

born: c. 1906
died: Aug. 2, 1996, age 90

Artist, animator.

Robert W. Youngquist had a 35-year career as a staff animator with the Walt Disney organization, from 1935 to 1970. Over the years, he worked on such features as SNOW WHITE AND THE SEVEN DWARFS (1937), FANTASIA (1940), CINDERELLA (1950), SLEEPING BEAUTY (1959), and THE SWORD AND THE STONE (1963).

Youngquist died of natural causes.

Zuckerman, George

born: Aug. 10, 1916, Brooklyn, NY
died: Sept. 30, 1996, Santa Monica, CA
educ: University of South Carolina

Screenwriter, mostly at Universal, during the 1940s and 1950s, playwright, novelist.

After graduating from college in 1940, George Zuckerman became the sports editor for the *Atlantic City Daily Word* , but his budding newspaper career was cut short by WWII, where he served in the military from 1941-45. Following his discharge, he tried fiction writing for a while before turning to screenwriting.

Zuckerman's early screenplays were minor collaborative efforts, such as TRAPPED (1949), SPY HUNT (1950), UNDER THE GUN (1951), YELLOW MOUNTAIN (1954), and RIDE CLEAR OF DIABLO (1954). Zuckerman's greatest success was writing the Douglas Sirk-directed WRITTEN ON THE WIND (1956). Several writers at Universal had been unsuccessful in adapting the Robert Wilder novel to the screen, and the studio chiefs were reluctant to invest more money in a project they felt was unfilmable, until producer Albert Zugsmith persuaded the powers to assign the project to Zuckerman. He produced a screenplay that was so good, the studio shot practically the first draft. Zuckerman had earlier scripted Sirk's TAZA, SON OF COCHISE (1954) and worked with him again after the success of WRITTEN ON THE WIND on THE TARNISHED ANGELS (1957). Zuckerman's original screenplays were for DAWN AT SOCORRO (1954), THE SQUARE JUNGLE (1955), and THE TATTERED DRESS (1957).

In his later years, Zuckerman wrote plays and novels.

No cause of death was reported.

MASTER INDEX FOR MPG ANNUALS

Listed below are the titles of all films reviewed since 1984, with their year of release in the US. This date will enable you to locate the *Motion Picture Guide* volume in which the film appears. All films released in 1984 can be found in volume IX of the original *Motion Picture Guide*. Films released during or after 1985 can be found in the *Motion Picture Guide Annual* for the year *following* the film's year of release (i.e. films of 1986 are reviewed in the 1987 Annual, films of 1987 in the 1988 Annual, etc.).

If a film has been reviewed, but is absent from the list below, the title in question was released prior to 1984 and may be found in the original, ten-volume set, which is arranged alphabetically by title.

A

A COR DO SEU DESTINO (SEE: COLOR OF DESTINY, THE)(1988)
A CORPS PERDU (SEE: STRAIGHT TO THE HEART)(1988)
A HORA DA ESTRELA (SEE: HOUR OF THE STAR)(1986)
A LA MODE (1994)
A NAGY GENERACIO (SEE: GREAT GENERATION, THE)(1986)
A RESZLEG (SEE: OUTPOST, THE)(1996)
ABDUCTED (1986)
ABOUT LAST NIGHT (1986)
ABOVE THE LAW (1988)
ABOVE THE RIM (1994)
ABRAXAS: GUARDIAN OF THE UNIVERSE (1993)
ABSOLUTE BEGINNERS (1986)
ABUSE (1996)
ABYSS, THE (1989)
ACCA (SEE: ASSA)(1988)
ACCIDENTAL TOURIST, THE (1988)
ACCOMPANIST, THE (1993)
ACCUMULATOR 1 (1995)
ACCUSED, THE (1988)
ACE VENTURA: PET DETECTIVE (1994)
ACE VENTURA: WHEN NATURE CALLS (1995)
ACES: IRON EAGLE III (1992)
ACHALGAZRDA KOMPOZITORIS MOGZAUROBA (SEE: YOUNG COMPOSER'S ODYSSEY)(1986)
ACQUA E SAPONE (1985)
ACROSS THE MOON (1995)
ACROSS THE SEA OF TIME: NEW YORK 3D (1995)
ACROSS THE TRACKS (1991)
ACT OF PIRACY (1988)
ACTION JACKSON (1988)
ADAM'S RIB (1992)
ADDAMS FAMILY VALUES (1993)
ADDAMS FAMILY, THE (1991)
ADDICTION, THE (1995)
ADJUSTER, THE (1992)
ADRENALIN: FEAR THE RUSH (1996)
ADUEFUE (1988)
ADULT EDUCATION (SEE: HIDING OUT)(1987)
ADVENTURES IN BABYSITTING (1987)
ADVENTURES IN DINOSAUR CITY (1992)
ADVENTURES IN SPYING (1992)
ADVENTURES OF A GNOME NAMED GNORM, THE (1994)
ADVENTURES OF BARON MUNCHAUSEN, THE (1989)
ADVENTURES OF FORD FAIRLANE, THE (1990)
ADVENTURES OF HERCULES (SEE: HERCULES II)(1985)
ADVENTURES OF HUCK FINN, THE (1993)
ADVENTURES OF MARK TWAIN, THE (1985)
ADVENTURES OF MATT THE GOOSEBOY, THE (1995)
ADVENTURES OF MILO AND OTIS, THE (1989)
ADVENTURES OF PINOCCHIO, THE (1996)
ADVENTURES OF PRISCILLA, QUEEN OF THE DESERT, THE (1994)
ADVENTURES OF THE AMERICAN RABBIT, THE (1986)
ADVOCATE, THE (1994)
AEROBICIDE (SEE: KILLER WORKOUT)(1987)
AFFAIR, THE (1996)
AFFENGEIL (1992)
AFRAID OF THE DARK (1992)
AFTER DARK, MY SWEET (1990)
AFTER HOURS (1985)
AFTER MIDNIGHT (1989)
AFTER SCHOOL (1989)
AFTERSHOCK (1990)
AGATHA CHRISTIE'S TEN LITTLE INDIANS (SEE: TEN LITTLE INDIANS)(1990)
AGE ISN'T EVERYTHING (1991)
AGE OF INNOCENCE, THE (1993)
AGENT ON ICE (1986)
AGNES OF GOD (1985)
AI CITY (1995)
AILEEN WUORNOS: THE SELLING OF A SERIAL KILLER (1994)
AILSA (1995)
AIR AMERICA (1990)
AIR UP THERE, THE (1994)
AIRBORNE (1993)
AIRHEADS (1994)
AKE AND HIS WORLD (1985)
AKIRA (1991)
AKIRA KUROSAWA'S DREAMS (SEE: DREAMS)(1990)
ALADDIN (1987)
ALADDIN (1992)
ALAMO BAY (1985)
ALAN & NAOMI (1992)
ALASKA (1996)
ALBERTO EXPRESS (1992)
ALEX (1996)
ALEXA (1989)
ALICE (1988)
ALICE (1990)
ALIENS (1986)
ALIEN3 (1992)
ALIEN FROM L.A. (1988)
ALIEN INTRUDER (1993)
ALIEN NATION (1988)
ALIEN PREDATOR (1987)
ALIEN SPACE AVENGER (SEE: SPACE AVENGER)(1991)
ALIENATOR (1990)
ALIVE (1993)
ALL-AMERICAN MURDER (1992)
ALL DOGS GO TO HEAVEN (1989)
ALL DOGS GO TO HEAVEN 2 (1996)
ALL I WANT FOR CHRISTMAS (1991)
ALL THE VERMEERS IN NEW YORK (1992)
ALL TIED UP (1994)
ALLAN QUATERMAIN AND THE LOST CITY OF GOLD (1987)
ALLIGATOR EYES (1990)
ALLIGATOR II: THE MUTATION (1991)
ALLNIGHTER, THE (1987)
ALLONSANFAN (1985)
ALMOST (1991)
ALMOST AN ANGEL (1990)
ALMOST BLUE (1993)
ALMOST DEAD (1995)
ALMOST HOLLYWOOD (1994)
ALMOST PREGNANT (1992)
ALOHA SUMMER (1988)
ALWAYS (1985)
ALWAYS (1989)
AMANDA AND THE ALIEN (1996)
AMANT, L (SEE: LOVER, THE)(1992)
AMATEUR (1995)
AMAZING GRACE AND CHUCK (1987)
AMAZING PANDA ADVENTURE, THE (1995)
AMAZON (1991)
AMAZON WOMEN ON THE MOON (1987)
AMAZONIA--THE CATHERINE MILES STORY (SEE: WHITE SLAVE)(1986)
AMAZONIA: VOICES FROM THE RAINFOREST (1993)
AMAZONS (1987)
AMBITION (1991)
AMBULANCE, THE (1993)
AMERICA 3000 (1986)
AMERICA'S DEADLIEST HOME VIDEO (1995)
AMERICAN ANTHEM (1986)
AMERICAN AUTOBAHN (1989)
AMERICAN BLUE NOTE (1991)
AMERICAN BOYFRIENDS (1990)
AMERICAN BUFFALO (1996)
AMERICAN COMMANDOS (1986)
AMERICAN COP (1995)
AMERICAN CYBORG: STEEL WARRIOR (1994)
AMERICAN DREAM (1992)
AMERICAN EAGLE (1990)
AMERICAN FABULOUS (1992)
AMERICAN FLYERS (1985)
AMERICAN FRIENDS (1993)
AMERICAN GOTHIC (1988)
AMERICAN HEART (1993)
AMERICAN JUSTICE (1986)
AMERICAN KICKBOXER 1 (1991)
AMERICAN ME (1992)
AMERICAN NIGHTMARES (SEE: COMBAT SHOCK)(1986)
AMERICAN NINJA (1985)
AMERICAN NINJA 2: THE CONFRONTATION (1987)
AMERICAN NINJA 3: BLOOD HUNT (1989)
AMERICAN NINJA 4: THE ANNIHILATION (1991)

AMERICAN PRESIDENT, THE (1995)
AMERICAN RICKSHAW (1991)
AMERICAN SHAOLIN: KING OF THE KICKBOXERS II (1993)
AMERICAN STRAYS (1996)
AMERICAN SUMMER, AN (1991)
AMERICAN TAIL: FIEVEL GOES WEST, AN (1991)
AMERICAN TAIL, AN (1986)
AMERICAN WAY, THE (SEE: RIDERS OF THE STORM)(1988)
AMERICAN YAKUZA (1995)
AMERICA'S DREAM (1996)
AMIGOS (1986)
AMITYVILLE 1992: IT'S ABOUT TIME (1992)
AMONG THE CINDERS (1985)
AMONGST FRIENDS (1993)
AMOS & ANDREW (1993)
ANA (1985)
ANCHORESS (1994)
AND GOD CREATED WOMAN (1988)
. . .AND GOD SPOKE (1994)
AND YOU THOUGHT YOUR PARENTS WERE WEIRD (1991)
ANDRE (1994)
ANDROID AFFAIR, THE (1995)
ANDY AND THE AIRWAVE RANGERS (SEE: ANDY COLBY'S INCREDIBLY AWESOME ADVENTURE)(1990)
ANDY COLBY'S INCREDIBLY AWESOME ADVENTURE (1990)
ANGEL AT MY TABLE, AN (1991)
ANGEL EYES (1993)
ANGEL 4: UNDERCOVER (1994)
ANGEL HEART (1987)
ANGEL IN RED (1991)
ANGEL OF DESTRUCTION (1994)
ANGEL RIVER (1986)
ANGEL 3: THE FINAL CHAPTER (1988)
ANGEL TOWN (1990)
ANGELA (1996)
ANGELFIST (1993)
ANGELS AND INSECTS (1996)
ANGELS IN THE OUTFIELD (1994)
ANGIE (1994)
ANGKOR-CAMBODIA EXPRESS (1986)
ANGLAGARD (SEE: HOUSE OF ANGELS)(1993)
ANGUISH (1988)
ANGUS (1995)
ANGUSTIA (SEE: ANGUISH)(1988)
ANIMAL BEHAVIOR (1990)
ANIMAL INSTINCTS (1992)
ANIMAL INSTINCTS 2 (1994)
ANIMAL INSTINCTS III: THE SEDUCTRESS (1996)
ANITA--DANCES OF VICE (1987)
ANJOS DA NOITE (SEE: NIGHT ANGELS)(1987)
ANNA (1996)
ANNA (1987)
ANNE FRANK REMEMBERED (1996)
ANNE TRISTER (1986)
ANNIE O (1996)
ANNIE'S COMING OUT (1985)
ANNIHILATORS, THE (1985)
ANOTHER DAY (SEE: QUARTIERE)(1987)
ANOTHER 48 HRS. (1990)
ANOTHER LOVE STORY (1986)
ANOTHER STAKEOUT (1993)
ANOTHER WOMAN (1988)
ANOTHER YOU (1991)
ANTONIA (SEE: ANTONIA'S LINE)(1996)
ANTONIA & JANE (1991)
ANTONIA'S LINE (1996)
APART FROM HUGH (1996)
APARTMENT ZERO (1989)
APEX (1994)
APOLLO 13 (1995)
APPOINTMENT WITH DEATH (1988)
APPOINTMENT WITH FEAR (1985)
APPRENTICE TO MURDER (1988)
APRES L'AMOUR (SEE: LOVE AFTER LOVE)(1994)
APRIL FOOL'S DAY (1986)
ARABIAN KNIGHT (1995)
ARACHNOPHOBIA (1990)
ARCADE (1994)
ARCHITECTURE OF DOOM, THE (1991)
ARCTIC HEAT (SEE: BORN AMERICAN)(1986)
ARENA (1991)
ARIA (1987)
ARIZONA DREAM (1995)
ARMAGEDDON: THE FINAL CHALLENGE (1995)
ARMED AND DANGEROUS (1986)
ARMED FOR ACTION (1992)
ARMED RESPONSE (1986)
ARMY OF DARKNESS (1993)
ARMY OF ONE (1994)
AROUND THE WORLD IN 80 WAYS (1987)
ARRIVAL, THE (1991)
ARRIVAL, THE (1996)
ART FOR TEACHERS OF CHILDREN (1995)
ART OF DYING, THE (1991)
ARTHUR 2: ON THE ROCKS (1988)
ARTHUR'S HALLOWED GROUND (1986)
ARTICLE 99 (1992)
ASCENT, THE (1995)
ASHES OF TIME (1995)
ASPEN EXTREME (1993)
ASSA (1988)
ASSAM GARDEN, THE (1985)
ASSASSIN, THE (SEE: POINT OF NO RETURN)(1993)
ASSASSINATION (1987)
ASSASSINATION GAME, THE (1993)
ASSASSINS (1995)
ASSAULT, THE (1986)
ASSAULT AT WEST POINT (1996)
ASSAULT OF THE KILLER BIMBOS (1988)
ASSISI UNDERGROUND, THE (1985)
ASSOCIATE, THE (1996)
ASYA'S HAPPINESS (1988)
AT CLOSE RANGE (1986)
. . . AT FIRST SIGHT (1996)
AT HOME WITH THE WEBBERS (1994)
AT MIDDLE AGE (1985)
AT PLAY IN THE FIELDS OF THE LORD (1991)
AT THE MAX (1991)
ATALIA (1985)
ATTACK OF THE 5'2" WOMEN (SEE: NATIONAL LAMPOON'S ATTACK OF THE 5'2" WOMEN)(1995)
ATTACK OF THE 60-FOOT CENTERFOLD (1995)
AU REVOIR, LES ENFANTS (1988)
AUF DER SONNENSEITE DES LEBENS (SEE: MISSING PIECES)(1996)
AUGUST (1996)
AUGUSTIN (1995)
AUNTIE LEE'S MEAT PIES (1992)
AURORA (SEE: QUALCOSA DI BIONDO)(1985)
AURORA ENCOUNTER, THE (1985)
AUTUMN (1988)
AVALON (1990)
AVA'S MAGICAL ADVENTURE (1994)
AVENGING ANGEL (1985)
AVENGING ANGEL (1995)
AVENGING FORCE (1986)
AVENTURERA (1996)
AVIATOR, THE (1985)
AWAKENINGS (1990)
AWFULLY BIG ADVENTURE, AN (1995)
AY, CARMELA! (1991)

B

B.O.R.N. (1989)
BA WANG BIE JI (SEE: FAREWELL MY CONCUBINE)(1993)
BABAR: THE MOVIE (1989)
BABE (1995)
BABE, THE (1992)
BABETTE'S FEAST (1987)
BABY BLOOD (SEE: EVIL WITHIN, THE)(1994)
BABY BOOM (1987)
BABY DOLL MURDERS, THE (1993)
BABY ON BOARD (1993)
BABY . . . SECRET OF THE LOST LEGEND (1985)
BABY-SITTERS CLUB, THE (1995)
BABYFEVER (1994)
BABY'S DAY OUT (1994)
BABYSITTER, THE (1995)
BACK IN ACTION (1994)
BACK IN THE U.S.S.R. (1992)
BACK TO BACK (1990)
BACK TO SCHOOL (1986)
BACK TO THE BEACH (1987)
BACK TO THE FUTURE (1985)
BACK TO THE FUTURE PART II (1989)
BACK TO THE FUTURE PART III (1990)
BACKBEAT (1994)
BACKDRAFT (1991)
BACKFIRE (1989)
BACKFIRE! (1995)
BACKLASH (1986)
BACKLASH: OBLIVION 2 (1996)
BACKSTREET DREAMS (1990)
BACKSTREET JUSTICE (1994)
BACKTRACK (1992)
BAD BEHAVIOR (1993)
BAD BLOOD (1995)
BAD BLOOD (1987)
BAD BOYS (1995)
BAD CHANNELS (1992)
BAD COMPANY (1986)
BAD COMPANY (1995)
BAD DREAMS (1988)
BAD GIRLS (1994)
BAD GIRLS (SEE: WHORE 2)(1994)
BAD GIRLS FROM MARS (1991)
BAD GUYS (1986)
BAD INFLUENCE (1990)
BAD JIM (1989)
BAD LIEUTENANT (1992)
BAD LOVE (1996)
BAD MEDICINE (1985)
BAD TASTE (1988)
BADKONAK-E SEFID (SEE: WHITE BALLOON, THE)(1996)
BAGDAD CAFE (1987)
BAIL JUMPER (1990)
BAJA (1996)
BAKFAT MONUI CHUN (SEE: BRIDE WITH WHITE HAIR, THE)(1994)
BAL NA VODI (SEE: HEY BABU RIBA)(1987)
BALBOA (1986)
BALLAD OF LITTLE JO, THE (1993)
BALLAD OF THE SAD CAFE, THE (1991)
BALLET (1995)
BALLISTIC (1995)
BALLOT MEASURE 9 (1995)

BALTO (1995)
BAND OF THE HAND (1986)
BANDIT QUEEN (1995)
BANDITS (1988)
BANK ROBBER (1993)
BANZAI RUNNER (1987)
BAR 51--SISTER OF LOVE (1986)
BAR GIRLS (1995)
BARAKA (1993)
BARB WIRE (1996)
BARBARIAN QUEEN (1985)
BARBARIAN QUEEN II: THE EMPRESS STRIKES BACK (1992)
BARBARIANS, THE (1987)
BARBARIC BEAST OF BOGGY CREEK PART II, THE (SEE: BOGGY CREEK II)(1985)
BARCELONA (1994)
BAREFOOT GEN (1995)
BARFLY (1987)
BARJO (1993)
BARTON FINK (1991)
BASHU, THE LITTLE STRANGER (1990)
BASIC INSTINCT (1992)
BASIC TRAINING (1985)
BASKET CASE 2 (1990)
BASKET CASE 3: THE PROGENY (1992)
BASKETBALL DIARIES, THE (1995)
BASQUIAT (1996)
BASTILLE (1985)
BAT 21 (1988)
BATMAN (1989)
BATMAN FOREVER (1995)
BATMAN: MASK OF THE PHANTASM (1993)
BATMAN RETURNS (1992)
BATON ROUGE (1996)
BATTERIES NOT INCLUDED (1987)
BAXTER (1991)
BEACH BALLS (1988)
BEACHES (1988)
BEANS OF EGYPT, MAINE, THE (1994)
BEANSTALK (1994)
BEAR, THE (1989)
BEAST, THE (1988)
BEASTMASTER 2: THROUGH THE PORTAL OF TIME (1992)
BEASTMASTER 3: THE EYE OF BRAXUS (1996)
BEAT, THE (1988)
BEATING HEART, A (1992)
BEATRICE (1988)
BEAUTE VOLEE (SEE: STEALING BEAUTY)(1996)
BEAUTIFUL DREAMERS (1992)
BEAUTIFUL GIRLS (1996)
BEAUTIFUL THING (1996)
BEAUTY AND THE BEAST (1991)
BEAVIS AND BUTT-HEAD DO AMERICA (1996)
BEBE'S KIDS (1992)
BECOMING COLETTE (1992)
BED & BREAKFAST (1992)
BED OF ROSES (1996)
BED YOU SLEEP IN, THE (1995)
BEDROOM EYES II (1990)
BEDROOM WINDOW, THE (1987)
BEER (1986)
BEETHOVEN (1992)
BEETHOVEN LIVES UPSTAIRS (1992)
BEETHOVEN'S 2ND (1993)
BEETLEJUICE (1988)
BEFORE AND AFTER (1985)
BEFORE AND AFTER (1996)
BEFORE SUNRISE (1995)
BEFORE THE RAIN (1995)
BEGINNER'S LUCK (1986)
BEING AT HOME WITH CLAUDE (1993)
BEING HUMAN (1994)
BELIEVERS, THE (1987)
BELIZAIRE THE CAJUN (1986)
BELL DIAMOND (1987)
BELLE EPOQUE (1993)
BELLY OF AN ARCHITECT, THE (1987)
BENEFIT OF THE DOUBT (1993)
BENJI THE HUNTED (1987)
BENNY & JOON (1993)
BERKELEY IN THE 60S (1996)
BERLIN AFFAIR, THE (1985)
BERNARD AND THE GENIE (1992)
BERRY GORDY'S THE LAST DRAGON (SEE: LAST DRAGON, THE)(1985)
BERSERKER (1988)
BERT RIGBY, YOU'RE A FOOL (1989)
BEST INTENTIONS, THE (1992)
BEST OF THE BEST (1989)
BEST OF THE BEST II (1993)
BEST OF THE BEST 3: NO TURNING BACK (1996)
BEST OF TIMES, THE (1986)
BEST SELLER (1987)
BETRAYAL (1995)
BETRAYAL OF THE DOVE (1993)
BETRAYED (1988)
BETSY'S WEDDING (1990)
BETTER OFF DEAD (1985)
BETTER OFF DEAD (1995)
BETTER TOMORROW, A (1994)
BETTY (1993)
BETTY BLUE (1986)
BETWEEN HEAVEN AND EARTH (1993)
BETWEEN THE TEETH (1994)
BEVERLY HILLBILLIES, THE (1993)
BEVERLY HILLS BRATS (1989)
BEVERLY HILLS COP II (1987)
BEVERLY HILLS COP III (1994)
BEWARE: CHILDREN AT PLAY (1996)
BEYOND DARKNESS (1992)
BEYOND DESIRE (1996)
BEYOND FORGIVENESS (1995)
BEYOND JUSTICE (1992)
BEYOND RANGOON (1995)
BEYOND SUSPICION (1994)
BEYOND THE CALL (1996)
BEYOND THE DOOR III (1991)
BEYOND THE LAW (1994)
BEYOND THE RISING MOON (SEE: STAR QUEST: BEYOND THE RISING MOON)(1990)
BEYOND THE WALLS (1985)
BEYOND THERAPY (1987)
BHAJI ON THE BEACH (1994)
BIAN ZHOU BIAN CHANG (SEE: LIFE ON A STRING)(1992)
BIG (1988)
BIG BAD JOHN (1990)
BIG BAD MAMA II (1987)
BIG BANG, THE (1991)
BIG BLUE, THE (1988)
BIG BLUE, THE (1989)
BIG BULLY (1996)
BIG BUSINESS (1988)
BIG CRIME WAVE, THE (1986)
BIG DIS, THE (1990)
BIG EASY, THE (1987)
BIG GIRLS DON'T CRY . . . THEY GET EVEN (1992)
BIG GREEN, THE (1995)
BIG MAN ON CAMPUS (1991)
BIG MAN, THE (SEE: CROSSING THE LINE)(1991)
BIG NIGHT (1996)
BIG PARADE, THE (1987)
BIG PICTURE, THE (1989)
BIG SHOTS (1987)
BIG SLICE, THE (1991)
BIG SQUEEZE, THE (1996)
BIG SWEAT, THE (1991)
BIG TOP PEE-WEE (1988)
BIG TOWN, THE (1987)
BIG TROUBLE (1986)
BIG TROUBLE IN LITTLE CHINA (1986)
BIG WARS (1996)
BIGFOOT: THE UNFORGETTABLE ENCOUNTER (1995)
BIKINI BISTRO (1995)
BIKINI CARWASH COMPANY II, THE (1993)
BIKINI CARWASH COMPANY, THE (1992)
BIKINI GENIE (SEE: WILDEST DREAMS)(1990)
BIKINI ISLAND (1991)
BIKINI SHOP, THE (SEE: MALIBU BIKINI SHOP)(1987)
BIKINI SUMMER (1991)
BIKINI SUMMER 2 (1992)
BILL & TED'S BOGUS JOURNEY (1991)
BILL & TED'S EXCELLENT ADVENTURE (1989)
BILLY BATHGATE (1991)
BILLY MADISON (1995)
BILOXI BLUES (1988)
BINGO (1991)
BIO-DOME (1996)
BIRD (1988)
BIRD ON A WIRE (1990)
BIRDCAGE, THE (1996)
BIRDS II: LAND'S END, THE (1994)
BIRDS OF PREY (1987)
BIRDS OF PREY (1988)
BIRUMA NO TATEGOTO (SEE: BURMESE HARP, THE)(1985)
BITTER HARVEST (1993)
BITTER MOON (1994)
BITTER SUGAR (1996)
BITTER VENGEANCE (1995)
BLACK AND WHITE (1986)
BLACK BEAUTY (1994)
BLACK BELT ANGELS (1995)
BLACK CAULDRON, THE (1985)
BLACK DAY BLUE NIGHT (1996)
BLACK FOX (1995)
BLACK ICE (1992)
BLACK IS . . . BLACK AIN'T (1995)
BLACK MAGIC WOMAN (1991)
BLACK MOON RISING (1986)
BLACK MOUNTAIN (1996)
BLACK MOUNTAIN ROAD, THE (SEE: BLACK MOUNTAIN)(1996)
BLACK OUT (1996)
BLACK RAIN (1989)
BLACK RAIN (1990)
BLACK ROBE (1991)
BLACK ROSE OF HARLEM (1996)
BLACK ROSES (1989)
BLACK SCORPION (1996)
BLACK SHEEP (1996)
BLACK SNOW (1994)
BLACK WATER (1994)
BLACK WIDOW (1987)
BLACKBELT (1992)
BLACKOUT (1988)
BLADE IN THE DARK, A (1986)
BLADES (1990)
BLAKE EDWARDS' SON OF THE PINK PANTHER (1993)
BLAME IT ON THE BELLBOY (1992)
BLANK CHECK (1994)

BLANKMAN (1994)
BLASTFIGHTER (1985)
BLAZE (1989)
BLESSING (1995)
BLIND CHANCE (1987)
BLIND DATE (1987)
BLIND DIRECTOR, THE (1986)
BLIND FURY (1990)
BLIND JUSTICE (1994)
BLIND TRUST (SEE: INTIMATE POWER)(1986)
BLIND VISION (1992)
BLINDFOLD: ACTS OF OBSESSION (1994)
BLINK (1994)
BLINK OF AN EYE (1992)
BLISS (1985)
BLOB, THE (1988)
BLOCK NOTES-DIE UN REGISTA-APPUNTI (SEE: INTERVISTA)(1987)
BLONDES HAVE MORE GUNS (1996)
BLOOD & DONUTS (1996)
BLOOD AND CONCRETE -- A LOVE STORY (1991)
BLOOD DINER (1987)
BLOOD GAMES (1991)
BLOOD IN THE FACE (1991)
BLOOD IN, BLOOD OUT (SEE: BOUND BY HONOR)(1993)
BLOOD OATH (SEE: PRISONERS OF THE SUN)(1991)
BLOOD OF HEROES (1990)
BLOOD ON THE BADGE (1992)
BLOOD ON THE MOON (SEE: COP)(1988)
BLOOD RED (1990)
BLOOD RELATIONS (1990)
BLOOD SALVAGE (1990)
BLOOD SCREAMS (1991)
BLOOD SISTERS (1987)
BLOODFIST (1989)
BLOODFIST VI: GROUND ZERO (1995)
BLOODFIST VII: MANHUNT (SEE: MANHUNT)(1995)
BLOODFIST VIII (SEE: HARD WAY OUT: BLOOD FIST VIII)(1996)
BLOODFIST V: HUMAN TARGET (1993)
BLOODFIST IV: DIE TRYING (1992)
BLOODFIST III: FORCED TO FIGHT (1992)
BLOODFIST II (1991)
BLOODHOUNDS OF BROADWAY (1989)
BLOODKNOT (1996)
BLOODMATCH (1991)
BLOODMOON (1991)
BLOODSPORT (1988)
BLOODSPORT II: THE NEXT KUMITE (1996)
BLOODSTONE: SUBSPECIES II (1993)
BLOODSUCKERS FROM OUTER SPACE (1987)
BLOODSUCKING PHAROAHS IN PITTSBURGH (1991)
BLOODY BIRTHDAY (1986)
BLOODY POM POMS (1988)
BLOODY WEDNESDAY (1987)
BLOODY WEEKEND (SEE: LOADED)(1996)
BLOWBACK (1991)
BLOWN AWAY (1994)
BLU ELETTRICO (SEE: ELECTRIC BLUE)(1988)
BLUE (1993)
BLUE (1994)
BLUE CHIPS (1994)
BLUE CITY (1986)
BLUE DESERT (1991)
BLUE FLAME (1995)
BLUE HEAT (SEE: LAST OF THE FINEST)(1990)
BLUE HEAVEN (1985)
BLUE IGUANA, THE (1988)
BLUE IN THE FACE (1995)
BLUE JEAN COP (SEE: SHAKEDOWN)(1988)
BLUE KITE, THE (1994)
BLUE MONKEY (1988)
BLUE SKY (1994)
BLUE STEEL (1990)
BLUE TIGER (1995)
BLUE TORNADO (1991)
BLUE VELVET (1986)
BLUE VILLA, THE (1995)
BLUES LA-CHOFESH HAGODOL (SEE: LATE SUMMER BLUES)(1988)
BLUSH (1996)
BOB MARLEY: TIME WILL TELL (1992)
BOB ROBERTS (1992)
BOCA (1995)
BOCA A BOCA (SEE: MOUTH TO MOUTH)(1996)
BODIES, REST & MOTION (1993)
BODILY HARM (1995)
BODY CHEMISTRY (1990)
BODY CHEMISTRY 4: FULL EXPOSURE (1995)
BODY CHEMISTRY III: POINT OF SEDUCTION (1994)
BODY CHEMISTRY II: THE VOICE OF A STRANGER (1992)
BODY COUNT (1996)
BODY LANGUAGE (1993)
BODY MELT (1994)
BODY MOVES (1991)
BODY OF EVIDENCE (1993)
BODY OF INFLUENCE (1993)
BODY OF INFLUENCE 2 (1996)
BODY PARTS (1991)
BODY PUZZLE (1994)
BODY SHOT (1995)
BODY SNATCHERS (1994)
BODY STROKES (1995)
BODY WAVES (1992)
BODYGUARD, THE (1992)
BOGGY CREEK II (1985)
BOGUS (1996)
BOILING POINT (1993)
BONEYARD, THE (1991)
BONFIRE OF THE VANITIES, THE (1990)
BOOK OF LOVE (1991)
BOOMERANG (1992)
BOOST, THE (1988)
BOPHA! (1993)
BORDER HEAT (1988)
BORN AMERICAN (1986)
BORN IN EAST L.A. (1987)
BORN NATTURUNNA (SEE: CHILDREN OF NATURE)(1994)
BORN OF FIRE (1987)
BORN ON THE FOURTH OF JULY (1989)
BORN TO BE WILD (1995)
BORN TO RIDE (1991)
BORN WILD (1995)
BORN YESTERDAY (1993)
BORROWER, THE (1991)
BOSNA! (1994)
BOSS' WIFE, THE (1986)
BOTTLE ROCKET (1996)
BOULEVARD (1995)
BOULEVARD OF BROKEN DREAMS (1994)
BOUND (1996)
BOUND AND GAGGED: A LOVE STORY (1993)
BOUND BY HONOR (1993)
BOUNTY HUNTER: 2002 (SEE: 2002: THE RAPE OF EDEN)(1994)
BOUNTY TRACKER (1993)
BOXING HELENA (1993)
BOY CALLED HATE, A (1996)
BOY IN BLUE, THE (1986)
BOY MEETS GIRL (1985)
BOY RENTS GIRL (SEE: CAN'T BUY ME LOVE)(1987)
BOY SOLDIER (1987)
BOY WHO COULD FLY, THE (1986)
BOY WHO CRIED BITCH, THE (1991)
BOYFRIEND SCHOOL, THE (SEE: DON'T TELL HER IT'S ME)(1990)
BOYFRIENDS AND GIRLFRIENDS (1988)
BOYS (1996)
BOYS LIFE (1994)
BOYS NEXT DOOR, THE (1996)
BOYS NEXT DOOR, THE (1985)
BOYS OF ST. VINCENT, THE (1994)
BOYS ON THE SIDE (1995)
BOYZ N THE HOOD (1991)
BRADDOCK: MISSING IN ACTION III (1988)
BRADY BUNCH MOVIE, THE (1995)
BRAIN, THE (1989)
BRAIN DAMAGE (1988)
BRAIN DEAD (1990)
BRAIN DONORS (1992)
BRAIN SMASHER. . . A LOVE STORY (1993)
BRAINSCAN (1994)
BRAM STOKER'S DRACULA (1992)
BRAVE LITTLE TOASTER, THE (1987)
BRAVEHEART (1995)
BRAVESTARR (1988)
BRAZIL (1985)
BREACH OF CONDUCT (1995)
BREACH OF TRUST (1996)
BREAK, THE (1995)
BREAKAWAY (1996)
BREAKFAST CLUB, THE (1985)
BREAKING ALL THE RULES (1985)
BREAKING IN (1989)
BREAKING POINT (1994)
BREAKING THE RULES (1992)
BREAKING THE WAVES (1996)
BREATHING FIRE (1992)
BREEDERS (1986)
BRENDA STARR (1992)
BRENNENDES GEHEIMNIS (SEE: BURNING SECRET)(1988)
BREWSTER'S MILLIONS (1985)
BRIDE, THE (1985)
BRIDE OF KILLER NERD (1992)
BRIDE OF RE-ANIMATOR, THE (1991)
BRIDE WITH WHITE HAIR 2, THE (1995)
BRIDE WITH WHITE HAIR, THE (1994)
BRIDGES OF MADISON COUNTY, THE (1995)
BRIEF HISTORY OF TIME, A (1992)
BRIGHT ANGEL (1991)
BRIGHT LIGHTS, BIG CITY (1988)
BRIGHTNESS (1988)
BRIGHTON BEACH MEMOIRS (1986)
BRILLIANT DISGUISE, A (1994)
BRITT ALLCROFT'S MAGIC ADVENTURES OF MUMFIE--THE MOVIE (1996)
BROADCAST BOMBSHELLS (1995)
BROADCAST NEWS (1987)
BROKEN ARROW (1996)
BROKEN HEARTS AND NOSES (SEE: CRIMEWAVE)(1985)
BROKEN MIRRORS (1985)
BROKEN NOSES (1992)
BROKEN TRUST (1995)
BROKEN VOWS (1994)
BRONX TALE, A (1993)
BRONX WAR, THE (1992)
BROTHER OF SLEEP (1996)
BROTHER'S KEEPER (1992)
BROTHERS MCMULLEN, THE (1995)

BROWN BREAD SANDWICHES (1991)
BROWNING VERSION, THE (1994)
BRUCE BROWN'S ENDLESS SUMMER II (SEE: ENDLESS SUMMER II: THE JOURNEY CONTINUES, THE)(1994)
BRUTAL FURY (1993)
BRUTE FORCE (SEE: EXPERT, THE)(1995)
BUDDIES (1985)
BUDDY FACTOR, THE (SEE: SWIMMING WITH SHARKS)(1995)
BUDDY'S SONG (1993)
BUFFALO GIRLS (1995)
BUFFY THE VAMPIRE SLAYER (1992)
BUFORD'S BEACH BUNNIES (1993)
BUGGED (1996)
BUGSY (1991)
BUILDING BOMBS (1991)
BULL DURHAM (1988)
BULLET IN THE HEAD (1994)
BULLETPROOF (1988)
BULLETPROOF (1996)
BULLETPROOF HEART (1995)
BULLETS OVER BROADWAY (1994)
BULLIES (1986)
BULLSEYE! (1991)
'BURBS, THE (1989)
BURGLAR (1987)
BURIAL OF THE RATS (1996)
BURKE AND WILLS (1985)
BURMESE HARP, THE (1985)
BURNDOWN (1990)
BURNING SEASON, THE (1995)
BURNING SECRET (1988)
BURNT BY THE SUN (1995)
BUSHWHACKED (1995)
BUSINESS AFFAIR, A (1995)
BUSTED UP (1986)
BUSTER (1988)
BUTCHER'S WIFE, THE (1991)
BUTTERFLY AND SWORD (SEE: COMET BUTTERFLY AND SWORD)(1994)
BUTTERFLY KISS (1996)
BUVOS VADASZ (SEE: MAGIC HUNTER)(1996)
BUY & CELL (1989)
BY THE SWORD (1994)
BYE BYE BABY (1989)
BYE BYE BLUES (1990)
BYE BYE, LOVE (1995)
BYGONES (1988)

C

C'EST ARRIVE PRES DE CHEZ VOUS (SEE: MAN BITES DOG)(1993)
CABEZA DE VACA (1992)
CABIN BOY (1994)
CABLE GUY, THE (1996)
CACTUS (1986)
CADDYSHACK II (1988)
CADENCE (1991)
CADILLAC GIRLS (1994)
CADILLAC MAN (1990)
CAFE AU LAIT (1994)
CAFE ROMEO (1992)
CAFFE ITALIA (1985)
CAGE (1989)
CAGE II: ARENA OF DEATH (1994)
CAGED FEAR (1992)
CAGED FURY (1990)
CAGED HEARTS (1995)
CAGED HEAT 2: STRIPPED OF FREEDOM (1994)
CAGED HEAT 3000 (1995)
CAGED IN PARADISO (1990)
CALENDAR (1994)
CALENDAR GIRL (1993)
CALIFORNIA CASANOVA (1991)
CALL ME (1988)
CALLING THE GHOSTS: A STORY ABOUT RAPE, WAR AND WOMEN (1996)
CAME A HOT FRIDAY (1985)
CAMERON'S CLOSET (1989)
CAMILLA (1994)
CAMILLE CLAUDEL (1989)
CAMORRA (1986)
CAMP NOWHERE (1994)
CAMPUS MAN (1987)
CAN IT BE LOVE (1992)
CAN'T BUY ME LOVE (1987)
CANAAN'S WAY (SEE: BLIND JUSTICE)(1994)
CANADIAN BACON (1995)
CANDY MOUNTAIN (1988)
CANDYMAN (1992)
CANDYMAN: FAREWELL TO THE FLESH (1995)
CANNIBAL! THE MUSICAL (1996)
CANNIBAL WOMEN IN THE AVOCADO JUNGLE OF DEATH (1989)
CANTERVILLE GHOST, THE (1996)
CANVAS (1992)
CAPE FEAR (1991)
CAPTAIN AMERICA (1992)
CAPTAIN NUKE AND THE BOMBER BOYS (1995)
CAPTAIN RON (1992)
CAPTIVE HEARTS (1988)
CAPTIVE IN THE LAND, A (1993)
CAPTIVE RAGE (1988)
CAPTIVES (1996)
CAR 54, WHERE ARE YOU? (1994)
CARAVAGGIO (1986)
CARE BEARS ADVENTURE IN WONDERLAND, THE (1987)
CARE BEARS MOVIE, THE (1985)
CARE BEARS MOVIE II: A NEW GENERATION (1986)
CAREER OPPORTUNITIES (1991)
CAREFUL (1993)
CARLITO'S WAY (1993)
CARMEN MIRANDA: BANANAS IS MY BUSINESS (1995)
CARNAGE (1986)
CARNAL CRIMES (1991)
CARNOSAUR (1993)
CARNOSAUR II (1995)
CARNOSAUR 3: PRIMAL SPECIES (1996)
CARO DIARIO (1994)
CAROLINE AT MIDNIGHT (1994)
CARPENTER, THE (1989)
CARPOOL (1996)
CARRIED AWAY (1996)
CARRINGTON (1995)
CASINO (1995)
CASPER (1995)
CASTLE FREAK (1995)
CASUAL SEX? (1988)
CASUALTIES OF WAR (1989)
CAT CHASER (1991)
CATCH THE HEAT (1987)
CATHOLIC BOYS (SEE: HEAVEN HELP US)(1985)
CAT'S EYE (1985)
CATWALK (1996)
CAUGHT (1987)
CAUGHT (1996)
CAVEGIRL (1985)
CB4 (1993)
CEASE FIRE (1985)
CELESTIAL CLOCKWORK (1996)
CELLAR DWELLER (1988)
CELLULOID CLOSET, THE (1996)
CELTIC PRIDE (1996)
CEMENT GARDEN, THE (1994)
CEMENTERIO DEL TERROR (1985)
CEMETERY CLUB, THE (1993)
CEMETERY MAN (1996)
CENTER OF THE WEB (1992)
CENTURY (1995)
CERTAIN FURY (1985)
C'EST LA VIE (1990)
CHAIN, THE (1985)
CHAIN GANG (1985)
CHAIN LETTERS (1985)
CHAIN OF DESIRE (1993)
CHAIN REACTION (1996)
CHAINED HEAT II (1993)
CHAINS OF GOLD (1992)
CHAINSAW HOOKERS (SEE: HOLLYWOOD CHAINSAW HOOKERS)(1988)
CHAIR, THE (1991)
CHALLENGERS, THE (1994)
CHAMBER, THE (1996)
CHAMELEON (1996)
CHAMELEON STREET (1991)
CHAMPAGNE SAFARI, THE (1996)
CHANCES ARE (1989)
CHAPLIN (1992)
CHARULATA (1995)
CHASE, THE (1994)
CHASERS (1994)
CHASING BUTTERFLIES (1996)
CHASING DREAMS (1989)
CHATTAHOOCHEE (1990)
CHEAP SHOTS (1991)
CHEATIN' HEARTS (1993)
CHECK IS IN THE MAIL, THE (1986)
CHECKING OUT (1989)
CHEERLEADER CAMP (SEE: BLOODY POM POMS)(1988)
CHEETAH (1989)
CHEKIST, THE (1996)
CHERRY 2000 (1985)
CHEYENNE WARRIOR (1994)
CHICAGO JOE AND THE SHOWGIRL (1990)
CHICKEN HAWK: MEN WHO LOVE BOYS (1994)
CHIDAMBARAM (1986)
CHILDREN OF A LESSER GOD (1986)
CHILDREN OF FURY (1996)
CHILDREN OF NATURE (1994)
CHILDREN OF NOISY VILLAGE, THE (1996)
CHILDREN OF THE CORN II: THE FINAL SACRIFICE (1993)
CHILDREN OF THE CORN III: URBAN HARVEST (1995)
CHILDREN OF THE CORN: THE GATHERING (1996)
CHILDREN OF THE DUST (SEE: GOOD DAY TO DIE, A)(1995)
CHILDREN OF THE NIGHT (1992)
CHILDREN, THE (1992)
CHILD'S PLAY (1988)
CHILD'S PLAY 2 (1990)
CHILD'S PLAY 3 (1991)
CHINA GIRL (1987)
CHINA MOON (1994)
CHINA O'BRIEN II (1992)
CHINA O'BRIEN (1991)
CHINA WHITE (1991)
CHINA: MOVING THE MOUNTAIN (SEE: MOVING THE MOUNTAIN)(1995)
CHING SE (SEE: GREEN SNAKE)(1994)
CHIPMUNK ADVENTURE, THE (1987)
CHOCOLATE WAR, THE (1988)
CHOKE CANYON (1986)

CHONGQING SENLIN (SEE: CHUNGKING EXPRESS)(1996)
CHOPPER CHICKS IN ZOMBIETOWN (1991)
CHOPPING MALL (1986)
CHORUS LINE, A (1985)
CHORUS OF DISAPPROVAL, A (1989)
CHRISTMAS REUNION, A (1994)
CHRISTOPHER COLUMBUS: THE DISCOVERY (1992)
CHRONICLE OF A DEATH FORETOLD (1987)
CHRONICLE OF THE WARSAW GHETTO UPRISING ACCORDING TO MAREK EDELMAN (1995)
C.H.U.D. II: BUD THE C.H.U.D. (1989)
CHUNG ON TSOU (SEE: CRIME STORY)(1994)
CHUNGKING EXPRESS (1996)
CHURCH, THE (1991)
CIA--CODE NAME ALEXA (1993)
C.I.A. II TARGET: ALEXA (1994)
CIAO, PROFESSORE! (1994)
CINEMA PARADISO (1990)
CIRCLE OF FRIENDS (1995)
CIRCUITRY MAN (1990)
CIRCUITRY MAN II (1994)
CIRCUMSTANCES UNKNOWN (1995)
CITIZEN RUTH (1996)
CITIZEN X (1995)
CITY AND THE DOGS, THE (1985)
CITY HALL (1996)
CITY LIMITS (1985)
CITY OF BLOOD (1988)
CITY OF HOPE (1991)
CITY OF JOY (1992)
CITY OF LOST CHILDREN, THE (1995)
CITY SLICKERS (1991)
CITY SLICKERS II: THE LEGEND OF CURLY'S GOLD (1994)
CITY UNPLUGGED (1995)
CITY ZERO (1991)
CLAIRE OF THE MOON (1993)
CLAN OF THE CAVE BEAR, THE (1986)
CLANDESTINOS (SEE: LIVING DANGEROUSLY)(1988)
CLARA'S HEART (1988)
CLASS ACT (1992)
CLASS ACTION (1991)
CLASS OF '61 (1995)
CLASS OF 1999 II: THE SUBSTITUTE (1994)
CLASS OF 1999 (1990)
CLASS OF NUKE 'EM HIGH 3: THE GOOD, THE BAD AND THE SUBHUMANOID (1995)
CLASS OF NUKE 'EM HIGH (1986)
CLASS OF NUKE 'EM HIGH PART 2: SUBHUMANOID MELTDOWN (1991)
CLASS RELATIONS (1986)
CLEAN AND SOBER (1988)
CLEAN SLATE (1994)
CLEAN, SHAVEN (1995)
CLEAR AND PRESENT DANGER (1994)
CLEARCUT (1992)
CLERKS (1994)
CLIENT, THE (1994)
CLIFFHANGER (1993)
CLIFFORD (1994)
CLIMATE FOR KILLING, A (1991)
CLIVE BARKER'S LORD OF ILLUSIONS (SEE: LORD OF ILLUSIONS)(1995)
CLOCKERS (1995)
CLOCKWISE (1986)
CLOSE MY EYES (1991)
CLOSE TO EDEN (1992)
CLOSER, THE (1991)
CLOSET LAND (1991)
CLUB EARTH (SEE: GALACTIC GIGOLO)(1988)
CLUB EXTINCTION (1991)
CLUB FED (1991)
CLUB LIFE (1987)
CLUB PARADISE (1986)
CLUB, THE (1994)
CLUBHOUSE DETECTIVES (1996)
CLUE (1985)
CLUELESS (1995)
COASTWATCHER (SEE: LAST WARRIOR, THE)(1989)
COBB (1994)
COBRA (1986)
COCA-COLA KID, THE (1985)
COCAINE WARS (1986)
COCKTAIL (1988)
COCOON (1985)
COCOON: THE RETURN (1988)
CODE NAME: CHAOS (1992)
CODE NAME: EMERALD (1985)
CODE NAME VENGEANCE (1989)
CODE NAME ZEBRA (1987)
CODE OF SILENCE (1985)
CODICE PRIVATO (SEE: PRIVAE ACCESS)(1988)
COEUR QUI BAT, UN (SEE: BEATING HEART, A)(1992)
COHEN AND TATE (1989)
COLD COMFORT FARM (1996)
COLD FEET (1990)
COLD FEVER (1996)
COLD HEAVEN (1992)
COLD JUSTICE (1992)
COLD LIGHT OF DAY (1996)
COLD STEEL (1987)
COLDBLOODED (1995)
COLLISION COURSE (1992)
COLONEL CHABERT (1994)
COLONEL REDL (1985)
COLONY, THE (1996)
COLOR ADJUSTMENT (1992)
COLOR OF DESTINY, THE (1988)
COLOR OF MONEY, THE (1986)
COLOR OF NIGHT (1994)
COLOR PURPLE, THE (1985)
COLORADO COWBOY: THE BRUCE FORD STORY (1995)
COLORS (1988)
COMBAT SHOCK (1986)
COMBINATION PLATTER (1993)
COME AND SEE (1986)
COME SEE THE PARADISE (1990)
COMEDIE! (SEE: COMEDY!)(1987)
COMEDY! (1987)
COMET BUTTERFLY AND SWORD (1994)
COMFORT OF STRANGERS, THE (1991)
COMIC MAGAZINE (1986)
COMING OUT UNDER FIRE (1994)
COMING TO AMERICA (1988)
COMING UP ROSES (1986)
COMMANDO (1985)
COMMANDO SQUAD (1987)
COMMENT FAIRE L'AMOUR AVEC UN NEGRE SANS SE FATIGUER (SEE: HOW TO MAKE LOVE TO A NEGRO WITHOUT GETTING TIRED)(1990)
COMMITMENTS, THE (1991)
COMMON BONDS (1992)
COMMUNION (1989)
COMO AGUA PARA CHOCOLATE (SEE: LIKE WATER FOR CHOCOLATE)(1993)
COMPANION, THE (1995)
COMPANY BUSINESS (1991)
COMPANY OF STRANGERS, THE (SEE: STRANGERS IN GOOD COMPANY)(1991)
COMPANY OF WOLVES, THE (1985)
COMPLEX WORLD (1992)
COMPROMISING POSITIONS (1985)
COMRADES (1987)
COMRADES IN ARMS (1992)
CONCIERGE, THE (SEE: FOR LOVE OR MONEY)(1993)
CONCRETE ANGELS (1987)
CONDITION RED (1996)
CONEHEADS (1993)
CONFESSIONS OF A HIT MAN (1994)
CONFESSIONS OF A SERIAL KILLER (1992)
CONGO (1995)
CONGRESS OF PENGUINS, THE (1995)
CONJUGAL BED, THE (1994)
CONSEIL DE FAMILLE (SEE: FAMILY BUSINESS)(1987)
CONSENTING ADULTS (1992)
CONSUMING PASSIONS (1988)
CONTACTO CHICANO (1986)
CONTAR HASTA TEN (1986)
CONUNDRUM (SEE: FRAME BY FRAME)(1996)
CONVENT, THE (1995)
CONVICT COWBOY (1995)
CONVICTION, THE (1994)
CONVICTS (1991)
COOK, THE THIEF, HIS WIFE & HER LOVER, THE (1989)
COOKIE (1989)
COOL AS ICE (1991)
COOL RUNNINGS (1993)
COOL SURFACE, THE (1994)
COOL WORLD (1992)
COP (1988)
COP AND A HALF (1993)
COP AND THE GIRL, THE (1985)
COP FOR THE KILLING, A (1995)
COPS AND ROBBERSONS (1994)
COPYCAT (1995)
CORPORATE AFFAIRS (1991)
CORRINA, CORRINA (1994)
COSMIC EYE, THE (1986)
COSMIC SLOP (1995)
COUCH TRIP, THE (1988)
COUNTDOWN (1985)
COUNTRY LIFE (1995)
COUPE DE VILLE (1990)
COURAGE MOUNTAIN (1990)
COURAGE UNDER FIRE (1996)
COURT OF THE PHARAOH, THE (1985)
COUSIN BOBBY (1992)
COUSINS (1989)
COVER ME (1995)
COVER STORY (1995)
COVER-UP (1991)
COVERT ASSASSIN (1994)
COW, THE (1995)
COWBOY WAY, THE (1994)
COWS (1994)
CRACK HOUSE (1989)
CRACKER: THE MADWOMAN IN THE ATTIC (1996)
CRACKERJACK (1995)
CRAFT, THE (1996)
CRASH AND BURN (1991)
CRASH LANDING: THE RESCUE OF FLIGHT 232 (SEE: THOUSAND HEROES, A)(1994)
CRAWLERS, THE (1994)
CRAWLSPACE (1986)
CRAZY BOYS (1987)
CRAZY FAMILY, THE (1986)
CRAZY JOE (SEE: DEAD CENTER)(1994)
CRAZY LOVE (SEE: LOVE IS A DOG FROM HELL)(1987)
CRAZY PEOPLE (1990)

CRAZYSITTER, THE (1995)
CREATION OF ADAM (1995)
CREATOR (1985)
CREATURE (1985)
CREEP (1995)
CREEPERS (1985)
CREEPOZOIDS (1987)
CREEPSHOW 2 (1987)
CREW, THE (1995)
CRI DU HIBOU, LE (SEE: CRY OF THE OWL, THE)(1992)
CRIME BROKER (1994)
CRIME LORDS (1991)
CRIME OF HONOR (1987)
CRIME STORY (1994)
CRIME WAVE (SEE: BIG CRIME WAVE, THE)(1986)
CRIME ZONE (1989)
CRIMES AND MISDEMEANORS (1989)
CRIMES OF THE HEART (1986)
CRIMEWAVE (1985)
CRIMINAL HEARTS (1996)
CRIMINAL LAW (1989)
CRIMINAL PASSION (1994)
CRIMSON TIDE (1995)
CRIMSON WOLF (1995)
CRISSCROSS (1992)
CRITICAL CONDITION (1987)
CRITTERS (1986)
CRITTERS 2: THE MAIN COURSE (1988)
CRITTERS 4 (1992)
CRITTERS 3 (1991)
"CROCODILE" DUNDEE (1986)
"CROCODILE" DUNDEE II (1988)
CROCODILES IN AMSTERDAM (1996)
CRONACA DI UNA MORTE ANNUNCIIATA (SEE: CHRONICLE OF A DEATH FORETOLD)(1987)
CRONOS (1994)
CROOKED HEARTS (1991)
CROOKLYN (1994)
CROSS MY HEART (1987)
CROSS MY HEART (1991)
CROSSCUT (1996)
CROSSING DELANCEY (1988)
CROSSING GUARD, THE (1995)
CROSSING THE BRIDGE (1992)
CROSSING THE LINE (1991)
CROSSING, THE (1992)
CROSSOVER DREAMS (1985)
CROSSROADS (1986)
CROW: CITY OF ANGELS, THE (1996)
CROW, THE (1994)
CRUCIBLE, THE (1996)
CRUDE OASIS, THE (1995)
CRUMB (1995)
CRUSH (1993)
CRUSH, THE (1993)
CRUSOE (1989)
CRY-BABY (1990)
CRY FREEDOM (1987)
CRY IN THE DARK, A (1988)
CRY IN THE NIGHT, A (1993)
CRY IN THE WILD, A (1991)
CRY OF THE OWL, THE (1992)
CRY, THE BELOVED COUNTRY (1995)
CRY WILDERNESS (1987)
CRYING GAME, THE (1992)
CRYSTAL HEART (1987)
CTHULHU MANSION (1992)
CUP FINAL (1992)
CURDLED (1996)
CURE, THE (1995)
CURFEW (1989)
CURFEW (1994)
CURLY SUE (1991)
CURSE, THE (1987)
CURSE IV: THE ULTIMATE SACRIFICE (1993)
CURSE OF THE CRYSTAL EYE (1993)
CURSE OF THE STARVING CLASS (1995)
CURSE III: BLOOD SACRIFICE (1991)
CURSE II: THE BITE (1988)
CURTIS'S CHARM (1996)
CUSTODIAN, THE (1994)
CUT AND RUN (1986)
CUTTHROAT ISLAND (1995)
CUTTING CLASS (1989)
CUTTING EDGE, THE (1992)
CYBER BANDITS (1995)
CYBER NINJA (1994)
CYBER TRACKER (1994)
CYBER TRACKER 2 (1995)
CYBERZONE (1995)
CYBORG (1989)
CYBORG 2 (1993)
CYBORG 3: THE RECYCLER (1995)
CYBORG SOLDIER (1995)
CYCLONE (1987)
CYRANO DE BERGERAC (1990)
LORD OF ILLUSIONS (1995)

D

D.O.A. (1988)
D3: THE MIGHTY DUCKS (1996)
DA (1988)
DA YUE BING (SEE: BIG PARADE, THE)(1987)
DAD (1989)
DADDY AND THE MUSCLE ACADEMY (1992)
DADDY NOSTALGIA (1991)
DADDY'S BOYS (1988)
DADDY'S DYIN' . . . WHO'S GOT THE WILL? (1990)
DADETOWN (1996)
DAENS (1996)
DAHONG DENGLONG GAOGAO GUA (SEE: RAISE THE RED LANTERN)(1992)
DALLAS CONNECTION, THE (1995)
DALLAS DOLL (1995)
DAMAGE (1992)
DAMNATION (1988)
DAMNED IN THE USA (1992)
DAMNED RIVER (1990)
DANCE MACABRE (1992)
DANCE ME OUTSIDE (1995)
DANCE OF THE DAMNED (1989)
DANCE WITH A STRANGER (1985)
DANCE WITH DEATH (1992)
DANCER, THE (1995)
DANCERS (1987)
DANCES WITH WOLVES (1990)
DANCING IN THE DARK (1986)
DANCING WITH DANGER (1994)
DANGER OF LOVE (1995)
DANGER ZONE, THE (1987)
DANGER ZONE II: REAPER'S REVENGE (1989)
DANGER ZONE III: STEEL HORSE WAR (1991)
DANGEROUS GAME (1993)
DANGEROUS HEART (1994)
DANGEROUS INDISCRETION (1995)
DANGEROUS LIAISONS (1988)
DANGEROUS MINDS (1995)
DANGEROUS PASSION (1996)
DANGEROUS PREY (1995)
DANGEROUS TOUCH (1994)
DANGEROUS WOMAN, A (1993)
DANGEROUS, THE (1995)
DANGEROUSLY CLOSE (1986)
DANIELLE STEELE'S "KALEIDOSCOPE" (SEE: KALEIDOSCOPE)(1994)
DANZON (1992)
DAO MA DAN (SEE: PEKING OPERA BLUES)(1986)
DARK ANGEL (SEE: I COME IN PEACE)(1990)
DARK ANGEL: THE ASCENT (1994)
DARK BACKWARD, THE (1991)
DARK DANCER, THE (1995)
DARK DEALER (1995)
DARK EYES (1987)
DARK FUTURE (1995)
DARK HALF, THE (1993)
DARK HORSE (1992)
DARK OBSESSION (1991)
DARK RIDER (1991)
DARK SECRETS (1996)
DARK SIDE OF GENIUS, THE (1995)
DARK SIDE OF THE MOON (1990)
DARK TOWER (1989)
DARK WIND, THE (1993)
DARK, THE (1994)
DARKMAN (1990)
DARKMAN 2: THE RETURN OF DURANT (1995)
DARKMAN III: DIE DARKMAN DIE (1996)
DARKNESS (1994)
DARKNESS IN TALLINN (SEE: CITY UNPLUGGED)(1995)
D.A.R.Y.L. (1985)
DAS HAUS AM FLUSS (1986)
DAS SCHWEIGEN DES DICHTERS (SEE: POET'S SILENCE, THE)(1987)
DATE WITH AN ANGEL (1987)
DAUGHTER OF DARKNESS (1994)
DAUGHTER OF THE NILE (1988)
DAUGHTERS OF THE DUST (1992)
DAVE (1993)
DAWANDEH (SEE: RUNNER, THE)(1991)
DAWNING, THE (1993)
DAY IN OCTOBER, A (1992)
DAY MY PARENTS RAN AWAY, THE (1994)
DAY OF ATONEMENT (1993)
DAY OF THE COBRA, THE (1985)
DAY OF THE DEAD (1985)
DAY THE SUN TURNED COLD, THE (1995)
DAY TO REMEMBER, A (SEE: TWO BITS)(1995)
DAY YOU LOVE ME, THE (1988)
DAYLIGHT (1996)
DAYS OF THUNDER (1990)
DAZED AND CONFUSED (1993)
DE AMOR Y DE SOMBRA (SEE: OF LOVE AND SHADOWS)(1996)
DE BRUIT ET DE FUREUR (SEE: SOUND AND FURY)(1988)
DE MISLUKKING (SEE: FAILURE, THE)(1986)
DE SABLE ET DE SANG (SEE: SAND AND BLOOD)(1989)
DE VLASCHAARD (SEE: FLAXFIELD, THE)(1985)
DEAD, THE (1987)
DEAD AGAIN (1991)
DEAD AIM (1990)
DEAD ALIVE (1993)
DEAD BADGE (1995)
DEAD-BANG (1989)
DEAD CALM (1989)
DEAD CENTER (1994)
DEAD CERTAIN (1992)
DEAD COLD (1996)
DEAD CONNECTION (1994)
DEAD-END DRIVE-IN (1986)
DEAD END KIDS (1986)
DEAD FUNNY (1995)
DEAD HEAT (1988)

DEAD MAN (1996)
DEAD MAN WALKING (1988)
DEAD MAN WALKING (1995)
DEAD MAN'S REVENGE (1994)
DEAD MATE (1989)
DEAD MEN DON'T DIE (1991)
DEAD OF WINTER (1987)
DEAD ON (1994)
DEAD ON: RELENTLESS II (1991)
DEAD ON SIGHT (1994)
DEAD PIT (1990)
DEAD POETS SOCIETY (1989)
DEAD POOL, THE (1988)
DEAD PRESIDENTS (1995)
DEAD RINGERS (1988)
DEAD SPACE (1991)
DEAD TIRED (SEE: GROSSE FATIGUE)(1995)
DEAD TO RIGHTS (1996)
DEAD WEEKEND (1996)
DEAD WOMEN IN LINGERIE (1991)
DEADBOLT (1992)
DEADFALL (1993)
DEADLINE (1987)
DEADLY BET (1992)
DEADLY CURRENTS (1992)
DEADLY CURRENTS (1994)
DEADLY DAPHNE'S REVENGE (1994)
DEADLY DREAMS (1988)
DEADLY EXPOSURE (1993)
DEADLY FRIEND (1986)
DEADLY ILLUSION (1987)
DEADLY MARIA (1995)
DEADLY OBSESSION (1989)
DEADLY OUTBREAK (1996)
DEADLY PASSION (1985)
DEADLY POSSESSION (1989)
DEADLY PREY (1987)
DEADLY PURSUIT (SEE: SHOOT TO KILL)(1988)
DEADLY RIVALS (1993)
DEADLY SECRET, THE (1994)
DEADLY STRANGERS (SEE: BORDER HEAT)(1988)
DEADLY TARGET (1994)
DEADLY TWINS (1988)
DEADTIME STORIES (1987)
DEALERS (1989)
DEAR GOD (1996)
DEATH AND THE MAIDEN (1994)
DEATH ARTIST, THE (1996)
DEATH BECOMES HER (1992)
DEATH BEFORE DISHONOR (1987)
DEATH BENEFIT (1996)
DEATH HOUSE (1992)
DEATH IN BRUNSWICK (1995)
DEATH MACHINE (1995)
DEATH MAGIC (1993)
DEATH MATCH (1994)
DEATH OF A SOLDIER (1986)
DEATH OF AN ANGEL (1985)
DEATH OF EMPEDOCLES, THE (1986)
DEATH OF MARIO RICCI, THE (1985)
DEATH PENALTY (SEE: SATAN KILLER, THE)(1993)
DEATH RING (1993)
DEATH SENTENCE (1986)
DEATH WARRANT (1990)
DEATH WISH 3 (1985)
DEATH WISH 4: THE CRACKDOWN (1987)
DEATH WISH V: THE FACE OF DEATH (1994)
DEATHROW GAMESHOW (1987)
DEATHSTALKER AND THE WARRIORS FROM HELL (1989)
DEATHSTALKER IV: MATCH OF TITANS (1992)
DEATHSTALKER II (1987)
DEBT, THE (SEE: VERONICO CRUZ)(1990)
DECEIT (1993)
DECEIVED (1991)
DECEIVERS, THE (1988)
DECEMBER (1991)
DECEMBER BRIDE (1994)
DECEPTION (1993)
DECLINE OF THE AMERICAN EMPIRE, THE (1986)
DECONSTRUCTING SARAH (1995)
DECOY (1995)
DEEP BLUES (1992)
DEEP COVER (1992)
DEEP DOWN (1995)
DEEPSTAR SIX (1989)
DEF BY TEMPTATION (1990)
DEF-CON 4 (1985)
DEFENCE OF THE REALM (1985)
DEFENDING YOUR LIFE (1991)
DEFENSELESS (1991)
DEJA VU (1985)
DELICATESSEN (1992)
DELIRIOUS (1991)
DELLAMORTE DELLAMORE (SEE: CEMETERY MAN)(1996)
DELOS ADVENTURE, THE (1987)
DELTA FORCE, THE (1986)
DELTA FORCE 2 (1990)
DELTA FORCE COMMANDO (1987)
DELTA FORCE COMMANDO 2 (1991)
DELTA FORCE 3: YOUNG COMMANDOS (1991)
DELTA HEAT (1992)
DELTA OF VENUS (1996)
DELUSION (1991)
DEMOLITION MAN (1993)
DEMOLITIONIST, THE (1996)
DEMON IN MY VIEW, A (1992)
DEMON KEEPER (1994)
DEMON KNIGHT (SEE: TALES FROM THE CRYPT: DEMON KNIGHT)(1995)
DEMON WIND (1990)
DEMONI 2--L'INCUBO RITORNA (SEE: DEMONS 2--THE NIGHTMARE RETURNS)(1986)
DEMONIC TOYS (1992)
DEMONS (1986)
DEMONS (1987)
DEMONS 2: THE NIGHTMARE RETURNS (1986)
DEMONSTONE (1990)
DENIAL (1991)
DENISE CALLS UP (1996)
DENNIS THE MENACE (1993)
DENTIST, THE (1996)
DER BEWEGTE MANN (SEE: MAYBE . . . MAYBE NOT)(1996)
DER BULLE UND DAS MAEDCHEN (SEE: COP AND THE GIRL, THE)(1985)
DER FLIEGER (SEE: FLYER, THE)(1987)
DER FREISCHUTZ (SEE: MAGIC HUNTER)(1996)
DER HIMMEL UBER BERLIN (SEE: WINGS OF DESIRE)(1987)
DER JOKER (SEE: LETHAL OBSESSION)(1988)
DER OLYMPISCHE SOMMER (SEE: OLYMPIC SUMMER, THE)(1994)
DER ROSENKONIG (1986)
DER TOD DES EMPEDOKLES (SEE: DEATH OF EMPEDOCLES, THE)(1988)
DERNIERE FRONTIERE (SEE: OUTPOST, THE)(1996)
DESERT BLOOM (1986)
DESERT HEARTS (1985)
DESERT KICKBOXER (1992)
DESERT STEEL (1994)
DESERT WARRIOR (1985)
DESIRE (1996)
DESIRE AND HELL AT SUNSET MOTEL (1992)
DESOLATION ANGELS (1996)
DESPERADO (1995)
DESPERATE HOURS (1990)
DESPERATE MOTIVE (1993)
DESPERATE MOVES (1986)
DESPERATE PREY (1995)
DESPERATE REMEDIES (1994)
DESPERATE TRAIL, THE (1994)
DESPERATELY SEEKING SUSAN (1985)
DESTINY (SEE: TIME OF DESTINY, A)(1988)
DESTINY TURNS ON THE RADIO (1995)
DETECTIVE (1985)
DETECTIVE KID, THE (SEE: GUMSHOE KID, THE)(1990)
DETECTIVE SCHOOL DROPOUTS (1986)
DEVIL IN A BLUE DRESS (1995)
DEVIL IN THE FLESH (1986)
DEVIL'S DAUGHTER, THE (1992)
DEVIL'S ODDS (SEE: WILD PAIR, THE)(1987)
DEVOTION (1996)
DIABOLIQUE (1996)
DIALOGUES WITH MADWOMEN (1994)
DIAMOND SKULLS (SEE: DARK OBSESSION)(1991)
DIARY OF A HITMAN (1992)
DICE RULES (1991)
DICK TRACY (1990)
DIE BLEIERNE ZEIT (SEE: MARIANNE AND JULIANE)(1994)
DIE EROTISCHE GESCHICHTEN (SEE: TALES OF EROTICA)(1996)
DIE HARD (1988)
DIE HARD 2: DIE HARDER (1990)
DIE HARD WITH A VENGEANCE (1995)
DIE KAMELIENDAME (SEE: LADY OF THE CAMELIAS)(1987)
DIE MACHT DER BILER: LENI RIEFENSTAHL (SEE: WONDERFUL, HORRIBLE LIFE OF LENI RIEFENSTAHL, THE)(1994)
DIE MITLAUFER (SEE: FOLLOWING THE FUHRER)(1986)
DIE REISE (SEE: JOURNEY, THE)(1986)
DIE WANNSEEKONFERENZ (SEE: WANNSEE CONFERENCE, THE)(1987)
DIE WATCHING (1993)
DIE XUE SHUANG XIONG (SEE: KILLER, THE)(1991)
DIGGER (1995)
DIGGSTOWN (1992)
DILLINGER (1995)
DILLINGER AND CAPONE (1995)
DIM SUM: A LITTLE BIT OF HEART (1985)
DINGO (1991)
DINOSAUR ISLAND (1994)
DIPLOMATIC IMMUNITY (1991)
DIRECT HIT (1994)
DIRT BIKE KID, THE (1986)
DIRTY DANCING (1987)
DIRTY LAUNDRY (1987)
DIRTY MONEY (1995)
DIRTY ROTTEN SCOUNDRELS (1988)
DISAPPEARANCE OF CHRISTINA, THE (1994)
DISCLOSURE (1994)
DISCRETION ASSURED (1994)
DISORDERLIES (1987)
DISORGANIZED CRIME (1989)
DISPARA (SEE: OUTRAGE)(1996)
DISTANT COUSINS (SEE: DESPERATE MOTIVE)(1993)
DISTANT THUNDER (1988)
DISTANT VOICES, STILL LIVES (1989)

DISTINGUISHED GENTLEMAN, THE (1992)
DISTURBANCE, THE (1990)
DISTURBED (1991)
DIVERTIMENTO (SEE: LA BELLE NOISEUSE)(1993)
DIVING IN (1991)
DIXIELAND DAIMYO (1986)
DO OR DIE (1992)
DO THE RIGHT THING (1989)
DOC HOLLYWOOD (1991)
DOCTEUR JEKYLL ET LES FEMMES (SEE: DR. JEKYLL)(1985)
DOCTEUR M. (SEE: CLUB EXTINCTION)(1991)
DR. ALIEN (1989)
DOCTOR AND THE DEVILS, THE (1985)
DR. BETHUNE (1993)
DR. CALIGARI (1990)
DR. GIGGLES (1992)
DR. HACKENSTEIN (1989)
DR. JEKYLL (1985)
DR. JEKYLL & MS. HYDE (1995)
DOCTOR MORDRID (1992)
DR. OTTO AND THE RIDDLE OF THE GLOOM BEAM (1986)
DR. PETIOT (1994)
DOCTOR, THE (1991)
DOES THIS MEAN WE'RE MARRIED? (1992)
DOG TAGS (1990)
DOGFIGHT (1991)
DOGFIGHTERS, THE (1996)
DOIN' TIME (1985)
DOIN' TIME ON PLANET EARTH (1989)
DOLLMAN (1991)
DOLLMAN VS. DEMONIC TOYS (1993)
DOLLS (1987)
DOLLY DEAREST (1992)
DOLORES CLAIBORNE (1995)
DOMINICK AND EUGENE (1988)
DOMINION (1995)
DOMINION TANK POLICE: PART 2 (1993)
DON JUAN DEMARCO (1995)
DON JUAN, MY LOVE (1991)
DON JUAN, MI QUERIDO FANTASMA (SEE: DON JUAN, MY LOVE)(1991)
DON'T HANG UP (1994)
DONA HERLINDA AND HER SON (1986)
DONOR UNKNOWN (1996)
DON'T BE A MENACE TO SOUTH CENTRAL WHILE DRINKING YOUR JUICE IN THE HOOD (1996)
DON'T DO IT! (1995)
DON'T LET YOUR MEAT LOAF (1996)
DON'T TALK TO STRANGERS (1995)
DON'T TELL HER IT'S ME (1990)
DON'T TELL MOM THE BABYSITTER'S DEAD (1991)
DOOM GENERATION, THE (1995)
DOOMED TO DIE (1985)
DOOMSDAY GUN (1995)
DOORS: THE SOFT PARADE - A RETROSPECTIVE, THE (1991)
DOORS, THE (1991)
DOPPELGANGER (1993)
DORMIRE (1985)
DOT AND THE KOALA (1985)
DOUBLE BLAST (1994)
DOUBLE CROSS (1994)
DOUBLE, DOUBLE, TOIL AND TROUBLE (1995)
DOUBLE DRAGON (1994)
DOUBLE EDGE (1992)
DOUBLE EXPOSURE (1994)
DOUBLE HAPPINESS (1995)
DOUBLE IDENTITY (1991)
DOUBLE IMPACT (1991)
DOUBLE LIFE OF VERONIQUE, THE (1991)
DOUBLE O KID, THE (1993)
DOUBLE OBSESSION (1994)
DOUBLE THREAT (1993)
DOUBLE TROUBLE (1992)
DOUBLE VISION (1992)
DOWN AND OUT IN BEVERLY HILLS (1986)
DOWN BY LAW (1986)
DOWN, OUT AND DANGEROUS (1996)
DOWN PERISCOPE (1996)
DOWN THE DRAIN (1990)
DOWN TWISTED (1989)
DOWNTOWN (1990)
DRACHENFUTTER (SEE: DRAGON'S FOOD)(1988)
DRACULA: DEAD AND LOVING IT (1995)
DRACULA RISING (1993)
DRACULA'S WIDOW (1988)
DRAGNET (1987)
DRAGON FIRE (1993)
DRAGON FURY (1995)
DRAGON: THE BRUCE LEE STORY (1993)
DRAGONFIGHT (1993)
DRAGONHEART (1996)
DRAGON'S FOOD (1988)
DRAGONWORLD (1994)
DREAM A LITTLE DREAM (1989)
DREAM A LITTLE DREAM 2 (1995)
DREAM GIRLS (1994)
DREAM LOVER (1986)
DREAM LOVER (1994)
DREAM MACHINE, THE (1991)
DREAM MAN (1995)
DREAM TEAM, THE (1989)
DREAMANIAC (1987)
DREAMCHILD (1985)
DREAMING OF RITA (1995)
DREAMS (1990)
DREI GEGEN DREI (1985)
DRIFTER, THE (1988)
DRIVE (1992)
DRIVING ME CRAZY (1991)
DRIVING MISS DAISY (1989)
DROP DEAD FRED (1991)
DROP SQUAD (1994)
DROP ZONE (1994)
DROWNING BY NUMBERS (1991)
DRUGSTORE COWBOY (1989)
DRY WHITE SEASON, A (1989)
D2: THE MIGHTY DUCKS (1994)
DU MICH AUCH (SEE: SAME TO YOU)(1987)
DUCKTALES: THE MOVIE--TREASURE OF THE LOST LAMP (1990)
DUDES (1988)
DUE OCCHI DIBOLICI (SEE: TWO EVIL EYES)(1990)
DUET FOR ONE (1986)
DUMB & DUMBER (1994)
DUMB DICKS (SEE: DETECTIVE SCHOOL DROPOUTS)(1986)
DUNE WARRIORS (1991)
DUNGEONMASTER (1985)
DUNSTON CHECKS IN (1996)
DUST (1985)
DUST DEVIL (1993)
DUTCH (1991)
DUTCH TREAT (1987)
DYING YOUNG (1991)
DYNAMO (1994)
TWO BITS (1995)

E

EAR, THE (1992)
EARTH GIRLS ARE EASY (1989)
EAST OF THE WALL (1986)
EASY WHEELS (1989)
EAT A BOWL OF TEA (1990)
EAT AND RUN (1986)
EAT DRINK MAN WOMAN (1994)
EAT THE PEACH (1987)
EATING (1991)
EBBTIDE (1994)
ECHO PARK (1986)
ECHOES OF PARADISE (1989)
ECLIPSE (1995)
ED (1996)
ED WOOD (1994)
EDDIE (1996)
EDDIE AND THE CRUISERS II: EDDIE LIVES! (1989)
EDGAR ALLAN POE'S MASQUE OF THE RED DEATH (SEE: MASQUE OF THE RED DEATH)(1990)
EDGE OF HELL, THE (SEE: ROCK 'N' ROLL NIGHTMARE)(1987)
EDGE OF HONOR (1991)
EDGE OF SANITY (1989)
EDIE & PEN (1996)
ED'S NEXT MOVE (1996)
EDWARD SCISSORHANDS (1990)
EDWARD II (1992)
EFFICIENCY EXPERT, THE (1992)
800 LEAGUES DOWN THE AMAZON (1993)
8 MAN (1995)
EIGHT MEN OUT (1988)
8 MILLION WAYS TO DIE (1986)
8 SECONDS (1994)
8 SECONDS TO GLORY (SEE: 8 SECONDS)(1994)
18 AGAIN! (1988)
84 CHARING CROSS ROAD (1987)
84 CHARLIE MOPIC (1989)
EIN BLICK--UND DIE LIEBE BRICHT AUS (1986)
EIN MANN WIE EVA (SEE: MAN LIKE EVA, A)(1985)
EIN VIRUS KENNT KEINE MORAL (SEE: VIRUS KNOWS NO MORALS, A)(1986)
EL AMOR BRUJO (1986)
EL AMOR ES UNA MUJER GORDA (SEE: LOVE IS A FAT WOMAN)(1988)
EL ANO DE LAS LUCES (SEE: YEAR OF AWAKENING, THE)(1987)
EL IMPERIO DE LA FORTUNA (SEE: REALM OF FORTUNE, THE)(1987)
EL MARIACHI (1993)
EL PATRULLERO (SEE: HIGHWAY PATROLMAN)(1993)
EL SILENCIO DE NETO (SEE: SILENCE OF NETO, THE)(1996)
EL TESORO DEL AMAZONES (SEE: TREASURE OF THE AMAZON, THE)(1985)
ELECTRA (1996)
ELECTRIC BLUE (1988)
ELENI (1985)
ELIMINATORS (1986)
ELLA (SEE: MONKEY SHINES: AN EXPERIMENT IN FEAR)(1988)
ELLIOT FAUMAN, PH.D. (1990)
ELSA (SEE: AILSA)(1995)
ELVIRA: MISTRESS OF THE DARK (1988)
EMANON (1987)
EMBRACE OF THE VAMPIRE (1995)
EMBRYOS (1985)
EMERALD FOREST, THE (1985)
EMINENT DOMAIN (1991)
EMMA (1996)
EMMANUELLE 5 (1987)
EMMANUELLE 4 (1985)
EMMANUELLE 6 (1992)
EMPIRE OF THE SUN (1987)

EMPIRE RECORDS (1995)
ENCHANTED APRIL (1992)
ENCINO MAN (1992)
END OF INNOCENCE, THE (1991)
END OF THE LINE (1988)
ENDANGERED (1994)
ENDLESS DESCENT (1991)
ENDLESS SUMMER II: THE JOURNEY CONTINUES, THE (1994)
ENEMIES, A LOVE STORY (1989)
ENEMY GOLD (1994)
ENEMY MINE (1985)
ENEMY TERRITORY (1987)
ENEMY UNSEEN (1991)
ENEMY WITHIN, THE (1995)
ENGLISH PATIENT, THE (1996)
ENID IS SLEEPING (SEE: OVER HER DEAD BODY)(1992)
ENORMOUS CHANGES AT THE LAST MINUTE (1985)
ENRICO IV (SEE: HENRY IV)(1985)
ENTANGLED (1993)
ENTERTAINING ANGELS: THE DOROTHY DAY STORY (1996)
EQUALIZER 2000 (1987)
EQUINOX (1993)
ERASER (1996)
ERIK THE VIKING (1989)
ERMO (1995)
ERNEST GOES TO CAMP (1987)
ERNEST GOES TO JAIL (1990)
ERNEST GOES TO SCHOOL (1994)
ERNEST RIDES AGAIN (1993)
ERNEST SAVES CHRISTMAS (1988)
ERNEST SCARED STUPID (1991)
ERNESTO CHE GUEVARA--THE BOLIVIAN DIARY (1996)
EROTIQUE (1995)
ESCAPE FROM . . . SURVIVAL ZONE (1992)
ESCAPE FROM THE BRONX (1985)
ESCAPES (1987)
ESCORT GIRL (SEE: HALF MOON STREET)(1986)
ESPECIALLY ON SUNDAY (1993)
ESPERAME EN EL CIELO (SEE: WAIT FOR ME IN HEAVEN)(1988)
ETERNITY (1995)
ETHAN FROME (1993)
ETZ HADOMIM TAFUS (SEE: UNDER THE DOMIM TREE)(1996)
EUROPA (SEE: ZENTROPA)(1992)
EUROPA, EUROPA (1991)
EVE OF DESTRUCTION (1991)
EVEN COWGIRLS GET THE BLUES (1994)
EVENING STAR, THE (1996)
EVERY BREATH (1994)
EVERY OTHER WEEKEND (1991)
EVERY TIME WE SAY GOODBYE (1986)
EVERYBODY WINS (1990)
EVERYBODY'S ALL-AMERICAN (1988)
EVERYBODY'S FINE (1991)
EVERYONE SAYS I LOVE YOU (1996)
EVERYTHING RELATIVE (1996)
EVIL CLUTCH (1992)
EVIL DEAD 2: DEAD BY DAWN (1987)
EVIL ED (1996)
EVIL HAS A FACE (1996)
EVIL SPIRITS (1991)
EVIL WITHIN, THE (1994)
EVILS OF THE NIGHT (1985)
EVITA (1996)
EVOLVER (1995)
EXCESSIVE FORCE (1993)
EXCESSIVE FORCE II: FORCE ON FORCE (1995)
EXECUTION PROTOCOL, THE (1993)
EXECUTIONERS (1995)
EXECUTIVE DECISION (1996)
EXILED IN AMERICA (1992)
EXIT (1996)
EXIT TO EDEN (1994)
EXORCIST III, THE (1990)
EXOTICA (1995)
EXPERT, THE (1995)
EXPERTS, THE (1989)
EXPLORERS (1985)
EXPOSURE (1991)
EXQUISITE TENDERNESS (SEE: SURGEON, THE)(1996)
EXTERMINATORS OF THE YEAR 3000, THE (1985)
EXTRAMUROS (1991)
EXTREME MEASURES (1996)
EXTREME PREJUDICE (1987)
EXTREME VENGEANCE (1994)
EXTREMITIES (1986)
EYE FOR AN EYE (1996)
EYE OF THE EAGLE (1987)
EYE OF THE EAGLE 3 (1992)
EYE OF THE EAGLE II: INSIDE THE ENEMY (1989)
EYE OF THE STORM (1992)
EYE OF THE STRANGER (1993)
EYE OF THE TIGER (1986)
EYE OF VICHY, THE (1996)
EYES OF A WITNESS (1994)
EYES OF AN ANGEL (1994)
EYES OF THE BEHOLDER (1993)
EYES OF THE SERPENT (1994)
EYEWITNESS TO MURDER (1993)
MAXIMUM RISK (1996)

F

FABULOUS BAKER BOYS, THE (1989)
FACE OF THE ENEMY (1990)
FACES OF WOMEN (1995)
FAILURE, THE (1986)
FAIR GAME (1985)
FAIR GAME (1986)
FAIR GAME (1991)
FAIR GAME (1995)
FAITH (1993)
FAITHFUL (1996)
FALCON AND THE SNOWMAN, THE (1985)
FALL TIME (1995)
FALLING, THE (SEE: ALIEN PREDATOR)(1987)
FALLING DOWN (1993)
FALLING FROM GRACE (1992)
FALSE IDENTITY (1990)
FAMILY, THE (1987)
FAMILY BUSINESS (1987)
FAMILY BUSINESS (1989)
FAMILY PRAYERS (1993)
FAMILY THING, A (1996)
FAMINE WITHIN, THE (1991)
FAN, THE (1996)
FANDANGO (1985)
FAR AND AWAY (1992)
FAR FROM HOME (1989)
FAR FROM HOME: THE ADVENTURES OF YELLOW DOG (1995)
FAR HARBOR (1996)
FAR NORTH (1988)
FAR OFF PLACE, A (1993)
FAR OUT MAN (1990)
FARAWAY, SO CLOSE (1993)
FAREWELL TO THE KING (1989)
FAREWELL, MY CONCUBINE (1993)
FARGO (1996)
FARINELLI (1995)
FARM, THE (SEE: CURSE, THE)(1987)
FARM OF THE YEAR (SEE: MILES FROM HOME)(1988)
FAST FOOD (1989)
FAST FORWARD (1985)
FAST GETAWAY (1991)
FAST GETAWAY 2 (1994)
FAST MONEY (1996)
FAT GUY GOES NUTZOID!! (1986)
FAT MAN AND LITTLE BOY (1989)
FATAL ATTRACTION (1987)
FATAL BEAUTY (1987)
FATAL BOND (1993)
FATAL FURY: THE MOTION PICTURE (1995)
FATAL INSTINCT (1992)
FATAL INSTINCT (1993)
FATAL JUSTICE (1993)
FATAL PAST (1994)
FATALLY YOURS (1996)
FATE (1992)
FATE (1996)
FATHER (1992)
FATHER AND SCOUT (1995)
FATHER HOOD (1993)
FATHER OF THE BRIDE (1991)
FATHER OF THE BRIDE PART II (1995)
FATHERLAND (1995)
FATHERS AND SONS (1992)
FATHER'S ON A BUSINESS TRIP (SEE: WHEN FATHER WAS AWAY ON BUSINES)(1985)
FAUST (1994)
FAUSTO (SEE: A LA MODE)(1994)
FAVOR, THE (1994)
FAVORITES OF THE MOON (1985)
FAVOUR, THE WATCH, AND THE VERY BIG FISH, THE (1992)
FEAR (1989)
FEAR (1996)
FEAR, ANXIETY AND DEPRESSION (1989)
FEAR OF A BLACK HAT (1994)
FEAR, THE (1995)
FEARLESS (1993)
FEAST OF JULY (1995)
FEDERAL HILL (1994)
FEDERICO FELLINI'S INTERVISTA (SEE: INTERVISTA)(1987)
FEDS (1988)
FEED (1992)
FEEL THE HEAT (SEE: CATCH THE HEAT)(1987)
FEELING MINNESOTA (1996)
FELDMANN CASE, THE (1987)
FELONY (1996)
FEMALE MISBEHAVIOR (1993)
FEMALIEN (1996)
FEMME FATALE (1991)
FEMME FONTAINE: KILLER BABE FOR THE C.I.A. (1995)
FEMMES DE PERSONNE (1986)
FENCE, THE (1995)
FERNGULLY: THE LAST RAINFOREST (1992)
FEROCIOUS FEMALE FREEDOM FIGHTERS (1989)
FERRIS BUELLER'S DAY OFF (1986)
FEUD, THE (1990)
FEVER PITCH (1985)
FEW DAYS WITH ME, A (1989)
FEW GOOD MEN, A (1992)
FIDDLEFEST: ROBERTA GUASPARI-TZAVARAS AND HER EAST HARLEM VIOLIN PROGRAM (SEE: SMALL WONDERS)(1996)
FIELD, THE (1990)
FIELD OF DREAMS (1989)

FIELD OF FIRE (1992)
FIFTH MONKEY, THE (1991)
50-50 (1993)
52 PICK-UP (1986)
FILOFAX (SEE: TAKING CARE OF BUSINESS)(1990)
FINAL ANALYSIS (1992)
FINAL APPROACH (1991)
FINAL CUT, THE (1996)
FINAL EMBRACE (1994)
FINAL EQUINOX, THE (1996)
FINAL EXECUTIONER, THE (1986)
FINAL IMPACT (1992)
FINAL JUDGMENT (1995)
FINAL JUSTICE (1985)
FINAL MISSION (1994)
FINAL ROUND (1994)
FINAL SACRIFICE, THE (SEE: QUEST FOR THE LOST CITY)(1994)
FINAL TAKE: THE GOLDEN AGE OF MOVIES (1986)
FINE MESS, A (1986)
FINE ROMANCE, A (1992)
FINEST HOUR, THE (1992)
FINISHING TOUCH, THE (1992)
FIORILE (1994)
FIRE AND ICE (1987)
FIRE BIRDS (1990)
FIRE FESTIVAL (SEE: HIMATSURI)(1985)
FIRE IN EDEN (SEE: TUSKS)(1990)
FIRE IN THE NIGHT (1986)
FIRE IN THE SKY (1993)
FIRE ON THE MOUNTAIN (1996)
FIRE THIS TIME, THE (1994)
FIRE WITH FIRE (1986)
FIREHAWK (1993)
FIREHEAD (1991)
FIREHOUSE (1987)
FIRES WITHIN (1991)
FIREWALKER (1986)
FIRING LINE, THE (1991)
FIRM, THE (1993)
FIRST DEGREE (1995)
FIRST KID (1996)
FIRST KNIGHT (1995)
FIRST POWER, THE (1990)
FIRST WIVES CLUB, THE (1996)
FISH CALLED WANDA, A (1988)
FISHER KING, THE (1991)
FIST FIGHTER (1989)
FIST OF HONOR (1993)
FIST OF STEEL (1993)
FIST OF THE NORTH STAR (1991)
FIST OF THE NORTH STAR (1996)
FIT TO KILL (1993)
FIVE CORNERS (1988)
FIVE HEARTBEATS, THE (1991)
FIX, THE (1985)
FLAME IN MY HEART, A (1990)
FLAMING EARS (1996)
FLANAGAN (1985)
FLASHBACK (1990)
FLATLINERS (1990)
FLATTERED (1996)
FLAXFIELD, THE (1985)
FLED (1996)
FLESH + BLOOD (1985)
FLESH AND BONE (1993)
FLESH GORDON 2 (SEE: FLESH GORDON MEETS THE COSMIC CHEERLEADERS)(1993)
FLESH GORDON MEETS THE COSMIC CHEERLEADERS (1993)
FLESHTONE (1994)
FLETCH LIVES (1989)
FLICKS (1987)
FLIGHT OF THE INNOCENT (1993)
FLIGHT OF THE INTRUDER (1991)
FLIGHT OF THE NAVIGATOR (1986)
FLINCH (1994)
FLINTSTONES CHRISTMAS CAROL, A (1995)
FLINTSTONES, THE (1994)
FLIPPER (1996)
FLIRT (1996)
FLIRTING (1992)
FLIRTING WITH DISASTER (1996)
FLOUNDERING (1994)
FLOWER OF MY SECRET, THE (1996)
FLOWERS IN THE ATTIC (1987)
FLUKE (1995)
FLY, THE (1986)
FLY AWAY HOME (1996)
FLY BY NIGHT (1994)
FLY II, THE (1989)
FLYER, THE (1987)
FOLKS! (1992)
FONG SAI-YUK (1993)
FOOD OF THE GODS II (SEE: GNAW: FOOD OF THE GODS II)(1989)
FOOL AND HIS MONEY, A (1995)
FOOL FOR LOVE (1985)
FOOLS OF FORTUNE (1990)
FOR A LOST SOLDIER (1994)
FOR A NIGHT OF LOVE (SEE: MANIFESTO)(1988)
FOR BETTER OR FOR WORSE (SEE: HONEYMOON ACADEMY)(1990)
FOR BETTER OR WORSE (1996)
FOR GOD AND COUNTRY (1995)
FOR KEEPS (1988)
FOR LOVE OR MONEY (1993)
FOR QUEEN AND COUNTRY (1989)
FOR THE BOYS (1991)
FOR THE MOMENT (1996)
FOR THOSE ABOUT TO ROCK (1992)
FORBIDDEN CHOICES (SEE: BEANS OF EGYPT, MAINE, THE)(1994)
FORBIDDEN DANCE, THE (1990)
FORBIDDEN QUEST, THE (1994)
FORBIDDEN SUN (1989)
FORBIDDEN ZONE: ALIEN ABDUCTION (1996)
FORCE OF CIRCUMSTANCE (1990)
FORCE, THE (1995)
FORCED MARCH (1990)
FORCED TO KILL (1994)
FORD FAIRLANE (SEE: ADVENTURES OF FORD FAIRLANE, THE)(1990)
FOREIGN BODY (1986)
FOREIGN CITY, A (1988)
FOREIGN FIELD, A (1994)
FOREIGN STUDENT (1994)
FOREST WARRIOR (1996)
FOREVER (1994)
FOREVER ACTIVISTS (1991)
FOREVER MARY (1991)
FOREVER YOUNG (1992)
FORGET MOZART! (1985)
FORGET PARIS (1995)
FORREST GUMP (1994)
FORT SAGANNE (1994)
FORTRESS (1993)
FORTUNES OF WAR (1994)
FORTY SQUARE METERS OF GERMANY (1986)
FOUETTE (1986)
FOUR ROOMS (1995)
4 TALES OF 2 CITIES (1996)
FOUR WEDDINGS AND A FUNERAL (1994)
1492: THE CONQUEST OF PARADISE (1992)
FOURTH PROTOCOL, THE (1987)
FOURTH WAR, THE (1990)
FOXFIRE (1996)
FRAME BY FRAME (1996)
FRAME UP (1991)
FRAMEUP (1995)
FRANCESCA (1987)
FRANCESCO (1994)
FRANCOIS TRUFFAUT: STOLEN PORTRAITS (1996)
FRANK & JESSE (1995)
FRANK AND OLLIE (1995)
FRANKENHOOKER (1990)
FRANKENSTEIN GENERAL HOSPITAL (1988)
FRANKENSTEIN SINGS (1995)
FRANKENSTEIN UNBOUND (1990)
FRANKIE AND JOHNNY (1991)
FRANKIE STARLIGHT (1995)
FRANKY AND HIS PALS (1991)
FRANTIC (1988)
FRATERNITY VACATION (1985)
FRAUDS (1993)
FREAKED (1993)
FREDDIE AS F.R.O.7 (1992)
FREDDIE THE FROG (SEE: FREDDIE AS F.R.O.7)(1992)
FREDDY'S DEAD: THE FINAL NIGHTMARE (1991)
FREE RIDE (1986)
FREE WILLY (1993)
FREE WILLY 2: THE ADVENTURE HOME (1995)
FREEDOM FIGHTERS (SEE: MERCENARY FIGHTERS)(1988)
FREEDOM ON MY MIND (1994)
FREEFALL (1994)
FREEJACK (1992)
FREEWAY (1996)
FREEWAY MANIAC, THE (1989)
FREEZE--DIE--COME TO LIFE (1990)
FRENCH KISS (1995)
FRENCH LESSON (1986)
FRENCH SILK (1994)
FRENCH TWIST (1996)
FRESH (1994)
FRESH HORSES (1988)
FRESHMAN, THE (1990)
FRIDAY (1995)
FRIDAY THE 13TH, PART V--A NEW BEGINNING (1985)
FRIDAY THE 13TH PART VI: JASON LIVES (1986)
FRIDAY THE 13TH PART VII--THE NEW BLOOD (1988)
FRIDAY THE 13TH PART VIII--JASON TAKES MANHATTAN (1989)
FRIED GREEN TOMATOES (1991)
FRIEND OF THE FAMILY (1995)
FRIEND OF THE FAMILY 2 (1996)
FRIENDS (1995)
FRIENDS, LOVERS AND LUNATICS (1989)
FRIENDSHIP'S DEATH (1988)
FRIGHT HOUSE (1990)
FRIGHT NIGHT (1985)
FRIGHT NIGHT--PART 2 (1989)
FRIGHTENERS, THE (1996)
FRINGE DWELLERS, THE (1986)
FRISK (1996)
FROG PRINCE, THE (SEE: FRENCH LESSON)(1986)
FROGTOWN II (1993)
FROM A WHISPER TO A SCREAM (SEE: OFFSPRING, THE)(1987)
FROM BEYOND (1986)
FROM DUSK TILL DAWN (1996)
FROM HOLLYWOOD TO DEADWOOD (1989)

FROM NINE TO FIVE (SEE: TWENTY SOMETHING)(1995)
FROM THE HIP (1987)
FROM THE JOURNALS OF JEAN SEBERG (1996)
FROSH: NINE MONTHS IN A FRESHMAN DORM (1994)
FROZEN ASSETS (1992)
FRUIT MACHINE, THE (SEE: WONDERLAND)(1988)
FUGITIVE RAGE (1996)
FUGITIVE, THE (1993)
FULL BODY MASSAGE (1996)
FULL FATHOM FIVE (1990)
FULL METAL JACKET (1987)
FULL MOON IN BLUE WATER (1988)
FUN (1995)
FUNERAL, THE (1996)
FUNLAND (1990)
FUNNY ABOUT LOVE (1990)
FUNNY BONES (1995)
FUNNY FARM (1988)
FUNNYMAN, THE (1996)
FURTHER ADVENTURES OF TENNESSEE BUCK, THE (1988)
FUTURE COP (SEE: TRANCERS)(1985)
FUTURE-KILL (1985)
FUTUREKICK (1991)
F/X (1986)
FX2 - THE DEADLY ART OF ILLUSION (1991)

G

G.I. EXECUTIONER, THE (1985)
GABY--A TRUE STORY (1987)
GALACTIC GIGOLO (1988)
GALAXIES ARE COLLIDING (1996)
GALAXIS (1995)
GAME, THE (1990)
GAMES OF LOVE, THE (SEE: LA COMEDIE-FRANCAISE OU L'AMOUR JOUE)(1996)
GANDAHAR (SEE: LIGHT YEARS)(1988)
GANG JUSTICE (1994)
GANG OF FOUR, THE (1989)
GANGLAND (SEE: VERNE MILLER)(1988)
GARBAGE PAIL KIDS MOVIE, THE (1987)
GARCON! (1985)
GARDEN OF SCORPIONS (1993)
GARDEN, THE (1990)
GARDENS OF STONE (1987)
GARGOYLES -- THE MOVIE: THE HEROES AWAKEN (1995)
GAS FOOD LODGING (1992)
GATE, THE (1987)
GATE II (1992)
GATOR BAIT II: CAJUN JUSTICE (1989)
GAZON MAUDIT (SEE: FRENCH TWIST)(1996)
GEBROKEN SPIEGELS (SEE: BROKEN MIRRORS)(1985)
GENUINE RISK (1991)
GEORGE BALANCHINE'S "THE NUTCRACKER" (1993)
GEORGE'S ISLAND (1991)
GEORGIA (1994)
GEORGIA (1995)
GERMAN SISTERS, THE (SEE: MARIANNE AND JULIANE)(1994)
GERMANY YEAR 90 NINE ZERO (1995)
GERMINAL (1994)
GERONIMO: AN AMERICAN LEGEND (1993)
GET BACK (1991)
GET ON THE BUS (1996)
GET SHORTY (1995)
GETAWAY, THE (1994)
GETTING AWAY WITH MURDER (1996)
GETTING EVEN (1986)
GETTING EVEN WITH DAD (1994)
GETTING IN (1994)
GETTING IT RIGHT (1989)
GETTING MARRIED IN BUFFALO JUMP (1992)
GETTING OUT (1995)
GETTYSBURG (1993)
GHETTOBLASTER (1989)
GHOST (1990)
GHOST AND THE DARKNESS, THE (1996)
GHOST BRIGADE (1995)
GHOST DAD (1990)
GHOST FEVER (1987)
GHOST IN THE MACHINE (1993)
GHOST IN THE SHELL (1996)
GHOST TOWN (1988)
GHOSTBUSTERS II (1989)
GHOSTS OF MISSISSIPPI (1996)
GHOULIES (1985)
GHOULIES IV (1994)
GHOULIES II (1988)
GHOULIES III: GHOULIES GO TO COLLEGE (1992)
GIFT (1993)
GIFTED, THE (1994)
GIG, THE (1985)
GILSODOM (1986)
GINGER AND FRED (1986)
GIRL, THE (1987)
GIRL FROM MARS, THE (1996)
GIRL IN A SWING, THE (1989)
GIRL IN THE CADILLAC (1995)
GIRL IN THE PICTURE, THE (1986)
GIRL 6 (1996)
GIRLFRIENDS (1996)
GIRLS JUST WANT TO HAVE FUN (1985)
GIRLS SCHOOL SCREAMERS (1986)
GIRLS TOWN (1996)
GIVING, THE (1992)
GLADIATOR (1992)
GLADIATOR COP: THE SWORDSMAN 2 (1995)
GLASS CAGE, THE (1996)
GLASS MENAGERIE, THE (1987)
GLASS SHIELD, THE (1995)
GLEAMING THE CUBE (1989)
GLENGARRY GLEN ROSS (1992)
GLIMMER MAN, THE (1996)
GLITCH (1989)
GLORY (1989)
GLORY BOYS, THE (1995)
GNAW: FOOD OF THE GODS II (1989)
GNOME NAMED GNORM, A (SEE: ADVENTURES OF A GNOME NAMED GNORM, THE)(1994)
GO FISH (1994)
GO MASTERS, THE (1985)
GOBOTS: BATTLE OF THE ROCK LORDS (1986)
GOD AFTON, HERR WALLENBERG (SEE: GOOD EVENING, MR. WALLENBERG)(1993)
GOD IS MY WITNESS (1994)
GOD'S ARMY (SEE: PROPHECY, THE)(1995)
GODFATHER, PART III, THE (1990)
GODS MUST BE CRAZY II, THE (1990)
GODZILLA 1985 (1985)
GODZILLA VS. BIOLLANTE (1992)
GOING AND COMING BACK (1985)
GOING HOME (1988)
GOING UNDER (1991)
GOING UNDERCOVER (1989)
GOKIBURI (SEE: TWILIGHT OF THE COCKROACHES)(1990)
GOLD DIGGERS: THE SECRET OF BEAR MOUNTAIN (1995)
GOLDEN BRAID, THE (1991)
GOLDEN CHILD, THE (1986)
GOLDEN DART HERO (1994)
GOLDEN EIGHTIES (1986)
GOLDEN GATE (1994)
GOLDEN GIRLS, THE (1995)
GOLDENEYE (1995)
GOLDY III: THE MAGIC OF THE GOLDEN BEAR (SEE: MAGIC OF THE GOLDEN BEAR: GOLDY III, THE)(1994)
GOLDY II: THE SAGA OF THE GOLDEN BEAR (1986)
GOOD DAY TO DIE, A (1995)
GOOD EVENING, MR. WALLENBERG (1993)
GOOD FATHER, THE (1987)
GOOD GIRLS DON'T (1995)
GOOD MAN IN AFRICA, A (1994)
GOOD MORNING, BABYLON (1987)
GOOD MORNING, VIETNAM (1987)
GOOD MOTHER, THE (1988)
GOOD OLD BOY (SEE: RIVER PIRATES, THE)(1994)
GOOD OLD BOYS, THE (1995)
GOOD SON, THE (1993)
GOOD WIFE, THE (1986)
GOOD WOMAN OF BANGKOK, THE (1991)
GOODBYE, CHILDREN (SEE: AU REVOIR LES ENFANTS)(1988)
GOODBYE, NEW YORK (1985)
GOODFELLAS (1990)
GOOFBALLS (1987)
GOOFY MOVIE, A (1995)
GOONIES, THE (1985)
GOR (1989)
GORDY (1995)
GORILLA BATHES AT NOON (1995)
GORILLAS IN THE MIST (1988)
GOSPEL ACCORDING TO VIC, THE (1986)
GOTCHA! (1985)
GOTHIC (1987)
GRACE OF MY HEART (1996)
GRAFFITI BRIDGE (1990)
GRAND CANYON (1991)
GRAND HIGHWAY, THE (1988)
GRANDMOTHER'S HOUSE (1989)
GRANNY, THE (1995)
GRASS HARP, THE (1996)
GRAVE, THE (1996)
GRAVEYARD SHIFT (1987)
GRAVEYARD SHIFT (1990)
GREAT AMERICAN SEX SCANDAL, THE (1994)
GREAT BALLS OF FIRE (1989)
GREAT BIKINI OFF-ROAD ADVENTURE, THE (1994)
GREAT DAY IN HARLEM, A (1995)
GREAT ELEPHANT ESCAPE, THE (1995)
GREAT GENERATION, THE (1986)
GREAT MOUSE DETECTIVE, THE (1986)
GREAT OUTDOORS, THE (1988)
GREAT WALL, A (1986)
GREAT WHITE HYPE, THE (1996)
GREEDY (1994)
GREEN CARD (1990)
GREEN MONKEY (SEE: BLUE MONKEY)(1988)
GREEN SNAKE (1994)
GREMLINS 2: THE NEW BATCH (1990)
GRIEF (1994)
GRIFTERS, THE (1990)
GRIM (1996)
GRIM PRAIRIE TALES (1990)
GROSS ANATOMY (1989)

GROSS MISCONDUCT (1995)
GROSSE FATIGUE (1995)
GROUND ZERO (1989)
GROUNDHOG DAY (1993)
GRUMPIER OLD MEN (1995)
GRUMPY OLD MEN (1993)
GRUNT! THE WRESTLING MOVIE (1985)
GUARDIAN, THE (1990)
GUARDIAN ANGEL (1994)
GUARDIAN OF HELL (1985)
GUARDING TESS (1994)
GUELWAAR (1993)
GUILIA E GUILIA (SEE: JULIA AND JULIA)(1988)
GUILTY AS CHARGED (1992)
GUILTY AS SIN (1993)
GUILTY BY SUSPICION (1991)
GUIMBA THE TYRANT (1996)
GUIMBA, UN TYRAN, UNE EPOQUE (SEE: GUIMBA THE TYRANT)(1996)
GUMBY: THE MOVIE (1995)
GUMSHOE KID, THE (1990)
GUN IN BETTY LOU'S HANDBAG, THE (1992)
GUNG HO (1986)
GUNMEN (1994)
GUNPOWDER (1987)
GUNRUNNER, THE (1989)
GUNS (1991)
GUNS OF HONOR (1994)
GUYVER II: DARK HERO, THE (1994)
GUYVER, THE (1992)
GYMKATA (1985)

H

H.P. LOVECRAFT'S LURKING FEAR (SEE: LURKING FEAR)(1994)
H.P. LOVECRAFT'S THE UNNAMABLE II: THE STATEMENT OF RANDOLPH CARTER (SEE: UNNAMABLE II, THE)(1993)
HAAKON HAAKONSEN (SEE: SHIPWRECKED)(1991)
HABITATION OF DRAGONS, THE (1995)
HACKERS (1995)
HAIL CAESAR (1994)
HAIL, MARY (1985)
HAIRDRESSER'S HUSBAND, THE (1992)
HAIRSPRAY (1988)
HALBMOND (SEE: HALFMOON)(1996)
HALF JAPANESE: THE BAND THAT WOULD BE KING (1993)
HALF MOON STREET (1986)
HALFBACK OF NOTRE DAME, THE (1996)
HALFMOON (1996)
HALLOWEEN IV: THE RETURN OF MICHAEL MYERS (1988)
HALLOWEEN 5: THE REVENGE OF MICHAEL MYERS (1989)
HALLOWEEN: THE CURSE OF MICHAEL MYERS (1995)
HALLOWEEN TREE, THE (1994)
HAMBURGER HILL (1987)
HAMBURGER. . . THE MOTION PICTURE (1986)
HAMLET (1990)
HAMLET (1996)
HAMOUN (1991)
HAND THAT ROCKS THE CRADLE, THE (1992)
HANDFUL OF DUST, A (1988)
HANDGUN (1995)
HANDMAID'S TALE, THE (1990)
HANDS OF STEEL (1986)
HANGFIRE (1991)
HANGIN' WITH THE HOMEBOYS (1991)
HANNAH AND HER SISTERS (1986)
HANNA'S WAR (1988)
HANOI HILTON, THE (1987)
HANS CHRISTIAN ANDERSEN'S THUMBELINA (1994)
HANUSSEN (1989)
HANY AZ ORA, VEKKER UR? (SEE: WHAT'S THE TIME, MR. CLOCK?)(1985)
HAPPILY EVER AFTER (1993)
HAPPY GILMORE (1996)
HAPPY HELL NIGHT (1992)
HAPPY HOUR (1987)
HAPPY NEW YEAR (1987)
HAPPY TOGETHER (1990)
HARD BOUNTY (1995)
HARD DRIVE (1994)
HARD HUNTED (1993)
HARD JUSTICE (1996)
HARD LABOUR (1994)
HARD PROMISES (1992)
HARD TARGET (1993)
HARD TICKET TO HAWAII (1987)
HARD TIMES (1988)
HARD TO DIE (1993)
HARD TO KILL (1990)
HARD TRAVELING (1985)
HARD TRUTH, THE (1994)
HARD VICE (1994)
HARD WAY OUT: BLOODFIST VIII (1996)
HARD WAY, THE (1991)
HARD-BOILED (1992)
HARDBODIES 2 (1986)
HARDCASE AND FIST (1989)
HARDWARE (1990)
HAREM (1985)
HARLEM DIARY: NINE VOICES OF RESILIENCE (1995)
HARLEM NIGHTS (1989)
HARLEY DAVIDSON AND THE MARLBORO MAN (1991)
HARMONY CATS (1994)
HARRIET THE SPY (1996)
HARRISON BERGERON (SEE: KURT VONNEGUT'S HARRISON BERGERON)(1995)
HARRY AND THE HENDERSONS (1987)
HARVEST OF FIRE (1996)
HARVEST, THE (1993)
HATE (1996)
HATTA ISHAAR AKHAR (SEE: CURFEW)(1994)
HAUNTED (1996)
HAUNTED HONEYMOON (1986)
HAUNTING FEAR (1991)
HAUNTING OF HAMILTON HIGH, THE (SEE: HELLO MARY LOU: PROM NIGHT II)(1987)
HAUNTING OF MORELLA, THE (1990)
HAUNTING OF SEACLIFF INN, THE (1995)
HAVANA (1990)
HAWK, THE (1993)
HE SAID, SHE SAID (1991)
HEAD OF THE FAMILY (1996)
HEAD OFFICE (1986)
HEADLESS BODY IN TOPLESS BAR (1996)
HEADS (1994)
HEAR MY SONG (1991)
HEAR NO EVIL (1993)
HEARING VOICES (1991)
HEART AND SOULS (1993)
HEART CONDITION (1990)
HEART IN WINTER, A (SEE: UN COEUR EN HIVER)(1993)
HEART OF DIXIE (1989)
HEART OF MIDNIGHT (1989)
HEARTBREAK HOTEL (1988)
HEARTBREAK RIDGE (1986)
HEARTBURN (1986)
HEARTS OF FIRE (1987)
HEARTSTONE (SEE: DEMONSTONE)(1990)
HEAT (1987)
HEAT (1995)
HEAT AND SUNLIGHT (1988)
HEATHCLIFF: THE MOVIE (1986)
HEATHERS (1989)
HEATSEEKER (1995)
HEAVEN AND EARTH (1990)
HEAVEN AND EARTH (1993)
HEAVEN HELP US (1985)
HEAVEN IS A PLAYGROUND (1992)
HEAVENLY BODIES (1985)
HEAVENLY CREATURES (1994)
HEAVENLY KID, THE (1985)
HEAVENLY PURSUITS (SEE: GOSPEL ACCORDING TO VIC, THE)(1986)
HEAVEN'S A DRAG (1995)
HEAVEN'S PRISONERS (1996)
HEAVY (1996)
HEAVYWEIGHTS (1995)
HECK'S WAY HOME (1996)
HEDD WYNN (1996)
HEIDI CHRONICLES, THE (1996)
HEIDI FLEISS HOLLYWOOD MADAM (1996)
HEIMAT (1985)
HELAS POUR MOI (1994)
HELL COMES TO FROGTOWN (1988)
HELL HIGH (1989)
HELL MASTER (1992)
HELL SQUAD (1986)
HELLBOUND (1995)
HELLBOUND: HELLRAISER II (1988)
HELLHOLE (1985)
HELLO AGAIN (1987)
HELLO MARY LOU: PROM NIGHT II (1987)
HELLRAISER (1987)
HELLRAISER 2 (SEE: HELLBOUND: HELLRAISER II)(1988)
HELLRAISER III: HELL ON EARTH (1992)
HELLRAISER IV (SEE: HELLRAISER: BLOODLINE)(1996)
HELLRAISER: BLOODLINE (1996)
HELLROLLER (1992)
HENRY & JUNE (1990)
HENRY: PORTRAIT OF A SERIAL KILLER (1989)
HENRY V (1989)
HER ALIBI (1989)
HERCULES II (1985)
HERDSMEN OF THE SUN (1991)
HERE COME THE LITTLES (1985)
HERO (1992)
HERO AND THE TERROR (1988)
HEROIC TRIO 2: EXECUTIONERS (SEE: EXECUTIONERS)(1995)
HEROIC TRIO, THE (1995)
HE'S A WOMAN, SHE'S A MAN (1995)
HE'S MY GIRL (1987)
HEXED (1993)
HEY BABU RIBA (1987)
HIDDEN, THE (1987)
HIDDEN II, THE (1994)
HIDDEN AGENDA (1990)
HIDDEN ASSASSIN (1996)
HIDDEN FEARS (1994)
HIDDEN OBSESSION (1993)
HIDDEN VISION (SEE: NIGHT EYES)(1990)
HIDEAWAY (1995)
HIDER IN THE HOUSE (1991)
HIDING OUT (1987)
HIE SHAN LU (SEE: BLACK MOUNTAIN)(1996)
HIGH DESERT KILL (1990)

HIGH HEELS (1991)
HIGH HOPES (1988)
HIGH LONESOME: THE STORY OF BLUEGRASS MUSIC (1994)
HIGH RISK (1995)
HIGH SCHOOL II (1994)
HIGH SCHOOL HIGH (1996)
HIGH SEASON (1988)
HIGH SPEED (1986)
HIGH SPIRITS (1988)
HIGH STAKES (1989)
HIGH STRUNG (1994)
HIGH TIDE (1987)
HIGHER LEARNING (1995)
HIGHLANDER (1986)
HIGHLANDER 2: THE QUICKENING (1991)
HIGHLANDER: THE FINAL DIMENSION (1995)
HIGHWAY PATROLMAN (1993)
HIGHWAY 61 (1992)
HIGHWAY TO HELL (1992)
HILLS HAVE EYES II, THE (1985)
HIMATSURI (1985)
HIMMO, KING OF JERUSALEM (1988)
HIRED TO KILL (1992)
HISTORY (1988)
HIT, THE (1985)
HIT LIST (1990)
HIT THE DUTCHMAN (1993)
HITCHER, THE (1986)
HITMAN (SEE: AMERICAN COMMANDOES)(1986)
HITMAN, THE (1991)
HIUCH HA'GDI (SEE: SMILE OF THE LAMB, THE)(1986)
HOCUS POCUS (1993)
HOFFA (1992)
HOL VOLT, HOL NEM VOLT (SEE: HUNGARIAN FAIRY TALE, A)(1989)
HOLCROFT COVENANT, THE (1985)
HOLD ME THRILL ME KISS ME (1993)
HOLLOW POINT (1996)
HOLLYWEIRD (SEE: FLICKS)(1987)
HOLLYWOOD BOULEVARD II (1991)
HOLLYWOOD CHAINSAW HOOKERS (1988)
HOLLYWOOD HARRY (1985)
HOLLYWOOD HOT TUBS II: EDUCATING CRYSTAL (1990)
HOLLYWOOD SHUFFLE (1987)
HOLLYWOOD VICE SQUAD (1986)
HOLLYWOOD ZAP! (1986)
HOLOGRAM MAN (1995)
HOLY MATRIMONY (1994)
HOMAGE (1996)
HOMBRE MIRANDO AL SUDESTE (SEE: MAN FACING SOUTHEAST)(1986)
HOME ALONE (1990)
HOME ALONE 2: LOST IN NEW YORK (1992)
HOME FOR THE HOLIDAYS (1995)
HOME FRONT (SEE: MORGAN STEWART'S COMING HOME)(1987)
HOME IS WHERE THE HART IS (1987)
HOME IS WHERE THE HEART IS (SEE: SQUARE DANCE)(1987)
HOME OF ANGELS (1994)
HOME OF OUR OWN, A (1993)
HOME SWEET HOME (1994)
HOMEBOY (1989)
HOMEBOYS (1992)
HOMECOMING (1996)
HOMER & EDDIE (1990)
HOMEWARD BOUND II: LOST IN SAN FRANCISCO (1996)
HOMEWARD BOUND: THE INCREDIBLE JOURNEY (1993)
HOMICIDAL IMPULSE (1992)
HOMICIDE (1991)
HONEY, I BLEW UP THE KID (1992)
HONEY, I SHRUNK THE KIDS (1989)
HONEYMOON ACADEMY (1990)
HONEYMOON IN VEGAS (1992)
HONG FEN (SEE: BLUSH)(1996)
HONG GAOLIANG (SEE: RED SORGHUM)(1988)
HONG KONG '97 (1994)
HONOR AND GLORY (1993)
HOOK (1991)
HOOP DREAMS (1994)
HOOSIERS (1986)
HOPE AND GLORY (1987)
HORROR SHOW, THE (1989)
HORSEMAN ON THE ROOF (1996)
HORSEPLAYER (1991)
HOSTAGE (1993)
HOSTAGE (1987)
HOSTAGE: DALLAS (SEE: GETTING EVEN)(1986)
HOSTAGE FOR A DAY (1994)
HOSTILE HOSTAGES (SEE: REF, THE)(1994)
HOSTILE INTENTIONS (1996)
HOSTILE TAKEOVER (1990)
HOT AND COLD (SEE: WEEKEND AT BERNIE'S)(1989)
HOT CHILD IN THE CITY (1987)
HOT CHILI (1986)
HOT CHOCOLATE (1992)
HOT PURSUIT (1987)
HOT RESORT (1985)
HOT SEAT (SEE: CHAIR, THE)(1989)
HOT SHOT (1987)
HOT SHOTS! (1991)
HOT SHOTS! PART DEUX (1993)
HOT SPOT, THE (1990)
HOT TARGET (1985)
HOT TO TROT (1988)
HOTEL COLONIAL (1987)
HOTEL NEW YORK (1985)
HOTEL SORRENTO (1995)
HOUR OF THE ASSASSIN (1987)
HOUR OF THE PIG, THE (SEE: ADVOCATE, THE)(1994)
HOUR OF THE STAR, THE (1986)
HOURGLASS (1996)
HOURS AND TIMES, THE (1992)
HOUSE (1986)
HOUSE ARREST (1996)
HOUSE IV (1992)
HOUSE IN THE HILLS, A (1993)
HOUSE OF ANGELS (1993)
HOUSE OF CARDS (1993)
HOUSE OF GAMES (1987)
HOUSE OF THE DARK STAIRWAY (SEE: BLADE IN THE DARK, A)(1986)
HOUSE OF THE SPIRITS, THE (1994)
HOUSE OF USHER, THE (1992)
HOUSE ON CARROLL STREET, THE (1988)
HOUSE ON THE EDGE OF THE PARK (1985)
HOUSE ON TOMBSTONE HILL, THE (1992)
HOUSE PARTY (1990)
HOUSE PARTY 3 (1994)
HOUSE PARTY 2 (1991)
HOUSE II: THE SECOND STORY (1987)
HOUSEGUEST (1995)
HOUSEHOLD SAINTS (1993)
HOUSEKEEPER, THE (1987)
HOUSEKEEPING (1987)
HOUSESITTER (1992)
HOUSEWIFE FROM HELL (1994)
HOW I GOT INTO COLLEGE (1989)
HOW THE WEST WAS FUN (1996)
HOW TO GET AHEAD IN ADVERTISING (1989)
HOW TO MAKE AN AMERICAN QUILT (1995)
HOW TO MAKE LOVE TO A NEGRO WITHOUT GETTING TIRED (1990)
HOW TO TOP MY WIFE (1995)
HOW U LIKE ME NOW (1993)
HOWARD THE DUCK (1986)
HOWARDS END (1992)
HOWLING TWO: YOUR SISTER IS A WEREWOLF (1985)
HOWLING III, THE (1987)
HOWLING IV . . . THE ORIGINAL NIGHTMARE (1988)
HOWLING 5: THE REBIRTH, THE (1989)
HOWLING VI - THE FREAKS (1991)
HOWLING: NEW MOON RISING, THE (1995)
H.P. LOVECRAFT'S NECRONOMICON: BOOK OF THE DEAD (SEE: NECRONOMICON: BOOK OF THE DEAD)(1996)
HUCK AND THE KING OF HEARTS (1994)
HUDSON HAWK (1991)
HUDSUCKER PROXY, THE (1994)
HUGH HEFNER: ONCE UPON A TIME (1992)
HUMAN SHIELD, THE (1992)
HUNCHBACK OF NOTRE DAME, THE (1996)
HUNG FAN KUI (SEE: RUMBLE IN THE BRONX)(1996)
HUNGARIAN FAIRY TALE, A (1989)
HUNK (1987)
HUNT FOR RED OCTOBER, THE (1990)
HUNTED, THE (1995)
HUNTER'S BLOOD (1987)
HUNTING (1992)
HUOZHE (SEE: TO LIVE)(1994)
HURRICANE SMITH (1992)
HUSBANDS AND LOVERS (1992)
HUSBANDS AND WIVES (1992)
HUSTRUER, 2--TI AR ETTER (SEE: WIVES--TEN YEARS AFTER)(1985)
HYENAS (1995)
HYPE! (1996)
HYPERSPACE (1990)
WINGS OF HONNEAMISE: ROYAL SPACE FORCE (1995)

I

BRIAN WILSON: I JUST WASN'T MADE FOR THESE TIMES (1995)
I AM CUBA (1995)
I AM MY OWN WOMAN (1994)
I CAN'T SLEEP (1995)
I COME IN PEACE (1990)
I DON'T BUY KISSES ANYMORE (1992)
I DON'T WANT TO TALK ABOUT IT (1994)
I JUST WASN'T MADE FOR THESE TIMES (SEE: BRIAN WILSON: I JUST WASN'T MADE FOR THESE TIMES)(1995)
I LIKE IT LIKE THAT (1994)
I LIKE TO PLAY GAMES (1995)
I LOVE A MAN IN A UNIFORM (SEE: A MAN IN UNIFORM)(1994)
I LOVE N.Y. (1987)
I LOVE TROUBLE (1994)
I LOVE YOU TO DEATH (1990)
I, MADMAN (1989)
I ONLY WANT YOU TO LOVE ME (1994)
I PHOTOGRAPHIA (SEE: PHOTOGRAPH, THE)(1987)
I SHOT ANDY WARHOL (1996)
I, THE WORST OF ALL (1995)
I WAS A TEENAGE T.V. TERRORIST (1987)
I WAS A TEENAGE ZOMBIE (1987)
ICE (1994)
ICE CREAM MAN (1995)
ICE PALACE, THE (1987)

ICE RUNNER, THE (1993)
ICH BIN MEINE EIGENE FRAU (SEE: I AM MY OWN WOMAN)(1994)
ICH UND ER (SEE: ME AND HIM)(1990)
ICH WILL DOCH NUR, DAS IHR MICH LIEBT (SEE: I ONLY WANT YOU TO LOVE ME)(1994)
ICICLE THIEF, THE (1990)
IDENTITY CRISIS (1991)
IDI I SMOTRI (SEE: COME AND SEE)(1986)
IF LOOKS COULD KILL (1991)
IF LUCY FELL (1996)
IL CASO MORO (SEE: MORO AFFAIR, THE)(1987)
IL DIAVOLO IN CORPO (SEE: DEVIL IN THE FLESH)(1986)
IL LADRO DI BAMBINI (SEE: STOLEN CHILDREN, THE)(1993)
IL MOSTRO (SEE: MONSTER, THE)(1996)
IL POSTINO (SEE: POSTMAN, THE)(1995)
I'LL DO ANYTHING (1994)
ILLEGAL IN BLUE (1995)
ILLEGALLY YOURS (1988)
ILLUSIONIST, THE (1985)
ILLUSIONS (1992)
ILLUSTRIOUS ENERGY (1988)
I'M GONNA GIT YOU SUCKA (1988)
I'M NOT RAPPAPORT (1996)
IMAGEMAKER, THE (1986)
IMAGEN LATENTE (SEE: LATENT IMAGE)(1988)
IMAGINARY CRIMES (1994)
IMMEDIATE FAMILY (1989)
IMMORTAL BELOVED (1994)
IMMORTAL COMBAT (1994)
IMMORTALS, THE (1996)
IMPORTANCE OF BEING EARNEST, THE (1992)
IMPORTED BRIDEGROOM, THE (1990)
IMPROMPTU (1990)
IMPROPER CONDUCT (1994)
IMPULSE (1990)
IN A GLASS CAGE (1989)
IN A MOMENT OF PASSION (1993)
IN BED WITH MADONNA (SEE: TRUTH OR DARE)(1991)
IN COUNTRY (1989)
IN CUSTODY (1994)
IN DE SCHADUW VAN DE OVERWINNING (SEE: SHADOW OF VICTORY)(1986)
IN GOLD WE TRUST (1992)
IN LOVE AND WAR (1996)
IN THE ARMY NOW (1994)
IN THE BLEAK MIDWINTER (SEE: MIDWINTER'S TALE, A)(1996)
IN THE COLD OF THE NIGHT (1991)
IN THE DEEP WOODS (1995)
IN THE EYE OF THE SNAKE (1994)
IN THE HANDS OF THE ENEMY (1994)
IN THE HEAT OF PASSION (1992)
IN THE HEAT OF PASSION 2: UNFAITHFUL (1994)
IN THE KINGDOM OF THE BLIND, THE MAN WITH ONE EYE IS KING (1995)
IN THE LAND OF THE DEAF (1994)
IN THE LINE OF DUTY: SIEGE AT MARION (SEE: CHILDREN OF FURY)(1996)
IN THE LINE OF FIRE (1993)
IN THE MOOD (1987)
IN THE MOUTH OF MADNESS (1995)
IN THE MOUTH OF THE WOLF (1988)
IN THE NAME OF THE EMPEROR (1995)
IN THE NAME OF THE FATHER (1993)
IN THE SHADOW OF KILIMANJARO (1986)
IN THE SHADOW OF THE STARS (1991)
IN THE SOUP (1992)
IN THE SPIRIT (1990)
IN THE WILD MOUNTAINS (1986)
IN TOO DEEP (1991)
IN WEITER FERNE SO NAH (SEE: FARAWAY, SO CLOSE)(1993)
INCIDENT AT OGLALA (1992)
INCREDIBLY TRUE ADVENTURES OF TWO GIRLS IN LOVE, THE (1995)
INDECENT BEHAVIOR (1993)
INDECENT BEHAVIOR 2 (1994)
INDECENT BEHAVIOR 3 (1995)
INDECENT OBSESSION, AN (1985)
INDECENT PROPOSAL (1993)
INDEPENDENCE DAY (1996)
INDIAN IN PARIS, AN (SEE: LITTLE INDIAN, BIG CITY)(1996)
INDIAN IN THE CUPBOARD, THE (1995)
INDIAN RUNNER, THE (1991)
INDIAN SUMMER (1993)
INDIANA JONES AND THE LAST CRUSADE (1989)
INDICTMENT: THE MCMARTIN TRIAL (1995)
INDIO (1990)
INDIO 2 - THE REVOLT (1992)
INDOCHINE (1992)
INFERNO IN DIRETTA (SEE: CUT AND RUN)(1986)
INFESTED (SEE: TICKS)(1994)
INFINITY (1991)
INFINITY (1996)
INHERITOR (1990)
INKWELL, THE (1994)
INNER CIRCLE, THE (1991)
INNER SANCTUM (1991)
INNER SANCTUM 2 (1994)
INNERSPACE (1987)
INNOCENT, THE (1988)
INNOCENT BLOOD (1992)
INNOCENT LIES (1995)
INNOCENT MAN, AN (1989)
INNOCENT MOVES (SEE: SEARCHING FOR BOBBY FISCHER)(1993)
INNOCENT VICTIM (1990)
INNOCENT, THE (1995)
INSIDE EDGE (1992)
INSIDE MONKEY ZETTERLAND (1993)
INSIDE OUT (1986)
INSIGNIFICANCE (1985)
INSOMNIACS (1986)
INSPECTOR LAVARDIN (1992)
INSTANT JUSTICE (1986)
INSTANT KARMA (1991)
INSTITUTE BENJAMENTA (1996)
INTENT TO KILL (1993)
INTERNAL AFFAIRS (1990)
INTERROGATION, THE (1990)
INTERSECTION (1994)
INTERVIEW WITH THE VAMPIRE (1994)
INTERVISTA (1987)
INTIMATE POWER (1986)
INTO THE NIGHT (1985)
INTO THE SUN (1992)
INTO THE WEST (1993)
INVADERS (1993)
INVADERS FROM MARS (1986)
INVASION OF THE SPACE PREACHERS (1992)
INVASION U.S.A. (1985)
INVISIBLE KID, THE (1988)
INVISIBLE: THE CHRONICLES OF BENJAMIN KNIGHT (1994)
IO SPERIAMO CHE ME LO CAVO (SEE: CIAO, PROFESSORE!)(1994)
I.Q. (1994)
IRON & SILK (1991)
IRON EAGLE (1986)
IRON EAGLE IV (1996)
IRON EAGLE III (SEE: ACES: IRON EAGLE III)(1992)
IRON EAGLE II (1988)
IRON MAZE (1991)
IRON MONKEY (1994)
IRON TRIANGLE, THE (1989)
IRON WILL (1994)
IRONWEED (1987)
IS-SLOTTET (SEE: ICE PALACE, THE)(1988)
IS THAT ALL THERE IS? (1995)
ISHTAR (1987)
ISLAND FURY (1994)
ISLAND OF DR. MOREAU, THE (1996)
ISTANBUL, KEEP YOUR EYES OPEN (1990)
ISTORIYA AS: KLYACHIMOL (SEE: ASYA'S HAPPINESS)(1988)
IT CAME FROM OUTER SPACE II (1996)
IT COULD HAPPEN TO YOU (1994)
IT COULDN'T HAPPEN HERE (1988)
IT DON'T PAY TO BE AN HONEST CITIZEN (1985)
IT RUNS IN THE FAMILY (1994)
IT TAKES TWO (1995)
IT'S ALL TRUE: BASED ON AN UNFINISHED FILM BY ORSON WELLES (1993)
IT'S ALIVE III: ISLAND OF THE ALIVE (1988)
IT'S MY PARTY (1996)
IT'S PAT (1994)
IVAN AND ABRAHAM (1994)
I'VE HEARD THE MERMAIDS SINGING (1987)

J

JACK (1996)
JACK & SARAH (1996)
JACK BE NIMBLE (1994)
JACK KEROUAC'S AMERICA (SEE: KEROUAC)(1985)
JACK THE BEAR (1993)
JACKALS (SEE: AMERICAN JUSTICE)(1986)
JACKNIFE (1989)
JACK-O (1995)
JACK'S BACK (1988)
JACOB'S LADDER (1990)
JACQUES AND NOVEMBER (1985)
JACQUOT (1993)
JACQUOT DE NANTES (SEE: JACQUOT)(1993)
JADE (1995)
JAG (1996)
JAGGED EDGE (1985)
JAILBIRD ROCK (1988)
JAKE SPEED (1986)
JAMES AND THE GIANT PEACH (1996)
JAMES JOYCE'S WOMEN (1985)
JAMON JAMON (1993)
JANE EYRE (1996)
JANUARY MAN, THE (1989)
JAR, THE (1995)
JASON GOES TO HELL: THE FINAL FRIDAY (1993)
JASON LIVES: FRIDAY THE 13TH PART VI (SEE: FRIDAY THE 13TH PART VII--THE NEW BLOOD)(1988)
JASON'S LYRIC (1994)
JATSZANI KELL (SEE: LILY IN LOVE)(1985)
JAWS: THE REVENGE (1987)
JE VOUS SALUE, MAFIA (SEE: HAIL MAFIA)(1985)
JEAN DE FLORETTE (1986)
JEAN DE FLORETTE 2 (SEE: MANON OF THE SPRING)(1986)
JEANNE, PUTAIN DU ROI (SEE: KING'S WHORE, THE)(1993)
JEFFERSON IN PARIS (1995)
JEFFREY (1995)
JEKYLL & HYDE (1995)
JENATSCH (1987)

JENNIFER EIGHT (1992)
JENNY KISSED ME (1985)
JERICHO FEVER (1994)
JERKY BOYS: THE MOVIE, THE (1995)
JERRY MAGUIRE (1996)
JERSEY GIRL (1994)
JESTER, THE (1987)
JESUS OF MONTREAL (1990)
JETSONS: THE MOVIE (1990)
JEWEL OF THE NILE, THE (1985)
JEZEBEL'S KISS (1990)
JFK (1991)
JIMMY HOLLYWOOD (1994)
JIMMY REARDON (SEE: NIGHT IN THE LIFE OF JIMMY REARDON, A)(1988)
JINGLE ALL THE WAY (1996)
JIT (1993)
JLG BY JLG (1995)
JO JO DANCER, YOUR LIFE IS CALLING (1986)
JOCKS (1987)
JOE VERSUS THE VOLCANO (1990)
JOE'S APARTMENT (1996)
JOEY BREAKER (1993)
JOHN CARPENTER'S ESCAPE FROM L.A. (1996)
JOHNNY BE GOOD (1988)
JOHNNY CIEN PESOS (SEE: JOHNNY 100 PESOS)(1996)
JOHNNY HANDSOME (1989)
JOHNNY MNEMONIC (1995)
JOHNNY 100 PESOS (1996)
JOHNNY SHORTWAVE (1996)
JOHNNY STECCHINO (1992)
JOHNNY SUEDE (1992)
JON JOST'S FRAMEUP (SEE: FRAMEUP)(1995)
JOSEPH CONRAD'S THE SECRET AGENT (1996)
JOSH AND S.A.M. (1993)
JOSH KIRBY . . . TIME WARRIOR!: EGGS FROM 70,000,000 B.C. (1996)
JOSH KIRBY . . . TIME WARRIOR!: JOURNEY TO THE MAGIC CAVERN (1996)
JOSH KIRBY . . . TIME WARRIOR!: LAST BATTLE FOR THE UNIVERSE (1996)
JOSH KIRBY . . . TIME WARRIOR!: PLANET OF THE DINO-KNIGHTS (1995)
JOSH KIRBY . . . TIME WARRIOR!: THE HUMAN PETS (1995)
JOSH KIRBY . . . TIME WARRIOR!: TRAPPED ON TOY WORLD (1996)
JOSHUA THEN AND NOW (1985)
JOSHUA TREE (SEE: WOMAN UNDONE, A)(1996)
JOURNEY, THE (1986)
JOURNEY OF AUGUST KING, THE (1995)
JOURNEY OF HONOR (1992)
JOURNEY OF HOPE (1991)
JOURNEY OF NATTY GANN, THE (1985)
JOURNEY TO SPIRIT ISLAND (1988)
JOY LUCK CLUB, THE (1993)
JU DOU (1991)
JUDE (1996)
JUDGE DREDD (1995)
JUDGEMENT IN STONE, A (SEE: HOUSEKEEPER, THE)(1987)
JUDGMENT IN BERLIN (1988)
JUDGMENT NIGHT (1993)
JUDICIAL CONSENT (1995)
JUICE (1992)
JULIA AND JULIA (1988)
JULIA HAS TWO LOVERS (1991)
JUMANJI (1995)
JUMPIN' AT THE BONEYARD (1992)
JUMPIN' JACK FLASH (1986)
JUNGLE BOOK, THE (1994)
JUNGLE FEVER (1991)
JUNGLE RAIDERS (1986)
JUNGLEGROUND (1995)
JUNIOR (1994)
JUPITER'S WIFE (1995)
JURASSIC PARK (1993)
JUROR, THE (1996)
JURY DUTY (1995)
JURY DUTY: THE COMEDY (SEE: GREAT AMERICAN SEX SCANDAL, THE)(1994)
JUST ANOTHER GIRL ON THE I.R.T. (1993)
JUST BETWEEN FRIENDS (1986)
JUST CAUSE (1995)
JUST LIKE A WOMAN (1994)
JUST LIKE IN THE MOVIES (1992)
JUST ONE OF THE GUYS (1985)
JUST YOUR LUCK (1996)
JUSTICE WOMEN (SEE: MIDNIGHT ANGEL)(1996)

K

K-9 (1989)
K2 (1992)
KADISBELLAN (SEE: SLINGSHOT, THE)(1994)
KAFKA (1991)
KALEIDOSCOPE (1994)
KALIFORNIA (1993)
KAMATA KOSHINKYOKU (SEE: FALL GUY)(1985)
KAMIKAZE TAXI (1996)
KANDYLAND (1988)
KANGAROO (1986)
KANSAS (1988)
KANSAS CITY (1996)
KAOS (1985)
KARATE KID PART II, THE (1986)
KARATE KID PART III, THE (1989)
KARATE TIGER 5 (SEE: AMERICAN SHAOLIN: KING OF THE KICKBOXERS II)(1993)
KARHOZAT (SEE: DAMNATION)(1988)
KARMA (1986)
KASPAR HAUSER (1996)
KAZAAM (1996)
KEROUAC (1985)
KEY EXCHANGE (1985)
KICK OR DIE (1992)
KICKBOXER (1989)
KICKBOXER 2: THE ROAD BACK (1991)
KICKBOXER 3: THE ART OF WAR (1992)
KICKBOXER 4: THE AGGRESSOR (1994)
KICKING AND SCREAMING (1995)
KID (1991)
KID IN KING ARTHUR'S COURT, A (1995)
KIDS (1995)
KIDS IN THE HALL: BRAIN CANDY (1996)
KIKA (1994)
KILIAN'S CHRONICLE (1995)
KILL CRAZY (1989)
KILL CRUISE (1992)
KILL LINE (1992)
KILL ME AGAIN (1990)
KILL-OFF, THE (1990)
KILL ZONE (1985)
KILL ZONE (1993)
KILLBOTS (SEE: CHOPPING MALL)(1986)
KILLER (SEE: BULLETPROOF HEART)(1995)
KILLER IMAGE (1992)
KILLER INSTINCT (SEE: MAD DOG COLL)(1993)
KILLER KLOWNS FROM OUTER SPACE (1988)
KILLER LOOKS (1994)
KILLER NERD (1991)
KILLER PARTY (1986)
KILLER TOMATOES EAT FRANCE! (1992)
KILLER TOMATOES STRIKE BACK (1991)
KILLER WORKOUT (1987)
KILLER, THE (1991)
KILLERS EDGE, THE (1991)
KILLING AFFAIR, A (1985)
KILLING BEACH, THE (1993)
KILLING EDGE, THE (SEE: INVADERS)(1993)
KILLING MAN, THE (1995)
KILLING OBSESSION (1994)
KILLING STREETS, THE (1991)
KILLING ZOE (1994)
KILLING ZONE, THE (1991)
KINDER KADER KOMMANDEURE (SEE: STRICTLY PROPAGANDA)(1993)
KINDERGARTEN COP (1990)
KINDRED, THE (1987)
KINEMA NO TENCHI (SEE: FINAL TAKE: THE GOLDEN AGE OF MOVIES)(1986)
KING AND HIS MOVIE, A (1986)
KING DAVID (1985)
KING KONG LIVES (1986)
KING LEAR (1988)
KING OF NEW YORK (1990)
KING OF THE HILL (1993)
KING OF THE KICKBOXERS, THE (1991)
KING OF THE STREETS (1986)
KING RALPH (1991)
KING SOLOMON'S MINES (1985)
KING'S WHORE, THE (1993)
KINGDOM, THE (1995)
KINGFISH: A STORY OF HUEY P. LONG (1995)
KINGPIN (1996)
KINJITE: FORBIDDEN SUBJECTS (1989)
KISS, THE (1988)
KISS BEFORE DYING, A (1991)
KISS GOODNIGHT, A (1994)
KISS ME A KILLER (1992)
KISS OF DEATH (1995)
KISS OF DEATH, THE (1994)
KISS OF THE SPIDER WOMAN (1985)
KISSINGER AND NIXON (1996)
KLASSENVERHALTNISSE (SEE: CLASS RELATIONS)(1986)
KNIGHT MOVES (1993)
KNIGHTS OF THE CITY (1985)
KOKAKU KIDOTAI (SEE: GHOST IN THE SHELL)(1996)
KOKS I KULISSEN (SEE: LADIES ON THE ROCKS)(1985)
KOMIKKU ZASSHI NANKA IRANI (SEE: COMIC MAGAZINE)(1986)
KONBU FINZE (SEE: TERRORIZERS, THE)(1987)
KONEKO MONGATARI (SEE: ADVENTURES OF MILO AND OTIS, THE)(1990)
KOOTENAI BROWN (SEE: SHOWDOWN AT WILLIAMS CREEK)(1991)
KORCZAK (1991)
KRAYS, THE (1990)
KRUSH GROOVE (1985)
KUFFS (1992)
KUNG FU MASTER (1989)
KUROI AME (SEE: BLACK RAIN)(1990)
KURT VONNEGUT'S HARRISON BERGERON (1995)
KVITEBJORN KONG VALEMAN (SEE: POLAR BEAR KING, THE)(1994)

L

L'ELEGANT CRIMINEL (1992)
L.627 (1994)
L.A. STREETFIGHTERS (SEE: NINJA TURF)(1986)

LA BAMBA (1987)
LA BELLE NOISEUSE (1991)
LA BOCA DEL LOBO (SEE: IN THE MOUTH OF THE WOLF)(1988)
L.A. BOUNTY (1989)
LA CAGE AUX FOLLES 3: THE WEDDING (1985)
LA CARTE DU TENDRE (SEE: MAP OF THE HUMAN HEART)(1993)
LA CASA CON LA SCALA NEL BUIO (SEE: BLADE IN THE DARK, A)(1986)
LA CASA NEL PARCO (SEE: HOUSE ON THE EDGE OF THE PARK)(1985)
LA CEREMONIE (1996)
LA CHASSE AUX PAPILLONS (1993)
LA CHEVRE (1985)
LA CHIESA (SEE: CHURCH, THE)(1991)
LA CIUDAD Y LOS PERROS (SEE: CITY AND THE DOGS, THE)(1987)
LA COMEDIE-FRANCAISE OU L'AMOUR JOUE (1996)
LA CONDANNA (SEE: CONVICTION, THE)(1994)
LA CORSA DELL'INNOCENTE (SEE: FLIGHT OF THE INNOCENT)(1993)
LA CORTE DE FARAON (SEE: COURT OF THE PHARAOH, THE)(1985)
LA DISCRETE (1992)
LA DOUBLE VIE DE VERONIQUE (SEE: DOUBLE LIFE OF VERONIQUE, THE)(1991)
LA DUEDA INTERNA (SEE: VERONICO CRUZ)(1990)
LA FAMIGLIA (SEE: FAMILY, THE)(1987)
LA FEMME NIKITA (1991)
LA FILLE SEULE (SEE: SINGLE GIRL, A)(1996)
LA FLOR DE MI SECRETO (SEE: FLOWER OF MY SECRET, THE)(1996)
LA FRACTURE DU MYOCARDE (SEE: CROSS MY HEART)(1991)
LA GLOIRE DE MON PERE (SEE: MY FATHER'S GLORY)(1991)
L.A. GODDESS (1993)
LA GRIETA (SEE: ENDLESS DESCENT)(1991)
LA GUERRE DES BOUTONS, CA RECOMMENCE (SEE: WAR OF THE BUTTONS, THE)(1996)
LA HAINE (SEE: HATE)(1996)
L.A. HEAT (1989)
LA HISTORIA OFICIAL (SEE: OFFICIAL STORY, THE)(1985)
LA LECTRICE (1989)
LA LEGENDA DEL RUDIO MALESE (SEE: JUNGLE RAIDERS)(1986)
LA LEI DEL DESEO (SEE: LAW OF DESIRE, THE)(1987)
LA MACHINE (SEE: MACHINE, THE)(1996)
LA MESSA E FINITA (SEE: MASS IS ENDED, THE)(1988)
LA MORT DE MARIO RICCI (SEE: DEATH OF MARIO RICCI, THE)(1985)
LA PASSION BEATRICE (SEE: BEATRICE)(1988)
LA PELICULA DEL REY (SEE: KING AND HIS MOVIE, A)(1986)
LA PESTE (SEE: PLAGUE, THE)(1993)
LA PROPRIETAIRE (SEE: PROPRIETOR, THE)(1996)
LA REINE MARGOT (SEE: QUEEN MARGOT)(1994)
LA SCARLATINE (1985)
LA SCORTA (1994)
LA SEGUA (1985)
L.A. STORY (1991)
LA VIE DE BOHEME (1993)
LA VIE EST RIEN D'AUTRE (SEE: LIFE AND NOTHING BUT)(1990)
L.A. WARS (1994)
LABYRINTH (1986)
LABYRINTH OF PASSION (1990)
L'ACCOMPAGNATRICE (SEE: ACCOMPANIST, THE)(1993)
L'ADDITION (1985)
LADIES CLUB, THE (1986)
LADIES OF THE LOTUS (1987)
LADIES ON THE ROCKS (1985)
LADRI DI SAPONETTE (SEE: ICICLE THIEF, THE)(1990)
LADY BEWARE (1987)
LADY DRAGON (1992)
LADY DRAGON 2 (1993)
LADY IN WAITING (1994)
LADY IN WHITE (1988)
LADY JANE (1986)
LADY OF THE CAMELIAS (1987)
LADYBIRD, LADYBIRD (1994)
LADYBUGS (1992)
LADYHAWKE (1985)
LAIR OF THE WHITE WORM, THE (1988)
LAKOTA WOMAN: SIEGE AT WOUNDED KNEE (1995)
LAMB (1995)
LAMBADA (1990)
LAMERICA (1995)
L'AMERIQUE DES AUTRES (SEE: SOMEONE ELSE'S AMERICA)(1996)
L'AMI DE MON AMIE (SEE: BOYFRIENDS AND GIRLFRIENDS)(1988)
LAMP, THE (SEE: OUTING, THE)(1987)
LAN FENGZHENG (SEE: BLUE KITE, THE)(1994)
LAND AND FREEDOM (1996)
LAND BEFORE TIME, THE (1988)
LAND BEFORE TIME III: THE TIME OF THE GREAT GIVING (1995)
LAND BEFORE TIME IV: JOURNEY THROUGH THE MISTS (1996)
LAND BEFORE TIME II: THE GREAT VALLEY ADVENTURE, THE (1994)
LAND OF DOOM (1986)
LANDSCAPE IN THE MIST (1990)
LANDSCAPE SUICIDE (1986)
LANDSLIDE (1992)
L'ANNEE DES MEDUSES (1987)
LAP DANCING (1995)
LARGER THAN LIFE (1996)
LARRY MCMURTRY'S STREETS OF LAREDO (1996)
LAS VEGAS WEEKEND (1985)
LASER MAN, THE (1988)
LASER MOON (1992)
LASSIE (1994)
LAST ACTION HERO (1993)
LAST BEST YEAR, THE (1995)
LAST BOY SCOUT, THE (1991)
LAST BUTTERFLY, THE (1993)
LAST CALL (1991)
LAST DANCE (1996)
LAST DAYS OF CHEZ NOUS, THE (1993)
LAST DAYS OF JOHN DILLINGER, THE (SEE: DILLINGER)(1995)
LAST DRAGON, THE (1985)
LAST EMPEROR, THE (1987)
LAST EXIT TO BROOKLYN (1989)
LAST FLIGHT TO HELL (1991)
LAST GASP (1995)
LAST GOOD TIME, THE (1995)
LAST HOUR, THE (1991)
LAST KLEZMER, THE (1994)
LAST KLEZMER: LEOPOLD KOZLOWSKI, HIS LIFE AND HIS MUSIC, THE (SEE: LAST KLEZMER, THE)(1994)
LAST MAN STANDING (1996)
LAST OF ENGLAND, THE (1987)
LAST OF THE DOGMEN (1995)
LAST OF THE FINEST, THE (1990)
LAST OF THE MOHICANS, THE (1992)
LAST PARTY, THE (1993)
LAST RESORT (1986)
LAST RIDE, THE (1991)
LAST RIDE, THE (1995)
LAST RITES (1988)
LAST SAMURAI, THE (1995)
LAST SEDUCTION, THE (1994)
LAST STRAW, THE (1987)
LAST SUMMER IN THE HAMPTONS (1995)
LAST SUPPER, THE (1996)
LAST TEMPTATION OF CHRIST, THE (1988)
LAST TIME OUT (1994)
LAST WARRIOR, THE (1989)
LATCHO DROM (1994)
LATE FOR DINNER (1991)
LATE SHIFT, THE (1996)
LATE SUMMER BLUES (1988)
LATENT IMAGE (1988)
LATINO (1985)
LAW OF DESIRE (1987)
LAWNMOWER MAN 2: JOBE'S WAR (SEE: LAWNMOWER MAN 2: BEYOND CYBERSPACE)(1996)
LAWNMOWER MAN 2: BEYOND CYBERSPACE (1996)
LAWNMOWER MAN, THE (1992)
LAWS OF GRAVITY (1992)
LAZARUS MAN, THE (1996)
LE CHATEAU DE MA MERE (SEE: MY MOTHER'S CASTLE)(1991)
LE CHENE (SEE: OAK, THE)(1993)
LE COMPLOT (SEE: TO KILL A PRIEST)(1989)
LE CRI DU PAPILLON (SEE: LAST BUTTERFLY, THE)(1993)
LE DECLIN DE L'EMPIRE AMERICAIN (SEE: DECLINE OF THE AMERICAN EMPIRE, THE)(1986)
LE DOCTEUR PETIOT (SEE: DR. PETIOT)(1994)
LE DUE VITE DI MATTIA PASCAL (SEE: TWO LIVES OF MATTIA PASCAL, THE)(1985)
LE GRAND BLEU (SEE: BIG BLUE, THE)(1988)
LE GRAND CHEMIN (SEE: GRAND HIGHWAY, THE)(1988)
LE GRAND PARDON II (SEE: DAY OF ATONEMENT)(1993)
LE HUSSARD SUR LE TOIT (SEE: HORSEMAN ON THE ROOF)(1996)
LE JEUNE MARIE (1985)
LE JUPON ROUGE (SEE: MANUELA'S LOVES)(1987)
LE LIEU DU CRIME (SEE: SCENE OF THE CRIME)(1986)
LE PAYS DES SOURDS (SEE: IN THE LAND OF THE DEAF)(1994)
LE PETIT AMOUR (SEE: KUNG FU MASTER)(1989)
LE POUVOIR DU MAL (SEE: POWER OF EVIL, THE)(1985)
LE RIDICULE (SEE: RIDICULE)(1996)
LE THE AU HAREM D'ARCHIMEDE (SEE: TEA IN THE HAREM OF ARCHIMEDE)(1985)
LEAGUE OF THEIR OWN, A (1992)
LEAN ON ME (1989)
LEAP OF FAITH (1992)
LEAPIN' LEPRECHAUNS! (1995)
LEATHER JACKETS (1992)
LEATHERFACE: THE TEXAS CHAINSAW MASSACRE III (1990)
LEAVING LAS VEGAS (1995)
LEAVING NORMAL (1992)
LEGAL EAGLES (1986)
LEGAL TENDER (1991)
LEGEND (1985)

LEGEND OF BILLIE JEAN, THE (1985)
LEGEND OF FONG SAI-YUK, THE (SEE: FONG SAI-YUK)(1993)
LEGEND OF GATOR FACE, THE (1996)
LEGEND OF SURAM FORTRESS (1985)
LEGEND OF THE OVERFIEND (1993)
LEGEND OF THE WHITE HORSE (1991)
LEGEND OF WOLF MOUNTAIN, THE (1993)
LEGENDS OF THE FALL (1994)
LEGENDS OF THE NORTH (1995)
LEKCE FAUST (SEE: FAUST)(1994)
LEMON SISTERS, THE (1990)
LENA'S HOLIDAY (1991)
L'ENFER (1994)
LEOLO (1993)
LEON (SEE: PROFESSIONAL, THE)(1994)
LEON THE PIG FARMER (1993)
LEONARD PART 6 (1987)
LEPRECHAUN (1993)
LEPRECHAUN 2 (1994)
LEPRECHAUN 3 (1995)
LES FAVORIS DE LA LUNE (SEE: FAVORITES OF THE MOON)(1985)
LES GUERISSEURS (SEE: ADUEFUE)(1988)
LES INNOCENTS (SEE: INNOCENT, THE)(1988)
LES MISERABLES (1995)
LES NOCES DE PAPIER (SEE: PAPER WEDDING)(1991)
LES NUITS FAUVES (SEE: SAVAGE NIGHTS)(1994)
LES PLOUFFE (1985)
LES PORTES TOURNANTES (SEE: REVOLVING DOORS, THE)(1988)
LES RENDEZ-VOUS DE PARIS (SEE: RENDEZVOUS IN PARIS)(1996)
LES SILENCES DU PALAIS (SEE: SILENCES OF THE PALACE, THE)(1996)
LES VEUFS (SEE: ENTANGLED)(1993)
LES VISITEURS (SEE: VISITORS, THE)(1996)
LES VISITEURS: ILS NE SONT PAS NES D'HIER! (SEE: VISITORS, THE)(1996)
LES VOLEURS (1996)
LES YEUX D'UN ANGE (SEE: EYES OF AN ANGEL)(1994)
LESS THAN ZERO (1987)
LESSONS OF DARKNESS (1995)
LET HIM HAVE IT (1991)
LET IT RIDE (1989)
L'ETAT SAUVAGE (1990)
LETHAL OBSESSION (1988)
LETHAL WEAPON (1987)
LETHAL WEAPON 3 (1992)
LETHAL WEAPON 2 (1989)
LET'S GET BIZZEE (1996)
LET'S GET HARRY (1987)
LETTER TO BREZHNEV (1986)
LETTER TO MY KILLER (1996)
LEVIATHAN (1989)
L'HOMME BLESSE (1985)
LIARS' CLUB, THE (1994)
LICENCE TO KILL (1989)
LICENSE TO DRIVE (1988)
LIE DOWN WITH DOGS (1995)
LIEBESTRAUM (1991)
LIFE AND DEATH OF CHICO MENDES, THE (SEE: BURNING SEASON,THE)(1995)
LIFE AND NOTHING BUT (1990)
LIFE AND TIMES OF ALLEN GINSBERG, THE (1994)
LIFE IS A LONG QUIET RIVER (1990)
LIFE IS CHEAP. . . BUT TOILET PAPER IS EXPENSIVE (1990)
LIFE IS SWEET (1991)
LIFE OF SIN, A (1993)
LIFE ON A STRING (1992)
LIFE ON THE EDGE (1992)
LIFE STINKS (1991)
LIFE WITH MIKEY (1993)
LIFEFORCE (1985)
LIFEFORM (1996)
LIGHT IN THE JUNGLE, THE (1992)
LIGHT OF DAY (1987)
LIGHT SLEEPER (1992)
LIGHT YEARS (1988)
LIGHTHORSEMEN, THE (1988)
LIGHTNING JACK (1994)
LIGHTNING--THE WHITE STALLION (1986)
LIGHTSHIP, THE (1986)
LIKE FATHER, LIKE SON (1987)
LIKE WATER FOR CHOCOLATE (1993)
LILY DALE (1996)
LILY IN LOVE (1985)
LILY WAS HERE (1992)
LIMIT UP (1989)
LINE KING: THE AL HIRSCHFELD STORY, THE (1996)
LINGUINI INCIDENT, THE (1992)
LINK (1986)
LION KING, THE (1994)
LIONHEART (1990)
LIONHEART (1991)
LIP GLOSS (1995)
LIPSTICK CAMERA, THE (1994)
LISA (1990)
LISTEN TO ME (1989)
LITTLE BIG LEAGUE (1994)
LITTLE BUDDHA (1994)
LITTLE DEATH, THE (1996)
LITTLE DORRIT (1988)
LITTLE FLAMES (1985)
LITTLE GIANTS (1994)
LITTLE HEROES (1991)
LITTLE INDIAN, BIG CITY (1996)
LITTLE MAN TATE (1991)
LITTLE MERMAID, THE (1989)
LITTLE MISS MILLIONS (1994)
LITTLE NEMO: ADVENTURES IN SLUMBERLAND (1992)
LITTLE NIKITA (1988)
LITTLE NOISES (1992)
LITTLE ODESSA (1995)
LITTLE PRINCESS, A (1995)
LITTLE RASCALS, THE (1994)
LITTLE SHOP OF HORRORS (1986)
LITTLE SISTER, THE (1985)
LITTLE SISTER (1992)
LITTLE STIFF, A (1994)
LITTLE THIEF, THE (1989)
LITTLE TREASURE (1985)
LITTLE VEGAS (1992)
LITTLE VERA (1988)
LITTLE WITCHES (1996)
LITTLE WOMEN (1994)
LIVE BY THE FIST (1993)
LIVE NUDE GIRLS (1996)
LIVE WIRE: HUMAN TIMEBOMB (1996)
LIVIN' LARGE (1991)
LIVING DANGEROUSLY (1988)
LIVING DAYLIGHTS, THE (1987)
LIVING END, THE (1992)
LIVING IN OBLIVION (1995)
LIVING ON TOKYO TIME (1987)
LIVING PROOF: HIV AND THE PURSUIT OF HAPPINESS (1994)
LIVING TO DIE (1991)
LO BALLO DA SOLA (SEE: STEALING BEAUTY)(1996)
LO ZIO INDEGNO (SEE: SLEAZY UNCLE, THE)(1991)
LOADED (1996)
LOCK 'N' LOAD (1991)
LOCK UP (1989)
LOCKED-UP TIME (1992)
L'ODEUR DE LA PAPAYE VERTE (SEE: SCENT OF GREEN PAPAYA, THE)(1994)
L'OEIL DE VICHY (SEE: EYE OF VICHY, THE)(1996)
LONDON (1994)
LONDON KILLS ME (1992)
LONE JUSTICE (1994)
LONE JUSTICE 2 (1995)
LONE JUSTICE: SHOWDOWN AT PLUM CREEK (1996)
LONE STAR (1996)
LONELY HEARTS (1992)
LONELY IN AMERICA (1993)
LONELY PASSION OF JUDITH HEARNE, THE (1988)
LONELY WIFE, THE (SEE: CHARULATA)(1995)
LONELY WOMAN SEEKS LIFE COMPANION (1990)
LONG DAY CLOSES, THE (1993)
LONG KISS GOODNIGHT, THE (1996)
LONG ROAD HOME, THE (1996)
LONG WALK HOME, THE (1991)
LONGSHOT, THE (1986)
LONGTIME COMPANION (1990)
LOOK WHO'S TALKING (1989)
LOOK WHO'S TALKING NOW (1993)
LOOK WHO'S TALKING TOO (1990)
LOOKING FOR EILEEN (1987)
LOOKING FOR RICHARD (1996)
LOOKING FOR TROUBLE (1996)
LOOSE CANNONS (1990)
LOOSE JOINTS (SEE: FLICKS)(1987)
LOOSE SCREWS (1985)
LORD OF THE FLIES (1990)
LORDS OF MAGICK, THE (1990)
LORDS OF THE STREET, THE (SEE: ADUEFUE)(1988)
LORENZO'S OIL (1992)
LOS INSOMNES (SEE: INSOMNIACS)(1986)
LOS MONJES SANGRIENTOS (SEE: BLOOD SCREAMS)(1991)
LOSER TAKE ALL (SEE: STRIKE IT RICH)(1990)
LOSER, THE HERO, THE (1985)
LOSING CHASE (1996)
LOSING ISAIAH (1995)
LOST ANGELS (1989)
LOST BOYS, THE (1987)
LOST EMPIRE, THE (1985)
LOST IN AMERICA (1985)
LOST IN YONKERS (SEE: NEIL SIMON'S LOST IN YONKERS)(1993)
LOST WORDS, THE (1994)
LOTTO LAND (1996)
LOTUS EATERS, THE (1995)
LOVE AFFAIR (1994)
LOVE AFTER LOVE (1994)
LOVE AND A .45 (1994)
LOVE AND HUMAN REMAINS (1995)
LOVE & MURDER (1991)
LOVE AT LARGE (1990)
LOVE, CHEAT & STEAL (1994)
LOVE CRIMES (1992)
LOVE FIELD (1992)
LOVE HURTS (1992)
LOVE IS A DOG FROM HELL (1987)
LOVE IS A FAT WOMAN (1988)
LOVE IS A GUN (1994)
LOVE IS ALL THERE IS (1996)
LOVE POTION NO. 9 (1992)
LOVE SONGS (1986)
LOVE TILL FIRST BLOOD (1986)

LOVE WITHOUT PITY (1991)
LOVE YOUR MAMA (1993)
LOVER, THE (1992)
LOVERBOY (1989)
LOVERS (1992)
LOVER'S KNOT (1996)
LOVERS' LOVERS (1994)
LOW BLOW (1986)
LOW DOWN DIRTY SHAME (1994)
LOW LIFE, THE (1996)
LOWER LEVEL (1992)
LOYALTIES (1986)
LUCAS (1986)
LUCKIEST MAN IN THE WORLD, THE (1989)
LUCKY LUKE (1994)
LUCKY LUKE: DAISY TOWN (1994)
LUNA PARK (1994)
LUNATIC, THE (1992)
LUNATICS, THE (1986)
LUNATICS: A LOVE STORY (1992)
L'UOMO DELLE STELLE (SEE: STAR MAKER, THE)(1996)
LUPIN III: THE MYSTERY OF MAMO (1995)
LURKING FEAR (1994)
LUST IN THE DUST (1985)
LYRICAL NITRATE (1991)

M

MADAME BUTTERFLY (1996)
ENGLISHMAN WHO WENT UP A HILL BUT CAME DOWN A MOUNTAIN, THE (1995)
M. BUTTERFLY (1993)
MA SAISON PREFEREE (1996)
MABOROSI (1996)
MABOROSI NO HIKARI (SEE: MABOROSI)(1996)
MAC (1993)
MAC AND ME (1988)
MACARONI (1985)
MACARTHUR'S CHILDREN (1985)
MACCHERONI (SEE: MACARONI)(1985)
MACHINE, THE (1996)
MACHINE DREAMS (1995)
MACHINE GUN BLUES (SEE: BLACK ROSE OF HARLEM)(1996)
MACK THE KNIFE (1990)
MACROSS II: THE MOVIE (1995)
MAD AT THE MOON (1993)
MAD DOG AND GLORY (1993)
MAD DOG COLL (1993)
MAD DOG TIME (1996)
MAD LOVE (1995)
MAD MAX BEYOND THUNDERDOME (1985)
MADAGASCAR SKIN (1996)
MADAME BOVARY (1991)
MADAME SOUSATZKA (1988)
MADAME WANG'S (1996)
MADDENING, THE (1996)
MADE IN AMERICA (1993)
MADE IN HEAVEN (1987)
MADE IN USA (1989)
MADHOUSE (1990)
MADNESS OF KING GEORGE, THE (1994)
MAGDALENE (1990)
MAGIC HUNTER (1996)
MAGIC IN THE MIRROR (1996)
MAGIC IN THE WATER (1995)
MAGIC KID, THE (1994)
MAGIC KID 2 (1994)
MAGICAL WORLD OF CHUCK JONES, THE (1992)
MAHABHARATA, THE (1990)
MAHJONG (1996)
MAID TO ORDER (1987)
MAID, THE (1991)
MAJIANG (SEE: MAHJONG)(1996)
MAJOR LEAGUE (1989)
MAJOR LEAGUE II (1994)
MAJOR PAYNE (1995)
MAKING MR. RIGHT (1987)
MAKING OF ". . . AND GOD SPOKE," THE (SEE: . . .AND GOD SPOKE)(1994)
MAKING THE CASE FOR MURDER: THE HOWARD BEACH STORY (SEE: SKIN)(1996)
MAKIOKA SISTERS, THE (1985)
MALA NOCHE (1985)
MALANDRO (1986)
MALAYUNTA (SEE: BAD COMPANY)(1986)
MALCOLM (1986)
MALCOLM X (1992)
MALENKAYA VERA (SEE: LITTLE VERA)(1989)
MALIBU BIKINI SHOP, THE (1987)
MALICE (1993)
MALICIOUS (1995)
MALLRATS (1995)
MALONE (1987)
MAMA, THERE'S A MAN IN YOUR BED (1990)
MAMBO KINGS, THE (1992)
MAMMA ROMA (1995)
MAN AND A WOMAN: 20 YEARS LATER, A (1986)
MAN BITES DOG (1993)
MAN BY THE SHORE, THE (1996)
MAN FACING SOUTHEAST (1986)
MAN FROM LEFT FIELD, THE (1994)
MAN IN LOVE, A (1987)
MAN IN THE ATTIC, THE (1996)
MAN IN THE MOON, THE (1991)
MAN IN UNIFORM, A (1994)
MAN INSIDE, THE (1990)
MAN LIKE EVA, A (1985)
MAN OF NO IMPORTANCE, A (1994)
MAN OF THE HOUSE (1995)
MAN OF THE YEAR (1996)
MAN ON FIRE (1987)
MAN OUTSIDE (1988)
MAN TROUBLE (1992)
MAN UNDER SUSPICION (1985)
MAN WHO ENVIED WOMEN, THE (1985)
MAN WITH A PLAN (1996)
MAN WITH ONE RED SHOE, THE (1985)
MAN WITH THE PERFECT SWING, THE (1996)
MAN WITHOUT A FACE, THE (1993)
MANCHURIAN AVENGER (1985)
MANDROID (1993)
MANGIATI VIVI (SEE: DOOMED TO DIE)(1985)
MANGLER, THE (1995)
MANHATTAN BABY (1986)
MANHATTAN BY NUMBERS (1994)
MANHATTAN MURDER MYSTERY (1993)
MANHATTAN PROJECT, THE (1986)
MANHUNT, THE (1986)
MANHUNTER (1986)
MANIAC COP (1988)
MANIAC COP 3: BADGE OF SILENCE (1993)
MANIAC COP 2 (1991)
MANIAC WARRIORS (1992)
MANIFESTO (SEE: NIGHT OF LOVE, A)(1988)
MANKILLERS (1987)
MANNEQUIN (1987)
MANNEQUIN TWO: ON THE MOVE (1991)
MANNER (SEE: MEN)(1985)
MANNY & LO (1996)
MANON (1987)
MANON OF THE SPRING (1987)
MAN'S BEST FRIEND (1993)
MANUELA'S LOVES (1987)
MANUFACTURING CONSENT: NOAM CHOMSKY AND THE MEDIA (1993)
MAP OF THE HUMAN HEART (1993)
MAPANTSULA (1989)
MARDI GRAS FOR THE DEVIL (1993)
MARI DE LA COIFFEUSE, LA (SEE: HAIRDRESSER'S HUSBAND, THE)(1992)
MARIANNE AND JULIANE (1994)
MARIA'S LOVERS (1985)
MARIA'S STORY (1991)
MARIE (1985)
MARK DACASCOS REDEMPTION: KICKBOXER 5 (SEE: REDEMPTION: KICKBOXER 5)(1996)
MARK TWAIN (SEE: ADVENTURES OF MARK TWAIN, THE)(1985)
MARKED FOR DEATH (1990)
MARQUIS (1993)
MARRIED PEOPLE, SINGLE SEX PART 2: FOR BETTER OR WORSE (1994)
MARRIED TO IT (1993)
MARRIED TO THE MOB (1988)
MARRYING MAN, THE (1991)
MARS ATTACKS! (1996)
MARSUPIALS: THE HOWLING III (SEE: HOWLING III, THE)(1987)
MARTHA & ETHEL (1995)
MARTHA AND I (1995)
MARTHA JELLNECK (1988)
MARTIAL LAW (1991)
MARTIAL LAW 2: UNDERCOVER (1992)
MARTIANS GO HOME! (1990)
MARTIN LAWRENCE YOU SO CRAZY (SEE: YOU SO CRAZY)(1994)
MARTIN'S DAY (1985)
MARUSA NO ONNA (SEE: TAXING WOMAN, A)(1987)
MARUSA NO ONNA II (SEE: TAXING WOMAN'S RETURN, A)(1988)
MARVIN'S ROOM (1996)
MARY REILLY (1996)
MARY SHELLEY'S FRANKENSTEIN (1994)
MASALA (1993)
MASCARA (1987)
MASK (1985)
MASK, THE (1994)
MASQUE OF THE RED DEATH (1990)
MASQUE OF THE RED DEATH, THE (1991)
MASQUERADE (1988)
MASS IS ENDED, THE (1988)
MASTERBLASTER (1987)
MASTERGATE (1995)
MASTERS OF MENACE (1991)
MASTERS OF THE UNIVERSE (1987)
MATA HARI (1985)
MATCH FACTORY GIRL, THE (1992)
MATERNAL INSTINCTS (1996)
MATEWAN (1987)
MATILDA (1996)
MATINEE (1993)
MATT RIKER (SEE: MUTANT HUNT)(1987)
MATTER OF DEGREES, A (1991)
MAURICE (1987)
MAUVAIS SANG (SEE: BAD BLOOD)(1987)
MAVERICK (1994)
MAXIE (1985)
MAXIM XUL (1991)
MAXIMUM BREAKOUT (1992)
MAXIMUM FORCE (1992)
MAXIMUM OVERDRIVE (1986)
MAY FOOLS (1990)
MAY WINE (1991)
MAYA LIN: A STRONG CLEAR VISION (1995)
MAYBE BABY (SEE: FOR KEEPS)(1988)

MAYBE . . . MAYBE NOT (1996)
MAZEPPA (1993)
MCBAIN (1991)
MCGUFFIN, THE (1985)
ME AND HIM (1990)
ME AND THE KID (1994)
ME AND THE MOB (1995)
ME & VERONICA (1993)
MEACHOREI HASORAGIM (SEE: BEOND THE WALLS)(1985)
MEAN SEASON, THE (1985)
MEATBALLS III (1987)
MEATBALLS 4 (1992)
MEDICINE MAN (1992)
MEDICINE RIVER (1994)
MEDITERRANEO (1992)
MEET THE APPLEGATES (1991)
MEET THE FEEBLES (1995)
MEET THE HOLLOWHEADS (1989)
MEETING VENUS (1991)
MEGAVILLE (1992)
MEIER (1987)
MELO (1988)
MEMED MY HAWK (1987)
MEMOIRS OF AN INVISIBLE MAN (1992)
MEMORIES OF ME (1988)
MEMPHIS BELLE (1990)
MEN. . . (1986)
MEN AT WORK (1990)
MEN DON'T LEAVE (1990)
MEN IN LOVE (1990)
MEN OF RESPECT (1991)
MEN OF WAR (1995)
MENACE II SOCIETY (1993)
MEN'S CLUB, THE (1986)
MERCENARY FIGHTERS (1988)
MERCY (1996)
MERLIN (1994)
MERLIN'S SHOP OF MAGICAL WONDERS (1996)
MERMAIDS (1990)
MERY PER SEMPRE (SEE: FOREVER MARY)(1991)
MESSAGE TO LOVE: THE ISLE OF WIGHT FESTIVAL (1996)
MESSENGER (1995)
MESSENGER OF DEATH (1988)
METAL AND MELANCHOLY (1995)
METAMORPHOSIS: THE ALIEN FACTOR (1993)
METEOR MAN, THE (1993)
METISSE (SEE: CAFE AU LAIT)(1994)
METROPOLITAN (1990)
MI VIDA LOCA--MY CRAZY LIFE (1994)
MIAMI BLUES (1990)
MIAMI RHAPSODY (1995)
MICHAEL (1996)
MICHAEL COLLINS (1996)
MICROCOSMOS (1996)
MIDNIGHT ANGEL (1996)
MIDNIGHT CABARET (1991)
MIDNIGHT CLEAR, A (1992)
MIDNIGHT COP (1989)
MIDNIGHT CROSSING (1988)
MIDNIGHT DANCERS (1996)
MIDNIGHT EDITION (1994)
MIDNIGHT FEAR (1992)
MIDNIGHT KISS (1993)
MIDNIGHT RUN (1988)
MIDNIGHT STING (SEE: DIGGSTOWN)(1992)
MIDNIGHT TEASE (1994)
MIDNIGHT TEASE 2 (1995)
MIDNIGHT 2: SEX, DEATH AND VIDEOTAPE (1993)
MIDWINTER'S TALE, A (1996)
MIGHTY APHRODITE (1995)
MIGHTY DUCKS, THE (1992)
MIGHTY MORPHIN POWER RANGERS: THE MOVIE (1995)
MIGHTY QUINN, THE (1989)
MIKAN NO TAIKYOKU (SEE: GO MASTERS, THE)(1985)
MIKEY (1992)
MILAGRO BEANFIELD WAR, THE (1988)
MILES FROM HOME (1988)
MILK MONEY (1994)
MILLE BOLLE BLU (1996)
MILLENNIUM (1989)
MILLER'S CROSSING (1990)
MILLION DOLLAR MYSTERY (1987)
MILLION TO JUAN, A (1995)
MILOU EN MAI (SEE: MAY FOOLS)(1990)
MILWR BYCHAN (SEE: BOY SOLDIER)(1987)
MINA TANNENBAUM (1995)
MINBO NO ONNA (SEE: MINBO - OR THE GENTLE ART OF JAPANESE EXTORTION)(1994)
MINBO - OR THE GENTLE ART OF JAPANESE EXTORTION (1994)
MIND, BODY & SOUL (1992)
MIND RIPPER (1996)
MINDWALK (1991)
MINDWARP (1992)
MINISTRY OF VENGEANCE (1989)
MIRACLE BEACH (1992)
MIRACLE MILE (1989)
MIRACLE ON 34TH STREET (1994)
MIRACLE, THE (1991)
MIRACLES (1987)
MIRROR HAS TWO FACES, THE (1996)
MIRROR IMAGES (1992)
MIRROR, MIRROR (1991)
MIRROR, MIRROR III: THE VOYEUR (1996)
MIRROR, MIRROR 2: RAVEN DANCE (1994)
MISADVENTURES OF MR. WILT, THE (1990)
MISCHIEF (1985)
MISERY (1990)
MISFIT BRIGADE, THE (1988)
MISHIMA (1985)
MISS FIRECRACKER (1989)
MISS MARY (1986)
MISS MONA (1987)
MISSING IN ACTION 2--THE BEGINNING (1985)
MISSING PARENTS (SEE: DAY MY PARENTS RAN AWAY, THE)(1994)
MISSING PIECES (1996)
MISSION, THE (1986)
MISSION: IMPOSSIBLE (1996)
MISSION KILL (1987)
MISSION OF JUSTICE (1992)
MISSISSIPPI BURNING (1988)
MISSISSIPPI MASALA (1992)
MR. AND MRS. BRIDGE (1990)
MR. BASEBALL (1992)
MR. DESTINY (1990)
MR. FROST (1990)
MR. HOLLAND'S OPUS (1996)
MR. ICE CREAM MAN (1996)
MISTER JOHNSON (1991)
MR. JONES (1993)
MR. LOVE (1986)
MR. NANNY (1993)
MR. NORTH (1988)
MR. PAYBACK (1995)
MR. SATURDAY NIGHT (1992)
MR. STITCH (1996)
MR. WONDERFUL (1993)
MR. WRITE (1994)
MR. WRONG (1996)
MISTRESS (1992)
MITT LIV SOM HUND (SEE: MY LIFE AS A DOG)(1987)
MITTEN INS HERZ (SEE: STRAIGHT THROUGH THE HEART)(1985)
MIXED NUTS (1994)
MO' BETTER BLUES (1990)
MO' MONEY (1992)
MOB WAR (1989)
MOBSTERS (1991)
MODEL BY DAY (1994)
MODERN AFFAIR, A (1996)
MODERN GIRLS (1986)
MODERN LOVE (1990)
MODERNS, THE (1988)
MOLL FLANDERS (1996)
MOM (1991)
MOM AND DAD SAVE THE WORLD (1992)
MOMMY (1995)
MONA LISA (1986)
MONEY FOR NOTHING (1993)
MONEY MAN (1993)
MONEY PIT, THE (1986)
MONEY TO BURN (1994)
MONEY TRAIN (1995)
MONEY TREE, THE (1993)
MONKEY BOY (1992)
MONKEY SHINES: AN EXPERIMENT IN FEAR (1988)
MONKEY TROUBLE (1994)
MONSIEUR HIRE (1989)
MONSTER DOG (1986)
MONSTER HIGH (1990)
MONSTER IN A BOX (1992)
MONSTER IN THE CLOSET (1987)
MONSTER SHARK (1986)
MONSTER SQUAD, THE (1987)
MONSTER, THE (1996)
MONSTERSHOW (1996)
MONTANA RUN, THE (1992)
MONTH BY THE LAKE, A (1995)
MOON 44 (1991)
MOON IN SCORPIO (1987)
MOON OVER PARADOR (1988)
MOON VALLEY (SEE: WEEKEND IN THE COUNTRY, A)(1996)
MOONLIGHT AND VALENTINO (1995)
MOONSHINE HIGHWAY (1996)
MOONSTRUCK (1987)
MORGAN STEWART'S COMING HOME (1987)
MORGEN GRAUEN (SEE: TIME TROOPERS)(1990)
MORNING AFTER, THE (1986)
MORNING GLORY (1993)
MORNING TERROR (SEE: TIME TROOPERS)(1990)
MORO AFFAIR, THE (1986)
MORONS FROM OUTER SPACE (1985)
MORTAL KOMBAT (1995)
MORTAL THOUGHTS (1991)
MORTUARY ACADEMY (1992)
MOSAIC PROJECT, THE (1995)
MOSQUITO (1995)
MOSQUITO COAST, THE (1986)
MOTEL VACANCY (SEE: TALKING WALLS)(1987)
MOTHER (1996)
MOTHER (1996)
MOTHER NIGHT (1996)
MOTHER OF KINGS (1996)
MOTHER'S BOYS (1994)
MOTHER'S PRAYER, A (1996)
MOTORAMA (1993)
MOUNTAINS OF THE MOON (1990)
MOUNTAINTOP MOTEL MASSACRE (1986)

MOUTH TO MOUTH (1996)
MOVERS AND SHAKERS (1985)
MOVIE HOUSE MASSACRE (1986)
MOVING (1988)
MOVING TARGETS (1987)
MOVING THE MOUNTAIN (1995)
MOVING VIOLATIONS (1985)
MRS. DOUBTFIRE (1993)
MRS. MUNCK (1996)
MRS. PARKER AND THE VICIOUS CIRCLE (1994)
MRS. WINTERBOURNE (1996)
MUCH ADO ABOUT NOTHING (1993)
MUI DU DU XANH (SEE: SCENT OF GREEN PAPAYA, THE)(1994)
MULHOLLAND FALLS (1996)
MULTIPLICITY (1996)
MUNCHIE (1992)
MUNCHIE STRIKES BACK (1994)
MUNCHIES (1987)
MUPPET CHRISTMAS CAROL, THE (1992)
MUPPET TREASURE ISLAND (1996)
MURDER BY NUMBERS (1990)
MURDER-IN-LAW (1993)
MURDER IN THE FIRST (1995)
MURDER ONE (1988)
MURDERED INNOCENCE (1996)
MURIEL'S WEDDING (1995)
MURPHY'S LAW (1986)
MURPHY'S ROMANCE (1985)
MUSIC BOX (1989)
MUSIC OF CHANCE, THE (1993)
MUTANT HUNT (1987)
MUTANT MAN (1996)
MUTANT ON THE BOUNTY (1989)
MUTANT SPECIES (1995)
MUTATOR (1991)
MUTE WITNESS (1995)
MUTILATOR, THE (1985)
MY AMERICAN COUSIN (1985)
MY ANTONIA (1995)
MY BEAUTIFUL LAUNDRETTE (1986)
MY BLUE HEAVEN (1990)
MY BOYFRIEND'S BACK (1993)
MY BROTHER'S WIFE (1994)
MY CHAUFFEUR (1986)
MY COUSIN VINNY (1992)
MY DARK LADY (1987)
MY DEMON LOVER (1987)
MY FAMILY: MI FAMILIA (1995)
MY FATHER IS COMING (1992)
MY FATHER, THE HERO (1994)
MY FATHER'S GLORY (1991)
MY FAVORITE SEASON (SEE: MA SAISON PREFEREE)(1996)
MY FELLOW AMERICANS (1996)
MY FIRST WIFE (1985)
MY GIRL (1991)
MY GIRL 2 (1994)
MY GRANDPA IS A VAMPIRE (1992)
MY HEROES HAVE ALWAYS BEEN COWBOYS (1991)
MY LEFT FOOT (1989)
MY LIFE (1993)
MY LIFE AND TIMES WITH ANTONIN ARTAUD (1995)
MY LIFE AS A DOG (1985)
MY LIFE'S IN TURNAROUND (1994)
MY LITTLE PONY (1986)
MY MAN ADAM (1986)
MY MOTHER'S CASTLE (1991)
MY NEIGHBOR TOTORO (1993)
MY NEW GUN (1992)
MY OWN PRIVATE IDAHO (1991)
MY SAMURAI (1993)
MY SCIENCE PROJECT (1985)
MY STEPMOTHER IS AN ALIEN (1988)
MY SWEET LITTLE VILLAGE (1985)
MY 20TH CENTURY (1989)
MY UNCLE'S LEGACY (1990)
MYSTERY DATE (1991)
MYSTERY OF ALEXINA, THE (1985)
MYSTERY OF RAMPO, THE (1995)
MYSTERY SCIENCE THEATER 3000: THE MOVIE (1996)
MYSTERY TRAIN (1989)
MYSTIC PIZZA (1988)
NIGHT OF LOVE, A (1988)

N

NADINE (1987)
NADJA (1995)
NAIL GUN MASSACRE (1988)
NAKED (1993)
NAKED CAGE, THE (1986)
NAKED GUN: FROM THE FILES OF POLICE SQUAD!, THE (1988)
NAKED GUN 33 1/3: THE FINAL INSULT (1994)
NAKED GUN 2 1/2: THE SMELL OF FEAR, THE (1991)
NAKED IN NEW YORK (1994)
NAKED KILLER (1995)
NAKED LUNCH (1991)
NAKED OBSESSION (1992)
NAKED SOULS (1996)
NAKED VENGEANCE (1986)
NAME OF THE ROSE, THE (1986)
NARROW MARGIN (1990)
NASTY GIRL, THE (1990)
NATIONAL LAMPOON'S ATTACK OF THE 5'2" WOMEN (1995)
NATIONAL LAMPOON'S CHRISTMAS VACATION (1989)
NATIONAL LAMPOON'S EUROPEAN VACATION (1985)
NATIONAL LAMPOON'S FAVORITE DEADLY SINS (1996)
NATIONAL LAMPOON'S LAST RESORT (1994)
NATIONAL LAMPOON'S LOADED WEAPON 1 (1993)
NATIONAL LAMPOON'S SENIOR TRIP (1995)
NATIVE SON (1986)
NATURAL BORN KILLERS (1994)
NATURE OF THE BEAST, THE (1995)
NAVIGATOR, THE (1989)
NAVY SEALS (1990)
NEA (1995)
NEAR DARK (1987)
NEAR MISSES (1992)
NECESSARY ROUGHNESS (1991)
NECO Z ALENKY (SEE: ALICE)(1988)
NECROMANCER (1989)
NECRONOMICON: BOOK OF THE DEAD (1996)
NECROPOLIS (1987)
NEEDFUL THINGS (1993)
NEIGHBOR, THE (1993)
NEIL SIMON'S LOST IN YONKERS (1993)
NEIL SIMON'S THE SLUGGER'S WIFE (SEE: SLUGGER'S WIFE, THE)(1985)
NEKROMANTIK (1995)
NELL (1994)
NELLY AND MONSIEUR ARNAUD (1996)
NELLY ET M. ARNAUD (SEE: NELLY AND MONSIEUR ARNAUD)(1996)
NEMESIS (1993)
NEMESIS 2: NEBULA (1995)
NEMESIS III: PREY HARDER (1996)
NEMESIS 3: TIME LAPSE (SEE: NEMESIS III: PREY HARDER)(1996)
NEON BIBLE, THE (1996)
NEON CITY (1992)
NEON MANIACS (1986)
NERVOUS TICKS (1993)
NET, THE (1995)
NETHERWORLD (1992)
NEUROSIA: 50 YEARS OF PERVERSITY (1996)
NEUROSIA: FUNFZIG JAHRE PERVERS (SEE: NEUROSIA: FIFTY YEARS OF PERVERSITY)(1996)
NEUROTIC CABARET (1991)
NEVER CRY DEVIL (SEE: NIGHT VISITOR)(1990)
NEVER LEAVE NEVADA (1991)
NEVER TALK TO STRANGERS (1995)
NEVER TOO YOUNG TO DIE (1986)
NEVERENDING STORY II: THE NEXT CHAPTER, THE (1991)
NEW ADVENTURES OF PIPPI LONGSTOCKING, THE (1988)
NEW AGE, THE (1994)
NEW CRIME CITY: LOS ANGELES 2020 (1994)
NEW EDEN (1994)
NEW JACK CITY (1991)
NEW JERSEY DRIVE (1995)
NEW KIDS, THE (1985)
NEW LIFE, A (1988)
NEW LIFE, A (1996)
NEW YEAR'S DAY (1989)
NEW YORK COP (1995)
NEW YORK STORIES (1989)
NEW YORK'S FINEST (1988)
NEWSIES (1992)
NEXT DOOR (1995)
NEXT KARATE KID, THE (1994)
NEXT OF KIN (1989)
NGATI (1987)
NI-LO-HO NU-ERH (SEE: DAUGHTER OF THE NILE)(1988)
NICE GIRLS DON'T EXPLODE (1987)
NICK OF TIME (1995)
NICKEL & DIME (1992)
NICKEL MOUNTAIN (1985)
NICO ICON (1996)
NIGHT AND DAY (1992)
NIGHT AND THE CITY (1992)
NIGHT ANGEL (1990)
NIGHT ANGELS (1987)
NIGHT EYES (1990)
NIGHT EYES III (1993)
NIGHT EYES 2 (1992)
NIGHT FIRE (1994)
NIGHT GAME (1989)
NIGHT IN THE LIFE OF JIMMY REARDON, A (1988)
NIGHT IS YOUNG, THE (SEE: BAD BLOOD)(1987)
NIGHT LIFE (1991)
'NIGHT, MOTHER (1986)
NIGHT OF THE CREEPS (1986)
NIGHT OF THE DEMONS (1989)
NIGHT OF THE DEMONS 2 (1994)
NIGHT OF THE LIVING DEAD (1990)
NIGHT OF THE RUNNING MAN (1994)
NIGHT OF THE SCARECROW (1996)
NIGHT OF THE SHARKS (1990)
NIGHT OF THE TWISTERS (1996)
NIGHT OF THE WARRIOR (1991)
NIGHT ON EARTH (1992)
NIGHT ON THE GALACTIC RAILROAD (1996)
NIGHT RHYTHMS (1992)
NIGHT SIEGE PROJECT: SHADOWCHASER 2 (1995)
NIGHT STALKER, THE (1987)
NIGHT TRAIN TO VENICE (1995)

NIGHT VISITOR (1990)
NIGHT WE NEVER MET, THE (1993)
NIGHT ZOO (1988)
NIGHTBREED (1990)
NIGHTFALL (1988)
NIGHTFLYERS (1987)
NIGHTFORCE (1987)
NIGHTMARE (1995)
NIGHTMARE ON ELM STREET 7 (SEE: WES CRAVEN'S NEW NIGHTMARE)(1994)
NIGHTMARE ON ELM STREET PART 2: FREDDY'S REVENGE, A (1985)
NIGHTMARE ON ELM STREET 3: DREAM WARRIORS, A (1987)
NIGHTMARE ON ELM STREET 4: THE DREAM MASTER, A (1988)
NIGHTMARE ON ELM STREET 5: THE DREAM CHILD, A (1989)
NIGHTMARE WEEKEND (1986)
NIGHTMARE'S PASSENGERS (1986)
NIGHTSCARE (1995)
NIGHTWARS (1988)
NIKI DE SAINT PHALLE: WHO IS THE MONSTER -- YOU OR ME? (1996)
NIKITA (SEE: LA FEMME NIKITA)(1991)
NINA TAKES A LOVER (1995)
9 1/2 NINJAS (1991)
NINE 1/2 WEEKS (1986)
9 DEATHS OF THE NINJA (1985)
NINE MONTHS (1995)
976-EVIL (1989)
976-EVIL II (1992)
1918 (1985)
1991: THE YEAR PUNK BROKE (1992)
1969 (1988)
90 DAYS (1986)
NINJA SCROLL (1995)
NINJA TURF (1986)
NIXON (1995)
NO CONTEST (1995)
NO DEAD HEROES (1987)
NO DESSERT DAD, 'TIL YOU MOW THE LAWN (1994)
NO ESCAPE (1994)
NO ESCAPE NO RETURN (1994)
NO HOLDS BARRED (1989)
NO MAN'S LAND (1987)
NO MERCY (1986)
NO MERCY (1995)
NO PLACE TO HIDE (1993)
NO RETREAT, NO SURRENDER (1986)
NO RETREAT, NO SURRENDER 3 - BLOOD BROTHERS (1991)
NO RETREAT, NO SURRENDER II (1989)
NO SAFE HAVEN (1989)
NO SECRETS (1991)
NO SKIN OFF MY ASS (1991)
NO SURRENDER (1986)
NO WAY OUT (1987)
NOBODY LOVES ME (1995)
NOBODY'S FOOL (1986)
NOBODY'S FOOL (1994)
NOBODY'S PERFECT (1990)
NOCE IN GALILEE (SEE: WEDDING IN GALILEE)(1988)
NOI TRE (SEE: WE THREE)(1985)
NOIR ET BLANC (SEE: BLACK AND WHITE)(1986)
NOIR ET BLANC (1991)
NOISES OFF (1992)
NOMADS (1985)
NORMA JEAN AND MARILYN (1996)
NORMAL LIFE (1996)
NORTH (1994)
NORTH SHORE (1987)
NOSTRADAMUS (1994)
NOSTRADAMUS KID, THE (1995)
NOT ANGELS BUT ANGELS (1995)
NOT BAD FOR A GIRL (1996)
NOT OF THIS EARTH (1988)
NOT OF THIS EARTH (1996)
NOT QUITE JERUSALEM (1985)
NOT SINCE CASANOVA (1988)
NOT WITHOUT MY DAUGHTER (1991)
NOTEBOOK ON CITIES AND CLOTHES (1991)
NOTHING BUT TROUBLE (1991)
NOTHING IN COMMON (1986)
NOTHING TO LOSE (SEE: DEATH IN BRUNSWICK)(1995)
NOVEMBER MEN (1994)
NOW AND THEN (1995)
NOWHERE TO HIDE (1987)
NOWHERE TO RUN (1989)
NOWHERE TO RUN (1993)
NUIT ET JOUR (SEE: NIGHT AND DAY)(1992)
#247 (SEE: MODERN AFFAIR, A)(1996)
NUMBER ONE FAN (1995)
NUMBER ONE WITH A BULLET (1987)
NUNS ON THE RUN (1990)
NUOVO CINEMA PARADISO (SEE: CINEMA PARADISO)(1990)
NUTCRACKER PRINCE, THE (1990)
NUTCRACKER: THE MOTION PICTURE (1986)
NUTS (1987)
NUTT HOUSE, THE (1995)
NUTTY PROFESSOR, THE (1996)

O

O BOBO (SEE: JESTER, THE)(1987)
O.C. AND STIGGS (1987)
OAK, THE (1993)
OBERST REDL (SEE: COLONEL REDL)(1985)
OBJECT OF BEAUTY, THE (1991)
OBLIVION (1994)
OBLIVION 2 (SEE: BACKLASH: OBLIVION 2)(1996)
OBSESSED (1989)
OCEAN DRIVE WEEKEND (1986)
OCI CIORNIE (SEE: DARK EYES)(1987)
OCTOBER 32ND (SEE: MERLIN)(1994)
ODD JOBS (1986)
ODDBALL HALL (1992)
OF LOVE AND SHADOWS (1996)
OF MICE AND MEN (1992)
OF UNKNOWN ORIGINS (SEE: BLACK SCORPION)(1996)
OFF AND RUNNING (1996)
OFF BEAT (1986)
OFF LIMITS (1988)
OFFERINGS (1989)
OFFICE PARTY (SEE: HOSTILE TAKEOVER)(1990)
OFFICIAL DENIAL (1994)
OFFICIAL STORY, THE (1985)
OFFRET-SA CRIFICATIO (SEE: SACRIFICE)(1986)
OFFSPRING, THE (1987)
OH . . . ROSALINDA!! (1995)
OH, WHAT A NIGHT (1992)
O.J. SIMPSON STORY, THE (1995)
OKOGE (1993)
OLD EXPLORERS (1991)
OLD GRINGO (1989)
OLD LADY WHO WALKED IN THE SEA, THE (1995)
OLD MAN AND THE SEA, THE (1995)
OLEANNA (1994)
OLIVER & COMPANY (1988)
OLIVIER, OLIVIER (1993)
OLYMPIC SUMMER, THE (1994)
OMEGA SYNDROME (1987)
ON DEADLY GROUND (1994)
ON THE BLOCK (1991)
ON THE EDGE (1985)
ON VALENTINE'S DAY (1986)
ONCE AROUND (1991)
ONCE BITTEN (1985)
ONCE UPON A CRIME (1992)
ONCE UPON A FOREST (1993)
ONCE UPON A TIME IN CHINA (1992)
ONCE UPON A TIME IN CHINA II (1994)
ONCE UPON A TIME IN CHINA III (1994)
ONCE UPON A TIME . . . WHEN WE WERE COLORED (1996)
ONCE WERE WARRIORS (1995)
ONE CRAZY NIGHT (1993)
ONE CRAZY SUMMER (1986)
ONE FALSE MOVE (1992)
ONE FINE DAY (1996)
ONE FOR SORROW, TWO FOR JOY (SEE: SIGNS OF LIFE)(1989)
ONE GOOD COP (1991)
ONE GOOD TURN (1996)
101 DALMATIANS (1996)
ONE LAST RUN (1992)
ONE LESS EGG TO FRY (1996)
ONE LOOK AND LOVE BEGINS (SEE: EIN BLICK--UND DIE LIEBE BRICHT AUS)(1987)
ONE MAGIC CHRISTMAS (1985)
ONE MAN'S JUSTICE (1996)
ONE MINUTE TO MIDNIGHT (1988)
ONE MORE SATURDAY NIGHT (1986)
ONE NIGHT ONLY (1986)
ONE NIGHT STAND (1996)
1-900 (1995)
ONE TOUGH BASTARD (SEE: ONE MAN'S JUSTICE)(1996)
ONE-WAY TICKET, A (1988)
ONLY THE BRAVE (1994)
ONLY THE BRAVE (1995)
ONLY THE LONELY (1991)
ONLY YOU (1992)
ONLY YOU (1994)
OPEN DOORS (1991)
OPEN FIRE (1995)
OPEN HOUSE (1987)
OPEN SEASON (1996)
OPERA DO MALANDRO (SEE: MALANDRO)(1986)
OPERATION DUMBO DROP (1995)
OPERATION GOLDEN PHOENIX (1994)
OPERATION INTERCEPT (1995)
OPPONENT, THE (1990)
OPPORTUNITY KNOCKS (1990)
OPPOSING FORCE (1987)
OPPOSITE SEX AND HOW TO LIVE WITH THEM, THE (1993)
OPTIONS (1989)
ORGANIZED CRIME & TRIAD BUREAU (1996)
ORIANE (1985)
ORIGINAL GANGSTAS (1996)
ORIGINAL INTENT (1992)
ORIGINAL SINS (1996)
ORLANDO (1993)
ORMENS VAG PA HALLEBERGET (SEE: SERPENT'S WAY)(1987)
ORPHANS (1987)
ORSON WELLES: THE ONE-MAN BAND (1996)
OSA (1985)
OSCAR (1991)
OTAC NA SLUZBENOH PUTU (SEE: WHEN FATHER WAS AWAY ON BUSINES)(1985)
OTELLO (1986)

OTHELLO (1995)
OTHER PEOPLE'S MONEY (1991)
OTHER WOMAN, THE (1992)
OTOKOWA TSURAIYOO TORAIJIRO KOKORO NO TABIJI (SEE: TORA-SAN GOES TO VIENNA)(1986)
OTRA HISTORIA DE AMOR (SEE: ANOTHER LOVE STORY)(1986)
OTRA VUELTA DE TUERCA (SEE: TURN OF THE SCREW)(1985)
OUR FATHER (1985)
OUT COLD (1989)
OUT FOR BLOOD (1992)
OUT FOR JUSTICE (1991)
OUT OF AFRICA (1985)
OUT OF ANNIE'S PAST (1995)
OUT OF BOUNDS (1986)
OUT OF CONTROL (1985)
OUT OF MY WAY (SEE: STORY OF FAUSTA)(1988)
OUT OF ORDER (1985)
OUT OF ROSENHEIM (SEE: BAGDAD CAFE)(1987)
OUT OF SIGHT (1995)
OUT OF SYNC (1995)
OUT OF THE RAIN (1991)
OUT ON A LIMB (1992)
OUT THERE (1996)
OUTBREAK (1995)
OUTER HEAT (SEE: ALIEN NATION)(1988)
OUTER LIMITS: SANDKINGS, THE (1996)
OUTFIT, THE (1993)
OUTING, THE (1987)
OUTPOST, THE (1996)
OUTRAGE (1996)
OUTRAGEOUS FORTUNE (1987)
OUTREMER (SEE: OVERSEAS)(1991)
OUTSIDE THE LAW (1995)
OUTSIDERS, THE (1987)
OVER EXPOSED (1990)
OVER GRENSEN (SEE: FELDMANN CASE, THE)(1987)
OVER HER DEAD BODY (1992)
OVER THE HILL (1993)
OVER THE SUMMER (1986)
OVER THE TOP (1987)
OVER THE WIRE (1996)
OVERBOARD (1987)
OVERKILL (1987)
OVERSEAS (1991)
OVIRI (SEE: WOLF AT THE DOOR, THE)(1986)
OX, THE (1992)

P

P.K. AND THE KID (1987)
P.O.W. THE ESCAPE (1986)
PACIFIC HEIGHTS (1990)
PACKAGE, THE (1989)
PAGEMASTER, THE (1994)
PAINT IT BLACK (1990)
PAINTED HERO (1996)
PAINTING THE TOWN (1992)
PALE BLOOD (1992)
PALE RIDER (1985)
PALERMO CONNECTION, THE (1991)
PALLBEARER, THE (1996)
PALOOKAVILLE (1996)
PAMELA PRINCIPLE, THE (1992)
PANAMA DECEPTION, THE (1992)
PANTHER (1995)
PANTHER SQUAD (1986)
PAPER MASK (1991)
PAPER WEDDING (1991)
PAPER, THE (1994)
PAPERBOY, THE (1994)
PAPERHOUSE (1989)
PARADISE (1991)
PARADISE LOST: THE CHILD MURDERS AT ROBIN HOOD HILLS (1996)
PARADISE MOTEL (1985)
PARALLEL LIVES (1995)
PARENTHOOD (1989)
PARENTS (1989)
PARIS, FRANCE (1994)
PARIS IS BURNING (1991)
PARIS WAS A WOMAN (1996)
PARISIAN ENCOUNTERS (SEE: RENDEZVOUS IN PARIS)(1996)
PARKING (1985)
PARTING GLANCES (1986)
PARTIR REVENIR (SEE: GOING AND COMING BACK)(1985)
PARTY CAMP (1987)
PARTY GIRL (1995)
PARTY PLANE (1991)
PASAJEROS DE UNA PESADILLA (SEE: MIGHTMARE'S PASSENGERS)(1986)
PASCALI'S ISLAND (1988)
PASOLINI, AN ITALIAN CRIME (SEE: WHO KILLED PASOLINI?)(1996)
PASOLINI, UN DELITTO ITALIANO (SEE: WHO KILLED PASOLINI?)(1996)
PASS THE AMMO (1988)
PASSED AWAY (1992)
PASSENGER 57 (1992)
PASSION FISH (1992)
PASSION OF DARKLY NOON, THE (1996)
PASSION TO KILL, A (1994)
PAST TENSE (1994)
PASTIME (1991)
PATAKIN (1985)
PATHFINDER (1990)
PATLABOR 2: MOBILE POLICE (1996)
PATLABOR: THE MOBILE POLICE (1995)
PATRIOT, THE (1986)
PATRIOT GAMES (1992)
PATTI ROCKS (1988)
PATTY HEARST (1988)
PATUL CONJUGAL (SEE: CONJUGAL BED, THE)(1994)
PAUL BOWLES: HALFMOON (SEE: HALFMOON)(1996)
PAUL BOWLES: THE COMPLETE OUTSIDER (1994)
PAVLOVA--A WOMAN FOR ALL TIME (1985)
PAYBACK (1991)
PAYBACK (1995)
PCU (1994)
PEACEMAKER (1990)
PEBBLE AND THE PENGUIN, THE (1995)
PEE-WEE'S BIG ADVENTURE (1985)
PEEPHOLE (1994)
PEGGY SUE GOT MARRIED (1986)
PEKING OPERA BLUES (1986)
PELICAN BRIEF, THE (1993)
PELLE THE CONQUEROR (1987)
PENITENT, THE (1988)
PENITENTIARY III (1987)
PENN & TELLER GET KILLED (1989)
PENTATHLON (1995)
PEOPLE UNDER THE STAIRS, THE (1991)
PEOPLE VS. LARRY FLYNT, THE (1996)
PEPI, LUCI, BOM AND OTHER GIRLS ON THE HEAP (1992)
PEPI, LUCI, BOM Y OTRAS CHICAS DEL MONTON (SEE: PEPI, LUCI, BOM AND OTHER GIRLS ON THE HEAP)(1992)
PERCY AND THUNDER (1995)
PEREZ FAMILY, THE (1995)
PERFECT (1985)
PERFECT CANDIDATE, A (1996)
PERFECT MATCH, THE (1987)
PERFECT MODEL, THE (1989)
PERFECT MURDER, THE (1990)
PERFECT WEAPON, THE (1991)
PERFECT WORLD, A (1993)
PERFECTLY NORMAL (1991)
PERIL (1985)
PERILS OF P.K., THE (1986)
PERMANENT RECORD (1988)
PERSONAL FOUL (1987)
PERSONAL JOURNEY WITH MARTIN SCORSESE THROUGH AMERICAN MOVIES, A (1996)
PERSONAL SERVICES (1987)
PERSUASION (1995)
PET SEMATARY (1989)
PET SEMATARY II (1992)
PET SHOP (1995)
PETER'S FRIENDS (1992)
PETIT CON (1985)
PHANTASM II (1988)
PHANTASM III: LORD OF THE DEAD (1994)
PHANTOM 2040: THE GHOST WHO WALKS (1996)
PHANTOM LOVER, THE (1995)
PHANTOM OF THE MALL: ERIC'S REVENGE (1989)
PHANTOM OF THE OPERA (1989)
PHANTOM OF THE RITZ (1992)
PHANTOM, THE (1996)
PHARAOH'S ARMY (1996)
PHAT BEACH (1996)
PHENOMENA (SEE: CREEPERS)(1985)
PHENOMENON (1996)
PHILADELPHIA (1993)
PHILADELPHIA ATTRACTION, THE (1985)
PHILADELPHIA EXPERIMENT 2, THE (1993)
PHOBIA (1988)
PHOENIX (1996)
PHONE CALL, THE (1991)
PHOTOGRAPH, THE (1987)
PHYSICAL EVIDENCE (1989)
PIANO LESSON, THE (1995)
PIANO, THE (1993)
PICCOLI FUOCHI (SEE: LITTLE FLAMES)(1985)
PICK-UP ARTIST, THE (1987)
PICKLE, THE (1993)
PICTURE BRIDE (1995)
PICTURES FROM A REVOLUTION (1992)
PIE IN THE SKY (1996)
PIGALLE (1995)
PIGS (1993)
PIG'S TALE, A (1996)
PIN (1989)
PINK CADILLAC (1989)
PINK NIGHTS (1985)
PINOCCHIO AND THE EMPEROR OF THE NIGHT (1987)
PINOCCHIO'S REVENGE (1996)
PIRANHA (1996)
PIRATES (1986)
PIT AND THE PENDULUM, THE (1991)
PIZZA MAN (1991)
PLACE FOR ANNIE, A (1994)
PLACE IN THE WORLD, A (1994)
PLACE OF WEEPING (1986)
PLAGUE, THE (1993)
PLANES, TRAINS, AND AUTOMOBILES (1987)
PLATOON (1986)
PLATOON LEADER (1988)
PLAY DEAD (1986)
PLAY MURDER FOR ME (1992)
PLAY NICE (1992)
PLAY TIME (1995)

PLAYBACK (1996)
PLAYBOYS, THE (1992)
PLAYER, THE (1992)
PLAYING AWAY (1986)
PLAYING FOR KEEPS (1986)
PLAYMAKER (1994)
PLEDGE NIGHT (1991)
PLENTY (1985)
PLOT AGAINST HARRY, THE (1990)
PLUGHEAD REWIRED: CIRCUITRY MAN II (SEE: CIRCUITRY MAN II)(1994)
POCAHONTAS (1995)
POCAHONTAS: THE LEGEND (1995)
POETIC JUSTICE (1993)
POET'S SILENCE, THE (1987)
POINT BREAK (1991)
POINT OF NO RETURN (1993)
POISON (1991)
POISON IVY (1992)
POISON IVY 2: LILY (1996)
POKAYANIYE (SEE: REPENTANCE)(1987)
POLAR BEAR KING, THE (1994)
POLICE (1986)
POLICE ACADEMY 7: MISSION TO MOSCOW (1995)
POLICE ACADEMY 2: THEIR FIRST ASSIGNMENT (1985)
POLICE ACADEMY 3: BACK IN TRAINING (1986)
POLICE ACADEMY 4: CITIZENS ON PATROL (1987)
POLICE ACADEMY 5: ASSIGNMENT MIAMI BEACH (1988)
POLICE ACADEMY 6: CITY UNDER SIEGE (1989)
POLTERGEIST II (1986)
POLTERGEIST III (1988)
POLYMORPH (1996)
POMPATUS OF LOVE, THE (1996)
PONTIAC MOON (1994)
POPCORN (1991)
POPE MUST DIE!, THE (SEE: POPE MUST DIET!, THE)(1992)
POPE MUST DIET!, THE (1992)
PORKY'S REVENGE (1985)
PORTE APERTE (SEE: OPEN DOORS)(1991)
PORTRAIT OF A LADY, THE (1996)
PORTRAITS OF A KILLER (1996)
PORTRAITS OF INNOCENCE (SEE: PORTRAITS OF A KILLER)(1996)
POSITIVE I.D. (1986)
POSSE (1993)
POSSESSED BY THE NIGHT (1994)
POSTCARDS FROM AMERICA (1995)
POSTCARDS FROM THE EDGE (1990)
POSTE AVANCE (SEE: OUTPOST, THE)(1996)
POSTMAN, THE (1995)
POTOMOK BELONGO BARSSA (SEE: DESCENDANT OF THE SNOW LEOPARD, THE)(1986)
POUND PUPPIES AND THE LEGEND OF BIG PAW (1988)
POUR SACHA (1992)
POUVOIR INTIME (SEE: INTIMATE POWER)(1986)
POWDER (1995)
POWER (1986)
POWER OF ATTORNEY (1995)
POWER OF EVIL, THE (1985)
POWER OF ONE, THE (1992)
PRANCER (1989)
PRAY FOR DEATH (1986)
PRAYER FOR THE DYING, A (1987)
PRAYER OF THE ROLLERBOYS (1991)
PREACHER'S WIFE, THE (1996)
PREDATOR (1987)
PREDATOR 2 (1990)
PREDICTIONS OF FIRE (1996)
PREHYSTERIA (1993)
PREHYSTERIA! 2 (1994)
PREHYSTERIA! 3 (1995)
PRELUDE TO A KISS (1992)
PRE-MADONNAS (1996)
PRESENCE, THE (1994)
PRESIDIO, THE (1988)
PRESUMED INNOCENT (1990)
PRETTY IN PINK (1986)
PRETTY SMART (1987)
PRETTY WOMAN (1990)
PRETTYKILL (1987)
PREY FOR THE HUNTER (1993)
PRICK UP YOUR EARS (1987)
PRIEST (1995)
PRIMAL FEAR (1996)
PRIMAL RAGE (1990)
PRIMAL SCREAM (1988)
PRIMARY MOTIVE (1992)
PRIMARY TARGET (1990)
PRIME RISK (1985)
PRIME TARGET (1991)
PRIMO BABY (1992)
PRINCE JACK (1985)
PRINCE OF DARKNESS (1987)
PRINCE OF TIDES, THE (1991)
PRINCES IN EXILE (1991)
PRINCESS ACADEMY, THE (1987)
PRINCESS AND THE GOBLIN, THE (1994)
PRINCESS BRIDE, THE (1987)
PRINCESS CARABOO (1994)
PRINCIPAL, THE (1987)
PRISON (1988)
PRISON PLANET (1993)
PRISON SHIP (SEE: STAR SLAMMER: THE ESCAPE)(1988)
PRISONERS OF THE SUN (1991)
PRIVATE ACCESS (1988)
PRIVATE FUNCTION, A (1985)
PRIVATE LESSONS--ANOTHER STORY (1994)
PRIVATE OBSESSION (1995)
PRIVATE RESORT (1985)
PRIVATE SHOW (1985)
PRIVATE WARS (1993)
PRIVILEGE (1991)
PRIZZI'S HONOR (1985)
PROBLEM CHILD (1990)
PROBLEM CHILD 2 (1991)
PROFESSION: NEO-NAZI (1995)
PROFESSIONAL, THE (1992)
PROFESSIONAL, THE (1994)
PROGRAM, THE (1993)
PROGRAMMED TO KILL (1987)
PROJECT: ALIEN (1991)
PROJECT: GENESIS (1994)
PROJECT: SHADOWCHASER (1992)
PROJECT: SHADOWCHASER 3000 (1995)
PROJECT X (1987)
PROJECT: METALBEAST (1995)
PROJECT: SHADOWCHASER 2 (SEE: NIGHT SIEGE PROJECT: SHADOWCHASER 2)(1995)
PROM NIGHT IV - DELIVER US FROM EVIL (1992)
PROM NIGHT III: THE LAST KISS (1989)
PROM NIGHT II (SEE: HELLO MARY LOU: PROM NIGHT II)(1987)
PROMISE, THE (1995)
PROMISED LAND (1988)
PROOF (1992)
PROPHECY, THE (1995)
PROPRIETOR, THE (1996)
PROSPERO'S BOOKS (1991)
PROTECTOR, THE (1985)
PROTEUS (1996)
PROVINCIAL ACTORS (1995)
PRZESLUCHANIE (SEE: INTERROGATION, THE)(1990)
PRZYPADEK (SEE: BLIND CHANCE)(1987)
PSY (SEE: PIGS)(1993)
PSYCHIC (1992)
PSYCHO III (1986)
PSYCHO COP 2 (1994)
PSYCHOS IN LOVE (1987)
PUBLIC ACCESS (1996)
PUBLIC ENEMIES (1996)
PUBLIC EYE, THE (1992)
PUERTO RICAN MAMBO (NOT A MUSICAL), THE (1992)
PULP FICTION (1994)
PULSE (1988)
PULSEBEAT (1986)
PUMP UP THE VOLUME (1990)
PUMPKINHEAD (1988)
PUMPKINHEAD 2: BLOOD WINGS (1994)
PUNCHLINE (1988)
PUNISHER, THE (1991)
PUPPET MASTER (1989)
PUPPET MASTER 4 (1993)
PUPPET MASTER 5: THE FINAL CHAPTER (1994)
PUPPET MASTER III: TOULON'S REVENGE (1991)
PUPPET MASTER II (1991)
PUPPET MASTERS, THE (SEE: ROBERT A. HEINLEIN'S THE PUPPET MASTERS)(1994)
PURE COUNTRY (1992)
PURE DANGER (1996)
PURE FORMALITY, A (1995)
PURE LUCK (1991)
PURPLE ROSE OF CAIRO, THE (1985)
PUSHED TO THE LIMIT (1992)
PUSHING HANDS (1995)
PYRATES (1991)
PYROMANIAC'S LOVE STORY, A (1995)

Q

Q&A (1990)
QIU JU (SEE: STORY OF QIU JU, THE)(1993)
QUALCOSA DI BIONDO (1985)
QUARREL, THE (1992)
QUARTIERE (1987)
QUEEN MARGOT (1994)
QUEEN OF HEARTS (1989)
QUEENS LOGIC (1991)
QUEST FOR THE LOST CITY (1994)
QUEST, THE (1996)
QUESTION OF COLOR, A (1993)
QUICK (1994)
QUICK AND THE DEAD, THE (1995)
QUICK CHANGE (1990)
QUICKSILVER (1986)
QUIET COOL (1986)
QUIET EARTH, THE (1985)
QUIGLEY DOWN UNDER (1990)
QUIZ SHOW (1994)

R

R.O.T.O.R. (1988)
RABID GRANNIES (1989)
RACE FOR GLORY (1989)
RACE THE SUN (1996)
RACE TO FREEDOM: THE UNDERGROUND RAILROAD (1995)
RACHEL PAPERS, THE (1989)
RACHEL RIVER (1989)
RAD (1986)

RADIO DAYS (1987)
RADIO FLYER (1992)
RADIO INSIDE (1995)
RADIOACTIVE DREAMS (1986)
RADIOLAND MURDERS (1994)
RAGE (1996)
RAGE AND HONOR (1993)
RAGE AND HONOR II: HOSTILE TAKEOVER (1993)
RAGE IN HARLEM, A (1991)
RAGE OF HONOR (1987)
RAGGEDY RAWNEY, THE (1990)
RAGING ANGELS (1995)
RAIN KILLER, THE (1991)
RAIN MAN (1988)
RAIN WITHOUT THUNDER (1993)
RAINBOW, THE (1989)
RAINBOW BRITE AND THE STAR STEALER (1985)
RAINING STONES (1994)
RAISE THE RED LANTERN (1992)
RAISING ARIZONA (1987)
RAISING CAIN (1992)
RAMBLING ROSE (1991)
RAMBO: FIRST BLOOD, PART II (1985)
RAMBO III (1988)
RAMPAGE (1992)
RAMPO (SEE: MYSTERY OF RAMPO, THE)(1995)
RAN (1985)
RANSOM (1996)
RAPA NUI (1994)
RAPID FIRE (1992)
RAPPIN' (1985)
RAPTURE, THE (1991)
RASPAD (1992)
RASPUTIN (1985)
RASPUTIN (1996)
RATBOY (1986)
RATTLED (1996)
RAVE REVIEW (1995)
RAVENHAWK (1996)
RAW DEAL (1986)
RAW JUSTICE (1994)
RAW NERVE (1991)
RAW TARGET (1996)
RAWHEAD REX (1987)
RE-ANIMATOR (1985)
READY TO WEAR (PRET-A-PORTER) (1994)
REAL BULLETS (1990)
REAL GENIUS (1985)
REAL MCCOY, THE (1993)
REALITY BITES (1994)
REALM OF FORTUNE, THE (1986)
REASON TO BELIEVE, A (1995)
REBEL (1985)
REBEL LOVE (1986)
REBRO ADAMA (SEE: ADAM'S RIB)(1992)
RECKLESS (1995)
RECKLESS KELLY (1994)
RECRUITS (1986)
RED (1994)
RED FIRECRACKER, GREEN FIRECRACKER (1995)
RED HEADED STRANGER (1987)
RED HEAT (1988)
RED HEAT (1988)
RED HOT (1995)
RED KISS (1986)
RED LINE (1996)
RED OCEAN (SEE: MONSTER SHARK)(1986)
RED ROCK WEST (1994)
RED SCORPION (1989)
RED SCORPION 2 (1996)
RED SHOE DIARIES 4: AUTO EROTICA (1994)
RED SONJA (1985)
RED SORGHUM (1988)
RED SUN RISING (1995)
RED SURF (1990)
RED X (SEE: STEPPING RAZOR - RED X)(1993)
REDEMPTION: KICKBOXER 5 (1996)
REDHEADS (SEE: DESPERATE PREY)(1995)
REDL EZREDES (SEE: COLONEL REDL)(1985)
REDWOOD CURTAIN (1995)
REF, THE (1994)
REFLECTING SKIN, THE (1991)
REFLECTIONS IN THE DARK (1995)
REFORM SCHOOL GIRLS (1986)
REFRIGERATOR, THE (1992)
REGARDING HENRY (1991)
REGENERATED MAN, THE (1994)
REINCARNATION OF GOLDEN LOTUS, THE (1990)
RELATIVE FEAR (1995)
RELENTLESS (1989)
RELENTLESS III (1993)
RELENTLESS 4: ASHES TO ASHES (1994)
RELENTLESS II (SEE: DEAD ON: RELENTLESS II)(1991)
REMAINS OF THE DAY, THE (1993)
REMANDO AL VIENTO (SEE: ROWING WITH THE WIND)(1988)
REMBETIKO (1985)
REMBRANDT LAUGHING (1989)
REMO WILLIAMS: THE ADVENTURE BEGINS . . . (1985)
REMOTE (1993)
REMOTE CONTROL (1988)
REMOTE CONTROL (1995)
RENAISSANCE MAN (1994)
RENDEZVOUS (1985)
RENDEZVOUS IN PARIS (1996)
RENEGADES (1989)
RENT-A-COP (1988)
RENT-A-KID (1995)
RENTED LIPS (1988)
REPENTANCE (1988)
REPLIKATOR (1994)
REPOSSESSED (1990)
REQUIEM FOR DOMINIC (1991)
REQUIEM FUR DOMINIC (SEE: REQUIEM FOR DOMINIC)(1991)
RESCUE, THE (1988)
RESCUERS DOWN UNDER, THE (1990)
RESERVOIR DOGS (1992)
RESIDENT ALIEN (1991)
RESISTANCE (1994)
RESTLESS CONSCIENCE, THE (1991)
RESTORATION (1995)
RESURRECTED, THE (1992)
RETALIATOR (SEE: PROGRAMMED TO KILL)(1987)
RETRIBUTION (1988)
RETURN (1986)
RETURN OF JAFAR, THE (1994)
RETURN OF JOSEY WALES, THE (1987)
RETURN OF SUPERFLY, THE (1990)
RETURN OF SWAMP THING, THE (1989)
RETURN OF THE GOD OF GAMBLERS (1995)
RETURN OF THE KILLER TOMATOES (1988)
RETURN OF THE LIVING DEAD (1985)
RETURN OF THE LIVING DEAD III (1993)
RETURN OF THE LIVING DEAD PART II (1988)
RETURN OF THE NATIVE, THE (1995)
RETURN OF THE TEXAS CHAINSAW MASSACRE, THE (SEE: TEXAS CHAINSAW MASSACRE: THE NEXT GENERATION)(1996)
RETURN TO FROGTOWN (SEE: FROGTOWN II)(1993)
RETURN TO HORROR HIGH (1987)
RETURN TO OZ (1985)
RETURN TO SALEM'S LOT, A (1988)
RETURN TO SNOWY RIVER (1988)
RETURN TO THE BLUE LAGOON (1991)
RETURN TO THE LOST WORLD (1994)
RETURN TO TWO MOON JUNCTION (1994)
RETURN TO WATERLOO (1985)
RETURNING, THE (1991)
REUNION (1991)
REVENGE (1990)
REVENGE (1986)
REVENGE OF THE INNOCENTS (SEE: SOUTH BRONX HEROES)(1985)
REVENGE OF THE NERDS 4: BOOGER'S WEDDING (1995)
REVENGE OF THE NERDS II: NERDS IN PARADISE (1987)
REVENGE OF THE TEENAGE VIXENS FROM OUTER SPACE, THE (1986)
REVERSAL OF FORTUNE (1990)
REVOLUTION (1985)
REVOLUTION! (1991)
REVOLVING DOORS, THE (1988)
RHAPSODY IN AUGUST (1991)
RHOSYN A RHITH (SEE: COMING UP ROSES)(1986)
RHYTHM THIEF (1995)
RICH GIRL (1991)
RICH IN LOVE (1993)
RICH MAN'S WIFE, THE (1996)
RICHARD III (1995)
RICHIE RICH (1994)
RICKY 1 (1988)
RICOCHET (1991)
RIDERS OF THE PURPLE SAGE (1996)
RIDERS OF THE STORM (1988)
RIDICULE (1996)
RIFF-RAFF (1993)
RIKKY AND PETE (1988)
RIKYU (1991)
RING OF FIRE (1991)
RING OF FIRE II: BLOOD AND STEEL (1993)
RING OF FIRE III: LION STRIKE (1995)
RING OF STEEL (1994)
RING OF THE MUSKETEERS (1994)
RISING SUN (1993)
RISK (1994)
RITA, SUE AND BOB TOO! (1987)
RIVER OF DEATH (1990)
RIVER OF GRASS (1995)
RIVER PIRATES, THE (1994)
RIVER RUNS THROUGH IT, A (1992)
RIVER WILD, THE (1994)
RIVERBEND (1990)
RIVER'S EDGE (1987)
ROAD HOME, THE (1996)
ROAD HOUSE (1989)
ROAD KILL USA (1994)
ROAD KILLERS, THE (1995)
ROAD TO GALVESTON, THE (1996)
ROAD TO RUIN (1992)
ROAD TO WELLVILLE, THE (1994)
ROAD TRIP (SEE: JOCKS)(1987)
ROADSIDE PROPHETS (1992)
ROALD DAHL'S MATILDA (SEE: MATILDA)(1996)
ROB ROY (1995)
ROBERT A. HEINLEIN'S THE PUPPET MASTERS (1994)
ROBIN HOOD: MEN IN TIGHTS (1993)
ROBIN HOOD: PRINCE OF THIEVES (1991)
ROBIN OF LOCKSLEY (1996)

ROBINSON'S GARDEN (1988)
ROBOCOP (1987)
ROBOCOP 2 (1990)
ROBOCOP 3 (1993)
ROBOT HOLOCAUST (1987)
ROBOT JOX (1990)
ROBOT WARS (1993)
ROCK-A-DOODLE (1992)
ROCK & ROLL COWBOYS (1992)
ROCK HUDSON'S HOME MOVIES (1993)
ROCK 'N' ROLL HIGH SCHOOL FOREVER (1991)
ROCK 'N' ROLL NIGHTMARE (1987)
ROCK SOUP (1992)
ROCK, THE (1996)
ROCKET GIBRALTAR (1988)
ROCKETEER, THE (1991)
ROCKIN' ROAD TRIP (1986)
ROCKY IV (1985)
ROCKY V (1990)
RODNIK DLIA ZHAZHDUSHCHIKH (SEE: SPRING FOR THE THIRSTY, A)(1988)
RODRIGO D. - NO FUTURE (1991)
RODRIGO D. - NO FUTURO (SEE: RODRIGO D. - NO FUTURE)(1991)
ROGER CORMAN'S FRANKENSTEIN UNBOUND (SEE: FRANKENSTEIN UNBOUND)(1990)
ROLLER BLADE (1986)
ROLLING STONES ROCK-AND-ROLL CIRCUS, THE (1996)
ROMANCE DA EMPREGADA (SEE: STORY OF FAUSTA)(1988)
ROMEO AND JULIET (SEE: WILLIAM SHAKESPEARE'S ROMEO + JULIET)(1996)
ROMEO IS BLEEDING (1994)
ROMERO (1989)
ROMPER STOMPER (1993)
ROOFTOPS (1989)
ROOKIE, THE (1990)
ROOKIE OF THE YEAR (1993)
ROOM WITH A VIEW, A (1986)
ROOMMATES (1995)
ROOTS OF EVIL (1992)
ROSA LUXEMBURG (1986)
ROSALIE GOES SHOPPING (1989)
ROSARY MURDERS, THE (1987)
ROSE GARDEN, THE (1989)
ROSEANNE: AN UNAUTHORIZED BIOGRAPHY (1995)
ROSENCRANTZ AND GUILDENSTERN ARE DEAD (1991)
ROSWELL: THE U.F.O. COVER-UP (1995)
ROTE OHREN SETZEN DURCH AFCHE (SEE: FLAMING EARS)(1996)
ROUGE (1990)
ROUGE BAISER (SEE: RED KISS)(1985)
ROUGE OF THE NORTH (1988)
ROUJIN-Z (1996)
ROUND MIDNIGHT (1986)
ROUND TRIP TO HEAVEN (1992)
ROVER DANGERFIELD (1992)
ROWING WITH THE WIND (1989)
ROXANNE (1987)
ROY COHN/JACK SMITH (1995)
ROYCE (1994)
RUBBERFACE (1995)
RUBIN & ED (1992)
RUBY (1992)
RUBY IN PARADISE (1993)
RUDE (1996)
RUDE AWAKENING (1989)
RUDY (1993)
RUDYARD KIPLING'S THE JUNGLE BOOK (SEE: JUNGLE BOOK, THE)(1994)
RULE #3 (1994)
RUMBLE IN THE BRONX (1996)
RUMPELSTILTSKIN (1987)
RUMPELSTILTSKIN (1996)
RUN (1991)
RUN OF THE COUNTRY, THE (1995)
RUNAWAY TRAIN (1985)
RUNAWAYS, THE (SEE: SOUTH BRONX HEROES)(1985)
RUNESTONE, THE (1992)
RUNNER, THE (1991)
RUNNING COOL (1993)
RUNNING FREE (1994)
RUNNING MAN, THE (1987)
RUNNING ON EMPTY (1988)
RUNNING OUT OF LUCK (1986)
RUNNING SCARED (1986)
RUSH (1991)
RUSH WEEK (1991)
RUSSIA HOUSE, THE (1990)
RUSSKIES (1987)
RUSTLERS' RHAPSODY (1985)
RUTANGA TAPES, THE (1991)
RUTHLESS PEOPLE (1986)
RYDER, P.I. (1986)

S

SABRINA (1995)
SABRINA, THE TEENAGE WITCH (1996)
SACRED HEARTS (1985)
SACRIFICE, THE (1986)
SADY SKORPIONA (SEE: GARDEN OF SCORPIONS)(1993)
SAFE (1995)
SAFE PASSAGE (1995)
SAIGON (SEE: OFF LIMITS)(1988)
SAIMT EL QUSUR (SEE: SILENCES OF THE PALACE, THE)(1996)
ST. ELMO'S FIRE (1985)
SAINT OF FORT WASHINGTON, THE (1993)
SAINTS AND SINNERS (1996)
SALAAM BOMBAY! (1988)
SALEM'S GHOST (SEE: WITCHCRAFT: SALEM'S GHOST)(1996)
SALMONBERRIES (1994)
SALOME (1986)
SALOME'S LAST DANCE (1988)
SALSA (1988)
SALUTE OF THE JUGGER, THE (SEE: BLOOD OF HEROES)(1990)
SALVADOR (1986)
SALVATION! (1987)
SAM & PHYLLIS (SEE: SUGARTIME)(1996)
SAM AND SARAH (1991)
SAMANTHA (1993)
SAME TO YOU (1987)
SAMMY AND ROSIE GET LAID (1987)
SAMURAI SHODOWN: THE MOTION PICTURE (1995)
SANCTUARY: THE MOVIE (1996)
SAND AND BLOOD (1989)
SANDLOT, THE (1993)
SANDMAN, THE (1996)
SANKOFA (1994)
SANS ESPOIR DE RETOUR (SEE: STREET OF NO RETURN)(1991)
SANS TOIT NI LOI (SEE: VAGABOND)(1985)
SANTA CLAUS: THE MOVIE (1985)
SANTA CLAUSE, THE (1994)
SANTA CLAWS (1996)
SANTA SANGRE (1990)
SANTA WITH MUSCLES (1996)
SARAFINA! (1992)
SARRAOUNIA (1994)
SATAN KILLER, THE (1993)
SATAN'S PRINCESS (1991)
SATIN VENGEANCE (SEE: NAKED VENGEANCE)(1986)
SATISFACTION (1988)
SATURDAY NIGHT AT THE PALACE (1987)
SATURDAY NIGHT SPECIAL (1994)
SATURDAY THE 14TH STRIKES BACK (1989)
SAVAGE BEACH (1990)
SAVAGE INSTINCT (1992)
SAVAGE ISLAND (1985)
SAVAGE LUST (1993)
SAVAGE NIGHTS (1994)
SAVE ME (1994)
SAVING GRACE (1986)
SAWBONES (1996)
SAXO (1988)
SAY ANYTHING (1989)
SAY YES (1986)
SCANDAL (1989)
SCANNER COP (1994)
SCANNER COP II: VOLKIN'S REVENGE (SEE: SCANNERS: THE SHOWDOWN)(1995)
SCANNERS: THE SHOWDOWN (1995)
SCANNERS III: THE TAKEOVER (1992)
SCANNERS II: THE NEW ORDER (1991)
SCARECROWS (1988)
SCARLET LETTER, THE (1995)
SCAVENGERS (1988)
SCENE OF THE CRIME (1986)
SCENES FROM A MALL (1991)
SCENES FROM THE CLASS STRUGGLE IN BEVERLY HILLS (1989)
SCENES FROM THE GOLDMINE (1988)
SCENT OF A WOMAN (1992)
SCENT OF GREEN PAPAYA, THE (1994)
SCHACHZUGE (SEE: KNIGHT MOVES)(1993)
SCHATTEN DER ENGEL (SEE: SHADOW OF ANGELS)(1996)
SCHINDLER'S LIST (1993)
SCHLAFES BRUDER (SEE: BROTHER OF SLEEP)(1996)
SCHOOL DAZE (1988)
SCHOOL SPIRIT (1985)
SCHOOL TIES (1992)
SCISSORS (1991)
SCORCHERS (1992)
SCORNED (1994)
SCOUT, THE (1994)
SCREAM (1996)
SCREAMERS (1996)
SCREAMPLAY (1986)
SCREAMTIME (1986)
SCREEN TEST (1986)
SCREWBALL HOTEL (1989)
SCREWFACE (SEE: MARKED FOR DEATH)(1990)
SCROOGED (1988)
SEA OF LOVE (1989)
SEARCH AND DESTROY (1995)
SEARCH FOR ONE-EYE JIMMY, THE (1996)
SEARCH FOR SIGNS OF INTELLIGENT LIFE IN THE UNIVERSE, THE (1991)
SEARCHING FOR BOBBY FISCHER (1993)
SEASON OF DREAMS (SEE: STACKING)(1987)
SEASON OF FEAR (1989)
SEBASTIAN STAR BEAR: FIRST MISSION (1993)
SECOND BEST (1994)
SECRET ADMIRER (1985)
SECRET ADVENTURES OF TOM THUMB, THE (1994)
SECRET AGENT 00-SOUL (1995)
SECRET AGENT, THE (SEE: JOSEPH CONRAD'S THE SECRET AGENT)(1996)
SECRET FRIENDS (1992)
SECRET GAMES (1992)
SECRET GAMES 2: THE ESCORT (1993)

SECRET GARDEN, THE (1993)
SECRET OF MY SUCCESS, THE (1987)
SECRET OF NIKOLA TESLA, THE (1985)
SECRET OF ROAN INISH, THE (1995)
SECRET OF THE SWORD, THE (1985)
SECRET PLACES (1985)
SECRET RAPTURE, THE (1994)
SECRETARY, THE (1995)
SECRETS & LIES (1996)
SECRETS IN THE ATTIC (1994)
SECRETS SECRETS (1985)
SECTION, THE (SEE: OUTPOST, THE)(1996)
SECUESTRO: A STORY OF A KIDNAPPING (1994)
SEDUCE ME (1994)
SEDUCED BY EVIL (1995)
SEDUCTION: THE CRUEL WOMAN (1989)
SEE NO EVIL, HEAR NO EVIL (1989)
SEE YOU IN THE MORNING (1989)
SEEDPEOPLE (1992)
SEGRETI SEGRETI (SEE: SECRETS SECRETS)(1985)
SENSATION (1995)
SENSE AND SENSIBILITY (1995)
SENSE OF FREEDOM, A (1985)
SENTIMIENTOS: MIRTA DE LINIERS A ESTAMBUL (1987)
SEPARATE LIVES (1995)
SEPARATE VACATIONS (1986)
SEPARATION (SEE: DON'T HANG UP)(1994)
SEPTEMBER (1987)
SERE CUALQUIER COSA PERO TE QUIERO (1986)
SGT. BILKO (1996)
SGT. KABUKIMAN N.Y.P.D. (1996)
SERIAL KILLER (1996)
SERIAL MOM (1994)
SERIOUS ABOUT PLEASURE (1995)
SERPENT AND THE RAINBOW, THE (1988)
SERPENT OF DEATH, THE (1991)
SERPENT'S LAIR (1996)
SERPENT'S WAY, THE (1987)
SESAME STREET PRESENTS: FOLLOW THAT BIRD (1985)
SET IT OFF (1996)
SETTA, LA (SEE: DEVIL'S DAUGHTER, THE)(1992)
SEVEN (1995)
SEVEN HOURS TO JUDGEMENT (1988)
SEVEN MINUTES IN HEAVEN (1986)
SEVENTH COIN, THE (1993)
SEVENTH SIGN, THE (1988)
SEVERED TIES (1992)
SEX AND ZEN (1993)
SEX APPEAL (1986)
SEX CRIMES (1992)
SEX, DRUGS AND DEMOCRACY (1995)
SEX, DRUGS, ROCK & ROLL (1991)
SEX, LIES, AND VIDEOTAPE (1989)
SEX O'CLOCK NEWS, THE (1986)
SEX OF THE STARS, THE (1994)
SEXUAL INTENT (1994)
SEXUAL OUTLAWS (1994)
SEXUAL RESPONSE (1992)
S.F.W. (1995)
SHADEY (1987)
SHADOW, THE (1994)
SHADOW OF ANGELS (1996)
SHADOW OF THE RAVEN, THE (1990)
SHADOW OF THE WOLF (1993)
SHADOW OF VICTORY (1986)
SHADOW PLAY (1986)
SHADOW WARRIORS (1996)
SHADOW YOU SOON WILL BE, A (1996)
SHADOWFORCE (1993)
SHADOWHUNTER (1993)
SHADOWLANDS (1993)
SHADOWS AND FOG (1992)
SHADOWS IN THE CITY (1991)
SHADOWS OF THE PEACOCK (SEE: ECHOES OF PARADISE)(1989)
SHADOWS RUN BLACK (1986)
SHADOWZONE (1990)
SHAG (1989)
SHAKEDOWN (1988)
SHAKES THE CLOWN (1992)
SHAKING THE TREE (1992)
SHALLOW GRAVE (1995)
SHAME (1988)
SHAME (1994)
SHAMELESS (1993)
SHAMELESS (1996)
SHANGHAI SURPRISE (1986)
SHANGHAI TRIAD (1995)
SHAO LIN POPEYE (1995)
SHARON'S SECRET (1996)
SHATTER DEAD (1994)
SHATTERED (1991)
SHATTERED IMAGE (1995)
SHAWSHANK REDEMPTION, THE (1994)
SHE (1985)
SHE-DEVIL (1989)
SHELTERING SKY, THE (1990)
SHERLOCK BONES, UNDERCOVER DOG (1994)
SHERLOCK: UNDERCOVER DOG (SEE: SHERLOCK BONES, UNDERCOVER DOG)(1994)
SHE'S BACK (1991)
SHE'S GOTTA HAVE IT (1986)
SHE'S HAVING A BABY (1988)
SHE'S OUT OF CONTROL (1989)
SHE'S THE ONE (1996)
SHINE (1996)
SHINING THROUGH (1992)
SHIPWRECKED (1991)
SHIRLEY VALENTINE (1989)
SHOCK 'EM DEAD (1991)
SHOCK TO THE SYSTEM, A (1990)
SHOCKER (1989)
SHOOT FOR THE SUN (1986)
SHOOT TO KILL (1988)
SHOOTFIGHTER 2: KILL OR BE KILLED! (1996)
SHOOTFIGHTER: FIGHT TO THE DEATH (1993)
SHOOTING ELIZABETH (1992)
SHOOTING PARTY, THE (1985)
SHOPPING (1996)
SHORT CIRCUIT (1986)
SHORT CIRCUIT 2 (1988)
SHORT CUTS (1993)
SHORT FILM ABOUT KILLING, A (1995)
SHORT FILM ABOUT LOVE, A (1995)
SHORT TIME (1990)
SHOT, THE (1996)
SHOUT (1991)
SHOW OF FORCE, A (1990)
SHOW, THE (1995)
SHOWDOWN (1993)
SHOWDOWN AT WILLIAMS CREEK (1991)
SHOWDOWN IN LITTLE TOKYO (1991)
SHOWGIRL MURDERS, THE (1996)
SHOWGIRLS (1995)
SHRIMP ON THE BARBIE, THE (1990)
SHRUNKEN HEADS (1994)
SHY PEOPLE (1988)
SIBAK (SEE: MIDNIGHT DANCERS)(1996)
SIBLING RIVALRY (1990)
SICILIAN, THE (1987)
SID AND NANCY (1986)
SIDE OUT (1990)
SIDEKICKS (1993)
SIDEWALK STORIES (1989)
SIESTA (1987)
SIGNE CHARLOTTE (SEE: SINCERELY CHARLOTTE)(1986)
SIGNS OF LIFE (1989)
SILENCE OF NETO, THE (1996)
SILENCE OF THE HAMS (1995)
SILENCE OF THE LAMBS, THE (1991)
SILENCER, THE (1993)
SILENCES OF THE PALACE, THE (1996)
SILENT ASSASSINS (1988)
SILENT FALL (1994)
SILENT HUNTER (1995)
SILENT NIGHT, DEADLY NIGHT 4: INITIATION (1991)
SILENT NIGHT, DEADLY NIGHT PART II (1987)
SILENT NIGHT, DEADLY NIGHT 5: THE TOY MAKER (1991)
SILENT NIGHT, DEADLY NIGHT 3: BETTER WATCH OUT! (1989)
SILENT TONGUE (1994)
SILENT TOUCH, THE (1993)
SILIP (1985)
SILK (1986)
SILK DEGREES (1994)
SILK 'N' SABOTAGE (1994)
SILK ROAD, THE (1992)
SILVER BRUMBY, THE (SEE: SILVER STALLION, THE)(1994)
SILVER CITY (1985)
SILVER STALLION, THE (1994)
SILVERADO (1985)
SILVERLAKE LIFE: THE VIEW FROM HERE (1994)
SIMPLE MEN (1992)
SIMPLE TWIST OF FATE, A (1994)
SIN VERGUENZA (SEE: SHAMELESS)(1993)
SINCERELY CHARLOTTE (1986)
SING (1989)
SINGLE GIRL, A (1996)
SINGLE WHITE FEMALE (1992)
SINGLES (1992)
SINS OF DESIRE (1993)
SINS OF THE NIGHT (1993)
SIOUX CITY (1994)
SIRENS (1994)
SISTER ACT (1992)
SISTER ACT 2: BACK IN THE HABIT (1993)
SISTER MY SISTER (1995)
SISTER OF LOVE (SEE: BAR 51--SISTER OF LOVE)(1986)
SISTER, SISTER (1988)
SISTERS (SEE: SOME GIRLS)(1989)
SIUNIN WONG FEI-HUNG TSI TITMALAU (SEE: IRON MONKEY)(1994)
SIX DAYS, SIX NIGHTS (1995)
SIX DEGREES OF SEPARATION (1993)
'68 (1988)
SIZZLE BEACH, U.S.A. (1986)
SJECAS LI SE DOLLY BELL? (SEE: DO YOU REMEBER DOLLY BELL?)(1986)
SKATEBOARD KID II, THE (1995)
SKATEBOARD KID, THE (1993)
SKEETER (1994)
SKELETON COAST (1989)
SKETCH ARTIST (1992)
SKETCH ARTIST II: HANDS THAT SEE (1995)
SKI PATROL (1990)
SKI SCHOOL (1991)
SKIN (1996)
SKIN ART (1994)
SKIN DEEP (1989)

SKINHEADS--THE SECOND COMING OF HATE (1990)
SKINNER (1995)
SKY BANDITS (1986)
SKYSCRAPER (1996)
SLACKER (1991)
SLAM DUNK ERNEST (1995)
SLAMDANCE (1987)
SLASH DANCE (1989)
SLAUGHTER HIGH (1987)
SLAUGHTER OF THE INNOCENTS (1994)
SLAUGHTERHOUSE (1988)
SLAUGHTERHOUSE ROCK (1988)
SLAVES OF NEW YORK (1989)
SLEAZY UNCLE, THE (1991)
SLEEP WITH ME (1994)
SLEEPAWAY CAMP 2: UNHAPPY CAMPERS (1988)
SLEEPAWAY CAMP 3: TEENAGE WASTELAND (1989)
SLEEPERS (1996)
SLEEPING CAR, THE (1990)
SLEEPING WITH STRANGERS (1994)
SLEEPING WITH THE ENEMY (1991)
SLEEPLESS IN SEATTLE (1993)
SLING BLADE (1996)
SLINGSHOT, THE (1994)
SLIPPING INTO DARKNESS (1989)
SLIPSTREAM (1990)
SLIVER (1993)
SLUGGER'S WIFE, THE (1985)
SLUMBER PARTY MASSACRE 3 (1992)
SLUMBER PARTY MASSACRE II (1987)
SMALL FACES (1996)
SMALL KILL (1993)
SMALL TIME (1991)
SMALL WONDERS (1996)
SMILE OF THE LAMB, THE (1986)
SMOKE (1995)
SMOOTH TALK (1985)
SMOOTH TALKER (1992)
SNAKEEATER (1989)
SNAKEEATER III . . . HIS LAW (1992)
SNAKEEATER II: THE DRUG BUSTER (1991)
SNAPPER, THE (1993)
SNEAKERS (1992)
SNIPER (1993)
SNO-LINE (1986)
SO I MARRIED AN AXE MURDERER (1993)
SOAPDISH (1991)
SOCIAL SUICIDE (SEE: PRE-MADONNAS)(1996)
SOCIETY (1992)
SODBUSTERS (1994)
SOFIA (1987)
SOFIE (1993)
SOFT KILL, THE (1994)
SOLAR CRISIS (1993)
SOLARBABIES (1986)
SOLDIER'S TALE, A (1992)
SOLDIER'S FORTUNE (1992)
SOLDIER'S REVENGE (1986)
SOLITAIRE FOR TWO (1996)
SOLO (1996)
SOME FOLKS CALL IT A SLING BLADE (1996)
SOME GIRLS (1989)
SOME KIND OF WONDERFUL (1987)
SOME MOTHER'S SON (1996)
SOMEONE ELSE'S AMERICA (1996)
SOMEONE TO LOVE (1988)
SOMEONE TO WATCH OVER ME (1987)
SOMETHING SPECIAL (1987)
SOMETHING TO DO WITH THE WALL (1991)
SOMETHING TO TALK ABOUT (1995)
SOMETHING WILD (1986)
SOMETIMES THEY COME BACK . . . AGAIN (1996)
SOMMERSBY (1993)
SON-IN-LAW (1993)
SON OF THE PINK PANTHER (SEE: BLAKE EDWARDS' SON OF THE PINK PANTHER)(1993)
SON OF THE SHARK, THE (1995)
SONDAGSBARN (SEE: SUNDAY'S CHILDREN)(1994)
SONG SPINNER, THE (1996)
SONIC OUTLAWS (1996)
SONNY BOY (1990)
SONS OF TRINITY (1996)
SORCERESS (1995)
SORORITY GIRLS AND THE CREATURES FROM HELL (1991)
SORORITY HOUSE MASSACRE (1986)
SORORITY HOUSE MASSACRE 2 (1992)
SORORITY HOUSE PARTY (1995)
SORRENTO BEACH (SEE: HOTEL SORRENTO)(1995)
SOUL MAN (1986)
SOULTAKER (1991)
SOUND AND FURY (1988)
SOURSWEET (1988)
SOUS LE SOLEIL DE SATAN (SEE: UNDER SATAN'S SUN)(1988)
SOUTH (1988)
SOUTH BEACH (1993)
SOUTH BEACH ACADEMY (1996)
SOUTH BRONX HEROES (1985)
SOUTH CENTRAL (1992)
SPACE 2074 (SEE: STAR QUEST: BEYOND THE RISING MOON)(1990)
SPACE AVENGER (1991)
SPACE JAM (1996)
SPACE RAGE (1987)
SPACEBALLS (1987)
SPACECAMP (1986)
SPACED INVADERS (1990)
SPANKING THE MONKEY (1994)
SPEAKING PARTS (1989)
SPECIALIST, THE (1994)
SPECIALMENTE LA DOMENICA (SEE: ESPECIALLY ON SUNDAY)(1993)
SPECIES (1995)
SPEECHLESS (1994)
SPEED (1994)
SPEED ZONE (1989)
SPELLBINDER (1988)
SPELLBREAKER: SECRET OF THE LEPRECHAUNS (1996)
SPIDER & ROSE (1996)
SPIDER AND THE FLY, THE (1994)
SPIES LIKE US (1985)
SPIKE AND MIKE'S FESTIVAL OF ANIMATION '95 (1995)
SPIKE OF BENSONHURST (1988)
SPIKER (1986)
SPIRIT OF THE EAGLE (1991)
SPIRITS (1992)
SPIRIT OF '76, THE (1991)
SPITFIRE (1995)
SPITFIRE GRILL, THE (1996)
SPLIT DECISIONS (1988)
SPLIT SECOND (1992)
SPLITTING HEIRS (1993)
SPONTANEOUS COMBUSTION (1990)
SPOORLOOS (SEE: VANISHING, THE)(1991)
SPOTSWOOD (SEE: EFFICIENCY EXPERT, THE)(1992)
SPRING FOR THE THIRSTY, A (1988)
SPY HARD (1996)
SPY WITHIN, THE (1995)
SPY WITHIN, THE (SEE: FLIGHT OF THE DOVE)(1995)
SQUAMISH FIVE, THE (1988)
SQUANDERERS, THE (SEE: RED LINE)(1996)
SQUANTO: A WARRIOR'S TALE (1994)
SQUARE DANCE (1987)
SQUEEZE, THE (1987)
STACKING (1987)
STAKEOUT (1987)
STALINGRAD (1995)
STAMMHEIM (1986)
STAND ALONE (1985)
STAND AND DELIVER (1988)
STAND BY ME (1986)
STAND-IN, THE (1985)
STAND OFF, THE (1996)
STANLEY AND IRIS (1990)
STANNO TUTTI BENE (SEE: EVERYBODY'S FINE)(1991)
STAR CRYSTAL (1986)
STAR MAKER, THE (1996)
STAR QUEST: BEYOND THE RISING MOON (1990)
STAR SLAMMER: THE ESCAPE (1988)
STAR TREK IV: THE VOYAGE HOME (1986)
STAR TREK V: THE FINAL FRONTIER (1989)
STAR TREK VI: THE UNDISCOVERED COUNTRY (1991)
STAR TREK: GENERATIONS (1994)
STAR TREK: FIRST CONTACT (1996)
STARCHASER: THE LEGEND OF ORIN (1985)
STARGATE (1994)
STARLIGHT HOTEL (1987)
STARS AND BARS (1988)
STARS FELL ON HENRIETTA, THE (1995)
STATE OF GRACE (1990)
STATIC (1985)
STATION, THE (1992)
STAY TUNED (1992)
STAYING TOGETHER (1989)
STAZIONE, LA (SEE: STATION, THE)(1992)
STEAL AMERICA (1992)
STEAL BIG, STEAL LITTLE (1995)
STEALING BEAUTY (1996)
STEALING HEAVEN (1989)
STEALING HOME (1988)
STEAMING (1985)
STEEL AND LACE (1991)
STEEL DAWN (1987)
STEEL FRONTIER (1995)
STEEL MAGNOLIAS (1989)
STEELE JUSTICE (1987)
STEELE'S LAW (1992)
STEFANO QUANTESTORIE (1994)
STELLA (1990)
STEPFATHER, THE (1987)
STEPFATHER 2: MAKE ROOM FOR DADDY (1989)
STEPHEN KING'S SOMETIMES THEY COME BACK (1991)
STEPHEN KING'S GRAVEYARD SHIFT (SEE: GRAVEYARD SHIFT)(1990)
STEPHEN KING'S SILVER BULLET (1985)
STEPHEN KING'S SLEEPWALKERS (1992)
STEPHEN KING'S THINNER (1996)
STEPMONSTER (1993)
STEPPING OUT (1991)
STEPPING RAZOR - RED X (1993)
STEWARDESS SCHOOL (1986)
STICK (1985)
STICKY FINGERS (1988)
STILL LIFE: THE FINE ART OF MURDER (1993)
STITCHES (1985)
STOLEN CHILDREN, THE (1993)

STONE COLD (1991)
STONED AGE, THE (1994)
STONEWALL (1996)
STOOGEMANIA (1986)
STOP! OR MY MOM WILL SHOOT (1992)
STORIA DI RAGAZZI E DI RAGAZZE (SEE: STORY OF BOYS AND GIRLS)(1991)
STORM (1989)
STORMS OF AUGUST, THE (1988)
STORMY MONDAY (1988)
STORMYYD AWST (SEE: STORMS OF AUGUST, THE)(1988)
STORY OF BOYS AND GIRLS (1991)
STORY OF FAUSTA, THE (1988)
STORY OF QIU JU, THE (1993)
STORY OF WOMEN (1989)
STORY OF XINGHUA, THE (1996)
STORYVILLE (1992)
STRAIGHT OUT OF BROOKLYN (1991)
STRAIGHT TALK (1992)
STRAIGHT THROUGH THE HEART (1985)
STRAIGHT TO HELL (1987)
STRAIGHT TO THE HEART (1988)
STRANDED (1987)
STRANGE DAYS (1995)
STRANGER, THE (1987)
STRANGER AMONG US, A (1992)
STRANGER BY NIGHT (1994)
STRANGER THINGS (SEE: FOR BETTER OR WORSE)(1996)
STRANGER, THE (1995)
STRANGERS IN GOOD COMPANY (1991)
STRANGLEHOLD (1994)
STRAPLESS (1989)
STRAWBERRY AND CHOCOLATE (1995)
STREET ASYLUM (1990)
STREET CRIMES (1992)
STREET FIGHTER (1994)
STREET FIGHTER II: THE ANIMATED MOVIE (1996)
STREET HUNTER (1991)
STREET JUSTICE (1989)
STREET KNIGHT (1993)
STREET LEGAL (SEE: LAST OF THE FINEST)(1990)
STREET OF NO RETURN (1991)
STREET SMART (1987)
STREET SOLDIERS (1991)
STREET STORY (1988)
STREET TRASH (1987)
STREET WARS (1994)
STREETCAR NAMED DESIRE, A (1996)
STREETS (1990)
STREETS OF GOLD (1986)
STREETS OF LAREDO (SEE: LARRY MCMURTRY'S STREETS OF LAREDO)(1996)
STREETWALKIN' (1985)
STRICTLY BALLROOM (1993)
STRICTLY BUSINESS (1991)
STRICTLY PROPAGANDA (1993)
STRIKE IT RICH (1990)
STRIKING DISTANCE (1993)
STRIKING POINT (1995)
STRIPPED TO KILL (1987)
STRIPPED TO KILL II: LIVE GIRLS (1989)
STRIPPER (1986)
STRIPTEASE (1996)
STRIPTEASER (1995)
STROKE OF MIDNIGHT (1991)
STUART SAVES HIS FAMILY (1995)
STUFF STEPHANIE IN THE INCINERATOR (1990)
STUFF, THE (1985)
STUPIDS, THE (1996)
SUBSPECIES (1991)
SUBSTANCE OF FIRE, THE (1996)
SUBSTITUTE WIFE, THE (1995)
SUBSTITUTE, THE (1996)
SUBSTITUTE, THE (SEE: SUBSTITUTE WIFE, THE)(1995)
SUBURBAN COMMANDO (1991)
SUBWAY (1985)
SUCCESSFUL MAN, A (1987)
SUDDEN DEATH (1985)
SUDDEN DEATH (1995)
SUGAR HILL (1994)
SUGARBABY (1985)
SUGARTIME (1996)
SUICIDE CLUB, THE (1988)
SUITE 16 (1996)
SUM OF US, THE (1995)
SUMMER (1986)
SUMMER (1988)
SUMMER CAMP (SEE: PIG'S TALE, A)(1996)
SUMMER CAMP NIGHTMARE (1987)
SUMMER HEAT (1987)
SUMMER HOUSE, THE (1993)
SUMMER RENTAL (1985)
SUMMER SCHOOL (1987)
SUMMER STORY, A (1988)
SUMMER VACATION: 1999 (1990)
SUNCHASER (1996)
SUNDAY'S CHILDREN (1994)
SUNDOWN: THE VAMPIRE IN RETREAT (1991)
SUNSET (1988)
SUNSET GRILL (1993)
SUNSET PARK (1996)
SUNSET STRIP (1985)
SUNSET STRIP (1992)
SUPER MARIO BROS. (1993)
SUPER, THE (1991)
SUPERCOP (1992)
SUPERFANTAGENIO (SEE: ALADDIN)(1987)
SUPERMAN IV: THE QUEST FOR PEACE (1987)
SUPERNATURALS, THE (1987)
SUPERSTAR: THE LIFE AND TIMES OF ANDY WARHOL (1991)
SUPERSTITION (1985)
SUR (SEE: SOUTH)(1988)
SUR LA TERRE COMME AU CIEL (SEE: BETWEEN HEAVEN AND EARTH)(1993)
SURE FIRE (1994)
SURE THING, THE (1985)
SURF NAZIS MUST DIE (1987)
SURF NINJAS (1993)
SURGEON, THE (1996)
SURPRISE PARTY (1985)
SURRENDER (1987)
SURVIVAL QUEST (1990)
SURVIVING PICASSO (1996)
SURVIVING THE GAME (1994)
SUSPECT (1987)
SUTURE (1994)
SWAN LAKE - THE ZONE (1991)
SWAN PRINCESS, THE (1994)
SWEEPER, THE (1996)
SWEET COUNTRY (1987)
SWEET DREAMS (1985)
SWEET HEARTS DANCE (1988)
SWEET JUSTICE (1993)
SWEET KILLING (1993)
SWEET LIBERTY (1986)
SWEET LIES (1989)
SWEET LORRAINE (1987)
SWEET MURDER (1993)
SWEET NOTHING (1996)
SWEET REVENGE (1987)
SWEET TALKER (1991)
SWEETIE (1989)
SWIMMER, THE (1988)
SWIMMING TO CAMBODIA (1987)
SWIMMING WITH SHARKS (1995)
SWING KIDS (1993)
SWINGERS (1996)
SWITCH (1991)
SWITCHING CHANNELS (1988)
SWOON (1992)
SWORD OF HEAVEN (1985)
SWORD OF HONOR (1994)
SWORDSMAN, THE (1993)
SYLVESTER (1985)
SYLVIA (1985)
SYNTHETIC PLEASURES (1996)
SZAMARKOHOGES (SEE: WHOOPING COUGH)(1987)
SZERELEM ELSO VERIG (SEE: LOVE TILL FIRST BLOOD)(1985)

T

ABDUCTED 2: THE REUNION (1995)
BAD MOON (1996)
T-FORCE (1995)
T2 (SEE: TERMINATOR 2: JUDGEMENT DAY)(1991)
TACONES LEJANOS (SEE: HIGH HEELS)(1991)
TAFFIN (1988)
TAI-PAN (1986)
TAILS YOU LIVE, HEADS YOU'RE DEAD (1996)
TAKEOVER, THE (1996)
TAKING CARE OF BUSINESS (1990)
TAKING OF BEVERLY HILLS, THE (1991)
TAKING THE HEAT (1994)
TALE OF GENJI, THE (1995)
TALE OF RUBY ROSE, THE (1987)
TALE OF SPRINGTIME, A (1992)
TALE OF WINTER, A (1994)
TALENT FOR THE GAME (1991)
TALES FROM THE CRYPT: DEMON KNIGHT (1995)
TALES FROM THE CRYPT PRESENTS BORDELLO OF BLOOD (1996)
TALES FROM THE DARKSIDE: THE MOVIE (1990)
TALES FROM THE HOOD (1995)
TALES OF EROTICA (1996)
TALES OF THE THIRD DIMENSION (1985)
TALK RADIO (1988)
TALKIN' DIRTY AFTER DARK (1991)
TALKING ABOUT SEX (1996)
TALKING TO STRANGERS (1988)
TALKING WALLS (1987)
TALL GUY, THE (1989)
TALL TALE: THE UNBELIEVABLE ADVENTURES OF PECOS BILL (1995)
TALONS OF THE EAGLE (1992)
TALVISOTA (1989)
TAMMY AND THE T-REX (1994)
TAMPOPO (1986)
TANGO AND CASH (1989)
TANGO BAR (1989)
TANK GIRL (1995)
TAP (1989)
TAPEHEADS (1988)
TARGET (1985)
TARGET (1996)
TAROT (1986)
TATIE DANIELLE (1991)
TATTOO BOY (1996)
TATTOO CONNECTION, THE (1994)
TAX SEASON (1990)

TAXI BLUES (1991)
TAXI DANCERS (1993)
TAXING WOMAN, A (1988)
TAXING WOMAN'S RETURN, A (1988)
TC 2000 (1993)
TEA IN THE HAREM OF ARCHIMEDE (1985)
TEARS IN THE RAIN (1994)
TED & VENUS (1991)
TEEN WITCH (1989)
TEEN WOLF (1985)
TEEN WOLF TOO (1987)
TEENAGE EXORCIST (1994)
TEENAGE MUTANT NINJA TURTLES (1990)
TEENAGE MUTANT NINJA TURTLES III (1993)
TEENAGE MUTANT NINJA TURTLES II: THE SECRET OF THE OOZE (1991)
TEKWAR (1995)
TELEPHONE, THE (1988)
TEMECULA (SEE: WEEKEND IN THE COUNTRY, A)(1996)
TEMP, THE (1993)
TEMPO DI UCCIDERE (SEE: TIME TO KILL)(1991)
TEMPOS DIFICEIS (SEE: HARD TIMES)(1988)
TEMPTATION (1994)
TEMPTATION OF A MONK, THE (1994)
TEMPTRESS (1995)
TEN LITTLE INDIANS (1990)
TENANTS, THE (1991)
TENDERFOOT, THE (SEE: BUSHWHACKED)(1995)
TEQUILA SUNRISE (1988)
TERESA'S TATTOO (1995)
TERMINAL BLISS (1992)
TERMINAL CHOICE (1985)
TERMINAL IMPACT (1996)
TERMINAL VELOCITY (1994)
TERMINATOR 2: JUDGMENT DAY (1991)
TERMINI STATION (1991)
TERROR AT THE OPERA (1991)
TERROR IN BEVERLY HILLS (1991)
TERROR WITHIN, THE (1989)
TERROR WITHIN II, THE (1991)
TERRORGRAM (1991)
TERRORVISION (1986)
TEST OF LOVE (SEE: ANNIE'S COMING OUT)(1985)
TESTAMENT (1988)
TETSUO: THE IRON MAN (1992)
TEXAS CHAINSAW MASSACRE PART 2, THE (1986)
TEXAS CHAINSAW MASSACRE: THE NEXT GENERATION (1996)
TEXAS PAYBACK (1996)
TEXAS TENOR: THE ILLINOIS JACQUET STORY (1992)
TEXASVILLE (1990)
THANK YOU AND GOOD NIGHT! (1992)
THAT NIGHT (1993)
THAT THING YOU DO! (1996)
THAT WAS THEN. . . THIS IS NOW (1985)
THAT'S ENTERTAINMENT! PART III (1994)
THAT'S LIFE! (1986)
THELMA & LOUISE (1991)
THEODORE REX (1996)
THERE GOES MY BABY (1995)
THERE GOES THE NEIGHBORHOOD (1993)
THEREMIN: AN ELECTRONIC ODYSSEY (1996)
THERE'S NOTHING OUT THERE (1992)
THERESE (1986)
THESE FOOLISH THINGS (SEE: DADDY NOSTALGIA)(1991)
THEY BITE (1996)
THEY LIVE (1988)
THEY STILL CALL ME BRUCE (1987)
THEY WATCH (1994)
THIEVES (SEE: LES VOLEURS)(1996)
THIN LINE BETWEEN LOVE AND HATE, A (1996)
THING CALLED LOVE, THE (1993)
THINGS CHANGE (1988)
THINGS TO DO IN DENVER WHEN YOU'RE DEAD (1995)
THINK BIG (1990)
35 UP (1992)
36 FILLETTE (1988)
THIRTY-TWO SHORT FILMS ABOUT GLENN GOULD (1994)
THIS BOY'S LIFE (1993)
THIS IS MY LIFE (1992)
THOUSAND HEROES, A (1994)
THOUSAND PIECES OF GOLD (1991)
THRASHIN' (1986)
THREE AMIGOS (1986)
THREE COLORS: BLUE (SEE: BLUE)(1993)
THREE COLORS: RED (SEE: RED)(1994)
THREE COLORS: WHITE (SEE: WHITE)(1994)
3:15, THE MOMENT OF TRUTH (1986)
THREE FOR THE ROAD (1987)
THREE FUGITIVES (1989)
THREE IFS AND A MAYBE (SEE: BIG SQUEEZE, THE)(1996)
THREE LIVES AND ONLY ONE DEATH (1996)
3 MEN AND A BABY (1987)
THREE MEN AND A CRADLE (1985)
3 MEN AND A LITTLE LADY (1990)
THREE MUSKETEERS, THE (1993)
3 NINJAS (1992)
3 NINJAS KICK BACK (1994)
3 NINJAS KNUCKLE UP (1995)
THREE O'CLOCK HIGH (1987)
THREE OF HEARTS (1993)
THREE WISHES (1995)
THREEPENNY OPERA, THE (SEE: MACK THE KNIFE)(1990)
THREESOME (1994)
THROUGH THE OLIVE TREES (1995)
THROW MOMMA FROM THE TRAIN (1987)
THUMBELINA (SEE: HANS CHRISTIAN ANDERSEN'S THUMBELINA)(1994)
THUNDER IN PARADISE 2 (1994)
THUNDER RUN (1986)
THUNDER WARRIOR (1986)
THUNDERHEART (1992)
TICKET (1987)
TICKS (1994)
TIDES OF WAR (1994)
TIE-DIED: ROCK 'N' ROLL'S MOST DEADICATED FANS (1995)
TIE ME UP! TIE ME DOWN! (1990)
TIE THAT BINDS, THE (1995)
TIGER CLAWS (1992)
TIGER HEART (1996)
TIGER WARSAW (1988)
TIGER'S TALE, A (1988)
TIGRERO: A FILM THAT WAS NEVER MADE (1994)
TIGRESS (1993)
TILL MURDER DO US PART (1994)
TILL THERE WAS YOU (1992)
TIM BURTON'S THE NIGHTMARE BEFORE CHRISTMAS (1993)
TIME AFTER TIME (1985)
TIME BOMB (1991)
TIME GUARDIAN, THE (1990)
TIME INDEFINITE (1993)
TIME OF DESTINY, A (1988)
TIME OF THE GYPSIES (1990)
TIME RUNNER (1993)
TIME TO DIE, A (1985)
TIME TO DIE, A (1991)
TIME TO KILL (1991)
TIME TO KILL, A (1996)
TIME TRACKERS (1989)
TIME TROOPERS (1990)
TIMECOP (1994)
TIMELESS (1996)
TIN CUP (1996)
TIN MEN (1987)
TIN SOLDIER, THE (1995)
TINA: WHAT'S LOVE GOT TO DO WITH IT (SEE: WHAT'S LOVE GOT TO DO WITH IT)(1993)
TITAN FIND (SEE: CREATURE)(1985)
TITO AND ME (1993)
TITO I YA (SEE: TITO AND ME)(1993)
TO BE THE BEST (1993)
TO CATCH A YETI (1995)
TO CROSS THE RUBICON (1995)
TO DENDRO POU PLIGONAME (SEE: TREE WE HURT, THE)(1987)
TO DIE FOR (1989)
TO DIE FOR (1995)
TO DIE FOR 2: SON OF DARKNESS (1991)
TO GILLIAN ON HER 37TH BIRTHDAY (1996)
TO GRANDMOTHER'S HOUSE WE GO (1995)
TO KILL A PRIEST (1989)
TO KILL A STRANGER (1985)
TO LIVE (1994)
TO LIVE AND DIE IN L.A. (1985)
TO PROTECT AND SERVE (1992)
TO RENDER A LIFE (1992)
TO SLEEP WITH A VAMPIRE (1993)
TO SLEEP WITH ANGER (1990)
TO THE DEATH (1993)
TO THE LIMIT (1995)
TO THE LIMIT (SEE: SIX DAYS, SIX NIGHTS)(1995)
TO WONG FOO, THANKS FOR EVERYTHING! JULIE NEWMAR (1995)
TOBE HOOPER'S NIGHT TERRORS (1995)
TOBY MCTEAGUE (1986)
TOGETHER ALONE (1992)
TOKYO DECADENCE (1993)
TOKYO POP (1988)
TOLLBOOTH (1996)
TOM AND HUCK (1995)
TOM AND JERRY - THE MOVIE (1993)
TOM & VIV (1994)
TOMB, THE (1986)
TOMBOY (1985)
TOMBSTONE (1993)
TOMCAT: DANGEROUS DESIRES (1993)
TOMMY BOY (1995)
TONARI NO TOTORO (SEE: MY NEIGHBOR TOTORO)(1993)
TONG TANA - A JOURNEY TO THE HEART OF BORNEO (1991)
TOO BEAUTIFUL FOR YOU (1989)
TOO FAST, TOO YOUNG (1996)
TOO MUCH SUN (1991)
TOO OUTRAGEOUS ANIMATION (1995)
TOO SCARED TO SCREAM (1985)
TOO YOUNG TO DIE? (1995)
TOP DOG (1995)
TOP GUN (1986)
TORA-SAN GOES TO VIENNA (1989)
TORCH SONG TRILOGY (1988)
TORMENT (1986)
TORN APART (1990)
TORRENTS OF SPRING (1990)
TOTAL ECLIPSE (1995)
TOTAL EXPOSURE (1991)
TOTAL RECALL (1990)

TOTO LE HEROS (1992)
TOUCH AND DIE (1992)
TOUCH AND GO (1986)
TOUCH OF A STRANGER (1990)
TOUGH AND DEADLY (1995)
TOUGH GUYS (1986)
TOUGH GUYS DON'T DANCE (1987)
TOUGHER THAN LEATHER (1988)
TOUR OF DUTY (SEE: BREACH OF CONDUCT)(1995)
TOUS LES MATINS DU MONDE (1992)
TOWARD THE TERRA (1995)
TOXIC AVENGER, THE (1985)
TOXIC AVENGER, PART II, THE (1989)
TOXIC AVENGER PART III: THE LAST TEMPTATION OF TOXIE, THE (1989)
TOY SOLDIERS (1991)
TOY STORY (1995)
TOYS (1992)
TRACES OF RED (1992)
TRACK 29 (1988)
TRACKS OF A KILLER (1996)
TRADING HEARTS (1988)
TRADING MOM (1994)
TRAIN OF DREAMS (1987)
TRAINED TO FIGHT (1992)
TRAINED TO KILL (1994)
TRAINSPOTTING (1996)
TRANCERS (1985)
TRANCERS 5: SUDDEN DETH (1994)
TRANCERS III: DETH LIVES (1992)
TRANCERS II: THE RETURN OF JACK DETH (1991)
TRANSFORMERS: THE MOVIE, THE (1986)
TRANSYLVANIA 6-5000 (1985)
TRANSYLVANIA TWIST (1989)
TRAPPED IN PARADISE (1994)
TRAPPED IN SPACE (1994)
TRAPS (1995)
TRAUMA (1994)
TRAVELLING AVANT (1988)
TRAVELLING NORTH (1988)
TRAXX (1988)
TREACHEROUS (1994)
TREASURE OF THE AMAZON, THE (1985)
TREE OF HANDS, THE (SEE: INNOCENT VICTIM)(1990)
TREE WE HURT, THE (1986)
TREES LOUNGE (1996)
TREMORS (1990)
TREMORS 2: AFTERSHOCKS (1996)
TRESPASS (1992)
TRIAL BY JURY (1994)
TRIAL, THE (1993)
TRIBULATION 99: ALIEN ANOMALIES UNDER AMERICA (1991)
TRICK OR TREAT (1986)
TRIGGER EFFECT, THE (1996)
TRIGGER FAST (1994)
TRIGGER HAPPY (SEE: MAD DOG TIME)(1996)
TRIP TO BOUNTIFUL, THE (1985)
TRIPLE IMPACT (1993)
TRIUMPH OF THE SPIRIT (1989)
TROIS COULEURS: BLANC (SEE: WHITE)(1994)
TROIS COULEURS: BLEU (SEE: BLUE)(1993)
TROIS COULEURS: ROUGE (SEE: RED)(1994)
TROLL (1986)
TROLL 3 (SEE: CRAWLERS, THE)(1994)
TROLL IN CENTRAL PARK, A (1994)
TROLL 2 (1992)
TROOP BEVERLY HILLS (1989)
TROP BELLE POUR TOI (SEE: TOO BEAUTIFUL FOR YOU)(1990)
TROPICAL HEAT (1993)
TROUBLE BOUND (1993)
TROUBLE IN MIND (1985)
TROUBLE WITH DICK, THE (1987)
TROUBLEMAKERS (1995)
TRUE BELIEVER (1989)
TRUE BLOOD (1989)
TRUE COLORS (1991)
TRUE CRIME (1995)
TRUE IDENTITY (1991)
TRUE LIES (1994)
TRUE LOVE (1989)
TRUE ROMANCE (1993)
TRUE STORIES (1986)
TRULY, MADLY, DEEPLY (1991)
TRUMAN (1996)
TRUST (1991)
TRUST ME (1989)
TRUST ME (1995)
TRUSTING BEATRICE (1993)
TRUTH ABOUT CATS AND DOGS, THE (1996)
TRUTH OR DARE (1991)
TRYST (1994)
TUCKER: THE MAN AND HIS DREAM (1988)
TUFF TURF (1985)
TULITIKKUTEHTAAN TYTTO (SEE: MATCH FACTORY GIRL, THE)(1992)
TUNE IN TOMORROW (1990)
TUNE, THE (1992)
TUNNEL VISION (1996)
TURK 182! (1985)
TURN OF THE SCREW (1985)
TURNER & HOOCH (1989)
TURTLE DIARY (1985)
TUSKEGEE AIRMEN, THE (1996)
TUSKS (1990)
TWEENERS (SEE: TRADING HEARTS)(1988)
TWELFTH NIGHT (1996)
TWELVE MONKEYS (1995)
TWENTY BUCKS (1993)
TWENTY DOLLAR STAR (1991)
24 HOURS TO MIDNIGHT (1992)
24TH INTERNATIONAL TOURNEE OF ANIMATION, THE (1994)
29TH STREET (1991)
TWENTY-ONE (1991)
TWENTY SOMETHING (1995)
TWICE DEAD (1989)
TWICE IN A LIFETIME (1985)
TWILIGHT OF THE COCKROACHES (1990)
TWIN PEAKS: FIRE WALK WITH ME (1992)
TWIN SISTERS (1992)
TWIN SITTERS (1995)
TWINS (1988)
TWIST (1993)
TWISTED (1991)
TWISTED JUSTICE (1990)
TWISTED OBSESSION (1990)
TWISTER (1989)
TWISTER (1996)
TWO-BITS & PEPPER (1996)
2 DAYS IN THE VALLEY (1996)
TWO DEATHS (1996)
TWO EVIL EYES (1990)
TWO FRIENDS (1996)
TWO GUYS TALKIN' ABOUT GIRLS (SEE: . . . AT FIRST SIGHT)(1996)
TWO IF BY SEA (1996)
TWO JAKES, THE (1990)
TWO LIVES OF MATTIA PASCAL, THE (1985)
TWO MOON JUNCTION (1988)
TWO MUCH (1996)
TWO SMALL BODIES (1994)
2020 TEXAS GLADIATORS (1985)
2002: THE RAPE OF EDEN (1994)
TWO TO TANGO (1989)
TWOGETHER (1995)
TYSON (1995)

U

UCHO (SEE: EAR, THE)(1992)
UFORIA (1985)
UHF (1989)
ULTERIOR MOTIVES (1993)
ULTIMATE DESIRES (1992)
ULTRAVIOLET (1992)
UMBRELLA WOMAN, THE (SEE: GOOD WIFE, THE)(1986)
UN COEUR EN HIVER (1993)
UN ETE INOUBLIABLE (SEE: UNFORGETTABLE SUMMER, AN)(1994)
UN HOMBRE DE EXITO (SEE: SUCCESSFUL MAN, A)(1987)
UN HOMBRE VIOLENTE (1986)
UN HOMME AMOUREUX (SEE: MAN IN LOVE, A)(1987)
UN HOMME ET UNE FEMME: VINGT ANS DEJA (SEE: MAN AND A WOMAN: 20 YEARS LATER, A)(1986)
UN INDIEN DAN LA VILLE (SEE: LITTLE INDIAN, BIG CITY)(1996)
UN LUGAR EN EL MUNDO (SEE: PLACE IN THE WORLD, A)(1994)
UN MONDE SANS PITIE (SEE: LOVE WITHOUT PITY)(1991)
UN PASAJE DE IDA (SEE: ONE-WAY TICKET, A)(1988)
UN WEEK-END SUR DEUX (SEE: EVERY OTHER WEEKEND)(1991)
UN ZOO LA NUIT (SEE: NIGHT ZOO)(1987)
UNA SOMBRA YA PRONTO SERAS (SEE: SHADOW YOU SOON WILL BE, A)(1996)
UNBEARABLE LIGHTNESS OF BEING, THE (1988)
UNBELIEVABLE TRUTH, THE (1990)
UNBORN II, THE (1994)
UNBORN, THE (1991)
UNCLE BUCK (1989)
UNCONSCIOUS (SEE: FEAR)(1986)
UNDER COVER (1987)
UNDER LOCK AND KEY (1995)
UNDER SATAN'S SUN (1988)
UNDER SIEGE (1992)
UNDER SIEGE 2: DARK TERRITORY (1995)
UNDER SUSPICION (1992)
UNDER THE BOARDWALK (1990)
UNDER THE CHERRY MOON (1986)
UNDER THE DOMIM TREE (1996)
UNDER THE GUN (1989)
UNDER THE HULA MOON (1996)
UNDERCOVER (1995)
UNDERCOVER BLUES (1993)
UNDERCOVER COP (1994)
UNDERNEATH, THE (1995)
UNDERSTUDY: GRAVEYARD SHIFT 2, THE (1996)
UNDERTOW (1996)
UNDYING LOVE (1991)
UNE FLAME DANS MON COEUR (SEE: FLAME IN MY HEART, A)(1990)
UNE NOUVELLE VIE (SEE: NEW LIFE, A)(1996)
UNEARTHING, THE (1994)
UNFAITHFUL (SEE: IN THE HEAT OF PASSION 2: UNFAITHFUL)(1994)
UNFINISHED BUSINESS (1985)
UNFINISHED BUSINESS. . . (1987)
UNFORGETTABLE (1996)
UNFORGETTABLE SUMMER, AN (1994)
UNFORGIVEN (1992)
UNHOLY, THE (1988)

UNHOOK THE STARS (1996)
UNINVITED, THE (1988)
UNINVITED (1993)
UNIVERSAL SOLDIER (1992)
UNKNOWN ORIGIN (1996)
UNLAWFUL ENTRY (1992)
UNNAMABLE II, THE (1993)
UNNAMABLE, THE (1988)
UNREMARKABLE LIFE, AN (1989)
UNSTRUNG HEROES (1995)
UNTAMED HEART (1993)
UNTERGANGENS ARKITEKTUR (SEE: ARCHITECTURE OF DOOM)(1991)
UNTIL THE END OF THE WORLD (1991)
UNTOUCHABLES, THE (1987)
UNVEILED (1994)
UNZIPPED (1995)
UP CLOSE AND PERSONAL (1996)
UP TO A CERTAIN POINT (1995)
UPHILL ALL THE WAY (1986)
URAMISTEN (SEE: PHILADELPHIA ATTRACTION, THE)(1985)
URANUS (1991)
URBAN CROSSFIRE (1994)
URGA (SEE: CLOSE TO EDEN)(1992)
UROTSUKIDOJI (SEE: LEGEND OF THE OVERFIEND)(1993)
USED PEOPLE (1992)
USUAL SUSPECTS, THE (1995)
UTZ (1993)

V

VACAS (SEE: COWS)(1994)
VAGABOND (1985)
VAGRANT, THE (1992)
VALENTINO RETURNS (1989)
VALET GIRLS (1987)
VALHALLA (1986)
VALLEY OF ABRAHAM, THE (1995)
VALMONT (1989)
VALS, THE (1985)
VAMP (1986)
VAMPIRE HUNTER D (1992)
VAMPIRE IN BROOKLYN (1995)
VAMPIRES AND OTHER STEREOTYPES (1995)
VAMPIRES IN HAVANA (1985)
VAMPIRE'S KISS (1989)
VAN GOGH (1992)
VANISHING, THE (1991)
VANISHING, THE (1993)
VANYA ON 42ND STREET (1994)
VASECTOMY: A DELICATE MATTER (1986)
VEGAS IN SPACE (1993)
VENDETTA (1986)
VENICE/VENICE (1992)
VENUS RISING (1996)
VERA (1987)
VERBRECHEN AM SEELENLEBEN EINES MENSCHENS (SEE: KASPAR HAUSER)(1996)
VERNE MILLER (1988)
VERONICO CRUZ (1990)
VERRIEGELTE ZEIT (SEE: LOCKED-UP TIME)(1992)
VERY BRADY SEQUEL, A (1996)
VERY CLOSE QUARTERS (1986)
VESNICKO MA STREDISKOVA (SEE: MY SWEET LITTLE VILLAGE)(1985)
V.I. WARSHAWSKI (1991)
VIA APPIA (1991)
VIBRATIONS (1995)
VICE ACADEMY (1989)
VICE ACADEMY PART 2 (1990)
VICE ACADEMY III (1991)
VICE VERSA (1988)
VICOLI E DELITTI (SEE: CAMORRA)(1986)
VICTIM OF DESIRE (1995)
VICTOR ONE (SEE: UNDERCOVER COP)(1994)
VIDEO DEAD (1987)
VIEW TO A KILL, A (1985)
VIKING SAGAS, THE (1996)
VILLA DEL VENERDI, LA (SEE: HUSBANDS AND LOVERS)(1992)
VILLAGE OF THE DAMNED (1995)
VILLE ETRANGERE (SEE: FOREIGN CITY, A)(1988)
VINCENT AND THEO (1990)
VINDICATOR (SEE: DESERT WARRIOR)(1985)
VIOLATED (1986)
VIOLENT BREED, THE (1986)
VIOLETS ARE BLUE (1986)
VIRGIN HIGH (1991)
VIRGIN QUEEN OF ST. FRANCIS HIGH, THE (1987)
VIRTUAL ASSASSIN (1995)
VIRTUAL COMBAT (1996)
VIRTUAL ENCOUNTERS (1996)
VIRTUOSITY (1995)
VIRUS (1996)
VIRUS KNOWS NO MORALS, A (1986)
VISA U.S.A. (1987)
VISION QUEST (1985)
VISIONS OF LIGHT: THE ART OF CINEMATOGRAPHY (1993)
VISITORS, THE (1996)
VISSZASZAMLALAS (SEE: COUNTDOWN)(1985)
VITAL SIGNS (1990)
VIVE L'AMOUR (1996)
VLCI BOUDA (SEE: WOLF'S HOLE)(1987)
VOICES FROM THE FRONT (1992)
VOLERE VOLARE (1993)
VOLUNTEERS (1985)
VOODOO DAWN (1991)
VOW TO KILL, A (1995)
VOYAGE EN DOUCE (1995)
VOYAGER (1992)
VOYEUR, THE (1994)
VROEGER IS DOOD (SEE: BYGONES)(1988)
VUKOVAR (1996)
VUKOVAR POSTE RESTANTE (SEE: VUKOVAR)(1996)

W

WAGONS EAST! (1994)
WAIT FOR ME IN HEAVEN (1988)
WAIT UNTIL SPRING, BANDINI (1991)
WAITING FOR THE MOON (1987)
WAITING TO EXHALE (1995)
WALK IN THE CLOUDS, A (1995)
WALK LIKE A MAN (1987)
WALK ON THE MOON, A (1987)
WALKER (1987)
WALKING AND TALKING (1996)
WALKING DEAD, THE (1995)
WALKING ON WATER (SEE: STAND AND DELIVER)(1988)
WALKING THE EDGE (1985)
WALL STREET (1987)
WALLACE AND GROMIT: THE BEST OF AARDMAN ANIMATION (1996)
WALTZING REGITZE (1991)
WANNSEE CONFERENCE, THE (1987)
WANTED: DEAD OR ALIVE (1987)
WAR AND LOVE (1985)
WAR AT HOME, THE (1996)
WAR BIRDS (1989)
WAR OF THE BUTTONS, THE (1996)
WAR OF THE ROSES, THE (1989)
WAR PARTY (1989)
WAR REQUIEM (1989)
WAR ROOM, THE (1993)
WAR ZONE (SEE: DEADLINE)(1987)
WAR, THE (1994)
WARDOGS (1987)
WARHEAD (1996)
WARLOCK (1991)
WARLOCK: THE ARMAGEDDON (1993)
WARM NIGHTS ON A SLOW MOVING TRAIN (1987)
WARM SUMMER RAIN, A (1989)
WARNING SIGN (1985)
WARRIOR QUEEN (1987)
WARRIOR SPIRIT (1995)
WARRIORS (1995)
WATCH IT (1993)
WATCH ME (1996)
WATCHERS (1988)
WATCHERS III (1994)
WATER (1985)
WATER AND SOAP (SEE: ACQUA E SAPONE)(1985)
WATER ENGINE, THE (1995)
WATERDANCE, THE (1992)
WATERLAND (1992)
WATERWORLD (1995)
WAVELENGTH (1996)
WAXWORK (1988)
WAXWORK II: LOST IN TIME (1992)
WAYNE'S WORLD (1992)
WAYNE'S WORLD 2 (1993)
WE THE LIVING (1989)
WE THINK THE WORLD OF YOU (1989)
WE THREE (1985)
WEDDING BAND (1990)
WEDDING BANQUET, THE (1993)
WEDDING GIFT, THE (1994)
WEDDING IN GALILEE (1988)
WEEDS (1987)
WEEKEND AT BERNIE'S (1989)
WEEKEND AT BERNIE'S II (1993)
WEEKEND IN THE COUNTRY, A (1996)
WEEKEND WARRIORS (1986)
WEININGER'S LAST NIGHT (1991)
WEININGERS NACHT (SEE: WEININGER'S LAST NIGHT)(1991)
WEIRD SCIENCE (1985)
WELCOME HOME (1989)
WELCOME HOME, ROXY CARMICHAEL (1990)
WELCOME IN VIENNA (1988)
WELCOME TO 18 (1986)
WELCOME TO GERMANY (1988)
WELCOME TO OBLIVION (1992)
WELCOME TO THE DOLLHOUSE (1996)
WENDY CRACKED A WALNUT (SEE: ALMOST)(1991)
WE'RE BACK! A DINOSAUR'S STORY (1993)
WE'RE NO ANGELS (1989)
WE'RE TALKIN' SERIOUS MONEY (1992)
WES CRAVEN'S NEW NIGHTMARE (1994)
WESTLER (SEE: EAST OF THE WALL)(1986)
WET AND WILD SUMMER (1993)
WETHERBY (1985)
WHALES OF AUGUST, THE (1987)
WHARF RAT, THE (1996)
WHAT ABOUT BOB? (1991)
WHAT COMES AROUND (1986)
WHAT EVER HAPPENED TO . . . (1995)
WHAT HAPPENED WAS . . . (1994)
WHAT WAITS BELOW (1986)
WHAT'S LOVE GOT TO DO WITH IT (1993)
WHATEVER IT TAKES (1986)

WHAT'S EATING GILBERT GRAPE? (1993)
WHAT'S THE TIME, MR. CLOCK? (1985)
WHEELS OF FIRE (SEE: DESERT WARRIOR)(1985)
WHEELS OF TERROR (SEE: MISFIT BRIGADE, THE)(1988)
WHEN A MAN LOVES A WOMAN (1994)
WHEN BILLY BROKE HIS HEAD . . . AND OTHER TALES OF WONDER (1995)
WHEN FATHER WAS AWAY ON BUSINESS (1985)
WHEN HARRY MET SALLY. . . (1989)
WHEN NATURE CALLS (1985)
WHEN NIGHT IS FALLING (1995)
WHEN THE BOUGH BREAKS (1995)
WHEN THE BULLET HITS THE BONE (1996)
WHEN THE PARTY'S OVER (1993)
WHEN THE RAVEN FLIES (1985)
WHEN THE WHALES CAME (1989)
WHEN THE WIND BLOWS (1988)
WHEN WE WERE KINGS (1996)
WHERE ANGELS FEAR TO TREAD (1992)
WHERE ARE THE CHILDREN? (1986)
WHERE SLEEPING DOGS LIE (1993)
WHERE THE DAY TAKES YOU (1992)
WHERE THE HEART IS (1990)
WHERE THE RED FERN GROWS, PART 2 (1994)
WHERE THE RIVER RUNS BLACK (1986)
WHERE THE RIVERS FLOW NORTH (1994)
WHERE'S THE MONEY, NOREEN? (1996)
WHEREVER YOU ARE (1988)
WHILE YOU WERE SLEEPING (1995)
WHISPERING, THE (1996)
WHISPERS (1991)
WHISPERS IN THE DARK (1992)
WHISTLE BLOWER, THE (1987)
WHITE (1994)
WHITE BALLOON, THE (1996)
WHITE FANG (1991)
WHITE FANG 2: MYTH OF THE WHITE WOLF (1994)
WHITE GHOST (1988)
WHITE GIRL, THE (1990)
WHITE HUNTER, BLACK HEART (1990)
WHITE LIGHT (1991)
WHITE MAN'S BURDEN (1995)
WHITE MEN CAN'T JUMP (1992)
WHITE MILE (1994)
WHITE MISCHIEF (1988)
WHITE NIGHTS (1985)
WHITE OF THE EYE (1988)
WHITE PALACE (1990)
WHITE SANDS (1992)
WHITE SLAVE (1986)
WHITE SQUALL (1996)
WHITE TIGER (1996)
WHITE TRASH (1992)
WHITE WATER SUMMER (1987)
WHITE WOLVES: A CRY IN THE WILD II (1993)
WHITE WOLVES II: LEGEND OF THE WILD (1996)
WHO DO I GOTTA KILL? (SEE: ME AND THE MOB)(1995)
WHO FRAMED ROGER RABBIT (1988)
WHO KILLED PASOLINI? (1996)
WHO SHOT PATAKANGO? (1992)
WHOLE WIDE WORLD, THE (1996)
WHOOPEE BOYS, THE (1986)
WHOOPING COUGH (1987)
WHORE (1991)
WHORE 2 (1994)
WHO'S HARRY CRUMB? (1989)
WHO'S THAT GIRL (1987)
WHO'S THE MAN? (1993)
WHY HAS BODHI-DHARMA LEFT FOR THE EAST? (1993)
WHY ME? (1990)
WICKED CITY (1995)
WICKED CITY, THE (1996)
WICKED GAMES (1994)
WICKED STEPMOTHER (1989)
WICKED, THE (1991)
WIDE EYED AND LEGLESS (SEE: WEDDING GIFT, THE)(1994)
WIDE SARGASSO SEA (1993)
WIDOW'S KISS (1996)
WIDOWS' PEAK (1994)
WIFE, THE (1996)
WIGSTOCK: THE MOVIE (1995)
WILD AT HEART (1990)
WILD BILL (1995)
WILD CACTUS (1993)
WILD GEESE II (1985)
WILD HEARTS CAN'T BE BROKEN (1991)
WILD ORCHID (1990)
WILD ORCHID 2: TWO SHADES OF BLUE (1992)
WILD PAIR, THE (1987)
WILD REEDS (1995)
WILD SIDE (1996)
WILD THING (1987)
WILD WEST, THE (1995)
WILD WHEELS (1992)
WILDCATS (1986)
WILDER NAPALM (1993)
WILDEST DREAMS (1990)
WILDFIRE (1992)
WILDROSE (1985)
WILLIAM SHAKESPEARE'S ROMEO + JULIET (1996)
WILLIES, THE (1991)
WILLOW (1988)
WILLS AND BURKE (1985)
WILLY MILLY (SEE: SOMETHING SPECIAL!)(1987)
WILT (SEE: MISADVENTURES OF MR. WILT, THE)(1990)
WIND (1992)
WIND, THE (1987)
WIND IN THE WILLOWS, THE (1996)
WINDOW TO PARIS (1995)
WINDRUNNER (1995)
WING CHUN (1996)
WINGS OF COURAGE (1995)
WINGS OF DESIRE (1987)
WINGS OF THE APACHE (SEE: FIRE BIRDS)(1990)
WINNERS TAKE ALL (1987)
WINTER IN LISBON, THE (1992)
WINTER PEOPLE (1989)
WINTER WAR, THE (SEE: TALVISOTA)(1989)
WIRED (1989)
WIRED TO KILL (1986)
WISDOM (1986)
WISE GUYS (1986)
WISECRACKS (1992)
WISH YOU WERE HERE (1987)
WISHFUL THINKING (1993)
WITCH HUNT (1995)
WITCH, THE (SEE: SUPERSTITION)(1985)
WITCHBOARD (1987)
WITCHBOARD 2: THE DEVIL'S DOORWAY (1993)
WITCHCRAFT (1989)
WITCHCRAFT III: THE KISS OF DEATH (1991)
WITCHCRAFT IV: VIRGIN HEART (1992)
WITCHCRAFT V: DANCE WITH THE DEVIL (1993)
WITCHCRAFT 6: THE DEVIL'S MISTRESS (1994)
WITCHCRAFT VII: JUDGMENT HOUR (1995)
WITCHCRAFT: SALEM'S GHOST (1996)
WITCHCRAFT VIII (SEE: SALEM'S GHOST)(1996)
WITCHCRAFT II: THE TEMPTRESS (1990)
WITCHES, THE (1990)
WITCHES OF EASTWICK, THE (1987)
WITCHFIRE (1986)
WITH HONORS (1994)
WITHIN THE ROCK (1996)
WITHNAIL & I (1987)
WITHOUT A CLUE (1988)
WITHOUT ANESTHESIA (1995)
WITHOUT MERCY (1996)
WITHOUT YOU, I'M NOTHING (1990)
WITNESS (1985)
WITNESS TO THE EXECUTION (1995)
WIT'S END (SEE: G.I. EXECUTIONER,T HE)(1985)
WITTGENSTEIN (1993)
WIVES--TEN YEARS AFTER (1985)
WIZARD, THE (1989)
WIZARD OF DARKNESS (1995)
WIZARD OF LONELINESS, THE (1988)
WIZARDS OF THE DEMON SWORD (1991)
WIZARDS OF THE LOST KINGDOM (1985)
WOLF (1994)
WOLF AT THE DOOR, THE (1987)
WOLF'S HOLE (1986)
WOLVES, THE (1996)
WOMAN AT WAR, A (1995)
WOMAN, HER MEN AND HER FUTON, A (1992)
WOMAN OBSESSED, A (1989)
WOMAN SCORNED: THE BETTY BRODERICK STORY, A (SEE: TILL MURDER DO US PART)(1994)
WOMAN UNDONE, A (1996)
WOMAN WITH A PAST (1994)
WOMAN'S TALE, A (1991)
WOMEN FROM THE LAKE OF SCENTED SOULS (1994)
WOMEN ON THE VERGE OF A NERVOUS BREAKDOWN (1988)
WOMEN'S PRISON MASSACRE (1986)
WONDERFUL, HORRIBLE LIFE OF LENI RIEFENSTAHL, THE (1994)
WONDERLAND (1988)
WONG FEI-HUNG (SEE: ONCE UPON A TIME IN CHINA)(1992)
WONG FEI-HUNG II (SEE: ONCE UPON A TIME IN CHINA II)(1994)
WONG FEI-HUNG III (SEE: ONCE UPON A TIME IN CHINA III)(1994)
WOODEN MAN'S BRIDE, THE (1995)
WOODSTOCK: THE DIRECTOR'S CUT (1994)
WOODSTOCK: THREE DAYS OF PEACE AND MUSIC (SEE: WOODSTOCK: THE DIRECTOR'S CUT)(1994)
WORKING GIRL (1988)
WORKING GIRLS (1986)
WORLD AND TIME ENOUGH (1995)
WORLD APART, A (1988)
WORLD GONE WILD (1988)
WORTH WINNING (1989)
WRAITH, THE (1986)
WRESTLING ERNEST HEMINGWAY (1993)
WRITE TO KILL (1991)
WRONG GUYS, THE (1988)
WRONG MAN, THE (1995)
WYATT EARP (1994)
WYROK SMIERCI (SEE: DEATH SENTENCE)(1986)

X

XIANG HUN NU (SEE: WOMEN FROM THE LAKE OF SCENTED SOULS)(1994)
XIYAN (SEE: WEDDING BANQUET, THE)(1993)
XTRO 2: THE SECOND ENCOUNTER (1991)
XTRO3 (1995)
XYZ MURDERS, THE (SEE: CRIMEWAVE)(1985)

Y

YAABA (1989)
YANKEE ZULU (1996)
YANZHI KOU (SEE: ROUGE)(1990)
YASEMIN (1988)
YASHA (1985)
YE SHAN (SEE: IN THE WILD MOUNTAINS)(1986)
YEAR MY VOICE BROKE, THE (1988)
YEAR OF AWAKENING, THE (1986)
YEAR OF THE COMET (1992)
YEAR OF THE DRAGON (1985)
YEAR OF THE GUN (1991)
YEAR OF THE WALL (SEE: PROMISE, THE)(1995)
YEARLING, THE (1994)
YEELEN (SEE: BRIGHTNESS)(1988)
YELLOW EARTH (1986)
YESTERDAY'S TARGET (1996)
YINGXIONG BENSE (SEE: BETTER TOMORROW, A)(1987)
YOU CAN'T HURRY LOVE (1988)
YOU ONLY DIE ONCE (SEE: DEAD MAN'S REVENGE)(1994)
YOU SO CRAZY (1994)
YOU'LL NEVER MAKE LOVE IN THIS TOWN AGAIN (1996)
YOUNG AMERICANS, THE (1994)
YOUNG COMPOSER'S ODYSSEY, A (1986)
YOUNG EINSTEIN (1989)
YOUNG EMMANUELLE, A (SEE: NEA)(1995)
YOUNG GUNS (1988)
YOUNG GUNS II (1990)
YOUNG NURSES IN LOVE (1989)
YOUNG POISONER'S HANDBOOK, THE (1996)
YOUNG SHERLOCK HOLMES (1985)
YOUNG SOUL REBELS (1991)
YOUNGBLOOD (1986)
YOUNGER & YOUNGER (1995)

Z

ZABUDNITE NA MOZARTA (SEE: FORGET MOZART!)(1985)
ZAMRI OUMI VOSKRESNI (SEE: FREEZE--DIE--COME TO LIFE)(1990)
ZANDALEE (1991)
ZARKORR! THE INVADER (1996)
ZEBRAHEAD (1992)
ZED & TWO NOUGHTS, A (1985)
ZELLY AND ME (1988)
ZENTROPA (1992)
ZERO BOYS, THE (1987)
ZERO PATIENCE (1994)
ZERO TOLERANCE (1995)
ZHONG AN SHI LU LING JI (SEE: ORGANIZED CRIME & TRIAD BUREAU)(1996)
ZINA (1985)
ZIPPERFACE (1993)
ZIVOT SA STRICEM (SEE: MY UNCLE'S LEGACY)(1990)
ZOEKEN NAAR EILEEN (SEE: LOOKING FOR EILEEN)(1987)
ZONE TROOPERS (1986)
ZONING (1986)
ZOO GANG, THE (1985)
ZOO RADIO (1991)
ZOOMAN (1995)
ZUCKERBABY (SEE: SUGARBABY)(1985)

FILMS BY COUNTRY OF ORIGIN

A bullet before the title indicates a film co-produced by more than one country

Argentina
- • OF LOVE AND SHADOWS
- SHADOW YOU SOON WILL BE, A

Australia
- • ALEX
- • GIRLFRIENDS
- SHINE
- SPIDER & ROSE
- TUNNEL VISION
- TWO FRIENDS
- • WILLIAM SHAKESPEARE'S ROMEO + JULIET

Austria
- • BROTHER OF SLEEP
- FLAMING EARS

Belgium
- • ANTONIA'S LINE
- • CELESTIAL CLOCKWORK
- DAENS
- • PASSION OF DARKLY NOON, THE
- • SUITE 16

Burkina Faso
- • GUIMBA THE TYRANT

Canada
- • ANNIE O
- BLOOD & DONUTS
- CHAMPAGNE SAFARI, THE
- CURTIS'S CHARM
- FOR THE MOMENT
- • FRAME BY FRAME
- • GETTING AWAY WITH MURDER
- GIRL FROM MARS, THE
- HECK'S WAY HOME
- • HEIDI FLEISS HOLLYWOOD MADAM
- • HOLLOW POINT
- IRON EAGLE IV
- JOHNNY SHORTWAVE
- • LEGEND OF GATOR FACE, THE
- • MAGIC HUNTER
- • MAN BY THE SHORE, THE
- • MAN IN THE ATTIC, THE
- • MOONSHINE HIGHWAY
- OUTER LIMITS: SANDKINGS, THE
- • PORTRAITS OF A KILLER
- ROBIN OF LOCKSLEY
- RUDE
- SCREAMERS
- SERIAL KILLER
- SONG SPINNER, THE
- STAND OFF, THE
- • TRACKS OF A KILLER
- UNDERSTUDY: GRAVEYARD SHIFT 2, THE
- WHEN THE BULLET HITS THE BONE
- • WILLIAM SHAKESPEARE'S ROMEO + JULIET

Chile
- • JOHNNY 100 PESOS
- • THREE LIVES AND ONLY ONE DEATH

China
- BLACK MOUNTAIN
- • BLUSH
- STORY OF XINGHUA, THE

Cuba
- BITTER SUGAR

Denmark
- • BREAKING THE WAVES
- • COLD FEVER

Finland
- • BREAKING THE WAVES
- • CONDITION RED

France
- • ADVENTURES OF PINOCCHIO, THE
- • ANNA
- • BREAKING THE WAVES
- MADAME BUTTERFLY
- • CELESTIAL CLOCKWORK
- • CEMETERY MAN
- • CHASING BUTTERFLIES
- • ERNESTO CHE GUEVARA—THE BOLIVIAN DIARY
- EYE OF VICHY, THE
- • FLOWER OF MY SECRET, THE
- FRANCOIS TRUFFAUT: STOLEN PORTRAITS
- FRENCH TWIST
- • GUIMBA THE TYRANT
- HATE
- HORSEMAN ON THE ROOF
- • JACK & SARAH
- • JANE EYRE
- • LA CEREMONIE
- • LA COMEDIE-FRANCAISE OU L'AMOUR JOUE
- LES VOLEURS
- LITTLE INDIAN, BIG CITY
- MA SAISON PREFEREE
- • MACHINE, THE
- • MAGIC HUNTER
- • MAN BY THE SHORE, THE
- • MICROCOSMOS
- • MR. STITCH
- • MONSTER, THE
- • NELLY AND MONSIEUR ARNAUD
- NEW LIFE, A
- • NIKI DE SAINT PHALLE: WHO IS THE MONSTER — YOU OR ME?
- • ORSON WELLES: THE ONE-MAN BAND
- • PHANTOM 2040: THE GHOST WHO WALKS
- • PROPRIETOR, THE
- RENDEZVOUS IN PARIS
- RIDICULE
- • SILENCES OF THE PALACE, THE
- SINGLE GIRL, A
- • SOMEONE ELSE'S AMERICA
- • STEALING BEAUTY
- • THREE LIVES AND ONLY ONE DEATH
- VISITORS, THE
- • WAR OF THE BUTTONS, THE
- • YOUNG POISONER'S HANDBOOK, THE

Germany
- • ADVENTURES OF PINOCCHIO, THE
- • BROTHER OF SLEEP
- • CHASING BUTTERFLIES
- • COLD FEVER
- • DEAD MAN
- FATE
- • FLIRT
- • GUIMBA THE TYRANT
- HALFMOON
- • HEIDI FLEISS HOLLYWOOD MADAM
- KASPAR HAUSER
- • LA CEREMONIE
- • LAND AND FREEDOM
- • MACHINE, THE
- MAYBE . . . MAYBE NOT
- • NELLY AND MONSIEUR ARNAUD
- NEUROSIA: 50 YEARS OF PERVERSITY
- NICO ICON
- • NIKI DE SAINT PHALLE: WHO IS THE MONSTER — YOU OR ME?
- • ORSON WELLES: THE ONE-MAN BAND
- • PARIS WAS A WOMAN
- • PASSION OF DARKLY NOON, THE
- • SURGEON, THE
- • TALES OF EROTICA
- • WOLVES, THE
- • YOUNG POISONER'S HANDBOOK, THE

Guatemala
- • SILENCE OF NETO, THE

Haiti
- • MAN BY THE SHORE, THE

Hong Kong
- • BLUSH
- CHUNGKING EXPRESS
- MIDNIGHT ANGEL
- ORGANIZED CRIME & TRIAD BUREAU
- • RUMBLE IN THE BRONX
- WICKED CITY, THE
- WING CHUN

Hungary
- • DOGFIGHTERS, THE
- • MAGIC HUNTER
- • OUTPOST, THE

Iceland
- • BREAKING THE WAVES
- • COLD FEVER
- • VIKING SAGAS, THE

India
- TARGET

Iran
- WHITE BALLOON, THE

Ireland
- • HARD WAY OUT: BLOODFIST VIII
- • SOME MOTHER'S SON

Israel
- UNDER THE DOMIM TREE

Italy
- • CEMETERY MAN
- • CHASING BUTTERFLIES
- • ENGLISH PATIENT, THE
- • JANE EYRE
- • LARGER THAN LIFE
- • MICROCOSMOS
- MILLE BOLLE BLU
- • MONSTER, THE
- • NELLY AND MONSIEUR ARNAUD

- • OUTRAGE
- • SONS OF TRINITY
- • STEALING BEAUTY
- WHO KILLED PASOLINI?

Japan
- BIG WARS
- • DEAD MAN
- • FLIRT
- • GHOST IN THE SHELL
- KAMIKAZE TAXI
- • LARGER THAN LIFE
- MABOROSI
- NIGHT ON THE GALACTIC RAILROAD
- PATLABOR 2: MOBILE POLICE
- ROUJIN-Z
- SANCTUARY: THE MOVIE
- • SGT. KABUKIMAN N.Y.P.D.
- STREET FIGHTER II: THE ANIMATED MOVIE

Mali
- • GUIMBA THE TYRANT

Mexico
- AVENTURERA
- • JOHNNY 100 PESOS
- • SOLO

Netherlands
- • ANTONIA'S LINE
- • BREAKING THE WAVES
- COLD LIGHT OF DAY
- CROCODILES IN AMSTERDAM

New Zealand
- • ALEX
- • GIRLFRIENDS
- • LOADED
- • PORTRAIT OF A LADY, THE

Norway
- • BREAKING THE WAVES

Philippines
- MIDNIGHT DANCERS

Poland
- MOTHER OF KINGS

Romania
- • FORBIDDEN ZONE: ALIEN ABDUCTION
- • JOSH KIRBY . . . TIME WARRIOR!: LAST BATTLE FOR THE UNIVERSE
- • MAGIC IN THE MIRROR
- • OUTPOST, THE

Russia
- • ANNA
- CHEKIST, THE
- • WOLVES, THE

South Africa
- • WARHEAD
- YANKEE ZULU

Spain
- BATON ROUGE
- • CELESTIAL CLOCKWORK
- • FLOWER OF MY SECRET, THE
- • LAND AND FREEDOM
- MOUTH TO MOUTH
- • OF LOVE AND SHADOWS
- • OUTRAGE
- • TWO MUCH

Sweden
- • BREAKING THE WAVES
- CHILDREN OF NOISY VILLAGE, THE
- EVIL ED

Switzerland
- • ERNESTO CHE GUEVARA—THE BOLIVIAN DIARY
- • MAGIC HUNTER
- • MICROCOSMOS
- • NIKI DE SAINT PHALLE: WHO IS THE MONSTER — YOU OR ME?
- • ORSON WELLES: THE ONE-MAN BAND
- SHADOW OF ANGELS

Taiwan
- MAHJONG
- VIVE L'AMOUR

Tunisia
- • SILENCES OF THE PALACE, THE

Turkey
- • PROPRIETOR, THE

U.K.
- • ADVENTURES OF PINOCCHIO, THE
- • AFFAIR, THE
- • ALL DOGS GO TO HEAVEN 2
- • ANGELS AND INSECTS
- • ANNE FRANK REMEMBERED
- • ANTONIA'S LINE
- AUGUST
- BEAUTIFUL THING
- BRITT ALLCROFT'S MAGIC ADVENTURES OF MUMFIE—THE MOVIE
- BUTTERFLY KISS
- CAPTIVES
- COLD COMFORT FARM
- CRACKER: THE MADWOMAN IN THE ATTIC
- • EMMA
- • ENGLISH PATIENT, THE
- FUNNYMAN, THE
- • GHOST IN THE SHELL
- • GIRLFRIENDS
- • HAUNTED
- • HEIDI FLEISS HOLLYWOOD MADAM
- INSTITUTE BENJAMENTA
- • JACK & SARAH
- • JANE EYRE
- JOSEPH CONRAD'S THE SECRET AGENT
- JUDE
- • LAND AND FREEDOM
- • LAWNMOWER MAN 2: BEYOND CYBERSPACE
- • LOADED
- MADAGASCAR SKIN
- • MESSAGE TO LOVE: THE ISLE OF WIGHT FESTIVAL
- • MICHAEL COLLINS
- MIDWINTER'S TALE, A
- • NEON BIBLE, THE
- • PASSION OF DARKLY NOON, THE
- • PERSONAL JOURNEY WITH MARTIN SCORSESE THROUGH AMERICAN MOVIES, A
- • PORTRAIT OF A LADY, THE
- PROTEUS
- ROLLING STONES ROCK-AND-ROLL CIRCUS, THE
- SECRETS & LIES
- SHAMELESS
- SHOPPING
- SMALL FACES
- SOLITAIRE FOR TWO
- • SOME MOTHER'S SON
- • SOMEONE ELSE'S AMERICA
- • STEALING BEAUTY
- • SUITE 16
- • TALES OF EROTICA
- TRAINSPOTTING
- • TWELFTH NIGHT
- TWO DEATHS
- WALLACE AND GROMIT: THE BEST OF AARDMAN ANIMATION
- • WAR OF THE BUTTONS, THE
- • WAVELENGTH
- WIND IN THE WILLOWS, THE
- • YOUNG POISONER'S HANDBOOK, THE

U.S.
- ABUSE
- ADRENALIN: FEAR THE RUSH
- • AFFAIR, THE
- ALASKA
- • ALL DOGS GO TO HEAVEN 2
- AMANDA AND THE ALIEN
- AMERICAN BUFFALO
- AMERICAN STRAYS
- AMERICA'S DREAM
- ANGELA
- • ANGELS AND INSECTS
- ANIMAL INSTINCTS III: THE SEDUCTRESS
- • ANNE FRANK REMEMBERED
- • ANNIE O
- APART FROM HUGH
- ARRIVAL, THE
- ASSAULT AT WEST POINT
- ASSOCIATE, THE
- . . . AT FIRST SIGHT
- BACKLASH: OBLIVION 2
- BAD LOVE
- BAD MOON
- BAJA
- BARB WIRE
- BASQUIAT
- BEASTMASTER 3: THE EYE OF BRAXUS
- BEAUTIFUL GIRLS
- BEAVIS AND BUTT-HEAD DO AMERICA
- BED OF ROSES
- BEFORE AND AFTER
- BERKELEY IN THE 60S
- BEST OF THE BEST 3: NO TURNING BACK
- BEWARE: CHILDREN AT PLAY
- BEYOND DESIRE
- BEYOND THE CALL
- BIG BULLY
- BIG NIGHT
- BIG SQUEEZE, THE
- BIO-DOME
- BIRDCAGE, THE
- BLACK DAY BLUE NIGHT
- BLACK OUT
- BLACK ROSE OF HARLEM
- BLACK SCORPION
- BLACK SHEEP
- BLONDES HAVE MORE GUNS
- BLOODKNOT
- BLOODSPORT II: THE NEXT KUMITE
- BODY COUNT
- BODY OF INFLUENCE 2
- BOGUS
- BOTTLE ROCKET
- BOUND
- BOY CALLED HATE, A
- BOYS
- BOYS NEXT DOOR, THE
- BREACH OF TRUST
- BREAKAWAY
- • BREAKING THE WAVES
- BROKEN ARROW
- BUGGED
- BULLETPROOF
- BURIAL OF THE RATS

CABLE GUY, THE
CALLING THE GHOSTS: A STORY ABOUT RAPE, WAR AND WOMEN
CANNIBAL! THE MUSICAL
CANTERVILLE GHOST, THE
CARNOSAUR 3: PRIMAL SPECIES
CARPOOL
CARRIED AWAY
CATWALK
CAUGHT
CELLULOID CLOSET, THE
CELTIC PRIDE
CHAIN REACTION
CHAMBER, THE
CHAMELEON
CHILDREN OF FURY
CHILDREN OF THE CORN: THE GATHERING
CITIZEN RUTH
CITY HALL
CLUBHOUSE DETECTIVES
• COLD FEVER
COLONY, THE
• CONDITION RED
COURAGE UNDER FIRE
CRAFT, THE
CRIMINAL HEARTS
CROSSCUT
CROW: CITY OF ANGELS, THE
CRUCIBLE, THE
CURDLED
D3: THE MIGHTY DUCKS
DADETOWN
DANGEROUS PASSION
DARK SECRETS
DARKMAN III: DIE DARKMAN DIE
DAYLIGHT
DEAD COLD
• DEAD MAN
DEAD TO RIGHTS
DEAD WEEKEND
DEADLY OUTBREAK
DEAR GOD
DEATH ARTIST, THE
DEATH BENEFIT
DELTA OF VENUS
DEMOLITIONIST, THE
DENISE CALLS UP
DENTIST, THE
DESIRE
DESOLATION ANGELS
DEVOTION
DIABOLIQUE
• DOGFIGHTERS, THE
DONOR UNKNOWN
DON'T BE A MENACE TO SOUTH CENTRAL WHILE DRINKING YOUR JUICE IN THE HOOD
DON'T LET YOUR MEAT LOAF
DOWN, OUT AND DANGEROUS
DOWN PERISCOPE
DRAGONHEART
DUNSTON CHECKS IN
ED
EDDIE
EDIE & PEN
ED'S NEXT MOVE
ELECTRA
• EMMA
• ENGLISH PATIENT, THE
ENTERTAINING ANGELS: THE DOROTHY DAY STORY
ERASER
EVENING STAR, THE
EVERYONE SAYS I LOVE YOU
EVERYTHING RELATIVE
EVIL HAS A FACE
EVITA
EXECUTIVE DECISION
EXIT
EXTREME MEASURES
EYE FOR AN EYE
FAITHFUL
FAMILY THING, A
FAN, THE
FAR HARBOR
FARGO
FAST MONEY
FATALLY YOURS
FEAR
FEELING MINNESOTA
FELONY
FEMALIEN
FINAL CUT, THE
FINAL EQUINOX, THE
FIRE ON THE MOUNTAIN
FIRST KID
FIRST WIVES CLUB, THE
FIST OF THE NORTH STAR
FLATTERED
FLED
FLIPPER
• FLIRT
FLIRTING WITH DISASTER
FLY AWAY HOME
FOR BETTER OR WORSE
• FORBIDDEN ZONE: ALIEN ABDUCTION
FOREST WARRIOR
4 TALES OF 2 CITIES
FOXFIRE
• FRAME BY FRAME
FREEWAY
FRIEND OF THE FAMILY 2
FRIGHTENERS, THE
FRISK
FROM DUSK TILL DAWN
FROM THE JOURNALS OF JEAN SEBERG
FUGITIVE RAGE
FULL BODY MASSAGE
FUNERAL, THE
GALAXIES ARE COLLIDING
GET ON THE BUS
• GETTING AWAY WITH MURDER
GHOST AND THE DARKNESS, THE
GHOSTS OF MISSISSIPPI
GIRL 6
• GIRLFRIENDS
GIRLS TOWN
GLASS CAGE, THE
GLIMMER MAN, THE
GRACE OF MY HEART
GRASS HARP, THE
GRAVE, THE
GREAT WHITE HYPE, THE
GRIM
HALFBACK OF NOTRE DAME, THE
HAMLET
HAPPY GILMORE
HARD JUSTICE
• HARD WAY OUT: BLOODFIST VIII
HARRIET THE SPY
HARVEST OF FIRE
• HAUNTED
HEAD OF THE FAMILY
HEADLESS BODY IN TOPLESS BAR
HEAVEN'S PRISONERS
HEAVY
HEIDI CHRONICLES, THE
• HEIDI FLEISS HOLLYWOOD MADAM
HELLRAISER: BLOODLINE
HIDDEN ASSASSIN
HIGH SCHOOL HIGH
• HOLLOW POINT
HOMAGE
HOMECOMING
HOMEWARD BOUND II: LOST IN SAN FRANCISCO
HOSTILE INTENTIONS
HOURGLASS
HOUSE ARREST
HOW THE WEST WAS FUN
HUNCHBACK OF NOTRE DAME, THE
HYPE!
I SHOT ANDY WARHOL
IF LUCY FELL
I'M NOT RAPPAPORT
IMMORTALS, THE
IN LOVE AND WAR
INDEPENDENCE DAY
INFINITY
ISLAND OF DR. MOREAU, THE
IT CAME FROM OUTER SPACE II
IT'S MY PARTY
JACK
JAG
JAMES AND THE GIANT PEACH
• JANE EYRE
JERRY MAGUIRE
JINGLE ALL THE WAY
JOE'S APARTMENT
JOHN CARPENTER'S ESCAPE FROM L.A.
JOSH KIRBY . . . TIME WARRIOR!: EGGS FROM 70,000,000 B.C.
JOSH KIRBY . . . TIME WARRIOR!: JOURNEY TO THE MAGIC CAVERN
• JOSH KIRBY . . . TIME WARRIOR!: LAST BATTLE FOR THE UNIVERSE
JOSH KIRBY . . . TIME WARRIOR!: TRAPPED ON TOY WORLD
JUROR, THE
JUST YOUR LUCK
KANSAS CITY
KAZAAM
KIDS IN THE HALL: BRAIN CANDY
KINGPIN
KISSINGER AND NIXON
• LA COMEDIE-FRANCAISE OU L'AMOUR JOUE
LAND BEFORE TIME IV: JOURNEY THROUGH THE MISTS
• LARGER THAN LIFE
LARRY MCMURTRY'S STREETS OF LAREDO
LAST DANCE
LAST MAN STANDING
LAST SUPPER, THE
LATE SHIFT, THE
• LAWNMOWER MAN 2: BEYOND CYBERSPACE
LAZARUS MAN, THE
• LEGEND OF GATOR FACE, THE
LET'S GET BIZZEE
LETTER TO MY KILLER
LIFEFORM
LILY DALE
LINE KING: THE AL HIRSCHFELD STORY, THE
LITTLE DEATH, THE
LITTLE WITCHES
LIVE NUDE GIRLS
LIVE WIRE: HUMAN TIMEBOMB
LONE JUSTICE: SHOWDOWN AT PLUM CREEK
LONE STAR

LONG KISS GOODNIGHT, THE
LONG ROAD HOME, THE
LOOKING FOR RICHARD
LOOKING FOR TROUBLE
LOSING CHASE
LOTTO LAND
LOVE IS ALL THERE IS
LOVER'S KNOT
LOW LIFE, THE
MAD DOG TIME
MADAME WANG'S
MADDENING, THE
• MAGIC IN THE MIRROR
• MAN IN THE ATTIC, THE
MAN OF THE YEAR
MAN WITH A PLAN
MAN WITH THE PERFECT SWING, THE
MANNY & LO
MARS ATTACKS!
MARVIN'S ROOM
MARY REILLY
MATERNAL INSTINCTS
MATILDA
MAXIMUM RISK
MERCY
MERLIN'S SHOP OF MAGICAL WONDERS
• MESSAGE TO LOVE: THE ISLE OF WIGHT FESTIVAL
MICHAEL
• MICHAEL COLLINS
MIND RIPPER
MIRROR HAS TWO FACES, THE
MIRROR, MIRROR III: THE VOYEUR
MISSING PIECES
MISSION: IMPOSSIBLE
MR. HOLLAND'S OPUS
MR. ICE CREAM MAN
• MR. STITCH
MR. WRONG
MODERN AFFAIR, A
MOLL FLANDERS
MONSTERSHOW
• MOONSHINE HIGHWAY
MOTHER
MOTHER
MOTHER NIGHT
MOTHER'S PRAYER, A
MRS. MUNCK
MRS. WINTERBOURNE
MULHOLLAND FALLS
MULTIPLICITY
MUPPET TREASURE ISLAND
MURDERED INNOCENCE
MUTANT MAN
MY FELLOW AMERICANS
MYSTERY SCIENCE THEATER 3000: THE MOVIE
NAKED SOULS
NATIONAL LAMPOON'S FAVORITE DEADLY SINS
NECRONOMICON: BOOK OF THE DEAD
NEMESIS III: PREY HARDER
• NEON BIBLE, THE
NIGHT OF THE SCARECROW
NIGHT OF THE TWISTERS
NORMA JEAN AND MARILYN
NORMAL LIFE
NOT BAD FOR A GIRL
NOT OF THIS EARTH
NUTTY PROFESSOR, THE
OFF AND RUNNING
ONCE UPON A TIME . . . WHEN WE WERE COLORED
ONE FINE DAY
ONE GOOD TURN
101 DALMATIANS
ONE LESS EGG TO FRY
ONE MAN'S JUSTICE
ONE NIGHT STAND
OPEN SEASON
ORIGINAL GANGSTAS
ORIGINAL SINS
OUT THERE
OVER THE WIRE
PAINTED HERO
PALLBEARER, THE
PALOOKAVILLE
PARADISE LOST: THE CHILD MURDERS AT ROBIN HOOD HILLS
• PARIS WAS A WOMAN
PEOPLE VS. LARRY FLYNT, THE
PERFECT CANDIDATE, A
• PERSONAL JOURNEY WITH MARTIN SCORSESE THROUGH AMERICAN MOVIES, A
• PHANTOM 2040: THE GHOST WHO WALKS
PHANTOM, THE
PHARAOH'S ARMY
PHAT BEACH
PHENOMENON
PHOENIX
PIE IN THE SKY
PIG'S TALE, A
PINOCCHIO'S REVENGE
PIRANHA
PLAYBACK
POISON IVY 2: LILY
POLYMORPH
POMPATUS OF LOVE, THE
• PORTRAIT OF A LADY, THE
• PORTRAITS OF A KILLER
PREACHER'S WIFE, THE
• PREDICTIONS OF FIRE
PRE-MADONNAS
PRIMAL FEAR
• PROPRIETOR, THE
PUBLIC ACCESS
PUBLIC ENEMIES
PURE DANGER
QUEST, THE
RACE THE SUN
RAGE
RANSOM
RASPUTIN
RATTLED
RAVENHAWK
RAW TARGET
RED LINE
RED SCORPION 2
REDEMPTION: KICKBOXER 5
RICH MAN'S WIFE, THE
RIDERS OF THE PURPLE SAGE
ROAD HOME, THE
ROAD TO GALVESTON, THE
ROCK, THE
• RUMBLE IN THE BRONX
RUMPELSTILTSKIN
SABRINA, THE TEENAGE WITCH
SAINTS AND SINNERS
SANDMAN, THE
SANTA CLAWS
SANTA WITH MUSCLES
SAWBONES
SCREAM
SEARCH FOR ONE-EYE JIMMY, THE
SGT. BILKO
• SGT. KABUKIMAN N.Y.P.D.
SERPENT'S LAIR
SET IT OFF
SHADOW WARRIORS
SHARON'S SECRET
SHE'S THE ONE
SHOOTFIGHTER 2: KILL OR BE KILLED!
SHOT, THE
SHOWGIRL MURDERS, THE
• SILENCE OF NETO, THE
SKIN
SKYSCRAPER
SLEEPERS
SLING BLADE
SMALL WONDERS
• SOLO
SOME FOLKS CALL IT A SLING BLADE
• SOME MOTHER'S SON
• SOMEONE ELSE'S AMERICA
SOMETIMES THEY COME BACK . . . AGAIN
SONIC OUTLAWS
• SONS OF TRINITY
SOUTH BEACH ACADEMY
SPACE JAM
SPELLBREAKER: SECRET OF THE LEPRECHAUNS
SPITFIRE GRILL, THE
SPY HARD
STAR MAKER, THE
STAR TREK: FIRST CONTACT
STEPHEN KING'S THINNER
STONEWALL
STREETCAR NAMED DESIRE, A
STRIPTEASE
STUPIDS, THE
SUBSTANCE OF FIRE, THE
SUBSTITUTE, THE
SUGARTIME
SUNCHASER
SUNSET PARK
• SURGEON, THE
SURVIVING PICASSO
SWEEPER, THE
SWEET NOTHING
SWINGERS
SYNTHETIC PLEASURES
TAILS YOU LIVE, HEADS YOU'RE DEAD
TAKEOVER, THE
TALES FROM THE CRYPT PRESENTS BORDELLO OF BLOOD
• TALES OF EROTICA
TALKING ABOUT SEX
TATTOO BOY
TERMINAL IMPACT
TEXAS CHAINSAW MASSACRE: THE NEXT GENERATION
TEXAS PAYBACK
THAT THING YOU DO!
THEODORE REX
THEREMIN: AN ELECTRONIC ODYSSEY
THEY BITE
THIN LINE BETWEEN LOVE AND HATE, A
TIGER HEART
TIME TO KILL, A
TIMELESS
TIN CUP
TO GILLIAN ON HER 37TH BIRTHDAY
TOLLBOOTH
TOO FAST, TOO YOUNG
• TRACKS OF A KILLER
TREES LOUNGE
TREMORS 2: AFTERSHOCKS
TRIGGER EFFECT, THE
TRUMAN

TRUTH ABOUT CATS AND DOGS, THE
TUSKEGEE AIRMEN, THE
• TWELFTH NIGHT
TWISTER
TWO-BITS & PEPPER
2 DAYS IN THE VALLEY
TWO IF BY SEA
• TWO MUCH
UNDER THE HULA MOON
UNDERTOW
UNFORGETTABLE
UNHOOK THE STARS
UNKNOWN ORIGIN
UP CLOSE AND PERSONAL
VENUS RISING
VERY BRADY SEQUEL, A
• VIKING SAGAS, THE
VIRTUAL COMBAT
VIRTUAL ENCOUNTERS
VIRUS
WALKING AND TALKING
WAR AT HOME, THE
• WARHEAD
WATCH ME
• WAVELENGTH
WEEKEND IN THE COUNTRY, A
WELCOME TO THE DOLLHOUSE
WHARF RAT, THE
WHEN WE WERE KINGS
WHERE'S THE MONEY, NOREEN?
WHISPERING, THE
WHITE SQUALL
WHITE TIGER
WHITE WOLVES II: LEGEND OF THE WILD
WHOLE WIDE WORLD, THE
WIDOW'S KISS
WIFE, THE
WILD SIDE
• WILLIAM SHAKESPEARE'S ROMEO + JULIET
WITCHCRAFT: SALEM'S GHOST
WITHIN THE ROCK
WITHOUT MERCY
• WOLVES, THE
WOMAN UNDONE, A
YESTERDAY'S TARGET
YOU'LL NEVER MAKE LOVE IN THIS TOWN AGAIN
ZARKORR! THE INVADER

Venezuela

• CELESTIAL CLOCKWORK

Wales

HEDD WYNN

Yugoslavia

• PREDICTIONS OF FIRE
VUKOVAR

FILMS BY DISTRIBUTOR

A&E HOME VIDEO
CRACKER: THE MADWOMAN IN THE ATTIC

A-PIX ENTERTAINMENT
ANIMAL INSTINCTS III: THE SEDUCTRESS
BODY COUNT
BODY OF INFLUENCE 2
CLUBHOUSE DETECTIVES
CROSSCUT
DARK SECRETS
DEMOLITIONIST, THE
EVIL ED
FUGITIVE RAGE
GRIM
LITTLE WITCHES
OUTRAGE
SUITE 16
SURGEON, THE
VIRTUAL COMBAT
WHISPERING, THE
WITCHCRAFT: SALEM'S GHOST
WITHIN THE ROCK

AAA/MYRIAD PICTURES
FRANCOIS TRUFFAUT: STOLEN PORTRAITS

ABKCO FILMS
ROLLING STONES ROCK-AND-ROLL CIRCUS, THE

ALLIANCE INTERNATIONAL
RUDE

AMAZING FANTASY ENTERTAINMENT
FEMALIEN
FORBIDDEN ZONE: ALIEN ABDUCTION
HEAD OF THE FAMILY
VIRTUAL ENCOUNTERS
ZARKORR! THE INVADER

AMERICAN HOME ENTERTAINMENT
SANTA CLAWS

ARENA HOME VIDEO
MIDNIGHT ANGEL

ARROW RELEASING
CATWALK
CONDITION RED
HOMAGE

ARROW VIDEO
FUNNYMAN, THE

ARTIFICIAL EYE
NELLY AND MONSIEUR ARNAUD
RENDEZVOUS IN PARIS

ARTISTIC LICENSE FILMS
COLD FEVER
NIKI DE SAINT PHALLE: WHO IS THE MONSTER — YOU OR ME?
PREDICTIONS OF FIRE
WIFE, THE

AUGUST ENTERTAINMENT/PWI
JOHNNY 100 PESOS

BELLWETHER FILMS
MAN WITH A PLAN

BENLA INC.
BAD LOVE

BMG VIDEO
BRITT ALLCROFT'S MAGIC ADVENTURES OF MUMFIE—THE MOVIE
FIST OF THE NORTH STAR
ONE GOOD TURN
SHAMELESS

BREAD & WATER PRODUCTIONS
SHOT, THE

BUENA VISTA
Walt Disney Productions
Hollywood Pictures
Touchstone Pictures

ASSOCIATE, THE
BEFORE AND AFTER
BEST OF THE BEST 3: NO TURNING BACK
BOYS
CELTIC PRIDE
D3: THE MIGHTY DUCKS
EDDIE
EVITA
FIRST KID
HOMEWARD BOUND II: LOST IN SAN FRANCISCO
HUNCHBACK OF NOTRE DAME, THE
JACK
JAMES AND THE GIANT PEACH
KAZAAM
LAST DANCE
LITTLE INDIAN, BIG CITY
MR. HOLLAND'S OPUS
MR. WRONG
MUPPET TREASURE ISLAND
101 DALMATIANS
PHENOMENON
PREACHER'S WIFE, THE
RANSOM
RICH MAN'S WIFE, THE
ROCK, THE
SPY HARD
TWO MUCH
UP CLOSE AND PERSONAL
WAR AT HOME, THE
WHITE SQUALL

CABIN FEVER ENTERTAINMENT
LARRY MCMURTRY'S STREETS OF LAREDO
LOVER'S KNOT
PAINTED HERO

CANOSA INC.
DESOLATION ANGELS

CAPITOL ENTERTAINMENT
SILENCES OF THE PALACE, THE

CASTLE HILL
DADETOWN
FAR HARBOR
LINE KING: THE AL HIRSCHFELD STORY, THE
TWO DEATHS

CBS VIDEO
STREETCAR NAMED DESIRE, A

CENTRAL PARK MEDIA
BIG WARS
NIGHT ON THE GALACTIC RAILROAD

CENTURY FILM PARTNERS INC.
BREAKAWAY

CFP DISTRIBUTION
BUTTERFLY KISS
FLIRT
HEAVY
HYPE!
LOSING CHASE
LOTTO LAND
LOW LIFE, THE
MONSTER, THE
POMPATUS OF LOVE, THE
YOUNG POISONER'S HANDBOOK, THE

CINEMA PARALLEL
CHEKIST, THE

CINEMA PRODUCTS VIDEO
DEVOTION

CINEMAGYAR HUNGAROFILM EXPORT LTD.
OUTPOST, THE

CINEPIX FILM PROPERTIES, INC.
PHARAOH'S ARMY

CINEVISTA HOME VIDEO
ABUSE

COLUMBIA
ALASKA
BOTTLE ROCKET
CABLE GUY, THE
CITY HALL
CRAFT, THE
EXTREME MEASURES
FLY AWAY HOME
FOR BETTER OR WORSE
GET ON THE BUS
GHOSTS OF MISSISSIPPI
HAMLET
HIGH SCHOOL HIGH
JERRY MAGUIRE
JUROR, THE
LONE STAR
MAXIMUM RISK

MIRROR HAS TWO FACES, THE
MULTIPLICITY
PEOPLE VS. LARRY FLYNT, THE
SOME MOTHER'S SON
SPITFIRE GRILL, THE
STRIPTEASE

COLUMBIA TRISTAR HOME VIDEO
MURDERED INNOCENCE
RAVENHAWK
SHOOTFIGHTER 2: KILL OR BE KILLED!
TEXAS CHAINSAW MASSACRE: THE NEXT GENERATION
VENUS RISING
YANKEE ZULU

CONCORDE PICTURES
SHOPPING

DEAD ALIVE HOME VIDEO
MR. ICE CREAM MAN
MUTANT MAN

DIMENSION
FROM DUSK TILL DAWN
HELLRAISER: BLOODLINE
HIDDEN ASSASSIN
SCREAM

DIMENSION HOME VIDEO
CHILDREN OF THE CORN: THE GATHERING

DISTRIBUTION LA FETE
SONG SPINNER, THE

DOVE INTERNATIONAL
BOY CALLED HATE, A
YOU'LL NEVER MAKE LOVE IN THIS TOWN AGAIN

EVERGREEN ENTERTAINMENT
HAUNTED
HOMECOMING
IMMORTALS, THE
STORY OF XINGHUA, THE
WEEKEND IN THE COUNTRY, A
WILD SIDE

FILMOPOLIS PICTURES
MA SAISON PREFEREE
TARGET

FINE LINE
CARRIED AWAY
DELTA OF VENUS
FEELING MINNESOTA
GRASS HARP, THE
KANSAS CITY
MOTHER NIGHT
NORMAL LIFE
SHINE
TWELFTH NIGHT

FIRST LOOK PICTURES
ANTONIA'S LINE
BIG SQUEEZE, THE
BITTER SUGAR
INFINITY

FIRST RUN FEATURES
BLUSH
CHAMPAGNE SAFARI, THE
CHILDREN OF NOISY VILLAGE, THE
EYE OF VICHY, THE
FIRE ON THE MOUNTAIN
GIRLFRIENDS
HALFMOON
MIDNIGHT DANCERS
NEUROSIA: 50 YEARS OF PERVERSITY

FM ENTERTAINMENT
BLOODSPORT II: THE NEXT KUMITE

FOREFRONT FILMS
SILENCE OF NETO, THE

FOX LORBER HOME VIDEO
WICKED CITY, THE

FOX SEARCHLIGHT
GIRL 6
JOSEPH CONRAD'S THE SECRET AGENT
LOOKING FOR RICHARD
SHE'S THE ONE
STEALING BEAUTY

FOXVIDEO
AMERICA'S DREAM

FULL MOON HOME VIDEO
BACKLASH: OBLIVION 2

GOETHE HOUSE NEW YORK
FATE

GOODTIMES ENTERTAINMENT
NIGHT OF THE TWISTERS

GOODTIMES HOME VIDEO
WIND IN THE WILLOWS, THE

GOTHAM ENTERTAINMENT
TATTOO BOY

GRAMERCY PICTURES
BARB WIRE
BOUND
COLD COMFORT FARM
FARGO
GRACE OF MY HEART
HATE
I'M NOT RAPPAPORT
JACK & SARAH
JUDE
LAND AND FREEDOM
MYSTERY SCIENCE THEATER 3000: THE MOVIE
PORTRAIT OF A LADY, THE
TRIGGER EFFECT, THE
WHEN WE WERE KINGS

HACHETTE PREMIERE ET CIE
MACHINE, THE

HALLMARK HOME ENTERTAINMENT
ANNIE O
BEYOND THE CALL
BOYS NEXT DOOR, THE
CANTERVILLE GHOST, THE
HALFBACK OF NOTRE DAME, THE
HARVEST OF FIRE
HECK'S WAY HOME
LEGEND OF GATOR FACE, THE
ROBIN OF LOCKSLEY

HBO HOME VIDEO
AFFAIR, THE
LATE SHIFT, THE
MISSING PIECES
NORMA JEAN AND MARILYN
OFF AND RUNNING
PARADISE LOST: THE CHILD MURDERS AT ROBIN HOOD HILLS
RASPUTIN
SUGARTIME
TRUMAN
TUSKEGEE AIRMEN, THE
WIDOW'S KISS

HORIZON UNLIMITED
NOT BAD FOR A GIRL

IN PICTURES
HEIDI FLEISS HOLLYWOOD MADAM

INTERNATIONAL FILM CIRCUIT
FROM THE JOURNALS OF JEAN SEBERG
MADAGASCAR SKIN

IRS RELEASING
ONCE UPON A TIME . . . WHEN WE WERE COLORED

J.M. PICTURES
ONE LESS EGG TO FRY

JOHN AARON RELEASING
FOR THE MOMENT

KEYSTONE PICTURES
WHITE TIGER

KINO INTERNATIONAL
GUIMBA THE TYRANT

KINO-EYE AMERICAN
SOME FOLKS CALL IT A SLING BLADE

KIT PARKER FILMS
ROUJIN-Z

KJM3 ENTERTAINMENT
MAN BY THE SHORE, THE

LEGACY RELEASING
ADRENALIN: FEAR THE RUSH
OPEN SEASON
SANTA WITH MUSCLES

LEISURE TIME FEATURES
KASPAR HAUSER

LEO
TALKING ABOUT SEX

LIVE ENTERTAINMENT
BEYOND DESIRE
DANGEROUS PASSION
DEAD COLD
DEADLY OUTBREAK
DOGFIGHTERS, THE
GIRL FROM MARS, THE
HOURGLASS
ONE MAN'S JUSTICE

PHANTOM 2040: THE GHOST WHO WALKS
PORTRAITS OF A KILLER
SAINTS AND SINNERS
SOUTH BEACH ACADEMY
TAKEOVER, THE
TRACKS OF A KILLER
WITHOUT MERCY

MALOFILM

BLOOD & DONUTS

MANGA ENTERTAINMENT

GHOST IN THE SHELL
PATLABOR 2: MOBILE POLICE

MCA/UNIVERSAL HOME VIDEO

BEASTMASTER 3: THE EYE OF BRAXUS
COLONY, THE
DARKMAN III: DIE DARKMAN DIE
DEATH BENEFIT
DONOR UNKNOWN
EVIL HAS A FACE
IT CAME FROM OUTER SPACE II
LAND BEFORE TIME IV: JOURNEY THROUGH THE MISTS
LETTER TO MY KILLER
MOTHER'S PRAYER, A
RATTLED
RED SCORPION 2
SHARON'S SECRET
TREMORS 2: AFTERSHOCKS

MGM/UA

ALL DOGS GO TO HEAVEN 2
BIO-DOME
BIRDCAGE, THE
FAMILY THING, A
FLED
HOUSE ARREST
IT'S MY PARTY
KINGPIN
LARGER THAN LIFE
MAD DOG TIME
MOLL FLANDERS
MULHOLLAND FALLS
2 DAYS IN THE VALLEY
UNFORGETTABLE

MGM/UA HOME VIDEO

HOW THE WEST WAS FUN
OUTER LIMITS: SANDKINGS, THE

MILESTONE FILMS

MABOROSI
TWO FRIENDS

MIRAMAX

BASQUIAT
BEAUTIFUL GIRLS
CAPTIVES
CITIZEN RUTH
CROW: CITY OF ANGELS, THE
CURDLED
DEAD MAN
DON'T BE A MENACE TO SOUTH CENTRAL WHILE DRINKING YOUR JUICE IN THE HOOD
EMMA
ENGLISH PATIENT, THE
EVERYONE SAYS I LOVE YOU
FLIRTING WITH DISASTER
HORSEMAN ON THE ROOF
JANE EYRE
LOADED
MARVIN'S ROOM
MOUTH TO MOUTH
OF LOVE AND SHADOWS
PALLBEARER, THE
PERSONAL JOURNEY WITH MARTIN SCORSESE THROUGH AMERICAN MOVIES, A
RIDICULE
SLING BLADE
SMALL WONDERS
STAR MAKER, THE
SUBSTANCE OF FIRE, THE
SWINGERS
TRAINSPOTTING
UNHOOK THE STARS
WALKING AND TALKING

MIRAMAX ZOE

FRENCH TWIST
MICROCOSMOS
VISITORS, THE

MONARCH HOME VIDEO

DESIRE
FATALLY YOURS
FINAL EQUINOX, THE
MAN WITH THE PERFECT SWING, THE
MERLIN'S SHOP OF MAGICAL WONDERS
PHOENIX
STAND OFF, THE
TOO FAST, TOO YOUNG

MTI HOME VIDEO

MIRROR, MIRROR III: THE VOYEUR
THEY BITE

NEW CITY RELEASING

TEXAS PAYBACK

NEW HORIZONS HOME VIDEO

BLACK ROSE OF HARLEM
BLACK SCORPION
BURIAL OF THE RATS
CARNOSAUR 3: PRIMAL SPECIES
CHILDREN OF FURY
DEATH ARTIST, THE
ELECTRA
HARD WAY OUT: BLOODFIST VIII
LONG ROAD HOME, THE
LOOKING FOR TROUBLE
NOT OF THIS EARTH
ONE NIGHT STAND
PIRANHA
SAWBONES
SHADOW WARRIORS
SHOWGIRL MURDERS, THE
SKIN
UNKNOWN ORIGIN
WHEN THE BULLET HITS THE BONE
WHITE WOLVES II: LEGEND OF THE WILD

NEW LINE

ADVENTURES OF PINOCCHIO, THE
BED OF ROSES
FAITHFUL
HEAVEN'S PRISONERS
IN LOVE AND WAR
ISLAND OF DR. MOREAU, THE
LAST MAN STANDING
LAWNMOWER MAN 2: BEYOND CYBERSPACE
LIVE WIRE: HUMAN TIMEBOMB
LONG KISS GOODNIGHT, THE
MICHAEL
RUMBLE IN THE BRONX
SET IT OFF
STUPIDS, THE
THEODORE REX
THIN LINE BETWEEN LOVE AND HATE, A

NEW LINE HOME VIDEO

FELONY
HARD JUSTICE
NECRONOMICON: BOOK OF THE DEAD
PIE IN THE SKY
POISON IVY 2: LILY
TERMINAL IMPACT
TOLLBOOTH
VIKING SAGAS, THE

NEW YORKER FILMS

ANNA
LA CEREMONIE
THREE LIVES AND ONLY ONE DEATH

NEW YORKER VIDEO

CHASING BUTTERFLIES
MILLE BOLLE BLU
SHADOW YOU SOON WILL BE, A

NORTHERN ARTS ENTERTAINMENT

HEADLESS BODY IN TOPLESS BAR
HEDD WYNN
SEARCH FOR ONE-EYE JIMMY, THE
WALLACE AND GROMIT: THE BEST OF AARDMAN ANIMATION

OCTOBER FILMS

BREAKING THE WAVES
CELESTIAL CLOCKWORK
CEMETERY MAN
FUNERAL, THE
GIRLS TOWN
SECRETS & LIES
SMALL FACES
SOMEONE ELSE'S AMERICA
WHITE BALLOON, THE

ORION

ARRIVAL, THE
DAENS
FAST MONEY
ORIGINAL GANGSTAS
PALOOKAVILLE
PHAT BEACH
SUBSTITUTE, THE
THEREMIN: AN ELECTRONIC ODYSSEY
TREES LOUNGE

ORION CLASSICS

ED'S NEXT MOVE
MAYBE . . . MAYBE NOT

ORION HOME VIDEO

ALEX
FRIEND OF THE FAMILY 2
GLASS CAGE, THE
RED LINE

PACIFIC ARTS

BERKELEY IN THE 60S

PARAMOUNT

BEAVIS AND BUTT-HEAD DO AMERICA

BLACK SHEEP
DEAR GOD
EVENING STAR, THE
EYE FOR AN EYE
FIRST WIVES CLUB, THE
GHOST AND THE DARKNESS, THE
HARRIET THE SPY
JOHN CARPENTER'S ESCAPE FROM L.A.
KIDS IN THE HALL: BRAIN CANDY
MAGIC IN THE MIRROR
MISSION: IMPOSSIBLE
MOTHER
PHANTOM, THE
PRIMAL FEAR
STAR TREK: FIRST CONTACT
STEPHEN KING'S THINNER
VERY BRADY SEQUEL, A

PARAMOUNT HOME VIDEO

BLOODKNOT
DEAD WEEKEND
DOWN, OUT AND DANGEROUS
FULL BODY MASSAGE
GALAXIES ARE COLLIDING
JAG
JOSH KIRBY . . . TIME WARRIOR!: EGGS FROM 70,000,000 B.C.
JOSH KIRBY . . . TIME WARRIOR!: JOURNEY TO THE MAGIC CAVERN
JOSH KIRBY . . . TIME WARRIOR!: LAST BATTLE FOR THE UNIVERSE
JOSH KIRBY . . . TIME WARRIOR!: TRAPPED ON TOY WORLD
MAN IN THE ATTIC, THE
MATERNAL INSTINCTS
MOONSHINE HIGHWAY
OUT THERE
PLAYBACK
ROAD TO GALVESTON, THE
SOLITAIRE FOR TWO
SPELLBREAKER: SECRET OF THE LEPRECHAUNS
TAILS YOU LIVE, HEADS YOU'RE DEAD
WHARF RAT, THE
WHERE'S THE MONEY, NOREEN?

PARAMOUNT/DOVE ENTERTAINMENT

WAVELENGTH

PAULIST PICTURES

ENTERTAINING ANGELS: THE DOROTHY DAY STORY

PHAEDRA CINEMA

TIMELESS

PM ENTERTAINMENT

PURE DANGER
RAGE
SKYSCRAPER
SWEEPER, THE
TIGER HEART

POLART

MOTHER OF KINGS

POLYGRAM VIDEO

COLD LIGHT OF DAY
EDIE & PEN
JUST YOUR LUCK
LITTLE DEATH, THE
PIG'S TALE, A

PONY CANYON INC.

KAMIKAZE TAXI

PYRAMIDE

NEW LIFE, A

REPUBLIC PICTURES HOME VIDEO

AMANDA AND THE ALIEN
ASSAULT AT WEST POINT
BAJA
BLACK DAY BLUE NIGHT
BREACH OF TRUST
EXIT
FINAL CUT, THE
FRAME BY FRAME
GRAVE, THE
LIVE NUDE GIRLS
MRS. MUNCK
NATIONAL LAMPOON'S FAVORITE DEADLY SINS
NIGHT OF THE SCARECROW
ROAD HOME, THE
RUMPELSTILTSKIN
SERIAL KILLER
SERPENT'S LAIR
TWO-BITS & PEPPER
UNDERTOW
WOMAN UNDONE, A
YESTERDAY'S TARGET

ROLLING THUNDER

CHUNGKING EXPRESS

ROXIE RELEASING

FREEWAY
NICO ICON
WHO KILLED PASOLINI?

SAMBA ENTERTAINMENT

SYNTHETIC PLEASURES

SAMUEL GOLDWYN COMPANY

AMERICAN BUFFALO
ANGELS AND INSECTS
AUGUST
BIG NIGHT
FOXFIRE
I SHOT ANDY WARHOL
LOVE IS ALL THERE IS

SAVOY PICTURES

GETTING AWAY WITH MURDER

SEVENTH ART

MAN OF THE YEAR
PERFECT CANDIDATE, A

SHADOW DISTRIBUTION

MAGIC HUNTER

SHADOWFAX FILM

AVENTURERA

SHOWCASE ENTERTAINMENT/LIVE HOME VIDEO

LIFEFORM

SHOWTIME NETWORKS

LILY DALE
SABRINA, THE TEENAGE WITCH

SOMETHING WEIRD VIDEO

ORIGINAL SINS

SONY CLASSICAL

MADAME BUTTERFLY

SONY MUSIC VIDEO

STREET FIGHTER II: THE ANIMATED MOVIE

SONY PICTURES CLASSICS

ANNE FRANK REMEMBERED
BEAUTIFUL THING
BROTHER OF SLEEP
CAUGHT
CELLULOID CLOSET, THE
DENISE CALLS UP
FLOWER OF MY SECRET, THE
LES VOLEURS
MANNY & LO
MIDWINTER'S TALE, A
WELCOME TO THE DOLLHOUSE
WHOLE WIDE WORLD, THE

SONY PICTURES ENTERTAINMENT

LAST SUPPER, THE

SOUTHERN STAR

SPIDER & ROSE

STARDANCE

DON'T LET YOUR MEAT LOAF

STRAND RELEASING

CURTIS'S CHARM
FRISK
MESSAGE TO LOVE: THE ISLE OF WIGHT FESTIVAL
NEON BIBLE, THE
SINGLE GIRL, A
STONEWALL
UNDER THE DOMIM TREE
VIVE L'AMOUR

TAI SENG VIDEO

ORGANIZED CRIME & TRIAD BUREAU
WING CHUN

TARA RELEASING

EVERYTHING RELATIVE
MODERN AFFAIR, A
VUKOVAR

TEMPE VIDEO

POLYMORPH
SANDMAN, THE

TREE FARM PICTURES

ANGELA

TRIBORO ENTERTAINMENT

LONE JUSTICE: SHOWDOWN AT PLUM CREEK
MOTHER
OVER THE WIRE
PUBLIC ACCESS
SONS OF TRINITY

TUNNEL VISION
WATCH ME

TRISTAR

FAN, THE
IF LUCY FELL
MARY REILLY
MATILDA
MRS. WINTERBOURNE
RACE THE SUN
SUNSET PARK

TRIUMPH RELEASING

SCREAMERS
SOLO
TO GILLIAN ON HER 37TH BIRTHDAY

TROMA TEAM VIDEO

CANNIBAL! THE MUSICAL

TROMA, INC.

BEWARE: CHILDREN AT PLAY
BLONDES HAVE MORE GUNS
BUGGED
SGT. KABUKIMAN N.Y.P.D.

TURNER HOME ENTERTAINMENT

FOREST WARRIOR
HEIDI CHRONICLES, THE
KISSINGER AND NIXON
LAZARUS MAN, THE
NECRONOMICON: BOOK OF THE DEAD
PASSION OF DARKLY NOON, THE
RIDERS OF THE PURPLE SAGE
UNDER THE HULA MOON

20TH CENTURY FOX

BROKEN ARROW
CHAIN REACTION
COURAGE UNDER FIRE
CRUCIBLE, THE
DOWN PERISCOPE
DUNSTON CHECKS IN
GREAT WHITE HYPE, THE
INDEPENDENCE DAY
JINGLE ALL THE WAY
ONE FINE DAY
THAT THING YOU DO!
TRUTH ABOUT CATS AND DOGS, THE
WILLIAM SHAKESPEARE'S ROMEO + JULIET

UNAPIX FILMS

AMERICAN STRAYS
MERCY

UNIVERSAL

BULLETPROOF
CHAMBER, THE
DAYLIGHT
DRAGONHEART
ED
FEAR
FLIPPER
FRIGHTENERS, THE
HAPPY GILMORE
NUTTY PROFESSOR, THE
QUEST, THE
SGT. BILKO
TALES FROM THE CRYPT PRESENTS BORDELLO OF BLOOD

VIDMARK

BLACK OUT
DEAD TO RIGHTS
DENTIST, THE
HOLLOW POINT
PINOCCHIO'S REVENGE
PUBLIC ENEMIES
RAW TARGET
REDEMPTION: KICKBOXER 5
SOMETIMES THEY COME BACK . . . AGAIN
VIRUS
WARHEAD
WOLVES, THE

VIDMARK ENTERTAINMENT

. . . AT FIRST SIGHT
IRON EAGLE IV
MADDENING, THE
PROTEUS
TALES OF EROTICA

VIRGIN VIDEO

UNDERSTUDY: GRAVEYARD SHIFT 2, THE

VIZ VIDEO

SANCTUARY: THE MOVIE

WARNER BROS.

BAD MOON
BIG BULLY
BOGUS
CARPOOL
DIABOLIQUE
ERASER
EXECUTIVE DECISION
GLIMMER MAN, THE
JOE'S APARTMENT
MARS ATTACKS!
MICHAEL COLLINS
MY FELLOW AMERICANS
PROPRIETOR, THE
SLEEPERS
SPACE JAM
SUNCHASER
SURVIVING PICASSO
SWEET NOTHING
TIME TO KILL, A
TIN CUP
TWISTER
TWO IF BY SEA
WAR OF THE BUTTONS, THE

WARNERVISION

CHAMELEON
CRIMINAL HEARTS
HOSTILE INTENTIONS
MIND RIPPER
MR. STITCH
NAKED SOULS
NEMESIS III: PREY HARDER
PRE-MADONNAS

WATER BEARER FILMS

APART FROM HUGH
CROCODILES IN AMSTERDAM
FLAMING EARS
SHADOW OF ANGELS

WOMEN MAKE MOVIES

CALLING THE GHOSTS: A STORY ABOUT RAPE, WAR AND WOMEN

XENON ENTERTAINMENT

LET'S GET BIZZEE

ZEITGEIST FILMS

INSTITUTE BENJAMENTA
PARIS WAS A WOMAN

ZIPPORAH FILMS

LA COMEDIE-FRANCAISE OU L'AMOUR JOUE

FILMS BY STAR RATING

All films in this volume are listed below by their star ratings. The ratings are:

★★★★★ = Masterpiece; ★★★★ = Excellent; ★★★ = Good; ★★ = Fair; ★ = Poor; No Star Rating = Without Merit

★★★★½

CHUNGKING EXPRESS
SECRETS & LIES

★★★★

BIG NIGHT
BLACK MOUNTAIN
CEMETERY MAN
COLD FEVER
DEAD MAN
FATE
JOHNNY 100 PESOS
LA CEREMONIE
LA COMEDIE-FRANCAISE OU L'AMOUR JOUE
LONE STAR
MILLE BOLLE BLU
PARADISE LOST: THE CHILD MURDERS AT ROBIN HOOD HILLS
PERSONAL JOURNEY WITH MARTIN SCORSESE THROUGH AMERICAN MOVIES, A
RENDEZVOUS IN PARIS
SILENCES OF THE PALACE, THE
SINGLE GIRL, A
THEREMIN: AN ELECTRONIC ODYSSEY

★★★½

AMERICA'S DREAM
ANGELA
ANNE FRANK REMEMBERED
AVENTURERA
BATON ROUGE
BEYOND THE CALL
BOUND
CALLING THE GHOSTS: A STORY ABOUT RAPE, WAR AND WOMEN
CHAMPAGNE SAFARI, THE
COLD COMFORT FARM
CRUCIBLE, THE
DADETOWN
DAENS
DESOLATION ANGELS
DEVOTION
EMMA
FARGO
FLOWER OF MY SECRET, THE
FLY AWAY HOME
FRANCOIS TRUFFAUT: STOLEN PORTRAITS
FREEWAY
FRIGHTENERS, THE
GIRL 6
HEAVY
HEIDI FLEISS HOLLYWOOD MADAM
I'M NOT RAPPAPORT
JAMES AND THE GIANT PEACH
JERRY MAGUIRE
KANSAS CITY
LAND AND FREEDOM
LIVE NUDE GIRLS
LOSING CHASE
MA SAISON PREFEREE
MADAME WANG'S
MAN WITH A PLAN
MANNY & LO
MESSAGE TO LOVE: THE ISLE OF WIGHT FESTIVAL
MICHAEL COLLINS
MOTHER
MOTHER OF KINGS
NEUROSIA: 50 YEARS OF PERVERSITY
NORMAL LIFE
PEOPLE VS. LARRY FLYNT, THE
PORTRAIT OF A LADY, THE
RIDICULE
ROLLING STONES ROCK-AND-ROLL CIRCUS, THE
SCREAM
SHINE
SILENCE OF NETO, THE
SKIN
SLING BLADE
SOMEONE ELSE'S AMERICA
SPIDER & ROSE
STORY OF XINGHUA, THE
THREE LIVES AND ONLY ONE DEATH
TRAINSPOTTING
TWO FRIENDS
UNHOOK THE STARS
WAR AT HOME, THE
WELCOME TO THE DOLLHOUSE
WHEN WE WERE KINGS

★★★

ADVENTURES OF PINOCCHIO, THE
AMERICAN BUFFALO
ANGELS AND INSECTS
ANNA
BEAUTIFUL GIRLS
BEAUTIFUL THING
BERKELEY IN THE 60S
BIG WARS
BOTTLE ROCKET
BREAKING THE WAVES
BROKEN ARROW
MADAME BUTTERFLY
CANTERVILLE GHOST, THE
CAUGHT
CELESTIAL CLOCKWORK
CELLULOID CLOSET, THE
CHEKIST, THE
CHILDREN OF NOISY VILLAGE, THE
CITY HALL
COLD LIGHT OF DAY
CRACKER: THE MADWOMAN IN THE ATTIC
CRAFT, THE
CURDLED
DEATH BENEFIT
DON'T BE A MENACE TO SOUTH CENTRAL WHILE DRINKING YOUR JUICE IN THE HOOD
ED'S NEXT MOVE
ENGLISH PATIENT, THE
ENTERTAINING ANGELS: THE DOROTHY DAY STORY
EVERYTHING RELATIVE
EVITA
EYE OF VICHY, THE
FAMILY THING, A
FAST MONEY
FROM THE JOURNALS OF JEAN SEBERG
GET ON THE BUS
GHOST AND THE DARKNESS, THE
GHOST IN THE SHELL
GIRLS TOWN
GLIMMER MAN, THE
HEDD WYNN
HEIDI CHRONICLES, THE
HUNCHBACK OF NOTRE DAME, THE
HYPE!
I SHOT ANDY WARHOL
INSTITUTE BENJAMENTA
JUDE
KASPAR HAUSER
KINGPIN
LITTLE INDIAN, BIG CITY
LOTTO LAND
LOVE IS ALL THERE IS
MABOROSI
MAN BY THE SHORE, THE
MARS ATTACKS!
MARVIN'S ROOM
MISSION: IMPOSSIBLE
MONSTER, THE
MONSTERSHOW
NECRONOMICON: BOOK OF THE DEAD
NELLY AND MONSIEUR ARNAUD
NEW LIFE, A
NICO ICON
NIKI DE SAINT PHALLE: WHO IS THE MONSTER — YOU OR ME?
NORMA JEAN AND MARILYN
ONCE UPON A TIME . . . WHEN WE WERE COLORED
ONE FINE DAY
ONE LESS EGG TO FRY
OUTPOST, THE
OUTRAGE
PASSION OF DARKLY NOON, THE
PERFECT CANDIDATE, A
PHARAOH'S ARMY
POLYMORPH
PRIMAL FEAR
RANSOM
RIDERS OF THE PURPLE SAGE
SAINTS AND SINNERS
SHADOW OF ANGELS
SMALL FACES
SOME FOLKS CALL IT A SLING BLADE
SOME MOTHER'S SON
SONG SPINNER, THE
STAR MAKER, THE
STAR TREK: FIRST CONTACT
SUGARTIME
SWEET NOTHING
SWINGERS
TARGET

TEXAS CHAINSAW MASSACRE: THE NEXT GENERATION
TIN CUP
TO GILLIAN ON HER 37TH BIRTHDAY
TREES LOUNGE
TRUMAN
TUNNEL VISION
TUSKEGEE AIRMEN, THE
TWISTER
2 DAYS IN THE VALLEY
UNDER THE DOMIM TREE
VERY BRADY SEQUEL, A
WALKING AND TALKING
WALLACE AND GROMIT: THE BEST OF AARDMAN ANIMATION
WHITE BALLOON, THE
WHOLE WIDE WORLD, THE
WICKED CITY, THE
WIFE, THE
WILD SIDE
YOUNG POISONER'S HANDBOOK, THE

★★½

ABUSE
AFFAIR, THE
ALASKA
ALEX
AMERICAN STRAYS
ANNIE O
ARRIVAL, THE
ASSOCIATE, THE
BASQUIAT
BED OF ROSES
BEFORE AND AFTER
BIG SQUEEZE, THE
BITTER SUGAR
BLACK DAY BLUE NIGHT
BLOODKNOT
BOY CALLED HATE, A
BOYS NEXT DOOR, THE
BROTHER OF SLEEP
BUGGED
BUTTERFLY KISS
CABLE GUY, THE
CANNIBAL! THE MUSICAL
CAPTIVES
CHAIN REACTION
CHASING BUTTERFLIES
CHILDREN OF FURY
COLONY, THE
CONDITION RED
COURAGE UNDER FIRE
CURTIS'S CHARM
D3: THE MIGHTY DUCKS
DANGEROUS PASSION
DARKMAN III: DIE DARKMAN DIE
DAYLIGHT
DEAD COLD
DEAD TO RIGHTS
DENTIST, THE
DOWN, OUT AND DANGEROUS
DRAGONHEART
EDIE & PEN
ERNESTO CHE GUEVARA—THE BOLIVIAN DIARY
EVERYONE SAYS I LOVE YOU
EVIL HAS A FACE
EXECUTIVE DECISION
FEAR
FINAL CUT, THE
FLATTERED
FLIRT
FLIRTING WITH DISASTER
4 TALES OF 2 CITIES
FRAME BY FRAME
FRENCH TWIST
FULL BODY MASSAGE
FUNERAL, THE
GHOSTS OF MISSISSIPPI
GIRLFRIENDS
GRACE OF MY HEART
GREAT WHITE HYPE, THE
HALFMOON
HAMLET
HARRIET THE SPY
HATE
HAUNTED
HEAVEN'S PRISONERS
HECK'S WAY HOME
HOLLOW POINT
HOMAGE
HOMECOMING
HORSEMAN ON THE ROOF
INDEPENDENCE DAY
ISLAND OF DR. MOREAU, THE
JAG
JANE EYRE
JOHN CARPENTER'S ESCAPE FROM L.A.
JOHNNY SHORTWAVE
JUST YOUR LUCK
KAMIKAZE TAXI
KIDS IN THE HALL: BRAIN CANDY
KISSINGER AND NIXON
LARRY MCMURTRY'S STREETS OF LAREDO
LAZARUS MAN, THE
LEGEND OF GATOR FACE, THE
LES VOLEURS
LET'S GET BIZZEE
LETTER TO MY KILLER
LINE KING: THE AL HIRSCHFELD STORY, THE
LIVE WIRE: HUMAN TIMEBOMB
LONE JUSTICE: SHOWDOWN AT PLUM CREEK
LONG KISS GOODNIGHT, THE
LOOKING FOR RICHARD
LOVER'S KNOT
LOW LIFE, THE
MACHINE, THE
MADAGASCAR SKIN
MAHJONG
MATILDA
MAYBE . . . MAYBE NOT
MERCY
MICHAEL
MIDWINTER'S TALE, A
MIRROR HAS TWO FACES, THE
MR. ICE CREAM MAN
MR. STITCH
MR. WRONG
MODERN AFFAIR, A
MOONSHINE HIGHWAY
MOTHER
MRS. MUNCK
MULHOLLAND FALLS
MUPPET TREASURE ISLAND
MYSTERY SCIENCE THEATER 3000: THE MOVIE
NATIONAL LAMPOON'S FAVORITE DEADLY SINS
NEON BIBLE, THE
NIGHT OF THE SCARECROW
NIGHT OF THE TWISTERS
NIGHT ON THE GALACTIC RAILROAD
NOT OF THIS EARTH
NUTTY PROFESSOR, THE
ORIGINAL GANGSTAS
ORIGINAL SINS
ORSON WELLES: THE ONE-MAN BAND
PALOOKAVILLE
PARIS WAS A WOMAN
PATLABOR 2: MOBILE POLICE
PINOCCHIO'S REVENGE
PREACHER'S WIFE, THE
PREDICTIONS OF FIRE
PROTEUS
RAGE
RASPUTIN
RATTLED
ROAD TO GALVESTON, THE
ROBIN OF LOCKSLEY
ROUJIN-Z
RUDE
SANCTUARY: THE MOVIE
SANDMAN, THE
SET IT OFF
SHE'S THE ONE
SHOPPING
SHOT, THE
SHOWGIRL MURDERS, THE
SONIC OUTLAWS
STEALING BEAUTY
STEPHEN KING'S THINNER
STONEWALL
STREET FIGHTER II: THE ANIMATED MOVIE
STREETCAR NAMED DESIRE, A
SUBSTANCE OF FIRE, THE
SUBSTITUTE, THE
SUITE 16
SURVIVING PICASSO
TALES OF EROTICA
TATTOO BOY
THAT THING YOU DO!
THEY BITE
THIN LINE BETWEEN LOVE AND HATE, A
TIMELESS
TRACKS OF A KILLER
TREMORS 2: AFTERSHOCKS
TWO DEATHS
VIVE L'AMOUR
VUKOVAR
WAR OF THE BUTTONS, THE
WHITE SQUALL
WHO KILLED PASOLINI?
WIND IN THE WILLOWS, THE
WING CHUN

★★

ALL DOGS GO TO HEAVEN 2
ANTONIA'S LINE
APART FROM HUGH
ASSAULT AT WEST POINT
. . . AT FIRST SIGHT
AUGUST
BACKLASH: OBLIVION 2
BAD MOON
BEAVIS AND BUTT-HEAD DO AMERICA
BEST OF THE BEST 3: NO TURNING BACK
BEWARE: CHILDREN AT PLAY
BEYOND DESIRE
BIRDCAGE, THE
BLACK OUT
BLACK SCORPION
BLUSH
BODY COUNT
BOYS
BREACH OF TRUST
BREAKAWAY
BULLETPROOF
CARRIED AWAY

CATWALK
CHAMELEON
CITIZEN RUTH
CROCODILES IN AMSTERDAM
CROSSCUT
DEADLY OUTBREAK
DEAR GOD
DELTA OF VENUS
DENISE CALLS UP
DESIRE
DIABOLIQUE
DOGFIGHTERS, THE
DONOR UNKNOWN
DOWN PERISCOPE
EDDIE
ERASER
EVENING STAR, THE
EVIL ED
EXIT
EXTREME MEASURES
FAN, THE
FATALLY YOURS
FEELING MINNESOTA
FIRE ON THE MOUNTAIN
FIRST KID
FIRST WIVES CLUB, THE
FLIPPER
FOR THE MOMENT
FROM DUSK TILL DAWN
GIRL FROM MARS, THE
GRASS HARP, THE
GRAVE, THE
GUIMBA THE TYRANT
HARD JUSTICE
HARVEST OF FIRE
HEADLESS BODY IN TOPLESS BAR
HELLRAISER: BLOODLINE
HIDDEN ASSASSIN
HOMEWARD BOUND II: LOST IN SAN FRANCISCO
IN LOVE AND WAR
INFINITY
IT'S MY PARTY
JACK
JACK & SARAH
JOSEPH CONRAD'S THE SECRET AGENT
JUROR, THE
LAND BEFORE TIME IV: JOURNEY THROUGH THE MISTS
LAST MAN STANDING
LATE SHIFT, THE
LIFEFORM
LILY DALE
LITTLE DEATH, THE
LOADED
LONG ROAD HOME, THE
MAD DOG TIME
MADDENING, THE
MAGIC HUNTER
MAN WITH THE PERFECT SWING, THE
MATERNAL INSTINCTS
MAXIMUM RISK
MICROCOSMOS
MIDNIGHT ANGEL
MIDNIGHT DANCERS
MR. HOLLAND'S OPUS
MOLL FLANDERS
MOTHER NIGHT
MOTHER'S PRAYER, A
MURDERED INNOCENCE
MY FELLOW AMERICANS
NAKED SOULS
NOT BAD FOR A GIRL
OF LOVE AND SHADOWS
ONE GOOD TURN
101 DALMATIANS
ONE MAN'S JUSTICE
ONE NIGHT STAND
ORGANIZED CRIME & TRIAD BUREAU
OUT THERE
OVER THE WIRE
PAINTED HERO
PHANTOM 2040: THE GHOST WHO WALKS
PHANTOM, THE
PHENOMENON
PIE IN THE SKY
PIRANHA
PRE-MADONNAS
PROPRIETOR, THE
PUBLIC ACCESS
PUBLIC ENEMIES
QUEST, THE
RAVENHAWK
RED SCORPION 2
RICH MAN'S WIFE, THE
ROAD HOME, THE
ROCK, THE
RUMBLE IN THE BRONX
SABRINA, THE TEENAGE WITCH
SANTA WITH MUSCLES
SAWBONES
SCREAMERS
SERIAL KILLER
SHADOW WARRIORS
SHADOW YOU SOON WILL BE, A
SHAMELESS
SHARON'S SECRET
SHOOTFIGHTER 2: KILL OR BE KILLED!
SKYSCRAPER
SLEEPERS
SMALL WONDERS
SOLO
SOMETIMES THEY COME BACK . . . AGAIN
SONS OF TRINITY
SPACE JAM
SPELLBREAKER: SECRET OF THE LEPRECHAUNS
SPITFIRE GRILL, THE
STAND OFF, THE
STRIPTEASE
STUPIDS, THE
SUNSET PARK
SWEEPER, THE
TAILS YOU LIVE, HEADS YOU'RE DEAD
TALKING ABOUT SEX
TERMINAL IMPACT
TEXAS PAYBACK
THEODORE REX
TOLLBOOTH
TRIGGER EFFECT, THE
TRUTH ABOUT CATS AND DOGS, THE
TWELFTH NIGHT
UNDERSTUDY: GRAVEYARD SHIFT 2, THE
UNDERTOW
UNFORGETTABLE
UNKNOWN ORIGIN
UP CLOSE AND PERSONAL
VIRTUAL COMBAT
VIRUS
VISITORS, THE
WARHEAD
WAVELENGTH
WHISPERING, THE
WIDOW'S KISS
WITHIN THE ROCK
WITHOUT MERCY
WOLVES, THE
WOMAN UNDONE, A
YESTERDAY'S TARGET

★½

BARB WIRE
BIG BULLY
BODY OF INFLUENCE 2
BOGUS
BRITT ALLCROFT'S MAGIC ADVENTURES OF MUMFIE—THE MOVIE
CARNOSAUR 3: PRIMAL SPECIES
CELTIC PRIDE
CHAMBER, THE
CRIMINAL HEARTS
DEMOLITIONIST, THE
ED
ELECTRA
FAITHFUL
FAR HARBOR
FOXFIRE
GETTING AWAY WITH MURDER
GRIM
HALFBACK OF NOTRE DAME, THE
HAPPY GILMORE
HOUSE ARREST
HOW THE WEST WAS FUN
IF LUCY FELL
JINGLE ALL THE WAY
JOSH KIRBY . . . TIME WARRIOR!: EGGS FROM 70,000,000 B.C.
JOSH KIRBY . . . TIME WARRIOR!: JOURNEY TO THE MAGIC CAVERN
JOSH KIRBY . . . TIME WARRIOR!: LAST BATTLE FOR THE UNIVERSE
KAZAAM
LARGER THAN LIFE
LAST DANCE
LAST SUPPER, THE
LAWNMOWER MAN 2: BEYOND CYBERSPACE
LITTLE WITCHES
MAN IN THE ATTIC, THE
MARY REILLY
MIND RIPPER
MOUTH TO MOUTH
MRS. WINTERBOURNE
OPEN SEASON
OUTER LIMITS: SANDKINGS, THE
PALLBEARER, THE
PLAYBACK
POISON IVY 2: LILY
POMPATUS OF LOVE, THE
PORTRAITS OF A KILLER
RACE THE SUN
RED LINE
RUMPELSTILTSKIN
SEARCH FOR ONE-EYE JIMMY, THE
SGT. BILKO
SPY HARD
SUNCHASER
SURGEON, THE
SYNTHETIC PLEASURES
TALES FROM THE CRYPT PRESENTS BORDELLO OF BLOOD
TIME TO KILL, A
TWO MUCH
WEEKEND IN THE COUNTRY, A
WILLIAM SHAKESPEARE'S ROMEO + JULIET
YOU'LL NEVER MAKE LOVE IN THIS TOWN AGAIN

ADRENALIN: FEAR THE RUSH

FILMS BY STAR RATING

AMANDA AND THE ALIEN
ANIMAL INSTINCTS III: THE SEDUCTRESS
BAD LOVE
BAJA
BEASTMASTER 3: THE EYE OF BRAXUS
BIO-DOME
BLACK ROSE OF HARLEM
BLACK SHEEP
BLONDES HAVE MORE GUNS
BLOOD & DONUTS
BLOODSPORT II: THE NEXT KUMITE
BURIAL OF THE RATS
CARPOOL
CHILDREN OF THE CORN: THE GATHERING
CLUBHOUSE DETECTIVES
CROW: CITY OF ANGELS, THE
DARK SECRETS
DEAD WEEKEND
DEATH ARTIST, THE
DON'T LET YOUR MEAT LOAF
DUNSTON CHECKS IN
EYE FOR AN EYE
FELONY
FEMALIEN
FINAL EQUINOX, THE
FIST OF THE NORTH STAR
FLED
FOR BETTER OR WORSE
FORBIDDEN ZONE: ALIEN ABDUCTION
FOREST WARRIOR
FRIEND OF THE FAMILY 2
FRISK
FUGITIVE RAGE
FUNNYMAN, THE
GALAXIES ARE COLLIDING
GLASS CAGE, THE
HARD WAY OUT: BLOODFIST VIII
HEAD OF THE FAMILY
HIGH SCHOOL HIGH
HOSTILE INTENTIONS
HOURGLASS
IMMORTALS, THE
IRON EAGLE IV
IT CAME FROM OUTER SPACE II
JOE'S APARTMENT
JOSH KIRBY . . . TIME WARRIOR!: TRAPPED ON TOY WORLD
LOOKING FOR TROUBLE
MAGIC IN THE MIRROR
MAN OF THE YEAR
MERLIN'S SHOP OF MAGICAL WONDERS
MIRROR, MIRROR III: THE VOYEUR
MISSING PIECES
MULTIPLICITY
MUTANT MAN
NEMESIS III: PREY HARDER
OFF AND RUNNING
PHAT BEACH
PHOENIX
PIG'S TALE, A
PURE DANGER
RAW TARGET
REDEMPTION: KICKBOXER 5
SANTA CLAWS
SGT. KABUKIMAN N.Y.P.D.
SERPENT'S LAIR
SOLITAIRE FOR TWO
SOUTH BEACH ACADEMY
TAKEOVER, THE
TIGER HEART
TOO FAST, TOO YOUNG
TWO-BITS & PEPPER
TWO IF BY SEA
UNDER THE HULA MOON
VENUS RISING
VIKING SAGAS, THE
VIRTUAL ENCOUNTERS
WATCH ME
WHARF RAT, THE
WHEN THE BULLET HITS THE BONE
WHERE'S THE MONEY, NOREEN?
WHITE TIGER
WHITE WOLVES II: LEGEND OF THE WILD
WITCHCRAFT: SALEM'S GHOST
YANKEE ZULU
ZARKORR! THE INVADER

NO STAR RATING

FLAMING EARS

FILMS BY GENRE

Films belonging to more than one genre are listed under each appropriate category

Action

BARB WIRE
BEASTMASTER 3: THE EYE OF BRAXUS
BEST OF THE BEST 3: NO TURNING BACK
BEYOND DESIRE
BLOODSPORT II: THE NEXT KUMITE
BODY COUNT
BREACH OF TRUST
BREAKAWAY
BROKEN ARROW
BULLETPROOF
CARNOSAUR 3: PRIMAL SPECIES
CHAIN REACTION
CRIMINAL HEARTS
CROSSCUT
CROW: CITY OF ANGELS, THE
DANGEROUS PASSION
DARKMAN III: DIE DARKMAN DIE
DAYLIGHT
DEADLY OUTBREAK
DEMOLITIONIST, THE
DOGFIGHTERS, THE
ERASER
EXECUTIVE DECISION
EXIT
FAST MONEY
FATALLY YOURS
FELONY
FINAL CUT, THE
FINAL EQUINOX, THE
FLED
FOREST WARRIOR
FUGITIVE RAGE
GLIMMER MAN, THE
GRIM
HARD JUSTICE
HARD WAY OUT: BLOODFIST VIII
HIDDEN ASSASSIN
HOSTILE INTENTIONS
IMMORTALS, THE
INDEPENDENCE DAY
IRON EAGLE IV
JINGLE ALL THE WAY
JOHN CARPENTER'S ESCAPE FROM L.A.
LAST MAN STANDING
LAWNMOWER MAN 2: BEYOND CYBERSPACE
LONG KISS GOODNIGHT, THE
MAXIMUM RISK
MIDNIGHT ANGEL
MISSION: IMPOSSIBLE
NEMESIS III: PREY HARDER
ONE MAN'S JUSTICE
ORIGINAL GANGSTAS
PHANTOM, THE
PHOENIX
POLYMORPH
PUBLIC ENEMIES
PURE DANGER
QUEST, THE
RAGE
RANSOM
RAVENHAWK
RAW TARGET
RED SCORPION 2
REDEMPTION: KICKBOXER 5
ROCK, THE
RUMBLE IN THE BRONX
SET IT OFF
SHADOW WARRIORS
SKYSCRAPER
SOLO
SUBSTITUTE, THE
SUBSTITUTE, THE
SWEEPER, THE
TAILS YOU LIVE, HEADS YOU'RE DEAD
TAKEOVER, THE
TERMINAL IMPACT
TEXAS PAYBACK
TIGER HEART
TOO FAST, TOO YOUNG
UNDER THE HULA MOON
VENUS RISING
VIRTUAL COMBAT
VIRUS
WARHEAD
WHARF RAT, THE
WHEN THE BULLET HITS THE BONE
WHITE TIGER
WICKED CITY, THE
WING CHUN
WITHOUT MERCY
WOLVES, THE
YANKEE ZULU

Adventure

ALASKA
BEASTMASTER 3: THE EYE OF BRAXUS
BLACK SCORPION
BROKEN ARROW
CHAIN REACTION
CLUBHOUSE DETECTIVES
DAYLIGHT
DRAGONHEART
ERASER
EXECUTIVE DECISION
FLIPPER
FOREST WARRIOR
GHOST AND THE DARKNESS, THE
HECK'S WAY HOME
HOMEWARD BOUND II: LOST IN SAN FRANCISCO
JOSH KIRBY . . . TIME WARRIOR!: EGGS FROM 70,000,000 B.C.
JOSH KIRBY . . . TIME WARRIOR!: JOURNEY TO THE MAGIC CAVERN
JOSH KIRBY . . . TIME WARRIOR!: LAST BATTLE FOR THE UNIVERSE
JOSH KIRBY . . . TIME WARRIOR!: TRAPPED ON TOY WORLD
LEGEND OF GATOR FACE, THE
MOLL FLANDERS
OFF AND RUNNING
PHANTOM, THE
QUEST, THE
ROCK, THE
SOLO
SPACE JAM
STAR TREK: FIRST CONTACT
STREET FIGHTER II: THE ANIMATED MOVIE
SUNCHASER
UNKNOWN ORIGIN
VIKING SAGAS, THE
WAR OF THE BUTTONS, THE
WHITE SQUALL
WHITE WOLVES II: LEGEND OF THE WILD

Animated

ALL DOGS GO TO HEAVEN 2
BEAVIS AND BUTT-HEAD DO AMERICA
BIG WARS
BRITT ALLCROFT'S MAGIC ADVENTURES OF MUMFIE—THE MOVIE
GHOST IN THE SHELL
HUNCHBACK OF NOTRE DAME, THE
JAMES AND THE GIANT PEACH
LAND BEFORE TIME IV: JOURNEY THROUGH THE MISTS
NIGHT ON THE GALACTIC RAILROAD
PATLABOR 2: MOBILE POLICE
PHANTOM 2040: THE GHOST WHO WALKS
ROUJIN-Z
SANCTUARY: THE MOVIE
SPACE JAM
STREET FIGHTER II: THE ANIMATED MOVIE
WALLACE AND GROMIT: THE BEST OF AARDMAN ANIMATION
WIND IN THE WILLOWS, THE

Biography

ANNE FRANK REMEMBERED
BASQUIAT
DAENS
ENTERTAINING ANGELS: THE DOROTHY DAY STORY
EVITA
FROM THE JOURNALS OF JEAN SEBERG
HEDD WYNN
I SHOT ANDY WARHOL
IN LOVE AND WAR
KASPAR HAUSER
MICHAEL COLLINS
NORMA JEAN AND MARILYN
ONCE UPON A TIME . . . WHEN WE WERE COLORED
PEOPLE VS. LARRY FLYNT, THE
RASPUTIN
SURVIVING PICASSO
TRUMAN
WHO KILLED PASOLINI?
WHOLE WIDE WORLD, THE

Children's

ADVENTURES OF PINOCCHIO, THE
ALASKA
ALL DOGS GO TO HEAVEN 2
ANNIE O
BEASTMASTER 3: THE EYE OF BRAXUS
BRITT ALLCROFT'S MAGIC ADVENTURES OF MUMFIE—THE MOVIE
CANTERVILLE GHOST, THE
CHILDREN OF NOISY VILLAGE, THE
CLUBHOUSE DETECTIVES

D3: THE MIGHTY DUCKS
DUNSTON CHECKS IN
ED
FIRST KID
FLIPPER
FLY AWAY HOME
HALFBACK OF NOTRE DAME, THE
HARRIET THE SPY
HECK'S WAY HOME
HOMEWARD BOUND II: LOST IN SAN FRANCISCO
HOUSE ARREST
HOW THE WEST WAS FUN
JAMES AND THE GIANT PEACH
JOSH KIRBY . . . TIME WARRIOR!: EGGS FROM 70,000,000 B.C.
JOSH KIRBY . . . TIME WARRIOR!: JOURNEY TO THE MAGIC CAVERN
JOSH KIRBY . . . TIME WARRIOR!: LAST BATTLE FOR THE UNIVERSE
JOSH KIRBY . . . TIME WARRIOR!: TRAPPED ON TOY WORLD
KAZAAM
LAND BEFORE TIME IV: JOURNEY THROUGH THE MISTS
LITTLE INDIAN, BIG CITY
LOOKING FOR TROUBLE
MAGIC IN THE MIRROR
MATILDA
MERLIN'S SHOP OF MAGICAL WONDERS
MUPPET TREASURE ISLAND
NIGHT OF THE TWISTERS
101 DALMATIANS
ROAD HOME, THE
ROBIN OF LOCKSLEY
SABRINA, THE TEENAGE WITCH
SANTA WITH MUSCLES
SONG SPINNER, THE
SPELLBREAKER: SECRET OF THE LEPRECHAUNS
STUPIDS, THE
THEODORE REX
WAR OF THE BUTTONS, THE
WHITE BALLOON, THE
WIND IN THE WILLOWS, THE

Comedy

ALL DOGS GO TO HEAVEN 2
AMANDA AND THE ALIEN
ASSOCIATE, THE
. . . AT FIRST SIGHT
BACKLASH: OBLIVION 2
BEAUTIFUL GIRLS
BEAUTIFUL THING
BED OF ROSES
BIG BULLY
BIG NIGHT
BIG SQUEEZE, THE
BIO-DOME
BIRDCAGE, THE
BLACK SHEEP
BLONDES HAVE MORE GUNS
BLOOD & DONUTS
BOGUS
BOTTLE ROCKET
BOYS NEXT DOOR, THE
BUGGED
BULLETPROOF
CABLE GUY, THE
CANNIBAL! THE MUSICAL
CARPOOL
CELESTIAL CLOCKWORK
CELTIC PRIDE
CHUNGKING EXPRESS
CITIZEN RUTH
COLD COMFORT FARM
COLD FEVER
CROCODILES IN AMSTERDAM
CURDLED
CURTIS'S CHARM
D3: THE MIGHTY DUCKS
DEAR GOD
DEATH ARTIST, THE
DENISE CALLS UP
DON'T BE A MENACE TO SOUTH CENTRAL WHILE DRINKING YOUR JUICE IN THE HOOD
DON'T LET YOUR MEAT LOAF
DOWN PERISCOPE
DUNSTON CHECKS IN
ED
EDDIE
EDIE & PEN
ED'S NEXT MOVE
EMMA
EVENING STAR, THE
EVERYONE SAYS I LOVE YOU
EVERYTHING RELATIVE
EVIL ED
FAITHFUL
FAMILY THING, A
FARGO
FEELING MINNESOTA
FIRST KID
FIRST WIVES CLUB, THE
FLATTERED
FLIRT
FLIRTING WITH DISASTER
FOR BETTER OR WORSE
4 TALES OF 2 CITIES
FRENCH TWIST
FRIGHTENERS, THE
FROM DUSK TILL DAWN
FUNNYMAN, THE
GALAXIES ARE COLLIDING
GETTING AWAY WITH MURDER
GIRL 6
GIRLFRIENDS
GREAT WHITE HYPE, THE
GUIMBA THE TYRANT
HAPPY GILMORE
HARRIET THE SPY
HEAD OF THE FAMILY
HECK'S WAY HOME
HIGH SCHOOL HIGH
HOLLOW POINT
HOUSE ARREST
HOW THE WEST WAS FUN
IF LUCY FELL
I'M NOT RAPPAPORT
IT'S MY PARTY
JACK
JACK & SARAH
JERRY MAGUIRE
JINGLE ALL THE WAY
JOE'S APARTMENT
KAZAAM
KIDS IN THE HALL: BRAIN CANDY
KINGPIN
LARGER THAN LIFE
LAST SUPPER, THE
LATE SHIFT, THE
LET'S GET BIZZEE
LITTLE INDIAN, BIG CITY
LIVE NUDE GIRLS
LOOKING FOR TROUBLE
LOVE IS ALL THERE IS
LOVER'S KNOT
LOW LIFE, THE
MAD DOG TIME
MADAME WANG'S
MAHJONG
MAN WITH A PLAN
MAN WITH THE PERFECT SWING, THE
MANNY & LO
MARS ATTACKS!
MATILDA
MAYBE . . . MAYBE NOT
MICHAEL
MIDWINTER'S TALE, A
MILLE BOLLE BLU
MIRROR HAS TWO FACES, THE
MISSING PIECES
MR. WRONG
MODERN AFFAIR, A
MONSTER, THE
MOTHER
MOUTH TO MOUTH
MRS. MUNCK
MRS. WINTERBOURNE
MULTIPLICITY
MUPPET TREASURE ISLAND
MY FELLOW AMERICANS
MYSTERY SCIENCE THEATER 3000: THE MOVIE
NATIONAL LAMPOON'S FAVORITE DEADLY SINS
NEUROSIA: 50 YEARS OF PERVERSITY
NUTTY PROFESSOR, THE
OFF AND RUNNING
ONE FINE DAY
101 DALMATIANS
OPEN SEASON
ORIGINAL SINS
OUT THERE
PALLBEARER, THE
PALOOKAVILLE
PHAT BEACH
PIE IN THE SKY
PIG'S TALE, A
POMPATUS OF LOVE, THE
PRE-MADONNAS
PURE DANGER
RACE THE SUN
RENDEZVOUS IN PARIS
SABRINA, THE TEENAGE WITCH
SANTA WITH MUSCLES
SEARCH FOR ONE-EYE JIMMY, THE
SGT. BILKO
SGT. KABUKIMAN N.Y.P.D.
SHE'S THE ONE
SHOT, THE
SOLITAIRE FOR TWO
SOMEONE ELSE'S AMERICA
SONS OF TRINITY
SOUTH BEACH ACADEMY
SPACE JAM
SPIDER & ROSE
SPY HARD
STRIPTEASE
STUPIDS, THE
SUNSET PARK
SWINGERS
TALES FROM THE CRYPT PRESENTS BORDELLO OF BLOOD
TALES OF EROTICA
TALKING ABOUT SEX
THAT THING YOU DO!
THEODORE REX
THEY BITE
THIN LINE BETWEEN LOVE AND HATE, A
TIN CUP

TOLLBOOTH
TRACKS OF A KILLER
TREES LOUNGE
TREMORS 2: AFTERSHOCKS
TRUTH ABOUT CATS AND DOGS, THE
TWELFTH NIGHT
TWO-BITS & PEPPER
2 DAYS IN THE VALLEY
TWO IF BY SEA
TWO MUCH
UNDER THE HULA MOON
UNHOOK THE STARS
VERY BRADY SEQUEL, A
VISITORS, THE
WALKING AND TALKING
WALLACE AND GROMIT: THE BEST OF AARDMAN ANIMATION
WEEKEND IN THE COUNTRY, A
WELCOME TO THE DOLLHOUSE
WHITE BALLOON, THE
WIFE, THE
YANKEE ZULU
YOUNG POISONER'S HANDBOOK, THE

Crime

AMERICAN BUFFALO
AMERICAN STRAYS
BAD LOVE
BAJA
BATON ROUGE
BEYOND DESIRE
BIG SQUEEZE, THE
BLACK OUT
BLACK ROSE OF HARLEM
BLACK SCORPION
BLOODKNOT
BODY COUNT
BOTTLE ROCKET
BOUND
BOY CALLED HATE, A
BREACH OF TRUST
CHAMBER, THE
CITY HALL
CONDITION RED
CRACKER: THE MADWOMAN IN THE ATTIC
CRIMINAL HEARTS
CROSSCUT
CURDLED
DANGEROUS PASSION
DEAD TO RIGHTS
DIABOLIQUE
DOWN, OUT AND DANGEROUS
ELECTRA
EVIL HAS A FACE
EYE FOR AN EYE
FARGO
FAST MONEY
FATALLY YOURS
FEELING MINNESOTA
FLED
FRAME BY FRAME
FREEWAY
FROM DUSK TILL DAWN
FUNERAL, THE
GHOST IN THE SHELL
GLASS CAGE, THE
GRAVE, THE
HARD JUSTICE
HEAVEN'S PRISONERS
HOLLOW POINT
HOSTILE INTENTIONS
HOURGLASS
IMMORTALS, THE
JAG
JOHNNY 100 PESOS
JUST YOUR LUCK
KAMIKAZE TAXI
KANSAS CITY
LA CEREMONIE
LAST MAN STANDING
LETTER TO MY KILLER
MAD DOG TIME
MAXIMUM RISK
MERCY
MIDNIGHT ANGEL
MOONSHINE HIGHWAY
MULHOLLAND FALLS
MURDERED INNOCENCE
NORMAL LIFE
ONE LESS EGG TO FRY
ONE MAN'S JUSTICE
ORGANIZED CRIME & TRIAD BUREAU
ORIGINAL GANGSTAS
PALOOKAVILLE
PORTRAITS OF A KILLER
PRIMAL FEAR
PUBLIC ENEMIES
RAVENHAWK
RAW TARGET
RED LINE
RUMBLE IN THE BRONX
SAINTS AND SINNERS
SANCTUARY: THE MOVIE
SGT. KABUKIMAN N.Y.P.D.
SET IT OFF
SHOOTFIGHTER 2: KILL OR BE KILLED!
SHOPPING
SOME FOLKS CALL IT A SLING BLADE
STAND OFF, THE
STRIPTEASE
SUGARTIME
SUNCHASER
TAILS YOU LIVE, HEADS YOU'RE DEAD
TAKEOVER, THE
TEXAS PAYBACK
THEODORE REX
TIMELESS
TOLLBOOTH
TOO FAST, TOO YOUNG
TUNNEL VISION
TWO-BITS & PEPPER
2 DAYS IN THE VALLEY
UNDER THE HULA MOON
VENUS RISING
WHARF RAT, THE
WHERE'S THE MONEY, NOREEN?
WITHOUT MERCY
YOUNG POISONER'S HANDBOOK, THE

Disaster

DAYLIGHT
NIGHT OF THE TWISTERS

Docudrama

FROM THE JOURNALS OF JEAN SEBERG
GHOSTS OF MISSISSIPPI
I SHOT ANDY WARHOL
KISSINGER AND NIXON
LATE SHIFT, THE
MAN OF THE YEAR
PERFECT CANDIDATE, A
SKIN
TRUMAN
TUSKEGEE AIRMEN, THE
WHO KILLED PASOLINI?

Documentary

ANNA
ANNE FRANK REMEMBERED
BERKELEY IN THE 60S
CALLING THE GHOSTS: A STORY ABOUT RAPE, WAR AND WOMEN
CATWALK
CELLULOID CLOSET, THE
CHAMPAGNE SAFARI, THE
ERNESTO CHE GUEVARA—THE BOLIVIAN DIARY
EYE OF VICHY, THE
FIRE ON THE MOUNTAIN
FRANCOIS TRUFFAUT: STOLEN PORTRAITS
FROM THE JOURNALS OF JEAN SEBERG
HEIDI FLEISS HOLLYWOOD MADAM
HYPE!
LA COMEDIE-FRANCAISE OU L'AMOUR JOUE
LINE KING: THE AL HIRSCHFELD STORY, THE
MESSAGE TO LOVE: THE ISLE OF WIGHT FESTIVAL
MICROCOSMOS
NICO ICON
NIKI DE SAINT PHALLE: WHO IS THE MONSTER — YOU OR ME?
NOT BAD FOR A GIRL
ORSON WELLES: THE ONE-MAN BAND
PARADISE LOST: THE CHILD MURDERS AT ROBIN HOOD HILLS
PARIS WAS A WOMAN
PERSONAL JOURNEY WITH MARTIN SCORSESE THROUGH AMERICAN MOVIES, A
PREDICTIONS OF FIRE
ROLLING STONES ROCK-AND-ROLL CIRCUS, THE
SMALL WONDERS
SONIC OUTLAWS
SYNTHETIC PLEASURES
THEREMIN: AN ELECTRONIC ODYSSEY
WHEN WE WERE KINGS
YOU'LL NEVER MAKE LOVE IN THIS TOWN AGAIN

Drama

ABUSE
AFFAIR, THE
ALEX
AMERICAN BUFFALO
AMERICA'S DREAM
ANGELA
ANGELS AND INSECTS
ANTONIA'S LINE
APART FROM HUGH
ASSAULT AT WEST POINT
AUGUST
AVENTURERA
BAD LOVE
BASQUIAT
BEAUTIFUL GIRLS
BEAUTIFUL THING
BED OF ROSES
BEFORE AND AFTER
BEYOND THE CALL
BIG BULLY
BIG NIGHT
BITTER SUGAR
BLACK MOUNTAIN
BLUSH
BOTTLE ROCKET
BOY CALLED HATE, A
BOYS

BOYS NEXT DOOR, THE
BREAKING THE WAVES
BROTHER OF SLEEP
BUTTERFLY KISS
MADAME BUTTERFLY
CAPTIVES
CARRIED AWAY
CAUGHT
CELESTIAL CLOCKWORK
CHAMBER, THE
CHASING BUTTERFLIES
CHEKIST, THE
CHILDREN OF FURY
CHUNGKING EXPRESS
CITIZEN RUTH
CITY HALL
COLD COMFORT FARM
COLONY, THE
COURAGE UNDER FIRE
CRAFT, THE
CRIMINAL HEARTS
CRUCIBLE, THE
CURTIS'S CHARM
DADETOWN
DARK SECRETS
DEAD TO RIGHTS
DEATH BENEFIT
DELTA OF VENUS
DENISE CALLS UP
DESOLATION ANGELS
DEVOTION
EDIE & PEN
ENGLISH PATIENT, THE
ENTERTAINING ANGELS: THE DOROTHY DAY STORY
EVENING STAR, THE
EVERYTHING RELATIVE
EYE FOR AN EYE
FAITHFUL
FAMILY THING, A
FAR HARBOR
FARGO
FATE
FEELING MINNESOTA
FLED
FLIRT
FLOWER OF MY SECRET, THE
FLY AWAY HOME
FOR THE MOMENT
4 TALES OF 2 CITIES
FOXFIRE
FRENCH TWIST
FRIEND OF THE FAMILY 2
FRISK
FULL BODY MASSAGE
FUNERAL, THE
GET ON THE BUS
GHOST AND THE DARKNESS, THE
GIRL FROM MARS, THE
GIRL 6
GIRLFRIENDS
GIRLS TOWN
GLASS CAGE, THE
GRACE OF MY HEART
GRASS HARP, THE
GUIMBA THE TYRANT
HALFMOON
HAMLET
HARVEST OF FIRE
HATE
HEADLESS BODY IN TOPLESS BAR
HEAVEN'S PRISONERS
HEAVY
HEIDI CHRONICLES, THE
HOMAGE
HOMECOMING
HORSEMAN ON THE ROOF
HOURGLASS
I SHOT ANDY WARHOL
I'M NOT RAPPAPORT
INFINITY
INSTITUTE BENJAMENTA
IT'S MY PARTY
JACK & SARAH
JAG
JANE EYRE
JERRY MAGUIRE
JOHNNY 100 PESOS
JOHNNY SHORTWAVE
JUDE
KANSAS CITY
KASPAR HAUSER
LA CEREMONIE
LAND AND FREEDOM
LAST DANCE
LES VOLEURS
LETTER TO MY KILLER
LILY DALE
LOADED
LONE STAR
LONG ROAD HOME, THE
LOOKING FOR RICHARD
LOSING CHASE
LOTTO LAND
LOVE IS ALL THERE IS
LOVER'S KNOT
LOW LIFE, THE
MA SAISON PREFEREE
MABOROSI
MAD DOG TIME
MADAGASCAR SKIN
MADAME WANG'S
MAGIC HUNTER
MAN BY THE SHORE, THE
MAN IN THE ATTIC, THE
MAN WITH THE PERFECT SWING, THE
MANNY & LO
MARVIN'S ROOM
MARY REILLY
MATERNAL INSTINCTS
MERCY
MICHAEL
MIDNIGHT DANCERS
MILLE BOLLE BLU
MR. HOLLAND'S OPUS
MODERN AFFAIR, A
MOLL FLANDERS
MONSTERSHOW
MOONSHINE HIGHWAY
MOTHER NIGHT
MOTHER OF KINGS
MOTHER'S PRAYER, A
MRS. MUNCK
MRS. WINTERBOURNE
MULHOLLAND FALLS
MURDERED INNOCENCE
NELLY AND MONSIEUR ARNAUD
NEON BIBLE, THE
NEW LIFE, A
NIGHT OF THE TWISTERS
NORMA JEAN AND MARILYN
NORMAL LIFE
OF LOVE AND SHADOWS
ONCE UPON A TIME . . . WHEN WE WERE COLORED
ONE LESS EGG TO FRY
ORIGINAL GANGSTAS
OUTPOST, THE
OUTRAGE
PAINTED HERO
PASSION OF DARKLY NOON, THE
PHARAOH'S ARMY
PHENOMENON
PLAYBACK
POMPATUS OF LOVE, THE
PORTRAIT OF A LADY, THE
PREACHER'S WIFE, THE
PRIMAL FEAR
PROPRIETOR, THE
PUBLIC ACCESS
PURE DANGER
RENDEZVOUS IN PARIS
RICH MAN'S WIFE, THE
RIDICULE
ROAD HOME, THE
ROAD TO GALVESTON, THE
RUDE
SAINTS AND SINNERS
SECRETS & LIES
SHADOW OF ANGELS
SHADOW YOU SOON WILL BE, A
SHAMELESS
SHINE
SHOPPING
SILENCE OF NETO, THE
SILENCES OF THE PALACE, THE
SINGLE GIRL, A
SLEEPERS
SLING BLADE
SMALL FACES
SOME FOLKS CALL IT A SLING BLADE
SOME MOTHER'S SON
SOMEONE ELSE'S AMERICA
SPITFIRE GRILL, THE
STAND OFF, THE
STAR MAKER, THE
STEALING BEAUTY
STONEWALL
STORY OF XINGHUA, THE
STREETCAR NAMED DESIRE, A
SUBSTANCE OF FIRE, THE
SUGARTIME
SUNCHASER
SUNSET PARK
SURVIVING PICASSO
SWEET NOTHING
SWINGERS
TALKING ABOUT SEX
TARGET
TATTOO BOY
THAT THING YOU DO!
THREE LIVES AND ONLY ONE DEATH
TIME TO KILL, A
TIMELESS
TO GILLIAN ON HER 37TH BIRTHDAY
TOLLBOOTH
TRAINSPOTTING
TREES LOUNGE
TRIGGER EFFECT, THE
TWELFTH NIGHT
TWO DEATHS
TWO FRIENDS
UNDER THE DOMIM TREE
UNFORGETTABLE
UNHOOK THE STARS
UP CLOSE AND PERSONAL
VIVE L'AMOUR
VUKOVAR
WAR AT HOME, THE

WAR OF THE BUTTONS, THE
WAVELENGTH
WELCOME TO THE DOLLHOUSE
WHITE BALLOON, THE
WHITE SQUALL
WIFE, THE
WILD SIDE
WILLIAM SHAKESPEARE'S ROMEO + JULIET
WOMAN UNDONE, A
YOUNG POISONER'S HANDBOOK, THE

Erotic

ANIMAL INSTINCTS III: THE SEDUCTRESS
BAD LOVE
BATON ROUGE
BEYOND DESIRE
CAUGHT
DARK SECRETS
DELTA OF VENUS
DESIRE
ELECTRA
EXIT
FEMALIEN
FORBIDDEN ZONE: ALIEN ABDUCTION
FRIEND OF THE FAMILY 2
GLASS CAGE, THE
LITTLE DEATH, THE
MAN IN THE ATTIC, THE
MIRROR, MIRROR III: THE VOYEUR
NAKED SOULS
OVER THE WIRE
PLAYBACK
POISON IVY 2: LILY
SAINTS AND SINNERS
SANTA CLAWS
SHOWGIRL MURDERS, THE
SUITE 16
TALES OF EROTICA
VIRTUAL ENCOUNTERS
WATCH ME
WITCHCRAFT: SALEM'S GHOST
WOMAN UNDONE, A

Fantasy

ADRENALIN: FEAR THE RUSH
ADVENTURES OF PINOCCHIO, THE
ANTONIA'S LINE
BLACK SCORPION
BRITT ALLCROFT'S MAGIC ADVENTURES OF MUMFIE—THE MOVIE
CANTERVILLE GHOST, THE
CELESTIAL CLOCKWORK
CEMETERY MAN
CRAFT, THE
CROW: CITY OF ANGELS, THE
DRAGONHEART
ELECTRA
GUIMBA THE TYRANT
INSTITUTE BENJAMENTA
JAMES AND THE GIANT PEACH
JOHNNY SHORTWAVE
JOSH KIRBY . . . TIME WARRIOR!: EGGS FROM 70,000,000 B.C.
JOSH KIRBY . . . TIME WARRIOR!: JOURNEY TO THE MAGIC CAVERN
JOSH KIRBY . . . TIME WARRIOR!: LAST BATTLE FOR THE UNIVERSE
JOSH KIRBY . . . TIME WARRIOR!: TRAPPED ON TOY WORLD
KAZAAM
LAWNMOWER MAN 2: BEYOND CYBERSPACE
LEGEND OF GATOR FACE, THE
MAGIC HUNTER
MAGIC IN THE MIRROR
MATILDA
MERLIN'S SHOP OF MAGICAL WONDERS
MICHAEL
MONSTERSHOW
MULTIPLICITY
PREACHER'S WIFE, THE
SABRINA, THE TEENAGE WITCH
SGT. KABUKIMAN N.Y.P.D.
SONG SPINNER, THE
SPELLBREAKER: SECRET OF THE LEPRECHAUNS
THEODORE REX
THREE LIVES AND ONLY ONE DEATH
TWO-BITS & PEPPER
WICKED CITY, THE

Historical

ANGELS AND INSECTS
ANNE FRANK REMEMBERED
ASSAULT AT WEST POINT
BLUSH
CHEKIST, THE
DAENS
EMMA
EYE OF VICHY, THE
GHOST AND THE DARKNESS, THE
HEDD WYNN
HORSEMAN ON THE ROOF
KASPAR HAUSER
LAND AND FREEDOM
MOLL FLANDERS
MOONSHINE HIGHWAY
MOTHER OF KINGS
RASPUTIN
RIDICULE
STONEWALL
TRUMAN
TUSKEGEE AIRMEN, THE
VIKING SAGAS, THE
WING CHUN

Horror

ADRENALIN: FEAR THE RUSH
BAD MOON
BEWARE: CHILDREN AT PLAY
BLOOD & DONUTS
BUGGED
CARNOSAUR 3: PRIMAL SPECIES
CEMETERY MAN
CHILDREN OF THE CORN: THE GATHERING
CRAFT, THE
CROW: CITY OF ANGELS, THE
DEATH ARTIST, THE
DENTIST, THE
EVIL ED
FRIGHTENERS, THE
FROM DUSK TILL DAWN
FUNNYMAN, THE
GRIM
HAUNTED
HEAD OF THE FAMILY
HELLRAISER: BLOODLINE
ISLAND OF DR. MOREAU, THE
LIFEFORM
LITTLE WITCHES
LOADED
MADDENING, THE
MARY REILLY
MERLIN'S SHOP OF MAGICAL WONDERS
MIND RIPPER
MIRROR, MIRROR III: THE VOYEUR
MR. ICE CREAM MAN
MOTHER
MUTANT MAN
NECRONOMICON: BOOK OF THE DEAD
NIGHT OF THE SCARECROW
ORIGINAL SINS
OUTER LIMITS: SANDKINGS, THE
PINOCCHIO'S REVENGE
PIRANHA
POLYMORPH
PROTEUS
RATTLED
RUMPELSTILTSKIN
SANDMAN, THE
SANTA CLAWS
SAWBONES
SCREAM
SERPENT'S LAIR
SOMETIMES THEY COME BACK . . . AGAIN
STEPHEN KING'S THINNER
SURGEON, THE
TALES FROM THE CRYPT PRESENTS BORDELLO OF BLOOD
TEXAS CHAINSAW MASSACRE: THE NEXT GENERATION
THEY BITE
TRACKS OF A KILLER
TREMORS 2: AFTERSHOCKS
UNDERSTUDY: GRAVEYARD SHIFT 2, THE
UNFORGETTABLE
UNKNOWN ORIGIN
WHISPERING, THE
WITCHCRAFT: SALEM'S GHOST
WITHIN THE ROCK

Martial Arts

BEST OF THE BEST 3: NO TURNING BACK
BLOODSPORT II: THE NEXT KUMITE
BODY COUNT
DEADLY OUTBREAK
DOGFIGHTERS, THE
FIST OF THE NORTH STAR
FOREST WARRIOR
HARD JUSTICE
HARD WAY OUT: BLOODFIST VIII
HIDDEN ASSASSIN
LIVE WIRE: HUMAN TIMEBOMB
MIDNIGHT ANGEL
QUEST, THE
RAVENHAWK
RAW TARGET
RED SCORPION 2
REDEMPTION: KICKBOXER 5
RUMBLE IN THE BRONX
SHOOTFIGHTER 2: KILL OR BE KILLED!
STREET FIGHTER II: THE ANIMATED MOVIE
TERMINAL IMPACT
TIGER HEART
VIRTUAL COMBAT
WARHEAD
WHITE TIGER
WING CHUN

Musical

ALL DOGS GO TO HEAVEN 2
AVENTURERA
CANNIBAL! THE MUSICAL
EVERYONE SAYS I LOVE YOU
EVITA
GRACE OF MY HEART
HUNCHBACK OF NOTRE DAME, THE

MESSAGE TO LOVE: THE ISLE OF WIGHT FESTIVAL
MUPPET TREASURE ISLAND
ROLLING STONES ROCK-AND-ROLL CIRCUS, THE
THAT THING YOU DO!

Mystery

BLACK DAY BLUE NIGHT
BODY OF INFLUENCE 2
CRACKER: THE MADWOMAN IN THE ATTIC
DEAD COLD
DEATH BENEFIT
DIABOLIQUE
FATALLY YOURS
FORBIDDEN ZONE: ALIEN ABDUCTION
GRAVE, THE
HEAVEN'S PRISONERS
MADDENING, THE
MAHJONG
MULHOLLAND FALLS
ONE NIGHT STAND
OVER THE WIRE
PUBLIC ACCESS
SHARON'S SECRET
TUNNEL VISION
UNFORGETTABLE
WHERE'S THE MONEY, NOREEN?
WHO KILLED PASOLINI?

Opera

MADAME BUTTERFLY

Political

ANNA
CHEKIST, THE
CITY HALL
JOHNNY SHORTWAVE
KAMIKAZE TAXI
KISSINGER AND NIXON
LAST SUPPER, THE
LET'S GET BIZZEE
LIVE WIRE: HUMAN TIMEBOMB
MAN BY THE SHORE, THE
MOTHER OF KINGS
OF LOVE AND SHADOWS
OUTPOST, THE
PERFECT CANDIDATE, A
SHADOW OF ANGELS
SILENCE OF NETO, THE
SONG SPINNER, THE
WHEN THE BULLET HITS THE BONE

Prison

BEYOND THE CALL
CAPTIVES
CONDITION RED
ROCK, THE

Religious

DAENS

Romance

AFFAIR, THE
AMANDA AND THE ALIEN
ANGELS AND INSECTS
. . . AT FIRST SIGHT
BEAUTIFUL GIRLS
BEAUTIFUL THING
BED OF ROSES
BIG SQUEEZE, THE
BLOOD & DONUTS
BLUSH
BOYS
MADAME BUTTERFLY
CAPTIVES
CARRIED AWAY
CAUGHT
CHUNGKING EXPRESS
COLD COMFORT FARM
CONDITION RED
DENISE CALLS UP
DEVOTION
ED'S NEXT MOVE
EMMA
ENGLISH PATIENT, THE
EVERYTHING RELATIVE
FLATTERED
FLOWER OF MY SECRET, THE
FOR BETTER OR WORSE
FOR THE MOMENT
FRENCH TWIST
GALAXIES ARE COLLIDING
HALFBACK OF NOTRE DAME, THE
HUNCHBACK OF NOTRE DAME, THE
IF LUCY FELL
IN LOVE AND WAR
INFINITY
JACK & SARAH
JANE EYRE
LOTTO LAND
LOVE IS ALL THERE IS
MADAGASCAR SKIN
MAHJONG
MODERN AFFAIR, A
MRS. WINTERBOURNE
NELLY AND MONSIEUR ARNAUD
NORMAL LIFE
OF LOVE AND SHADOWS
ONE FINE DAY
ONE LESS EGG TO FRY
ONE NIGHT STAND
PALLBEARER, THE
PIE IN THE SKY
POMPATUS OF LOVE, THE
PROPRIETOR, THE
RENDEZVOUS IN PARIS
SHE'S THE ONE
SOLITAIRE FOR TWO
STEALING BEAUTY
STORY OF XINGHUA, THE
TIMELESS
TIN CUP
TO GILLIAN ON HER 37TH BIRTHDAY
TRUTH ABOUT CATS AND DOGS, THE
TWELFTH NIGHT
TWO IF BY SEA
TWO MUCH
UNDER THE DOMIM TREE
UP CLOSE AND PERSONAL
WALKING AND TALKING
WEEKEND IN THE COUNTRY, A
WHOLE WIDE WORLD, THE
WILLIAM SHAKESPEARE'S ROMEO + JULIET

Science Fiction

AMANDA AND THE ALIEN
ARRIVAL, THE
BACKLASH: OBLIVION 2
BARB WIRE
BIG WARS
DARKMAN III: DIE DARKMAN DIE
DEAD WEEKEND
DEMOLITIONIST, THE
FEMALIEN
FINAL EQUINOX, THE
FLAMING EARS
FORBIDDEN ZONE: ALIEN ABDUCTION
GHOST IN THE SHELL
GRIM
INDEPENDENCE DAY
ISLAND OF DR. MOREAU, THE
IT CAME FROM OUTER SPACE II
JOHN CARPENTER'S ESCAPE FROM L.A.
JOSH KIRBY . . . TIME WARRIOR!: EGGS FROM 70,000,000 B.C.
JOSH KIRBY . . . TIME WARRIOR!: JOURNEY TO THE MAGIC CAVERN
JOSH KIRBY . . . TIME WARRIOR!: LAST BATTLE FOR THE UNIVERSE
JOSH KIRBY . . . TIME WARRIOR!: TRAPPED ON TOY WORLD
LAWNMOWER MAN 2: BEYOND CYBERSPACE
LIFEFORM
MACHINE, THE
MARS ATTACKS!
MIND RIPPER
MR. STITCH
NAKED SOULS
NEMESIS III: PREY HARDER
NOT OF THIS EARTH
OUT THERE
OUTER LIMITS: SANDKINGS, THE
PATLABOR 2: MOBILE POLICE
PHOENIX
PIRANHA
POLYMORPH
PROTEUS
ROUJIN-Z
SCREAMERS
SHADOW WARRIORS
STAR TREK: FIRST CONTACT
SYNTHETIC PLEASURES
THEODORE REX
THEY BITE
TREMORS 2: AFTERSHOCKS
UNKNOWN ORIGIN
VENUS RISING
VIRTUAL COMBAT
WICKED CITY, THE
WITHIN THE ROCK
YESTERDAY'S TARGET
ZARKORR! THE INVADER

Sports

ALEX
ANNIE O
CELTIC PRIDE
D3: THE MIGHTY DUCKS
ED
EDDIE
GREAT WHITE HYPE, THE
HALFBACK OF NOTRE DAME, THE
KINGPIN
MAN WITH THE PERFECT SWING, THE
REDEMPTION: KICKBOXER 5
SOUTH BEACH ACADEMY
SUNSET PARK
TIN CUP

Spy

DOGFIGHTERS, THE
HIDDEN ASSASSIN
JOSEPH CONRAD'S THE SECRET AGENT

MISSION: IMPOSSIBLE
MOTHER NIGHT
SPY HARD

Thriller

ADRENALIN: FEAR THE RUSH
AMERICAN STRAYS
ARRIVAL, THE
BAJA
BARB WIRE
BATON ROUGE
BLACK DAY BLUE NIGHT
BLACK OUT
BLOODKNOT
BODY OF INFLUENCE 2
BOUND
BREACH OF TRUST
BURIAL OF THE RATS
CABLE GUY, THE
CHAIN REACTION
CHAMBER, THE
CHAMELEON
CLUBHOUSE DETECTIVES
COLD LIGHT OF DAY
COLONY, THE
CURDLED
DEAD COLD
DEADLY OUTBREAK
DEATH ARTIST, THE
DEATH BENEFIT
DEMOLITIONIST, THE
DESIRE
DIABOLIQUE
DONOR UNKNOWN
DOWN, OUT AND DANGEROUS
ERASER
EVIL HAS A FACE
EXIT
EXTREME MEASURES
EYE FOR AN EYE
FAN, THE
FEAR
FELONY
FINAL CUT, THE
FRAME BY FRAME
FREEWAY
FUGITIVE RAGE
GLIMMER MAN, THE
HARD WAY OUT: BLOODFIST VIII
HOLLOW POINT
INDEPENDENCE DAY
JOHNNY 100 PESOS
JOSEPH CONRAD'S THE SECRET AGENT
JUROR, THE
JUST YOUR LUCK
LA CEREMONIE
LES VOLEURS
LETTER TO MY KILLER
LITTLE DEATH, THE
LIVE WIRE: HUMAN TIMEBOMB
LOADED
LONG KISS GOODNIGHT, THE
MACHINE, THE
MADDENING, THE
MATERNAL INSTINCTS
MISSION: IMPOSSIBLE
MR. STITCH
MOTHER
NAKED SOULS
OFF AND RUNNING
ONE GOOD TURN
ONE NIGHT STAND
ORGANIZED CRIME & TRIAD BUREAU
OUTRAGE
OVER THE WIRE
POISON IVY 2: LILY
PORTRAITS OF A KILLER
PRIMAL FEAR
PUBLIC ACCESS
RANSOM
RATTLED
RED LINE
RICH MAN'S WIFE, THE
SAWBONES
SERIAL KILLER
SERPENT'S LAIR
SET IT OFF
SHADOW WARRIORS
SHAMELESS
SHARON'S SECRET
SHOWGIRL MURDERS, THE
SKYSCRAPER
SPIDER & ROSE
SUITE 16
TAILS YOU LIVE, HEADS YOU'RE DEAD
TRACKS OF A KILLER
TRIGGER EFFECT, THE
TUNNEL VISION
TWISTER
2 DAYS IN THE VALLEY
UNDERTOW
VIRUS
WHEN THE BULLET HITS THE BONE
WIDOW'S KISS
WILD SIDE
WOLVES, THE
WOMAN UNDONE, A

War

AFFAIR, THE
COURAGE UNDER FIRE
EYE OF VICHY, THE
FIRE ON THE MOUNTAIN
FOR THE MOMENT
HEDD WYNN
IN LOVE AND WAR
IRON EAGLE IV
JAG
LAND AND FREEDOM
PHARAOH'S ARMY
VUKOVAR
WARHEAD

Western

BACKLASH: OBLIVION 2
CANNIBAL! THE MUSICAL
DEAD MAN
LARRY MCMURTRY'S STREETS OF LAREDO
LAST MAN STANDING
LAZARUS MAN, THE
LONE JUSTICE: SHOWDOWN AT PLUM CREEK
LONG ROAD HOME, THE
RIDERS OF THE PURPLE SAGE
SONS OF TRINITY

FILMS BY MPAA RATING

The Motion Picture Association of America (MPAA) currently grades films according to the following codes:

G GENERAL AUDIENCES (All ages admitted)
PG PARENTAL GUIDANCE SUGGESTED (Some material may not be suitable for children)
PG-13 PARENTS STRONGLY CAUTIONED (Some material may be inappropriate for children under 13)
R RESTRICTED (Under 17 requires accompanying parent or adult guardian)
NC-17 NO CHILDREN UNDER 17 ADMITTED
NR NOT RATED

G

ADVENTURES OF PINOCCHIO, THE
ALL DOGS GO TO HEAVEN 2
HALFBACK OF NOTRE DAME, THE
HOMEWARD BOUND II: LOST IN SAN FRANCISCO
HUNCHBACK OF NOTRE DAME, THE
LAND BEFORE TIME IV: JOURNEY THROUGH THE MISTS
MAGIC IN THE MIRROR
MICROCOSMOS
MUPPET TREASURE ISLAND
101 DALMATIANS
SMALL WONDERS
SPELLBREAKER: SECRET OF THE LEPRECHAUNS

PG

ALASKA
ANNE FRANK REMEMBERED
ANNIE O
AUGUST
BEASTMASTER 3: THE EYE OF BRAXUS
BED OF ROSES
BIG BULLY
BOGUS
BOYS NEXT DOOR, THE
CARPOOL
CLUBHOUSE DETECTIVES
COLD COMFORT FARM
D3: THE MIGHTY DUCKS
DEAR GOD
DUNSTON CHECKS IN
ED
EMMA
EVITA
FIRST KID
FIRST WIVES CLUB, THE
FLIPPER
FLY AWAY HOME
FOREST WARRIOR
GRASS HARP, THE
HARRIET THE SPY
HARVEST OF FIRE
HOMECOMING
HOUSE ARREST
INFINITY
JAMES AND THE GIANT PEACH
JANE EYRE
JINGLE ALL THE WAY
JOSH KIRBY . . . TIME WARRIOR!: EGGS FROM 70,000,000 B.C.
JOSH KIRBY . . . TIME WARRIOR!: JOURNEY TO THE MAGIC CAVERN
JOSH KIRBY . . . TIME WARRIOR!: LAST BATTLE FOR THE UNIVERSE
JOSH KIRBY . . . TIME WARRIOR!: TRAPPED ON TOY WORLD
KAZAAM
LARGER THAN LIFE
LEGEND OF GATOR FACE, THE
LILY DALE
LITTLE INDIAN, BIG CITY
LONE JUSTICE: SHOWDOWN AT PLUM CREEK
LOOKING FOR TROUBLE
MATILDA
MICHAEL
MISSING PIECES
MR. HOLLAND'S OPUS
ONCE UPON A TIME . . . WHEN WE WERE COLORED
ONE FINE DAY
PHANTOM, THE
PHENOMENON
PIG'S TALE, A
PREACHER'S WIFE, THE
RACE THE SUN
ROAD HOME, THE
SABRINA, THE TEENAGE WITCH
SANTA WITH MUSCLES
SGT. BILKO
SPACE JAM
STUPIDS, THE
THAT THING YOU DO!
THEODORE REX
TRUMAN
TWELFTH NIGHT
TWO-BITS & PEPPER
UP CLOSE AND PERSONAL
WAR OF THE BUTTONS, THE
WHEN WE WERE KINGS
WHITE WOLVES II: LEGEND OF THE WILD
WHOLE WIDE WORLD, THE
YANKEE ZULU

PG-13

ARRIVAL, THE
ASSAULT AT WEST POINT
ASSOCIATE, THE
BACKLASH: OBLIVION 2
BEAVIS AND BUTT-HEAD DO AMERICA
BEFORE AND AFTER
BIO-DOME
BLACK SHEEP
BOYS
CABLE GUY, THE
CELTIC PRIDE
CHAIN REACTION
CHILDREN OF FURY
COLONY, THE
CRUCIBLE, THE
DAYLIGHT
DEATH BENEFIT
DENISE CALLS UP
DOWN PERISCOPE
DRAGONHEART
EDDIE
EDIE & PEN
ENTERTAINING ANGELS: THE DOROTHY DAY STORY
EVENING STAR, THE
FAMILY THING, A
FOR BETTER OR WORSE
FOR THE MOMENT
GHOSTS OF MISSISSIPPI
HAMLET
HAPPY GILMORE
HIGH SCHOOL HIGH
I'M NOT RAPPAPORT
IN LOVE AND WAR
INDEPENDENCE DAY
IRON EAGLE IV
IT CAME FROM OUTER SPACE II
JACK
JOE'S APARTMENT
KINGPIN
LAWNMOWER MAN 2: BEYOND CYBERSPACE
LETTER TO MY KILLER
LOOKING FOR RICHARD
MARS ATTACKS!
MARVIN'S ROOM
MATERNAL INSTINCTS
MIRROR HAS TWO FACES, THE
MISSION: IMPOSSIBLE
MR. WRONG
MOLL FLANDERS
MOONSHINE HIGHWAY
MOTHER
MOTHER'S PRAYER, A
MRS. WINTERBOURNE
MULTIPLICITY
MY FELLOW AMERICANS
MYSTERY SCIENCE THEATER 3000: THE MOVIE
NEW LIFE, A
NUTTY PROFESSOR, THE
PALLBEARER, THE
PORTRAIT OF A LADY, THE
PRE-MADONNAS
QUEST, THE
RATTLED
ROAD TO GALVESTON, THE
ROUJIN-Z
SHINE
SOLO
SPITFIRE GRILL, THE

SPY HARD
STAR TREK: FIRST CONTACT
STREET FIGHTER II: THE ANIMATED MOVIE
TIGER HEART
TO GILLIAN ON HER 37TH BIRTHDAY
TREMORS 2: AFTERSHOCKS
TRUTH ABOUT CATS AND DOGS, THE
TUSKEGEE AIRMEN, THE
TWISTER
TWO MUCH
VERY BRADY SEQUEL, A
VIRUS
WHERE'S THE MONEY, NOREEN?
WHITE SQUALL
WILLIAM SHAKESPEARE'S ROMEO + JULIET
WOLVES, THE
ZARKORR! THE INVADER

R

ADRENALIN: FEAR THE RUSH
AFFAIR, THE
AMANDA AND THE ALIEN
AMERICAN BUFFALO
AMERICAN STRAYS
ANGELS AND INSECTS
ANIMAL INSTINCTS III: THE SEDUCTRESS
. . . AT FIRST SIGHT
BAD LOVE
BAD MOON
BAJA
BARB WIRE
BASQUIAT
BEAUTIFUL GIRLS
BEAUTIFUL THING
BEST OF THE BEST 3: NO TURNING BACK
BEWARE: CHILDREN AT PLAY
BEYOND DESIRE
BEYOND THE CALL
BIG NIGHT
BIG SQUEEZE, THE
BIRDCAGE, THE
BLACK DAY BLUE NIGHT
BLACK OUT
BLACK ROSE OF HARLEM
BLACK SCORPION
BLONDES HAVE MORE GUNS
BLOOD & DONUTS
BLOODKNOT
BLOODSPORT II: THE NEXT KUMITE
BODY COUNT
BODY OF INFLUENCE 2
BOTTLE ROCKET
BOUND
BOY CALLED HATE, A
BREACH OF TRUST
BREAKAWAY
BREAKING THE WAVES
BROKEN ARROW
BROTHER OF SLEEP
BUGGED
BULLETPROOF
BURIAL OF THE RATS
CANNIBAL! THE MUSICAL
CAPTIVES
CARNOSAUR 3: PRIMAL SPECIES
CARRIED AWAY
CAUGHT
CELLULOID CLOSET, THE
CEMETERY MAN
CHAMBER, THE
CHAMELEON
CHILDREN OF THE CORN: THE GATHERING
CHUNGKING EXPRESS
CITIZEN RUTH
CITY HALL
COLD LIGHT OF DAY
CONDITION RED
COURAGE UNDER FIRE
CRAFT, THE
CRIMINAL HEARTS
CROSSCUT
CROW: CITY OF ANGELS, THE
CURDLED
DAENS
DARKMAN III: DIE DARKMAN DIE
DEAD COLD
DEAD MAN
DEAD TO RIGHTS
DEAD WEEKEND
DEADLY OUTBREAK
DEATH ARTIST, THE
DEMOLITIONIST, THE
DENTIST, THE
DEVOTION
DIABOLIQUE
DOGFIGHTERS, THE
DONOR UNKNOWN
DON'T BE A MENACE TO SOUTH CENTRAL WHILE DRINKING YOUR JUICE IN THE HOOD
DOWN, OUT AND DANGEROUS
ED'S NEXT MOVE
ELECTRA
ENGLISH PATIENT, THE
ERASER
EVERYONE SAYS I LOVE YOU
EVIL ED
EVIL HAS A FACE
EXECUTIVE DECISION
EXIT
EXTREME MEASURES
EYE FOR AN EYE
FAITHFUL
FAN, THE
FARGO
FAST MONEY
FEAR
FEELING MINNESOTA
FELONY
FEMALIEN
FINAL CUT, THE
FIST OF THE NORTH STAR
FLED
FLIRTING WITH DISASTER
FLOWER OF MY SECRET, THE
FORBIDDEN ZONE: ALIEN ABDUCTION
FOXFIRE
FRAME BY FRAME
FREEWAY
FRENCH TWIST
FRIGHTENERS, THE
FROM DUSK TILL DAWN
FUGITIVE RAGE
FULL BODY MASSAGE
FUNERAL, THE
FUNNYMAN, THE
GALAXIES ARE COLLIDING
GET ON THE BUS
GETTING AWAY WITH MURDER
GHOST AND THE DARKNESS, THE
GIRL 6
GIRLS TOWN
GLASS CAGE, THE
GLIMMER MAN, THE
GRACE OF MY HEART
GRAVE, THE
GREAT WHITE HYPE, THE
GRIM
HARD JUSTICE
HARD WAY OUT: BLOODFIST VIII
HAUNTED
HEAD OF THE FAMILY
HEAVEN'S PRISONERS
HELLRAISER: BLOODLINE
HIDDEN ASSASSIN
HOLLOW POINT
HOMAGE
HORSEMAN ON THE ROOF
HOSTILE INTENTIONS
HOURGLASS
I SHOT ANDY WARHOL
IF LUCY FELL
IMMORTALS, THE
ISLAND OF DR. MOREAU, THE
IT'S MY PARTY
JACK & SARAH
JERRY MAGUIRE
JOHN CARPENTER'S ESCAPE FROM L.A.
JOSEPH CONRAD'S THE SECRET AGENT
JUDE
JUROR, THE
JUST YOUR LUCK
KANSAS CITY
KIDS IN THE HALL: BRAIN CANDY
LAST DANCE
LAST MAN STANDING
LAST SUPPER, THE
LATE SHIFT, THE
LIFEFORM
LITTLE WITCHES
LIVE NUDE GIRLS
LIVE WIRE: HUMAN TIMEBOMB
LOADED
LONE STAR
LONG KISS GOODNIGHT, THE
LOSING CHASE
LOVE IS ALL THERE IS
LOVER'S KNOT
LOW LIFE, THE
MAD DOG TIME
MAN IN THE ATTIC, THE
MANNY & LO
MARY REILLY
MAXIMUM RISK
MAYBE . . . MAYBE NOT
MERCY
MICHAEL COLLINS
MIDWINTER'S TALE, A
MIND RIPPER
MR. STITCH
MODERN AFFAIR, A
MOTHER NIGHT
MOUTH TO MOUTH
MRS. MUNCK
MULHOLLAND FALLS
MURDERED INNOCENCE
NAKED SOULS
NATIONAL LAMPOON'S FAVORITE DEADLY SINS
NECRONOMICON: BOOK OF THE DEAD
NEMESIS III: PREY HARDER
NIGHT OF THE SCARECROW
NORMA JEAN AND MARILYN
NORMAL LIFE
NOT OF THIS EARTH
OF LOVE AND SHADOWS
OFF AND RUNNING
ONE GOOD TURN
ONE MAN'S JUSTICE
ONE NIGHT STAND

OPEN SEASON
ORIGINAL GANGSTAS
OUTRAGE
OVER THE WIRE
PAINTED HERO
PALOOKAVILLE
PASSION OF DARKLY NOON, THE
PEOPLE VS. LARRY FLYNT, THE
PHAT BEACH
PIE IN THE SKY
PINOCCHIO'S REVENGE
PIRANHA
PLAYBACK
POISON IVY 2: LILY
PORTRAITS OF A KILLER
PRIMAL FEAR
PROPRIETOR, THE
PROTEUS
PUBLIC ENEMIES
PURE DANGER
RAGE
RANSOM
RASPUTIN
RAVENHAWK
RAW TARGET
RED LINE
RED SCORPION 2
REDEMPTION: KICKBOXER 5
RICH MAN'S WIFE, THE
RIDICULE
ROCK, THE
RUDE
RUMBLE IN THE BRONX
RUMPELSTILTSKIN
SAINTS AND SINNERS
SAWBONES
SCREAM
SCREAMERS
SECRETS & LIES
SERIAL KILLER
SERPENT'S LAIR
SET IT OFF
SHADOW WARRIORS
SHAMELESS
SHARON'S SECRET
SHE'S THE ONE
SHOOTFIGHTER 2: KILL OR BE KILLED!
SHOT, THE
SHOWGIRL MURDERS, THE
SKYSCRAPER
SLEEPERS
SLING BLADE
SMALL FACES
SOLITAIRE FOR TWO
SOME MOTHER'S SON
SOMEONE ELSE'S AMERICA
SOMETIMES THEY COME BACK . . . AGAIN
SOUTH BEACH ACADEMY
STAR MAKER, THE
STEALING BEAUTY
STEPHEN KING'S THINNER
STRIPTEASE
SUBSTANCE OF FIRE, THE
SUBSTITUTE, THE
SUGARTIME
SUNCHASER
SUNSET PARK
SURGEON, THE
SURVIVING PICASSO
SWEEPER, THE
SWINGERS
TAILS YOU LIVE, HEADS YOU'RE DEAD
TAKEOVER, THE
TALES FROM THE CRYPT PRESENTS BORDELLO OF BLOOD
TALES OF EROTICA
TERMINAL IMPACT
TEXAS CHAINSAW MASSACRE: THE NEXT GENERATION
TEXAS PAYBACK
THIN LINE BETWEEN LOVE AND HATE, A
TIME TO KILL, A
TIN CUP
TOLLBOOTH
TOO FAST, TOO YOUNG
TRACKS OF A KILLER
TRAINSPOTTING
TREES LOUNGE
TRIGGER EFFECT, THE
2 DAYS IN THE VALLEY
TWO DEATHS
TWO IF BY SEA
UNDER THE HULA MOON
UNDERSTUDY: GRAVEYARD SHIFT 2, THE
UNDERTOW
UNFORGETTABLE
UNHOOK THE STARS
UNKNOWN ORIGIN
VENUS RISING
VIKING SAGAS, THE
VIRTUAL COMBAT
VISITORS, THE
WALKING AND TALKING
WAR AT HOME, THE
WARHEAD
WATCH ME
WAVELENGTH
WEEKEND IN THE COUNTRY, A
WELCOME TO THE DOLLHOUSE
WHARF RAT, THE
WHEN THE BULLET HITS THE BONE
WHISPERING, THE
WHITE TIGER
WIDOW'S KISS
WIFE, THE
WILD SIDE
WITHIN THE ROCK
WITHOUT MERCY
WOMAN UNDONE, A
YESTERDAY'S TARGET

NC-17

DELTA OF VENUS

NR

ABUSE
ALEX
AMERICA'S DREAM
ANGELA
ANNA
ANTONIA'S LINE
APART FROM HUGH
AVENTURERA
BATON ROUGE
BERKELEY IN THE 60S
BIG WARS
BITTER SUGAR
BLACK MOUNTAIN
BLUSH
BRITT ALLCROFT'S MAGIC ADVENTURES OF MUMFIE—THE MOVIE
BUTTERFLY KISS
MADAME BUTTERFLY
CALLING THE GHOSTS: A STORY ABOUT RAPE, WAR AND WOMEN
CANTERVILLE GHOST, THE
CATWALK
CELESTIAL CLOCKWORK
CHAMPAGNE SAFARI, THE
CHASING BUTTERFLIES
CHEKIST, THE
CHILDREN OF NOISY VILLAGE, THE
COLD FEVER
CRACKER: THE MADWOMAN IN THE ATTIC
CROCODILES IN AMSTERDAM
CURTIS'S CHARM
DADETOWN
DANGEROUS PASSION
DARK SECRETS
DESIRE
DESOLATION ANGELS
DON'T LET YOUR MEAT LOAF
ERNESTO CHE GUEVARA—THE BOLIVIAN DIARY
EVERYTHING RELATIVE
EYE OF VICHY, THE
FAR HARBOR
FATALLY YOURS
FATE
FINAL EQUINOX, THE
FIRE ON THE MOUNTAIN
FLAMING EARS
FLATTERED
FLIRT
4 TALES OF 2 CITIES
FRANCOIS TRUFFAUT: STOLEN PORTRAITS
FRIEND OF THE FAMILY 2
FRISK
FROM THE JOURNALS OF JEAN SEBERG
GHOST IN THE SHELL
GIRL FROM MARS, THE
GIRLFRIENDS
GUIMBA THE TYRANT
HALFMOON
HATE
HEADLESS BODY IN TOPLESS BAR
HEAVY
HECK'S WAY HOME
HEDD WYNN
HEIDI CHRONICLES, THE
HEIDI FLEISS HOLLYWOOD MADAM
HOW THE WEST WAS FUN
HYPE!
INSTITUTE BENJAMENTA
JAG
JOHNNY 100 PESOS
JOHNNY SHORTWAVE
KAMIKAZE TAXI
KASPAR HAUSER
KISSINGER AND NIXON
LA CEREMONIE
LA COMEDIE-FRANCAISE OU L'AMOUR JOUE
LAND AND FREEDOM
LARRY MCMURTRY'S STREETS OF LAREDO
LAZARUS MAN, THE
LES VOLEURS
LET'S GET BIZZEE
LINE KING: THE AL HIRSCHFELD STORY, THE
LITTLE DEATH, THE
LONG ROAD HOME, THE
LOTTO LAND
MA SAISON PREFEREE
MABOROSI
MACHINE, THE
MADAGASCAR SKIN
MADAME WANG'S
MADDENING, THE
MAGIC HUNTER

MAHJONG
MAN BY THE SHORE, THE
MAN OF THE YEAR
MAN WITH A PLAN
MAN WITH THE PERFECT SWING, THE
MERLIN'S SHOP OF MAGICAL WONDERS
MESSAGE TO LOVE: THE ISLE OF WIGHT FESTIVAL
MIDNIGHT ANGEL
MIDNIGHT DANCERS
MILLE BOLLE BLU
MIRROR, MIRROR III: THE VOYEUR
MR. ICE CREAM MAN
MONSTER, THE
MONSTERSHOW
MOTHER
MOTHER OF KINGS
MUTANT MAN
NELLY AND MONSIEUR ARNAUD
NEON BIBLE, THE
NEUROSIA: 50 YEARS OF PERVERSITY
NICO ICON
NIGHT OF THE TWISTERS
NIGHT ON THE GALACTIC RAILROAD
NIKI DE SAINT PHALLE: WHO IS THE MONSTER — YOU OR ME?
NOT BAD FOR A GIRL
ONE LESS EGG TO FRY
ORGANIZED CRIME & TRIAD BUREAU
ORIGINAL SINS
ORSON WELLES: THE ONE-MAN BAND
OUT THERE
OUTER LIMITS: SANDKINGS, THE
OUTPOST, THE
PARADISE LOST: THE CHILD MURDERS AT ROBIN HOOD HILLS
PARIS WAS A WOMAN
PATLABOR 2: MOBILE POLICE
PERFECT CANDIDATE, A
PERSONAL JOURNEY WITH MARTIN SCORSESE THROUGH AMERICAN MOVIES, A
PHANTOM 2040: THE GHOST WHO WALKS
PHARAOH'S ARMY
PHOENIX
POLYMORPH
POMPATUS OF LOVE, THE
PREDICTIONS OF FIRE
PUBLIC ACCESS
RENDEZVOUS IN PARIS
RIDERS OF THE PURPLE SAGE
ROBIN OF LOCKSLEY
ROLLING STONES ROCK-AND-ROLL CIRCUS, THE
SANCTUARY: THE MOVIE
SANDMAN, THE
SANTA CLAWS
SEARCH FOR ONE-EYE JIMMY, THE
SGT. KABUKIMAN N.Y.P.D.
SHADOW OF ANGELS
SHADOW YOU SOON WILL BE, A
SHOPPING
SILENCE OF NETO, THE
SILENCES OF THE PALACE, THE
SINGLE GIRL, A
SKIN
SOME FOLKS CALL IT A SLING BLADE
SONG SPINNER, THE
SONIC OUTLAWS
SONS OF TRINITY
SPIDER & ROSE
STAND OFF, THE
STONEWALL
STORY OF XINGHUA, THE
STREETCAR NAMED DESIRE, A
SUITE 16
SWEET NOTHING
SYNTHETIC PLEASURES
TALKING ABOUT SEX
TARGET
TATTOO BOY
THEREMIN: AN ELECTRONIC ODYSSEY
THEY BITE
THREE LIVES AND ONLY ONE DEATH
TIMELESS
TUNNEL VISION
TWO FRIENDS
UNDER THE DOMIM TREE
VIRTUAL ENCOUNTERS
VIVE L'AMOUR
VUKOVAR
WALLACE AND GROMIT: THE BEST OF AARDMAN ANIMATION
WHITE BALLOON, THE
WHO KILLED PASOLINI?
WICKED CITY, THE
WIND IN THE WILLOWS, THE
WING CHUN
WITCHCRAFT: SALEM'S GHOST
YOU'LL NEVER MAKE LOVE IN THIS TOWN AGAIN
YOUNG POISONER'S HANDBOOK, THE

FILMS BY PARENTAL RECOMMENDATION (PR)

AA – good for children; A – acceptable for children;
C – cautionary, some scenes may be objectionable for children; O – objectionable for children

AA

ALEX
ANNIE O
CANTERVILLE GHOST, THE
CHILDREN OF NOISY VILLAGE, THE
CLUBHOUSE DETECTIVES
ED
FLY AWAY HOME
FOREST WARRIOR
GIRL FROM MARS, THE
HALFBACK OF NOTRE DAME, THE
HECK'S WAY HOME
HOMEWARD BOUND II: LOST IN SAN FRANCISCO
HOW THE WEST WAS FUN
JOSH KIRBY . . . TIME WARRIOR!: EGGS FROM 70,000,000 B.C.
JOSH KIRBY . . . TIME WARRIOR!: JOURNEY TO THE MAGIC CAVERN
JOSH KIRBY . . . TIME WARRIOR!: TRAPPED ON TOY WORLD
KAZAAM
LAND BEFORE TIME IV: JOURNEY THROUGH THE MISTS
MAGIC IN THE MIRROR
MUPPET TREASURE ISLAND
NIGHT ON THE GALACTIC RAILROAD
101 DALMATIANS
PERSONAL JOURNEY WITH MARTIN SCORSESE THROUGH AMERICAN MOVIES, A
ROAD HOME, THE
ROBIN OF LOCKSLEY
SANTA WITH MUSCLES
SONG SPINNER, THE
SPACE JAM
SPELLBREAKER: SECRET OF THE LEPRECHAUNS
WHITE BALLOON, THE
WIND IN THE WILLOWS, THE

A

ADVENTURES OF PINOCCHIO, THE
ALASKA
ALL DOGS GO TO HEAVEN 2
ANNE FRANK REMEMBERED
ASSOCIATE, THE
BACKLASH: OBLIVION 2
BARB WIRE
BEASTMASTER 3: THE EYE OF BRAXUS
BED OF ROSES
BERKELEY IN THE 60S
BEYOND THE CALL
BIG BULLY
BOGUS
BOYS NEXT DOOR, THE
BRITT ALLCROFT'S MAGIC ADVENTURES OF MUMFIE—THE MOVIE
MADAME BUTTERFLY
CARPOOL
CATWALK
CHAMPAGNE SAFARI, THE
CHASING BUTTERFLIES
COLD FEVER
D3: THE MIGHTY DUCKS
DEAR GOD
DRAGONHEART
DUNSTON CHECKS IN
EMMA
ENTERTAINING ANGELS: THE DOROTHY DAY STORY
ERNESTO CHE GUEVARA—THE BOLIVIAN DIARY
EVERYONE SAYS I LOVE YOU
FIRE ON THE MOUNTAIN
FIRST KID
FLIPPER
FOR THE MOMENT
FROM THE JOURNALS OF JEAN SEBERG
HARRIET THE SPY
HARVEST OF FIRE
HOMECOMING
HOUSE ARREST
HUNCHBACK OF NOTRE DAME, THE
INFINITY
INSTITUTE BENJAMENTA
IT CAME FROM OUTER SPACE II
JACK
JAMES AND THE GIANT PEACH
JANE EYRE
JINGLE ALL THE WAY
JOSH KIRBY . . . TIME WARRIOR!: LAST BATTLE FOR THE UNIVERSE
KISSINGER AND NIXON
LA COMEDIE-FRANCAISE OU L'AMOUR JOUE
LARGER THAN LIFE
LEGEND OF GATOR FACE, THE
LILY DALE
LINE KING: THE AL HIRSCHFELD STORY, THE
LITTLE INDIAN, BIG CITY
LONE JUSTICE: SHOWDOWN AT PLUM CREEK
LOOKING FOR TROUBLE
MAN OF THE YEAR
MAN WITH A PLAN
MATILDA
MESSAGE TO LOVE: THE ISLE OF WIGHT FESTIVAL
MICROCOSMOS
MR. HOLLAND'S OPUS
NIGHT OF THE TWISTERS
ONCE UPON A TIME . . . WHEN WE WERE COLORED
ONE FINE DAY
OUTER LIMITS: SANDKINGS, THE
PARIS WAS A WOMAN
PATLABOR 2: MOBILE POLICE
PERFECT CANDIDATE, A
PHANTOM 2040: THE GHOST WHO WALKS
PHANTOM, THE
PIG'S TALE, A
PREACHER'S WIFE, THE
RACE THE SUN
ROLLING STONES ROCK-AND-ROLL CIRCUS, THE
ROUJIN-Z
SABRINA, THE TEENAGE WITCH
SMALL WONDERS
SONIC OUTLAWS
SONS OF TRINITY
SPITFIRE GRILL, THE
STUPIDS, THE
TARGET
THAT THING YOU DO!
THEODORE REX
THEREMIN: AN ELECTRONIC ODYSSEY
TRUMAN
TWELFTH NIGHT
UP CLOSE AND PERSONAL
WALLACE AND GROMIT: THE BEST OF AARDMAN ANIMATION
WHITE WOLVES II: LEGEND OF THE WILD
WHOLE WIDE WORLD, THE
WING CHUN
YANKEE ZULU

C

AFFAIR, THE
AMANDA AND THE ALIEN
AMERICAN BUFFALO
AMERICAN STRAYS
AMERICA'S DREAM
ANGELA
ANGELS AND INSECTS
ANNA
ANTONIA'S LINE
APART FROM HUGH
ARRIVAL, THE
ASSAULT AT WEST POINT
. . . AT FIRST SIGHT
AUGUST
AVENTURERA
BAD LOVE
BAD MOON
BASQUIAT
BATON ROUGE
BEAUTIFUL GIRLS
BEAUTIFUL THING
BEAVIS AND BUTT-HEAD DO AMERICA
BEFORE AND AFTER
BEYOND DESIRE
BIG NIGHT
BIG SQUEEZE, THE
BIG WARS
BIO-DOME
BIRDCAGE, THE
BITTER SUGAR
BLACK MOUNTAIN
BLACK OUT
BLACK SHEEP
BLONDES HAVE MORE GUNS
BLOODKNOT
BLOODSPORT II: THE NEXT KUMITE
BLUSH

BODY COUNT
BOTTLE ROCKET
BOUND
BOYS
BREACH OF TRUST
BROKEN ARROW
BROTHER OF SLEEP
CABLE GUY, THE
CALLING THE GHOSTS: A STORY ABOUT RAPE, WAR AND WOMEN
CAPTIVES
CAUGHT
CELESTIAL CLOCKWORK
CELLULOID CLOSET, THE
CELTIC PRIDE
CHAIN REACTION
CHAMBER, THE
CHEKIST, THE
CHILDREN OF FURY
CHUNGKING EXPRESS
CITIZEN RUTH
CITY HALL
COLD COMFORT FARM
COLONY, THE
COURAGE UNDER FIRE
CRACKER: THE MADWOMAN IN THE ATTIC
CRAFT, THE
CROCODILES IN AMSTERDAM
CROSSCUT
CROW: CITY OF ANGELS, THE
CRUCIBLE, THE
CURDLED
CURTIS'S CHARM
DADETOWN
DAENS
DANGEROUS PASSION
DARKMAN III: DIE DARKMAN DIE
DAYLIGHT
DEAD COLD
DEAD MAN
DEAD TO RIGHTS
DEADLY OUTBREAK
DEATH BENEFIT
DENISE CALLS UP
DESIRE
DEVOTION
DONOR UNKNOWN
DON'T BE A MENACE TO SOUTH CENTRAL WHILE DRINKING YOUR JUICE IN THE HOOD
DOWN, OUT AND DANGEROUS
DOWN PERISCOPE
EDDIE
EDIE & PEN
ED'S NEXT MOVE
ENGLISH PATIENT, THE
ERASER
EVENING STAR, THE
EVERYTHING RELATIVE
EVIL HAS A FACE
EVITA
EXECUTIVE DECISION
EXTREME MEASURES
EYE FOR AN EYE
EYE OF VICHY, THE
FAITHFUL
FAMILY THING, A
FAN, THE
FAR HARBOR
FARGO
FAST MONEY
FATALLY YOURS
FELONY
FINAL CUT, THE
FINAL EQUINOX, THE
FIRST WIVES CLUB, THE
FLATTERED
FLED
FLIRT
FLIRTING WITH DISASTER
FLOWER OF MY SECRET, THE
FOR BETTER OR WORSE
4 TALES OF 2 CITIES
FOXFIRE
FRANCOIS TRUFFAUT: STOLEN PORTRAITS
FRIGHTENERS, THE
FULL BODY MASSAGE
FUNERAL, THE
GALAXIES ARE COLLIDING
GET ON THE BUS
GETTING AWAY WITH MURDER
GHOST AND THE DARKNESS, THE
GHOST IN THE SHELL
GHOSTS OF MISSISSIPPI
GIRLFRIENDS
GIRLS TOWN
GLIMMER MAN, THE
GRACE OF MY HEART
GRASS HARP, THE
GRAVE, THE
GREAT WHITE HYPE, THE
GUIMBA THE TYRANT
HALFMOON
HAMLET
HAPPY GILMORE
HARD JUSTICE
HARD WAY OUT: BLOODFIST VIII
HEAVEN'S PRISONERS
HEAVY
HEDD WYNN
HEIDI CHRONICLES, THE
HEIDI FLEISS HOLLYWOOD MADAM
HIDDEN ASSASSIN
HIGH SCHOOL HIGH
HOLLOW POINT
HOMAGE
HORSEMAN ON THE ROOF
HYPE!
IF LUCY FELL
I'M NOT RAPPAPORT
IN LOVE AND WAR
INDEPENDENCE DAY
IRON EAGLE IV
ISLAND OF DR. MOREAU, THE
IT'S MY PARTY
JACK & SARAH
JAG
JERRY MAGUIRE
JOE'S APARTMENT
JOHN CARPENTER'S ESCAPE FROM L.A.
JOHNNY SHORTWAVE
JOSEPH CONRAD'S THE SECRET AGENT
JUDE
JUROR, THE
JUST YOUR LUCK
KANSAS CITY
KIDS IN THE HALL: BRAIN CANDY
LA CEREMONIE
LAND AND FREEDOM
LARRY MCMURTRY'S STREETS OF LAREDO
LAST DANCE
LAST SUPPER, THE
LATE SHIFT, THE
LAWNMOWER MAN 2: BEYOND CYBERSPACE
LAZARUS MAN, THE
LES VOLEURS
LET'S GET BIZZEE
LETTER TO MY KILLER
LIVE WIRE: HUMAN TIMEBOMB
LOADED
LONE STAR
LONG KISS GOODNIGHT, THE
LONG ROAD HOME, THE
LOOKING FOR RICHARD
LOSING CHASE
LOTTO LAND
LOVE IS ALL THERE IS
LOVER'S KNOT
LOW LIFE, THE
MA SAISON PREFEREE
MABOROSI
MAD DOG TIME
MADAGASCAR SKIN
MADAME WANG'S
MADDENING, THE
MAGIC HUNTER
MAN BY THE SHORE, THE
MAN IN THE ATTIC, THE
MAN WITH THE PERFECT SWING, THE
MANNY & LO
MARS ATTACKS!
MARVIN'S ROOM
MARY REILLY
MATERNAL INSTINCTS
MAXIMUM RISK
MERCY
MERLIN'S SHOP OF MAGICAL WONDERS
MICHAEL
MICHAEL COLLINS
MIDNIGHT ANGEL
MIDWINTER'S TALE, A
MILLE BOLLE BLU
MIRROR HAS TWO FACES, THE
MISSING PIECES
MISSION: IMPOSSIBLE
MR. WRONG
MODERN AFFAIR, A
MOLL FLANDERS
MONSTER, THE
MONSTERSHOW
MOONSHINE HIGHWAY
MOTHER
MOTHER
MOTHER NIGHT
MOTHER OF KINGS
MOTHER'S PRAYER, A
MRS. MUNCK
MRS. WINTERBOURNE
MULTIPLICITY
MURDERED INNOCENCE
MY FELLOW AMERICANS
MYSTERY SCIENCE THEATER 3000: THE MOVIE
NATIONAL LAMPOON'S FAVORITE DEADLY SINS
NELLY AND MONSIEUR ARNAUD
NEMESIS III: PREY HARDER
NEON BIBLE, THE
NEW LIFE, A
NICO ICON
NIKI DE SAINT PHALLE: WHO IS THE MONSTER — YOU OR ME?
NORMAL LIFE
NOT BAD FOR A GIRL
NOT OF THIS EARTH
NUTTY PROFESSOR, THE
OF LOVE AND SHADOWS
OFF AND RUNNING
ONE LESS EGG TO FRY
ONE MAN'S JUSTICE
OPEN SEASON

ORGANIZED CRIME & TRIAD BUREAU
ORIGINAL GANGSTAS
ORSON WELLES: THE ONE-MAN BAND
OUT THERE
OUTPOST, THE
PAINTED HERO
PALLBEARER, THE
PALOOKAVILLE
PASSION OF DARKLY NOON, THE
PHARAOH'S ARMY
PHENOMENON
PHOENIX
PIE IN THE SKY
PIRANHA
POISON IVY 2: LILY
POMPATUS OF LOVE, THE
PORTRAIT OF A LADY, THE
PREDICTIONS OF FIRE
PRE-MADONNAS
PRIMAL FEAR
PROPRIETOR, THE
PUBLIC ACCESS
PUBLIC ENEMIES
QUEST, THE
RAGE
RANSOM
RASPUTIN
RATTLED
RAVENHAWK
RED SCORPION 2
REDEMPTION: KICKBOXER 5
RENDEZVOUS IN PARIS
RICH MAN'S WIFE, THE
RIDERS OF THE PURPLE SAGE
RIDICULE
ROAD TO GALVESTON, THE
RUDE
RUMBLE IN THE BRONX
SCREAM
SCREAMERS
SEARCH FOR ONE-EYE JIMMY, THE
SECRETS & LIES
SGT. BILKO
SERPENT'S LAIR
SET IT OFF
SHADOW WARRIORS
SHADOW YOU SOON WILL BE, A
SHARON'S SECRET
SHE'S THE ONE
SHINE
SHOOTFIGHTER 2: KILL OR BE KILLED!
SHOPPING
SHOT, THE
SILENCE OF NETO, THE
SILENCES OF THE PALACE, THE
SINGLE GIRL, A
SKIN
SLEEPERS
SLING BLADE
SMALL FACES
SOLITAIRE FOR TWO
SOLO
SOME FOLKS CALL IT A SLING BLADE
SOME MOTHER'S SON
SOMEONE ELSE'S AMERICA
SOUTH BEACH ACADEMY
SPIDER & ROSE
STAND OFF, THE
STAR MAKER, THE
STAR TREK: FIRST CONTACT
STEPHEN KING'S THINNER
STONEWALL
STORY OF XINGHUA, THE
STREET FIGHTER II: THE ANIMATED MOVIE
STREETCAR NAMED DESIRE, A
STRIPTEASE
SUBSTANCE OF FIRE, THE
SUBSTITUTE, THE
SUGARTIME
SUNCHASER
SUNSET PARK
SURVIVING PICASSO
SWEEPER, THE
SWINGERS
SYNTHETIC PLEASURES
TAILS YOU LIVE, HEADS YOU'RE DEAD
TAKEOVER, THE
TERMINAL IMPACT
THIN LINE BETWEEN LOVE AND HATE, A
THREE LIVES AND ONLY ONE DEATH
TIGER HEART
TIME TO KILL, A
TIMELESS
TIN CUP
TO GILLIAN ON HER 37TH BIRTHDAY
TOO FAST, TOO YOUNG
TRACKS OF A KILLER
TREES LOUNGE
TREMORS 2: AFTERSHOCKS
TRIGGER EFFECT, THE
TRUTH ABOUT CATS AND DOGS, THE
TUNNEL VISION
TUSKEGEE AIRMEN, THE
TWISTER
TWO-BITS & PEPPER
2 DAYS IN THE VALLEY
TWO FRIENDS
TWO IF BY SEA
TWO MUCH
UNDER THE DOMIM TREE
UNDER THE HULA MOON
UNDERSTUDY: GRAVEYARD SHIFT 2, THE
UNFORGETTABLE
UNHOOK THE STARS
UNKNOWN ORIGIN
VENUS RISING
VERY BRADY SEQUEL, A
VIKING SAGAS, THE
VIRTUAL COMBAT
VIRUS
VISITORS, THE
VIVE L'AMOUR
VUKOVAR
WALKING AND TALKING
WAR AT HOME, THE
WAR OF THE BUTTONS, THE
WARHEAD
WAVELENGTH
WEEKEND IN THE COUNTRY, A
WELCOME TO THE DOLLHOUSE
WHARF RAT, THE
WHEN WE WERE KINGS
WHERE'S THE MONEY, NOREEN?
WHISPERING, THE
WHITE SQUALL
WICKED CITY, THE
WIFE, THE
WILLIAM SHAKESPEARE'S ROMEO + JULIET
WOLVES, THE
WOMAN UNDONE, A
YESTERDAY'S TARGET
YOUNG POISONER'S HANDBOOK, THE
ZARKORR! THE INVADER

O

ABUSE
ADRENALIN: FEAR THE RUSH
ANIMAL INSTINCTS III: THE SEDUCTRESS
BAJA
BEST OF THE BEST 3: NO TURNING BACK
BEWARE: CHILDREN AT PLAY
BLACK DAY BLUE NIGHT
BLACK ROSE OF HARLEM
BLACK SCORPION
BLOOD & DONUTS
BODY OF INFLUENCE 2
BOY CALLED HATE, A
BREAKAWAY
BREAKING THE WAVES
BUGGED
BULLETPROOF
BURIAL OF THE RATS
BUTTERFLY KISS
CANNIBAL! THE MUSICAL
CARNOSAUR 3: PRIMAL SPECIES
CARRIED AWAY
CEMETERY MAN
CHAMELEON
CHILDREN OF THE CORN: THE GATHERING
COLD LIGHT OF DAY
CONDITION RED
CRIMINAL HEARTS
DARK SECRETS
DEAD WEEKEND
DEATH ARTIST, THE
DELTA OF VENUS
DEMOLITIONIST, THE
DENTIST, THE
DESOLATION ANGELS
DIABOLIQUE
DOGFIGHTERS, THE
DON'T LET YOUR MEAT LOAF
ELECTRA
EVIL ED
EXIT
FATE
FEAR
FEELING MINNESOTA
FEMALIEN
FIST OF THE NORTH STAR
FLAMING EARS
FORBIDDEN ZONE: ALIEN ABDUCTION
FRAME BY FRAME
FREEWAY
FRENCH TWIST
FRIEND OF THE FAMILY 2
FRISK
FROM DUSK TILL DAWN
FUGITIVE RAGE
FUNNYMAN, THE
GIRL 6
GLASS CAGE, THE
GRIM
HATE
HAUNTED
HEAD OF THE FAMILY
HEADLESS BODY IN TOPLESS BAR
HELLRAISER: BLOODLINE
HOSTILE INTENTIONS
HOURGLASS
I SHOT ANDY WARHOL
IMMORTALS, THE
JOHNNY 100 PESOS
KAMIKAZE TAXI
KASPAR HAUSER
KINGPIN
LAST MAN STANDING

LIFEFORM
LITTLE DEATH, THE
LITTLE WITCHES
LIVE NUDE GIRLS
MACHINE, THE
MAHJONG
MAYBE . . . MAYBE NOT
MIDNIGHT DANCERS
MIND RIPPER
MIRROR, MIRROR III: THE VOYEUR
MR. ICE CREAM MAN
MR. STITCH
MOUTH TO MOUTH
MULHOLLAND FALLS
MUTANT MAN
NAKED SOULS
NECRONOMICON: BOOK OF THE DEAD
NEUROSIA: 50 YEARS OF PERVERSITY
NIGHT OF THE SCARECROW
NORMA JEAN AND MARILYN
ONE GOOD TURN
ONE NIGHT STAND
ORIGINAL SINS
OUTRAGE
OVER THE WIRE
PARADISE LOST: THE CHILD MURDERS AT ROBIN HOOD HILLS
PEOPLE VS. LARRY FLYNT, THE
PHAT BEACH
PINOCCHIO'S REVENGE
PLAYBACK
POLYMORPH
PORTRAITS OF A KILLER
PROTEUS
PURE DANGER
RAW TARGET
RED LINE
ROCK, THE
RUMPELSTILTSKIN
SAINTS AND SINNERS
SANCTUARY: THE MOVIE
SANDMAN, THE
SANTA CLAWS
SAWBONES
SGT. KABUKIMAN N.Y.P.D.
SERIAL KILLER
SHADOW OF ANGELS
SHAMELESS
SHOWGIRL MURDERS, THE
SKYSCRAPER
SOMETIMES THEY COME BACK . . . AGAIN
SPY HARD
STEALING BEAUTY
SUITE 16
SURGEON, THE
SWEET NOTHING
TALES FROM THE CRYPT PRESENTS BORDELLO OF BLOOD
TALES OF EROTICA
TALKING ABOUT SEX
TATTOO BOY
TEXAS CHAINSAW MASSACRE: THE NEXT GENERATION
TEXAS PAYBACK
THEY BITE
TOLLBOOTH
TRAINSPOTTING
TWO DEATHS
UNDERTOW
VIRTUAL ENCOUNTERS
WATCH ME
WHEN THE BULLET HITS THE BONE
WHITE TIGER
WHO KILLED PASOLINI?
WIDOW'S KISS
WILD SIDE
WITCHCRAFT: SALEM'S GHOST
WITHIN THE ROCK
WITHOUT MERCY
YOU'LL NEVER MAKE LOVE IN THIS TOWN AGAIN

NAME INDEX

Individuals included in the cast or credit sections of the film reviews in this volume are listed below. Names are arranged alphabetically by function as follows:

Actors
Animators
Art Directors
Associate Producers
Casting
Choreographers
Cinematographers
Co-producers
Costumes
Directors
Editors
Executive Producers
Makeup/ FX makeup
Music Composers
Producers
Production Designers
Screenwriters
Set Decorators
Sound
Source Authors
Special Effects
Stunts

ACTORS

Aaron, Caroline
BIG NIGHT
BOYS NEXT DOOR, THE
HOUSE ARREST
MODERN AFFAIR, A
Aaron, Victor
BULLETPROOF
SUNCHASER
Aarons, Bonnie
DEAR GOD
Abassi, Riz
HAMLET
Abbot, Bernie
CAUGHT
Abbot, Tommy
CAUGHT
Abbott, Bruce
BLACK SCORPION
DEMOLITIONIST, THE
Abbott, John
YOUNG POISONER'S HANDBOOK, THE
Abbott, Tracey
WHISPERING, THE
Abdelmoujoud, Latifa
SUITE 16
Abdillah, Shion
SHOPPING
Abe, Y. Hiro
HOURGLASS
Abel, Dominique
CELESTIAL CLOCKWORK
Abelew, Alan
DON'T BE A MENACE TO SOUTH CENTRAL WHILE DRINKING YOUR JUICE IN THE HOOD
Abell, Alistair
FOR THE MOMENT
Abell, Tim
FUGITIVE RAGE
OVER THE WIRE
Abercrombie, Ian
RATTLED
Abernathy, Abby
SOME FOLKS CALL IT A SLING BLADE
Abot, Didier
RIDICULE
Abou-Keer, Rebekah
BOGUS
Aboulela, Amir
BARB WIRE
Abraham, Falconer
RUDE
Abraham, Richard
FUGITIVE RAGE
Abrahams, Doug
BIG BULLY
Abrams, George
SANDMAN, THE
Abrams, Jeffrey
DIABOLIQUE
Abrams, Patsy Grady
FIRST KID
Abrego, Olga
HATE
Abril, Victoria
BATON ROUGE
FRENCH TWIST
Accolas, Raymond
MAXIMUM RISK
Accornero, Roberto
WHO KILLED PASOLINI?
Acheson, James
KAZAAM
Ackert, Ramin
WHISPERING, THE
Ackland, Joss
D3: THE MIGHTY DUCKS
SHAMELESS
SURVIVING PICASSO
Ackley, Don
DADETOWN
Acosta, Eric
CROW: CITY OF ANGELS, THE
Acovone, Jay
CROSSCUT
FOXFIRE
INDEPENDENCE DAY
Acquah, Janice
SECRETS & LIES
Acri, Elena Louise
MUTANT MAN
Acuna, Wanda
EYE FOR AN EYE
Adair-Rios, Mark
COURAGE UNDER FIRE
Adams, Camille James
GETTING AWAY WITH MURDER
Adams, Chris
DARKMAN III: DIE DARKMAN DIE
Adams, Diane
STRIPTEASE
Adams, Ernie
FAMILY THING, A
Adams, Jacob
MR. HOLLAND'S OPUS
Adams, Jane
KANSAS CITY
Adams, Jason
MOTHER
Adams, Jay
PEOPLE VS. LARRY FLYNT, THE
Adams, Joey
BIO-DOME
Adams, Joey Lauren
MICHAEL
Adams, Lynne
GRACE OF MY HEART
Adams, Mason
ASSAULT AT WEST POINT
NOT OF THIS EARTH
Adams, Polly
JUROR, THE
Adams, Rick
RACE THE SUN
Adams, Steve
DEVOTION
Adamson, Chris
SHAMELESS
Adamson, Larina
JERRY MAGUIRE
Adcox, Thomas
IT CAME FROM OUTER SPACE II
Addis, Gailyn
OUT THERE
Addis, Richard
SPITFIRE GRILL, THE
Addison, Amanda
AMERICA'S DREAM
Addison, Walter
FAN, THE
GREAT WHITE HYPE, THE
Addy, Wesley
BEFORE AND AFTER
HARVEST OF FIRE
MODERN AFFAIR, A
Ade, Dayo
RUDE
Ade, Herbie
BEAUTIFUL GIRLS
Adejugbe, Ayo
LAWNMOWER MAN 2: BEYOND CYBERSPACE
Adel, Bruce
HEAD OF THE FAMILY
Adelist, Jack
DEADLY OUTBREAK
Adell, Traci
PLAYBACK
Adi, Alexandra
EDDIE
Adjani, Isabelle
DIABOLIQUE
Adler, Jerry
GETTING AWAY WITH MURDER
Adler, Joanna
PROPRIETOR, THE
Adler, Michael
DON'T BE A MENACE TO SOUTH CENTRAL WHILE DRINKING YOUR JUICE IN THE HOOD
Adonis, Frank
JUROR, THE
Adrisani, Emilio
STAR MAKER, THE

Affleck, Casey
RACE THE SUN
Agashe, Mohan
TARGET
Agnew, Iain
BREAKING THE WAVES
Agnew, Valerie
HYPE!
Agostini, Diana
I'M NOT RAPPAPORT
Agoun, Nabil
MADAME BUTTERFLY
Agullo, Neus
LAND AND FREEDOM
Agut, Alicia
FLOWER OF MY SECRET, THE
Ahern, Jim
KINGPIN
Ahlquist, Jane
TWO FRIENDS
Ahmed, Ahmed
EXECUTIVE DECISION
SWINGERS
Ahn, Ralph
LAWNMOWER MAN 2: BEYOND CYBERSPACE
Ahumada, Alfredo
JOHNNY 100 PESOS
Ahumada, Helena
JOHNNY 100 PESOS
Ai Ya
SOMEONE ELSE'S AMERICA
Aiello, Danny
CITY HALL
ROAD HOME, THE
2 DAYS IN THE VALLEY
TWO MUCH
Aiello, Rick
ROAD HOME, THE
Aikman, Troy
JERRY MAGUIRE
Ailiya
BLACK MOUNTAIN
Aimee, Chantal
CELESTIAL CLOCKWORK
Ainslie, Jean
SECRETS & LIES
Airlie, Andrew
FEAR
HOMEWARD BOUND II: LOST IN SAN FRANCISCO
Aitken, Marcella Vitalainai
TWO MUCH
Ajimi, Karima
SILENCES OF THE PALACE, THE
Akai, Hidekazu
MABOROSI
Akerstream, Marc
RUMBLE IN THE BRONX
Akin, Philip
FLY AWAY HOME
STUPIDS, THE
Akins, Joe
JACK
Akiyama, Denis
EXTREME MEASURES
Akler, Rhea
VIRUS
Akomah, Jeffrey
VIRUS
Alabi, Yetunde
BOGUS
Alacchi, Carl
HOLLOW POINT
UNDERSTUDY: GRAVEYARD SHIFT 2, THE
Aladren, Andres
LAND AND FREEDOM
Alaia, Azzedine
CATWALK
Alaimo, Marc
DEAD TO RIGHTS
Alamia, Giovanni
STAR MAKER, THE
Alanna, Judy
PROPRIETOR, THE
Alaouie, Affifi
DEAD WEEKEND
Alarcon, Luis
JOHNNY 100 PESOS
Alba, Jessica Marie
VENUS RISING
Albanese, Brett
MURDERED INNOCENCE
Alber, Kevin
BURIAL OF THE RATS
SHOWGIRL MURDERS, THE
Alberici, Fabio
CEMETERY MAN
Albert, Eddie
GIRL FROM MARS, THE
Albert, Edward
GIRL FROM MARS, THE
Albert, Marv
CELTIC PRIDE
EDDIE
Albert, Renee
DEAR GOD
Albertini, Michel
NELLY AND MONSIEUR ARNAUD
Albrecht, Richard
JUDE
Albright, Ariauna
POLYMORPH
Albright, Brad
DON'T LET YOUR MEAT LOAF
Alcaniz, Fina
LAND AND FREEDOM
Alda, Alan
EVERYONE SAYS I LOVE YOU
FLIRTING WITH DISASTER
Alday, Luis
EVITA
Alden, Andrew
LAST MAN STANDING
LIFEFORM
Aldredge, Tom
HARVEST OF FIRE
Aldrich, Dell
MICHAEL
WHOLE WIDE WORLD, THE
Aldunate, Gabriel
JOHNNY 100 PESOS
Aled, Gruffuld
HEDD WYNN
Alejandrino, Alberto
ASSOCIATE, THE
Alen, Brit
DAENS
Aleong, Aki
CABLE GUY, THE
QUEST, THE
Ales, John
NUTTY PROFESSOR, THE
SPY HARD
Alesi, Filippo
STAR MAKER, THE
Alessandro, Anthony
FUNERAL, THE
Alessi, Joseph
INSTITUTE BENJAMENTA
Alessi, Mike
ARRIVAL, THE
Alexander, Adriana
BARB WIRE
Alexander, Anton
CEMETERY MAN
Alexander, Cory
EDDIE
Alexander, Dorothea
YOUNG POISONER'S HANDBOOK, THE
Alexander, Gabriel
DON'T BE A MENACE TO SOUTH CENTRAL WHILE DRINKING YOUR JUICE IN THE HOOD
Alexander, J.C.
MATILDA
Alexander, Jane
STAR MAKER, THE
Alexander, Jason
DUNSTON CHECKS IN
FOR BETTER OR WORSE
HUNCHBACK OF NOTRE DAME, THE
LAST SUPPER, THE
Alexander, Robert
BASQUIAT
Alexander, Wayne
MR. WRONG
Alexander, Zoe
LITTLE WITCHES
Alexander-Willis, Hope
DEAR GOD
Alfavo, Alberto
JERRY MAGUIRE
Alfonsi, Claudio
WHO KILLED PASOLINI?
Ali, Angela
CAUGHT
Ali Mete, Hasan
FLIRT
Ali, Muhammad
WHEN WE WERE KINGS
Alice, Mary
BED OF ROSES
Aliseo, Enza
MILLE BOLLE BLU
Alisharan, Jason
HALFBACK OF NOTRE DAME, THE
Aljinovic, Boris
FLIRT
Allain, Stephanie
BOY CALLED HATE, A
Allain-Marcus, Wade
BOY CALLED HATE, A
Allee, John
PHOENIX
Allen, B.
WITCHCRAFT: SALEM'S GHOST
Allen, Bill
LAZARUS MAN, THE
Allen, Bonita
CHAMBER, THE
Allen, Carlo
CABLE GUY, THE
Allen, Clint
KINGPIN
Allen, David
LAND AND FREEDOM
Allen, Geri
KANSAS CITY
Allen, Jay Presson
CELLULOID CLOSET, THE
Allen, Joan
CRUCIBLE, THE
Allen, Keith
CAPTIVES
TRAINSPOTTING
Allen, Kevin
TRAINSPOTTING
Allen, Mozelle Hawkins
PREACHER'S WIFE, THE
Allen, Peg
LAST DANCE

Allen, Penelope
LOOKING FOR RICHARD
Allen, Penny
WAR AT HOME, THE
Allen, Robin Lindsley
THAT THING YOU DO!
Allen, Rosalind
MOTHER
PINOCCHIO'S REVENGE
Allen, Sage
ED
Allen, Todd
PINOCCHIO'S REVENGE
Allen, Tommy
RANSOM
Allen, Woody
EVERYONE SAYS I LOVE YOU
Allende, Gonzalo
OF LOVE AND SHADOWS
Allerson, Alexander
SHADOW OF ANGELS
Alley, Tom
SWINGERS
Alliger, Richard
UP CLOSE AND PERSONAL
Allin, Eugene
MAXIMUM RISK
Allison, Don
NIGHT OF THE TWISTERS
WHERE'S THE MONEY, NOREEN?
Allport, Christopher
SWEEPER, THE
Allred, Corbin
JOSH KIRBY . . . TIME WARRIOR!: EGGS FROM 70,000,000 B.C.
JOSH KIRBY . . . TIME WARRIOR!: JOURNEY TO THE MAGIC CAVERN
JOSH KIRBY . . . TIME WARRIOR!: LAST BATTLE FOR THE UNIVERSE
JOSH KIRBY . . . TIME WARRIOR!: TRAPPED ON TOY WORLD
Almagor, Gila
UNDER THE DOMIM TREE
Almendral, Ami
EVERYONE SAYS I LOVE YOU
Almengor, Oscar Javier
SILENCE OF NETO, THE
Alonso, Maria Conchita
CAUGHT
Alpert, Arnie
LAST MAN STANDING
Alpert, Mike
DESOLATION ANGELS
Alphenaar, Carel
CROCODILES IN AMSTERDAM
Alster, Pamela
SGT. KABUKIMAN N.Y.P.D.
Alterman, Idan
DEADLY OUTBREAK
Althanova, Jana
HIDDEN ASSASSIN
Altman, Bruce
TO GILLIAN ON HER 37TH BIRTHDAY
Altman, Chelsea
FIRST WIVES CLUB, THE
Alto, Bobby
LOVE IS ALL THERE IS
Alvalos, Luis
LONE JUSTICE: SHOWDOWN AT PLUM CREEK
Alvarado, Christina
TRIGGER EFFECT, THE
Alvarado, Trini
FRIGHTENERS, THE
Alvaredo, Daniel
OF LOVE AND SHADOWS
Alvarez, Abraham
DEATH BENEFIT
Alvarez, Elizabeth
ONE GOOD TURN
Alvarez, George
HEAVY
Alvarez, Joshua
MATILDA
Alvarez, Rafael
WALKING AND TALKING
Alza, Walter
STUPIDS, THE
Alzenberg, Juanita
OF LOVE AND SHADOWS
Amador, Nattacha
CURDLED
Amandes, Tom
LONG KISS GOODNIGHT, THE
Amaral, Nicole
PHAT BEACH
Amatller, Xavier
LAND AND FREEDOM
Amato, Paul
JOHNNY SHORTWAVE
UNDERSTUDY: GRAVEYARD SHIFT 2, THE
Amatrudo, Ed
TOLLBOOTH
UP CLOSE AND PERSONAL
Ambrose, Paul
MADAME WANG'S
Ambrose, Tangie
THIN LINE BETWEEN LOVE AND HATE, A
Ambuehl, Cindy
BODY COUNT
Amendola, Claudio
HORSEMAN ON THE ROOF
WHO KILLED PASOLINI?
Amendola, Tony
LONE STAR
Ames, Kenner
BOGUS
HOMECOMING
Amis, Suzy
ONE GOOD TURN
Ammann, Renee
GREAT WHITE HYPE, THE
Amor, Jay
CURDLED
Amos, David
TAKEOVER, THE
Amos, Emma
SECRETS & LIES
Amos, John
FOR BETTER OR WORSE
Amross, Jim
STUPIDS, THE
Amsterdam, Lisa
JERRY MAGUIRE
Anastasio, Leo
POLYMORPH
Anastos, Ernie
INDEPENDENCE DAY
Ancelin, Cyril
HATE
Anders, Jentri
BERKELEY IN THE 60S
Anders, Kimberly
PIG'S TALE, A
Anders, Luana
AMERICAN STRAYS
Andersen, Jennifer
DEMOLITIONIST, THE
Anderson, Arthur
I'M NOT RAPPAPORT
Anderson, Brent
LILY DALE
PAINTED HERO
Anderson, Brittany
PREACHER'S WIFE, THE
Anderson, Carol
STUPIDS, THE
Anderson, Charlotte
WHITE SQUALL
Anderson, Cheryl
WOMAN UNDONE, A
Anderson, Daniel
BODY OF INFLUENCE 2
Anderson, Dawn
HYPE!
Anderson, Deke
FELONY
Anderson, Elizabeth
PAINTED HERO
ZARKORR! THE INVADER
Anderson, Erich
FINAL CUT, THE
INFINITY
Anderson, Georgia
TWO FRIENDS
Anderson, Ian
ROLLING STONES ROCK-AND-ROLL CIRCUS, THE
Anderson, Jo
DAYLIGHT
Anderson, Joseph
MR. HOLLAND'S OPUS
Anderson, Louie
MR. WRONG
Anderson, Maxi
SPY HARD
Anderson, Norm
DADETOWN
Anderson, Pamela
BARB WIRE
NAKED SOULS
Anderson, Roy T.
WHERE'S THE MONEY, NOREEN?
Anderson, Sharon
FARGO
Anderson, Stanley
CITY HALL
PRIMAL FEAR
Anderson, Steven
MOTHER
Anderson, Tommy
BIG BULLY
Anderson, Whitney
PIG'S TALE, A
Anderson-Gunter, Jeffery
DON'T BE A MENACE TO SOUTH CENTRAL WHILE DRINKING YOUR JUICE IN THE HOOD
Andolini, Michael
FAN, THE
Andrade, Billy
KINGPIN
Andre, Benita
HARD JUSTICE
SHARON'S SECRET
Andre, Jill
GHOSTS OF MISSISSIPPI
Andreoni, Marc
MACHINE, THE
Andreozzi, Jack
MOTHER
Andreu, Simon
HIDDEN ASSASSIN
Andrews, Anthony
HAUNTED
Andrews, Emily
BEYOND THE CALL
Andrews, Guiseppe
INDEPENDENCE DAY
Andrews, Naveen
ENGLISH PATIENT, THE
Andrews, Real
MAD DOG TIME

RED SCORPION 2
Andriole, David
BARB WIRE
Androgyn, Ichgola
NEUROSIA: 50 YEARS OF PERVERSITY
Androsky, Carol
THAT THING YOU DO!
Andrucci, Fred
RUMBLE IN THE BRONX
Anello, Frank
BEAUTIFUL GIRLS
Anello, Gary
HEAD OF THE FAMILY
Angarano, Michael
I'M NOT RAPPAPORT
Angel, Vanessa
KINGPIN
Angela, Sharon
TALES OF EROTICA
Angelin
NELLY AND MONSIEUR ARNAUD
Angell, Vincent
LOOKING FOR RICHARD
Anglade, Jean-Hugues
MAXIMUM RISK
NELLY AND MONSIEUR ARNAUD
Aniston, Jennifer
SHE'S THE ONE
Anka, Paul
MAD DOG TIME
Ann, Debora
PHAT BEACH
Annabi, Noureddine
SILENCES OF THE PALACE, THE
Annamalai, Satchu
GHOST AND THE DARKNESS, THE
Anoro, Manel
LAND AND FREEDOM
Anselmo, Robert M.
ROCK, THE
Ansley, Anessa
DADETOWN
Ansley, Zach
SLEEPERS
Ansley-Purpura, Michael
DADETOWN
Ant, Adam
LOVER'S KNOT
Anthony, Horacio
GLASS CAGE, THE
Anthony, Lysette
DEAD COLD
Anthony, Marc
BIG NIGHT
SUBSTITUTE, THE
Anthony, Mark
MADAGASCAR SKIN
Anthony, Nicholas
LAZARUS MAN, THE
Anthony, Nigel
ROUJIN-Z
Antin, Steve
IT'S MY PARTY
Antman, Tina Catharina
BEYOND DESIRE
Antoine, Vinessa
ANNIE O
Antoinette, Cecelia
DON'T LET YOUR MEAT LOAF
Antoinio, Larry
THAT THING YOU DO!
Anton, Katja
CEMETERY MAN
Antonios, Kim
TWO FRIENDS
Antoniuk, Mark
RUMBLE IN THE BRONX
Antunes, Nuno
ANNIE O
Anwar, Gabrielle
GRAVE, THE
Anzaldo III, Sebastian
CITIZEN RUTH
Apergis, Andreas
HOLLOW POINT
Apicella, John
MIND RIPPER
NORMA JEAN AND MARILYN
Apisa, Bob
COURAGE UNDER FIRE
EXECUTIVE DECISION
FLED
Apparcel, Father Greg
ENTERTAINING ANGELS: THE DOROTHY DAY STORY
Appel, Alex
GETTING AWAY WITH MURDER
Appel, Peter
BIG NIGHT
EXTREME MEASURES
SLEEPERS
Applebaum, Bill
VERY BRADY SEQUEL, A
Applegate, Christina
MARS ATTACKS!
Applegate, Jeremy
CABLE GUY, THE
Applegate, Phyllis
MOTHER
Aprea, John
SUNSET PARK
Araiza, Armando
JOHNNY 100 PESOS
Arana, Tomas
FIRST KID
Arancio, Lawrence
EXTREME MEASURES
Aranda-Richards, Dave
RAGE
Aranha, Ray
CITY HALL
Aras, Ruta
FAST MONEY
Araskog, Julie
BASQUIAT
EDDIE
Arbona, Gilles
PROPRIETOR, THE
Archer, Anne
MAN IN THE ATTIC, THE
Archie, Brent
MR. HOLLAND'S OPUS
Archison, Wayne
MUTANT MAN
Arcos, Maria Gentil
AVENTURERA
Ardant, Fanny
FRANCOIS TRUFFAUT: STOLEN PORTRAITS
RIDICULE
Ardi, Richard
BAD LOVE
Arditi, Pierre
HORSEMAN ON THE ROOF
Ardolino, Isaac
HIGH SCHOOL HIGH
Arenales, Pablo
SILENCE OF NETO, THE
Aresco, Joey
SAWBONES
Argenziano, Carmen
BROKEN ARROW
Argiro, Vinny
MARS ATTACKS!
Argo, Katherine
PROPRIETOR, THE
Argo, Victor
CONDITION RED
FUNERAL, THE
Arias, Imanol
FLOWER OF MY SECRET, THE
Arilla, Ricard
LAND AND FREEDOM
Aris, Tim
RACE THE SUN
Arisco, David
TOLLBOOTH
Arizmendi, Yareli
UP CLOSE AND PERSONAL
Arizona, Mooky
HOUSE ARREST
Arkin, Alan
HECK'S WAY HOME
MOTHER NIGHT
Arlys, Dimitra
IT'S MY PARTY
Arm, Mark
HYPE!
Armani, Giorgio
CATWALK
Armiger, Martin
TWO FRIENDS
Armitage, Alison
JERRY MAGUIRE
Armor, Gene
TIGER HEART
Armstrong, Brett
HAPPY GILMORE
Armstrong, Chris
SHOPPING
Armstrong, Curtis
BIG BULLY
SPY HARD
Armstrong, David
GHOSTS OF MISSISSIPPI
Armstrong, Louis E.
GHOSTS OF MISSISSIPPI
Armstrong, Ronald K.
BUGGED
Armus, Sidney
I'M NOT RAPPAPORT
Arnaud, Tony
MANNY & LO
Arndt, Jacques
OF LOVE AND SHADOWS
Arnett, Kathryn
MR. HOLLAND'S OPUS
Arnett, Will
ED'S NEXT MOVE
Arney, Randall
CHAIN REACTION
Arning, Tina
SPY HARD
Arnold, Annette
TREES LOUNGE
Arnold, Madison
LOOKING FOR RICHARD
Arnold, Roddy
WITCHCRAFT: SALEM'S GHOST
Arnold, Steve
APART FROM HUGH
Arnold, Tobias
YOUNG POISONER'S HANDBOOK, THE
Arnold, Tom
BIG BULLY
CARPOOL
STUPIDS, THE
Arnold, Tracy
SHOT, THE
Arnold, Victor
TREES LOUNGE

Aron, Laszlo
RASPUTIN
Arone, James
MOTHER'S PRAYER, A
Aronson, Steve
CITY HALL
Arquette, Alexis
DEAD WEEKEND
FRISK
SOMETIMES THEY COME BACK . . . AGAIN
Arquette, David
BEAUTIFUL GIRLS
SCREAM
Arquette, Lewis
WILD SIDE
Arquette, Patricia
FLIRTING WITH DISASTER
INFINITY
JOSEPH CONRAD'S THE SECRET AGENT
Arredondo, Cesar
JOHNNY 100 PESOS
Arrington, Timothy
OPEN SEASON
Arta
WITHOUT MERCY
Arthur, Beatrice
FOR BETTER OR WORSE
Arthur, Greg
TUNNEL VISION
Arthur, Jacqueline
CHAIN REACTION
Artist Formerly Known as Docky, The
KINGPIN
Artura, Michael
SGT. KABUKIMAN N.Y.P.D.
Artz, Gregg
EXECUTIVE DECISION
Arvanites, Steven
ED'S NEXT MOVE
Asano, Tadanobu
MABOROSI
Ashbourne, Lorraine
JACK & SARAH
Asher, Vanessa Lee
BARB WIRE
Ashforth, Justin
CITY HALL
Ashker, John
BLACK SHEEP
Ashley, Craig
TUNNEL VISION
Ashton, John
FAST MONEY
HIDDEN ASSASSIN
Ashton-Griffiths, Roger
PORTRAIT OF A LADY, THE
Askoldov, Alexander
CHASING BUTTERFLIES
Aslen, Abdelazziz
MADAME BUTTERFLY
Aso, Yuri
FLIRT
Aspen, Jennifer
SOMETIMES THEY COME BACK . . . AGAIN
VERY BRADY SEQUEL, A
Assad, Richard
MARS ATTACKS!
MOTHER
Assante, Armand
STRIPTEASE
Assante, Marco
STRIPTEASE
Assayas, Olivier
FRANCOIS TRUFFAUT: STOLEN PORTRAITS
Asti, Adriana
WHO KILLED PASOLINI?
Astilean, Dan
MAGIC IN THE MIRROR
Astin, John
FRIGHTENERS, THE
Astin, Mackenzie
EVENING STAR, THE
IN LOVE AND WAR
WIDOW'S KISS
Astin, Sean
COURAGE UNDER FIRE
LOW LIFE, THE
Aston, Emily
BUTTERFLY KISS
Astrachan, Joshua
ED'S NEXT MOVE
Astruc, Alexandre
FRANCOIS TRUFFAUT: STOLEN PORTRAITS
Atasanoff, Pete
FROM DUSK TILL DAWN
Atherton, Doran
LARRY MCMURTRY'S STREETS OF LAREDO
Atherton, Heidi
BLOODKNOT
Atherton, William
BIO-DOME
RAVENHAWK
SAINTS AND SINNERS
Atkin, Harvey
STUPIDS, THE
Atkine, Feodor
THREE LIVES AND ONLY ONE DEATH
Atkins, Allan
SMALL FACES
Atkins, Amy
CITY HALL
Atkins, Christopher
IT'S MY PARTY
Atkins, Dan
MERCY
Atkins, Eileen
COLD COMFORT FARM
JACK & SARAH
Atkins, John
HYPE!
Atkinson, Fort
EYE FOR AN EYE
MAN OF THE YEAR
Attanasio, Joseph
SLEEPERS
Attenborough, Charlotte
JANE EYRE
Attenborough, Richard
HAMLET
WAVELENGTH
Atterton, Edward
FAR HARBOR
Attili, Antonella
STAR MAKER, THE
Atwood, Dana
NEON BIBLE, THE
Auberjonois, Tessa
I'M NOT RAPPAPORT
Aubier, Pascal
CHASING BUTTERFLIES
Aubry, Sophie
NEW LIFE, A
Aubu
SGT. KABUKIMAN N.Y.P.D.
Auchelli, Marcelo Alejandro
EVITA
Audcoeur, Sylvie
FRENCH TWIST
Audiberti, Joan
PROPRIETOR, THE
Audiello, Massimo
I SHOT ANDY WARHOL
Audran, Stephanie
MAXIMUM RISK
Auerman, Nadja
CATWALK
August, Lance
EXECUTIVE DECISION
Auguste, Ailo
MAN BY THE SHORE, THE
Augustus, Sherman
RUMPELSTILTSKIN
Aumiller, Gary
MURDERED INNOCENCE
Aumont, Jean-Pierre
PROPRIETOR, THE
Aumont, Tina
NICO ICON
Aurbach, Gary
SWINGERS
Aurel, Jean
FRANCOIS TRUFFAUT: STOLEN PORTRAITS
Aurelius, Marcus
BLACK ROSE OF HARLEM
WILD SIDE
Aussedat, Pierre
VISITORS, THE
Austin, Michele
SECRETS & LIES
Austin, Paul
FLIRT
PALOOKAVILLE
Austin, Simon
SHOPPING
Austin-Olsen, Shaun
EXTREME MEASURES
Auteuil, Daniel
LES VOLEURS
MA SAISON PREFEREE
Authier, Jaques
MAXIMUM RISK
Avedon, Loren
VIRTUAL COMBAT
Avelar, Socorro
SOLO
Averlant, Eric
VISITORS, THE
Averlont, Erik
ADVENTURES OF PINOCCHIO, THE
Avery, Rick
STUPIDS, THE
Aviel, Shimon
MOTHER NIGHT
Aviles, Angel
LOW LIFE, THE
Avital, Mili
DEAD MAN
Ayari, Ramia
SILENCES OF THE PALACE, THE
Ayer, Debbon
I SHOT ANDY WARHOL
Ayers, Chad
STRIPTEASE
Aykroyd, Dan
CELTIC PRIDE
FEELING MINNESOTA
GETTING AWAY WITH MURDER
MY FELLOW AMERICANS
SGT. BILKO
Aylward, Rory J.
COURAGE UNDER FIRE
Azaiez, Samy
ENGLISH PATIENT, THE
Azaria, Hank
BIRDCAGE, THE
Azcuy, Ana
UP CLOSE AND PERSONAL

Azerot, Alain
MACHINE, THE
Azhari, Ayu
WITHOUT MERCY
Azito, Tony
NECRONOMICON: BOOK OF THE DEAD
Azman, Jank
WHARF RAT, THE
Azoulay, Didier
CELESTIAL CLOCKWORK
Azzouz, Ichraf
SILENCES OF THE PALACE, THE
B'tiste, I'ilana
IT CAME FROM OUTER SPACE II
B., Lisa
SERPENT'S LAIR
B.C.
HECK'S WAY HOME
Babalis, Mia
FUNERAL, THE
Babatunde, Akin
ROAD TO GALVESTON, THE
Babatunde, Obba
MULTIPLICITY
NECRONOMICON: BOOK OF THE DEAD
THAT THING YOU DO!
Babb, Sean
PIG'S TALE, A
Babbin, Barbara
CABLE GUY, THE
CABLE GUY, THE
Babe, Fabienne
LES VOLEURS
Babes in Toyland
NOT BAD FOR A GIRL
Bacall, Lauren
LINE KING: THE AL HIRSCHFELD STORY, THE
MIRROR HAS TWO FACES, THE
MY FELLOW AMERICANS
Bacarella, Mike
PRIMAL FEAR
Bach, Jason
ARRIVAL, THE
Bachman, Porstein
VIKING SAGAS, THE
Bacino, Joe
RANSOM
Bacon, Beaumont
JERRY MAGUIRE
Bacon, Kevin
SLEEPERS
Bacon, Rebecca
PIG'S TALE, A
Badalucco Jr., Joe
RANSOM
Badalucco, Michael
BASQUIAT
TWO IF BY SEA
Badin, Jean
THREE LIVES AND ONLY ONE DEATH
Badland, Annette
ANGELS AND INSECTS
CAPTIVES
Badov, Vladimir
BURIAL OF THE RATS
Badreya, Sayed
INDEPENDENCE DAY
KINGPIN
Baer, G. Gordon
FUGITIVE RAGE
Baer, Harry
SHADOW OF ANGELS
Baetens, Karel
DAENS
Baez, Joan
BERKELEY IN THE 60S
MESSAGE TO LOVE: THE ISLE OF WIGHT FESTIVAL
Bagby, Ben
EDDIE
Bagby, Michelle
EDDIE
Bagenal, Philip
SHOPPING
Bagley, Lori
KINGPIN
Bagley, Ross
EYE FOR AN EYE
INDEPENDENCE DAY
Bahktiari, Mohammad
WHITE BALLOON, THE
Bahns, Maxine
SHE'S THE ONE
Bahri, Lotfi
MADAME BUTTERFLY
Bahri, Taoufic
SILENCES OF THE PALACE, THE
Bahul, Milan
DRAGONHEART
Bailey, Blake
HEAD OF THE FAMILY
Bailey, D'Army
PEOPLE VS. LARRY FLYNT, THE
Bailey, Dennis
MAN OF THE YEAR
Bailey, Kevin
TOLLBOOTH
Bailey, Kimberly Marie
EDDIE
Bailey, Kirk
BLACK DAY BLUE NIGHT
Bailey, Lacy
SLING BLADE
Bailey, Laura
MIRROR HAS TWO FACES, THE
Bailey-Gates, Charles
AMERICAN STRAYS
SURGEON, THE
Bailhache, Pierette Pompom
CHASING BUTTERFLIES
Baillargeon, Denise
DARKMAN III: DIE DARKMAN DIE
Bailous, Michael
LIFEFORM
Bain, Susan
BIG BULLY
Baines, Bob
SPIDER & ROSE
Baines, Dennis
ABUSE
Baio, Jimmy
MIRROR HAS TWO FACES, THE
Baitz, Jon Robin
ONE FINE DAY
Bajema, Don
BAD LOVE
Bajon, Megan
BLONDES HAVE MORE GUNS
Baker, Bart
BODY OF INFLUENCE 2
Baker, Becky Ann
I'M NOT RAPPAPORT
WHITE SQUALL
Baker, Bob
PURE DANGER
Baker, Bradley
SPACE JAM
Baker, Carroll
JUST YOUR LUCK
Baker, Diane
CABLE GUY, THE
COURAGE UNDER FIRE
Baker, Don
PERFECT CANDIDATE, A
Baker, Frank
YOUNG POISONER'S HANDBOOK, THE
Baker, Gere
DESIRE
Baker, Joe Don
FELONY
GRASS HARP, THE
MARS ATTACKS!
Baker, Jordan
CITY HALL
JOHN CARPENTER'S ESCAPE FROM L.A.
Baker, Kathy
TO GILLIAN ON HER 37TH BIRTHDAY
Baker, Mike
MR. ICE CREAM MAN
Baker, Ray
EXECUTIVE DECISION
FINAL CUT, THE
Baker, Thom
DRAGONHEART
Baker, Tim
VIRTUAL COMBAT
Baker-Hall, Philip
LITTLE DEATH, THE
Bakija, Bianca
TREES LOUNGE
Bakke, Brenda
LONE JUSTICE: SHOWDOWN AT PLUM CREEK
Bako, Marta
DOGFIGHTERS, THE
Balaban, Bob
LATE SHIFT, THE
PIE IN THE SKY
Balasko, Josiane
FRENCH TWIST
Baldalucco, Michael
SEARCH FOR ONE-EYE JIMMY, THE
Baldasare, Nick
THEY BITE
Baldi, Jim
MUTANT MAN
Baldvinsson, Jon
VIKING SAGAS, THE
Baldwin, Adam
INDEPENDENCE DAY
LOVER'S KNOT
SAWBONES
Baldwin, Alec
GHOSTS OF MISSISSIPPI
HEAVEN'S PRISONERS
JUROR, THE
LOOKING FOR RICHARD
STREETCAR NAMED DESIRE, A
Baldwin, C. B.
SHOWGIRL MURDERS, THE
Baldwin, Charles Jason
PARADISE LOST: THE CHILD MURDERS AT ROBIN HOOD HILLS
Baldwin, Daniel
MULHOLLAND FALLS
TREES LOUNGE
YESTERDAY'S TARGET
Baldwin, Elizabeth
MIRROR, MIRROR III: THE VOYEUR
Baldwin, Floyd
SHOWGIRL MURDERS, THE
Baldwin, Stephen
BIO-DOME
DEAD WEEKEND
FLED
UNDER THE HULA MOON
Baldwin, William
CURDLED
Bale, Christian
JOSEPH CONRAD'S THE SECRET AGENT
PORTRAIT OF A LADY, THE
Balicki, Ron
BARB WIRE

Balint, Eszter
TREES LOUNGE
Balk, Fairuza
CRAFT, THE
ISLAND OF DR. MOREAU, THE
TOLLBOOTH
Ball, Christopher
CLUBHOUSE DETECTIVES
Ball, Meaghan
PORTRAITS OF A KILLER
Ballam, Michael
CLUBHOUSE DETECTIVES
Ballantine, Sara
NUTTY PROFESSOR, THE
Ballard, Nora
FLY AWAY HOME
Ballerini, Edoardo
I SHOT ANDY WARHOL
I'M NOT RAPPAPORT
PALLBEARER, THE
Ballesteros, Marita
SHADOW YOU SOON WILL BE, A
Ballinger, Christopher
EVENING STAR, THE
Ballou, Howard
TIME TO KILL, A
Balmaceda, Madeline
EVERYONE SAYS I LOVE YOU
Balsan, Humbert
PROPRIETOR, THE
Balthazar, Jimmie Lee
EVENING STAR, THE
Bambo, Dana
LAST MAN STANDING
Bancroft, Anne
HOMECOMING
SUNCHASER
Bandemer, John
FARGO
Banderas, Antonio
BATON ROUGE
EVITA
OF LOVE AND SHADOWS
OUTRAGE
TWO MUCH
Bandey, Paul
VISITORS, THE
Bandy, Kevin
MAN OF THE YEAR
Bangun, Advent
WITHOUT MERCY
Banko, Jennifer
BARB WIRE
Banks, Boyd
BLACK SHEEP
Banks, Gene
EDDIE
Banks, Jonathan
FLIPPER
Banks, Lenore
HEAVEN'S PRISONERS
Banks, Nancy
SURGEON, THE
Bannister, Daniel D.
EDDIE
Bannister, Reggie
DEMOLITIONIST, THE
Bannon, James
JACK & SARAH
Baptiste, Frederic
VISITORS, THE
Baranski, Christine
BIRDCAGE, THE
Barba, Jacqueline
BEAVIS AND BUTT-HEAD DO AMERICA
Barba, Norberto
SOLO
Barbeau, Adrienne
BURIAL OF THE RATS
Barbee, Buzz
EYE FOR AN EYE
Barber, Gillian
HALFBACK OF NOTRE DAME, THE
MATERNAL INSTINCTS
Barbie Liberation Organization, The
SONIC OUTLAWS
Barbour, Bruce Paul
SPY HARD
Barbour, Kathy
GRACE OF MY HEART
MATILDA
Barboza, Richard
TALES OF EROTICA
Barclay, Caroline
BLACK DAY BLUE NIGHT
WITHIN THE ROCK
Bard, Bartley
HOW THE WEST WAS FUN
Bardacke, Frank
BERKELEY IN THE 60S
Bardem, Javier
MOUTH TO MOUTH
Bardy, Gyorgy
MAGIC HUNTER
Barge, Gene
CHAIN REACTION
Barillaro, William
GET ON THE BUS
SPY HARD
Baringo, Jose Luis
BATON ROUGE
Barish, Natalie
UP CLOSE AND PERSONAL
Barker, Bob
HAPPY GILMORE
Barker, Edhem
TRIGGER EFFECT, THE
Barker, Rick
KINGPIN
RUMPELSTILTSKIN
Barker, Ron
VIRTUAL COMBAT
Barker, William Joseph
NIGHT OF THE SCARECROW
Barkin, Ellen
FAN, THE
MAD DOG TIME
Barklem, Nick
YANKEE ZULU
Barkley, Charles
SPACE JAM
Barkus, C. J.
TATTOO BOY
Barlow, John Perry
SYNTHETIC PLEASURES
Barlow, Roxane
FIRST WIVES CLUB, THE
Barlow, Tim
MARY REILLY
Barnes, Adilah
SHARON'S SECRET
Barnes, Barbara
ROUJIN-Z
Barnes, Barry
MICHAEL COLLINS
MOLL FLANDERS
Barnes, Christopher Daniel
PIG'S TALE, A
VERY BRADY SEQUEL, A
Barnes, Donna
RUMPELSTILTSKIN
Barnes, Fred
GETTING AWAY WITH MURDER
INDEPENDENCE DAY
Barnes, Georgia-Troy
GIRLFRIENDS
Barnes, Isaiah
DON'T BE A MENACE TO SOUTH CENTRAL WHILE DRINKING YOUR JUICE IN THE HOOD
Barnes, Juian
MARS ATTACKS!
Barnes, Rick Tyler
BLACK SCORPION
Barnes, Ron
ZARKORR! THE INVADER
Barnes, Susan
NATIONAL LAMPOON'S FAVORITE DEADLY SINS
Barnes, Suzanne
CLUBHOUSE DETECTIVES
Barnes-Hopkins, Barbara
CURTIS'S CHARM
Barnett, Charlie
THEY BITE
Barnett, Craig
ERASER
Barnett, Slade
CARNOSAUR 3: PRIMAL SPECIES
Barnett, Steven R.
SHARON'S SECRET
Barney, Bruce
SGT. KABUKIMAN N.Y.P.D.
Barnhouse-Diekman, Billie
CITIZEN RUTH
Barnot, Perry
EXIT
Barnun, Billie
SPY HARD
Baro, Amparo
MOUTH TO MOUTH
Baron, Bridgett
EVIL HAS A FACE
Baron, Daniel
FIRST KID
Baron, Joanne
DENTIST, THE
HOURGLASS
Baron, Matthew
STRIPTEASE
Barondes, Elizabeth
ADRENALIN: FEAR THE RUSH
FULL BODY MASSAGE
NIGHT OF THE SCARECROW
NOT OF THIS EARTH
Barone, Anita
TAKEOVER, THE
Baroody, Gerald
DADETOWN
Barr, Jason
KIDS IN THE HALL: BRAIN CANDY
Barr, Jean-Marc
BREAKING THE WAVES
Barr, Sharon
GALAXIES ARE COLLIDING
Barr, Steve
KAZAAM
Barrado, Lupe
BATON ROUGE
Barranco, Maria
MOUTH TO MOUTH
Barrault, Veronique
FRENCH TWIST
Barraza, Jana
CHAMBER, THE
Barrera, Cindy
BULLETPROOF

Barrera, David
EYE FOR AN EYE
INFINITY
Barrera, Pilar
BATON ROUGE
Barrett, Eileen
DEVOTION
Barrett, Jennifer
SANDMAN, THE
Barrett, Kashi
KAZAAM
Barrett, Sean
ROUJIN-Z
Barrett, Sunshine
BEWARE: CHILDREN AT PLAY
Barrie, Lester
DON'T BE A MENACE TO SOUTH CENTRAL WHILE DRINKING YOUR JUICE IN THE HOOD
Barrie, Max
NATIONAL LAMPOON'S FAVORITE DEADLY SINS
Barrientos, Maria
BLACK OUT
Barron, Jude
SOME FOLKS CALL IT A SLING BLADE
Barron, Oliver
ADVENTURES OF PINOCCHIO, THE
Barron, Rosalie
SOME FOLKS CALL IT A SLING BLADE
Barrow, Lance
TIN CUP
Barrow, Stacy
SLING BLADE
Barry, Alan
SOME MOTHER'S SON
Barry, Brent
JERRY MAGUIRE
Barry, Cristopher
SUGARTIME
Barry, Guerin
FATALLY YOURS
Barry, Michelle
FEMALIEN
VIRTUAL ENCOUNTERS
Barry, Raymond J.
CHAMBER, THE
HEADLESS BODY IN TOPLESS BAR
Barry, Thom
HIGH SCHOOL HIGH
INDEPENDENCE DAY
Barry, Thomas
GHOSTS OF MISSISSIPPI
Barry, Toni
PROTEUS
ROUJIN-Z
Barry, Tony
TWO FRIENDS
Barrymore, Drew
EVERYONE SAYS I LOVE YOU
SCREAM
Barrymore Jr., Sidney J.
KINGPIN
Barsky, Brett
JUROR, THE
Bart, Peter
YOU'LL NEVER MAKE LOVE IN THIS TOWN AGAIN
Bartel, Cheryl
SAWBONES
Bartel, Paul
BASQUIAT
DEATH ARTIST, THE
JOHN CARPENTER'S ESCAPE FROM L.A.
Bartellini, Francesca
PORTRAIT OF A LADY, THE
Bartik, Oldrich
KASPAR HAUSER

Bartlett, Bonnie
DEAD TO RIGHTS
GHOSTS OF MISSISSIPPI
Bartlett, Cal
MAN OF THE YEAR
Bartlett, Jamie
WARHEAD
Bartlett, Keith
JACK & SARAH
Bartley, Jim
WAR OF THE BUTTONS, THE
Barton, Neil
CHAMBER, THE
Barton, Rodger
IN LOVE AND WAR
Bartsch, Angelika
BROTHER OF SLEEP
Bartunkova, Dana
KASPAR HAUSER
Baruch, Rabbi Robert K.
BIRDCAGE, THE
Barwise, John
RAW TARGET
Basaraba, Gary
STRIPTEASE
Basco, Derek
SGT. BILKO
Basco, Dion
RACE THE SUN
Bascom, Roderick
DUNSTON CHECKS IN
Bashoff, Blake
BIG BULLY
Baskin, Elya
FOREST WARRIOR
SPY HARD
Basler, Antoine
NEW LIFE, A
RENDEZVOUS IN PARIS
Basque, Priscilla K.
BUGGED
Bass, Bobby
MY FELLOW AMERICANS
Bass, Phonz
FLED
Bass Sr., L. D.
GHOSTS OF MISSISSIPPI
Bassadouk, Zaid
HALFMOON
Bassett, Linda
HAUNTED
MARY REILLY
Bassett, Peter
DESOLATION ANGELS
Bassey, Jennifer
DUNSTON CHECKS IN
Bastiani, Billy
BEYOND DESIRE
SAINTS AND SINNERS
Baston, Susan
GET ON THE BUS
Batalla, Rick
ERASER
Batanova, Katiya
BURIAL OF THE RATS
Bateman, Justine
DEATH ARTIST, THE
Bates, Azura
FLY AWAY HOME
Bates, Brannon
FLED
Bates, Jo
FEAR
Bates, Joe
SABRINA, THE TEENAGE WITCH
Bates, John
ANIMAL INSTINCTS III: THE SEDUCTRESS

Bates, Jonathan
FLY AWAY HOME
Bates, Kathy
DIABOLIQUE
LATE SHIFT, THE
WAR AT HOME, THE
Bates, Paul
PREACHER'S WIFE, THE
Bates, Tina M.
PEOPLE VS. LARRY FLYNT, THE
Bateso, Simon
SHOPPING
Bateson, David
BREAKING THE WAVES
Batinkoff, Randall
WALKING AND TALKING
Batson, Susan
GIRL 6
Batt, Paul
WAR OF THE BUTTONS, THE
Battaglia, John
MUTANT MAN
Battaglia, Joseph Anthony
EDDIE
Battista, Bobbie
GETTING AWAY WITH MURDER
Battle, John S.
EDDIE
Bau, C.J.
PRE-MADONNAS
STAR TREK: FIRST CONTACT
Bauchau, Patrick
SERPENT'S LAIR
Bauer, Belinda
NECRONOMICON: BOOK OF THE DEAD
POISON IVY 2: LILY
Bauer, Doug
PEOPLE VS. LARRY FLYNT, THE
Bauer, Richard
SUNCHASER
Bauer, Steven
BODY COUNT
PRIMAL FEAR
WILD SIDE
Bauerle, Christine
SOUTH BEACH ACADEMY
STRIPTEASE
Bauguil, Alain
HORSEMAN ON THE ROOF
Baum, Van
SET IT OFF
Baum, Vincent
SET IT OFF
Baumgartner, Franz
KASPAR HAUSER
Bautista, Marty
MATILDA
Bautista, Perla
MIDNIGHT DANCERS
Baxter, Jeffrey
SYNTHETIC PLEASURES
Baxter, Lynsey
COLD LIGHT OF DAY
Baxter, Tommie
EVERYONE SAYS I LOVE YOU
Baxter, Trevor
COLD COMFORT FARM
Bay, Frances
HAPPY GILMORE
Bayari, Murat
TWO FRIENDS
Baye, Nathalie
FRANCOIS TRUFFAUT: STOLEN PORTRAITS
MACHINE, THE
Bayer, Gary
TRIGGER EFFECT, THE

Bayer, Michael
DOWN, OUT AND DANGEROUS
Bayle, Gerard
HORSEMAN ON THE ROOF
Bayliss, John
MAXIMUM RISK
Baynaud, Erwan
MACHINE, THE
Baynes, Hetty
TALES OF EROTICA
Bazin, Janine
FRANCOIS TRUFFAUT: STOLEN PORTRAITS
Be, Yoshio
LAWNMOWER MAN 2: BEYOND CYBERSPACE
Beach, Adam
BOY CALLED HATE, A
Beach, Lisa
SCREAM
Beach, Michael
DANGEROUS PASSION
FAMILY THING, A
Beale, Simon Russell
HAMLET
Beals, Jennifer
SEARCH FOR ONE-EYE JIMMY, THE
Beals, Stephen
DADETOWN
Beamon, Brance H.
TIME TO KILL, A
Bean, Henry
VENUS RISING
Bean, Richard
NEW LIFE, A
Bean, Sean
SHOPPING
Beart, Emmanuelle
MISSION: IMPOSSIBLE
NELLY AND MONSIEUR ARNAUD
Beasley, Adam
CABLE GUY, THE
Beasley, Allyce
ENTERTAINING ANGELS: THE DOROTHY DAY STORY
RUMPELSTILTSKIN
Beasley, Barth
THAT THING YOU DO!
Beasley, Bill
CABLE GUY, THE
Beasley, Christine
CABLE GUY, THE
Beasley, Devon
CABLE GUY, THE
Beasley, Eloise
PREACHER'S WIFE, THE
Beasley-Prime, Yolanda
PREACHER'S WIFE, THE
Beatty, Bruce
DUNSTON CHECKS IN
Beatty, Jon
LOW LIFE, THE
Beatty, Nancy
EXTREME MEASURES
HARRIET THE SPY
LOSING CHASE
Beatty, Ned
AFFAIR, THE
LARRY MCMURTRY'S STREETS OF LAREDO
Beatty, Rick
BREAKAWAY
Beatty, Zatella
ARRIVAL, THE
Beaubian, Susan
RATTLED
Beauchene, Willie
KINGPIN
Beaudin, Glen
SOMETIMES THEY COME BACK . . . AGAIN
Beaudoin, Michelle
SABRINA, THE TEENAGE WITCH
Beaulieu, Trace
MYSTERY SCIENCE THEATER 3000: THE MOVIE
Beaumont, Rob
SOME FOLKS CALL IT A SLING BLADE
Beautier, Philippe
CELESTIAL CLOCKWORK
Bebb, Richard
COLD COMFORT FARM
Bechdholt, Curtis
ANNIE O
Bechir, Damian
SOLO
Bechtelheimer, Marian Lamb
UP CLOSE AND PERSONAL
Beck, Barbara
INDEPENDENCE DAY
Beck, Henry Cabot
I SHOT ANDY WARHOL
Beck, John
BLACK DAY BLUE NIGHT
Beck, Kimberly
INDEPENDENCE DAY
Beck, Michael
FOREST WARRIOR
Beck, Noelle
SUBSTITUTE, THE
Beck, Rufus
MAYBE . . . MAYBE NOT
Becker, Ben
BROTHER OF SLEEP
Becker, Gerry
ERASER
EXTREME MEASURES
Becker, Herbert
SGT. KABUKIMAN N.Y.P.D.
Becker, Samantha
PIG'S TALE, A
Becker, Stacy
SPITFIRE GRILL, THE
Beckett, Linda
SECRETS & LIES
Beckford, Ruth
AMERICA'S DREAM
Beckinsale, Kate
COLD COMFORT FARM
HAUNTED
Bedard, Dana
ARRIVAL, THE
Bedard, George
KINGPIN
Bedelia, Bonnie
HOMECOMING
Bedford, Kurtis
SCREAM
Bednar, Petr
ADVENTURES OF PINOCCHIO, THE
Bednarski, Claire
D3: THE MIGHTY DUCKS
Beecham, Jake
PIG'S TALE, A
Beeman, Terry
ERASER
Beene, Dan
CHAMBER, THE
Beer, Daniel
TALKING ABOUT SEX
Beer, Ingrid
JERRY MAGUIRE
Beer, Phillip
HAPPY GILMORE
Beesley, Nina
CHAIN REACTION
Beezer, Leighton
HYPE!
Begansky, Jennifer
ABUSE
Begley Jr., Ed
CHILDREN OF FURY
HOURGLASS
LATE SHIFT, THE
SANTA WITH MUSCLES
Behar, Fabien
RIDICULE
Behar, Joy
LOVE IS ALL THERE IS
Behrens, Bernard
MOTHER NIGHT
Behrens, Yeniffer
EXIT
Beilstein, Eric
MR. ICE CREAM MAN
Bekavac, John
FOR THE MOMENT
Beks, Jakob
ANTONIA'S LINE
Belafonte, Harry
KANSAS CITY
Belafonte, Shari
HEIDI CHRONICLES, THE
Belcher, James
MAN WITH THE PERFECT SWING, THE
Belcher, Patricia
EYE FOR AN EYE
LAWNMOWER MAN 2: BEYOND CYBERSPACE
NATIONAL LAMPOON'S FAVORITE DEADLY SINS
WOMAN UNDONE, A
Belcon, Natalie Venetia
GRACE OF MY HEART
Belfiore, Brauno
QUEST, THE
Belfquih, Mohammed
HALFMOON
Belgaeid, Abdelaziz
SILENCES OF THE PALACE, THE
Belgrader, Andre
BIG NIGHT
Belhassan, Sondos
HALFMOON
Belhassen, Sondess
ENGLISH PATIENT, THE
Belitzky, Joe
THEY BITE
Belk, Sid
SOLO
Belkhadra, Karim
HATE
Bell Calloway, Vanessa
DAYLIGHT
Bell, Dan
SHOT, THE
Bell, Darryl M.
BLACK SCORPION
Bell, Doron
HALFBACK OF NOTRE DAME, THE
Bell, Drake
JERRY MAGUIRE
NEON BIBLE, THE
Bell, Fiona
TRAINSPOTTING
Bell, James
ROBIN OF LOCKSLEY
Bell, John
CITIZEN RUTH
Bell Jr., Robert R.
TIME TO KILL, A
Bell, Marshall
TOO FAST, TOO YOUNG

Bell, Melissa
TAILS YOU LIVE, HEADS YOU'RE DEAD
Bell, Michael
HOMEWARD BOUND II: LOST IN SAN FRANCISCO
THIN LINE BETWEEN LOVE AND HATE, A
Bell, Monica
EVERYTHING RELATIVE
Bell, Nicholas
SHINE
Bell, Thom
KIDS IN THE HALL: BRAIN CANDY
Bell, Tobin
SERIAL KILLER
Bell, Tyrone
EDDIE
Bella, Rachael
CRUCIBLE, THE
Bellamy, Anne
SERIAL KILLER
Bellamy, Bill
FLED
Bellamy, Diana
DIABOLIQUE
GHOSTS OF MISSISSIPPI
Bellamy, Ned
PIG'S TALE, A
Bellar, Clara
RENDEZVOUS IN PARIS
Belle, Camilla
POISON IVY 2: LILY
Bellemare, Pierre
THREE LIVES AND ONLY ONE DEATH
Bellier, Michel
HORSEMAN ON THE ROOF
Bellin, Thomas
NATIONAL LAMPOON'S FAVORITE DEADLY SINS
Bellini, Paul
KIDS IN THE HALL: BRAIN CANDY
Bellio, Seron
DEAR GOD
Bello, Teodorina
RANSOM
Bellows, Gil
BLACK DAY BLUE NIGHT
SUBSTANCE OF FIRE, THE
Belushi, James
JINGLE ALL THE WAY
RACE THE SUN
Belzer, Richard
GET ON THE BUS
GIRL 6
MISSING PIECES
NOT OF THIS EARTH
OFF AND RUNNING
VERY BRADY SEQUEL, A
Beme, Sylvie
SUITE 16
Bemer, Garrett
ANGELA
Ben Ammar, Zahira
SILENCES OF THE PALACE, THE
Ben Mhamed, Nabil
HATE
Ben Othman, Khedija
SILENCES OF THE PALACE, THE
Ben Rabiaa, Rachida
SILENCES OF THE PALACE, THE
Ben Saad, Jalel
SILENCES OF THE PALACE, THE
Ben Saidane, Fatma
SILENCES OF THE PALACE, THE
Ben-Victor, Paul
MAXIMUM RISK
RED SCORPION 2
Benaiche, Wilfred
ADVENTURES OF PINOCCHIO, THE
MACHINE, THE
Bender, Candace Camille
BARB WIRE
WILD SIDE
Bender, Dominik
FLIRT
Bendetti, Michael
AMANDA AND THE ALIEN
Bendidi, Naguime
LES VOLEURS
Benedetti, Carla
MILLE BOLLE BLU
Benedict, Chase
PAINTED HERO
Benedict, Dirk
ALASKA
Benedict, Fritz
FIRE ON THE MOUNTAIN
Benedict, Jewel
PHENOMENON
Benes, Rudolph
DELTA OF VENUS
Benezet-Brown, Caroline
I SHOT ANDY WARHOL
Benfield, John
BEAUTIFUL THING
101 DALMATIANS
Benigni, Roberto
MONSTER, THE
Bening, Annette
MARS ATTACKS!
Benitez, Mike
SUBSTITUTE, THE
Benjamin, Selma
TALKING ABOUT SEX
Benjaminson, Scott
CHAIN REACTION
Bennett, Alan
IN LOVE AND WAR
WIND IN THE WILLOWS, THE
Bennett, Charles E.
KAZAAM
Bennett, Charles Edward
DON'T BE A MENACE TO SOUTH CENTRAL WHILE DRINKING YOUR JUICE IN THE HOOD
Bennett, Fran
FOXFIRE
Bennett, Henry
SPIDER & ROSE
Bennett, Jeff
LAND BEFORE TIME IV: JOURNEY THROUGH THE MISTS
PHANTOM 2040: THE GHOST WHO WALKS
Bennett, Lloyd "Benny"
GHOSTS OF MISSISSIPPI
Bennett, Lynette
FULL BODY MASSAGE
Bennett, Matt
SURGEON, THE
Bennett, Maureen
WAR OF THE BUTTONS, THE
Bennett, Nallie
SPIDER & ROSE
Bennett, Nigel
DARKMAN III: DIE DARKMAN DIE
WHERE'S THE MONEY, NOREEN?
Bennett, Paul
MICHAEL COLLINS
Bennett, Simon
MADAGASCAR SKIN
Bennett, Tamara Nicole
PHAT BEACH
Benrubi, Abraham
OUT THERE
TWISTER
Benseman, Steph
SGT. BILKO
Benson, Alan
MONSTERSHOW
Benson, Chris
FLY AWAY HOME
TWO IF BY SEA
Benson, Kelly
FINAL CUT, THE
Benson-Wald, Deborah
DEAR GOD
2 DAYS IN THE VALLEY
Benstock, Shari
PARIS WAS A WOMAN
Bental, Dotan
PHAT BEACH
Bentley, Marcus
SHAMELESS
Benton, Craig
TRUMAN
Benton, Kevin
CELTIC PRIDE
Benureau, Didier
VISITORS, THE
Benza, A.J.
RANSOM
Bercovici, Luca
BIG SQUEEZE, THE
Berdy, Magaly
MAN BY THE SHORE, THE
Berenger, Tom
SUBSTITUTE, THE
Beresford, Simon
JANE EYRE
Beresford, Trilby
LAST DANCE
Berg, Adam
FOREST WARRIOR
Berg, Peter
GIRL 6
GREAT WHITE HYPE, THE
Berg, Pia
EVIL ED
Bergansky, Chuck
LOVE IS ALL THERE IS
Bergen, Bob
SPACE JAM
Bergenholtz, Marie
EVIL ED
Berger, Anna
MOTHER NIGHT
Berger, Debra Joy
ORIGINAL SINS
Berger, Leslie
WHOLE WIDE WORLD, THE
Berger, Melissa
SUNSET PARK
Bergin, Michael
PROPRIETOR, THE
PROPRIETOR, THE
Bergin, Patrick
LAWNMOWER MAN 2: BEYOND CYBERSPACE
Bergin, Polly
ONCE UPON A TIME . . . WHEN WE WERE COLORED
Bergin, York
I'M NOT RAPPAPORT
Bergman, Harold
EXIT
Bergman, Mary Kay
HUNCHBACK OF NOTRE DAME, THE
Bergman, Teddy
STRIPTEASE

Bergschneider, Christopher
HEAD OF THE FAMILY
Bergstrom, Linda
CHILDREN OF NOISY VILLAGE, THE
Berkeley, Xander
BARB WIRE
BULLETPROOF
DEAD TO RIGHTS
FAMILY THING, A
POISON IVY 2: LILY
WITHIN THE ROCK
Berkley, Elizabeth
FIRST WIVES CLUB, THE
WHITE WOLVES II: LEGEND OF THE WILD
Berling, Charles
NELLY AND MONSIEUR ARNAUD
RIDICULE
Berlinger, Warren
THAT THING YOU DO!
Berman, Chris
EDDIE
Berman, Marc
RIDICULE
Bern, Mina
EVERYTHING RELATIVE
I'M NOT RAPPAPORT
Bernadini, Ida
FUNERAL, THE
Bernales, Aldo
JOHNNY 100 PESOS
Bernard, Ed
PINOCCHIO'S REVENGE
Bernard, Jason
DOWN, OUT AND DANGEROUS
Bernard, Paul
MR. HOLLAND'S OPUS
Bernardi, Robin
NIGHT OF THE SCARECROW
Bernardo, Michael
SHOOTFIGHTER 2: KILL OR BE KILLED!
VIRTUAL COMBAT
Bernbaum, Sharon
MAXIMUM RISK
Bernert, Marcel
FRANCOIS TRUFFAUT: STOLEN PORTRAITS
Bernet, Chopper
CROSSCUT
Bernhard, Sandra
LATE SHIFT, THE
Bernhardt, Cliff
BLOODSPORT II: THE NEXT KUMITE
Bernhardt, Daniel
BLOODSPORT II: THE NEXT KUMITE
Bernhardt, Dirk
BLOODSPORT II: THE NEXT KUMITE
Bernhardt, Kevin
IMMORTALS, THE
Bernheim, Shirl
I'M NOT RAPPAPORT
Bernier, Michele
FRENCH TWIST
Berns, Gerald
ERASER
Bernsen, Corbin
BAJA
DENTIST, THE
GREAT WHITE HYPE, THE
TAILS YOU LIVE, HEADS YOU'RE DEAD
Bernstein, Allen
RANSOM
Bernstein, David
MICHAEL
Bernstein, Nils
HYPE!

Beron, David
ENTERTAINING ANGELS: THE DOROTHY DAY STORY
Berrills, Gene
SOME MOTHER'S SON
Berrington, Elizabeth
SECRETS & LIES
Berroyer, Jackie
LITTLE INDIAN, BIG CITY
Berry, Christine Louise
CRAFT, THE
Berry, Glen
BEAUTIFUL THING
Berry, Halle
EXECUTIVE DECISION
GIRL 6
RACE THE SUN
RICH MAN'S WIFE, THE
Berry, Lloyd
FINAL CUT, THE
Berry, Stephanie
GIRLS TOWN
Berry, Tom
SCREAMERS
Berryhill, Betsy
PHENOMENON
Berryman, Michael
SPY HARD
Bertelle, Ralph
FAN, THE
Bertelson, Sonya
FAN, THE
Berthoud, Jerome
VISITORS, THE
Bertin, Brenda
DAENS
Bertin, Gaston
DAENS
Bertin, Roland
LA COMEDIE-FRANCAISE OU L'AMOUR JOUE
Bertolino, Allison
FLIPPER
Bertorelli, Tony
WHO KILLED PASOLINI?
Bertram, Laura
BOYS NEXT DOOR, THE
NIGHT OF THE TWISTERS
Berube, Michelle
FROM DUSK TILL DAWN
Besch, Bibi
RATTLED
Besgrove, Robert C.
ROCK, THE
Beskow, Andreas
EVIL ED
Besnehard, Dominique
LITTLE INDIAN, BIG CITY
Best, C. Dale
SURGEON, THE
Best, James Homer
GHOSTS OF MISSISSIPPI
Best, Leah
PUBLIC ENEMIES
Bestelli, Mara
EVITA
Beswick, Martine
NIGHT OF THE SCARECROW
Betker, Carrie
KIDS IN THE HALL: BRAIN CANDY
Betoule, Regis
LES VOLEURS
Bettin, Val
ENTERTAINING ANGELS: THE DOROTHY DAY STORY
Bettles, Thomas
DEAD MAN

Bettman, Gary M.
TALKING ABOUT SEX
Betts, Daniel
CANTERVILLE GHOST, THE
Beugg, Linda
SOME FOLKS CALL IT A SLING BLADE
Beugg, Michael
LOW LIFE, THE
SOME FOLKS CALL IT A SLING BLADE
Beuth, Robert Alan
NORMA JEAN AND MARILYN
Bevine, Victor
STAR TREK: FIRST CONTACT
Bevington, Sean
MR. HOLLAND'S OPUS
Bevins, Christopher
TUSKEGEE AIRMEN, THE
Bevis, Leslie
OUT THERE
Bexton, R. Allan
ZARKORR! THE INVADER
Bey, Turhan
VIRTUAL COMBAT
Beyer, Hermann
KASPAR HAUSER
Beyer, Troy
EDDIE
LITTLE DEATH, THE
Beymer, Richard
FOXFIRE
LITTLE DEATH, THE
Bezace, Didier
LES VOLEURS
Bianchi, Shelley
BOGUS
Bianco, Mario
MILLE BOLLE BLU
Biase, Michael
CELTIC PRIDE
Biasi, Dennis
MR. HOLLAND'S OPUS
Biasucci, Dean
JERRY MAGUIRE
Biberstein, Tara Nichelle
QUEST, THE
Bick, Susie
FLIRT
Bickford, Christopher Anthony
ANNIE O
Bicskei, Istvan
RASPUTIN
Bidasha, Neena
FROM DUSK TILL DAWN
Bidasha, Veena
FROM DUSK TILL DAWN
Bidenko, Kris
TWO FRIENDS
Biechler, Merri
MAN OF THE YEAR
Biehn, Michael
BREACH OF TRUST
FRAME BY FRAME
ROCK, THE
Bieri, Ramon
GHOSTS OF MISSISSIPPI
Bierko, Craig
LONG KISS GOODNIGHT, THE
Biester, Jorg
FLIRT
Big Bad Voodoo Daddy
SWINGERS
Big Daddy Wayne
SET IT OFF
Bigagli, Claudio
MILLE BOLLE BLU
Bigelow, Pixie
MAN IN THE ATTIC, THE

Biggham, Anthony
PREACHER'S WIFE, THE
Biggs, Casey
BROKEN ARROW
Biggs-Dawson, Roxann
DARKMAN III: DIE DARKMAN DIE
Bigham, Lexie
HIGH SCHOOL HIGH
UP CLOSE AND PERSONAL
Biko, Chris
YANKEE ZULU
Bilcher, Brian
SGT. KABUKIMAN N.Y.P.D.
Bill, Tony
BARB WIRE
Billa, Salvatore
STAR MAKER, THE
Billings, Dawn Ann
VIRTUAL COMBAT
Billings, Earl
FAN, THE
Billington, Steve
THAT THING YOU DO!
Bilson, David
ERASER
Bindea, Alexandra
OUTPOST, THE
Binder, Gabi
PASSION OF DARKLY NOON, THE
Binkley, James
MAN IN THE ATTIC, THE
TAILS YOU LIVE, HEADS YOU'RE DEAD
Binks, Andrew
RED SCORPION 2
Binoche, Juliette
ENGLISH PATIENT, THE
HORSEMAN ON THE ROOF
Biondi, John
MAN WITH THE PERFECT SWING, THE
Biondi, Lynda
MILLE BOLLE BLU
Birch, Thora
ALASKA
Bird, Bill
RAVENHAWK
Bird, Larry
CELTIC PRIDE
SPACE JAM
Birdsall, Jim
TRUMAN
Birdsong, Richard
PEOPLE VS. LARRY FLYNT, THE
Birk, Raye
BIG SQUEEZE, THE
Birman, Matt
VIRUS
Birmingham, Kari
FRISK
Birznieks, David
EXECUTIVE DECISION
Bisagli, Claudio
WHO KILLED PASOLINI?
Bishop, Charlene
SMALL WONDERS
Bishop, Ed
FUNNYMAN, THE
Bishop, Joey
MAD DOG TIME
Bishop, Kevin
MUPPET TREASURE ISLAND
Bishop, Larry
MAD DOG TIME
Bishop, Patrick Francis
HARD JUSTICE
Bishop, Troy
SCREAM

Bisig, Gary
HARVEST OF FIRE
Bisley, Steve
TWO FRIENDS
Bissainthe, Toto
MAN BY THE SHORE, THE
Bissell, James
MY FELLOW AMERICANS
Bisset, Jacqueline
LA CEREMONIE
Bissonette, Joel
DARKMAN III: DIE DARKMAN DIE
Bista, Henryk
MOTHER OF KINGS
Bitskey, Tibor
MAGIC HUNTER
Bitzelberger, Rick
BEWARE: CHILDREN AT PLAY
Bjelland, Kat
NOT BAD FOR A GIRL
Blachly, Bill
MAN WITH A PLAN
Blachly, Tom
MAN WITH A PLAN
Black, Christi
MARS ATTACKS!
Black, Jack
BIO-DOME
CABLE GUY, THE
FAN, THE
MARS ATTACKS!
Black, James
MAN WITH THE PERFECT SWING, THE
Black, Joan Jett
FRISK
Black, Karen
CHILDREN OF THE CORN: THE GATHERING
Black, Leon
SHOPPING
Black, Lucas
GHOSTS OF MISSISSIPPI
SLING BLADE
Black, Pauline
FUNNYMAN, THE
Black, Tre
PHAT BEACH
Black, Trevor
CURTIS'S CHARM
Blackburn, Ken
FRIGHTENERS, THE
Blackburn, Richard
GETTING AWAY WITH MURDER
IN LOVE AND WAR
SUGARTIME
WHARF RAT, THE
Blacker, David
TAILS YOU LIVE, HEADS YOU'RE DEAD
Blackmon, Harlow
MAN WITH THE PERFECT SWING, THE
Blackner, Danny
MUPPET TREASURE ISLAND
Blackstone, Don
HYPE!
Blackwell, Chuck
ROLLING STONES ROCK-AND-ROLL CIRCUS, THE
Blackwood, John
BEYOND THE CALL
Blackwood, Sharon
NEON BIBLE, THE
Blacque, Taurean
FLED
Blaine, Charlene
TALKING ABOUT SEX
Blair, Dani
PINOCCHIO'S REVENGE

Blair, David
HAMLET
Blair, Kimberly
OVER THE WIRE
Blair, Linda
SCREAM
Blair, Michael L.
CAPTIVES
Blair, Pamela
BEAVIS AND BUTT-HEAD DO AMERICA
BEFORE AND AFTER
Blaisdell, Brad
EXECUTIVE DECISION
GREAT WHITE HYPE, THE
Blaisdell, Nesbitt
MRS. WINTERBOURNE
PALOOKAVILLE
Blake, Andre
DON'T LET YOUR MEAT LOAF
Blake, Clement
FAST MONEY
IT CAME FROM OUTER SPACE II
Blake, Geoffrey
ENTERTAINING ANGELS: THE DOROTHY DAY STORY
ENTERTAINING ANGELS: THE DOROTHY DAY STORY
WAR AT HOME, THE
Blake, Joel
ASSOCIATE, THE
Blake Jr., John
SMALL WONDERS
Blake, Scott
EXIT
Blaki
SONS OF TRINITY
Blanc, Francoise
HORSEMAN ON THE ROOF
Blanc, Mateo
SINGLE GIRL, A
Blanc, Michel
MONSTER, THE
Blanchard, Dan
DADETOWN
Blanchard, Kathleen
JOHN CARPENTER'S ESCAPE FROM L.A.
Blanchard, Rachel
IRON EAGLE IV
Blanchard-Power, Christie
NUTTY PROFESSOR, THE
Blanchet, Narda
CHASING BUTTERFLIES
Blaney, Keith
STRIPTEASE
Blatnik, Mary
MONSTERSHOW
Blatt, Stuart
SERPENT'S LAIR
Blaze, Tommy
RUMPELSTILTSKIN
Bledsoe, Drew
JERRY MAGUIRE
Blessed, Brian
HAMLET
Blessed Roscoe
LOVE IS ALL THERE IS
Blethyn, Brenda
SECRETS & LIES
Blevins, James
LOW LIFE, THE
Blich, Riki
UNDER THE DOMIM TREE
Blick, Jonathan
FRIGHTENERS, THE
Blicker, Jason
HOLLOW POINT
IRON EAGLE IV

Bliss, Lucille
SCREAM
Blitz, Amanda
SUGARTIME
Blitz, Jacob
SMALL WONDERS
Blitz, Renessa
SUGARTIME
Bloch, Scotty
EVERYONE SAYS I LOVE YOU
Block, Cody
PEOPLE VS. LARRY FLYNT, THE
Block, Kurt
HYPE!
Block, Larry
BIG NIGHT
Blocker, Dirk
NIGHT OF THE SCARECROW
Blom, Dan
MIND RIPPER
Blond, Susan
MADAME WANG'S
Blonde Fox, The
SGT. KABUKIMAN N.Y.P.D.
Blondell, Brian
NORMAL LIFE
Blood Circus
HYPE!
Bloom, Claire
DAYLIGHT
SHAMELESS
Bloomfield, Angela
FRIGHTENERS, THE
Blount, Corie
EDDIE
Blow, Joey
SOME FOLKS CALL IT A SLING BLADE
Blucas, Marcus P.
EDDIE
Blues Traveler
KINGPIN
Blum, Conradin
BROTHER OF SLEEP
Blum, Mark
DENISE CALLS UP
LOW LIFE, THE
Blum, Max E.
MATILDA
Blume, Edith
BED OF ROSES
Bluteau, Lothaire
I SHOT ANDY WARHOL
Bluthal, John
SPELLBREAKER: SECRET OF THE LEPRECHAUNS
Bluto, John
GLIMMER MAN, THE
Blythe, Charlotte
ANGELA
Boa, Bruce
FOR THE MOMENT
SCREAMERS
Bobbie, Walter
EDIE & PEN
FIRST WIVES CLUB, THE
Bobbitt, Russell
SGT. BILKO
Bobby, Anne
BEAUTIFUL GIRLS
JUROR, THE
Boboras, Peter
JOHNNY SHORTWAVE
Bobsled
NOT BAD FOR A GIRL
Boccia, Luis
EVITA
Bocelli, Dick
ARRIVAL, THE
Bockner, Martin
JOHNNY SHORTWAVE
Bodanis, Kelly
SUGARTIME
Boden, Petra
FARGO
Bodie, W. Paul
SHOOTFIGHTER 2: KILL OR BE KILLED!
Bodison, Wolfgang
FREEWAY
Bodnar, Jenna
FRIEND OF THE FAMILY 2
Boehlke, Bain
FARGO
Boen, Earl
DENTIST, THE
NORMA JEAN AND MARILYN
WITHIN THE ROCK
Boes, Richard
DEAD MAN
TREES LOUNGE
Bofshever, Michael
FAN, THE
Bogdanovich, Antonia
EVENING STAR, THE
WHOLE WIDE WORLD, THE
Bogdanovich, L. B.
WHISPERING, THE
Bogomaz, Dumitru
FORBIDDEN ZONE: ALIEN ABDUCTION
Bogosian, Eric
BEAVIS AND BUTT-HEAD DO AMERICA
SUBSTANCE OF FIRE, THE
Bogue, Kevin
EVERYONE SAYS I LOVE YOU
Bogues, Muggsy
EDDIE
SPACE JAM
Bohanon, Greer
THIN LINE BETWEEN LOVE AND HATE, A
Bohn III, Parker
KINGPIN
Bohn, Tim
SHARON'S SECRET
Bohne, Bruce
FARGO
Bohrer, Corinne
HEIDI FLEISS HOLLYWOOD MADAM
Boisson, Christine
NEW LIFE, A
Boje, Steffan
JANE EYRE
Bojkovic, Svetlana
VUKOVAR
Boksenbaum, Anna V.
CRUCIBLE, THE
Bolande, Gene
MY FELLOW AMERICANS
Bolender, Bill
INFINITY
Bolin, Kimberly
BAD LOVE
Boll, Bill
SOME FOLKS CALL IT A SLING BLADE
Boll, Sidonie
UNFORGETTABLE
Bollain, Iciar
LAND AND FREEDOM
Bollen, Paul
BAD LOVE
Bologna, Joseph
LOVE IS ALL THERE IS
Bologna, Sam
CHAMBER, THE
Bolongna, Gabriel
LOVE IS ALL THERE IS
Bompoil, Michel
SINGLE GIRL, A
Bonacelli, Paolo
MILLE BOLLE BLU
Bonafoux, Jose
OF LOVE AND SHADOWS
Bonanni, Paolo
WHO KILLED PASOLINI?
Bonato, Giuseppe
IN LOVE AND WAR
Bonaza, Vito
TALKING ABOUT SEX
Bond, Julie
ROBIN OF LOCKSLEY
Bonds, De'Aundre
GET ON THE BUS
SUNSET PARK
Bondurant, Eugene
SAINTS AND SINNERS
Bondy, Chris
DARKMAN III: DIE DARKMAN DIE
Bondy, Sy
OFF AND RUNNING
Bone, Kristen
LONG KISS GOODNIGHT, THE
Bonet, Wilma
JACK
Bonham Carter, Helena
TWELFTH NIGHT
Bonilla, Michelle
DUNSTON CHECKS IN
RICH MAN'S WIFE, THE
Bonk, Ron
SANDMAN, THE
Bonnaire, Sandrine
LA CEREMONIE
Bonner, Frank
COLONY, THE
Bono, Sonny
FIRST KID
Bonora, Corrado
OUTRAGE
Bonshor, Walker
SURGEON, THE
Bonucci, Emilio
IN LOVE AND WAR
Bonvoisin, Bernie
HATE
Bookston, Alex
BARB WIRE
Boone, Daniel
SGT. KABUKIMAN N.Y.P.D.
Boone Jr., Mark
TREES LOUNGE
Boone, Walker
DARKMAN III: DIE DARKMAN DIE
Boorman, Telshe
FRENCH TWIST
Booth, Andrew
TUNNEL VISION
Booth, Art
MY FELLOW AMERICANS
Booth, Lauren
IN LOVE AND WAR
Booth, Rulan
REDEMPTION: KICKBOXER 5
Boothby, Ian
HAPPY GILMORE
Bordet, Jean Yves
SUITE 16
Borgeaud, Nelly
NEW LIFE, A
Borgnine, Ernest
ALL DOGS GO TO HEAVEN 2
MERLIN'S SHOP OF MAGICAL WONDERS
Borgos, Gil
BARB WIRE
Borinsky, Marek
DELTA OF VENUS

Boris, Angel
EXIT
Boris, Nicoletta
MILLE BOLLE BLU
Borkan, Gene
BOUND
Borkowski, Andrzei
MISSION: IMPOSSIBLE
Boros, Julia
MAGIC IN THE MIRROR
Borrego, Amaryllis
JERRY MAGUIRE
Borrego, James
LONE STAR
Borrego, Jesse
LONE STAR
Bosch, Jordi
MOUTH TO MOUTH
Bosco, Mario
SLEEPERS
Bosco, Philip
FIRST WIVES CLUB, THE
Bose, Miguel
FRENCH TWIST
Bose, T'Fani
EDDIE
Bosley, Randall
KAZAAM
Bosley Sr., Freeman
TRUMAN
Bosley, Todd
JACK
Boss, Sarah
SLING BLADE
Bossell, Simon
SPIDER & ROSE
Bossley, Caitlin
JUDE
Bosso, Jorge Oscar
SONS OF TRINITY
Bostany, Donna
MURDERED INNOCENCE
Bostwick, Barry
SPY HARD
Bostwick, Lois
TALKING ABOUT SEX
Boswell, Charles
DANGEROUS PASSION
Boswell, Sunni
EXECUTIVE DECISION
Bosworth, Brian
BLACK OUT
ONE MAN'S JUSTICE
VIRUS
Bothe, Detlef
BROTHER OF SLEEP
Botngard, Monia
EVIL ED
Bottoms, Timothy
HOURGLASS
Bou-Sliman, Noelle
CHAIN REACTION
Bouajila, Sami
SILENCES OF THE PALACE, THE
Boucher, Mary
WHISPERING, THE
Bouchez, Elodie
PROPRIETOR, THE
Boudova, Nela
COLD LIGHT OF DAY
Boudreau, Michelle
EXECUTIVE DECISION
Bougouma, Mame
DON'T LET YOUR MEAT LOAF
Boujdouni, Abdel-Moulah
HATE
Boulianne, Roxanne
FOR THE MOMENT
Boulogne, Ari
NICO ICON
Boulogne, Edith
NICO ICON
Bourdon, Didier
MACHINE, THE
Bourguignon, Didier
HORSEMAN ON THE ROOF
Bourkowska, Anna
WHITE BALLOON, THE
Bourland, Kevin
NORMA JEAN AND MARILYN
Bourn, Andrew M.
FRISK
Bouslough, Cecelia
SANDMAN, THE
Bouslough, Douglas
SANDMAN, THE
Bousquet, Jean
MA SAISON PREFEREE
Boutefeu, Nathalie
NEW LIFE, A
Boutsikaris, Dennis
SURVIVING PICASSO
Boutte, Duane
STONEWALL
Bouvier, Jean-Pierre
MA SAISON PREFEREE
Bouzouita, Sabah
SILENCES OF THE PALACE, THE
Bowden, Peter
TWO FRIENDS
Bowe, David
CABLE GUY, THE
ROCK, THE
Bowechop, Leonard
DEAD MAN
Bowen, Christopher
COLD COMFORT FARM
Bowen, Dennis
NORMA JEAN AND MARILYN
Bowen, Julie
HAPPY GILMORE
MULTIPLICITY
Bowen-Wallace, Marquis
PREACHER'S WIFE, THE
Bowens, Malik
WHEN WE WERE KINGS
Bowens, R. B.
ONE MAN'S JUSTICE
Bower, Adrian
JUDE
Bower, Kay
CHILDREN OF THE CORN: THE GATHERING
Bowerman, Bill
FIRE ON THE MOUNTAIN
Bowers, Daniel
BEAUTIFUL THING
Bowes, Michelle
YANKEE ZULU
Bowie, David
BASQUIAT
Bowie, Sean
FOR THE MOMENT
Bowles, Paul
HALFMOON
Bowling, John
TATTOO BOY
Bown, Paul
JUDE
Box, Joey
BROKEN ARROW
Boxer, Stephen
MARY REILLY
Boyadjian, Amandine
VISITORS, THE
Boyadjian, Yohan
VISITORS, THE
Boyce, Brandon
PUBLIC ACCESS
Boyce, Todd
AFFAIR, THE
Boyce, Valerie
SUGARTIME
Boyd, Alexandra
MR. HOLLAND'S OPUS
Boyd, Barbara
BEST OF THE BEST 3: NO TURNING BACK
Boyd, Blake
CABLE GUY, THE
FIRST KID
Boyd, Cameron
MANNY & LO
Boyd, Leslie
TWO IF BY SEA
Boyd, Niven
JACK & SARAH
Boyd, Sissy
GRACE OF MY HEART
Boyell, Brian
SECRETS & LIES
Boyer, Christopher
ZARKORR! THE INVADER
Boyer, Jan
LOW LIFE, THE
Boyer, John
MR. HOLLAND'S OPUS
Boylan, Matthew
HOLLOW POINT
Boyle, Christopher
SANTA CLAWS
Boyle, Daniel
FRISK
Boyle, Jeri
FAMILY THING, A
Boyle, Lara Flynn
BIG SQUEEZE, THE
Boyle, Lisa
CRIMINAL HEARTS
NUTTY PROFESSOR, THE
Boyle, Mary Beth
SANTA CLAWS
Boyle, Peter
SURGEON, THE
Bozian, James
UNHOOK THE STARS
Bozzi, Gene
MUTANT MAN
Braaten, Heather
BOGUS
Bracco, Elizabeth
TREES LOUNGE
Bracken, Eddie
ASSAULT AT WEST POINT
Bracken, Heather
FUNERAL, THE
Brackin, Allena
PUBLIC ENEMIES
Bradford, Chris
ANNIE O
Bradford, Jesse
WILLIAM SHAKESPEARE'S ROMEO + JULIET
Bradford, Richard
CHAMBER, THE
Bradley, Charlotte
MOLL FLANDERS
Bradley, David
EXIT
HARD JUSTICE

Bradley, Doug
HELLRAISER: BLOODLINE
PROTEUS
Bradley, Harold
DAYLIGHT
Bradley, John
INDEPENDENCE DAY
Bradley, Shawn
SPACE JAM
Bradshaw, Anderson C.
QUEST, THE
Bradshaw, Richard
MAN WITH THE PERFECT SWING, THE
Brady, Don
HEAVEN'S PRISONERS
Brady, Ian
CHAMBER, THE
Brady, John
MYSTERY SCIENCE THEATER 3000: THE MOVIE
Brady, Monica
SMALL FACES
Brady, Moya
MARY REILLY
Braga, Sonia
LARRY MCMURTRY'S STREETS OF LAREDO
TWO DEATHS
Bragg, Allan
SGT. BILKO
Bragg, Bobby
FUGITIVE RAGE
Braid, Hilda
101 DALMATIANS
Braiden, Des
MOLL FLANDERS
Brame, Charles L.
HAPPY GILMORE
Brammall, Bridget
LOADED
Branagh, Kenneth
ANNE FRANK REMEMBERED
HAMLET
LOOKING FOR RICHARD
Branaman, Rustam
HEADLESS BODY IN TOPLESS BAR
Brandenburg, Larry
FARGO
Brando, Marlon
ISLAND OF DR. MOREAU, THE
Brandon, Terrell
EDDIE
Brandoni, Luis
SHADOW YOU SOON WILL BE, A
Brandt, Carlo
RIDICULE
Brandt, Hank
KINGPIN
Branzea, Nicu
STUPIDS, THE
Braschi, Nicoletta
MONSTER, THE
WHO KILLED PASOLINI?
Brasco, Dante
FIST OF THE NORTH STAR
Braswell, Mitch
MY FELLOW AMERICANS
Brathwaite, Glenise
PHAT BEACH
Brathwaite, Nicole
CELTIC PRIDE
Bratt, Benjamin
WOMAN UNDONE, A
Braugher, Andre
GET ON THE BUS
PRIMAL FEAR
TUSKEGEE AIRMEN, THE
Braun, Craig
ASSOCIATE, THE
Braun, Eddie
TUSKEGEE AIRMEN, THE
Braunstein, Jeff
FLY AWAY HOME
Braverman, A. Kent
DEAR GOD
Braverman, Amy
WALKING AND TALKING
Braverman, Marvin
DEAR GOD
Bravo, Michele
ARRIVAL, THE
Bravo, Rodolfo
JOHNNY 100 PESOS
Brawley, Jason
CARNOSAUR 3: PRIMAL SPECIES
Bray, Wilfred
WHARF RAT, THE
Brazeau, Andre
BLONDES HAVE MORE GUNS
Brazzel, Greg
BLACK SCORPION
Breathnach, Paraic
MICHAEL COLLINS
Breedlove, Cassondra M.
PREACHER'S WIFE, THE
Breen, Nora
GIRLFRIENDS
Breen, Patrick
BRITT ALLCROFT'S MAGIC ADVENTURES OF MUMFIE—THE MOVIE
4 TALES OF 2 CITIES
SWEET NOTHING
Breit, Mark
WHISPERING, THE
Bremner, Ewen
TRAINSPOTTING
Bren, Jonathan
LILY DALE
Brennan, Laura
MICHAEL COLLINS
Brennan, Pat
BODY OF INFLUENCE 2
Brennan, Terry
MAN WITH THE PERFECT SWING, THE
Brenneman, Amy
DAYLIGHT
FEAR
Brenner, Dori
INFINITY
Brentano, A.J.
ED'S NEXT MOVE
Brentley, Justin
BEST OF THE BEST 3: NO TURNING BACK
Bresee, Bobbie
PRE-MADONNAS
Breslau, Ben
HIGH SCHOOL HIGH
Breslau, Jeremy
HIGH SCHOOL HIGH
Breslau, Susan
HIGH SCHOOL HIGH
Brett, Jeremy
MOLL FLANDERS
SHAMELESS
Brett, Nick
CHAMBER, THE
Brettschneider, Mark
THAT THING YOU DO!
Breuler, Robert
CRUCIBLE, THE
Brewer, Brad
RANSOM
Brewer, Charlie
BROKEN ARROW
Brewster, Shawn
HARD WAY OUT: BLOODFIST VIII
Breymann, Andrew
BLACK SHEEP
Breznahan, Kevin
4 TALES OF 2 CITIES
Breznahan, Tom
HEADLESS BODY IN TOPLESS BAR
Brezner, Josh
WHISPERING, THE
Brialy, Jean-Claude
MONSTER, THE
Brian, Rick
DESIRE
Briand, Ludwig
LITTLE INDIAN, BIG CITY
Briant, Shane
TUNNEL VISION
Briaux, Herve
PROPRIETOR, THE
Brice, Ron
BASQUIAT
Bridge Dance Theater, The
PIE IN THE SKY
Bridges, Beau
KISSINGER AND NIXON
LOSING CHASE
OUTER LIMITS: SANDKINGS, THE
Bridges, Dylan
OUTER LIMITS: SANDKINGS, THE
Bridges, Jeff
MIRROR HAS TWO FACES, THE
WHITE SQUALL
Bridges, Krista
BLOODKNOT
KIDS IN THE HALL: BRAIN CANDY
Bridges, Lloyd
OUTER LIMITS: SANDKINGS, THE
Bridgewater, Stephen W.
LARRY MCMURTRY'S STREETS OF LAREDO
Briers, Richard
HAMLET
MIDWINTER'S TALE, A
Briggs, DeWitte
SOME FOLKS CALL IT A SLING BLADE
Briggs, Karen
SMALL WONDERS
Briggs, Michael
SERIAL KILLER
Briggs, Richard
UNKNOWN ORIGIN
Bright, Linda Marie
ORIGINAL GANGSTAS
Bright, Richard
BEAUTIFUL GIRLS
SWEET NOTHING
Bright, Susie
BOUND
CELLULOID CLOSET, THE
Brill, Fran
CITY HALL
Brill, Herbert
D3: THE MIGHTY DUCKS
Brill, Mary
D3: THE MIGHTY DUCKS
Brill, Steven
D3: THE MIGHTY DUCKS
Brilliant, Michele
FIRST WIVES CLUB, THE
Brimley, Wilford
MY FELLOW AMERICANS
Bringelson, Mark
DEAD MAN
Brinkley, Ritch
AMANDA AND THE ALIEN
Brinkmann, Robert
TRUTH ABOUT CATS AND DOGS, THE

Brinton, Malone
MATILDA
Briole, Vera
SINGLE GIRL, A
Brion, Francoise
NELLY AND MONSIEUR ARNAUD
Briones Jr., Effrain
WAR AT HOME, THE
Brisbin, David
LATE SHIFT, THE
Briscoe, Brent
SLING BLADE
SOME FOLKS CALL IT A SLING BLADE
Briscoe, Mary
STREET FIGHTER II: THE ANIMATED MOVIE
Briston, Patrick
DEATH ARTIST, THE
Bristow, Douglas
TERMINAL IMPACT
Bristow, Gary
SOUTH BEACH ACADEMY
Britos, Lenno
ANNIE O
Britt, Rod
CRAFT, THE
DESIRE
RAGE
Britton, Christopher
TAILS YOU LIVE, HEADS YOU'RE DEAD
Broadbent, Jim
JOSEPH CONRAD'S THE SECRET AGENT
Broadway, Christophe
TUNNEL VISION
Brochtrup, Bill
ARRIVAL, THE
MAN OF THE YEAR
Brock, Jeyer
THEY BITE
Brock, Phil
MERCY
Brock, Vince
TEXAS CHAINSAW MASSACRE: THE NEXT GENERATION
Brockman, Ungela
FROM DUSK TILL DAWN
Broderick, Beth
MAN OF THE YEAR
MATERNAL INSTINCTS
Broderick, Brendan
DEATH ARTIST, THE
Broderick, Charles
CELTIC PRIDE
Broderick, Golda
JANE EYRE
Broderick, Matthew
CABLE GUY, THE
INFINITY
Brodesser, Dorothy
CRUCIBLE, THE
Brodie, Raymond
JACK & SARAH
Brody, Adrien
SOLO
Brody, Heather Atwood
EDDIE
Brody, Kathryn
PIE IN THE SKY
Brolin, James
TRACKS OF A KILLER
Brolin, Josh
BED OF ROSES
FLIRTING WITH DISASTER
Bronsky, Brick
QUEST, THE
SGT. KABUKIMAN N.Y.P.D.
Bronte, Laura
ORIGINAL SINS

Brook, Jayne
ED
Brook, Laura
MISSION: IMPOSSIBLE
Brook, Peter
LOOKING FOR RICHARD
Brooke, Jayne
LAST DANCE
Brooker, Gary
EVITA
Brookhurst, Michelle
FOXFIRE
Brooks, Alan
SKYSCRAPER
Brooks, Albert
MOTHER
Brooks, Angelle
ONE MAN'S JUSTICE
Brooks, Arthur
INDEPENDENCE DAY
Brooks, David
HYPE!
MAGIC IN THE MIRROR
Brooks, Dina
PUBLIC ACCESS
Brooks, J. Cynthia
LIVE WIRE: HUMAN TIMEBOMB
Brooks, James
MR. ICE CREAM MAN
Brooks, Lucy Avery
MIRROR HAS TWO FACES, THE
Brooks, Nick
IN LOVE AND WAR
Brooks, Richard
BLACK ROSE OF HARLEM
CHAMELEON
CROW: CITY OF ANGELS, THE
SUBSTITUTE, THE
Brooks, Sally Ann
SGT. BILKO
Brophy, Anthony
SOME MOTHER'S SON
Brosnan, Pierce
MARS ATTACKS!
MIRROR HAS TWO FACES, THE
Brothers, Dr. Joyce
DEAR GOD
LOVER'S KNOT
SPY HARD
Broussard, Rebecca
MARS ATTACKS!
Brower, David
FIRE ON THE MOUNTAIN
Brown, Andre Rosey
BARB WIRE
FIST OF THE NORTH STAR
ONE GOOD TURN
Brown, Ashley
RUDE
Brown, B.J.
LAST DANCE
Brown, Bobby
THIN LINE BETWEEN LOVE AND HATE, A
Brown, Bryan
FULL BODY MASSAGE
Brown, Christopher
ONE MAN'S JUSTICE
Brown, Clancy
DONOR UNKNOWN
Brown, Darren
RANSOM
Brown, Derec
HEDD WYNN
Brown, Dorothy Recasner
EDDIE
Brown, Dwier
GALAXIES ARE COLLIDING

Brown, Edmond
EXECUTIVE DECISION
Brown, Elijah R.
KIDS IN THE HALL: BRAIN CANDY
Brown, Eric Martin
FIRST WIVES CLUB, THE
Brown, Ernie
MOTHER
Brown, Howard
POISON IVY 2: LILY
Brown III, Dr. Hosea
GET ON THE BUS
Brown, James
WHEN WE WERE KINGS
Brown, Jason
LOOKING FOR TROUBLE
Brown, Jim
MARS ATTACKS!
ORIGINAL GANGSTAS
Brown, John Fraser
WATCH ME
Brown Jr., Oscar
ORIGINAL GANGSTAS
Brown, Julia Montgomery
TWO IF BY SEA
Brown, Julie
OUT THERE
SPY HARD
Brown, Julie Caitlin
LOVER'S KNOT
Brown, Katherine Dora
POISON IVY 2: LILY
Brown, Kathy Sue
SLING BLADE
Brown, Kedar
MAXIMUM RISK
Brown, Kristofor
BEAVIS AND BUTT-HEAD DO AMERICA
Brown, Lennox
FAN, THE
Brown, Leon Addison
ASSOCIATE, THE
Brown, Marvin
RANSOM
Brown, Norman Patrick
BLACK DAY BLUE NIGHT
Brown, Pat Crawford
BAD LOVE
Brown, Paul
BUTTERFLY KISS
Brown, Randy
EDDIE
Brown, Robin Joi
FINAL EQUINOX, THE
Brown, Rosey
DEMOLITIONIST, THE
KINGPIN
PURE DANGER
Brown, Sharon
MISSING PIECES
Brown, Steven
PREACHER'S WIFE, THE
Brown, Tony
FAMILY THING, A
Brown, W. Earl
SCREAM
Brown, Winston
ANNIE O
Brown, Wren
HELLRAISER: BLOODLINE
Browne, Bernard
EXTREME MEASURES
Browne, Jackson
NICO ICON
Browne, Roscoe Lee
DEAR GOD
FOREST WARRIOR
POMPATUS OF LOVE, THE

Browne, Victor
I SHOT ANDY WARHOL
Broyden, Jimmy
UNFORGETTABLE
Brozova, Katerina
KASPAR HAUSER
Brucato, Christina
WELCOME TO THE DOLLHOUSE
Bruce, Alison
ALEX
Bruce, Carol
LAND BEFORE TIME IV: JOURNEY THROUGH THE MISTS
Bruce, Virginia
MADAME WANG'S
Bruck, Nils
FLIRT
Brugnini, Achille
PORTRAIT OF A LADY, THE
Brune, Jackie
NAKED SOULS
Bruneau, Philippe
LITTLE INDIAN, BIG CITY
Bruneau, Sharon
NEMESIS III: PREY HARDER
Brunet, Marc
LITTLE INDIAN, BIG CITY
Brunetti, Ted
ASSOCIATE, THE
Bruni, Carla
CATWALK
Brunner, Michael
TERMINAL IMPACT
Brunner, Robert
GRACE OF MY HEART
Bruno, Kim
MR. ICE CREAM MAN
Bruno, Tina
BIG NIGHT
Bruns, Philip
TRIGGER EFFECT, THE
Bruns, Phillip
ED
Brunsin, Jerry
PREACHER'S WIFE, THE
Bruskotter, Eric
FAN, THE
Bruton, Cheryl L.
THAT THING YOU DO!
Bruzzo, Alicia
SHADOW YOU SOON WILL BE, A
Bryan, Gordon
SGT. KABUKIMAN N.Y.P.D.
Bryan, John Cajun
APART FROM HUGH
Bryan, Zachery Ty
FIRST KID
Bryant, Ardie
NORMA JEAN AND MARILYN
Bryant, Michael
HAMLET
Bryant, Molly
BIO-DOME
Bryant, Walter
PALOOKAVILLE
Bryce, Scott
UP CLOSE AND PERSONAL
Bryggman, Larry
LOOKING FOR RICHARD
Bryniarski, Bruno
CURTIS'S CHARM
Bryson, Ed
GHOSTS OF MISSISSIPPI
Bryson, Eric
ELECTRA
Bubik, Istvan
RASPUTIN

Bucaro, Joe
ED
Bucci, Joe
EXIT
Buccille, Ashley
PHENOMENON
Buccio, Julian
SOLO
Buchanan, Chris
LIVE WIRE: HUMAN TIMEBOMB
WARHEAD
Buchanan, Yvonne
MUTANT MAN
Buchar, Dian
CANNIBAL! THE MUSICAL
Buchman, Jessica
SWINGERS
Buchner, Fern
UP CLOSE AND PERSONAL
Buck, Waltrudis
EVERYONE SAYS I LOVE YOU
Buckley, Brad
TUNNEL VISION
Buckman, Phil
GREAT WHITE HYPE, THE
VERY BRADY SEQUEL, A
Buckner, Wendy
NOT OF THIS EARTH
Buda, Santino
MRS. WINTERBOURNE
Buday, Zoltan
SURGEON, THE
Buddeke, Kate
EVIL HAS A FACE
Buechler, John
NOT OF THIS EARTH
Buell, Bill
WELCOME TO THE DOLLHOUSE
Buelvas, Andy
ED'S NEXT MOVE
Buena, Rico
DARK SECRETS
Buencamino, Nonie
MIDNIGHT DANCERS
Buescher, Julianne
SKIN
Buffolino, Vinnie
MATILDA
Bugin, Harry
CITY HALL
Buglewicz, Kayla
MADDENING, THE
Buhagiar, Valerie
JOHNNY SHORTWAVE
Bujeau, Christian
MACHINE, THE
VISITORS, THE
Bujold, Genevieve
ADVENTURES OF PINOCCHIO, THE
Bukatman, Scott
SYNTHETIC PLEASURES
Bukowski, Julien
RIDICULE
Bukowski, Marta
TIMELESS
Bulimia Banquet
NOT BAD FOR A GIRL
Bull
PROPRIETOR, THE
Bullen, Joe
TIME TO KILL, A
Bullock, Gary
TIGER HEART
Bullock, Sandra
IN LOVE AND WAR
TIME TO KILL, A
TWO IF BY SEA

Bumatai, Ray
UNDER THE HULA MOON
Bumgarner, Sean
FRISK
Bumpass, Rodger
BIO-DOME
Bunch, Betty
MARS ATTACKS!
Bunker, Clive
ROLLING STONES ROCK-AND-ROLL CIRCUS, THE
Bunn, Sharon
EVENING STAR, THE
Bunster, Patricio
JOHNNY 100 PESOS
Burch, Liz
TUNNEL VISION
Burda, Donald
MAXIMUM RISK
Burdette, Nicole
PALOOKAVILLE
Burgard, Christopher
FULL BODY MASSAGE
Burge, Christopher
FIRST WIVES CLUB, THE
Burgel, Patrick
VISITORS, THE
Burgess, Don
EVENING STAR, THE
Burgess, Michael
RACE THE SUN
Burgess, Tom
HEAVEN'S PRISONERS
Burk, Shay
DEMOLITIONIST, THE
Burke, Delta
MATERNAL INSTINCTS
Burke, Gregory
SUBSTANCE OF FIRE, THE
Burke, Harold
TAILS YOU LIVE, HEADS YOU'RE DEAD
Burke, Michael
TRUTH ABOUT CATS AND DOGS, THE
Burke, Michael Reilly
MARS ATTACKS!
Burke, Robert John
FLED
FLIRT
IF LUCY FELL
STEPHEN KING'S THINNER
Burke, Toni
STREET FIGHTER II: THE ANIMATED MOVIE
Burke, William
MADAGASCAR SKIN
Burkette, Michele
BLACK SHEEP
Burkhardt, Gerry
EVERYONE SAYS I LOVE YOU
Burkholder, Scott
EDIE & PEN
MY FELLOW AMERICANS
SUNSET PARK
Burkley, Dennis
TIN CUP
Burks, Jernard B.
PREACHER'S WIFE, THE
Burmester, Leo
LONE STAR
NEON BIBLE, THE
TRUMAN
Burnes, Albert J.
KANSAS CITY
Burnett, Anthony
PREACHER'S WIFE, THE
Burnett, Judge David
PARADISE LOST: THE CHILD MURDERS AT ROBIN HOOD HILLS

Burnett, Judith
ERNESTO CHE GUEVARA—THE BOLIVIAN DIARY
Burnette, Billy
CARNOSAUR 3: PRIMAL SPECIES
Burnette, Olivia
EYE FOR AN EYE
Burnham, Mark
INFINITY
Burns, Catherine Lloyd
MICHAEL
Burns, Diann
PRIMAL FEAR
Burns, Don
MR. HOLLAND'S OPUS
Burns, Edward
SHE'S THE ONE
Burns, Jennifer
JOSH KIRBY . . . TIME WARRIOR!: EGGS FROM 70,000,000 B.C.
JOSH KIRBY . . . TIME WARRIOR!: JOURNEY TO THE MAGIC CAVERN
JOSH KIRBY . . . TIME WARRIOR!: LAST BATTLE FOR THE UNIVERSE
JOSH KIRBY . . . TIME WARRIOR!: TRAPPED ON TOY WORLD
Burns, Jim
DADETOWN
Burns, Kelly
WATCH ME
Burns, Martha
BOYS NEXT DOOR, THE
Burns, R.J.
MUTANT MAN
Burns, Vincent
RANSOM
Burr, Britt
MULHOLLAND FALLS
Burrell, Kim
LET'S GET BIZZEE
Burrell, Scott
EDDIE
Burrell, Sheila
COLD COMFORT FARM
JANE EYRE
Burress, Hedy
FOXFIRE
Burroughs, Gloria
DON'T LET YOUR MEAT LOAF
Burrows, Stephen
DEATH ARTIST, THE
SPY HARD
Burruano, Luigi Maria
STAR MAKER, THE
Burruss, Iris
KAZAAM
Burse, Denise
BASQUIAT
JUROR, THE
Bursill, Tina
SPIDER & ROSE
Burstyn, Ellen
SPITFIRE GRILL, THE
Burt, Earl R.
BEAUTIFUL GIRLS
Burton, Corey
HUNCHBACK OF NOTRE DAME, THE
Burton, Jennifer
WATCH ME
Burton, Jennifer Leigh
DESIRE
Burton, Kate
AUGUST
FIRST WIVES CLUB, THE
Burton, LeVar
STAR TREK: FIRST CONTACT
YESTERDAY'S TARGET
Burton, Mark
BIO-DOME
Burton, Tony
BLACK ROSE OF HARLEM
Burton, Ursula
SGT. BILKO
Burton, Vernon P.
HIGH SCHOOL HIGH
Burton, Warren
HARD WAY OUT: BLOODFIST VIII
Bury, Karl
OUT THERE
Buscemi, Lucian
TREES LOUNGE
Buscemi, Michael
TREES LOUNGE
Buscemi, Steve
FARGO
JOHN CARPENTER'S ESCAPE FROM L.A.
KANSAS CITY
SEARCH FOR ONE-EYE JIMMY, THE
TREES LOUNGE
Busey, Gary
BLACK SHEEP
CARRIED AWAY
Busey, Jake
FRIGHTENERS, THE
TWISTER
Busfield, Timothy
FIRST KID
Bush, Brantley
SET IT OFF
Bush, Tommy
FAMILY THING, A
MARS ATTACKS!
Bushman, Marisa Guttman
SMALL WONDERS
Bushwick Bill
ORIGINAL GANGSTAS
Bussemaker, Reinout
ANTONIA'S LINE
Buster
GRACE OF MY HEART
Bustos, Enrique
OF LOVE AND SHADOWS
Bustos, Mario
JOHNNY 100 PESOS
Buta, Janos
RASPUTIN
Butcher, Jim
HEIDI FLEISS HOLLYWOOD MADAM
Butler, Calvin
STAND OFF, THE
Butler, Dan
FAN, THE
Butler, David
NATIONAL LAMPOON'S FAVORITE DEADLY SINS
Butler, Holly
LOOKING FOR TROUBLE
Butler, Jermaine Mauriece
EDDIE
Butler, Larry
ANIMAL INSTINCTS III: THE SEDUCTRESS
Butler, Richard
BASQUIAT
Butler, Tom
MATERNAL INSTINCTS
ROBIN OF LOCKSLEY
Butler, William
SLEEPERS
Butler, Yancy
FAST MONEY
Buttner, Bennie
BLONDES HAVE MORE GUNS
Butto, Chuck
RAGE
Buxtorf, Clementine
RIDICULE
Buza, George
OPEN SEASON
Buzick III, William
RED LINE
Bybee, Klair
JERRY MAGUIRE
Byers, Aggie
KINGPIN
Byers, Jessica
KINGPIN
Byers, John Mark
PARADISE LOST: THE CHILD MURDERS AT ROBIN HOOD HILLS
Byers, Julie
KINGPIN
Byers, Melissa
PARADISE LOST: THE CHILD MURDERS AT ROBIN HOOD HILLS
Bygott, Peter
HAMLET
Bynum, Nate
PEOPLE VS. LARRY FLYNT, THE
Byrd, David
LAWNMOWER MAN 2: BEYOND CYBERSPACE
Byrd, Eugene
DEAD MAN
SLEEPERS
Byrd, Pamela
TATTOO BOY
Byrd, Thomas Jefferson
GET ON THE BUS
GIRL 6
SET IT OFF
Byrne, Allie
MIDWINTER'S TALE, A
Byrne, Gabriel
DEAD MAN
MAD DOG TIME
Byrne, Gerry Robert
PEOPLE VS. LARRY FLYNT, THE
Byrne, Karl
WAR OF THE BUTTONS, THE
Byrne, Liam
SOME MOTHER'S SON
Byrne, Michael P.
FAN, THE
THAT THING YOU DO!
Byrne, Peter
TIMELESS
Byrne, Sabrina
ANNIE O
Byron, Don
KANSAS CITY
Byron, Kathleen
EMMA
Byun, Susan
SGT. KABUKIMAN N.Y.P.D.
Caan, James
BOTTLE ROCKET
BOY CALLED HATE, A
BULLETPROOF
ERASER
Caan, Scott
BOY CALLED HATE, A
Caan, Sheila
BOY CALLED HATE, A
Cabal, Lillian
CLUBHOUSE DETECTIVES
Caballero, Joseph Luis
PRIMAL FEAR
Cabot, Joe
SANDMAN, THE
Cabral, Eva
OF LOVE AND SHADOWS
Cabrera, Susan
SHADOW YOU SOON WILL BE, A

Cabrillana, Miguel
LAND AND FREEDOM
Caciola, Jim
VIRTUAL ENCOUNTERS
Caddell, Debbie
EDDIE
Cadell, Simon
COLD LIGHT OF DAY
Cadiente, Jeff
SAINTS AND SINNERS
Cadieux, Jason
IRON EAGLE IV
Cafe Orchestra
MICHAEL COLLINS
Cafferty, Jack
CITY HALL
Cage, Nicolas
ROCK, THE
Cahill, Jo-Anne
RACE THE SUN
Cahill, Robin
DEAD TO RIGHTS
Cahill, Sally
HARRIET THE SPY
Caicedo, Donny
BOTTLE ROCKET
EVENING STAR, THE
Caicedo, Eddie
MULHOLLAND FALLS
Cain, Lukas
TIME TO KILL, A
Cain, William
MIRROR HAS TWO FACES, THE
SUBSTANCE OF FIRE, THE
Caitlin, Faith
SPITFIRE GRILL, THE
Cajano, Pasquale
BIG NIGHT
SLEEPERS
Calaba, Kevin
MR. HOLLAND'S OPUS
Calabrese, Pino
STAR MAKER, THE
Calamity Jane
NOT BAD FOR A GIRL
Caldecott, Todd
FEAR
Calder, Judith
ASSOCIATE, THE
Calderon, Paul
CONDITION RED
LOTTO LAND
SWEET NOTHING
Calderon Torres, Angelina
LARRY MCMURTRY'S STREETS OF LAREDO
Caldwell, Brendan
WAR OF THE BUTTONS, THE
Caldwell, L. Scott
DANGEROUS PASSION
Caldwell, Sandra
WHERE'S THE MONEY, NOREEN?
Cale, John
NICO ICON
Calfa, Don
NECRONOMICON: BOOK OF THE DEAD
Calhoun Jr., Lawrence
SET IT OFF
Calhoun, Savannah
SANTA CLAWS
Calil, George
TIGER HEART
Calip, Demetrius
EDDIE
Call, R.D.
LAST MAN STANDING
Callahan, Dick
FLY AWAY HOME
GETTING AWAY WITH MURDER
MOONSHINE HIGHWAY
Callahan, John
MARVIN'S ROOM
Callahan, Mars
THAT THING YOU DO!
Callan, Geoff
SET IT OFF
Callan, Monica
SPITFIRE GRILL, THE
Callaway, Sage
PHENOMENON
Calleja, Sergi
LAND AND FREEDOM
Callow, Simon
JAMES AND THE GIANT PEACH
Calloway, Vaness Bell
AMERICA'S DREAM
Calnor, B.J.
FRISK
Caloz, Michael
QUEST, THE
SCREAMERS
Calvani, Riccardo
WHO KILLED PASOLINI?
Calvert, Jennifer
PROTEUS
Calvo, Yayo
BATON ROUGE
Camacho, Art
TIGER HEART
Camacho, Luis
BIRDCAGE, THE
Cambra, Lali
LAND AND FREEDOM
Cameron, Alister
SOLITAIRE FOR TWO
Cameron, Candace
SHARON'S SECRET
Cameron, Dave
HAPPY GILMORE
Cameron, Doug
MATERNAL INSTINCTS
Cameron, Matt
HYPE!
Cameron, Michael
ERASER
Cameron, Rhona
FUNNYMAN, THE
Camilletti, Robert
CARNOSAUR 3: PRIMAL SPECIES
Camp, Colleen
ASSOCIATE, THE
HOUSE ARREST
Camp, Hamilton
ALL DOGS GO TO HEAVEN 2
Camp, Judson
SEARCH FOR ONE-EYE JIMMY, THE
Campanella, Joseph
GLASS CAGE, THE
Campbell, Amelia
TRUMAN
Campbell, Bill
LOVER'S KNOT
OUT THERE
UNDER THE HULA MOON
Campbell, Bruce
DEMOLITIONIST, THE
JOHN CARPENTER'S ESCAPE FROM L.A.
Campbell, Desmond
BEYOND THE CALL
WHARF RAT, THE
Campbell, J. Kenneth
MARS ATTACKS!
Campbell, J. Marvin
AMANDA AND THE ALIEN
Campbell, Joe
MR. HOLLAND'S OPUS
Campbell, Katie
PORTRAIT OF A LADY, THE
Campbell, Keith
SPY HARD
Campbell, Ken Hudson
DOWN PERISCOPE
Campbell, Monica
DEAR GOD
Campbell, Naomi
CATWALK
GIRL 6
Campbell, Neil
TWO FRIENDS
Campbell, Neve
CANTERVILLE GHOST, THE
CRAFT, THE
SCREAM
Campbell, Rob
CRUCIBLE, THE
LONE JUSTICE: SHOWDOWN AT PLUM CREEK
Campbell, Rory
DELTA OF VENUS
Campbell, Ross
SONG SPINNER, THE
Campbell, Scott Michael
HOMECOMING
Campbell, Tisha
HOMEWARD BOUND II: LOST IN SAN FRANCISCO
Campese, Renato
WHO KILLED PASOLINI?
Campion, Lisa
MANNY & LO
Campiti, Vince
THEY BITE
Campos, Cristian
JOHNNY 100 PESOS
Campos, Victor
MURDERED INNOCENCE
Camroux, Ken
HAPPY GILMORE
TRACKS OF A KILLER
Camus, Sophie
PROPRIETOR, THE
Canaan, Brigitte
HORSEMAN ON THE ROOF
Canada, Ron
LONE STAR
PINOCCHIO'S REVENGE
Canavan, Kristie J.
THAT THING YOU DO!
Cancelier, Urbain
RIDICULE
Cane, Russ
SHAMELESS
Canerday, Natalie
SLING BLADE
Canfield, Gene
BIG NIGHT
Cannavale, Bobby
I'M NOT RAPPAPORT
Canning, Lisa
SCREAM
Cannon, Mookie
DON'T LET YOUR MEAT LOAF
Cannon, Sylvia "Small Frie"
FIRST KID
Cannon, Wanda
FOR THE MOMENT
Canova, Alberto
SILENCES OF THE PALACE, THE
Cansino, Richard
MIRROR, MIRROR III: THE VOYEUR
Cantatore, Raffaele
LAND AND FREEDOM
Cantillon, Colum
BIG BULLY

Cantrell, Jerry
JERRY MAGUIRE
Canty, Freda
DON'T LET YOUR MEAT LOAF
Canuel, Lindsay
EVERYONE SAYS I LOVE YOU
Cao Lei
BLUSH
Capaldi, Peter
CAPTIVES
Capers, Virginia
TRUMAN
Capiche, Harrison
DADETOWN
Capizzi, Bill
BULLETPROOF
ED
Capodice, John
FATALLY YOURS
INDEPENDENCE DAY
PHANTOM, THE
Capone, Tony
CITY HALL
Caporali, Marco
WHO KILLED PASOLINI?
Capra, Francis
KAZAAM
Caprari, Tony
REDEMPTION: KICKBOXER 5
TERMINAL IMPACT
YANKEE ZULU
Capron, Brian
EMMA
101 DALMATIANS
Capshaw, Kate
4 TALES OF 2 CITIES
Caputo, Jay
ED
Cara, Tiffany
SOUTH BEACH ACADEMY
Caramitru, Ion
MISSION: IMPOSSIBLE
TWO DEATHS
Carasco, Rene
DONOR UNKNOWN
Carcano, Alvaro
SOLO
Cardinahl, Jessika
INDEPENDENCE DAY
Cardinal, Ben
ALASKA
HOW THE WEST WAS FUN
WOLVES, THE
Cardona, Richard
STREET FIGHTER II: THE ANIMATED MOVIE
Carey, Ann
FLIPPER
Carey, Don
STREET FIGHTER II: THE ANIMATED MOVIE
Carey Jr., Harry
SUNCHASER
Carhart, Timothy
AMERICA'S DREAM
BLACK SHEEP
Cariou, Len
EXECUTIVE DECISION
MAN IN THE ATTIC, THE
Carliez, Michel
HORSEMAN ON THE ROOF
Carlin, George
LARRY MCMURTRY'S STREETS OF LAREDO
Carlin, Tony
NUTTY PROFESSOR, THE
Carlisle, Karen
SOME MOTHER'S SON

Carlisle, Steve
FLED
MY FELLOW AMERICANS
Carlo, Ismael "East"
ERASER
Carlone, Alessandro
WHO KILLED PASOLINI?
Carlson, Les
BEYOND THE CALL
MOONSHINE HIGHWAY
Carlson, Leslie
GIRL FROM MARS, THE
SONG SPINNER, THE
Carlson, Lillian
BIG BULLY
Carlson, Velletta
MARS ATTACKS!
Carlsson, Ewa
CHILDREN OF NOISY VILLAGE, THE
Carlsson-Wollbruck, Carl
LAWNMOWER MAN 2: BEYOND CYBERSPACE
Carlton, Brian
BREAKAWAY
Carlton, Jordan
MR. HOLLAND'S OPUS
Carlton, Kaili
MR. HOLLAND'S OPUS
Carlton, Robert
BOYS
Carlton, Tom
GHOST IN THE SHELL
STREET FIGHTER II: THE ANIMATED MOVIE
Carlyle, Robert
TRAINSPOTTING
Carman, Dale
ED'S NEXT MOVE
Carmichael, Jocelyne
HORSEMAN ON THE ROOF
Carmichael, Katy
MIDWINTER'S TALE, A
Carnaghi, Roberto
SHADOW YOU SOON WILL BE, A
Carneiro, Cesar
QUEST, THE
Carnes, Tara
GIRLS TOWN
Carniero, Cesar
SHOOTFIGHTER 2: KILL OR BE KILLED!
Caro, Norman
SOLITAIRE FOR TWO
YOUNG POISONER'S HANDBOOK, THE
Carol, Madalyn
RUMPELSTILTSKIN
Carol, Seraiah
ORIGINAL GANGSTAS
Carola, Linda
KINGPIN
Caron, Jean-Luc
VISITORS, THE
Carothers, Mariann V.
PHENOMENON
Carpenter, Charisma
JOSH KIRBY . . . TIME WARRIOR!: LAST BATTLE FOR THE UNIVERSE
Carpenter, David
GHOSTS OF MISSISSIPPI
Carpenter, Fred
MURDERED INNOCENCE
Carpenter, Jana
ROUJIN-Z
Carpenter, Violet
TOLLBOOTH
Carpenter, Willie C.
RATTLED
Carpentier, Yannick
CHASING BUTTERFLIES

Carpino, Phallon
EXTREME MEASURES
MRS. MUNCK
Carr, Darleen
PIRANHA
Carr, Michael
BEYOND DESIRE
Carr, Trent
CURTIS'S CHARM
Carra, Gloria
SHADOW YOU SOON WILL BE, A
Carradine, Calista
FUGITIVE RAGE
Carradine, Ever
FOXFIRE
Carradine, Keith
2 DAYS IN THE VALLEY
Carradine, Robert
JOHN CARPENTER'S ESCAPE FROM L.A.
Carral, DeVonn
MR. ICE CREAM MAN
Carrasco, Carlos
GLASS CAGE, THE
LIFEFORM
Carrasco, Jonathan
IT CAME FROM OUTER SPACE II
KAZAAM
Carraway, Patricia
GLIMMER MAN, THE
Carre, Isabelle
HORSEMAN ON THE ROOF
Carremo, Ignacio
OUTRAGE
Carreon-Reyes, Julio
LARRY MCMURTRY'S STREETS OF LAREDO
Carrera, Barbara
LOVE IS ALL THERE IS
SAWBONES
Carrera, James
BEYOND DESIRE
Carrere, Tia
HIGH SCHOOL HIGH
HOLLOW POINT
HOSTILE INTENTIONS
IMMORTALS, THE
Carreri, Steve
FAITHFUL
Carrero, Sara
SMALL WONDERS
Carrey, Jim
CABLE GUY, THE
Carrier, Corey
ADVENTURES OF PINOCCHIO, THE
Carrillo, Elpidia
DANGEROUS PASSION
Carroll, Cecilley
HARRIET THE SPY
HECK'S WAY HOME
Carroll, Christopher
NATIONAL LAMPOON'S FAVORITE DEADLY SINS
PRIMAL FEAR
Carroll, Deryl
NAKED SOULS
Carroll, J. Winston
BLOOD & DONUTS
Carroll, Justin
DARK SECRETS
Carroll, Kevin
ED'S NEXT MOVE
Carroll, Rocky
GREAT WHITE HYPE, THE
Carrot Top
PURE DANGER
Carrozza, Costantino
STAR MAKER, THE

Carson, Dane
PHANTOM, THE
Carson, Lisa
LET'S GET BIZZEE
Carson, Price
MULHOLLAND FALLS
Carter, Adrienne
HOMEWARD BOUND II: LOST IN SAN FRANCISCO
Carter, Alex
MAN IN THE ATTIC, THE
MOONSHINE HIGHWAY
Carter, Arwen
FOXFIRE
Carter, Cecil
REDEMPTION: KICKBOXER 5
Carter, Doyle
MAN WITH THE PERFECT SWING, THE
Carter, Finn
GHOSTS OF MISSISSIPPI
Carter, Jack
PRE-MADONNAS
Carter, Jamaal
ONE MAN'S JUSTICE
Carter, James
KANSAS CITY
Carter, Julius
COURAGE UNDER FIRE
Carter, Ki-Jana
JERRY MAGUIRE
Carter, Michael Patrick
BLACK SHEEP
Carter, Mitch
CHILDREN OF FURY
Carter, Nell
GRASS HARP, THE
PROPRIETOR, THE
Carter, Pam
CITIZEN RUTH
Carter, Rick
PREACHER'S WIFE, THE
Carter, Ron
KANSAS CITY
Carter, T. K.
YESTERDAY'S TARGET
Cartlidge, Katrin
BREAKING THE WAVES
Caruso, Johnny
AMANDA AND THE ALIEN
Carvalho, Betty
DEAR GOD
Carvell, Marium
EXTREME MEASURES
Carver, Brent
SONG SPINNER, THE
Carvey, Dana
SHOT, THE
Carville, James
PEOPLE VS. LARRY FLYNT, THE
Casado, Desire
BED OF ROSES
Casal, Lou
PURE DANGER
Casares, Maria
SOMEONE ELSE'S AMERICA
Cascone, Nicholas
EYE FOR AN EYE
UP CLOSE AND PERSONAL
Case, D.S.
SHOWGIRL MURDERS, THE
Casella, Mark
FLIPPER
Casella, Max
SGT. BILKO
Casey, Bernie
ONCE UPON A TIME . . . WHEN WE WERE COLORED
Casey, Eileen
EVERYONE SAYS I LOVE YOU
Casey, Kelly M.
MR. HOLLAND'S OPUS
Casey, Michele
SWEET NOTHING
Casey, Sue
VERY BRADY SEQUEL, A
Cashman, Dan
PRE-MADONNAS
Casiano, Deena
DEATH ARTIST, THE
Casimiri, Luciano
KIDS IN THE HALL: BRAIN CANDY
Casnoff, Phillip
SAINTS AND SINNERS
Cass Sr., David S.
LARRY MCMURTRY'S STREETS OF LAREDO
Cassaro, Nancy
MOTHER'S PRAYER, A
Cassavetes, John
PERSONAL JOURNEY WITH MARTIN SCORSESE THROUGH AMERICAN MOVIES, A
Cassavetes, Nick
BLACK ROSE OF HARLEM
Cassel, Jean-Pierre
LA CEREMONIE
Cassel, Seymour
BAD LOVE
MRS. MUNCK
TOLLBOOTH
TREES LOUNGE
Cassel, Vincent
HATE
Cassell, Paul
BED OF ROSES
Cassella, Mark
BULLETPROOF
ED
Casseus, Gabriel
GET ON THE BUS
LONE STAR
Cassidy, Joanna
CHAIN REACTION
Cassidy, Patrick
HOW THE WEST WAS FUN
Cassin, Barry
SOME MOTHER'S SON
Cassini, Frank
FINAL CUT, THE
SURGEON, THE
Cassini, John
GIRL FROM MARS, THE
Cassity, Richard
MIDNIGHT DANCERS
Castaing, Dany
HORSEMAN ON THE ROOF
Castaldo, Craig
RANSOM
Castaneda, Erika
SMALL WONDERS
Castaneda, Wendy
SMALL WONDERS
Castel, Lou
THREE LIVES AND ONLY ONE DEATH
Castellaneta, Dan
ALL DOGS GO TO HEAVEN 2
Castellanos, Alma Rosa
CELESTIAL CLOCKWORK
Castellanos, Theodora
TWO MUCH
Castellanos, Vincent
CROW: CITY OF ANGELS, THE
Castellitto, Sergio
STAR MAKER, THE
Castelnuovo, Nino
ENGLISH PATIENT, THE
Castens, Matthew Nathan
BEAUTIFUL GIRLS
Castillo, Enrique
MARS ATTACKS!
Castillo, Gabriel
JOHN CARPENTER'S ESCAPE FROM L.A.
Castillo, Gonzalo
LONE STAR
Castle, Charlene
MR. WRONG
Castle, Robert
FUNERAL, THE
Castle, Robert W.
BIG NIGHT
Castranovo, T.J.
DONOR UNKNOWN
Castro, Felix
DARK SECRETS
Cat, Holly
FEMALIEN
Catalano, Lidia Leonor
EVITA
Cater, John
RASPUTIN
Cates, Helen
LARRY MCMURTRY'S STREETS OF LAREDO
WHOLE WIDE WORLD, THE
Cathcart, Cathy
FUGITIVE RAGE
Catillon, Brigitte
PROPRIETOR, THE
Cattell, Christine
LAST DANCE
MR. WRONG
Cattino, Joelle
HORSEMAN ON THE ROOF
Cattrall, Kim
HEIDI CHRONICLES, THE
LIVE NUDE GIRLS
UNFORGETTABLE
Caty, Caren
RUMPELSTILTSKIN
Catzan, Jeniya
UNDER THE DOMIM TREE
Catzaras, Helene
SILENCES OF THE PALACE, THE
Cauldwell, Brendan
MOLL FLANDERS
Caulfield, Maxwell
BACKLASH: OBLIVION 2
Causwell, Duane
EDDIE
Cavalier, Christine
SANTA CLAWS
Cavalier, Jason
QUEST, THE
SCREAMERS
Cavalieri, Michael
LAST MAN STANDING
Cavallo, Mike
KINGPIN
Cavallo, Victor
WHO KILLED PASOLINI?
Cavanagh, Robert
COLD LIGHT OF DAY
Cavanaugh, Christina
JERRY MAGUIRE
Cavanaugh, Christine
DOWN, OUT AND DANGEROUS
Cavanaugh, Michael
DEAD TO RIGHTS
Cavanaugh, Tim
BEFORE AND AFTER
Cavanaugh, Timothy Patrick
SHADOW WARRIORS

Cavanno, Thomas
THEY BITE
Cavazos, Lumi
BOTTLE ROCKET
Cavelhosa, Fernando
NEUROSIA: 50 YEARS OF PERVERSITY
Caven, Ingrid
MA SAISON PREFEREE
SHADOW OF ANGELS
Caviezel, James
ED
ROCK, THE
Cawthorn, Lisa
PAINTED HERO
Cayol, Viviane
HORSEMAN ON THE ROOF
Cayouette, Laura
EVENING STAR, THE
Caywood, Stephen
FIRST KID
Cazenove, Christopher
PROPRIETOR, THE
Cease, Jonathan
MATILDA
Cease, Raina
MATILDA
Ceballos, Cedric
EDDIE
Ceballos, Jennifer
GIRL 6
Ceballos, Rene
EVERYONE SAYS I LOVE YOU
Cecchi, Carlo
HORSEMAN ON THE ROOF
STEALING BEAUTY
Cecchinato, Antonio
SINGLE GIRL, A
Cecere, Vince
SHOOTFIGHTER 2: KILL OR BE KILLED!
Cecillon, Bruno
HORSEMAN ON THE ROOF
Cedar, Larry
PINOCCHIO'S REVENGE
Cedillo, Julio
BOTTLE ROCKET
Cee, Frank
FUNERAL, THE
Celaya, Santi
LAND AND FREEDOM
Cele, Henry
GHOST AND THE DARKNESS, THE
Celedonio, Maria
FOXFIRE
SUBSTITUTE, THE
Celeiro, Luis
BITTER SUGAR
Celeste, Jimi
DADETOWN
Celik, George
STREET FIGHTER II: THE ANIMATED MOVIE
Celio, Teco
ADVENTURES OF PINOCCHIO, THE
Cellucci, Claire
MAXIMUM RISK
Cepeda, Laura
BATON ROUGE
Cephers, Troy
FAN, THE
Ceron, Laura
BIG SQUEEZE, THE
Cerone, Mike
KINGPIN
Cerruti, Nino
CATWALK
Cerullo, Al
BED OF ROSES
ERASER

Cerullo Jr., Al
JUROR, THE
Cervantes, Gandong
MIDNIGHT DANCERS
Cervantes, Gary
UNDER THE HULA MOON
Cervi, Valentina
PORTRAIT OF A LADY, THE
Cesari, Elio
CEMETERY MAN
Chaback, J.J.
GHOSTS OF MISSISSIPPI
RANSOM
Chabat, Alain
FRENCH TWIST
Chabrol, Claude
FRANCOIS TRUFFAUT: STOLEN PORTRAITS
Chada, Jennifer
NORMAL LIFE
Chadha, Gurinder
STUPIDS, THE
Chadwick, Marc
DAYLIGHT
Chaet, Mark
LETTER TO MY KILLER
Chagall, Rachel
LAST SUPPER, THE
Chagrin, Nicolas
RIDICULE
Chakravarty, Baroon
TARGET
Chalke, Sarah
ROBIN OF LOCKSLEY
Chalker, Dennis
ROCK, THE
Chaltiel, Zachary
BED OF ROSES
Chalupa, Pavel
DELTA OF VENUS
Chamay, Laure
NELLY AND MONSIEUR ARNAUD
Chamberlain, Dennis
LIFEFORM
Chamberlain, Jennifer
KASPAR HAUSER
Chamberlain, Matthew
FRIGHTENERS, THE
Chambers, Carrie
DESIRE
Chambers, Emma
WIND IN THE WILLOWS, THE
Chambers, Justin
HARVEST OF FIRE
Chambers, Marie
EYE FOR AN EYE
Chambers, Stan
ZARKORR! THE INVADER
Chambers, Steve
MY FELLOW AMERICANS
Champion, Beth
SPIDER & ROSE
Champion, Michael
RAVENHAWK
Champnella, Julie
STUPIDS, THE
Chan, "Piggy"
CHUNGKING EXPRESS
Chan, Darryl
MISSING PIECES
Chan, Henry
KISSINGER AND NIXON
Chan, Jackie
RUMBLE IN THE BRONX
Chan, Michael Paul
IMMORTALS, THE

Chan, Victor
GETTING AWAY WITH MURDER
Chancel, Judith
RENDEZVOUS IN PARIS
Chancer, John
FUNNYMAN, THE
GRIM
Chanda
DARK SECRETS
Chandler, Damon
DON'T LET YOUR MEAT LOAF
Chandler, Jared
PHANTOM, THE
Chandler, John
SHARON'S SECRET
Chandler, Kyle
MULHOLLAND FALLS
Chandler, Susan
BEWARE: CHILDREN AT PLAY
Chanel, David
INDEPENDENCE DAY
Chaney, Dirk
PREACHER'S WIFE, THE
Chang Chen
MAHJONG
Chang, Corey Ann
PHAT BEACH
Chang Kuo-chu
MAHJONG
Chang, Ray
DUNSTON CHECKS IN
Channing, Carol
LINE KING: THE AL HIRSCHFELD STORY, THE
Channing, Stockard
EDIE & PEN
FIRST WIVES CLUB, THE
LILY DALE
MOLL FLANDERS
UP CLOSE AND PERSONAL
Chant, Holley
CROW: CITY OF ANGELS, THE
Chantry, Art
HYPE!
Chao, Harvey
FRAME BY FRAME
Chao Te
MAHJONG
Chapa, Damian
SAINTS AND SINNERS
Chapa, Ricco
SAINTS AND SINNERS
Chapanond, Chai
QUEST, THE
Chapin, Miles
ASSOCIATE, THE
PEOPLE VS. LARRY FLYNT, THE
Chaplin, Ben
TRUTH ABOUT CATS AND DOGS, THE
Chaplin, Carmen
MA SAISON PREFEREE
Chaplin, Chang Ching Peng
QUEST, THE
Chaplin, Geraldine
JANE EYRE
Chapman, Brent
HAPPY GILMORE
Chapman, Brock
UNFORGETTABLE
Chapman, Justin
JINGLE ALL THE WAY
Chapman, Reverend Leonard
CITY HALL
Chapman, Robert
TIME TO KILL, A
Chappelle, Dave
NUTTY PROFESSOR, THE

Chappuis, Alexandre
NELLY AND MONSIEUR ARNAUD
Charattanawet, Jodie
QUEST, THE
Charbonneau, Patricia
PORTRAITS OF A KILLER
Chardiet, Jon
TOO FAST, TOO YOUNG
Charles, Annie
ROBIN OF LOCKSLEY
Charles, Josh
GRAVE, THE
NORMA JEAN AND MARILYN
PIE IN THE SKY
Charles, Nancy Linehan
NORMA JEAN AND MARILYN
Charles, Ray
SPY HARD
Charles, Timothy
LIFEFORM
Charnley, Hetta
MIDWINTER'S TALE, A
Charpentier, Mark
KINGPIN
Charters, Mychelle
RAW TARGET
Chartian, Cristian
SILENCES OF THE PALACE, THE
Chartrand, Lauro
RUMBLE IN THE BRONX
Charvat, Milan
KASPAR HAUSER
Charvin, S.J.
STREET FIGHTER II: THE ANIMATED MOVIE
Chase, Genevieve
TWO MUCH
Chase, John
PROTEUS
Chase, Johnie
EXTREME MEASURES
MRS. WINTERBOURNE
Chase, Johnnie
GETTING AWAY WITH MURDER
Chase, Sharon D.
EYE FOR AN EYE
Chase, Vincent
BLACK SCORPION
Chatel, Peter
SHADOW OF ANGELS
Chatman, Glenndon
ERASER
Chattman, Dwayne
SGT. BILKO
Chatton, Charlotte
HELLRAISER: BLOODLINE
Chavez, Mildred
SILENCE OF NETO, THE
Chavis, Karen
ANIMAL INSTINCTS III: THE SEDUCTRESS
Chaykin, Marc
STRIPTEASE
Chaykin, Maury
SUGARTIME
Chazal, Marie-Anne
VISITORS, THE
Cheeka, Cecil
DEAD MAN
Cheeseman, Ken
CRUCIBLE, THE
Chen Chao-jung
VIVE L'AMOUR
Chen, Ivy
MAHJONG
Chen, Joan
WILD SIDE
Chen, Nancy
LAWNMOWER MAN 2: BEYOND CYBERSPACE
Cheney, Heather
JERRY MAGUIRE
Cheng, Mark
MIDNIGHT ANGEL
Cher
FAITHFUL
Cherif, Med Iamine
SILENCES OF THE PALACE, THE
Cherney, Kaethe
IN LOVE AND WAR
Chernov, Jacqueline
FIRST KID
Cherpaw, Melody
TALES FROM THE CRYPT PRESENTS BORDELLO OF BLOOD
Cherry, Vivian
EVERYONE SAYS I LOVE YOU
Cheshier, Lydell M.
CABLE GUY, THE
GREAT WHITE HYPE, THE
Cheshire, Denise
ED
Chesnutt, Vic
SLING BLADE
Chesser, Bethany
THAT THING YOU DO!
Chesson-Fohl, Peyton
FIRST KID
Chester, Craig
FRISK
I SHOT ANDY WARHOL
Chester, Vanessa Lee
HARRIET THE SPY
Chestnut, Cyrus
KANSAS CITY
Chetoui, Habib
ENGLISH PATIENT, THE
Cheung, George
WHITE TIGER
Cheung, Jacky
WICKED CITY, THE
Cheung, Roy
ORGANIZED CRIME & TRIAD BUREAU
WICKED CITY, THE
Chevalia, Kevin
HOMEWARD BOUND II: LOST IN SAN FRANCISCO
Chevillard, Paul
HORSEMAN ON THE ROOF
Chevit, Maurice
RIDICULE
Chevolleau, Richard
RUDE
Chi, Chao-Li
NUTTY PROFESSOR, THE
Chi Hoang Cai
MARS ATTACKS!
Chi-Lites, The
ORIGINAL GANGSTAS
Chianese, Dominic
IF LUCY FELL
LOVE IS ALL THERE IS
Chiang, George
STUPIDS, THE
Chiba, Sonny
BODY COUNT
Chibas, Marissa
GETTING AWAY WITH MURDER
Chidley, Suzie
HEAD OF THE FAMILY
Chief Moon, Byron
ALASKA
Chieffo, Michael
BIG SQUEEZE, THE
ED
WOMAN UNDONE, A
Chignoli, Roberto
JOHNNY 100 PESOS
Chignoli, Valeria
JOHNNY 100 PESOS
Child, Bob
FIRST KID
Child, Buffalo
BOY CALLED HATE, A
Childers, Mary Ann
PRIMAL FEAR
Childress, Wade
PROPRIETOR, THE
Childs, Brenda J.
PREACHER'S WIFE, THE
Chiles, Linden
FLY AWAY HOME
Chiles, Lois
CURDLED
Chilivis, Taryn
KINGPIN
Chimento, Jim
BODY COUNT
Chin, Brady
ONE MAN'S JUSTICE
Chinchilla, Indira
SILENCE OF NETO, THE
Ching, Chan Man
RUMBLE IN THE BRONX
Chinlund, Nick
ERASER
LETTER TO MY KILLER
Chinn, Lori Tan
RANSOM
Chiofalo, Domingo
EVITA
Chiquete, Charles
ERASER
Chiriac, Horin
FORBIDDEN ZONE: ALIEN ABDUCTION
Chirkinian, Frank
TIN CUP
Chisem, James
EVIL HAS A FACE
Chisholm, Anthony
LET'S GET BIZZEE
Chisholm, Jesse James
JACK
Chittell, Emily
WHITE SQUALL
Chivers, Jeff
HOMEWARD BOUND II: LOST IN SAN FRANCISCO
Chivichyan, Gokor
BLOODSPORT II: THE NEXT KUMITE
Chivulescu, Alina
FORBIDDEN ZONE: ALIEN ABDUCTION
Cho, J. Moki
RACE THE SUN
Cho, Margaret
IT'S MY PARTY
Cho, Master Lee Il
BLOODSPORT II: THE NEXT KUMITE
Cho Tat-Wah
MIDNIGHT ANGEL
Choate, Tim
LIVE NUDE GIRLS
Choc, Eva
GIRLFRIENDS
Choe, Dean
UNFORGETTABLE
Chong, Marcus
PURE DANGER
Chong, Precious
GRACE OF MY HEART
Chong, Robbi
FATALLY YOURS

Chontos, Matthew J.
MIRROR, MIRROR III: THE VOYEUR
Chouchanian, Jack
PHENOMENON
Chow, Allan
BEYOND THE CALL
Chow, Ho
HARRIET THE SPY
Chow, Janis
PINOCCHIO'S REVENGE
Chow, Michael
BASQUIAT
Chow, Valerie
CHUNGKING EXPRESS
Chowdhry, Ranjit
GIRL 6
I'M NOT RAPPAPORT
Chris, Marilyn
TREES LOUNGE
Chriss, Sandra
KAZAAM
Christensen, Alisa
BAD LOVE
IMMORTALS, THE
MULHOLLAND FALLS
Christensen, David
OVER THE WIRE
Christensen, Jeff
WHARF RAT, THE
Christensen, Katrina
CITIZEN RUTH
Christian, Wolf
DRAGONHEART
Christiansen, Helena
CATWALK
Christiansen, Nynne
WHITE SQUALL
Christianson, Brandon
JERRY MAGUIRE
Christie, Dawn
MAN OF THE YEAR
Christie, Julianne
NUTTY PROFESSOR, THE
Christie, Julie
DRAGONHEART
HAMLET
Christie, Rab
SMALL FACES
Christine, Wanda
FAMILY THING, A
Christoffel, David
MAXIMUM RISK
Christofferson, Debra
UNDER THE HULA MOON
Christopher, Bojesse
SOMETIMES THEY COME BACK . . . AGAIN
Christopher, Dennis
IT'S MY PARTY
NECRONOMICON: BOOK OF THE DEAD
Chuay
BLOODSPORT II: THE NEXT KUMITE
Chung, Lily
MIDNIGHT ANGEL
Churchett, Stephen
SECRETS & LIES
Ciacci, Claudio
OF LOVE AND SHADOWS
Cialini, Julie Lynn
SOUTH BEACH ACADEMY
Ciandre, Conrod
CURTIS'S CHARM
Cianni, Dennis
ONE LESS EGG TO FRY
Ciano, Philip
LAST MAN STANDING
Ciarametaro, Laurie
DONOR UNKNOWN
Ciarcia, John "ChaCha"
FUNERAL, THE
Ciarfalio, Carl
SPY HARD
TRIGGER EFFECT, THE
Cicetti, Rick
DEATH BENEFIT
Cifuentes, Anna
BOTTLE ROCKET
Cigelj, Jadranka
CALLING THE GHOSTS: A STORY ABOUT RAPE, WAR AND WOMEN
Cikatic, Branko
SKYSCRAPER
Cilurzo, Stephen
HIGH SCHOOL HIGH
Cimarosa, Tano
STAR MAKER, THE
Cinabro, Stephen
EVIL HAS A FACE
Cintron, Monique
CONDITION RED
Cioffoletti, John
KINGPIN
Cippola, Sal
DADETOWN
Cisneros, Roman
HOSTILE INTENTIONS
SAWBONES
Cisse, Salif
DON'T LET YOUR MEAT LOAF
Ciu, Chelsea Madison
CRIMINAL HEARTS
Civale, Kevin
KINGPIN
Claes, Jappe
DAENS
Claffin, James
CLUBHOUSE DETECTIVES
Clami, Jean-Pierre
VISITORS, THE
Clancy, Brian
CURTIS'S CHARM
Clancy, Claude
MICHAEL COLLINS
Clapp, Gordon
STAND OFF, THE
Clapton, Eric
ROLLING STONES ROCK-AND-ROLL CIRCUS, THE
Clardy, Larry
KAZAAM
Clark, Adam
HARD JUSTICE
Clark, Anthony
HOURGLASS
ROCK, THE
Clark, Brett
SHOOTFIGHTER 2: KILL OR BE KILLED!
Clark, Dorian "Joe"
TALES FROM THE CRYPT PRESENTS BORDELLO OF BLOOD
Clark, James
ERASER
Clark, Larry
DEMOLITIONIST, THE
Clark, Lynn
MY FELLOW AMERICANS
Clark, Madison
FROM DUSK TILL DAWN
Clark, Mara
CRUCIBLE, THE
Clark, Matt
MOTHER
RAVENHAWK
Clark, Mickey
ABUSE
Clark, Patrick James
INFINITY
Clark, Richard
CHILDREN OF FURY
Clark, Shaun R.
TWO IF BY SEA
Clark, Tyrone
KANSAS CITY
Clarke, Angela
LAND AND FREEDOM
Clarke, Hope
BASQUIAT
Clarke, Jeff
STUPIDS, THE
Clarke, Jordan
WHITE SQUALL
Clarke, Lenny
TWO IF BY SEA
Clarke, Melinda
MULHOLLAND FALLS
Clarkin, Tony
MICHAEL COLLINS
Clarkson, Helene
BLOOD & DONUTS
Clarkson, Patricia
PHARAOH'S ARMY
Clatterbuck, Tamara
SET IT OFF
Clausen, Anja
WHITE SQUALL
Clavier, Christian
VISITORS, THE
Claxton, Richard
ADVENTURES OF PINOCCHIO, THE
Clay, Andrew
NATIONAL LAMPOON'S FAVORITE DEADLY SINS
Cleaver, Eldridge
BERKELEY IN THE 60S
Cleere, John
WAR OF THE BUTTONS, THE
Clegg, David
MR. HOLLAND'S OPUS
Cleghorne, Ellen
DEAR GOD
MR. WRONG
Cleland, Nicholas
SANDMAN, THE
Clem, Frank
GET ON THE BUS
PHARAOH'S ARMY
Clemens, Roger
KINGPIN
Clement, Aixa
LETTER TO MY KILLER
Clemente, Francesco
CATWALK
Clements, Ed
STAND OFF, THE
Clendenin, Bob
EYE FOR AN EYE
KAZAAM
Clennon, David
GRACE OF MY HEART
Cleo, Thomas
THAT THING YOU DO!
Cleyrergue, Berthe
PARIS WAS A WOMAN
Cliff, Nicola
FRIGHTENERS, THE
Clifford, Cheryl
DESOLATION ANGELS
ORIGINAL SINS
Clift, Eleanor
GETTING AWAY WITH MURDER
INDEPENDENCE DAY
Clifton, Jake
PAINTED HERO

Clifton, Prasitt
RACE THE SUN
Clinton, Roger
BIO-DOME
SPY HARD
Clooney, George
FROM DUSK TILL DAWN
ONE FINE DAY
Close, Glenn
ANNE FRANK REMEMBERED
MARS ATTACKS!
MARY REILLY
101 DALMATIANS
Clotworthy, Robert
PHOENIX
Cloud, Lauren
BEWARE: CHILDREN AT PLAY
Clout, Bob
SUGARTIME
Clow, Stuart
SUGARTIME
WHERE'S THE MONEY, NOREEN?
Clown, Roger
BOGUS
HARRIET THE SPY
Cluff, Jennifer
SPIDER & ROSE
Cluzet, Francois
HORSEMAN ON THE ROOF
Clyde, Craig
CHILDREN OF FURY
Clyde, Jeremy
KASPAR HAUSER
Coady, Frank J.
BODY OF INFLUENCE 2
Coates, Conrad
RUDE
Coates, Kim
BREACH OF TRUST
CARPOOL
OUTER LIMITS: SANDKINGS, THE
UNFORGETTABLE
Cobb, Kristi
FIRST KID
Cobb, Mel
PASSION OF DARKLY NOON, THE
Cobbs, Bill
ED
FIRST KID
GHOSTS OF MISSISSIPPI
THAT THING YOU DO!
Coble, Eric
FLATTERED
Cobo, Luis
LONE STAR
Coburn, James
ERASER
NUTTY PROFESSOR, THE
Coca, Richard
LONE STAR
TRUTH ABOUT CATS AND DOGS, THE
Cochrane, Rory
LOW LIFE, THE
Cockburn, David
SPIDER & ROSE
Cockrum, Dennis
GLIMMER MAN, THE
Cocktails, Johnny
SPY HARD
Coda, Frank
YOUNG POISONER'S HANDBOOK, THE
Codora, Eric
BODY COUNT
Coe, Ashley
LARRY MCMURTRY'S STREETS OF LAREDO
Coe, Richard E.
MATILDA
Coecho, Otto
SOME FOLKS CALL IT A SLING BLADE
Coelho, Otto
LOW LIFE, THE
Coen, Ricardo
WARHEAD
Coeur, Paul
PORTRAITS OF A KILLER
Coffee, Robert
LAST MAN STANDING
Coffey, John
WAR OF THE BUTTONS, THE
Coffey, Judy
WHARF RAT, THE
Coffield, Kelly
JERRY MAGUIRE
Coffin Break
HYPE!
Coffin, Fred
STREETCAR NAMED DESIRE, A
Coffin, William Sloane
MAN WITH A PLAN
Cohen, Alice
GRACE OF MY HEART
Cohen, Ari
FOR THE MOMENT
Cohen, Carl
DADETOWN
Cohen, Joshua D.
NOT OF THIS EARTH
Cohen, Joyce
INDEPENDENCE DAY
Cohen, Kaipo
UNDER THE DOMIM TREE
Cohen, Kyle
DRAGONHEART
Cohen, Leonard
MESSAGE TO LOVE: THE ISLE OF WIGHT FESTIVAL
Cohen, Lynn
EVERYTHING RELATIVE
I SHOT ANDY WARHOL
WALKING AND TALKING
Cohen, Marc
LONG KISS GOODNIGHT, THE
Cohen, Nicole Ann
HIGH SCHOOL HIGH
Cohen, Olga
DEADLY OUTBREAK
Cohen, Scott
WHARF RAT, THE
Cohen, Steve
WALKING AND TALKING
Cohendy, Christiane
HORSEMAN ON THE ROOF
Cohn, Nurith
ANGELA
Cohrs, Yvonne M.
DEMOLITIONIST, THE
Cojocaru, Lucian
JOSH KIRBY . . . TIME WARRIOR!: TRAPPED ON TOY WORLD
Colajemma, Angelo
STAR MAKER, THE
Colangeli, Giorgio
WHO KILLED PASOLINI?
Colaw, Cassie
MATILDA
Colazzo, Dianne
HEAD OF THE FAMILY
Colby, James
LOOKING FOR RICHARD
Colceri, Tim
ERASER
RAGE
SWEEPER, THE
Cole, Eric Michael
MR. HOLLAND'S OPUS
WHITE SQUALL
Cole, Gary
VERY BRADY SEQUEL, A
Cole, George
MARY REILLY
Cole, Jennifer
SOUTH BEACH ACADEMY
Cole, Kevin
SOLO
Cole, Sidney
SHOPPING
Coleby, Robert
PHANTOM, THE
Coleman, Baoan
HIGH SCHOOL HIGH
Coleman, Charlotte
YOUNG POISONER'S HANDBOOK, THE
Coleman, Cy
LINE KING: THE AL HIRSCHFELD STORY, THE
Coleman, Fritz
GLIMMER MAN, THE
Coleman, George
PREACHER'S WIFE, THE
Coleman, Gwen
DON'T LET YOUR MEAT LOAF
Coleman, Kari
MULTIPLICITY
Coleman, Signy
NECRONOMICON: BOOK OF THE DEAD
Colerider-Krugh, Kyle
PRIMAL FEAR
Coles, Emma
TWO FRIENDS
Coles, Mary Ann
GETTING AWAY WITH MURDER
Coles, Stan
BOGUS
Coletta, Louis
SEARCH FOR ONE-EYE JIMMY, THE
Colin, Margaret
INDEPENDENCE DAY
Colin, Suzanne
SUITE 16
Collado, Adrian
EVITA
Collett, Lisanne
HAPPY GILMORE
Collette, Toni
EMMA
PALLBEARER, THE
Collier, Eugene
TRIGGER EFFECT, THE
Collingridge, Christina
CAPTIVES
Collins, Alma
PHAT BEACH
Collins, Christina
BEYOND THE CALL
EXTREME MEASURES
Collins, Eryn
BIG BULLY
Collins, George
HOW THE WEST WAS FUN
Collins, Greg
CROSSCUT
DEAD WEEKEND
INDEPENDENCE DAY
ROCK, THE
SHARON'S SECRET
SOLO
Collins, Jennifer
NAKED SOULS
Collins, Joan
LINE KING: THE AL HIRSCHFELD STORY, THE
MIDWINTER'S TALE, A

Collins, Joely
ANNIE O
Collins, Kerry
JERRY MAGUIRE
Collins, Kim
LIFEFORM
Collins, Michelle
DARKMAN III: DIE DARKMAN DIE
Collins, Niall
WAR OF THE BUTTONS, THE
Collins, Pat
ERASER
Collins, Paul
EXECUTIVE DECISION
MOTHER
Collins, Rick
SGT. KABUKIMAN N.Y.P.D.
Collins, Rickey D'Shon
JACK
Collins, Ross
PUBLIC ACCESS
Collins, Stephen
FIRST WIVES CLUB, THE
Collins, Thom
MAN OF THE YEAR
Collver, Marc
BARB WIRE
Colon, Miriam
LARRY MCMURTRY'S STREETS OF LAREDO
LONE STAR
Colouris, Keith
SOUTH BEACH ACADEMY
Colquitt, Ken
CHAMBER, THE
Colquitt, Marquis Ramone
FAMILY THING, A
Colston, Robert
PREACHER'S WIFE, THE
Colton, Jacque Lynn
HOMECOMING
Coltorti, Ennio
WHO KILLED PASOLINI?
Coltrane, Robbie
CRACKER: THE MADWOMAN IN THE ATTIC
Coluca, Teddy
WELCOME TO THE DOLLHOUSE
Columbo, Michael
TALKING ABOUT SEX
Colvin, Kay
MICHAEL
Colvin, Shawn
GRACE OF MY HEART
Combs, Gil
MR. WRONG
Combs, Jeffrey
FELONY
FRIGHTENERS, THE
NECRONOMICON: BOOK OF THE DEAD
NORMA JEAN AND MARILYN
Comden, Danny
DUNSTON CHECKS IN
Comer, Anjanette
LARRY MCMURTRY'S STREETS OF LAREDO
Comerford, Jon
STAND OFF, THE
Compean, Carlos
LARRY MCMURTRY'S STREETS OF LAREDO
Comploj, Ruggero
MIRROR HAS TWO FACES, THE
Compte, Maurice
SUBSTITUTE, THE
Compton, David
PEOPLE VS. LARRY FLYNT, THE
Compton, Norm
FAN, THE
Compton, O'Neal
DESIRE
DIABOLIQUE
Conde, Natalie
MAGIC HUNTER
Condon, Chris
WHITE SQUALL
Cone, Tyler
TEXAS CHAINSAW MASSACRE: THE NEXT GENERATION
Cone, Tyler Shea
WAR AT HOME, THE
Conley, Jack
CHAMBER, THE
EDIE & PEN
Conlon, Mark
CRAFT, THE
SHARON'S SECRET
Connel, Robert
FUGITIVE RAGE
Connelly, Jennifer
FAR HARBOR
MULHOLLAND FALLS
OF LOVE AND SHADOWS
Conner, Van
HYPE!
Connery, Sean
DRAGONHEART
ROCK, THE
Connick Jr., Harry
INDEPENDENCE DAY
Connolly, Andrew
SHAMELESS
Connolly, Billy
MUPPET TREASURE ISLAND
Connors, Michael
DOWN PERISCOPE
PINOCCHIO'S REVENGE
Conrad, David
GHOST IN THE SHELL
STREET FIGHTER II: THE ANIMATED MOVIE
Conrad, Elizabeth
BLONDES HAVE MORE GUNS
Conrad, Robert
JINGLE ALL THE WAY
Conrad, Roy
BLACK OUT
FAN, THE
Conrad, Sid
GLIMMER MAN, THE
Conrad, Stevi
FEMALIEN
Conrath, Malcolm
RENDEZVOUS IN PARIS
Conroy, Brendan
MOLL FLANDERS
Conroy, Frances
CRUCIBLE, THE
NEON BIBLE, THE
Consolo, Adam
CABLE GUY, THE
Consolo, Louis Charles
KINGPIN
Constable, Paulette
CRACKER: THE MADWOMAN IN THE ATTIC
Constantine, Dorothy
BIRDCAGE, THE
Constantine, Michael
JUROR, THE
STEPHEN KING'S THINNER
Constantinou, Chris
SHOPPING
Constanzo, Robert
FOR BETTER OR WORSE
Conti, Tom
SOMEONE ELSE'S AMERICA
Contreras, Luis
LAST MAN STANDING
UNDER THE HULA MOON
Contreras, Patricio
OF LOVE AND SHADOWS
Contreres, Yanira
WHEN THE BULLET HITS THE BONE
Conway, Blake
LAZARUS MAN, THE
Conway, Denis
MICHAEL COLLINS
Conway, Kevin
LARRY MCMURTRY'S STREETS OF LAREDO
LAWNMOWER MAN 2: BEYOND CYBERSPACE
LOOKING FOR RICHARD
STUPIDS, THE
Conway, Tim
DEAR GOD
Coogan, Colm
MICHAEL COLLINS
Coogan, Scott
WELCOME TO THE DOLLHOUSE
Cook, Ancel
DOWN PERISCOPE
Cook, Carole
FAST MONEY
Cook, Christopher
I SHOT ANDY WARHOL
Cook, Dale "Apollo"
RAW TARGET
Cook, Dean
ADVENTURES OF PINOCCHIO, THE
Cook, Joanne
BUTTERFLY KISS
Cook, Joe
EXECUTIVE DECISION
Cook, Jonathan Teague
I'M NOT RAPPAPORT
Cook, Larry
PRIMAL FEAR
Cook, Rachael Leigh
CARPOOL
Cook, Ron
SECRETS & LIES
Cook, Xavier
DON'T BE A MENACE TO SOUTH CENTRAL WHILE DRINKING YOUR JUICE IN THE HOOD
Cooke, Darlene
OPEN SEASON
Cooke, Matt
IRON EAGLE IV
STAND OFF, THE
"Cookie"
HEIDI FLEISS HOLLYWOOD MADAM
Coolidge, Jennifer
DEATH ARTIST, THE
NOT OF THIS EARTH
Coolio
DEAR GOD
PHAT BEACH
Cooney, Cinckevin
INDEPENDENCE DAY
Cooney, Kevin
LIFEFORM
WOMAN UNDONE, A
Cooper, Bobby
UNHOOK THE STARS
Cooper, Camille
LAWNMOWER MAN 2: BEYOND CYBERSPACE
Cooper, Chris
BOYS
LONE STAR
PHARAOH'S ARMY

TIME TO KILL, A
Cooper, Chuck
JUROR, THE
Cooper, Connie
EVENING STAR, THE
Cooper, Dennis
FRISK
Cooper, Garry
BEAUTIFUL THING
Cooper, Helmar Augustus
PREACHER'S WIFE, THE
Cooper, Kahlena
TALKING ABOUT SEX
Cooper, Ken
TALKING ABOUT SEX
Cooper, Kenn
PRE-MADONNAS
Cooper, Malcolm
SOLITAIRE FOR TWO
Cooper, Matt
LAST SUPPER, THE
Cope, Kenneth
CAPTIVES
Copeland, Anthony Dean
PREACHER'S WIFE, THE
Copeland, Bill
VIRUS
Copeland, Jay
BURIAL OF THE RATS
Copeman, Michael
FLY AWAY HOME
MOONSHINE HIGHWAY
Copemen, Michael
WHERE'S THE MONEY, NOREEN?
Copley, Paul
CRACKER: THE MADWOMAN IN THE ATTIC
JUDE
Coppage, Walter
TRUMAN
Coppin, Tyler
RACE THE SUN
Copping, John
UNDERSTUDY: GRAVEYARD SHIFT 2, THE
Coppola, Francis Ford
PERSONAL JOURNEY WITH MARTIN SCORSESE THROUGH AMERICAN MOVIES, A
Coppola, Sam
PALOOKAVILLE
Coppolo, Marc
JACK
Coraci, Frank
MURDERED INNOCENCE
Corbalis, Brendan
STONEWALL
Corbeau, Igor
ANTONIA'S LINE
Corbett, Michael
WHOLE WIDE WORLD, THE
Corbin, Barry
CURDLED
SOLO
Corbin, Freeman O.
MR. HOLLAND'S OPUS
Corcoran, Aisling
MOLL FLANDERS
Corday, Bill
MOTHER NIGHT
Cordeiro, Michael
LAST MAN STANDING
Cordelier, Magali
SUITE 16
Cordes, Michel
HORSEMAN ON THE ROOF
Corduner, Allan
NORMA JEAN AND MARILYN

Core, Natalie
DUNSTON CHECKS IN
Corey, Irwin
I'M NOT RAPPAPORT
JACK
Corinne, Shanna
DENTIST, THE
Cork, Malcolm
TUNNEL VISION
Corkery, K.C.
ED
Corkum, Roland
UNFORGETTABLE
Corley, Pat
ALL DOGS GO TO HEAVEN 2
Corley, Sharron
SUBSTITUTE, THE
Corman, Dick
THAT THING YOU DO!
Corman, Maddie
BOYS
MR. WRONG
SWINGERS
Cornejo, Muriel
JOHNNY 100 PESOS
Cornelius, Janice
LET'S GET BIZZEE
Cornick, Glenn
ROLLING STONES ROCK-AND-ROLL CIRCUS, THE
Cornoe, Antoni
LOW LIFE, THE
Cornwell, Judy
WIND IN THE WILLOWS, THE
Corone, Antoni
STRIPTEASE
Coronel, Xavier
TOLLBOOTH
Corr, Andrea
EVITA
Corraface, George
JOHN CARPENTER'S ESCAPE FROM L.A.
Correa, Madelin
SGT. KABUKIMAN N.Y.P.D.
Correia, Don
EVERYONE SAYS I LOVE YOU
Corrente, Michael
KINGPIN
Corrigan, Kevin
PALLBEARER, THE
TREES LOUNGE
WALKING AND TALKING
Cort, Bud
THEODORE REX
Cortes, Joaquin
FLOWER OF MY SECRET, THE
Cortes, Pep
LAND AND FREEDOM
Cortese, Dan
. . . AT FIRST SIGHT
PUBLIC ENEMIES
WEEKEND IN THE COUNTRY, A
Cortez, Luis
MIDNIGHT DANCERS
Cosby, Bill
JACK
Cosenza, Catherine
LOVE IS ALL THERE IS
Cosmo, James
EMMA
TRAINSPOTTING
Cossack, Peter
DON'T LET YOUR MEAT LOAF
Cossette, Lorne
DARKMAN III: DIE DARKMAN DIE
TWO IF BY SEA
Costa, Derrick J.
MIRROR, MIRROR III: THE VOYEUR

Costa Gavras, Constantin
STUPIDS, THE
Costallos, Suzanne
LOTTO LAND
Costanzo, Denis
MAXIMUM RISK
Costas, Bob
OPEN SEASON
Costello, Luke
GETTING AWAY WITH MURDER
Costello, Matt
SMALL FACES
Costello, Tracey
GHOSTS OF MISSISSIPPI
Costelloe, John
KAZAAM
Costner, Kevin
TIN CUP
Cotamanis, Constantin
MAGIC IN THE MIRROR
Cote, Jean Luke
WHARF RAT, THE
Cote, Laurence
LES VOLEURS
Cote, Tina
BARB WIRE
Cothran Jr., John
MR. WRONG
Cotie, Robert
JOHNNY SHORTWAVE
Cottel, Clee
CHAMBER, THE
Cotter, Wayne
SPY HARD
Cotto, Delilah
GIRL 6
Cotton, James
PHENOMENON
Cottone, Rosolino
STAR MAKER, THE
Cottrell, Mickey
HELLRAISER: BLOODLINE
Couer, Paul
SONG SPINNER, THE
Coughlan, Sarah Kaite
PINOCCHIO'S REVENGE
Coulibaly, Fatoumata
GUIMBA THE TYRANT
Coulouris, Keith
BEASTMASTER 3: THE EYE OF BRAXUS
Coulsen, Bernie
SURGEON, THE
Coulter, Steve
EDDIE
TIME TO KILL, A
Coulthard, Raymond
ENGLISH PATIENT, THE
Council, Richard
I'M NOT RAPPAPORT
Countryman, Michael
RANSOM
Courier, David
EYE FOR AN EYE
Court, Jake
ADVENTURES OF PINOCCHIO, THE
Courtney, Emily
LARRY MCMURTRY'S STREETS OF LAREDO
Courtney, Lorna
BEWARE: CHILDREN AT PLAY
Courtney, Stacy
COLONY, THE
Cousin, David E.
SGT. BILKO
Cousy, Bob
CELTIC PRIDE

Couts, George
GLIMMER MAN, THE
Covay, Cab
PHENOMENON
Coverdale, John
EVITA
Covert, Alan
HAPPY GILMORE
Covert, Allen
BULLETPROOF
Covert, Michael
RED SCORPION 2
Cowan, Chris
HARD WAY OUT: BLOODFIST VIII
Cowan, Richard
MADAME BUTTERFLY
Cowan, Sabrina
CURDLED
Cowans, Adger
I'M NOT RAPPAPORT
Cowell, Chris
DEMOLITIONIST, THE
Cowgill, Danielle
SANDMAN, THE
Cowgill, David
STAR TREK: FIRST CONTACT
Cowie, David
FOR THE MOMENT
Cowl, Richard
LAST DANCE
Cowles, Matthew
JUROR, THE
Cox, Arthur
YOUNG POISONER'S HANDBOOK, THE
Cox, Brain
CHAIN REACTION
Cox, Brian
GLIMMER MAN, THE
LONG KISS GOODNIGHT, THE
Cox, Courteney
SCREAM
Cox, Darryl
BOTTLE ROCKET
Cox, Janine
SABRINA, THE TEENAGE WITCH
Cox, Jennifer
WEEKEND IN THE COUNTRY, A
Cox, Jennifer Elise
SOMETIMES THEY COME BACK . . . AGAIN
VERY BRADY SEQUEL, A
Cox, Joseph
SHOOTFIGHTER 2: KILL OR BE KILLED!
Cox, Nicholas
MATILDA
Cox, Nikki
GLIMMER MAN, THE
Cox, Richard
LOOKING FOR RICHARD
Cox, Ron L.
CITY HALL
Cox, Sam
HALFMOON
Coyle, Eliza
D3: THE MIGHTY DUCKS
Coyle, J. Stephen
JAMES AND THE GIANT PEACH
Coyne, Jonathan
SECRETS & LIES
Coyne, Kathleen
DEAD TO RIGHTS
Coyote, Peter
UNFORGETTABLE
Cozart, Cylk
ERASER
Crackerbash
HYPE!
Cracknell, Ruth
SPIDER & ROSE
Craft, Paula
SILENCES OF THE PALACE, THE
Cragg, Melvin
BREACH OF TRUST
Craig, Cathy
THEY BITE
Craig, Charmaine
BULLETPROOF
Craig, Rebecca
EMMA
IN LOVE AND WAR
Craighead, Robert
ZARKORR! THE INVADER
Cramer, Grant
PUBLIC ENEMIES
Cramer, Rick
SPY HARD
Cramer, Scott
DADETOWN
Crane, Darreck
STRIPTEASE
Crane, Greg
PIG'S TALE, A
Crane, Rachel
TWO-BITS & PEPPER
Cranford, Georgia
TOLLBOOTH
Cranham, Kenneth
BED OF ROSES
Cranitch, Lorcan
CRACKER: THE MADWOMAN IN THE ATTIC
Cranshaw, Patrick
EVERYONE SAYS I LOVE YOU
Cranston, Bryan
THAT THING YOU DO!
Crapps, Will
TIME TO KILL, A
Craven, James
D3: THE MIGHTY DUCKS
Craven, Matt
BREACH OF TRUST
FINAL CUT, THE
JUROR, THE
WHITE TIGER
Craven, Mimi
LAST DANCE
Cravens, Rutherford
LARRY MCMURTRY'S STREETS OF LAREDO
Craver, Haskel
BOTTLE ROCKET
ROAD TO GALVESTON, THE
Crawford, Chris
ONE LESS EGG TO FRY
Crawford, Cindy
CATWALK
Crawford, Hendrick
TERMINAL IMPACT
Crawford, Rachael
RUDE
Crawford, Rachel
CURTIS'S CHARM
Crawford, Rufus
BEYOND THE CALL
Crawley, Amos
NIGHT OF THE TWISTERS
Creed-Miles, Charlie
YOUNG POISONER'S HANDBOOK, THE
Creeden, Jack
DADETOWN
Creel, Monica
RATTLED
Crenshaw, Nesba
GRIM
Crescendo
SHOWGIRL MURDERS, THE
Crescenzo, Jim
HAPPY GILMORE
Crespin, Claudia
PHENOMENON
Crestjo, Mike
FINAL CUT, THE
UNFORGETTABLE
Creswell, Robyn
SMALL WONDERS
Crewson, Wendy
TO GILLIAN ON HER 37TH BIRTHDAY
Cribben, Mik
BEWARE: CHILDREN AT PLAY
Crider, Dave
HYPE!
Crider, Missy
BOY CALLED HATE, A
Crisafi, Giorgio
WHO KILLED PASOLINI?
Criscuolo, Lou
EDDIE
Crisp, Quentin
CELLULOID CLOSET, THE
DESOLATION ANGELS
Cristos
FROM DUSK TILL DAWN
Crivello, Anthony
INDEPENDENCE DAY
Crnkovich, Thomas
SGT. KABUKIMAN N.Y.P.D.
Croccolo, Carlo
IN LOVE AND WAR
Crockett, Ellie
MARY REILLY
Croft, Alyson
GREAT WHITE HYPE, THE
Crognale, Gino
DEMOLITIONIST, THE
FROM DUSK TILL DAWN
Cromartie Davis, Betty
PREACHER'S WIFE, THE
Cromartie, Hayward
PREACHER'S WIFE, THE
Cromwell, James
ERASER
PEOPLE VS. LARRY FLYNT, THE
STAR TREK: FIRST CONTACT
Cronauer, Gail
CARRIED AWAY
Crone, Penny
DAYLIGHT
Cronenberg, David
BLOOD & DONUTS
EXTREME MEASURES
MOONSHINE HIGHWAY
STUPIDS, THE
Cronin, Charlie
JERRY MAGUIRE
Cronin, Jim
TIMELESS
Cronyn, Hume
MARVIN'S ROOM
Crook, Danny
TO GILLIAN ON HER 37TH BIRTHDAY
Crook, Richard
STUPIDS, THE
Crooke, Leland
AMERICAN STRAYS
Cropper, Anna
AFFAIR, THE
Cros, Garvin
RUMBLE IN THE BRONX
Crosbie, Annette
SOLITAIRE FOR TWO
Crosby, Doug
FUNERAL, THE

Cross, Bill
SUGARTIME
Cross, David
CABLE GUY, THE
DEATH ARTIST, THE
TRUTH ABOUT CATS AND DOGS, THE
Crossea, Constance
LITTLE WITCHES
Crossett, William
RICH MAN'S WIFE, THE
Crossley, Amanda
SECRETS & LIES
Crosz, Anna
RASPUTIN
Crotsley, Don
SANTA CLAWS
Croucher, Brian
SHOPPING
Crouse, Lindsay
ARRIVAL, THE
JUROR, THE
NORMA JEAN AND MARILYN
Crover, Dale
HYPE!
Crow, Gregory L.
PARADISE LOST: THE CHILD MURDERS AT ROBIN HOOD HILLS
Crowder, Randy
TOO FAST, TOO YOUNG
WILD SIDE
Crowe, Alice
JERRY MAGUIRE
Crowe, Joan
EYE FOR AN EYE
Crowe, Russell
FOR THE MOMENT
Crowell, Hank
LARRY MCMURTRY'S STREETS OF LAREDO
Crowl, Tom
ARRIVAL, THE
DARK SECRETS
Crowley, Donncha
WAR OF THE BUTTONS, THE
Crowley, John
WAR OF THE BUTTONS, THE
Crowley, Mart
CELLULOID CLOSET, THE
Crudup, Billy
EVERYONE SAYS I LOVE YOU
SLEEPERS
Cruise, Tom
JERRY MAGUIRE
MISSION: IMPOSSIBLE
Crumbley, Melia
SMALL WONDERS
Crume, Louis Seeger
FLIPPER
STRIPTEASE
TWO MUCH
Crumley Jr., James M.
TIME TO KILL, A
Crump, Charles M.
PEOPLE VS. LARRY FLYNT, THE
Crusaders, The
WHEN WE WERE KINGS
Cruttwell, Greg
2 DAYS IN THE VALLEY
Cruz, Alexis
LARRY MCMURTRY'S STREETS OF LAREDO
Cruz, Francesca
BIRDCAGE, THE
Cruz, Gary W.
INDEPENDENCE DAY
Cruz, Michael Brian
SMALL WONDERS
Cruz, Raymond
SUBSTITUTE, THE
UP CLOSE AND PERSONAL
Cryer, Ed
DADETOWN
Cryer, Jon
POMPATUS OF LOVE, THE
Cryer, Suzanne
SOME FOLKS CALL IT A SLING BLADE
Crystal, Billy
HAMLET
Csakanyi, Eszter
MAGIC HUNTER
Cser, Nancy
BLOODKNOT
Csurka, Laszlo
RASPUTIN
Cuban, Mark
TALKING ABOUT SEX
Cudlitz, Michael
D3: THE MIGHTY DUCKS
Cuellar Jr., Gilbert R.
LONE STAR
Cuk, Vladimir
CELTIC PRIDE
Culea, Melinda
DOWN, OUT AND DANGEROUS
Cullen, Max
SPIDER & ROSE
Culp, Clint
DEAD WEEKEND
Culp, Robert
SPY HARD
Culp, Steven
DONOR UNKNOWN
JAMES AND THE GIANT PEACH
NORMA JEAN AND MARILYN
Cumberbatch, Scott Owen
EDDIE
Cumming, Alan
EMMA
Cummings, Emery
DADETOWN
Cummings, Jim
ALL DOGS GO TO HEAVEN 2
HUNCHBACK OF NOTRE DAME, THE
Cummings, Jimmy
ED'S NEXT MOVE
Cummings, Richard
EVERYONE SAYS I LOVE YOU
Cummins, Gregory Scott
SUNCHASER
Cummins, Scott
NORMAL LIFE
Cunningham, Anthony
WAR OF THE BUTTONS, THE
Cunningham, Colin
ROBIN OF LOCKSLEY
Cunningham, Danny
LOADED
Cunningham, John
LAST DANCE
Cunningham, Liam
JUDE
WAR OF THE BUTTONS, THE
Cunningham, Matthew Z.
THEY BITE
Cunnington, Ceri
HEDD WYNN
Cuomo, Eduardo
WHO KILLED PASOLINI?
Cupae, Sam
ANIMAL INSTINCTS III: THE SEDUCTRESS
Cupisti, Barbara
CEMETERY MAN
Cupo, Patrick
DEAD WEEKEND
Cur, D.
ORIGINAL SINS
Curan, Marianne
MATILDA
Curcuro, Robert M.
CELTIC PRIDE
Curran, Angela
SECRETS & LIES
Curran, Chris
MOLL FLANDERS
Curran, Dominic
SECRETS & LIES
Curran, Todd
IN LOVE AND WAR
Curran, Tony
CAPTIVES
Currie, Brian
BIO-DOME
CARNOSAUR 3: PRIMAL SPECIES
Currie, Gordon
BLOOD & DONUTS
Curry, Dick
CAUGHT
Curry, Julian
RASPUTIN
Curry, Michael Todd
CRIMINAL HEARTS
Curry, Tamara
MARS ATTACKS!
Curry, Tim
LOVER'S KNOT
MUPPET TREASURE ISLAND
Curtin, Cathy
ED'S NEXT MOVE
Curtis, Anthony
GLASS CAGE, THE
Curtis Hall, Vondie
BROKEN ARROW
HEAVEN'S PRISONERS
Curtis, Jamie Lee
HEIDI CHRONICLES, THE
HOUSE ARREST
Curtis, Mickey
KAMIKAZE TAXI
Curtis, Robin
SANTA WITH MUSCLES
Curtis, Tony
CELLULOID CLOSET, THE
IMMORTALS, THE
Curto, Vinnie
BARB WIRE
Curto, Vinny
UNHOOK THE STARS
Curzi, Pierre
STAND OFF, THE
Cusack, Ann
BIRDCAGE, THE
MULTIPLICITY
MY FELLOW AMERICANS
Cusack, Dick
CHAIN REACTION
EVIL HAS A FACE
Cusack, Joan
MR. WRONG
TWO MUCH
Cusack, John
CITY HALL
Cusack, Sinead
STEALING BEAUTY
Cushman, Mary
DADETOWN
Cushna, Stephanie
AMERICAN STRAYS
Cut Killer
HATE
Cuthbertson, Callum
BREAKING THE WAVES

Cutlas, Burdie
BIO-DOME
Cutler, Allen
AMANDA AND THE ALIEN
CROSSCUT
HALFBACK OF NOTRE DAME, THE
Cutler, Wendy
PRIMAL FEAR
Cutrona, Ryan
GLIMMER MAN, THE
QUEST, THE
Cuttel, Lou
NORMA JEAN AND MARILYN
Cutts, Dale
REDEMPTION: KICKBOXER 5
Cybulski, Artur
NORMA JEAN AND MARILYN
Cyphers, Harvey L.
WAR AT HOME, THE
Cyr, Myriam
I SHOT ANDY WARHOL
Czerny, Henry
MISSION: IMPOSSIBLE
Czypionka, Hansa
KASPAR HAUSER
d'Abo, Maryam
SOLITAIRE FOR TWO
d'Abo, Olivia
LIVE NUDE GIRLS
D'Addario, Jason
KIDS IN THE HALL: BRAIN CANDY
D'Agostino, Lisa
CABLE GUY, THE
d'Amboise, Charlotte
PREACHER'S WIFE, THE
D'Ambrose, Camille
BEAUTIFUL GIRLS
D'Amore, Renato
SONS OF TRINITY
D'Andrea, Al
FATALLY YOURS
D'Angelo, Beverly
EDIE & PEN
EYE FOR AN EYE
WIDOW'S KISS
D'Angelo, Sonny
LAST MAN STANDING
D'Angerio, Joe
NORMA JEAN AND MARILYN
D'Aquila, Diane
BEYOND THE CALL
D'Arbanville, Patti
FAN, THE
D'Arcangelo, Allan
HEAVY
D'Ayala, Maria
MILLE BOLLE BLU
D'Oench, Peter
UP CLOSE AND PERSONAL
D'Oliveira, Damon
BOGUS
GETTING AWAY WITH MURDER
D'Onofrio, Elizabeth
WHOLE WIDE WORLD, THE
D'Onofrio, Joseph
CAUGHT
PALLBEARER, THE
D'Onofrio, Vincent
FEELING MINNESOTA
WHOLE WIDE WORLD, THE
d'Staic, Liam
MICHAEL COLLINS
Da Pozza, Walter
WHO KILLED PASOLINI?
Da Silva, Eric
DELTA OF VENUS
Da Silva, Jo
LIVE WIRE: HUMAN TIMEBOMB
WARHEAD
Daans, Lara
ELECTRA
Dacascos, Mark
ISLAND OF DR. MOREAU, THE
REDEMPTION: KICKBOXER 5
Dafoe, Willem
BASQUIAT
ENGLISH PATIENT, THE
Dagg, Cory
UNFORGETTABLE
Dahan, Armand
EDDIE
FIRST WIVES CLUB, THE
Dahl, Dirk
WHISPERING, THE
Dahlberg, Christopher
WAR AT HOME, THE
Dahy, Clarence
RACE THE SUN
Dailey, Rod
PHANTOM, THE
Daily, Dan
DAYLIGHT
Dain, Joseph
PUBLIC ENEMIES
Daish, Charles
HAMLET
Daiz, Maria
FROM DUSK TILL DAWN
Dakota
INDEPENDENCE DAY
Daley, James
JUDE
Dalglish, Robin
DOGFIGHTERS, THE
Dallesandro, Joe
BAD LOVE
Dalmat, Jose-Philippe
HATE
Dalool, Abe
SOME FOLKS CALL IT A SLING BLADE
Dalton, Darren
PURE DANGER
WOLVES, THE
Dalton, John
PROPRIETOR, THE
Dalton, Kristen
SWEEPER, THE
Daltrey, Roger
ROLLING STONES ROCK-AND-ROLL CIRCUS, THE
Daly, Carol
BLONDES HAVE MORE GUNS
Daly, Tim
ASSOCIATE, THE
DENISE CALLS UP
Damant, Andree
HATE
Dambuza, Nathan
CAPTIVES
Damian, Kristian
EDDIE
Damian, Luis
JERRY MAGUIRE
Damon, Matt
COURAGE UNDER FIRE
Damsyik, Him
WITHOUT MERCY
Damus, Mike
PIG'S TALE, A
Dan, Andy
JOHNNY SHORTWAVE
Danare, Malcolm
INDEPENDENCE DAY
Dance, Charles
MICHAEL COLLINS
SURGEON, THE
UNDERTOW
Danchimah, Godfrey C.
CHAIN REACTION
ORIGINAL GANGSTAS
Dando, Bill
MAN WITH THE PERFECT SWING, THE
Dando, Evan
HEAVY
Danes, Claire
TO GILLIAN ON HER 37TH BIRTHDAY
WILLIAM SHAKESPEARE'S ROMEO + JULIET
Dangerfield, Marcia
CHILDREN OF FURY
Dani Girl
ORIGINAL GANGSTAS
Daniel, Eugene
DOWN PERISCOPE
Daniel, Greg
DESIRE
Daniel, Gregg
LAWNMOWER MAN 2: BEYOND CYBERSPACE
MARS ATTACKS!
Daniel, Kevan
APART FROM HUGH
Daniels, Ben
BEAUTIFUL THING
Daniels, Bo
FAN, THE
Daniels, Gary
FIST OF THE NORTH STAR
RAGE
WHITE TIGER
Daniels, James
ROAD TO GALVESTON, THE
Daniels, Jeff
FLY AWAY HOME
101 DALMATIANS
2 DAYS IN THE VALLEY
Daniels, Jennifer
LOVE IS ALL THERE IS
Daniels, Mark
MR. HOLLAND'S OPUS
Daniels, Max
TUSKEGEE AIRMEN, THE
Daniels, William
SKIN
Danielson, Kurt
HYPE!
Dann, Dennis
OF LOVE AND SHADOWS
Dannell-Foran, Stuart
WAR OF THE BUTTONS, THE
Danner, Blythe
HOMAGE
Danon, Leslie
SOMETIMES THEY COME BACK . . . AGAIN
WHISPERING, THE
Danova, Yelena
INDEPENDENCE DAY
Danton, Mitch
DOWN PERISCOPE
Danton, Steve
EVENING STAR, THE
Dapkunaite, Ingeborga
MISSION: IMPOSSIBLE
Dara, Olu
KANSAS CITY
Darblay, Jeanne-Marie
PROPRIETOR, THE
Darbo, Patrika
FAST MONEY
HOUSE ARREST
DaRe, Eric
TAKEOVER, THE

Darling, Tony
BEAVIS AND BUTT-HEAD DO AMERICA
Darmstaedter, David
TOO FAST, TOO YOUNG
Darrigo, Paul
CARNOSAUR 3: PRIMAL SPECIES
Darrius, Armand
COURAGE UNDER FIRE
Dash, Kevin
SHARON'S SECRET
Dash, Ray
BREAKAWAY
Datillo-Hayward, Kristin
. . . AT FIRST SIGHT
Dauder, Jordi
LAND AND FREEDOM
Daugherty, Brad
EDDIE
Dautremay, Jean
LA COMEDIE-FRANCAISE OU L'AMOUR JOUE
Davael, Kiami
MATILDA
Davenport, Johnny Lee
CHAIN REACTION
Davenport, Laura
TWO DEATHS
Davey, Billy
PROTEUS
Davi, Robert
BODY COUNT
DELTA OF VENUS
DOGFIGHTERS, THE
David, Alan
CRACKER: THE MADWOMAN IN THE ATTIC
David, Angel
CITY HALL
David, Brent
PARADISE LOST: THE CHILD MURDERS AT ROBIN HOOD HILLS
David, Jonathan
BAD LOVE
David, Keith
EYE FOR AN EYE
LARGER THAN LIFE
David, Lawrence
MIDNIGHT DANCERS
Davidovich, Lolita
FOR BETTER OR WORSE
HARVEST OF FIRE
Davidson, Bret
LAZARUS MAN, THE
Davidson, Elizabeth
MOTHER'S PRAYER, A
Davidson, Jaye
CATWALK
Davidson, Scott
PARADISE LOST: THE CHILD MURDERS AT ROBIN HOOD HILLS
Davidtz, Embeth
MATILDA
Davies, Ann
MIDWINTER'S TALE, A
Davies, Jeremy
TWISTER
Davies, John
PAINTED HERO
Davies, John S.
ROAD TO GALVESTON, THE
Davies, Matthew
MADAGASCAR SKIN
Davies, Mitchell
BREACH OF TRUST
Davies, Tom
UNFORGETTABLE
Davies, Vincent Paul
CRACKER: THE MADWOMAN IN THE ATTIC
Davies, Virginia
MADAGASCAR SKIN
Davila, Azalea
MULHOLLAND FALLS
PRIMAL FEAR
UNFORGETTABLE
Davila, Michael
QUEST, THE
Davis, Andy
BOYS
Davis, Benford
BODY COUNT
Davis, Craig
ADRENALIN: FEAR THE RUSH
Davis, Dale
EDDIE
Davis, Dan
TATTOO BOY
Davis, Dan R.
MR. ICE CREAM MAN
Davis, Don S.
ALASKA
FAN, THE
Davis, Duane
BOY CALLED HATE, A
GREAT WHITE HYPE, THE
Davis, Eddie
PEOPLE VS. LARRY FLYNT, THE
Davis, Elizabeth
HYPE!
Davis, Frank
CABLE GUY, THE
Davis, Geena
LONG KISS GOODNIGHT, THE
Davis, Hannah
SECRETS & LIES
Davis, Heather
OFF AND RUNNING
Davis, Hope
MR. WRONG
Davis, J.J.
ABUSE
Davis, Jason
BIO-DOME
Davis, Jesse
KANSAS CITY
Davis, Jesse Ed
ROLLING STONES ROCK-AND-ROLL CIRCUS, THE
Davis, Jim
FRISK
Davis, Joe
DEAD WEEKEND
Davis, Joy
EDDIE
Davis Jr., Darvel
PREACHER'S WIFE, THE
Davis, Marianne
NORMA JEAN AND MARILYN
Davis, Mary Bond
PREACHER'S WIFE, THE
Davis, Michael
PEOPLE VS. LARRY FLYNT, THE
Davis, Miles
MESSAGE TO LOVE: THE ISLE OF WIGHT FESTIVAL
Davis, Nathan
CHAIN REACTION
DUNSTON CHECKS IN
Davis, Neriah
DUNSTON CHECKS IN
Davis, Ossie
GET ON THE BUS
I'M NOT RAPPAPORT
Davis, Philip
SECRETS & LIES
Davis, Robert
PEOPLE VS. LARRY FLYNT, THE
Davis, Stephen
TUNNEL VISION
Davis, Steve
GHOST IN THE SHELL
STREET FIGHTER II: THE ANIMATED MOVIE
Davis, Ted
NATIONAL LAMPOON'S FAVORITE DEADLY SINS
NOT OF THIS EARTH
Davis, Travis Kyle
MRS. MUNCK
Davis, V.C.
LIVE NUDE GIRLS
Davis, Victoria
WELCOME TO THE DOLLHOUSE
Davis, Viola
SUBSTANCE OF FIRE, THE
Davis, William B.
UNFORGETTABLE
Davis, Yonda
NAKED SOULS
Davison, Bruce
CRUCIBLE, THE
DOWN, OUT AND DANGEROUS
GRACE OF MY HEART
HOMAGE
IT'S MY PARTY
WIDOW'S KISS
Davison, Michelle
CHAMBER, THE
Daw, Joseph A.
POLYMORPH
Dawe, Emily
SPIDER & ROSE
Dawson, Frederick
MR. WRONG
Dawson, Kim
ARRIVAL, THE
Day, Gary
GIRL FROM MARS, THE
TUNNEL VISION
Day, Philipa
ENGLISH PATIENT, THE
Day-Lewis, Daniel
CRUCIBLE, THE
Dayan, Ami
DEADLY OUTBREAK
De Angelis, Rosemary
JUROR, THE
De Baer, Jean
ASSOCIATE, THE
de Banzie, Lois
DUNSTON CHECKS IN
de Bernal, Fernecio
SOLO
De Bisogno, Vittorio
WHO KILLED PASOLINI?
De Bonis, Marcia
EXTREME MEASURES
De Bont, Anneke
TWISTER
de Brauw, Elsie
ANTONIA'S LINE
de Broux, Lee
DEATH BENEFIT
SKYSCRAPER
de Bruyn, Erik
ANTONIA'S LINE
De Cadenet, Amanda
GRACE OF MY HEART
de Candia, Mario
MILLE BOLLE BLU

de Chauvigny, Emmanuel
CHASING BUTTERFLIES
De Cormier, Louise
SPITFIRE GRILL, THE
De Filippi, Carlo
WHO KILLED PASOLINI?
De Francovich, Massimo
WHO KILLED PASOLINI?
De Giorgio, Paolo
WHO KILLED PASOLINI?
de Graaf, Marina
ANTONIA'S LINE
de Graeve, Marjolaine
PROPRIETOR, THE
De Grazia, Alfonzo
SHADOW YOU SOON WILL BE, A
de Groot, Boudewijn
COLD LIGHT OF DAY
De Gruccio, Nick
JOSH KIRBY . . . TIME WARRIOR!: JOURNEY TO THE MAGIC CAVERN
de Jonge, Marc
LITTLE INDIAN, BIG CITY
De Klerk, Bryan
WARHEAD
De La Fontaine, Jacqui
JACK
De La Maza, Rolando
WILD SIDE
De La Personne, Frank
PROPRIETOR, THE
De La Rosa, Nelson
ISLAND OF DR. MOREAU, THE
De Lancie, John
MISSING PIECES
De Laria, Lea
FIRST WIVES CLUB, THE
de Lavallade, Carmen
LONE STAR
De Lemeny, Nadia
GRIM
De Leon, Gigi
BOGUS
De Leon, Marita
BIG SQUEEZE, THE
de Maldonado-Bostock, Carlos
NICO ICON
de Muynck, Viviane
SUITE 16
De Nicola, Krum
WHO KILLED PASOLINI?
De Niro, Drena
GRACE OF MY HEART
De Niro, Robert
FAN, THE
MARVIN'S ROOM
SLEEPERS
De Nys, Crispen
LIVE WIRE: HUMAN TIMEBOMB
De Otezza Ortiz, Luis
SONS OF TRINITY
De Palma, Brian
PERSONAL JOURNEY WITH MARTIN SCORSESE THROUGH AMERICAN MOVIES, A
de Palma, Rossy
FLOWER OF MY SECRET, THE
de Pauw, Josse
PASSION OF DARKLY NOON, THE
De Pina, Sabrina
PHAT BEACH
de Prume, Cathryn
MRS. WINTERBOURNE
De Ray, Devin
PHAT BEACH
de Rochambeau, Angelique
ORIGINAL SINS
de Saint Phalle, Niki
NIKI DE SAINT PHALLE: WHO IS THE MONSTER — YOU OR ME?
de Salvo, Brian
MOLL FLANDERS
De Shields, Andre
EXTREME MEASURES
De Somber, Joel
HARVEST OF FIRE
De Souza, Edward
JANE EYRE
De Toth, Andre
PERSONAL JOURNEY WITH MARTIN SCORSESE THROUGH AMERICAN MOVIES, A
de Turckheim, Charlotte
PROPRIETOR, THE
de Vasquez, Juan Carlos
FEMALIEN
De Veaux, Nathaniel
HOMEWARD BOUND II: LOST IN SAN FRANCISCO
de Victor, Claudio
UNFORGETTABLE
De Villiers, Lisa
LIVE WIRE: HUMAN TIMEBOMB
De Young, Cliff
CRAFT, THE
JAG
Deacon, Robert
FLIPPER
TOLLBOOTH
Dead Moon
HYPE!
Deadrick Jr., Vince
COLONY, THE
Deadrick Sr., Vince
BROKEN ARROW
Deak, Michael S.
BEASTMASTER 3: THE EYE OF BRAXUS
DeAlessandro, Mark
DAYLIGHT
Deam, Jack
YOUNG POISONER'S HANDBOOK, THE
Dean, Erin
PIG'S TALE, A
Dean, Everett
EVIL HAS A FACE
Dean, Jennifer
STUPIDS, THE
Dean, Karyn J.
CRAFT, THE
Dean, Loren
MRS. WINTERBOURNE
PASSION OF DARKLY NOON, THE
Dean, Patrick
DON'T LET YOUR MEAT LOAF
Dean, Rick
BLACK SCORPION
CARNOSAUR 3: PRIMAL SPECIES
Dean, Ron
CHAIN REACTION
EYE FOR AN EYE
Deare, Morgan
MISSION: IMPOSSIBLE
DeBaer, Jean
PALLBEARER, THE
DeBarge, Flotilla
MERCY
DeBark, Yvonne
SONS OF TRINITY
DeBoeck, Antje
DAENS
deBoer, Nicole
KIDS IN THE HALL: BRAIN CANDY
Debrane, Michel
CELESTIAL CLOCKWORK
Debrosse, Eric
HORSEMAN ON THE ROOF
Decegli, Nicholas
FUNERAL, THE
Decker, Steve
ROCK, THE
Decker, Susan
MANNY & LO
Deckert, Blue
MAN WITH THE PERFECT SWING, THE
MICHAEL
Decleir, Jan
ANTONIA'S LINE
DAENS
DeClie, Xavier
ADRENALIN: FEAR THE RUSH
NEMESIS III: PREY HARDER
Ded, Jiri
DELTA OF VENUS
Dedet, Yann
FRANCOIS TRUFFAUT: STOLEN PORTRAITS
Deeg, Michael
SGT. KABUKIMAN N.Y.P.D.
Deekin, Ted
HAPPY GILMORE
Deezen, Eddie
SPY HARD
Deezer D.
GREAT WHITE HYPE, THE
DeFina, Don
WHARF RAT, THE
Deftones
CROW: CITY OF ANGELS, THE
Degan, Shea
CITIZEN RUTH
Degand, Johanne
MAN BY THE SHORE, THE
Degass, Andre
CONDITION RED
Degen, Yves
DAENS
DeGeneres, Ellen
MR. WRONG
Deger, Vicky
HEIDI FLEISS HOLLYWOOD MADAM
DeGivray, Claude
FRANCOIS TRUFFAUT: STOLEN PORTRAITS
DeGraff-Arenas, Patrice
EXIT
Degtyarenko, Eugeni
BURIAL OF THE RATS
DeHart, Wayne
TIME TO KILL, A
DeJongh, Jules
GRIM
Dekker, Eric
FRISK
Del Corral, Pedro Diaz
BATON ROUGE
Del Grande, Louis
SUGARTIME
Del Llano, Pedro
CELESTIAL CLOCKWORK
Del Mar, Maria
MOONSHINE HIGHWAY
TAILS YOU LIVE, HEADS YOU'RE DEAD
Del Negro, Vinny
EDDIE
Del Rey, Maria
SPY HARD
Del Rosario, Alex
MIDNIGHT DANCERS
Del Sherman, Barry
INDEPENDENCE DAY
Del Toro, Benicio
BASQUIAT

FAN, THE
FUNERAL, THE
Delagarde, Katia
VISITORS, THE
Delamere, Louise
SHAMELESS
DeLance, John
MULTIPLICITY
DeLancie, John
RAVENHAWK
Delaney, Kim
SERIAL KILLER
Delaney, Leon
DANGEROUS PASSION
Delaney, Rory
TWO FRIENDS
Delano, Diane
RATTLED
Delano, Lee
BIRDCAGE, THE
Delany, Dana
DEAD TO RIGHTS
FLY AWAY HOME
LIVE NUDE GIRLS
Delany, Grainne
SOME MOTHER'S SON
Delassanoro, Mark
FATALLY YOURS
DeLaurentis, Jimmy
MUTANT MAN
DelBono, Robert
DADETOWN
Delegall, Bob
SAINTS AND SINNERS
DeLeon, Luke
ADVENTURES OF PINOCCHIO, THE
Delerm, Graziella
NELLY AND MONSIEUR ARNAUD
Deleron, Tony
SHOOTFIGHTER 2: KILL OR BE KILLED!
Delgado, Kim
EDDIE
Delien, Lisa
SANTA CLAWS
Delizia, Melissa
INFINITY
Dell, Howard
HALFBACK OF NOTRE DAME, THE
Dell Jr., Gabriel
SOMETIMES THEY COME BACK . . . AGAIN
Della, Jay
SUNSET PARK
Dellar, Lois
BIG BULLY
Delmont, Jim
CITIZEN RUTH
Delofski, Sevilla
TWO DEATHS
Delpi, Jacques
THREE LIVES AND ONLY ONE DEATH
Delpy, Albert
MAN BY THE SHORE, THE
RIDICULE
Deluise, Dom
ALL DOGS GO TO HEAVEN 2
DeLuise, Dom
RED LINE
DeLuise, Michael
SHOT, THE
DeMangus, Louise
PRE-MADONNAS
DeMaree, Richard
SGT. KABUKIMAN N.Y.P.D.
Dembele, Habib
GUIMBA THE TYRANT
Demeger, Robert
YOUNG POISONER'S HANDBOOK, THE
Demers, Todd
TIME TO KILL, A
Demerus, Ellen
CHILDREN OF NOISY VILLAGE, THE
Demidio, Regis
BLONDES HAVE MORE GUNS
Demir, Alex
WATCH ME
Demme, Jonathan
THAT THING YOU DO!
Demolon, Pascal
LAND AND FREEDOM
DeMoss, Darcy
DEATH ARTIST, THE
FORBIDDEN ZONE: ALIEN ABDUCTION
Dempsey, Brendan
MOLL FLANDERS
Dempsey, Patrick
BLOODKNOT
DeMunn, Jeffrey
PHENOMENON
Dench, Judi
HAMLET
JACK & SARAH
Denchev, Kliment
HOLLOW POINT
Deneuve, Catherine
LES VOLEURS
MA SAISON PREFEREE
Denga, Andrei
MAXIMUM RISK
Denize, Eric
VISITORS, THE
Denman, Tony
FARGO
Denmark, Brenda Thomas
WALKING AND TALKING
Dennehey, Brian
WILLIAM SHAKESPEARE'S ROMEO + JULIET
Dennehy, Elizabeth
LAZARUS MAN, THE
Dennehy, J. Kelly
LOOKING FOR TROUBLE
Denney, David
LARRY MCMURTRY'S STREETS OF LAREDO
Denney, Nora
TRUMAN
Dennis, Jon
KINGPIN
Denny, Paul
TUNNEL VISION
Dent, Chester
SOME FOLKS CALL IT A SLING BLADE
Dente, Joey
SPY HARD
Denton, Lucas
LOSING CHASE
Denzler, Cynthia
WHISPERING, THE
DePalma, Vincent
SKYSCRAPER
TIGER HEART
Depardieu, Gerard
BOGUS
FRANCOIS TRUFFAUT: STOLEN PORTRAITS
HAMLET
HORSEMAN ON THE ROOF
JOSEPH CONRAD'S THE SECRET AGENT
MACHINE, THE
UNHOOK THE STARS
Depardieu, Julie
MACHINE, THE
Depp, Johnny
DEAD MAN
DePriest, Teresa
FIRST WIVES CLUB, THE
Derbyshire, Jan
DEVOTION
Dereppe, Claude
RIDICULE
Derey, Mike
LIFEFORM
Dern, Bruce
DOWN PERISCOPE
LAST MAN STANDING
MOTHER'S PRAYER, A
MRS. MUNCK
MULHOLLAND FALLS
Dern, Laura
CITIZEN RUTH
Derocker, Jeff
EVERYONE SAYS I LOVE YOU
DeRose, Chris
BREAKAWAY
Deruddere, Vic
SUITE 16
Des Barres, Michael
WIDOW'S KISS
Desai, Shelly
BARB WIRE
CROW: CITY OF ANGELS, THE
JOHN CARPENTER'S ESCAPE FROM L.A.
DeSantis, Stanley
BIRDCAGE, THE
FAN, THE
TRUTH ABOUT CATS AND DOGS, THE
Desarthe, Gerard
DAENS
Desert, Alex
SWINGERS
Desny, Ivan
LES VOLEURS
Despotovich, Nada
JERRY MAGUIRE
Desroses, Thierry
LITTLE INDIAN, BIG CITY
Desselle, Natalie
SET IT OFF
DeStaebler, David
MANNY & LO
DeStefano, Juliehera
FIRST WIVES CLUB, THE
PREACHER'S WIFE, THE
Destrey, John
SURGEON, THE
Destry, John
HAPPY GILMORE
Detmers, Maruschka
HIDDEN ASSASSIN
Detroit, Michael
PEOPLE VS. LARRY FLYNT, THE
Devancker, Frederic
STUPIDS, THE
Deveaux, Nathaniel
UNFORGETTABLE
Devenie, Stuart
FRIGHTENERS, THE
Devine, Aidan
IRON EAGLE IV
Devine, Christine
CABLE GUY, THE
INDEPENDENCE DAY
Devine, Loretta
PREACHER'S WIFE, THE
DeVito, Danny
MARS ATTACKS!

MATILDA
SPACE JAM
Devitt, Conor
HARRIET THE SPY
Devitt, Matthew
FUNNYMAN, THE
Devlin, Alan
WAR OF THE BUTTONS, THE
Devlin, Billy
ROCK, THE
Devlin, Carolyn
TWO FRIENDS
Devlin, Chris
HOURGLASS
Devlin, Christopher Mathew
PURE DANGER
Devlin, Leslie
RANSOM
Devnarain, Jack
GHOST AND THE DARKNESS, THE
Devney, James
CITIZEN RUTH
Dewey, John
LIFEFORM
Dewhurst, Colleen
LINE KING: THE AL HIRSCHFELD STORY, THE
DeWolf, Paul
KINGPIN
Dey, Janet
EYE FOR AN EYE
Deyle, John
BEFORE AND AFTER
DeYoung, Cliff
SUBSTITUTE, THE
Dheran, Bernard
RIDICULE
Di Carmine, Maurizio
WHO KILLED PASOLINI?
Di Carpegna, Allegra
IN LOVE AND WAR
Di Ciaula, Clarizio
WHO KILLED PASOLINI?
Di Donna, Gian
FUNERAL, THE
Di Maggio, John
EDDIE
Di Mambro, Joseph
TWO IF BY SEA
Di Marco, Dyanne
ELECTRA
Di Mazzarelli, Carmelo
STAR MAKER, THE
Di Modica, Maryanne
CELTIC PRIDE
Di Pinto, Nicola
STAR MAKER, THE
di Tomassi, Stefano
CEMETERY MAN
Diakun, Alex
SURGEON, THE
Dial, Rick
SLING BLADE
Diallo, Lamine
GUIMBA THE TYRANT
Diamond, Joe
APART FROM HUGH
Diarra, Helene
GUIMBA THE TYRANT
Diaz, Cameron
FEELING MINNESOTA
LAST SUPPER, THE
SHE'S THE ONE
Diaz, Edith
FAN, THE
Diaz, Guillermo
GIRLS TOWN
HIGH SCHOOL HIGH
I'M NOT RAPPAPORT
STONEWALL
Diaz, Julio
SILENCE OF NETO, THE
Diaz, Rafael
BATON ROUGE
LAND AND FREEDOM
DiBenedetto, Giovanni
DAENS
DiBenedetto, John
SLEEPERS
DiBenedetto, Tony
DANGEROUS PASSION
Diblasio, Raffi
INFINITY
DiCaprio, Leonardo
MARVIN'S ROOM
WILLIAM SHAKESPEARE'S ROMEO + JULIET
DiCenzo, George
DOWN, OUT AND DANGEROUS
DiCicco, Bobby
ALL DOGS GO TO HEAVEN 2
Dick, Andy
CABLE GUY, THE
Dickens, Joanna
COLD LIGHT OF DAY
Dickens, Kim
PALOOKAVILLE
Dickenson, Bonnie
FRISK
Dickerson, Jacqueline
BULLETPROOF
Dickerson, Lori Lynn
BLOODSPORT II: THE NEXT KUMITE
Dickinson, Angie
MADDENING, THE
Dickinson, James
CELTIC PRIDE
Dickinson, Luke
BLACK SHEEP
Dicko, Solo
HATE
Dickson, Jain
STAND OFF, THE
DiCocco, Paulie
THAT THING YOU DO!
Didawick, Dawn
I SHOT ANDY WARHOL
Didi, Evelyne
CELESTIAL CLOCKWORK
die Gottliche, Tima
NEUROSIA: 50 YEARS OF PERVERSITY
Diego, Gabino
TWO MUCH
Diehl, John
AMANDA AND THE ALIEN
FOXFIRE
GRAVE, THE
LAZARUS MAN, THE
MIND RIPPER
TIME TO KILL, A
Diehl, Veronique
MAXIMUM RISK
Diekman, Mark
BEWARE: CHILDREN AT PLAY
Dierdorf, Dan
JERRY MAGUIRE
Dierkop, Charlie
TOO FAST, TOO YOUNG
Dietlein, Marsha
RUMPELSTILTSKIN
Dignan, Stephen
BOTTLE ROCKET
Dijon, Rocky
ROLLING STONES ROCK-AND-ROLL CIRCUS, THE
Dikker, Ellen
ANTONIA'S LINE
Dill, Deena
LAST DANCE
Dillane, Stephen
TWO IF BY SEA
Dillinger, Darlene
THAT THING YOU DO!
Dillon, Brook
FRISK
Dillon, Hugh
CURTIS'S CHARM
Dillon, Kevin
CRIMINAL HEARTS
Dillon, Matt
BEAUTIFUL GIRLS
GRACE OF MY HEART
Dillon, Melinda
ENTERTAINING ANGELS: THE DOROTHY DAY STORY
Dillon, Thom
CLUBHOUSE DETECTIVES
Dilts, Liz
PUBLIC ACCESS
Dilworth, Grant
FOR THE MOMENT
DiMaggio, Lou
RICH MAN'S WIFE, THE
Dimitri, Nick
DANGEROUS PASSION
Dimopoulos, Stephen
HAPPY GILMORE
Dimvale, Misu
OUTPOST, THE
Dingo, Ernie
WEEKEND IN THE COUNTRY, A
Dini, Bob
DOWN PERISCOPE
Dinsdale, Reece
HAMLET
Diola, Jay
SWINGERS
Dionisi, Stefano
MILLE BOLLE BLU
Diot, Maureen
FRENCH TWIST
DiPego, Justin
PHENOMENON
Dirty Mac, The
ROLLING STONES ROCK-AND-ROLL CIRCUS, THE
Dispina, Teresa
BIG SQUEEZE, THE
Ditson, Harry
COLD COMFORT FARM
Divac, Ana
EDDIE
Divac, Vlade
EDDIE
Divoff, Andrew
ADRENALIN: FEAR THE RUSH
BACKLASH: OBLIVION 2
Dixon, Benjamin J.
MR. HOLLAND'S OPUS
Dixon, Maggie Wade
TIME TO KILL, A
Dixon, Reverend Phil
SWINGERS
Dixon-Green, Rosebud
TIME TO KILL, A
DJ Tim
SHOPPING
Djola, Badja
HEAVEN'S PRISONERS
Dlada, Mbali
YANKEE ZULU
Doan, C.R.
GHOSTS OF MISSISSIPPI

Dobrowsky, Frantz
LIVE WIRE: HUMAN TIMEBOMB
Dobry, Karel
MISSION: IMPOSSIBLE
Dobson, Peter
BIG SQUEEZE, THE
DEAD COLD
FRIGHTENERS, THE
NORMA JEAN AND MARILYN
Dobtcheff, Vernon
JUDE
Docky
KINGPIN
Dodd, Ken
HAMLET
Dodge, Edgar
MAN WITH A PLAN
Dodley, Lewis
CITY HALL
RANSOM
Doduk, Alex
ROAD HOME, THE
Doe, Leonardo
DADETOWN
Doering, Erica
LITTLE WITCHES
Doggart, Evelyn
MARY REILLY
Doggett, Walter
CHAIN REACTION
Dogherty, Bob
BREAKING THE WAVES
Doherty, Conan
MR. HOLLAND'S OPUS
Doherty, Matt
D3: THE MIGHTY DUCKS
Dokic, Maya
MISSION: IMPOSSIBLE
Dolan, Michael
COURAGE UNDER FIRE
Dolce, Domenico
STAR MAKER, THE
Dole, Bob
OVER THE WIRE
Dolezar, Gerald
DADETOWN
Doll, Cheryl
SHAMELESS
Dollaghan, Patrick
UNDER THE HULA MOON
Dolle, Gaston
LITTLE INDIAN, BIG CITY
Dollson, Ed
PUBLIC ENEMIES
Doman, John
BEAVIS AND BUTT-HEAD DO AMERICA
Dombasle, Arielle
CELESTIAL CLOCKWORK
LITTLE INDIAN, BIG CITY
THREE LIVES AND ONLY ONE DEATH
Domiano, Patricia
MAN OF THE YEAR
Dominguez, Claudio
LAND AND FREEDOM
Don, Carl
RANSOM
Donahower, James
DELTA OF VENUS
Donahue, Elinor
DEAR GOD
Donahue, Joe
MERCY
Donald, Juli
SHARON'S SECRET
Donald, William L.
GHOSTS OF MISSISSIPPI
Donato, Charles
DEAD TO RIGHTS
Dondertman, John
CURTIS'S CHARM
Done, Jason
ENGLISH PATIENT, THE
Donella, Chad
LONG KISS GOODNIGHT, THE
Donis, Renato
CEMETERY MAN
Donnell, Evans
PEOPLE VS. LARRY FLYNT, THE
Donnelly, Kate
TRAINSPOTTING
Donnelly, Kathy
THEY BITE
Donovan
MESSAGE TO LOVE: THE ISLE OF WIGHT FESTIVAL
Donovan, Jeffrey
SLEEPERS
Donovan, Martin
FLIRT
PORTRAIT OF A LADY, THE
Donovan, Tate
AMERICA'S DREAM
Donzell, James
TAKEOVER, THE
Doolan, Trish
MOTHER'S PRAYER, A
Dooley, Brian
PORTRAITS OF A KILLER
Dooley, Paul
OUT THERE
Doonan, Paul
SMALL FACES
Doors, The
MESSAGE TO LOVE: THE ISLE OF WIGHT FESTIVAL
Dopman, Susu
SGT. KABUKIMAN N.Y.P.D.
Dore, Mike
SHOOTFIGHTER 2: KILL OR BE KILLED!
Doresa, Reginald
LONG KISS GOODNIGHT, THE
Dorff, Stephen
I SHOT ANDY WARHOL
Dorish, John
RANSOM
Dorkin, Cody
COLONY, THE
Dorman, John
DONOR UNKNOWN
Dorn, Michael
AMANDA AND THE ALIEN
STAR TREK: FIRST CONTACT
VIRTUAL COMBAT
Dorsey, Diane
NORMAL LIFE
Dorsey, Kevin
ADVENTURES OF PINOCCHIO, THE
Dorval, Adrien
ALASKA
Dorza, Don
ROAD HOME, THE
Dost, Bano
FLIRT
Dotson, Rhonda
MAN OF THE YEAR
Dotten, Irv L.
GREAT WHITE HYPE, THE
Dottermans, Els
ANTONIA'S LINE
Doucette, Suzanne
MISSION: IMPOSSIBLE
Dougal, Miles
BARB WIRE
Douglas, Alice
HAUNTED
Douglas, Angela
HAMLET
Douglas, Hazel
YOUNG POISONER'S HANDBOOK, THE
Douglas, Illeana
4 TALES OF 2 CITIES
GRACE OF MY HEART
Douglas, Jeff
SHOWGIRL MURDERS, THE
Douglas, Jonathan
DADETOWN
Douglas, Malcolm
MICHAEL COLLINS
Douglas, Michael
GHOST AND THE DARKNESS, THE
Douglas, Paul
TWISTER
Douglas, Robin
HOMEWARD BOUND II: LOST IN SAN FRANCISCO
TALES FROM THE CRYPT PRESENTS BORDELLO OF BLOOD
UNFORGETTABLE
Douglas, Sam
MISSION: IMPOSSIBLE
Douglas, Sarah
DEMOLITIONIST, THE
Douglass, Charles
DANGEROUS PASSION
Douglass, Diane
FLY AWAY HOME
GETTING AWAY WITH MURDER
Doukoure, Cheik
LITTLE INDIAN, BIG CITY
Doumani Jr., Frederick Malick
BEYOND DESIRE
Dourdan, Gary
SUNSET PARK
Dourif, Brad
BLACK OUT
PHOENIX
Dow, Bill
BIG BULLY
Dow, Lauren
IT CAME FROM OUTER SPACE II
Dowd, Ned
BOTTLE ROCKET
Dowe, Don
RUMPELSTILTSKIN
Dowie, Freda
BUTTERFLY KISS
JUDE
Dowling, Bairbre
WAR OF THE BUTTONS, THE
Down, Angela
EMMA
Down, Dru
ORIGINAL GANGSTAS
Down, Lesley-Anne
BEASTMASTER 3: THE EYE OF BRAXUS
Downer, Wayne
BEYOND THE CALL
Downey, Ferne
TWO IF BY SEA
Downie, Louise
CRACKER: THE MADWOMAN IN THE ATTIC
Dowse, Denise
BIO-DOME
Dowson, Mike
DEAD MAN
Doyle, Chris
FOREST WARRIOR
LAST MAN STANDING
Doyle, David
ADVENTURES OF PINOCCHIO, THE
Doyle, Patrick
MIDWINTER'S TALE, A

Doyle, Shawn
DARKMAN III: DIE DARKMAN DIE
LONG KISS GOODNIGHT, THE
Doyle, Tad
HYPE!
Doyle, Tracey
MICHAEL
Doyle-Murray, Brian
MULTIPLICITY
Dr. Dre
SET IT OFF
Draber, Etienne
RIDICULE
Drago, Billy
MAD DOG TIME
MIRROR, MIRROR III: THE VOYEUR
PHOENIX
TAKEOVER, THE
Drake, Bebe
NORMA JEAN AND MARILYN
Drake, Jessica
TRUMAN
Drake, Judith
NECRONOMICON: BOOK OF THE DEAD
RUMPELSTILTSKIN
Drake, Nancy
HECK'S WAY HOME
Drakeford, Deborah
MAN IN THE ATTIC, THE
Draper, Aurora
SCREAM
Draper, Tell
CHAIN REACTION
Dreger, Reg
SUGARTIME
Dremann, Beau
SHARON'S SECRET
Drescher, Fran
JACK
Dreschler, Adam
FATALLY YOURS
Drew, Sheron
VIRTUAL ENCOUNTERS
Drewy, Chris
WAR AT HOME, THE
Dreyer, Dianne
MICHAEL
Dreyfus, Jean-Claude
ADVENTURES OF PINOCCHIO, THE
SHADOW OF ANGELS
Dreyfuss, Richard
JAMES AND THE GIANT PEACH
MAD DOG TIME
MR. HOLLAND'S OPUS
Driscoll, Delaney
CITIZEN RUTH
Driscoll, Eddie
NOT OF THIS EARTH
Driscoll, Tim
CITIZEN RUTH
Driver, Minnie
BIG NIGHT
SLEEPERS
Drogo, Martin
EVITA
Drose, Robert
EVIL ED
Drouot, Jean-Claude
ADVENTURES OF PINOCCHIO, THE
Drozda, Peter
HIDDEN ASSASSIN
Drum, Paul
DADETOWN
Drummond, Alice
WALKING AND TALKING
Drummond, Charles
MAXIMUM RISK
Drummond, John
CHAIN REACTION
Drummond, Tam
PEOPLE VS. LARRY FLYNT, THE
Druxman, Adam
FAN, THE
Dryhurst, Nia
HEDD WYNN
du Jannerand, Philippe
RIDICULE
Du Plessis, J. D.
TERMINAL IMPACT
Du Re, Flo
MOTHER
Duarte, Herbie
WELCOME TO THE DOLLHOUSE
Dube, Lilian
YANKEE ZULU
Dubin, Brad Joseph
WIDOW'S KISS
Dubois, Jean-Yves
PROPRIETOR, THE
DuBois, Marta
BLACK OUT
Dubouche, Gerard
HORSEMAN ON THE ROOF
Ducato, Onofrio
STAR MAKER, THE
Ducey, John
HIGH SCHOOL HIGH
RUMPELSTILTSKIN
Duchene, Deborah
SUGARTIME
Duchesne, Albert
FRANCOIS TRUFFAUT: STOLEN PORTRAITS
Duchkova, Eva
DELTA OF VENUS
Duckworth, George
DEAD MAN
Duckworth, Todd
GIRL FROM MARS, THE
SUGARTIME
Duclos, Philippe
MAGIC HUNTER
Dudgeon, Alex
MR. HOLLAND'S OPUS
Dudley, Bronson
TREES LOUNGE
Dudley, Lucas
SOLO
Duell, William
PALOOKAVILLE
Duerr, Nancy
OFF AND RUNNING
Duff, Denice
PHOENIX
Duffert, Nicola
SHAMELESS
Duffy, Donna M.
BULLETPROOF
Duffy, J.S.
SMALL FACES
Duffy, Quinn
NUTTY PROFESSOR, THE
PLAYBACK
Duffy, Thomas
FAN, THE
Duffy, Thomas F.
INDEPENDENCE DAY
Dugan, Dennis
HAPPY GILMORE
Dugan, Marion
CABLE GUY, THE
MATILDA
Dugan, Tom
HELLRAISER: BLOODLINE
Duge, Melissa
TIMELESS
Duhame, Zack
MULTIPLICITY
Duhler, Christine
MIDNIGHT ANGEL
Dukakis, Olympia
MR. HOLLAND'S OPUS
MOTHER
Duke, Patty
HARVEST OF FIRE
Duke, Robin
MULTIPLICITY
Dukes, David
FLED
NORMA JEAN AND MARILYN
Dulli, Gregory
BEAUTIFUL GIRLS
Dumas, Jean-Claude
HORSEMAN ON THE ROOF
Dumas, Roger
NEW LIFE, A
Dumaurier, Francis
BASQUIAT
BEAVIS AND BUTT-HEAD DO AMERICA
Dumochel, Steve
SUBSTITUTE, THE
Dumouchel, Steve
MARVIN'S ROOM
Dun, Dennis
UP CLOSE AND PERSONAL
VENUS RISING
Dunaway, Faye
CHAMBER, THE
DUNSTON CHECKS IN
Dunbar, Adrian
CRACKER: THE MADWOMAN IN THE ATTIC
Dunbar, Dorian
TRIGGER EFFECT, THE
Dunbar, Ted
PREACHER'S WIFE, THE
Duncan, Alexe
OPEN SEASON
Duncan, Andy
THAT THING YOU DO!
Duncan, Arlene
EXTREME MEASURES
Duncan, Bruce
THEY BITE
Duncan, Bunk
LARRY MCMURTRY'S STREETS OF LAREDO
Duncan, Christopher B.
ORIGINAL GANGSTAS
Duncan, Kelly
KAZAAM
Duncan, Lindsay
CITY HALL
Duncan, Rachel
ONE MAN'S JUSTICE
RUMPELSTILTSKIN
Duncanson, Jon
PRIMAL FEAR
Dundas, Jennifer
FIRST WIVES CLUB, THE
Dunlap, Cirocco
JAMES AND THE GIANT PEACH
Dunlop, David
BOGUS
Dunlop, Marissa
JANE EYRE
Dunlop, William
WHARF RAT, THE
Dunn, Colleen
EVERYONE SAYS I LOVE YOU

Dunn, Kevin
CHAIN REACTION
JAG
Dunn, Nora
LAST SUPPER, THE
Dunn, Roger
HOMECOMING
LEGEND OF GATOR FACE, THE
Dunn, Ryan
LIFEFORM
Dunn, Silk Willie
SUNSET PARK
Dunne, Martin
WAR OF THE BUTTONS, THE
Dunne, Robin
ROAD HOME, THE
Dunne, Roger
OPEN SEASON
Dunphy, Jerry
INDEPENDENCE DAY
Dunst, Kirsten
MOTHER NIGHT
Dunster, Wilson
YANKEE ZULU
Dunye, Cheryl
GIRLFRIENDS
Duong, Anh
I SHOT ANDY WARHOL
Dupois, Starletta
LET'S GET BIZZEE
ROAD TO GALVESTON, THE
Duppin, Andy
GIRL 6
Dupree, Stephen
PEOPLE VS. LARRY FLYNT, THE
Dupuis, Diana
MAHJONG
Dupuis, Roy
SCREAMERS
Duran, Dan
MAXIMUM RISK
Duran, Gonzalo
OUTRAGE
Duran, Ignacio
BATON ROUGE
Duran, Reynaldo
CROW: CITY OF ANGELS, THE
Durand, Brandon
KAZAAM
Durand, Jared
BOGUS
Durbin, John
TRUMAN
Durek, Jaroslav
KASPAR HAUSER
Duret, Marc
HATE
During, Allison Joy
SMALL WONDERS
Duringer, Annemarie
SHADOW OF ANGELS
Durning, Charles
GRASS HARP, THE
LAND BEFORE TIME IV: JOURNEY THROUGH THE MISTS
LAST SUPPER, THE
ONE FINE DAY
SPY HARD
Dury, Ian
CROW: CITY OF ANGELS, THE
Dushku, Eliza
RACE THE SUN
Dutton, Charles S.
GET ON THE BUS
TIME TO KILL, A
Duval, James
INDEPENDENCE DAY

Duvall, Clea
LITTLE WITCHES
Duvall, Robert
FAMILY THING, A
PHENOMENON
SLING BLADE
Duvall, Shelley
PORTRAIT OF A LADY, THE
Duvall, Wayne
BAJA
FAN, THE
MY FELLOW AMERICANS
Duvernay, Natalie
PHAT BEACH
Dvorak, Daniel
DELTA OF VENUS
Dvorakova, Alice
KASPAR HAUSER
Dwyer, David
EDDIE
FLED
PEOPLE VS. LARRY FLYNT, THE
Dwyer, Jack
TUSKEGEE AIRMEN, THE
Dwyer, Kerry
TWO FRIENDS
Dwyer, Michael
MICHAEL COLLINS
Dye, Dale
MISSION: IMPOSSIBLE
SGT. BILKO
WITHIN THE ROCK
Dye, Steven
DON'T LET YOUR MEAT LOAF
Dyer, Clint
SHOPPING
Dyer, Dwight
LIFEFORM
Dyer, Dwight Brad
PRIMAL FEAR
Dyer, Richard
CELLULOID CLOSET, THE
Dyer, Sharon
KIDS IN THE HALL: BRAIN CANDY
Dykes, Joseph
QUEST, THE
Dykstra, Jan
SWINGERS
Dylan, Paige
GRACE OF MY HEART
Dysart, Richard
TRUMAN
Dywik, Peter
CHILDREN OF NOISY VILLAGE, THE
Eadie, Victor
TRAINSPOTTING
Earl, Danny
MADAGASCAR SKIN
Earle, Frankie
DADETOWN
Earnhart, Stephen
CHILDREN OF THE CORN: THE GATHERING
Eastin, Steve
ED
SWEEPER, THE
Eastman, Marilyn
SANTA CLAWS
Easton, Elliot
DOWN PERISCOPE
Easton, Sheena
ALL DOGS GO TO HEAVEN 2
Eastwood, Clint
PERSONAL JOURNEY WITH MARTIN SCORSESE THROUGH AMERICAN MOVIES, A
Eaton, Eddie
BLOODSPORT II: THE NEXT KUMITE

Eaton, Marion
WHOLE WIDE WORLD, THE
Eberhard, Fabrice
RIDICULE
Ebersole, Christine
BLACK SHEEP
PIE IN THE SKY
Ebersole, Drew
INFINITY
Ebner, Eva
NEUROSIA: 50 YEARS OF PERVERSITY
Ebony, Jo-Ann
EDDIE
Eccleston, Christopher
CRACKER: THE MADWOMAN IN THE ATTIC
JUDE
Echanove, Juan
FLOWER OF MY SECRET, THE
Echols, Damien Wayne
PARADISE LOST: THE CHILD MURDERS AT ROBIN HOOD HILLS
Echols, Pan
PARADISE LOST: THE CHILD MURDERS AT ROBIN HOOD HILLS
Eckert, David
PRIMAL FEAR
Eckman, Chris
HYPE!
Eckstrom, Lauren
TWO-BITS & PEPPER
Eda-Young, Barbara
SUBSTANCE OF FIRE, THE
Eddy, M. Caroline
APART FROM HUGH
Eddy, Sonya
HIGH SCHOOL HIGH
Edelman, Gregg
FIRST WIVES CLUB, THE
Edelman, Jeff
MURDERED INNOCENCE
Edelman, Steve
FARGO
Eden, Richard
PUBLIC ENEMIES
Edenetti, Nick
ORIGINAL GANGSTAS
Edfeldt, Catti
CHILDREN OF NOISY VILLAGE, THE
Edfeldt, Tove
CHILDREN OF NOISY VILLAGE, THE
Edgar, William
MADAME WANG'S
Edgerton, Joel
RACE THE SUN
Edmonds, Michael
FULL BODY MASSAGE
Edmonds, Samantha
YOUNG POISONER'S HANDBOOK, THE
Edmund, Justin Pierre
PREACHER'S WIFE, THE
Edmunds, Dartanyan
THIN LINE BETWEEN LOVE AND HATE, A
Edney, Beatie
AFFAIR, THE
Edney, Tyus
EDDIE
Edson, Richard
BAD LOVE
Edwards, Chris
EXTREME MEASURES
Edwards, D'Urville
SANDMAN, THE
Edwards, Daryl
ASSOCIATE, THE
Edwards, Eric
SGT. BILKO

Edwards, Frank
FRIGHTENERS, THE
Edwards, James L.
POLYMORPH
SANDMAN, THE
Edwards, Jeillo
BEAUTIFUL THING
Edwards, Rob
HAMLET
Edwards, Valerie Inez
PREACHER'S WIFE, THE
Edwards, Victoria
TRUTH ABOUT CATS AND DOGS, THE
Efroni, Yehuda
DEADLY OUTBREAK
Egan, Maggie
EXECUTIVE DECISION
Egelhof, Kurt
GHOST AND THE DARKNESS, THE
LIVE WIRE: HUMAN TIMEBOMB
Eggar, Samantha
PHANTOM, THE
Eggert, Fritz
ENGLISH PATIENT, THE
Eggert, Nicole
AMANDA AND THE ALIEN
DEMOLITIONIST, THE
Eggleston, Devin
ED'S NEXT MOVE
Eggleton, Mathew
LOADED
Eginton, Zack
EYE FOR AN EYE
RATTLED
Egoyan, Atom
STUPIDS, THE
Ehrlich, Christina
GRACE OF MY HEART
Eichenberger, Merrill
BREAKAWAY
Eichhorn, Lisa
FIRST KID
MODERN AFFAIR, A
Eichling, James
EVIL HAS A FACE
Eiding, Paul
BIO-DOME
Eilber, Janet
CRAFT, THE
Einhorn, Faryn
TRUTH ABOUT CATS AND DOGS, THE
Eirek, Sten
ELECTRA
Eisenberg, Kristy K.
SHOOTFIGHTER 2: KILL OR BE KILLED!
Eisenberg, Ned
LAST MAN STANDING
Eisenberg, Shawn
MRS. WINTERBOURNE
Eisenschitz, Anne-Marie
CHASING BUTTERFLIES
Eisermann, Andre
BROTHER OF SLEEP
KASPAR HAUSER
Eisner, David
EXTREME MEASURES
Ejdus, Predrag
SOMEONE ELSE'S AMERICA
VUKOVAR
Ek, Anders
EVIL ED
Ekstrand, Laura
I SHOT ANDY WARHOL
El Mecky, Khaldoun
CROCODILES IN AMSTERDAM
Elam, Greg
CHAMBER, THE
Elam, Ousaun
BROKEN ARROW
RUMPELSTILTSKIN
Elboim, Yehuda
DEADLY OUTBREAK
Eldard, Ron
LAST SUPPER, THE
SLEEPERS
Elder, Paul
LATE SHIFT, THE
Eldridge, Craig
BEYOND THE CALL
LONG KISS GOODNIGHT, THE
MRS. WINTERBOURNE
Eldridge, Kevin
EXECUTIVE DECISION
Eleniak, Erika
TALES FROM THE CRYPT PRESENTS BORDELLO OF BLOOD
Elevins, Shanah S.
DEMOLITIONIST, THE
Elfman, Bodhi Pine
VERY BRADY SEQUEL, A
Elfvin, Hanna
EVIL ED
Elg, Taina
MIRROR HAS TWO FACES, THE
Elgort, Arthur
CATWALK
Eli, Lovie
TALES FROM THE CRYPT PRESENTS BORDELLO OF BLOOD
Elias, Carmen
FLOWER OF MY SECRET, THE
Elias, Hector
MR. WRONG
Elias, Rick
THAT THING YOU DO!
Eliopoulos, Paul
SPY HARD
Eliot, Su
SECRETS & LIES
Eliot, Tom
AMERICAN STRAYS
Elise, Kimberly
SET IT OFF
Elizondo, Hector
DEAR GOD
Ellerinei
NORMA JEAN AND MARILYN
Elliot, Caroline
UNFORGETTABLE
Elliot, Deanna
APART FROM HUGH
Elliot, Shawn
CAUGHT
Elliott, Alison
SPITFIRE GRILL, THE
Elliott, Chris
KINGPIN
Elliott, David James
JAG
Elliott, Larry
EVENING STAR, THE
Elliott, Mike
BLACK SCORPION
Elliott, Patricia
CRIMINAL HEARTS
Elliott, Peter
ISLAND OF DR. MOREAU, THE
Elliott, Peter Anthony
PRE-MADONNAS
Elliott, Sam
FINAL CUT, THE
WOMAN UNDONE, A
Ellis, Ananda
SOMEONE ELSE'S AMERICA
Ellis, Aunjanue
ED'S NEXT MOVE
GIRLS TOWN
Ellis, Chris
THAT THING YOU DO!
Ellis, Gwen
HEDD WYNN
Ellis, James
SPELLBREAKER: SECRET OF THE LEPRECHAUNS
Ellis, Jimmy
HAMLET
Ellis, John
PUBLIC ACCESS
Ellis, Salle
CHILDREN OF THE CORN: THE GATHERING
ROAD TO GALVESTON, THE
Ellis, Shawn
PUBLIC ACCESS
Ellis, Tracey
CROW: CITY OF ANGELS, THE
Ellison, Disraeli
CHAMBER, THE
Ellison, Tara
POISON IVY 2: LILY
Ellwand, Gregg
SUGARTIME
Elrod, Lu
HIGH SCHOOL HIGH
Elwes, Cary
TWISTER
Elwood, Rich
HAPPY GILMORE
Emane, Virginie
SINGLE GIRL, A
Embry, Ethan
THAT THING YOU DO!
WHITE SQUALL
Embry, Gordon
SET IT OFF
Emergency Broadcast Network
SONIC OUTLAWS
Emerson, Jonathan
MARS ATTACKS!
Emerson, Patrick
REDEMPTION: KICKBOXER 5
Emerson, Lake & Palmer
MESSAGE TO LOVE: THE ISLE OF WIGHT FESTIVAL
Emery, Gideon
LIVE WIRE: HUMAN TIMEBOMB
Emingholz, Heinz
BROTHER OF SLEEP
Emmerich, Noah
BEAUTIFUL GIRLS
Emori, Hiroko
BIG WARS
Emoto, Akira
MABOROSI
Empie, Ken
THAT THING YOU DO!
Empson, Tameka
BEAUTIFUL THING
Endino, Jack
HYPE!
Endoso, Kenny
LAWNMOWER MAN 2: BEYOND CYBERSPACE
Endsley, Andrew
LIFEFORM
Eng, Arthur
FRAME BY FRAME
STUPIDS, THE
Eng, Tara
MR. HOLLAND'S OPUS
Engel, Bernie
EDDIE

England, Audie
DELTA OF VENUS
ONE GOOD TURN
VENUS RISING
England, Gary
TWISTER
England, Peter
HAUNTED
English, Alex
EDDIE
English, Andrew
DOWN PERISCOPE
SPY HARD
English, Tiara
DON'T BE A MENACE TO SOUTH CENTRAL WHILE DRINKING YOUR JUICE IN THE HOOD
PHAT BEACH
Englund, Morgan
CARNOSAUR 3: PRIMAL SPECIES
Ennis, Paul
CROSSCUT
Enomoto, Ken
MY FELLOW AMERICANS
Enos III, John
ROCK, THE
Enos, John
RAVENHAWK
Enos, Lakeya
PREACHER'S WIFE, THE
Enos, Taleah
PREACHER'S WIFE, THE
Enriquez, Mercedes
HARRIET THE SPY
Entius, Yolanda
CROCODILES IN AMSTERDAM
Entwhistle, John
ROLLING STONES ROCK-AND-ROLL CIRCUS, THE
Epper, Curtis
CHAMBER, THE
Epper, Gary
BROKEN ARROW
Epperson, Van
HEAD OF THE FAMILY
Epps, Omar
DON'T BE A MENACE TO SOUTH CENTRAL WHILE DRINKING YOUR JUICE IN THE HOOD
Epstein, Jon
ADRENALIN: FEAR THE RUSH
NEMESIS III: PREY HARDER
Erb, Billy
I SHOT ANDY WARHOL
Erickson, Anne W.
BEAUTIFUL GIRLS
Erickson, Ethan
TWO-BITS & PEPPER
Erickson, Nick
MAHJONG
Erikson, Kaj-Eric
GIRL FROM MARS, THE
Eriksson, Sigfrid
CHILDREN OF NOISY VILLAGE, THE
Erin, Bryn
LAST SUPPER, THE
Eriquel, Mercedes
SUBSTITUTE, THE
Erker, Joe
TRUMAN
Ermey, R. Lee
FRIGHTENERS, THE
UNDER THE HULA MOON
Ernest, Loetta
BULLETPROOF
Erskine, Howard
STEPHEN KING'S THINNER
Ertmanis, Victor
BLOODKNOT
STUPIDS, THE
Ervini, Simone
CEMETERY MAN
Erwin, Bill
JUST YOUR LUCK
Erwin, Gail
CITIZEN RUTH
Erwin, Jhene
NIGHT OF THE TWISTERS
Eschke, Volker
NEUROSIA: 50 YEARS OF PERVERSITY
Escobar, Miguel
KAZAAM
Escott, Anthony
FLAMING EARS
Eskell, Diana
SOLITAIRE FOR TWO
Espinoza, Gil
HIGH SCHOOL HIGH
Ester, Ruddy
SHOOTFIGHTER 2: KILL OR BE KILLED!
Ester, Will
ROAD HOME, THE
Estevez, Emilio
D3: THE MIGHTY DUCKS
MISSION: IMPOSSIBLE
WAR AT HOME, THE
Estevez, Joe
BREAKAWAY
DARK SECRETS
RED LINE
Estevez, Paloma
WAR AT HOME, THE
Estevez, Renee
ENTERTAINING ANGELS: THE DOROTHY DAY STORY
WAR AT HOME, THE
Estrada, Angelina
BIG SQUEEZE, THE
Estudillo, Cristobal
LAND AND FREEDOM
Esumi, Makiko
MABOROSI
Etaadili, Abderrahim
HALFMOON
Etheredge, Jeanette
JACK
Ettinger, Cynthia
DOWN, OUT AND DANGEROUS
Ettinger, Robert
SYNTHETIC PLEASURES
Eugene, Wesley
DON'T BE A MENACE TO SOUTH CENTRAL WHILE DRINKING YOUR JUICE IN THE HOOD
Evangelista, Anton
RANSOM
Evans, Art
GREAT WHITE HYPE, THE
Evans, Danielle
PORTRAITS OF A KILLER
Evans, Grey
HEDD WYNN
Evans, John
101 DALMATIANS
Evans, Matt
LEGEND OF GATOR FACE, THE
Evans, Scott
FIRST KID
Evans, Stacey
LETTER TO MY KILLER
Evans, Troy
ED
FRIGHTENERS, THE
PHENOMENON
WOMAN UNDONE, A
Evans, Wanda Lee
TRIGGER EFFECT, THE
UP CLOSE AND PERSONAL
Evengelista, Daniella
ROAD HOME, THE
Evenson, Wayne
FARGO
Everett, Barbara
LOOKING FOR RICHARD
Everett, Jacqui
BUGGED
Everett, Lee
NATIONAL LAMPOON'S FAVORITE DEADLY SINS
THAT THING YOU DO!
Everett, Pamela
EVERYONE SAYS I LOVE YOU
Everett, Rupert
CEMETERY MAN
DUNSTON CHECKS IN
Everett, Tom
MY FELLOW AMERICANS
Everhart, Angie
MAD DOG TIME
TALES FROM THE CRYPT PRESENTS BORDELLO OF BLOOD
Everitt, Benjamin
DON'T BE A MENACE TO SOUTH CENTRAL WHILE DRINKING YOUR JUICE IN THE HOOD
Evers, Darrell
GHOSTS OF MISSISSIPPI
Evers, James Van
GHOSTS OF MISSISSIPPI
Evers, Keanan K.
GHOSTS OF MISSISSIPPI
Evers-Everette, Nicole
GHOSTS OF MISSISSIPPI
Everson, Cory
FELONY
Ewald, Patrick
WHISPERING, THE
Ewell, Dwight
FLIRT
STONEWALL
Ewert, Mark
FRISK
Ewing, Patrick
SPACE JAM
Eyiam, Eshref
GIRLFRIENDS
Eyjolfsson, Gunnar
VIKING SAGAS, THE
Eynon, Jeremy
EYE FOR AN EYE
Eyre, Peter
SURVIVING PICASSO
Ezzeldin, Cherif
PROPRIETOR, THE
Fabbri, Valeria
IN LOVE AND WAR
Faber, Matthew
PALLBEARER, THE
STONEWALL
WELCOME TO THE DOLLHOUSE
Fabian
UP CLOSE AND PERSONAL
Fabian, Romeo Rene
HOSTILE INTENTIONS
Fabio
EDDIE
MAN OF THE YEAR
SPY HARD
Fabrini, Flavio
ARRIVAL, THE
Facinelli, Peter
ANGELA
FOXFIRE

Fadda, Matteo
MILLE BOLLE BLU
Fager, Tommy
WELCOME TO THE DOLLHOUSE
Fagerbakke, Bill
HUNCHBACK OF NOTRE DAME, THE
Fahey, Jeff
DARKMAN III: DIE DARKMAN DIE
SERPENT'S LAIR
SWEEPER, THE
Fairbass, Craig
PROTEUS
Fairchild, Morgan
CRIMINAL HEARTS
VENUS RISING
Fairchild, Ray
BIG BULLY
Fairman, Blain
ROUJIN-Z
Fairman, Blair
PATLABOR 2: MOBILE POLICE
Fairman, Michael
GREAT WHITE HYPE, THE
LATE SHIFT, THE
Faison, Frankie
MOTHER NIGHT
RICH MAN'S WIFE, THE
STUPIDS, THE
Faith, Dani
JACK
Faithfull, Marianne
ROLLING STONES ROCK-AND-ROLL CIRCUS, THE
SHOPPING
Falchi, Anna
CEMETERY MAN
Falco, Anthony
SGT. KABUKIMAN N.Y.P.D.
Falco, Edie
FUNERAL, THE
Falcon
PROPRIETOR, THE
Fallon, Siobhan
STRIPTEASE
Falvo, Antonio
WHO KILLED PASOLINI?
Fan, Jing-Ma
MADAME BUTTERFLY
Fan Siu-Wong
ORGANIZED CRIME & TRIAD BUREAU
Fancy, Richard
LAWNMOWER MAN 2: BEYOND CYBERSPACE
Fann, Al
SHARON'S SECRET
Fann, Emma
MIRROR HAS TWO FACES, THE
Faraci, Mary Jo
FLIPPER
Faraci, Richard
RUMBLE IN THE BRONX
Faragallah, Ramsey
ED'S NEXT MOVE
Farago, Matt
MURDERED INNOCENCE
Farentino, James
BULLETPROOF
Farfel, Roy
RANSOM
Fargas, Antonio
CELLULOID CLOSET, THE
DON'T BE A MENACE TO SOUTH CENTRAL WHILE DRINKING YOUR JUICE IN THE HOOD
Farina, Dennis
EDDIE
Faris, John
BLONDES HAVE MORE GUNS
Farkas, Zsanett
EVITA
Farley, Chris
BLACK SHEEP
Farley, John
BLACK SHEEP
Farley, Kevin P.
BLACK SHEEP
Farley, Rupert
YOUNG POISONER'S HANDBOOK, THE
Farley, Sid
FRIEND OF THE FAMILY 2
Farmer, Bill
SPACE JAM
Farmer, Cyrus
ONE MAN'S JUSTICE
Farmer, Gary
DEAD MAN
MOONSHINE HIGHWAY
Farmer, Loren
WHARF RAT, THE
Farmer, Mary
DADETOWN
Farmer, Nicole
WHARF RAT, THE
Farnham, Euclid
MAN WITH A PLAN
Farnham, Priscilla
MAN WITH A PLAN
Farrell, Nicholas
HAMLET
MIDWINTER'S TALE, A
TWELFTH NIGHT
Farrell, Richard
HARD WAY OUT: BLOODFIST VIII
Farrell, Sharon
BEYOND DESIRE
Farrell, Shea
MR. WRONG
Farrelly, Kathy
KINGPIN
Farrelly, Mariann
KINGPIN
Farrelly, Nancy
KINGPIN
Farris, Lorraine
I SHOT ANDY WARHOL
Farrow, Yvonne
VERY BRADY SEQUEL, A
Farwell, Dane
PHANTOM, THE
Faskett, Tawnya
RED LINE
Fassari, Antonello
WHO KILLED PASOLINI?
Fassbinder, Rainer Werner
SHADOW OF ANGELS
Fastbacks, The
HYPE!
Fat Jack
HAPPY GILMORE
Fateyev, Alexei
BOGUS
Faulkner, James
WAVELENGTH
Faulkner, Peter
CRACKER: THE MADWOMAN IN THE ATTIC
Faustina
ORIGINAL SINS
Favreau, Joan
SWINGERS
Favreau, Jon
JUST YOUR LUCK
SWINGERS
Faxon, Brad
KINGPIN
Faynes, Arthur
TWO FRIENDS
Fazaa, Kamel
SILENCES OF THE PALACE, THE
Fazio, Santo
FUNERAL, THE
Fazzani, Beya
SILENCES OF THE PALACE, THE
Fearon, Ray
HAMLET
Feather, Jim
JOHNNY SHORTWAVE
MRS. WINTERBOURNE
Fechter, Randy
THAT THING YOU DO!
Fedorenko, Valerij
FATE
Fedorov, Oleg
MISSION: IMPOSSIBLE
Feeney, Caroleen
DENISE CALLS UP
JOHN CARPENTER'S ESCAPE FROM L.A.
Feeney, Moira
MR. HOLLAND'S OPUS
Fega, Russ
MOTHER
Feiden, Margo
LINE KING: THE AL HIRSCHFELD STORY, THE
Feiffer, Jules
LINE KING: THE AL HIRSCHFELD STORY, THE
Feig, Paul
MY FELLOW AMERICANS
SABRINA, THE TEENAGE WITCH
THAT THING YOU DO!
Fein, Amanda
MATILDA
Fein, Caitlin
MATILDA
Fein, Doren
ED
RAGE
Feldman, Corey
RED LINE
SOUTH BEACH ACADEMY
TALES FROM THE CRYPT PRESENTS BORDELLO OF BLOOD
Feldman, Mindy
SOUTH BEACH ACADEMY
Feldstein, Don
DEAR GOD
Feliciano, Jose
FARGO
Felix, Karina
BUGGED
Fellowes, Julian
JANE EYRE
Felszeghy, Tibor
DOGFIGHTERS, THE
Fendley, Danny
ARRIVAL, THE
Feni, Bechir
SILENCES OF THE PALACE, THE
Fenner, Richie
COLONY, THE
Feore, Colm
CHAMPAGNE SAFARI, THE
TRUMAN
WHERE'S THE MONEY, NOREEN?
Fequiere, Andal
PREACHER'S WIFE, THE
Fera, Vince
BOGUS
Ferar, Anthony
KAZAAM
Ferchland, Andrew J.
FAN, THE

Ferency, Adam
MOTHER OF KINGS
Ferens, Sandra
HOMEWARD BOUND II: LOST IN SAN FRANCISCO
Ferguson, Chamblee
LILY DALE
Ferguson, J. Don
EDDIE
FLED
Ferguson, Kikka
TALES FROM THE CRYPT PRESENTS BORDELLO OF BLOOD
Ferguson, Matthew
ENGLISH PATIENT, THE
Ferguson, Meresa T.
PEOPLE VS. LARRY FLYNT, THE
Ferguson, Steve
SGT. KABUKIMAN N.Y.P.D.
Feria, Augusto
BITTER SUGAR
Feringa, Jeff
KANSAS CITY
Fernandez, Alberto
BATON ROUGE
Fernandez, Dario
OF LOVE AND SHADOWS
Fernandez, Juan
EXECUTIVE DECISION
MAD DOG TIME
NECRONOMICON: BOOK OF THE DEAD
SAINTS AND SINNERS
Fernandez, Michelle
EDDIE
Fernandez, Rene-Andre
HORSEMAN ON THE ROOF
Fernetz, Charlene
SABRINA, THE TEENAGE WITCH
Ferns, Alex
GHOST AND THE DARKNESS, THE
Ferraez, Marcos Antonio
DEAD WEEKEND
Ferrante, Antonio
WHO KILLED PASOLINI?
Ferrari, Jean-Paul
SUITE 16
Ferrari, Paul
BLONDES HAVE MORE GUNS
Ferraro, Brianna
RUMPELSTILTSKIN
Ferraro, Brittani
RUMPELSTILTSKIN
Ferraro, Simona
WHO KILLED PASOLINI?
Ferre, Enriqueta
LAND AND FREEDOM
Ferre, Gianfranco
CATWALK
Ferreira, Elena
OUTRAGE
Ferrell, Andrea
JERRY MAGUIRE
Ferrell, Conchata
MY FELLOW AMERICANS
Ferrell, Will
DEATH ARTIST, THE
Ferrelli, Robert J.
HEAD OF THE FAMILY
ZARKORR! THE INVADER
Ferrer, Jose Luis
BASQUIAT
Ferrer, Leilani Sarelle
BREACH OF TRUST
Ferrer, Lupitz
CURDLED
Ferreri, Joseph
DESIRE
Ferretti, Alberta
CATWALK
Ferretti, Daniele
STAR MAKER, THE
Ferrier, Dennis
LAST DANCE
Ferrini, Sheila
CRUCIBLE, THE
Ferris, Pam
MATILDA
Ferro, Dan
SGT. BILKO
Ferry, David
NIGHT OF THE TWISTERS
STUPIDS, THE
Fesos, Andras
DOGFIGHTERS, THE
Feyer, Jonathan
MATILDA
Feynman, Michelle
INFINITY
Fiarbairn, Trevor
GIRLFRIENDS
Fick, Chris
FAN, THE
Fickle, Malindi
EVERYTHING RELATIVE
Fidele, Jon
FROM DUSK TILL DAWN
Fido, Jonny
TWO IF BY SEA
Field, Arabella
POMPATUS OF LOVE, THE
Field, Chelsea
FLIPPER
Field, David
GIRLFRIENDS
Field, Iris
EYE FOR AN EYE
Field, James
TUSKEGEE AIRMEN, THE
Field, Sally
EYE FOR AN EYE
HOMEWARD BOUND II: LOST IN SAN FRANCISCO
Field, Todd
TWISTER
WALKING AND TALKING
Fielding, Mark
RUMBLE IN THE BRONX
Fields, Danny
NICO ICON
Fields, Edith
COLONY, THE
LOVE IS ALL THERE IS
NORMA JEAN AND MARILYN
Fields, Robert
AMERICAN STRAYS
GETTING AWAY WITH MURDER
Fiennes, Joseph
STEALING BEAUTY
Fiennes, Ralph
ENGLISH PATIENT, THE
Fierstein, Harvey
CELLULOID CLOSET, THE
EVERYTHING RELATIVE
INDEPENDENCE DAY
Figura, Kasia
TOO FAST, TOO YOUNG
Filar, Gil
IN LOVE AND WAR
Filardi, Jason
CRAFT, THE
Filz, Flip
ANTONIA'S LINE
Fimple, Dennis
DOWN PERISCOPE
Finch, Gil
LET'S GET BIZZEE
Finch, Mark
FRISK
Findejs, Milan
KASPAR HAUSER
Findlay, Deborah
JACK & SARAH
Findlay, Freddy
RASPUTIN
Findlay, Joy
ED'S NEXT MOVE
Finley, Cameron
LARRY MCMURTRY'S STREETS OF LAREDO
Finley, Margot
D3: THE MIGHTY DUCKS
Finn, Carina
TREES LOUNGE
Finn, John
CITY HALL
TRUMAN
Finnegan, John
MARS ATTACKS!
Finnegan, Neil
PROTEUS
Finnerty, John "Spike"
RANSOM
Finney, Brian
IMMORTALS, THE
SAWBONES
Finti, Andrei
OUTPOST, THE
Fiore, Chris
FATALLY YOURS
Fiorentini, Marco
CEMETERY MAN
Fiorentino, Linda
LARGER THAN LIFE
UNFORGETTABLE
Fiorenza, Vincenzo
STAR MAKER, THE
Firestone, Roy
JERRY MAGUIRE
1st Baptist Church Choir
ORIGINAL GANGSTAS
Firth, Colin
ENGLISH PATIENT, THE
Firth, Robert
PROTEUS
Fiscella, Andrew
FUNERAL, THE
Fischer, Don
DESIRE
EXECUTIVE DECISION
FAN, THE
STAR TREK: FIRST CONTACT
Fischetti, Diane
SGT. KABUKIMAN N.Y.P.D.
Fischler, Patrick
TWISTER
Fish, Nancy
DANGEROUS PASSION
Fishburne, Laurence
FLED
TUSKEGEE AIRMEN, THE
Fisher, Andrena
PEOPLE VS. LARRY FLYNT, THE
Fisher, Frances
STRIPTEASE
Fisher, George
GLIMMER MAN, THE
SET IT OFF
TWO-BITS & PEPPER
Fisher, Jason Zone
EVIL HAS A FACE
Fisher, Jodie
BODY OF INFLUENCE 2

Fisher, John V.
WATCH ME
Fisher, La Tanya M.
TRUTH ABOUT CATS AND DOGS, THE
Fisher, Scott
MRS. MUNCK
Fisher, Tricia Leigh
HOSTILE INTENTIONS
Fisk, Steve
HYPE!
Fite, Mark
INDEPENDENCE DAY
Fitz, Peter
FLIRT
Fitzgerald, Annie
FATALLY YOURS
Fitzgerald, Bettye
MAN WITH THE PERFECT SWING, THE
Fitzgerald, Ciaran
SOME MOTHER'S SON
Fitzgerald, Dan
TOLLBOOTH
Fitzgerald, Dennis
JERRY MAGUIRE
MOONSHINE HIGHWAY
Fitzgerald, Glenn
FLIRTING WITH DISASTER
MANNY & LO
Fitzgerald, Gregg
WAR OF THE BUTTONS, THE
Fitzgerald, John Jay
ROUJIN-Z
Fitzgerald, Lewis
SPIDER & ROSE
Fitzgerald, Stan
SANDMAN, THE
Fitzhugh, Adam
MR. HOLLAND'S OPUS
Fitzpatrick, Colleen
HIGH SCHOOL HIGH
Fitzpatrick, John J.
BOYS
Fitzpatrick, Kevin
TERMINAL IMPACT
Fitzpatrick, Michael
GRIM
Fitzpatrick, Richard
HOMECOMING
IN LOVE AND WAR
TWO IF BY SEA
WHEN THE BULLET HITS THE BONE
Fitzpatrick, Robert
IT'S MY PARTY
Fitzpatrick, Steve
JAG
Fitzpatrick, Tony
NORMAL LIFE
PRIMAL FEAR
Flack, Herbert
DAENS
Flacks, Diane
KIDS IN THE HALL: BRAIN CANDY
Flaherty, Jim
BEAVIS AND BUTT-HEAD DO AMERICA
Flaherty, Joe
HAPPY GILMORE
PIG'S TALE, A
Flaherty, Lanny
SOMEONE ELSE'S AMERICA
Flanagan, Fionnula
SOME MOTHER'S SON
Flanagan III, Lewis
CHILDREN OF THE CORN: THE GATHERING
Flanders, Keeley
SECRETS & LIES
Flanery, Sean Patrick
GRASS HARP, THE
JUST YOUR LUCK
Flatman, Barry
OPEN SEASON
Flea
JUST YOUR LUCK
Fleck, John
RAVENHAWK
Fleeks, Eric
PHAT BEACH
Fleishaker, Joe
SGT. KABUKIMAN N.Y.P.D.
Fleiss, Heidi
HEIDI FLEISS HOLLYWOOD MADAM
Fleiss, Noah
MOTHER'S PRAYER, A
Fleming, Peter
MRS. WINTERBOURNE
ROAD HOME, THE
Fleming, Raissa
FOXFIRE
Fleming, Victoria
TRIGGER EFFECT, THE
Flemming, Peter
ANNIE O
Flemyng, Jason
STEALING BEAUTY
Flender, Rodman
BLACK SCORPION
CARNOSAUR 3: PRIMAL SPECIES
CRIMINAL HEARTS
Fletcher, Barry
BODY COUNT
Fletcher, Dexter
JUDE
SHOOTFIGHTER 2: KILL OR BE KILLED!
Fletcher, Gary Don
SLING BLADE
Fletcher, Louise
EDIE & PEN
HIGH SCHOOL HIGH
MULHOLLAND FALLS
TOLLBOOTH
2 DAYS IN THE VALLEY
Fletcher, Sherry Josand
CITIZEN RUTH
Flett, Katrina
TWO MUCH
Fleugel, Darlanne
DARKMAN III: DIE DARKMAN DIE
Flippin, Lucy Lee
MOTHER
Floberg, Bjorn
VIKING SAGAS, THE
Flock, John
SOLO
Flockhart, Calista
BIRDCAGE, THE
Flood, Staci
CABLE GUY, THE
Flop
HYPE!
Flores, Abraham
FAN, THE
Flores, Victoria
MR. WRONG
Flores, Von
DARKMAN III: DIE DARKMAN DIE
FRAME BY FRAME
Flores-Recinos, Carlos
HIGH SCHOOL HIGH
Flotats, Josep Maria
MOUTH TO MOUTH
Flower, Buck
FAST MONEY
FOREST WARRIOR
Floyd, David
SGT. KABUKIMAN N.Y.P.D.
Floyd, Helen E.
TIME TO KILL, A
Floyd, Susan
BIG NIGHT
Flueger, Valerie
PHANTOM, THE
Flum, Steven
LET'S GET BIZZEE
Flynn, Barbara
CRACKER: THE MADWOMAN IN THE ATTIC
Flynn, Bill
LIVE WIRE: HUMAN TIMEBOMB
Flynn, F. J.
BLACK DAY BLUE NIGHT
Flynn, Herbie
KINGPIN
Flynn, Jackie
KINGPIN
Flynn, James K.
EDDIE
Flynn, Kimberly
STRIPTEASE
Flynn, Miriam
LETTER TO MY KILLER
Flynn, Neil
CHAIN REACTION
Flynn, Tony
SOME MOTHER'S SON
Flynt, Larry
PEOPLE VS. LARRY FLYNT, THE
Flynt, Stephanie Bell
CHAMBER, THE
Foch, Nina
IT'S MY PARTY
Foerder, Preston
4 TALES OF 2 CITIES
Fogarty, Mary
MISSING PIECES
Fogel, Donna Jean
BED OF ROSES
Fogerty, Tonya
WHISPERING, THE
Fogleman, John N.
PARADISE LOST: THE CHILD MURDERS AT ROBIN HOOD HILLS
Fogwill, Vera
EVITA
Fois, Vanni
WHO KILLED PASOLINI?
Folch, Maria
LAND AND FREEDOM
Foley, David
KIDS IN THE HALL: BRAIN CANDY
Foley, Macka
ED
Foley, Tom Sean
MY FELLOW AMERICANS
Folland, Alison
BEFORE AND AFTER
Fonda, Bridget
CITY HALL
GRACE OF MY HEART
Fonda, Peter
GRACE OF MY HEART
JOHN CARPENTER'S ESCAPE FROM L.A.
PAINTED HERO
Fondacaro, Phil
TALES FROM THE CRYPT PRESENTS BORDELLO OF BLOOD
Fong, Leslie
LIVE WIRE: HUMAN TIMEBOMB
Fong, Patrick
MR. HOLLAND'S OPUS
Fong, Tig
ELECTRA

Fontayne, Fine Time
BUTTERFLY KISS
Fontes, Evelyn
JERRY MAGUIRE
Fontes, Wayne
JERRY MAGUIRE
Foote, Horton
LILY DALE
Foote Jr., Horton
INFINITY
For Real
GRACE OF MY HEART
Foraker, Lois
NATIONAL LAMPOON'S FAVORITE DEADLY SINS
Forbes, Kate
SUBSTANCE OF FIRE, THE
Forbes, Michelle
BLACK DAY BLUE NIGHT
JOHN CARPENTER'S ESCAPE FROM L.A.
Forbes, Miranda
JANE EYRE
Force, Jeffrey
INFINITY
Forch, Amaya
JOHNNY 100 PESOS
Ford, Carl Kwaku
GIRLS TOWN
Ford, Faith
WEEKEND IN THE COUNTRY, A
Ford, Hazen G. F.
OFF AND RUNNING
Ford, Jack
ROCK, THE
Ford, Jeffery
LAST DANCE
Ford, John
PERSONAL JOURNEY WITH MARTIN SCORSESE THROUGH AMERICAN MOVIES, A
Ford, Maria
BLACK ROSE OF HARLEM
BURIAL OF THE RATS
GLASS CAGE, THE
NECRONOMICON: BOOK OF THE DEAD
SHOWGIRL MURDERS, THE
Ford, Michael James
MICHAEL COLLINS
Ford, Paul N.
PARADISE LOST: THE CHILD MURDERS AT ROBIN HOOD HILLS
Ford, Steve
ERASER
Foree, Ken
DENTIST, THE
Foreman, George
WHEN WE WERE KINGS
Foreman, Julie
UP CLOSE AND PERSONAL
Forest, Denis
ERASER
Foresta, Molly Gia
SMALL WONDERS
Forke, Farrah
NATIONAL LAMPOON'S FAVORITE DEADLY SINS
Forlani, Claire
BASQUIAT
ROCK, THE
Formica, Fabiana
CEMETERY MAN
Forner, Michael
PHENOMENON
Forrest, Brett
SHAMELESS
Forrest, Frederic
ONE NIGHT STAND
Forristal, Susan
GETTING AWAY WITH MURDER
Forsgren, Ken
BARB WIRE
Forshaw, Weasel
LARRY MCMURTRY'S STREETS OF LAREDO
Forslund, Jenny
EVIL ED
Forss, Gun
EVIL ED
Forster, Robert
ORIGINAL GANGSTAS
Forsyth, Rosemary
DAYLIGHT
Forsythe, William
BEYOND DESIRE
IMMORTALS, THE
PALOOKAVILLE
ROCK, THE
SUBSTITUTE, THE
Fortier, Laurie
TO GILLIAN ON HER 37TH BIRTHDAY
Fortin, Andre
FUGITIVE RAGE
Fossat, Michael
CABLE GUY, THE
Foster, Adam
ARRIVAL, THE
Foster, Frances
JUROR, THE
Foster, Meg
BACKLASH: OBLIVION 2
Foster, Neil
SUGARTIME
Foster, Steffen
SUNSET PARK
Foster, Tiffany
BIG BULLY
Fourie, Dean
REDEMPTION: KICKBOXER 5
Fourmond, Stephane
RIDICULE
Fournier, Mireille
GLIMMER MAN, THE
Foviau, Karine
NELLY AND MONSIEUR ARNAUD
Fow, Paul
MAN OF THE YEAR
Fowler, Cate
YOUNG POISONER'S HANDBOOK, THE
Fowler, Joe
INDEPENDENCE DAY
Fowler, Shea
BOTTLE ROCKET
Fowlkes, Curtis
KANSAS CITY
Fox, Colin
DAYLIGHT
IN LOVE AND WAR
MRS. WINTERBOURNE
OPEN SEASON
Fox, David
VIRUS
Fox, Grethe
WARHEAD
Fox, Huckleberry
PHARAOH'S ARMY
Fox, Kerry
AFFAIR, THE
Fox, Kirk
CRIMINAL HEARTS
INFINITY
TRIGGER EFFECT, THE
Fox, Kitty
FREEWAY
Fox, Michael J.
FRIGHTENERS, THE
HOMEWARD BOUND II: LOST IN SAN FRANCISCO
MARS ATTACKS!
Fox, Phil
SOLITAIRE FOR TWO
Fox, Rick
EDDIE
Fox, Robert
ROBIN OF LOCKSLEY
Fox, Vivica
DON'T BE A MENACE TO SOUTH CENTRAL WHILE DRINKING YOUR JUICE IN THE HOOD
Fox, Vivica A.
INDEPENDENCE DAY
SET IT OFF
TUSKEGEE AIRMEN, THE
Foxworth, Bobby J.
EYE FOR AN EYE
Foxx, Jamie
GREAT WHITE HYPE, THE
TRUTH ABOUT CATS AND DOGS, THE
Fraim, Tracy
FEAR
Frain, James
RASPUTIN
Frakes, Jonathan
STAR TREK: FIRST CONTACT
Franciosa, Tony
CITY HALL
Francis, Ann
LOVER'S KNOT
Francis, David
HOLLOW POINT
Francis, Eddie
RICH MAN'S WIFE, THE
Francis, Geff
JACK & SARAH
Francisco, R.S.
MIDNIGHT DANCERS
Franck, Carole
PROPRIETOR, THE
Francks, Don
BOGUS
HARRIET THE SPY
HECK'S WAY HOME
Franco, Chris
RUMBLE IN THE BRONX
Franco, Ramon
HOSTILE INTENTIONS
Franek, Clem "Mandingo"
KINGPIN
Frank, Elan
DEADLY OUTBREAK
Frank, Jay
MR. HOLLAND'S OPUS
Frank, Jessica
HOUSE ARREST
Frank, Kevin
GETTING AWAY WITH MURDER
Frank, Tony
LARRY MCMURTRY'S STREETS OF LAREDO
LONE STAR
ROAD TO GALVESTON, THE
Franke, Peter
BROTHER OF SLEEP
Frankel, Mark
SOLITAIRE FOR TWO
Frankel, Shelley
EVERYONE SAYS I LOVE YOU
Franklin, Cherie
EYE FOR AN EYE
Franklin, Phyllis
MAN OF THE YEAR
Franklin, Shyheim
ORIGINAL GANGSTAS
PREACHER'S WIFE, THE

Franz, Dennis
AMERICAN BUFFALO
CHILDREN OF FURY
Franz, Elizabeth
PALLBEARER, THE
STEPHEN KING'S THINNER
SUBSTANCE OF FIRE, THE
Franz, Robert
SOMEONE ELSE'S AMERICA
Franzen, Charlie
NEON BIBLE, THE
Fraser, Andrew
BEAUTIFUL THING
Fraser, Brendan
MRS. WINTERBOURNE
PASSION OF DARKLY NOON, THE
Fraser, Brent
LITTLE DEATH, THE
Fraser, David
TAILS YOU LIVE, HEADS YOU'RE DEAD
Fraser, Duncan
ALASKA
RED SCORPION 2
UNFORGETTABLE
Fraser, Hugh
101 DALMATIANS
Fraser, Laura
SMALL FACES
Fraser, Xuan
RUDE
Frater, Vna Zen
TALKING ABOUT SEX
Frazen, Diane
DEAR GOD
Frazier, Frank L.
HAPPY GILMORE
Frazier, Guyle
RUMBLE IN THE BRONX
Frazier, Scott
SYNTHETIC PLEASURES
Frazier, Walt
EDDIE
Frechette, Peter
FIRST WIVES CLUB, THE
HEIDI CHRONICLES, THE
Frederick, Leon
GREAT WHITE HYPE, THE
Frederick, William
GHOST IN THE SHELL
Fredericks, David
BREACH OF TRUST
FEAR
RUMBLE IN THE BRONX
Fredericks, Kayla
MATILDA
Fredericks, Kelsey
MATILDA
Fredericks, Kyle
BLACK SCORPION
Frederickson, Amanda
TWO FRIENDS
Frederickson, Gray
HEAVEN'S PRISONERS
Fredricksen, Cully
STAR TREK: FIRST CONTACT
Fredrickson, Fred
SGT. KABUKIMAN N.Y.P.D.
Free
MESSAGE TO LOVE: THE ISLE OF WIGHT FESTIVAL
Freed, Sam
STEPHEN KING'S THINNER
Freels, Shari
GIRL 6
Freeman, Aisha
PORTRAITS OF A KILLER
Freeman, Alan "Fluff"
SHAMELESS
Freeman, Eddie
MURDERED INNOCENCE
Freeman, Jonathan
ASSOCIATE, THE
Freeman Jr., Al
ASSAULT AT WEST POINT
ONCE UPON A TIME . . . WHEN WE WERE COLORED
Freeman, K. Todd
ERASER
HOUSE ARREST
Freeman, Kathleen
. . . AT FIRST SIGHT
Freeman, Morgan
CHAIN REACTION
MOLL FLANDERS
Freeman, Nathaniel
GIRLS TOWN
RANSOM
Freeman, Paul
HORSEMAN ON THE ROOF
Freeman, Terrance
TIME TO KILL, A
Freeman, Yvette
NORMA JEAN AND MARILYN
Freifield, Brian
FAN, THE
Frejo, Brian
BOY CALLED HATE, A
French, Arthur
ASSOCIATE, THE
French, Colby
COLONY, THE
French, Dawn
ADVENTURES OF PINOCCHIO, THE
French, Kari
BAD LOVE
French, Leigh
GHOSTS OF MISSISSIPPI
French, Michael Bryan
GLIMMER MAN, THE
French, Patricia
LAST DANCE
French, Richard
DEMOLITIONIST, THE
Frerichs, Reed
COURAGE UNDER FIRE
WAR AT HOME, THE
Fresh, Doug E.
LET'S GET BIZZEE
Fresu, Maria Elena
CEMETERY MAN
Freund, Gisele
PARIS WAS A WOMAN
Frewer, Matt
KISSINGER AND NIXON
LAWNMOWER MAN 2: BEYOND CYBERSPACE
Frey, Glenn
JERRY MAGUIRE
Frey-Jarecki, Nancy
KINGPIN
Fricke, Grayson
GRASS HARP, THE
Fricker, Brenda
MOLL FLANDERS
TIME TO KILL, A
Fridjohn, Anthony
LIVE WIRE: HUMAN TIMEBOMB
Fridley, Tom
PHENOMENON
Fridmanovich, Maria
SGT. KABUKIMAN N.Y.P.D.
Friedman, Daniel H.
CHAIN REACTION
Friedman, Michael
FOREST WARRIOR
Friedman, Michael Charles
FIST OF THE NORTH STAR
Friedman, Nora
SMALL WONDERS
Friedman, Peter
I SHOT ANDY WARHOL
I'M NOT RAPPAPORT
Friedman, Roberto
FRISK
Friel, Vincent
TRAINSPOTTING
Friend, Bob
MISSION: IMPOSSIBLE
Friend, Tom
JERRY MAGUIRE
Friesen, John
FLY AWAY HOME
TWO IF BY SEA
Friessen, Peggy
TRUMAN
Frisch, Aaron
NEON BIBLE, THE
Frisk, Curt
CELTIC PRIDE
Frissung, Jean-Claude
SINGLE GIRL, A
Fritsch, Hannes
LAST MAN STANDING
Fritsch, Regina
BROTHER OF SLEEP
Fritts, David
TRUMAN
Fritz, Felicia
EDDIE
Fritz, Nikki
BURIAL OF THE RATS
FUGITIVE RAGE
SHOWGIRL MURDERS, THE
Frolov, Constantine
RASPUTIN
Frost, Roger
YOUNG POISONER'S HANDBOOK, THE
Frost, Sadie
MAGIC HUNTER
SHOPPING
Frot, Dominique
LA CEREMONIE
Frotscher, Donna
THEY BITE
Fry, Benjamin
WAVELENGTH
Fry, Kevin
ERASER
Fry, Stephen
COLD COMFORT FARM
Frye, Charlie
THAT THING YOU DO!
Frye, Hardy
BERKELEY IN THE 60S
Frye, Soleil Moon
PIRANHA
Frye, Stephen
LONE JUSTICE: SHOWDOWN AT PLUM CREEK
Fryharski, C. A.
ORIGINAL SINS
Fuchs, Jason
FLIPPER
Fuchs, Kenneth
UP CLOSE AND PERSONAL
Fuchsl, Peter
BROTHER OF SLEEP
Fuentes, Andre
BIRDCAGE, THE
Fuentes, Daisy
CURDLED
Fugees, The
WHEN WE WERE KINGS

Fuhrer, Judy
SGT. KABUKIMAN N.Y.P.D.
Fujimoto, Yuzuru
BIG WARS
Fujita, Tomoko
FLIRT
Fujiwara, Toshizo
FLIRT
Fulger, Holly
LOVER'S KNOT
Fuller, Jonathan
SKYSCRAPER
Fuller, Kurt
FAN, THE
Fuller, Sam
PERSONAL JOURNEY WITH MARTIN SCORSESE THROUGH AMERICAN MOVIES, A
Fuller, William
FULL BODY MASSAGE
Fulton, John
TWO IF BY SEA
Fumanal, Jose
RIDICULE
Funari, Giuseppe
STAR MAKER, THE
Fung, Theresa
BOGUS
Fuqua, Joseph
ED'S NEXT MOVE
Furey, John
WOLVES, THE
Furla, Vera
MILLE BOLLE BLU
Furlong, Edward
BEFORE AND AFTER
GRASS HARP, THE
Furlong, John
LAZARUS MAN, THE
Furphy, Carol
MUTANT MAN
Furst, Stephanie
JERRY MAGUIRE
Furtak, Evelyn
DESIRE
Furuya, Fumio
SGT. KABUKIMAN N.Y.P.D.
Fusco, Anthony
ERASER
Fusco, Joe
MAN OF THE YEAR
Futterman, Dan
BIRDCAGE, THE
FAR HARBOR
Fychan, Catrin
HEDD WYNN
Fyfe, Jim
FRIGHTENERS, THE
Fylking, Gert
EVIL ED
Gabana, Stefano
STAR MAKER, THE
Gabay, Eli
TALES FROM THE CRYPT PRESENTS BORDELLO OF BLOOD
Gabela, Glen
GHOST AND THE DARKNESS, THE
Gabison, David
VISITORS, THE
Gabor, Zsa Zsa
VERY BRADY SEQUEL, A
Gabriel, Ron
LOSING CHASE
SUGARTIME
Gabteni, Choukri
HATE

Gaffney, Mo
BOGUS
SHOT, THE
Gage, John
BERKELEY IN THE 60S
Gage, Melanie A.
GRACE OF MY HEART
Gagliarducci, Nicholas
SWINGERS
Gail, Max
FOREST WARRIOR
Gail, Scanlon
WOMAN UNDONE, A
Gainer, James F.
CITY HALL
Gaines, Boyd
I'M NOT RAPPAPORT
Gainey, M.C.
CITIZEN RUTH
FAN, THE
ONE MAN'S JUSTICE
Gainsbourg, Charlotte
JANE EYRE
Gal, Lizi
BREACH OF TRUST
Gal, Yoram
DEADLY OUTBREAK
Galash, T.J.
FOXFIRE
Gale, James
TEXAS CHAINSAW MASSACRE: THE NEXT GENERATION
Gale, Lorena
MATERNAL INSTINCTS
Galeota, Jimmy
CLUBHOUSE DETECTIVES
Galeota, Michael
CLUBHOUSE DETECTIVES
RATTLED
Galespie, Ian M.
VERY BRADY SEQUEL, A
Galiena, Anna
THREE LIVES AND ONLY ONE DEATH
Galiente, Rocky Reyna
LAST MAN STANDING
Galindo, Josep
LAND AND FREEDOM
Galko, Balazs
DOGFIGHTERS, THE
Gallacher, David
BREAKING THE WAVES
Gallacher, Tom
SMALL FACES
Gallagher, Bronagh
MARY REILLY
Gallagher, David
PHENOMENON
Gallagher, David Drew
INFINITY
NORMA JEAN AND MARILYN
Gallagher, Fiona
JUROR, THE
Gallagher, James
MATILDA
Gallagher, Megan
CROSSCUT
Gallagher, Pat
FELONY
Gallagher, Peter
LAST DANCE
TO GILLIAN ON HER 37TH BIRTHDAY
Gallagher, Susan
LOOKING FOR TROUBLE
Gallagher, Trevor
MATILDA
Gallaher, Timothy
LOW LIFE, THE

Gallant, Shannon
TWO-BITS & PEPPER
Gallardo, Camillo
OF LOVE AND SHADOWS
Gallatin, Chase
PAINTED HERO
Gallegos, Scott
FOXFIRE
Gallegos, Timothy
LAST MAN STANDING
Galleri, Jean-Pierre
MAXIMUM RISK
Galliano, John
CATWALK
Galligan, Patrick
VIRUS
Gallo, Vincent
ANGELA
FUNERAL, THE
PALOOKAVILLE
Gallop, Tom
JERRY MAGUIRE
Galloway, Carole
SUGARTIME
Galloway, Sheena
TALES FROM THE CRYPT PRESENTS BORDELLO OF BLOOD
Gallus, Agi
UNDERSTUDY: GRAVEYARD SHIFT 2, THE
Gallusz, Nikolett
RASPUTIN
Gamba, Francesca
CEMETERY MAN
Gamble, Mason
BAD MOON
SPY HARD
Gambon, Michael
MARY REILLY
TWO DEATHS
WIND IN THE WILLOWS, THE
Game, Dave
UP CLOSE AND PERSONAL
Gamelin, Eugine
RASPUTIN
Gamelin, Herve
SINGLE GIRL, A
Gamelin, Joa
MRS. WINTERBOURNE
Gammon, James
LARRY MCMURTRY'S STREETS OF LAREDO
TRUMAN
Gamy, Yvonne
HORSEMAN ON THE ROOF
Ganatra, Nitin Chandra
SECRETS & LIES
Gandolfini, James
JUROR, THE
Gandy, Elizabeth
TRIGGER EFFECT, THE
Ganger, Toby Scott
BLACK SHEEP
Gannascoli, Joseph R.
BASQUIAT
Gannon, Russell
BEYOND DESIRE
Gano, Tara
VISITORS, THE
Ganon, Kwame
DON'T BE A MENACE TO SOUTH CENTRAL WHILE DRINKING YOUR JUICE IN THE HOOD
Gansar, Lynn
BODY COUNT
Gant, Richard
CITY HALL
ED
GLIMMER MAN, THE

Gantt, Leland
AFFAIR, THE
Garber, Victor
FIRST WIVES CLUB, THE
MARVIN'S ROOM
Garbi, Avner
SAWBONES
Garbus, Martin
DEAR GOD
Garces, Jennifer
JACK
Garcia, Abraham
FLOWER OF MY SECRET, THE
Garcia, Alejandro
JUROR, THE
Garcia, Aymee
STRIPTEASE
Garcia, Domonique
PHAT BEACH
Garcia, Ernest
FROM DUSK TILL DAWN
Garcia, Hector
BOTTLE ROCKET
Garcia, Henri
PROPRIETOR, THE
Garcia, Jerry
RAVENHAWK
Garcia, Kaci
FOXFIRE
Garcia, Leo
DONOR UNKNOWN
Garcia, Marie Victoria
LET'S GET BIZZEE
Garcia, Nelson
SHOOTFIGHTER 2: KILL OR BE KILLED!
Garcia, Sergio
LAND AND FREEDOM
Garcia, Stella
EYE FOR AN EYE
Gardener, Micah
CARPOOL
Gardien, Isabelle
LA COMEDIE-FRANCAISE OU L'AMOUR JOUE
Gardiner, James
BOYS
Gardiner, Mark
FLED
Gardner, Dionne
LAST DANCE
Gardner, Jake
I'M NOT RAPPAPORT
Gardner, Jeff
LIFEFORM
Gardner, Karl D.
FLED
Gardner, Terry
LAZARUS MAN, THE
Garen, Danna
ARRIVAL, THE
Garfield, Allen
DIABOLIQUE
WILD SIDE
Garfield, Andrea
MISSING PIECES
Garfield, J. D.
LAZARUS MAN, THE
Garfield, Julie
MOTHER'S PRAYER, A
Garganese, Michael
BREAKAWAY
Gargiulo, Lulu
HYPE!
Garguier, Claire
RIDICULE
Garito, Ken
ASSAULT AT WEST POINT
Garland, Roseline
IN LOVE AND WAR
Garmon, Huw
HEDD WYNN
Garner, Hunter
PIG'S TALE, A
Garner, Jack
LARRY MCMURTRY'S STREETS OF LAREDO
MY FELLOW AMERICANS
Garner, James
LARRY MCMURTRY'S STREETS OF LAREDO
MY FELLOW AMERICANS
Garner, Jennifer
HARVEST OF FIRE
Garofalo, Janeane
CABLE GUY, THE
KIDS IN THE HALL: BRAIN CANDY
LARGER THAN LIFE
TRUTH ABOUT CATS AND DOGS, THE
Garp, Memory
EVIL ED
Garr, Nicholas
DUNSTON CHECKS IN
Garr, Teri
MICHAEL
Garrett, Brad
SPY HARD
Garrett, Jean
ABUSE
Garrett, Kimberley M.
PREACHER'S WIFE, THE
Garrett, Leif
WHISPERING, THE
Garrett, Spencer
GHOSTS OF MISSISSIPPI
Garrido, Joaquin
SOLO
Garris, Mick
STUPIDS, THE
Garrison, Andy
MOTHER
Garrison, Bill
DADETOWN
Garrison, Larry
MULHOLLAND FALLS
Garruba, Sammy
I'M NOT RAPPAPORT
Garson, Willie
KINGPIN
MARS ATTACKS!
ROCK, THE
Gartin, Christopher
TREMORS 2: AFTERSHOCKS
Garvey, Ray
EVERYONE SAYS I LOVE YOU
Gary, Mitzi
BUGGED
Gas Huffer
HYPE!
Gass, Kyle
BIO-DOME
CABLE GUY, THE
Gassman, Vittorio
SLEEPERS
Gaston, Michael
CRUCIBLE, THE
RANSOM
Gates, Daryl
HEIDI FLEISS HOLLYWOOD MADAM
Gati, Kathleen
DOGFIGHTERS, THE
Gatkin, Sergei
BURIAL OF THE RATS
Gaulke, James
FARGO
Gaultier, Jean-Paul
CATWALK
Gauny, Jerry
CHAMBER, THE
Gaup, Mikkel
BREAKING THE WAVES
Gautier, Jean-Yves
THREE LIVES AND ONLY ONE DEATH
Gautreaux, David
DEAD TO RIGHTS
DOGFIGHTERS, THE
Gava, Cassandra
LAST MAN STANDING
Gaver, Duffy
ROCK, THE
Gavia, Raquel
LARRY MCMURTRY'S STREETS OF LAREDO
Gavin, Don
TWO IF BY SEA
Gayle, Karen
IRON EAGLE IV
Gaylor, Anna
VISITORS, THE
Gaylord, Lisa
SHOOTFIGHTER 2: KILL OR BE KILLED!
Gaynes, George
CRUCIBLE, THE
Gayton, Clark
KANSAS CITY
Gazelle, Wendy
UNDERSTUDY: GRAVEYARD SHIFT 2, THE
Gazzara, Ben
DOGFIGHTERS, THE
Gecks, Joe
LOADED
Geddings, Lex D.
RANSOM
Gee, David Michael
CHAIN REACTION
Geer, Ellen
PHENOMENON
Geer, Faith
I SHOT ANDY WARHOL
Geer, Noel
SABRINA, THE TEENAGE WITCH
Gehrke, Steven R.
KINGPIN
Geier, Paul
RANSOM
Gelb, Arthur
LINE KING: THE AL HIRSCHFELD STORY, THE
Gelfant, Alan
CROW: CITY OF ANGELS, THE
Gelli, Cesare
MILLE BOLLE BLU
Gelman, Kimiko
MOTHER
Gemmill, Charles
CITY HALL
Genaro, Tony
BIG SQUEEZE, THE
CRAFT, THE
PHENOMENON
Genelin, Nora
BURIAL OF THE RATS
Genesse, Bryan
LIVE WIRE: HUMAN TIMEBOMB
TERMINAL IMPACT
Genest, Claude
HOLLOW POINT
Gennaro, Gianluca
CEMETERY MAN
Gennaro, Maria
STRIPTEASE

Gennaro, Mimmo
STAR MAKER, THE
Gentile, Guillermo
UP CLOSE AND PERSONAL
Gentili, Dino
WHO KILLED PASOLINI?
Gentili, Robert
FATALLY YOURS
TOO FAST, TOO YOUNG
Gentle, Elizabeth
TWO FRIENDS
Gentry, Tony W.
DON'T LET YOUR MEAT LOAF
Genuardi, Pietro
CEMETERY MAN
George, Eric
SUNSET PARK
George, Richard
GHOST IN THE SHELL
George, Tami-Adrian
SGT. BILKO
Georgia Mass Choir & Band
PREACHER'S WIFE, THE
Georgiades, James
RANSOM
Gera, Zoltan
MAGIC HUNTER
Geralden, James
CHAMBER, THE
Gerbel, Charles
TALES OF EROTICA
Gerber, Kathy
ABUSE
Gerber, Martin
QUEST, THE
Gere, Richard
PRIMAL FEAR
Gerety, Peter
MRS. WINTERBOURNE
SLEEPERS
SURVIVING PICASSO
Germain, Kareen
PLAYBACK
Germaine, Bruce
PUBLIC ACCESS
German, Felix
BITTER SUGAR
Germond, Jack
INDEPENDENCE DAY
Gershon, Charles
FLED
Gershon, Gina
BEST OF THE BEST 3: NO TURNING BACK
BOUND
Gershon, Molli D.
FLED
Gerstein, Lisa
IF LUCY FELL
Gertz, Jami
TWISTER
Gesner, Cynthia Farrelly
KINGPIN
Gesner, Zen
KINGPIN
Gesualdi, Gil
SOUTH BEACH ACADEMY
Getty, Balthazar
WHITE SQUALL
Getz, John
LATE SHIFT, THE
PAINTED HERO
Geurin, Margie
DADETOWN
Gherardi, Anna Maria
STEALING BEAUTY
Ghili, Abdel Ahmed
HATE
Ghisalberti, Juan Jose
SHADOW YOU SOON WILL BE, A
Giacomini, Gino
DARKMAN III: DIE DARKMAN DIE
Giaimo, Anthony
BIRDCAGE, THE
STRIPTEASE
Giambalvo, Louis
DEAD TO RIGHTS
Gianasi, Rick
SGT. KABUKIMAN N.Y.P.D.
Giannell, Steve
INDEPENDENCE DAY
Giannini, Cheryl
I'M NOT RAPPAPORT
Giannini, Jimm
NORMA JEAN AND MARILYN
Gibb, Donald
BLOODSPORT II: THE NEXT KUMITE
MISSING PIECES
Gibbs, Andree
SOMETIMES THEY COME BACK . . . AGAIN
Gibbs, David
BLACK OUT
LAWNMOWER MAN 2: BEYOND CYBERSPACE
Gibbs, Harry
TRUMAN
Gibbs, Keith
CABLE GUY, THE
CELTIC PRIDE
Gibbs, Matyelok
JACK & SARAH
Gibbs, Nigel
TRUTH ABOUT CATS AND DOGS, THE
UP CLOSE AND PERSONAL
Gibbs, Okley
CITIZEN RUTH
Gibis, Tom
BEAUTIFUL GIRLS
Gibney, Jennifer
SOME MOTHER'S SON
Gibney, Mitchell Thomas
DONOR UNKNOWN
Gibney, Susan
GREAT WHITE HYPE, THE
Gibson, Darryl
SET IT OFF
Gibson, Henry
BIO-DOME
MOTHER NIGHT
Gibson, Lance
RUMBLE IN THE BRONX
Gibson, Mel
RANSOM
Gibson, Moses
EDDIE
Gidden, Yvonne
HAMLET
Gidley, Pamela
BAD LOVE
LITTLE DEATH, THE
Gieger, Yamit
SUGARTIME
Gielgud, John
HAMLET
HAUNTED
LOOKING FOR RICHARD
PORTRAIT OF A LADY, THE
SHINE
Gien, Pamela
LAST SUPPER, THE
Gifford, Frank
JERRY MAGUIRE
Gifford, Grant
DADETOWN
Gifford, Jim
DADETOWN
Gifford, Justin
GHOST AND THE DARKNESS, THE
Gifford, Kathie Lee
FIRST WIVES CLUB, THE
Gifford, Patrick
GHOST AND THE DARKNESS, THE
Gifford, Samantha
DADETOWN
Gil, Ariadna
CELESTIAL CLOCKWORK
Gil, Damian
WHISPERING, THE
Gil, Jorge
SHOOTFIGHTER 2: KILL OR BE KILLED!
Gilbert, J. Renee
MERLIN'S SHOP OF MAGICAL WONDERS
Gilbert, John
BURIAL OF THE RATS
Gilbert, Mark
PREACHER'S WIFE, THE
Gilbert, Patrick
STREET FIGHTER II: THE ANIMATED MOVIE
Gilbert, Taylor
TWISTER
Gilbert, Valerie
DADETOWN
Gilborn, Steven
DUNSTON CHECKS IN
VERY BRADY SEQUEL, A
Gilbreath, Mildred J.
TIME TO KILL, A
Gildea, Christina
TREES LOUNGE
Gildea, Sean P.
KINGPIN
Giles, Jerry
IT CAME FROM OUTER SPACE II
Giles, Nancy
I'M NOT RAPPAPORT
Gilhorn, Steven
LATE SHIFT, THE
Gill, Brendan
LINE KING: THE AL HIRSCHFELD STORY, THE
Gillan, Tony
I'M NOT RAPPAPORT
Gillen, Aidan
SOME MOTHER'S SON
Gillen, Michelle
UP CLOSE AND PERSONAL
Gillette, Anita
LARGER THAN LIFE
SHE'S THE ONE
Gillette, Chris
VIRUS
Gilliam, Seth
ASSAULT AT WEST POINT
COURAGE UNDER FIRE
Gilliard Jr., Larry
ASSOCIATE, THE
LOTTO LAND
Gillies, Isabel
I SHOT ANDY WARHOL
Gillin, Tim
TRUMAN
Gillot, Nick
RASPUTIN
Gilman-Frederick, Dieffyd
MR. HOLLAND'S OPUS
Gilmore, Doug
BOGUS
Gilmore, Gary
ROLLING STONES ROCK-AND-ROLL CIRCUS, THE

Gilmore, Kim
PROPRIETOR, THE
Gilpin, Jack
JUROR, THE
Gilroy, Tom
GIRLS TOWN
LAND AND FREEDOM
Gilvezan, Don
COLONY, THE
Gimbrere, Mark
SOME FOLKS CALL IT A SLING BLADE
Gimenez, Hernan
SHADOW YOU SOON WILL BE, A
Gimpel, Erica
FLIRT
Ginsberg, Allen
BERKELEY IN THE 60S
Ginsberg, Haras
ED'S NEXT MOVE
Ginter, Lindsay
CHILDREN OF FURY
Giordano, Andrea "Andi"
SGT. KABUKIMAN N.Y.P.D.
Giordano, Elizabeth
WARHEAD
Giordano, Joe
MUTANT MAN
Giordano, Jonathan
EVERYONE SAYS I LOVE YOU
Gioris, Penelope
BLOODKNOT
Giotta, Kathy
ABUSE
Giraldi, Aldo
DARK SECRETS
Giralo, Steve
DOWN PERISCOPE
Girardin, Michael
JAMES AND THE GIANT PEACH
Giraudeau, Bernard
NEW LIFE, A
RIDICULE
Girl Trouble
HYPE!
Girling, Cindy
DEVOTION
Gironda, Dominic
BREAKAWAY
Girotti, Massimo
MONSTER, THE
Giscome, Marcelo
SGT. KABUKIMAN N.Y.P.D.
Gish, Annabeth
BEAUTIFUL GIRLS
LAST SUPPER, THE
Gitchell, Chief Inspector Gary
PARADISE LOST: THE CHILD MURDERS AT ROBIN HOOD HILLS
Gitlin, Todd
BERKELEY IN THE 60S
Gitlis, Ivry
ROLLING STONES ROCK-AND-ROLL CIRCUS, THE
Giuliani, Rudolph W.
EDDIE
Giuntoli, Neil
UP CLOSE AND PERSONAL
Gladman, Joe
BOGUS
Glasco, Joe
BASQUIAT
Glaser, Jake
KAZAAM
Glass, Rachel
LAST DANCE
Glass, Ron
IT'S MY PARTY
Glassco, Briony
PATLABOR 2: MOBILE POLICE
Glasser, Isabel
MOTHER
SURGEON, THE
Glassman, Andrew
UP CLOSE AND PERSONAL
Glassman, Howard
GETTING AWAY WITH MURDER
Glassman, Jim
ZARKORR! THE INVADER
Glazer, Eugene Robert
IT'S MY PARTY
Gleason, James
MOTHER
SAWBONES
Gleason, Joanna
EDIE & PEN
MR. HOLLAND'S OPUS
Gleason, Mary Pat
CRUCIBLE, THE
INFINITY
Gleeson, Brendan
MICHAEL COLLINS
Gleeson, Redmond
ENTERTAINING ANGELS: THE DOROTHY DAY STORY
Glen, Doug
TALKING ABOUT SEX
Glen, Edward
PATLABOR 2: MOBILE POLICE
Glendinning, Katie
FLED
Glenn, Scott
COURAGE UNDER FIRE
EDIE & PEN
Glines, Kermit
MAN WITH A PLAN
Glitter
DARK SECRETS
Glogovac, Nebojsa
VUKOVAR
Gloster, Jim
EDDIE
Glover, Bruce
NIGHT OF THE SCARECROW
Glover, Crispin
DEAD MAN
PEOPLE VS. LARRY FLYNT, THE
Glover, Danny
AMERICA'S DREAM
Glover, Don
CHILDREN OF FURY
Glover, Joan
NEON BIBLE, THE
Glover, John
ASSAULT AT WEST POINT
Glover, Zachary Simmons
EDDIE
Gmeindl, Billa
FLAMING EARS
Gmeindl, Norbert
FLAMING EARS
Gnadinger, Mathias
MAGIC HUNTER
Gnecco, Luis
JOHNNY 100 PESOS
Gobert, Boy
SHADOW OF ANGELS
Godbold, Catherine
ALEX
Goddard, Beth
BEAUTIFUL THING
Goddard, Trevor
FAST MONEY
YESTERDAY'S TARGET
Godreche, Judith
NEW LIFE, A
RIDICULE
Godunov, Alexander
DOGFIGHTERS, THE
Goethals, Angela
JERRY MAGUIRE
Goetz, John E.
LOVER'S KNOT
Goetz, Kevin
NORMA JEAN AND MARILYN
Goetz, Peter Michael
INFINITY
Goggins, Walton
PAINTED HERO
Gogin, Michael Lee
SPY HARD
Goin, Garry
FAMILY THING, A
Goines, Jesse D.
DEATH ARTIST, THE
Gold, Glori
PHAT BEACH
Gold, Harvey
FEAR
Gold, L. Harvey
ROBIN OF LOCKSLEY
Gold, Luann
TALKING ABOUT SEX
Gold, Shannon
DESOLATION ANGELS
Goldberg, Adam
HOMEWARD BOUND II: LOST IN SAN FRANCISCO
Goldberg, Eric
LINE KING: THE AL HIRSCHFELD STORY, THE
Goldberg, Jackie
BERKELEY IN THE 60S
Goldberg, Whoopi
ASSOCIATE, THE
BOGUS
CELLULOID CLOSET, THE
EDDIE
GHOSTS OF MISSISSIPPI
TALES FROM THE CRYPT PRESENTS BORDELLO OF BLOOD
THEODORE REX
Goldblum, Jeff
GREAT WHITE HYPE, THE
INDEPENDENCE DAY
MAD DOG TIME
Golden, Dan
BURIAL OF THE RATS
FUGITIVE RAGE
Golden II, Norman D.
AMERICA'S DREAM
Golden, Renee
DEAD TO RIGHTS
Goldenhersh, Heather
I'M NOT RAPPAPORT
Golder, Margery
ANGELS AND INSECTS
Goldfarb, Daniel
MURDERED INNOCENCE
Goldin, Joshua
INFINITY
Goldman, Gloria
ED'S NEXT MOVE
Goldman, Jill
BAD LOVE
Goldring, Danny
CHAIN REACTION
Goldschmidt, Judy
MERCY
Goldsmith, Carianne
PINOCCHIO'S REVENGE
Goldsmith, Gwen
PALLBEARER, THE

Goldstein, Allan
VIRUS
Goldstein, Edward
STRIPTEASE
Goldstein, Harel
DEADLY OUTBREAK
Goldstein, Jenette
DEAD TO RIGHTS
Goldstein, Jonathan
BODY OF INFLUENCE 2
Goldstone, Dana
NORMA JEAN AND MARILYN
Goldthwait, Bobcat
OUT THERE
Goldwyn, Tony
BOYS NEXT DOOR, THE
SUBSTANCE OF FIRE, THE
TRUMAN
Golino, Valeria
JOHN CARPENTER'S ESCAPE FROM L.A.
Golov, Brett
AMANDA AND THE ALIEN
Golovin, Igor
CHEKIST, THE
Golz, Glenn
FRISK
Gomer, Emlyn
HEDD WYNN
Gomez, Carlos
HOSTILE INTENTIONS
STREETCAR NAMED DESIRE, A
Gomez, Casim
BUGGED
Gomez, Cristina
SMALL WONDERS
Gomez, Glenn
HEAVEN'S PRISONERS
Gomez, Henry
MAXIMUM RISK
Gomez, Jaime
SOLO
Gomez, Panchito
SAINTS AND SINNERS
Gomez, Rick
MERCY
Gomez, Sylvia
PRIMAL FEAR
Gomez-Preston, Reagan
JERRY MAGUIRE
Gong, Michael Gregory
ERASER
Gontha, H. Rudy
QUEST, THE
Gonyeo, Gloria
DADETOWN
Gonzalez, Adoni
LAND AND FREEDOM
Gonzalez, Anthony Richard
BIRDCAGE, THE
Gonzalez, Barbara
LOTTO LAND
Gonzalez, Clifton
SGT. BILKO
Gonzalez, Daniel
COURAGE UNDER FIRE
Gonzalez, Delia
GRACE OF MY HEART
Gonzalez Gonzalez, Clifton
ONE MAN'S JUSTICE
Gonzalez, Jose Luis
LAND AND FREEDOM
Gonzalez, Mares
JOHNNY 100 PESOS
Gonzalez, Maricela
LONE STAR
Good, Melanie
DESIRE
ONE GOOD TURN
Goodall, Caroline
WHITE SQUALL
Goode, Cheryl
BOYS
Goode, Conrad
BULLETPROOF
Goode, Frank
DON'T LET YOUR MEAT LOAF
Gooden, Cara
MY FELLOW AMERICANS
Goodhart, Donna
SANDMAN, THE
Goodin, Mark
PERFECT CANDIDATE, A
Gooding, Ben
BEAUTIFUL GIRLS
Gooding Jr., Cuba
JERRY MAGUIRE
TUSKEGEE AIRMEN, THE
Goodman, Henry
MARY REILLY
Goodman, John
MOTHER NIGHT
PIE IN THE SKY
STREETCAR NAMED DESIRE, A
Goodman-Hill, Tom
IN LOVE AND WAR
Goodrich, Justin
BIG BULLY
Goodson, Ludy
THEY BITE
Goodwill, Sarah
WHERE'S THE MONEY, NOREEN?
Goodwin, Alexander
I'M NOT RAPPAPORT
Goos, Jeffrey L.
CITIZEN RUTH
Goossen, Greg
CHAMBER, THE
Gopnik, Adam
LINE KING: THE AL HIRSCHFELD STORY, THE
Gordon, Abraham
CARNOSAUR 3: PRIMAL SPECIES
Gordon, Dan
SOME MOTHER'S SON
Gordon, Eve
HEIDI CHRONICLES, THE
Gordon, Jade
GRACE OF MY HEART
Gordon, Joel
RUDE
Gordon, Mark
YOUNG POISONER'S HANDBOOK, THE
Gordon, Mary Kathleen
YESTERDAY'S TARGET
Gordon, Meredith
FLED
Gordon, Mitchell
EDDIE
Gordon, Stuart
ARRIVAL, THE
Gordon-Levitt, Joseph
JUROR, THE
Gore II, George O.
EDDIE
Gorham, Mel
CURDLED
Gori, Evelina
MILLE BOLLE BLU
Goric, Voyo
FATALLY YOURS
Gorlitsky, Lisa
. . . AT FIRST SIGHT
Gorman, Bill
DADETOWN
Gorman, Cliff
SKIN
Gorov, Kiril
RASPUTIN
Gorry, David
MICHAEL COLLINS
Gosselin, Marc
EXTREME MEASURES
Gossett Jr., Louis
IRON EAGLE IV
Gossett, Robert
PHOENIX
Gossom Jr., Thom
CHAMBER, THE
Gosztonyi, Janos
RASPUTIN
Gottlieb, Heather
WALKING AND TALKING
Gottschall, Ruth
EVERYONE SAYS I LOVE YOU
Gotz, Stu
FEMALIEN
Gould, Clio
SHOPPING
Gould, Dana
MY FELLOW AMERICANS
Gould, David
SWINGERS
Gould, Elliott
BOY CALLED HATE, A
4 TALES OF 2 CITIES
Gould, Graydon
MISSION: IMPOSSIBLE
ROUJIN-Z
Gould, Harold
LOVER'S KNOT
Gould, Nancy
CROCODILES IN AMSTERDAM
Gould, Richard
WELCOME TO THE DOLLHOUSE
Goulet, Robert
LINE KING: THE AL HIRSCHFELD STORY, THE
MR. WRONG
Gowans, Kirsty
TWO FRIENDS
Goya, Ilinca
JOSH KIRBY . . . TIME WARRIOR!: EGGS FROM 70,000,000 B.C.
Goyvaerts, Andrew
WAR OF THE BUTTONS, THE
Goznobi, Abdul
HIGH SCHOOL HIGH
Graas, John Christian
LAZARUS MAN, THE
Grace, Anna
GIRLS TOWN
I SHOT ANDY WARHOL
Grace, April
HEADLESS BODY IN TOPLESS BAR
Grace, Catherine
TALKING ABOUT SEX
Grace, Nickolas
TWO DEATHS
Grace, Wayne
LAZARUS MAN, THE
Gradilone, Michael
ANIMAL INSTINCTS III: THE SEDUCTRESS
Graf, Allan
LAST MAN STANDING
Graf, David
CITIZEN RUTH
Graff, Sasha
JANE EYRE
Graham, Aimee
FROM DUSK TILL DAWN

Graham, Alissa
MATILDA
Graham, Amanda
MATILDA
Graham, Ashley Anne
SHADOW WARRIORS
Graham, Beverly
TOO FAST, TOO YOUNG
Graham, Billy
BUGGED
Graham, Currie
PORTRAITS OF A KILLER
Graham, Donald
MURDERED INNOCENCE
Graham, Gary
NECRONOMICON: BOOK OF THE DEAD
Graham, Gerrit
NATIONAL LAMPOON'S FAVORITE DEADLY SINS
Graham, Ginny
UP CLOSE AND PERSONAL
Graham, Heather
ENTERTAINING ANGELS: THE DOROTHY DAY STORY
SWINGERS
Graham, Holter
FLY AWAY HOME
Graham, Leslie
UNFORGETTABLE
Graham, Lyla
DOWN, OUT AND DANGEROUS
Graham, Peter
DARKMAN III: DIE DARKMAN DIE
Graham, Ronny
SUBSTANCE OF FIRE, THE
Graham, Samaria
CHILDREN OF THE CORN: THE GATHERING
Graham, Sasha
POLYMORPH
Graham, Stuart
MICHAEL COLLINS
Graham, Tiffiny Money
PREACHER'S WIFE, THE
Grahm, Marcus
ANIMAL INSTINCTS III: THE SEDUCTRESS
Grainger, Gawn
AUGUST
Grammer, Kelsey
DOWN PERISCOPE
GALAXIES ARE COLLIDING
Grana, Sam
SUGARTIME
Grandi, Maria
WHO KILLED PASOLINI?
Graney, Oliver
BEFORE AND AFTER
Granger, Farley
CELLULOID CLOSET, THE
Granger, Philip
FINAL CUT, THE
WHITE TIGER
Granier, Oliver
CELESTIAL CLOCKWORK
Grant, Beth
NORMA JEAN AND MARILYN
TIME TO KILL, A
Grant, Brian
EDDIE
IMMORTALS, THE
Grant, Charles
PLAYBACK
Grant, Clare
ISLAND OF DR. MOREAU, THE
Grant, Crystal Celeste
LAWNMOWER MAN 2: BEYOND CYBERSPACE
Grant, David Marshall
CHAMBER, THE
LAZARUS MAN, THE
Grant, Dennis
CITIZEN RUTH
Grant, Hugh
EXTREME MEASURES
Grant, Jennifer
EVENING STAR, THE
Grant, Jessica Brooks
BED OF ROSES
Grant, Lee
IT'S MY PARTY
SUBSTANCE OF FIRE, THE
Grant, Omar
SMALL WONDERS
Grant, Richard E.
COLD LIGHT OF DAY
JACK & SARAH
PORTRAIT OF A LADY, THE
TWELFTH NIGHT
Grant, Rodney A.
SUBSTITUTE, THE
Grant, Sandra P.
SURGEON, THE
Grant, Sean
EVERYONE SAYS I LOVE YOU
Grassini, Alessandro
OUTRAGE
Grateful Dead, The
BERKELEY IN THE 60S
Gratzer, Hans
SHADOW OF ANGELS
Grau, Ernesto
LAND AND FREEDOM
Graubard, Dave
BREAKAWAY
Graves, Karron
CRUCIBLE, THE
Gray, Amee
CRUCIBLE, THE
Gray, Andy
SMALL FACES
Gray, Bruce
SPY HARD
UP CLOSE AND PERSONAL
Gray, Christopher
FEAR
Gray, Diva
EVERYONE SAYS I LOVE YOU
Gray, Erin M.
MATILDA
Gray, John
MARS ATTACKS!
Gray, Linda
LAND BEFORE TIME IV: JOURNEY THROUGH THE MISTS
Gray, Marc
RACE THE SUN
Gray, Mike
CHAIN REACTION
Gray, Spalding
DIABOLIQUE
Grayson, C.J.
BIG BULLY
Grayson, Jerry
PROTEUS
STRIPTEASE
Graziano, John
SGT. KABUKIMAN N.Y.P.D.
Graziosi, Paolo
WHO KILLED PASOLINI?
Greco, Joe
NUTTY PROFESSOR, THE
Greco, Marco
SLEEPERS
Greco, Maurizio
WHO KILLED PASOLINI?
Greco, Paul
CABLE GUY, THE
IF LUCY FELL
LOVE IS ALL THERE IS
Green, Adolph
SUBSTANCE OF FIRE, THE
Green, Colton
EVERYONE SAYS I LOVE YOU
Green, Crystal Laws
FAMILY THING, A
Green, Danny
KINGPIN
Green, Fanni
I'M NOT RAPPAPORT
Green, Jaquita
ED
Green, Johnny
JOSH KIRBY . . . TIME WARRIOR!: LAST BATTLE FOR THE UNIVERSE
Green, Melrose Larry
EDDIE
Green, Reginald
DON'T BE A MENACE TO SOUTH CENTRAL WHILE DRINKING YOUR JUICE IN THE HOOD
Green, Rodney
DON'T LET YOUR MEAT LOAF
Green, Seth
TO GILLIAN ON HER 37TH BIRTHDAY
Greenbaum, Wesley
NEUROSIA: 50 YEARS OF PERVERSITY
Greenberg, Ari
FIRST WIVES CLUB, THE
Greenblatt, William
HOMECOMING
Greenbud, Sid
KINGPIN
Greenbury, Andrew
KINGPIN
Greenbury, Nicholas
KINGPIN
Greene, B.J.
BODY COUNT
Greene, Ellen
MURDERED INNOCENCE
ONE FINE DAY
Greene, Erika
THAT THING YOU DO!
Greene, John
FUGITIVE RAGE
Greene Jr., Benjamin
PEOPLE VS. LARRY FLYNT, THE
Greene, Katherine
MR. ICE CREAM MAN
Greene, Michele
HOW THE WEST WAS FUN
Greene, Peter
RICH MAN'S WIFE, THE
Greenhouse, Kate
VIRUS
Greenhut, Jennifer
CRAFT, THE
Greening, Mary
ENTERTAINING ANGELS: THE DOROTHY DAY STORY
Greenly, Theo
JERRY MAGUIRE
Greenquist, Brad
ASSAULT AT WEST POINT
BLACK OUT
Greenstein, Oded
DEADLY OUTBREAK
Greenwald, Alex
PIG'S TALE, A
Greenwalt, Evan
CHILDREN OF THE CORN: THE GATHERING

Greenwood, Kathryn
KIDS IN THE HALL: BRAIN CANDY
Greer, Larry
TRUMAN
Greeves, Peter
MUPPET TREASURE ISLAND
Gregan, Karen S.
BAJA
Gregory, Cezette
EDDIE
Gregory, Goliath
MATILDA
Gregory, Ian
NORMA JEAN AND MARILYN
PINOCCHIO'S REVENGE
Gregory, Michael
ERASER
Gregson Wagner, Natasha
HIGH SCHOOL HIGH
Gregus, Luba
ABUSE
Greist, Kim
HOMEWARD BOUND II: LOST IN SAN FRANCISCO
Grenier, Zach
MAXIMUM RISK
MOTHER NIGHT
Grennan, Emmett
FRIEND OF THE FAMILY 2
ZARKORR! THE INVADER
Grennell, Aiden
MICHAEL COLLINS
Gress, Googie
INFINITY
Gress, Googy
KINGPIN
Grettve, Sten
EVIL ED
Grevill, Laurent
JACK & SARAH
Grey, Jennifer
LOVER'S KNOT
PORTRAITS OF A KILLER
Grey, Joel
VENUS RISING
Greyeyes, Michael
RUDE
Gribble, Bill
LARRY MCMURTRY'S STREETS OF LAREDO
Grieco, Richard
DEMOLITIONIST, THE
Grier, Pam
JOHN CARPENTER'S ESCAPE FROM L.A.
MARS ATTACKS!
ORIGINAL GANGSTAS
SERIAL KILLER
Griesemer, Ida
SPITFIRE GRILL, THE
Griesemer, John
CRUCIBLE, THE
LONE STAR
Grifasi, Joe
HEAVY
ONE FINE DAY
Grifell, Maruja
AVENTURERA
Griffin, Douglas
BODY COUNT
Griffin, John
EVERYONE SAYS I LOVE YOU
Griffin, Kathy
CABLE GUY, THE
Griffin, Katie
ELECTRA
Griffin, S.A.
BED OF ROSES
Griffin, Susan
BERKELEY IN THE 60S
Griffis, Robert
PUBLIC ENEMIES
Griffith, Andy
SPY HARD
Griffith, Kirk
LARRY MCMURTRY'S STREETS OF LAREDO
Griffith, Melanie
MULHOLLAND FALLS
TWO MUCH
Griffith, Thomas Ian
HOLLOW POINT
Griffiths, Lydia
HEDD WYNN
Griffiths, Michael
TIMELESS
Griffiths, Peter
TWO FRIENDS
Griffiths, Rachel
JUDE
Griffiths, Roger Ashton
JUDE
Griffus, Milissa
TEXAS PAYBACK
Grillo, Aldo
BATON ROUGE
Grillo, Amanda
TRIGGER EFFECT, THE
Grillo, John
CRACKER: THE MADWOMAN IN THE ATTIC
JACK & SARAH
Grimes, Frank
WAR OF THE BUTTONS, THE
Grimes, Tammy
MODERN AFFAIR, A
Grimshaw, Jim
PEOPLE VS. LARRY FLYNT, THE
Grindley, Anne
BEWARE: CHILDREN AT PLAY
Grinnell, Gail
PARADISE LOST: THE CHILD MURDERS AT ROBIN HOOD HILLS
Grippo, Carmine
LAST MAN STANDING
Griswold, Kenny
KINGPIN
KINGPIN
Grober, Lee
WITCHCRAFT: SALEM'S GHOST
Grobon, Guillemette
PROPRIETOR, THE
SINGLE GIRL, A
Grochau, Robert
DOWN PERISCOPE
Grodenchik, Max
RUMPELSTILTSKIN
Gross, Arye
MOTHER NIGHT
Gross, Brian
TIGER HEART
Gross, Magdalena
GIRLFRIENDS
Gross, Mary
EVENING STAR, THE
Gross, Michael
SOMETIMES THEY COME BACK . . . AGAIN
TREMORS 2: AFTERSHOCKS
Gross, Richard
CHILDREN OF THE CORN: THE GATHERING
CROSSCUT
PHENOMENON
Grossman, De'Prise
ZARKORR! THE INVADER
Groth, Robin
INDEPENDENCE DAY
Grove, Rick
MOTHER
Grover, George
FRIGHTENERS, THE
Grover, Max
FRIGHTENERS, THE
Grover, Stanley
EXECUTIVE DECISION
Grow, Lincoln
SPITFIRE GRILL, THE
Grow, Louise
SPITFIRE GRILL, THE
Gruault, Jean
FRANCOIS TRUFFAUT: STOLEN PORTRAITS
Grube, Thomas
TIMELESS
Grudgeon, Sarah
BREAKING THE WAVES
Gruenenfelder, Kim
BODY OF INFLUENCE 2
Gruffyd, Arwel
HEDD WYNN
Grunberg, Greg
PALLBEARER, THE
TRIGGER EFFECT, THE
Gruschka, Bela
VISITORS, THE
Gu Zhifen
BLUSH
Guan Lina
CHUNGKING EXPRESS
Guardino, Charles
SAINTS AND SINNERS
Guarrera, Alessandro
STAR MAKER, THE
Guaspari-Tzavaras, Roberta
SMALL WONDERS
Guastaferro, Joe
CHAIN REACTION
Guber, Elizabeth
BIO-DOME
CRAFT, THE
Gudge, Naomi
ANGELS AND INSECTS
Gudluvin, Giovanni
LET'S GET BIZZEE
Gudmundson, Jon
PIG'S TALE, A
Guegan, Philippe
HORSEMAN ON THE ROOF
Guerin, Michael
DENTIST, THE
Gueron, Ivan
LIFEFORM
PINOCCHIO'S REVENGE
Guerra, Castulo
LAWNMOWER MAN 2: BEYOND CYBERSPACE
Guerra, Saverio
NATIONAL LAMPOON'S FAVORITE DEADLY SINS
SLEEPERS
Guerrero, Eduardo Jose
SILENCE OF NETO, THE
Guerria, Lance
FUNERAL, THE
Guerrieri, Giorgio
STAR MAKER, THE
Guertchikoff, Louba
LITTLE INDIAN, BIG CITY
Guesmi, Samir
HALFMOON
Guess, Alvaleta
BIG NIGHT

Guest, Nicholas
ADRENALIN: FEAR THE RUSH
LATE SHIFT, THE
RAVENHAWK
Guez, Marine
RIDICULE
Gugino, Carla
HOMEWARD BOUND II: LOST IN SAN FRANCISCO
MICHAEL
WAR AT HOME, THE
Gugushe, Biski
ANNIE O
SABRINA, THE TEENAGE WITCH
Guhl, Sher
TWO FRIENDS
Guichard II, Vernon
FAN, THE
Guida, Tony
OPEN SEASON
Guidera, Anthony
ROCK, THE
Guijar, Francisco
BATON ROUGE
Guijar, Paco
BATON ROUGE
Guilfoyle, Paul
CELTIC PRIDE
EXTREME MEASURES
HEAVEN'S PRISONERS
LOOKING FOR RICHARD
MANNY & LO
RANSOM
STRIPTEASE
Guillard Jr., Larry
TREES LOUNGE
Guillaume, Robert
FIRST KID
SPY HARD
Guillen-Cuervo, Fernando
MOUTH TO MOUTH
Guilliard, Leontine
UP CLOSE AND PERSONAL
Guillier, Azur
HORSEMAN ON THE ROOF
Guillory, Bennet
AMERICA'S DREAM
TUSKEGEE AIRMEN, THE
Guinee, Tim
BEAVIS AND BUTT-HEAD DO AMERICA
BLACK DAY BLUE NIGHT
COURAGE UNDER FIRE
4 TALES OF 2 CITIES
LILY DALE
POMPATUS OF LOVE, THE
Guinness, Rowena
FIST OF THE NORTH STAR
ONE GOOD TURN
Guitierez, Therese Marie
CURDLED
Guittonneau, Catherine
SINGLE GIRL, A
Gulino, John P.
GLIMMER MAN, THE
Gullotta, Leo
STAR MAKER, THE
Gummersall, Devon
INDEPENDENCE DAY
IT'S MY PARTY
Gundrum, G. Gunny
DADETOWN
Guneratne, Anthony
SOME FOLKS CALL IT A SLING BLADE
Gunn, Heather
FULL BODY MASSAGE
Gunn, Janet
CARNOSAUR 3: PRIMAL SPECIES
QUEST, THE
SWEEPER, THE
Gunn, Jessica
HAPPY GILMORE
Gunter, Ben
THEY BITE
Gunther, Dan
DENISE CALLS UP
Gunther, Michael
FRISK
Gunton, Bob
BROKEN ARROW
GLIMMER MAN, THE
MISSING PIECES
Guo Zhiqiang
BLACK MOUNTAIN
Gurland, Robert
SYNTHETIC PLEASURES
Gurney, Robin
FRISK
Gurwitch, Annabelle
CABLE GUY, THE
Gusevs, Rob
MRS. WINTERBOURNE
Gusner, Amina
FLIRT
Gutierrez, Bo
SANDMAN, THE
Gutierrez, Miguel
BITTER SUGAR
Gutierrez, Studio
JACK
Gutowski, Rita
SANDMAN, THE
Guy, Damon
LONE STAR
Guy, Dejuan
ONE MAN'S JUSTICE
SAINTS AND SINNERS
Guy, Jasmine
AMERICA'S DREAM
Guyer, Cindy
MIRROR HAS TWO FACES, THE
Guyer, Murphy
CITY HALL
Guzaldo, Joe
EVIL HAS A FACE
Guzman, Jesus Alberto
JERRY MAGUIRE
Guzman, Luis
LOTTO LAND
SUBSTITUTE, THE
Guzman, Patricia
JOHNNY 100 PESOS
Guzzo, Francesco
STAR MAKER, THE
Haas, Lukas
BOYS
EVERYONE SAYS I LOVE YOU
MARS ATTACKS!
Haas, Mark
FLATTERED
Haas, Oona
ANGELS AND INSECTS
Haas, Victoria
POISON IVY 2: LILY
Haas, Vita
ANGELS AND INSECTS
Haberle, Sean
SURGEON, THE
Habl, Karel
KASPAR HAUSER
Hachey, Lyne
TALES FROM THE CRYPT PRESENTS BORDELLO OF BLOOD
Hack, Olivia
VERY BRADY SEQUEL, A
Hackel, Leor Livneh
MATILDA
Hackett, Bill
FIRE ON THE MOUNTAIN
Hackett, Jonathan
BREAKING THE WAVES
Hackett, Kevin Dean
EXIT
Hackford, Rio
SWINGERS
Hackman, Charlotte
LAST DANCE
Hackman, Gene
BIRDCAGE, THE
CHAMBER, THE
EXTREME MEASURES
Hadary, Jonathan
TIME TO KILL, A
Haddigan, Mark
101 DALMATIANS
Haddock, Paula
PEOPLE VS. LARRY FLYNT, THE
Haddon, Laurence
INFINITY
Hadfield, Mark
MIDWINTER'S TALE, A
Hadji-Lazaro, Francois
CEMETERY MAN
Hadler, Carsten
NEUROSIA: 50 YEARS OF PERVERSITY
Hadley, Joey
PEOPLE VS. LARRY FLYNT, THE
Hadley, Lisa Ann
JERRY MAGUIRE
Hafler, Max
MICHAEL COLLINS
Hafsi, Saima
SILENCES OF THE PALACE, THE
Hagan, Jennifer
JACK
Hagan, Kevin
EVERYONE SAYS I LOVE YOU
Hagane, Tomoko
GIRL 6
Hageboeck, T.J.
ROCK, THE
Hagen, Claire
FUGITIVE RAGE
Hagen, Julia
MARY REILLY
Hagen, Molly
DENTIST, THE
SOMETIMES THEY COME BACK . . . AGAIN
Hagen, Ross
FUGITIVE RAGE
OVER THE WIRE
Hager, Dave
LAST DANCE
Haggerty, Bob
CELTIC PRIDE
Haggerty, Julie
WIFE, THE
Hagiwara, Michael
JOSH KIRBY . . . TIME WARRIOR!: JOURNEY TO THE MAGIC CAVERN
Hagler, Nik
LARRY MCMURTRY'S STREETS OF LAREDO
Hagon, Garrick
MISSION: IMPOSSIBLE
Hahn, Jessica
AMANDA AND THE ALIEN
Haiduc, Ion
MAGIC IN THE MIRROR
SPELLBREAKER: SECRET OF THE LEPRECHAUNS
Haiduk, Stacey
YESTERDAY'S TARGET

Hail, Mack
MR. ICE CREAM MAN
Haines, Gibby
DEAD MAN
Hair, Donny
HARD WAY OUT: BLOODFIST VIII
Hairston, Kiyoko M
MIRROR HAS TWO FACES, THE
Hajek, Stanislav
KASPAR HAUSER
Haji, Takaya
SANCTUARY: THE MOVIE
Halaby, John R.F.
WATCH ME
Halbert, Stephen
DELTA OF VENUS
Haler, Ted
RUMPELSTILTSKIN
Haley, Brian
MARS ATTACKS!
Haley, Jack
EDDIE
Haley, R.M.
BED OF ROSES
Halfhide Jr., Gerald
DON'T LET YOUR MEAT LOAF
Halgas, George
EDDIE
Hall, Albert
COURAGE UNDER FIRE
GET ON THE BUS
GREAT WHITE HYPE, THE
Hall, Angela
BOYS
Hall, Ann Marie
PEOPLE VS. LARRY FLYNT, THE
Hall, Anthony
SUNSET PARK
Hall, Anthony Michael
DEATH ARTIST, THE
GRAVE, THE
Hall, Betty Lynn
SLING BLADE
Hall, Bug
STUPIDS, THE
Hall, Carrie
DESIRE
Hall, Davis
I SHOT ANDY WARHOL
Hall, Hanna
HOMECOMING
Hall, Irma P.
FAMILY THING, A
Hall, J. D.
PHANTOM 2040: THE GHOST WHO WALKS
Hall, Landon
BODY OF INFLUENCE 2
LITTLE WITCHES
OVER THE WIRE
Hall, Lois
LETTER TO MY KILLER
Hall, Philip Baker
EYE FOR AN EYE
Hall, Randy
LAST MAN STANDING
RAVENHAWK
Hall, Rick
MY FELLOW AMERICANS
Hall, Ron
BLOODSPORT II: THE NEXT KUMITE
RAW TARGET
Hall, Sara Caitlin
ANGELA
Hall, Tonya
DEMOLITIONIST, THE
Hall, Vondie Curtis
WILLIAM SHAKESPEARE'S ROMEO + JULIET
Hallahan, Charles
EXECUTIVE DECISION
FAN, THE
RICH MAN'S WIFE, THE
Halldorsson, Gisli
COLD FEVER
Hallheden, Karin
EVIL ED
Halliday, Courtney
DON'T LET YOUR MEAT LOAF
Hallier, Lori
MOONSHINE HIGHWAY
NIGHT OF THE TWISTERS
Hallowell, Todd
RANSOM
Halme, Tony
FIST OF THE NORTH STAR
Halpern, Lisa
NUTTY PROFESSOR, THE
Halpin, Luke
FLIPPER
Halston, Julie
JUROR, THE
Halston, Rodger
CARNOSAUR 3: PRIMAL SPECIES
CRIMINAL HEARTS
UNKNOWN ORIGIN
Halton, Jack
ABUSE
Halvorson, Brad
SWINGERS
Hama, Stuart
WHISPERING, THE
Hamada, Cheryl
CHAIN REACTION
Hambline, Russell
TIME TO KILL, A
Hamburger, Philip
LINE KING: THE AL HIRSCHFELD STORY, THE
Hamill, Mark
PHANTOM 2040: THE GHOST WHO WALKS
Hamill, Pete
ONE FINE DAY
Hamill, Rita
MOLL FLANDERS
Hamilton, Allen
CHAIN REACTION
Hamilton, Barbara
BOGUS
Hamilton, Emily
HAUNTED
Hamilton, Eugenia
DUNSTON CHECKS IN
Hamilton, George
PLAYBACK
Hamilton, Josh
PROPRIETOR, THE
Hamilton, Lalaneya
LITTLE WITCHES
Hamilton, Linda
MOTHER'S PRAYER, A
Hamilton, Lisa Gay
PALOOKAVILLE
Hamilton, Mark
ZARKORR! THE INVADER
Hamilton, Paula
SHAMELESS
Hamilton, Quancetia
BOGUS
Hamilton, Rich
BEWARE: CHILDREN AT PLAY
Hamilton, Thomas J.
SHARON'S SECRET
Hamilton-Montoute, Khalia
PREACHER'S WIFE, THE
Hamlin, Harry
CELLULOID CLOSET, THE
Hamm, Nick
HEIDI FLEISS HOLLYWOOD MADAM
Hammer, Ben
SLEEPERS
Hammer, M.C.
ONE MAN'S JUSTICE
Hammerbox
HYPE!
Hammil, John
INFINITY
Hammill, John
FATALLY YOURS
Hammond, Brandon
FAN, THE
MARS ATTACKS!
ROAD TO GALVESTON, THE
Hammond, Darrell
CELTIC PRIDE
Hammond, Gabrielle
RACE THE SUN
Hammond, John
STREET FIGHTER II: THE ANIMATED MOVIE
Hammond, Roger
JOSEPH CONRAD'S THE SECRET AGENT
Hammond, Vincent
NECRONOMICON: BOOK OF THE DEAD
Hammons, Brian
TIN CUP
Hampton, Colonel Bruce
SLING BLADE
Hampton, James
SLING BLADE
Hamrick, Ashley
MR. HOLLAND'S OPUS
Hamrouni, Abdellatif
ENGLISH PATIENT, THE
Hamud, Mensur
SWINGERS
Han Guichen
BLACK MOUNTAIN
Han, Maggie
OPEN SEASON
Han, Ong Soo
BLOODSPORT II: THE NEXT KUMITE
QUEST, THE
Hanau, Sasha
MARY REILLY
Hancisse, Thierry
LA COMEDIE-FRANCAISE OU L'AMOUR JOUE
Hancke, Rik
DAENS
Handler, Evan
RANSOM
Handy, Bill
SHARON'S SECRET
Handy, Craig
KANSAS CITY
Haney, Anne
MOTHER
Haney, Kate Ann
PHAT BEACH
Haney, Tony
JAMES AND THE GIANT PEACH
Hanft, Helen
ASSOCIATE, THE
Hankin, Mitchell
DESIRE
Hanks, Colin
THAT THING YOU DO!
Hanks, Elizabeth
THAT THING YOU DO!

Hanks, Tom
CELLULOID CLOSET, THE
THAT THING YOU DO!
Hanley, Joe
MICHAEL COLLINS
Hanley, Roberta
DELTA OF VENUS
TOLLBOOTH
TREES LOUNGE
Hanley, Tres
GRIM
Hanlin, Joe
BREAKAWAY
Hanlon, Peter
ANNIE O
MATERNAL INSTINCTS
Hann-Byrd, Adam
DIABOLIQUE
Hannah, Bob
FLED
NEON BIBLE, THE
Hannah, Daryl
TWO MUCH
Hannah, John
FINAL CUT, THE
MADAGASCAR SKIN
Hannan, Carolynn
DADETOWN
Hannock, Patty
MACHINE, THE
Hannon, Joey
FUNERAL, THE
Hanova, Irena
DELTA OF VENUS
Hanover, Donna
PEOPLE VS. LARRY FLYNT, THE
RANSOM
Hansen, Juliana
LAND BEFORE TIME IV: JOURNEY THROUGH THE MISTS
Hansen, Nicole
EXIT
Hansen, T.J.
VIRTUAL ENCOUNTERS
Hanson, Geoff
ARRIVAL, THE
Hanson, Heather
TALES FROM THE CRYPT PRESENTS BORDELLO OF BLOOD
Hanson, Kevin
ROBIN OF LOCKSLEY
Hansson, Sanna
EVIL ED
Hansudi, Eddy
WITHOUT MERCY
Hanusova, Natasa
COLD LIGHT OF DAY
Hara, Chikako
FLIRT
Harada, Shuichi
MABOROSI
Haraldson, Rurik
VIKING SAGAS, THE
Harazim, Donna
TALKING ABOUT SEX
Harden, Marcia Gay
FAR HARBOR
FIRST WIVES CLUB, THE
SPITFIRE GRILL, THE
SPY HARD
Hardie, James
GREAT WHITE HYPE, THE
Hardie, Kate
JACK & SARAH
Hardin, Ian
CANNIBAL! THE MUSICAL
Hardin, Jerry
ASSOCIATE, THE
GHOSTS OF MISSISSIPPI
STREETCAR NAMED DESIRE, A
Hardin, Melora
CHAMELEON
Harding, D. Garnet
BEYOND THE CALL
EXTREME MEASURES
Harding, Jan Leslie
4 TALES OF 2 CITIES
Harding, Tonya
BREAKAWAY
Hardman, Karl
SANTA CLAWS
Hardman-Broughton, Ann
EVENING STAR, THE
Hardy, Dona
CABLE GUY, THE
Hardy, Gerard
RIDICULE
Hardy, John
EXECUTIVE DECISION
Hardy, John W.
CHAIN REACTION
Hardy, Jonathan
TUNNEL VISION
Hardy, Trishalee
WOMAN UNDONE, A
Hardy, William
LARRY MCMURTRY'S STREETS OF LAREDO
MAN WITH THE PERFECT SWING, THE
Harewood, David
SHAMELESS
Hargreaves, Missy
EDIE & PEN
Harker, Susannah
SURVIVING PICASSO
Harker, Wiley
TRUMAN
Harkins, Kelley
MUTANT MAN
Harkness, Julie L.
THAT THING YOU DO!
Harlan, Frank
HYPE!
Harley, Graham
SUGARTIME
Harley, Jim
GHOSTS OF MISSISSIPPI
Harley, Robert
SOLITAIRE FOR TWO
Harman, Brett
COLONY, THE
Harman, Sylvia
EDDIE
Harmon, Linda
SPY HARD
Harmon, Mark
LAST SUPPER, THE
LONG ROAD HOME, THE
Harmstorf, Raimund
VIKING SAGAS, THE
WOLVES, THE
Harnesk, Johan
EVIL ED
Harnos, Christine
HELLRAISER: BLOODLINE
Harper, Hill
GET ON THE BUS
Harper, James
DOWN PERISCOPE
ONE MAN'S JUSTICE
WIDOW'S KISS
Harper, Jessica
BOYS
Harper, Kate
PASSION OF DARKLY NOON, THE
Harper, Russel
HOUSE ARREST
Harper, Tess
CHILDREN OF FURY
ROAD TO GALVESTON, THE
Harpur, Elizabeth
BOGUS
STAND OFF, THE
Harrell, James
FAMILY THING, A
MICHAEL
Harrelson, Brett
PEOPLE VS. LARRY FLYNT, THE
Harrelson, Woody
KINGPIN
PEOPLE VS. LARRY FLYNT, THE
SUNCHASER
Harries, Davyd
BEAUTIFUL THING
Harries, Susan
MADAGASCAR SKIN
Harrington, Chelsea
MULHOLLAND FALLS
Harrington, Cheryl Francis
SGT. BILKO
Harris, Alisa
CLUBHOUSE DETECTIVES
Harris, Asa
FAMILY THING, A
Harris, Baxter
ASSOCIATE, THE
Harris, Becky
THEY BITE
Harris, Bob L.
RIDERS OF THE PURPLE SAGE
Harris, Brett
ANGELS AND INSECTS
Harris, Bruklin
GIRLS TOWN
Harris, Carli
SOLITAIRE FOR TWO
Harris, Cristi
NIGHT OF THE SCARECROW
Harris, Danielle
DAYLIGHT
Harris, David
NATIONAL LAMPOON'S FAVORITE DEADLY SINS
Harris, Ed
EYE FOR AN EYE
RIDERS OF THE PURPLE SAGE
ROCK, THE
Harris, Jackie
KIDS IN THE HALL: BRAIN CANDY
TAILS YOU LIVE, HEADS YOU'RE DEAD
Harris, James
SUNSET PARK
Harris, Jared
DEAD MAN
I SHOT ANDY WARHOL
Harris, Julie
CARRIED AWAY
Harris, Lara
DOGFIGHTERS, THE
Harris, Laura
HALFBACK OF NOTRE DAME, THE
Harris, Lisa
ED'S NEXT MOVE
Harris, Mark
OFF AND RUNNING
Harris, Mel
SHARON'S SECRET
Harris, Michael
MR. STITCH
Harris, Neil Patrick
MAN IN THE ATTIC, THE
Harris, Ramsey
FAMILY THING, A

Harris, Randy "Roughhouse"
GREAT WHITE HYPE, THE
Harris, Ricky
HIGH SCHOOL HIGH
Harris, Rosemary
HAMLET
LOOKING FOR RICHARD
Harris, Rutha
PREACHER'S WIFE, THE
Harris, Samantha
D3: THE MIGHTY DUCKS
Harris, Shawntae
KAZAAM
Harris, Steve
ROCK, THE
Harris, Virginia
RAVENHAWK
Harrison, Cynthia
COLONY, THE
Harrison, Dale
CURTIS'S CHARM
Harrison, Gavin
PUBLIC ENEMIES
Harrison, Gene
RANSOM
Harrison, Gregory
IT'S MY PARTY
Harrison, John
TEXAS CHAINSAW MASSACRE: THE NEXT GENERATION
Harrison, Lois
JOHNNY SHORTWAVE
Harrison, Mickey
MR. WRONG
Harrison, Tim
MICHAEL
Harrod, David
MICHAEL
TUSKEGEE AIRMEN, THE
Harrold, Jamie
GETTING AWAY WITH MURDER
I SHOT ANDY WARHOL
Harry, Deborah
HEAVY
PHANTOM 2040: THE GHOST WHO WALKS
Harscheid, Karla
FAMILY THING, A
Hart, Amia
PREACHER'S WIFE, THE
Hart, Anita
BLACK SCORPION
Hart, Christopher Paul
SGT. BILKO
Hart, Emily
IF LUCY FELL
Hart, Ian
LAND AND FREEDOM
MICHAEL COLLINS
Hart, Ingrid
KIDS IN THE HALL: BRAIN CANDY
Hart, Joanne
KAZAAM
Hart, Joe
TIMELESS
Hart, Judith
CITIZEN RUTH
Hart, Kitty Carlisle
LINE KING: THE AL HIRSCHFELD STORY, THE
Hart, Linda
OFF AND RUNNING
TIN CUP
Hart, Melissa Joan
SABRINA, THE TEENAGE WITCH
Hart, Nikki
FAN, THE
Hart, Roderick
EVITA
Harte, Ken
BLOODSPORT II: THE NEXT KUMITE
Hartf, Bethany
THAT THING YOU DO!
Harth, C. Ernst
BREACH OF TRUST
Hartig, Meg
HEAVY
Hartig, Zandy
HEAVY
Hartley, Andrew
WHITE SQUALL
Hartley, Clabe
HARD JUSTICE
Hartley, Hal
FLIRT
Hartman, Phil
JINGLE ALL THE WAY
SGT. BILKO
Hartman, Ron
GETTING AWAY WITH MURDER
Hartman, Tara
PINOCCHIO'S REVENGE
WOMAN UNDONE, A
Hartman, Thomas
MIRROR HAS TWO FACES, THE
Hartmann, John Richard
RANSOM
Hartwell, Taea
FRIGHTENERS, THE
Harvey, Bob
MR. WRONG
NIGHT OF THE SCARECROW
Harvey, Claire Marie
TALES FROM THE CRYPT PRESENTS BORDELLO OF BLOOD
Harvey, David
STAND OFF, THE
Harvey, Don
LAST DANCE
SAWBONES
Harvey, Ellie
HAPPY GILMORE
Harvey, Eric Laray
TWISTER
Harvey, Pat
HIGH SCHOOL HIGH
Harvey, Robert
BOY CALLED HATE, A
LAZARUS MAN, THE
RUMPELSTILTSKIN
Harvey, Terrence
SECRETS & LIES
Harvey, Tom
MRS. WINTERBOURNE
Hasfal-Schou, Topaz
BREACH OF TRUST
TALES FROM THE CRYPT PRESENTS BORDELLO OF BLOOD
Hashimoto, Kikuko
MABOROSI
Hashimoto, Kuni
RACE THE SUN
Haskell, Susan
MRS. WINTERBOURNE
Hastings, Flynn
FRISK
Hastings, Melanie
FIRST KID
Hatcher, Granville
EXECUTIVE DECISION
Hatcher, Teri
HEAVEN'S PRISONERS
2 DAYS IN THE VALLEY
Hatchett, Patti
PEOPLE VS. LARRY FLYNT, THE
Hatem, Rosine "Ace"
BLACK SCORPION
Hathaway, Amy
COURAGE UNDER FIRE
Hatley, Carla
SCREAM
Hatosy, Sean
SLEEPERS
Hattstrom, Niklas
EVIL ED
Hauer, Rutger
MR. STITCH
Hauff, Thomas
MOTHER NIGHT
STAND OFF, THE
Hauge, Fredrik
EVIL ED
Haughey, Daniel
I SHOT ANDY WARHOL
Haughland, William
MOTHER NIGHT
Haugk, Charlie
CELTIC PRIDE
Hauman, Constance
MADAME BUTTERFLY
Hauser, Thomas
WHEN WE WERE KINGS
Hauser, Wings
ORIGINAL GANGSTAS
Hausman, Willo
CAUGHT
FAMILY THING, A
Have, Scott
STAR TREK: FIRST CONTACT
Haven, Todd
TO GILLIAN ON HER 37TH BIRTHDAY
Hawes, Joseph
ROCK, THE
Hawkes, John
FROM DUSK TILL DAWN
NIGHT OF THE SCARECROW
Hawkins, Thomas "Kirk"
LAST DANCE
Hawkins, Virginia
DOWN, OUT AND DANGEROUS
Hawks, Howard
PERSONAL JOURNEY WITH MARTIN SCORSESE THROUGH AMERICAN MOVIES, A
Hawks, Sunny
DEAR GOD
Hawley, Richard
CAPTIVES
Hawn, Goldie
EVERYONE SAYS I LOVE YOU
FIRST WIVES CLUB, THE
Hawthorne, Denys
EMMA
Hawthorne, Elizabeth
ALEX
FRIGHTENERS, THE
Hawthorne, Nigel
TWELFTH NIGHT
Hawtrey, Kay
IN LOVE AND WAR
KIDS IN THE HALL: BRAIN CANDY
TWO IF BY SEA
Hay, John
FIRE ON THE MOUNTAIN
Hayakawa, Rosalia
FROM DUSK TILL DAWN
Hayami, Sho
SANCTUARY: THE MOVIE
Hayashi, Henry
SGT. BILKO
SHARON'S SECRET
Hayden, Dennis
BEYOND DESIRE

Hayden, Julie
CABLE GUY, THE
Hayden, Luke
MICHAEL COLLINS
Hayden, Maria
MOLL FLANDERS
Hayek, Salma
FLED
FROM DUSK TILL DAWN
Hayes, Annie
SECRETS & LIES
Hayes, David
SUBSTITUTE, THE
Hayes, Deryl
HOMEWARD BOUND II: LOST IN SAN FRANCISCO
Hayes, Devalle
EVERYONE SAYS I LOVE YOU
Hayes, Hillary
STAR TREK: FIRST CONTACT
Hayes, Isaac
BACKLASH: OBLIVION 2
FLIPPER
ONCE UPON A TIME . . . WHEN WE WERE COLORED
Hayes, James H.
GREAT WHITE HYPE, THE
Hayes, Kevin
UNFORGETTABLE
Hayes, Reginald C.
FAMILY THING, A
Hayes, Roland
EVERYONE SAYS I LOVE YOU
Hayes, Tara
ANIMAL INSTINCTS III: THE SEDUCTRESS
Hayman, Jeri
DEADLY OUTBREAK
Haynes, Billy
CHAIN REACTION
Haynes, Curtis Tyler
GHOSTS OF MISSISSIPPI
Haynes, Roy
PREACHER'S WIFE, THE
Hays, Robert
HOMEWARD BOUND II: LOST IN SAN FRANCISCO
Haysbert, Dennis
WIDOW'S KISS
Hayter, Charles
BLOOD & DONUTS
Hayward, Charles
DEAD TO RIGHTS
Hayward, Kristin Dattilo
INFINITY
Hayward, Rachel
FINAL CUT, THE
Haywood, Chris
ALEX
Haywood, Idella
ORIGINAL GANGSTAS
Hazenwinkel, Nicolette
BOGUS
Hazlett, Barbara
SANDMAN, THE
He Saifei
BLUSH
Headley, Shari
PREACHER'S WIFE, THE
Headly, Glenne
MR. HOLLAND'S OPUS
SGT. BILKO
2 DAYS IN THE VALLEY
Heald, Anthony
TIME TO KILL, A
Healy, Patrick
KINGPIN

Heard, Cordis
HEAVY
Heard, Harry
FUNNYMAN, THE
Heard, Jamie
FUNNYMAN, THE
Heard, John
BEFORE AND AFTER
MY FELLOW AMERICANS
Hearn, Ann
WAR AT HOME, THE
Hearn, George
ALL DOGS GO TO HEAVEN 2
Hearst, Patricia
BIO-DOME
Heater, Jerry J.
EDDIE
Heath, Darrell
BARB WIRE
DON'T BE A MENACE TO SOUTH CENTRAL WHILE DRINKING YOUR JUICE IN THE HOOD
Heath, Sharon
DEVOTION
Heathman, Ron
HYPE!
Heaton, Tom
SURGEON, THE
Heche, Anne
JUROR, THE
PIE IN THE SKY
WALKING AND TALKING
WILD SIDE
Hecht, Beverly
WELCOME TO THE DOLLHOUSE
Hecht, Gina
ONE NIGHT STAND
Hecht, Lawrence
SCREAM
Hecht, Marlen
MANNY & LO
Hecht, Paul
FIRST WIVES CLUB, THE
Heckart, Eileen
FIRST WIVES CLUB, THE
Heckendorn, Thierry
NELLY AND MONSIEUR ARNAUD
Hecker, Gary
ED
Hedaya, Dan
DAYLIGHT
FIRST WIVES CLUB, THE
FREEWAY
MARVIN'S ROOM
RANSOM
Heddings, Sandy
EDDIE
Hedhili, Amel
SILENCES OF THE PALACE, THE
Hedison, Alexandra
RICH MAN'S WIFE, THE
Hedman, Helen
FIRST KID
Hedren, Tippi
CITIZEN RUTH
Heesch, Martin
BROTHER OF SLEEP
Heffernan, John
EXTREME MEASURES
Hegarty, Ruth
WAR OF THE BUTTONS, THE
Hegel, Jon
CANNIBAL! THE MUSICAL
Heggins, Amy
FIRST WIVES CLUB, THE
Heggs, Ryan
KINGPIN

Heggs, William
KINGPIN
Hehir, Peter
TWO FRIENDS
Heimbigue, Eric
APART FROM HUGH
Heimbold, Joanna
DEAR GOD
Heinze, Dirk K.
ELECTRA
Heisler, Tommy
LIFEFORM
Helde, Annette
ALL DOGS GO TO HEAVEN 2
STAR TREK: FIRST CONTACT
Heldenbergh, Johan
ANTONIA'S LINE
Helgenberger, Marg
FRAME BY FRAME
Hell, Kevin
SOME FOLKS CALL IT A SLING BLADE
Helland, J. Roy
BIRDCAGE, THE
Hellberg, Jurgen
TERMINAL IMPACT
Heller, Chip
NATIONAL LAMPOON'S FAVORITE DEADLY SINS
PUBLIC ENEMIES
Heller, Sally
GIRLFRIENDS
Helm, Levon
FEELING MINNESOTA
Helman, Bonnie
IT CAME FROM OUTER SPACE II
Helmayr, Susana
FLAMING EARS
Helme, Simone
SUITE 16
Helton, Martin E.
FRISK
Hembd, Austin Samuel
EVENING STAR, THE
Hemblen, David
CHAMPAGNE SAFARI, THE
FLY AWAY HOME
HOLLOW POINT
MAXIMUM RISK
SONG SPINNER, THE
Hemby, Dee Dee
. . . AT FIRST SIGHT
Hemeyer, Tracy
PORTRAITS OF A KILLER
Hemingway, Margaux
BAD LOVE
Hemingway, Mariel
BAD MOON
Heminway, Tobin
LOW LIFE, THE
Hemmings, Thoywell
WHARF RAT, THE
Hemon, Olivier
LITTLE INDIAN, BIG CITY
Hendershott, Adam
CELTIC PRIDE
Henderson, Adam
ROUJIN-Z
Henderson, Dante Lamar
BIRDCAGE, THE
Henderson, Dennis Neil
FAN, THE
Henderson, Fred
ROBIN OF LOCKSLEY
Henderson, G. Ja'ron
GHOSTS OF MISSISSIPPI
Henderson, Ian
SHAMELESS

Henderson, Meredith
SONG SPINNER, THE
Henderson, Michael
TALKING ABOUT SEX
Henderson, Shriley
TRAINSPOTTING
Henderson, Tonia
BODY COUNT
Hendrix, Elaine
LOVER'S KNOT
Hendrix, Jimi
MESSAGE TO LOVE: THE ISLE OF WIGHT FESTIVAL
Hendrix, Kim
TIME TO KILL, A
Hendrix, Sharon
MARS ATTACKS!
Henin, Fernando Agustin
EVITA
Henke, Brad
FAN, THE
MR. WRONG
Henley, Susan
LONG KISS GOODNIGHT, THE
Hennecke, Joan
CITIZEN RUTH
Hennessy, Jill
I SHOT ANDY WARHOL
Hennig, Kate
LOSING CHASE
MRS. WINTERBOURNE
Hennigan, Dee
ROAD TO GALVESTON, THE
Hennigan, Mary
PORTRAITS OF A KILLER
Hennigan, Sean
LILY DALE
Henriksen, Lance
BAJA
DEAD MAN
FELONY
MIND RIPPER
Henritze, Bette
HARVEST OF FIRE
Henry, Carolyn
PREACHER'S WIFE, THE
Henry, David
EVITA
Henry, Frida
SILENCE OF NETO, THE
Henry, Gregg
SHARON'S SECRET
Henry, Linda
BEAUTIFUL THING
Henshall, Douglas
ANGELS AND INSECTS
Hensley Paradee, Janelle
BLACK SCORPION
Henson, Garette Ratliff
D3: THE MIGHTY DUCKS
Henstridge, Natasha
ADRENALIN: FEAR THE RUSH
MAXIMUM RISK
Henteloff, Alex
NORMA JEAN AND MARILYN
Henwood, Edward
CANNIBAL! THE MUSICAL
Hepburn, Katharine
LINE KING: THE AL HIRSCHFELD STORY, THE
Herbert, Sylvie
RIDICULE
Herbert, Vernon
REDEMPTION: KICKBOXER 5
Herbst, Becky
DONOR UNKNOWN
Herd, Harold
TRUMAN
Herd, Patricia
STREETCAR NAMED DESIRE, A
Herd, Richard
SGT. BILKO
YESTERDAY'S TARGET
Herman, Mike
SOME FOLKS CALL IT A SLING BLADE
Herman, Paul
FAN, THE
SLEEPERS
Herman, Rabbi Howard S.
MIRROR HAS TWO FACES, THE
Hermann, Irm
SHADOW OF ANGELS
Hernandez, Anthony
MATILDA
Hernandez, Gabriela
JOHNNY 100 PESOS
Hernandez, Hugo
JACK
Hernandez, Johnny Vatos
FROM DUSK TILL DAWN
Hernandez, Jonathan
MR. WRONG
Hernandez, Lita
GRACE OF MY HEART
Hernandez, Marco
TREMORS 2: AFTERSHOCKS
Hernandez, Mary Jane R.
LONE STAR
Hernandez, Sergio
JOHNNY 100 PESOS
Hernandez, Thom Adcox
ENTERTAINING ANGELS: THE DOROTHY DAY STORY
Hernandezo, Ingrid
SILENCE OF NETO, THE
Herpich, Russ
HEAD OF THE FAMILY
Herrera, Maria
MATERNAL INSTINCTS
Herrington, Suzanne
MULTIPLICITY
Herron, Nalona
FIST OF THE NORTH STAR
Hershey, Barbara
PALLBEARER, THE
PORTRAIT OF A LADY, THE
Hertford, Brighton
EVIL HAS A FACE
Heske, Habby
QUEST, THE
Heslov, Grant
BIRDCAGE, THE
BLACK SHEEP
Hess, Joe
HEAVEN'S PRISONERS
TWO MUCH
Hess, Sandra
BEASTMASTER 3: THE EYE OF BRAXUS
Hesser, Kira Spencer
MATILDA
Hester, Kyle
LAST DANCE
Heston, Charlton
ALASKA
HAMLET
Hewes, Michael
GHOSTS OF MISSISSIPPI
Hewitt, Don
MISSING PIECES
SLEEPERS
Hewitt, Heather
THAT THING YOU DO!
Hewitt, Jennifer Love
HOUSE ARREST
Hewitt, Jery
LOVE IS ALL THERE IS
Hewitt, Paul
ED
Hewitt, Reine
ED'S NEXT MOVE
Heyn, Orville
BOGUS
Hiatt, Paul
SGT. KABUKIMAN N.Y.P.D.
Hibbert, Edward
EVERYONE SAYS I LOVE YOU
FIRST WIVES CLUB, THE
Hickenlooper Sr., George
LOW LIFE, THE
Hickey, James
SOME MOTHER'S SON
Hickey, John Benjamin
EDDIE
Hickey, Paul
MICHAEL COLLINS
MOLL FLANDERS
Hickey, William
LOVE IS ALL THERE IS
MADDENING, THE
Hicks, Danny
DEMOLITIONIST, THE
Hicks, Dwight
JACK
ROCK, THE
Hicks, Jonathan P.
GREAT WHITE HYPE, THE
Hicks, Kevin
BLOODKNOT
Hicks, Letitia
NORMAL LIFE
Hicks, Taral
PREACHER'S WIFE, THE
Hickson, Louise
GRIM
Hidalgo, Maria Lujan
EVITA
Hiegel, Catherine
FRENCH TWIST
Higgins, Clare
SMALL FACES
Higgins, Fiona
SOME MOTHER'S SON
Higgins, John
SOME MOTHER'S SON
Higgins, John Michael
LATE SHIFT, THE
Higgins, Mike
SPELLBREAKER: SECRET OF THE LEPRECHAUNS
Higginson, Torri
ENGLISH PATIENT, THE
WHEN THE BULLET HITS THE BONE
High, Mark
FINAL CUT, THE
Highet, Fiona
STUPIDS, THE
Hilario, Jonathan
PIG'S TALE, A
Hild, Jim
PEOPLE VS. LARRY FLYNT, THE
Hildebrand, Heiderose
FLAMING EARS
Hiler, Katherine
I'M NOT RAPPAPORT
Hill, Bernard
GHOST AND THE DARKNESS, THE
MADAGASCAR SKIN
Hill, Cherie
THAT THING YOU DO!
Hill, Christi
FLY AWAY HOME
Hill, Hollis
SPY HARD

Hill, Ian
EVITA
Hill, James
BIRDCAGE, THE
SHOPPING
Hill, James Michael
FLED
Hill, Lamar
LET'S GET BIZZEE
Hill, Matt
BIG BULLY
TALES FROM THE CRYPT PRESENTS BORDELLO OF BLOOD
Hill, Melanie
SHOPPING
Hill, Myfanwy
COLD COMFORT FARM
Hill, Nick
BLOODSPORT II: THE NEXT KUMITE
RAW TARGET
Hill, Rick
DEAR GOD
Hill, Steven
WHERE'S THE MONEY, NOREEN?
Hill, Teresa
BIO-DOME
Hill, William
ASSOCIATE, THE
JUROR, THE
STRIPTEASE
Hillboldt, Lise
NORMA JEAN AND MARILYN
Hillerman, John
VERY BRADY SEQUEL, A
Hillhouse, Brenda
FROM DUSK TILL DAWN
Hilliard, David
BERKELEY IN THE 60S
Hilliard, Sherry
KIDS IN THE HALL: BRAIN CANDY
Hillwood, Amanda
LAWNMOWER MAN 2: BEYOND CYBERSPACE
Hilman, Gale
JERRY MAGUIRE
Hilton, Lorraine
JUDE
Hilton, Sherri
TIME TO KILL, A
Hinds, Ciaran
AFFAIR, THE
MARY REILLY
SOME MOTHER'S SON
Hines, Ben
FAN, THE
Hines, Bruce
FAN, THE
Hines, Damon
ONCE UPON A TIME . . . WHEN WE WERE COLORED
Hines, E'Dena
MOLL FLANDERS
Hines, Gregory
MAD DOG TIME
PREACHER'S WIFE, THE
Hines, Robert
MIDWINTER'S TALE, A
Hines, Sharon
CAPTIVES
Hines, Teacel
MOLL FLANDERS
Hines, Tom
DEAR GOD
Hingle, Pat
LARGER THAN LIFE
TRUMAN
Hinkle, Marin
I'M NOT RAPPAPORT
Hinkley, Tommy
CABLE GUY, THE
Hinzman, Bill
SANTA CLAWS
Hiona, Sam
FRIEND OF THE FAMILY 2
Hipp, Paul
FUNERAL, THE
Hirasawa, Jillian
GETTING AWAY WITH MURDER
Hiroyuki-Tagawa, Cary
WHITE TIGER
Hirsch, David
CITIZEN RUTH
Hirsch, Judd
INDEPENDENCE DAY
Hirschfeld, Al
LINE KING: THE AL HIRSCHFELD STORY, THE
Hirschfeld, Dolly Hass
LINE KING: THE AL HIRSCHFELD STORY, THE
Hirschfeld, Nina
LINE KING: THE AL HIRSCHFELD STORY, THE
Hirt, Christianne
FOR THE MOMENT
GIRL FROM MARS, THE
Hitchcock, Michael
HOUSE ARREST
Hlusicka, Karel
KASPAR HAUSER
Ho, Danny
RUDE
Ho, Don
JOE'S APARTMENT
Ho, Michael
BOGUS
Ho, Vic
HARRIET THE SPY
Hoag, Jan
DENTIST, THE
Hobbs Jr., Johnnie
UP CLOSE AND PERSONAL
Hobbs, Pan
PARADISE LOST: THE CHILD MURDERS AT ROBIN HOOD HILLS
Hobbs, Roy
GETTING AWAY WITH MURDER
Hobbs, Terry
PARADISE LOST: THE CHILD MURDERS AT ROBIN HOOD HILLS
Hobson, Thomas
CLUBHOUSE DETECTIVES
Hocine, Alain
RIDICULE
Hocke, Bernard
BEWARE: CHILDREN AT PLAY
RATTLED
Hocke, Mette
WHITE SQUALL
Hocking, Kristen
WOLVES, THE
Hodder, Angus
ANGELS AND INSECTS
Hodge, Aldis
BED OF ROSES
Hodge, Edwin
LONG KISS GOODNIGHT, THE
Hodge, Kate
DESIRE
Hodge, Mike
MIRROR HAS TWO FACES, THE
RANSOM
Hodges, David U.
TIME TO KILL, A
Hodges, Fulton
LET'S GET BIZZEE
Hodges, Tom
MICHAEL
Hodson, Biddy
LOADED
Hodson, Ed
EVERYONE SAYS I LOVE YOU
Hoes, Hans
CROCODILES IN AMSTERDAM
Hofert, Earl
BEAVIS AND BUTT-HEAD DO AMERICA
Hofesh, Mali
HARD JUSTICE
Hoffman, Dustin
AMERICAN BUFFALO
SLEEPERS
Hoffman, Jackie
PIG'S TALE, A
Hoffman, Linda
DENTIST, THE
Hoffman, Marlon
TRUMAN
Hoffman, Pato
RAVENHAWK
Hoffman, Philip Seymour
TWISTER
Hoffman, Thom
COLD LIGHT OF DAY
Hoffmann, Gaby
EVERYONE SAYS I LOVE YOU
Hoffmann, Gloria
MARS ATTACKS!
Hofheimer, Charlie
BOYS
Hofschneider, Marco
ISLAND OF DR. MOREAU, THE
Hogan, Bosco
SOME MOTHER'S SON
Hogan, Gabriel
HALFBACK OF NOTRE DAME, THE
Hogan, Heather
LAND BEFORE TIME IV: JOURNEY THROUGH THE MISTS
Hogan, Hulk
SANTA WITH MUSCLES
SPY HARD
Hogan, Michael
BOYS NEXT DOOR, THE
Hogan, Paul
FLIPPER
Hogan, Stephen
SOME MOTHER'S SON
Hogenboom, Leo
ANTONIA'S LINE
Hogg, Ian
RASPUTIN
Hogue, Jim
SPITFIRE GRILL, THE
Hojat, Ali
HIGH SCHOOL HIGH
Holberg, Rebecca
DEAR GOD
Holbrook, Hal
CARRIED AWAY
Holcombe, Gary
TRUMAN
Holden, Darelle Porter
MARS ATTACKS!
Holden, Jill
BULLETPROOF
Holder, Chris
NAKED SOULS
Holder, Geoffrey
LINE KING: THE AL HIRSCHFELD STORY, THE
Holder, Janice
PEOPLE VS. LARRY FLYNT, THE
Holder, Tim
SLING BLADE

Holdsworth, Michelle
HAPPY GILMORE
Hole
NOT BAD FOR A GIRL
Holgado, Ticky
FRENCH TWIST
Holguin, Danny
TEXAS PAYBACK
Holiday, Brenda
DARK SECRETS
Holiday, John E.
WITCHCRAFT: SALEM'S GHOST
Holihan, Ryan
AMANDA AND THE ALIEN
Holladay, David
IT'S MY PARTY
Holland, Penny
MATILDA
Hollander, Barbara
EVERYONE SAYS I LOVE YOU
Hollander, Tom
SOME MOTHER'S SON
Holliday, Charlie
UP CLOSE AND PERSONAL
Holliday, Polly
MR. WRONG
Hollimon, Greg
FAMILY THING, A
Hollingbery, Vilma
YOUNG POISONER'S HANDBOOK, THE
Hollings, Ernest F.
CITY HALL
Hollister, Reed
BAD LOVE
Hollitt, Raye
JAG
Hollo, Eric
DARKMAN III: DIE DARKMAN DIE
Holloman II, Sterling
PREACHER'S WIFE, THE
Holloway, Ann
KIDS IN THE HALL: BRAIN CANDY
Holloway, Christopher
CHAIN REACTION
Holly, Lauren
BEAUTIFUL GIRLS
DOWN PERISCOPE
Holm, Ian
BIG NIGHT
Holm, Sharon
PATLABOR 2: MOBILE POLICE
Holman, Bruce E.
BROKEN ARROW
Holman, Mark
PURE DANGER
Holman, Max
PURE DANGER
Holmes, Brittany Ashton
DEATH BENEFIT
Holmes, Lian-Marie
CRUCIBLE, THE
Holmes, Mai-Lis
WITCHCRAFT: SALEM'S GHOST
Holmes, Meredyth
FORBIDDEN ZONE: ALIEN ABDUCTION
Holmes, Michael
BLACK DAY BLUE NIGHT
Holmes, Prudence Wright
KINGPIN
Holmes, Wendell
LOTTO LAND
Holmquist, Kirsten
ENTERTAINING ANGELS: THE DOROTHY DAY STORY
Holofcener, Lawrence
WALKING AND TALKING
Holt, Bryant
MURDERED INNOCENCE
Holt, Clayton
FAN, THE
Holt, Larry
LAST MAN STANDING
Holt, Lester D.
PRIMAL FEAR
Holt, Mette
WHISPERING, THE
Holton, Mark
RUMPELSTILTSKIN
Holtzman, Merrill
ED'S NEXT MOVE
Holub, Hugh
DESIRE
Holzle, Richard
LITTLE INDIAN, BIG CITY
Holzman, Winnie
JERRY MAGUIRE
Homar, Lluis
CELESTIAL CLOCKWORK
Homer, Dru
UNHOOK THE STARS
Hon Chun
MIDNIGHT ANGEL
Hones, Samantha
MARY REILLY
Honeyben, John
WITHOUT MERCY
Honeywell, Helen
GIRL FROM MARS, THE
HAPPY GILMORE
Hong, James
BLOODSPORT II: THE NEXT KUMITE
INFINITY
MISSING PIECES
SOUTH BEACH ACADEMY
Hong, Vera
RACE THE SUN
Hong-Louie, Ed
HOMEWARD BOUND II: LOST IN SAN FRANCISCO
Hood, Gavin
LIVE WIRE: HUMAN TIMEBOMB
REDEMPTION: KICKBOXER 5
Hooker, Buddy Joe
ARRIVAL, THE
MULHOLLAND FALLS
Hooks, Brian
HIGH SCHOOL HIGH
PHAT BEACH
Hooks, Michael
FLED
Hooks, Robert
FLED
Hooper, Alex
MADAGASCAR SKIN
Hooper, David
RUMBLE IN THE BRONX
Hooper, Donna
I'M NOT RAPPAPORT
Hoopes, Melanie
TWISTER
Hootkins, William
ISLAND OF DR. MOREAU, THE
Hooton, James
CAPTIVES
Hoover, Elva Mai
LOSING CHASE
Hoover, Grant
BIG BULLY
Hoover, Howard
WHERE'S THE MONEY, NOREEN?
Hoover, Tom
POLYMORPH
SANDMAN, THE
Hope, Jade
COLD LIGHT OF DAY
Hopkins, Anthony
AUGUST
SURVIVING PICASSO
Hopkins, Bo
PAINTED HERO
TEXAS PAYBACK
Hopkins, Jermaine "Huggy"
PHAT BEACH
Hopkins, Nicky
ROLLING STONES ROCK-AND-ROLL CIRCUS, THE
Hopkins, Rand
PEOPLE VS. LARRY FLYNT, THE
Hopkins, Rosanne
SURGEON, THE
Hopkins, Tony
FRIGHTENERS, THE
Hopkins, Virgil Graham
NEON BIBLE, THE
Hopkins, Wendy
STUPIDS, THE
Hopper, Dennis
BASQUIAT
CARRIED AWAY
Horan, Fielding
BOGUS
Horan, Gerard
MIDWINTER'S TALE, A
Horan, Leslie
PRE-MADONNAS
WIDOW'S KISS
Horhn, John A.
GHOSTS OF MISSISSIPPI
Hornish, Rudy
DOWN PERISCOPE
GALAXIES ARE COLLIDING
Horowitz, Jude
SHOT, THE
Horse, Mike
AMERICAN STRAYS
Horsford, Anna Maria
DEAR GOD
ONCE UPON A TIME . . . WHEN WE WERE COLORED
ONE FINE DAY
SET IT OFF
WIDOW'S KISS
Horsting, J.R.
STAR TREK: FIRST CONTACT
Horton, Jeffery
SMALL WONDERS
Horton, John
STEPHEN KING'S THINNER
Horton, Michael
STAR TREK: FIRST CONTACT
Horton, Peter
DEATH BENEFIT
2 DAYS IN THE VALLEY
Horton, Richard
BUGGED
Horton, Stefanie-Erin
SMALL WONDERS
Horton, Victoria
THEY BITE
Horvath, Barbara
RASPUTIN
Horvath, Lou
ISLAND OF DR. MOREAU, THE
Hosea, Bobby
INDEPENDENCE DAY
Hoskins, Basil
COLD COMFORT FARM
Hoskins, Bob
JOSEPH CONRAD'S THE SECRET AGENT
MICHAEL

Hostmyer, Tracy
IN LOVE AND WAR
Hoty, Tony
RANSOM
Houghton, Mark
MISSION: IMPOSSIBLE
Houicha, Sabrina
HATE
Houlihan, Mike
EVIL HAS A FACE
Hounslow, David
CAPTIVES
Hourani, Ned
RAW TARGET
House, Candy
EDDIE
House, Christal L.
GREAT WHITE HYPE, THE
House, Dale E.
LAWNMOWER MAN 2: BEYOND CYBERSPACE
House, Daniel
HYPE!
Houston, Cissy
PREACHER'S WIFE, THE
Houston, Gary
FARGO
Houston, Hollis
TRUMAN
Houston, Teretha G.
PREACHER'S WIFE, THE
Houston, Whitney
PREACHER'S WIFE, THE
Hoven, Adrian
SHADOW OF ANGELS
Howard, Arliss
BEYOND THE CALL
TALES OF EROTICA
Howard, Cheryl
RANSOM
Howard, Clint
BARB WIRE
FIST OF THE NORTH STAR
RATTLED
SANTA WITH MUSCLES
SAWBONES
THAT THING YOU DO!
UNHOOK THE STARS
Howard, David S.
SUBSTANCE OF FIRE, THE
Howard, F.A.J.
FOREST WARRIOR
Howard, Jean Speegle
BLACK SHEEP
MATILDA
MY FELLOW AMERICANS
Howard, Kate
SHAMELESS
Howard, Kelly
BODY OF INFLUENCE 2
Howard, Kyle
HOUSE ARREST
Howard, Nancy
ARRIVAL, THE
Howard, Nicola
JANE EYRE
Howard, Rance
COLONY, THE
GHOSTS OF MISSISSIPPI
INDEPENDENCE DAY
MARS ATTACKS!
SGT. BILKO
TIGER HEART
Howard, Shawn Michael
CABLE GUY, THE
SUNSET PARK
Howard, Siri
WELCOME TO THE DOLLHOUSE
Howard, Terrence
MR. HOLLAND'S OPUS
Howard, Terrence DaShon
SUNSET PARK
Howard, William
GHOSTS OF MISSISSIPPI
Howe, Brian
SPY HARD
Howe, Susan
PEOPLE VS. LARRY FLYNT, THE
Howe, Trenton
KIDS IN THE HALL: BRAIN CANDY
Howell, C. Thomas
HOURGLASS
PURE DANGER
SHAMELESS
SWEEPER, THE
Howell, Katherine
JAMES AND THE GIANT PEACH
Howell, Neva
MY FELLOW AMERICANS
Howell, Philippa
CRACKER: THE MADWOMAN IN THE ATTIC
Howell, William
BLACK SHEEP
Howitt, Peter
SOME MOTHER'S SON
Howsen, Terry
RUMBLE IN THE BRONX
Howze, Zakee
FAITHFUL
Hoxby, Scott
BULLETPROOF
MY FELLOW AMERICANS
Hoy, Linda
LETTER TO MY KILLER
Hoyt, John
FUNERAL, THE
Hrachovinova, Marta
COLD LIGHT OF DAY
Hresko, Randy
LAST DANCE
Hric, Peter
DRAGONHEART
Hromek, Justin
KINGPIN
Hrubesova, Marketa
DELTA OF VENUS
Hruza, Oldrich
DELTA OF VENUS
Hsu, Talun
BODY COUNT
Huang, Ying
MADAME BUTTERFLY
Huang Zhiming
CHUNGKING EXPRESS
Hubbard, Dana S.
DON'T LET YOUR MEAT LOAF
Hubbard, Walter C.
DEMOLITIONIST, THE
Hubbell, J.P.
JOSH KIRBY . . . TIME WARRIOR!: TRAPPED ON TOY WORLD
Hubble, Kathy
RUMBLE IN THE BRONX
Huber, Charles
SKYSCRAPER
Huber, Lotti
NEUROSIA: 50 YEARS OF PERVERSITY
Huber, Rhys
HOMEWARD BOUND II: LOST IN SAN FRANCISCO
Huberth, Jon
MODERN AFFAIR, A
Hubley, Georgia
I SHOT ANDY WARHOL
Hubley, Whip
EXECUTIVE DECISION
VERY BRADY SEQUEL, A
Huculak, Maggie
WHERE'S THE MONEY, NOREEN?
Huddleston, David
JOE'S APARTMENT
Hudnell, Kevin
SOME FOLKS CALL IT A SLING BLADE
Hudson, David
ISLAND OF DR. MOREAU, THE
Hudson, Ernie
JUST YOUR LUCK
SUBSTITUTE, THE
Hudson, Gary
SERIAL KILLER
TEXAS PAYBACK
Hudson, Judy
RANSOM
Hudson, Linden
MAN WITH THE PERFECT SWING, THE
Hudson, Stephanie
FEMALIEN
Huertas, Jon
EXECUTIVE DECISION
Huertas, Luisa
JUROR, THE
Huff, Brent
BACKLASH: OBLIVION 2
Huff, Thomas J.
ERASER
Huffman, Jon
FLED
Huffman, Rosanna
TRIGGER EFFECT, THE
Hughes, Angee
LILY DALE
Hughes, Christopher Shepard
MATILDA
Hughes, Frank John
FUNERAL, THE
Hughes, Helen
NIGHT OF THE TWISTERS
Hughes, Howard
SHAMELESS
Hughes, John E.
GIRLFRIENDS
Hughes, Laura
COLD FEVER
Hughes, Mica
GIRL 6
Hughes, Robert
RACE THE SUN
Hughes, Shannon
MATILDA
Hughes, Stuart
BOGUS
Hughes, Suzan
KINGPIN
Hughson, Randy
RUDE
Hugo, Peter
YANKEE ZULU
Hugo, Tara
IN LOVE AND WAR
Hugot, Marceline
DUNSTON CHECKS IN
Hulce, Tom
HEIDI CHRONICLES, THE
HUNCHBACK OF NOTRE DAME, THE
Hules, Endre
CRAFT, THE
Hulin, Dominique
VISITORS, THE
Hulin, Steve
BEST OF THE BEST 3: NO TURNING BACK

Hull, Ross
IRON EAGLE IV
Hulne, Patrick
CELTIC PRIDE
Hulne, Peter A.
CELTIC PRIDE
Hult, Chloe
BIO-DOME
Humphreys, Alf
ANNIE O
BIG BULLY
Humphreys, Alfred E.
ROBIN OF LOCKSLEY
Humphreys, Judith
HEDD WYNN
Humphries, Harry
ROCK, THE
Hung, Catherine
WING CHUN
Hungan, Joseph
WITHOUT MERCY
Hunley, Sarah
GHOSTS OF MISSISSIPPI
Hunt, Bonnie
GETTING AWAY WITH MURDER
JERRY MAGUIRE
Hunt, Brad
ED
MULHOLLAND FALLS
Hunt, Eamonn
WAR OF THE BUTTONS, THE
Hunt, Giles
SAWBONES
Hunt, Helen
TWISTER
Hunt, Jerry
TIME TO KILL, A
Hunt, Leigh
PUBLIC ACCESS
Hunt, Neil
BARB WIRE
NORMA JEAN AND MARILYN
Hunter, Bill
RACE THE SUN
Hunter, Ciara
TALES FROM THE CRYPT PRESENTS BORDELLO OF BLOOD
Hunter, J. Michael
FIRST KID
Hunter, Lionel
LIVE WIRE: HUMAN TIMEBOMB
Hunter, Moray
JUDE
Huntington, Sam
HARVEST OF FIRE
Hunyudkurti, Istvan
RASPUTIN
Hupp, Jana Marie
INDEPENDENCE DAY
Huppert, Isabelle
LA CEREMONIE
Huraib, Karel
KASPAR HAUSER
Hurlburt, Carolyn
CLUBHOUSE DETECTIVES
Hurley, Elizabeth
SHAMELESS
Hurley, Kevin
NORMAL LIFE
Hurley, Kieran
MOLL FLANDERS
Hurley, Melissa
THAT THING YOU DO!
Hurst, Bob
DEMOLITIONIST, THE
Hurst, Doug
MURDERED INNOCENCE
Hurst, Michelle
I SHOT ANDY WARHOL
Hurt, John
DEAD MAN
Hurt, Mary Beth
FROM THE JOURNALS OF JEAN SEBERG
Hurt, William
JANE EYRE
MICHAEL
Hurtado, Mark
MERLIN'S SHOP OF MAGICAL WONDERS
Hus, Martin
HIDDEN ASSASSIN
Huss, Jennifer
POLYMORPH
Huss, Toby
BEAVIS AND BUTT-HEAD DO AMERICA
DEAR GOD
DOWN PERISCOPE
JERRY MAGUIRE
Hussey, John
LILY DALE
MICHAEL
REDEMPTION: KICKBOXER 5
Huston, Candace
MADDENING, THE
Huston, Michael
ED'S NEXT MOVE
Huston, Patricia
HEAVEN'S PRISONERS
Hutcherson, Warren
LAST SUPPER, THE
Hutchins, Jalil
DON'T LET YOUR MEAT LOAF
Hutchins, Walter L.
TIME TO KILL, A
Hutchinson, Fiona
RAGE
Hutchinson, Harry
MOTHER
Hutchinson, Michelle
FARGO
Hutchinson, Tim
SUNSET PARK
Hutchison, Doug
TIME TO KILL, A
Hutchison, Joe
PARADISE LOST: THE CHILD MURDERS AT ROBIN HOOD HILLS
Hutchison, Tad
HYPE!
Hutson, Candace
LAND BEFORE TIME IV: JOURNEY THROUGH THE MISTS
Hutt, Grady
NORMAL LIFE
Hutton, Lauren
MISSING PIECES
Hutton, Timothy
BEAUTIFUL GIRLS
SUBSTANCE OF FIRE, THE
Hyacinth, Rommel
LOW LIFE, THE
Hyatt, Pam
LEGEND OF GATOR FACE, THE
Hyatt, Ron
SOUTH BEACH ACADEMY
Hyatt, Ron Jeremy
MR. STITCH
Hyde-White, Alex
UNKNOWN ORIGIN
Hylands, Scott
HALFBACK OF NOTRE DAME, THE
Hylton, Ramiah
RUDE
Hyross, Ingrid
MIRROR, MIRROR III: THE VOYEUR
Hytner, Steve
DOWN, OUT AND DANGEROUS
Hytower, Roy
FAMILY THING, A
Iacona, Joe
DADETOWN
Ibanez, Teresa
FLOWER OF MY SECRET, THE
Ibarra, Jesse
FAN, THE
Ibrahim, Majed
EXECUTIVE DECISION
Ichida, Hiromi
MABOROSI
Ideishi, Randy
BLACK SCORPION
Idle, Eric
MISSING PIECES
Idol, Billy
MAD DOG TIME
Iervolino, Dimitri
WELCOME TO THE DOLLHOUSE
Ifull, Ross
BEYOND THE CALL
Iglesias, Agustin
JOHNNY 100 PESOS
Iijima, Junji
FLIRT
Ikeda, Edmund
SUBSTANCE OF FIRE, THE
Ikeda, Morito
FLIRT
Ikeuchi, Mansaku
FLIRT
Illouz, Maurice
LITTLE INDIAN, BIG CITY
Illusion, Justin
TERMINAL IMPACT
WARHEAD
Imada, Jeff
JOHN CARPENTER'S ESCAPE FROM L.A.
Imershein, Deidre
SKYSCRAPER
Imhoff, Gary
SKYSCRAPER
Imperioli, Michael
FLIRT
GIRL 6
GIRLS TOWN
I SHOT ANDY WARHOL
LAST MAN STANDING
SWEET NOTHING
TREES LOUNGE
Imrie, Celia
MIDWINTER'S TALE, A
Ince, Elizabeth
PUBLIC ACCESS
Inclan, Miguel
AVENTURERA
Indri, Christina
MADAME WANG'S
Indtrasathit, Vichai
QUEST, THE
Ineson, Ralph
SHOPPING
Ing, Ivo
ORIGINAL SINS
Ingham, Barrie
JOSH KIRBY . . . TIME WARRIOR!: EGGS FROM 70,000,000 B.C.
JOSH KIRBY . . . TIME WARRIOR!: JOURNEY TO THE MAGIC CAVERN
JOSH KIRBY . . . TIME WARRIOR!: LAST BATTLE FOR THE UNIVERSE
JOSH KIRBY . . . TIME WARRIOR!: TRAPPED ON TOY WORLD
Ingle, John
LAND BEFORE TIME IV: JOURNEY THROUGH THE MISTS

Ingolin, Tyler
FRISK
Ingram, Richard
MICHAEL COLLINS
Ingrassia, Jon
MAD DOG TIME
SWEEPER, THE
Innes, Timothy
FRISK
Inoue, Takashi
MABOROSI
Insanto, Diana Lee
BARB WIRE
Inscoe, Joe
FIRST KID
LAST DANCE
Insdorf, Annette
FRANCOIS TRUFFAUT: STOLEN PORTRAITS
Iommi, Tony
ROLLING STONES ROCK-AND-ROLL CIRCUS, THE
Iosseliani, Otar
CHASING BUTTERFLIES
Ip Choi Nam
QUEST, THE
Irene, Bernard
MRS. MUNCK
Irizarry, Gloria
SUBSTANCE OF FIRE, THE
Irney, Frank
NORMA JEAN AND MARILYN
Irons, Jeremy
STEALING BEAUTY
Ironside, Michael
PORTRAITS OF A KILLER
RED SCORPION 2
TOO FAST, TOO YOUNG
Irsay, Jim
JERRY MAGUIRE
Irsay, Meg
JERRY MAGUIRE
Irvin, Sam
BACKLASH: OBLIVION 2
Irving, Amy
CARRIED AWAY
I'M NOT RAPPAPORT
Irving, Martha
TWO IF BY SEA
Irving, Richard
MARS ATTACKS!
Irwin, Jennifer
MRS. WINTERBOURNE
Isaacs, Jason
DRAGONHEART
SHOPPING
SOLITAIRE FOR TWO
Isaacson, Ben
GHOST IN THE SHELL
Isaak, Chris
GRACE OF MY HEART
THAT THING YOU DO!
Isakovic, Boris
VUKOVAR
Ischiale, Maddalena
CEMETERY MAN
Iscovich, Joshua
DEAR GOD
Isherwood, Jim
MICHAEL COLLINS
Ishida, Jim
DUNSTON CHECKS IN
Ishizuka, Kumiko
FLIRT
Ishmael, Marvin
OPEN SEASON
Islam, Champa
TARGET
Islam, Sirajul
EDDIE
IF LUCY FELL
Isler, Seth
BOY CALLED HATE, A
CHAMBER, THE
Isyanov, Ravil
TWO DEATHS
Itkin, Steve
I SHOT ANDY WARHOL
Ito, Robert
HOLLOW POINT
Ittleson, Stephanie
SWINGERS
Itzin, Gregory
DEAD TO RIGHTS
Iures, Marcel
MISSION: IMPOSSIBLE
Ivanek, Zeljko
ASSOCIATE, THE
COURAGE UNDER FIRE
INFINITY
TRUMAN
WHITE SQUALL
Ivanov, Victor
GLIMMER MAN, THE
Ivar, Stan
ED
Iversen, Roseanna
SET IT OFF
Ives, Nathaniel
WHITE SQUALL
Ivony, Zsofia
RASPUTIN
Ivory Ocean
VENUS RISING
Izzard, Eddie
JOSEPH CONRAD'S THE SECRET AGENT
J., Ray
MARS ATTACKS!
Jace, Michael
FAN, THE
GREAT WHITE HYPE, THE
Jacelone, Pete
POLYMORPH
Jacks, Robert
TEXAS CHAINSAW MASSACRE: THE NEXT GENERATION
Jackson, Billy
FRIGHTENERS, THE
Jackson, Bo
CHAMBER, THE
Jackson, Dana
PAINTED HERO
Jackson, Dee Jay
HAPPY GILMORE
SURGEON, THE
Jackson, Douglas Robert
CABLE GUY, THE
Jackson, Ernestine
GIRLS TOWN
Jackson, Jaime
PEOPLE VS. LARRY FLYNT, THE
Jackson, Jeanine
CRAFT, THE
Jackson, Jim
DEATH ARTIST, THE
Jackson, Joaquin
LARRY MCMURTRY'S STREETS OF LAREDO
Jackson, John
MONSTERSHOW
Jackson, John M.
GLIMMER MAN, THE
SPITFIRE GRILL, THE
Jackson, Josh
ROBIN OF LOCKSLEY
Jackson, Joshua
D3: THE MIGHTY DUCKS
Jackson, Kevin
BOGUS
Jackson, Kurt
GRACE OF MY HEART
Jackson, Lauren
ALEX
Jackson, Leonard
BASQUIAT
PALOOKAVILLE
Jackson, Mark
EDDIE
Jackson, Mary
FAMILY THING, A
Jackson, Michael Alexander
PREACHER'S WIFE, THE
Jackson, Nicole
KAZAAM
Jackson, Roger
SCREAM
Jackson, Rowdy
FINAL EQUINOX, THE
Jackson, Samuel L.
ASSAULT AT WEST POINT
GREAT WHITE HYPE, THE
LONG KISS GOODNIGHT, THE
SEARCH FOR ONE-EYE JIMMY, THE
TIME TO KILL, A
TREES LOUNGE
Jackson, Stephen
WHARF RAT, THE
Jackson, Stoney
FAN, THE
Jackson, Stuart
SPITFIRE GRILL, THE
Jackson, Tim
HECK'S WAY HOME
Jacobi, Derek
HAMLET
LOOKING FOR RICHARD
Jacobs, Claire Mari
BED OF ROSES
Jacobsen, Ann-Mari
SGT. KABUKIMAN N.Y.P.D.
Jacobsen, Colombe
D3: THE MIGHTY DUCKS
Jacobsen, Peter
TIN CUP
Jacobson, Peter
ED'S NEXT MOVE
Jacobsson, Anders
EVIL ED
Jacoby, Ellen
TWO MUCH
Jacox Jr., David
BIG BULLY
Jacquinot, Stephanie
SUITE 16
Jadrnicek, Kristin
FUGITIVE RAGE
Jaeck, Scott
JAG
Jaeger, Frederick
COLD COMFORT FARM
Jaffe, Jerry
DADETOWN
Jaffee, Alicia
GRACE OF MY HEART
Jaffer, Azmine
PROPRIETOR, THE
Jaffrey, Sakina
DAYLIGHT
Jagersky, Brian
MAXIMUM RISK
Jagger, Mick
ROLLING STONES ROCK-AND-ROLL CIRCUS, THE

Jahme, Carol
MOLL FLANDERS
Jaimes, Marabina
ALL DOGS GO TO HEAVEN 2
HIGH SCHOOL HIGH
Jakub, Lisa
INDEPENDENCE DAY
PIG'S TALE, A
Jamal, A.J.
DON'T BE A MENACE TO SOUTH CENTRAL WHILE DRINKING YOUR JUICE IN THE HOOD
Jamar, Travon
DON'T BE A MENACE TO SOUTH CENTRAL WHILE DRINKING YOUR JUICE IN THE HOOD
James, Brion
AMERICAN STRAYS
LAZARUS MAN, THE
James, Clifton
LONE STAR
James, Don
FAMILY THING, A
James, Fraser
AFFAIR, THE
SHOPPING
James, Geraldine
MOLL FLANDERS
James, Godfrey
MAGIC IN THE MIRROR
SPELLBREAKER: SECRET OF THE LEPRECHAUNS
James, Harri
NIGHT OF THE SCARECROW
James, Hawthorne
HEAVEN'S PRISONERS
James, Heinrich
STAR TREK: FIRST CONTACT
James, Jack
HEDD WYNN
James, Jamie
DOWN PERISCOPE
James, Ken
BEYOND THE CALL
FLY AWAY HOME
James, Matthew
TATTOO BOY
James, Michael Gaylord
CHAIN REACTION
James, Nia
SPY HARD
James, Robert
COLD COMFORT FARM
James, Stephen
DAYLIGHT
James, Steve
ABUSE
James, Tim
FUNNYMAN, THE
James-Young, Sandra
CAPTIVES
Jameson, Nick
EXECUTIVE DECISION
Jamieson, Kathy
BUTTERFLY KISS
CRACKER: THE MADWOMAN IN THE ATTIC
Jamieson, Will
CITIZEN RUTH
Jamison, Michael
DON'T LET YOUR MEAT LOAF
Jamison, Porter
DEMOLITIONIST, THE
Jane, Thomas
CROW: CITY OF ANGELS, THE
Janina
BROTHER OF SLEEP
Janis, Conrad
CABLE GUY, THE
Janisse, Carrie
DESIRE
Janke, Linda Williams
MR. HOLLAND'S OPUS
Janketic, Mihajlo
VUKOVAR
Jannelli, Romano
WHO KILLED PASOLINI?
Janney, Allison
ASSOCIATE, THE
BIG NIGHT
FAITHFUL
WALKING AND TALKING
Jansen, Jim
BIRDCAGE, THE
Jansen, Joann
MICHAEL
Jansen, Tom
SUITE 16
Jao, Radmar Agana
PHANTOM, THE
Jara, Jose
JUROR, THE
Jaramillo, Naomi
DEMOLITIONIST, THE
Jarman, Duncan
PROTEUS
Jarman, Otto
SOLITAIRE FOR TWO
Jarmusch, Jim
SLING BLADE
Jarrett, Arnella
EDDIE
Jarrett, Phillip
STUPIDS, THE
VIRUS
WHEN THE BULLET HITS THE BONE
Jarvel, Siria
JOHNNY SHORTWAVE
Jarvis, David
PATLABOR 2: MOBILE POLICE
Jarvis, Peter
BOGUS
Jasecko, Steve
SANDMAN, THE
Jasey, Jen
TALES FROM THE CRYPT PRESENTS BORDELLO OF BLOOD
Jasienski, Peter
NECRONOMICON: BOOK OF THE DEAD
Jason, Peter
DEMOLITIONIST, THE
GLIMMER MAN, THE
JOHN CARPENTER'S ESCAPE FROM L.A.
RAGE
Jasper, Megan
HYPE!
Jaworski, Stephanie
BEWARE: CHILDREN AT PLAY
Jay, John
FIRE ON THE MOUNTAIN
Jay, Rob
TIME TO KILL, A
Jay, Tony
ALL DOGS GO TO HEAVEN 2
HUNCHBACK OF NOTRE DAME, THE
Jay, Tyler
ROAD HOME, THE
Jaye, Billy
ASSOCIATE, THE
Jbara, Gregory
ONE FINE DAY
Jean-Baptiste, Marianne
SECRETS & LIES
Jean-Thomas, David
DOWN, OUT AND DANGEROUS
Jedell, Cara
GIRLFRIENDS
Jeffers, Juliette
SURGEON, THE
Jefferson II, Terry Ricardo
JACK
Jefferson, Jemar Jewann
FIRST KID
Jefferson, Summer Ross
AMERICA'S DREAM
Jefferson, Winter Elaine
AMERICA'S DREAM
Jeffrey, Peter
RASPUTIN
Jeffrey, Ron
THAT THING YOU DO!
Jeffrey, Susan
LAST DANCE
Jeffreys, Chuck
GIRL 6
Jeffries, Ray
BREAKING THE WAVES
Jeffries, Todd
ARRIVAL, THE
COLONY, THE
EXECUTIVE DECISION
Jefry, Abel
NELLY AND MONSIEUR ARNAUD
Jenkel, Brad
IF LUCY FELL
Jenkins, Carol
GIRL 6
Jenkins, Daniel
SHAMELESS
Jenkins, John
ANGELS AND INSECTS
Jenkins, Ken
COURAGE UNDER FIRE
EXECUTIVE DECISION
FLED
LAST DANCE
LAST MAN STANDING
Jenkins, Noam
EXTREME MEASURES
Jenkins, Richard
BOYS NEXT DOOR, THE
EDDIE
FLIRTING WITH DISASTER
Jenney, Lucinda
GRACE OF MY HEART
LATE SHIFT, THE
STEPHEN KING'S THINNER
Jennings, Brent
CHILDREN OF THE CORN: THE GATHERING
Jennings, Byron
TIME TO KILL, A
Jennings, Dev
FIRE ON THE MOUNTAIN
Jennings, Rory
AFFAIR, THE
Jennison, Gordon
HEAD OF THE FAMILY
Jensen, Belinda
ARRIVAL, THE
Jensen, Jim
GIRL 6
Jensen, Todd
WARHEAD
Jeremy, Ron
HEIDI FLEISS HOLLYWOOD MADAM
RED LINE
THEY BITE
Jerome, Howard
SUGARTIME
WHEN THE BULLET HITS THE BONE
Jerome, Timothy
EVERYONE SAYS I LOVE YOU
Jeskova, Gabriela
KASPAR HAUSER

Jessie
PUBLIC ACCESS
Jessop, Jack
KIDS IN THE HALL: BRAIN CANDY
WHEN THE BULLET HITS THE BONE
Jessup, Jack
GETTING AWAY WITH MURDER
Jeter, Michael
BOYS NEXT DOOR, THE
Jethro Tull
MESSAGE TO LOVE: THE ISLE OF WIGHT FESTIVAL
ROLLING STONES ROCK-AND-ROLL CIRCUS, THE
Jett, Joan
NOT BAD FOR A GIRL
Jewesbury, Edward
MIDWINTER'S TALE, A
Jewison, Norman
STUPIDS, THE
Jiang Wenli
STORY OF XINGHUA, THE
JiBi
HATE
Jick, Andy
CELTIC PRIDE
Jimenez, Gladys
SAWBONES
Jimenez, Hector
KAZAAM
Jimenez, Jose
EVIL ED
Jimenez, Rosa
TWO MUCH
Jin, Elaine
MAHJONG
Jin Lianhua
BLACK MOUNTAIN
Jirankova, Nina
COLD LIGHT OF DAY
Jirku, Christine
SHADOW OF ANGELS
Jirouskova, Olga
LITTLE INDIAN, BIG CITY
Jiroyan, Arsene
MACHINE, THE
Joachim, Suzy
MATERNAL INSTINCTS
UNFORGETTABLE
Jobert, Sylvie
NELLY AND MONSIEUR ARNAUD
Joganic, Alex
MY FELLOW AMERICANS
Johannsdottir, Margret Helga
VIKING SAGAS, THE
Johansson, Fredrik
EVIL ED
Johansson, Hunter
MANNY & LO
Johansson, Karsten
MANNY & LO
Johansson, Melanie
MANNY & LO
Johansson, Scarlett
IF LUCY FELL
MANNY & LO
Johansson, Vanessa
MANNY & LO
Johansson, Veronika
RENDEZVOUS IN PARIS
John, Gottfried
INSTITUTE BENJAMENTA
John, Tommy
EVERYONE SAYS I LOVE YOU
Johnny Cocktails
STRIPTEASE
Johnson, Ajia Mignon
KANSAS CITY
Johnson, Angela
BODY COUNT
Johnson, Anthony "A.J."
GREAT WHITE HYPE, THE
Johnson, Avery
EDDIE
Johnson, Ben
EVENING STAR, THE
Johnson, Blake
CHAMBER, THE
Johnson, Bobby
FEMALIEN
Johnson, Bonnie
MANNY & LO
Johnson, Brad
LONE JUSTICE: SHOWDOWN AT PLUM CREEK
Johnson, C. David
LEGEND OF GATOR FACE, THE
Johnson, Calvin
HYPE!
Johnson, Caroline Key
NATIONAL LAMPOON'S FAVORITE DEADLY SINS
Johnson, Clark
RUDE
Johnson, Derek C.
BUGGED
Johnson, Don
TIN CUP
Johnson, Geordie
ENGLISH PATIENT, THE
Johnson, Georgann
WOMAN UNDONE, A
Johnson, Gilbert Ivan
CHAMBER, THE
Johnson, Greg
ALEX
Johnson II, Ian
WILD SIDE
Johnson, Jeff "J.J."
CITIZEN RUTH
Johnson, Jeffrey Paul
KAZAAM
Johnson, Johna
MULHOLLAND FALLS
Johnson, Karl
YANKEE ZULU
Johnson, Kimberly Ann
APART FROM HUGH
Johnson, Kirsten
KIDS IN THE HALL: BRAIN CANDY
Johnson, Lamont
GREAT WHITE HYPE, THE
JERRY MAGUIRE
Johnson, Larry
DON'T LET YOUR MEAT LOAF
EDDIE
SPACE JAM
Johnson, Linda Calvin
TIME TO KILL, A
Johnson, Lionel
ORIGINAL SINS
Johnson, Liz
AMANDA AND THE ALIEN
Johnson, Mark W.
PEOPLE VS. LARRY FLYNT, THE
Johnson, Mark Whitman
TIME TO KILL, A
Johnson, Melissa
MANNY & LO
Johnson, Michael James
JERRY MAGUIRE
Johnson, Michelle
GLIMMER MAN, THE
WHEN THE BULLET HITS THE BONE
Johnson, Paul
SUNSET PARK
Johnson, Penny
DEATH BENEFIT
ROAD TO GALVESTON, THE
Johnson, Rick
ED
JERRY MAGUIRE
MULHOLLAND FALLS
Johnson, Ron
FAST MONEY
Johnson, Sam
BEAVIS AND BUTT-HEAD DO AMERICA
Johnson, Scott
WHISPERING, THE
Johnson, Shorty
APART FROM HUGH
Johnson, Sid
CHAMBER, THE
Johnson, Stacii Jae
THIN LINE BETWEEN LOVE AND HATE, A
Johnson, Tony T.
ARRIVAL, THE
Johnson, Valentino
SPY HARD
Johnson, Wesley
FOXFIRE
Johnson, William
STREET FIGHTER II: THE ANIMATED MOVIE
Johnston, Andrew
HAPPY GILMORE
Johnston, Jeff
PEOPLE VS. LARRY FLYNT, THE
Johnston, John Dennis
FOREST WARRIOR
Johnston, Justine
BOGUS
EYE FOR AN EYE
Johnston, Justine A.
MULTIPLICITY
Johnston, Katelynd
FOR THE MOMENT
Johnston, Melissa
FIRST KID
Johnston, Shaun
HOW THE WEST WAS FUN
Johnston Ulrich, Kim
RUMPELSTILTSKIN
Johnstone, Nahanni
MAN IN THE ATTIC, THE
SUGARTIME
Jokovic, Mirjana
VUKOVAR
Jolie, Angelina
FOXFIRE
LOVE IS ALL THERE IS
Jolly, Arthur
ORIGINAL SINS
Joly, Antonin Lebas
RIDICULE
Jonas, Johonna
VIKING SAGAS, THE
Jones, Alan
MR. ICE CREAM MAN
Jones, Alesia
EYE FOR AN EYE
Jones, Andras
DEMOLITIONIST, THE
Jones, Andy
KIDS IN THE HALL: BRAIN CANDY
Jones, Angela
CURDLED
Jones, Angela L.
PREACHER'S WIFE, THE
Jones, Antar
LET'S GET BIZZEE
Jones, Anthony
STRIPTEASE

Jones, Arlen
UNFORGETTABLE
Jones, Brian
ROLLING STONES ROCK-AND-ROLL CIRCUS, THE
Jones, Catherine
TUNNEL VISION
Jones, Catherine Zeta
PHANTOM, THE
Jones, Celvia
DON'T LET YOUR MEAT LOAF
Jones, Cherylyn
EVERYONE SAYS I LOVE YOU
Jones, Christopher
MAD DOG TIME
Jones, Eddie
LETTER TO MY KILLER
Jones, Emrys
LOOKING FOR RICHARD
Jones, Freddie
COLD COMFORT FARM
Jones, Gary
HOMEWARD BOUND II: LOST IN SAN FRANCISCO
Jones, Griff Rhys
ADVENTURES OF PINOCCHIO, THE
Jones, Harry
MUPPET TREASURE ISLAND
Jones, Heather
EDDIE
Jones, J.O.
HEDD WYNN
Jones, Jake-Ann
DON'T LET YOUR MEAT LOAF
Jones, James
HEAD OF THE FAMILY
Jones, James Earl
FAMILY THING, A
LOOKING FOR RICHARD
Jones, Jamie
HARRIET THE SPY
Jones, Jeffrey
CRUCIBLE, THE
Jones, Jennifer L.
MY FELLOW AMERICANS
Jones, John Christopher
SUBSTANCE OF FIRE, THE
Jones, John Marshall
SGT. BILKO
Jones, John Stevens
SLEEPERS
Jones Jr., Tedero
DON'T BE A MENACE TO SOUTH CENTRAL WHILE DRINKING YOUR JUICE IN THE HOOD
Jones, Karen
LARRY MCMURTRY'S STREETS OF LAREDO
Jones, Ken
JUDE
Jones, Kevin
DEADLY OUTBREAK
Jones, Kimberly Faith
SERIAL KILLER
Jones, Mal
FLIPPER
TOLLBOOTH
Jones, Mark
DON'T LET YOUR MEAT LOAF
Jones, Michael K.
LONG KISS GOODNIGHT, THE
Jones, Michelle
HIGH SCHOOL HIGH
Jones, Mickey
IT CAME FROM OUTER SPACE II
SLING BLADE
SUNCHASER
TIN CUP
Jones, Morris Vernon
PREACHER'S WIFE, THE
Jones, Neal
LOOKING FOR RICHARD
Jones, O-Lan
MARS ATTACKS!
Jones, Pirie
DEAD TO RIGHTS
Jones, Retha
NUTTY PROFESSOR, THE
Jones, Richard A.
LONE STAR
Jones, Richard T.
BLACK ROSE OF HARLEM
TRIGGER EFFECT, THE
Jones, Rick
FOXFIRE
Jones, Ricky
SOLITAIRE FOR TWO
Jones, Ruth
EMMA
Jones, Sam
AMERICAN STRAYS
TEXAS PAYBACK
Jones, Seth
BIG NIGHT
Jones, Sharon Lee
JOSH KIRBY . . . TIME WARRIOR!: TRAPPED ON TOY WORLD
Jones, Stephanie
RUMPELSTILTSKIN
Jones, Stephanie Astalos
NEON BIBLE, THE
Jones, Steven Anthony
JACK
Jones, Teresa Wells
HOURGLASS
Jones, Tom
MARS ATTACKS!
Jones, Tony
OFF AND RUNNING
Jones, Tracey Cherelle
DON'T BE A MENACE TO SOUTH CENTRAL WHILE DRINKING YOUR JUICE IN THE HOOD
Jones, Tracy
TWO IF BY SEA
Jones, Waddy
REDEMPTION: KICKBOXER 5
Jones, William
PHANTOM, THE
Jones, William James
EXECUTIVE DECISION
Jonsson, Bill
CHILDREN OF NOISY VILLAGE, THE
Jonsson, Magnus
VIKING SAGAS, THE
Jordae, Janine
FROM DUSK TILL DAWN
Jordan, Aaron
PREACHER'S WIFE, THE
Jordan, Alan
SHOOTFIGHTER 2: KILL OR BE KILLED!
Jordan, Ashleigh
FAMILY THING, A
Jordan, Derwin
EXTREME MEASURES
Jordan, Diana
JERRY MAGUIRE
Jordan, Don
MOTHER NIGHT
Jordan, Elizabeth
KINGPIN
Jordan, Jack
SANDMAN, THE
Jordan, Jeremy
BIO-DOME
Jordan, John
KINGPIN
Jordan, Joshua
PREACHER'S WIFE, THE
Jordan, Leslie
MISSING PIECES
Jordan, Michael
SPACE JAM
Jordan, Monty
ARRIVAL, THE
Jordan, Peter
HECK'S WAY HOME
Jordan, Robert
PRIMAL FEAR
Jordan, Rose Merry
PREACHER'S WIFE, THE
Jordan, Tom
MOLL FLANDERS
Jordan, William
KINGPIN
Jordan, Yakin Manassah
PREACHER'S WIFE, THE
Josefina
BROTHER OF SLEEP
Joseph, Clifton
RUDE
Joseph, Edward Francis
RANSOM
Joseph, Kevin
MERCY
Joseph, Tiffany
PREACHER'S WIFE, THE
Joseph, Todd
DESIRE
Josepher, Wendel
TWISTER
Joshua, Lilyr
HEDD WYNN
Jourdan, Ines
SUITE 16
Jourdan, Sylvie
SUITE 16
Journot, Jean-Paul
HORSEMAN ON THE ROOF
Joy, Mary
GIRLS TOWN
Joy, Robert
HARRIET THE SPY
MODERN AFFAIR, A
PHARAOH'S ARMY
Joyce, Christopher
GHOST IN THE SHELL
Joyce, Christopher A.
SWINGERS
Joyce, Ella
SET IT OFF
Joyce, James J.
INDEPENDENCE DAY
Joyce, Jennifer Judith
DEATH ARTIST, THE
Joyce, Mike
LIVE WIRE: HUMAN TIMEBOMB
Joyce, Thomas
MRS. WINTERBOURNE
Joyner, Mario
SGT. KABUKIMAN N.Y.P.D.
Joyner, Michelle
PAINTED HERO
Jozefson, Jack
FATALLY YOURS
Juanas, Paco
I SHOT ANDY WARHOL
Juarbe, Israel
DEAR GOD
Jubinville, Kevin
FLY AWAY HOME

Judd, Ashley
NORMA JEAN AND MARILYN
NORMAL LIFE
PASSION OF DARKLY NOON, THE
TIME TO KILL, A
Judd, John
EVIL HAS A FACE
Judd, Rainer
JACK
Jude, Patrick
SUGARTIME
Judell, Brandon
NEUROSIA: 50 YEARS OF PERVERSITY
Judge, Mike
BEAVIS AND BUTT-HEAD DO AMERICA
Judkins, Johnny
TUSKEGEE AIRMEN, THE
Julien, Martin
STAND OFF, THE
Julio, Don
KINGPIN
Julius-Scott, Alice
TIME TO KILL, A
Juliusson, Theodor
VIKING SAGAS, THE
Junco, Tito
AVENTURERA
Jupp, Ed
RANSOM
Jurasek, Josef
KASPAR HAUSER
Jurasik, Peter
LATE SHIFT, THE
Jurgensen, Randy
JUROR, THE
Juricek, Zdenek
BREACH OF TRUST
Jussim, Jared
JERRY MAGUIRE
Juszczakiewicz, Michal
MOTHER OF KINGS
Jutras, Richard
HOLLOW POINT
MOTHER NIGHT
k funk
GIRL 6
Kaal, Jim
CITIZEN RUTH
Kabasares, Kennedy
CABLE GUY, THE
Kabo, Olga
BURIAL OF THE RATS
Kaczmarek, Jane
CHAMBER, THE
Kadamba
GRIM
MARY REILLY
Kagan, Elaine
SHARON'S SECRET
Kagy, Tom
SLING BLADE
Kahan, Judith
MULTIPLICITY
Kahn, Douglas
SONIC OUTLAWS
Kahn, Heather
GETTING AWAY WITH MURDER
Kahn, Jeff
CABLE GUY, THE
Kahn, Karen
BLACK SHEEP
Kahn, Rakeem
GHOST AND THE DARKNESS, THE
Kaidanovsky, Alexander
MAGIC HUNTER
Kain, Amber
MERCY

Kaiser, Suki
FINAL CUT, THE
RED SCORPION 2
Kaiser, Suzi
GIRL FROM MARS, THE
Kaitan, Elizabeth
SOUTH BEACH ACADEMY
SPY HARD
VIRTUAL ENCOUNTERS
Kaku, Michio
SYNTHETIC PLEASURES
Kaleem, Claudia
PHAT BEACH
Kalem, Toni
AMERICAN STRAYS
Kaler, Berwick
JUDE
Kalifi, Mohsen
WHITE BALLOON, THE
Kalil, Kymberly
JERRY MAGUIRE
Kalinina, Daria
WELCOME TO THE DOLLHOUSE
Kaliski, Mike
AMERICAN STRAYS
Kallaanvaara, Mikael
EVIL ED
Kalmic, Lazar
SOMEONE ELSE'S AMERICA
Kalodimos, Demetria
LAST DANCE
Kalpatru, Debria
SHADOW OF ANGELS
Kalvoda, Radim
DELTA OF VENUS
Kam Seung-Yuk
MIDNIGHT ANGEL
Kaman, Rob
MAXIMUM RISK
Kamerling, Antonie
SUITE 16
Kamin, Daniel Tucker
AMERICA'S DREAM
Kampmann, Steven
MULTIPLICITY
Kanakaredes, Melina
LONG KISS GOODNIGHT, THE
Kandel, Jack
CHAIN REACTION
Kandel, Paul
HUNCHBACK OF NOTRE DAME, THE
Kane, Bob
PHANTOM, THE
Kane, Carol
AMERICAN STRAYS
BIG BULLY
PALLBEARER, THE
SUNSET PARK
THEODORE REX
TREES LOUNGE
Kane, Ivan
BOUND
NORMA JEAN AND MARILYN
Kane, Kathleen
PEOPLE VS. LARRY FLYNT, THE
Kaneshiro, Takeshi
CHUNGKING EXPRESS
Kanewsky, Alexander
MAXIMUM RISK
Kanfer, Stefan
LINE KING: THE AL HIRSCHFELD STORY, THE
Kang, Sang
SHOOTFIGHTER 2: KILL OR BE KILLED!
Kani, John
GHOST AND THE DARKNESS, THE
Kankuja, Nathalie
EVIL ED

Kant, Paul
ENGLISH PATIENT, THE
Kantner, China
EVENING STAR, THE
GRACE OF MY HEART
Kapelos, John
LATE SHIFT, THE
Kapetan, George
TWO MUCH
Kaplan, Arkadij
MAXIMUM RISK
Kaplan, Curt
ED
Kaplan, Cynthia
ED'S NEXT MOVE
Kaplan, Ira
I SHOT ANDY WARHOL
Kaplan, Jonathan Charles
JOSH KIRBY . . . TIME WARRIOR!: LAST BATTLE FOR THE UNIVERSE
Kaplan, Rick
ED'S NEXT MOVE
Kaplan, Vivienne
FRIGHTENERS, THE
Kapp, Alex
MOTHER'S PRAYER, A
Karan, Allison
DADETOWN
Karen, Anna
BEAUTIFUL THING
Karen, James
PIRANHA
UP CLOSE AND PERSONAL
Karger, Jodi
SERIAL KILLER
Karriem, Khadijah
DON'T LET YOUR MEAT LOAF
Karris, Laura
SABRINA, THE TEENAGE WITCH
Kartalian, Buck
JOSH KIRBY . . . TIME WARRIOR!: TRAPPED ON TOY WORLD
ROCK, THE
Kartheiser, Vincent
ALASKA
Kartovsky, John
ABUSE
Karz, Jimmy
MATILDA
Kasem, Casey
MR. WRONG
Kasem, Jean
MR. WRONG
Kash, Daniel
VIRUS
Kash, George
MAXIMUM RISK
Kashiyama, Gohki
MABOROSI
Kashkar, Andray
DEADLY OUTBREAK
Kaske, Scott
BIRDCAGE, THE
Kasper, Gary
FINAL EQUINOX, THE
JOSH KIRBY . . . TIME WARRIOR!: EGGS FROM 70,000,000 B.C.
Kaspszak, Edward
BEAUTIFUL GIRLS
Kass, Trevor
LIVE WIRE: HUMAN TIMEBOMB
Kassir, John
SPY HARD
TALES FROM THE CRYPT PRESENTS BORDELLO OF BLOOD
Kassovitz, Mathieu
HATE

Kassovitz, Peter
HATE
Kaszas, Geza
DOGFIGHTERS, THE
Kates, Bernard
PHANTOM, THE
Katims, Robert
PALLBEARER, THE
Katkin, Brian
BURIAL OF THE RATS
Katsulas, Andreas
EXECUTIVE DECISION
Katsuyama, Gerry
MAN WITH THE PERFECT SWING, THE
Katt, Nicky
TIME TO KILL, A
Katt, William
PIRANHA
RATTLED
TOLLBOOTH
Katz, Judah
BLOODKNOT
LONG KISS GOODNIGHT, THE
Katz, Sarah
BEAUTIFUL GIRLS
Katz-Norrod, Barbara
SANDMAN, THE
Katzman, Lon E.
MAXIMUM RISK
Kauders, Sylvia
CITY HALL
Kaufman, Charlotte
SGT. KABUKIMAN N.Y.P.D.
Kaufman, Jeffrey
RANSOM
Kaufman, Lily Hayes
SGT. KABUKIMAN N.Y.P.D.
Kaufman, Lisbeth
SGT. KABUKIMAN N.Y.P.D.
Kaufman, Melinda Wade
4 TALES OF 2 CITIES
Kaufman, Patricia
SGT. KABUKIMAN N.Y.P.D.
Kaufman Sr., Stanley L.
SGT. KABUKIMAN N.Y.P.D.
Kaulback, Brian
MAXIMUM RISK
SUGARTIME
Kavafian, Ani
SMALL WONDERS
Kavafian, Ida
SMALL WONDERS
Kavanagh, John
SOME MOTHER'S SON
Kavanagh, Owen
BREAKING THE WAVES
Kavanagh, Thomas
WAR OF THE BUTTONS, THE
Kavanaugh, Charles
PUBLIC ACCESS
Kawakami, Tim
GREAT WHITE HYPE, THE
Kawamura, Kotoko
HIGH SCHOOL HIGH
Kay, Hadley
BLOOD & DONUTS
Kay, Joe
LAST MAN STANDING
Kay, Jolene
FOREST WARRIOR
Kaye, David
HAPPY GILMORE
Kaye, Ivan
COLD COMFORT FARM
Kayman, Lee
BEWARE: CHILDREN AT PLAY
Kazan, Elia
PERSONAL JOURNEY WITH MARTIN SCORSESE THROUGH AMERICAN MOVIES, A
Kazan, Laine
ASSOCIATE, THE
Kazan, Lainie
LOVE IS ALL THERE IS
Kazan, Sandra
CAUGHT
Kazuya, Takahashi
KAMIKAZE TAXI
Keach, Stacy
AMANDA AND THE ALIEN
JOHN CARPENTER'S ESCAPE FROM L.A.
Keane, Brian
IF LUCY FELL
Keane, James
LETTER TO MY KILLER
PHENOMENON
Kearney, Charles
BREAKING THE WAVES
Kearney, Gerard
WAR OF THE BUTTONS, THE
Kearns, Liam
MATILDA
Kearns, Michael
IT'S MY PARTY
MOTHER'S PRAYER, A
Keating, Michael
WAVELENGTH
Keaton, Diane
FIRST WIVES CLUB, THE
MARVIN'S ROOM
Keaton, Michael
MULTIPLICITY
Keats, Ele
MOTHER
WHITE WOLVES II: LEGEND OF THE WILD
Keawkalaya, Joseph
DOWN PERISCOPE
Keegan, Andrew
INDEPENDENCE DAY
PIG'S TALE, A
Keehen, Virginia
DENTIST, THE
Keeley, David
SUGARTIME
Keen, Pat
COLD COMFORT FARM
Keenan, Harvey
DEAR GOD
Keene, Christopher J.
HIGH SCHOOL HIGH
Keene, Jason
DANGEROUS PASSION
Keener, Catherine
BOYS
WALKING AND TALKING
Keener, Eliott
BODY COUNT
GHOSTS OF MISSISSIPPI
Keenleyside, Eric
TALES FROM THE CRYPT PRESENTS BORDELLO OF BLOOD
Keeshan, Bob
STUPIDS, THE
Keeslar, Mark
STUPIDS, THE
Keeslar, Matt
STREETCAR NAMED DESIRE, A
Kehar, Jan
KASPAR HAUSER
Kehela, Steve
SGT. BILKO
Kehler, Jack
AMERICAN STRAYS
DEATH BENEFIT
MY FELLOW AMERICANS
SERPENT'S LAIR
SHOT, THE
Kei
CURTIS'S CHARM
Kein, Paula
PROPRIETOR, THE
Keiser, Jeff
BREAKAWAY
Keita
NAKED SOULS
Keita, Bala Moussa
GUIMBA THE TYRANT
Keitel, Harvey
FROM DUSK TILL DAWN
Keith, Brian
ENTERTAINING ANGELS: THE DOROTHY DAY STORY
NATIONAL LAMPOON'S FAVORITE DEADLY SINS
Keith, David
FAMILY THING, A
OFF AND RUNNING
Keith, Paul
MISSING PIECES
Keith, Warren
FARGO
Kellehen, Tim
TUSKEGEE AIRMEN, THE
Kelleher, Tim
BIRDCAGE, THE
EXECUTIVE DECISION
INDEPENDENCE DAY
Kelleher, Timothy
UNDERSTUDY: GRAVEYARD SHIFT 2, THE
Keller, Audrey
MR. ICE CREAM MAN
Keller, Mary Page
COLONY, THE
Keller, Melissa
D3: THE MIGHTY DUCKS
Keller, Ryan
MR. ICE CREAM MAN
Keller, Tiffany
MR. ICE CREAM MAN
Kellerman, Sally
IT'S MY PARTY
Kelley, Bill
FLIPPER
Kelley, Sheila
ONE FINE DAY
SECRETS & LIES
Kellner, Catherine
HARVEST OF FIRE
Kells, Ken
ROCK, THE
Kelly
BUTTERFLY KISS
Kelly, Aidan
MICHAEL COLLINS
Kelly, Bebihinn
HARD WAY OUT: BLOODFIST VIII
Kelly, Brendan
ROCK, THE
Kelly, Daniel Hugh
TUSKEGEE AIRMEN, THE
Kelly, David Patrick
FLIRTING WITH DISASTER
FUNERAL, THE
HEAVY
LAST MAN STANDING
Kelly, Desmond
FRIGHTENERS, THE
Kelly, Emma
HEDD WYNN

Kelly, Frank
WAR OF THE BUTTONS, THE
Kelly, Ian
IN LOVE AND WAR
Kelly, Jean Louisa
HARVEST OF FIRE
MR. HOLLAND'S OPUS
Kelly, Jill
VIRTUAL ENCOUNTERS
Kelly, Joseph Patrick
ROCK, THE
Kelly, KC
FRIGHTENERS, THE
Kelly, Kevin James
SWINGERS
Kelly, Lesley
UNDERSTUDY: GRAVEYARD SHIFT 2, THE
Kelly, Michele
GIRL 6
Kelly, Mike
D3: THE MIGHTY DUCKS
Kelly, Moira
ENTERTAINING ANGELS: THE DOROTHY DAY STORY
UNHOOK THE STARS
Kelly, Paula
ONCE UPON A TIME . . . WHEN WE WERE COLORED
Kelly, Peter
DADETOWN
Kelly, Rae'ven
AMERICA'S DREAM
GHOSTS OF MISSISSIPPI
Kelly, Rae'ven Larrymore
TIME TO KILL, A
Kelly, Ritamarie
WALKING AND TALKING
Kelly, Robin
SURGEON, THE
Kelly S.J., Reverend Joseph
CITY HALL
Kelly-Young, Leonard
DOWN, OUT AND DANGEROUS
ED
Kelpine, Dan
TWISTER
Kelso, Mo
STUPIDS, THE
Kemble, Mark
ARRIVAL, THE
Kemler, Andrew
CANNIBAL! THE MUSICAL
Kemp, Gary
MAGIC HUNTER
Kemp, Jeremy
ANGELS AND INSECTS
Kemp, Martin
DESIRE
Kempf, Robert Louis
FAN, THE
Kemsley, Victoria
DUNSTON CHECKS IN
Kendall, Katherine
SWINGERS
Kenderesi, Tibor
RASPUTIN
Kennedy, Beth
PHENOMENON
Kennedy, David
GRIM
Kennedy, Jaime
WILLIAM SHAKESPEARE'S ROMEO + JULIET
Kennedy, Jamie
SCREAM
Kennedy, Maria Doyle
MOLL FLANDERS
Kennedy, Ryan
JACK
SCREAM
Kenney, Bob
PRIMAL FEAR
Kenney, Kaitlyn
LAST DANCE
Kennington, Brian
GETTING AWAY WITH MURDER
Kenny, John
MICHAEL COLLINS
Kenny, Tom
DEAD WEEKEND
OUT THERE
Kennylside, Erick
ANNIE O
Kensit, Patsy
ANGELS AND INSECTS
GRACE OF MY HEART
TUNNEL VISION
Kent, Allan
DEAR GOD
Kent, Ryan
ALASKA
Kent, Steven
HIGH SCHOOL HIGH
Keogh, Doreen
SOME MOTHER'S SON
Keogh, Jimmy
SOME MOTHER'S SON
Kepros, Nicholas
ASSOCIATE, THE
Kern, Dan
PHOENIX
Kernan, Anthony
CAPTIVES
Kerner, Jeannette
D3: THE MIGHTY DUCKS
Kerner, Jerry
D3: THE MIGHTY DUCKS
Kerr, Kenny
ASSOCIATE, THE
Kerr, Patrick
ED
Kerr, William
MY FELLOW AMERICANS
Kerrigan, Lodge
SEARCH FOR ONE-EYE JIMMY, THE
Kerry, John
VENUS RISING
Kerry, Margaret
PUBLIC ACCESS
Kertesz, Marta
DOGFIGHTERS, THE
Kerwin, Brian
GETTING AWAY WITH MURDER
IT CAME FROM OUTER SPACE II
JACK
Kerz, Louise
LINE KING: THE AL HIRSCHFELD STORY, THE
Kessler, Anne
LA COMEDIE-FRANCAISE OU L'AMOUR JOUE
Kestner, Boyd
ENTERTAINING ANGELS: THE DOROTHY DAY STORY
Kevorkian, Soseh
CHAIN REACTION
EVIL HAS A FACE
Key, Elizabeth
BLONDES HAVE MORE GUNS
Key, Jennifer
MATILDA
Key, Tara
I SHOT ANDY WARHOL
Keyes, Irwin
BACKLASH: OBLIVION 2
PURE DANGER
Keys, Christopher
MIRROR HAS TWO FACES, THE
Khakh, Robert
EVERYONE SAYS I LOVE YOU
Khali, Simbi
THIN LINE BETWEEN LOVE AND HATE, A
Khalil, Christel
MATILDA
Khan, Shaheen
CAPTIVES
Kharashkevich, Alexander
CHEKIST, THE
Kheireddine, Abdellatif
SILENCES OF THE PALACE, THE
Khelif, Samir
HATE
Khokhlushkina, Inna
BURIAL OF THE RATS
Khouth, Gabe
HECK'S WAY HOME
Khozianov, Victor
RASPUTIN
Kidd, Ken
PEOPLE VS. LARRY FLYNT, THE
Kidder, Margot
BLOODKNOT
PHANTOM 2040: THE GHOST WHO WALKS
Kidman, Nicole
PORTRAIT OF A LADY, THE
Kidnie, James
BREACH OF TRUST
Kiel, Richard
HAPPY GILMORE
Kier, Udo
ADVENTURES OF PINOCCHIO, THE
BARB WIRE
BREAKING THE WAVES
4 TALES OF 2 CITIES
Kieser, Father Ellwood E.
ENTERTAINING ANGELS: THE DOROTHY DAY STORY
Kilbert, Tony
SCREAM
Kiley, Richard
PHENOMENON
Kilgore, John
BUGGED
Kilguss, Jessie
CRUCIBLE, THE
Killer, Turi
STAR MAKER, THE
Killinger, Marion
I'M NOT RAPPAPORT
Kilmer, Val
GHOST AND THE DARKNESS, THE
ISLAND OF DR. MOREAU, THE
Kilpatrick, Patrick
BEASTMASTER 3: THE EYE OF BRAXUS
ERASER
LAST MAN STANDING
Kilroy, Colette
CHILDREN OF FURY
Kim, Derek
INDEPENDENCE DAY
Kim, Gena
WILD SIDE
Kim, Karen
COLONY, THE
Kim, Kim
EYE FOR AN EYE
Kim, Teisha
HARRIET THE SPY
Kim, Walter
POISON IVY 2: LILY
Kimball, Frederic
LOOKING FOR RICHARD

Kimbrough, Charles
HUNCHBACK OF NOTRE DAME, THE
Kimmell, Todd
SGT. KABUKIMAN N.Y.P.D.
Kinder, Kirk
DON'T BE A MENACE TO SOUTH CENTRAL WHILE DRINKING YOUR JUICE IN THE HOOD
King, Asha J.
LAST DANCE
King, B.B.
WHEN WE WERE KINGS
King, Beth
DADETOWN
King, Chantel
NAKED SOULS
King, Chris
THEY BITE
King, Courtney
MOLL FLANDERS
King, Davidson
KAZAAM
King, Diana
WHEN WE WERE KINGS
King, Don
WHEN WE WERE KINGS
King, Ellery
DEAR GOD
King, Glenn
RANSOM
King, Jeffrey
MARS ATTACKS!
King Jr., Martin Luther
BERKELEY IN THE 60S
King, Larry
LONG KISS GOODNIGHT, THE
OPEN SEASON
King, Lorna
TWO FRIENDS
King, Regina
JERRY MAGUIRE
THIN LINE BETWEEN LOVE AND HATE, A
King, Sonny H.
ERASER
King, Yolanda
AMERICA'S DREAM
GHOSTS OF MISSISSIPPI
Kingi, Henry
BARB WIRE
Kingi Jr., Henry
RANSOM
Kingsley, Ben
TWELFTH NIGHT
Kinley, Catherine
PROPRIETOR, THE
Kinmont, Kathleen
TEXAS PAYBACK
THAT THING YOU DO!
Kinnear, Greg
DEAR GOD
Kinney, David
DADETOWN
Kinney, Terry
FLY AWAY HOME
SLEEPERS
Kino, Lloyd
CABLE GUY, THE
Kinsley, Mike
BIRDCAGE, THE
Kinzie, David
MIRROR HAS TWO FACES, THE
Kiper, Mel
JERRY MAGUIRE
Kiraly, Istvan
DOGFIGHTERS, THE
Kirayama-Lem, James
SHARON'S SECRET

Kirby, Bruno
SLEEPERS
Kirby, Chae
JAMES AND THE GIANT PEACH
Kirishima, Max
WHITE TIGER
Kirk, Heather
FIRST KID
Kirkconnell, John
WHITE TIGER
Kirkland, Eric Jerome
GRACE OF MY HEART
Kirkland, Mirabelle
RIDICULE
Kirkpatrick, Vanessa
CRACKER: THE MADWOMAN IN THE ATTIC
Kirouac Jr., Roland
HARRIET THE SPY
Kirshenbaum, Debra
LONG KISS GOODNIGHT, THE
SUGARTIME
Kirshner, Mia
CROW: CITY OF ANGELS, THE
GRASS HARP, THE
Kirwan, Dervla
WAR OF THE BUTTONS, THE
Kiser, Terry
FOREST WARRIOR
HOURGLASS
Kishi, Jon W.
BROKEN ARROW
Kisicki, Jim
DIABOLIQUE
Kiss, Andy
FLATTERED
Kiss, Ferenc David
RASPUTIN
Kiss, Irene
BASQUIAT
Kissoon, Jeffrey
HAMLET
Kitaen, Tawny
PLAYBACK
Kitao
QUEST, THE
Kitchen, Anthony D-Wayne
WAR AT HOME, THE
Kitchen, Megan
NIGHT OF THE TWISTERS
Kitt, Eartha
HARRIET THE SPY
Kitt, Sam
EVIL HAS A FACE
Kiuchi, Midori
MABOROSI
Kivel, Barry
BOUND
ONE FINE DAY
Kiviaho, Rik
QUEST, THE
Kizer, Jeff
HARVEST OF FIRE
Kizzier, Heath
SONS OF TRINITY
Klaffke, Jakob
FLIRT
Klassen, Tina
BIG BULLY
Klastorin, Michael
PEOPLE VS. LARRY FLYNT, THE
Klein, Jacqueline
GETTING AWAY WITH MURDER
Klein, Larry
GRACE OF MY HEART
Klein, Leslie
FRIGHTENERS, THE

Klein, Robert
ONE FINE DAY
Klein, Spencer
MOTHER
Klein, Trude
EVERYONE SAYS I LOVE YOU
Kleinbaum, Rabbi Sharon
EVERYTHING RELATIVE
Kleine, Joe
EDDIE
Kleyla, Brandon
CHILDREN OF THE CORN: THE GATHERING
Klieman, Rikki
CABLE GUY, THE
Kliman, Lou
HAPPY GILMORE
Klimaszewski, Diane
SPY HARD
TIGER HEART
Klimaszewski, Elaine
SPY HARD
TIGER HEART
Kline, Jim
IT'S MY PARTY
Kline, Jurex
WITHOUT MERCY
Kline, Kevin
HUNCHBACK OF NOTRE DAME, THE
LOOKING FOR RICHARD
Kling, Heidi
D3: THE MIGHTY DUCKS
Klinger, Herb
BEWARE: CHILDREN AT PLAY
Klug, Mary
CELTIC PRIDE
Klugman, Jack
DEAR GOD
Klumm, Kenneth
DADETOWN
Klvana, Kathryn
TOLLBOOTH
Klyn, Vincent
FINAL EQUINOX, THE
RAVENHAWK
Kmetko, Steve
FIRST KID
IT'S MY PARTY
Knape, Anne Sophie
CHILDREN OF NOISY VILLAGE, THE
Knapp, David
IT'S MY PARTY
Knatchbull, Melissa
MISSION: IMPOSSIBLE
Knaup, Herbert
BROTHER OF SLEEP
Knepper, Robert
EVERYONE SAYS I LOVE YOU
Knight, Byran
MUTANT MAN
Knight, Jack
ENTERTAINING ANGELS: THE DOROTHY DAY STORY
Knight, Lisa Renee
BOGUS
Knight, Nic
JANE EYRE
Knight, Rosalind
SOLITAIRE FOR TWO
Knight, Shirley
DIABOLIQUE
Knight, Trenton
FOREST WARRIOR
Knight, Tuesday
FAN, THE
Knight, Wayne
CHAMELEON
SPACE JAM

Knight, William
DARK SECRETS
WITCHCRAFT: SALEM'S GHOST
ZARKORR! THE INVADER
Knoller, Ohad
UNDER THE DOMIM TREE
Knotts, Don
BIG BULLY
Knowlton, Steve
FIRE ON THE MOUNTAIN
Knox, Mickey
CEMETERY MAN
Knudsen, Mark
SWEEPER, THE
Ko Yu-lun
MAHJONG
Kobayashi, Dian
DONOR UNKNOWN
Kober, Jane
SGT. KABUKIMAN N.Y.P.D.
Kober, Jeff
ONE MAN'S JUSTICE
Koch, Edward
EDDIE
Koch, Edward I.
CITY HALL
FIRST WIVES CLUB, THE
Koch, Sebastian
FLIRT
Koci, Paavel
ADVENTURES OF PINOCCHIO, THE
Kocsis, Melinda
KINGPIN
Kodar, Oja
ORSON WELLES: THE ONE-MAN BAND
Koenig, Danielle
CRAFT, THE
Koenig, Jack
PROPRIETOR, THE
Koffman, Susan
BLOOD & DONUTS
Kohl, Tonia
FRISK
Kohler, Kurt
EXECUTIVE DECISION
Kohn, Barbara
MAN WITH A PLAN
Kohn, Joan
CHAIN REACTION
Kokenyessy, Agi
RASPUTIN
Kokernot, Larissa
FARGO
Kokkos, Yannis
LA COMEDIE-FRANCAISE OU L'AMOUR JOUE
Kokotakis, Nick
NUTTY PROFESSOR, THE
Koldenhoven, Darlene
SPY HARD
Kollenda, Anna
YOUNG POISONER'S HANDBOOK, THE
Kollenda, Katja
YOUNG POISONER'S HANDBOOK, THE
Kolosko, Stefan
FLIRT
Komenich, Rich
CHAIN REACTION
Komlos, Andras
RASPUTIN
Komorowska, Liliana
SCREAMERS
Koncak, Jon
EDDIE
Koncz, Gabor
RASPUTIN
Kondracke, Morton
GETTING AWAY WITH MURDER
INDEPENDENCE DAY
Kondrashoff, Kim
TALES FROM THE CRYPT PRESENTS BORDELLO OF BLOOD
Konn, Armin
MAXIMUM RISK
Konowal, Brian
GIRL 6
Konrad, Kristof
INDEPENDENCE DAY
Kooij, Paul
ANTONIA'S LINE
Koon, Christine Lameisha
PREACHER'S WIFE, THE
Koon, Rebecca
TIME TO KILL, A
Kopache, Thomas
GHOSTS OF MISSISSIPPI
Kopczynski, Anthony
CHAMBER, THE
Kopelow, Michael
ONE GOOD TURN
Kopf, Kim
WITCHCRAFT: SALEM'S GHOST
Kopman, Micha
CEMETERY MAN
Koppel, Bernie
MISSING PIECES
Koprova, Misa
CABLE GUY, THE
Kopyc, Frank
DUNSTON CHECKS IN
Kordina, Julia
FLAMING EARS
Korf, Anita
ARRIVAL, THE
Korkes, Jon
GETTING AWAY WITH MURDER
Korman, Harvey
JINGLE ALL THE WAY
Korn, Alan
SONIC OUTLAWS
Kornbluth, Josh
JACK
Korognai, Karoly
DOGFIGHTERS, THE
Korthaze, Richard
I'M NOT RAPPAPORT
Korvin, Veronika
ED'S NEXT MOVE
Kosala, Joe
CHAIN REACTION
PRIMAL FEAR
Koskoff, Sarah
THAT THING YOU DO!
Kostelka, Lubomir
KASPAR HAUSER
Kostis, Peter
TIN CUP
Kotcheff, Alexandra
HIDDEN ASSASSIN
Kotcheff, Thomas
HIDDEN ASSASSIN
Koteas, Elias
SUGARTIME
Kotecki, Robert
ONE MAN'S JUSTICE
Kotite, Richie
JERRY MAGUIRE
Kotoske, Tamar
BIG NIGHT
Kottke, Austin
BLACK SHEEP
SPY HARD
Kotto, Yaphet
TWO IF BY SEA
Kounde, Hubert
HATE
Kousi, Katherine
BIO-DOME
Kovacicova, Sandra
DRAGONHEART
Kovacs, Geza
STAND OFF, THE
Kovacs, Patricia
RASPUTIN
Koval, Vladimir
ADVENTURES OF PINOCCHIO, THE
Kovar, Mikey
CARPOOL
Kove, Martin
FINAL EQUINOX, THE
WITHOUT MERCY
Kowalchuk, Tannis
HECK'S WAY HOME
Koyama, Johnny
HARD JUSTICE
Kozak, John
SUGARTIME
Kozibraska, Vaclav
KASPAR HAUSER
Kozuharov, Stefan
GIRLFRIENDS
Kraemer, Roxanne
PORTRAITS OF A KILLER
Kraen, Gary
PEOPLE VS. LARRY FLYNT, THE
Kraft, Jamey
SANDMAN, THE
Kraft, Joy
FLIRT
Kraft, Kevin
DUNSTON CHECKS IN
ED
Kraft, Michael
RENDEZVOUS IN PARIS
Kraft, Scott
FOR THE MOMENT
STUPIDS, THE
Kragen, Ken
LATE SHIFT, THE
Kraisman, Gabriel
EVITA
Krakowski, Jane
MRS. WINTERBOURNE
Kral, Josef
DELTA OF VENUS
Kramer, Connie
MONSTERSHOW
Kramer, Eric Allen
HIGH SCHOOL HIGH
Kramer, Grant
SANTA CLAWS
Kramer, Robert
ERNESTO CHE GUEVARA—THE BOLIVIAN DIARY
Kramer, Ted
THAT THING YOU DO!
Kramme, Anthony
BLACK SCORPION
Kranich, Rainer
NEUROSIA: 50 YEARS OF PERVERSITY
Krantz, Peter
SUGARTIME
Kranz, Bob
SHOOTFIGHTER 2: KILL OR BE KILLED!
Kraus, Jena
WAR AT HOME, THE
Krause, Brian
NAKED SOULS
WITHIN THE ROCK
Krause, Jamie
BEWARE: CHILDREN AT PLAY
Krauss, Jim
HIDDEN ASSASSIN

Kravitz, Steven
BLACK SCORPION
Krawic, Michael
FIRST KID
MULHOLLAND FALLS
Krawlicky, Joe "Smokey"
KINGPIN
Krebbs, Nathalie
HORSEMAN ON THE ROOF
Krebs, Joey
POISON IVY 2: LILY
Kreemer, Ladislav
KASPAR HAUSER
Krelle, Raquel
ROCK, THE
Krevoy, Cecile
BIO-DOME
KINGPIN
Krieg, Jim
CHILDREN OF THE CORN: THE GATHERING
Kriesa, Chris
MY FELLOW AMERICANS
Kriesa, Christopher
DENTIST, THE
MR. WRONG
ONE MAN'S JUSTICE
TIGER HEART
Krifa, Kamel
MAXIMUM RISK
Krifa, Mechket
SILENCES OF THE PALACE, THE
Krige, Alice
DONOR UNKNOWN
INSTITUTE BENJAMENTA
STAR TREK: FIRST CONTACT
Krinsky, Tamara Lee
STAR TREK: FIRST CONTACT
Krisea, Chris
HEAVEN'S PRISONERS
Kristen, Marta
HARVEST OF FIRE
Kristensen, Lene
WHITE SQUALL
Kristiansen, Tori
TRIGGER EFFECT, THE
Kristiansen, Tyra
TRIGGER EFFECT, THE
Kristjansson, David
VIKING SAGAS, THE
Kristof, Ivo
DRAGONHEART
Kristofer, Jason
FEAR
Kristofferson, Kris
LONE STAR
MESSAGE TO LOVE: THE ISLE OF WIGHT FESTIVAL
PHARAOH'S ARMY
ROAD HOME, THE
Krol, Joachim
MAYBE . . . MAYBE NOT
Kroll, Michael
WALKING AND TALKING
Kromfeld, Stan
MURDERED INNOCENCE
Krondofer, Birge
FLAMING EARS
Kronenberg, Bruce
MISSING PIECES
Kronish, Steve
COLONY, THE
Kroot, Matt
JACK
Krouse, Doug
TUSKEGEE AIRMEN, THE
Krowchuk, Chad
HECK'S WAY HOME

Krueger, Kirsten
JERRY MAGUIRE
Kruk, John
FAN, THE
Kruk, Tony
TIMELESS
Krupa, Olek
ERASER
Kruse, Doug
HARD JUSTICE
Kryn, Luzi
NEUROSIA: 50 YEARS OF PERVERSITY
Krystyan, Vieslav
DARKMAN III: DIE DARKMAN DIE
Ksouri, Khaled
HALFMOON
Kubelka, Luise
FLAMING EARS
Kubota, Takayuki
BOTTLE ROCKET
Kucera, Jan
KASPAR HAUSER
Kudrow, Lisa
MOTHER
Kuleshov, Vladimir
BURIAL OF THE RATS
Kulhavy, Vladimir
COLD LIGHT OF DAY
Kulich, Vladimir
BREACH OF TRUST
NECRONOMICON: BOOK OF THE DEAD
RED SCORPION 2
Kulo, Heming
EVIL ED
Kunis, Mila
PIRANHA
Kunneke, Evelyn
NEUROSIA: 50 YEARS OF PERVERSITY
Kunstlich, Sarah
SUITE 16
Kunz, Simon
YOUNG POISONER'S HANDBOOK, THE
Kupel, Chris
SANDMAN, THE
Kurlander, Tom
INFINITY
Kurtz, Swoosie
CITIZEN RUTH
Kurup, Shishir
TRIGGER EFFECT, THE
Kusatsu, Clyde
NATIONAL LAMPOON'S FAVORITE DEADLY SINS
SPY HARD
Kusenko, Nick
CHAIN REACTION
Kushner, Jill Tara
MIRROR HAS TWO FACES, THE
Kusiak, Ron
MR. ICE CREAM MAN
Kuskabe, Yo
MADAME BUTTERFLY
Kuss, Richard
DEAD TO RIGHTS
Kutsunku, Yuri
BURIAL OF THE RATS
Kvasnicka, Jiri
ADVENTURES OF PINOCCHIO, THE
Kvinsland, Craig
DEAD WEEKEND
Kwong, Kenny
SCREAM
Kwong, Peter
THEODORE REX
Kwong, Richard
MISSING PIECES

Kyle, Alexandra
EYE FOR AN EYE
TIME TO KILL, A
Kyris, Marco
MRS. WINTERBOURNE
L'Heureux, Gerard
UNHOOK THE STARS
L7
NOT BAD FOR A GIRL
La Brecque, Patrick
LAWNMOWER MAN 2: BEYOND CYBERSPACE
La Fleur, Art
FIRST KID
La Marca, Gina
EXIT
La Marche, Maurice
ALL DOGS GO TO HEAVEN 2
La Pena, E J De
JINGLE ALL THE WAY
La Sardo, Robert
ONE MAN'S JUSTICE
Labasse, Laurent
HATE
LaBelle, Rob
CITY HALL
Labelle, Yvan
BOGUS
Labine, Kyle
BIG BULLY
Labine, Tyler
ROBIN OF LOCKSLEY
SABRINA, THE TEENAGE WITCH
Labiosa, David
BULLETPROOF
LaBreque, Paul
MIRROR HAS TWO FACES, THE
Labyorteaux, Patrick
JAG
LaCamara, Carlos
INDEPENDENCE DAY
Lacatus, Carmen
FORBIDDEN ZONE: ALIEN ABDUCTION
JOSH KIRBY . . . TIME WARRIOR!: EGGS FROM 70,000,000 B.C.
LaCause, Sebastian
ERASER
Lacey, Ingrid
FUNNYMAN, THE
IN LOVE AND WAR
Lacey, Joe
101 DALMATIANS
Lacey, Joyce
BEAUTIFUL GIRLS
LaCharles, Arkan V.
I'M NOT RAPPAPORT
Lachenay, Robert
FRANCOIS TRUFFAUT: STOLEN PORTRAITS
Lachens, Catherine
FRENCH TWIST
Lackey, Gina
DEMOLITIONIST, THE
Lacombe, Gerard
HORSEMAN ON THE ROOF
Lacopo, Jay
. . . AT FIRST SIGHT
Lacroix, Ghalia
SILENCES OF THE PALACE, THE
LaCroix, Tyler
DADETOWN
Lacy, Ross
INDEPENDENCE DAY
Ladan, Katya
TWO IF BY SEA
Ladd, Diane
GHOSTS OF MISSISSIPPI

MOTHER
MRS. MUNCK
Ladislav, Patrick
LOW LIFE, THE
Ladizinsky, Nicholas
GALAXIES ARE COLLIDING
Ladman, Cathy
MY FELLOW AMERICANS
Laffan, Pat
WAR OF THE BUTTONS, THE
Lafferty, Sandra Ellis
NORMA JEAN AND MARILYN
LaForme, John
BODY OF INFLUENCE 2
Lagerfeld, Karl
CATWALK
Lageson, Lincoln
EDIE & PEN
Lagpacan, Samantha
HEAVEN'S PRISONERS
Lahier-Bertrand, Lysiane
SUITE 16
Lahti, Christine
PIE IN THE SKY
WEEKEND IN THE COUNTRY, A
Lahti, Gary
MODERN AFFAIR, A
Lai, Leon
WICKED CITY, THE
Laibl, Jan
DELTA OF VENUS
Lairana, Monica
EVITA
Laird, Kathy
SONG SPINNER, THE
Laird, Trevor
SECRETS & LIES
Lake, Bill
WHERE'S THE MONEY, NOREEN?
Lake, Jason
SHAMELESS
Lake, Ricki
MRS. WINTERBOURNE
Lalande, Francois
VISITORS, THE
Lally, James
BIRDCAGE, THE
Lam, Jennifer
FIRST WIVES CLUB, THE
Lam, Morgan
RUMBLE IN THE BRONX
Lam, Sarah
HAMLET
LaMarr, Phil
BIO-DOME
SAWBONES
Lamarre, Jean Claude
BASQUIAT
DENISE CALLS UP
SWEET NOTHING
Lamberg, Adam
I'M NOT RAPPAPORT
Lambert, Christopher
ADRENALIN: FEAR THE RUSH
Lambert, Ed
MARS ATTACKS!
Lambert, Mark
JUDE
Lambert, Michael Ian
QUEST, THE
Lamontagne, Cynthia
CABLE GUY, THE
FLIRTING WITH DISASTER
Lamoth, Don
MARS ATTACKS!
Lampley, Oni Faida
LONE STAR
Lampreave, Chus
FLOWER OF MY SECRET, THE
Lancaster, Ellen
BEFORE AND AFTER
Lancaster, Erica
KIDS IN THE HALL: BRAIN CANDY
Lancaster, James
ENTERTAINING ANGELS: THE DOROTHY DAY STORY
Lancaster, Kate
UNFORGETTABLE
Lancione, Elisa
WHO KILLED PASOLINI?
Land, Janet
GETTING AWAY WITH MURDER
Landau, Juliet
THEODORE REX
Landau, Martin
ADVENTURES OF PINOCCHIO, THE
CITY HALL
Landergren, Ulf
EVIL ED
Landers, Matt
DOWN PERISCOPE
Landers, Michael
EDIE & PEN
Landey, Clayton
ERASER
Landi, Sal
BULLETPROOF
SAINTS AND SINNERS
Landis, Matthew
FRISK
Landis, Max
STUPIDS, THE
Landon, Judy
FATALLY YOURS
Landry, Charle
JUROR, THE
Lane, Bernie
LOW LIFE, THE
Lane, Campbell
FINAL CUT, THE
Lane, Chilton
MATERNAL INSTINCTS
Lane, Diane
JACK
MAD DOG TIME
STREETCAR NAMED DESIRE, A
Lane, Laura
TALES OF EROTICA
Lane, Nathan
BIRDCAGE, THE
BOYS NEXT DOOR, THE
Lang, Antoina
MAYBE . . . MAYBE NOT
Lang, Fritz
PERSONAL JOURNEY WITH MARTIN SCORSESE THROUGH AMERICAN MOVIES, A
Lang, Perry
DEAD WEEKEND
Lang, Robert
RASPUTIN
SOME MOTHER'S SON
Lang, Stephen J.
LONE STAR
Langa, Steven
FATALLY YOURS
Langdon, Libby
KINGPIN
Lange, Jessica
STREETCAR NAMED DESIRE, A
Lange, Kelly
SPY HARD
Langella, Frank
EDDIE
Langenkamp, Heather
DEMOLITIONIST, THE
Langer, A.J.
JOHN CARPENTER'S ESCAPE FROM L.A.
Langerud, Jake
EVENING STAR, THE
Langford, Lisa
SWEET NOTHING
Langford, Lisa Louise
SPITFIRE GRILL, THE
Langham, Wallace
MICHAEL
Langlois, Lisa
FINAL CUT, THE
WHITE TIGER
Langlois, Riel
FOR THE MOMENT
Langston, Corinne
SUGARTIME
Langton, Brooke
SWINGERS
Lanier, Jane
MERCY
MICHAEL
Lanier, Jaron
SYNTHETIC PLEASURES
Lanier, Monique
CHILDREN OF FURY
Lankford, Kim
MISSING PIECES
Lanning, Dianne
BLONDES HAVE MORE GUNS
Lansbury, David
TRUMAN
Lanzafame, Rosario
STAR MAKER, THE
Lanzello, Marissa
TREES LOUNGE
Laoyant, Cherdpong
QUEST, THE
LaPaglia, Anthony
CHAMELEON
TREES LOUNGE
Lapchinski, Larissa
EXTREME MEASURES
SUGARTIME
Lapina, Natalia
BEYOND DESIRE
Lapinto, Gina
BEYOND DESIRE
Laplante, Jaie
FRISK
Lapotaire, Jane
SURVIVING PICASSO
Lapuzza, John
CITIZEN RUTH
Lara, Carlos
INDEPENDENCE DAY
Lara, Joe
FINAL EQUINOX, THE
LIVE WIRE: HUMAN TIMEBOMB
WARHEAD
Laresca, Vincent
ASSOCIATE, THE
BASQUIAT
EXTREME MEASURES
I'M NOT RAPPAPORT
SUBSTITUTE, THE
WILLIAM SHAKESPEARE'S ROMEO + JULIET
Large, Adam
SUGARTIME
Larimore, Jason
CABLE GUY, THE
Larkin, Bob
SAINTS AND SINNERS

Larkin, Chris
ANGELS AND INSECTS
JANE EYRE
Larkin, Linda
BASQUIAT
Larkin, Sheena
HOLLOW POINT
Larkins, Tommy
KINGPIN
Laroque, Michele
NELLY AND MONSIEUR ARNAUD
LaRose, Melba
DADETOWN
LaRou, Elizabeth
GREAT WHITE HYPE, THE
Larreta, Augusto
SHADOW YOU SOON WILL BE, A
Larriva, Tito
FROM DUSK TILL DAWN
Larsen, Wolf
TRACKS OF A KILLER
Larson, Darrell
EYE FOR AN EYE
Larson, Jill
WHITE SQUALL
Larson, Roberta
CITIZEN RUTH
Larsson, Henrik
CHILDREN OF NOISY VILLAGE, THE
Larusso, Vincent A.
D3: THE MIGHTY DUCKS
Lasaki, Dominique
SOMEONE ELSE'S AMERICA
LaSardo, Robert
NATIONAL LAMPOON'S FAVORITE DEADLY SINS
TIGER HEART
Lascher, David
WHITE SQUALL
Laser
DEMOLITIONIST, THE
Laser, Dieter
KASPAR HAUSER
Laseur, Petra
ANTONIA'S LINE
Laska, Ray
PURE DANGER
Laskawy, Harris
GLIMMER MAN, THE
Laskey, Kathleen
LEGEND OF GATOR FACE, THE
Laskin, Michael
NORMA JEAN AND MARILYN
UP CLOSE AND PERSONAL
LaSorda, Tommy
ED
HOMEWARD BOUND II: LOST IN SAN FRANCISCO
Lassalle, Jacques
LA COMEDIE-FRANCAISE OU L'AMOUR JOUE
Lasser, Abe
GHOST IN THE SHELL
Lassick, Sidney
FREEWAY
Lastewka, Alex
NIGHT OF THE TWISTERS
Lastewka, Thomas
NIGHT OF THE TWISTERS
Latessa, Dick
SUBSTANCE OF FIRE, THE
Latimore, Joseph
DOWN PERISCOPE
Latour, Francois
MAN BY THE SHORE, THE
Latsko, Lawrence
SANDMAN, THE

Latter, Greg
REDEMPTION: KICKBOXER 5
Lauchu, Carlos
SPY HARD
Lauer, Andy
SCREAMERS
Laughlin, Stephanie
DON'T LET YOUR MEAT LOAF
Lauper, Cyndi
OFF AND RUNNING
Lauren, Andrew
FAR HARBOR
Lauren, Ashlee
JACK
Lauren, Greg
TIME TO KILL, A
Lauren, Honey
FATALLY YOURS
Lauren, Kate
SHOPPING
Lauren, Veronica
HOMEWARD BOUND II: LOST IN SAN FRANCISCO
Laurence, Ashley
FELONY
Laurence, David
TEXAS CHAINSAW MASSACRE: THE NEXT GENERATION
Laurence, Paula
LINE KING: THE AL HIRSCHFELD STORY, THE
Laurenson, James
COLD LIGHT OF DAY
Laurents, Arthur
CELLULOID CLOSET, THE
Lauria, Dan
INDEPENDENCE DAY
SKIN
Laurie, Hugh
101 DALMATIANS
Laurie, Piper
GRASS HARP, THE
ROAD TO GALVESTON, THE
Laurin, Christian
STAND OFF, THE
Laurin, Marie
BURIAL OF THE RATS
Lauter, Ed
BREACH OF TRUST
MULHOLLAND FALLS
RATTLED
RAVENHAWK
SWEEPER, THE
TUSKEGEE AIRMEN, THE
Lautner, Kathrin
SWEEPER, THE
TWO-BITS & PEPPER
Lavan, Jonathan
NORMAL LIFE
Lavan, Rene
BITTER SUGAR
TOLLBOOTH
Lavanant, Dominique
MONSTER, THE
Lavandeira, Florent
HATE
Laverty, Frank
MICHAEL COLLINS
Laverty, Paul
LAND AND FREEDOM
Lavery, Patrick
EVERYONE SAYS I LOVE YOU
Lavin, Jim
MODERN AFFAIR, A
Law, Jude
SHOPPING
Law, May
MIDNIGHT ANGEL

Law, Phyllida
EMMA
Lawless, Fenton
GHOSTS OF MISSISSIPPI
I SHOT ANDY WARHOL
Lawless, Lucy
GIRLFRIENDS
Lawlor, Sean
SOME MOTHER'S SON
Lawlor, Tom
MOLL FLANDERS
Lawrence, Brandon
COLONY, THE
Lawrence, Claudia
CEMETERY MAN
Lawrence, Elizabeth
CRUCIBLE, THE
Lawrence, Enoch
WAR AT HOME, THE
Lawrence, Marc
FROM DUSK TILL DAWN
Lawrence, Martin
THIN LINE BETWEEN LOVE AND HATE, A
Lawrence, Nathan
DEATH BENEFIT
Lawrence, Scott
CELTIC PRIDE
Lawrence, Sharon
HEIDI CHRONICLES, THE
Lawrence, Shawn
BEYOND THE CALL
SUGARTIME
WHARF RAT, THE
Lawrence, Tiffany
BARB WIRE
Lawson, Adele
BUTTERFLY KISS
Lawson, Cristina Anzu
BEST OF THE BEST 3: NO TURNING BACK
Lawson, Eric
RUMPELSTILTSKIN
Lawson, Jacque
FROM DUSK TILL DAWN
Lawson, Ray
EDDIE
Lawson, Shannon
HECK'S WAY HOME
STAND OFF, THE
Lawther, Chas
IRON EAGLE IV
Lawyer, Cheryl
BODY OF INFLUENCE 2
Lax, Lisa
PEOPLE VS. LARRY FLYNT, THE
Lazalier, Jeff
TWISTER
LaZar, John
NIGHT OF THE SCARECROW
OVER THE WIRE
Lazenby, George
FATALLY YOURS
Le Bihan, Francoise
SUITE 16
Le Brocq, Christine
YANKEE ZULU
Le Dantec, Jean-Guillaume
VISITORS, THE
Le Doux, Michelle Suzanne
FARGO
Le John, Lawrence
BODY COUNT
Le Maitre, Martin
TERMINAL IMPACT
le Masne, Christophe
HORSEMAN ON THE ROOF
Le Roux, Annette Renee
APART FROM HUGH

Le Roux, Lieneke
CROCODILES IN AMSTERDAM
Le Vessier, Jean-Jacques
RIDICULE
Lea, Ron
IRON EAGLE IV
Leach, Steven
BREAKING THE WAVES
Leachman, Cloris
BEAVIS AND BUTT-HEAD DO AMERICA
Leacock, Richard
ANNIE O
Leaf, Richard
JACK & SARAH
MARY REILLY
Leahs, Michael
SPY HARD
Leal, Jack
BLACK DAY BLUE NIGHT
Leary, Denis
NATIONAL LAMPOON'S FAVORITE DEADLY SINS
NEON BIBLE, THE
TWO IF BY SEA
Leary, James
THAT THING YOU DO!
Leary, Timothy
SYNTHETIC PLEASURES
Leasca, Tom
KINGPIN
Leavens, Chris
MRS. MUNCK
Leavy, Pat
MOLL FLANDERS
Lebanz, William
BREAKAWAY
Lebas-Joly, Antonin
HORSEMAN ON THE ROOF
LeBlanc, Matt
ED
LeBon, Yasmine
CATWALK
LeBrock, Kelly
TRACKS OF A KILLER
Lechner, Geno
FLIRT
Leckner, Brian
SGT. BILKO
LeClair, Paul
INDEPENDENCE DAY
LeClaire, Marie-Charlotte
LITTLE INDIAN, BIG CITY
Lederer, Helen
SOLITAIRE FOR TWO
Ledoyen, Virginie
LA CEREMONIE
MAHJONG
SINGLE GIRL, A
Lee, Anthony
AMERICAN STRAYS
SHOPPING
Lee, Bianca
JACK & SARAH
Lee, Carman
WICKED CITY, THE
Lee, Casey
DON'T BE A MENACE TO SOUTH CENTRAL WHILE DRINKING YOUR JUICE IN THE HOOD
TALKING ABOUT SEX
Lee, Christopher
FUNNYMAN, THE
STUPIDS, THE
Lee, Damon
EXECUTIVE DECISION
Lee, Dana
WHITE TIGER
Lee, Danny
ORGANIZED CRIME & TRIAD BUREAU
Lee, Darren
EVERYONE SAYS I LOVE YOU
Lee, Don
MICHAEL
Lee, Donald
STREET FIGHTER II: THE ANIMATED MOVIE
Lee, Elizabeth
ORGANIZED CRIME & TRIAD BUREAU
Lee, Eric
BLOODSPORT II: THE NEXT KUMITE
Lee Fai
ORGANIZED CRIME & TRIAD BUREAU
Lee, James
SHOOTFIGHTER 2: KILL OR BE KILLED!
Lee, Jeamin
RACE THE SUN
Lee, Jeff
BUGGED
Lee, Jennifer
GIRL 6
Lee, Jesse
VERY BRADY SEQUEL, A
Lee, John
MURDERED INNOCENCE
Lee, Joie
GET ON THE BUS
Lee, Joie Susannah
GIRL 6
Lee, Kaiulani
BEFORE AND AFTER
Lee Kang-sheng
VIVE L'AMOUR
Lee, Leo
ONE MAN'S JUSTICE
Lee, Mary
CABLE GUY, THE
Lee, Nikki
FAN, THE
Lee, Paul
HARRIET THE SPY
WHERE'S THE MONEY, NOREEN?
Lee, Piu Fan
MARY REILLY
Lee, Rob
FEMALIEN
VIRTUAL ENCOUNTERS
Lee, Sheryl
HOMAGE
MOTHER NIGHT
Lee, Sophia
JACK & SARAH
Lee, Spike
GIRL 6
WHEN WE WERE KINGS
Lee, Stephen
BLACK SCORPION
CARNOSAUR 3: PRIMAL SPECIES
Lee, Tim
SUGARTIME
Lee, Waise
WING CHUN
Leeder, Stephen
TWO FRIENDS
Leeds, Andrew Harrison
PIG'S TALE, A
Leeds, Phil
TWO MUCH
Lees, John
DAYLIGHT
Leese, Lindsay
KIDS IN THE HALL: BRAIN CANDY
Leeves, Jane
JAMES AND THE GIANT PEACH
Lefebvre, John
SUGARTIME
LeFevour, Rick
CHAIN REACTION
LeFevre, Adam
BEAUTIFUL GIRLS
MIRROR HAS TWO FACES, THE
SEARCH FOR ONE-EYE JIMMY, THE
LeGault, Lance
BLACK OUT
Legein, Marc
DAENS
Legner, Vaclav
KASPAR HAUSER
LeGros, James
BOYS
INFINITY
LOW LIFE, THE
Leguillou, Lisa
EVERYONE SAYS I LOVE YOU
Leguizamo, John
EXECUTIVE DECISION
FAN, THE
WILLIAM SHAKESPEARE'S ROMEO + JULIET
Lehman, Barry
TUSKEGEE AIRMEN, THE
Lehman, Kristin
ALASKA
Lehman, Lillian
SAWBONES
Lehoczki, Bela
BREAKAWAY
Leidelmeyer, Rory
KAZAAM
Leierth, Camela
EVIL ED
Leigh, Coco
MARS ATTACKS!
Leigh, Houston
FROM DUSK TILL DAWN
Leigh, Jennifer Jason
KANSAS CITY
Leigh, John
FRIGHTENERS, THE
Leigh, Summer
FEMALIEN
Leigh, Terrance
RUMBLE IN THE BRONX
Leitch, Donovan
I SHOT ANDY WARHOL
Lejohn, Lawrence J.
PHAT BEACH
Leland, Brad
PAINTED HERO
Lelievre, Philippe
NELLY AND MONSIEUR ARNAUD
Lelliott, Jeremy
JACK
LeMat, Paul
CHILDREN OF FURY
Lemercier, Valerie
VISITORS, THE
Lemiere, Tony
HORSEMAN ON THE ROOF
Lemkau, Catherine
CHAIN REACTION
Lemmon, Amy
ARRIVAL, THE
Lemmon, Jack
GETTING AWAY WITH MURDER
GRASS HARP, THE
HAMLET
MY FELLOW AMERICANS
WEEKEND IN THE COUNTRY, A
Lemoine, Klodi
SHOOTFIGHTER 2: KILL OR BE KILLED!
Lemole, Samantha
SWINGERS

Lemon, Genevieve
GIRLFRIENDS
Lemper, Ute
BOGUS
Lemus, Eva Tamargo
SILENCE OF NETO, THE
Lenk, Christy
UNHOOK THE STARS
Lenkowsky, Philip
DONOR UNKNOWN
Lennix, Harry
GET ON THE BUS
Lennon, Jarrett
SURGEON, THE
Lennon, John
ROLLING STONES ROCK-AND-ROLL CIRCUS, THE
Lennox, Jordan
RUMBLE IN THE BRONX
Lent, Nicholas
MANNY & LO
Lenz, Joy
STEPHEN KING'S THINNER
Lenzini, Dan
PEOPLE VS. LARRY FLYNT, THE
Leon
PURE DANGER
Leon, Bernie
JOHNNY SHORTWAVE
Leon, Tara
SPY HARD
Leonard, Lu
MAN OF THE YEAR
Leonard, Robert Sean
BOYS NEXT DOOR, THE
Leone, Joseph
DADETOWN
Leonetti, Elisa
FAITHFUL
PURE DANGER
Leoni, Tea
FLIRTING WITH DISASTER
Leonidoff, Derek
FIRST KID
Leopard, Michael
RATTLED
LePage, Jerome
PALOOKAVILLE
LePlat, Ted
YANKEE ZULU
Lerer, Sergio
EVITA
Lerigny, Matthew
SONG SPINNER, THE
Lerner, Michael
LAST MAN STANDING
Leroy, Philippe
IN LOVE AND WAR
Leroy, Zoaunne
GHOSTS OF MISSISSIPPI
LeRoy, Zoaunne
RICH MAN'S WIFE, THE
Lesa, Anita
OF LOVE AND SHADOWS
Lesa, Anthony
ANIMAL INSTINCTS III: THE SEDUCTRESS
Leske, Diego
EVITA
OF LOVE AND SHADOWS
Lesley, Bradley Jay
BOY CALLED HATE, A
Leslie, Lorelei
SOUTH BEACH ACADEMY
Lester, Adrian
AFFAIR, THE
Lester, Eleese
LONE STAR
Lester, Noble Lee
SGT. KABUKIMAN N.Y.P.D.
Lester, Wallace
KINGPIN
Lett, Dan
FRAME BY FRAME
SUGARTIME
Letts, Dennis
ROAD TO GALVESTON, THE
Leung, Angile
MIDNIGHT ANGEL
Leung Chiu-Wai, Tony
CHUNGKING EXPRESS
Leung, Ken
WELCOME TO THE DOLLHOUSE
Leung, Kwok-Wing
HARRIET THE SPY
Levani
INDEPENDENCE DAY
Levantal, Francois
HATE
Levels, Calvin
SKYSCRAPER
WITHIN THE ROCK
Leveque, Stephane
SUITE 16
Levering, Cliff
SPITFIRE GRILL, THE
Leverone, Bertha
MRS. WINTERBOURNE
Levin, Susan
MUTANT MAN
Levine, Allison
BEAUTIFUL GIRLS
Levine, Floyd
NORMA JEAN AND MARILYN
Levine, Jerry
GHOSTS OF MISSISSIPPI
Levine, Robert
ASSOCIATE, THE
Levinson, Brian
MATILDA
Levinson, Daniel
ELECTRA
Levinson, Jordan
WALKING AND TALKING
Levisetti, Emile
CRIMINAL HEARTS
UNKNOWN ORIGIN
Levitt, John
SOLITAIRE FOR TWO
Levy, Eugene
MULTIPLICITY
Levy, Rob
EVITA
Levy, Salvador
UP CLOSE AND PERSONAL
Levy, Scott
DEATH ARTIST, THE
Levy, Veronique
SUITE 16
Lewallen, Raymond
SLING BLADE
Lewandowski, Ed
SANTA CLAWS
Lewandowski, Terri
SANTA CLAWS
Lewarne, Andrew
STAND OFF, THE
Lewart, Thomas
EVIL ED
Lewin, June
CRUCIBLE, THE
Lewis, Al
FAST MONEY
SOUTH BEACH ACADEMY
Lewis, Arron
TATTOO BOY
Lewis, Bob
FIRE ON THE MOUNTAIN
Lewis, Bret
FAN, THE
Lewis, Brittney
UNHOOK THE STARS
Lewis, Charlotte
GLASS CAGE, THE
Lewis, Clea
DIABOLIQUE
RICH MAN'S WIFE, THE
Lewis, Deidre
GRACE OF MY HEART
Lewis, Denice D.
NECRONOMICON: BOOK OF THE DEAD
Lewis, Dierdre
CONDITION RED
Lewis, Doreen H.
APART FROM HUGH
Lewis, Elbert
LILY DALE
Lewis, Fred
FELONY
Lewis, Gilbert
VIRTUAL COMBAT
Lewis, Greg
DEAR GOD
TAKEOVER, THE
Lewis, Ira
LOOKING FOR RICHARD
Lewis, Jenifer
GIRL 6
PREACHER'S WIFE, THE
Lewis, Jenny
FOXFIRE
Lewis, Joe
KINGPIN
Lewis, Jonathan Everett
BLACK SHEEP
Lewis, Juliette
EVENING STAR, THE
FROM DUSK TILL DAWN
Lewis, Keith
OVER THE WIRE
Lewis, Kristina
HOMEWARD BOUND II: LOST IN SAN FRANCISCO
Lewis, Lightfield
JERRY MAGUIRE
Lewis, Lucien
SUNSET PARK
Lewis, Nathan Lee
FAMILY THING, A
Lewis, Phill
ONCE UPON A TIME . . . WHEN WE WERE COLORED
Lewis, Rachel
SECRETS & LIES
Lewis, Rhoda
AUGUST
Lewis, Richard
WEEKEND IN THE COUNTRY, A
Lewis, Rosalie V.
PRIMAL FEAR
Lewis, Roy
WHEN THE BULLET HITS THE BONE
Lewis, Sharon M.
RUDE
Lewis, Skylar
PALOOKAVILLE
Lewis, Timothy
ORIGINAL GANGSTAS
Lewis, Victor
KANSAS CITY
Lewkowitz, Jerry
DADETOWN

Lexsee, Richard
FAMILY THING, A
Leysen, Johan
DAENS
Leza, Concha
OUTRAGE
Leza, Daniel
DELTA OF VENUS
Lezinska, Sonia
LITTLE INDIAN, BIG CITY
Lhermitte, Thierry
LITTLE INDIAN, BIG CITY
Li Bassi, Giorgio
STAR MAKER, THE
Lia, Rita
STAR MAKER, THE
Liagre, Thierry
VISITORS, THE
Liang, Ning
MADAME BUTTERFLY
Liang Zhen
CHUNGKING EXPRESS
Libby, Brian
ENTERTAINING ANGELS: THE DOROTHY DAY STORY
ERASER
Liberatore, Lou
IT'S MY PARTY
Libman, Dan
HOW THE WEST WAS FUN
Lichfield, Patrick
SHAMELESS
Lichtenson, Gregory
CAUGHT
Lidberg, Adam
CHILDREN OF THE CORN: THE GATHERING
Lidington, Bruce
IN LOVE AND WAR
Liebenberg, Lee Ann
WARHEAD
Lieber, Paul
ENTERTAINING ANGELS: THE DOROTHY DAY STORY
Lieberman, Alexandra
CHASING BUTTERFLIES
Lieberman, Edward
HAPPY GILMORE
Lieu, Kim
HARRIET THE SPY
Lifante Ruiz, Jose
SONS OF TRINITY
Lifford, Tina
AMERICA'S DREAM
STREETCAR NAMED DESIRE, A
Lifton, James Ian
MIRROR, MIRROR III: THE VOYEUR
Lightbourne, Camelia
QUEST, THE
Lighthouse, Marilyn
IRON EAGLE IV
Lillard, Matthew
SCREAM
Lillard, Tom
EYE FOR AN EYE
Lilley, Clint
PHANTOM, THE
Lilly, Robin
BEWARE: CHILDREN AT PLAY
Lim, Anderson
BLONDES HAVE MORE GUNS
Lim, Yohan
GIRL 6
Lima, Danny
ELECTRA
MAXIMUM RISK
Lima, Sam
DEAR GOD

Lin, Ben
IF LUCY FELL
Lin, Bill
I SHOT ANDY WARHOL
Lin, Brigitte
CHUNGKING EXPRESS
Lina, Boguslav
MOTHER OF KINGS
Linares, Aida
FIRST WIVES CLUB, THE
Lincoln, Toni
EXIT
Lind, Eleanor Joy
MOONSHINE HIGHWAY
Linda
YOU'LL NEVER MAKE LOVE IN THIS TOWN AGAIN
Lindbjerg, Lalaina
ANNIE O
SABRINA, THE TEENAGE WITCH
Linde, Betty
HALFBACK OF NOTRE DAME, THE
HAPPY GILMORE
Linden, Hal
COLONY, THE
Lindine, Jack
INFINITY
Lindman, Joakim
EVIL ED
Lindo, Allan
EDDIE
Lindo, Delroy
BROKEN ARROW
FEELING MINNESOTA
RANSOM
Lindon, Vincent
HATE
Lindsay, Helen
MISSION: IMPOSSIBLE
Lindsay, J. Dean
TWISTER
Lindsey, Joseph
PUBLIC ENEMIES
Lindsey, Minnie Summers
EYE FOR AN EYE
Lindsley, Blake
GLIMMER MAN, THE
SWINGERS
Lineback, Richard
TIN CUP
TWISTER
Lineham, Danny
FRIGHTENERS, THE
Ling, Bai
DEAD WEEKEND
Link, Ron
FLATTERED
Linklater, Richard
BEAVIS AND BUTT-HEAD DO AMERICA
Linn, Rex
CHILDREN OF FURY
LONG KISS GOODNIGHT, THE
PUBLIC ENEMIES
TIN CUP
Linn, Teri Ann
PURE DANGER
Linney, Laura
PRIMAL FEAR
Lins, Daniel
BROTHER OF SLEEP
Linz, Alex D.
ONE FINE DAY
Lions, Nathalie
SUITE 16
Liotta, Ray
UNFORGETTABLE

Lipe, Dan
LAWNMOWER MAN 2: BEYOND CYBERSPACE
Lipinski, Eugene
HARRIET THE SPY
Lipko, Terry J.
SANDMAN, THE
Lipman, David
MRS. WINTERBOURNE
Lipnicki, Jonathan
JERRY MAGUIRE
Lippin, Renee
THAT THING YOU DO!
Lippincott, Pucky
KINGPIN
Lir, Jiri
KASPAR HAUSER
Lisa, Romana
BLONDES HAVE MORE GUNS
Lishman, Carmen
FLY AWAY HOME
Lisi, Joe
MARVIN'S ROOM
TREES LOUNGE
Liska, Stephen
DIABOLIQUE
Liss, Richard
GETTING AWAY WITH MURDER
MAN IN THE ATTIC, THE
Lister Jr., Tiny
BARB WIRE
PHAT BEACH
THIN LINE BETWEEN LOVE AND HATE, A
Liszewski, Janie
FROM DUSK TILL DAWN
Lithgow, John
HOLLOW POINT
TUSKEGEE AIRMEN, THE
Little, David
GIRLFRIENDS
Little, Mark Anthony
LOW LIFE, THE
Little, Rich
LATE SHIFT, THE
Little Richard
LATE SHIFT, THE
Littman, Julian
EVITA
Litwin, Peter
HYPE!
Liu, Ernest
FROM DUSK TILL DAWN
Liu, Lucy Alexis
JERRY MAGUIRE
Liufau, Sidney
VERY BRADY SEQUEL, A
Livingston, Barry
RATTLED
Livingston, John
MR. WRONG
Livingston, Rick
GALAXIES ARE COLLIDING
Livingston, Ron
LOW LIFE, THE
SOME FOLKS CALL IT A SLING BLADE
SWINGERS
Livley, Ernie
MULHOLLAND FALLS
Liza
KINGPIN
YOU'LL NEVER MAKE LOVE IN THIS TOWN AGAIN
Ljoka, Daniel J.
ARRIVAL, THE
Ljoka, Linda
ARRIVAL, THE
Ljung, Cecilia
EVIL ED

Ljungberg, Magnus
QUEST, THE
Llano, Marie
RIDICULE
Lleo, Gracia
BATON ROUGE
Lleras, Anibal
SOMEONE ELSE'S AMERICA
SWEET NOTHING
Lloyd, Caleb
LOADED
Lloyd, Devin
TIME TO KILL, A
Lloyd, Emily
UNDER THE HULA MOON
Lloyd, Eric
DUNSTON CHECKS IN
Lloyd, Hugh
AUGUST
Lloyd, Jake
JINGLE ALL THE WAY
UNHOOK THE STARS
Lloyd, Jennifer
4 TALES OF 2 CITIES
Lloyd, May
ALEX
Lloyd, Sam
DEATH ARTIST, THE
Lloyd Sr., Sam
SPITFIRE GRILL, THE
Lloyd, Stephanie
FIRST KID
Lo Bianco, Tony
JUROR, THE
Lobato, Alisha
MR. ICE CREAM MAN
Lobato, Cheriesa
MR. ICE CREAM MAN
Lobato, Nathan
MR. ICE CREAM MAN
Lobell, Anna
STRIPTEASE
Lobst, Anne
GIRLFRIENDS
Locane, Amy
CARRIED AWAY
CRIMINAL HEARTS
Locarro, Joe
EVERYONE SAYS I LOVE YOU
Lochhead, Liz
SMALL FACES
Locke, Howard
THAT THING YOU DO!
Lockhart, June
COLONY, THE
OUT THERE
Lockwood, Gary
NIGHT OF THE SCARECROW
Lockwood, Vera
LOVE IS ALL THERE IS
RUMPELSTILTSKIN
Lodato, Tiziana
STAR MAKER, THE
Lodge, Roger
FAN, THE
Lodwig, Loni
DADETOWN
Loewitsch, Klaus
SHADOW OF ANGELS
Lofberg, Per
EVIL ED
Loffler, Gianin
SAINTS AND SINNERS
Loftin, Lennie
SLEEPERS
Loftus, Terry
WARHEAD

Logan, Ed
CELTIC PRIDE
Logan, Kristopher
NATIONAL LAMPOON'S FAVORITE DEADLY SINS
Logan, Phyllis
SECRETS & LIES
Logan, Stacey Ann
MISSING PIECES
Logan, Stacy
NORMAL LIFE
Logan, Tom
SMALL FACES
Loggia, Kristina
LOW LIFE, THE
Loggia, Robert
INDEPENDENCE DAY
LINE KING: THE AL HIRSCHFELD STORY, THE
Loggins, Ben
BOTTLE ROCKET
Logue, Donal
BAJA
DEAR GOD
DIABOLIQUE
EYE FOR AN EYE
GRAVE, THE
JERRY MAGUIRE
Lohman, Lenore
DAYLIGHT
Lohmeyer, Gerd
KASPAR HAUSER
Lohmeyer, Peter
KASPAR HAUSER
Lohr, Aaron
D3: THE MIGHTY DUCKS
Loi Gao Li
SOMEONE ELSE'S AMERICA
Lok Ying-Kwan
MIDNIGHT ANGEL
Lokcinski, Tadek
HATE
Lomax, David
FARGO
GIRL 6
Lombard, Carol
SPY HARD
Lombard, Karina
LAST MAN STANDING
Lommel, Ulli
SHADOW OF ANGELS
Londberg, Robert
EXECUTIVE DECISION
London, Jeremy
WHITE WOLVES II: LEGEND OF THE WILD
Long, Anni
PHENOMENON
Long, Brad
EXIT
Long, Howie
BROKEN ARROW
Long, Jeanie
SPY HARD
Long, Joseph
IN LOVE AND WAR
Long, Shelley
VERY BRADY SEQUEL, A
Long, Thang
HATE
Longbois, Frederic
CELESTIAL CLOCKWORK
Longe, Jerry
TRUMAN
Longfellow, J.
FUGITIVE RAGE
Longmore, Jeffrey
BUTTERFLY KISS

Longo, Tony
ERASER
TAKEOVER, THE
Longoni, Theresa
BROTHER OF SLEEP
Lonnebro, Harald
CHILDREN OF NOISY VILLAGE, THE
Lonow, Mark
CITY HALL
Lonsdale, Michael
NELLY AND MONSIEUR ARNAUD
Loomis
BIO-DOME
Loovey, Peter
ZARKORR! THE INVADER
Lopata, Chris
RANSOM
Lopez, Angel de Andres
BATON ROUGE
Lopez, Carmen
CURDLED
Lopez, Fredrick
LARRY MCMURTRY'S STREETS OF LAREDO
Lopez, Ignacio
OF LOVE AND SHADOWS
Lopez, Irene Olga
DONOR UNKNOWN
Lopez, Jennifer
JACK
Lopez, Jorge Rivera
OF LOVE AND SHADOWS
Lopez, Miguel
ISLAND OF DR. MOREAU, THE
Lopez, Seidy
SOLO
Lopez Sr., Anthony
EDDIE
Lopez, Trini
PRE-MADONNAS
Lord, Kris
RUMBLE IN THE BRONX
Lord, Lisa
DONOR UNKNOWN
LETTER TO MY KILLER
Loree, Brad
FINAL CUT, THE
Lorentz, Nick
GHOST AND THE DARKNESS, THE
Lorenz, Christopher
FLY AWAY HOME
Lorien, Jeff
HYPE!
Loris, Kristin
FUGITIVE RAGE
Lorit, Jean-Pierre
NELLY AND MONSIEUR ARNAUD
Lott, Kurt
BLACK SCORPION
Lottimer, Eb
BLACK ROSE OF HARLEM
Lou, Marius
LAND AND FREEDOM
Louderback, Richard
MR. STITCH
Louganis, Greg
IT'S MY PARTY
Loughlin, Terry
TIME TO KILL, A
Loughran, Jonathan
BULLETPROOF
Loughran, Susan
TEXAS CHAINSAW MASSACRE: THE NEXT GENERATION
Louis, Justin
BLOOD & DONUTS
Louiso, Todd
JERRY MAGUIRE

LETTER TO MY KILLER
ROCK, THE
Love, Andrew
FAMILY THING, A
Love Battery
HYPE!
Love, Courtney
BASQUIAT
FEELING MINNESOTA
NOT BAD FOR A GIRL
PEOPLE VS. LARRY FLYNT, THE
Love, Faizon
DON'T BE A MENACE TO SOUTH CENTRAL WHILE DRINKING YOUR JUICE IN THE HOOD
THIN LINE BETWEEN LOVE AND HATE, A
Love Jr., John W.
ROCK, THE
Love, Victor
IT'S MY PARTY
Lovelace, Fred
CITIZEN RUTH
Lovell, Clare
ANGELS AND INSECTS
Lovell, Jacqueline
ANIMAL INSTINCTS III: THE SEDUCTRESS
FEMALIEN
HEAD OF THE FAMILY
VIRTUAL ENCOUNTERS
Lovell, Jenny
ANGELS AND INSECTS
Lovell, Marilynn
GHOSTS OF MISSISSIPPI
Lovelle, Herb
GETTING AWAY WITH MURDER
MAXIMUM RISK
Lover, Jill
DEAR GOD
Lovett, Conor
MOLL FLANDERS
Lovett, Marjorie
BIRDCAGE, THE
FAN, THE
Lovitt, Gorden
ADVENTURES OF PINOCCHIO, THE
Lovitz, Jon
GREAT WHITE HYPE, THE
HIGH SCHOOL HIGH
Lovstrom, Peter
INSTITUTE BENJAMENTA
Low, Elizabeth
NAKED SOULS
Low, Victor
ANTONIA'S LINE
Lowe, Alex
HAUNTED
Lowe, Cheryl
MR. ICE CREAM MAN
Lowe, Lawrence
ONE MAN'S JUSTICE
Lowe, Rob
MULHOLLAND FALLS
Lowell, Carey
4 TALES OF 2 CITIES
Lowell, Sara
CABLE GUY, THE
Lowens, Curt
NECRONOMICON: BOOK OF THE DEAD
Lowensohn, Elina
BASQUIAT
FLIRT
I'M NOT RAPPAPORT
Lowenthal, Mark
MY FELLOW AMERICANS
Lowery, Gary
GET ON THE BUS
PEOPLE VS. LARRY FLYNT, THE
Lowery, Marcella
PREACHER'S WIFE, THE
Lowry, Joan D.
RANSOM
Lowry, Joe
WAR AT HOME, THE
Loyen, Benedicte
RENDEZVOUS IN PARIS
Lozano, Mario
SHADOW YOU SOON WILL BE, A
Lucas, Brian
TERMINAL IMPACT
Lucas, Dylan
BLACK SHEEP
Lucas, Eric
MONSTERSHOW
Lucas, George
PERSONAL JOURNEY WITH MARTIN SCORSESE THROUGH AMERICAN MOVIES, A
Lucas, Maites
LAND AND FREEDOM
Lucas, Monique
FRANCOIS TRUFFAUT: STOLEN PORTRAITS
Lucas, Peter Jozef
INDEPENDENCE DAY
Lucas, Steve
STAND OFF, THE
Lucas, Will
PHARAOH'S ARMY
Lucchesi, Andy
BIO-DOME
Lucey, Dorothy
MY FELLOW AMERICANS
Luchak, Joan
MRS. WINTERBOURNE
Lucia, Charles "Chip"
EDIE & PEN
Luciano, Lucky
COURAGE UNDER FIRE
Lucibello, Robert
HORSEMAN ON THE ROOF
Lucienne, Jennifer
PHAT BEACH
Lucking, William
TRIGGER EFFECT, THE
Lucky Starr
GIRLFRIENDS
Lucy, Tom
PROTEUS
Luduena, William
JOHN CARPENTER'S ESCAPE FROM L.A.
Ludwig, Salem
I'M NOT RAPPAPORT
Luenell
ROCK, THE
Luft, Robert
ANNIE O
Lugo, Frank
MR. WRONG
Lugo, Frank R.
RATTLED
Lukats, Andor
MAGIC HUNTER
Lukesov, Barbara
KASPAR HAUSER
Lukin, Matt David
BLACK SHEEP
Lum, Benjamin
BLACK DAY BLUE NIGHT
Lum, Joanie
PRIMAL FEAR
Lumbley, Carl
AMERICA'S DREAM
Lumley, Joanna
COLD COMFORT FARM
JAMES AND THE GIANT PEACH
Luna, Francia
MR. ICE CREAM MAN
Luna, Olga
LONE STAR
Lunachicks
NOT BAD FOR A GIRL
Lund, Janet
VIRUS
Lund, Jordan
BAD LOVE
GHOSTS OF MISSISSIPPI
Lunday, Russel
JERRY MAGUIRE
Lundberg, Michael
VERY BRADY SEQUEL, A
Lundgren, Dolph
HIDDEN ASSASSIN
Lundin, Stacy
KINGPIN
Lundquist, Verne
HAPPY GILMORE
Lundstrom, Goran
EVIL ED
Lundy, Jessica
STUPIDS, THE
Lung, Tong
UNFORGETTABLE
Lung, Tony
RED SCORPION 2
Lunghi, Cherie
CANTERVILLE GHOST, THE
JACK & SARAH
Luniz
ORIGINAL GANGSTAS
Luong, Kathleen
2 DAYS IN THE VALLEY
Lupien, Tabitha
BOGUS
Lupo, Tom
KINGPIN
Lupone, Patti
SONG SPINNER, THE
LuPone, Robert
MODERN AFFAIR, A
PALOOKAVILLE
Lupu, Rodica
MAGIC IN THE MIRROR
Lurie, Evan
SHADOW WARRIORS
Lurie, Jeff
JERRY MAGUIRE
Lurie, John
JUST YOUR LUCK
Lusiak, Gloria
BLONDES HAVE MORE GUNS
Lustig, Aaron
LATE SHIFT, THE
MOTHER'S PRAYER, A
PINOCCHIO'S REVENGE
Lute, Trudie
CROCODILES IN AMSTERDAM
Lutes, Eric
BODY COUNT
Lux, Billy
ABUSE
MERCY
Lyden, Mona
DEAR GOD
Lydon, Gary
MICHAEL COLLINS
Lye, Mark
HAPPY GILMORE
Lyell, Dennis R.
MULTIPLICITY
Lykov, Alexander
RASPUTIN
Lyman, Will
CELTIC PRIDE

CRUCIBLE, THE
WELCOME TO THE DOLLHOUSE
Lynam, Harris M.
APART FROM HUGH
Lynch, Edward
JACK
Lynch, Jack
WAR OF THE BUTTONS, THE
Lynch, Jalil
GIRL 6
Lynch, John
MOLL FLANDERS
SOME MOTHER'S SON
Lynch, John Carroll
BEAUTIFUL GIRLS
FAN, THE
FARGO
Lynch, Kelly
HEAVEN'S PRISONERS
Lynch, Kerry
LAST MAN STANDING
Lynch, Pauline
TRAINSPOTTING
Lynch, Richard
NECRONOMICON: BOOK OF THE DEAD
Lynch, Torie
ZARKORR! THE INVADER
Lynde, Janice
MISSING PIECES
Lyndes, Bruce
MAN WITH A PLAN
Lynn, Chuck
LIFEFORM
Lynn, Corrie
SANDMAN, THE
Lynn, Daria
TALKING ABOUT SEX
Lynn, Dave
BEAUTIFUL THING
Lynn, Jaliyl
CITY HALL
Lynn, Marc
NORMA JEAN AND MARILYN
RICH MAN'S WIFE, THE
Lynn, Vickie
HEAD OF THE FAMILY
Lynne, Christy
SURGEON, THE
Lynskey, Melanie
FRIGHTENERS, THE
Lyon, Matt
QUEST, THE
Lyon, Nelson
BAJA
Lyonne, Natasha
EVERYONE SAYS I LOVE YOU
Lyons, Gene
PEOPLE VS. LARRY FLYNT, THE
Lyons, James
FRISK
I SHOT ANDY WARHOL
Lyons, Jennifer
TIGER HEART
Lyons, Paul
LAST MAN STANDING
Lytle, Jill
KINGPIN
Lyttle, Archer
RACE THE SUN
Maara, Dell
RANSOM
Mabius, Eric
HARVEST OF FIRE
I SHOT ANDY WARHOL
WELCOME TO THE DOLLHOUSE
Mac, Bernie
DON'T BE A MENACE TO SOUTH CENTRAL WHILE DRINKING YOUR JUICE IN THE HOOD
GET ON THE BUS
Macaggi, Danilo
OUTRAGE
Macaluso, Dee
LONE STAR
Macarenko, Gloria
MATERNAL INSTINCTS
Macario, Jacqueline
MURDERED INNOCENCE
Macaulay, Marc
SHOOTFIGHTER 2: KILL OR BE KILLED!
UP CLOSE AND PERSONAL
Macaulay, Mark
TOLLBOOTH
MacCaughey, Scott
HYPE!
MacCreedy, David
CAPTIVES
MacDonald, Ann Marie
GETTING AWAY WITH MURDER
MacDonald, Bill
EXTREME MEASURES
LONG KISS GOODNIGHT, THE
MacDonald, George
CELTIC PRIDE
MacDonald, Gordon
LOOKING FOR RICHARD
MacDonald, James G.
BROKEN ARROW
FAN, THE
MacDonald, Jennifer
DEAD WEEKEND
HEADLESS BODY IN TOPLESS BAR
MacDonald, Jock
LETTER TO MY KILLER
MacDonald, Karen
CRUCIBLE, THE
Macdonald, Kelly
TRAINSPOTTING
MacDonald, Kerry
GETTING AWAY WITH MURDER
MacDonald, Norm
PEOPLE VS. LARRY FLYNT, THE
MacDonnell, Sarah
DOWN, OUT AND DANGEROUS
FATALLY YOURS
MacDowell, Andie
MICHAEL
MULTIPLICITY
Mace, Cynthia
BOGUS
MacGregor, Eduardo
SONS OF TRINITY
Mach, Gary
EVIL HAS A FACE
Machine, Tony
PALLBEARER, THE
MacInnis, Cheryl
FLY AWAY HOME
MacInnis, Kimberly
FRISK
MacIntosh, Keegan
HOMEWARD BOUND II: LOST IN SAN FRANCISCO
Mack, Kendra
SMALL WONDERS
Mack, Michael
SUNSET PARK
Mackall, Steve
ALL DOGS GO TO HEAVEN 2
Mackay, James
FRISK
MacKay, Lizbeth
MARVIN'S ROOM
WHITE SQUALL
MacKechnie, Keith
NORMA JEAN AND MARILYN
Mackenzie, J.C.
HEAVY
Mackenzie, Peter
THEODORE REX
Mackintosh, Steven
TWELFTH NIGHT
Macklin, Albert
DAYLIGHT
GRACE OF MY HEART
MacLachlan, Janet
BIG SQUEEZE, THE
PINOCCHIO'S REVENGE
TUSKEGEE AIRMEN, THE
MacLachlan, Kyle
MAD DOG TIME
MOONSHINE HIGHWAY
TRIGGER EFFECT, THE
MacLachlan, Samantha
ENTERTAINING ANGELS: THE DOROTHY DAY STORY
SET IT OFF
MacLaine, Shirley
CELLULOID CLOSET, THE
EVENING STAR, THE
MRS. WINTERBOURNE
MacMillan, Donald
HAPPY GILMORE
MacMillian, Weston
FINAL CUT, THE
MacNeill, Peter
FRAME BY FRAME
MacNeille, Tress
HOMEWARD BOUND II: LOST IN SAN FRANCISCO
LAND BEFORE TIME IV: JOURNEY THROUGH THE MISTS
Macone, Ron
LOVE IS ALL THERE IS
Macpherson, Elle
IF LUCY FELL
JANE EYRE
MIRROR HAS TWO FACES, THE
Macri, Don
DADETOWN
MacVittie, Bruce
LOOKING FOR RICHARD
STONEWALL
MacWilliams, Jennifer
SHARON'S SECRET
Macy, William H.
CHILDREN OF FURY
DOWN PERISCOPE
FARGO
GHOSTS OF MISSISSIPPI
MR. HOLLAND'S OPUS
Madame Alex
HEIDI FLEISS HOLLYWOOD MADAM
Madaus, Jimmy
MADAME WANG'S
Madden, Kimberly
HOLLOW POINT
Maddock, Suzanne
LAND AND FREEDOM
Madias, Jim
TWO FRIENDS
Madigan, Amy
RIDERS OF THE PURPLE SAGE
Madison
DAYLIGHT
Madland, Michael
JACK
Madonna
EVITA
GIRL 6
Madrid, Robert
DONOR UNKNOWN

Madriz, Hidegar Garcia
CELESTIAL CLOCKWORK
Madrona, Victor
PHANTOM, THE
Madsen, Dolly
ALASKA
Madsen, Michael
MULHOLLAND FALLS
RED LINE
Madsen, Virginia
GHOSTS OF MISSISSIPPI
JUST YOUR LUCK
Madvig, Cynthia
DON'T BE A MENACE TO SOUTH CENTRAL WHILE DRINKING YOUR JUICE IN THE HOOD
DUNSTON CHECKS IN
Maelen, Christian
RANSOM
Maffia, Roma
ERASER
HEIDI CHRONICLES, THE
Mafham, Dominic
ENGLISH PATIENT, THE
Magdalena, Deborah
STRIPTEASE
Magdalin, Sara
MATILDA
Magem, Josep
LAND AND FREEDOM
Magimel, Benoit
HATE
LES VOLEURS
SINGLE GIRL, A
Magnan, Philippe
RIDICULE
Magnante, Rick
FAN, THE
Magnes, Bruno
MAXIMUM RISK
Magni, Marcello
ADVENTURES OF PINOCCHIO, THE
Magnin, Claire
VISITORS, THE
Magnuson, Ann
BEFORE AND AFTER
Maguire, Oliver
SOME MOTHER'S SON
Maguire, Tobey
4 TALES OF 2 CITIES
Magwili, Dom
DEAR GOD
Mahan, Larry
LARRY MCMURTRY'S STREETS OF LAREDO
Mahaney, Matthew
ERASER
Maher, Chris
EXECUTIVE DECISION
Maher, Joseph
MARS ATTACKS!
SURVIVING PICASSO
Mahl, Fiona
ISLAND OF DR. MOREAU, THE
Mahmud-Bey, Sheik
JOE'S APARTMENT
Mahogany, Kevin
KANSAS CITY
Mahon, Michael
BACKLASH: OBLIVION 2
JOSH KIRBY . . . TIME WARRIOR!: LAST BATTLE FOR THE UNIVERSE
OUT THERE
Mahoney, John
PRIMAL FEAR
SHE'S THE ONE
Mahoney, Mike
HARD WAY OUT: BLOODFIST VIII
Mahrer, Mike
ROCK, THE
Maiga, Mouneissa
GUIMBA THE TYRANT
Mailer, Norman
WHEN WE WERE KINGS
Mailhouse, Robert
GLIMMER MAN, THE
Maille, Maite
NEW LIFE, A
Mainprize, James
MAN IN THE ATTIC, THE
Mainwaring, Karin
GIRLFRIENDS
Mainz, Steven
LETTER TO MY KILLER
Maitland, Alice
ANGELS AND INSECTS
Maitland, Beth
MR. HOLLAND'S OPUS
Maitland, Carol
TALKING ABOUT SEX
Maitland, Hannah
ANGELS AND INSECTS
Majean, Bruno
IN LOVE AND WAR
Major, Mary
BIRDCAGE, THE
Makeba, Miriam
WHEN WE WERE KINGS
Makenzie, Sam
MOUTH TO MOUTH
Makkar, Joseph
EXECUTIVE DECISION
Makkena, Wendy
DEATH BENEFIT
Malahide, Patrick
LONG KISS GOODNIGHT, THE
TWO DEATHS
Malashevskaya, Elena A.
RASPUTIN
Malcomson, Paula
DUNSTON CHECKS IN
Maldonado, Aixa
DENTIST, THE
Maleczech, Ruth
ANGELA
CRUCIBLE, THE
SLEEPERS
Maleczen, Ruth
TALES OF EROTICA
Malek-Yonan, Rosie
UP CLOSE AND PERSONAL
Malgarini, Gloria M.
MARS ATTACKS!
Malicano, Pat
NAKED SOULS
Malin, Emma Griffiths
MARY REILLY
Malina, Joshua
INFINITY
Malina, Robert
DEAR GOD
Malinger, Ross
HOMEWARD BOUND II: LOST IN SAN FRANCISCO
Malis Callaway, Claire
MOTHER'S PRAYER, A
Malizia, Tina
SANDMAN, THE
Malkin, Sam
BLOOD & DONUTS
MAN IN THE ATTIC, THE
Malkina, Lilian
ADVENTURES OF PINOCCHIO, THE
Malkovich, John
MARY REILLY
MULHOLLAND FALLS
PORTRAIT OF A LADY, THE
Malla, Coque
OUTRAGE
Mallon, Brian
SOME MOTHER'S SON
Mallon, Jim
MYSTERY SCIENCE THEATER 3000: THE MOVIE
Malloy, Christopher
PREACHER'S WIFE, THE
Malloy, Dallas
JERRY MAGUIRE
Malloy, David "Skippy"
MY FELLOW AMERICANS
Malloy, Jessica
PREACHER'S WIFE, THE
Malloy, Matt
BOYS
Malmer, Danne
EVIL ED
Malmer, Therese
EVIL ED
Malnai, Zsuzsa
RASPUTIN
Malone, Russell
KANSAS CITY
Maloney, Michael
HAMLET
MIDWINTER'S TALE, A
Maloney, Peter
ASSAULT AT WEST POINT
CRUCIBLE, THE
EXTREME MEASURES
Malota, Michael
SOMETIMES THEY COME BACK . . . AGAIN
Malota, Peter
QUEST, THE
Maltine, Ovo
NEUROSIA: 50 YEARS OF PERVERSITY
Maman, Isabelle
SUITE 16
Mamodeally, Ozdemir
BEAUTIFUL THING
Man in't Veld, Hans
ANTONIA'S LINE
Manalanson, Leonard
MIDNIGHT DANCERS
Manas, Archero
OUTRAGE
Mancini, Ray "Boom Boom"
SEARCH FOR ONE-EYE JIMMY, THE
Mancuso, Nick
TAKEOVER, THE
Mancuso, Penny
HOLLOW POINT
Mandac, Tracy Leanne
FAN, THE
Mandel, Jules
TALKING ABOUT SEX
Mandelstam, Ruan
YANKEE ZULU
Mandola, Tony
CHAMELEON
Mandon, Jeff
MY FELLOW AMERICANS
Mandvi, Aasif
EDDIE
Mandylor, Costas
CROSSCUT
DELTA OF VENUS
FIST OF THE NORTH STAR
PORTRAITS OF A KILLER
VENUS RISING
Mandylor, Louis
QUEST, THE
Maneri, Sal
PALLBEARER, THE

Manesh, Marshall
BARB WIRE
KAZAAM
Manette, Alex
NAKED SOULS
Manfull, Helen
KINGPIN
Mangan, Kevin
MARS ATTACKS!
Mangan, Margaret
HARD WAY OUT: BLOODFIST VIII
Manheim, Camryn
ERASER
Maniaci, Jim
HARD JUSTICE
ROCK, THE
Mankai, Sonia
ENGLISH PATIENT, THE
Manker, Paulus
BROTHER OF SLEEP
Mankiewicz, Christopher
ERASER
Manley, Felix
SECRETS & LIES
Mann, Dieter
KASPAR HAUSER
Mann III, Fred C.
EVERYONE SAYS I LOVE YOU
Mann, Leslie
CABLE GUY, THE
LAST MAN STANDING
SHE'S THE ONE
Mann, Nathalie
RIDICULE
Mann, Traci
SGT. KABUKIMAN N.Y.P.D.
Mann, Vinny
SHOPPING
Mann, William
SGT. KABUKIMAN N.Y.P.D.
Mannell, Larry
KIDS IN THE HALL: BRAIN CANDY
Manning, Christine
MAXIMUM RISK
Manning, Danny
EDDIE
Manojlovic, Miki
SOMEONE ELSE'S AMERICA
Manojlovic, Zorka
SOMEONE ELSE'S AMERICA
Manoogian, Peter
ARRIVAL, THE
Manson, Ted
LAST DANCE
Mansour, Arash
HATE
Mantegna, Joe
EYE FOR AN EYE
FOR BETTER OR WORSE
NATIONAL LAMPOON'S FAVORITE DEADLY SINS
STEPHEN KING'S THINNER
UP CLOSE AND PERSONAL
Mantel, Brownen
MOTHER NIGHT
Mantel, Henriette
VERY BRADY SEQUEL, A
Mantell, Michael
BED OF ROSES
Mantle, Doreen
IN LOVE AND WAR
Mantz, Delphine T.
EVERYONE SAYS I LOVE YOU
Manver, Kiti
FLOWER OF MY SECRET, THE
Manville, Lesley
SECRETS & LIES

Manzano, Miguel
AVENTURERA
Manzano, Roxanne
ED'S NEXT MOVE
Manzo, Carlos Martin
WILLIAM SHAKESPEARE'S ROMEO + JULIET
Manzo, Chema
OUTRAGE
Manzullo, Richard
CROSSCUT
Mapa, Alec
SUBSTANCE OF FIRE, THE
Mapes, Roy
APART FROM HUGH
Maples Trump, Marla
EXECUTIVE DECISION
Mappin, Jefferson
BEYOND THE CALL
Mappin, John
DARK SECRETS
Mara, Mary
BOUND
Marais, Jean
STEALING BEAUTY
Maranda, Michael
DEMOLITIONIST, THE
Marangoni, Giovanni
TWO FRIENDS
Marcano, Fabian
SMALL WONDERS
Marcelin, Michele
MAN BY THE SHORE, THE
Marcelli, Enzo
WHO KILLED PASOLINI?
Marchand, Mitchell
DON'T BE A MENACE TO SOUTH CENTRAL WHILE DRINKING YOUR JUICE IN THE HOOD
Marchand, Nancy
DEAR GOD
Marcil, Vanessa
ROCK, THE
Marcotulli, Bruno
ONE MAN'S JUSTICE
SPY HARD
Marcoux, Manon
QUEST, THE
Marcq, Nicholas
WAVELENGTH
Marcus, Dominic
ERASER
Marcus, Jo
KINGPIN
Marcus, Trula
SUNSET PARK
Marder, Jordan
DOWN PERISCOPE
Marean, Simone
CRUCIBLE, THE
Mares, Vaclav
KASPAR HAUSER
Marescotti, Ivano
MONSTER, THE
WHO KILLED PASOLINI?
Margo, Guy
GET ON THE BUS
Margolis, Mark
I SHOT ANDY WARHOL
PALLBEARER, THE
Margolis, Robert
ED'S NEXT MOVE
Margolyes, Miriam
COLD COMFORT FARM
JAMES AND THE GIANT PEACH
Margoni, Elizabeth
HORSEMAN ON THE ROOF

Margoyles, Miriam
WILLIAM SHAKESPEARE'S ROMEO + JULIET
Marhoffer-Bains, Maria
TALES FROM THE CRYPT PRESENTS BORDELLO OF BLOOD
Mariah, Katherine
FATALLY YOURS
Marich, Marietta
CHILDREN OF THE CORN: THE GATHERING
Marich, Michael
RICH MAN'S WIFE, THE
Marid, Robert
UNDER THE HULA MOON
Marie, Bobbie
FEMALIEN
Marie, Lisa
MARS ATTACKS!
Marie, Louisa
RANSOM
Marie, Stephanie
VISITORS, THE
Marie-Bergan, Judith
RAGE
Marin, Cheech
FROM DUSK TILL DAWN
GREAT WHITE HYPE, THE
TIN CUP
Marina, Ivana
JERRY MAGUIRE
Marinakis, Vardis
NEUROSIA: 50 YEARS OF PERVERSITY
Marinelli, Joe
DONOR UNKNOWN
Marini, Martin
BOY CALLED HATE, A
Marinker, Peter
PATLABOR 2: MOBILE POLICE
Marino, Ann Marie
ONE LESS EGG TO FRY
Marino, Joseph
EXIT
Marino, Max
JOHNNY 100 PESOS
Marino, Vincent
EXTREME MEASURES
SUGARTIME
Marioles, Ian
SUBSTITUTE, THE
Marioni, Laura
HORSEMAN ON THE ROOF
Maris, Ada
2 DAYS IN THE VALLEY
Marius, Robert
RAW TARGET
Mark, Dana
OFF AND RUNNING
Mark, Emmanuel
JOHNNY SHORTWAVE
Markese, Don
THAT THING YOU DO!
Markham, Kika
CRACKER: THE MADWOMAN IN THE ATTIC
Markham, Monte
. . . AT FIRST SIGHT
PIRANHA
Markinson, Brian
UP CLOSE AND PERSONAL
Markland, Ted
LAST MAN STANDING
Markle, Stephen
VIRUS
Markowitz, Bud
DEAR GOD
Marks, Alan T.
WARHEAD

Marks, Bridget
DEADLY OUTBREAK
Marks, Glenn
SHAMELESS
Markus, Iren
RASPUTIN
Marley, Ben
RED LINE
RUMPELSTILTSKIN
Marley, Jake
. . . AT FIRST SIGHT
Marlow, Metin
SECRETS & LIES
Marlowe, Melissa
EDDIE
Marmana, Sebastia
LAND AND FREEDOM
Marner, Carmela
MISSION: IMPOSSIBLE
Marondo, Marcel
HATE
Marques, Teddy
HATE
Marquette, Christopher
SWEET NOTHING
Marquette, Ron
PUBLIC ACCESS
Marquis, Suzy
LITTLE INDIAN, BIG CITY
NELLY AND MONSIEUR ARNAUD
Marr, Kevin
ORIGINAL SINS
Marra, Emilia
WHO KILLED PASOLINI?
Marren, Christopher
MAN IN THE ATTIC, THE
Marrero, Andre
WARHEAD
Mars, Kenneth
CITIZEN RUTH
LAND BEFORE TIME IV: JOURNEY THROUGH THE MISTS
Mars, Rainbeau
PEOPLE VS. LARRY FLYNT, THE
Marsala, Giovanni
WHO KILLED PASOLINI?
Marsden, James
PUBLIC ENEMIES
Marsden, Jason
WHITE SQUALL
Marsh, Alan
PATLABOR 2: MOBILE POLICE
Marsh, Ali
MIRROR HAS TWO FACES, THE
Marsh, Isabella
MARY REILLY
Marsh, Michelle
RAVENHAWK
Marsh, Ray
TUNNEL VISION
Marsh, Toni
CHILDREN OF THE CORN: THE GATHERING
Marsh, Walter
GIRL FROM MARS, THE
SURGEON, THE
Marsh, William
PROTEUS
Marshall, Andy
RUDE
Marshall, Barbara
DEAR GOD
Marshall, Caleb
BEYOND THE CALL
Marshall, David Anthony
DEMOLITIONIST, THE
Marshall, Dean
RUDE
Marshall, Kathleen
DEAR GOD
GETTING AWAY WITH MURDER
Marshall, Michael
PREACHER'S WIFE, THE
Marshall, Paula
FAMILY THING, A
Marshall, Stephen
WHOLE WIDE WORLD, THE
Marsili, Fiorenzo
CEMETERY MAN
Marston, Nathaniel
CRAFT, THE
LOVE IS ALL THERE IS
Martell, Arlene
EVERYONE SAYS I LOVE YOU
Martelli, Laura
IN LOVE AND WAR
Martells, Cynthia
DUNSTON CHECKS IN
MODERN AFFAIR, A
Marten, Ethan Edward
EDDIE
Marten, Jonathan
EDDIE
Martens, Rica
WELCOME TO THE DOLLHOUSE
Marth, Chris
MR. HOLLAND'S OPUS
Marti, Flavio
CEMETERY MAN
Marti, Gerald
DAENS
Martial, Jean-Michel
MAN BY THE SHORE, THE
Martin, Alfredo
EVITA
OF LOVE AND SHADOWS
Martin, Anderson
FLED
Martin, Andrea
BOGUS
Martin, Barrett
HYPE!
Martin, Barry
JANE EYRE
Martin, Charles
EDDIE
Martin, Dan
DONOR UNKNOWN
Martin, Deena
SWINGERS
Martin, Duane
DOWN PERISCOPE
Martin, Elizabeth
WELCOME TO THE DOLLHOUSE
Martin, George
ASSOCIATE, THE
ONE FINE DAY
Martin, Gilbert
CAPTIVES
Martin, Helen
DON'T BE A MENACE TO SOUTH CENTRAL WHILE DRINKING YOUR JUICE IN THE HOOD
Martin, Jacqueline
PREACHER'S WIFE, THE
Martin, John Benjamin
LAWNMOWER MAN 2: BEYOND CYBERSPACE
Martin, John L.
LARRY MCMURTRY'S STREETS OF LAREDO
Martin Jr., James
DOWN PERISCOPE
Martin, Ken Patrick
DUNSTON CHECKS IN
Martin, Lauren
ARRIVAL, THE
Martin, Lewis
FRIGHTENERS, THE
Martin, Louise
ELECTRA
Martin, Martin
KANSAS CITY
Martin, Rudolph
TALES OF EROTICA
Martin, Steve
SGT. BILKO
Martin, Steven
BEAUTIFUL THING
Martin, Tina
SPELLBREAKER: SECRET OF THE LEPRECHAUNS
Martin, Varona
SONS OF TRINITY
Martindale, Margo
GHOSTS OF MISSISSIPPI
MARVIN'S ROOM
Martinez, A
ONE NIGHT STAND
WHERE'S THE MONEY, NOREEN?
Martinez, Carina
LONE STAR
Martinez, Chuck
NOT OF THIS EARTH
Martinez, Daniel
JUROR, THE
Martinez, Edgar
SUBSTANCE OF FIRE, THE
Martinez, Eduardo
LONE STAR
Martinez, Harold Jose
LOW LIFE, THE
Martinez, Lizzie Curry
LONE STAR
Martinez, Marc
LAND AND FREEDOM
Martinez, Olivier
HORSEMAN ON THE ROOF
Martinez, Steve
BLOODSPORT II: THE NEXT KUMITE
Martinez, Vanessa
LARRY MCMURTRY'S STREETS OF LAREDO
LONE STAR
Martiniz, Charles
UP CLOSE AND PERSONAL
Marty & Elayne
SWINGERS
Maruyama, Karen
DUNSTON CHECKS IN
SAWBONES
Marzan, Rick
ERASER
Marzano, Joe
ONE LESS EGG TO FRY
Marzavan, Daniela
MAGIC IN THE MIRROR
Mascarino, Pierrino
DOWN PERISCOPE
Masciarelli, Stefano
CEMETERY MAN
MILLE BOLLE BLU
Mascis, J.
GRACE OF MY HEART
Mashita, Nelson
INDEPENDENCE DAY
Masini, Henri
SUITE 16
Mason, Anthony
EDDIE
Mason, Bob
MARY REILLY

Mason, Cynthia
CABLE GUY, THE
Mason, Hilary
HAUNTED
Mason, Margery
101 DALMATIANS
Mason, Marsha
2 DAYS IN THE VALLEY
Mason, Ruthann
ARRIVAL, THE
Mason, Tom
MATERNAL INSTINCTS
Massabo, Claire
HORSEMAN ON THE ROOF
Massaro, Maurice
ABUSE
Masse, Sylvain
SCREAMERS
Massee, Michael
LOW LIFE, THE
ONE FINE DAY
Massett, Patrick
RUMPELSTILTSKIN
Massey, Anna
ANGELS AND INSECTS
HAUNTED
Massey, Athena
NUTTY PROFESSOR, THE
VIRTUAL COMBAT
Masson, Jean-Claude
SINGLE GIRL, A
Masson, William
COLD COMFORT FARM
Masten, Gordon
QUEST, THE
Master, Grant
SECRETS & LIES
Masters, George
PALLBEARER, THE
Masters, Giles
GHOST AND THE DARKNESS, THE
Masters, Kevin
FRISK
Masterson, Mary Stuart
BED OF ROSES
HEAVEN'S PRISONERS
LILY DALE
Mastier, Rafaeil
SILENCES OF THE PALACE, THE
Mastrogiorgio, Daniel
SLEEPERS
Mastroianni, Chiara
MA SAISON PREFEREE
THREE LIVES AND ONLY ONE DEATH
Mastroianni, Marcello
THREE LIVES AND ONLY ONE DEATH
Masur, Richard
MULTIPLICITY
Matacena, Orestes
BITTER SUGAR
Matarazzo, Heather
WELCOME TO THE DOLLHOUSE
Matchett, Leigh
FEMALIEN
Matheron, Virginie
HORSEMAN ON THE ROOF
Matheson, Joe
SUGARTIME
Matheson, Michelle
KINGPIN
Matheson, Tim
BLACK SHEEP
TAILS YOU LIVE, HEADS YOU'RE DEAD
VERY BRADY SEQUEL, A
Mathews, Hrothgar
HOMEWARD BOUND II: LOST IN SAN FRANCISCO
Mathews, Thom
RAVENHAWK
Mathis, Carmen
DON'T LET YOUR MEAT LOAF
Mathis, Samantha
BROKEN ARROW
JACK & SARAH
Mathou, Jacques
RIDICULE
Matlen, Roy
SAINTS AND SINNERS
Matlin, Marlee
IT'S MY PARTY
Maton, Andy
PORTRAITS OF A KILLER
Matshikiza, John
YANKEE ZULU
Matsushige, Yutaka
FLIRT
Matteo, Mona
JOHNNY SHORTWAVE
Mattes, Eva
BROTHER OF SLEEP
Matthau, Walter
GRASS HARP, THE
I'M NOT RAPPAPORT
Matthew, James
ANIMAL INSTINCTS III: THE SEDUCTRESS
Matthews, Betty
PREACHER'S WIFE, THE
Matthews, Duane
DEAR GOD
Matthews, Hillary
KINGPIN
SAWBONES
Matthews, Jon
INDEPENDENCE DAY
Matthews, Phil
STREET FIGHTER II: THE ANIMATED MOVIE
Matthewson, Mary
DADETOWN
Matthewson, Robert
DADETOWN
Mattioli, Maurizio
MILLE BOLLE BLU
Mattos, Tony A.
PHENOMENON
Matute, Sara
OUTRAGE
Maud, Julian
CAPTIVES
Mauduech, Julie
HATE
Maugans, Wayne
SEARCH FOR ONE-EYE JIMMY, THE
Maupin, Armistead
CELLULOID CLOSET, THE
Maura, Carmen
BATON ROUGE
Maurel-Sithole, Linda
EVERYONE SAYS I LOVE YOU
Mavimbela, Isaac
LIVE WIRE: HUMAN TIMEBOMB
Maxey, Dawn
MULTIPLICITY
NORMAL LIFE
THAT THING YOU DO!
Maxwell, Larry
PUBLIC ACCESS
Maxwell, Norman "Max"
EDDIE
Maxwell, Timothy
CHAIN REACTION
May, Debra
TWO FRIENDS
May, Jay
THEY BITE
May, Marin
PIG'S TALE, A
May-Ladd, Gabriela
NATIONAL LAMPOON'S FAVORITE DEADLY SINS
Mayall, Rik
WIND IN THE WILLOWS, THE
Mayer, Marvy
WATCH ME
Mayerson, Jordan
BIO-DOME
Mayes, Sally
CITY HALL
Mayfield, Julie
BOTTLE ROCKET
Maynard, Emilia
SMALL WONDERS
Maynard, Rebecca
JOHNNY SHORTWAVE
Mayo, Deborah
MURDERED INNOCENCE
Mays, Jamal A.
COURAGE UNDER FIRE
Mays, Jefferson
LOW LIFE, THE
SOME FOLKS CALL IT A SLING BLADE
Mazar, Debi
BAD LOVE
GIRL 6
TREES LOUNGE
Mazursky, Paul
FAITHFUL
2 DAYS IN THE VALLEY
Mazzeo, Joseph
MUTANT MAN
Mazzola, Robert
WILD SIDE
Mazzone, George
THEY BITE
Mazzorana, Maria
GIRLFRIENDS
McAfee, Scott
LAND BEFORE TIME IV: JOURNEY THROUGH THE MISTS
McAleer, Des
BUTTERFLY KISS
McAliskey, Deirdre
SOME MOTHER'S SON
McAllister, Jacqueline
GIRL 6
McAllister, Shawn
LOOKING FOR TROUBLE
McAlpine, Bob
MRS. WINTERBOURNE
McAlpine, James
DEATH BENEFIT
McArt, Don
TWO MUCH
McArthur, Alex
SHARON'S SECRET
McAtee, Jeff
LAST DANCE
McAuley, Anne
BODY COUNT
McAuley, Nichole
NUTTY PROFESSOR, THE
McBee, Deron
SKYSCRAPER
McBride, Chi
FRIGHTENERS, THE
McBride, Christian
KANSAS CITY
McBride, Geoff
FLY AWAY HOME
McBride, Michael
LAST MAN STANDING

McCabe, Michael
WARHEAD
McCabe, Mike
MICHAEL COLLINS
McCabe, Morgan
EVIL HAS A FACE
McCabe, Vinnie
MICHAEL COLLINS
McCaffrey, James
TRUTH ABOUT CATS AND DOGS, THE
McCain, Ben
BIO-DOME
McCain, Butch
BIO-DOME
McCain, Frances Lee
SCREAM
McCairbe, Roman
MICHAEL COLLINS
McCall, Phil
BREAKING THE WAVES
McCallany, Holt
FLIRT
SEARCH FOR ONE-EYE JIMMY, THE
McCallum, Heather
HOW THE WEST WAS FUN
McCalmont, John
EVENING STAR, THE
McCann, Brian
NORMAL LIFE
McCann, Donal
STEALING BEAUTY
McCann, Mary
SLEEPERS
McCann, Sean
IRON EAGLE IV
McCardie, Brian
GHOST AND THE DARKNESS, THE
McCarthy, Andrew
EVERYTHING RELATIVE
MULHOLLAND FALLS
McCarthy, Brid
WAR OF THE BUTTONS, THE
McCarthy, Eoin
LAND AND FREEDOM
McCarthy, Eugene
KAZAAM
McCarthy, Jenny
STUPIDS, THE
McCarthy, Julianna
DEAD TO RIGHTS
DEATH ARTIST, THE
FRIGHTENERS, THE
McCarthy, Michael C.
LATE SHIFT, THE
McCarthy, Paul
SGT. KABUKIMAN N.Y.P.D.
McCarthy, Sheila
HOUSE ARREST
McCarthy, Tom
UP CLOSE AND PERSONAL
McCarty, Michael
DEAD MAN
DUNSTON CHECKS IN
McCaul, Jarel
ARRIVAL, THE
McCauley, James Michael
JUROR, THE
McClain, David
DEAD TO RIGHTS
McClanahan, Rue
DEAR GOD
McClaughlin, Danny
BEWARE: CHILDREN AT PLAY
McClellan, Charlie
FRIGHTENERS, THE
McClellan, Kathleen
ASSOCIATE, THE
McCloskey, Eileen
MOLL FLANDERS
McCloud, Damon
EVERYONE SAYS I LOVE YOU
McClure, Jim
WOMAN UNDONE, A
McClure, Marc
THAT THING YOU DO!
McClure, Molly
UNDER THE HULA MOON
McClure, Nancy
HAPPY GILMORE
McClure, Shaler
SGT. KABUKIMAN N.Y.P.D.
McClurg, Edie
UNDER THE HULA MOON
McColl, Karen
SMALL FACES
McCollum, J.P.
APART FROM HUGH
McColm, Matt
RED SCORPION 2
McComas, Lorissa
PIRANHA
TIGER HEART
McConaughey, Matthew
LARGER THAN LIFE
LONE STAR
TEXAS CHAINSAW MASSACRE: THE NEXT GENERATION
TIME TO KILL, A
McConnaughey, Aaron A.
PREACHER'S WIFE, THE
McConnell, John
BODY COUNT
McConnochie, Mark
SMALL FACES
McCook, Elias Perkins
SECRETS & LIES
McCord, Constance
ANGELA
McCord, Gary
TIN CUP
McCormack, Eilidh
SMALL FACES
McCormick, Allan
TUSKEGEE AIRMEN, THE
McCormick, Catherine
LOADED
McCormick, Larry
FLY AWAY HOME
McCourt, Joe
MR. ICE CREAM MAN
McCourt, Malachy
SHE'S THE ONE
McCoy, Larry
BULLETPROOF
McCoy, Matt
FAST MONEY
McCoy, Sylvester
SPELLBREAKER: SECRET OF THE LEPRECHAUNS
McCracken, Bob
SKYSCRAPER
McCrae, Scooter
ORIGINAL SINS
McCready, Kevin Neil
RANSOM
McCredie, Colin
SMALL FACES
McCulloch, Bruce
KIDS IN THE HALL: BRAIN CANDY
McCulloch, Robin
SUGARTIME
McCullough, Lisa
BLOODSPORT II: THE NEXT KUMITE
DAYLIGHT
FATALLY YOURS
McCullough, Suli
CABLE GUY, THE
DON'T BE A MENACE TO SOUTH CENTRAL WHILE DRINKING YOUR JUICE IN THE HOOD
McCullough, Tommy
TIME TO KILL, A
McCurdy, Jadi
GET ON THE BUS
McCurdy, Jonathan
BEST OF THE BEST 3: NO TURNING BACK
McDaniel, Chad Edward
PHAT BEACH
McDaniel, Dentis
EXECUTIVE DECISION
McDaniels, Paulette
FAMILY THING, A
McDermott, David
BASQUIAT
McDermott, Dean
BLOODKNOT
IRON EAGLE IV
McDermott, Tom
CRUCIBLE, THE
SUBSTANCE OF FIRE, THE
McDonald, Belle
CELTIC PRIDE
McDonald, Bill
CELTIC PRIDE
McDonald, Bruce
CURTIS'S CHARM
Mcdonald, Chris
TUSKEGEE AIRMEN, THE
McDonald, Christopher
BEST OF THE BEST 3: NO TURNING BACK
CELTIC PRIDE
HAPPY GILMORE
HOUSE ARREST
RICH MAN'S WIFE, THE
UNFORGETTABLE
McDonald, Gary
SECRETS & LIES
McDonald, Jeffrey
GRACE OF MY HEART
McDonald, Kevin
KIDS IN THE HALL: BRAIN CANDY
McDonald, Marilyn
EXTREME MEASURES
McDonald, Michael James
CARNOSAUR 3: PRIMAL SPECIES
CRIMINAL HEARTS
DEATH ARTIST, THE
SAWBONES
McDonald, Mick
CITIZEN RUTH
McDonald, Samantha
TWISTER
McDonald, Steven
GRACE OF MY HEART
McDonald, Tim
JERRY MAGUIRE
McDonell, Tim
IN LOVE AND WAR
McDonnell, Mary
INDEPENDENCE DAY
WOMAN UNDONE, A
McDonnell, Tim
SOME MOTHER'S SON
McDonough, Marty
BOYS
McDonough, Neal
ONE MAN'S JUSTICE
STAR TREK: FIRST CONTACT
McDormand, Frances
FARGO
LONE STAR
PALOOKAVILLE
PRIMAL FEAR

McDougall, Martin
AFFAIR, THE
PATLABOR 2: MOBILE POLICE
McDowall, Roddy
FATALLY YOURS
GRASS HARP, THE
IT'S MY PARTY
UNKNOWN ORIGIN
McDowell, A. V.
PEOPLE VS. LARRY FLYNT, THE
McDowell, Malcolm
FIST OF THE NORTH STAR
SURGEON, THE
YESTERDAY'S TARGET
McDurmont, Todd
MY FELLOW AMERICANS
McElhinney, Ian
HAMLET
MICHAEL COLLINS
SMALL FACES
McElhone, Natascha
SURVIVING PICASSO
McEneaney, Mickey
SOME MOTHER'S SON
McEneaney, Paddy
SOME MOTHER'S SON
McEnroe, Anne
PIG'S TALE, A
McEvoy, Mary
MOLL FLANDERS
McFadden, Barney
MOTHER'S PRAYER, A
McFadden, Davenia
EDDIE
McFadden, Gates
STAR TREK: FIRST CONTACT
McFadden, Joseph
SMALL FACES
McFarland, Bob
CARNOSAUR 3: PRIMAL SPECIES
CRIMINAL HEARTS
NOT OF THIS EARTH
SHOWGIRL MURDERS, THE
McFee, Dwight
UNFORGETTABLE
McFerran, Douglas
CAPTIVES
McGaharn, Michael
BLONDES HAVE MORE GUNS
McGaw, Patrick
FUNERAL, THE
McGee, Bobby
UNDER THE HULA MOON
McGee, Carl A.
HEAVEN'S PRISONERS
McGee, Curtis
SUNSET PARK
McGee, Diane
THAT THING YOU DO!
McGee, Gwen
BULLETPROOF
McGee, Jack
QUEST, THE
RUMPELSTILTSKIN
McGee, Rev. Corey
PREACHER'S WIFE, THE
McGee-Davis, Trina
BIRDCAGE, THE
DAYLIGHT
McGill, Bruce
BLACK SHEEP
COURAGE UNDER FIRE
McGill, Everett
MY FELLOW AMERICANS
McGill, Michael
MOTHER NIGHT
McGinley, John C.
MOTHER
ROCK, THE
SET IT OFF
McGinley, Sean
MICHAEL COLLINS
McGinley, Ted
TAILS YOU LIVE, HEADS YOU'RE DEAD
McGiver, Boris
ASSOCIATE, THE
McGlone, Mike
ED
SHE'S THE ONE
McGoohan, Patrick
PHANTOM, THE
TIME TO KILL, A
McGough, Peter
BASQUIAT
McGovern, Mick
EDDIE
McGovern, Terry
JACK
McGowan, Rose
BIO-DOME
SCREAM
McGowan, Tom
BIRDCAGE, THE
McGrath, Derek
CHAMELEON
McGrath, Elizabeth
BUTTERFLY KISS
McGrath, Matt
SUBSTANCE OF FIRE, THE
McGrath, Noelle
MOTHER
McGregor, Elizabeth
SMALL FACES
McGregor, Ewan
EMMA
TRAINSPOTTING
McGregor, Nathan
TUNNEL VISION
McGrew, LaConte
TIME TO KILL, A
McGuire, Russ
DEMOLITIONIST, THE
McGurk, Jamie
MR. WRONG
McHale, Christopher
SUNSET PARK
McHattie, Stephen
THEODORE REX
McHenry, Dyer
HEAD OF THE FAMILY
ZARKORR! THE INVADER
McHugh, Jason
CANNIBAL! THE MUSICAL
McHugh, Joanne
EVERYONE SAYS I LOVE YOU
McHugh, John
HARD WAY OUT: BLOODFIST VIII
McIlvain, Terry
PAINTED HERO
McInerney, Bernie
ASSOCIATE, THE
McInnerny, Tim
101 DALMATIANS
McIntosh, Keegan
ROAD HOME, THE
McIntosh, Kelly
BOGUS
McIntosh, Lisa
SMALL FACES
McIvor, Emma
MOLL FLANDERS
McKay, Christina
I SHOT ANDY WARHOL
McKay, Cole
BEST OF THE BEST 3: NO TURNING BACK
McKay, David
BUGGED
McKay, Don
HALFBACK OF NOTRE DAME, THE
MATERNAL INSTINCTS
ROAD HOME, THE
McKay, Michael
FROM DUSK TILL DAWN
McKean, Michael
EDIE & PEN
JACK
POMPATUS OF LOVE, THE
McKechnie, Elizabeth
COLD LIGHT OF DAY
McKee, Justin
PAINTED HERO
McKee, Lonette
DANGEROUS PASSION
McKellaig, Ronnie
BREAKING THE WAVES
McKellen, Ian
COLD COMFORT FARM
JACK & SARAH
RASPUTIN
McKenna, Alex
STUPIDS, THE
WOMAN UNDONE, A
McKenna, Joseph
LONG KISS GOODNIGHT, THE
McKenna, Robert
LET'S GET BIZZEE
McKenna, Susie
JACK & SARAH
McKennah, Brandon
GHOSTS OF MISSISSIPPI
McKenzie, Candace
PINOCCHIO'S REVENGE
McKenzie, Dean
RED SCORPION 2
RUMBLE IN THE BRONX
McKenzie, Mark
WARHEAD
McKenzie, Nicolette
ROUJIN-Z
McKenzie, Sean
JUDE
McKern, Roger
HEDD WYNN
McKernan, Peter
LIFEFORM
McKerras, Ross
FULL BODY MASSAGE
McKidd, Kevin
SMALL FACES
TRAINSPOTTING
McKinney, Bill
IT CAME FROM OUTER SPACE II
LONE JUSTICE: SHOWDOWN AT PLUM CREEK
McKinney, Gregory
ERASER
JAG
McKinney, Mark
KIDS IN THE HALL: BRAIN CANDY
McKinnon, Jake
FROM DUSK TILL DAWN
McKinstry, Michael
CRUCIBLE, THE
McKnight, Brian
WHEN WE WERE KINGS
McKnight, Elizabeth
MOLL FLANDERS
McKnight, Esau
SPY HARD
McKnight, Wil
ANGELA
McLane, Brian
FULL BODY MASSAGE

McLaren, Mike
PEOPLE VS. LARRY FLYNT, THE
TIME TO KILL, A
McLarty, Jim
FRIGHTENERS, THE
McLaughlin, Brian
DENTIST, THE
McLaughlin, Ellen
EVERYTHING RELATIVE
McLaughlin, John
GETTING AWAY WITH MURDER
INDEPENDENCE DAY
MISSION: IMPOSSIBLE
McLaughlin, Lee
RAVENHAWK
McLaughlin, Magael
MOLL FLANDERS
McLaughlin, Mark Thomas
BLACK SHEEP
McLaughlin, Rebecca
CRAFT, THE
McLean, Dwayne
WHERE'S THE MONEY, NOREEN?
McLean, Geoffrey
TWO IF BY SEA
McLellan, Angus
LIFEFORM
McLellan, B.J.
LOSING CHASE
McLellan, Margarette
THEY BITE
McLellan, Zoe
MR. HOLLAND'S OPUS
McLendon, Maria
SOUTH BEACH ACADEMY
McLeod, Jacqueline
STUPIDS, THE
McLeod, Ken
VIRTUAL COMBAT
McLish, Rachel
RAVENHAWK
McMahan, Leonard
ROCK, THE
McMains, Cody
BIG BULLY
McManus, Jennifer
PUBLIC ACCESS
McMillan, Norma
BIG BULLY
McMillan, Sara
FOR THE MOMENT
McMillan, Travis
THEY BITE
McMillan, William Lyle
FLED
McMurray, Sam
DEAR GOD
McMurtrey, Joan
DEATH BENEFIT
McNab, Garvy
HEAD OF THE FAMILY
McNally, David
PORTRAITS OF A KILLER
McNamara, Brenda
WAR OF THE BUTTONS, THE
McNamara, Pat
SEARCH FOR ONE-EYE JIMMY, THE
SLEEPERS
McNamara, Rosemary
BEAVIS AND BUTT-HEAD DO AMERICA
McNamara, Yvonne
WAR OF THE BUTTONS, THE
McNeal, Heidi
FROM DUSK TILL DAWN
McNeal, Joyce
LETTER TO MY KILLER
McNeeley, Todd
TATTOO BOY
McNeese, Carter
BOYS
McNeill, Robert
FRIGHTENERS, THE
McNeilly, Paul
SHOPPING
McNew, James
I SHOT ANDY WARHOL
McNinch, Jeff
DADETOWN
McNulty, Kevin
MATERNAL INSTINCTS
McNulty, Tom
JOHN CARPENTER'S ESCAPE FROM L.A.
McPhail, Marnie
STAR TREK: FIRST CONTACT
McPherson, Coco
I SHOT ANDY WARHOL
McPherson, Graham
LONG KISS GOODNIGHT, THE
NIGHT OF THE TWISTERS
McPherson, Mark
NUTTY PROFESSOR, THE
McQuade, Kris
TWO FRIENDS
McQuarrie, Stuart
TRAINSPOTTING
McQueen, Chad
RED LINE
McQueen, Cordell
WARHEAD
McRobbie, Peter
ASSOCIATE, THE
BIG NIGHT
HARVEST OF FIRE
NEON BIBLE, THE
PALOOKAVILLE
McSorley, Gerard
MICHAEL COLLINS
SOME MOTHER'S SON
McStay, Michael
JACK & SARAH
McSwain, David
COURAGE UNDER FIRE
McSwain, Monica
EVERYONE SAYS I LOVE YOU
McTague, Gary T.
EDDIE
McTigue, Tom
LOVER'S KNOT
McWhirter, Jillian
HARD WAY OUT: BLOODFIST VIII
RAGE
McZala, Csaba
BOGUS
Mead, Courtland
HELLRAISER: BLOODLINE
Mead, Geoff
REDEMPTION: KICKBOXER 5
Mead, Taylor
NEUROSIA: 50 YEARS OF PERVERSITY
Meader, Derek
MISSING PIECES
Meadows, Ron
CRACKER: THE MADWOMAN IN THE ATTIC
Meaney, Colm
WAR OF THE BUTTONS, THE
Meara, Anne
SEARCH FOR ONE-EYE JIMMY, THE
Mears, Derek
DEMOLITIONIST, THE
Mechoso, Julio
WHITE SQUALL
Medak, Karen
GALAXIES ARE COLLIDING
Meddeb, Sonia
SILENCES OF THE PALACE, THE
Medford, Robert
WATCH ME
Medianik, Sveltlana
MAXIMUM RISK
Medina, Armand
DEMOLITIONIST, THE
Medina, David
IT'S MY PARTY
Medina, Hugo
JOHNNY 100 PESOS
Medina, James
WHITE SQUALL
Medioni, Patrick
HATE
HORSEMAN ON THE ROOF
Medlock, Ken
LAST MAN STANDING
Medrano, Frank
BOGUS
FAN, THE
SLEEPERS
Medway, Heather
SERPENT'S LAIR
Meek, Joe
CHAMBER, THE
Meeks, Edith
DADETOWN
Meeks, Trevor
PUBLIC ENEMIES
Meertens, Conrad
SLEEPERS
Megan, Anna
SOME MOTHER'S SON
Megard, Mathias
RENDEZVOUS IN PARIS
Megill, Sheelah
SURGEON, THE
Mehler, Tobias
SABRINA, THE TEENAGE WITCH
Mehlman, Michael
RASPUTIN
Mehta, Ajay
MERCY
Meier, Ron
BLONDES HAVE MORE GUNS
Meier, Shane
QUEST, THE
Meiga, Cheick Oumar
GUIMBA THE TYRANT
Meinze, Ernest
TERMINAL IMPACT
Meisels, Annie
LOVE IS ALL THERE IS
Meisle, William
SUBSTANCE OF FIRE, THE
Meity
WITHOUT MERCY
Mekas, Jonas
NICO ICON
Meko, Jerry
SGT. KABUKIMAN N.Y.P.D.
Meldrum, Wendel
SONG SPINNER, THE
Melen, Charlotte
CRUCIBLE, THE
Melendres, Nathan
FRISK
Melgosa, Fernando
BATON ROUGE
Melinand, Monique
THREE LIVES AND ONLY ONE DEATH
Melis, Simone
WHO KILLED PASOLINI?
Melleny, Victor
REDEMPTION: KICKBOXER 5

Mellerine, Celeste
BODY COUNT
Melnick, Daniel
CELLULOID CLOSET, THE
Melon, Michael
DANGEROUS PASSION
Meloni, Christopher
BOUND
Meloni, Costantino
WHO KILLED PASOLINI?
Melson, Sara
LOW LIFE, THE
Melton, Barry
BERKELEY IN THE 60S
Melton, Karin
FLAMING EARS
Melvins
HYPE!
Mendecino, Gerry
SUGARTIME
Mendelsohn, Ben
MERLIN'S SHOP OF MAGICAL WONDERS
Mendelson, Michael
MR. HOLLAND'S OPUS
Mendez, Azalea
LONE STAR
Mendillo, Stephen
FIRST WIVES CLUB, THE
LONE STAR
Mendizabal, Ricardo
SILENCE OF NETO, THE
Mendl, Michael
BROTHER OF SLEEP
Mendoza, Arthur
LAWNMOWER MAN 2: BEYOND CYBERSPACE
Mendoza, Lucia
CITY HALL
Menegazzo, Bettina
EVITA
Menendez, Natalin
OUTRAGE
Meneses, Alex
AMANDA AND THE ALIEN
IMMORTALS, THE
Meneses, Herbert
SILENCE OF NETO, THE
Menglet, Alex
GIRLFRIENDS
Menglets, Maya
BURIAL OF THE RATS
Menom, Aaron
LOOKING FOR TROUBLE
Mentiply, Sydney
SURGEON, THE
Menuez, Stephanie
LAWNMOWER MAN 2: BEYOND CYBERSPACE
Menville, Scott
NORMA JEAN AND MARILYN
Menza, Gina
SLEEPERS
Meoli, Christian
LOW LIFE, THE
Mer, Juliano
UNDER THE DOMIM TREE
Mercedes, Ana
ENTERTAINING ANGELS: THE DOROTHY DAY STORY
Mercer, Ian
CRACKER: THE MADWOMAN IN THE ATTIC
Mercier, Claire
SUITE 16
Mercier, Denis
BOGUS
Mercurio, Micole
NORMA JEAN AND MARILYN
2 DAYS IN THE VALLEY
Mercury, Bruce
FINAL EQUINOX, THE
Merdis, Thomas
TIME TO KILL, A
Meredíz, Olga
EVITA
MARVIN'S ROOM
Mergenthaler, Carl
FAN, THE
Merideth, Candice
PHAT BEACH
Merino, David
FAITHFUL
Merito, Simona
STAR MAKER, THE
Merkerson, S. Epatha
MOTHER'S PRAYER, A
Merlet, Valentin
LA CEREMONIE
Mermans, Marilou
DAENS
Merrick, Gordie
KINGPIN
Merrill, Cynthia
NIGHT OF THE SCARECROW
Merrill, Dina
OPEN SEASON
Merring, Rick
LAST MAN STANDING
Merrison, Clive
ENGLISH PATIENT, THE
Merson, Susan
PHENOMENON
Mertens, Fried
CROCODILES IN AMSTERDAM
Merwin, David
APART FROM HUGH
Mescolii, Fraco
MILLE BOLLE BLU
Mescollini, Franco
MONSTER, THE
WHO KILLED PASOLINI?
Mese, John
NIGHT OF THE SCARECROW
Meserve, Tom
THEY BITE
Meskimen, Jim
DEAR GOD
Mesnick, William
EYE FOR AN EYE
Messaline, Peter
MAXIMUM RISK
Messina, Gabriella
EVERYTHING RELATIVE
Messina, Orina
JANE EYRE
Messina, Tony
SGT. KABUKIMAN N.Y.P.D.
Metcalf, Laurie
DEAR GOD
Metcalf, Mark
RAGE
STUPIDS, THE
Metcalf, Toby
PAINTED HERO
Metcalfe, Robert
UNFORGETTABLE
Metellus, Mireille
MAN BY THE SHORE, THE
Method Man
GREAT WHITE HYPE, THE
Meullerleile, Marianne
LOW LIFE, THE
Meuwissen, Wim
DAENS
Meyer, Bess
NECRONOMICON: BOOK OF THE DEAD
Meyer, Brandon
WHISPERING, THE
Meyer, Breckin
CRAFT, THE
JOHN CARPENTER'S ESCAPE FROM L.A.
Meyer, Dina
DRAGONHEART
Meyer, Jeffrey
LARRY MCMURTRY'S STREETS OF LAREDO
Meyer, Pattie
SGT. KABUKIMAN N.Y.P.D.
Meyering Jr., Ralph
SAWBONES
Meyers, Larry John
UP CLOSE AND PERSONAL
Meyers, Lou
PASSION OF DARKLY NOON, THE
Mezieres, Myriam
MOUTH TO MOUTH
Mezzi, Khaoula
SILENCES OF THE PALACE, THE
Mezzoprete, Daniele
CEMETERY MAN
Miano, Robert
FUNERAL, THE
Micco, Sammy
SGT. BILKO
Miceli, Antonio
STAR MAKER, THE
Michael, Christopher
CABLE GUY, THE
SOLO
Michael, David
TIGER HEART
Michael, George
TIN CUP
Michaeli, Dani
FUGITIVE RAGE
ORIGINAL SINS
Michaels, Al
HOMEWARD BOUND II: LOST IN SAN FRANCISCO
JERRY MAGUIRE
Michaels, Beau
RAVENHAWK
Michaels, Joe
STREET FIGHTER II: THE ANIMATED MOVIE
Michaels, Roxanna
BAJA
Michaels, Suzanne
RICH MAN'S WIFE, THE
Michalak, Cathren
GIRLFRIENDS
Michalchuk, Steve
BEYOND THE CALL
Michalski, Jeff
CABLE GUY, THE
DEAR GOD
Michelucci, Bob
SANTA CLAWS
SANTA CLAWS
Michelucci, Dawn
SANTA CLAWS
Michelucci, Diana
SANTA CLAWS
Michetti, Emidio
HOLLOW POINT
Michl, Keith
ABUSE
Mick, Gabriel
HARVEST OF FIRE
I SHOT ANDY WARHOL

Mickaelian, Kyle
COURAGE UNDER FIRE
Middlekoop, George
GHOST AND THE DARKNESS, THE
Middleton, Lorraine
TIME TO KILL, A
Midler, Bette
FIRST WIVES CLUB, THE
Mientka, Dennis
SPITFIRE GRILL, THE
Mif
STUPIDS, THE
Migliozzi, Emilio
QUEST, THE
Mignemi, Mimmo
WHO KILLED PASOLINI?
Mihok, Dash
FOXFIRE
SLEEPERS
WILLIAM SHAKESPEARE'S ROMEO + JULIET
Mikels, John
FAMILY THING, A
Mikhalkov, Anna
ANNA
Mikhalkov, Nikita
ANNA
Mikol, Leslie
CHAIN REACTION
Milan, George
MERLIN'S SHOP OF MAGICAL WONDERS
Milan, Thomas
NAKED SOULS
Milano, Alyssa
FEAR
POISON IVY 2: LILY
PUBLIC ENEMIES
Milburn, Oliver
LOADED
Milburne, Estelle
EVIL ED
Miled, Salah
ENGLISH PATIENT, THE
Miles, Helen
EVERYONE SAYS I LOVE YOU
Miles, Marc
LAZARUS MAN, THE
Miles, Maria
COLD COMFORT FARM
Miles, Sylvia
DENISE CALLS UP
Miley, Brett
EMMA
Milford, Penelope
NORMAL LIFE
Milhoan, Michael
EXECUTIVE DECISION
MULTIPLICITY
PHENOMENON
TIN CUP
Milholland, Kathy
APART FROM HUGH
Millan, Arturo
I'M NOT RAPPAPORT
Millar, Bruce
LIVE WIRE: HUMAN TIMEBOMB
Millbern, David
AMANDA AND THE ALIEN
DEAD WEEKEND
Miller, "Pig"
EDDIE
Miller, Angela
SCREAM
Miller, Aurora J.
MR. HOLLAND'S OPUS
Miller, Candace
DAYLIGHT
Miller, Cara
TALKING ABOUT SEX
Miller, Carlton
NORMAL LIFE
Miller, Claude
FRANCOIS TRUFFAUT: STOLEN PORTRAITS
Miller, Dennis
TALES FROM THE CRYPT PRESENTS BORDELLO OF BLOOD
Miller, Ed
TALKING ABOUT SEX
Miller, Haley
BOTTLE ROCKET
Miller, Jason
MURDERED INNOCENCE
Miller, Jennifer
TERMINAL IMPACT
Miller, Joel
MOTHER NIGHT
Miller, Johnny
ASSOCIATE, THE
MR. WRONG
Miller, Jonny Lee
TRAINSPOTTING
Miller, Larry
DEAR GOD
NUTTY PROFESSOR, THE
Miller, Laura
EVITA
Miller, Mark
FRISK
Miller, Mary Linn
SGT. KABUKIMAN N.Y.P.D.
Miller, Michael Ray
IT CAME FROM OUTER SPACE II
Miller, Mike
BERKELEY IN THE 60S
Miller, Naguanda
PREACHER'S WIFE, THE
Miller, Randy
BUGGED
Miller, Rhonda G.
BAD LOVE
Miller, Roxanne
FEMALIEN
Miller, Sherry
SABRINA, THE TEENAGE WITCH
STUPIDS, THE
Miller, Stephen E.
ALASKA
Milligan, Tuck
HEAVEN'S PRISONERS
Milliken, Sean
ANNIE O
ROBIN OF LOCKSLEY
Millington, Jim
MAXIMUM RISK
Millman, Gabriel
EVERYONE SAYS I LOVE YOU
Mills, Angela
FLED
Mills, Brad
ARRIVAL, THE
Mills, Christian Dyer
HIGH SCHOOL HIGH
Mills, Frank
YOUNG POISONER'S HANDBOOK, THE
Mills, Jim
MR. ICE CREAM MAN
Mills, John
HAMLET
Mills, Sheila
TALES FROM THE CRYPT PRESENTS BORDELLO OF BLOOD
Mills, Stephen
GLIMMER MAN, THE
Milner, Joel
SOME FOLKS CALL IT A SLING BLADE
Milo, Jack
THAT THING YOU DO!
Milostnik, Franko
RACE THE SUN
Miltsakakis, Stefanos
MAXIMUM RISK
QUEST, THE
Mimura, Daniel
MICHAEL
Minatel, Tiffini
DADETOWN
Minchenberg, Richard
ONE GOOD TURN
RATTLED
Mineo, John
EVERYONE SAYS I LOVE YOU
Minerd, Dean
ARRIVAL, THE
Minervini, Gina
ENTERTAINING ANGELS: THE DOROTHY DAY STORY
Mingle, Joe
CELTIC PRIDE
Minjares, Joe
RATTLED
Minnick, Joshua
MR. HOLLAND'S OPUS
Minogue, Kylie
BIO-DOME
Minor, Asia
GIRLS TOWN
Minor, Bob
DANGEROUS PASSION
Minor, Rita
DUNSTON CHECKS IN
Minor, Willie
TUSKEGEE AIRMEN, THE
Minot, Anna
CONDITION RED
Mintello, Frank
ERASER
Minter, Kelly Jo
RICH MAN'S WIFE, THE
Minter, Kristin
LOVER'S KNOT
Miosky, Mark
KINGPIN
Miou
SOMEONE ELSE'S AMERICA
Miou-Miou
LITTLE INDIAN, BIG CITY
Miquel, Jean-Pierre
LA COMEDIE-FRANCAISE OU L'AMOUR JOUE
Mirand, Alex
CLUBHOUSE DETECTIVES
Miranda, Diana
NOT OF THIS EARTH
Miranda, Robert
DESIRE
ERASER
Mirer, Rick
JERRY MAGUIRE
Mirren, Helen
LOSING CHASE
SOME MOTHER'S SON
Mischwitzky, Gertrud
NEUROSIA: 50 YEARS OF PERVERSITY
Mishaud, Michael
ONE MAN'S JUSTICE
Misner, Susan
EVERYONE SAYS I LOVE YOU
Misskelley, Jessie Lloyd
PARADISE LOST: THE CHILD MURDERS AT ROBIN HOOD HILLS

PARADISE LOST: THE CHILD MURDERS AT ROBIN HOOD HILLS
Misskelley, Shelby
PARADISE LOST: THE CHILD MURDERS AT ROBIN HOOD HILLS
Mistry, Jimi
HAMLET
Mitchell, Beverley
CROW: CITY OF ANGELS, THE
Mitchell, Darrin
TIME TO KILL, A
Mitchell, Daryl
SGT. BILKO
THIN LINE BETWEEN LOVE AND HATE, A
Mitchell, Delores
PREACHER'S WIFE, THE
Mitchell, Don "Mazi"
DON'T BE A MENACE TO SOUTH CENTRAL WHILE DRINKING YOUR JUICE IN THE HOOD
Mitchell, Gavin
BREAKING THE WAVES
Mitchell, Gene
TAKEOVER, THE
Mitchell, Gregory
EVERYONE SAYS I LOVE YOU
Mitchell, Herb
NORMA JEAN AND MARILYN
Mitchell, John Cameron
GIRL 6
Mitchell, Joni
MESSAGE TO LOVE: THE ISLE OF WIGHT FESTIVAL
Mitchell, June
SECRETS & LIES
Mitchell, Katherine
FAMILY THING, A
Mitchell, Kevin
PREACHER'S WIFE, THE
Mitchell, Kirby
BIRDCAGE, THE
Mitchell, Kirsty
SMALL FACES
Mitchell, Lizan
PREACHER'S WIFE, THE
Mitchell, Mitch
ROLLING STONES ROCK-AND-ROLL CIRCUS, THE
Mitchell, Phillip
PREACHER'S WIFE, THE
Mitchell, Rick
TWISTER
Mitchell, Sam
EDDIE
Mitchell, Sharon A.
PREACHER'S WIFE, THE
Mitchell, Thomas
GETTING AWAY WITH MURDER
RUDE
Mitchum, Carrie
VIRTUAL COMBAT
Mitchum, Robert
DEAD MAN
Mitri, Charles
TALKING ABOUT SEX
Miu Kiu-Wai
MIDNIGHT ANGEL
Mix, Victor
JOHNNY 100 PESOS
Mixon, Bernard
FAMILY THING, A
Mixon, Jamal
NUTTY PROFESSOR, THE
Miyeni, Eric
REDEMPTION: KICKBOXER 5
Mizel, Courtney
BIO-DOME
Mizgalski, Michael
TALKING ABOUT SEX
Mizrahi, Isaac
CATWALK
Mizuno, Natsumi
FLIRT
Mockus Jr., Tony
NORMAL LIFE
Modderno, Craig
GREAT WHITE HYPE, THE
Moeller, Ralf
VIKING SAGAS, THE
Moertl, Michael G.
INDEPENDENCE DAY
Moffat, Donald
EVENING STAR, THE
Moffat, Jane
TWO IF BY SEA
Moffat, Katherine
SPY HARD
Moffatt, Jim
JERRY MAGUIRE
Moffett, D.W.
LITTLE DEATH, THE
STEALING BEAUTY
Mohammakhani, Aida
WHITE BALLOON, THE
Mohler, Robert
EVIL HAS A FACE
Mohr, Daria
CROCODILES IN AMSTERDAM
Mohr, Jay
FOR BETTER OR WORSE
JERRY MAGUIRE
Mohsen, Mohammad
NUTTY PROFESSOR, THE
Moinot, Michel
EVERYONE SAYS I LOVE YOU
Mol, Gretchen
FUNERAL, THE
GIRL 6
Moldovan, Jeff
TWO MUCH
Molina, Alfred
BEFORE AND AFTER
DEAD MAN
Molina, Noel
BATON ROUGE
Molina, Pep
LAND AND FREEDOM
Molina, Rolando
EYE FOR AN EYE
RICH MAN'S WIFE, THE
Moll, Richard
GLASS CAGE, THE
JINGLE ALL THE WAY
Molla, Jordi
FLOWER OF MY SECRET, THE
Mollenhauer, Heidi
HUNCHBACK OF NOTRE DAME, THE
Mollison, JoAn
MIRROR HAS TWO FACES, THE
Molloy, Dearbhla
LOADED
Molloy, Leigh
DEAR GOD
Moloney, Aedin
CAPTIVES
Momo, Joseph
HATE
Momtchilova, Nathalia
SAWBONES
Monaco, Ralph
FATALLY YOURS
Monahan, Jeff
LONE STAR
Mondragon, Jorge
AVENTURERA
Mone, Brian
KINGPIN
Mongold, James
DEMOLITIONIST, THE
Monich, Timothy F.
TIME TO KILL, A
Monjo, Justin
TUNNEL VISION
Monk, Art
JERRY MAGUIRE
Monk, Debra
BED OF ROSES
EXTREME MEASURES
FIRST WIVES CLUB, THE
MRS. WINTERBOURNE
SUBSTANCE OF FIRE, THE
Mono Men, The
HYPE!
Monoson, Lawrence
BLACK ROSE OF HARLEM
Monro, Lochlyn
GIRL FROM MARS, THE
Monroe, Betsy
DENTIST, THE
Monroe, Christian
MUTANT MAN
Monroe Jr., Samuel
DON'T BE A MENACE TO SOUTH CENTRAL WHILE DRINKING YOUR JUICE IN THE HOOD
Monroe, Midori Diane
SMALL WONDERS
Monroe, Poppy Cee Jay
PIG'S TALE, A
Monroe, Steve
NUTTY PROFESSOR, THE
Monroy, Grant
DADETOWN
Monroy-Marquez, Anthony
SGT. BILKO
Monsion, Tim
FAN, THE
Monson, Lex
PREACHER'S WIFE, THE
Montague, Helene
MOLL FLANDERS
WAR OF THE BUTTONS, THE
Montana, Rick
FUGITIVE RAGE
Montano, Felix
MAN OF THE YEAR
Montano, Fran
SPY HARD
Montel, Virginie
HATE
Monteleone, Mike
INDEPENDENCE DAY
Montgomery, Bud
PHAT BEACH
Montgomery, Michael
LAST DANCE
Monti, Mario
TWO FRIENDS
Montorsi, Stefania
MILLE BOLLE BLU
Montoute, Edouard
HATE
Moodie, Andrew
RUDE
Moody, Bill
CAPTIVES
Moody Blues, The
MESSAGE TO LOVE: THE ISLE OF WIGHT FESTIVAL
Moog, Robert
THEREMIN: AN ELECTRONIC ODYSSEY
Moolman, George
REDEMPTION: KICKBOXER 5

Moon, Brett
GETTING AWAY WITH MURDER
Moon, J. Antonio
FAMILY THING, A
Moon, Keith
ROLLING STONES ROCK-AND-ROLL CIRCUS, THE
Moon, Ryan
GETTING AWAY WITH MURDER
Moon, Warren
JERRY MAGUIRE
Moor, Andrea
GIRLFRIENDS
Moore, Angela
TWO IF BY SEA
Moore, Bob
BOYS
Moore, Carlene
LAST DANCE
Moore, Chante
FAN, THE
Moore, Dana
EVERYONE SAYS I LOVE YOU
Moore, Demi
HUNCHBACK OF NOTRE DAME, THE
JUROR, THE
STRIPTEASE
Moore, Diane
PARADISE LOST: THE CHILD MURDERS AT ROBIN HOOD HILLS
Moore, Dudley
WEEKEND IN THE COUNTRY, A
Moore, Edwina
AMANDA AND THE ALIEN
UP CLOSE AND PERSONAL
Moore, Emma Louise
DELTA OF VENUS
Moore, Frank
BLOOD & DONUTS
LONG KISS GOODNIGHT, THE
Moore, Helene
INFINITY
Moore, Herman
JERRY MAGUIRE
Moore, Ian
SLING BLADE
Moore, Jack
INDEPENDENCE DAY
Moore, Joel
FOXFIRE
Moore, John Rixey
EXECUTIVE DECISION
Moore, Julianne
SURVIVING PICASSO
Moore, Kirk
MIRROR HAS TWO FACES, THE
Moore, Lisa
FAST MONEY
Moore, Lisa Bronwyn
HOLLOW POINT
Moore, Mary Tyler
FLIRTING WITH DISASTER
Moore, Max
SYNTHETIC PLEASURES
Moore, Mickie
MRS. MUNCK
Moore, Perry
TUSKEGEE AIRMEN, THE
Moore, Polly
SHOPPING
Moore, Rob
JERRY MAGUIRE
Moore, Robyn
RACE THE SUN
Moore, Roger
QUEST, THE
Moore, Tedde
MAN IN THE ATTIC, THE
Moore, Todd
PARADISE LOST: THE CHILD MURDERS AT ROBIN HOOD HILLS
Moore, Valerie
SUGARTIME
Moorer, Margo
FLED
Mora, Daniel Edward
FAST MONEY
Mora-Arriaga, David
TWO MUCH
Mora-Arriaga, Jose
TWO MUCH
Mora-Arriaga, Levis
TWO MUCH
Morace, Eric
PALLBEARER, THE
Morales, Aida
SMALL WONDERS
Morales, Eugenio
JOHNNY 100 PESOS
Morales, Juan Arnoldo
JERRY MAGUIRE
Morales, Rauol
JUROR, THE
Moran, Dan
MAXIMUM RISK
Moran, Erin
DEAR GOD
Moran, Gigi
DEMOLITIONIST, THE
Moran, Janet
MOLL FLANDERS
Moran, Julie
INDEPENDENCE DAY
Moran, Linda
DESOLATION ANGELS
Moran, Maria Julia
CROW: CITY OF ANGELS, THE
Moran, Mark
LOW LIFE, THE
Moran, Michael
MOTHER NIGHT
SLEEPERS
Moran, Rob
KINGPIN
Moranis, Rick
BIG BULLY
More, Desiree
SPY HARD
Moreau, Jeanne
PROPRIETOR, THE
Moreau, Jennie
I'M NOT RAPPAPORT
Moreau, Marguerite
D3: THE MIGHTY DUCKS
Moreau, Muguette
BOGUS
Moreau, Yolande
HORSEMAN ON THE ROOF
Morehouse, Ed
CITIZEN RUTH
Morell, Marisa
INDEPENDENCE DAY
Morelli, Vince
CITIZEN RUTH
Moreno, Belita
DEATH BENEFIT
Moreno, Carlos
HORSEMAN ON THE ROOF
Moreno, Desi
EXTREME MEASURES
GIRL 6
Moreno, Ken
CHAIN REACTION
Moreno, Rene
BIO-DOME
Moreno, Rita
WHARF RAT, THE
Moret, Julie
LOOKING FOR RICHARD
Moretti, Michele
MA SAISON PREFEREE
Morettini, Mark
CHAIN REACTION
Morfogen, George
ASSOCIATE, THE
SUBSTANCE OF FIRE, THE
Morgan, Branden R.
BLACK SHEEP
Morgan, C.W.
SCREAM
Morgan, Cass
BED OF ROSES
Morgan, Chad
WAR AT HOME, THE
Morgan, Cindy
AMANDA AND THE ALIEN
DEAD WEEKEND
OUT THERE
Morgan, Diana
ERASER
Morgan, Frank
HAMLET
Morgan Jr., Tommy
DON'T BE A MENACE TO SOUTH CENTRAL WHILE DRINKING YOUR JUICE IN THE HOOD
Morgan, Judson
SHARON'S SECRET
Morgan, Julie
STAR TREK: FIRST CONTACT
Morgan, Lisa
DON'T BE A MENACE TO SOUTH CENTRAL WHILE DRINKING YOUR JUICE IN THE HOOD
Morgan, Mariana
DEAR GOD
Morgan, Molly
TRIGGER EFFECT, THE
Morgan, Rhian
AUGUST
Morgan, Ron
SPY HARD
Morgan, Tracy
THIN LINE BETWEEN LOVE AND HATE, A
Morgenroth, Robert
GETTING AWAY WITH MURDER
Morgenstern, Danny
I SHOT ANDY WARHOL
Morgenstern, Madeleine
FRANCOIS TRUFFAUT: STOLEN PORTRAITS
Mori, Giovanna
MILLE BOLLE BLU
Mori, Jeanne
MARS ATTACKS!
Moriarty, Cathy
FOXFIRE
Moriarty, Edmund
HAUNTED
Moriarty, Michael
COURAGE UNDER FIRE
Morikawa, Toshiyuki
BIG WARS
Morin, Donald
ROBIN OF LOCKSLEY
Morison, Akiko
FINAL CUT, THE
SURGEON, THE
TRACKS OF A KILLER
Morita, Pat
BLOODSPORT II: THE NEXT KUMITE
SPY HARD

Moritz, Rosemary
ARRIVAL, THE
Morley, Susannah
COLD COMFORT FARM
Morlidge, Roger
ENGLISH PATIENT, THE
Mornet, Midori
MADAME BUTTERFLY
Moro, Christian
HATE
Moroff, Mike
FROM DUSK TILL DAWN
Morris, Alex
EVENING STAR, THE
ROAD TO GALVESTON, THE
Morris, Anita
OFF AND RUNNING
Morris, Aubrey
TALES FROM THE CRYPT PRESENTS BORDELLO OF BLOOD
Morris, Chloe
CITY HALL
Morris, Eileen
EVENING STAR, THE
Morris, Elliott
KINGPIN
Morris, Eric
EYE FOR AN EYE
Morris, Garrett
BLACK ROSE OF HARLEM
BLACK SCORPION
SANTA WITH MUSCLES
Morris, Howard
IT CAME FROM OUTER SPACE II
Morris, Iona
ONCE UPON A TIME . . . WHEN WE WERE COLORED
Morris, Jane
DEAR GOD
EYE FOR AN EYE
Morris, Jim
CHAMPAGNE SAFARI, THE
Morris, Keith
DON'T BE A MENACE TO SOUTH CENTRAL WHILE DRINKING YOUR JUICE IN THE HOOD
Morris, Ray K.
DUNSTON CHECKS IN
Morris, Sarah Ann
LETTER TO MY KILLER
Morris, Virginia
DEAD TO RIGHTS
NORMA JEAN AND MARILYN
Morrisette, Ledge
HYPE!
Morrisey, Lori
VIRTUAL ENCOUNTERS
Morrison, Alisha
HARRIET THE SPY
Morrison, Bill
SANDMAN, THE
Morrison, Brent
BIG BULLY
Morrison, James H.
BIRDCAGE, THE
Morrison, Jim
MESSAGE TO LOVE: THE ISLE OF WIGHT FESTIVAL
Morrison, Sterling
NICO ICON
Morrison, Temuera
BARB WIRE
ISLAND OF DR. MOREAU, THE
Morrissey, Joe
BREAKAWAY
Morrissey, Paul
NICO ICON
Morrone, Dina
BOGUS
Morrow, Rob
LAST DANCE
MOTHER
Morrow, Sharonlyn
TWISTER
Morse, David
EXTREME MEASURES
LONG KISS GOODNIGHT, THE
ROCK, THE
Morse, James Paul
COURAGE UNDER FIRE
Morse, Robin
FIRST WIVES CLUB, THE
PALLBEARER, THE
Morshower, Glenn
DEATH BENEFIT
JAG
Mortensen, Viggo
DAYLIGHT
PASSION OF DARKLY NOON, THE
PORTRAIT OF A LADY, THE
Mortenson, John
HYPE!
Mortimer, Emily
GHOST AND THE DARKNESS, THE
Morton, George
FUNNYMAN, THE
Morton, Joe
EXECUTIVE DECISION
LONE STAR
SKIN
Morton, Johnnie
JERRY MAGUIRE
Moseley, Robin
JUROR, THE
Moseley, Stacey
WELCOME TO THE DOLLHOUSE
Mosely, Jeff
JAMES AND THE GIANT PEACH
Mosely, Page
YESTERDAY'S TARGET
Moses, Paul
QUEST, THE
Moses, Ramon
ED'S NEXT MOVE
Moses, William R.
EVIL HAS A FACE
Mosley, Roger E.
THIN LINE BETWEEN LOVE AND HATE, A
Mosner, Donald
FRISK
Moss, Haylie
THEY BITE
Moss, Kate
CATWALK
Moss, Michael H.
FLED
Moss, Rebecca
THEY BITE
Moss, Tegan
BIG BULLY
Mosshammer, Jack
MRS. WINTERBOURNE
Most, Donnie
HOURGLASS
Mostel, Josh
MADDENING, THE
Mother Love
SURGEON, THE
Motriuc, Christian
MAGIC IN THE MIRROR
Mott, Zachary
DIABOLIQUE
Mousseau, Steve
STAND OFF, THE
Mouton, Benjamin
TIME TO KILL, A
WHOLE WIDE WORLD, THE
Mouzon, Alphonse
THAT THING YOU DO!
Mowod, John
SANTA CLAWS
Moxley, Gina
MOLL FLANDERS
Moyer, Betty
FOXFIRE
Moyle, Jim
BROKEN ARROW
Moynihan, Joseph
TRUMAN
Moynihan, Joseph Patrick
MARS ATTACKS!
Mozzatta, Kathleen
FEMALIEN
Mr. T.
SPY HARD
Mudd, John
PALLBEARER, THE
Muddle, Wm. J. "Billy Bob"
CITIZEN RUTH
Mudhoney
HYPE!
Mudwimin
NOT BAD FOR A GIRL
Muel, Jean-Paul
VISITORS, THE
Mueller, Julia
4 TALES OF 2 CITIES
NOT OF THIS EARTH
Mueller, Marcus
SOUTH BEACH ACADEMY
Mueller, Maureen
LARGER THAN LIFE
Mueller, Michael
MAN OF THE YEAR
Mueller-Stahl, Armin
SHINE
THEODORE REX
Muellerleile, Marianne
CHAMELEON
ENTERTAINING ANGELS: THE DOROTHY DAY STORY
EXECUTIVE DECISION
INFINITY
NORMA JEAN AND MARILYN
Muggli, Debbie
NEMESIS III: PREY HARDER
Mui, Anita
RUMBLE IN THE BRONX
Mujica, Rene
TALKING ABOUT SEX
Mukherji, Kevin
NORMAL LIFE
Mula, Tom
CHAIN REACTION
Mulheren, Michael
FAITHFUL
Mulhern, Matt
INFINITY
SUNCHASER
Mulholland, Declan
WAR OF THE BUTTONS, THE
Mulkey, Chris
BROKEN ARROW
DEAD COLD
FAN, THE
FOXFIRE
Mull, Martin
EDIE & PEN
HOW THE WEST WAS FUN
JINGLE ALL THE WAY
Mull, Wendy
EDIE & PEN

Mullan, Peter
TRAINSPOTTING
Mullane, Liz
FRIGHTENERS, THE
Mullany, Terry
KINGPIN
Mullarkey, Neil
SOLITAIRE FOR TWO
Mullen, Gary Paul
MICHAEL COLLINS
Mullen, Jennifer
SANDMAN, THE
Muller, Jurgen
LAND AND FREEDOM
Muller, Stephan
MAXIMUM RISK
Muller, Turk
CHAIN REACTION
PRIMAL FEAR
Mullin, Linn
BOTTLE ROCKET
Mullin, Mark
MERCY
Mullion, Annabel
MISSION: IMPOSSIBLE
Mulroney, Dermot
KANSAS CITY
TRIGGER EFFECT, THE
Mulroney, Kieran
IMMORTALS, THE
SPITFIRE GRILL, THE
Mulrooney, Kelsey
NORMA JEAN AND MARILYN
Mulryan, Pat
SOME MOTHER'S SON
Mulvey, Brians "Joker"
MICHAEL COLLINS
Mulvihill, Carmella
CRUCIBLE, THE
Mumm, Jonathan
TRIGGER EFFECT, THE
Mumy, Seth
DEAR GOD
Munafo, Tony
DAYLIGHT
Munch, Tony
MRS. WINTERBOURNE
SUGARTIME
Muncz, Paul
DEMOLITIONIST, THE
Mundi, Coati
GIRL 6
Munic, Robert Paul
TALES FROM THE CRYPT PRESENTS BORDELLO OF BLOOD
Munn, Brian
MOLL FLANDERS
Munoz, Daniel
LAND AND FREEDOM
Munoz, Gloria
FLOWER OF MY SECRET, THE
Munoz, Richard T.
CHAMBER, THE
Munsen, Michael
SANDMAN, THE
Munson, Warren
EXECUTIVE DECISION
Muratore, Robert
CANNIBAL! THE MUSICAL
Murdoch, Lachlan
KIDS IN THE HALL: BRAIN CANDY
Murdock, George
CROSSCUT
Muriel, Marisol
FLOWER OF MY SECRET, THE
Murnik, Peter
IT'S MY PARTY
PHOENIX
Murph, Henry
BROKEN ARROW
Murphy, Andrew
ONE GOOD TURN
Murphy, Brittany
FREEWAY
Murphy, Cathy
CAPTIVES
MOLL FLANDERS
Murphy, Charlie
POMPATUS OF LOVE, THE
Murphy, Danny
KINGPIN
Murphy, Dennis
ARRIVAL, THE
Murphy, Eddie
NUTTY PROFESSOR, THE
Murphy, Eric
VIRUS
Murphy, Harry
CHILDREN OF FURY
Murphy, Johnny
WAR OF THE BUTTONS, THE
Murphy, Karen
SMALL FACES
Murphy, Katy
BUTTERFLY KISS
Murphy, Kevin
MYSTERY SCIENCE THEATER 3000: THE MOVIE
Murphy, Lynne
TWO FRIENDS
Murphy, Martin
MICHAEL COLLINS
Murphy, Mary
CITY HALL
Murphy, Michael
KANSAS CITY
Murphy, Rosemary
TUSKEGEE AIRMEN, THE
Murphy, Tom
MICHAEL COLLINS
Murra, Shirley
APART FROM HUGH
Murray, Bill
KINGPIN
LARGER THAN LIFE
SPACE JAM
Murray, Brendan
HARD WAY OUT: BLOODFIST VIII
Murray, Brian
CITY HALL
Murray, Christopher
NORMA JEAN AND MARILYN
Murray, David
KANSAS CITY
Murray, Forrest
SPITFIRE GRILL, THE
Murray, J.J.
WHARF RAT, THE
Murray, Joel
CABLE GUY, THE
Murray, Melissa
JUROR, THE
Murrell, Lindsay
BEYOND THE CALL
Murtagh, John
SMALL FACES
Murtagh, Kate
RATTLED
Murtaugh, James
LETTER TO MY KILLER
Muser, Wolf
FINAL EQUINOX, THE
Musgrave, Robert
BOTTLE ROCKET
Mushtaghi, Mina
CURTIS'S CHARM
Musselman, Rusty
RIDERS OF THE PURPLE SAGE
Mussenden, Isis
DAYLIGHT
Musser, Larry
SURGEON, THE
Musters, Moral
CROCODILES IN AMSTERDAM
Mustillo, Louis
HELLRAISER: BLOODLINE
Mychelle, Terez
DON'T LET YOUR MEAT LOAF
Myers, David
BLONDES HAVE MORE GUNS
Myers, Jason
IF LUCY FELL
Myers, Jonathan Rhys
MICHAEL COLLINS
Myers, Kim
HELLRAISER: BLOODLINE
Myers, Lou
TIN CUP
Myers, Marjory
MONSTERSHOW
Myers, Richard
BLONDES HAVE MORE GUNS
Myers, Tim
COLD COMFORT FARM
Myers, Troy
EVERYONE SAYS I LOVE YOU
Myles Sr., Herman
HEAVEN'S PRISONERS
N'Diaye, Maimouna
CHASING BUTTERFLIES
Naber, Joey
EXECUTIVE DECISION
MOTHER
Nacco, John
GRACE OF MY HEART
Nadeau, Claire
NELLY AND MONSIEUR ARNAUD
Nader, Michael
FLED
Naebig, Kurt
SKIN
Naessens, Glen
DESIRE
Nagase, Masatoshi
COLD FEVER
FLIRT
Nagel, Bill
FIST OF THE NORTH STAR
Nagy, Ivan
HEIDI FLEISS HOLLYWOOD MADAM
Nagy, Mari
OUTPOST, THE
Nahaku, Don
VERY BRADY SEQUEL, A
Nahan, Stu
GREAT WHITE HYPE, THE
Nahon, Philippe
HATE
Nahtanaba, Jan
RAVENHAWK
Nail, Jimmy
EVITA
Naito, Takashi
MABOROSI
Nakada, Kazuhiro
SANCTUARY: THE MOVIE
Nakadai, Tatsuya
WICKED CITY, THE
Nakagami, Chika
KAMIKAZE TAXI
Nakagawa, Hirofumi
FLIRT

Nakahara-Wallett, Kellye
BLACK DAY BLUE NIGHT
Nakamura, Seami
HIGH SCHOOL HIGH
Nalbandian, Al
JACK
JAMES AND THE GIANT PEACH
Nalewicki, Stephen
DAYLIGHT
Name, Billy
NICO ICON
Nance, Jack
DEMOLITIONIST, THE
LITTLE WITCHES
Nance, Richard
LARRY MCMURTRY'S STREETS OF LAREDO
Nann, Erika
NORMA JEAN AND MARILYN
Nanty, Isabelle
VISITORS, THE
Nantz, Jim
TIN CUP
Naomi
FAST MONEY
Napes, Boris
RIDICULE
Napier, Charles
CABLE GUY, THE
FELONY
HARD JUSTICE
ORIGINAL GANGSTAS
Napier, Marshall
RACE THE SUN
SPIDER & ROSE
Naples, Toni
FUGITIVE RAGE
Napoli, Francisco
EVITA
Napolitano, Sister
LITTLE WITCHES
Narain, Kuldeep
LAST DANCE
Nardi, Laura
IN LOVE AND WAR
Nardone, Chris
DADETOWN
Nardone, Terry
DADETOWN
Nardoni, Tiziano
CEMETERY MAN
Narita, Richard
DOWN, OUT AND DANGEROUS
Nascarella, Arthur
GIRL 6
Nash, Larry
LETTER TO MY KILLER
Nash, Temple
BOTTLE ROCKET
Nashold MD, Blaine
PEOPLE VS. LARRY FLYNT, THE
Nassar, Mark
FAITHFUL
FIRST KID
Nasser, Jamil
PREACHER'S WIFE, THE
Natale, Anthony
JERRY MAGUIRE
MR. HOLLAND'S OPUS
Natale, Greg
NUTTY PROFESSOR, THE
Nathan, John
ROCK, THE
SGT. KABUKIMAN N.Y.P.D.
Natwick, Myron
GALAXIES ARE COLLIDING
Naubert, Louise
MAXIMUM RISK
Nauffts, Geoffrey
INFINITY
Naughton, Daragh
WAR OF THE BUTTONS, THE
Naughton, David
MIRROR, MIRROR III: THE VOYEUR
Naughton, James
FIRST KID
FIRST WIVES CLUB, THE
PROPRIETOR, THE
Naughton, Tina
UNDER THE HULA MOON
Naujoks, Ingo
BROTHER OF SLEEP
Navarra, Vincent
STAR MAKER, THE
Navarro, Anthony Babe
MAN WITH THE PERFECT SWING, THE
Navarro, Demetrius
BIG SQUEEZE, THE
INFINITY
Navarro, Pep
LAND AND FREEDOM
Navedo, Andrea
GIRL 6
Navratilova, Sona
DELTA OF VENUS
Nay, A.J.
ERASER
Naylor, Mary Neal
PEOPLE VS. LARRY FLYNT, THE
Nayyar, Harsh
BEAVIS AND BUTT-HEAD DO AMERICA
FIRST WIVES CLUB, THE
PREACHER'S WIFE, THE
Neal, Billie
GIRL 6
SWEET NOTHING
Neal, Scott
BEAUTIFUL THING
Neal, Wade
HYPE!
Nealon, Kevin
HAPPY GILMORE
Neary, Chantel
JUDE
Neary, John
KINGPIN
Neath, Robin
MADAGASCAR SKIN
Nederlof, Joan
CROCODILES IN AMSTERDAM
Nedorost, Josef
DELTA OF VENUS
Neeld, Lisa
SANDMAN, THE
Neenan, Audrie
NORMA JEAN AND MARILYN
Neeson, Liam
BEFORE AND AFTER
MICHAEL COLLINS
Negativland
SONIC OUTLAWS
Negri, Patty
FATALLY YOURS
Negron, Olivia
EVERYTHING RELATIVE
Negron, Taylor
BIO-DOME
MR. STITCH
Neil, Richard
BLONDES HAVE MORE GUNS
Neill, Pamela S.
PRE-MADONNAS
Neill, Patti
TALKING ABOUT SEX
Neilson, David
SECRETS & LIES
Neilson, Phil
FUNERAL, THE
Neilson, Richard
SOME MOTHER'S SON
Nelkin, Stacey
EVERYTHING RELATIVE
Nelles, John
MAXIMUM RISK
Nelles, John E.
FLY AWAY HOME
Nelligan, Kate
MOTHER'S PRAYER, A
UP CLOSE AND PERSONAL
Nellis Jr., Le'roy
WAR AT HOME, THE
Nelson, Clay
FRIGHTENERS, THE
Nelson, Clement
FOR THE MOMENT
Nelson, Craig T.
GHOSTS OF MISSISSIPPI
I'M NOT RAPPAPORT
Nelson, Danny
TIME TO KILL, A
Nelson, Kasey
MR. HOLLAND'S OPUS
Nelson, Kelly
DARK SECRETS
PRE-MADONNAS
Nelson, Marcus H.
WAR AT HOME, THE
Nelson, Mark
FIRST WIVES CLUB, THE
Nelson, Michael J.
MYSTERY SCIENCE THEATER 3000: THE MOVIE
Nelson, Morely
FIRE ON THE MOUNTAIN
Nelson, Novella
GIRL 6
MANNY & LO
MERCY
Nelson, Sandra
HALFBACK OF NOTRE DAME, THE
MATERNAL INSTINCTS
Nelson, Sean
AMERICAN BUFFALO
Nelson, Suzy
BERKELEY IN THE 60S
Nemcova, Andrea
DELTA OF VENUS
Nemec, Corin
WAR AT HOME, THE
WHITE WOLVES II: LEGEND OF THE WILD
Nemec, Lois
CITIZEN RUTH
Nemethy, Ferenc
RASPUTIN
Nemo
BASQUIAT
Nemo, Henry
WHISPERING, THE
Nene, Sibongile
TAILS YOU LIVE, HEADS YOU'RE DEAD
Neogard, Lena
EVIL ED
Neri, Francesca
OUTRAGE
Neri, Georges
HORSEMAN ON THE ROOF
Nerlino, Joanne
SPY HARD
Nesbitt, James
JUDE

Nesbitt-Dufort, Angela
TALES FROM THE CRYPT PRESENTS BORDELLO OF BLOOD
Nesnow, Joe
DOWN, OUT AND DANGEROUS
Nest, Tilo
KASPAR HAUSER
Nestor, Eddie
TRAINSPOTTING
Netter, David
YESTERDAY'S TARGET
Nettles, Irene
ONE MAN'S JUSTICE
Neubert, Keith
SONS OF TRINITY
THAT THING YOU DO!
Neuborne, Burt
PEOPLE VS. LARRY FLYNT, THE
Neuenschwander, Bria
JACK
Neufeld, Beverly
LETTER TO MY KILLER
Neuhaus, Ingo
EXECUTIVE DECISION
ROCK, THE
Neuman, John G.
DEMOLITIONIST, THE
Neumann, Margarete
FLAMING EARS
Neumann, Nadine
BROTHER OF SLEEP
Neuwirth, Bebe
ADVENTURES OF PINOCCHIO, THE
ALL DOGS GO TO HEAVEN 2
ASSOCIATE, THE
Nevada Belle
SGT. KABUKIMAN N.Y.P.D.
Neville, Aaron
FAN, THE
MULHOLLAND FALLS
Neville, Gordon
EVITA
Neville, John
HIGH SCHOOL HIGH
SONG SPINNER, THE
Nevin, Katrina
CRUCIBLE, THE
Nevinson, Gennie
TUNNEL VISION
New, Lori
TO GILLIAN ON HER 37TH BIRTHDAY
UP CLOSE AND PERSONAL
Newbern, George
EVENING STAR, THE
FAR HARBOR
THEODORE REX
Newell, Douglas
HAPPY GILMORE
Newman, Barry
DAYLIGHT
Newman, Danny
SHOPPING
Newman, Edwin
MY FELLOW AMERICANS
Newman, Eric Neal
INDEPENDENCE DAY
Newman, Erica C.
COURAGE UNDER FIRE
Newman Jr., David "Fathead"
KANSAS CITY
Newman, Lorraine
JINGLE ALL THE WAY
Newman, Richard
GIRL FROM MARS, THE
SURGEON, THE
Newman, William
CRAFT, THE

Newmar, Julie
BACKLASH: OBLIVION 2
Newmark, Charles
TREES LOUNGE
Newmeyer, Lisa
TEXAS CHAINSAW MASSACRE: THE NEXT GENERATION
Newsom, David
BOYS
Newsom, Paul
PUBLIC ENEMIES
Newton, Huey
BERKELEY IN THE 60S
Newton, Joe
HYPE!
Newton, Thandie
LOADED
Newton-John, Olivia
IT'S MY PARTY
Ng, Carol
STUPIDS, THE
Ng, Carrie
MAHJONG
Ng Man Tat
MIDNIGHT ANGEL
Nguyen Ba Hau, Therese
MADAME BUTTERFLY
Nguyen Khac, Long
SINGLE GIRL, A
Nial, Thomas
EDDIE
Niang, Medard
HATE
Niarchos Jr., Ted
STRIPTEASE
Nic-Nam
PHAT BEACH
Nichol, Scott
SUGARTIME
Nicholas, David J.
JACK & SARAH
Nicholas, Eileen
TRAINSPOTTING
Nicholas, Lisa
DADETOWN
Nicholas, Stephen
GLASS CAGE, THE
Nicholls-King, Melanie
RUDE
Nichols, Dave
TAILS YOU LIVE, HEADS YOU'RE DEAD
Nichols, David
GETTING AWAY WITH MURDER
Nichols, Paula
THAT THING YOU DO!
Nichols, Stephen
PHOENIX
Nichols, Taylor
HEADLESS BODY IN TOPLESS BAR
NORMA JEAN AND MARILYN
SERPENT'S LAIR
Nicholsen, Jack
IRON EAGLE IV
Nicholson, Jack
EVENING STAR, THE
MARS ATTACKS!
Nicholson, Julie
SHAMELESS
Nicholson, Mil
SPY HARD
Nicholson, Nick
RAW TARGET
Nicholson, Skylar
FEMALIEN
Nick, Desiree
NEUROSIA: 50 YEARS OF PERVERSITY
Nickel, Jochen
BROTHER OF SLEEP

Nickerson, Jimmy
MY FELLOW AMERICANS
Nicklaus, Jill
EVERYONE SAYS I LOVE YOU
Nickles, Michael A.
BAJA
Nicksay, Lily
UP CLOSE AND PERSONAL
Nickson, Julia
WHITE TIGER
Nicoli, Vincenzo
IN LOVE AND WAR
Nicosia, Elia
STAR MAKER, THE
Nicosia, Joseph A.
PHENOMENON
Nicotero, Greg
DEMOLITIONIST, THE
Niculescu, Mihai
JOSH KIRBY . . . TIME WARRIOR!: JOURNEY TO THE MAGIC CAVERN
Nielsen, Brigitte
BODY COUNT
Nielsen, Leslie
SPY HARD
Nieves, Benny
CITY HALL
Nignan, Diane
PROPRIETOR, THE
Nikaidoh, Miho
FLIRT
Nilsson, Kurt
EVIL ED
Nimier, Gaby
SERIAL KILLER
TALKING ABOUT SEX
Nims, Mina
HIGH SCHOOL HIGH
Ning, Tony
KIDS IN THE HALL: BRAIN CANDY
Nino, Miguel
CHAIN REACTION
Nipote, Joe
EDIE & PEN
Nirvana
HYPE!
Nishold, Bryon Lee
BOY CALLED HATE, A
Nistor, Stelian
MAGIC IN THE MIRROR
Nitschke, Ronald
SONS OF TRINITY
Nittalo, Horacio
SHADOW YOU SOON WILL BE, A
Nitzer, Alexis
HORSEMAN ON THE ROOF
MACHINE, THE
Niu, Chia-Ching
SOMEONE ELSE'S AMERICA
Niven, Barbara
FOREST WARRIOR
FOXFIRE
Nix, Beau
EDDIE
Nixon, Ademeyi E.
LET'S GET BIZZEE
Nixon, Beverly S.
PREACHER'S WIFE, THE
Nixon, Cynthia
MARVIN'S ROOM
Nixon, Dorothy
DADETOWN
Niznik, Stephanie
DEAR GOD
Noah, James
BLACK SHEEP
Noakes, Tony
BREAKAWAY

DENTIST, THE
Noble, James
THEY BITE
Nocera, Jonathan
BED OF ROSES
Nocerino, Anthony
GIRL 6
Noday, Patt
EDDIE
Nodine, Dr. Calvin F.
LINE KING: THE AL HIRSCHFELD STORY, THE
Noelle
VIRTUAL ENCOUNTERS
Noff, R. L.
DEADLY OUTBREAK
Nogaro, Angela
RICH MAN'S WIFE, THE
Nogulich, Natalija
EYE FOR AN EYE
LAZARUS MAN, THE
SHOT, THE
Nolan, Barry
BIRDCAGE, THE
INDEPENDENCE DAY
RAGE
Nolan, Bill
FLIPPER
Nolan, Conor
HARD WAY OUT: BLOODFIST VIII
Nolan, Matt
MOTHER
Nolan, Michael
MURDERED INNOCENCE
Noland, Charles
UP CLOSE AND PERSONAL
WOMAN UNDONE, A
Nolasco, Elvis
I'M NOT RAPPAPORT
Nolin, Rachel
FULL BODY MASSAGE
Nolot, Jacques
MA SAISON PREFEREE
Nolte, Brawley
MOTHER NIGHT
RANSOM
Nolte, Nick
MOTHER NIGHT
MULHOLLAND FALLS
Nomura, Christopheren
MADAME BUTTERFLY
Nomvete, Pamela
LIVE WIRE: HUMAN TIMEBOMB
Nonas-Barnes, Aurora
SMALL WONDERS
Noonan, John Ford
FLIRTING WITH DISASTER
Noonan, Tom
WIFE, THE
Noone, Elisabeth
FIRST KID
Noone, Kathleen
CITIZEN RUTH
SERPENT'S LAIR
Norasingh, Santy
MADAME BUTTERFLY
Norat, Max
FAITHFUL
Nordfjord, Simon
DELTA OF VENUS
Nordkvist, Elisabeth
CHILDREN OF NOISY VILLAGE, THE
Nordling, Jeffrey
D3: THE MIGHTY DUCKS
Norfleet, Susan
JERRY MAGUIRE
Norling, Mark
PUBLIC ACCESS
Norman, Mary M.
PEOPLE VS. LARRY FLYNT, THE
Norman, Paul
ANNIE O
Norman, Walter
CROSSCUT
Norman, Zack
CROSSCUT
Norris, Chuck
FOREST WARRIOR
Norris, Dean
DEATH BENEFIT
IT CAME FROM OUTER SPACE II
Norris, Kimberly
RAVENHAWK
Norry, Marilyn
SURGEON, THE
Norseworthy, Robert
LARRY MCMURTRY'S STREETS OF LAREDO
North, Alan
I'M NOT RAPPAPORT
LONG KISS GOODNIGHT, THE
North, Barnaby
FUNNYMAN, THE
North, John
DEAD MAN
North, Oliver
PERFECT CANDIDATE, A
Northam, Jeremy
EMMA
Norton, Brad
KINGPIN
Norton, Edward
EVERYONE SAYS I LOVE YOU
PEOPLE VS. LARRY FLYNT, THE
PRIMAL FEAR
Norwood Jr., Willie
ONCE UPON A TIME . . . WHEN WE WERE COLORED
Noseworthy, Jack
BARB WIRE
TRIGGER EFFECT, THE
Nossek, Ralph
JANE EYRE
JOSEPH CONRAD'S THE SECRET AGENT
Notaro, Frank
REDEMPTION: KICKBOXER 5
WARHEAD
Noto, Paolo
STAR MAKER, THE
Nottingham, Wendy
MARY REILLY
SECRETS & LIES
Nottle, Dean
TUNNEL VISION
Nouri, Azdine
QUEST, THE
Novack, Adam
WILD SIDE
Novak, Frank
INDEPENDENCE DAY
Novak, John
DARKMAN III: DIE DARKMAN DIE
ROAD HOME, THE
Novak, Mel
DEAR GOD
Novak, Steven
HEAD OF THE FAMILY
ZARKORR! THE INVADER
Novello, Don
JACK
ONE NIGHT STAND
Novikoff, Garry
ORIGINAL SINS
Novo, Nancho
FLOWER OF MY SECRET, THE
Now, Michael
FRISK
Nucci, Danny
BIG SQUEEZE, THE
ERASER
HOMAGE
ROCK, THE
Nuckles-Holt, Gary
PREACHER'S WIFE, THE
Nunez, Alexandra
TOLLBOOTH
Nunez, Debrah
MICHAEL
Nunez Jr., Miguel A.
THIN LINE BETWEEN LOVE AND HATE, A
Nunn, Bill
AFFAIR, THE
BULLETPROOF
EXTREME MEASURES
Nunn, Mike
SHOOTFIGHTER 2: KILL OR BE KILLED!
Nunziato, Elisabeth
PHENOMENON
Nurkiewicz, Gabriella
MUTANT MAN
Nurkiewicz, Jonathan
MUTANT MAN
Nurses, The
ROLLING STONES ROCK-AND-ROLL CIRCUS, THE
Nuttall, Jeff
CAPTIVES
Nutter, Mark
MICHAEL
Nwamba, Richard
GHOST AND THE DARKNESS, THE
Nyandeni, Thembi
REDEMPTION: KICKBOXER 5
Nye, Michael
HIGH SCHOOL HIGH
Nye, Ted
BOY CALLED HATE, A
Nyerges, Chadd
AMANDA AND THE ALIEN
Nyswaner, Ron
CELLULOID CLOSET, THE
O'Boto, Isadora
DEAR GOD
O'Brien, Austin
LAWNMOWER MAN 2: BEYOND CYBERSPACE
O'Brien, Doc
HEDD WYNN
O'Brien, Kevin
KINGPIN
O'Brien, Kieran
CRACKER: THE MADWOMAN IN THE ATTIC
O'Brien, Peter
MICHAEL COLLINS
O'Brien, Phil
LAND AND FREEDOM
O'Brien, Shauna
FRIEND OF THE FAMILY 2
FUGITIVE RAGE
OVER THE WIRE
O'Brien, Skip
BLACK SHEEP
VERY BRADY SEQUEL, A
O'Brien, Trevor
HOMECOMING
LAWNMOWER MAN 2: BEYOND CYBERSPACE
O'Bryan, Sean
DEAR GOD
PHENOMENON
O'Byrne, Kehli
PIRANHA

O'Connell, Colette
HOURGLASS
O'Connell, Deirdre
LIFEFORM
O'Connell, Drew
HIGH SCHOOL HIGH
O'Connell, Jack
ANGELA
BIG NIGHT
O'Connell, James
CABLE GUY, THE
O'Connell, Jerry
JERRY MAGUIRE
JOE'S APARTMENT
O'Connell, R.D. "Cuz"
CITIZEN RUTH
O'Connell, Raoul
FRISK
LIFEFORM
O'Connor, Dan
AMANDA AND THE ALIEN
O'Connor, Dennis
TWO IF BY SEA
O'Connor, Gladys
FLY AWAY HOME
HARRIET THE SPY
LONG KISS GOODNIGHT, THE
O'Connor, Helen
SPIDER & ROSE
O'Connor, Jim
ABUSE
O'Connor, Mark
SMALL WONDERS
O'Connor, Raymond
ROCK, THE
O'Connor, Terrence
NORMA JEAN AND MARILYN
O'Conor, Hugh
YOUNG POISONER'S HANDBOOK, THE
O'Donnell, Addie
RANSOM
O'Donnell, Annie
BLACK SHEEP
O'Donnell, Anthony
BREAKING THE WAVES
SECRETS & LIES
O'Donnell, Chris
CHAMBER, THE
IN LOVE AND WAR
O'Donnell, David
TRIGGER EFFECT, THE
O'Donnell, Hugh
SOME MOTHER'S SON
O'Donnell, Rosie
BEAUTIFUL GIRLS
HARRIET THE SPY
O'Donoghue, James
WELCOME TO THE DOLLHOUSE
O'Donoghue, Louis
HAPPY GILMORE
O'Donoghue, Maurice
WAR OF THE BUTTONS, THE
O'Donoghue, Ronan
SOME MOTHER'S SON
O'Donohue, John
CABLE GUY, THE
O'Donovan, Jerome X.
CITY HALL
O'Farrell, Conor
TRIGGER EFFECT, THE
O'Grady, Gail
CELTIC PRIDE
O'Grady, Rynagh
MOLL FLANDERS
O'Hallaran, Tim
FINAL CUT, THE
O'Hanlon, Ardal
MOLL FLANDERS
O'Hara, David
SOME MOTHER'S SON
O'Hara, Jenny
MOTHER'S PRAYER, A
O'Heir, Jim
ED
O'Herlihy, Gavan
HIDDEN ASSASSIN
O'Kane, Louise
SMALL FACES
O'Keefe, Doug
GETTING AWAY WITH MURDER
WHEN THE BULLET HITS THE BONE
O'Keefe, John
SWEET NOTHING
O'Keefe, Michael
EDIE & PEN
GHOSTS OF MISSISSIPPI
O'Keeffe, Doug
JOHNNY SHORTWAVE
O'Leary, Alan
FRIGHTENERS, THE
O'Leary, Derek
WAR OF THE BUTTONS, THE
O'Leary, Ger
MICHAEL COLLINS
O'Leary, Helen
WAR OF THE BUTTONS, THE
O'Leary, Jer
SOME MOTHER'S SON
O'Leary, John
MY FELLOW AMERICANS
O'Looney, Michael
CITY HALL
O'Malley, Bingo
DIABOLIQUE
O'Malley, Jim
SWEEPER, THE
O'Malley, Kate
SECRETS & LIES
O'Malley, Kathleen
BLACK SHEEP
O'Malley, Kevin
WAR OF THE BUTTONS, THE
O'Mealy, Mary Kay
MR. HOLLAND'S OPUS
O'Meara, Caroline
SWINGERS
O'Neal, Ron
ORIGINAL GANGSTAS
O'Neal, Ryan
FAITHFUL
O'Neal, Shaquille
KAZAAM
O'Neal, Tatum
BASQUIAT
O'Neal, Ty
D3: THE MIGHTY DUCKS
O'Neill, Chris
FAITHFUL
O'Neill, Jennifer
BAD LOVE
O'Neill, Michael
NORMA JEAN AND MARILYN
SUNCHASER
O'Neill, Owen
MICHAEL COLLINS
O'Neill, Patrick
PIG'S TALE, A
O'Neill, Ryan J.
MOTHER'S PRAYER, A
O'Neill, Sean
SGT. KABUKIMAN N.Y.P.D.
O'Neill, Terry
DRAGONHEART
O'Pelka, Michael
SGT. KABUKIMAN N.Y.P.D.
O'Plotnik, Brent
PUBLIC ENEMIES
O'Quinn, Terry
JAG
PRIMAL FEAR
SHADOW WARRIORS
O'Rawe, Geraldine
SOME MOTHER'S SON
O'Reilly, Cyril
CARNOSAUR 3: PRIMAL SPECIES
O'Reilly, Harry
CABLE GUY, THE
O'Rourke, Mick
RANSOM
O'Ryan, Heather
BLACK SCORPION
O'Shaughnessy, Brian
WARHEAD
O'Steen, Michael
EVERYONE SAYS I LOVE YOU
O'Sullivan, Aisling
MICHAEL COLLINS
O'Sullivan, Anne
MIRROR HAS TWO FACES, THE
O'Sullivan, Billy
ROBIN OF LOCKSLEY
O'Sullivan, Frank
MICHAEL COLLINS
WAR OF THE BUTTONS, THE
O'Sullivan, Michael S.
SOME MOTHER'S SON
O'Toole, Matt
LAST MAN STANDING
Oakes, Lee
DAYLIGHT
DRAGONHEART
Oakley, Vern
MODERN AFFAIR, A
Oates, Stephen
RANSOM
Obata, Yoshi
STRIPTEASE
Oberly, Charlet
FLIRTING WITH DISASTER
Obodzinski, Gayle
SPY HARD
Obradovich, Lorie
CITIZEN RUTH
Occhipinti, Andrea
WHO KILLED PASOLINI?
Ochoa, Jorge
OF LOVE AND SHADOWS
Ochoa, Steven
CRUCIBLE, THE
Ochsenknecht, Uwe
KASPAR HAUSER
Oden, Carroll
WHISPERING, THE
Odenkirk, Bob
CABLE GUY, THE
TRUTH ABOUT CATS AND DOGS, THE
Odent, Christophe
HORSEMAN ON THE ROOF
Odom, Todd
DOWN PERISCOPE
Oglesby, Randy
INDEPENDENCE DAY
Ohsugi, Ren
MABOROSI
Ohtaki, Shinya
BIG WARS
Oida, Yoshi
MADAME BUTTERFLY
Ok, Anne
GIRL 6
Okumoto, Yuji
HARD JUSTICE

Olafsdottir, Margret
VIKING SAGAS, THE
Olafson, Hinrik
VIKING SAGAS, THE
Olafsson, Egill
VIKING SAGAS, THE
Olafsson, Magnus
VIKING SAGAS, THE
Olawumi, Olumiji Aina
PIG'S TALE, A
Oldham, Todd
CATWALK
Oldman, Gary
BASQUIAT
Oleson, Nick
TEXAS PAYBACK
Oliensis, Adam
POMPATUS OF LOVE, THE
Oliney, Alan
RAVENHAWK
Oliva, Ignazio
STEALING BEAUTY
Oliver, Dave
THAT THING YOU DO!
Oliver, Jessica
MR. ICE CREAM MAN
Oliver, John
FEAR
Oliver, Mindy
MR. ICE CREAM MAN
Oliveri, Antonio
CAUGHT
Oliveri, Dominick
CAUGHT
Olives, Lola
LAND AND FREEDOM
Olivier, Frank
DESOLATION ANGELS
Olivierio, Silvio
UNDERSTUDY: GRAVEYARD SHIFT 2, THE
Olkewicz, Walter
SURGEON, THE
Ollivier, Lilia
CHASING BUTTERFLIES
Olmez, Gahit
CROCODILES IN AMSTERDAM
Olmos, Edward James
CAUGHT
Olmsted, Jeff
ABUSE
Olohan, John
WAR OF THE BUTTONS, THE
Olsen, Ashley
HOW THE WEST WAS FUN
Olsen, Katherine
DUNSTON CHECKS IN
Olsen, Lizzie
HOW THE WEST WAS FUN
Olsen, Mary Kate
HOW THE WEST WAS FUN
Olsson, Roger
EVIL ED
Olsson, Sven-Erik
EVIL ED
Olstead, Renee
LARRY MCMURTRY'S STREETS OF LAREDO
Olyphant, Timothy
FIRST WIVES CLUB, THE
Omilami, Elizabeth
LAST DANCE
TIME TO KILL, A
Ono, Yoko
ROLLING STONES ROCK-AND-ROLL CIRCUS, THE
Onorati, Peter
DONOR UNKNOWN
Onorato, Marzio
STAR MAKER, THE
Onrubia, Cynthia
EVERYONE SAYS I LOVE YOU
Ophuls, Marcel
FRANCOIS TRUFFAUT: STOLEN PORTRAITS
Opinato, Mario
BODY COUNT
Oppenheim, Misty L.
MATILDA
Oppenheimer, Allan
PHANTOM 2040: THE GHOST WHO WALKS
Orange, Thomas
ADVENTURES OF PINOCCHIO, THE
Orantes, Patricia
SILENCE OF NETO, THE
Orban, Judith
FLY AWAY HOME
MAN IN THE ATTIC, THE
Orel, Rostislav
RACE THE SUN
Orella, Francesc
LAND AND FREEDOM
Orfani, Fereshteh Sadr
WHITE BALLOON, THE
Orgolini, Lisa
TWO DEATHS
Oribe
CATWALK
Orita, Denise
SECRETS & LIES
Orlan
SYNTHETIC PLEASURES
Orlandini, Hal
TERMINAL IMPACT
Ormond, Julia
CAPTIVES
Ornstein, Michael
MAN OF THE YEAR
Orr, Christopher
D3: THE MIGHTY DUCKS
Orrach, Joe
EVERYONE SAYS I LOVE YOU
Orsatti, Noon
ED
Orser, Leland
INDEPENDENCE DAY
JOHN CARPENTER'S ESCAPE FROM L.A.
LIFEFORM
PHOENIX
PIRANHA
Orsini, Umberto
WHO KILLED PASOLINI?
Ortega, Chick
LITTLE INDIAN, BIG CITY
Ortega, Jimmy
FOREST WARRIOR
LAST MAN STANDING
Ortel, Peter
HEAVY
Orth, Zak
PALLBEARER, THE
WILLIAM SHAKESPEARE'S ROMEO + JULIET
Ortiz, Humberto
ONE MAN'S JUSTICE
Ortiz, John
RANSOM
SGT. BILKO
Ortlieb, Jim
CHAIN REACTION
Orwig, Bob
GET ON THE BUS
Osborne, Andrew
SGT. KABUKIMAN N.Y.P.D.
Osborne, Buzz
HYPE!
Osborne, Holmes
TRUMAN
Osborne Jr., Holmes
THAT THING YOU DO!
Osborne, William
COLD COMFORT FARM
Osgood, Nathan
MISSION: IMPOSSIBLE
Oshima, Yukari
MIDNIGHT ANGEL
Osment, Haley Joel
BOGUS
Osorio, Ismael
EVITA
Osorio, Rafael
RANSOM
Osorlo, Armando
AVENTURERA
Osser, Jonathan
MY FELLOW AMERICANS
Osterberg, Ollie
BEAUTIFUL GIRLS
Ostertag, Greg
EDDIE
Osterwald, Bibi
GLIMMER MAN, THE
PHANTOM 2040: THE GHOST WHO WALKS
Ostevic, Gabriel
RUMBLE IN THE BRONX
Osti, Mattia
WHO KILLED PASOLINI?
Ostow, Mary
ZARKORR! THE INVADER
Ostrin, Gregg
ARRIVAL, THE
Ostrosky, Beth
FLIRTING WITH DISASTER
Ostroukhov, Pavel
BURIAL OF THE RATS
Ostrow, Mary
ENTERTAINING ANGELS: THE DOROTHY DAY STORY
Oswald, John
SONIC OUTLAWS
Oswalt, Patton
DOWN PERISCOPE
Otaki, Hitoe
PLAYBACK
Otegui, Juan Jose
FLOWER OF MY SECRET, THE
Otis, Billy
WHERE'S THE MONEY, NOREEN?
Otokiti, Adam
HIGH SCHOOL HIGH
Otsuki, Tamayo
DON'T BE A MENACE TO SOUTH CENTRAL WHILE DRINKING YOUR JUICE IN THE HOOD
Ottamano, Fred
EXIT
Ouerghi, Najia
SILENCES OF THE PALACE, THE
Oughterson, Scott
STRIPTEASE
Outerbridge, Jen Sung
QUEST, THE
Outerbridge, Peter
FOR THE MOMENT
Outlaw, Paul
BASQUIAT
Overby, Rhonda
UP CLOSE AND PERSONAL
Overmyer, Tom
WITCHCRAFT: SALEM'S GHOST

Overton, Rick
GALAXIES ARE COLLIDING
Owen, Chris
BLACK SHEEP
Owen, Clive
RICH MAN'S WIFE, THE
Owen, Nancy Lea
PEOPLE VS. LARRY FLYNT, THE
Owens, C. Wayne
MARS ATTACKS!
Owens, Gary
SPY HARD
Owens, Susie
THEY BITE
Owsley, Steven
MAN WITH THE PERFECT SWING, THE
Oxenberg, Jan
CELLULOID CLOSET, THE
Ozasky, Robert
FARGO
Pabros, Marcella
JACK
Pacey, Peter
YOUNG POISONER'S HANDBOOK, THE
Pacheco M.D., Ferdie
GREAT WHITE HYPE, THE
Pachicano, Lee Andrew
WAR AT HOME, THE
Pacho, Andrew
EVERYONE SAYS I LOVE YOU
Pachorek, Richard
INDEPENDENCE DAY
Pachoso, Steven Clark
FOXFIRE
Pacific, Jerry
STRIPTEASE
Pacino, Al
CITY HALL
LOOKING FOR RICHARD
Pack, Roger Lloyd
YOUNG POISONER'S HANDBOOK, THE
Padayachee, Kaycey
GHOST AND THE DARKNESS, THE
Paden, Rev. Kenneth
PREACHER'S WIFE, THE
Padgett, Daniel R.
BOTTLE ROCKET
Paetty, Scott
ASSAULT AT WEST POINT
Pagan, Saida
PEOPLE VS. LARRY FLYNT, THE
Page, Jordan
PROTEUS
Page, La Wanda
DON'T BE A MENACE TO SOUTH CENTRAL WHILE DRINKING YOUR JUICE IN THE HOOD
Page, Patrick
SUBSTANCE OF FIRE, THE
Pages, Jean-Francois
HORSEMAN ON THE ROOF
Pahernik, Albin
EVITA
Pai, Liana
ASSOCIATE, THE
POMPATUS OF LOVE, THE
Pai, Lianna
FLIRT
Paidle, Renee
BULLETPROOF
Pailhas, Geraldine
SUITE 16
Pain, Didier
VISITORS, THE
Pais, Josh
I'M NOT RAPPAPORT
Paisley, Ray
WHARF RAT, THE
Pajot, Olivier
NELLY AND MONSIEUR ARNAUD
Palac, Lisa
SYNTHETIC PLEASURES
Paladino, Dennis
FOREST WARRIOR
Palagonia, Al
GIRL 6
Palatsi, Ma Eugenia
LAND AND FREEDOM
Palatsi, Pepa
LAND AND FREEDOM
Palau, Jose
FLOWER OF MY SECRET, THE
Palazzi, Henriette
HORSEMAN ON THE ROOF
Palazzo, Tony
STAR MAKER, THE
Palermo, Anthony
SERPENT'S LAIR
Palermo, Vivian
INDEPENDENCE DAY
Palevsky, Joy
SGT. KABUKIMAN N.Y.P.D.
Palin, Michael
WIND IN THE WILLOWS, THE
Palladino, Aleska
MANNY & LO
Pallana, Dipak
BOTTLE ROCKET
Pallana, Kumar
BOTTLE ROCKET
Pallas, Laura
EVITA
Palma, Andrea
AVENTURERA
Palmer, Andrew
STAR TREK: FIRST CONTACT
Palmer, Darryl
MRS. MUNCK
Palmer, Jim
BROKEN ARROW
LAST MAN STANDING
PEOPLE VS. LARRY FLYNT, THE
Palmer, Nick
SGT. KABUKIMAN N.Y.P.D.
Palmer, Richard
WILD SIDE
Palmieri, Mark
MANNY & LO
Palminteri, Chazz
DIABOLIQUE
FAITHFUL
MULHOLLAND FALLS
Palomino, Carlos
CRIMINAL HEARTS
Paltrow, Gwyneth
EMMA
PALLBEARER, THE
Palumbi Jr., Ron
KINGPIN
Palumbo, Pasquale
STAR MAKER, THE
Pandolfo, Tony
DEAD TO RIGHTS
Panetta, Alicia
DARKMAN III: DIE DARKMAN DIE
Pang, Andrew
SUBSTANCE OF FIRE, THE
Pankhurst, Patrick
BLACK SHEEP
Pankin, Stuart
BIG BULLY
DOWN, OUT AND DANGEROUS
STRIPTEASE
Panos, Lia
EDDIE
Panther
PROPRIETOR, THE
Panther, Puven
TUNNEL VISION
Panthere
PHAT BEACH
Pantoliano, Joe
BOUND
IMMORTALS, THE
Paola, Jimmy
BREAKAWAY
Paoli, Cecile
KASPAR HAUSER
Papajohn, Michael
ERASER
NAKED SOULS
Papatakis, Nico
NICO ICON
Papp, Joseph
LINE KING: THE AL HIRSCHFELD STORY, THE
Paquin, Anna
FLY AWAY HOME
JANE EYRE
Paradise, James
NECRONOMICON: BOOK OF THE DEAD
Paragon, John
RICH MAN'S WIFE, THE
Parati, Tim
PEOPLE VS. LARRY FLYNT, THE
TIME TO KILL, A
Pare, Michael
BAD MOON
Paredes, Marisa
FLOWER OF MY SECRET, THE
THREE LIVES AND ONLY ONE DEATH
Parenago, Steven
BASQUIAT
Parent, Monique
DARK SECRETS
MIRROR, MIRROR III: THE VOYEUR
Pares, Cecile
RENDEZVOUS IN PARIS
Parhm, Sean
LAWNMOWER MAN 2: BEYOND CYBERSPACE
Parilo, Markus
STUPIDS, THE
TWO IF BY SEA
Paris, Gerald
101 DALMATIANS
Paris, Janie
PEOPLE VS. LARRY FLYNT, THE
Paris, Livia Daza
GIRLFRIENDS
Parise, Claudio
WHO KILLED PASOLINI?
Parise, Sandy
SANDMAN, THE
Park, Peyton
LARRY MCMURTRY'S STREETS OF LAREDO
MICHAEL
Park, Steve
FARGO
SGT. BILKO
Parke, Evelyn
EYE FOR AN EYE
Parker, Andrea
JAG
Parker, Anthony Ray
FRIGHTENERS, THE
Parker, Carl
PHENOMENON
Parker, Carl D.
DANGEROUS PASSION
Parker, Corey
MOTHER'S PRAYER, A

Parker, Doug
WARHEAD
Parker, Ginny
LAST DANCE
Parker, Judith
JANE EYRE
Parker, Lauren
JERRY MAGUIRE
Parker, Leni
SCREAMERS
Parker, Mary-Louise
PORTRAIT OF A LADY, THE
SUGARTIME
Parker, Nicole
HALFBACK OF NOTRE DAME, THE
RUDE
Parker, Norman
UP CLOSE AND PERSONAL
Parker, Pam
THEY BITE
Parker, Paula Jai
DON'T BE A MENACE TO SOUTH CENTRAL WHILE DRINKING YOUR JUICE IN THE HOOD
GET ON THE BUS
Parker, Rick
DARKMAN III: DIE DARKMAN DIE
Parker, Robert
FIRE ON THE MOUNTAIN
Parker, Sarah Jessica
EXTREME MEASURES
FIRST WIVES CLUB, THE
IF LUCY FELL
MARS ATTACKS!
SUBSTANCE OF FIRE, THE
Parker-Jones, Jill
BOTTLE ROCKET
LARRY MCMURTRY'S STREETS OF LAREDO
Parkes, Gerard
MOTHER NIGHT
Parks, Andrew
MIRROR HAS TWO FACES, THE
Parks, Michael
FROM DUSK TILL DAWN
Parlani, Cesar
OF LOVE AND SHADOWS
Parlato, Michael
DEADLY OUTBREAK
Parnes, Fred
MATILDA
Parnes, Mitch
PURE DANGER
Parnes, Phillip
I'M NOT RAPPAPORT
Parodi, Aldo
JOHNNY 100 PESOS
Parolisi, Phil
LOOKING FOR RICHARD
RANSOM
Parrello, Maria Rosa
STAR MAKER, THE
Parrillo, Benjamin John
THAT THING YOU DO!
Parrish, Sally
MARVIN'S ROOM
Parry, Alan
GIRLFRIENDS
Parson, Eboni
KAZAAM
Parson, Ron O.J.
PRIMAL FEAR
Parsons, Danielle
KINGPIN
Parsons, Estelle
LOOKING FOR RICHARD
Partain, Dan
PHENOMENON
Partington, David J.
DOWN, OUT AND DANGEROUS
Pas, Michael
ANTONIA'S LINE
DAENS
Pascal, Lucien
RIDICULE
Pasco, Nicholas
GETTING AWAY WITH MURDER
Pasdar, Adrian
POMPATUS OF LOVE, THE
Pashalinski, Lola
I SHOT ANDY WARHOL
Pashkow, Matt
INDEPENDENCE DAY
Paskel, Eric
INDEPENDENCE DAY
Pasqualone, Rick
TALES OF EROTICA
Pasquesi, David
CHAIN REACTION
Pass, Cyndi
SERIAL KILLER
Passaro, Chris
CROSSCUT
Passeri, Vito
CEMETERY MAN
WHO KILLED PASOLINI?
Passoni, Valentin
NEUROSIA: 50 YEARS OF PERVERSITY
Pastko, Earl
BLOOD & DONUTS
Pastor, Rosana
LAND AND FREEDOM
Pastore, Vincent
SUNSET PARK
WALKING AND TALKING
Pastorelli, Robert
ERASER
MICHAEL
Pater, Jacques
HORSEMAN ON THE ROOF
Patiro, Charlie
MUTANT MAN
Patocka, Jiri
ADVENTURES OF PINOCCHIO, THE
Paton, Angela
EYE FOR AN EYE
Paton, Lance
DARKMAN III: DIE DARKMAN DIE
Paton, Sarena
FLY AWAY HOME
Patric, Jason
SLEEPERS
Patrick, Barbara
WITHIN THE ROCK
Patrick, Nick
LOADED
Patrick, Robert
STRIPTEASE
Pattak, Cory
DIABOLIQUE
Pattee, Richard
ARRIVAL, THE
Patterson, Carlos
DON'T LET YOUR MEAT LOAF
Patterson, Frank
MICHAEL COLLINS
Patterson, John
INFINITY
Patterson, Jonathan
CHILDREN OF THE CORN: THE GATHERING
Patterson, Joshua
CHILDREN OF THE CORN: THE GATHERING
Patterson, Pat
KIDS IN THE HALL: BRAIN CANDY
Patterson, Scott
BOY CALLED HATE, A
Patterson, Sheila
ROAD HOME, THE
Patterson, Willie "Spaceman"
TALES OF EROTICA
Pattison, John
DEAD MAN
Patton, Josh
FROM DUSK TILL DAWN
Patton, Tom
WHISPERING, THE
Patton, Tyler
SPY HARD
Patton, Will
FLED
SPITFIRE GRILL, THE
TOLLBOOTH
Pattoni, Suzanna
PROPRIETOR, THE
Paul, Adam
NORMA JEAN AND MARILYN
Paul, Alexandra
PIRANHA
SPY HARD
Paul, Brian
DARKMAN III: DIE DARKMAN DIE
Paul, Gary
BIG SQUEEZE, THE
Paul, Maximillian
PASSION OF DARKLY NOON, THE
Paul, Megan
FOREST WARRIOR
Paul, Randall
MISSION: IMPOSSIBLE
Paul, Richard
GLASS CAGE, THE
PEOPLE VS. LARRY FLYNT, THE
Paul, Richard Joseph
BACKLASH: OBLIVION 2
Paul, Talia
IT'S MY PARTY
Paul, Tina
EVERYONE SAYS I LOVE YOU
EVERYONE SAYS I LOVE YOU
Paulsen, Rob
LAND BEFORE TIME IV: JOURNEY THROUGH THE MISTS
Paulson, David
BOYS
Pauperas, Mark
KINGPIN
Pauthe, Serge
HORSEMAN ON THE ROOF
Pauzer, Irene
MAXIMUM RISK
MRS. WINTERBOURNE
Pavitt, Bruce
HYPE!
Pavlic, Chris
CROSSCUT
Pavlidis, Harry
RACE THE SUN
Pavlokovic, Anthony
BIG BULLY
Paxton, Bill
EVENING STAR, THE
LAST SUPPER, THE
TWISTER
Paxton, John
BARB WIRE
LAST MAN STANDING
Paxton, Robert
EYE OF VICHY, THE
Paxton, Tajamika
DON'T LET YOUR MEAT LOAF
Paxton, Vivian
MAN OF THE YEAR

Paymer, David
CARPOOL
CITY HALL
UNFORGETTABLE
Payne, Allan
TUSKEGEE AIRMEN, THE
Payne, Brandy
MIRROR, MIRROR III: THE VOYEUR
Payne, Bruce
NECRONOMICON: BOOK OF THE DEAD
ONE MAN'S JUSTICE
Payne, Frankie
FRISK
Payne II, Carl Anthony
ED
Payne, Julie
SPY HARD
Payne, Kathy
FLED
Pays, Amanda
SOLITAIRE FOR TWO
Payton, Gary
EDDIE
Payton, Nicholas
KANSAS CITY
Paz, Sergio
SILENCE OF NETO, THE
Peabody, Dossy
CRUCIBLE, THE
Peaks, Pandora
STRIPTEASE
Pearl, Aaron
ANNIE O
Pearl Jam
HYPE!
Pearl, Julie R.
CHAIN REACTION
Pearl, Phoebe
MATILDA
Pearlman, Bill
LAZARUS MAN, THE
Pearlman, Dina
GIRL 6
Pearlman, Stephen
FIRST WIVES CLUB, THE
Pearlstein, Randy
MIRROR HAS TWO FACES, THE
Pearson, Brandi
WITCHCRAFT: SALEM'S GHOST
Pearson, John
BEYOND THE CALL
MAXIMUM RISK
Pearson, Malechi
DEAD TO RIGHTS
Peart, Kamela
JACK
Pecchia, David
TALKING ABOUT SEX
Pechan, Rudolf
MISSION: IMPOSSIBLE
Pechaty, Petr
DELTA OF VENUS
Pecheur, Sierra
EYE FOR AN EYE
Peck, Anthony
CARNOSAUR 3: PRIMAL SPECIES
Peck, Bob
SURVIVING PICASSO
Peck, Brian
PUBLIC ENEMIES
Peck, Gregory
PERSONAL JOURNEY WITH MARTIN SCORSESE THROUGH AMERICAN MOVIES, A
Peck, Jim
PEOPLE VS. LARRY FLYNT, THE
Peck, Jonathon
SOMEONE ELSE'S AMERICA
Peddie, Roy A.
THEY BITE
Pederson, Randy
KINGPIN
Pedlow, Jessica
ANNIE O
Peduto, Ralph
ROCK, THE
Peeples, Nia
MR. STITCH
Peery, Sara
BOGUS
Peet, Amanda
ONE FINE DAY
SHE'S THE ONE
Peeters, Filip
ANTONIA'S LINE
Peeters, Mark
DAENS
Pegram, Nigel
PROTEUS
Peirano, Tomiko
MR. HOLLAND'S OPUS
Peiro, Teddy
EVITA
Peldon, Ashley
BLACK SCORPION
CRUCIBLE, THE
Pellegrino, Pino
STAR MAKER, THE
Pelletier, Paul
KINGPIN
Pellicer, Antonio
LAND AND FREEDOM
Pellicer, Felicio
LAND AND FREEDOM
Pelligra, Biagio
WHO KILLED PASOLINI?
Pellington, Mark
JERRY MAGUIRE
Pemberton, Diana
STAND OFF, THE
Pemberton, Robert
SGT. KABUKIMAN N.Y.P.D.
Pena, Candela
MOUTH TO MOUTH
Pena, Elizabeth
IT CAME FROM OUTER SPACE II
LONE STAR
Pena, Lanell
LARRY MCMURTRY'S STREETS OF LAREDO
Pena, Michael
MY FELLOW AMERICANS
Pena, William
JOHN CARPENTER'S ESCAPE FROM L.A.
Pendleton, Austin
ASSOCIATE, THE
MIRROR HAS TWO FACES, THE
PROPRIETOR, THE
SGT. BILKO
2 DAYS IN THE VALLEY
TWO MUCH
Pendleton, Sha-ri
UNKNOWN ORIGIN
Penkov, Nikolai
BURIAL OF THE RATS
Penn, Arthur
PERSONAL JOURNEY WITH MARTIN SCORSESE THROUGH AMERICAN MOVIES, A
Penn, Chris
FIST OF THE NORTH STAR
FUNERAL, THE
MULHOLLAND FALLS
UNDER THE HULA MOON
Penner, Jonathan
DOWN PERISCOPE
LAST SUPPER, THE
Penner, Ralph
ABUSE
Pennington, Jessica
ED
Penry-Jones, Rupert
COLD COMFORT FARM
Penuel, Pete
MY FELLOW AMERICANS
Pepper, Leah
BED OF ROSES
Peragine, Antoinette
. . . AT FIRST SIGHT
Peralta, Diego
SILENCE OF NETO, THE
Peralta, Oscar
HOSTILE INTENTIONS
Percival, Chaille
THAT THING YOU DO!
Percival, Michael
101 DALMATIANS
Pere, Wayne
EYE FOR AN EYE
Pereira, Christian
MACHINE, THE
Perella, Marco
LONE STAR
MAN WITH THE PERFECT SWING, THE
TUSKEGEE AIRMEN, THE
Perelman, Jessica
AMERICAN STRAYS
Perenski, Tony
TEXAS CHAINSAW MASSACRE: THE NEXT GENERATION
Perez, George
TIN CUP
Perez, Jesse
KAZAAM
Perez, Jose
OFF AND RUNNING
Perez, Krystal
SMALL WONDERS
Perez, Luis Martin
EVERYONE SAYS I LOVE YOU
EVERYONE SAYS I LOVE YOU
Perez, Manny
COURAGE UNDER FIRE
Perez, Miguel
UP CLOSE AND PERSONAL
Perez, Pierre
LES VOLEURS
Perez, Roberto
LIVE WIRE: HUMAN TIMEBOMB
Perez, Vincent
CROW: CITY OF ANGELS, THE
Perkins, Clare
SECRETS & LIES
Perkins, Jennifer
DEAR GOD
Perkins, Millie
CHAMBER, THE
HARVEST OF FIRE
NECRONOMICON: BOOK OF THE DEAD
Perl, Orli
UNDER THE DOMIM TREE
Perlich, Max
BEAUTIFUL GIRLS
GRAVE, THE
HOMEWARD BOUND II: LOST IN SAN FRANCISCO
Perlin, Linda
NORMAL LIFE
Perlman, Itzhak
EVERYONE SAYS I LOVE YOU
SMALL WONDERS
Perlman, Navah
EVERYONE SAYS I LOVE YOU

Perlman, Rhea
CARPOOL
MATILDA
SUNSET PARK
Perlman, Ron
ISLAND OF DR. MOREAU, THE
LAST SUPPER, THE
MR. STITCH
PHANTOM 2040: THE GHOST WHO WALKS
Perman, Mark
FIRST WIVES CLUB, THE
Perra, J.W.
HEAD OF THE FAMILY
Perri, Paul
FUNERAL, THE
HELLRAISER: BLOODLINE
Perrier, Jean-Francois
LA CEREMONIE
Perrin, Anelique
PHAT BEACH
Perrineau, Harold
FLIRT
WILLIAM SHAKESPEARE'S ROMEO + JULIET
Perrino, Joe
JUROR, THE
SLEEPERS
Perron, Fred
HAPPY GILMORE
Perrone, David
JOHN CARPENTER'S ESCAPE FROM L.A.
Perrotta, Toni
DUNSTON CHECKS IN
Perry, Bruce
MERLIN'S SHOP OF MAGICAL WONDERS
Perry, Connie
CELTIC PRIDE
Perry, Elliot
EDDIE
Perry, Felton
SWEEPER, THE
Perry, Io
HIGH SCHOOL HIGH
Perry, John Bennett
EVENING STAR, THE
INDEPENDENCE DAY
Perry Jr., Ernest
DUNSTON CHECKS IN
SKIN
Perry, Kate
SOME MOTHER'S SON
Perry, Luke
AMERICAN STRAYS
NORMAL LIFE
Perry, Marilyn Sue
DON'T LET YOUR MEAT LOAF
Perry, Pamela
FINAL CUT, THE
Perry, Sean
DADETOWN
Perry, Virginia
PUBLIC ACCESS
Perthold, Sabine
FLAMING EARS
Pertwee, Sean
SHOPPING
Pesce, Frank
ORIGINAL GANGSTAS
Pesci, Lori
SANDMAN, THE
Pesko, David
BAD LOVE
Petchlor, Chatpong "Jim"
PHANTOM, THE
Pete Escovedo with the New Morty Show
JACK
Peterman, Melissa
FARGO
Peters, Austin
PHANTOM, THE
Peters, Brock
GHOSTS OF MISSISSIPPI
Peters, Daniel Joe
BLACK SHEEP
Peters, Jeremy
COLD COMFORT FARM
Peters, John
101 DALMATIANS
Peters, Lance
PROTEUS
Peters, Robert
MULHOLLAND FALLS
Peters, Roberta
CITY HALL
Peters, Wendi
IN LOVE AND WAR
Petersen, William
FEAR
MULHOLLAND FALLS
Peterson, Brandon Scott
MIRROR, MIRROR III: THE VOYEUR
Peterson, Charles
HYPE!
Peterson, Chris
WHARF RAT, THE
Peterson, Eric
VIRUS
Peterson, Fred
LOOKING FOR TROUBLE
Peterson, Gunnar
MY FELLOW AMERICANS
Peterson, Jennifer
DEAR GOD
Peterson, Kimberlee
HOMECOMING
Peterson, Paul
ABUSE
Peterson, Roger
MARS ATTACKS!
Petersson, Soren
CHILDREN OF NOISY VILLAGE, THE
Petifer, Brian
MIDWINTER'S TALE, A
Petit-Jacques, Isabelle
RIDICULE
Peto, Fanni
RASPUTIN
Petracci, Bob
ARRIVAL, THE
Petri, Suzanne
EVIL HAS A FACE
Petrocelli, Antonio
WHO KILLED PASOLINI?
Petrone, Shana
EXIT
Petrov, Misho
GIRLFRIENDS
Petrucci, Maria
IN LOVE AND WAR
Petrucci, Massimiliano
WHO KILLED PASOLINI?
Petter III, Stanley D.
NUTTY PROFESSOR, THE
Pettet, Kristen
EVERYONE SAYS I LOVE YOU
Petti, John
MURDERED INNOCENCE
Pettiet, Christopher
BOYS
CARRIED AWAY
Pettit, Mark
MADAGASCAR SKIN
Petty, Ross
EXTREME MEASURES
Petursdottir, Bryndis
VIKING SAGAS, THE
Petzoldt, Paul
FIRE ON THE MOUNTAIN
Peyrelon, Michel
VISITORS, THE
Peyser, Penny
LATE SHIFT, THE
Pfaff, Brent
BODY COUNT
Pfeifer, Chuck
BASQUIAT
Pfeifer, Friedl
FIRE ON THE MOUNTAIN
Pfeiffer, Bryan
MAN WITH A PLAN
Pfeiffer, Dedee
UP CLOSE AND PERSONAL
Pfeiffer, Michaela
BROTHER OF SLEEP
Pfeiffer, Michelle
ONE FINE DAY
TO GILLIAN ON HER 37TH BIRTHDAY
UP CLOSE AND PERSONAL
Pfeiffer, Todd
DEAD MAN
Pflieger, Jean
SERIAL KILLER
Pham, Thi
MAN WITH THE PERFECT SWING, THE
Phares, Rick
HEAD OF THE FAMILY
Phelan, Anthony
TUNNEL VISION
Phelan, David
MISSION: IMPOSSIBLE
Phelan, Walter
FROM DUSK TILL DAWN
Phelps, David
DADETOWN
TRUTH ABOUT CATS AND DOGS, THE
Phifer, Mekhi
HIGH SCHOOL HIGH
TUSKEGEE AIRMEN, THE
Philbin, Regis
OPEN SEASON
Phillip, Alain
MAXIMUM RISK
Phillippe, Ryan
LIFEFORM
WHITE SQUALL
Phillips, Angie
MANNY & LO
Phillips, Bill
SWINGERS
Phillips, Bruce
ALEX
Phillips, Don
LONE STAR
Phillips, Jeff
INDEPENDENCE DAY
Phillips, Jo
PHANTOM, THE
Phillips Jr., Don
BOTTLE ROCKET
Phillips, Julianne
BIG BULLY
WHERE'S THE MONEY, NOREEN?
Phillips, Karen
BEAVIS AND BUTT-HEAD DO AMERICA
Phillips, Lauren Leigh
FAMILY THING, A
Phillips, Leslie
AUGUST

Phillips, Leslie Ann
TALES FROM THE CRYPT PRESENTS BORDELLO OF BLOOD
Phillips, Lou Diamond
COURAGE UNDER FIRE
HOURGLASS
UNDERTOW
WHARF RAT, THE
Phillips, Madelon
MERLIN'S SHOP OF MAGICAL WONDERS
Phillips, Martin
MICHAEL COLLINS
Phillips, Neville
JOSEPH CONRAD'S THE SECRET AGENT
101 DALMATIANS
Phillips, Peg
HOW THE WEST WAS FUN
Phillips, Rod
CHAMBER, THE
Phillips, Rodger L.
ANGELA
Phillips, Sarah
SHOPPING
Phills, Bobby
EDDIE
Philson, Ava P.
LAST DANCE
Phuvan, Ann
SGT. KABUKIMAN N.Y.P.D.
Piamonti, Pee Wee
SPY HARD
Pianeta, Rosa
WHO KILLED PASOLINI?
Piatgorsky, Sacha
CHASING BUTTERFLIES
Picardo, Robert
OUT THERE
STAR TREK: FIRST CONTACT
Picatto, Alexandra
COLONY, THE
Piccirillo, Mike
THAT THING YOU DO!
Pichler, Joe
FAN, THE
Pickens, David
TUSKEGEE AIRMEN, THE
Pickens, Jimmy Ray
COURAGE UNDER FIRE
Pickens Jr., James
GHOSTS OF MISSISSIPPI
SHARON'S SECRET
SLEEPERS
Picker, Josh
ALEX
Pickett, Blaine
PEOPLE VS. LARRY FLYNT, THE
Pickett, Blake
THEY BITE
Pickett, Cindy
PAINTED HERO
Pickett, Jay
RUMPELSTILTSKIN
Pickett, Tom
TALES FROM THE CRYPT PRESENTS BORDELLO OF BLOOD
Pickles, Christina
GRACE OF MY HEART
WILLIAM SHAKESPEARE'S ROMEO + JULIET
Pickren, Richard
EVIL HAS A FACE
Picoy, Kane
JAG
Piddington, Jerry
BLOODSPORT II: THE NEXT KUMITE
Piddock, James
MULTIPLICITY
Piddock, Jim
INDEPENDENCE DAY
Pieczka, Franciszek
MOTHER OF KINGS
Pieczynski, Krzysztof
CHAIN REACTION
Piedimonte, Andrea
EVERYONE SAYS I LOVE YOU
Pieiller, Jacques
THREE LIVES AND ONLY ONE DEATH
Piemonte, Pee Wee
BARB WIRE
Pienkoski, Brian
DADETOWN
Pieraccini, Carmen
SMALL FACES
Pierce, Brock
FIRST KID
Pierce, Denney
REDEMPTION: KICKBOXER 5
Pierce, Scott
LAST MAN STANDING
Pierce, Tony
BIG BULLY
Pierce, Wendell
GET ON THE BUS
SLEEPERS
Pierpoint, Eric
LITTLE WITCHES
Pierre, Herve
HORSEMAN ON THE ROOF
Pierrot, Frederic
LAND AND FREEDOM
Piersig, Max
IRON EAGLE IV
Pietri, Frank
EVERYONE SAYS I LOVE YOU
Pietropinto, Angela
WELCOME TO THE DOLLHOUSE
Pilato, Joseph
DEMOLITIONIST, THE
FATALLY YOURS
Pilato, Timothy
ED'S NEXT MOVE
Pilavin, Barbara
BAD LOVE
Pileggi, Mitch
RAVENHAWK
Pillet, Marie
RIDICULE
Pillsbury, Drew
MULHOLLAND FALLS
Pinard, Miki-Lou
MADAME BUTTERFLY
Pinchot, Bronson
COURAGE UNDER FIRE
FIRST WIVES CLUB, THE
IT'S MY PARTY
Pinckes, Craig
CHAMBER, THE
Pine, Larry
BEFORE AND AFTER
GIRL 6
Pine, Robert
INDEPENDENCE DAY
Pinette, John
DEAR GOD
Pingleton, Susan
JERRY MAGUIRE
Pingue, Joe
MAXIMUM RISK
Pinkett, Jada
NUTTY PROFESSOR, THE
SET IT OFF
Pinkham, Sheila
CRUCIBLE, THE
Pinney, Patrick
HUNCHBACK OF NOTRE DAME, THE
Pino, Mariangelo
. . . AT FIRST SIGHT
Pinsent, Leah
VIRUS
Pinsolle, Pauline
LITTLE INDIAN, BIG CITY
Pinto, Johnny
OFF AND RUNNING
Pionilla, Nadja
RACE THE SUN
Piperno, Giacomo
WHO KILLED PASOLINI?
Pire, Felix A.
DEAR GOD
IT'S MY PARTY
Pirelli, Gregory
FUNERAL, THE
Piretti, Walter
WHO KILLED PASOLINI?
Pirkle, Joan
CITIZEN RUTH
Pirkle, Mac
PEOPLE VS. LARRY FLYNT, THE
Pirnie, Alex
THEY BITE
Piro, Salvatore
SLEEPERS
Piro, Sandro
STAR MAKER, THE
Piros, Joanna
UNFORGETTABLE
Pisana, Jennifer
BOGUS
LONG KISS GOODNIGHT, THE
Pisano, Jennifer
WHEN THE BULLET HITS THE BONE
Pisarenkov, Albert
EDDIE
Piscopo, Joe
OPEN SEASON
TWO-BITS & PEPPER
Pisier, Marie-France
FRANCOIS TRUFFAUT: STOLEN PORTRAITS
Pitillo, Maria
DEAR GOD
Pitoniak, Anne
BED OF ROSES
Pitt, Brad
SLEEPERS
Pitta, Zsanne
WELCOME TO THE DOLLHOUSE
Pitts, Jane
THEY BITE
Pitts, Ron
BIRDCAGE, THE
FAN, THE
INDEPENDENCE DAY
Pitts, Ronald
DEAD TO RIGHTS
Pittu, David
ED'S NEXT MOVE
Piven, Byrne
LOVER'S KNOT
WAVELENGTH
Piven, Jeremy
LARGER THAN LIFE
WAVELENGTH
Piyo
ARRIVAL, THE
Pizza, Cathy
BLONDES HAVE MORE GUNS
Pizzuti, Riccardo
SONS OF TRINITY
Place, Mary Kay
CITIZEN RUTH
MANNY & LO

Place, Patricia
BLACK SHEEP
Plana, Tony
LONE STAR
PRIMAL FEAR
Planche, Val
PORTRAITS OF A KILLER
Planchon, Roger
LA COMEDIE-FRANCAISE OU L'AMOUR JOUE
Plank, Scott
AMERICAN STRAYS
SAINTS AND SINNERS
Plante, Carol Ann
AMANDA AND THE ALIEN
Platt, Howard
NORMA JEAN AND MARILYN
ROCK, THE
Platt, Oliver
EXECUTIVE DECISION
TIME TO KILL, A
Platts, Diana
DARKMAN III: DIE DARKMAN DIE
Plaxin, Eduard
BURIAL OF THE RATS
Plimpton, Eufemia
SWINGERS
Plimpton, George
WHEN WE WERE KINGS
Plimpton, Martha
BEAUTIFUL GIRLS
I SHOT ANDY WARHOL
I'M NOT RAPPAPORT
Plon, Harold
MULTIPLICITY
Plon, Richard
MULTIPLICITY
Plovtsev, Alexander
RASPUTIN
Plowright, Joan
JANE EYRE
MR. WRONG
101 DALMATIANS
SURVIVING PICASSO
Plummer, Amanda
BUTTERFLY KISS
FINAL CUT, THE
FREEWAY
Plummer, Glenn
SUBSTITUTE, THE
UP CLOSE AND PERSONAL
Pniewski, Mike
PEOPLE VS. LARRY FLYNT, THE
TIME TO KILL, A
Podemski, Jennifer
BOGUS
Podhursky, Zdenek
ADVENTURES OF PINOCCHIO, THE
Podowski, Debbie
SURGEON, THE
Podwal, Michael
EYE FOR AN EYE
Pohlkotte, Tanya
NATIONAL LAMPOON'S FAVORITE DEADLY SINS
Poindexter, Jeris Lee
DEAR GOD
SET IT OFF
Poindexter, Larry
VIRTUAL COMBAT
Pointer, Chandra
DON'T LET YOUR MEAT LOAF
Pointer, Mike
IT'S MY PARTY
Pointer, Priscilla
CARRIED AWAY
Poitier, Pam
ABUSE
Polanco, Iraida
RANSOM
Polata, Ladislav
DELTA OF VENUS
Poletti, Stephen
BODY OF INFLUENCE 2
Polhamus, Boyd
PAINTED HERO
Polhemus, Josiah
TRUTH ABOUT CATS AND DOGS, THE
Polis, Joel
IT'S MY PARTY
SERIAL KILLER
Polisensky, Karel
DELTA OF VENUS
Polish, Mark
HELLRAISER: BLOODLINE
Polish, Michael
HELLRAISER: BLOODLINE
Polito, Jon
HOMEWARD BOUND II: LOST IN SAN FRANCISCO
JUST YOUR LUCK
Polito, Monica
SLEEPERS
Polito, Nino
EYE FOR AN EYE
Polizos, Vic
ERASER
Pollack, Yvonne
DEAR GOD
Pollak, Kevin
CHAMELEON
HOUSE ARREST
THAT THING YOU DO!
Pollan, Claire
FRIEND OF THE FAMILY 2
Pollard, Michael J.
MAD DOG TIME
Polley, Michael
SUGARTIME
Pollick, Marlon
LOOKING FOR RICHARD
Pollio, Silvio
ANNIE O
Pollock, Alexander
BIG BULLY
Polo, Miro
UNKNOWN ORIGIN
Polo, Teri
ARRIVAL, THE
Poloa, Pouono M.
BLOODSPORT II: THE NEXT KUMITE
Pols, Ed
CROCODILES IN AMSTERDAM
Polson, Larry
EYE FOR AN EYE
Poluyan, Alexi
CHEKIST, THE
Polycarpou, Peter
EVITA
Polyi, Stevo
MR. STITCH
Polynice, Olden
EDDIE
Pomerantz, Edward
CAUGHT
Pomerantz, Marnie
PALLBEARER, THE
Pomeroy, William
FRIGHTENERS, THE
Pompili, Manuele
MILLE BOLLE BLU
Poncela, Eusebio
SHADOW YOU SOON WILL BE, A
Pond, Rachel
EDDIE
Ponds, Jim
BOTTLE ROCKET
Poneman, Jonathan
HYPE!
Ponte, John Negro
RACE THE SUN
Pontecorvo, Gillo
STUPIDS, THE
Pontidis, Telly
WELCOME TO THE DOLLHOUSE
Pontrelli, John D.
BIRDCAGE, THE
Pooley, Olaf
BEASTMASTER 3: THE EYE OF BRAXUS
Poor, Bray
GIRL 6
Pop, Iggy
CROW: CITY OF ANGELS, THE
DEAD MAN
Pope, Francis
SHOPPING
Pope, Howard
FRISK
Pope, Peggy
SUBSTITUTE, THE
Popescu, Valentin
SERPENT'S LAIR
Popper, John
KINGPIN
Poppick, Eric
NORMA JEAN AND MARILYN
Poppy
MARS ATTACKS!
Porcaro, Reno
IN LOVE AND WAR
Porfido, Steven
BIRDCAGE, THE
Porster, Mary
NORMA JEAN AND MARILYN
Port, George
FRIGHTENERS, THE
Porter, Charles
CELTIC PRIDE
Porter, Duane
REDEMPTION: KICKBOXER 5
Porter, Katherine Anne
PORTRAIT OF A LADY, THE
Porter, Ken
TWO FRIENDS
Porter, Linda
TRUTH ABOUT CATS AND DOGS, THE
Porter, Russell B.
ANNIE O
Porter, Steven M.
NATIONAL LAMPOON'S FAVORITE DEADLY SINS
Portero, Paco
LITTLE INDIAN, BIG CITY
Portillo, Zoila
SILENCE OF NETO, THE
Portman, Natalie
BEAUTIFUL GIRLS
EVERYONE SAYS I LOVE YOU
MARS ATTACKS!
Portnow, Richard
BOGUS
DONOR UNKNOWN
Porto, Lidia
LARRY MCMURTRY'S STREETS OF LAREDO
Portrait
GRACE OF MY HEART
Posey, Parker
BASQUIAT
FLIRT
FRISK

Pospisil, Eric
BIG BULLY
UNFORGETTABLE
Post, Ryan
PEOPLE VS. LARRY FLYNT, THE
Poster, Tom
BLACK OUT
YESTERDAY'S TARGET
Postlethwaite, Pete
DRAGONHEART
JAMES AND THE GIANT PEACH
SUITE 16
WILLIAM SHAKESPEARE'S ROMEO + JULIET
Potenza, Josephine
DADETOWN
Potter, Carol
TIGER HEART
Potter, Jay
BEFORE AND AFTER
Potter, Madeleine
HARVEST OF FIRE
SPELLBREAKER: SECRET OF THE LEPRECHAUNS
Potter, Miles
SUGARTIME
Potter, Monica
BULLETPROOF
Potter, Tim
YOUNG POISONER'S HANDBOOK, THE
Potts, Tony
RANSOM
Potworowska, Mimi
MARY REILLY
MISSION: IMPOSSIBLE
Pouget, Ely
LAWNMOWER MAN 2: BEYOND CYBERSPACE
Poujol, Olivier
RENDEZVOUS IN PARIS
Poulas, Mitch
LOVE IS ALL THERE IS
Poulis, Jeffrey W.
FLY AWAY HOME
Poulsen, Rob
PHANTOM 2040: THE GHOST WHO WALKS
Pouncie, Ocie
MY FELLOW AMERICANS
Poupaud, Melvil
THREE LIVES AND ONLY ONE DEATH
Poustie, Greg
WARHEAD
Powell, Amy
BIRDCAGE, THE
Powell, Brittney
FLED
THAT THING YOU DO!
Powell, Charles
SCREAMERS
Powell, Gary
MICHAEL COLLINS
Powell, Randy
TALKING ABOUT SEX
Power, Peter
TUNNEL VISION
Powers, Alexandra
LAST MAN STANDING
Powers, Shane
BLACK SCORPION
Powledge, Dave
EDIE & PEN
RAGE
Pownall, Leon
HOW THE WEST WAS FUN
Pozzi, Claudia
WHO KILLED PASOLINI?

Prada, Anthony
MA SAISON PREFEREE
Prado, Toribio
DUNSTON CHECKS IN
Prael, Bill
CHILDREN OF THE CORN: THE GATHERING
Prairie, Timmy
LOOKING FOR RICHARD
Prater, Will
PHENOMENON
Prather, Vrenika
REDEMPTION: KICKBOXER 5
Prati, Sandro
CEMETERY MAN
Prats, Jaime
LAND AND FREEDOM
Prats, Jose Luis
LAND AND FREEDOM
Pratt, Jane
KINGPIN
Pratt, Lisa
OVER THE WIRE
Pratt, Mitzie
RANSOM
Pratt, Ramya
GIRLS TOWN
Pratt, Susan
BEFORE AND AFTER
Praxel, Karen
THAT THING YOU DO!
Preddy, Robby
FLED
Preler, Ross
WARHEAD
Prendergast, Shaun
MIDWINTER'S TALE, A
Prentice, Ernie
GIRL FROM MARS, THE
HOMEWARD BOUND II: LOST IN SAN FRANCISCO
Prescott, Jennifer
CITY HALL
Presha, Krishna
PREACHER'S WIFE, THE
Presnell, Harve
CHAMBER, THE
FARGO
LARGER THAN LIFE
WHOLE WIDE WORLD, THE
Press, Graham
TERMINAL IMPACT
Pressley, Brenda
CITY HALL
Pressman, David
INDEPENDENCE DAY
Pressman, Lawrence
LATE SHIFT, THE
SUNCHASER
Preston, J. A.
HARVEST OF FIRE
Preston, Kelly
CITIZEN RUTH
CURDLED
FROM DUSK TILL DAWN
JERRY MAGUIRE
MRS. MUNCK
Preston, Matt
SHOWGIRL MURDERS, THE
Preston, William
CRUCIBLE, THE
I'M NOT RAPPAPORT
Prevost, Nikywa
SOME FOLKS CALL IT A SLING BLADE
Prianti, Judy
SGT. KABUKIMAN N.Y.P.D.
Price, Denise
CHAIN REACTION

Price, Isabel
UNFORGETTABLE
Price, Kevin
MR. ICE CREAM MAN
Price, Lloyd
WHEN WE WERE KINGS
Price, Nicole
EDDIE
Price, Richard
RANSOM
Price, Sue
NEMESIS III: PREY HARDER
Price, Tom
HYPE!
Price, Val P.
PARADISE LOST: THE CHILD MURDERS AT ROBIN HOOD HILLS
Primeau, Suzanne
DARKMAN III: DIE DARKMAN DIE
Prince, Daisy
EVERYONE SAYS I LOVE YOU
Prince, Faith
BIG BULLY
Prince, Steven Chester
LARRY MCMURTRY'S STREETS OF LAREDO
Prine, Andrew
SERIAL KILLER
Prinze Jr., Freddie
TO GILLIAN ON HER 37TH BIRTHDAY
Procanik, Jerry
HEAVEN'S PRISONERS
Procter, Emily
JERRY MAGUIRE
Proctor, Kelly
FOR THE MOMENT
Proctor, Phil
BIO-DOME
Proctor, Toby
MAN IN THE ATTIC, THE
Proctor, Tom
UNHOOK THE STARS
Proctor, William
BULLETPROOF
Proietti, Gigi
MILLE BOLLE BLU
Props, Rene
POMPATUS OF LOVE, THE
Prosky, Andy
UP CLOSE AND PERSONAL
Prosky, John
NUTTY PROFESSOR, THE
PHANTOM, THE
Prosky, Robert
CHAMBER, THE
ROAD HOME, THE
Proudstar, Jon
BOY CALLED HATE, A
Proval, David
PHANTOM, THE
Provenza, Paul
SHOT, THE
Provenzano II, Danny
SGT. KABUKIMAN N.Y.P.D.
Provvidenti, Pippo
STAR MAKER, THE
Prozzo, Michael
LAST MAN STANDING
Prulhiere, Timi
DEAR GOD
MARS ATTACKS!
Pryce, Jonathan
EVITA
SHOPPING
Pryeres, Demitri
FUNERAL, THE
Pryor, Ashlee Jordan
COURAGE UNDER FIRE

Pryor, Jim
DADETOWN
Pryor, Nicholas
CHAMBER, THE
EXECUTIVE DECISION
Pryor, Richard
MAD DOG TIME
Prysor, Manon
HEDD WYNN
Pufah, Jeff
MOTHER NIGHT
Pugh, Rhys
ZARKORR! THE INVADER
Pugh, Willard
UNDER THE HULA MOON
Pugliesi, Antonello
STAR MAKER, THE
Pugsley, Don
LETTER TO MY KILLER
Pujol, Eric
HATE
Pujol, Martine
MAXIMUM RISK
Pulitzer, C.C.
RATTLED
Pulkkinen, Jane
CRUCIBLE, THE
Pullman, Bill
INDEPENDENCE DAY
MR. WRONG
Pulman, Scott
ONE MAN'S JUSTICE
Punzo, Patrizia
CEMETERY MAN
Pupella, Massimo
STAR MAKER, THE
Pupo, Jorge
BITTER SUGAR
Purcell, Lee
LONG ROAD HOME, THE
Purdy-Green, Carolyn
ARRIVAL, THE
Purefoy, Shaun
PREACHER'S WIFE, THE
Puri, Om
GHOST AND THE DARKNESS, THE
TARGET
Purrer, Ursula
FLAMING EARS
Purves-Smith, Esther
PORTRAITS OF A KILLER
Pustil, Jeff
IRON EAGLE IV
TAILS YOU LIVE, HEADS YOU'RE DEAD
Putnam, George
INDEPENDENCE DAY
Puzova, Elena
BURIAL OF THE RATS
Pyatkiv, Alexander
BURIAL OF THE RATS
Qissi, Abdel
QUEST, THE
Quaid, Dennis
DRAGONHEART
Quaid, Randy
INDEPENDENCE DAY
KINGPIN
LARRY MCMURTRY'S STREETS OF LAREDO
LAST DANCE
MOONSHINE HIGHWAY
WOMAN UNDONE, A
Quain, Loray
HEAD OF THE FAMILY
Quarry, Michael
DON'T LET YOUR MEAT LOAF
Quarterman, Saundra
FAMILY THING, A
Quarzell, Rocco
IN LOVE AND WAR
Quatrocchi, Rori
STAR MAKER, THE
Queen, Bronwyn
TALKING ABOUT SEX
Queen Latifah
SET IT OFF
Queensberry, Ann
JANE EYRE
Queffelec, Ed
MAXIMUM RISK
Quercia, Boris
JOHNNY 100 PESOS
Queypo, Kalani
JUROR, THE
Quezaza, Marco
JUROR, THE
Quick, Diana
RASPUTIN
Quigley, Bernadette
BEFORE AND AFTER
Quigley, Gerry
EXTREME MEASURES
HARRIET THE SPY
WHERE'S THE MONEY, NOREEN?
Quigley, Linnea
BURIAL OF THE RATS
Quigley, Mary
GALAXIES ARE COLLIDING
Quilligan, Veronica
HALFMOON
Quinlan, Ian
CITY HALL
Quinn, Aidan
HAUNTED
LOOKING FOR RICHARD
MICHAEL COLLINS
Quinn, Christopher J.
MERCY
Quinn, Danielle
MOTHER
Quinn, Glenn
LIVE NUDE GIRLS
Quinn, J.C.
GETTING AWAY WITH MURDER
Quinn, James W.
PINOCCHIO'S REVENGE
Quinn, John Michael
ENTERTAINING ANGELS: THE DOROTHY DAY STORY
Quinn, Ken
STUPIDS, THE
Quinn, Mariah
I SHOT ANDY WARHOL
Quinn, Marian
HEAVY
Quinn, Patrice Pitman
FAMILY THING, A
Quinn, Patrick Neil
FULL BODY MASSAGE
Quintana, Miguel
LAND AND FREEDOM
Quintero, Carlos
SOLO
Rabattidevalle, Laurence
SUITE 16
Rabbit, Johnny
POISON IVY 2: LILY
Raci, Paul
GLIMMER MAN, THE
Racicot, Jody
MOONSHINE HIGHWAY
Racki, Branko
MAXIMUM RISK
Racki, Robert
ELECTRA
WHERE'S THE MONEY, NOREEN?
Rader-Duval, Dean
LAST MAN STANDING
Radick, Jeremy
GIRL FROM MARS, THE
Radinger, Sian
HAMLET
Radoaca, Constantin
MAGIC IN THE MIRROR
Radon, Peter
WHARF RAT, THE
Rae, Bette
MOTHER
Rae, Cassidy
NATIONAL LAMPOON'S FAVORITE DEADLY SINS
Raeder, Louise
CHILDREN OF NOISY VILLAGE, THE
Rafalowicz, Alex
SHINE
Rafferty, Wendell
SLING BLADE
Raffin, Gina
CHAIN REACTION
Rafraf, Zohra
SILENCES OF THE PALACE, THE
Ragas, Roef
BREAKING THE WAVES
Ragno, Angela
OF LOVE AND SHADOWS
Ragno, Joseph
DAYLIGHT
PHANTOM, THE
Ragsdale, William
NATIONAL LAMPOON'S FAVORITE DEADLY SINS
Rahman, Mujibur
EDDIE
IF LUCY FELL
Rail, Jason
FRISK
Railsback, Steve
BARB WIRE
Raimi, Ted
SHOT, THE
Rajab, Robert Ben
ROCK, THE
Rajczi, Adrienne
RASPUTIN
Rajkumar, Stephen
ORIGINAL SINS
Rajskub, Mary Lynn
TRUTH ABOUT CATS AND DOGS, THE
Rakenzes, Mark
ARRIVAL, THE
Rakerd, Cliff
FARGO
Rallo, Aniceto
LAND AND FREEDOM
Ralph, Sheryl Lee
BOGUS
LOVER'S KNOT
Rambis, Kurt
EDDIE
Rameau, Patrick
MAN BY THE SHORE, THE
Ramer, Henry
SCREAMERS
Ramirez, Efren
KAZAAM
Ramirez, Jesus
LONE STAR
Ramirez, Juan
CHAIN REACTION
Ramirez, Roberto Roman
PEOPLE VS. LARRY FLYNT, THE
Ramon, Eulalia
OUTRAGE

Ramos, Armando
SHOOTFIGHTER 2: KILL OR BE KILLED!
Ramos, Danny
MIDNIGHT DANCERS
Ramos, Jennifer
GIRL 6
Ramos, Loyda
RICH MAN'S WIFE, THE
Ramos, Luis Antonio
HOSTILE INTENTIONS
SAWBONES
Ramos, Rudy
DANGEROUS PASSION
Ramos, Sophia
GIRLFRIENDS
Ramsay, Anne
FINAL CUT, THE
Ramsay, Bruce
CURDLED
HELLRAISER: BLOODLINE
Ramsey, Ben "Killa"
ZARKORR! THE INVADER
Ramsey, David
NUTTY PROFESSOR, THE
VERY BRADY SEQUEL, A
Ramsey, Kennya J.
THAT THING YOU DO!
Ramsey, Melanie
HAMLET
Ramsey, Remak
TRUMAN
Ranallo, Nicole
BEAUTIFUL GIRLS
Ranaszkiewicz, Julia
DAENS
Ranaudo, Gianna
FAITHFUL
Randall, Shannon
BODY OF INFLUENCE 2
Randazzo, Steven
BASQUIAT
FAITHFUL
TREES LOUNGE
WHARF RAT, THE
Randle, Kenneth
NATIONAL LAMPOON'S FAVORITE DEADLY SINS
Randle, Scott
DON'T BE A MENACE TO SOUTH CENTRAL WHILE DRINKING YOUR JUICE IN THE HOOD
Randle, Theresa
GIRL 6
SPACE JAM
Randolph, Chase
SHOOTFIGHTER 2: KILL OR BE KILLED!
Ranftl, Sarina L.
DEAR GOD
Rangel, Paco
LAND AND FREEDOM
Rankin, Claire
TWO IF BY SEA
Ransom, Tim
COURAGE UNDER FIRE
Raoul, Dale
DEATH BENEFIT
NATIONAL LAMPOON'S FAVORITE DEADLY SINS
Rapaport, Michael
BEAUTIFUL GIRLS
Raphael, Sally Jessy
ASSOCIATE, THE
Rapp, Anthony
ASSAULT AT WEST POINT
TWISTER
Rappaport, Michael
PALLBEARER, THE
Rappaport, Sheeri
LITTLE WITCHES
Rappazo, Carmela
SGT. BILKO
Rasche, David
DEAD WEEKEND
OUT THERE
PIE IN THE SKY
Rashad, Phylicia
ONCE UPON A TIME . . . WHEN WE WERE COLORED
Rasicot, Dr. James
PARADISE LOST: THE CHILD MURDERS AT ROBIN HOOD HILLS
Raskin, Mindy Lee
IN LOVE AND WAR
Raskin, Paul
HAPPY GILMORE
Rasmussen, Castagna
PUBLIC ENEMIES
Rasner, Robert L.
CABLE GUY, THE
Raso, Michael L.
POLYMORPH
Ratchford, Jeremy
FLY AWAY HOME
MOONSHINE HIGHWAY
STUPIDS, THE
WHERE'S THE MONEY, NOREEN?
Rathburn, Roger
UP CLOSE AND PERSONAL
Ratliff, Elden
D3: THE MIGHTY DUCKS
FOXFIRE
Ratner, Ben
BREACH OF TRUST
Rauch, Siegfried
SONS OF TRINITY
Rauscher, Aurore
RENDEZVOUS IN PARIS
Rauth, Heloise
HATE
Ravelo, Caridad
BITTER SUGAR
CURDLED
Raven, Elsa
ONE NIGHT STAND
Ravera, Gina
GET ON THE BUS
Ravesteijn, Thyrza
ANTONIA'S LINE
Rawlins, Adrian
BREAKING THE WAVES
Ray, Connie
MY FELLOW AMERICANS
VERY BRADY SEQUEL, A
Ray, Fred Olen
FUGITIVE RAGE
Ray, Gene Anthony
EDDIE
Ray, Mickey
VIRTUAL ENCOUNTERS
Ray, Nicholas
PERSONAL JOURNEY WITH MARTIN SCORSESE THROUGH AMERICAN MOVIES, A
Ray, William Earl
TUSKEGEE AIRMEN, THE
Rayford, Ernest
LET'S GET BIZZEE
Raymond, Didier
LES VOLEURS
Raymond, Sid
TWO MUCH
Raymond, Simmi
BOGUS
Rea, Louise
COLD COMFORT FARM
Rea, Stephen
MICHAEL COLLINS
Read, Andrew
JACK & SARAH
Read, James
HARVEST OF FIRE
Read, Kimberly
FUGITIVE RAGE
Read, Peter
JOHNNY SHORTWAVE
Reader, Kim
TALKING ABOUT SEX
Readman, Andrew
101 DALMATIANS
Ready, Paul
ANGELS AND INSECTS
Reagan, Ronald
BERKELEY IN THE 60S
Reagh, Juliet
TALES FROM THE CRYPT PRESENTS BORDELLO OF BLOOD
Reardon, Mary
CRUCIBLE, THE
Rebhorn, James
IF LUCY FELL
INDEPENDENCE DAY
MY FELLOW AMERICANS
UP CLOSE AND PERSONAL
WHITE SQUALL
Rector, Jeff
FRIEND OF THE FAMILY 2
Redding, Carl S.
RANSOM
Redding, Lynne
RANSOM
Reddy, Brian
BIRDCAGE, THE
PRIMAL FEAR
Reddy, Teddy
GHOST AND THE DARKNESS, THE
Redfern, Ross
CURTIS'S CHARM
Redford, Robert
UP CLOSE AND PERSONAL
Redgate, Sheila
WATCH ME
Redglare, Rockets
BASQUIAT
TREES LOUNGE
Redgrave, Lynn
SHINE
Redgrave, Vanessa
LOOKING FOR RICHARD
MISSION: IMPOSSIBLE
WIND IN THE WILLOWS, THE
Redhouse, Thomas
BLACK DAY BLUE NIGHT
Redman, Christopher
KIDS IN THE HALL: BRAIN CANDY
Redman, Clare
ANGELS AND INSECTS
Redman, Joshua
KANSAS CITY
Redmond, Siobhan
CAPTIVES
Redpath, Barbara Lynn
KIDS IN THE HALL: BRAIN CANDY
Redwine, Tim
TWO-BITS & PEPPER
Redwood, John Henry
MR. HOLLAND'S OPUS
Redwood, Manning
AFFAIR, THE
Reece, Joanna
DARKMAN III: DIE DARKMAN DIE
Reed, A. Doran
SUNSET PARK

Reed, Allyson
NORMA JEAN AND MARILYN
Reed, Cindy
MR. ICE CREAM MAN
Reed, Darryl Alan
ONE MAN'S JUSTICE
Reed, Don
DON'T BE A MENACE TO SOUTH CENTRAL WHILE DRINKING YOUR JUICE IN THE HOOD
Reed, Fawn
FIRST KID
KAZAAM
Reed, Jennifer A.
APART FROM HUGH
Reed, Julie
ARRIVAL, THE
Reed, Lucia
DADETOWN
Reed, Oliver
PEOPLE VS. LARRY FLYNT, THE
Reed, Rondi
EYE FOR AN EYE
STREETCAR NAMED DESIRE, A
Reed, Shanna
RATTLED
Rees, Clive
BODY OF INFLUENCE 2
Rees, Jed
FEAR
FINAL CUT, THE
Rees, Roger
SUBSTANCE OF FIRE, THE
Reese, Ahmad
CABLE GUY, THE
DON'T BE A MENACE TO SOUTH CENTRAL WHILE DRINKING YOUR JUICE IN THE HOOD
Reese, Della
THIN LINE BETWEEN LOVE AND HATE, A
Reese, Julianna
HEIDI FLEISS HOLLYWOOD MADAM
Reese, Matt
SANDMAN, THE
Reeves, Altameza
KAZAAM
Reeves, Christine
BEYOND THE CALL
Reeves, Dale
BEAVIS AND BUTT-HEAD DO AMERICA
Reeves, Freddy "Doc Ice"
DON'T LET YOUR MEAT LOAF
Reeves, John
BOYS
Reeves, Keanu
CHAIN REACTION
FEELING MINNESOTA
Reeves, Nania
PURE DANGER
Reeves, Saskia
BUTTERFLY KISS
Reevis, Steven
FARGO
Refoy, Niall
TWO DEATHS
Regan, Mary
GIRLFRIENDS
Regen, Stuart
FOXFIRE
Regev, Gabriel
GETTING AWAY WITH MURDER
Reghanti, Jed
CROSSCUT
Regina, Paul
IT'S MY PARTY
SHARON'S SECRET
Regine, Ed "The Machine"
CELTIC PRIDE

Regis, Ed
SYNTHETIC PLEASURES
Regnery, Jon
DEAD WEEKEND
Reguerraz, Jean Pierre
OF LOVE AND SHADOWS
Regunaga, Leandro
SHADOW YOU SOON WILL BE, A
Reibel, Aladin
SINGLE GIRL, A
Reibel, Steven
OFF AND RUNNING
Reichmeister, Mimi
LITTLE WITCHES
Reid, Adam
KIDS IN THE HALL: BRAIN CANDY
Reid, Eileen
MOLL FLANDERS
Reid, Fiona
BLOOD & DONUTS
BOGUS
Reid, Glenn
DON'T LET YOUR MEAT LOAF
Reid, J.R.
EDDIE
Reid, L'Hua
HEIDI FLEISS HOLLYWOOD MADAM
Reid, Noah
IN LOVE AND WAR
Reid, Phil
HEDD WYNN
Reid, R.D.
HOMECOMING
Reid, Tanya
PHAT BEACH
Reigert, Peter
PIE IN THE SKY
Reighn, Carl Nick
ANGELA
Reilly, Desmond
BREAKING THE WAVES
Reilly, Joanne
SMALL FACES
Reilly, John C.
BOYS
Reilly, Sean
SLEEPERS
Reilly, Thomas J.
JERRY MAGUIRE
Reimers, Monroe
RACE THE SUN
Reiner, Rob
FIRST WIVES CLUB, THE
FOR BETTER OR WORSE
MAD DOG TIME
Reiner, Tracy
THAT THING YOU DO!
Reinger, Scott
EXIT
Reinhardt, Christine
APART FROM HUGH
Reinhardt, Markus
DEATH ARTIST, THE
Reinhold, Judge
WHARF RAT, THE
Reinken, Jim
CITIZEN RUTH
Reis, Michelle
WICKED CITY, THE
Reischel, John
BEWARE: CHILDREN AT PLAY
Reiswig, Isaac
PHENOMENON
Reitzell, Brian
GRACE OF MY HEART
Remar, James
ONE GOOD TURN
PHANTOM, THE
QUEST, THE
SURGEON, THE
Remini, Leah
PHANTOM 2040: THE GHOST WHO WALKS
Remy, Judith
PROPRIETOR, THE
Renaldo, Rique
BAJA
Renard, Carmen
OF LOVE AND SHADOWS
Rendon, Kevin
I SHOT ANDY WARHOL
Renee, Shana
KAZAAM
Renfro, Brad
SLEEPERS
Renko, Serge
RENDEZVOUS IN PARIS
Renna, Melinda
BOTTLE ROCKET
EVENING STAR, THE
Renna, Patrick
SOMETIMES THEY COME BACK . . . AGAIN
Rennard, Deborah
KAZAAM
Renner, Nicholas John
MR. HOLLAND'S OPUS
Rennie, Callum Keith
CURTIS'S CHARM
UNFORGETTABLE
Rennison, Colleen
CARPOOL
UNFORGETTABLE
Reno, Jean
MISSION: IMPOSSIBLE
VISITORS, THE
Reno, Susan
GLIMMER MAN, THE
Renshaw, John
PUBLIC ACCESS
Repo-Martell, Lisa
ENGLISH PATIENT, THE
Restell, Kimberly
HAPPY GILMORE
Reubens, Paul
DUNSTON CHECKS IN
MATILDA
Revach, Zev
QUEST, THE
Revell, Sophie
COLD COMFORT FARM
Revill, Clive
DELTA OF VENUS
Revilla, Raydeen
CABLE GUY, THE
Rey, Jose
PINOCCHIO'S REVENGE
Reyes, Carlos
LITTLE INDIAN, BIG CITY
Reyes Jr., Ernie
WHITE WOLVES II: LEGEND OF THE WILD
Reyes, Julian
BAJA
CABLE GUY, THE
Reyes, Mary Anna
BARB WIRE
Reyes, Pia
FORBIDDEN ZONE: ALIEN ABDUCTION
Reyes, Randy
SOLO
Reyes, Richard
BOTTLE ROCKET
LONE STAR

Reymond, Jacob
HORSEMAN ON THE ROOF
Reynolds, Bob
TUNNEL VISION
Reynolds, Burt
CITIZEN RUTH
MAD DOG TIME
MADDENING, THE
STRIPTEASE
Reynolds, Colleen
GETTING AWAY WITH MURDER
Reynolds, Debbie
MOTHER
Reynolds, James "Hooks"
HEAVEN'S PRISONERS
Reynolds, Marian
DON'T BE A MENACE TO SOUTH CENTRAL WHILE DRINKING YOUR JUICE IN THE HOOD
Reynolds, Michael J.
EXTREME MEASURES
FLY AWAY HOME
Reynolds, Robert
TUNNEL VISION
Reynolds, Ryan
SABRINA, THE TEENAGE WITCH
Reynolds, Simon
EXTREME MEASURES
LOSING CHASE
WHERE'S THE MONEY, NOREEN?
Reynoldson, Rondel
UNFORGETTABLE
Reynoso, Juan "Rambo"
KAZAAM
Rhames, Ving
MISSION: IMPOSSIBLE
STRIPTEASE
Rhapsody
IT'S MY PARTY
Rhea, Alan
SGT. KABUKIMAN N.Y.P.D.
Rhee, Phillip
BEST OF THE BEST 3: NO TURNING BACK
Rheingold, Howard
SYNTHETIC PLEASURES
Rhoades, Michael
SUGARTIME
Rhodes, Michael
MRS. MUNCK
Rhodin, Hannes
EVIL ED
Rhodin, Joel
EVIL ED
Rhodin, Olof
EVIL ED
Rhoze, Tim
ORIGINAL GANGSTAS
Rhyne, John Thomas
TWISTER
Rhyne, Miranda Stuart
ANGELA
WALKING AND TALKING
Rhys-Davies, John
GREAT WHITE HYPE, THE
Riave, Andrea
DESIRE
Ribisi, Giovanni
MIND RIPPER
THAT THING YOU DO!
Rice, Brett
FLED
Rice, Gina
CITY HALL
Rice, Nicholas
STUPIDS, THE
SUGARTIME
Rich, Allan
JACK
NATIONAL LAMPOON'S FAVORITE DEADLY SINS
RICH MAN'S WIFE, THE
TWO MUCH
Rich, Daniella
TREES LOUNGE
Rich, Katie
JAG
Richard, Jean-Louis
FRANCOIS TRUFFAUT: STOLEN PORTRAITS
Richard the Ox
BASQUIAT
Richards, A.J.
SANDMAN, THE
Richards, Ann
FLATTERED
Richards, Dave
ZARKORR! THE INVADER
Richards, George
OFF AND RUNNING
Richards, Joe
TALKING ABOUT SEX
Richards, Keith
ROLLING STONES ROCK-AND-ROLL CIRCUS, THE
Richards, Sal
LOVE IS ALL THERE IS
Richards, Ted
STREET FIGHTER II: THE ANIMATED MOVIE
Richardson, Anna Louise
HOMECOMING
WHERE'S THE MONEY, NOREEN?
Richardson, Burton
REDEMPTION: KICKBOXER 5
Richardson, Dougie
JOHNNY SHORTWAVE
Richardson, Jackie
BOGUS
EXTREME MEASURES
HARRIET THE SPY
MAXIMUM RISK
Richardson, Jay
FUGITIVE RAGE
Richardson, Joely
101 DALMATIANS
Richardson, Kevin
BOY CALLED HATE, A
Richardson, Kevin M.
ALL DOGS GO TO HEAVEN 2
BOUND
Richardson, LaTanya
LONE STAR
Richardson, Lee
TRUMAN
Richardson, Miranda
EVENING STAR, THE
KANSAS CITY
Richardson, Salli
GREAT WHITE HYPE, THE
ONCE UPON A TIME . . . WHEN WE WERE COLORED
Riche, Clive
CEMETERY MAN
Richert, Nick
ONE MAN'S JUSTICE
Richette, Jean-Pierre
LITTLE INDIAN, BIG CITY
Richey, Jeff D.
WAR AT HOME, THE
Richie, Lionel
PREACHER'S WIFE, THE
Richings, Julian
SONG SPINNER, THE
Richman, Jonathan
KINGPIN
Richmond, Krissy
EVERYONE SAYS I LOVE YOU
Richmond, Mitch
EDDIE
Richmond, Werner
MAN WITH THE PERFECT SWING, THE
Richwood, Patrick
DEAR GOD
Rickard, Matthew
IT'S MY PARTY
Rickman, Alan
MICHAEL COLLINS
RASPUTIN
Ricotta, Vincenzo
IN LOVE AND WAR
Riddelle, Frances
IN LOVE AND WAR
Ridder, Nancy Ann
SCREAM
Riddoch, Billy
TRAINSPOTTING
Ridgely, Robert
MULTIPLICITY
THAT THING YOU DO!
Ridgle, Elston
INDEPENDENCE DAY
Riefsnyder, Kyle
BREACH OF TRUST
Riegert, Peter
INFINITY
Riehle, Richard
EXECUTIVE DECISION
FAN, THE
GHOSTS OF MISSISSIPPI
LONE JUSTICE: SHOWDOWN AT PLUM CREEK
TOO FAST, TOO YOUNG
Riemann, Katja
MAYBE . . . MAYBE NOT
Riffel, Rena
STRIPTEASE
Rifkin, Ron
I'M NOT RAPPAPORT
NORMA JEAN AND MARILYN
SUBSTANCE OF FIRE, THE
Rigg, Rebecca
JERRY MAGUIRE
TUNNEL VISION
Rigney, Daniel
ISLAND OF DR. MOREAU, THE
Rijxman, Lineke
ANTONIA'S LINE
Riker, William
PALOOKAVILLE
Riley, Chuck
GALAXIES ARE COLLIDING
Riley, Claire
BIG BULLY
Riley, Forbes
PHOENIX
Riley, Gary John
FEAR
Riley, Lisa Jane
BUTTERFLY KISS
Riley, Michael
HECK'S WAY HOME
Riley, Paul B.
FRISK
Riley, Rebecca
ONE GOOD TURN
Rimmer, Danny
JERRY MAGUIRE
Rimoux, Alain
PROPRIETOR, THE
Ringleh, Ned
ED'S NEXT MOVE
Ringwald, Molly
BAJA
SOME FOLKS CALL IT A SLING BLADE

Rini, Peter
JUROR, THE
SLEEPERS
Rinski, Chaim
DEADLY OUTBREAK
Riojas, Juan A.
ROCK, THE
Riordan, Daniel
JINGLE ALL THE WAY
Riordan, Kevin
VIRUS
Riordan, Mike
TEXAS PAYBACK
Rios, Christian
SMALL WONDERS
Ripa, Kelly
MARVIN'S ROOM
Ripolles, Jose Antonio
LAND AND FREEDOM
Ripper, Lori
LARRY MCMURTRY'S STREETS OF LAREDO
Rippon, Todd
FRIGHTENERS, THE
Rippy, Leon
ARRIVAL, THE
Rise, Yogi
WAR AT HOME, THE
Risler, Florence
SUITE 16
Risler, Veronica Ferrari
EVITA
Risley, Michael
TWO IF BY SEA
Rispoli, Michael
HOMEWARD BOUND II: LOST IN SAN FRANCISCO
JUROR, THE
Rissien, Edward
SWINGERS
Rissien, Jenna
SWINGERS
Ristholm, Carina
EVIL ED
Ristic, Suzanne
ANNIE O
Ristow, Trevor
MIRROR HAS TWO FACES, THE
Ritchie, Jim
TIME TO KILL, A
Ritchie, Perry
TIME TO KILL, A
Ritter, John
COLONY, THE
SLING BLADE
Ritz, James
RANSOM
Ritz, Mike
TIN CUP
Ritzenberg, Sam
JACK
Riva, Maria
LINE KING: THE AL HIRSCHFELD STORY, THE
Rivas, Geoffrey
EYE FOR AN EYE
HOSTILE INTENTIONS
SAWBONES
Rive, Patricia
ARRIVAL, THE
DOGFIGHTERS, THE
Rivera, Emilio
CABLE GUY, THE
DONOR UNKNOWN
RAGE
Rivera, Janice
BULLETPROOF
MARS ATTACKS!
Rivera, Patricia
JOHNNY 100 PESOS
Rivera, Rene
BASQUIAT
Rivers, Glenn "Doc"
EDDIE
Rivers, Victor
FLED
Riviera, Spencer
MR. HOLLAND'S OPUS
Riviere, Julien
LES VOLEURS
Rivierre, Corinne
SUITE 16
Rivkin, Michael
CABLE GUY, THE
SHOT, THE
Rivo, Phil
SGT. KABUKIMAN N.Y.P.D.
Rixon, Cheryl
DARK SECRETS
Roach, Daryl
PLAYBACK
Roach, Martin
EXTREME MEASURES
Roach, Pat
PORTRAIT OF A LADY, THE
Roarke, John
COURAGE UNDER FIRE
Robards, Jason
LINE KING: THE AL HIRSCHFELD STORY, THE
Robards, Sam
BEAUTIFUL GIRLS
DONOR UNKNOWN
Robb, Charles
PERFECT CANDIDATE, A
Robb, R.D.
MATILDA
Robbins, Garry
STUPIDS, THE
Robbins, Jacqueline
HOW THE WEST WAS FUN
Robbins, Janna
MOTHER
Robbins, John Franklyn
EMMA
Robbins, Joyce
HOW THE WEST WAS FUN
Robbins, Rex
ASSOCIATE, THE
Robbins, Ron
FINAL EQUINOX, THE
Roberson, David
CARNOSAUR 3: PRIMAL SPECIES
Roberson, Greg
PEOPLE VS. LARRY FLYNT, THE
Robert, Gerry
PALOOKAVILLE
Robert, Jeffrey
CRACKER: THE MADWOMAN IN THE ATTIC
Robert, Lionel
HORSEMAN ON THE ROOF
Roberts, Allison
COLD COMFORT FARM
Roberts, Anghaard
HEDD WYNN
Roberts, Arthur
FRIEND OF THE FAMILY 2
HARD JUSTICE
NOT OF THIS EARTH
Roberts, Bill
PATLABOR 2: MOBILE POLICE
Roberts, Billie Dee
JUDE
Roberts, Burke
LIFEFORM
Roberts, Damian
FRISK
Roberts, Dave
SHOPPING
Roberts, Denise
TWO FRIENDS
Roberts, Douglas
WOMAN UNDONE, A
Roberts, Dylan Jones
HEDD WYNN
Roberts, Eric
AMERICAN STRAYS
CABLE GUY, THE
GLASS CAGE, THE
HEAVEN'S PRISONERS
IMMORTALS, THE
IT'S MY PARTY
PUBLIC ENEMIES
Roberts, Francesca P.
EYE FOR AN EYE
Roberts, Geraint
HEDD WYNN
Roberts, Guto
HEDD WYNN
Roberts, Ian
TERMINAL IMPACT
Roberts, J.N.
BROKEN ARROW
Roberts, Jeremy
BLACK OUT
PHOENIX
Roberts, Jimmy
TIN CUP
Roberts, Julia
EVERYONE SAYS I LOVE YOU
MARY REILLY
MICHAEL COLLINS
Roberts, Ken
SURGEON, THE
Roberts, Kim
EXTREME MEASURES
Roberts, Kimberly
BLACK SCORPION
Roberts, Mario
BROKEN ARROW
Roberts, Mark
BULLETPROOF
Roberts, Rick
MAN IN THE ATTIC, THE
MOONSHINE HIGHWAY
Roberts, Steve
SYNTHETIC PLEASURES
Roberts, T.J.
TIGER HEART
Roberts, Tracy
OFF AND RUNNING
Roberts, Trevor
ANNIE O
Roberts, Valerie
LITTLE WITCHES
Robertson, Alan
ROAD HOME, THE
Robertson, Cliff
JOHN CARPENTER'S ESCAPE FROM L.A.
Robertson, George R.
BOYS NEXT DOOR, THE
Robertson, Iain
SMALL FACES
Robertson, Jenny
BOYS NEXT DOOR, THE
Robertson, Robert
BREAKING THE WAVES
Robertson, Shauna
HIGH SCHOOL HIGH
Robertson, Shelley
PINOCCHIO'S REVENGE
Robertson, Struan
MERLIN'S SHOP OF MAGICAL WONDERS

Robertz, Wren
RED SCORPION 2
Robie, Wendy
GLIMMER MAN, THE
Robillard, Kim
FAN, THE
SURGEON, THE
Robin
YOU'LL NEVER MAKE LOVE IN THIS TOWN AGAIN
Robin, Diane
GRACE OF MY HEART
Robin, Michel
LA COMEDIE-FRANCAISE OU L'AMOUR JOUE
Robinow, Anthony J.
MOTHER NIGHT
Robins, Laila
LIVE NUDE GIRLS
Robins, Paul Michael
FRIEND OF THE FAMILY 2
Robinson, Alexia
NUTTY PROFESSOR, THE
Robinson, Andrea
SGT. BILKO
Robinson, Charlie
SET IT OFF
Robinson, Eartha D.
EDDIE
Robinson, Eddie
LONE STAR
Robinson III, Charles Knox
CABLE GUY, THE
Robinson, Karen
RUDE
Robinson, Larry
SGT. KABUKIMAN N.Y.P.D.
TIMELESS
Robinson, Leon
ONCE UPON A TIME . . . WHEN WE WERE COLORED
Robinson, Marc Jason
WATCH ME
Robinson, Michael
BEWARE: CHILDREN AT PLAY
FRIGHTENERS, THE
Robinson, Michelle
PEOPLE VS. LARRY FLYNT, THE
Robinson, Wendy
THIN LINE BETWEEN LOVE AND HATE, A
Robles, Walter
SET IT OFF
Robson, Sterling
BEAUTIFUL GIRLS
Robson, Wade J.
KAZAAM
Robson, Wayne
GETTING AWAY WITH MURDER
STAND OFF, THE
TWO IF BY SEA
Roca
LAND AND FREEDOM
Rocco, Alex
THAT THING YOU DO!
Roces, Pinky
RAW TARGET
Rocha, Kali
CRUCIBLE, THE
Roche, Brogan
CRAFT, THE
Roche, Eugene
EXECUTIVE DECISION
Rochefort, Jean
RIDICULE
Rochefort, Julien
LA CEREMONIE
Roches, The
WEEKEND IN THE COUNTRY, A
Rochon, Bill
LAST MAN STANDING
Rochon, Debbie
SANTA CLAWS
Rochon, Lela
CHAMBER, THE
Rock 'n' Roll High School
NOT BAD FOR A GIRL
Rock, Chris
IMMORTALS, THE
SGT. BILKO
Rockmore, Clara
THEREMIN: AN ELECTRONIC ODYSSEY
Rockwell, Sam
BASQUIAT
MERCY
SEARCH FOR ONE-EYE JIMMY, THE
Rocovsky, Petr
DELTA OF VENUS
Rodd, Everett
VIRTUAL ENCOUNTERS
Rodd, Everett J.
FEMALIEN
Roderick, Rachelle
HIGH SCHOOL HIGH
Roderick, Sue
HEDD WYNN
Rodger, Kate
POISON IVY 2: LILY
Rodgers, Michael
DENTIST, THE
Rodgers, R.E.
ED'S NEXT MOVE
Rodman, Dennis
EDDIE
Rodrick, Michael
DESOLATION ANGELS
Rodrigo, Al
BIRDCAGE, THE
GREAT WHITE HYPE, THE
Rodrigo, Daniel
FUGITIVE RAGE
Rodriguez, Arlene
TAKEOVER, THE
Rodriguez, Augustin
LET'S GET BIZZEE
Rodriguez, Eliott
UP CLOSE AND PERSONAL
Rodriguez, Kristina
SOUTH BEACH ACADEMY
Rodriguez, Manny
EYE FOR AN EYE
Rodriguez, Marco
HIGH SCHOOL HIGH
SERIAL KILLER
Rodriguez, Roland
LARRY MCMURTRY'S STREETS OF LAREDO
Rodriguez, Valente
BIG SQUEEZE, THE
ED
RICH MAN'S WIFE, THE
Rodway, Norman
MOTHER NIGHT
Rody, David
BEST OF THE BEST 3: NO TURNING BACK
Roe, Channon
BIO-DOME
LOW LIFE, THE
Roe, Matt
BLACK SCORPION
Roe, Owen
MICHAEL COLLINS
Roe, Valerie
SOME MOTHER'S SON
Roebuck, Daniel
HOUSE ARREST
LATE SHIFT, THE
Roeder, Aaron
HYPE!
Roeder, Peggy
ENTERTAINING ANGELS: THE DOROTHY DAY STORY
Roemer, Bill
SUGARTIME
Roeser, Rob
HEAD OF THE FAMILY
Rogers, Ashley M.
SWINGERS
Rogers, Debra
GET ON THE BUS
Rogers, Greg
FINAL CUT, THE
Rogers, John Brian
RANSOM
Rogers, Johnny
ONE MAN'S JUSTICE
Rogers, Lisa
TWO FRIENDS
Rogers, Lori
FOXFIRE
Rogers, Michael
HIDDEN ASSASSIN
MISSION: IMPOSSIBLE
Rogers, Mimi
FULL BODY MASSAGE
MIRROR HAS TWO FACES, THE
TREES LOUNGE
Rogers, Reg
I SHOT ANDY WARHOL
PRIMAL FEAR
Rogers, Rick
PEOPLE VS. LARRY FLYNT, THE
Rogers, Steve
RAW TARGET
Rogers, Theotis
FAMILY THING, A
Rogers, Wayne
GHOSTS OF MISSISSIPPI
Rogness, Scott
THAT THING YOU DO!
Rohde, Armin
MAYBE . . . MAYBE NOT
Rohmer, Eric
FRANCOIS TRUFFAUT: STOLEN PORTRAITS
Rohner, Clayton
NAKED SOULS
Roisman, Harper
CABLE GUY, THE
Roisum, Ted
MR. HOLLAND'S OPUS
Rojas, Teresa Maria
BITTER SUGAR
Rojo, Ruben
AVENTURERA
Rolan, Alain
SINGLE GIRL, A
Rolf, Frederick
ASSOCIATE, THE
EVERYONE SAYS I LOVE YOU
Rolf, Sean
VENUS RISING
Rolle, Esther
MY FELLOW AMERICANS
Rolling Stones, The
ROLLING STONES ROCK-AND-ROLL CIRCUS, THE
Rollins, Francesca
MY FELLOW AMERICANS
Rollwage, Ursula
NEUROSIA: 50 YEARS OF PERVERSITY
Rolman, Quinto
IN LOVE AND WAR
Rolston, Mark
BEST OF THE BEST 3: NO TURNING BACK

DAYLIGHT
ERASER

Roman, Frank
MR. WRONG

Roman, Jacques
RIDICULE

Romani, Joan Pau
LAND AND FREEDOM

Romano, Andy
CHAMELEON
ERASER
FAST MONEY
GETTING AWAY WITH MURDER
GHOSTS OF MISSISSIPPI

Romano, Christy
EVERYONE SAYS I LOVE YOU

Romano, Frank
SGT. BILKO

Romano, Larry
CITY HALL
LOVE IS ALL THERE IS
SLEEPERS

Romano, Rino
GETTING AWAY WITH MURDER
LOSING CHASE
SUGARTIME

Romanov, Joseph
LIFEFORM

Romanov, Stephanie
SPY HARD

Rome, Florence
LINE KING: THE AL HIRSCHFELD STORY, THE

Rome, Lance
CITIZEN RUTH

Romeo, Ina
JOHN CARPENTER'S ESCAPE FROM L.A.

Romer, Dorte
BREAKING THE WAVES

Romero, Thomas G.
BAJA

Romic, Monica
VUKOVAR

Romoli, Maruizio
CEMETERY MAN

Ronan, Paul
FAITHFUL

Rondel, Stephen M.
APART FROM HUGH

Rondell, Ronald R.
STAR TREK: FIRST CONTACT

Rondinella, Clelia
MILLE BOLLE BLU
STAR MAKER, THE

Rone, Doria
DARK SECRETS

Roodner, Uri
INSTITUTE BENJAMENTA

Roofthooft, Dirk
SUITE 16

Rooker, Michael
TRIGGER EFFECT, THE

Rooney, Mickey
ROAD HOME, THE

Rooney, Ted
CELTIC PRIDE

Roos, Camilla Overbye
WHITE SQUALL

Root, Amanda
JANE EYRE

Root, Stephen
NIGHT OF THE SCARECROW
ROAD TO GALVESTON, THE

Roper, Deidra "Spin"
KAZAAM

Rorker, Tina
APART FROM HUGH

Rosales, Thomas
TREMORS 2: AFTERSHOCKS

Rosales, Tom
LAST MAN STANDING

Rosandic, Milan
IN LOVE AND WAR

Rosario, Jose
TREMORS 2: AFTERSHOCKS

Rosario, Jose Ramon
SOMEONE ELSE'S AMERICA
SUBSTANCE OF FIRE, THE

Rosario, Willie
EVERYONE SAYS I LOVE YOU

Rosato, Tony
KISSINGER AND NIXON
SUGARTIME

Rose, Bettina
TIME TO KILL, A

Rose, Enid
HIDDEN ASSASSIN

Rose, Leigh
MY FELLOW AMERICANS

Rose, Michael
WILD SIDE

Roselius, John
JAG
MARS ATTACKS!
NORMA JEAN AND MARILYN

Rosen, Dan
LAST SUPPER, THE

Rosen, Emily
JAMES AND THE GIANT PEACH

Rosen, Michaela
BROTHER OF SLEEP

Rosen, Ruth
BERKELEY IN THE 60S

Rosenberg, Erin
DEADLY OUTBREAK

Rosenberg, Sarah
FOXFIRE

Rosenblum, Gregorio
BOYS

Rosenblum, Sheri
SWINGERS

Rosenblum, Stasea
SWINGERS

Rosenfeld, Donald
PROPRIETOR, THE

Rosengren, Clive
THAT THING YOU DO!

Rosenhaus, Drew
JERRY MAGUIRE

Rosenthal, Amy Lynn
SOUTH BEACH ACADEMY

Rosenthal, Carol
SGT. BILKO

Rosenthal, Jeffrey Dean
BARB WIRE

Rosenthal, Joy
DEAR GOD

Rosenthal, Murray
ABUSE

Roshell, Antoine
FAMILY THING, A

Roshetnikova, Natasha
RASPUTIN

Rosling, Tara
EXTREME MEASURES

Ross, Annie Louise
TRAINSPOTTING

Ross, Bruce
EXECUTIVE DECISION

Ross, Burl
FOXFIRE

Ross, Chelcie
CHAIN REACTION
EVIL HAS A FACE

Ross, David
MARY REILLY

Ross, Gene
ED

Ross, Hugh
TRAINSPOTTING

Ross, Jeffrey
CELTIC PRIDE

Ross, Jesse Sky
DIABOLIQUE

Ross, Jonathan
PAINTED HERO

Ross, Jordan
JERRY MAGUIRE

Ross, Justin Jon
BIG BULLY

Ross, Lee
ENGLISH PATIENT, THE
SECRETS & LIES

Ross, Marion
EVENING STAR, THE

Ross, Matt
ED'S NEXT MOVE

Ross, Natalie
TALES FROM THE CRYPT PRESENTS BORDELLO OF BLOOD

Ross, Raymond
JUDE

Ross, Ricco
MISSION: IMPOSSIBLE
PROTEUS

Ross, Sandi
TWO IF BY SEA

Ross, Tracee Ellis
FAR HARBOR

Rossall, Kerry
CROW: CITY OF ANGELS, THE

Rossellini, Isabella
BIG NIGHT
FUNERAL, THE

Rossi, Feliciano Tello
LITTLE INDIAN, BIG CITY

Rossi, George
IN LOVE AND WAR

Rossi, Leo
BEYOND DESIRE
FELONY

Rossi, Reanna Lynn
ANIMAL INSTINCTS III: THE SEDUCTRESS

Rossignon, Christophe
HATE

Rossman, Michael
BERKELEY IN THE 60S

Rossovich, Rick
BLACK SCORPION
FATALLY YOURS

Rostom, Hichem
ENGLISH PATIENT, THE
SILENCES OF THE PALACE, THE

Rota, Carlo
MAXIMUM RISK

Rotblatt, Janet
CRAFT, THE

Rote, Edward
ERASER
LAST MAN STANDING

Roth, Mark
KINGPIN

Roth, Tim
CAPTIVES
EVERYONE SAYS I LOVE YOU

Rothaar, Will
LETTER TO MY KILLER

Rothberg, Elise
CROSSCUT
Rothery, Teryl
SURGEON, THE
Rothhaar, Michael
NUTTY PROFESSOR, THE
Rothhaar, Will
AMERICAN STRAYS
KINGPIN
Rothlein, William
SWEET NOTHING
Rothman, John
ASSOCIATE, THE
Rothrock, Cynthia
EYE FOR AN EYE
Rothschild, Ami
ARRIVAL, THE
Rotondi, Lisa
JERRY MAGUIRE
Rotter, Clara
LINE KING: THE AL HIRSCHFELD STORY, THE
Rougeux, Greg
DADETOWN
Roundtree, Richard
ONCE UPON A TIME . . . WHEN WE WERE COLORED
ORIGINAL GANGSTAS
THEODORE REX
Rouse, Mitch
TRUTH ABOUT CATS AND DOGS, THE
Roussos, Bianca
GIRLFRIENDS
Rowe, Douglas
COLONY, THE
Rowe, Leanne
JANE EYRE
Rowe, Tonia
SET IT OFF
Rowell, Victoria
BARB WIRE
Rowland, Oscar
CHILDREN OF FURY
Rowland, Paige
GLIMMER MAN, THE
Rowlands, Dave
UNHOOK THE STARS
Rowlands, Gena
NEON BIBLE, THE
UNHOOK THE STARS
Rowley, Ryan
DEMOLITIONIST, THE
Roy, Allen
JOHNNY SHORTWAVE
Roy, Christian
LITTLE INDIAN, BIG CITY
Roy, Deep
UNDER THE HULA MOON
Roy Gerson Orchestra, The
ASSOCIATE, THE
Roy, Gloria
TALES FROM THE CRYPT PRESENTS BORDELLO OF BLOOD
Royal, Allan
BLOODKNOT
Royle, Amanda
TWO DEATHS
Royo, Asuncion
LAND AND FREEDOM
Royston, D.J.
SLING BLADE
Rozand, Pascal
HORSEMAN ON THE ROOF
Rozen, Robert
TALES FROM THE CRYPT PRESENTS BORDELLO OF BLOOD
Rubenstein, John
NORMA JEAN AND MARILYN

Rubin, Barbara
LIVE WIRE: HUMAN TIMEBOMB
Rubin, Daniel
SURGEON, THE
Rubin, Jennifer
LITTLE WITCHES
RED SCORPION 2
SAINTS AND SINNERS
SCREAMERS
Rubin, Loren
BARB WIRE
Rubin, Martin
BEAUTIFUL GIRLS
Rubinek, Saul
OPEN SEASON
Rubinstein, John
MERCY
Rubinstein, Zelda
LITTLE WITCHES
LOVER'S KNOT
Ruby, Amanda
SANDMAN, THE
Ruchaud, Frederique
HORSEMAN ON THE ROOF
Ruche, Christian
MACHINE, THE
Ruck, Alan
TWISTER
Rudall, Nicholas
CHAIN REACTION
Rudd, Paul
WILLIAM SHAKESPEARE'S ROMEO + JULIET
Rude, Lea
FRISK
Rudebeck, Johan
EVIL ED
Ruderman, Eduardo
EVITA
Rudner, Rita
WEEKEND IN THE COUNTRY, A
Rudnick, Paul
CELLULOID CLOSET, THE
Rudolph, Lars
FLIRT
Rudolph, Sebastian
ENGLISH PATIENT, THE
Rudrud, Kristin
FARGO
Ruedelstein, Joan
HIGH SCHOOL HIGH
Ruf, Eric
PROPRIETOR, THE
Ruff, Kerry
TALKING ABOUT SEX
Ruffalo, Mark
DENTIST, THE
MIRROR, MIRROR III: THE VOYEUR
Ruffelle, Frances
SECRETS & LIES
Ruffini, Gene
EXTREME MEASURES
Ruggiero, Beth
SOME FOLKS CALL IT A SLING BLADE
Ruggles, Steve
GALAXIES ARE COLLIDING
Ruginis, Vyto
BAD LOVE
BROKEN ARROW
PHENOMENON
Ruhring, Peter
ENGLISH PATIENT, THE
Ruivivar, Anthony
RACE THE SUN
Ruiz Garcia, Juan
SONS OF TRINITY
Rummler, Bob
CHAMBER, THE

Rumph, Sky
GHOSTS OF MISSISSIPPI
Runarsdottir, Valgerdur
VIKING SAGAS, THE
Rundgren, Todd
THEREMIN: AN ELECTRONIC ODYSSEY
Runnette, Sean
TWO IF BY SEA
RuPaul
FLED
MOTHER'S PRAYER, A
VERY BRADY SEQUEL, A
Rupp, Debra Jo
SGT. BILKO
Rupp, Jacob
BIG BULLY
Ruschak, Mike
BEAVIS AND BUTT-HEAD DO AMERICA
Ruscio, Al
PHANTOM, THE
Ruscio, Elizabeth
DEATH BENEFIT
UP CLOSE AND PERSONAL
Rush, Barbara
WIDOW'S KISS
Rush, Geoffrey
SHINE
Rush, Lee
PARADISE LOST: THE CHILD MURDERS AT ROBIN HOOD HILLS
Rush, Maggie
GIRL 6
Rushbrook, Claire
SECRETS & LIES
Rushent, Martin
HYPE!
Rushing, Lance
BEASTMASTER 3: THE EYE OF BRAXUS
Rushton, Kevin
BEYOND THE CALL
MAXIMUM RISK
Rusich, Stellina
ROAD HOME, THE
UNFORGETTABLE
Ruskin, Morris
WHISPERING, THE
Ruskin, Sheila
RASPUTIN
Russ, Matej
PREDICTIONS OF FIRE
Russell, Catherine
SOLITAIRE FOR TWO
Russell, Cheri Rae
LITTLE WITCHES
Russell, Christopher
WHISPERING, THE
Russell, Gerry
LOOKING FOR TROUBLE
Russell, Grant
SHOPPING
Russell Jr., Anthony
SKIN
Russell, Ken
TALES OF EROTICA
Russell, Kurt
EXECUTIVE DECISION
JOHN CARPENTER'S ESCAPE FROM L.A.
Russell, Lisa Marie
TRUTH ABOUT CATS AND DOGS, THE
Russell, Theresa
PUBLIC ENEMIES
Russell, William Jess
NECRONOMICON: BOOK OF THE DEAD
Russell-Woloshin, Carol
PEOPLE VS. LARRY FLYNT, THE
Russi, Celeste
LOVE IS ALL THERE IS

Russo, Colton
CELTIC PRIDE
Russo, Daniel
HORSEMAN ON THE ROOF
Russo, Gianni
STRIPTEASE
Russo, James
AMERICAN STRAYS
CONDITION RED
Russo, John A.
SANTA CLAWS
Russo, Julia Ann
SANTA CLAWS
Russo, Mary Lou
SANTA CLAWS
Russo, Michael
BARB WIRE
MY FELLOW AMERICANS
PURE DANGER
Russo, Rene
RANSOM
TIN CUP
Russom, Leon
LONG ROAD HOME, THE
PHANTOM, THE
Rutherford, Maxwell
WHISPERING, THE
Rutkoski, Bill
PURE DANGER
Rutledge, Paul
ELECTRA
Ryan, Amanda
JUDE
Ryan, Andy
ROCK, THE
Ryan, Bridgit
PALOOKAVILLE
Ryan, Dave
THAT THING YOU DO!
Ryan, Eveanna
WAR OF THE BUTTONS, THE
Ryan, Ger
MOLL FLANDERS
WAR OF THE BUTTONS, THE
Ryan, James
REDEMPTION: KICKBOXER 5
Ryan, John
PEOPLE VS. LARRY FLYNT, THE
Ryan, John Fergus
PEOPLE VS. LARRY FLYNT, THE
Ryan, John P.
BOUND
Ryan, Jonathan
MOLL FLANDERS
Ryan, Joseph R.
PRIMAL FEAR
Ryan, Ken
LONG KISS GOODNIGHT, THE
Ryan, Lisa Dean
HOSTILE INTENTIONS
Ryan, Mark
EVITA
Ryan, Meg
COURAGE UNDER FIRE
Ryan, Mitchell
ED
RAVENHAWK
Ryan, Rusty
WHARF RAT, THE
Ryan, Seana
NAKED SOULS
Ryan, Steve
I'M NOT RAPPAPORT
Ryane, Jenafor
UNFORGETTABLE
Rychtarik, Edward
DELTA OF VENUS
Rydbeck, Whitney
VERY BRADY SEQUEL, A
Ryder, Richard
ABUSE
Ryder, Rob
EDDIE
Ryder, Winona
BOYS
CRUCIBLE, THE
LOOKING FOR RICHARD
Ryerson, Ann
LATE SHIFT, THE
Rylance, Mark
ANGELS AND INSECTS
INSTITUTE BENJAMENTA
Rymer, Steven
TERMINAL IMPACT
S., Rony
WITHOUT MERCY
Sabatino, Joe
JAG
Sabri, Hend
SILENCES OF THE PALACE, THE
Saccio, Thomas
MIRROR HAS TWO FACES, THE
Sach, Terence
IN LOVE AND WAR
Sachs, Hugh
SHAMELESS
Sack, Graham
DUNSTON CHECKS IN
PIG'S TALE, A
Sack, Lauren R.
BUGGED
Sackeroff, Mae
NEUROSIA: 50 YEARS OF PERVERSITY
Sacks, Emma
SMALL WONDERS
Sadeli, Jimmy
RACE THE SUN
Sadler, Nicholas
SAWBONES
TWISTER
Sadler, Nick
LAST SUPPER, THE
Sadler, William
SOLO
TALES FROM THE CRYPT PRESENTS BORDELLO OF BLOOD
Sadoti, Sabrina
EXIT
Sagal, Joe
BARB WIRE
Sagal, McNally
HIGH SCHOOL HIGH
MOTHER'S PRAYER, A
Sagalle, Jonathan
DEADLY OUTBREAK
Sage, Bill
BOYS
FLIRT
I SHOT ANDY WARHOL
IF LUCY FELL
Sage, David
BIRDCAGE, THE
GALAXIES ARE COLLIDING
Sahagun, Elena
TIGER HEART
Sahay, Vikram
HOLLOW POINT
Sahely, Ed
ELECTRA
MAXIMUM RISK
Sahlin, Anna
CHILDREN OF NOISY VILLAGE, THE
Saint-Louis, Douveline
MAN BY THE SHORE, THE
Sakasitz, Amy
HOUSE ARREST
Sakura, Matsuko
MABOROSI
Sakurai, Kitao
BEST OF THE BEST 3: NO TURNING BACK
Salas, Tania
OUTRAGE
Salatino, Brian
ANIMAL INSTINCTS III: THE SEDUCTRESS
Salazar, Leonard
WIDOW'S KISS
Salazar, Randy
MAN WITH THE PERFECT SWING, THE
Salcedo, Jose Manuel
JOHNNY 100 PESOS
Saldivar, Laura
FULL BODY MASSAGE
Saleem, Damon
LIFEFORM
Salem, Kario
MR. STITCH
Salenger, Meredith
VENUS RISING
Salerno, Mary Jo
MODERN AFFAIR, A
Salerno, Randy
PRIMAL FEAR
Salerno, Tiffany
LOVER'S KNOT
WHISPERING, THE
Salers, Joelle
DEMOLITIONIST, THE
Sales, Leander
DON'T LET YOUR MEAT LOAF
Salguero, Randal
FAN, THE
Salguero, Sophia
DIABOLIQUE
SUBSTANCE OF FIRE, THE
Sali, Curtis
FOR THE MOMENT
Salinger, Diane
ONE NIGHT STAND
Salisbury, Benjamin
D3: THE MIGHTY DUCKS
Salley, John
EDDIE
Salling, Mark
CHILDREN OF THE CORN: THE GATHERING
Salmon, Colin
CAPTIVES
Salmon, Kelly
SOLITAIRE FOR TWO
Salsedo, Frank Stonoma
BOY CALLED HATE, A
Saltzman, Avery
IN LOVE AND WAR
Salvallon, Fred
ROCK, THE
Salwen, Hal
DENISE CALLS UP
Sam, Pamela
HARVEST OF FIRE
Samaha, John
GIRLFRIENDS
Samara
HEAD OF THE FAMILY

Samel, Knut
PASSION OF DARKLY NOON, THE
Samel, Udo
KASPAR HAUSER
Samie, Catherine
FRENCH TWIST
LA COMEDIE-FRANCAISE OU L'AMOUR JOUE
Samie, Celine
LA COMEDIE-FRANCAISE OU L'AMOUR JOUE
Sammel, Richard
HORSEMAN ON THE ROOF
Sammut, Norbert
HORSEMAN ON THE ROOF
Samper, Emilia
LAND AND FREEDOM
Samples, William
HAPPY GILMORE
Sampson, John
RUMBLE IN THE BRONX
Sampson, Tony
ANNIE O
Samuel, Nicole Ann
WHITE SQUALL
San Miguel, Carlos
FEMALIEN
San Narciso, Luis
BATON ROUGE
San, Raul
SHOOTFIGHTER 2: KILL OR BE KILLED!
Sanchez, Carlos
SOME FOLKS CALL IT A SLING BLADE
Sanchez, Joanna
LARRY MCMURTRY'S STREETS OF LAREDO
UP CLOSE AND PERSONAL
Sanchez, Johnny
FIRST WIVES CLUB, THE
Sanchez, Octavio O.
WAR AT HOME, THE
Sanchez-Gijon, Aitana
MOUTH TO MOUTH
Sancho, Roberto
JOHNNY 100 PESOS
Sandaydiego, Vivienne
CURDLED
Sandberg, Bert
D3: THE MIGHTY DUCKS
Sandell, Julian
SHOPPING
Sander, Casey
CROSSCUT
Sanderford, John
BLACK SCORPION
Sanders, Deion
CELTIC PRIDE
Sanders, Derrick
WAR AT HOME, THE
Sanders, Jay O.
DAYLIGHT
Sanders, Jeff
CHAMBER, THE
SPY HARD
Sanders, Kim
GIRLFRIENDS
Sanders, Sydney
OFF AND RUNNING
Sanderson, Catherine
BEAUTIFUL THING
CAPTIVES
Sanderson, Jim
FAMILY THING, A
Sanderson, William
FOREST WARRIOR
LAST MAN STANDING
LONE JUSTICE: SHOWDOWN AT PLUM CREEK
PHOENIX
Sandiarin, Silva
WITHOUT MERCY
Sandiford, Hadley
OPEN SEASON
Sandler, Adam
BULLETPROOF
HAPPY GILMORE
Sandler, Barry
CELLULOID CLOSET, THE
Sandler, Mallory
HIGH SCHOOL HIGH
Sandmann, Antoinette
BLONDES HAVE MORE GUNS
Sandoval, Carlos
ROCK, THE
Sandoval, Cha-Cha
JERRY MAGUIRE
Sandoval, Miguel
BREACH OF TRUST
DANGEROUS PASSION
MRS. WINTERBOURNE
UP CLOSE AND PERSONAL
Sandrelli, Stefania
OF LOVE AND SHADOWS
STEALING BEAUTY
Sands, Peter
NORMA JEAN AND MARILYN
Sandulescu, Ilana
MAGIC IN THE MIRROR
Sandy, J. Craig
FLY AWAY HOME
Saneyoshi, Isako
KAMIKAZE TAXI
Sanford, Garwin
CHILDREN OF FURY
MATERNAL INSTINCTS
UNFORGETTABLE
Sanford, Isabel
ORIGINAL GANGSTAS
Sanford, Jason
UP CLOSE AND PERSONAL
Sangster, Jim
HYPE!
Sanguinetti, Jane
ROCK, THE
Sansom, Noel
OUTRAGE
Sanson, Kathy
EVERYONE SAYS I LOVE YOU
Sansone, Patricia
MERLIN'S SHOP OF MAGICAL WONDERS
Santesmases, Rosario
OUTRAGE
Santi, Lisa
WITHOUT MERCY
Santiago, Renoly
DAYLIGHT
Santiago, Socorro
ASSOCIATE, THE
HEAVEN'S PRISONERS
Santoni, Reni
LATE SHIFT, THE
Santos, Bert
BIG SQUEEZE, THE
Santususso, Steve
JUROR, THE
Sanvido, Guy
CURTIS'S CHARM
Saorin, Desire
HORSEMAN ON THE ROOF
Sapienza, Al
MR. STITCH
Sapp, Eric
FRISK
Sara, Mia
BLACK DAY BLUE NIGHT
MADDENING, THE
POMPATUS OF LOVE, THE
UNDERTOW
Sarachu, Cesar
INSTITUTE BENJAMENTA
Sarafian, Richard
BOUND
Sarandon, Chris
EDIE & PEN
TALES FROM THE CRYPT PRESENTS BORDELLO OF BLOOD
Sarandon, Susan
CELLULOID CLOSET, THE
JAMES AND THE GIANT PEACH
Sarcev, Ursula
NEMESIS III: PREY HARDER
Sardella, Andrew
BEYOND THE CALL
Sargeant, Lindsay
QUEST, THE
Sarosiak, Ronn
DARKMAN III: DIE DARKMAN DIE
VIRUS
Sarosian, Ron
ELECTRA
Sartain, Gailard
OPEN SEASON
SPITFIRE GRILL, THE
Sasagawa, Shigezo
SANCTUARY: THE MOVIE
Saslow, Jerry
FAN, THE
Sass, Jeffrey W.
SGT. KABUKIMAN N.Y.P.D.
Sass, Zachary Daniel
SGT. KABUKIMAN N.Y.P.D.
Sassano, Marcella
MATILDA
Sasso, William
ANNIE O
HAPPY GILMORE
HOMEWARD BOUND II: LOST IN SAN FRANCISCO
Sato, Garret T.
BULLETPROOF
Sato, Masaharu
BIG WARS
SANCTUARY: THE MOVIE
Sauerwein, Ralph
BROTHER OF SLEEP
Sauls, Christa
DENTIST, THE
Saulsberry, Michael
GRACE OF MY HEART
Saunders, Jacqulyn V.
PREACHER'S WIFE, THE
Saunders, Jennifer
MIDWINTER'S TALE, A
MUPPET TREASURE ISLAND
Saunders, Lois
SCREAM
Sauval, Catherine
LA COMEDIE-FRANCAISE OU L'AMOUR JOUE
LA COMEDIE-FRANCAISE OU L'AMOUR JOUE
Savadier, Russell
YANKEE ZULU
Savage, John
AMERICAN STRAYS
BEAUTIFUL THING
ONE GOOD TURN
RED SCORPION 2
TAKEOVER, THE
WHITE SQUALL
Savage, Mimi
RATTLED

Savenkoff, Elizabeth Carol
ROBIN OF LOCKSLEY
Saville, David
YOUNG POISONER'S HANDBOOK, THE
Savini, Tom
DEMOLITIONIST, THE
FROM DUSK TILL DAWN
MR. STITCH
Savino, Joe
MOLL FLANDERS
Savio, Mario
BERKELEY IN THE 60S
Saviola, Camille
MR. WRONG
SUNSET PARK
Savitt, Daniel
BODY COUNT
Savoy, Jerry
GETTING AWAY WITH MURDER
Savoy, Suzanne
MAN WITH THE PERFECT SWING, THE
Sawa, Devon
NIGHT OF THE TWISTERS
ROBIN OF LOCKSLEY
Sawaki, Ikuya
BIG WARS
Sawalha, Julia
MIDWINTER'S TALE, A
Sawatsky, Sarah
GIRL FROM MARS, THE
Sawyer, Connie
IT CAME FROM OUTER SPACE II
Saxon, John
FROM DUSK TILL DAWN
Saxon, Rolf
AFFAIR, THE
MISSION: IMPOSSIBLE
Saxon, Sylvia
TALKING ABOUT SEX
Saxton, Richard
FLY AWAY HOME
Sbarge, Raphael
ABUSE
INDEPENDENCE DAY
Sbrocca, Theya
HOURGLASS
Scacchi, Greta
EMMA
RASPUTIN
Scagnetti, Franca
WHO KILLED PASOLINI?
Scaldati, Franco
STAR MAKER, THE
Scanlon, James
JUDE
Scanlon, Patricia
FLIRT
PURE DANGER
Scannell, Kevin
LATE SHIFT, THE
Scarabelli, Michele
COLONY, THE
Scarber, Sam
DEAD WEEKEND
ERASER
TAKEOVER, THE
Scarborough, Adrian
MIDWINTER'S TALE, A
Scarborough, Victoria
CAPTIVES
Scardino, Hal
MARVIN'S ROOM
Scarduzio, Nick
GALAXIES ARE COLLIDING
Scarface
ORIGINAL GANGSTAS
Scarpa, Daniel
FUNERAL, THE
Scarpa, Renata
SONS OF TRINITY
Scarpati, Giulio
WHO KILLED PASOLINI?
Scarry, Rick
GREAT WHITE HYPE, THE
Scarwid, Diana
NEON BIBLE, THE
TRUMAN
Scelfo, Leonora
SCREAM
Scerri, Joseph
SGT. KABUKIMAN N.Y.P.D.
Schaal, Wendy
OUT THERE
Schacter, David
ABUSE
Schade, Birge
BROTHER OF SLEEP
Schadrack, Chris
PEOPLE VS. LARRY FLYNT, THE
Schaech, Johnathon
POISON IVY 2: LILY
THAT THING YOU DO!
Schaefer, Brent
SOLO
Schaeffer, Eric
IF LUCY FELL
Schafer, Frank
NEUROSIA: 50 YEARS OF PERVERSITY
Schaff, Edmond
SET IT OFF
Schanley, Tom
COURAGE UNDER FIRE
Schaub, Will
EXECUTIVE DECISION
Schayes, Danny
EDDIE
Schedeen, Anne
HEAVEN'S PRISONERS
Scheer, Mary
NOT OF THIS EARTH
Scheib, Ingrid
NEUROSIA: 50 YEARS OF PERVERSITY
Scheine, Raynor
EXTREME MEASURES
FIRST KID
LAST MAN STANDING
Schell, Dustin
FRISK
Scheller, Damion
INFINITY
Schendler, Frank
FLIRT
Schenkel, Chris
KINGPIN
Scherer, Glenn
EXIT
Schiavelli, Vincent
PEOPLE VS. LARRY FLYNT, THE
ROAD HOME, THE
TWO MUCH
Schiff, Nathan
ONE LESS EGG TO FRY
Schiff, Richard
ARRIVAL, THE
CITY HALL
GRACE OF MY HEART
MICHAEL
TRIGGER EFFECT, THE
Schiffer, Claudia
CATWALK
Schiffler, Carrie
PORTRAITS OF A KILLER
Schill, Patricia
FINAL CUT, THE
Schiller, Anja
KASPAR HAUSER
Schintzius, Dwayne
EDDIE
Schipek, Dietmar
FLAMING EARS
Schipper, Sebastian
ENGLISH PATIENT, THE
Schlatter, Charlie
ED
Schlei, Lincoln
SOME FOLKS CALL IT A SLING BLADE
Schlesinger, John
CELLULOID CLOSET, THE
Schloss, Arleen
FLAMING EARS
Schlossberg, Katie
MULTIPLICITY
Schmid, Kyle
VIRUS
Schmid, Max
ABUSE
Schmidt, Kenneth
LETTER TO MY KILLER
Schmidtke, Ned
CHAIN REACTION
Schmittler, Jake
MOTHER
Schmitz, Peter
FARGO
Schmitzer, Jiff
KASPAR HAUSER
Schmoeller, David
ARRIVAL, THE
Schnabel, Esther G.
BASQUIAT
Schnabel, Jack
BASQUIAT
Schnabel, Lola
BASQUIAT
Schnabel, Olatz Maria
BASQUIAT
Schnabel, Stella
BASQUIAT
Schnass, Jorg
PROPRIETOR, THE
Schneider, Carol
EVERYTHING RELATIVE
Schneider, Charles
ZARKORR! THE INVADER
Schneider, David
MISSION: IMPOSSIBLE
Schneider, Glennon
SOME FOLKS CALL IT A SLING BLADE
Schneider, John
NIGHT OF THE TWISTERS
Schneider, Maria
JANE EYRE
Schneider, Mark
VENUS RISING
Schneider, Michael
SOLITAIRE FOR TWO
Schneider, Rabbi Marc
SUBSTANCE OF FIRE, THE
Schneider, Rob
ADVENTURES OF PINOCCHIO, THE
DOWN PERISCOPE
Schneider, Robert
BROTHER OF SLEEP
Schneider, Susan
ABUSE
Schnidelhauer, Peter
ELECTRA
Schnur, Max
DAENS
Schnurr, Vikki
EVERYONE SAYS I LOVE YOU
Schoenaerts, Julien
DAENS

Schoene, Patrick
MADAME WANG'S
Schoppman, Rosemary
BROKEN ARROW
Schornagel, Jurgen
BROTHER OF SLEEP
Schossig, Alicia
MR. ICE CREAM MAN
Schott, Bob
HEAD OF THE FAMILY
Schrader, Maria
FLIRT
Schram, Bitty
CAUGHT
ONE FINE DAY
PALLBEARER, THE
Schramm, Bitty
MARVIN'S ROOM
Schreiber, Liev
BIG NIGHT
DENISE CALLS UP
RANSOM
SCREAM
WALKING AND TALKING
Schreiner, Peter
PRIMAL FEAR
Schrenk, Todd
PALLBEARER, THE
Schroeder, Barbet
MARS ATTACKS!
Schroeder, Sandi
MIRROR HAS TWO FACES, THE
Schroeder, Todd
ELECTRA
Schrum, Peter
DEAD MAN
Schub, Steven
CAUGHT
Schubert, Samantha
RED SCORPION 2
Schuelke, David
HELLRAISER: BLOODLINE
Schuelke, Jimmy
HELLRAISER: BLOODLINE
Schuler, Thomas
DESIRE
Schulman, Molly
IF LUCY FELL
Schulte, F. Joseph
LOW LIFE, THE
Schultz, Albert
MAXIMUM RISK
Schultz, Dwight
STAR TREK: FIRST CONTACT
Schulz, Kenneth
LAST DANCE
Schumacher, Carroll
FUGITIVE RAGE
Schumacher, Wendy
ANIMAL INSTINCTS III: THE SEDUCTRESS
FUGITIVE RAGE
Schuster, Leon
YANKEE ZULU
Schwartz, Juan
CANNIBAL! THE MUSICAL
Schwartz, Myke
BROKEN ARROW
Schwartz, Stefan
SOLITAIRE FOR TWO
Schwartz, Tara
THAT THING YOU DO!
Schwary, Brian
MIRROR HAS TWO FACES, THE
Schwarzenegger, Arnold
ERASER
JINGLE ALL THE WAY
Schweickhardt, Kurt
FARGO
Schweiger, Til
MAYBE . . . MAYBE NOT
Schwieterman, Jan Patrick
WHISPERING, THE
Schwimmer, David
PALLBEARER, THE
Schwimmer, Rusty
DOWN, OUT AND DANGEROUS
LONE JUSTICE: SHOWDOWN AT PLUM CREEK
TWISTER
Schwoeble, Kurt
FEMALIEN
Sciacca, Thom
MURDERED INNOCENCE
Scibelli, Carlo
MIRROR HAS TWO FACES, THE
Scimone, Emilio
STAR MAKER, THE
Scimone, Spiro
STAR MAKER, THE
Scionti, Stefano
FUGITIVE RAGE
Scionti, Steve
FRIEND OF THE FAMILY 2
Sciorra, Annabella
FUNERAL, THE
NATIONAL LAMPOON'S FAVORITE DEADLY SINS
Sciullo, Vincent
MRS. MUNCK
Scofield, Paul
CRUCIBLE, THE
Scola, Paulo
HIDDEN ASSASSIN
Scolari, Peter
THAT THING YOU DO!
Scorsese, Martin
PERSONAL JOURNEY WITH MARTIN SCORSESE THROUGH AMERICAN MOVIES, A
Scott, Adam
HELLRAISER: BLOODLINE
STAR TREK: FIRST CONTACT
Scott, Alan
EDDIE
Scott, Campbell
BIG NIGHT
Scott, Carly
FOREST WARRIOR
Scott, Clive
LIVE WIRE: HUMAN TIMEBOMB
Scott, Dave
FELONY
Scott, Esther
CRAFT, THE
LOW LIFE, THE
WOMAN UNDONE, A
Scott, Ford
BULLETPROOF
Scott, Gayle
JUROR, THE
SLEEPERS
Scott, Joe "Nub"
DON'T BE A MENACE TO SOUTH CENTRAL WHILE DRINKING YOUR JUICE IN THE HOOD
Scott, John-Clay
ED
Scott, Jordan
WHITE SQUALL
Scott, Judith
DUNSTON CHECKS IN
Scott, Kennan
PREACHER'S WIFE, THE
Scott, Lee
DON'T BE A MENACE TO SOUTH CENTRAL WHILE DRINKING YOUR JUICE IN THE HOOD
Scott, Lisa Marie
GLASS CAGE, THE
Scott, Monica
SHOPPING
Scott, Ninka
COLD COMFORT FARM
Scott, Steven
CABLE GUY, THE
Scott, Thomas
CABLE GUY, THE
Scott Thomas, Kristin
ANGELS AND INSECTS
ENGLISH PATIENT, THE
MICROCOSMOS
MISSION: IMPOSSIBLE
POMPATUS OF LOVE, THE
Scott, Tim
LONE JUSTICE: SHOWDOWN AT PLUM CREEK
Scott, Tom Everett
THAT THING YOU DO!
Scott, Victoria
KINGPIN
Scotto, Rosanna
RANSOM
Scozzesi, Delores
TALKING ABOUT SEX
Screaming Trees
HYPE!
Scriba, Mik
DON'T BE A MENACE TO SOUTH CENTRAL WHILE DRINKING YOUR JUICE IN THE HOOD
Scribner, Don
FRIEND OF THE FAMILY 2
Scroggins, Omar Sharif
FAITHFUL
Scuderi, Pasquale
BREAKAWAY
Scurti, John
BEAUTIFUL GIRLS
Sczepaniak, Jeremy
CITIZEN RUTH
Seagal, Steven
EXECUTIVE DECISION
GLIMMER MAN, THE
Seager, Eddy
PORTRAIT OF A LADY, THE
Seago, Terry
PUBLIC ENEMIES
Seale, Bobby
BERKELEY IN THE 60S
Seale, Douglas
PALOOKAVILLE
Seale, Orlando
HAMLET
Sealy, Malik
EDDIE
Sealy-Smith, Alison
RUDE
Searle, John
BERKELEY IN THE 60S
Searls, Peter
FRISK
Sears, Djanet
STAND OFF, THE
Seaton, Geoff
DEMOLITIONIST, THE
Seaweed
HYPE!
Sebastian, John
MESSAGE TO LOVE: THE ISLE OF WIGHT FESTIVAL
Secher, Pierre
PEOPLE VS. LARRY FLYNT, THE

Secor, Kyle
CHILDREN OF FURY
Seda, Jon
DEAR GOD
PRIMAL FEAR
SUNCHASER
Seddon, Dave
LAND AND FREEDOM
Sedgwick, Kyra
LOSING CHASE
LOW LIFE, THE
PHENOMENON
Sedlacek, Zdenek
DELTA OF VENUS
Sefty, Gerard
VISITORS, THE
Segal, Amy
BURIAL OF THE RATS
Segal, George
CABLE GUY, THE
FLIRTING WITH DISASTER
IT'S MY PARTY
MIRROR HAS TWO FACES, THE
Segal, Peter
MY FELLOW AMERICANS
Segall, Pamela
. . . AT FIRST SIGHT
BED OF ROSES
PHANTOM 2040: THE GHOST WHO WALKS
SGT. BILKO
Seganti, Paolo
EVERYONE SAYS I LOVE YOU
Segel, Gil
LAST SUPPER, THE
Seghers, Mil
ANTONIA'S LINE
Segni, Pedro
SHADOW YOU SOON WILL BE, A
Segura, Consol
LAND AND FREEDOM
Segura, Santiago
TWO MUCH
Sehill, Thoraya
ENGLISH PATIENT, THE
Seibel, Lynn Phillip
D3: THE MIGHTY DUCKS
Seibel, Mary
CHAIN REACTION
EVIL HAS A FACE
Seibert, Peter
FIRE ON THE MOUNTAIN
Seidman-Lockamy, Rachel
TO GILLIAN ON HER 37TH BIRTHDAY
Seiler, Terry S.
FRISK
Seitz, Alex
HOUSE ARREST
Seixas, Charles
ELECTRA
Seki, Tomokazu
SANCTUARY: THE MOVIE
Seko, President Mobuto Sese
WHEN WE WERE KINGS
Selby, David
D3: THE MIGHTY DUCKS
HEADLESS BODY IN TOPLESS BAR
WHITE SQUALL
Selby, Deborah
TALKING ABOUT SEX
Selby, Nicholas
AFFAIR, THE
Seldes, Marian
TRUMAN
Selleck, Tom
OPEN SEASON
Sellers, Diane
LAST DANCE
Sellers, Victoria
HEIDI FLEISS HOLLYWOOD MADAM
Sellors, Mark
SOME FOLKS CALL IT A SLING BLADE
Selya, John
EVERYONE SAYS I LOVE YOU
Selznick, Daniel Mayer
LINE KING: THE AL HIRSCHFELD STORY, THE
Semenoff, Ariel
VISITORS, THE
Semler, Willy
JOHNNY 100 PESOS
Semple, Colin
SMALL FACES
Sempliner, Claywood
MODERN AFFAIR, A
Seneca, Joe
TIME TO KILL, A
Senescu, Cathryne
THAT THING YOU DO!
Senger, Frank
MAXIMUM RISK
Sengotta, Will
ANNIE O
FEAR
Senour, Jeffrey
EXECUTIVE DECISION
Senteno, Jose
JUROR, THE
Senzy, Arthur
CRAFT, THE
Serano, Greg
RICH MAN'S WIFE, THE
Serao, Lello
WHO KILLED PASOLINI?
Serbedzija, Rade
TWO DEATHS
Sereys, Jacques
HORSEMAN ON THE ROOF
LA COMEDIE-FRANCAISE OU L'AMOUR JOUE
Sergheyev, Igor
CHEKIST, THE
Sergue, Gerard
RIDICULE
Seritsani, Bob
YANKEE ZULU
Serna, Assumpta
CRAFT, THE
HIDDEN ASSASSIN
Serrano, Nestor
CITY HALL
DAYLIGHT
Serrault, Michel
NELLY AND MONSIEUR ARNAUD
Serre, Josephine
JANE EYRE
Sersale, Gaetano
WHO KILLED PASOLINI?
Sessions, Bob
FUNNYMAN, THE
Sessions, John
ADVENTURES OF PINOCCHIO, THE
MIDWINTER'S TALE, A
Sessoms, Stanley
JERRY MAGUIRE
Seth, Roshan
SOLITAIRE FOR TWO
Setterfield, Valda
EVERYONE SAYS I LOVE YOU
Settles, Jeremy
MR. ICE CREAM MAN
Setzer, Brian
GREAT WHITE HYPE, THE
7 Year Bitch
HYPE!
Severance, Joan
BLACK SCORPION
Severin, Gerhard
FLIRT
Sevigny, Chloe
TREES LOUNGE
Sevilla, Joelle
HORSEMAN ON THE ROOF
Sevilla, Ninon
AVENTURERA
Sewell, Rufus
COLD COMFORT FARM
HAMLET
Seweryn, Andrzej
LA COMEDIE-FRANCAISE OU L'AMOUR JOUE
Sexton Jr., Brendan
WELCOME TO THE DOLLHOUSE
Seymour, Dave
MICHAEL COLLINS
Seymour, Dorin
ERASER
Seymour, Raul
IT'S MY PARTY
Seymour, William
BASQUIAT
Sfar, Med Chedly
SILENCES OF THE PALACE, THE
Sframeli, Francesco
STAR MAKER, THE
Shackelford, David
KINGPIN
Shadix, Glenn
DUNSTON CHECKS IN
MULTIPLICITY
Shaefer, Steve
FARGO
Shaeffer, David
MISSION: IMPOSSIBLE
Shafer, Deidra
MAN OF THE YEAR
Shafer, Dirk
MAN OF THE YEAR
Shafer, Jonathan
DADETOWN
Shafer, Pamela
ENTERTAINING ANGELS: THE DOROTHY DAY STORY
Shaff, Edmund L.
LATE SHIFT, THE
Shahani, Mohammad
WHITE BALLOON, THE
Shaifer, Andrew
BULLETPROOF
CABLE GUY, THE
Shakinovsky, Larry
LIVE WIRE: HUMAN TIMEBOMB
Shale, Kerry
CRACKER: THE MADWOMAN IN THE ATTIC
JUDE
Shalet, Victoria
HAUNTED
Shalhoub, Tony
BIG NIGHT
Shallo, Karen
BIG NIGHT
Shamata, Chuck
SUGARTIME
VIRUS
Shamshak, Sam
NORMA JEAN AND MARILYN
Shanahan, Eileen
MURDERED INNOCENCE
Shannon, Michael J.
AFFAIR, THE
Shannon, Mike
CHAIN REACTION

Shannon, Molly
LAWNMOWER MAN 2: BEYOND CYBERSPACE
Shanta, James
WEEKEND IN THE COUNTRY, A
Shapiro, Joe B.
UP CLOSE AND PERSONAL
Shapiro, Marcia
AMANDA AND THE ALIEN
DESIRE
Shapiro, Rick
PURE DANGER
Sharif, Aaliyan
SMALL WONDERS
Sharp, Glenn
ARRIVAL, THE
Sharp, Matthew
IN LOVE AND WAR
Sharp, Richard D.
MISSION: IMPOSSIBLE
Sharp, Thom
SPY HARD
Sharpe, April
STRIPTEASE
Shatner, Melanie
UNKNOWN ORIGIN
Shattuck, Shari
SPY HARD
Shaver, Helen
CRAFT, THE
OPEN SEASON
OUTER LIMITS: SANDKINGS, THE
TREMORS 2: AFTERSHOCKS
Shaw, Andy
PRIMAL FEAR
Shaw, Bernard
GETTING AWAY WITH MURDER
Shaw, Bill
SHOOTFIGHTER 2: KILL OR BE KILLED!
Shaw, Fiona
JANE EYRE
Shaw, Joe-Norman
SURGEON, THE
Shaw, John
HAPPY GILMORE
Shaw, Michael
SOLITAIRE FOR TWO
Shaw, Pamela
SWINGERS
Shaw, Stan
DAYLIGHT
Shawn, Wallace
ALL DOGS GO TO HEAVEN 2
HOUSE ARREST
WIFE, THE
Shay, Diane
BARB WIRE
Shay, Jimmy
KINGPIN
Shay, Monica
KINGPIN
Shaye, Lin
KINGPIN
LAST MAN STANDING
Shea, Jack
PEOPLE VS. LARRY FLYNT, THE
Shea, John
WEEKEND IN THE COUNTRY, A
Shearer, Chris
BAJA
GRACE OF MY HEART
WHOLE WIDE WORLD, THE
Shearer, Ian
NEON BIBLE, THE
Shearer, Jack
STAR TREK: FIRST CONTACT
UP CLOSE AND PERSONAL
Sheedy, Ally
ONE NIGHT STAND
Sheehy, Joan
SOME MOTHER'S SON
Sheel
EXIT
Sheen, Charlie
ALL DOGS GO TO HEAVEN 2
ARRIVAL, THE
Sheen, Lucy
SECRETS & LIES
Sheen, Martin
ENTERTAINING ANGELS: THE DOROTHY DAY STORY
WAR AT HOME, THE
Sheen, Michael
MARY REILLY
Sheen, Ruth
SECRETS & LIES
YOUNG POISONER'S HANDBOOK, THE
Sheerin, John
TWO FRIENDS
Sheffer, Craig
BLOODKNOT
GRAVE, THE
Sheirl, Angela Hans
FLAMING EARS
Shelby, Larita
BLACK SHEEP
Sheldon, Jack
DEAR GOD
Sheldon, Jana
FUNNYMAN, THE
Shellen, Stephen
RUDE
STAND OFF, THE
Shelley, Dave
BASQUIAT
Shelton, Deborah
DESIRE
Shelton, Marc
RICH MAN'S WIFE, THE
Shen, Freda Foh
GLIMMER MAN, THE
Shend
CAPTIVES
Shenkman, Ben
ERASER
Shepard, Chaz Lamar
SET IT OFF
Shepard, Robert
MERCY
Shepard, Sam
LARRY MCMURTRY'S STREETS OF LAREDO
LILY DALE
Shephard, Mike
NEUROSIA: 50 YEARS OF PERVERSITY
Shepherd, Chaz
PIG'S TALE, A
Shepherd, Chaz Lamar
NUTTY PROFESSOR, THE
Shepherd, Jessica
FARGO
Shepherd, John
DOWN PERISCOPE
Shepherd, Peter
MIND RIPPER
Shepherd, Simon
TALES OF EROTICA
Shepherd, Suzanne
PALOOKAVILLE
TREES LOUNGE
Sheppard, Angel
THAT THING YOU DO!
Sheppard, Mark
LOVER'S KNOT
Sheppard, W. Morgan
SOMETIMES THEY COME BACK . . . AGAIN
Sher, Antony
YOUNG POISONER'S HANDBOOK, THE
Sherbanee, Maurice
EYE FOR AN EYE
Sheridan, Jim
MOLL FLANDERS
Sheridan, Kent
SUGARTIME
Sheridan, Mary Elizabeth
UP CLOSE AND PERSONAL
Sheridan, Nicollete
SPY HARD
Sherlock, Di
SECRETS & LIES
Sherlock, Simon
ENGLISH PATIENT, THE
Sherman, Charley
CHAIN REACTION
Sherman, Cosimo
INFINITY
Sherrie, Michael
SOME MOTHER'S SON
Sherrill, David
UNHOOK THE STARS
Sherrom, Tony Scott
CHAMBER, THE
Sherry, James
BIG BULLY
Sherwin, Candy
PLAYBACK
Sherwin, Steven
WATCH ME
Sheveleva, Nina
ED'S NEXT MOVE
Shibaji, Maria
SGT. KABUKIMAN N.Y.P.D.
Shield, Harvey
BARB WIRE
Shields, Brooke
FREEWAY
Shier, Ivor
MR. WRONG
Shih Kien
MIDNIGHT ANGEL
Shimerman, Armin
EYE FOR AN EYE
Shimizu, Jenny
FOXFIRE
Shinas, Sofia
HOURGLASS
Shlesinger, Bob
MURDERED INNOCENCE
Shock, Nina
HARRIET THE SPY
Shoemaker, Timothy
CHILDREN OF FURY
Shondalon
GIRLS TOWN
Shook, Howard
TATTOO BOY
Shore, Pauly
BIO-DOME
Short, James
ERASER
ONE MAN'S JUSTICE
Short, John
ASSOCIATE, THE
RANSOM
Short, Martin
MARS ATTACKS!
Short, Rhodes
BREAKAWAY
Short, Sylvia
BIRDCAGE, THE
DEAD TO RIGHTS

Short, Wade
THAT THING YOU DO!
Shouse, Janine
MR. HOLLAND'S OPUS
Shrapnel, John
101 DALMATIANS
TWO DEATHS
Shreeman, Andy
LOVE IS ALL THERE IS
Shriner, Kin
DEATH ARTIST, THE
Shriner, Wyl
FOREST WARRIOR
Shropshire, Anne
FIRST WIVES CLUB, THE
Shuain Hui
SOMEONE ELSE'S AMERICA
Shub, Vivienne
BOYS
Shue, Elisabeth
TRIGGER EFFECT, THE
Shue, Matt
FEMALIEN
Shufford, Kimberly
ORIGINAL GANGSTAS
Shuki, Ron
DEADLY OUTBREAK
Shumaker, Helen
JACK
Shuman, Danielle
GIRLFRIENDS
Shure, Paul
THEREMIN: AN ELECTRONIC ODYSSEY
Shuster, Paul
MONSTERSHOW
Shuster, Rick
ERASER
Shuttelworth, Daryl
PORTRAITS OF A KILLER
Sib, Joe
BIO-DOME
Sibertin-Blanc, Jean-Chretien
SINGLE GIRL, A
Sible, Todd
KAZAAM
Siciliano, Francesco
STEALING BEAUTY
WHO KILLED PASOLINI?
Sidaway, Marlene
BEAUTIFUL THING
Sidney, Sylvia
MARS ATTACKS!
Sie, James
CHAIN REACTION
Siebert, Ed
CHAMBER, THE
Siedhoff, Joost
YOUNG POISONER'S HANDBOOK, THE
Siedman, Albert
TALKING ABOUT SEX
Siegal, Dan
HYPE!
Siegel, Eric
BOY CALLED HATE, A
MY FELLOW AMERICANS
Siegel, Lilian
FRANCOIS TRUFFAUT: STOLEN PORTRAITS
Siegel, Liza
TALKING ABOUT SEX
Siegel, Stacey
MR. HOLLAND'S OPUS
Siemaszko, Casey
BLACK SCORPION
PHANTOM, THE
Siemaszko, Nina
SAWBONES
Sierra, Miguel
CITY HALL
Sierra, Victor
BED OF ROSES
Sievers, Gary
PUBLIC ENEMIES
Siff, Helen
JOSH KIRBY . . . TIME WARRIOR!: LAST BATTLE FOR THE UNIVERSE
Sifuentes, Kevin
INDEPENDENCE DAY
Sigall, Eve
HIGH SCHOOL HIGH
Sigloch, Matt
COURAGE UNDER FIRE
Signoracci, Bob
DADETOWN
Signorelli, Tom
JUROR, THE
SLEEPERS
Sigrist, Lori
DEAR GOD
Sigrist, Terri
DEAR GOD
Sigurdsson, Gudrandur
VIKING SAGAS, THE
Silbar, Margaret
PRE-MADONNAS
Silberg, Nicolas
LA COMEDIE-FRANCAISE OU L'AMOUR JOUE
Silberschneider, Johannes
KASPAR HAUSER
Silke, Liam
HARD WAY OUT: BLOODFIST VIII
Sillas, Karen
FLIRT
Silva, Henry
MAD DOG TIME
Silva Jr., Anthony J.
VERY BRADY SEQUEL, A
Silva, Rebeca
MARS ATTACKS!
Silver, Kitty
ISLAND OF DR. MOREAU, THE
Silver, Michael Buchman
EYE FOR AN EYE
Silver, Ron
ARRIVAL, THE
DEADLY OUTBREAK
GIRL 6
KISSINGER AND NIXON
Silver, Susan
HYPE!
Silver-Smith, Rhea
MERCY
Silverfish
NOT BAD FOR A GIRL
Silverman, Jonathan
. . . AT FIRST SIGHT
Silvers, Catherine
SGT. BILKO
Silvers, Dean
MANNY & LO
Silvers, Forrest
MANNY & LO
Silvers, Tyler
MANNY & LO
Silverstein, Margarette
WIDOW'S KISS
Silyn, Lilio
HEDD WYNN
Simels, Robert
CABLE GUY, THE
Simeoni, Valentino
WHO KILLED PASOLINI?
Simmons, J.K.
EXTREME MEASURES
FIRST WIVES CLUB, THE
Simmons, Katrina
EDDIE
Simmons, Lisa
RUMPELSTILTSKIN
Simmons, Peter
BEST OF THE BEST 3: NO TURNING BACK
Simmons, Ronald
ROCK, THE
Simmons, Sue
FIRST WIVES CLUB, THE
Simms, Lise
DENTIST, THE
Simms, Mark
FINAL CUT, THE
Simms, Tashia
MATERNAL INSTINCTS
Simon, Eric
HOURGLASS
Simon, Lou
BARB WIRE
Simon, Susanna
FLIRT
Simon, Tania
GIRLFRIENDS
Simon, Todd
THAT THING YOU DO!
Simonds, David Hamilton
4 TALES OF 2 CITIES
Simpkin, Paul
SOLITAIRE FOR TWO
Simpson, Gary
BEASTMASTER 3: THE EYE OF BRAXUS
Simpson, Tina May
FINAL EQUINOX, THE
Sims, Joan
CANTERVILLE GHOST, THE
Sinacori, Joseph
EDDIE
Sinbad
FIRST KID
HOMEWARD BOUND II: LOST IN SAN FRANCISCO
JINGLE ALL THE WAY
Sinclair, Judy
GETTING AWAY WITH MURDER
Sinclair, Liz
BED OF ROSES
Sinclair, Malcolm
YOUNG POISONER'S HANDBOOK, THE
Sinden, Donald
CANTERVILLE GHOST, THE
Singer, Marc
BEASTMASTER 3: THE EYE OF BRAXUS
Singleton, Steven
SMALL FACES
Singleton, Vernel
EDDIE
Sinise, Gary
RANSOM
TRUMAN
Sinko, Akos Istvan
DOGFIGHTERS, THE
Sinko, Laszlo
RASPUTIN
Sinnott, Dave
VIRTUAL COMBAT
Sir Robert Fossett's Circus
ROLLING STONES ROCK-AND-ROLL CIRCUS, THE
Siragusa, Peter
DUNSTON CHECKS IN
Siravo, Joseph
SEARCH FOR ONE-EYE JIMMY, THE
WALKING AND TALKING

Sirianni, Nicolas
MR. HOLLAND'S OPUS
Sirico, Tony
EVERYONE SAYS I LOVE YOU
SEARCH FOR ONE-EYE JIMMY, THE
Sirius, R.U.
SYNTHETIC PLEASURES
Sirk, Douglas
PERSONAL JOURNEY WITH MARTIN SCORSESE THROUGH AMERICAN MOVIES, A
Sirtis, Marina
STAR TREK: FIRST CONTACT
Siskind, Carol
ABUSE
Sisto, Jeremy
WHITE SQUALL
Sisto, Rocco
ERASER
Sit, Alien
RUMBLE IN THE BRONX
Sitler, Linn
PEOPLE VS. LARRY FLYNT, THE
Sivac, Nusreta
CALLING THE GHOSTS: A STORY ABOUT RAPE, WAR AND WOMEN
Sizemore, Tom
BAD LOVE
Sjogren, Olof
CHILDREN OF NOISY VILLAGE, THE
Skaggs, Jimmie F.
BACKLASH: OBLIVION 2
Skahill, Don William
FARGO
Skalbania, Nelson K.
FINAL CUT, THE
Skarsgard, Stellan
BREAKING THE WAVES
Skeen, Charlie
RAVENHAWK
Skelton, Sean
ROCK, THE
Skewes, Michael
CHAIN REACTION
NORMAL LIFE
Skinner, Rob
HYPE!
Skinner, Vikki
FUGITIVE RAGE
Skipper, Pat
HELLRAISER: BLOODLINE
INDEPENDENCE DAY
Skolimowski, Jerzy
MARS ATTACKS!
Skvar, Jan
KASPAR HAUSER
Skwire, Kate
MUTANT MAN
Skyler
WHISPERING, THE
Slack, Ben
DEATH BENEFIT
Slade, Gloria
MAXIMUM RISK
Slade, Max
SWEEPER, THE
Slade, Robert G.
FOR THE MOMENT
Slagle, G. John
GREAT WHITE HYPE, THE
Slater, Christian
BED OF ROSES
BROKEN ARROW
Slater, Ford
DADETOWN
Slater, Richard
SGT. KABUKIMAN N.Y.P.D.
Slattery, John
CITY HALL
ERASER
LILY DALE
SLEEPERS
Slaughter, Ginger
THAT THING YOU DO!
Slavik, Oldrich
KASPAR HAUSER
Slavin, Millie
ONE NIGHT STAND
Slavin, Randall
PRIMAL FEAR
PUBLIC ACCESS
Slaza, Carrie
FUNERAL, THE
Sleet, Jackson
DOWN PERISCOPE
Slegers, Bart
SUITE 16
Slivnikov, Anatoly
RASPUTIN
Sloane, Charles
MAN OF THE YEAR
Sloman, Roger
COLD LIGHT OF DAY
Slonimsky, Nicolas
THEREMIN: AN ELECTRONIC ODYSSEY
Slotnick, Joseph
TWISTER
Slovak, Jan
ADVENTURES OF PINOCCHIO, THE
Slowik, Matthew
BIG BULLY
Smain
THREE LIVES AND ONLY ONE DEATH
Smal, Andrei
MAXIMUM RISK
Small, Constance
PREACHER'S WIFE, THE
Small, Ralph
SUGARTIME
Smallwood, Tucker
BIO-DOME
BLACK SHEEP
Smallwood, Vivian "Rappin' Granny"
DON'T BE A MENACE TO SOUTH CENTRAL WHILE DRINKING YOUR JUICE IN THE HOOD
Smart, Jen
EDIE & PEN
Smarz, Nena
BOTTLE ROCKET
Smee, Anthony
ENGLISH PATIENT, THE
Smerling, Heather
ENTERTAINING ANGELS: THE DOROTHY DAY STORY
Smigel, Robert
HAPPY GILMORE
Smirnow, Evan
IN LOVE AND WAR
Smit, Nick
WARHEAD
Smith, A.C.
KANSAS CITY
Smith, Aaron Thell
CROW: CITY OF ANGELS, THE
Smith, Alfred
ROAD TO GALVESTON, THE
Smith, Allen J.
HIGH SCHOOL HIGH
Smith, Allison
. . . AT FIRST SIGHT
Smith, Amber
FAITHFUL
FUNERAL, THE
MIRROR HAS TWO FACES, THE
Smith, Amy
KIDS IN THE HALL: BRAIN CANDY
Smith, Anna Nicole
SKYSCRAPER
Smith, Bee-Be
NATIONAL LAMPOON'S FAVORITE DEADLY SINS
SUNSET PARK
Smith, Benjamin Kimball
JERRY MAGUIRE
Smith, Brenda
EYE FOR AN EYE
Smith, Brian
BREAKING THE WAVES
Smith, Britta
MOLL FLANDERS
Smith, Brittany Alyse
PINOCCHIO'S REVENGE
Smith, Brooke
KANSAS CITY
TREES LOUNGE
Smith, Charles Martin
FINAL CUT, THE
LARRY MCMURTRY'S STREETS OF LAREDO
ROAD HOME, THE
Smith, Corbitt
INFINITY
Smith, Cotter
LIFEFORM
Smith, Daniel
INSTITUTE BENJAMENTA
SECRETS & LIES
Smith, Danny
SUGARTIME
Smith, Dylan
SUGARTIME
Smith, Ed
CROSSCUT
Smith, Florence
MIRROR, MIRROR III: THE VOYEUR
Smith, Forrie
LAZARUS MAN, THE
Smith, Fred
THEY BITE
Smith, Gloria K.
CITY HALL
Smith, Gregory
BIG BULLY
HARRIET THE SPY
Smith, Gregory Edward
SPELLBREAKER: SECRET OF THE LEPRECHAUNS
Smith, Hank
GHOST IN THE SHELL
STREET FIGHTER II: THE ANIMATED MOVIE
Smith, Harold W.
BUGGED
Smith, J.W.
DON'T BE A MENACE TO SOUTH CENTRAL WHILE DRINKING YOUR JUICE IN THE HOOD
Smith, Jack
SANTA CLAWS
Smith, James
PEOPLE VS. LARRY FLYNT, THE
Smith, Jamie Renee
CHILDREN OF THE CORN: THE GATHERING
MAGIC IN THE MIRROR
Smith, John Paul
SHOOTFIGHTER 2: KILL OR BE KILLED!
Smith, Joseph
FRISK
Smith Jr., Eddie Bo
CHAIN REACTION
ORIGINAL GANGSTAS

Smith, Julie
BEAUTIFUL THING
THEY BITE
Smith, Keith
GIRL 6
Smith, Kim
TALES OF EROTICA
Smith, Kimani Ray
RUMBLE IN THE BRONX
Smith, Kurtwood
BROKEN ARROW
CITIZEN RUTH
TIME TO KILL, A
Smith, Lane
WAR AT HOME, THE
Smith, Larry
DEADLY OUTBREAK
Smith, Leslie E.
EXECUTIVE DECISION
Smith, Lindzee
NEUROSIA: 50 YEARS OF PERVERSITY
Smith, Liz
HAUNTED
SECRETS & LIES
Smith, Lois
LARGER THAN LIFE
TRUMAN
TWISTER
Smith, Maggie
FIRST WIVES CLUB, THE
Smith, Margaret
BOUND
Smith, Mark
RANSOM
SWINGERS
Smith, Mel
TWELFTH NIGHT
Smith, Michael Bailey
BEST OF THE BEST 3: NO TURNING BACK
Smith, Michele Lonsdale
DEVOTION
Smith, Miriam
BIG BULLY
Smith, Monica
MANNY & LO
Smith, Patrick
ALEX
Smith, Patty
SPITFIRE GRILL, THE
Smith, Richard Kee
BLOODSPORT II: THE NEXT KUMITE
Smith, Robin
REDEMPTION: KICKBOXER 5
Smith, Roger Guenveur
GET ON THE BUS
Smith, Ron Clinton
EDDIE
Smith, Sam
JERRY MAGUIRE
Smith, Seth
JACK
Smith, Shawnee
LOW LIFE, THE
Smith, Sheila Greer
SMALL FACES
Smith, Steve W.
WHERE'S THE MONEY, NOREEN?
Smith, Toukie
PREACHER'S WIFE, THE
Smith, Tyler
JACK
Smith, Will
INDEPENDENCE DAY
Smith, Windland
LOVE IS ALL THERE IS
Smith, Zae
DON'T LET YOUR MEAT LOAF

Smith-Cameron, J.
FIRST WIVES CLUB, THE
HARRIET THE SPY
MODERN AFFAIR, A
PROPRIETOR, THE
Smith-Lotenero, Rose
KINGPIN
Smitham, Pam
ANGELS AND INSECTS
Smitrovich, Bill
GHOSTS OF MISSISSIPPI
INDEPENDENCE DAY
PHANTOM, THE
TRIGGER EFFECT, THE
Smolanoff, Bruce
SLEEPERS
SWEET NOTHING
Smollett, Jurnee
JACK
Smyrl, David Langston
PREACHER'S WIFE, THE
Sneed Sr., Troy L.
PREACHER'S WIFE, THE
Snider, Peter
SUGARTIME
Snipes, Wesley
AMERICA'S DREAM
FAN, THE
Snodgress, Carrie
DEATH BENEFIT
PHANTOM 2040: THE GHOST WHO WALKS
Snow, Dottie
LAST DANCE
Snow, Gary
OFF AND RUNNING
Snow, Rachel
MATILDA
Snow, Raven
DELTA OF VENUS
Snow, Tony
BIRDCAGE, THE
Snow, Victoria
IRON EAGLE IV
Snowden, Anthony
ORIGINAL GANGSTAS
Snyder, Drew
FAN, THE
Snyder, John
ERASER
Snyder, Kim
RANSOM
Snyder, Rick
TUSKEGEE AIRMEN, THE
Sobczyk, Lydia
DADETOWN
Sobel, Barry
THAT THING YOU DO!
Sobolov, David
UNFORGETTABLE
Sobule, Jill
GRACE OF MY HEART
Soda Pop
BIO-DOME
Soedjarvo, Agoes
ISLAND OF DR. MOREAU, THE
PHANTOM, THE
Sogliuzzo, Andre
LOOKING FOR RICHARD
Sokolow, Betsy
MICHAEL
Sola, Miguel Angel
SHADOW YOU SOON WILL BE, A
Solari, Corrado
STAR MAKER, THE
Solari, Sky
MULHOLLAND FALLS

Solberg, Russell
FAST MONEY
Soler, Aldana Garcia
EVITA
Soles, P.J.
OUT THERE
Solis, Christina
DONOR UNKNOWN
HOSTILE INTENTIONS
Solomon, Adam
MIND RIPPER
Solomonoff, Henry
THEREMIN: AN ELECTRONIC ODYSSEY
Some Velvet Sidewalk
HYPE!
Somerville, Geraldine
CRACKER: THE MADWOMAN IN THE ATTIC
HAUNTED
Sommer, Josef
CHAMBER, THE
LETTER TO MY KILLER
Sommer, Robert
DAYLIGHT
Somoza, Luis Lopez
AVENTURERA
Son, D. Ruby
BOGUS
Son, Joe
SHOOTFIGHTER 2: KILL OR BE KILLED!
Song Xiuling
BLUSH
Sonnleitner, Sherry
PORTRAITS OF A KILLER
Sonshine
PHAT BEACH
Soo, Betsy
PHOENIX
Sood, Veena
SURGEON, THE
Soosar, Jenni
KIDS IN THE HALL: BRAIN CANDY
Soper, Mark
PHENOMENON
UNDERSTUDY: GRAVEYARD SHIFT 2, THE
Soren, Tabitha
CABLE GUY, THE
Sorenson, Cindy L.
JOSH KIRBY . . . TIME WARRIOR!: JOURNEY TO THE MAGIC CAVERN
Sorgi, Erica
JERRY MAGUIRE
Soriano, Pepe
SHADOW YOU SOON WILL BE, A
Sorich, Mike
GHOST IN THE SHELL
Sorlano Perez, Ana
SONS OF TRINITY
Sorrentino, Byran
MUTANT MAN
Sorvino, Mira
BEAUTIFUL GIRLS
NORMA JEAN AND MARILYN
SWEET NOTHING
TALES OF EROTICA
Sorvino, Paul
LOVE IS ALL THERE IS
WILLIAM SHAKESPEARE'S ROMEO + JULIET
Soteriou, Mia
SECRETS & LIES
Soto, Joe
DOWN PERISCOPE
Soto, Talisa
SUNCHASER
Soualem, Zinedine
HATE

Souchon, Janine
NELLY AND MONSIEUR ARNAUD
Soucie, Kath
PHANTOM 2040: THE GHOST WHO WALKS
SPACE JAM
Soundgarden
HYPE!
Sousa, Michael R.
BOGUS
Souter, Anthony
HATE
South, Robin
LITTLE WITCHES
Southerland, Boots
LAZARUS MAN, THE
Souvlis, Alexandra
GIRLFRIENDS
Sowerby, Jane
DEVOTION
Spacek, Sissy
BEYOND THE CALL
GRASS HARP, THE
LARRY MCMURTRY'S STREETS OF LAREDO
Spacey, Kevin
LOOKING FOR RICHARD
TIME TO KILL, A
Spade, David
BLACK SHEEP
Spade, Isabelle
RIDICULE
Spader, James
2 DAYS IN THE VALLEY
Spaghetti, Eddie
HYPE!
Spain, Chris
KINGPIN
Spall, Timothy
HAMLET
SECRETS & LIES
Span, Stanley M.
CHAIN REACTION
Spangler, Donna
MATILDA
Spangler, Shirley
COLONY, THE
Spano, Joe
PRIMAL FEAR
Sparber, Herschel
BIRDCAGE, THE
Spargue, Bill
SOME FOLKS CALL IT A SLING BLADE
Sparks, Adrian
IT CAME FROM OUTER SPACE II
Sparks, Adrien
RAVENHAWK
Sparks, Carrie Cain
RUMBLE IN THE BRONX
Sparks, Donita
NOT BAD FOR A GIRL
Sparks, Lee
FIRST KID
Sparks, Willis
SUBSTITUTE, THE
Sparrow, Walter
JANE EYRE
Spates, David
LOOKING FOR TROUBLE
SUBSTITUTE, THE
Speakman, Jeff
DEADLY OUTBREAK
Spears, Aries
JERRY MAGUIRE
Speight Jr., Richard
AMANDA AND THE ALIEN
DEAD WEEKEND
INDEPENDENCE DAY
OUT THERE
Spellos, Peter
BAD LOVE
BOUND
Spencer, Chris
DON'T BE A MENACE TO SOUTH CENTRAL WHILE DRINKING YOUR JUICE IN THE HOOD
Spencer, David
FAMILY THING, A
Spencer, Joel
TATTOO BOY
Spencer, John
ROCK, THE
Spencer, Octavia
TIME TO KILL, A
Spengler, Sanja
FATE
Sperandeo, Tony
STAR MAKER, THE
Sperber, Brian
APART FROM HUGH
Sperberg, Fritz
LAZARUS MAN, THE
Spheeris, "Gypsy"
BLACK SHEEP
Spielvogel, Laurent
MONSTER, THE
Spinella, Stephen
FAITHFUL
Spiner, Brent
INDEPENDENCE DAY
PHENOMENON
PIE IN THE SKY
STAR TREK: FIRST CONTACT
Spinners, The
WHEN WE WERE KINGS
Spinuzza, Doug
CROSSCUT
Spitale, Filippo
STAR MAKER, THE
Spivak, Alice
IF LUCY FELL
Spivey, Shannon
EDDIE
Spoor, Carolien
ANTONIA'S LINE
Spore, Richard
I'M NOT RAPPAPORT
Sporleder, Gregory
MIND RIPPER
ROCK, THE
TWISTER
Spradlin, G.D.
LONG KISS GOODNIGHT, THE
RIDERS OF THE PURPLE SAGE
Spriggs, Elizabeth
JOSEPH CONRAD'S THE SECRET AGENT
Spybey, Dina
BIG NIGHT
FIRST WIVES CLUB, THE
STRIPTEASE
Squires, Alex
SECRETS & LIES
Squires, Lauren
SECRETS & LIES
Squires, Sade
SECRETS & LIES
Srbova, Michaela
DELTA OF VENUS
Srivastava, Anian
TARGET
St. Cecilia Choir
PREACHER'S WIFE, THE
St. Clair, Taylore
FEMALIEN
St. Claire, Taylore
VIRTUAL ENCOUNTERS
St. Espirit, Patrick
TEXAS PAYBACK
St. James, David
BLACK SHEEP
St. John, Jill
OUT THERE
St. John, Michael
ROBIN OF LOCKSLEY
St. John, Trevor
BIO-DOME
St. Macary, Hubert
PROPRIETOR, THE
St. Michael, Jody
HELLRAISER: BLOODLINE
St. Onge, Janet
SPITFIRE GRILL, THE
St. Onge, Korrine
TALES FROM THE CRYPT PRESENTS BORDELLO OF BLOOD
St. Paule, Irma
EVERYTHING RELATIVE
LOVE IS ALL THERE IS
TREES LOUNGE
St. Pierre, Dave
UNFORGETTABLE
St. Ryan, John
HEIDI CHRONICLES, THE
SWEEPER, THE
St. Vincent, Ryk
TIME TO KILL, A
Stabler, Steve
KINGPIN
Stacey, Paul
YOUNG POISONER'S HANDBOOK, THE
Stack, Don
SANTA WITH MUSCLES
Stack, Robert
BEAVIS AND BUTT-HEAD DO AMERICA
Stack, Timothy
DEAR GOD
Stacy, Daniel Chas
DEAD MAN
Stadler, Craig
TIN CUP
Stadvec, Michael
DENTIST, THE
PUBLIC ENEMIES
SOMETIMES THEY COME BACK . . . AGAIN
Staff, Kathy
MARY REILLY
Stafford, Paul
ANNIE O
Stahelski, Chad
BLOODSPORT II: THE NEXT KUMITE
Stahl, Andrew
PEOPLE VS. LARRY FLYNT, THE
Stahl, Andy
TIME TO KILL, A
Stahl, Lasse
CHILDREN OF NOISY VILLAGE, THE
Stahl, Lisa
JERRY MAGUIRE
Stahl, Rene
BARB WIRE
Stahl, Richard
GHOSTS OF MISSISSIPPI
Stallings, Jim
GHOSTS OF MISSISSIPPI
Stallone, Frank
PUBLIC ENEMIES
Stallone, Sage
DAYLIGHT
FATALLY YOURS
Stallone, Sylvester
DAYLIGHT

Stander, Jennifer
FAN, THE
Stanford, Alan
MICHAEL COLLINS
MOLL FLANDERS
Stanger, Len
MODERN AFFAIR, A
Stanger-Ortiz, Jason
SMALL WONDERS
Stanger-Ortiz, Matthew
SMALL WONDERS
Stanley, Christopher
CROSSCUT
Stanley, Taylor
CRUCIBLE, THE
Stanners, Tamara
BIG BULLY
Stanphill, Kimberly
BEASTMASTER 3: THE EYE OF BRAXUS
Stansfield, Claire
MIND RIPPER
Stanton, Harry Dean
DOWN PERISCOPE
PLAYBACK
Stanton, Robert
STRIPTEASE
Stanton, Sophie
BEAUTIFUL THING
Stanton, William
2 DAYS IN THE VALLEY
Stapleton, Jean
LILY DALE
MICHAEL
Star, Lisa
INDEPENDENCE DAY
Starger, Golde
JERRY MAGUIRE
Stark, Don
HEAVEN'S PRISONERS
STAR TREK: FIRST CONTACT
Starks, Carol
MIDWINTER'S TALE, A
Starks, John
EDDIE
Starks, Michael D.
NUTTY PROFESSOR, THE
SGT. BILKO
Starman, Cameron
CABLE GUY, THE
Starr, Beau
MOONSHINE HIGHWAY
WHARF RAT, THE
Starr, Fredro
SUNSET PARK
Starr, Gary
TALES FROM THE CRYPT PRESENTS BORDELLO OF BLOOD
Starr, Melinda
SWINGERS
Starr, Mike
JAMES AND THE GIANT PEACH
JUST YOUR LUCK
TWO IF BY SEA
Starr, Pat
MISSION: IMPOSSIBLE
Staskel, James
UNDER THE HULA MOON
States, Marcia
DADETOWN
States, Sarah
DADETOWN
Statham, Ellen
NOT OF THIS EARTH
Staubdulieh, Anthony
RED SCORPION 2
Staunton, Imelda
TWELFTH NIGHT

Stavin, Mary
DESIRE
Stay, Richard
IT CAME FROM OUTER SPACE II
Stea, Kevin Alexander
BIRDCAGE, THE
Stead, John
LONG KISS GOODNIGHT, THE
Steadman, Alison
SECRETS & LIES
Stedelin, Claudia
THAT THING YOU DO!
Steed, Evin
SMALL WONDERS
Steed, Jairus
SMALL WONDERS
Steed, Zelton
EDDIE
Steele, Jeremy
THEY BITE
Steele, Richard
GREAT WHITE HYPE, THE
Steele, Vanessa
TUNNEL VISION
Steen, Jan
ANTONIA'S LINE
Steenburgen, Mary
GRASS HARP, THE
Stefansdottir, Ingibjorg
VIKING SAGAS, THE
Stefanson, Leslie
MIRROR HAS TWO FACES, THE
Steiger, Jacqueline
MATILDA
Steiger, Rod
CARPOOL
MARS ATTACKS!
OUT THERE
Stein, Ben
HOUSE ARREST
Stein, Gayle
DADETOWN
Stein, Jonathan "Earl"
KINGPIN
Stein, Mary
MAN OF THE YEAR
Stein, Saul
HEAVEN'S PRISONERS
Steinberg, Eric
STAR TREK: FIRST CONTACT
Steinberg, Margot
IN LOVE AND WAR
PROTEUS
Steinem, Gloria
FIRST WIVES CLUB, THE
Steinhardt, Arnold
SMALL WONDERS
Steinhauer, Friedrich
NEUROSIA: 50 YEARS OF PERVERSITY
Steinmetz, Richard
SKYSCRAPER
Stellrecht, Skip
MULTIPLICITY
Stelmack, Andrew
SUGARTIME
Stempel, Dyanne
BREAKAWAY
Stenborg, Helen
MARVIN'S ROOM
Stensland, Athena
NOT OF THIS EARTH
Stephane, Idwig
DAENS
Stephen, Jeffrey J.
BROKEN ARROW
Stephens, Anaar
SMALL WONDERS

Stephens, Glyn
MRS. WINTERBOURNE
Stephens, Joshua
SMALL WONDERS
Stephens, Perry
NORMA JEAN AND MARILYN
TWO-BITS & PEPPER
Stephens, Toby
TWELFTH NIGHT
Sterbling, Philip
MR. ICE CREAM MAN
Sterling, Jim
JOE'S APARTMENT
Sterling, Maury
BULLETPROOF
Sterling, Mindy
MAN OF THE YEAR
Stern, Daniel
CELTIC PRIDE
Stern, Dawn
ORIGINAL GANGSTAS
Stern, Isaac
SMALL WONDERS
Stern, Kate
MISSING PIECES
Stern, Leonard
MISSING PIECES
Stern, Stewart
CELLULOID CLOSET, THE
Stern, Susan
CITIZEN RUTH
Steveman, Kaj
EVIL ED
Stevens, Arkay
THIN LINE BETWEEN L OVE AND HATE, A
Stevens, Brittany English
GRACE OF MY HEART
Stevens, C. B.
OVER THE WIRE
Stevens, Connie
LOVE IS ALL THERE IS
Stevens, Dana
EXTREME MEASURES
Stevens, Fisher
COLD FEVER
POMPATUS OF LOVE, THE
Stevens, James Castle
COLONY, THE
Stevens, Joe
LARRY MCMURTRY'S STREETS OF LAREDO
LONE STAR
TEXAS CHAINSAW MASSACRE: THE NEXT GENERATION
Stevens, Lisa
RUMBLE IN THE BRONX
Stevens, Lita
GRACE OF MY HEART
Stevens, Robbi
MARY REILLY
Stevens, Sally
SPY HARD
Stevens, Sara
JANE EYRE
Stevens, Shadoe
DEATH ARTIST, THE
Stevens, Sharon
DADETOWN
Stevens, Stella
VIRTUAL COMBAT
Stevenson, Charles
SGT. BILKO
Stevenson, Cynthia
LIVE NUDE GIRLS
Stevenson Jr., Charles C.
UP CLOSE AND PERSONAL

Stevenson, Juliet
EMMA
PARIS WAS A WOMAN
Stevenson, Parker
NOT OF THIS EARTH
Stevenson, Patrick
RED SCORPION 2
Stevenson, Tyrone
TERMINAL IMPACT
Stevie, Gillian
JOHNNY SHORTWAVE
Steward, Renee
RAW TARGET
Steward, Sam
PARIS WAS A WOMAN
Stewardson, Matthew
REDEMPTION: KICKBOXER 5
Stewart, Amanda Payton
KIDS IN THE HALL: BRAIN CANDY
Stewart, Anthoni
WITCHCRAFT: SALEM'S GHOST
Stewart, Bill
101 DALMATIANS
Stewart, Bobby
ANNIE O
Stewart, Duncan
NEON BIBLE, THE
Stewart, French
BROKEN ARROW
Stewart, Guy
FOR THE MOMENT
Stewart, Jackie
SLING BLADE
TIME TO KILL, A
Stewart, Jamie
SLING BLADE
Stewart, Kathy
FAN, THE
Stewart, Lynne Marie
DUNSTON CHECKS IN
Stewart, Malcolm
MATERNAL INSTINCTS
Stewart, Nils
BLOODSPORT II: THE NEXT KUMITE
Stewart, Nils Allen
BARB WIRE
DEMOLITIONIST, THE
Stewart, Patrick
CANTERVILLE GHOST, THE
STAR TREK: FIRST CONTACT
Stewart, Paule
BULLETPROOF
Stewart, Robert
ANNIE O
Stewart, Scott
SLING BLADE
Stewart, Sheri Mann
MY FELLOW AMERICANS
Stewart, Todd
EXTREME MEASURES
Stewart, Tonea
TIME TO KILL, A
Sthare, Ingrid
SOMETIMES THEY COME BACK . . . AGAIN
Stidham, Daniel T.
PARADISE LOST: THE CHILD MURDERS AT ROBIN HOOD HILLS
Stier, Hans Martin
FLIRT
VIKING SAGAS, THE
Stiers, David Ogden
EVERYONE SAYS I LOVE YOU
HUNCHBACK OF NOTRE DAME, THE
Stiffel, Aya
UNDER THE DOMIM TREE
Stiggers Jr., Willie James
PREACHER'S WIFE, THE
Stiller, Amy
CABLE GUY, THE
Stiller, Ben
CABLE GUY, THE
FLIRTING WITH DISASTER
FOR BETTER OR WORSE
HAPPY GILMORE
IF LUCY FELL
Stillman, Richard
DADETOWN
Stillman, Tom
THIN LINE BETWEEN LOVE AND HATE, A
Stilwell, Dick
CHAMBER, THE
Stimpson, Catharine R.
PARIS WAS A WOMAN
Stinton, Colin
IN LOVE AND WAR
Stivi, Alon
HARD JUSTICE
Stocci, Roberto
MILLE BOLLE BLU
Stock, Emma
FIRST KID
Stock, Jesse
GLIMMER MAN, THE
Stock, Michael
FRISK
Stock-Poynton, Amy
LITTLE DEATH, THE
Stockbridge, Peter
SECRETS & LIES
SHAMELESS
Stocker, Emily
TWO FRIENDS
Stockton, Rose
FARGO
Stockwell, Alec
STAND OFF, THE
Stockwell, Dean
MR. WRONG
NAKED SOULS
Stofer, Dawn
BIG BULLY
Stofford, Randy
DEMOLITIONIST, THE
Stohl, Hank
DIABOLIQUE
Stohn, Alex
KINGPIN
Stohn, Mary
KINGPIN
Stoica, Luana
MAGIC IN THE MIRROR
Stoilob, Nickolai
SAWBONES
Stojanovich, Christina
COURAGE UNDER FIRE
Stojkovic, Andjela
SOMEONE ELSE'S AMERICA
Stokes, Allan R.
TUSKEGEE AIRMEN, THE
Stole, Mink
DEATH ARTIST, THE
Stoltz, Eric
GRACE OF MY HEART
JERRY MAGUIRE
2 DAYS IN THE VALLEY
Stolze, Lena
BROTHER OF SLEEP
Stone, Chris
UP CLOSE AND PERSONAL
Stone, Dee Wallace
BEST OF THE BEST 3: NO TURNING BACK
FRIGHTENERS, THE
Stone, Doug
GHOST IN THE SHELL
Stone, Fred
NORMAL LIFE
Stone, Jonathan
INSTITUTE BENJAMENTA
Stone, Matthew
CANNIBAL! THE MUSICAL
Stone, Michael
ERASER
ONE MAN'S JUSTICE
Stone, Sharon
DIABOLIQUE
LAST DANCE
Stoneham, John
ELECTRA
Stoneham Jr., John
ELECTRA
STUPIDS, THE
Storey, Howard
TRACKS OF A KILLER
Storey, John
INDEPENDENCE DAY
Storey, Ptosha
ROAD TO GALVESTON, THE
Stork, Tommy
LITTLE WITCHES
Stormare, Peter
FARGO
Storms, Michael
IF LUCY FELL
TREES LOUNGE
Storms, Pamela
DADETOWN
Stothard, Lisa
KINGPIN
Stoudamire, Robert Earl
FIRST KID
Stout, Justin
MATILDA
Stovall, Craig
PUBLIC ACCESS
Stowe, Jane
SHOWGIRL MURDERS, THE
Stracuzzi, Grazio
MILLE BOLLE BLU
Stradalova, Jana
DELTA OF VENUS
Strahan, Paul
RAW TARGET
Strain, Julie
BAD LOVE
DARK SECRETS
RED LINE
Straite-McClure, Luke
MR. STITCH
Stram, Henry
ANGELA
SLEEPERS
Strand, Scott
LAST MAN STANDING
Stransky, Charles
DANGEROUS PASSION
TALKING ABOUT SEX
Stransky, Oldrich
DELTA OF VENUS
Strasser, Michael
GHOSTS OF MISSISSIPPI
LAST MAN STANDING
Stratas, Fabian
EVITA
Stratford, Judith
SPIDER & ROSE
Strathairn, David
BEYOND THE CALL
MOTHER NIGHT
STAND OFF, THE
Strathairn, Tay
LONE STAR

Stratton, W.K.
JAG
Strauss, Lee
INDEPENDENCE DAY
Strauss, Louis
MOTHER NIGHT
Strauss, Stacy
DEAD WEEKEND
Strecker, Scott
THAT THING YOU DO!
Streep, Meryl
BEFORE AND AFTER
MARVIN'S ROOM
Streisand, Barbra
MIRROR HAS TWO FACES, THE
Streit, Alexander
CRUCIBLE, THE
Strick, Frank
PURE DANGER
Strickland, Gail
MOTHER'S PRAYER, A
Strickland, Stephanie
TIME TO KILL, A
Stripling, Randy
LONE STAR
Stroden, Kipp
KINGPIN
Stroganov, Bev
NEUROSIA: 50 YEARS OF PERVERSITY
Stromer, Eric A.
GRACE OF MY HEART
Strong, Brenda
CRAFT, THE
Strong, Johnny
GLIMMER MAN, THE
Strong, Mark
CAPTIVES
Strong, Peter
DANGEROUS PASSION
Strong, Shiloh
FOXFIRE
Stroock, Gloria
MISSING PIECES
Strother, Frederick
UP CLOSE AND PERSONAL
Stroud, Don
CRIMINAL HEARTS
SAWBONES
UNKNOWN ORIGIN
Strozier, Henry
FIRST KID
Strozier, Scott
STAR TREK: FIRST CONTACT
Strudom, Julie
YANKEE ZULU
Struhar, Hans Georg
ROCK, THE
Struycken, Carel
BACKLASH: OBLIVION 2
OUT THERE
Struyken, Carel
UNDER THE HULA MOON
Strzalkwoski, Henry
RAW TARGET
Stuart, Laird
TOLLBOOTH
Stuart, Roxana
ANGELA
Stubbs, Imogen
JACK & SARAH
TWELFTH NIGHT
Stube, Brian
KINGPIN
Stuber, Kathy
THAT THING YOU DO!
Studen, Stacy
GLIMMER MAN, THE
Studer, Karen
NEMESIS III: PREY HARDER
Studer, Robert
BROTHER OF SLEEP
Studi, Wes
LARRY MCMURTRY'S STREETS OF LAREDO
LONE JUSTICE: SHOWDOWN AT PLUM CREEK
Study, Lomax
JOSH KIRBY . . . TIME WARRIOR!: JOURNEY TO THE MAGIC CAVERN
Stuhr, Jerzy
MOTHER OF KINGS
Stumm, Michael
I SHOT ANDY WARHOL
Sturges, Shannon
. . . AT FIRST SIGHT
PRE-MADONNAS
Su, John Alan
RACE THE SUN
Suarez, Jeremy
JERRY MAGUIRE
Suarez, Lisa
LONE STAR
Suarez, Manny
UP CLOSE AND PERSONAL
Suarez, Patti Davis
UP CLOSE AND PERSONAL
Subert, Gaston
MISSION: IMPOSSIBLE
Sucharetza, Marla
FAN, THE
LOVER'S KNOT
Suchet, David
EXECUTIVE DECISION
Suchoka, Anna Grazyna
DAENS
Sudduth, Skipp
ERASER
Sues, Alan
DEATH ARTIST, THE
Sugar, Bert Randolph
GREAT WHITE HYPE, THE
Sugar, J.B.
ANNIE O
Suggs, Harold
MAN WITH THE PERFECT SWING, THE
Suij, Crispyn Duplisia
APART FROM HUGH
Sulipeck, Joey
PEOPLE VS. LARRY FLYNT, THE
Sullivan, Charlotte
HARRIET THE SPY
LEGEND OF GATOR FACE, THE
Sullivan, Hannah
FLIRT
Sullivan, John
SUBSTANCE OF FIRE, THE
Sullivan, Justin
SCREAM
Sullivan, Nancy
RATTLED
Sullivan, Sophia
JACK & SARAH
Sullivan, Stacy
JOSH KIRBY . . . TIME WARRIOR!: LAST BATTLE FOR THE UNIVERSE
Sulocki, Kim
EVIL ED
Summers, Amanda
MATILDA
Summers, Bunny
MERLIN'S SHOP OF MAGICAL WONDERS
Summers, Kristin
MATILDA
Summers, Sian
HEDD WYNN
Sumner, John
FRIGHTENERS, THE
Sumter, Stacie
MIRROR HAS TWO FACES, THE
Sundgren, Carina
EVIL ED
Sunni
DUNSTON CHECKS IN
Supersuckers, The
HYPE!
Sus, Victoria
EVITA
Susi, Carol Ann
EDIE & PEN
Susman, Shantha
SMALL WONDERS
Susman, Todd
JUROR, THE
Sussman, Ben
MERLIN'S SHOP OF MAGICAL WONDERS
Sutera, Paul
VERY BRADY SEQUEL, A
Sutherland, Claudette
MAN OF THE YEAR
Sutherland, Donald
HOLLOW POINT
TIME TO KILL, A
Sutherland, Kendra
JACK
Sutherland, Kiefer
EYE FOR AN EYE
4 TALES OF 2 CITIES
FREEWAY
HOURGLASS
TIME TO KILL, A
Sutherland, Mac
SGT. KABUKIMAN N.Y.P.D.
Sutton, Patrick
TIME TO KILL, A
Suwarino, Titi
WITHOUT MERCY
Suzuki, Seijun
COLD FEVER
Svanc, Milan
DELTA OF VENUS
Svegen, Asa
EVIL ED
Svensson, Ingwar
CHILDREN OF NOISY VILLAGE, THE
Svihlik, Frantisek
DELTA OF VENUS
Svoboda, Sabine
FLIRT
Svornic, Skye
YANKEE ZULU
Swain, Charles
CHAMBER, THE
Swain, Howard
NIGHT OF THE SCARECROW
Swank, Hilary
SOMETIMES THEY COME BACK . . . AGAIN
Swansburg, Jim
SABRINA, THE TEENAGE WITCH
Swanson, Eric
EDIE & PEN
Swanson, Jackie
BACKLASH: OBLIVION 2
Swanson, Kristy
PHANTOM, THE
Swanson, Parker
TRIGGER EFFECT, THE
Swanson, Rochelle
DEADLY OUTBREAK
Swanson, Scott
HALFBACK OF NOTRE DAME, THE
Swanson, Tighe
LOVE IS ALL THERE IS

Swarbrick, Carol
NORMA JEAN AND MARILYN
Swarts, Cheryl
EXTREME MEASURES
LOSING CHASE
Swash, Joe
ADVENTURES OF PINOCCHIO, THE
Swedberg, Heidi
UP CLOSE AND PERSONAL
Sweeney, Birdy
MOLL FLANDERS
Sweeney, Garry
SMALL FACES
Sweeney, Steve
CELTIC PRIDE
Sweeney, Warren
NORMA JEAN AND MARILYN
Sweet, Vonte
AMERICAN STRAYS
Swenson, Jeep
BULLETPROOF
Swenson, Mark
HIGH SCHOOL HIGH
Swift, David
JACK & SARAH
Swift, Keith
MR. HOLLAND'S OPUS
Swike, Jacqueline
ORIGINAL GANGSTAS
Swing, Catherine
WHERE'S THE MONEY, NOREEN?
Swinscoe, Steve
CAPTIVES
Swit, Loretta
FOREST WARRIOR
Sy, Javanni
OPEN SEASON
Syal, Meera
BEAUTIFUL THING
Sylbert, Richard
MULHOLLAND FALLS
Sylver, Brett
MAN OF THE YEAR
Sylvester, Michelle
ANGELS AND INSECTS
Sylwetser, Mary
CURTIS'S CHARM
Symons-Sutcliffe, Alex
MADAGASCAR SKIN
Syms, Richard
SECRETS & LIES
Syp, Miranda
BOYS
Szarvas, Jozsef
OUTPOST, THE
Szekatsch, Gabriele
FLAMING EARS
Szekely, Miklos B.
RASPUTIN
Szekeres, Thomas
HAMLET
Szekhelyi, Joszef
DOGFIGHTERS, THE
Szigeti, Cynthia
MAN OF THE YEAR
UP CLOSE AND PERSONAL
Szokol, Peter
RASPUTIN
T'Kaye, Eileen
MAGIC IN THE MIRROR
Tab, Joe
ELECTRA
Tabata, Tetsuya
FLIRT
Tabone, Elyse
GIRLFRIENDS
Tacher, Alyssa
CURDLED
Tackett, Kellie Jo
MISSING PIECES
Tad
HYPE!
Taenaka, James Katsuki
LOW LIFE, THE
Taffone, Daniele
WHO KILLED PASOLINI?
Tagawa, Cary-Hiroyuki
PHANTOM, THE
Tager, Aron
CURTIS'S CHARM
WHERE'S THE MONEY, NOREEN?
Tager, Joshua
FRISK
Taghmaoui, Said
HATE
Tainton, Kelly
EVIL ED
Tait, Tristan
LARRY MCMURTRY'S STREETS OF LAREDO
Taj Mahal
ONCE UPON A TIME . . . WHEN WE WERE COLORED
ROLLING STONES ROCK-AND-ROLL CIRCUS, THE
Takagi, Miyako
KAMIKAZE TAXI
Takei, George
BACKLASH: OBLIVION 2
KISSINGER AND NIXON
Takeshi, Caesar
KAMIKAZE TAXI
Talbot, Annie
DOWN PERISCOPE
Talbot, Tamarah
HEAD OF THE FAMILY
Talbott, Michael
OUT THERE
Taliferro, Michael
THIN LINE BETWEEN LOVE AND HATE, A
Talley, Andre Leon
CATWALK
Talmadge, Victor
NAKED SOULS
Talor, Venesa
FEMALIEN
Talwar, Sanjay
EXTREME MEASURES
Tam, Anika
SMALL WONDERS
Tambakis, Peter Anthony
RANSOM
Tambor, Jeffrey
BIG BULLY
Tamburro, Chuck
LONG KISS GOODNIGHT, THE
Tamburro, Michael
GLIMMER MAN, THE
Tammi, Tom
SHE'S THE ONE
Tamparo, Fred
LOOKING FOR TROUBLE
Tan, Philip
BLOODSPORT II: THE NEXT KUMITE
Tanaka, Hideyuki
BIG WARS
Tanaka, Sara
RACE THE SUN
Tang, Sikay
DON'T LET YOUR MEAT LOAF
Tang Tsung-sheng
MAHJONG
Tangkilisan, Diaz
WITHOUT MERCY
Tann, Tyrone
TRIGGER EFFECT, THE
Tanner, Antwon
SUNSET PARK
Tanner, Jan
CHILDREN OF FURY
Tanner, Richard
GLIMMER MAN, THE
Tanti, Melissa
FLY AWAY HOME
Tanzillo, Pat
SPY HARD
Tape-beatles, The
SONIC OUTLAWS
Tarantina, Brian
ASSOCIATE, THE
BED OF ROSES
SWEET NOTHING
Tarantino, Filippo
STAR MAKER, THE
Tarantino, Quentin
FROM DUSK TILL DAWN
GIRL 6
Tarassachvili, Thamar
CHASING BUTTERFLIES
Taravella, Rosie
NORMA JEAN AND MARILYN
Tarigan, Anna M.
WITHOUT MERCY
Tarr, Trevor A.
SOME FOLKS CALL IT A SLING BLADE
Tarwater, James
RAVENHAWK
Tash, Diana
DENTIST, THE
Tassoni, Angela
WITCHCRAFT: SALEM'S GHOST
Taste
MESSAGE TO LOVE: THE ISLE OF WIGHT FESTIVAL
Tata, Joe E.
BAD LOVE
Tate, Lahmard
DON'T BE A MENACE TO SOUTH CENTRAL WHILE DRINKING YOUR JUICE IN THE HOOD
Tate, Nick
BED OF ROSES
Tate, Rod
JERRY MAGUIRE
Tatum, Bradford
BLACK SCORPION
DOWN PERISCOPE
WITHIN THE ROCK
Taub, Melissa
LITTLE WITCHES
Tavare, Jay
EXECUTIVE DECISION
Tavarez-Terrero, Andres
SMALL WONDERS
Tavel, Sebastien
HATE
Tavernier, Bertrand
FRANCOIS TRUFFAUT: STOLEN PORTRAITS
Tavin, Erin
CRAFT, THE
Taxier, Arthur
LATE SHIFT, THE
Tay, Sharon
INDEPENDENCE DAY
Taylor, Amber
COLD LIGHT OF DAY
LAST SUPPER, THE
Taylor, Andy
KINGPIN

Taylor, Billy
SMALL WONDERS
Taylor, Christine
CRAFT, THE
VERY BRADY SEQUEL, A
Taylor, Corey Joshua
ERASER
Taylor, Courtney
TRACKS OF A KILLER
Taylor, Cyril
IN LOVE AND WAR
Taylor, Diana
LAST DANCE
Taylor, Frank Hoyt
GHOSTS OF MISSISSIPPI
Taylor, Helen
GETTING AWAY WITH MURDER
Taylor, Holland
ONE FINE DAY
Taylor, Jerel
TRUMAN
Taylor, Jocelyn
GIRLFRIENDS
Taylor, Joseph Lyle
GIRL 6
Taylor Jr., Charles Earl "Spud"
ONCE UPON A TIME . . . WHEN WE WERE COLORED
Taylor, Lili
COLD FEVER
GIRLS TOWN
I SHOT ANDY WARHOL
RANSOM
Taylor, Myra Lucretia
EVERYONE SAYS I LOVE YOU
Taylor, Noah
SHINE
Taylor, Raph
IN LOVE AND WAR
Taylor, Raymond
ORIGINAL GANGSTAS
Taylor, Regina
COURAGE UNDER FIRE
FAMILY THING, A
Taylor, Renee
LOVE IS ALL THERE IS
Taylor, Rip
VIRTUAL COMBAT
Taylor, Robert
SOME MOTHER'S SON
Taylor, Rod
OPEN SEASON
Taylor, Steven
BIG BULLY
Tcherkassoff, Alexandre
CHASING BUTTERFLIES
te Selle, Truus
ANTONIA'S LINE
CROCODILES IN AMSTERDAM
Teague, Marshall
COLONY, THE
ROCK, THE
Teed, Jill
FINAL CUT, THE
Teehan, Nicola
MOLL FLANDERS
Teer, Domini
PARADISE LOST: THE CHILD MURDERS AT ROBIN HOOD HILLS
Tefkin, Blaire
BAD LOVE
Tejero, Lisa
CHAIN REACTION
Telford, Jo
EVERYONE SAYS I LOVE YOU
Tello, Joseph
GHOSTS OF MISSISSIPPI
Tempo, Soul
PREACHER'S WIFE, THE
ten Bruggencate, Catherine
ANTONIA'S LINE
ten Holt, Jaap
CROCODILES IN AMSTERDAM
Ten Years After
MESSAGE TO LOVE: THE ISLE OF WIGHT FESTIVAL
Tench, John
JOHNNY SHORTWAVE
UNDERSTUDY: GRAVEYARD SHIFT 2, THE
Tenenbaum, Brian
BOTTLE ROCKET
Tennant, David
JUDE
Tennant, Susie
HYPE!
Tennant, Victoria
EDIE & PEN
Tenney, Jon
PHANTOM, THE
Tennor, Adria
FIRST WIVES CLUB, THE
Teo
BARB WIRE
Teodosiu, Valentin
OUTPOST, THE
Terada, Minori
MABOROSI
Terdre, Matthew
TWO DEATHS
Termo, Leonard
SERIAL KILLER
Ternisiern, Pascal
MACHINE, THE
Terracina, Nydia Rodriguez
CHAIN REACTION
Terrance, John
MERLIN'S SHOP OF MAGICAL WONDERS
Terranove, Umberto
STAR MAKER, THE
Terrel, Cedrick
WHISPERING, THE
Terrell, Tommy
DOWN PERISCOPE
Terry, Kim
EVENING STAR, THE
Terry, Kirk D.
FAN, THE
Terry, Paul
JAMES AND THE GIANT PEACH
Tertyask, Russ
SHADOW WARRIORS
Tessler, Karl
TWO DEATHS
Tetreau, David
BREAKAWAY
Teuber, Karl-Heinz
BLONDES HAVE MORE GUNS
Tewes, Lauren
IT CAME FROM OUTER SPACE II
Texada, Tia
FROM DUSK TILL DAWN
Thalbach, Katharina
KASPAR HAUSER
Thaler, Emma
NATIONAL LAMPOON'S FAVORITE DEADLY SINS
Thalken, Meg
FAMILY THING, A
Thall, Benj
HOMEWARD BOUND II: LOST IN SAN FRANCISCO
Tharp, Hunter
PAINTED HERO
Thayil, Kim
HYPE!
The Gits
HYPE!
Thedford, Marcello
DAYLIGHT
Theiss, Richard
EXIT
Thelen, Jodi
PLAYBACK
Theodore, Diana
VERY BRADY SEQUEL, A
Theremin, Leon
THEREMIN: AN ELECTRONIC ODYSSEY
Theron, Charlize
THAT THING YOU DO!
2 DAYS IN THE VALLEY
Theroux, Earl
LETTER TO MY KILLER
Theroux, Justin
I SHOT ANDY WARHOL
Thewlis, David
DRAGONHEART
ISLAND OF DR. MOREAU, THE
JAMES AND THE GIANT PEACH
Thibault, Carl
WOMAN UNDONE, A
Thibaut Jr., Robbie
BIO-DOME
Thibeau, Robby
KINGPIN
Thicke, Alan
OPEN SEASON
Thierree, Aurelia
PEOPLE VS. LARRY FLYNT, THE
Thigpen, Father William M.
MULHOLLAND FALLS
Thigpen, Lynne
BOYS NEXT DOOR, THE
Thigpen, Sandra
CABLE GUY, THE
CURDLED
LAST DANCE
Thioune, Fatou
HATE
Thirion, Aude
MACHINE, THE
Thom, Ben
HAMLET
Thomas, Alex
DON'T BE A MENACE TO SOUTH CENTRAL WHILE DRINKING YOUR JUICE IN THE HOOD
Thomas, Brenda
CITY HALL
Thomas, David Jean
WITCHCRAFT: SALEM'S GHOST
Thomas, Diane
DADETOWN
Thomas, Gail
BEAVIS AND BUTT-HEAD DO AMERICA
Thomas, George
MADAGASCAR SKIN
Thomas, Henry
RIDERS OF THE PURPLE SAGE
Thomas III, Johnny
GRACE OF MY HEART
MATILDA
Thomas, Isa
HARVEST OF FIRE
WALKING AND TALKING
Thomas, Jack C.
BEST OF THE BEST 3: NO TURNING BACK
Thomas, Jay
MR. HOLLAND'S OPUS
Thomas, Jeff
KINGPIN

Thomas, Jennifer
DESOLATION ANGELS
Thomas, John Norman
SOMEONE ELSE'S AMERICA
Thomas, Jonathan Taylor
ADVENTURES OF PINOCCHIO, THE
Thomas, Ken
MARS ATTACKS!
Thomas, Leonard
GIRL 6
TIME TO KILL, A
Thomas, Lindsay
ANGELS AND INSECTS
Thomas, Monty
GHOSTS OF MISSISSIPPI
Thomas, Pat
WIDOW'S KISS
Thomas, Peyton
WHITE SQUALL
Thomas, Preston
KINGPIN
Thomas, Ray Anthony
I'M NOT RAPPAPORT
Thomas, Rev. Lawrence K.
PREACHER'S WIFE, THE
Thomas, Richard
DOWN, OUT AND DANGEROUS
Thomas, Robert
HIDDEN ASSASSIN
LONG KISS GOODNIGHT, THE
Thomas, Robin
CHAMELEON
Thomas, Rufus
FAMILY THING, A
Thomas, Sarah
MADAGASCAR SKIN
Thomas, Sean Patrick
COURAGE UNDER FIRE
Thomas, Ulisa A.
PREACHER'S WIFE, THE
Thomerson, Tim
NEMESIS III: PREY HARDER
Thomlison, Alec
MRS. WINTERBOURNE
Thompson, Brian
DRAGONHEART
Thompson, Charles E.
SUNSET PARK
Thompson, Dar
BEASTMASTER 3: THE EYE OF BRAXUS
Thompson, Don
SURGEON, THE
Thompson, Glen
FOR THE MOMENT
Thompson, Hugh
MAXIMUM RISK
Thompson, Ian
ROUJIN-Z
Thompson, Jack
BROKEN ARROW
LAST DANCE
Thompson, John Robert
BEST OF THE BEST 3: NO TURNING BACK
Thompson, Kenan
D3: THE MIGHTY DUCKS
Thompson, Mark
CABLE GUY, THE
INDEPENDENCE DAY
SET IT OFF
Thompson, Scott
KIDS IN THE HALL: BRAIN CANDY
Thompson, Shawn Taylor
EVENING STAR, THE
Thompson, Sophie
EMMA
Thompson, Susanna
AMERICA'S DREAM
GHOSTS OF MISSISSIPPI
Thompson, Teri
BREAKAWAY
Thompson, Trent Nicholas
BEAUTIFUL GIRLS
Thomson, Anna
ANGELA
I SHOT ANDY WARHOL
Thomson, John
YOUNG POISONER'S HANDBOOK, THE
Thomson, Scott
TWISTER
Thomson, Tess
CRACKER: THE MADWOMAN IN THE ATTIC
Thoolan, Gerard
COLD LIGHT OF DAY
Thorne, Angela
COLD COMFORT FARM
Thorne, Callie
ED'S NEXT MOVE
Thorne, Tracy
JACK & SARAH
Thorns, Tricia
CAPTIVES
Thornton, Billy Bob
DEAD MAN
OUT THERE
SLING BLADE
SOME FOLKS CALL IT A SLING BLADE
Thornton, David
IF LUCY FELL
OFF AND RUNNING
UNHOOK THE STARS
Thornton, Patricia
GALAXIES ARE COLLIDING
Thornton, Shannon
JERRY MAGUIRE
Thorp, William
LAST DANCE
Thorsen, Sven-Ole
VIKING SAGAS, THE
Thorson, Russ
APART FROM HUGH
Thrainsson, Gudmundur
VIKING SAGAS, THE
Thrasher, Sibel
TALES FROM THE CRYPT PRESENTS BORDELLO OF BLOOD
Thrush, Michelle
DEAD MAN
Thunderwolf, Christopher
DEMOLITIONIST, THE
Thurman, Bill
PAINTED HERO
Thurman, Dechen
TRUTH ABOUT CATS AND DOGS, THE
Thurman, Uma
BEAUTIFUL GIRLS
4 TALES OF 2 CITIES
TRUTH ABOUT CATS AND DOGS, THE
Thurston, Robert
ROBIN OF LOCKSLEY
Tian Shaojun
STORY OF XINGHUA, THE
Tibbetts, Stephen
HAPPY GILMORE
Tichy, Daniel
DELTA OF VENUS
Ticotin, Nancy
EVERYONE SAYS I LOVE YOU
FIRST WIVES CLUB, THE
RANSOM
Ticotin, Rachel
WHARF RAT, THE
Tiefenbach, Dov
BEYOND THE CALL
HARRIET THE SPY
Tiernan, Andrew
TWO DEATHS
Tiernan, Michael
SURGEON, THE
Tierney, Jacob
NEON BIBLE, THE
Tierney, Lawrence
2 DAYS IN THE VALLEY
Tierney, Maura
MERCY
PRIMAL FEAR
Tietsort, Steve
ARRIVAL, THE
Tiffany
YOU'LL NEVER MAKE LOVE IN THIS TOWN AGAIN
Tiffe, Angelo
TEXAS PAYBACK
Tigar, Kenneth
PRIMAL FEAR
RAGE
Tighe, Darren
JUDE
Tighe, Kevin
RACE THE SUN
Tignini, Eric G.
PHENOMENON
Tilbrook, Paula
BUTTERFLY KISS
Tilden, Leif
LIFEFORM
Tiller, Patrick
TOO FAST, TOO YOUNG
Tilly, Grant
ALEX
Tilly, Jennifer
AMERICAN STRAYS
BOUND
EDIE & PEN
HOUSE ARREST
POMPATUS OF LOVE, THE
Timbes, Graham
BODY COUNT
TIME TO KILL, A
Timmins, Cali
TAKEOVER, THE
Timsit, Patrick
LITTLE INDIAN, BIG CITY
Timtsunik, Leonid
BURIAL OF THE RATS
Tiny Ron
LAST MAN STANDING
Tiny Tim
MESSAGE TO LOVE: THE ISLE OF WIGHT FESTIVAL
Tipp, Marilyn
CITIZEN RUTH
Tippo, Patti
BARB WIRE
Tipton, Christine
DADETOWN
Tirelli, Jaime
LOTTO LAND
PREACHER'S WIFE, THE
Tirey, Amandda
TATTOO BOY
Tirgrath, Lori
BEWARE: CHILDREN AT PLAY
Tirico, Mike
JERRY MAGUIRE
Tisch, Steve
DEAR GOD
Tisdale, Wayman
EDDIE
Tissot, Marc
PROPRIETOR, THE
To, Brian
IT'S MY PARTY

Tobeck, Joel
GIRLFRIENDS
Tobolowsky, Stephen
GLIMMER MAN, THE
HOMEWARD BOUND II: LOST IN SAN FRANCISCO
Toccalinos, Alejandro
OF LOVE AND SHADOWS
Tocha, Paolo
FIST OF THE NORTH STAR
Toda, Toshi
DON'T BE A MENACE TO SOUTH CENTRAL WHILE DRINKING YOUR JUICE IN THE HOOD
HOURGLASS
Todd, Beverly
SURGEON, THE
Todd, Sonia
SHINE
Todd, Tony
BEASTMASTER 3: THE EYE OF BRAXUS
ROCK, THE
Todeschini, Bruno
MA SAISON PREFEREE
Todhunter, Chad
ROBIN OF LOCKSLEY
Todisco, Mario
PALOOKAVILLE
Toeman, Claire
JACK & SARAH
Toji, Marcus
DEAR GOD
Tokoro, Mihoko
MY FELLOW AMERICANS
Toledano, Valerie
PROPRIETOR, THE
Toledo, Denise Maria
DONOR UNKNOWN
Toles-Bey, John
EXTREME MEASURES
TALES OF EROTICA
Tolkein, Daniela
ADVENTURES OF PINOCCHIO, THE
Tolkin, Theadora
ARRIVAL, THE
Tolson, Billy
LARRY MCMURTRY'S STREETS OF LAREDO
Tolsty
LITTLE INDIAN, BIG CITY
Tom, Audrey
MOLL FLANDERS
Toma, Luke
LOOKING FOR RICHARD
Tomanovich, Dara
BIO-DOME
Tomazewski, Thomas
PROPRIETOR, THE
Tome, Gregg
FAN, THE
Tomei, Adam
INDEPENDENCE DAY
Tomei, Marisa
UNHOOK THE STARS
Tomlin, Lily
CELLULOID CLOSET, THE
FLIRTING WITH DISASTER
GETTING AWAY WITH MURDER
Tomlinson, Ricky
BUTTERFLY KISS
Tomlinson, Ryan
ONE MAN'S JUSTICE
Tommassini, Luca
BIRDCAGE, THE
EVITA
Tompkins, Judy
MONSTERSHOW
Toms, Rick
ROCK, THE
Tong, Kaity
CITY HALL
Tonken, Eric
BEWARE: CHILDREN AT PLAY
Tony V.
CELTIC PRIDE
Toolan, Rebecca
ANNIE O
SURGEON, THE
Tooley, Jenni
BOTTLE ROCKET
Toomer, Omari
SMALL WONDERS
Toor, Ravinder
FEAR
TALES FROM THE CRYPT PRESENTS BORDELLO OF BLOOD
Tootoosis, Gordon
ALASKA
LONE STAR
Topacio, Soxy
MIDNIGHT DANCERS
Topor, Roland
THREE LIVES AND ONLY ONE DEATH
Torgerson, Carla
HYPE!
Torn, Rip
DOWN PERISCOPE
FOR BETTER OR WORSE
LETTER TO MY KILLER
Tornatore, Peppino
STAR MAKER, THE
Torrance, Ingrid
BIG BULLY
Torre, Roma
CITY HALL
Torres, Diego
SHADOW YOU SOON WILL BE, A
Torres, Gina
BED OF ROSES
SUBSTANCE OF FIRE, THE
Torres, Jenique
SLEEPERS
Torres, Monica
TRIGGER EFFECT, THE
Torreton, Philippe
LA COMEDIE-FRANCAISE OU L'AMOUR JOUE
NEW LIFE, A
Torrisi, Bruno
STAR MAKER, THE
Torry, Guy
DON'T BE A MENACE TO SOUTH CENTRAL WHILE DRINKING YOUR JUICE IN THE HOOD
SUNSET PARK
Torry, Joe
FLED
Torti, Robert
THAT THING YOU DO!
Toth, Andras
DOGFIGHTERS, THE
Toth, Geza
OUTPOST, THE
Toth, Ildiko
MAGIC HUNTER
Toth, Tamas
RASPUTIN
Toth, Wayne
FROM DUSK TILL DAWN
Touati, Kamel
MADAME BUTTERFLY
SILENCES OF THE PALACE, THE
Toub, Shaun
BROKEN ARROW
EXECUTIVE DECISION
Touihiri, Wahid
MADAME BUTTERFLY
Touliatos, George
FINAL CUT, THE
RED SCORPION 2
TRACKS OF A KILLER
Touma, Yumi
BIG WARS
Toumarkine, Francois
HATE
Toumi, Abdelkerim
SILENCES OF THE PALACE, THE
Tourek, Mike
CITIZEN RUTH
Tournie, Mark Estrada
MAXIMUM RISK
Toussaint, Lorraine
AMERICA'S DREAM
Towb, Harry
MOLL FLANDERS
Towery, Russell
BOTTLE ROCKET
Towles, Tom
NORMAL LIFE
ROCK, THE
Townsel, William Carvell
WAR AT HOME, THE
Townsend, Isabelle
LAZARUS MAN, THE
Townsend, Jim
ROAD HOME, THE
Townsend, Joe
EVITA
Townsend, Ruth
HEAD OF THE FAMILY
Townsend, Stanley
MOLL FLANDERS
Townshend, Pete
ROLLING STONES ROCK-AND-ROLL CIRCUS, THE
Toy, Patty
DENTIST, THE
SHARON'S SECRET
Toyoda, Tony
STRIPTEASE
Toyon, Stacy Rae
TIME TO KILL, A
Trachtenberg, Michelle
HARRIET THE SPY
Tracy, Stan
PALOOKAVILLE
Trager, Josiah
WELCOME TO THE DOLLHOUSE
Trainor, Mary Ellen
EXECUTIVE DECISION
Trainor, Saxon
MAGIC IN THE MIRROR
Trammel, Sam
HARVEST OF FIRE
Tran, Cindy
MATILDA
Tran, Emerson
INFINITY
Tran, Sonny
BOGUS
Tran, Tuan
WAR AT HOME, THE
Trandifar, Claudiu
JOSH KIRBY . . . TIME WARRIOR!: EGGS FROM 70,000,000 B.C.

Trang, Thuy
CROW: CITY OF ANGELS, THE
SPY HARD
Tranghese, Paul
DOWN PERISCOPE
PHAT BEACH
Tranter, John
JANE EYRE
Traore, Falaba Issa
GUIMBA THE TYRANT
Trapp, Robin
EXIT
Trapp, Valerie
MR. STITCH
Trask, Richard
FIRST KID
Trautwig, Al
EDDIE
Travanti, Daniel J.
SKIN
Travers, Sean
TWO FRIENDS
Traversari, Gabriel
TWO MUCH
Traverzo, Susanna Gabriela
SMALL WONDERS
Travis, Nancy
BOGUS
Travis, Randy
EDIE & PEN
Traviss, Sheila
DEATH ARTIST, THE
Travolta, John
BROKEN ARROW
MICHAEL
PHENOMENON
Travolta, Margaret
CHAIN REACTION
MICHAEL
Traylor, Craig Lamar
MATILDA
Treas, Terri
YANKEE ZULU
Trebek, Alex
SPY HARD
Trebicka, Jirina
MISSION: IMPOSSIBLE
Treco, Lindsay
FLIPPER
Tree, Michael
SMALL WONDERS
Tregloan, Peter
GRIM
Trejo, Danny
FROM DUSK TILL DAWN
Tremblay, Denis
EVITA
Tremblay, Lyne
STAND OFF, THE
Trentino, Peggy
VIRTUAL COMBAT
Trese, Adam
PALOOKAVILLE
Treser, Gretchen
KINGPIN
Trevan, Tim
UNKNOWN ORIGIN
Treves, Frederick
SHAMELESS
Treviglio, Leonardo
STEALING BEAUTY
Trevino, Lee
HAPPY GILMORE
Trice, Judy Pryor
SLING BLADE
Tricky, Paula
BLACK SCORPION
Trieste, Leopoldo
STAR MAKER, THE
Trifunovic, Sergej
SOMEONE ELSE'S AMERICA
Triggelis, Takis
QUEST, THE
Trillin, Calvin
MICHAEL
Tripe, Donald
KIDS IN THE HALL: BRAIN CANDY
Trippel, Dieter R.
ERASER
Triska, Jan
PEOPLE VS. LARRY FLYNT, THE
Tritt, Travis
SGT. BILKO
Tritter, Wes
HOW THE WEST WAS FUN
Tritton, Harry
SPIDER & ROSE
Trittschuh, R. Bruce
SANDMAN, THE
Trock, Greg
MOTHER'S PRAYER, A
Tronto, Marilise
TIMELESS
Tropicana, Carmelita
GIRLFRIENDS
Trotter, Kate
BLOODKNOT
Trousdale, Gary
HUNCHBACK OF NOTRE DAME, THE
Trowell, Katherine
WHERE'S THE MONEY, NOREEN?
Troxell, Richard
MADAME BUTTERFLY
Troy, Lesley-Camille
GIRL 6
Troy, Louise
MISSING PIECES
Trudell, John
EXTREME MEASURES
True, Jim
FAR HARBOR
NORMAL LIFE
True, Rachel
CRAFT, THE
Truffaut, Ewa
FRANCOIS TRUFFAUT: STOLEN PORTRAITS
Truffaut, Laura
FRANCOIS TRUFFAUT: STOLEN PORTRAITS
Truly Jr., Dr. William
TIME TO KILL, A
Truman, Jeff
RACE THE SUN
Trump, Donald
ASSOCIATE, THE
EDDIE
Trump, Ivana
FIRST WIVES CLUB, THE
Trussell, Paul
SECRETS & LIES
Trussler, Menna
AUGUST
Truter, Gregor
ENGLISH PATIENT, THE
Tsao, Andrew
MAHJONG
Tshudy, Benjamin
RATTLED
Tshudy, Michael
RATTLED
Tsouladze, Francoise
CHASING BUTTERFLIES
Tsui, Mung-Ling
HARRIET THE SPY
Tsui Siu Keung
WING CHUN
Tsujitani, Kouji
BIG WARS
Tsuru, Hiromi
SANCTUARY: THE MOVIE
Tubert, Marcelo
TREMORS 2: AFTERSHOCKS
Tucci, Christine
BIG NIGHT
Tucci, Maria
SWEET NOTHING
Tucci, Stanley
BIG NIGHT
MODERN AFFAIR, A
Tuccillo, Liz
ED'S NEXT MOVE
Tucker, Charles J.
CURDLED
Tucker, Joe
CAPTIVES
SECRETS & LIES
Tucker, Jonathan
SLEEPERS
TWO IF BY SEA
Tucker, Kendra
SURGEON, THE
Tuitavuki, Charlie
SOLO
Tuite, Danielle
WAR OF THE BUTTONS, THE
Tulaine, Lynn
SGT. BILKO
Tull, Patrick
SLEEPERS
Tullo, Anthony
VIRUS
Tumbuan, Frans
WITHOUT MERCY
Tung, Bill
RUMBLE IN THE BRONX
Tunie, Tamara
CITY HALL
Tunney, Eric
KIDS IN THE HALL: BRAIN CANDY
Tunney, Robin
CRAFT, THE
RIDERS OF THE PURPLE SAGE
Tupou, Manu
TAKEOVER, THE
Turbiville, Tom
FLED
NEON BIBLE, THE
Turco, Paige
POMPATUS OF LOVE, THE
Turenne, Louis
ASSOCIATE, THE
HELLRAISER: BLOODLINE
Turesson, Willy
CHILDREN OF NOISY VILLAGE, THE
Turjeman, Dan
DEADLY OUTBREAK
Turk, Art
LOOKING FOR TROUBLE
Turki, Rim
ENGLISH PATIENT, THE
Turlington, Christy
CATWALK
Turnbull, Ross Colvin
JUDE
Turner, Bree
DUNSTON CHECKS IN
Turner, David
MAXIMUM RISK
Turner, Dennis
PEOPLE VS. LARRY FLYNT, THE
Turner, Emma
JUDE

Turner, Jim
JOE'S APARTMENT
POMPATUS OF LOVE, THE
Turner, John
RASPUTIN
Turner, Jonathan A.
JACK
Turner, Leonard
CABLE GUY, THE
Turner, Mike
ZARKORR! THE INVADER
Turner, Raymond
AMANDA AND THE ALIEN
Turner, Steve
HYPE!
Turner, Steven Neil
BLACK SHEEP
Turner, Tonya
TATTOO BOY
Turner, Trisha
TATTOO BOY
Turner-Cray, Susan
JAMES AND THE GIANT PEACH
Turney, Elizabeth
ANGELS AND INSECTS
Turney, Jack
ANGELS AND INSECTS
Turney, Nicky
ANGELS AND INSECTS
Turnham, Jenny
MR. WRONG
Turturro, Aida
DENISE CALLS UP
SEARCH FOR ONE-EYE JIMMY, THE
SLEEPERS
TALES OF EROTICA
Turturro, John
GIRL 6
GRACE OF MY HEART
SEARCH FOR ONE-EYE JIMMY, THE
SUGARTIME
Turturro, Nick
SEARCH FOR ONE-EYE JIMMY, THE
Turturro, Olinda
FAITHFUL
Tury, Adam
GRIM
Tuttle, Fred
MAN WITH A PLAN
Tuttle, Joe
MAN WITH A PLAN
Twa, Kate
BIG BULLY
DEVOTION
Twardowski, Jason
BOGUS
Tweed, Shannon
ELECTRA
Tydings, Alexandra
SUNCHASER
Tyler, Liv
HEAVY
STEALING BEAUTY
THAT THING YOU DO!
Tyler, Twain
SET IT OFF
Tyrrell, Susan
DEMOLITIONIST, THE
Tyson, Barbara
FINAL CUT, THE
Tyson, Cicely
ROAD TO GALVESTON, THE
Tyson, Pamala
LAST DANCE
Tyson, Richard
GLASS CAGE, THE
KINGPIN
PHARAOH'S ARMY
Tyukodi, Anthony
ELECTRA
Tzavaras, Nicholas
SMALL WONDERS
Tzi Ma
CHAIN REACTION
Ubach, Alanna
DENISE CALLS UP
JUST YOUR LUCK
LOVE IS ALL THERE IS
Udy, Larry
ENTERTAINING ANGELS: THE DOROTHY DAY STORY
Uecker, Bob
HOMEWARD BOUND II: LOST IN SAN FRANCISCO
Uffelman, Sarah
SGT. KABUKIMAN N.Y.P.D.
Uganiza, Adriane Napualani
RACE THE SUN
Uhler, Mike
THAT THING YOU DO!
Ukranian Shumka Dancers, The
SONG SPINNER, THE
Ulbrich, Lutz
NICO ICON
Ulizzi, Benny
TWO FRIENDS
Ullrick, Sharon
BEFORE AND AFTER
Ulrich, Beth
FUGITIVE RAGE
Ulrich, Skeet
BOYS
CRAFT, THE
LAST DANCE
SCREAM
Underwood, Blair
SET IT OFF
Ungar, Benjamin
SUBSTANCE OF FIRE, THE
Unger, Bela
RASPUTIN
Unger, Joe
NIGHT OF THE SCARECROW
Ungerman, William
SOLO
Uno, Conrad
HYPE!
Upendran, Panicker
RANSOM
Upson, Leslie
JERRY MAGUIRE
Urb, Tarmo
BASQUIAT
Urena, Arturo Soto
AVENTURERA
Urge Overkill
KINGPIN
Urich, Robert
LAZARUS MAN, THE
Urla, Joe
SLEEPERS
Urrutia, Paulina
JOHNNY 100 PESOS
Ursin, David
JERRY MAGUIRE
Urso, Guila
SINGLE GIRL, A
Vacca, Augusto
WHO KILLED PASOLINI?
Vacca, Capt. Michael "Chewy"
INDEPENDENCE DAY
Vaccaro, Brenda
MIRROR HAS TWO FACES, THE
Vadim, David
PALLBEARER, THE
RANSOM
Vagliardo, Theresa
MURDERED INNOCENCE
Vagner, Milan
KASPAR HAUSER
Vahle, Dirk
LIFEFORM
Vail, John
THEY BITE
Vail, Justina
CARNOSAUR 3: PRIMAL SPECIES
JERRY MAGUIRE
NAKED SOULS
Vail, Valerie
KASPAR HAUSER
Valadie, Dominique
SINGLE GIRL, A
Valdez, Manuel
LARRY MCMURTRY'S STREETS OF LAREDO
Valencia, Mathew
LAWNMOWER MAN 2: BEYOND CYBERSPACE
Valente, Antoinette
TRUTH ABOUT CATS AND DOGS, THE
Valentine, Michael
MATILDA
Valentine, Scott
CARNOSAUR 3: PRIMAL SPECIES
PHANTOM 2040: THE GHOST WHO WALKS
Valentine, Steve
MARS ATTACKS!
Valentino
CATWALK
Valenzuela, Pepe
LAND AND FREEDOM
Valim, Mark
PHENOMENON
Valinsky, Martin
GRACE OF MY HEART
Valk, Blair
DEAD WEEKEND
EXECUTIVE DECISION
Vallai, Peter
MAGIC HUNTER
Vallance, Jason
PUBLIC ACCESS
Vallas, Peter
EXIT
Vallette, Franklin
ZARKORR! THE INVADER
Valo, Laurent
RIDICULE
Valoppi, Jennifer
UP CLOSE AND PERSONAL
Valpy, Rebecca
STEALING BEAUTY
Valverde, Rodrigo
OUTRAGE
Van Alyn, Abigail
JACK
van Ammelrooy, Willeke
ANTONIA'S LINE
Van Bergen, Lewis
PINOCCHIO'S REVENGE
Van Blankenstein, Tyler
BIG BULLY
Van Dam, Carlo
ANTONIA'S LINE
Van Damme, Jean-Claude
MAXIMUM RISK
QUEST, THE
van der Groen, Dora
ANTONIA'S LINE
Van Der Merwe, Tolla
YANKEE ZULU
van der Meulen, Evert
CROCODILES IN AMSTERDAM

van der Post, Becky
SHOPPING
Van Deventer, Marie
YANKEE ZULU
Van Dien, Casper
BEASTMASTER 3: THE EYE OF BRAXUS
Van Dohlen, Lenny
TOLLBOOTH
van Dousselaere, Michel
ANTONIA'S LINE
Van Dusen, Bob
ZARKORR! THE INVADER
Van Exel, Nick
EDDIE
Van Hart, Ron
MAXIMUM RISK
Van Holt, Brian
VERY BRADY SEQUEL, A
Van Horn, Patrick
SWINGERS
Van Hoven, Keith
WARHEAD
Van Impe, Koen
DAENS
Van Keeken, Frank
MAXIMUM RISK
Van Kuijk, Fred
DAENS
Van Landingham, Jack
WITCHCRAFT: SALEM'S GHOST
Van Lear, Phillip Edward
FAMILY THING, A
Van Lier, Heidi
PUBLIC ACCESS
Van Lieshout, Justin
MRS. WINTERBOURNE
Van Luchene, Filip
DAENS
van Nitsen, Valerie
SUITE 16
van Overloop, Veerle
ANTONIA'S LINE
Van Patten, Dick
LOVE IS ALL THERE IS
Van Patten, James
DON'T BE A MENACE TO SOUTH CENTRAL WHILE DRINKING YOUR JUICE IN THE HOOD
Van Patten, Joyce
INFINITY
Van Peebles, Mario
SOLO
Van Peebles, Melvin
FIST OF THE NORTH STAR
Van Rensberg, Daniel
WARHEAD
van Sauers, Marielle
SUITE 16
Van Snellenberg, Jared
HAPPY GILMORE
Van Sprang, Alan
FRAME BY FRAME
Van Varenberg, Kristopher
QUEST, THE
Van Vladricken, James
SGT. KABUKIMAN N.Y.P.D.
Van Zyl, Julius
YANKEE ZULU
Vance, Courtney B.
AFFAIR, THE
BOYS NEXT DOOR, THE
LAST SUPPER, THE
PREACHER'S WIFE, THE
TUSKEGEE AIRMEN, THE
Vance, Gregg D.
PHAT BEACH
Vandeberghe, Tim
CITIZEN RUTH
Vandenberg, Dominique
BARB WIRE
Vander, Musetta
BACKLASH: OBLIVION 2
UNDER THE HULA MOON
Vanderbugh, Gillian
STUPIDS, THE
Vandersall, Hal
SANDMAN, THE
Vandusen, Andrew
GIRLS TOWN
Vaneck, Pierre
PROPRIETOR, THE
Vannice, Nicki
HEIDI CHRONICLES, THE
Vannicola, Joanne
IRON EAGLE IV
Vanzi, Alessandra
PORTRAIT OF A LADY, THE
STEALING BEAUTY
WHO KILLED PASOLINI?
Varga, Richie
ERASER
Vargas, John
SUNSET PARK
Vargas, Jorge
ANNIE O
Vargas, Manuela
FLOWER OF MY SECRET, THE
Vargas, Valentina
HELLRAISER: BLOODLINE
Vari, Eva
EVITA
Varkonyi, Andras
RASPUTIN
Varszegi, Rudolf
DOGFIGHTERS, THE
Vartan, Michael
PALLBEARER, THE
Vasa
EVIL ED
Vasey, John
SAWBONES
Vasgersian, Ed
CROSSCUT
Vasquez, Nelson
EXTREME MEASURES
GIRL 6
Vasquez, Randy
DEMOLITIONIST, THE
Vasut, Marek
DELTA OF VENUS
MISSION: IMPOSSIBLE
Vaughan, Peter
CRUCIBLE, THE
JOSEPH CONRAD'S THE SECRET AGENT
Vaughn, Gwyn
HEDD WYNN
Vaughn, John Michael
FUGITIVE RAGE
Vaughn, Kelly
DON'T BE A MENACE TO SOUTH CENTRAL WHILE DRINKING YOUR JUICE IN THE HOOD
Vaughn, Ned
COURAGE UNDER FIRE
TUSKEGEE AIRMEN, THE
Vaughn, Robert
JOE'S APARTMENT
Vaughn, Shirley
BUTTERFLY KISS
Vaughn, Terri J.
BLACK SCORPION
CARNOSAUR 3: PRIMAL SPECIES
DON'T BE A MENACE TO SOUTH CENTRAL WHILE DRINKING YOUR JUICE IN THE HOOD
Vaughn, Vernon
SWINGERS
Vaughn, Vince
JUST YOUR LUCK
SWINGERS
Vaugier, Emmanuelle
HALFBACK OF NOTRE DAME, THE
Vavrik, Tamas
DOGFIGHTERS, THE
Vavrina, Bruce
MAN IN THE ATTIC, THE
Vavrova, Dana
BROTHER OF SLEEP
Vayne
PHAT BEACH
Veasey, John
ANGELS AND INSECTS
Vedder, Eddie
HYPE!
Vega, Alexa
GHOSTS OF MISSISSIPPI
GLIMMER MAN, THE
TWISTER
Vega III, Juan
LONE STAR
Vega, Tata
SPY HARD
Vejmelkova, Eva
DRAGONHEART
Velasco, Rafael
SOLO
Velazquez, Dolores
EYE FOR AN EYE
Velazquez, Pablo
EYE FOR AN EYE
Veldman, Salsh
TALES OF EROTICA
Velez, Jose Ruiz
AVENTURERA
Velez, Lauren
CITY HALL
Velvet, Sherry
NEON BIBLE, THE
Venables, Bruce
SPIDER & ROSE
Vener, Scott
PHAT BEACH
Vennema, John C.
CITY HALL
Venokur, Johnny
HOURGLASS
Venora, Diane
SUBSTITUTE, THE
SURVIVING PICASSO
WILLIAM SHAKESPEARE'S ROMEO + JULIET
Ventimiglia, John
ANGELA
EXTREME MEASURES
FUNERAL, THE
GIRLS TOWN
TREES LOUNGE
Venture, Richard
COURAGE UNDER FIRE
TRUMAN
Venturi, Ken
TIN CUP
Vercruyssen, Frank
DAENS
Verdon, Gwen
MARVIN'S ROOM
Verduzco, Abraham
SOLO
Verduzco, Danny
CROW: CITY OF ANGELS, THE
Verell, Jack
SAWBONES

Verginella, Deborah
FLY AWAY HOME
Verica, Tom
DEAD TO RIGHTS
Verley, Bernard
NEW LIFE, A
Vermeir, Gary
TWO IF BY SEA
Vermuellen, Herbie
REDEMPTION: KICKBOXER 5
Vernet, Claire
LA COMEDIE-FRANCAISE OU L'AMOUR JOUE
Vernon, Kate
BLOODKNOT
Veronica, Christina
THEY BITE
Verow, Todd
FRISK
Versace, Gianni
CATWALK
Verveen, Arie
CAUGHT
Vhay, Daniel J.
MR. HOLLAND'S OPUS
Vial, Pierre
VISITORS, THE
Viala, Florence
LA COMEDIE-FRANCAISE OU L'AMOUR JOUE
Viancos, Claudio
JOHNNY 100 PESOS
Viard, Karin
HATE
Vicent, Manolo
LAND AND FREEDOM
Vichi, Gerry
CITY HALL
Vickers, Kerri
TRIGGER EFFECT, THE
Victor, Harry
GRACE OF MY HEART
Victor, James
EXECUTIVE DECISION
LARRY MCMURTRY'S STREETS OF LAREDO
Victor, Katherine
FUGITIVE RAGE
Vidal, Christina
WELCOME TO THE DOLLHOUSE
Vidal, Gore
CELLULOID CLOSET, THE
Vidan, Richard
VENUS RISING
Vidarte, Walter
OUTRAGE
Vidler, Susan
TRAINSPOTTING
Vierra, Zack
STAND OFF, THE
Vigeant, Edward
DADETOWN
Vigil, Selene
HYPE!
Vigoda, Abe
LOVE IS ALL THERE IS
Vila, Juan Rodriguez
SOMEONE ELSE'S AMERICA
Vilan, Mayte
BITTER SUGAR
Vilar, Tracy
GRACE OF MY HEART
SUNSET PARK
Vilarrasa, Carles
LAND AND FREEDOM
Villalonga, Marthe
MA SAISON PREFEREE
Villamil, Servando
EVITA
Villani, Michael
UP CLOSE AND PERSONAL
Villanova, Marco
THAT THING YOU DO!
Villanueva, Larry
BITTER SUGAR
Villar, Celita
HORSEMAN ON THE ROOF
Villari, Libby
CHILDREN OF THE CORN: THE GATHERING
WHOLE WIDE WORLD, THE
Villegas, Billy
MUTANT MAN
Villegas, Victor
BUGGED
Villeneuve, Dale
UNFORGETTABLE
Villiers, James
WAVELENGTH
WIND IN THE WILLOWS, THE
Vinay, Kevin
DIABOLIQUE
Vince, Pruitt Taylor
BEAUTIFUL GIRLS
HEAVY
UNDER THE HULA MOON
Vincent, Bastien
THREE LIVES AND ONLY ONE DEATH
Vincent, Craig
TEXAS PAYBACK
Vincent, E. Duke
OFF AND RUNNING
Vincent, Ernie
EYE FOR AN EYE
Vincent, Eugenie
I SHOT ANDY WARHOL
Vincent, Frank
SHE'S THE ONE
Vincent, Jan-Michael
BODY COUNT
RED LINE
Vincent, Johnny
FUGITIVE RAGE
Vincent, Leonard
CHAMBER, THE
Vincent, Sam
DEAD TO RIGHTS
Vincent, Teddy
EYE FOR AN EYE
Vint, Alan
WHARF RAT, THE
Viotto, Regina
MIRROR HAS TWO FACES, THE
Viront, James
SANDMAN, THE
Viscuso, Sal
DENTIST, THE
PINOCCHIO'S REVENGE
Visser, Angela
SPY HARD
Vitale, Fabrizio
WHO KILLED PASOLINI?
Vitar, Mike
D3: THE MIGHTY DUCKS
Viterbi, Emanuelle Carucci
PORTRAIT OF A LADY, THE
Viterelli, Joe
AMERICAN STRAYS
BLACK ROSE OF HARLEM
ERASER
HEAVEN'S PRISONERS
Vitoria, Adrian
VENUS RISING
Vitry, Mathilde
HATE
NELLY AND MONSIEUR ARNAUD
Vittet, Judith
NELLY AND MONSIEUR ARNAUD
Viva
NICO ICON
Vivan, Gigi
IN LOVE AND WAR
Vivat, Tracy
ABUSE
Viviani, Vittorio
MILLE BOLLE BLU
Vivich, Brian
SANDMAN, THE
Vivona, Jerome
EVERYONE SAYS I LOVE YOU
Vlach, Oldrich
KASPAR HAUSER
Vlachos, George
FIRST WIVES CLUB, THE
Vlahos, Sam
BIG SQUEEZE, THE
LONE STAR
Vlaskova, Lida
ADVENTURES OF PINOCCHIO, THE
Voda, Bogdan
JOSH KIRBY . . . TIME WARRIOR!: TRAPPED ON TOY WORLD
Voe, Sandra
BREAKING THE WAVES
Vogel, Carlo
GIRL 6
Vogel, Tony
MISSION: IMPOSSIBLE
Voges, Quinton
WARHEAD
Voight, Jon
MISSION: IMPOSSIBLE
Vokolin, Pavel
HIDDEN ASSASSIN
Vollans, Michael
BOGUS
FLY AWAY HOME
Vollereaux, Sonia
LITTLE INDIAN, BIG CITY
Volokh, Ilia
EXECUTIVE DECISION
Volpe II, Robert
SGT. KABUKIMAN N.Y.P.D.
Voltaire
ED'S NEXT MOVE
Volton
SABRINA, THE TEENAGE WITCH
Volz, Nedra
GREAT WHITE HYPE, THE
von Arnim, Piero
RACE THE SUN
Von Bargen, Dan
LOOKING FOR RICHARD
Von Bargen, Daniel
BEFORE AND AFTER
BROKEN ARROW
STEPHEN KING'S THINNER
TRUMAN
von Briel, Ronette
DON'T LET YOUR MEAT LOAF
Von Dohlen, Lenny
ENTERTAINING ANGELS: THE DOROTHY DAY STORY
ONE GOOD TURN
von Franckenstein, Clement
DARK SECRETS
Von Franckenstein, Clement
EVENING STAR, THE
von Glatz, Ilse
UNDERSTUDY: GRAVEYARD SHIFT 2, THE

Von Hasperg, Ila
SHADOW OF ANGELS
von Praunheim, Rosa
NEUROSIA: 50 YEARS OF PERVERSITY
Von Ryzin, Henrik
FROM DUSK TILL DAWN
von Sohlern, Gilbert
BROTHER OF SLEEP
Von Watts, Hamilton
NUTTY PROFESSOR, THE
von Woltor, Sula
MUTANT MAN
Vonnegut, Kurt
MOTHER NIGHT
Vosburgh, Tilly
SHOPPING
Vosloo, Arnold
DARKMAN III: DIE DARKMAN DIE
Voss, Brian
KINGPIN
Voughn, Adam
BULLETPROOF
Vouyer, Vince
VIRTUAL ENCOUNTERS
Vrana, Vlasta
HOLLOW POINT
HYPE!
MOTHER NIGHT
Vraney, Mike
HYPE!
Vreeken, Ron
ISLAND OF DR. MOREAU, THE
Vriends, Brian
SPIDER & ROSE
Vriesendorp, Esther
ANTONIA'S LINE
Vrooman, Spencer
BOYS
Vuletic, Jenny
GIRLFRIENDS
Vydra, Vaclav
ADVENTURES OF PINOCCHIO, THE
Waagfjord, Thorir
VIKING SAGAS, THE
Waara, Scott
EYE FOR AN EYE
Waco, Laurel
FRISK
Waddell, Tom
BROKEN ARROW
Waddington, Peter
SECRETS & LIES
Wade, Geoffrey
CITY HALL
Wade, Jonathan Cabot
FIRST KID
Wade, Maggie
GHOSTS OF MISSISSIPPI
Wade, Virgil
BUGGED
Wadell, Karen
FRAME BY FRAME
Wadham, Julian
ENGLISH PATIENT, THE
JOSEPH CONRAD'S THE SECRET AGENT
Wadling, Magnus
EVIL ED
Wadsworth, Oliver
ED'S NEXT MOVE
Wady, Tabitha
WAVELENGTH
Wafford, Rowland
MR. STITCH
Wagner, Christopher
LARRY MCMURTRY'S STREETS OF LAREDO
Wagner, Jeannine
SPY HARD
Wagner, Lori
DARK SECRETS
Wagner, Natasha
MIND RIPPER
Wagner, Rachel
KINGPIN
Wagner, Thomas
ASSOCIATE, THE
PINOCCHIO'S REVENGE
Wagner, Tom
HOMEWARD BOUND II: LOST IN SAN FRANCISCO
Wahlberg, Donnie
RANSOM
Wahlberg, Mark
FEAR
Waid, Jeffrey
COURAGE UNDER FIRE
Waite, Michael
FRISK
Waite, Ralph
HOMEWARD BOUND II: LOST IN SAN FRANCISCO
Waites, Jim
TWO FRIENDS
Wajacs, Michael
KAZAAM
Wajsbrot, Rywka
HATE
Wakefield, Colin
SOLITAIRE FOR TWO
Walch, Hynden
ANGELA
JERRY MAGUIRE
Wale
DELTA OF VENUS
Walkabouts, The
HYPE!
Walken, Christopher
BASQUIAT
FUNERAL, THE
LAST MAN STANDING
WILD SIDE
Walker, Ally
BED OF ROSES
KAZAAM
Walker, Amanda
ENGLISH PATIENT, THE
Walker, Andy
TRIGGER EFFECT, THE
Walker, Charles
SET IT OFF
THIN LINE BETWEEN LOVE AND HATE, A
Walker, Chris
FUNNYMAN, THE
Walker, David
SMALL FACES
Walker, Eammon
SHOPPING
Walker, Jake
LAZARUS MAN, THE
Walker, Jimmy
OPEN SEASON
Walker, John Patrick
SUBSTANCE OF FIRE, THE
Walker, Julie
BUTTERFLY KISS
Walker, Liza
SOLITAIRE FOR TWO
WAVELENGTH
Walker, Marcy
TALKING ABOUT SEX
Walker, Peggy Walton
LAST DANCE
Walker, Peter
IF LUCY FELL
Walker, Polly
EMMA
Walker, Robert
EVERYONE SAYS I LOVE YOU
Wall, Jared
KIDS IN THE HALL: BRAIN CANDY
Wall, Robert
DADETOWN
Wallace, Billye Ree
MOTHER
Wallace, George D.
MULTIPLICITY
Wallace, Jim
MAN WITH A PLAN
Wallace, Julie
SANTA CLAWS
Wallace, Leighanne
MY FELLOW AMERICANS
Wallace, Matt
FLED
Wallace Stone, Dee
ROAD HOME, THE
Wallace, Will
EVENING STAR, THE
Wallace, William
SOLO
Wallach, Eli
ASSOCIATE, THE
TWO MUCH
Wallach, Katherine
ASSOCIATE, THE
Waller, Philip
EDIE & PEN
Wallraff, Diego
OF LOVE AND SHADOWS
Walls, Kevin Patrick
SCREAM
Walper, Sandy
WHOLE WIDE WORLD, THE
Walsh, Barry
WAR OF THE BUTTONS, THE
Walsh, Gerry
MOLL FLANDERS
Walsh, Gwynyth
GIRL FROM MARS, THE
Walsh, J.T.
BLACK DAY BLUE NIGHT
EXECUTIVE DECISION
LITTLE DEATH, THE
LOW LIFE, THE
SLING BLADE
SOME FOLKS CALL IT A SLING BLADE
Walsh, James
FATALLY YOURS
Walsh, Jerry
FAITHFUL
Walsh, Kate
NORMAL LIFE
Walsh, Kenneth
KISSINGER AND NIXON
Walsh, M. Emmet
CRIMINAL HEARTS
PORTRAITS OF A KILLER
WILLIAM SHAKESPEARE'S ROMEO + JULIET
Walsh, Mandy
LAND AND FREEDOM
Walsh, Martin
BEAUTIFUL THING
Walsh, Marty
ARRIVAL, THE
Walsh, Matthew Jason
SANDMAN, THE
Walsh, Wendy
CABLE GUY, THE
FLY AWAY HOME
INDEPENDENCE DAY
Walston, Ray
HOUSE ARREST

Walstrom, Owen
FINAL CUT, THE
RUMBLE IN THE BRONX
Walter, Jayne
EXECUTIVE DECISION
Walter, Lisa Ann
EDDIE
Walter, Miroslav
HIDDEN ASSASSIN
Walter, Sarah
SMALL WONDERS
Walter, Tracey
FIST OF THE NORTH STAR
LARGER THAN LIFE
MATILDA
Walter, Tracy
ENTERTAINING ANGELS: THE DOROTHY DAY STORY
Walters, Alexander
DUNSTON CHECKS IN
Walters, Barbara
LINE KING: THE AL HIRSCHFELD STORY, THE
Walters, Mark
EVENING STAR, THE
LILY DALE
Walters, Melora
AMERICAN STRAYS
ERASER
Walters, Susan
. . . AT FIRST SIGHT
GALAXIES ARE COLLIDING
Walters, Toddy
CANNIBAL! THE MUSICAL
Walters, Zaquarii
CHAMBER, THE
Walton, Bill
CELTIC PRIDE
Walton, Jim
MRS. MUNCK
Walton, Kacky
PEOPLE VS. LARRY FLYNT, THE
Walton, Steven
TWO FRIENDS
Wampetich, Nandor
RASPUTIN
Wan, Al
BARB WIRE
Wan, Diana
SMALL WONDERS
Wang Anqing
BLACK MOUNTAIN
Wang Chi-tsan
MAHJONG
Wang Dawei
BLACK MOUNTAIN
Wang Ji
BLUSH
Wang, Luoyong
DAYLIGHT
Wang Po-sen
MAHJONG
Wang Rouli
BLUSH
Wang Zhiwen
BLUSH
Wanlass, Lynn
RIDERS OF THE PURPLE SAGE
Warburton, David
FOR THE MOMENT
Warburton, Patrick
AMERICAN STRAYS
Ward, Andra
BEST OF THE BEST 3: NO TURNING BACK
Ward, Christy
SLING BLADE
Ward, Fred
CHAIN REACTION
TREMORS 2: AFTERSHOCKS
Ward, James K.
GALAXIES ARE COLLIDING
Ward, Jeff
GIRL 6
Ward, Kirk
FAN, THE
Ward, Lyman
INDEPENDENCE DAY
SERIAL KILLER
Ward, Megan
JOE'S APARTMENT
Ward, Sela
MY FELLOW AMERICANS
Ward, Tom
PUBLIC ENEMIES
Ward, Vincent
SHOT, THE
Ward, Wayne
STUPIDS, THE
Ward, Zacharias
ED
Warden, Jack
ED
Warden, Judi
DADETOWN
Warder, Frederick
EVITA
MUPPET TREASURE ISLAND
Ware, Liane
BEAUTIFUL THING
Wark, John
BREAKING THE WAVES
Warkov, Jordan
CARPOOL
Warlock, Dick
RAVENHAWK
Warne, Andrew
INDEPENDENCE DAY
Warner, David
BEASTMASTER 3: THE EYE OF BRAXUS
FELONY
FINAL EQUINOX, THE
NAKED SOULS
NECRONOMICON: BOOK OF THE DEAD
RASPUTIN
Warner, Malcolm Jamal
TUSKEGEE AIRMEN, THE
Warner, Rick
UP CLOSE AND PERSONAL
Warnick, Kim
HYPE!
Warren, Dexter
INDEPENDENCE DAY
Warren, Jean
YOUNG POISONER'S HANDBOOK, THE
Warren, Jennifer Leigh
GRACE OF MY HEART
Warren, Kiersten
INDEPENDENCE DAY
PAINTED HERO
Warren, Matthew
LOW LIFE, THE
Warren, Mervyn
PREACHER'S WIFE, THE
Warren, Nancy
WHERE'S THE MONEY, NOREEN?
Warrington, Don
HAMLET
Warry-Smith, Dan
LEGEND OF GATOR FACE, THE
LONG KISS GOODNIGHT, THE
Warshay, Diane
BARB WIRE
Warwick, Richard
JANE EYRE
Wash, Kevin
STAND OFF, THE
Washington, Denzel
COURAGE UNDER FIRE
PREACHER'S WIFE, THE
Washington III, Irving Eugene
GRACE OF MY HEART
Washington, Isaiah
GET ON THE BUS
GIRL 6
Washington, Kory
ROAD TO GALVESTON, THE
Washington, Sharon
LONG KISS GOODNIGHT, THE
Washington, Warren "Zubari"
DON'T BE A MENACE TO SOUTH CENTRAL WHILE DRINKING YOUR JUICE IN THE HOOD
Washio, Isako
FIST OF THE NORTH STAR
Wasler, Mark "Chief"
KINGPIN
Wasscher, Alexandra
MAGIC HUNTER
Wasser, Ed
DARK SECRETS
Wasserbaum, Mikhail
CHEKIST, THE
Wasserman, Jerry
MATERNAL INSTINCTS
RED SCORPION 2
Wasserman, Mark
LOVE IS ALL THERE IS
Wasson, Craig
HARVEST OF FIRE
Watabe, Takeshi
SANCTUARY: THE MOVIE
Watanabe, Gedde
THAT THING YOU DO!
Watanabe, Naomi
MABOROSI
Waters Jr., Harry
BIG BULLY
Waters, Julia
SPY HARD
Waters, Maxine
SPY HARD
Waterston, Sam
ASSAULT AT WEST POINT
PROPRIETOR, THE
Watier, Fany
HORSEMAN ON THE ROOF
Watkins, Debra
SLEEPERS
Watkins, Jack
COURAGE UNDER FIRE
Watkins, Paul A.
WAR AT HOME, THE
Watkins, Sophie
FRIGHTENERS, THE
Watson, Art
PAINTED HERO
Watson, Emily
BREAKING THE WAVES
Watson, Henry
UNFORGETTABLE
Watson, Kevin
ORIGINAL GANGSTAS
Watson, Kristina
SUGARTIME
Watson, Mark
MATILDA
Watson, Robert Keith
UP CLOSE AND PERSONAL
Watson, Theresa
SECRETS & LIES

Watson, Virginia
DON'T BE A MENACE TO SOUTH CENTRAL WHILE DRINKING YOUR JUICE IN THE HOOD
Watson, Woody
EVENING STAR, THE
Watthaub, Ali Abdul
DON'T LET YOUR MEAT LOAF
Watts, Charlie
ROLLING STONES ROCK-AND-ROLL CIRCUS, THE
Watts, Naomi
CHILDREN OF THE CORN: THE GATHERING
Watts, Rolonda
GIRL 6
STUPIDS, THE
Waxel, John
FRISK
Waxman, Al
BOGUS
IRON EAGLE IV
Wayans, Craig
DON'T BE A MENACE TO SOUTH CENTRAL WHILE DRINKING YOUR JUICE IN THE HOOD
Wayans, Damien
DON'T BE A MENACE TO SOUTH CENTRAL WHILE DRINKING YOUR JUICE IN THE HOOD
Wayans, Damon
BULLETPROOF
CELTIC PRIDE
GREAT WHITE HYPE, THE
Wayans, Keenen Ivory
DON'T BE A MENACE TO SOUTH CENTRAL WHILE DRINKING YOUR JUICE IN THE HOOD
GLIMMER MAN, THE
Wayans, Kim
DON'T BE A MENACE TO SOUTH CENTRAL WHILE DRINKING YOUR JUICE IN THE HOOD
TALKING ABOUT SEX
Wayans, Marlon
DON'T BE A MENACE TO SOUTH CENTRAL WHILE DRINKING YOUR JUICE IN THE HOOD
Wayans, Shawn
DON'T BE A MENACE TO SOUTH CENTRAL WHILE DRINKING YOUR JUICE IN THE HOOD
WC
SET IT OFF
Weary, A.C.
EYE FOR AN EYE
Weatherred, Michael
CHILDREN OF FURY
VERY BRADY SEQUEL, A
Weathers, Carl
DANGEROUS PASSION
HAPPY GILMORE
Weaver, Celeste
ROCK, THE
Weaver, Dennis
TWO-BITS & PEPPER
Weaver, Lee
JUST YOUR LUCK
Weaver, Linda
SANDMAN, THE
Weaver, Paul
ENTERTAINING ANGELS: THE DOROTHY DAY STORY
Webb, Bunty
LOSING CHASE
Webb, David
FRISK
WARHEAD
YANKEE ZULU
Webb, Gregory
LIFEFORM
UNDER THE HULA MOON
Webb, Simon
HAPPY GILMORE
Webb, Spud
EDDIE
Webb, Veronica
CATWALK
Webb, Zachary
BIG BULLY
HAPPY GILMORE
Webber, John
BEFORE AND AFTER
Weber, Andrea
EVERYTHING RELATIVE
Weber, Ben
MIRROR HAS TWO FACES, THE
TWISTER
Weber, Laura L.
PHAT BEACH
Weber, Rudolf
MIRROR, MIRROR III: THE VOYEUR
Webster, Derek
INDEPENDENCE DAY
JOSH KIRBY . . . TIME WARRIOR!: EGGS FROM 70,000,000 B.C.
JOSH KIRBY . . . TIME WARRIOR!: JOURNEY TO THE MAGIC CAVERN
JOSH KIRBY . . . TIME WARRIOR!: LAST BATTLE FOR THE UNIVERSE
JOSH KIRBY . . . TIME WARRIOR!: TRAPPED ON TOY WORLD
Webster, Jeff
I SHOT ANDY WARHOL
Webster, John
DADETOWN
Weckesser, Henry
MR. ICE CREAM MAN
Weclawek, Stefan
ADVENTURES OF PINOCCHIO, THE
Wedan, Stephen
MY FELLOW AMERICANS
Wedekind, Thorsten
LIVE WIRE: HUMAN TIMEBOMB
Wedgeworth, Ann
WHOLE WIDE WORLD, THE
Weeden, Bill
SGT. KABUKIMAN N.Y.P.D.
Weekes, Laura
BLACK SHEEP
MOTHER
VERY BRADY SEQUEL, A
Weeks, Bob
KINGPIN
Weeks, Jimmie Ray
DEAD MAN
Weeks, Kim
DEAD TO RIGHTS
Weeks, Perdita
COLD LIGHT OF DAY
HAMLET
Wehr, John
ASSAULT AT WEST POINT
Weider, Anita
WHITE SQUALL
Weigand, Jon David
IT'S MY PARTY
STAR TREK: FIRST CONTACT
Weigel, Ute
SOUTH BEACH ACADEMY
Weil, Robert
SHE'S THE ONE
Weills, David
WITCHCRAFT: SALEM'S GHOST
Weinberg, Jack
BERKELEY IN THE 60S
Weinberger, Harry
TALKING ABOUT SEX
Weiner, Danielle
PINOCCHIO'S REVENGE
Weiner, Eric
ED'S NEXT MOVE
Weiner, John
ORIGINAL SINS
Weinger, Lauren Kate
SGT. BILKO
Weinstein, Josh
MARS ATTACKS!
Weintraub, Craig Morris
MURDERED INNOCENCE
Weintraub, Helene
ED'S NEXT MOVE
Weir, Malachi B.
BUGGED
Weis, Venesa
EVITA
Weisman, Adam
BIO-DOME
Weiss, Michael T.
FREEWAY
Weiss, Shaun
D3: THE MIGHTY DUCKS
Weiss, Zohren
101 DALMATIANS
Weisser, Morgan
LONG ROAD HOME, THE
MOTHER
Weisser, Norbert
ADRENALIN: FEAR THE RUSH
CHILDREN OF FURY
NEMESIS III: PREY HARDER
RIDERS OF THE PURPLE SAGE
Weisser, Rene
AMANDA AND THE ALIEN
Weisz, Rachel
CHAIN REACTION
STEALING BEAUTY
Weitzenbock, Katia
LITTLE INDIAN, BIG CITY
Weizman, Eli
DEADLY OUTBREAK
Welch, Debbie
SMALL FACES
Welch, Eric
UNDER THE HULA MOON
Welch, Tahnee
I SHOT ANDY WARHOL
Welch, Wally
LARRY MCMURTRY'S STREETS OF LAREDO
Welcome, V. Ranaldo
PREACHER'S WIFE, THE
Weld, Tuesday
FEELING MINNESOTA
Weldon, Julia
BEFORE AND AFTER
Welker, Frank
HUNCHBACK OF NOTRE DAME, THE
Weller, Frederick
BASQUIAT
STONEWALL
Weller, Peter
SCREAMERS
Welles, Orson
ORSON WELLES: THE ONE-MAN BAND
PERSONAL JOURNEY WITH MARTIN SCORSESE THROUGH AMERICAN MOVIES, A
Welles, Shannon
SWEEPER, THE
Wellington, James
TOO FAST, TOO YOUNG
Wellington, Madison
MY FELLOW AMERICANS
Welliver, Titus
MULHOLLAND FALLS

Wells, Briant
MR. WRONG
Wells, Dawn
LOVER'S KNOT
Wells, Jason
EVIL HAS A FACE
Wells, Julie C.
EDDIE
Wells, Mell
MOTHER
Wells, Robert
ORIGINAL SINS
Wells, Vanessa J.
INDEPENDENCE DAY
TRUTH ABOUT CATS AND DOGS, THE
Wells, Vernon
HARD JUSTICE
Welsh, Finlay
BREAKING THE WAVES
TRAINSPOTTING
Welsh, Irvine
TRAINSPOTTING
Welsh, Kenneth
PORTRAITS OF A KILLER
Welsh, Tom
LOADED
Weltmann, Sandor
HATE
Welton, Sean
PHAT BEACH
Wenban, Amanda
RACE THE SUN
Wendel, Elmarie
RUMPELSTILTSKIN
Wendel, J.C.
YESTERDAY'S TARGET
Wendenius, Crispin Dickson
CHILDREN OF NOISY VILLAGE, THE
Wendt, Alyssa
FRISK
Wenger, Allan
ROUJIN-Z
Wenner, Darryl
TERMINAL IMPACT
Wenner, Jann
JERRY MAGUIRE
Wentworth, Alexandra
JERRY MAGUIRE
Werner, Darryl
WARHEAD
Werner, Roy
FAST MONEY
NUTTY PROFESSOR, THE
Wescott, Don
FARGO
Wesley, John
COLONY, THE
Wesley, Melina
BURIAL OF THE RATS
Wessof, Lloyd
FAST MONEY
Wesson, Eileen
ZARKORR! THE INVADER
Wesson, Jessica
FLIPPER
West, Billy
SPACE JAM
West, Dominic
SURVIVING PICASSO
WAVELENGTH
West, Gregory
SURGEON, THE
West, John
FELONY
West, Kevin
BIO-DOME
SANTA WITH MUSCLES

West, Pamela
LAWNMOWER MAN 2: BEYOND CYBERSPACE
West, Red
FELONY
West, Samuel
JANE EYRE
West, Tegan
GRACE OF MY HEART
Westcott, Genevieve
FRIGHTENERS, THE
Westenberg, Robert
BEFORE AND AFTER
Westenskow, Mike
CHILDREN OF FURY
Westergaard, Joyce
BODY OF INFLUENCE 2
Weston, Celia
FLIRTING WITH DISASTER
Weston, Eric
BODY COUNT
Weston, Jeff
BACKLASH: OBLIVION 2
Weston, Terry
SANTA CLAWS
Westwood, Julie
CRACKER: THE MADWOMAN IN THE ATTIC
Westwood, Karen
EMMA
Whalen, Jim
RANSOM
Whalen, Sean
CABLE GUY, THE
THAT THING YOU DO!
TWISTER
Whaley, Frank
BROKEN ARROW
HOMAGE
Whalin, Justin
WHITE WOLVES II: LEGEND OF THE WILD
Whately, Kevin
ENGLISH PATIENT, THE
Wheaton, Wil
MR. STITCH
PIE IN THE SKY
Wheeldon, Steven
CITIZEN RUTH
Wheeler, Aaron
SOME FOLKS CALL IT A SLING BLADE
Wheeler, Andrew
BIG BULLY
SURGEON, THE
Wheeler, Ed
DAYLIGHT
Wheeler, Ira
ASSOCIATE, THE
Wheeler, Joe
TEXAS PAYBACK
Wheeler, Lisa
MIRROR HAS TWO FACES, THE
Wheeler-Nicholson, Dana
DENISE CALLS UP
POMPATUS OF LOVE, THE
Whelan, Gary
MICHAEL COLLINS
MOLL FLANDERS
Whelker, Frank
LAND BEFORE TIME IV: JOURNEY THROUGH THE MISTS
Whipp, Joseph
SCREAM
SHARON'S SECRET
Whipple, Sam
GREAT WHITE HYPE, THE
ROCK, THE

Whirry, Shannon
EXIT
PLAYBACK
Whitaker, Damon
MR. HOLLAND'S OPUS
SAINTS AND SINNERS
Whitaker, Duane
NIGHT OF THE SCARECROW
WITHIN THE ROCK
Whitaker, Forest
PHENOMENON
Whitbeck, Allison
JACK
Whitchurch, Philip
ENGLISH PATIENT, THE
White, Betty
WEEKEND IN THE COUNTRY, A
White, Carl
CITY HALL
White, Danny
WHARF RAT, THE
White, Devoy
TRIGGER EFFECT, THE
White, Dwain L.
PREACHER'S WIFE, THE
White, Earl
BLOODSPORT II: THE NEXT KUMITE
NEMESIS III: PREY HARDER
White, Freeman
FAN, THE
White, Gregory
VERY BRADY SEQUEL, A
White, Ian
TWO IF BY SEA
White, Jack
D3: THE MIGHTY DUCKS
White, James A.
PEOPLE VS. LARRY FLYNT, THE
White, James D.
MIDWINTER'S TALE, A
White, Jeffrey
DADETOWN
White, John
LEGEND OF GATOR FACE, THE
TAILS YOU LIVE, HEADS YOU'RE DEAD
White, Karen Malina
ONCE UPON A TIME . . . WHEN WE WERE COLORED
White, Kerry
PEOPLE VS. LARRY FLYNT, THE
White, Kevin
GLIMMER MAN, THE
MR. STITCH
White, Loni
ARRIVAL, THE
White, Michael Jai
2 DAYS IN THE VALLEY
White, Michole
COURAGE UNDER FIRE
White, Mike
JERRY MAGUIRE
White, Peter
MR. WRONG
MOTHER
White, Rhonda Stubbins
SUNSET PARK
White, Ron
FRAME BY FRAME
KISSINGER AND NIXON
SCREAMERS
White, Rory
WAR OF THE BUTTONS, THE
White, Sebastian
NECRONOMICON: BOOK OF THE DEAD
White, Steve
BULLETPROOF
GET ON THE BUS
OPEN SEASON

White, Susan Ellen
SANTA CLAWS
Whitehead, Robert
LIVE WIRE: HUMAN TIMEBOMB
REDEMPTION: KICKBOXER 5
Whitelaw, Billie
JANE EYRE
Whitfield, June
JUDE
Whitfield, Lynn
THIN LINE BETWEEN LOVE AND HATE, A
Whitfield, Mark
KANSAS CITY
Whitfield, Martin
DON'T LET YOUR MEAT LOAF
Whitfield, Mitchell
SGT. BILKO
Whitfield, Myla
DON'T LET YOUR MEAT LOAF
Whitfield, Peter
INSTITUTE BENJAMENTA
Whitford, Bradley
MY FELLOW AMERICANS
Whitlock, Isiah
EVERYONE SAYS I LOVE YOU
Whitlock Jr., Isiah
EDDIE
Whitlock, Lee
SHOPPING
Whitman, Mae
INDEPENDENCE DAY
ONE FINE DAY
Whitney, Ann
CHAIN REACTION
Whitney, Jane
MOTHER'S PRAYER, A
Whittaker, Jonathan
SUGARTIME
Whittemore, Connie
HEAVEN'S PRISONERS
Whittemore, Libby
FLED
Who, The
MESSAGE TO LOVE: THE ISLE OF WIGHT FESTIVAL
ROLLING STONES ROCK-AND-ROLL CIRCUS, THE
Whorley, Billy
PIRANHA
Whyle, James
LIVE WIRE: HUMAN TIMEBOMB
Whyte, Mal
MICHAEL COLLINS
MOLL FLANDERS
SOME MOTHER'S SON
Whyte, Scott
D3: THE MIGHTY DUCKS
Wickes, Mary
HUNCHBACK OF NOTRE DAME, THE
Wickham, Saskia
ANGELS AND INSECTS
Wicki, Amy
MUTANT MAN
Wickware, Scott
WHARF RAT, THE
Widdoes, Kathleen
COURAGE UNDER FIRE
Widierker, Jack
DEADLY OUTBREAK
Wieder, Anna Marie
RANSOM
Wiener, Joshua
INFINITY
Wiessner, Joe
MUTANT MAN
Wiest, Dianne
ASSOCIATE, THE
BIRDCAGE, THE

Wigdor, Geoff
SLEEPERS
Wigge, Jenny
EVIL ED
Wiggins, Wiley
BOYS
Wight, Peter
SECRETS & LIES
Wike, Tony
CITIZEN RUTH
Wilbee, Codie Lucas
SURGEON, THE
Wilcox, Ralph
LAST DANCE
Wilcox, Shannon
DANGEROUS PASSION
DEAR GOD
Wilde, Adam
FEMALIEN
Wilde, Adrienne
DEAR GOD
Wilde, Bob
UNFORGETTABLE
Wilder, Billy
PERSONAL JOURNEY WITH MARTIN SCORSESE THROUGH AMERICAN MOVIES, A
Wilder, James
TOLLBOOTH
Wilder, Steve
JOSH KIRBY . . . TIME WARRIOR!: EGGS FROM 70,000,000 B.C.
Wilderson, Wayne
INDEPENDENCE DAY
Wilding, Chris
ANNIE O
Wildman, Valerie
DEAR GOD
MARS ATTACKS!
RUMPELSTILTSKIN
Wilequet, Alex
DAENS
Wiles, Michael Shamus
UP CLOSE AND PERSONAL
Wiley, Bill
THAT THING YOU DO!
Wiley, Edward
CANTERVILLE GHOST, THE
CHILDREN OF FURY
Wilhelm, Wimie
ANTONIA'S LINE
Wilhelmsson, Hans
EVIL ED
Wilhite, Jason
FOXFIRE
Wilhoite, Kathleen
TALES OF EROTICA
Wilkerson, Jerry
SANDMAN, THE
Wilkerson, Mary
SANDMAN, THE
Wilkey, Jim
LAST MAN STANDING
Wilkie, Rich
NORMAL LIFE
Wilkins, Claudia
D3: THE MIGHTY DUCKS
Wilkinson, Tom
GHOST AND THE DARKNESS, THE
Wilkof, Lee
ASSOCIATE, THE
Wilks, Audra
FIRST KID
Willes, Christine
BIG BULLY
Willett, Chad
ANNIE O

Williams, Aaron
CHAIN REACTION
Williams, Afram Bill
CHAIN REACTION
Williams, Berta J.
PREACHER'S WIFE, THE
Williams, Billy Dee
DANGEROUS PASSION
Williams, Brenda
PUBLIC ENEMIES
Williams, Brent J.
LOW LIFE, THE
SOME FOLKS CALL IT A SLING BLADE
Williams, Brian
DANGEROUS PASSION
Williams Brothers, The
GRACE OF MY HEART
Williams, Bruce
SET IT OFF
Williams, Burt
PUBLIC ACCESS
Williams, Cress
2 DAYS IN THE VALLEY
Williams, Curtis
DEAR GOD
Williams, Cynda
BLACK ROSE OF HARLEM
CONDITION RED
SWEEPER, THE
TALES OF EROTICA
Williams, Cynthia
LAST DANCE
Williams, D. Chance
UNHOOK THE STARS
Williams, David Brian
TIME TO KILL, A
Williams, Dijon S.
GHOSTS OF MISSISSIPPI
Williams, Doug
NUTTY PROFESSOR, THE
Williams, Doug MacArthur
FIRST KID
Williams, Earl
STUPIDS, THE
Williams, Ellis
EYE FOR AN EYE
GLIMMER MAN, THE
LAWNMOWER MAN 2: BEYOND CYBERSPACE
Williams, Gareth
FULL BODY MASSAGE
PALOOKAVILLE
Williams, Gus
CELTIC PRIDE
Williams, Harland
DOWN PERISCOPE
Williams, Heathcote
COLD LIGHT OF DAY
Williams, Herb
EDDIE
Williams, Ian Patrick
DEAD TO RIGHTS
Williams III, Clarence
IMMORTALS, THE
ROAD TO GALVESTON, THE
Williams, Jacqueline
FAMILY THING, A
Williams, John "Hot Rod"
EDDIE
Williams, Johnny
EDDIE
VIRTUAL COMBAT
Williams Jr., Clarence
PRIMAL FEAR
Williams, Junior
RUDE
Williams, Keith Leon
FAN, THE

Williams, Kelli
WAVELENGTH
Williams, Kimberly
WAR AT HOME, THE
Williams, Malinda
HIGH SCHOOL HIGH
SUNSET PARK
THIN LINE BETWEEN LOVE AND HATE, A
Williams, Mark
101 DALMATIANS
Williams, Michael W.
HIGH SCHOOL HIGH
Williams, Patrick
THEY BITE
Williams, Paul
HEADLESS BODY IN TOPLESS BAR
PHANTOM 2040: THE GHOST WHO WALKS
Williams, Phil
GHOST IN THE SHELL
STREET FIGHTER II: THE ANIMATED MOVIE
Williams, Philip
BOGUS
TWO IF BY SEA
Williams, Robin
BIRDCAGE, THE
HAMLET
JACK
JOSEPH CONRAD'S THE SECRET AGENT
Williams, Shirley
TATTOO BOY
Williams, Sioned Jones
HEDD WYNN
Williams, Stacey
JERRY MAGUIRE
Williams, Steve
THEY BITE
Williams, Timothy
TIGER HEART
Williams, Treat
LATE SHIFT, THE
MULHOLLAND FALLS
PHANTOM, THE
Williams, Vanessa
ERASER
MOTHER
Williams, Victor
PREACHER'S WIFE, THE
Williams, Walt
EDDIE
Williamson, Fred
FROM DUSK TILL DAWN
ORIGINAL GANGSTAS
Williamson, Paul
EMMA
Williamson, Scott
PLAYBACK
Williamson, Stace
AMERICAN STRAYS
Williard, Carol
DEAR GOD
Williby, Erin
FIRST KID
Willingham, Nobel
UP CLOSE AND PERSONAL
Willinton, Curt
SURGEON, THE
Willis, Bruce
LAST MAN STANDING
Willis, Cher
ANIMAL INSTINCTS III: THE SEDUCTRESS
Willis, Jimmy
THAT THING YOU DO!
Willis, Michael
SOMEONE ELSE'S AMERICA
Willis, Mirron E.
INDEPENDENCE DAY
Willis, Rumer
STRIPTEASE
Willis, Troy
INDEPENDENCE DAY
Wills, Jerry
RIDERS OF THE PURPLE SAGE
Wills, Sheila
BLACK OUT
Willson, Paul
WHARF RAT, THE
Wilmot, David
MICHAEL COLLINS
Wilon, Nitza
WALKING AND TALKING
Wilson, Aloysius
MURDERED INNOCENCE
Wilson, Andrew
BOTTLE ROCKET
Wilson, Brad
KAZAAM
Wilson, Brian
THEREMIN: AN ELECTRONIC ODYSSEY
Wilson, Bridgette
UNHOOK THE STARS
Wilson, Chandra
LONE STAR
Wilson, Cheryl
UNFORGETTABLE
Wilson, Chris
THAT THING YOU DO!
Wilson, Debra
GIRL 6
Wilson, Don "The Dragon"
HARD WAY OUT: BLOODFIST VIII
VIRTUAL COMBAT
Wilson, Drew
BLACK SHEEP
Wilson, Elizabeth
BOYS NEXT DOOR, THE
Wilson, George
BEST OF THE BEST 3: NO TURNING BACK
Wilson, Jody
SUBSTITUTE, THE
TOLLBOOTH
Wilson, Jonathan
KIDS IN THE HALL: BRAIN CANDY
SUGARTIME
Wilson, Kristen
BULLETPROOF
GIRL 6
POMPATUS OF LOVE, THE
Wilson, Kristin
GET ON THE BUS
Wilson, Lenny
PRIMAL FEAR
Wilson, Luke
BOTTLE ROCKET
Wilson, Mara
MATILDA
Wilson, Mark
FLY AWAY HOME
Wilson, Michael
FRISK
Wilson, Miss Ruby
PEOPLE VS. LARRY FLYNT, THE
Wilson, Mychal
POISON IVY 2: LILY
Wilson, Owen
CABLE GUY, THE
Wilson, Owen C.
BOTTLE ROCKET
Wilson, Pasean
STRIPTEASE
Wilson, Patricia
NUTTY PROFESSOR, THE
Wilson, Paul D.
FAMILY THING, A
Wilson, Peta
WOMAN UNDONE, A
Wilson, Raleigh
MOONSHINE HIGHWAY
Wilson, Reno
GREAT WHITE HYPE, THE
SGT. BILKO
Wilson, Rita
JINGLE ALL THE WAY
THAT THING YOU DO!
Wilson, Rod
ELECTRA
Wilson, Ruby
CHAMBER, THE
Wilson, Scott
MOTHER
QUEST, THE
Wilson, Sheri-D
ROBIN OF LOCKSLEY
Wilson, Stuart
EDIE & PEN
Wilson, Teddy
BOTTLE ROCKET
Wilson, Victor
DEATH ARTIST, THE
Wilson, Yvette
DON'T BE A MENACE TO SOUTH CENTRAL WHILE DRINKING YOUR JUICE IN THE HOOD
Wimmer, Brian
MADDENING, THE
Winbush, Camille
ERASER
Wincott, Jeff
WHEN THE BULLET HITS THE BONE
Wincott, Michael
BASQUIAT
DEAD MAN
Winde, Beatrice
LONE STAR
Windsor, Bob
DARKMAN III: DIE DARKMAN DIE
HARRIET THE SPY
STAND OFF, THE
Winer, Rosie
HOUSE ARREST
Wineshmutz, Jeff
SGT. KABUKIMAN N.Y.P.D.
Winfield, Chris
WATCH ME
Winfield, J. Jason
EXIT
Winfield, Paul
LEGEND OF GATOR FACE, THE
MARS ATTACKS!
ORIGINAL GANGSTAS
Winfrey, Jonathan
BLACK SCORPION
CARNOSAUR 3: PRIMAL SPECIES
Wing, Leslie
FRIGHTENERS, THE
Wingate, David
EDDIE
Wingdom, William
CHILDREN OF THE CORN: THE GATHERING
Wingert, Sally
FARGO
Winkel, Natalie
BROTHER OF SLEEP
Winkler, Henry
SCREAM
Winkler, Mel
CITY HALL
Winley, Robert
PINOCCHIO'S REVENGE

Winling, Jean-Marie
HORSEMAN ON THE ROOF
Winningham, Mare
BOYS NEXT DOOR, THE
LETTER TO MY KILLER
Winslet, Kate
HAMLET
JUDE
Winston, Ellis
QUEST, THE
Winston, Hattie
SUNSET PARK
Winston, Matt
JOSH KIRBY . . . TIME WARRIOR!: JOURNEY TO THE MAGIC CAVERN
Wint, Maurice Dean
CURTIS'S CHARM
Winter, Gordon
SECRETS & LIES
Winters, Gloria Jackson
CHAMBER, THE
Winters, Scott
PEOPLE VS. LARRY FLYNT, THE
Winters, Shelley
HEAVY
MRS. MUNCK
PORTRAIT OF A LADY, THE
Winther, Michael
INDEPENDENCE DAY
Winton, Dale
TRAINSPOTTING
Wirth, Billy
VENUS RISING
Wisdom, Robert
LIFEFORM
THAT THING YOU DO!
Wise, Alan
NICO ICON
Wise, Jim
DEATH ARTIST, THE
Wise, Robert
STUPIDS, THE
Wiseman, Michael
BLACK SCORPION
WAR AT HOME, THE
Wisniewski, Andreas
MISSION: IMPOSSIBLE
Withers, Googie
SHINE
Withers, Jane
HUNCHBACK OF NOTRE DAME, THE
Withers, Margery
SECRETS & LIES
Witherspoon, Reese
FEAR
FREEWAY
Witkin, Jacob
FAST MONEY
SAWBONES
Witkowska, Kryska
LIVE WIRE: HUMAN TIMEBOMB
Witt, Alicia
CITIZEN RUTH
MR. HOLLAND'S OPUS
Witt, Katarina
JERRY MAGUIRE
Witt, Maurice Dean
RUDE
Witt, Thomas
REDEMPTION: KICKBOXER 5
Witter, Diane
IN LOVE AND WAR
Wixted, Kevin
MAGIC IN THE MIRROR
Woerner, Natalia
MACHINE, THE
Wojcik, Magda Teresa
MOTHER OF KINGS
Wolchok, James Marshall
GHOSTS OF MISSISSIPPI
Wold, Ty
THEY BITE
Wolf, Fred
BLACK SHEEP
Wolf, J.
DEMOLITIONIST, THE
Wolf, Joe
EDDIE
Wolf, Kelly
EDIE & PEN
INFINITY
Wolf, Lynn
WATCH ME
Wolf, Rita
GIRL 6
Wolf, Scott
EVENING STAR, THE
WHITE SQUALL
Wolfe, Jeff
BLOODSPORT II: THE NEXT KUMITE
Wolfe, Joanne
KINGPIN
Wolff, Helma
NICO ICON
Wolff, William
DEAR GOD
Wolford, Josh
FOREST WARRIOR
HOUSE ARREST
Wolfson, Conrad
ED'S NEXT MOVE
Wolk, Andrew Michael
SGT. KABUKIMAN N.Y.P.D.
Wolos-Fonteno, David
ERASER
Wolvett, Gordon Michael
RUDE
Wonderly, Kim
JACK
Wong, Albert
GLIMMER MAN, THE
Wong, Anthony
ORGANIZED CRIME & TRIAD BUREAU
Wong, B.D.
EXECUTIVE DECISION
Wong, Byron
HARRIET THE SPY
Wong, Daniel May
RANSOM
Wong, Faye
CHUNGKING EXPRESS
Wong, Gary
RUMBLE IN THE BRONX
Wong, James
INDEPENDENCE DAY
Wong, Justin
D3: THE MIGHTY DUCKS
Wong, Kea
SABRINA, THE TEENAGE WITCH
Wong, Melvin
MIDNIGHT ANGEL
Wong, Parkman
ORGANIZED CRIME & TRIAD BUREAU
Wong, Paul
SHOPPING
Wong, Peter
QUEST, THE
Wong, William
HARD JUSTICE
Wood, Andrew T.
FIRST KID
Wood, Ashley Ann
BLOODKNOT
Wood, Bennett
PEOPLE VS. LARRY FLYNT, THE
Wood, Bonnie
SCREAM
Wood, Bret
EDDIE
Wood, Elijah
FLIPPER
Wood, John
JANE EYRE
RASPUTIN
Wood, Katherine
GHOSTS OF MISSISSIPPI
Wood, Tara
EDDIE
Woodall, Edward
EMMA
Woodard, Alfre
PRIMAL FEAR
STAR TREK: FIRST CONTACT
Woodard, Charlayne
CRUCIBLE, THE
EYE FOR AN EYE
Woodbine, Bokeem
FREEWAY
ROCK, THE
Woodbury, Judith
NUTTY PROFESSOR, THE
Woodeson, Nicholas
CRACKER: THE MADWOMAN IN THE ATTIC
Woodin, John
KINGPIN
Woodley, Al
BUGGED
Woodley, David
TUNNEL VISION
Woods, Barbara Alyn
DEAD WEEKEND
STRIPTEASE
Woods, James
FOR BETTER OR WORSE
GHOSTS OF MISSISSIPPI
Woods, Kevin Jamal
AMERICA'S DREAM
Woods, Lesley
COLONY, THE
Woods, Mimi
GHOST IN THE SHELL
Woods, Tyler
FOR THE MOMENT
Woodson, Jackie
GIRLFRIENDS
Woodthorpe, Peter
JANE EYRE
Woodward, Sean
ADVENTURES OF PINOCCHIO, THE
Woodward, Tim
SOME MOTHER'S SON
Woodyard, Shawn D.
MY FELLOW AMERICANS
Wooley, Rachel
MR. HOLLAND'S OPUS
Woolrich, Abel
SOLO
Woolson, Michael
WIDOW'S KISS
Woolvet, Gordon Michael
LEGEND OF GATOR FACE, THE
Wordham, Gary R.
JUROR, THE
Woren, Dan
STAR TREK: FIRST CONTACT
Worley, Darlene
CABLE GUY, THE
Worrell, Fred
DADETOWN
Worsley, Julia
EVITA

Worth, Nicholas
BARB WIRE
DEAD WEEKEND
HIGH SCHOOL HIGH
Worthing, Deborah
ONE MAN'S JUSTICE
Worthington, Deborah
DESIRE
Worthington, Reid
SPY HARD
Worthington, Wendy
NORMA JEAN AND MARILYN
Worthly, Ross
WHISPERING, THE
Worthy, Rick
TRIGGER EFFECT, THE
Wostry, Florian
BROTHER OF SLEEP
Wotton, Phillip
MAXIMUM RISK
MR. STITCH
Wouassi, Felicite
HATE
Wrangler, Greg
DEAD WEEKEND
VENUS RISING
Wreck, Becky
NOT BAD FOR A GIRL
Wright, Ben
TIN CUP
Wright, Blake
HYPE!
Wright, Brian
BASQUIAT
Wright, Bruce
RICH MAN'S WIFE, THE
TWISTER
Wright, Burt
SGT. KABUKIMAN N.Y.P.D.
Wright, David Grant
BEASTMASTER 3: THE EYE OF BRAXUS
Wright, Gary
LIVE WIRE: HUMAN TIMEBOMB
Wright, Herbert Leslie
SHAMELESS
Wright, Io Tillett
ANGELA
TREES LOUNGE
Wright, Jack
BARB WIRE
Wright, Janet
BEYOND THE CALL
Wright, Jeff
HIGH SCHOOL HIGH
Wright, Jeffrey
BASQUIAT
FAITHFUL
Wright, Julie
EXECUTIVE DECISION
Wright, Kimberly L.
PREACHER'S WIFE, THE
Wright, Matt
HYPE!
Wright, Patrick
HOURGLASS
Wright, Robin
MOLL FLANDERS
Wright, Steve
FUNNYMAN, THE
Wright, Steven
FOR BETTER OR WORSE
Wright, Tom
MY FELLOW AMERICANS
Wright, Wayne
PRIMAL FEAR
Wu Nien-jen
MAHJONG

Wuhl, Robert
MISSING PIECES
OPEN SEASON
Wuhrer, Kari
BEYOND DESIRE
STEPHEN KING'S THINNER
Wulf, Mary Kay
INFINITY
Wunder, Graig
APART FROM HUGH
Wyand, Carole
DOWN, OUT AND DANGEROUS
Wyatt, Dale
DELTA OF VENUS
Wycherley, Don
MICHAEL COLLINS
Wylie, Adam
ALL DOGS GO TO HEAVEN 2
Wylie, John
BEFORE AND AFTER
Wyman, Bill
ROLLING STONES ROCK-AND-ROLL CIRCUS, THE
Wynands, Dan
ERASER
Wyson, Edmund
NORMAL LIFE
Xie Yuan
BLACK MOUNTAIN
Xing Yangchun
BLUSH
Xu, Tony
CRACKER: THE MADWOMAN IN THE ATTIC
Xuereb, Emanuel
TALES OF EROTICA
Xuereb, Emmanuel
GRIM
Xuereb, Salvator
BARB WIRE
MR. STITCH
Yaconi, Vittorio
JOHNNY 100 PESOS
Yagher, Jeff
MY FELLOW AMERICANS
Yajima, Kenishi
KAMIKAZE TAXI
Yakunina, Valentina
MISSION: IMPOSSIBLE
Yakusho, Keji
KAMIKAZE TAXI
Yakusho, Koji
KAMIKAZE TAXI
Yamada, Meikyoh
FLIRT
Yamaguchi, Kenji
FLIRT
Yamaguchi, Masahiro
SGT. KABUKIMAN N.Y.P.D.
Yamazaki, Tetsushi
FLIRT
Yan Shi
SOMEONE ELSE'S AMERICA
Yanan, Don
ZARKORR! THE INVADER
Yanez, Eduardo
STRIPTEASE
Yang, Ginny
ASSOCIATE, THE
Yang Kuei-mei
VIVE L'AMOUR
Yannatos, Michalis
SOMEONE ELSE'S AMERICA
Yanne, Jean
HORSEMAN ON THE ROOF
Yannis, Suzy
BUTTERFLY KISS

Yanofsky, Louise
WALKING AND TALKING
Yares, Coco
ANNIE O
Yarlett, Claire
BLACK OUT
Yarmush, Michael
LOSING CHASE
Yassira
GIRLS TOWN
Yasutake, Patti
DEAD TO RIGHTS
ROAD TO GALVESTON, THE
STAR TREK: FIRST CONTACT
Yates, Ashley
VIRTUAL ENCOUNTERS
Yates, Gary
FLED
Yates, Jack
ROCK, THE
Yates, Paul
FRIGHTENERS, THE
Yea, Helena
BIG BULLY
HAPPY GILMORE
Yeager, Biff
HEADLESS BODY IN TOPLESS BAR
Yeager, Caroline
GETTING AWAY WITH MURDER
Yedidia, Mario
JACK
JAMES AND THE GIANT PEACH
Yee, Derek
BLONDES HAVE MORE GUNS
Yee, Nancy
GLIMMER MAN, THE
Yen, Donnie
WING CHUN
Yen, Tricia
VIRTUAL ENCOUNTERS
Yenque, Teresa
EXTREME MEASURES
Yeoh, Michelle
WING CHUN
Yerro, Mayte
EVITA
Yesso, Don
HEAVEN'S PRISONERS
Yesz
PHAT BEACH
Yeung, Bolo
SHOOTFIGHTER 2: KILL OR BE KILLED!
Yharra, Karina
RAVENHAWK
Yi Fan-Wai
ORGANIZED CRIME & TRIAD BUREAU
Yim Chau-Wah
MIDNIGHT ANGEL
Yin Jimei
BLUSH
Yip, Cecilia
ORGANIZED CRIME & TRIAD BUREAU
Yip, Francoise
RUMBLE IN THE BRONX
Yli-Loumi, Caroline
MRS. WINTERBOURNE
Yoakam, Dwight
LITTLE DEATH, THE
PAINTED HERO
SLING BLADE
Yoeman, Matt
MAN WITH THE PERFECT SWING, THE
Yohnka, Merritt
FAST MONEY
York, Brian
BLONDES HAVE MORE GUNS
York, Jennifer
THAT THING YOU DO!

York, Michael
NOT OF THIS EARTH
York, Rachel
ONE FINE DAY
Yorke, Carl Gabriel
LETTER TO MY KILLER
Yosephsberg, Yorman
DEADLY OUTBREAK
Yoshino, Sayaka
MABOROSI
Young, Benny
FUNNYMAN, THE
Young, Bobby
FEMALIEN
Young, Bruce
NORMAL LIFE
PHENOMENON
Young, Camie
TALKING ABOUT SEX
Young, Dey
EXECUTIVE DECISION
LETTER TO MY KILLER
PIE IN THE SKY
Young, Eric
NORMAL LIFE
Young Fresh Fellows, The
HYPE!
Young, Harrison
CHILDREN OF THE CORN: THE GATHERING
Young, Howard
BEST OF THE BEST 3: NO TURNING BACK
Young, James
NICO ICON
Young, K. Addison
FLED
Young, Karen
DAYLIGHT
WIFE, THE
Young, Kate
DIABOLIQUE
Young, Keone
JACK
STRIPTEASE
Young, Neil
ISLAND OF DR. MOREAU, THE
Young, Patrick
COURAGE UNDER FIRE
Young, Queline
DON'T BE A MENACE TO SOUTH CENTRAL WHILE DRINKING YOUR JUICE IN THE HOOD
Young, Ricardo Miguel
FIRST KID
Young, Russell
BOYS
Young, Sean
EVIL HAS A FACE
PROPRIETOR, THE
Young, Sharon
BREAKAWAY
Young, Steve James
FOR THE MOMENT
Young, Victor
MRS. WINTERBOURNE
Young, Vincent
MODERN AFFAIR, A
Yrola, Genevieve
GIRL 6
Yu, Eri
FLIRT
Yu, Linda
PRIMAL FEAR
Yu Ming
MIDNIGHT ANGEL
Yuan, Ron Winston
WHITE TIGER
Yuen King Tan
WING CHUN
Yuen, Russell
FRAME BY FRAME
HOLLOW POINT
Yuen Woo Ping
WICKED CITY, THE
Yule, Ian
TERMINAL IMPACT
WARHEAD
Yulin, Harris
LOOKING FOR RICHARD
MULTIPLICITY
TRUMAN
Yurchis, Rasa
FOXFIRE
Yusko, Kelly
ED'S NEXT MOVE
Yustman, Odette
DEAR GOD
Yuzna, Brian
DENTIST, THE
NECRONOMICON: BOOK OF THE DEAD
Z'Dar, Robert
RED LINE
Zabelicka, Eva
KASPAR HAUSER
Zabka, William
SHOOTFIGHTER 2: KILL OR BE KILLED!
Zabriskie, Grace
FAMILY THING, A
PASSION OF DARKLY NOON, THE
Zacapa, Daniel
PHENOMENON
UP CLOSE AND PERSONAL
Zachar, Robert L.
STAR TREK: FIRST CONTACT
Zachary, Jude
BREACH OF TRUST
FINAL CUT, THE
Zagaria, Anita
ADVENTURES OF PINOCCHIO, THE
Zagarino, Frank
TERMINAL IMPACT
WARHEAD
WITHOUT MERCY
Zaghbib, Naoufel
SILENCES OF THE PALACE, THE
Zago, Catherine
PORTRAIT OF A LADY, THE
Zagon, Marty
CABLE GUY, THE
Zahedi, Caveh
CITIZEN RUTH
Zahn, Steve
RACE THE SUN
THAT THING YOU DO!
Zahner, Sigrid K.
PRIMAL FEAR
Zahonero, Coraly
LA COMEDIE-FRANCAISE OU L'AMOUR JOUE
NELLY AND MONSIEUR ARNAUD
Zahoryin, Tracy
DUNSTON CHECKS IN
Zahrn, Will
CHAIN REACTION
Zahrouni, Salem
MADAME BUTTERFLY
Zajonc, Bobby
CABLE GUY, THE
Zakir, Said
HALFMOON
Zal, Roxana
RED LINE
Zamattio, Alessandro
CEMETERY MAN
Zamperla, Rinaldo
CEMETERY MAN
Zamprogna, Dominic
IRON EAGLE IV
Zana, Stanley
LITTLE INDIAN, BIG CITY
Zanardi, Bruno
RIDICULE
Zane, Billy
PHANTOM, THE
Zane, Lora
LIVE NUDE GIRLS
Zapasiewicz, Zbigniew
MOTHER OF KINGS
Zapata, Carmen
STREETCAR NAMED DESIRE, A
Zappa, William
PHANTOM, THE
Zardo, Giuseppe
STAR MAKER, THE
Zavala, Rio
CHAIN REACTION
Zavayna, Ken
ED
Zawadska, Valerie
DELTA OF VENUS
Zazee, Dewar
TALES OF EROTICA
Zboyovski, Matt
MY FELLOW AMERICANS
Zebrowski, Brett
FIRST KID
Zee, Eric Michael
INDEPENDENCE DAY
Zeek, Dawn
IT CAME FROM OUTER SPACE II
Zeelenberg, Dirk
ANTONIA'S LINE
Zegarac, Dusica
VUKOVAR
Zekman, Pam
CHAIN REACTION
Zeller, Jacques-Francois
RIDICULE
Zellweger, Renee
JERRY MAGUIRE
LOW LIFE, THE
TEXAS CHAINSAW MASSACRE: THE NEXT GENERATION
WHOLE WIDE WORLD, THE
Zelniker, Michael
WITHIN THE ROCK
Zem, Roschdy
MA SAISON PREFEREE
Zeman, Richard
HOLLOW POINT
MOTHER NIGHT
Zemanek, Timm
FLY AWAY HOME
SUGARTIME
Zepeda, Jimmy
PIG'S TALE, A
Zeper, Fran Waller
ANTONIA'S LINE
Zeppieri, Richard
HOLLOW POINT
Zetlin, Barry
DOGFIGHTERS, THE
Zette, Bernard
DELTA OF VENUS
Zhang Guoli
STORY OF XINGHUA, THE
Zhang Liwei
BLUSH
Zhao Gang
BLACK MOUNTAIN
Zhao, Wen-Juan
MADAME BUTTERFLY

Zhao Xiaorui
BLACK MOUNTAIN
Zhou Jianying
BLUSH
Zhu Jiyong
BLUSH
Zibetti, Roberto
STEALING BEAUTY
Zick, Leo
JERRY MAGUIRE
Ziegelmeyer, Larry
PINOCCHIO'S REVENGE
Ziegler, Gunter
VIKING SAGAS, THE
Ziegler, Tessa
YANKEE ZULU
Ziesmer, Jerry
JERRY MAGUIRE
Zima, Yvonne
BED OF ROSES
EXECUTIVE DECISION
LONG KISS GOODNIGHT, THE
Zimbo
ARRIVAL, THE
Zimmer, Diana
EXTREME MEASURES
Zimmerman, Joey
BEASTMASTER 3: THE EYE OF BRAXUS
Zindel, Bill
FRISK
Zinser, Marion
HEAVEN'S PRISONERS
Zion
WILD SIDE
Zion, Rabbi Joel
PALLBEARER, THE
Zipgun
HYPE!
Ziskie, Daniel
DANGEROUS PASSION
Ziskine, Mikhael
MAXIMUM RISK
Zitelli, Pam
POLYMORPH
Zitner, Alan
PHANTOM, THE
Zito, Chuck
FUNERAL, THE
HEAVEN'S PRISONERS
JUROR, THE
RED LINE
Zold, Edward
FRISK
Zollar, James
KANSAS CITY
Zolotin, Adam
JACK
Zorich, Louis
MISSING PIECES
Zouheir, Asmna
SILENCES OF THE PALACE, THE
Zubar, Jennifer
MAN BY THE SHORE, THE
Zubatov, Alexander
THEY BITE
Zuber, Melanie
MRS. WINTERBOURNE
Zucker, Charlotte
HIGH SCHOOL HIGH
Zuckerman, Donald
LOW LIFE, THE
Zuiderhoek, Olga
CROCODILES IN AMSTERDAM
Zuk, Marla
MANNY & LO
Zuniga, Jose
FLIRT
RANSOM
STRIPTEASE
Zuo Songshen
CHUNGKING EXPRESS
Zurk, Steve
SUBSTITUTE, THE
Zwiener, Michael
BIG BULLY

ANIMATORS

Baxter, James
HUNCHBACK OF NOTRE DAME, THE
Berry, Paul
JAMES AND THE GIANT PEACH
Boomerang
ROUJIN-Z
Brothers Quay, The
INSTITUTE BENJAMENTA
Burgess, Dave
HUNCHBACK OF NOTRE DAME, THE
Cervone, Tony
SPACE JAM
Chiasson, Claude
LAND BEFORE TIME IV: JOURNEY THROUGH THE MISTS
Edmonds, Russ
HUNCHBACK OF NOTRE DAME, THE
Eguchi, Marisuke
NIGHT ON THE GALACTIC RAILROAD
STREET FIGHTER II: THE ANIMATED MOVIE
Feiss, David
ALL DOGS GO TO HEAVEN 2
Finn, Will
HUNCHBACK OF NOTRE DAME, THE
Fucile, Tony
HUNCHBACK OF NOTRE DAME, THE
Galieote, Danny
HUNCHBACK OF NOTRE DAME, THE
Gleeson, Patrick
LAND BEFORE TIME IV: JOURNEY THROUGH THE MISTS
Griffith, Gregory
HUNCHBACK OF NOTRE DAME, THE
Husband, Ron
HUNCHBACK OF NOTRE DAME, THE
Ikeuchi, Toshio
ROUJIN-Z
Kaplan, Yvette
BEAVIS AND BUTT-HEAD DO AMERICA
Kim, Jae Joong
BEAVIS AND BUTT-HEAD DO AMERICA
Kim, Jong Ho
BEAVIS AND BUTT-HEAD DO AMERICA
Kise, Kazuchika
GHOST IN THE SHELL
PATLABOR 2: MOBILE POLICE
Kodama, Takao
NIGHT ON THE GALACTIC RAILROAD
Kubo, Hidemi
SANCTUARY: THE MOVIE
Lee, Choon Man
BEAVIS AND BUTT-HEAD DO AMERICA
Maeda, Minoru
STREET FIGHTER II: THE ANIMATED MOVIE
Matsuhara, Yuji
ROUJIN-Z
Merell, Mike "Moe"
HUNCHBACK OF NOTRE DAME, THE
Murase, Shuko
STREET FIGHTER II: THE ANIMATED MOVIE
Nakasaki, Mitsumochi
ROUJIN-Z
Nishikubo, Toshihiko
GHOST IN THE SHELL
PATLABOR 2: MOBILE POLICE
Okiura, Hiroyuki
GHOST IN THE SHELL
Park, Jun Nam
BEAVIS AND BUTT-HEAD DO AMERICA
Park, Nick
WALLACE AND GROMIT: THE BEST OF AARDMAN ANIMATION
Perkins, Bill
SPACE JAM
Poem Cinema
ROUJIN-Z
Pruiksma, David
HUNCHBACK OF NOTRE DAME, THE
Prynoski, Chris
BEAVIS AND BUTT-HEAD DO AMERICA
Shimizu, Keizou
BIG WARS
Smith, Bruce
SPACE JAM
Takada, Akemi
PATLABOR 2: MOBILE POLICE
Tippe, Ron
SPACE JAM
Tsuruyama, Osamu
PHANTOM 2040: THE GHOST WHO WALKS
Waterman, Todd
ALL DOGS GO TO HEAVEN 2
Wombat
ROUJIN-Z
Yuuki, Masami
PATLABOR 2: MOBILE POLICE
Zielinski, Kathy
HUNCHBACK OF NOTRE DAME, THE
Zombie, Rob
BEAVIS AND BUTT-HEAD DO AMERICA

ART DIRECTORS

Aaron, Fanee
IMMORTALS, THE
Acevedo, John
DARK SECRETS
Adams, Charmian
TWO DEATHS
Aguilar, Jose Luis
SOLO
Alesch, Stephen
PALLBEARER, THE
Alex, Jennifer
TREES LOUNGE
Allen, Aram
NECRONOMICON: BOOK OF THE DEAD
Ammerlaan, Harry
ANTONIA'S LINE
Arditti, Carlos
TWO MUCH
Arnold, Steve
LONG KISS GOODNIGHT, THE
Arnold, William
PRIMAL FEAR
RICH MAN'S WIFE, THE
Atkins, Shawn
GIRLFRIENDS
Atwell, Michael
MAD DOG TIME
PIE IN THE SKY
TO GILLIAN ON HER 37TH BIRTHDAY
Austerberry, Paul Denham
EXTREME MEASURES
HARRIET THE SPY
KIDS IN THE HALL: BRAIN CANDY
Babic, Branimir
RASPUTIN

Baker, Joshua Meath
EMMA
Bangham, Humphrey
AUGUST
JACK & SARAH
Barbasso, Maria Teresa
DRAGONHEART
Bartraw, Damon L.
MUTANT MAN
Basaldua, Emilio
SHADOW YOU SOON WILL BE, A
Basile, Pier-Luigi
DAYLIGHT
Beal, Charles
FIRST WIVES CLUB, THE
Beal, Charley
JUROR, THE
Becket, George
JAG
Berger, Linda
LATE SHIFT, THE
Berke, Mayne
FAN, THE
GRACE OF MY HEART
Berke, Mayne Schuyler
FROM DUSK TILL DAWN
Berman, Danielle
BLACK ROSE OF HARLEM
DEATH ARTIST, THE
SAWBONES
Berner, Ted
DEAD MAN
Billerman, Mark
BOY CALLED HATE, A
Black, Kyler
LONE STAR
Blake, Perry Andelin
BULLETPROOF
Boes, Bill
JAMES AND THE GIANT PEACH
Bolton, Gregory
DEAR GOD
MULHOLLAND FALLS
Bomba, David J.
CHAIN REACTION
EYE FOR AN EYE
Borck, Peter
SPITFIRE GRILL, THE
Bosher, Dennis
JANE EYRE
Boyd, Tim
WHEN THE BULLET HITS THE BONE
Bradette, Jacques
OPEN SEASON
Bradford, Dennis
DIABOLIQUE
PREACHER'S WIFE, THE
Breen, Charles
CROW: CITY OF ANGELS, THE
FLED
Brisco, Ellee Wynn
LOVE IS ALL THERE IS
Brock, Ian
DARKMAN III: DIE DARKMAN DIE
STAND OFF, THE
Brooks, Karen
BREACH OF TRUST
Bruce, John
I SHOT ANDY WARHOL
Buckland, Jeff
BEAVIS AND BUTT-HEAD DO AMERICA
Buckley, Gae
CRAFT, THE
MY FELLOW AMERICANS
TIN CUP
Bucklin, John
LARRY MCMURTRY'S STREETS OF LAREDO
Burian-Mohr, Christopher
GHOSTS OF MISSISSIPPI
TIN CUP
Burmann, Wolfgang
FLOWER OF MY SECRET, THE
Buschmann, Robyn
DENTIST, THE
YESTERDAY'S TARGET
Butcher, Charles
MOTHER
Byggdin, Doug
UNFORGETTABLE
Cabrera, Charley
AMANDA AND THE ALIEN
Cabrera, Leah
DEMOLITIONIST, THE
Campbell, Pat
SMALL FACES
Capaletti, Tom
HOSTILE INTENTIONS
Carew-Watts, Antonia
BREAKAWAY
Carey, Matthew
SHARON'S SECRET
Carriker-Thayer, Teresa
MIRROR HAS TWO FACES, THE
Cassells, Jeremy
MOTHER
Cassie, Alan
MUPPET TREASURE ISLAND
Castillo, Juan Carlos
JOHNNY 100 PESOS
Cavedon, Liz
DESIRE
Chambliss, Scott
CELLULOID CLOSET, THE
Chariton, Laura
MERLIN'S SHOP OF MAGICAL WONDERS
Check, Ed
JOE'S APARTMENT
Chen Yiyun
BLUSH
Childs, Martin
PORTRAIT OF A LADY, THE
Chodak, Randy
RED SCORPION 2
SURGEON, THE
Christov, Anthony B.
LAND BEFORE TIME IV: JOURNEY THROUGH THE MISTS
Chunsuttiwat, Chaiyan "Lek"
QUEST, THE
Chusid, Barry
LAST MAN STANDING
Clark, Karen M.
BEYOND THE CALL
Cobbold, Caroline
JANE EYRE
Cochrane, Sandy
CARPOOL
Cohen, Mark
DEAD WEEKEND
Constant, Kevin
2 DAYS IN THE VALLEY
Cooper, Steve
COURAGE UNDER FIRE
Corciova, Ioana
SPELLBREAKER: SECRET OF THE LEPRECHAUNS
Cormack, Jill
ALEX
Cornwell, Chris
BLACK SHEEP
HOUSE ARREST
Crone, Bruce
JOHN CARPENTER'S ESCAPE FROM L.A.
SGT. BILKO
Cronkhite, Kendal
JAMES AND THE GIANT PEACH
Crowe, Desmond
HAMLET
Crugnola, Aurelio
ENGLISH PATIENT, THE
Cruse, William M.
EXECUTIVE DECISION
Cui, Junde
STORY OF XINGHUA, THE
Curry, Carla
CHILDREN OF THE CORN: THE GATHERING
Curtis, Beth
FUNERAL, THE
TIMELESS
Dabe, Marc
FIRST KID
Dancklefsen, Diane
CAPTIVES
Danielsen, Dins
BARB WIRE
Darrow, Harry
D3: THE MIGHTY DUCKS
Davenport, Dennis
LONG KISS GOODNIGHT, THE
MRS. WINTERBOURNE
de Chauvigny, Emmanuel
CHASING BUTTERFLIES
Devine, Michael
SCREAMERS
Devlin, Conor
SOME MOTHER'S SON
Devoe, Jea
ASSAULT AT WEST POINT
Dexter, John
MARS ATTACKS!
Diamond, Gary
CROW: CITY OF ANGELS, THE
Diers, Don
BIO-DOME
Dobroschke, Vera
PASSION OF DARKLY NOON, THE
Dopaso, Andrea
BOUND
PIG'S TALE, A
Dou Guoxiang
BLACK MOUNTAIN
Doyle, Alta Louise
MAN IN THE ATTIC, THE
Druda, Martin
SOUTH BEACH ACADEMY
Duffield, Tom
BIRDCAGE, THE
Dupre, Susan
4 TALES OF 2 CITIES
Durrell Jr., William J.
SPY HARD
Dvorak, Daniel
DELTA OF VENUS
Earl, Richard
EVITA
Edwards-Bonilla, Le'ce
ONE MAN'S JUSTICE
PHAT BEACH
Ellis, Tim
SOLITAIRE FOR TWO
Epstein, Margarette
HEAD OF THE FAMILY
Eyres, Ricky
TWELFTH NIGHT
Ferguson, David
TAILS YOU LIVE, HEADS YOU'RE DEAD
Fernandez, Javier
BATON ROUGE

Fitzpatrick, David
UNDER THE HULA MOON
Fleming, Jerry N.
BOTTLE ROCKET
Fleming, Zdenek
COLD LIGHT OF DAY
Fleury, Jared
RAGE
Fojo, Richard
SUBSTITUTE, THE
Forrest, Kim
HECK'S WAY HOME
Fort, Michelle
UNKNOWN ORIGIN
Fox, K. C.
DANGEROUS PASSION
Fox, Michael L.
ED
Fraser, Eric
HOMEWARD BOUND II: LOST IN SAN FRANCISCO
Galie, Nathan
CANNIBAL! THE MUSICAL
Gallacher, Tracey
TRAINSPOTTING
Galvin, Tim
SLEEPERS
Gantly, Arden
MICHAEL COLLINS
Geleng, Antonello
CEMETERY MAN
Georgieva, Prolet Spasova
MIND RIPPER
Ghenea, Viorel
MAGIC IN THE MIRROR
Gillies, Rebecca
WAVELENGTH
Ginn, Jeff
GETTING AWAY WITH MURDER
Glotz, Michel
MADAME BUTTERFLY
Goetz, David
HUNCHBACK OF NOTRE DAME, THE
Goldfield, Daniel
HEAVY
Goldstein, Robert
BOUND
Gould, David
SWINGERS
Gracie, Ian
ISLAND OF DR. MOREAU, THE
Graham, Angelo
JACK
Grimsman, Geoffrey S.
ONCE UPON A TIME . . . WHEN WE WERE COLORED
Grundy, Peter
MRS. MUNCK
Guedon, John
BAD LOVE
Guerra, Robert
CITY HALL
Guidery, Wendy
FIST OF THE NORTH STAR
Haack, Mark
TWO IF BY SEA
Haas, Nathan
CHILDREN OF FURY
Haley, Sheila
TALES FROM THE CRYPT PRESENTS BORDELLO OF BLOOD
Halter, Steven
RED LINE
Hambidge, James
LOADED
Hamel, Francois
HORSEMAN ON THE ROOF
Hamlin, Greg
EXIT
Hamrick, Roswell
PALOOKAVILLE
WALKING AND TALKING
Hardwick, Doug
WILLIAM SHAKESPEARE'S ROMEO + JULIET
Hardy, Kenneth A.
FOR BETTER OR WORSE
Harlan, Chase
JUST YOUR LUCK
SANTA WITH MUSCLES
Harrison, Richard
HAPPY GILMORE
Hartley, Clayton
JERRY MAGUIRE
Harwell, Helen
VIRTUAL COMBAT
Hausman, Shawn
PEOPLE VS. LARRY FLYNT, THE
Hennah, Dan
FRIGHTENERS, THE
Henry, Chris
LILY DALE
Heya, Kyoko
MABOROSI
Hix, Kim
FLIPPER
Hobbs, Richard
RACE THE SUN
Hohenberg, Deborah A.
FRISK
Hole, Frederick
MISSION: IMPOSSIBLE
Holland, Page
RIDERS OF THE PURPLE SAGE
Holloway, Jim
COLD COMFORT FARM
Hsu Wing-choi
ORGANIZED CRIME & TRIAD BUREAU
Hubbard, Geoff
MULTIPLICITY
Hudolin, Richard
FEAR
Hudson, Denise
AMERICAN STRAYS
Hudson, Steve
WAVELENGTH
Hugon, Jean-Michel
EVITA
Isenor, Barry
VIRUS
Jackson, John
MONSTERSHOW
James, Lauree S.
TALKING ABOUT SEX
Jefferds, Vincent
SAINTS AND SINNERS
Jenkins, Katy
WHISPERING, THE
Johanna, Rosslyn
PHOENIX
Johnson, Bo
LARGER THAN LIFE
THEODORE REX
Johnson, Brad
NIGHT OF THE SCARECROW
Johnson, Richard L.
EVENING STAR, THE
KANSAS CITY
Juliusson, Karl
BREAKING THE WAVES
Jurek, Ingrid
BLOOD & DONUTS
Kasarda, John
RANSOM
Kato, Hiroshi
SANCTUARY: THE MOVIE
Kelly, John Michael
LAWNMOWER MAN 2: BEYOND CYBERSPACE
Kelly, Monroe
HEAVEN'S PRISONERS
LAST DANCE
Keywan, Alicia
BOGUS
Kibel, Jessica
ED'S NEXT MOVE
King, John
IN LOVE AND WAR
MARY REILLY
Klassen, David
SPACE JAM
Klaus, Sonja
SHAMELESS
Klewais, Willem
PASSION OF DARKLY NOON, THE
Klicius, Galius
UNDERTOW
Knipp, Jeff
CABLE GUY, THE
TRIGGER EFFECT, THE
TRUTH ABOUT CATS AND DOGS, THE
Kobayashi, Reiko
DON'T BE A MENACE TO SOUTH CENTRAL WHILE DRINKING YOUR JUICE IN THE HOOD
Kosko, Gary
BOYS
TRUMAN
Kozak, Lana
ANNIE O
TRACKS OF A KILLER
Kussin, Lori
FUGITIVE RAGE
LaMarre, Helene
HOLLOW POINT
Lamont, Michael
IN LOVE AND WAR
MARY REILLY
Lanfranchi, Damien
MAXIMUM RISK
Lanson, Ken
CHAMELEON
Lapp, Elizabeth
STRIPTEASE
Larson, Ken
HELLRAISER: BLOODLINE
RUMPELSTILTSKIN
TREMORS 2: AFTERSHOCKS
Lavery, Sarah
WIFE, THE
Lazan, David
THIN LINE BETWEEN LOVE AND HATE, A
Lebredt, Gordon
FRAME BY FRAME
HOMECOMING
Lee Pao-ling
VIVE L'AMOUR
Lee, Robert E.
JOSH KIRBY . . . TIME WARRIOR!: JOURNEY TO THE MAGIC CAVERN
JOSH KIRBY . . . TIME WARRIOR!: TRAPPED ON TOY WORLD
Lev, Lisa
LEGEND OF GATOR FACE, THE
Lin Chaoxing
BLUSH
Lipton, Dina
CELTIC PRIDE
MR. HOLLAND'S OPUS
Lisiecki, Robert
ABUSE
Locke, Alan
FOXFIRE

Lohman, Melissa P.
GIRLS TOWN
Lombard, Janet
LIVE WIRE: HUMAN TIMEBOMB
Long, Joan
BODY COUNT
Longacre, Kerry
CROSSCUT
Louderback, Richard
MR. STITCH
Love, Lonnie
POLYMORPH
Lubin, David
SCREAM
MacAulay, Don
WHITE TIGER
Maclean, Catriona
FUNNYMAN, THE
Maclean, Don Marshall
FAR HARBOR
Macleod, Janet
ELECTRA
Magoori, Mihoko
NIGHT ON THE GALACTIC RAILROAD
Malchus, Scott
LIFEFORM
Maly, Martin
HIDDEN ASSASSIN
Mann, Steven
BEWARE: CHILDREN AT PLAY
Mansbridge, Mark
ROCK, THE
UP CLOSE AND PERSONAL
Marchitelli, Maurizio
MILLE BOLLE BLU
Maric, Miodrag
VUKOVAR
Marshall, Loraine
WIND IN THE WILLOWS, THE
Martinet, Rachel
MIRROR, MIRROR III: THE VOYEUR
Marty, Jack
LILY DALE
Marz, Volker
NEUROSIA: 50 YEARS OF PERVERSITY
Massey, Brian
CRIMINAL HEARTS
PUBLIC ENEMIES
Masters, Giles
GHOST AND THE DARKNESS, THE
Matolin, Jiri
ADVENTURES OF PINOCCHIO, THE
Matsuoka, Hajime
STREET FIGHTER II: THE ANIMATED MOVIE
Matteo, Rocco
STUPIDS, THE
Matthews, William F.
BULLETPROOF
Maxey, Caty
FAITHFUL
SHE'S THE ONE
Mayman, Lee
SUNCHASER
SUNSET PARK
Mays, Aaron
BLACK SCORPION
NOT OF THIS EARTH
Mazuer, Lori Yvonne
LETTER TO MY KILLER
McAllister, Don
BEYOND DESIRE
McAvoy, Ed
ROCK, THE
McCrae, Jamie
TAKEOVER, THE
McDaniel, Jennifer
FATALLY YOURS
McDonald, Jeffrey D.
BIG NIGHT
McGahey, Michelle
RACE THE SUN
McIntosh, Mary Olivia
ENTERTAINING ANGELS: THE DOROTHY DAY STORY
McKinstry, Jonathan
MICHAEL COLLINS
Menchions, Douglasann
BIG BULLY
Mercier, Daniel
LA CEREMONIE
Merewether, Janet
GIRLFRIENDS
Merritt, Michael
SKIN
Messina, Philip
ASSOCIATE, THE
FEELING MINNESOTA
NEON BIBLE, THE
Middleton, Louise
SONG SPINNER, THE
Miles, Rupert
BUTTERFLY KISS
Miller, Bruce Alan
PHENOMENON
UP CLOSE AND PERSONAL
Miller, Chris
RATTLED
Minty, David
CANTERVILLE GHOST, THE
Moerhle, Peter
BRITT ALLCROFT'S MAGIC ADVENTURES OF MUMFIE—THE MOVIE
Morahan, Jim
MARY REILLY
Morley, Deborah
CRACKER: THE MADWOMAN IN THE ATTIC
Moulinet, Louis
SHOWGIRL MURDERS, THE
Moving Jim
PROTEUS
Muller, Anja
BROTHER OF SLEEP
Muszynski, Suzan A.
PHAT BEACH
Myers, Richard
MONSTERSHOW
Nedza, Jim
FAMILY THING, A
Neely, Keith
DUNSTON CHECKS IN
Nezda, James
PEOPLE VS. LARRY FLYNT, THE
O'Brien, William
BROKEN ARROW
O'Dell, Dean A.
LOSING CHASE
O'Neil, Larry
DESOLATION ANGELS
Obratzov, Grigory
CHEKIST, THE
Oderigo, Graciela
OF LOVE AND SHADOWS
Ogura, Hiromasa
GHOST IN THE SHELL
PATLABOR 2: MOBILE POLICE
Olexiewicz, Dan
TWISTER
Olszewski, Adam
OUT THERE
Otis, Anna
DON'T LET YOUR MEAT LOAF
Paine, William
BIG SQUEEZE, THE
Palermo, Rafael
OUTRAGE
Palormo, Cynthia
OVER THE WIRE
Panahi, Jafar
WHITE BALLOON, THE
Papalia, Greg
NUTTY PROFESSOR, THE
Parente, Jack
MURDERED INNOCENCE
Parker, Chuck
STEPHEN KING'S THINNER
Parks, Michael
IRON EAGLE IV
Patton, Nancy
GLIMMER MAN, THE
MR. WRONG
Pecur, Nenad
ADRENALIN: FEAR THE RUSH
Pederson, Diana
SWINGERS
Peregrino, Jun
RAW TARGET
Phillips, Jim
FOR THE MOMENT
Pitrel, Alain
NELLY AND MONSIEUR ARNAUD
Platow, Andrej
WOLVES, THE
Platow, Leonid
WOLVES, THE
Ponturo, Giuseppe
HATE
Potter, Chuck
GRAVE, THE
Pouille, Hubert
DAENS
Qiu Weiming
CHUNGKING EXPRESS
Quinn, Catherine
HALFBACK OF NOTRE DAME, THE
ROBIN OF LOCKSLEY
Raglan, Rex
ALASKA
Ralph, John
101 DALMATIANS
Ramon, Manuel
HARD JUSTICE
Ranch, Leon
MOTHER'S PRAYER, A
Randolph, Virginia
JERRY MAGUIRE
Raubertas, Jonathan Alexandre
CARRIED AWAY
Reade-Hill, Ian
ADVENTURES OF PINOCCHIO, THE
Reading, Anthony
ADVENTURES OF PINOCCHIO, THE
Reynaud, Vincent
LAWNMOWER MAN 2: BEYOND CYBERSPACE
Rhee, Judy
FLIRTING WITH DISASTER
Rice, Teddi
RAVENHAWK
Richardson, Mark
RAGE
Richarz, Walter
BROTHER OF SLEEP
Ricker, Mark
SUBSTANCE OF FIRE, THE
Ridpath, James
PROTEUS
Riley, Sam
EMMA
Ritenour, Scott
GREAT WHITE HYPE, THE

Riva, Alison
ANGELS AND INSECTS
INSTITUTE BENJAMENTA
Roberts, Nanci B.
WOMAN UNDONE, A
Robertson, Rachael
MADAGASCAR SKIN
Robinson, Cliff
MICHAEL COLLINS
Rogness, Peter
BEAUTIFUL GIRLS
MARVIN'S ROOM
Rothschild, Andrew
JUDE
Rubin, Edward L.
SUNCHASER
Runningen, Stephen
BEASTMASTER 3: THE EYE OF BRAXUS
Sage, Jefferson
BED OF ROSES
Saint-Loubert, Bernadette
PROPRIETOR, THE
Sakellaropoulo, Zoe
MOTHER NIGHT
Saklad, Steve
BEFORE AND AFTER
Salvitti, Thomas
PURE DANGER
SKYSCRAPER
Sanchez, Virgil
BEST OF THE BEST 3: NO TURNING BACK
Sandefur, David
SWEEPER, THE
Sasaki, Hiroshi
ROUJIN-Z
Schell, Jeffrey "Tex"
INFINITY
Schillinger, Thom
PHANTOM 2040: THE GHOST WHO WALKS
Schmidt, O. Jochen
KASPAR HAUSER
Schmidt, Phil
GIRL FROM MARS, THE
Schroeder, Barry
WHITE WOLVES II: LEGEND OF THE WILD
Scott, Jeanette
MAN WITH THE PERFECT SWING, THE
Seagers, Chris
WAR OF THE BUTTONS, THE
Seesselberg, Wolf
SOMEONE ELSE'S AMERICA
Sharps, Ted
GALAXIES ARE COLLIDING
Sharpton, Leanne
MERCY
Shaw Jr., Robert K.
EDDIE
Sherman, James
TALES OF EROTICA
Shuster, Paul
MONSTERSHOW
Sica, Domenico
STEALING BEAUTY
Silver, Amy
SWEET NOTHING
Simakis, Elizabeth
PRE-MADONNAS
Simmonds, Steve
MOLL FLANDERS
Simpson, C.J.
BASQUIAT
Sizemore, Troy
NORMA JEAN AND MARILYN
VERY BRADY SEQUEL, A
Skinner, William Ladd
ERASER

Smith, Deborah
SOME FOLKS CALL IT A SLING BLADE
Smith, Easton Michael
HEIDI CHRONICLES, THE
Smith, Russell
TUSKEGEE AIRMEN, THE
Sofitsi, Chrysoula
BEAUTIFUL THING
Solares, Ana
SILENCE OF NETO, THE
Solondz, Lori
WELCOME TO THE DOLLHOUSE
Spain Winfrey, Mary
CARNOSAUR 3: PRIMAL SPECIES
Spalt, Johannes
GALAXIES ARE COLLIDING
Stabley, Anthony
ARRIVAL, THE
Stary, Milan
DELTA OF VENUS
Steffensen, Paul
HARVEST OF FIRE
Stein, David
BIG NIGHT
Stensel, Carl
BIO-DOME
Stevenson, Mark
YOUNG POISONER'S HANDBOOK, THE
Stokes, Janet
STREETCAR NAMED DESIRE, A
Stone, Malcolm
GHOST AND THE DARKNESS, THE
Strawn, Mick
KAZAAM
Sulzberg, Bruce
PUBLIC ACCESS
Svoboda, Jano
DRAGONHEART
Tanner, Stacy
CONDITION RED
Targownik, Tom
HIGH SCHOOL HIGH
Taylor, Deane
ALL DOGS GO TO HEAVEN 2
Teegarden, Jim
INDEPENDENCE DAY
Thomas, Lisette
PHANTOM, THE
Thompkins, Leslie
MAXIMUM RISK
Timoner, Dean
HOURGLASS
Tissandier, Hugues
VISITORS, THE
Tocci, James
MICHAEL
Tomkins, Alan
101 DALMATIANS
Tomkins, Gary
HAUNTED
Toolin, Philip
MATILDA
Tougas, Ginger
I'M NOT RAPPAPORT
Townsend, Chris
SHOPPING
Toyon, Richard
TIME TO KILL, A
Vacek, Karel
KASPAR HAUSER
Valle, Luis
MOUTH TO MOUTH
Van Der Pol, Rein
ANNE FRANK REMEMBERED
Ventenilla, Mario R.
SEARCH FOR ONE-EYE JIMMY, THE

Vetter, Jay
KINGPIN
Vint IV, Jessie
ZARKORR! THE INVADER
Walker, Claire Christine
IT CAME FROM OUTER SPACE II
Wall, Kaki
WILD SIDE
Walsh, Frank
JOSEPH CONRAD'S THE SECRET AGENT
Wareham, Terry
WHARF RAT, THE
Warnke, John
CRUCIBLE, THE
ONE FINE DAY
Warren, Tom
EVERYONE SAYS I LOVE YOU
EXTREME MEASURES
Webster, Dan
DOWN PERISCOPE
THAT THING YOU DO!
Wendling, Maya
NELLY AND MONSIEUR ARNAUD
Westfelt, Lasse
CHILDREN OF NOISY VILLAGE, THE
White, Kevin
MR. STITCH
White, Nicholas
UNDERSTUDY: GRAVEYARD SHIFT 2, THE
Wiesel, Karin
FLIRT
Wilkins, Thomas P.
FARGO
Wilkinson, Ron
STAR TREK: FIRST CONTACT
Wilson, Ray
TERMINAL IMPACT
Wolfson, Gregory
PLAYBACK
Wong, Oliver
RUMBLE IN THE BRONX
Worthington, Mark
CHAMBER, THE
Wratten, Alison
BEAUTIFUL THING
Young, Warren Alan
WATCH ME
Yu Wei-yen
MAHJONG
Zabonik, Mark
FAST MONEY
Zachary, James R.
BLACK OUT
Zak, Lucinda
SUGARTIME
Zalay, Daniel
MADAME BUTTERFLY
Zuelske, Mark
MISSING PIECES

ASSOCIATE PRODUCERS

Abaunza, Bonnie
PHANTOM, THE
Ackerman, Noah
FIRST WIVES CLUB, THE
Adkiins, Dorothea
FIRST KID
Ahmad, Maher
CHAIN REACTION
Albright, Ariauna
POLYMORPH
SANDMAN, THE
Alexander, Juan
MOUTH TO MOUTH
Alexander, Tara
SANTA CLAWS

Alsop, Scott
MRS. MUNCK
Altschul, Fernando
TRIGGER EFFECT, THE
Amato, Michael
BLACK ROSE OF HARLEM
Andrews, Steve
ENGLISH PATIENT, THE
Andriole, David
BAD LOVE
Anthony, Lysette
DEAD COLD
Astrachan, Joshua
ED'S NEXT MOVE
Atkins, D.J.
MERCY
Auty, Chris
STEALING BEAUTY
Baha Eddine Attia, Ahmed
MADAME BUTTERFLY
Baird, David
BLOODKNOT
UNDERTOW
Ballon, Daphne
GIRL FROM MARS, THE
Barone, Ermanno
ROAD HOME, THE
Bates, Kenny
ROCK, THE
Beaulieu, Trace
MYSTERY SCIENCE THEATER 3000: THE MOVIE
Beckman, Chris
BAD LOVE
Bell, Carolynne
CURTIS'S CHARM
Bell, Geraint
BEASTMASTER 3: THE EYE OF BRAXUS
Ben Yishay, Aria
HARD JUSTICE
Berlatsky, David
PUBLIC ENEMIES
Bernstein, Stan
JUST YOUR LUCK
Beugg, Michael
LOW LIFE, THE
Beyda, Katherine E.
CELTIC PRIDE
Bibo, Heinz
CEMETERY MAN
Bigham, Jim
SHOOTFIGHTER 2: KILL OR BE KILLED!
Bilek, Jan
ADVENTURES OF PINOCCHIO, THE
HIDDEN ASSASSIN
Blumenthal, Raymond
MAN BY THE SHORE, THE
Boehm, Richard
DOGFIGHTERS, THE
Borza II, Donald
ROAD HOME, THE
Braitman, Wendy
CELLULOID CLOSET, THE
Braschi, Gianluigi
MONSTER, THE
Breidenbach, Kelly
DRAGONHEART
Brock, Deborah
ONE MAN'S JUSTICE
Brody, Dennis
BARB WIRE
Bronchtein, Henry
FAITHFUL
Brooks, Simon
PROTEUS
Bryant, Sheri
DENTIST, THE
Byrne, Alex
GRAVE, THE
Callon, Trudi
AMERICAN STRAYS
Cannold, Jay
FUNERAL, THE
Capra III, Frank
ERASER
Carillo, Julio
BITTER SUGAR
Carrere, Tia
IMMORTALS, THE
Carrillo, Purita
BITTER SUGAR
Cartensen, Kira
NATIONAL LAMPOON'S FAVORITE DEADLY SINS
Carty, Kate
THEREMIN: AN ELECTRONIC ODYSSEY
Caruso, Frank
JOHNNY SHORTWAVE
Cathell, Cevin
TEXAS CHAINSAW MASSACRE: THE NEXT GENERATION
Chambers, Larry
PRE-MADONNAS
Chapman, Freddye
ONCE UPON A TIME . . . WHEN WE WERE COLORED
Chaskin, Janis Rothbard
DELTA OF VENUS
Chea, Claudio
BITTER SUGAR
Chen, Joan
WILD SIDE
Cikatic, Branko
SKYSCRAPER
Clark, Terri
MOLL FLANDERS
Cohen, Stacy
BEST OF THE BEST 3: NO TURNING BACK
Colina, Luis
LAST SUPPER, THE
WHOLE WIDE WORLD, THE
Collins, Jeff
MAN OF THE YEAR
Colville-Reeves, Audrey
JOHNNY SHORTWAVE
Conner, Jeff
CROW: CITY OF ANGELS, THE
Conroy, Daneen Lagrone
STRIPTEASE
Cordish, Jonathan
WIFE, THE
Corrao, Angelo
LINE KING: THE AL HIRSCHFELD STORY, THE
Couturie, Kathryn
ED
Cracchiolo, Dan
TALES FROM THE CRYPT PRESENTS BORDELLO OF BLOOD
Criscione, Michael
BLOODSPORT II: THE NEXT KUMITE
Crooks, Harold
CHAMPAGNE SAFARI, THE
Cuddihy, Christopher
MRS. MUNCK
Curtiss, Alan
MICHAEL
Daniel, Sarah
BUTTERFLY KISS
MADAGASCAR SKIN
Daniels, Gary
RAGE
Davis, Kellie
TIN CUP
Davis, Peaches
THIN LINE BETWEEN LOVE AND HATE, A
De Marco, Frank
THEREMIN: AN ELECTRONIC ODYSSEY
Degus, Robert J.
SET IT OFF
Desclos, Gena
HOMEWARD BOUND II: LOST IN SAN FRANCISCO
Diamant, Limor
MAXIMUM RISK
Diamond, Paul
TWO MUCH
Diana, Juanita
DEADLY OUTBREAK
Donato, Raffaele
PERSONAL JOURNEY WITH MARTIN SCORSESE THROUGH AMERICAN MOVIES, A
DuPre', Paula
JINGLE ALL THE WAY
Eberle, Jake
CHILDREN OF THE CORN: THE GATHERING
Eckert, John M.
FLY AWAY HOME
Ehrenzweig, Michael
CELLULOID CLOSET, THE
Elvin, William M.
TIME TO KILL, A
Esposito, John
DEMOLITIONIST, THE
Esteban, Marta
LAND AND FREEDOM
Euling, Philip
INFINITY
Fahey, Jeff
SWEEPER, THE
Fanfarra, Stephen
BLOOD & DONUTS
Ferguson, Scott
FAMILY THING, A
HEAVY
PEOPLE VS. LARRY FLYNT, THE
Ferreri, Marcella
GIRLFRIENDS
Fitzgibbon, Coleen
FROM THE JOURNALS OF JEAN SEBERG
Foster, Jan
LONE STAR
Franchini, Paula
OF LOVE AND SHADOWS
Freud, Karin
TIN CUP
Friedman, Laura
HOUSE ARREST
Gaines, David
2 DAYS IN THE VALLEY
Gains, Herbert W.
DRAGONHEART
Gannage, Antoine
NELLY AND MONSIEUR ARNAUD
Garcillan, Fernando
TWO MUCH
Garland, Mark
MODERN AFFAIR, A
Gavras, Michele Ray
CEMETERY MAN
Gaye, Nora
RAVENHAWK
Gayne, Matthew
DELTA OF VENUS
Gering, Craig
MARVIN'S ROOM
Gillespie, John
VIRUS
Gilmore, William
JUST YOUR LUCK

Glennon, James
LIFEFORM
Glickman, Jonathan
BEFORE AND AFTER
Gochanour, Mitch
ROLLING STONES ROCK-AND-ROLL CIRCUS, THE
Goebel, Lawrence
SERIAL KILLER
Goode, Christopher
FLIRTING WITH DISASTER
Goodman, David
TOLLBOOTH
Graf, Patricia
PRIMAL FEAR
Grant, Casey
CARPOOL
Grazia, Tony
PAINTED HERO
Greenspan, David
SGT. KABUKIMAN N.Y.P.D.
Grey, Donna
EMMA
Griffith, Howard
ROAD TO GALVESTON, THE
Groff, Lee Ann
BAJA
Guare, John
MARVIN'S ROOM
Gueritz, Joanna
COLD COMFORT FARM
Guinness, Laurence
GHOST IN THE SHELL
Gusick, Ned
ED
Guzman, Yelena
PRE-MADONNAS
Hahn, Colleen
FAR HARBOR
Halaczinsky, Thomas
CALLING THE GHOSTS: A STORY ABOUT RAPE, WAR AND WOMEN
Hamilton, Matthew
STONEWALL
Hankin, Mitchell
DESIRE
Hawley, Richard
PROPRIETOR, THE
Haxall, Lee
LONE JUSTICE: SHOWDOWN AT PLUM CREEK
Heller, Paula
LAST MAN STANDING
Henwood, Edward
CANNIBAL! THE MUSICAL
Herrington, Suzanne
MULTIPLICITY
Heydemann, Klaus
CONDITION RED
Hida, Mitsuhisa
STREET FIGHTER II: THE ANIMATED MOVIE
Hlinomaz, Bonnie
PREACHER'S WIFE, THE
Hobbs, Jessica
GIRLFRIENDS
Holt, James
BLACK OUT
VIRTUAL COMBAT
Hopkins, Ian
CAPTIVES
Howard, Kelsey T.
BREACH OF TRUST
FINAL CUT, THE
Hsu, Carleen L.
FLIRT
Huber, Charles
SKYSCRAPER
Hunt, Abigail
SILENCE OF NETO, THE
Ibuki, Makoto
GHOST IN THE SHELL
Ichaso, Mari
BITTER SUGAR
Imperato, Michele
BIRDCAGE, THE
Indig, Mark
MR. WRONG
Irving, Brian
SABRINA, THE TEENAGE WITCH
Ivers, Jeff
WAR AT HOME, THE
Jablow, Michael
MUPPET TREASURE ISLAND
Jackson, Rowdy
FINAL EQUINOX, THE
Jewison, Michael
BOGUS
Johnson, Bill
HIGH SCHOOL HIGH
Johnson, Gary
CHAMELEON
Joyce, Bernadette
DARKMAN III: DIE DARKMAN DIE
Kalman, Ernest
MODERN AFFAIR, A
Kassim, Sami
BOY CALLED HATE, A
Katz-Norrod, Barbara
SANDMAN, THE
Katzman, Jon
BIO-DOME
Kauffman, Gary
MANNY & LO
Kelly, Brian
THEREMIN: AN ELECTRONIC ODYSSEY
Khan, Michael Alan
HEAVEN'S PRISONERS
Kikumoto, Jan
NOT OF THIS EARTH
Kleiman, Felix
BURIAL OF THE RATS
Kliot, Jason
WELCOME TO THE DOLLHOUSE
Knowlton, Kathryn
EYE FOR AN EYE
Koenig, Kip
BIO-DOME
Koltai, Peter
MAGIC HUNTER
Kornylo, Lacia
MAGIC HUNTER
Kostich, Alex
BURIAL OF THE RATS
Krell, Amy
WOMAN UNDONE, A
Kretchmer, John T.
DUNSTON CHECKS IN
Kristofferson, Tracy
PHARAOH'S ARMY
Kuroiwa, Hisami
FLIRT
Kurtzman, Anne
DEMOLITIONIST, THE
Lambeth, Welch
STEPHEN KING'S THINNER
Lang, Michael
BOTTLE ROCKET
Laramie, Bernie
CHAMELEON
Larsson, Christina
TREES LOUNGE
Lecallier, Adeline
HATE
Lee Jr, Donald J.
MICHAEL
Leonhardt, Ute
PORTRAIT OF A LADY, THE
Levin, Mitchell
CRUCIBLE, THE
Levinson, Joshua
MATILDA
Lichtenstein, Adam
MERCY
Linardos, George
PEOPLE VS. LARRY FLYNT, THE
Llorens, Antonio
BATON ROUGE
Lofaro, Phil
HUNCHBACK OF NOTRE DAME, THE
Luciano, Melanie
JUST YOUR LUCK
Ludwig, Avram
SWINGERS
Lunne, Joe
LARRY MCMURTRY'S STREETS OF LAREDO
Lutz, Brian
JUST YOUR LUCK
Mack, Thomas
CITY HALL
Maltha, San Fu
SUITE 16
Mandzuka, Zlatko
VUKOVAR
Manriquez, Jenny
GALAXIES ARE COLLIDING
Manton, Marcus
FOREST WARRIOR
Manzella, Ray
BARB WIRE
Marcano, Scott
BIO-DOME
Marcotte, Jean-Roche
MAN BY THE SHORE, THE
Marcus, Jeff
MAN OF THE YEAR
Margolis, Bruce
LAZARUS MAN, THE
Marin, Mindy
2 DAYS IN THE VALLEY
Markovsky, Dessie
IT'S MY PARTY
Marlow, David
SHAMELESS
Martin, Gordon
CHAMPAGNE SAFARI, THE
Martin, Spencer
EXECUTIVE DECISION
Mastandrea, Nicholas C.
SCREAM
Mazauric, Bernard
SUITE 16
McAree, Roy
FIST OF THE NORTH STAR
McCann, Sean
DESOLATION ANGELS
McCarthy, Jeff
BIO-DOME
McCord, Todd
MAN WITH THE PERFECT SWING, THE
McCrum-Abdo, C. Cory M.
AMERICA'S DREAM
McGuinness, Thomas Carl
WITHIN THE ROCK
McLindon, James
KANSAS CITY
Mellin, Robyn
WITCHCRAFT: SALEM'S GHOST
Mendel, J. Michael
JERRY MAGUIRE

Mendez, Caryn
CELLULOID CLOSET, THE
Menzies, Kathy L.
D3: THE MIGHTY DUCKS
Merrifield, Doug
FLIPPER
Merrifield, Marta
RAGE
Meyer, Alison
LILY DALE
Meyer, Juana
BEYOND DESIRE
Millar, Miles
WAVELENGTH
Miller, Anna C.
HELLRAISER: BLOODLINE
Miller, Linda H.
SPITFIRE GRILL, THE
Miller, Lori
OPEN SEASON
Miller, Terry
2 DAYS IN THE VALLEY
Milne, Sheila Fraser
JUDE
Mirisch, Richard
TALES FROM THE CRYPT PRESENTS BORDELLO OF BLOOD
Mirren, Helen
SOME MOTHER'S SON
Moarefi, Kim
BED OF ROSES
Mooradian, Greg
FAN, THE
Moore, Amy
GRIM
Moore, Mary Katherine
PHANTOM 2040: THE GHOST WHO WALKS
Moran, Lisa
EVITA
Morgan, Cindy
AMANDA AND THE ALIEN
DEAD WEEKEND
OUT THERE
Morgan, John
BLOODKNOT
Morgenthau, H. Ben
LOW LIFE, THE
Morse, Richard
MAN WITH A PLAN
Muller, Michael
BREAKAWAY
Munafo, Tony
DAYLIGHT
Murphy, Kevin
MYSTERY SCIENCE THEATER 3000: THE MOVIE
Murphy, Richard G.
MAXIMUM RISK
QUEST, THE
Nedivi, Udi
NORMA JEAN AND MARILYN
Neely, Heather
FIRST WIVES CLUB, THE
Nelson, Ted
LARRY MCMURTRY'S STREETS OF LAREDO
Newman, Eric
BLACK SHEEP
Nices, Samsung
MADAME BUTTERFLY
Nimerfro, Scott
TALES FROM THE CRYPT PRESENTS BORDELLO OF BLOOD
Norris, Rebecca
FOREST WARRIOR
Norris, Steve
WAR OF THE BUTTONS, THE

Nottage, Cirri
GIRL 6
O'Brien, Lorenzo
ARRIVAL, THE
O'Brien, Molly
MAN WITH A PLAN
O'Hagan, Nick
SOLITAIRE FOR TWO
Odem, Terry
THAT THING YOU DO!
Olen, Brigid
LIVE WIRE: HUMAN TIMEBOMB
TERMINAL IMPACT
WARHEAD
Oord, Riete
HEIDI FLEISS HOLLYWOOD MADAM
Ormiers, Jean-Luc
DAENS
Page, Wayne Nelson
BIO-DOME
Palaggi, Marisa
SONS OF TRINITY
Palermo, Tony
LAZARUS MAN, THE
Palladino, Dante
VUKOVAR
Pang, Jacy
CHUNGKING EXPRESS
Pantoliano, Joe
IMMORTALS, THE
Parda, Joseph
ONE LESS EGG TO FRY
Pearl, Steven
. . . AT FIRST SIGHT
Perry, Craig
FIRST WIVES CLUB, THE
Peters, Maria
DAENS
Pina, Kevin
BERKELEY IN THE 60S
Pine, Angel
DEAR GOD
HOMEWARD BOUND II: LOST IN SAN FRANCISCO
Pistor, Julie
HARRIET THE SPY
Pope, Joe
LILY DALE
Porter, Aldric La'auli
RANSOM
Porter, Sarah
FAR HARBOR
Pos, Hans
DAENS
Powers, Thom
MERCY
Price, Iona
MIDWINTER'S TALE, A
Quinn, Colin
CELTIC PRIDE
Rajewski, Nadia
ELECTRA
Ramsey, Scott
WIFE, THE
Raskin, Larry
GIRL FROM MARS, THE
Redman, David
YOUNG POISONER'S HANDBOOK, THE
Reshoeft, Heidrun
PORTRAIT OF A LADY, THE
Richards, Peter
WAR AT HOME, THE
Riordan, Mike
TEXAS PAYBACK
Ripps, Hillary Anne
4 TALES OF 2 CITIES

Rivera-Mitchell, Cristal
DON'T BE A MENACE TO SOUTH CENTRAL WHILE DRINKING YOUR JUICE IN THE HOOD
Roberts, Bob
TIGER HEART
Roberts, T.J.
TIGER HEART
Rocca, Alain
HATE
Rodgers, Elizabeth
PHARAOH'S ARMY
Rogers, James B.
KINGPIN
Rohovit, Troy
CLUBHOUSE DETECTIVES
Romine, Jennifer
PARIS WAS A WOMAN
Rosenberg, Marc
SERPENT'S LAIR
Rosenberg, Scott
BEAUTIFUL GIRLS
Rowell, Jack
MAN WITH A PLAN
Rudd, Rebekah
101 DALMATIANS
Rudnick, Arnold
PRIMAL FEAR
Rychtarik, Sara
GIRLFRIENDS
Sahlein, Steve Tyler
NIGHT OF THE SCARECROW
Sanchez, Carlos H.
CHAIN REACTION
Sanders, Jack Frost
QUEST, THE
Sax, Gary
SOUTH BEACH ACADEMY
Sayad, Helen
CATWALK
Schiff, Nathan
ONE LESS EGG TO FRY
Schlei, Bradford L.
SWINGERS
Schram, Dave
DAENS
Schuler, Carol
ONE MAN'S JUSTICE
Schuler, Thomas
ONE MAN'S JUSTICE
Schuth, Andrei
BAD LOVE
Sciorra, Annabella
FUNERAL, THE
Sears, Elliot
MODERN AFFAIR, A
Segal, Amy
BURIAL OF THE RATS
Sekiguchi, Takeshi
STREET FIGHTER II: THE ANIMATED MOVIE
Sherman, Janine
BULLETPROOF
Sherman, Mark
MR. WRONG
Shirazi, Donna
PHAT BEACH
Shulman, Marcia
SAINTS AND SINNERS
Shwarzstein, Meyer
SERIAL KILLER
Sicilia, Gail
GETTING AWAY WITH MURDER
Simmons, Russell
FUNERAL, THE
Sjogren, Pat
RED LINE

Slane, Heath
TALKING ABOUT SEX
Smith, Amy
THEREMIN: AN ELECTRONIC ODYSSEY
Smith, Anna Nicole
SKYSCRAPER
Smith, Mike
SANTA CLAWS
Snauffer, Doug
POLYMORPH
Snow, Karen
CHAMBER, THE
FEAR
Sprey, Jetse
CROCODILES IN AMSTERDAM
St. Clair, Beau
RACE THE SUN
Steward, Lisa
JERRY MAGUIRE
Stillerman, Joel
BEAUTIFUL GIRLS
Stirgwolt, Karen
DEAR GOD
Stitt, Deborah
SPITFIRE GRILL, THE
Stone, Robert
THEREMIN: AN ELECTRONIC ODYSSEY
Strick, Frank
HOURGLASS
PURE DANGER
Stronach, John
ALASKA
Sugiyama, Megumu
STREET FIGHTER II: THE ANIMATED MOVIE
Sukeof, Yasushi
GHOST IN THE SHELL
Takiyama, Masao
LAWNMOWER MAN 2: BEYOND CYBERSPACE
Thaler, Jonas
OUT THERE
Theodoulou, Stella
RIDERS OF THE PURPLE SAGE
Thomas, Tamar
MIDWINTER'S TALE, A
Tonelli, Melissa Cahill
PARIS WAS A WOMAN
Townsend, Jim
ROAD HOME, THE
Tripet, David
ARRIVAL, THE
Tucker-Davies, Teresa
CHAIN REACTION
Turnbull, Mark
PORTRAIT OF A LADY, THE
Van Der Meer, Gerrit
SLEEPERS
Van Der Sluis, Wouter
ANNE FRANK REMEMBERED
Van Varenberg, Eugene
MAXIMUM RISK
QUEST, THE
Vandeleene, Catherine
SUITE 16
Velis, Louisa
RANSOM
Vicente, Joana
WELCOME TO THE DOLLHOUSE
Villahermosa, Vivian
RAW TARGET
Vincent, Jan-Michael
RED LINE
Waldman, Barry
ROCK, THE
Walsh, Fran
FRIGHTENERS, THE
Waxman, Michael
CELTIC PRIDE
Webb, Gregory
UNDER THE HULA MOON
Wein, Joel
EXIT
Weisler, Michele
TRIGGER EFFECT, THE
Wexler, Michael
GRAVE, THE
Whaley, Frank
HOMAGE
White, Michelle
RED SCORPION 2
Whyte, Justine
BLOOD & DONUTS
Wielochowski, Ron
TEXAS PAYBACK
Wiessner, John T.
MUTANT MAN
Williams, Vikki
FLED
Wilson, Andrew
BOTTLE ROCKET
Wincott, Jeff
WHEN THE BULLET HITS THE BONE
Winther, Peter
INDEPENDENCE DAY
Withrington, Alan
ALEX
Wlodarkiewicz, Mark Jan
FRISK
Wodoslawsky, Stefan
SCREAMERS
Woertz, Gregory G.
CROW: CITY OF ANGELS, THE
Wolk, Andrew
SGT. KABUKIMAN N.Y.P.D.
Woodruff, Dan
MADAME WANG'S
Wright, Jane
HEAVY
Wright, Jeff
HIGH SCHOOL HIGH
Wright Jr., Tom
IMMORTALS, THE
Yamazaki, Hiroshi
GHOST IN THE SHELL
Yeung, Bolo
SHOOTFIGHTER 2: KILL OR BE KILLED!
Z'Dar, Robert
RED LINE
Zaentz, Paul
ENGLISH PATIENT, THE
Zide, Warren
JINGLE ALL THE WAY
Zimmerman, Ulrike
FLAMING EARS
Zisman, Leonard
FOREST WARRIOR

CASTING

Aikens, Stuart
GIRL FROM MARS, THE
RED SCORPION 2
Aikins, Stuart
HALFBACK OF NOTRE DAME, THE
Albright, Ariauna
POLYMORPH
Alderman, Jane
SKIN
Allen, Jennifer
TWO FRIENDS
Allen, Michelle
BAD MOON
Anderson, Linda
LET'S GET BIZZEE
Andreas, Shelly
SKIN
Aquila, Deborah
MOTHER
PHANTOM, THE
PRIMAL FEAR
VERY BRADY SEQUEL, A
Aquila, Debora
BLACK SHEEP
Arenas, Ed
SHOOTFIGHTER 2: KILL OR BE KILLED!
Artz & Cohen
FOR BETTER OR WORSE
Artz, Mary Gail
ALASKA
LAST MAN STANDING
LETTER TO MY KILLER
THIN LINE BETWEEN LOVE AND HATE, A
Ashton-Barson, Julie
FLIPPER
Bankert, Lisa
INFINITY
Barden, Kerry
AMERICAN BUFFALO
I SHOT ANDY WARHOL
PALLBEARER, THE
PALOOKAVILLE
STONEWALL
Barry, Matthew
MARS ATTACKS!
UNHOOK THE STARS
Bartlett, Carolyn
AUGUST
Basker, Pamela
JUST YOUR LUCK
Beach, Lisa
CITIZEN RUTH
Benson, Annette
ADVENTURES OF PINOCCHIO, THE
Bestrop, Juel
CABLE GUY, THE
HEIDI CHRONICLES, THE
Bialy, Sharon
LAZARUS MAN, THE
MR. HOLLAND'S OPUS
RACE THE SUN
Biras, Jeanne
MACHINE, THE
Blanc, Celina
VISITORS, THE
Blick, Tammara
FULL BODY MASSAGE
Bluestein, Susan
RIDERS OF THE PURPLE SAGE
Booker, Susan
LAZARUS MAN, THE
Bowdan, Jack
EVERYTHING RELATIVE
Bowen, Deirdre
BLOOD & DONUTS
FLY AWAY HOME
KISSINGER AND NIXON
MAN IN THE ATTIC, THE
Brace, John
DUNSTON CHECKS IN
EXTREME MEASURES
Bramon Garcia, Risa
TWISTER
Bresler, Jacov
HARD JUSTICE
Breuls, Peter
SUITE 16
Bronkowitz, Xavier
POLYMORPH

Brooksbank, Steven
ARRIVAL, THE
SHARON'S SECRET
Brown, Deborah
MAXIMUM RISK
Brown, Lisa
BUGGED
Brown-Karman, Jackie
ONCE UPON A TIME . . . WHEN WE WERE COLORED
Bucci, Rosina
HOLLOW POINT
IRON EAGLE IV
Budin, J.
NEMESIS III: PREY HARDER
Bullington, Perry
HEAD OF THE FAMILY
JOSH KIRBY . . . TIME WARRIOR!: EGGS FROM 70,000,000 B.C.
JOSH KIRBY . . . TIME WARRIOR!: JOURNEY TO THE MAGIC CAVERN
JOSH KIRBY . . . TIME WARRIOR!: LAST BATTLE FOR THE UNIVERSE
JOSH KIRBY . . . TIME WARRIOR!: TRAPPED ON TOY WORLD
SPELLBREAKER: SECRET OF THE LEPRECHAUNS
ZARKORR! THE INVADER
Burch, Jackie
DIABOLIQUE
Burrows, Victoria
FRIGHTENERS, THE
HOW THE WEST WAS FUN
LOVER'S KNOT
RUMPELSTILTSKIN
TALES FROM THE CRYPT PRESENTS BORDELLO OF BLOOD
Byatt, Wally
AUGUST
Cameron, John
MURDERED INNOCENCE
Campobasso, Craig
ORIGINAL GANGSTAS
Cannon, Reuben
FLY AWAY HOME
GET ON THE BUS
Carol, Robin
GRAVE, THE
Casas, Yvonne
CURDLED
Cassel, Ferne
BAD LOVE
CELTIC PRIDE
DOWN PERISCOPE
Cavanno Productions
THEY BITE
Chadwick, Bette
HECK'S WAY HOME
Chambers, Beth
EDDIE
Chamian, Denise
CHAMELEON
Chamion, Denise
WIDOW'S KISS
Champion, Fern
SPY HARD
Chappelle, Aleta
NUTTY PROFESSOR, THE
Charbonneau, Nan
NORMAL LIFE
Charkham, Beth
PORTRAIT OF A LADY, THE
Chavanne, Brian
JAMES AND THE GIANT PEACH
Chenoweth, Ellen
FAITHFUL
SLEEPERS
Claman, Barbara
BEASTMASTER 3: THE EYE OF BRAXUS

Clydesdale, Ross
KIDS IN THE HALL: BRAIN CANDY
Cobe, Lori
ANIMAL INSTINCTS III: THE SEDUCTRESS
BODY OF INFLUENCE 2
WATCH ME
Cohen, Barbara
ALASKA
LAST MAN STANDING
LETTER TO MY KILLER
THIN LINE BETWEEN LOVE AND HATE, A
Colbert, Joanna
BULLETPROOF
HAPPY GILMORE
Coley, Aisha
GIRL 6
Colquhoun, Mary
AFFAIR, THE
ASSOCIATE, THE
COURAGE UNDER FIRE
TRUMAN
Comerford, Jon
BEYOND THE CALL
STAND OFF, THE
Connection III/In House
PHAT BEACH
Continental Casting
DAENS
Crittenden, Dianne
KAZAAM
Crowley, Suzanne
MUPPET TREASURE ISLAND
DaMota, Billy
FELONY
Daniels, Glenn
LAWNMOWER MAN 2: BEYOND CYBERSPACE
Davidson, Leeza
HARD JUSTICE
Davis, Kimberly
CAUGHT
Davis, Leo
MARY REILLY
Davis, Noel
COLD COMFORT FARM
JANE EYRE
Dawson, Eric
LONE JUSTICE: SHOWDOWN AT PLUM CREEK
Debbie Manwiller Associates
GLIMMER MAN, THE
Dietz, Liane
NAKED SOULS
DiGiaimo, Louis
JUROR, THE
SLEEPERS
SONS OF TRINITY
WHITE SQUALL
Dixon, Pam
CRAFT, THE
Duchman, Yonit
SHOOTFIGHTER 2: KILL OR BE KILLED!
Dunas, Dorian
FAST MONEY
Dunlop, Eddie
EDDIE
Dupont, Pennie
VIKING SAGAS, THE
Dutton, Nan
JAG
Edelman, Abra
BLACK DAY BLUE NIGHT
BREACH OF TRUST
NIGHT OF THE SCARECROW
WHITE TIGER
Edfeldt, Catti
CHILDREN OF NOISY VILLAGE, THE

Essary, Lisa
FAR HARBOR
Estrada, Maria
ALL DOGS GO TO HEAVEN 2
Ettinger, Wendy
LAND AND FREEDOM
Fenton, Mike
MUPPET TREASURE ISLAND
Fertig, Steven
IT'S MY PARTY
Feuer, Howard
BEFORE AND AFTER
BOGUS
MULTIPLICITY
STEALING BEAUTY
THAT THING YOU DO!
Figgis, Susie
LAND AND FREEDOM
MICHAEL COLLINS
Finger, Leonard
ASSAULT AT WEST POINT
STEPHEN KING'S THINNER
Fink, Jakki
TALES OF EROTICA
Finn, Mali
CHAMBER, THE
EYE FOR AN EYE
LITTLE DEATH, THE
MISSION: IMPOSSIBLE
TIME TO KILL, A
Finnegan, Bonnie
MIRROR HAS TWO FACES, THE
Fitzpatrick, Peter
TALKING ABOUT SEX
Flamand, Jean-Claude
HATE
Forry, Ann
RUMBLE IN THE BRONX
Fothergil, Janey
JOSEPH CONRAD'S THE SECRET AGENT
Fox, Celestia
ANGELS AND INSECTS
101 DALMATIANS
STEALING BEAUTY
TWO DEATHS
WAVELENGTH
Foy, Nancy
BOUND
LATE SHIFT, THE
MRS. WINTERBOURNE
NORMA JEAN AND MARILYN
Francis, Linda
FIST OF THE NORTH STAR
ONE GOOD TURN
TOLLBOOTH
WITHIN THE ROCK
Frazier, Carrie
DEAR GOD
JOHN CARPENTER'S ESCAPE FROM L.A.
Frisby, Jane
SHOPPING
Gabriel, Tedra
PINOCCHIO'S REVENGE
Gallegos, Dennis
TWO-BITS & PEPPER
Garcia, Risa Bramon
FLIRTING WITH DISASTER
Garo, Alberte
NELLY AND MONSIEUR ARNAUD
Garver, Elisa
MOTHER
Gerusi, Tina
LEGEND OF GATOR FACE, THE
Gerussi, Tina
HOMECOMING
LOSING CHASE
MAN IN THE ATTIC, THE
Giella, David
EDDIE

Glaser, Jan
BLACK ROSE OF HARLEM
BLACK SCORPION
CARNOSAUR 3: PRIMAL SPECIES
DEATH ARTIST, THE
HARD WAY OUT: BLOODFIST VIII
PIRANHA
SAWBONES
UNKNOWN ORIGIN
WHITE WOLVES II: LEGEND OF THE WILD
Goldberg, Mary
MICHAEL
Goldstein, Brett
SWEET NOTHING
Goodman, Elisa
BLACK DAY BLUE NIGHT
BREACH OF TRUST
NIGHT OF THE SCARECROW
WHITE TIGER
Gosschalk, Job
ANTONIA'S LINE
Goulder, Ann
FUNERAL, THE
WELCOME TO THE DOLLHOUSE
Gray, Russell
. . . AT FIRST SIGHT
BAJA
GRACE OF MY HEART
ROAD HOME, THE
Greenspan, Harriet
PLAYBACK
Guish, Michelle
ENGLISH PATIENT, THE
YOUNG POISONER'S HANDBOOK, THE
Gurland, Robin
JAMES AND THE GIANT PEACH
Hampton, Iris
FOREST WARRIOR
Hans Kemma Casting
SUITE 16
Harkins, Pat
SMALL FACES
Harris, Olivia
BOYS NEXT DOOR, THE
HARVEST OF FIRE
Havens, Geno
IMMORTALS, THE
Haynes, Rene
IN LOVE AND WAR
Heilbrun, Mikie
FAR HARBOR
Hendel, Karen
DEAD TO RIGHTS
DEATH BENEFIT
Henderson, Cathy
REDEMPTION: KICKBOXER 5
SERIAL KILLER
Henderson, Judy
POMPATUS OF LOVE, THE
Herold, Paula
PREACHER'S WIFE, THE
Hewitt, Claire
SUGARTIME
Hirschfield, Marc
NATIONAL LAMPOON'S FAVORITE DEADLY SINS
Hirshenson, Janet
AMERICA'S DREAM
GHOSTS OF MISSISSIPPI
MR. WRONG
RANSOM
SGT. BILKO
SPACE JAM
Hoffman, Alphy
PHAT BEACH
Hopkins, Billy
AMERICAN BUFFALO
FLIRT
I SHOT ANDY WARHOL
PALLBEARER, THE
PALOOKAVILLE
ROCK, THE
STONEWALL
Horning, Annette
GRAVE, THE
Hubbard, John
EVITA
JAMES AND THE GIANT PEACH
LOADED
MOLL FLANDERS
SHAMELESS
WAR OF THE BUTTONS, THE
Hubbard, Ros
EVITA
JAMES AND THE GIANT PEACH
LOADED
MOLL FLANDERS
SHAMELESS
WAR OF THE BUTTONS, THE
Huff, Vickie
RAVENHAWK
Huffman, Phyllis
BOYS NEXT DOOR, THE
HARVEST OF FIRE
Hughes, Jennifer
MISSING PIECES
Hughes, Julie
MERCY
Hughes Moss Casting
BEAVIS AND BUTT-HEAD DO AMERICA
Hughes-Moss Ltd.
OFF AND RUNNING
Huzzar, Elaine J.
FROM DUSK TILL DAWN
TWO MUCH
Hymson, Beth
CHILDREN OF FURY
Ireland, Simone
HAMLET
JUDE
MADAGASCAR SKIN
Isaacson, Donna
BROKEN ARROW
CRUCIBLE, THE
Jacobson, Dean
PUBLIC ACCESS
Jacoby, Justine
FULL BODY MASSAGE
Jaffe, Sheila
AMERICAN STRAYS
DENISE CALLS UP
IF LUCY FELL
Jenkins, Jane
AMERICA'S DREAM
GHOSTS OF MISSISSIPPI
MR. WRONG
RANSOM
SGT. BILKO
SPACE JAM
Jobbins, Sheridan
ALEX
Johnson, Amanda Mackey
FLED
Johnston, Ed
OPEN SEASON
TIN CUP
Jones, Caro
ENTERTAINING ANGELS: THE DOROTHY DAY STORY
IT CAME FROM OUTER SPACE II
Joseph, Rosalie
JACK
Kaplan, Darlene
MAN IN THE ATTIC, THE
Kaplan, Meredith
WAVELENGTH
Karsian, Kerry
BEASTMASTER 3: THE EYE OF BRAXUS
Kassel, Kenneth
NEMESIS III: PREY HARDER
Kaufman, Avy
LONE STAR
WALKING AND TALKING
Keigley, Liz
BOTTLE ROCKET
CARRIED AWAY
Kelsay, Carol
SABRINA, THE TEENAGE WITCH
Kemna, Hans
ANTONIA'S LINE
Kennedy, Lora
CROW: CITY OF ANGELS, THE
ONE FINE DAY
Kent, Rody
LILY DALE
Kerbel, Diane
SUGARTIME
Klapper, Stephanie
ASSAULT AT WEST POINT
Klein, Beth
BEYOND THE CALL
FRAME BY FRAME
MOONSHINE HIGHWAY
MRS. MUNCK
WHARF RAT, THE
Kleinman, Marsha
MOTHER'S PRAYER, A
STREETCAR NAMED DESIRE, A
Klopper, Nancy
RICH MAN'S WIFE, THE
Knight, Eileen Mack
GREAT WHITE HYPE, THE
Knoll, Robyn
LOVE IS ALL THERE IS
Kock, Bernhard
BROTHER OF SLEEP
Kohn, Linda
PIG'S TALE, A
Kordos, Richard S.
NORMAL LIFE
Koster, Dorothy
HOURGLASS
Koudhaei, Adel
SILENCES OF THE PALACE, THE
Kozak, Sid
MATERNAL INSTINCTS
Kressel, Lynn
CANTERVILLE GHOST, THE
I'M NOT RAPPAPORT
LARRY MCMURTRY'S STREETS OF LAREDO
Kurtzman, Wendy
CARRIED AWAY
HOUSE ARREST
INDEPENDENCE DAY
Lamb, Irene
ADVENTURES OF PINOCCHIO, THE
INSTITUTE BENJAMENTA
Lambert, Ruth
HUNCHBACK OF NOTRE DAME, THE
Laurence, Rosanne
TRACKS OF A KILLER
Lawson, Karen
REDEMPTION: KICKBOXER 5
Lecker, Marjorie
ELECTRA
VIRUS
Lee, Tony
DON'T BE A MENACE TO SOUTH CENTRAL WHILE DRINKING YOUR JUICE IN THE HOOD
Lefko, Carol
DENTIST, THE
LeModeln, Ltd.
SANDMAN, THE

Lemon, Mike
CONDITION RED
Leustig, Elisabeth
HIGH SCHOOL HIGH
KANSAS CITY
UNDER THE HULA MOON
Levin, Gail
JERRY MAGUIRE
LARGER THAN LIFE
Levine, Jean
TEXAS PAYBACK
Levitt, Heidi
LOW LIFE, THE
ROCK, THE
Lewis, Carol
SUBSTITUTE, THE
UNFORGETTABLE
Lewis, Ellen
BIRDCAGE, THE
DEAD MAN
FAN, THE
Lewis, Marty
LOOKING FOR TROUBLE
Liberman, Meg
NATIONAL LAMPOON'S FAVORITE DEADLY SINS
Lieberman, Amy
MAD DOG TIME
Liebling, Terry
SUNCHASER
Limon, Blanca Esthela
JOHNNY 100 PESOS
Lippens, Amy
STUPIDS, THE
Liroff, Marci
SPITFIRE GRILL, THE
Louden, Cheryl
TOLLBOOTH
Lowry-Johnson, Junie
STAR TREK: FIRST CONTACT
Lowy, Linda
DUNSTON CHECKS IN
EXTREME MEASURES
Lyons, John
CITY HALL
FARGO
STRIPTEASE
MacDonald, Robert
HEAD OF THE FAMILY
JOSH KIRBY . . . TIME WARRIOR!: EGGS FROM 70,000,000 B.C.
JOSH KIRBY . . . TIME WARRIOR!: JOURNEY TO THE MAGIC CAVERN
JOSH KIRBY . . . TIME WARRIOR!: LAST BATTLE FOR THE UNIVERSE
JOSH KIRBY . . . TIME WARRIOR!: TRAPPED ON TOY WORLD
SPELLBREAKER: SECRET OF THE LEPRECHAUNS
ZARKORR! THE INVADER
Maci, Alejandro
OF LOVE AND SHADOWS
Mackey, Amanda
CHAIN REACTION
EXECUTIVE DECISION
Maisier, Francine
FEELING MINNESOTA
Maisler, Francine
PEOPLE VS. LARRY FLYNT, THE
Mallen, Leah
FINAL CUT, THE
Mamade
LITTLE INDIAN, BIG CITY
Manwiller, Debi
PIE IN THE SKY
Margiotta, Karen
ONE MAN'S JUSTICE
SCREAMERS
Margiotta, Margaret
DESIRE
Margiotta, Mary
DESIRE
ONE MAN'S JUSTICE
SCREAMERS
Marin, Mindy
2 DAYS IN THE VALLEY
Marquette SPI
SANTA CLAWS
Mazauric, Caroline
SUITE 16
McCaffrey, Valerie
ISLAND OF DR. MOREAU, THE
MOTHER NIGHT
McCann, Hank
SURGEON, THE
McCarthy, Jeanne
LILY DALE
MARS ATTACKS!
McConnell, Megan
HOMEWARD BOUND II: LOST IN SAN FRANCISCO
McSweeney, Tom
REDEMPTION: KICKBOXER 5
ROAD HOME, THE
SANTA WITH MUSCLES
Melton, Pat
YANKEE ZULU
Menidrey, Francoise
VISITORS, THE
Middleton, Joseph
ED
FIRST KID
HEADLESS BODY IN TOPLESS BAR
HOMAGE
LAST DANCE
MULHOLLAND FALLS
Miller, Vera
HOLLOW POINT
Mitchell, Ed
MAGIC IN THE MIRROR
SOMETIMES THEY COME BACK . . . AGAIN
Moidon, Frederique
HORSEMAN ON THE ROOF
PROPRIETOR, THE
SINGLE GIRL, A
Moiselle, Nuala
SOME MOTHER'S SON
Montgomery, Rick
BARB WIRE
BIO-DOME
KINGPIN
LOW LIFE, THE
MR. STITCH
Moore, Tracey
DON'T LET YOUR MEAT LOAF
Morones, Bob
BEYOND DESIRE
Moss, Barry
MERCY
MISSING PIECES
Moulevrier, Gerard
NELLY AND MONSIEUR ARNAUD
Mullane, Liz
ALEX
Mullinar, Liz
TUNNEL VISION
Murt, Hayley
SMALL FACES
Nance, Cheryl
AUGUST
Nasri, Michel
LES VOLEURS
Nayor, Nancy
TRIGGER EFFECT, THE
Nettles, Joyce
BREAKING THE WAVES
HAUNTED
RASPUTIN
Newberg, Bruce H.
EDIE & PEN
O'Loughlin, Meryl
TREMORS 2: AFTERSHOCKS
Octobon, Nicole
SUITE 16
Ogilvie, Heather
ALEX
Orchen, Kim
BOY CALLED HATE, A
Orenstein, Fern
RED SCORPION 2
Pagano, Rik
PIE IN THE SKY
Paladini, Mark
SPY HARD
Palo, Linda Phillips
JACK
Papsidera, John
2 DAYS IN THE VALLEY
Parada, Dan
BARB WIRE
BIO-DOME
KINGPIN
LOW LIFE, THE
Parks, Ellen
FLIRTING WITH DISASTER
MANNY & LO
Partiot, Isabelle
MADAME BUTTERFLY
Passero, Jeffery
NECRONOMICON: BOOK OF THE DEAD
POISON IVY 2: LILY
Pemrick, Donald Paul
AMANDA AND THE ALIEN
CHILDREN OF THE CORN: THE GATHERING
CROSSCUT
DEAD WEEKEND
EXIT
GLASS CAGE, THE
OUT THERE
VENUS RISING
YESTERDAY'S TARGET
Pereira, Vanessa
HAMLET
JUDE
Perkins, Mike
PAINTED HERO
Phillips-Palo, Linda
HEAVEN'S PRISONERS
Pierce, Shancy
CLUBHOUSE DETECTIVES
Pollock, Patsy
MISSION: IMPOSSIBLE
Poole, Gilly
MUPPET TREASURE ISLAND
Pope, Judith
PAINTED HERO
Proctor, Carl
PROTEUS
Pryor, Andy
BEAUTIFUL THING
TRAINSPOTTING
Rack, Pamela
OF LOVE AND SHADOWS
WILD SIDE
Ray, Johanna
FROM DUSK TILL DAWN
TWO MUCH
Ray, Robyn
MAGIC IN THE MIRROR
SOMETIMES THEY COME BACK . . . AGAIN
Rea, Karen
MY FELLOW AMERICANS

SOLO
UNDERTOW

Reece, Pam
ANGELA

Reed, Andrea
DON'T BE A MENACE TO SOUTH CENTRAL WHILE DRINKING YOUR JUICE IN THE HOOD

Reed, Robi
SOMEONE ELSE'S AMERICA

Reed-Humes, Robi
DON'T BE A MENACE TO SOUTH CENTRAL WHILE DRINKING YOUR JUICE IN THE HOOD
SET IT OFF
SUNSET PARK

Rene, Keely
VIRTUAL ENCOUNTERS

Reyes, Carlos
LITTLE INDIAN, BIG CITY

Reynolds, Simone
CANTERVILLE GHOST, THE
JACK & SARAH

Rhodes, Shari
ED
FIRST KID
HOMAGE
LAST DANCE
MULHOLLAND FALLS

Robitaille, Lucie
SCREAMERS

Rona, Nadia
HOLLOW POINT

Roos, Fred
JACK

Rose, Patricia
BODY COUNT

Rosenthal, Laura
DEAD MAN
NEON BIBLE, THE
SHE'S THE ONE

Ross, Marcia
LIVE NUDE GIRLS
101 DALMATIANS

Rousseau, Richard
LAND AND FREEDOM

Rousselot, Renee
MATILDA
PHENOMENON

Rubin, David
ENGLISH PATIENT, THE
MATILDA
UP CLOSE AND PERSONAL
WILLIAM SHAKESPEARE'S ROMEO + JULIET

Rush, Patrick
NATIONAL LAMPOON'S FAVORITE DEADLY SINS

Sale, Beth
TOLLBOOTH

Sandrich, Cathy
EXECUTIVE DECISION
FLED

Sandrich, Kathy
CHAIN REACTION

Sands, Jill Greenberg
HARRIET THE SPY

Schamberger, Christa
LIVE WIRE: HUMAN TIMEBOMB
TERMINAL IMPACT

Schiff, Laura
BIG SQUEEZE, THE
BURIAL OF THE RATS
DEAD COLD
HOSTILE INTENTIONS
ONE NIGHT STAND
TRACKS OF A KILLER

Schroth, Sabine
KASPAR HAUSER

Schweber, Emily
FOXFIRE

Selway, Mary
EMMA
GHOST AND THE DARKNESS, THE

Shaner, Dan
DOWN, OUT AND DANGEROUS
MATERNAL INSTINCTS
ROAD TO GALVESTON, THE
TAILS YOU LIVE, HEADS YOU'RE DEAD
WHERE'S THE MONEY, NOREEN?

Shannon, Jane
BLACK SHEEP
PRIMAL FEAR

Shawn, Sue
DELTA OF VENUS

Shirazi, Donna
PHAT BEACH

Shopmaker, Susan
ED'S NEXT MOVE

Shull, Jennifer
EVENING STAR, THE

Shulman, Marcia
SAINTS AND SINNERS
SEARCH FOR ONE-EYE JIMMY, THE

Siciliano, Pat
VIRTUAL ENCOUNTERS

Sikes, Mark
PURE DANGER
RAGE
SKYSCRAPER
SWEEPER, THE
TIGER HEART

Simkin, Margery
BEAUTIFUL GIRLS
DAYLIGHT
DRAGONHEART

Simon, Meg
BED OF ROSES
JOE'S APARTMENT
SUBSTANCE OF FIRE, THE

Skalbania, Audrey
FINAL CUT, THE

Skoff, Melissa
DONOR UNKNOWN
EVIL HAS A FACE
HIDDEN ASSASSIN
PAINTED HERO

Slater, Mary Jo
ARRIVAL, THE
SHARON'S SECRET

Smith, Jane Shannon
MOTHER
PHANTOM, THE
VERY BRADY SEQUEL, A

Smith, Kathy A.
BLACK OUT
PHOENIX
TAKEOVER, THE

Smith, Laurel
HELLRAISER: BLOODLINE
LIFEFORM
WHOLE WIDE WORLD, THE

Smith, Suzanne
AMERICAN BUFFALO
FLIRT
I SHOT ANDY WARHOL
PALLBEARER, THE
PALOOKAVILLE
STONEWALL

Snik, Jeanette
CROCODILES IN AMSTERDAM

Soulam, Roz
CLUBHOUSE DETECTIVES

Stalmaster, Lynn
CARPOOL
TO GILLIAN ON HER 37TH BIRTHDAY

Starger, Ilene
FIRST WIVES CLUB, THE
MARVIN'S ROOM

Steinberg, Dawn
DOGFIGHTERS, THE

Stern, Adrienne
GIRLFRIENDS
GIRLS TOWN

Stern and Parriss
SECRETS & LIES

Stevens, Gail
AFFAIR, THE
BEAUTIFUL THING
CAPTIVES
CRACKER: THE MADWOMAN IN THE ATTIC
TRAINSPOTTING

Stewart, Karen Lindsay
COLD LIGHT OF DAY

Stone, Anrea
HELLRAISER: BLOODLINE

Style, Emma
SOLITAIRE FOR TWO

Surma, Ron
STAR TREK: FIRST CONTACT

Swan, Leslie
PORTRAITS OF A KILLER
SONG SPINNER, THE

Swee, Daniel
CRUCIBLE, THE

Tackett, Sarah
SLING BLADE

Tait, Anne
FOR THE MOMENT

Tannenbaum, Paul
TOLLBOOTH

Tarzia, James
BEST OF THE BEST 3: NO TURNING BACK
QUEST, THE

Taylor, Judy
D3: THE MIGHTY DUCKS
JINGLE ALL THE WAY
WAR AT HOME, THE

Taylor, Juliet
BIRDCAGE, THE
EVERYONE SAYS I LOVE YOU
MARY REILLY

Telsey, Bernard
MODERN AFFAIR, A

Thaler, Todd
BOYS
HEAVY
MIRROR HAS TWO FACES, THE
NATIONAL LAMPOON'S FAVORITE DEADLY SINS
TWO IF BY SEA

Thomas, Victoria
FAMILY THING, A
MARS ATTACKS!
PASSION OF DARKLY NOON, THE
TIN CUP

Thompson, Sheila
DARK SECRETS

Thurm, Joel
IT'S MY PARTY

Tillman, Mark
. . . AT FIRST SIGHT
COLONY, THE

Timmermann, Bonnie
ERASER

Todd, Joy
HOMECOMING

Tolan, Cindy
ANGELA

Trevis, Sarah
EMMA
GHOST AND THE DARKNESS, THE

Ulrich, Robert J.
LONE JUSTICE: SHOWDOWN AT PLUM CREEK
Valsecchi, Marta
LAND AND FREEDOM
Vernieu, Mary
FREEWAY
LONG KISS GOODNIGHT, THE
Vogel, Barbara
BROTHER OF SLEEP
Von Tonder, Marina
REDEMPTION: KICKBOXER 5
Walken, Georgianne
AMERICAN STRAYS
DENISE CALLS UP
IF LUCY FELL
Walken/Jaffe
GETTING AWAY WITH MURDER
TREES LOUNGE
Walker, Clare
IN LOVE AND WAR
JAG
MOONSHINE HIGHWAY
MRS. MUNCK
PLAYBACK
SPELLBREAKER: SECRET OF THE LEPRECHAUNS
Warren, Jane
WARHEAD
Weiner, Judith
DANGEROUS PASSION
Weitz, Jori
TALES OF EROTICA
Whitworth, J.L.
SHOWGIRL MURDERS, THE
Wieder, Susan
BOY CALLED HATE, A
Wilmot, Jill
ROUJIN-Z
Wolff, Gerald I.
MIRROR, MIRROR III: THE VOYEUR
Wolff, Gerald
FINAL EQUINOX, THE
PUBLIC ENEMIES
Yeskel, Ronnie
LONG KISS GOODNIGHT, THE
Yoelin, Naomi
NOT OF THIS EARTH
Young, Rhonda
PLAYBACK
Zaitseva, Marina
BURIAL OF THE RATS
Zane, Bonnie
LAST SUPPER, THE
Zane, Debra
FEAR
LAST SUPPER, THE
TRUTH ABOUT CATS AND DOGS, THE
Zimmerman, Jeremy
IN LOVE AND WAR
Zuckerbrod, Gary
LIVE NUDE GIRLS
Zuckerman, Dori
PORTRAITS OF A KILLER

CHOREOGRAPHERS

Adamo, Diane
CANNIBAL! THE MUSICAL
Basil, Toni
THAT THING YOU DO!
Brandstrup, Kim
ANGELS AND INSECTS
Daniele, Graciela
EVERYONE SAYS I LOVE YOU
de Meriche, Julien
AVENTURERA
Derricks, Marguerite Pomerhn
STRIPTEASE
Donovan
DON'T BE A MENACE TO SOUTH CENTRAL WHILE DRINKING YOUR JUICE IN THE HOOD
Elkin, Ian
FOR THE MOMENT
Johnson, Louis
TALES OF EROTICA
Lefton, Sue
EMMA
Litvinov, Victor
SONG SPINNER, THE
McDonald, Bruce
MR. HOLLAND'S OPUS
Moore, Valerie
SUGARTIME
Paterson, Vincent
BIRDCAGE, THE
EVITA
Pichlyk, John
SONG SPINNER, THE
Robinson, Eartha D.
EDDIE
Rosemund, Philip S.
CANNIBAL! THE MUSICAL
Sevilla, Ninon
AVENTURERA

CINEMATOGRAPHERS

Abouchar, Chantal
GIRLFRIENDS
Ackroyd, Barry
ANNE FRANK REMEMBERED
LAND AND FREEDOM
Adamek, Witold
MOTHER OF KINGS
Adefarasin, Remi
CAPTIVES
Aguirresarobe, Javier
OUTRAGE
Ahern, Lloyd
LAST MAN STANDING
Ahlberg, Mac
LATE SHIFT, THE
VERY BRADY SEQUEL, A
Aim, Pierre
HATE
Albert, Arthur
HAPPY GILMORE
ONE NIGHT STAND
Alberti, Maryse
TALES OF EROTICA
WHEN WE WERE KINGS
TWO MUCH
Alcaine, Jose Luis
TWO MUCH
Alexander, T.
TAKEOVER, THE
Alissov, Vadim
ANNA
Allred, Randall
APART FROM HUGH
Almond, Alan
LOADED
Alonzo, John A.
GRASS HARP, THE
Altman, Robert Reed
LOOKING FOR TROUBLE
Ameen, Samuel
WHISPERING, THE
Amoros, Juan
MOUTH TO MOUTH
SONS OF TRINITY
Anchia, Juan Ruiz
ADVENTURES OF PINOCCHIO, THE
Anderson, Eric
PINOCCHIO'S REVENGE
Anderson, Jamie
JUROR, THE
Araya, Mario
DEVOTION
Arbogast, Thierry
HORSEMAN ON THE ROOF
MA SAISON PREFEREE
RIDICULE
Arguelles, Fernando
HIDDEN ASSASSIN
MIND RIPPER
Aronovich, Ricardo
CELESTIAL CLOCKWORK
Aronson, John
BLACK ROSE OF HARLEM
GLASS CAGE, THE
HARD WAY OUT: BLOODFIST VIII
WHITE WOLVES II: LEGEND OF THE WILD
Arredondo, Jose Luis
JOHNNY 100 PESOS
Arvanitis, Yorgos
SOMEONE ELSE'S AMERICA
Attewell, Warrick
GIRL FROM MARS, THE
Aviv, Nurith
PARIS WAS A WOMAN
Bachmann, Harald
CURTIS'S CHARM
Baer, Hanania
SHOOTFIGHTER 2: KILL OR BE KILLED!
Baffa, Christopher
CRIMINAL HEARTS
DEATH ARTIST, THE
PIRANHA
SAWBONES
SOMETIMES THEY COME BACK . . . AGAIN
Bailey, John
EXTREME MEASURES
Baker, Ian
CHAMBER, THE
Bakke, Eric
YOU'LL NEVER MAKE LOVE IN THIS TOWN AGAIN
Ballhaus, Michael
SLEEPERS
Baratier, Diane
RENDEZVOUS IN PARIS
Barham, Jim
MAN WITH THE PERFECT SWING, THE
Barklage, Jeff
FLATTERED
Barrow, Michael
CAUGHT
HEAVY
Bartkowiak, Andrzej
MIRROR HAS TWO FACES, THE
OFF AND RUNNING
Bartlett, Michael
NIKI DE SAINT PHALLE: WHO IS THE MONSTER — YOU OR ME?
Bartoli, Adolfo
BACKLASH: OBLIVION 2
FORBIDDEN ZONE: ALIEN ABDUCTION
HEAD OF THE FAMILY
MAGIC IN THE MIRROR
SPELLBREAKER: SECRET OF THE LEPRECHAUNS
Baum, Jurgen
ONE MAN'S JUSTICE
PHAT BEACH
Beato, Affonso
FLOWER OF MY SECRET, THE
Ben Youssef, Youssef
SILENCES OF THE PALACE, THE

Benison, Peter
NIGHT OF THE TWISTERS
Bennett, Robert
HYPE!
Bernstein, Steven
BULLETPROOF
CURDLED
Berry, S. Torriano
BUGGED
Berryman, Ross
CHAMELEON
Berta, Renato
SHADOW OF ANGELS
Biddle, Adrian
101 DALMATIANS
Blakey, Ken
PURE DANGER
RAGE
SWEEPER, THE
Blick, John
FRIGHTENERS, THE
Blofson, Richard
LINE KING: THE AL HIRSCHFELD STORY, THE
Bode, Ralf
STREETCAR NAMED DESIRE, A
Bollinger, Alun
FRIGHTENERS, THE
Bonk, Ron
SANDMAN, THE
Bonvillain, Michael
SAINTS AND SINNERS
Bookwalter, J.R.
POLYMORPH
Bota, Rick
BARB WIRE
GLIMMER MAN, THE
Box, Harry
SHOWGIRL MURDERS, THE
Boyd, Russell
TIN CUP
Braham, Henry
SOLITAIRE FOR TWO
Brandt, Russ
DON'T BE A MENACE TO SOUTH CENTRAL WHILE DRINKING YOUR JUICE IN THE HOOD
NECRONOMICON: BOOK OF THE DEAD
PLAYBACK
Bridges, David
CROSSCUT
PAINTED HERO
Brinkmann, Robert
CABLE GUY, THE
TRUTH ABOUT CATS AND DOGS, THE
Burgess, Don
EVENING STAR, THE
Burr, David
PHANTOM, THE
RACE THE SUN
Burstyn, Thomas
SURGEON, THE
Burum, Stephen H.
MISSION: IMPOSSIBLE
Bush, Dick
MAN IN THE ATTIC, THE
Butler, Bill
FLIPPER
Byers, Frank
MAD DOG TIME
Calloway, Tom
NIGHT OF THE SCARECROW
Cameron, Paul
LAST SUPPER, THE
Campbell, John J.
4 TALES OF 2 CITIES
Candillo, Alan
SHOT, THE
Capener, Brian
YESTERDAY'S TARGET
Carchrae, Andy
MESSAGE TO LOVE: THE ISLE OF WIGHT FESTIVAL
Cardone, Michael
BLACK DAY BLUE NIGHT
Caso, Alan
ED
Cawley, Sarah
GIRLFRIENDS
MERCY
Champetier, Caroline
SINGLE GIRL, A
Chan, Joe
WICKED CITY, THE
Chan Kwong-hung
ORGANIZED CRIME & TRIAD BUREAU
Chapman, Michael
PRIMAL FEAR
SPACE JAM
Charters, Rodney
FRAME BY FRAME
Chea, Claudio
BITTER SUGAR
Chemaly, Pierre
FINAL EQUINOX, THE
Christensen, T. C.
CLUBHOUSE DETECTIVES
Clabaugh, Richard
CHILDREN OF THE CORN: THE GATHERING
Collister, Peter
DUNSTON CHECKS IN
Conroy, Jack
HOMEWARD BOUND II: LOST IN SAN FRANCISCO
Conversi, Fabio
LITTLE INDIAN, BIG CITY
Corradi, Pio
ERNESTO CHE GUEVARA—THE BOLIVIAN DIARY
Coulter, Mick
NEON BIBLE, THE
Cousin, Lionel
GUIMBA THE TYRANT
Cribben, Mik
BEWARE: CHILDREN AT PLAY
Crosby, Floyd
CHAMPAGNE SAFARI, THE
Crudo, Richard
AMERICAN BUFFALO
LOW LIFE, THE
Curtis, Oliver
MADAGASCAR SKIN
Czapsky, Stefan
MATILDA
Daniel, Bill
SONIC OUTLAWS
Daniels, Mark
FROM THE JOURNALS OF JEAN SEBERG
Davey, John
LA COMEDIE-FRANCAISE OU L'AMOUR JOUE
David, Zoltan
DONOR UNKNOWN
Davis, Elliot
GET ON THE BUS
LARGER THAN LIFE
Davis, Michael
BEASTMASTER 3: THE EYE OF BRAXUS
De Battista, Gerard
FRENCH TWIST
de Borman, John
PASSION OF DARKLY NOON, THE
SMALL FACES
de Menil, Francois
NIKI DE SAINT PHALLE: WHO IS THE MONSTER — YOU OR ME?
Deakins, Roger
COURAGE UNDER FIRE
FARGO
DeKeyzer, Bruno
WAR OF THE BUTTONS, THE
Del Ruth, Thomas
DEAD TO RIGHTS
JAG
Delic, Mario
CALLING THE GHOSTS: A STORY ABOUT RAPE, WAR AND WOMEN
DeMarco, Frank
THEREMIN: AN ELECTRONIC ODYSSEY
Deming, Peter
JOE'S APARTMENT
DeSalvo, Joe
WIFE, THE
Deschanel, Caleb
FLY AWAY HOME
DeSegonzac, Jean
NORMAL LIFE
Di Palma, Carlo
MONSTER, THE
Dickinson, Douglas
ABUSE
Dill, Bill
LET'S GET BIZZEE
DiPalma, Carlo
EVERYONE SAYS I LOVE YOU
Doob, Nicolas
PERFECT CANDIDATE, A
Dorfman, Bruce
RAW TARGET
Doyle, Christopher
CHUNGKING EXPRESS
Drago, Juan
MADAME WANG'S
Draper, Rob
SPITFIRE GRILL, THE
Drummond, Randy
WELCOME TO THE DOLLHOUSE
Dryburgh, Stuart
GIRLFRIENDS
LONE STAR
PORTRAIT OF A LADY, THE
Duca, Gurd
FLAMING EARS
Dumas, Ray
CHAMPAGNE SAFARI, THE
Duncan, Donald
ALEX
Dunn, Andrew
CRUCIBLE, THE
Edamitsu, Hiroaki
STREET FIGHTER II: THE ANIMATED MOVIE
Edwards, Eric
FLIRTING WITH DISASTER
Eggby, David
DAYLIGHT
DRAGONHEART
Egilsson, Eagle
DELTA OF VENUS
Elkin, Ian
FOR THE MOMENT
Elliott, Paul
TRUMAN
Elswit, Robert
BOYS
PALLBEARER, THE
Erickson, Nils
MIRROR, MIRROR III: THE VOYEUR
Escoffier, Jean-Yves
CROW: CITY OF ANGELS, THE
GRACE OF MY HEART
JACK & SARAH

PERSONAL JOURNEY WITH MARTIN SCORSESE THROUGH AMERICAN MOVIES, A
Evans, Blake
BODY COUNT
Everitt, Tim
FATALLY YOURS
Fash, Mike
ENTERTAINING ANGELS: THE DOROTHY DAY STORY
Fauntleroy, Don E.
FELONY
LILY DALE
Fellous, Maurice
FRANCOIS TRUFFAUT: STOLEN PORTRAITS
Fenner, John
MUPPET TREASURE ISLAND
Fernandes, Joao
FOREST WARRIOR
ROAD TO GALVESTON, THE
Fernandez, Angel Luis
BATON ROUGE
Fester, Rick
JOHNNY SHORTWAVE
Fine, Russell
GIRLS TOWN
POMPATUS OF LOVE, THE
Fischer, Jens
CHILDREN OF NOISY VILLAGE, THE
Fortunato, Ron
BASQUIAT
IF LUCY FELL
SKIN
Fraker, William A.
ISLAND OF DR. MOREAU, THE
Francesco, William
MURDERED INNOCENCE
Franco, David
HOLLOW POINT
Fresco, Robert
ROAD HOME, THE
Fridriksson, Fridrik Thor
COLD FEVER
Fujimoto, Tak
THAT THING YOU DO!
Furusawa, Toshifumi
SYNTHETIC PLEASURES
Garcia, Ron
GREAT WHITE HYPE, THE
PIG'S TALE, A
Geddes, David
COLONY, THE
George, Geoff
BLACK SCORPION
George, Lazlo Gyuriko
MATERNAL INSTINCTS
Gfelner, Michael
MERLIN'S SHOP OF MAGICAL WONDERS
SANTA WITH MUSCLES
Gibbons, Rodney
SCREAMERS
Glennon, James
CITIZEN RUTH
LIFEFORM
MRS. MUNCK
Goebert, Chip
YOU'LL NEVER MAKE LOVE IN THIS TOWN AGAIN
Goldblatt, Stephen
STRIPTEASE
Goldsmith, Paul
WHEN WE WERE KINGS
Goldstein, Eric J.
NAKED SOULS
Gonzalez, Carlos
ORIGINAL GANGSTAS
Goozee, Gerald R.
ELECTRA
WHEN THE BULLET HITS THE BONE
Gorman, W.J.
DADETOWN
Gourley, Susan
CHAMPAGNE SAFARI, THE
Graver, Gary
FRIEND OF THE FAMILY 2
Graves, Chris
CANNIBAL! THE MUSICAL
Green, Jack N.
TWISTER
Greenberg, Adam
ERASER
Greenberg, Robbie
SUNSET PARK
Gribble, David
QUEST, THE
Griffin, Garrett
LOVER'S KNOT
Grunther, Jeffrey
LINE KING: THE AL HIRSCHFELD STORY, THE
Gruszynski, Alexander
CRAFT, THE
MAXIMUM RISK
Gurfinkel, David
UNDER THE DOMIM TREE
Guthe, Manfred
STUPIDS, THE
Haarmann, Lorenz
NEUROSIA: 50 YEARS OF PERVERSITY
Hahn, Marcus
DEMOLITIONIST, THE
SYNTHETIC PLEASURES
Haitkin, Jacques
BIG SQUEEZE, THE
BLOODSPORT II: THE NEXT KUMITE
FIST OF THE NORTH STAR
ONE GOOD TURN
RATTLED
TWO-BITS & PEPPER
Hammer, Victor
DOWN PERISCOPE
Harper, Virgil
TREMORS 2: AFTERSHOCKS
Harris, Frank
SKYSCRAPER
Hazan, Jack
MESSAGE TO LOVE: THE ISLE OF WIGHT FESTIVAL
Heinl, Bernd
IT'S MY PARTY
PIE IN THE SKY
Hennings, David
D3: THE MIGHTY DUCKS
Hermann, Karl
AMERICA'S DREAM
Hinricks, Rodger
NIKI DE SAINT PHALLE: WHO IS THE MONSTER — YOU OR ME?
Hinzman, Bill
SANTA CLAWS
Hirsch, Ernst
NIKI DE SAINT PHALLE: WHO IS THE MONSTER — YOU OR ME?
Holahan, Paul
BOY CALLED HATE, A
Holahan, Philip
NOT OF THIS EARTH
Holender, Adam
I'M NOT RAPPAPORT
Holland, Keith
DARK SECRETS
Holt, Gary
LAZARUS MAN, THE
Howe, Matthew
DESOLATION ANGELS
ORIGINAL SINS
Huneck, John
DESIRE
ONE MAN'S JUSTICE
Imi, Tony
SHOPPING
Ingle Jr., Tom
FUNNYMAN, THE
Ioussov, Vadim
ANNA
Irwin, Mark
KINGPIN
ROBIN OF LOCKSLEY
SCREAM
STAND OFF, THE
Isaacks, Levie
DENTIST, THE
TEXAS CHAINSAW MASSACRE: THE NEXT GENERATION
WHARF RAT, THE
Isaacks, Pierre
DOGFIGHTERS, THE
Jacobsson, Anders
EVIL ED
James, Peter
DIABOLIQUE
LAST DANCE
Jannelli, Tony
NATIONAL LAMPOON'S FAVORITE DEADLY SINS
Jansons, Maris
HALFBACK OF NOTRE DAME, THE
HECK'S WAY HOME
Jewett, Thomas
FAST MONEY
SERIAL KILLER
TALKING ABOUT SEX
Johnson, Bruce Douglas
PUBLIC ACCESS
Johnson, Hugh
WHITE SQUALL
Jones, Alan
LOVE IS ALL THERE IS
Jowdat, Farzad
WHITE BALLOON, THE
Jur, Jeffrey
UNFORGETTABLE
Kaminski, Janusz
JERRY MAGUIRE
Kane, Adam
WITHIN THE ROCK
Karavaev, Elisbar
ANNA
Katz, Stephen
LETTER TO MY KILLER
SHARON'S SECRET
Kaufmann, Judith
NICO ICON
Keating, Kevin
WHEN WE WERE KINGS
Kelemen, Fred
FATE
Kelsch, Ken
ASSAULT AT WEST POINT
BIG NIGHT
CONDITION RED
FUNERAL, THE
Kemper, Victor J.
EDDIE
JINGLE ALL THE WAY
Kennan, Wayne
FOR BETTER OR WORSE
Kenny, Francis
HARRIET THE SPY
THIN LINE BETWEEN LOVE AND HATE, A
Kerrigan, Lodge
SEARCH FOR ONE-EYE JIMMY, THE

Kershaw, Glenn
. . . AT FIRST SIGHT
Khondji, Darius
EVITA
STEALING BEAUTY
Kibbe, Gary B.
JOHN CARPENTER'S ESCAPE FROM L.A.
Kiefer, Douglas
CHAMPAGNE SAFARI, THE
Kiehl, Stuart
PRE-MADONNAS
Kiesser, Jan
BAD MOON
Kimmel, Adam
BEAUTIFUL GIRLS
BED OF ROSES
Kirsten, Sven
BEYOND DESIRE
Klimov, Vladimir
BURIAL OF THE RATS
Klosinski, Edward
MOTHER OF KINGS
Kloss, Paul
HEIDI FLEISS HOLLYWOOD MADAM
Kloss, Thomas
FEAR
Knowland, Nic
INSTITUTE BENJAMENTA
MESSAGE TO LOVE: THE ISLE OF WIGHT FESTIVAL
Koltai, Lajos
MOTHER
Koren, Avi
DEADLY OUTBREAK
Kossak, Andreas
WATCH ME
Kovacs, Laszlo
MULTIPLICITY
Kozachik, Pete
JAMES AND THE GIANT PEACH
Krueger, Tom
MANNY & LO
Kuras, Ellen
ANGELA
I SHOT ANDY WARHOL
Kurita, Toyomichi
HOMECOMING
INFINITY
WOMAN UNDONE, A
Kyle, Kyle C.
NOT BAD FOR A GIRL
Lachman, Ed
THEREMIN: AN ELECTRONIC ODYSSEY
Lambert, John
HOURGLASS
Langley, Norman
MESSAGE TO LOVE: THE ISLE OF WIGHT FESTIVAL
Lanser, Roger
MIDWINTER'S TALE, A
WEEKEND IN THE COUNTRY, A
Lapine, Jean
BEYOND THE CALL
Lapoirie, Jeanne
LES VOLEURS
Lau, Andrew
WICKED CITY, THE
Lau Wai-Keung
CHUNGKING EXPRESS
Lay, Dwight
MUTANT MAN
Layton, Vernon
HIGH SCHOOL HIGH
Le Mener, Jean-Yves
VISITORS, THE
Leacock, Robert
CATWALK
LOOKING FOR RICHARD
Lebechev, Pavel
ANNA
Lebovitz, Jim
PHAT BEACH
Lecca, Franco
WHO KILLED PASOLINI?
Lee, Mark
WING CHUN
Lee, Philip
GALAXIES ARE COLLIDING
Lehn, Kenneth
FIRE ON THE MOUNTAIN
Leiterman, Richard
HOW THE WEST WAS FUN
LeMener, Jean Yves
FRANCOIS TRUFFAUT: STOLEN PORTRAITS
Lenoir, Denis
JOSEPH CONRAD'S THE SECRET AGENT
NEW LIFE, A
Lent, Dean
VIKING SAGAS, THE
Leonetti, John R.
SPY HARD
Leonetti, Matthew F.
FLED
STAR TREK: FIRST CONTACT
Lerner, Murray
MESSAGE TO LOVE: THE ISLE OF WIGHT FESTIVAL
Lesnie, Andrew
SPIDER & ROSE
TWO IF BY SEA
Letarte, Pierre
SUGARTIME
Levey, Chuck
SEARCH FOR ONE-EYE JIMMY, THE
Levin, Moshe
HARD JUSTICE
Levy, Peter
BROKEN ARROW
WAR AT HOME, THE
Leweth, Herman
FLAMING EARS
Lewiston, Denis
CANTERVILLE GHOST, THE
Li, Jiaguo
STORY OF XINGHUA, THE
Li Lung-yu
MAHJONG
Li Yi-hsu
MAHJONG
Liao Pen-jung
VIVE L'AMOUR
Lighthill, Stephen
BERKELEY IN THE 60S
EVIL HAS A FACE
OPEN SEASON
Liman, Doug
SWINGERS
Lindenlaub, Karl Walter
INDEPENDENCE DAY
UP CLOSE AND PERSONAL
Lindley, John
MICHAEL
Lindstrom, Rolf
CHILDREN OF NOISY VILLAGE, THE
Linsey, Philip
BLOODKNOT
Linzey, Philip
OUTER LIMITS: SANDKINGS, THE
Litz, David
TATTOO BOY
Lively, Gary
HELLRAISER: BLOODLINE
Lively, Gerry
MOTHER
NECRONOMICON: BOOK OF THE DEAD
WITHOUT MERCY
Llewellyn, Wes
SOUTH BEACH ACADEMY
Lloyd, Walt
FEELING MINNESOTA
Lohmann, Dietrich
MACHINE, THE
Lombardi, Cris
THEREMIN: AN ELECTRONIC ODYSSEY
Lubezki, Emmanuel
BIRDCAGE, THE
Lubtchansky, William
CHASING BUTTERFLIES
Luther, Igor
COLD LIGHT OF DAY
Ma, Jingle
RUMBLE IN THE BRONX
Macat, Julio
MY FELLOW AMERICANS
NUTTY PROFESSOR, THE
Machado, Thierry
MICROCOSMOS
Machuel, Laurent
THREE LIVES AND ONLY ONE DEATH
Maeda, Yasuo
NIGHT ON THE GALACTIC RAILROAD
Maibaum, Paul
DOWN, OUT AND DANGEROUS
Makin, David A.
KIDS IN THE HALL: BRAIN CANDY
Maloney, Denis
BAJA
WITCHCRAFT: SALEM'S GHOST
Maniaci, Teodoro
PREDICTIONS OF FIRE
Mankofsky, Isidore
HEIDI CHRONICLES, THE
Manley, Hong
TALES OF EROTICA
Marchetti, Mauro
CEMETERY MAN
Marco, Armand
MAN BY THE SHORE, THE
Markowitz, Barry
SLING BLADE
Martin, Tony
MERLIN'S SHOP OF MAGICAL WONDERS
Marzano, Joe
ONE LESS EGG TO FRY
Mathe, Tibor
MAGIC HUNTER
Mauch, Thomas
ORSON WELLES: THE ONE-MAN BAND
Maxwell, Joe Caramico
ZARKORR! THE INVADER
May, Bradford
DARKMAN III: DIE DARKMAN DIE
Mayers, Michael
DENISE CALLS UP
Maysles, Albert
WHEN WE WERE KINGS
McAlpine, Don
WILLIAM SHAKESPEARE'S ROMEO + JULIET
McGarvey, Seamus
BUTTERFLY KISS
McGuire, Maurice
TIGER HEART
McKay, Kevin
RED LINE
McLean, Nicky
MADDENING, THE
Melville, Alexander
PHOENIX
Melville, Mark
PHOENIX

Mendencevic, Suki
POISON IVY 2: LILY
Menges, Chris
MICHAEL COLLINS
Menzies Jr., Peter
TIME TO KILL, A
Michelson, Paul
REDEMPTION: KICKBOXER 5
Mickens, Mike
UNKNOWN ORIGIN
Middleton, Chris
WAVELENGTH
Middleton, Gregory
WHITE TIGER
Miller, David
VIRTUAL COMBAT
Milsome, Doug
RUMPELSTILTSKIN
SUNCHASER
Minsky, Charles
DEAR GOD
KAZAAM
Mokri, Amir M.
EYE FOR AN EYE
Molgaut, Valery
CHEKIST, THE
Montaner, Carlos
BREAKAWAY
Monti, Felix
OF LOVE AND SHADOWS
SHADOW YOU SOON WILL BE, A
Mooradian, George
ADRENALIN: FEAR THE RUSH
NEMESIS III: PREY HARDER
RAVENHAWK
Morgenthau, Kramer
SMALL WONDERS
SYNTHETIC PLEASURES
Morris, Mark
TEXAS PAYBACK
Morrisey, Kevin
HEADLESS BODY IN TOPLESS BAR
Morse, Richard
MAN WITH A PLAN
Mullen, M. David
DEAD COLD
SHADOW WARRIORS
Muller, Robby
BREAKING THE WAVES
DEAD MAN
Munzi, Maximo
BLONDES HAVE MORE GUNS
Muratore, Robert
CANNIBAL! THE MUSICAL
Murphy, Fred
FAITHFUL
FAMILY THING, A
Murphy, Paul
TUNNEL VISION
Mutarevic, Sead
WILD SIDE
Mutarevic, Sean
AMERICAN STRAYS
Myers, Richard
MONSTERSHOW
Nakabori, Masao
MABOROSI
Narita, Hiro
ARRIVAL, THE
JAMES AND THE GIANT PEACH
Navarro, Guillermo
FROM DUSK TILL DAWN
LONG KISS GOODNIGHT, THE
Nelson, Peter
ED'S NEXT MOVE
Nepomniaschy, Alex
ASSOCIATE, THE
MRS. WINTERBOURNE

Neumann, Margarete
FLAMING EARS
Neuwirth, Manfred
FLAMING EARS
New, Robert C.
IT CAME FROM OUTER SPACE II
Nicholson, Lynn
MR. ICE CREAM MAN
Nicholson, Rex
MODERN AFFAIR, A
Norr, Chris
TIMELESS
Nowell, David B.
EXIT
Nuridsany, Claude
MICROCOSMOS
O'Brien, John
MAN WITH A PLAN
Ohashi, Rene
KISSINGER AND NIXON
Ohno, Azusa
BODY OF INFLUENCE 2
HOSTILE INTENTIONS
Okada, Daryn
BIG BULLY
BLACK SHEEP
Okazaki, Hideo
ROUJIN-Z
Ondricek, Miroslav
PREACHER'S WIFE, THE
Orieux, Ronald
TUSKEGEE AIRMEN, THE
Orton, Ray
HEDD WYNN
Othmer, Zakaela Rachel
EVERYTHING RELATIVE
Papamichael, Phedon
BIO-DOME
PHENOMENON
UNHOOK THE STARS
Parmet, Phil
UNDER THE HULA MOON
Parnell, Feliks
SERPENT'S LAIR
Pau, Massimino
MILLE BOLLE BLU
Pei, Edward
LARRY MCMURTRY'S STREETS OF LAREDO
Penney, Julian
TWO FRIENDS
Perennou, Marie
MICROCOSMOS
Peters, John
SHAMELESS
Petersen, Curtis
IRON EAGLE IV
PORTRAITS OF A KILLER
RED SCORPION 2
Petkovic, Aleksandar
VUKOVAR
Phillips, Alex
AVENTURERA
Phillips, David
LITTLE DEATH, THE
Phillips, Garry
GIRLFRIENDS
Pierce-Roberts, Tony
HAUNTED
SURVIVING PICASSO
Pizer, Larry
PROPRIETOR, THE
Pope, Bill
BOUND
Pope, Dick
SECRETS & LIES
Pratt, Roger
IN LOVE AND WAR

Priestley, Tom
TALES FROM THE CRYPT PRESENTS BORDELLO OF BLOOD
Prinzi, Frank
GRAVE, THE
SHE'S THE ONE
Protat, Francois
SONG SPINNER, THE
TAILS YOU LIVE, HEADS YOU'RE DEAD
Quinlan, Dick
ANNIE O
LOSING CHASE
MOONSHINE HIGHWAY
Quinn, Declan
CARRIED AWAY
Ragalyi, Elemer
RASPUTIN
Raha, Barun
TARGET
Rance III, Floyd
DON'T LET YOUR MEAT LOAF
Reid, Francis
PERSONAL JOURNEY WITH MARTIN SCORSESE THROUGH AMERICAN MOVIES, A
Reiker, Tami
FAR HARBOR
4 TALES OF 2 CITIES
GIRLFRIENDS
Remin, Katarzyna
NICO ICON
Reshovsky, Marc
SET IT OFF
Richman, Robert
PARADISE LOST: THE CHILD MURDERS AT ROBIN HOOD HILLS
Richmond, Anthony B.
FIRST KID
IMMORTALS, THE
ROLLING STONES ROCK-AND-ROLL CIRCUS, THE
Richmond, Anthony R.
FULL BODY MASSAGE
Richmond, Tom
HOMAGE
MR. STITCH
MOTHER NIGHT
Rinzler, Lisa
TREES LOUNGE
Roach, Neil
HARVEST OF FIRE
LONE JUSTICE: SHOWDOWN AT PLUM CREEK
Robin, Jean-Francois
NELLY AND MONSIEUR ARNAUD
SUITE 16
Rocha, Claudio
WHOLE WIDE WORLD, THE
Rodgers, Adam
PROTEUS
Roebuck, Ernest Paul
ANIMAL INSTINCTS III: THE SEDUCTRESS
Roll, Gernot
KASPAR HAUSER
MAYBE . . . MAYBE NOT
Rossotto, Andrea V.
CARNOSAUR 3: PRIMAL SPECIES
Rousselot, Philippe
MARY REILLY
PEOPLE VS. LARRY FLYNT, THE
Russell, Ward
LAWNMOWER MAN 2: BEYOND CYBERSPACE
Ryffel, Hughes
MICROCOSMOS
Sakamoto, Yoshinao
KAMIKAZE TAXI

Salzman, Bernard
SABRINA, THE TEENAGE WITCH
Sarossey, Paul
BLOOD & DONUTS
Sass, James Robert
YANKEE ZULU
Savides, Harris
HEAVEN'S PRISONERS
Sayeed, Malik Hassan
GIRL 6
Schaaf, Geoff
BLACK OUT
Schaefer, Roberto
JUST YOUR LUCK
Schiller, Greta
PARIS WAS A WOMAN
Schlair, Doron
PHARAOH'S ARMY
Schreiber, Nancy
PERSONAL JOURNEY WITH MARTIN SCORSESE THROUGH AMERICAN MOVIES, A
Schwartzman, John
MR. WRONG
ROCK, THE
Seager, Chris
BEAUTIFUL THING
COLD COMFORT FARM
STONEWALL
Seale, John
ENGLISH PATIENT, THE
GHOSTS OF MISSISSIPPI
Seresin, Michael
CITY HALL
Sergovici, Viorel
JOSH KIRBY . . . TIME WARRIOR!: EGGS FROM 70,000,000 B.C.
JOSH KIRBY . . . TIME WARRIOR!: JOURNEY TO THE MAGIC CAVERN
JOSH KIRBY . . . TIME WARRIOR!: TRAPPED ON TOY WORLD
Serra, Eduardo
JUDE
Shaw, Steven
DANGEROUS PASSION
Shirai, Hisao
GHOST IN THE SHELL
Shreiber, Nancy
CELLULOID CLOSET, THE
Shugleit, Eugene
WOLVES, THE
Sigel, Newton Thomas
FOXFIRE
TRIGGER EFFECT, THE
Simmons, John
ONCE UPON A TIME . . . WHEN WE WERE COLORED
Simpson, Geoffrey
SHINE
SOME MOTHER'S SON
Sinkovics, Geza
PRE-MADONNAS
Sitkovics, Geza
UNDERTOW
Slovis, Michael
BREACH OF TRUST
Smith, Doyle
WIDOW'S KISS
Smitty, Allen
FEMALIEN
Sobocinski, Piotr
MARVIN'S ROOM
RANSOM
Sourioux, Michel
FRANCOIS TRUFFAUT: STOLEN PORTRAITS
Southon, Mike
FINAL CUT, THE
Sova, Peter
SGT. BILKO
Spencer, Brenton
WHERE'S THE MONEY, NOREEN?
Spencer, James
FUGITIVE RAGE
Spiller, Michael
FLIRT
4 TALES OF 2 CITIES
WALKING AND TALKING
Spinotti, Dante
MIRROR HAS TWO FACES, THE
STAR MAKER, THE
Standefer, Rufus
LOTTO LAND
Stanley, Richard
MESSAGE TO LOVE: THE ISLE OF WIGHT FESTIVAL
Stapleton, Oliver
KANSAS CITY
ONE FINE DAY
Stassen, Willy
ANTONIA'S LINE
Steiger, Ueli
HOUSE ARREST
Stein, Peter
MISSING PIECES
Stewart, Charles
MESSAGE TO LOVE: THE ISLE OF WIGHT FESTIVAL
Stewart, Rod
LIVE WIRE: HUMAN TIMEBOMB
TERMINAL IMPACT
WARHEAD
Stok, Witold
TWO DEATHS
Stone, Barry
RUDE
UNDERSTUDY: GRAVEYARD SHIFT 2, THE
Stone, Robert
THEREMIN: AN ELECTRONIC ODYSSEY
Stonehouse, Jeff
MYSTERY SCIENCE THEATER 3000: THE MOVIE
Strasburg, Ivan
AFFAIR, THE
CRACKER: THE MADWOMAN IN THE ATTIC
Sturme, Sibylle
NICO ICON
Suarez, Ramon
SILENCE OF NETO, THE
Suhrstedt, Tim
TO GILLIAN ON HER 37TH BIRTHDAY
Sunara, Igor
TALES OF EROTICA
Surtees, Bruce
SUBSTITUTE, THE
Suschitzky, Peter
MARS ATTACKS!
Suslov, Misha
PUBLIC ENEMIES
Taczanowski, Hubert
YOUNG POISONER'S HANDBOOK, THE
Takahashi, Akihiko
PATLABOR 2: MOBILE POLICE
Tarver, John
LEGEND OF GATOR FACE, THE
Tattersall, David
MOLL FLANDERS
THEODORE REX
Taylor, Christopher
DEATH BENEFIT
LIVE NUDE GIRLS
Thiriet, Michel
LA CEREMONIE
Thomas, John
FREEWAY
NORMA JEAN AND MARILYN
PALOOKAVILLE
VENUS RISING
Thompson, Jamie
NATIONAL LAMPOON'S FAVORITE DEADLY SINS
Thomson, Alex
EXECUTIVE DECISION
HAMLET
Thorin, Donald
FIRST WIVES CLUB, THE
Tickner, Clive
TWELFTH NIGHT
Tidy, Frank
BOYS NEXT DOOR, THE
CHAIN REACTION
GETTING AWAY WITH MURDER
Tieche, Gary
AMANDA AND THE ALIEN
BAD LOVE
DEAD WEEKEND
OUT THERE
Timberlake, Stephen
MAN OF THE YEAR
Tittel, Volker
HALFMOON
Toll, John
JACK
Tonelli, Renato
PARIS WAS A WOMAN
Torigoe, Kazushi
SANCTUARY: THE MOVIE
Tougas, Kirk
CHAMPAGNE SAFARI, THE
Tovoli, Luciano
BEFORE AND AFTER
Trauttmansdorff, Andreas
JOHNNY SHORTWAVE
Tromie, Brett
THEY BITE
Trow, Alan
GRIM
Tufano, Brian
TRAINSPOTTING
Turowski, Ron
LITTLE WITCHES
Tutanes, George
MIDNIGHT DANCERS
Tynes, Jim
MADAME WANG'S
Van Haren Noman, Eric
MOTHER'S PRAYER, A
Van Oostrum, Kees
LONG ROAD HOME, THE
STEPHEN KING'S THINNER
Vanden Ende, Walther
DAENS
Vargas, Henry
TOLLBOOTH
Vasile, Vivi Dragan
JOSH KIRBY . . . TIME WARRIOR!: LAST BATTLE FOR THE UNIVERSE
OUTPOST, THE
Vidgeon, Robin
AUGUST
Vilsmaier, Joseph
BROTHER OF SLEEP
Von Sternberg, Nicolas
VIRUS
Wages, William
CHILDREN OF FURY
RIDERS OF THE PURPLE SAGE
Wakeford, Kent
4 TALES OF 2 CITIES
SOME FOLKS CALL IT A SLING BLADE
Walker, Howard
OVER THE WIRE

Walling, Christopher
SOLO
Walsh, David M.
CARPOOL
Watanabe, Makoto
SWEET NOTHING
Watkin, David
BOGUS
JANE EYRE
Watkins, Greg
FRISK
Watson, Jerry
BEST OF THE BEST 3: NO TURNING BACK
Webb, William G.
PERSONAL JOURNEY WITH MARTIN SCORSESE THROUGH AMERICAN MOVIES, A
Weber, Alicia
EDIE & PEN
Welt, Philippe
MADAME BUTTERFLY
Westman, Tony
ALASKA
Wexler, Haskell
MULHOLLAND FALLS
RICH MAN'S WIFE, THE
Whitehead, Peter
NIKI DE SAINT PHALLE: WHO IS THE MONSTER — YOU OR ME?
Whittaker, Mike
MESSAGE TO LOVE: THE ISLE OF WIGHT FESTIVAL
Williams, Bob
SGT. KABUKIMAN N.Y.P.D.
Wilson, Ian
EMMA
Wisbred, Lester
VIRTUAL ENCOUNTERS
Wolski, Dariusz
FAN, THE
Wong Wing-hang
ORGANIZED CRIME & TRIAD BUREAU
Wood, Oliver
CELTIC PRIDE
MR. HOLLAND'S OPUS
2 DAYS IN THE VALLEY
Worrall, Bruce
TRACKS OF A KILLER
Wouthuysen, Bernd
CROCODILES IN AMSTERDAM
Yacker, Fawn
PARIS WAS A WOMAN
Yeoman, Robert
BOTTLE ROCKET
SUBSTANCE OF FIRE, THE
Young, Roderick
WHEN WE WERE KINGS
Zeng Nianping
BLUSH
Zhou Xiaowen
BLACK MOUNTAIN
Zitzermann, Bernard
ANGELS AND INSECTS
LA CEREMONIE
NIKI DE SAINT PHALLE: WHO IS THE MONSTER — YOU OR ME?
Zsigmond, Vilmos
GHOST AND THE DARKNESS, THE

CO-PRODUCERS

Ader-Brown, Jamie
HEIDI FLEISS HOLLYWOOD MADAM
Airoldi, Conchita
CEMETERY MAN
Alexander, Elizabeth W.
BIG NIGHT
Alexander, Stephen
SOLITAIRE FOR TWO
Allred, Randall
APART FROM HUGH
Alsobrook, Allen
SET IT OFF
Alsobrook, James
RAVENHAWK
Amatullo, Tony
CHAMELEON
Anderson, Kurt
ONE MAN'S JUSTICE
Andrews, John
BEAVIS AND BUTT-HEAD DO AMERICA
Avellan, Elizabeth
FROM DUSK TILL DAWN
Baden-Powell, Sue
LARGER THAN LIFE
Bahoric, Carol
TUSKEGEE AIRMEN, THE
Bak, Frank
SUITE 16
Baldwin, Johanna
SOMEONE ELSE'S AMERICA
Balsan, Humbert
SURVIVING PICASSO
Band, Albert
BACKLASH: OBLIVION 2
Barnett, Laura
FAR HARBOR
Baumgartner, Karl
INSTITUTE BENJAMENTA
Beasley, William
CABLE GUY, THE
Beer, Jeffrey
LOTTO LAND
Berg, Barry
GREAT WHITE HYPE, THE
MOTHER
Berk, Daniel Zelik
PUBLIC ENEMIES
Bernhardt, Kevin
IMMORTALS, THE
Bertolli, John
KINGPIN
Beugg, Michael
SOME FOLKS CALL IT A SLING BLADE
Binder, Chuck
LAST DANCE
Bishop, Dennis
EVENING STAR, THE
Bishop, Larry
MAD DOG TIME
Blomquist, Alan C.
BEAUTIFUL GIRLS
Blum, Jennifer
JINGLE ALL THE WAY
Blumenthal, Jason
DUNSTON CHECKS IN
Boam, Jeffrey
PHANTOM, THE
Bourne, Timothy M.
PREACHER'S WIFE, THE
Bowler, Simon
MAN OF THE YEAR
Brandman, Steven J.
HEIDI CHRONICLES, THE
Brandstein, Jonathan
WAR AT HOME, THE
Brigham, Chris
BEFORE AND AFTER
EXTREME MEASURES
Broderick, Suzanne
THIN LINE BETWEEN LOVE AND HATE, A
Bromiley Jr., Bill
BLACK ROSE OF HARLEM
UNKNOWN ORIGIN
Brown, G. Mac
MICHAEL
Brown, Harriet
SERPENT'S LAIR
Brown, Kevin Kelly
BLOODKNOT
Brown, Martin
WILLIAM SHAKESPEARE'S ROMEO + JULIET
Brown, Stephen
ERASER
Brubaker, James D.
NUTTY PROFESSOR, THE
Bufford, Takashi
SET IT OFF
Buonincontri, Cara
SUNSET PARK
Burke, Jim
KINGPIN
2 DAYS IN THE VALLEY
Burrell, Peter J.
ENTERTAINING ANGELS: THE DOROTHY DAY STORY
Capp, Dixie J.
SCREAM
Capra III, Frank
GHOSTS OF MISSISSIPPI
Carr, Warren
HAPPY GILMORE
Carraro, Bill
OFF AND RUNNING
Carraro, William C.
THIN LINE BETWEEN LOVE AND HATE, A
Carson, L.M. Kit
BOTTLE ROCKET
Cartlidge, William F.
HAUNTED
Cathell III, Ed
BEYOND DESIRE
Chase, Debra Martin
PREACHER'S WIFE, THE
Chernov, Jeffrey
FIRST KID
Chow, Roberta
RUMBLE IN THE BRONX
Clark, Jason
MAXIMUM RISK
Cociasu, Mihail
OUTPOST, THE
Cohen, Andrew
SOLITAIRE FOR TWO
Collett, Alexander
TALES FROM THE CRYPT PRESENTS BORDELLO OF BLOOD
Comeaga, Cristian
OUTPOST, THE
Conli, Roy
HUNCHBACK OF NOTRE DAME, THE
Cook, Christopher
BOYS NEXT DOOR, THE
Corn, Kahane
HEIDI FLEISS HOLLYWOOD MADAM
Counihan, Judy
ANTONIA'S LINE
Cozell, Michael
DENISE CALLS UP
Cremata, Jud
BREAKAWAY
Cryer, Jon
POMPATUS OF LOVE, THE
Cuddy, M. Charles
SANTA WITH MUSCLES
Curi, Pamela S.
DEVOTION
Daigler, Gary
DIABOLIQUE
David, Peter
BACKLASH: OBLIVION 2

Davidson, Boaz
WILD SIDE
Day, Janet
AUGUST
Di Dionisio, Dino
CEMETERY MAN
Dion, Debra
BACKLASH: OBLIVION 2
Dix, Gregory
HARD JUSTICE
Dobbs, Frank Q.
LARRY MCMURTRY'S STREETS OF LAREDO
Donahue, Chris
ENTERTAINING ANGELS: THE DOROTHY DAY STORY
Dowlatabadi, Zahra
LAND BEFORE TIME IV: JOURNEY THROUGH THE MISTS
Drago, Billy
MIRROR, MIRROR III: THE VOYEUR
PHOENIX
Duchowny, Bobby
BOY CALLED HATE, A
Durkos, Stephanie
MRS. MUNCK
Dutton, Lisa
HYPE!
Dysinger, Elaine
BIO-DOME
Edmonds, Don
FAST MONEY
Eick, David
DARKMAN III: DIE DARKMAN DIE
Eilts, Mary
RED SCORPION 2
Elliot, Mike
ONE NIGHT STAND
Ellis, Kirk
GRASS HARP, THE
Esposito, Jon
FROM DUSK TILL DAWN
Etheridge, Dan
BIO-DOME
LOW LIFE, THE
Ewing, Michael
MY FELLOW AMERICANS
Ezralow, Marc
FREEWAY
Favreau, Jon
SWINGERS
Ferguson, Scott
PALOOKAVILLE
Fields, Karyn
EXECUTIVE DECISION
Fischer, Carl
YANKEE ZULU
Fischer, Marc S.
FOXFIRE
Flynn, Michael
CROW: CITY OF ANGELS, THE
Forland, Kristian
BEYOND DESIRE
Forsyth, Kelley
GIRLS TOWN
TREES LOUNGE
Fottrell, Michael
VERY BRADY SEQUEL, A
Frederickson, Gray
HEAVEN'S PRISONERS
Fry, Carla
LONG KISS GOODNIGHT, THE
Fukuda, Kayo
SANCTUARY: THE MOVIE
Gains, Herbert W.
DAYLIGHT
Gainville, Rene
ASSOCIATE, THE
Gale, David
SUGARTIME
Galin, Mitchell
STEPHEN KING'S THINNER
Gardner, Cynthia
LIFEFORM
Gardner, Tony
LIFEFORM
Garfinkle, Jerry
SOUTH BEACH ACADEMY
Geissler, Deiter
ADVENTURES OF PINOCCHIO, THE
Gesualdo, Cathy
GLASS CAGE, THE
Giarraputo, Jack
BULLETPROOF
HAPPY GILMORE
Gillespie, John
ELECTRA
WHEN THE BULLET HITS THE BONE
Gloor, Luciano
CHASING BUTTERFLIES
Goddard, Melissa
POISON IVY 2: LILY
Goldberg, Daniel
LATE SHIFT, THE
Goldfine, Phillip
DENTIST, THE
PUBLIC ENEMIES
SOMETIMES THEY COME BACK . . . AGAIN
Goncalves, Helder
VIRUS
Goodwill, Jonathan
WHERE'S THE MONEY, NOREEN?
Gray, Russell
BAJA
Green, Sarah
AMERICAN BUFFALO
Greene, Justis
HOMEWARD BOUND II: LOST IN SAN FRANCISCO
Gund, George
COLD FEVER
Gunn, Andrew
EDDIE
Hadida, Samuel
ADVENTURES OF PINOCCHIO, THE
Haley, Michael
BED OF ROSES
Hamburger, Kevin
LOVER'S KNOT
Hammerel, Paula
DOGFIGHTERS, THE
Hampton, Christopher
JOSEPH CONRAD'S THE SECRET AGENT
Hampton, Sanford
FOREST WARRIOR
Hampton, Tim
ADVENTURES OF PINOCCHIO, THE
Hansen, Kirk Edward
HEAD OF THE FAMILY
Harbert, Tim
MOLL FLANDERS
Hargett, Hester
DAYLIGHT
DRAGONHEART
Hart, Joe
TIMELESS
Hawkins, Diana
IN LOVE AND WAR
Hazan, Alex
HARD JUSTICE
Headley, Mark
MIRROR, MIRROR III: THE VOYEUR
Helfant, Michael A.
ASSOCIATE, THE
Helgeland, Axel
BREAKING THE WAVES
Hellerman, Paul
FROM DUSK TILL DAWN
Herz, Michael
BLONDES HAVE MORE GUNS
Higby, Morgan
TALKING ABOUT SEX
Higgins, Jean
MY FELLOW AMERICANS
Hill, Grant
GHOST AND THE DARKNESS, THE
Hool, Conrad
FLIPPER
Huberty, Martin
UP CLOSE AND PERSONAL
Huggard, Richard
FRISK
Imperato, Thomas
FIRST WIVES CLUB, THE
Isaac, Margaret French
FAN, THE
James, Judith
MR. HOLLAND'S OPUS
James, Tim
FUNNYMAN, THE
Jayanti, Vikram
WHEN WE WERE KINGS
Jimirro, James
NATIONAL LAMPOON'S FAVORITE DEADLY SINS
Johnson, Broderick
LOVE IS ALL THERE IS
Jones, Damian
DEAD WEEKEND
Jones, Dennis E.
SURGEON, THE
Jones, Steven A.
NORMAL LIFE
Kahn, Sheldon
SPACE JAM
Kalmbach, Scott
GRAVE, THE
Kane, Mary
SUNSET PARK
Kardos, Ferenc
MAGIC HUNTER
Katims, Jason
PALLBEARER, THE
Katz, Al
TALES FROM THE CRYPT PRESENTS BORDELLO OF BLOOD
Kaufman, Lloyd
BLONDES HAVE MORE GUNS
Kavanaugh, Derek
DEATH BENEFIT
Kazan, Nicholas
MATILDA
Kelemen, Fred
FATE
Kelly, Tim
LOVE IS ALL THERE IS
Kennerly, Mark
DON'T LET YOUR MEAT LOAF
King, Lisa
DEVOTION
Kirn, Summer Ku'ulei
RACE THE SUN
Kirtland Silverman, Kathy
MATERNAL INSTINCTS
Kitrosser, Martin
SERIAL KILLER
Knell, Catalaine
CARRIED AWAY
Koch, Karen
DEAD MAN
OPEN SEASON

Koll, Bjoern
PARIS WAS A WOMAN
Kolmel, Rainer
YOUNG POISONER'S HANDBOOK, THE
Komine, Aki
NECRONOMICON: BOOK OF THE DEAD
Koper, Peter
HEADLESS BODY IN TOPLESS BAR
Kosove, Andrew A.
LOVE IS ALL THERE IS
Kramer, Jeremy
GLASS CAGE, THE
Kurtzman, Robert
FROM DUSK TILL DAWN
Labowitz, Amy
POISON IVY 2: LILY
Ladd, Diane
MOTHER
Ladd, Kelliann
VERY BRADY SEQUEL, A
Lahti, Ed
SHARON'S SECRET
Lancaster, Joanna
WILD SIDE
Langestraat, Rob
BREAKING THE WAVES
Larouziere, Patricia
EVERYTHING RELATIVE
Lauritson, Peter
STAR TREK: FIRST CONTACT
Leifer, Neil
GREAT WHITE HYPE, THE
Lemisch, Amy
PREACHER'S WIFE, THE
Lepetit, Jean Francois
JANE EYRE
Lepetit, Jean-Francois
WHO KILLED PASOLINI?
Lerner, Danny
DEADLY OUTBREAK
Levin, Nava
HARRIET THE SPY
Levine, Janet
BAD LOVE
Liguori, Peter
BIG NIGHT
Lindstrom, Lisa
UP CLOSE AND PERSONAL
Liroff, Marci
SPITFIRE GRILL, THE
Lombardo, Antonino
ANTONIA'S LINE
Ludlow, Jose
SOLO
Lumpkin, Michael
CELLULOID CLOSET, THE
MacDonald, Joe
FOR THE MOMENT
MacDonald, Michael
ADVENTURES OF PINOCCHIO, THE
TWO IF BY SEA
Majewski, Lech
BASQUIAT
Mark, Gordon
ALASKA
Marmion, Yves
MAGIC HUNTER
Martin, Jonathon Komack
PINOCCHIO'S REVENGE
Martin, Rob
ZARKORR! THE INVADER
Matovich Jr., Mitchel J.
PRE-MADONNAS
McAboy, Scott
PURE DANGER
RAGE
SKYSCRAPER
TWO-BITS & PEPPER
McCann, Hank
BLOODKNOT
McDaniel, Darin
FATALLY YOURS
McDermott, Mickey
WAR AT HOME, THE
McDonnell, Ed
GLIMMER MAN, THE
McLaglen, Mary
ONE FINE DAY
SGT. BILKO
McLeod, Erin
FEELING MINNESOTA
McMinn, Robert
PRIMAL FEAR
Medjuck, Joe
LATE SHIFT, THE
Merims, Adam J.
FREEWAY
Merrifield, Marta
SWEEPER, THE
TIGER HEART
Merzbach, Susan
RANSOM
Michael, Terence
IF LUCY FELL
Mickleberry, William
WOMAN UNDONE, A
Miller, Lori
LAST SUPPER, THE
Millichap, Paulette
ONCE UPON A TIME . . . WHEN WE WERE COLORED
Minot, Dinah
BLACK SHEEP
Molito, Tom
PAINTED HERO
Morris, Redmond
MICHAEL COLLINS
Morrow, Carrie
DON'T BE A MENACE TO SOUTH CENTRAL WHILE DRINKING YOUR JUICE IN THE HOOD
LITTLE DEATH, THE
Morse, Terry
TO GILLIAN ON HER 37TH BIRTHDAY
Moskalyk, Tony
DELTA OF VENUS
Mouton, Benjamin
WHOLE WIDE WORLD, THE
Mulay, James
JINGLE ALL THE WAY
Myers, Michael Scott
WHOLE WIDE WORLD, THE
Nadler, James
MAN IN THE ATTIC, THE
Newman, Carroll
HOUSE ARREST
Nichols, David
WAR OF THE BUTTONS, THE
Nicolaou, Panos C.
UNHOOK THE STARS
O'Dwyer, Colleen
LAZARUS MAN, THE
O'Neal, Brian E.
PHAT BEACH
Okamoto, Haruo
SANCTUARY: THE MOVIE
Oliensis, Adam
POMPATUS OF LOVE, THE
Orent, Kerry
FLIRTING WITH DISASTER
Palef, Bonnie
MARVIN'S ROOM
Partland, Dan
PERFECT CANDIDATE, A
WELCOME TO THE DOLLHOUSE
Peak, Kearie
DEAR GOD
Pentecost, James
HOMEWARD BOUND II: LOST IN SAN FRANCISCO
Peterson, Clark
DEAD COLD
Pham, Caroline
ERASER
Phillips, Don
INFINITY
ONE GOOD TURN
Platt, Oliver
BIG NIGHT
Poe, Amos
DEAD WEEKEND
Pokorny, Diana
CRUCIBLE, THE
Polaire, Michael
EYE FOR AN EYE
Polk, Curtis
SPACE JAM
Purcell, Evelyn
WOMAN UNDONE, A
Pustin, Bruce S.
JERRY MAGUIRE
Raynr, David
THIN LINE BETWEEN LOVE AND HATE, A
Redman, David
FUNNYMAN, THE
Resnick, Gina
SOLO
Reynolds, Raimond
HOMAGE
Rhoden, Lisa
BITTER SUGAR
Ribeiro, Chantal
LOVE IS ALL THERE IS
Ridpath, Deborah
IF LUCY FELL
Ripp, Adam
PUBLIC ACCESS
Robert, Yves
WAR OF THE BUTTONS, THE
Robinson, Keith
WHEN WE WERE KINGS
Robinson, Todd
WHITE SQUALL
Rodnunsky, Serge
FINAL EQUINOX, THE
Rosboch, Ettore
CHASING BUTTERFLIES
Rose, Jacobus
BAD MOON
Rosen, Brian
JAMES AND THE GIANT PEACH
Rosen, Dan
LAST SUPPER, THE
Rosenberg, Phillip
DEATH BENEFIT
Rosenthal, James R.
SANTA WITH MUSCLES
Roth, Helen
EVERYONE SAYS I LOVE YOU
Ryman, John
GALAXIES ARE COLLIDING
Sabusawa, Randy
FUNERAL, THE
Sai, Haruo
SANCTUARY: THE MOVIE
Sanders, Tim
FRIGHTENERS, THE
Schaeffer, Eric
IF LUCY FELL

Schenkman, Richard
POMPATUS OF LOVE, THE
Schofield, John D.
JERRY MAGUIRE
Schroeder, Adam
MARVIN'S ROOM
MOTHER
RANSOM
Schuler, Carol
DESIRE
Schuster, Leon
YANKEE ZULU
Schwartz, Ellen H.
DEAR GOD
Scoon, Mark
ADRENALIN: FEAR THE RUSH
Scott, Deborah
BEST OF THE BEST 3: NO TURNING BACK
Scotta, Carole
YOUNG POISONER'S HANDBOOK, THE
Sechrest, Steve
ZARKORR! THE INVADER
Segan, Allison Lyon
BROKEN ARROW
Seig, Matthew
KANSAS CITY
Selick, Henry
JAMES AND THE GIANT PEACH
Seligman, Guy
CHASING BUTTERFLIES
Seydoux, Michel
ANNA
Shepherd, Peter
MIND RIPPER
Shields, Brent
HARVEST OF FIRE
Shuman, Ira
BULLETPROOF
MR. WRONG
Silberg, David
SANTA WITH MUSCLES
Silliphant, Stirling
GRASS HARP, THE
Simmons, Rudd
BOYS
Simons, Edward
ADVENTURES OF PINOCCHIO, THE
Singleton, Ralph
LAST MAN STANDING
Skillman, Ted
PERFECT CANDIDATE, A
WELCOME TO THE DOLLHOUSE
Slot, Marianne
BREAKING THE WAVES
Smecchia, Lilia
CHASING BUTTERFLIES
Smith, Iain
MARY REILLY
Soisson, Joel
FIST OF THE NORTH STAR
Solberg, Russell
FAST MONEY
Speiser, Aaron
PRE-MADONNAS
Spezzi, Darlene
FLIPPER
Squires, Herb
RACE THE SUN
Stathakis, Jonathan
EXIT
Steinhauer, Robert Bennett
STREETCAR NAMED DESIRE, A
Stephen, Elizabeth Guber
D3: THE MIGHTY DUCKS
Stewart, Patrick
CANTERVILLE GHOST, THE
Stone, Andrew
CITIZEN RUTH
Subotsky, Milton
SOMETIMES THEY COME BACK . . . AGAIN
Sudzin, Jeffrey
BOUND
Swicord, Robin
MATILDA
Syvan, Lemore
SUBSTANCE OF FIRE, THE
Tabrizi, Alexander
BLOODSPORT II: THE NEXT KUMITE
Tana, Gabrielle
SOMEONE ELSE'S AMERICA
Taubert, Clifton
ONCE UPON A TIME . . . WHEN WE WERE COLORED
Taylor, Geoffrey
FAITHFUL
Teitler, William
MR. HOLLAND'S OPUS
Tejada-Flores, Miguel
TAILS YOU LIVE, HEADS YOU'RE DEAD
Thaler, Jonas
AMANDA AND THE ALIEN
Thomas, David C.
KANSAS CITY
Thompson, Barnaby
KIDS IN THE HALL: BRAIN CANDY
Thompson, Ron Stacker
AMERICA'S DREAM
Tinchat, Maurice
CHASING BUTTERFLIES
Tomiyama, Katsue
INSTITUTE BENJAMENTA
Tornell, Lisa
CRAFT, THE
Tse, Simon
GLASS CAGE, THE
Tuchinsky, Galina
RASPUTIN
Turrow, Randolf
NAKED SOULS
Tyler, Ashley
AMERICA'S DREAM
Ueda, Ayao
SANCTUARY: THE MOVIE
Upton, Mike
NOT OF THIS EARTH
SAWBONES
Van Vogelpoel, Peter
BREAKING THE WAVES
Vanderbeek, Susan
EDIE & PEN
Vaughn, Edward E.
SPITFIRE GRILL, THE
Virgo, Clement
RUDE
Vogel, Sarah
GIRLS TOWN
TREES LOUNGE
Vogt, Pete
HYPE!
Von Ganaith, Ira
LA CEREMONIE
Wadhwan, Raju
WITHOUT MERCY
Wadsworth, Gil
TWO-BITS & PEPPER
Waldburger, Ruth
MAGIC HUNTER
Weathers, Carl
DANGEROUS PASSION
Webb, Gordon
SPACE JAM
Weimer, Lynn
PIG'S TALE, A
Weisler, Michele
SAINTS AND SINNERS
Whitcher, Patricia
HIGH SCHOOL HIGH
White, Whitney
MULTIPLICITY
Whitley, Patrick
LEGEND OF GATOR FACE, THE
Wilson, Brad
FAMILY THING, A
Wilson, Stanley
DOWN PERISCOPE
GALAXIES ARE COLLIDING
Wingate, Ann
PORTRAIT OF A LADY, THE
Wisnievitz, David
MARVIN'S ROOM
Wooll, Nigel
WHITE SQUALL
Wright, Richard S.
KIDS IN THE HALL: BRAIN CANDY
Yavner, Cyrus
ARRIVAL, THE
Yetman, Ches
FOR THE MOMENT
Yu, Martin
LOW LIFE, THE
Zanitsch, Noel
DENTIST, THE
SERIAL KILLER
Zannoni, Giovannella
JANE EYRE
Zicree, Marc
LAZARUS MAN, THE
Zimmerman, Ray
BOTTLE ROCKET

COSTUMES

Aboitiz, Marisa
BAD LOVE
Adams, Valari
DON'T BE A MENACE TO SOUTH CENTRAL WHILE DRINKING YOUR JUICE IN THE HOOD
Alderson, Angela Dawn
DEMOLITIONIST, THE
Aldredge, Theoni V.
FIRST WIVES CLUB, THE
MIRROR HAS TWO FACES, THE
MRS. WINTERBOURNE
STREETCAR NAMED DESIRE, A
Allen, Marit
DEAD MAN
Allyson, Dana
TRIGGER EFFECT, THE
Altman, Barbara
LOOKING FOR TROUBLE
Alvargonzalez, Ana
LAND AND FREEDOM
Amos, Dorothy
FOREST WARRIOR
MOTHER'S PRAYER, A
Anacker, Kristen
BAJA
GLASS CAGE, THE
NAKED SOULS
Anderson, ChoAhnne
HALFMOON
Appel, Deena
FULL BODY MASSAGE
April, Renee
MOTHER NIGHT
Armani, Giorgio
STEALING BEAUTY
Arthur, Loyce
MURDERED INNOCENCE

Aslin, Jill
STAND OFF, THE
Atwood, Colleen
JUROR, THE
MARS ATTACKS!
THAT THING YOU DO!
Aubrey, Juslene
LOOKING FOR TROUBLE
B., Sandy
PAINTED HERO
Bafaloukos, Eugenie
FEELING MINNESOTA
Bakker, Trysha
MAN IN THE ATTIC, THE
Baranova, Elena
YESTERDAY'S TARGET
Barett, Kym
WILLIAM SHAKESPEARE'S ROMEO + JULIET
Beale, Sara
ALEX
Beavan, Jenny
JANE EYRE
Becker, Susan
SGT. BILKO
Benbrook, Wendy
ONE GOOD TURN
Bergin, Joan
SOME MOTHER'S SON
Bernice, Jenny
DEVOTION
Bertram, Susan
GRACE OF MY HEART
Bilbrough, Miro
GIRLFRIENDS
Bimek, Daniela
NEUROSIA: 50 YEARS OF PERVERSITY
Binder, Gabi
PASSION OF DARKLY NOON, THE
Bogers, Linda
COLD LIGHT OF DAY
Boies, Shelly
ADRENALIN: FEAR THE RUSH
NEMESIS III: PREY HARDER
Bonmati, Nereida
MOUTH TO MOUTH
Bordone, Beatrice
STAR MAKER, THE
Bourbigot, Chantal
MAN BY THE SHORE, THE
Boyle, Consolata
MARY REILLY
MOLL FLANDERS
Breckl, Janos
OUTPOST, THE
Bridges, Mark
NIGHT OF THE SCARECROW
Bright, John
TWELFTH NIGHT
Bronson, Tom
SPY HARD
Bronson-Howard, Aude
HEAVEN'S PRISONERS
Brown, Paul
ANGELS AND INSECTS
Brown, Winnie D.
AMERICA'S DREAM
ONCE UPON A TIME . . . WHEN WE WERE COLORED
Bruno, Richard
ERASER
Bryan, Jennifer
FLED
Bryant, Katherine Jane
PALOOKAVILLE
Burden, Howard
CANTERVILLE GHOST, THE
SHOPPING
Burke, Kristin M.
WITHIN THE ROCK
Burrows, Rosemary
101 DALMATIANS
Busalacchi, Shelly
RAVENHAWK
Bush, Robin Michel
JOHN CARPENTER'S ESCAPE FROM L.A.
Byrne, Alexandra
HAMLET
Campbell, Glenne
UNFORGETTABLE
Canter, Nina
JUST YOUR LUCK
Carin, Kate
SMALL FACES
Carter, Ruth
GREAT WHITE HYPE, THE
SUNCHASER
Carulli, Maria
OUTRAGE
Cassady, Janet
FROM THE JOURNALS OF JEAN SEBERG
Casterline, Thomas
DAYLIGHT
DRAGONHEART
Castro, Eduardo
THIN LINE BETWEEN LOVE AND HATE, A
WOMAN UNDONE, A
Ceo, Mari-An
SHOT, THE
TREES LOUNGE
Channeson, Jill
TRUMAN
Clancy, Michael
STONEWALL
Clark, Julie
ANIMAL INSTINCTS III: THE SEDUCTRESS
Cole, Michelle
EDIE & PEN
Corrigan, Lucy W.
BEAUTIFUL GIRLS
BOYS
Coulibaly, Kandjoura
GUIMBA THE TYRANT
Cox, Betsy
MY FELLOW AMERICANS
PHENOMENON
PRIMAL FEAR
Crabtree, Ane
IF LUCY FELL
Cronenberg, Denise
SUGARTIME
Crowley, Bob
CRUCIBLE, THE
Culotta, Sandi
DOWN, OUT AND DANGEROUS
Cunliffe, Shay
LONE STAR
MULTIPLICITY
D'Arcy, Timothy
DEAD TO RIGHTS
Darragh, Barbara
FRIGHTENERS, THE
David, Charlotte
CHASING BUTTERFLIES
Davis, Holly
RUMPELSTILTSKIN
De Benedetto, Beatriz
OF LOVE AND SHADOWS
de Laugardiere, Anne
PROPRIETOR, THE
De Nekker, Yvonne
TERMINAL IMPACT
De Toro, Kathleen
VENUS RISING
Dee, Patte
PRE-MADONNAS
Delgato, Ricardo
FUGITIVE RAGE
Delta Burke Design
MATERNAL INSTINCTS
DeSanto, Susie
CHILDREN OF FURY
ONE FINE DAY
Detoro, Kathleen
DONOR UNKNOWN
Deveau, Marie-Sylvie
FLY AWAY HOME
OPEN SEASON
Dicks-Mireaux, Odile
CAPTIVES
Dillon, Rudy
TREMORS 2: AFTERSHOCKS
Dimitrov, Olga
TWO IF BY SEA
Dinulesco, Laura
DEADLY OUTBREAK
Donati, Danilo
MONSTER, THE
Dorleac, Jean-Pierre
LILY DALE
Doron, Rona
UNDER THE DOMIM TREE
Dottori, Catia
MILLE BOLLE BLU
Dresbach, Terry
PIG'S TALE, A
UNFORGETTABLE
Drew, Laurie
WHERE'S THE MONEY, NOREEN?
Dunn, John
BASQUIAT
Duplaga, Marie
VIRUS
Dyehouse, Lisa
PURE DANGER
RAGE
SKYSCRAPER
SWEEPER, THE
TIGER HEART
Eastern Costume Rental
THEY BITE
Echanove, Juan
FLOWER OF MY SECRET, THE
Echerd, Jim
LARRY MCMURTRY'S STREETS OF LAREDO
LONE JUSTICE: SHOWDOWN AT PLUM CREEK
Engelsman, Julie Rae
TALES OF EROTICA
England, Emma
BLOOD & DONUTS
England, Judith
ELECTRA
WHEN THE BULLET HITS THE BONE
Ennis, Elizabeth
NOT OF THIS EARTH
Eshelman, Melinda
SAINTS AND SINNERS
Eshelman, Mindy
FUNERAL, THE
Espinoza, Charmian
DESIRE
Evan-Ivy, Gail
ENTERTAINING ANGELS: THE DOROTHY DAY STORY
Evans, Leesa
LAST SUPPER, THE
Everberg, Kirsten
CROW: CITY OF ANGELS, THE
FEAR

Everett, Dany
AUGUST
JACK & SARAH
Everton, Deborah
CRAFT, THE
LAWNMOWER MAN 2: BEYOND CYBERSPACE
STAR TREK: FIRST CONTACT
Falguiere, Ellen
SHOOTFIGHTER 2: KILL OR BE KILLED!
Fedyszyn, Joan
SEARCH FOR ONE-EYE JIMMY, THE
Fenner, Betty
HARD JUSTICE
Fernandez, Estella
SOLO
Ferrin, Ingrid
MR. WRONG
TIME TO KILL, A
Ferry, April
ASSOCIATE, THE
Feschi, Andrea
DOGFIGHTERS, THE
Field, Patricia
SUBSTITUTE, THE
Fielder, Roseanne
IMMORTALS, THE
Fien, Pennie
ONE MAN'S JUSTICE
Filipe, Ruy
LIVE WIRE: HUMAN TIMEBOMB
Fleming, Rachael
BUTTERFLY KISS
TRAINSPOTTING
Flynt, Cynthia
BED OF ROSES
PREACHER'S WIFE, THE
Folsey, Erin
FAR HARBOR
Fomina, Nelly
BURIAL OF THE RATS
Fort, Mary Jane
INFINITY
Fraisse, Claire
MA SAISON PREFEREE
France, Marie
BULLETPROOF
Frogley, Louise
EXECUTIVE DECISION
PIE IN THE SKY
WAR OF THE BUTTONS, THE
Froiland, Linda
MYSTERY SCIENCE THEATER 3000: THE MOVIE
Fungfuang, Rattana
BLOODSPORT II: THE NEXT KUMITE
Garcia, Magdalena
SILENCES OF THE PALACE, THE
Gardiner, Lizzy
BOUND
Gasc, Christian
MADAME BUTTERFLY
RIDICULE
Geaghan, Debbie
SURGEON, THE
Gearon, Ida
NECRONOMICON: BOOK OF THE DEAD
Gellman, Judy
GETTING AWAY WITH MURDER
Giguere, Edi
DENISE CALLS UP
WALKING AND TALKING
Gill, Tanya
AMERICAN STRAYS
Gillibrand, Nikky
INSTITUTE BENJAMENTA
Glynn, Gloria
GRAVE, THE
Goldsmith, Laura
FOXFIRE
Goldstein, Jess
SUBSTANCE OF FIRE, THE
Graef, Vicki
HOMAGE
Granata, Dona
KANSAS CITY
LOVE IS ALL THERE IS
Gresham, Gloria
GHOSTS OF MISSISSIPPI
SLEEPERS
Grifel, Carolyn
GIRLS TOWN
LOTTO LAND
POMPATUS OF LOVE, THE
Hall, Douglas
SLING BLADE
Hanafin, Hope
FAITHFUL
HOUSE ARREST
KAZAAM
Hannan, Mary Claire
BIO-DOME
CELTIC PRIDE
Harris, Caroline
MIDWINTER'S TALE, A
WAVELENGTH
Harris, Enid
LETTER TO MY KILLER
Heimann, Betsy
JERRY MAGUIRE
2 DAYS IN THE VALLEY
Heinze, Gudrun
JOHNNY SHORTWAVE
Helgenson, Mari
FAST MONEY
Hendrawan, Harry
WITHOUT MERCY
Hernandez, Sandra
GET ON THE BUS
GIRL 6
Hester, Nazhat
LIFEFORM
Hickman, Celestine
MIRROR, MIRROR III: THE VOYEUR
Hirsch, Alison
WILD SIDE
Hiscox, Maureen
GIRL FROM MARS, THE
Hofinger, Ute
BROTHER OF SLEEP
Hogard, Bruce
PHANTOM, THE
Holdich, Charlotte
SOMEONE ELSE'S AMERICA
Hood, Rosalea
TUNNEL VISION
Hooey, Mathew Clayton
SCREAM
Hopper, Deborah
DEAR GOD
Hornung, Richard
CITY HALL
Hovis, Angela Sembera
MAN WITH THE PERFECT SWING, THE
Howe, Monica
NEON BIBLE, THE
Huete, Lala
TWO MUCH
Hurley, Fran
CONDITION RED
Hurley, Jay
JINGLE ALL THE WAY
SKIN
Iglesias, Maria Jose
OUTRAGE
Ilyevtseva, Tatyana
BURIAL OF THE RATS
Ireland, Druh
BREACH OF TRUST
FINAL CUT, THE
Iturregui, Leonardo
MERCY
Jacobsen, Matthew
FLIPPER
SOME FOLKS CALL IT A SLING BLADE
Jaleh
MR. STITCH
Jamison-Tanchuck, Francine
COURAGE UNDER FIRE
Jenkins, Katy
WHISPERING, THE
Jennings, Melanie
LEGEND OF GATOR FACE, THE
TAILS YOU LIVE, HEADS YOU'RE DEAD
Jensen, Judi
PINOCCHIO'S REVENGE
Jesneck, Tim
ANIMAL INSTINCTS III: THE SEDUCTRESS
Jett, Elizabeth
EXIT
HOSTILE INTENTIONS
MIND RIPPER
Jimenez, Jolie Anna
DELTA OF VENUS
Johnson, Lisa
SHAMELESS
Jones, Nena
WATCH ME
Jorry, Corinne
LA CEREMONIE
NELLY AND MONSIEUR ARNAUD
Jusid, Margarita
SHADOW YOU SOON WILL BE, A
Kalfus, Renee Ehrlich
EVENING STAR, THE
Kalinian, Maral
CARNOSAUR 3: PRIMAL SPECIES
DEATH ARTIST, THE
Kaplan, Michael
DIABOLIQUE
LONG KISS GOODNIGHT, THE
Katany, Fabienne
FRENCH TWIST
Katsaras, Jo
REDEMPTION: KICKBOXER 5
Kaufman, Susan
. . . AT FIRST SIGHT
EVIL HAS A FACE
Keating, Trish
CARPOOL
TALES FROM THE CRYPT PRESENTS BORDELLO OF BLOOD
Keech-Swerling, Karen
PUBLIC ENEMIES
Kelemen, Fred
FATE
Kelly, Bridget
TRUTH ABOUT CATS AND DOGS, THE
Kelly, Lyn
RED SCORPION 2
Kelsall, Colleen
LAST DANCE
RICH MAN'S WIFE, THE
Kemp, Lynda
KISSINGER AND NIXON
Kennedy, Eileen
HELLRAISER: BLOODLINE
King, Daniele
IT'S MY PARTY
Kitamura, Michiko
MABOROSI

Krausa, John
PROTEUS
Kreiner, Jillian Ann
BEYOND DESIRE
PLAYBACK
Kurland, Jeffrey
EVERYONE SAYS I LOVE YOU
Landau, Natasha
HEADLESS BODY IN TOPLESS BAR
RASPUTIN
Landry, Noreen
BLOODKNOT
DARKMAN III: DIE DARKMAN DIE
Lapper, Vincent
LITTLE WITCHES
Lavadenz, Agda
AMERICAN STRAYS
Lavery, Gwen
DARK SECRETS
FRIEND OF THE FAMILY 2
LaVoi, Greg
SHARON'S SECRET
Lawson, Merrie
FIST OF THE NORTH STAR
FREEWAY
ONE MAN'S JUSTICE
Lee, Esther
SHOWGIRL MURDERS, THE
Lee, Franne
SWEET NOTHING
Lee, Tonya
MUTANT MAN
Leonard, Karin
CONDITION RED
Leterrier, Catherine
VISITORS, THE
Lettieri, Alfonsina
CEMETERY MAN
Lewis, Robin
ED
Liu Jianhua
BLUSH
Ljung, Katharina
EVIL ED
Loats, Dana
TAKEOVER, THE
Lovaas, Lisa
PHANTOM, THE
Lucci, Mike
SANTA CLAWS
Luo Chung-hung
VIVE L'AMOUR
Lutter, Ellen
FLIRTING WITH DISASTER
Lyall, Susan
EXTREME MEASURES
SHE'S THE ONE
MacDonald, Aleida
GETTING AWAY WITH MURDER
MacKay, Lynne
BEYOND THE CALL
Madden, Betty Pecha
HEIDI CHRONICLES, THE
Maginnis, Molly
EDDIE
Major, Ross
SPIDER & ROSE
Makovsky, Judianna
WHITE SQUALL
Malin, Mary
BROKEN ARROW
Martynova, Nina
WOLVES, THE
Maslansky, Stephanie
JOE'S APARTMENT
Massone, Nicoletta
HOLLOW POINT
Matheson, Linda
MRS. MUNCK
May, Mona
HIGH SCHOOL HIGH
Mazon, Graciela
FROM DUSK TILL DAWN
McBride, Elizabeth
MICHAEL
McKay, Marcelle
WITCHCRAFT: SALEM'S GHOST
McKinley, Tom
CITIZEN RUTH
McManus, Jennifer
GALAXIES ARE COLLIDING
PUBLIC ACCESS
McMullen, Gail
WHOLE WIDE WORLD, THE
McPherson, Winkie
HIDDEN ASSASSIN
Meachem, Stewart
LOADED
YOUNG POISONER'S HANDBOOK, THE
Melgaard, Mimi
LITTLE DEATH, THE
Meltzer, Ileane
MAD DOG TIME
TUSKEGEE AIRMEN, THE
Meus, Loret
SUITE 16
Mezcua, Hugo
FLOWER OF MY SECRET, THE
Michel, Michelle
BREAKAWAY
Millenotti, Maurizio
ADVENTURES OF PINOCCHIO, THE
CEMETERY MAN
Miller, Roxanne
FEMALIEN
Mingenbach, Louise
ONE NIGHT STAND
SPITFIRE GRILL, THE
Mirojnick, Ellen
GHOST AND THE DARKNESS, THE
MULHOLLAND FALLS
Mirojnik, Ellen
TWISTER
Moffie, Lisa
ORIGINAL GANGSTAS
Monoghan, Tish
HAPPY GILMORE
Montaldo, Elisabetta
WHO KILLED PASOLINI?
Montel, Virginie
HATE
Montgomery, Morgan
TRACKS OF A KILLER
Moore, Dan
LAST MAN STANDING
Moore, Robert
COLONY, THE
Moore, Tami
PIRANHA
Mor, Tami
BLACK ROSE OF HARLEM
Moriceau, Norma
ISLAND OF DR. MOREAU, THE
Morris, Camille
CLUBHOUSE DETECTIVES
Morris, Tania
PORTRAITS OF A KILLER
Mueller, Michael
MAN OF THE YEAR
Mulholland, Vicky
SABRINA, THE TEENAGE WITCH
Murray, Abigail
PROPRIETOR, THE
Mussenden, Isis
DAYLIGHT
Myers, Ruth
BOGUS
EMMA
Nadoolman, Deborah
STUPIDS, THE
Neil, Warden
DENTIST, THE
WEEKEND IN THE COUNTRY, A
Newhall, Deborah
AMERICAN BUFFALO
Nguyen, Ha
NORMA JEAN AND MARILYN
NUTTY PROFESSOR, THE
STEPHEN KING'S THINNER
Nick, Desiree
NEUROSIA: 50 YEARS OF PERVERSITY
Nieradzik, Anushia
JOSEPH CONRAD'S THE SECRET AGENT
Nixon, Barb
WHITE TIGER
Nixon, Kathryn
WIFE, THE
Nolin, Stephanie
HOMEWARD BOUND II: LOST IN SAN FRANCISCO
Norton, Rosanna
BARB WIRE
VERY BRADY SEQUEL, A
Nosella, Karen
ROBIN OF LOCKSLEY
O. K. Uniforms
BUGGED
Oditz, Carol
TIN CUP
Ohanneson, Jill
BLACK SHEEP
Orlandi, Daniel
FAN, THE
Palmer, Barbara
WIDOW'S KISS
Panova, Alina
DUNSTON CHECKS IN
Papio, Ariadna
CELESTIAL CLOCKWORK
Paredes, Marisa
FLOWER OF MY SECRET, THE
Parker, Jennifer
MANNY & LO
Parker, Rodger
SOLITAIRE FOR TWO
Partridge, Wendy
HOW THE WEST WAS FUN
Pasternak, Beth
CURTIS'S CHARM
Patch, Karen
BOTTLE ROCKET
Paterson, Candy
HAUNTED
Patterson, Janet
PORTRAIT OF A LADY, THE
Paunescu, Oana
JOSH KIRBY . . . TIME WARRIOR!: EGGS FROM 70,000,000 B.C.
JOSH KIRBY . . . TIME WARRIOR!: JOURNEY TO THE MAGIC CAVERN
JOSH KIRBY . . . TIME WARRIOR!: LAST BATTLE FOR THE UNIVERSE
JOSH KIRBY . . . TIME WARRIOR!: TRAPPED ON TOY WORLD
MAGIC IN THE MIRROR
SPELLBREAKER: SECRET OF THE LEPRECHAUNS
Pehrsson, Inger
CHILDREN OF NOISY VILLAGE, THE
Perkins, Kari
TEXAS CHAINSAW MASSACRE: THE NEXT GENERATION
Petrovici, Viorica
MAGIC IN THE MIRROR

Phillips, Arianne
4 TALES OF 2 CITIES
PEOPLE VS. LARRY FLYNT, THE
Phillips, Erica Edell
CABLE GUY, THE
Pistek, Theodor
PEOPLE VS. LARRY FLYNT, THE
Polcsa, Juliet
BIG NIGHT
Porro, Joseph
INDEPENDENCE DAY
MAXIMUM RISK
QUEST, THE
Portillo, Claudia
TWO-BITS & PEPPER
Powell, Anthony
101 DALMATIANS
Powell, Sandy
MICHAEL COLLINS
Powell-Parker, Marianne
DESOLATION ANGELS
Preston, Grania
CARRIED AWAY
FIRST KID
WAR AT HOME, THE
Price, Maria
SECRETS & LIES
Priest, Heather
HEAD OF THE FAMILY
Prudhomme, Monique
ALASKA
BIG BULLY
Puisto, Susana
UNDER THE HULA MOON
Pye, Celia
HEDD WYNN
Radakovic, Julia
WIND IN THE WILLOWS, THE
Radovanov, Christine
CHILDREN OF THE CORN: THE GATHERING
Ramon Fiddler, Rina
PIRANHA
UNKNOWN ORIGIN
Ramsey, Carol
SUNSET PARK
SURVIVING PICASSO
Ramsey, Van Broughton
LONE JUSTICE: SHOWDOWN AT PLUM CREEK
ROAD TO GALVESTON, THE
Range, Wendy
AMANDA AND THE ALIEN
DEAD WEEKEND
Rapin, Martine
LITTLE INDIAN, BIG CITY
Rasmussen, Manon
BREAKING THE WAVES
Raynor, Mary Partridge
HOMECOMING
Read, Bobbie
EYE FOR AN EYE
MISSING PIECES
OFF AND RUNNING
ROCK, THE
Reichle, Luke
DOWN PERISCOPE
GLIMMER MAN, THE
Reimers, Nadine
MOTHER
Remy, Diemut
KASPAR HAUSER
Ren Zhiwen
BLACK MOUNTAIN
Renaissance Goddess Unlimited
ORIGINAL SINS
Richt, Tami
EXIT
Riggs, Rita
BAD MOON
UNDERTOW
Robbins, Gayle Alden
MODERN AFFAIR, A
Roberts, Amy
COLD COMFORT FARM
Robinson, David
I SHOT ANDY WARHOL
Robinson, Jane
HAUNTED
LARGER THAN LIFE
Roche, Michael
JOSH KIRBY . . . TIME WARRIOR!: EGGS FROM 70,000,000 B.C.
JOSH KIRBY . . . TIME WARRIOR!: LAST BATTLE FOR THE UNIVERSE
JOSH KIRBY . . . TIME WARRIOR!: TRAPPED ON TOY WORLD
SPELLBREAKER: SECRET OF THE LEPRECHAUNS
Rodgers, Aggie Guerard
JACK
MR. HOLLAND'S OPUS
Roldan, Damita J.
SERIAL KILLER
Rose, Penny
EVITA
IN LOVE AND WAR
MISSION: IMPOSSIBLE
Rosenberg, Sharon
IT CAME FROM OUTER SPACE II
Rosenblatt, Jana
PHARAOH'S ARMY
Rosenfeld, Hilary
CAUGHT
Roswell, Arthur
BOYS NEXT DOOR, THE
Roth, Allison
RED LINE
Roth, Ann
BEFORE AND AFTER
BIRDCAGE, THE
ENGLISH PATIENT, THE
Rubeo, Mayes C.
ARRIVAL, THE
Ruhm, Jane
MATILDA
Ruskin, Judy L.
MOTHER
Ryack, Rita
FAN, THE
RANSOM
Sacks, Renee Alaina
BEST OF THE BEST 3: NO TURNING BACK
Safier, Beverly Nelson
CURDLED
Saint Anne, Jacqueline
NORMAL LIFE
Saldutti, Gary J.
SCREAM
Sanchez, Vicki
HARVEST OF FIRE
Schclair, Julia
TEXAS PAYBACK
Schlaich, Anne
HALFMOON
Schrader, M.T.
NEUROSIA: 50 YEARS OF PERVERSITY
Schreiner, Charmian
BIG SQUEEZE, THE
Schure, Joyce
IRON EAGLE IV
Schwarzer, Suzanne
VIRTUAL COMBAT
Scott, Deborah L.
TO GILLIAN ON HER 37TH BIRTHDAY
Seeman, Tanya
NATIONAL LAMPOON'S FAVORITE DEADLY SINS
Segal, Israel
LIVE NUDE GIRLS
Sequeira, Luis
MOONSHINE HIGHWAY
Sheppard, Anna
DRAGONHEART
Silverman, Julie
HOURGLASS
Simmons, Charmaine
FOR BETTER OR WORSE
Simmons, Paul
ASSAULT AT WEST POINT
Sircus, Maura
ED'S NEXT MOVE
Slinger, Julie
JAMES AND THE GIANT PEACH
Slotnik, Sara Jane
HEAVY
Smith, Polly
MUPPET TREASURE ISLAND
Squarciapino, Franca
HORSEMAN ON THE ROOF
Stat-Tyskiewicz, Gabriela
MOTHER OF KINGS
Stauch, Bonnie
BLACK DAY BLUE NIGHT
BODY OF INFLUENCE 2
Stauch, Bonnie Ann
SAWBONES
SOMETIMES THEY COME BACK . . . AGAIN
Stephensen, Tessa
UNHOOK THE STARS
Stevenson, Tammy
TALKING ABOUT SEX
Stewart, Marlene
SPACE JAM
Stjernsward, Louise
STEALING BEAUTY
Stolz, Mary Kay
NATIONAL LAMPOON'S FAVORITE DEADLY SINS
Summers, Cynthia
MATERNAL INSTINCTS
Sussman, Howard
MADDENING, THE
Symons, Annie
MADAGASCAR SKIN
Szakacs, Gyorgyi
MAGIC HUNTER
Tait, Pamela
BEAUTIFUL THING
VIKING SAGAS, THE
Talsky, Ron
BLACK OUT
Tarasova, Marina
WOLVES, THE
Tavernier, Elisabeth
LES VOLEURS
MACHINE, THE
Tax, Jan
DAENS
Temime, Jany
ANTONIA'S LINE
Tempest, Frances
AFFAIR, THE
Thalheimer, Mona
PHAT BEACH
Thomas, Todd
ANGELA
Thomson, Tamara
WHITE WOLVES II: LEGEND OF THE WILD
Tillman, Kimberly A.
D3: THE MIGHTY DUCKS

Tompkins, Joe I.
FAMILY THING, A
Toth, Melissa
WELCOME TO THE DOLLHOUSE
Turturice, Robert
JAG
Tynan, Tracy
CHAMBER, THE
Tyrrell, Genevieve
SWINGERS
Van Flandern, Constance
GIRLFRIENDS
Vega-Vasquez, Sylvia
CHAMELEON
SET IT OFF
Verhoeven, Anne
PASSION OF DARKLY NOON, THE
Vogel, Vanessa
BOY CALLED HATE, A
Vogt, Mary
THEODORE REX
Von Martius, Katharina
MAYBE . . . MAYBE NOT
Von Mayrhauser, Jennifer
I'M NOT RAPPAPORT
Vuskovic, Loreto
JOHNNY 100 PESOS
Wachsler, Susan
PHOENIX
Wade, Sheila
DON'T LET YOUR MEAT LOAF
Wagner, Cathryn
CROSSCUT
LOVER'S KNOT
SANTA WITH MUSCLES
Wakefield, Louise
SHINE
Waller, Elizabeth
TWO DEATHS
Weiss, Julie
MARVIN'S ROOM
Welker, Alexandra
FLIRT
LOW LIFE, THE
Westover, Alex
FUNNYMAN, THE
White, Delphine
KIDS IN THE HALL: BRAIN CANDY
Wilson, Margot
RACE THE SUN
Winston, Mary Ellen
MISSING PIECES
Wolfe, Paki
POISON IVY 2: LILY
Wolsky, Albert
GRASS HARP, THE
STRIPTEASE
UP CLOSE AND PERSONAL
Wood, Durina
RIDERS OF THE PURPLE SAGE
Wright, Jocelyn F.
LOSING CHASE
Wurmser, Gloria
SILENCE OF NETO, THE
Wyman, Tami Mor
UNKNOWN ORIGIN
Yamin, Mandana
OVER THE WIRE
Yano, Kei
FRAME BY FRAME
Yao Huiming
CHUNGKING EXPRESS
Yates, Janty
CRACKER: THE MADWOMAN IN THE ATTIC
JUDE
Ynocencio, Jo
DEATH BENEFIT
Zakowska, Donna
HARRIET THE SPY
PALLBEARER, THE
Zech, Ushi
SURGEON, THE
Zimelman, Jodi
ZARKORR! THE INVADER
Zitrick, Kelly
TOLLBOOTH
Zophres, Mary
FARGO
KINGPIN

DIRECTORS

Abey, Dennis
WIND IN THE WILLOWS, THE
Adler, Gilbert
TALES FROM THE CRYPT PRESENTS BORDELLO OF BLOOD
Alexander, Jason
FOR BETTER OR WORSE
Allen, Woody
EVERYONE SAYS I LOVE YOU
Almodovar, Pedro
FLOWER OF MY SECRET, THE
Altman, Robert
KANSAS CITY
Anders, Allison
GRACE OF MY HEART
Anderson, Kurt
DEAD COLD
Anderson, Paul
SHOPPING
Anderson, Wes
BOTTLE ROCKET
Andreef, Christina
GIRLFRIENDS
Anthony, Robert
WITHOUT MERCY
Apon, Annette
CROCODILES IN AMSTERDAM
Apramian, Lisa Rose
NOT BAD FOR A GIRL
Apted, Michael
EXTREME MEASURES
Argueta, Luis
SILENCE OF NETO, THE
Armstrong, Andy
MOONSHINE HIGHWAY
Armstrong, Ronald K.
BUGGED
Arnold, Frank
JOSH KIRBY . . . TIME WARRIOR!: LAST BATTLE FOR THE UNIVERSE
JOSH KIRBY . . . TIME WARRIOR!: TRAPPED ON TOY WORLD
Assayas, Olivier
NEW LIFE, A
Attenborough, Richard
IN LOVE AND WAR
Aubrey, Jay
LOOKING FOR TROUBLE
Auerbach, Gary
JUST YOUR LUCK
Avary, Roger
MR. STITCH
Avery, Rick
DEADLY OUTBREAK
Avnet, Jon
UP CLOSE AND PERSONAL
Bacon, Kevin
LOSING CHASE
Baigelman, Steven
FEELING MINNESOTA
Baird, Stuart
EXECUTIVE DECISION
Baker, Mark H.
LIFEFORM
Balasko, Josiane
FRENCH TWIST
Baldwin, Craig
SONIC OUTLAWS
Ballard, Carroll
FLY AWAY HOME
Barba, Norberto
SOLO
Barclay, Paris
AMERICA'S DREAM
DON'T BE A MENACE TO SOUTH CENTRAL WHILE DRINKING YOUR JUICE IN THE HOOD
Barish, Leora
VENUS RISING
Barmettler Jr., J.J.
WITCHCRAFT: SALEM'S GHOST
Barr, Douglas
FRAME BY FRAME
Barreto, Bruno
CARRIED AWAY
Barron, Steve
ADVENTURES OF PINOCCHIO, THE
Battle, Murray
STAND OFF, THE
Bay, Michael
ROCK, THE
Beaumont, Gabrielle
BEASTMASTER 3: THE EYE OF BRAXUS
Becker, Harold
CITY HALL
Bell, Dan
SHOT, THE
Bellisario, Donald P.
JAG
Bender, Jack
LONE JUSTICE: SHOWDOWN AT PLUM CREEK
Benedict, Terry
PAINTED HERO
Benigni, Roberto
MONSTER, THE
Benjamin, Richard
MRS. WINTERBOURNE
Bennett, Bill
SPIDER & ROSE
TWO IF BY SEA
Benson, Michael
PREDICTIONS OF FIRE
Beresford, Bruce
LAST DANCE
Berger, Howard
ORIGINAL SINS
Bergman, Andrew
STRIPTEASE
Bergman, Martin
WEEKEND IN THE COUNTRY, A
Berlinger, Joe
PARADISE LOST: THE CHILD MURDERS AT ROBIN HOOD HILLS
Bertolucci, Bernardo
STEALING BEAUTY
Betuel, Jonathan
THEODORE REX
Bianchi, Edward
OFF AND RUNNING
Bill, Tony
BEYOND THE CALL
Bishop, Larry
MAD DOG TIME
Blair, Jon
ANNE FRANK REMEMBERED
Bloom, Jason
BIO-DOME
Bochner, Hart
HIGH SCHOOL HIGH

Bockner, Michael
JOHNNY SHORTWAVE
Bogart, Paul
HEIDI CHRONICLES, THE
Bologna, Joseph
LOVE IS ALL THERE IS
Bond, Timothy
NIGHT OF THE TWISTERS
Bonniere, Rene
HALFBACK OF NOTRE DAME, THE
Bookwalter, J. R.
POLYMORPH
Bookwalter, J.R.
SANDMAN, THE
Bowen, John
DARK SECRETS
Boyle, Danny
TRAINSPOTTING
Braddock, Reb
CURDLED
Bradshaw, Randy
SONG SPINNER, THE
Branagh, Kenneth
HAMLET
MIDWINTER'S TALE, A
Bravo, Edgar
VENUS RISING
Bressan Jr., Arthur J.
ABUSE
Breziner, Salome
TOLLBOOTH
Bright, Matthew
FREEWAY
Broderick, Matthew
INFINITY
Brooks, Albert
MOTHER
Broomfield, Nick
HEIDI FLEISS HOLLYWOOD MADAM
Brothers Quay, The
INSTITUTE BENJAMENTA
Bruce, James
HEADLESS BODY IN TOPLESS BAR
Burns, Edward
SHE'S THE ONE
Burr, Jeff
NIGHT OF THE SCARECROW
Burton, Kenneth J.
MERLIN'S SHOP OF MAGICAL WONDERS
Burton, Tim
MARS ATTACKS!
Buscemi, Steve
TREES LOUNGE
Cammell, Donald
WILD SIDE
Campbell, Graeme
MAN IN THE ATTIC, THE
Campion, Anna
LOADED
Campion, Jane
PORTRAIT OF A LADY, THE
TWO FRIENDS
Card, Lamar
SHADOW WARRIORS
Cardone, J.S.
BLACK DAY BLUE NIGHT
Carpenter, John
JOHN CARPENTER'S ESCAPE FROM L.A.
Carver, Steve
WOLVES, THE
Cassavetes, Nick
UNHOOK THE STARS
Castle, Nick
MR. WRONG
Celantano, Jeff
UNDER THE HULA MOON
Chabrol, Claude
EYE OF VICHY, THE
LA CEREMONIE
Chamchoum, Georges
TIGER HEART
Chapman, Michael
VIKING SAGAS, THE
Chechik, Jeremiah
DIABOLIQUE
Chik Ki Yee
MIDNIGHT ANGEL
Ching, Lipo
WATCH ME
Chionglo, Mel
MIDNIGHT DANCERS
Christian, Roger
FINAL CUT, THE
Chubbuck, Lyndon
NAKED SOULS
Cicoritti, Gerard
UNDERSTUDY: GRAVEYARD SHIFT 2, THE
Cimino, Michael
SUNCHASER
Clay, Carl
LET'S GET BIZZEE
Clucher, E.B.
SONS OF TRINITY
Cochran, Stacy
BOYS
Coen, Joel
FARGO
Cohen, Eli
UNDER THE DOMIM TREE
Cohen, Larry
ORIGINAL GANGSTAS
Cohen, Rob
DAYLIGHT
DRAGONHEART
Cole, Henry
SHAMELESS
Collins, John Laurence
BRITT ALLCROFT'S MAGIC ADVENTURES OF MUMFIE—THE MOVIE
Coninx, Stijn
DAENS
Cook, Luis
WALLACE AND GROMIT: THE BEST OF AARDMAN ANIMATION
Cook, Troy
PHOENIX
TAKEOVER, THE
Coppola, Francis Ford
JACK
Coraci, Frank
MURDERED INNOCENCE
Corcoran, Bill
PORTRAITS OF A KILLER
Corrente, Michael
AMERICAN BUFFALO
Couturie, Bill
ED
Covert, Michael
AMERICAN STRAYS
Craven, Wes
SCREAM
Cribben, Mik
BEWARE: CHILDREN AT PLAY
Crowe, Cameron
JERRY MAGUIRE
Cutler, R.J.
PERFECT CANDIDATE, A
Cyran, Catherine
HOSTILE INTENTIONS
SAWBONES
Dahl, John
UNFORGETTABLE
Dale, Holly
BLOOD & DONUTS
Dash, Sean
BREAKAWAY
David, Pierre
SERIAL KILLER
Davies, Terence
NEON BIBLE, THE
Davis, Andrew
CHAIN REACTION
De Bont, Jan
TWISTER
De Cerchio, Tom
CELTIC PRIDE
De Leon, Marcus
BIG SQUEEZE, THE
De Palma, Brian
MISSION: IMPOSSIBLE
DeLaurentis, Suzanne
MUTANT MAN
Demme, Ted
BEAUTIFUL GIRLS
Densham, Pen
MOLL FLANDERS
Deruddere, Dominique
SUITE 16
DeVito, Danny
MATILDA
Diamonde, Lucian S.
FORBIDDEN ZONE: ALIEN ABDUCTION
Dickerson, Ernest
BULLETPROOF
Dindo, Richard
ERNESTO CHE GUEVARA—THE BOLIVIAN DIARY
Douglas, Illeana
4 TALES OF 2 CITIES
Draskovic, Boro
VUKOVAR
Dryfoos, Susan W.
LINE KING: THE AL HIRSCHFELD STORY, THE
Duchowny, Roger
IT CAME FROM OUTER SPACE II
Dugan, Dennis
HAPPY GILMORE
Duguay, Christian
SCREAMERS
Duke, Bill
AMERICA'S DREAM
Dunne, Griffin
4 TALES OF 2 CITIES
Dunye, Cheryl
GIRLFRIENDS
Dupeyron, Francois
MACHINE, THE
Edel, Uli
RASPUTIN
Elikann, Larry
MOTHER'S PRAYER, A
Ellin, Doug
PHAT BEACH
Ellis, David R.
HOMEWARD BOUND II: LOST IN SAN FRANCISCO
Emmerich, Roland
INDEPENDENCE DAY
Enyedi, Ildiko
MAGIC HUNTER
Ephron, Nora
MICHAEL
Epstein, Rob
CELLULOID CLOSET, THE
Erman, John
BOYS NEXT DOOR, THE
Esposito, Joe
SOUTH BEACH ACADEMY

Estevez, Emilio
WAR AT HOME, THE
Eubanks, Corey Michael
TWO-BITS & PEPPER
Evans, David Mickey
FIRST KID
Everitt, Tim
FATALLY YOURS
TOO FAST, TOO YOUNG
Farino, Ernest
JOSH KIRBY . . . TIME WARRIOR!: JOURNEY TO THE MAGIC CAVERN
Farrelly, Bobby
KINGPIN
Farrelly, Peter
KINGPIN
Fearnley, Neill
GIRL FROM MARS, THE
Ferrara, Abel
FUNERAL, THE
Finch, Nigel
STONEWALL
Fitzgerald, Jon
APART FROM HUGH
Fleming, Andrew
CRAFT, THE
Fleury, Clive
TUNNEL VISION
Foldes, Lawrence D.
PRE-MADONNAS
Foldy, Peter
WIDOW'S KISS
Foley, James
CHAMBER, THE
FEAR
Forman, Milos
PEOPLE VS. LARRY FLYNT, THE
Frakes, Jonathan
STAR TREK: FIRST CONTACT
Frankenheimer, John
ISLAND OF DR. MOREAU, THE
Franklin, Howard
LARGER THAN LIFE
Frears, Stephen
MARY REILLY
Fresco, Rob
EVIL HAS A FACE
Fridriksson, Fridrik Thor
COLD FEVER
Friedberg, Rick
SPY HARD
Friedman, Jeffrey
CELLULOID CLOSET, THE
Frost, Harvey
TRACKS OF A KILLER
Fry, Benjamin
WAVELENGTH
Furie, Sidney J.
HOLLOW POINT
IRON EAGLE IV
Fywell, Tim
NORMA JEAN AND MARILYN
Gage, Beth
FIRE ON THE MOUNTAIN
Gage, George
FIRE ON THE MOUNTAIN
Gallo, Fred
BLACK ROSE OF HARLEM
Gans, Christophe
NECRONOMICON: BOOK OF THE DEAD
Gardner, Herb
I'M NOT RAPPAPORT
Gast, Leon
WHEN WE WERE KINGS
Gayton, Joe
MIND RIPPER
George, Terry
SOME MOTHER'S SON

Gibson, Brian
JUROR, THE
Gieras, Gregory
WHISPERING, THE
Gilbert, Lewis
HAUNTED
Gillard, Stuart
OUTER LIMITS: SANDKINGS, THE
Ginsberg, Milton Moses
CATWALK
Giordana, Marco Tullio
WHO KILLED PASOLINI?
Glaser, Paul Michael
KAZAAM
Golden, Dan
BURIAL OF THE RATS
Goldenberg, Michael
BED OF ROSES
Goldman, Jill
BAD LOVE
Goldstein, Allan A.
BLACK OUT
VIRUS
Goleszowski, Richard
WALLACE AND GROMIT: THE BEST OF AARDMAN ANIMATION
Gomer, Steve
SUNSET PARK
Gordon, Bryan
PIE IN THE SKY
Gordon, Keith
MOTHER NIGHT
Gordon, Rachel
MIRROR, MIRROR III: THE VOYEUR
Gorris, Marleen
ANTONIA'S LINE
Gothar, Peter
OUTPOST, THE
Goursaud, Anne
POISON IVY 2: LILY
Gout, Alberto
AVENTURERA
Graef-Marino, Gustavo
JOHNNY 100 PESOS
Grant, Brian
IMMORTALS, THE
Grant, Julian
ELECTRA
Gray, F. Gary
SET IT OFF
Gray, John
GLIMMER MAN, THE
Grossman, Adam
SOMETIMES THEY COME BACK . . . AGAIN
Haas, Philip
ANGELS AND INSECTS
Haid, Charles
CHILDREN OF FURY
RIDERS OF THE PURPLE SAGE
Hail, Mack
MR. ICE CREAM MAN
Hallstrom, Lasse
CHILDREN OF NOISY VILLAGE, THE
Hamilton, Dean
ROAD HOME, THE
Hampton, Christopher
JOSEPH CONRAD'S THE SECRET AGENT
Hanks, Tom
THAT THING YOU DO!
Harada, Masato
KAMIKAZE TAXI
Harlin, Renny
LONG KISS GOODNIGHT, THE
Harling, Robert
EVENING STAR, THE
Harrison, John
DONOR UNKNOWN

Harron, Mary
I SHOT ANDY WARHOL
Hart, Chris
TIMELESS
Hartley, Hal
FLIRT
Haywood-Carter, Annette
FOXFIRE
Hedden, Rob
COLONY, THE
Heller, Barbara
GIRLFRIENDS
Hemmings, David
LONE JUSTICE: SHOWDOWN AT PLUM CREEK
Hendershot, Eric
CLUBHOUSE DETECTIVES
Henkel, Kim
TEXAS CHAINSAW MASSACRE: THE NEXT GENERATION
Henson, Brian
MUPPET TREASURE ISLAND
Henson, Robby
PHARAOH'S ARMY
Herek, Stephen
MR. HOLLAND'S OPUS
101 DALMATIANS
Hertel, Gene
SHOWGIRL MURDERS, THE
Herz, Michael
SGT. KABUKIMAN N.Y.P.D.
Herzfeld, John
2 DAYS IN THE VALLEY
Heston, Fraser C.
ALASKA
Hexter, Russ
DADETOWN
Hickenlooper, George
LOW LIFE, THE
SOME FOLKS CALL IT A SLING BLADE
Hicks, Scott
SHINE
Hill, Walter
LAST MAN STANDING
Hiller, Arthur
CARPOOL
Hippolyte, Gregory
ANIMAL INSTINCTS III: THE SEDUCTRESS
Hlavin, John
FLATTERED
Hoblit, Gregory
PRIMAL FEAR
Hoffman, Michael
ONE FINE DAY
Hofmeyr, Gray
YANKEE ZULU
Hogan, David
BARB WIRE
Holcomb, Rod
DEAD TO RIGHTS
Holland, Tom
STEPHEN KING'S THINNER
Holofcener, Nicole
WALKING AND TALKING
Hooks, Kevin
FLED
Hopkins, Anthony
AUGUST
Hopkins, Stephen
GHOST AND THE DARKNESS, THE
Hovis, Michael
MAN WITH THE PERFECT SWING, THE
Howard, Ron
RANSOM
Howe, Matthew
ORIGINAL SINS

Howell, C. Thomas
HOURGLASS
PURE DANGER
Hsu, Talun
BODY COUNT
Huddles, John
FAR HARBOR
Hudlin, Reginald
GREAT WHITE HYPE, THE
Hughes, Bronwen
HARRIET THE SPY
Huston, Danny
MADDENING, THE
Huston, Jimmy
WHARF RAT, THE
Hytner, Nicholas
CRUCIBLE, THE
Ichaso, Leon
BITTER SUGAR
Iosseliani, Otar
CHASING BUTTERFLIES
Ireland, Dan
WHOLE WIDE WORLD, THE
Irmas, Matthew
EDIE & PEN
Irvin, Sam
BACKLASH: OBLIVION 2
OUT THERE
Ivory, James
SURVIVING PICASSO
Jablin, David
NATIONAL LAMPOON'S FAVORITE DEADLY SINS
Jackson, Peter
FRIGHTENERS, THE
Jacobson, Mandy
CALLING THE GHOSTS: A STORY ABOUT RAPE, WAR AND WOMEN
Jacobsson, Anders
EVIL ED
Jacquot, Benoit
SINGLE GIRL, A
Jarmusch, Jim
DEAD MAN
Jean, Mark
HOMECOMING
Jelincic, Karmen
CALLING THE GHOSTS: A STORY ABOUT RAPE, WAR AND WOMEN
Jensen, Johnny E.
LAZARUS MAN, THE
Jewison, Norman
BOGUS
Joanou, Phil
HEAVEN'S PRISONERS
Johnston, Aaron Kim
FOR THE MOMENT
Jones, Amy Holden
RICH MAN'S WIFE, THE
Jones, Mark
RUMPELSTILTSKIN
Jordan, Glenn
STREETCAR NAMED DESIRE, A
Jordan, Neil
MICHAEL COLLINS
Judge, Mike
BEAVIS AND BUTT-HEAD DO AMERICA
Kaczender, George
MATERNAL INSTINCTS
Kaneko, Shusuke
NECRONOMICON: BOOK OF THE DEAD
Kanganis, Charles T.
RACE THE SUN
Kaplan, Betty
OF LOVE AND SHADOWS
Kaplan, Mindy
DEVOTION

Kass, Sam Henry
SEARCH FOR ONE-EYE JIMMY, THE
Kassovitz, Mathieu
HATE
Kaufman, Lloyd
SGT. KABUKIMAN N.Y.P.D.
Kaurismaki, Mika
CONDITION RED
Keen, Bob
PROTEUS
Kelemen, Fred
FATE
Kennedy, Michael
RED SCORPION 2
ROBIN OF LOCKSLEY
King, Zalman
DELTA OF VENUS
Kitakubo, Hiroyuki
ROUJIN-Z
Kitchell, Mark
BERKELEY IN THE 60S
Kleiser, Randal
IT'S MY PARTY
Koepp, David
TRIGGER EFFECT, THE
Kore-eda, Hirokazu
MABOROSI
Korty, John
LONG ROAD HOME, THE
Kotcheff, Ted
HIDDEN ASSASSIN
Kroll, Jon
AMANDA AND THE ALIEN
Krueger, Lisa
MANNY & LO
Kurtzman, Robert
DEMOLITIONIST, THE
Kwapis, Ken
DUNSTON CHECKS IN
L'Ecuyer, John
CURTIS'S CHARM
Ladd, Diane
MRS. MUNCK
Laloggia, Frank
MOTHER
Lam, Ringo
MAXIMUM RISK
Landis, John
STUPIDS, THE
Lavin, Julianna
LIVE NUDE GIRLS
Lawrence, Martin
THIN LINE BETWEEN LOVE AND HATE, A
Leacock, Robert
CATWALK
Leary, Denis
NATIONAL LAMPOON'S FAVORITE DEADLY SINS
Leconte, Patrice
RIDICULE
Lee, Damian
WHEN THE BULLET HITS THE BONE
Lee, Iara
SYNTHETIC PLEASURES
Lee, Spike
GET ON THE BUS
GIRL 6
Lehmann, Michael
TRUTH ABOUT CATS AND DOGS, THE
Leigh, Mike
SECRETS & LIES
Leker, Larry
ALL DOGS GO TO HEAVEN 2
Lerner, Dan
LONE JUSTICE: SHOWDOWN AT PLUM CREEK

Lerner, Murray
MESSAGE TO LOVE: THE ISLE OF WIGHT FESTIVAL
Lester, Mark
PUBLIC ENEMIES
Levant, Brian
JINGLE ALL THE WAY
Levinson, Barry
SLEEPERS
Levy, Scott
PIRANHA
UNKNOWN ORIGIN
Li Shaohong
BLUSH
Lieberman, Robert
D3: THE MIGHTY DUCKS
Liman, Doug
SWINGERS
Lindsay-Hogg, Michael
ROLLING STONES ROCK-AND-ROLL CIRCUS, THE
Loach, Ken
LAND AND FREEDOM
Lord, Peter
WALLACE AND GROMIT: THE BEST OF AARDMAN ANIMATION
Lowry, Dick
SKIN
Luhrmann, Baz
WILLIAM SHAKESPEARE'S ROMEO + JULIET
Lyman, Michel
PHANTOM 2040: THE GHOST WHO WALKS
Lynn, Jonathan
SGT. BILKO
Macartney, Syd
CANTERVILLE GHOST, THE
Macdonald, Hettie
BEAUTIFUL THING
MacKinnon, Gillies
SMALL FACES
Mak Tai Kit
WICKED CITY, THE
Makin, Kelly
KIDS IN THE HALL: BRAIN CANDY
Mallon, Jim
MYSTERY SCIENCE THEATER 3000: THE MOVIE
Mandel, Robert
SUBSTITUTE, THE
Mandelberg, Artie
WHERE'S THE MONEY, NOREEN?
Mangold, James
HEAVY
Mann, Farhad
LAWNMOWER MAN 2: BEYOND CYBERSPACE
Manos, Mark
JOSH KIRBY . . . TIME WARRIOR!: EGGS FROM 70,000,000 B.C.
Marcus, Mitch
BOY CALLED HATE, A
Margolin, Stuart
HOW THE WEST WAS FUN
Markowitz, Robert
TUSKEGEE AIRMEN, THE
Marks, Ross Kagan
HOMAGE
Marshall, Garry
DEAR GOD
Marshall, Penny
PREACHER'S WIFE, THE
Martin, Richard
WHITE TIGER
Martin, Steven M.
THEREMIN: AN ELECTRONIC ODYSSEY
Martino, Raymond
SKYSCRAPER

Marzano, Joe
ONE LESS EGG TO FRY
Masterson, Peter
LILY DALE
Matheson, Tim
TAILS YOU LIVE, HEADS YOU'RE DEAD
Matthau, Charles
GRASS HARP, THE
Matthews, Paul
GRIM
May, Bradford
DARKMAN III: DIE DARKMAN DIE
Mazursky, Paul
FAITHFUL
McCann, Tim
DESOLATION ANGELS
McClary, J. Michael
ANNIE O
McDonald, Michael James
DEATH ARTIST, THE
McDonald, Rodney
DESIRE
McGrath, Douglas
EMMA
McKay, Jim
GIRLS TOWN
McNaughton, John
NORMAL LIFE
Medina, Nicholas
FRIEND OF THE FAMILY 2
OVER THE WIRE
Mehrez, Alan
BLOODSPORT II: THE NEXT KUMITE
Merchant, Ismail
PROPRIETOR, THE
Merhi, Joseph
RAGE
SWEEPER, THE
Merriweather, George
BLONDES HAVE MORE GUNS
Meyers, Janet
LETTER TO MY KILLER
Michels, Barbara Rose
GIRLFRIENDS
Mikhalkov, Nikita
ANNA
Miller, Allan
SMALL WONDERS
Miller, Harvey
GETTING AWAY WITH MURDER
Miller, Michael
DANGEROUS PASSION
Miller, Rebecca
ANGELA
Miner, Steve
BIG BULLY
Minghella, Anthony
ENGLISH PATIENT, THE
Mitterrand, Frederic
MADAME BUTTERFLY
Moleon, Rafael
BATON ROUGE
Mones, Paul
SAINTS AND SINNERS
Montesi, Jorge
BLOODKNOT
Morrissey, Paul
MADAME WANG'S
Moses, Harry
ASSAULT AT WEST POINT
Munchkin, Richard W.
TEXAS PAYBACK
Murlowski, John
SANTA WITH MUSCLES
Myers, Richard
MONSTERSHOW

Newby, Chris
MADAGASCAR SKIN
Nichols, Mike
BIRDCAGE, THE
Nicolaou, Ted
MAGIC IN THE MIRROR
SPELLBREAKER: SECRET OF THE LEPRECHAUNS
Noonan, Tom
WIFE, THE
Norris, Aaron
FOREST WARRIOR
Nosseck, Noel
DOWN, OUT AND DANGEROUS
Nunn, Trevor
TWELFTH NIGHT
Nuridsany, Claude
MICROCOSMOS
O'Brien, John
MAN WITH A PLAN
Oakley, Vern
MODERN AFFAIR, A
Ofteringer, Susanne
NICO ICON
Olivera, Hector
SHADOW YOU SOON WILL BE, A
Osborne, Aaron
ZARKORR! THE INVADER
Oshii, Mamoru
GHOST IN THE SHELL
PATLABOR 2: MOBILE POLICE
Othenin-Girard, Dominique E.
BEYOND DESIRE
Pacino, Al
LOOKING FOR RICHARD
Palud, Herve
LITTLE INDIAN, BIG CITY
Panahi, Jafar
WHITE BALLOON, THE
Park, Nick
WALLACE AND GROMIT: THE BEST OF AARDMAN ANIMATION
Parker, Alan
EVITA
Parker, Christine
GIRLFRIENDS
Parker, Trey
CANNIBAL! THE MUSICAL
Pascal, Michel
FRANCOIS TRUFFAUT: STOLEN PORTRAITS
Paskaljevic, Goran
SOMEONE ELSE'S AMERICA
Pate, Jonas
GRAVE, THE
Pavone, Michael
CHAMELEON
Payne, Alexander
CITIZEN RUTH
Payne, David
CRIMINAL HEARTS
Payson, John
JOE'S APARTMENT
Peake, Peter
WALLACE AND GROMIT: THE BEST OF AARDMAN ANIMATION
Pearce, Richard
FAMILY THING, A
Pearl, Steven
. . . AT FIRST SIGHT
Peck, Raoul
MAN BY THE SHORE, THE
Pellizzari, Monica
GIRLFRIENDS
Pereira, Manuel Gomez
MOUTH TO MOUTH
Perennou, Marie
MICROCOSMOS

Perfili, Virginia
MIRROR, MIRROR III: THE VOYEUR
Peterson, Kristine
REDEMPTION: KICKBOXER 5
Petrie, Daniel
KISSINGER AND NIXON
Petrie, Donald
ASSOCIATE, THE
Pierson, Frank
TRUMAN
Piper, Brett
THEY BITE
Piznarski, Marc
DEATH BENEFIT
Poe, Amos
DEAD WEEKEND
Poire, Jean-Marie
VISITORS, THE
Pollack, Sharon
EVERYTHING RELATIVE
Pompucci, Leone
MILLE BOLLE BLU
Pope, Angela
CAPTIVES
Pope, Tim
CROW: CITY OF ANGELS, THE
Pray, Doug
HYPE!
Pressman, Michael
TO GILLIAN ON HER 37TH BIRTHDAY
Prior, David A.
FELONY
Purcell, Evelyn
WOMAN UNDONE, A
Purrer, Ursula
FLAMING EARS
Pytka, Joe
SPACE JAM
Pyun, Albert
ADRENALIN: FEAR THE RUSH
NEMESIS III: PREY HARDER
RAVENHAWK
Rafelson, Bob
TALES OF EROTICA
Raimondi, Paul
CROSSCUT
Ramis, Harold
MULTIPLICITY
Randel, Tony
FIST OF THE NORTH STAR
ONE GOOD TURN
RATTLED
Rappaport, Mark
FROM THE JOURNALS OF JEAN SEBERG
Rappeneau, Jean-Paul
HORSEMAN ON THE ROOF
Rash, Steve
EDDIE
Ray, Fred Olen
FUGITIVE RAGE
Ray, Sandip
TARGET
Red, Eric
BAD MOON
UNDERTOW
Reeves, Matt
PALLBEARER, THE
Reid, Tim
ONCE UPON A TIME . . . WHEN WE WERE COLORED
Reiner, Jeffrey
SERPENT'S LAIR
Reiner, Rob
GHOSTS OF MISSISSIPPI
Rhee, Phillip
BEST OF THE BEST 3: NO TURNING BACK

Rhodes, Michael
ENTERTAINING ANGELS: THE DOROTHY DAY STORY
Richards, Cybil
FEMALIEN
VIRTUAL ENCOUNTERS
Riddett, Dave Alex
WALLACE AND GROMIT: THE BEST OF AARDMAN ANIMATION
Ridley, Philip
PASSION OF DARKLY NOON, THE
Roberts, John
WAR OF THE BUTTONS, THE
Rodnunsky, Serge
FINAL EQUINOX, THE
Rodriguez, Robert
FROM DUSK TILL DAWN
Roeg, Nicolas
FULL BODY MASSAGE
TWO DEATHS
Rogozhkin, Alexander
CHEKIST, THE
Rohmer, Eric
RENDEZVOUS IN PARIS
Roper, Mark
LIVE WIRE: HUMAN TIMEBOMB
WARHEAD
Ross, Benjamin
YOUNG POISONER'S HANDBOOK, THE
Rubino, John
LOTTO LAND
Ruiz, Raul
THREE LIVES AND ONLY ONE DEATH
Russell, Chuck
ERASER
Russell, David O.
FLIRTING WITH DISASTER
Russell, Ken
TALES OF EROTICA
Russo, John A.
SANTA CLAWS
Ryman, John
GALAXIES ARE COLLIDING
Sabella, Paul
ALL DOGS GO TO HEAVEN 2
Sales, Leander
DON'T LET YOUR MEAT LOAF
Salwen, Hal
DENISE CALLS UP
Samson, Barry
HARD WAY OUT: BLOODFIST VIII
YESTERDAY'S TARGET
Sandiff-Wetzler, Gwen
PHANTOM 2040: THE GHOST WHO WALKS
Sanford, Arlene
VERY BRADY SEQUEL, A
Sargent, Joseph
LARRY MCMURTRY'S STREETS OF LAREDO
Sarin, Vic
LEGEND OF GATOR FACE, THE
Sassone, Oley
PLAYBACK
Saura, Carlos
OUTRAGE
Sautet, Claude
NELLY AND MONSIEUR ARNAUD
Sayles, John
LONE STAR
Schaeffer, Eric
IF LUCY FELL
Schamoni, Peter
NIKI DE SAINT PHALLE: WHO IS THE MONSTER — YOU OR ME?
Scheirl, Angela Hans
FLAMING EARS
Schenkel, Carl
SURGEON, THE
Schenkman, Richard
POMPATUS OF LOVE, THE
Schiller, Greta
PARIS WAS A WOMAN
Schipek, Dietmar
FLAMING EARS
Schlaich, Frieder
HALFMOON
Schlesinger, John
COLD COMFORT FARM
EYE FOR AN EYE
Schmid, Daniel
SHADOW OF ANGELS
Schnabel, Julian
BASQUIAT
Schneider, Jane
GIRLFRIENDS
Schroeder, Barbet
BEFORE AND AFTER
Schroeder, Michael
GLASS CAGE, THE
Schumacher, Joel
TIME TO KILL, A
Scorsese, Martin
PERSONAL JOURNEY WITH MARTIN SCORSESE THROUGH AMERICAN MOVIES, A
Scott, Campbell
BIG NIGHT
Scott, Michael
HECK'S WAY HOME
SHARON'S SECRET
Scott, Ridley
WHITE SQUALL
Scott, Tony
FAN, THE
Seed, Paul
AFFAIR, THE
Segal, Peter
MY FELLOW AMERICANS
Sehr, Peter
KASPAR HAUSER
Seidelman, Arthur Allan
HARVEST OF FIRE
Seidelman, Susan
TALES OF EROTICA
Selick, Henry
JAMES AND THE GIANT PEACH
Shadyac, Tom
NUTTY PROFESSOR, THE
Shafer, Dirk
MAN OF THE YEAR
Shaner, Pete
LOVER'S KNOT
Shapiro, Alan
FLIPPER
Shelly, Adrienne
4 TALES OF 2 CITIES
Shelton, Ron
TIN CUP
Shepard, Richard
MERCY
Shire, Talia
ONE NIGHT STAND
Silovic, Vassili
ORSON WELLES: THE ONE-MAN BAND
Simpson, Jane
LITTLE WITCHES
Simpson, Megan
ALEX
Singer, Bryan
PUBLIC ACCESS
Sinofsky, Bruce
PARADISE LOST: THE CHILD MURDERS AT ROBIN HOOD HILLS
Sinyor, Gary
SOLITAIRE FOR TWO
Sissoko, Cheick Oumar
GUIMBA THE TYRANT
Sjogren, John
RED LINE
Smith, Brian J.
BODY OF INFLUENCE 2
Smith, John N.
SUGARTIME
Smith, Roy Allen
LAND BEFORE TIME IV: JOURNEY THROUGH THE MISTS
Soavi, Michele
CEMETERY MAN
Solondz, Todd
WELCOME TO THE DOLLHOUSE
Speiser, Aaron
TALKING ABOUT SEX
Spence, Greg
CHILDREN OF THE CORN: THE GATHERING
Spheeris, Penelope
BLACK SHEEP
Sprackling, Simon
FUNNYMAN, THE
Spring, Tim
RAW TARGET
Sproxton, David
WALLACE AND GROMIT: THE BEST OF AARDMAN ANIMATION
Stern, Leonard
MISSING PIECES
Stevens, Andrew
VIRTUAL COMBAT
Stevens, Fisher
4 TALES OF 2 CITIES
Stiller, Ben
CABLE GUY, THE
Streisand, Barbra
MIRROR HAS TWO FACES, THE
Sugii, Gisaburo
NIGHT ON THE GALACTIC RAILROAD
STREET FIGHTER II: THE ANIMATED MOVIE
Sullivan, Daniel
SUBSTANCE OF FIRE, THE
Sullivan, Kevin Rodney
AMERICA'S DREAM
Sullivan, Tim
JACK & SARAH
Takacs, Tibor
SABRINA, THE TEENAGE WITCH
Takizawa, Toshifumi
BIG WARS
Talbot, Robert
HEAD OF THE FAMILY
Tamahori, Lee
MULHOLLAND FALLS
Tassie, Paul
PIG'S TALE, A
Taylor, Alan
PALOOKAVILLE
Taylor, Rene
LOVE IS ALL THERE IS
Techine, Andre
LES VOLEURS
MA SAISON PREFEREE
Tenney, Kevin S.
PINOCCHIO'S REVENGE
Thomas, Betty
LATE SHIFT, THE
Thornton, Billy Bob
SLING BLADE
Title, Stacy
LAST SUPPER, THE
Tlatli, Moufida
SILENCES OF THE PALACE, THE

Tong Kwei Lai
RUMBLE IN THE BRONX
Tornatore, Giuseppe
STAR MAKER, THE
Torres, Fina
CELESTIAL CLOCKWORK
Tors, Peter
LOOKING FOR TROUBLE
Toubiana, Serge
FRANCOIS TRUFFAUT: STOLEN PORTRAITS
Trousdale, Gary
HUNCHBACK OF NOTRE DAME, THE
Troyano, Ela
GIRLFRIENDS
Trueba, Fernando
TWO MUCH
Tsai Ming-liang
VIVE L'AMOUR
Tucci, Stanley
BIG NIGHT
Tunnicliffe, Gary J.
WITHIN THE ROCK
Turner, Larry
TATTOO BOY
Turner, Paul
HEDD WYNN
Turteltaub, Jon
PHENOMENON
Twohy, David
ARRIVAL, THE
Ungar, George
CHAMPAGNE SAFARI, THE
Uno, Michael Toshiyuki
ROAD TO GALVESTON, THE
Unwin, Dave
WIND IN THE WILLOWS, THE
Van Damme, Jean-Claude
QUEST, THE
van den Berg, Rudolf
COLD LIGHT OF DAY
Van Peebles, Melvin
TALES OF EROTICA
Van Taylor, David
PERFECT CANDIDATE, A
Verheyen, Jan
LITTLE DEATH, THE
Verow, Todd
FRISK
Vilsmaier, Joseph
BROTHER OF SLEEP
Viner, Michael
YOU'LL NEVER MAKE LOVE IN THIS TOWN AGAIN
Virgo, Clement
RUDE
von Alberti, Irene
HALFMOON
von Praunheim, Rosa
NEUROSIA: 50 YEARS OF PERVERSITY
Von Trier, Lars
BREAKING THE WAVES
Voss, Kurt
BAJA
Wachowski, Andy
BOUND
Wachowski, Larry
BOUND
Walsh, John
ED'S NEXT MOVE
Ward, David S.
DOWN PERISCOPE
Watanabe, Takashi
SANCTUARY: THE MOVIE
Waugh, Ric Roman
EXIT
Wein, Yossi
TERMINAL IMPACT

Wilkinson, Charles
BREACH OF TRUST
Wilson, Hugh
FIRST WIVES CLUB, THE
Wilson, Michael Henry
PERSONAL JOURNEY WITH MARTIN SCORSESE THROUGH AMERICAN MOVIES, A
Wilson, S.S.
TREMORS 2: AFTERSHOCKS
Wimmer, Kurt
ONE MAN'S JUSTICE
Wincer, Simon
PHANTOM, THE
Winer, Harry
HOUSE ARREST
Winfrey, Jonathan
BLACK SCORPION
CARNOSAUR 3: PRIMAL SPECIES
Winick, Gary
SWEET NOTHING
Winkless, Terence H.
NOT OF THIS EARTH
WHITE WOLVES II: LEGEND OF THE WILD
Winterbottom, Michael
BUTTERFLY KISS
CRACKER: THE MADWOMAN IN THE ATTIC
JUDE
Wise, Kirk
HUNCHBACK OF NOTRE DAME, THE
Wiseman, Frederick
LA COMEDIE-FRANCAISE OU L'AMOUR JOUE
Wong Kar-Wai
CHUNGKING EXPRESS
Wong, Kirk
ORGANIZED CRIME & TRIAD BUREAU
Woo, John
BROKEN ARROW
Wortmann, Sonke
MAYBE . . . MAYBE NOT
Wright, Alexander
FAST MONEY
Wuhl, Robert
OPEN SEASON
Yagher, Kevin
HELLRAISER: BLOODLINE
Yaitanes, Gregory
HARD JUSTICE
Yang, Edward
MAHJONG
Yin Li
STORY OF XINGHUA, THE
Young, Robert M.
CAUGHT
Yuen Woo Ping
WING CHUN
Yuzna, Brian
DENTIST, THE
NECRONOMICON: BOOK OF THE DEAD
Zaks, Jerry
MARVIN'S ROOM
Zaorski, Janusz
MOTHER OF KINGS
Zeffirelli, Franco
JANE EYRE
Zetlin, Barry
DOGFIGHTERS, THE
Zhou Xiaowen
BLACK MOUNTAIN
Ziller, Paul
SHOOTFIGHTER 2: KILL OR BE KILLED!
Zlotoff, Lee David
SPITFIRE GRILL, THE
Zwick, Edward
COURAGE UNDER FIRE

EDITORS

Abe, Hirohide
KAMIKAZE TAXI
Abel, Doug
4 TALES OF 2 CITIES
Adair, Sandra
TEXAS CHAINSAW MASSACRE: THE NEXT GENERATION
Akers, George
JOSEPH CONRAD'S THE SECRET AGENT
Albert, Ross
BLACK SHEEP
Alexander, Tara
SANTA CLAWS
Alk, Howard
MESSAGE TO LOVE: THE ISLE OF WIGHT FESTIVAL
Allred, Randall
APART FROM HUGH
Amundsen, Michael
CLUBHOUSE DETECTIVES
Amundson, Peter
DAYLIGHT
DRAGONHEART
Anderson, William
DOWN PERISCOPE
LOOKING FOR RICHARD
Andreson, Judy
ANNIE O
Angelo, Lou
PIG'S TALE, A
Anwar, Tariq
CRUCIBLE, THE
Appleby, George
GIRL FROM MARS, THE
Armstrong, Ronald K.
BUGGED
Arrley, Richmond
WIFE, THE
Attia, Kahena
GUIMBA THE TYRANT
Azul, Baker
DARK SECRETS
Baird, Stuart
EXECUTIVE DECISION
Baragli, Nino
MONSTER, THE
Barnier, Luc
MADAME BUTTERFLY
NEW LIFE, A
Barrere, Robert
HEADLESS BODY IN TOPLESS BAR
Barrett, Clive
WAVELENGTH
Barry, Dick
DOGFIGHTERS, THE
Bartczak, Jozef
MOTHER OF KINGS
Bartels-Vandagriff, Janet
DANGEROUS PASSION
Barton, Sean
ADVENTURES OF PINOCCHIO, THE
Baskin, Sonny
BIG SQUEEZE, THE
FIST OF THE NORTH STAR
Bassett, Craig
WAR AT HOME, THE
Basswood, Ronald
FRIEND OF THE FAMILY 2
Bastille, Ned
LOOKING FOR RICHARD
Baubeau, Roland
LITTLE INDIAN, BIG CITY
Baumgarten, Alan
LOSING CHASE

Beason, Eric L.
MADDENING, THE
UNFORGETTABLE
Beatty, David
TUSKEGEE AIRMEN, THE
Beckman, Peregrine
VIRTUAL ENCOUNTERS
Bedford, James Gavin
DELTA OF VENUS
Beldin, Dale
STUPIDS, THE
Berdan, Brian
AMANDA AND THE ALIEN
Berenbaum, Michael
BASQUIAT
Berger, Howard
ORIGINAL SINS
Berger, Peter E.
HOMEWARD BOUND II: LOST IN SAN FRANCISCO
Bergstresser, John
UNKNOWN ORIGIN
Berlatsky, David
PUBLIC ENEMIES
Berlinger, Joe
PARADISE LOST: THE CHILD MURDERS AT ROBIN HOOD HILLS
Bernard, Nena
TWO MUCH
Berner, Alexander
BROTHER OF SLEEP
Bestman, Dave
RAW TARGET
Beyda, Kent
JINGLE ALL THE WAY
Bilcock, Jill
WILLIAM SHAKESPEARE'S ROMEO + JULIET
Blangsted, David
HOW THE WEST WAS FUN
Bloecher, Michael
YESTERDAY'S TARGET
Bloom, John
FIRST WIVES CLUB, THE
LAST DANCE
Bloom, S.J.
HEIDI FLEISS HOLLYWOOD MADAM
Blythe, Terry
LONE JUSTICE: SHOWDOWN AT PLUM CREEK
Bock, Larry
JUST YOUR LUCK
Bockner, Michael
JOHNNY SHORTWAVE
Boisson, Noelle
HORSEMAN ON THE ROOF
MACHINE, THE
Bonanni, Mauro
MILLE BOLLE BLU
Bonnot, Francoise
WEEKEND IN THE COUNTRY, A
Bookwalter, J. R.
SANDMAN, THE
Bookwalter, J.R.
POLYMORPH
Bornstein, Ken
BEASTMASTER 3: THE EYE OF BRAXUS
Bouwmeester, Henni
SOME FOLKS CALL IT A SLING BLADE
Bowers, George
PREACHER'S WIFE, THE
Boyle, Peter
TWELFTH NIGHT
Bradley, Michael
ALL DOGS GO TO HEAVEN 2
Brandenburger, Elfe
NICO ICON
Brandt, Byron "Buzz"
SKIN
Brandt-Burgoyne, Anita
LETTER TO MY KILLER
VERY BRADY SEQUEL, A
Bravo, Edgar
VENUS RISING
Brenner, David
FEAR
INDEPENDENCE DAY
Bressan Jr., Arthur J.
ABUSE
Bretherton, David
CITY HALL
Bricker, Randolph K.
HELLRAISER: BLOODLINE
Bricmont, Wendy Greene
RACE THE SUN
RICH MAN'S WIFE, THE
Brochu, Donald
CHAIN REACTION
Brown, O. Nicholas
PHANTOM, THE
Brown, Robert
GHOST AND THE DARKNESS, THE
Brunjes, Ralph
HIDDEN ASSASSIN
MAN IN THE ATTIC, THE
SUGARTIME
Buba, Pasquale
LOOKING FOR RICHARD
Buckley, Norman
CAUGHT
SAWBONES
Burton, Joseph
LET'S GET BIZZEE
Butler, Bill
OF LOVE AND SHADOWS
Byrne, Barry
FEMALIEN
Cabreros, Ron
FAST MONEY
TOO FAST, TOO YOUNG
Cahn, Daniel
DARKMAN III: DIE DARKMAN DIE
Cambas, Jacqueline
MRS. WINTERBOURNE
Cambern, Donn
GLIMMER MAN, THE
Cannon, Bruce
CARRIED AWAY
Caplin, Joan
GIRLFRIENDS
Carroll, Bryan H.
PHANTOM, THE
Carter, John
SET IT OFF
THIN LINE BETWEEN LOVE AND HATE, A
Carter-Giez, Krysia
FIRE ON THE MOUNTAIN
Cecchini, Pietro
MUTANT MAN
Chamberlain, Felix
ZARKORR! THE INVADER
Chan Kar-fei
RUMBLE IN THE BRONX
Chang, William
CHUNGKING EXPRESS
Chavance, Pascale
SINGLE GIRL, A
Chestnut, Scott
UNFORGETTABLE
Cheung, Peter
RUMBLE IN THE BRONX
Chew, Richard
THAT THING YOU DO!
Chiate, Debra
HARRIET THE SPY
Choi Hung
ORGANIZED CRIME & TRIAD BUREAU
Christen, Ueli
MAYBE . . . MAYBE NOT
Cibelli, Chris
CHILDREN OF THE CORN: THE GATHERING
Cioffi, Louis
CARNOSAUR 3: PRIMAL SPECIES
Clark, Jim
MARVIN'S ROOM
Coates, Anne V.
STRIPTEASE
Coburn, Arthur
SUNSET PARK
Cohen, Bette Jane
MOTHER
Cole, Stan
HEIDI CHRONICLES, THE
Colina, Luis
LAST SUPPER, THE
WHOLE WIDE WORLD, THE
Comets, Jacques
MAN BY THE SHORE, THE
Conrad, Scott
FIRE ON THE MOUNTAIN
SOLO
Cook, Bruce
TAKEOVER, THE
Cooper, Christopher
KIDS IN THE HALL: BRAIN CANDY
Corrao, Angelo
AMERICA'S DREAM
LINE KING: THE AL HIRSCHFELD STORY, THE
Cotte, Camille
SILENCES OF THE PALACE, THE
Coughlin, Cari
DOWN, OUT AND DANGEROUS
ROAD TO GALVESTON, THE
Craven, Garth
ONE FINE DAY
Cribben, Michael
BEWARE: CHILDREN AT PLAY
Curtis, Tracy
WHISPERING, THE
D'Antonio, Joanne
CHAMELEON
D'Augustine, Joe
SUNCHASER
Dagnen, John David
TEXAS PAYBACK
Dangar, Henry
SPIDER & ROSE
Daniel, Bill
SONIC OUTLAWS
Daniel, Danniel
CROCODILES IN AMSTERDAM
Danner, Lowell
VIRTUAL ENCOUNTERS
Das, Poppy
HEAD OF THE FAMILY
Davalos, Raul
FRAME BY FRAME
Davies, Freeman
LAST MAN STANDING
Davis, Mona
PERFECT CANDIDATE, A
TALES OF EROTICA
Davis, Roderick
DEATH ARTIST, THE
WITHIN THE ROCK
Day, Mark
COLD COMFORT FARM
Day, Paul G.
ELECTRA
De La Bouillerie, Hubert
CELTIC PRIDE

Dean, Rod
AMERICAN STRAYS
HELLRAISER: BLOODLINE
DeGraff, Monty
AMERICA'S DREAM
Del Mar, Martin
OVER THE WIRE
Denisova, Tamara
CHEKIST, THE
Dindo, Richard
ERNESTO CHE GUEVARA—THE BOLIVIAN DIARY
Diver, William
SOMEONE ELSE'S AMERICA
Djokic, Lazar
HEAD OF THE FAMILY
Doerfer, Andrew
CHILDREN OF FURY
Dorn, Dody
EXIT
Driscoll, Ryan L.
FUNNYMAN, THE
Ducsay, Bob
TREMORS 2: AFTERSHOCKS
Duffner, J. Patrick
MICHAEL COLLINS
Dufour, Joelle
GUIMBA THE TYRANT
Duncan, Daniel
BEYOND DESIRE
PINOCCHIO'S REVENGE
Dutta, Dulal
TARGET
Eberlein, Matt
PLAYBACK
SOUTH BEACH ACADEMY
Eliopoulos, Nicholas
LOVE IS ALL THERE IS
Ellerman, Daria
SABRINA, THE TEENAGE WITCH
Elliot, Michael
TALES OF EROTICA
Ellis, Peter B.
ORIGINAL GANGSTAS
Elmiger, Suzy
BIG NIGHT
Errington, Mac
TERMINAL IMPACT
Everitt, Tim
FATALLY YOURS
Fairservice, Don
BEAUTIFUL THING
Fanfarra, Stephen
BLOOD & DONUTS
Fardoulis, Monique
LA CEREMONIE
Farr, Glenn
NORMA JEAN AND MARILYN
Farrell, Neil
HAMLET
MIDWINTER'S TALE, A
Faugno, Frank
ROAD HOME, THE
Fedele, Jody
ANIMAL INSTINCTS III: THE SEDUCTRESS
BODY OF INFLUENCE 2
Fillios, Danielle
JOHNNY 100 PESOS
Finkle, Claudia
RATTLED
UNDERTOW
Fitzgerald, Jon
APART FROM HUGH
Flaer, Howard
TWO-BITS & PEPPER
Flaum, Seth
OPEN SEASON
RASPUTIN
Fletcher, James
VENUS RISING
Fletcher, William
MRS. WINTERBOURNE
Folsey Jr., George
BULLETPROOF
ENTERTAINING ANGELS: THE DOROTHY DAY STORY
Forbes, Doug
PORTRAITS OF A KILLER
SONG SPINNER, THE
Foster, Ruth
ROLLING STONES ROCK-AND-ROLL CIRCUS, THE
Francis-Bruce, Richard
ROCK, THE
Frank, Peter
JOE'S APARTMENT
Fraticelli, Franco
CEMETERY MAN
Frazen, Robert
DEATH BENEFIT
Frazier, Jimmy B.
SURGEON, THE
Freeman, David
WAR OF THE BUTTONS, THE
Freeman, Jeff
CRAFT, THE
Freund, Jay
ASSAULT AT WEST POINT
Friedman, Jeffrey
CELLULOID CLOSET, THE
Fruchtman, Lisa
TRUMAN
Gahan, Linda
GIRLFRIENDS
Garber, Tony
ALL DOGS GO TO HEAVEN 2
Gardner, Eric
BREAKAWAY
Garland, Glenn
HOSTILE INTENTIONS
Gast, Leon
WHEN WE WERE KINGS
Ghaffari, Earl
HYPE!
Gibby, Gwyneth
BLACK SCORPION
Gilbert, John
BURIAL OF THE RATS
HARD WAY OUT: BLOODFIST VIII
LOADED
PIRANHA
WHITE WOLVES II: LEGEND OF THE WILD
Ginsberg, Milton Moses
CATWALK
Giordano, Martine
LES VOLEURS
MA SAISON PREFEREE
Glassman, Arnold
CELLULOID CLOSET, THE
Glatstein, Bert
HARVEST OF FIRE
JOSH KIRBY . . . TIME WARRIOR!: LAST BATTLE FOR THE UNIVERSE
Glinka, Gunter
BEAVIS AND BUTT-HEAD DO AMERICA
Goard, David
LEGEND OF GATOR FACE, THE
Goddard, Bill
HALFBACK OF NOTRE DAME, THE
ROBIN OF LOCKSLEY
Goldenberg, William
LONG KISS GOODNIGHT, THE
Goodman, Joel
LAWNMOWER MAN 2: BEYOND CYBERSPACE
Goodspeed, Margie
SPITFIRE GRILL, THE
Gorchow, Michelle
4 TALES OF 2 CITIES
Gorshow, Michelle
NATIONAL LAMPOON'S FAVORITE DEADLY SINS
Gotlieb, Mallory
CURDLED
Gottlieb, Jay
OVER THE WIRE
Gourson, Jeff
HAPPY GILMORE
Graef, Susan
IF LUCY FELL
SHE'S THE ONE
Green, Bruce
PHENOMENON
TWO IF BY SEA
Greenbury, Christopher
BIO-DOME
KINGPIN
Greenwald, David
THEREMIN: AN ELECTRONIC ODYSSEY
Gregory, John
SECRETS & LIES
Greutert, Kevin
SHOT, THE
Grieve, Neil
UNDERSTUDY: GRAVEYARD SHIFT 2, THE
Grossman, Marc
DELTA OF VENUS
Guinee, Margaret
FAR HARBOR
Gunderson, Quincy
WOMAN UNDONE, A
Gutowski, Joseph
FLED
LITTLE DEATH, THE
Haas, Belinda
ANGELS AND INSECTS
Hache, Joelle
RIDICULE
Hackford, Taylor
WHEN WE WERE KINGS
Hai Kit-Wai
CHUNGKING EXPRESS
Haigis, Jack
LOTTO LAND
Hall, Alex
GIRLS TOWN
Halsey, Colleen
D3: THE MIGHTY DUCKS
PIE IN THE SKY
Halsey, Richard
EDDIE
Hambling, Gerry
EVITA
WHITE SQUALL
Hammouda, Kerim
SILENCES OF THE PALACE, THE
Handorf, Heidi
KASPAR HAUSER
Hanley, Dan
RANSOM
Hardin, Ian
CANNIBAL! THE MUSICAL
Harrington, Patricia
LOOKING FOR TROUBLE
Hart, Chris
TIMELESS
Hartley, Hal
FLIRT

Hartmann, Susanne
KASPAR HAUSER
Harvey, Marshall
BIG BULLY
DON'T BE A MENACE TO SOUTH CENTRAL WHILE DRINKING YOUR JUICE IN THE HOOD
Healey, Leslie
PASSION OF DARKLY NOON, THE
Henderson, Alastair
YANKEE ZULU
Henderson, Wilton
FAR HARBOR
JINGLE ALL THE WAY
Henson, Robby
PHARAOH'S ARMY
Herring, Craig
MULTIPLICITY
Herring, Pam
MULTIPLICITY
Hewitt, David
WITHOUT MERCY
Hickenlooper, George
SOME FOLKS CALL IT A SLING BLADE
Hill, Mike
RANSOM
Hilton, Simon
SHAMELESS
Himoff, Kathryn
LIVE NUDE GIRLS
OF LOVE AND SHADOWS
Hirakubo, Masahiro
TRAINSPOTTING
Hirsch, Paul
MISSION: IMPOSSIBLE
Hitner, Harry
MIND RIPPER
Hoenig, Dov
CHAIN REACTION
Holden, David
RIDERS OF THE PURPLE SAGE
Hollyn, Norman
MAD DOG TIME
Holmes, Christopher
CROSSCUT
RUMPELSTILTSKIN
Honess, Peter
EYE FOR AN EYE
Hoover, Claudia
BLACK DAY BLUE NIGHT
Horvitch, Andy
BACKLASH: OBLIVION 2
Hovis, Michael
MAN WITH THE PERFECT SWING, THE
Howe, Matthew
ORIGINAL SINS
Hoy, Maysie
FREEWAY
MRS. MUNCK
Hubert, Axel
BEYOND THE CALL
Hunter, Martin
ARRIVAL, THE
Hutshing, Joe
BROKEN ARROW
JERRY MAGUIRE
Innes, Louise
FOXFIRE
Iosseliani, Otar
CHASING BUTTERFLIES
Ivanovic, Snezana
VUKOVAR
Jablow, Michael
FOR BETTER OR WORSE
MUPPET TREASURE ISLAND
Jackson, J.J.
SHOWGIRL MURDERS, THE
Jacobsson, Anders
EVIL ED
Jakubowicz, Alain
DEADLY OUTBREAK
WARHEAD
Janett, Georg
ERNESTO CHE GUEVARA—THE BOLIVIAN DIARY
Jaynes, Roderick
FARGO
Jeffs, Christine
GIRLFRIENDS
Jenet, Veronika
PORTRAIT OF A LADY, THE
Johnson, Bill
INFINITY
MYSTERY SCIENCE THEATER 3000: THE MOVIE
Jones, Robert C.
CITY HALL
Jordan, Lawrence
VIKING SAGAS, THE
Juergens, Mark
SEARCH FOR ONE-EYE JIMMY, THE
Jympson, John
HAUNTED
Kahn, Sheldon
SPACE JAM
Kakesu, Shuichi
GHOST IN THE SHELL
PATLABOR 2: MOBILE POLICE
Kaplan, Mindy
DEVOTION
Karen, Debra
LARRY MCMURTRY'S STREETS OF LAREDO
Karlsson, Steingrimur
COLD FEVER
Karmel, Pip
SHINE
Kassovitz, Mathieu
HATE
Katkin, Brian
BLACK ROSE OF HARLEM
CRIMINAL HEARTS
Katz, Virginia
SERPENT'S LAIR
Kaurismaki, Mika
CONDITION RED
Kavanagh, Tony
ALEX
Kelber, Catherine
VISITORS, THE
Kelemen, Fred
FATE
Kelley, Terry
BEAVIS AND BUTT-HEAD DO AMERICA
Kemp, Andy
WIND IN THE WILLOWS, THE
Keneshea, Ellen
HUNCHBACK OF NOTRE DAME, THE
Kenessey, Heidi
GIRLFRIENDS
Kennedy, Patrick
MR. WRONG
Keramidas, Harry
FIRST KID
Kern, David
ORIGINAL GANGSTAS
Kerr, William
MY FELLOW AMERICANS
Keuhnelian, Janice
FAR HARBOR
Khan, Michael
TWISTER
King, Dave
CAPTIVES
Kirkman, David
DADETOWN
Klein, Robin
ROLLING STONES ROCK-AND-ROLL CIRCUS, THE
Klevin, Sloane
MR. STITCH
Klingman, Lynzee
MATILDA
Klocek, Donald
SMALL WONDERS
Knue, Michael
CROW: CITY OF ANGELS, THE
Knue, Michael N.
LILY DALE
Kobrin, Rob
ALASKA
WITHOUT MERCY
Koehler, Bonnie
ASSOCIATE, THE
Koslowsky, John
JAG
Krajewski, Guido
NICO ICON
Kramer, John
CHAMPAGNE SAFARI, THE
Krattenmacher, Thomas
NIKI DE SAINT PHALLE: WHO IS THE MONSTER — YOU OR ME?
Kurson, Jane
BED OF ROSES
Kwei, James
4 TALES OF 2 CITIES
GRACE OF MY HEART
Kwong Chi-Leung
CHUNGKING EXPRESS
Kyle, Kyle C.
NOT BAD FOR A GIRL
Labik, Ludwig
WOLVES, THE
Lack, Christiane
CELESTIAL CLOCKWORK
Ladizinsky, Ivan
GALAXIES ARE COLLIDING
Lafferty, John
GLASS CAGE, THE
Lah, Nika
PREDICTIONS OF FIRE
Lambert, Robert K.
ED
Landis, Evan
VIRUS
Langlois, L. James
CARPOOL
Langlois, Yves
HOLLOW POINT
SCREAMERS
Lanza, Tony
BODY COUNT
Lategen, Johan
YANKEE ZULU
Laub, Marc
STEPHEN KING'S THINNER
Laubscher, Tiny
YANKEE ZULU
Lawrence, Chris
HEDD WYNN
Lawrence, Neil
BEAVIS AND BUTT-HEAD DO AMERICA
Lawrence, Stephen
KISSINGER AND NIXON
Lawson, Tony
MICHAEL COLLINS
TWO DEATHS
Lebenzon, Christopher
MARS ATTACKS!
LeCompte, Rick
BLONDES HAVE MORE GUNS

Leighton, Robert
GHOSTS OF MISSISSIPPI
Leirer, Barry B.
COLONY, THE
Leonard, David
PALOOKAVILLE
Lepselter, Alisa
WALKING AND TALKING
Lerea, Yaffa
LOW LIFE, THE
Levin, Sidney
GRASS HARP, THE
LARGER THAN LIFE
Levy-Hinte, Jeffrey
WHEN WE WERE KINGS
Lewis, Thomas
MURDERED INNOCENCE
Lichtenstein, Adam
MERCY
Likovich, Donald
UNDER THE HULA MOON
Linder, Stu
SLEEPERS
Ling, Ewa J.
SOLITAIRE FOR TWO
Link, John F.
QUEST, THE
Linnman, Susanne
CHILDREN OF NOISY VILLAGE, THE
Littleton, Carol
DIABOLIQUE
Lloyd, Doug H.
WIDOW'S KISS
Lo, Mayin
FUNERAL, THE
Loewenthal, Daniel
SHADOW WARRIORS
Lombardo, Tony
SGT. BILKO
London, Andrew
EVIL HAS A FACE
London, Melody
ANGELA
Lopez, Eduardo
SHADOW YOU SOON WILL BE, A
Lossignol, Frederic
EYE OF VICHY, THE
Lottman, Evan
MISSING PIECES
Louwrier, Wim
ANTONIA'S LINE
Lovejoy, Stephen
TALES FROM THE CRYPT PRESENTS BORDELLO OF BLOOD
Lovitt, Bert
BEST OF THE BEST 3: NO TURNING BACK
Lowenthal, Dan
VIRTUAL ENCOUNTERS
Lowenthal, Daniel
DEAD COLD
LIVE WIRE: HUMAN TIMEBOMB
Lussier, Patrick
D3: THE MIGHTY DUCKS
SCREAM
MacDonald, Kate
JOSH KIRBY . . . TIME WARRIOR!: JOURNEY TO THE MAGIC CAVERN
Mackie, Alex
SUBSTITUTE, THE
Maganini, Elena
INFINITY
NORMAL LIFE
Maggi, Susan
RUDE
Majoros, Eszter
OUTPOST, THE
Makiej, Jim
LOW LIFE, THE
Malanowski, Tony
FELONY
Malkin, Barry
JACK
Mandelberg, Neil
WHERE'S THE MONEY, NOREEN?
Mansell, Edward
AUGUST
Manton, Marcus
FOREST WARRIOR
Marcus, Andrew
SURVIVING PICASSO
Marden, Richard
JANE EYRE
Mark, Tony
VIRTUAL COMBAT
Markey, Mary Jo
. . . AT FIRST SIGHT
Markinson, Keith
WITCHCRAFT: SALEM'S GHOST
Marrinson, William D.
SANTA WITH MUSCLES
Martin, Dominique
FRANCOIS TRUFFAUT: STOLEN PORTRAITS
Martin, Pamela
ED'S NEXT MOVE
SUBSTANCE OF FIRE, THE
Martin, Richard
BREACH OF TRUST
Marzano, Joe
ONE LESS EGG TO FRY
Matthews, Peter
GRIM
Mattiussi, Roger
STAND OFF, THE
Mazur, Lara
HECK'S WAY HOME
Mazzola, Frank
WILD SIDE
Mazzucato, Paolo
DEMOLITIONIST, THE
McCabe, Anne
GIRLFRIENDS
McCann, Tim
DESOLATION ANGELS
McElroy, Jim
LONE JUSTICE: SHOWDOWN AT PLUM CREEK
McKay, Craig
SOME MOTHER'S SON
McKay, Jim
GIRLS TOWN
McLaughlin, Gary
PAINTED HERO
McLean, Michael S.
IT CAME FROM OUTER SPACE II
McMahon, Pat
MOONSHINE HIGHWAY
Menell, Jon
TATTOO BOY
Menke, Sally
MULHOLLAND FALLS
Merlin, Claudine
FRENCH TWIST
Meshelski, Thomas
BLACK DAY BLUE NIGHT
Meshover, William J.
QUEST, THE
Michael, Stephen
MATERNAL INSTINCTS
Miller, Allan
SMALL WONDERS
Miller III, Harry B.
DONOR UNKNOWN
Miller, Jim
2 DAYS IN THE VALLEY
Miller, Peter
FUGITIVE RAGE
Milmore, M. Watanabe
PARADISE LOST: THE CHILD MURDERS AT ROBIN HOOD HILLS
Minasian, Armen
DOWN PERISCOPE
Mirkovich, Steve
BROKEN ARROW
GHOST AND THE DARKNESS, THE
THEODORE REX
Mirrione, Stephen
SWINGERS
Mitchell, James D.
LAWNMOWER MAN 2: BEYOND CYBERSPACE
Mittelman, Gina
RATTLED
Mock, Kevin
SKYSCRAPER
TIGER HEART
Moritz, David
BOTTLE ROCKET
EVENING STAR, THE
Morris, Jonathan
LAND AND FREEDOM
Morris, Lorne
BURIAL OF THE RATS
Morrisey, Ken
ADRENALIN: FEAR THE RUSH
NEMESIS III: PREY HARDER
Morse, Susan E.
EVERYONE SAYS I LOVE YOU
Moss, Thomas V.
ALL DOGS GO TO HEAVEN 2
Mueller, Niels
SWEET NOTHING
Murawski, Bob
NIGHT OF THE SCARECROW
Murch, Walter
ENGLISH PATIENT, THE
Myers, Richard
MONSTERSHOW
Myers, Stephen
OUT THERE
SANTA WITH MUSCLES
SOMETIMES THEY COME BACK . . . AGAIN
Myhrstad, Stein
TRACKS OF A KILLER
Nallin, Michael
MADAME WANG'S
Nassour, Tony
YOU'LL NEVER MAKE LOVE IN THIS TOWN AGAIN
Navarro, Jess
MIDNIGHT DANCERS
Nedd-Friendly, Priscilla
EVENING STAR, THE
Neil-Fisher, Debra
DEAR GOD
UP CLOSE AND PERSONAL
Nelson, Christopher
DEAD TO RIGHTS
LAZARUS MAN, THE
Newby, Chris
MADAGASCAR SKIN
Nielson, Steve
BODY COUNT
FORBIDDEN ZONE: ALIEN ABDUCTION
HEAD OF THE FAMILY
Nishiide, Eiko
ROUJIN-Z
Nord, Richard
FLED
GETTING AWAY WITH MURDER
PHAT BEACH
Northrop, Jan
LIFEFORM

Novak, Peter
SGT. KABUKIMAN N.Y.P.D.
O'Brien, John
MAN WITH A PLAN
O'Connor, Dennis M.
LOVE IS ALL THERE IS
RAVENHAWK
O'Meara, Timothy
BAD MOON
GRASS HARP, THE
Oblath, Carol
WATCH ME
Ohshima, Tomoyo
MABOROSI
Oliver, Jim
CANTERVILLE GHOST, THE
LONG ROAD HOME, THE
Ottman, John
PUBLIC ACCESS
Oxman, Alan
WELCOME TO THE DOLLHOUSE
Paige, Meredith
EVERYTHING RELATIVE
Paine, Emily
I'M NOT RAPPAPORT
Pan, Kant
COLD LIGHT OF DAY
SUITE 16
Panahi, Jafar
WHITE BALLOON, THE
Pankow, Bill
FUNERAL, THE
MAXIMUM RISK
Percy, Lee
BEFORE AND AFTER
Peroni, Geraldine
KANSAS CITY
MICHAEL
Petersen, Tom
BLACK SCORPION
Phillips, Melanie Anne
PRE-MADONNAS
Pillsbury, Suzanne
CONDITION RED
MODERN AFFAIR, A
MURDERED INNOCENCE
Pincus, David
ONCE UPON A TIME . . . WHEN WE WERE COLORED
Pineyro, Yvette
BITTER SUGAR
Pinyero, Gloria
SILENCE OF NETO, THE
Poitevin, Catherine
ERNESTO CHE GUEVARA—THE BOLIVIAN DIARY
Polakow, Michael E.
KAZAAM
SOMETIMES THEY COME BACK . . . AGAIN
Poll, Jon
DUNSTON CHECKS IN
Pollard, Sam
GIRL 6
Powen, Chen
MAHJONG
Praskina, Eleonora
ANNA
Pray, Doug
HYPE!
Priego, Alfredo Rosas
AVENTURERA
Prior, Jim
HELLRAISER: BLOODLINE
ONE NIGHT STAND
Prior, Peck
FLIPPER
Puett, Dallas
EXECUTIVE DECISION
Quaglia, Massimo
STAR MAKER, THE
Rabinowitz, Jay
DEAD MAN
MOTHER NIGHT
Rae, Dan
RASPUTIN
Ransley, David
WHEN THE BULLET HITS THE BONE
Rappaport, Mark
FROM THE JOURNALS OF JEAN SEBERG
Rawley, Fabienne
DEAD WEEKEND
Ray, Kimberly
TIN CUP
Reamer, Keith
I SHOT ANDY WARHOL
LONE JUSTICE: SHOWDOWN AT PLUM CREEK
Redman, Anthony
CROW: CITY OF ANGELS, THE
Rees, Charles
NEON BIBLE, THE
Refn, Anders
BREAKING THE WAVES
Reichwein, Michiel
ANTONIA'S LINE
Reitano, Robert
JUROR, THE
Represa, Guillermo
MOUTH TO MOUTH
Reticker, Meg
HEAVY
Reynolds, William
CARPOOL
Ricard, Florence
MICROCOSMOS
Richards, John
STONEWALL
Richardson, Nancy
HOMECOMING
Riddle, Scott
PURE DANGER
Riegel, Tatiana S.
LOVER'S KNOT
Rigo, Maria
MAGIC HUNTER
Rivkin, Stephen
BOGUS
Robinson, Keith
WHEN WE WERE KINGS
Robison, Michael
OUTER LIMITS: SANDKINGS, THE
Rodd, Miles
FINAL EQUINOX, THE
Rodriguez, Robert
FROM DUSK TILL DAWN
Rodriquez, Freddie
GIRLFRIENDS
Rokob, Magdolna
HALFMOON
Roose, Ronald
HOUSE ARREST
Rose, Margarete
HALFMOON
Rosen, Dan
POMPATUS OF LOVE, THE
Rosenbloom, David
PRIMAL FEAR
Rosenblum, Steven
COURAGE UNDER FIRE
Rosenstock, Harvey
GRACE OF MY HEART
MOTHER
Ross, Rebecca
NAKED SOULS
Rostock, Susanne
CALLING THE GHOSTS: A STORY ABOUT RAPE, WAR AND WOMEN
Roth, Christopher
DENTIST, THE
NECRONOMICON: BOOK OF THE DEAD
Rotter, Stephen A.
PREACHER'S WIFE, THE
Roulston, George
BLOODKNOT
Rouse, Christopher
TAILS YOU LIVE, HEADS YOU'RE DEAD
WHARF RAT, THE
Rowland, Geoffrey
ENTERTAINING ANGELS: THE DOROTHY DAY STORY
Roy, Rita
FOR THE MOMENT
Rubacky, Louise
FULL BODY MASSAGE
Rubell, Paul
ISLAND OF DR. MOREAU, THE
Ruscio, Michael
BOY CALLED HATE, A
EDIE & PEN
Russell, Esther
BAD LOVE
Russell, Robin
FINAL CUT, THE
Russell, Xavier
TALES OF EROTICA
Russo, Bill
TWO FRIENDS
Sacco, Frank
HOURGLASS
Salcedo, Jose
BATON ROUGE
FLOWER OF MY SECRET, THE
Sales, Leander
DON'T LET YOUR MEAT LOAF
Sales, Leander T.
GET ON THE BUS
Salfas, Stan
PALLBEARER, THE
WOMAN UNDONE, A
San Mateo, Juan Ignacio
OUTRAGE
Sanders, Gregory
JOSH KIRBY . . . TIME WARRIOR!: EGGS FROM 70,000,000 B.C.
JOSH KIRBY . . . TIME WARRIOR!: TRAPPED ON TOY WORLD
MAGIC IN THE MIRROR
SPELLBREAKER: SECRET OF THE LEPRECHAUNS
Sanford, Kate
AMERICAN BUFFALO
Sauter, Keith
NECRONOMICON: BOOK OF THE DEAD
Savitt, Jill
TRIGGER EFFECT, THE
Sayles, John
LONE STAR
Scalia, Pietro
STEALING BEAUTY
Scharf, William
TO GILLIAN ON HER 37TH BIRTHDAY
Scheirl, Angela Hans
FLAMING EARS
Schiller, Greta
PARIS WAS A WOMAN
Schink, Peter
BARB WIRE
Schmidt, Arthur
BIRDCAGE, THE
CHAIN REACTION
Schmidt, Wayne
TALKING ABOUT SEX
VIRTUAL COMBAT

Schoonmaker, Thelma
GRACE OF MY HEART
PERSONAL JOURNEY WITH MARTIN SCORSESE THROUGH AMERICAN MOVIES, A
Schultz, Michael
AMERICA'S DREAM
Scott, John
TUNNEL VISION
Sears, Eric
SPY HARD
Seelig, Douglas
BLOODSPORT II: THE NEXT KUMITE
Selkirk, Jamie
FRIGHTENERS, THE
Selver, Veronica
BERKELEY IN THE 60S
Selwyn, Lionel
SHAMELESS
Semel, Stephen
TRUTH ABOUT CATS AND DOGS, THE
Semilian, Julian
SERIAL KILLER
Seydor, Paul
TIN CUP
Shaine, Rick
EXTREME MEASURES
OFF AND RUNNING
THEODORE REX
Sharfin, Gary
DENISE CALLS UP
Sharp, Colleen
MANNY & LO
Shaw, Ron
TIGER HEART
Sheldon, Greg
MESSAGE TO LOVE: THE ISLE OF WIGHT FESTIVAL
Shepard, Mike
NEUROSIA: 50 YEARS OF PERVERSITY
Shik, Danny
UNDER THE DOMIM TREE
Ship, Trudy
MR. HOLLAND'S OPUS
101 DALMATIANS
Shropshire, Terilyn A.
POISON IVY 2: LILY
Siciliano, Antonio
SONS OF TRINITY
Sider, Larry
INSTITUTE BENJAMENTA
Silver, Barry
MAN OF THE YEAR
Silvi, Roberto
MADDENING, THE
Simmons, David
STREETCAR NAMED DESIRE, A
Simpson, Claire
FAN, THE
Sinofsky, Bruce
PARADISE LOST: THE CHILD MURDERS AT ROBIN HOOD HILLS
Sjogren, John
RED LINE
Slater, Ian
SGT. KABUKIMAN N.Y.P.D.
Smith, Gary L.
NIGHT OF THE TWISTERS
Smith, Mary Ann
JOSH KIRBY . . . TIME WARRIOR!: LAST BATTLE FOR THE UNIVERSE
Smith, Nicholas C.
FAITHFUL
FLY AWAY HOME
Smith, Paul Martin
CANTERVILLE GHOST, THE
Smith, Scott
SHARON'S SECRET
Solomon, Ken
MAN OF THE YEAR
Sopel, Anne
YOUNG POISONER'S HANDBOOK, THE
Speer, Mark
VIRTUAL COMBAT
Staenberg, Zach
BOUND
Stanzler, Wendey
I'M NOT RAPPAPORT
Steen, Vagn L.
FLATTERED
Steininger, Karen
ANNE FRANK REMEMBERED
Steinkamp, William
HEAVEN'S PRISONERS
TIME TO KILL, A
Stellar Jr., James
NOT OF THIS EARTH
Stephen, Mary
RENDEZVOUS IN PARIS
Stevenson, Michael A.
HOMEWARD BOUND II: LOST IN SAN FRANCISCO
Stevenson, Scott
HATE
Stiven, David
SHOPPING
Stothart, John
AFFAIR, THE
Sullivan, Brett
BLOOD & DONUTS
Sung Shin-cheng
VIVE L'AMOUR
Symons, James R.
HIGH SCHOOL HIGH
MOLL FLANDERS
Tal, Omer
HARD JUSTICE
SHOOTFIGHTER 2: KILL OR BE KILLED!
Taylor, Warren
LAND BEFORE TIME IV: JOURNEY THROUGH THE MISTS
Tedeschi, David
SILENCE OF NETO, THE
Tellefsen, Christopher
FLIRTING WITH DISASTER
PEOPLE VS. LARRY FLYNT, THE
Tent, Kevin
HOMAGE
ONE GOOD TURN
Teschner, Peter
LATE SHIFT, THE
TOLLBOOTH
Thibault, Michael
DESIRE
ONE MAN'S JUSTICE
Thiedot, Jacqueline
NELLY AND MONSIEUR ARNAUD
Thomas, Scott
SMALL FACES
Thompson, Stacia
SYNTHETIC PLEASURES
Timar, Peter
OUTPOST, THE
Tlatli, Moufida
SILENCES OF THE PALACE, THE
Toniolo, Camilla
BOYS
Travis, Neil
MOLL FLANDERS
Trejo, Paul
GRAVE, THE
Trent, Kevin
CITIZEN RUTH
Trevor, Richard
IMMORTALS, THE
Trirogoff, Kristina
LITTLE WITCHES
Troch, Ludo
DAENS
Troeger, Adreas
SYNTHETIC PLEASURES
Trombetta, Leo
SAINTS AND SINNERS
Tronick, Michael
ERASER
Trouillet, Catherine
CELESTIAL CLOCKWORK
Uchida, Kerry
WHITE TIGER
Uelmen, Larry
MR. ICE CREAM MAN
Urioste, Frank J.
EXECUTIVE DECISION
Van Peebles, Melvin
TALES OF EROTICA
Van Wyck, Gerrie
YANKEE ZULU
Vander Meulen, Kert
BLACK OUT
Vandermeulen, Kert
REDEMPTION: KICKBOXER 5
Verow, Todd
FRISK
Victor, Paulette Renee
MIRROR, MIRROR III: THE VOYEUR
PHOENIX
Volk, Paul G.
SWEEPER, THE
Von Hasperg, Ila
IT'S MY PARTY
SHADOW OF ANGELS
Von Oelffen, Petra
UNHOOK THE STARS
Wagner, Christian
FAN, THE
Wagner, George
MADAME WANG'S
Wahrman, Wayne
2 DAYS IN THE VALLEY
Waite, Trevor
BUTTERFLY KISS
CRACKER: THE MADWOMAN IN THE ATTIC
JUDE
Walker, Lesley
EMMA
IN LOVE AND WAR
JACK & SARAH
MARY REILLY
Walsh, Martin
FEELING MINNESOTA
Ware, Annabel
MADAGASCAR SKIN
Warner, Mark
CHAMBER, THE
FAMILY THING, A
Warnow, Stan
MESSAGE TO LOVE: THE ISLE OF WIGHT FESTIVAL
Warren, Jeff
IRON EAGLE IV
Warschilka, Edward A.
JOHN CARPENTER'S ESCAPE FROM L.A.
Watson, Earl
GREAT WHITE HYPE, THE
Webb, Stan
JAMES AND THE GIANT PEACH
Webb, William
PROPRIETOR, THE
Webber, Liz
PROTEUS
Webster, Craig
CURTIS'S CHARM

Wedeles, Rodolfo
THREE LIVES AND ONLY ONE DEATH
Weisberg, Steven
CABLE GUY, THE
Werner, Jeff
MIRROR HAS TWO FACES, THE
Westerlund, Einar
MESSAGE TO LOVE: THE ISLE OF WIGHT FESTIVAL
Wheeler, John W.
BOYS NEXT DOOR, THE
STAR TREK: FIRST CONTACT
White, Brent
MATILDA
White, Peter
MOTHER'S PRAYER, A
Williams, Kate
TREES LOUNGE
Winborne, Hughes
SLING BLADE
Winick, Gary
4 TALES OF 2 CITIES
Wiseman, Frederick
LA COMEDIE-FRANCAISE OU L'AMOUR JOUE
Wolf, Jeffrey
BEAUTIFUL GIRLS
Worland, Chris
RAGE
Wright, John
BROKEN ARROW
Yamaoka, Jon
PRE-MADONNAS
Yasunaga, Gail
BAJA
Young, Amy
INFINITY
Young, William
DON'T BE A MENACE TO SOUTH CENTRAL WHILE DRINKING YOUR JUICE IN THE HOOD
Yoyotte, Marie-Josephe
MICROCOSMOS
ORSON WELLES: THE ONE-MAN BAND
Zanuso, Cecilia
WHO KILLED PASOLINI?
Zapata, Joan
HYPE!
Zhao, Yihua
STORY OF XINGHUA, THE
Zhong Furong
BLACK MOUNTAIN
Zhou Xinxia
BLUSH
Ziehl, Scott
RED LINE
Zimmerman, Don
NUTTY PROFESSOR, THE
Zubeck, Gary
RED SCORPION 2

EXECUTIVE PRODUCERS

Abbott, Elliot
GETTING AWAY WITH MURDER
PREACHER'S WIFE, THE
Abramoff, Jack
RED SCORPION 2
Abramoff, Robert
RED SCORPION 2
Adelson, Gary
HIDDEN ASSASSIN
Aert, Christian Moey
MAN OF THE YEAR
Aglion, Michael D.
WIFE, THE
Agrama, Frank
AMERICAN STRAYS
Airoldi, Conchita
CEMETERY MAN
Allard, Tony
BOY CALLED HATE, A
Allen, Joseph
BASQUIAT
Almodovar, Agustin
FLOWER OF MY SECRET, THE
Amatullo, Tony
2 DAYS IN THE VALLEY
Amin, Mark
. . . AT FIRST SIGHT
DENTIST, THE
IRON EAGLE IV
MADDENING, THE
PINOCCHIO'S REVENGE
SOMETIMES THEY COME BACK . . . AGAIN
Amritraj, Ashok
ELECTRA
VIRUS
WHEN THE BULLET HITS THE BONE
Andrews, Dale
RED SCORPION 2
Apatow, Judd
CELTIC PRIDE
Armato, Leonard
KAZAAM
Assouma, Rachel
SHADOW WARRIORS
Avary, Roger
MR. STITCH
Ayala, Fernando
SHADOW YOU SOON WILL BE, A
Baer, Willi
BLACK DAY BLUE NIGHT
Bailin, Marc
MODERN AFFAIR, A
Bakalar, Steven
SUBSTITUTE, THE
Baldwin, Alec
HEAVEN'S PRISONERS
Bambihill, Michael
CONDITION RED
Bancroft, Shelly
PASSION OF DARKLY NOON, THE
Band, Albert
ZARKORR! THE INVADER
Band, Charles
BACKLASH: OBLIVION 2
JOSH KIRBY . . . TIME WARRIOR!: EGGS FROM 70,000,000 B.C.
JOSH KIRBY . . . TIME WARRIOR!: JOURNEY TO THE MAGIC CAVERN
JOSH KIRBY . . . TIME WARRIOR!: LAST BATTLE FOR THE UNIVERSE
JOSH KIRBY . . . TIME WARRIOR!: TRAPPED ON TOY WORLD
MAGIC IN THE MIRROR
SPELLBREAKER: SECRET OF THE LEPRECHAUNS
Barber, Gary
BAD MOON
BIG BULLY
DIABOLIQUE
TWO IF BY SEA
Barker, Clive
HELLRAISER: BLOODLINE
Barnholtz, Barry
PROTEUS
PUBLIC ENEMIES
SOMETIMES THEY COME BACK . . . AGAIN
Barone, Tracy
MY FELLOW AMERICANS
Barreto, Bruno
CARRIED AWAY
Baruc, Robert
GRIM
LITTLE WITCHES
Baruc, Robert E.
DEMOLITIONIST, THE
Bascom, Donna
WELCOME TO THE DOLLHOUSE
Baumgartner, Craig
HIDDEN ASSASSIN
Beach, Jim
PASSION OF DARKLY NOON, THE
Beaucaire, J.E.
EVERYONE SAYS I LOVE YOU
Becker, Richard
. . . AT FIRST SIGHT
Beece, Debby
HARRIET THE SPY
Beigel, Herbert
HEAVY
Belafonte, Harry
AFFAIR, THE
Belfort, Jordan
SANTA WITH MUSCLES
Bellisario, Donald P.
JAG
Bender, Lawrence
FROM DUSK TILL DAWN
Benitez, Cesar
MOUTH TO MOUTH
Bennett, C. Casey
HELLRAISER: BLOODLINE
Bennett, Robert M.
TOLLBOOTH
Beretta, Grace
MERLIN'S SHOP OF MAGICAL WONDERS
Bernt, Heather
LIVE NUDE GIRLS
Berrigan, Frances
PARIS WAS A WOMAN
Berwin, Dorothy
WALKING AND TALKING
Bevan, Tim
FARGO
Binder, Chuck
DIABOLIQUE
Birnbaum, Roger
BEFORE AND AFTER
MAXIMUM RISK
Blatt, Daniel H.
KISSINGER AND NIXON
Bleiberg, Ehud
BAJA
Blum, Mark
LOW LIFE, THE
Blumenthal, Jason
BIO-DOME
Boboras, Peter
JOHNNY SHORTWAVE
Boladian, Armen
MIRROR, MIRROR III: THE VOYEUR
Bold, Edgar
YANKEE ZULU
Botwick, Terry
GIRL FROM MARS, THE
Bouix, Bernard
HORSEMAN ON THE ROOF
MACHINE, THE
UNHOOK THE STARS
Bowie, David
MAGIC HUNTER
Boyle, Barbara
BOTTLE ROCKET
Bozman, Ron
EDDIE
Bradley, Paul
PROPRIETOR, THE
SURVIVING PICASSO
Brandman, Michael
HEIDI CHRONICLES, THE

Brant, Peter
BASQUIAT
Bregman, Martin
MATILDA
Breznahan, Tom
HEADLESS BODY IN TOPLESS BAR
Brill, Steven
D3: THE MIGHTY DUCKS
Brillstein, Bernie
BULLETPROOF
CABLE GUY, THE
CELLULOID CLOSET, THE
HAPPY GILMORE
Brody, Tod Scott
MARVIN'S ROOM
Broke, Richard
COLD COMFORT FARM
Brooks, Eric
ORIGINAL GANGSTAS
Brooks, James L.
BOTTLE ROCKET
Brost, Frederic W.
GETTING AWAY WITH MURDER
Brown, Kevin Kelly
COLONY, THE
Brownstein, Jerome
FLIRT
Brundig, Reinhard
COLD FEVER
FLIRT
Brunton, Colin
BLOOD & DONUTS
RUDE
Buhai, Jeff
EDDIE
Burdis, Ray
PASSION OF DARKLY NOON, THE
Burg, Mark
DON'T BE A MENACE TO SOUTH CENTRAL WHILE DRINKING YOUR JUICE IN THE HOOD
LITTLE DEATH, THE
Burke, Delta
MATERNAL INSTINCTS
Burke, Graham
PHANTOM, THE
Burke, Martyn
SUGARTIME
Burns, William F.
NIGHT OF THE TWISTERS
Bursteen, Alan B.
FORBIDDEN ZONE: ALIEN ABDUCTION
Burstein, Alan
FRIEND OF THE FAMILY 2
Bushnell, Scott
KANSAS CITY
Cady, Fitch
CARPOOL
Calderwood, Andrea
SMALL FACES
Camon, Alessandro
CROW: CITY OF ANGELS, THE
Campoy, Eduardo
BATON ROUGE
Cantillon, Elizabeth
SUNSET PARK
Caracciolo, Joseph M.
COURAGE UNDER FIRE
SUNCHASER
Carraro, William
MISSING PIECES
Cascante, Gregory
WHOLE WIDE WORLD, THE
Cavan, Susan
MAGIC HUNTER
Cazes, Lila
VENUS RISING
Chackler, David
ORIGINAL GANGSTAS
Chambers, Michael
FUNERAL, THE
Chan Pui-Wah
CHUNGKING EXPRESS
Chapman, Jan
TWO FRIENDS
Chase, Debra Martin
COURAGE UNDER FIRE
Cheng Zhigu
BLUSH
Chesler, Lewis B.
BLOODKNOT
UNDERTOW
Chetwynd, Lionel
KISSINGER AND NIXON
Christiansen, Bob
BEYOND THE CALL
Ciolino, Rose
MERLIN'S SHOP OF MAGICAL WONDERS
Claybourne, Doug
JACK
Cohen, Annette
STAND OFF, THE
Cohen, Barney
SABRINA, THE TEENAGE WITCH
Cohen, Joseph
IRON EAGLE IV
Colichman, Paul
AMANDA AND THE ALIEN
DEAD WEEKEND
OUT THERE
VENUS RISING
Collier, Barry
WITHIN THE ROCK
Connery, Sean
ROCK, THE
Cooper, David
LAST SUPPER, THE
Coote, Greg
PHANTOM, THE
Copeland III, Miles A.
AMANDA AND THE ALIEN
DEAD WEEKEND
EXIT
OUT THERE
VENUS RISING
YESTERDAY'S TARGET
Coppola, Francis Ford
HAUNTED
Corbett, David J.
PHANTOM 2040: THE GHOST WHO WALKS
Corman, Cis
MIRROR HAS TWO FACES, THE
Corman, Roger
BLACK ROSE OF HARLEM
BLACK SCORPION
BURIAL OF THE RATS
DEATH ARTIST, THE
HARD WAY OUT: BLOODFIST VIII
NOT OF THIS EARTH
ONE NIGHT STAND
PIRANHA
SAWBONES
UNKNOWN ORIGIN
Cort, Robert W.
ARRIVAL, THE
ASSOCIATE, THE
BOYS
KAZAAM
TWO MUCH
Costa, Gerard
CELESTIAL CLOCKWORK
Cotone, Mario
STAR MAKER, THE
Couturie, Bill
ED
Crane, Peter
LILY DALE
Craven, Wes
MIND RIPPER
Cummins, Jack
DOWN PERISCOPE
Curran Wexelblatt, Linda
LILY DALE
Cutler, Devora
SUBSTITUTE, THE
Dahl, Rick
UNFORGETTABLE
Dammico, Cico
TOO FAST, TOO YOUNG
Dammico, Stefano
PORTRAITS OF A KILLER
TOO FAST, TOO YOUNG
Danon, Marcello
BIRDCAGE, THE
Dante, Joe
PHANTOM, THE
Daou, Diane
BODY COUNT
Dattila, Robert
CARRIED AWAY
David, Pierre
DEAD COLD
Davis, Gail
RAVENHAWK
Davis, Jim
RAVENHAWK
Davis, John
DANGEROUS PASSION
DENISE CALLS UP
De La Torre, Dale
FIRST KID
De Laurentiis, Raffaella
DAYLIGHT
De Luca, Michael
LAST MAN STANDING
LONG KISS GOODNIGHT, THE
Decker, Emily
DEVOTION
Demme, Jonathan
DESOLATION ANGELS
Densham, Pen
OUTER LIMITS: SANDKINGS, THE
DePasse, Suzanne
LARRY MCMURTRY'S STREETS OF LAREDO
Devlin, C. Tad
D3: THE MIGHTY DUCKS
Deyhle, Rolf
SURGEON, THE
Di Dionisio, Dino
CEMETERY MAN
Dimbort, Danny
DEADLY OUTBREAK
FOREST WARRIOR
HARD JUSTICE
IMMORTALS, THE
LIVE WIRE: HUMAN TIMEBOMB
TERMINAL IMPACT
WARHEAD
WILD SIDE
Dion, Debra
JOSH KIRBY . . . TIME WARRIOR!: EGGS FROM 70,000,000 B.C.
JOSH KIRBY . . . TIME WARRIOR!: JOURNEY TO THE MAGIC CAVERN
JOSH KIRBY . . . TIME WARRIOR!: LAST BATTLE FOR THE UNIVERSE
JOSH KIRBY . . . TIME WARRIOR!: TRAPPED ON TOY WORLD
SPELLBREAKER: SECRET OF THE LEPRECHAUNS
Ditchfield, Bruce
FATALLY YOURS

Donner, Richard
TALES FROM THE CRYPT PRESENTS BORDELLO OF BLOOD
Douglas, Michael
GHOST AND THE DARKNESS, THE
Doumanian, Jean
EVERYONE SAYS I LOVE YOU
Duncan, Patrick Sheane
MR. HOLLAND'S OPUS
Dunne, Griffin
JOE'S APARTMENT
Durkin, Bill
CAUGHT
East, Guy
AUGUST
LARGER THAN LIFE
Eberts, Jake
JAMES AND THE GIANT PEACH
Edelman, Pierre
WIFE, THE
Egoyan, Atom
CURTIS'S CHARM
Eiferman, Loren
PARADISE LOST: THE CHILD MURDERS AT ROBIN HOOD HILLS
Einhorn, Steve
POISON IVY 2: LILY
Elders, Kevin
RAVENHAWK
Elliott, Mike
LOOKING FOR TROUBLE
Elwes, Cassian
BAD LOVE
Emmerich, Roland
INDEPENDENCE DAY
Emmerich, Ute
INDEPENDENCE DAY
Ephron, Delia
MICHAEL
Epstein, Allen
HOW THE WEST WAS FUN
Epstein, Brad
ED
Eralp, Osman
PROPRIETOR, THE
Erickson, C.O.
BLACK SHEEP
Estes, Larry
WEEKEND IN THE COUNTRY, A
Faber, George
STONEWALL
Falk, David
SPACE JAM
Farber, Sid
MURDERED INNOCENCE
Faure, Brigitte
SINGLE GIRL, A
Faure, Michel
MICROCOSMOS
Fay, William
INDEPENDENCE DAY
Feifer, Jerry
WITCHCRAFT: SALEM'S GHOST
Feldman, Edward S.
101 DALMATIANS
Fellner, Eric
FARGO
Felsberg, Ulrich
LAND AND FREEDOM
Ferns, W. Paterson
STAND OFF, THE
Ferrari, Stefano
THEODORE REX
Ferri, Elda
MONSTER, THE
Field, Ted
ARRIVAL, THE
ASSOCIATE, THE
BOYS
KAZAAM
TWO MUCH
Figgis, Mike
FOXFIRE
Finch, Charles
MADDENING, THE
Finnegan, Bill
ED
Fitzpatrick, Robert
IT'S MY PARTY
Foote, Hallie
LILY DALE
Foreman, John
UP CLOSE AND PERSONAL
Forsythe, William
BEYOND DESIRE
Frain, Andy
GHOST IN THE SHELL
Fraser-Baigelman, Gayle
BOGUS
Fremes, John
DEMOLITIONIST, THE
LITTLE WITCHES
WITHIN THE ROCK
Fridriksson, Fridrik Thor
COLD FEVER
Friedman Block, Lisa
MATERNAL INSTINCTS
Friedman, Laura
FOXFIRE
Friedman, Stephen
MOTHER
Friendly, David
CHAMBER, THE
Fries, Charles W.
SCREAMERS
Fuchs, Fred
HAUNTED
Fujimura, Tetsu
SGT. KABUKIMAN N.Y.P.D.
Gale, David
BEAVIS AND BUTT-HEAD DO AMERICA
Gallagher, Patrick F.
FELONY
Gallagher, Stephen
PREDICTIONS OF FIRE
Gallin, Sandy
FLY AWAY HOME
Garcia, Pelayo
BITTER SUGAR
Garcillan, Fernando
MOUTH TO MOUTH
Gatien, Peter
FAITHFUL
Gautier, Philippe
MICROCOSMOS
Gavigan, Sean
HEADLESS BODY IN TOPLESS BAR
Gelber, Stephen
JUST YOUR LUCK
Gelin, Xavier
WAR OF THE BUTTONS, THE
Genetti, Dan
DON'T BE A MENACE TO SOUTH CENTRAL WHILE DRINKING YOUR JUICE IN THE HOOD
LITTLE DEATH, THE
Gernert, Walter
ANIMAL INSTINCTS III: THE SEDUCTRESS
BODY OF INFLUENCE 2
Gerrie, Malcolm
MESSAGE TO LOVE: THE ISLE OF WIGHT FESTIVAL
Gibson, Ben
LOADED
MADAGASCAR SKIN
Gigliotto, Donna
EMMA
Gil, Edmundo
BATON ROUGE
Giler, David
TALES FROM THE CRYPT PRESENTS BORDELLO OF BLOOD
Ginsburg, David
DONOR UNKNOWN
Ginsburg, David R.
RASPUTIN
Ginzberg, Yitzhak
BAJA
Giuliano, Peter
SLEEPERS
Giustra, Frank
BEST OF THE BEST 3: NO TURNING BACK
Glattes, Wolfgang
LARGER THAN LIFE
Glickman, Jonathan
CELTIC PRIDE
Glover, Danny
AMERICA'S DREAM
Goddard, Melissa
SHARON'S SECRET
Godsick, Christopher
BROKEN ARROW
Gold, Eric L.
BULLETPROOF
Goldschmidt, Ernst
OF LOVE AND SHADOWS
Golin, Steve
PIG'S TALE, A
Goodale, Robert D.
MAGIC HUNTER
Gottlieb, Hildy
HEAVEN'S PRISONERS
Gray, Bill
HECK'S WAY HOME
Gray, F. Gary
SET IT OFF
Green, Jim
HOW THE WEST WAS FUN
Greenhut, Robert
PREACHER'S WIFE, THE
Greenstein, Scott
ENGLISH PATIENT, THE
Greenwald, Martin W.
FAST MONEY
Grey, Brad
BULLETPROOF
CABLE GUY, THE
CELLULOID CLOSET, THE
HAPPY GILMORE
Gros, Robert
STREETCAR NAMED DESIRE, A
Gross, H. Daniel
PAINTED HERO
Grunstein, Pierre
FRENCH TWIST
Guinness, Laurence
PATLABOR 2: MOBILE POLICE
ROUJIN-Z
Guinzburg, Kate
ONE FINE DAY
Gurvitz, Marc
CABLE GUY, THE
Haas III, Jim
MUTANT MAN
Hafkamp, Eric
CROCODILES IN AMSTERDAM
Hallowell, Todd
RANSOM
Halmi Jr., Robert
LARRY MCMURTRY'S STREETS OF LAREDO
Halsted, Dan
FREEWAY

Harari, Sasha
HIGH SCHOOL HIGH
Harris, Ed
RIDERS OF THE PURPLE SAGE
Harris, Lynn
BED OF ROSES
Hart, Paula
SABRINA, THE TEENAGE WITCH
Hartwick, Joseph
BED OF ROSES
STRIPTEASE
Hashimoto, Richard
TRUTH ABOUT CATS AND DOGS, THE
Hauer, Rutger
MR. STITCH
Hausman, Michael
FAMILY THING, A
Head, Sally
CRACKER: THE MADWOMAN IN THE ATTIC
Hell, Kevin
SOME FOLKS CALL IT A SLING BLADE
Heller, Peter
BARB WIRE
Herman, Mike
SOME FOLKS CALL IT A SLING BLADE
Hernandez, Carlos
LOTTO LAND
Herrero, Gerardo
LAND AND FREEDOM
Herz, Michael
BUGGED
Hewitt, Caroline
YOUNG POISONER'S HANDBOOK, THE
Hibbin, Sally
LAND AND FREEDOM
Hickenlooper, George
LOW LIFE, THE
Hill, Andrew
DANGEROUS PASSION
Hill, Walter
TALES FROM THE CRYPT PRESENTS BORDELLO OF BLOOD
Hinton, Gregory
IT'S MY PARTY
Hitchcock, Paul
MISSION: IMPOSSIBLE
Ho, Leonard
RUMBLE IN THE BRONX
Hoberman, David
MR. WRONG
Hodge, Jim B.
UNDER THE HULA MOON
Hoffman, Yvette
MR. ICE CREAM MAN
Hohoff, Christian
FATE
Hookstratten, Ed
UP CLOSE AND PERSONAL
Hool, Lance
FLIPPER
Hope, Ted
GIRLFRIENDS
Horibuchi, Seiji
SANCTUARY: THE MOVIE
Hornstein, Marty
STAR TREK: FIRST CONTACT
Hoskins, Bob
JOSEPH CONRAD'S THE SECRET AGENT
Huddles, Gary
FAR HARBOR
Huddles, John
FAR HARBOR
Hunt, Anjanantre
RAW TARGET
Hurd, Gale Ann
SUGARTIME
Ichise, Taka
FIST OF THE NORTH STAR
NECRONOMICON: BOOK OF THE DEAD
Inagaki, Hiroshi
STREET FIGHTER II: THE ANIMATED MOVIE
Irving, Amy
CARRIED AWAY
Iscovich, Mario
DEAR GOD
MULHOLLAND FALLS
Iseki, Satoru
FLIRT
Jablin, David
NATIONAL LAMPOON'S FAVORITE DEADLY SINS
Jackson, David A.
PORTRAITS OF A KILLER
James, Judith
KISSINGER AND NIXON
Jao, Jim
WING CHUN
Javitz, Barbara
WITHIN THE ROCK
Jensen, Peter Aalbaek
COLD FEVER
Jiang Feng-chyi
VIVE L'AMOUR
Johnson, Patrick Read
DRAGONHEART
Jonsson, Lars
BREAKING THE WAVES
Kallberg, Kenneth J.
DOGFIGHTERS, THE
Kaplan, Avaram Butch
LAWNMOWER MAN 2: BEYOND CYBERSPACE
Kaplan, Caroline
4 TALES OF 2 CITIES
Kaufman, Kenneth
CHILDREN OF FURY
SKIN
Kaufman, Lloyd
BUGGED
Kazanjian, Howard
RATTLED
Kehela, Karen
CHAMBER, THE
FEAR
NUTTY PROFESSOR, THE
Kelleher, Tim
FIRST KID
Kelly, Alexandra
CANNIBAL! THE MUSICAL
Kemler, Andrew
CANNIBAL! THE MUSICAL
Kemp, Ralph
HAUNTED
Kempin, Geoff
MESSAGE TO LOVE: THE ISLE OF WIGHT FESTIVAL
Kenneally, Rob
WEEKEND IN THE COUNTRY, A
Kesten, Stephen F.
STEPHEN KING'S THINNER
Kidney, Ric
CHAMBER, THE
Kilik, Jon
GIRL 6
SAINTS AND SINNERS
Kimmel, Sidney
MOTHER
Kirkpatrick, David
BIG NIGHT
RASPUTIN
Kitt, Sam
EVIL HAS A FACE
Kleeman, Jeff
HAUNTED
Koch Jr., Howard W.
PRIMAL FEAR
Konrad, Cathy
BEAUTIFUL GIRLS
Konvitz, Jeffrey
BLOODSPORT II: THE NEXT KUMITE
Korda, David
BLACK DAY BLUE NIGHT
SURGEON, THE
Krane, Jonathan D.
MICHAEL
PHENOMENON
Kreloff, Mark
SOUTH BEACH ACADEMY
Kroopf, Scott
ASSOCIATE, THE
BOYS
MR. HOLLAND'S OPUS
Kugler, Harry
MAYBE . . . MAYBE NOT
Kurosawa, Mitsuru
BODY COUNT
Kushner, Donald
ADVENTURES OF PINOCCHIO, THE
GRAVE, THE
WHOLE WIDE WORLD, THE
La Travese, Anne Marie
NIGHT OF THE TWISTERS
La Voo, George
FRISK
Ladd, Diane
MRS. MUNCK
Lancelot, Patrick
MICROCOSMOS
Lane, Steve
LAWNMOWER MAN 2: BEYOND CYBERSPACE
Last, Bob
PERSONAL JOURNEY WITH MARTIN SCORSESE THROUGH AMERICAN MOVIES, A
Lauria, Dan
FAITHFUL
Law, Lindsay
ANGELS AND INSECTS
I SHOT ANDY WARHOL
PALOOKAVILLE
Lawenda, Jeff
PAINTED HERO
Lawrence, Martin
THIN LINE BETWEEN LOVE AND HATE, A
Layton, Mel
LIVE NUDE GIRLS
Lazar, Andrew
UNFORGETTABLE
Lazare, Andre
MICROCOSMOS
Lee, Damian
ELECTRA
Lee, Danny
ORGANIZED CRIME & TRIAD BUREAU
Lee, Spike
GET ON THE BUS
Leff, Adam
BIO-DOME
Leiberson, Sandy
ROLLING STONES ROCK-AND-ROLL CIRCUS, THE
Leipzig, Adam
TWO MUCH
Lemmon, Jack
WEEKEND IN THE COUNTRY, A
Leonard, Harvey
SOUTH BEACH ACADEMY
Lerner, Avi
DEADLY OUTBREAK

FOREST WARRIOR
HARD JUSTICE
HOLLOW POINT
IMMORTALS, THE
LIVE WIRE: HUMAN TIMEBOMB
WARHEAD
WILD SIDE

Levett, Ashley
SHAMELESS

Levi, Jean-Pierre Ramsay
EYE OF VICHY, THE

Levinson, Larry
LARRY MCMURTRY'S STREETS OF LAREDO

Levitt, Zane W.
FIST OF THE NORTH STAR

Lewis, Butch
ONCE UPON A TIME . . . WHEN WE WERE COLORED

Lewis, Jerry
NUTTY PROFESSOR, THE

Lewis, Richard B.
OUTER LIMITS: SANDKINGS, THE

Liber, Rodney
DUNSTON CHECKS IN

Links, James E.
THEY BITE

Lipsky, Mark
NUTTY PROFESSOR, THE

Little, Dwight H.
BROKEN ARROW

Littler, Lawrence
BEWARE: CHILDREN AT PLAY

Littman, Robert
FULL BODY MASSAGE

Locke, Peter
ADVENTURES OF PINOCCHIO, THE
GRAVE, THE
WHOLE WIDE WORLD, THE

Lord, Peter
WALLACE AND GROMIT: THE BEST OF AARDMAN ANIMATION

Lynn, Tony
GLASS CAGE, THE
PLAYBACK

MacDonald, Laurie
TRIGGER EFFECT, THE
TWISTER

MacDonald, Peter
QUEST, THE

Machlis, Neil
BIRDCAGE, THE

Machuel, Herve
OF LOVE AND SHADOWS

MacRory, Avril
MESSAGE TO LOVE: THE ISLE OF WIGHT FESTIVAL

Maddalena, Marianne
SCREAM

Madden, David
ASSOCIATE, THE

Maddock, Brent
TREMORS 2: AFTERSHOCKS

Madigan, Amy
RIDERS OF THE PURPLE SAGE

Malott, Richard A.
CLUBHOUSE DETECTIVES

Mann, Robert
DESIRE

Manpearl, Stephan
MAD DOG TIME

March, Donald
MAN IN THE ATTIC, THE

Markey, Patrick
BOGUS

Marks, Ross Kagan
HOMAGE

Marsil, Stephane
WAR OF THE BUTTONS, THE

Martin, Alan
PROTEUS

Mason, Morgan
MR. STITCH

Mayes, Lee R.
MULTIPLICITY

McAree, Roy
WHITE TIGER

McCabe, Colin
PERSONAL JOURNEY WITH MARTIN SCORSESE THROUGH AMERICAN MOVIES, A

McClain, Kimberly
TOO FAST, TOO YOUNG

McCormick, Patrick
JUROR, THE

McCracken, Cameron
YOUNG POISONER'S HANDBOOK, THE

McDonald, Carolyn
AMERICA'S DREAM

McGrath, Judith
JOE'S APARTMENT

McHugh, Jason
CANNIBAL! THE MUSICAL

McMillan, Michael
GIRL FROM MARS, THE

McMurtry, Larry
LARRY MCMURTRY'S STREETS OF LAREDO

McRae, Peter
LAWNMOWER MAN 2: BEYOND CYBERSPACE

Meek, Scott
WALKING AND TALKING

Mehrez, Diane
BLOODSPORT II: THE NEXT KUMITE

Meistrich, Larry
SLING BLADE

Mejia, Alejandra
DARK SECRETS

Memel, Jana Sue
4 TALES OF 2 CITIES

Meron, Neil
MY FELLOW AMERICANS

Meyer, Irwin
LILY DALE

Miao, Brenda
DEAD TO RIGHTS

Michelucci, Bob
SANTA CLAWS

Miguel, Isidro
OF LOVE AND SHADOWS

Milchan, Arnon
TIN CUP

Miller, William E.
PHANTOM 2040: THE GHOST WHO WALKS

Mittweg, Rolf
DELTA OF VENUS

Miyahara, Teruo
GHOST IN THE SHELL

Molen, Gerald R.
TRIGGER EFFECT, THE
TWISTER

Morgan, Peter
POISON IVY 2: LILY
SHARON'S SECRET

Morrison, Steve
AUGUST

Mortorff, Lawrence
GRAVE, THE

Moszkowicz, Martin
MAYBE . . . MAYBE NOT

Munchkin, Richard W.
BREAKAWAY

Nakamura, Masaya
SGT. KABUKIMAN N.Y.P.D.

Nathanson, Michael
BOGUS
SUNCHASER

Nau, Robert
TOO FAST, TOO YOUNG

Nemeth, Stephen
DENISE CALLS UP

Neufeld, Mace
WOMAN UNDONE, A

Nevins, Sheila
PARADISE LOST: THE CHILD MURDERS AT ROBIN HOOD HILLS

Newirth, Charles
GHOSTS OF MISSISSIPPI
PHENOMENON

Newton, Joseph
IRON EAGLE IV

Nichols, David
RACE THE SUN
WAR OF THE BUTTONS, THE

Nielsen, Leslie
SPY HARD

Nolin, Michael
DELTA OF VENUS

North, Steve
VUKOVAR

Nozik, Michael
SHE'S THE ONE

Nugent, Ginny
CRAFT, THE

O'Donnell, John
NIGHT ON THE GALACTIC RAILROAD

O'Neal, Shaquille
KAZAAM

O'Sullivan, Morgan
MOLL FLANDERS

Offsay, Jerry
DIABOLIQUE

Ogden, Jennifer
RICH MAN'S WIFE, THE

Ogiens, Michael
LAZARUS MAN, THE

Oldham, Rocky
MESSAGE TO LOVE: THE ISLE OF WIGHT FESTIVAL

Olsberg, Jonathon
TWO DEATHS

Ommidvar, Abdullah
JOHNNY 100 PESOS

Ordesky, Mark
MOTHER NIGHT

Ormond, Julia
CALLING THE GHOSTS: A STORY ABOUT RAPE, WAR AND WOMEN

Osborne, Barrie M.
FAN, THE

Ossana, Diana
LARRY MCMURTRY'S STREETS OF LAREDO

Ouedraogo, Idrissa
GUIMBA THE TYRANT

Palaggi, Ezio
SONS OF TRINITY

Palmer, Patrick
MRS. WINTERBOURNE

Panzarella, Patrick
FUNERAL, THE

Pappas, George
LOVE IS ALL THERE IS

Parent, Mary
SET IT OFF

Parker, Jonathan
FATALLY YOURS

Parkes, Walter
TRIGGER EFFECT, THE
TWISTER

Parsons, Steve
FUNNYMAN, THE

Patchett, Tom
CHILDREN OF FURY
SKIN
Patel, Sharad
ADVENTURES OF PINOCCHIO, THE
Paul, Steven
WHISPERING, THE
Pavlic, Bobbie
CROSSCUT
Pavlic, John
CROSSCUT
Pearlman, Jennifer L.
MERCY
Peck, Mitchell
BIO-DOME
Pedas, Jim
CAUGHT
Pedas, Ted
CAUGHT
Peel, Jonathan
WIND IN THE WILLOWS, THE
Pelecanos, George P.
CAUGHT
Perfili, Virginia
MIRROR, MIRROR III: THE VOYEUR
Perlmutter, David M.
BLOODKNOT
UNDERTOW
Perry, Steve
EXECUTIVE DECISION
Peyser, Michael
MATILDA
Pfeffer, Andrew
WILD SIDE
Pfeiffer, Michelle
ONE FINE DAY
Pillsbury, Sarah
LETTER TO MY KILLER
Pinchuk, Sheldon
IT CAME FROM OUTER SPACE II
Pleshette, Lynn
MARY REILLY
Porush, Danny
SANTA WITH MUSCLES
Poster, Meryl
PALLBEARER, THE
Potter, Barr B.
ADRENALIN: FEAR THE RUSH
Powell, Nik
NEON BIBLE, THE
Powell, Norman S.
LAZARUS MAN, THE
Preuss, Ruben
TAILS YOU LIVE, HEADS YOU'RE DEAD
Price, Frank
TUSKEGEE AIRMEN, THE
Pringle, Bob
LAWNMOWER MAN 2: BEYOND CYBERSPACE
Rachmil, Michael
GLIMMER MAN, THE
Raimi, Sam
DARKMAN III: DIE DARKMAN DIE
Ray, Melanie
YESTERDAY'S TARGET
Redford, Robert
SHE'S THE ONE
Rehne, Robert
WOMAN UNDONE, A
Reisman, Linda
MOTHER NIGHT
Reitman, Ivan
LATE SHIFT, THE
Reuther, Steven
GHOST AND THE DARKNESS, THE
Reynolds, Don
GIRL FROM MARS, THE
Rice, Tracie Graham
WAR AT HOME, THE
Rich, Paul
HELLRAISER: BLOODLINE
TOLLBOOTH
Riethmuller, Pit
ORSON WELLES: THE ONE-MAN BAND
Risher, Sara
IN LOVE AND WAR
LAST MAN STANDING
Robbins, Lance
DEATH ARTIST, THE
TRACKS OF A KILLER
Robbins, Lance H.
BLACK SCORPION
CRIMINAL HEARTS
HOSTILE INTENTIONS
NOT OF THIS EARTH
SAWBONES
Robers, Wayne M.
NIGHT OF THE TWISTERS
Rodriguez, Robert
FROM DUSK TILL DAWN
Ronson, Rena
TOLLBOOTH
Root, Antony
COLD COMFORT FARM
Rose, Lee
MOTHER'S PRAYER, A
Rosemont, David A.
LONG ROAD HOME, THE
RIDERS OF THE PURPLE SAGE
Rosen, Phillip L.
DELTA OF VENUS
Rosen, Robert L.
SPY HARD
Rosenberg, Rick
BEYOND THE CALL
DEATH BENEFIT
Rosenberg, Tom
KIDS IN THE HALL: BRAIN CANDY
Rosenblum, Paul
ADRENALIN: FEAR THE RUSH
NEMESIS III: PREY HARDER
Rosenfeld, Donald
CATWALK
SURVIVING PICASSO
Rosenman, Howard
CELLULOID CLOSET, THE
Rosetti, Richard P.
GLASS CAGE, THE
PLAYBACK
Ross, Ken
SPACE JAM
Ross, Mark
SWEET NOTHING
Rotenberg, Michael
BIO-DOME
WEEKEND IN THE COUNTRY, A
Roth, Joe
BEFORE AND AFTER
Rothschild, Richard Luke
LAST DANCE
Rotman, David
DRAGONHEART
Rowe, Frank D.
PRE-MADONNAS
Rowe, Tom
BOY CALLED HATE, A
Rozema, Patricia
CURTIS'S CHARM
Rubin, Bob
ASSAULT AT WEST POINT
Rudnick-Polstein, Claire
ISLAND OF DR. MOREAU, THE
Russell, Chuck
ERASER
Russell, Neil
DEAD TO RIGHTS
Russo, John A.
SANTA CLAWS
Rutowski, Richard
FREEWAY
Rydell, Guy
SAINTS AND SINNERS
S., Sam
WITHOUT MERCY
Sackman, Jeff
WHEN THE BULLET HITS THE BONE
Saewitz, Anita
CALLING THE GHOSTS: A STORY ABOUT RAPE, WAR AND WOMEN
Saidiner, Mara
SOUTH BEACH ACADEMY
Sakai, Akio
STREET FIGHTER II: THE ANIMATED MOVIE
Sakai, Richard
BOTTLE ROCKET
Salbot, Sophie
GUIMBA THE TYRANT
Salkind, Morton
FINAL EQUINOX, THE
PHOENIX
Samaha, Elie
HOLLOW POINT
Sameth, David
I'M NOT RAPPAPORT
Samples, Keith
BIG NIGHT
CHAMELEON
HOUSE ARREST
KINGPIN
2 DAYS IN THE VALLEY
WIDOW'S KISS
Sanford, Linda
BEWARE: CHILDREN AT PLAY
Sanford, Midge
LETTER TO MY KILLER
Saperstein, Richard
LONG KISS GOODNIGHT, THE
Saredi, Christa
COLD FEVER
Sasaki, Shiro
HOMECOMING
Savage, Nigel
SOLITAIRE FOR TWO
Saviano, John
NORMAL LIFE
Schamus, James
GIRLFRIENDS
Scheinman, Andrew
EXTREME MEASURES
Scheuer, Walter
SMALL WONDERS
Schifman, Aron
BREAKAWAY
Schlei, Brad
SOME FOLKS CALL IT A SLING BLADE
Schlissel, Charles J.D.
CELTIC PRIDE
Schminke, Frederick
ABUSE
Schon, Jeffrey
PHANTOM 2040: THE GHOST WHO WALKS
Schroeder, Adam
FIRST WIVES CLUB, THE
Schroeder, Barbet
DESOLATION ANGELS
Schuler, Thomas
DESIRE
Schwartzman, Jack
ONE NIGHT STAND

Scorsese, Martin
GRACE OF MY HEART
Scott, Allan
TWO DEATHS
Scott, Jeffrey
GHOSTS OF MISSISSIPPI
Scott, Ridley
WHITE SQUALL
Sedgwick, Kyra
LOSING CHASE
Segall, Stu
BEASTMASTER 3: THE EYE OF BRAXUS
FAST MONEY
Sehring, Jonathan
4 TALES OF 2 CITIES
Sellers, Dylan
BIG BULLY
Senft, Elvira
MAYBE . . . MAYBE NOT
Shapiro, Len
MAD DOG TIME
Shavick, James
ROAD HOME, THE
Shelly, Adrienne
4 TALES OF 2 CITIES
Shelton, Ron
OPEN SEASON
Sherlock, Bruce
PHANTOM, THE
Shields, Brent
BOYS NEXT DOOR, THE
CANTERVILLE GHOST, THE
Shigenobu, Yutaka
MABOROSI
Shivas, Mark
CAPTIVES
JUDE
SMALL FACES
TWO DEATHS
Short, Trevor
DEADLY OUTBREAK
HARD JUSTICE
IMMORTALS, THE
LIVE WIRE: HUMAN TIMEBOMB
TERMINAL IMPACT
WARHEAD
WILD SIDE
Shuster, Harry
SANTA WITH MUSCLES
Shwarztenn, Meyer
SONG SPINNER, THE
Siciliano, Pat
FEMALIEN
Siegel, David
ORIGINAL SINS
Siegler, Bill
ASSAULT AT WEST POINT
Siegler, Gary
LOW LIFE, THE
Sighvatsson, Sigurjon
KIDS IN THE HALL: BRAIN CANDY
PIG'S TALE, A
Silver, Joel
TALES FROM THE CRYPT PRESENTS BORDELLO OF BLOOD
Silvey, Tina
NOT BAD FOR A GIRL
Simmons, Jack
MADAME WANG'S
Simo, Sandor
OUTPOST, THE
Simon, Randy
LOVER'S KNOT
Simpson, Paige
FOXFIRE
Sinbad
FIRST KID

Singer, Bryan
PUBLIC ACCESS
Singh, Anant
CAPTIVES
Siriez, Catherine
FRANCOIS TRUFFAUT: STOLEN PORTRAITS
Sjoquist, Peter
PHANTOM, THE
Skotchdopole, James W.
FAN, THE
Skouras, Marjorie
BOY CALLED HATE, A
Sladek, Daniel Jakub
HIDDEN ASSASSIN
Slan, Jon
KISSINGER AND NIXON
Sloss, John
AMERICAN BUFFALO
LONE STAR
Smith, Greg
TWELFTH NIGHT
Smith, Jack
SANTA CLAWS
Sofronski, Bernard
HARVEST OF FIRE
Soloman, Maury
CALLING THE GHOSTS: A STORY ABOUT RAPE, WAR AND WOMEN
Sonenberg, David
WHEN WE WERE KINGS
Speiser, Aaron
TALKING ABOUT SEX
Spielberg, Steven
TWISTER
Sproxton, David
WALLACE AND GROMIT: THE BEST OF AARDMAN ANIMATION
Stadvec, Michael
DENTIST, THE
Staggs, Marlon
BEST OF THE BEST 3: NO TURNING BACK
Steinberg, David
KIDS IN THE HALL: BRAIN CANDY
Steinberg, Lori
MARVIN'S ROOM
Stitt, Warren G.
SPITFIRE GRILL, THE
Stoff, Erwin
CHAIN REACTION
FEELING MINNESOTA
Stone, Oliver
FREEWAY
Stonestrom, Eric
YOUNG POISONER'S HANDBOOK, THE
Straight, Robert H.
GALAXIES ARE COLLIDING
Strange, Michael
BREACH OF TRUST
WHITE TIGER
Stroh, Ernst
BLACK OUT
Stroller, Louis A.
ROCK, THE
Strong III, Michael
FINAL CUT, THE
Stuart, William
ROCK, THE
Suer, Ferris
BLONDES HAVE MORE GUNS
Sullivan, Irene
EVERYTHING RELATIVE
Sun, David
MAHJONG
Sussman, Peter
MAN IN THE ATTIC, THE
Swerdlow, Ezra
FIRST WIVES CLUB, THE

Sylbert, Anthea
TRUMAN
Szonyi, Sandor
OUTPOST, THE
Tabet, Sylvio
BEASTMASTER 3: THE EYE OF BRAXUS
Tadross, Michael
ERASER
Talmadge, William
NAKED SOULS
Tapert, Robert
DARKMAN III: DIE DARKMAN DIE
Tarantino, Quentin
CURDLED
FROM DUSK TILL DAWN
Taylor, Michael
BOTTLE ROCKET
Teitler, William
LOOKING FOR RICHARD
UNFORGETTABLE
Terkuhle, Abby
JOE'S APARTMENT
Tierney, Kevin
SONG SPINNER, THE
Till, Stewart
JUDE
Tisch, Steve
LONG KISS GOODNIGHT, THE
Todman Jr., Bill
BAD MOON
DIABOLIQUE
TWO IF BY SEA
Toffler, Van
BEAVIS AND BUTT-HEAD DO AMERICA
Troyano, Ela
GIRLFRIENDS
Tsui Hark
WICKED CITY, THE
Turner, Clive
LAWNMOWER MAN 2: BEYOND CYBERSPACE
Turrow, Randolf
ROAD HOME, THE
Uemura, Tetsu
PATLABOR 2: MOBILE POLICE
Underwood, Ron
TREMORS 2: AFTERSHOCKS
Unger, Bill
FAN, THE
Usami, Ken
SANCTUARY: THE MOVIE
Valovich, Dennis
BLONDES HAVE MORE GUNS
Van Effenterre, Bertrand
FRANCOIS TRUFFAUT: STOLEN PORTRAITS
Van Relim, Tim
VIKING SAGAS, THE
Vane, Dick
PHANTOM, THE
Vane, Richard
JINGLE ALL THE WAY
Vitale, Ruth
MOTHER NIGHT
Volkenborn, Klaus
MANNY & LO
Von Furstenberg, Molly
MAYBE . . . MAYBE NOT
Wachowski, Andy
BOUND
Wachowski, Larry
BOUND
Waddell, Alasdair
PROTEUS
Walker, John
CHAMPAGNE SAFARI, THE

Wall, Anthony
I SHOT ANDY WARHOL
STONEWALL
Wallack, Kathryn
SABRINA, THE TEENAGE WITCH
Watanabe, Shigeru
GHOST IN THE SHELL
Watanabe, Yoshinori
BODY COUNT
Watson, John
OUTER LIMITS: SANDKINGS, THE
Wechsler, Nick
TREES LOUNGE
Weingrod, Herschel
TOLLBOOTH
Weinstein, Bob
BEAUTIFUL GIRLS
CROW: CITY OF ANGELS, THE
EMMA
ENGLISH PATIENT, THE
FLIRTING WITH DISASTER
PALLBEARER, THE
SCREAM
Weinstein, Harvey
BEAUTIFUL GIRLS
CROW: CITY OF ANGELS, THE
EMMA
ENGLISH PATIENT, THE
FLIRTING WITH DISASTER
PALLBEARER, THE
SCREAM
Weinstein, Paula
TRUMAN
Weintraub, Leonard
MURDERED INNOCENCE
Weiss, Robert K.
BLACK SHEEP
Wells, Audrey
TRUTH ABOUT CATS AND DOGS, THE
Welsh, Richard
BOYS NEXT DOOR, THE
CANTERVILLE GHOST, THE
HARVEST OF FIRE
Werner, Avi
TERMINAL IMPACT
Wernick, Sandy
BULLETPROOF
HAPPY GILMORE
Whitmore II, Preston A.
FLED
Wichard, Gary
BLACK OUT
ONE MAN'S JUSTICE
VIRUS
Wiley, Gareth
FUNNYMAN, THE
Willat, Boyd
HEADLESS BODY IN TOPLESS BAR
Willenson, Seth
FOREST WARRIOR
Williams, Robert
TUSKEGEE AIRMEN, THE
Windisch, Ingrid
MACHINE, THE
Winfield, John
GRASS HARP, THE
Witliff, Bill
LONE JUSTICE: SHOWDOWN AT PLUM CREEK
Wolf, Daniel
CATWALK
Wolstenholme, John
FAR HARBOR
Woods, Cary
SWINGERS
Woods, Michael
TAKEOVER, THE
Woolley, Stephen
NEON BIBLE, THE
Worth, Marvin
NORMA JEAN AND MARILYN
Yamashina, Makoto
PATLABOR 2: MOBILE POLICE
Yorn, Julie Silverman
TREES LOUNGE
Yoshizaki, Michiyo
BASQUIAT
Young, Harry
GIRL FROM MARS, THE
Zacharias, Steven
EDDIE
Zadan, Craig
MY FELLOW AMERICANS
Zaleski, Simon
DAENS
Zane, Chuck
DARK SECRETS
Zanuck, Richard D.
CHAIN REACTION
Zemeckis, Robert
FRIGHTENERS, THE
TALES FROM THE CRYPT PRESENTS BORDELLO OF BLOOD
Ziegler, Regina
TALES OF EROTICA
Zinnemann, Tim
ISLAND OF DR. MOREAU, THE
Zuckerman, Leslie
LOW LIFE, THE

MAKEUP/FX MAKEUP

Abrums, Stephen
DEAR GOD
Adams, Susie
EMMA
Alchemyfx
BACKLASH: OBLIVION 2
Allsop, Christine
MADAGASCAR SKIN
Altamura, Dee Dee
ED
Alterian Studios
HIGH SCHOOL HIGH
Alterian Studios, Inc.
CRAFT, THE
ROCK, THE
Anderson, ChoAhnne
HALFMOON
Anderson, David Leroy
NUTTY PROFESSOR, THE
Anderson, Lance
ISLAND OF DR. MOREAU, THE
Animated Engineering
ED
Arias, Richard
RIDERS OF THE PURPLE SAGE
Armstrong, Linda
MUPPET TREASURE ISLAND
Armstrong, Lynda
MICHAEL COLLINS
101 DALMATIANS
Arrindell, Lisa
BUGGED
Arroy, Elena
SOME FOLKS CALL IT A SLING BLADE
Artus, Eckart
REDEMPTION: KICKBOXER 5
Ashley-Collins, Beverley
YOU'LL NEVER MAKE LOVE IN THIS TOWN AGAIN
Aspinall, Jennifer
BASQUIAT
Athayde, Pamela
FOR THE MOMENT
Atherton, David
LARRY MCMURTRY'S STREETS OF LAREDO
Bachman, Cynthia
DEATH BENEFIT
PIG'S TALE, A
Bain-Partin, Imelda
GIRL FROM MARS, THE
Baker, Jennifer
WIFE, THE
Baker, Lori
PHOENIX
Baker, Lori Ann
TAKEOVER, THE
Baker, Rick
JOHN CARPENTER'S ESCAPE FROM L.A.
NUTTY PROFESSOR, THE
Bani, Any Umar
WITHOUT MERCY
Barber, Lynn
FLED
Barlova, Libuse
COLD LIGHT OF DAY
Barrett, Dave
NOT OF THIS EARTH
Bart Mixon's Monster Fixins
WITCHCRAFT: SALEM'S GHOST
Bartels, Anni
REDEMPTION: KICKBOXER 5
Barton, David
WOMAN UNDONE, A
Baurens, Muriel
LITTLE INDIAN, BIG CITY
VISITORS, THE
Bayless, John R.
TO GILLIAN ON HER 37TH BIRTHDAY
Beatty, Sandy
LOW LIFE, THE
Beck, Kenneth Michael
ONE GOOD TURN
Benaiche, Sophie
HATE
Benevides, Rob
I SHOT ANDY WARHOL
Berger, Howard
FROM DUSK TILL DAWN
Berkeley, Kathleen
MAD DOG TIME
Berkeley, Ron
MAD DOG TIME
Beveridge, Christine
HAUNTED
JACK & SARAH
TWELFTH NIGHT
Bitar, Kamar
FROM DUSK TILL DAWN
Black, Jean A.
BEFORE AND AFTER
Blake, John
FARGO
Blumberg, Angela
MURDERED INNOCENCE
Blundeli, Christine
SECRETS & LIES
Booth, Nigel
ENGLISH PATIENT, THE
Bosch, Derrick
COLD LIGHT OF DAY
Bottin, Rob
MISSION: IMPOSSIBLE
Bram, Dominique
PHAT BEACH
Branche, Stacye
PHAT BEACH
Branche, Stacye P.
THIN LINE BETWEEN LOVE AND HATE, A
Brezner, Josh
VENUS RISING

Brezner, Mike
VENUS RISING
Brown, Henry
BUGGED
Brown, Linda A.
UNFORGETTABLE
Buacharern, Shutchai "Tym"
FEMALIEN
Buchanan, Ann
TWO DEATHS
Buchner, Fern
EVERYONE SAYS I LOVE YOU
UP CLOSE AND PERSONAL
Buck, Janice
MUTANT MAN
Buechler, John
FREEWAY
PIRANHA
Buechler, John Carl
NOT OF THIS EARTH
Buechler, Lynn
NOT OF THIS EARTH
Buono, Lisa
NECRONOMICON: BOOK OF THE DEAD
RUMPELSTILTSKIN
Buren, Trudy
CROCODILES IN AMSTERDAM
Burke, Michele
MOLL FLANDERS
Burke-Winter, Michele
JERRY MAGUIRE
Burwell, Lois
MISSION: IMPOSSIBLE
Bushell, Sandie
TWO FRIENDS
Busoiu, Dana
JOSH KIRBY . . . TIME WARRIOR!: EGGS FROM 70,000,000 B.C.
JOSH KIRBY . . . TIME WARRIOR!: JOURNEY TO THE MAGIC CAVERN
JOSH KIRBY . . . TIME WARRIOR!: TRAPPED ON TOY WORLD
Byot, Evelyne
CHASING BUTTERFLIES
SINGLE GIRL, A
Cabral, Susan
LAST DANCE
Camara, Norma
ROLLING STONES ROCK-AND-ROLL CIRCUS, THE
Campayno, Joe
DIABOLIQUE
Campbell, Lynn
MIRROR HAS TWO FACES, THE
Cannistraci, Jay
OFF AND RUNNING
SUBSTITUTE, THE
Cannom, Greg
STEPHEN KING'S THINNER
Carbone, Marilyn
DEAD TO RIGHTS
MISSING PIECES
Carter-Narcisse, Marietta
GREAT WHITE HYPE, THE
TIME TO KILL, A
Cate, Russell
TRUMAN
Chapuis-Asselin, Francoise
SOMEONE ELSE'S AMERICA
Chase, Ken
SPY HARD
Chin, Judy
FLIRT
I SHOT ANDY WARHOL
Choi, Jane
ED'S NEXT MOVE
Clements, Caroline
INSTITUTE BENJAMENTA
Cooper, Sandy
HOMEWARD BOUND II: LOST IN SAN FRANCISCO
Coplin, Shannon
ELECTRA
Cornelius, Pia
WARHEAD
Cossu, Walter
ADVENTURES OF PINOCCHIO, THE
Cotton, Becky
FIST OF THE NORTH STAR
SERIAL KILLER
Coudouloux, Eva
TAILS YOU LIVE, HEADS YOU'RE DEAD
Crean, Kara
MODERN AFFAIR, A
Criswell, Christina
WHITE WOLVES II: LEGEND OF THE WILD
Cush, Fionaugh
UNKNOWN ORIGIN
D'Alonzo, Roxy
SCREAMERS
D'Amore, Hallie
CHAIN REACTION
GHOSTS OF MISSISSIPPI
PHENOMENON
PRIMAL FEAR
da Paz, Sergio
HALFMOON
Dahl, Elizabeth
BAJA
Daily, Wade
BEST OF THE BEST 3: NO TURNING BACK
Darensky, Roman
WOLVES, THE
Davies-Irvine, Cathie
BLOOD & DONUTS
Davison, Diana
TRACKS OF A KILLER
Dawn, Gray
SANTA CLAWS
Dawn, Jeff
ERASER
De Rossi, Giannetto
DAYLIGHT
DRAGONHEART
Deak, Michael S.
BACKLASH: OBLIVION 2
SPELLBREAKER: SECRET OF THE LEPRECHAUNS
Degennes, Nicolas
PROPRIETOR, THE
DeHaven, Bonita
SUNSET PARK
Del Russo, Marie
OFF AND RUNNING
Delprete, Marie
DENISE CALLS UP
Demers, Nicole
BREACH OF TRUST
Demetriades, Aliki
MATERNAL INSTINCTS
Depp, Lori
VENUS RISING
Deruelle, Michel
LES VOLEURS
Devetta, Linda
ROLLING STONES ROCK-AND-ROLL CIRCUS, THE
Diaz, Ken
JACK
Diaz, Suzanne
SAINTS AND SINNERS
WIDOW'S KISS
Dion, Michele
MAN BY THE SHORE, THE
Dipersio, Jane
SEARCH FOR ONE-EYE JIMMY, THE
Dominguez, Ramon Diego
HIDDEN ASSASSIN
Donne, Naomi
BOYS
CRUCIBLE, THE
I'M NOT RAPPAPORT
Doss, Kathy
BOY CALLED HATE, A
Down, Victoria
BIG BULLY
FEAR
TALES FROM THE CRYPT PRESENTS BORDELLO OF BLOOD
Dupuis, Stephan
FRISK
Eagan, Lynne
SPITFIRE GRILL, THE
Earnshaw, Tina
EMMA
HAMLET
Edmonds, Stan
ALASKA
Egorova, Zinaida
WOLVES, THE
Eisele, Beate
LIFEFORM
Elek, Zoltan
QUEST, THE
Ellis, Earl
SOMETIMES THEY COME BACK . . . AGAIN
Engelen, Paul
GHOST AND THE DARKNESS, THE
Engelman, Leonard
CHAMBER, THE
Evans, Kris
CHILDREN OF FURY
FLIPPER
Ferrante, Anthony
DENTIST, THE
VIRTUAL COMBAT
Fink, Jill
BAD LOVE
Fletcher, Joanne
FINAL EQUINOX, THE
Forgacs, Erzsebet
MAGIC HUNTER
Fossberg, Ragna
VIKING SAGAS, THE
Foster, John
NOT OF THIS EARTH
Fouche, Debra
WARHEAD
Fournier, Marie Lastennet
NELLY AND MONSIEUR ARNAUD
Frampton, Robert
FUNNYMAN, THE
Friedman, Alan
STREETCAR NAMED DESIRE, A
Fry, Elisabeth
FREEWAY
SOMETIMES THEY COME BACK . . . AGAIN
Fry, Elizabeth
WITHIN THE ROCK
Fry, Kelcey
TOLLBOOTH
Frye, Joanne
GRIM
Fuller, Leslie
JUROR, THE
G., Shauna
TALKING ABOUT SEX
G., Tony
WOMAN UNDONE, A

Gaffney, Magdalen
PORTRAIT OF A LADY, THE
Gallis, Winnie
DAENS
Garber, Jake
STAR TREK: FIRST CONTACT
Gardner, Tony
CRAFT, THE
HIGH SCHOOL HIGH
ROCK, THE
Gastineau, Jacques
VISITORS, THE
Gatchell, Valerie
ANGELA
Gayo, Judith
RIDICULE
Gerard, Cedric
LES VOLEURS
MA SAISON PREFEREE
Gerhardt, Pat
ROCK, THE
Germain, Michael
ASSOCIATE, THE
BOGUS
EDDIE
Gibson, Anita
GIRL 6
Gleason, Kelly
ANGELA
Gooley, Nikki
RACE THE SUN
Gordon, Sally
TUNNEL VISION
Gore, Kelly Raye
PUBLIC ENEMIES
Gorton, Neil
GRIM
Gosselin, Karl
SCREAMERS
Gosselin, Ronny
SCREAMERS
Graham, Bettina
FUNNYMAN, THE
Graham, Kathleen
LOSING CHASE
Gravfort, Sanne
BREAKING THE WAVES
Green, Patricia
BOYS NEXT DOOR, THE
Greene, Kimberly
KINGPIN
Greenmum, Sam
VIRTUAL COMBAT
Griffin, Glen
MYSTERY SCIENCE THEATER 3000: THE MOVIE
Griffin Jr., Frank H.
THAT THING YOU DO!
Gruzka, Liz
IRON EAGLE IV
Guan Lina
CHUNGKING EXPRESS
Gundlach, Patricia
DENTIST, THE
Hagood, Martin "Vinnie"
MR. HOLLAND'S OPUS
Haines, Ted
ONE MAN'S JUSTICE
Hall, Keith
BEASTMASTER 3: THE EYE OF BRAXUS
Hall, Mindy
EVENING STAR, THE
Hamilton, A. Scott
WHEN THE BULLET HITS THE BONE
Hamilton, Jeffrey
CRAFT, THE
Hamlin, Marjory
FRIGHTENERS, THE

Hammond, Diane
GIRL 6
Hammond, Fae
LOADED
Hancock, Mike
MULHOLLAND FALLS
Haney, Kevin
CHAMBER, THE
CHAMELEON
KISSINGER AND NIXON
Hannaman, Peggy
IMMORTALS, THE
Hansson, Sanna
EVIL ED
Hardin, Brad
NOT OF THIS EARTH
PIRANHA
Harper, Bernadette
AMANDA AND THE ALIEN
Harper, Robert
LILY DALE
Hart, Christine
LONG KISS GOODNIGHT, THE
MRS. WINTERBOURNE
Hauge, Fredrik
EVIL ED
Haynes, Lesley
WHERE'S THE MONEY, NOREEN?
Helgestad, Sharin
ROAD TO GALVESTON, THE
Helland, J. Roy
BIRDCAGE, THE
Henderson, Camille
TREMORS 2: AFTERSHOCKS
Henderson, Donna L.
BARB WIRE
Henri-Perez, Dominique
WAR OF THE BUTTONS, THE
Henriques, Ed
MIRROR HAS TWO FACES, THE
Hernandez, Juan Pedro
FLOWER OF MY SECRET, THE
Hicks, Lori
LONE STAR
Hole, Gina
WHITE TIGER
Holland, Desne
LAST SUPPER, THE
TRIGGER EFFECT, THE
Holley, Fran
ALEX
Houle, Julie
TWO IF BY SEA
Howell, Abiiba
CHILDREN OF THE CORN: THE GATHERING
Howell, Abiiba S.
AMERICA'S DREAM
Hughes, Melanie
HOUSE ARREST
Hunt, Michael
GLASS CAGE, THE
Hurt, Joseph P.
ASSAULT AT WEST POINT
Hyeronimus, Anne
HELLRAISER: BLOODLINE
Hyman, France
UNDER THE DOMIM TREE
Iacaponi, Enrico
CEMETERY MAN
Iacoponi, Nilo
STEALING BEAUTY
Ilson, Sharon
BED OF ROSES
BROKEN ARROW
STRIPTEASE
Image Animation
SOLO

Jabour, Shonagh
SUGARTIME
Jackson DuCane, Andrea
MYSTERY SCIENCE THEATER 3000: THE MOVIE
Jackson, John E.
MULHOLLAND FALLS
MULTIPLICITY
Jacquetta
SOLITAIRE FOR TWO
Jakots, Katalin
DOGFIGHTERS, THE
James, Whitney L.
CELTIC PRIDE
Jayne, Selina
LARRY MCMURTRY'S STREETS OF LAREDO
Jaziri, Fatma
SILENCES OF THE PALACE, THE
Jeen, Corey
HOSTILE INTENTIONS
Jenae, Jori
PURE DANGER
SKYSCRAPER
TIGER HEART
Jim Henson's Creature Shop
ENGLISH PATIENT, THE
Johnson, Bill "Splat"
FLED
Johnson, Elisa
BEAUTIFUL THING
Johnson, Megan
FUGITIVE RAGE
Johnston, Graham
TRAINSPOTTING
Jordan, Cindy
SOUTH BEACH ACADEMY
Jorfald, Jennifer
BREAKING THE WAVES
Josefczyk, Jeannee
FIRST KID
Joslin, Valerie
FATALLY YOURS
K.N.B. Effects Group
KINGPIN
K.N.B. EFX Group
FROM DUSK TILL DAWN
Kaigler, Donna
PAINTED HERO
Kail, James R.
DOWN PERISCOPE
Kallos, Connie
ORIGINAL GANGSTAS
Kang, Soo Y.
WHISPERING, THE
Karridene, Kathleen
VIRTUAL COMBAT
Kastner-Delago, Eileen
FOXFIRE
Kelly, Stacy Stewart
HEAVEN'S PRISONERS
Kennedy, Gail
HOW THE WEST WAS FUN
Kent, Irene
GETTING AWAY WITH MURDER
Kevin Yagher Productions
TALES FROM THE CRYPT PRESENTS BORDELLO OF BLOOD
King, Helen
CRACKER: THE MADWOMAN IN THE ATTIC
Kirkman, Patricia
WAR OF THE BUTTONS, THE
Kleitsch, Todd
4 TALES OF 2 CITIES
Knezev, Maribeth
BLOODKNOT

Knight, Amanda
MISSION: IMPOSSIBLE
Knyrim, Roy
FIST OF THE NORTH STAR
Kohl, Martina
POISON IVY 2: LILY
Kolar, Francis
MOTHER
Kolodkina, Nina
BURIAL OF THE RATS
Kulow, Heidi
WELCOME TO THE DOLLHOUSE
Kupko, Yvonne DePatis
MAN OF THE YEAR
Kurtzman, Robert
FROM DUSK TILL DAWN
L.M.C.
WATCH ME
La Mia Denaver, Deborah
GHOSTS OF MISSISSIPPI
2 DAYS IN THE VALLEY
Laden, Bob
STEPHEN KING'S THINNER
Lamar, Kristin
TEXAS PAYBACK
Lamm, Toby
DOWN, OUT AND DANGEROUS
Lange, David
POLYMORPH
Lapierre, Nicole
HOLLOW POINT
LaPorte, Steve
MY FELLOW AMERICANS
Larsen, Deborah
MICHAEL
NORMA JEAN AND MARILYN
Latinopolous, Margie
BREAKAWAY
Laudati, Michael
FAITHFUL
Laurence, Chris
NATIONAL LAMPOON'S FAVORITE DEADLY SINS
Lavau, Joel
HORSEMAN ON THE ROOF
Lavergne, Didier
FRENCH TWIST
Leavitt, Geoff
TOO FAST, TOO YOUNG
Lederman, Nicki
CAUGHT
Ledermann, Nicki
PALOOKAVILLE
Ledermann, Nicki Jasny
WALKING AND TALKING
Lee, Mi Yeoun
MAN OF THE YEAR
Lee, Tracy
SHAMELESS
Lema, Tammy
WHOLE WIDE WORLD, THE
Levy, Myrav
IT CAME FROM OUTER SPACE II
Liddiard, Dennis
EXECUTIVE DECISION
Liddiard, Gary
LAST MAN STANDING
Llewellyn, Amanda
BLOODSPORT II: THE NEXT KUMITE
Loader, Traci
ELECTRA
VIRUS
Lopatorska, Aurelia
MOTHER OF KINGS
Lopez, Maria Laura
OF LOVE AND SHADOWS
Louie, Pearl
PORTRAITS OF A KILLER
RED SCORPION 2
Love, Lisa
FINAL CUT, THE
Loveland, Juliet
EXIT
Lovell, Judy
PHANTOM, THE
Lundstrom, Goran
EVIL ED
Luzy, Richard
MR. STITCH
Macaluso, Jerry
FIST OF THE NORTH STAR
Magical Media Industries
NOT OF THIS EARTH
Mahan, Shane Patrick
ISLAND OF DR. MOREAU, THE
Mansano, Roy
IT CAME FROM OUTER SPACE II
Marazzi, Alfredo
OUTRAGE
Marchenski, Lili
SABRINA, THE TEENAGE WITCH
Margolis-Moos, Angela
CITIZEN RUTH
Markowitz, Cheryl Ann
LETTER TO MY KILLER
Marks, K.C.
NEMESIS III: PREY HARDER
Martinez, Gregorio
BATON ROUGE
Martinez, Sunshine
BUGGED
Martz, Neal
BIG NIGHT
DEAD MAN
Massie, Stephanie
BLACK SCORPION
DEATH ARTIST, THE
Masters, Todd
ARRIVAL, THE
RICH MAN'S WIFE, THE
Mathai, Judy
NIGHT OF THE SCARECROW
Matz, Carlann
BLACK DAY BLUE NIGHT
Mayer, Lisa
MAN OF THE YEAR
Mays, Sarah
NEON BIBLE, THE
Mazur, Bernadette
CITY HALL
FIRST WIVES CLUB, THE
McCann, Robert
SMALL FACES
McComas, Tania
HEIDI CHRONICLES, THE
McCormack, Linda
HOMECOMING
McCoy, James L.
BLACK SHEEP
McEwan, Anne
LAND AND FREEDOM
McGill, Maureen
BUTTERFLY KISS
McIntosh, Todd
VERY BRADY SEQUEL, A
McMurray, Frances
MRS. MUNCK
McNally, Brenda
AMERICAN BUFFALO
McNulty, Deborah
ONE MAN'S JUSTICE
ME*FX
SOMETIMES THEY COME BACK . . . AGAIN
Melazzo, Linda
FAMILY THING, A
Mercer, Martin
PHOENIX
Mercer, Randy Houston
MIRROR HAS TWO FACES, THE
Messina, Patricia
DUNSTON CHECKS IN
Michaels, Myke
FOREST WARRIOR
Milars, Lydia
AMERICAN STRAYS
Minkin, Stacy
PUBLIC ACCESS
Minns, Cheri
BIRDCAGE, THE
MULTIPLICITY
Mixon, Bart J.
SOMETIMES THEY COME BACK . . . AGAIN
Monaci, Gina
4 TALES OF 2 CITIES
Montagna, Peter
HIGH SCHOOL HIGH
Montgomery, Jennifer
DEAD WEEKEND
OUT THERE
Montgomery, Nancy
UNDER THE HULA MOON
Monzani, Sara
JANE EYRE
Monzani, Sarah
ANGELS AND INSECTS
EVITA
WHITE SQUALL
Moore, Marjolein
FRIEND OF THE FAMILY 2
OVER THE WIRE
Moos, Angela Margolis
INFINITY
Mora, Alfredo
SOLO
Moreira, Luciana
GIRLFRIENDS
Morot, Adrien
SCREAMERS
Morrison, Bill
SANDMAN, THE
Morse, Mary Kay
SHARON'S SECRET
Mosel, Gregory
BEWARE: CHILDREN AT PLAY
Mowat, Donald J.
EXTREME MEASURES
FLY AWAY HOME
HARRIET THE SPY
Mueller, Elfi
FLAMING EARS
Mungle, Matthew
PRIMAL FEAR
Mungle, Matthew W.
GHOSTS OF MISSISSIPPI
MULHOLLAND FALLS
MULTIPLICITY
Murdock, Judy
GET ON THE BUS
Myre, Brigette
JUST YOUR LUCK
Myrick, Bill
TAKEOVER, THE
Naidenov, Kristo
MIND RIPPER
Naostepad, Dick
COLD LIGHT OF DAY
Nardella, Marie
STAND OFF, THE
Neal, Robin L.
EYE FOR AN EYE
Nealy-Dobbie, Jaquline
WAR AT HOME, THE

Neill, Ve
MATILDA
Nelson, Chris
TALES FROM THE CRYPT PRESENTS BORDELLO OF BLOOD
Nelson, Christopher
TALES FROM THE CRYPT PRESENTS BORDELLO OF BLOOD
Nelson, Dave
ED
Newman, Jan
SURGEON, THE
Nguyen, Thi Loan
MADAME BUTTERFLY
LA CEREMONIE
Nick, Cheryl
D3: THE MIGHTY DUCKS
Nicotero, Greg
FROM DUSK TILL DAWN
Niehuse, Heiner
BROTHER OF SLEEP
Nieradzik, Dorka
COLD COMFORT FARM
Nishio, Yukiko
MABOROSI
Nogaro, Angela
DONOR UNKNOWN
RICH MAN'S WIFE, THE
Nonjui, Shecheep
BLOODSPORT II: THE NEXT KUMITE
Nye, Ben
PEOPLE VS. LARRY FLYNT, THE
Nye Jr., Ben
MR. WRONG
O'Reilly, Valli
MARS ATTACKS!
O., Dianne
LAWNMOWER MAN 2: BEYOND CYBERSPACE
Oppenheim, Geri B.
NUTTY PROFESSOR, THE
Orme, Shirley
DARK SECRETS
Orosz, Imre
MAGIC HUNTER
Ospina, Ermahn
FROM DUSK TILL DAWN
Ostrom, Inger
ANIMAL INSTINCTS III: THE SEDUCTRESS
Ottaviano, Joanne M.
TREES LOUNGE
Owen, Peter
BIRDCAGE, THE
PORTRAIT OF A LADY, THE
Page, Barbara
CLUBHOUSE DETECTIVES
Pala, Ann
BULLETPROOF
Palmer, Carla
CELTIC PRIDE
LONE JUSTICE: SHOWDOWN AT PLUM CREEK
Parker, Daniel
HORSEMAN ON THE ROOF
IN LOVE AND WAR
Parsons, Patricia
GALAXIES ARE COLLIDING
Patterson, Cristina
LITTLE WITCHES
Paxton, Vivian
MAN OF THE YEAR
Pebbles
SHOPPING
Peitzman, Pamela
MOTHER'S PRAYER, A
Petersen, Jane
ALEX

Philipp, Rith
BROTHER OF SLEEP
Phillips, Kelly
UNDERTOW
Phillips, Pamela
SANTA WITH MUSCLES
Phillips, Robert I.
MYSTERY SCIENCE THEATER 3000: THE MOVIE
Phillips, Scott
NOT OF THIS EARTH
Pierre, Eric
LITTLE INDIAN, BIG CITY
Pleijzier, Brigitte
SUITE 16
Poharnok, Ivan
MAGIC HUNTER
Polita, Eric A.
SWINGERS
Porter, Yolanda
SAWBONES
Poulsen-Wells, Amanda
BODY COUNT
Pra
JOHNNY SHORTWAVE
Proud, Trefor
SHAMELESS
Pryor, Beverly Jo
PHAT BEACH
Ptak, Sheryl Leigh
CABLE GUY, THE
Quatolas Rubio, Jose
SONS OF TRINITY
Quist, Gerald
MR. HOLLAND'S OPUS
SGT. BILKO
Racz, Constanza
JOHNNY 100 PESOS
Rae, Ronda
VIRTUAL ENCOUNTERS
ZARKORR! THE INVADER
Ragland, Diana
BLACK ROSE OF HARLEM
Rail, Jason
FRISK
Raskin-Smaling, Carol
SHOOTFIGHTER 2: KILL OR BE KILLED!
Regan, Patricia
FUNERAL, THE
Reiner, Susan
RATTLED
Ricci, Gina G.
LOVE IS ALL THERE IS
Roberts, Lisa
HAPPY GILMORE
Robillard, Gil
LITTLE INDIAN, BIG CITY
Rodgers, Lynn
DELTA OF VENUS
Rodier, Suzanne
BOUND
EDIE & PEN
Roeg, Steff
CANTERVILLE GHOST, THE
Roney, Marie
YANKEE ZULU
Roseanu, Dana
MAGIC IN THE MIRROR
Rosita
WITHOUT MERCY
Roylance, Bron
PEOPLE VS. LARRY FLYNT, THE
Ryan, Bob
MOTHER
Ryder, James
PUBLIC ENEMIES
Sacca Jr., Jim
BEYOND DESIRE

Samodral, Linda
AMERICAN STRAYS
Samuel, Jordan
LEGEND OF GATOR FACE, THE
Sander, Helga
KASPAR HAUSER
Sandling, Palah
HEAD OF THE FAMILY
Sarris Jr., Manny
BOTTLE ROCKET
Savini, Tom
MR. STITCH
Sazani, Victoria
TWO-BITS & PEPPER
Scheeley, Anne
EVIL HAS A FACE
Schlegelmich, Kuno
HORSEMAN ON THE ROOF
Schneider, Janine
GRIM
Schon, Karin
BROTHER OF SLEEP
Schopke, Mia
KASPAR HAUSER
Schwartz, Carol
SCREAM
Scott, Ashley
WILD SIDE
Sewell, Jan
AFFAIR, THE
ANTONIA'S LINE
CAPTIVES
Sforza, Fabrizio
ENGLISH PATIENT, THE
Shaw, Lindy
YOUNG POISONER'S HANDBOOK, THE
Sheen, Edna
COURAGE UNDER FIRE
PREACHER'S WIFE, THE
Shepard, Blake
SET IT OFF
Shircone, Jenny
RASPUTIN
Shircore, Jenny
MARY REILLY
MIDWINTER'S TALE, A
Sicova, Adrianna
UNDERSTUDY: GRAVEYARD SHIFT 2, THE
Sicova, Andrea
UNDERSTUDY: GRAVEYARD SHIFT 2, THE
Silva, Rea Ann
SET IT OFF
Silvi, Maurizio
DRAGONHEART
WILLIAM SHAKESPEARE'S ROMEO + JULIET
Simons, Jef
GLIMMER MAN, THE
Smallhorn, Leslie
ROLLING STONES ROCK-AND-ROLL CIRCUS, THE
Smarz, Nena
BOTTLE ROCKET
Smith, Christina
UNHOOK THE STARS
Smith, Dorothy
STUPIDS, THE
Smith, Gord
EXTREME MEASURES
Smith, Gordon J.
TRUMAN
Snell, Richard
FAN, THE
JAMES AND THE GIANT PEACH
Sobeck, John
TWO MUCH

Soler, Karmele
MOUTH TO MOUTH
Sorenson, Frances
MANNY & LO
SOTA FX
CHILDREN OF THE CORN: THE GATHERING
Sotirova, Anastasia "Sia"
MIND RIPPER
Southcoutt, Barbara
HEDD WYNN
Southern, Katherine
BEYOND THE CALL
Steele, Christine M.
GRACE OF MY HEART
Stern, Molly R.
SWINGERS
Steve Johnson's XFX
DEAD MAN
Steve Johnson's XFXf
ERASER
Stone, Ava
MAN IN THE ATTIC, THE
Striepeke, Daniel C.
THAT THING YOU DO!
Sun Bin
BLUSH
Sun Hongkui
BLUSH
Surprenant, Thomas E.
SET IT OFF
Tal, Mira
DEADLY OUTBREAK
Tarpin, Marina
AMERICAN STRAYS
Taylor, Anni
TERMINAL IMPACT
Teague, Peggy
DANGEROUS PASSION
Tebeau, Scott
RICH MAN'S WIFE, THE
Tempia, Norman
ED
Temple, Phyllis
COLONY, THE
Thomas, Todd
SUBSTANCE OF FIRE, THE
Tilk, Joy
FAST MONEY
Tisseur, Benoit
SCREAMERS
Tomasino, Michael
JUST YOUR LUCK
Tomasino, Michael "Mic"
KAZAAM
Tooker, Melanie
DEMOLITIONIST, THE
Toth, Lillian
SKIN
Tso, Pauline
RUMBLE IN THE BRONX
Tsuruba, Howard
MERLIN'S SHOP OF MAGICAL WONDERS
Tunnicliffe, Gary
CHILDREN OF THE CORN: THE GATHERING
HELLRAISER: BLOODLINE
SOLO
Turi, Josh
ORIGINAL SINS
Tuskes, Alan
WITCHCRAFT: SALEM'S GHOST
van de Wardt, Marly
SUITE 16
van den Abbeele, Eddy
PASSION OF DARKLY NOON, THE
Vigen, Ricoh
APART FROM HUGH
Vogel, Alexis
NAKED SOULS
Voss, Cheryl
SUBSTITUTE, THE
Vulich, John
NECRONOMICON: BOOK OF THE DEAD
Walder, Jennifer
HARVEST OF FIRE
Walsh, Seamus
WITCHCRAFT: SALEM'S GHOST
Wanstall, Tania
SHOWGIRL MURDERS, THE
UNKNOWN ORIGIN
Warbin, Tracy
FAR HARBOR
HEAVY
IF LUCY FELL
SUBSTANCE OF FIRE, THE
Warburton, Amanda
JUDE
Weaver, Linda
SANDMAN, THE
Weaver, Samantha
HOURGLASS
LITTLE DEATH, THE
Weisinger, Allen
MARVIN'S ROOM
PALLBEARER, THE
RANSOM
Weiss, Jamie Sue
NORMAL LIFE
West, Cherry
HEDD WYNN
Westmore, June
LATE SHIFT, THE
Westmore, Kandace
JOHN CARPENTER'S ESCAPE FROM L.A.
Westmore, Michael
STAR TREK: FIRST CONTACT
Wheeler, Scott
STAR TREK: FIRST CONTACT
White, Barry
DON'T LET YOUR MEAT LOAF
White, Doug
MERLIN'S SHOP OF MAGICAL WONDERS
Whobrey, Nacoma
BODY OF INFLUENCE 2
Wiemer, Ann
CROSSCUT
Wilder, Barbara
NAKED SOULS
Wilder, Brad
TWISTER
Willett, Suzanne
FULL BODY MASSAGE
Williams, Cindy J.
BEAUTIFUL GIRLS
Williams, Daphne
LIVE WIRE: HUMAN TIMEBOMB
Williams, Gigi
ABUSE
Williams, Sandy
MIRROR, MIRROR III: THE VOYEUR
Williams, Veronica
GIRLFRIENDS
Wilson, Beau
PAINTED HERO
Wilson, Joan
DON'T LET YOUR MEAT LOAF
Wilson, Rod
LAZARUS MAN, THE
Winston, Stan
ISLAND OF DR. MOREAU, THE
Wirgler, Maureen
ADRENALIN: FEAR THE RUSH
Wirgler, Maurine
RAVENHAWK
Wittun, Lyssa
DON'T BE A MENACE TO SOUTH CENTRAL WHILE DRINKING YOUR JUICE IN THE HOOD
Wolski McNulty, Debra
DESIRE
Wood, Natalie
LAWNMOWER MAN 2: BEYOND CYBERSPACE
Wraith, Geralyn
KIDS IN THE HALL: BRAIN CANDY
Wright, Erin
APART FROM HUGH
Wright, Tori
PROTEUS
Wright, Victoria
WAVELENGTH
Yagher, Kevin
FAN, THE
HELLRAISER: BLOODLINE
RUMPELSTILTSKIN
Yonemoto, Judy
PINOCCHIO'S REVENGE
Yonemoto, Judy Kaye
LOVER'S KNOT
York, Patty
LILY DALE
Zamit, Suzie
INSTITUTE BENJAMENTA
Zamprioli, Gino
CEMETERY MAN
Zanetti, Cinzia
NATIONAL LAMPOON'S FAVORITE DEADLY SINS
Zoe
IT'S MY PARTY
Zoller, Debbie
2 DAYS IN THE VALLEY
Zoltan
MAXIMUM RISK
Zurlo, Rosemarie
EVERYONE SAYS I LOVE YOU
Zvorsky, Nicola
CARNOSAUR 3: PRIMAL SPECIES

MUSIC COMPOSERS

Abramovitch, Barron
TRACKS OF A KILLER
Adler, Brian
DEATH BENEFIT
Adzinikolov, Tony
CALLING THE GHOSTS: A STORY ABOUT RAPE, WAR AND WOMEN
Allen, Richard
DESIRE
Angell, Peitor
MAN OF THE YEAR
Arnold, David
INDEPENDENCE DAY
Arriagada, Jorge
THREE LIVES AND ONLY ONE DEATH
Artemyev, Eduard
ANNA
BURIAL OF THE RATS
Bacon, Michael
LOSING CHASE
Bajda, Srecko
PREDICTIONS OF FIRE
Baker, Michael Conway
ROAD HOME, THE
Balanescu, Alexander
ANGELS AND INSECTS
Band, Richard
HEAD OF THE FAMILY
JOSH KIRBY . . . TIME WARRIOR!: EGGS FROM 70,000,000 B.C.
JOSH KIRBY . . . TIME WARRIOR!: JOURNEY TO THE MAGIC CAVERN

JOSH KIRBY . . . TIME WARRIOR!: LAST BATTLE FOR THE UNIVERSE
JOSH KIRBY . . . TIME WARRIOR!: TRAPPED ON TOY WORLD
ZARKORR! THE INVADER

Barber, Billy
MYSTERY SCIENCE THEATER 3000: THE MOVIE

Barber, Stephen
GALAXIES ARE COLLIDING

Barnes, John
DON'T BE A MENACE TO SOUTH CENTRAL WHILE DRINKING YOUR JUICE IN THE HOOD

Barone, Marcus
GLASS CAGE, THE

Barton, Todd
FIRE ON THE MOUNTAIN

Bates, Tyler
CRIMINAL HEARTS

Battishill, Arlene
DEVOTION

Bauer, Rolf
WOLVES, THE

Beal, Jeff
LOVE IS ALL THERE IS

Beamer, Keola
FAR HARBOR

Bell, Darron
TATTOO BOY

Bell, David
LONE JUSTICE: SHOWDOWN AT PLUM CREEK

Bellis, Richard
HOW THE WEST WAS FUN
WHERE'S THE MONEY, NOREEN?

Bellon, Roger
PRE-MADONNAS

Beltrami, Marco
SCREAM
WHISPERING, THE

Bergeaud, David
DONOR UNKNOWN
HEIDI FLEISS HOLLYWOOD MADAM

Bergman, Efrem
DARK SECRETS

Bernstein, Charles
RUMPELSTILTSKIN

Bernstein, Elmer
BULLETPROOF
PERSONAL JOURNEY WITH MARTIN SCORSESE THROUGH AMERICAN MOVIES, A

Bernstein, Peter
MOTHER

Berry, Adam
FRIEND OF THE FAMILY 2
FUGITIVE RAGE

Bicat, Nick
PASSION OF DARKLY NOON, THE

Black, George
FINAL EQUINOX, THE

Blackstone, Wendy
TALES OF EROTICA

Blanchard, Terence
ASSAULT AT WEST POINT
GET ON THE BUS

Blondheim, George
HALFBACK OF NOTRE DAME, THE
RED SCORPION 2

Bloom, Bill
SEARCH FOR ONE-EYE JIMMY, THE

Blue, Frankie
OUT THERE

Boardman, Chris
TALES FROM THE CRYPT PRESENTS BORDELLO OF BLOOD

Boll, Bill
LOW LIFE, THE
SOME FOLKS CALL IT A SLING BLADE

Boneheads, The
MADAME WANG'S

Bonezzi, Bernardo
BATON ROUGE
MOUTH TO MOUTH

Boswell, Simon
JACK & SARAH

Botti, Chris
CAUGHT

Bowers, Richard
DEAD COLD

Bradley, Foster
DON'T LET YOUR MEAT LOAF

Bragg, Billy
WALKING AND TALKING

Brahem, Anouar
SILENCES OF THE PALACE, THE

Breuer, Torsten
MAYBE . . . MAYBE NOT

Bricusse, Leslie
LAND BEFORE TIME IV: JOURNEY THROUGH THE MISTS

Bridgman, David
GIRLFRIENDS

Brosse, Dirk
DAENS

Broughton, Bruce
CARRIED AWAY
HOMEWARD BOUND II: LOST IN SAN FRANCISCO
HOUSE ARREST
INFINITY
JAG

Bryant, John
ANNIE O

Buenoamino, Nonog
MIDNIGHT DANCERS

Bunka, Roman
HALFMOON

Burwell, Carter
CELLULOID CLOSET, THE
CHAMBER, THE
FARGO
FEAR
JOE'S APARTMENT

Butch
MADAME WANG'S

Calasso, Michael
CHUNGKING EXPRESS

Cale, John
BASQUIAT
I SHOT ANDY WARHOL

Camilo, Michel
TWO MUCH

Capponi, Claudio
JANE EYRE

Carothers, Craig
RED LINE

Carpenter, John
JOHN CARPENTER'S ESCAPE FROM L.A.

Cesario, John
FLATTERED

Chabrol, Matthieu
LA CEREMONIE

Chan, Frankie
CHUNGKING EXPRESS

Chang, Gary
CHILDREN OF FURY
ISLAND OF DR. MOREAU, THE
SUBSTITUTE, THE

Chartrand, Denis
CHAMPAGNE SAFARI, THE

Cheek, Todd
DON'T LET YOUR MEAT LOAF

Clarke, James
APART FROM HUGH

Clarke, Stanley
EDDIE
ROAD TO GALVESTON, THE

Clinton, George S.
BEYOND THE CALL
DELTA OF VENUS
VIKING SAGAS, THE

Cloquet, Simon
ORSON WELLES: THE ONE-MAN BAND

Cohen, Larry
VIRUS

Coil
FRISK

Coleman, Graeme
BREACH OF TRUST
PORTRAITS OF A KILLER
WHITE TIGER

Colombier, Michel
BARB WIRE
FOXFIRE

Colvin, Shawn
EDIE & PEN

Conde, Antonio Diaz
AVENTURERA

Conti, Bill
SPY HARD

Convertino, Michael
BED OF ROSES
MOTHER NIGHT
PIE IN THE SKY

Cooder, Ry
LAST MAN STANDING

Copeland, Stewart
BOYS
PALLBEARER, THE

Corbeil, Normand
SCREAMERS

Coulais, Bruno
MICROCOSMOS

Coulanges, Amos
MAN BY THE SHORE, THE

Country Joe and the Fish
BERKELEY IN THE 60S

Covell, James
SANTA WITH MUSCLES

Cox, Rick
BAD LOVE

Cozzi, Michael
AMANDA AND THE ALIEN

Cruel Sea
SPIDER & ROSE

Cutler, Miriam
WITCHCRAFT: SALEM'S GHOST

D'Andrea, John
STREET FIGHTER II: THE ANIMATED MOVIE

Daring, Mason
LETTER TO MY KILLER
LONE STAR
OFF AND RUNNING

Davey, Shaun
TWELFTH NIGHT

David, Tonton
LITTLE INDIAN, BIG CITY

Davies, Victor
FOR THE MOMENT

Davis, Aaron
RUDE

Davis, Carl
ANNE FRANK REMEMBERED

Davis, Don
BOUND

Day, Jeff
MR. ICE CREAM MAN

De Sica, Manuel
CEMETERY MAN

DeBelles, Greg
SABRINA, THE TEENAGE WITCH
Debney, John
CARPOOL
CHAMELEON
LAZARUS MAN, THE
Dejean, Dominique
MAN BY THE SHORE, THE
Delia, Joe
FUNERAL, THE
Dickson, Andrew
SECRETS & LIES
SOMEONE ELSE'S AMERICA
Dikker, Loek
BAD MOON
DiMichele, Gary
BIG NIGHT
Donaggio, Pino
BACKLASH: OBLIVION 2
Dorff, Steve
MOONSHINE HIGHWAY
Doyle, Patrick
HAMLET
MRS. WINTERBOURNE
Duca, Gurd
FLAMING EARS
Duhamel, Antoine
RIDICULE
Dunne, James Patrick
DEAR GOD
Edelman, Randy
DAYLIGHT
DIABOLIQUE
DOWN PERISCOPE
DRAGONHEART
QUEST, THE
Edwards, Steve
BLOODSPORT II: THE NEXT KUMITE
WITHOUT MERCY
Elegeert, Yves
COLD LIGHT OF DAY
Elfman, Danny
DARKMAN III: DIE DARKMAN DIE
EXTREME MEASURES
FREEWAY
FRIGHTENERS, THE
MARS ATTACKS!
MISSION: IMPOSSIBLE
TALES FROM THE CRYPT PRESENTS BORDELLO OF BLOOD
Elias, Jonathan
SKIN
Elkins, Boris
BUGGED
Elliot, Bill
FOREST WARRIOR
Ellis, Charles
PHARAOH'S ARMY
Emmett, Vince
PHARAOH'S ARMY
Endelman, Stephen
ED
FLIRTING WITH DISASTER
English, Paul
MAN WITH THE PERFECT SWING, THE
Erms, Sebastien
RENDEZVOUS IN PARIS
Ett, Allen
MUTANT MAN
Faulkner, John
HARD WAY OUT: BLOODFIST VIII
Febre, Louis
RAGE
SERIAL KILLER
TWO-BITS & PEPPER
Fennell, Tony
WITHIN THE ROCK

Fenton, George
HEAVEN'S PRISONERS
IN LOVE AND WAR
LAND AND FREEDOM
MARY REILLY
MULTIPLICITY
Ferguson, Jay
TREMORS 2: AFTERSHOCKS
Fiedel, Brad
RASPUTIN
Flint, Cheryl
GIRLFRIENDS
Folk, Robert
LAWNMOWER MAN 2: BEYOND CYBERSPACE
MAXIMUM RISK
THEODORE REX
Formosa, Ric
TUNNEL VISION
Frank, David Michael
TAILS YOU LIVE, HEADS YOU'RE DEAD
Franke, Christopher
PUBLIC ENEMIES
SOLO
SURGEON, THE
Friedman, Robert
PHARAOH'S ARMY
Frizzell, John
BEAVIS AND BUTT-HEAD DO AMERICA
RICH MAN'S WIFE, THE
UNDERTOW
Funton, George
CRUCIBLE, THE
Gallegos, Jose
SILENCE OF NETO, THE
Gallegos, Maurice
SILENCE OF NETO, THE
Galloway, Derek
LET'S GET BIZZEE
Gammons, Rod
WITHIN THE ROCK
Garcia, Roel A.
CHUNGKING EXPRESS
Gaudette, Claude
IMMORTALS, THE
VIRTUAL COMBAT
Gee, Kay
SUNSET PARK
Gibbs, Richard
. . . AT FIRST SIGHT
FIRST KID
Giffin, Philip
SHARON'S SECRET
Gintrowski, Przemyslaw
MOTHER OF KINGS
Glass, Philip
JOSEPH CONRAD'S THE SECRET AGENT
Glennie-Smith, Nick
ROCK, THE
TWO IF BY SEA
Glorified Magnified
GIRLFRIENDS
Goldberg, Barry
BEST OF THE BEST 3: NO TURNING BACK
Goldenthal, Elliot
MICHAEL COLLINS
TIME TO KILL, A
Goldsmith, Jerry
CHAIN REACTION
CITY HALL
EXECUTIVE DECISION
GHOST AND THE DARKNESS, THE
STAR TREK: FIRST CONTACT
Goldsmith, Joel
ONE GOOD TURN
RATTLED
Goldsmith, Jonathan
KISSINGER AND NIXON
STAND OFF, THE

Golia, Vinny
SERPENT'S LAIR
Golson, Benny
ED'S NEXT MOVE
Gonzalez, John
TIGER HEART
Gonzalez, Joseph Julian
CURDLED
Goodman, Miles
DUNSTON CHECKS IN
LARGER THAN LIFE
SUNSET PARK
Gore, Michael
EVENING STAR, THE
Goren, Yoav
WATCH ME
Gorgoni, Adam
TOLLBOOTH
Graham, John
AMERICAN STRAYS
Greer, Ken
WHEN THE BULLET HITS THE BONE
Greer, Scott
FATALLY YOURS
Gregson-Williams, Harry
FULL BODY MASSAGE
WHOLE WIDE WORLD, THE
Gross, Andrew
BIO-DOME
Gross, Charles
FAMILY THING, A
Grossman, Larry
BRITT ALLCROFT'S MAGIC ADVENTURES OF MUMFIE—THE MOVIE
Grusin, Dave
MULHOLLAND FALLS
Guard, Barrie
SHAMELESS
Gunning, Christopher
AFFAIR, THE
Guo Wenjing
BLUSH
Guru
GIRLS TOWN
Haber, Itai
LIVE WIRE: HUMAN TIMEBOMB
Hale, Ken
NORMAL LIFE
Halfpenny, Jim
SKYSCRAPER
TEXAS PAYBACK
Hames, Frank
ANNIE O
Hamlisch, Marvin
MIRROR HAS TWO FACES, THE
MISSING PIECES
OPEN SEASON
Hammer, Jan
BEASTMASTER 3: THE EYE OF BRAXUS
MODERN AFFAIR, A
Hanes, Wendell
DON'T LET YOUR MEAT LOAF
Hardy, John E. R.
HEDD WYNN
Harle, John
BUTTERFLY KISS
Harris, Johnny
RAVENHAWK
Hart, Joseph V.
TIMELESS
Hartley, Richard
STEALING BEAUTY
Haskell, Jimmie
DOGFIGHTERS, THE
Hassell, Jon
WILD SIDE

Hayen, Todd
MERLIN'S SHOP OF MAGICAL WONDERS
YESTERDAY'S TARGET
Henriksson & Lindh
EVIL ED
Hidden Faces
UNDER THE HULA MOON
Hill, John
POMPATUS OF LOVE, THE
Hirschfelder, David
SHINE
TUNNEL VISION
Holbek, Joachim
BREAKING THE WAVES
Holden, Mark
BEYOND DESIRE
Holdridge, Lee
HARVEST OF FIRE
TUSKEGEE AIRMEN, THE
Holland, Deborah
OUT THERE
VENUS RISING
Holmes Brothers, The
LOTTO LAND
Holton, Nigel
NAKED SOULS
Hopkins, Anthony
AUGUST
Horner, James
COURAGE UNDER FIRE
LAND BEFORE TIME IV: JOURNEY THROUGH THE MISTS
RANSOM
SPITFIRE GRILL, THE
TO GILLIAN ON HER 37TH BIRTHDAY
Horunzhy, Valdimir
ORIGINAL GANGSTAS
Hosono, Haruomi
NIGHT ON THE GALACTIC RAILROAD
Howard, James Newton
EYE FOR AN EYE
JUROR, THE
ONE FINE DAY
PRIMAL FEAR
SPACE JAM
TRIGGER EFFECT, THE
Howarth, Alan
DENTIST, THE
Huensberg, Gottfried
SHADOW OF ANGELS
Hufsteter, Steven
UNHOOK THE STARS
Hughes, David A.
PROTEUS
SOLITAIRE FOR TWO
Hunter, Steve
DEAD WEEKEND
Hunter, Todd
ALEX
Hus, Walter
SUITE 16
Iglesias, Alberto
FLOWER OF MY SECRET, THE
OUTRAGE
Isham, Mark
FLY AWAY HOME
LAST DANCE
Itakura, Fumi
ROUJIN-Z
James, Sidney
SUGARTIME
Jankowski, Lech
INSTITUTE BENJAMENTA
Jarre, Maurice
SUNCHASER
Johnston, Adrian
JUDE
Johnston, Freedy
KINGPIN
Johnston, Phillip
FAITHFUL
Kaczmarek, Jan A. P.
FELONY
Kamen, Michael
JACK
MR. HOLLAND'S OPUS
101 DALMATIANS
STONEWALL
Kander, John
BOYS NEXT DOOR, THE
Karpman, Laura
LOVER'S KNOT
Katche, Manu
LITTLE INDIAN, BIG CITY
Katoh, Michiaki
BIG WARS
Kauderer, Emilio
PLAYBACK
Kawai, Kenji
GHOST IN THE SHELL
PATLABOR 2: MOBILE POLICE
Kawasaki, Masahiro
KAMIKAZE TAXI
Kempel, Arthur
ARRIVAL, THE
RIDERS OF THE PURPLE SAGE
Kent, Rolfe
CITIZEN RUTH
MERCY
Kilar, Wojiech
PORTRAIT OF A LADY, THE
Kiner, Kevin
BLACK SCORPION
CARNOSAUR 3: PRIMAL SPECIES
EXIT
LIFEFORM
Kiti, El Houssaine
HALFMOON
Klein, Larry
GRACE OF MY HEART
Korven, Mark
CURTIS'S CHARM
Kosinski, Richard
MAGIC IN THE MIRROR
SPELLBREAKER: SECRET OF THE LEPRECHAUNS
Kraut, Alexander
NEUROSIA: 50 YEARS OF PERVERSITY
WOLVES, THE
Kravat, Amanda
IF LUCY FELL
Krol, Mitchell D.
ELECTRA
Laibach
PREDICTIONS OF FIRE
Landers, Tim
TALKING ABOUT SEX
Lane, Robert
YOUNG POISONER'S HANDBOOK, THE
Lanois, Daniel
SLING BLADE
Lauderdale, Jim
GALAXIES ARE COLLIDING
Lay, James
MUTANT MAN
Lennertz, Christopher
PIRANHA
UNKNOWN ORIGIN
Lerios, Cory
STREET FIGHTER II: THE ANIMATED MOVIE
Leroy and the Lifters
MADAME WANG'S
Levay, Sylvester
DEAD TO RIGHTS
Levi, Eric
VISITORS, THE
Levine, William
SPELLBREAKER: SECRET OF THE LEPRECHAUNS
Licht, Daniel
HELLRAISER: BLOODLINE
NECRONOMICON: BOOK OF THE DEAD
WOMAN UNDONE, A
Lifton, Jimmy
MIRROR, MIRROR III: THE VOYEUR
TAKEOVER, THE
Liu, Weigong
STORY OF XINGHUA, THE
Lockhart, Robert
COLD COMFORT FARM
NEON BIBLE, THE
LoDuca, Joseph
NECRONOMICON: BOOK OF THE DEAD
London, Frank
EVERYTHING RELATIVE
Loya, Marcos
HOSTILE INTENTIONS
Lubbock, Jeremy
DEAR GOD
Lundmak, Erik
ANIMAL INSTINCTS III: THE SEDUCTRESS
Lupito, Jun
RAW TARGET
Lurie, Evan
4 TALES OF 2 CITIES
MONSTER, THE
TREES LOUNGE
Lurie, John
MANNY & LO
Macchia, Frank
MERLIN'S SHOP OF MAGICAL WONDERS
Mainetti, Stefano
HIDDEN ASSASSIN
SONS OF TRINITY
Malou, Manuel
FRENCH TWIST
Mancina, Mark
MOLL FLANDERS
TWISTER
Mann, Marc
MIRROR, MIRROR III: THE VOYEUR
Mansfield, David
STREETCAR NAMED DESIRE, A
TRUMAN
Manzie, Jim
NIGHT OF THE SCARECROW
Marinelli, Anthony
ONE MAN'S JUSTICE
PIG'S TALE, A
2 DAYS IN THE VALLEY
Marotta, Rick
PAINTED HERO
Mason, Harvey
DEADLY OUTBREAK
Mason, Janette
PARIS WAS A WOMAN
Massari, John
REDEMPTION: KICKBOXER 5
McCarthy, Dennis
COLONY, THE
McCullough, Paul
SANTA CLAWS
McHugh, David
TALES OF EROTICA
McLaren, Malcolm
CATWALK
McNaughton, Robert
NORMAL LIFE
McNeely, Joel
FLIPPER

Meeks, Robert
LET'S GET BIZZEE
Melillo, Stephen
THEY BITE
Melnick, Peter Rodgers
LILY DALE
Menken, Alan
HUNCHBACK OF NOTRE DAME, THE
Mentors, The
MADAME WANG'S
Metallica
PARADISE LOST: THE CHILD MURDERS AT ROBIN HOOD HILLS
Miller, Marcus
GREAT WHITE HYPE, THE
Miller, Randy
DARKMAN III: DIE DARKMAN DIE
Miller, Steve
SAINTS AND SINNERS
Ming-Chang, Chen
MABOROSI
Moloney, Paddy
TWO IF BY SEA
Montes, Osvaldo
SHADOW YOU SOON WILL BE, A
Moon, Guy
VERY BRADY SEQUEL, A
Moore, Thurston
HEAVY
Morell, Steven
HEAD OF THE FAMILY
Morricone, Ennio
STAR MAKER, THE
WHO KILLED PASOLINI?
Mothersbaugh, Mark
BIG SQUEEZE, THE
BOTTLE ROCKET
HAPPY GILMORE
LAST SUPPER, THE
Mounsey, Rob
DANGEROUS PASSION
Mulligan, Gerry
I'M NOT RAPPAPORT
Murphy, John
PROTEUS
Nagari, Benny
UNDER THE DOMIM TREE
Nash the Slash
BLOOD & DONUTS
Natale, Lou
GIRL FROM MARS, THE
MAN IN THE ATTIC, THE
Newborn, Ira
HIGH SCHOOL HIGH
LATE SHIFT, THE
Newman, David
BIG BULLY
JINGLE ALL THE WAY
MATILDA
NUTTY PROFESSOR, THE
PHANTOM, THE
Newman, Randy
JAMES AND THE GIANT PEACH
MICHAEL
Newman, Thomas
AMERICAN BUFFALO
PEOPLE VS. LARRY FLYNT, THE
PHENOMENON
UP CLOSE AND PERSONAL
Nieto, Jose
OF LOVE AND SHADOWS
Northey, Craig
KIDS IN THE HALL: BRAIN CANDY
O'Brien, Gerald
PHANTOM 2040: THE GHOST WHO WALKS
Ober, Gene
WHITE WOLVES II: LEGEND OF THE WILD
Ogawa, Michio
ROUJIN-Z
Orban, Gyorgy
OUTPOST, THE
Oryema, Geoffrey
LITTLE INDIAN, BIG CITY
Ottman, John
CABLE GUY, THE
PUBLIC ACCESS
Paniagua, Gregorio
MAGIC HUNTER
Parker, Trey
CANNIBAL! THE MUSICAL
Parsons/Haines
FUNNYMAN, THE
Pasqua, Alan
MURDERED INNOCENCE
Passengers
GHOST IN THE SHELL
Patterson, Shawn
DEMOLITIONIST, THE
Pavlov, Dimitry
CHEKIST, THE
Peake, Don
BODY COUNT
HARD JUSTICE
Peters, Randolph
HECK'S WAY HOME
Petit, Jean-Claude
HORSEMAN ON THE ROOF
Petrone, Mike
FLATTERED
Pettus, Charlton
IF LUCY FELL
Petty, Tom
SHE'S THE ONE
Pheloung, Barrington
SHOPPING
Phillips, Shawn
ABUSE
Phranque
MADAME WANG'S
Piersanti, Franco
MILLE BOLLE BLU
Plumeri, Terry
BLACK OUT
Poledouris, Basil
CELTIC PRIDE
IT'S MY PARTY
WAR AT HOME, THE
Pollak, Andres
JOHNNY 100 PESOS
Portal, Michel
MACHINE, THE
Portman, Rachel
ADVENTURES OF PINOCCHIO, THE
EMMA
MARVIN'S ROOM
PALOOKAVILLE
WAR OF THE BUTTONS, THE
Pottorf, Rob
MR. ICE CREAM MAN
Powell, Reg
ALASKA
BAJA
Powell, Reginald
JOSH KIRBY . . . TIME WARRIOR!: EGGS FROM 70,000,000 B.C.
JOSH KIRBY . . . TIME WARRIOR!: JOURNEY TO THE MAGIC CAVERN
JOSH KIRBY . . . TIME WARRIOR!: LAST BATTLE FOR THE UNIVERSE
JOSH KIRBY . . . TIME WARRIOR!: TRAPPED ON TOY WORLD
Prado, Damaso Perez
AVENTURERA
Prahi, Kvarteto Mesta
SINGLE GIRL, A
Pray For Rain
BOY CALLED HATE, A
Preston, Don
SAWBONES
Prince
GIRL 6
Pronje, Zane
YANKEE ZULU
Puccini, Giacomo
MADAME BUTTERFLY
Raben, Peer
SHADOW OF ANGELS
Rabin, Trevor
GLIMMER MAN, THE
Rachtman, Karyn
HEADLESS BODY IN TOPLESS BAR
Ragland, Robert O.
TOO FAST, TOO YOUNG
WARHEAD
Ranaldo, Lee
FRISK
Ray, Satyajit
TARGET
Redford, J.A.C.
D3: THE MIGHTY DUCKS
Reinhardt, Justin
SWINGERS
Renzetti, Joe
BLONDES HAVE MORE GUNS
Revell, Graeme
CRAFT, THE
CROW: CITY OF ANGELS, THE
FLED
FROM DUSK TILL DAWN
RACE THE SUN
Ridgeback Studios
PHOENIX
Riedel, Georg
CHILDREN OF NOISY VILLAGE, THE
Rifle, Ned
FLIRT
Riparetti, Tony
ADRENALIN: FEAR THE RUSH
FAST MONEY
NEMESIS III: PREY HARDER
Risse, Michel
GUIMBA THE TYRANT
Rivas, Fernando
GIRLFRIENDS
Rivera, Nicholas
LITTLE WITCHES
Robbins, Richard
PROPRIETOR, THE
SURVIVING PICASSO
Robinson, J. Peter
MIND RIPPER
Robinson, Peter Manning
MADDENING, THE
SOMETIMES THEY COME BACK . . . AGAIN
Roger, Normand
CHAMPAGNE SAFARI, THE
Rohatyn, Michael
ANGELA
Rona, Jeff
WHITE SQUALL
Rose, Earl
MAD DOG TIME
Rosenbaum, Joel
JOHNNY SHORTWAVE
Rosenman, Leonard
MRS. MUNCK
Ross, William
BLACK SHEEP
EVENING STAR, THE
MY FELLOW AMERICANS
TIN CUP

Roth, Adam
NATIONAL LAMPOON'S FAVORITE DEADLY SINS
Rubini, Michel
BLOODKNOT
Rushen, Patrice
AMERICA'S DREAM
Safan, Craig
LONG ROAD HOME, THE
MR. WRONG
Saidiner, Grant
SOUTH BEACH ACADEMY
Sanders, Rich
CANNIBAL! THE MUSICAL
Sandman, Mark
JUST YOUR LUCK
Sanko, Anton
LIVE NUDE GIRLS
Saranec, Chris
HOURGLASS
Sarde, Philippe
LES VOLEURS
MA SAISON PREFEREE
NELLY AND MONSIEUR ARNAUD
Sauvageot, Pierre
GUIMBA THE TYRANT
Schell, Johnny Lee
BLACK DAY BLUE NIGHT
Schifrin, Lalo
MISSION: IMPOSSIBLE
Schipek, Dietmar
FLAMING EARS
Schnabel, Julian
BASQUIAT
Schneider, Norbert J.
BROTHER OF SLEEP
Scott, Tom
MOTHER'S PRAYER, A
Sekacz, Ilona
ANTONIA'S LINE
Selmeczy, Gyorgy
OUTPOST, THE
Shaiman, Marc
BOGUS
FIRST WIVES CLUB, THE
GHOSTS OF MISSISSIPPI
MOTHER
Sharifi, Jamshied
HARRIET THE SPY
Shire, David
HEIDI CHRONICLES, THE
LARRY MCMURTRY'S STREETS OF LAREDO
ONE NIGHT STAND
Shore, Howard
BEFORE AND AFTER
LOOKING FOR RICHARD
STRIPTEASE
THAT THING YOU DO!
TRUTH ABOUT CATS AND DOGS, THE
Shragge, Lawrence
MATERNAL INSTINCTS
NIGHT OF THE TWISTERS
SONG SPINNER, THE
Siegel, David
ORIGINAL SINS
Silvestri, Alan
ERASER
LONG KISS GOODNIGHT, THE
SGT. BILKO
Sklair, Sam
TERMINAL IMPACT
Snow, Mark
DOWN, OUT AND DANGEROUS
FRAME BY FRAME
Sonis, Dan
SHOT, THE
Sorret, Ludovico
WIFE, THE
Sprayberry, Robert
WIDOW'S KISS
Stamper, Michael
PHARAOH'S ARMY
Stern, Philip
UNDERSTUDY: GRAVEYARD SHIFT 2, THE
Stern, Steven M.
SWEET NOTHING
Stewart, David A.
BEAUTIFUL GIRLS
Stone, Christopher L.
FIST OF THE NORTH STAR
STUPIDS, THE
Storey, Michael
WAVELENGTH
Strobel, Frank
YOUNG POISONER'S HANDBOOK, THE
Sublett, Joe
BLACK DAY BLUE NIGHT
Sumen, Mauri
CONDITION RED
Sures, Ron
BODY OF INFLUENCE 2
Swell
4 TALES OF 2 CITIES
Sydnor, Charles
LAZARUS MAN, THE
Syrewicz, Stanislas
YANKEE ZULU
Tavera, Michael
LAND BEFORE TIME IV: JOURNEY THROUGH THE MISTS
Taylor, Jeffrey
FLIRT
Tejada, Manuel
BITTER SUGAR
Tenney, Dennis Michael
GRIM
PINOCCHIO'S REVENGE
tomandandy
MR. STITCH
Towns, Colin
CAPTIVES
WIND IN THE WILLOWS, THE
Troost, Ernest
CANTERVILLE GHOST, THE
Troutman, Roger
THIN LINE BETWEEN LOVE AND HATE, A
Truyman, Stefan
COLD LIGHT OF DAY
Tsung Ding-yat
ORGANIZED CRIME & TRIAD BUREAU
Turner, Simon Fisher
LOADED
Tyng, Christopher
ASSOCIATE, THE
CROSSCUT
FAR HARBOR
KAZAAM
LITTLE DEATH, THE
NATIONAL LAMPOON'S FAVORITE DEADLY SINS
SHADOW WARRIORS
Tyrell, Steve
ONCE UPON A TIME . . . WHEN WE WERE COLORED
van der Meulen, Henk
CROCODILES IN AMSTERDAM
Van Peebles, Melvin
TALES OF EROTICA
Vanelli, Ross
FINAL CUT, THE
Varner, Tom
SAINTS AND SINNERS
Vitarelli, Joseph
EVIL HAS A FACE
SUBSTANCE OF FIRE, THE
Vlad, Alessio
JANE EYRE
von Goisern, Hubert
BROTHER OF SLEEP
Wait, Robert
BREAKAWAY
Walden, W.G. Snuffy
HOMAGE
HOMECOMING
Waldman, Peter
MIRROR, MIRROR III: THE VOYEUR
Walker, Daniel
ANIMAL INSTINCTS III: THE SEDUCTRESS
Walker, Jim
RED LINE
Walker, Shirley
IT CAME FROM OUTER SPACE II
JOHN CARPENTER'S ESCAPE FROM L.A.
Wall, Lee
4 TALES OF 2 CITIES
Walsh, Matthew Jason
POLYMORPH
SANDMAN, THE
Warren, Mervyn
WHARF RAT, THE
Wastall, Julian
CRACKER: THE MADWOMAN IN THE ATTIC
Watters, Mark
ALL DOGS GO TO HEAVEN 2
Webber, Andrew Lloyd
EVITA
Welsman, John
ROBIN OF LOCKSLEY
Wenger, Brahm
HOLLOW POINT
Whelan, Bill
SOME MOTHER'S SON
Wiedlin, Jane
AMANDA AND THE ALIEN
Wilkinson, K. Alexander
PURE DANGER
SHOOTFIGHTER 2: KILL OR BE KILLED!
SWEEPER, THE
Williams, Alan
CLUBHOUSE DETECTIVES
Williams, David
CHILDREN OF THE CORN: THE GATHERING
Williams, John
SLEEPERS
Williams, Joseph
LEGEND OF GATOR FACE, THE
POISON IVY 2: LILY
Williams, Patrick
GRASS HARP, THE
WEEKEND IN THE COUNTRY, A
Willner, Hal
KANSAS CITY
THEREMIN: AN ELECTRONIC ODYSSEY
Wilson, Nancy
JERRY MAGUIRE
Winkless, Jeff
NOT OF THIS EARTH
Wiseman, Debbie
HAUNTED
Wisoff, Jill
WELCOME TO THE DOLLHOUSE
Wood, Ollie
FEMALIEN
VIRTUAL ENCOUNTERS
Wurman, Alex
GRAVE, THE
Wurst, David
BLACK ROSE OF HARLEM
DEATH ARTIST, THE

LOOKING FOR TROUBLE
SHOWGIRL MURDERS, THE
Wurst, Eric
BLACK ROSE OF HARLEM
DEATH ARTIST, THE
LOOKING FOR TROUBLE
SHOWGIRL MURDERS, THE
Yared, Gabriel
ENGLISH PATIENT, THE
Young, Christopher
NORMA JEAN AND MARILYN
SET IT OFF
UNFORGETTABLE
Young, Neil
DEAD MAN
Yuill, Jimmy
MIDWINTER'S TALE, A
Zaza, Paul
IRON EAGLE IV
Zeane, John
SMALL FACES
Zeretzke, John
SPELLBREAKER: SECRET OF THE LEPRECHAUNS
Zhao Jiping
BLACK MOUNTAIN
Zimmer, Hans
BROKEN ARROW
FAN, THE
MUPPET TREASURE ISLAND
PREACHER'S WIFE, THE
ROCK, THE
TWO DEATHS
WHOLE WIDE WORLD, THE
Zourabichvili, Nicolas
CHASING BUTTERFLIES

PRODUCERS

Abel-Bey, Gay
BUGGED
Abey, Dennis
WIND IN THE WILLOWS, THE
Abrams, Jeffrey
PALLBEARER, THE
Abramson, Richard
THEODORE REX
Adler, Gilbert
TALES FROM THE CRYPT PRESENTS BORDELLO OF BLOOD
Ahlberg, Julie
FULL BODY MASSAGE
Albert, Cari-Esta
TRUTH ABOUT CATS AND DOGS, THE
Albert, Trevor
MULTIPLICITY
Alia, Phyllis
MURDERED INNOCENCE
Allcroft, Britt
BRITT ALLCROFT'S MAGIC ADVENTURES OF MUMFIE—THE MOVIE
Almagor, Gila
UNDER THE DOMIM TREE
Altman, Robert
KANSAS CITY
Amiel, Alan
SHOOTFIGHTER 2: KILL OR BE KILLED!
Amritraj, Ashok
BLACK OUT
VIRTUAL COMBAT
Anciano, Dominic
PASSION OF DARKLY NOON, THE
Andrews, Anthony
HAUNTED
Annaud, Monique
FRANCOIS TRUFFAUT: STOLEN PORTRAITS
Antoine, Dominique
ORSON WELLES: THE ONE-MAN BAND
Apatow, Judd
CABLE GUY, THE
Apramian, Lisa Rose
NOT BAD FOR A GIRL
Argueta, Luis
SILENCE OF NETO, THE
Armstrong, Andy
MOONSHINE HIGHWAY
Arntzen, Becky
MOONSHINE HIGHWAY
Attal, Yves
MONSTER, THE
Attenborough, Richard
IN LOVE AND WAR
Attia, Ahmed Baha Eddine
SILENCES OF THE PALACE, THE
Aubrey, Jay
LOOKING FOR TROUBLE
Austin, Stephanie
LONG KISS GOODNIGHT, THE
Avalon, Phil
TUNNEL VISION
Avnet, Jon
D3: THE MIGHTY DUCKS
UP CLOSE AND PERSONAL
Bachrach, Doro
TRUMAN
Bacino, Mark
HOW THE WEST WAS FUN
Badalato, Bill
BROKEN ARROW
Baden-Powell, Sue
THEODORE REX
Baer, Rick
LIFEFORM
Baer, Thomas
FRAME BY FRAME
Baer, Willi
SURGEON, THE
Bahr, Helga
SOMEONE ELSE'S AMERICA
Baines, Julie
BUTTERFLY KISS
MADAGASCAR SKIN
Baird, T. A.
BLOODKNOT
Baitz, Jon Robin
SUBSTANCE OF FIRE, THE
Baker, Mark H.
LIFEFORM
Baker, Martin G.
MUPPET TREASURE ISLAND
Baldwin, Craig
SONIC OUTLAWS
Balian, Haig
COLD LIGHT OF DAY
Balsan, Humbert
PROPRIETOR, THE
Baran, Jack
HOMECOMING
Bardet, Pierre-Olivier
MADAME BUTTERFLY
LA COMEDIE-FRANCAISE OU L'AMOUR JOUE
Barnathan, Michael
JINGLE ALL THE WAY
Barnett, Bill
DEADLY OUTBREAK
Barratier, Christophe
MICROCOSMOS
Barron, David
HAMLET
MIDWINTER'S TALE, A
Bartlett, Helen
BEYOND THE CALL
Baruch, Jonathan
. . . AT FIRST SIGHT
Bates, Dan
FINAL EQUINOX, THE
PHOENIX
Battishill, Arlene
DEVOTION
Battista, Franco
SCREAMERS
Baum, Carol
FLY AWAY HOME
Beattie, Alan
SURGEON, THE
Becker, Harold
CITY HALL
Becker, Louis
LITTLE INDIAN, BIG CITY
Belzberg, Leslie
STUPIDS, THE
Benedetti, Robert
CANTERVILLE GHOST, THE
Benedict, Terry
PAINTED HERO
Benigni, Roberto
MONSTER, THE
Benitez, Cesar
MOUTH TO MOUTH
Bennett, Michael
ONCE UPON A TIME . . . WHEN WE WERE COLORED
Benson, Michael
PREDICTIONS OF FIRE
Bentsvi, Yakov
BLACK OUT
Bergendahl, Waldemar
CHILDREN OF NOISY VILLAGE, THE
Berger, Howard
ORIGINAL SINS
Bergman, Martin
WEEKEND IN THE COUNTRY, A
Berlinger, Joe
PARADISE LOST: THE CHILD MURDERS AT ROBIN HOOD HILLS
Berman, Rick
STAR TREK: FIRST CONTACT
Bernardi, Barry
LIVE NUDE GIRLS
NIGHT OF THE SCARECROW
Berner, Fred
GREAT WHITE HYPE, THE
Berri, Claude
FRENCH TWIST
Berrigan, Frances
PARIS WAS A WOMAN
Berry, Tom
SCREAMERS
Bettman, Gary M.
TALKING ABOUT SEX
Bice, Patricia
TIMELESS
Bill, Tony
BEYOND THE CALL
Binder, John
LAZARUS MAN, THE
Birnbaum, Roger
CELTIC PRIDE
FIRST KID
RICH MAN'S WIFE, THE
Black, Shane
LONG KISS GOODNIGHT, THE
Black, Todd
DUNSTON CHECKS IN
FAMILY THING, A
Blair, Jon
ANNE FRANK REMEMBERED
Blazin, Milan
PREDICTIONS OF FIRE

Boboras, Peter
JOHNNY SHORTWAVE
Bockner, Michael
JOHNNY SHORTWAVE
Bojilov, Jordan
SHADOW OF ANGELS
Bolt, Jeremy
SHOPPING
Bonivento, Claudio
WHO KILLED PASOLINI?
Bookwalter, J.R.
POLYMORPH
SANDMAN, THE
Borchers, Donald P.
DEMOLITIONIST, THE
LITTLE WITCHES
Borchiver, Richard
KISSINGER AND NIXON
Borden, Bill
GET ON THE BUS
Borden, Christopher
GIRLFRIENDS
Bordier, Patrick
MACHINE, THE
Boros, Stuart
BOUND
Bourgois, Dominique
LA COMEDIE-FRANCAISE OU L'AMOUR JOUE
Bowden, Helen
GIRLFRIENDS
Bowman, Rick
SWEET NOTHING
Boyle, Barbara
MRS. MUNCK
PHENOMENON
Bradshaw, Randy
SONG SPINNER, THE
Branaman, Rustam
HEADLESS BODY IN TOPLESS BAR
Branco, Paulo
THREE LIVES AND ONLY ONE DEATH
Brandes, Richard
DEAD COLD
Brauner, Wolf
WOLVES, THE
Brayton, Marian
DEAD TO RIGHTS
Bressan Jr., Arthur J.
ABUSE
Brett, Jonathan
TALES OF EROTICA
Breuls, Paul
SUITE 16
Brick, Richard
CAUGHT
Brillion, Frederic
RIDICULE
Broderick, Matthew
INFINITY
Broderick, Patricia
INFINITY
Brooks, James L.
JERRY MAGUIRE
Brooks, Paul
PROTEUS
Broomfield, Nick
HEIDI FLEISS HOLLYWOOD MADAM
Brouwer, Chris
COLD LIGHT OF DAY
Bruce, Lisa
SEARCH FOR ONE-EYE JIMMY, THE
Bruck, Arnold H.
UNDERSTUDY: GRAVEYARD SHIFT 2, THE
Bruckheimer, Jerry
ROCK, THE
Bryce, Ian
TWISTER
Burg, Andy
ALASKA
Burg, Mark
EDDIE
Burgess, Andre
WAVELENGTH
Burke, Ed
SOME MOTHER'S SON
Burns, Edward
SHE'S THE ONE
Burton, Kenneth J.
MERLIN'S SHOP OF MAGICAL WONDERS
Burton, Tim
JAMES AND THE GIANT PEACH
MARS ATTACKS!
Bushell, David L.
SLING BLADE
Calderon, Guillermo
AVENTURERA
Calderon, Pedro A.
AVENTURERA
Caleb, Ruth
STONEWALL
Camp, Alida
ONE NIGHT STAND
Cannon, Reuben
GET ON THE BUS
Canter, Ross
MRS. WINTERBOURNE
Cappe, Syd
GALAXIES ARE COLLIDING
Carcassonne, Philippe
RIDICULE
SINGLE GIRL, A
Carden, Jim
DADETOWN
Carlucci, Anne
DEAD TO RIGHTS
Carmody, Don
LATE SHIFT, THE
Carpenter, Fred
MURDERED INNOCENCE
Carraro, Bill
TUSKEGEE AIRMEN, THE
Cassavetti, Patrick
EMMA
Cecchi Gori, Rita
STAR MAKER, THE
WHO KILLED PASOLINI?
Cecchi Gori, Vittorio
STAR MAKER, THE
WHO KILLED PASOLINI?
Celal, T.
LA COMEDIE-FRANCAISE OU L'AMOUR JOUE
Chan Yi-Kan
CHUNGKING EXPRESS
Chang, Terence
BROKEN ARROW
Channing-Williams, Simon
JACK & SARAH
SECRETS & LIES
Charny, Ruth
GRACE OF MY HEART
Chen Kunming
BLUSH
Chesser, Chris
SURGEON, THE
Chubbuck, Ivana
NAKED SOULS
Chubbuck, Lyndon
NAKED SOULS
Chung Hu-pin
VIVE L'AMOUR
Cimino, Michael
SUNCHASER
Cinelli, Frank
BEYOND DESIRE
Clark-Hall, Steve
SMALL FACES
Clarke, Sally
ZARKORR! THE INVADER
Clay, Carl
LET'S GET BIZZEE
Cleitman, Rene
HORSEMAN ON THE ROOF
UNHOOK THE STARS
Clements, Jack
FOR THE MOMENT
Clermont, Nicolas
HOLLOW POINT
Coates, John
WIND IN THE WILLOWS, THE
Coatsworth, David
SUGARTIME
Cochran, Lisa M.
BEASTMASTER 3: THE EYE OF BRAXUS
Codikow, Stacy
UNDER THE HULA MOON
Coen, Ethan
FARGO
Cohen, Joseph Newton
SOLO
Cohn, Elie
WILD SIDE
Collins, Rocky
MERCY
Colpaert, Carl-Jan
WHOLE WIDE WORLD, THE
Columbus, Chris
JINGLE ALL THE WAY
Colwell, Thom
4 TALES OF 2 CITIES
Conrad, Rick
DESIRE
Cook, Cheryl
TAKEOVER, THE
Cook, Troy
PHOENIX
Cooper, Matt
LAST SUPPER, THE
Coppola, Francis Ford
JACK
Corman, Julie
WHITE WOLVES II: LEGEND OF THE WILD
Corman, Roger
CARNOSAUR 3: PRIMAL SPECIES
Corsi, Tilde
CEMETERY MAN
Cort, Robert W.
MR. HOLLAND'S OPUS
Cowan, Rob
JUROR, THE
Craven, Jonathan
MIND RIPPER
Crichton, Michael
TWISTER
Cross, Pippa
AUGUST
JACK & SARAH
Crowe, Cameron
JERRY MAGUIRE
Cruise, Tom
MISSION: IMPOSSIBLE
Cundiff, Greg
JUST YOUR LUCK
Cunningham, Sandra
CURTIS'S CHARM
Curtis, Bruce Cohn
WIDOW'S KISS
Curtis, Madelyn
LIFEFORM

Cutler, R.J.
PERFECT CANDIDATE, A
D'Oliveira, Damon
RUDE
D'Onofrio, Vincent
WHOLE WIDE WORLD, THE
Dahl, Liccy
MATILDA
Daniel, Sean
MICHAEL
Danon, Leslie
WHISPERING, THE
Dash, Sean
BREAKAWAY
Dauman, Florence
PERSONAL JOURNEY WITH MARTIN SCORSESE THROUGH AMERICAN MOVIES, A
David, Pierre
DENTIST, THE
SERIAL KILLER
Davies, Shan
HEDD WYNN
Davis, Andrew
CHAIN REACTION
Davis, John
CHAMBER, THE
COURAGE UNDER FIRE
DAYLIGHT
GRASS HARP, THE
Davis, Richard
SABRINA, THE TEENAGE WITCH
Davison, Boaz
HARD JUSTICE
Day, Janette
JACK & SARAH
de Clermont-Tonnerre, Antoine
SOMEONE ELSE'S AMERICA
De Laurentiis, Dino
UNFORGETTABLE
De Laurentiis, Martha
UNFORGETTABLE
De Laurentiis, Raffaella
DRAGONHEART
De Nave, Caterina
GIRLFRIENDS
De Niro, Robert
FAITHFUL
MARVIN'S ROOM
de Pourtales Davis, Gigi
FAR HARBOR
de Weers, Hans
ANTONIA'S LINE
Dean, Rod
AMERICAN STRAYS
DeFaria, Christopher
TREMORS 2: AFTERSHOCKS
Degass, Andre
CONDITION RED
DeLaurentis, Suzanne
MUTANT MAN
Demme, Jonathan
THAT THING YOU DO!
Densham, Pen
LARGER THAN LIFE
MOLL FLANDERS
DePew, Gary
CHILDREN OF THE CORN: THE GATHERING
Dern, Jonathan
ALL DOGS GO TO HEAVEN 2
Devien, Matt
BAD LOVE
DeVito, Danny
FEELING MINNESOTA
MATILDA
SUNSET PARK
Devlin, Dean
INDEPENDENCE DAY
Dezaki, Satoshi
BIG WARS
Di Novi, Denise
JAMES AND THE GIANT PEACH
Diamant, Moshe
MAXIMUM RISK
QUEST, THE
Dickerson, Albert T.
YESTERDAY'S TARGET
Dickerson III, Albert
VENUS RISING
Donen, Joshua
GREAT WHITE HYPE, THE
Dow, Tony
IT CAME FROM OUTER SPACE II
Draizin, Doug
SPY HARD
du Plantier, Daniel Toscan
MADAME BUTTERFLY
Dubinet, Ann
LITTLE DEATH, THE
Dubovsky, Dana
PUBLIC ENEMIES
Duchowny, Roger
IT CAME FROM OUTER SPACE II
Duff, James
WAR AT HOME, THE
Dunye, Cheryl
GIRLFRIENDS
Duvall, Robert
FAMILY THING, A
Eaton, Andrew
JUDE
Edwards, James L.
SANDMAN, THE
Eichinger, Bernd
MAYBE . . . MAYBE NOT
Eilts, Mary
MATERNAL INSTINCTS
Einbinder, Scott
BLACK DAY BLUE NIGHT
Eisenman, Morrie
SUBSTITUTE, THE
Elliott, Mike
BLACK ROSE OF HARLEM
BLACK SCORPION
CRIMINAL HEARTS
DEATH ARTIST, THE
NOT OF THIS EARTH
PIRANHA
SAWBONES
UNKNOWN ORIGIN
Ellis, Riley Kathryn
FIRST KID
Engelman, Bob
KAZAAM
Ephron, Nora
MICHAEL
Epstein, Rob
CELLULOID CLOSET, THE
Erman, John
BOYS NEXT DOOR, THE
Estes, Larry
AMANDA AND THE ALIEN
DEAD WEEKEND
OUT THERE
YESTERDAY'S TARGET
Estevez, Emilio
WAR AT HOME, THE
Etchegaray, Francoise
RENDEZVOUS IN PARIS
Etheridge, Dan
4 TALES OF 2 CITIES
Evan, Eitan
UNDER THE DOMIM TREE
Evans, Robert
PHANTOM, THE
Evans, Stephen
TWELFTH NIGHT
Fahey, Murray
GIRLFRIENDS
Falick, Steven
HEADLESS BODY IN TOPLESS BAR
Feifer, Michael
WITCHCRAFT: SALEM'S GHOST
Feldsher, Paul
BOYS
Fengler, Michael
SHADOW OF ANGELS
Field, Fern
COLONY, THE
Field, Ted
MR. HOLLAND'S OPUS
Filley, Jonathan
BIG NIGHT
Finch, Randy
SUBSTANCE OF FIRE, THE
Finerman, Wendy
FAN, THE
Fisher, Mary Ann
HARD WAY OUT: BLOODFIST VIII
Fitzgerald, Jon
APART FROM HUGH
Flacks, Stephen R.
UNDERSTUDY: GRAVEYARD SHIFT 2, THE
Flock, John
SOLO
Foster, Gary
BIG BULLY
TIN CUP
Fox, Keith
LAWNMOWER MAN 2: BEYOND CYBERSPACE
Fradis, Anatoly
BURIAL OF THE RATS
Franck, Eric
SHADOW OF ANGELS
Franco, Larry
MARS ATTACKS!
Frand, Harvey
LAZARUS MAN, THE
Frankfurt, Peter
BOYS
Friedberg, Rick
SPY HARD
Friedman, Jeffrey
CELLULOID CLOSET, THE
Friendly, David T.
COURAGE UNDER FIRE
DAYLIGHT
Fry, Benjamin
WAVELENGTH
Fuchs, Carol
ALASKA
Fuchs, Fred
JACK
Fujiwara, Masamichi
SANCTUARY: THE MOVIE
Gage, Beth
FIRE ON THE MOUNTAIN
Gage, George
FIRE ON THE MOUNTAIN
Gallagher, Bob
SOUTH BEACH ACADEMY
Gamble, Tom
TOO FAST, TOO YOUNG
Garcia, Esther
FLOWER OF MY SECRET, THE
Gardner, Eric
BREAKAWAY
Garnett, Tony
BEAUTIFUL THING

Garroni, Andrew
ANIMAL INSTINCTS III: THE SEDUCTRESS
BODY OF INFLUENCE 2
Gast, Leon
WHEN WE WERE KINGS
Geoffray, Jeff
PINOCCHIO'S REVENGE
Gerlach, Phil
ALEX
Gerrans, Jon
FRISK
Gieras, Gregory
WHISPERING, THE
Gil, Jaime Comas
OUTRAGE
Gilbert, Lewis
HAUNTED
Gilford, Hilary
4 TALES OF 2 CITIES
Gillott, Nick
RASPUTIN
Gitlin, Mimi Polk
WHITE SQUALL
Glaser, Paul Michael
KAZAAM
Glatzer, Peter
GRAVE, THE
Goetzman, Gary
THAT THING YOU DO!
Golchan, Frederic
ASSOCIATE, THE
Gold, Eric L.
DON'T BE A MENACE TO SOUTH CENTRAL WHILE DRINKING YOUR JUICE IN THE HOOD
Goldberg, Daniel
SPACE JAM
Golden, Noah
TALES OF EROTICA
Goldstein, David
DEADLY OUTBREAK
Goldstein, Harel
DEADLY OUTBREAK
Goldstein, Judy
SUNCHASER
Goldwyn Jr., Samuel
PREACHER'S WIFE, THE
Golin, Steve
PORTRAIT OF A LADY, THE
SLEEPERS
Goncalves, Helder
ELECTRA
WHEN THE BULLET HITS THE BONE
Goodman, Gregory
PIG'S TALE, A
Goodwin, Richard
OF LOVE AND SHADOWS
Gordon, Keith
MOTHER NIGHT
Gordon, Mark
BROKEN ARROW
Gozu, Naoe
MABOROSI
Grant, Julian
ELECTRA
WHEN THE BULLET HITS THE BONE
Gray, Valerie
HECK'S WAY HOME
Grazer, Brian
CHAMBER, THE
FEAR
NUTTY PROFESSOR, THE
RANSOM
SGT. BILKO
STUPIDS, THE
Greene, Justis
OUTER LIMITS: SANDKINGS, THE
Greene, Peter
PAINTED HERO
Greenfield, Barry
SHARON'S SECRET
Greenfield, Michael
EXIT
Greenhut, Robert
EVERYONE SAYS I LOVE YOU
Greif, Leslie
HEAVEN'S PRISONERS
MADDENING, THE
Griffiths, Keith
INSTITUTE BENJAMENTA
Grillo, Michael
TRIGGER EFFECT, THE
Grisham, John
TIME TO KILL, A
Gund III, George
SYNTHETIC PLEASURES
Gurian, Paul
VIKING SAGAS, THE
Haas, Belinda
ANGELS AND INSECTS
Hackford, Taylor
WHEN WE WERE KINGS
Hadar, Ronnie
HOSTILE INTENTIONS
Hadge, Michael
LOOKING FOR RICHARD
Hadida, Samuel
NECRONOMICON: BOOK OF THE DEAD
Haft, Steven
EMMA
LAST DANCE
Hagen, Stephanie
CHILDREN OF FURY
Hagopian, B. Kipling
RANSOM
Hahn, Don
HUNCHBACK OF NOTRE DAME, THE
Haines, Randa
FAMILY THING, A
Hamawatari, Tsuyoshi
PATLABOR 2: MOBILE POLICE
Hamilton, Dean
ROAD HOME, THE
Hamori, Andras
MAGIC HUNTER
Hanley, Chris
FREEWAY
TREES LOUNGE
Hanna, Stuart
WHISPERING, THE
Hansen, Kirk Edward
ZARKORR! THE INVADER
Hansen, Lisa M.
CARRIED AWAY
Hara, Masato
NIGHT ON THE GALACTIC RAILROAD
Hardin, Ian
CANNIBAL! THE MUSICAL
Hargrave, Cynthia
BOTTLE ROCKET
Harlin, Renny
LONG KISS GOODNIGHT, THE
Harman Jr., J. Boyce
SKIN
Harris, J. Todd
DENISE CALLS UP
Hart, Chris
TIMELESS
Harvey, Bruce
PORTRAITS OF A KILLER
Hassid, Daniel
GRACE OF MY HEART
Hassig, Kirk
AMERICAN STRAYS
Hausman, Michael
PEOPLE VS. LARRY FLYNT, THE
Hazlett, David
LOADED
Hecht, Marlen
MANNY & LO
Heller, Barbara
GIRLFRIENDS
Helvey, Steven
HYPE!
Heminway, Tobin
LOW LIFE, THE
Hendershot, Dicklyn
CLUBHOUSE DETECTIVES
Hendershot, Eric
CLUBHOUSE DETECTIVES
Henry, Noble
FRIEND OF THE FAMILY 2
FUGITIVE RAGE
Henschke, Frank
PASSION OF DARKLY NOON, THE
Henson, Brian
MUPPET TREASURE ISLAND
Henson, Robby
PHARAOH'S ARMY
Herlihy, Joyce
ANGELS AND INSECTS
Herman, Vicky
LETTER TO MY KILLER
Hertzberg, Paul
CARRIED AWAY
POISON IVY 2: LILY
Herz, Michael
SGT. KABUKIMAN N.Y.P.D.
Hess, Oliver G.
DOGFIGHTERS, THE
Heus, Richard
RACE THE SUN
Hewitt, Caroline
LOADED
Heyman, Norma
JOSEPH CONRAD'S THE SECRET AGENT
MARY REILLY
Hickenlooper, George
SOME FOLKS CALL IT A SLING BLADE
Hill, Debra
JOHN CARPENTER'S ESCAPE FROM L.A.
Hill, Walter
LAST MAN STANDING
Ho, Kitman
GHOST AND THE DARKNESS, THE
Hoban, Steven
BLOOD & DONUTS
Hoffman, Susan
BEFORE AND AFTER
Holmes, Richard
SOLITAIRE FOR TWO
Hope, Ted
FLIRT
SHE'S THE ONE
WALKING AND TALKING
Horowitz, Jude
SHOT, THE
Hovis, Angela Sembera
MAN WITH THE PERFECT SWING, THE
Hovis, Michael
MAN WITH THE PERFECT SWING, THE
Howard, Andy
FOREST WARRIOR
Howard, Ron
CHAMBER, THE
STUPIDS, THE
Howe, Matthew
ORIGINAL SINS
Hsu Li-kong
VIVE L'AMOUR
Hu, Marcus
FRISK

Hudnell, Kevin
SOME FOLKS CALL IT A SLING BLADE
Huete, Cristina
TWO MUCH
Huggins, Erica
BOYS
Hughes, John
101 DALMATIANS
Hunt, David
RAW TARGET
Hurd, Gale Anne
GHOST AND THE DARKNESS, THE
Hurley, Elizabeth
EXTREME MEASURES
Hyman, Kevin
MAGIC IN THE MIRROR
Ichaso, Leon
BITTER SUGAR
Ikin, Bridget
LOADED
Imai, Kenichi
STREET FIGHTER II: THE ANIMATED MOVIE
Impens, Dirk
DAENS
Inomata, Koichiro
SANCTUARY: THE MOVIE
Ireland, Dan
WHOLE WIDE WORLD, THE
Irmas, Matthew
EDIE & PEN
Isaacs, Stanley
WITHIN THE ROCK
Ishikawa, Mitsuhisa
GHOST IN THE SHELL
PATLABOR 2: MOBILE POLICE
Ito, Umeo
SANCTUARY: THE MOVIE
Iyadomi, Ken
GHOST IN THE SHELL
Jacks, James
MICHAEL
Jackson, George
THIN LINE BETWEEN LOVE AND HATE, A
Jackson, Peter
FRIGHTENERS, THE
Jacobson, Mandy
CALLING THE GHOSTS: A STORY ABOUT RAPE, WAR AND WOMEN
James, Judith Rutherford
MAD DOG TIME
Jenkel, Brad
BIO-DOME
IF LUCY FELL
Jensen, Peter Aalbaek
BREAKING THE WAVES
Jewison, Norman
BOGUS
Johnson, Dave Alan
CHAMELEON
Johnston, Aaron Kim
FOR THE MOMENT
Jordan, Glenn
STREETCAR NAMED DESIRE, A
Jossen, Barry
HOMEWARD BOUND II: LOST IN SAN FRANCISCO
Josten, Walter
PINOCCHIO'S REVENGE
Juso, Galliano
OUTRAGE
Justice, Milton
LOSING CHASE
Kahn, Mary
GIRL FROM MARS, THE
Kalin, Tom
I SHOT ANDY WARHOL
Kallberg, Kevin
DOGFIGHTERS, THE
Kane, Mary
FUNERAL, THE
Kane, Thomas
RIDERS OF THE PURPLE SAGE
Kaplan, Betty
OF LOVE AND SHADOWS
Kaplan, Susan
SMALL WONDERS
Karlsen, Elizabeth
NEON BIBLE, THE
Karmitz, Marin
LA CEREMONIE
Karnowski, Tom
ADRENALIN: FEAR THE RUSH
NEMESIS III: PREY HARDER
Kash, Samantha
WATCH ME
Kastner, Elliott
LOVE IS ALL THERE IS
Kastner, Ron
ANGELA
SUBSTANCE OF FIRE, THE
Katz, Marty
MR. WRONG
Katz, Perry
FLIPPER
Kaufman, Lloyd
SGT. KABUKIMAN N.Y.P.D.
Kaufman, Paul A.
LOVER'S KNOT
Kazanjian, Howard
JAG
Kazawa, Yasuhisa
ROUJIN-Z
Keener, Matt
MAN OF THE YEAR
Kelley, David E.
TO GILLIAN ON HER 37TH BIRTHDAY
Kelly, Alexandra
CANNIBAL! THE MUSICAL
Kennedy, Kathleen
TWISTER
Kent, Rolfe
MERCY
Kerner, Jordan
D3: THE MIGHTY DUCKS
UP CLOSE AND PERSONAL
Key Jr., Don
OVER THE WIRE
Keytsman, Alan
PASSION OF DARKLY NOON, THE
Kidney, Ric
FEAR
Kikukawa, Yukio
BIG WARS
Kimatian, Paul
WHARF RAT, THE
Kimaz, Nicolas T.
SHADOW WARRIORS
King, Karen A.
RUDE
Kirkpatrick, David
EVENING STAR, THE
Kitchell, Mark
BERKELEY IN THE 60S
Klein, Robin
ROLLING STONES ROCK-AND-ROLL CIRCUS, THE
Kleiser, Randal
IT'S MY PARTY
Klik, Jon
BASQUIAT
Knell, Catalaine
POISON IVY 2: LILY
Knoller, David
AMERICA'S DREAM
Kokin, Kenneth
PUBLIC ACCESS
Kolar, Evzen
DELTA OF VENUS
Komine, Aki
FIST OF THE NORTH STAR
Konkov, Oleg
CHEKIST, THE
Konrad, Cathy
CITIZEN RUTH
SCREAM
Konvitz, Jeffrey
SPY HARD
Kopelson, Anne
ERASER
Kopelson, Arnold
ERASER
Koslow, Michael
BEWARE: CHILDREN AT PLAY
Kottenbrook, Carol
BLACK DAY BLUE NIGHT
Koules, Oren
MRS. WINTERBOURNE
SET IT OFF
Krevoy, Brad
BIO-DOME
GLASS CAGE, THE
IF LUCY FELL
KINGPIN
WAR AT HOME, THE
Kroopf, Scott
KAZAAM
Kuhn, Robert
TEXAS CHAINSAW MASSACRE: THE NEXT GENERATION
Kuhn, Tom
UNDERTOW
Kyle, Kyle C.
NOT BAD FOR A GIRL
Labib, Jean
LA COMEDIE-FRANCAISE OU L'AMOUR JOUE
Ladd Jr., Alan
PHANTOM, THE
VERY BRADY SEQUEL, A
LaLoggia, Nicole Shay
SWINGERS
Lambros, Alana H.
SABRINA, THE TEENAGE WITCH
Lancaster, David
WOMAN UNDONE, A
Lang, Rocky
WHITE SQUALL
Langley, John
WILD SIDE
Lappin, Arthur
SOME MOTHER'S SON
Later, Adria
HOW THE WEST WAS FUN
Lavery, Ron
DARK SECRETS
Lawrence, Robert
DOWN PERISCOPE
Lazar, Andrew
BOUND
Leahy, Michael
INFINITY
Lee, Bonni
JOE'S APARTMENT
Lee, Damian
VIRUS
WHEN THE BULLET HITS THE BONE
Lee, Raymond
WICKED CITY, THE
Lee, Spike
GIRL 6
Legrand, Gilles
RIDICULE

Leipzig, Adam
ASSOCIATE, THE
Lenox, John Thomas
LILY DALE
Lerner, Danny
LIVE WIRE: HUMAN TIMEBOMB
TERMINAL IMPACT
WARHEAD
Lerner, Murray
MESSAGE TO LOVE: THE ISLE OF WIGHT FESTIVAL
Lester, David
TIN CUP
Lester, Mark
PUBLIC ENEMIES
Levine, Johnna
VENUS RISING
Levitt, Zane W.
BIG SQUEEZE, THE
ONE GOOD TURN
Levy, Michael I.
EYE FOR AN EYE
Lewis, Richard B.
LARGER THAN LIFE
MOLL FLANDERS
Lhermitte, Thierry
LITTLE INDIAN, BIG CITY
Licht, Andrew
CABLE GUY, THE
Lifton, Jimmy
FINAL EQUINOX, THE
MIRROR, MIRROR III: THE VOYEUR
PHOENIX
Lindemann, Adam
SOME FOLKS CALL IT A SLING BLADE
Links, William J.
THEY BITE
Lipper, Ken
CITY HALL
Liu, Ming
STORY OF XINGHUA, THE
Lobell, Mike
STRIPTEASE
LoCash, Robert
HIGH SCHOOL HIGH
Lodato, Doug
PHARAOH'S ARMY
Lovell, Dyson
JANE EYRE
Lowry, Hunt
TIME TO KILL, A
Loze, Matthew
PIG'S TALE, A
Lucchesi, Gary
PRIMAL FEAR
Luhrmann, Baz
WILLIAM SHAKESPEARE'S ROMEO + JULIET
Lundstrom, Goran
EVIL ED
Lurie, Jeffrey
FOXFIRE
Maass, John
CURDLED
Macaulay, Scott
WIFE, THE
MacBride, Demetra J.
DEAD MAN
Macdonald, Andrew
TRAINSPOTTING
MacKinnon, Billy
SMALL FACES
MacLean, Robert
RED SCORPION 2
MacLeod, Douglas
SONG SPINNER, THE
Magee, Doug
BEYOND THE CALL
Magnien, Richard
SILENCES OF THE PALACE, THE
Mak Chi Sin
WICKED CITY, THE
Mallet, Yvette
MICROCOSMOS
Mallon, Jim
MYSTERY SCIENCE THEATER 3000: THE MOVIE
Mancuso Jr., Frank
FLED
Mandzuka, Danka Muzdeka
VUKOVAR
Manoogian, Peter
NATIONAL LAMPOON'S FAVORITE DEADLY SINS
Manulis, John Bard
FOXFIRE
WEEKEND IN THE COUNTRY, A
Marignac, Martine
CHASING BUTTERFLIES
Mark, Laurence
JERRY MAGUIRE
Markey, Patrick
ASSOCIATE, THE
Marks, Julian
TAILS YOU LIVE, HEADS YOU'RE DEAD
WHERE'S THE MONEY, NOREEN?
Marmot, Janine
INSTITUTE BENJAMENTA
Marsh, John P.
FOXFIRE
Marshall, Penny
GETTING AWAY WITH MURDER
Martin, Jonathan Komack
. . . AT FIRST SIGHT
Martin, Steven M.
THEREMIN: AN ELECTRONIC ODYSSEY
Martinelli, Gabriella
WILLIAM SHAKESPEARE'S ROMEO + JULIET
Marvin, Ira
LONG ROAD HOME, THE
Marzano, Joe
ONE LESS EGG TO FRY
Matsumoto, Ken
GHOST IN THE SHELL
Matthau, Charles
GRASS HARP, THE
Matthews, Elizabeth
GRIM
Mattingly, Jonna
4 TALES OF 2 CITIES
Mayersohn, Paul
OF LOVE AND SHADOWS
Maynard, John
LOADED
Maynard, Richard
NORMAL LIFE
Mazkouri, Kurosh
WHITE BALLOON, THE
Mazor, David
WALLACE AND GROMIT: THE BEST OF AARDMAN ANIMATION
Mazur, Derek
HECK'S WAY HOME
McCann, Tim
DESOLATION ANGELS
McCarthy, Lyn
SPIDER & ROSE
McDermott, Liz
BIG SQUEEZE, THE
McGinnis, Scott
WITHIN THE ROCK
McHenry, Douglas
THIN LINE BETWEEN LOVE AND HATE, A
McHugh, Jason
CANNIBAL! THE MUSICAL
McMillin, Steve
ABUSE
McNamara, James J.
FLIPPER
McQueen, Chad
RED LINE
Medjuck, Joe
SPACE JAM
Medoff, Mark
HOMAGE
Mehrez, Alan
BLOODSPORT II: THE NEXT KUMITE
Meltzer, Michael
SOMETIMES THEY COME BACK . . . AGAIN
Merchant, Ismail
SURVIVING PICASSO
Merhi, Joseph
PURE DANGER
RAGE
SKYSCRAPER
SWEEPER, THE
TIGER HEART
TWO-BITS & PEPPER
Merriweather, George
BLONDES HAVE MORE GUNS
Mertens, Thomas
NICO ICON
Messenger, Gary L.
RATTLED
Messmer, Fredy
ORSON WELLES: THE ONE-MAN BAND
Mestres, Ricardo
101 DALMATIANS
Mestres, Richard
JACK
Meyer, Andreas
KASPAR HAUSER
Michaels, Lorne
BLACK SHEEP
KIDS IN THE HALL: BRAIN CANDY
Michels, Barbara Rose
GIRLFRIENDS
Michelucci, Bob
SANTA CLAWS
Migdall, Suzanne
SOUTH BEACH ACADEMY
Mikhalkov, Nikita
ANNA
Milchan, Arnon
BOGUS
CARPOOL
MIRROR HAS TWO FACES, THE
SUNCHASER
TIME TO KILL, A
Miller, R. Paul
LONE STAR
Miller, Richard
HEAVY
Miller, Robert A.
CRUCIBLE, THE
Mimon, Tzury
HARD JUSTICE
Mindel, Allan
BED OF ROSES
PIE IN THE SKY
Mitchell, Verna
TOO FAST, TOO YOUNG
Mizuo, Yoshimasa
GHOST IN THE SHELL
Mones, Paul
SAINTS AND SINNERS
Montagu, Carolyn
TWO DEATHS
Montgomery, Monty
PORTRAIT OF A LADY, THE
Moore, Leanne
DONOR UNKNOWN

HEIDI CHRONICLES, THE
Morgan, Andre E.
HEAVEN'S PRISONERS
Morrow, Barry
RACE THE SUN
Moses, Harry
ASSAULT AT WEST POINT
Mosher, Gregory
AMERICAN BUFFALO
Most, Jeff
CROW: CITY OF ANGELS, THE
Motoya, Yoshiaki
ROUJIN-Z
Moyer, Todd
BARB WIRE
Mruvka, Alan
LEGEND OF GATOR FACE, THE
Mueller, Jeffrey A.
CABLE GUY, THE
Mulvehill, Charles
CITY HALL
Munchkin, Richard W.
TEXAS PAYBACK
Muraglia, Silvio
HIDDEN ASSASSIN
Murphey, Michael S.
REDEMPTION: KICKBOXER 5
Murray, Forrest
SPITFIRE GRILL, THE
Myerink, Victoria Paige
PRE-MADONNAS
Myers, Richard
MONSTERSHOW
Nanas, Herb
MOTHER
2 DAYS IN THE VALLEY
Nasso, Julius R.
GLIMMER MAN, THE
Nathanson, Michael
CARPOOL
TIME TO KILL, A
Navarrete, Patricia
JOHNNY 100 PESOS
Neal, Gub
CRACKER: THE MADWOMAN IN THE ATTIC
Netter, Gil
HIGH SCHOOL HIGH
Ng Ming Toi
MIDNIGHT ANGEL
Nichols, Mike
BIRDCAGE, THE
Nicksay, Dick
UP CLOSE AND PERSONAL
Nickson, Robert
SEARCH FOR ONE-EYE JIMMY, THE
Nicolaides, Steve
BOY CALLED HATE, A
Nolin, Michael
FULL BODY MASSAGE
MR. HOLLAND'S OPUS
Nomura, Kazufumi
ROUJIN-Z
Nunnari, Gianni
FROM DUSK TILL DAWN
O'Brien, John
MAN WITH A PLAN
O'Brien, Rebecca
LAND AND FREEDOM
O'Hara, Robin
WIFE, THE
O'Neal, Cleveland
PHAT BEACH
Oakley, Vern
MODERN AFFAIR, A
Obst, Lynda
ONE FINE DAY
Odell, Nigel
FUNNYMAN, THE
Olivera, Hector
SHADOW YOU SOON WILL BE, A
Olivieri, Steve
DESOLATION ANGELS
Oristrell, Joaquin
MOUTH TO MOUTH
Orthel, Rolf
CROCODILES IN AMSTERDAM
Ostrow, Randy
BASQUIAT
Ozarai, Andras
OUTPOST, THE
Pacino, Al
LOOKING FOR RICHARD
Paleologos, Nicholas
GHOSTS OF MISSISSIPPI
Paloian, Nancy
WEEKEND IN THE COUNTRY, A
Parfitt, David
TWELFTH NIGHT
Parker, Alan
EVITA
Parker, Brian
MAN IN THE ATTIC, THE
Parker, Trey
CANNIBAL! THE MUSICAL
Parkinson, Tom
ALEX
Pasolini, Uberto
PALOOKAVILLE
Patel, Raju
ADVENTURES OF PINOCCHIO, THE
Patrick, Robert
WITHIN THE ROCK
Paul, D.J.
POMPATUS OF LOVE, THE
Paul, Steven
HOURGLASS
Paulson, Dan
SUNSET PARK
Paunescu, Oana
BACKLASH: OBLIVION 2
JOSH KIRBY . . . TIME WARRIOR!: EGGS FROM 70,000,000 B.C.
JOSH KIRBY . . . TIME WARRIOR!: JOURNEY TO THE MAGIC CAVERN
JOSH KIRBY . . . TIME WARRIOR!: LAST BATTLE FOR THE UNIVERSE
JOSH KIRBY . . . TIME WARRIOR!: TRAPPED ON TOY WORLD
SPELLBREAKER: SECRET OF THE LEPRECHAUNS
Paunescu, Vlad
BACKLASH: OBLIVION 2
JOSH KIRBY . . . TIME WARRIOR!: EGGS FROM 70,000,000 B.C.
JOSH KIRBY . . . TIME WARRIOR!: JOURNEY TO THE MAGIC CAVERN
JOSH KIRBY . . . TIME WARRIOR!: LAST BATTLE FOR THE UNIVERSE
JOSH KIRBY . . . TIME WARRIOR!: TRAPPED ON TOY WORLD
MAGIC IN THE MIRROR
SERPENT'S LAIR
SPELLBREAKER: SECRET OF THE LEPRECHAUNS
Pavone, Michael
CHAMELEON
Peach, Patrick
MOTHER
Penotti, John
I'M NOT RAPPAPORT
Pepin, Richard
PURE DANGER
RAGE
SKYSCRAPER
SWEEPER, THE
TIGER HEART
TWO-BITS & PEPPER
Pereira, Manuel Gomez
MOUTH TO MOUTH
Perrin, Jacques
MICROCOSMOS
Peters, Jon
MY FELLOW AMERICANS
Phillips, Diana
JOE'S APARTMENT
Picker, David V.
CRUCIBLE, THE
Pina, Jaime
BITTER SUGAR
Pisacane, Annette
NICO ICON
Platt, Polly
BOTTLE ROCKET
EVENING STAR, THE
Pollack, Sharon
EVERYTHING RELATIVE
Pollock, Dale
MRS. WINTERBOURNE
SET IT OFF
Polone, Judith A.
HOUSE ARREST
Pompian, Paul
DANGEROUS PASSION
HIDDEN ASSASSIN
Powell, Marykay
HARRIET THE SPY
TO GILLIAN ON HER 37TH BIRTHDAY
Prescott, Michael
RUMPELSTILTSKIN
Pressman, Edward R.
CITY HALL
CROW: CITY OF ANGELS, THE
ISLAND OF DR. MOREAU, THE
Price, Frank
GETTING AWAY WITH MURDER
Prieto, Ignacio
JOHNNY 100 PESOS
Prior, Ted
FELONY
Puig, Raul
CURDLED
Purrer, Ursula
FLAMING EARS
Puttnam, David
WAR OF THE BUTTONS, THE
Radcliffe, Mark
JINGLE ALL THE WAY
Radin, Paul
GHOST AND THE DARKNESS, THE
Raimondi, Jane
CROSSCUT
Ramis, Harold
MULTIPLICITY
Raskov, Daniel
OPEN SEASON
Rattner, Larry J.
BAJA
Rauch, Paul
LOVER'S KNOT
Ravine, Vince
FAST MONEY
Ray, Fred Olen
FUGITIVE RAGE
Ray, Melanie
EXIT
Re, John Lawrence
WALLACE AND GROMIT: THE BEST OF AARDMAN ANIMATION
Reid, Tim
ONCE UPON A TIME . . . WHEN WE WERE COLORED
Reidy, Kevin
WHOLE WIDE WORLD, THE

Reiss, Jonathan
BAD LOVE
Reitman, Ivan
SPACE JAM
Renzi, Maggie
LONE STAR
Resnik, Jon
POMPATUS OF LOVE, THE
Rhee, Phillip
BEST OF THE BEST 3: NO TURNING BACK
Rich, Lee
BIG BULLY
Richardson, Mike
BARB WIRE
Riedel, Guy
NORMA JEAN AND MARILYN
Risi, Marco
MILLE BOLLE BLU
Roberts, Nancy
TREMORS 2: AFTERSHOCKS
Robinson, James G.
BAD MOON
DIABOLIQUE
TWO IF BY SEA
Roe, Bob
ROAD TO GALVESTON, THE
Roe, Jack
DOWN, OUT AND DANGEROUS
Roeg, Luc
TWO DEATHS
Roessell, David
DARKMAN III: DIE DARKMAN DIE
Roloff, Stephen
NIGHT OF THE TWISTERS
Roman, John L.
EVIL HAS A FACE
Romoli, Gianni
CEMETERY MAN
Rose, David
SOMEONE ELSE'S AMERICA
Rose, Sherrie
SHOT, THE
Rosenbush, Barry
GET ON THE BUS
Rosenfeld, Donald
PROPRIETOR, THE
Rosenthal, Jane
FAITHFUL
MARVIN'S ROOM
Rosser, Brandon
SLING BLADE
Rossignon, Christophe
HATE
Rothberg, Jeff
BOGUS
Rotman, David
FOR BETTER OR WORSE
Roy, Sally
ED'S NEXT MOVE
Rubenstein, Richard P.
STEPHEN KING'S THINNER
Rubino, John
LOTTO LAND
Rubino, Michael J.
LOTTO LAND
Ruby, Joe
RUMPELSTILTSKIN
Ruddy, Albert S.
HEAVEN'S PRISONERS
Rudin, Scott
FIRST WIVES CLUB, THE
MARVIN'S ROOM
MOTHER
RANSOM
Russell, Kurt
JOHN CARPENTER'S ESCAPE FROM L.A.
Russo, Aaron
MISSING PIECES
OFF AND RUNNING
Ryerson, Sean
NIGHT OF THE TWISTERS
Saavedra, Craig
. . . AT FIRST SIGHT
Sabella, Paul
ALL DOGS GO TO HEAVEN 2
Saidiner, Grant
SOUTH BEACH ACADEMY
Sakai, Richard
JERRY MAGUIRE
Sales, Leander
DON'T LET YOUR MEAT LOAF
Samantha, Elie
IMMORTALS, THE
Samples, Keith
EVENING STAR, THE
Samtani, Gope T.
WITHOUT MERCY
Samuels, Ron
RAVENHAWK
Sarde, Alain
LES VOLEURS
MA SAISON PREFEREE
NELLY AND MONSIEUR ARNAUD
Sarkissian, Arthur
LAST MAN STANDING
Sassone, Joseph
PLAYBACK
Sassoon, Elan
HOMAGE
Saxon, Edward
THAT THING YOU DO!
Schamoni, Peter
NIKI DE SAINT PHALLE: WHO IS THE MONSTER — YOU OR ME?
Schamus, James
SHE'S THE ONE
WALKING AND TALKING
Scheinman, Andrew
GHOSTS OF MISSISSIPPI
Scheirl, Angela Hans
FLAMING EARS
Scheuer, Walter
SMALL WONDERS
Schifman, Aron
TEXAS PAYBACK
Schiller, Greta
PARIS WAS A WOMAN
Schipek, Dietmar
FLAMING EARS
Schlaich, Frieder
HALFMOON
Schmidt, Arne L.
CHAIN REACTION
Schmoeller, Gary
ADRENALIN: FEAR THE RUSH
NEMESIS III: PREY HARDER
Schoenberg, Steven
BLACK OUT
Scholtz, Andre
YANKEE ZULU
Schroeder, Barbet
BEFORE AND AFTER
Schulz-Keil, Wieland
MAGIC HUNTER
Schwartz, Lloyd J.
VERY BRADY SEQUEL, A
Schwartz, Sherwood
VERY BRADY SEQUEL, A
Schwenker, Kenneth
CONDITION RED
Scott, Jane
SHINE
Seagal, Steven
GLIMMER MAN, THE
Seligmann, Guy
CHEKIST, THE
Selkirk, Jamie
FRIGHTENERS, THE
Sender, Julie Bergman
RICH MAN'S WIFE, THE
Sereny, Julia
STAND OFF, THE
Settles, Jeremy A.
MR. ICE CREAM MAN
Shamberg, Michael
FEELING MINNESOTA
MATILDA
SUNSET PARK
Shapiro-Jackson, Shauna
PORTRAITS OF A KILLER
Shapter, Bill
BEAUTIFUL THING
Shavick, James
TRACKS OF A KILLER
Shaw, Denise
BED OF ROSES
PIE IN THE SKY
Shepard, Richard
MERCY
Sher, Stacey
FEELING MINNESOTA
MATILDA
Sheridan, Jim
SOME MOTHER'S SON
Shuster, Brian
SANTA WITH MUSCLES
Siciliano, Pat
VIRTUAL ENCOUNTERS
Sighvatsson, Joni
BASQUIAT
Silver, Joel
EXECUTIVE DECISION
Silvers, Dean
FLIRTING WITH DISASTER
MANNY & LO
Simmons, Russell
NUTTY PROFESSOR, THE
Simonds, Robert
BULLETPROOF
HAPPY GILMORE
Simons, Edward
LAWNMOWER MAN 2: BEYOND CYBERSPACE
Simpkins, Victor
SWINGERS
Simpson, Don
ROCK, THE
Simpson, Peter R.
IRON EAGLE IV
Sinclair, Shelly
TATTOO BOY
Singer, Joseph M.
COURAGE UNDER FIRE
DAYLIGHT
Sinofsky, Bruce
PARADISE LOST: THE CHILD MURDERS AT ROBIN HOOD HILLS
Sinyor, Gary
SOLITAIRE FOR TWO
Skalski, Mary Jane
GIRLFRIENDS
Small, Thomas
VENUS RISING
Smith, Brian J.
BODY OF INFLUENCE 2
Smith, Jack
SANTA CLAWS
Smith, Roy Allen
LAND BEFORE TIME IV: JOURNEY THROUGH THE MISTS
Smith, Thomas G.
ARRIVAL, THE
Smithson, John
AFFAIR, THE

Smulski, Andrzej
MOTHER OF KINGS
Sneller, Jeffrey
ADVENTURES OF PINOCCHIO, THE
Soavi, Michele
CEMETERY MAN
Soisson, Joel
INFINITY
Solondz, Todd
WELCOME TO THE DOLLHOUSE
Sonenberg, David
WHEN WE WERE KINGS
Spears, Ken
RUMPELSTILTSKIN
Spiegel, Larry
SUNCHASER
Spillman, Darin
SHOWGIRL MURDERS, THE
Stabler, Steve
BIO-DOME
GLASS CAGE, THE
IF LUCY FELL
KINGPIN
WAR AT HOME, THE
Stark, Jim
COLD FEVER
Starke, John
I'M NOT RAPPAPORT
Steele, Jim
ARRIVAL, THE
SUBSTITUTE, THE
Stewart, Olivia
NEON BIBLE, THE
Stigwood, Robert
EVITA
Stiliades, Nicolas
GALAXIES ARE COLLIDING
Stone, Matthew
CANNIBAL! THE MUSICAL
Stone, Nancy Rae
HELLRAISER: BLOODLINE
Stone, Oliver
PEOPLE VS. LARRY FLYNT, THE
Strauss, Peter E.
BEST OF THE BEST 3: NO TURNING BACK
Streisand, Barbara
MIRROR HAS TWO FACES, THE
Stuckmeyer, John V.
RATTLED
Sugar, Larry
ANNIE O
HALFBACK OF NOTRE DAME, THE
ROBIN OF LOCKSLEY
Sutton III, John
DONOR UNKNOWN
Swedlin, Rosalie
ED
Talbot, Robert
HEAD OF THE FAMILY
Tan, Jimmy
BLUSH
Tanaka, Susumu
KAMIKAZE TAXI
Tanen, Nancy Graham
MARY REILLY
Tanen, Ned
MARY REILLY
Tang, Richard Wong
MIDNIGHT DANCERS
Tapper, Cara
LIVE NUDE GIRLS
Tashiro, Atsumi
NIGHT ON THE GALACTIC RAILROAD
Taylor, Michael
MRS. MUNCK
PHENOMENON
Taylor, Sam
YOUNG POISONER'S HANDBOOK, THE
Tedesco, Maurizio
MILLE BOLLE BLU
Tennant, Victoria
EDIE & PEN
Teper, Meir
FROM DUSK TILL DAWN
Terkuhle, Abby
BEAVIS AND BUTT-HEAD DO AMERICA
Terzian, Alain
VISITORS, THE
Textor, Douglas
AMERICAN STRAYS
Thomas, Bradley
KINGPIN
Thomas, Jeremy
STEALING BEAUTY
Thomas, Jim
EXECUTIVE DECISION
Thomas, John
EXECUTIVE DECISION
Thomas, Nigel
SHAMELESS
Thompson, David M.
AFFAIR, THE
CAPTIVES
Threadgil, Tina
DEATH BENEFIT
Thurm, Joel
IT'S MY PARTY
Tisch, Steve
DEAR GOD
Tokofsky, Jerry
GRASS HARP, THE
Torres, Fina
CELESTIAL CLOCKWORK
Tse, Simon
BODY COUNT
Tubbenhauer, Graeme
SPIDER & ROSE
Tung, Barbie
RUMBLE IN THE BRONX
Ungar, George
CHAMPAGNE SAFARI, THE
Unozawa, Shin
PATLABOR 2: MOBILE POLICE
Vachon, Christine
I SHOT ANDY WARHOL
STONEWALL
Vajna, Andrew G.
EVITA
Van Leeuwen, Chako
PIRANHA
Van Peebles, Melvin
TALES OF EROTICA
Van Taylor, David
PERFECT CANDIDATE, A
Vance, Marilyn
LEGEND OF GATOR FACE, THE
Vasconcellos, Ronaldo
TALES OF EROTICA
Vecchio, Joseph M.
SUNCHASER
Veitch, John
FLY AWAY HOME
Verroust, Pascal
MAN BY THE SHORE, THE
Villa, Sug
CATWALK
Villard, Dimitri
IN LOVE AND WAR
Vilsmaier, Joseph
BROTHER OF SLEEP
Vince, Robert
BREACH OF TRUST
FINAL CUT, THE
WHITE TIGER
Vince, William
BREACH OF TRUST
FINAL CUT, THE
WHITE TIGER
Vincent, Tony
BODY COUNT
Viner, Michael
YOU'LL NEVER MAKE LOVE IN THIS TOWN AGAIN
von Alberti, Irene
HALFMOON
Wagner, David A.
POLYMORPH
Wagner, Paula
MISSION: IMPOSSIBLE
Wald, Jeff
2 DAYS IN THE VALLEY
Wang Po Ming
WING CHUN
Ward, Kelly
ALL DOGS GO TO HEAVEN 2
Watson, John
LARGER THAN LIFE
MOLL FLANDERS
Watson-Wood, Peter
SHAMELESS
Waxman, Jeff
PAINTED HERO
Wayans, Keenen Ivory
DON'T BE A MENACE TO SOUTH CENTRAL WHILE DRINKING YOUR JUICE IN THE HOOD
Weaver, Linda
SANDMAN, THE
Webb, William
ONE MAN'S JUSTICE
Webber, Melanie
MODERN AFFAIR, A
Webster, Paul
PALLBEARER, THE
Wedner, Ellen
BEWARE: CHILDREN AT PLAY
Weide, Robert B.
MOTHER NIGHT
Weinberg, Larry
LAST SUPPER, THE
Weinberger, Charles
HEADLESS BODY IN TOPLESS BAR
Weinman, Richard
PAINTED HERO
Weintraub, Fred
UNDERTOW
Weiss, Andrea
PARIS WAS A WOMAN
White, Steve
LIVE NUDE GIRLS
NIGHT OF THE SCARECROW
Wick, Douglas
CRAFT, THE
Wilkinson, Jennifer
MODERN AFFAIR, A
Williamson, Fred
ORIGINAL GANGSTAS
Willoughby, Robert
FELONY
Windelov, Vibeke
BREAKING THE WAVES
Winer, Harry
HOUSE ARREST
Winick, Gary
SWEET NOTHING
Winkler, Irwin
JUROR, THE
Winters, David
BODY COUNT
Wise, David
BEASTMASTER 3: THE EYE OF BRAXUS

Wiseman, Frederick
LA COMEDIE-FRANCAISE OU L'AMOUR JOUE
Witrock, William
DARK SECRETS
Wizan, Joe
DUNSTON CHECKS IN
Wolfe, Steven J.
TOLLBOOTH
Wolper, David L.
SURVIVING PICASSO
Woods, Cary
BEAUTIFUL GIRLS
CITIZEN RUTH
SCREAM
Woolley, Stephen
MICHAEL COLLINS
Worth, Marvin
DIABOLIQUE
Wyman, Brad
BARB WIRE
FREEWAY
TREES LOUNGE
Wyndham-Davies, June
AUGUST
Yaeger, Karen
GIRLFRIENDS
Yamashita, Tatsumi
BIG WARS
Yang, Janet
PEOPLE VS. LARRY FLYNT, THE
Yellen, Mark
BIG SQUEEZE, THE
FIST OF THE NORTH STAR
ONE GOOD TURN
Yoshida, Toshifumi
SANCTUARY: THE MOVIE
Young, Irwin
CAUGHT
Young, Mark
ALL DOGS GO TO HEAVEN 2
Young, Sally
MOTHER'S PRAYER, A
Yu, Martin
4 TALES OF 2 CITIES
Yu Wei-yen
MAHJONG
Yuen Woo Ping
WING CHUN
Yuzna, Brian
NECRONOMICON: BOOK OF THE DEAD
Zaentz, Saul
ENGLISH PATIENT, THE
Zag, Roland
ORSON WELLES: THE ONE-MAN BAND
Zalaznick, Lauren
GIRLS TOWN
Zanuck, Lili Fini
MULHOLLAND FALLS
Zanuck, Richard D.
MULHOLLAND FALLS
Zarpas, Chris
LITTLE DEATH, THE
Zehnder, Kirk
FLATTERED
Ziehl, Scott
RED LINE
Zingarelli, Italo
SONS OF TRINITY
Zollo, Frederick
GHOSTS OF MISSISSIPPI
Zucker, David
HIGH SCHOOL HIGH
Zuckerman, Donald
LOW LIFE, THE

PRODUCTION DESIGNERS

Abbe-Vannier, Michele
MADAME BUTTERFLY
Abel, Gene
FOREST WARRIOR
Adam, Ken
BOGUS
Ahmad, Maher
CHAIN REACTION
OFF AND RUNNING
Aird, Gilles
HOLLOW POINT
MAN BY THE SHORE, THE
Allen, James
MOTHER'S PRAYER, A
MRS. MUNCK
Alsina, Gustav
DEAD WEEKEND
HEADLESS BODY IN TOPLESS BAR
Altman, Stephen
KANSAS CITY
Amaral, Roy Alan
DOWN, OUT AND DANGEROUS
Amies, Caroline
JOSEPH CONRAD'S THE SECRET AGENT
Ammon, Ruth
NATIONAL LAMPOON'S FAVORITE DEADLY SINS
Amor, Bobby
MADDENING, THE
Ancona, Amy
HOMAGE
Andrews, Sara
DONOR UNKNOWN
Arrighi, Luciana
SURVIVING PICASSO
Auckland-Snow, Brian
HAUNTED
Barclay, William
SHE'S THE ONE
Barkska, Teresa
MOTHER OF KINGS
Barry, Brenden
TOLLBOOTH
Bartholomew Jr., Sidney Jackson
KINGPIN
Bauert, Monika
MAYBE . . . MAYBE NOT
Baugh, Michael
RIDERS OF THE PURPLE SAGE
Beatty, John Lee
SUBSTANCE OF FIRE, THE
Becher, Sophie
TWELFTH NIGHT
Beeton, William
TAILS YOU LIVE, HEADS YOU'RE DEAD
Ben Yishay, Aria
HARD JUSTICE
Bennett, Charles
FLED
Bennett, Joseph
JUDE
Bennett, Laurence
STEPHEN KING'S THINNER
Berman, Danielle
ZARKORR! THE INVADER
Beswick, Wayne
DEAD WEEKEND
Bishop, Dan
BOYS
LONE STAR
Bissell, James
MY FELLOW AMERICANS
TIN CUP
Blackie, John
SONG SPINNER, THE
Blake, Perry Andelin
HAPPY GILMORE
Blass, David
FRIEND OF THE FAMILY 2
Blatt, Stuart
SERPENT'S LAIR
Block, Susan
WELCOME TO THE DOLLHOUSE
Bolles, Susan
DENISE CALLS UP
Bolton, Michael
HOMEWARD BOUND II: LOST IN SAN FRANCISCO
Bose, Ashoke
TARGET
Botella, Juan
TWO MUCH
Bourne, Mel
STRIPTEASE
Bowin, Claire
WILD SIDE
Boyd, Tim
VIRUS
Bradshaw, Christopher J.
JACK & SARAH
Branco, Ze
LES VOLEURS
Braverman, Diamond Jim
SHOT, THE
Brenner, Albert
DEAR GOD
Brezeski, Bill
MATILDA
Brisbin, David
CHAMBER, THE
Brock, Ian
STAND OFF, THE
Brodie, Bill
UNDERTOW
Bromley, Karen
BOYS NEXT DOOR, THE
KISSINGER AND NIXON
Bronzi, Francesco
STAR MAKER, THE
Bulgarelli, Enzo
SONS OF TRINITY
Burchiellaro, Giantito
MONSTER, THE
Burt, Donald
KAZAAM
Burton, Linda
LAST SUPPER, THE
OPEN SEASON
Butcher, Robert
SHOOTFIGHTER 2: KILL OR BE KILLED!
Cabrera, Charley
DEMOLITIONIST, THE
Calinascu, Vali
JOSH KIRBY . . . TIME WARRIOR!: EGGS FROM 70,000,000 B.C.
JOSH KIRBY . . . TIME WARRIOR!: JOURNEY TO THE MAGIC CAVERN
JOSH KIRBY . . . TIME WARRIOR!: LAST BATTLE FOR THE UNIVERSE
JOSH KIRBY . . . TIME WARRIOR!: TRAPPED ON TOY WORLD
Calinescu, Valentin
FORBIDDEN ZONE: ALIEN ABDUCTION
Cameron, Allan
ADVENTURES OF PINOCCHIO, THE
Canter, Markus
SOLO
Caplan, Sal
SHADOW WARRIORS
Capra, Bernt
INFINITY
Carlson, Jonathan
MOTHER

Carp, Jean-Philippe
BARB WIRE
Cauley, Eve
BOUND
WAR AT HOME, THE
Cavedon, Jane
DESIRE
Ceder, Elayne Barbara
ORIGINAL GANGSTAS
PAINTED HERO
Chalon, Luc
THREE LIVES AND ONLY ONE DEATH
Chambers, Karissa
FEMALIEN
Chang, Justo
SILENCE OF NETO, THE
Chang, William
CHUNGKING EXPRESS
Chapman, David
TWO IF BY SEA
Charette, Cynthia
NORMA JEAN AND MARILYN
VERY BRADY SEQUEL, A
Cheng, Mayling
JAG
Chitty, Alison
SECRETS & LIES
Clausen, Michael
ONCE UPON A TIME . . . WHEN WE WERE COLORED
Clay, Jim
WAR OF THE BUTTONS, THE
Cleitman, Rene
MACHINE, THE
Clinker, Nigel
BEASTMASTER 3: THE EYE OF BRAXUS
Cohen, Lester
HARRIET THE SPY
TALES OF EROTICA
Collins, Carmel
SOLITAIRE FOR TWO
Conner, Chuck
JUST YOUR LUCK
SANTA WITH MUSCLES
Conti, Carlos
MA SAISON PREFEREE
NELLY AND MONSIEUR ARNAUD
Conway, Jeremy
UP CLOSE AND PERSONAL
Corciova, Radu
SPELLBREAKER: SECRET OF THE LEPRECHAUNS
Corenblith, Michael
DOWN PERISCOPE
RANSOM
Cowan, Robert
SWEEPER, THE
Cowan, Roger
PIRANHA
Cowley, Anthony
AMERICA'S DREAM
Cox, Jeff
CONDITION RED
Craig, Stuart
ENGLISH PATIENT, THE
IN LOVE AND WAR
MARY REILLY
Creber, William
SPY HARD
Cristante, Ivo
HELLRAISER: BLOODLINE
RUMPELSTILTSKIN
TREMORS 2: AFTERSHOCKS
Cross, Paul
MADAGASCAR SKIN
Cruz, Villamor
LIFEFORM

Cummings, Howard
ASSAULT AT WEST POINT
LONG KISS GOODNIGHT, THE
SPITFIRE GRILL, THE
TRIGGER EFFECT, THE
Dagort, Phil
STUPIDS, THE
Dague, Claire
CELESTIAL CLOCKWORK
Danielsen, Dins
HEIDI CHRONICLES, THE
Davis, Dan
BEAUTIFUL GIRLS
EDDIE
MICHAEL
De Rouin, Colin
JOSH KIRBY . . . TIME WARRIOR!: EGGS FROM 70,000,000 B.C.
JOSH KIRBY . . . TIME WARRIOR!: JOURNEY TO THE MAGIC CAVERN
JOSH KIRBY . . . TIME WARRIOR!: LAST BATTLE FOR THE UNIVERSE
JOSH KIRBY . . . TIME WARRIOR!: TRAPPED ON TOY WORLD
DeGovia, Jackson
MULTIPLICITY
Del Rosario, Linda
BAD MOON
Deprez, Therese
I SHOT ANDY WARHOL
STONEWALL
DeScenna, Linda
FAMILY THING, A
Deskin, Andrew
FOR THE MOMENT
DeVico, Robert
POISON IVY 2: LILY
Devine, Colleen
PHAT BEACH
Di Minico, John
BAD LOVE
Dilley, Leslie
DIABOLIQUE
Diss, Eileen
AUGUST
Djurkovic, Maria
YOUNG POISONER'S HANDBOOK, THE
Dobbin, Simon
THIN LINE BETWEEN LOVE AND HATE, A
Dobrowolski, Marek
CRAFT, THE
Doernberg, David
GIRLS TOWN
Dondertman, John
CURTIS'S CHARM
FINAL CUT, THE
Doumbia, Boubacar
GUIMBA THE TYRANT
Dunphy, Barbara
SUGARTIME
Durham, Russell
LOOKING FOR TROUBLE
Dusek, Helmut
WITCHCRAFT: SALEM'S GHOST
Earnest, Randal
UNDER THE HULA MOON
Eatwell, Brian
HIDDEN ASSASSIN
TALES OF EROTICA
Edwards, Le'Ce
ANIMAL INSTINCTS III: THE SEDUCTRESS
Elliot, Bill
FOR BETTER OR WORSE
Elliott, William
NUTTY PROFESSOR, THE
Endley, David
FUNNYMAN, THE
GRIM

Ennist, Melodie
MERLIN'S SHOP OF MAGICAL WONDERS
Ensley, David
LONG ROAD HOME, THE
Faccello, Abel
OF LOVE AND SHADOWS
Fenner, John
HAUNTED
Ferenczfy-Kovacs, Attila
MAGIC HUNTER
Fernandez, Benjamin
DAYLIGHT
DRAGONHEART
Fhlanncha, Sinead Nie
HARD WAY OUT: BLOODFIST VIII
Flannery, Seamus
FLY AWAY HOME
Fleming, Bill
HECK'S WAY HOME
RUDE
Fleming, Jerry
BLACK DAY BLUE NIGHT
LIVE NUDE GIRLS
Flemming, Zdenek
DELTA OF VENUS
Fleury, Jared
TIGER HEART
Fontana, Michael T. J.
EXIT
Foreman, Ron
SUBSTITUTE, THE
Fox, J. Rae
BIG SQUEEZE, THE
Frick, John Allen
WHOLE WIDE WORLD, THE
Friedberg, Mark
4 TALES OF 2 CITIES
I'M NOT RAPPAPORT
Fulton, Larry
TIME TO KILL, A
Ganz, Armin
LITTLE DEATH, THE
Gillespie, John
ELECTRA
Giminez, Raul
SHADOW OF ANGELS
Ginn, Jeff
BEYOND THE CALL
Ginnever, Jodi
LITTLE WITCHES
Gorrara, Perri
SCREAMERS
Gorton, Assheton
101 DALMATIANS
Gottlieb, Max
SHOPPING
Gould-Galliers, Bob
BRITT ALLCROFT'S MAGIC ADVENTURES OF MUMFIE—THE MOVIE
Graber, Jennifer
FRISK
Grant, Mike
PROTEUS
Graysmark, John
COURAGE UNDER FIRE
Greville-Morris, Caroline
WAVELENGTH
Groom, Bill
PREACHER'S WIFE, THE
Gropman, David
MARVIN'S ROOM
ONE FINE DAY
Gross, Holger
BROKEN ARROW
Gutteres, Candi
PINOCCHIO'S REVENGE

Haberecht, Barbara
LILY DALE
Haggerty, M. Nord
AMANDA AND THE ALIEN
OUT THERE
Hall, Roger
JANE EYRE
Halvorson, Brad
SWINGERS
Hampton, Peter J.
WHITE SQUALL
Hanan, Michael
MISSING PIECES
Hanania, Caroline
MOLL FLANDERS
Hanna, Ed
BLOODKNOT
HOMECOMING
MOONSHINE HIGHWAY
Hardwicke, Catherine
2 DAYS IN THE VALLEY
Harpman, Fred
STREETCAR NAMED DESIRE, A
Harvey, Tim
HAMLET
MIDWINTER'S TALE, A
Harwell, Helen
FUGITIVE RAGE
OVER THE WIRE
Hebert, Jacques
HOURGLASS
Hedge, David
CANNIBAL! THE MUSICAL
Heinrichs, Rick
FARGO
Hendrickson, Stephen
EYE FOR AN EYE
Hermer-Bell, Lindsey
LOSING CHASE
Heslup, William
HAPPY GILMORE
Higgins, Douglas
ALASKA
SURGEON, THE
Hinds, Marcia
LARGER THAN LIFE
Hobbs, Christopher
NEON BIBLE, THE
Holt, Paul
AMERICAN STRAYS
Howells, Michael
EMMA
Huang, David
LOVER'S KNOT
TEXAS PAYBACK
Hunter, Clark
FIST OF THE NORTH STAR
IT'S MY PARTY
SLING BLADE
Iacovelli, John
NATIONAL LAMPOON'S FAVORITE DEADLY SINS
Iida, Fumio
ROUJIN-Z
Jackness, Andrew
ASSOCIATE, THE
BIG NIGHT
Jackson, John
MONSTERSHOW
Jamison, Peter
BLACK SHEEP
HOUSE ARREST
Javor, Lorand
DOGFIGHTERS, THE
Jefferds, Vincent
COLONY, THE
SAINTS AND SINNERS
Jelambi, Sandi
CELESTIAL CLOCKWORK
Jenkins, Katy
WHISPERING, THE
Jessup, Harley
JAMES AND THE GIANT PEACH
Johansson, Arni Poll
COLD FEVER
John, Tom
MIRROR HAS TWO FACES, THE
Johnson, Martin
LAND AND FREEDOM
Johnston, Michael
BIO-DOME
Kaczenski, Chester
FIRST KID
Kahn, Eric
BLACK SCORPION
Kanter, Peter
PRE-MADONNAS
Kavelin, John
SABRINA, THE TEENAGE WITCH
Kay, Alistair
LOADED
Keen, Gregory P.
KIDS IN THE HALL: BRAIN CANDY
Keita, Baba
GUIMBA THE TYRANT
Kelemen, Fred
FATE
Kempster, Victor
THAT THING YOU DO!
Kenney, Bill
ERASER
Kernke, Jennifer
ANGELS AND INSECTS
INSTITUTE BENJAMENTA
Khell, Zsolt
OUTPOST, THE
Kilvert, Lilly
CRUCIBLE, THE
GHOSTS OF MISSISSIPPI
Kinetikon Pictures
PREDICTIONS OF FIRE
King, Robb Wilson
SET IT OFF
King, Trae
CRIMINAL HEARTS
PUBLIC ENEMIES
Kirkland, Geoffrey
SPACE JAM
Kljakovic, Miljen
RASPUTIN
SOMEONE ELSE'S AMERICA
Kortekaas, Niek
SUITE 16
Kraner, Doug
EXTREME MEASURES
MR. WRONG
Krantz, Michael
POMPATUS OF LOVE, THE
Kretschmer, John
GRAVE, THE
Kusakova, Ludmila
BURIAL OF THE RATS
LaFranche, Damien
MR. STITCH
Lagola, Charles
FUNERAL, THE
Lalande, Guy
MATERNAL INSTINCTS
Lambon, Jon-Jon
YANKEE ZULU
Larkin, Peter
FIRST WIVES CLUB, THE
Lee, Steve
CLUBHOUSE DETECTIVES
Legler, Steven
WOMAN UNDONE, A
Leigh, Dan
BASQUIAT
Levine, Jeremy
MIND RIPPER
Levy, Eitan
UNDER THE DOMIM TREE
Lineweaver, Stephen
JERRY MAGUIRE
Lipton, Dina
MAD DOG TIME
Littaua, Edgar Martin
MIDNIGHT DANCERS
Lomofsky, Sharon
MANNY & LO
Longmire, Susan
MAN IN THE ATTIC, THE
Loquasto, Santo
EVERYONE SAYS I LOVE YOU
Love, Lonnie
SANDMAN, THE
Lowe, Georgina
SECRETS & LIES
Luczyc-Wyhowski, Hugo
AFFAIR, THE
MacLeod, Zoe
SMALL FACES
Major, Grant
FRIGHTENERS, THE
GIRLFRIENDS
Major, Ross
SPIDER & ROSE
Marcus, Caryn
BOY CALLED HATE, A
Marsh, Stephen
CELTIC PRIDE
TRUMAN
Marsh, Terence
EXECUTIVE DECISION
Marshall, Cathy T.
MODERN AFFAIR, A
Martin, Catherine
WILLIAM SHAKESPEARE'S ROMEO + JULIET
Martin, Gregory
RAGE
Martin, Maggie
FAR HARBOR
Martishius, Walter
THEODORE REX
Maruyawa, Hiroshi
KAMIKAZE TAXI
Maussion, Ivan
LITTLE INDIAN, BIG CITY
RIDICULE
Mayhew, Ina
GET ON THE BUS
GIRL 6
Maynard, Jef
MYSTERY SCIENCE THEATER 3000: THE MOVIE
McAteer, James
FRAME BY FRAME
HOMECOMING
McCabe, Stephen
BED OF ROSES
McDonald, Leslie
JINGLE ALL THE WAY
McDowell, Alex
CROW: CITY OF ANGELS, THE
FEAR
McKernin, Kathleen
VENUS RISING
Meerdink, Doug
UNKNOWN ORIGIN

Melton, Gregory
TALES FROM THE CRYPT PRESENTS BORDELLO OF BLOOD
Meuller, Michael
MAN OF THE YEAR
Michelucci, Bob
SANTA CLAWS
Miller, Bruce Alan
SCREAM
Milo
BACKLASH: OBLIVION 2
Moe, David
BLOOD & DONUTS
WHERE'S THE MONEY, NOREEN?
Montaldo, Elisabetta
WHO KILLED PASOLINI?
Montiel, Cecilia
FROM DUSK TILL DAWN
Moore, Jay
GETTING AWAY WITH MURDER
Morley, Martin
HEDD WYNN
Morris, Brian
EVITA
Mullins, Peter
CANTERVILLE GHOST, THE
Musky, Jane
CITY HALL
Myers, Richard
MONSTERSHOW
Myhre, John
FOXFIRE
Nall, Roger
VIRTUAL COMBAT
Nava
BLACK ROSE OF HARLEM
BLACK SCORPION
CARNOSAUR 3: PRIMAL SPECIES
DEATH ARTIST, THE
NOT OF THIS EARTH
SHOWGIRL MURDERS, THE
Nemec III, Joseph
TWISTER
Nemirsky, Michael
PORTRAITS OF A KILLER
New Collectivism
PREDICTIONS OF FIRE
Nichols, David
MR. HOLLAND'S OPUS
Niculescu, Cristian
MAGIC IN THE MIRROR
OUTPOST, THE
Niehus, Vicki
SHINE
Norsworthy, Ron
LOVE IS ALL THERE IS
Novotny, Michael
ARRIVAL, THE
Olson, Steve
4 TALES OF 2 CITIES
Oppewall, Jeannine
PRIMAL FEAR
RICH MAN'S WIFE, THE
Osborne, Aaron
DON'T BE A MENACE TO SOUTH CENTRAL WHILE DRINKING YOUR JUICE IN THE HOOD
SOMETIMES THEY COME BACK . . . AGAIN
Otis, Anna
DON'T LET YOUR MEAT LOAF
Ouellette, Dan
WIFE, THE
Palermo, Rafael
OUTRAGE
Papamichael Sr., Phedon
UNHOOK THE STARS
Parnet, Claude
FRENCH TWIST
Pastor, Debbie
TEXAS CHAINSAW MASSACRE: THE NEXT GENERATION
Paterson, Owen
RACE THE SUN
Patterson, Janet
GIRLFRIENDS
PORTRAIT OF A LADY, THE
TWO FRIENDS
Paul, Rick
NORMAL LIFE
Paul, Victoria
SUNCHASER
SUNSET PARK
Paull, Lawrence G.
JOHN CARPENTER'S ESCAPE FROM L.A.
SGT. BILKO
Pearce, Michael
BODY OF INFLUENCE 2
HOSTILE INTENTIONS
SAWBONES
Pearl, Linda
PIE IN THE SKY
TO GILLIAN ON HER 37TH BIRTHDAY
Pearson, Rob
UNFORGETTABLE
Perretti, William J.
BEST OF THE BEST 3: NO TURNING BACK
Perrin, Bryce
VIKING SAGAS, THE
Peters, Paul
PHANTOM, THE
Pouille, Hubert
PASSION OF DARKLY NOON, THE
Pratt, Anthony
MICHAEL COLLINS
Preovolos, Nicholas
LETTER TO MY KILLER
PIG'S TALE, A
Prim, Bernard
FRENCH TWIST
Quinn, Kave
TRAINSPOTTING
Ramos, Steve
PURE DANGER
SKYSCRAPER
Ramsey, Nina
OFF AND RUNNING
Randall, Gary
PLAYBACK
Random, Ida
FAN, THE
Raubertas, Peter Paul
CARRIED AWAY
Raymond, Deborah
CHAMELEON
WITHIN THE ROCK
Recht, Ray
SEARCH FOR ONE-EYE JIMMY, THE
Reynolds, Norman
MISSION: IMPOSSIBLE
Rice, Charles
LET'S GET BIZZEE
Ridley, Leith
TERMINAL IMPACT
Ridolfi, Paola
LOTTO LAND
Roberts, AnnMarie
HEAD OF THE FAMILY
Roberts, Rick
HOW THE WEST WAS FUN
Robertson, Cathy
DEVOTION
Robinson, Marc
WATCH ME
Roelfs, Jan
JUROR, THE
Roloff, Stephen
NIGHT OF THE TWISTERS
Rosen, Charles
ENTERTAINING ANGELS: THE DOROTHY DAY STORY
GREAT WHITE HYPE, THE
MOTHER
Rosenblatt, Jana
PHARAOH'S ARMY
Rosenfeld, Hilary
CAUGHT
Rosenzweig, Steve
FLIRT
TREES LOUNGE
Roshko, Ariel
DEADLY OUTBREAK
Ross, Anne
MERCY
Roth, Ernest H.
LAWNMOWER MAN 2: BEYOND CYBERSPACE
Rubeo, Bruno
EVENING STAR, THE
Ryan, M. Kevin
ANNIE O
Ryder, William V.
DENTIST, THE
YESTERDAY'S TARGET
Sage, Jefferson
NATIONAL LAMPOON'S FAVORITE DEADLY SINS
Sakash, Evelyn
MRS. WINTERBOURNE
Sandell, William
GLIMMER MAN, THE
LAZARUS MAN, THE
Santini, Bruno
PROPRIETOR, THE
Saro, E. Colleen
RAVENHAWK
Scanlon, James
PHOENIX
TAKEOVER, THE
Schaetzle, Terri
ONE MAN'S JUSTICE
PHAT BEACH
Schell, Jeffrey T.
FULL BODY MASSAGE
Schnell, Curtis A.
ED
Scholl, Oliver
INDEPENDENCE DAY
Schoppe, James
DEATH BENEFIT
Schwartz, Ruben
CROCODILES IN AMSTERDAM
Scott, Elisabeth A.
BAJA
GLASS CAGE, THE
NAKED SOULS
Scott, Gerald
APART FROM HUGH
Scott, Jan
HARVEST OF FIRE
Seguin, Francois
GRACE OF MY HEART
MOTHER NIGHT
Sessler, Jan
PUBLIC ACCESS
Seymour, Sharon
CABLE GUY, THE
TRUTH ABOUT CATS AND DOGS, THE
Shaw, Michael
HEAVY
Sherman, Richard
DEAD TO RIGHTS

Shohan, Naomi
FEELING MINNESOTA
Shuster, Paul
MONSTERSHOW
Silvestri, Gianni
STEALING BEAUTY
Sinclair, Kim
ALEX
Sjostrum, Lee
MERLIN'S SHOP OF MAGICAL WONDERS
Smith, Deborah
LOW LIFE, THE
Smith, Rusty
DUNSTON CHECKS IN
ONE NIGHT STAND
Sole, Alfred
WIDOW'S KISS
Soto, Liliana
BITTER SUGAR
Spence, Steve
MAXIMUM RISK
QUEST, THE
Spier, Carol
JOE'S APARTMENT
Standefer, Robin
PALLBEARER, THE
Starski, Allan
DAENS
Steele, Jon Gary
EDIE & PEN
Stepeck, Timothy S.
SHARON'S SECRET
Stevenson, Mark
BEAUTIFUL THING
Stewart, Jane Ann
CITIZEN RUTH
Stoddart, John
HEAVEN'S PRISONERS
LAST DANCE
Stopkewich, Lynn
BREACH OF TRUST
Storer, Stephen
CHILDREN OF FURY
D3: THE MIGHTY DUCKS
Stover, Garreth
LATE SHIFT, THE
PHENOMENON
Strawn, Mick
NIGHT OF THE SCARECROW
Strazovec, Val
MUPPET TREASURE ISLAND
Stringer, Tony
SHAMELESS
Strober, Carol
ONE GOOD TURN
Stuhler, Anne
PALOOKAVILLE
WALKING AND TALKING
Sylbert, Paul
GRASS HARP, THE
Sylbert, Richard
MULHOLLAND FALLS
Talpers, Daniel
AMERICAN BUFFALO
ANGELA
Tangkilisan, Hendro
WITHOUT MERCY
Tankus, Zeev
TWO-BITS & PEPPER
Tapper, Amy
SWEET NOTHING
Tatopoulos, Patrick
INDEPENDENCE DAY
Tavoularis, Dean
JACK
Taylor, Don
TWO DEATHS
Thomas, Brent
OUTER LIMITS: SANDKINGS, THE
RED SCORPION 2
Thomas, Ian
BIG BULLY
Thomas, Wynn
MARS ATTACKS!
Thompson, Kevin
FLIRTING WITH DISASTER
PROPRIETOR, THE
Thornton, Malcolm
COLD COMFORT FARM
Tilley, Quenby
BODY COUNT
Tollotson, John
BREAKAWAY
Tomkins, Leslie
WHITE SQUALL
Tougas, Ginger
IF LUCY FELL
Townsend, Jeffrey
FAITHFUL
Tremblay, Anthony
EVIL HAS A FACE
IT CAME FROM OUTER SPACE II
NECRONOMICON: BOOK OF THE DEAD
Turzer, Harald
HALFMOON
Vallow, Kristin
ED'S NEXT MOVE
Van De Coolwijk, Robert
REDEMPTION: KICKBOXER 5
YANKEE ZULU
Vance, James D.
CARPOOL
Vanflanderan, Connie
4 TALES OF 2 CITIES
Varod, David
WARHEAD
Vasels, Phillip
RATTLED
Vernacchio, Dorian
CHAMELEON
WITHIN THE ROCK
Vetter, Arlan Jay
BLACK OUT
Vigeant, J. Edward
DADETOWN
Von Brandenstein, Patrizia
PEOPLE VS. LARRY FLYNT, THE
Wagener, Christiaan
TUSKEGEE AIRMEN, THE
Walker, Graham "Grace"
ISLAND OF DR. MOREAU, THE
Walker, Stuart
CAPTIVES
Walsh, Thomas A.
FLIPPER
Wanek, Jerry
LARRY MCMURTRY'S STREETS OF LAREDO
Wareham, Terry
WHERE'S THE MONEY, NOREEN?
Warner, Pam
FREEWAY
ROAD TO GALVESTON, THE
Warner, Phil
TUNNEL VISION
Wasco, David
BOTTLE ROCKET
Washington, Dennis
HIGH SCHOOL HIGH
Watabe, Takashi
GHOST IN THE SHELL
Weatherby, Jo
GIRLFRIENDS
Wedner, Ellen
BEWARE: CHILDREN AT PLAY
Welch, Bo
BIRDCAGE, THE
Wheeler, W. Brooke
SERIAL KILLER
White, Cary
LONE JUSTICE: SHOWDOWN AT PLUM CREEK
White, Michael
ROCK, THE
Wihak, Marian
LEGEND OF GATOR FACE, THE
Wilkinson, Chris
CRACKER: THE MADWOMAN IN THE ATTIC
Williams, Sherman
CURDLED
Wilson, Andrew
HALFBACK OF NOTRE DAME, THE
ROAD HOME, THE
ROBIN OF LOCKSLEY
Wilson, David
SOME MOTHER'S SON
Wilson, Raymond
LIVE WIRE: HUMAN TIMEBOMB
Wissner, Gary
LAST MAN STANDING
Wurtzel, Stuart
BEFORE AND AFTER
GHOST AND THE DARKNESS, THE
Zachery, John
VIRTUAL ENCOUNTERS
Zea, Kristi
SLEEPERS
Zehetbauer, Rolf
BROTHER OF SLEEP
Ziembicki, Bob
DEAD MAN
Zimmerman, Herman
STAR TREK: FIRST CONTACT

SCREENWRITERS

Adler, Gilbert
TALES FROM THE CRYPT PRESENTS BORDELLO OF BLOOD
Aguilar, Lou
ELECTRA
Albert, Jeff
LIVE WIRE: HUMAN TIMEBOMB
TERMINAL IMPACT
WARHEAD
Alcott, Todd
JUST YOUR LUCK
Alexander, Scott
PEOPLE VS. LARRY FLYNT, THE
Alexandre, Michel
LES VOLEURS
Alfieri, Richard
HARVEST OF FIRE
Allcroft, Britt
BRITT ALLCROFT'S MAGIC ADVENTURES OF MUMFIE—THE MOVIE
Allen, Jim
LAND AND FREEDOM
Allen, Woody
EVERYONE SAYS I LOVE YOU
Almagor, Gila
UNDER THE DOMIM TREE
Almodovar, Pedro
FLOWER OF MY SECRET, THE
Altman, Robert
KANSAS CITY
Amendolare, Nicholas
HARD JUSTICE
Amini, Hossein
JUDE

Anders, Allison
GRACE OF MY HEART
Anderson, Paul
SHOPPING
Anderson, Wes
BOTTLE ROCKET
Andreef, Christina
GIRLFRIENDS
Angelella, Michael
MOTHER
Anthony, Robert
WITHOUT MERCY
Apatow, Judd
CELTIC PRIDE
Apon, Annette
CROCODILES IN AMSTERDAM
Applegate Jr., William
PURE DANGER
SKYSCRAPER
SWEEPER, THE
TIGER HEART
Apramian, Lisa Rose
NOT BAD FOR A GIRL
Aptekman, Igor
LITTLE INDIAN, BIG CITY
Argueta, Luis
SILENCE OF NETO, THE
Armitage, George
LATE SHIFT, THE
Armstrong, Andy
MOONSHINE HIGHWAY
Armstrong, Mike
TWO IF BY SEA
Armstrong, Ronald K.
BUGGED
Asmussen, Peter
BREAKING THE WAVES
Assayas, Olivier
NEW LIFE, A
Atkins, Peter
FIST OF THE NORTH STAR
HELLRAISER: BLOODLINE
Aubrey, Jay
LOOKING FOR TROUBLE
Auerbach, Gary
JUST YOUR LUCK
Augustyn, Joe
EXIT
Avary, Roger
MR. STITCH
Azema, Jean-Pierre
EYE OF VICHY, THE
Baigelman, Steven
FEELING MINNESOTA
Baitz, Jon Robin
SUBSTANCE OF FIRE, THE
Baker, Mark H.
LIFEFORM
Balasko, Josiane
FRENCH TWIST
Baldwin, Craig
SONIC OUTLAWS
Barboni, Marcotullio
SONS OF TRINITY
Barhydt, Frank
KANSAS CITY
Barish, Leora
VENUS RISING
Barmettler, Joseph John
PURE DANGER
RAGE
Barmettler Jr., Joseph John
WITCHCRAFT: SALEM'S GHOST
Barr, Douglas
FRAME BY FRAME
Barrie, Michael
NATIONAL LAMPOON'S FAVORITE DEADLY SINS

Barron, Steve
ADVENTURES OF PINOCCHIO, THE
Basichis, Gordon
BREACH OF TRUST
Bass, Kim
THIN LINE BETWEEN LOVE AND HATE, A
Battishill, Arlene
DEVOTION
Battle, Murray
STAND OFF, THE
Baynac, Jacques
CHEKIST, THE
Beaton, Hilary
GIRLFRIENDS
Beaujour, Jerome
SINGLE GIRL, A
Beaulieu, Trace
MYSTERY SCIENCE THEATER 3000: THE MOVIE
Beauman, Phil
DON'T BE A MENACE TO SOUTH CENTRAL WHILE DRINKING YOUR JUICE IN THE HOOD
Beebe, Dick
LAZARUS MAN, THE
Bell, Dan
SHOT, THE
Bellisario, Donald P.
JAG
Bello, Steve
SKIN
Benedek, Tom
ADVENTURES OF PINOCCHIO, THE
Benedetti, Robert
CANTERVILLE GHOST, THE
Benedict, Terry
PAINTED HERO
Benigni, Roberto
MONSTER, THE
Bennett, Bill
SPIDER & ROSE
Benson, Michael
PREDICTIONS OF FIRE
Benvenuti, Leo
SPACE JAM
Berg, James
VERY BRADY SEQUEL, A
Berger, Howard
ORIGINAL SINS
Berger, Stephen
CHILDREN OF THE CORN: THE GATHERING
Bergman, Andrew
STRIPTEASE
Bergman, Martin
WEEKEND IN THE COUNTRY, A
Berlin, Jefferson
ANNIE O
Berlinger, Joe
PARADISE LOST: THE CHILD MURDERS AT ROBIN HOOD HILLS
Berman, Barry
ADVENTURES OF PINOCCHIO, THE
Berman, Rick
STAR TREK: FIRST CONTACT
Bernd, Art
WOLVES, THE
Bernhardt, Kevin
IMMORTALS, THE
Bertheaud, Stan
PAINTED HERO
Berzins, Andrew Rai
BLOOD & DONUTS
Besset, Jean-Marie
PROPRIETOR, THE
Betsuyaku, Minoru
NIGHT ON THE GALACTIC RAILROAD

Betuel, Jonathan
THEODORE REX
Biderman, Ann
PRIMAL FEAR
Bigelow, Kathryn
UNDERTOW
Bing, Lou
ORGANIZED CRIME & TRIAD BUREAU
Biondi, Lee
NATIONAL LAMPOON'S FAVORITE DEADLY SINS
Bishop, Larry
MAD DOG TIME
Black, Shane
LONG KISS GOODNIGHT, THE
Blair, Jon
ANNE FRANK REMEMBERED
Blair, Rikki Beadle
STONEWALL
Blanc, Michel
MONSTER, THE
Blaustein, Barry W.
NUTTY PROFESSOR, THE
Blinn, William
BOYS NEXT DOOR, THE
Bloom, Steve
JAMES AND THE GIANT PEACH
Blount Jr, Roy
LARGER THAN LIFE
Boam, Jeffrey
PHANTOM, THE
Boboras, Peter
JOHNNY SHORTWAVE
Bockner, Michael
JOHNNY SHORTWAVE
Bodar, Adam
OUTPOST, THE
Bogner, Nicholas
LITTLE DEATH, THE
Bohem, Leslie
DAYLIGHT
Bold, Chris
HARD JUSTICE
Bologna, Joseph
LOVE IS ALL THERE IS
Bolotnick, Troy
RED SCORPION 2
Bond, Jonathan
SANTA WITH MUSCLES
Bonitzer, Pascal
LES VOLEURS
MA SAISON PREFEREE
THREE LIVES AND ONLY ONE DEATH
Bookwalter, J.R.
SANDMAN, THE
Boorman, Telsche
CELESTIAL CLOCKWORK
FRENCH TWIST
Bortman, Michael
CHAIN REACTION
Bourla, David
YESTERDAY'S TARGET
Boyce, Frank Cottrell
BUTTERFLY KISS
Bradbury, Malcolm
COLD COMFORT FARM
Braddock, Reb
CURDLED
Braga, Brannon
STAR TREK: FIRST CONTACT
Branagh, Kenneth
HAMLET
MIDWINTER'S TALE, A
Brandes, Richard
DEAD COLD
Breckman, Andy
SGT. BILKO

Breen, Patrick
4 TALES OF 2 CITIES
Bressan Jr., Arthur J.
ABUSE
Brett, Jonathan
TALES OF EROTICA
Breziner, Salome
TOLLBOOTH
Bright, Matthew
FREEWAY
Brill, Steven
D3: THE MIGHTY DUCKS
Brodbin, Kevin
GLIMMER MAN, THE
Broderick, Brendan
DEATH ARTIST, THE
Broderick, Patricia
INFINITY
Brooks, Adam
4 TALES OF 2 CITIES
Brooks, Albert
MOTHER
Brosnan, John
PROTEUS
Brothers Quay, The
INSTITUTE BENJAMENTA
Bruneau, Philippe
LITTLE INDIAN, BIG CITY
Bryan, Mark
ANNIE O
Bufford, Takashi
SET IT OFF
Buford, Kenny
THIN LINE BETWEEN LOVE AND HATE, A
Buhai, Jeff
EDDIE
Buntzman, Mark
PRE-MADONNAS
Burg, Andy
ALASKA
Burke, Martyn
SUGARTIME
Burns, Edward
SHE'S THE ONE
Burnstein, Jim
D3: THE MIGHTY DUCKS
Burton, Kenneth J.
MERLIN'S SHOP OF MAGICAL WONDERS
Buscemi, Steve
TREES LOUNGE
Bythewood, Reggie Rock
GET ON THE BUS
Caceres, Gerardo
JOHNNY 100 PESOS
Caldwell, Helen
UNHOOK THE STARS
Cammell, Donald
WILD SIDE
Campion, Anna
LOADED
Cardone, J.S.
BLACK DAY BLUE NIGHT
Carlson, Christopher
HOMECOMING
Carpenter, Fred
MURDERED INNOCENCE
Carpenter, John
JOHN CARPENTER'S ESCAPE FROM L.A.
Carr, Benjamin
HEAD OF THE FAMILY
ZARKORR! THE INVADER
Carriere, Jean-Claude
HORSEMAN ON THE ROOF
Carter, Bill
LATE SHIFT, THE
Carter Jr., Ken
MAGIC IN THE MIRROR

Casano, Denise
GIRLS TOWN
Casella, Marty
ONE NIGHT STAND
Cassavetes, Nick
UNHOOK THE STARS
Catran, Ken
ALEX
Celantano, Jeff
UNDER THE HULA MOON
Cerami, Vincenzo
MONSTER, THE
Chabrol, Claude
LA CEREMONIE
Chaiken, Ilene
BARB WIRE
Champnella, Eric
EDDIE
Chang, Justo
SILENCE OF NETO, THE
Chaplin, Paul
MYSTERY SCIENCE THEATER 3000: THE MOVIE
Chapman, Richard
MY FELLOW AMERICANS
Charouhas, Elisa J.
PRE-MADONNAS
Chetwynd, Lionel
KISSINGER AND NIXON
Chevallier, Francois
DAENS
Chudnow, Dick
SPY HARD
Cicoritti, Gerard
UNDERSTUDY: GRAVEYARD SHIFT 2, THE
Cirillo, Patrick
SURGEON, THE
Clark, Richard
HALFBACK OF NOTRE DAME, THE
Clavier, Christian
VISITORS, THE
Clay, Carl
LET'S GET BIZZEE
Clifton, Patrick
JOSH KIRBY . . . TIME WARRIOR!: EGGS FROM 70,000,000 B.C.
SPELLBREAKER: SECRET OF THE LEPRECHAUNS
Cochran, Stacy
BOYS
Coen, Ethan
FARGO
Coen, Joel
FARGO
Cohen, Barney
SABRINA, THE TEENAGE WITCH
Cohen, Eli
UNDER THE DOMIM TREE
Colick, Lewis
BULLETPROOF
GHOSTS OF MISSISSIPPI
Colleary, Michael
DARKMAN III: DIE DARKMAN DIE
Companeez, Nina
HORSEMAN ON THE ROOF
Coninx, Stijn
DAENS
Connolly, John
EDDIE
Cook, Douglas S.
ROCK, THE
Cook, Lius
WALLACE AND GROMIT: THE BEST OF AARDMAN ANIMATION
Cook, Troy
PHOENIX

Cooney, Michael
TRACKS OF A KILLER
Cooper, Paul W.
ONCE UPON A TIME . . . WHEN WE WERE COLORED
Copel, Ken
. . . AT FIRST SIGHT
Coraci, Frank
MURDERED INNOCENCE
Corlet, Rachel
VISITORS, THE
Corley, David
SOLO
Covell, David
LEGEND OF GATOR FACE, THE
Covert, Michael
AMERICAN STRAYS
Craven, Jonathan
MIND RIPPER
Crichton, Michael
TWISTER
Crooks, Harold
CHAMPAGNE SAFARI, THE
Crowe, Cameron
JERRY MAGUIRE
Crowe, Christopher
FEAR
Cryer, Jon
POMPATUS OF LOVE, THE
Custodio, Alvaro
AVENTURERA
Cyran, Catherine
HOSTILE INTENTIONS
Dalton, Darren
HOURGLASS
Danon, Leslie
WHISPERING, THE
Dash, Sean
BREAKAWAY
David, Peter
BACKLASH: OBLIVION 2
Davies, Terence
NEON BIBLE, THE
De Leon, Marcus
BIG SQUEEZE, THE
Deasy, Frank
CAPTIVES
Degass, Andre
CONDITION RED
Delaubre, Yves
CELESTIAL CLOCKWORK
DeLaurentis, Suzanne
MUTANT MAN
DeMonaco, James
JACK
Dennis, Gill
RIDERS OF THE PURPLE SAGE
Densham, Pen
MOLL FLANDERS
Devlin, Dean
INDEPENDENCE DAY
Dexter, Pete
MICHAEL
MULHOLLAND FALLS
Didion, Joan
UP CLOSE AND PERSONAL
Dietz, Frank
MAGIC IN THE MIRROR
NAKED SOULS
Dimster-Denk, Dennis
HARD JUSTICE
TERMINAL IMPACT
DiMuccio, Brian
DEMOLITIONIST, THE
LITTLE WITCHES
Dindo, Richard
ERNESTO CHE GUEVARA—THE BOLIVIAN DIARY

DiPego, Gerald
PHENOMENON
Donnelly, Mark
WIDOW'S KISS
Douglas, Illeana
4 TALES OF 2 CITIES
Dowdy, Jeffrey
LOOKING FOR TROUBLE
Draskovic, Boro
VUKOVAR
Draskovic, Maja
VUKOVAR
Dryfoos, Susan W.
LINE KING: THE AL HIRSCHFELD STORY, THE
Drysdale, Lee
SWEET NOTHING
DuBos, David
PLAYBACK
Duff, James
WAR AT HOME, THE
Dugan, Michael Feit
PUBLIC ACCESS
Duncan, Patrick Sheane
COURAGE UNDER FIRE
MR. HOLLAND'S OPUS
Dunne, Griffin
4 TALES OF 2 CITIES
Dunne, John Gregory
UP CLOSE AND PERSONAL
Dunye, Cheryl
GIRLFRIENDS
Dupeyron, Francois
MACHINE, THE
Dwyer, Jim
FRISK
Edwards, James L.
POLYMORPH
Ehrin, Kerry
MR. WRONG
Elders, Kevin
RAVENHAWK
Elfont, Harry
VERY BRADY SEQUEL, A
Eliacheff, Caroline
LA CEREMONIE
Ellin, Doug
PHAT BEACH
Ellis, Kirk
GRASS HARP, THE
Ellis, Trey
TUSKEGEE AIRMEN, THE
Emery, Caroline
VISITORS, THE
Emmerich, Roland
INDEPENDENCE DAY
Enbom, John
LOW LIFE, THE
Entius, Yolanda
CROCODILES IN AMSTERDAM
Enyedi, Ildiko
MAGIC HUNTER
Ephron, Delia
MICHAEL
Ephron, Nora
MICHAEL
Epperson, Tom
FAMILY THING, A
Epstein, David
PALOOKAVILLE
Epstein, Rob
CELLULOID CLOSET, THE
Eubanks, Corey Michael
TWO-BITS & PEPPER
Evans, Bentley Kyle
THIN LINE BETWEEN LOVE AND HATE, A
Evans, David Mickey
ED
Everitt, Tim
TOO FAST, TOO YOUNG
Factor, Nicholas
SABRINA, THE TEENAGE WITCH
Fanaro, Barry
KINGPIN
Fassbinder, Rainer Werner
SHADOW OF ANGELS
Favreau, Jon
SWINGERS
Fenjves, Pablo
AFFAIR, THE
Ferguson, Larry
MAXIMUM RISK
Fessler, Michel
RIDICULE
Fieschi, Jacques
NELLY AND MONSIEUR ARNAUD
Filardi, Peter
CRAFT, THE
Filon, Rick
REDEMPTION: KICKBOXER 5
Finch, Charles
DENTIST, THE
Finly, Steve A.
SHADOW WARRIORS
Fleming, Andrew
CRAFT, THE
Fleury, Clive
TUNNEL VISION
Foldes, Lawrence D.
PRE-MADONNAS
Foldy, Peter
WIDOW'S KISS
Foote, Horton
LILY DALE
Ford, Christian
KAZAAM
Forrester, Brent
STUPIDS, THE
Frank, Scott
HEAVEN'S PRISONERS
Freed, Donald
OF LOVE AND SHADOWS
Fresco, Rob
EVIL HAS A FACE
Fridriksson, Fridrik Thor
COLD FEVER
Friedberg, Jason
SPY HARD
Friedberg, Rick
SPY HARD
Friedman Block, Lisa
MATERNAL INSTINCTS
Friedman, Brent V.
EXIT
NECRONOMICON: BOOK OF THE DEAD
Friedman, Jeffrey
CELLULOID CLOSET, THE
Friedman, Josh
CHAIN REACTION
Frumkes, Roy
SUBSTITUTE, THE
Fry, Benjamin
WAVELENGTH
Gage, Beth
FIRE ON THE MOUNTAIN
Gans, Christophe
NECRONOMICON: BOOK OF THE DEAD
Ganz, Lowell
MULTIPLICITY
Gardner, Eric
BREAKAWAY
Gardner, Herb
I'M NOT RAPPAPORT
Garner, Helen
TWO FRIENDS
Gayton, Joe
BULLETPROOF
Geddie, Bill
UNFORGETTABLE
Gems, Jonathan
MARS ATTACKS!
Geoffrion, Robert
HOLLOW POINT
George, Terry
SOME MOTHER'S SON
Giacosa, Giuseppe
MADAME BUTTERFLY
Gilbert, Lewis
HAUNTED
Gill, Andy K.
LET'S GET BIZZEE
Gilroy, Tony
EXTREME MEASURES
Giordana, Marco Tullio
WHO KILLED PASOLINI?
Glazer, Mitch
OFF AND RUNNING
Goldenberg, Michael
BED OF ROSES
Goldman, Bo
CITY HALL
Goldman, William
CHAMBER, THE
GHOST AND THE DARKNESS, THE
Goldsman, Akiva
TIME TO KILL, A
Goldstein, Harel
DEADLY OUTBREAK
Goleszowski, Richard
WALLACE AND GROMIT: THE BEST OF AARDMAN ANIMATION
Goluboff, Bryan
AFFAIR, THE
Goodman, Dan
BLONDES HAVE MORE GUNS
Gordon, Bryan
PIE IN THE SKY
Gordon, Reuben
BLACK OUT
Gordon, Stuart
DENTIST, THE
Gorris, Marleen
ANTONIA'S LINE
Gothar, Peter
OUTPOST, THE
Goyer, David S.
CROW: CITY OF ANGELS, THE
Grace, Anna
GIRLS TOWN
Graef-Marino, Gustavo
JOHNNY 100 PESOS
Graham, Bruce
DUNSTON CHECKS IN
Graham, Sam
NIGHT OF THE TWISTERS
Grall, Andre
MAN BY THE SHORE, THE
Gray, Barry
BEST OF THE BEST 3: NO TURNING BACK
Green, Walon
ERASER
Greif, Leslie
MADDENING, THE
Grossman, Adam
SOMETIMES THEY COME BACK . . . AGAIN
Gurian, Paul
VIKING SAGAS, THE
Gurskis, Dan
FULL BODY MASSAGE

Guthrie, Mary
BLONDES HAVE MORE GUNS
Haas, Belinda
ANGELS AND INSECTS
Haas, Philip
ANGELS AND INSECTS
Haddock, Chris
HECK'S WAY HOME
Hadley, Dylan Kelsey
WHITE WOLVES II: LEGEND OF THE WILD
Hail, Mack
MR. ICE CREAM MAN
Hale, Mary
MULTIPLICITY
Haller, Peg
NORMAL LIFE
Hampton, Christopher
JOSEPH CONRAD'S THE SECRET AGENT
MARY REILLY
Hanks, Tom
THAT THING YOU DO!
Harada, Masato
KAMIKAZE TAXI
Harling, Robert
EVENING STAR, THE
FIRST WIVES CLUB, THE
Harrigan, Stephen
LONE JUSTICE: SHOWDOWN AT PLUM CREEK
Harris, Bruklin
GIRLS TOWN
Harris, Selwin
ANIMAL INSTINCTS III: THE SEDUCTRESS
Harris, Timothy
SPACE JAM
Harrison, John
DONOR UNKNOWN
Harron, Mary
I SHOT ANDY WARHOL
Hart, Chris
TIMELESS
Hart, Jacobsen
RAGE
Hart, Jerry Juhljim
MUPPET TREASURE ISLAND
Hartley, Hal
FLIRT
Harvey, Bruce
PORTRAITS OF A KILLER
Harvey, Jonathan
BEAUTIFUL THING
Hauty, Chris
HOMEWARD BOUND II: LOST IN SAN FRANCISCO
Hayes, Carey
DOWN, OUT AND DANGEROUS
Hayes, Chad
DOWN, OUT AND DANGEROUS
Hedden, Rob
COLONY, THE
Hein, Adrie
BURIAL OF THE RATS
Heller, Milly
GIRLFRIENDS
Hendershot, Eric
CLUBHOUSE DETECTIVES
Hendra, Tony
GREAT WHITE HYPE, THE
Henkel, Ken
TEXAS CHAINSAW MASSACRE: THE NEXT GENERATION
Henson, Robby
PHARAOH'S ARMY
Herd, Dale
CARRIED AWAY
VIKING SAGAS, THE
Herlihy, Tim
HAPPY GILMORE
Herzfeld, John
2 DAYS IN THE VALLEY
Hexter, Russ
DADETOWN
Hickenlooper, George
LOW LIFE, THE
Higson, Charles
SUITE 16
Hill, Debra
JOHN CARPENTER'S ESCAPE FROM L.A.
Hill, Walter
LAST MAN STANDING
Hiscock, Norm
KIDS IN THE HALL: BRAIN CANDY
Hitchcock, Michael
HOUSE ARREST
Hlavin, John
FLATTERED
Hodge, John
TRAINSPOTTING
Hofmeyr, Gray
YANKEE ZULU
Holden, Michael
LITTLE DEATH, THE
Holofcener, Nicole
WALKING AND TALKING
Holtz Jr., Lou
CABLE GUY, THE
Homer, Mark
SHARON'S SECRET
Hopkins, John
DUNSTON CHECKS IN
Housley, John
DADETOWN
Hovis, Michael
MAN WITH THE PERFECT SWING, THE
Howard-Hammerstein, Jane
LONG ROAD HOME, THE
Howe, Matthew
ORIGINAL SINS
Howell, C. Thomas
HOURGLASS
Hubbell, Chris
NIGHT OF THE TWISTERS
Huddles, John
FAR HARBOR
Hughes, John
101 DALMATIANS
Husky, Rick
CHILDREN OF FURY
Huston, Jimmy
WHARF RAT, THE
Hutchinson, Ron
ISLAND OF DR. MOREAU, THE
TUSKEGEE AIRMEN, THE
Iborra, Juan Luis
MOUTH TO MOUTH
Ichaso, Leon
BITTER SUGAR
Ignon, Alexander
RANSOM
Illica, Luigi
MADAME BUTTERFLY
Imai, Kenichi
STREET FIGHTER II: THE ANIMATED MOVIE
Inglis, Raul
BREACH OF TRUST
FINAL CUT, THE
Iosseliani, Otar
CHASING BUTTERFLIES
Isaacs, Jill
NORMA JEAN AND MARILYN
Ito, Kazunori
GHOST IN THE SHELL
NECRONOMICON: BOOK OF THE DEAD
PATLABOR 2: MOBILE POLICE
Jackson, Peter
FRIGHTENERS, THE
Jacobsson, Anders
EVIL ED
Jacquot, Benoit
SINGLE GIRL, A
Jaffa, Rick
EYE FOR AN EYE
Jarmusch, Jim
DEAD MAN
Jean, Mark
HOMECOMING
Jhabvala, Ruth Prawer
SURVIVING PICASSO
Johnson, Dave Alan
CHAMELEON
Johnson, Mark Steven
BIG BULLY
Johnson, Monica
MOTHER
Johnston, Aaron Kim
FOR THE MOMENT
Jones, Amy Holden
RICH MAN'S WIFE, THE
Jones, Bridget
MYSTERY SCIENCE THEATER 3000: THE MOVIE
Jones, Ed
CARRIED AWAY
Jones, Laura
PORTRAIT OF A LADY, THE
Jones, Mark
RUMPELSTILTSKIN
Jordan, Neil
MICHAEL COLLINS
Jordon III, Eugene
LET'S GET BIZZEE
Joyner, Courtney
PUBLIC ENEMIES
Judge, Mike
BEAVIS AND BUTT-HEAD DO AMERICA
Kane, John
BRITT ALLCROFT'S MAGIC ADVENTURES OF MUMFIE—THE MOVIE
Kanefsky, Rolf
RED LINE
Kaplan, Deborah
VERY BRADY SEQUEL, A
Kaplan, E. Jack
MY FELLOW AMERICANS
Kaplan, Ed
DEAR GOD
Kaplan, Mindy
DEVOTION
Karaszewski, Larry
PEOPLE VS. LARRY FLYNT, THE
Kass, Sam Henry
SEARCH FOR ONE-EYE JIMMY, THE
Kassovitz, Mathieu
HATE
Katims, Jason
PALLBEARER, THE
Katz, Al
TALES FROM THE CRYPT PRESENTS BORDELLO OF BLOOD
Kaufman, Lloyd
SGT. KABUKIMAN N.Y.P.D.
Kazan, Nicholas
MATILDA
Kelemen, Fred
FATE
Kelleher, Tim
FIRST KID
Kellett, Robert
HAUNTED

Kelley, David E.
TO GILLIAN ON HER 37TH BIRTHDAY
Kiarostami, Abbas
WHITE BALLOON, THE
Kimball, Frederic
LOOKING FOR RICHARD
King, Chloe
POISON IVY 2: LILY
Kirkpatrick, Karey
JAMES AND THE GIANT PEACH
Kirtland Silverman, Kathy
MATERNAL INSTINCTS
Klein, Steven
QUEST, THE
Kleiser, Randal
IT'S MY PARTY
Knop, Patricia Louisianna
DELTA OF VENUS
Koenig, Kip
BIO-DOME
Koepp, David
MISSION: IMPOSSIBLE
TRIGGER EFFECT, THE
Koide, Kazumi
BIG WARS
Kong, China
WILD SIDE
Koper, Peter
HEADLESS BODY IN TOPLESS BAR
Kornfield, Randy
BLOODKNOT
JINGLE ALL THE WAY
Koslow, Ron
LAST DANCE
Kramer, John
CHAMPAGNE SAFARI, THE
Krinkle, Henry
FRIEND OF THE FAMILY 2
Kroll, Jon
AMANDA AND THE ALIEN
Krueger, Lisa
MANNY & LO
Krum Raymond, Dorrie
SANTA WITH MUSCLES
Kurtzman, Andrew
DOWN PERISCOPE
Kwong Man-Wai
MIDNIGHT ANGEL
Kyle, Kyle C.
NOT BAD FOR A GIRL
L'Ecuyer, John
CURTIS'S CHARM
La Voo, George
FRISK
Ladd, Diane
MRS. MUNCK
LaGravenese, Richard
MIRROR HAS TWO FACES, THE
Laing, Nancy
PORTRAITS OF A KILLER
Lane, Brian Allen
GIRL FROM MARS, THE
Lanier, Kate
SET IT OFF
Larrabee, John
SKYSCRAPER
Lavin, Julianna
LIVE NUDE GIRLS
Lawrence, Martin
THIN LINE BETWEEN LOVE AND HATE, A
Lawton, J.F.
CHAIN REACTION
Le Bel, Pauline
SONG SPINNER, THE
Leary, Denis
TWO IF BY SEA

Leavitt, Charles
SUNCHASER
Ledoux, Trish
SANCTUARY: THE MOVIE
Lee, Damian
ELECTRA
WHEN THE BULLET HITS THE BONE
Lee, Ricardo
MIDNIGHT DANCERS
Lee, Tony
ROAD TO GALVESTON, THE
Leigh, Mike
SECRETS & LIES
Leight, Warren
DEAR GOD
Lembeck, Ann
NATIONAL LAMPOON'S FAVORITE DEADLY SINS
Levinson, Barry
SLEEPERS
Levy, Brian
HYPE!
Lhermitte, Thierry
LITTLE INDIAN, BIG CITY
Li Shaohong
BLUSH
Lifton, Jimmy
PHOENIX
Lindgren, Astrid
CHILDREN OF NOISY VILLAGE, THE
Lipper, Ken
CITY HALL
Llwyd, Alan
HEDD WYNN
LoCash, Robert
HIGH SCHOOL HIGH
Lord, Peter
WALLACE AND GROMIT: THE BEST OF AARDMAN ANIMATION
Loucka, David
EDDIE
Lucas, Steve
CHAMPAGNE SAFARI, THE
Luhrmann, Baz
WILLIAM SHAKESPEARE'S ROMEO + JULIET
Lumley, Vernon
FORBIDDEN ZONE: ALIEN ABDUCTION
Lundstrom, Goran
EVIL ED
Maass, John
CURDLED
MacKinnon, Billy
SMALL FACES
MacKinnon, Gillies
SMALL FACES
Madden, Henry
BODY COUNT
Maddock, Brent
TREMORS 2: AFTERSHOCKS
Maddox, Larry
RAW TARGET
Magee, Doug
BEYOND THE CALL
COLD LIGHT OF DAY
Mallon, Jim
MYSTERY SCIENCE THEATER 3000: THE MOVIE
Mamet, David
AMERICAN BUFFALO
Mandel, Babaloo
MULTIPLICITY
Mangold, James
HEAVY
Mann, Farhad
LAWNMOWER MAN 2: BEYOND CYBERSPACE

Marcano, Scott
BIO-DOME
Marcus, Mitch
BOY CALLED HATE, A
Martell, William C.
VIRTUAL COMBAT
Martin, Anne-Marie
TWISTER
Martin, Steven M.
THEREMIN: AN ELECTRONIC ODYSSEY
Martin, Yves Andre
HIDDEN ASSASSIN
Marzano, Joe
ONE LESS EGG TO FRY
Masiel, David
CROSSCUT
Mata, Fred
SANTA WITH MUSCLES
Matacena, Orestes
BITTER SUGAR
Matheson, Chris
MR. WRONG
Matthews, Paul
GRIM
Mauldin, Nat
PREACHER'S WIFE, THE
Maupin, Armistead
CELLULOID CLOSET, THE
May, Elaine
BIRDCAGE, THE
Mayer, Lise
SUITE 16
Mazur, Dan
NIGHT OF THE SCARECROW
McCann, Tara
BURIAL OF THE RATS
McCann, Tim
DESOLATION ANGELS
McCoy, Karen
SWEEPER, THE
McCullogh, Bruce
KIDS IN THE HALL: BRAIN CANDY
McDaniel, Darin
FATALLY YOURS
McDonald, Kevin
KIDS IN THE HALL: BRAIN CANDY
McDonald, Michael James
DEATH ARTIST, THE
McDonald, Rodney
DESIRE
McDowell, Michael
STEPHEN KING'S THINNER
McGhee-Anderson, Kathleen
SUNSET PARK
McGovern, Jimmy
CRACKER: THE MADWOMAN IN THE ATTIC
McGrath, Douglas
EMMA
McKay, Jim
GIRLS TOWN
McKewin, Vince
FLY AWAY HOME
McKinney, Mark
KIDS IN THE HALL: BRAIN CANDY
McMurtry, Larry
LARRY MCMURTRY'S STREETS OF LAREDO
McPherson, Scott
MARVIN'S ROOM
PORTRAITS OF A KILLER
McQuarrie, Christopher
PUBLIC ACCESS
Mecchi, Irene
HUNCHBACK OF NOTRE DAME, THE
Medoff, Mark
HOMAGE

Melbourne, Gordon
WHITE TIGER
Mellott, Greg
SHOOTFIGHTER 2: KILL OR BE KILLED!
Meredith, Anne
LOSING CHASE
Merriweather, George
BLONDES HAVE MORE GUNS
Michaeli, Dani
FUGITIVE RAGE
Michels, Barbara Rose
GIRLFRIENDS
Mickleberry, William
WOMAN UNDONE, A
Migeon, Celine
VISITORS, THE
Mihic, Gordan
SOMEONE ELSE'S AMERICA
Mikhalkov, Nikita
ANNA
Miller, Arthur
CRUCIBLE, THE
Miller, Chris
MULTIPLICITY
Miller, David Keith
GLASS CAGE, THE
Miller, Harvey
GETTING AWAY WITH MURDER
Miller, Rebecca
ANGELA
Milling, William R.
SOUTH BEACH ACADEMY
Mills, Jim
MR. ICE CREAM MAN
Mills, Sherry
ADVENTURES OF PINOCCHIO, THE
Minahan, Daniel
I SHOT ANDY WARHOL
Miner, Michael
LAWNMOWER MAN 2: BEYOND CYBERSPACE
Minghella, Anthony
ENGLISH PATIENT, THE
Minot, Susan
STEALING BEAUTY
Mirochnitchenko, Serguei
ANNA
Mitchell, Gene
TAKEOVER, THE
Mitchell, Julian
AUGUST
Mitchell, Keith
EDDIE
Mittleman, Phil
MIND RIPPER
Moleon, Rafael
BATON ROUGE
Mones, Paul
QUEST, THE
SAINTS AND SINNERS
Monteleone, Enzo
OUTRAGE
Montgomery, Sam
SAWBONES
Moore, Charles Philip
BLACK ROSE OF HARLEM
NOT OF THIS EARTH
Moore, Ronald D.
STAR TREK: FIRST CONTACT
Morris, Ben
PHAT BEACH
Morris, Charles
DEADLY OUTBREAK
Morrissey, Paul
MADAME WANG'S
Morrow, Barry
RACE THE SUN

Moses, Harry
ASSAULT AT WEST POINT
Mruvka, Alan
LEGEND OF GATOR FACE, THE
Mulholland, Jim
NATIONAL LAMPOON'S FAVORITE DEADLY SINS
Munson, Craig
MR. WRONG
Murphy, Kevin
MYSTERY SCIENCE THEATER 3000: THE MOVIE
Murphy, Tab
HUNCHBACK OF NOTRE DAME, THE
Myers, Michael Scott
WHOLE WIDE WORLD, THE
Myers, Richard
MONSTERSHOW
Myers, Scott
ALASKA
Nadeau, Gary
JACK
Nanus, Susan
HARVEST OF FIRE
Nathan, Mort
KINGPIN
Nathanson, Jeff
FOR BETTER OR WORSE
Nelson, Carl
TALKING ABOUT SEX
Nelson, Michael J.
MYSTERY SCIENCE THEATER 3000: THE MOVIE
Nevius, Craig J.
BLACK SCORPION
Newby, Chris
MADAGASCAR SKIN
Ni Zhen
BLUSH
Nicolaou, Ted
SPELLBREAKER: SECRET OF THE LEPRECHAUNS
Nigh, Alison
OUT THERE
Noonan, Tom
WIFE, THE
Norville, John
TIN CUP
Nunn, Trevor
TWELFTH NIGHT
Nuridsany, Claude
MICROCOSMOS
O'Bannon, Dan
SCREAMERS
O'Bannon, Sean
FUGITIVE RAGE
O'Brien, John
MAN WITH A PLAN
O'Leary, Keith
ROAD HOME, THE
O'Neal, Brian E.
PHAT BEACH
Odier, Daniel
CELESTIAL CLOCKWORK
Oedekerk, Steve
NUTTY PROFESSOR, THE
Ofteringer, Susanne
NICO ICON
Ogita, Yoshihisa
MABOROSI
Ohlsson, Christer
EVIL ED
Oliensis, Adam
POMPATUS OF LOVE, THE
Olivera, Hector
SHADOW YOU SOON WILL BE, A
Olsen, Arne
ALL DOGS GO TO HEAVEN 2

Oristrell, Joaquin
MOUTH TO MOUTH
Ormsby, Alan
SUBSTITUTE, THE
Osborne, Andrew
SGT. KABUKIMAN N.Y.P.D.
Ossana, Diana
LARRY MCMURTRY'S STREETS OF LAREDO
Otomo, Katsuhiro
ROUJIN-Z
Pacino, Al
LOOKING FOR RICHARD
Page, Brian
TEXAS PAYBACK
Paine, Nick
JOSH KIRBY . . . TIME WARRIOR!: TRAPPED ON TOY WORLD
Palminteri, Chazz
FAITHFUL
Palud, Herve
LITTLE INDIAN, BIG CITY
Paoli, Dennis
DENTIST, THE
Park, Nick
WALLACE AND GROMIT: THE BEST OF AARDMAN ANIMATION
Parker, Alan
EVITA
Parker, Christine
GIRLFRIENDS
Parker, Trey
CANNIBAL! THE MUSICAL
Parks, Jay
NIGHT ON THE GALACTIC RAILROAD
Parks, Suzan-Lori
GIRL 6
Pascal, Michel
FRANCOIS TRUFFAUT: STOLEN PORTRAITS
Passes, Alan
INSTITUTE BENJAMENTA
Passoni, Valentin
NEUROSIA: 50 YEARS OF PERVERSITY
Pate, Jonas
GRAVE, THE
Pate, Josh
GRAVE, THE
Pavone, Michael
CHAMELEON
Paxton, Robert
EYE OF VICHY, THE
Payne, Alexander
CITIZEN RUTH
Payne, David
CRIMINAL HEARTS
Payson, John
JOE'S APARTMENT
Peake, Peter
WALLACE AND GROMIT: THE BEST OF AARDMAN ANIMATION
Pearce, Craig
WILLIAM SHAKESPEARE'S ROMEO + JULIET
Peck, Raoul
MAN BY THE SHORE, THE
Pehl, Mary Jo
MYSTERY SCIENCE THEATER 3000: THE MOVIE
Pelletier, Chantal
CELESTIAL CLOCKWORK
Pereira, Manuel Gomez
MOUTH TO MOUTH
Perennou, Marie
MICROCOSMOS
Pernecker, Chantal
VISITORS, THE

Gianneschi, Michael
EVIL HAS A FACE
Gibeson, Bruce
FOR BETTER OR WORSE
Gilstrap, Joyce Anne
TRUMAN
Giovanni, Judi
FIRST KID
Goddard, Richard
BROKEN ARROW
Goldman, Dina
MANNY & LO
Goldman, Gina
BAD LOVE
Gould, Robert
LAZARUS MAN, THE
Graves, Regina
LOVE IS ALL THERE IS
Griffith, Clay A.
JERRY MAGUIRE
Gullickson, Mary
AMERICAN STRAYS
Haigh, Nancy
MARS ATTACKS!
Hallenbeck, Casey
MRS. WINTERBOURNE
Hand, John
SOLITAIRE FOR TWO
Harris, Mike
KIDS IN THE HALL: BRAIN CANDY
Hart, Jay
PHENOMENON
Hart, Lisa
LIVE WIRE: HUMAN TIMEBOMB
TERMINAL IMPACT
Hasmann, Klaus
PIE IN THE SKY
Hicks, John Alan
MIRROR HAS TWO FACES, THE
Holinko, Roberta J.
EDDIE
Hollands, Sy
HAUNTED
Hotte, Paul
HOLLOW POINT
Howard, Alison
FAST MONEY
Howitt, Peter
MISSION: IMPOSSIBLE
Hurte, Mary
DARK SECRETS
Huwaert, Frederick
DAENS
Jackson, Courtney
ONE MAN'S JUSTICE
Jacobson, Chad
SWEET NOTHING
Jacobson, Jacqueline
NATIONAL LAMPOON'S FAVORITE DEADLY SINS
Jaquest, David
SCREAMERS
Jenkins, Katy
WHISPERING, THE
Jensen, Dea
LAST SUPPER, THE
Job, Ann
FOREST WARRIOR
Johanna, Rosslyn
PHOENIX
Johannsson, Arni Pall
VIKING SAGAS, THE
Johnson, Bradford
KINGPIN
Kasch, Brian
SUNSET PARK

Keith, Katterina
MATERNAL INSTINCTS
ROBIN OF LOCKSLEY
Kensinger, Bob
VERY BRADY SEQUEL, A
Kirshbaum, Traci
BIG SQUEEZE, THE
FIST OF THE NORTH STAR
IT'S MY PARTY
ONE GOOD TURN
SLING BLADE
Klopp, Kathe
JOHN CARPENTER'S ESCAPE FROM L.A.
Kuchera, Tedd
ALASKA
Kuljian, Anne
CROW: CITY OF ANGELS, THE
ONE FINE DAY
LaHaye, Simon
MOTHER NIGHT
Lambie, Jim
ELECTRA
Lane, Mark
HAPPY GILMORE
Lanier, Jessica
AMERICAN BUFFALO
ASSOCIATE, THE
Lavoie, Carol
STUPIDS, THE
Lederman, Diane
FUNERAL, THE
I SHOT ANDY WARHOL
Lee, Dayna
DEAD MAN
Less, Megan
LOSING CHASE
Lewis, Garrett
DEAR GOD
ERASER
Lipsitt, Katie
VENUS RISING
Lombardo, Lance
SET IT OFF
Loucks, Cal
OPEN SEASON
Lucas, Kathy
MAD DOG TIME
Lundin, Beth Ann
BODY OF INFLUENCE 2
Lusignan, Jeanne
DON'T BE A MENACE TO SOUTH CENTRAL WHILE DRINKING YOUR JUICE IN THE HOOD
MacAvin, Josie
MICHAEL COLLINS
MacDonald, Lin
HOMEWARD BOUND II: LOST IN SAN FRANCISCO
MacFadyen, Lesley Ann
JOHNNY SHORTWAVE
MacKenzie, Margaux
TRACKS OF A KILLER
MacLean, Christine
MAN IN THE ATTIC, THE
Mailing, Bruce
FRAME BY FRAME
March, Marvin
EXECUTIVE DECISION
Markic, Laci
ADRENALIN: FEAR THE RUSH
Marti, Christian
HORSEMAN ON THE ROOF
Martin, Maggie
CABLE GUY, THE
TRUTH ABOUT CATS AND DOGS, THE
McCulley, Anne D.
MOTHER

McCullough, Doug
STAND OFF, THE
WHERE'S THE MONEY, NOREEN?
McElvin, Ric
FAMILY THING, A
TIN CUP
McGary, Kristen
ONCE UPON A TIME . . . WHEN WE WERE COLORED
McGill, Melodi
PORTRAITS OF A KILLER
McIntosh, Mary
GREAT WHITE HYPE, THE
McMillan, Stephenie
ENGLISH PATIENT, THE
IN LOVE AND WAR
MARY REILLY
McSherry, Rose Marie
TALES FROM THE CRYPT PRESENTS BORDELLO OF BLOOD
Meisenbach, Kurt
DONOR UNKNOWN
Menyhart, Agnes
DOGFIGHTERS, THE
Messina, Kristen Toscano
BOUND
Messina, Kristin
NEON BIBLE, THE
Michaels, Mickey S.
DOWN PERISCOPE
Mirkin, Miguel
DEADLY OUTBREAK
Moroney, Nicola
HARD WAY OUT: BLOODFIST VIII
Mowat, Doug
MISSING PIECES
Muller, Jodi
BAJA
Munch, Barbara
JACK
Murphy, Michael
ED'S NEXT MOVE
Murray, Jim
HOW THE WEST WAS FUN
Myers, Troy
PUBLIC ENEMIES
Nash, Barry
WARHEAD
Nay, Maria A.
PEOPLE VS. LARRY FLYNT, THE
Nejman, Jennifer
HARD JUSTICE
Nothnagel, Ian
SABRINA, THE TEENAGE WITCH
Nourafchan, Tori
DANGEROUS PASSION
Nye, Nancy
CRAFT, THE
O'Donnell, Elaine
EVERYONE SAYS I LOVE YOU
O'Hara, Karen A.
GHOSTS OF MISSISSIPPI
Padli, Ujang
WITHOUT MERCY
Paizis, Melanie
. . . AT FIRST SIGHT
Parente, Jack
MURDERED INNOCENCE
Parker, Dominic
IRON EAGLE IV
Pearl, Linda
TO GILLIAN ON HER 37TH BIRTHDAY
Pelegrin, Miguel Lopez
FLOWER OF MY SECRET, THE
Peters, Kathryn
HIGH SCHOOL HIGH
NUTTY PROFESSOR, THE

Petersen, Beau
LETTER TO MY KILLER
PIG'S TALE, A
Peterson, Barbara
SUBSTITUTE, THE
TWO MUCH
Peterson, Kristin
DEATH BENEFIT
Peyton, Robin
D3: THE MIGHTY DUCKS
Pierrat, Catherine
LA CEREMONIE
Pierson, Catherine
DENISE CALLS UP
Pineau, Marthe
FOXFIRE
Pinholster, Katie
FLED
Pitrel, Alain
MA SAISON PREFEREE
Polito-Gaulke, Jennifer
MATILDA
Pope, Leslie A.
JUROR, THE
Pope, Natali
BEST OF THE BEST 3: NO TURNING BACK
Posnansky, Tessa
THIN LINE BETWEEN LOVE AND HATE, A
Poulik, Michele
SCREAM
Quertier, Jill
PORTRAIT OF A LADY, THE
Raney, Susan
BIG NIGHT
Rau, Gretchen
BEFORE AND AFTER
CRUCIBLE, THE
Ravins, Mava
BLOOD & DONUTS
Razmofsky, Peter
TAILS YOU LIVE, HEADS YOU'RE DEAD
Reiss, Ron
TWISTER
Reynolds-Wasco, Sandy
BOTTLE ROCKET
Rivas, Jaime
ARRIVAL, THE
Robbins, Wendy
JOHNNY SHORTWAVE
Roberts, Jane
HEDD WYNN
Rodarte, Cecelia
BEASTMASTER 3: THE EYE OF BRAXUS
Rollins, Leslie E.
FIRST WIVES CLUB, THE
Rosemarin, Hilton
BOGUS
GHOST AND THE DARKNESS, THE
Rosenkranz, Roland
NATIONAL LAMPOON'S FAVORITE DEADLY SINS
Roux, Emelia
REDEMPTION: KICKBOXER 5
Rouxel, Jacques
HORSEMAN ON THE ROOF
Rubino, Beth
SLEEPERS
Samson, Jim
DUNSTON CHECKS IN
Sanchez, Jorge Lara
SOLO
Savage, Sue
TUSKEGEE AIRMEN, THE
Schlesinger, David
FLIPPER
Schneider, Crista
ED
Schutt, Debra
BED OF ROSES
Scoppa Jr., Justin
FAITHFUL
Scott, Carolyn
SOME MOTHER'S SON
Scott, Jeanette
WAR AT HOME, THE
Seckinger, Caroline
ANGELA
Seirton, Michael
DIABOLIQUE
Seitz, Betrand
VISITORS, THE
Serdena, Gene
CHAIN REACTION
2 DAYS IN THE VALLEY
Sessions, Lisa K.
4 TALES OF 2 CITIES
Sharp, Melanie
FATALLY YOURS
Sherrill, Dan
SAWBONES
Shewchuk, Steven
TWO IF BY SEA
Siegel, Yvette
FEELING MINNESOTA
Sigmond, Shana
WILD SIDE
Sim, Gordon
HARRIET THE SPY
Simmonet, Jean-Michel
CHASING BUTTERFLIES
Simpson, Rick
EVENING STAR, THE
SGT. BILKO
Slagter, Cynthia Anne
BLACK SCORPION
Sleiter, Cinzia
STEALING BEAUTY
Spheeris, Linda
BLACK SHEEP
HOUSE ARREST
Stacy, Mary
FLED
Steinberg, Sue L.
POISON IVY 2: LILY
Strack, Eva
YANKEE ZULU
Stull, Christopher
MAN WITH THE PERFECT SWING, THE
Suchatanont, Kuladee "Gai"
QUEST, THE
Sullivan, Kate
KAZAAM
Sutton, Linda Lee
DOWN, OUT AND DANGEROUS
Tapper, Amy
FLIRT
Taylor, Michael
LONG KISS GOODNIGHT, THE
Turk, Pamela
MIRROR HAS TWO FACES, THE
Turlure, Philippe
EVITA
Vail, Bill
RIDERS OF THE PURPLE SAGE
Ventenilla, Mario R.
SEARCH FOR ONE-EYE JIMMY, THE
Verheyen, Marieken
CROCODILES IN AMSTERDAM
Virgin, Karen
CURDLED
Wakefield, Simon
MUPPET TREASURE ISLAND
Wang Zesheng
BLUSH
Ward, Barbard
UNHOOK THE STARS
Wargo, Michael
DEAD TO RIGHTS
Weathered, Paul R.
GIRL 6
Webb, Mark Andrew
FOR THE MOMENT
Wells, Amy
PEOPLE VS. LARRY FLYNT, THE
PHANTOM, THE
Whateley, Totty
EMMA
Wheeler, C. Ford
FLIRTING WITH DISASTER
PROPRIETOR, THE
Wiesel, Karin
JOE'S APARTMENT
Wilcox, Elizabeth
UNFORGETTABLE
Wilkinson, Mary
VIRUS
Winter, Alyssa
EXTREME MEASURES
Woollard, Joanne
101 DALMATIANS
Worth, Lea
RACE THE SUN
Wright, Terri L.
WHOLE WIDE WORLD, THE
Xie Xinsheng
BLUSH
Yatsko, Kate
PALLBEARER, THE
Zisswiller, Maurice
SUITE 16
Zucker, Harriet
SHE'S THE ONE
Zuleta, Lily
ANIMAL INSTINCTS III: THE SEDUCTRESS

SOUND

Aaron, Steve
FLIPPER
Ahmadi, Said
WHITE BALLOON, THE
Ailetcher, Jon
BAJA
FAST MONEY
Alberghini, Roberto
MIND RIPPER
Alderton, Chris
TWO FRIENDS
Alexander, Tara
SANTA CLAWS
Allen, David
RASPUTIN
Allen, Mark
TWO-BITS & PEPPER
Alper, Gary
EVERYONE SAYS I LOVE YOU
Alverez, David
FAR HARBOR
Anderson, Arnold
MAN OF THE YEAR
Anderson Jr., Robert
CHAIN REACTION
SGT. BILKO
Anderson, Richard L.
DAYLIGHT
Andres, John
LINE KING: THE AL HIRSCHFELD STORY, THE
Andrianos, Agamemnon
JACK
JAMES AND THE GIANT PEACH

Archer, Lee
BEASTMASTER 3: THE EYE OF BRAXUS
Arnardi, Vincent
FRANCOIS TRUFFAUT: STOLEN PORTRAITS
LITTLE INDIAN, BIG CITY
Arnold, Doug
FOREST WARRIOR
Arroyo, Antonio
SILENCE OF NETO, THE
SYNTHETIC PLEASURES
Asman, Bub
ERASER
Astakhov, Nikolay
CHEKIST, THE
Attal, Remy
MA SAISON PREFEREE
Aubry, Kim
THEREMIN: AN ELECTRONIC ODYSSEY
Axtell, Douglas
EVENING STAR, THE
SUNCHASER
TRUTH ABOUT CATS AND DOGS, THE
Bacca, Paul
PHAT BEACH
Bacigalupe, Maria Teresa
JOHNNY 100 PESOS
Bailey, Greg
MESSAGE TO LOVE: THE ISLE OF WIGHT FESTIVAL
Bailey, Ronald
BUTTERFLY KISS
PARIS WAS A WOMAN
Baker, Beau
PERSONAL JOURNEY WITH MARTIN SCORSESE THROUGH AMERICAN MOVIES, A
Barbeau, Philippe
MICROCOSMOS
Barnett, Charles
HEADLESS BODY IN TOPLESS BAR
Barnett, Joe
CARNOSAUR 3: PRIMAL SPECIES
Barosky, Michael
CRUCIBLE, THE
PALLBEARER, THE
Bates, Jonathan
IN LOVE AND WAR
Batut, Eric J.
ALASKA
FEAR
SURGEON, THE
UNFORGETTABLE
Beckett, Ray
LAND AND FREEDOM
Beemer, Bob
INDEPENDENCE DAY
Behlmer, Anna
EVITA
Bender, Lon E.
COURAGE UNDER FIRE
Benoit, Marc
WHITE TIGER
Benson, John
BEAVIS AND BUTT-HEAD DO AMERICA
Bentley, Peter
BODY COUNT
Benton, Bill W.
INDEPENDENCE DAY
Berger, Mark
ENGLISH PATIENT, THE
Berman, Sandy
MULTIPLICITY
Bertrand, Claude
CELESTIAL CLOCKWORK
Bindel, Tim
MR. STITCH
Birnbaum, Richard
HARVEST OF FIRE
Black, Trevor
DOWN, OUT AND DANGEROUS
Blackwell, Charles
NICO ICON
Blank, Donny
BOY CALLED HATE, A
Boisseau, Martin
GUIMBA THE TYRANT
Bombey, Dirk
ANTONIA'S LINE
SUITE 16
Borcoman, Tiberiu
JOSH KIRBY . . . TIME WARRIOR!: EGGS FROM 70,000,000 B.C.
JOSH KIRBY . . . TIME WARRIOR!: JOURNEY TO THE MAGIC CAVERN
JOSH KIRBY . . . TIME WARRIOR!: TRAPPED ON TOY WORLD
MAGIC IN THE MIRROR
Borrero, Felipe
BOUND
SUNSET PARK
Boullieme, Nadine
JOHNNY 100 PESOS
Boyes, Christopher
ERASER
ROCK, THE
Boyle, Thomas P.
BLACK SCORPION
SAWBONES
TOO FAST, TOO YOUNG
Brasher, John
SOMETIMES THEY COME BACK . . . AGAIN
WITHIN THE ROCK
Braun, Arnold
HOURGLASS
VIRTUAL COMBAT
Bridgeman, Hank
CHAMPAGNE SAFARI, THE
Brisseau, Daniel
MR. STITCH
SUITE 16
Brown, Lance
KAZAAM
WHOLE WIDE WORLD, THE
Brownrigg, Stacy
BOTTLE ROCKET
Bruce, Raoul A.
PERSONAL JOURNEY WITH MARTIN SCORSESE THROUGH AMERICAN MOVIES, A
Buch, Chuck
IT CAME FROM OUTER SPACE II
Buchanan, Jack
MAN IN THE ATTIC, THE
Buckle, Rudi
AUGUST
Burton, Willie
BLACK SHEEP
Butler, William
MATERNAL INSTINCTS
Butterworth, Syd
SPIDER & ROSE
Byer, Allan
BASQUIAT
FARGO
GIRL 6
Cameron, Doug
CLUBHOUSE DETECTIVES
Cannella, Tony
SHOOTFIGHTER 2: KILL OR BE KILLED!
Cantamessa, Gene
BIRDCAGE, THE
Cantamessa, Steve
PRIMAL FEAR
Carben, Rainer
KASPAR HAUSER
Carden, Carl
SHOOTFIGHTER 2: KILL OR BE KILLED!
TOLLBOOTH
Carmona, Alejandra
FATE
Carpenter, Chris
INDEPENDENCE DAY
Carwardine, Bruce
BOGUS
EXTREME MEASURES
KIDS IN THE HALL: BRAIN CANDY
Causey, Thomas
JOHN CARPENTER'S ESCAPE FROM L.A.
LARGER THAN LIFE
STAR TREK: FIRST CONTACT
Cerda, Sophia
EYE OF VICHY, THE
Chandler, Michael
KINGPIN
Chapman, Gibbs
SONIC OUTLAWS
Chen Weixiong
CHUNGKING EXPRESS
Chevallier, Eric
HORSEMAN ON THE ROOF
Child, Jeremy
COLD LIGHT OF DAY
Chin, Sarah
PERSONAL JOURNEY WITH MARTIN SCORSESE THROUGH AMERICAN MOVIES, A
Chornow, David
GREAT WHITE HYPE, THE
Choudhury, Gautam K.
SMALL WONDERS
Coffey, Linda
PERSONAL JOURNEY WITH MARTIN SCORSESE THROUGH AMERICAN MOVIES, A
Cooney, Tim
D3: THE MIGHTY DUCKS
Cottance, Bruno
HATE
Crain, Brian
WHITE WOLVES II: LEGEND OF THE WILD
Cranston, Lamont
ORIGINAL SINS
Creagh, Gethin
LOADED
Cridlin, Paul
WAR OF THE BUTTONS, THE
Cristianini, Jacqueline
MIND RIPPER
Crozier, David
MISSION: IMPOSSIBLE
TWELFTH NIGHT
Cunningham, Garry
COLONY, THE
FIRST KID
Dallimonti, Andrea
CEMETERY MAN
Dalmasso, Dominique
HATE
Daly, Bill
FAITHFUL
MISSING PIECES
Daniel, David O.
CARRIED AWAY
PAINTED HERO
Daniell, Roger
SPACE JAM
David, Israel
UNDER THE DOMIM TREE
Davies, Malcolm
GRIM

Davis, Dane
BOUND
Davis, Richard
JUST YOUR LUCK
Dawson, Marcus
MIRROR, MIRROR III: THE VOYEUR
Day, Brian
TAILS YOU LIVE, HEADS YOU'RE DEAD
Day, Bryan
MRS. MUNCK
WHARF RAT, THE
De Aguirre, Marcos
JOHNNY 100 PESOS
de la Fuente, Salvador
SOLO
Deaf by Dawn
EVIL ED
Defever, Gene
WHEN WE WERE KINGS
Dehr, Jim
LIVE NUDE GIRLS
Dejbodi, Mehdi
WHITE BALLOON, THE
Deschaine, Robert
ALL DOGS GO TO HEAVEN 2
Devenney, Mary Jo
UNDER THE HULA MOON
Devlin, Peter
CURDLED
Devulder, Eric
MAN BY THE SHORE, THE
Dewan, Matthew
YOU'LL NEVER MAKE LOVE IN THIS TOWN AGAIN
Diaz, Jose Luis
OF LOVE AND SHADOWS
Dior, Rick
GIRLFRIENDS
MESSAGE TO LOVE: THE ISLE OF WIGHT FESTIVAL
DiSimon, Giovanni
MAN OF THE YEAR
WEEKEND IN THE COUNTRY, A
Doc
EVIL ED
Doheny, Roberta
PRE-MADONNAS
Dolenz, Richard
SANDMAN, THE
Doni, Alberto
SONS OF TRINITY
Duke, Margaret
GALAXIES ARE COLLIDING
Dweck, Ezra
WITHIN THE ROCK
Eber, Robert
ERASER
FOR BETTER OR WORSE
GHOSTS OF MISSISSIPPI
Edwards, Mark
WIND IN THE WILLOWS, THE
Edwards, Robert
ANNE FRANK REMEMBERED
Einolf, James
PHOENIX
TAKEOVER, THE
VIRTUAL COMBAT
Ellis, Mary H.
FLED
Embry, Henry
ELECTRA
Espinoza, Roberto
JOHNNY 100 PESOS
Evans, Yekaterina
CHASING BUTTERFLIES
Farner, Dirk
HEIDI FLEISS HOLLYWOOD MADAM
Faruolo, Carlos
MOUTH TO MOUTH
Fasal, John
SURGEON, THE
Felburg, Craig
BAD LOVE
Fiege, William M.
BIO-DOME
HEIDI CHRONICLES, THE
Flageollet, William
MADAME BUTTERFLY
Flick, Stephen Hunter
MAD DOG TIME
Flick, William
PERSONAL JOURNEY WITH MARTIN SCORSESE THROUGH AMERICAN MOVIES, A
Foglia, Joe
MADDENING, THE
SUBSTITUTE, THE
Fowler, Mick E.
SHARON'S SECRET
Francis, Kirk
MR. HOLLAND'S OPUS
TIN CUP
Frankley, Cameron
HARRIET THE SPY
Friedgen, Mark
CHAMELEON
Frisk, Curt
CELTIC PRIDE
NORMAL LIFE
Gabor, Craig
MURDERED INNOCENCE
Galt, Nigel
PASSION OF DARKLY NOON, THE
Gamet, Pierre
HORSEMAN ON THE ROOF
MACHINE, THE
TWO MUCH
Ganton, Douglas
FLY AWAY HOME
GETTING AWAY WITH MURDER
LONG KISS GOODNIGHT, THE
Garcia, Jose Antonio
CHAMBER, THE
NUTTY PROFESSOR, THE
Garcia, Vince
BARB WIRE
Garfield, Hank
HIGH SCHOOL HIGH
LAST DANCE
MY FELLOW AMERICANS
Gauthier, Glen
HARRIET THE SPY
MAXIMUM RISK
TWO IF BY SEA
Geesin, Ron
MESSAGE TO LOVE: THE ISLE OF WIGHT FESTIVAL
Geisinger, Joe
CROW: CITY OF ANGELS, THE
Gerhardt, Alan
REDEMPTION: KICKBOXER 5
Gervais, Didier
MADAME BUTTERFLY
Gilad, Chaim
DARKMAN III: DIE DARKMAN DIE
Gitman, Mike
SOME FOLKS CALL IT A SLING BLADE
Glossop, Peter
HAMLET
INSTITUTE BENJAMENTA
MIDWINTER'S TALE, A
PORTRAIT OF A LADY, THE
Goldstein, Daniel
BATON ROUGE
Goldstein, Jacob
ED
Gomillion, Tim
SUNSET PARK
Gonzalez, Freddy
JOHNNY 100 PESOS
Gooch, Don
BIG SQUEEZE, THE
Goodman, Richard
SCREAM
Granel, Stephanie
MADAME BUTTERFLY
Green, Andy
THEREMIN: AN ELECTRONIC ODYSSEY
Greenhorn, Jim
COLD COMFORT FARM
TWO DEATHS
Griffith, Patrick M.
DEMOLITIONIST, THE
GLASS CAGE, THE
HEAD OF THE FAMILY
LITTLE WITCHES
ZARKORR! THE INVADER
Griffiths, Frank
RED SCORPION 2
Groult, Francois
SOMEONE ELSE'S AMERICA
Gunter, Chat
BEST OF THE BEST 3: NO TURNING BACK
Guske, Michael
YOU'LL NEVER MAKE LOVE IN THIS TOWN AGAIN
Gynn, Kip
UNDERTOW
Halaby, John R.F.
FEMALIEN
WATCH ME
Halbert, Peter
PUBLIC ENEMIES
Halbert, Stephen
DELTA OF VENUS
GRACE OF MY HEART
WOMAN UNDONE, A
Hales, John
ROLLING STONES ROCK-AND-ROLL CIRCUS, THE
Hall, Mike
TWO-BITS & PEPPER
Hamza, Cameron
ONE NIGHT STAND
SOMETIMES THEY COME BACK . . . AGAIN
Happ, Simon
MAYBE . . . MAYBE NOT
Harpaz, Chen
EVERYTHING RELATIVE
Harris, Mark
COURAGE UNDER FIRE
Haststone, Graham V.
FLOWER OF MY SECRET, THE
Hawkins, Jim
FOXFIRE
Hayder, Hamo
KASPAR HAUSER
Haywood, Gareth
MESSAGE TO LOVE: THE ISLE OF WIGHT FESTIVAL
Hazanavicius, Claude
MOTHER NIGHT
Hazen, John
CURTIS'S CHARM
Hedges, Michael
LOADED
Hedin, Wendy
FLIRTING WITH DISASTER
Hennequin, Dominique
FRENCH TWIST
RIDICULE
Hennessy, Karla
DEATH ARTIST, THE

Henrici, Peter
HALFMOON
Heywood, Phil
MAHJONG
Hidderley, Thomas
HOMECOMING
LEGEND OF GATOR FACE, THE
ONE FINE DAY
TIME TO KILL, A
Hliddal, Peter
ONE FINE DAY
TIME TO KILL, A
WHEN WE WERE KINGS
Hodge, Greg
GIRLFRIENDS
Holding, Mark
MADAGASCAR SKIN
Honda, Yasunori
ROUJIN-Z
Horgan, Kieran
MICHAEL COLLINS
MOLL FLANDERS
Howe, Matthew
ORIGINAL SINS
Howell, Lee
ADRENALIN: FEAR THE RUSH
Howell-Thornhill, Rosa
ASSOCIATE, THE
FUNERAL, THE
JOE'S APARTMENT
Hoylman, Walter
DEATH BENEFIT
Hsin Chiang-sheng
VIVE L'AMOUR
Hu Ding-yi
VIVE L'AMOUR
Hudson, Linden
MAN WITH THE PERFECT SWING, THE
Hu Dongzhi
BLACK MOUNTAIN
Hughesdon, Fred
ROLLING STONES ROCK-AND-ROLL CIRCUS, THE
Humphreys, Gerry
IN LOVE AND WAR
Hunt, Charles R.
GIRLS TOWN
Husby, David
BAD MOON
FOR THE MOMENT
Hutcherson, Marty
SOMETIMES THEY COME BACK . . . AGAIN
WITHIN THE ROCK
Iorillo, Victor
KAZAAM
Jackson, Pat
CELLULOID CLOSET, THE
Jackson, Robert
AMERICAN BUFFALO
Jacobsson, Anders
EVIL ED
Janiger, Robert
KAZAAM
John, David
WAR OF THE BUTTONS, THE
Johnson, Jon
KINGPIN
Johnson, Leon
STAND OFF, THE
Johnson, Randall
IT'S MY PARTY
Johnson-Porter, Dana
ALL DOGS GO TO HEAVEN 2
Joseph, Adam
PUBLIC ACCESS
Judkins, Fred
HOMEWARD BOUND II: LOST IN SAN FRANCISCO
Judkins, Ronald
AMERICAN BUFFALO
PHENOMENON
Kaiser, Reinhold
BROTHER OF SLEEP
Kaplan, William B.
DOWN PERISCOPE
FAN, THE
Karas, Michael
PARADISE LOST: THE CHILD MURDERS AT ROBIN HOOD HILLS
Karjalainen, Pekka
CONDITION RED
Karp, Judy
NATIONAL LAMPOON'S FAVORITE DEADLY SINS
Kaye, Simon
GHOST AND THE DARKNESS, THE
IN LOVE AND WAR
Kazarian, Richard
WOLVES, THE
Kelly, Charles
DONOR UNKNOWN
Kelson, David
BOYS
MATILDA
Kennedy, Andy
PROTEUS
Kessel, Jay
SEARCH FOR ONE-EYE JIMMY, THE
King, Clark David
DUNSTON CHECKS IN
EXECUTIVE DECISION
Kirschner, David
HOUSE ARREST
TO GILLIAN ON HER 37TH BIRTHDAY
Kitinski, Gabriel
MIRROR, MIRROR III: THE VOYEUR
Kitinski, Nick
MIRROR, MIRROR III: THE VOYEUR
Kjartansson, Kjartan
COLD FEVER
Konken, Stephan
HALFMOON
Kortwich, Gunther
SHADOW OF ANGELS
Koven, Gus
GIRLS TOWN
Kozy, William
MODERN AFFAIR, A
Krah, Regina
FATE
Kramer, Louis
SMALL FACES
Kremer, Tony
MR. ICE CREAM MAN
Kuchenbecker, Eckhard
YOUNG POISONER'S HANDBOOK, THE
Kunej, Damjan
PREDICTIONS OF FIRE
Kunin, Drew
DEAD MAN
Kurland, Peter
FIRST WIVES CLUB, THE
Kushner, Jeff
ORIGINAL SINS
SLING BLADE
Lacroix, Michael
WHERE'S THE MONEY, NOREEN?
Laforce, Jean-Pierre
LES VOLEURS
Laine, Paul
RIDICULE
Lamps, Gerard
MACHINE, THE
Landaker, Gregg
TWISTER
Laneri, Stephen
CHILDREN OF FURY
Lang, John
RUDE
Langevin, Owen
STUPIDS, THE
Lanhout, Erik
CROCODILES IN AMSTERDAM
Lanza, Mark A.
PUBLIC ACCESS
Larrea, Robert Taz
FATALLY YOURS
GIRLS TOWN
I SHOT ANDY WARHOL
Lax, Mike
MESSAGE TO LOVE: THE ISLE OF WIGHT FESTIVAL
Lay, James
MUTANT MAN
Lazarowitz, Les
JUROR, THE
PREACHER'S WIFE, THE
Le Roux, Jean-Philippe
ADVENTURES OF PINOCCHIO, THE
Ledford, Paul
SLING BLADE
Lee, David
GETTING AWAY WITH MURDER
ISLAND OF DR. MOREAU, THE
KISSINGER AND NIXON
RACE THE SUN
Lenoir, Pierre
NELLY AND MONSIEUR ARNAUD
Leroux, Bernard
MICROCOSMOS
VISITORS, THE
Level, Guy
MADAME BUTTERFLY
Levy, Jerome
VISITORS, THE
Liang Da
CHUNGKING EXPRESS
Liang Lizhi
CHUNGKING EXPRESS
Libby, Shirley
ROAD TO GALVESTON, THE
Lightstone, Richard
MRS. WINTERBOURNE
SET IT OFF
Lindauer, Jack
MAN OF THE YEAR
Lindfors, Kauko
CONDITION RED
Lindsay, Peter
JOSEPH CONRAD'S THE SECRET AGENT
LOADED
MUPPET TREASURE ISLAND
Linkow, Daryl
AMERICAN STRAYS
Litecky, Bruce
MAXIMUM RISK
Livecchi, Al
PARIS WAS A WOMAN
Lockett, Tommy
LIFEFORM
Lockman, Ed
WHEN WE WERE KINGS
Loffredi, Massimo
STAR MAKER, THE
Long, Ron
AMERICAN STRAYS
Lonsdale, Michael
CATWALK
Loo, Ao
IRON EAGLE IV
OPEN SEASON

Lopez, Art
CHAMPAGNE SAFARI, THE
FRISK
WITCHCRAFT: SALEM'S GHOST
Lorrain, Pierre
LITTLE INDIAN, BIG CITY
Loublier, Jean-Paul
DAENS
NELLY AND MONSIEUR ARNAUD
Louw, Nico
LIVE WIRE: HUMAN TIMEBOMB
TERMINAL IMPACT
Loyola, Gloria
JOHNNY 100 PESOS
Lynn, John
BEAVIS AND BUTT-HEAD DO AMERICA
Maayan, Yehuda
BLACK DAY BLUE NIGHT
PHARAOH'S ARMY
MacMillan, David
HOUSE ARREST
Madigan, David
ALEX
Magal, Itzhak "Ike"
MOTHER
RIDERS OF THE PURPLE SAGE
Maitland, Dennis
DIABOLIQUE
MARS ATTACKS!
Maitland Sr., Dennis L.
MULTIPLICITY
Maitland, Tod A.
CITY HALL
SLEEPERS
Manton, Richard
CAPTIVES
Marcuse, Gary
CHAMPAGNE SAFARI, THE
Markovsky, Dessie
TO GILLIAN ON HER 37TH BIRTHDAY
Martinez, Juan Carlos
WIFE, THE
Maslow, Steve
TWISTER
Mateos, Javier
AVENTURERA
Mather, Tom
SUGARTIME
Matheson, Bryan
BLONDES HAVE MORE GUNS
Matthews, Don H.
LAST SUPPER, THE
Matthews, Jeff
HEDD WYNN
McCart, Kathleen
MULHOLLAND FALLS
McDuffie, Mike
MESSAGE TO LOVE: THE ISLE OF WIGHT FESTIVAL
McKay, John
GIRLFRIENDS
McLaughlin, Jan
HEAVY
McMillan, Bill
BLOODKNOT
McNabb, Mark Hopkins
MR. WRONG
MOTHER'S PRAYER, A
Meagher, Jay
STEPHEN KING'S THINNER
Megill, John
TRACKS OF A KILLER
Meiselmann, Peter
DOGFIGHTERS, THE
LOW LIFE, THE
NIGHT OF THE SCARECROW
SOME FOLKS CALL IT A SLING BLADE
Melson, Mac
CHILDREN OF THE CORN: THE GATHERING
Menz, Bernardo
FLOWER OF MY SECRET, THE
Michael, Danny
BED OF ROSES
MARVIN'S ROOM
RANSOM
Midgley, John
BEAUTIFUL THING
HIDDEN ASSASSIN
Miller, Tony
WHEN WE WERE KINGS
Mitchell, Patrick
BEYOND DESIRE
Mitchison, Clive
ROUJIN-Z
Molinari, David
THEY BITE
Monahan, Daniel D.
DESIRE
FIST OF THE NORTH STAR
HOSTILE INTENTIONS
ONE MAN'S JUSTICE
SERIAL KILLER
Moore, Michael
FULL BODY MASSAGE
STREETCAR NAMED DESIRE, A
Moran, Andrew
GIRLFRIENDS
Morelle, Henri
DAENS
Morse, Richard
MAN WITH A PLAN
Mortazavi, Mojtaba
WHITE BALLOON, THE
Moser, Stuart
CAPTIVES
Moss, Oliver
GET ON THE BUS
SUGARTIME
Mugel, Jean-Paul
LES VOLEURS
MA SAISON PREFEREE
MONSTER, THE
Munro, Chris
EMMA
Murch, Walter
ENGLISH PATIENT, THE
Murphy, Jennifer
WAR AT HOME, THE
Murray, Alan Robert
ERASER
Musu, Francois
NEW LIFE, A
Naunas, Thomas A.
MYSTERY SCIENCE THEATER 3000: THE MOVIE
Nelson, Andy
EVITA
Nelson, Steve
FEELING MINNESOTA
Nelson, Tom
BEFORE AND AFTER
EXTREME MEASURES
MIRROR HAS TWO FACES, THE
Newman, Chris
ENGLISH PATIENT, THE
PEOPLE VS. LARRY FLYNT, THE
Nichol, Richard
SCREAMERS
Nicolson, Colin
ANGELS AND INSECTS
SHOPPING
TRAINSPOTTING
Nielsen, Scott
LINE KING: THE AL HIRSCHFELD STORY, THE
Novick, Ed
RICH MAN'S WIFE, THE
O'Connell, Kevin
ROCK, THE
TWISTER
O'Mara, T.J.
SHE'S THE ONE
Obermeyer, David
EVIL HAS A FACE
Oddo, J. Paul
SKIN
Orloff, Lee
LAST MAN STANDING
Ornitz, Kim
DEAD TO RIGHTS
HEAVEN'S PRISONERS
IMMORTALS, THE
MOTHER
RAVENHAWK
2 DAYS IN THE VALLEY
Osmo, Ben
PHANTOM, THE
Oswin, Martin
MAHJONG
Palmieri, Riccardo
OUTRAGE
Pardula, Rolf
FLIRTING WITH DISASTER
Parker, David
ENGLISH PATIENT, THE
Patillo, Mike
ONCE UPON A TIME . . . WHEN WE WERE COLORED
Patrick, Benjamin
AMERICAN STRAYS
WILD SIDE
Patsos, Julia
MIRROR HAS TWO FACES, THE
Patterson, Geoffrey
LETTER TO MY KILLER
MICHAEL
NECRONOMICON: BOOK OF THE DEAD
TWISTER
Patterson, Jay
CITIZEN RUTH
Patton, Rick
HAPPY GILMORE
Paturet, Mark
WHEN WE WERE KINGS
Paul, Tom
PERSONAL JOURNEY WITH MARTIN SCORSESE THROUGH AMERICAN MOVIES, A
WIFE, THE
Pavlin, Boris
PREDICTIONS OF FIRE
Pearce, Steuart
SPITFIRE GRILL, THE
Peek, Hammond
FRIGHTENERS, THE
Perreault, Andre
LAZARUS MAN, THE
Phillips, Mark
YANKEE ZULU
Pi, Rudy
COURAGE UNDER FIRE
Plain, Andrew
SPIDER & ROSE
Poirier, Laurent
THREE LIVES AND ONLY ONE DEATH
Poirier, Sylvia
CHAMPAGNE SAFARI, THE
Popovic, Sergei
WHISPERING, THE
Pospisil, John
JOHN CARPENTER'S ESCAPE FROM L.A.
Post, Wim
ANTONIA'S LINE

Powell, Daryl
HOW THE WEST WAS FUN
Powers, David
WALKING AND TALKING
Prentice, Henry
WARHEAD
Price, Matthew
LOTTO LAND
Primot, Alain
HORSEMAN ON THE ROOF
Pritchett, John Patrick
KANSAS CITY
LONE JUSTICE: SHOWDOWN AT PLUM CREEK
THAT THING YOU DO!
TRIGGER EFFECT, THE
Pullman, Jeff
FLIRT
Quaglio, Laurent
MICROCOSMOS
Raguseo, Angelo
CEMETERY MAN
Rangon, Joel
GUIMBA THE TYRANT
Ratajczak, Paul
BIG SQUEEZE, THE
LIFEFORM
PAINTED HERO
Rauchsberg, Matt
OVER THE WIRE
Raves, Phillip
NIGHT OF THE SCARECROW
Razpopov, Emile
IT'S MY PARTY
TO GILLIAN ON HER 37TH BIRTHDAY
Reinhardt, Bill
ANIMAL INSTINCTS III: THE SEDUCTRESS
BODY OF INFLUENCE 2
Reti, Janos
OUTPOST, THE
Reyes, Ramon
MIDNIGHT DANCERS
Ribier, Pascal
RENDEZVOUS IN PARIS
Richards, Colin
MESSAGE TO LOVE: THE ISLE OF WIGHT FESTIVAL
Richards, George
SECRETS & LIES
Richardson, Tim
GIRL FROM MARS, THE
Ritchie, D. J.
AMANDA AND THE ALIEN
DEAD WEEKEND
OUT THERE
Ritchie, Gary
MULHOLLAND FALLS
Robbins, Bill
BLACK SCORPION
VENUS RISING
Robinson, Buck
CARNOSAUR 3: PRIMAL SPECIES
Rogers, Steve
SWEET NOTHING
Romano, Joe
LOVE IS ALL THERE IS
Ronne, David
BROKEN ARROW
SPY HARD
Rosin, Urmas
LOSING CHASE
Rousseau, Gerard
THREE LIVES AND ONLY ONE DEATH
Rousseau, Patrick
HOLLOW POINT
Rowell, Jack
MAN WITH A PLAN
Rozett, Mark
HEIDI FLEISS HOLLYWOOD MADAM
Rualt, Jean-Charles
VISITORS, THE
Rubay, Geoff
DRAGONHEART
Rue, Edward Earl
DANGEROUS PASSION
Russell, Greg P.
ROCK, THE
Russell, Sam
LINE KING: THE AL HIRSCHFELD STORY, THE
Rydstrom, Gary
JAMES AND THE GIANT PEACH
Sabat, James J.
I'M NOT RAPPAPORT
STRIPTEASE
Sain, Didier
PROPRIETOR, THE
Sales, Leander
DON'T LET YOUR MEAT LOAF
Salkin, Douglas
FEMALIEN
Samuels, Alan B.
DARK SECRETS
SWINGERS
Sanchez, Michael
OPEN SEASON
Sands, Kevin
PORTRAITS OF A KILLER
Sarokin, William
BIG NIGHT
Sartor, Max
JOHNNY SHORTWAVE
Sawade, Peter
CHAMPAGNE SAFARI, THE
Scaduto, Jeffrey W. "Spud"
POLYMORPH
Scharf, Larry
CHILDREN OF THE CORN: THE GATHERING
Schexnayder, Richard
LAWNMOWER MAN 2: BEYOND CYBERSPACE
RATTLED
Schiefelbein, John
TUNNEL VISION
Schliessler, Jochen
BREACH OF TRUST
Schneider, Peter
PALOOKAVILLE
Schroeder, Mark
RUMBLE IN THE BRONX
Scibelli, Ann
SET IT OFF
Segeler, Lothar
NICO ICON
Sephton, Robert L.
HOMEWARD BOUND II: LOST IN SAN FRANCISCO
Sharrock, Ivan
ENGLISH PATIENT, THE
MESSAGE TO LOVE: THE ISLE OF WIGHT FESTIVAL
STEALING BEAUTY
Shepard, Mike
NEUROSIA: 50 YEARS OF PERVERSITY
Shepard, Randal
WHEN WE WERE KINGS
Shepherd, Gary
SOME FOLKS CALL IT A SLING BLADE
Sheridan, Bob
WHISPERING, THE
Sigal, Matthew
DENISE CALLS UP
SYNTHETIC PLEASURES
Sigurdsson, Sigurdur
VIKING SAGAS, THE
Silviu, Camil
JOSH KIRBY . . . TIME WARRIOR!: EGGS FROM 70,000,000 B.C.
JOSH KIRBY . . . TIME WARRIOR!: JOURNEY TO THE MAGIC CAVERN
Simmons, Brian
CANTERVILLE GHOST, THE
SOME MOTHER'S SON
Sipos, Istvan
MAGIC HUNTER
Slinguff, Jim
TEXAS PAYBACK
Smith, David Ashley
ROLLING STONES ROCK-AND-ROLL CIRCUS, THE
Smith, J. Byron
ORIGINAL GANGSTAS
Smith, Joel E.
PINOCCHIO'S REVENGE
SHOWGIRL MURDERS, THE
Smith, Lee
PORTRAIT OF A LADY, THE
Smith, Phil
CRACKER: THE MADWOMAN IN THE ATTIC
Smith, William
CARNOSAUR 3: PRIMAL SPECIES
Smyles, Tony
DENTIST, THE
PINOCCHIO'S REVENGE
Snodgrass, Harry E.
FLIPPER
Sound Dimensions
BUGGED
Spiess, Raymond E.
SKYSCRAPER
Springman, Stefan
ANGELA
Stafeckis, Roger
RUMBLE IN THE BRONX
SABRINA, THE TEENAGE WITCH
Stambler, Bruce
GHOST AND THE DARKNESS, THE
Stavropulos, Jorge
SHADOW YOU SOON WILL BE, A
Stein, Jonathan "Earl"
KINGPIN
RIDERS OF THE PURPLE SAGE
UNHOOK THE STARS
Steinberg, Ricardo
BATON ROUGE
Stephenson, David
JANE EYRE
QUEST, THE
Stergar, Reinhard
DAYLIGHT
DRAGONHEART
TRUMAN
Steveman, Kaj
EVIL ED
Stevenson, Roger
BOY CALLED HATE, A
Stoll, Nelson
CABLE GUY, THE
Strauss, Irin
GIRLS TOWN
MANNY & LO
MERCY
Streit, Per
BREAKING THE WAVES
Stuebe, Jim
BULLETPROOF
CRAFT, THE
Susch, Eric
DESOLATION ANGELS
Sutton, Larry
BIG BULLY

CARPOOL
TALES FROM THE CRYPT PRESENTS BORDELLO OF BLOOD

Szabo, Scott
TEXAS CHAINSAW MASSACRE: THE NEXT GENERATION

Takahashi, Yoshiteru
SYNTHETIC PLEASURES

Tanaka, Kenji
GIRLFRIENDS

Tanenbaum, Jim
VERY BRADY SEQUEL, A

Tattersall, Jane
RUDE

Taylor, Christopher
BLACK ROSE OF HARLEM
UNKNOWN ORIGIN

Taylor, Marlowe
MONSTERSHOW

Taylor, Steve
WAVELENGTH

Taz, Rob
SEARCH FOR ONE-EYE JIMMY, THE

Tegelman, Jussi
FINAL EQUINOX, THE

Thabet, Faouzi
SILENCES OF THE PALACE, THE

Thai, Roland
TIME TO KILL, A

Thom, Randy
CHAIN REACTION

Thomasson, Jean-Bernard
LA CEREMONIE

Thomson, John J.
WHERE'S THE MONEY, NOREEN?

Thornton, James
BEAUTIFUL GIRLS
RUMPELSTILTSKIN

Tibbo, Stephen A.
LITTLE DEATH, THE
SAINTS AND SINNERS

Timan, Noah
GIRLS TOWN

Tipton, John
LINE KING: THE AL HIRSCHFELD STORY, THE

Tise, Edward
ENTERTAINING ANGELS: THE DOROTHY DAY STORY
EYE FOR AN EYE
GLIMMER MAN, THE

Toma, Pat
DON'T BE A MENACE TO SOUTH CENTRAL WHILE DRINKING YOUR JUICE IN THE HOOD
HARD JUSTICE

Tovsky, Bruce
ABUSE

Tracy, Brian
BODY COUNT

Trautman, Paul
PIG'S TALE, A

Trevis, Martin
JUDE

Tromer, Michael
OFF AND RUNNING

Trouette, Valerie
HATE

Tu Tu-chih
MAHJONG

Tukiendorf, Jens
NICO ICON

Tulli, Vincent
HATE

Tzouris, William
ED'S NEXT MOVE

Ulano, Mark
FROM DUSK TILL DAWN

Urmson, Paul
DOWN PERISCOPE

van Eijden, Roberto
COLD LIGHT OF DAY

Van Slyke, David F.
HARRIET THE SPY

Van Taylor, David
PERFECT CANDIDATE, A

Varga, Thomas
NEON BIBLE, THE

Villand, Claude
VISITORS, THE

Vionnet, Michel
SINGLE GIRL, A

Volonte, Tony
FROM THE JOURNALS OF JEAN SEBERG

Waddell, Rick
MAD DOG TIME
RAVENHAWK
TREMORS 2: AFTERSHOCKS

Waelder, David
FRIEND OF THE FAMILY 2
FUGITIVE RAGE

Wagner, David
POLYMORPH
SANDMAN, THE

Wakabayashi, Kazuhiro
GHOST IN THE SHELL

Wald, Robert Alan
GLIMMER MAN, THE
THIN LINE BETWEEN LOVE AND HATE, A

Wangler, Christian
SOMEONE ELSE'S AMERICA

Wannberg, Jeff
MR. STITCH

Wdowczak, Pawel
IF LUCY FELL
SUBSTANCE OF FIRE, THE

Webb, James E.
EDDIE

Webb Jr., James E.
DEAR GOD
MULHOLLAND FALLS

Weber, L. Mo
EDIE & PEN
MADDENING, THE
SOMETIMES THEY COME BACK . . . AGAIN
WITHIN THE ROCK
WOMAN UNDONE, A

Weir, Tom
FINAL EQUINOX, THE

Wells, Richard
WHEN WE WERE KINGS

Wester, Keith A.
ROCK, THE

Weston, Ken
EVITA
HAUNTED
JACK & SARAH
WHITE SQUALL

Wexler, Jeff
INDEPENDENCE DAY
JERRY MAGUIRE

Whitcher, Jeffrey
CARNOSAUR 3: PRIMAL SPECIES

White, Ed
FREEWAY
HELLRAISER: BLOODLINE
ONE GOOD TURN
RATTLED

White, Michael J.
GRIM

Whittaker, David A.
DAYLIGHT

Wiemer, Marshall
. . . AT FIRST SIGHT
CROSSCUT

Wilborn, Charles
UP CLOSE AND PERSONAL

Williams, Glenn
FAMILY THING, A

Willingham, Ken
LARRY MCMURTRY'S STREETS OF LAREDO

Wilson, Ian
PROTEUS

Wilson, Stuart
SOLITAIRE FOR TWO

Winter, Brent
SOUTH BEACH ACADEMY

Winter, Clive
LONE STAR
MARY REILLY
101 DALMATIANS

Wirtz, Aad
SOMEONE ELSE'S AMERICA

Wiseman, Frederick
LA COMEDIE-FRANCAISE OU L'AMOUR JOUE

Wlodarkiewicz, Mark Jan
FRISK

Wolfe, Alex
WELCOME TO THE DOLLHOUSE

Wood, Art
FINAL EQUINOX, THE

Woods, Craig
NATIONAL LAMPOON'S FAVORITE DEADLY SINS
POISON IVY 2: LILY

Woolfson, John
BLOOD & DONUTS

Woolfson, Robert
VIRUS

Wu Ling
BLUSH

Yaffe, David Barr
THIN LINE BETWEEN LOVE AND HATE, A

Yang Ching-an
VIVE L'AMOUR

Yang Jing-an
VIVE L'AMOUR

Yao, Guoqiang
STORY OF XINGHUA, THE

Yarkoni, Eli
DEADLY OUTBREAK

Yewdall, David Lewis
NECRONOMICON: BOOK OF THE DEAD

Yokomizo, Masatoshi
MABOROSI

Young, Rob
HOMEWARD BOUND II: LOST IN SAN FRANCISCO
WILLIAM SHAKESPEARE'S ROMEO + JULIET

Zahm, Barbara
PARIS WAS A WOMAN

Zaini, Kang Rizal
WITHOUT MERCY

Zampagni, Gianni
WHO KILLED PASOLINI?

Zappala, Joe
HARD JUSTICE
TREMORS 2: AFTERSHOCKS

Zarantash, Shane
WHEN WE WERE KINGS

Zeigermann, Volker
HALFMOON

Zhang, Ye
MUTANT MAN

SOURCE AUTHORS

Abrahams, Peter
FAN, THE

Allard, Harry
STUPIDS, THE
Allende, Isabel
OF LOVE AND SHADOWS
Almagor, Gila
UNDER THE DOMIM TREE
Anderson, Kurt
DEAD COLD
Angelou, Maya
AMERICA'S DREAM
Apatow, Judd
CELTIC PRIDE
Aramaki, Yoshio
BIG WARS
Archie Comics
SABRINA, THE TEENAGE WITCH
Armstrong, Mike
TWO IF BY SEA
Auerbach, Gary
JUST YOUR LUCK
Austen, Jane
EMMA
Avery, Tex
SPACE JAM
Baitz, Jon Robin
SUBSTANCE OF FIRE, THE
Band, Charles
BACKLASH: OBLIVION 2
Barboni, Marcotullio
SONS OF TRINITY
Barish, Leora
VENUS RISING
Barr, James O.
CROW: CITY OF ANGELS, THE
Bean, Henry
VENUS RISING
Belasco, David
MADAME BUTTERFLY
Bell, Dan
SHOT, THE
Belletto, Rene
MACHINE, THE
Bend Team
EVIL ED
Bercovici, Leonardo
PREACHER'S WIFE, THE
Berman, Rick
STAR TREK: FIRST CONTACT
Bertolucci, Bernardo
STEALING BEAUTY
Blumenthal, Jason
BIO-DOME
Bodar, Adam
OUTPOST, THE
Boehm, Richard
DOGFIGHTERS, THE
Bookwalter, J.R.
POLYMORPH
SANDMAN, THE
Boon, Louis-Paul
DAENS
Bouileau, Pierre
DIABOLIQUE
Bowles, Paul
HALFMOON
Boyce, Frank Cottrell
BUTTERFLY KISS
Bradbury, Ray
IT CAME FROM OUTER SPACE II
Brady, Michael
TO GILLIAN ON HER 37TH BIRTHDAY
Braga, Brannon
STAR TREK: FIRST CONTACT
Brandes, Richard
DEAD COLD
Brandys, Kasimierz
MOTHER OF KINGS
Brill, Steven
D3: THE MIGHTY DUCKS
Bronte, Charlotte
JANE EYRE
Brosnan, John
PROTEUS
Brown, Rosellen
BEFORE AND AFTER
Browning, Ricou
FLIPPER
Bufford, Takashi
SET IT OFF
Buhai, Jeff
EDDIE
Burke, James Lee
HEAVEN'S PRISONERS
Burnford, Sheila
HOMEWARD BOUND II: LOST IN SAN FRANCISCO
Burnstein, Jim
D3: THE MIGHTY DUCKS
Byatt, A.S.
ANGELS AND INSECTS
Capote, Truman
GRASS HARP, THE
Carcaterra, Lorenzo
SLEEPERS
Carpenter, John
JOHN CARPENTER'S ESCAPE FROM L.A.
Carter, Bill
LATE SHIFT, THE
Castle, Nick
JOHN CARPENTER'S ESCAPE FROM L.A.
Cayatte, Andre
MIRROR HAS TWO FACES, THE
Cerami, Vincenzo
MONSTER, THE
Cercone, Janus
ED
Chaiken, Ilene
BARB WIRE
Charouhas, Elisa J.
PRE-MADONNAS
Chekhov, Anton
AUGUST
Chernuchin, Michael S.
ERASER
Ching, Lipo
WATCH ME
Clarke, John Henrik
AMERICA'S DREAM
Cole, Henry
SHAMELESS
Collodi, Carlo
ADVENTURES OF PINOCCHIO, THE
Connolly, John
EDDIE
Conrad, Joseph
JOSEPH CONRAD'S THE SECRET AGENT
Cook, Douglas
ROCK, THE
Cook, T. S.
TUSKEGEE AIRMEN, THE
Cooper, Dennis
FRISK
Coscarelli, Dan
BEASTMASTER 3: THE EYE OF BRAXUS
Cowden, Jack
FLIPPER
Custodio, Alvaro
AVENTURERA
Dahl, Roald
JAMES AND THE GIANT PEACH
MATILDA
Danon, Leslie
WHISPERING, THE
Danon, Marcello
BIRDCAGE, THE
Defoe, Daniel
MOLL FLANDERS
Densham, Pen
LARGER THAN LIFE
MOLL FLANDERS
Dexter, Pete
MULHOLLAND FALLS
Dick, Philip K.
SCREAMERS
Diehl, William
PRIMAL FEAR
Doel, Frances
BLACK ROSE OF HARLEM
Duberman, Martin
STONEWALL
Duder, Tessa
ALEX
Duff, James
WAR AT HOME, THE
Durrenmatt, Friedrich
COLD LIGHT OF DAY
Dux, Frank
QUEST, THE
Early, Jack
DEAD TO RIGHTS
Elfont, Harry
VERY BRADY SEQUEL, A
Enbom, John
LOW LIFE, THE
Essex, Harry
IT CAME FROM OUTER SPACE II
Falk, Lee
PHANTOM 2040: THE GHOST WHO WALKS
PHANTOM, THE
Fassbinder, Rainer Werner
SHADOW OF ANGELS
Feifer, Jerry
WITCHCRAFT: SALEM'S GHOST
Feynman, Richard
INFINITY
Filardi, Peter
CRAFT, THE
Fitzhugh, Louise
HARRIET THE SPY
Fontana, Randy
FEMALIEN
Foote, Horton
LILY DALE
Freleng, Friz
SPACE JAM
Freudberg, Judy
LAND BEFORE TIME IV: JOURNEY THROUGH THE MISTS
Friedberg, Jason
SPY HARD
Friedman, Josh
CHAIN REACTION
Fumimura, Sho
SANCTUARY: THE MOVIE
Gaines, William M.
TALES FROM THE CRYPT PRESENTS BORDELLO OF BLOOD
Gale, Bob
TALES FROM THE CRYPT PRESENTS BORDELLO OF BLOOD
Garcia, Pelayo
BITTER SUGAR
Gardner, Herb
I'M NOT RAPPAPORT
Gayton, Joe
BULLETPROOF
Geiss, Tony
LAND BEFORE TIME IV: JOURNEY THROUGH THE MISTS

Geller, Bruce
MISSION: IMPOSSIBLE
Gems, Jonathan
MARS ATTACKS!
Gibbons, Stella
COLD COMFORT FARM
Gilmore, Joseph
RATTLED
Giono, Jean
HORSEMAN ON THE ROOF
Giordana, Marco Tullio
WHO KILLED PASOLINI?
Glaser, Paul Michael
KAZAAM
Glatzer, Peter
GRAVE, THE
Goldsmith, Olivia
FIRST WIVES CLUB, THE
Goldstein, Mark
BACKLASH: OBLIVION 2
Grahame, Kenneth
WIND IN THE WILLOWS, THE
Green, George Dawes
JUROR, THE
Green, Walon
ERASER
Grey, Zane
RIDERS OF THE PURPLE SAGE
Griffin, Tom
BOYS NEXT DOOR, THE
Griffith, Charles B.
DEATH ARTIST, THE
NOT OF THIS EARTH
Grimm, The Brothers
RUMPELSTILTSKIN
Grisham, John
CHAMBER, THE
TIME TO KILL, A
Haft, Steven
LAST DANCE
Hanna, Mark
NOT OF THIS EARTH
Hara, Buronson
FIST OF THE NORTH STAR
Hara, Tetsuo
FIST OF THE NORTH STAR
Hardy, Thomas
JUDE
Harrison, Jim
CARRIED AWAY
Hart, Jacobsen
SWEEPER, THE
Hauty, Chris
HOMEWARD BOUND II: LOST IN SAN FRANCISCO
Heilbroner, David
DEATH BENEFIT
Heller, Milly
GIRLFRIENDS
Herbert, James
HAUNTED
Hiaasen, Carl
STRIPTEASE
Hicks, Scott
SHINE
Hickson, Julie
HOMEWARD BOUND II: LOST IN SAN FRANCISCO
Hiken, Nat
SGT. BILKO
Hill, Andrew
DANGEROUS PASSION
Hodgson, Joel
MYSTERY SCIENCE THEATER 3000: THE MOVIE
Holman, Michael Thomas
BASQUIAT
Holzer, Erika
EYE FOR AN EYE
Hopkins, John
DUNSTON CHECKS IN
Hugo, Victor
HUNCHBACK OF NOTRE DAME, THE
Hume, Cyril
RANSOM
Huston, Jimmy
WHARF RAT, THE
Ichaso, Leon
BITTER SUGAR
Ikegami, Ryoichi
SANCTUARY: THE MOVIE
Isaacson, Walter
KISSINGER AND NIXON
James, Henry
PORTRAIT OF A LADY, THE
Johnson, Kenneth
D3: THE MIGHTY DUCKS
Johnson, Patrick Read
DRAGONHEART
Jones, Chuck
SPACE JAM
Judge, Mike
BEAVIS AND BUTT-HEAD DO AMERICA
Kaplan, Deborah
VERY BRADY SEQUEL, A
Kaplan, Mindy
DEVOTION
Kikuchi, Hideyuki
WICKED CITY, THE
Kikushima, Ryuzo
LAST MAN STANDING
Kimatian, Paul
WHARF RAT, THE
King, Stephen
CHILDREN OF THE CORN: THE GATHERING
SOMETIMES THEY COME BACK . . . AGAIN
STEPHEN KING'S THINNER
Koepp, David
MISSION: IMPOSSIBLE
Konig, Ralf
MAYBE . . . MAYBE NOT
Koslow, Ron
LAST DANCE
Kurosawa, Akira
LAST MAN STANDING
Kurtzman, Anne
DEMOLITIONIST, THE
Kurtzman, Robert
DEMOLITIONIST, THE
FROM DUSK TILL DAWN
LaGravenese, Richard
MIRROR HAS TWO FACES, THE
Lange, David
SANDMAN, THE
Lawrence, Martin
THIN LINE BETWEEN LOVE AND HATE, A
Leary, Denis
TWO IF BY SEA
Leff, Adam
BIO-DOME
Leffland, Ella
MRS. MUNCK
Lembeck, Ann
TWO IF BY SEA
Lewis, Jerry
NUTTY PROFESSOR, THE
Leyland, Crash
FINAL CUT, THE
Lishman, Bill
FLY AWAY HOME
Logan, Bey
WHITE TIGER
Long, John L.
MADAME BUTTERFLY
Loucka, David
EDDIE
Lovecraft, H. P.
NECRONOMICON: BOOK OF THE DEAD
Ma Mei-ping
RUMBLE IN THE BRONX
Maibaum, Richard
RANSOM
Majewski, Lech
BASQUIAT
Mamet, David
AMERICAN BUFFALO
Mann, Farhad
LAWNMOWER MAN 2: BEYOND CYBERSPACE
Marshall, James
STUPIDS, THE
Marszalek, John F.
ASSAULT AT WEST POINT
Martin, George R. R.
OUTER LIMITS: SANDKINGS, THE
Martin, Valerie
MARY REILLY
Masamune, Shirow
GHOST IN THE SHELL
Mason, Robert
SOLO
McCarthy, Francis X.
BOGUS
McCullough, David
TRUMAN
McGann, Michael
SPELLBREAKER: SECRET OF THE LEPRECHAUNS
McMurtry, Larry
EVENING STAR, THE
LARRY MCMURTRY'S STREETS OF LAREDO
McPherson, Scott
MARVIN'S ROOM
Merchant, Ismail
PROPRIETOR, THE
Meredith, Anne
LOSING CHASE
Mikhalkov, Nikita
ANNA
Miller, Arthur
CRUCIBLE, THE
Miller, Chris
MULTIPLICITY
Mitchell, Julian
AUGUST
Miyamoto, Teru
MABOROSI
Miyazawa, Kenji
NIGHT ON THE GALACTIC RAILROAD
Molinaro, Edouard
BIRDCAGE, THE
Mooney, William
DONOR UNKNOWN
Moore, Ronald D.
STAR TREK: FIRST CONTACT
Morrissey, Paul
MADAME WANG'S
Murphy, Tab
HUNCHBACK OF NOTRE DAME, THE
Mutrux, Floyd
MULHOLLAND FALLS
Nagel, James
IN LOVE AND WAR
Narcejac, Thoams
DIABOLIQUE
Nash, Alanna
UP CLOSE AND PERSONAL
Nathan, Robert
PREACHER'S WIFE, THE

Neiderman, Andrew
MADDENING, THE
Nin, Anais
DELTA OF VENUS
Noonan, Tom
WIFE, THE
O'Neal, Brian E.
PHAT BEACH
O'Neal, Cleveland
PHAT BEACH
Oakley, Vern
MODERN AFFAIR, A
Oates, Joyce Carol
FOXFIRE
Ogata, Hideo
BIG WARS
Olsen, Arne
RED SCORPION 2
Ondaatje, Michael
ENGLISH PATIENT, THE
Osburn, Charles
WOLVES, THE
Otomo, Katsuhiro
ROUJIN-Z
Oury, Gerard
MIRROR HAS TWO FACES, THE
Palmer, Michael
EXTREME MEASURES
Palminteri, Chazz
FAITHFUL
Panahi, Jafar
WHITE BALLOON, THE
Parrent, Joanne
YOU'LL NEVER MAKE LOVE IN THIS TOWN AGAIN
Pate, Jonas
GRAVE, THE
Pate, Josh
GRAVE, THE
Peck, Mitchell
BIO-DOME
Pepperman, Paul
BEASTMASTER 3: THE EYE OF BRAXUS
Pergaud, Louis
WAR OF THE BUTTONS, THE
Petraglia, Sandro
WHO KILLED PASOLINI?
Poe, Amos
DEAD WEEKEND
Pogue, Charles Edward
DRAGONHEART
Poiret, Jean
BIRDCAGE, THE
Price Ellis, Novalyne
WHOLE WIDE WORLD, THE
Pronzini, Bill
TAILS YOU LIVE, HEADS YOU'RE DEAD
Puryear, Tony
ERASER
Quinn, Colin
CELTIC PRIDE
Raimi, Sam
DARKMAN III: DIE DARKMAN DIE
Rendell, Ruth
LA CEREMONIE
Rheaume, John
BACKLASH: OBLIVION 2
Rice, Tim
EVITA
Richards, Ken
ED
Richmond, Bill
NUTTY PROFESSOR, THE
Roemer Jr., William F.
SUGARTIME
Rothberg, Jeff
BOGUS
Roy, Prafulla
TARGET
Ruckman, Ivy
NIGHT OF THE TWISTERS
Rulli, Stefano
WHO KILLED PASOLINI?
Russo, Vito
CELLULOID CLOSET, THE
Salmon, Beth
WATCH ME
Salter, James
BOYS
Samantha, Elie
IMMORTALS, THE
Sayles, John
PIRANHA
Scerbanenco, Giorgio
OUTRAGE
Schaeffer, Eric
IF LUCY FELL
Schmidt, Arne L.
CHAIN REACTION
Schneider, Robert
BROTHER OF SLEEP
Schwartz, Sherwood
VERY BRADY SEQUEL, A
Sclavi, Tiziano
CEMETERY MAN
Seaman, Rick
CHAIN REACTION
Seltzer, Aaron
SPY HARD
Shahbazi, Parviz
WHITE BALLOON, THE
Shakespeare, William
HAMLET
TWELFTH NIGHT
WILLIAM SHAKESPEARE'S ROMEO + JULIET
Sherwood, Robert E.
PREACHER'S WIFE, THE
Siciliano, Enzo
WHO KILLED PASOLINI?
Sloane, Bernard
SURGEON, THE
Smith, Dodie
101 DALMATIANS
Smith, Wayne
BAD MOON
Soriano, Osvaldo
SHADOW YOU SOON WILL BE, A
Spiridakis, Tony
IF LUCY FELL
Standiford, Les
VIRUS
Stoker, Bram
BURIAL OF THE RATS
Su Tong
BLUSH
Suddeth, Hreg
BACKLASH: OBLIVION 2
Talbot, Robert
HEAD OF THE FAMILY
Talen, Julie
HARRIET THE SPY
Taulbert, Clifton
ONCE UPON A TIME . . . WHEN WE WERE COLORED
Taylor, Greg
HARRIET THE SPY
Taylor, Ronald B.
LONG ROAD HOME, THE
Thornton, Billy Bob
SLING BLADE
Tong, Stanley
RUMBLE IN THE BRONX
Toole, John Kennedy
NEON BIBLE, THE
Topps
MARS ATTACKS!
Tornatore, Giuseppe
STAR MAKER, THE
Tozer, Katherine
BRITT ALLCROFT'S MAGIC ADVENTURES OF MUMFIE—THE MOVIE
Van Damme, Jean-Claude
QUEST, THE
Veber, Francis
BIRDCAGE, THE
Villard, Henry S.
IN LOVE AND WAR
Voigt, Cynthia
HOMECOMING
Vonnegut, Kurt
MOTHER NIGHT
Walser, Robert
INSTITUTE BENJAMENTA
Walsh, Matthew Jason
SANDMAN, THE
Ward, Kelly
ALL DOGS GO TO HEAVEN 2
Wasserstein, Wendy
HEIDI CHRONICLES, THE
Webber, Andrew Lloyd
EVITA
Weisberg, David
ROCK, THE
Weiss, Arthur
FLIPPER
Wells, H.G.
ISLAND OF DR. MOREAU, THE
Welsh, Irvine
TRAINSPOTTING
Westlake, Donald E.
TWO MUCH
Wexler, Michael
GRAVE, THE
Wilde, Oscar
CANTERVILLE GHOST, THE
Williams, Robert
TUSKEGEE AIRMEN, THE
Wilson, Hugh
DOWN PERISCOPE
Wimmer, Kurt
WOLVES, THE
Winski, Norman
MAN IN THE ATTIC, THE
Winterbottom, Michael
BUTTERFLY KISS
Woolrich, Cornell
MRS. WINTERBOURNE
Wright, Richard
AMERICA'S DREAM
Young, Mark
ALL DOGS GO TO HEAVEN 2
Yuuki, Masami
PATLABOR 2: MOBILE POLICE
Zacharias, Steve
EDDIE
Zaillian, Steven
MISSION: IMPOSSIBLE
Zazubrin, V.
CHEKIST, THE
Zemeckis, Robert
TALES FROM THE CRYPT PRESENTS BORDELLO OF BLOOD
Zetlin, Barry
DOGFIGHTERS, THE
Zimmerman, Paul
MODERN AFFAIR, A

SPECIAL EFFECTS

1st Effects
INSTITUTE BENJAMENTA

Abades, Reyes
LAND AND FREEDOM
OUTRAGE
Abe, Ken'ichi
ROUJIN-Z
Acevedo, Angel L.
BUGGED
Adamson, Andrew
TIME TO KILL, A
Alba, Eric
SABRINA, THE TEENAGE WITCH
Allder, Nick
MUPPET TREASURE ISLAND
Andersen, Lars
BREAKING THE WAVES
Any Effects
SOLITAIRE FOR TWO
Arbogast, Roy
CHAIN REACTION
Arcolio, Marc
UNHOOK THE STARS
Atlanta Film Effects
THEY BITE
Available Light Ltd.
TALES FROM THE CRYPT PRESENTS BORDELLO OF BLOOD
Baker, Don
BROKEN ARROW
Baker, John
DRAGONHEART
Balsmeyer, Randall
GIRL 6
TALES OF EROTICA
Barkan, Sam
EVIL HAS A FACE
SKIN
Barker, David J.
BEYOND DESIRE
Barnbrook, Jacquie
KAZAAM
Barron, Craig
DUNSTON CHECKS IN
Bartalos, Gabe
LITTLE WITCHES
PINOCCHIO'S REVENGE
Barton, David
NEMESIS III: PREY HARDER
Baur, Tassilo
FATALLY YOURS
Bawden, Ron
TWO-BITS & PEPPER
Beauchamp, Wayne
CHILDREN OF THE CORN: THE GATHERING
Becker, Martin
LETTER TO MY KILLER
Belardinelli, Charles
FROM DUSK TILL DAWN
MAD DOG TIME
Bell, Doug
HARRIET THE SPY
Bellissimo, T. "Brooklyn"
BULLETPROOF
FROM DUSK TILL DAWN
SET IT OFF
Bellissimo/Belardinelli Effects, Inc.
FROM DUSK TILL DAWN
MAD DOG TIME
Benjamin, Al
RUMBLE IN THE BRONX
Bennett, Jack D.
HARVEST OF FIRE
LONE STAR
Benson, Steven R.
SPY HARD
Bentley, Gary
FLED
Berman, Richard
BOGUS
Bickerton, Angus
ADVENTURES OF PINOCCHIO, THE
Bird, Jan
MR. STITCH
Bitar, Kamar
SCREAM
Blitstein, David
ED
GHOSTS OF MISSISSIPPI
MICHAEL
PHENOMENON
Blue Sky Productions
JOE'S APARTMENT
Board, Jason
HARRIET THE SPY
Boss Film Studios
MULTIPLICITY
Bosseau, John
EXIT
Botsford, Diana Dru
FROM DUSK TILL DAWN
Boyington, Paul
OUTER LIMITS: SANDKINGS, THE
Brayham, Peter
CRACKER: THE MADWOMAN IN THE ATTIC
Breheny, Steve
HEDD WYNN
Bresin, Marty
DOWN PERISCOPE
JOHN CARPENTER'S ESCAPE FROM L.A.
Brink, Connie
BIG NIGHT
EVERYONE SAYS I LOVE YOU
PREACHER'S WIFE, THE
Brink, Conrad
SOMEONE ELSE'S AMERICA
Brink, Jeff
SOMEONE ELSE'S AMERICA
Brisdon, Stuart
CAPTIVES
TWO DEATHS
Buechler, John Carl
BURIAL OF THE RATS
CARNOSAUR 3: PRIMAL SPECIES
Buena Vista Special Effects
BIG BULLY
FIRST KID
Buena Vista Visual Effects
FEAR
JAMES AND THE GIANT PEACH
JOHN CARPENTER'S ESCAPE FROM L.A.
PHANTOM, THE
Burr, Tassilo
TOO FAST, TOO YOUNG
Burton, Rob
PRIMAL FEAR
C.O.R.E. Digital Pictures
FLY AWAY HOME
Cameron, Mageara
CRAFT, THE
PHENOMENON
Cammaert, Jim
PORTRAITS OF A KILLER
Campfens, Jon
KIDS IN THE HALL: BRAIN CANDY
Carlucci, Lou
BIO-DOME
BOUND
DEAD MAN
GLASS CAGE, THE
PIG'S TALE, A
UNKNOWN ORIGIN
WAR AT HOME, THE
WIDOW'S KISS
Caudle, Lyn
LARRY MCMURTRY'S STREETS OF LAREDO
Cavanaugh, Lawrence James
LAST MAN STANDING
CB
BARB WIRE
Ceglia, Frank
FULL BODY MASSAGE
IMMORTALS, THE
SCREAM
WOMAN UNDONE, A
Chamberlayne, Andrew
FINAL CUT, THE
WHITE TIGER
Champion, Neal
GRIM
Chandler, Estee
LONG KISS GOODNIGHT, THE
Cheap Tricks
THEY BITE
Cheng Xiaolong
CHUNGKING EXPRESS
Cicchirillo, Sam
MIRROR, MIRROR III: THE VOYEUR
Cineffects Productions Inc.
SCREAMERS
Cinesite
LAWNMOWER MAN 2: BEYOND CYBERSPACE
SPACE JAM
Class A Special Effects
KAZAAM
Clayton, Guy
CELTIC PRIDE
NORMAL LIFE
Clifford, Geoff
JANE EYRE
Clowers, Wes
CITIZEN RUTH
Cohen, Gary
HIDDEN ASSASSIN
Conway, Richard
ENGLISH PATIENT, THE
IN LOVE AND WAR
MARY REILLY
Cook, Phil
PHOENIX
Coplan, Ted
SERIAL KILLER
Corbould, Chris
GHOST AND THE DARKNESS, THE
Cordero, Laurnecio "Chov"
WILLIAM SHAKESPEARE'S ROMEO + JULIET
Corridori, Giovanni
MONSTER, THE
Cory, Phil
GALAXIES ARE COLLIDING
Cosgrove, Ryal
SCREAMERS
Cowan, David
UNFORGETTABLE
Cox, Brian
ISLAND OF DR. MOREAU, THE
Craig, Louis
HOLLOW POINT
Craig, Ron
IRON EAGLE IV
VIRUS
Cresswell, Rick
LIVE WIRE: HUMAN TIMEBOMB
TERMINAL IMPACT
WARHEAD
YANKEE ZULU
Criswell Productions
THEODORE REX

Crosman, Peter
BROKEN ARROW
Cundom, Tom
OF LOVE AND SHADOWS
Cutler, Rory
RED SCORPION 2
CWI
FRISK
D'Amico, Gary
LAST DANCE
D'Arcy, Robin
ARRIVAL, THE
Dalton, Burt
CHAMBER, THE
NUTTY PROFESSOR, THE
Daniels, Peter
UNHOOK THE STARS
David Allen Productions
BACKLASH: OBLIVION 2
Davis, Nick
CHAIN REACTION
De Bono, Yves
EVITA
MICHAEL COLLINS
de Laveleye, Olivier
ANTONIA'S LINE
Deak, Michael S.
ZARKORR! THE INVADER
Demetrau, Georges
HORSEMAN ON THE ROOF
MACHINE, THE
Deng Weijue
CHUNGKING EXPRESS
Digital Armageddon
POLYMORPH
Digital Domain
ISLAND OF DR. MOREAU, THE
SGT. BILKO
Digital Drama
NOT OF THIS EARTH
Ding Yunda
CHUNGKING EXPRESS
Dion, Dennis
HEAVEN'S PRISONERS
HOUSE ARREST
DiSarro, Mark
LITTLE DEATH, THE
Dolson, Mark
BEWARE: CHILDREN AT PLAY
Donen, Peter
EXECUTIVE DECISION
Dorney, Roger
CROW: CITY OF ANGELS, THE
Doublin, Anthony
CARNOSAUR 3: PRIMAL SPECIES
Dream Quest Images
PRIMAL FEAR
ROCK, THE
Drisden, Stuart
YOUNG POISONER'S HANDBOOK, THE
Duboi
VISITORS, THE
Dutton, Syd
BIRDCAGE, THE
HIGH SCHOOL HIGH
Edlund, Richard
MULTIPLICITY
Effects Associates
EMMA
Ellingson, Andre
LAZARUS MAN, THE
Elswit, Helen
SPACE JAM
Engel, Volker
INDEPENDENCE DAY
England, Chrissie
101 DALMATIANS
Escott, Anthony
FLAMING EARS
Estes, Ken
STEPHEN KING'S THINNER
Ettema, Dale
JOHN CARPENTER'S ESCAPE FROM L.A.
Excalibur
MAGIC HUNTER
VISITORS, THE
Faen, Laurie
TWO FRIENDS
Fangmeier, Stefen
TWISTER
Farfan, Federico
SOLO
Farhat, Jon
DEAD MAN
NUTTY PROFESSOR, THE
Farino, Ernest
SCREAMERS
Farnham, Bob
BLACK SCORPION
Ferri, Peter
JOHNNY SHORTWAVE
Film Effects, Inc.
KIDS IN THE HALL: BRAIN CANDY
Finance, Charles L.
ARRIVAL, THE
Fioritto, Larry
BEST OF THE BEST 3: NO TURNING BACK
BREAKAWAY
CROSSCUT
MOTHER
PUBLIC ENEMIES
RATTLED
2 DAYS IN THE VALLEY
Fisher, Scott R.
HIGH SCHOOL HIGH
Fisher, Thomas L.
HIGH SCHOOL HIGH
Flash Film Works
DEMOLITIONIST, THE
Foley, Maurice
MOLL FLANDERS
Forbes, Scott
TRUTH ABOUT CATS AND DOGS, THE
Fort, Daniel A.
FROM DUSK TILL DAWN
Foury, Pierre
HATE
Francis, Jim
FUNNYMAN, THE
GRIM
Frazee, Terry D.
ERASER
STAR TREK: FIRST CONTACT
Frazier, John
TWISTER
FTS EFX, Inc.
BIO-DOME
DEAD MAN
Fuentes, Larry
JAG
Gajdecki, John
DARKMAN III: DIE DARKMAN DIE
OUTER LIMITS: SANDKINGS, THE
Galich, Steve
SGT. BILKO
TIME TO KILL, A
Garmsen, Lutz
HALFMOON
Gibbs, George
101 DALMATIANS
Gibson, Charles
KAZAAM
Gill, Danny
BOY CALLED HATE, A
FOR BETTER OR WORSE
Gillis, Alec
TREMORS 2: AFTERSHOCKS
Goedecke, Mike
VENUS RISING
YESTERDAY'S TARGET
Gorton, Neill
FUNNYMAN, THE
Grasmere Jr., Robert A.
ED
Gray, John E.
BARB WIRE
Griffin, Robin
CRAFT, THE
Griswold, Albert
ASSOCIATE, THE
Grossberg, Wendy
JOSH KIRBY . . . TIME WARRIOR!: TRAPPED ON TOY WORLD
Gutierrez, Gary
JACK
Habros, Robert
THEODORE REX
Haines, Paul
IMMORTALS, THE
JERRY MAGUIRE
Hakian, Josh
PHAT BEACH
Hall, Allen L.
LONG KISS GOODNIGHT, THE
Hall, Bob
HARRIET THE SPY
Hanan, Michael Z.
ISLAND OF DR. MOREAU, THE
Harovas, Perry
BLACK SCORPION
Harris, Tom
PROTEUS
Hart, James M.
MR. WRONG
Hart, Walter
STUPIDS, THE
Hartigan, Beverly
ONE MAN'S JUSTICE
THIN LINE BETWEEN LOVE AND HATE, A
Hartigan, John
DEMOLITIONIST, THE
DUNSTON CHECKS IN
GRACE OF MY HEART
HELLRAISER: BLOODLINE
IT CAME FROM OUTER SPACE II
LITTLE WITCHES
VIKING SAGAS, THE
Hasegawa, Toshio
GHOST IN THE SHELL
Henry, Erik
CELTIC PRIDE
Hesseyh, Russ
DEATH BENEFIT
Hodgson, Robert
EXTREME MEASURES
Hollander, Richard E.
DOWN PERISCOPE
Hoshiba
GHOST IN THE SHELL
Houston, Kent
MARY REILLY
Howard, Adam
STAR TREK: FIRST CONTACT
Howard, Jeff
LAND BEFORE TIME IV: JOURNEY THROUGH THE MISTS
Howell, Eric
MYSTERY SCIENCE THEATER 3000: THE MOVIE
Hubin, Philippe
MA SAISON PREFEREE
Huffman, Linus
RAVENHAWK

Hughes, Dave
BEAVIS AND BUTT-HEAD DO AMERICA
Hughes, Evan Green
HEDD WYNN
Hutchinson, Peter
CANTERVILLE GHOST, THE
HAUNTED
WAR OF THE BUTTONS, THE
Illusion Arts, Inc.
BIRDCAGE, THE
BOGUS
HIGH SCHOOL HIGH
Image Animation
PROTEUS
WITHIN THE ROCK
Image Animation Canada
LEGEND OF GATOR FACE, THE
Industrial Light & Magic
DAYLIGHT
DRAGONHEART
ERASER
MARS ATTACKS!
MISSION: IMPOSSIBLE
101 DALMATIANS
STAR TREK: FIRST CONTACT
TWISTER
Ingram, Steve
FRIGHTENERS, THE
Inns, Garth
ADVENTURES OF PINOCCHIO, THE
International Creative Effects
SPY HARD
Jacobs, Evan
SOMETIMES THEY COME BACK . . . AGAIN
Jacobsen, Morten
BREAKING THE WAVES
Jarman, Duncan
PROTEUS
Jarvis, Jeff
MAXIMUM RISK
Jenkins, Christopher
HUNCHBACK OF NOTRE DAME, THE
Jim Henson's Creature Shop
ADVENTURES OF PINOCCHIO, THE
101 DALMATIANS
Jiritano, Drew
ANGELA
PALOOKAVILLE
SUBSTANCE OF FIRE, THE
John Gejdecki, Ltd.
KIDS IN THE HALL: BRAIN CANDY
Johnson, Scott
WHISPERING, THE
Johnson, Steve
SURGEON, THE
Johnston, Gerry
MICHAEL COLLINS
Jolliffe, Brock
ELECTRA
LEGEND OF GATOR FACE, THE
Jones, Ed
SPACE JAM
Jones, J. B.
OFF AND RUNNING
Jones, Paul
LEGEND OF GATOR FACE, THE
MIND RIPPER
Jones, Richard
SUBSTITUTE, THE
TWO MUCH
Kalman, Steve
SANDMAN, THE
Karogian, Marijan
ADRENALIN: FEAR THE RUSH
Kavanagh, Michael
BEYOND THE CALL
EXTREME MEASURES
MOONSHINE HIGHWAY
MRS. WINTERBOURNE
TAILS YOU LIVE, HEADS YOU'RE DEAD
WHERE'S THE MONEY, NOREEN?
Kelsey, David
CRAFT, THE
KINGPIN
Kelt, Mike
COLD COMFORT FARM
Kerrigan, Richard
HELLRAISER: BLOODLINE
KFX
FAITHFUL
Kim, Jung
LAND BEFORE TIME IV: JOURNEY THROUGH THE MISTS
King, Jeremy
COLD COMFORT FARM
Kirshoff, Steve
BEFORE AND AFTER
CITY HALL
FAITHFUL
GIRL 6
Kiser, Rodman
FAMILY THING, A
PEOPLE VS. LARRY FLYNT, THE
Klavir, Pini
DEADLY OUTBREAK
Kline II, Henry
MAXIMUM RISK
KNB EFX Group
DEMOLITIONIST, THE
Knoll, John
MISSION: IMPOSSIBLE
Knowlton, Peter
FLIPPER
Kobielski, Kaz
GETTING AWAY WITH MURDER
Kocar, Paul
TAKEOVER, THE
Koneval, Kevin
FIRST KID
Kozachik, Pete
JAMES AND THE GIANT PEACH
Krejcik, David
DELTA OF VENUS
Krejcik, Vaclav
DELTA OF VENUS
Kuehn, Brad
FLIPPER
Kwiatek, Mark
BEWARE: CHILDREN AT PLAY
La Bounta, Henry
TWISTER
Lacrosse, Boyd
JOSH KIRBY . . . TIME WARRIOR!: EGGS FROM 70,000,000 B.C.
JOSH KIRBY . . . TIME WARRIOR!: JOURNEY TO THE MAGIC CAVERN
Lambert, Michael
FOREST WARRIOR
Landerer, Gregory C.
BLACK ROSE OF HARLEM
PIRANHA
Landry, Tim
JAG
Langevin, Arthur
HARRIET THE SPY
Lantieri, Michael
MARS ATTACKS!
MATILDA
Larsen, Rolf
UNHOOK THE STARS
Lee, Ed
KAZAAM
Lemaire, Jean-Francois
LITTLE INDIAN, BIG CITY
Lemon, Lynda
JAMES AND THE GIANT PEACH
Lennick, Michael
BLOOD & DONUTS
Lessa, Michael
JOHN CARPENTER'S ESCAPE FROM L.A.
MR. WRONG
Lidstone, Tim
HARRIET THE SPY
Linberg, Craig
BUGGED
Lockwood, Dean
ALASKA
BIG BULLY
Lorimer, Alan E.
LARGER THAN LIFE
MY FELLOW AMERICANS
PHANTOM, THE
Lowe, Dennis
ENGLISH PATIENT, THE
Ludwig, Heinz
KASPAR HAUSER
Lundstrom, Goran
EVIL ED
Mack, Kevin
ISLAND OF DR. MOREAU, THE
Magical Media Industries
CARNOSAUR 3: PRIMAL SPECIES
Malivoire, Martin
FLY AWAY HOME
GETTING AWAY WITH MURDER
MAXIMUM RISK
SUGARTIME
Malzahn, Richard
BLACK DAY BLUE NIGHT
Marangoni, Albert
STREETCAR NAMED DESIRE, A
Mariella, John
FLY AWAY HOME
Markman, Elliot
BROKEN ARROW
Markwell, John
JUDE
Marr, Kevin
ORIGINAL SINS
Martynov, Boris
BURIAL OF THE RATS
Mason, Grant
TRAINSPOTTING
Mass. Illusion
ERASER
McCarthy, Kevin
CHAMELEON
CHILDREN OF FURY
FAST MONEY
FUGITIVE RAGE
HARD JUSTICE
McClellan, Charlie
FRIGHTENERS, THE
McClung, Patrick
SGT. BILKO
McGeoch, Norman
RACE THE SUN
McGovern, Mickey
JAMES AND THE GIANT PEACH
McKinnon, Jake the Snake
PUBLIC ACCESS
McLeod, John
ADRENALIN: FEAR THE RUSH
JACK
McMurray, Gregory L.
JINGLE ALL THE WAY
McMurray, Laird
MRS. MUNCK
TWO IF BY SEA
Meinardus, Michael
LAWNMOWER MAN 2: BEYOND CYBERSPACE
ROCK, THE

Merriam, Chad
KAZAAM
Mertz, Tom
VERY BRADY SEQUEL, A
Mettox, Bruce
RATTLED
Michelucci, Bob
SANTA CLAWS
Milinac, John
BEFORE AND AFTER
Miller, David
NIGHT OF THE SCARECROW
Miller, Dean
DON'T BE A MENACE TO SOUTH CENTRAL WHILE DRINKING YOUR JUICE IN THE HOOD
Miller, Douglas
SOMETIMES THEY COME BACK . . . AGAIN
Mitchell, James
MARS ATTACKS!
Mohagen, Craig
JAMES AND THE GIANT PEACH
Molina
FLOWER OF MY SECRET, THE
Montefusco, Shirley
TO GILLIAN ON HER 37TH BIRTHDAY
Montefusco, Vincent
TO GILLIAN ON HER 37TH BIRTHDAY
Montgomery, Peter
CHAMBER, THE
FEAR
FLED
Moore, Randy E.
BOTTLE ROCKET
EVENING STAR, THE
PAINTED HERO
Moreau, Frederic
HORSEMAN ON THE ROOF
Mouligne, Jean-Marc
VISITORS, THE
Movie Arms Management
DEAD WEEKEND
Munro, Alan
BOGUS
Murakami, Mutsu
GHOST IN THE SHELL
Murphy, Karen
FLIPPER
Murphy, Paul
D3: THE MIGHTY DUCKS
FARGO
MYSTERY SCIENCE THEATER 3000: THE MOVIE
Nakano, Minoru
MABOROSI
Nary, Ronald
GREAT WHITE HYPE, THE
Natali, Germano
MONSTER, THE
Nefzer, Uli
PASSION OF DARKLY NOON, THE
Nejaglov, Nickolai
WOLVES, THE
Nelmes, Mark
MARY REILLY
Nelson, Kimberly K.
JOHN CARPENTER'S ESCAPE FROM L.A.
Newkirk, Dale
PHOENIX
Nicholson, Lyn
MISSION: IMPOSSIBLE
Nixon, Rodney
BAJA
Nowak, Zygmunt
MOTHER OF KINGS
Okun, Jeffrey A.
LONG KISS GOODNIGHT, THE
Olson, Jeff
STAR TREK: FIRST CONTACT
Oosthuizen, Heather
TERMINAL IMPACT
Ornec, Tim
CANNIBAL! THE MUSICAL
Orr, Bill
HAPPY GILMORE
HOMEWARD BOUND II: LOST IN SAN FRANCISCO
Ostiguy, Richard
SCREAMERS
Ota, Noriyuki
GHOST IN THE SHELL
Ottesen, Daniel
JUROR, THE
Ottesen, John
I'M NOT RAPPAPORT
JUROR, THE
Ottesen, Ron
I'M NOT RAPPAPORT
Owens, Michael
101 DALMATIANS
Paller, David
RUMBLE IN THE BRONX
Paller, Gary
SURGEON, THE
UNFORGETTABLE
Parks, Stan
BIRDCAGE, THE
Pepiot, Ken
EXECUTIVE DECISION
GLIMMER MAN, THE
Perfili, Virginia
MIRROR, MIRROR III: THE VOYEUR
Performance Solutions
KIDS IN THE HALL: BRAIN CANDY
Performance World
LAST SUPPER, THE
Petino, Steve
DESIRE
Pike, Kevin
DONOR UNKNOWN
EYE FOR AN EYE
Pinney, Clay
INDEPENDENCE DAY
PM Effects
MYSTERY SCIENCE THEATER 3000: THE MOVIE
Powers, Don
BREAKAWAY
Price, Jamie
DOWN PERISCOPE
Pride, Tad
RACE THE SUN
Pritchett, Darrell
SPACE JAM
Pupulin, Yves
MAGIC HUNTER
R/Greenberg Associates West, Inc.
DEAD MAN
Rader, Scott
STAR TREK: FIRST CONTACT
Rainone, Thomas C.
NECRONOMICON: BOOK OF THE DEAD
NIGHT OF THE SCARECROW
Ralston, Ken
PHENOMENON
Ramboz, Eve
CELESTIAL CLOCKWORK
Ramsey, Joe
FAN, THE
Rappaport, Mark
HEAD OF THE FAMILY
JOSH KIRBY . . . TIME WARRIOR!: EGGS FROM 70,000,000 B.C.
JOSH KIRBY . . . TIME WARRIOR!: JOURNEY TO THE MAGIC CAVERN
JOSH KIRBY . . . TIME WARRIOR!: LAST BATTLE FOR THE UNIVERSE
JOSH KIRBY . . . TIME WARRIOR!: TRAPPED ON TOY WORLD
MAGIC IN THE MIRROR
OUT THERE
SPELLBREAKER: SECRET OF THE LEPRECHAUNS
Ray, Kelley R.
CRAFT, THE
Reedy, James
CHAIN REACTION
Reedyk, Rae
MATERNAL INSTINCTS
SABRINA, THE TEENAGE WITCH
TRACKS OF A KILLER
Reynolds, Lisa
NEON BIBLE, THE
Rhythm & Hues Studios
KAZAAM
Ricci, Brian
CRUCIBLE, THE
Riggs, Bob
MR. HOLLAND'S OPUS
Riley, Steven
JAMES AND THE GIANT PEACH
Roberts, David
RACE THE SUN
Roberts, Larry
ONE GOOD TURN
SAINTS AND SINNERS
SKYSCRAPER
TRIGGER EFFECT, THE
Robertson, Stuart
BEFORE AND AFTER
Romanoff, Lisa
PRE-MADONNAS
Rompre, Normand
BEAVIS AND BUTT-HEAD DO AMERICA
Rosengrant, John
GHOST AND THE DARKNESS, THE
Ross, Ted
FOR THE MOMENT
STUPIDS, THE
Routly, Lee
HOW THE WEST WAS FUN
Ruano Rogriguez, Midro
SONS OF TRINITY
Rundell, Steve
THAT THING YOU DO!
Ryba, Tom
MULTIPLICITY
PRIMAL FEAR
Rylander, Eric
RICH MAN'S WIFE, THE
WILD SIDE
Sampson, Sean
BLOOD & DONUTS
Samuels, Brian
MULTIPLICITY
Sanchez, Virgil
RATTLED
Sancho, Roberto
JOHNNY 100 PESOS
Schaab, Wally
PHANTOM, THE
Schaedler, Gary
GHOSTS OF MISSISSIPPI
Schaffer, Clark
FIST OF THE NORTH STAR
Scheirer, Clayton
HAPPY GILMORE
Schlenz, Maurine
NEMESIS III: PREY HARDER
Scott, J. Alan
ISLAND OF DR. MOREAU, THE
Settles, Jeremy
MR. ICE CREAM MAN

Shatkov, Rafik
BURIAL OF THE RATS
Shea, Mike
HEAVEN'S PRISONERS
Shelley, Bob
ASSAULT AT WEST POINT
FLED
ORIGINAL GANGSTAS
Sindicich, Thomas F.
JAMES AND THE GIANT PEACH
Skotak, Dennis
UNKNOWN ORIGIN
Skotak, Robert
UNKNOWN ORIGIN
Smith, Douglas
INDEPENDENCE DAY
Smith, Neil
VIRTUAL COMBAT
Smith, Tom
MUPPET TREASURE ISLAND
Snow Business
INSTITUTE BENJAMENTA
Sonderhoff, Terry
TALES FROM THE CRYPT PRESENTS BORDELLO OF BLOOD
Sony Pictures Imageworks
CABLE GUY, THE
CRAFT, THE
JAMES AND THE GIANT PEACH
PHENOMENON
Soper, Carolyn
FEAR
Sota FX
FIST OF THE NORTH STAR
SPFX Unlimited
LONG KISS GOODNIGHT, THE
SPY HARD
Squires, Scott
DRAGONHEART
Stan Winston Studios
GHOST AND THE DARKNESS, THE
Stargate Films Inc.
FINAL EQUINOX, THE
Steers, Tony
TRAINSPOTTING
Steinheimer, R. Bruce
LAST MAN STANDING
Stempel, Bruno
UNDER THE HULA MOON
Stewart, Chuck
SPY HARD
UP CLOSE AND PERSONAL
Stifanich, John
IF LUCY FELL
Stivaletti, Sergio
CEMETERY MAN
Stone, Bob
MIRROR, MIRROR III: THE VOYEUR
Storvick, Tim
FEAR
TALES FROM THE CRYPT PRESENTS BORDELLO OF BLOOD
Straus, James
DRAGONHEART
Street IV, J. D.
SHARON'S SECRET
Stroweis, Jacques
BROKEN ARROW
Sturm, Dieter
BEAUTIFUL GIRLS
Stutsman, Richard
VERY BRADY SEQUEL, A
Sullivan, John
ERASER
Sullivan, Peter Michael
COURAGE UNDER FIRE
Swanger, Paul "Cowboy"
MUTANT MAN
Sweeney, Matt
CABLE GUY, THE
Szilagyi, Peter
MAGIC HUNTER
T.R.I.X. Unlimited Special Effects
HIGH SCHOOL HIGH
Tangkilisan, Hendro
WITHOUT MERCY
Taylor, Bill
BIRDCAGE, THE
HIGH SCHOOL HIGH
Terranova, Frank
POLYMORPH
Thompson, Mike
GREAT WHITE HYPE, THE
Thompson, Richard
BROKEN ARROW
Tippett, Phil
DRAGONHEART
Tippett Studio
TREMORS 2: AFTERSHOCKS
Trifunovich, Neil
BOGUS
Trinquier, Jean-Louis
LITTLE INDIAN, BIG CITY
Trost, Ron
BAJA
HOSTILE INTENTIONS
KAZAAM
RUMPELSTILTSKIN
Tunnicliffe, Gary J.
AMANDA AND THE ALIEN
WITHIN THE ROCK
Turi, Josh
ORIGINAL SINS
Turoff, Michael
JOE'S APARTMENT
Ultimate Effects
DUNSTON CHECKS IN
SERIAL KILLER
THIN LINE BETWEEN LOVE AND HATE, A
van Couwelaar, Steven
ANTONIA'S LINE
van der Poel, Claire
BAJA
Van Perre Jr., I.J.
FOXFIRE
Van Vliet, John T.
TALES FROM THE CRYPT PRESENTS BORDELLO OF BLOOD
Van Zeebroeck, Bruno
CROW: CITY OF ANGELS, THE
Vasquez, Gabriel
BAJA
Vazquez, Bob
FIRST KID
VCE, Inc.
BOGUS
Vendetta FX
SHOPPING
VIFX
CELTIC PRIDE
DOWN PERISCOPE
FIRST WIVES CLUB, THE
Vision Crew Unlimited
SOMETIMES THEY COME BACK . . . AGAIN
Viskocil, Joseph
INDEPENDENCE DAY
Vogel, Matt
BOYS
FIRST WIVES CLUB, THE
RIDERS OF THE PURPLE SAGE
Wake, John
MR. STITCH
Ward, Tom
DEAR GOD
MULHOLLAND FALLS
THAT THING YOU DO!
Wardlow, Keith
HAPPY GILMORE
Warner Digital Effects
ERASER
MARS ATTACKS!
Warren, Jon
SOMETIMES THEY COME BACK . . . AGAIN
Watkins, David
QUEST, THE
Watts, Chris
EXTREME MEASURES
MATILDA
Wedge, Chris
JOE'S APARTMENT
Wenger, Cliff
MISSING PIECES
West, Kit
DAYLIGHT
DRAGONHEART
Wheatley, Ken
CHILDREN OF THE CORN: THE GATHERING
Whibley, Alan
RASPUTIN
Whitcher, Jerry
SAWBONES
White, Paul
VIKING SAGAS, THE
Wiessenhaan, Hary
CROCODILES IN AMSTERDAM
Williams, David
HEDD WYNN
Williams, Joss
HAMLET
WHITE SQUALL
Witzmann, Andrea
FLAMING EARS
Wixson, Amy Hollywood
JAMES AND THE GIANT PEACH
Woodruff Jr., Tom
TREMORS 2: AFTERSHOCKS
XFX
SURGEON, THE
Yager, Juliette
JOHN CARPENTER'S ESCAPE FROM L.A.
Yagher, Kevin
RUMPELSTILTSKIN
Yeatman, Hoyt
ROCK, THE
Yuricich, Richard
MISSION: IMPOSSIBLE
Yutaka, "Matrix"
GHOST IN THE SHELL
Zaharov, Sergei
WOLVES, THE
Zakarian, Louis
BUGGED
Zannotti, Albert
SANTA WITH MUSCLES
Zargarpour, Habib
TWISTER
Zarro, Richard M.
BLACK SHEEP
Zsalek, Gyula
MAGIC HUNTER

STUNTS

Aguilar, George
BIG NIGHT
PALLBEARER, THE
Aiello III, Danny
SPITFIRE GRILL, THE
Akerstream, Marc
ROAD HOME, THE
RUMBLE IN THE BRONX

TRACKS OF A KILLER

Albu, Ioan
JOSH KIRBY . . . TIME WARRIOR!: EGGS FROM 70,000,000 B.C.
JOSH KIRBY . . . TIME WARRIOR!: JOURNEY TO THE MAGIC CAVERN

Alon, Roy
JUDE

Amiel, Alan
SHOOTFIGHTER 2: KILL OR BE KILLED!

Anagnos, Bill
EVERYONE SAYS I LOVE YOU

Anders, Ed
BAD LOVE
BODY COUNT

Anderson, Chris
TUNNEL VISION

Anderson, Greg
BEYOND DESIRE

Andre, Charles
FEAR

Armstrong, Andy
MOONSHINE HIGHWAY
TRUMAN

Arnett, M. James
BARB WIRE

Ateah, Scott
BREACH OF TRUST
FINAL CUT, THE
TRACKS OF A KILLER

Avery, Rick
STUPIDS, THE

Bahr, Thom
TWO MUCH

Baldwin, Danny
GHOST AND THE DARKNESS, THE

Barker, Rick
KINGPIN

Bates, Ken
ADRENALIN: FEAR THE RUSH
LAWNMOWER MAN 2: BEYOND CYBERSPACE
ROCK, THE

Baumert, Hank
FOREST WARRIOR

Bianco, Marco
STAND OFF, THE
SUGARTIME

Blackwell, Richard
BEFORE AND AFTER

Borden, Chuck
PHOENIX

Boswell, Glenn
ISLAND OF DR. MOREAU, THE
RACE THE SUN

Boyle, Marc
HAUNTED

Boyum, Steve
MR. HOLLAND'S OPUS

Bradford, Andy
YOUNG POISONER'S HANDBOOK, THE

Bradley, Dan
INDEPENDENCE DAY

Brady, Michael T.
GRACE OF MY HEART

Bragg, Bobby
FUGITIVE RAGE
OVER THE WIRE

Branche, George
ADVENTURES OF PINOCCHIO, THE

Braun, Eddie
ARRIVAL, THE

Brayham, Peter
CRACKER: THE MADWOMAN IN THE ATTIC

Brown, Bobby
RAVENHAWK

Brown, Bruce
FRIGHTENERS, THE

Brubaker, Tony
FIRST KID
TUSKEGEE AIRMEN, THE

Bryant, Kurt
BIO-DOME
DENTIST, THE
DESIRE
ONE MAN'S JUSTICE
THIN LINE BETWEEN LOVE AND HATE, A

Bucossi, Peter
BEAUTIFUL GIRLS
CAUGHT
FAITHFUL
PALOOKAVILLE

Burton, Billy
PHANTOM, THE

Cadiente, Jeff
PHENOMENON
SAINTS AND SINNERS

Camacho, Art
VIRTUAL COMBAT

Capella, Rocky
FIST OF THE NORTH STAR
JAMES AND THE GIANT PEACH

Cardwell, Shane
HOLLOW POINT
IRON EAGLE IV
MRS. MUNCK

Carliez, Michel
HORSEMAN ON THE ROOF

Cass Sr, David S.
LARRY MCMURTRY'S STREETS OF LAREDO

Cassidy, Mike
MULTIPLICITY

Cecere, Tony
SCREAM

Celis, Fernando
BEASTMASTER 3: THE EYE OF BRAXUS

Chan, Jackie
RUMBLE IN THE BRONX

Coleman, Doug
BEFORE AND AFTER
CROW: CITY OF ANGELS, THE
FLIPPER
UP CLOSE AND PERSONAL

Combs, Gary
DEAR GOD
EDDIE

Combs, Gil
MR. WRONG

Crane, Simon
HAMLET
101 DALMATIANS

Croughwell, Charlie
IT CAME FROM OUTER SPACE II
MICHAEL

Crowther, Graham
JANE EYRE

Cudney, Cliff
BOUND

Curtis, Clive
CAPTIVES

Dacascos, Mark
REDEMPTION: KICKBOXER 5

Dashnaw, Jeffrey J.
PIG'S TALE, A
RICH MAN'S WIFE, THE

Davidson, Brett
SAWBONES

Davidson, Steve M.
LONG KISS GOODNIGHT, THE

Davis, B. J.
BODY COUNT

Davis, Gary
DOWN, OUT AND DANGEROUS

Davison, Steve
FROM DUSK TILL DAWN

Davison, Tim
BULLETPROOF
TALES FROM THE CRYPT PRESENTS BORDELLO OF BLOOD

Deadrick Jr., Vince
MIRROR HAS TWO FACES, THE

Derrick, Ben
SABRINA, THE TEENAGE WITCH

Deweir, Tom
HELLRAISER: BLOODLINE

Dixon, Shane
BLACK SHEEP
SUNSET PARK
TALES FROM THE CRYPT PRESENTS BORDELLO OF BLOOD

Donne, Joe
MARS ATTACKS!

Doty, Baxter
MAN WITH A PLAN

Doumitrescu, Dogu
JOSH KIRBY . . . TIME WARRIOR!: TRAPPED ON TOY WORLD

Dowdall, Jim
ENGLISH PATIENT, THE
LOADED
MARY REILLY
SHOPPING

Dunne, Joe
DEATH BENEFIT
MISSING PIECES

Eirikson, Tom
HOW THE WEST WAS FUN

Elam, Greg Wayne
GHOSTS OF MISSISSIPPI

Ellis, Annie
HOMEWARD BOUND II: LOST IN SAN FRANCISCO

Epstein, Jon
AMANDA AND THE ALIEN

Farfel, Roy
ANGELA
EVERYONE SAYS I LOVE YOU

Farnsworth, Diamond
JAG

Ferguson, Bill
BREACH OF TRUST
MATERNAL INSTINCTS
UNFORGETTABLE

Ferrara, Frank
MARVIN'S ROOM

Fierro, James
EVIL HAS A FACE

Fife, Randy
LAST DANCE

Fioramonti, Glory
CRAFT, THE

Forrestal, Terry
BREAKING THE WAVES
TRAINSPOTTING

Forsayeth, Rick
TAILS YOU LIVE, HEADS YOU'RE DEAD

Foxworth, Bobby J.
EYE FOR AN EYE
PUBLIC ENEMIES

Gatot & Group
WITHOUT MERCY

Genesse, Bryan
LIVE WIRE: HUMAN TIMEBOMB

Gilbert, Mickey
NUTTY PROFESSOR, THE
TIME TO KILL, A

Gilbert, Troy
FREEWAY

Gill, Jack
FIRST WIVES CLUB, THE
JACK

Graf, Alan
BROKEN ARROW

Guegan, Philippe
HATE
Hanlan, Ted
BOGUS
KIDS IN THE HALL: BRAIN CANDY
Hewitt, Jery
ASSOCIATE, THE
BIRDCAGE, THE
EXTREME MEASURES
FARGO
LOVE IS ALL THERE IS
UP CLOSE AND PERSONAL
Hice, Freddie
CABLE GUY, THE
MY FELLOW AMERICANS
Hollands, Sy
HAUNTED
Hooker, Buddy Joe
ARRIVAL, THE
MULHOLLAND FALLS
Howell, Chris
HOURGLASS
HOUSE ARREST
Hutchinson, Rawn
CROSSCUT
MOTHER
Imada, Jeff
JOHN CARPENTER'S ESCAPE FROM L.A.
KAZAAM
Jackson, Ernie
HOMEWARD BOUND II: LOST IN SAN FRANCISCO
Jacox, David
TALES FROM THE CRYPT PRESENTS BORDELLO OF BLOOD
Jansen, Roly
LIVE WIRE: HUMAN TIMEBOMB
TERMINAL IMPACT
WARHEAD
YANKEE ZULU
Jensen, Gary
MAD DOG TIME
Jensen, Jeff
COLONY, THE
HIDDEN ASSASSIN
SHARON'S SECRET
Johnson, Bjorn
LAST SUPPER, THE
Johnston, Keii
UNDER THE HULA MOON
Jolly, Arthur M.
TREES LOUNGE
Judkins, Terri Sue
UNHOOK THE STARS
Kasper, Gary
FINAL EQUINOX, THE
Kimler, Kay
BAJA
Kives, Gyorgy
DOGFIGHTERS, THE
Kramer, Joel
ERASER
Lahoda, Ladislav
ADVENTURES OF PINOCCHIO, THE
LeFevour, Rick
CELTIC PRIDE
FAMILY THING, A
LeRosa, Kevin
TUSKEGEE AIRMEN, THE
Logan, Stacy
EVIL HAS A FACE
Lucescu, Steve
FRAME BY FRAME
Lundin, Justin
LAZARUS MAN, THE
Makaro, J.J.
BIG BULLY
Malesci, Artie
OFF AND RUNNING
Mansker, Eric
HARD JUSTICE
McClennon, Rusty
FIRST KID
McDancer, Buck
DEADLY OUTBREAK
McKay, Cole
BLACK OUT
BLACK SCORPION
RATTLED
SKYSCRAPER
McLean, Dwayne
BLOOD & DONUTS
McLean, Larry
MRS. WINTERBOURNE
McLoughlin, Fiona
MOLL FLANDERS
Meier, John
FLED
Mey, Gavin
REDEMPTION: KICKBOXER 5
Michaels, Wayne
CAPTIVES
Milinac, Carl
HARD WAY OUT: BLOODFIST VIII
Minor, Bob
DANGEROUS PASSION
LETTER TO MY KILLER
ORIGINAL GANGSTAS
SET IT OFF
Morgan, Gary
WHITE WOLVES II: LEGEND OF THE WILD
Mourino, Edgard
SGT. KABUKIMAN N.Y.P.D.
Muzila, Tom
SOLO
Nagys, Giedrius
UNDERTOW
Neilson, Phil
BOYS
JUROR, THE
STRIPTEASE
Nicholas, Ray
MOLL FLANDERS
O'Dell, Phil
TAKEOVER, THE
Omega, Winston
CROSSCUT
FIST OF THE NORTH STAR
Orsatti, Ernie
ED
PRIMAL FEAR
SGT. BILKO
TO GILLIAN ON HER 37TH BIRTHDAY
TRUTH ABOUT CATS AND DOGS, THE
Palmisano, Conrad
CARPOOL
Papajohn, Michael
BOY CALLED HATE, A
Paul, Gary
BIG SQUEEZE, THE
ONE GOOD TURN
POISON IVY 2: LILY
Picerni, Charles
MAXIMUM RISK
Picerni, Chuck
FAN, THE
Picerni Sr., Charles
2 DAYS IN THE VALLEY
Picerni, Steve
FAN, THE
Pock, Bernie
WAR AT HOME, THE
Powell, Greg
MICHAEL COLLINS
MISSION: IMPOSSIBLE
WAR OF THE BUTTONS, THE
Powell, Nick
JACK & SARAH
MUPPET TREASURE ISLAND
Quinn, Fenton
CLUBHOUSE DETECTIVES
Quinn, Ken
HARRIET THE SPY
UNDERSTUDY: GRAVEYARD SHIFT 2, THE
Racki, Branko
GETTING AWAY WITH MURDER
TWO IF BY SEA
WHERE'S THE MONEY, NOREEN?
Rampe, J. Suzanne
OUT THERE
Randall, Glenn
SUBSTITUTE, THE
Randall Jr., Glenn
DOWN PERISCOPE
Razatos, Spiro
LAWNMOWER MAN 2: BEYOND CYBERSPACE
PURE DANGER
RAGE
SWEEPER, THE
Reid, Alison
HARRIET THE SPY
HOMECOMING
Renfro, Bryan
MAN IN THE ATTIC, THE
Rhee, Simon
BEST OF THE BEST 3: NO TURNING BACK
Richardson, Burton
REDEMPTION: KICKBOXER 5
Robotham, John
VERY BRADY SEQUEL, A
Rogers, Mic
TWISTER
Rondel, R.A.
MATILDA
Rondell, Ronald R.
STAR TREK: FIRST CONTACT
Ross, Debby Lynn
WOMAN UNDONE, A
Rosso, Pierre
SUITE 16
Rozato, Spiro
TOO FAST, TOO YOUNG
Russo, Mike
CITY HALL
Ruyard, Michael
JACK
Salvitti, John Paul
SHOOTFIGHTER 2: KILL OR BE KILLED!
Sarna, Michael
PUBLIC ENEMIES
Scherer, Michael
SCREAMERS
Scott, John
PORTRAITS OF A KILLER
Scott, Walter
CHAIN REACTION
CRUCIBLE, THE
DUNSTON CHECKS IN
Serna, Michael John
HARD JUSTICE
Silver, Spike
WILD SIDE
Siverio, Manny
SOMEONE ELSE'S AMERICA
Smith, Lonnie
NEON BIBLE, THE
Solberg, Russell
FAST MONEY
Speaker, Dan
WITCHCRAFT: SALEM'S GHOST
Speaker, Dave
WITCHCRAFT: SALEM'S GHOST

Stacey, Eddie
IN LOVE AND WAR
WHITE SQUALL
Statham, Patrick
BLACK SCORPION
UNKNOWN ORIGIN
VENUS RISING
Stefanich, Mark
QUEST, THE
Stein, Ron
COURAGE UNDER FIRE
Stivi, Alon
HARD JUSTICE
Stone, Joe
NATIONAL LAMPOON'S FAVORITE DEADLY SINS
Stoneham Jr., John
ELECTRA
VIRUS
Strikhanerut, Seng Kawee
QUEST, THE
Stuart, Monty
RIDERS OF THE PURPLE SAGE
Tabatabai, Mohammed
RED SCORPION 2
Taylor, Rocky
EVITA
Thomas, Betty
ALASKA
Tong, Stanley
RUMBLE IN THE BRONX
Towery, Russell
BOTTLE ROCKET
EVENING STAR, THE
FOXFIRE
Townsend, Andy
WHEN THE BULLET HITS THE BONE
Trella, Tim
DEAD WEEKEND
KINGPIN
PEOPLE VS. LARRY FLYNT, THE
Tsui Chung-Sun
MIDNIGHT ANGEL
Turner, Tierre
DONOR UNKNOWN
Vickers, James
CURDLED
Virtue, Danny
GIRL FROM MARS, THE
Walsh, Alan
MOLL FLANDERS
Ward, Jeff
BASQUIAT
GET ON THE BUS
GIRL 6
HIGH SCHOOL HIGH
RANSOM
Waters, Chuck
MOTHER'S PRAYER, A
Watkins, Eddie L.
GREAT WHITE HYPE, THE
Watson, Mike
PAINTED HERO
Waugh, Fred
SPY HARD
Wayton, Gary
WIDOW'S KISS
Webb, Chris
CRACKER: THE MADWOMAN IN THE ATTIC
Werner, Mark
FATALLY YOURS
Weston, Paul
DAYLIGHT
DRAGONHEART
VIKING SAGAS, THE
Whinery, Webster
CHAMBER, THE
Wilder, G. Scott
TALES FROM THE CRYPT PRESENTS BORDELLO OF BLOOD
Wilder, Glen
HEAVEN'S PRISONERS
Woodbury, Rod
WAVELENGTH
Woodruff, Rod
SOLITAIRE FOR TWO
Woolsey, Brent
HAPPY GILMORE
WILLIAM SHAKESPEARE'S ROMEO + JULIET
Yohnka, Merritt
TRIGGER EFFECT, THE
Zagarino, Frank
WITHOUT MERCY
Zamperla, Neno
CEMETERY MAN
Ziker, Dick
EXECUTIVE DECISION
GLIMMER MAN, THE

REVIEW ATTRIBUTION

Films reviewed in this volume are listed below by the author of the review

Bartholomew, David
LOW LIFE, THE
WAR OF THE BUTTONS, THE

Camp, Brian
BIG WARS
GET ON THE BUS
GHOST IN THE SHELL
LAST MAN STANDING
MAXIMUM RISK
MIDNIGHT ANGEL
NIGHT OF THE TWISTERS
NIGHT ON THE GALACTIC RAILROAD
ORGANIZED CRIME & TRIAD BUREAU
PATLABOR 2: MOBILE POLICE
ROUJIN-Z
SANCTUARY: THE MOVIE
SET IT OFF
SPACE JAM
STREET FIGHTER II: THE ANIMATED MOVIE
SURVIVING PICASSO
WICKED CITY, THE
WING CHUN

Cassady Jr., Charles
ANNIE O
... AT FIRST SIGHT
BIG SQUEEZE, THE
BLACK OUT
BRITT ALLCROFT'S MAGIC ADVENTURES OF MUMFIE--THE MOVIE
FLATTERED
FRAME BY FRAME
HARD WAY OUT: BLOODFIST VIII
HAUNTED
HECK'S WAY HOME
JAG
JOSH KIRBY ... TIME WARRIOR!: JOURNEY TO THE MAGIC CAVERN
JOSH KIRBY ... TIME WARRIOR!: LAST BATTLE FOR THE UNIVERSE
KAMIKAZE TAXI
LET'S GET BIZZEE
LOOKING FOR TROUBLE
MERLIN'S SHOP OF MAGICAL WONDERS
MOONSHINE HIGHWAY
NEMESIS III: PREY HARDER
OPEN SEASON
OUTPOST, THE
PIE IN THE SKY
PIRANHA
PLAYBACK
PORTRAITS OF A KILLER
RAW TARGET
RED LINE
ROBIN OF LOCKSLEY
SABRINA, THE TEENAGE WITCH
SHOT, THE
SILENCE OF NETO, THE
SONG SPINNER, THE
SPELLBREAKER: SECRET OF THE LEPRECHAUNS
TALES OF EROTICA
TATTOO BOY
TIMELESS
UNDERSTUDY: GRAVEYARD SHIFT 2, THE
UNDERTOW
WHEN THE BULLET HITS THE BONE
WIDOW'S KISS
WIND IN THE WILLOWS, THE
YESTERDAY'S TARGET

Celeste, Reni
ANGELA
BASQUIAT
BERKELEY IN THE 60S
BLACK MOUNTAIN
BUTTERFLY KISS
INSTITUTE BENJAMENTA
JAMES AND THE GIANT PEACH
PORTRAIT OF A LADY, THE
SILENCES OF THE PALACE, THE
TARGET
THEREMIN: AN ELECTRONIC ODYSSEY

Chris, Cynthia
EVITA
HEIDI FLEISS HOLLYWOOD MADAM
I SHOT ANDY WARHOL

Contreras, Sandra
AVENTURERA
MAN BY THE SHORE, THE

Dearman, Jill
CONDITION RED
EVERYTHING RELATIVE
FAR HARBOR
LONG ROAD HOME, THE
MADDENING, THE
SHADOW WARRIORS
WILD SIDE

Faust, M.
AMERICA'S DREAM
ANTONIA'S LINE
ASSOCIATE, THE
BAD MOON
BEAVIS AND BUTT-HEAD DO AMERICA
BEYOND THE CALL
BLOODSPORT II: THE NEXT KUMITE
BOGUS
BREAKAWAY
BURIAL OF THE RATS
D3: THE MIGHTY DUCKS
DEATH ARTIST, THE
DON'T LET YOUR MEAT LOAF
EDIE & PEN
ENTERTAINING ANGELS: THE DOROTHY DAY STORY
EXIT
FEELING MINNESOTA
FUNNYMAN, THE
GLIMMER MAN, THE
JUST YOUR LUCK
LAND AND FREEDOM
LAND BEFORE TIME IV: JOURNEY THROUGH THE MISTS
LILY DALE
LOVER'S KNOT
MACHINE, THE
MILLE BOLLE BLU
MODERN AFFAIR, A
NICO ICON
NORMA JEAN AND MARILYN
NOT BAD FOR A GIRL
PASSION OF DARKLY NOON, THE
PEOPLE VS. LARRY FLYNT, THE
SANTA WITH MUSCLES
SECRETS & LIES
SHAMELESS
STREETCAR NAMED DESIRE, A
TALKING ABOUT SEX
TWISTER
2 DAYS IN THE VALLEY
VIRTUAL ENCOUNTERS

Fox, Ken
WAR AT HOME, THE

French, Kenneth
CANTERVILLE GHOST, THE
KISSINGER AND NIXON
LITTLE DEATH, THE
MICHAEL COLLINS
REDEMPTION: KICKBOXER 5
SKIN

Galens, David
DARKMAN III: DIE DARKMAN DIE
JINGLE ALL THE WAY
NAKED SOULS
NOT OF THIS EARTH

Gingold, Michael
ARRIVAL, THE
BOYS
BUGGED
CARNOSAUR 3: PRIMAL SPECIES
CHILDREN OF THE CORN: THE GATHERING
COLD LIGHT OF DAY
CRAFT, THE
CROW: CITY OF ANGELS, THE
CURDLED
DEMOLITIONIST, THE
DRAGONHEART
EVIL ED
FRIGHTENERS, THE
HEAD OF THE FAMILY

HELLRAISER: BLOODLINE
LIFEFORM
LITTLE WITCHES
MIND RIPPER
MIRROR, MIRROR III: THE VOYEUR
MR. ICE CREAM MAN
MR. STITCH
MUTANT MAN
NECRONOMICON: BOOK OF THE DEAD
NIGHT OF THE SCARECROW
ORIGINAL GANGSTAS
ORIGINAL SINS
PHAT BEACH
PINOCCHIO'S REVENGE
POLYMORPH
PROTEUS
RUMBLE IN THE BRONX
RUMPELSTILTSKIN
SANDMAN, THE
SANTA CLAWS
SCREAMERS
SOMETIMES THEY COME BACK ... AGAIN
STEPHEN KING'S THINNER
SURGEON, THE
TALES FROM THE CRYPT PRESENTS BORDELLO OF BLOOD
THEY BITE
TREMORS 2: AFTERSHOCKS
WITHIN THE ROCK
ZARKORR! THE INVADER

Grant, Edmond

CHUNGKING EXPRESS
KANSAS CITY
MARS ATTACKS!

Greene, Kent

FROM DUSK TILL DAWN
TREES LOUNGE

Joseph, Andrew

JUDE
MABOROSI

Kaufman, Seth

BODY OF INFLUENCE 2
FUGITIVE RAGE
ONE GOOD TURN
RUDE
SUITE 16

Kelleher, Ed

ANNE FRANK REMEMBERED
CAUGHT
COLD COMFORT FARM
GHOSTS OF MISSISSIPPI
GRACE OF MY HEART
HYPE!
ISLAND OF DR. MOREAU, THE
JACK & SARAH
MADAME BUTTERFLY
MESSAGE TO LOVE: THE ISLE OF WIGHT FESTIVAL
MULHOLLAND FALLS
UNHOOK THE STARS
WHEN WE WERE KINGS

Lovece, Frank

BEAUTIFUL THING
BLACK SCORPION
BLUSH
CHAIN REACTION
FLIPPER
HUNCHBACK OF NOTRE DAME, THE
MAGIC HUNTER
PARIS WAS A WOMAN
SEARCH FOR ONE-EYE JIMMY, THE
SYNTHETIC PLEASURES
TIME TO KILL, A
TOLLBOOTH
VERY BRADY SEQUEL, A

Mandros, Chris

CHILDREN OF NOISY VILLAGE, THE
IMMORTALS, THE
LARRY MCMURTRY'S STREETS OF LAREDO
SOME FOLKS CALL IT A SLING BLADE
STORY OF XINGHUA, THE
SUGARTIME
TUSKEGEE AIRMEN, THE

McDonagh, Maitland

CEMETERY MAN

Milenski, Aaron

ASSAULT AT WEST POINT
BOUND
DEVOTION
GIRL 6
GLASS CAGE, THE
JOHNNY 100 PESOS
LITTLE INDIAN, BIG CITY
LIVE NUDE GIRLS
LONE JUSTICE: SHOWDOWN AT PLUM CREEK
MAN WITH A PLAN
MONSTERSHOW
ONCE UPON A TIME ... WHEN WE WERE COLORED
PHARAOH'S ARMY
SONIC OUTLAWS
SPIDER & ROSE
STAR MAKER, THE
TEXAS CHAINSAW MASSACRE: THE NEXT GENERATION

Monder, Eric

ALL DOGS GO TO HEAVEN 2
AMERICAN STRAYS
BED OF ROSES
BEFORE AND AFTER
BIG BULLY
BIO-DOME
BITTER SUGAR
BOTTLE ROCKET
BROKEN ARROW
BROTHER OF SLEEP
CABLE GUY, THE
CARRIED AWAY
CITIZEN RUTH
CITY HALL
COLD FEVER
COURAGE UNDER FIRE
CURTIS'S CHARM
DADETOWN
DEAD MAN
DELTA OF VENUS
DENISE CALLS UP
DESOLATION ANGELS
DIABOLIQUE
DON'T BE A MENACE TO SOUTH CENTRAL WHILE DRINKING YOUR JUICE IN THE HOOD
DOWN PERISCOPE
ED
ERASER
ERNESTO CHE GUEVARA--THE BOLIVIAN DIARY
EVERYONE SAYS I LOVE YOU
EXECUTIVE DECISION
EXTREME MEASURES
FAITHFUL
FAMILY THING, A
FAN, THE
FATE
FIRST KID
FLIRT
FOR THE MOMENT
4 TALES OF 2 CITIES
FRENCH TWIST
FROM THE JOURNALS OF JEAN SEBERG
FUNERAL, THE
GETTING AWAY WITH MURDER
GIRLFRIENDS
GUIMBA THE TYRANT
HALFMOON
HAPPY GILMORE
HEAVY
HOMAGE
HOMEWARD BOUND II: LOST IN SAN FRANCISCO
HORSEMAN ON THE ROOF
JANE EYRE
JOE'S APARTMENT
JUROR, THE
KINGPIN
LA CEREMONIE
LA COMEDIE-FRANCAISE OU L'AMOUR JOUE
LAWNMOWER MAN 2: BEYOND CYBERSPACE
LES VOLEURS
LOADED
LONE STAR
LOOKING FOR RICHARD
MA SAISON PREFEREE
MADAME WANG'S
MAHJONG
MARY REILLY
MERCY
MICHAEL
MICROCOSMOS
MIRROR HAS TWO FACES, THE
MR. WRONG
NELLY AND MONSIEUR ARNAUD
NEW LIFE, A
NIKI DE SAINT PHALLE: WHO IS THE MONSTER -- YOU OR ME?
NUTTY PROFESSOR, THE
ONE LESS EGG TO FRY
ONE NIGHT STAND
PALOOKAVILLE

PARADISE LOST: THE CHILD MURDERS AT ROBIN HOOD HILLS
PERFECT CANDIDATE, A
POMPATUS OF LOVE, THE
PREACHER'S WIFE, THE
PREDICTIONS OF FIRE
RENDEZVOUS IN PARIS
RICH MAN'S WIFE, THE
ROCK, THE
ROLLING STONES ROCK-AND-ROLL CIRCUS, THE
SGT. KABUKIMAN N.Y.P.D.
SHINE
SINGLE GIRL, A
SMALL WONDERS
SOLO
SPITFIRE GRILL, THE
STEALING BEAUTY
SUBSTANCE OF FIRE, THE
SUNSET PARK
SWEET NOTHING
SWINGERS
THEODORE REX
THIN LINE BETWEEN LOVE AND HATE, A
THREE LIVES AND ONLY ONE DEATH
TRUTH ABOUT CATS AND DOGS, THE
TWELFTH NIGHT
TWO FRIENDS
UNFORGETTABLE
UP CLOSE AND PERSONAL
VUKOVAR
WALLACE AND GROMIT: THE BEST OF AARDMAN ANIMATION
WELCOME TO THE DOLLHOUSE
WHITE BALLOON, THE
WIFE, THE
YOU'LL NEVER MAKE LOVE IN THIS TOWN AGAIN

Nicastro, Nicholas

CELTIC PRIDE
DAYLIGHT
GREAT WHITE HYPE, THE
KAZAAM
MOLL FLANDERS
STRIPTEASE
TIN CUP

Noh, David

ANGELS AND INSECTS
AUGUST
BEAUTIFUL GIRLS
BIG NIGHT
CATWALK
CELESTIAL CLOCKWORK
CELLULOID CLOSET, THE
EVENING STAR, THE
EYE FOR AN EYE
FIRST WIVES CLUB, THE
FOXFIRE
FRISK
HARRIET THE SPY
HATE
HEADLESS BODY IN TOPLESS BAR
HEAVEN'S PRISONERS
INFINITY
IT'S MY PARTY
MAN OF THE YEAR
MANNY & LO
MATILDA
MAYBE ... MAYBE NOT
MIDNIGHT DANCERS
MIDWINTER'S TALE, A
MOTHER NIGHT
MOUTH TO MOUTH
101 DALMATIANS
RACE THE SUN
RIDICULE
SOME MOTHER'S SON
STONEWALL
UNDER THE DOMIM TREE
WALKING AND TALKING
YOUNG POISONER'S HANDBOOK, THE

O'Bradovich, Donica

CHILDREN OF FURY
LOSING CHASE
NEUROSIA: 50 YEARS OF PERVERSITY
SHOPPING

Pardi, Robert

ABUSE
AMANDA AND THE ALIEN
ANIMAL INSTINCTS III: THE SEDUCTRESS
APART FROM HUGH
BAD LOVE
BAJA
BATON ROUGE
BEASTMASTER 3: THE EYE OF BRAXUS
BEST OF THE BEST 3: NO TURNING BACK
BEYOND DESIRE
BLOOD & DONUTS
BLOODKNOT
BODY COUNT
BOY CALLED HATE, A
BREACH OF TRUST
CHASING BUTTERFLIES
CLUBHOUSE DETECTIVES
COLONY, THE
CRACKER: THE MADWOMAN IN THE ATTIC
CROCODILES IN AMSTERDAM
CROSSCUT
DAENS
DANGEROUS PASSION
DARK SECRETS
DEAD COLD
DEAD TO RIGHTS
DEAD WEEKEND
DEADLY OUTBREAK
DEATH BENEFIT
DENTIST, THE
DESIRE
DOGFIGHTERS, THE
DONOR UNKNOWN
DOWN, OUT AND DANGEROUS
ED'S NEXT MOVE
ELECTRA
EVIL HAS A FACE
FAST MONEY
FATALLY YOURS
FINAL EQUINOX, THE
FIST OF THE NORTH STAR
FLAMING EARS
FLOWER OF MY SECRET, THE
FOR BETTER OR WORSE
FOREST WARRIOR
FRANCOIS TRUFFAUT: STOLEN PORTRAITS
FRIEND OF THE FAMILY 2
FULL BODY MASSAGE
GALAXIES ARE COLLIDING
GIRL FROM MARS, THE
GRIM
HARD JUSTICE
HARVEST OF FIRE
HEDD WYNN
HEIDI CHRONICLES, THE
HIDDEN ASSASSIN
HOLLOW POINT
HOMECOMING
HOURGLASS
HOW THE WEST WAS FUN
INDEPENDENCE DAY
IRON EAGLE IV
IT CAME FROM OUTER SPACE II
JOSH KIRBY ... TIME WARRIOR!: EGGS FROM 70,000,000 B.C.
JOSH KIRBY ... TIME WARRIOR!: TRAPPED ON TOY WORLD
LAZARUS MAN, THE
LETTER TO MY KILLER
LIVE WIRE: HUMAN TIMEBOMB
LOVE IS ALL THERE IS
MAGIC IN THE MIRROR
MAN IN THE ATTIC, THE
MAN WITH THE PERFECT SWING, THE
MATERNAL INSTINCTS
MISSING PIECES
MOTHER
MOTHER'S PRAYER, A
MRS. MUNCK
MURDERED INNOCENCE
NATIONAL LAMPOON'S FAVORITE DEADLY SINS
OF LOVE AND SHADOWS
OFF AND RUNNING
ONE MAN'S JUSTICE
OUT THERE
OUTRAGE
OVER THE WIRE
PAINTED HERO
PHANTOM 2040: THE GHOST WHO WALKS
PHOENIX
PIG'S TALE, A
POISON IVY 2: LILY
PUBLIC ACCESS
PUBLIC ENEMIES
RATTLED
RAVENHAWK
RED SCORPION 2
RIDERS OF THE PURPLE SAGE
ROAD HOME, THE
ROAD TO GALVESTON, THE
SAINTS AND SINNERS
SAWBONES
SHADOW OF ANGELS
SHADOW YOU SOON WILL BE, A

SHARON'S SECRET
SHOOTFIGHTER 2: KILL OR BE KILLED!
SOLITAIRE FOR TWO
SONS OF TRINITY
SOUTH BEACH ACADEMY
STAND OFF, THE
SUBSTITUTE, THE
SUNCHASER
TAILS YOU LIVE, HEADS YOU'RE DEAD
TAKEOVER, THE
TERMINAL IMPACT
TOO FAST, TOO YOUNG
TRACKS OF A KILLER
TRUMAN
TUNNEL VISION
TWO MUCH
UNDER THE HULA MOON
UNKNOWN ORIGIN
VENUS RISING
VIKING SAGAS, THE
VIRTUAL COMBAT
VIRUS
VIVE L'AMOUR
WARHEAD
WATCH ME
WAVELENGTH
WHARF RAT, THE
WHERE'S THE MONEY, NOREEN?
WHISPERING, THE
WHITE WOLVES II: LEGEND OF THE WILD
WILLIAM SHAKESPEARE'S ROMEO + JULIET
WITCHCRAFT: SALEM'S GHOST
WITHOUT MERCY
WOLVES, THE
WOMAN UNDONE, A
YANKEE ZULU

Puchalski, Steve

AMERICAN BUFFALO
BACKLASH: OBLIVION 2
BEWARE: CHILDREN AT PLAY
BLONDES HAVE MORE GUNS
CANNIBAL! THE MUSICAL
CAPTIVES
CRIMINAL HEARTS
NORMAL LIFE
SCREAM

Riley, Phil

AFFAIR, THE
BLACK SHEEP
BULLETPROOF
CARPOOL
CHAMBER, THE
CRUCIBLE, THE
DUNSTON CHECKS IN
EMMA
FEAR
FELONY
FEMALIEN
FLED
FLIRTING WITH DISASTER
FLY AWAY HOME
FORBIDDEN ZONE: ALIEN ABDUCTION
FREEWAY
GIRLS TOWN
HALFBACK OF NOTRE DAME, THE
HIGH SCHOOL HIGH
HOUSE ARREST
IF LUCY FELL
JACK
JOHN CARPENTER'S ESCAPE FROM L.A.
LARGER THAN LIFE
LATE SHIFT, THE
LOTTO LAND
MR. HOLLAND'S OPUS
MRS. WINTERBOURNE
MUPPET TREASURE ISLAND
ONE FINE DAY
OUTER LIMITS: SANDKINGS, THE
PHANTOM, THE
RANSOM
SERPENT'S LAIR
SHE'S THE ONE
SLEEPERS
STAR TREK: FIRST CONTACT
STUPIDS, THE
THAT THING YOU DO!
TO GILLIAN ON HER 37TH BIRTHDAY
TRIGGER EFFECT, THE
TWO IF BY SEA

Royce, Brenda Scott

ADVENTURES OF PINOCCHIO, THE
DEAR GOD
I'M NOT RAPPAPORT
PURE DANGER
RAGE
SWEEPER, THE
WHITE SQUALL

Rubenstein, Leonard

CHEKIST, THE
EYE OF VICHY, THE
FIRE ON THE MOUNTAIN
MOTHER OF KINGS

Scheinfeld, Michael

ADRENALIN: FEAR THE RUSH
ALASKA
ALEX
ANNA
BIRDCAGE, THE
BLACK DAY BLUE NIGHT
BLACK ROSE OF HARLEM
BREAKING THE WAVES
CHAMELEON
GRASS HARP, THE
HAMLET
HOSTILE INTENTIONS
IN LOVE AND WAR
JOSEPH CONRAD'S THE SECRET AGENT
KASPAR HAUSER
LEGEND OF GATOR FACE, THE
LONG KISS GOODNIGHT, THE
MONSTER, THE
MOTHER
MY FELLOW AMERICANS
MYSTERY SCIENCE THEATER 3000: THE MOVIE
ORSON WELLES: THE ONE-MAN BAND
PERSONAL JOURNEY WITH MARTIN SCORSESE THROUGH AMERICAN MOVIES, A
PRE-MADONNAS
QUEST, THE
SERIAL KILLER
SGT. BILKO
SHOWGIRL MURDERS, THE
SKYSCRAPER
SPY HARD
TEXAS PAYBACK
TIGER HEART
TWO DEATHS
TWO-BITS & PEPPER
VISITORS, THE
WHITE TIGER

Seulowitz, Robert

BARB WIRE
MULTIPLICITY
PHENOMENON

Thomajan, Dale

CALLING THE GHOSTS: A STORY ABOUT RAPE, WAR AND WOMEN
CHAMPAGNE SAFARI, THE
ENGLISH PATIENT, THE
FARGO
LAST SUPPER, THE
MADAGASCAR SKIN
MARVIN'S ROOM
NEON BIBLE, THE
PROPRIETOR, THE
SLING BLADE
SMALL FACES
WHO KILLED PASOLINI?
WHOLE WIDE WORLD, THE

Trenz, Brandon

FINAL CUT, THE
GHOST AND THE DARKNESS, THE
GRAVE, THE
JERRY MAGUIRE
KIDS IN THE HALL: BRAIN CANDY
LAST DANCE
MAD DOG TIME
PALLBEARER, THE
PRIMAL FEAR
TRAINSPOTTING

Westberg, Jenny

MISSION: IMPOSSIBLE

Yellin, Todd

BOYS NEXT DOOR, THE
LINE KING: THE AL HIRSCHFELD STORY, THE
RASPUTIN
SOMEONE ELSE'S AMERICA
WEEKEND IN THE COUNTRY, A

Zonis, Nadia

EDDIE
JOHNNY SHORTWAVE

OUR CONTRIBUTORS

A.J. Andrew Joseph has a degree in East Asian Studies from Harvard University and is completing an MFA in film production at Columbia University. He has translated a variety of articles on Asian cinema.

A.M. Aaron Milenski is assistant director of admissions at Oberlin College. In addition to loving obscure and independent film, he is a guitarist and songwriter for The Palindromes. His wife, Jill, is an artist.

B.C. Brian Camp is the programming director at CUNY-TV in New York. He has written for *Animation World, Asian Cult Cinema, Film Comment, Film Library Quarterly, Outre,* and *Sightlines.* He was educated in film production at Hunter College and in cinema studies at New York University.

B.R. Brenda Scott Royce is a freelance entertainment writer and award-winning playwright. She is the author of *Lauren Bacall: A Bio-Bibliography, Hogan's Heroes: A Complete Reference,* and numerous articles.

B.T. Brandon Trenz is a freelance writer based in Detroit, Michigan. He is also a former contributing editor of the reference series *Contemporary Theater, Film and Television,* published by Gale Research.

C.C. Charles Cassady Jr. has worked as a columnist and freelance movie reviewer for various publications around the world. He has contributed reviews to *Video Reference Book Series, TV Guide Entertainment Network,* and is the movie columnist of *The Morning Journal,* the daily newspaper of Lorain, Ohio.

C.Ch. Cynthia Chris currently lives in San Diego. Her writing has appeared in *Afterimage, exposure, High Performance,* and *The Independent.* She is working toward a Ph.D in Communication at the University of California, San Diego.

C.M. Chris Mandros has a B.A. in Mass Communications from Towson State University. He lives in Baltimore, works for States News Service, and writes about film and video.

D.B. David Bartholomew is the Film Specialist for the New York Public Library's Theater Collection at Lincoln Center. He is also a freelance video consultant, writer, film critic, and editor.

D.G. David Galens is an editor, author, and musician. He edits *Contemporary Authors on CD* and *Drama for Students* at Gale Research. He also plays guitar in the Detroit-based band, the Civilians.

D.N. David Noh was born and raised in Hawaii, where a childhood viewing of GONE WITH THE WIND at a Cinerama theater instilled in him a lifelong love of movies. Educated in film on both coasts, he is a writer living in New York

D.O. Donica O'Bradovich is a text writer for the Listings section of *TV Guide* and a freelance writer of movie reviews.

D.T. Dale Thomajan is the author of *From Cyd Charisse to Psycho: A Book of Movie Bests* and the editor of the book *Great Movie Lines.* His articles on film have appeared in *Film Comment, The Village Voice,* and *Spy.*

E.G. Edmond Grant is editor of *The Motion Picture Guide.* He previously served as a staff writer for *TV Guide* and as managing editor of *Movies on TV.* He produces "Media Funhouse," a weekly NYC cable-access television program.

E.K. Ed Kelleher is associate editor of *Film Journal International.* As Edouard Dauphin, he created the "Drive-In Saturday" column in *Creem* magazine. His screenwriting credits include seven produced features, and he has lectured on film at the School of Visual Arts and New York University.

E.M. Eric Monder is the author of *George Sidney* (Greenwood Press, 1994) and has contributed articles to *The New York Times, Film Comment, Cinemania* and the Directors Guild of America Magazine. He lives in Manhattan with his wife, Kathi Patterson, who is also a writer and filmmaker.

F.L. Frank Lovece is the author of several books about television, including *The X-Files Declassified, Taxi: The Official Fan's Guide,* and *The Television Yearbook 1990-91.* He has also written for such periodicals as *Penthouse, Premiere,* and *New York.* He is chief film critic for Baseline.

J.D. Jill Dearman is a playwright and director whose work has been produced by Performance Space 122, Nada, Dixon Place, and other NYC venues. She is currently in pre-production on her first feature film, *The Great Bravura.*

J.F. Joe Frazzetta has written for *Films in Review,* and was a movie database researcher at *TV Guide.*

J.W. Jenny Westberg, a mother of four, lives in Portland, Oregon.

K.F. Ken Fox is associate editor of *The Motion Picture Guide* and the associate movies editor at *TV Guide Entertainment Network,* a World Wide Web-based entertainment magazine.

K.Fr. Kenneth French is a librarian in the areas of reference and special collections. He lives in New Jersey with his wife and son.

K.G. Kent Greene is a Jersey City, NJ-based writer on film, TV, and popular culture. His work has appeared in *The Village Voice, American Film,* and *Cineaste.* He is also the content editor of STRANGE FUN, a provocative website devoted to fantastic screen entertainment.

L.R. Leonard Rubenstein is the author of *The Great Spy Films* and co-editor of *The Cineaste Interviews.* He is a contributor to *World Film Directors, The Encyclopedia of Film, Political Companion to American Film,* and other reference books.

M.F. M. Faust is proprietor of Mondo Video, the coolest video store in Buffalo, NY. He has written about movies for *Video Movie Guide, Movies on TV and Videocassete, The Complete Guide to Videocassette Movies, Video Digest, Video* magazine, Baseline, and *The Buffalo News.*

M.G. Michael Gingold is the managing editor of *Fangoria* magazine, for which he has written since 1988. He has contributed reviews to such books as *The Blockbuster Video Guide* and Steven Scheuer's *Movies on TV and Videocassette.*

M.M. Maitland McDonagh is the movies editor at *TV Guide Entertainment Network,* the World Wide Web-based arts and entertainment magazine, and the author of three books: *Broken Mirrors/Broken Minds, Filmmaking on the Fringe,* and *The 50 Most Erotic Films of All Time.* She has written on film for a variety of publications.

M.S. Michael Scheinfeld is currently a senior writer at *TV Guide,* and since 1985 has been a contributor to *Leonard Maltin's Movie and Video Guide.* His reviews and articles have also appeared in *Films in Review* and *Laserviews* magazine.

N.N. Nicholas Nicastro is a filmmaker and critic whose work has appeared in *The New York Times, Film Comment, The New York Observer, Publisher's Weekly,* and *Heterodoxy.* He currently lives in upstate New York.

N.Z. Nadia Zonis is a writer and editor in New York.

P.R. Phil Riley has a degree in philosophy and has done graduate work in film and television criticism. He lives in Austin, Texas.

R.C. Reni Celeste is a freelance writer who is currently working on her PhD in the Visual and Cultural Studies program at the University of Rochester.

R.P. Robert Pardi was managing editor and chief film critic of four editions of *Movies on TV.* He is the author of *Movie Blockbusters* and *Who's Who in Cable and TV,* co-wrote *The Complete Guide to Videocassette Movies,* and contributed to *The International Dictionary of Films and Filmmakers.*

R.S. Robert Seulowitz holds an M.Div. from the Union Theological Seminary, MhD from Universal Life Church, and a CNE from Drake Institute. He has worked in publishing as a production manager and editor.

S.C. Sandra Contreras writes the Movie Dailies column for *TV Guide Entertainment Network.*

S.K. Seth Kaufman is the senior editor of *TV Guide Entertainment Network.* He has written for *The New York Times, The New York Post, People,* and *The New York Observer.* He co-wrote a song for the film ED'S NEXT MOVE.

S.P. Steven Puchalski is the editor/publisher of *Shock Cinema* magazine. A collection of his cult film reviews, entitled *Slimetime,* has recently been published in England, and he is a regular contributor to *Fangoria* and *Sci-Fi Channel Entertainment.*

T.Y. Todd S. Yellin is an independent filmmaker who, in 1993, became the only person ever to film Tibetan refugees escaping over the Himalayas into Nepal. He now writes in the depths of Brooklyn.